THE ENCYCLOPEDIA OF
AMERICAN CRIME

THE ENCYCLOPEDIA OF
AMERICAN CRIME

By
CARL SIFAKIS

SMITHMARK

THE ENCYCLOPEDIA OF AMERICAN CRIME

Copyright © 1982 by Facts on File, Inc.

This edition published in 1992 by SMITHMARK
Publishers Inc., 16 East 32nd Street, New York, NY
10016.

SMITHMARK books are available for sales promotion and
premium use. For details, write or call the manager of
special sales, SMITHMARK Publishers Inc., 16 East 32nd
Street, New York, NY 10016; (212) 532-6600.

Library of Congress Cataloging-in-Publication Data

Sifakis, Carl.
    The encyclopedia of American crime / by Carl Sifakis.
      p.   cm.
    Includes index.
    ISBN 0-8317-2767-5 : $19.98
      1. Crime—United States—Encyclopedias.   I. Title.
HV6789.S54   1992
364.973'03—dc20   92-17112
                              CIP

Printed in the United States of America

9 8 7 6 5

For Maria Balluff

ACKNOWLEDGEMENTS

Special thanks concerning this book must be given to Ed Knappman, who thought of the idea and made it work; to Howie Langer, who thought of me; to Joe Reilly, a most determined copy editor with his six eternal questions—who, what, when, where, why and how; Mimi Clifford, whose enthusiasm for the book was equaled by her proofreading zeal for rooting out errors; and Nancy Fishelberg and Ophelia Batalion, who were most supportive. And of course to my wife, Maria-Luise, whose encouragement, researching, editing and constant checking of facts often passed what should have been the limits of endurance.

CONTENTS

INTRODUCTION

The history of crime in America is quite simply the history of America. When criminals began arriving in the New World, America, unlike the nations of Europe, had virtually no social structure, customs, or institutions of its own. As America grew into a nation, criminals adapted themselves to the emerging institutions, flourished with them, worked within them, corrupted them, and, some might even say, were corrupted *by* them. Criminality started immediately with the arrival of the first white man. If the Viking sagas are given credence, there were eight murders on day one of the white man's appearance in North America.

New York City became a symbol of urban crime well before the end of the 18th century. Although there are earlier commentaries on crime in the city, an observation by New York printer-journalist John Holt in 1762 is especially illustrative. Holt wrote of "such various attempts to rob, and so many Robberies actually committed, having of late been very frequent within the Circuits of this City, both Day and Night; it is become hazardous for any person to walk in the latter."

Holt's words sound much like a 1990s New York newspaper editorial demanding something be done to solve the crime problem. What becomes apparent to any serious student of crime in America is the myth of the "good old days." In Philadelphia in the 18th century, newspapers spoke in awe of the most fearful of all criminals, "those nocturnal Sons of Violence." And even in the good old days, the best of neighborhoods quickly went to hell. That was true of Cherry Street, that wondrous New York thoroughfare lined with splendid mansions, where George Washington resided at the corner of Franklin Square after his inauguration as president of the United States and where, a few doors away, John Hancock lived. Together they strolled amid the street's fragrant cherry trees and spoke of the American dream. Yet within a few short decades, Cherry Street had degenerated into an area jammed with miserable tenements and inhabitants steeped in poverty, vice, and criminality. Cherry Street became the domain of the early Irish street gangs, and no honest citizen dared venture where Washington had once casually ambled.

Crime soon developed into an "organized" activity, as gangs found allies and protectors among the aspiring politicians of the day. The politicians realized that, properly used, the gangs could win and maintain power for them by intimidating voters at election time. The gangs continued to work with political machines for about 100 years, until approximately the start of World War I.

By that time, reform movements had taken root in most big cities, and politicians realized that the great street gangs—such as New York's primarily Jewish Eastman gang and the equal-numbered Italian Five Points gang under Paul Kelly—had turned into a liability. No longer could the gangs rob and kill (often to order according to detailed price lists) and expect New York's Tammany Hall or its equivalent political machines in other cities to protect them. With their members subject to frequent arrests and imprisonment, the great gangs started to disintegrate.

What saved the gangs from total collapse was a unique development in American history: Prohibition. The Noble Experiment began shortly after the close of World War I, and suddenly, the disintegrating criminal gangs were revived. The attempt to legislate morality was doomed to failure, and in a sad by-product of this ill-advised attempt, the seeds of organized crime were sown. Where once the criminals had been popular just with the politicians, they now became accepted by the public as a whole; the bootleggers were the public's saviors, supplying them with forbidden drink. Al Capone, the "bootleg king" of Chicago, was cheered at baseball games, while Herbert Hoover, the president of the United States, was booed.

More importantly, the revenues from bootlegging provided the gangsters with wealth they never had accumulated before. No longer could the politicians buy them; now they could and would buy the politicians. In Chicago, Capone would boast about how he owned the police. In New York, a young Frank Costello would tell his superior, Lucky Luciano, that the mob owned the police commissioner. Society nurtured the new underworld criminals of the 1920s and then bewailed the relatively insignificant "public enemies" of the 1930s, reflecting a total misunderstanding of the era's crime problem. That misunderstanding continues to the present day.

Not only do we fail to see the genuine menace of crime, but we panic over illusions, particularly the specter of a rising crime wave in the 1970s and 1980s and on into the 1990s. We demand that something be done about crime, that dangerous criminals be put away, ignoring the old lessons that prisons do not reform criminals but generally make them into worse ones. Undoubtedly, one reason for this return to a tougher attitude is racial bias. Today's prison populations in general have darker skins. Crime is currently personified by rowdy black youths in high tops. In our prejudice, we see the root problems of crime as an ethnic matter. And in a sense it is, since crime springs from ghettos and ghettos tend to be inhabited by ethnic minorities. When the Irish were the first people jammed into the original ghettos of American cities, they were responsible for the bulk of the crime wave. After the Jews and Italians arrived, they became the nation's leading gangsters. When in history has most of the crime in America (except for white-collar crime) *not* sprung from the ghettos?

Any crime reporter is familiar with the attitude that has been described as "Irish cop morality": "Why are these people like animals? Why don't they pull themselves out of the slime the way we did?" Certainly the Irish did, but it took them about a century. Many second- and third-generation Jews do not even know of their heritage of criminality in America, making that one of the nation's best-kept secrets. And according to an ethnic self-delusion, spoken not without a measure of pride among Jews, those among them who became the power-wielding criminals remained in the background, letting others carry out the violence. This myth is clearly contradicted in the persons of such brutal thugs and killers as Monk Eastman, Crazy Butch, Johnny Spanish, Little Kishky, Ike the Blood, Kid Jigger, Kid Dahl, Big Jack Zelig, Gyp the Blood, Lefty Louis, Whitey Lewis, Yoske Nigger, Charley the Cripple, Johnny Levinsky, and Dopey Benny; and in a succeeding era by Kid Dropper, Little Augie, Legs Diamond, Dutch Schultz, Waxey Gordon, Meyer Lansky, Bugsy Siegel, Pretty Amberg, Louis Lepke, Gurrah Shapiro, Abe Reles, Pittsburgh Phil Strauss, and Buggsy Goldstein. Many drew their first blood as juvenile muggers, preying on citizens alarmed by the crime wave in their time and insisting things had been better in the good old days. (The identities of some gangsters are lost because they adopted Irish-sounding names. Even the celebrated Monk Eastman, born Edward Osterman, often called himself Edward Delaney, and the notorious turn-of-the-century Italian gang leader Paolo Vaccarelli was likewise better known as Paul Kelly. It was part of the prejudice of the day that even these criminals thought they had to have good Irish names to be gangsters!)

Of course, the public *has* reason to believe that we are in the midst of a great crime wave. Each year, new statistics bear it out. But according to Thornstein Sellin, the "dean of criminal statisticians," the United States "has the worst crime statistics of any major country in the Western world." Sophia M. Robinson of the Columbia School of Social Work declared, "The FBI's figures are not worth the paper they are printed on."

Yet, year after year headlines proclaim: SERIOUS CRIMES UP 9 PERCENT (or some such) FOR THE YEAR IN FBI REPORT. The headlines are almost replays of the headlines from previous years. Such statements naturally encourage the public perception of a soaring crime wave. But is crime really on the rise? Almost as often as the FBI figures show a rise in *reported* crimes, the National Crime Survey of the Bureau of Justice Statistics, a hardly noticed but highly respected study, finds no crime wave. The survey, which polls more than 130,000 persons in some 60,000 households across the country to compile statistics on both reported and unreported crimes, frequently measures a *decline* in crime. There have been periods over a five-year span in which the FBI's studies have shown a steady rise while the survey has shown a steady, if small, decline. Generally, too, the survey reports three times as many crimes as does the FBI.

The explanation for the difference between the FBI's findings and those of the National Crime Survey may well be that crime has remained fairly constant in recent years, while the *reporting* of crime to law enforcement agencies has increased. Unquestionably, the reporting of rapes has increased, as police have devised techniques for relieving at least some of the emotional distress of the victims and as more women find the courage and support to fight back. Furthermore, more crimes are being reported to take advantage of insurance coverage.

However, facts are not important in public perception. The public *knows* crime has gone up compared with the good old days. That perception is firmly rooted, and its causes are not difficult to find.

One reason is that, in the past several decades, the public has become better informed. The average person today probably watches one to one and a half hours of news on television each day, far more time than was ever spent reading newspapers in the prevideo age. Crime news is driven home much more forcefully—and in vivid color. This is not to say that the public would be better off uninformed. Television played a similar role during the Vietnam War, subjecting viewers night after night to the horrors of that tragic conflict. As a result, TV was more instrumental in ending the nation's involvement in Vietnam than were the numerous antiwar demonstrations.

Today, television sickens viewers with crime reports. There is something antiseptic about a three-paragraph news story of a killing. It is quite different to show a murder corpse being carted off, with close-ups of bloodstains on a floor or sidewalk. In the good old days, people rarely saw anything like this. Therefore, says the person in the street, crime now must indeed be worse.

This public misconception naturally carries over into the political arena, with politicians seeking to outdo each other by promising to "get tough with criminals." At the same time as courts are ordering prison populations reduced because of overcrowding, the politicians talk of taking violent criminals off the streets and locking them up. In an era of reduced government spending, various politicians are calling for new prisons. Yet while it costs a minimum of $20,000 a year to house a convict in an existing facility, the per-prisoner cost of providing new accommodations is $70,000 to $100,000 a year. Of course, the politicians realize what they propose could never be done on the scale that would be necessary to take care of the overflow, but the idea represents a "quick fix" for the public's worry.

Focusing on the criminal justice system, which has proven incapable of stopping crime in the past, inhibits any serious discussion of the problem. For years now, the Federal Drug Enforcement Administration has made numerous arrests of major drug dealers in the United States and abroad, and long prison terms have been handed out. Still, the country is flooded with heroin and cocaine, and their impact on the crime rate is staggering. An addict often requires $200 or more a day to support his or her habit. Ultimately, how can the user get the necessary drugs except by stealing and assaulting victims in the process? Researchers at Temple University found that 243 heroin users in Baltimore had committed more than half a million crimes over an 11-year period, an annual average of two hundred per criminal. Sooner or later, rather than emphasizing the "Lock 'em up and throw away the key" attitude, it will become necessary to begin a serious dialogue about other solutions. Until an effective method of dealing with the drug problem is implemented, addicts will go on committing vast numbers of crimes.

A genuine effort will have to be made to come up with proper standards of probation, parole, and sentencing of criminals. New York District Attorney Robert M. Morgenthau notes that the law metes out the harshest sentences to second- and third-time offenders, many of whom are by that time in their late twenties—an age when, the records show, a criminal's illegal activities generally diminish. "From the standpoint of fairness, that's the fairest way to do it," Morgenthau stresses. "But actually he's less of a danger to society than the guy who's twenty-two or twenty-three years old, is more active, and has fewer convictions."

It is not the purpose of this book to attempt to solve the crime problem, but it is important to try to note some of the fallacies of many of the remedies. President Ronald Reagan's labeling of crime as an "American epidemic," requiring a sweeping overhaul of federal criminal laws to "redress the imbalance between the rights of the accused and the rights of the innocent," particularly missed the point. Reagan proposed new drug-trafficking crackdowns (which in retrospect did little, if anything) and bail-tightening procedures, and also endorsed legislative proposals that would permit judges to order convicted criminals to make restitution to their victims. This last point would require serious study, since it would offer new opportunities for frame-ups by giving victims a financial motivation to positively identify suspects, a matter few proponents have yet addressed.

Police claim that their hands are tied, that no matter how many arrests they make, the courts continue to put criminals back on the streets. But is this not an attempt to draw attention away from the fact that the police make an arrest in only one crime out of five? Furthermore, this 20 percent ratio is bloated with arrests for "easy" cases, those of murder, aggravated assault, and rape, in which the identities of the perpetrators are often readily established.

The need for a more systematized analysis of the history of crime in America is readily apparent, but it is not an easy field to study. Facts about crime are more obscure than in most other subject fields. Indeed, some crime myths have become so imbedded in our culture that it is probably too late at this date to separate fact from fiction. It may be a hopeless struggle to try to prove that John Dillinger never used a wooden gun to break out of jail. Some of the most-respected references to this day inaccurately report that Al Capone was born in Naples, when, in fact, his birthplace was Brooklyn, New York.

Criminals lie not only about their deeds but about their lives as well. Efforts to obtain birth and death dates of criminals are often frustrating. They give different birth places and dates at different times, perhaps in an attempt to assume other identities or to cloud the truth and avoid being deported. The result is confusion. Deaths are not always reported. Criminals, certainly more so than old soldiers, seem to just fade away.

Police have been known to misrepresent facts, and, when convenient, the great historians of crime—news reporters—have also stretched the truth, sometimes entertainingly so. The pressure in the newspaper profession for a "fresh angle" undoubtedly has led some reporters to embellish their facts. Paul Schoenstein, one of New York's leading newspaper editors, once said his favorite reporters were those who came back with news stories in which at least the addresses didn't turn out to be in the middle of the Hudson River!

Reporters have gained reputations, or at least some journalistic rewards, by catering to the public's appetite for sensationalism. The vehicle for their fame has been the "piped" newspaper crime story, the origin of the term deriving from the location of New York police headquarters near Chinatown, where people could journey to dreamland puffing on an opium pipe.

Some of the most fanciful stories have been produced on out-of-town assignments, which provide police reporters with their greatest joy: the chance to escape police headquarters and their city rooms. There is a convenient division of labor on such jobs, whereby only one reporter covers the news sources while the rest play cards. At a given moment, all the reporters get the same facts and call their offices at the same time so that no one gets a lead on the rest. Even more importantly, expense accounts cover lavish living and allow for padding of such imaginary items as hip boots to traipse around with police in swampy areas.

According to a story often told at the Columbia University School of Journalism, in the days when New York City had a dozen-odd newspapers, police reporters were sent to New Jersey to cover a particularly important murder. After several weeks, the investigation began to peter out and the city editors started making rumbles about the reporters returning home. Faced with the loss of their journalistic vacations, the reporters came up with a ruse: One of them obtained a rusted gun that could not be traced and buried it in the backyard of a suspect. Naturally, the police were tipped off and there was a new break in the story, which kept the boys in New Jersey for another week until it was determined that the gun was not linked to the case.

It is the frequent capers of this sort that cloud the history of crime and make the serious student's task all the harder. Crime is sensational enough, bizarre enough, certainly important enough, and sometimes even entertaining enough to require no more than, as Sergeant Joe Friday used to say on TV's long-running "Dragnet" series, "Just the facts, ma'am."

A work attempting to cover the full gamut of crime in America is, of necessity, highly selective. With a mere 2,000 entries, how does one cover just murder, with 20,000 known cases a year? Only those killings that in some way have become "classics" can be recorded here. Although more words have been written on the Hall-Mills murders than on any other criminal case up to the 1920s, it remains, in essence, a singularly common crime: the murder of a married man and his paramour, to use the vocabulary of the day, while on a tryst. A sensational trial and a not-guilty verdict have given it a special niche in America's criminal history. The Snyder-Gray case also lives in our memories, even though it was another rather ordinary murder, a married woman and her lover killing the lady's husband, a crime repeated perhaps hundreds of times a year. Still, we remember Snyder-Gray not for what they were—especially Judd Gray, a particularly weak man with little inclination for killing—but for what we the public made of them. In the 1920s, the murder they committed was labeled "one of the great crimes of the century," a phrase found with monotonous regularity in tabloid headlines.

I have always paid particular attention to recording "firsts" in this work. Along with the Vikings' early acts of killing is included the case of John Billington, who was convicted of the first murder in the Plymouth colony. Also included are murders of a particularly bizarre nature or those with some important symbolic or historical relevance.

Other murder cases are included because they were trailblazers in such fields as an establishment of insanity pleas or, on a slightly more exotic level, set precedents involving murders by sleepwalkers or victims of hypnotists. The mass murderers of America are also here, including such wholesale practitioners of death as H. H. Holmes, Johann Hoch, Albert Fish, Earle Nelson, Howard Unruh, Charles Starkweather, Carl Panzram, Edmund Kemper, Richard Speck, Charles Whitman, Dean Corll, Joseph Gacy, Albert DeSalvo (the Boston Strangler), and many others—all "serial killers" before that phrase came into vogue. More recent examples of this awesome type of murderer follow later in this section.

In the Old West, it is striking to note how little separated the lawmen from the bandits; in fact, many readily and frequently passed from one role to the other. Men like Wyatt Earp and Wild Bill Hickok are presented here, warts and all—indeed, with little but warts showing. Such other folk heroes as the James brothers and Billy the Kid, examined objectively, lose the redeeming qualities often attributed to them.

Any detailed study of the public enemies in the 1930s shows most of them to have been overglamorized, with the possible exception of John Dillinger and one or two others. In the process of deglamorizing them, also inevitably deglamorized are those who built the myths around them while they ignored and indeed denied the existence and growth of an organized crime syndicate. Fame in the field of crime is fickle, sticking to some and deserting others. Today, Baron Lamm, a giant among bank robbers, is little remembered, although his influence on Dillinger, who never met him, was enormous.

Even among genuine heroes, fame can prove to be shortlived. Few Americans today recognize the name of Ed Morrell, possibly the most tortured and, later, the most respected convict in the nation's penal history. When he eventually was pardoned, a prison warden wept for joy with him. Excuses are made for

Jesse James, and the railroads that he plundered are cast as villains, but James was certainly a cold-blooded murderer. At the same time, the California Outlaws, led by such men as Morrell, Chris Evans and the Sontag brothers, are described in superficial histories as cutthroats, while the true villain of the day, the Southern Pacific Railroad, escapes censure.

Also included are important prosecutors and defense attorneys, not all Darrows perhaps, but many of them colorful, brilliant, and, in some cases, devious. In examining these practitioners of the law as well as looking at judges and police officers, the inequities in America's judicial history become apparent.

Moral judgments aside, the events and people—the killers, thieves, madams, whores, crooked and honest lawmen and judges, political bosses, syndicate gangsters, and even victims—in the annals of crime are worth studying because they are, perhaps much more than we wish to admit, reflections of ourselves and the society we have created. Certainly, the latter element is very true about the infamous financial depredations that marked the 1980s, which now has come to be recognized as the "decade of greed." Financial swindlers appeared on a scale never before seen in America—certainly neither in terms of the money grabbed nor to the extent that those conned represented the supposed business brains of the financial world. Even teenagers demonstrated the ability to gouge Wall Street.

Barry Minkow: Teenage Wolf of Wall Street

One cunning teenager who left Wall Streeters with red faces— to say nothing of flattened portfolios—was Barry Minkow, who, at the tender age of 16, launched his own rug-cleaning business in his parents' garage in Reseda, California—clearly a laudable example of a budding entrepreneur. In less than four years, the still barely postadolescent punk engineered a stock scam that conned top Wall Street firms with a bald-faced ploy no different than the classic one used by legendary swindler Charles Ponzi— that of robbing Peter to pay Paul.

Ponzi was known to his gullible victims as the "man who invented money." Barry was hailed in the financial press as the kid wonder who "invented profits." Barry did not find profits the old-fashioned way by working for them; he didn't work at it at all. Far from building up a tiny company into a financial giant worth $200 million, Barry's work ethic never produced an honest dime ever. "There was," said one Minkow biographer, "always a quality about Barry that suggested he held an MBA from the Dada School of Business."

Barry's rug-cleaning business was rather humorously called ZZZZ Best, hinting perhaps at just a bit of dreamlike quality. Even for the lowest of business ethics, young Barry trailblazed dishonest ways of raising capital. He blithely set up burglaries to collect insurance money. He hit on his grandmother for $2,000 and then stole her pearls by way of a thank-you. He also forged $13,000 worth of money orders from a liquor firm.

By such methods, ZZZZ Best soon boasted an impressive balance sheet. Then, in 1985, Barry struck it rich with an unending flow of income. He opened up a merchant's account at a local bank, which gave him the right to take credit card payments, with ready cash paid to him by the bank. Occasionally, some sharp-eyed customer noticed he was billed for something he hadn't ordered or received, and Barry responded by throwing a tantrum about crooked employees forging the slips on him. Barry then immediately coughed up refunds and blithely kited other accounts to make up the difference—and more.

This was all still relatively small potatoes for Barry, who had learned enough from his high school economics classes to know that to really make money, he had to float stock in his company. The catch was that this required an outside firm to authenticate the claims of his company's worth. Happily, there was just such a firm, named Interstate Appraisal Services, which actually was just another creation of Barry's fertile imagination. He installed as head of this bogus firm a weirdo friend who had a passion for guns, Adolf Hitler, and Nazi SS jewelry. Although Minkow was Jewish, he had no problem working with a Nazi weirdo and another odd character, a 275-pound albino who was facing charges concerning cocaine and calling himself the "ultimate white man."

Business, Barry understood, was business. And Interstate's monkey business, its only business, was confirming ZZZZ Best's contracts, which allegedly came from insurance companies to repair fire-and-water damages in large buildings. These orders had to have an air of confidentiality about them, Minkow said, because if others learned of the insurance companies' liabilities, they would be deluged with further claims.

The phony revenues attested to by Interstate convinced banks and investors to put money into ZZZZ Best. And, of course, early investors made money, since later batches of suckers paid the freight for them.

Even as late as 1986, Barry got away without having to exhibit a single site of a ZZZZ Best project. Finally, an auditor for Ernst & Whitney put his foot down, requiring authentication of the company's projects and assets. In a merry act worthy of a Marx Brothers routine, Barry and the boys leased office space and put up signs declaring that ZZZZ Best was fixing up the premises. Actually, the work was turned over to an outside contractor, who got a big bonus for doing the chores incognito—but after all, what did ZZZZ Best itself know about doing any real restoring work? The scam went over like a charm, and the auditor was pacified.

Barry's grand scam rocketed to wild success. He was idolized in newspaper stories, fussed over on Oprah Winfrey's show, and was ripe for a triumphal entrance on Wall Street. Personally he led the life of a nouveau millionaire—plus. He spent money on anything that brought him attention, such as fielding a girls' softball team and paying spectators as much as $1,000 each to cheer his players on. Barry evidently fostered a deep hatred for his parents, so he put them on the company payroll just so he could enjoy making them squirm by threatening to fire them. In his love life, he acquired a girlfriend who stayed true to him despite his constant attempts to humiliate her. Barry, with the mark of the supreme con man, knew how to pick his victims.

Of course, the best victims of all were out in that great, gullible stock market. Barry hired the securities firm of Rooney, Pace—a company destined for destruction in the aftermath of the ZZZZ Best mess—to take his company public in December 1986. In three months, fevered speculation raised the value of the shares to $64 million, and in another month, to $100 million. Then ZZZZ Best value went to $200 million—on nothing at all. When the downfall came, all that creditors and stockholders could find were assets that went for $62,000 at auction.

That downfall did not come from any discovery of the nonexistence of those big-ticket fire-and-water insurance jobs, but rather from Barry's outrageous credit card capers. His biographer, Daniel Akst, a former reporter for the *Los Angeles Times* and the *Wall Street Journal,* had early on fallen for Minkow's scam operation and had written a laudatory article in 1985 that greatly propelled the myth of Barry's acumen. But in May 1987, he unearthed the credit card skulduggery, which appeared in a story headlined: BEHIND "WHIZ KID" IS A TRAIL OF FALSE CREDIT CARD BILLINGS. The story appeared on May 22, 1987, and the next day, the shares of ZZZZ Best nose-dived 28 percent. Panic ensued, and further investigation revealed that the "kid emperor" of Wall Street had no clothes. ZZZZ Best went to zero.

Twenty-two-year-old Barry Minkow's downfall was complete in December 1988 when he was convicted on 57 counts of fraud and sentenced to 25 years in prison. *Barron's,* the financial weekly, summed up Barry Minkow's colossal con: "ZZZZ Best had earned a chapter in the long history of financial scams written by the eighties."

Dennis Levine: Inside Hustler

If a brazen youth could con supposedly savvy Wall Streeters, surely more sophisticated crooks could do far better. Dennis Levine was the first to reveal the extent of grand theft in the "Avarice is beautiful" '80s. The 33-year-old hustler broke open the 1986 Ivan Boesky scandal involving insider trading that victimized innocent stockholders. In all, millionaire hardball stock trader and arbitrageur Boesky offered to pay Levine, a whiz kid managing director of the investment banking firm of Drexel Burnham Lambert, a total of $2.4 million for his illegal stock tips. That tidy fortune hardly represented a major portion of Levine's criminal profits. Through a secret bank account in the Bahamas, he traded illegally in well over 50 stocks in his own right and accumulated $12.6 million in dirty profits, thanks to information about the companies before the public learned of it—following to the letter the definition of insider trading. Illustrative of how easily Levine made his killings were his 1985 activities in Nabisco stock. With his inside knowledge, Levine merely made two phone calls concerning the stock and strolled off with close to $3 million in booty.

Later, Levine admitted, "That was the insanity of it all. It wasn't that hard. . . . You get bolder and bolder, and it gets easier, and you make more and more money, and it feeds upon itself. And looking back . . . I realize that I was sick, that it became an addiction, that I lived for the high of making those trades, of doing the next deal, making the bigger deal."

When finally caught for securities fraud, perjury, and tax evasion, Levine gave up $11.6 million of his illicit profits and served 15 months in prison. He had gotten off with light prison time by agreeing to expose Boesky and other financial wheeler-dealers with whom he had worked.

Ivan Boesky: The "Ivan the Terrible" of Stock Deals

Ivan Boesky had, up to the time of his own exposure, been known as Ivan the Terrible, famed and feared as a high-rolling stock speculator wagering tens of millions on risky security deals. Boesky arrived on Wall Street in 1966, the son of Russian immigrants from Detroit, having graduated from law school four years earlier. After a stint with an investment firm and then a brokerage house, Boesky jumped into arbitrage, risking huge sums by buying and selling stocks that were about to be merged or taken over by other companies. When he accumulated $700,000, he launched his own arbitrage firm. In a little over a decade, Boesky's worth skyrocketed to about $2 billion, little of it acquired legally.

He was now one of the most important men in financial America, sporting a 200-acre estate and 10-bedroom mansion in affluent Westchester County and maintaining a lavish Manhattan apartment from which he directed many of his deals. Boesky paid handsomely for insider tips, making a fortune on those supplied by Levine until the latter was nailed by the government and sought to save himself by informing on others, especially Boesky.

Now, like Levine, Boesky desperately sought a deal with the government to nail yet other Wall Street crooks. Boesky agreed to pay a penalty of $100 million for violation of security laws. Ivan the Terrible cooperated with investigators by allowing them to tape his telephone conversations as he carried out trading shenanigans. It was a sting operation that caused numerous heads to roll; Drexel, one of the most powerful financial institutions on Wall Street, plummeted to virtual collapse.

In the end, Boesky was rewarded with a light, three-year prison term. Boesky insisted he was "deeply ashamed" of his acts, but numerous observers noted that the $100 million penalty, although up to then the largest of its type in history, hardly dented his wealth. It appeared that Boesky had driven a hard bargain with the government, even though it was likely that after his release, Boesky figured to find his fortune under steady attack by ex-partner and shareholder lawsuits.

Michael Milken: King of the Junk Bonds

What Ivan Boesky proved in the end was that he was hardly even close to being the biggest crook in American finance. Specifically, Boesky could point to Michael R. Milken, the

Michael Milken, "king of the junk bonds," was forced to give back well over $1 billion in fines and restitution but remained a millionaire.

"junk bond" chief at Drexel, who was nailed through Boesky's cooperation.

Milken had risen to fame as the main force creating the huge market for junk bonds, the high-yield, high-risk debt securities that marked the corporate takeover boom of the 1980s. Milken did not go down easily, spending an estimated $1 million a month for several years fighting the federal government's case against him. He finally reversed his tactics and pleaded guilty in 1990 to six felony counts involving securities fraud and agreed to pay the lion's share of a cash settlement by himself and his cohorts, which was eventually fixed at $1.3 billion in fines and restitution costs to settle claims by fraud victims.

Still, there were those who objected to the deal, insisting that Milken had forced the government to drop the more serious charges of racketeering and insider trading. They also complained about his being allowed to keep about $125 million of his personal fortune. In addition, his immediate family maintained more than $300 million in assets, meaning that the settlement could leave the convicted junk bond king something like $5 billion. Milken drew a ten-year prison term, with sentencing Judge Kimba M. Wood declaring, "When a man of your power in the financial world, at the head of one of the most important investment banking houses in this country, repeatedly conspires to violate, and violates, securities and tax laws in order to achieve more power and wealth for himself and his wealthy clients, and commits financial crimes that are particularly hard to detect, a significant prison term is required in order to deter others." Nevertheless, Milken could win parole after serving only one-third of the sentence.

Jake Butcher: The $700 Million Bank Man

While some legal experts have insisted that the Milken prison sentence is "too severe," it hardly matches the term given Jacob "Jake" Franklin Butcher, a former Democratic candidate for governor of Tennessee and organizer of the 1982 World's Fair in Knoxville. Considered a respected figure in Tennessee banking circles, Butcher defrauded his own banks (he controlled 26 in Tennessee and Kentucky) of millions of dollars so that many of them failed and went bankrupt. Butcher's depredations, which financed his flamboyant life-style—such as the purchase of such high-priced "toys" as a 60-foot yacht for a mere $400,000— ended up costing the Federal Deposit Insurance Corporation (FDIC) well over $700 million, with Butcher and his wife having personal debits of more than $200 million.

It was said at the time that by his actions alone, Butcher had destroyed the deep-held faith that people had put in their banks since the reforms of the 1930s. The public grasped clearly the threats to their banks and savings and that they would have to pay for FDIC losses through their taxes. As a result, there was universal praise for the sentence imposed on Butcher—two 20-year concurrent terms, the maximum allowed.

Charles Keating, Jr.: The $2.6 Billion Savings and Loan Con Man

The Butcher case and the Wall Street insider trading mess set the stage for the burgeoning savings and loan scandal that hit

Charles Keating, Jr., caused the greatest of all savings and loans cons, shaking the Senate establishment with his huge political contributions, in return for expected favors.

the nation's finances in the late 1980s, highlighted by the case of Charles H. Keating, Jr., and its subsequent exposure of the U.S. Senate's so-called Keating Five. No case outraged the American public more than the reports of unfettered S&L officials living high on the hog with depositors' and investors' money. What clearly upset the public was not only that Keating could engage in the financial finagling that would eventually cost the taxpayers some $2.6 billion but that, thanks to his political contributions, Keating was able to enlist the aid of five U.S. senators in a questionable meeting with bank examiners on his behalf. The five senators were Alan Cranston of California, John Glenn of Ohio, Donald W. Riegle of Michigan, and Dennis DeConcini of Arizona, all Democrats, and John McCain of Arizona, Republican.

Keating had started out in 1984 by having American Continental, which he had formed, buy up the Lincoln Savings and Loan of California for $51 million. Two years later, in March 1986, the Federal Home Loan Bank in San Francisco began an examination of Lincoln's rapid growth by way of wild investment activities. Within a couple of months, examiners were asking Washington officials to crack down on Lincoln for its peculiar accounting and loan procedures. But by November 1986, the five U.S. senators were meeting with the examiners on behalf of free-contributing Keating. Thus, it was not until May 1987 that examiners finally were able to recommend that the S&L be seized.

Nothing happened for almost another year until finally, on April 13, 1989, American Continental filed for bankruptcy, its millions in junk bonds now worthless. Many Lincoln investors had been misled into thinking the junk bonds were government insured. By now it was apparent that the bailout would cost $2.6 billion, the most expensive in history.

In February 1991, the Senate Ethics Committee announced a "verdict" on the Keating Five, stating there was "substantial credible evidence" of misconduct by Senator Cranston (which resulted later in a severe rebuke from the Senate). Riegle and DeConcini were found to have given the appearance of impropriety, but no further action was taken against them, and Glenn and McCain were criticized less severely.

After a four-month trial concluding in December 1991, Keating was convicted of securities fraud and was sentenced by a Los Angeles judge to ten years in prison and fined $250,000, a punishment that drew cheers from Keating victims present in the court. With federal charges still pending and Keating still facing many civil lawsuits, the case figures to be on the front pages for some years yet.

Rev. Jim Bakker: "Praise the Lord" for Suckers

If bankers and Wall Streeters represented the unbridled greed in the 1980s, their activities were matched in some televangelist circles—and most particularly in the hectic sexual and Ponzi-like schemes of the Reverend Jim Bakker. Bakker had built up a

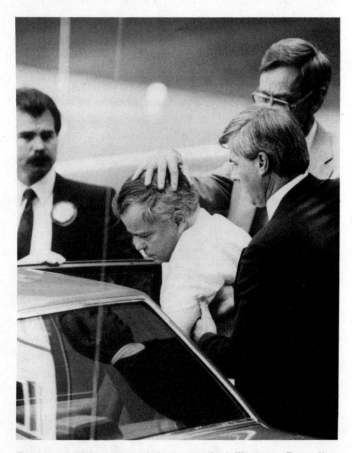

Besides being exposed for sexual dalliances, Rev. Jim Bakker was sentenced to 45 years for fraud and conspiracy, and was denounced by the judge who said the public was "sick of being saps for money-grubbing preachers."

vast television network that reached over 13 million American household, the PTL (for Praise the Lord, or People That Love).

It was a sexual dalliance that precipitated Bakker's downfall. In December 1980, the youthful-looking Bakker had met a 21-year-old comely brunette named Jessica Hahn, a secretary at a Pentecostal church in Massapequa, New York, during a visit to Clearwater, Florida. At the time, Bakker's 19-year marriage to his wife, Tammy Faye, who co-hosted his religious television show, was having a rough going. Bakker and Hahn had sex, and to hear Hahn tell of it, she suffered great emotional distress as a result of the encounter. In any event, her pain and suffering were so great that $265,000 was to be paid to her as compensation for her silence.

Bakker's secret remained safe for a time; the story was eventually broken in the *Charlotte* (N.C.) *Observer*, a newspaper near the headquarters of the PTL network. As well as loosening gossipy tongues, the scandal triggered an investigation on the whereabouts of the PTL ministry's assets. In addition to the television show featuring Jim and Tammy Faye, the PTL empire included Heritage USA, a Christian resort complex and amusement park in Fort Mill, South Carolina. In the PTL's peak year, the ministry took in $129 million, and in the recent few years, it had garnered $158 million by offering promises of lifetime vacations—which Bakker could not provide. Instead, huge sums were diverted to the couple, which allowed the Bakkers to live in opulence. In March 1987, Bakker was forced to resign his ministry and later was charged with fraud and conspiracy. At his trial (with Tammy Faye—by now regarded as something of an American original—vowing to stand by her man), a former reservation supervisor at Heritage USA said that in the last year of Bakker's regime at PTL, between 1,300 and 3,700 lifetime contributors had been turned away every month from lodgings that had been promised but did not exist.

Bakker was convicted on all 24 counts charged against him and was sentenced to 45 years in prison and fined $500,000. He would not be eligible for parole for 10 years. In passing sentence, U.S. District Judge Robert Potter said, "Those of us who do have religion are sick of being saps for money-grubbing preachers and priests. I just feel like there was massive fraud here, and it's going to have to be punished."

Once again, Tammy Faye promised to stand by her man, but she later filed for divorce and planned to marry a businessman who likewise divorced his wife. In the meantime, Hahn had appeared on the cover of *Playboy* magazine and was paid an estimated $750,000 for a photo display and an interview in which she informed readers that "I'm not a bimbo." She later devoted her talents to hosting a late-night show advising viewers via special 800 numbers how to find "love."

Until about 1970, perpetrators of such white-collar financial crimes seldom went to prison, as their activities were not regarded as akin to the acts of a criminal with a gun, but this policy changed with the verdict that prison sentences might deter others from similar activities.

One youthful fraud operator, Cortes Randell, who, like Barry Minkow, rode a stock with little or no assets into the share price stratosphere, got eight months in Allenwood federal prison. This did not prove to be a discouragement, because he soon launched another financial fraud—during his prison stay. Along with a deputy assistant secretary of labor, Randell sold unregistered securities and used fake financial statements to get loans. Randell got a seven-year term for that one.

In 1991, the CBS news program "60 Minutes" reported that Dennis Levine of the insider-trading scandals of the 1980s had, after his release from prison, introduced clients of his newly formed consulting business to con men, supposedly to help them in financial deals. Among those Levine vouched for, the program said, was a former fellow prisoner who had done time with him in Lewisburg penitentiary in Pennsylvania. Levine told "60 Minutes" that he had not informed clients about the man's past, saying he would have been "a hypocrite" to make such a disclosure, considering his own record. Several Levine clients indicated they had paid money to people recommended by Levine but had received no aid in return. Levine insisted that the CBS report was "unbalanced," and that he was trying to change his reputation since finishing his prison term. Indeed, he was spending much time lecturing business school students on ethics.

Danny Ferris: Con Game from a Prison Cell

Perhaps the classic case of the failure of prison as a cure for con men was offered on another 1991 "60 Minutes" exposé, in what the media has dubbed the "nationwide jailhouse shopping network." This scam of scams was thought up by Danny Ferris, a notorious crook doing time for murder. For more than four years, Ferris made local and free 800 calls from a phone placed in his cell in Miami's Dade County jail, which was legally required to provide inmates with telephone access.

Ferris ordered all sorts of merchandise over the phone, an estimated $2 million worth, using credit card numbers that had been retrieved from hotel trash and the like. He then had the goods sent to accomplices on the outside who sold the loot and split the profits with Ferris. Ferris ordered in wholesale lots such items as camcorders, Rolex watches, gourmet gift baskets, gold and silver coins, and champagne.

Later, he said, "I split right half with everybody. I mean, I never took more than half. I got robbed a lot, but again, you kind of take it on the chin. You know what I mean? It was like you said, 'Heck, it was all free.' "

Embarrassed jail officials, stymied that they could not legally deprive Ferris of his telephone rights, staged raids on his cell and confiscated hundreds of credit card numbers. Unfortunately, he retained one number and used that to place a newspaper ad and a telephone answering service number in *USA Today*, offering $89.95 worth of cosmetics for a mere $19.95. Orders came in to an 800 number, but no cosmetics were ever shipped out. Still, Ferris got what he was after—a new batch of credit card numbers.

Eventually, he got five years for credit card fraud tacked on to his previous life term, and he was transferred to a tougher state prison, which controlled his telephone call habit. But, meanwhile, back at the Dade County jail, other inmates were engaging in Ferris's routine, one operating from the master's old cell. Finally, jail officials removed in-cell telephones, requiring pris-

oners to make all calls in open corridors, and it remained to be seen if the Danny Ferris legacy could really be squashed.

Serial Killers: Murder for Recreation

If finagling in the financial field produces an endless supply of incorrigible con men, the annals of murder provide a seemingly deadly parade of "serial killers," a term that came into being in the early 1980s, with the notorious Theodore Bundy generally regarded as being the "godfather" of them all. As stated earlier in this introduction, up until then, we were limited to the term "mass murderers" to describe the wholesale practitioners of death. In an effort to categorize serial killers, researchers have come up with numerous theories or behavior patterns in such murderers. The true serial killers, say experts, are "recreational killers," for whom profit or sexual motives do not exist or are of minor consequence. They butcher their victims at random, literally for the "sport" of killing. Only about 10 percent of serial killers are "social killers," that is, operating with one or more accomplices in either the same or mixed sexual groupings.

More importantly, we are told, is the fact that serial killers— far more than their counterparts among average murderers— have histories of aberrant symptoms in their childhood behavior, such as persistent bed-wetting, arson, and cruelty to pets and other animals. However, as psychologists have pointed out, human behaviors and character traits are usually well set between the ages of two and five. To expect society to mobilize for a war on serial killers on the basis of such theories demands too much of the criminal justice system and especially of the police, whose ability to investigate strong serial killer hints is woeful, to say the least. When parents of youths who turned out to be victims of Dean Corll, an infamous serial killer of the 1970s, complained to Houston, Texas, police by the dozens that their sons were missing, the force took no pains investigating, simply informing the worried relatives that the boys had probably run off and "joined those hippies in California." Before he was himself killed, Corll proceeded to kill at least 27 victims—with the Houston police blissfully unaware of a mass murderer loose in the city.

Jeffrey Dahmer: The Underinvestigated Killer

Similarly, in a more recent case, 31-year-old Jeffrey L. Dahmer was convicted in February 1992 of the murder of 15 young men and boys (plus another one in a later prosecution), most of them killed right in his apartment. Once again, far from being on the alert for a serial killer as more and more young people disappeared, the Milwaukee police did nothing to catch Dahmer early on—and actually were subjected to national outrage as being virtually guilty themselves of ignorant complicity *before* the fact! In one case, a Dahmer victim escaped naked and bloodied from the killer's apartment and raced screaming into the street. Three police officers who "investigated" simply decided the matter was no more than a quarrel between gay lovers and turned the victim back over to Dahmer without so much as checking out his apartment. Dahmer took his victim in tow and

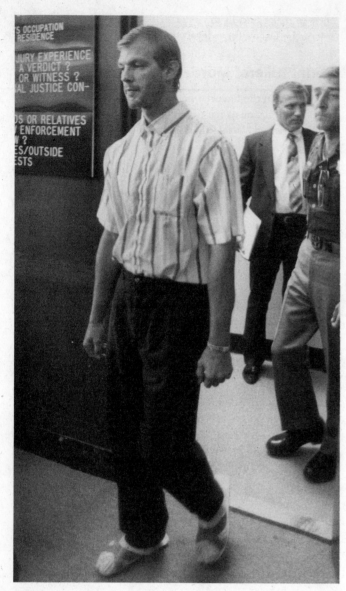

Jeffrey Dahmer, killer of 16 young men and boys, was actually caught once by Milwaukee police but was inexplicably let go.

butchered him a few hours later. It was charged that if the victim had been white, rather than a member of a minority—in this case, a Laotian—the police would have been more competent in their investigation.

Meanwhile, Dahmer went on luring victims to his home, drugging them, killing them, and then dismembering their bodies. In some cases, he attempted to perform primitive lobotomies on his victims by drilling holes in their heads in an effort to make them into zombie-like sex slaves. Dahmer also engaged in frightful practices of cannibalism and necrophilia, descriptions of which are best left for medical texts.

Ted Bundy: The Handsome Monster

In many cases, and certainly in the cases of both Corll and Dahmer, the serial killer has the behavior patterns of a "creep,"

in the descriptions of neighbors. In other instances, however, the serial killer comes across much differently. Ted Bundy seemed atypical, judging by the general perception of a serial killer as a "human monster." As one journalist noted: "The moment he stepped into the courtroom in Utah . . . those who saw him for the first time agreed with those who had known him for all of his twenty-eight years: There must have been some terrible mistake."

It was no mistake, as Robert Keppel, an expert who had worked on serial killer investigations, noted: "Bundy [later] said he had a Ph.D. in serial killing. He taught us that a serial killer can appear to be absolutely normal, the guy next door. It's very simple: He liked to kill."

Ted Bundy was to leave a scar on the American psyche from 1974 to 1989, when he finally was executed in Florida. His first batch of kills, eight of them, started in 1974 as the young women disappeared from Seattle streets. They had been lured into a beige Volkswagen by a presentable young man named Ted. A police computer search turned up nearly 3,000 owners of light-colored Volkswagens in Seattle, and Bundy's name cropped up among them. But while many were questioned and checked on, Bundy was not. Why should he have

Serial killer Ted Bundy conducted a large part of his own legal defense.

been? He was of impeccable character, with numerous good points:

- He had worked as a counselor at a crisis clinic.
- He had become an assistant director of the Seattle Crime Prevention Advisory Commission.
- He had written a rape prevention pamphlet for women.
- He had gotten a letter of commendation from the governor of Washington for once capturing a purse snatcher in a shopping mall.

Bundy was very active in the Republican party and won the title of Mr. Up-and-Coming Republican. A former state party chairman who knew Bundy well and recruited him as his assistant said: "If you can't trust someone like Ted Bundy, you can't trust anyone—your parents, your wife, anyone."

Presumably, Seattle lost a fine resource when Bundy left the city and moved on to Salt Lake City and became a Mormon. The killings went with him.

Bundy's first arrest came in October 1975 when a 19-year-old woman identified him in a police lineup as the man who had tried to handcuff her and pull her into his car one night in Murray, Utah. Bundy had been picked up for a traffic violation, and when handcuffs were found in the car, police thought back to the attempted kidnapping of the young woman. Bundy was convicted in the case and given a one- to fifteen-year prison sentence. While the case was pending, police in Colorado became convinced Bundy had murdered Caryn Campbell, a nurse who had been vacationing in Aspen almost a year earlier. Campbell had been missing for five weeks before her body turned up in a snowbank. She had been raped, bludgeoned to death, and then ravaged by wild animals almost beyond recognition.

Bundy was extradited to Colorado but was never to stand trial for the Campbell murder. Instead he escaped twice. The first break occurred when Bundy was alone in a room in the county courthouse in Aspen. He jumped from a second-story window and disappeared, not to be recaptured until a week later. Although Bundy was being charged with a vile crime, his exploit made him a folk hero in some quarters, a bizarre public reaction that would resurface on future occasions. Six months later, still awaiting trial, Bundy outwitted his jailers again, this time wiggling through a lighting panel in the ceiling of his cell. The opening was only 18 inches wide, and in order to make good his escape, Bundy had managed to trim down 35 pounds.

While authorities pressed their search for the fugitive, Bundy made his way across the country to Tallahassee, Florida. Using a phony name and stolen cars and credit cards, he moved into a rooming house on the outskirts of Florida State University. The lodging was just four blocks from the Chi Omega sorority house.

Less than two weeks after making it to Florida, Bundy invaded the sorority house. He was dressed in black and carried a heavy wooden club. Two coeds were to die in the house. They were found to have been gnawed badly, but unlike Campbell, they bore bite marks not from wild animals but from their wild *human* attacker. Particularly gnawed up was Lisa Levy, who bore teeth marks on one of her breasts and on her buttocks. She had been beaten, bitten, and strangled to death in her bed. Another

sorority sister, Margaret Bowman, met the same grisly fate. The bite marks, investigators realized, were appalling evidence of the killer's rampaging fervor at the moment of the kills.

Levy and Bowman were not the only victims in the Chi Omega house that night. Another coed was also attacked and beaten unconscious, but she recovered.

Meanwhile, Bundy moved on like a wraith in the night, and six blocks farther on, a young actress was beaten and raped in her bed. She also survived but could offer no description of her attacker.

During the ensuing investigation, several residents in Bundy's rooming house became suspects in the case, although Bundy did not. He evidently was considered a cut above the rest. At the time, the fact that Bundy had very crooked teeth went unnoticed but would be noted later on.

Three weeks after the sorority house invasion, Bundy stole a white van and drove to Jacksonville, where he attempted to abduct a 14-year-old girl. He was forced to drive off when the girl's brother appeared. The brother and sister were quick enough to make a note of the van's license plate.

Three days later, 12-year-old Kimberly Leach disappeared from her Lake City junior high school in the middle of the day. Her corpse was not found for two months. When it was found, Kimberly was described as having been the victim of "homicidal violence to the neck region."

By now, police in Washington State, Utah, Colorado, and Florida were coming to grasp that a *single* killer was responsible for at least 18 murders in their areas. Bundy had been the prime suspect in the Campbell murder in Colorado, and he was now being sought for many others as well. He moved on to Pensacola, driving yet another stolen VW and unaware that the FBI had just listed him on its Ten Most Wanted list. The car Bundy was driving was recognized by police as a stolen vehicle, and he was seized as he tried to flee on foot. At first, the police did not know whom they had caught, as Bundy gave a false name. But they did know that the suspect was someone to be regarded as being involved in other cases as well: They found the plates from the van in which the driver had tried to abduct the 14-year-old Jacksonville girl.

Thirty-six hours after Bundy's arrest, he was identified. The authorities had hit the jackpot!

Florida authorities charged Bundy with the murders of Lisa Levy and Margaret Bowman. An impression made of Bundy's teeth showed that his crooked bite marks matched perfectly with those found on Lisa Levy's buttocks.

Bundy pleaded not guilty for the Chi Omega murders and became celebrated again by those with a twisted maudlin viewpoint when, as an ex-law student, he conducted part of his own defense. It took the jury just seven hours to find Bundy guilty on a variety of counts. The teeth bite evidence was the most damning, but in addition, a hair in the panty hose mask worn during the attack of the actress the same night as the sorority house killings was found to be indistinguishable from Bundy's.

When asked if he had anything to say before sentencing, Bundy, with tears in his eyes, declared: "I find it somewhat absurd to ask for mercy for something I did not do. The sentence is not a sentence of me. It's a sentence of someone who is not standing here today."

Bundy's mother was quoted as saying, "There will be appeal after appeal after appeal."

Even the judge exhibited a certain sympathy for Bundy when passing the death sentence; and then, in a bizarre way, he reinforced Bundy's near folk-hero image by saying: "Take care of yourself, young man. I say that to you sincerely. It's a tragedy to this court to see such a total waste of humanity. You'd have made a good lawyer. I bear you no animosity, believe me. But you went the wrong way, partner. Take care of yourself."

On a radio talk show, one commentator wondered if the judge would have been just as proud to have Bundy give his daughter driving lessons.

A year later, Bundy was convicted of the murder of Kimberly Leach, whose body had been found half-buried near a state park. The van he had been driving at the time contained leaves and soil matching samples near the burial site. Also, bloodstains in the van matched the blood type of the murdered girl.

There were a number of appeals put forward by Bundy. In the process, he accumulated a large body of people who felt he was innocent, including a number of lawyers and journalists who had followed the trials.

The string ran out at last for Bundy in early 1989. In a final interview, Bundy confessed to a total of 28 additional murders. On the night of his electrocution, there were 100 newspeople circulating the crowd assembled outside the prison. It was one of a few cases where those favoring execution far outnumbered those opposed. Signs raised in celebration bore messages such as BUCKLE UP, BUNDY. IT'S THE LAW and ROAST IN PEACE.

Douglas Clark: The "Sunset Slayer"

Ted Bundy was to leave his mark in the chronicles of serial killings in many ways, particularly as an inspiration to "copy-cat" criminals. It is apparent that a sometime factory worker named Douglas Daniel Clark—the "Sunset Slayer"—had been much impressed by Bundy's murder spree and sought to imitate it. His murders, often in company of his lover, Carol Mary Bundy, started in 1980 and were far more ghoulish than those of his role model.

Calling himself the "king of the one-night stands," he dated either women older than himself or young girls between the ages of 10 and 15. However, sexual liaisons, even kinky ones, hardly sated his desires, which ran to dark reflections on rape, mutilation, murder, and necrophilia. In 1980, Clark met Carol Bundy, a vocational nurse in Burbank, who at age 37 was a half-dozen years older than he, and she became a willing partner in his gruesome activities. When their game turned deadly, Carol cruised the Sunset Strip looking for prostitutes—with a strong preference for blondes—for Clark to murder and *then* engage in depraved sexual acts. Clark and Carol rang up about ten known murders in this fashion; at times, the heads of their decapitated victims were stored in a refrigerator for later gory fun and games. In one case, Carol later confessed making up one face

with cosmetics, saying, "We had a lot of fun with her. I washed her up like a Barbie with makeup."

Typical of Clark's killings were those of two half-sisters, 16-year-old Cynthia Chandler and 15-year-old Gina Narano, who vanished from a beach. They were later found on the side of the Ventura Freeway in Los Angeles, each shot in the head. Gleefully, Clark described to Carol how he had forced sex with the girls before killing them.

Carol clearly had become a murder slave for Clark, a fairly common occurrence for female consorts of serial killers, but she was also responsible for his eventual capture. In the past, she had had a romantic attachment with an apartment house super-intendent and part-time singer in country and western bars, John Robert Murray. In a date with Murray after her murderous involvement with Clark, a liquored-up Carol let too much slip out about Clark and their doings. Murray said he might well go to the police about it all, a prospect that threw Carol into a panic. On August 5, 1980, she set up a midnight rendezvous with Murray in his van near the bar where he was doing a gig. She shot him in the head. Murray's body turned up four days later with nine stab wounds and deep slashes across the but-tocks. The head was missing, removed by Carol and Clark to prevent any ballistics identification.

Two days after the discovery of the corpse, Carol sank into a state of depression, crying out on her job to another nurse, "I can't take it anymore. I'm supposed to save lives, not take them." Her co-worker reported her comments to the police, who arrested Carol and in a search of her home found shocking pictures involving Clark and young girls. Clark was arrested at his job, where police found a pistol that ballistics tests linked to five of the known victims of the Sunset Slayer.

According to Carol, Clark claimed he had killed at least 50 young women both before and after meeting her and that he hoped to hit 100 before he was inevitably caught.

At his trial, Clark tried to shift the Sunset slayings to Carol and victim Murray, claiming it was they who were ardent fans of Ted Bundy. The jury believed otherwise. Clark was sentenced to death and joined the growing list of condemned waiting for years for the resumption of executions in California. Carol Bundy first claimed insanity but then admitted her part in some of the slayings, including that of John Murray, and was sen-tenced to a total of 52 years in prison.

Bianchi and Buono: The "Hillside Strangler" Duo

If the Sunset Slayer was a member of a Ted Bundy admiration society, it is equally true that the West Coast's "Hillside Strangler" drew his—or, more accurately, their—inspiration from Caryl Chessman, California's notorious "Red Light Ban-dit" of the 1940s. Chessman's modus operandi was to approach couples parked in lonely spots, flashing a red light resembling that on a police car. He robbed the drivers and sometimes took off with the women and forced them to perform sexual acts with him.

Chessman never killed his victims, but the Hillside Strangler murdered ten women starting in 1977. What prevented the police from catching him sooner was the fact that the Hillside Strangler was not one man but two—cousins Kenneth Bianchi, born in 1952, and the older Angelo Buono, Jr., born in 1935. At times, they killed together, and at others, separately. They first planned out their murder rampage after a long drinking bout in which they speculated how it would feel to kill someone. (There may have been some modesty here, as to this day, it is not clear if actually one or both had previously committed murders on their own.) Both decided that Chessman's method of pretending to be a law officer was the perfect way to grab women.

Their technique was to stop women motorists or streetwalkers, flash badges, demand identification, and force them into their car, supposedly an undercover police vehicle. The women were invariably raped, sodomized, and then strangled to death. Most of the bodies were left in spots where they were certain to be found. The bodies were generally washed cleaned—apparently on Buono's planning—so as to leave no clues for the police to follow.

After a while, Bianchi decided a change of scenery was called for, and he moved up to the state of Washington, where, in Bellingham, he procured work as a security guard. Eventually, he was linked to the murders of two young women who had been lured by him to investigate a nonexistent house-sitting job. A search of Bianchi's home turned up evidence tying him to the killings, and cooperation with California authorities linked him to at least five Hillside Strangler slayings. Fearful of a possible death penalty in Washington State, Bianchi offered to identify his cousin as the "real" Hillside Strangler. Based on Bianchi's evidence, Buono was convicted in 1983 of nine murders. Despite Buono's care in always fixing up the death scene after one of the pair's murders—he always cleaned his home after Bianchi left so that no fingerprints of any victims were found—a meticulous scientific search turned up a single eyelash from one of the dead. Also, some strands of fiber from a chair in Buono's home were discovered on one body.

One witness in the Buono trial was 27-year-old Catherine Lorre, who identified the two cousins as the men who had stopped her on a Hollywood street in the late 1970s and demanded identification. She had produced her driver's license, next to which was a picture of herself as a little girl sitting on the lap of her proud father, actor Peter Lorre. Bianchi testified that he decided not to try to ensnare her, for fear that murdering the daughter of a celebrity might produce too much heat on the homicidal partners.

Buono was sentenced to nine terms of life imprisonment without parole, while Bianchi was returned to Washington State to a life sentence with no possibility of parole before 2005.

Like several other serial murderers, the Hillside Strangler— or at least Bianchi—also did manage a romantic liaison with a woman drawn to him because of his crimes, such as Carol Bundy was to Douglas Clark. While Bianchi was in California prior to Buono's trial, a 23-year-old poet and aspiring playwright named Veronica Lynn Compton sought Bianchi's opinion of her new play about a female serial killer. Correspondence and conversa-

tions followed, which revealed how close Veronica's tastes came to serial killing. Bianchi then concocted a plan to spring him from his own guilty verdict in the Bellingham murders by having Veronica strangle a woman and leave specimens of Bianchi's semen at the scene to convince authorities that the real killer was still at large.

Compton visited Bianchi in prison and got from him a book in which he had hidden part of a rubber glove containing his semen. Compton went to Bellingham and attempted a murder but botched the job. She was convicted and was sent to prison with no hope of parole before 1994. For a time, she continued to correspond with Bianchi, but finally her ardor for him cooled, and she shifted to a correspondence with Douglas Clark, then in San Quentin waiting execution as the Sunset Slayer. A typical ghoulish passage in one letter to Clark read: "Our humor is unusual. I wonder why others don't see the necrophilic aspects of existence as we do."

In July 1988, Veronica escaped from the women's prison at Gig Harbor, Washington, and disappeared.

Perhaps the most perplexing serial killer of all has been Henry Lee Lucas, now under death sentence in Texas for the murder of a female hitchhiker. How many people has Lucas killed? The estimates are controversial, especially since he kept escalating his own claims, as he confessed to killing 50, 75, 100, 150, 360, and then finally 500.

In 1960, at the age of 23, Lucas started a 20- to 40-year sentence for murdering his mother in Tecumseh, Michigan. Part of his term was spent in a hospital for the criminally insane, but he was paroled in 1970. He was promptly charged with kidnapping two teenage girls and went back to state prison, being paroled in 1975. Lucas went west, killing a number of people—the exact count is in dispute—dumping bodies in canyons and riverbeds, and on open prairies.

Late in 1976, Lucas teamed up with another serial killer, Ottis Elwood Toole, whom he had met in a Florida soup kitchen. Ironically, both men at first viewed the other as a potential murder victim, but each soon came to realize they had so much in common and could accomplish so much more as a murderous duo. According to statements by both men, they crisscrossed the country on an unending death spree. Eventually, they returned to Florida where they picked up Toole's nephew, Frank Powell, and his ten-year-old niece, Becky Powell.

The quartet hit the road, and the awesome acts Frank Powell witnessed proved enough to send him to a mental institution in 1983. The foursome broke up in 1982 with Toole and a shaken Powell returning to Florida while Lucas and Becky moved on together. The young girl never lived to be 15. Two years after they first met, Lucas stabbed her to death, at times saying it was because she slapped him and at others admitting to attempting to have sex with her. At that point, Lucas was living with casual acquaintances and simply shrugged that the girl had run off with a truck driver.

Lucas was taken into custody in 1983 by police as an ex-convict charged with possession of a handgun. After four nights in jail, Lucas announced, "I've done some bad things." And the confessions spewed out, ever escalating.

It's anybody's guess—including Lucas's—how many murders he committed. He did lead authorities in various states to a great number of corpses. Officially, Lucas has only been convicted of five murders, with about two dozen pending. Most of his claims have been denounced as "hoaxes," but some law enforcement officers remain convinced he killed in excess of a hundred victims. Unfortunately, Lucas's killing mate, Toole, can hardly be a source for reliable confirmation, since many of his own claims to murders he committed have proved to be lies. He claimed to have killed—gruesomely—six-year-old Adam Walsh, whose story was later filmed in the movie *Adam*. Most lawmen discount his confession. In another instance, Toole admitted to having killed a woman in Colorado Springs. When police disputed his story, he shrugged, "Okay, if you say I didn't kill her, maybe I didn't."

It is quite possible that neither Lucas nor Toole know where their real acts ended and their fantasies of murders they so wanted to commit began. How many murders did Toole, now serving 20 years in Florida, commit? The easy answer is many; the hard answer is how many.

The "Green River Killer": The One They Couldn't Catch

Quite possibly the most prolific unidentified serial killer is the "Green River Killer," so called because the 49 victims attributed to him (or her) were dumped in or near Washington State's Green River. All the victims died starting on January 21, 1982, when 16-year-old Leann Wilcox of Tacoma was found strangled eight miles from Seattle. Then, in the fall of 1984, the parade of corpses abruptly stopped. There have been no further attributable Green River killings since then, but a law enforcement Green River Task Force has remained in place to find the killer. The force has, to date, been unsuccessful but has in the process solved 7 unrelated murders and 3 rapes. For some time before his execution, Ted Bundy was used as an adviser to the task force, but he contributed little and was clearly motivated by a desire to postpone his own death sentence.

Why did the Green River Killer stop? Some have speculated that he died or was in prison or a mental institution, his crimes unsuspected. Another theory held by a number of authorities was that he simply moved elsewhere. These experts note that in 1985, a series of murders started in San Diego, California, that seemed related to the Green River cases. The number attributed to the unknown San Diego serial killer ranged from 10 to perhaps 18 at recent count. This would raise the combined toll to anywhere from 59 to 67.

Serial Killer Death Toll: 3,500 a Year

That number is, sadly, hardly outlandish. According to an FBI estimate, of the 5,000 murder victims whose killers are not apprehended each year, at least 3,500 are believed to be the victims of serial killers. This would allow for a great many Green River types on the loose. Some observers believe we are in the midst of an "epidemic of homicidal mania," and they point

especially to the barbarity of the crimes committed. However, the crimes committed by mass murderers of an earlier era, such as at the turn of the century, were probably equally as gruesome. What has changed is the loss of inhibitions by the media in reporting the bizarre sexual practices of the serial killers. Oddly, the Victorian era eschewed such frightful details but allowed descriptions of cannibalism only—which was presumably considered rather "nonsexual."

Today, we also accept the media's description of recent murders as "crimes of the century," so much so that we can embrace one or more annually. Actually, some murders achieve this status because of the social significance attached to the particular crime.

Jean Harris: "He Done Her Wrong"

Certain cases rise little above the level of the tawdry in their bare facts but take on special import because of the role they play in the social attitudes affecting the American scene. Many crime aficionados would eschew Jean Harris's murder of famous "Scarsdale Diet" doctor Herman Tarnower as hardly a major event in the annals of homicide. She shot him, made no real effort to escape, was easily apprehended, and insisted it was an accident

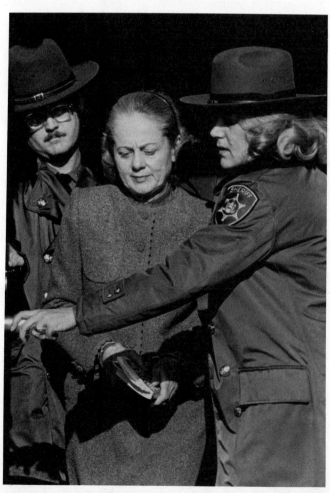

The case of Jean Harris's murder of the famous "Scarsdale Diet" doctor, Herman Tarnower, energized many women in their demands for social equality in court.

Dr. Tarnower's best-seller was said by authorities to have greatly increased his ability to attract female admirers, much to Jean Harris's anger.

in a lover's quarrel. However, the Harris-Tarnower case had an important impact on the nation's views, occurring as it did on the tide of rising female expectations and demands for social equality with men. For decades, legal verdicts in cases where men had killed unfaithful wives or lovers in the "heat of the moment" were seldom harsh at the hands of courts and juries. Jean Harris represented fair turnaround, or, as one female put it in a switch on a popular refrain, "He done her wrong."

On March 10, 1980, Dr. Tarnower, the 69-year-old cardiologist and author of the best-selling book *The Complete Scarsdale Medical Diet,* which brought him millions, was shot and killed in the bedroom of his luxurious home in Purchase, New York. The police were summoned by the Tarnower maid and picked up 56-year-old Jean S. Harris before she drove away.

Harris, a cultured woman and headmistress of the exclusive Madeira School for Girls in McLean, Virginia, had had a torrid love affair with Tarnower for 14 years. Known to her students as Integrity Harris, she had spent many weekends and vacations with the doctor and had helped him in the writing of his book. Over the years, Tarnower had spoken often of marriage to Harris but had even called off an impending wedding on one occasion. During the years, Harris had shut her eyes to the more than 30 relationships Tarnower had maintained with other women, and she had tolerated other women's nightclothes, underwear, cosmetics, and the like, which littered the Tarnower bedroom.

But it was Mrs. Lynne Tryforos, 18 years younger than Harris, whom the headmistress came to regard as her main threat. The pair carried on a fierce struggle for the doctor's affections, cutting up each other's clothes, and Harris accused Tryforos of making obscene phone calls. Harris contemplated plastic surgery to regain the doctor's affections.

Just a few days before Tarnower's death, Harris mailed him a letter from Virginia, calling Tryforos a "dishonest adultress . . . a slut and a psychotic whore."

Hoping to spend the weekend with Tarnower, Harris drove up from Virginia and arrived in advance of her letter. She and the doctor got into a violent argument in the bedroom after Harris came across a nightgown and hair curlers belonging to some other woman. In the ensuing struggle, Harris pulled a .32-caliber handgun from her purse, and the doctor began pushing her and was heard to cry out, "Get out of here. You're crazy." Four shots were fired, and Tarnower keeled over, bleeding profusely. He died about an hour later in the hospital. Meanwhile, Harris gave a rambling statement to the police who apprehended her. "He wanted to live," she said. "I wanted to die." She claimed she had carried the revolver and a number of amphetamines to give her courage, saying she had planned to persuade Tarnower to shoot her and that her shooting of him (with three hits) had been accidental.

Harris's three-month-long trial started in November 1980 and was a field day for the gossipy press, as much testimony centered on Tarnower's life-style and love affairs. Much was made of the intimate clothing so many women had left behind. At one point, even Harris's own underwear was introduced as evidence, much to her discomfort.

Although many women sympathized with Harris and felt she had been subjugated by Tarnower, the jury of eight women and four men found that she had deliberately set out to kill the lover who had spurned her. On March 20, 1981, she was sentenced to a mandatory term of 15 years to life imprisonment. An attempt to gain clemency, which was supported by many women, failed, and she remains confined at Bedford Hills Correctional Facility, not eligible for release until 1996. Harris has been active in prison reform and, in 1988, wrote a book entitled *They Always Calls Us Ladies* about her prison experience.

Charles Stuart: The Not-So-Heroic Husband

Another murder case that deeply infected the social scene was the 1989 shooting of 29-year-old Charles Stuart and his 30-year-old wife, Carol. It was to stir racial tensions in Boston, since the Stuarts were white and the killer was supposedly black.

According to the story Charles Stuart gave police at the time, he and his seven-month-pregnant wife had just left a childbirth class at Brigham and Women's Hospital on October 23, 1989, when a gun-wielding black man jumped into their car. Stuart recounted that the assailant had ordered him to drive to an inner-city neighborhood where he robbed them. The assailant, Stuart said, shot Carol in the head and Charles in the stomach before fleeing. Stuart managed to maintain consciousness and called the police on his cellular car telephone. Tapes of his dramatic call for help and the frantic police search for the car were broadcast on radio and television stations from coast to coast.

When the wounded couple was found, they were hurried to the hospital, but Carol Stuart died the next day. Her baby, named Christopher, was delivered by cesarean section but lived only 17 days. Slowly, Charles Stuart recovered, and the hunt was on for the black killer. It was no exaggeration to say that racial hysteria gripped the city. Black leaders criticized city police, Mayor Raymond Flynn, and the local media for their response to the case. The mayor ordered 100 extra officers into the predominantly black Mission Hill neighborhood where the Stuarts had been located. Residents told of police breaking into their apartments and routinely stopping and frisking young black men.

On December 28, Charles Stuart identified a black man in a lineup as resembling the man who had shot him and his wife. Shortly thereafter, there was a stunning twist in the case, when Stuart's brother, Matthew, implicated Charles in the shooting. He said that as part of an arrangement he had made with Charles, he had driven to the area of the shooting and picked up Carol's purse, together with a revolver that Charles apparently had used to shoot his wife and then wound himself.

Matthew Stuart said he had thrown the evidence into the Pines River in the suburb of Revere. Police recovered the purse and a .38-caliber revolver, which turned out to be the murder weapon.

With the police now zeroing in on him, Charles Stuart killed himself by jumping from a bridge into Boston Harbor. It seemed that Stuart's motives had been at least twofold: He had taken out a large amount of life insurance on his wife and appeared to have had a romantic involvement with a young woman who had worked in a store he had managed.

Benson Family Murders: A Not-So-Ideal Son

During the 1980s—the decade of greed—it was inevitable that much sharp focus would involve the scandals and homicides among the rich and famous, the Benson family murders in Florida being a case in point.

Mrs. Margaret Benson, the 58-year-old widow and heiress to a $10 million tobacco fortune after the death of her wealthy husband in 1980, moved herself and her grown children to a life of self-indulgent ease in Naples, Florida. She supported her children, a married daughter, Carol Lynn Benson Kendall, her older son, Steven, and her young adopted son, Scott. Of the boys, Steven—seemingly the ideal son—was by far the more responsible and dependable and had taken charge of managing the family's affairs. Twenty-one-year-old Scott, by contrast, was always a problem, given to violence and the use of drugs, snorting cocaine and inhaling nitrous oxide (laughing gas). Given to expensive clothes and flashy sports cars, Scott had difficulty living within a $7,000-a-month allowance. On occasion, he beat his mother and sister, and once the police had to haul him away to a drug-treatment center. Still, the members of the Benson family remained loyal and loving to him.

In 1985, Steven bought himself a $215,000 home complete with tennis court and swimming pool, which aroused his mother's suspicions about how he could afford to do so. She began to suspect he had been skimming money from a company the family owned. She made plans to have an audit conducted and hinted at disinheriting Steven. One summer day in 1985, the family was climbing into their Chevrolet Suburban van for a drive when Steven said he had forgotten something and reentered the Benson mansion. While he was gone, two pipe bombs went off in the van. Sixty-three-year-old Mrs. Benson and young Scott died instantly, and Carol was badly injured.

After recovering, Carol told investigators that Steven had made no effort to aid her after the explosion and had shown little emotion at the scene. He was eventually charged with murder. At Steven's 1986 trial, Carol shocked the court by revealing that Scott Benson was actually her illegitimate son and that her mother—actually Scott's grandmother—had adopted him.

Steven Benson's defense was that the pipe bombs had probably been made by the drug-crazed Scott, who was seeking to destroy the family. The pipe bombs, the defense argued, must have gone off sooner than Scott had expected them to. However, prosecution witnesses contradicted that line of reasoning; one of them testified that Steven had once declared he had learned how to make pipe bombs several years before. A purchase order for materials used for such devices was found to bear Steven's finger- and palm prints.

While no one had actually seen Steven plant the bombs, the circumstantial evidence was strong enough for the jury to quickly bring in a guilty verdict. Steven, then 35, was sentenced to two consecutive terms of life imprisonment with no parole for at least 50 years.

The Bloomingdale-Morgan Affair: Perversion in High Places

A sex scandal that caused considerable dismay in the Reagan White House—and concluded with a later savage murder that was judged to be unconnected to the scandal itself—was the Bloomingdale-Morgan affair. The scandal erupted when a beautiful playgirl-model filed a $10 million palimony suit in 1982. Thirty-year-old Vicki Morgan filed the claim against multimillionaire Alfred Bloomingdale and later against his estate, charging she had long been "kept" by him for sexual perversions and sadomasochistic orgies. Bloomingdale was the scion of the Bloomingdale's department store family and a longtime friend of Ronald Reagan. His wife, Betsy, was a particularly close friend of the president's wife, Nancy.

Alfred Bloomingdale extended his fame and fortune by developing the Diners Club credit card. He also was for a time a Hollywood agent and producer and was a big booster of actor Reagan's prominence in state and later national politics. After Reagan became president, Bloomingdale, as a member of Reagan's "kitchen cabinet" of political advisers, harbored hopes of becoming ambassador to France. However, he got no such position, and it was said later by some observers that this was because the public image-conscious president was obviously

The Bloomingdale-Vicki Morgan affair bared perversions in high political and social circles.

aware of his pal's swinging life-style. A year later, Bloomingdale became a member of Reagan's Foreign Intelligence Advisory Board, composed of "trustworthy and distinguished citizens outside the government" who reviewed the operations of U.S. intelligence and counterintelligence agencies.

Early in 1982, the 66-year-old Bloomingdale came down with throat cancer and was hospitalized. It was during this period that his wife discovered that her husband had been providing Vicki Morgan with a monthly allowance of $18,000. Furious, Mrs. Betsy Bloomingdale had the payments stopped. Morgan countered by filing a $5 million palimony suit, claiming she was Bloomingdale's confidante, business partner, and traveling companion. She shortly raised the ante another $5 million for Betsy's act of cutting off her $18,000 stipend.

Before the case came to court, Bloomingdale died, on August 20, 1982. The following month, a court threw out most of the $10 million claim, declaring the relationship had been no more than that of a "wealthy, older paramour and a young, well-paid mistress." The judge permitted to stand Morgan's claim that she had a written contract guaranteeing her a $10,000 payment each month as a partner in Bloomingdale's business interests.

While litigation against the Blooingdale estate continued, the depressed and angry Morgan moved into a North Hollywood condominium, which she eventually shared with an old friend, Marvin Pancoast, a homosexual with major psychological problems of his own. The condominium became the site of frequent drug and drinking bouts and arguments between the two about money.

On July 7, 1983, Pancoast used a baseball bat to beat Morgan to death. He notified the police and confessed to the crime, but later recanted.

Meanwhile, the embarrassing political fallout continued when a criminal lawyer announced he had been asked to represent Pancoast at his trial and said he had videotapes showing Bloomingdale and Morgan in group and sadomasochistic sex with a number of top government officials. The lawyer said one person so involved "would definitely embarrass the president, just like Mr. Bloomingdale did."

Shortly thereafter, he insisted the tapes had been stolen, which led to his being charged with the filing of a false report. Most observers thought it most likely that there never had been any tapes.

Pancoast pleaded innocent by reason of insanity; records indicated he had been diagnosed over the past 13 years as masochistic, manic-depressive, and psychotic-depressive. It turned out he had once even confessed to the Sharon Tate and related murders, which actually were committed by the murderous Charles Manson family. Besides thus trying to discredit Pancoast's previous confession, the defense also stressed that others had had reasons to murder Morgan because of her claims of depraved sex with government officials. The jury rejected such theories and convicted Pancoast. He was sentenced to 26 years to life in prison.

In December 1984, a jury finally ordered the Bloomingdale estate to pay $200,000 to Morgan's estate, on the grounds that Bloomingdale had promised in a letter in February 1982 to pay $240,000 for her to spend time with him in the hospital during his terminal illness. Morgan had received $40,000 before these funds also had been cut off. Under the law, the money went to Morgan's 15-year-old son.

Sydney Biddle Barrows: The "Mayflower Madam"

The 1980s infatuation with the sins of the rich and famous extended even into the world of prostitution, a field that was withering not so much due to a rise in morals but because, as one practitioner put it, "the sexual revolution is killing us. There are just too many women willing to just give it away."

Thus, the nation's tabloids were thrilled by the appearance of Sydney Biddle Barrows—the "Mayflower Madam." For the scandal-minded press, the story harkened back to the glorious old days of high-paid sex, "little black books," and erudite madams. Intellectually, the swooning press declared, Barrows could have held her own with Polly Adler, the "Madam Elite" of the 1930s and 1940s. Sydney Barrows also added a new dimension in class, *Social Register* charm, and grace, being a descendant of two *Mayflower* Pilgrims.

Thirty-two-year-old Barrows was indicted in December 1984 in New York City for promoting prostitution in the guise of a temporary-employment agency, through which she ran three escort services that actually were expensive call-girl operations. The press was much impressed that the call girls she trained garnered as much as $2,000 a night, in her 20-woman, $1 million-a-year business.

When the tabloids uncovered her connection with the *Mayflower* (which linked her with Elder William Brewster, the minister who had played a leading role in the 1620 Plymouth Rock landing), they quickly dubbed her the Mayflower Madam.

Barrows pleaded guilty in July 1985 to a lesser charge of fourth-degree promotion of prostitution and paid a $5,000 fine. The press saw this as a plea bargain deal to suppress those eternal little black books. In fact, under the agreement, the prosecution returned seized documents that bore information about her clients, said to include "scores of prominent businessmen."

Sydney Biddle Barrows, the "Mayflower Madam," marked the return to the glorious old days of high-paid sex, little black books, erudite madams, and best-seller confessions.

Now famous, Barrows appeared on the "Donahue" television show unrepentant and complaining that nobody had gone to jail in the state in the last 100 years for what she had done. She earned the attention of the press by writing about her call-girl business: "As I saw it, this was a sector of the economy that was crying out for the application of good management skills—not to mention a little common sense and decency." She expressed the opinion that all women are prostitutes since they withhold favors from their husbands when they are angry. But she assured the eager public that, in her own life, "I am monogamous and rather old-fashioned."

Barrows did qualify as a trailblazer in the world's oldest profession by employing only well-informed, articulate women and letting her ladies choose the nights they wished to work. She even allowed clients to pay for services *after* they were rendered, truly a revolutionary practice in the field.

Barrows was a graduate of New York's Fashion Institute of Technology and had studied business management and merchandising. After a stint as a fashion buyer, she got a job through a friend answering the phone for an escort service. She decided she could do it better with her own service, one with very special wrinkles.

Barrows would not even concede that her *Mayflower* ancestors necessarily would have censured her activities. "Had they lived in a more enlightened era," she opined, "they would have understood that the private behavior of consenting adults is not the business of the state."

When TV host Phil Donahue wondered what Barrows's grandmother—who died only after her arrest and conviction—had thought about it all, Barrows answered, "She was not amused."

Her postbusiness activities proved most rewarding for Barrows. A book on her career soared to the best-seller lists and was condensed in a top women's magazine, and she remained much sought after for financially rewarding television appearances.

Sydney Barrows most likely would have readily conceded that crime does not pay. She hardly would have had to say the same about sex.

Mafia Update: The Fall of John Gotti

Even if sex does pay, can it be said that being in the Mafia still does? Certainly commencing with the death of J. Edgar Hoover in 1972, organized crime has been put under considerable distress by the FBI and other agencies now free of the restraining yoke of Hoover, who, for his own reasons, refused to do battle with the Mafia (see his entry).

Throughout the 1980s, mafiosi in New England, New Jersey, New York, Chicago, Philadelphia, Kansas City, Cleveland, and many other locals have been jailed on a scale never before witnessed.

Thus, the federal government claimed in 1992 that the power of the mob had finally been broken with the conviction of John Gotti, the boss of the Gambino crime family, the biggest and most powerful mob family in the nation. Some seasoned observers felt otherwise, pointing out that this boast has been made every five or ten years by law enforcement since the days of

John Gotti, the so-called Teflon Don, speeds away from court after one of his acquittals, before he was finally nailed in early 1992.

racket buster Thomas E. Dewey in New York in the 1930s. Al Capone's imprisonment in 1931 was supposed to finish off the Chicago mob, but it prospered even more thereafter. Then later in the 1930s, it was the convictions of a number of top mobsters, especially Charles "Lucky" Luciano. Five years after that, it was the smashing of Murder Inc., the assassination unit of the mob, and the execution of Louis "Lepke" Buchalter, the only ruling crime syndicate boss ever put to death legally. In the early 1950s, the exposures made by the Kefauver crime hearings were to mark once again the death knell of the mob. The disclosures by informer Joe Valachi were to have the same effect in the 1960s, and so on.

Still the mob thrived, even though constantly under pressure to change leaders. While being harassed by the law, the mobsters had plenty of muscle left to engage in internal warfare for control, a sure indication that there remained plenty worth fighting for. Among those to fall in this manner was Paul Castellano, the head of the Gambino crime family, who was labeled the "boss of bosses" by the media.

Castellano was the handpicked successor of Carlo Gambino, easily the most brilliant of the more recent crime bosses and perhaps an equal of the legendary Luciano and Meyer Lansky. Gambino, who died in 1976, arranged for his brother-in-law Castellano to take over the nation's most powerful crime family. Castellano was not popular with mafiosi either within his group or in other families, and he was "whacked out" in December 1985, along with his top aide, Thomas Bilotti.

The hit was masterminded by John Gotti, considered the top capo, or lieutenant, in the Gambinos. He was destined to become a near folk hero to the public as the "Dapper Don," wearing $2,000 suits and apparently immune from successful prosecution. He gained the nickname Teflon Don when three times he won not-guilty verdicts for his activities.

Finally, in April 1992, on the fourth try, prosecutors succeeded in convicting him, with the strong likelihood the 52-year-old crime boss will never see freedom again—no matter how long he lives. Gotti had been betrayed by one of his most-trusted aides, Sammy "the Bull" Gravano, who sought leniency for himself even though he had committed 19 murders, mostly all mob hits but perhaps a few for personal pleasure.

Actually, Gotti most likely would have been convicted without Gravano's testimony, which included the information that Gotti and he had sat in a car watching the Castellano hit. Gotti was nailed by audiotapes that stripped bare his brutality and activities as a Mafia boss, the latter being one of the specific charges against him. In one conversation, Gotti was recorded as saying to a cohort: "And every time we got a partner that don't agree with us, we kill him. You go to the boss and your boss kills him. He kills 'em. He O.K.'s it."

It was John Gotti's mouth even more that the Bull's words that convicted him.

With the court victory, U.S. Attorney Andrew J. Maloney and top FBI officials declared organized crime to be in its death throes—again that old refrain. But other authorities involved in the war on organized crime predicted the Gotti conviction would have no effect whatsoever.

The Gambino crime family is estimated to have up to

400 "made men," or "wise guys." Virtually all of them are believed to be millionaires. It is hardly likely that the mobsters would fold up their tent with so much money to be made. One estimate is that the family takes in $500 million a year, not even including drug-trafficking revenues.

Despite the government claims, there has never been a period when the Mafia hasn't had more applicants than it needed. For every made man, there are an estimated ten "associates" eager to join. And in a sense, some experts say, prosecutions actually are the lifeblood of the organization because they create golden chances for advancement. There is a new boss, a new underboss, a new capo, a new soldier every time there is a top-level conviction or erasure.

Prosecutions cannot eliminate the mob, not when there are millions of illicit dollars to be made daily. Continuous prosecution of narcotics criminals has similarly not stopped the flow of drugs into the United States, the fear of punishment being ignored when the rewards are so great. The most educated guess is that organized crime remains with us and will continue to be a growth industry.

Computer Fraud: New High-Tech Thefts

We can likewise expect newer crimes to develop in the modern age, especially in the computer world. A swindler can commit computer fraud once he or she learns the code or password that will activate the system to be robbed. Then all the scam artist has to do is link up a keyboard terminal to a touch tone telephone and start issuing orders to the computer. Banks are most vulnerable to computer frauds. One bank employee programmed his institution's computer to shift $120,000 from various depositors' accounts to those belonging to a couple of friends. Another diverted more than $1 million, which he needed to play the horses, with a computerized handicapping system that turned out to be far less effective that his theft methods. The Internal Revenue Service has also suffered computer theft. One programmer set up a system that funneled unclaimed tax credits to a relative's account. Another set up a system that diverted checks being held for taxpayers whose mailing addresses could not be determined—to his own account.

The only computer swindles we know about are those that have been exposed. We don't know about those that have proved to be too good to be discovered. We may never know them.

According to one expert who requests anonymity, it is only a matter of time until some major institution or corporation collapses and it is discovered that it has been drained of all its ready cash assets. Computer scams thus may become the ultimate growth industry.

Sperm Fraud: Praying on Desperate, Would-Be Parents

There are still more blatant new crimes developing as various technologies advance, even in such unlikely matters as artificial insemination, as revealed in a shocking 1992 case. According to his claims, Virginia "sperm doctor" Cecil B. Jacobson, an infertility specialist, helped scores of desperate, infertile women by supplying them with sperm through an "extensive, carefully regulated donor program" involving physical, mental, and social characteristics. However, it developed that the doctor himself was the only donor and that he produced the sperm in the privacy of his office bathroom shortly before each patient arrived at his clinic.

Jacobson referred to himself as "the baby maker" and boasted that "God doesn't give you babies—I do." Some parents started to discover just how right he was. One couple testified in the 55-year-old doctor's trial that they became suspicious and shocked by their daughter's first baby pictures. "We pulled them out of the envelope and both went, 'Whoa, who does she look like?' " the mother said. "And we both had the same feeling—she looked a lot like Dr. Jacobson."

DNA tests showed that the doctor had fathered 15 children for his patients, but the belief was that there were several dozen more who were so duped but had refused to come forward for testing. Jacobson was said to have gotten fees of about $5,000 in many cases.

But at the time of Jacobson's conviction, there were no laws prohibiting a doctor from donating sperm to a patient or impregnating an unwitting woman with his sperm. Under those circumstances, Jacobson had to be charged with more straightforward counts of criminal fraud involving the use of telephones and the U.S. mail. At the time of his conviction, the doctor faced punishment of up to 280 years in prison and fines of up to $500,000.

New crime marches on.

THE ENCYCLOPEDIA OF
AMERICAN CRIME

A

ABBANDANDO, Frank "The Dasher" (1910-1942): Murder, Inc. killer

One of Murder, Inc.'s most prolific killers, Frank "the Dasher" Abbandando got his nickname, according to one version, on one of his early hits. He pointed his gun at a huge waterfront character and pulled the trigger, but the weapon didn't fire. Abbandando then made a mad dash to get away, with his intended victim lumbering after him. According to the story, Abbandando ran around a building so fast that he actually came up behind the man. This time he got him with three slugs in the back. Even if this story is legend, it is matter of fact that during the 1930s, Abbandando did a remarkable job of littering the streets of Brooklyn with corpses. No accurate statistics on his kills were ever kept, but he was known to have been involved in probably 50 or so. When he wasn't knocking off mob victims, the Dasher spent his free time raping young girls in the Brownsville and Ocean Hill sections of Brooklyn. In one case he "squared up" with a girl's family by tossing them $25, "or otherwise I buy you all tombstones."

When finally brought to justice as a result of the testimony of informer Abe Reles and several other gang members who turned into stoolies, Abbandando was probably the most unrepentant of the hired killers in court. At one stage in the Dasher's trial, the judge ordered a court officer to stand between himself and Abbandando on the witness stand after the defendant threatened to kill him right in his own court. Still, the Dasher's lawyer tried to cast him in the best possible light, pointing out he had indeed been a star at second base for the Elmira team—the Elmira Reformatory team that was. In his summation he pleaded for the Dasher in the fair name of baseball, arguing: "Ballplayers don't kill people. In all my experience I cannot think of a single baseball player who ever killed anybody—at least so viciously as in this case."

The athletic assassin went to the electric chair on February 19, 1942.

See also: *Murder, Inc.; Abe Reles.*

ABBOTT, Burton W. (1928-1957): Murderer

The defendant in one of California's most sensational kidnap-murder trials, 29-year-old Burton W. Abbott was the object of an even more sensational execution, which offered grim proof of the finality of the death sentence.

On April 28, 1955, 14-year-old Stephanie Bryan disappeared in Berkeley, Calif. after walking a classmate home. Thirteen days after the hunt for the girl began, the police found one of Stephanie's schoolbooks in a field outside of town. On the evening of July 15, Georgia Abbott was rummaging in the basement of her home when she found a purse and identification card bearing the name of the missing girl. She rushed upstairs and blurted out news of her find to her husband, Burton, and a dinner guest. Police were summoned and a careful search of the premises revealed a number of Stephanie's schoolbooks, her brassiere and her glasses. Neither Burton nor Georgia Abbott could explain the presence of the girl's possessions, but Abbott pointed out that his garage had served as a polling place in May and that anyone of scores of people might have used the opportunity to hide the items on his property.

While the police remained suspicious, they had no other evidence to link Abbott to the girl's disappearance. The Abbotts owned a weekend cabin in the Trinity Mountains, some 300 miles away, and on a hunch, investigators visited the area. Dogs led them to a shallow grave that contained the badly decomposed body of Stephanie Bryan. She had been bludgeoned to death and her panties tied around her neck. Abbott was arrested and charged with kidnapping and murder.

While the case against Abbott was circumstantially strong, the prosecution had difficulty establishing a direct link between the suspect and the victim. However, scientific examination showed that hairs and fibers found in Abbott's car matched those from the girl's head and clothing. Still, there were enough doubts in the case to cause the jury to deliberate for seven days before finding Abbott guilty. He was sentenced to die in the gas chamber. Insisting on his innocence, Abbott filed appeal after appeal, but each was turned down. He was, however, granted several stays—some only hours before his scheduled execution—to launch yet another appeal.

On March 14, 1957 Abbott's last appeal failed and he was taken to the gas chamber at San Quentin. At 11:15 a.m. the tiny gas pellets were exploded beneath Abbott's chair. Just then the telephone "hot line" from Gov. Goodwin Knight's office buzzed Warden Harry Teets. "Hold the execution," a governor's assistant ordered. Warden Teets explained it was too late—the gas had been released. Gov. Knight had ordered a stay for one hour, for a reason never officially explained. It didn't matter. At 11:25 Abbott was dead.

Since then the Abbott case has often been cited by forces opposing capital punishment, not because of the merits of his claim of innocence, but as stark evidence that once the state takes away a person's life, it cannot restore that life.

ABILENE, KANSAS: See *Shame of Abilene.*

ABOLITIONIST Riots

Riots against abolitionists were common in the pre-Civil War North, but in New York City such commotions were often engineered by the gangsters of the Bowery and the Five Points in order to provide opportunities for general looting and mischief.

Several minor episodes occurred in 1833, followed by numerous bloody riots the subsequent year. On July 7, 1834 anti-abolitionist mobs attacked a chapel on Chatham Street and the Bowery Theater. Finally routed by the police, the rioters stormed down Rose Street, then a fashionable thoroughfare of mansions, and attacked the home of Lewis Tappan, a leading antislaver. Tappan escaped but most of the furniture in his house was heaved into the street, doused with oil and set on fire. As the mob ripped pictures from the wall, one rioter suddenly stopped another from throwing a painting on the bonfire. "It's Washington! For God's sake, don't burn Washington!" The mob took up the chant, and the painting was held aloft by a group of thugs who respectfully escorted it to the veranda of a house not under attack, where it was fervently guarded during the rest of the riot.

The worst of the year's violence took place three days later, when the leaders of the anti-abolitionist gangs declared they would destroy any house in the Five Points area that didn't put a candle in the window in denunciation of abolition. By evening, candles flickered from almost every window but still a dozen buildings were set ablaze and looted. The rioters attacked St. Phillip's Negro Church on Center Street and completely gutted it. A house next door to the church and three across the street were also destroyed. As smoke spread throughout the district, the gangsters turned their frenzy on houses of prostitution, and the occupants of five of them were dragged outside and forced to watch their homes and belongings burned. The women were stripped, passed out to the gang and horribly mistreated. Blacks were pulled from their homes or hiding places and tortured, and an Englishman had both eyes gouged out and his ears cut off.

When troops arrived on the scene a little after one o'clock in the morning, the mob fled. The following night rioters gutted a church on Spring Street whose pastor had supported the antislavery movement, and then barricaded the streets, vowing to battle the soldiers to the death. But when the troops moved on the barricades, the mob turned and ran. For a time thereafter, the riots against abolitionists ceased, resuming in the 1850s.

ABRAMS, Big Mike (?-1898): Murderer

While the Chinese of New York's Chinatown have fought many savage tong wars among themselves, through the years they have tried to avoid violent conflicts with whites. The opposite was not the case, however. White killers were familiar denizens of the Chinatown alleys, always ready to eliminate any man's enemy for a shockingly reasonable price. The most notorious of this ilk was Big Mike Abrams, who roamed the area performing beatings and killings for pay. When work was slow, Abrams would take to street muggings, which, besides earning his keep, further enhanced his reputation.

Big Mike sometimes operated opium-smoking dens on Pell Street and in Coney Island and in his later years settled for a small percentage from such establishments, while contributing nothing to their operation. The fact that a man was a client of one of these dens, however, did not afford him protection in the event Big Mike was offered cash to slug or kill him. Big Mike's most-celebrated murders were the knife decapitations of three Chinese before the horrified eyes of onlookers on Pell Street.

Even the dread hatchet men of the tongs feared Big Mike, but finally one of them, Sassy Sam of the Hip Sing Tong, got drunk on rose wine and rice brandy and attacked the awesome killer. Big Mike happened to be unarmed at the time and fled down Pell Street, with Sassy Sam in hot pursuit waving a long ceremonial sword.

Big Mike lost considerable stature after that display of vulnerability. While he did regain a measure of respect by removing the head of Ling Tchen, one of the chiefs of the Hip Sing Tong, the unthinkable—the elimination of Big Mike—began to be considered. Within a month of the death of Ling Tchen, police found Big Mike dead in bed, his room filled with gas. The windows and door to his room had been sealed from the outside and a line of thin hose from a gas jet in the hall had been stuffed in the keyhole of Big Mike's door.

The Hip Sings were generally credited with killing Big Mike, but the tong never acknowledged the deed, apparently fearful of retribution from other white gangsters.

ACCARDO, Anthony Joseph (1906-   ): Chicago mob leader

Today, it may be somewhat hard to believe that someone like "Joe Batters," who, as a young tough, gained his sobriquet for his proficiency with a baseball bat and who served as one of Al Capone's bodyguards, could become the boss of the Chicago mob and be described by his syndicate supporters as having "more brains before breakfast than Al Capone had all day."

Accardo's rise in the Chicago underworld was rapid. When Capone first went to jail for a brief stay in 1929 and named Jake Guzik in charge of administration and Frank Nitti in charge of operations, Accardo was installed as the head of "enforcement." Under him were such brutal characters as Machine Gun Jack McGurn, Tough Tony Capezio, Screwy John Moore, Sam "Golf Bag" Hunt, Red Forsyth and Jimmy Belcastro, the King of the Bombers. Tough Tony continued to grow in stature in the gang, and when Nitti committed suicide in 1943 rather than go to prison, Accardo became the acknowledged head of the Chicago mob.

At various stages in the 1950s and 1960s, Accardo reportedly had his powers wrested away by Sam "Momo" Giancana, but it is unclear how much Accardo gave up under force and how much he relinquished willingly.

Accardo was always reputed as a leader who believed in iron-clad obedience in the lower ranks but a sharing of power at the top. Under his rule the level of violence in the Chicago underworld dropped to near zero, especially compared to the old Capone days. However, enforcement against alleged informers and those who tried to steal from the syndicate remained strict and awesome. Such was the fate in 1961 of one William "Action" Jackson, a collector for the mob who had developed "sticky" fingers. Action got particularly brutal treatment, ending up stripped naked and hanging by his chained feet from a meat hook in the basement of a Cicero gambling joint. He was beaten on the lower body and genitals with a baseball bat, carved up with a razor and had his eyes burned out with a blowtorch. Following that treatment he was further dissected, and then pictures were taken of his corpse (he had died, according to the coroner's report, not of his wounds but of shock) and distributed in mob centers as a warning of what was in store for a thief.

Accardo's personal fairness, by underworld standards, was of the same sort that inspired so much loyalty in many of Capone's adherents. Noted for his pool playing, Accardo was once victimized in a $1,000 bet by a pool hustler who had wedged up the table and then adjusted his technique accordingly to beat the crime chief. When the hustler was exposed, Accardo blamed only himself. "Let the bum go," he said. "He cheated me fair and square." Accardo's behavior in such matters won him a great amount of affection.

But Accardo also proved most resourceful in dealing with the drug problem, which much of the national syndicate and the Mafia had ruled out of bounds. Some families disobeyed the rule but others enforced it rigorously, killing any who disobeyed or cutting them off from legal and support aid if they were caught. Accardo's solution was to ban all narcotics dealings, but he also ordered that all those involved in dope be given $200 a week out of family funds to help make up their losses.

This "taking care of everybody" approach helped to pacify the Chicago mob; by comparison, gangland murders became much more common in New York, with its five greedy Mafia families. This record of peace may well have been shattered by the 1975 murder of Sam Giancana, but a number of underworld sources insist Accardo was not behind the murder. According to them, the Giancana killing was "a CIA operation all the way," designed to prevent him from speaking about the agency's use of the underworld in a Castro assassination plot.

By the late 1970s Accardo, a multimillionaire, was reportedly in semiretirement, living the good life as he traveled from Florida to the West Coast to Chicago looking after his enormous legitimate investments. According to the FBI, the mob's operational authority in Chicago had shifted to Joe Aiuppa, an Accardo gunman buddy from the old days.

See also: *Sam "Momo" Giancana.*

ACCIDENT Faking: Insurance swindle

Over the years faking accidents to swindle insurance companies has developed into a thriving business. There is no way to gauge accurately the extent of this crime since insurance industry figures are themselves suspect; many observers claim that the companies have a vested interest in minimizing the extent of fraud to deter other attempts and to defend their rate structures. Some calculations of accident frauds place the figure between $20 million and $100 million a year, with most estimates falling in the upper range. It was estimated that one insurance gang in Birmingham, Ala. cleared several million dollars over a seven-year period. Such insurance rings sometimes buy duplicates of legitimate X rays from doctors and then use them to bolster phony claims of industrial, auto and personal injuries.

One of the most incredible operations of this kind worked out of Kirksville, Mo. The swindle involved doctors, lawyers, osteopaths, nurses, insurance agents, a county sheriff, farmers and businessmen. Sixty-six of them were eventually convicted and sentenced. The racket was run by a crooked insurance agent. He favored realism in staging his phony claims; claimants had their wrists broken with crank handles and their fingers smashed with hammers. An osteopath would be called in to compound such injuries by manipulating the bones of the hand and giving injections designed to cause infections. In some cases miscalculations resulted in amputations, but these only increased the size of the award. The men, women and children who willingly pose as the accident victims in such plots are often of limited intelligence, but they are also usually poor and the pool of these volunteer victims increases dramatically during periods of high unemployment.

Faked pedestrian accidents have long been a mainstay of the racket. Sometimes both the victim and the driver are in collusion, but most fakers prefer to utilize an honest driver who can stand up to rigorous investigation because he really is innocent. "Floppers" and "divers" are used when the motorist is not a willing partner in the swindle. A flopper is a person who is adept at feigning being hit by a car going around a corner. Perpetrators insist this is not as hard to do as it would appear. The flopper simply stands in the street and starts crossing as the car makes its turn. Under such circumstances the car is moving relatively slowly, and the flopper bounces off the front fender and flips his body backward to the ground. As the crowd starts to gather, the flopper moan and groans. The premium flopper is one who has an old fracture, preferably a skull fracture since the break will show up in an X ray no matter how old it is1 The flopper is naturally schooled in the art of faking serious injury. Just before the accident he will bite his lip open and dab some of the blood into his ear.

"Divers" are considered finer artists than floppers because their act seems more convincing. They work at night so that witnesses can't really see what is happening. As a car approaches, the diver runs into the street and in a crouching position slams the car door with his hand as hard as he can. The resulting loud noise quickly attracts onlookers as the diver lies on the ground, doing the same moaning and groaning act as the flopper.

One of the most bizarre accident swindles involved a father of identical twins. One child was normal but the other quite retarded. Rather than put the unfortunate child into an institution, the father decided to use him as a prop for a swindle scheme. He would take his normal child into stores and when no one was looking, he'd knock something off a shelf and have the child start screaming as though he had been hit on the head. The father would then create a scene and storm out of the store. Later, he would file suit against the store, charging the accident had permanently damaged his child's brain. As proof, he would produce the retarded twin. Settlements were hastily arranged since no company dared take such a case to a jury. The racket worked a number of times until an investigator making a routine check visited the family's home while the parents were out and saw the normal child playing in the backyard.

ADAMS, Albert J. (1844-1907): Numbers king

A famous and colorful New York City gambler, known as the Policy King, Al Adams was the boss of the most extensive numbers game operation in the city.

Dishonesty has been the keynote of policy games from the time they started in England during the 1700s to the present, but Adams gave them a new wrinkle, not only bilking the public but also swindling other numbers operators in order to take over their businesses.

Adams came to New York from his native Rhode Island in the early 1870s and first worked as a railroad brakeman, a job he found much too taxing. He soon became a runner in a policy game operated by Zachariah Simmons. Duly impressed by Adams' penchant for deviousness, the older man took him in as a partner. Adams developed many ways to rig the game to reduce the winners' payoff. After Simmons died, Adams took over his operation and eventually became the boss of the New York policy racket. At the time, there were scores of independent operators. It was common practice for independent policy men to "lay off" numbers that had been bet too heavily for comfort. They would simply shift part of the action to another operator who had light play on the number, thus spreading the risk. When these operators tried to lay off a heavily played number with Adams, he would note the number and claim he already had too much action on it. He would then lay off the same number around the city, even if he actually had little or no action on it. Thus, a number of operators would become vulnerable to that number. Adams' next move was to fix the results so the heavily played number came out, hitting the owners of many policy shops with devastating losses. To make their payoffs, the operators had to seek loans from Adams, who exacted a partnership as the price of a loan, ultimately kicking the operators out entirely. Some policy operators he simply refused to help, forcing them to make their payoffs (many to Adams' undercover bettors) by dipping into the cash reserved for bribes to politicians and the police. Losing their protection, they were immediately shut down, and Adams simply moved in.

In time, it was estimated that Adams ran between 1,000 and 1,100 policy shops in the city. Over the years his payments to the Tweed Ring totaled in the millions. Even after Tweed fell and reformers came in, Adams was able to operate with the connivance of the police. It was not until 1901 that law enforcement authorities were forced to take action against his nefarious operations, raiding his headquarters. Adams was sent to Sing Sing, where he served more than a year.

When he came out, Adams found that he no longer controlled the New York policy game. The battle for control of the business was turning exceedingly violent, and Adams, who had always operated with bribes and trickery, neither needed nor wanted to be involved in wars to the death. He lived out the next few years in luxury in the Ansonia Hotel and amassed a great fortune through land speculation. However, he was estranged from his family, who was ashamed of his past criminality and blamed him for their inability to lead normal, respectable lives. On October 1, 1907 Adams committed suicide in his apartment.

See also: *Numbers Racket*.

ADLER, Polly (1900-1962): New York madam

Often called the last of the great madams, Polly Adler achieved such a measure of esteem that in the 1930s and 1940s she was regarded as one of New York City's most illustrious "official greeters." As she said in her memoirs, "I could boast a clientele culled not only from *Who's Who* and the *Social Register*, but from *Burke's Peerage* and the *Almanach de Gotha*." Her clients, of course, were not limited to high society; they included politicians, police, writers and gangsters. Among the latter were Dutch Schultz, Frank Costello and Lucky Luciano. The first two were regarded by Polly and her girls as lavish spenders. Luciano was not. If a girl sent by Polly to Luciano's suite in the Waldorf Towers thought she would do much better than the standard $20 fee, she was disillusioned. Luciano might stuff an extra $5 in her bra at the conclusion of a session, but that was all. As he later recalled: "I didn't want to do nothin' different. What do you think I was gonna do—spoil it for everybody?"

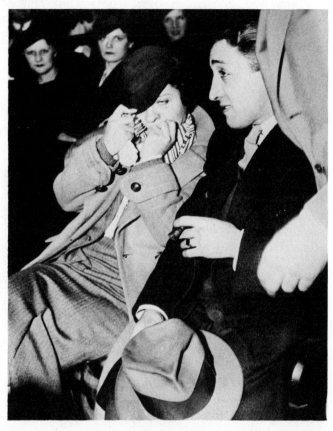

The flamboyant Polly Adler managed to appear dowdyish whenever hauled into court on vice charges, a far cry from the way she paraded with her girls through the Broadway nightclubs.

Polly almost always used the real names of her clients when introducing them to her girls; the clients did not object, knowing that their secret was safe with Polly. When Dutch Schultz was on the run from the law in 1933 because of an income tax evasion charge drawn by a young federal prosecutor named Thomas E. Dewey, there were 50,000 wanted posters on him. The gang chief nevertheless continued his regular two or three visits a week to Polly's place and was never betrayed.

Despite some memorable police raids, Polly generally operated with little interference out of lavish apartments in Manhattan's fashionable East 50s and 60s. Long laudatory descriptions of the decor in her opulent "homes" appeared in various publications. One establishment at Madison Avenue and East 55th Street was described as having a living room done up in "Louis XVI," a taproom in a military motif colored in red, white and blue and a dining room that suggested the interior of a seashell. All the baths and "workrooms" were finished in peach and apple green. Free food was always offered and the bar did a thriving business. Many men dropped in just for refreshments and a stimulating chat with the loquacious madam.

Polly became a celebrity in her own right. Interviewed by the press, she commented on various past and present events. Her opinion on Prohibition: "They might as well have been trying to dry up the Atlantic with a post-office blotter." Offer the people what they want, she said, and they will buy it. It was a philosophy that served her as well in her field as it did the bootleggers in their area. Madam Adler routinely made the gossip columns and was a regular at nightclub openings, where she would create a sensation marching in with a bevy of her most beautiful girls. She later recalled: "The clubs were a display window for the girls. I'd make a newspaper column or two, the latest Polly Adler gag would start the rounds and, no matter where we happened to go, some of the club patrons would follow after us and end the evening at the house."

Polly Adler retired from the business in 1944. Encouraged by a number of writer friends, including Robert Benchley, she pursued a writing career after taking a number of college courses, and by the time of her death in 1962, she had become something of a literary light. In her later years Adler, an acknowledged expert on matters sexual, was a dinner companion of Dr. Alfred Kinsey.

ADONIS, Joe (1902-1972): Syndicate gangster

A member of the governing board of the national crime syndicate from its inception in the early 1930s, Joe Adonis, or simply Joey A., remained a power until he was deported in 1953. While Adonis always insisted that he was born in this country, he was, in fact, born in Montemarano, Italy, on November 22, 1902. Joseph Doto entered the country illegally and adopted the name Adonis to pay tribute to what he regarded to be his handsome looks. After joining a New York street gang, Adonis formed a teenage friendship with the future big names in American crime—Albert Anastasia, Vito Genovese and Lucky Luciano. By the mid-1920s Adonis was the head of the Broadway Mob, which controlled the flow of bootleg liquor in mid-Manhattan, the richest market in the country. While he was the operating head of the mob, he may not have been the real brains, since his partners included Luciano and Frank Costello. However, Adonis continued to rise in the hierarchy of organized crime because he was loyal and never overambitious. He became a trusted member of the board of the national syndicate, settling disputes between various criminal factions and issuing murder contracts, among other duties. Abe Reles, the informer in the Murder, Inc. case, once told authorities, "Cross Joey Adonis and you cross the national combination." When Luciano went to prison, he left Adonis in nominal charge of the combination's affairs, but he added,

"Cooperate with Meyer." Meyer was Meyer Lansky, who became the chief officer in the combination. Adonis proved smart enough to know how to take orders.

Following the end of Prohibition, Adonis extended his domain to include not only the waterfront and gambling rackets in Manhattan but those in Brooklyn and New Jersey as well. He also masterminded a number of jewel thefts, an avocation that amused his big-time confederates. It seemed like a dangerous enterprise but it made Adonis happy. Despite a long career in crime, he did not go to jail until 1951, when, after the Kefauver Committee hearings, he pleaded guilty in New Jersey to violation of the state's gambling laws and received a two-year sentence. In 1956, Adonis, facing federal perjury charges, accepted a deportation order, after his true birthplace had been discovered. Thereafter, he lived out his days lavishly in Milan, Italy, still maintaining ties with the underworld in America and occasionally meeting with Luciano, who resided— also in exile—in Naples.

See also: *Broadway Mob, Meyer Lansky, Lucky Luciano.*

ADORNO, George (1959-   ): Youthful murderer

The case history of George Adorno is frequently cited as an example of the breakdown of the criminal justice system in the prosecution of juvenile crime. Adorno first ran afoul of the legal system at the age of four, when he set his sister on fire. After 16 subsequent arrests for theft, Adorno—age 15—was charged with triple murder, which he confessed to before a New York City district attorney in the presence of his sister. The sister had been summoned because Adorno's mother, an immigrant from Puerto Rico, did not speak any English. A juvenile court judge threw out the confession, however, because the mother had not been present. With the murder charge dropped, the judge found Adorno guilty of a lesser offense of robbery, ordered his confinement for three years and, as required by law, had his complete criminal record, including the three murder charges, sealed.

After serving half his sentence, Adorno was released. Nineteen days later, he shot to death Steven Robinson, a black law student who drove a cab to finance his education. When Justice Burton Roberts sentenced him to 15 years to life for the Robinson murder, he commented: "Nothing ever happened to Adorno. He plays the courts like a concert player plays the piano. Is there ever a time when a red light goes on and you say, 'We have to control this person'? So, at age sixteen, he finally gets a three-year sentence and he is out in eighteen months." Under Justice Roberts' sentence, the maximum permitted by the youth's plea of guilty, Adorno became eligible for parole after 8½ years.

See also: *Juvenile Delinquency.*

ADULTERY

One of the most-unenforced laws in the country is that concerning the crime of adultery, which, with certain variations in state laws, may be described as sexual intercourse by a married person with someone other than his wife or her husband. In some states adultery is committed only when the married person is the woman.

New York Penal Law defines the crime as "the sexual intercourse of two persons, either of whom is married to a third person. The offense is deemed a misdemeanor and is punishable by imprisonment in a penitentiary or county jail, for not more than six months or by a fine of not more than two hundred and fifty dollars, or by both." A few states, among them South Dakota, Oklahoma and Vermont, allow for a five-year prison term; in several others, small fines (as low as $10 in Maryland) are the limit of punishment. Such penalties caused Judge Morris Ploscowe to wonder "why legislatures have bothered to include adultery in their penal system if the enjoyment of extramarital intercourse may at most result in a small fine."

The law is, of course, generally incapable of controlling voluntary sexual behavior. According to Dr. Alfred Kinsey, strict enforcement of sex statutes would result in the jailing of 95 percent of the population.

AGE And Crime

Crime, especially violent crime, is for the young in body, not just the young in heart. Perhaps as many as three out of every four street crimes are committed by persons under the age of 25. This phenomenon is hardly a new one; the average Western outlaw was shockingly young. Billy the Kid, who was reputed to have killed several men by the time of his 21st birthday, was more the rule than the exception. A criminal act does require a good amount of daring, vigor and rebelliousness, and as Peter W. Lewis and Jack Wright, Jr. point out in *Modern Criminal Justice,* "Society is not often plagued by daring, rebellious old people."

Some of the statistics are shocking indeed. Children under the age of 15 commit more total crimes than do adults over 25. About one-third of all violent crimes are the work of the under-18 group. The under-25 group commits about four out of five robberies, burglaries, larceny-thefts and car thefts; three out of every five forcible rapes; and about half of all murders, non-negligent manslaughters and aggravated assaults. Thus, it is fair to speak of what one observer has called a "tidal wave of young criminality." It is impossible to judge whether this represents a break with the past or just reflects age-old patterns, since there are no reliable statistics for the 19th century— much less earlier times—to match with those of the present-day *Uniform Crime Reports.* But it might be pointed out that while organized crime today is largely an over-25 activity, in the 19th century this violent business was largely controlled by the young. The Daybreak Boys, a brutal New York gang, were composed of mostly 20-year-old and younger criminals. Certainly today's school violence must go far to equal that of the Walsh School feud in Chicago from 1881 to 1905.

Much of the "crime wave" that supposedly enveloped the United States from the 1960s onward has been little more

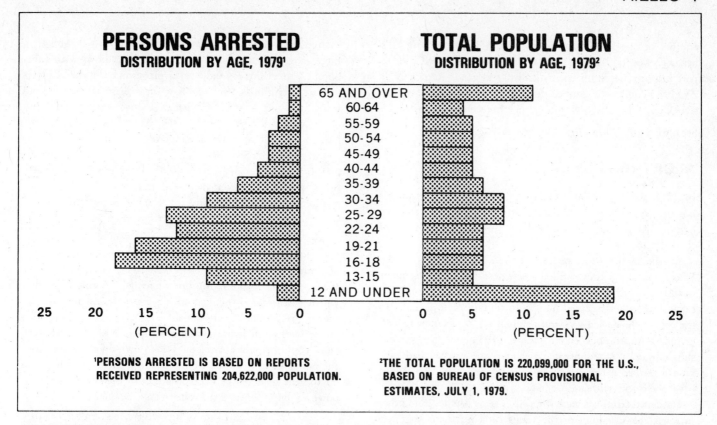

PERSONS ARRESTED
DISTRIBUTION BY AGE, 1979[1]

TOTAL POPULATION
DISTRIBUTION BY AGE, 1979[2]

65 AND OVER
60-64
55-59
50-54
45-49
40-44
35-39
30-34
25-29
22-24
19-21
16-18
13-15
12 AND UNDER

25   20   15   10   5   0
(PERCENT)

0   5   10   15   20   25
(PERCENT)

[1]PERSONS ARRESTED IS BASED ON REPORTS
RECEIVED REPRESENTING 204,622,000 POPULATION.

[2]THE TOTAL POPULATION IS 220,099,000 FOR THE U.S.,
BASED ON BUREAU OF CENSUS PROVISIONAL
ESTIMATES, JULY 1, 1979.

Percentage of persons arrested within age groups, based on FBI statistics, shows that the years of prime criminal activity run from 13 through 34.

than a logical development of the age-crime relationship. Irresponsible statements by politicians and law enforcement officials have tended to confirm public fear of a new crime wave. The simple fact is that as a result of the postwar baby boom, the under-25 age group has grown far faster than the rest of the population and, as always, the increasing number of youngsters have committed an increasing number of crimes.

Further complicating the use of age-crime statistics are other factors that strongly affect them. For instance, the high crime rate produced by under-15 and under-25 black youths is in part influenced by urbanization. All studies show that the violent crime rate for young blacks who have moved from the South to large urban cities in the North and Midwest is far higher than that for young blacks on a nationwide basis.

Clearly, a study of the relationship between age and crime is necessary as a method for understanding the problem but it hardly provides an answer to it.

See also: *Daybreak Boys, Juvenile Delinquency, Walsh School Feud.*

AH Hoon (?-1909): Murder victim

The tong wars of New York's Chinatown were fought with more than guns, hatchets and snickersnee. They were also fought with insult, loss of face and wit. In the 1909-10 war between the Hip Sings and the On Leongs, some of the most telling blows were struck by the celebrated comic Ah Hoon, who was a member of the On Leongs. Ah Hoon used his performances at the venerable old Chinese Theater on Doyers Street to savage the Hip Sings. Finally, the Hip Sings could take no more insults to their honor and passed the death

sentence on the comic. They announced publicly that Ah Hoon would be assassinated on December 30. The On Leongs vowed he would not be. And even the white man got into the act. A police sergeant and two patrolmen appeared on stage with Ah Hoon on December 30. The performance went off without a hitch, and immediately after, Ah Hoon was escorted back to his boarding house on Chatham Square. He was locked in his room and several On Leongs took up guard duty outside the door. Ah Hoon was safe. The only window in his room faced a blank wall across a court.

The On Leongs started celebrating this new loss of face by the Hip Sings, who sulked as the On Leongs paraded through Chinatown. When Ah Hoon's door was unlocked the next morning, his shocked guards found him dead, shot through the head. Subsequent investigation revealed a member of the Hip Sings had been lowered on a chair by a rope from the roof and had shot the comic using a gun equipped with a silencer. Now, the Hip Sings paraded through Chinatown. Ah Hoon's killer was never found.

See also: *Bloody Angle, Bow Kum, Mock Duck, Tong Wars.*

AIELLO, Joseph (1891-1930): Chicago mobster

Joseph Aiello and his brothers, Dominick, Antonio and Andrew, were enemies of Al Capone in the struggle for control of organized crime in Chicago. Aiello tried to have Capone killed in somewhat novel ways, e.g., attempting to bribe a restaurant chef $10,000 to put prussic acid in Capone's soup and, on another occasion, offering a reward of $50,000 for Big Al's head. These efforts called for extraordinary vengeance on Capone's part and he ordered his enemy killed "real good." On October 23, 1930 Aiello was gunned down on North Kolmar Avenue, struck by 59 bullets, weighing altogether well over a pound.

See also: *Louis "Little New York" Campagna.*

ALCATRAZ Prison

In 1868 the U.S. War Department established a prison for hostiles and deserters on a stark little island in San Francisco harbor. The Indians called it "Alka-taz"—the lonely "Island of the Pelicans."

By the 1930s Alcatraz had outlived its usefulness to the War Department, but it filled a new need for the Department of Justice, which wanted a "superprison to hold supercriminals," because there just seemed no way to contain them securely in the rest of the nation's federal penitentiaries. The new federal prison on Alcatraz opened on January 1, 1934 under the wardenship of James A. Johnston. Although the warden had previously earned a reputation as a "penal reformer," he would rule "the Rock" with an iron hand.

Hardened criminals were shipped in large batches from other prisons, the schedules of the trains carrying them kept top secret. The first batch, the so-called Atlanta Boys Convoy,

excited the public's imagination, conjuring up wild stories of huge gangster armies plotting to attack the convoy with guns, bombs, flamethrowers and even airplanes in order to free scores of deadly criminals. But the first mass prisoner transfer and those following it went off without a single hitch; by the end of the year, the prison, now called America's Devil's Island, housed over 250 of the most dangerous federal prisoners in the country. The city of San Francisco, which had fought the establishment of a superprison on Alcatraz, now found it had a prime tourist attraction; picture postcards of Alcatraz by the millions—invariably inscribed, "Having wonderful time—wish you were here"—were mailed from the city.

The prisoners, however, wished they were almost anywhere else. Johnston followed the principle of "maximum security and minimum privileges." There were rules, rules, rules, which made Alcatraz into a living but silent hell. A rule of silence, which had to be abandoned after a few years as unworkable, meant the prisoners were not allowed to speak to each other either in the cell house or the mess hall. A single whispered word could bring a guard's gas stick down on a prisoner. But the punishment could be worse; he might instead be marched off to "the hole" to be kept on a diet of bread and water for however long it pleased the warden and the guards.

A convict was locked up in his Alcatraz cell 14 hours a day, every day without exception. Lockup was at 5:30, lights out

U.S. Coast Guard aerial photo of Alcatraz furthers its "superprison" image. In truth, it proved to be a crumbling, inefficient institution.

was at 9:30 and morning inspection at 6:30. There was no trustee system, and thus no way a convict could win special privileges. While good behavior won no favors, bad behavior was punished with water hosing, gas stick beatings, special handcuffs that tightened with every movement, a strait jacket that left a man numb with cramps for hours, the hole, a bread-and-water diet and, worst of all, the loss of "good time," by which all federal prisoners could have 10 days deducted from their sentence for every 30 days with no infractions. But this harsh treatment proved too much for the prisoners and too difficult for the guards to enforce, even with an incredible ratio of one guard for every three prisoners. Within four years the rule of silence started to be modified and some other regulations were eased.

Incredibly, despite the prison's security and physical isolation, there were numerous attempts to escape from Alcatraz, but none were successful. In 1937 two convicts, Ralph Roe and Teddy Cole, got out of the workshop area during a heavy fog, climbed a Cyclone fence 10 feet high and then jumped from a bluff 30 feet into the water. They were never seen again, but there is little doubt they were washed to sea. The tide ran very fast that day and the nearest land was a mile and a quarter away through 40° water. The fact that the two men, habitual criminals, were never arrested again makes it almost certain that they died. Probably the closest anyone came to a successful escape occurred during a 1946 rebellion plotted by a bank robber named Bernie Coy. During the 48 hours of the rebellion, five men died and 15 more were wounded, many seriously, before battle-trained Marines stormed ashore and put an end to the affair. Escape attempts proved particularly vicious on Alcatraz because convicts with so little hope of release or quarter were much more likely to kill guards during a break.

Many more prisoners sought to escape the prison by suicide and several succeeded. Those who failed faced long stays in the hole after being released from the prison hospital. Others escaped the reality of Alcatraz by going insane. According to some estimates, at least 60 percent of the inmates were insane. It remains a moot point whether Al Capone, who arrived there in 1934 from the Atlanta Penitentiary, where he had been serving an 11-year sentence for tax evasion, won parole in 1939 because of the advanced state of his syphilitic condition or because he too had gone stir crazy like so many others.

Alcatraz in the 1930s housed not only the truly notorious and dangerous prisoners but also many put there for vindictive reasons, such as Robert Stroud, the Birdman of Alcatraz, who, along with Rufus "Whitey" Franklin, was one of the most ill-treated prisoners in the federal penal system. The inmate roster included the tough gangsters who truly belonged, like Doc Barker, and those who did not, like Machine Gun Kelly, who had never even fired his weapon at anyone. There were also such nontroublesome convicts as former public enemy Alvin "Creepy" Karpis.

Over the years there were many calls for the closing of Alcatraz. Some did so in the name of economy, since it cost twice as much to house a prisoner on Alcatraz than in any other federal prison. Sen. William Langer even charged the government could board inmates "in the Waldorf Astoria cheaper."

By the 1950s Alcatraz had lost its reputation as an escape-proof prison and had become known simply as a place to confine prisoners deemed to be deserving of harsher treatment.

By the time "the Rock" was finally phased out as a federal prison in 1963, it was a crumbling mess and prisoners could easily dig away at its walls with a dull spoon.

See also: *Alcatraz Prison Rebellion, Alcatraz Push-ups, Atlanta Boys Convoy, Rufus "Whitey" Franklin, James A. Johnston, James Lucas, Rule of Silence, Robert Stroud.*

ALCATRAZ Prison Rebellion

The 1946 Alcatraz Prison Rebellion was a misnomer. It was nothing more or less than a cunning prison escape plot by six men based on the release of the other prisoners in order to confuse and distract the authorities. The attempted breakout, which was foiled after 48 hours, was bloody: five men died and 15 others were wounded, many seriously. To quell the so-called rebellion, trained sharpshooters were flown in from other prisons and battle-trained U.S. Marines stormed ashore under the command of Gen. Joseph "Vinegar Joe" Stilwell and Frank Merill, of the famous World War II Marauders.

The mastermind of the plot was one of the least likely of convicts, 46-year-old Bernie Coy, who still had another 16 years to serve for bank robbery. The warden and guards regarded Coy as little more than a Kentucky hillbilly bandit. Coy, however, had spotted a critical weakness in the Alcatraz security system; as a cellhouse orderly, he saw that he could overpower the tier guard, release a few confederates and work his way up to a gun gallery, a floor-to-ceiling cage of bars behind which was housed the one man with weapons in the entire building. The only time this armed guard stepped out of the cage was to inspect D Block, the dreaded isolation section. On May 2, according to a detailed plan, Coy was waiting for the guard when he left the cage and overcame him in a fierce hand-to-hand battle. Inside the gun gallery there was an ample supply of weapons and ammunition.

From here on, Coy's plan was simple. He and his confederates captured all nine guards in the building and placed them in two cells. They then released most of the other convicts but barred the doors so that they could not follow them. Under cover of the resulting confusion, the escapers intended to use hostages to get across the prison yard, seize the prison launch and speed across the bay before an alarm could be sounded. On the mainland, cars would be waiting for them, thanks to the connections of Joseph Paul "Dutch" Cretzer, one of Coy's accomplices. Besides Cretzer, a bank robber, murderer and former Public Enemy No. 4, Coy's accomplices included: Sam Shockley, a mental defective and close friend of Cretzer; Marvin Hubbard, a gangling Alabama gunman and close friend of Coy; Miran Edgar "Buddy" Thompson, a robber, murderer and jailbreak artist who previously had escaped from eight prisons; and Clarence Carnes, a 19-year-old Choctaw Indian serving 99 years for kidnapping a farmer across a state line after escaping from a prison where he was doing time for murder.

The plot failed because a prison guard—against orders—had failed to return one corridor key to its place on a keyboard. The escapers then jammed the lock trying to force it open with other keys. Soon, the convicts' timetable ran out and the prison launch left. Coy, accompanied by Hubbard, left Cretzer in charge of the hostages, ordering that none of them be killed, and went off to communicate with Warden James A. Johnston over the prison phone system. Coy had come up with a desperate alternative plan to use the guard hostages to get into the staff living compound, where the guards' families, including 30 young girls, lived. With these hostages, Coy was sure the authorities would have to let him and his confederates off the island.

Back with the hostages, Cretzer knew better. He realized that as soon as the convicts headed in the direction of the family area, the guards on the walls would cut loose, killing the escapers and the guard hostages as well. There was no way the guards would let their families be taken. Besides, Cretzer wanted to kill all the guards. He had not told Coy that he had already killed a guard in a gunfight and that the prison authorities had the body. Cretzer had nothing to lose. Moreover, the deranged Shockley and the cunning Thompson kept goading Cretzer to kill all the guards. Thompson realized that if all nine were dead, there would be nobody alive who could name him as one of the escapers. Only Carnes, obedient to Coy and Hubbard, was opposed. Suddenly, Cretzer exploded in a murderous fury. He fired shot after shot into the two cells holding the guards. All went down. Then he ordered Carnes to go inside to make sure all were dead. Carnes went in at gunpoint and saw most of the guards were alive, but he reported that all were dead. Actually, only one was dead; of the remaining eight, five were gravely wounded and three had escaped injury completely, though they feigned death.

When Coy returned from talking with Warden Johnston, who had stalled for time, he discovered Cretzer's mass shooting. Without the guard hostages, Coy knew there could be no escape. Furious over how their carefully laid plans had been destroyed, Coy and Hubbard stalked Cretzer, who in turn hunted them. Meanwhile, news of the mass break attempt and wild rumors spread throughout San Francisco. Thousands lined the waterfront to watch as 80 Marines stormed ashore in full battle dress and guard sharpshooters slipped into the prison. They found the hostages, including one already dead, and brought them out. The seriously wounded five had compresses pressed over their wounds. Some unknown convict had treated them, undoubtedly saving the lives of at least three or four, and then slipped away, never to be identified.

More guard sharpshooters were sent in. Holes were cut in the roof of the building and grenades heaved inside, forcing most prisoners back to their own cell blocks, among them Thompson, Carnes and Shockley. But the remaining trio, Cretzer, Coy and Hubbard, evaded the grenade blasts by moving into the darkened utility corridors, concrete trenches below the cell blocks where plumbing and electric wires were buried. Even gas grenades dropped through the ventilator shafts could not dislodge them or stop them from firing at the guards stalking them.

The trio of convicts did not find each other until almost the end. By then Cretzer had been wounded by bomb shrapnel and Coy by gunfire. According to Clark Howard's *Six Against the Rock* (1977), the most definitive study of the escape, it was Cretzer—not the guards—who killed Coy, jumping out of the shadows and shooting him in the neck, shoulders and face. Cretzer tried to kill Hubbard as well but raced off as guards closed in. Hubbard dragged Coy off into a dark tunnel and remained with him until he died. In the meantime Cretzer was cornered by guards, who finally killed him with grenades and gunfire, 41 hours after the great escape attempt had started. Several hours later, four guards caught up with Hubbard. He died in a barrage of fire, taking one rifle slug in the left eye and another in the left temple.

The investigation that followed the great escape attempt focused on the brutal conditions in the prison. It was found that one prisoner, Whitey Franklin, who had attempted an escape back in 1938 with two others and had received an added life sentence for killing a guard, had spent every day since his conviction, more than seven years, in the hole.

It was almost an anticlimax when the three survivors of the ill-fated plot were brought to trial. Carnes got life to go along with his 99 years, and on December 3, 1948 Thompson and the obviously insane Shockley became the first two men to die in San Quentin's new gas chamber.

See also: *Bernard Coy, Joseph Paul "Dutch" Cretzer, Rufus "Whitey" Franklin, James A. Johnston, Sam Richard Shockley, Miran Edgar "Buddy" Thompson.*

ALCATRAZ Push-Ups: Prison "currency"

While Alcatraz had the deserved reputation of being America's toughest federal prison, there were a couple of seemingly odd exceptions to the rugged regimen that produced one of the strangest and most unique practices in American penology. Alcatraz became known as the *best* prison for "eats and smokes." Federal regulations called for a minimum of 2,000 calories per prisoner per day, but on Alcatraz the average was kept between 3,100 and 3,600 daily calories. When Mrs. Homer Cummings, the wife of the attorney general, visited "the Rock" in the mid-1930s, she was served the standard convict dinner—soup, beefaroni, beans, cabbage, onions, chili pods, hot biscuits, ice cream, iced tea and coffee—and exclaimed: "Why, this is more than we eat at home!" It was estimated that the average convict gained 15 to 20 pounds during his stay in the prison, and some put on 40 pounds or more.

Along with this rather lavish menu, Alcatraz had a bountiful smoking program. Each prisoner was issued three packs of cigarettes a week, and when that supply was gone, he could get all the loose tobacco he wanted from free dispensers to roll his own. Thus, in Alcatraz cigarettes lost the currency value and bribing power they enjoyed in other institutions. As a result, the curious practice of paying debts, such as those incurred in gambling games, with so many push-ups developed. This allowed the prisoners to have some action and offered something of an antidote for their overfeeding.

See also: *Alcatraz Prison.*

ALCOHOL

Drinking, drunkenness and alcoholism are significant factors contributing to crime in the United States. Each year there are about three million arrests for drunkenness and drunk driving and for vagrancy, disorderly conduct and other activities that usually involve drunkenness. These so-called direct alcoholism arrests may well account for 30 to 40 percent of all arrests made. Many far more serious crimes are also committed "under the influence," ranging from personal assault to armed robbery and murder. There are no reliable statistics measuring the exact correlation between drinking and homicide, but any veteran police officer knows that a great many domestic quarrels and "in the home murders," the leading category of homicides, are preceded by heavy drinking by one or more of the participants.

A 1974 study divided 3,510 men between the ages of 20 and 30 into drinking and nondrinking categories. The men were asked if they had committed a number of crimes, including car theft, breaking and entering, shoplifting, face-to-face stealing and armed robbery. Among the nondrinkers 16 percent had engaged in shoplifting and five percent admitted to breaking and entering. The incidence of all the other types of crime was statistically nonexistent. Among the drinkers in the study, the number of law breakers increased as the survey moved from light or moderate drinkers to heavy users of alcohol.

In the heaviest drinkers category, 18 percent reported engaging in breaking and entering, 56 percent in shoplifting, nine percent in car theft, five percent in stealing and two percent in armed robbery.

In a 1974 nationwide study of 191,400 inmates at state correctional facilities, 43 percent said they had been drinking at the time they committed the crime of which they were convicted. About half of these described their drinking as heavy.

Criminologists have long debated whether these and other studies demonstrate whether a person who is under the influence of alcohol will violate laws that he would not violate if he were not intoxicated. No definite conclusions are possible, but there is considerable evidence indicating that a drinker will behave in a "class" manner. Thus, among the middle class and advancing up the socioeconomic ladder, there is generally little economic basis for the commission of crime, especially violent crime, and the tendency is for drunkenness to result in such behavior as singing, telling dirty stories and crying. On the other hand, in the ghettos and among the lower socioeconomic classes, the economic basis for crime increases and there

is a far greater tendency to turn from "happy drunkenness" to the starting of fights and the violation of criminal laws.

Further reading: *Fundamentals of Criminal Investigation* by Charles O'Hara.

ALDERISIO, Felix "Milwaukee Phil" (1922-1971): Hit man

Regarded by many as the top hit man of the Chicago mob, Felix "Milwaukee Phil" Alderisio was popularly given credit for designing the "hitmobile," a car especially geared for committing murder with the least possible interference. Among what may be called its optional features were switches that would turn out the car's front or rear lights to confuse police tails. Another innovation was a secret compartment in a backrest that not only held murder weapons but contained clamps to anchor down handguns, shotguns or rifles for more steady shooting while the vehicle was in motion. Although the Chicago police insisted that Milwaukee Phil was the executioner in well over a dozen gangland hits, no murder charge against him was ever proven. He was, however, finally convicted of extortion and died in prison in 1971.

ALDERMEN'S Wars: Chicago political killings

Even for Chicago, a city noted for its gangland killings and battles, the so-called Aldermen's Wars, between 1916 and 1921, stand out for sheer savagery. In all, 30 men died in the continuous five-year battle fought for control of the 19th, or "Bloody," Ward, which encompassed the city's Little Italy. The political forces that controlled the 19th were entitled to the huge payoffs coming out of Little Italy for various criminal enterprises. With the coming of Prohibition, the production of moonshine alcohol became the area's "cottage industry" and an important source of illicit alcohol for the entire city.

The 19th had been controlled by Johnny "de Pow" Powers, an incorrigible saloonkeeper, protector of criminals and graft-taking alderman from the 1890s on. Despite the transition of much of the area from Irish to Italian, Powers was able to maintain his control and met no serious challenge until 1916, when Anthony D'Andrea mounted a bid against James Bowler, junior alderman from the 19th and a Powers henchman. D'Andrea was less than a pillar of civic virtue himself, although he was a prominent leader in many Italian fraternal societies and a labor union official. The *Chicago Tribune* reported: "Anthony Andrea is the same Antonio D'Andrea, unfrocked priest, linguist, and former power in the old 'red light' district, who in 1903 was released from the penitentiary after serving 13 months on a counterfeit charge. D'Andrea's name has also been connected with a gang of Italian forgers and bank thieves who operated at one time all over the country."

The killings commenced in February 1916. Frank Lombardi, a Powers ward heeler, was shot dead in a saloon. D'Andrea lost his election battle that year, as well as another one in 1919 and a final one in 1921, a direct race against Powers. During all that time, corpses of supporters on both sides filled the streets, and a number of bombings took place, including one set off on the front porch of Powers' home. The Powers forces retaliated with the bombing of a D'Andrea rally, severely injuring five persons. There were subsequent bombings of D'Andrea's headquarters and the home of one of his lieutenants.

One day in March 1921, Paul Labriola, a Powers man who was a court bailiff, walked to work with some apprehension because his name had been listed on the Dead Man's Tree, a poplar on Loomis Street on which both factions had taken to posting the names of slated victims, a grim form of psychological warfare. At Halsted and Congress, Labriola passed four D'Andrea gunmen; as he started across the intersection, he was cut down by a volley of shots. One of the four gunmen walked over to their victim, straddled his body and pumped three more revolver shots into him. Later that day the same four gunmen killed cigar store owner Harry Raimondi, a former D'Andrea man who had switched sides. While the killings and bombings continued, Alderman Bowler declared:

> Conditions in the 19th Ward are terrible. Gunmen are patrolling the streets. I have received threats that I was to be 'bumped off' or kidnapped. Alderman Powers' house is guarded day and night. Our men have been met, threatened and slugged. Gunmen and cutthroats have been imported from New York and Buffalo for this campaign of intimidation. Owners of halls have been threatened with death or the destruction of their buildings if they rent their places to us. It is worse than the Middle Ages.

The killings continued after D'Andrea's third election defeat, despite his announcement that he was through with 19th Ward politics. In April 1921 a man named Abraham Wolfson who lived in the apartment across the hall from D'Andrea got a threatening letter that read in part: "You are to move in 15 days. We are going to blow up the building and kill the whole D'Andrea family. He killed others and we are going to do the same thing. We mean business. You better move and save many lives."

Wolfson showed the note to D'Andrea and then moved out. This gave D'Andrea's enemies what they wanted, an empty apartment from which to watch him. On May 11, just after his bodyguard had driven off, D'Andrea was gunned down as he was about to enter his building.

D'Andrea was the wars' 28th victim. There were to be two more, Andrew Orlando and Joseph Sinacola, D'Andrea's Sicilian "blood brother," both of whom had sworn to avenge their boss' death. Orlando was killed in July and Sinacola in August.

There was only one prosecution for any of the 30 murders committed during the Aldermen's Wars, that of Bloody Angelo Genna for the street corner slaying of Paul Labriola. But nothing much came of it. The numerous witnesses to the murder belatedly realized they hadn't seen a thing.

See also: *Dead Man's Tree.*

ALLEN, Bill (?-1882): Murderer

A Chicago black man named Bill Allen had the distinction of being hunted by the largest "posse" in American history. On November 30, 1882 Allen killed one black and wounded another, and later that evening he murdered Patrolman Clarence E. Wright, who tried to arrest him. Three days after the incident Allen was located in the basement of a house by Patrolman Patrick Mulvihill, but the fugitive shot Mulvihill through a window and fled. Soon, 200 policemen were scouring the black district of Chicago for Allen. By mid-afternoon, according to a contemporary account, "Upwards of 10,000 people armed with all sorts of weapons from pocket pistols and pitchforks to rifles, were assisting the police in the hunt." At 3:30 that afternoon, Sgt. John Wheeler found Allen in the backyard of a house on West Kinzie Street and killed him in a gunfight. Allen's body was taken in a patrol wagon to the Desplaines police station, and somehow the rumor started that he had been arrested rather than killed. A lynch mob of thousands quickly formed, and when a few officers tried to break up the crowd, they were threatened. "The crowd," one report of the event said, "became frenzied and threatened to tear down the station. Threats and promises were all in vain, and a serious riot seemed inevitable. Chief Doyle mounted the wagon and assured the crowd that the Negro was really dead. They hooted and yelled, shouting that the police were concealing the man and encouraging each other to break in the windows of the station."

The police chief then came up with a way of placating the mob. Allen's body was stripped, laid out on a mattress and put on view through a barred window where it could be seen at the side of the station. A line was formed, and "the crowd passed in eager procession, and were satisfied by a simple glance at the dull, cold face. All afternoon that line moved steadily along, and the officers were busily occupied in keeping it in order. The crowd increased rather than diminished, and until darkness settled down, they were still gazing at the dead murderer. After dark a flaring gas jet at the head of the body brought it out in strong relief, and all night long the line of curious people filed by for a glimpse of the dead." It was 48 hours before Allen's body could be taken off display.

ALLEN, John (c.1830-?): "Wickedest Man in New York"

One of the most notorious dives in New York City during the 1850s and 1860s—on a par with such later infamous resorts as the Haymarket, Paresis Hall and McGuirk's Suicide Hall—was John Allen's Dance House at 304 Water Street. Allen himself became widely known as "the Wickedest Man in New York," a sobriquet pinned on him first by Oliver Dyer in *Packard's Monthly.* What brought down the wrath of Dyer and other crusading journalists was not simply the vulgarity and depravity of Allen's establishment but his peronal background. Allen came from a pious upper New York state family; three of his brothers were ministers, two Presbyterian preachers and the other a Baptist. He himself had initially pursued a similar ministerial career but soon deserted the Union Theological Seminary for the pleasures and profits of the flesh.

With his new wife, John Allen opened a dance hall-brothel on Water Street, stocking it with 20 prostitutes famed for wearing bells on their ankles and little else. In 10 years of operation, the Allens banked more than $100,000, placing them among the richest vice operators in the city.

John Allen rented out his dance hall-bordello for prayer meetings and obligingly provided sinners at 25 or 50 cents a head.

Despite his desertion of the cloth, Allen never entirely shed his religious training. While he was a drunk, procurer and thief and was suspected of having committed more than one murder, Allen insisted on providing his lurid establishment with an aura of holiness. All the cubicles in which his ladies entertained customers were furnished with a Bible and other religious tracts. Regular clients were often rewarded with gifts of the New Testament. Before the dance hall opened for business at 1 p.m., Allen would gather his flock of musicians, harlots, bouncers and barkeeps and read passages out of the Scriptures. Hymn singing was a ritual; the favorite of Allen's hookers was "There is Rest for the Weary," apparently because it held out a more serene existence for the ladies in the life hereafter.

> There is rest for the weary,
> There is rest for you.
> On the other side of Jordan,
> In the sweet fields of Eden,
> Where the Tree of Life is blooming,
> There is rest for you.

Eventually, when a group of uptown clergymen took over Allen's resort for prayer meetings, it looked as if the religious aspect of the dance hall had gotten out of hand. Allen had apparently embraced religion entirely, and a lot of uptown devout began attending these meetings to bear witness to the reformation of sinners—especially John Allen. Alas, exposes in several newspapers turned up the sad intelligence that Allen, rather than undergoing a religious rebirth, had actually leased out his establishment to the ministers for $350 a month and seemingly provided some newly reformed sinners for 25 or 50 cents a head.

In time, the revivalist movement faded and Allen attempted to return his resort to its former infamy, only to find the criminal element no longer had faith in him, figuring anyone so religiously inclined might be untrustworthy. The last public record of Allen was his arrest, along with his wife and some of his prostitutes, for robbing a seaman. Shortly thereafter, the dance hall closed.

Allen's fate is obscured by contradictory legends. One had him finally undergoing a complete reformation and even taking up the cloth, but another placed "the Wickedest Man in New York" practicing his tawdry business in a different city under an assumed name. None of these stories has ever been confirmed.

ALLEN, Lizzie (1840-1896): Chicago madam

Next to the fabulous Carrie Watson, Lizzie Allen was Chicago's most successful madam during the 19th century. A native of Milwaukee, she came to Chicago in 1858, at the age of 18, with the clear intention of becoming a madam. She went to work at Mother Herrick's Prairie Queen and, unlike most of the other girls, did not squander her earnings on men. After a stint at another leading brothel, the Senate, Allen opened a house on Wells Street staffed by three prostitutes. Despite the modest nature of the enterprise, she prospered there. Like most other brothel owners, Lizzie was burned out in the Great Chicago Fire of 1871, but she is credited with being the first back in business. She recruited a large staff of unemployed harlots and put them to work in a new house on Congress Street while the carpenters were still working to complete it. With that jump on the competition, Allen accumulated a large fortune and soon became one of the most important madams in the city. In 1878 she formed a relationship with a "solid man," the colorful Christopher Columbus Crabb, and with him as her lover and financial adviser, she flourished still more. In fact, Lizzie Allen was regarded by one local tabloid as "the finest looking woman in Chicago."

In 1888 Allen and Crabb built a 24-room mansion on Lake View Avenue to use as a plush brothel, but police interference doomed the enterprise. They then built an imposing double house at 2131 South Dearborn, which they named the House of Mirrors. Costing $125,000, it was one of the most impressive brothels of its day. (The house was destined to even greater fame under the Everleigh sisters, who took it over in 1900 and made it the most-celebrated bawdy house in America.) Lizzie Allen operated the mansion until 1896, when, in poor health, she retired, leasing the property to Effie Hankins. She signed over all her real estate to Crabb and named him the sole beneficiary in her will. The estate was estimated to be worth between $300,000 and $1 million. When Lizzie Allen died on September 2, 1896, she was buried in Rosehill Cemetery. Her tombstone was inscribed, "Perpetual Ease."

See also: *Christopher Columbus Crabb, Everleigh Sisters, Prairie Queen.*

ALLEN Massacre, The: Courtroom shoot-out

The bloodiest confrontation ever to take place in an American courtroom occurred on March 14, 1912 at the Carroll County Courthouse in Hillsville, Va. The Allen clan of the Blue Ridge Mountain area believed in its own code of behavior built around making moonshine, shooting revenuers and—certainly—paying no taxes. One day in 1911 a peace officer arrested a member of the clan for moonshining. Floyd Allen, the uncle of the accused, knocked the officer down and helped his nephew to escape. Uncle Floyd subsequently was charged with assault. It was an unheard-of event—nobody had every dared arrest Floyd Allen before.

The Allen clan immediately began informing citizens throughout the county that Floyd Allen was innocent and had better be found so. It soon became evident that no one in the county was about to find Allen guilty of anything, and the state came up with the legally questionable ploy of importing jurors from elsewhere in Virginia. Floyd Allen was readily found guilty by the imported jurors. At 9 a.m. on March 14, the court convened for sentencing. As Judge Thornton L. Massie started speaking, some 17 Allen men entered the courtroom and stationed themselves at strategic positions. The judge finished his speech and sentenced Floyd Allen to one year. Floyd then addressed the court. "Gentlemen," he said, "I ain't goin'."

With that statement, Floyd Allen pulled out two guns and started shooting: where and at whom varies with each account. Most say that Floyd shot and killed Judge Massie. But some credit his brother Sidna with that killing. In any event, 17 Allens started shooting; some only shot at the ceiling or into the floor and most of the shooting was done by Floyd, Sidna and Floyd's son Claude. In less than 60 seconds at least 75 shots were fired and six people killed—the judge, the sheriff, the commonwealth attorney, a spectator, a juror and a woman witness, ironically for the defense. Eight others were wounded. Among the Allens only Floyd was wounded and he was able to hobble off to a nearby hotel, where he was later taken into custody. This too must have surprised the Allens, who obviously thought their show of force would be enough to allow Floyd to walk from the courtroom. Sidna Allen was so nonchalant about the entire matter that when he ran out of ammunition, he went across the street to buy more in a hardware store. It was closed because the owner was in court.

Virginia authorities moved in rapidly to suppress the Allens once and for all. Floyd and his son Claude were sentenced to death for murder and electrocuted on March 28, 1913. Sidna got 15 years. All the other Allens got lesser sentences; some had insisted they had fired in the air or at the floor, trying deliberately not to kill anyone but merely create panic. A few came up with a novel defense: because the gunsmoke was so thick, it was impossible to aim, and therefore, if anyone was killed, it was purely an accident.

After serving 13 years, Sidna Allen received a pardon in 1926 from Gov. (later Sen.) Harry F. Byrd.

In his memoirs, Sidna insisted the shootings had all been unpremeditated and were originally intended as a bluff to free Floyd Allen. He also claimed the clan had been the object of political persecution in the county for some time. After Sidna's release the Allen clan argued that his pardon indicated the state had admitted they had been framed.

ALLISON, Clay (1840-1887): Gunfighter

One of the most notorious of the Western gunfighters, Clay Allison was not an outlaw in the ordinary sense of the word. He called himself a "shootist," apparently in an attempt to indicate he was a professional, like an artist or a dentist. Allison lived on the fringe of the law and according to a personal code governed more by his own belief in honor than by the strictures of the law. Invariably, this meant he killed men "that deserved killin'." In a morbid sense, he may have contributed some of the most entertaining—to observers rather than to victims—shootings in Western lore.

One of his more famous duels was with a gunman named Chunk Colbert in 1874. The pair sat eyeball to eyeball in a New Mexico Territory eatery, staring each other down and stirring their coffee with the muzzles of their six-guns. Soon each reholstered his piece and continued to eat. Colbert made the first move to draw but Allison shot him dead just above the right eye. On another occasion Allison led a lynching party against a man named Kennedy who was suspected of killing his own young daughter. Some bones were found on the Kennedy ranch, but there was no definite determination that the bones were human. The matter was still in dispute after the lynching, but that didn't stop Allison from cutting off the dead man's head, impaling it on a pike and riding 29 miles to Cimarron, Kan. to his favorite watering hole, Henry Lambert's saloon.

Allison could best be described as a part-time maniac, since between his vicious killings he was generally a well-mannered rancher. There might have been some excuse for his behavior, however. He had joined the Confederate Army in his native Tennessee but was discharged after sustaining a blow on his skull, which was said to have made him intermittently epileptic and at other times maniacal. After the Civil War, he punched cattle and finally set up the first of his several ranches.

What troubled other men about Allison was his unpredictability. In 1875, although a rancher, he sided with the homesteaders in their battles, clearly out of a sense of fair play, an attitude that enraged other ranchers and stock associations. At the same time Allison was a bitter racist, and in New Mexico he killed a number of Mexican "outlaws." Few, however, even considered challenging him for any of his deeds.

Allison continued to devise duels that bordered on lunacy. He once indulged in a fast-draw contest with a gunman named Mace Bowman. After Bowman continually outdrew him, Allison suggested they pull off their boots, strip down to their underwear and take turns shooting at each other's bare feet to see who danced best under fire. Remarkably, the confrontation ended without bloodshed after several hours, each man giving in to exhaustion.

Contemporary drawing depicts Clay Allison's famous shoot-out with another notorious gunman, Chunk Colbert.

When he got into yet another dispute, Allison arranged to do battle naked in a grave in which each adversary would be armed with a Bowie knife. Both agreed to purchase a tombstone and the winner would see to it that the stone of the loser was suitably engraved. While waiting for the delivery of the tombstone, Allison picked up a wagonload of supplies from Pecos, Tex. to bring back to his ranch. When a sack of grain fell from the moving wagon, he tried to grab it and toppled to the ground. A wagon wheel rolled over his neck, breaking it and killing him.

It was a bizarre ending to a violent life for a man credited, by various counts, with the deaths of 15 to 21 men. A Kansas newspaper had a difficult time trying to evaluate the life of Clay Allison and whether he was "in truth a villain or a gentleman." That was "a question that many never settled to their own satisfaction. Certain it is that many of his stern deeds were for the right as he understood that right to be."

See also: *Chunk Colbert.*

ALLISON, Dorothy (1925-): Crime-solving psychic

Among the various psychics who have made the popular press in recent years, one American psychic, a housewife from Nutley, N. J., ranks above all others as having some apparent crime-solving ability. Dorothy Allison's visions of peaceful landscapes

containing unfound bodies have turned out to be, as *Newsweek* labeled them, "close approximations of grisly reality." In the past dozen years or so, Mrs. Allison has been consulted by police in well over 100 cases and, by her own count, has helped solve 13 killings and find more than 50 missing persons. Many police departments have expressed wholehearted, if befuddled, gratitude. "Seeing is believing," said Anthony Tortora, head of the missing persons division of the Bergen County N.J. sheriff's office. "Dorothy Allison took us to within 50 yards of where the body was found. She's quite a gal."

Some of Mrs. Allison's "finds" have been accident victims and others have been the victims of foul play. In September 1977 two of her finds turned up in different states just one day apart. She pinpointed a swamp area in New Jersey where 17-year-old Ronald Stica would be found and was able to tell police prior to the discovery of the body that he had been stabbed to death. The day before, the body of 14-year-old Susan Jacobson, missing two years, had turned up inside an oil drum in an abandoned boat yard in Staten Island, N.Y. Mrs. Allison had described the corpse site—although she had never been to Staten Island—as a swampy area, with "twin church steeples and two bridges—but one not for cars" nearby. She said she also saw the letters M A R standing alone. All the elements were there, including the letters M A R painted in red on a nearby large rock.

Perhaps Mrs. Allison's most amazing case was one that began at about 6:30 p.m. on Thursday, July 22, 1976, when

Deborah Sue Kline left her job as a hospital aide, got in her car and started for her home in Waynesboro, Pa. She never got there. Months of police investigations proved fruitless. Jane Kline, the girl's mother, finally contacted Mrs. Allison, who agreed to come to Pennsylvania. Quite naturally, the first thing the mother asked was if her daughter was still alive. By the end of the day, Mrs. Allison told her the answer: Debbie was dead. Mrs. Allison put on Debbie's graduation ring "to help me feel her presence." She toured the area with police, reporters and a friend of the Klines.

After a while, she was able to reconstruct the crime. She saw Debbie driving home from the hospital and two cars, a yellow one and a black one, forcing her off the road. According to a local newspaper account: "She was taken from her car in one of the other cars to a place where she was molested. She was taken to another place where she was killed with a knife wound. I saw [at the death site] yellow signs, a dump, burnt houses and a swimming pool. I could see her skeleton. It was not underground. The word 'line' or 'lion' came to me."

On January 26, 1977, three days after Dorothy Allison had returned home, police located the body of Debbie Kline. It was not buried and was in an area where junk was dumped. There were no "burnt houses" but the spot was just off the Fannettsburg-Burnt Cabins Road. In the area were yellow traffic signs warning motorists of steep grades on the road. Near the body was a discarded plastic swimming pool. There was no "lion" but there was a "line"—150 feet away was the line between Huntington and Franklin counties. And Debbie had been stabbed to death.

Then the police confronted a suspect, in jail at the time on another rape charge. His name was Richard Lee Dodson. Dodson broke down and led them to where the body had been found. He and another man, Ronald Henninger, were charged with the crime. Ken Peiffer, a reporter for the *Record Herald,* said: "She told me, among other clues later proven accurate, the first names of the two men involved, Richard and Ronald. She even told me that one of the men had a middle name of Lee or Leroy."

The police of Washington Township, who were in charge of the case, made Dorothy Allison an honorary member of the police department. The citation given to her reads in part, "Dorothy Allison, through psychic powers, provided clues which contributed to the solving of the crime."

Of course, not all of Dorothy Allison's efforts have been triumphs. She was the first psychic called in by Randolph Hearst after daughter Patty disappeared in Berkeley, Calif. Mrs. Allison turned up little of value while on the West Coast. Still, Hearst did not scoff. "Dorothy couldn't locate Patty," he said, "but she is honest and reputable. I wouldn't laugh at it."

ALLMAN, John (?-1877): The Cavalryman Killer

The prototypal Western cavalryman bad guy, according to a Hollywood historian, "Bad John Allman did as much to make John Ford a great movie director as did John Wayne." The point may have been stretched, but John Allman was just about the worst killer the U.S. Army contributed to the West.

A native of Tennessee, Allman was a violent character throughout his Army career. There is some speculation that Allman was not his original name, that he had served elsewhere in uniform under another identity or two until it became wise to change it.

There is no record of exactly how many men Allman killed—"not countin' injuns," as they said in the cavalry. In any case, his last spree substantially reduced the population of the Arizona Territory. In the summer of 1877 Allman got into an argument during a poker game in the cavalry barracks at Prescott, Ariz. When the pistol smoke cleared, Allman and the pot were gone and two Army sergeants were dead. A posse soon started out after Bad John and got close to him, close enough for two of its members, Billy Epps and Dave Groat, to be killed by him. Still on the run, Allman was recognized, or at least thought he had been recognized, by two woodcutters, and he promptly shot them dead. Late in August, about two weeks after he had killed the woodcutters, Allman, tired, hungry and broke, rode into Yuma. When he rode out, a bartender named Vince Dundee was dead, and Allman had the contents of the till and as many bottles of whiskey as a man could tote. In Williams, Ariz. Deputy Sheriff Ed Roberts spotted Allman in a saloon, but Bad John's gun was quicker; on his way out, the cavalryman killer stepped right over the dying lawman.

Sheriff Ullman of Coconino County turned over the job of apprehending Allman to a bizarre group of bounty hunters referred to by the press as Outlaw Exterminators, Inc. The Exterminators consisted of five bounty hunters who specialized in going after "dead or alive" quarries and bringing them in dead rather than alive. However, Allman was a hard man to run to ground. Low on bullets, he killed a sheepherder named Tom Dowling for his gun and ammunition. Next he kidnapped a 13-year-old white girl named Ida Phengle and a 12-year-old Hopi girl and raped them both. Allman eventually freed his two young captives but soon found himself pursued by various lawmen, the Exterminators and a Hopi war party. In the end, it was Clay Calhoun, one of the Exterminators, who located Allman among some deserted Indian cliff dwellings on October 11, 1877. According to Calhoun, whose version of what happened was the only one reported, he brought down Allman in a stirring gun fight. This dramatic scenario is hard to credit since Allman had been shot four times, in the mouth, chest, stomach and groin, all in a nice neat line. Any of those shots would have grounded Allman, making the alignment of wounds most unusual for a shoot-out. Some speculated that Allman had more likely been shot while asleep. But speculation aside, the important thing was that Bad John Allman's bloody reign of terror was over, and the particulars of how it happened didn't trouble many people in Arizona.

See also: *Outlaw Exterminators, Inc.*

ALMODOVAR, Louisa (1919-1942): Murder victim

Terry Almodovar had the misfortune of strangling his estranged wife to death on a certain hill in Central Park in New York City, thereby achieving unlikely fame in botany texts. If he had done it almost anywhere else in the park, in fact on the other side of the same hill, he might not have gone to the electric chair.

When Louisa's body was found on November 2, 1942, the police were certain the murder had been committed either by a park marauder or by the woman's husband. Terry Almodovar insisted that at the time of the murder, fixed at between 9 and 10 o'clock the night before, he was at a dance hall several blocks away. No less than 22 girls backed him up, saying he was there the whole time. The truth was that he had slipped away long enough to kill his wife, whom he had secretly offered to meet in the park. Her death was desirable because he had been offered marriage by a very wealthy widow.

Almodovar didn't realize the trouble he was in when the police took his suit and gave it to Dr. Alexander O. Gettler of the Medical Examiner's Office. Dr. Gettler made a spectrogram of the dirt from Terry's trousers and another of the dirt from where the body was found. The elements of both were exactly the same. Still, Almodovar insisted he hadn't been in Central Park the night of the murder or at any time within the previous two years. But Dr. Gettler also found some grass spikelets in the suspect's cuffs; these were identified as *Panicum dicoth milleflorium,* and they matched perfectly with similar grass spikelets found at the murder scene. Almodovar insisted they must have been picked up somewhere else—perhaps in Tremont Park in the Bronx, where he'd been recently. At this point Joseph J. Copeland, a professor of botany at City College of New York, took over. This particular kind of grass, *Panicum dicoth,* was extremely rare in the New York area. It grew in three areas in Westchester County, two in Long Island—but only one in New York City: a small section of a hill in Central Park, and not even on the other side of the same hill where the murder had been committed. Confronted with the evidence, Almodovar suddenly remembered he'd gone through Central Park just a couple of months before, in September. Copeland, however, knew that *Panicum dicoth* is a late bloomer. Most of the spikelets found in Almodovar's cuffs couldn't have gotten there before October 10 and probably not before October 15. But they most certainly could have got there on November 1.

The science of botany sent Terry Almodovar to the electric chair on March 9, 1943.

ALTA, Utah: Lawless mining town

For a time, Alta, Utah Territory sported a sign that read, "WELCOME TO THE MEANEST LITTLE TOWN IN THE WEST." The small silver-mining town in the foothills of Utah's Rustler Mountains lived up to its motto. In its heyday during the 1870s, Alta had 26 saloons and a cemetery touted as the largest in any town of that size.

While avalanches claimed the lives of many miners, the largest contingent of corpses buried in the Alta cemetery were the more than 100 victims of gun battles. In 1873 a stranger dressed in black came to town and announced he had the power to resurrect all of the town's dead gunmen. The miners, a superstitious lot, speculated that such a development would only lead to a lot of bullets flying about in vengeance shootouts and opted for the status quo. They raised $2,500 in a community collection as a gift for the "resurrection man" contingent on his leaving Alta permanently.

By the early 1900s Alta was a ghost town, its ore mined out, but today it thrives in a new reincarnation as a popular ski resort.

ALTERIE, Louis "Two Gun" (1892-1935): Gangster

The Dion O'Banion gang that dominated Chicago's North Side during the early years of Prohibition was particularly noted for its zaniness (it once "rubbed out" a horse for killing one of its members in a riding mishap), but even for this bunch, Louis "Two Gun" Alterie was wacky. Alterie, whose real name was Leland Verain, owned a ranch in Colorado but came east to join up with O'Banion's gambling and bootlegging operations. He wore two pistols, one on each hip, Wild West-style, and always boasted of his perfect marksmanship with either his left or right hand, often shooting out the lights in saloons to prove his point.

It was Alterie, it was said, who insisted that revenge was required after a leading member of the gang, Nails Morton, had been thrown by a horse in Lincoln Park and kicked to death. He led the gang to the riding stable and there they kidnapped the horse, took it to the scene of Morton's demise and shot it to death. Alterie was so incensed by the "murder" of his comrade that he first punched the hapless horse in the snout before turning his gun on it.

When Dion O'Banion was assassinated by Capone gunmen, Two Gun Alterie went wild. In a tearful performance at the funeral, Alterie raged to reporters: "I have no idea who killed Deanie, but I would die smiling if only I had a chance to meet the guys who did, any time, any place they mention and I would get at least two or three of them before they got me. If I knew who killed Deanie, I'd shoot it out with the gang of killers before the sun rose in the morning." Asked where the duel should be fought, he suggested Chicago's busiest corner, Madison and State streets, at noon. Mayor William E. Dever was enraged when he heard of Alterie's words. "Are we still abiding by the code of the Dark Ages?" he demanded.

Earl "Little Hymie" Weiss, successor to O'Banion as head of the mob, ordered Alterie to cool off, stating that because of his rantings political and police pressure was being put on the gang's operations on the North Side. Alterie nodded grandly with a big wink and stayed quiet for about a week. Then he swaggered into a Loop nightclub frequented by reporters and gangsters and, brandishing his two pistols, boasted loudly:

"All 12 bullets in these rods have Capone's initials carved on their noses. And if I don't get him, Bugs, Hymie or Schemer will."

For Weiss, who was trying to keep peace with Capone until the right time to strike, Alterie's blustering was just too much. He ordered Bugs Moran to "move" Alterie. Moran went to the cowboy gangster and growled: "You're getting us in bad. You run off at the mouth too much."

Alterie recognized an invitation to leave town when he heard one and returned to his ranch in Colorado, ending his participation in the Chicago gang wars. When he finally came back to Chicago on a visit in 1935, the O'Banion gang had been wiped out except for Moran, and he was no longer a power. Apparently, just for old time's sake, somebody shot Alterie to death.

See also: *Animal Lynching, George "Bugs" Moran, Samuel J. "Nails" Morton, Charles Dion "Deanie" O'Banion.*

ALTGELD, John P. (1847-1902): Illinois governor

John P. Altgeld, elected governor of Illinois in 1892, was the main player in the final act of the 1886 Haymarket affair, in which a dynamite bomb killed seven policemen and two civilians and wounded 130 others. Altgeld, a wealthy owner of business property, announced he would hear arguments for pardoning three anarchists who had been sentenced to long prison terms for their alleged part in the affair; but no one expected him to free them because it would be an act of political suicide. Four other anarchists had already been hung as a result of Haymarket, and another had committed suicide in his cell.

In June 1893 Altgeld issued a long analysis of the Haymarket trial, attacking the trial judge, Joseph E. Gary, for ruling the prosecution did not have to identify the bomb-thrower or even prove that the actual murderer had been influenced by the anarchist beliefs of the defendants. "In all the centuries during which government has been maintained among men and crime has been punished, no judge in a civilized country has ever laid down such a rule before." Altgeld also referred to the judge's obvious bias in constantly attacking the defendants before the jury. He then issued full pardons for Samuel Fielden, Michael Schwab and Oscar Neebe, declaring them and the five dead men innocent.

While Altgeld was hailed by labor spokesmen, most newspapers condemned him bitterly. The *New York World* caricatured him as an acolyte worshipping the bomb-wielding black-robed figure of an anarchist. The *Chicago Tribune* denounced Altgeld, who was German, as "not merely an alien by birth, but an alien by temperament and sympathies. He has apparently not a drop of pure American blood in his veins. He does not reason like an American, nor feel like one." The governor was also hanged in effigy.

Altgeld ignored such criticisms, being content he was "merely doing right," but his act turned out to be political suicide. In 1896 he ran for the U.S. Senate but was defeated. Clarence

Darrow later tried to set him up in practice as an associate, but Altgeld, no longer rich, was a tired man, and he died in obscurity six years later. His memory was neglected until Vachel Lindsay placed a poem, "The Eagle That Is Forgotten," on his grave; it read in part:

> Where is that boy, that Heaven-born Bryan,
> That Homer Bryan, who sang from the West?
> Gone to join the shadows with Altgeld the eagle,
> Where the kings and the slaves and the troubadours rest. . . .

See also: *Clarence Darrow, Haymarket Affair.*

ALVORD, Burt (1866-1910?): Lawman and outlaw

A notorious law officer turned bad, Burt Alvord seems to have enjoyed long simultaneous careers as a lawman and bandit. The son of a roving justice of the peace, Alvord was a youth in Tombstone during the time of the vaunted gunfight at the O.K. Corral. Although only 15, he was astute enough to spot one of the underlying motives for the battle—control of the county sheriff's office, with the special duty of collecting taxes, which might or might not be turned over to the treasury.

When the celebrated lawman John Slaughter was elected sheriff of Cochise County in 1886, Alvord, who was 20 at the time, became his chief deputy and began building a solid reputation as an enforcer of the law, tracking down numerous rustlers and other thieves. There is little doubt, however, that during the same period he was also an outlaw. In time, Slaughter, an honest man, became disenchanted with his deputy. Yet when the sheriff retired from his post in 1890, no crimes had been pinned on Alvord. In the mid-1890s Alvord switched from wearing a badge to rustling cattle in Mexico. But by 1899 he was a constable in Willcox, Arizona Territory despite some murders under his belt. Here Alvord teamed up with Billie Stiles to pull off a number of train robberies and other holdups. The entire Alvord-Stiles gang was captured after a train robbery near Cochise in September 1899, but they escaped from jail and went back in business. Alvord and Stiles were caught again in 1903 but once more broke free. After that, Alvord tried to fake their deaths, even sending coffins allegedly carrying their remains to Tombstone. The trick failed, and the law kept hunting for the two outlaw chiefs. Finally, the Arizona Rangers swept into Mexico in 1904 and cornered Alvord at Nigger Head Gap. Alvord was wounded and brought back to Arizona. This time he spent two years in prison. Thereafter, Alvord's record becomes murky. He was spotted, according to various stories, all over Latin America and even in Jamaica. When a canal worker in Panama died in 1910, he was said to be Alvord, but the identification was not conclusive.

See also: *Billie Stiles.*

AMATUNA, Samuzzo "Samoots" (1898-1925): Chicago gangster and murderer

One of Chicago's most colorful and brutal gangsters during the

1920s, Samuzzo "Samoots" Amatuna for a time held a power base from which he challenged Al Capone's control of crime in the city. In the end, however, Samoots was more remembered for the changes his death brought about in the practices of Chicago-area barber shops.

A professional fiddler and a fop, Samoots was one of the first to conceal a weapon in an instrument case, using this technique with three confederates in the attempted murder of a musicians' union business agent. The proud possessor of 200 monogrammed silk shirts, he once took off in pursuit of the driver of a Chinese laundry delivery wagon after one of his shirts was returned scorched. Samoots pulled his gun to shoot the frightened driver, but at the last moment he was overcome by a spark of humanity and shot the driver's horse instead.

Samoots became the chief bodyguard for the notorious Terrible Gennas, who controlled much of the city's homemade bootleg racket. As they were wiped out or scattered one by one, Samoots moved up in power and in 1925 he seized control of the Unione Siciliane. This group had been a lawful fraternal organization up to the turn of the century, but from then on, it became more and more a front for the criminal operations of Mafia forces. Chicago had the largest number of branches of the Unione, whose 40,000 members represented a potent force as well as an organization to be looted through various rackets, such as manipulation of pension funds. For years the Unione was under the control of Mike Merlo, who knew how to keep peace among the various criminal combines, but after his death in 1924 the Unione presidency became a hot seat. Bloody Angelo Genna took over as president, only to be murdered in May 1925.

Al Capone, who was not a Sicilian and thus not eligible for membership, wanted to place his *consigliere*, Tony Lombardo, in the office but decided to wait for an election. In the meantime Samoots walked into the Unione's offices with two armed confederates, Abe "Bummy" Goldstein and Eddie Zion, and declared himself elected. Capone was furious at the effrontery, but he soon had more reason to hate Samoots as the latter moved to open a chink in Capone's booze and other operations.

However, Samoots had other enemies such as the O'Banion Irish gang, which was still in power on the North Side even after the death of its leader. On November 13, 1925 Samoots, planning to go to the opera with his fiancee, Rose Pecorara, dropped into a Cicero barbershop for a shave. He was reclining in a barber's chair with a towel over his face when two assassins, believed to be Jim Doherty and Schemer Drucci of the O'Banions, marched in. One of the gunmen fired four shots but, remarkably, missed Samoots with every shot. The frightened target bolted from the barber's chair and tried to dodge four bullets from the second gunman. Each of these shots hit home, and the assassins strode out, leaving their victim near death. Rushed to a hospital, Samoots asked to marry his fiancee from his hospital bed but died before the ceremony started.

Within a few weeks Samoots' aides, Goldstein and Zion, were also killed, and the way was open for Capone's man, Lombardo, to take over the Unione. After Samoots' death, which was the second recent Chicago barbershop assassination,

it became common practice for barbers dealing with a gangster clientele never to cover their faces with a towel and to position the chair so that it always faced the entrance. This local custom did not spread to New York, where some two decades later Albert Anastasia was gunned down under similar circumstances.

AMBERG, Louis "Pretty" (1898-1935): Racketeer and murderer

From the late 1920s until his own violent demise in 1935, Louis "Pretty" Amberg was New York's best-known killer, having dispatched over 100 victims. Thanks to cunning and dumb luck, however, he was never so much as saddled with a stiff fine for any of his or his brother Joe's murders, although his achievements were common knowledge. His technique of stuffing victims into laundry bags, alive but trussed up in such a way that they strangled themselves, was immortalized by Damon Runyon in several stories in which Pretty Amberg was featured in a thinly fictionalized form.

Pretty, so named because of his ugliness, was brought to America from Russia by his fruit peddler parents. By the age of 10 he was terrorizing his home territory of Brownsville in Brooklyn, New York City, an area that bowed only to genuine toughness and meanness. Young Pretty developed a unique fruit-selling technique: he would kick on a door until the resident opened up and then shove handfuls of fruit and vegetables forward and snarl, "Buy." People bought.

By the time he was 20, Pretty was *the* terror of Brownsville. He was now so ugly that a representative from Ringling Brothers offered him a job with the circus as the missing link. It is the mark of Pretty's intellect or sense of humor that he often bragged about the offer. However, Pretty didn't accept the job because of his involvement in the loansharking business with his brother. Unlike the banks of Brownsville, the Ambergs turned no one down for a loan, but at 20 percent interest a week. Pretty would watch his brother count out the amount of the loan and growl, "I will kill you if you don't pay us back on time."

The Amberg brothers soon became so successful in loansharking that they shifted their operations to around Borough Hall in downtown Brooklyn. The brothers did not desert Brownsville, however. Pretty stalked Pitkin Avenue; for amusement he would walk into a cafeteria and spit in someone's soup. If the diner protested, Pretty would spill the whole bowl in his lap. Even Buggsy Goldstein, shortly to become a prize killer in the fledgling Murder, Inc., once took the soup treatment in silence. Famous Murder, Inc. informer Abe Reles later said, "The word was that Pretty was nutty."

Pretty Amberg's continuing ties with Brownsville were not based solely on sentiment. He took control of all bootlegging in the area, and speakeasies took Pretty's booze or none at all, a business practice Pretty established with a few bombings and frequent use of a lead pipe.

Soon, Pretty was wallowing in money, and he became a lavish-spending, if rather grotesque, figure in New York's night life. Waiters fawned over him because he never tipped less than $100. He was a regular at the Central Park Casino, where in time he became a nodding acquaintance of the city's playboy mayor, James J. Walker. It was Runyon who reported that when the mayor first saw Pretty, he vowed to stay off booze.

Pretty expanded his rackets to include laundry services for Brooklyn businesses. His rates were rather high, but his sales approach was particularly forceful. It was at this time that laundry bags stuffed with corpses started littering Brooklyn streets. One victim was identified as a loanshark debtor of the Ambergs who owed a grand total of $80. Pretty was arrested for that one, but he just laughed: "I tip more than that. Why'd I kill a bum for a lousy 80 bucks?" In fact, it was Pretty's philosophy to kill men who were indebted to him for small amounts so that their loss of life would not cause him to have to write off a major capital investment. It also made an excellent object lesson for more substantial debtors. And while the police knew the particulars, they could not prove them in court and Pretty went free.

By the early 1930s Pretty was considered among the most successful racketeers in the city, one who could withstand any inroads by other kingpins, such as Dutch Schultz and Legs Diamond. Once, Schultz told him, "Pretty, I think I'm going to come in as your partner in Brooklyn."

"Arthur," Pretty was quoted as replying, "why don't you put a gun in your mouth and see how many times you can pull the trigger."

Pretty was famous for such pithy comments. Another big racketeer, Owney Madden, mentioned to Pretty one day that he'd never visited Brownsville in his life and thought he would come out some time and "let you show me the sights." Pretty was carving up a steak at the moment. "Tell you what, Owney," he said matter-of-factly while continuing his meal, "if I ever see you in Brownsville, I'll cut your heart out on the spot." He was even more direct with Legs Diamond, whom he buddied around with. "We'll be pals, Jack," Pretty told Diamond, "but if you ever set foot in Brownsville, I'll kill you and your girl friend and your missus and your whole damn family."

With the end of Prohibition, however, such threats proved insufficient. Dutch Schultz, without his former bootleg rackets, was down to only a multimillion dollar numbers racket centered in Harlem, and he kept casting greedy glances over at Brooklyn and the Amberg loanshark operations around Borough Hall. Pretty had by now firmly established himself in the laundry business, but loansharking remained his principal source of funds. He was therefore hardly overjoyed in 1935 when Schultz ensconced his top lieutenants, Frank Dolak and Benny Holinsky, in a new loan office just a block away from the Amberg enterprise. When Pretty stormed into the place, the pair glared back at him defiantly. "We ain't afraid of you," Holinsky said, and Dolak echoed, "That's right, we ain't afraid of you." The statements qualified as famous last words because 24 hours later their bodies, riddled with bullets, were found on a Brooklyn street.

The Ambergs and the Schultz forces faced off for total war.

The first to go was Joey Amberg, who was ambushed by Schultz' gunmen. In October 1935 both Amberg and Schultz died. Some historians have insisted that each man was responsible for the other's death. According to this theory Amberg had paid professional killers $25,000 down to kill Schultz and promised them $25,000 more upon completion of the job. In the meantime, however, the fire department, responding to an alarm, found a blazing automobile on a Brooklyn street. In the back seat of the car was the body of a man roasted beyond all recognition, with wire wrapped around his neck, arms and legs. It took a few days for a positive identification: it was Pretty Amberg. But by the time the identification was made, a couple of killers had gunned down Dutch Schultz in a Newark chop house.

Despite the war, it is not certain that Amberg was killed by Schultz. A more convincing theory attributed Pretty's passing to a gang of armed robbers he had joined and offended by insisting on taking virtually all the loot for himself. Another view held that both Amberg and Schultz were "put to sleep" by the increasingly dominant national crime syndicate bossed by Lucky Luciano and Meyer Lansky.

But whoever was to blame, Pretty Amberg was dead, and as a *Brooklyn Eagle* reporter observed, "There was joy in Brownsville."

AMEER Ben Ali: See "Old Shakespeare."

AMERICAN Protective League: Vigilantes

With the possible exception of the Sons of Liberty, formed during the American Revolution, the World War I American Protective League (APL) was probably this country's most abusive and lawless patriotic vigilante group. The league was the brainchild of A. M. Briggs, a Chicago advertising executive, who in March 1917 wrote Bureau of Investigation Chief A. Bruce Bielaski to suggest the formation of a volunteer group of patriotic Americans who would aid the bureau in its national defense duties. Not the most perceptive of officials, Bielaski enthusiastically approved the idea, and divisions of the APL were established in every large city in the country, soon achieving a membership of 250,000.

APL members paid their own expenses and sported badges that read, "American Protective League, Secret Service Division." The words "Secret Service" were removed following the protest of the secretary of the treasury, but Attorney General Thomas W. Gregory defended the league and its patriotic purpose despite the fact that the organization exhibited the worst attributes of a vigilante movement, had a callous disregard of civil rights and even committed lynchings.

In 1917 in Butte, Mont., armed masked men, generally believed to have been league members, invaded the boarding house room of Frank Little, a member of the general executive board of the Industrial Workers of the World (IWW), dragged him out into the night and hanged him from a railroad trestle for what was regarded as his unpatriotic beliefs and actions. The Little hanging did not receive particularly bad press. While the *New York Times* called the lynching "deplorable and detestable," it also noted that "IWW agitators are in effect, and perhaps in fact, agents of Germany. The Federal government should make short work of these treasonable conspirators against the United States." A Western newspaper declared Butte had "disgraced itself like a gentleman." And on the floor of the House of Representatives, a congressman wondered if those who gave no allegiance to this nation "have any right to 'squeal' when citizens of this country hang one of them occasionally?"

President Woodrow Wilson felt it necessary to warn of "the great danger of citizens taking the law into their own hands," but he did nothing to force Gregory and Bielaski to repudiate the APL. The league continued to make illegal arrests and searches, and its members continually gave the impression they were federal officers. Labor leaders attacked the APL, citing instances of it being used by employers to intimidate strikers. When veteran members of the Bureau of Investigation scoffed at these "voluntary detectives," they were warned that such "slurs" could result in their dismissal.

In August and September of 1918 the league, cooperating with the Bureau of Investigation, the Army and local draft boards, launched a great war against "slackers" and deserters, men who failed to answer the call to service after registering for the draft. Small roundup experiments using local police and APL members proved successful in Pittsburgh, Boston and Chicago. Early in September a three-day roundup was staged in New York City. Newspapers ran notices reminding all men between 21 and 31 that they were required to carry their draft cards on their person and that all others should carry proof of their age. No warning, however, was given of an impending roundup. At 7 a.m. on September 3, 1918, a task force of 1,350 soldiers, 1,000 sailors, several hundred policemen and 2,000 APL members struck. During the next three days 50,000 men were hustled out of theaters and restaurants, plucked off street corners and from trolley cars and seized in railway stations and poolhalls. Workers were stopped by bayonet-wielding soldiers as they left work. All were jammed into bull pens for interrogation, left for hours without food and refused the right to make telephone calls to establish their innocence. Frightened wives of out-of-town visitors reported their husbands as kidnapped.

The seizures in general and those by the APL in particular were sharply criticized. The *New York World* condemned "this monstrous invasion of human rights." In the Senate, California Sen. Hiram Johnson said that "to humiliate 40,000 citizens, to shove them with bayonets, to subject them to prison and summary military force, merely because they are 'suspects,' is a spectacle never before presented in the Republic."

The weight of public opinion turned against the APL following the roundups, which resulted in the estimated induction of 1,500 men into the service. President Wilson demanded a report from Attorney General Gregory, who informed the President that he took full and complete responsibility for the raids and that they would continue, although he did deplore

the use of extralegal methods. Wilson seemed incapable of moving against Gregory and the APL, but in November 1918 the war ended, eliminating the need for confrontation.

The American Protective League formally dissolved on February 1, 1919.

AMERICAN Tragedy, An: See Chester Gillette.

ANASTASIA, Albert (1903-1957): Syndicate gang leader and murderer

The Lord High Executioner of Murder, Inc., Albert Anastasia rose to the top levels of the national crime syndicate and remained there until he himself was murdered in a hit as efficient as any of the countless ones he carried out or planned.

Immediately upon his arrival in the United States in 1920, Anastasia and his brother, Tough Tony Anastasio, became active on the crime-ridden Brooklyn docks and gained a position of power in the longshoremen's union. He demonstrated a penchant for murder at the snap of a finger, an attitude that was not altered even after he spent 18 months in the Sing Sing death house during the early 1920s for killing another longshoreman. He was freed when, at a new trial, the four most important witnesses against him could not be located, a situation that proved permanent.

For Anastasia the solution to any problem was homicide. So it was hardly surprising that he and Louis "Lepke" Buchalter were installed as the executive heads of the enforcement arm of Murder, Inc. The victim toll of Murder, Inc. has been estimated as low as 63 and as high as 400 or 500. Unlike Lepke and many other members of the operation, Anastasia escaped punishment. In a "perfect case" against him, the main prosecution witness—again—vanished. This disappearance of witnesses was a regular occurrence in the Anastasia story, as were killings to advance his career. When in 1951 Anastasia aspired to higher things, he took over the Mangano family, one of New York's five crime families, by murdering Phil Mangano and making Vincent Mangano a permanent missing person.

Anastasia became known as the Mad Hatter because his killings were so promiscuous. He had always been a devoted follower of others, mainly Lucky Luciano and Frank Costello. His devotion to Luciano was legendary. In 1930, when Luciano decided to take over crime in America by destroying the two old-line Mafia factions headed by Giuseppe "Joe the Boss" Masseria and Salvatore Maranzano, he outlined his plan to Anastasia because he knew the Mad Hatter would kill for him. Anastasia promptly grabbed Luciano in a bear hug and kissed him on both cheeks. He said: "Charlie, I been waiting for this day for at least eight years. You're gonna be on top if I have to kill everybody for you. With you there, that's the only way we can have any peace and make the real money."

Anastasia's killer instincts could be contained as long as Luciano and Costello were around to control him, but Luciano

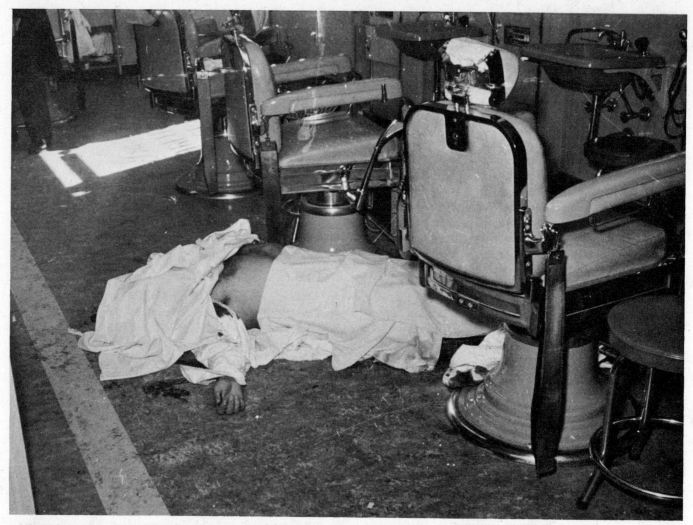

Albert Anastasia, Lord High Executioner of Murder, Inc., was gunned down in a Manhattan hotel barber shop with all the efficiency he himself exhibited in numerous killings.

was deported in 1946 and a few years later Costello became bogged down by continuous harassment from the authorities. Now in charge of his own crime family, Anastasia really turned kill-crazy. In 1952 he even had a young Brooklyn salesman named Arnold Schuster killed after watching Schuster bragging on television about how he had recognized bank robber Willie Sutton and brought about his capture. "I can't stand squealers!" Anastasia screamed and then ordered his men, "Hit that guy!"

The Schuster killing violated a principal rule of the underworld, We only kill each other. Outsiders—prosecutors, reporters, the general public—were not to be killed unless the very life of the organization was threatened. That clearly was not the case in the Schuster murder. The rest of the underworld, even Anastasia's friends Luciano (now in Italy) and Costello, were horrified, but they dared not move on him because they needed him as a buffer against a new force within the crime structure. Vito Genovese, long number two under Luciano, was making a grab for greater power. Between him and that goal stood Anastasia, a man who had hated him for years. Secretly, Genovese brought to his banner Anastasia's

underboss, Carlo Gambino, a frail-looking mobster with unbridled ambition of his own, who in turn recruited Joe Profaci and his Brooklyn crime family.

Before Genovese could move against Anastasia, he needed more support, and he could not move without the tacit agreement of Meyer Lansky, the highest-ranking Jewish member of the national syndicate. Normally, Lansky would not have supported Genovese under any circumstances; their ethnic bitterness was one of the underworld's longest-standing feuds. But Anastasia had recently given Lansky reason to hate him even more. In 1957 Lansky was in full control of gambling in Cuba through his close personal and financial arrangements with that country's dictator, Fulgencio Batista. As was his style of always enhancing his own base within the underworld, Lansky gave a piece of the action to Miami crime boss Santo Trafficante and a number of other Italian-American mobsters. When Anastasia learned of Lansky's largesse, he started to put pressure on him for a huge cut.

Under these circumstances Lansky, who previously had preferred to let Genovese and Anastasia bleed each other to death, okayed the elimination of the latter.

Early on the morning of October 25, 1957, Anastasia entered the barbershop of the Park Sheraton Hotel in New York City and sat down for a quick haircut, shutting his eyes. Anastasia's bodyguard took his car to an underground garage and then conveniently went off for a little stroll. Moments after Anastasia sat down in the barber's chair, two men entered the shop with scarves over their faces. Arthur Grasso, the shop owner, was standing at the entrance by the cash register. He was told, "Keep your mouth shut if you don't want your head blown off." The two men moved to Anastasia's chair and shoved the barber aside. If Anastasia's eyes had been open, he would have seen them in the mirror. Suddenly, both guns roared.

Anastasia leaped out of the chair with the first volley and weaved on his feet. Then he saw his attackers and lunged at them—in the mirror. He took several more shots, one in the back of the head, and collapsed dead on the floor.

Officially, the Anastasia killing remains unsolved, although it is known that Joe Profaci gave the contract for the killing to the three homicidal Gallo brothers from Brooklyn.

The double-dealing continued after the Anastasia murder, with Gambino breaking off from Genovese and making his peace with Luciano, Costello and Lansky. A desperate Genevese called an underworld summit meeting at Apalachin, N.Y. to justify the elimination of Anastasia, who, he said, had become so murder-crazed that he had imperiled the entire organization. That meeting ended in disaster following a state police raid, and six months after that, Genovese was arrested on a narcotics rap, one which much of the underworld regarded as a setup. The inside word was that the setup was arranged by Gambino, Luciano, Costello and Lansky. At any rate, Genovese was effectively removed from the scene.

See also: *Anthony "Tough Tony" Anastasio; Apalachin Conference; Frank Costello; Thomas E. Dewey; Carlo Gambino; Vito Genovese; Charles "Lucky" Luciano; Murder, Inc.; S.S.* Normandie; *Frank Scalice; Arnold Schuster; Frederick J. Tenuto.*

ANASTASIO, Anthony "Tough Tony" (1906-1963): Waterfront racketeer

From the 1930s until his death from natural causes in 1963, Tough Tony Anastasio ruled the New York waterfront with an iron hand as a vice president of the International Longshoremen's Association and head of Local 1814. Much of his real authority derived from the power and reputation of his murderous brother, Albert Anastasia. While Tony kept the original spelling of his last name, he never hesitated to point out he was Albert's brother in order to enhance his own position. Ever loyal to Albert, Tony once cornered a reporter from the *New York World-Telegram and Sun* and asked: "How come you keep writing all those bad things about my brother Albert? He ain't killed nobody in your family . . . yet."

Because would-be rivals knew Tough Tony had the full weight of the mob behind him, they never seriously challenged him. As a result, Tony's word was law. During World War II he could order, with Lucky Luciano's approval, the sabotaging of the French luxury liner SS *Normandie* to panic federal authori-

ties into seeking underworld assistance to help protect the New York waterfront. It was apparently in return for this "good work" that Luciano was transferred from Dannemora to a far less restrictive prison and, after the war, was pardoned by Gov. Thomas E. Dewey. Following Luciano's release Tony had an army of longshoremen on a Brooklyn pier to keep away reporters and others while the top gangland figures gathered to bid Luciano farewell on the day he was being deported to Italy.

See also: *Charles "Lucky" Luciano, SS Normandie.*

ANATOMY and Crime

The idea that criminals differ from noncriminals in certain anatomical traits was first expounded by an Italian named Cesare Lombroso, often considered to be the father of criminology. According to Lombroso, such differences turned up in various parts of the body, with criminals typically possessing such features as a long lower jaw, a flattened nose, a scanty beard and an asymmetrical cranium. He did not claim that these stigmata or anomalies themselves caused crime, but rather that they pointed to personalities predisposed to criminal patterns of behavior. Above all, Lombroso insisted that deviations in the shape of the cranium were the most critical.

Over the years Lombroso's views fell into disrepute, but in the 1930s an American anthropologist, E. A. Hooton, attempted to resurrect the Lombrosian theory. He measured thousands of prisoners and a few nonprisoners and found what he considered to be deviations between the two groups. From these studies he concluded, in his *Crime and the Man* (1939), that "the primary cause of crime is biological inferiority." However, other studies failed to find significant differences in physical traits between criminals and noncriminals and the Lombrosian revival gained little support.

Further reading: "Physical Factors in Criminal Behavior" by W. Norwood East in the *Journal of Clinical Psychopathy* 8 (1946):7-36.

ANDREWS, Shang (c. late 19th century): Publisher

During the 1870s and 1880s a sporting character named Shang Andrews launched a series of publications that chronicled the doings of Chicago's prostitutes.

The Walter Winchell-style tidbits were read as avidly by ladies of the evening as the *Chicago Tribune's* social pages were by matrons of prominence. Portraying the ravages of the profession, they are, no doubt of sociological value today. The following quotations are taken from the *Chicago Street Gazette*, which like *Sporting Life, Chicago Life* and *Chicago Sporting Gazette* among others, made up the Andrews publication list:

Lottie Maynard should not be so fresh with other girls' lovers, or she will hear something to her disadvantage.

Ada Huntley is now happy—she has a new lover—Miss Fresh from Pittsburgh.

Lizzie Allen has put on her fall coat of veneer and varnish, and she is now the finest looking woman in Chicago.

Eva Hawkins is on one of her drunks again.

Miss Kit Thompson of 483 South Clark had better let up on taking other girls' men in her room and buying booze for them.

Lulu Lee, the little streetwalker, has gone into a house to endeavor and reform herself, but we think it will prove a failure.

Lizzie Moss has got sober.

What has become of Bad Millie?

May Willard, why don't you take a tumble to yourself and not be trying to put on so much style around the St. Marks Hotel, for very near all of the boys are on to you; and when you register, please leave the word "New York" out, for we know it's from the Bridewell you are.

We are happy to inform the public that the old-timer, Frankie Warner, has left the city.

Mary McCarthy has gone to the insane asylum.

The true identity of gutter journalist Shang Andrews was never definitely established.

ANDREWS Committee:
Police corruption inquiry

During the 1890s a spate of investigations around the country revealed that most large cities—Atlanta, Kansas City, Baltimore, Chicago, Los Angeles, San Francisco and Philadelphia—had just as much police corruption as had been found in New York City by the Lexow Committee. Of all the panels set up to hold investigations, the Andrews Committee, which examined the Philadelphia police, had one real distinction: it proved that a city consistently under Republican Party rule could have just as corrupt a police force as any under Democratic Party rule, including that of Tammany Hall.

At the urging of the Citizens' Municipal Association of Philadelphia, a bipartisan reform group, the committee was set up in 1895 by the Pennsylvania Senate with Sen. William H. Andrews of Crawford County as its chairman. In a devastating report issued in May 1897, the committee accused the police of being no more than political agents of various Republican Party factions. Police officers labored hard to see to it that the voters voted right, or not at all. Ballots containing the "wrong" votes were discarded by the hundreds. In some cases policemen got into the booths with voters to make sure they cast their ballots "according to the rules."

In exchange for these and other services rendered to politicians, well-connected officers were exempt from even the threat of departmental discipline and therefore could freely engage in brutality and harassment of citizens as well as offer protection to gambling and prostitution interests. The Andrews Committee's findings were never seriously challenged, but very little came of them. The city's public safety director, while admitting the police orce's entanglement with city politics, promised only to deal with the problem in the future. It proved to be an unkept promise. General Smedley D. Butler, appointed public safety director in 1923, found that many, if not most, of Philadelphia's patrolmen were pocketing $150 to $200 a month in payoffs.

See also: *Lexow Committee.*

ANIMAL Criminals

The history of crime and justice in America is replete with examples of dumb animals being charged and often punished for alleged illegal acts. Perhaps the most famous episode occurred in Erwin, Tenn. in 1916, when a circus elephant named Mary was charged with murder after running amok and killing a man. The dumb beast was hanged from a railroad derrick before a cheering crowd of 5,000 persons. Whether Mary deserved capital punishment might be legally debated on the grounds that she did not know right from wrong, but there are numerous cases of animals being trained to follow a life of crime.

In Chicago in 1953, a resourceful bird fancier trained her pet magpie to enter rooms in a nearby hotel and bring back any bright object it found. The heavy jewelry losses were driving the house detectives crazy, but they were unable to turn up any leads. If it were not for the fact that one day the magpie entered the room of a woman guest who was a particularly light sleeper, the bird fancier and her pet might still be at their winged larceny. The woman, taking a nap after lunch, was awakened by a low noise. She saw a bird flying around the room as though looking for something. It swooped down and picked up a diamond ring lying on a table. When the bird flew out the window, the woman jumped up and got to the window in time to see the bird flying into a neighboring flat. She told her story to the police, and although dubious, they raided the apartment. Their doubts were allayed when they found a fortune in jewelry. The lady bird-lover tearfully admitted all. She had spent arduous years training her bird because magpies, although notorious thieves, can seldom be taught to bring what they steal to a specific spot. Usually they drop their loot in any place that strikes their fancy.

Then there was the case of the chimp cat-burglar. For months in 1952 householders in a New York City neighborhood were being plagued by a series of odd burglaries. In some instances the victims lived in apartments 15 stories up and there seemed to be no means of entry other than a window. One day the son of a city detective happened to see a small figure round a rooftop corner. At first he thought it was a child, but when he looked around the corner, he saw an ape. The boy watched the animal climb through the open skylight of a shop. When it emerged within a matter of seconds, it was carrying a sack around its neck, packed nearly full. The boy followed the chimp and saw it disappear into a run-down house on another street. He ran home and told his father. Shortly thereafter, the owner of the long-armed, light-fingered animal stood before a judge and told a strange story.

While abroad he had bought a chimpanzee for his children. Chimps are probably the brightest of animals next to humans and his was one of the smartest, he said. He named the chimp Socrates. But then his fortunes took a sudden dive, and it became difficult to provide for his family's needs. One day Socrates went foraging by himself. When he returned, he was munching on a piece of bread and carrying a bagful of pastries. Realizing what had happened, the owner decided to exploit the chimp's latent talents. Socrates was a quick learner and his master designed a special sack he could use to carry the swag in. Before long, Socrates had the family back in the chips again. The upshot of the case was jail for the chimp owner and a zoo for Socrates.

See also: *Animal Lynching.*

Further reading: *The Criminal Prosecution and Capital Punishment of Animals* by E. R. Evans.

ANIMAL Lynching

The lynching of animals—cats, dogs, horses, cows, bulls etc.—has a long and brutal history in the United States, but on September 13, 1916 an all-time low in man's inhumanity to beast was reached when Mary, a circus elephant that had killed three men, was hanged from a railroad derrick in Erwin, Tenn. The first attempt to lynch the animal ended after two hours when the derrick's steel cable broke and Mary came crashing down to earth. The second try was successful, and much to the satisfaction of 5,000 spectators, the dumb beast paid the human price demanded for its crimes.

It was not uncommon in the West to kill horses or cattle deemed to have been responsible for the loss of human life. And even the Chicago underworld got into the act. When the celebrated Nails Morton was thrown by a riding horse and killed in Lincoln Park in 1924, his buddies in Dion O'Banion's gang abducted the animal from its stable at gunpoint and took it to the spot where Nails had been killed. There the poor creature was executed, as each of the gangsters solemnly shot it in the head.

During the last century more restraint was shown toward a steer over which an argument regarding its ownership had arisen. Shooting broke out and when the smoke cleared, six men were dead or dying. Because the incident was such a tragedy, it was felt that something other than death was required. The animal was branded with the word MURDER and allowed to live on as grim reminder of the awful occurrence.

See also: *Louis "Two Gun" Alterie, Samuel J. "Nails" Morton.*

ANNENBERG, Moses L. (1878-1942): Gambling information czar

Moe Annenberg rose from Chicago's South Side slums to become, for a time, the possessor of the largest individual income of any person in the nation. Using methods not everyone considered legal, he was able to capitalize on two American traits, the desire to read newspapers and the eagerness to bet. However, like Al Capone, he ended up in prison for income tax evasion. For the year 1932 the government said Annenberg owed $313,000; he had paid $308. For 1936 Annenberg owed an estimated $1,692,000; he had paid $475,000. Together with interest and penalties his unpaid taxes totaled $9.5 million. And just as was true with Capone, Annenberg's income tax problems were merely a logical consequence of his other activities.

Annenberg, who had cut his teeth in the early Chicago circulation wars, was, in the words of William Randolph Hearst,

a "circulation genius." That "genius" meant selling newspapers with an army of sluggers, overturning the competition's delivery trucks, burning their newspapers and roughing up dealers who sold papers under the impression that it was a free country. Moe first worked in the circulation department of the *Chicago Tribune* and later switched his allegiance to Hearst's new papers in town, the *American* and the *Examiner,* serving as circulation manager of the latter from 1904 to 1906. The roster of Moe's sluggers read like a future public enemies list. A typical Annenberg hireling was Frank McErlane. Former Chicago newspaperman George Murray later wrote of the Annenberg-McErlane Alliance: "McErlane went on to become the most vicious killer of his time. Moe Annenberg went on to become father of the ambassador to the Court of St. James."

Moving up in the Hearst organization, Annenberg became one of the highest-paid circulation men in the country. His arrangement with Hearst gave him the right to engage in private business dealings on the side, which included his incursion into the racing information field, on both a legal and an illegal basis. In 1922 he bought the *Daily Racing Form* and by 1926 his various enterprises had become so vast that he quit Hearst and struck out on his own. In a matter of a few years, he had gathered in his domain the *New York Morning Telegraph, Radio Guide, Screen Guide* and the Nation-Wide News Service. He also took over the century-old *Philadelphia Inquirer* and through it became a power in Republican Party politics. According to Annenberg, because these activities occurred during a Democratic era, they got him in trouble with the law. Others said that Nation-Wide News Service gave him his great legal problems, as well as huge profits. The service received its information from telegraph and telephone wires hooked into 29 race tracks and from those tracks into 223 cities in 39 states, where thousands of poolrooms and bookie joints operated in violation of local laws. Annenberg became the fifth largest customer of American Telephone and Telegraph, exceeded only by the three press associations and RCA.

The flow of money simply gushed in, becoming so large that, as the *New York Times* reported, "it apparently did not seem worth while to give the government its share." In 1939 Moe and his only son, Walter, were indicted. Walter pleaded not guilty and Moe attacked the charges against him as politically motivated. But finally, in what some observers called great paternal devotion, Moe declared: "It's the best gamble. I'll take the rap." Moe was in his 60s, and his lawyers were hopeful that his guilty plea would lead to the dropping of charges against his son. The gamble paid off. Moe Annenberg drew a three-year prison term and made a $9.5 million settlement with the government.

Nation-Wide News folded up and Moe Annenberg was succeeded as the country's racing information czar by James M. Ragen, who founded Continental Press Service. Walter Annenberg remained a great publishing power and society figure and went on to become ambassador to England under President Richard Nixon.

See also: *James M. Ragen.*

Further reading: *My Last Million Readers* by Emile Gauvreau.

ANSELMI and Scalise: Gangsters

It is impossible to record the criminal activities of Albert Anselmi without also discussing those of John Scalise, the worst pair of killers during the bloody 1920s. Anselmi and Scalise grew up together, played together, worked together, killed together and, fittingly, were slaughtered together. The two resembled that other inseparable pair Mutt and Jeff; Anselmi was short and bulky, Scalise tall and thin. It was this duo who brought to the Chicago underworld the old Sicilian custom of rubbing bullets with garlic; if the shots failed to kill, the resulting gangrene allegedly would. Anselmi and Scalise's medical knowledge was somewhat faulty, although the same could not be said about their homicidal prowess, which was proficient even by Chicago standards.

While in their twenties, Anselmi and Scalise were forced to flee their native Marsala because of a murder charge. The pair turned up in Chicago during the early 1920s and went to work for the Terrible Gennas, a family of killers who had established themselves as the leading bootleggers in the Midwest. Since the Gennas also hailed from Marsala, they welcomed the two to their bosom, having a constant need for reliable torpedoes. Anselmi and Scalise were single-minded of purpose: they planned to make a million dollars each, which they felt would give them enough to fix the case against them in Sicily and allow them to return as rich men. Their killing services came high, but they were extremely efficient. For one killing the Gennas rewarded each of the pair with $10,000 and a $3,000 diamond ring. Scalise, the more romantic of the two, sent his ring to his sweetheart in Sicily. Anselmi reportedly sold his to a jeweler at the point of a gun for $4,000.

Anselmi and Scalise introduced a degree of double-dealing unknown even in the Chicago underworld. True innovators, they introduced the "handshake hit," whereby the short, fat Anselmi would shake hands with the unsuspecting victim and lock his right hand in a tight grip. With the victim's gun hand incapacitated, the taller Scalise would quickly step forward and shoot him in the head. The shorter Anselmi always did the holding because he had a grip of iron and Scalise did the shooting because his height enabled him to get in a head shot regardless of how tall the victim was. Anselmi and Scalise were definitely two of three killers involved in the 1924 assassination of Dion O'Banion, the leading Irish gangster of the era, in which the usually careful gang leader was caught off guard in a handshake just before the funeral of a leading Italian underworld figure.

Some of their other killings were legendary. One victim held his hands in prayer and begged to be spared. They shot off his hands before putting a bullet in his brain. Anselmi and Scalise probably sprayed more pedestrian-mobbed streets than any other pair of kill-happy gunners. They gunned down gangland rivals and police officers with equal ferocity. Once, in the company of several other killers, they noticed that their bullet-filled victim lying on a street managed to raise his head. Chagrined that he was not dead, the two rushed back across the street and, before dozens of witnesses, finished the job.

The only time Anselmi and Scalise wavered in obeying the orders of the Gennas was when they were told to kill Al Capone, for they realized their ultimate reward for such an act would be their own deaths. Instead, they informed Capone of the Gennas' plan and became Capone men while ostensibly still working for the Gennas. When it finally came time for Capone to erase the Gennas, Anselmi and Scalise "set up" one of the brothers and took an active part in killing another.

Capone now welcomed the pair openly into his organization, making them two of his most important bodyguards and gunners. When the mob boss offered to make peace with Hymie Weiss and the rest of the O'Banion gang, his terms proved entirely acceptable. Weiss made only one stipulation: Anselmi and Scalise had to be turned over to the gang for killing Dion O'Banion. Capone rejected the deal, declaring, "I wouldn't do that to a yellow dog."

Several legal attempts were made to get Anselmi and Scalise. They were once charged with the killing of two police detectives, but after three trials, involving a great number of threats against witnesses and jurors, they went free, remarkably, on the ground that they had merely been resisting unwarranted police aggression.

In 1929 they were arrested for taking part in the infamous St. Valentine's Day Massacre, but by the time their trial date arrived, they too had been murdered. How they died is no secret. Capone staged a party in honor of the pair and Joseph "Hop Toad" Giunta, whom he had recently installed as president of Unione Siciliana. At the height of the banquet, Capone stopped the festivities, accused the trio of plotting to murder him and, after having them tied up, beat all three to death with a heavy Indian club. They may well have been conspiring against Capone, but it is just as possible that Capone decided to kill the trio because he feared they were getting too important. Anselmi and Scalise had been appointed as bodyguards for Giunta in his new rule, but Scalise had quickly relegated Giunta to the background and had taken direct charge of the organization's affairs. He was heard to brag, "I am the most powerful man in Chicago." And Anselmi chimed in, "We the big shot now."

It was a fitting collective singular. Anselmi and Scalise, who had so often killed together, died together.

See also: *Alphonse "Scarface Al" Capone, Genna Brothers, Antonio "the Scourge" Lombardo, Charles Dion "Deanie" O'Banion, St. Valentine's Day Massacre*

ANTI-Horse Thief Association

A vigilante organization, the Anti-Horse Thief Association was formed at Fort Scott during 1859 to battle the marauders plaguing the border states. After the Civil War these outlaw elements, using sprawling, poorly policed Indian Territory as their base, swept into Kansas and other states to run off herds of horses and cattle. Because of the strength of the outlaws, few lawmen would pursue them further than Marion County in Kansas, and the work fell to the Anti-Horse Thief Associations that proliferated in Kansas and other states. They generally dispensed instant justice on the trail when they caught the rustlers. As the West was tamed and the incidence of horse thievery dropped, the organization stayed on as a social group. Well into the 20th century it was common for a chapter to announce somberly at an annual meeting that no horse thieves had been apprehended during the previous 12 months, a record worthy of a great celebration.

See also: *Horse Stealing.*

APACHE Gangs: Mythical Indian outlaw bands

Without doubt one of the most fertile subjects for foreigners' misconceptions of conditions in America has always been crime. This has been true not merely because of purple reporting by several popular writers but also because of the inaccurate opinions of many experts. Typical was the work of Dr. Edmond Locord, one of the great criminologists of France in the early part of this century. Writing in the preface of a book on crime in 1925, Locard discussed crime in various parts of the world; of America he said: "In Texas and California even today one meets roving bands of redskins who live by extortion, pillage, and rapine. They are the Apaches." Thus, foreigners visiting the United States in that period spoke fearsomely of traveling in "Apache Gang" country.

The "Apache dancers," depicting the ways of the brutal French underworld, also derived their name from popular 19th century misconceptions of the generally peaceful Apaches.

APACHE Indian Job: Gangland bombing

Using bombs as a "convincer" has long been a practice of the underworld. Today, organized crime makes great use of firebombs, particularly for what is known in the underworld as an Apache Indian job: when a building is so thoroughly burned that little remains standing other than a chimney and a few smoking timbers, as in the case of Indian burnings of settlers' cabins.

Such firebombings have been common in recent years in New York City to convince, for example, restaurateurs to pay tribute to the little-known but lucrative parsley racket. Restaurants that don't serve parsley with every meal, and indeed with a number of mixed drinks, can look forward to an Apache raid.

Apache Indian jobs have reappeared in the West recently. In 1980 the Montana State Crime Control Commission reported that a New York "parsley king" was involved in restaurant firebombings in that state.

See also: *Parsley Racket.*

APACHE Kid (1867-?): Rapist, robber, murderer

The Apache Kid conducted the worst one-man reign of terror the Arizona Territory and perhaps the entire West ever saw. Until age 20 the Apache Kid adapted well to the white man's

Originally a sergeant of scouts, the Apache Kid (center) later went on an orgy of robbery, rape, kidnapping and murder, becoming the most-hunted Indian outlaw in the Arizona Territory.

world, becoming a sergeant of scouts at the San Carlos Agency under Al Sieber, Arizona's famed Indian fighter. When his father was murdered, tribal law required the young Indian to avenge the crime, and under that law, it would be a legal execution. Although Sieber warned him that such revenge would be illegal under the white man's law, the Apache Kid slipped away with a few followers, located his quarry near a creek and stabbed him to death. The young Indian then surrendered to Sieber, but becoming fearful of his treatment in a hostile white court, he escaped with his followers. After two years on the run, the Apache Kid returned to face a court-martial. He was convicted but won a pardon from President Grover Cleveland. Incensed by this action, the local Indian haters promptly indicted the Kid and several of his band on charges of having killed a whiskey drummer who was trying to sell "fire water" to their people. The Apache Kid was found guilty and given seven years in prison, a remarkably short sentence that indicated the case against him was either weak or that the crime itself was considered by many to be justified. On November 1, 1889 the Apache Kid was being escorted to the prison at Yuma when he overwhelmed his two guards, Sheriff Glen Reynolds and Deputy Bill Holmes, killed them and made his escape. From then on, the Apache Kid became the scourge of the state, leaving a bloody trail of robbery, rape and murder. He struck blindly, victimizing Indians as well as whites. He took many squaws, and when he tired of them, he cut their throats. Prospectors were robbed and murdered in their mountain cabins; lonely ranches were attacked and their inhabitants killed. It was impossible to get an accurate count of the number of white girls he kidnapped, raped and killed because he was blamed whenever a lone Indian committed a crime, but there was no doubt that most such victims were his. Even a $5,000 bounty on his head failed to stop him, although several whites and Indians alike tried and died in the effort.

The terror ended abruptly in 1894. One night Ed Clark, a prospector and former chief of Wallapai Scouts, awakened at his camp north of Tucson to see an Indian brave and a squaw trying to steal his horse. Clark shot the woman and badly wounded the Indian, who fled. Clark, whose partner, Billy Diehl, had been killed by the Apache Kid five years earlier, was sure he recognized him. He was equally positive that he had gotten in a killing shot and that the Apache Kid had crawled in some hole to die. Clark's story was plausible, but it was more likely that the Apache Kid realized the tale of his fate gave him the perfect opportunity to fade away. There seems little doubt that he took a squaw, went into the Sierra Madre in Mexico and raised a family. He was recognized and spoken to by a number of reliable witnesses well into the 20th century.

Further reading: *Lone War Trail of Apache Kid* by Earle F. Forrest and Edwin B. Hill.

APALACHIN Conference: Underworld convention

A much-publicized fiasco, the great underworld conference held at Apalachin, N.Y. on November 14, 1957 was in its own way as important for its impact on crime in America as the famous Atlantic City crime meeting in 1929. However, while Atlantic City was famous for what it did, Apalachin's chief significance was what it did not do, namely propel Vito Genovese into the number one spot in the syndicate hierarchy. More accurately, the Apalachin meeting destroyed Genovese, and in hindsight, it is impossible not to regard the events as brilliantly stage-managed.

The bare-bones history of the conference is rather clear-cut. It came three weeks after the barbershop assassination of Albert Anastasia, which was arranged by Genovese as part of his plan to become "boss of bosses" both in New York and the nation. Genovese called the conference among other reasons, to justify Anastasia's death and relieve the heat he was getting for the attempt on Frank Costello's life a few months earlier. Most of all, he wanted his position as the syndicate's top man affirmed. But that was against the wishes of other powerful forces.

As it happened, the meeting at the 58-acre estate of mobster Joseph Barbara, Sr. never got off the ground. Before real discussions started, a raid by state police sent the participants scurrying. It was a ludicrous scene: immaculately tailored crime bosses, mostly in their fifties or older and no longer fleet of foot, climbed out windows or bolted through back doors and went racing through woods, burrs and undergrowth in a frantic attempt to escape. How many did is not known, but 58 were caught. The arrest roster bore the names of men whom various law enforcement agencies had tried to corner for years: Genovese, Trafficante, Profaci, Magliocco, Bonanno, Scalish, DeSimone, Riela, Magaddino, Gambino, Miranda, Catena, Ida, Zito, Civello, Colletti, Ormento, Galante. Of the 58, 50 had been arrested some time in their lives; 35 had convictions and 23 had served prison sentences. Eighteen had been involved in murder case investigations; 15 had been arrested for narcotics violations, 30 for gambling, 23 for illegal use of firearms. Newspapers wondered if anyone still thought the Mafia didn't exist.

The public assumption was that the Apalachin meeting was intended as the forum for presenting Genovese with his crown, and much was made of the fact that a total of $300,000 was found on the arrested crime bosses. This, the theory went, was "envelope money" to be given to Genovese. There was considerable reason to dispute that view, however. Few of the participants ever went about with anything less than a fat "roll," and it was known that Carlo Gambino was ready to announce he brought no money for Genovese. Gambino had cooperated with Genovese in the Anastasia assassination in order to take over the latter's crime family, but he had no intention of gaining Genovese as an overboss.

In short, Apalachin seemed likely to produce fireworks and perhaps even open warfare. All of that, however, could be avoided if the meeting were boycotted or sabotaged. The first alternative was partially accomplished, the second completely. Unless one holds to the theory that the crime leaders from Chicago, Detroit and San Francisco had escaped during the raid or were still "on the way," their absence was noteworthy. Lucky Luciano, from his exile in Italy, lobbied strongly against the meeting with some of these people (his voice was still powerful in those very cities), and he coached others on their behavior at the conference, especially Carlo Gambino. Frank Costello also begged off on the grounds that he was constantly being tailed by the authorities. As treasurer for the syndicate, Meyer Lansky was supposed to show but developed, he said, a sore throat that kept him in Florida.

All these absences pointed up the lack of unanimity facing Genovese. And then came the fiasco of the raid—nothing so degrading had ever happened in the underworld's history. Vito Genovese, it was concluded, had led the crime bosses to disaster. The extent of the fury against Genovese was pointed up in a tapped telephone conversation later between Sam Giancana, then head of the Chicago syndicate, and Steve Magaddino, his Buffalo, N.Y. counterpart:

Magaddino: "It never would've happened in your place."

Giancana: "You're fuckin' right it wouldn't. This is the safest territory in the world for a big meet. . . . We got three towns just outside of Chicago with the police chiefs in our pocket. We got this territory locked up tight."

Magaddino's comments were less than gracious considering it was he who had suggested to Genovese that the meeting be held at Apalachin. Host Barbara was a lieutenant in Magaddino's crime family. If Genovese had the feeling he had been set up, there was considerable justification. How much so he did not realize until he and a number of his aides were indicted for narcotics conspiracy six months later. The chief testimony against Genovese was provided by a two-bit heroin pusher named Nelson Cantellops. That an unimportant Puerto Rican street operator could have the goods on a big man like Genovese did not seem logical, but the government gleefully used his testimony to convict the crime boss.

Shortly before he died, Lucky Luciano revealed the secret behind the Cantellops testimony. He said Cantellops had in the past worked for Chicago's Sam Giancana and for Meyer Lansky, both of whom had missed the Apalachin conclave. The pusher had received a $100,000 payoff from Luciano, Gambion, Lansky and Costello. For his $25,000, Costello had insisted that among those convicted had to be Vincente "the Chin" Gigante, the triggerman in the Genovese-inspired attempt on his life.

Apalachin had indeed been the first nail in Genovese's coffin. The coup de grace followed in 1959, when he was sentenced to prison for 15 years. He would die there in 1969.

See also: *Joseph Barbara, Sr.; Vito Genovese.*

ARBUCKLE, Roscoe "Fatty" (1887-1933): Accused murderer

Roscoe "Fatty" Arbuckle was at the peak of his career as a comedian, regarded second only to Chaplin, when he was arrested in 1921 for the rape-killing of a delicate young actress named Virginia Rappe, which came to be regarded as Holly-

wood's worst scandal. The three trials that followed laid bare facts about Arbuckle's private life. What had been amusing on screen for an almost 300-pound buffoon assumed sinister aspects off screen. Somehow the knowledge that Arbuckle had the back seat of his $25,000 Rolls Royce equipped with a built-in toilet came across as more animalistic than humorous when associated with an alleged rapist-murderer.

The facts in the death of 25-year-old Virginia Rappe have never been entirely clear, the picture having been muddled by Hollywood movie studios anxious to protect their investment in a hot comic property. Bribes were paid and witnesses disappeared or changed their stories. But what is clear is that Arbuckle, straight from working on three films without a day off, headed for a session of relaxation in San Francisco with a party of friends, among them Virginia Rappe, who had recently moved up to starring roles on the basis of her delicate beauty rather than any acting ability. Her pretty face at the moment graced the sheet music of "Let Me Call You Sweetheart."

According to some accounts, Virginia thoroughly disliked Arbuckle but kept his company because she felt the fat comedian could aid her career, a common enough belief among aspiring starlets. The young actress was present at a wild party—some later described it as an orgy—that took place in Fatty's St. Francis Hotel suite on September 5, 1921. During the revelry Fatty seized Virginia and hustled her into the bedroom, with the actress showing some or no resistance, according to the conflicting testimony of the witnesses. But what happened next was not disputed.

For 20 minutes no sound was heard from the bedroom and the others in the party simply passed knowing glances. Suddenly, there were hysterical screams and Virginia cried, "I'm dying, he's killing me, I'm dying!"

Arbuckle then walked out of the room wearing Virginia's hat and giggling. "Go in and get her dressed and take her back to her hotel. She makes too much noise."

When the others looked into the bedroom, they saw Virginia's nude, bloody body lying among her ripped clothes. "He hurt me. Roscoe hurt me," she cried. "I'm dying, I'm dying. Roscoe did it."

Arbuckle was unimpressed by Virginia's ravings. "She's acting it up," he said. "She's always been a lousy actress." He warned those present he would throw her out the 12th-story window unless she stopped moaning. Several other women carried Virginia down the hall to another room. Three days later she died.

The three trials of Fatty Arbuckle for felony rape and murder were legal curiosities. At first, courtroom descriptions of what Arbuckle had done were considered so shocking that they were passed back and forth in writing. The official version that Virginia's bladder had been ruptured when the fat man had forced intercourse on her was hardly the complete story. Finally, a witness testified that after the incident Arbuckle had laughingly told others at the party that he had jammed a large jagged piece of ice into her vagina. Later, there was talk about a champagne bottle as well.

The first two trials ended in hung juries, voting 10 to two for acquittal and then 10 to two for conviction. The third trial resulted in a not-guilty verdict, after the jury had deliberated only six minutes. In addition to setting the comedian free, the panel added: "Acquittal is not enough for Roscoe Arbuckle. We feel a great injustice has been done him and there was not the slightest proof to connect him in any way with the commission of any crime." The jurors then stuck around to have their pictures taken with the grateful comic.

While the air was filled with charges that witnesses and jury members had been bribed, the studios set up plans to relaunch Arbuckle's film career. However, it soon became apparent that although a California court had cleared him, the rest of the country did not feel the same way. Theater owners reported that the comedian's unreleased movies would play to empty houses, and his films were junked. Arbuckle spent the next 10 years knocking around in vaudeville and playing second-rate cabarets. He was allowed to direct some minor films under the name of William Goodrich, while he implored the studios to give him another chance. Finally, in 1933 Warner Brothers signed him to do some two-reelers. He finished the first one in New York on June 29. "This is the happiest day of my life," he said. The next morning he was found dead in his hotel room bed of a heart attack.

ARGOS Lectionary: Rare manuscript

One of the most-valued Greek manuscripts possessed by an American university is the University of Chicago's Argos Lectionary, a book of parchment leaves containing excerpts from the Bible arranged for church services. The book was purchased by the school in 1930 from the manager of an underworld-controlled nightclub, who had phoned and offered to sell "a Bible with an odd history."

The nightclub manager, however, had something else in mind when he referred to its "odd history." Prohibition-era gunmen had placed their hands on the Bible when they swore their oath of allegiance to Al Capone. The university's experts recognized it as a ninth or 10th century work—and a masterpiece of singular scholarly import.

ARIZONA Rangers

Formed much later than the Texas Rangers, the Arizona Rangers were organized in 1901 to assist local officials in maintaining law and order. Headed by Capt. Burton C. Mossman, the 12- to 14-man force achieved a noteworthy record. While aimed at stopping outlaws and rustlers in general, the Arizona Rangers probably would not have been formed had it not been for the depredations of a vicious outlaw and murderer named Augustine Chacon, a 30-notch gunman. The Rangers got their man and many more before being disbanded in 1910, probably in recognition of the fact that the use of such a force was justified only in an era of widespread lawlessness. By doing so, the Arizona Rangers avoided the later criticism of the Texas Rangers as an organization that had outlived its usefulness. Such early groups as the Arizona Rangers and the New Mexico Rangers set the precedent for the present state police organizations.

See also: *Burt Alvord, Burton C. Mossman.*

ARKANSAS Tom: See Roy Daugherty.

ARKANSAS Toothpick: Murder weapon

The popular concept of backwoods feuding and killing is of mountain boys blasting away at each other with their trusty shotguns. True, they all carried shotguns or rifles, but as in the Hatfield-McCoy feud, many of the killings were done with a stiletto-type dagger known as an Arkansas Toothpick, the hillbillies' favorite for a "silent job."

ARLINGTON, Josie (1864-1914): Madam

Mary Deubler, better known professionally as Josie Arlington, was perhaps New Orleans' most famous madam. She was certainly regarded as the classiest and her house, the Arlington, gained a reputation as the gaudiest and grandest of bordellos. Her achievement was somewhat remarkable, however, considering her early years in the trade. For nine years, starting at the age of 17, she worked in various brothels on Customhouse Street and Basin Street under the name of Josie Alton. She never stayed long in one place because of her proclivity for brawling with the other girls. In 1886 she engaged in a fierce fight with another prostitute, Beulah Ripley. Josie lost much of her hair, while Beulah staggered from the battle minus her lower lip and half an ear. In 1888 Josie opened her own place at No. 172 Customhouse Street, a house known for having the most quarrelsome residents on the street. The profits enabled Josie to support her lover, Philip Lobrano, who lived in the house, and several members of her family. Lobrano was quite outspoken about relatives living off the income of his women like "a flock of vultures." In 1890, during a fierce brawl in the house involving Josie and all her girls, Lobrano shot and killed Josie's brother, Peter Deubler. New Orleans being New Orleans, Lobrano was acquitted by the courts.

Changing her name to Lobrano d'Arlington, Josie turned over a new leaf. She kicked out her lover, dismissed all her battling prostitutes and announced that henceforth she would fill her establishment with the most gracious of foreign ladies who would entertain only gentlemen of refinement and impeccable taste.

The *Mascot,* a tabloid that reported the doings of the red-light district, trumpeted: "Society is graced by the presence of a bona-fide baroness, direct from the Court at St. Petersburg. The baroness is at present residing incog. at the Chateau Lobrano d'Arlington, and is known as La Belle Stewart." The baroness was soon exposed as being a hoochy-koochy dancer and circus specialist who had graced the Midway at the Chicago World's Fair. Many of Josie Arlington's other imports also proved to be imposters. Despite this, her lavish brothel thrived and when Storyville, a quasi-legal red-light district, was established, Josie opened the Arlington, which was just about the most discriminating in Storyville. Over the next decade Josie Arlington amassed a considerable fortune, which allowed her to buy a mansion in the most fashionable part of New Orleans.

MISS
JOSIE ARLINGTON

225 Basin Street   Phone 1888

The Arlington

Nowhere in this country will you find a more complete and thorough sporting establishment than the Arlington.

Absolutely and unquestionably the most decorative and costly fitted out sporting palace ever placed before the American public.

The wonderful originality of everything that goes to fit out a mansion makes it the most attractive ever seen in this and the old country.

Miss Arlington recently went to an expense of nearly $5,000 in having her mansion renovated and replenished.

Within the great walls of the Arlington will be found the work of great artists from Europe and America. Many articles from the Louisiana Purchase Exposition will also be seen.

One of Madam Arlington's ads in the *Blue Book*, a turn-of-the-century guide to whoring in New Orleans, heralds the ultimate in brothel furnishings and decor.

Josie also started to get religion, sending a niece to be educated in a convent. While still in her early forties, she bought a plot in Metarie Cemetery and erected an $8,000 tomb of red marble, with two large flambeaux on top and a crosscut in the back. There was a copper door and carved on it, in bas-relief, was the figure of a kneeling woman, her arms filled with flowers.

Josie leased out the Arlington in 1909 and retired from the business. She died in 1914, at the age of 50, by then Storyville's most-storied madam. Even in death, Josie entertained, in a fashion, the citizenry of New Orleans. The city installed a red traffic light on the street by Metarie Cemetery, and during the night its red glow cast on the two flambeaux gave the illusion of a red light shining over the renowned madam's tomb. Crowds gathered each night to enjoy the spectacle, and nightly sight-seeing tours all paused at the cemetery for the show. The city eventually replaced the red light with a white one, making the traffic light one of the most confusing ever installed. In 1924 Josie's niece had the madam's bones transferred to a receiving vault and the gaudy tomb was sold.

See also: *Storyville*.

ARNOLD, Keith: See Gerald Craft.

ARNOLD, Stephen (c. 1770-?): Murderer

Men and women suffering from varying degrees of lunacy have committed murders, and depending on the prevailing mores of their societies, they have received varying punishments. Stephen Arnold, in an event marked by high drama, was one of the first in America to win leniency due to insanity. As a thirtyish schoolteacher in Cooperstown, N.Y., he was a perfectionist who would fly into a mad rage whenever a pupil made a spelling error. When in 1805 his six-year-old niece, Betsy Van Amburgh, misspelled "gig," Arnold lost all control of himself, seized a club and beat her to death. Then comprehending what he had done, he fled Cooperstown for Pittsburgh, Pa., where he took up a new identity. Caught later that year, he was returned to Cooperstown to be tried for murder. Since his lawyer could not dispute the obvious facts of the crime, Arnold was convicted in short order and sentenced to be hanged.

Arnold's execution day was a banner event in Cooperstown, with thousands from the surrounding area converging on the town for the big show. According to a contemporary account, marching bands, a company of artillery and a full battalion of infantry led Arnold to the gallows. Flowers and bunting decorated the caissons and even the gallows. While Arnold stood with the noose around his neck, a minister launched into an hour-long sermon on the sins of men letting their tempers race unchecked. Much of the admonishments were quotations from Arnold himself. Now, with the obligatory matters taken care of, the hangman stepped forward—the crowd tensed . . . suddenly the sheriff moved to the condemned man and ceremoniously flung the noose from Arnold's neck. Before the stunned onlookers, the sheriff then read a reprieve for Arnold that he had received from the governor earlier in the morning. The sheriff had let the execution charade continue for three reasons: to show his disagreement with the chief executive's act; to force Arnold to experience the terror of execution for his murderous sin; and not to disappoint entirely the thousands gathered for the event. The crowd's disappointment was great nonetheless, and there was some speculation that the sheriff had acted as he did only so that the local merchants and tavern keepers could still profit from what would prove to be a non-event. Amidst all the bickering on that point, the concept of temporary insanity and the pros and cons of it were lost on most of the crowd. Arnold was later pardoned for the same reason.

ARREST, Citizen's

A private citizen has just as much right to arrest a lawbreaker as does a police officer, but these so-called citizen's arrests are actually rife with legal danger to the person making them. A private citizen can arrest another for a crime that is committed or attempted in his or her presence. In addition, a private citizen can arrest a person who has committed a felony even though it was not perpetrated in the arresting citizen's presence. The arresting citizen must inform the person he is arresting of the arrest and, without undue delay, take him or her before a magistrate or hand him or her over to a police officer. Everything will then have been handled properly—provided the person arrested is later found guilty. If he or she is acquitted or the charges are dropped, the citizen making the arrest can be sued for false arrest, not an uncommon occurrence. As a result, most legal authorities strongly counsel against a citizen's arrest except under the most certain of circumstances.

ARREST Procedures

Arrest is the taking or detainment of a person by legal authority, preferably by an officer of the law acting with a warrant, a written order signed by a magistrate stating the reason for the arrest. An officer can also make an arrest without a warrant if the crime is a misdemeanor, or lesser offense, committed in his presence or a felony, or major offense, that he may not have witnessed but has reasonable cause to believe the person being arrested has committed.

As soon as the arrested person arrives at the station house, he or she is booked. Booking is the entry of the charge into what is called the "arrest book," more popularly known as the police blotter. At this point, the defendant officially learns the exact charge against him, but in practice, the average person often is so frightened he doesn't grasp the exact words or the desk officer mumbles in such a manner that the accused can't make out the officer's words.

Next comes an "order for admittance and property receipt." The arrested person empties his pockets; everything is itemized and put in an envelope. As a rule, wristwatches may be kept.

Regulations in the average jail permit an arrested person to send local telephone messages to his or her relatives, friends, employer and a lawyer. "Messages" is indeed the right word, since in most places the police make the calls for you. If the arrested person is well behaved, the police wink at the rules and let him or her personally use the phone and even make as many calls as desired. If the arrestee gets nasty, the police will make the call, or at least they say they will. Unfortunately, they sometimes will inform the arrestee the line is busy. The Constitution provides no guarantee that a telephone can't be busy.

If charged with a felony or a misdemeanor, the arrestee is fingerprinted and "mugged." A person can refuse to be fingerprinted, but in most places one can't get bail without going through the procedure. Four sets of fingerprints are made: two for the local police files, one for the state capital and another for the FBI. Four photographs—"mug shots"—are taken, two front view and one left and one right profile. If the arrested person is later found innocent or the charges are dropped, he or she has the right to demand the return of the prints. Some officers make a point of not doing this, instead offering a phony set of prints. In some states a court order is needed to get back such prints. It's often wise to have a lawyer get a court order even where it is not required; few officers will play games when a court order is involved.

After the arrested person has been booked, printed and mugged, he or she is brought into court for arraignment. Usually, the police are required to bring an arrested person before a judge within 24 hours, but in some areas the rule isn't rigidly enforced. Over a weekend an arrestee can often spend three nights locked up, and there are numerous cases of persons being held two or three weeks before arraignment. At times, court arraignment is used only in felony cases. In any case, the formal charge is made at arraignment, and at the same time, or possibly at a later hearing, the arrested person pleads either guilty or innocent. A magistrate then hears the police case and decides whether it's strong enough to hold the arrested person for the grand jury. If not, the magistrate will dismiss the charge.

The grand jury hearing a case does not necessarily call the defendant before it. It may simply hear the police side and decide that a crime has been committed and that the defendant could have committed it. The grand jury is a body of 12 to 23 citizens, with the average number around 19. For a verdict, 12 jury members must agree. If the grand jury decides there is enough evidence to bring a defendant to trial, it issues a "true bill," or indictment. After that, the defendant is permitted to alter his or her plea, and the judge will set new bail, either larger or smaller, depending on what is deemed appropriate.

For a misdemeanor the arrestee or may not be arraigned in court the next day. In many cities, at the time of booking, the desk officer will order the arrested person to be in court on a given date, possibly two or three weeks later. By agreement with the courts, the police are empowered to collect bail in misdemeanor cases according to fixed rates and allow the defendant's release. Bail is solely for the purpose of guaranteeing that the accused will appear at his or her trial. If the defendant can't raise bail, for either a felony or a misdemeanor charge, it's back to jail, possibly for a long stay until the case comes to court.

See also: *Bail.*

ARSON

If any crime in America can be described as out of control, it is arson. At the end of the 1970s, arson was responsible for killing 1,000 persons and injuring 10,000 more each year. The cost to insurance companies was over $1.6 billion. From 1970 to 1977 the number of fires due to arson jumped from

120,000 to 240,000. A Senate investigations subcommittee warned, "Long thought by the public to be a sporadic act of greed, arson has evolved into a way of life in many metropolitan areas." The committee said landlords and other building owners who saw property values dropping often overinsured their properties and then arranged to have them burned down by professional firebugs or ghetto gangs in order to obtain quick insurance windfalls.

Pyromania, the act of a compulsive fire-setter, may not have increased as fast as arson for money, but it too is growing. In fact, insurance arsonists are at times the inspiration for pyromaniacs. The South Bronx in New York City has become an arsonist's playground; while many fires are definitely started by paid arsonists, many of the borough's fires are the work of pyromaniacs looking for a thrill. In one case a pyromaniac came all the way from Texas to set blazes in the Bronx because, as he said, "I know I'll be safe doing it there."

Pyromania is a difficult illness to diagnose and one that shows few social patterns.

• The Chicago area had a rash of fires set in 27 different buildings. It turned out to be the work of one of the community's most-respected physicians, a dedicated doctor who still made house calls.

• When a large building on the campus of the University of Michigan was set afire, a respected faculty member was apprehended for the crime.

• A Georgia orphanage burned to the ground, and the arsonist turned out to be a society matron who had worked hard to raise money for its construction in the first place. "When I get the urge to set a fire," she declared when caught, "nothing I can do stops me."

Few arsonists start fires with any desire to kill people. They know it will happen sooner or later, but the thought doesn't stop them from committing their crimes.

Recent history's worst proven case of arson was the Ringling Brothers Barnum and Bailey Circus fire in 1944 in Hartford, Conn., in which 168 men, women and children perished. Eventually, a 15-year-old circus roustabout was found to have set the fire. He was caught some six years later after he set another big blaze in East St. Louis. The pyromaniac couldn't really explain why he had started the circus fire; all that could be established was that he had felt picked on by his bosses and that he had had a lifelong preoccupation with fire.

By and large, pyromaniacs can be said to share one or more of four common characteristics: (1) a resentment of authority; (2) the urge for destruction; (3) an inability to show resentment directly; and (4) extremely poor sexual adjustment. One of the leading authorities on the subject, Dr. Nolan D. C. Lewis, has observed: "The pyromaniac can give no rational motive for his incendiary acts. Even though he is aware that he may cause property damage worth hundreds of thousands of dollars, perhaps even be responsible for the deaths of innocent women and children, he feels he *must* set fires. I know of cases where such people have rushed into police stations shouting, 'Stop me before I set another fire!' "

There is considerable evidence to indicate that compulsive arsonists can be cured. In their landmark study, *Pathological Firesetting,* Drs. Nolan Lewis and Helen Yarnell traced 1,071 convicted pyromaniacs. Only 138 of the pyromaniacs had received psychiatric treatment specifically designed to solve their problem. Of these, Lewis and Yarnell concluded, not one was still setting fires.

ASHBY, James (c.1830): Riverboat gambler

While the Mississippi was noted for many colorful riverboat gamblers, none was more amazing than old James Ashby, a grizzled sharper skilled at suckering others who superficially seemed much more polished.

Ashby would work with a young confederate, pretending to be father and son returning home after selling off some stock at market. The bumpkin-appearing "son" looked like a perfect victim, easily inveigled into trying his luck at cards, and Ashby pretended to be a fiddle-playing old man teetering on the brink of senility. While the son was gambling, Ashby guzzled white lightning and played snatches of tunes on his fiddle, bemoaning that he no longer remembered how the complete version went. His son proved less dim-witted than he looked, winning hand after hand in defiance of all the odds. "Not for a long time," one historian of the river wrote, "did the gamblers learn that the tunes were signals." Whereupon Ashby retired from Mississippi activities, having grown wealthy by outsharping the sharpers.

ASHLEY, John (1895-1924): Everglades gangster

Still regarded as a folk hero in the Florida Everglades, John Ashley headed an unlikely band of criminals who, from 1915 to 1924, robbed a total of 40 banks and stole close to a million dollars. Small-town bankers lived in dread of the sight of the Ashley gang bouncing into town in a Model T and out again with the loot, often waving a gin bottle at the citizens as they went. They were also expert hijackers. Rumrunners, not a spineless sort, blanched when Ashley and his crew mounted one of their transports. A state official called Ashley the worst menace to Florida since the war with the Seminoles. The newspapers likened him to Jesse James, and there was indeed a resemblance save that James never flaunted the law quite as openly as John Ashley.

Once the Ashley gang pulled a job, they would separate and head for the Everglades, where no man alive could track John Ashley, a "cracker" who could move through the swamps with the assurance of an urban pedestrian on well-marked city streets. The story was often told of the time a posse of 12 men went after Ashley when he was alone in the swamp. They failed to catch him but ended up racing out of the swamp panic-stricken, two of them wounded. They suddenly had realized that Ashley was tracking them instead of the other way around.

It was exploits of this sort that made Ashley a hero to a great many crackers who inhabited the pine and palmetto backwoods of Florida. He became a symbol of their resentment toward an encroaching civilization, and a popular belief was that Ashley killed only when he was forced to, lived a life of crime only because he was forced into it. And besides, he sure stuck it to all those the crackers detested—the townies, the revenuers, the police, even them big-city rumrunners importing that foreign stuff and taking away white lightnin' markets. In that last endeavor, the Ashley gang did what the U.S. Coast Guard had failed to do. They virtually halted rumrunning between Bimini, a little spit of sand in the Bahamas, and much of Florida's east coast. The smugglers lost so much liquor to the Ashley gang that they transferred their activities elsewhere.

Perhaps what made the gang so engaging was the fact they did their work so haphazardly; in fact, they were just too lazy to do any advance planning. When Ashley robbed a bank, often the extent of his casing the job was to check the bank's hours to make sure it would be open when he got there. Once when the Ashley mob hit a bank in Stuart, Fla. without bothering to bring along a getaway car, they had an excellent reason: no member of the gang at the time knew how to drive! Ashley figured there'd be someone in the bank who had a car parked outside. Which was exactly how things worked out.

Ashley did get caught a couple of times: following one bank robbery, a member of his own gang accidentally shot him in the eye while firing at pursuers. Ashley was captured as he staggered around on the edge of a swamp, clutching his eye and half-crazed with pain. After that, he wore a glass eye.

Instead of being tried for the bank robbery, Ashley was shipped to Miami to stand trial for the murder of a Seminole Indian subchief. There was no hard evidence against Ashley, and he was almost certainly innocent of the murder. The crackers of the swamp knew what was behind it all: the land sellers wanted someone convicted of the killing because they didn't want any Indian trouble scaring away buyers. So why not pin it on John Ashley?

The Ashley gang was incensed and determined to free its leader. Ashley's brother Bob actually made his way into the jailhouse and killed a guard, but he was forced to flee before reaching his brother's cell and was killed shortly thereafter in a fight with police. The frustrated gang then sent an "ultimatum" to the city of Miami that brought the Ashleys nationwide fame. Addressed to the local sheriff, its exact words were:

Dear Sir,

We were in your city at the time one of gang Bob Ashley was brutely shot to death by your officers and now your town can expect to feel the results of it any hor. and if John Ashley is not fairly delt with and given a fair trial and turned loose simply for the life of a God-damn Seminole Indian we expect to shoot up the hole God-damn town regardless to what the results might be. we expect to make our apearance at a early date.

The Ashley Gang

It is doubtful the course of Miami justice bent because of this threat, but among the crackers there was a knowing nod of

the heads when the murder charge against Ashley was nol-prossed. However, Ashley was convicted of bank robbery and sentenced to 17 years in prison. In a short time, he escaped and returned to take command of his gang.

In 1924 Ashley, tired of bank jobs and the like, pulled one of the most fabulous crimes of the century, though it is little remembered today because the loot turned out to be disappointingly small. During this period of Prohibition most of the rumrunners drew their supplies from the West End Settlement in the Bimini Islands. Ashley decided that instead of going through all the trouble involved in waylaying the rumrunners, it would be a lot less tiring to go to West End and rob whatever money the rumrunners brought there. John and his crew hit the island late one afternoon and within two hours cleaned out all the money the liquor suppliers had on hand. It was the first time in over 100 years that an American pirate had raided a British crown colony, but Ashley wasn't particularly interested in the distinction. What bothered him was that his master coup had netted a mere $8,000. Just hours before the gang hit the island, an express boat carrying $250,000 in cash had left for Nassau.

Ashley went back to bank robbing, but the end was near. The police now had a stoolpigeon within the gang. His identity has never been established with certainty, but it is widely believed to have been Clarence Middleton, a drug addict member of the gang. The police got a tip in February 1924 that Ashley's father, who'd recently jumped bail on a moonshining charge, was holed up not far from the Ashley home, and that John Ashley was going to visit him.

The hideout was attacked, and Old Man Ashley was killed and a few others wounded. John Ashley, however, escaped. The same source then informed the police that the gang was heading for Jacksonville. A roadblock with a chain and some lanterns was set up at the Sebastian Bridge. It was dark when the Ashley gang's car pulled up. All four men in it—Ashley, Hanford Mobley, Ray Lynn and Clarence Middleton—got out to inspect what they thought was a construction job. A score of gun muzzles were leveled on them. They started to raise their hands.

What happened next is a mystery. The official version is that Ashley made a move for his gun. Twenty law officers fired, and four of the most-wanted men in Florida died. According to another version, told by the crackers, Ashley and the others were handcuffed and then shot to death. This story claims that when their bodies were brought to the funeral parlor, all the dead men's wrists bore the marks of handcuffs.

ASSASSINATION

Political assassination came late upon the American scene. The first assassination attempt against a U.S. president occurred in 1835 as Andrew Jackson was strolling out of the Capitol. Richard Lawrence, an out-of-work painter, stepped out from behind a pillar and fired two pistols at Jackson, both of which misfired. Lawrence was judged deranged and committed to an insane asylum, although Jackson remained convinced the would-be assassin's act had been part of a Whig conspiracy to kill him.

The next attack on a U.S. president was the assassination of Abraham Lincoln by John Wilkes Booth in 1865. Besides Booth, who was killed by pursuing troops, four others—Lewis Paine, George Atzerodt, David Herold and Mrs. Mary Surratt—were hanged and several others sent to prison. What followed can best be summarized by a phrase from James McKinley's *Assassination in America*, "After Lincoln, the deluge." While Andrew Johnson was president, 13 political officeholders were shot at and 12 of them killed. During Ulysses S. Grant's two terms, from 1869 to 1877, there were 20 attacks, resulting in 11 deaths.

Assassinations became a part of American political life from the late 19th century on. Some important assassinations and attempts included:

1881: President James A. Garfield was shot in Washington, D.C. on March 13 by a disappointed office seeker, Charles Julius Gaiteau. Garfield died on September 29 and Gaiteau was hanged in June 1882.

1901: President William McKinley was shot in Buffalo, New York on September 6 by Leon Czolgosz. McKinley died on September 14 and Czolgosz was executed the following month.

In what many experts regard as the greatest crime photo ever taken, New York Mayor William J. Gaynor is shown seconds after he was shot by a disgruntled city employee in 1910 aboard an ocean liner as he prepared to sail for Europe. Gaynor survived. When Charles Chapin, city editor of the *Evening World,* saw the picture he exclaimed, "Look, what a wonderful thing! Blood all over him—and exclusive too!"

1910: New York Mayor William J. Gaynor was shot and badly wounded by James J. Gallagher, a disgruntled city employee, but the mayor recovered.

1912: Former President Theodore Roosevelt was shot in Milwaukee by a demented man named John N. Shrank, but Roosevelt was saved when the passage of the bullet was slowed by a folded 50-page speech and the spectacle case in his pocket. The bullet nevertheless, penetrated the former President's chest in too dangerous a position ever to be removed. Shrank was confined in mental institutions until his death in 1943.

1933: President-elect Franklin D. Roosevelt was shot at in Miami, Fla. on February 15 by Joseph Zangara. The shot missed Roosevelt and instead hit and fatally wounded Chicago Mayor Anton J. Cermak. Some historians insist Zangara never intended to shoot Roosevelt (despite his own claims to that effect) but had been hired by elements of the Capone mob to get rid of Cermak. The mayor himself clung to that belief on his deathbed. Zangara died in the electric chair in March 1933.

1935: Sen. Huey P. Long of Louisiana was shot and killed by Dr. Carl Austin Weiss, who in turn was cut down by Long's bodyguards.

1950: On November 1 two Puerto Rican nationalists, Oscar Collazo and Griselio Torresola, attempted to storm Blair House to assassinate President Harry S Truman. They never reached Truman but killed a guard, Leslie Coffelt. Torresola was also killed and Collazo wounded. Collazo was sentenced to life imprisonment. In 1979 President Carter granted him clemency and he returned to Puerto Rico.

1963: President John F. Kennedy was shot to death in Dallas, Tex. by Lee Harvey Oswald. Oswald was later assassinated by Jack Ruby while in police custody.

1965: Malcolm X was shotgunned to death in New York City on February 21 by three assassins as he addressed his Organization of Afro-American Unity. Thomas "15X" Johnson and Norman "3X" Butler, both reputed Black Muslim enforcers, and Talmadge Hayer were all convicted of murder and given life imprisonment.

1968: Dr. Martin Luther King, Jr. was gunned down in Memphis, Tenn. on April 4 by James Earl Ray, who was convicted of the shooting and sentenced to 99 years in prison.

1968: Sen. Robert F. Kennedy was fatally shot in Los Angeles on June 5 by Sirhan Sirhan, who was subsequently convicted of the murder and sentenced to life imprisonment.

1972: Alabama Gov. George Wallace was shot and permanently paralyzed in Laurel, Md. on May 15 by Arthur H. Bremer. Bremer was sentenced to 53 years in prison.

1975: An adherent of Charles Manson, Lynette Alice "Squeaky" Fromme, pointed a gun at President Gerald Ford in Sacramento, Calif. on September 5, but she was immediately seized by a Secret Service agent. Fromme received a sentence of life imprisonment.

1975: In the second attempt on President Ford's life in 17 days, Sara Jane Moore fired a revolver at him in San Francisco, Calif. on September 22 but an onlooker shoved the gun off target. Moore was sentenced to life in prison.

1981: President Ronald Reagan was shot in the left lung on March 30 by 25-year-old John W. Hinckley, Jr., who fired a total of six shots at the President as he left a Washington, D.C., hotel. Reagan's press secretary, a Secret Service guard and a city policeman were also severely wounded. Reagan recovered.

ASSAULT And Battery

Assault and battery are two distinct crimes and the distinction is most valuable in the prosecution of criminals. Assault involves the threat or the attempt to use force or violence on another, but its commission does not require the actual use of force. Battery constitutes the actual use of force.

Legally, the distinction is most important, for without it, a holdup man who does not actually manhandle or touch his victim would not be guilty of any crime other than, say, robbery or attempted robbery. Thus, the mere waving of a fist in a person's face constitutes assault, and the employment of that fist raises the crime to assault and battery.

ASTOR Place Riots

One of the worst riots in New York City's history started on May 10, 1849, ostensibly as an outgrowth of a rather silly theatrical feud between the English tragedian William Charles Macready and the American actor Edwin Forrest. Actually, the riots were fomented by a notorious political rogue, Capt. Isaiah Rynders, who capitalized on the poor's general class hatred and anti-British feeling to regain a measure of public power following the unexpected defeat of his Democratic Party in 1848.

Macready had been chosen instead of Forrest to perform in *Macbeth* at the Astor Place Opera House. When the English actor appeared on stage, he was met by a mob who had gathered in response to a fiery tirade by Capt. Rynders and one of his chief lieutenants, Edward Z. C. Judson, better known as Ned Buntline. Rynders' thugs broke up the performance by hurling rotten eggs, pennies and even chairs onto the stage. Others threw pieces of paper filled with gunpowder in the chandeliers. Macready was driven from the stage but no one was injured. The noted actor was induced by the righteous element, led by Washington Irving and John Jacob Astor, to try once more on May 10, but Rynders was again prepared.

Offering free drinks, passes and rabble-rousing handbills, Rynders produced a crowd of 10,000 to 15,000. Twenty of Rynders' thugs entered the theater with orders to kidnap the hated foreigner right off the stage. However, the police foiled the plot and locked them all up in the basement, where they unsuccessfully tried to burn down the building. Meanwhile, the mob outside was running wild. They bombarded the barricaded windows of the theater with cobblestones gathered from a nearby sewer excavation and ripped down street lamps to use as clubs, plunging the area into darkness.

The police managed to evacuate the building and got Mac-

ready out wearing a disguise, but they couldn't contain the rioting. When Edward Judson was arrested, the mob turned even more violent. Officers were stoned to their knees, and the Seventh Regiment was called into action. Even the cavalrymen were knocked off their horses and the infantry fell back on the sidewalk on the east side of the Opera House. When the crowd tried to seize their muskets, the soldiers were ordered to fire and several volleys tore into the rioters, who fell by the dozens. Twenty-three persons were killed, and the injury list on both sides totaled more than 120.

The mobs returned the following night determined to wreck and burn the Opera House, but they were driven off by reinforced troops and artillery, which had been set up to sweep Broadway and the Bowery. For several days thereafter, crowds gathered in front of the New York Hotel, where Macready had been staying, calling on him to come out and be hanged. However, the actor had rushed to New Rochelle on May 10 and gone on by train to Boston, where he sailed for England, never to return to America.

For his part in fomenting the trouble, Edward Judson was fined $250 and sentenced to a year in the penitentiary. Rynders also was tried for inciting to riot. At the farcical trial, prosecution witnesses retraced the genesis of the plot back to Rynder's Empire Club, where the original plotting had been done, but they could not recall anything involving him directly. The jury acquitted Rynders in two hours and 10 minutes.

See also: *Edward Z. C. Judson.*

ATLANTA Boys Convoy: Mass shipment of convicts

On January 1, 1934 the former military prison on Alcatraz island in San Francisco Bay officially became a federal penitentiary. In the months that followed, this "super cage to hold super criminals" began drawing the worst inmates from other federal prisons, the troublemakers and those most likely to attempt an escape.

It was decided to ship these dangerous convicts en masse in convoy form from each prison. The first of these, called the Atlanta Boys Convoy, caused an immense amount of excitement throughout the country. On August 14, 1934, 53 tough convicts were taken from their cells in Atlanta Penitentiary, chained hand and foot and loaded into a train composed of special steel coaches with barred windows and wire-meshed doors. This came in a year when the hysteria over gangsters had reached its zenith. Once the plan to move "the Atlanta boys" became public, there were wild rumors of huge underworld armies mobilizing armored cars, flamethrowers, machine guns and even aircraft to free the convicts.

The government took measures that were appropriate for a military operation in hostile territory. The prisoners were chained to their chairs and refused toilet privileges other than on a carefully planned schedule. While the train's route was unannounced, the mysterious closings of certain stations along the way led to public speculation.

At Alcatraz, Warden James A. Johnston was kept constantly informed of the train's progress. He stayed up the entire night of the 13th tracking the route on a large map. When the train neared Oakland, it was shifted away from the city's busy terminal and switched to a little-used railway yard at Tiburon. The cars were run straight onto a ferry barge and escorted to the Rock by the Coast Guard. The prisoners were in terrible shape, having been chained in close quarters where they could hardly move and certainly couldn't sleep. All were caked in grime and sweat, and most suffered swollen feet from the irons and could hardly walk.

Their bitter journey was over, but their ordeal in the most restrictive federal prison in history was just beginning. When all were finally locked in their cells, Warden Johnston wired Attorney General Homer Cummings, "FIFTY THREE CRATES OF FURNITURE FROM ATLANTA RECEIVED IN GOOD CONDITION—INSTALLED—NO BREAKAGE."

See also: *Alcatraz Prison.*

ATLANTA Children Murders

Over a period of 24 months, from mid-1979 to mid-1981, a total of 29 young blacks, most of whom were considerably under the age of 20, disappeared in Atlanta, Ga. Twenty-eight of them were found dead. The string of murders terrified the city and galvanized the rest of the country into outpourings of support and sympathy. The main national effort came in the form of green ribbons, "symbolizing life," which appeared on millions of lapels everywhere, worn by blacks and whites. Even shopping bag ladies in New York City were seen wearing the ribbons as well as green-lettered buttons proclaiming "SAVE THE CHILDREN."

Vice President George Bush journeyed to Atlanta to demonstrate an extraordinary degree of national concern. President Ronald Reagan announced the authorization of a $1.5 million grant to aid the investigation, and huge rewards were offered for information leading to the capture of the killer or killers. Celebrities, such as Frank Sinatra and Sammy Davis, Jr., contributed money to pay for investigations and aid to the families of the victims, and thousands of letters containing checks, dollar bills and even coins streamed into Atlanta.

The official manhunt was marked by bickering between local and federal investigators. FBI Director William H. Webster riled local feelings when he announced that four of the cases, apparently unrelated to the others, had been solved. The next day a bureau agent in Macon, Ga. said the four children had been killed by their parents. This brought an angry outcry from the public, demanding to know why no arrests had been made. None were made, Atlanta Mayor Maynard Jackson said, because there was not enough evidence to justify an arrest. He complained the FBI head had undermined the public's confidence in the investigation.

A large proportion of the deaths were so similar they indicated the likelihood that many of the victims had died by the same hand or hands. Nineteen of the 28 were believed to have died from strangulation or other forms of asphyxiation. Nine were found in rivers, nude or almost nude. More than a dozen had traces of similar fibers, from a blanket or carpet, on their bodies. Evidence of dog hairs was found on a number of the bodies.

Numerous suspects, some found thousands of miles from Atlanta, were quizzed, but without success. Finally, on June 3, 1981 23-year-old Wayne B. Williams was standing in an Atlanta phone booth when FBI agents appeared and "insisted," according to Williams, that he come downtown for questioning. Word of his interrogation spread quickly through Atlanta and for the first time many felt the hunt for the mass killer might be over. However, after being held for 12 hours, Williams, who had worked as a TV cameraman and part-time talent scout and booking agent, was released. Publicly, officials said there was insufficient evidence to hold him, but privately they implied he was still a definite suspect.

It appears that Williams was picked up because investigators feared he might destroy suspected criminal evidence. During his interrogation Williams submitted to three lie detector tests, which, he later said he was told, indicated "all my answers were deceptive." The findings, Williams explained to the press, might have been caused by his nervousness. Following his release, authorities obtained a warrant to search Williams' home and confiscated a yellow blanket and a purple robe and collected samples of dog hairs and fibers from a bedspread and carpet.

Williams had first come to police attention on May 22. Around 3 a.m. officers staking out a bridge across the Chattahoochee River stopped his car after hearing a loud splash in the water. According to the police, when asked if he had thrown anything into the river, Williams said he had dumped some garbage. However, he subsequently insisted, "I told them I had dropped nothing in the river." Two days later, the body of 27-year-old Nathaniel Cater floated to shore about a mile downstream from the bridge, within 500 yards of where the body of 21-year-old Jimmy Ray Payne had been found the month before.

On June 21 Williams was arrested and charged with murdering Cater. An Atlanta grand jury indicted him on July 17 for both the Payne and Cater slayings. Clearly, the authorities acted as though several of the killings had been solved. In August, Williams pleaded not guilty to the charges.

By September, when the new school year started, there had been no further unaccountable murders of young blacks. Teachers reported that unlike the previous year there was hardly any talk among the pupils about the unsolved murders. A 12-year-old boy, Owen Malone, was quoted as saying: "It seems like it's over. Last year we talked a lot about the case; we got safety tips. The students were afraid of getting snatched." But this year, he observed, "It was all right."

On February 27, 1982 Williams was convicted of the two murders and sentenced to life imprisonment.

ATLANTIC City Conference: Underworld convention

Perhaps the most important criminal conference of the American underworld was held during three days in May 1929 in Atlantic City. Its deliberations were certainly more important than even the famous conference called in Havana by the deported Lucky Luciano in 1946 or those scheduled for the ill-fated conference in Apalachin, N.Y. in 1957.

The meeting was hosted by the boss of Atlantic City, Nucky Johnson, who was able to guarantee no police interference. For three days the overlords of American crime discussed their future plans in the Hotel President's conference rooms and various hospitality suites, which Johnson kept stocked with whiskey, food and hostesses.

Chicago's Al Capone and his "brain," Greasy Thumb Guzik, attended the conference. Other delegates included King Solomon of Boston, Nig Rosen and Boo-Boo Hoff of Philadelphia, Moe Dalitz and Chuck Polizzi of Cleveland, Abe Bernstein of Detroit's Purple Gang, John Lazia (representing Tom Pendergast) of Kansas City and Longy Zwillman of New Jersey. The biggest contingent represented New York and included Johnny Torrio, Luciano, Frank Costello, Joe Adonis, Louis Lepke, Dutch Schultz, gambler Frank Erickson, Meyer Lansky, Vince Mangano, Frank Scalise and Albert Anastasia. Notably absent and uninvited were the two New York Mafia leaders then engaged in a bloody battle to decide who would be the so-called boss of bosses—Giuseppe "Joe the Boss" Masseria and Salvatore Maranzano. Both were what Luciano and others among the new crop of Italian gangsters referred to contemptuously as "Mustache Petes," men who failed to understand the need to work with non-Italian crime leaders.

At the convention, plans were laid for criminal activity following the end of Prohibition, and it was decided that the gangs would emphasize getting into the legitimate end of the bootlegging business by acquiring distilleries, breweries and import franchises. "After all," Luciano said, "who knew more about the liquor business than us?" It was also determined that gambling would become a major enterprise. The country was sliced up into exclusive franchises for both purposes. Groundwork for deals with Moses Annenberg, who controlled the dissemination of horse racing news, was laid. Labor and protection rackets were also plotted. One thing everyone agreed upon was that all these activities would be apportioned peacefully. The earlier success of the Seven Group on peacefully resolving the bootlegging wars was held up as a model for the future.

It was further agreed that gang violence had to be cooled down. Capone was lectured on the pointless folly of incidents such as the bloody St. Valentine's Day Massacre, which produced far too much publicity and heat for comfort. Under pressure from the other gang leaders, Capone even agreed to submit to arrest and a short jail term for some minor offense in order to reduce the heat. All the participants concurred that the next logical step would be the establishment of a national crime syndicate; in fact, the meeting ended on this harmonious note. The call for reduced violence was meant seriously, but all understood that the Luciano-Lansky group would have to use considerable force to wrest control from the old Mafia dons. At this task they did not fail.

While the Atlantic City Conference was earthshaking in its effect on the development of American crime syndicates, historians have always been impressed or amused by how casual some of the deliberations were. Many took place on the beach, with the top mobsters in America walking barefoot through the water, their pants legs rolled up, somberly dividing an empire and deciding who was to live and who was to die.

See also: *Seven Group*.

ATTICA Prison Riot

If not the most violent prison riot in American penal history, the uprising at the Attica State Correctional Facility, 40 miles east of Buffalo, N.Y., in September 1971 was certainly one of the most tragic and most controversial. The riot was finally smashed by a massive assault of 1,500 heavily armed sheriff's deputies, state troopers and prison guards during which 28 prisoners and nine guards being held hostage were killed. State officials claimed that the guards had had their throats cut by the convicts and that one of them had been emasculated.

The riot began on September 9, when about 1,000 prisoners among the inmate population of 2,254 seized a portion of the prison compound, in the process taking more than 30 guards and civilian workers captive. The convicts presented a series of demands, including higher wages and greater political and religious freedom. In addition, they demanded total amnesty and no reprisals for the riot. Negotiations took place between the inmates and Russell G. Oswald, the state commissioner of corrections. Most of the deliberations were handled through the liaison of an "observers committee," consisting of representatives of government, several newspapers, the radical Young Lords and Black Muslims and other social and professional groups.

Oswald accepted most of the prisoners' demands but refused to fire Attica Superintendent Vincent Mancusi and rejected total amnesty. Gov. Nelson Rockefeller also refused the amnesty demand and rejected the requests of the observers committee that he come to Attica and personally join in the negotiations.

Early on the morning of September 13, Oswald read an ultimatum that listed his concessions and demanded the release of the hostages. The prisoners answered by displaying a number of the hostages with knives held to their throats. The bloody but successful assault followed. During the 24 hours after the assault, state officials made much of the convicts' violence and the sadistic murders of the hostages during the attack. Then came the official autopsies, which showed that none of the dead hostages had had their throats cut and none had been mutilated. All had been shot. In further contradiction of the state version, it was found that the prisoners had been in possession of no guns. All the hostages apparently had

Photo shows police and correction officers attempting to re-establish security at Attica, while dead and wounded inmates lie on the catwalks. Some of the wounded did not receive medical treatment for four hours.

been killed in the crossfire of the police attackers.

Angered state officials summoned other medical examiners to check the findings of the Monroe County medical examiner, Dr. John F. Edland, who reported state troopers had stood over him while he performed the autopsies, evidently to guard against any cover-up of the supposed throat-slashing evidence. Commissioner Oswald, who previously had told reporters that "atrocities were committed on the hostages," could not believe Dr. Edland's findings. According to one newspaper, "He suggested that some sinister force—conceivably—motivated Dr. Edland to heap blame and shame on the authorities who decided to storm the prison." The other medical examiners called in were also subjected to close observation but concurred in Dr. Edland's findings.

After long public hearings a congressional sub-committee issued a report in June 1973 that criticized the methods used by prison officials and the police and condemned the brutality and inadequate medical treatment given wounded convicts after the attack. Previously, a nine-member citizens fact-finding committee, chaired by Robert B. McKay, dean of New York University Law School, had filed a final report that condemned Rockefeller's failure to go to Attica as well as the chaotic nature of the attack. The committee declared the riot was a spontaneous uprising stemming from legitimate grievances.

The autopsies' findings, as well as the later reports, stunned the small village where the prison stood and most of the guards lived. Hatred towards the prisoners shifted to angry disbelief and in many cases to vitriolic accusations that the authorities had recklessly risked lives by ordering the retaking of the prison.

Several indictments followed and on December 30, 1976 Gov. Hugh L. Carey pardoned seven former Attica inmates and commuted the sentence of an eighth in a move to "close the book" on the bloody uprising. He also declared that no disciplinary action would be taken against 20 law officers who had participated in the attack.

The closing of the book was not complete, however. In 1977 the first of a series of lawsuits was filed on behalf of a number of guards who were taken hostage and relatives of hostages who were killed. They contended law enforcement officials used excessive force in retaking the prison and asked $20 million in damages. The trial was delayed a full year after appellate courts ruled the state had to produce the "debriefing" statements the guards and troopers made shortly after the riot. Another delay, possibly for a year or more, was indicated when appeals were filed on behalf of 19 guards and troopers who had been cited for contempt by the trial judge after they took the Fifth Amendment on questions concerning the retaking of the prison.

The name Attica and the attending stain would remain in the public's conscience for years to come.

AURORA, Nevada: Lawless mining town

As far as gold-mining towns went, Aurora, Nev. may not have been much more violent than others, but because accurate records were kept in Aurora, statistics offer considerable evidence on how wild the West really was. Founded in 1860, Aurora's heyday lasted only four years and then the gold seams ran out, but in that time, it managed to bury exactly 65 persons in its graveyard. Half were described as the victims of gunshot and the rest expired of such afflictions as knife wounds, mining mishaps and "accidents." Aurora lasted another 90 years as a ghost town; the last of its buildings were vandalized in the 1950s.

AUTO Theft

The cost of the stolen car racket in America is now put at over $4 billion a year, and that figure only includes direct monetary loss, excluding the higher insurance premiums all automobile owners must pay. A motor vehicle is stolen every 29 seconds, and the annual total is now close to one million, double the total in 1967. Generally, cars are stolen for the salvage value of their parts rather than for direct resale. An automobile that sells for $10,000 can be taken apart and its component parts sold for almost twice that amount.

While it is true that most auto thefts are perpetrated by teenage joyriders and the large majority of stolen cars are recovered—although often with considerable damage done to them—the recovery rate for professionally stolen cars is close to zero. It is not unusual for a ring of auto thieves to steal and dispose of as many as 2,000 vehicles a year. Some cars are stolen to order; e.g., a ring furnishes autos on specific order from a dealer for immediate delivery to customers. At no time does any of the hot cars have to grace the dealer's lot. Most professional car theft rings have sufficient artistry to alter motor numbers in a manner that will deceive every test but fluoroscope analysis.

Probably the most prolific auto thief was Gabriel "Bla Bla" Vigorito, who masterminded a highly efficient organization in the 1930s, 40s and 50s. Bla Bla—so named because of his incessant boasting about his family—did a land office business in hot cars, shipping more than $250,000 worth to Norway alone in the 1930s. He also transported altered stolen vehicles to Russia and Persia and shipped a special order to a warlord general in Sinkiang Province, China.

Standard operating procedure for car thieves is the salvage racket. Auto graveyards and body shops are searched for wrecks of late-model cars already written off by insurance companies. The thieves buy the wrecks for a pittance; but more importantly, they buy a good and legal title. Then they steal duplicate models of each wreck, install the salvaged serial plate, restamp the motors to coincide with the salvage documents and attach salvaged license plates. The stolen car now has a complete new identity.

While the resale of stolen cars can be profitable, the "chop shop" racket has really come of age, as criminals have learned that on a nationwide black market the sale of parts from completely dismantled stolen cars can be even more lucrative. Once a stolen car has been reduced to its parts, no identification is possible. Just as important is the fact that the gang's operations can undergo a much greater division of labor, so that various members of the outfit do not even know each other. For instance, a spotter merely locates a likely candidate for a theft and then disappears from the scene. The actual heister then shows up to drive the car away to a drop, and another driver sees that the vehicle reaches the chop house. The choppers do their job without ever coming into contact with the sellers, who move the parts back into commerce.

If identification numbers were put on all body components, a responsibility auto manufacturers have resisted, chop shop operators would find life much more difficult. Cynical car thieves claim that automakers have a vested interest in the stolen car racket's continued existence since it puts hundreds of thousands of motorists back in the market well ahead of schedule.

See also: *Dyer Act.*

AVERILL, James (?-1889): Lynch victim

Jim Averill, whose lynching along with Cattle Kate Watson helped foment Wyoming's Johnson County War of the 1890s, may or may not have had a shady past when he took advantage of the Homestead Act and settled on the banks of the Sweetwater. There are conflicting reports about his background, but in that respect, he differed little from many of the homesteaders seeking a new start in life. There was even a report that he had attended or been a graduate of Cornell University, or some similar institution of learning. But it was evident that Averill was an articulate man and he soon became the spokesman of the homesteaders in the Sweetwater Valley. He wrote blistering letters to the *Casper Daily Mail* in which he condemned the power of the cattle barons. When Averill became a leader in a futile fight to stop passage of the Maverick Bill, under which all unbranded cattle were made the property of the Stockmen's Association, it was clear the big cattlemen had to silence him. They did so by lynching Averill and an enterprising prostitute friend of his, Cattle Kate, who had set up a one-girl brothel in a cabin near his. The story the stockmen planted was that Cattle Kate was a big-time bandit queen and Averill her top aide and that the two of them were running a massive rustling operation. The twin lynching proved to be only the opening move in an effort to clear the range of homesteaders, or "rustlers," and led to the Johnson County War.

See also: *Cattle Kate, Johnson County War.*

B

BACA, Elfego (1865-1945): Gunfighter and lawman

In his native New Mexico Territory, Baca, at 19, was the chief participant and main target of one of the truly memorable gun battles of the frontier West. At the time, Frisco, a town in western New Mexico was constantly being terrorized by cowboys from the Slaughter spread. Among other things the cowhands castrated a Mexican for a prank and then used another man for target practice when he tried to intervene. These stories were told to Baca by his brother-in-law, who was deputy sheriff of Frisco.

Enraged, Baca put on his brother-in-law's badge and on November 30, 1884 headed for Frisco. He found the town living in terror and being constantly shot up by cowboys. When one of them shot Baca's hat off, the self-appointed deputy promptly arrested him. The next day 80 cowboys descended on Frisco to get the "dirty little Mex." Baca placed all the women and children in the church and prepared to meet his attackers in an ancient adobe hut. The gunplay started at 9 a. m. and continued for 36 hours, during which time an estimated 4,000 bullets were poured into the shack. The plucky Baca killed four of his assailants, wounded eight others and came through the battle unscathed. When two regular lawmen appeared, the remaining cowboys retreated and Baca was placed under arrest. Baca was tried twice in connection with the great shoot-out, but even in the Anglo courts, he was found innocent. A hero to his people, Baca was later elected sheriff of Socorro County and enjoyed a political career of 50 years.

BADGER Game: Sex swindle

The badger game is an ancient con, worked in many variations in every land. The standard modus operandi is simple: man picks up woman; woman takes him to a room; woman's "husband" comes in suddenly, confronts lovers and demands satisfaction. He gets it in the form of the frightened lover's money.

Perhaps the greatest organizer of the badger game was a notorious 19th century New York City gangster named Shang Draper, who was also an accomplished bank robber. In the 1870s Draper operated a saloon on Sixth Avenue at 29th Street. From it he directed the activities of 30 women and girls in a combined badger and panel game operation headquartered at a house in the vicinity of Prince and Wooster streets.

In the panel game, a thief would sneak into the room while the woman and her male friend were occupied in bed and steal the man's money and valuables from his discarded clothing. The sneak thief would gain entry to the room through a hidden panel in the wall out of sight from the bed.

However, if the man appeared really prosperous, Draper preferred working the badger game, because the stakes were potentially much higher. Draper added a new wrinkle to the game by using young girls, from age nine to about 14. Instead of an angry husband breaking into the room, the young girl's irate "parents" would burst in. The "mother" would immediately seize the child and smash her face, usually her blows would be hard enough to make the child bleed from the nose or mouth. While this convincing act was taking place, the equally angry "father" would shove his fist under the man's nose and say, "I'm going to put you in prison for a hundred years!"

Men victimized by this technique often could be induced to pay thousands in hush money. Draper himself loved to tell about how he stood in a telegraph office with a quivering out-of-towner waiting for his bank to wire him $9,000 so he could pay off a badger game. It was estimated that Draper's badger game conned 100 or more men each month. The police finally broke up Draper's racket in the early 1880s, but the hardy badger game easily survived the demise of his operation.

Another colorful practitioner was a Philadelphian known as "Raymond the Cleric," who found the pose of a betrayed minister-husband to be more lucrative. While he prayed in a corner for divine forgiveness for his errant spouse and her sinful lover, a couple of "members of his congregation" would appear a bit more threatening, and the sinner usually demonstrated his repentance with a hefty contribution.

To this day, the badger game, in its pure form and in dozens of variations, is one of the country's most widely practiced confidence games, although given the compromising position of the victim, one that rarely comes to the attention of the police.

See also: *Panel Houses.*

BADMAN From Bodie: Western bogeyman

During the last three decades of the 19th century, Western mothers would scare their mischievous children into line by invoking the specter of the "Badman from Bodie," who had to have a victim every day. Unlike the more traditional bogeyman, the Badman from Bodie was rooted in reality. Bodie, Calif. was one of the West's most lawless towns reportedly averaging at least one killing a day for 20 years. Even if that estimation was somewhat off, threatening nasty children with the Badman from Bodie was apparently an effective instrument of parental control.

See also: *Bodie, California*

BAGMAN: Payoff man

Originally, the word "bagman" was applied to commercial travelers, or salesmen, in England during the 18th century. At first, it was used with the same connotation in America, but the term was gradually applied more to underworld figures who carried large cases or bags in which they toted off stolen goods. These fences often had to pay off the police to operate and carried the bribe money in their bags. Bagman was soon used to describe either the man paying a bribe or the one accepting and subsequently dividing it among all the parties involved.

For years during the heyday of the Capone mob, one of the chores of Jake "Greasy Thumb" Guzik was to sit nightly in Chicago's St. Hubert's Old English Grill and Chop House and hand over money to district police captains or the sergeants who collected the graft for them, as well as the bagmen for various mayors and their aides. Another famous bagman was Joe Cooney, better known as Joe the Coon. He dispensed money within New York City police headquarters for the emerging Lucky Luciano-Frank Costello-Meyer Lansky-Joe Adonis crime empire. It was one thing to distribute payoffs to lower-ranking police officers and politicians but quite another to bring payoffs directly into the office of the police commissioner, as Lucky Luciano was later to reveal. Cooney was chosen for the job because, as a red-haired freckle-faced Irishman, it was easy for him to enter the commissioner's office each week in a maintenance man's uniform to hand over the sum of $10,000 in small bills (later said to have increased to $20,000 a week

during the tenures of Joseph A. Warren and Grover A. Whalen). Joe the Coon carried the money in a plain brown bag as though it were his lunch. To make him even more inconspicuous, Luciano instructed Joe to change a light bulb occasionally.

During the Kefauver Committee crime hearings in 1950-51, Frank Bals, named seventh deputy police commissioner during the reign of Mayor Bill O'Dwyer, admitted (and subsequently retracted) to the committee that while his duties and those of his staff of 12 were to gather intelligence about gambling and corruption in the police department, he and his men played a far different role. Bals stated that they were actually bagmen for the New York Police Department, collecting payoffs from gamblers and doling out the funds throughout police headquarters.

The most famous bag lady in criminal history was Virginia Hill, that bedmate of gangsters, who promptly carried off much of their money to secret bank accounts in Switzerland.

BAIL

Bail is a method whereby a person awaiting trial on a criminal charge is allowed to go free upon the posting of security sufficient to ensure his appearance in court. Most state constitutions specifically provide for the right to bail in all cases except capital crimes. Since the majority of persons arrested cannot come up with sufficient cash to cover a bail bond, they must patronize a surety company or professional bondsmen to obtain bail. The legal cost for such a bond may be five or 10 percent of the bail, but many bondsmen demand and get more. These bondsmen justify their exorbitant fees by claiming that because their business involves such a high risk, they would go broke if they had a half-dozen "skips"—persons who fail to make an appearance at the appropriate time—in quick succession.

Exposes of the bail bond racket are common. Criminologists H. E. Barnes and N. K. Teeters state: "Professional bondsmen are usually parties to a questionable, if not downright corrupt, political system and usually have no appreciable assets with which to go to bail for those who must later appear for another hearing. They offer what is called a *straw bond,* that is, they present evidence that collateral exists which is nonexistent or is insufficient for the purpose." In one instance a bondsman in New York City offered as security a piece of property that, according to its street address, would have been in the middle of the Hudson River. Bondsmen have also been found to use the same property as security for 15 to 20 defendants concurrently. In cases where a defendant skipped, a small bribe generally could get the record of the bond removed and the security returned to the bondsman.

In the old days bondsmen were legally permitted to solicit business openly and aggressively; in the process, they put the storied ambulance chaser to shame. Cops in almost every station house tipped off bondsmen whenever there was a bailable arrest, and some even passed out bondsmen's business cards. Sometimes, thanks to a cooperative arresting officer, a bondsman could get to the station before the officer brought in the prisoner for booking. In most jurisdictions today, a bondsman must wait until somebody comes and asks him to put up a bond. Of course, many bondsmen have their methods of circumventing the legal obstacles to soliciting business. They often hire runners to hang around the courthouse and whisper to relatives of prisoners, "I can see that you get a bond fast." If the person bites, the runner guides him to the bondsman. Trying to prove a bondsman hired a runner is, as authorities have found, practically impossible.

When a bondsman posts a bond, he gets all the security he can from the defendant. He will take possession of such things as automobile ownership papers and bankbooks, requiring the accused to sign an agreement that no money may be withdrawn from the account without the bondsman's signature as well. Call girls must often put up their jewelry and furs. Bondsmen have also taken such items as manufacturing dies, bulletproof vests, guns, war souvenirs, pornographic collections, rare comic books, out-of-print books and toupees. One legendary New York bondsman was said to specialize in exceptionally hot items including packets of heroin, police pistols and badges, blackmail material, phony draft cards, stolen license plates and bogus ration books. The tale is often told that he made a fortune renting out counterfeiting plates he was holding against a client's $25,000 bail.

Organized crime has never had any trouble rasing bail; a gang will often use one or more bondsmen to handle its bail business. Stitch McCarthy, who for years held the title of Bail Baron of New York, was a close friend of Jack "Legs" Diamond and did most of the bail bonding for Diamond and his men. Once, Mad Dog Coll went gunning for Diamond when Legs was out on bail and McCarthy became frightened that Diamond might skip out to avoid a fatal battle. Magnanimously, McCarthy insisted Diamond hide out in his home.

Large bonds are meaningless for top crime figures. On one occasion Johnny Torrio's devoted mother paraded into federal district court and calmly peeled off 97 $1,000 bills, four $500 bills and 10 $100 bills to make a cool $100,000 bail for her mobster son. Torrio kissed mom on the cheek and they walked out.

A major criticism of the bail system is that the poor are generally victimized since they usually are unable to provide enough security to satisfy a bondsman. One answer to this—although a judge who resorts to it risks being labeled a low-bail jurist—is to limit the bail to the fee that would normally be paid to a bondsman. For the poor the incentive of getting back the equivalent of the bondsman's fee is sufficient to guarantee reappearance. While critics of low bail protest the system simply returns criminals to the streets, they seldom concern themselves about the abuses of high bail. A 43-year-old truck driver in New York who was held on $75,000 bail for two charges of murder remained in jail for 14 months. He was then proved totally innocent. Had he been from a higher-income group, he would not have been falsely imprisoned for over a year.

The worst abuse of high bail is its use by prosecutors to set a climate for plea bargaining. Legal experts agree that a defendant kept in jail suffers from depression about his fate and becomes less resistant to the prosecution's offer of a lighter sentence, especially when time served is credited against the term involved.

See also: *Arrest Procedures*.

BAILEY, F. Lee (1933-   ): Defense attorney

Not quite as flamboyant as some other present-day criminal defense lawyers, such as Richard "Racehorse" Haynes and Percy Foreman, F. Lee Bailey is nonetheless recognized as one of the best in the business. Virtually a specialist on homicide, he has, at least until recent years, flown from case to case, around the country in his own private jet, causing courtroom foes and some of the more staid members of the bar to nickname him "The Flying Mouth."

Bailey has proven to be a miracle worker in court: he freed Dr. Sam Sheppard after he had been convicted of murdering his wife when represented by other well-regarded attorneys; he won acquittal for Army Capt. Ernest L. Medina on charges of killing South Vietnamese civilians at My Lai; and perhaps most remarkably of all, he prevailed upon the state of Massachusetts to try Albert DeSalvo, the notorious Boston Strangler, on noncapital charges.

Of course, Bailey has had some notable failures—because, his supporters say, he refuses to run away from the really tough cases. Thus, he lost the Patricia Hurst case and one out of two murder cases against Dr. Carl Coppolino. In his courtroom oratory Bailey lacks the bombast typical of some of today's leading defense lawyers. He is not given to cheap moralizing and has been described by *Newsweek* magazine "as unsentimental as a cat, and equally predatory." Bailey is also cunning. In pre-1972 murder cases—before the Supreme Court temporarily halted the death penalty—he went out of his way to get prosecutors to smile amiably during the trial. "To ask for the death penalty successfully," he explained, "a prosecutor must be like an Old Testament figure—deeply serious, righteously angry. No smiling man can properly ask for another man's death."

Of course, Bailey is accomplished at what has been long recognized as a defense lawyer's most important function: picking the right jurors. In the first Coppolino trial, one of his notable successes, he asked prospective jurors if they would be prejudiced because the defendant "may have stepped out of line" during his marriage. One man replied, "I step out of line myself occasionally." When the courtroom laughter subsided, the man added, "You look like you might have played around a little yourself."

"Right there and then," Bailey later said, "I knew he was my man, and I grabbed him. For some reason, the prosecution didn't challenge. And when the jury went out, my man dragged his chair to the window and said, 'I vote not guilty. Call me when the rest of you are ready to agree with me.'"

However, Bailey does not rely on such lucky happenstance. At many of his trials he posts beside him a hypnotist aide who advises him on juror selection and who allegedly is able to tell Bailey how a potential female juror will react to a lawyer based on the way she crosses her legs when answering questions.

Some observers say that in recent years the glow has rubbed off Bailey. He reputedly was chosen to defend Patty Hearst only because the family's first choice, Racehorse Haynes, had asked for double the fee Bailey wanted. But Bailey's detractors are no doubt motivated, in large part, by jealousy. His reputation with the public is probably best typified by one prospective juror's comment under questioning: "I think the man's guilty already. He wouldn't have the most important lawyer in the U.S. otherwise."

See also: *Anthony H. DeSalvo, Patricia Hearst.*

BAKER, Cullen M. (1838-1868): Outlaw and murderer

A sallow-faced killer, Cullen Baker did most of his "Civil War fighting" as the head of a Texas gang of outlaws who called themselves Confederate Irregulars in the years immediately after Appomattox. The band was really little more than a group of farm looters, but they pacified their fellow Texans by occasionally killing some Yankee soldiers or upstart "nigger police."

Baker hadn't been much of a patriot during the war. He had been drafted into the Confederate Army in Cass County, where he had lived since the age of four. Actually, being drafted had its advantages: since he had killed a man in Arkansas two years earlier, the Army provided a good hiding place for Baker. He soon deserted, however. After killing two Union soldiers in Spanish Bluffs, Tex., Baker figured a good place to hide would be in Lincoln's army, so he joined the Union cause. Not long after, he deserted again and joined a group of Confederate irregulars. After the war Baker saw no reason to stop his activities. He and his gang of vicious gunmen terrorized much of Texas, preying mostly on local farmers. They were still regarded in some circles as local heroes because they were pursued by Northern troops and black police, several of whom they killed in various fights.

Late in 1867, Bill Longley, a young gunfighter on the run from the law, joined the irregulars. He was to become the infamous Wild Bill Longley. Young Longley stayed with Baker about a year, leaving just before Baker's death. During that period Baker had developed a strong liking for a girl named Belle Foster, who did not return his attention but instead focused her affection on a crippled schoolteacher named Thomas Orr. In December 1868 Baker kidnapped Orr at gunpoint and hung him from a tree. Fortunately for Orr, he was found before he strangled to death. This act set local opinion against Baker. Trying to hang Orr hardly qualified as an anti-Yankee act. Orr and a posse of local citizens took off after Baker, and when they cornered him, Orr was given the privilege of shooting him full of holes, permanently dissolving Baker's Confederate Irregulars.

See also: *William P. Longley.*

BAKER, Joseph (?-1800): Pirate and murderer

Pirates who plied their murderous trade along the American coast around 1800 had one modus operandi that was particularly insidious as well as effective. Used by the free-lance pirate Joseph Baker, it called for a sailor to sign aboard a small vessel, subvert a few of the crew, kill the honest sailors in a mutiny and sail for pirate waters, where the craft and cargo could be disposed of at a handsome profit.

Little is known of Baker's early career except that he was a Canadian whose real name apparently was Boulanger. For Baker, piracy was definitely profitable until he tried it on Capt. William Wheland of the schooner *Eliza*. Having joined the small crew, Baker, with the aid of two other sailors named Berrouse and LaCroix, killed the first mate and wounded Capt. Wheland. Wheland was allowed to live after promising that he would sail the ship into pirate waters, since Baker's seamanship did not extend to the art of navigation. A cunning captive, Wheland awaited the proper moment and then managed to lock Baker's confederates below deck. Seizing an axe, the captain drove Baker high into the rigging of the ship and forced him to remain there for 16 days in a deadly game of cat and mouse. By that time Wheland was able to bring his vessel into port. On May 9, 1800 pirates Baker, Berrouse and LaCroix were hanged in Philadelphia.

BAKER, Rosetta (1866-1930): Murder victim

Few murder trial verdicts were ever based so much on racial stereotypes as that in the Rosetta Baker case, although this was one of the few times the decision went in favor of a member of a minority.

A wealthy San Francisco widow in her sixties, the woman was found dead by her Chinese houseboy, Liu Fook. In the course of their investigation, detectives zeroed in on Liu Fook, who was about the same age as the victim, as the only logical suspect. Witnesses revealed that Liu Fook and his "boss missy" had quarreled often, and on the day of the murder, he had scratches on his face and an injured finger—as though it had been bitten. In addition to that, a broken heel and a shirt button found on the floor beside the body belonged to the houseboy.

In spite of this and still more incriminating evidence, the jury at Liu Fook's trial in 1931 acquitted him. Some of the jurors said they had simply been swayed by the defense lawyer's repeated insistence that Liu Fook could not have been guilty because no Chinese employed in this country had ever murdered his employer. Immediately after the trial, Liu Fook took a fast boat for Hong Kong.

BAKER Estate: Great swindle

One of the most lucrative and enduring swindles in American

history began just after the Civil War with the establishment of the first of numerous Baker Estate associations. These associations were joined and supported by victims conned into believing they were the rightful heirs to a $300 million fortune in Philadelphia.

The fortune was entirely imaginary, but one association after another roped in suckers with claims that the estate was just about settled. Exactly how much money victims lost to the criminal operators of the fraud is difficult to calculate; the best estimate is that some 40 different Baker Estate associations took at least a half-million persons for a minimum of $25 million in "legal expenses" during the peak years of the fraud, from 1866 to 1936. During that period the estate swindle had very little interference from the law, but finally in 1936 the federal government launched a vigorous effort to stamp it out through many arrests and a massive publicity campaign. Since then similar con games have appeared from time to time, but none has ever been as successful as the Baker Estate swindle was during its early years.

BAKER'S Confederate Irregulars: See Cullen M. Baker.

BALL, Joe (1892-1938): Mass murderer

When it came to ghoulishness, an ex-bootlegger and tavern owner named Joe Ball, of Elmendorf, Tex., was exceptional even for a mass murderer.

In the 1930s Ball ran the Sociable Inn, a watering hole famous for two tourist attractions: the most beautiful waitresses for miles around and the pet alligators Ball kept in a pond in back of the establishment. The high point of the day was feeding time for the alligators, which Ball turned into a regular show, often feeding a live stray dog or cat to the slithering reptiles. It was a performance that could drive even the strongest men to drink, which made the 'gators as good for business as the pretty waitresses.

Ball's waitresses seemed to be a fickle lot, disappearing without a word to any of the customers. Naturally, they told Ball. Some were getting married, others had sick mothers, still others left for new jobs. Ball was never very enlightening. He merely shrugged and said philosophically, "They come, they go."

Exactly how many really went was never fully established. Later, police were able to find some of the waitresses alive, but 12 or 14 were never found. Most or all of the missing women were murdered by Ball so he would not be hampered in his constant search for a new romance. Some of them had become pregnant and demanded that Ball "do the right thing." His concept of the right thing was to axe them to death. Then, as later evidence would show, he often chopped up the body and fed the incriminating pieces to the alligators.

In 1937 the family of Minnie Mae Gotthardt wrote the local police complaining they had not heard from her for a long time. Some officers dropped in to see Ball. He set up drinks for them and explained that Minnie Mae had left to take another job. A short while later, the police came around again, wondering what happened to another waitress named Julia Turner. She left for the same reason, Ball said. That didn't wash too well because Julia had not packed any of her belongings. However, when Ball explained Julia had had a fight with her roommate and left without packing because he had given her $500 to help out, the law was placated. Then two more waitresses were listed among the missing and the Texas Rangers entered the case. They began compiling a list of Ball's former waitresses and found quite a few who could not be accounted for; their relatives had no idea of where they were.

The investigators were clearly suspicious of Ball but failed to break him down. However, an old black handyman and cook who had worked for Ball for years proved less resistant to the lawmen's questions and confessed helping his boss kill some of the women and dispose of their bodies. He said he did so because he was fearful that Ball would kill him if he refused. When the lawmen showed up at the inn on September 24, 1938, seeking the barrel in which Ball said he kept meat for feeding the alligators, the tavern owner realized the game was up. Before the officers could stop him, Ball rang up a "no sale" on the cash register, pulled out a revolver and shot himself in the head, dying instantly.

The handyman got two years for being an accessory after the fact, and the alligators were carted off to the San Antonio Zoo.

BANANA War: Battle for control of organized crime

The Banana War of 1964-69 was the most recent significant effort by the head of a leading Mafia family to seize control of the major portion of organized crime. The attack was led by the aging Joseph C. Bonanno, Sr., the head of the small but efficient crime family known by his nickname as the Bananas family.

Joe Bananas' crime interests extended from New York to Canada, Arizona and California; however, as he watched many of the older dons fade away, he decided to strike out for greater glory and illegal revenues. He launched plans to eliminate in one swoop such old-time powers as New York's Tommy Lucchese and Carlo Gambino, Buffalo's Steve Magaddino and even Los Angeles' Frank DeSimone. Bananas involved in the plot an old ally, Giuseppe Magliocco, who agreed despite misgivings and ill health. His loyalty to Bananas was unquestioned. Unfortunately for Bananas, Magliocco passed the hit assignment to an ambitious younger underboss named Joe Colombo, who readily accepted but immediately reported to the other side, seeking a reward. Colombo was rewarded with the leadership of the late Joe Profaci's Brooklyn crime family. But the dons and board members of the Mafia were still faced with the Joe Bananas problem. At a moment's notice he could put 100 gunmen on the streets of Brooklyn and Manhattan. There might be a bloodbath of a magnitude unseen since the days of Capone in the 1920s and the Genovese move for power in the 1950s.

Bananas and Magliocco were summoned to a peace meeting by the underworld commission. Bananas contemptuously didn't show. Magliocco did and begged for mercy. The syndicate leaders decided to let him live, swayed by the fact that he obviously lacked the guts to continue a war and was so ill he would not live long in any case. He was fined $50,000 and stripped of his power, which went to Colombo. A few months later, he died of a heart attack.

Bananas took off for his strongholds out West and in Canada, ignoring a second order to appear before the commission. In October 1964 he returned to Manhattan under a grand jury summons. On the night of October 21, he had dinner with his lawyers. Afterwards as he stepped from a car on Park Avenue, he was seized by two gunmen, shoved into another car and taken away. The newspapers assumed Bananas had been executed.

However, the commission was treating Bananas, an important don, carefully, apparently realizing his death would provoke a full-scale war. If Bananas was frightened, he did not show it. He realized he was in a tight spot and offered a deal. He would retire from the rackets, give up control of his family and move to Arizona. He proposed that his son, Salvatore "Bill" Bonanno, take over, but the proposal was rejected out of hand. The commission members decided Bananas should retire and so should his son. They would pick his successor. Bananas could do little but agree.

When Joe Bananas reappeared in May 1966—19 months after his disappearance—the newspapers treated it as a sort of a second coming, but more importantly, Bananas, instead of retiring, began expanding his family activities into Haiti, working tightly with the Duvalier regime. Meanwhile, the national commission appointed Gaspar DiGregorio to take over Bananas' family, a move that split the group. Many loyalists insisted on sticking with Joe Bananas, and if they could not have him, then his son, Bill.

With a war threatening, DiGregorio called for a peace meeting with Bill Bonanno. It was set for a house on Troutman Street in Brooklyn. When Bill arrived, several riflemen and shotgunners opened up on him and his men. The Bananas gang fired back, but in the dark, everyone's aim was off and there were no casualties.

DiGregorio's failure enraged the national commission and he was removed from power and replaced by a tougher leader, Paul Sciacca. Sciacca couldn't prevent the Bananas forces from striking, and several of his men were wounded in various attacks, with three being machine-gunned to death in a Queens restaurant. Eventually, five others on either side died.

A heart attack in 1968 finally slowed Joe Bananas, and he flew off to his home in Tucson, Ariz. He sent word to his foes that he had decided to retire. But the commission viewed the message as an old and unbelievable story and they continued the war. On several occasions bombs were planted at the Joe Bananas' home as well as the homes of his allies in Arizona. Finally, however, peace was achieved.

The Bananas family kept control of its Western interests, but Sciacca, and later Natale Evola, was accepted as the East Coast boss. The war was over. In 1980 Joe Bananas, at the age of 75, was convicted of conspiracy to interfere with a federal grand jury's investigation of his two sons' business operations. By that time Bill Bonanno was in prison for a parole violation. Joe Bananas' dream of power had ended.

It may be that the other Mafia chiefs learned something from the conflict. When another tough mafioso named Carmine Galante started a violent push for power in the late 1970s, he was summarily executed, without ever receiving the opportunity to appear before the board to explain himself.

See also: *Joseph Colombo, Sr.*

BANCO: Swindle

A swindle whose name careless writers often misspelled as "bunco", which was later applied to all types of confidence games.

Banco was based on the old English gambling pastime of eight-dice cloth. Sharpsters who introduced it in America usually converted it into a card game, which could be manipulated more easily than dice. It was very prevalent in the Western gold fields during the 1850s until California vigilantes drove out the gamblers using it to swindle miners. About 1860 banco was introduced in New York City, where the two greatest practitioners of the art—George P. Miller, the King of the Banco Men, and Hungry Joe Lewis—amassed fortunes.

In its card game variation, banco was played on a layout of 43 spaces—42 were numbered and 13 of those contained stars. The remaining space was blank. The 29 unstarred numbers were winning ones, being worth from $2 up to $5,000, depending on the size of the bank. Each player received eight cards numbered from one to six, with the total number in his hand representing the prize. However, if a number with a star came up, he got no prize but could draw again by putting up a certain amount of money. The sucker would generally be allowed to win at first—with no money actually changing hands—until he was ahead a few hundred to a few thousand dollars. Then he would be dealt number 27 which was the so-called conditional prize, meaning he had to stake a sum equal to the amount owed him and draw again or lose all his "winnings." Naturally, he would be dealt a blank or starred card and thereby lose everything.

The pattern of play just described was automatic since the entire banco game was a phony, being played in a "skinning dive" in which all but one of the players were actually confidence operators. The only person not in on the scheme was the sucker who had been steered there.

Miller and Hungry Joe specialized in victimizing bankers, businessmen and other prominent personages. Not only did these victims have plenty of money to lose, they also were likely to be too embarrassed to go to the police. In 1882, Hungry Joe wormed his way into an acquaintanceship with Oscar Wilde, then on a lecture tour of the country. Over several dinners he boasted of the money he had won at banco and then steered the writer to a game. The confidence man later bragged that he had taken Wilde for close to $7,000.

Wilde himself, perhaps in a face-saving exercise, later insisted he had lost only $1,500 in cash and had taken care of the rest with a check on which he had stopped payment once he discovered the play was dishonest. Banco died out not because of a dearth of potential victims but rather because con men found they could attract more suckers to fixed horse races or stock market swindles.

BANDITTI Of The Plains, The: Book

Probably the most explosive book ever to come out of the West, *The Banditti of the Plains* by Asa C. Mercer was a hard-hitting account of the brutal Johnson County War in 1892 between cattlemen and homesteaders.

THE

Banditti of the Plains

— OR THE —

Cattlemen's Invasion of Wyoming in 1892

[THE CROWNING INFAMY OF THE AGES.]

By A. S. MERCER.

Title page of *The Banditti of the Plains,* which charged some of Wyoming's greatest cattlemen with mass murder. The book was ruthlessly suppressed and even the copy at the Library of Congress vanished.

Mercer, born in 1839, was a longtime editor, author and lawmaker on the frontier. In *Banditti* he placed the blame for the war on some of the richest and most powerful cattlemen of Wyoming, various state officials and even President Benjamin Harrison, whom he accused of being in sympathy with the stockmen. He charged that many important men—naming names and supplying details—were guilty of a long list of crimes from bribery to genocide.

The book itself had a most violent life from the time it appeared in the winter of 1893. It was ruthlessly suppressed and its plates were destroyed. Copies of the book were burned and even the one in the Library of Congress disappeared. At one point, Mercer was jailed for a time for sending "obscene matter" through the mails. Somehow a few copies survived over the years and in 1954 the University of Oklahoma Press reprinted the book. Thanks to that printing, it can be found today in many libraries. The motion picture *Shane* has been described as being "straight out of *The Banditti of the Plains.*"

As for Mercer, he wrote other books and pamphlets but nothing as potent as *Banditti*. He died in relative obscurity in 1917.

See also: *Johnson County War.*

BANK Robberies

The first bank robbery—actually a burglary, since it did not involve the use of threats or violence—in America was pulled by an Englishman named Edward Smith (alias Edward Jones, alias James Smith, alias James Honeyman). Using duplicate keys obtained by a method never fully explained, he entered two doors of the City Bank on Wall Street in New York City on March 19, 1831 and stole $245,000. Because of his free spending and tips from informers, Smith was apprehended quickly and $185,000 of the loot was recovered. On May 11, 1831 he was sentenced to five years at hard labor in Sing Sing, which was a rather light sentence considering the terms handed out later to other bank thieves. It appears Smith was treated somewhat leniently because his crime was unique and the authorities were not prepared to deal with it.

In the ensuing years bank robberies became commonplace. Daylight robberies were the mode of the West, with the first jobs being pulled by the Reno gang, the Jesse James gang, the Youngers and others. In the East the more common practice was nighttime burglaries, including safecrackings, of which the leading practitioners were the notorious George Leonidas Leslie, George Miles Bliss and Mark Shinburn. Bliss and Shinburn led the Bliss Bank Ring, which was especially noted for bribing the police in New York City with a percentage of the loot from each job. In the famous $1.75 million robbery of the Ocean Bank in 1869, the Bliss gang paid a total of $132,300 in bribes to guarantee a nonsolution to the case.

In the 20th century the daylight robberies of the Wild West migrated to the East. The first really great practitioner of the craft, one who stressed meticulous planning, was Herman K. "Baron" Lamm, an ex-Prussian army officer who brought discipline and precision to the field. Lamm never robbed a bank without first drawing up a detailed floor plan of the institution and running his men through a series of full rehearsals, sometimes using a complete mock-up of the bank's interior. His men were drilled in their assignments on a minute-by-minute basis, and they were required to leave a job at a scheduled moment, regardless of the amount of loot scooped up by then. Getaways were staged with equal preciseness. A skilled driver, often a veteran of the car-racing circuit, followed a chart pasted on the dashboard showing the escape route marked block by block, with speedometer readings and alternate turns. Lamm tested each route in various weather conditions. After 13 years of successful bank robberies without a hitch, Lamm was killed in a 1930 robbery that went wrong for freak reasons. In prison, two survivors of his gang were permitted to join a mass escape engineered by what would become the Dillinger mob on the understanding that they would teach Dillinger the details of Baron Lamm's methods.

In the 1930s the bank-robbery business was taken over by the public enemies, led by the likes of Dillinger, Creepy Karpis, the Barker brothers and Baby Face Nelson. The FBI's success in running down these bank-robbing and kidnapping gangs did much to enhance the public image of that previously unimpressive organization.

Since then, probably the only great bank robber has been Slick Willie Sutton, famous for his alleged quote on why he robbed banks: "Because that's where the money is."

Looking at crime statistics, one would conclude that bank robbery is a much more serious problem today than in the 1930s. The dollar take, now totaling between $30 and $40 million annually, far exceeds that of the 1930s and the number of robberies is up many times. However, considering inflation, population expansion, the hugh growth of bank branches in the suburbs—just off main highways—we can see why the crime has apparently increased. The professionals, in fact, have more or less dropped out of the field, leaving it to amateurs, crackpots and persons seized by little more than a sudden impulse to raise money. And where is the money? Still in banks.

Some experts feel that only persons of limited intelligence try to rob banks today because the sophisticated antirobbery devices and other security measures now in use limit the take to a measly average of $1,500 and almost always lead to the capture of the culprit. A random sample of recent robberies supports that conclusion.

- In Queens, New York City an unemployed shoe salesman walked into a bank and handed a teller a note demanding "all your tens, twenties and thirties." When he left, he was followed by a bank officer as he went by foot to a motel a block away from the scene of the crime. He was arrested by police within 15 minutes.
- In Salt Lake City a would-be robber walked up to a teller and asked her to hand over all the money. As she was gathering it up, he fainted.
- In Los Angeles two shotgun-armed robbers made everyone lie down on the floor of the bank. When there was nobody left to gather up the money, the pair hesitated a moment and then fled in panic.

The typical bank robber, according to New York City police and the FBI, is an unemployed man in his early to mid-20s, often in need of money for debts or drugs. In many cases, especially in Manhattan, the bandit does not show a gun and, indeed, sometimes does not even have one. He simply passes over a note demanding the teller's money or makes a verbal threat.

Most banks instruct tellers to hand over the cash in such instances, rather than risk a shooting situation. However, tellers, being human, react in different ways. One teller became so unnerved that she plopped a wastebasket over her head as a form of protection. The shocked bandit charged out of the bank. In another case a teller by force of habit counted and recounted the money before handing it over to the patient robber.

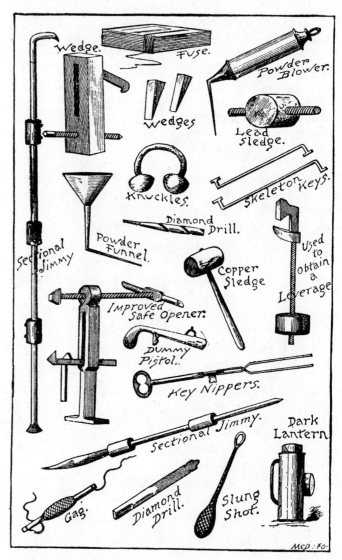

A 19th century bank burglar's kit included a gag and slung shot to use on watchmen, but the more common procedure was to bribe them.

An FBI official in Los Angeles has called modern bank robbers "young and dumb. By dumb I mean not wise in the ways of the professional holdup man. We've had guys write holdup notes on the back of their own utility bills. Or run out of a bank so excited they can't find their getaway car."

Another FBI man observed: "Twenty years ago the bank robber was looked up to by the other inmates in prison. He was a big shot, and bank robbery was viewed as the class robbery. Not any more."

Because of the changing nature of bank robbers, the FBI in recent years has been reducing its involvement in such cases. Under criticism that such crimes are trivial, easy to solve and do little other than add to the agency's solved total, the agency has been moving more into the field of organized crime and white-collar crime. Embezzlers steal three to five times as much as bank robbers.

Bank officials have objected to the FBI's withdrawal from the field, however, not so much because the agency is needed that often but because they fear general knowledge of this will simply encourage more attempts. But the fact is that with new antirobbery devices the banks can pretty much take care of themselves. One innovation is a money wrapper that dispenses tear gas. The teller simply activates the device before handing the money over. In an Atlanta, Ga. bank a 19-year-old happily stuffed $5,000 in his waistband and raced out the door. The next moment he collapsed in a coughing, crying fit, ripping at his clothes as he rolled around in the parking lot. By the time he was captured, the young robber had torn off every stitch of clothing.

Consider also the sad plight of two robbers who took money that a teller had secretly doused with a vial of malodorous liquid hidden in the money wrapper. As they drove away, a foul odor infested the car, and in desperation, they abandoned it and ran, still holding the money. But the money will never be spent—it smells too bad.

See also: *Bank Robberies—Bounties, Bliss Bank Ring, John Dillinger, Edward Green, Jug Markers, Herman "Baron" Lamm, George Leonidas Leslie, Little Joker, Safecracking, Mark Shinburn.*

BANK Robberies—Bounties

In 1928 a strange invitation to murder was unwittingly issued by a group dedicated to the prevention of crime. At the time, Texas was being plagued by a rash of bank robberies that law enforcement officials were unable to solve. Finally, the state's desperate bankers came up with what was thought to be the perfect deterrent. The Texas Bankers Association had printed and posted in every bank in the state a notice that read:

REWARD

$5,000 for *Dead* Bank Robbers
Not One Cent For Live Ones

In short order, several bank robbers turned up very dead and rewards were paid out to the local lawmen who brought in the bodies in what was very much a throwback to the bounty system of the Old West. The bankers were happy, and the lawmen were happy. But a Texas Ranger named Frank Hamer, who was to win fame later as the stalker and killer of outlaws Bonnie Parker and Clyde Barrow, was unhappy. Hamer wondered why all the bank robbers had been killed late at night.

He also wondered why local lawmen were making all the kills rather than Texas Rangers or U.S. marshals, both of whom had a fairly good record of bringing bank robbers to justice.

Hamer dug into the background of a number of cases and found the "bank robbers" were types such as loners, town bums, drifters passing through or young men who had been drunk earlier in the evening of their demise. The Ranger unearthed evidence that these so-called bank robbers had been framed and murdered by crooked lawmen who then collected the rewards. It soon became apparent that there were "murder rings" at work collecting the rewards. When Hamer went to law enforcement officials with his findings, he met with stubborn disbelief. He tried appealing to the Texas Bankers Association for a withdrawal of the reward system. Again, he was rebuffed.

Hamer took his findings to the leading newspapers of the state, including an accusation that the bankers were "bringing about the execution of men by illegal means and for money." The ensuing headlines broke the scandal wide open and led to a grand jury investigation that handed down indictments against two men accused of being the leaders of one of the several murder rings. Hamer arrested them and they subsequently confessed. Only then did the bankers admit their scheme had caused the death of innocent men; the terms of the reward offer were changed to require positive proof that a bank robbery had taken place.

BANKRUPTCY Fraud

In recent years bankruptcy scams have become one of the most lucrative activities of organized crime. According to U.S. Justice Department sources, crime syndicates pull off at least 250 such capers every year, each one involving at least $250,000 in goods and materials.

As the racket is generally worked by the New York Mafia crime families, a new company is set up with a "front man" who has no criminal record. "Nut money" of at least $30,000 is deposited in a bank to establish credit, and the company starts ordering supplies that are quickly paid for in full. However, as the orders are increased, the payments slow down a bit until finally a huge order is placed. As soon as these supplies arrive, they are either sold off at extremely low rates or transferred to other business outlets. The nut money is then pulled out of the bank and the operators simply disappear. All the creditors can find is a bankrupt shell of a company.

Perhaps the classic bankruptcy scam was pulled by members of the Vito Genovese crime family, who once took control of a large New York meat wholesale business by advancing the company cash and then insisting on putting in their own president to safeguard the loan. After becoming established, the Mafia operators needed only 10 days to work a $1.3 million swindle. They bought up huge amounts of poultry and meat on credit and sold them off at lowered prices. The mob then pulled out, blithely ordering the cowed management to go into bankruptcy.

BANNACK, Montana Territory:
Gold rush town

The site of the Montana Territory's first big gold strike, Bannack was such a violent town in the 1860s that it became "the town nobody wanted." Because territorial borders at the time were imprecise, for a while Bannack was part of Oregon and then Idaho. In 1864 it finally became part of Montana and was even the territorial capital for a period. Murder and thievery were common in Bannack since the time the prospectors panned gold from Grasshopper Creek in 1862. The greatest crook of them all was Henry Plummer, who served both as the local sheriff and the head of a huge gang called the Innocents, which committed almost all the crimes in the area. Plummer planned the gang's jobs and then, as sheriff, proved singularly ineffective at solving any of the crimes. It took the dreaded rope of the Montana Vigilantes to clear up wrongdoing in the area, and they did so by hanging Plummer—from a scaffold he had built himself for executing lawbreakers—and a large number of his Innocents.

After a long spell of noose justice, tranquility prevailed in Bannack. As the gold ran out, the town began to decay. Today, it is a ghost town with just a few well-preserved relics, such as the jail Plummer built.

See also: *John X. Beidler, Henry Plummer, Vigilantes of Montana.*

BARBARA, Joseph, Sr. (1905-1959):
Apalachin conference host

Almost as shadowy as the complete story of the infamous underworld conference at Apalachin, N. Y., in 1957 is the personal history of its host, Joseph Barbara, Sr., at whose rambling estate the meeting took place. Barbara, who was to rise to the rank of lieutenant in the Magaddino crime family in Buffalo, N.Y., came to the United States from Sicily at the age of 16, and his first job was apparently that of an underworld enforcer. He was arrested in a number of murder cases, once being caught in possession of a submachine gun that had been used in a gang murder in New York. He was also arrested for a number of murders in Pennsylvania. A typical victim was racketeer Sam Wichner, who was lured to Barbara's home in 1933 to confer with Barbara, Santo Volpe and Angelo Valente, Wichner's silent partners in a bootlegging operation. Police said, but couldn't prove, that Barbara strangled Wichner. During his entire career Barbara was only convicted of one crime: the illegal acquisition of 300,000 pounds of sugar in 1946.

After that, Barbara was ostensibly nothing more than a beer and soft drink distributor. He himself insisted he was in poor health and could do nothing more. In fact, virtually all of the 60-odd participants in the 1957 underworld meeting claimed they had gone to Barbara's home to pay a call because he was a cardiac patient. It "just happened," they insisted, that they all picked the same day for their visit.

Investigators were thwarted in their efforts to question Barbara after the Apalachin raid because of his insistence that he was too ill to testify. Finally, the State Investigation Commission sent its own heart specialist to examine Barbara and in May 1959 a state supreme court justice ordered him to appear before the commission. The following month, however, Barbara died of a heart attack. At the time he was living in a new home in Endicott. His 58-acre estate in Apalachin had been sold for use as a tourist attraction.

See also: *Apalachin Conference.*

BARBE, Warren Gilbert (?-1925):
Murder victim

To his neighbors in Berkeley, Calif., Charles Henry Schwartz was a remarkable individual. He was a master chemist and during World War I he'd been a spy in Germany for the Allies. After the war he'd taken an important post in a German chemical plant, where he had discovered a process for the manufacture of artificial silk. He smuggled the process into the United States and set up a hush-hush experimental laboratory, in which he often worked into the night. It sounded impressive, but it was all hogwash. Least of all was he a master chemist. But Schwartz found plenty of people willing to give him money in exchange for a piece of the process. When he produced no silk, however, some of his backers started to grumble and talk of fraud.

In 1925 Schwartz began to take an avid interest in a different science—human anatomy. He cultivated a friendship with a traveling evangelist named Warren Gilbert Barbe. Although the facial features of the two men were very dissimilar, they were of the same overall size. Late in July, Barbe disappeared from his usual haunts, but no one gave it a thought. He most likely got the "call" and had "gone into the wilderness" to preach. Meanwhile, Schwartz was very busy in his laboratory. He said he was almost finished with his process and he worried that some international cartel might try to stop his work. He took out a $200,000 insurance policy on his life and allowed no one to enter the laboratory.

In the lab he was very busy altering the dead evangelist into a stand-in corpse for himself. He burned away a section of the corpse's chest because he had a scar in his own chest. He pulled out two teeth from the upper jaw to match his own dental characteristics. He punctured the eyeballs to solve the problem of different color eyes. But all these he regarded as extra precautions, since he planned to blow up his laboratory in order to really make the corpse unidentifiable. In fact, he believed the entire building would be destroyed in the explosion. He soaked the laboratory with several gallons of benzol which, when detonated, would take care of the building and the evidence. Schwartz set up a timing device and left. He couldn't afford to be seen at the site of the explosion. But he stayed close enough to hear the clanging fire trucks approaching as he stepped into a taxi.

Hiding out in Oakland, Schwartz was shocked to discover he was wanted for murder. The body, hardly singed, had been identified. Even three religious pamphlets bearing Barbe's name had survived the blaze. An incompetent chemist, Schwartz didn't realize that benzol fumes rise very slowly. Several more minutes would have been needed to set off the fire properly. A flop as a chemist, an anatomist and a murderer, Schwartz did better in his final endeavor: suicide.

See also: *Insurance Frauds.*

BARKER, Arizona Clark "Kate" Or "Ma" (?1871-1935): Outlaw or mother of outlaws

Kate, or Ma, Barker remains one of the enigmas of the underworld. Was she the brains, indeed the queen mother, of one of the most violent gangs of the 1930s, or was she just a dumpy little old lady whom many of the gangsters of the era considered just plain "Mom"? One version, which belongs to Hollywood and the FBI, presents us with an iron mistress who was feared by her murderous sons as well as numerous other members of the Barker-Karpis gang and who died, Tommy Gun in hand, in a fabled shoot-out with federal agents. A different viewpoint, held by other members of the underworld, portrays a doting, worried—although at times ill-tempered—mother whose sole concern was always the safety of her brood. Whatever the truth was, the fact is that Ma Barker was never on any official list of public enemies and indeed was never charged with a crime during her lifetime.

Born to Scotch-Irish parents about 1871 in the Ozark Mountain area near Springfield, Mo.—the area that nurtured Jesse and Frank James—she was saddled with the unlikely name of Arizona, which friends soon shortened to "Arrie" and she herself later switched to Kate. One of her greatest experiences in childhood was seeing Jesse James ride by one day, and she cried with youthful anguish when "that dirty coward" Bob Ford killed Jesse in 1882. The year 1892 was doubly bad for Kate; the Dalton gang was cut down at Coffeyville, Kan. and Kate married an itinerant farm laborer named George Barker. It was not a happy marriage. Kate realized that a penniless sharecropper could never be much of an inspiration for the four boys—Herman, Lloyd, Arthur and Fred—who were born of the union. As the boys grew up in a series of tar paper shacks, Kate made it clear to Barker that she would run the family and she would guide the boys' upbringing. George Barker merely shrugged.

Brought up in this impoverished environment, the boys soon started turning up regularly on police blotters. Ma Barker frequently managed to get her sons released, sometimes weeping hysterically and at other times screaming. As late as 1915, Ma was able to get her eldest, Herman, freed from a highway robbery charge. In the following years the Barkers turned to bank robbery. According to later FBI accounts, Ma planned all the jobs and the boys and their buddies executed them. Ma supposedly ran things with iron discipline, making the boys memorize a "getaway chart." She herself was said to drive around all the surrounding roads, checking the times needed on them under all weather conditions. During the actual commission of a crime, Ma would once more become the doting mother, weeping for fear that her sons might be hurt. Ma was also said to dominate the gang's personal lives, refusing to allow the presence of any girl friends. This, to be sure, was nonsense. All of the gang's hideouts were always awash with whores, and Ma did nothing about it. Things hardly could have been otherwise, given the character of her sons and the other top gangsters she sheltered, such as Al Spencer, Ray Terrill, Earl Thayer, Frank Nash, Francis Keating, Tommy Holden and Alvin "Creepy" Karpis.

"Ma" Barker was either "a veritable beast of prey," as J. Edgar Hoover claimed, or just a dumpy little old mom to a bunch of gangsters, as the latter said.

Karpis probably best presented the underworld version of the real Ma Barker. He wrote in his memoirs:

> Ma was always *somebody* in our lives. Love didn't enter into it really. She was somebody we looked after and took with us when we moved from city to city, hideout to hideout.
>
> It's no insult to Ma's memory that she just didn't have the brains or know-how to direct us on a robbery. It wouldn't have occurred to her to get involved in our business, and we always made a point of only discussing our scores when Ma wasn't around. We'd leave her at home when we were arranging a job, or we'd send her to a movie. Ma saw a lot of movies.

In 1927 son Herman was stopped by police near Wichita, Kan. after a robbery. When one officer leaned down to look in Herman's car window, Herman grabbed the policeman around the neck and fired a pistol into his head. A cop on the other side of the car cut loose at Barker, so filling him with bullets that the gangster turned his weapon on himself and finished the job. This development, according to J. Edgar Hoover in a bit of colorful prose, caused Ma to change "from an animal mother of the she-wolf type to a veritable beast of prey." Thereafter, according to the FBI version of events, Ma planned a near-endless string of bank robberies, the kidnappings of millionaires William A. Hamm, Jr. and Edward George Bremer and the murder of her "loving man," Arthur Dunlop. The best evidence indicates that Dunlop was murdered by Ma's sons and other members of the gang, with total disregard for Ma's feelings, because they suspected him of being a "squealer." The FBI claim that Ma was the brain behind the Hamm kidnapping is somewhat tarnished by the fact that the agency first arrested and caused the wrongful prosecution of Roger Touhy and his "Terribles" for the offense before discovering its mistake and correctly pinning the charge on the Barker-Karpis gang.

By 1935 the gang was being intensively pursued by the FBI and other law enforcement agencies. On January 16 Ma and her youngest and favorite son, Freddie, were traced to a cottage hideout at Lake Weir, Fla. A four-hour gun battle ensued, and both Freddie and Ma were shot to death. The official version had Ma manning a submachine gun in the battle, but this is debatable. Freddie was found with 14 bullets in him, indicating he was obviously in the line of fire. There is a discrepancy on how many bullets were in Ma, however. Some accounts said three and others only one—and that one self-inflicted. Cynics have charged that the FBI, having killed a dumpy, insignificant middle-aged woman, quickly promoted her into "Bloody Mama."

See also: *Barker Brothers, Alvin "Creepy" Karpis, Shotgun George Ziegler.*

BARKER Brothers: Public enemies

Easily the worst collection of criminal brothers in 20th century America were the Barkers, or the "Bloody Barkers," as the newspapers not inappropriately called them. Indeed, J. Edgar Hoover called the Barker-Karpis gang "the toughest mob we ever cracked." This characterization was close to the truth, whether or not Ma Barker herself, the so-called Bloody Mama was included. There is considerable controversy over whether Ma Barker was really much of a criminal, but there is no doubt that her brood of four boys—Herman, born 1894; Lloyd, born 1896; Arthur—or "Doc" or "Dock"—born 1899; and Fred, born 1902—were a bloodthirsty lot. Of the four, Doc Barker was probably the leader, the one who commanded the respect of other prominent gangsters of the day.

Doc was both fearless and cold-blooded and often killed without provocation or warning. Once when his brother Freddie and a few others of the gang wanted another gang member, William J. Harrison, rubbed out, Doc jumped at the assignment. He took Harrison at gunpoint to an abandoned barn near Ontarioville, Ill., shot him to death and after saturating him and the surrounding area of the barn with gasoline, set fire to the whole thing. He then wrote a note to several of the gang members hiding out in Florida: "I took care of that business for you boys. It was done just as good as if you had

did it yourself. I am just like Standard Oil—always at your service. Ha, Ha!"

After several brushes with the law on minor—by Barker family standards—charges, Doc was sentenced to life imprisonment at the Oklahoma State Penitentiary for the murder of a night watchman during a robbery in 1920. In 1927 Herman Barker took his own life after being severely wounded in a shoot-out with police following a robbery. The next severe blow to the Barker family came when Lloyd Barker was arrested for a 1932 mail robbery and sentenced to 25 years in Leavenworth. This left only Freddie free.

Next to Doc, Freddie was the deadliest of the Barkers. He had a rather loose attitude towards killing. Once in Monett, Mo., he and another gangster, Bill Weaver, broke into a garage to steal a car for use in a job. Freddie got behind the wheel and Weaver slid the garage door open to find himself facing a policeman with gun drawn. Freddie leaned out of the window and promptly shot the officer dead. He later moralized, "That's what comes from stealing these goddamn cars all the time." Freddie did a considerable amount of time for that killing but he was eventually freed after Ma Barker haunted the parole board, wardens and governors and reputedly spent a significant amount of money.

When Freddie rejoined his mother following his release, he brought with him Alvin "Creepy" Karpis, who proved to be the most important leader of the gang. Each had a mutual respect for the other and they worked well as a team. Ma Barker was equally taken with Karpis and treated him almost as another son, perhaps because she now only had Freddie on the loose. In the meantime, however, Ma also worked on freeing Doc. Remarkably, Doc won a banishment pardon from the governor, which meant he could go free provided he left the state of Oklahoma. J. Edgar Hoover raged over the pardon and even more over the treatment afforded Doc's partner-in-crime, Volney Davis, who was granted an unbelievable "two-year leave of absence."

The Barker-Karpis gang, headed by Creepy, Doc and Freddie, was now ready for full operation. They pulled off an unparalleled number of bank robberies and the like and then moved into the lucrative new field of kidnapping. Their two major jobs were the abductions of William A. Hamm, Jr. and Edward George Bremer, which netted the gang a total of $300,000 in ransoms. Many have claimed Ma Barker was the master planner of both crimes, but none of the facts support this conclusion. Hoover credited the plan to a member of the Barker-Karpis gang named Jack Peifer, while according to Karpis, the Bremer job was the brainchild of Harry Sawyer, a flamboyant character who ran much of the crime in St. Paul, Minn. In all, there were about 25 or 26 members of the Barker-Karpis gang, and Doc and Freddie Barker were only slightly more equal than the rest. None regarded Ma Barker as their leader but did feel she was valuable for renting hideouts and handling payoffs to corrupt officials.

The Hamm and Bremer kidnappings were to prove the downfall of the Barkers and the rest of the gang, triggering one of the most persistent manhunts in history, during which the members were picked off one by one.

On January 8, 1935 Doc Barker was captured by FBI agents led by the legendary Melvin Purvis, the man who got Dillinger. The authorities located Doc by shadowing women he was known to have been in contact with. Eight days later, Freddie Barker was traced to a cottage at Lake Weir in northern Florida, where he was hiding with Ma Barker. Both were killed in a four-hour shoot-out, although there are some reports that Ma Barker actually shot herself when she saw her favorite son riddled with bullets.

In January 1939, Doc Barker, long a troublemaker at Alcatraz, attempted an escape from what was known as America's Devil's Island. He made it into the water before his skull was smashed and his left leg broken by guards' bullets. In the prison hospital he murmured: "I was a fool to try it. I'm all shot to hell." He died the following day, January 14, and was buried in a potter's field on the California mainland.

That left Lloyd Barker the last living brother. He remained in prison until 1947. Two years later, after returning home from his job at a filling station-snack shop, he was shot to death by his wife, with whom he had been feuding.

See also: *Arizona Clark "Kate" or "Ma" Barker, Alvin "Creepy" Karpis, Dr. Joseph Patrick Moran, Shotgun George Ziegler.*

BARNES, Leroy "Nicky" (1933–   ): Harlem narcotics king

Born in Harlem of a poor family, Barnes rose rags-to-riches fashion to criminal stardom and what could well be called the position of the first King of the Black Mafia.

He was definitely the King of Harlem. As the *New York Times Magazine* reported: "Checking in at Shalimar, the Gold Lounge, or Small's . . . he will be bowed to, nodded to, but not touched." The juke always got a steady play of "Baaad, Baaad Leroy Brown," which, say Barnes' fans, was written for him. "It's like the Godfather movie," according to a New York police detective who also described Barnes wading through mobs of admirers "being treated like the goddamn Pope."

This idolatry of Barnes was, in a sense, a celebration because he was one of the first blacks to come out on top in the underworld as organized criminal activity shifted—and is still shifting—from Italians to other minority groups. Barnes' rise to power was in large part due to his alliance with Crazy Joey Gallo, a maverick of the Mafia who taught Barnes how to organize a drug empire.

Barnes and Gallo met in New York state's Greenhaven Prison, where the former was doing time for narcotics violations and the latter for extortion. Gallo fed Barnes inside information about the drug world of Harlem, how it was supplied and how one man could take control of it. When Gallo was released, it was agreed that the two would work together. In exchange, Barnes would supply the Brooklyn gangster with black "troops" when he needed them. When Barnes was released, he began importing, with Gallo's help, large amounts of heroin directly from Italian sources. Barnes then set up his own network of "millworkers," who cut the heroin, and deliverers. This gave him control of heroin distribution over large areas in upstate New York, New Jersey, Pennsylvania and even into Canada. Barnes also moved to take over actual street operation in Harlem. Italians were replaced by blacks without bloodshed, also apparently due to Gallo muscle.

In the process Nicky Barnes became not just rich but flamboyantly so, walking around with incredible bankrolls. During one of his arrests, $130,000 cash was found in the trunk of his automobile, of which he had many. Among his possessions were a Mercedes Benz and a Citroen Maserati, and police department files were admittedly incomplete in recording his Cadillacs, Lincoln Continentals and Thunderbirds. Barnes had several apartments in Manhattan, another in the fashionable Riverdale area of the Bronx and at least two in New Jersey. These residences were, of course, in addition to the working apartments Barnes maintained for his drug operation. The *Times* reported that the operations of a typical Barnes heroin plant involved more than a dozen young women and two men. "The . . . women . . . are lined up along the sides of a huge sheet of plate glass that, propped up on pieces of furniture, has become a table. The women are naked, to insure that they will not be tempted to conceal any of the powder they are working over. The lieutenants, trusted, dressed, do not even look at the women. Their eyes, like the eyes of the women, are on the small pyramids of white powder heaped on the plate glass." It would take some 16 hours to cut the heroin. "In those 16 hours, 10 kilos of pure heroin brought from a wholesaler by a trusted representative of one of New York City's major drug dealers for $150,000 has become worth about $630,000. For the dealer, the night's expenses have run about $170,000, including the cash fees to the women and their apartment guardians. Thus the dealer has cleared about $460,000 in profits—all in cash—in an operation that he financed, sanctioned, and arranged, but in which he had no physical part."

While Barnes openly led a lavish life, proving anything against him was not easy. He paid taxes on a quarter of a million dollars in annual "miscellaneous income." Although the IRS insisted he owed much more, substantiating it would not be easy. Barnes had always been good at avoiding conviction; he had a record of 13 arrests but only one had led to a sentence (an abbreviated one) behind bars. This ability to avoid the law's retribution made Barnes something of a cult figure in Harlem and beyond. "Sure, that's the reason the kids loved the guy and wanted to be like him," a newsweekly quoted a federal narcotics agent as saying. "Mr. Untouchable—that's what they called him—was rich, but he was smart too, and sassy about it. The bastard loved to make us cops look like idiots."

Unlike his worshipers, Barnes probably was smart enough to know he'd eventually fall, and in 1978 he did, thanks to a federal narcotics strike force. When brought up for sentencing that year, Barnes rose, squared his shoulders and smiled faintly when he was given life imprisonment plus a $125,000 fine. Barnes appeared to take his fate well, as though, to some observers, he was taking pride in the pivotal role he had played in shifting underworld power from Italians to blacks. The severity of the sentence was fitting. It was as though his importance was being certified by the courts and, according to one reporter, "making him a sort of Muhammed Ali of crime or, even better, the black man's Al Capone."

See also: *Crazy Joe Gallo.*

BARON Of Arizona: See James Addison Reavis.

BARREL Murders: Early Mafia execution style

The "barrel murders" started turning up in America around 1870. The modus operandi of these killings, which occurred in several large cities, was always the same. A victim, invariably an Italian, would be killed—either shot, strangled or stabbed—and then stuffed into a barrel, which was then either deposited on a street corner or empty lot or else shipped by rail to a nonexistent address in another city.

It was the barrel murders that first alerted authorities to the existence of the Mafia. The murder technique started by coincidence with the arrival of a fierce pack of brothers, half-brothers and brothers-in-law from Corleone, Sicily, the Morellos. Over the next three decades more than 100 barrel murders were traced to the Morellos, who finally abandoned the technique because all such murders merely advertised their criminal activities. Even worse, free-lance non-Italian murderers were using the barrel method to divert suspicion from themselves to Italian gangsters.

See also: *Morello Family.*

BARRIE, Peter Christian "Paddy" (1888-1935): Horse race fixer

Without doubt the most successful horce race fixer in the United States was Paddy Barrie, a skilled "dyer" who applied his handiwork to swindle bettors out of some $6 million from 1926 to 1934.

Barrie's system was perhaps the simplest ever used to fix races. He would buy two horses, one with a very good record and the other a "dog." Then he would "repaint" the fast horse to look like the slow one and enter it in a race under the latter's name. Based on the past performance record of the slow horse, the ringer would generally command odds of 50 to one or even more; because it really outclassed its opponents, the horse would usually win the race easily. Using stencils, bleaches, special dyes and dental instruments, Barrie changed the identity of a champion horse, Aknahton, and ran it under three less-distinguished names at four tracks—Havre de Grace, Agua Caliente, Bowie and Hialeah. The horse made five killings for a gambling syndicate Barrie was working with. It was a feat that led the gamblers to call him "Rembrandt."

The Pinkerton Detective Agency finally unmasked Barrie following an investigation that was started after a leader in the betting syndicate, Nate Raymond, made a drunken spectacle of himself in Broadway clubs and was heard bragging about a "bagged race" worked by an "artist" from England named Paddy. The Pinkertons queried Scotland Yard and learned that a master dyer named Paddy Barrie had disappeared from the British Isles some years previous. An alert went out for Barrie, but he managed to elude capture for another two years by doing the same thing to himself that he did to horses, adopting disguises and changing his name frequently. One day a Pinkerton operative recognized him at Saratoga race track in New York, and he was bundled off to jail.

Oddly, the laws on horse race gambling and fixing were rather lax and Barrie appeared to have broken no law other than having entered the United States illegally. He was deported back to his native Scotland, where he died less than six month later of a "broken heart," according to a sensational British tabloid, due to constant surveillance aimed at guaranteeing he would never be able to ring another horse.

Because of Barrie's depredations, American tracks adopted such precautions as lip tattoos and other methods of identification to make the ringing in of other horses almost impossible. However, since foreign horses have not been so identified they have been used as ringers in recent years. The disclosure of such fixes has led to close checks on the identification of foreign horses.

BARROW, Clyde: See Bonnie and Clyde.

BARTER, Rattlesnake Dick (1834-1859): Stagecoach robber

Few criminal reputations in the Old West were more enhanced by the Eastern writers whose flowery prose graced the pages of such 19th century publications as *New York Weekly, Harper's Monthly* and the torrent of dime novels and paperbacks than Rattlesnake Dick's.

The real-life Rattlesnake Dick Barter was more wooly than wild, and, alas, hardly an archbadman of the West. Barter was, on the whole, quite incompetent. According to the legend-makers, he was named Rattlesnake Dick because he was so dangerous and devious. No doubt the fact that he was an Englishman operating outside the American law was enough to give him a certain romantic aura. However, Rattlesnake Dick was downright prosaic in comparison with many native American badmen of the period. The real story behind his name was that he had prospected for a short time at Rattlesnake Bar in the Northern Mines area of California. Rattlesnake Dick soon decided, however, that it was easier to steal gold than to dig for it. Here the legend-makers were right, although they failed to note that Rattlesnake Dick had never made a dime at his digs. In 1856, after some small-time stage holdups, Barter hit on what was to prove the most brilliant and, at the same time, most comic criminal scheme of his career. To give him credit due, he masterminded the $80,000 robbery of the Yreka Mine's mule train and managed to organize a gang for that purpose. Rattlesnake Dick did not take part in the actual robbery, which was left to George Skinner and some others, possibly explaining why that part of the scheme worked so well. The Yreka Mine mule train had been regarded as immune from robbers because the mules would always tire out halfway down the mountains and thus make pursuit too easy. Rattlesnake Dick's plan called for him and George Skinner's brother, Cyrus, to meet the robbers on the mountain trail with fresh mules. Clever though the plan was, it left the execution of this phase to Rattlesnake Dick. When George Skinner and his gunmen reached the rendezvous point, there was not a fresh mule in sight. It developed that Rattlesnake Dick and Cy Skinner were already in jail. They had been caught, drunk, trying to steal some mules.

Under the circumstances all George Skinner could think to do was bury most of the stolen gold nuggets and then head off with his crew for some high living over at Folsom. That's where Wells Fargo agents caught up with them. George Skinner was shot dead while in bed with a screaming prostitute and the rest of the gang was similarly liquidated. But with them died the secret of where the stolen gold was buried. Shortly thereafter, Rattlesnake Dick and Cy Skinner broke jail by walking out an open door and went looking for the buried loot. Following an unsuccessful search for it, the pair returned to the stagecoach-robbing business. After some of their hold-ups netted the pair less than $20, Cy Skinner decided he had had enough of the criminal genius of Rattlesnake Dick and went his separate way. Barter continued his bush-league hold-ups until he was shot and killed by a pursuing posse in July 1859. But the legend of Rattlesnake Dick as California's worst bandit between the eras of Murieta and Vasquez lives on, enhanced by the fact that today treasure hunters still scour the California hills for Dick's buried gold.

BASS, Sam (1851-1878): Outlaw

> Sam Bass was born in Indiana, it was his native home;
> At the age of seventeen young Sam began to roam.
> Sam first came out to Texas, a cowboy for to be—
> A kinder-hearted fellow you seldom ever see.
> From "The Ballad of Sam Bass"

Kinder-hearted or not, Sam Bass was an outlaw. While he "came out of Texas, a cowboy for to be," young Bass found life dull and soon opted for crime. He and two other characters, Joel Collins and Jack Davies, went in for some "easy rustling," taking on 500 cattle on consignment, driving them to market in Kansas in 1876 and then neglecting to settle up with the Texas ranchers who had hired them. With their loot as capital, the trio became pimps and opened a whorehouse in Deadwood, Dakota Territory, a place described as "the most degraded den of infamy that ever cursed the Earth." With that sort or recommendation, the brothel did a thriving business. Nonetheless, Bass, Collins and Davies drank and gambled away their income faster than their prostitutes could make it; so the trio and three of their best bordello customers, Bill Heffridge, Jim Berry and Tom Nixon, formed an outlaw gang and held up a number of stagecoaches. On September 19, 1877 the gang made a big score, robbing a Union Pacific train of $60,000.

With a $10,000 stake, Bass returned to Denton County,

Tex. and started a new gang, becoming a folk hero in the process. While he was not exactly a Robin Hood, Bass was loose with the money he stole and if there was one way for a gunman to become popular in Texas, it was for him to be a free spender. For a time, Bass proved to be a real will-o-the-wisp, impossible for the law to corner and remarkably skillful at extracting hospitality from Texans who looked upon him with affection. As the reward money mounted, however, Bass became a marked man. Finally, one of his own band, Jim Murphy, whose family often gave Bass refuge on their ranch, betrayed him by informing the law that the gang planned a bank robbery in Round Rock. While Murphy ducked for shelter, ambushers killed an outlaw named Seaborn Barnes and shot Sam Bass off his horse. Another outlaw, Frank Jackson, rode back through a fusillade of fire to rescue Bass and carry him out of town.

Photograph shows outlaw Sam Bass (center), although its authenticity has been disputed.

Bass was found by pursuers the next day; he was lying under a tree, near death. While he clung to life, Texas Rangers questioned him about his accomplices and the location of the loot he was believed to have buried. Bass would not respond, saying only: "Let me go. The world is bobbing around." He died on his 27th birthday. Some treasure hunters still search for the Bass loot, although it is more than likely that the dying Bass told Jackson where to find it. The "Ballad of Sam Bass" is still a Texas favorite and the outlaw's grave at Round Rock remains an attraction.

See also: *Frank Jackson, Jim Murphy.*

BASSITY, Jerome (?1870-1929): Whoremaster

During the long history of prostitution in San Francisco's Barbary Coast, Jerome Bassity stands out as perhaps the owner of more brothels than any other single person in that city. Although he was described by the press as being a "study in depravity" with an intelligence only slightly higher than that of a chimpanzee, Bassity was the veritable lord of the red-light district. In the heyday of the corrupt Ruef machine, especially during the three terms of Mayor Eugene Schmitz from 1901 to 1907, Bassity, whose real name was said to be Jere McGlane, was far and away the most potent figure in the San Francisco underworld.

The newspapers singled him out for special condemnation. The *San Francisco Bulletin* invited its readers to "look at the low, cunning lights in the small, rapacious, vulture-like eyes; look at that low, dull-comprehending brow; the small sensual mouth; the soft puffy fingers with the weak thumb, indicating how he seeks ever his own comfort before others, how his will works only in fits and starts." Despite such publicity, Bassity operated with little or no restraint, from about the turn of the century until 1916, save for two years—1907 to 1909—during a reform administration. In 1909 Mayor P. H. McCarthy took office on a platform designed to "make San Francisco the Paris of America." Bassity aided that cause by operating a 100-cubicle brothel called the Parisian Mansion. While McCarthy was in office it was openly acknowledged that the city was really ruled by a triumvirate: the mayor, police commissioner and bar owner Harry P. Flannery and Bassity.

In addition to his brothels, Bassity owned dance halls and other dives, including a notorious Market Street deadfall called the Haymarket that even the streetwalkers refused to enter. Bassity had an interest in the income of at least 200 prostitutes and his own income was estimated to be around $10,000 a month, no trifling sum for the period. A dandy dresser and "diamond ring stud," Bassity reportedly went to bed with a diamond ring on each of his big toes. In his own brothels he claimed and exercised his seigniorial rights whenever a young girl or virgin arrived, but by and large, Bassity patronized his competitors' establishments. His patronage practically amounted to sabotage since he was generally drunk, always armed and frequently concluded a night of debauchery by shooting out the lights or seeing how close he could fire shots to the harlots' toes. Bassity bragged that he squandered most of his income on clothes, jewelry and debauchery, but he predicted the flow of money would never end. In 1916, foreseeing the success of reform efforts to shut down the Barbary Coast, Bassity retired from the sex racket and headed for Mexico, where he unsuccessfully attempted a takeover of the Tijuana race track. He was later charged but not prosecuted for a swindle in California. When he died in 1929, after what was described as "California's most sinful life," he left an estate of less than $10,000.

See also: *Abraham Ruef.*

BATH, Michigan : School bombing

One of the most hideous crimes ever committed in America was the slaying of 37 school children in 1927 by Andrew Kehoe, the mad bomber of Bath, Mich.

The background to the case was pieced together by the police after the fact, because Kehoe himself did not survive the crime. Kehoe was a farmer, but not a very successful one, barely scraping by even in boom years. When the community of Bath decided to build a new schoolhouse, property owners were assessed a special levy. Kehoe's tax bite came to $300. After he paid up, he no longer could meet his mortgage and faced imminent loss of his house. "It's that school tax," he would tell anyone who would listen. "If it hadn't been for the $300 I had to pay, I'd have the money. That school never should have been built."

Kehoe feuded with school board officials, accusing them of squandering the taxpayers' money. He started telling people he'd have his revenge for that. Night after night Kehoe would be seen near the school. It turned out that he was sneaking in the building and spending hours planting dynamite in safe hiding places.

At 9:43 a.m. on May 18, 1927, the whole building shook. The second floor of the north wing rose in the air and came down, crushing the first floor in an avalanche of battered wreckage. In all, 37 school children and one teacher died, and some 43 others were very seriously injured.

The explosion brought the townspeople running, while Andy Kehoe sat and watched the whole horrible scene from his parked car. Among the rescuers was the head of the school board, heroically risking his life to bring injured children out of the tottering wreckage. He kept at it until Kehoe beckoned him over to his car. Andy Kehoe still had one more murder card to play. As the school official placed his foot on the running board of the car, Kehoe turned a switch and a violent explosion killed the last two victims of the mad bomber of Bath.

BATS: Prostitutes

"Batting" remains one of the most common forms of streetwalking. A bat is a prostitute who works the streets only at night in sections that are respectable by day. In Chicago during the 1870s, for example, a respectable woman could readily traverse such downtown streets as Randolph, Dearborn and East Monroe during the day and fear no untoward incident. At night, however, she could well be accosted by men in search of a harlot. The hookers operated out of "marble front" business buildings, residing there but remaining undercover until after dark and then venturing forth to entice still available businessmen.

Bats prefer working respectable streets because the fees earned are much better than along more vice-ridden streets. Bats too are generally far nicer looking than their competitors in the business. Typical bat streets in the early 1980s in New York are Lexington Avenue and Madison Avenue from the low 40s to about 48th Street, the so-called prime meat market row.

BATTAGLIA, Sam "Teets" (1908-1973): Syndicate gangster

Perhaps the craziest and certainly the deadliest of the four notorious Battaglia brothers who were members of the Chicago mobs, Sam Battaglia was a graduate of the notorious juvenile 42 Gang.

A burglar from the age of 16 and later a muscleman for the mob, he was arrested 25 times, beginning in 1924, on various armed robbery charges and at least seven homicide charges. A hugh barrel of a youth, nicknamed Teets because of his muscular chest, Battaglia gained his first major notoriety when he was arrested in the fall of 1930 on a charge of robbing at gunpoint $15,500 worth of jewelry from the wife of the mayor of Chicago, Mrs. William Hale Thompson. Adding insult to injury, Teets appropriated the gun and badge of her policeman chauffeur. However, a positive identification could not be made, and Teets went free when he insisted he was watching a movie at the time of the robbery and a half dozen witnesses insisted they were watching him watching the movie.

The robbery occurred on November 17, and, between then and the end of the year, Teets was involved in one fatal killing and one attempted killing. In ensuing years he became one of the mob's most reliable machine gunners and, despite a reputation for being a bit zany, moved steadily up the syndicate ladder. By the 1950s he was the virtual king of the mob's "juice," or loansharking, rackets and supervised a number of gambling joints and prostitution rings.

Sam Battaglia, a tough out of Chicago's Patch district who was always considered stronger on brawn than brains, became a millionaire and the owner of a luxury horse-breeding farm and country estate in Kane County, Ill. In 1967 Battaglia was finally sent away for 15 years on extortion charges; yet he was considered, pending his release, the likely head of the Chicago mob.

See also: *Forty-two Gang.*

BAYONNE-ABRIEL Gang: New Orleans waterfront killers

A small band of burglars, wharf rats and professional murderers that terrorized New Orleans in the 1860s, the Bayonne-Abriel gang made up in viciousness what they lacked in numbers. According to one story, the gang once stole a row boat and, after discovering the boat was missing an oar, went out and killed another sailor just for his oars. While they occasionally functioned as shanghaiiers, their main operation was a lucrative racket supplying seamen with everything from women and drugs to murder services. It was such a murder-for-hire service that eventually eliminated both leaders, Vincent Bayonne and Pedro Abriel, and led to the gang's dissolution.

Early in June 1869 the mate of a Spanish bark offered Bayonne and Abriel the kingly sum of $6 to kill a sailor who had earned his enmity. With such a prize at stake, Bayonne and Abriel decided to handle the job themselves rather than share it with any of their followers. The pair lured the sailor into a dive for a few drinks and then all three headed down to the levee "for some fun." Fun for the sailor turned out to be getting batted over the head with a club wielded by Bayonnne. When Bayonne raised his arm to strike the unconscious man again, Abriel stopped him and said, "Let me finish him."

Bayonne refused, and Abriel struck him in assertion of his rights. The pair struggled fiercely for several minutes until Abriel knocked Bayonne out. By that time the sailor was stirring. Abriel then stabbed him 17 times and heaved the body into the river. Abriel and Bayonne reconciled afterwards but made the mistake of revealing the details of their vicious crime to a man named Isadore Boyd. Boyd's testimony was instrumental in getting the pair convicted and on May 14, 1871, hanged.

BEACHY, Hill: See Lloyd Magruder.

BEADLE, William (?-1782): Murderer

As a murderer, Weathersfield, Conn.'s William Beadle achieved lasting local notoriety not only because of the horrendous nature of his crime but also because of the way he kept coming back to remind local residents of what he'd done. It appeared later than William had planned to wipe out his family—his wife and five children, aged six to 11— for some time. Finally, one night as they slept, he crept upstairs, struck each in the head with an axe and then cut their throats. After this bloodletting, Beadle returned to the kitchen downstairs and sat in a chair at the table. He picked up two pistols, placed one in each ear and pulled both triggers at the same time. The victims were all buried in the town cemetary, but the townspeople had to decide what to do with Beadle. They determined he should be buried secretly and a grave was dug in the frozen December ground down by the river. However, an overflow the following spring disinterred the body. Beadle was again buried secretly, but this time a dog dug up the corpse. Finally, on the third try, the murderer's body stayed buried.

BEAN, Roy (c.1825-1902): Saloonkeeper and judge

Billing himself as the "law west of the Pecos," Roy Bean of Texas was without question the most unusual and colorful jurist ever to hold court in America. Bean dispensed justice between poker hands in his saloon-courtroom. He would open a proceeding by declaring: "Hear Ye! Hear Ye! This honorable court's now in session and if any galoot wants a snort before we start, let him step up and name his pizen."

A native of Kentucky, Bean had been a trader, bartender and Confederate guerrilla during the Civil War. (He organized the Free Rovers in the New Mexico Territory, which local residents soon began calling the Forty Thieves, an indication of how much of the booty went to the Confederate cause.) In his late fifties, fat, bewhiskered and whiskey-sodden, Bean ambled into the tent town of Vinegaroon in 1882 and got

Judge Roy Bean dispensed his special brand of Texas justice seated on a beer keg outside his saloon.

himself appointed justice of the peace, perhaps because he had a copy of the *1879 Revised Statutes of Texas*. When the road gangs moved on from Vinegaroon, Bean went to Langtry, a stopover point on the Southern Pacific. Here Bean, first by appointment and then by elections held in his saloon, was to dispense his bizarre justice for 20 years.

Judge Bean had all sorts of profitable lines. He got $5 a head officiating at inquests, $2 performing marriages and $5 granting divorces. When higher-ups informed him he did not have the authority to divorce people, he was unimpressed. "Well, I married 'em, so I guess I got a right to unmarry 'em if it don't take." When a railroad man with a good record, meaning he was a regular paying customer at Bean's saloon, was hauled in for killing a Chinese laborer, the judge leafed through his dog-eared legal guide and then released the prisoner, ruling, "There ain't a damn line here nowheres that makes it illegal to kill a Chinaman." And when another friend of the judge was charged with shooting a Mexican, Bean's finding was that "it served the deceased right for getting in front of a gun."

Having himself appeared in other courts on occasion, Bean knew that judges from time to time made very flowery speeches, and he endeavored to do the same, adding a flourish or two of his own. Passing sentence on a cattle rustler once, he intoned:

> You have been tried by 12 good men and true, not of your peers but as high above you as heaven is of hell, and they have

said you are guilty. Time will pass and seasons will come and go. Spring with its wavin' green grass and heaps of sweet-smellin' flowers on every hill and in every dale. Then sultry Summer, with her shimmerin' heat-waves on the baked horizon. And Fall, with her yeller harvest moon and the hills growin' brown and golden under a sinkin' sun. And finally Winter, with its bitin', whinin' wind, and all the land will be mantled with snow. But you won't be here to see any of 'em; not by a damn sight, because it's the order of this court that you be took to the nearest tree and hanged by the neck till you're dead, dead, dead, you olive-colored son of a billy goat.

In 1896 a lamentable oversight occurred in Bean's reelection campaign. He ended up with more votes than there were eligible voters, and as a result, the authorities awarded the office to his hated opponent, Jesus P. Torres. Bean was undaunted by this development and continued to handle cases that originated on his side of town. He died in 1902, a victim of his own rum as much as old age.

See also: *Benedict's Sentence.*

BEAUCHAMP, Jereboam O. (1803-1826): Murderer

Few murderers shocked, and yet typified, the genteel antebellum South more than Jereboam O. Beauchamp. A brilliant young lawyer from a leading Kentucky family, Beauchamp created quite a stir in society when he married Ann Cooke, a somewhat withered belle of 38; Beauchamp was but 21. Beside the disparity in age, there were other complications, such as Ann's well-known affair with a leading political figure, Col. Solomon P. Sharp. In 1826 Sharp, a former state attorney general, ran for reelection to the Kentucky House of Representatives. During the campaign Sharp's foes dredged up his old affair with Ann, fully publicizing her charges at the time that he had seduced and impregnated her.

It was stale gossip, but even at this late date, Beauchamp decided Ann's honor had to be avenged. He challenged Sharp, who had maintained a strict silence on the matter, to a duel. Sharp refused, and Beauchamp considered this breach of behavior almost as heinous as his sexual escapade with a woman who was then unmarried.

One day early in 1826, Beauchamp donned a red hood and appeared at the colonel's door. When Sharp appeared, Beauchamp stabbed him to death and fled. However, he had been readily recognized by his garments and was quickly cast into jail in Frankfort. Ann visited him daily and proclaimed her eternal gratitude for the avenging of her honor. After Beauchamp was sentenced to hang in July, the couple decided to commit suicide together. Ann smuggled in some poison to the cell, but they succeeded only in getting themselves a bit sick.

Jereboam's execution was scheduled for July 7, and the two were permitted to breakfast together. When they were alone, they took turns plunging a knife into each other's stomach. Beauchamp held Ann in his arms as she died, but he did not die. Bleeding profusely, he was dragged from the cell by embarrassed guards, still clinging to his dead wife. It was decided that his execution would go on even though it was not certain if the bleeding prisoner would be able to stand on the scaffold.

Thousands of spectators lined the way to the gallows, fully expecting to see the condemned man sitting on his own coffin in an open cart, as was the custom of the day. Instead, Beauchamp was bundled in a blanket, still clutching his wife's body, and transported in a closed carriage. Once the crowd was appraised of his condition and the circumstances surrounding it, it was appeased. This was truly something different.

Hushed whispers of satisfaction swept through the crowd when Beauchamp managed to climb the steps of the gallows. He weaved precariously, while a band played a favorite selection of the period, "Bonaparte's Retreat from Moscow," as Beauchamp's last request. His final words were; "Farewell, child of sorrow! For you I have lived; for you I die!"

Husband and wife were buried in a common grave. Chiseled in the stone slab was a poem Ann had composed in the death cell:

> He heard her tale of matchless woe,
> And burning for revenge he rose,
> And laid her base seducer low,
> And struck dismay to virtue's foe.
>
> Daughter of virtue! Moist thy tear.
> This tomb of love and honor claim;
> For thy defense the husband here,
> Laid down in youth his life and fame.

BECK, Dave (1894-   ):
Labor union leader

In the early 1950s David D. Beck was one of the most powerful and respected labor union leaders in the United States. He was president of the country's largest single union, the 1.4 million member International Brotherhood of Teamsters. He was a rich man whose friendship was sought by business executives and statesmen. He boasted that management almost unanimously hailed him as a cooperative labor leader sympathetic to its problems. He was also greedy on a monumental scale.

In his younger years Beck was noted as an aggressive labor leader and an effective bargainer. Founder of the Western Conference of Teamsters, he negotiated contracts that became standards for labor settlements throughout the rest of the country. When he became president of the union in 1952, he had seemingly achieved the pinnacle of success, although he had to share his union powers in several areas with tough James R. Hoffa, chairman of the Teamsters Central States Conference. In fact, Hoffa once boasted: "Dave Beck? Hell, I was running it while he was playing big shot. He never knew the score."

Beck knew the score, however, when it came to milking union funds to become a millionaire. He took loans from the union treasury, which he never repaid. With the aid of money from the union, he built for himself an elegant house in the suburbs of Seattle, featuring an artificial waterfall in the back yard and a basement movie theater. He sold it to the Teamsters at twice what it cost to build and then got it back from the union rent-free for his lifetime use. He put the bite on large companies for personal "loans" and gained the reputation of being able to walk off with anything not nailed down.

Beck's downfall came in a confrontation with the Senate Select Committee on Improper Activities in the Labor or Management Field, chaired by Sen. John McClellan of Arkansas with a young Robert F. Kennedy as chief counsel. The McClellan Committee did much to expose the greed of a number of union officials who had often allied themselves with underworld figures and had looted union treasuries for personal gain. Many union officials squirmed under the inquiry, but none more so than the Teamster leadership. Beck, like others, was to infer that the committee and especially the chief counsel were "antilabor," but he came before the investigation declaring: "I have nothing to fear. My record is an open book." He then proceeded to invoke the Fifth Amendment more than 200 times.

In summing up the committee declared:

> The fall of Dave Beck from a position of eminence in the labor-union movement is not without sadness. When named to head this rich and powerful union, he was given an opportunity to do much good for a great segment of American working men and women. But when temptation faced Dave Beck, he could not turn his back. His thievery in the final analysis became so petty that the committee must wonder at the penuriousness of the man. What would cause a man in such circumstances to succumb to the temptation of using union funds to pay for six pairs of knee drawers for $27.54, or

a bow tie for $3.50? In Beck's case, the committee must conclude that he was motivated by an uncontrollable greed.

Exposure of Beck's greed caused him to leave the hearings a broken man. He would soon be imprisoned, although he tried to fend off this fate by refunding huge sums of money to the Teamsters' treasury. By May 1, 1957 he had returned some $370,000, but the next day, with only a few days remaining before the statute of limitations expired, he was indicted on charges of income tax evasion.

Jimmy Hoffa replaced him as president on February 20, 1958, and Beck drew a long prison term. When he came out, he was still worth a considerable amount of money and had intact his $50,000 lifetime pension from the union. Beck still owed the government $1.3 million in back taxes, and the Treasury Department had the right to seize any and all of his assets to satisfy the claim. However, in 1971 John B. Connolly, secretary of the treasury under President Richard Nixon, approved a plan for a moratorium on the payment of the debt. The Teamsters became Nixon's strongest booster in the labor movement.

BECK, Martha (1920-1951): Lonely hearts killer

Together with Raymond Martinez Fernandez, 280-pound Martha Beck became infamous in the 1940s as one of the Lonely Hearts Killers. Although the pair was charged with only three murders, they were suspected of committing 17 others.

Both Fernandez and Beck were social misfits who joined several lonely hearts clubs seeking companionship. In addition to companionship, Fernandez sought money from women he became acquainted with. When Fernandez and Beck met through the auspices of a club, they teamed up to make a business of swindling women. While Fernandez wooed the women, Martha played the role of his sister. They mulcted scores of women and simply killed those who proved uncooperative or troublesome. The murders that tripped the pair up were those of Mrs. Janet Fay, a 60-year-old Albany, N.Y. widow, and Mrs. Delphine Downing, an attractive 41-year-old widow from Grand Rapids, Mich., and her 20-month-old child.

Mrs. Fay traveled as fast as she could to Valley Stream, Long Island to meet her husband-to-be (Fernandez) and his sister (Beck) after selling her home in Albany. Once the pair was sure they had all the woman's money, they beat her to death with a hammer and buried her in the cellar of a rented house. The killers then traveled to Grand Rapids and similarly stripped Mrs. Downing of much of her wealth. After feeding her sleeping pills, Fernandez then shot her to death. A few days later Martha Beck drowned the woman's child in the bathtub. The murderous pair then buried both corpses under cement in the cellar.

That chore completed the couple went off to a movie. When they returned, they found the police inside the Downing home. Suspicious neighbors had not seen the woman around for a few days and notified the authorities. Since the cement in the cellar had not yet dried, the bodies were quickly found. The police also discovered traces of the late Mrs. Fay's belongings in the couples' possession and soon obtained a confession to the New York murder as well. Since New York had a death penalty and Michigan did not, the two were tried for the Fay killing. After a 44-day trial, in which the sexual aberrations of Fernandez and Beck provided a field day for the sensational press, they were sentenced to death. On March 8, 1951—their final day of life—Fernandez received a message from Beck that she still loved him, news he exclaimed, that made him "want to burst with joy." Martha Beck was granted her last request. Before she was executed in Sing Sing's electric chair, she had her hair meticulously curled.

The lonely hearts murders led to the tightening of restrictions on the operations of lonely hearts clubs, but most lawmakers conceded little safeguards could be established to protect foolish and romantic people from being swindled and even killed for love's sake.

BECKER, Charles (1869-1915): Corrupt policeman and murderer

In the 1890s novelist Stephen Crane witnessed a tall, brawny policeman walk up to a prostitute and start beating her to a pulp when she refused to share the proceeds of her last business transaction. Crane would write about this brutish patrolman in his novel titled *Maggie: A Girl of the Streets,* but the real-life officer, Charles Becker, would go on to commit far worse offenses. Becker was known as "the crookedest cop who ever stood behind a shield," no mean accomplishment in the sordid history of New York City police corruption.

He rose to the rank of lieutenant, became personal assistant to dapper police Commissioner Rhinelander Waldo, perhaps the most inept holder of that office before or since, and was in charge of the department's special crime squad. In addition to his police function, Becker was also the protege of Tammany Hall leader Tim Sullivan and aspired to succeed him. Becker used his position to handle all payoffs to the police and politicians from gamblers, prostitutes and other vice operators. His special squad as well as outside gangsters were employed to enforce the payoff rules, providing protection to those who paid and retribution to those who refused.

One gambler who attempted to stand up to Becker was Herman Rosenthal, who ran a betting joint on West 45th Street. Fearful that Rosenthal would set a bad example for other gamblers, Becker kept intensive pressure on him, but the tactic boomeranged. Rosenthal started telling his troubles to reporter Herbert Bayard Swope of the *New York World* and to Charles S. Whitman, Republican district attorney of Manhattan. Soon, Becker realized his position was threatened. He turned to his top underworld henchman, Big Jack Zelig, to take care of Rosenthal before he did any more talking. At the moment, Zelig was in jail, but Becker used his influence to free him. Zelig then arranged for four gunmen— Gyp the

Blood, Lefty Louie, Dago Frank and Whitey Lewis—to handle the hit.

The four botched a few attempts, and the frightened Rosenthal sent word to Becker and Zelig that he was finished talking and would leave New York. However, Rosenthal had already talked too much, and on July 16, 1912, the four killers brought him down in a fusillade of bullets outside the Hotel Metropole on West 43rd Street.

An investigation was ordered, and Commissioner Waldo put Becker in charge. With amazing nerve, Becker instructed the police to "lose" the license number of the murderers' car and even attempted to hide an eyewitness to the crime in a police station jail cell. Through a tipster, District Attorney Whitman learned of the witness and, with the help of his own investigators, seized him in a scuffle in the station house.

Eventually, the killers were caught and, in hope of saving their own necks, talked, implicating Zelig. Zelig, in turn, realized his best chance to avoid execution also lay in talking, and he informed on Becker. Allowed free on bail, Zelig was shot and killed by another gangster. However, Whitman, who saw the Rosenthal case as a way of purging police graft and perhaps promoting himself into the governorship, still presented enough evidence to have the four killers convicted and sentenced to death and convicted Becker of being the instigator of the killing.

Becker was granted a new trial amid clear indications that Whitman had promised rewards to various prosecution witnesses in return for their aid in convicting a police officer. Nonetheless, he was found guilty once again and was sentenced to death. As Becker's execution date drew near, his only hope was to obtain clemency from the governor, but unfortunately for him, Whitman had since been elected to that office. He ignored a plea from Becker's wife, who remained faithful to her husband to the end.

Becker's friends insisted that he had been "jobbed" and, whatever his sins, had not masterminded the Rosenthal murder. After Becker was electrocuted on July 7, 1915, in what was probably Sing Sing's clumsiest execution, his wife had attached to the top of his coffin a silver plate with the following inscription:

CHARLES BECKER
MURDERED JULY 7, 1915
BY GOVERNOR WHITMAN

The plate was finally removed when the police convinced Mrs. Becker that she could be prosecuted for criminal libel.

See also: *Stephen Crane.*

BECKER, Jennie (1881-1922): Murder victim

Abe Becker was certain he had committed the perfect crime when he bashed in his wife's skull, buried her in a pit and poured corrosive alkali over her body. Instead, it became a criminal-medical text classic. On the night of the murder in April 1922, Becker had taken his wife, Jennie, to a party at a friend's house in New York City and played the role of a loving

spouse, stuffing her with canapes, grapes, figs and almonds. On the way home, he lured Jennie out of the car by pretending to have motor trouble. He then struck her over the head with a wrench and carried her dead body to a prepared grave, where he doused it with alkali. In the ensuing months Becker explained his wife's disappearance by saying she'd run off with another man. He was not even too concerned when the police found Jennie's body, or what they thought was her body, five months later. Proving it would be another matter. The alkali had rendered the body unrecognizable.

In desperation, the police turned the corpse over to the medical examiner's office. Experts found that the alkali had not totally destroyed the stomach. They found the woman had eaten grapes, figs, almonds and some meat-spread sandwiches—the very things Becker had lovingly fed his wife at the party. Becker was undoubtedly frightened now, but he kept insisting the body was not his wife's. Figs are figs, grapes are grapes and almonds are almonds—some other woman had simply eaten the same type of food, he contended. Denials proved worthless, however. Laboratory examination of the meat spread found it matched exactly with the meat spread prepared by the party hostess—according to a private family recipe. Becker died in the electric chair in April 1924.

BECKETT Sisters: White slave kidnap victims

During the early 1800s, no kidnapping of young girls by the infamous Mississippi River procurers excited the American public as much as that of two teenage sisters, Rose and Mary Beckett of St. Louis, who were abducted by the notorious Sam Purdy gang.

It was the custom of these river procurers to buy up young girls from their impoverished parents and transport them down the Mississippi by flatboat to Natchez, where they were sold at auction to whoremasters from various Southern cities. Only when they could not find enough willing girls available to be "sold down the river"—hence the origin of the phrase—did the procurers go in for actual kidnapping. Such was the fate of the Beckett girls, who wound up at Natchez in early 1805 and were sold off after spirited bidding by various bordello keepers and "floating hog pen" operators. The girls were sold as a set for $400 to the proprietor of a notorious New Orleans establishment called The Swamp.

Here the girls were incarcerated and here they would have remained had it not been for a reformer named Carlos White, who had tracked the Purdy gang from St. Louis and scoured the New Orleans fleshpots for the Beckett sisters. A man of action, White used force to rescue the two sisters from The Swamp, shooting one of their guards to death and pistol-whipping another while the girls climbed out a window and escaped.

White eventually reunited the pair with their parents and, unlike the fate of most "ruined girls," the Beckett Sisters became famous heroines of the day.

See also: *Sam Purdy.*

BECKWOURTH, Jim (1800-1866 or 1867): Black mountaineer and thief

Trader, scout and all-around frontiersman, Jim Beckwourth was easily the most famous of the black adventurers of the West.

Beckwourth was born in Virginia, the son of Sir Jennings Beckwith (who was descended from minor Irish aristocrats) and a mulatto slave woman. In 1822 Beckwourth (the spelling he adopted) appeared in Missouri as a free black man. Two years later, he joined Gen. William Ashley's expedition to the Rocky Mountains. It is difficult to measure Beckwourth's accomplishments because his own accounts make him easily the greatest Indian fighter and squaw lover of all time; yet his reputation grew quickly, and migrants coming West in wagon trains bid high for his services as a guide through the Sierras. Beckwourth also did a thriving business supplying these migrants with horses. To that end, he formed the biggest gang of horse thieves in California's history, together with famed mountain men Old Bill Williams and Pegleg Smith. The gang's greatest raid occurred in 1840, when, with a large band of Indians, they slipped undetected over Cajon Pass. On May 14 Juan Perez, the administrator at San Gabriel Mission, reported to the authorities that every ranch in the valley from San Garbirel to San Bernardino had been stripped of its horse stock. Although posses occasionally caught up to the horse thieves, they were beaten off. Finally, a posse of 75 men under Gov. Jose Antonio Carillo cornered the gang at Resting Springs. In the ensuing gun battle, Beckwourth justified the tales of his prowess with a gun, killing or wounding several members of the posse. Scores of horses were killed and others so badly wounded they had to be destroyed, but Beckwourth and company still got away with over 1,200 head.

Eventually, Beckwourth turned to ranching, managing to build up his stock with stolen horses until 1855, when he barely got out of the state ahead of vigilantes out to hang him. He moved to the Colorado Territory, scouted again for the Army and later took up city life in Denver as a storekeeper. This activity bored him, and in 1864 he went back to the wilderness, acting as a guide for John M. Chivington in the infamous Sand Creek Massacre. Perhaps unwisely, Beckwourth then started trading with the Indians again, and in 1866 he was allegedly poisoned by the Crows while visiting their village. Other reports have him dying in 1867 near Denver.

See also: *Thomas L. "Pegleg" Smith, William S. "Old Bill" Williams.*

BEGGING

The practice, or perhaps more correctly the profession, of begging doubtlessly goes back to prehistoric times. It appeared in America almost with the first settlers and it continues to the present day. In New York one resourceful entrepreneur, after years of successful panhandling, opened a school in 1979 to teach the art of begging. (Lesson One: On the subway, pick out one target, stand before him and whine loudly, "Please!" If that doesn't work, get on one knee and continue to plead until he does give.)

There have been many legendary beggars in American history. One of the most successful during the 1920s was New York City's "Breadline Charlie," who eschewed use of a harness or other equipment to make him appear crippled or helpless. Instead, he carried in his pocket small chunks of stale bread, and when in a crowd, he would drop a piece on the sidewalk. Then he would "discover" it, let out a scream of ecstasy and gobble it down as though he hadn't eaten in days. This pitiful scene always touched the hearts and purses of passersby.

An earlier faker, George Gray, had earned, by his own confession, at least $10,000 a year for many years around the turn of the century thanks to his incredible ability to feign an epileptic fit or a heart attack, usually in front of the residence of a well-to-do Manhattanite. After one of his many arrests, Gray was taken by police to Presbyterian Hospital, where doctors pronounced him "a curiosity of nature in that he possesses the power of accelerating or retarding his heart action at will." A businessman named Jesse L. Strauss gave police a considerable argument when they tried to roust Gray as he lay writhing on the sidewalk. Strauss had his money in hand and was ready to give it to the unfortunate man so that he could seek medical attention. Gray was wanted as the era's most professional "fit-thrower" by police in a dozen Eastern cities.

Robert I. Ingles was an energetic beggar who toured the country for years on a regular begging beat until his death in a charity ward in New York during the 1950s. On his person was found a pass book showing he had $2,500 in a Manhattan bank. In due course, it was found he had 42 other savings accounts with a total value of well over $100,000.

Rose Dym (born Anna Dym), a nightmarishly homely daughter of a retired Brooklyn pushcart peddler, hit the bright-light district in 1929. She was 17 then, a stage-struck little autograph hunter. Almost immediately, she developed a knack for making a pest of herself and people gave her whatever she asked for just to get rid of her. Soon, she was asking for money. Her technique worked so well that after a while, she would accept folding money only. Celebrities quailed at Rose's glance. Jack Dempsey once fled his own restaurant when she walked in to put the touch on his customers. In time, Broadway Rose prospered to the extent that she could refuse donations from nobodies with the admonition, "Go get yourself a reputation, jerk, before I'll take your scratch."

Probably the most profitable approach used today is a beggar in a business suit who embarrassedly tells victims he has lost his wallet and needs commuter fare home. Since home is a far way off, a minimum bite is $5. While such a routine can be most remunerative, it probably will never earn the profits attained by a New York beggar who used to pose as a leper. He was a tall, gaunt, olive-skinned man who'd haunt shadowy alleys and emerge only when he saw a prospective sucker coming along. "Mister . . . I'm a leper . . . Will you drop some money on the sidewalk for me? . . . Will you, please? . . . For a poor leper?'' All this time, the "leper" would keep moving toward his quarry, his arms outstretched—and many a poor soul was known to have reacted by dropping his entire wallet and then racing out of harm's way.

BEHAN, John (c.1840-?): Lawman and Wyatt Earp foe

John Behan was sheriff of Cochise County, Ariz. for only a year from 1881 to 1882, but since that was the period of the Earp-Clanton feud and such events as the gunfight at the O.K. Corral, he is accorded much more attention in Western lore than the average crooked sheriff of the day. Behan was a firm enemy of Wyatt Earp, the bone of contention between them being the sheriff's office, which Behan had and Earp wanted. Most sheriffs devoted the bulk of their time to collecting county taxes, leaving the gunfighting to their deputies. Remuneration for the job was largely a percentage of the tax collection which combined with a reasonable amount of graft from road-building and other contracts that a sheriff often controlled, could make such a lawman wealthy. At the time, the sheriff's job in Cochise County was worth $30,000 a year and Behan made $40,000.

In his fight to retain control of the office, Behan represented the cowboy and rustler element, or Democratic Party, while Earp represented the saloonkeeper/gambler-townie interests, or generally the Republican forces. It is against this background that events such as the O.K. Corral shoot-out must be seen. To win the support of the out-county elements, Behan allied himself with the Clanton forces and hired some of their gunmen to help in the collection of taxes. Elimination of the Clantons would weaken Behan's hold on his office. Behan tried to stop the shoot-out at the O.K. but was contemptuously ignored by the Earps and Doc Holliday. He could do nothing to prevent the magnificent duel, or callous slaughter, depending on one's viewpoint, that followed.

Despite the killing of one Clanton and two McLowery brothers, the Earps failed to wipe out their enemies, and in the end, they were driven out of Tombstone by a combination of legal charges and public opinion. Behan's triumph was short-lived, however. In 1882 he faced charges of financial irregularities and stepped down. After leaving office, he was indicted for continuing to collect taxes after his term.

Behan disappeared before the indictment could be served and nothing was heard about him for a few years. In 1887 he surfaced as a turnkey at the Yuma Penitentiary, where he became something of a hero by helping to quell a prison riot, although in the uproar he locked the warden in with a bunch of knife-brandishing convicts. No effort was made to return him to Cochise County for prosecution. Two years later, Behan came under another cloud when he was suspected of helping some convicts escape. For the second time in his life, Behan found it prudent to fade from the scene.

See also: *Wyatt Earp, O.K. Corral.*

BEIDLER, John X. (1831-1890): Montana vigilante hangman

In the 1860s John Beidler's "long rope" became the terror of Montana's bad men, and Beidler became known as the most zealous vigilante that ever looped a noose. In one six-week period 26 outlaws were hanged and Beidler's rope did the job in every case.

Beidler, a plump, walrus-faced man, was born in Montjoy, Pa. of German stock. Even to his friends in the West, he was known as a rather joyless person. Some biographers are unsure how much of Beidler's appetite for hanging sprang from a respect for law and order and how much from a morbid pleasure in hanging people. But whatever else was said about Beidler, he was certainly brave enough in taking credit for his acts. He never wore a mask, as did so many other vigilantes. If some of the "boys" ever wanted to get even with him, they knew where to find him.

Beidler's first vigilante act took place in Kansas, where, as the head of a posse, he disabled a gang of lawbreakers by firing a howitzer loaded with printer's type at them. In contradiction to the general description of his somberness, Beidler said, as the victims painfully dug the type slugs out of their bodies, that he saw no need for a necktie party, pointing out they could become good citizens now that "they have the opportunity to learn to read." A few years later, in the Alder Gulch-Bannack area of lawless Montana, Beidler came to the fore as the hanging vigilante. His victims included all the important badmen in the area. Beidler's style was casual in most cases: a handy tree limb or corral gate, the noose tightened and a box kicked out from under the victim's feet. With the coming of more organized law and order, the need for Beidler's long rope ended, and he became a businessman and saloon keeper, later serving as collector of customs for Idaho and Montana. He held that post until his death on January 22, 1890 in Helena.

See also: *Bannack, Montana Territory; Vigilantes of Montana.*

BELL, Tom (1825-1856): Outlaw doctor

Known as the Outlaw Doc, Tom Bell, whose real name was Thomas J. Hodges, is believed to have been the only physician to ride the Western bandit trail. On a criminal job he would carry as many implements as a doctor would carry on a house visit, in one case totaling up to six revolvers and a like number of knives and, presumably because of his superior medical knowledge, a chest protector fashioned from sheet iron.

Born in Rome, Tenn., Bell took part in the Mexican War. During that period he was trained as a doctor and emerged as a fully qualified practitioner. Bell followed the '49ers to California in search of gold but came up empty. He supported himself by gambling at cards, now and then taking time out to treat a gunshot victim. Exactly how or why he turned to crime is not know, but in 1855 he was doing time for theft in Angel Island Prison. There he befriended a vicious criminal named Bill Gristy, and within a matter of weeks the pair engineered an escape. The two then organized their own outlaw gang with five other hard cases and began pulling stage holdups.

On August 12, 1856 Bell and his confederates attempted to hold up the Camptonville-Marysville stage, which had $100,000 in gold bullion aboard. They killed a woman passenger and wounded two men but were beaten back by the stage's shotgun guards who killed two of them. The murder of the woman passenger sparked a huge manhunt for the bandits. There were legal posses under assorted lawmen and illegal posses of vigilantes who vowed to reach the killers first and mete out fast Western justice. By the end of September, Gristy had been arrested and, under threat of being handed over to a lynch mob, had turned stoolpigeon in his jail cell, identifying Doc Bell as the main culprit. The official and unofficial posses were quickly back on the trail in a race to locate Bell first. The sheriff of Stockton came in a close second. He found Doc on October 4, 1856 dangling from a tree on the Nevada City road.

BELLI, Melvin (1907-   ): Lawyer

One of the most successful lawyers of the modern era, San Francisco's Melvin Belli is famed for winning huge settlements for his clients in damage suits. In criminal cases his record is far more pedestrian. In the opinion of most of his peers, Belli did poorly in his defense of Jack Ruby after the killing of Lee Harvey Oswald. Belli has represented other criminal defendants, from Berkeley demonstrators to topless dancers, but his true forte is negligence cases.

BENDER Family: Mass murderers

The Hell Benders, as they came to be called, were the most murderous family America ever produced. They robbed as a family, killed as a family and may well have been slaughtered together as a family. When the Benders moved into Cherryvale in southeastern Kansas during the early 1870s, no one thought ill of them, and in fact, most of the young blades around were much impressed by the beauty of young Kate Bender, whose age was around 18 or 20.

The family consisted of Old Man William John, aged about 60, Ma Bender (no Christian name has ever been ascribed to her), young Kate and her brother, John, who, while older in years, was certainly less mature mentally than his sister. He was actually a moron whose main activity in life appeared to be cackling insanely.

The family maintained a log cabin outside of town consisting of one large room divided by a canvas curtain. They served drink and meals to travelers on one side of the curtain and slept on the other side. At night, they set up some beds on the public side to put up travelers wishing to stay the night. If they served meals to someone they knew, the Benders were most hospitable and sent them cheerfully on their way. However, if the patron was a lone traveler and looked like he had money, he never left the Bender cabin alive. Kate would sit him down on a bench against the canvas curtain and presumably flirt with him until he was smitten—in the most literal sense of the word. Either Old Man Bender or moronic John would be on the other side of the canvas, and when they made out the outline of the man's head, they would bash it in with a sledgehammer.

The dead man would be taken down to the cellar through a trap door and stripped of all money and valuables. Later, the victim would be buried on the grounds around the house, and Ma Bender would plant flowers over the spot.

The Benders last victim was a Dr. William H. York of Fort Scott, Kan. Passing through Cherryvale in March 1873, he asked for a place where he could eat and perhaps stay the night and was directed to the Benders. When he disappeared, his brother, a lawyer named Colonel A. M. York, followed his trail. He traced Dr. York to Cherryvale and no further. The Benders told Colonel York that his brother had never come to their place. Kate Bender invited the colonel to sit a while and she would fix him a cup of tea. She offered him a seat by the canvas, but York said he wanted to ride on past Cherryvale to see if he could pick up his brother's trail. Then John came in with a jug of cider and suggested the lawyer have a swig before leaving. York refused the offer and said he wanted to cover some ground before night fell. If he failed to pick up his brother's trail, he announced, he would be coming back.

The next day a neighbor rode past the Bender place and noted the door was open and the family wagon nowhere in sight. He went inside and discovered the Benders had gone, belongings and all. When Colonel York returned to Cherryvale, the trail gone cold, he was informed of the facts. A group of men went out to the Bender place. They looked in the cellar and found some loose dirt there. They dug and discovered the body of Dr. York.

They started digging around the cabin and found 10 other bodies, all with their skulls crushed. The Benders had something like a two-day start, but if they were in their wagon, they still might be caught. A posse of seven men headed by Colonel York started out to scour the surrounding area in the hopes of finding the fugitive family. When they came back some weeks later, they said they had failed to find the Benders. But the posse members were downright uncommunicative about where they had been; they didn't seem to want to talk about it. Colonel York lost interest in hunting for the murderous family, and took his brother's body with him for reburial.

The news of the Hell Benders spread from coast to coast. Souvenir hunters descended on Cherryvale and soon leveled the Bender place to the ground. Nails and boards said to be from the Benders' house sold for high prices in New York and San Francisco. Months passed, then years, but none of the four Benders turned up. Of course, there was a rash of false identifications. In 1889 Leroy Dick of Cherryvale traveled to Michigan and identified Mrs. Almira Griffith and her daughter, Mrs. Sarah Eliza Davis, as Ma Bender and Kate. They were returned to Kansas, and out of 13 persons, seven agreed with Dick's identification. Proof was then produced that one of the women had been married in Michigan in 1872, and the case against the two women was dropped. There were a number of other false identifications, all of which proved unreliable.

In 1909 George Downer lay dying in a Chicago suburb. He called for his lawyer, and in his last hour, Downer told the lawyer and his wife that he had been a member of the posse that had killed the Benders. After catching up with them, the posse had butchered the family so badly they felt they could not reveal the facts; they therefore buried the Benders in a 20-foot well and covered them over with dirt. In 1910 a man named Harker, dying in a New Mexico cow camp, confessed he too had helped kill the Benders. He also mentioned the 20-foot well—at that time Downer's confession had not yet become common knowledge. Harker said the posse had taken several thousand dollars from the bodies of the Benders, money they believed to have been stolen from the victims. As late as 1940 the same story surfaced from another source, George Stark, who said his late father had made an identical confession to him but had pledged him to secrecy until after his death.

Were the confessions true? After the 1909 and 1910 confessions a search was made for the well in the area identified by Downer and Harker. But the area had long since been planted with corn. If the Benders were there, they had been plowed under.

Of all the missing members of the Hell Benders, William "Old Man" Bender (c. 1813-1884?) is worth special mention since, if any of the family did survive the manhunt for them and was not killed, it was the elder Bender. If that was what happened, Old Man Bender died in 1884, 11 years after he had fled Kansas. In that year an aged individual who answered to his description and spoke with a German accent, as Bender had, was seized in the Montana Territory for a murder near Salmon, Idaho Territory. The victim's skull had been crushed from behind with a blunt instrument. The method, plus the suspect's physical appearance and the fact that he grew sullen when the name Bender was mentioned, convinced the arresting officers that they had the much-sought Old Man Bender.

The suspect was clamped in ankle irons and tossed in the Salmon jail while the authorities back in Kansas were notified to send someone to make an identification. The next morning the old man was dead. In a desperate effort to escape, he had tried to cut off his foot and had bled to death. Since there was no ice house in town, the sheriff's deputies tried to preserve the body in a calcifying pool. It didn't work, and by the time witnesses arrived from Kansas, identification was no longer possible.

However, since it seemed like a waste to give up such an attraction as a heinous murderer, the dead man's skull, identified as "Bender's skull," was put on display in the Buckthorn Saloon in Salmon, where it remained, an object of many toasts, until the onset of Prohibition in 1920. Then it, like the rest of the Benders, disappeared.

BENEDICT'S Sentence: Judge's speech

Probably the most famous judicial speech ever made in the Old West was the death sentence pronounced by Judge Kirby Benedict and referred to with solemn awe as Benedict's Sentence.

Benedict was an extremely learned man who was appointed to the Supreme Court of New Mexico by President Franklin Pierce in 1853. Previously, he had spent all his adult life in Illinois, where he was a highly regarded member of the bar and a friend of both Abraham Lincoln and Stephen A. Douglas. On the New Mexico bench, Benedict handed down several opinions that are often cited as examples of fine judicial writing, but he is unquestionably best remembered for his sentencing in Taos of Jose Maria Martin. Martin had been convicted of a particularly heinous murder, a verdict with which Benedict fully concurred. Jude Benedict addressed the prisoner as follows:

Jose Maria Martin, stand up. Jose Maria Martin, you have been indicted, tried and convicted, by a jury of your countrymen, of the crime of murder, and the Court is now about to pass upon you the dread sentence of the law. As a usual thing, Jose Maria Martin, it is a painful duty for the Judge of a court of justice to pronounce upon a human being the sentence of death. There is something horrible about it, and the mind of the Court naturally revolts at the performance of such a duty. Happily, however, your case is relieved of all such unpleasant features and the Court takes the positive pleasure in sentencing you to death!

You are a young man, Jose Maria Martin; apparently of good physical condition and robust health. Ordinarily, you might have looked forward to many years of life, and the Court has no doubt you have, and have expected to die at a green old age; but you are about to be cut off in consequence of your own act. Jose Maria Martin, it is now the springtime, in a little while the grass will be springing up green in these beautiful valleys, and, on these broad mesas and mountain sides, flowers will be blooming; birds will be singing their sweet carols, and nature will be pleasant and men will want to stay; but none of this for you, Jose Maria Martin; the flowers will not bloom for you, Jose Maria Martin; the birds will not carol for you, Jose Maria Martin; when these things come to gladden the senses of men, you will be occupying a space about six feet by two beneath the sod, and the green grass and those beautiful flowers will be growing above your lowly head.

The sentence of the Court is that you be taken from this place to the county jail; that you be kept there safely and securely confined, in the custody of the sheriff, until the day appointed for your execution. (Be very careful, Mr. Sheriff, that he have no opportunity to escape and that you have him at the appointed place at the appointed time); that you be so kept, Jose Maria Martin until—(Mr. Clerk, on what day of the month does Friday about two weeks from this time come? "March 22nd, your honor.") Very well, until Friday, the 22nd day of March, when you will be taken by the sheriff from your place of confinement to some safe and convenient spot within the county (that is in your discretion, Mr. Sheriff, you are only confined to the limits of this county), and that you there be hanged by the neck until you are dead, and the Court was about to add, Jose Maria Martin, 'May God have mercy on your soul,' but the Court will not assume the responsibility of asking an allwise Providence to do that which a jury of your peers has refused to do. The Lord couldn't have mercy on your soul. However, if you affect any religious belief, or are connected with any religious organization, it might be well for you to send for your priest or minister, and get from him—

well—such consolation as you can, but the Court advises you to place no reliance upon anything of that kind! Mr. Sheriff, remove the prisoner.

The only footnote to Judge Benedict's sentence was that Jose Maria Martin did escape and never paid the supreme penalty.

See also: *Roy Bean.*

BENI, Jules (?-1861): Outlaw

An ageless and larcenous Frenchman, Jules Beni operated a trading post near Lodgepole Creek, Colorado Territory around 1850, where anything went with no questions asked. An Eastern reporter called it the "wickedest city on the plains." It wasn't much of a city until a stage station was built next to it and a small settlement sprung up around it. The city became known as Julesburg in honor of old Beni.

The real joke was putting Beni in charge of the stagecoach station; instantly, the line was plagued by holdups. Considering that the bandits always seemed to know which stages carried important money and which didn't, it was only a matter of time until Beni came under suspicion. Beni was dismissed and replaced by Jack Slade, one of the most notorious killers the West ever produced. Needless to say, Slade and Beni did not get along, especially as Beni went about his stagecoach robbing a little more obviously now. The scene was set for a showdown, and Jack Slade came out second best. Beni blasted him with a shotgun and left him for dead, but miraculously, Slade recovered after the doctors had given up on him. That was lucky for Beni because the local citizens had taken him in custody and were getting set to hang him, founder of Julesburg or not. When Slade pulled through Beni was released after promising to vacate the area. He did, only to return about a year later. According to one account—Slade's—Beni tried to kill his adversary again. In any event, whether Beni found Slade or Slade found Beni, the fact was that Slade captured the Frenchman, tied him to a fence post, and used him for target practice. Then Slade killed Beni and cut off his ears as souvenirs. According to most accounts, Slade used one ear as a watch fob and sold the other for drinking money.

Today, Julesburg is a quiet little town of about 25,000 persons with very little of the wickedness that its founders had bequeathed it.

See also: *Joseph "Jack" Slade.*

BERGDOLL, Grover Cleveland (1893-1966): World War I draft dodger

No draft dodger in American history was as infamous as Grover Cleveland Bergdoll, a handsome Philadelphia millionaire playboy who refused to report to his local draft board in 1917. Bergdoll was not captured until January 1920, eventually, he was sentenced to five years imprisonment. In a bizarre escape, Bergdoll talked his military escort into allowing him to retrieve a gold cache of $105,000 he said was hidden in his home, took them there and then eluded them. Over the next

two decades the federal government spent millions of dollars trying to recapture him. Private "vigilantes" tried to kidnap, lynch or murder him. During this time Bergdoll flitted between America and various hideouts in Europe, but remarkably, he spent a large portion of the time hidden in the family mansion in Philadelphia with his wife and children.

An overview of newspaper headlines perhaps best illustrates the comic quality of the desperate hunt. Some read:

SEAS SEARCHED IN BERGDOLL HUNT . . . BERGDOLL DISGUISED AS WOMAN POSSIBLY . . . SEARCH FRUITLESS . . . BANKER COUNSELS PATIENCE IN BERGDOLL CASE: HAS NO CLUE TO THE FUGITIVE . . . INDIANA MARSHAL SAYS DRAFT DODGER WENT INTO KENTUCKY . . . MAN IN FEMALE GARB TAKEN FOR BERGDOLL . . . BERGDOLL NEARING MEXICO . . . SEEK BERGDOLL IN MOHAWK TOWNS . . . BERGDOLL SUSPECT FREED . . . BERGDOLL CAPTURE HOAX OF SUMMER . . . ONEONTA PRISONER NOT BERGDOLL . . . BERGDOLL REPORTED NEAR CITY . . . BERGDOLL 'ARRESTED' AGAIN

Perhaps the most frantic headline of all appeared in the *New York Times:* BERGDOLL'S INITIALS AND ARROW ON TREE.

Finally tiring of the chase, Bergdoll—who had slipped in and out of the country at least a half-dozen times—surrendered on May 27, 1939, sailing into New York aboard the German liner *Bremen.* Reports said he had fled Hitler's Germany to avoid being drafted into the army there. However, as an American citizen, Bergdoll was not subject to German military service. Bergdoll's case was debated in Congress and pressure was put on President Franklin D. Roosevelt to deny amnesty that had been granted to all other draft evaders and deserters. Bergdoll was sentenced to a total of seven years at hard labor. He was released early in 1944. Nineteen years later, suffering mental deterioration, he was confined to a psychiatric hospital in Richmond, Va. He died there on January 27, 1966.

BERGER, Meyer (1898-1959): Reporter

Although totally lacking the flamboyance of such other great crime reporters as Ike White, Charles MacArthur and Ben Hecht, Meyer "Mike" Berger was probably the greatest of his or any other day. He brought a sense of quiet, self-effacing dignity and a devotion to accuracy for which the field was hardly renowned. All doors were open to Berger, whether they belonged to distinguished citizens or secretive mobsters. Whenever a rampaging horde of crime reporters from the more than 10 New York City newspapers then in existence would descend on the home of a well-known citizen drawn into a criminal investigation, they would shove Berger to the front and announce: "This is Mr. Meyer Berger of the *New York Times.* He would like to ask some questions." This same respect for the *Times* man was shown in a most unusual way by Arthur (Dutch Schultz) Flegenheimer after the reporter had covered one of his many trials. An incensed Schultz sought out Berger, demanded to know if he had written the story in which someone was quoted as saying Dutch was a "pushover for a blonde." Quaking, Berger admitted he was. "Pushover for a blonde!" the gangster raged. "What kind of language is that to use in the *New York Times?*"

Berger was nominated for a Pulitzer Prize in 1932 for his stories on Al Capone's Chicago trial that had captured the character of America's most famous gangster far better than the more so-called definitive efforts. When Abe Reles, the Murder Inc. informer, "went out the window" of a Coney Island hotel in which he was being held under police "safekeeping," Berger climbed out on the ledge where Reles would have stood—if indeed he had gone willingly—and told his readers what Reles saw and heard and what he must have felt. Berger won a Pulitzer Prize for his brilliant coverage of the 1949 shooting of 13 persons in Camden, N.J. by an insane veteran named Howard Unruh. The reporter followed the mad killer's trail, talking to 50 persons who had watched segments of Unruh's movements. The account, written in two and a half hours and running 4,000 words, was printed in the *Times* without any editorial changes.

When Berger died nine years later, very few of his colleagues knew that he had given his prize money to Unruh's aged mother.

BERKMAN, Alexander (1870-1936): Anarchist and would-be assassin

In one of the most tortured assassination attempts ever, anarchist Alexander Berkman tried but failed to kill a leading industrialist of the late 19th century.

Few men were more hated by labor and radical forces in this country than Henry Clay Frick, chairman and strongman of the Carnegie Steel Co., who was blamed as much or more for the company's abysmal working conditions as his partner, Andrew Carnegie.

During the terrible Homestead Steel Strike of 1892, Carnegie left for a vacation in Scotland to avoid being around when the great labor crisis erupted over the workers' refusal to accept a reduction in wages. Carnegie wanted the strike crushed by any means and no one was more capable and indeed eager to do so than Frick. He recruited a private army of 300 Pinkertons and fortified the company's mills at Homestead, Pa. Then, under cover of night, he sent the Pinkertons by barge up the Monongahela River. They opened fire on the strikers without warning, killing several, including a small boy, and wounding scores of others. The strikers countered with burning oil, dynamite and homemade cannon. With his army stymied, Frick turned to the governor for aid and 8,000 militiamen were dispatched to the scene.

During the stalemate Frick continued his opposition to unionization despite a rising anger in the country. On July 23, 1892 Frick was in his private office with his chief aide, John Leishman, planning company strategy when a young man posing as an agent for a New York "employment firm" received permission to enter.

Actually, the man was 21-year-old Alexander Berkman, a fiery anarchist and lover of another famous anarchist, Emma Goldman. Berkman was outraged at Frick's behavior during the strike and resolved to assassinate him as an act of liberation on behalf of his working comrades. He first tried to do so by making a bomb but failed to produce a workable model. Emma then went into the streets as a prostitute to raise money in order to buy a gun. She was picked up by a kindly older man who guessed her amateur status and sent her home with $10. With that, Berkman bought the assassination weapon.

Anarchist Alexander Berkman is shown after his assassination attempt on steel magnate Henry Clay Frick during the Homestead Steel Strike of 1892.

The actual attempt was best described by a contemporary account in *Harper's Weekly:*

Mr. Frick had been sitting with his face half turned from the door, his right leg thrown over the arm of his chair . . . and almost before he had realized the presence of a third party in the room, the man fired at him. The aim had been for the brain, but the sudden turning of the chairman spoiled it, and the bullet ploughed its way into the left side of his neck. The shock staggered Mr. Frick. Mr. Leishman jumped up and faced the assailant. As he did so another shot was fired and a second bullet entered Mr. Frick's neck, but on the left side. Again the aim had been bad. Mr. Leishman, who is a small man, sprang around the desk, and just as the assailant was firing the third time, he seized his hand and threw it upward and back. The bullet embedded itself in the ceiling back of where the man was standing . . . Mr. Frick recovered almost instantly from the two shots and ran to the assistance of Leishman, who was grappling with the would-be assassin . . . The exertion made the blood spurt from his wounds and it dyed the clothing of the assailant.

The struggle lasted fully two minutes. Not a word was spoken by any one, and no cry had been uttered. The fast-increasing crowd in the street looked up at it open-mouthed and apparently paralyzed (Frick's upper-floor office could be readily seen into from across the street). There were no calls for the police and no apparent sign of excitement, only spell-bound interest. The three men swayed to and fro in struggle, getting all the time nearer to the windows. Once the assailant managed to shake himself loose, but before he could bring his revolver again into play, Mr. Leishman knocked his knees from under him, and the combined weight of himself and Mr. Frick bore the man to the floor. In the fall, he succeeded in loosening one hand and with it he drew an old-fashioned dirk-knife from his pocket and began slashing with it. He held it in his left hand. Mr. Frick was trying to hold him on that side. Again and again, the knife plunged into Mr. Frick until seven distinct wounds had been made, and then Mr. Frick succeeded in catching and holding the arm.

At the first sign of the knife the crowd in the street seemed to recover itself and there were loud calls of "Police!" "Fire!" The clerks in the main office recovered from their stupefaction, and rushed pell-mell into the office of their chief. Deputy Sheriff May, who happened to be in the office, was in the lead. He drew a revolver, and was about to use it, when Mr. Frick cried: "Don't shoot! Don't kill him! The law will punish him." The deputy's hand was seized and held by one of the clerks, while half a dozen others fell on the prostrate assailant. The police were in the office in a few minutes and took the man away. Fully two thousand people had gathered in the street, and there were cries of "Shoot him! Lynch him!"

Despite a total of nine wounds, Frick was back at his desk within a week, but Berkman spent 14 years in prison before being pardoned in 1906. Like most acts of terrorism, his attack on Frick had not helped the intended beneficiaries. In fact, the strikers generally denounced the act, though many with seemingly little conviction. From 1906 until 1919, when they were deported in the Red Scare roundups, Berkman and Goldman became the primary spokesmen for American anarchism. They were sent back to their native Russia, where they were welcomed by the new Soviet government, but the incompatibility of anarchism and communism soon forced them both to leave. Berkman settled first in Sweden, then Germany and finally in France. He continued his anarchist writing and organizing and edited many of Goldman's works. He did some translating and ghostwriting for European and American publishers but needed contributions from friends and comrades to survive. Both despondent and ill, he committed suicide in 1936. H. L. Mencken wrote of Berkman that he was a "transparently honest man . . . a shrewder and a braver spirit than has been seen in public among us since the Civil War."

BERKOWITZ, David R.:
See "Son of Sam."

BERMAN, Otto "Abbadabba" (1889-1935):
Policy game fixer

Few rackets have ever produced as much money for underworld coffers as the numbers game, and although the profit slice is 40 percent or more, crime bosses have always searched for ways to give the suckers even less of a break.

Otto "Abbadabba" Berman was for a time a magician at this, as his nickname indicates. During the 1930s Berman devised a system for rigging the results of the game so that only a lesser-played number would win. He worked for Dutch Schultz, the crime czar who controlled the bulk of the numbers game in New York, including most of the action in black Harlem. At the time, the winning number was derived from the betting statistics at various race tracks. The underworld could not control the figures at the New York tracks, but during the periods when those courses were closed, the number was based on the results from tracks that the underworld had successfully infiltrated, such as New Orleans' Fair Grounds, Chicago's Hawthorne and Cincinnati's Coney Island. Berman was able to figure out how much money to put into the mutual machines to have a low-played number come out. It was estimated that Abbadabba's magic added 10 percent to every million dollars a day the underworld took in.

In 1935 Dutch Schultz was assassinated by vote of the Luciano-Lansky national crime syndicate, allegedly because Schultz had announced he intended to kill Thomas E. Dewey, whose racket-busting activities were hampering underworld operations. Luciano especially was concerned about the ramifications of killing a man of Dewey's stature. His concern, however, was no doubt heightened by the opportunity he saw to take over the Schultz numbers racket. Schultz and three of his favorite underlings were cut down at the Palace Chophouse in Newark while having dinner. Unfortunately for the mob, one of those shot with Schultz was Berman. His loss was to cost the mob literally millions of dollars a year, for while others tried to imitate the technique of what Luciano's aide, Vito Genovese, called "the Yid adding machine," few approached even a fraction of his results.

See also: *Numbers Racket, Dutch Schultz.*

BERRETT-MOLWAY Taxi Cab Case:
Murder trial

The murder trial of two men, Clement Molway and Louis Berrett, both Boston taxi drivers, in February 1934 is memorable for the sobering second thoughts it caused the jury. Eight undisputed eyewitnesses identified the pair as the men who murdered an employee of the Paramount Theatre in Lynn, Mass. Just before the case was to go to the jury, a man convicted with two others in another robbery-murder confessed to the crime. Berrett and Molway were freed and won compensation. Newspapers widely reported the deep impression made on the jurors, who admitted they would have convicted the innocent men. Typical was the following comment of the jury foreman, Hosea E. Bradstreet:

> Those witnesses were so positive of their identification that it was only natural that we should be misled. While I sat at the trial I somehow hated the thought of sending those two men to the electric chair; but we were sworn to perform our duty and we would have done it—to the best of our ability. . . . This trial has taught me one thing. Before I was a firm believer in capital punishment, I'm not now.

BERTILLON System: Criminal identification method

From the mid-1880s through 1904 or 1905 the standard method of criminal identification in the United States was the system invented in 1883 by Alphonse Bertillon, a Frenchman. Bertillon concluded there were 12 measurements on an adult that do not change, such as the length and width of the head, the length of the left foot, left forearm and left little finger, and so on. Criminals were photographed and measured according to this method and records were compiled on the assumption that no two people would every look alike and have exactly the same measurements. There were several flaws in the Bertillon system, not the least being that more than one arresting officer often made entry of a subject's "pedigree" and the material would be contradictory. The real death knell for the system came when two prisoners lodged in the same penitentiary were found to have the same Bertillon measurements, looked alike and even had virtually the same names. The Will West-William West case was the prime factor in convincing law authorities to switch to fingerprinting as an identification method.

See also: *Fingerprinting, "West Brothers."*

BETHEA, Rainey (1914-1936): Last publicly executed man

The last public execution in America was held in 1936. The victim was a 22-year-old black man named Rainey Bethea, and his execution at Owensboro, Ky. remains one of the most shameful episodes in U.S. history.

Because Rainey had killed a 70-year-old white woman, public opinion was at a fever pitch, and the county sheriff, a woman named Florence Thompson, decided to stage the execution in an open field so that thousands of witnesses could be accommodated. By the night before the execution, Owensboro was swamped with visitors from all over the country; by dawn more than 20,000 persons had gathered at the execution site. Only six blacks were present—virtually all the local blacks had fled the town during the previous night's drunken revelry, which was punctuated by calls for a mass lynching. Each time the hangman tested the scaffold, it snapped open to the appreciative cheers of the crowd. Bethea reached the scaffold at 5:12 a.m. and the execution moved briskly, authorities now fearing the crowd might get out of hand. When the bolt snapped, a

joyous roar swept over the field and the crowd surged closer. Souvenir hunters almost immediately attacked the dangling, still-warm body, stripping off pieces of the condemned man's clothing and in some instances trying to carve out chunks of flesh. Meanwhile, doctors fought their way through the melee to certify Bethea's death and then cried out that his heart was still beating. The spectators groaned and pulled back, waiting. Bethea was finally pronounced dead at 5:45, and once more the souvenir hunters charged forward, a great scuffle taking place for possession of the death hood.

See also: *Executions, Public.*

BICKFORD, Maria (1823-1845): Murder victim

The murder of Maria Bickford by Albert Tirrell in Boston on October 27, 1845 was noteworthy because the young man was of the Weymouth Tirrells, one of New England's wealthiest and most socially prominent families. However, the case was to become even more noteworthy since it represented the first effective use of sleepwalking as a defense.

The 25-year-old Tirrell was the bane of his family. Although married, he was notorious for picking up a whore and going off with her for a week or longer at a time. In one of the family's constant efforts to get Albert to reform, they sent him on the road as a representative for one of the Tirrell businesses, Tirrell's Triumphant Footwear. Exactly how providing Albert with such an ideal opportunity for whoring would lead to his reformation was, at least in retrospect, a mystery. In New Bedford, Mass., he met 23-year-old Maria Bickford and was soon pursuing his usual desires. But in the case of this woman, it was a matter of true love; Tirrell brought Bickford back to Boston, ensconcing her in a waterfront flat where he could visit her regularly, while continuing to pretend to his family that he had indeed become a solid citizen.

However, the Tirrell-Bickford love affair was not a quiet one. They screamed, fought, got drunk frequently and eventually were evicted for boisterous behaviour. Tirrell's conduct became the talk of Boston. The family could no longer ignore this, and finally, Tirrell's wife and brother-in-law brought criminal charges of adultery against him. In the year 1845 in Boston, adultery was a word spoken only in whispers. Indeed, the act was punishable by a fine and six months imprisonment. Even worse, a convicted man would almost certainly be treated as a pariah, shunned by society. Painfully aware of this, Tirrell was most contrite when visited in his cell by the family. "He implored his young wife for forgiveness," says an account of the day. The fact that he was in the process of "drying out" added to the heart-rending scene. Finally, on October 20 the family, including Tirrell's wife and brother-in-law, capitulated. They withdrew the charges and the prodigal son was turned loose upon signing a bond promising to "keep the peace and observe propriety in his behavior."

Back home for an hour, Tirrell kissed his wife and said he had to go out "on business." Like a homing pigeon, he headed for the house of Joel Lawrence on Cedar Lane in the Beacon

Hill district, where Maria Bickford had taken up residence. Tirrell brought with him a demijohn of rum. During the reunion of the lovers that followed, landlord Lawrence later said that he thought the house was falling down. Eventually, the lovers quieted a bit until the following evening. Then the revelry started again but soon turned into a nasty quarrel when Tirrell found some letters written to Maria by a new admirer. Over the next several evenings the pair's frolicking was increasingly interrupted by harsh arguments, a matter compounded when a Miss Priscilla Moody from down the hall, unaware that Tirrell was around one afternoon, dropped by to ask Maria to help her out since she had two gentlemen calling on her shortly. When Tirrell erupted in anger, Maria just laughed and said if she did anything like that, it would just be "funning."

The Tirrell-Bickford funning came to an end at 4:30 the morning of October 27. Smoke was seen pouring out of Maria's window, and the landlord, who had been awakened about an hour earlier by another of the incessant screaming matches between the lovers, broke in. Someone had deliberately set fire to the room. It was not Maria. She was laying on the floor, totally nude, her throat slit almost from ear to ear. When Lawrence viewed the scene, he shouted out, "Where's Albert?"

Albert had headed for the Boston docks, he joined a ship's crew and sailed away as a common seaman. It was not until February 27, 1846 that he was apprehended aboard the schooner *Cathay* in New York and returned to Boston to face murder charges. There was little reason to doubt that Tirrell would be convicted. There were witnesses who saw him leave the Lawrence house moments before the fire. Those who had seen him testified that he wore no shirt under his coat—his bloody shirt had been found in the murder room. An acquaintance of Tirrell's, Sam Head, told of how young Albert had turned up at his home and asked, "Sam—how came I here?" He stank of rum.

With such a strong case against him, Tirrell was considered as good as convicted. Nevertheless, the Tirrell family decided to strive mightily to save the errant son, recoiling in horror from the stigma that would attach to all if Albert were hanged for murder. The Honorable Rufus B. Choate was retained to defend Albert. Choate, then at the height of his oratorical powers, was rightly considered a courtroom wizard, but everyone was convinced that in this case he was espousing a hopeless cause. It would take a miracle to save Tirrell. Which was exactly what Choate came up with.

Choate stunned the court when he conceded that his client had indeed killed "this unfortunate woman." However, the lawyer said, "I will prove that he cannot be held responsible under the law because he was asleep at the time." While the courtroom buzzed with an argument never heard before in an American court of law, Choate continued:

> I do not mean, of course, that he was asleep in the usual physical sense. He was mentally asleep. Although he was capable of physical movement and action, he had no knowledge or judgment of what he was doing. His mental and moral faculties were in deepest slumber. He was a man in somnambulism, acting in a dream. Gentlemen, I will show that the defendant Tirrell has been a sleepwalker since early youth, and

that while in a condition of somnambulism that often lasted for many hours, he performed feats of almost incredible complexity and dexterity.

Witness after witness took the stand to tell of Tirrell's past sleepwalking escapades and accomplishments. His mother said her son had first shown sleepwalking tendencies at the age of three. He had been found in the kitchen sound asleep smearing jam on the walls. He started sleepwalking regularly. Mrs. Tirrell took to tying her son to his bed, but the boy showed a slumbrous ability to untie knots he could not undo when awake. After the lad had been discovered to have climbed out of his bedroom window and perched precariously on the porch roof, Mrs. Tirrell, according to the testimony of a workman, ordered an iron grill over the window "to keep the tyke from killing himself."

The family physician reported that at the age of 10, the sleepwalking boy, barefoot and in only his nightgown, had been found in the late hours of a winter night just as he completed building a snowman. "The boy came near dying of pneumonia as a result of that," the doctor testified.

According to the evidence presented, Tirrell's sleepwalking escapades became less frequent in adulthood but tended to be more dangerous and violent. His wife Cynthia awoke one night to find him trying to strangle her. Her desperate screams awakened him, and he expressed surprise and contrition, begged her forgiveness and then lapsed into a peaceful sleep. A sailor from the *Cathay* told of watching the sleeping and stark-naked Tirrell cross the ice-covered deck of the vessel, climb high in the mast and then come down safely, all the while acting "like a man in his sleep."

Lawyer Choate then recalled the words of Samuel Head, who had seen Tirrell shortly after Maria Bickford's murder. "He seemed like a man coming out of a stupor. He said, 'Sam, how came I here?' "

Despite the prosecution's attempts to knock down Choate's unique defense of his client, the jury was duly impressed. It took less than two hours to bring in a verdict that established a legal milestone. Albert Tirrell was found not guilty and freed. As time passed, the Tirrell verdict did not sit well with the public, which clearly felt the family money had gotten him off. A man who could slit a pretty girl's throat and—allegedly—not remember it was, general opinion held, more likely rum-soaked than in a somnambulistic trance. Finally, bowing to public opinion, the family had Albert confined where he would no longer be a danger, sleeping or awake.

See also: *Sleepwalking and Crime.*

BICYCLE Police

Late in the 19th century most big-city police departments found they could not adequately patrol their communities with just police on foot or on horseback. What they needed was a "motorized" force on bicycle. Typical was the New York Bicycle Squad formed in 1895 after Police Commissioner Theodore Roosevelt angrily declared the traffic of "steam carriages," the forerunner of the automobile; huge horse-drawn trucks; and bicycles had made Eighth Avenue and the waterfront area unsafe for pedestrians. To regulate traffic in these areas, he assigned bicycles to four officers. The speed limit for all vehicles was set at eight miles an hour and speeders were flagged down by a traffic cop on a bike who would demand to see the driver's license.

By 1902 the Bicycle Squad was enlarged to 100 men, and Police Commissioner Thomas Andrew could proudly announce a total of 1,366 arrests that year of "civilian wheelmen who persisted in risking the lives and limbs of others by 'scorching' along the Central Park drives." He added that a great many of these "bicyclist-scorchers were also of that despicable breed known as 'mashers.'"

A New York City bicycle cop runs down one of the new automobile "speed demons" around the turn of the century.

By 1910 the horseless carriages had ceased being the mere playthings of the very wealthy and eccentric and were starting to choke the city streets. The Bicycle Squad did heroic work trying to contain these automobile "speed demons." It did not occur to anyone until 1912 to provide the police with automobiles so that they could give chase to other such vehicles. In that year the Traffic Division was established. Still, the Bicycle Squad hung on, providing sundry services until finally being abandoned in 1934. Rather than sell hundreds of bicycles to commercial dealers, the police auctioned them off to city kids, with some of the police bikes going for a mere 25 cents.

BIDDLE Brothers: Murderers and death-row escapees

Ed and Jack Biddle escaped from the Allegheny County Jail on January 30, 1902, 16 days before they were to be executed for the killing of a store owner and a police detective. When details of the escape became known, it scandalized Pittsburgh and much of the rest of the country since the escape was engineered by 26-year-old Katherine Scoffel, the warden's wife.

She had come to their death cells a month earlier, as was her custom to try to bring religion to doomed men and had fallen in love with Ed Biddle, eight years her junior. Mrs. Scoffel supplied the brothers with guns and hacksaws and led them to freedom through the warden's home, which had a private entrance to the institution. She had drugged her husband so he would be asleep and made sure their four children were not home at the time.

Two guards were shot superficially and another was overpowered during the breakout, when they were found, the alarm was sounded. The warden, apprised of the facts, notified the police of the Biddle brothers' escape and told them to arrest his wife as an accomplice. Then he wrote a letter of resignation, gathered up his children and left the prison for the last time.

Meanwhile, the three fugitives made it as far as Butler, Pa., switching from the carriage Mrs. Scoffel had secured for them to a stolen sleigh. They were stopped by a seven-man roadblock, and in a furious gun battle 26-year-old Jack Biddle was shot dead. Ed Biddle was hit three times in the lung. As he was dying, Katherine Scoffel begged him to shoot her. He did so, but while Biddle died a few hours after being taken into custody, Mrs. Scoffel survived. When she recovered, she was tried and sentenced to serve two years in the penitentiary of which she had once been the first lady. Asked during her trial how a woman of her standing could love a vicious criminal like Ed Biddle, she said: "I can forgive anything he's done. Except one. I can forgive his killings, his robberies, anything. But I cannot forgive him for failing to kill me so that I could be with him forever in death."

Katherine Scoffel was released from prison in 18 months and lived until 1926, ostracized and in disgrace. Often through the years, she would see an advertisement in a newspaper for a performance of a melodrama about the case. It was called *The Biddle Boys* and played to capacity houses for many years.

BIG Store: Major confidence game operation

Prior to 1900, swindles were pretty much "short cons" in which the victim was cheated for a few dollars, perhaps a few hundred and occasionally a few thousand. It was difficult to keep the sucker in tow long enough to make a really big killing. Buck Boatright, an ingenious gambler and the originator of a little con game called the smack, solved this problem by devising the most elaborate and successful confidence racket ever invented.

Boatright's plan was to set up a permanent base of operations, either an office or a store with seemingly respectable or authentic trimmings as well as many employees and "customers." Here the sucker could be skinned with near-scientific precision. Boatright set up his operation with the backing of a number of con men who became his partners. The first requirement was to establish a protected territory in which police and politicians would cooperate for either a flat payoff or a percentage of the take. Boatright's selection was Webb City, Mo., where in 1900 he opened what was to become known as the Big Store.

Boatright's operation was a fake gambling club, featuring among other things fixed sporting events (generally foot races or fights). So convincing was the atmosphere in Boatright's establishment, which soon spawned a branch in Council Bluffs, Iowa, that a sucker almost never suspected he was losing his money in a completely play-act arena where everyone except the victim was a member of the gang.

After the sucker was roped in by being allowed to win a few small bets, he then was informed of a big fix and induced to bet thousands, only to watch as something unforeseen went wrong. In a footrace or fight the participant the victim was betting on might suddenly "drop dead," triggering a false panic since such sporting events were illegal. In other cases the victim would be kissed off when the two operators who suckered him in, and who allegedly lost their money with his, got into an argument that would end with one pulling a gun and "killing" the other. In this play-acted "sting" the shot con man would slump to the floor with blood gushing from his mouth. This would really be chicken blood secreted in a pouch in the man's mouth and bitten open at the right moment. It was an act well calculated to put the sucker "on the run" since, while he had intended only to break the law against illegal betting, he now believed he was an accessory to murder.

Although the big store would seem to be an operation that could fleece only the most gullible, it was carried off with such convincing performances that many men of business and wealth were easily taken, never for a moment suspecting a swindle. Perhaps the greatest of all big store operators was Lou Blonger, a master fixer, who for four decades made Denver, Colo. the "con man's capital of America."

See also: *Dollar Store, Smack Game.*

BIGAMY

Few crimes are as welcome to newspaper editors as bigamy, the act of ceremonially marrying another person when already legally married. Although the typical state statute exacts up to five years imprisonment for the offense, few bigamists are ever punished, usually getting off with a stern lecture provided they make amends by speedily annulling the illegitimate marriage. Meanwhile, the newspapers have their human interest story, especially when, as often happens, the bigamist's spouses violently denounce or attack one another.

One such case involved two women who went at each other in a Chicago courthouse corridor, pulling hair, gouging and biting. "I'm still in love with him," wife number one announced to reporters, after the two battling women were separated. "I'll help him all I can." Which is how things turned out. Since he was her husband first, she got him while the second wife got only an annulment. Triumphantly, in fact, wife number one paid the $500 fine her errant husband faced for his misdeeds.

It is not unusual to find a bigamist with six or eight spouses who still does not end up with a prison sentence, unless he or she is also guilty of stealing his or her spouses' money or defrauding them of their fortunes. Few prosecuting attorneys will expend much energy on bigamy complaints because as many as a dozen investigators would have to be put on a single bigamy case full time to clear the tangled web. Another discouraging factor is that bigamists often have wives and families in different states. As a result, for every bigamist finally hauled into court, possibly as many as a hundred or more go free and undetected.

Many bigamists have bizarre or zany reasons for committing the crime. Often, they have concocted and sold their spouses wildly improbable tales to sustain their deception. This was the case of a Washington woman who married two Canadian navy seamen, assuring each that she had a twin sister who had married the other. When it was discovered that both "twins" had identical cuts on a finger, her double life was exposed.

Courting exposure, indeed, seems very common among bigamists. A gray-haired 52-year-old night watchman was clapped in the county jail in New Haven, Conn. for having two wives—living a mere block from each other. He was exposed when a long distance call for one wife mistakenly went to the other. One Michigan bigamist got caught when his wife went by a photographer's shop and spotted a picture of her husband and a stunning young bride. A Massachussets man's bigamy was revealed when two of his wives met in court while both were bringing action against him for nonsupport.

Harried bigamists often find themselves mired deep in serious crime before long. The "flying lothario" of Memphis made the headlines from coast to coast after it was found he kept one wife in Tennessee and another in California, commuting back and forth each week by plane in order to spend weekdays in Memphis and weekends in Los Angeles. Travel costs murdered him, and he finally confessed to stealing $19,000 from the Memphis firm where he worked as a cashier.

Few bigamists are exceptionally attractive. In fact, some of the country's most successful bigamists are bald and fortyish, both in age and waistline. Master swindler and bigamist Sigmund Engel was only coming into his prime when he was arrested at the age of 73. At the other end of the scale was a 17-year-old schoolboy who had already walked up the aisle three times, evidently incapable of saying no to older women.

Probably the only way to end bigamy would be to enact a proposal made in recent years by several district attorneys that a central national office be established to receive notice of and record every marriage made anywhere in the country. In addition, every person being married would have to be fingerprinted. Obviously, while this would effectively stop the bigamists, the proposal's disregard for American concepts of civil liberties outweighs its usefulness as a measure to eliminate bigamy.

BILER Avenue: Chicago vice district

From the 1870s until the turn of the century, Pacific Avenue, nicknamed Biler Avenue, was "one of the most disreputable streets in the city, built up with hastily constructed tenements which were occupied by the most depraved of men and women, black, white and mixed." Yet it was still held in particular fondness by the reigning political powers. Biler Avenue and its side streets were filled with bordellos of the lowest class and lowest price in the city. A typical establishment was Dan Webster's big groggery and bagnio at Nos. 130-132, which the *Chicago Times* called an "infernal hell hole. There it is that the rottenest, vilest, filthiest strumpets, black and white, reeking with corruption, are bundled together, catering indiscriminately to the lust of all." What made the activities of the establishment most noteworthy was, as the *Times* discovered, that the building was owned by Michael C. Hickey, the superintendent of police. Because of the stir caused by the *Times* expose, Hickey was hauled before the Police Board for trial, but he was acquitted of any wrongdoing since there was no way a superintendent of police could possibly have known about the character of his tenants. An even more startling revelation was that an entire block on Harrison Street was the property of Mayor Carter Harrison.

"Our Carter" the *Times* said, "owns the entire block between Clark Street and Pacific Avenue. On the corner of Clark, and running west to the middle of the block, stands a hotel. The other half of the block is occupied by four or five ordinary frame houses. One is used for a lager-beer saloon, another for a restaurant, still another for a tobacco store, a fourth as a hotel on a small scale, and right among these, as snug as a bug, Our Carter has allowed a number of gay damsels to nestle down, and they are rather homely ones at that."

Even that last withering comment was not enough to keep Carter Harrison from becoming a five-term mayor. Biler Avenue thus typified Chicago's tolerance of political venality, an attitude that was to last for many decades.

See also: *Carter Harrison.*

BILLEE, John (?-1890): Western murderer

The idea of bringing in a badman dead or alive was an Old West concept that did not usually apply to deputy federal marshals. For each prisoner brought back, the marshal was paid the sum of $2 plus a mileage allowance of six cents per mile going and 10 cents coming back provided he had his man. Out of this sum, the marshal had to pay all his own expenses and feed his prisoner. However, if he lost his prisoner or was forced to kill him, the lawman lost his fee and mileage allowance! The system encouraged marshals to try their best to keep their quarry alive.

A noted case that underscored the point involved John Billee, who killed a man named W. P. Williams in April 1888 and buried the corpse in a ravine in the Kiamichi Mountains. Federal deputies caught up with Billee in a wide sweep during which they also netted four other wanted men. On their way back to Fort Smith, deputies Perry DuVall, Will Ayers and James Wilkerson stopped with their prisoners to spend the night at a deserted two-room cabin outside Muskogee, Oklahoma in Indian Territory.

Deputy Ayers, with three prisoners chained to him, bedded down in the front room along with Deputy DuVal, who had Billee in tow. Deputy Wilkerson and the fifth prisoner slept in the small rear room of the cagin. About 3 a.m. Billee worked out of one of his handcuffs and managed to reach DuVal's revolver. He fired but in the darkness only succeeded in wounding DuVall in the head. He then turned the gun on Ayers before the deputy had a chance to react out of his sleep, shooting him in the right nipple. Meanwhile Wilkerson had rolled over into a sitting position in the doorway of the next room and Billee put a shot into his back. Ayers then lunged at the outlaw and battled Billee to keep him from getting off another shot. While this was going on, Wilkerson leveled his own gun and aimed carefully at the outlaw, trying to get off an incapacitating, rather than a fatal, shot, which he did. By keeping Billee alive long enough for him to meet his doom on the gallows at Fort Smith on January 16, 1890, the three wounded deputies were able to collect their fee for the outlaw.

BILLINGTON, John (?-1630): America's first murderer

Even before the Pilgrims landed at Plymouth Rock in 1620, Capt. Miles Standish had already had his fill of one John Billington aboard the *Mayflower.* Standish reprimanded Billington, a foul-mouthed brawler from the London slums, and eventually was forced to make an example of the man by having his feet and neck tied together. There is no evidence that this punishment had any lasting effect on Billington, who became the scourge of the Plymouth colony, starting feuds with a number of settlers.

One Pilgrim who refused to knuckle under to Billington's bullying was John Newcomen, a neighbor, and the pair became mortal enemies. Finally, one day in 1630 Billington ambushed Newcomen while he was out in the woods hunting, shooting him dead with a blunderbuss from behind a rock. Billington was quickly seized, tried by the Pilgrims and summarily hanged. Ironically, many Americans today proudly trace their ancestry back to the *Mayflower* and Billington, the American colonies' first murderer.

BILLY The Kid (1859-1881): Outlaw

There has probably been more written about Billy the Kid than any other outlaw, which perhaps explains why so little of his true story can be accurately reconstructed.

Hyperbole has been added to lies until we are left with a portrait of a young outlaw said to have killed 21 men during his 21 years. The number is an exaggeration. He did not kill a man at the age of 12 for insulting his mother as is often stated. Probably the first man the New York-born youngster—whose real name is believed to have been either William Bonney or Henry McCarty—killed was a bully named Frank "Windy" Cahill, who had called him a "pimp and a son of a bitch." Billy gunned him down on the spot. He was arrested but almost immediately escaped from jail. In fact, he frequently escaped from jails, which probably helped to give him a romantic air. There was certainly nothing romantic about his looks. He was small, with prominent front teeth and a short, fuzzy upper lip, almost a harelip, which gave him a perpetual smile. He smiled when he killed and his smile made him look pathological, which he probably was. One moment he was good-natured and the next he displayed an explosive temper.

Famous "flopped, " i.e., reversed, portrait of Billy the Kid started the legend that he was left-handed.

Beginning in his early teens, Billy supported himself by gambling and, when the cards ran wrong, by stealing anything from clothes to cattle. After his mother died in 1874, Billy was completely on his own. Following the Cahill killing and a few others, according to some historians, Billy hired out as a cowboy to an English gentleman rancher, John Tunstall.

It was a smart move by Tunstall since Billy had been stealing his stock. Billy looked upon the Englishman as a father figure, even though Tunstall was only five or six years older. Tunstall, on the other hand, said he saw good in Billy and was determined to make a man out of him. When the Lincoln County War for much of the New Mexico Territory backcountry and the Pecos Valley broke out soon afterwards, Tunstall became a leading figure on one side. Allied with Alexander McSween and cattle king John Chisum against the business interests of the county dominated by Lawrence G. Murphy, James J. Dolan and James H. Riley, Tunstall turned out to be the first major casualty, shot down in February 1878 by gunmen supposedly deputized to arrest him on a trumped up charge.

Billy saw the killing from a distance but could do nothing about it. He was deeply affected by Tunstall's murder. "He was the only man that ever treated me like I was free-born and white," he said. Over Tunstall's grave he swore, "I'll get every son-of-a-bitch who helped kill John if it's the last thing I do."

With that pledge Billy the Kid became the chief killer of the Lincoln County War, lining up with McSween. When the opposing forces besieged the town of Lincoln for several days, Billy killed numerous enemies. McSween was murdered during the siege and his death ended the war, as Chisum saw he lacked the power to win by himself. Billy the Kid went back to rustling and organized a gang of gunfighters and cutthroats. He robbed Chisum's cattle as well as others'. Eventually, Gov. Lew Wallace offered an amnesty to all participants in the Lincoln County War, and for a time, Billy considered accepting it. But he was leery of the "formality" of the trial he would have to face and stayed on the loose. He permanently lost his chance to go straight after killing a lawman.

Billy and his gang killed several more men over the next year or so but suffered their losses as well. Sheriff Pat Garrett stalked Billy and in one ambush killed Billy's close friend Tom O'Folliard, whom he mistook for the Kid. In December 1880 Charlie Bowdre died in an ambush at Stinking Springs, New Mexico Territory. Trapped by Garrett and his posse, Billy and several of his confederates were forced to surrender. Billy was convicted of the murder of Sheriff William Brady and sentenced to hang. Confined in a top-floor room of the Lincoln County Courthouse, he made a sensational escape, killing deputies James Bell, whom he liked, and sadistic Bob Olinger, whom he hated. He shot Olinger down like a dog in the street outside the courthouse and fled.

Billy was a hero to those who shared his sympathies in the Lincoln County War and to Mexicans, among whom he often hid out.

Finally, Garrett located Billy the Kid hiding at old Fort Sumner. When Billy walked into a darkened room, Garrett shot him down without giving him a chance to surrender. He was buried in a common grave with his two buddies, O'Folliard and Bowdre. The gravestone bore the inscription "Pals."

After Billy the Kid died, the legend-makers went to work. The first book about him appeared three weeks after his death. Most of his biographers probably had never been west of New York. Sheriff Garrett contributed a volume, which greatly

An enthusiastic *Police Gazette* artist was so awed by the Kid's exploits that he awarded him two right hands.

built up Billy and in the process, of course, the man who had gotten him. Serious students of Billy the Kid have been mystified by his place in the folklore of the country. His crimes were largely unimaginative and cold-blooded. He lacked the verve and style that marked Jesse James, for instance, and seldom inspired the loyalty that James did.

See also: *Charlie Bowdre, Patrick Floyd Garrett, Joe Grant, Lincoln County War, Tom O'Folliard, Robert Olinger, Dave Rudabaugh, John Tunstall.*

BINAGGIO, Charles (1909-1950): Political leader and murder victim

The murder of Charley Binaggio and his number one muscleman, Charley Gargotta, on April 6, 1950 shocked Kansas City, Mo., where Binaggio was the acknowledged political and crime boss. He was found stretched out in a swivel chair at the First District Democratic Club, his face blood-soaked and four bullets in his head. Garotta lay on the floor nearby, the same number of slugs in his head. Overlooking the grisly scene were large portraits of President Harry Truman and Gov. Forrest Smith. The bullet wounds in the heads of both men were

arranged in two straight rows, or "two deuces." In dice parlance, this is called Little Joe. It is also the insignia the underworld stamps on welshers when it wants the world to know that the murder was done by the mob. Clearly, Binaggio had welshed on a promise to the national crime syndicate.

Only 41 at the time of his murder, Binaggio was recognized as a political "comer." He had been born in Beaumont, Tex. As a youngster he became a drifter and was arrested twice in Denver for carrying a concealed weapon and for vagrancy. At age 23 Binaggio landed in Kansas City and joined the operations of North Side leader Johnny Lazia, who delivered votes for Democratic boss Tom Pendergast. Lazia's reward was control of gambling, vice, liquor and racing wires in the North Side. Binaggio continued to climb the criminal ladder even after Lazia's assassination in 1934. By 1944 he controlled all the North Side wards.

In 1946 Binaggio made a splash on the national scene when President Truman ordered a purge of Congressman Roger C. Slaughter for voting against administration bills. Truman called in Jim Pendergast, the late Tom's nephew successor, and ordered the nomination of Enos Axtell. Slaughter lost in the primary, but the *Kansas City Star* soon charged wholesale ballot fraud. During several probes launched on both the national and state level, a woman election watcher was shot to death on the porch of her home. Just before state hearings were scheduled to start, the safe at City Hall in Kansas City was dynamited and fraudulent ballot evidence was destroyed.

Both the ballot frauds and the City Hall bombing were believed to have been masterminded by Binaggio. However, he was never indicted and only one minor hanger-on, "Snags" Klein, went to prison, for a short term. Thereafter, a power struggle broke out between Jim Pendergast and Binaggio. The former proved to be lacking the astuteness of his late uncle and by 1948 it was obvious that Kansas City was becoming Binaggio's town. However, Binaggio still needed a lot of funds to beat Pendergast's entrenched machine, and he spread the word throughout the underworld that once his man was elected governor, he would give gambling and other "wide-open" interests free rein in the state. More than $200,000 flowed in from gangland sources to help Binaggio's plans. Forrest Smith was elected governor and Binaggio claimed credit. But Binaggio found he could not deliver on his promise to the underworld, a fact that was now common knowledge. A St. Louis newspaper broke the story that the understanding he had with the underworld called for opening up both Kansas City and St. Louis, but that the St. Louis police commissioner had blocked every one of his moves. Binaggio was forced to stall for time on his underworld agreement. The time expired, and it was obvious that Binaggio was in deep trouble. The mobs had realized that their $200,000 was a write-off. All that remained was the payoff. It was Little Joe for Binaggio and Gargotta.

BIOFF, Willie Morris (1900-1955): Labor racketeer and stool pigeon

A noted union racketeer and ex-pimp, Willie Bioff masterminded, with George Browne, the Chicago syndicate's extortion of an estimated $6.5 million from the Hollywood movie studios in the 1930s. Bioff was eventually convicted because of the crusading activities of right-wing columnist Westbrook Pegler, who discovered Bioff as a "guest of honor" at a lavish Hollywood party and remembered him as a two-bit panderer during his own apprenticeship as a Chicago reporter.

Bioff became a pimp no later than the age of 10, when he began collecting money from other schoolboys for enjoying the favors of his "girls" on a table at the local poolhall. By his mid-teens Bioff had an entire string of prostitutes working for him and was a familiar sight in Chicago's vice-ridden Levee area, wearing gaudy silk shirts and offering a girl for every purpose. While Bioff knew the virtue of paying for police protection, some of his activities proved just too much, and he served jail time for brutalizing his prostitutes. Yet somehow, as just seemed to happen in Chicago, Bioff escaped serving one six-month term he was sentenced to.

In the meantime, while maintaining his vice activities, Bioff moved up in the Capone mob as a union slugger, a job he performed so well that he was promoted steadily up the ladder, eventually being installed by the mob as president of the International Alliance of Theatrical Stage Employes and Motion Picture Operators. In this position, Bioff teamed up with George Browne to terrorize studio executives by threatening to shut down all moviemaking. The result was enormous payoffs by the movie moguls to Bioff, Browne and numerous other members of the Capone syndicate.

It was at this stage that Pegler started digging into Bioff's record and publicizing his unsavory past. Despite charges of Pegler's antiunionism, Bioff was forced to serve his old six-month vice sentence, although while doing his time in the Chicago House of Correction, he was provided with a private office and a tub of iced beer renewed each day.

Thanks to Pegler's efforts Bioff and Browne were convicted in 1941 of violating antiracketeering laws. Each of the pair drew a 10-year sentence. It was not a fate either appreciated, and both testified for the government in the prosecution of many top members of the syndicate, men like Frank Nitti, Phil D'Andrea, Paul Ricca, Charlie Gioe, Lou Kaufman and John Roselli.

The defense attacked Bioff's character and demanded to know why he had lied to previous grand juries. "I am just a low, uncouth person," he replied sadly. "I'm a low-type sort of man."

Because of his testimony the top members of the Chicago syndicate went to prison. The exception was Nitti who committed suicide instead. As these crime figures went in, Bioff and Browne went out. Browne ran and hid. Bioff also traveled, finally settling in Phoenix, Ariz. under the name of William Nelson.

Bioff's nature was to court the centers of power, and in 1952 he and his wife contributed $5,000 to the senatorial campaign of a department store heir named Barry Goldwater. After the election a warm friendship developed between Arizona's new senator and Bioff-Nelson. Just two weeks before Bioff's untimely demise, Goldwater, an accomplished Air Force pilot, flew Bioff and his wife to Las Vegas and back. On November 4, 1955, Bioff went out the kitchen door of his home and climbed into his small pickup truck. His wife waved to him. Bioff waved back, then tramped on the starter. There was a blast and a flash. The truck was demolished, as was Willie Bioff. It was a little late in coming, but syndicate vengeance had been exacted.

See also: *Procuring*

BIRD Cage Theatre: Tombstone night spot and "shooting gallery"

One of the more-wicked establishments in Tombstone, Ariz. during the 1880s was the Bird Cage Theatre. A performance of *H.M.S. Pinafore* might grace its stage while harlots plied their trade in 12 tiny balcony boxes. An act more in keeping with the place was the appearance of Fatima, who belly-danced to raucous Western acclaim in 1882

The owners of the theater, Bill and Lottie Hutchinson,

made it a rule that the audience had to check their shooting irons upon entering, but unfortunately, the regulation was not always obeyed, often with tragic consequences. In one wild shoot-out 12 men were reportedly left dead. Care was required in the selection of the repertoire, since if too evil a villain appeared on the stage, he might soon be forced to dodge lead from outraged members of the audience. There is no accurate record of the numbers of fatalities that occurred in the Bird Cage, but while it never equaled the fabulous Oriental Saloon as a shooting gallery, it certainly provided the setting for a good many death scenes on both sides of the footlights.

See also: *Tombstone, Arizona Territory.*

BIRDMAN Of Alcatraz: See Robert Franklin Stroud.

BISBEE (Arizona) Kidnapping

Without doubt, the largest mass kidnapping in American history occurred in 1917 in Bisbee, Ariz., once the greatest copper boom town in the country. In that year the Industrial Workers of the World, or Wobblies, staged a general strike, which, given the economy of the town, meant primarily a strike against Phelps-Dodge Copper. What happened next is not in dispute by labor historians. The company bankrolled an operation by Sheriff Harry Wheeler that gathered the largest posse in the West's history to run the strikers out of town. In a midnight raid more than 2,000 strikers were rounded up; some 1,200 of them were jammed into cattle cars and shipped off across the desert into New Mexico. This mass abduction broke the strike and started the Wobblies on a steady decline within the union movement. As for the criminal aspects—the action was clearly an act of kidnapping—Phelps-Dodge was credited with using its gigantic financial power in Arizona to ensure that not a single man went to prison for the outrageous act.

BISBEE Massacre: Robbery carnage

Probably few robberies exercised the West more than what became known as the infamous Bisbee Massacre, which some historians have claimed marked the swing of the Arizona Territory from anarchy to law and order.

On the evening of December 8, 1883, five masked men rode into the mining town of Bisbee and dismounted at the store of A. A. Castanda. They wore long overcoats to cover the rifles they carried. Two of the men entered the store, which was about to close. There were six customers still inside and one of them, J. C. Tappenier, reached for his gun when he saw the intruders produce their rifles. He went down in a blast of rifle fire that alerted the whole town. As curious townsfolk poured into the street to see what was going on, three lookouts outside the store started shooting to clear them away. Two men and a woman were killed in the raking fire, bringing the total death count to four, with several others wounded, before the five thieves rode out of town with $3,000 in cash and various pieces of jewelry.

A sheriff's posse from Tombstone took off in pursuit of the bandits, numbering among its ranks a tracker named John Heath. Some thought Heath did an excellent job of getting the posse to run in circles. Suspicion also focused on him for a number of other reasons, one being a report that he had been suspected of heading an outlaw gang some time earlier in Brewery Gulch.

In the view of many in the Old West, confession did not cleanse the soul. John Heath was dragged from Tombstone's jail and lynched for his part in the Bisbee Massacre despite the fact that his confession led to the capture of five other perpetrators.

These suspicions were not unfounded. Once jailed and subjected to some persuasion, Heath admitted knowing about the robbery plans. It was not clear whether he was merely in on the planning or had indeed done most of it, but in any event, Heath was now "cooperative" and spilled out the names of those involved: Daniel Kelley, Daniel Dowd, James "Tex" Howard, William Delaney and Comer Sample. After some months all five were rounded up given a speedy trial and sentenced to hang.

Heath, without whose admissions the others would not have been apprehended, was extended leniency and given a life sentence. Arizonians found it difficult to accept this concept of law and order. Western beliefs did not hold that a man's soul was made any less black through confession. On February 22, 1884 an irate mob of several hundred broke into the Tombstone jail, and when they were finished, John Heath dangled lifeless from a telegraph pole. In the cemetery at Tombstone, Heath's marker can still be read. "John Heath, taken from County Jail and lynched by Bisbee mob in Tombstone, Feb. 22nd, 1884."

See also: *Daniel Kelley.*

BISMARCK Hall: New York dive

Of all the vicious establishments that abounded in New York's Bowery in the post-Civil War period, one that had a uniquely Old World flavor was Bismarck Hall. Low physically as well as morally, the Hall had an annex in a string of cavelike rooms buried under the sidewalk where ladies employed in the dive could entertain gentlemen. Following an Old World custom, the operator of the dive supposedly often "bought" his inmates by paying them a small sum of money binding them to him for several years. While such an agreement, of course, would have had little standing in court, its terms were quite well enforced; the girls were not allowed off the premises unless they left a "deposit" that guaranteed their return. Bismarck Hall achieved a measure of renown when Grand Duke Alexis of Russia, visiting it in the 1870s while slumming, or, as the practice was then known, "elephant hunting," recognized a Russian countess who had fallen on hard times and was working there as a "waiter girl." According to the story, he bought the freedom of this unnamed noblewoman and took her back to Russia and her former position of grace.

BLACK Bart (1830-1917?): Stagecoach robber

One of the most colorful, daring and unconventional bandits of the Old West was Charles E. Bolton, better known as Black Bart, the poet laureate of outlawry. By the best count, he pulled 27 stagecoach holdups in California from 1874 to 1883. But he prided himself on never robbing a stagecoach passenger. After each robbery Black Bart would send the coach on its way and then stroll off on foot, since he greatly disliked horses. Wearing a duster and a flour-sack mask and carrying an empty shotgun, he would step out into the road and shout to the stage driver, "Throw down your box or die." Sometimes he would issue orders to his men in the bushes to open fire if the driver refused. The driver would see a half-dozen rifles in the shadows and would do as he was told. Actually, the rifles were never more than broomstick handles. After each holdup Black Bart would leave behind bits of doggerel that won him a reputation as a poet. One typical poem read:

> Here I lay me down to sleep
>
>> To await the coming morrow
>> Perhaps success, perhaps defeat
>> And everlasting sorrow
>>
>> I've labored long and hard for bred (sic)
>> For honor and for riches
>> But on my corns too long you've tred
>> You fine-haired Sons of Bitches
>>
>> Let come what will, I'll try it on
>> My condition can't be worse

> And if there's money in that box
> 'Tis munny in my purse.
> Black Bart, the Po-8.

Black Bart was captured on November 3, 1883, after a robbery that had netted him $4,800. A rider came by during the robbery and fired at the outlaw, forcing him to flee so rapidly he dropped his handkerchief. Detectives traced the laundry mark, F.O.X. 7, until it led them to a man named Charles E. Bolton in San Francisco. The *San Francisco Bulletin* described him as "a distinguished-looking gentleman who walked erect as a soldier and carried a gold-knobbed cane." At first, Bolton denied being Black Bart but finally confessed. He was sentenced to 10 years in San Quentin but was released on January 21, 1888, with time off for good behavior. When a reporter asked him if he intended to go on writing poetry, Black Bart snapped, "Young man, didn't you just hear me say I will commit no more crimes?" According to the report, which had a romantic air, Wells Fargo settled an annuity on Black Bart for his agreement to rob no more stagecoaches. There is no additional information about him. One account had him living out his days in Nevada, and another said he died in 1917 in New York City.

BLACK Dahlia (1925-1947): Murder victim

The 1947 case of Elizabeth Short, better known as the Black Dahlia, is unsolved but still actively pursued, principally because it has had more "confessions" than any other case in California history.

In a sense, Elizabeth Short was typical of the young girls who flooded Los Angeles: she was from a broken home, with an unhappy lovelife, consumed with a desire for a Hollywood career. She had, as they said in Hollywood, a gimmick. She always dressed completely in black. It was one way to grab attention, but she certainly had others. She understood the meaning of the casting couch and would go to bed with any man who had even the most tenuous connection with the studios. They started calling her the Black Dahlia, and in the zany world of moviemaking, she might eventually have gained enough of a reputation to make it despite a lack of acting ability.

On January 15, 1947 her nude corpse was found in a garbage-strewn vacant lot in a Los Angeles suburb. She had been badly mutilated and her body had been crudely cut in half. Deep into the thigh of the 22-year-old victim, the killer had carved the initials "BD," presumably for Black Dahlia. It took the police some time to identify the severed corpse as Elizabeth Short, or the Black Dahlia, but no time at all to make several arrests. The murder seemed to excite the public and produced a rash of confessions. In fact, the police were overwhelmed by men and women coming forward to claim credit for the brutal act. Most of the confessions were soon discounted because the self-proclaimed murderers demonstrated a lack of knowledge about various aspects of the case. Yet, still more confessors came forward. One woman walked into a station house and said "The Black Dahlia stole my man, so I killed her and cut her up." A husband whose wife had deserted him said he was the killer in the hope that if he made himself notorious and got his picture in the papers, his wife would return to him. Another sent the police a letter made out of pasted-up letters from magazines, offering to meet them and give them information. He signed the message "Black Dahlia Avenger." But he never kept the rendezvous. Another writer sent a message reading: "Here are Dahlia's belongings. Letter to follow." Enclosed were Elizabeth Short's Social Security card and birth certificate and her address book—with one page missing. Unfortunately, no letter followed. The most promising confession appeared to be that made by a 29-year-old Army corporal, who talked loudly and convincingly of knowing her. He appeared quite knowledgeable about the facts of the case and insisted, "When I get drunk, I get rough with women." After an intensive investigation, the police wrote him off as an unbalanced personality. As the confessions continued to pour in, all efforts to keep an accurate count were dropped, and to this day the Black Dahlia case remains unsolved.

BLACK Hand: Extortion racket

"The Society of the Black Hand" was one of the sillier journalistic hoaxes of its time. Contrary to what newspapers of the era published, there was no such Society of the Black Hand, but that was undoubtedly of little comfort to Black Hand victims.

Recalcitrant victims of this extortion racket were shot, poisoned, dynamited or maimed; more pliant targets willingly turned over their funds after receiving a demand for money usually outlined at the bottom with a hand that had been dipped in black ink, a menacing sight sure to produce an icy feeling around a victim's heart. Actually, there once had been a Society of the Black Hand—not in New York, not in Italy, not even in Sicily, but in Spain. It originated in the days of the Inquisition, when like such genuine Italian secret societies as the Camorra and Mafia, it was organized as a force of good, trying to fight the oppression of its day. In later centuries the Mafia and the Camorra turned into criminal bodies, while the Society of the Black Hand in Spain simply withered away. But for New York City newspapermen, *La Mano Nera,* or the Black Hand, had a nice ring to it; it was easy to remember and lurid. Thus was reborn the Black Hand. Reporters and some detectives wasted their time trying to trace suspects' family trees to tie them to some Black Hand Society. In reality, the Black Hand was simply an extortion racket practiced in the Little Italy sections of numerous American cities. The senders would threaten the recipient or his family and would warn that they would kill or maim a family member as a starter. Usually, the letter was signed with some sort of ominous symbol, such as a skull and crossbones or knives, hatchets or sabers dripping blood. Once the newspapers publicized the symbol of a black hand, that symbol became standard.

Certainly, Black Handers, many of whom were Mafia and Camorra gangsters, often killed if they did not receive their payoff, although more often they might at first catch a victim's child and cut off a finger as a convincer. A typical victim of a Black Hand operation was a wealthy Brooklyn butcher named Gaetano Costa, who in 1905 got a Black Hand letter that read: "You have more money than we have. We know of your wealth and that you are alone in this country. We want $1,000, which you are to put in a loaf of bread and hand to a man who comes in to buy meat and pulls out a red handkerchief." Costa, unlike his neighbors, refused to pay and was shot dead one morning as he worked behind his counter. His killers were never caught, although it was suspected that gangsters working for Lupo the Wolf, a Black Hand chieftain in Italian Harlem, were behind it.

Lupo was regarded as the biggest Black Hander in New York City, and years later, an infamous Murder Stable, which he owned on East 107th Street in Manhattan, was discovered to be the burial place for at least 60 victims, many of them individuals who had refused to pay Black Hand extortion demands. Lupo's power sprang from his shrewd use of terror. Strutting around Italian Harlem, the man exuded cruelty, and it was the custom for residents, at the very mention of his name, to cross themselves and extend their fingers in an effort to ward off his spell.

Within Italian-American society almost anyone could be a Black Hand victim. While on a triumphal engagement at the Metropolitan Opera shortly before World War I, tenor Enrico Caruso got a Black Hand demand for $2,000, which he paid, regarding an appeal to the police as useless if not foolhardy. However, his payment of the money led to a new demand for $15,000 more. This time the tenor notified the authorities because he realized paying the money would only lead to further, even greater demands. Under police direction, Caruso left the money beneath the steps of a factory as the extortionists had ordered. When two prominent Italian businessmen tried to retrieve the loot, they were arrested. Both went to prison in one of the few successful prosecutions of Black Hand criminals. Caruso was kept under guard for a number of years thereafter on the theory that he faced Black Hand retribution, but it never came, because his extortioners were no more than independent operators who had no connection with a crime family or the nonexistent Society of the Black Hand.

A New Orleans Black Hander, Paul Di Cristina, considered himself so immune from interference by the law that he delivered his Black Hand notes in person. His victims always quaked and paid—all except Pietro Pepitone, a grocer. He informed Di Cristina's strong-arm men that he would not pay. So the boss came around personally to collect. When Di Cristina alighted from his wagon in front of the grocer's store, Pepitone picked up a shotgun, stepped out on the sidewalk and blasted the Black Hander to death.

It has been estimated that at least 80 different Black Hand gangs operated in Chicago, totally unrelated to one another except that their messages to their victims were always the same, "Pay or Die."

Virtually all the Black Hand gangs were wiped out or disappeared around 1920. The leaders of the Cardinelli Black

Handers were executed in Chicago; the DiGiovanni mob leaders were convicted in Kansas City, Lupo the Wolf got 30 years in New York, albeit for counterfeiting rather than Black Hand crimes. Some observers of the crime scene have attributed the decline of the Black Hand racket to the rise of the big-money rackets under the scourge of Prohibition; there was so much more money available in bootlegging, rumrunning and hijacking that the extortionists couldn't be bothered anymore with what was by comparison a penny-ante racket. However, that was hardly the whole answer. The fact was that Prohibition brought the Italian immigrants into close contact with the feared police for the first time. Most Little Italy sections around the country turned alcohol making into a "cottage industry," with its attendant odors, smoke and fumes. That meant the neighborhood policeman had to be paid off. And when you paid off a man, you had the right to ask him for a favor, such as taking care of this Black Hander who was bothering you.

See also: *Enrico Caruso, Death Corner, Lupo the Wolf, Shotgun Man, White Hand Society.*

BLACK Maria: Police van

The Black Maria (pronounced Ma-ri-ah) police van originated in Boston, Mass. In 1847 a newspaper informed its readers that a "new Black Maria" had been put into service. There is no record of Black Marias necessarily being painted black; the origin of the term most likely referred to huge a huge black woman, Maria Lee, who ran a lodging house for sailors during the period. Since the woman was generally called Black Maria and her establishment was among the most unruly in the city, it was assumed that a police van loaded with boisterous offenders was coming from Black Maria's.

BLACK Sox Scandal: Baseball betting coup

Before 1919 the fixing of baseball games for betting purposes was by no means unheard of. But in that year it went too far: the "unthinkable" happened; a World Series was fixed by eight star players for the Chicago White Sox who managed to lose the series to the underdog Cincinnati Redlegs five games to three (the series that year was being played in an experimental nine-game set).

All the details of what was to be called the Black Sox Scandal were never fully exposed, primarily because there was an attempted cover-up by the baseball establishment, in general, and White Sox owner Charles A. Comiskey, in particular. The offending players were not even suspended until there were only three games left to play in the following season, when confessions by three players to the grand jury forced Comiskey to act.

The throwing of the series appears to have been thought of initially by Chicago first baseman Charles Arnold "Chick" Gandil, who passed the word to Boston gamblers that he could line up several teammates for a lucrative killing. The other players involved were Eddie Cicotte and Claude Williams, star pitchers who between them had won 52 games during the season; left fielder Shoeless Joe Jackson; center fielder Oscar Felsch; third baseman George "Buck" Weaver; shortstop Charles "Swede" Risbergand; and utility infielder Fred McMullin. The gamblers first approached were Joseph "Sport" Sullivan of Boston and William "Sleepy Bill" Burns of New York. Because they felt they needed more capital to finance a gigantic killing, they approached the country's leading gambler, Arnold "the Brain" Rothstein. It is debatable whether or not Rothstein entered the plot or turned them down and then simply went ahead and bet at least $60,000 on Cincinnati (and collected $270,000) because he knew the fix was in and saw no need to pay out any bribe money himself. In any event, the main operator behind the fix became Abe Attell, the ex-featherweight boxing champion. A caller to Attell's hotel suite in Cincinnati later told of seeing money stacked on every horizontal surface in the room, on tables, dresser tops and chair seats, after the Reds won the first game.

In the first two games Cicotte's invincible "shine ball" failed him and he was knocked out in the fourth inning; Williams was uncharacteristically wild and lost 4-2. By the end of the second game, rumors of the fix were rampant and the Reds were big favorites to take the series. It was impossible to find a professional bookmaker who would bet on Chicago, that action being played strictly by amateur bettors. It took a year-long grand jury investigation to crack the case, with confessions coming from Jackson, Cicotte and Williams. Comiskey was forced to fire all the players except Gandil, who had already "retired."

Testimony showed that most of the players had gotten $5,000 for their parts in the fix, while Gandil had kept $35,000 for himself. How many hundreds of thousands the gamblers made was never really determined. When several of the players left the grand jury room, a group of small boys awaited them. One said to Shoeless Joe Jackson: "It ain't true, is it, Joe?"

"Yes, boys," the outfielder replied, "I'm afraid it is."

The conversation has come down in folklore as the boy wailing plaintively, "Say it ain't so, Joe."

Another bit of folklore is that the baseball establishment excised this cancer as quickly as possible. In fact, the baseball magnates provided legal aid to the players, and indeed, the jury acquitted them and carried some of the defendants out of the courtroom on their shoulders. However, Judge Kenesaw Mountain Landis, appointed commissioner to oversee the integrity of "the Game," was not satisfied. He never let any of the players don a Comiskey uniform again.

See also: *Arnold Rothstein.*

BLACKBEARD (?-1718): Pirate

No pirate in American history enjoys quite as ferocious a reputation as Edward Teach (or Thack or Thatch) of the 14 wives and the pigtailed beard. A contemporary pirate historian, Capt. Charles Johnson, offered the following description:

> This beard was black, which he suffered to grow of an extravagant length, as to breadth, it came up to his eyes. He was accustomed to twist it with ribbons, in small tails . . . and

J.B. POWER. N.Y.

An old print depicts the bloody end of Blackbeard the Pirate.

turn them about his ears. In time of action he wore a sling over his shoulders, with three brace of pistols hanging in holsters like bandoliers, and stuck slow-burning lighted matches under his hat, which, appearing on each side of his face, his eyes naturally looking fierce and wild, made him altogether such a figure that imagination cannot form an idea of a fury from hell to look more frightful.

Not much is known about Blackbeard's early life. He was generally believed to have been born in Bristol, England, although some claimed he was from Jamaica or the Carolinas and "of very creditable parents." Blackbeard himself boasted his parents were even bigger rascals than he, keeping a grog-shop and specializing in giving sailors knockout drops and then shanghaiing them. In any event, Blackbeard went to sea at a young age and served on English privateers during Queen Anne's War (1702-13), eventually gathering a group of cut-throats on a ship of his own. When peace came, Blackbeard turned pirate and came to command five ships and crews totaling 400 to 500. By 1716 Blackbeard enjoyed the protection of Carolina Gov. Charles Eden, who thereafter shared in a portion of the booty taken. Blackbeard preyed on shipping all along the American coast line from New England down to the West Indies. In one of his more daring raids, he once blockaded the port of Charleston, S. C., finally accepting a ransom in drugs and medications.

Under a pardon granted by Gov. Eden, Blackbeard became a familiar figure in what is now North Carolina. At the time he had 13 wives, scattered around various ports. In Bath, N.C. he took bride number 14, a blonde-haired girl just turned 15. The marriage barely outlasted the honeymoon when Blackbeard brought a number of his ruffians along for a visit at his new in-laws' plantation. His young wife finally fled and hid with friends. Despite the pirates' lavish spending, the people of Bath soon were disenchanted with Blackbeard, finding that he and his crew made free with their houses and women and demanded all kinds of requisitions from them. Despairing because of the pirate's close ties to the royal governor, several Carolinians appealed to Gov. Alexander Spotswood of Virginia for help. Spotswood could not interfere in another colony but resolved to do something about Blackbeard at sea, since the pirate was notorious for attacking Virginian shipping. Spotswood commissioned a young lieutenant named Robert Maynard to conduct a hunt. Maynard finally located the pirate at anchor near Ocracoke Island, off North Carolina. On November 21, 1718 Blackbeard was killed in a fierce battle in which he took five bullets and 25 cutlass wounds before a seaman struck him from behind and sliced his head off. When Maynard sailed back to Virginia, Blackbeard's bloody head was hung by the hair from the bowsprit of his ship for all to see.

Stories of Blackbeard's buried treasure have tantalized fortune hunters for 250 years. Legend places some of his many hoards in such locations as Ocracoke Island; the Isles of Shoals off New Hampshire; Plum Point, N.C.; under the Blackbeard Tree on the island of New Providence in the Bahamas; Ossabaw Island Ga.; under a walnut in Burlington, N.J.; and the island of Trinidad. None has ever been found.

See also: *Major Stede Bonnet, Piracy.*

BLACKMAIL

Blackmail, the extortion of money from a victim by threats of public disclosure, censure or exposure to ridicule, is not a frequent crime, if judged by the numbers reported to the police. In one year the New York district attorney reported only four cases had reached his office. However, during that same period three of the larger detective agencies in the city handled more than 50 cases, none of which had been reported to the authorities—and at the time, there were also 300 private detectives in the city. Since even a small agency will get eight or 10 blackmail cases a year, it is evident that police statistics on the crime are meaningless, with perhaps only one in 20 or 50 cases reported. Furthermore, there is no way of measuring how many other victims are too frightened even to enlist the service of a private agency and instead pay off.

Most blackmail cases are based on modern versions of the badger game and involve the sexual misadventures of the victim, complete with pictures. The second largest category is probably homosexual cases, and many of the remainder relate to business shenanigans. A classic example of the latter involved a Brooklyn businessman who faked company expenses to beat the Internal Revenue Service on his income. Unfortunately for him, the businessman let his secretary help with the doctoring, and shortly afterward, the secretary decided she would work only from 11:30 a.m. until 3:00 p.m., with two hours or so for lunch. She doubled her own salary, the balance being off the books. Ironically, the secretary ran afoul of the tax men and the blackmail case came to light.

Many blackmailers are free lancers such as a brother and sister team who blackmailed a university professor in Massachusetts for $21,000 by claiming that he had fathered the woman's son or a prostitute who milked the son of a former governor for $40,000. However, there have been a number of organized blackmail rings. The most successful of these was the Forcier-Gaffney gang, which extracted at least $2 million from wealthy homosexuals over a period of 15 years. The ring was smashed when one victim finally had the courage to go to the police. Organized crime often uses blackmail in its bankruptcy scams, first getting something on a businessman and using it as a wedge to become his "partner." At the petty end of professional blackmailers was a Midwestern ring that concentrated on housewives who shopped in supermarkets. They spied on the women until they spotted one slipping small items into her purse or coat pocket. Outside the store they would confront her under the guise of being police detectives. They would settle for all the money the woman had on her plus, of course, the groceries.

Blackmail is a crime with a long history. According to the Greek historian Xenophon, blackmailing was so pervasive some 2,300 years ago that many prominent and wealthy citizens of Athens went into exile to escape the exactions of its perpetrators. He also tells us of another victim who subsequently lost all his money in a commercial venture and thus, happily, no longer was compelled to live in fear of the blackmailers. Even today that is probably the most foolproof protection.

BLISS Bank Ring: Criminal-police alliance

Crime's golden age in America started with the end of the Civil War, as thousands of wastrels and rogues schooled in the rough-and-tumble of wartime criminality came home determined never to work for a living again. While great gangs had existed in the cities long before the war, the crime specialist emerged during the postwar period. Mobs formed to practice one particular brand of crime, and among the most highly rewarded were the bank burglar gangs. Since the great street gangs had often allied themselves with political protectors and carried out many chores for them, such as winning elections through voter intimidation, it was only logical that the new crime mobs would work with the authorities.

The Bliss Bank Ring, bossed by two leading thieves, George Miles Bliss and Mark Shinburn, was probably the biggest bank mob to appreciate the virtue of working with the law. It was common practice for the Bliss gang to pay off the police with about 10 percent of the loot, somewhat less if the score was exceptionally large. "If we spoil them with too much money," Shinburn said, "they won't be hungry for more."

They hardly needed to worry. The appetite of the police seemed insatiable, and they often squabbled about their individual shares. Capt. John Young, Chief of the Detective Bureau of the New York Police Department, finally quit in disgust rather than share the $17,500 cut given him by the Bliss forces for one robbery. The extent of the gang's involvement in police bribery was perhaps best exhibited after Young's departure. Bliss lobbied openly for Detective Jim Irving to be put in charge of the bureau, personally stating his case to Boss Tweed of Tammany Hall. The friction over bribes within the bureau was such, he warned, that some disgruntled member might go to reform-minded Samuel Tilden with the facts. "Put Detective Jim Irving at the head of the Detective Bureau," Bliss told Tweed, "and you'll switch the whole business to safety. If not, I can't say what will happen."

Tweed saw the merits in Bliss' argument, and Irving was given the post, whereupon the bank ring entered its most prosperous period. With the cooperation of the police, the ring pulled off the famous $2.75 million raid on the Ocean Bank located at Fulton and Greenwich streets, in 1869. The following breakdown of bribes paid to police was revealed later by confessions:

James Irving, head of Detective Bureau	$17,000
John McCord, detective	$17,000
George Radford, detective	$17,000
James Kelso, detective	$17,000
Philip Farley, detective	$17,000

John Jordan, captain of the Sixth Precinct and later	
superintendent of police	$17,000
George Elder, detective	$17,000
Inspector Johnson	$1,800
One other detective	$1,000
Frank Houghtaling, clerk of Jefferson Market	
Police Court	$10,000
John Browne	$500
Total	$132,000

For this sum of money the police not only did not harrass the Bliss gang but also performed yeoman service in trying to pin the job on the George Leonidas Leslie gang, an outfit notorious for being niggardly in the payment of bribes.

The Bliss Ring survived even the fall of Boss Tweed in 1873, but when Thomas F. Byrnes became head of the Detective Bureau in 1880 and outlawed the alliance between the police and the bank burglars, the gang fell apart. Many members were arrested and Bliss himself was captured and sentenced to prison for the robbery of a Vermont bank. Penniless when released, he spent his final years writing exposes of crime. Only Shinburn survived the ring's demise, fleeing to Europe, where for years he lived the life of a count, having bought the title with the proceeds of some of his crimes.

See also: *Mark Shinburn.*

BLOODY Angle: New York murder site

During the great tong wars fought in the early 20th century in New York's Chinatown, the area became a sort of an armed camp. Mott Street became the stronghold of the On Leong Tong, while Pell Street belonged to the Hip Sing Tong. Doyers Street was a sort of no man's land with a certain sharp turn that journalists labeled the Bloody Angle. The police later estimated that more men were murdered there than at any other spot in New York City and most likely the entire U.S. Only the foolhardy ventured past it after dark. The Bloody Angle was ideal for an ambush, with too abrupt a turn for a pedestrian to see ahead. Armed with a snickersnee, or hatchet, sharpened to a razor's edge, a *boo how doy,* or hatchet man, could strike before the victim had time to cry out, lay the weapon across his throat and flee through an arcade to safety.

See also: *Ah Hoon, Bow Kum, Mock Duck, Snickersnee, Tong Wars.*

BLOODY Tubs: Criminal gang

One of the most vicious gangs in Baltimore, Md. during the mid-1800s, the Bloody Tubs sold their election-influencing services to the highest political bidder. They earned their name from their habit of dunking political opponents in the slaughterhouse tubs. Like another vicious gang of criminals, the Bloody Inks, whose turf extended from Baltimore to Philadelphia, they so terrified voters with their brutal methods that many persons were afraid to come to the polls.

The heyday of both the Bloody Tubs and the Bloody Inks ran from 1857 to 1870. By the end of this period, their crimes were so outrageous that even the most callous politicians could

no longer offer them protection or make use of their services. Stripped of their political protection, the Bloody Tubs fell to the mercy of police "head smashers" and retired from the field.

BLUE-SKY Laws

In 1911 the state of Kansas passed the first law to protect the public from the marketing of deceitful stock or shares in worthless, often imaginary enterprises. The blue-sky nickname was given to them by a state legislator who demanded that the rules placed on investment concerns "should be as far reaching as the blue sky." The Kansas law and those enacted by other states were vigorously challenged by investment and banking interests until the Supreme Court upheld them in a 1917 ruling. The High Court bolstered the nickname by denouncing fraudulent investment schemes "which have no more basis than so many feet of 'blue sky.'"

BODIE, California: Lawless gold-mining camp

Gold placers were first discovered in Bodie in 1859, but since the town was isolated on the eastern slope of the Sierra Nevada, it didn't boom until 1870, when rich veins started showing up. The population quickly mushroomed to some 15,000, drawn by what would eventually prove to be some $100 million worth of ore over the next two decades. With fortunes to be made and stolen overnight, Bodie became perhaps the most lawless, corrupt and vice-ridden town in the West. Three breweries working 24 hours a day, were needed to service some 35 saloons. There were also some 60 bordellos in action on a 24-hour basis, home, according to one historian's account, to no less than 1,800 prostitutes. With a total population of only 15,500, it was clear what the remaining 13,200 were doing when they weren't drinking, digging or killing each other. Violent deaths in such an atmosphere were understandably frequent, and in fact, it was said that Bodie always had "a man for breakfast." Men were killed for their gold in arguments over who paid for the last beer, for being line-jumpers at brothels and, now and then, in disputes about the facts of some previous killing. When one entire Sunday passed without a fatality, folks in Bodie spoke with pride of the "Christian spirit" that had overtaken the town.

Bodie did not live long enough to be tamed. After 1880 the gold finds became less lucrative and by the turn of the century much of the town was empty and forlorn. Some slight mining activity continued up to World War II, but most of the town's well-preserved but unused wooden structures were burned in a fire in 1932. Today Bodie is nothing more than a ghost town with a bloody past.

See also: *Badman from Bodie*

BOLBER-PETRILLO Murder Ring

The Bolber-Petrillo murder ring, which reaped a fortune from insurance killings in the Italian community of Philadelphia during the 1930's, is an excellent example of why murder statistics are not to be trusted. The ring disposed of an estimated 30 to 50 victims before police suspicions over just one or two brought about the killers' downfall. From a statistical viewpoint, the case is often cited as an indication that the generally accepted figure of 20,000 murder victims a year may be greatly understated and that a truer figure would be 20,000 known homicides a year and 20,000 undiscovered ones.

Neither Dr. Morris Bolber nor his two cousins, Paul and Herman Petrillo, were much interested in such a statistical overview, being content to rake in a goodly income from the occupation of murder during the Depression, a period when most forms of business were hardly rewarding.

The original murder scheme was hatched by Dr. Bolber and Paul Petrillo in 1932, when they decided to have Petrillo seduce the wife of one of the doctor's patients, Mrs. Anthony Giscobbe. The woman had often complained to Dr. Bolber of her husband's infidelities. When she fell in love with Petrillo, she also rather enthusiastically agreed to a plan to kill her husband for the $10,000 insurance on his life. Since the errant Mr. Giscobbe often staggered home dead drunk, it was a relatively simple matter to undress him and leave him all night by an open window in the dead of winter. Eventually, the husband succumbed to pneumonia and the grieving widow and Dr. Bolber each netted $5,000. Perhaps the only sad development for the widow was that immediately upon completion of this financial transaction, Paul Petrillo lost all amorous interest in her. The slick-haired Petrillo had moved on to conquer new lonely wives, all of whom had husbands not long for this world.

Since the plotters found that few Italian husbands carried much, if any, insurance, they decided to add a new wrinkle to the operation by recruiting Petrillo's cousin, Herman Petrillo, an actor of some accomplishment with church groups, to impersonate the husbands and apply for insurance. Naturally, the wives were required to screen their husbands' mail and weed out all insurance correspondence. After a few premium payments were made, the husbands were efficiently dispatched. A roofer named Lorenzo was heaved off an eight-story building by the Petrillos in an on-the-job accident that doubled the payment on his life. To make the death more convincing, the Petrillos gave the roofer some French post cards before shoving him off the roof, making it rather obvious that the victim had been distracted by them when he misstepped.

After a dozen or so murders, the plotters recruited a valuable new accomplice, Carino Favato, a faith healer known as the Witch in her own bailiwick. The Witch had murdered three of her own husbands and apparently been consulted by female clients who wished to be rid of their spouses. The Witch poisoned them for a price. However, when Dr. Bolber pointed out that she had erred grievously by not adding the insurance wrinkle to the operation, the Witch was duly impressed, and readily agreed to a liaison and was able to supply the names of quite a few potential victims.

The ring went busily about committing murder, most often by poison or by Dr. Bolber's favorite method, "natural means," a canvas bag filled with sand that, when artfully applied, caused a fatal cerebral hemorrhage without any telltale marks. By 1937 the ring's death toll may easily have approached 50, at least 30 of which were rather well documented later on.

A recently released convict in need of money called on Herman Petrillo with a scheme by which they could both make money. Herman was not impressed, mainly because he already had a very good thing going. "Dig up somebody we can murder for some insurance and you can make some dough with us," he told the ex-convict earnestly. The ex-con was frightened of murder and informed the police. The ring's members were rounded up, and with unseemly eagerness, each agreed to inform on all the others in the hope of gaining leniency. Although some wives went to prison, others were permitted to turn state's evidence. Dr. Bolber and the Witch were sentenced to life imprisonment and the Petrillos were executed.

BOLLES, Don (1929-1976): Murder victim

Don Bolles, award-winning investigative reporter for the *Arizona Republic,* was fatally wounded when a bomb exploded in his car on June 2, 1976. He died 11 days later after having lost both legs and his right arm in the explosion. At the time of the explosion, Bolles told eyewitnesses and paramedics that he "was working on a Mafia story." He also said "John Adamson did it" and mentioned "Emprise," a Buffalo, N. Y. sports conglomerate that had been linked to organized crime and operated dog racing tracks in Arizona. Adamson was a 32-year-old professional racing dog owner.

In December, Adamson confessed a murder-for-hire plot, implicating Max Dunlap, a wealthy Pnoenix contractor, and James Robison, a Phoenix plumber. Adamson signed a statement alleging that Dunlap had hired him for $10,000 to kill Bolles because his writings had irritated Kemper Marley, Sr. a 74-year-old rancher and wholesale liquor distributor and one of the richest man in the state. Adamson also claimed Dunlap wanted the reporter killed before Bolles made a scheduled trip to San Diego the following month. The significance of the trip was never established. According to Adamson, he invited Bolles to a Phoenix hotel and then placed a bomb under his car. His statement further declared that Robison detonated the explosive charge from several hundred feet away by use of a radio transmitter.

After Bolles' death, a group of journalists called Investigative Reporters and Editors, Inc. came to the state and wrote about corruption and other criminal matters. Meanwhile, Adamson was allowed to plead guilty to second-degree murder and was sentenced to 20 years and two months. Dunlap and Robison were convicted in 1977 of first-degree murder, mainly on Adamson's testimony, and were sentenced to death. In February 1980 the convictions of the two men, still professing their innocence, were overturned by the Arizona Supreme Court because the trial judge had not permitted the defense to question Adamson about his criminal activities unrelated to the murder.

The state announced plans to retry the pair but in June 1980 asked for dismissal of the charges "without" prejudice because Adamson had refused to testify against them. Adamson indicated he wished a better deal for himself. He was retried alone and found guilty. The state announced plans to push for the death sentence and then allow Adamson to serve a life term if he would once more agree to testify. Many observers felt, however, the Bolles murder case would never be brought to a satisfactory conclusion.

Don Bolles remains the only American reporter believed to have been killed by what is considered "organized crime." *Chicago Tribune* reporter Jake Lingle suffered the same fate in 1930, but his death was not due to his endeavors as a journalist but rather to his own criminal involvement in the rackets.

BOLTON, Charles E.: See Black Bart.

BOMBINGS (Aerial): See Bootlegging.

BONANNO, Joseph C.: See Banana War.

BONNET, Jeanne (1841-1876): Gangster

Also known as the Little Frog Catcher, Jeanne Bonnet was a bizarre character who founded one of California's strangest criminal gangs, composed only of women. Jeanne got her nickname from the way she made an honest living—catching frogs in the marshes of San Mateo County. She had other unusual habits, including wearing men's clothing and regularly visiting the leading bagnios of the Barbary Coast. Whether her interests were truly or solely sexual became a cloudy issue in view of later events. She formed a gang of women recruited from the brothels, from which they all fled on a single night. A dozen of them joined her, holing up in a shack on the San Francisco waterfront south of Market Street. They lived by robbing, stickups, shoplifting and other forms of thievery, swearing off prostitution completely and having nothing to do with men, except, of course, as victims. The gang crumbled in less than a year, however, when Jeanne Bonnet was found shot to death with a bullet through her heart. The police concluded she had been murdered by one or more of the pimps whose ladies she had taken, thus ending an early, if criminal, experiment in women's liberation.

BONNET, Major Stede (c.1670-1718): The Gentleman Pirate

Aside from Blackbeard, Major Stede Bonnet, the so-called Gentleman Pirate, was probably the worst scourge in American coastal waters during the early 1700s, the halcyon years of piracy. Blackbeard's reputation for violence was largely exaggerated, while Bonnet was, in fact, more of a bloodthirsty killer than a gentleman. In pirate legend, it is Blackbeard who made victims walk the plank and then laughed hideously as the poor souls struggled in the water and finally submerged. Actually, it was never proven that Blackbeard made anyone walk the plank. Bonnet, on the other hand, did, having read hundreds of pirate stories and decided that was one of the things a bloody pirate should do.

The information on Bonnet's life is sketchy and not necessarily trustworthy. He was supposedly a man of good family and education who had fought in Queen Anne's War until it ended in 1713, when he retired in middle age to an estate he had bought on the island of Barbados. For no apparent reason, he decided to turn pirate. One historian of the period assures us he "was driven to it by a nagging wife." In any event, Bonnet went about becoming a buccaneer in a most unpiratical fashion: he bought and outfitted a vessel with his own money.

Shortly thereafter, he formed an alliance with Blackbeard, a valuable ally since he was under the protection of Carolina Gov. Charles Eden. Blackbeard's interest in Bonnet seemed limited to the latter's possession of a vessel that was worth adding to his fleet. Blackbeard insisted on bringing Bonnet aboard his own vessel, *Queen Anne's Revenge,* as number two in charge of all pirate activities. It apparently took Bonnet some time to figure out that Blackbeard had simply appropriated his ship and put one of his own men in charge.

Eventually, Bonnet got another vessel and started a one-man crime wave of the sea, looting ships from New England to the Spanish Main. Like Blackbeard, Bonnet maintained control of his crew through threats and violence. Bonnet's crew required merciless discipline, perhaps because the men had little respect for their captain's seamanship. Once when Blackbeard cheated Bonnet out of his share of booty and set sail, Bonnet started out for what is now North Carolina in pursuit but instead wound up in Bermuda.

When Blackbeard was killed on November 21, 1718, Bonnet became a most-hunted buccaneer along the Atlantic Coast. He lasted only until the following December 18, when he was hanged in Charleston. Bonnet had been easily captured after running his ship aground.

See also: *Blackbeard, Piracy.*

BONNEY, William H.: See Billy the Kid.

BONNIE And Clyde: Public enemies

As professional thieves, Bonnie and Clyde—Bonnie Parker and Clyde Barrow—never qualified as public enemies. Most of their thefts were of the minor-league variety: grocery stores, filling stations, luncheonettes and a few small-town banks. Their greatest haul was no more than $3,500. But they were brutal, killing at least 13 persons and escaping police ambushes with incredible pluck.

In a sense, Clyde Barrow was cut from a heroic mold, unlike many other gangsters of the 1930s, such as Baby Face Nelson, Pretty Boy Floyd and even John Dillinger. When trapped, he never abandoned his woman, often fighting his way back to her and leading her to safety. It was an odd relationship: a homosexual and a near nymphomaniac.

Born in extreme poverty in Texas in 1909, Clyde followed his older brother into crime, first stealing turkeys and then graduating to cars. The pair committed several robberies in the Dallas area. Finally, after holding up a gas station in Denton, Texas, they were forced to make a 90-mile-an-hour run from the police with Clyde behind the wheel. Buck was shot during the chase, and when Clyde wrecked the car in a ditch, he left Buck for the law, fearing his brother would bleed to death otherwise. Buck got five years.

In January 1930 Clyde met 90-pound, golden-haired 19-year-old Bonnie Parker, who was "sort of married" to a convict, Roy Thornton, serving 99 years for murder. Bonnie described herself in that period as "bored crapless." They started living together, and Clyde tried to support them by playing the saxophone. It was a futile effort and he quickly reverted to robbery. It wasn't long before Dallas lawmen arrested Clyde for a burglary in Waco: he had left his fingerprints behind. The judge sentenced him to two years.

Buck Barrow escaped from prison and he and his wife, Blanche, joined up with Bonnie. On a visit soon afterwards, Bonnie passed a narrow-handle .38 Colt through the jail bars to Clyde. After he made his break, Bonnie stayed put for a while to keep the law occupied. The law caught up with Clyde in Ohio.

This time Barrow was sent to the prison farm at Eastham, Tex., one of the most brutal institutions in the state. Clyde endured many tortures there and became a far more hardened criminal and a confirmed homosexual. He served 20 months, gaining a pardon after his mother tearfully pleaded his cause with Gov. Ross Sterling. Clyde Barrow said he would never see the inside of a prison again. "I'll die first," he said, and he was right.

Following Clyde's release, Bonnie teamed up with him on various robberies, but after a confrontation with the police, they became separated and Bonnie was caught. She served three months for the robbery of a car the couple had seized trying to escape. Clyde went on committing robberies and killed his first two lawmen in Atoka, Okla.

When Bonnie rejoined him, they fell in with a gunman named Ray Hamilton, an incorrigible young thief and killer who in many ways was a more spectacular criminal than Clyde. His relationship with Bonnie and Clyde, however, was more meaningful than just the addition of greater firepower on their holdups. Hamilton regularly slept with Bonnie and at times with Clyde as well. It was, by all accounts, a well-adjusted triangle, at least for brief periods. Eventually, the sexual pressures probably became too much for the three and Hamilton would break away. Both Bonnie and Clyde apparently needed a more submissive love partner; Hamilton was just too tough to give them their way. After leaving them the last time, he pulled off a long string of crimes and several jail-breaks before finally dying in the electric chair in 1935.

While Bonnie's and Clyde's robberies continued to be on the minor side, their escapades were often extremely violent. They stuck up a butcher, and when the man came at Clyde with a cleaver, Clyde avoided the blow and emptied his gun into him. In November 1932 the pair held up a filling station and kidnapped the attendant, William Daniel Jones. After learn-

ing who his captors were, Jones joined up with them and replaced Ray Hamilton in their affections. He later described his experience as "18 months of hell."

Meanwhile, Buck Barrow had been in and out of jail again, this time pardoned by the new governor, Mrs. Miriam "Ma" Ferguson, who had granted pardons to some 2,000 felons during an earlier term. With Buck and Blanche in tow, the gang now numbered five and was ready for the big time. Brandishing newly obtained machine guns, they held up a loan company office in Kansas City. They had been identified and their exploits made front-page news from coast to coast, which pleased Bonnie no end. She deluged newspapers with samples of her "poetry." Editors eagerly printed her poem "The Story of Suicide Sal." They also printed pictures of her smoking a cigar and brandishing a machine gun. Bonnie said these were "horsing around" pictures and she resented the light in which the newspapers had put them. During their getaways the gang often kidnapped lawmen, one of whom was Chief of Police Percy Boyd. When they let him go, Bonnie told Boyd: "Tell the public I don't smoke cigars. It's the bunk."

Bonnie and Clyde are snapped in a playful mood. Gag photos such as these did much to capture the public's attention.

They fought their way out of a trap in Joplin, Mo., killing two officers, but it was apparent that the gang could not continue to escape capture or death. In July 1933 the gang was hiding out in the deserted fair grounds in Dexter, Iowa when a posse closed in. Buck Barrow was fatally wounded and Blanche captured. Bonnie and Jones were also wounded, but Clyde got both of them away.

In the next few months, Bonnie and Clyde killed four more lawmen. During this period Jones took the first opportunity to desert them. When picked up in late 1933, he told of his incredible career of crime and suffering with the pair and begged to be sent to prison, where he would be safe from Bonnie and Clyde. The law obliged.

Bonnie knew the end was near. She mailed newspapers "The Ballad of Bonnie and Clyde," which concluded:

> The road gets dimmer and dimmer,
> Sometimes you can hardly see,
> Still it's fight man to man,
> And do all you can,
> For they know they can never be free.
>
> If they try to act like citizens,
> And rent them a nice little flat,
> About the third night they are invited to fight
> By a submachine-gun rat-tat-tat.
>
> They don't think they are too tough or desperate,
> They know the law always wins,
> They have been shot at before
> But they do not ignore
> That death is the wages of sin.
>
> From heartbreaks some people have suffered,
> From weariness some people have died,
> But take it all and all,
> Our troubles are small,
> Till we get like Bonnie and Clyde.
>
> Some day they will go down together,
> And they will bury them side by side.
> To a few it means grief,
> To the law it's relief
> But it's death to Bonnie and Clyde.

The pair stayed on the run until May 23, 1934, when they attempted to hook up with Henry Methvin, a convict they had freed once while busting out Ray Hamilton in a daring prison raid. With the law closing in on all sides, they felt Methvin was the only one left outside of family whom they could trust. But Methvin sold them out, informing the law about a roadside rendezvous he was to have with them. In exchange, he was not prosecuted for charges pending against him in Louisiana and Texas.

A trap was set up at Gibland, La., near the Texas border, under the command of Capt. Frank Hamer of the Texas Highway Patrol, an ex-Texas Ranger who for the past 3½ months had been assigned exclusively to tracking down Bonnie and Clyde. Hamer and five other lawmen waited at an embankment armed with a Browning automatic rifle, three automatic shotguns and two rifles.

Bonnie and Clyde drove up to the rendezvous site. Clyde was driving in his socks; Bonnie was munching on a sandwich. They had in their car a shotgun, a revolver, 11 pistols, three Browning automatic rifles and 2,000 rounds of ammunition.

There is some argument about whether they were given a chance to surrender or even knew they had run into a trap. The lawmen opened fire and the pair died instantly. They dug 25 bullets out of Clyde and 23 out of Bonnie.

See also: *Frank Hamer, Ray Hamilton.*

BOODLE Gang: Early New York hijackers

It may well be that the American crime of hijacking was originated by an 1850s New York street gang known as the Boodle Gang. These toughs raided food provision wagons that passed through their area on the lower West Side. When the wagons started detouring around the Boodle Gang's territory, they descended on the Centre (later changed to Center) Market and became the most efficient of the butcher cart mobs. About a dozen thugs would ride up to a large butcher shop and charge inside. Seizing a whole carcass of beef, they would fling it on their cart and then whip their horses at breakneck speed down the street. The gang's activities did not meet with disfavor in their neighborhood since immediately after a raid a number of stores would offer meats at bargain prices.

In the 1860s the Boodlers perfected their methods and invaded the financial district to rob messengers of their money and securities, a haul more rewarding than meat carcasses. In January 1866 two gang members knocked down a messenger, grabbed his satchel and escaped on a speeding butcher's cart with $14,000 in cash. As they fled, the gang stopped all pursuit by clogging up Beekman Street with three other carts.

The technique was a perfect model for the hijackers of the following century. The police were not particularly successful at rounding up the Boodlers, but the gang eventually disappeared because it could not withstand the depredations of other area gangs, especially the Potashes, who sought to reserve the best criminal activities and territories for themselves.

BOOK Whippings

During Colonial days books that were deemed offensive were also considered "criminal" in themselves and therefore subject to criminal punishment in addition to being burned. In a typical Massachusetts case, a book was sentenced "to be publicly whipt with 40 stripes, save one, and then burnt." In 1754 the hangman was assigned to perform that same task on a pamphlet that criticized the court. The public punishment was carried out in the middle of Boston's King Street.

BOORN Brothers: Wrong men convicted of murder

The case of the Boorn brothers has been cited countless times by those warning against the perils of both capital punishment and false confessions.

In 1819 the village of Manchester in Vermont was rocked by a murder trial, described at the time as being "attended by such multitudes" that it had to be held in the Congregational church since the court house was "by a very great deal too small." Seven years earlier, during the War of 1812, a man named Russell Colvin had disappeared from his home after 18 years of a presumably happy marriage that produced a string of numerous and presumably happy children. Folks thought it odd at the time but did nothing about it until old Amos Boorn had a dream in 1819 that was to become most famous. Old Amos was the uncle of Colvin's wife. Three times on a single night in May, Colvin appeared in the old man's dream and informed him that he had been murdered and was willing to name names and places. His murderers, the spirit announced, were Stephen and Jesse Boorn, his brothers-in-law and Amos' own nephews. The murder place was the Boorn farm and "I'm buried there under the stump of a tree."

By October the brothers had been tried, convicted and sentenced to death. Naturally, the state of Vermont had more evidence that just Uncle Amos' dream. Buried in the earth inside the Boorn barn had been found a large knife, a penknife and a button. The knives were identified by Mrs. Colvin as the property of her husband. Then there were the bones found by a dog digging at the base of a stump on the farm. The first announcement was that they "might have been human." Two doctors later said they belonged to an animal, but they had to admit that two toenails found among the bones had "the appearance of belonging to a human foot." Then Jesse, in shackles for three months, made a confession and his brother Stephen followed some weeks later. According to Stephen's written admission, they had murdered Colvin after a fierce argument, buried him, dug up his bones some years later and "throwed them in the river."

At their trial both brothers repudiated their confessions, insisting they had made them simply as a bid for clemency when they saw how inflamed public opinion against them was. Their mother, Mrs. Barney Boorn, was ex-communicated from the Baptist church. The state legislature was then petitioned for a commutation of the sentences to life imprisonment. The petition was granted Jesse but denied his brother, who was slated to hang January 28, 1820.

One of the Boorns' attorneys attempted a final gamble; he decided to advertise for Russell Colvin. An advertisement thus appeared in the *Rutland Herald* under the headline MURDER:

> Printers of newspapers throughout the United States are desired to publish that Stephen Boorn, of Manchester, in Vermont, is sentenced to be executed for the murder of Russell Colvin, who has been absent about seven years. Any person who can give information of said Colvin, may save the life of an innocent by making immediate communication.

There followed a short description of the supposed victim. Among the newspapers that picked up the item was the *New York Post,* and it was read aloud one night in a New York hotel to James Whelpley, a former Manchester resident, who began telling stories about the village idiot Colvin. Within earshot of Whelpley was Taber Chadwick. Chadwick realized that his brother-in-law, William Polhemus, who owned a farm in Dover, N.J., had working for him a weak-minded man who called himself Russell Colvin. In late December 1819 Colvin was returned to Manchester. There he confronted Stephen Boorn, whose legs were still fettered in irons.

Colvin looked at the fetters and asked, "What's them for?"

"Because they say I killed you," Stephen said.

"You never did," Russell said in all seriousness. "Jesse threw a shoe at me once, but it didn't hurt me any."

The case was reopened and the Boorns were cleared. In 1820 the brothers petitioned the legislature for compensation for their false conviction and close call with the hangman. Their request was turned down. It was pointed out that both brothers had made false confessions, no matter how desperate their situation, which had helped to convict them.

BOOT Hill

Almost all Americans believe that every gunslinging Western community had its Boot Hill, where all the victims of lead poisoning were buried. The fact is that the "Boot Hill industry" is a 20th century development. There really was only one Boot Hill and that was at Dodge City. The name referred to a slight rise used as a temporary burial spot and alluded to the custom of burying a corpse there with his boots curled up and placed under his head as a sort of permanent pillow. In due course, Dodge's Prairie Grove Cemetery was completed, and in 1879 the 25 or so inhabitants of Boot Hill were transferred to the new burial grounds.

Most communities didn't know they were supposed to have a Boot Hill until they read modern Western novels and aw movies about the Wild West and became aware of the demands of the tourist industry. Along with newly christened Boot Hills came such graveyard graffiti as "Died of lead poisoning" and, for a cattle rustler, "Too many irons in the fire." One of the superattractions of the West is the 20th century Boot Hill in Tombstone, Ariz., where visitors are welcomed to the burial sites of Tom and Frank McLowery and Billie Clanton, who all died in the famous gunfight at the O.K. Corral. With a certain pride it is claimed that among the graveyard's residents are Dan Dowd, Red Sample, Tex Howard, Bill DeLaney and Dan Kelly, all of whom were "hanged legally," an accomplishment of sorts. In one of the more exploitative events at Tombstone, one promoter tried to sell square-inch plots of Boot Hill cemetery but was squelched by the city council.

See also: *Lester Moore.*

BOOTH, John Wilkes: See Abraham Lincoln—Assassination.

BOOTLEGGING

Bootlegging was and is a major pastime in America. Because it remains an illegal enterprise, however, no reliable figures on its scope have ever been established.

The term bootlegging derives from the custom of the early Indian traders who carried a bottle of liquor in their boot since such traffic with the red man was either illegal or frowned upon. Hence, a bootlegger came to mean a person engaged in illegal liquor deliveries. Naturally, bootleggers thrived most during Prohibition, from January 16, 1920 until repeal of the 18th Amendment on December 3, 1933. The best guess was that during the Prohibition period Americans annually consumed at least 100 million gallons of bootleg liquor.

Great profits were derived from bootlegging during Prohibition. In the larger cities powerful bootlegging gangs arose to meet demand and to fight bloody wars for control of the huge income. Much of the liquor was smuggled across the border from Canada or Mexico or brought in by boat. Many of the gangs found it necessary to produce their own alcohol to assure themselves of a steady supply and established illegal distilleries and breweries, activities that would be impossible without political and police cooperation.

Prohibition made possible the rise of the "Chicago gangster" and the domination of that city and the entire Midwest by the Capone gang, but only after the gang had eliminated many tough competitors, such as the Dion O'Banion mob and the Bloody Gennas. It has been estimated that more than 1,000 men died as a result of the bootleg wars in Chicago alone.

In Williamson County, Ill. another bloody war was fought, perhaps even more constant and murderously inventive than those in Chicago, Detroit, Philadelphia or New York. It was also the scene of an incredible American first. On November 12, 1926 the farmhouse belonging to a prominent family of bootleggers was subjected to an aerial bombing by a rival bootlegging family. Three projectiles were dropped, but since all failed to explode, no damage occurred and there were no complaints and no arrests. Still, it was the first and only time real bombs were dropped from a plane in the United States in a genuine effort to destroy human life.

Many of the great American fortunes derived from bootlegging activities, as leading businesses, like the criminals themselves, could not resist the lure of huge revenues. In 1930 a federal grand jury uncovered the largest liquor ring of the era.

The U.S. Coast Guard stopped thousands of boats attempting to bring in bootleg liquor. Despite many shoot-outs and arrests most rumrunners easily reached the shore.

Thirty-one corporations and 158 individuals were cited in Chicago, New York, Cleveland, Detroit, St. Louis, Philadelphia, St. Paul, Minneapolis, Los Angeles and North Bergen, N.J. and charged with the diversion of more than seven million gallons of alcohol in seven years. Their total business in bootlegging was put in excess of $50 million.

With the repeal of Prohibition, bootlegging did not simply fade away. Bootleggers have always operated and probably always will. By not paying alcohol taxes the bootlegger is able to put out a more reasonably priced product of "mountain dew," or "white lightning." In 1958 the government seized 15,000 stills, although by the 1970s the figure stood at about only 10 percent of that figure. It is difficult, however, to dismiss bootlegging and moonshining as playful larks; hundreds of tipplers of bootlegged alcohol die each year from poisoning.

One of the more frightful instances occurred in Atlanta, Ga. in October 1951, when a bootlegger used 54 gallons of methyl alcohol to mix up a large batch of moonshine. The liquor was sold all over Atlanta, some to an Auburn Avenue nightclub. One Sunday night a man named Eliza Foster walked into the club and downed a shot. A half hour later he dropped dead. He was the first to go. A little while after that, two more went. A man died in his car, a bottle of this same batch on the seat beside him. Another casualty, a little old lady, died in her rocking chair, a bottle of the bad liquor lying spilled at her feet. In all, 13 people died that day, and hundreds of others, feeling miserable and some already blind or writhing on stretchers, jammed into Grady Memorial Hospital. Tortured, frightened people fell to their knees in prayer, expecting to die, and by Monday night 14 more had passed away, raising the total to 27. By the end of the week, there were 35 dead—three were children. The figure finally reached 42. There was no reliable estimate of the number of people who went blind. Altogether, however, at least 500 persons were seriously affected. After the mass poisonings the sale of legal whiskey went up 51.2 percent in Atlanta. But the tragedy in that city was not an unusual event. Just two weeks later eight persons in Revere, Mass. died from another batch of poisoned liquor.

There are no accurate national figures on how many deaths are caused each year by poisoned moonshine, but the number of deaths plus those permanently blinded or paralyzed is certainly in the hundreds. Moonshining operations and stills are turned up not only in the backwoods but in the big cities as well. In virtually all these cases a frightening disrespect for human life is exhibited. Producers seeking to cut costs often dilute their moonshine with rubbing alcohol. Some shortcut artists even add lye to the whiskey to give it a sting, and even more callous individuals mix in ether and fuel oil.

Some experts calculate that as much as 20 percent of all alcohol consumed in this country is illicit moonshine, basing their estimates on the government's open admission that it finds no more than one-third to one-half of all illegal stills, a figure that others believe high.

See also: *Hams, Prohibition, Rum Row.*

BORDEN, Lizzie (1860-1927): Accused murderess

A well-respected, religious spinster of 32, Lizzie Borden of Fall River, Mass. became without doubt America's most-celebrated accused female murderer, charged with the 1892 killing of her father Andrew, and her stepmother, Abby.

On August 3 of that year, Mr. and Mrs. Borden were both taken ill with severe stomach pains. Lizzie had bought some prussic acid just a short time before, but no connection was ever developed.

Between 9 and 9:30 on August 4, a hot, sweltering morning, someone entered a second-story bedroom of the Borden house and axed Abby Borden to death, bashing her skull 19 times. At the time, Lizzie's sister Emma was away from home, and the only ones known to be in the house besides the victim were Lizzie and Bridget Sullivan, the Irish maid. If either of them was the murderer, they certainly concealed it from the other for the next hour to 90 minutes, each going about their business without indicating any knowledge of the body in the bedroom. At about 10:30 Andrew Borden returned home from his business activities. He lay down on a sofa in the downstairs sitting room to take a nap, and the murderer crept up on him and hit him 10 times with an axe, killing him.

The police charged Lizzie Borden with committing the crimes, strictly on circumstantial evidence, not all of it very strong. For one thing, although the walls of both murder rooms were splashed with blood, no blood was found on Lizzie or her clothes. There was a theory that Lizzie had stripped naked to do the deeds and then had put her clothes back on, but that certainly would have involved a great risk of her being seen by the maid. The authorities claimed but never really proved that Lizzie had burned a dress in the kitchen stove a few days after the murders.

After being held in jail for nearly a year, Lizzie was subjected to a 13-day trial, with the entire nation hanging on every word. Rather than play down the gruesome nature of the murders, her defense attorney stressed this aspect. He then pointed to the prim, very feminine, charity-minded Lizzie and said: "To find her guilty, you must believe she is a fiend. Gentlemen, does she look it?"

The verdict in the case of Lizzie Borden, perhaps this country's most enduring cause celebre, was not guilty. The jury had needed only an hour to arrive at it.

Lizzie made one statement to the press expressing her elation but then refused to say any more, even though reporters parked in front of the Borden home for weeks and weeks, searching for more morsels to feed their hungry readers. Lizzie enjoyed a considerable public sympathy during her ordeal and through her acquittal, but over the years public opinion seemed to turn, with more and more people regarding her as guilty. After a time she was considered guilty, as the popular rhyme went, of the charge that she "gave her mother forty whacks."

Lizzie and Emma inherited their parents' $500,000 estate, but they soon sold the house and moved into a lavish mansion in Fall River. Lizzie returned to her charitable works. Although she demanded anonymity, it is believed she financed several college educations.

In 1905 Emma moved out of the mansion after an argument. She too had lived under a cloud and there was even speculation that she was the killer. At the time of the murder, Emma had been staying overnight with friends, but some authorities on the Borden case insisted she could have returned home, committed the crimes and returned to her friends unseen.

The sisters never spoke again. When Lizzie died in 1927, she left nothing to Emma. Aside from some bequests to servants, she willed the bulk of her estate, $30,000 in cash and large holdings in stocks, to the Animal Rescue Leagues of Fall River and Washington, D.C. She was buried in the family plot beside her mother, father and stepmother.

BORDENMANIA: Impact of Lizzie Borden case

No murder case in American history caused more public repercussions than that involving Lizzie Borden, the 32-year-old spinster who was tried and acquitted of killing her father and stepmother with an axe in their home in Fall River, Mass. in 1892. The case was the subject of an endless number of books, magazine articles and newspaper accounts. Edmund Pearson explained the public's fascination with the case may have resulted from its very "purity." The murders, and Lizzie's guilt or innocence, were uncomplicated by such sins as ambition, robbery, greed, lust or other usual homicidal motives. Innocent or guilty, Lizzie became an American heroine.

The verse and doggerel on the case varied from the anonymous children's jump rope rhyme:

> Lizzie Borden took an ax
> And gave her mother forty whacks;
> When she saw what she had done,
> She gave her father forty-one.

to A. L. Bixby's almost endearing:

> There's no evidence of guilt,
>   Lizzie Borden,
> That should make your spirit wilt,
>   Lizzie Borden;
> Many do not think that you,
> Chopped your father's head in two,
> It's so hard a thing to do,
>   Lizzie Borden.

The *New York Times* informed its readers that controversy over Lizzie Borden's innocence or guilt was directly responsible for 1,900 divorces. Such was the grip of "Bordenmania" on the entire nation.

BORNE, Henry: See Dutch Henry.

BOSTON, Patience (1713-1735): First woman hanged in Maine

In Puritan New England, Patience Boston was often cited from the pulpit as proof of how one sin begets another. She was first caught lying, then swearing, then being drunk, then stealing and finally committing murder. In 1735 Boston killed eight-year-old Benjamin Trot of Falmouth by picking him up and throwing him down a well to drown after he had accidentally tramped on her toe. There was only a minimum of debate about sparing her life because she was a woman, a fact certainly outweighed by her heinous past record as a liar, curser, drunk and petty thief. She was hanged in York on July 24, 1735, the first woman to suffer that fate in what is now Maine.

BOSTON Police Strike

On September 9, 1919 a union of policemen in Boston went on strike; 1,117 out of 1,544 patrolmen walked off their jobs after the police commissioner refused to recognize their right to join the American Federation of Labor (AFL). Under an unusual law, the police commissioner was appointed by the governor of the state rather than the mayor of the city and thus had much more freedom. Although Mayor Andrew J. Peters and a citizens committee made compromise proposals on pay and working conditions to head off the strike, the police commissioner rejected them. The resulting strike left Boston virtually unprotected and riots, robberies and lootings followed.

Before the strike began, Mayor Peters and James J. Storrow, the head of the citizens committee, had urged Gov. Calvin Coolidge to act, but he had refused. When rioting broke out, the mayor called out Boston contingents of the militia, established order and broke the strike. Then Gov. Coolidge ordered the commissioner to take charge of the police once more and called out the entire Massachusetts militia. With the police union defeated, AFL head Samuel Gompers tried to win back the jobs of the strikers, who had all been fired. Coolidge responded with a statement that made him famous, won him the vice-presidential nomination in 1920 and paved the way for his subsequent succession to the presidency. "There is no right to strike against the public safety by anybody, anywhere, any time," Coolidge said.

BOSTON Strangler: See Albert H. DeSalvo.

BOTKIN, Cordelia (1854-1910): Poisoner

A poisoner convicted in one of the most sensational trials of the 1890s, Cordelia Botkin may well have been, as the Sunday supplement writers later referred to her, the original Red Hot Mama. Certainly her triangle love affair earned her a reputation as a truly wanton woman as well as a murderess.

A stocky, fleshy woman living in San Francisco, she nonetheless seemed to have all the charms necessary to lure a successful journalist named John Presley Dunning away from his wife and child for a life of gambling and whoring. In 1896 Dunning's wife had had enough and returned to her parents in Dover, Del. While that should have pleased Botkin, she still feared Dunning's wife might someday lure him back, and she deluged Mrs. Dunning with anonymous threatening letters, advising her against trying to rejoin her husband.

In 1898 Dunning got an assignment covering the Spanish-American War, and Botkin grew more certain he would not return to her. Her depression gave way to murderous thoughts. She went out and bought a box of chocolates, a lace handkerchief and two ounces of arsenic. She spent several hours inserting arsenic into each piece of candy. She enclosed the handkerchief and a note that read "With love to yourself and baby—Mrs. C." and tied up the whole package with pink ribbons. The next day she mailed the "gift" to Mrs. Mary Dunning in Delaware.

When the box arrived, Mrs. Dunning puzzled over the identify of the "Mrs. C." who had sent the candy. She thought of several people it might have been. But having a sweet tooth, she didn't hesitate long before polishing off the box. Her sister, Mrs. Joshua Deane, joined in. Twenty-four hours later both women were dead. The deaths did not help Botkin's lovelife, however, because the box of candy was eventually traced back to her in San Francisco.

After a lurid trial that satisfied even the most avid readers of the sensational press, she was found guilty of murder on December 31, 1898 and sentenced to life imprisonment. She died in San Quentin in 1910.

BOUNTIES: See Bank Robberies— Bounties; John Billee; Outlaw Exterminators, Inc.

BOUNTY Jumping: Civil War racket

During the Civil War enterprising individuals and organized gangs reaped a fortune collecting bounties for enlisting in the Union Army and then immediately deserting. The cycle would then be repeated, generally in another congressional district or state, for amounts that varied from $100 to as much as $1,000.

One specialist in this racket was caught after 32 enlistments and desertions, a record that drew him a four-year prison term. A notorious Chicago underworld character named Mike McDonald operated a bounty racket on an organized basis, recruiting hoodlums to sign up for service. McDonald collected a commission each time and shuttled the men around to different areas for repeat tries, keeping track of his "campaigns" on a large war map with tacks indicating where each hoodlum was assigned. Profits from this racket provided McDonald with the capital to set up several gambling houses after the war.

There are some estimates that perhaps neraly half of all desertions from the Union Army, which totaled 268,000, were really cases of bounty jumping. While such figures are most likely too high, considering the large number of draftee desertions, they are at least indicative of how widespread the crime was.

See also: *Michael Cassius "Mike" McDonald.*

BOW Kum (1889-1909): Murder victim

Bow Kum, meaning "Little Sweet Flower," was a beautiful slave girl of 15 when she was illegally brought into the United States by a wealthy San Francisco Chinese, Low Hee, who had paid a Canton slave merchant the unheard of sum of $3,000 for her. The American authorities found out about Bow Kum some three years later and despite Low Hee's valid bill of sale, placed her in a home. Bow Kum was finally released when she married another man, Tchin Len, who took her to New York. A dispute broke out between Low Hee and Tchin Len on the matter of compensation and soon involved three groups: the On Leong Tong, an alliance of the Hip Sing Tong and a fraternal organization called the Four Brothers. These groups were already at odds on such matters as the control of gambling in various parts of New York's Chinatown. As the dispute appeared beyond settlement, the On Leongs murdered Bow Kum on April 15, 1909, and the first of Chinatown's great tong wars broke out.

One typical killing spree took place in the venerable Chinese Theater on Doyers Street on New Year's night during a supposed truce in the fighting that had been arranged for the biggest Chinese celebration of the year. The performance went along smoothly until a celebrant in the audience suddenly tossed a bunch of lighted firecrackers into the air. This caused a brief commotion before things quieted down. As the audience filed out at the end of the performance, five men remained in their seats. They all had bullets in their heads. The banging of the firecrackers had drowned out the cracks of the revolvers of five Hip Sings behind five On Leongs.

Police estimates of casualties during the war were put at about 350 before the tongs came to a peace settlement in late 1910 and the war over Little Sweet Flower ended.

See Also: *Ah Hoon, Bloody Angle, Mock Duck, Tong Wars.*

BOWDRE, Charlie (c.1853-1880): Accomplice of Billy the Kid

Charlie Bowdre's grave is among the most visited in the country, but only because he shares it in common with Billy the Kid. They, together with another of the Kid's sidekicks, Tom O'Folliard, lie in Old Fort Sumner, N.M. under a stone marker bearing the inscription "Pals."

Bowdre, somewhat older than the Kid, seems to have always been fascinated by him. A cowboy drifter, he settled in New Mexico Territory in the late 1870s and married a pretty Mexican girl named Manuela. He apparently wanted to retire from the wild life, but with the outbreak of the Lincoln County War, he took up his guns on behalf of the Tunstall-McSween group and joined forces with Billy the Kid. By the time the war ended, Bowdre was convinced that Billy was the smartest and toughest man ever to ride a horse. When the Kid said they were going into the cattle-rustling trade, Bowdre went along without question. But his blind faith in Billy came to an abrupt halt on December 21, 1880, when a posse headed by Pat Garrett cornered the Kid's gang in a deserted farmhouse at Stinking Springs. In the gunfight that ensued Billy shoved Bowdre, who had been hit five times, through the door of the house, saying: "They have murdered you, Charlie, but you can get revenge. Kill some of the sons of bitches before you go." Bowdre lived only long enough to pick up another couple of bullets; lunge forward mumbling, "I wish . . . I wish"; and die. A short while later, Billy the Kid surrendered to Garrett. The gunfight at Stinking Springs perhaps gives the inscription "Pals" an ironic twist.

See also: *Billy the Kid, Patrick Floyd Garrett, Lincoln County War.*

BOWERS, J. Milton (1843-1904): Accused murderer

The Bowers case, involving a handsome young San Francisco doctor who lost three wives to early deaths, was one of the 19th century's most sensational, controversial and protracted. The doctor, J. Milton Bowers, was convicted of murder and later cleared, although not to the satisfaction of the police or a substantial portion of the public.

Bowers' third wife, 29-year-old Cecelia, had been ill for two months before dying from what appeared to be an abscess of the liver. Dr. Bowers appeared appropriately grief-stricken over the death of his wife of three years. But an anonymous letter triggered an investigation, and an autopsy was ordered. When the body was found to contain phosphorus, Bowers was charged with murder. He was pilloried in the press, and the public seemed obsessed with the fact that Cecelia was the third of Bowers' wives to die after a short-lived marriage. In addition, all three had been duly insured. There were also charges that Bowers was a criminal abortionist. At Bowers' trial much damning evidence was presented by his brother-in-law, Henry Benhayon, who testified that the doctor had prevented his wife from receiving outside care during much of her illness. Bowers was convicted of first-degree murder and incarcerated pending a decision on his appeal for a new trial.

In October 1887 Henry Benhayon was found dead in a rooming house. Police discovered a bottle of potassium cyanide and three suicide notes. One of the notes, addressed to the coroner, confessed that Benhayon had poisoned Mrs. Bowers. While this sensational development appeared to clear Dr. Bowers, the police were not convinced that the suicide note was genuine or that Benhayon's death was a suicide. Tracing purchases of potassium cyanide, the police located a druggist who identified one John Dimmig as a purchaser. They then discovered that Dimmig had visited Bowers in his jail cell.

Although he denied having bought the poison or being involved in Benhayon's death, Dimmig was charged with murder. The first trial ended in a hung jury. In the meantime, Dr. Bowers' motions for a new trial were rejected. Dimmig was tried again in late 1888 and acquitted. In August 1889 Dr. Bowers was released from jail, where he had been confined for four years. He eventually married a fourth time, and when he died in 1904 at the age of 61, the murder of Cecelia Bowers was still being carried in police files as "unsolved."

BOWERY Boys: Early New York gang

One of the toughest gangs in New York during the early 1800s was the famed Bowery Boys, who, as native Americans, did battle with the dreaded Irish gangs, especially the Dead Rabbits and their satellites. On occasion, they also fought the police.

Unlike the other great gangs, the Bowery Boys were not loafers and bums—except on Sundays and holidays. Nor were they criminals, except once in a while, until the Civil War. The average Bowery Boy was a burly ruffian who worked as a butcher or apprentice mechanic or perhaps a bouncer in a Bowery saloon or dance cellar. Almost always, he was a volunteer fireman, an avocation that gave the Bowery Boys important political pull since the firemen were strong allies of Tammany Hall and thus had important influence on the running of city government. The Bowery Boys were especially valuable allies on election day when their rough activities often determined voting results.

The Bowery Boys' hatred of Irish gangs and of foreigners in general was implacable, and they campaigned strongly for those candidates who ran against naturalization laws and favored their repeal so that Irish voters could be stripped of their citizenship. The Bowery Boys worked on behalf of such candidates with blackjacks in hand and voted early and often themselves in every election.

The Bowery Boys' greatest fight was a two-day battle on July 4 and 5, 1857, when allied with forces of the anti-Irish Native American Party, they withstood an invasion of the Bowery by the Dead Rabbits and the Plug Uglies and other gangs from the Five Points area. With more than 1,000 combatants taking part, the police lacked sufficient manpower or backbone to stop the fighting throughout the first day and much of the second. Officially, eight gang members died and another 100 were injured, but it was known that both sides dragged off a considerable number of corpses for secret burials in their own bailiwicks.

During the Draft Riots the Bowery Boys took part in much of the criminality loosed on the city. After that, the gang splintered into various smaller groups, almost all involved in illegal pursuits.

See also: *Dead Rabbits, Draft Riots.*

BOWIE Knife

Fashioned either by the famed Jim Bowie or his brother Rezin P. Bowie, the bowie knife was the West's most popular close-combat weapon before being supplanted by the six-shooter. The Mississippi pirates disemboweled their victims with it; the early river gamblers settled disputes with it; the Texas Rangers carried it as a sidearm, and the men of the mountains and the West hunted with it, slaughtered animals with it, cut wood with it and ate with it.

The knife was baptized in blood by Jim Bowie in the famous Sandbar Duel fought on the Mississippi near Natchez in 1827. Jim Bowie, appearing only as a second for one of the participants, joined in a murderous melee that broke out and killed a second for the rival party with a 15-inch-blade knife. He butchered his opponent so efficiently that word of his wicked weapon spread rapidly. The homemade knife had originally been fashioned from a large blacksmith's rasp, but given its new notoriety, the Bowie brothers sent it to a Philadelphia cutlery manufacturer who shaped and polished it to their instructions and christened it a bowie knife.

An authentic bowie knife was anywhere from 15 to 20 inches in overall length with a blade of nine to 15 inches, sharpened only on one side to the curve of the tip and then on both sides to the tip. A handguard of brass allowed the knife wielder to thrust or parry and slide his hand down over the blade as the situation required. Weighing two pounds or more, it could be used for brute force or deft lethality.

Once the weapon became popular, more than a dozen cutlers started producing it, each claiming to have been the originator. There was, however, no dispute over the knife's intended use. A Sheffield, England manufacturer catered to the market perfectly by inscribing on the blade the legend "America Can and Must be Ruled by Americans."

See also: *Sandbar Duel.*

BOYD, Jabez (?-1845): Murderer

Eventually to be known as the American Jekyll and Hyde, Jabez Boyd was always judged to be a highly religious man in his community, but it appears that he used his church-going activities to learn when potential victims would be abroad with sums of money on their person or in their homes. He would then strike accordingly.

One night in 1845, Boyd waylaid Wesley Patton in Westchester, Pa. When Patton resisted and possibly recognized Boyd, the latter clubbed him to death. Unknown to Boyd, another man witnessed the crime and identified him. When Boyd was apprehended the next day, was sitting in a church pew "with a hymn book in his hand, and from which he was singing with apparent composure." He was hanged forthwith.

When four decades later Robert Louis Stevenson created *The Strange Case of Dr. Jekyll and Mr. Hyde,* an enterprising American journalist tried to resurrect Boyd as the source of Stevenson's inspiration. This thesis had and has nothing to recommend it other than increased circulation, since Stevenson was known to have based his tale of "man's double being" on Deacon William Brodie, an 18th century Scotsman who, while a respected member of the Edinburgh town council, led a gang of criminals.

BOYLE, W. A. "Tony" (1902-   ): Labor leader and murderer

In labor's worst murder scandal during recent years, rivaling the disappearance of ex-Teamsters boss Jimmy Hoffa, United Mine Workers (UMW) President Tony Boyle was convicted of the 1969 murder of union rival Joseph Yablonski and Yablonski's wife and daughter. On December 31, 1969, seven months after the 59-year-old Yablonski, a union rebel, announced he would oppose Boyle for the UMW leadership, he, his wife, Margaret, 57, and their daughter Charlotte, 25, were shot to death while they slept in their Clarksville, Pa. home.

Boyle, angered by the grass roots opposition to his reign, ordered Yablonski's assassination after a heated board meeting in Washington the previous June. The plot began to unravel when William Turnblazer, a lawyer and former UMW District 19 president, admitted his role in the conspiracy. He testified that the order was given as Boyle, Turnblazer and Albert Pass stood outside an elevator. At his first trial in 1974 in Media, Pa. Boyle insisted no such meeting had taken place, but he was found guilty. Three others pleaded guilty, including Pass, who was sentenced to three consecutive life prison terms. Boyle got the same sentence.

Boyle's conviction was overturned by the Pennsylvania Supreme Court because the presentation of certain evidence had not been permitted. A retrial in 1978 ended with the same verdict, and the same sentence was again imposed on Boyle, then 77 and suffering from heart disease.

BRADY Gang: Public enemies

Although they are little remembered now, the Brady gang were the most sought criminals in the United States, following the fall of such 1930s gangsters as Dillinger, Baby Face Nelson, Pretty Boy Floyd, Bonnie and Clyde and the Barker-Karpis mob. By eradicating the Brady gang, the FBI disarmed the critics of its methods. Before that, J. Edgar Hoover had been attacked on the floor of the U. S. Senate as being a personal coward, the FBI had been criticized for killing John Dillinger without giving him a "chance"; and when Hoover made his famed foray to New Orleans to arrest Alvin Karpis personally, the newspapers gleefully reported that none of the host of FBI agents making the arrest had thought of bringing along a pair of handcuffs.

The Brady gang began in Indiana during the early 1930s, when three former lonewolves—Al Brady, Clarence Shaffer and James Dalhover—teamed up to terrorize the Midwest. While the other public enemies fell one by one, Brady and his two friends left a trail of holdups of banks and other establishments during which they killed two clerks and three police officers. They had been captured once but had escaped jail and by the end of 1937 were the most-hunted men in the country. Feeling the "heat," the trio moved into virgin territory in Maine. In October 1937 they entered a sporting goods store in Bangor and asked for two revolvers of a certain make. The clerk waiting on them recognized the three as the Brady gang and said the weapons would be in stock the following week. On October 12, 1937, the trio returned and were recognized by an employee, who immediately pulled a hidden cord that caused a suspended show card to drop in the store window. At that instant four FBI men, guns drawn, jumped from hiding places under the counter and surprised the gangsters, who turned and charged out the door. They were immediately hit with a hail of bullets fired by 16 other FBI agents hidden across the street. Brady and Shaffer died instantly; Dalhover lived long enough to be executed. More importantly, the FBI received no criticism for the ambush of the gang. In part, that was because none of the gangsters ever exhibited the verve and flair of John Dillinger. But it was also true that the public took the Brady gang for what they were, brutal murderers. The days of romanticizing public enemies was over.

BRANDING: Punishment for crime

Branding as a punishment for crimes was never as widely used in the New World as in Europe, but it was a standard form of punishment in Colonial America. In the Massachusetts colony the wearing of signs or initials on a person's outermost garment was in effect a method of symbolic branding. Thus, in Boston in 1639 Richard Wilson had to wear a T for theft of "money and diverse small things" from his master, and about the same time in Plymouth, Katheren Aines, a married woman, was required to wear a B for bawd "for her unclean and laciviouse behavior with . . . William Paule."

A number of crimes were considered so heinous that branding was mandatory even for a first offense. Burglary of a dwelling house called for the letter B to be branded on a culprit's forehead. A second such offense required a second branding and whipping. A third offense called for the death penalty. Counterfeiting was considered such a danger that the offender was branded on his right cheek with an F for forger. It was presumed that such a branding would be proper warning to any potential victims to beware of their money or supposed legal records.

With proper application, branding of course produced a permanent scar, but the punishment was considered so awesome that several constables took to using a light touch or an iron not heated sufficiently to destroy the tissue.

Officially, the branding iron was last used on Jonathan Walker, who in 1844 had the letters S.S. (for slave stealer) burned into the palm of his right hand: however, the practice of branding continued as an acceptable form of punishment in the informal miners courts in the West and in the military, especially during the Civil War. On October 10, 1863 a Union artillery brigade held a mass branding of those being drummed out of the service for deserting their batteries. The brigade was assembled in the form of a hollow square facing inward, with a battery forge in the center. A battery blacksmith heated irons, and the letter D was burned into the convicted men's left hips. Significantly, the army had by this time restricted branding to relatively unseen parts of the body. Miners courts, acting in a lawless environment, were not as lenient. Generally, these courts believed in only two penalties, hanging and expulsion from the community. When this later punishment was decreed, the convicted man was often branded on the forehead, face or hands to give due warning to other communities of his unsavory character. This extralegal form of punishment disappeared by the 1880s and 1890s.

See also: *Jonathan Walker.*

Further reading: *Crime and Punishment in Early Massachusetts* by Edwin Powers.

BRAS Coupe (?-1837): Slave outlaw

In the 1820s one of the most famous slaves in New Orleans was Squier, an exceptionally talented Bamboula dancer. His master was Gen. William de Buys, well known as an indulgent slave owner. The general was all the more indulgent of a famous slave like Squier. He taught Squier to shoot and let him go hunting alone in the forests and swamps. A big and powerful man, Squier became adept at firing a rifle with either hand, something that would stand him in good stead later on. He also became accustomed to the feeling of freedom. So much so, that he ran away. When he was caught, he escaped again. In 1834 Squier was shot by a patrol of planters hunting slaves in the swamps, and his right arm was amputated. As soon as his would was healed, Squier ran away again, determined never to be retaken. He organized a gang of escaped blacks and—what truly terrified New Orleans—some renegade whites. Now known as Bras Coupe, the escaped slave led his gang on frequent robbery and murdering raids around the outskirts of New Orleans. For nearly three years Bras Coupe was the scourge of New Orleans, a hobgoblin used by mothers and nurses to frighten their children. The New Orleans *Picayune* described him as "a semi-devil and fiend in human shape" and called his life "one of crime and depravity." What frightened the slave owners most, of course, was the fact that Bras Coupe became a hero to the other blacks. They endowed Bras Coupe with superhuman powers. In the instant folklore that sprung up around him, the veritable superman was fireproof and, having now lost his one weak arm, invulnerable to wounds. Hunters who tried to take him in the swamp stood in awe as their bullets flattened against his chest while he laughed. Sometimes the bullets whizzed off Bras Coupe's chest and came flying back at the hunters. When a detachment of soldiers invaded his lair, they were swallowed up in a cloud of mist and never seen again. Bras Coupe was said to paralyze with a mere glance and to nourish himself on human flesh.

Bras Coupe's mythic qualities were tarnished on April 6, 1837, when he was shot by two hunters. But he escaped and it was assumed, would surely survive since he knew all the miraculous herbs that could be found in the swamps. On July 19 of the same year, the legend came to a tawdry end. A Spanish fisherman, Francisco Garcia, long considered to be in league with the slave-outlaw, brought Bras Coupe's body into New Orleans on a mule-drawn cart. He said Bras Coupe had fired on him from the shore of the Bayou St. John. Infuriated, Garcia said he had come ashore and beat the slave renegade's brains out with a club. The weight of evidence, however pointed to the conclusion that Bras Coupe had been murdered as he slept in Garcia's hut. Garcia demanded the $2,000 reward that had been posted for the outlaw; but however much the whites had feared the man they called the Brigand of the Swamp, they had little stomach for the Spaniard's act. He was given only $250 and told to leave. The body of Bras Coupe was displayed for two days in the Place d'Armes so that several thousand slaves could be brought to view it as an object lesson.

BREAKENRIDGE, William (1846-1931): Western lawman

An opponent of the Earps, Deputy Sheriff Billy Breakenridge of Tombstone was a "survivor" of the Tombstone feuds and certainly one of the few lawmen ever to hire known outlaws to act as his bodyguards.

A native of Wisconsin, Breakenridge served in the U.S. Cavalry and later made an unsuccessful attempt at prospecting. In 1880 he was a deputy to Sheriff John Behan, a law officer often at odds with Wyatt Earp and accused of being in league with the notorious Clantons and Curly Bill Brocius, the leaders of the "cowboy element," which was more or less a synonym for rustlers. Breakenridge's main duty was the collection of taxes, an occupation not noted for longevity in the area around Tombstone. To solve this problem, Breakenridge approached Curly Bill and asked him to act as his bodyguard while he made his rounds in outlaw territory. On the surface, Curly Bill's agreement appeared to be a lark, but it was far more likely that the outlaw was interested in cementing his relations with Behan.

In all the violence of the Tombstone feuds, including the famous gunfight at the O. K. Corral, Breakenridge, although not loved by the Earp faction, at least managed to avoid antagonizing the Earps to the point of provking a showdown. As a result, and in spite of the "Behan stain," Breakenridge continued to hold down various law enforcement jobs, working as a U.S. marshal and as a special agent for the Southern Pacific Railroad. He died in 1931, six years after a much-publicized "reconciliation" with Wyatt Earp.

See also: *John Behan.*

BREDELL, Baldwin: See Counterfeiting.

BREMER, Arthur Herman (1950-   ): Would-be assassin

On the afternoon of May 15, 1972, George Wallace was campaigning at a Laurel, Md. shopping center in his quest for the Democratic presidential nomination. He left the bulletproof podium and was shaking hands with people when a young blond man called several times, "Hey, George, over here!" Wallace moved toward that area and the youth pulled a gun and fired several shots at Wallace, hitting him four times. In the ensuing struggle with Wallace's guards, the assassin emptied his weapon, and wounding three others, all of whom recovered. Wallace himself remained paralyzed afterwards because of a bullet that lodged near the spinal column

The would-be assassin was identified—how soon was to be a matter of some concern later—as Arthur H. Bremer, a young man in his twenties who had been a janitor's assistant and a busboy in Milwaukee, Wis. In November 1971 Bremer had been charged by Milwaukee police with carrying a concealed weapon, but this was reduced to a disorderly conduct charge and the gun confiscated. Shortly thereafter, he went out and bought two other guns.

On March 1, 1972 Bremer started following the Wallace campaign trail. During that period he spent about $5,000, although his total earnings for 1971-72 came to only $1,611. At times, he left the Wallace trail. On April 7 and 8 he stayed at the Waldorf-Astoria Hotel in New York, where Hubert Humphrey was staying. Bremer then traveled to Ottawa, Canada, where he stayed at the expensive Lord Elgin. He also checked into a number of motor inns along the Wallace campaign route. Where he got the money for the bills has remained a mystery, especially since it was established that he had not received any money from his parents.

As is customary in such cases, Bremer was intially reported to be a "loner," but that does not appear to have been very accurate. He had quite a few friends in Milwaukee, including Dennis Cassini, an individual officials never got to question. He was found dead of a heroin overdose, his body locked in the trunk of his own automobile. Although this was reported to the FBI, there is no indication that its director, L. Patrick Gray, ordered any inquiry into the matter. Other odd facts or circumstances developed. Bremer had been seen in Ludington, Mich. in the company of a man described as having a "New Joisey brogue." Roger Gordon, who was a former member of the Secret Army Organization (SAO), a right-wing intelligence organization, said the man was Anthony Ulasewicz, a White House operative later to win fame in the Watergate scandal. Gordon later left the country.

There were prominent reports that White House aide Charles W. Colson ordered E. Howard Hunt (two more Watergate personalities) to break into Bremer's apartment and plant Black Panther Party and Angela Davis literature. More explosive than that charge was the allegation that the order was given within one hour of the attempt to kill Wallace.

Commenting on these details in an interview with Barbara Walters, Wallace said: "So I just wondered, if that were the case, how did anyone know where he lived within an hour after I was shot?"

A practical political result of the attempted assassination of Wallace was to force him out of the 1972 race, in which he was expected to run as a third party candidate. A week before the election, voters were polled on how they would have voted had Wallace run. The results were Nixon, 44 percent; McGovern, 41 percent; Wallace, 15 percent. Such a result, because of how the vote broke down, would likely have thrown the election into the House of Representatives, where Wallace would have had considerable influence. With Wallace out of the race, virtually all his supporters went to President Nixon.

Arthur Bremer has steadfastly refused to state why he shot Wallace. He was sentenced to 63 years, over objections by his attorneys that he was unbalanced. He has been described as a loner in the Maryland State Penitentiary, working in the print shop.

"Bremer does not give interviews," Warden George Collins said in 1979. "In fact, he won't even see his mother. She came in all the way from Milwaukee at Christmas, and he talked to her for about five minutes and went on back down inside. He just doesn't want to be bothered. He just doesn't want any hassle." The warden did add Bremer was "a very good inmate, so far as obeying institution rules is concerned."

BRENNAN, Molly (?1853-1875): Murder victim

A dance hall girl at the Lady Gay gambling saloon in Sweetwater, Tex., Molly Brennan participated in a love triangle that provided Western folklore and Hollywood with one of the most oft-used cliches ever.

A character named Melvin King who was a sergeant with the 4th Cavalry when he wasn't beating up or shooting up folks, was romantically inclined toward Molly. Once while on leave, King rode up to Kansas to visit friends, which put him far out of sight and out of mind for Molly, who then took an interest in a civilian scout for the Army named Bat Masterson. Returning from his leave, King was already in a foul mood, having come out second best in a dispute with Wyatt Earp, and he was spoiling for a fight. When he heard about Molly's fickleness, he rode hell-for-leather towards Sweetwater. King stormed into the Lady Gay to find Molly and Bat on the dance floor. Masterson barely had time to unclinch from Molly as King drew his gun. At the same time King fired, Molly threw her body in front of Masterson and took the bullet in her stomach. King's second shot shattered Masterson's pelvis, but as Bat was falling, he drew his .45 and shot King dead. Molly Brennan died shortly afterward as a result of her wound.

An unkind chronicler said that out of respect for Molly, Bat Masterson avoided all romantic entanglements for a month. Considering the condition of Masterson's pelvis, this was almost certainly both untrue and ungracious. It became the custom at the Lady Gay for the men to toast the memory of Molly Brennan, and her sacrifice went on to be reenacted in scores of Hollywood shoot-em-ups.

BRIEFCASE Agents: Early FBI men

During the early years of the FBI, agents were not permitted, under ordinary circumstances, to carry a gun or make an arrest, other than those an average citizen could make. If they needed to arrest someone, they were required to seek local assistance. Such restrictions on federal agents made sense in terms of preventing the rise of a national police force, but in actual practice they led the underworld to regard the FBI as an impotent force. FBI men became known as "briefcase agents," because that was about the only equipment they could carry. The requirement that the FBI seek local assistance in making arrests proved to be a serious drawback because of the widespread corruption among many local police departments. By the time agents arrived to arrest a suspect, he often had already fled the scene thanks to the local police "pipeline." The FBI was forced to select carefully among the various jurisdictions before attempting an arrest.

While the rise of the public enemies brought about some demands for unshackling the briefcase agents, two crimes in particular led to federal passage of a package of crime laws by 1934 that widened the scope of the FBI and gave its agents the right to care firearms and make arrests. These were the Lindbergh baby kidnapping and the Kansas City Massacre.

BRIGGEN, Joseph (c.1850-1903): Mass murderer

One of this country's most awesome mass murderers, Joseph Briggen committed his crimes for many years on a small ranch in a remote California valley.

Briggen barely made a living on his Sierra Morena Ranch. Certainly he was never prosperous enough to keep more than one hired hand at a time. In fact, were it not for his prime Berkshire swine, for which he almost invariably won the coveted blue ribbon at the state fair in Sacramento, Briggen's ranching would probably have been considered a total loss.

At state fair time, however, he was in his glory, his prize swine attracting top dollar. When he was asked about how he raised them, Briggen would say the secret was all in their care and feeding. But his recipe for the latter was something he would share with no one, other than to say they got prime feed only.

There was good reason for Briggen to guard his secret. The truth was a grisly story. He hired homeless men as his helpers, recruiting them on a customary trip to the Embarcadero section of San Francisco. A down-and-outer would jump at the chance for a good job with room and board and Briggen could keep him several weeks if not months before the man would demand his back pay. Then Briggen would kill him, chop up the body and feed it to his prize swine. In his twisted mind, Briggen had become convinced it was this diet of human flesh that made his swine prize winners. He was finally exposed in early 1902, when his newest hired hand, a youth named Steve Korad, who had arrived very enthusiastic about finding work, looked around his room and found two severed human fingers from a previous victim that Briggen had carelessly dropped behind the bed. Korad raced off in the night and notified the law. When authorities dug up Briggen's ranch, their search turned up the bones of at least a dozen victims, but they were sure they had not found them all. The pigpen itself yielded up several bones, including one dead man's skull.

Briggen was convicted in August 1902 and sentenced to life. He died in San Quentin shortly thereafter.

BRIGGS, Hattie (c.1880-1890s): Madam

In vice-ridden Chicago during the 1880s and 1890s, the most famous madams were Carrie Watson and Lizzie Allen, but a black madam ("as ugly as anyone could imagine," according to one contemporary account) named Hattie Briggs enjoyed almost equal notoriety, being the subject of a never-ending string of newspaper articles.

Six feet tall and weighing about 225 pounds, Hattie cut an

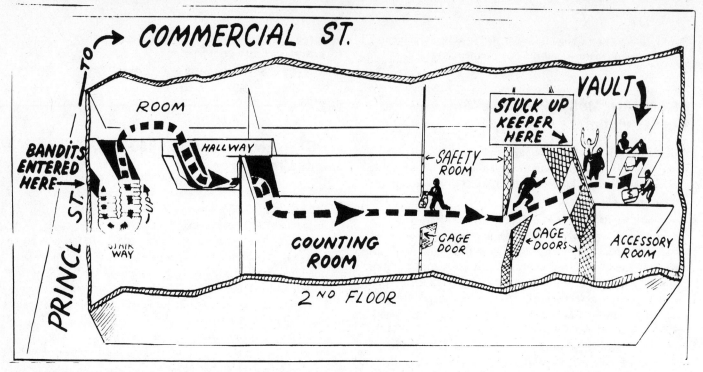

A diagram shows the route taken by the bandits in the Great Brink's Robbery in 1950, which netted them $2.7 million in cash, checks and securities.

arresting figure in the long scarlet coat she always wore. She ran two brothels, one on Clark Street and another on Custom House Place, where her girls were available for 25 cents. However, rare indeed was the customer who got out of either of these dens without being robbed. Scorning such slow-moving, indirect robbery methods as the sliding panels used in some other establishments, Hattie's technique was quick and most direct. She would simply seize a customer and slam him up against a wall a few times, strip him of his money and toss him out into the street. Although Hattie was raided several times a week, she got off with minor fines; few victimized customers cared to appear in court to testify against her.

While the newspapers constantly wrote exposes of her activities, it took the police some 10 years to drive her from the city; some cynical newsmen saw this as proof of police corruption. Indeed, Hattie's downfall resulted more from her insulting the police than from her breaking the law. In the early 1890s Hattie took a young black thief and gambler, William Smith, as a lover. She set him up in the saloon business and dressed him gaudily in patent-leather shoes with white spats, lavender pants, white vest, yellow shirt, bright blue coat and, of course, a silk hat. She adorned him with diamond pins and rings. Smith soon became very "big for his britches" and bragged that Hattie intended to make him the "biggest black boy in Chicago." Indeed, Hattie announced that she was making so much money she intended to buy up all the brothels and saloons in the city's vice centers for Smith, elect him mayor and abolish the police force.

This may have been the insult the police could not abide because a force of 20 patrolmen raided Smith's main saloon and, following a desperate battle, arrested the great man and 22 of his henchmen. After Smith's liquor license was revoked,

the still-smarting police turned their rage on Hattie Briggs, arresting her 10 to 20 times a day with blanket warrants. After lasting about half a month, Hattie finally hired a moving van and shipped off her girls and their bedding to a new place in suburban Lemont. According to later reports, Hattie moved south to a place where the law was said to be more considerate of hard-working madams.

See also: *Panel House.*

BRINK'S Robbery

The Great Brink's Robbery of 1950 was two years in the making. For 24 months, 11 middle-aged Bostonians, seven of them heretofore no more than petty thieves, worked on the robbery of the Brink's North Terminal Garage. They entered the garage at night and walked about in their stocking feet, measuring distances, locating doors, determining which way they opened, all beneath unsuspecting guards. On one occasion they removed the locks from the doors, fitted keys to them and then replaced the locks. They even went so far as to break into a burglar alarm company in order to make a closer study of the alarm system used by Brink's. In December 1949 they ran through a complete dress rehearsal. Finally, they decided they were ready.

On the appointed day, January 17, 1950, the bandits entered the garage dressed in simulated Brink's uniforms, rubber Halloween masks and crepe-soled shoes or rubber overshoes. They made their way to the counting room and relieved five very surprised employees of $2.7 million in cash, checks and securities. The cash alone came to $1,218,211. In less than 15 minutes they were gone.

The plan had been to keep a low profile for six years until

the statute of limitations ran out, but one of the bandits, Joseph "Specs" O'Keefe, felt he had been gypped out of his fair share. He demanded another $63,000. The others refused but then started worrying he would turn informer. A professional hit man, Elmer "Trigger" Burke, was assigned to shut O'Keefe up permanently. Burke chased O'Keefe through the streets of Boston in a wild nighttime shoot-out, firing at him with a machine gun. O'Keefe was wounded in the arm and chest but escaped although Burke was sure he had finished him off. The hit man was seized by police before he could correct his error.

O'Keefe took offense at the effort to kill him and eventually started talking to the law; by then the FBI had spent $25 million investigating the caper. As as result of O'Keefe's talking to the police, eight of the plotters were convicted and given life sentences.

In 1980 an $18 million movie titled *The Brink's Job* was released. It was played partly for laughs. On hand for the showing in Boston were two of the three surviving members of the original bandit group. Both had served 14 years for the crime before being released.

"I'm glad they made something light out of it," said 72-year-old Thomas "Sandy" Richardson. "Yeah, people need a few laughs these days."

Seventy-year-old Adolph "Jazz" Maffie wasn't completely sold. "I thought it was all right. But only thing is that it wasn't that much fun. That was hard work, that kind of job."

"Yeah" Sandy said.

See also: *Elmer "Trigger" Burke.*

BRISTOL Bill (c.1840): Bank robber and counterfeiter

Perhaps one of the most mysterious criminals in American history was the notorious Bristol Bill, who operated during the 1840s in New York and Boston. His true identity was never known to police in this country, although the London police know exactly who he was. They refused to reveal it, however, because Bill's influential father, a member of the British Parliament, did not want the family name dishonored. It was established that Bristol Bill had escaped from the British penal colony in Sydney, Australia; his true identity had not been known there either.

In New York, Bristol Bill teamed up with another ex-Sidney prisoner, James Stuart, better known as English Jim, who had served 12 years down under. It was later estimated that the pair robbed more banks in the area from New York to Boston than any other criminals of their era.

By the late 1840s, after several close brushes with pursuing detectives, they decided to pursue their calling in the relative safety of Vermont. Within a matter of several weeks during the fall of 1849, they robbed six banks, floated a huge quantity of counterfeit money and swindled a number of businessmen. However, the small-town police of Vermont proved sharper than their big-city brethren and captured Bristol Bill. English Jim escaped, fleeing to California, where he became one of that state's top criminals before being captured and hanged by

vigilantes. Bristol Bill was sent to prison for 14 years. His later life proved as enigmatic as his earlier history, and his true identity was never learned on this side of the Atlantic.

BROADWAY Mob: Rumrunners

One of the most important components that eventually were merged into the national crime syndicate was the Broadway Mob of the 1920s. Officially run by Joe Adonis (his real name was Joseph Doto but he went under the name "Adonis" because he was proud of his looks), the Broadway gang boasted a board of directors that included such future big shots as Frank Costello and Lucky Luciano. It totally controlled the flow of bootleg liquor in the great center of Manhattan.

Luciano brought in the Bug and Meyer Mob, run by Meyer Lansky and Bugsy Siegel, to provide protection for the gang's convoys. Adonis and Costello soon decided that it made more sense and was cheaper to bring Lansky and Siegel in as partners. This new interethnic Broadway Mob soon dominated bootlegging in New York, supplying good whiskey to all the top speakeasies, including Jack White's, Jack and Charlie's "21" Club, the Silver Slipper, Sherman Billingsley's Stork Club and others. While not all the whiskey was "right off the boat" as claimed, even the liquor produced in Waxey Gordon's Philadelphia distilleries was far better than the local rotgut. The Broadway Mob invested in some of the best speakeasies and thus had a special interest in keeping the liquor supplies of good quality. It was through the workings of the Broadway Mob that the syndicate's top mobsters came to own some of Manhattan's most valuable real estate, a situation unchanged even to the present day.

See also: *Joe Adonis.*

BROCIUS, William B. "Curly Bill" (1857-1882): Western outlaw

A brutal outlaw whose real name was William B. Graham, Curly Bill Brocius, or Brocious, was the most important gunfighter in the Clanton gang and, as such was frequently at odds in Tombstone with the Earps. Curly Bill was probably the one Clanton man Earp feared most, and it was said the Earps provoked the famous or infamous gunfight at the O. K. Corral because Brocius was not around.

When Old Man Clanton died, Curly Bill became the de facto leader of the gang, having far more ability, brains and guts than Ike Clanton. He would have been a more imposing outlaw except for a lack of ambition. Curly Bill preferred commiting crimes that required little effort on his part. He was quite content to capture a Mexican muleteer in the hills, take all his money and torture him to death.

Brocius killed Marshall Fred White on the streets of Tombstone in a confrontation with that lawman and his deputy, Virgil Earp. It was a matter of dispute whether Curly Bill killed the marshal with a cunning maneuver of his six-gun as he was handing it over to White or whether White caused his own death by seizing the gun by the barrel. Virgil Earp said it was murder; a jury decided on accidental death.

In July 1881 two Clanton gunmen, Bill Leonard and Harry Head, were killed trying to hold up the store of William and Isaac Haslett in Hauchita, New Mexico Territory. The brothers were hailed as heroes, but they didn't have much time to enjoy their fame before Curly Bill and Johnny Ringo rode into town and shot them both dead. Later that same month Brocius led his men on a particularly vicious murder spree, ambushing a Mexican trail herd in the San Luis Pass and killing 14 *vaqueros*. Actually, six of the victims fell in the first volley and the rest surrendered, only to be tortured to death before their cattle were driven off.

After the O.K. Corral gunfight, Curly Bill took part in an assassination attempt on Virgil Earp and the successful ambush of Morgan Earp, both for handsome pay provided by Ike Clanton. After those killings and a couple of stagecoach robberies, Brocius, in one of the frequent ironies of law enforcement in Tombstone, was sent off to the hills armed with a warrent for the arrest of Wyatt Earp that had been issued by Earp's foe Sheriff John Behan. Earp was in the hills at the same time looking for Brocius. Their respective bands met at Iron Springs, a waterhole in the Whetstone Mountains. Earp told Brocius he was taking him in, and Curly Bill said he had a warrant for Earp. The latter ended this legal impasse by blowing Brocius to pieces with a double blast from his shotgun.

See also: *Joseph Isaac "Ike" Clanton, Newman H. "Old Man" Clanton, Wyatt Earp.*

BROKEN Homes And Crime

For years the broken home, one altered by divorce, desertion or death, has been considered a major cause of delinquency and subsequent criminal behavior by children. Overall, various studies have indicated that 40 percent of juvenile delinquents give or take 10 percent or so, come from broken homes, which is at least double the percentage of children from broken homes in the general population. Among male delinquents in cases closed by the Los Angeles Probation Department, 58 percent of those institutionalized came from broken homes.

However, it has become apparent on the basis of several studies that the judicial process tends to select children from broken homes for institutionalization, adding an important distortion to the figures. More recent studies have concluded that the impact of a broken home may not be very significant on white males, although some researchers insist there is an important impact on white females and on blacks compared to whites in general. But even in these cases, the differences may be more apparent than real, as is suggested in a 1972 Florida study by Roland J. Chilton and Gerald E. Markle. It found that the so-called differences in delinquency rates between white boys and girls are primarily in the areas of ungovernability, truancy and running away from home and that statistical differences between the sexes virtually disappear for behavior that would be considered a crime if committed by an adult.

Among black children distinctions between the seriousness of the offense tend to disappear, suggesting that for black youths the home situation may be less significant as a cause of major misconduct, which is considerably higher among blacks than among whites. The Florida study found that in low-income families, white or black, the seriousness of the offense was not determined by the family situation, suggesting that the family's overall economic condition rather than its composition is more relevant to the development of delinquency.

BROOKS, William L. "Buffalo Bill" (?1832-1874): Lawman and horse thief

There are those who say that William Brooks could have been the greatest and most efficient lawman the West had ever seen before he himself went bad.

The life of Brooks, called Buffalo Bill because his prowess as a buffalo hunter nearly equaled that of William F. Cody, is steeped in controversy. Little is known about his early life, although he was apparently born in Ohio. Brooks' story really begins in the late 1860s, when he was reputed to have killed several men in gunfights. After a stint as a stage driver, he became marshal of Newton, Kan. in 1872, reportedly at the age of 40. The town wanted a "mature man" for the job and Brooks seemed to fit the bill. Yet some biographers insist he was in his twenties at the time. Brooks' six-guns made quite an impression in Newton, and he was soon offered the chance to clean up Dodge City. In his first month on the job there, Brooks was involved in some 15 gunfights, killing or wounding numerous "hard cases." One of the men he killed had four brothers, who then came gunning for Brooks; with just four shots—according to the legend—Brooks dispatched them all.

In any event, Brooks had gone far in taming Dodge and had he continued, Wyatt Earp would never have gotten the opportunity to achieve his later fame there. However, power seemed to have corrupted Brooks. He killed a few men he ought not have, one for merely being his rival for the affections of a dance hall girl. Brooks then backed down in a shoot-out with a tough character named Kirk Jordan and left Dodge. Some say it was this loss of face that turned Brooks bad and led him to engage in many illegal enterprises. According to one popular story, Brooks made a try for the marshal's job in Butte, Mont., but his reputation and an opponent named Morgan Earp defeated him. The legend says Brooks' defeat rankled him to the point that he went gunning for Morgan Earp and was killed in a classic gunfight at high noon, with the two men firing at once and one dropping in the dust. That would have been a far more glorious ending for Buffalo Bill Brooks than what actually happened.

The facts are that no such duel ever took place—Brooks' time ran out long before the alleged fight. In early 1874 he returned to his old employer, the Southwestern Stage Co., as a driver. A few months later, the company lost its mail contract to a competitor, and Brooks was out of a job. Late in June 1874 a number of mules and horses belonging to the competing company were stolen. About a month after that, Brooks and two others were arrested for the thefts. Before they could be brought to trial, they were lynched the night of July 29, 1874. Brooks' motive, it became apparent, was to cripple the rival company and win back the mail contract for his former employer. All in all, it was an ignoble end for the man who just two years before had been known as the toughest gun in Dodge City.

BROWN, Hendry (?1850-1884): Lawman and outlaw

Several men in the history of the West have made a transition from outlaw to lawman or vice versa, but Hendry Brown seemed to flit back and forth so much it was difficult to say which one he was at any particular time.

Brown was first heard of when he was operating in Texas as an illegal whiskey peddler. He said then that he had been a lawman in the panhandle, which may or may not have been true. What is true is that later on he did some posse duty with the McSween forces during the Lincoln County War in New Mexico, which might have qualified him as a lawman except that he spent a good deal of this time riding with Billy the Kid.

After the Lincoln County War cooled, Brown split from Billy the Kid, deciding that the outlaw life offered little promise of longevity. He drifted over to Tascosa, Tex., where he magically ended up as town constable. But that activity soon bored Brown and he hit the outlaw trail, working his way up to Kansas. After a while, Brown figured that the lawman game was, all in all, a better bet, and using his credentials as a constable in Texas, he became a deputy marshal at Caldwell. He killed a couple of men in the line of duty and soon picked up the marshal's star. He was holding that job when in 1884 fickleness overtook him again. With three confederates he plotted out a bank robbery at Medicine Lodge in April of that year. It was a bloody affair, with Brown gunning down the bank president and another member of the gang killing a teller. The four bandits fled but they never made it back to cover in Caldwell. A hard-riding and fast-shooting posse cornered them and took them back to the local jail. They never survived the night—a large mob overwhelmed the guards and hanged all four from the same tree.

BROWN, Sam (?-1861): Virginia City killer

Vicious even by the standards of the frontier, Sam Brown was said to have killed some 13 men in the streets and barrooms of Virginia City, Nev. The stocky red-bearded killer always carried a huge bowie knife slung from his gun belt. Proficient with the use of both knife and revolver, Brown killed without provocation. There is no record of him ever challenging a man as well armed as himself, and he never invited anyone to do fair battle. He killed only when he knew he was in no danger himself. One of his more revolting crimes took place in a C Street saloon in 1861. A pleasant young miner named McKen-

zie accidentally bumped his elbow at the bar. Brown turned to see who had offended him and spotted McKenzie, a man Brown knew had not been around long enough to make any close friends who would stand up for him. Seizing the youth by the throat, Brown, according to a contemporary account, "ran a knife into his victim, and then turned it around, completely cutting the heart out, then wiped his bloody knife and lay down on a billiard table and went to sleep."

Finally, Brown picked the wrong would-be victim, a farmer named Vansickle. On July 6 1861, Brown's birthday, the killer boasted between whiskeys that he would "have a man for supper." He decided on Vansickle, who quickly made off for his farm, with Brown in bloodthirsty pursuit. By the time Brown reached the farmhouse, Vansickle had just enough time to dash inside and grab a shotgun. When the farmer came back to his doorway with the weapon, Brown, not relishing such resistance, climbed back on his horse and rode off to town. However, Vansickle was not prepared to let the matter rest. He decided he'd have to kill Brown to prevent him from trying again. As Brown dismounted in front of a saloon, Vansickle rode up. A contemporary account states, "Upon seeing his pursuer, mortal terror seized upon the ruffian; abject, unutterable fear sealed his lips; a spasmodic, agonizing yell of despair forced itself from his mouth. . . ." Vansickle leveled his shotgun and blasted his tormentor with both barrels. An inquest the next day found that Vansickle "had shown good sense, and, instead of deserving punishment, he should be rewarded for having thus rid the community of this brutal and cowardly villain."

BROWN, William: See Alexander William Holmes.

BROWN'S Hole: Western outlaw refuge

Brown's Hole was one of the great Western outlaw hideouts, lying some 250 southwest of Hole in the Wall. Accessible only by little-known roads that wound through deserts and over mountains, it lay at the junction of what is now eastern Utah, western Colorado and southern Wyoming. Brown's Hole, rather than Hole in the Wall, was Butch Cassidy's favorite hideout. It was here that the scattered elements of Cassidy's Wild Bunch knew they could always renew contact. What Butch liked best about it was that "the tax collector doesn't come around too often."

BROWNSVILLE Affair: Mass punishment

One of America's most callous miscarriages of justice occurred in 1906 after an unidentified group of men shot up stores and homes around Fort Brown in Brownsville, Tex., where three companies of black soldiers were stationed. The shootings happened around midnight on August 13 and resulted in the death of a local resident and the severe wounding of a policeman. Despite the fact that the incident had taken place in the dark, a number of witnesses said the shooting had been done by soldiers, and the following morning some cartridges of U.S. Army specifications were found outside the fort. The company commanders instituted an immediate inspection of all the soldiers' rifles but concluded none had been fired, and an inventory check indicated that none of the fort's cartridges were missing.

Several grand jury and military inquiries failed to pin the blame on any specific individuals. On October 4 President Theodore Roosevelt ordered an ultimatum be read to the troops, who had since been transferred to Fort Reno, warning that all would be ordered discharged "without honor" unless they handed over the guilty parties. When all continued to maintain their innocence, the entire group of 167 enlisted men were accused of a "conspiracy of silence" and discharged "without honor." None were afforded any opportunity to confront their accusers and none were ever proved guilty of being involved in the crime. The Senate Committee on Military Affairs later held hearings that were critical of the President's actions, and a military court of inquiry in 1909 announced that 14 of the soldiers would be allowed to reenlist, but the reasoning behind this decision was not revealed. The record of the discharges stood for 66 years until September 22, 1972, when Secretary of the Army Robert F. Froehlke issued a directive changing them from "without honor" to "honorable."

BUCCIERI, Fiore "Fifi" (1904-1973): Syndicate killer

A top enforcer for the Chicago syndicate, Fiore "Fifi" Buccieri was considered to be mob leader Sam Giancana's personal hit man. No complete record of Fifi's kills have been recorded, although federal agents who had bugged a house in Florida being used to plan a murder heard Buccieri reminisce about a number of killings. Among other principles he espoused was that ammunition for shotguns used in an assassination should be "fresh." Fifi was particularly lighthearted about the gruesome demise of William "Action" Jackson, a 300-pound collector for the mob's loansharking operation who was suspected of holding out some of the money and of being an informant for federal authorities. Jackson was hung from a meat hook, stripped and shot in the knee. Then, Buccieri recalled, the boys decided "to have a little bit of fun." Jackson was worked over with ice picks, baseball bats and a blow torch. Fifi got hold of an electric cattle prod and jammed it up Jackson's rectum. The fat victim lived for two days, but even at that, Fifi was "sorry the big slob died so soon." Buccieri took photographs of the mutilated corpse and passed them around as reminders to other mobsters not to stray from mob rule.

Fifi was a graduate of Chicago's worst juvenile gang, the 42ers. He was a hulking, gravel-voiced punk who attracted younger kids by his dapper dress and his affection of wearing wide-brimmed hats similar to those worn by movie gangsters. He attached himself to another up-and-coming 42er, Sam Giancana, who eventually rose to the top position in the Chicago

outfit. Fifi became Giancana's personal executioner and his loyal ally during the power struggles for mob leadership.

The law never made Buccieri crack. During one federal probe investigators tried to elicit mob information by questioning Fifi about his brother Frank, also involved in mob affairs. They even questioned Fifi about the fact that his brother had a girl friend who had been a Playboy bunny and a centerfold nude in *Playboy* magazine and that he had given her a horse as a present. Fifi's answer, which became a classic in underworld circles was, "I take the Fifth on the horse and the broad."

Fifi died of cancer in 1973 and Giancana was assassinated two years later. There was speculation at the time that the mob—if the Giancana killing was a mob caper and not a CIA operation, as the underworld has insisted— would never have dared move against Giancana while Fifi Buccieri was alive.

BUCHALTER, Louis "Lepke" (1897-1944): Syndicate leader and murderer

The only national crime czar and kingpin of the rackets ever to go to the electric chair, Louis "Lepke" Buchalter graduated from sneak thievery during his youth on New York's Lower East Side to become one of the founders of the national crime syndicate. Through control of the tailors and cutters unions, Lepke milked millions from the New York garment industry. Part of Lepke's power sprung from his control of Murder, Inc., the Brooklyn "troop" of specialist killers who serviced the syndicate. Thus, Thomas E. Dewey referred to Lepke as "the worst industrial racketeer in America," and J. Edgar Hoover called him "the most dangerous criminal in the United States."

In the early 1920s, while most gangsters were attracted by the huge fortunes to be made in booze, Lepke chose a different route to underworld fame and wealth. He and another thug, Jacob "Gurrah" Shapiro, linked up with the era's top labor racketeer, "Little Augie" Orgen, to offer strike-breaking services to garment industry employers. Little Augie was shot dead in 1927, but Lepke and Shapiro prospered, especially after refining their operations so that they could serve both sides, assuming the added duties of union organizers and eventually taking control of union locals.

The union racketeers extended their operations to control the bakery drivers union and levied a penny "tax" per loaf on bakers to guarantee their products got to market fresh. To greater or lesser degrees, Lepke moved into other industries, especially in league with Tommy Lucchese, a mobster with close ties to Lucky Luciano. Their extortion rackets expanded to tough on such businesses as handbags, shoes, millinery, poultry, cleaning and dyeing, leather, restaurants and others until it was estimated legitimate businesses were paying Lepke up to $10 million a year just so they could operate without trouble.

The Lucchese connection gave Lepke an "in" with the budding crime syndicate being formed by Luciano, Meyer Lansky, Frank Costello, Joe Adonis, Dutch Schultz and others. The new organization recognized the need for an enforcement branch within its framework. Lepke was put in charge of it, with Albert Anastasia as second in command. The choice of Anastasia was obvious; he was a madman whose philosophy could be summed up in three words—kill, kill, kill. And the election of Lepke over him was equally logical. Lepke was the greatest exponent of violence in the rackets; an associate once noted "Lep loves to hurt people." Under Lepke and Anastasia the enforcement branch, later dubbed Murder, Inc. by the newspapers, carried out hundreds of hits for the syndicate.

Lepke courted trouble with the law, living lavishly and relishing the spotlight. Thomas Dewey, then an ambitious special prosecutor, zeroed in on him once he had convicted Luciano. And while Dewey went after him for bakery extortion, the federal government stalked him for restraint-of-trade violations. Then the federal Narcotics Bureau began gathering proof that Lepke was the head of a narcotics-smuggling operation that was involved in massive bribing of U.S. customs agents. Free on bail, Lepke decided to go into hiding. While a nationwide manhunt was organized to catch him, he continued to control his union rackets from various Brooklyn hideouts, where he was being hidden by Anastasia.

The continued manhunt, however, put extraordinary pressure on the entire syndicate and hamstrung their operations. Mayor Fiorello LaGuardia turned the screw even tighter by ordering his police commissioner, Lewis Valentine, to go to war on "hoodlums." The problem got so bad that it was brought to the attention of Luciano, then confined at Dannemora Prison but still the top voice in the organization. Luciano agreed that Lepke had to give himself up, but there was a problem: Lepke realized Dewey could convict him of enough charges to keep him in prison for life. Therefore, Luciano decided that Lepke would have to be fooled into surrendering. He arranged for an emissary Lepke trusted, Moe "Dimples" Wolensky, to carry a message that a deal had been worked out with J. Edgar Hoover whereby if he surrendered directly to the FBI chief, he would be tried on the federal narcotics charge only and not handed over to Dewey.

Lepke bought the story and surrendered on a Manhattan street to gossip columnist Walter Winchell and Hoover. As soon as he entered their car and Hoover spoke to him, Lepke realized he had been double-crossed. Lepke was convicted on federal charges of narcotics conspiracy and sentenced to 14 years at Leavenworth but was then turned over to Dewey who succeeded in getting another conviction that resulted in a 39-year-to-life sentence.

Unfortunately for Lepke, while he was behind bars, the story of Murder, Inc. broke, mainly because of information supplied by squealer, Abe Reles, one of the group's leading killers. Lepke was tied in as the leader of the killer troop and was specifically linked to the 1936 murder of a Brooklyn candy store owner named Joe Rosen, a former trucker in the garment district who had been forced out of business by Lepke. Instead of bearing his loss in silence, Rosen began making noise about going to the district attorney's office. Lepke handed out a contract on Rosen to two of his chief aides, Mendy Weiss and

Louis Capone, and to Pittsburgh Phil Strauss. Rosen ended up with 17 bullets in his corpse.

Even though Reles was killed in a mysterious fall from a window in a hotel where he was being kept under police guard, authorities had more than enough evidence to convict Lepke, Weiss and Capone (Strauss had already been sentenced to death for another murder). Through various appeals, Lepke staved off execution until March 1944. Shortly before his death the newspapers were filled with speculation that Lepke was talking about corrupt political and labor officials he had had dealings with and that if he really "opened up" he could blow the roof off the country, among other things delivering what one newspaper called "a prominent labor leader, powerful in national politics, as a man who had inspired several crimes." In thinly disguised sidebar stories, that labor leader was readily identifiable as Sidney Hillman, then an intimate adviser to President Franklin D. Roosevelt. Lepke himself was quoted as saying: "If I would talk, a lot of big people would get hurt. When I say big, I mean big. The names would surprise you."

The manhunt for Louis "Lepke" Buchalter was among the most intensive ever, one that ended only when other leaders of organized crime betrayed him.

The *New York Mirror* reported, "It is said Lepke offered material to Governor Dewey that would make him an unbeatable presidential candidate."

On the afternoon of the execution, Lepke released his version of the facts. He had his wife read a statement that he had dictated: "I am anxious to have it clearly understood that I did not offer to talk and give information in exchange for any promise of commutation of my death sentence. I did not ask for that! . . . The one and only thing I have asked for is to have a commission appointed to examine the facts. If that examination does not show that I am not guilty, I am willing to go to the chair, regardless of what information I have given or can give."

Clearly Lepke had given some information, but it had not been enough, and now he was eager to inform the syndicate he was not going to talk about crime matters. If he did, he realized, no member of his family would be spared.

On March 4, 1944 Lepke silently followed Capone and Weiss to the chair.

See also: *Thomas E. Dewey; Jewish Mafia; Murder, Inc.; Jacob "Little Augie" Orgen; Jacob "Gurrah" Shapiro; Walter Winchell.*

BUCHANAN, Dr. Robert (?1855-1895): Murderer

Dr. Robert Buchanan, one of New York's most famous 19th century killers, was a vain murderer who modeled his crime on a similar one committed by a young medical student, Carlyle Harris, for which the latter went to the chair. Dr. Buchanan, possessing higher scientific knowledge than that of a mere medical student, improved on Harris' method but also went to the chair.

Buchanan's background is a bit murky. He had lied about his age and education so that he could practice medicine in Canada without a license. When he got caught, he went to Chicago for a couple of years and then returned to Halifax, Nova Scotia, where he married the daughter of a wealthy manufacturer. Buchanan talked his in-laws into sending him to Edinburgh, Scotland to complete his medical education. When he returned, he and his wife moved to New York, where he set up a modest practice in Greenwich Village.

By 1890 when he divorced his wife and sent her back to Nova Scotia, Buchanan had developed a taste for the seamier side of life and had formed an attachment with big, fat, ugly Annie Sutherland, who lived in the Village but ran a call house in Newark. Annie had one very redeeming quality: she had $50,000 in the bank. When he proposed marriage, Annie Sutherland jumped at the chance. For her, marrying a doctor meant respectability. For Dr. Buchanan, the marriage meant $50,000.

About that time the Carlyle Harris case was coming to trial. Harris, a medical student had secretly married a young girl named Helen Potts. After tiring of her, he disposed of Helen by poisoning her with morphine. He had been caught because a doctor noticed her pupils were pin points, the universal sign of morphine poisoning.

One evening Buchanan was drinking in Macomber's, a Vil-

lage watering hole. He slammed a fist on the bar and said: "And I tell you Carlyle Harris was a fool! If Harris had known anything about medicine, he could have gotten away with it easily."

"How, Doc?" a drinking companion asked.

"Never mind," said Buchanan. "We of the profession cannot have laymen mindful of such information."

Buchanan would say no more, but he was in fact to put his opinion to the test. In 1892 he announced he was going to Edinburgh by himself, but four days before he was scheduled to leave, he canceled the trip because his wife had taken sick. Buchanan promptly called in not one but two other physicians to treat her. Both of them were with her when she died. Clearly, the doctors had no reason to view the woman's death as anything other than apoplexy, the result of a cerebral hemorrhage, their patient did not appear to have been poisoned since her pupils were not contracted. Apoplexy and morphine poisoning produced similar symptoms except for that one basic difference: in apoplexy there is no change in the pupils of the eyes, but in morphine poisoning the pupils greatly contract.

Some of Mrs. Buchanan's friends, from her brothel in Newark, were sure the doctor had not only married her for her money but had also killed her for it. Although the police wouldn't listen to such shady characters maligning an apparently respectable medical man, Ike White, a star reporter for the *New York World* who had a reputation for breaking cases, did listen. He had worked on the Carlyle Harris case he was intrigued by the story of a doctor who had married a madam.

White asked the physicians who had attended Mrs. Buchanan about her symptoms and raised the possibility of morphine poisoning, he was told that the woman's pupils had definitely not contracted. An average investigator or reporter might have given up right there, but White kept checking. He discovered that a mere three months after Mrs. Buchanan's death, the doctor had announced he was going to Edinburgh. Instead, he went back to Nova Scotia and remarried his first wife. The major difference in the doctor's present marital condition was that he was $50,000 better off. There was a story here and White knew it.

He also knew that in the 1890s, before the psychiatric couch came into vogue, the average man imparted his deepest secrets to either his priest or his bartender. He also knew that Dr. Buchanan was not a churchgoer. This theory is what finally led the reporter to Macomber's. He talked with Old Man Macomber about a number of things, including sports, current events, murders—especially the Carlyle Harris case—and people in the neighborhood who had died, such as Mr. Buchanan. Finally, the matter of Dr. Buchanan's statement about Harris' stupidity was raised.

"Now how could Harris not have been found out?" White said derisively.

The bartender leaned forward. "The doc told me," he said. "One night he said he wouldn't tell anybody how it could be done, but by closing time he was so plastered he whispered to me that if I'd set up one for him, he'd tell just me. I did and he said, 'If you've ever been to the eye doctor, and he's put drops in your eyes, chances are the eye drops were atropine, which makes the pupils dilate or enlarge. If Harris had used some atropine when he gave his wife the morphine, his wife's eyes would have ended up looking normal, and no one would have suspected."

White ran his story, and Dr. Buchanan was indicted. An autopsy showed that his wife had in fact been killed by morphine poisoning. At his trial the prosecution went so far as to kill a cat in the courtroom with morphine and then administer atropine to show how the pin pointing could be prevented.

On July 1, 1895 Dr. Buchanan went to the electric chair as a result of drunken remarks he never remembered making.

See also: *Isaac DeForest "Ike" White.*

BUCK Gang: Indian murderers

The Rufus Buck gang, five semi-literate, half-black, half-Creek Indians, lasted only two weeks in the old Indian territory of Arkansas-Oklahoma. While their crimes were shocking, they are best remembered by the enemies they made.

Rufus Buck and his four confederates—Lewis Davis, Sam Sampson, Maoma July and Luckey Davis—were all under the age of 20 when they started their depredations on July 28, 1895. A deputy marshal made the mistake of looking at them suspiciously and died in a hail of rifle fire. Over the next 13 days they carried out a series of holdups of stores and ranches around Fort Smith and committed several rapes, in one case threatening to drown a woman's babies unless she submitted. They held up a drummer, or salesman, named Callahan and gave him a "sporting chance" to escape if he could outrun their fire. He did, and in frustration, the gang turned their guns on Callahan's young black helper, killing him without the same sporting offer.

Not only whites but Creek Indians as well were incensed by the gang's actions. On August 10 the five were trapped in a grove outside of Muskogee where they were dividing some loot. The posse that tracked them down was composed of lawmen and a company of Creek Light Horse (Indian police).

They were brought to trial before Hanging Judge Parker, although the Creeks sorely wanted to try the gang and mete out Indian justice. None of the gang or their five appointed lawyers had much to say. One attorney's total summation was: "May it please the court and the gentlemen of the jury, you have heard the evidence. I have nothing to say." The jury rendered its verdict without even sitting down in the jury room and the five were duly hanged on July 1, 1896.

After the execution a picture of Rufus Buck's mother was found in his cell. On the back of it he had written this poem:

MY dreAM—
i,dremP'T, i, wAs, in, HeAven,
Among, THe Angels, FAir:
i,d, neAr, seen, none, so HAnd-
some,
THAT TWine, in goLden, HAir:
THeY, Looked, so, neAT,
And; sAng, so, sweeT

And, PLAY,d, THe, THe, goL-
den, HArp,
i, wAs, ABouT, To, Pick, An,
Angel ouT,
And, TAke, Her, To, mY HeaRT:
BuT, THe, momenT, i, BegAn,
To, PLea,
i,THougHT, oF, You, mY, Love,
THere, Was, none, i,d seen,
so, BeAuTiFuLL,
On, eArTH, or, HeAven, ABove.
gooDl By, My Dear, Wife . . anD
MoTHer

All. so. My sisTers.
RUFUS, BUCK
Youse. Truley

We are told by one of Hanging Judge Parker's more maudlin biographers that the poem "brought tears to Parker's dimming eyes."

See also: *Isaac C. "Hanging Judge" Parker.*

BUCKMINSTER, Fred (1863-1943): Con man

One of the most fabled of American con men Fred Buckminster started on the "bunco trail" while still a teenager. He was to be a swindler the rest of his life, completing his last prison term at the age of 75. In an era of hard money, he stole a minimum of $3 million.

He worked for 20 years with another fabulous fraud, Artist Yellow Kid Weil, together developing and pulling off some of the most famous con games of all time. They worked variations of the "fixed" prize fight and horse race swindles, utilizing a "big store," or phony betting shop, to trim the suckers. Everyone in the establishment other than the victim was a fake, betting and collecting on phony races. On some occasions Buckminster and Weil would turn things around and swindle a genuine betting parlor; one of them would get the results of a race at the Western Union office while the other placed a bet before the hotel bookie joint received the results. They swindled "Palmer House" Ryan, operator of the Stockade, a horse-betting establishment in the woods outside Chicago, by having a railroad engineer toot out the winner in code as his train passed the Stockade.

Buckminster discovered early in his career that the easiest person to cheat was another thief, amateur or professional. He victimized dishonest bankers, seeking out those who had been accused of cheating customers. He would pose as a depositor with some stocks that he would leave for safekeeping and then would permit himself to be "swindled" out of them after the banker was fed false information that the stock had suddenly ballooned in value.

As Buckminster once put it, "When I see a crook, I see nothing but dollar signs."

Buckminster's greatest swindle of other swindlers was a racket he worked with Kid Dimes, a leading gimmick man who fixed roulette wheels for crooked gambling houses. Buckminster was probably the first man to "fix" a fixed roulette wheel. In 1918 the Kid was busy rigging a wheel for the King George Club, a crooked gambling joint in Chicago's Loop area populated by con men who steered suckers there nightly.

The wheel Kid Dimes constructed allowed the croupier to let the ball stop in any of three numbers he desired, giving him complete control in picking red or black, odd or even or the winning set of numbers. On Buckminster's instructions, Kid Dimes added another button at the customer's end of the table that would cancel out the croupier's choice and magnetize the ball into the number 8 slot.

Outfitting himself in a 10-gallon hat, Buckminster posed as a Texan looking for some gambling action and soon was steered into the King George. With a con man at each elbow, he began playing the wheel. Despite their egging and his swagger about being a Texas oilman, he made only small bets. The house let him win a few while the con men kept working on him to set up a killing. Finally, Fred rose to the bait. He plunked down a roll of $10,000 on a bet covering numbers 7 through 12. The odds against Fred winning were 5-to-1. But of course there was no danger of that. Then just before the croupier rolled his roll, Fred tossed a fat $1,000 bill on number 8 "for good luck."

As the wheel spun, the croupier hit the secret button that guaranteed the ball would stop in a safe number in the 30s. At the same time, Fred pushed his button, canceling out the croupier's action. The little ball came to rest on number 8.

A loud cry went up in the place. Nobody had seen a hit like that. Five-to-1 on the combination bet and 35-to-1 on the number bet paid a total profit of $85,000. The croupier was stunned. A hurried conference was held, but Buckminster was relaxed. With so many suckers in the place, the house could do nothing but pay off. Others pounded on his back, congratulating him. Fred announced he hadn't had enough and continued to play further until he lost back $5,000. In the process, he also removed the secret button from under the table. Then he walked out, promising the con men to return the next evening. Naturally, he did not come back.

The gambling house owners were furious and sent for Kid Dimes to explain what went wrong. Kid Dimes was a picture of innocence as he inspected the table. He emerged from under the table holding a dead battery. Shaking his head in disdain, he said: "Why don't you people change batteries at least once a week to be safe? At a dime a throw you ought to even be able to afford to change batteries every night."

Over the next decade, whenever things cooled down, Buckminster and Kid Dimes worked that racket on several gambling houses. Buckminster once estimated it netted close to $750,000.

Despite his successes, Buckminster spent a great many of his adult years in prison. He was acutely aware of how greatly the odds favored the police over the crook. "A copper can make a thousand mistakes but a crook only one to get put away," he said sadly when he got out of prison the last time. At the age of 76, Buckminster retired from the rackets. In 1941 he did a series of memoirs for a detective magazine. He raised one of the checks given him for the use of his byline from $100 to $1,000 and cashed it. The publishing house took it philosophically and did not prosecute. Sending a dying old man back to prison made little sense, and it did seem a little late for Buckminster to alter his ways.

See also: *Joseph "Yellow Kid" Weil.*

BUFFALINO, Russell A. (1903–): Mob leader

Although labeled by the McClellan Committee as "one of the most ruthless and powerful leaders of the Mafia in the United States," Russell A. Buffalino has remained a prime example of the shadowy crime kingpin about whom much is suspected but little proved. Centering his activities around Pittstown Pa., Buffalino has long been considered the Mafia "family boss" of organized crime in much of that state. His activities reportedly have also extended into upstate New York and New Jersey, where he has been described as an active participant in labor racketeering and a behind-the-scenes power in Teamsters' affairs. It is known that the government has long regarded Buffalino as the prime suspect in ordering the "disappearance" of ex-Teamster head Jimmy Hoffa. He also has reputedly been involved in peddling drugs and fencing stolen jewelry. Although he had a record of arrests dating back to 1927 on such charges as receiving stolen goods, petty larceny and conspiracy to obstruct justice, he was not convicted of a serious offense until 1977, when he was sentenced to four years for extortion after threatening a man who owed $25,000 to a jeweler. The evidence against Buffalino was uncovered as part of the federal government's efforts to link him to the possible murder of Hoffa.

BUFFALOING: Method of police brutality in the old west

Described several times in Western lore as "the gentle art of bending a revolver barrel around a lawbreaker's skull," buffaloing was a common treatment given cowboys by vicious "townie" lawmen. Two confirmed practitioners of the method were Wild Bill Hickok and Wyatt Earp. This technique was rarely anything other than pure brutality, since the victim was generally in custody and disarmed when the "head creasing" took place. The term evidently derived from the contemptuous attitude many lawmen had toward cowboys, regarding them as so dimwitted that they were as easy targets for a slugging as a buffalo was for a hunter's gun. Earp carried the practice to such excess that one Texas cattleman put a $1,000 bounty on his head because of his treatment of the rancher's cowboys.

See also: *George Hoyt.*

BUG And Meyer Mob: Early Lansky gang

Started in 1921 by Meyer Lansky, who was the brains, and Bugsy Siegel, who provided the muscle, the Bug and Meyer Mob was the forerunner of Murder, Inc.

Lansky and Siegel had been inseparable buddies since childhood in New York City. Together they formed a stolen car combine, in time supplying cars to various gangs. As their gang of tough Jewish hoods grew, Lansky began renting out drivers for the cars and then hit men who might be needed. They also took on the job of protecting bootleg gangs' booze convoys, occasionally hijacking shipments for another gang. The Bug and Meyer Mob's rates were high, and in time some bootleggers figured out it would be cheaper simply to bring them into the operation and give them a slice of the take.

Lucky Luciano, thanks to a friendship with Lansky that was to last his lifetime, made good use of the mob. The Bug and Meyer forces protected Luciano from assassination until he was ready to move against the "Mustache Petes" of the old Mafia forces. As the head of a group of Jewish gunmen posing as police detectives, Siegel assassinated Salvatore Maranzano, thereby making Luciano the number one Italian gangster in the country. After that, the need for the Bug and Meyer Mob ended and all its members moved on to lucrative positions with the newly established Luciano-Lansky crime syndicate.

Years later when Lansky attempted to gain refuge from U.S. law in Israel, he tried to paint the Bug and Meyer Mob as just a collection of poor Jewish boys he had organized to protect other Jews from the vicious Irish gangs of the period. This revisionist version of history has little evidence to support it. The Bug and Meyer Mob was a group of killers, the first of organized crime's Murder, Inc. troops, and many of its "graduates" played godfatherly roles when the Brooklyn version of that organization was established in the 1930s under Lepke and Anastasia.

See also: *Meyer Lansky, Benjamin "Bugsy" Siegel.*

BUGGING: See Wiretapping and Bugging.

BULETTE, Julia (1832-1867): Madam and murder victim

Julia Bulette was the reigning madam of Virginia City, Nev. during the town's wide-open mining days and her murder in 1867 became a *cause celebre* of the time. In a larger sense, it marked the beginning of the taming of the West.

It is hard to separate fact from legend when talking about Julia. In later years it was believed that she was buried in a solid silver coffin, that a parlor car on the Virginia and Truckee Railroad was named in her honor, that she was enormously rich and that she charged as much as $1,000 a night for her company. Probably only the last two items were really true.

This beauty of Creole origin turned up in Virginia City in 1859, when it was no more than a town of clapboard houses and tents inhabited by 6,000 miners and a handful of women.

Julia immediately set up business as a prostitute, starting to entertain men as soon as a floor was laid for her cabin, while other grateful miners went about putting up the walls and roof. Julia's enterprise flourished and within a year she employed six other girls to handle business. She opened a parlor house that became the town's center of elegance, one that offered French cuisine and wines and had fresh flowers brought in daily from the West Coast by Wells Fargo. Julia was made an honorary member of the Virginia City Fire Co., the only woman so honored, and on the Fourth of July, she led the parade through town, riding a fire truck adorned with roses.

Much beloved by miners, mine owners and railroad tycoons, Julia was frequently pictured as the prostitute with the Golden Heart. Her praises were often sung by a young reporter for the *Territorial Enterprise* who had just adopted the pen name of Mark Twain. During the Civil War she was one of the biggest contributors to and fund raisers for the Sanitation Fund, the Red Cross of its day. When a fever epidemic hit the area, Julia turned her pleasure palace into a hospital and pawned much of her jewelry and furs to raise money to care for and feed the sick. After the sickness passed, the establishment returned to its fabled bagnio status.

During her early years in town, Julia always sat in the orchestra of the local theater surrounded by a swarm of admirers but with the arrival of more virtuous ladies and gentlemen in Virginia City, she was forced to sit in a box on the side, curtained off from their cold stares. Civilization was coming to the West and Julia's days as queen of Virginia City society were clearly coming to an end.

On January 20, 1867 Julia was found strangled in her bed, most of her valuables gone. She had been murdered by either a thief or a client.

The miners of Virginia City were outraged. Quickly, suspect after suspect, 12 in all, were arrested, questioned and finally released after proving their innocence. Had one been judged guilty in those angry days just following murder, a lynching would have resulted, despite the attitudes of the more righteous elements.

Unable to bring the culprit to justice, the men of Virginia City gave Julia Bulette the biggest funeral the town had ever seen. All mines, mills and stores were shut down and draped in black bunting. Led by the fire company and the Metropolitan Brass Band, the cortege paraded through town with hundreds of weeping men in the line of march. We are told that the respectable women of the town shuttered their windows for fear of seeing their own husbands in the procession. After Julia's body was laid in the ground, the band marched back to town, playing the rollicking "The Girl I Left Behind Me."

Several months after the murder, the culprit, John Millain, described in the local press as a "trail louse," was captured following an attempt to rob and kill another madam. Many of Julia's jewels and other prize possessions were found on him. Despite his claims that others were responsible for the murder, Millain was convicted after a quick trial.

The community attitude toward Millain was probably best

reflected in the district attorney's summation to the jury:

> Although this community has, in times past, seen blood run
> like water, yet in most cases there was some cause brought
> forward in justification of the deed, some pretext. But on the
> morning of the 20th of January last, this community, so har-
> dened by previous deeds of blood, was struck dumb with
> horror by a deed which carried dread to the heart of everyone—a
> deed more fiendish, more horrible than ever before perpetrated
> on this side of the snowy Sierra. Julia Bulette was found lying
> dead in her bed, foully murdered, and stiff and cold in her
> clotted gore. True, she was a woman of easy virtue. Yet hund-
> reds in this city have had cause to bless her name for her many
> acts of kindness and charity. So much worse the crime. That
> woman probably had more real, warm friends in this commu-
> nity than any other; yet there was found at last a human being
> so fiendish and base as to crawl to her bedside in the dead hour
> of the night, and with violent hands, beat and strangle her to
> death—not for revenge, but in order to plunder her of these
> very articles of clothing and jewelry we see before us. What
> inhuman, unparalled barbarity!

That philosophy reflected the thinking of virtually the entire male population of Virginia City, but not that of some of
the women. During his confinement in jail, many of the good
ladies of the area virtually lionized Millain, bringing him
delicacies to fortify his spirits. A woman's committee went so
far as to circulate a petition for commutation of his sentence.
The *Territorial Enterprise* was incensed by the effort, commenting: "We believe that the man will be hung. If he is not, we
do not know where a fit subject for hanging is to be found."

After Millain was sentenced to be hanged on April 24,
1868, so many people wished to attend the event that it had to
be shifted to a great natural ampitheater one mile to the north
of the city. On that day all the mines on the Comstock shut
down once again; it was the second major holiday Julia Bulette
had provided.

BUMMERS: Western gang

The Bummers were an organized band of outlaws who robbed,
raped and terrorized Auraria, Colorado Territory from about
1855 to 1860, much as the Plummer gang did a few years later
in Bannack, Montana Territory.

In 1860 the Bummers were wiped out by a vigilante committee of just 10 townsmen in alliance with the local sheriff, who
made no pretense about observing legal niceties. The sheriff
whose name went unrecorded by the chroniclers of the day,
would approach two or three Bummers and arrest them on
some minor charge, and since the outlaws knew they would be
released shortly, they offered no resistance, right up to the
moment when a noose was suddenly slipped around their necks.
After a few such multiple hangings, the Bummers who hadn't
been hung fled and law and order came to Auraria.

BUNCH, Eugene "Captain Gerald" (?1850-1889): Train robber

A former schoolteacher who decided there was more money in
robbing trains, Eugene Bunch became the notorious Captain

Gerald, scourge of the railroads of Texas, Louisiana and Mississippi during the 1880s.

He staged his first robbery in 1888, when he climbed aboard
a Southern Express train outside New Orleans and quietly
informed the express car guard that he would blow his brains
out if he didn't open the safe. Departing with $10,000 in
currency and bonds, he told the guard to inform the railroad
line that Captain Gerald would be back. Wanted posters described this Captain Gerald as "soft-spoken." After he gained
notoriety and a certain popularity with a few more robberies,
Bunch was described by the newspapers as being "handsome
and daring."

Bunch moved on to Texas, where he became a society darling and extremely popular with the ladies. He passed himself
off as a Captain Bunch, a former newspaper editor from Virginia, and he spent an honest six months running a local
newspaper. Bunch also had a torrid affair with the daughter of
a former governor of Texas. When the train-robbing urge hit
him again, Bunch ended up in Mississippi and the girl followed him, dutifully awaiting his return from each holdup. By
now, however, Pinkerton detectives were closing in on Captain Gerald and had even connected him with Captain Bunch.

In 1889 Bunch ceased his lone wolf operations and recruited
five gunfighters to form a gang. One was captured and betrayed
the gang's hiding place on a small island in a Mississippi
swamp. Bunch and two of his gang were ambushed while they
were eating. His two confederates were shot before they could
even rise from the table. Attempting to make a run for it,
Bunch was shot dead in a spirited gun battle. The revelations
about Captain Bunch, needless to say, sent shock waves through
Texas society.

BUNTLINE, Ned: See Edward Z. C. Judson.

BURDELL, Dr. Harvey (1811-1857): Murder victim

The murder of Dr. Harvey Burdell was New York's most
sensational case during the 1850's, marked by too many suspects and too many motives, and ending with the public paying
P. T. Barnum a fortune to view a baby whose claim to fame
was not having been fathered by the late dentist Burdell.

In 1857 Dr. Burdell, at the age of 46, was no pillar of
righteousness in the community. When the police relayed
news of Burdell's murder to his own brother, Theo, the man
declared, "I am not surprised, for he was a dirty"—here even
the more sensational of the city's press concealed the words—
.............!"

As the police pressed their investigation, they found that no
one seemed to have a good word to say about the departed
wealthy dentist. He was described as a sly scoundrel, an accomplished thief, a slick cheat, a welsher, a cheap swindler, a
liar "whose word was not worth a cough," a man who quarreled with everyone including his patients. One redoubtable
Irishman even insisted Burdell had been a secret agent in the

pay of the British government. And why not? Anything was possible when speaking of a man who could woo a girl; go to the church to marry her; pull her father aside and say the wedding was off unless he was paid $20,000; and indeed call the wedding off if no agreement in principle was reached.

Dr. Burdell was paid back in full by his murderer; he died in painful and lingering fashion. He had been stabbed 12 times, and sometime during that ritual, in between or afterward, the murderer or murderess paused to strangle him for good measure. He was found in the master bedroom of his Bond Street home by a young boy who came each morning to make a fire in the fireplace. The boy had trouble pushing open the door to the bedroom, and the obstruction turned out to be Burdell's body. The place was spattered with blood.

There were three other people living in the Burdell mansion. One was a comely widow, Mrs. Emma Cunningham, who, on a sublet deal with the dentist, rented out rooms to boarders. She was about the most distressed person the police found. When informed of the crime, she shrugged and said, "Well those things happen."

A bachelor businessman, John J. Eckel, who rented a room in the house, was not quite as heartbroken. In fact, a contemporary historian insisted he danced a jig when he learned of Burdell's passing. The other tenant was George Snodgrass, who was the son of a Presbyterian minister, a shy and effeminate-looking youth, broke into a big smile when told about the murder and supposedly went out to celebrate, got drunk and tried to attack a hulking longshoreman. Snodgrass was to become a prime suspect after the police found various female undergarments, which he evidently liked to wear, secreted in his rooms. This struck the lawmen as somehow highly significant in a murder investigation.

But there were other major suspects. Dr. Burdell was known to owe a bundle to Honest John Burke, the crookedest gambler in town. Honest John took the loss of his money quite well when informed of his patsy's death. As a matter of fact, he ordered drinks set up for everyone in his favorite tavern, including the officers who brought him the tidings. A rich old Connecticut Yankee, Spawl, now living in New York, had much the same reaction as Honest John, although he didn't spend any money to exhibit his joy. Dr. Burdell had also pursued his daughter, Miss Lucy Spawl, until Spawl sent him away. Burdell had become so incensed that he beat up the old man.

Unfortunately for the police, Honest John, Spawl and several other suspects all had alibis for the time of the murder. This left authorities with the three persons living in the Burdell mansion, Cunningham, Eckel and Snodgrass. And in fact, since the house was shut tight from the inside and the fireplace boy had his own key to get in, the murder certainly appeared to be an inside job. If it hadn't been, then how had the killer entered and left?

Mrs. Cunningham became a prime suspect when she suddenly laid claim to a widow's portion of Burdell's estate, stating she had married him secretly a short time before his murder. She even produced a rather senile minister to attest to the

marriage. Yes, the minister said, he had married the woman to a Harvey Burdell. But he wasn't at all sure if this Burdell fellow resembled the deceased. In fact, the minister allowed that the groom looked a little like roomer Eckel.

The coroner decided there wasn't all that strong a case against any of the three alone; so he ruled all three were involved in the murder and should be charged. The prosecutor in the case was A. Oakley Hall, a district attorney who was later to become the most rapacious and, according to some, the most dishonest district attorney in the history of New York City, known as O.K. Haul. But at this stage of the game, Hall was merely out to make a name for himself so he could pave the way for his future misdeeds.

Mrs. Cunningham was to be tried first, under Hall's plan, and her supposed confederates later. One reason for this was that doctors had found Burdell had been stabbed by a left-handed person—and Mrs. Cunningham, or Mrs. Burdell, was left-handed. But aside from that detail and motive and opportunity, there was little direct evidence linking the woman with the crime.

All the while the district attorney was presenting his case, the defendant sat in a chair demurely knitting little blue and pink things. Finally, Hall had had enough and he protested this bizarre behavior. Emma's lawyer, Henry L. Clinton, a descendant of a former vice-president of the United States, defended his client's action. Mrs. Burdell—as he insisted on calling her—was pregnant and would soon be giving birth to the deceased's child.

In the end, that as much as anything caused the jury to bring in a not-guilty verdict. With the woman free, the prosecution gave up efforts to convict the two men. The men quickly disappeared, but Mrs. Cunningham-Burdell stayed much in evidence, pressing her claim to the Burdell fortune. Now that she was with child, she stood to inherit virtually the entire estate. Her pregnancy, however, had an odd quality to it. She seemed to grow bigger, but she would not permit her doctor to examine her. She was, she said, of the old, old school and no male hands would ever touch her body.

Finally, the doctor decided he was being used and went to the district attorney to say he suspected the woman was stuffing her dress with cushions. The authorities put a watch on her and soon found she was dickering to buy a new-born baby. She offered a young unmarried girl about to give birth $1,000 if she would slip her baby right over to the Burdell home. The girl took the money, and as soon as her baby was born, it was sent over to the alleged Mrs. Burdell, who planned to inform her doctor that a little event had happened during the night. But the police were watching and stormed into the bedroom of the bogus mother-to-be and arrested her.

Many people thought that since Mrs. Cunningham wasn't pregnant, it somehow meant she had indeed murdered Burdell. But the fact was she had been acquitted of that charge. Fraud charges were brought against her but they were later dropped. The Burdell case was to remain unsolved, although for many years the press continued to present various theories. The *Police Gazette* came out with an exclusive that the murderer was a man named Lewis, who had just been executed in New Jersey for another murder. Lewis had told the Gazette that he had done the job by mistake, meaning to kill another Burdell.

Whoever did kill Dr. Burdell, now firmly established as New York's favorite murder victim, never paid for his sins, but at least the guilty party did not gain financially from his or her crime. The only one to make out well moneywise was the bogus Burdell baby. Her mother, already $1,000 ahead on the deal, rented her out for $25 a week to P.T. Barnum, who displayed the tot at his museum for all the eager New Yorkers wishing to see what a baby impostor looked like.

BURKE, Elmer "Trigger" (1917-1958): Hit man

In the 1950s the most reliable hit man used by the underworld was Elmer "Trigger" Burke, who often said there were only two things in this world that he loved—money and machine guns. In trouble as a youth, he was advised by his older hoodlum brother, Charlie, to join the Army in order to avoid being sent to prison for the robbery of a New York City grocery. Fighting in Europe during World War II, he distinguished himself, earning his nickname of Trigger by storming a German machine-gun nest and killing eight enemy soldiers. When his lieutenant reached the scene, he found Burke still blazing away and told him to stop because "those bastards are dead."

"You're goddamn right they are," Burke replied, slinging his weapon.

When Burke returned to his native Hell's Kitchen in New York City, he again moved in mob circles and through his brother's good offices became a freelance killer for a number of gangs. These killings he handled with precision, but he proved less adept at committing his own robberies. He was sentenced to two years at Sing Sing for a liquor store holdup. While Burke was in prison, his brother was murdered. The police nabbed a man named George Goll for the job but released him for insufficient evidence. Via the grapevine, Burke informed Goll that he did not believe the accusation against him. When he got out of prison, he found Goll on a Manhattan street and put two bullets into the back of his head.

Burke also committed a number of other murders mostly on paid assignments but occasionally gratis. He apparently killed Edward "Poochy" Walsh on July 23, 1952 out of nothing more than personal pique. He entered a bar where Poochy was holding forth, stuck a revolver in his face and blew his victim away with three slugs. "Don't call me Trigger no more," he said. "Call me Killer."

For the rest of Trigger Burke's days before his arrest, he was a wanted man, but he remained readily available to the underworld for hit duty. In June 1954 Burke was assigned to eradicate Joseph "Specs" O'Keefe, reputedly a wayward member of the gang that had pulled the $2.7 million Brinks robbery and believed to be about ready to provide the police with details and names of those involved. It was one of the few jobs Burke messed up. In a wild machine-gun spree through the streets of Boston, Burke loosed blast after blast at the fleeing O'Keefe but managed only to wound him. O'Keefe survived and identified his attacker. Trigger Burke became the most-hunted outlaw of the era for all of 24 hours.

Contrary to expectations, Burke did not leave Boston; he apparently had more assignments. The next day another hoodlum, George O'Brien, was found fatally wounded just three miles from the scene of the Burke-O'Keefe shooting spree. And that evening a Boston detective arrested Burke "on suspicion." Burke looked at him and said, "You've made a better pinch than you think, copper."

Burke was clapped in the 104-year-old Suffolk County Prison on Charles Street and remained there until he was able to escape three months later with the help of two gunmen who broke into the prison through a carriage shed and two unused emergency doors.

Burke's escape electrified the nation, but his freedom was short-lived. A year later, he was captured by the FBI in Charleston, S.C. while waiting for a bus. He was unarmed and offered no resistance. Burke's attorneys resisted efforts to extradite him to New York for the Walsh killing, insisting he go instead to Massachusetts to face charges of carrying a machine gun and breaking out of jail. New York won out. On January 9, 1958 Burke went to the electric chair, after a last meal of a giant steak followed by a half dozen cigars. He spent his remaining hours going over 144 newspaper clippings of his exploits. Burke advised the warden to preserve them all "for history's sake."

See also: *Brink's Robbery.*

BURKE, William (1870-?): "Philadelphia's Jean Valjean"

William Burke was one of the most tragic figures in American criminality, whose fate earned him the title of Philadelphia's Jean Valjean. Burke did not, however, enjoy the final happiness of his fictional counterpart. In his early years in Boston Burke had a different nickname, the Prince of Flatworkers, which he had earned by robbing an estimated 300 to 400 houses and apartments in that city. Finally caught, he served seven years in the Charlestown state prison under another name.

Upon completion of his sentence Burke settled in Philadelphia, where he lived an honest life and saved up enough to open a cigar store. He married and in 1911 was elected to the city council on a reform slate. Burke might have continued his upright life with his past shrouded in secrecy had not a former fellow convict from Charlestown recognized him. The man blackmailed Burke to the point that he finally resigned from office and confessed his criminal record, retiring then to a bitter obscurity.

BURNS, Robert Elliott (1890-1965): Chain gang fugitive

Author of *I Am a Fugitive from a Georgia Chain Gang,* Robert Elliott Burns, through his book and a subsequent movie about his life, was responsible for the exposure and eventually the end of the inhumane Georgia chain gang system.

Out of a job as a World War I veteran, Burns, together with two strangers, burglarized $5.80 from a grocery store. For this crime he was sentenced to six-to-10 years on the chain gang. In June 1922 Burns made a dramatic escape and was not located until 1930, by which time he had risen to a high post on a magazine in Chicago. Burns voluntarily returned to Georgia after being promised by state officials that he would get a pardon. Instead, he was returned to the chain gang. Burns then did what no other prisoner had done—he escaped the chain gang a second time, assuming a double life in New Jersey. During this period Burns began writing magazine articles describing his personal story and exposing chain gang conditions. These articles were expanded into a book, and in 1932 a movie about his prison life starring Paul Muni evoked much public sympathy.

Georgia officials, however, were outraged. Finally locating Burns later than year, they demanded his extradition. New Jersey Gov. A. Harry Moore held a special hearing in the Senate Chamber of the State House at Trenton. Heading Burns' defense was Clarence Darrow, and the hearing soon turned into a trial of Georgia's penal system. Described in chilling detail was the "sweat box," a barrel with iron staves on top, in which "insolent" prisoners were kept, often with near-fatal results. It was revealed that prison cages built for 18 men actually housed 34 convicts. Bolstered with endorsements by several other governors, Gov. Moore rejected the extradition request. Burns was a free man inside New Jersey. Still Georgia did not cease its efforts to recapture its most-publicizing fugitive. In 1941, Gov. Eugene Talmadge tried again to win custody of Burns, citing improvements made in the penal system. These claims were countered by penal reformers who said the changes were in name only, not in fact.

In 1945, Gov. Ellis Arnall finally ended the chain gang system and invited Burns to return to Georgia. He did and Arnall immediately commuted his sentence to time served. A free man at last, Burns returned to his New Jersey home and thereafter continued to lend support to penal reform movements until his death 10 years later.

See also: *Chain Gangs.*

BURNS, William J. (1858-1932): Detective

Few detectives in history have led as checkered a career as William J. Burns, founder of the detective agency that bears his name. He was also the "star of the United States Secret Service" and later the discredited head of the Bureau of Investigation, forerunner of the present FBI. Both in government and private work, Burns may have been the most-politicized detective the country has ever seen. Samuel Gompers, the head of the American Federation of Labor, regarded him as an enemy of labor, a frame-up man and faker of evidence. Yet during their head-on clash over the 1910 bombing of the *Los Angeles Times* building, it was Gompers who lost face when the McNamara brothers, two labor officials, were convicted of the

murderous plot. Burns emerged to great accolades, with the *New York Times* referring to him as "the greatest detective certainly, and perhaps the only really great detective, the only detective of genius whom the country has produced."

Similarly the great attorney, Clarence Darrow, who also tangled with Burns in the McNamara case, came within an eyelash of being sent to prison on a charge of jury tampering. But during his career Burns himself narrowly missed being imprisoned on such charges as kidnapping and jury tampering, once being lucky to escape with a mere fine against his agency for keeping under surveillance the jurors in the trial of oil man Harry Sinclair. Throughout his career, Burns served the establishment, or at least those elements within the establishment he deemed proper. Generally, this meant those with a strong antilabor bias and pro-Eastern Republican leanings.

Few could quarrel with Burns' early detective career as a member of the U. S. Secret Service, when he cracked many important counterfeiting cases, especially the Bredell-Taylor ring. In 1905 Burns was put in charge of investigating the great Western land fraud, in which tens of thousands of acres of public lands were illegally fenced or bought under false representations. Through Burns' efforts Oregon Sen. John H. Mitchell and Oregon Rep. John N. Williamson, both Republicans, were convicted and right-wing Republicans never forgave Burns. Years later, considerable evidence indicated that some of the investigations and prosecutions were so corrupt and politically tainted that many regarded them as worse than the charges brought against those eventually convicted.

In 1906 Burns left government service to conduct an investigation of corruption in San Francisco one that would ultimately wreck the machine and send Boss Abe Ruef to prison. Later, he cracked the *Los Angeles Times* bombing, which many regarded as the greatest bit of detective work in American history, by tracing bomb fragments to the McNamara brothers. However, Burns' stunning accomplishment in the case became somewhat tarnished when, some say at the instigation of *Times* owner Harrison Gray Otis, he attempted to prove the McNamara's lawyer, Clarence Darrow, had attempted to bribe two jurors. The charge was a bit far fetched considering Darrow was at the time preparing to have the McNamara brothers plead guilty in order to save them from execution.

The move failed when Darrow, taking over his own case in summation, made a speech lasting a day and a half that has been cited as matching the eloquence of William Jennings Bryan's "Cross of Gold" oration. "Burns!" Darrow sneered throughout. "Burns with his pack of hounds. The steel trust with its gold. All arrayed against me. I stood alone for the poor and weak. Will it be the gray dim walls of San Quentin? My life has been all too human, but I have been a friend to the helpless. I have cried their cause."

Near the conclusion, Darrow cried: "Oh, you wild insane members of the steel trust . . . . Oh, you bloodhounds of detectives who do your masters' evil bidding. Oh, you district attorneys. You know not what you do."

Right then, it was said, Burns knew he was beaten. The jury came in with a not-guilty verdict after only one ballot.

Another trial for the alleged bribing of the second juror ended in a hung jury, and the local authorities, Otis and Burns gave up their attempt to jail Darrow.

Despite this defeat, Burns' detective agency was flourishing. He had succeeded in wresting the plum of the profession, the contract with the American Bankers Association for the protection of its 11,000 member banks, from the much larger and more powerful Pinkertons. Burns' disdain for the Pinkertons was limitless. He regarded his competitors as cowardly, taking on only "safe" cases and never going against local public opinion. To Burns' credit, he was willing to buck public opinion in the case of a young Jewish businessman in Georgia, Leo Frank, who was convicted of raping and murdering a 14-year-old white girl, Mary Phagan, and sentenced to death. During their investigation Burns and one of his assistants were almost lynched by a mob. Because of evidence uncovered by the detectives, Frank's death sentence was commuted, but he was later kidnapped from his prison cell and hanged.

From 1912 through the war years, Burns compiled an impressive record of uprooting political corruption in a number of states, leading to indictments of many lawmakers and political figures. In 1913 he exposed bribe taking in Canada in the Quebec Legislature.

In 1921 Burns was appointed to a position that should have been the capstone of his career, head of the Bureau of Investigation, then an organization that was inept at best and corruption-ridden at worst. It cannot be said that Burns improved matters; in fact, the bureau became overrun with agents urged on Burns by the very figures who were to become involved in the Teapot Dome Scandal. About the only laudable accomplishment of the bureau under Burns was an effective prosecution of the Ku Klux Klan, which Burns had come to hate in the aftermath of the Leo Frank case. However, his famed ability to detect fraud and graft failed him completely as the "Ohio Gang" took over during the Harding Administration. Burns apparently saw nothing while corrupt friends of Harding looted the Veteran's Bureau and the Alien Property Claims Bureau. The former bloodhound failed to uncover Secretary of the Interior Albert Fall's blatant selling off of the Teapot Dome and Elk Hills government oil reserves to the highest bribers.

In 1924 Burns resigned in disgrace and was succeeded by a young assistant, J. Edgar Hoover. Burns remained on the front pages as head of his private agency, he was accused in 1927 of jury tampering in the acquittal of oilman Henry Sinclair, charged as one of the bribers of Secretary of the Interior Fall. Burns had accepted an assignment from Sinclair to keep the jurors under surveillance. An angry federal judge ruled that the jury shadowing was itself a form of jury tampering.

Burns' angry response, which perhaps all too well summarized his own career, was, "My men didn't do anything for Harry Sinclair that I haven't done for the federal government hundreds of times!"

Burns died in April 1932.

See also: *Leo Frank, Land Frauds,* Los Angeles Times *Bombing, Gaston Bullock Means, Earl Rogers.*

BURR-HAMILTON Duel

The most famous duel in this country's history was between Alexander Hamilton and Vice President Aaron Burr on the banks of the Hudson River at Weehawken, N.J. on July 11, 1804.

There had been a festering hatred between the two men since 1801, when Hamilton refused to join in the conspiracy to keep Thomas Jefferson from the presidency and persuaded a number of key Federalist congressmen to choose Jefferson in the runoff against Burr, whom Hamilton called "a cold-blooded Cataline." At the signal, Burr fired, and Hamilton tumbled forward mortally wounded. Hamilton's gun had discharged into the air, and many of his supporters claimed he had deliberately fired high. A coroner's jury called for Burr's arrest, but he fled to the South. After the duel, Hamilton's reputation was enhanced, while Burr became an outcast. A typical poem attacking him read:

> Oh Burr, oh Burr, what hast thou done,
> Thou hast shooted dead great Hamilton!
> You hid among a bunch of thistle
> And shooted him dead with a great hoss pistol!

BURROW, Rube (1856-1890): Train robber and murderer

Reuben Houston Burrow, the leader of the notorious Burrow gang of the 1880s, developed the same sort of mystique that Jesse James enjoyed. The balladeers and legend-makers, for instance, celebrated the time Rube and brother Jim drove off the miserly banker out to foreclose on a widow's mortgage; of course, they also robbed him for their own gain.

A daring criminal, Rube several times pulled off one of the most difficult of criminal endeavors: robbing a train single-handed. Generally, however, he worked with a gang that included his brother James, another pair of brothers, Will and Leonard Brock, and various other "hard cases."

The Burrow brothers were born in Alabama and eventually moved to Texas, where they led rather tranquil existences as small farmers for about 14 years before suddenly turning to crime, perhaps because of tales they had heard about a so-called glamorous and lately lamented outlaw named Sam Bass. In any event, they went about robbing trains until they became the subject of ballads, especially after the brothers made a habit of robbing the same train at the same spot on a number of occasions. In February 1888 the Burrows were captured, but Rube broke jail and escaped. With an accomplice named Lewis Waldrip, who may have been Leonard Brock, Rube spent most of the next several months trying to break Jim Burrow out of his Little Rock, Ark. prison, but his brother died there from consumption in December. Forced eastward by his pursuers, Rube Barrow continued his train-robbing activities in Florida and Alabama. In 1890 he pulled one of his lone wolf jobs. As he confidently strode to his horse to ride off once more into the darkness, a Southern Express detective took his head off with a shotgun blast.

BURTON, Mary (?-?): False informer

An 18th century prostitute and thief named Mary Burton had a more chilling record as an informer than even the girls involved in the Salem witchcraft hysteria. Finding herself in prison in 1741, Burton, also known as Margaret Kelly, sought and won her freedom by concocting a story about an imaginary "Negro criminal plot" in New York City. Because blacks, slave and free, comprised a large segment of the population, any talk of concerted action by them provoked fears on the part of the whites. Given that climate, the general rule was that any testimony by a white woman, regardless of her character or motive, was sufficient to convict a black. Mary Burton also found that every new accusation she made added to her prestige. As a result, 71 blacks were transported away, 20 were hanged and 14 others were burned at the stake. As was the case in the Salem executions, the general dignity with which many of the condemned died finally sparked doubt in the public's mind and Mary Burton's charges were later simply ignored.

BURTS, Matthew (1878-1925): Train robber

A minor member of the notorious Burt Alvord-Billy Stiles outlaw band, Burts deserves an entry of his own since, thanks to a cunning strategem by law officers, he was responsible for the gang's complete breakup.

Burts was suspected of being one of the robbers who held up the Southern Pacific train near Cochise, Arizona Territory on September 9, 1899 but it couldn't be proved. Constable Grover of Pearce devised what might be called a reverse undercover operation: he hired Burts as a deputy. Totally unsuspecting any ulterior motive, the dim-witted Burts, got rip-roarin' drunk with Grover and his cronies and slowly spilled out details of the robbery until he had made what amounted to a complete confession and had named all the other robbers. With Alvord and Stiles identified, the days of their criminal enterprises were numbered. For being an unwitting informer, Burts was rewarded with a prison term instead of the rope. He served his time and then moved on to California, where he engaged in the cattle business. Despite years of honest living, Burts still died violently; he was shot dead in 1925 in a grazing rights dispute with a neighboring rancher.

See also: *Burt Alvord, Billie Stiles.*

BUSHWHACKER

Originally bushwhacker had no more meaning than backwoodsman, but the backwoods became the scene of so much criminal violence, starting with the 18th century depredations of Joseph Hare, Sam Mason and the Harpe brothers along the Natchez Trace, that every bushwhacker had to be regarded as a potential attacker. By the time of the maraudings of Quantrill and his Raiders during the Civil War, bushwhacker had already come to mean a backwoods outlaw.

BUSTER From Chicago (?-1931): Hit man

Perhaps the most brutal and efficient hit man the Mafia ever had was known simply as "Buster from Chicago." Because of his prowess at murder, he was imported into New York by the Maranzano forces to do battle with the dominant power of Giuseppe "Joe the Boss" Masseria during the Castellammarese War of 1930-1931. In true Hollywood fashion, no one ever knew Buster's real identity, and his appearance belied that of a professional killer. He looked and dressed like a college boy and carried with him, in the proper Chicago tradition, a submachine gun in a violin case. How many men he killed during that war or earlier in Chicago was never determined, but Buster had a reputation of always succeeding in a hit and doing it with a flair that other gangsters admired. On an assignment to "take out" Peter "the Clutching Hand" Morello, Buster found him and a visitor in Morello's office. He shot Morello, but his victim was tough. He got up and danced around the office trying to avoid further shots. Getting into the spirit of things, Buster backed off and for a while tried to wing Morello shooting gallery style before finally finishing him for good. Then, without a word, Buster turned to the visitor, one Giuseppe Pariano, who had stood frozen during the macabre scene, and killed him also.

Joe Valachi, the celebrated informer, marveled at Buster's shooting ability, which was equally masterful with machine guns, pistols or shotguns. Buster was the main shotgunner in the shooting of two top Masseria aides. Alfred Mineo and Steve Ferrigno, cut down in the Bronx on November 5, 1930. After the hit he and the two other gunmen with him scattered, but a police officer cut him off just a block from the murder scene. Excitedly, Buster told him there had been a shooting down the street. The officer raced that way and Buster the other. Another of Buster's victims was James Catania, alias Joe Baker, who was killed on February 3, 1931 as he stood on a street corner talking to his wife. Buster had been loathe to do the shooting in front of the victim's wife but couldn't resist such an open target. He was proud of the fact that every shot hit the victim and none the woman.

Buster lived through the Castellammarese War and the victory of Maranzano, but when Maranzano died in a 1931 plot that brought Lucky Luciano to real power, Buster's days were numbered, probably because he was not respectful toward the Mafia captains. He was amused by, rather than in awe of, the structure and rituals of the Mafia. In September 1931 the nonbeliever was killed in a poolhall on the Lower East Side and his body toted away for dumping. Just as Buster's early history is a mystery, so too is his final resting place.

See also: *Joseph Valachi.*

BUTTERWORTH, Mary (1686-1775): Counterfeiter

One of the first successful counterfeiting rings in America was masterminded by a woman, probably the first of her sex to practice the art in the New World. In 1716 30-year-old Mary Butterworth started her monumental fraud right in her own kitchen in the Plymouth colony, copying the Rhode Island pound "bills of credit." Using a hot iron and some starched muslin, she simply reproduced the image onto a blank paper.

With several confederates of artistic bent, she filled in the images with quill pens and then passed them on through a pipeline, which included a local justice who was above suspicion.

It is impossible to establish any firm money figure on the scope of the profits realized, but the bills reportedly caused considerable financial havoc in Rhode Island, and the operation must have been extensive. The so-called kitchen counterfeiters stayed in existence for seven years before Mary Butterworth was arrested along with a half-dozen others. However, while a number of bogus bills were found and the counterfeiter's tools located in the woman's kitchen, no hard evidence could be produced proving the bills had been there. Eventually, Butterworth and the others were released for lack of evidence. She was closely watched for many years thereafter to prevent any resumption of the counterfeiting. Thus, tranquility was restored to the New England financial scene.

BYRNES, Thomas F. (1842-1910): New York police inspector

Although he served briefly as chief of police in New York City, Thomas F. Byrnes really made his mark while serving as chief of detectives and chief inspector of the force in the 1880s and 1890s, during which time he was easily the most-renowned American policeman of the era. What he lacked in honesty he more than made up for in flamboyance. It has been said that Byrnes embodied all that was good and all that was bad in the 19th century policeman.

Born in Ireland in 1842, he was brought to New York as a child. During the Civil War he fought for two years in the Union Army before joining the police force in 1863. By 1870 he had moved up to captain, a rank generally achieved only by playing according to the accepted rules, which meant collecting bribes and passing along the proper share to police higher-ups and to the right politicians at Boss Tweed's Tammany Hall. In 1880 Byrnes became head of the Detective Bureau after solving the record $3 million robbery of the Manhattan Bank. He had rounded up most of the loot and several of the burglars, and been applauded by Tammany for his work, especially since the Leslie mob, which pulled the job, had neglected to fork over the standard police-politician cut for such a caper, generally 10 percent of the take.

As head of the Detective Bureau, Byrnes outlawed such cooperation between crooks and police and set as his first goal the elimination of bank robberies in the Wall Street area. He had received more than acclaim after solving the Manhattan Bank job. Several grateful bankers had gotten together and "invested" a large sum of money for him from which he collected the profits. This was not to be considered a reward because rewards had to be approved by and shared with police superiors, not to mention that a certain percentage of rewards had to be given to the police pension fund. Byrnes appreciated the sentiments of the bankers and decided to show his gratitude by ordering all professional criminals to stay out of the Wall Street area. To enforce this edict, he ordered his men to arrest or at least blackjack any professional thief found south of Fulton Street, the demarcation known to criminals as Byrnes' Dead Line.

Byrnes further aided the prominent bankers and stockbrokers by always proving cooperative in hushing up any personal scandals. If he reduced the incidence of major crimes in the Wall Street area, Byrnes was also responsible for a novel treatment of crime elsewhere in the city. He more or less legalized crime, or more precisely, he kept it within acceptable limits by using some criminals to oversee or suppress other criminals, giving each a protected area in which to operate. In return, for this right, the criminals paid Byrnes far less than the previous levels of graft but were required to perform certain other duties on request. For instance, if a prominent person had his pocket picked or was robbed by foodpads, all Byrnes had to do was ask for the return of the loot and it was on his desk within 24 hours.

A gullible public regarded such feats as examples of keen detective work, and overall, Byrnes' stature was enhanced. Byrnes appreciated the value of public relations and became a romantic figure in print. He collaborated on a number of books, and one of his own, *Professional Criminals of America* became a best-seller. In his day, Byrnes got as much mileage out of denouncing foreign-born anarchists as did J. Edgar Hoover upon his discovery of the Communist menace.

Byrnes realized that if he catered to a privileged few, he had carte blanche to do whatever he wished with all others. In the 1880s he was considered second only to Inspector Alexander "Clubber" Williams in his devotion to the practice of the third degree. Byrnes was, to journalist Lincoln Steffens, "Simple, no complication at all—a man who would buy you or beat you, as you might choose, but get you he would."

Byrnes' downfall came about in the mid-1890s because of the opposition of reformer Theodore Roosevelt, at the time a member of the four-man board of police commissioners, and because of the findings of the Lexow Committee. Writing to Henry Cabot Lodge, Roosevelt announced: "I think I shall move against Byrnes at once. I thoroughly distrust him, and cannot do any thorough work while he remains. It will be a hard fight, and I have no idea how it will come out."

As it was, Byrnes retired about a month later, in June of 1895. He had had a particularly trying time before the Lexow Committee, which heard testimony indicating that Byrnes permitted widespread corruption within the Detective Bureau. His men were notorious for refusing to undertake robbery investigations unless the victim first posted a reward. Byrnes was personally pressed to explain how he had accumulated $350,000 in real estate, $292,000 in his wife's name. His top salary had been $5,000 a year and no more than a quarter of his huge estate could be attributed to the "gratuities" of the Wall Street crowd.

Despite these embarrassments, Byrnes made a pitch at staying on as chief of police, assuring Roosevelt and the other reformers that he could run a department free of all corruption. His own failings, he said, were due to being trapped in a foul system. His offer was rejected.

See also: *Bliss Bank Ring, Dead Line, Old Shakespeare.*

C

CACKLE-BLADDER: Con man's trick

Probably the most efficient method ever devised by confidence men to "blow the mark off," i.e., to get rid of a victim after fleecing him is the use of a "cackle-bladder." The victim is lured into a supposedly sure thing such as betting on what he is assured to be a fixed horse race. He is steered to a phony betting parlor where everyone is an actor playing a role, from the supposed tellers to the bettors winning and losing fortunes. Naturally, the horse he bets on loses, but before the mark can remonstrate another supposed loser, who is actually in on the scheme, turns on the con man playing the role of the chief conspirator. He screams he has been ruined, pulls a gun and shoots the con man dead. There seems no doubt the man is dead as blood literaly gushes from his mouth. Everyone starts to scatter, and so does the bilked victim. Not only has he lost his money, but even worse, he's now involved in a homicide. Sometimes the supposed murderer will flee with the mark, even conning the sucker into leaving the city with him. Eventually, of course, the mark decides he is better off to part company with a man who has committed murder and who could now drag him into prison as an accessory.

This type of scam is made convincing through the use of a cackle-bladder, a tiny bag of chicken blood concealed in the mouth and bitten open at the appropriate moment. The gimmick was also used in the last century at fixed running races and boxing matches as well, where the "sure thing" runner or boxer the sucker had bet on seemed to drop dead. Since gambling on such races or fights was illegal and all the bettors were therefore liable to imprisonment, everyone, including the gullible victim, fled when the faking runner or boxer dropped.

While the cackle-bladder is only used on rare occasions in contemporary confidence games, it remains a favorite with insurance accident fakers, who use the dramatic spurt of blood to convince witnesses that they have really been injured.

CALAMITY Jane (1852-1903): Woman "outlaw"

Few works touching on female criminality in America and especially in the West fail to include Martha Jane Cannary, best known as Calamity Jane. However, her inclusion in such studies is a miscarriage of justice, since it has been clearly demonstrated that the extent of her lawless behavior was limited to disorderly conduct, drunkenness and stints of prostitution, such as her 1875 tour of duty at E. Coffey's "hog farm" near Fort Laramie.

Calamity's "autobiography" is full of shoot-'em-up exploits and, of course, a torrid love affair with Wild Bill Hickok. Actually, it is doubtful that Hickok ever considered this muscular, big-boned girl who dressed like a man anything other than an occasional member of his entourage. After Hickok's death in 1876 Calamity Jane became a living legend: "the White Devil of the Yellowstone," as one dime novel called her. The last 25 years of her life were spent peddling her autobiography and other books about her for a few pennies, whoring and appearing in various Wild West shows, from which she was invariably fired for drunkenness. In 1900 a newspaper editor found her sick in a brothel and nursed her back to health. Calamity was dying in a hotel room in Terry, not far from Deadwood, South Dakota in the summer of 1903. On August 2 her eyes fluttered open and she asked the date. Upon being told, she nodded and said: "It's the 27th anniversary of Bill's [Hickok's] death. Bury me next to Bill." They did and recorded her death on August 2, although she had not died until August 3. But then the facts never have been permitted to cloud the Calamity Jane legend.

See also: *Wild Bill Hickok*.

CALICO Jim (?-1897?): Shanghai operator

Shanghaiing of men was an old San Francisco custom and one

Public drunk and prostitute Calamity Jane picked up occasional change in her last years posing for tourists at the gravesite of her "lover," Wild Bill Hickok.

of its most proficient practitioners, along with the infamous Shanghai Kelly, was Calico Jim. A Chilean whose real name was said to be Reuben, Jim ran a saloon and crimping joint at Battery Point, from which a great many men were sent on long sea voyages. During the 1890s the San Francisco police received so many complaints against Jim that they began paying him close attention. Evidently not close enough, however, because a policeman sent to arrest him didn't come back. Another tried and also never returned. A total of six police officers went to the saloon and disappeared; all had taken a sea cruise, compliments of Calico Jim. Feeling now that his days in the business were limited, Jim sold out and returned to his native Chile.

It was many months before the policemen made their way back to home port. It has been said that they pooled their money, drew lots and sent one of their number off to Chile to hunt down Calico Jim. After many months of hunting, according to the story, the policeman found Jim on a street corner in Callao, Chile and shot him six times, one for each officer he had shanghaied. There is some doubt about the truth of this

account, although it gained a great deal of currency. For years the police department insisted there was no record of six officers being shanghaied. But jaded citizens of San Francisco contended they knew a cover-up when they heard one.

See also: *Shanghai Kelly.*

CALIFORNIA Outlaws: Anti-railroad band

Perhaps the nearest thing this country ever saw to the Robin Hood legend was the California Outlaws, a misnomer for the small ranchers and mountain people of the San Joaquin Valley who did battle in the latter part of the 19th century with the Southern Pacific Railroad, or the "Octopus," as it was commonly known and described in the Frank Norris novel of that title. The railroad was laying its tracks through several Western states, and from its standpoint, all intervening land had to be acquired for this purpose, no matter by what means. If the railroad passed through farmland or the home of some settler, the property was condemned, and the helpless owner had to accept the pittance offered him or get nothing. The railroad imported gunmen from the East to do battle for it, and any act committed by the company was considered legal, including such atrocities as the "slaughter of Mussel Slough," in which seven settlers were shot and killed in 1880. The result was a virtual civil war, as the landowners of the San Joaquin Valley banded together to fight the "enveloping tentacles of the Octopus engulfing their lands," as one historian put it. Undercover agents of the railroad moved in among the settlers to spy on and single out troublemakers to be dealt with.

Under their leaders, Chris Evans and the Sontag brothers, George and John, the California Outlaws began robbing Southern Pacific trains. They would stop the trains on lonely stretches and, ignoring the passengers and the U.S. mails, rob only the railroad's safe in the express car. The raids went on for years. Railroad detectives under the notorious Big Bill Smith and lawmen under U.S. Marshal George C. Gard engaged in an unseemly bounty competition for bringing in, or more often killing, individual members of the Outlaws. In time, the Outlaws dwindled down to a band of 24 men, plus a 25th named Ed Morrell who worked as a spy for them among the railroad detectives. Morrell, later immortalized by Jack London in *The Star Rover*, was able to save the Outlaws from several traps, but after he was exposed, the band was destroyed. John Sontag was killed in a shoot-out with a posse of railroad gunmen. Chris Evans went to prison under a life sentence; and George Sontag died attempting to escape from Folsom Prison. Ed Morrell, later to become famous as the most tortured prisoner in the history of American penology, drew a life term but was pardoned in 1907.

See also: *Christopher Evans, Ed Morrell, Sontag Brothers.*

CAMPAGNA, Louis "Little New York" (1900-1955): Gangster

Considered by Al Capone to be his most reliable bodyguard, Louis "Little New York" Campagna was a stubby little mobster who, thanks more to his steel nerves than his brainpower, rose to the top echelon of syndicate crime.

During the Chicago Mob's movie studio extortion days, Campagna walked into a jail and stiffened a wilting gang member, Willie Bioff, who had announced he wanted to quit the rackets. In a menacing voice few could equal, Campagna said, "Whoever quits us, quits feet first." Later, after Bioff cracked, sending several top syndicate men, including Campagna, to prison, Little New York always bemoaned the fact that his associates had vetoed a "feet first" proposal regarding Bioff.

Al Capone had imported Campagna in 1927 from New York, where he had cut his criminal teeth as a teenager in the Five Points gang and been convicted of bank robbery at 19. Capone dubbed him Little New York merely to demonstrate his ability to import all the gunners he needed. Campagna soon demonstrated his nerve following an unsuccessful plot by the Aiello brothers to assassinate Capone. Shortly thereafter, Joseph Aiello and one of his gunmen were taken to the Chi-

cago Detective Bureau lockup. Campagna promptly surrounded the bureau with a dozen gunmen and he and two others approached the building, shifting weapons from holsters to side pockets. A policeman recognized Campagna and, realizing he was laying siege to the building, sounded the alarm. A score of detectives rushed out to seize the trio and hustled them into the building before their accomplices could come to their aid.

Campagna was lodged in a cell next to Aiello while a detective who understood the Sicilian dialect posed as a prisoner in another cell. He heard Campagna say: "You're dead, dear friend, you're dead. You won't get up to the end of the street still walking."

Aiello was quaking with fear. "Can't we settle this?" he pleaded. "Give me fourteen days and I'll sell my stores, my house and everything and quit Chicago for good. Can't we settle it? Think of my wife and baby."

Campagna was unmoved. "You dirty rat! You've broken faith with us twice now. You started this. We'll finish it."

It was no idle threat. When Aiello was later found shot down on the street, 59 slugs, more than a pound of bullets, were dug out of his body.

At the height of the assassination scare against Capone, the gang boss made Campagna his main bodyguard. At night, the devoted little killer slept on a cot just outside Capone's bedroom door. Anyone going in would have to climb over Campagna's body.

In the 1930s and early 1940s, Campagna became a key figure in the mob's union rackets and extortion plots against Hollywood movie studios. Along with six others, Campagna was convicted of conspiracy to extort $1 million from studio executives and sentenced to 10 years. He served one-third of his sentence and was paroled to a firestorm of protest by Chicago newspapers. In later years Campagna played the role of a gentleman farmer on an 800-acre spread near Fowler, Ind. He died of a heart attack aboard a pleasure cruiser off Miami in 1955.

CAMPBELL, Bertram (1886-1946): Wrong man

The case of Bertram Campbell demonstrates as well as any the near impossibility of achieving adequate compensation for wrongfully convicted individuals.

Before his conviction, Campbell had been a securities salesman and customer's man for several New York brokerage houses. In February 1938, New York City police detectives visited Campbell in his apartment in Freeport, Long Island and brought him to the city for questioning. There five bank tellers identified him as a forger who had recently cashed two checks for $4,160 under the name of George Workmaster. He was convicted of the charge and served three years and four months of a five- to 10-year sentence in Sing Sing, all the time maintaining his innocence. Released on parole late in 1941, Campbell, a sick and broken man, eked out a rather miserable existence as a bookkeeper. In early 1945 he happened to read a newspaper story that the FBI had arrested a forger in Kentucky. The man's method of operation brought Campbell up sharply. It fitted perfectly with the one used in the crimes of which he had been convicted. Campbell contacted a lawyer, who learned that the forger had been brought to New York for arraignment. The lawyer rounded up the five bank employees and took them to see the forger, Alexander D. L. Thiel. Three of them immediately admitted they had been in error, that Thiel was the man.

Thiel, now a drug addict, readily confessed. To the FBI he had been "Mr. X," who in 40 years had duped banks the country over for upwards of $600,000. After months of delay Campbell was pardoned and awarded $40,000 for earnings lost and $75,000 for disgrace and humiliation suffered. All in all, it seemed about as satisfactory a conclusion to a sad case as was possible. However, Campbell's tribulations were not over. Nassau County officials slapped Campbell with a $4,000 bill for welfare payments made to his wife while he had been wrongfully imprisoned. Then, just 82 days after he had won the $115,000, Campbell died of a stroke, which doctors speculated was the result of the strain of his years in prison.

See also: *Alexander Thiel.*

CANADA Bill: See William "Canada Bill" Jones.

CANAL Street: Buffalo vice center

"For sheer wickedness, vice and crime there is no need to go any further west than here," a 19th century historian said of Canal Street in Buffalo, N.Y. It was quite a claim to make about a thoroughfare but two blocks long.

Born with the Erie Canal, Canal Street was set off on a jutting piece of land, segregated from the rest of Buffalo by 40 feet of murky water. On quiet summer nights Buffalonians could stroll casually along the canal and gaze across at the street that never lost its light from dusk to dawn. They could hear boisterous noises of ribaldry and wonder if at that moment, somewhere on Canal Street, someone was in the process of being killed, a likely occurrence on a street that boasted 93 saloons, three combination grocery-saloons and 15 dives known as concert halls. More than half these establishments had portions of their premises given over to prostitution, with an estimated 400 practitioners of that art on hand around the clock.

Canal Street grew up with the Erie Canal, which cut across New York state and linked up the Hudson with the Great Lakes. The street sucked gold from the rugged sailors of the Lakes and the lusty canalers and in return provided a bawdiness unrivaled even in the tenderloin sections of far bigger cities. An early clergyman thundered from his pulpit that it should be called Market Street because the fruits of any vice

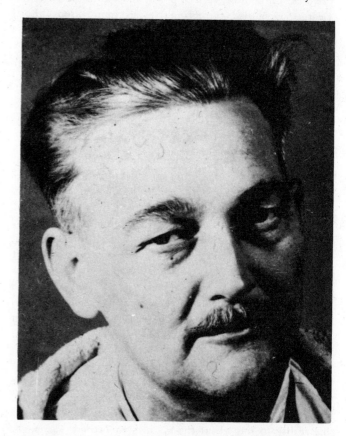

Often cited as an example of the dangers of faulty eye witness testimony, Bertram Campbell(left, was identified as a forger by five bank tellers and sent to prison. Later, Alexander Thiel (right), a professional check passer, was determined to be the guilty party.

could be purchased along its cobble-stoned length. The ladies of Canal Street knew how to get a man's money; and they were not averse to slitting his throat if need be. In the end, the residents of the street usually got every penny a man had, leaving him without even enough with which to buy a mug of beer. Canal Street was said to be the birthplace of the word "mugging." When a man had been so sheared that he didn't even have the price of a mug of beer, he would walk outside and waylay a passerby or "mug" him.

The worst dives on Canal Street were those places on the East Side whose rear areas extended on wooden pilings over the canal. Unsuspecting canalers and lakers were hustled there by painted women who charged exorbitant prices for their services. However, if a man had money, but was uncooperative about parting with it, he was fed an overdose of knockout drops. He then was hauled into a backroom, stripped of all his clothes and dumped naked down a slicked wooden chute into the canal with hardly an incriminating splash. Eventually he would turn up floating face down in the murky water. The police would know no more than that he had been killed in one of about 100 places and listed the victim as a "floater." In one week in 1863 no less than 14 floaters were fished out of the canal, five on one morning alone.

Canal Street lived on protection. One time there was a report, undoubtedly true, that several leading politicians had had a little two-day party in one of the street's leading bordellos, which helped explain why no concerted effort was made to drive out the scarlet women. For many years about all the politicians would grant the citizens of Buffalo was a segregation ruling that denied such ladies the right to go any further uptown than the liberty pole, which marked the entrance to Buffalo proper in those days. So long as the prostitutes remained in the Canal Street area, they were safe.

In 1870 a young reformer named Grover Cleveland was elected sheriff of Erie County after making campaign promises to clean up Canal Street. Cleveland tried to keep his word but was singularly ineffective. The saloon keepers and brothel owners of the street paid out so much money to the right political forces in Buffalo that Cleveland's campaign was fruitless. If he made arrests politically controlled judges immediately released the prisoners for "lack of evidence." Cleveland went on to become president of the United States. He was once asked what was the greatest disappointment of his life; he stated that it was not failing to be reelected president in 1888 but rather being unable to wipe out the scourge of Canal Street.

Both before and after Cleveland, Canal Street went its own murderous way, regarding all type of crime as hardly worthy of special notice. When Fat Charley Ott, the proprietor of The Only Theater, a sort of combination concert hall, saloon, dance hall and assignation hotel, came to a bad end, the street handled it in typical fashion. Fat Charley had a propensity for padding the bill of a client who appeared in possession of less than all his faculties. One sweltering night in the 1890s, he made the mistake of trying it on a certain bearded laker. After letting out an angry howl that filled the Only, the laker reached across the bar, seized Fat Charley by the hair and with brute force hauled Charley to him. Like many a lakeman, he carried a Spanish knife, a nasty, two-edged slicer that was worn up the sleeve, attached by a leather thong. He whipped it out. Fat Charley struggled to get loose, but his unhappy patron wasn't letting go. At the time, there were some two dozen other patrons in the Only. They gaped in motionless horror as the bearded lakeman decapitated Charley Ott with one swipe.

The murderer strode out of the Only as the other customers froze. Someone allowed that perhaps the police should be informed. Others agreed but suggested that perhaps they should have a drink in memory of the dear departed. They had one, another and then another. When in due course the police arrived, the Only was empty save for the two parts of Fat Charley, a looted till and scores of empty liquor bottles. And some wag had even left a sign on the door that read CLOSED ON ACCOUNT OF ILLNESS.

It was said, not without good reason, that the females of Canal Street were far more deadly than the males. There was, for instance, Gallow May Moore, a blonde hellion who could throw her garter stiletto with unerring accuracy; any man who tried to leave her without paying the premiums could count on awesome retribution. Her favorite trick was to pin an unchivalrous gentleman to a wall with a stiletto, empty his pockets, kiss him goodbye and leaving him dangling as she went out to live it up on his roll, with enough set aside for a new knife.

Then there was Frosty Face Emma, described as a handsome woman much sought after by men. She had, however, one disconcerting habit. For a time she could drink liquor as though she had a hollow leg, and a gentleman would wait impatiently for her to enter a more compliant phase, which unfortunately never happened. At a certain level of consumption, she turned into a vicious man-hater. A man's only hope was that he had not as yet adjourned with her to a more secluded atmosphere before she exploded. Otherwise, there was little chance he would be seen alive again. One historian states Emma assassinated at least seven lovers and cut up many others. The law never did get anything on Emma, however. Her victims couldn't or wouldn't talk and Canal Street had its own rules: nobody ever told anything to the law about anybody.

Fittingly, Emma got her just deserts in a knife battle with a redhead called Deadly Dora. If there was one thing Dora wouldn't tolerate, it was another woman stealing a man from her. She had latched on to a blue-eyed Swedish sailor for whom she developed a genuine affection. Emma tried to cut in and knives flashed. They fished Emma's body out of the canal a few days later.

A time came when Buffalonians could thank the girls of Canal Street for preventing the city from being overrun by prostitutes. It happened during Pan-American Year, when all Buffalo was in a Mardi Gras spirit in celebration of the turn of the century. Up till then the several hundred prostitutes in and around Canal Street had the territory to themselves, but with the celebration hundreds of sinful ladies from New York City headed for the bonanza town of the North. One day, bag and baggage, they poured from a train at the Terrace railroad station, directly across from the canal, and attempted to move in.

The women were all colorfully dressed and canalers paused in their labors to give them a cheering welcome. They circulated among the men with friendly words that happy days had indeed come to Buffalo. The gay arrival, however, also had been seen by the women of Canal Street, and like an army, they swarmed out of the dives and bordellos to descend on the train station. Many carried stillettos, clubs, planks or chairs.

It was a battle the likes of which Buffalo had never seen before. Before it was over, close to 100 ladies were in various degrees of undress. A dedicated reporter counted eight females stripped totally raw. Two dozen girls had to be hospitalized, many with awful knife slashes across their faces. The paddy wagon made a total of 32 trips to the Franklin Street Station, hauling off battling participants. By nightfall the battle was over, and the New York ladies, no match for the denizens of Canal Street, jammed back into the station and took the next train out.

Pan-American Year was the last really big one for Canal Street. Buffalo was changing. Erie Canal traffic was dipping, and as the railroads took over more, fewer and fewer Great Lakes freighters docked. Consequently, fewer sailors and canalers hit Canal Street. The joints began to shutter. In 1908 a citizens' movement increased the pressure on the police to clean up Canal Street once and for all. Raids increased, and foreign immigrants began to flood into Canal Street, soon outnumbering the criminal element. In 1915 the name of the street was changed to Dante Place. In peculiarly American style, the area became an ordinary slum, breeding its own type of vice and crime. But the whores and whoremasters were gone and Canal Street, with its incredible century of murder, mayhem, vice and corruption, was just a memory.

See also: *Floaters, Mugging, Yorky of the Great Lakes.*

CANDELARIA, Nevada: Lawless mining town

Of all the mining camps that sprang up in Nevada in the 1860s and 70s, Candelaria deserves special mention because for a quarter of a century it officially had only seven murders. That was remarkable for a town which boasted 10 whorehouses running around the clock and which sold whiskey by the gallon. In fact, fatal shootings were extremely common and recorders of the town's history put the death toll in the several hundreds. More so than any other mining camp where the law was seldom found, the public relations-minded authorities of Candelaria were inclined to write off almost any shooting as a matter of self-defense. Of the seven killings officially listed as murders, none was ever solved.

CANTON, Frank M. (1849-1927): Outlaw, lawman and vigilante leader

One of the villains or heroes of the Johnson County War in Wyoming Territory, depending on one's outlook, Frank M.

Canton was proof that an evil man who was good to the right people could do all right for himself in the Old West.

While his early life was at the time a mystery, Canton turned up in Wyoming in 1880 and became a small rancher; two years later, he was elected sheriff. As a lawman, he ran up an impressive record tracking down rustlers, although some objected that many of the so-called rustlers were in no shape to answer formal charges after facing Canton's six-guns. After two terms Canton found himself voted out of office. He was so bitter that when approached by Wyoming's wealthy stockmen to head up their vigilante war against rustlers in Johnson County, Canton accepted even though he knew the real objective of the war was to intimidate the small ranchers responsible for electing him to office. These ranchers, actually homesteaders with a few head of cattle, had incurred the wrath of the absentee cattle barons of Cheyenne, who were determined to rewrite the traditional law of the range that a maverick, or unbranded, steer belonged to the man with the longest rope. With Major Frank Wolcott, Canton led the big cattlemen's paid vigilantes in numerous attacks and lynchings in Johnson County. They were finally beaten, however, by a ragtag but straight-shooting army of homesteaders, who won the sympathy of most of the nation.

During the period of the Johnson County War, Canton, slender, cold-eyed and sinister looking in a long capelike coat, was described by a companion as a man who "only thought of guns and killings . . . they seemed to be on his mind all the time . . . he couldn't sleep. He was always jumping up and saying . . . 'Do you hear them? . . . Get on your guns.' But it wasn't anything—just the wind or the horses."

The fact that Canton was able to switch sides with so few second thoughts can be partially explained by the gunfighter ethics of the day. However, it was later proved that he had switched sides more than once. Canton's real name was Joseph Horner, the son of a Virginia doctor who came to Texas after the Civil war. By his mid-twenties Horner had run up a criminal record of bank robbery, rustling and assault with intent to kill. In 1874 he fled Texas after killing a soldier in a saloon brawl. Between that time and his appearance in Wyoming, Horner had engaged in a number of illegal enterprises. After his Wyoming days—there was no way he could remain there, being generally regarded as a hired killer—Horner, using the name Canton, became an undersheriff in Pawnee County, Okla. and then a deputy U.S. marshal in Alaska. He later returned to the States and was employed by the Texas Cattle Raisers' Association. It has been suggested that through this organization's good offices a long-missing fugitive named Joe Horner received a pardon from the governor of Texas. Perhaps in deference to the feelings of ill-will back in Wyoming, it was not revealed that Horner was Canton until he died in 1927.

See also: *Cattle Kate, Nathan D. Champion, Johnson County War, Red Sash Gang.*

CAPITAL Punishment

When on January 17, 1977 Gary Gilmore was led before a

firing squad and shot to death, the execution marked the return of capital punishment in the United States after a 10-year hiatus.

It is often assumed that executions stopped because of a ruling by the U.S. Supreme Court, but in fact, executions ceased basically because of a combination of public disapproval and the growing reluctance of juries to convict in cases involving mandatory death sentences. Thus, while there were 152 executions in 1947, the number dropped to seven by 1965 and to just one in 1967. It was only at this stage that the Supreme Court agreed to hear arguments in two cases challenging the basic precepts of capital punishment. Certainly, the strongest evidence that the High Court follows election results or public opinion can be seen in its rulings concerning capital punishment, both pro and con. In 1967 public opinion was overwhelmingly opposed to the death penalty, and the High Court was eventually to rule that way. When by 1976 public opinion shifted in the opposite direction, the Court veered toward that view, even while admitting that the primary argument always made for the death penalty, that it is a deterrent to murder and other capital crimes, was faulty.

Capital punishment in the American colonies was patterned after the English system, but the early settlers, with some lamentable exceptions, soon broke away from the full implementation of the death penalty for such crimes as witchcraft, blasphemy, fornication, various "crimes against nature" and "man stealing." Murder and thievery, major or petty, remained firm cause for execution.

In 1834 Pennsylvania banned public executions, and in 1847 Michigan became the first state to abolish the death penalty. Other states joined the abolition movement, although the death penalty made a strong comeback during periods of great wars, the Civil War and the two world wars. By 1971 39 of the 54 U.S. jurisdictions (the 50 states, the District of Columbia, Puerto Rico, the Virgin Islands and the federal jurisdiction) carried the death penalty on the books for as many as eight capital crimes: espionage, treason, murder, rape, kidnapping, arson, train wrecking and robbery. In most states the number of offenses for which the penalty was imposed ranged from one to four.

The principal argument presented by advocates of capital punishment is that it satisfies society's need for retribution and retaliation and serves as a deterrent to the commission of murder. Moreover, it is the only certain process for the elimination of deviants. The arguments of the abolitionists are many. It is a weapon used primarily against the blacks and other racial minorities and the poor ("Rich men never burn" is a death house saying). As a deterrent, they insist, capital punishment doesn't work. In some states the murder rate actually decreased when the death penalty was abolished. Overall, it appears that the murder rate in states with or without the death penalty is, over a period of time, about the same. In states where murders do increase (both in states with and without capital punishment), the causes for the increase are apparently due to societal or cultural variations or changes. If a state moves to a greater heterogenous mix, the murder rate will go up, death penalty or no. Abolitionists also argue against the deterrent theory on the ground that the crimes it punishes result from irrational impulses, not cool calculation. As Gary Gilmore commented about his murder of two young strangers: "Murder is just a thing of itself, a rage, and rage is not reason, so why does it matter who? It vents a rage." Most of the men who have been on death row insisted they murdered without any thought of the consequences. Furthermore, it has been shown that mass murderers move blithely from states without the death penalty to states with it.

There have even been a number of murders committed because the death penalty exists. According to the Washington Research Project, an Oklahoma farmer who had shot to death a total stranger simply explained to police, "I was tired of living." In 1961 a convicted Oklahoma murderer, James French, who had been tried three times for one homicide, strangled his cellmate in order to speed his own execution along. In 1938 Robert West, who had helped build Missouri's gas chamber, killed a young girl and, after turning himself in, said his only motive for murdering the victim was to be able to die in the gas chamber. When John Spenkelink died in the electric chair in May 1979, he became the first person executed in Florida in 15 years. A later study of the six-month period before and after his execution, when the public controversy about the issue was at its peak, showed that homicides in the state increased 14 percent.

Opponents of the death penalty also argue for rehabilitation over execution. Probably no prison warden would deny that murderers are often the most easily rehabilitated and best-behaved convicts. Additionally, cases of murder committed by paroled murderers are most rare, especially when compared with repeaters of other types of crimes.

It was against this background that in 1972 the Supreme Court ruled the death penalty as practiced was unconstitutional, in violation of the Eighth Amendment ban on cruel and unusual punishment, particularly in the way judges and juries arbitrarily and infrequently imposed it. The immediate impact of the Court's decision was that the death sentence for 648 men and women then on death row was commuted to life imprisonment. Almost immediately, supporters of capital punishment launched a counterattack. By 1976 public opinion, upset by sensational murders little different from those of earlier years, had turned once more in favor of the death penalty.

A not-unmindful Supreme Court took the hint and announced in a new ruling the same year that execution methods in the U.S. were not inherently "cruel and unusual" punishment as prohibited by the Constitution. The Court even cited various public opinion polls indicating that Americans favored capital punishment by a two-to-one margin. However, at the same time, the Supreme Court agreed there was little proof the death penalty deters the commission of capital crimes. Fundamentally, the Court decreed that retribution and punishment alone were sufficient reasons to impose the death penalty. In other words, the concept of the state "getting even" for killing by killing had become a worthwhile value. Left unanswered by the Court was how, if society has the right to take a life as retribution, this could fail to reinforce a murderer in his firm belief that he has a right to "get even" with his victim. Surveys indicate that 84 percent of all homicides are motivated by the murderer's desire to exact retribution for some real or imagined offense committed by the victim.

The reimposition of the death penalty in the United States puts this country in the opposite camp from such Western nations, 41 in all, as England, West Germany, Italy, Switzerland, the Netherlands, Israel, the Dominican Republic, Honduras, Costa Rica and Ecuador. Among the United State's bedfellows are the Soviet Union and other Iron Curtain countries, China, Libya, Iraq, Iran, Castro's Cuba, Chile and Saudi Arabia.

Perhaps remarkably, the Supreme Court has never regarded execution in itself as "cruel and unusual punishment" when the possibility of error is considered. Proponents of the death penalty give assurances that the liklihood of a mistake can be ruled out because the judicial process in capital cases is allegedly so much more exact, thus eliminating the type of error that turns up in so many "wrong man" cases involving lesser crimes. Of course, innocent men have been executed. Years afterward, official decrees of one sort or another have cleared some of the Mollie Maguires, the Haymarket martyrs and Sacco and Vanzetti, but these are cause celebres. As many legal authorities have commented, the interest in clearing the average innocent man after he is executed dwindles to nil. What we are left with is some of the more bizarre ways innocent persons have been saved from execution. In 1894 Will Purvis was saved from hanging in Mississippi simply because the knot around his neck slipped and he dropped unharmed. The execution was postponed because the onlookers became unruly, some taking it as a sign from the Divine that Purvis was innocent. In the period before his execution was rescheduled, Purvis escaped from custody and surrendered only when a new governor agreed to commute his sentence to life imprisonment. Twenty-two years later, in 1920, Purvis was proven innocent by a deathbed confession of the real murderer, whose story was found to check in every detail. For his tribulations, Purvis was awarded $5,000 by the state legislature.

In Florida in 1902 J. B. Brown mounted the scaffold still protesting his innocence for having murdered one Harry Wesson. Chagrined officials called off the execution when the sheriff, as required by law, started reading the death warrant and discovered that through a clerical error it listed as the man to be executed not Brown but the foreman of the jury that had convicted him. While officials argued about whether or not to proceed with the execution, Brown's ordeal on the scaffold created a nationwide stir, and the governor bowed to demands that the condemned man's sentence be commuted to life. In 1913 a man named J. J. Johnson confessed on his deathbed that it was he who had killed Wesson, even revealing where

he'd hidden some of the victim's personal effects. Brown was pardoned and awarded compensation of $2,492, to be paid in $25 monthly installments.

See also: *Execution, Methods of.*

Further reading: *The Death Penalty in America,* edited by Hugo A. Bedau; *Capital Punishment,* edited by Thorsten Sellen.

CAPONE, Alphonse "Scarface Al" (1899-1947): Gang leader

Al Capone was a mindless, brutal and obscure Brooklyn hood in his teens, but by the age of 26 he had become the most powerful crime boss of his day and could boast that he "owned" Chicago, that city of gangsters, during the Prohibition years.

At its zenith the Capone mob had probably upward of 1,000 members, most of them experienced gunmen, but this represented only a portion of Capone's overall empire. Capone often proclaimed, "I own the police," and it was true. Few estimates would place less than half the police on the mob's payroll in one way or another. Capone's hold on the politicians was probably greater. He had "in his pocket" aldermen, state's attorneys, mayors, legislators, governors and even congressmen.

Mug shot of Al Capone was taken in 1929 in Philadelphia, where he allowed the police to arrest him in order to "take off some heat" brought on by the St. Valentine's Day Massacre.

The Capone organization's domination of Chicago and such suburban areas as Cicero, Ill. was absolute. When Capone wanted a big vote in elections, he got out the vote; when he wanted to control the election returns, his gangsters intimidated and terrorized thousands of voters. The politicians he put in power were expected to act the way the Big Fellow desired. The mayor of Cicero once took an independent action. Capone caught him on the steps of City Hall and beat him to a pulp; a police officer standing nearby had to look elsewhere to avoid seeing the violence.

Capone was born in Brooklyn in 1899 and attended school through the sixth grade, when he beat up his teacher, got beaten by the principal and quit. After that, he learned his lessons in the streets, especially with the tough teenage James Street gang, run by an older criminal, Johnny Torrio, as a subsidiary of the notorious Five Points Gang, to which Capone eventually graduated. Among his closest friends, both in school and in the gang, was a kid who grew up to become a major crime boss, Lucky Luciano, and the two remained lifelong friends.

When he was in his late teens, Capone was hired by Torrio as a bouncer in a saloon-brothel he ran in Brooklyn. Capone picked up a huge scar on his left cheek in an altercation with a tough hood named Frank Galluccio, who slashed him with a knife in a dispute about a girl. Later, Capone would claim he got the wound serving with the "Lost Battalion" in France during World War I, but he was never in the Army.

In 1920 Torrio, who had relocated in Chicago to help his uncle, Big Jim Colosimo, the city's leading whoremaster, ply his trade, summoned Capone to come and help him. What Torrio wanted to do was take advantage of Prohibition and gain control of the booze racket, an endeavor that promised profits in the millions. But he was being thwarted by Colosimo, who was so rich and content he saw no need to expand. Torrio soon decided Colosimo would have to be eliminated so that he could use Big Jim's organization for his criminal plans. He and Capone plotted Colosimo's murder and imported New York talent to do the job.

The Torrio-Capone combine was then on the move, taking over some mobs that bowed to their threats and going to war with those that failed to cooperate. Their biggest coup was the assassination in 1924 of Dion O'Banion, the head of the largely Irish North Side Gang, utilizing the talents of Frankie Yale of Brooklyn, the same man who had rubbed out Colosimo. However, the O'Banion killing resulted in all-out war with the rest of the North Siders. Torrio was badly shot in an ambush and hovered near death in a hospital for days. When he got out in February 1925, he told Capone, "Al, it's all yours," and retired back to Brooklyn with an estimated $30 million.

It was a sobering experience for the 26-year-old Capone, who found he now needed to use brains instead of muscle to run things. He had to become a top executive, bossing a firm employing more than 1,000 persons with a weekly payroll of over $300,000. He demonstrated he could do this as well as work with other ethnic groups, such as the Jews, the Irish, the Poles and the blacks. Capone appreciated any man provided he was a hustler, crook or killer, and he never discriminated against any of them because of their religion, race or national origin, being perhaps the underworld's first equal opportunity employer.

Capone's secret of success was to limit his mob's activities mainly to rackets that enjoyed strong demand from the public: liquor, gambling and prostitution. Give the people what they want and you have to gain a measure of popularity. Al Capone was cheered when he went to the ball park. Herbert Hoover was not.

Capone surrounded himself with men in whom he could place his trust, a quality he in turn inspired in many of his underlings. He was even smart enough to hire Galluccio, the thug who had scarred him, as a bodyguard, an act that demonstrated to the underworld the Big Fellow's magnanimity. Still, he faced many assassination attempts, including an effort to poison his soup. In September 1926 the O'Banions sent an entire convoy of cars loaded with machine-gunners past Capone's Cicero hotel headquarters. They poured in 1,000 rounds but Capone escaped injury.

One by one, Capone had his North Side enemies eliminated, and he did the same to others who resisted bending to his will. His most famous killing involved treachery within his own organization. Hop Toad Giunta and Capone's two most competent killers, John Scalise and Albert Anselmi, were showing signs of planning to go independent. Capone invited them to a banquet in their honor and, at the climax of the evening, produced an Indian club with which he bashed their brains in.

By this time, Capone started to look invincible, but he erred terribly when he ordered the St. Valentine's Day massacre in an effort to kill Bugs Moran, the last major force among the old O'Banions. Seven men were machine-gunned to death by Capone hit men masquerading as police officers. Suddenly, the public had had enough of the savage bootleg wars. Washington began applying intense pressure, and while he could not be convicted of murder, Capone was nailed for income tax evasion and sentenced to the federal prison at Atlanta for 11 years.

He was transferred to Alcatraz in 1934 and within a few years his health began to deteriorate. When released in 1939, he was a helpless paretic, a condition generally attributed to the ravages of syphillis contracted in his early whorehouse days. Chances are he had also gone "stir crazy," a common fate among Alcatraz inmates.

Capone retired to his mansion in Miami Beach, no longer capable of running the Chicago mob. For several years he wavered between lucidity and mental inertia. He died on January 25, 1947.

Al Capone had left an imprint on America and the rest of the world. Even in the minds of foreigners, he was the "Chicago gangster" personified. His impact on Chicago was significant and long lasting. During his reign Capone ordered the extermination of more than 500 men, and an estimated 1,000 died in his bootleg wars. The pattern of violence he set and the organization he built did not disappear with either his imprisonment or death. It is still not dead.

See also: *Anthony Joseph Accardo; Joseph Aiello; Alcatraz Prison; Louis "Two Gun" Alterie; Anselmi and Scalise; Bootlegging; Louis "Little New York" Campagna, Frank Capone, James Capone, Ralph "Bottles" Capone; Cicero, Ill.; Vincent "Schemer" Drucci; Five Points Gang; Genna Brothers; Great Depression; Jake "Greasy Thumb" Guzik; Hawthorne Inn; Mike "de Pike" Heitler; Herbert Hoover; Alfred "Jake" Lingle; Antonio "the Scourge" Lombardo; James Lucas; "Count" Victor Lustig; Machine Gun Jack McGurn; George "Bugs" Moran; Eliot Ness; Frank Nitti; Charles Dion "Deanie" O'Banion; Pineapple Primary; Paul "the Waiter" Ricca; John Torrio; Roger "Terrible" Touhy; Hymie Weiss; White Hand Gang; Frank J. Wilson; Frankie Yale.*

CAPONE, Frank (1895-1924): Brother of Al Capone

Had Frank (Salvatore) Capone, Al Capone's elder brother, survived until the latter's climb to the pinnacle of power, it might well be that he would have been just as famous—Frank Capone's killer instincts and savagery exceeded those of his brother. Despite Al's acknowledged ruthlessness, he was a man who would try to deal before he tried to kill. Frank Capone never exhibited such patience. "You never get no back talk from no corpse," he used to say, a sentiment made all the more ominous by his quiet, almost bankerlike demeanor.

Frank's labors and those of his mentor Johnny Torrio on behalf of brother Al were generally employed in situations where persuasion had failed and force was called for. Such was the case in the 1924 city election in Cicero, Ill., where the Democratic Party had actually dared to mount a serious effort against the Torrio/Capone-backed regime of Joseph Z. Klenha. What ensued on April 1 was one of the most terror-filled elections in American history. Frank Capone showed his great ability as a political campaigner by leading an assault on election eve against the Democratic candidate for town clerk, William K. Pflaum, beseiging him in his office, roughing him up and finally destroying his office. At polling places during the balloting, a thug would sidle up to a voter waiting in line to cast his or her ballot and inquire as to the person's preferences. If the voter gave the wrong answer, the thug ripped the ballot from the person's hand and marked it properly. The thug then waited, fingering a revolver, until the voter dropped the ballot into the box. Voters who still protested were simply slugged and carried from the polling place to vote another day. When honest election officials and poll watchers objected, they too were slugged, kidnapped and held until the voting ended. Three men were shot dead and another had his throat cut. A policeman was blackjacked: Michael Gavin, a Democratic campaign worker, was shot in both legs and carted off to be held prisoner in the basement of a mob-owned hotel in Chicago. Eight other balky Democrats kept him company and ministered to his wounds.

By late afternoon a group of honest citizens appealed to the courts for assistance and County Judge Edmund K. Jarecki swore in 70 Chicago policemen as deputy sheriffs. Over the next several hours officers and Capone's followers fought a series of battles. A police squad commanded by Detective Sgt. William Cusick pulled up in front of a polling place near the Hawthorne works of the Western Electric Co. where Al and Frank Capone, Charles Fischetti, a cousin, and Dave Hedlin were "campaigning" with drawn revolvers. In that era unmarked police cars were long limousines no different in appearance from the type gangsters used, and Al Capone, Fischetti and Hedlin hesitated at the sight of the vehicle, unsure whether its occupants were police officers or merely gangsters who supported the anti-Klenha ticket. Frank Capone exhibited no such inhibitions and immediately opened fire on an officer at virtually point-blank range. Frank missed and the officer and another policeman responded with double blasts from their shotguns, killing the elder Capone instantly. Al Capone fled the scene.

Frank Capone was given the biggest underworld funeral Chicago had seen up till then, even eclipsing that of Big Jim Colosimo a few years earlier. His coffin was silver-plated, satin-lined and surrounded by $20,000 worth of flowers. The *Chicago Tribune* called the affair fitting enough for a "distinguished statesman." In deference to the sad occasion, every saloon, gambling joint and whorehouse in Cicero closed down for two solid hours. But perhaps the crowning tribute to Frank Capone was the election returns. The entire Klenha slate was swept back into office by overwhelming margins.

CAPONE, James (1887-1952): Brother of Al Capone and lawman

Referred to by the newspapers as the "white sheep" of the family, James Capone was not precisely a model citizen—except in comparison. He disappeared from the Capone family fold in 1905, when he was 18, and considering what later became of the other Capone brothers, it was probably a good thing. Jim Capone did not surface again until 1940, when—broke, missing an eye and unable to support a wife and several children—he wrote to Ralph Capone, still a mighty power in the Chicago mob. He later visited with Ralph, who thereafter sent him monthly support checks, and with Al, who was in sickly retirement in Florida. Only then did Jim's wife learn for the first time that her husband was the brother of the notorious Al Capone. The newspapers also soon learned the facts, at least as Jim Capone told them. According to Jim's own account, he had spent most of his years as an enforcer of the law and was known in Nebraska as Richard James "Two-Gun" Hart because of his prowess with a gun. The loss of an eye he falsely attributed to a gunfight with gangsters.

While the newspapers played up this white sheep story, the real facts were hardly as flattering to Two-Gun Hart. Capone-Hart had joined a circus and later bummed all over the United States and Central America. In 1919 he dropped off a freight in Homer, Neb. and settled there. He married Kathleen Winch, the daughter of a grocer, and eventually had four sons. During this period he told such vivid tales of his war exploits, although he had never served in the armed forces, that the awed local American Legion post made him their commander.

Hart's popularity was such that he was named the town's marshal and after two years became a state sheriff. In 1922 he joined the Indian Service as a special officer supervising the Omaha and Winnebago tribes to prevent the sale of liquor to them. Hart earned a reputation for cruelty to the Indians and was eventually transferred to Sioux City, Iowa, where he killed an Indian in a saloon brawl but was not prosecuted. It was in a later melee with other Indians that Hart lost an eye. Transferred to Idaho, he was charged with yet another murder, but the case was finally dropped.

Returning to his marshal's job in Homer, Hart eventually lost his badge when store owners began noticing steady shrinkage of their stocks. As marshal, Hart was furnished keys to all business places. He also lost his position as commander of the American Legion post when other members finally thought of asking for proof of his war record. When he couldn't even prove he was a veteran, he was expelled. Without income and evicted from one house for nonpayment of rent, the Hart family went on relief. It was then that Hart got in touch with the other Capones. With the help he received from them and the money he got for telling his fanciful stories to the newspapers, Hart-Capone was able to live out the rest of his years in reasonable comfort, although by the time of his death in 1952 he was totally blind.

CAPONE, Ralph "Bottles" (1893-1974): Brother of Al Capone

The most durable of the Capone brothers, Ralph "Bottles" Capone was a loyal aide to his younger brother Al, and like the mob chieftain, he did a stretch for income tax evasion. Afterward, he got out, Ralph rejoined the Capone mob. In 1950 the United Press stated that "in his own right [Ralph Capone] is now one of the overlords of the national syndicate which controls gambling, vice and other rackets." That statement was somewhat of an exaggeration. Ralph was always given a position of honor within the group as well as excellent sources of income, partly to provide for Big Al's sickly retirement in Florida after his release from prison. But Ralph was never on the same level as the leaders of the national syndicate, such as Lucky Luciano or Meyer Lansky, or the heads of the Chicago mob, such as Tony Accardo, Paul Ricca, Jake Guzik and Sam Giancana.

Part of Ralph's income through the years came from his longtime legitimate business: distributing bottled water in Chicago, an activity that won him the nickname Bottles. Ralph's investment in bottling plants stemmed from a plan Al had devised to gain monopoly control of the soda water and ginger ale used in mixed drinks.

In the early 1950s Ralph was questioned by the Kefauver Committee at great length. A short while later, his son, Ralph, Jr., committed suicide. Young Ralph had been haunted by the Capone name through school and a long string of jobs and he had always tried to keep his identity secret but without success. The Capone name was not easily shaken by either the son or the father. Even in his eighties, Ralph Capone was still being described as an important member of the mob.

CAR Barn Gang

The Car Barn Gang, the last gang in America to declare open war on the police, was clearly an organization born in the wrong era. The Car Barners harkened back to the post-Civil War days when criminal bands operated in most big cities on the basis of pure terror and often engaged in pitched battles or vindictive strikes against the police. Organized in late 1911 in New York City, the Car Barners recruited mostly the young toughs who infested the East River docks, fighting, stealing and rolling drunks. As a gang, they became vicious gunmen and highwaymen, staging daring daylight robberies and holding up trolley-cars with the same Wild West techniques used in earlier days on stagecoaches.

The first the police knew of the existence of an organized gang was the appearance of placards near the old car barns around Second Avenue and East 97th Street. The signs read:

Notice
COPS KEEP OUT!
NO POLICEMAN WILL HEREAFTER
BE ALLOWED IN THIS BLOCK
By Order of
THE CAR BARN GANG.

The police soon learned the Car Barners were most serious about their edict after a half-dozen officers who had ventured into the forbidden zone were either stabbed or had their skulls fractured. Following that, the police never patrolled the area in groups of less than four or five, leading to the vaudevillian comic's famous joke that the police were insisting on police protection.

The primary captain of the Car Barners was one Big Bill Lingley, widely renowned as a burglar and desperado. He seldom ventured forth with less than two revolvers, a blackjack and a slungshot, which he used to attack a likely citizen or a police officer. Big Bill's principal confederate was Freddie Muehfeldt, a youth who, although from a good family and a background of considerable Sunday School work, at age 17 had taken up a wastrel life on the docks. Big Bill determined to make over Muehfeldt, who became known as the Kid, in his own image. They became the twin terrors of the Car Barners' domain from East 90th Street to 100th and from Third Avenue to the East River. Almost by themselves, they were said to make the area as unsafe for honest folk as the notorious Hell's Kitchen section.

The Car Barn Gang ranged far afield in their depredations and would often make an incredible sweep robbing saloons from Manhattan's 14th Street all the way up to the Bronx. The Kid would simply walk behind the bar and tap the till while Big Bill and a dozen or so stalwarts isolated the bouncers. If a barkeep objected to the Kid's action, he would receive a liquor bottle across his skull from the teenaged gangster. Often the saloon keepers who got advanced warning of the approach of the Car Barners, realizing that resistance was foolhardy, would reduce the amount of cash in the till and hope the gangsters would be mollified with their take.

Meanwhile, the war between the Car Barners and the police raged on. Finally, the police strong-arm squad was sent into the area to clean out the gang. They clubbed the gangsters unmercifully, but neither side could get the better of the other as long as Big Bill and the Kid were in the forefront of the battles. Eventually, however, the pair killed a Bronx liquor dispenser making a valiant effort to protect his receipts and were arrested for murder.

Big Bill and the Kid, not yet 21, were executed for the

crime, and by the onset of World War I, the dispirited Car Barners collapsed under persistent police attacks.

CARDIFF Giant: Scientific hoax

The Cardiff Giant, allegedly the fossilized remains of an authentic giant who in ancient times walked the earth in the area of what has become New York state, was one of the most lucrative hoaxes in history.

George Hull, a former cigar maker from Binghampton, N.Y., conceived the plot to create the the giant. In 1868 he obtained a five-ton block of gypsum in Iowa and had it fashioned into the shape of a huge man by a stonecutter in Chicago. He then shipped the statue to the farm of a cousin, William Newell, near Cardiff, N.Y., where after a year the latter duly "discovered" it. It is not clear whether the pair had first concocted their plot as a swindle or if, as he would later state, Hull had had the giant built to ridicule clergymen who were always quoting from Genesis about a supersized race—"There were giants in the earth in those days."

A Syracuse newspaper headlined the find as "A Wonderful Discovery," and the pair pitched a tent and began exhibiting the giant, charging five cents for a view. News of the find flashed across the country and indeed around the world. Thousands swarmed to see it and admission was raised to 50 cents and then to $1. Meanwhile, most experts were convinced the Cardiff Giant was genuine. Two Yale professors, a paleontologist and a chemist, agreed it was a true fossil. The director of the New York State Museum thought the giant was really a statue but indeed most ancient and the "the most remarkable object yet brought to light in this country." Others, including Oliver Wendell Holmes and Ralph Waldo Emerson, concurred. Still, a few were doubtful; the president of Cornell University felt the giant was made of gypsum and thought there were hints of a sculptor's chisel. But the crowds, now arriving by special trains, continued to grow, and P.T. Barnum, the great showman, offered $60,000 to lease the object from Newell for three months. The farmer refused. Undeterred, Barnum hired a sculptor, Professor Carl C. F. Otto, to make an exact copy of the giant.

When Hull and Newell brought their giant to New York in 1871 for exhibit, they discovered Barnum was already displaying his version in Brooklyn. While they hauled Barnum into court, newspapermen were tracing Hull's activities and uncovered his purchase of gypsum in Iowa. They located the stonecutter in Chicago, one Edward Salle, who admitted to carving the giant, aging it with sand, ink and sulfuric acid and punching pores into it with darning needles. Faced with the growing evidence of fraud, Hull confessed. Barnum now was able to avoid prosecution by claiming all he had done was show the hoax of a hoax.

Thanks to their fraud, Hull and Newell netted about $33,000 after building expenses of $2,200. Barnum, who continued showing his version for years, made much more. Today, the Cardiff Giant, Hull's authentic fake, is on display at the Farmers' Museum in Cooperstown, N.Y.

CARDINELLA, Salvatore "Sam" (1880-1921): Murderer

One of the most terrifying and obese criminals in Chicago history and chief of a gang that even the beer barons of Prohibition were fearful of crossing, Sam Cardinella was the mastermind of an incredible plot of self-resuscitation. Known as Il Diavolo, or "The Devil," Cardinella was one of the city's most powerful Black Handers until police cracked down on that racket, whereupon he and his gang turned to banditry and violent crime. Il Diavolo's top triggerman was Nicholas Viana, better known as the Choir Boy, an accomplished murderer at the age of 18. The gang committed 20 murders and well over 100 holdups before Cardinella, Viana and Frank Campione were captured and sentenced to be hanged. But the Cardinella story did not end there.

In his death cell at the Cook County Jail, Cardinella went on a hunger strike and lost 40 pounds. Only 11 minutes before Cardinella was slated to die, police Lt. John Norton, who had apprehended him, received a telephone tip that Cardinella's friends "are going to revive him after the execution." Norton quickly gathered a squad of detectives and hurried to the prison, posting men at the rear entrances where the bodies were taken out. A hearse turned into the alley and stopped. The officers surrounded the vehicle and opened the back door. Inside were a doctor and a nurse, dressed in white.

"What does a dead man need with medical attention?" Norton wanted to know, but he got no answer. The hearse contained a rubber mattress filled with hot water and heated by pads attached to batteries. At the head of the bed was an oxygen tank. There was also a basket jammed with hot-water bottles and a shelf loaded with syringes and stimulants.

Rushing into the jail, Norton found Cardinella laid out on a slab and his relatives eagerly signing papers for possession of the body. Norton bluntly announced that the body would be held for 24 hours, and though Cardinella's relatives screamed in anger, they were powerless.

Later, medical men agreed Cardinella's neck had not been broken when the trap was sprung: his body had been too light. Death had resulted from choking. The doctors said that had sufficient heat been applied to the body quickly, he might have been revived.

CARLTON, Handsome Harry (?-1888): Murderer

Handsome, blue-eyed Harry Carlton was a dapper murderer who had a date with the hangman late in 1888. However, after his sentence had been pronounced, the New York legislature decided that no convicted murderer would be hanged after June 4, 1888 and that from January 1 of the following year on, the state would use the electric chair for capital punishment. The lawmakers' intention was that anyone with a death sentence who was still alive on June 4 would be executed the next year in the electric chair. But that was not the way they had written the statute. Instead, the law was phrased to say that nobody could be hanged after June 4, 1888 and that "electrocution shall apply to all convictions punishable by death on or after January 1st." Carlton's lawyer was quick to spot the loophole. He demanded that Handsome Harry be freed. Death happened to be the only punishment on the books for murder—unless the jury recommended mercy, which in Handsome Harry's case it had not. If a person committed murder, as Harry had, and got no sympathy from the jury, he or she had to die. However unintentionally, the language of the new law stated that persons who committed murder before June 4, 1888 not only could not be hanged but moreover could not be punished at all.

Handsome Harry became an instant worldwide cause celebre and his case shook the very foundation of law in New York state. If he were let go, it would mean that for a seven-month period murder was legal in the state! The dispute was rushed to the Supreme Court. In a marked departure from the High Court's traditional respect for legalisms, it ruled that while the interpretation of the law by Carlton's attorney might be technically correct, no slipup by the legislature could be allowed to endanger human lives. Hanging, the Supreme Court held, remained in force until replaced by the electric chair. On a gray morning two days before Christmas, Carlton swung from the gibbet in the Tombs courtyard in New York City. After the execution a newspaper commented, "We are not at all sure that this hanging was entirely legal but it certainly was justice."

See also: *Howe and Hummel*.

CARNIVAL Gyps

Probably half the people in this country visit a carnival or fair of some kind during the course of a year; yet the so-called games of skill or chance they play are obviously among the most lucrative gyps practiced today. None of the games played are susceptible to being beaten, either by skill or chance. All of them are or can be rigged. The television program "60 Minutes" once devoted an entire segment to the exposure of just one gyp game, "razzle," an involved form of gambling in which the customer can never win.

The "gaff," or fix, is applied to every game or built right into it, as is the case with various coin-pitch games in which a player wins a prize if his coin lands inside a square or circle without touching a line. In this game valuable prizes can theoretically be won, but the house percentage has been mathematically worked out as 80 percent—compared to a little over one percent for casino dice, 2.5 to five percent for roulette and 15 percent or so for one-armed bandits.

Milk bottle toss is a notorious gaff game, although the proprietor or a shill, or phony player, will always be seen winning. The object of the game is to knock six imitation milk bottles off a podium with three baseballs. Knocking them down is not sufficient—they must be knocked completely off the table. The key to the gyp is that three of the six bottles arranged in pyramid form are lead-weighted at the bottom.

When these three are placed at the bottom row, or base, they will do no more than fall over even when hit directly, and the player loses. Yet it's relatively simple for the operator of the game to demonstrate how easy it is to win. He throws the three baseballs and the six bottles topple to the floor, but his assistant has simply stacked the six bottles so that three non lead-weighted bottles are on the bottom row and the weighted ones are on top. A mere brushing will topple the weighted bottles to the floor.

Even games with a guaranteed prize are gaffed. The most common variation of this is the "string game," in which all prizes are attached to strings that feed into a crossbar, or collar. The player pulls a tab for one of the strings on the opposite side of the collar and wins whatever prize pops up. The operator demonstrates the honesty of the game by grabbing all the strings on the other side of the collar and pulling them so that every prize, including very valuable ones, jump up to tempt the public. The trick: the strings attached to the valuable ones are "dead-enders," reaching the collar but not extending to any of the tabs on the other side.

One of the most exotic gaffed games, and a very popular one at big carnivals because it seemingly can't be fixed, is the "mouse game." The public bets on which of 60 numbered holes a mouse will enter, and the prize is quite a good one. A mouse is placed on a wheel, covered with a tin can and spun around vigorously so that when liberated, it is weaving almost drunkenly. Then completely unrehearsed, the mouse heads for the numbered holes. Meanwhile, the operator of the game has made a quick survey of the board and judged whether more money is bet on odd or even numbers. With a foot pedal, he simply closes either the odd or even holes, thereby greatly increasing the house's winnings, especially if the mouse enters an unplayed number. If the mouse, staggering around the holes, butts his head against a closed-off hole, it simply backs off and heads for another opening. This does not look suspicious to the public because the mouse has been moving erratically all along. Finally, the creature enters a hole. Whether or not there is money bet on it, the house almost always wins much more than it loses.

CARPENTER, Richard (1929-1956): Murderer

The object of one of the greatest manhunts in American criminal history, Richard Carpenter was the real life villain of Hollywood's *The Desperate Hours,* holding a Chicago family hostage and forcing them to hide him in a drama reported in headlines around the world after he was finally caught.

The Sunday supplements still carry stories of Carpenter as a prime example of a "mama's boy" turned killer. His probation report showed he was passionately fond of his mother and would always come to her as a child, sit on her lap and moan, "Mother, I'm terribly lonely."

In 1951 Carpenter had begun to make excursions into crime. He was finally arrested for pulling a gun on a taxi driver and robbing him of $8; he got a year in jail. On her visits to the prison, Carpenter's mother brought him cakes and other sweets, which he shared with nobody. He made no friends among his fellow prisoners. His cellmates tagged him Mama's Boy and savagely never let him forget it. When Carpenter was released, he vowed never to fool around with crime or guns again. He became a cabbie, earning about $80 a week. His streak of puritanism showed through when he refused any fare to a gambling joint or brothel. He remained his lone wolf self but occasionally would take his sisters and a girl cousin to a skating rink or the movies. While he couldn't skate, he didn't approve of the girls going out alone at night. Carpenter always bought clothes for the girls, although he neglected himself to the point of going around in tatters. In addition, he always kept his grandfather supplied with three cigars a day. Suddenly, his thin veneer of sanity cracked.

On December 4 1953 Carpenter stole a car, which he later wrecked, and held up a grocery for $100. From that day on, he never returned to his home or saw his family. He ran up a string of over 70 heists and became a cop killer in August 1955, gunning down a police detective who attempted to arrest him on a Chicago subway. Once, he was recognized and almost caught in a downtown movie theater by an off-duty policeman named Clarence Kerr, who happened to be there with his wife. When Kerr ordered Carpenter into the lobby and demanded identification, Carpenter faked a stumble and came up shooting, hitting Kerr in the chest and wounding him badly. Kerr was able to fire one shot off at the fleeing Carpenter, injuring him in the leg. Before passing out, Kerr gasped to his wife: "It was Carpenter—Carpenter—I know it was Carpenter."

The manhunt for Carpenter, pressed by Chicago police for over a year, intensified, with the fugitive's picture splashed across television screens. While police cars wailed through the streets, Carpenter took refuge in the house of a truck driver and his family and threatened to kill them all unless they kept him hidden. But Carpenter was really not that much of a menace to his captives. He yearned for a family environment and ended up trusting the truck driver and his wife too much. They managed to elude his watch long enough to get out of the house and call the police. Within minutes 30 police cars surrounded the house. Carpenter was able to flee through a barrage of bullets and made it across the roof to another building, where he took refuge in a room. When police burst in on him, Carpenter tried unsuccessfully to pretend he was the real occupant of the room.

After his arrest, he said: "I'm sorry about one thing—I didn't do a single thing to make my mother and my sisters proud. It was a lousy life I led—but it is too late now. . . . I'll go to the chair, but I hope I can see my mother before I die."

Carpenter got his wish before dying in the electric chair on March 16, 1956.

CARROLL'S Orgy: Prohibition offense

What may have been the silliest arrest in the entire era of

Prohibition, but one with tragic personal consequences, was that of Broadway producer Earl Carroll for an "orgy" held on February 22, 1926 at the Earl Carroll Theatre after a performance of his *Vanities*.

With typical Broadway irreverence, Carroll was honoring the Countess Vera Cathcart, who had just beaten an Immigration Service effort to prevent her from remaining in this country on the grounds of "moral turpitude" because of her sensational divorce from the Earl of Cathcart. Climaxing the party onstage, a bathtub was filled with champagne and a nude model climbed in while men eagerly waited to fill their glasses or at least ogle at the naked beauty. When reports of the big bash got out, producer Carroll was hauled before a federal grand jury to explain his unique violation of the Volstead Act. Carroll tried to avoid prosecution by declaring there was no champagne in the bathtub, merely ginger ale. For this heinous distortion, he was convicted of perjury, fined $2,000 and sentenced to the federal prison at Atlanta for a year and a day. Carroll suffered a nervous breakdown on the way to the penitentiary. Because of his mental state, his fellow prisoners were ordered never to mention bathtubs in his presence. He was released after serving four months.

CARSON, Ann (1790-1838): Counterfeiter

A strange set of circumstances turned Ann Carson into one of early America's most notorious female criminals. The daughter of a naval officer, she was the lovely and vivacious wife of Army Capt. John Carson, who disappeared in 1810 on a mission in the West against the Indians. Carson was listed as presumed dead. In 1812 Ann Carson met Army Lt. Richard Smith, who was stationed near her home in Philadelphia. After a short courtship they were married and lived happily until January 20, 1816, when her first husband arrived at his home and banged loudly on the door. He told Smith who he was. Smith, who later insisted he had been confused, drew a revolver and shot Carson dead. Within days Smith was brought to trial and it was soon evident that everyone assumed he had killed Carson rather than give up his wife.

While the trial was going on, Ann Carson made a desperate attempt to kidnap the governor of Pennsylvania, Simon Snyder, and hold him as a hostage to gain her second husband's release. She failed and Smith was convicted and, on February 4, 1816, hanged. Ann Carson lost all respect for law and order and became the head of a band of hardened criminals. Drawing on her military background, she organized the gang under strict regulations that made them most effective. While they engaged in some violent crimes, Ann Carson's gang were most competent at counterfeiting, passing notes for six years with brilliant efficiency. After they were finally rounded up, all were given long prison terms in 1823. Ann Carson died in Philadelphia Prison in 1838 while working on her memoirs.

CARUSO, Enrico (1873-1921): Black hand extortion victim

Few Italians coming to America around the turn of the 20th

century expected to escape the terrors and tribulations they had experienced at the hands of criminals in their native country. Rich or poor they could expect threats on their lives—so-called Black Hand threats that promised death unless they paid money. These were not the work of any "Black Hand Society" but extortions performed by the Mafia or other criminals, and not even the most famous were immune. During a triumphal engagement at the Metropolitan Opera shortly before World War I, the great Italian tenor Enrico Caruso received a Black Hand letter, with the imprint of a black hand and a dagger, demanding $2,000. The singer quietly paid, considering an appeal to the police both useless and foolhardy.

However, when this payment was followed by a new demand for $15,000, Caruso knew he had no choice but to go to the police. If he did not, he realized the criminals would continue to increase their demands and drain him dry. Caruso had been instructed to leave the money under the steps of a factory, and after the police set a trap, he did so. Two prominent Italian businessmen were seized when they tried to retrieve the loot. The two were convicted of extortion and sent to prison—one of the few successful prosecutions of Black Hand criminals. Even so, Caruso was considered to be in such great danger in case the criminals sought their usual vengeance on an informer that he was kept under police and private detective protection, both in this country and in Europe, for several years.

See also: *Black Hand*.

CASEY, James P. (?-1856): Murderer

One of the most famous and infamous victims of the San Francisco Committee of Vigilance, James Casey was the editor of the *Sunday Times* and a member of the city's Board of Supervisors during what many regard as the most politically corrupt decade in San Francisco's history. Ruffians, outlaws, thieves and murderers controlled the city in the 1850s and were protected by equally crooked politicians, one of whom was Casey.

An arch rival of Casey was James King, editor of the *Evening Bulletin,* who publicized Casey's involvement with corrupt elements and his previous history, which included serving 18 months in Sing Sing prison for larceny. In 1855 King's voice was the most virulent in calling for the reestablishment of the 1851 vigilance committee to clean up the city. On May 14, 1856 King launched a vigorous attack against Casey and said he deserved "having his neck stretched." As King left his newspaper's offices later that day, Casey accosted him, shoved a revolver against his chest and ordered him to "draw and defend yourself." Casey then shot and mortally wounded his foe without even giving him a chance to draw a weapon, which in any case he did not have. After the shooting Casey was taken into custody. However, fearing the political powers would permit him to escape justice, the vigilance committee swung into action. A thousand men enrolled in a special armed force, and militiamen guarding Casey in jail wired their resignation to the governor, stacked their arms and joined the vigilantes. King clung to life for six days before dying on May 20. He was

buried two days later, with an estimated 15,000 to 20,000 men and women following his body to the grave. By the time the last of the throng returned to the city, Casey and another murderer, Charles Cora, were hanged from the windows of the vigilante headquarters on makeshift gallows.

Casey's political friends buried him and had inscribed on his tombstone, "May God Forgive My Persecutors." It should also be noted that in the two months following Casey's execution, not a single murder occurred in San Francisco, a period of tranquility never again experienced in that city.

Drawing shows James Casey being conveyed through heckling San Franciscans to be hanged by the vigilance committee.

CASSIDY, Butch (1866-1937?): Outlaw leader

Robert LeRoy Parker, alias Butch Cassidy, is without doubt the most romantic character to come out of the outlaw West. He combined the daring of Jesse James with the free spirit of Bill Doolin and, indeed, his Wild Bunch had much in common with the latter's Oklahombres. What is most amazing about Parker's appeal is that he never killed anyone and American hero worship has usually been reserved for more efficient bloodletters. But Cassidy had other ingratiating qualities. He could prevent Kid Curry from shooting a resisting railroad express car guard by saying: "Let him alone, Kid. A man with his nerve deserves not to be shot." In 1894, when Cassidy was convicted of horse stealing and sentenced to two years, he requested permission to leave his jail cell unescorted for the night before he was to be transferred to the state prison. "I give you my word I'll be back." Incredibly, permission was granted and sure enough the next morning Cassidy returned. He never revealed where he went or whom he visited; he simply turned in his guns and went off to prison.

Born in 1866 in Utah Territory, young Bob Parker was raised on his Mormon father's remote ranch. As a teenager he came under the influence of an old-time rustler named Mike Cassidy and rode with him in the early 1880s in Colorado. Later, he went to work for a mining outfit in Telluride, Colo., and fell in with bad company, taking up rustling and pulling small bank jobs. Strictly speaking, Cassidy's Wild Bunch was not formed until his release from prison in 1896, although his earlier gang, which included the likes of Tom McCarty and Matt Warner, was cut from the same fun-loving mold.

In 1896 Cassidy (Parker had by then adopted the name of his old mentor) turned up in a desperado haven called Brown's Hole. There and in Hole in the Wall, he met many other young criminals who became part of the loosely-knit Wild Bunch. They included Kid Curry (Harvey Logan), the Sundance Kid (Harry Longbaugh), Harry Tracy, Matt Warner, Elzy Lay, Deaf Charley Hanks and Ben Kilpatrick. From the very first, Cassidy was regarded as the leader of the gang, commanding respect as much by being able to exercise restraint as by his more than competent shooting. He was a superb planner of crimes and had the gift for being able to use the best ideas of others, especially Elzy Lay, who was probably the smartest of the group and Cassidy's best and most-trusted friend.

The Wild Bunch's first important train robbery, after a number of bank jobs and stock thefts, was that of a Union Pacific train near Wilcox, Wyo. on June 2, 1899. The gang detached the express car and blasted it open with a dynamite charge, enough to get in but not to kill a plucky guard inside who was determined to resist. Throughout his career Cassidy could boast he had never killed a man, although the same could not be said for the rest of his gang despite his best efforts to restrain them. The Wilcox robbery netted $30,000. The Wild Bunch quickly pulled three more train robberies and Cassidy's fame spread. While Pinkerton detectives tracked him, the Union Pacific considered another way of containing Cassidy—offering to buy him off by obtaining a pardon for him and giving him a job as an express guard at a very high salary, presumably as a no-show job. Cassidy himself probably queered that deal by robbing yet another train just as negotiations through intermediaries were beginning.

The railroad then sent its own band of gunfighters after Cassidy and his gang. Equipped with high-powered rifles, these man hunters took up the chase utilizing a high-speed train. A number of the gang were either killed or arrested, and Cassidy realized it was only a matter of time until he too would be run into the ground. In late 1901 Cassidy, accompanied by the Sundance Kid and his lady, the celebrated Etta Place, fled to New York and the following year headed for South America. Much has been speculated about the relationship between Etta, Butch and Sundance, but there is little doubt that Etta was basically Sundance's woman. Butch once told an acquaintance, "She was the best housekeeper in the Pampas, but she was a whore at heart."

Etta was also the hard-riding partner who joined with the two men on their many holdups in Argentina. In between jobs Butch and Sundance flirted with going straight and became close friends with a young mining man, Percy Seibert, who in time came to learn their identities, a secret he kept. Cassidy often spoke earnestly to Seibert about changing his life, and the mining man encouraged him. In 1907 Etta Place returned to the States for reasons of health. Sundance took her back but rejoined Cassidy in 1908. Forced to move on because they had been identified, the pair went to Bolivia, where, according to more or less the official Pinkerton version, they were killed in 1911 by Bolivian troops after being cornered following a robbery. In a variation of this story the Sundance Kid was killed but Cassidy escaped and eventually returned to the United States.

Seibert identified two American bank robbers killed in Bolivia as Cassidy and Sundance. But his identification was rebutted in a 1975 book—*Butch Cassidy, My Brother*—by Butch Cassidy's sister, Lula Parker Betenson, who insisted her brother came home and lived out a good life until his death in the 1930s. According to his sister, Cassidy visited his family on a number of occasions and rendezvoused many times with his old buddies Warner and Lay, who had mended their ways. She said Butch felt that Seibert had willfully misidentified the two bandits just to give him and Sundance another chance. Overall, the evidence appears that Cassidy did not die in Bolivia, but that he returned around 1910, married and spent some time in the Mexican Revolution as a mercenary, all under the name of William Thadeus Phillips. If Cassidy was Phillips, he died in Spangle, Wash. in 1937.

See also: *Brown's Hole, Hole in the Wall, Kid Curry, Ben Kilpatrick, Elzy Lay, Etta Place, Sundance Kid, Matt Warner.*

CASTELLAMMARESE War: Mafia power struggle

During much of the 1920s the Mafia in New York was dominated by one man, Giuseppe "Joe the Boss" Masseria, who could quite logically be considered the "boss of bosses." However, Masseria was a crude, obscene leader who was increasingly hated by the young, second-generation mafiosi around town. They resented what they considered his stupidity and insistence on putting personal power and the old Sicilian virtues of "respect" and "dignity" ahead of the quest for money. Like other old "Mustache Petes," Masseria was violently opposed to working with the powerful, non-Italian gangs, even though the high profits of such cooperation were obvious.

What these young rebels objected to even more was the needless and constant struggle for power within the Mafia. Under these old-time gang leaders, Mafia gunmen not only fought other ethnic groups but also warred among themselves, with Sicilians battling Neapolitans and, even worse, Sicilians battling Sicilians who had immigrated from other parts of the island or from other villages.

By 1928 Masseria had become concerned about the growing power of Mafiosi from the west coast Sicilian town of Castellammare del Golfo. Several of these Castellammarese rose to power in other American cities, especially Cleveland and Buffalo, but their main source of strength lay in Brooklyn, where many of the rackets were controlled by Salvatore Maranzano, a tough mafioso in his own right who aspired to the title of boss of bosses himself. Soon, the war for control of New York rackets broke out between the two groups.

In the Masseria organization were such rising talents as Lucky Luciano, Vito Genovese, Frank Costello, Albert Anastasia, Joe Adonis, Carlo Gambino and Willie Moretti. Under the Maranzano banner were such future crime leaders as Joe Profaci, Joe Bonanno, Tommy Lucchese, Gaetano Gagliano and Joe Magliocco. However, few of these men owed much allegiance to their respective bosses, wanting only for the Castellammarese War, as the struggle was called, to be brought to a conclusion.

Thus, while Masseria men killed Maranzano supporters and vice versa, a secret underground developed in the two camps, attracting men who realized that both leaders would have to be eliminated to achieve the peace needed to organize crime the way they knew it should be. The leader in this rebellion was Lucky Luciano, who developed a strong rapport with his young counterparts in the Maranzano organization, especially with Tommy Lucchese, who kept him informed of all secret developments.

Finally, Luciano planned and carried out the assassination of Joe the Boss in a Coney Island restaurant. Luciano, then number two in command to Masseria, simply stepped into the men's room just before four of his supporters, Vito Genovese, Joe Adonis, Albert Anastasia and Bugsy Siegel, loaned to Luciano for the operation by his closest Jewish confederate, Meyer Lansky, walked in and gunned down Joe the Boss.

When the police arrived, Joe the Boss was dead, and Luciano, having emerged from the men's room, was unhelpful. The standard report quoted in newspapers around the country was that Luciano said he had heard the shooting and "as soon as I finished drying my hands, I walked out to see what it was all about." A bit of journalistic censorship was involved. Luciano's actual comment was: "I was in the can taking a leak. I always take a long leak."

With Masseria eliminated, Luciano and his cohorts contacted Maranzano with a peace offering, one that was accepted with the clear understanding that Maranzano was now the boss of bosses. However, Maranzano was smart enough to realize that what had happened to Masseria would also happen to him unless he struck first. He therefore planned a series of assassinations that would eliminate not only Luciano and his second-in-command, Vito Genovese, but also many others, including Al Capone in Chicago, Willie Moretti, Joe Adonis, Frank Costello and Dutch Schultz, one of Luciano's non-Italian

associates. According to his battle plan, Maranzano would emerge from such a bloodbath as the undisputed crime boss in America.

However, Luciano and Lansky anticipated Maranzano's moves, and on September 10, 1931, just hours before a psychopathic killer named Vincent "Mad Dog" Coll was to begin the Maranzano purge, four Jewish gangsters supplied by Lansky walked into Maranzano's office in the guise of detectives and shot and stabbed Maranzano to death.

The Castellammarese War thus ended with the two contending forces vanquished. The young rebels under Lucky Luciano took over. While Luciano made use of such terms as "Cosa Nostra," or "our thing," as a sort of Mafia carryover, the day of the Mafia was really finished. The new crime boss formed lasting alliances with non-Italian gangsters, and the national crime syndicate, or "organized crime," was born, taking control and continuing to this day.

See also: *Charles "Lucky" Luciano, Salvatore Maranzano, Giuseppe "Joe the Boss" Masseria, Night of the Sicilian Vespers.*

CASTRATION As Punishment

Castration is a much-discussed and little-used method of punishment for criminality. There are no overall statistics available, and the best that can be determined is that during the 20th century it has been used several hundred times in California and less frequently in some other states. Because of new interpretations of existing law and malpractice, it is highly unlikely to be used much in the future, although one occasionally reads a newspaper item of a prisoner being offered or indeed suggesting the use of castration as an alternate to a long prison term. In California in 1975 two convicted child molesters, Paul de la Haye and Joseph Kenner, requested they be castrated instead of being given what was likely to be a life sentence. The sentencing judge readily agreed, but the operations were canceled when the urologist retained to perform them was advised by a group of colleagues at University Hospital in San Diego that he most likely would be open to a lawsuit for assault and battery and probably would not be covered by malpractice insurance. The county urological society gave the doctor the same advice.

Aside from these legal restrictions there is a growing philosophical opposition to the practice, despite an occasional flamboyant outburst by an isolated jurist. The sentiment is probably best summarized by Aryeh Neier, executive director of the American Civil Liberties Union, in a recent book entitled *Crime and Punishment:* "But an overriding purpose of the criminal law should be to prevent citizens from committing physical violence against each other. It cannot be useful to that end for the state to set an example of violence against its own citizens. If prison is more barbarous to the victim, at least citizens cannot readily mimic the state by holding other citizens behind bars."

The last reported case of castration appears to have been in Colorado in 1972.

CAT Burglar

A general public misconception is that a so-called catman, or cat burglar, is an acrobatic daredevil who burglarizes private homes. Very few of these talented criminals would waste their skills on so pedestrian a target, even if it was the mansion of a millionaire. The cat burglar's habitat is the urban skyscraper, which he climbs by means of ropes and scaling ladders. His targets are jewelry salesrooms, fur shops and cash-heavy businesses deemed safe from window-entry burglary because of their location on high floors.

A catman of extraordinary ability was a character named Slippery Augie Smith, who plagued businesses and baffled New York City police in the 1950s and 1960s. The police suspected they had catman trouble after an epidemic of baffling burglaries. There were no signs of forcible entry, and insurance companies were balking at paying claims for so many burglary losses. At first, the heists looked like inside jobs. In three instances bookkeepers who had the combinations of rifled safes were fired. It struck the police as odd, however, that three trusted employees should all go bad at about the same time.

Then one Saturday night, protective agency patrolmen answering an automatic alarm on West 28th Street came across an intruder on the 14th floor and raced after him down a corridor. Without hesitation the man crawled through an open window at the front of the building, hung from the sill for a moment and, to the officers' horror, let go. The guards called for an ambulance and went to the street to help remove the gory remains. The only trouble was there were no remains— just a moccasin. When the police arrived a few minutes later, the only explanation seemed to be that the burglar had fallen 14 stories and walked away. The agency patrolmen swore they'd seen the man disappear from the ledge.

The mystery was finally solved when the other moccasin was found on the 13th floor under a heavy pivot window that swung out from the middle of the frame. The thief had dropped to this open slanted window directly below and slid down it like a chute into the 13th floor hallway. While the guards were rushing to the street, the catman had blithely made his getaway over the roof.

The next weekend the catman went into action again. Fifteen Persian lamb coats were stolen from the same building where he had put on his high-diving act. Unable to make off with all the loot in one trip, he stashed 10 of the coats under a water tower on the roof. The police found the coats and immediately staked lookouts all around, hoping to nab the thief when he returned for the rest of the haul. But the catman apparently surveyed the scene from another roof and spotted the police trap. After several futile nights the police gave up and returned the coats to the owner. The very next night, the catman struck and made off with the same 10 coats.

Months marked by more improbably burglaries went by before the police got a break. Finally, they received a tip from the desk clerk at a hotel on 27th Street that a salesman guest was renting a top-floor room by the week but occupied it only from Friday night to Monday morning. The routine made no sense since salesmen don't do any business in the garment area on weekends; moreover, if someone wanted a room for a fling on the town, he'd be more likely to rent space nearer the Times Square area. After obtaining a search warrant, police entered the hotel room. A fast check indicated they had found their catman. The room contained a cache of ropes, ladders and stolen loot, including those elusive Persian lamb coats.

When Slippery Augie, a 23-year-old ex-sailor, strolled into the room a few hours later, he found himself under arrest, with no chance to make a fast break to the window. Realizing he faced a long prison stretch, Augie talked, not without an air of pride. He said he got his thrills suspended high above the street. He also explained how he had been able to make his safecracking robberies look like inside jobs. "Most of these businessmen were so sure nobody could get into their places except through the door, which was protected by burglar alarms, they would leave the safe combination around someplace handy," he said. "Some pasted them in the upper left-hand drawer of their desks. Others filed the figures under S."

CATANIA Curse: Fate of Mafia victim's family

A Sunday supplement phrase invented to describe the sorry plight of the Catanias, father and son, who met the same fate at the hands of Mafia executioners 29 years apart, it nevertheless reflects the primitive law of survival pervading that criminal organization.

Joe Catania was a Mafia capo who ran the southern Brooklyn docks area in 1902. This position made him extremely valuable to New York's first Mafia family, the Morellos, in their counterfeit money distribution setup. The bogus money was printed in Sicily and then concealed in olive oil shipments that wre sent to Catania's piers. From there the bills went to Pittsburgh, Buffalo, Chicago and New Orleans, where they were passed by Mafia organizations. The only threat to the arrangement was Catania himself, whose increasing addiction to the bottle weakened his sense of discretion. When his saloon remarks became too open, Catania was subject to a special Mafia trial—one that the defendant knew nothing about—and his execution was ordered. His body was found near the Gowanus docks inside a barrel, his throat slit from ear to ear. He had also been so savagely beaten that all major bones in his body were broken, a clear Mafia signal for all to maintain silence.

At the time of his father's assassination, Joseph "Joe the Baker" Catania was only a babe in arms. He grew up in the rackets, as was his right since he was related by blood to the Morello family. On February 3, 1931, just after he kissed his wife goodbye, Joe the Baker was gunned down in the Bronx by Joe Valachi and the mysterious "Buster from Chicago." Much was made about Joe the Baker being a victim of the Masseria-Maranzano war for control of New York, but the fact was that Catania had been marked for death when his father died. It was a Mafia custom that members of a family were supposed to avenge killings of their kin. Joe the Baker, therefore, was supposed to kill his father's assassins. On the other hand, when someone in the Mafia had cause to eliminate Joe the Baker for reasons unrelated to his father's killing, in this case his hijacking of certain bootleg whiskey trucks, they found ready allies among the kin of old Joe Catania's murderers.

CATTLE Kate (1862-1889): Prostitute and alleged rustler

Ella Watson, known as Cattle Kate, was an enterprising young prostitute from Kansas who settled in the Wyoming cow country. With a partner of sorts, Jim Averill, she did a thriving business in cattle, which was the coin of the realm for cowboys paying her for services rendered.

Rendering of the lynching of Cattle Kate and Jim Averill appeared in a publication sympathetic with the interests of the big cattlemen.

It would of course have been highly unusual if the cowboys limited their payments to cows they held clear title to. For a time, Cattle Kate was tolerated by all, including the big stockmen, who understood that men on the range needed certain diversions and cattle losses of this sort were merely the price of doing business, that era's equivalent of cheating on expense accounts. However, the blizzards of 1888 thinned out the herds, and the big stockmen felt they could no longer stand

such losses. One July day in 1889 a wealthy and arrogant cattleman named Albert Bothwell and 10 others decided to do something about the matter. They kidnapped Cattle Kate from her cabin, picked up Averill, who had become something of a spokesman for the small homesteaders fencing off the wide-open range, and threatened to hang them. It appears there was no real plan for a lynching but rather just a desire to frighten the duo. Unfortunately for them, neither Cattle Kate nor Averill took the threats seriously, even when nooses were put around their necks. They were then shoved into space, apparently just to carry the scare tactics a step further. But as the pair slowly strangled, no one made a move to cut them down. The lynchings stirred up an outcry from citizens that Bothwell and his friends had not anticipated, but Bothwell's fellow stockmen hastily came up with a new justification for the act. Stories were planted in the friendly Cheyenne press that Cattle Kate was a mean, gun-toting bandit queen and Averill her business manager. They were accused of systematically looting the range, with her red-light activities a mere cover for their crimes. Cattle Kate became a criminal adventuress worthy of front-page coverage in even the *Police Gazette*. The *Cheyenne Weekly Mail* observed that the lynchings indicated the time had come "when men would take the law into their own hands." The whitewash, the cattle barons soon saw, was effective enough cover for them to launch a major attack on the homesteaders in Johnson County, Wyo. Others were accused of running rustling operations similar to Cattle Kate's and, it was said, would have to be dealt with. Thus, the lynching of a 26-year-old prostitute provided the rationale for what was to become the Johnson County War.

See also: *James Averill, Johnson County War.*

CATTLE Rustling

The principal business of the American West was cattle raising, and, quite naturally, the number one crime was cattle rustling. Actually, the Indians did much of the early stealing, mainly because they realized that if the white man could not keep his cattle, he could not occupy the Indian hunting grounds. Many Indians also felt that stealing cattle made up in some small way for the newcomers' slaughter of the buffalo. In due course, it became the main illegal activity of many outlaws. Mexican bandits frequently raided the Texan and later the American side of the Rio Grande and, according to official claims made to the Mexican government, rustled 145,298 cattle from the King and Kennedy ranches. Turnabout seemed fair play. Numerous Texas stockmen built their vast herds by stealing animals from Mexican-owned ranches on either side of the border. Often going to Mexico on a "buying trip" meant stealing great herds and swimming them across the Rio Grande at night. Such herds, in fact, came to be called "wet stock."

Having so accumulated much of their herds, these same stockmen were nonetheless enraged by the relatively insignificant losses caused by other American rustlers. Yet, cattle rustling never provoked the venom that horse stealing did. The stealing of one neighbor's stock by another, however, was universally condemned, unless the other was a hated absentee owner, in which case the prohibition did not apply. A small rancher often would start his herd using a "rope with a wide loop," an accepted practice when restricted to unbranded animals. As Bill Nye wrote in his *Laramie Boomerang* in 1883: "A guileless tenderfoot came to Wyoming, leading a single steer and carrying a branding iron. Now he is the opulent possessor of 600 head of fine cattle—the ostensible progeny of that one steer."

The great cattle wars were essentially fought by the hired guns of big ranchers out to eliminate thefts by smaller ranchers and cowboys seeking "to get a start in the business." This type of conflict was epitomized by Wyoming's bloody Johnson County War, which took place in an area where local jurors simply would not convict local citizens for cutting a few animals out of a big ranchman's stock. Many alleged rustlers died of "hemp fever" for no other reason than that they had arrived on the scene at the wrong time. Just a few years earlier the very men now doing the "stringing up" had been committing the same crimes; in fact, that's how they had gotten started in the business. In the end, cattle rustling was stamped out by these extreme measures. "Range detectives," who were often no more than hired guns, barbed wire fences and the forceful closing of the range put an end to this traditional method of breaking into the ranching business.

See also: *Johnson County War, Wet Stock.*

CAVE-IN-ROCK Pirates

The great commercial route that opened the frontier in the early 19th century was down the Ohio and Mississippi rivers to the port of New Orleans. The two rivers teemed with pirates who falsely marked the channels so that rafts and keelboats would run aground or crash into the rocks. When this wasn't practical, the boats were attacked from skiffs and canoes. The most treacherous stretch was on the Kentucky shore of the Ohio from Red Bank to Smithland, where the king of the local pirates was Bully Wilson.

A Virginian, Wilson set up his headquarters in a cave near the head of Hurricane Bars. Beckoning thirsty travelers to shore was the following sign:

WILSON'S LIQUOR VAULT
and
HOUSE FOR ENTERTAINMENT

The unwary who paused there rarely resumed their voyage. Wilson's place was known as Cave-in-Rock, and the only visitors who could stop there in safety were pirates, robbers, slave stealers and murderers. And if they were alone and were known to have a hoard of loot with them, they were not particularly safe either. But the main purpose of Cave-in-Rock was to prey on river traffic, and Bully Wilson always had 80 to 100 men ready to swoop down on helpless vessels. Whenever a craft was taken, all aboard were killed, and the boat, manned by a pirate crew, would sail on to New Orleans to sell its goods. The river pirates dominated the waterways until the mid-1820s, when the boatmen organized to fight back.

In July 1824 the crews of about a dozen flatboats, about 80 men in all, hid in the cargo box of a single boat and floated down the river. The boat was soon attacked by a force of about 30 pirates, coming out in canoes and skiffs. As the pirates swept aboard the flatboat, the hidden men stormed out of the cargo box. Ten pirates were killed and another 12 captured. They were blindfolded and forced to walk the plank in 20 feet of water. As the helpless men surfaced, crewmen armed with rifles stood on the cargo box and shot them. The end result of such punitive expeditions finally broke the power of Bully Wilson and other pirates, so that the waterways were relatively free of piracy and safe for commerce after 1825.

See also: *Colonel Plug, Piracy.*

CENTER Street: New York vice district

Currently the site of New York Police Headquarters, Center Street had an unwholesome history. Its creation traces back to the financial crisis of the winter of 1807-08, when business virtually ground to a halt because of the weather. The out-of-work elements were near starvation, and because of mob riots for jobs and food, the city began its first public works program to create employment. Large work gangs were set to draining and filling a pond and marshland known as the Collect. When the work was finally completed and the earth settled, the area was opened for settlement. The first street created was called Collect Street; later, it was renamed Rynders Street for Captain Isaiah Rynders, the corrupt political boss of the Sixth Ward and protector of the gangsters that inhabited the Five Points section. For well over half a decade, the street was known as one of the wickedest in the city and contained virtually nothing but saloons and brothels. Even with a determined effort to rid the area of vice, unsavory elements remained when most of the worst dives were closed and the name changed to Centre Street (later altered to Center). But the real cleanup was not made until police headquarters was situated there and the criminals decided to move a few blocks away.

CERMAK, Anton J. (1873-1933): Chicago mayor and murder victim

Mayor Anton J. Cermak of Chicago was with Franklin D. Roosevelt in Miami on February 15, 1933 when Joseph Zangara attempted to assassinate the President-elect and fatally shot Cermak instead. Cermak became a martyr.

At the time he was shot, Cermak cried, "The President, get him away!" He told Roosevelt, "I'm glad it was me instead of you." Roosevelt, who cradled the wounded mayor, said: "I held him all the way to the hospital and his pulse constantly improved. . . . I remember I said, 'Tony, keep quiet—don't move—it won't hurt you if you keep quiet and remain perfectly still.'"

Cermak lingered for three weeks. From his deathbed the mayor expounded a theory, long held by some historians after his death, that he, not Roosevelt, was the intended victim all the time. Judge John H. Lyle, probably as knowledgeable as any non-Mafia man on the subject of Chicago crime, stated categorically, "Zangara was a Mafia killer, sent from Sicily to do a job and sworn to silence." It was not an outlandish theory, the concept of the sacrificial hit man having a long history in the annals of the Mafia.

In theory, Cermak was a great reformer, but that must be measured in light of what constituted reform in Chicago. Born in Prague and brought to America when he was one year old, Cermak went into politics at any early age and soon won the nickname Ten Percent Tony, since that figure was said to be his standard skim in kickbacks and other deals. By the time Cermak had served three terms in the state legislature, he was worth $1 million. Before he took office as mayor, his net worth was $7 million. In the words of a contemporary writer, Cermak was guilty of using "surreptitious means such as wire taps, mail drops, surveillance and stool pigeons to ferret out information concerning the weaknesses and foibles of administrative and political friends, taking great pains to learn the identities of his enemies."

Cermak did not attempt to purge Chicago of gangsterism but only of the Capone element, which he sought to replace with others who had supported his campaign, headed by Gentleman Teddy Newberry. Some writers have claimed that Cermak moved to take over all crime in Chicago after the imprisonment of Al Capone. Later court testimony indicated that the mayor had dispatched some "tough cops" to eradicate Frank Nitti, Capone's regent during his absence. Nitti was searched, found to be unarmed and was about to be handcuffed when an officer leveled his gun at the gangster and shot him three times in the neck and back. The officer then shot himself in the finger. Nitti was taken to the hospital to die, and the police announced he had been wounded while resisting arrest, as the officer's injured finger proved. Unfortunately for the mayor, Nitti recovered and a full-scale war ensued, one of the early victims being Cermak's favorite gangster, Newberry. At the time, Cermak was taking the sun in Florida on a rather extended vacation, said to have been so arranged to keep him away from the Capone gangsters. Cermak had left Chicago for Florida on December 21, 1932, and he was still there February 15, 1933. Some cynics suggested that the mayor was seeking the protective wing of the President-elect to stay alive. Others contended that Cermak was merely cementing relations with the incoming administration and just possibly talking to Roosevelt's campaign manager, James J. Farley, about an indictment said to be pending against him for income tax evasion.

Zangara, who had been overwhelmed by guards and the crowd after firing the shots, died in the electric chair on March 21, 1933. He insisted Roosevelt was the man he had meant to kill.

See also: *Joseph Zangara.*

CERO-GALLO Case: Wrong man case

In one of the most-twisted "wrong man" cases in history, Gangi Cero, a young Italian seaman was found guilty of murder in Massachusetts and sentenced to die in September 1928. Cero's sympathetic employer, Samuel Gallo, provided his own lawyer, who unsuccessfully tried to save the defendant. On the night scheduled for the execution, a witness was found who identified the murderer as Gallo. Cero was granted a reprieve. Gallo was then indicted and both he and Cero were brought to trial together. Cero was quickly found not guilty, but Gallo was convicted. Gallo, however, won a new trial, and after the main witness against him left the country, he too was acquitted.

CHADWICK, Cassie (1857-1907): Swindler

One of the most audacious swindles ever worked in this country was accomplished in the 1890s by a Canadian woman and incorrigible thief, Mrs. Cassie Chadwick, who married into Cleveland society. She was, she hinted, the illegitimate daughter of Andrew Carnegie, the steel magnate. In fact, she did more than hint—she flashed all sorts of promissory notes supposedly signed by Carnegie and then deposited some $7 million worth of allegedly valid securities in a Cleveland bank. She told the banker to keep her secret, which meant, of course, that the news spread like wildfire throughout the banking community and soon among the city's social set. Clearly, Mrs. Chadwick was somebody, and she was invited to the best functions. Bankers too volunteered their services without asking. Yes, Mrs. Chadwick acknowledged, she might be able to use a little loan or two against future payments from her tycoon father. She took a few small loans, all under $100,000, and repaid them promptly by taking out other loans from different banks and private lenders. She then went whole hog, borrowing millions. Mrs. Chadwick paid high interest, but with all that Carnegie money behind her, she seemed good for it.

The hoax was simplicity itself, being so outrageous that it was never questioned. Certainly, no one was going to approach Carnegie for confirmation. The Chadwicks now traveled frequently to Europe and, when they were in Cleveland, entertained lavishly. Mrs. Chadwick was also a leading public benefactor. In less than a decade, it was later estimated, she took banks and private lenders for upwards of $20 million dollars.

The bubble burst in 1904, when the *Cleveland Press* heard of a Boston creditor who had become dubious about getting his money back. The newspaper checked on Mrs. Chadwick's background and found out her real name was Elizabeth Bigley, a convicted forger who had been pardoned in 1893 by Ohio Gov. William McKinley. When the news came out, Charles T. Beckwith, president of the Citizens National Bank of Oberlin, to whose institution Mrs. Chadwick owed $1.25 million, promptly keeled over from heart failure. There was a run on the bank and on scores of others that were found to have made loans to the woman.

Mrs. Chadwick, who was in New York on a spending spree when the unpleasantness surfaced, was arrested and extradited back to Cleveland, where she was tried and sentenced to 10 years in prison. She died there in 1907. It was believed at the time of her death that many of her victims had still not come forth, some individuals hoping to avoid ridicule and the banks to avoid runs. Remarkably, there were still those who firmly believed that Mrs. Chadwick was indeed Carnegie's daughter and that he would in due course make good on her debts. All of which made Cassie Chadwick's swindle among the most enduring ever concocted.

CHAIN Gangs

The use of chain gangs for convict labor was not, as the public now generally believes, an invention of the Southern states; the custom was practiced in both the North and in England during the 18th century. The Southern states, having used the method to some extent in antebellum years, embraced the custom wholeheartedly in the post-Civil War era as an important source of revenue during their financial distress. Convicts were turned over to leasees, who not only chained a prisoner's two legs together but chained him as well to several other prisoners, lessening the chances of escape. Public protests against the inhumane treatment of chain gang convicts led to a sharp reduction of the practice. However, the advent of the automobile and the need for many new roads led to a great resurgence of chain gang labor; by the early part of the 20th century, a major part of the prisoner force in several states labored in road gangs. Exposes of conditions became common, the most potent being that written by an escaped convict, Robert Elliott Burns, who authored *I Am a Fugitive from a Georgia Chain Gang*, a best-selling book that was made into an important movie in the 1930s. Reform pressures no doubt forced some states to reduce greatly or discontinue chain gangs, but in truth, their virtual elimination was due to a form of "automation." New road-making machinery simply rendered chain gang labor obsolete.

In the late 1940s Georgia became the last state to eliminate the practice, although in later years it was still reported to exist for small details of brief duration.

See also: *Robert Elliott Burns, Convict Labor System.*

CHAMPION, Nathan D. (1857-1892): Victim of Johnson County War

Even today in some quarters of Wyoming, the name of Nate Champion is a hallowed one, that of a man killed solely because he defied the great cattle barons. Others regard him as a cunning rustler, the head of the notorious Red Sash Gang that allegedly stole thousands of head of cattle. Whatever the truth may be, it is certain that he was on a "death list" composed by the executive committee of the Wyoming Stock Growers' Association on the basis of "nominations" received from members.

Champion, a powerfully built man, had been a trailherder for several years until the early 1880s when he collected his pay after a drive and settled in Johnson County. Similar to many others, Champion became a homesteader and built up a little herd of cattle, thus earning the enmity of the cattle barons,

who wanted an open range for their huge herds. These absentee cattlemen sent Pinkerton agents onto the range and were assured by them that there was organized rustling of their stock in Johnson County, mainly the work of the Red Sash Gang bossed by Nate Champion. Other observers believed that the charge was a self-serving lie and the only connection Champion had with any mythical Red Sashers was the fact that he, like a great many other homesteaders who came up from Texas, wore a *vaquero*-type red sash.

In the early morning hours of April 11, 1892, a small army of about 50 gunmen, most hired for the occasion, attacked Champion's cabin, which he shared with a cowboy named Nick Ray. Ray went outside in the snow to chop some wood and was cut down by a hail of bullets. Champion rushed out and hauled the severely wounded Ray to safety. He then kept up a barrage of fire that held off his attackers. By afternoon Ray had died, but so had two of the invaders and several others were wounded. During lulls in the battle Champion kept a diary of his ordeal. One entry read:

"Boys, there is bullets coming like hail. They are shooting from the table and river and back of the house." Another: "Boys, I feel pretty lonesome just now. I wish there was someone here with me so we could watch all sides at once." The final entry was made that evening, about 12 hours after the first attack. "Well, they have just got through shelling the house like hail. I heard them splitting wood. I guess they are going to fire the house to-night. I think I will make a break when night comes, if alive. Shooting again. It's not night yet. The house is all fired. Goodbye, boys, if I never see you again."

Champion signed his pathetic diary and then charged out the back door, firing two guns. How many bullets cut him down could not be determined because his dead body was strung up and used for target practice. Later, 28 bullets were removed from the body. Champion's slayers also pinned a card on the body—"Rustlers beware."

The killings of Champion and Ray were the opening shots in the Johnson County War, one in which the cattle barons' mercenary army would go down to ignoble defeat. Because a reporter accompanying the stockmen's hired army found their victim's diary, Nate Champion was to emerge as the folk hero of the struggle.

See also: *Johnson County War, Red Sash Gang.*

CHAPIN, Charles E.: See Rose Man of Sing Sing.

CHAPMAN, Gerald (1892- or 1893-1926): Robber and murderer

The term "Public Enemy No. 1" was first coined by a newspaperman to describe Gerald Chapman, the most popular criminal in the country for a time in the 1920s. When his picture was flashed in movie newsreels, the audience responded with thunderous applause, a phenomenon not repeated until Franklin D. Roosevelt was perceived by moviegoers in the 1930s as the savior of the nation.

Even the *New York Times,* on April 7, 1923, editorialized under the heading "Something Almost Heroical":

> It is getting to be rather difficult to keep in mind that fact that Gerald Chapman is a thoroughly bad man, whose right place is in jail. The difficulty arises from the fact that in his battle with the law he shows qualities—courage, persistence, ingenuity and skill—which it is impossible not to admire. The result is that unless one is careful one finds one's self hoping that he isn't caught, and, so great are the odds against him, that the struggle seems somehow unfair. . . . The temptation is strong to lament that such a man should make of his abilities and peculiarities such miserable employment as devoting them to theft. There must be some explanation of that, however, and the probability is that he is defective. But it does seem hard that his punishment for his crimes should be increased because of his attempts to evade it. That he hates imprisonment is only human, and that he takes desperate risks in his efforts to get out is rather to his credit than his discredit—from every standpoint except the safety of society.

Thus did the *Times* come down on the side of law and order, but it was a close decision.

Gerald Chapman had that way about him. An accomplished criminal a dozen or so years older than Chapman, Dutch Anderson, similarly impressed with young Chapman when both were doing time in New York's Auburn Prison, taught him all he knew about committing crimes and was eventually to become his willing underling. When the pair got out within two months of each other, they teamed up as con men and made about $100,000 trimming suckers in Chicago with varied swindles. They returned to New York City to live the high life, with their hotel suite a parade ground for showgirls, whores and impressionable young things.

In 1921 they got together with an old Auburn crony, Charley Loeber, and robbed a mail truck in New York City in a daring escapade with Chapman jumping from a moving car onto the running board of the truck and, gun in hand, forcing the driver to stop. The trio made off with five sacks of registered mail containing $1,424,129 in cash and securities, the greatest mail theft up to that time.

Chapman and Anderson fenced the securities slowly while living the good life, but Loeber proved incapable of handling the fruits of such a big-time heist and was caught disposing of his loot. When he was nabbed, he implicated Chapman and Anderson, and unaware of any danger, they were easily captured. The pair had been on a jaunt upstate, robbing five banks just to stay in shape.

Taken to the main post office building for questioning, Chapman made his first electrifying attempt at an escape. In the midst of the interrogation of Anderson and himself, Chapman, in the middle of a yawn, leaped from his chair; said, "Sorry, gentlemen"; and dashed to a window, stepped over the sill and disappeared.

"He's jumped," someone yelled, and everyone rushed to the window. However, they did not see what they had expected on the ground 75 feet below. There was no spread-eagled body.

Gerald Chapman might have escaped had not a detective noticed a cleaning woman in a building across the street frantically pointing to one side. Chapman had stepped onto a ledge and wormed his way down to another open window. He was captured four offices away.

Both men were convicted and sentenced to 25 years in the Atlanta Penitentiary. Chapman refused to testify, but one of his lawyers, Grace F. Crampton, reported later:

> Chapman's philosophy of life excused his crimes. He told me that he did not believe it as sinful to hold up a mail truck or rob a store as it was to speculate on Wall Street and probably steal money from widows and orphans and poorly paid teachers. "At least we do not take money from poor people," he said to me. "What we steal hurts nobody. Everything that is sent by mail or express is fully insured and in the end the sender loses nothing. The man who comes out the winner on Wall Street is respected, and he is envied for his yachts and cars and homes, while we are hunted and despised. I think I am the more honorable of the two.

After seven months in Atlanta, Chapman escaped. He feigned illness by drinking a disinfectant, overpowered a guard and went out the window using bedsheets for a ladder. He was free only two days before being cornered by a posse and shot in the arm, hip and back. One bullet had penetrated his kidney. He was taken back to the prison hospital for a real reason this time. Yet, though it was feared he might die, Chapman escaped the same way six days later. The authorities were sure they would find his body shortly, but Chapman made a clean break.

Two months later, Dutch Anderson tunneled out of Atlanta, and the team was back in business as two of the most-wanted men in the country. The *Times* was not the only publication having difficulty managing restraint in its admiration of Chapman. Meanwhile, Chapman, separated for security reasons from Anderson, made the mistake of teaming up with one Walter J. Shean, the black-sheep son of a wealthy hotel owner and a fledgling criminal. They attempted to hold up a department store in New Britain, Conn., on October 12, 1924, and in the process one of the bandits shot and killed a police officer. Shean was captured and, with some pride, proclaimed, "My pal was Gerald Chapman."

Finally, Chapman was caught in December in Muncie, Ind. and returned to federal prison under incredibly tight security. For a time the government refused to turn over Chapman to Connecticut for trial, fearing he would escape, but finally it relented. The trial was an event that had the country going haywire. Chapman fan clubs sprang up, and at least four or five bouquets arrived each day at the front door of the prison where he was kept during the trial.

It didn't help Chapman, nor did his claim that he had never been in New Britain and never even met Shean. He was found guilty and sentenced to death.

Meanwhile, Dutch Anderson was going off his rocker. Convinced that Chapman had been betrayed by a man named Ben Hance, who had once shielded the pair in Muncie. Anderson killed Hance and his wife. He then tried to assassinate Shean, but he was too well guarded and Anderson could not get near him. Anderson was finally recognized by a policeman in Muskegon, Mich. Both went for their guns at the same time, and each killed the other.

Chapman's execution was postponed a couple of times. In his death cell he whiled away the time writing epigrams ("The more we learn, the less we discover we know") and poetry (his favorite poet was Shelley). A poem of his, "Reward," was released by one of his lawyers, who said, "I do this because I don't want people to think Chapman was merely a bandit with nothing in his head." It read in part:

> Comes peace at last! The drums have beat disray,
>   No armistice of hours, but ever and ever
> The slow dispersing legions of decay,
>   Under the muffled skies, tell all is over.
> Returns the husbandman, returns the lover,
>   To reap the quiet harvest of alway,
> The bright-plumed stars those wide fields
>   May not cover
> Though wings beat on forever and a
>   day. . . .

Chapman was hanged on April 6, 1926.

CHAPMAN, Mrs. James (1874-1922): Murder victim

When on December 27, 1922 Mr. and Mrs. James A. Chapman opened a package they thought was a Christmas present arriving late in the mail, the parcel exploded in Mrs. Chapman's face, fatally injuring her and crippling her husband. Thus began a case that the Wisconsin Supreme Court, in rejecting the convicted murderer's appeal, was to call unrivaled for being "so replete with scientific presentation of actualities." And indeed, the bomb murderer, John Magnuson, never did have a chance, as one clue after another, developed in brilliant scientific fashion, blared his guilt.

The wrapping paper the dynamite package came in had been burst apart in the explosion and much of it was stained with blood and powder, but the handwritten name and address had only been torn apart. These scraps were turned over to John F. Tyrrell, then considered the country's number one examiner of questioned documents. Tyrrell reassembled the writing, which read, "J. A. Chapman, R. 1, Marsfilld, (sic) Wis." From this tiny scrap of evidence Tyrrell reached a startling number of conclusions. The writing was stilted, as though the writer had deliberately attempted to disguise it. Tyrrell studied the spacing, slope, alignment, pressure and rhythm of the script and determined this was not the case. It had been written the best its author, who was not used to writing very much, could manage. The misspelling of the town name indicated the writer had simply spelled it phonetically. Tyrrell concluded the writer was a foreigner, most likely a Swede. There was only one Swede in the community, John Magnuson, and he had had a long-running dispute with Chapman concerning a creek drain.

Tyrrell had only begun to make conclusions. He also determined the writing had been done with a medium smooth-pointed fountain pen. The ink was an odd mixture, mostly Carter's black ink with a slight trace of Sanford's blue-black fluid ink. When postal inspectors armed with a search warrant inspected the Magnuson home, they found that the man's daughter had a fountain pen with the very point Tyrrell had described. She always used Sanford's ink but had loaned her bottle of ink to a schoolmate who, when it ran dry, had refilled it with Carter's black ink, producing the exact mixture Tyrrell had discovered on the death package.

Then the iron-bomb remnants were turned over to two professors at the University of Wisconsin, who polished them and matched their tell-tale properties with metal found in Magnuson's barn workshop. Fragments of the wood portions of the bomb were sent to Arthur Koehler, a wood expert who was to give vital testimony in the Lindbergh kidnapping. He identified the wood as elm. On the floor of his workshop, Magnuson had elm lumber and wood shavings with the same cellular structure as the scraps from the bomb.

The jury convicted Magnuson on the very first ballot, and given the mound of scientific evidence, it was hardly surprising that the high court of Wisconsin saw no reason to set aside his life sentence.

CHAPMAN, John T. (1832-?): Train robber

A respected resident of Reno and superintendent of a Sunday school, John Chapman, together with Jack Davis, masterminded the robbery of the Central Pacific's Train No. 1 on November 4, 1870, the first train holdup in the Far West.

Chapman's arrest for the robbery, which occurred near Verdi, Nev. came as a shock to the good folks of Reno, who never suspected him of being anything other than a pillar of the community. True, it was known that he was often in the company of a deadbeat and gambler named Jack Davis, but it was assumed he was out to save the soul of that sharper. The facts were the other way around; Davis had introduced Chapman to a number of hard cases ready to make some money in any logical six-gun manner. When Chapman unveiled a plan to hold up a train, something the Reno gang had pioneered just four years earlier in Indiana, they all agreed enthusiastically. Since such robberies were not common at the time, the gang had little trouble. They boarded the train just as it was about to pull out of Verdi, overpowered the conductor and engineer and forced their way into the express car after uncoupling that car and the engine from the rest of the train. The messenger in the express car gave up without a struggle, and the gang broke into treasure boxes containing $41,600 in coins and escaped with their loot.

Chapman and Davis hadn't counted on their accomplices acting like cowpokes at trail's end, spending money so fast that they had to attract the attention of the Wells Fargo detectives. Under intensive questioning, two of the gang confessed and led detectives to some of the buried loot. Davis and Chapman were arrested, stunning Reno. Chapman put on a defiant front, denying all, but Davis saw that was useless and confessed. Davis got 10 years, but Chapman was given 20.

On September 28, 1871, nine months after he had gone to prison, Chapman led three of his men in a prison break; however, he and two of the others were recaptured after a brief period and given an extra year for their escape. The former Sunday school superintendent served his entire sentence. Upon his release he advised the current crop of train robbers to cease their wicked ways and find God. With that, he dropped from sight, although he was named as a likely suspect in several train holdups, including two in widely separated places within eight hours of each other.

See also: *Jack Davis.*

CHAPMAN, Mark David (1955-): Murderer of John Lennon

The murder of 40-year-old rock star John Lennon, a former member of the Beatles, on December 8, 1980 by Mark David Chapman was a long time in the making. Chapman had waited all that wintry day and evening in front of the Dakota, a celebrated New York apartment building, where the singer and his wife, Yoko Ono, lived. He had come prepared for the weather, wearing two pairs of long underwear, a jacket, an overcoat and a hat. He also carried a .38-caliber Charter Arms revolver.

Chapman had been living in Honolulu since 1977, arriving there from Decatur, Ga., his home state, and had apparently been afflicted with John Lennon fantasies for a considerable period. Lennon's wife was Japanese, and although Chapman's wife was not Japanese, she was of Japanese descent. In the fall of 1980 Chapman decided to "retire," at the age of 25. After all, Lennon was retired. Later, a psychiatrist would testify that the more Chapman imitated Lennon, "the more he came to believe he was John Lennon." He eventually began to look upon Lennon as a "phony."

In September 1980 Chapman sold a Norman Rockwell lithograph for $7,500, paid off a number of debts and kept $5,000 for "a job" he had to do. He contacted the Federal Aviation Administration to inquire about the best way to transport a revolver by plane. He was advised that he should put the gun in his baggage but was warned that the change in air pressure could damage any bullets. When Chapman left his job as a security guard at a Honolulu condominium development for the last time, he scrawled the name John Lennon on the sign-out sheet. On October 29 he flew to New York, taking a gun but no bullets.

Frustrated in New York by an inability to obtain bullets for his weapon or to gain accesss to Lennon, Chapman left on November 12 or 13 to return to Honolulu. After his arrival there he made an appointment at the Makiki Mental Health Clinic for November 26 but didn't keep it. On December 6 he flew back to New York.

Two days later, Chapman waited outside the Dakota for Lennon to appear. About 4:30 p.m. the singer and his wife left the building. When he saw the couple, Chapman held up his copy of Lennon's recently released *Double Fantasy* album, and Lennon stopped to autograph it. After the Lennons departed, the doorman asked Chapman why he lingered, and he said he wanted to wait to get Yoko Ono's autograph as well.

At 11 p.m. Lennon and his wife returned. Chapman stepped out of the darkness and said, "Mr. Lennon." As Lennon turned, Chapman fired his revolver five times. Four bullets struck Lennon, killing him. When the police arrived, Chapman was reading his copy of *Catcher in the Rye* by J. D. Salinger.

A few weeks later, John W. Hinckley, Jr. recited into a tape recorder: "I just want to say goodbye to the old year, which was nothing, total misery, total death. John Lennon is dead, the world is over, forget it." In March 1981 Hinckley attempted to assassinate President Ronald Reagan.

Chapman pleaded guilty to the Lennon killing. On August 24, 1981, appearing in court with what looked to be a bulletproof vest underneath his T-shirt, evidently to protect him from possible retribution by distraught Lennon fans, he was sentenced to 20 years to life. Under New York state law he would have to stay in prison for 20 years before becoming eligible for parole.

CHAPPLEAU, Joseph Ernst (1850-1911): Murderer

Joseph Chappleau was the first man sentenced to die in the electric chair, but he escaped that fate in 1889 when the new-fangled instrument of death was not completed in time for his execution, and his sentence was commuted to life imprisonment. In his memoirs, the famous warden of Sing Sing, Lewis E. Lawes, later credited Chappleau with doing more to shape his philosophy of modern penology than any other man. While Lawes was a rookie guard at Clinton Prison in New York in 1905, Chappleau was credited with saving his life in a prison yard melee.

A New York farmer, Chappleau had been found guilty of the murder of a neighbor named Tabor over some poisoned cows. The real motive for the murder, according to local gossip, was not the poisoning of the cows but an affair between Tabor and Chappleau's wife. Once his sentence had been commuted, Chappleau became a prisoner uniquely popular with other convicts and the guards. None regarded him as a true criminal but rather a man trapped by fate. Lawes came to regard Chappleau as the perfect example of a murderer not likely ever to commit another crime and perhaps the best possible argument against capital punishment, a penalty Chappleau had escaped for purely technical reasons. When Chappleau died in the prison hospital at Clinton in 1911, guards and prisoners alike declared their happiness that he had been released from the burdens of his life.

See also: *William Kemmler, Lewis E. Lawes.*

CHARLTON Street Gang: Hudson River pirates

In early New York virtually all pirate activity was restricted to the East River, where the prime loot was the stores of relatively small craft. On the West Side, only a daring bunch of ruffians called the Charlton Street Gang worked the Hudson River, but they did it with a vengeance, actually flying the Jolly Roger and making forays as far upriver as Poughkeepsie, attacking riverside mansions and even kidnapping men, women and children for ransom. In the 1860s the Charlton Streeters found the pickings on their side of Manhattan slim because the Hudson piers were reserved for ocean vessels and shippers kept an army of watchmen on duty to protect their property. With looting in the immediate city area not very rewarding, gang leaders were forced to cast their eyes upstream. It is doubtful if their ambitions would ever have become as grandiose as they did without the inspiration of an attractive but deadly haridan named Sadie the Goat. She convinced them in 1869 that to be successful river pirates, they had to have a first-class sloop of their own, one that could outrun pursuers. The gang promptly went out and stole one.

The gang flew the Jolly Roger from the masthead, finding that its appearance frightened residents along the Hudson from the Harlem River to Poughkeepsie and tended to encourage flight rather than resistance. The Charlton Streeters soon had a lucrative enterprise going, looting farmhouses and mansions. Learning that Julius Caesar had once been held for ransom by pirates, Sadie involved the gang in kidnapping. She cut a sinister figure pacing the deck, issuing orders. According to the sensationalist press of the day, Sadie on several occasions made men walk the plank in proper piratical style.

After a number of murders had been committed, the desperate riverside residents finally organized vigilante posses to battle the pirates. Their ranks thinned by a number of musket battles, the Charlton Streeters returned to their home base and restricted their activities to more ordinary urban crimes. Sadie the Goat left the group in disgust with its timidity.

See also: *Gallus Mag, Piracy.*

CHECK Passing

Not long ago a professional check passer, a forger who writes worthless checks, in New York, was asked why he only passed his rubbery works of art in bars and taverns. Paraphrasing Willie Sutton, who supposedly said one robs banks "because that's where the money is," the check passer declared, "Because that's where the crooks are." The check passer's technique was simple enough, relying as it did on human greed. He would enter a saloon, appearing well bombed, and hoist a few. Then he would produce what appeared to be his paycheck drawn on the account of a well-known local firm and in an apparent stupor, ask the bartender to cash it. Normally, the barkeep would be reluctant to cash a check for an unknown party, but since in this case the customer could barely stand erect, he would find it too appetizing to pass up. The bartender would cash the check and invariably shortchange the purported drunk $10 or $20, figuring he was too far gone to notice. The check passer would hoist one more and stagger out of the place, heading for another bar to repeat his routine.

The check passer stated he generally could cash eight to 10 bad checks an evening and get turned down in no more than two or three places. He had found a new wrinkle to make one of this country's most common and easiest crimes even easier.

Check forgery is so common, in fact, that no one really knows how extensive it is. Spokesmen for surety companies have put the losses at $400 million to $1 billion, and those estimates are probably too low, since a great many businesses have one to a dozen bad checks tucked away unreported. With the value of checks written annually now totaling a few trillion dollars, the bogus-check business is currently the most lucrative field available to a smooth-mannered con man, or even to people with a lot less finesse.

In Washington, D.C., a few years ago, a 14-year-old boy walked into a small store and made a few inexpensive purchases with a government check that eventually bounced. It had been stolen, but the shopkeeper had no one to blame but himself. The rightful recipient was an 83-year-old woman and the check had been clearly marked, "Old Age and Survivor's Insurance."

Once, in Cleveland, Ohio, the story goes, a bad-check artist handed a bank clerk a check to cash after signing it "Santa Claus." He got his money.

Another comic check passer liked to sign his phony masterpieces, "N. O. Good." No one every caught on—in time. And a Bedford, Ind. grocer, who was not too quick, accepted a check signed "U. R. Hooked." Fun-loving check passers have used bum checks drawn on such institutions as the East Bank of the Mississippi.

The interesting fact about all these cases is the ridiculous chances the bad-check writer will take, so sure is he that the sucker will bite at his bait. Not all forgers are so cocky and contemptuous of their victims, but these incidents do point out what check passers have learned: with the proper approach and in many cases, without, a person can have far less trouble cashing a bad check than a good one.

The professional operator runs into absolutely no trouble 95 percent of the time as long as he has a gimmick to distract suspicion. A California forger cashed 200 bad checks by pretending to be a physician. He found that by passing checks that carried such corner notations as "In Payment for Tonsils" or "Balance over Blue Cross," he was seldom questioned. In big cities he often entered a store dressed in a doctor's white coat in order to give the impression that he had just stepped out of his office in a nearby building to get a check cashed.

One of the most prolific bogus-check passers was Courtney Townsend Taylor, who was most active in the 1940s and 1950s. In Chicago he once went down a certain street and cashed a check in every other store the whole length of the street. On the return trip he hit all the stores he had missed. Caught once in Mobile, Ala., he pulled a fountain pen from his pocket while he was being frisked for a weapon and said: "This is the only gun I need. I can get all the money I want with it."

Nobody knows how many rubber-check artists are operating, but one estimate placed the figure at around 2,500 full timers. Roughly two-thirds of all phony checks sent to the FBI are quickly identified as the work of known forgers by examining a file of about 60,000 current fraudulent check signatures. The rest are the product of amateurs.

Check passing is the type of crime that gets into a practitioner's blood. Rapists and muggers may slow down over the years and quit by the time they start graying at the temples. Check passers simply mellow. Their dignified look turns into a plus. Although in his seventies, Joseph W. Martin had no trouble separating thousands of dollars from gullible check cashers until his arrest in 1952 by the FBI. An actor, Martin had actually played in more than 500 motion pictures during more honest times, including a 1932 film in which he portrayed President Warren Harding. As a check passer, he simply carried on acting. His favorite technique was turning up at bar association meetings and cashing checks with his "colleagues." He was arrested in New York while posing as a lawyer from Nebraska attending a meeting of the American Bar Association in the Waldorf-Astoria.

Experts consider the late Alexander Thiel the most accomplished forger of modern times. Also high on the list is Frederick Emerson Peters. However, the great-granddaddy of all check chiselers clearly was Jim the Penman, who was born Alonzo James Whitman in 1854. He dissipated an inherited fortune, amassed an illegal million, became a state senator in Minnesota, received an honorary degree from Hamilton College and was almost elected to its board of trustees. He also passed thousands of bad checks. During his career, Jim the Penman was arrested 43 times, indicted 27, convicted 11. Once while doing a stretch in Auburn Prison, he was assigned to teach in the prison school—until it was discovered he was teaching forgery.

See also: *Frederick Emerson Peters, Alexander Thiel.*

CHEROKEE Bill (1876-1896): Holdup man and murderer

It was often said that the man Hanging Judge Isaac Parker most enjoyed sending to the gallows was Crawford Goldsby, a part-Cherokee, part-white, part-Mexican and part-Negro murderer better known as Cherokee Bill, who killed 13 men before his 20th birthday.

Goldsby came to live with a foster mother at Fort Gibson, Okla. when he was seven years old. The woman imbued the boy with the credo: "Stand up for your rights. Don't let anybody impose on you." When he was 18, he followed her advice. He shot a man who beat him up at a dance. The man lived, but Goldsby fled to Indian Territory and soon joined the outlaw band of Bill and Jim Cook. In June 1894 the Cooks and Goldsby shot their way out of a posse trap after Goldsby killed a member of the law party, Sequoyah Houston.

After that, the killings came fast, and Crawford became known and hunted as Cherokee Bill. The young killer had a dozen notches on his gun before he was betrayed by a couple of supposed friends while he was paying a courting call on a young girl. The duo, Ike Rogers and Clint Scales, clubbed him unconscious and collected $1,300 in reward money. Cherokee Bill was speedily tried before Judge Parker for just one of his crimes and sentenced to be hanged. However, his lawyer succeeded in delaying the execution through several appeals. While the murderer was still being held in his prison cell, he somehow got hold of a gun and attempted to make an escape. The attempt failed, although Cherokee Bill did kill a prison guard, Lawrence Keating, the father of four children.

The escape effort roused Judge Parker to a fit of anger. He blamed the guard's death on the U.S. Supreme Court and told reporters that the High Court's obsession with the "flimsiest technicalities" was allowing the 60 "murderers" then in his Fort Smith jail to fight off their executions—Cherokee Bill among them. Parker brought the outlaw to trial for the guard's murder without waiting for the outcome of his appeal on the previous conviction. The judge found Cherokee Bill guilty of this second charge and sentenced him to death, but again the execution was forestalled by appeals. Finally, though, the first appeal went against the defendant, and on March 17, 1896, with Judge Parker watching the execution from his office window, Cherokee Bill mounted the gallows. Asked if he had any last words, the young murderer replied, "I came here to die, not to make a speech." Cherokee Bill paid for his 13 murders, but it appeared later that he was responsible for one more. Ike Rogers, one of the men who betrayed him, was murdered. The crime was believed to have been the work of Cherokee Bill's young brother, Clarence Goldsby, in an act of vengeance. If Clarence was the killer, he was never brought to justice.

See also: *Isaac C. "Hanging Judge" Parker.*

CHERRY Hill Gang: Gay Nineties criminals

A vicious bunch of thieves and killers, the Cherry Hill Gang were the "dandies" of the New York underworld in the 1890s. Members of the gang were seldom seen in other than dress suits and often carried walking sticks, metal-weighted of course. Disguised in the height of fashion, they found it easy to get within striking range of a well-heeled gentleman and attack before their victim had a chance to be alarmed.

The Cherry Hillers were also responsible for provoking others to crime out of envy. Other gangs often tried to match their sartorial splendor and would go to any lengths to do so. When the Batavia Street Gang announced plans to hold a ball at New Irving Hall, the Cherry Hillers announced they were obtaining new wardrobes for the occasion. As hosts, the Batavians felt required to match or surpass the Cherry Hillers in dress. To raise funds the night before the gala social affair, the gangsters smashed a window of Segal's jewelry store on New Chambers Street and carried off 44 gold rings. They sold them the following morning, but more than a dozen of the gangsters were caught by police as they were being fitted for new suits at a Division Street tailor shop. On the night of the big event, the leading lights of the Batavia Street Gang languished in the Tombs while the elegant dandies of Cherry Hill were once again the hit of the ball.

CHESSMAN, Caryl (1921-1960): Executed sex offender

During the 1950s the case of Caryl Chessman produced one of the most intense anticapital punishment campaigns in history. Certainly no case since that of Sacco and Vanzetti produced such furor. Protests came from all levels of society. Millions of persons in Brazil, 2.5 million in Sao Paulo alone, and thousands more in Switzerland signed petitions pleading for his life. The Queen of Belgium made a special plea for Chessman, as did Aldous Huxley, Pablo Casals, Eleanor Roosevelt, Dr. Karl Menninger, Arthur Koestler, Andre Maurois and Francois Mauriac. Added to those names were Max Ascoli, Harry Elmer Barnes, Ray Bradbury, Norman Corwin, William Inge, Norman Mailer, Dwight MacDonald, Clifford Odets, Christopher Isherwood, Carey McWilliams, Billy Graham, Harry Golden and Robert Frost.

In January 1948 Chessman, then 27, had been on parole for just six weeks from California's Folsom Prison when he was arrested in Los Angeles as the suspected Red-Light Bandit. This marauder approached victims parked in lonely spots, flashing a red light resembling that of a police car. He would rob the driver and sometimes drive off with the woman and force her to perform sexual acts with him. Chessman made a confession, which he later said had been extracted from him by police torture.

He was found guilty under California's "Little Lindbergh" law, which provided for the death penalty in cases of kidnapping "with bodily harm." Chessman had killed nobody and had held nobody for ransom. Since the jury brought in a verdict of guilty without a recommendation of mercy, he was automatically sentenced to death in the gas chamber. There were many who thought Chessman's punishment was excessive for a felon who had not murdered anyone.

Chessman was sent to death row at San Quentin, and his first execution date was set for March 28, 1952. Then began the famous drama of Cell 2455, Death Row. That prison address became the title of a best-selling book by Chessman, which sold a half-million copies and was translated into a dozen languages. It was one of four he would write, often smuggling out manuscripts after he had been forbidden to publish any further. With the success of his first book, Chessman retained a group of lawyers to help him with his appeals, which previously he had handled on his own, having "read or skimmed 10,000 law books."

The fight went on for 12 years. It finally ended in defeat when Gov. Edmund G. Brown, a stated opponent of capital punishment, insisted his hands were tied and he would not save Chessman. By then Chessman had survived eight scheduled dates of execution, some by only a matter of hours. On May 2, 1960 he entered the gas chamber at San Quentin. At that moment federal Judge Louis E. Goodman granted Chessman's attorneys a delay of at least 30 minutes to argue their case. He asked his secretary to telephone the warden at San Quentin. As the prison number passed through several persons, a digit was inadvertently omitted. After being verified, the number had to be redialed. By the time the call was put through, Associate Warden Louis Nelson said the cyanide pellets had just been dropped.

Inside the gas chamber, Caryl Chessman had turned to a female supporter who was there was a witness, and his lips formed a final message: "Take it easy . . . It's all right . . . Tell Rosalie [one of his attorneys] goodbye. . . ."

After the pellets dropped, Chessman managed to strain at the binds in order to see if his message had been understood. The woman, a reporter, nodded. Chessman half-smiled and winked.

Convict-author Caryl Chessman (left) appears in court in 1957 in a futile attempt to win a new trial.

Chessman had one more signal to give. Just before he lost consciousness, he turned to reporter Will Stevens of the *San Francisco Examiner*. He had agreed to give the newsman a signal if a gas chamber death was a form of agony. Chessman moved his head up and down, staring at Steens. It was the signal that death in the gas chamber was agony.

One news account of the execution started, "Sex-terrorist Carol Chessman ended his 12-year fight for life today with a wink and a smile."

CHICAGO Amnesia: Discouragement of witnesses

During the gang wars in Chicago during the 1920s, successful prosecution of murderers and other lawbreakers often proved almost impossible. The gangsters themselves never would impart information to the police, even when dying. Despite the fact that a number of eyewitnesses might step forward initially to do their civic duty, by the time of the trial these witnesses almost invariably had been "reached" by bribes, threats or outright attempts on their lives. As a result, some witnesses even had trouble remembering their own names on the stand. Gang leader Dion O'Banion, an accomplished practitioner of the art of witness discouragement, observed puckishly: "We have a new disease in town. It's called Chicago amnesia."

CHICAGO Fire Looting

Without question the greatest rampage of criminality sparked by an American disaster occurred during the 24 hours of the Great Chicago Fire on October 8-9, 1871.

The *Chicago Post* perhaps best set the scene:

> The people were, mad. Despite the police—indeed, the police were powerless—they crowded upon frail coigns of vantage, as fences and high sidewalks propped on wooden piles, which fell beneath their weight, and hurled them, bruised and bleeding, in the dust. They stumbled over broken furniture and fell, and were trampled under foot. Seized with wild and causeless panics, they surged together, backwards and forwards, in the narrow streets, cursing, threatening, imploring, fighting to get free. Liquor flowed like water; for the saloons were broken open and despoiled, and men on all sides were to be seen frenzied with drink. . . . Everywhere dust, smoke, flame, heat, thunder of falling shouts, braying of trumpets, wind, tumult, and uproar.

And into this human cauldron the criminals swarmed. Hoodlums, prostitutes, thieves hunting alone or in packs snatched all they wanted from drays and carriages. They broke into stores and homes and stuffed their pockets with money and jewelry. Men ran about wearing as many as a dozen women's rings and bracelets. They broke into saloons and guzzled down liquor to fortify their criminal daring. "They smashed windows with their naked hands," the *Post* reported, "regardless of the wounds inflicted, and with bloody fingers rifled till and shelf and cellar, fighting viciously for the spoils of their forage. Women, hollow-eyed and brazen-faced, with filthy drapery tied over them, their clothes in tatters and their feet in trodden-over slippers, moved here and there—scolding, stealing, fighting; laughing at the beautiful and splendid crash of walls and falling roofs."

When the courthouse caught fire, guards released 350 prisoners from the basement jail and then watched helplessly as they descended in a single horde on a jewelry store and looted every stone, every watch in the place. William Walker, a Chicago reporter, added his eyewitness account:

> As the night wore on, and the terrors aggregated into an intensity of misery, the thieves, amateur and professional, dropped all pretense at concealment and plied their knavish calling undaunted by any fear of immediate retribution. They would storm into stores, smash away at the safes, and if, as happily was almost always the case, they failed to effect an opening, they would turn their attention to securing all of value from the stock that could conveniently be made away with, and then slouch off in search of further booty. The promise of a share in the spoils gave them the assistance of rascally express-drivers, who stood with their wagons before doors of stores, and waited as composedly for a load of stolen property to be piled in as if they were receiving the honestly-acquired goods of the best man in town. . . . The scenes of robbery were not confined to the sacking of stores. Burglars would raid into the private dwellings that lay in the track of the coming destruction, and snatch . . . anything which their practical senses told them would be of value. Interference was useless. The scoundrels . . . were inflamed with drink, and were alarmingly demonstrative in the flourishing of deadly weapons. Sometimes women and children, and not infrequently men, would be stopped as they were bearing from their homes objects of especial worth, and the articles would be torn from their grasp by gangs of these wretches.

Besides the looting, which the authorities were unable to thwart, trouble developed from a new source. By the time the conflagration was burning itself out on the night of October 9, firebugs took to the streets trying to start new blazes, some for the thrill of it and others because they had seen how fire created opportunities for looting. Seven men were shot after being caught setting fires and another was stoned to death by an angry mob, his body left on the street as a warning to others. For the next 13 days Chicago was patrolled by 2,400 regular and special policemen, six companies of state militia and four companies of U.S. Army troops, all under Gen. Phil Sheridan, who placed the city under martial law. Perhaps the most significant comment on the aftermath of the Chicago Fire was a historian's observation that "no part of Chicago was rebuilt more quickly than the saloons, brothels, gambling-houses, and other resorts and habitations of the underworld."

CHICAGO May (1876-1935): Queen of the Badger Game

May Churchill Sharpe did not invent the badger game, whereby a gentleman is invited to a lady's room to be "done for" and ends up being "done out" of his money through blackmail or simple robbery, but she was its most accomplished practitioner in the 1890s.

Born in Dublin, Ireland in 1876, May Sharpe spent six years in a convent school before running off to America, with 60 pounds from her father's strongbox as traveling money. Within a year after arriving in New York in the spring of 1889, she was living the fast life as the mistress of Dal Churchill. Churchill eventually married her and took her west. He was "a robber, highwayman, safecracker, cattle rustler and general all-round crook," according to May, and also a member of the Dalton gang. May was sublimely happy for an exciting year. Then Dal fouled up a train robbery and ended up hanging from vigilantes' rope near Phoenix, Ariz.

Widowed at 15, May went to Chicago, where with her looks she became the Queen of the Badger Game. At first, she operated as a loner, choosing her victims from hotels, night spots and other places where good-time Charlies congregated. Because of the publicity involved and the resultant effect on their families, most of the men who took her to a hotel wouldn't dream of going to the police after she had robbed them. May would also steal a sucker's valuable papers and write him, asking if he remembered the gay time they almost had together and wondering if he wanted his papers back. She would threaten, if ignored, to take the matter up with the wives. The tactic got results, and the errant husbands would give the money to an underworld pickup man sent by May. She would then deliver the papers. She never double-crossed a sucker a second time. She took him in the badger game and then once with a spot of blackmail, but then she let him off the hook.

Later, May took to using male accomplices and an older woman posing as her mother. The "mother" would catch May and her gentleman and shriek for help, which would come in the form of a hulking relative or neighbor. There would be no escape for the unfortunate victim until he paid. By her 16th birthday Chicago May had made $100,000 and by 17 she had run that up to $300,000.

Deciding the really big money was in New York, May transferred her operations there in the early 1890s. She frequented a famous criminal hangout, Considine's, which was also a slumming spot for sportsmen and literary and theatrical personalities. One evening she spotted a bushy-haired man with a drooping mustache. Thinking of him as a likely victim, she inquired about his identity and learned he was the celebrated author Mark Twain. May immediately started boning up on her Tom Sawyer and Huck Finn, and one night, done up in finery, she strolled over to Twain and introduced herself as Lady May Avery of England. She said she so admired Twain's work and had to meet him. The next evening Lady Avery dined with Twain and amused him greatly. It was well known that Twain was highly appreciative of the spicier things in life and May expected him to jump at the bait when she invited him to visit her in Connecticut. Twain's eyes twinkled, but he shook his head.

"I'm sorry, dear lady," he said, "but I'm off to Washington in the morning and then am going West for an extended period."

Chicago May was crushed. However, the real crusher came when Twain got up to leave. He kissed her hand and whispered to her: "May I thank you, my dear lady, for a most amusing time. Of course, I don't believe a word of your story that you are an English noblewoman."

Such defeats were rare for May, especially after she formed a business relationship with police Sgt. Charles Becker, New York's notorious cop-crook who was to die in the electric chair for murder. Becker fed May victims and took a 25 percent cut of the revenues.

A few years after the turn of the century, Becker advised Chicago May to pull out of New York because of an impending reform wave, and she moved to London, where she met the accomplished bank robber Eddie Guerin. She helped him rob some $250,000 from the Paris branch of the American Express Co. However, the couple had a falling out and were eventually caught by French police. Eddie Guerin was sent to Devil's Island, from which he later made a sensational escape. May did a short stint in an English jail for transporting the American Express loot to London and then was kicked out of the country. She returned to the United States, but she was pushing 40. Hard-living had left her with wrinkles, puffs and rheumy eyes. There was no way she could be the Chicago May of the badger game.

The road the rest of the way was down. There were a number of arrests and convictions for various thefts, even petty larceny. For a time, May's fortunes picked up. She ran what she called a "nice house" in Philadelphia, where she used to entertain the prostitutes with tales of her exploits as Chicago May. However, a reform movement put her out of business.

Rather belatedly, May came to the conclusion that crime did not pay and wrote her autobiography in 1928. In an amused air, she noted: "My old friends, in the police write me letters of encouragement. Christians feel called upon to send me platitudes. Reformers insist upon drawing their pet theories to my attention. Professional crooks berate and praise me. Beggars importune me. Sycophants lather me with adulation. The rich . . . and others . . . patronize me."

But May was actually trying to live in her past. Her real life was nothing like that. The last newspaper clipping about her tells the whole story. She was arrested in Detroit during the early 1930s for soliciting male pedestrians, asking the bargain price of $2. She died a few years later.

CHICAGO Piano: Tommy gun

The Chicago Piano, or Tommy Gun, first gained underworld acceptance in the Chicago gang wars of the 1920s. Some historians insist its first use came in the shooting of Jim Doherty and Tom Duffy, gunmen of the O'Donnell gang, and William H. McSwiggin, an assistant state's attorney, on April 27, 1926 in front of the Pony Inn in Cicero. Supposedly, Al Capone handled the weapon personally. However, the likelihood is that the Chicago Piano was introduced by the Polish Saltis-McErlane gang that controlled the Southwest Side of Chicago. After Joe Saltis and Frank McErlane demonstrated the Chicago Piano's awesome potential, every Chicago gangster wanted one. And it was easy to see why. The weapon was light, weighing only 8½ pounds, easy to operate and could fire up to a thousand .45-caliber cartridges a minute. Furthermore, it cost a mere $175 by mail order. When the federal government slapped controls on the sale of the guns, gangsters still managed to get all they wanted through a thriving black market, although the price soared to thousands of dollars.

CHICAGO Street Gazette: See Shang Andrews.

CHICAGO Times: Sensationalist newspaper

If any one 19th century newspaper can be singled out as the most devoted to the coverage of crime news, it would have to be the *Chicago Times,* which was founded in 1854 to promote the political career of Sen. Stephen A. Douglas, a role it continued to fulfill until it was sold to Cyrus H. McCormick, the reaper manufacturer, in 1860. A year later, McCormick sold the newspaper to Wilbur F. Storey of Vermont, who made it into an antiwar publication upon the issuance of the Emancipation Proclamation, which Storey regarded as a deceitful act because it switched the war's aims. To silence Storey's blasts at President Lincoln, Gen. Ambrose Burnside seized the *Times,* provoking one of the great civil liberties controversies of the Civil War. Mobs formed at the *Times* to support the Army action, while Copperhead forces swarmed around the *Chicago Tribune* office and threatened to burn down that newspaper's building unless the *Times* was allowed to publish. Tempers were dampened when Lincoln revoked Gen. Burnside's order of suppression, and the *Times* appeared again.

However, it was after the war that the *Times* emerged, under Storey, as one of the great muckraking and crusading newspapers, carrying on a steady fight against crime and political corruption, exposing the growing accommodation between the underworld and politicians and identifying reputable citizens who allowed their property to be used for immoral purposes. Storey's staff reporters originated or popularized many phrases that were to become criminal vernacular. The word "racket" appears to have been born in the *Times* on October 24, 1876, when the newspaper carried a story which noted that "big thieves are boldly traversing our streets by day, planning their racket." The *Times* headline style on criminal matters was certainly colorful as well as prejudicial. When on September 10, 1872 a notorious hoodlum named Christopher Rafferty was found guilty of the murder of Patrolman Patrick O'Meara, Storey's paper turned nearly poetic with the following headline:

SHUT OFF HIS WIND
A Satisfactory Job for Jack Ketch at Last.

The Hangman's Rope Awarded to
Christopher Rafferty.

Now, Do Not Reprieve Nor Pardon Him,
Nor Give Him a New Trial.

And, in the Name of All That's Decent,
Don't Commute His Sentence.

The Jury Concludes, in Just Twenty Minutes,
To String the Ruffian Up.

Perhaps an even more colorful headline, one still quoted in journalistic circles, appeared on November 27, 1875; it read:

JERKED TO JESUS
Four Senegambian Butchers Were
Wafted to Heaven on Yes-
terday from Scaffolds.

Two of Them, in Louisiana, Died with
the Sweet Confidence of
Pious People.

While Yet Two Others, in Mississippi, Expired
Exhorting the Public to Beware of
Sisters-In-Law.

Sometimes Storey's outspoken attitudes on crime and moral-

ity got him in deep trouble. When the noted burlesque actress Lydia Thompson appeared at Crosby's Opera House with her troupe of "English Blondes," the *Times* denounced the young maids for "capering lasciviously and uttering gross indecencies." The *Times* added that Miss Thompson was not much better than a common strumpet and that Chicagoans would do well to run her out of their city. When Storey refused to retract the statements, Miss Thompson caught him in front of his home on Wabash Avenue and beat him severely with a horsewhip.

CHICKEN Ranch: The best little whorehouse in Texas

A Texas institution that was around almost as long as the Alamo, the Chicken Ranch was never a ranch during all its 129 years of existence, although chickens sometimes pecked around its front yard. Its last and most famous proprietor, gun-toting Miss Edna Milton, called the establishment in La Grange a boarding house. The boarders were all very attractive young women in cocktail dresses, and their guests included any man who happened to have $10. The Chicken Ranch was closed down in 1973 after a television newsman from Houston publicized what many people in Texas knew it to be, and the "expose" eventually forced the governor to order it shuttered.

The Chicken Ranch went on to live again in a highly successful Broadway musical called *The Best Little Whorehouse in Texas,* with Miss Edna acting as an adviser for the show and doing a short walk-on part. The newsman whose story doomed the ranch, Marvin Zindler, was portrayed on Broadway as Melvin P. Thorpe, a crusading reporter with an American flag necktie. In 1978 the Small Business Administration ordered an auction of the ranch's fixtures. A bag of brass tokens bearing the legend "Good for All Night" sold for $30.

CHINESE Riots

When the Chinese first arrived in this country about 1850, they were greeted warmly, especially in San Francisco, where they worked for very low wages as household servants and menials. Within a year or two, as their numbers increased, the Chinese became one of the most-hated ethnic groups because they allegedly took jobs away from "Americans," mostly other ethnics who had also come to America from foreign shores. The wanton killing of Chinese probably was even less hindered by legal sanctions than the slaughter of Indians or Mexican "greasers." The saying "not having a Chinaman's chance" had a very awesome meaning for a "chink," "heathen," "celestial," "coolie," "moon face" or "slant-eyes" meeting a white man with a gun. Riots became common, with particularly bloody ones occurring in Los Angeles, San Francisco, Denver, Seattle, Rock Springs, Wyo. and Pierce City, Idaho. Cities like Tacoma, Wash. expelled their entire Chinese populations. The main opposition to the Chinese was economic, since such employers as the Union Pacific preferred to hire Chinese because, besides being docile, they worked for low pay and were satisfied with a bowl of rice. However, their large numbers and their insistence on maintaining their own customs—an attitude not really different than those of all other ethnis—became an added irritant. Not surprisingly, the Chinese were unmoved by efforts to Christianize them, one missionary observing, "They were unable to distinguish between our mobs and our Christian workers and could not be expected to favor or tolerate our religion. They had no way of knowing that Christianity was a religion of love, not one of bowie knife, insult, and the worst oppression the world has yet seen." Henry Ward Beecher's comment was more sarcastic: "We have clubbed them, stoned them, burned their houses and murdered some of them; yet they refuse to be converted. I do not know any way, except to blow them up with nitroglycerin, if we are ever to get them to Heaven."

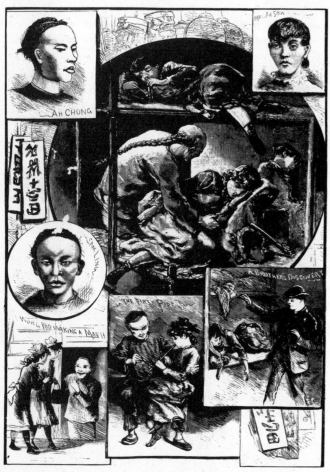

Scandal sheets of the 19th century constantly fanned public opinion against the Chinese by depicting their alleged corrupting influence on young white females.

It would probably be impossible to try to estimate the hundreds or thousands of Chinese who were murdered by whites in this country during the 19th century since most newspapers did not regard the killing of a Chinese as newsworthy. Diaries of 49ers in California constantly refer in passing to the killing of a "chink" here or there. Practically no white man was ever convicted of killing a Chinese; the crude Texas judge Roy Bean once dismissed a case because he said he found no statutory restriction against the activity. Lawmen in general showed no inclination to ascertain the facts in the violent death of any Chinese. Perhaps the 19th century attitude in the West is best summed up in a ballad still popular around the turn of the century:

> Old John Martin Duffy was judge of the court
> In a small mining town in the West;
> Although he knew nothing about rules of the law,
> At judging he was one of the best.
>
> One night in the winter a murder occurred,
> And the blacksmith was accused of the crime;
> We caught him red-handed and give him three trials,
> But the verdict was "guilty" each time.
>
> Now he was the only good blacksmith we had
> And we wanted to spare him his life,
> So Duffy stood up in the court like a lord
> And with these words he settled the strife:
>
> "I move we dismiss him, he's needed in town";
> Then he spoke out these words which have gained him renown:
> "We've got two Chinese laundrymen, everyone knows;
> Why not save the poor blacksmith and hang one of those?"

Eventually, anti-Chinese violence petered out, although not for any commendable reason. First, President Chester A. Arthur signed a bill suspending Chinese immigration. Second, the focus of bigotry shifted to newer immigrant groups, such as the Japanese.

See also: *Roy Bean*.

Los Angeles

One of California's bloodiest and most barbaric mob actions occurred on October 24, 1871, when a huge group of whites—men, women and children—rampaged through Calle de los Negros, or "Nigger Alley," which had become the city's Chinatown. Ostensibly, the reason for the riot was to avenge the death of a white who had been killed in the cross fire of fighting between two rival Chinese gangs, or tongs. But it was clear that this was little more than a rationale for an explosion of racially motivated violence. On the day of the riot, hundreds of people charged through Nigger Alley smashing windows and battering down doors. Any Chinese seized was beaten or stabbed. When one Chinese man broke free of his tormentors and tried to run away, he was shot down in the street. Having thus tasted blood, the crowd grabbed another Chinese and hauled him through the streets to a corral, where they hanged him. Other victims were pulled over the cobblestoned streets with a rope around their necks until they died.

Perhaps the most shocking killing, one that drew international attention, was that of an elderly Chinese doctor named Gene Tong. When caught by the mob, he pleaded to be spared and offered several thousand dollars he was carrying in exchange for his life. The rioters just laughed and hanged him anyway. As the old man was choking to death, several women in the crowd stepped forward and ripped off his trousers to get at his money. Someone also severed his ring finger with a bowie knife when a diamond ring would not slip off readily.

The death toll in the 1871 massacre was placed at 20 to 25, with many more injured, and it was estimated that the rioters had robbed and looted every room, every strongbox, every trunk in all Chinatown. A grand jury investigation condemned the mob for "disgracing our city" and charged that the authorities had failed to perform their duty properly, but not one person was ever brought to trial. Not surprisingly therefore, a few years later, after the first initial shock and revulsion had passed, Anti-Coolie Clubs began to spring up in the city. Finally stung by charges of intolerance, the officials of Los Angeles did something: they changed the name of Nigger Alley to Los Angeles Street.

Pierce City, Idaho Territory

Compared to some anti-Chinese massacres, the slaughter at Pierce City, Idaho Territory was, as one participant put it, "small potatoes." However, it is most illustrative of the brutal and inhuman attitude of whites towards Orientals.

On September 10, 1885 the body of a white merchant, D. M. Frazier, was found "chopped to pieces in his own store." A vigilante mob was formed quickly and on no apparent evidence, deduced the crime had been committed by two Chinese merchants who were in competition with the victim. The Chinese partners were seized and tortured until each accused the other of committing the crime. The verdict was that both should be hanged, and as long as they were hanging them, the vigilantes thought it would be a good idea to get rid of three other undesirable Chinese—a gambler; a barber, described as "hard featured" and a "parasite," meaning a local camp prostitute. Cooler heads among the mob convinced the others that the five should be turned over to the law so that they could be tried formally before being hanged. That night when a half-dozen lawmen set out with the prisoners for the county seat, they were stopped by a large mob of masked men who abducted the five. It seems some discussion among the vigilantes had led to the conclusion that the three additional prisoners would most likely not be hanged for the murder and that perhaps the confessions extracted from the two merchants by torture might also be disallowed in a courtroom. Direct action would solve that problem, and all five were hanged, if somewhat inefficiently and slowly, from a pole placed between the forks of two pine trees. The incident triggered wholesale expulsions of Chinese from a number of Idaho towns with the tacit approval of high government officials.

When news of the lynchings spread, the Department of State received a protest from the Chinese government, but it was six months before the territorial governor E. A. Stevenson, arrived in Pierce City to launch an investigation. The "investigation" consisted solely of talking to anti-Chinese elements and announcing he had failed to discover the identities of any perpetrators of the lynchings. He did express regret at the hangings but added, "The Chinese hanged were the identical parties, who so cruelly, shockingly and brutally murdered without the least provocation (except jealousy) one of the best citizens of Idaho." The governor also insisted that deportation was the only solution to the Chinese problem, since "their low, filthy habits, their high-binder piratical societies, together with their low dens of infamy, prostitution and opium smoking, have disgusted our people."

After the Pierce City affair a prodeportation movement seemed to be gaining ground in Washington, but by this time a new wave of immigrants, this one from Japan, had started to arrive and hostility was shifted away from the Chinese to meet this new menace. Deportation of the Chinese was forgotten, and they went on to become one of the most law-abiding ethnic groups in America.

Rock Springs, Wyoming Territory

As terrible as the slaughter was in the Los Angeles Chinese massacre of 1871, it did not compare with the mob riot in Rock Springs, Wyoming Territory in 1885.

When the main line of the Union Pacific was completed in 1869, many of the Chinese laborers settled in the railroad town of Rock Springs. In 1885 there were 500 Chinese in Rock Springs, the great majority working in the Union Pacific coal mines. In fact, the Chinese were the majority in the mines, and this led to friction as unemployment grew in the white community. When on September 2 a white miner and two Chinese got into an altercation underground, the fighting soon spread in the shaft among other miners, leaving one Chinese killed and three others severely injured. Word of the battle was passed above ground and a heavily armed mob of white miners formed for the destruction of Chinatown. The Chinese had no reason to expect an attack and were easily routed from their dugouts and shacks. One white miner's diary recalled, "Bullets followed the fleeing Chinese and sixteen of them were killed brutally, while the other casualties met an even more horrible fate the same evening when some of the citizens satisfied their murderous instincts and inhumanly slew the few remaining Chinese for the money which their victims had hidden on their persons, after setting fire to the buildings to hide their crimes." The entire Chinatown section was burned to the ground and "the smell that arose from the smoking ruins was horribly suggestive of burning flesh." Overall, the death toll was put at 50, or 10 percent of the Chinese community.

The *Rock Springs Independent* put out an extra edition the following day and sided with the anti-Chinese forces. It especially complimented saloon operators for shutting down during the riot: "It cannot be said that a 'drunken mob' drove out the Chinamen. Everyone was sober, and we did not see a case of drunkness. All of the stores in town were closed, and men, women and children were out watching the hurried exit of John Chinaman and everyone seemed glad to see them on the wing."

Because of demands by the Union Pacific, federal troops were called in and took over the task of feeding the destitute Chinese wandering about the countryside. Many of the men involved in the massacre were identified; instead of being prosecuted, they were paid off by the railroad, given train tickets and "strongly advised" by the commander of the troops to leave the state. The federal troops remained on duty in Rock Springs for the next 13 years, finally departing at the start of the Spanish-American War in 1898.

CHIVINGTON, John M. (1821-1894): Leader of massacre

The minister-soldier who commanded the infamous Sand Creek Indian Massacre in 1864, John Chivington was court-martialed but acquitted. To escape further military justice, he resigned from the Army. Most authorities on Chivington say that he was hated the rest of his life, unable to escape the stigma of his deeds, unable to find employment. The truth, however, was that the man once tried for the wanton slaughter of 450 Indian men, women and children later became a lawman. For many years until his death, he held the job of undersheriff in Denver, Colo., where he did his duty, so it is said, with honor and fairness and was respected by all those who worked with him.

CHOCTAW Legacy, The: Con game

Fleecing Indians became a major sport for con men during the 1930s. Most of these swindles were based on telling the victims that under old treaties Indians were entitled to $1,000 each for their deceased relatives and that the only thing needed was to get an enabling act through Congress. The Indians could finance the lobbying necessary to pass the act for a mere $5 apiece.

A notorious sharper, Odie Moore, worked the scheme to perfection in Neshoba County, Miss., promising the Indians great rewards due them because of the breaking of the Dancing Rabbit Treaty of 1839. Since there had been wide intermarriage between whites and Choctaws over the decades, thousands of white suckers added their $5 contributions. Moore's fanciful association managed to come up with a slogan, promising "$1,000 for every dollar." A number of young whites even sought out girls with traces of Choctaw blood in them to get on the promised gravy train.

Moore's victims gave and gave from the time he started his swindle in 1930 until his death in 1945, and even after that, many remained sure their promised windfall would soon be forthcoming.

CHOWCHILLA School Bus Kidnapping

The greatest kidnap for ransom plot in terms of numbers of victims in the United States took place on July 15, 1976 near the town of Chowchilla, Calif. By blocking the road with a van, three stocking-masked armed men stopped a school bus containing 19 girls and seven boys returning from a summer school session. While one of the three masked men drove the bus off and hid it in a dried-out creek bed, the 26 children and the bus driver were herded into the van used for the blockade

and a second van driven up from a hiding place. The driver and the children, who ranged in age from six to 14 years, were driven around for more than 11 hours and finally brought to a rock quarry near Livermore, less than 100 miles from the kidnap site.

There they were all transferred to a large moving van that had been buried in an isolated section of the quarry. Tarpaulins were stretched from the two small vans to the roof of the buried van so that the prisoners could not see where they were. A hole had been cut in the roof of the buried van, and the children were forced to climb down a ladder into their underground prison. Before each child was transferred, his or her name and age were recorded and a personal item or bit of clothing was taken, obviously for proof later that the kidnappers indeed held them prisoner.

The bus driver was given a flashlight and ordered into the moving van, which was then sealed off with large sheets of metal, plywood, dirt and other debris. The van, 25 feet long and eight feet wide, had been well furnished for accommodation of the prisoners, containing a portable toilet and supplies of water, bread, potato chips and breakfast cereal. There were a number of matresses, and ventilation was provided by four-inch rubber tubing, with air pumped in and out by two battery-driven fans.

Later that day a police air search located the abandoned school bus, but there was no trace of the children, and terror gripped the Chowchilla area. Twenty-four hours went by without a ransom demand from the kidnappers, who were apparently determined to fuel the parents' anxiety further so that the state would be forced to make payment immediately. However, the kidnappers' plans went awry when, 16 hours after their imprisonment in the large van, the driver and some of the older children managed to dig their way out. When all the children were pulled free, the group walked towards lights in the distance. They found a quarry employee, who immediately called the police. The Chowchilla children's ordeal was over.

It took the authorities 12 days to round up the three kidnappers involved. The day before the kidnapping a woman had jotted down the license number—1C91414—of a small van near what was to prove to be the site of the abduction. She had become suspicious of the van's occupants. The school bus driver underwent voluntary hypnosis and was able to recall the license number of one of the vans—1C91414—and all but one digit of the other. The numbers were eventually traced to an Oakland car dealer, and the large buried van to a Palo Alto firm, which had sold it to one Mark Hall. Employees at the Palo Alto and Oakland firms identified the purchaser from photographs as Frederick Newhall Woods, IV, the son of the owner of the rock quarry. Some of the children recalled hearing their abductors use the names Fred and James, and since Woods was known to be close friends with two brothers named James and Richard Allen Schoenfeld, sons of a prominent Atherton podiatrist, warrants were issued for them as well. Richard Allen Schoenfeld surrendered to authorities on July 23, and his older brother was captured on July 29. On the same day,

Woods was arrested by Royal Canadian Mounted Police in Vancouver.

The defendants chose a court trial rather than a jury trial, feeling that jurors would be hostile because the victims had been children. Evidence indicated that the trio had worked on the details of the kidnapping for an entire year before setting it in motion. All three were convicted of 24 counts of kidnapping and three of kidnapping with bodily harm. Richard Allen Schoenfeld got life imprisonment, and brother James and Woods drew life with a stipulation barring parole.

CHRISTIE, Ned (?1867-1892): Indian outlaw

Along with the Apache Kid, Ned Christie, a full-blooded Cherokee, became one of the most-wanted Indian outlaws in the West.

A bright youth, Christie served in the Cherokee tribal legislature, but in 1885 he became an outlaw in a big way. For some unknown reason, he killed Deputy U.S. Marshal Dan Maples and vanished into the Cookson Hills of the Oklahoma Indian Territory. In that area he functioned as a horse thief, rumrunner, bandit and murderer, although there is no doubt that, as was the case with the Apache Kid, just about any crime committed in the territory by a young Indian was pinned on him.

Photograph of the lifeless body of Indian outlaw Ned Christie nailed up to an old door became the most popular pinup in the Oklahoma Territory during the 1890s.

It took Hanging Judge Parker's deputies seven years to catch up with Ned, who was cornered by U.S. marshals Heck Thomas and Paden Tolbert in a log fort near Tahlequah on November 1, 1892. Finding Ned and flushing him out were two different matters, however, as the fort was close to impregnable. The marshals sent all the way to Kansas for an Army cannon and then set about the task of blasting out the Indian outlaw with the aid of about 20 reinforcements. They pumped an estimated 2,000 bullets into the fortress that did no damage at all; the cannon proved even less helpful. The logs held firm and the cannon balls had the disconcerting habit of bouncing back at the besiegers. Twenty-four hours of battle had not added up to a day of glory for the law. Finally, the attackers used dynamite to breach the walls. Although shell-shocked, the Indian came out fighting, riding hard and pumping away with his Winchester. With some 20 guns trained on him, Ned Christie was blasted off his mount, full of holes and dead.

The killing of Oklahoma's most-wanted Indian desperado deserved special artistic commemoration. His body was allowed to harden somewhat into a pre-rigor mortis pose, propped up against an old door with his rifle cradled in his hands, and then his picture was taken. Ned Christie became the most popular pinup in Oklahoma during the 1890s.

See also: *Heck Thomas*.

CICERO, Ill.: Mob-controlled Chicago suburb

In the heyday of the Capone mob, Cicero was known as the syndicate's town. Al Capone's private guard in Cicero totaled about 800 gunmen, while the town's police force numbered about 50. Any officer who considered standing up to the Capone gang thought twice because every official from the mayor down to the dogcatcher was believed to follow Capone's orders without question. Once when the mayor dared to displease Capone, the mob chieftain knocked His Honor down on the steps of the town hall and kicked him unmercifully in the groin. A Cicero policeman watched the entire procedure, reportedly looking quite embarrassed.

In 1924 the Democrats dared to put up candidates opposing the Klenha slate, which with bipartisan backing had ruled the town for three terms. The Capone forces sent in hundreds of gangsters to guarantee the proper election results. On the eve of the election, William F. Pflaum, the Democratic candidate for town clerk, was roughed up in his office and the place was totally wrecked. On election day gangsters in seven-passenger black limousines patrolled the streets, terrorizing the citizenry. Persons known to favor the Democrats were beaten. Capone men walked up and down lines of voters asking people how they intended to vote. If they gave a wrong answer, their ballots would be snatched from their hands and marked properly by the mobsters. Then a Capone hood, fingering a revolver in his coat pocket, would stand beside the voter until he or she dropped the ballot into the box. Honest poll watchers and election officials were simply kidnapped and held until the polls closed. A Democratic campaign worker, Michael Gavin, was shot through both legs; policemen were blackjacked.

Terrified Cicero citizens appealed to the courts for aid. Cook County Judge Edmund K. Jarecki deputized 70 Chicago patrolmen, nine squads of motorized police and five squads of detectives and sent them to the beleaguered town. That afternoon and evening pitched battles were fought between gangsters and police. Frank Capone, Al's brother, took aim at officers piling out of an unmarked black limousine and squeezed the trigger of his automatic, but it clicked on an empty chamber. Before he could pull the trigger again, two lawmen blasted him with their shotguns.

When Al buried Frank a few days later, he could at least console himself with the knowledge that his brother had not died in vain. The Klenha slate carried the election by a huge margin.

See also: *Al Capone, Frank Capone, Hawthorne Inn.*

CIMARRON County Seat War

While the Cimarron County Seat War in Kansas in 1889 may not have been the most murderous of the struggles of this kind, it has often been cited as the prototype of the county seat wars that bloodied Kansas and several other states during the land boom era, especially in the 1880s.

In October 1887 Cimmaron had been voted the seat of Gray County, a decision that did not please Asa T. Soule, a leading citizen of Ingalls, the town that had competed with Cimarron for the designation. Soule had invested heavily in Ingalls real estate and knew that if Ingalls became the county seat, his holdings would soar in value. At the time, custom dictated that the possession of the county court records established the legal location of the county seat. Promising a $1,000 reward, Soule got Sheriff Bill Tilghman to deputize a gang of hired guns and go after the records. Tilghman and more than a dozen gunfighters, including Neal Brown and Jim and Tom Masterson, arrived in Cimarron in the early hours of January 13, 1889. While several stood guard outside, the two Mastersons and Brown broke into the courthouse and began hauling out the records. They had almost completed the job when a Cimarron resident spotted them and sounded the alarm. The awakened Cimarron citizenry pushed guns out of scores of windows and opened fire. Four Ingalls invaders went down in the fusillade. Their bodies were tossed into a wagon loaded with the court records and the invaders fled. The Mastersons and Brown were left trapped inside the courthouse. A gunfight consumed the entire next day, with more than 200 armed men keeping the trio pinned down. Talk of lynching filled the air after a resident died and three others were badly hurt, but in the end, nothing happened. By that time two of the trapped men had been identified as Mastersons, and the news of their plight went out over the telegraph lines, reaching their noted brother, Bat Masterson, in Denver. He immediately wired Cimarron warning the townspeople to release the trio or he would lead an army of gunfighters to level the town. It was no idle threat. Bat commanded the loyalty of scores of noted gunmen, such as the Earps, Doc Holliday, Luke Short and others, men whom ordinary citizens could never stand up to. Thus, the following morning the trapped trio was allowed to leave town under a flag of truce.

By its forceful action, Ingalls did indeed become the county seat and held on to this honor until 1893, when it was passed back to Cimarron following another election. On this occasion there was no warring, however. Hard economic times had punctured the land bubble. Within a few years the populations of both Cimarron and Ingalls dropped to a few hundred souls each, and the bitter struggle had proved meaningless.

See also: *County Seat Wars.*

CINCINNATI Riots

A common public perception in 19th century big-city America was that enforcement agencies and the courts were corrupt and that criminals could often buy their freedom or mild sentences. This view, hardly unjustified, led to the organization of many vigilance committees and to frequent and bloody riots.

One of the worst of these took place in Cincinnati, Ohio in 1884. The public had been outraged by the actions of the criminal courts, which in the previous year had sentenced to death only four persons out of 50 convicted of capital crimes. On March 28, 1884 a huge mob stormed the jail where two youths who had been let off with manslaughter convictions were being held. They lynched the pair and were finally dispersed by a militia company. The following night mobs formed again to perform additional acts of "instant justice." Stores were looted of guns, the jail attacked and the courthouse set afire and almost totally destroyed. The rioters were eventually driven off after a pitched battle with troops. Violence continued the third day, a Sunday, and that night the mobs, which now contained large numbers of criminals protesting for law and order and looting stores at the same time, again battled the militia. Soldiers were rushed in from all parts of the state and streets were barricaded to isolate the mobs. Vicious fighting continued for three more days before the barricades could be removed and street-car service restored. The death toll in the rioting was at least 45 persons with 138 more badly injured. Despite the riots, Cincinnati retained its reputation as a wide-open city during the immediate ensuing years.

CIRCUS Grifting

Compared to circuses in other countries, the American version has relied much more on criminal enterprises and fake exhibits and less on talented performers. A prime source of revenue in 19th century circuses was gambling, particularly such crooked pastimes as the shell game, three-card monte and eight-dice cloth. Some seemingly ran independently of the circus management, but all paid a certain percentage of their take for the right to operate on the circus grounds. For these circus cons to thrive required four basic ingredients: grifters, victims, a dishonest circus management and public officials open to bribes. None were ever hard to come by.

The arrival of a circus in a community meant that within the next day or two many residents would find themselves swindled out of much of their ready cash, just as several church sermons the previous Sunday had warned. What the gambling grifters didn't take, circus shortchangers and pickpockets would. As late as 1900, many of the small circuses that traveled about the country still made each ticket seller pay up to $35 a week for the job because shortchanging the excited "rubes" on ticket sales was so easy and profitable. The pickpocketing franchise was sold to professional thieves, and to assist them in their chores, the master of ceremonies would make it a point to warn patrons about pickpockets. As a result, most men would quickly feel their wallets and thus reveal to the watchful crooks in which pocket they carried their cash. When a circus pulled up stakes, the grifters would ride out in the "privilege car," one lined with steel to protect them from angered rubes taken by the gambling grifts.

Criminologists have attributed the dishonest inclinations of the American circus to its more mobile existence compared to its European counterparts, especially the English circus, which stayed rooted in one place for much longer periods of time. The footloose lifestyle of American circuses encouraged a criminal business thrust. Many circuses in early years were ideal fences for stolen horses. Knowing they would be gone from an area the next day, circus employees became notorious for stealing from farms, barns and clotheslines.

Any one-shot method for improving profits would do. Balloon sellers typically hired an assistant to blow tacks at balloons in order to create an instant demand by howling children for a second or third sale. Many of the exhibits were outright frauds, particularly in small circuses, which used grifters because they could be paid far less than, for example, talented acrobats. Thus, the "Siamese twins" were simply two individuals held together by a flesh-colored belt while on display. As soon as that exhibit closed, the twins could hurry off, one to be perhaps a clown and the other to work, say, at the refreshment stand.

Circus grifting was an accepted practice in virtually all circuses until the 1880s and in all except Ringling's up to 1900. By as late as 1930, only the large circuses were free of grifting. The change did not come about as a result of a sudden reformation of the circuses or because public officials were less willing to take bribes or due to any growing sophistication among the customers. In earlier years a circus changed its name frequently so that it could return the following year to a community which it had angered on a previous trip. But as circuses grew, their very name became more of an asset than the revenues brought in by grifting. Faced with the necessity of making a choice, the bigger outfits, reluctantly, gave up grifting.

See also: *Carnival Gyps, Shell Game, Three-Card Monte.*

CIUCCI, Vincent (1925-1962): Murderer

The Ciucci case is often cited by critics of the court system as an example of justice delayed. Vincent Ciucci of Chicago was found guilty of having murdered his wife and three young children because he had fallen in love with an 18-year-old girl and wanted his freedom. He chloroformed his wife and three children on the night of December 4, 1953 and then shot each in the head. After the killings he set his apartment ablaze, apparently in the futile hope that the flames would eradicate all evidence of the shootings.

Although the case seemed open-and-shut and the jury quickly found Ciucci guilty, the wheels of justice moved slowly. Ingenious appeals and constant applications for commutation kept Ciucci alive for almost nine years until his execution in 1962. While these delays did not equal the 12 years on death row served by California's Caryl Chessman, the Ciucci case was criticized from all sides, by those who felt constant appeals were making a mockery of the death penalty and by opponents of capital punishment who condemned a system of justice that could make any defendant go through such a long ordeal. The Ciucci case contributed to the public's disenchantment with capital punishment in the 1960s, an attitude not reversed until the mid-1970s, when the death penalty once more became regarded as the cure-all for crime.

CIVIL War Gold Hoax

Perhaps the most audacious illegal money scheme of the Civil War period was perpetrated by a professional newspaperman, Joseph Howard, city editor of the *Brooklyn Eagle,* who concocted a false proclamation by President Abraham Lincoln. The hoax, in the words of one witness, "angered Lincoln more than almost any other occurrence of the war period."

Working with a reporter named Francis A. Mallison, Howard forged an Associated Press dispatch of the supposed proclamation that began, "In all seasons of exigency it becomes a nation carefully to scrutinize its line of conduct, humbly to approach the Throne of Grace, and meekly to implore forgiveness, wisdom, and guidance." The document, recounting the military stalemate in Virginia and disastrous news from Louisiana, called for a national day of "fasting, humiliation and prayer" eight days hence, on May 26, 1864. The real crushing news in the proclamation was the drafting of an additional 400,000 men.

Howard realized such a doleful pronouncement would shake the financial community to its roots, upset the stock market and undoubtedly cause a rise in the price of gold. Days before he and Mallison unleashed their hoax, Howard bought a considerable amount of gold on margins, much of it apparently under other names, so that the best estimate of his profits could only be put at "many, many thousands of dollars."

The schemers used young boys to deliver the bogus AP dispatch to various New York newspapers. The news was so startling that several of the publications decided to confirm the facts before printing the story. However, two papers, the *World* and the *Journal of Commerce,* were pressed by deadlines and tore down their makeup at the last moment to get the story out. Quite as Howard had expected, the stock exchange "was thrown into a violent fever." The price of gold instantly shot up 10 percent. Fortunes were made and lost before the hoax was exposed.

Incensed by the false story, President Lincoln, Secretary of State William H. Seward and Secretary of War Edwin M. Stanton ordered the two newspapers seized. Only two days later, on May 20, the trail led to Howard and Mallison when it became apparent that the newspapers had been the victims rather than the perpetrators of an act that in Stanton's words "distinguished [them] by the violence of their opposition to the Administration."

The clearing of the newspapers led to a firestorm of protest against President Lincoln's initial seizure of them. Lincoln, locked in a battle for renomination and reelection, found the charges of suppression of the free press particularly embarrassing. Almost forgotten in the controversy were the culprits, Howard and Mallison, who were confined in Fort Lafayette. Finally, Howard's father, an elder of Henry Ward Beecher's church, prevailed upon the famous minister to petition Lincoln for mercy. Beecher told Lincoln that the 35-year-old Howard was "the only spotted child of a large family" and his only guilt was "the hope of making some *money*." Finally, after the culprits had been confined for less than three months, Lincoln ordered their release.

The freeing of the gold hoaxers may not have been as magnanimous as it appeared on the surface. Ironically, when the report of the phony proclamation was published, an as yet unreleased proclamation lay on Lincoln's desk. It called for the draft of 300,000 more men. When Lincoln saw the adverse effect of the bogus report on the people and on the financial markets, he postponed all call-up plans for an additional two months.

CLAIBORNE, Billy (1860-1882): Gunfighter and rustler

Billy Claiborne is most noted as a survivor of the gunfight at the O.K. Corral.

Claiborne was a young gunslinger who insisted on being called Billy the Kid after the death of the more famous bearer of that name in July 1881. It is recorded that each of the three men who laughed in Claiborne's face over that pretension paid with their lives. The last doubter to die was Jim Hickey, and Claiborne was arrested for his murder. Incarcerated in San Pedro, Arizona Territory, Claiborne, a member of the Clanton gang of rustlers, was busted out of jail by Ike Clanton and the McLowery brothers on October 22, 1881. At the time, a showdown was fast approaching with the Earp forces, and Ike Clanton undoubtedly wanted all the guns he could get.

Claiborne's two guns proved of questionable value. The gunfight at the O.K. Corral took place four days later, and as nearly as can be determined, Claiborne got off one or two wild shots in the general direction of Virgil Earp and then fled for the sanctuary of C. S. Fly's photography studio. Ike Clanton

himself had little ground for complaint since he also sought shelter there while his brother Billy and the McLowery brothers were being gunned down.

It was a while before Claiborne again insisted on being referred to as Billy the Kid. While drunk in Tombstone's Oriental Saloon on November 14, 1882, he made the same demand of Buckskin Frank Leslie, a pitiless gunfighter who may well have killed more of the Clanton gang than the Earps ever did. Leslie, then serving as a sort of combination barman and bouncer, stepped outside on the street with Billy the Kid, II and shot him dead. Claiborne had managed to live to be one year older than his self-proclaimed namesake.

See also: *Buckskin Frank Leslie, O.K. Corral, Oriental Saloon.*

CLAIM Jumping

Few crimes in the mining communities of the West were considered more reprehensible than that of claim jumping, stealing another man's goldfield property before he had a chance to record it officially.

Filing a claim was not really the legalistic ritual it might seem. The district recorder was often a merchant or saloon keeper, and once a man had filed his claim, he still had to protect it. A typical sign read, "CLAME NOTISE—Jim Brown of Missoury takes this ground; jumpers will be shot." If by chance Brown or a counterpart did shoot a jumper, a miners court would readily clear him and most likely set up a bottle for him at the local saloon. Claim jumpers were not treated leniently. A frequent punishment called for a jumper to have his ears cut off so that, said one miner's diary, he would "not hear about no more strikes." When a stranger showed up in gold-strike country, he would not be welcomed if he had a reputation as a claim jumper. "Preventative hangings" were not unheard of in such circumstances. Overall, however, it must be said that the miners and their courts generally settled claim-jumping problems in a fair and equitable manner. When the law became fully established years later, few miners court findings were ever upset.

See also: *Soapy Smith.*

CLANTON, Joseph Isaac "Ike" (?-1887): Outlaw

Son of the notorious Old Man Clanton, Ike became nominal head of the Clanton gang following the death of his father in July 1881, but he was not that strong a personality and ranked no better than second in command to Curly Bill Brocius. While Ike Clanton hated the Earps and others of the "townie/gambler" element and plotted against them, he never really sought a confrontation with them. In the noted gunfight at the O.K. Corral on October 26, 1881, Ike aligned with Billy Claiborne, the McLowery brothers and his younger brother Billy against the Earps and Doc Holliday. Ike begged that the shooting be stopped and then fled, leaving Billy Clanton and the McLowerys to be killed. A few months later, Ike was involved in the plan to kill Virgil Earp, and although it failed, the shooting left Virgil maimed for life. While Ike was not present when Morgan Earp was murdered in March 1882, there is little doubt he was in on the planning.

After the Earps left Tombstone later that same year under considerable pressure from the citizens, Ike Clanton and brother Finn became scarce in the area as well, and rumor had it that Wyatt Earp must have killed Ike. Within a year, however, Ike was back at work rustling cattle, continuing to operate without trouble from the law until the new sheriff of Apache County, Commodore Perry Owens, led a posse that trapped the Clanton rustlers at their camp on the Blue River. Finn Clanton was captured and received a long prison term, but Ike fought to the end and was killed.

See also: *Wyatt Earp, O.K. Corral, Commodore Perry Owens.*

CLANTON, Newman H. "Old Man" (?-1881): Outlaw clan leader

A Texan of a hazy but definitely bloody past, Newman "Old Man" Clanton settled his family in the 1870s on a ranch at Lewis Springs, Arizona Territory, which was stocked with a constantly changing supply of stolen cattle. Old Man Clanton directed the lawless activities of the family and numerous hangers-on. The Clanton gang swept into Mexico and Texas to undertake robberies of stagecoaches and bullion pack trains. Besides his three sons, Ike, Finn and young Billy, important members of the gang included such cutthroats as Johnny Ringo, Curly Bill Brocius and the McLowery brothers, Tom and Frank. Clanton also maintained a spy network on both sides of the border that advised him on potential victims. One of the Old Man's worst depredations was the Guadalupe Canyon Massacre in July 1881, in which he and his men slaughtered 19 Mexicans escorting a mule train loaded with $75,000 in silver bullion. That vicious act made Old Man Clanton just about the most hated of all *gringos.* But about two weeks later, a large posse of Mexicans ambushed the old man and five of his gang as they were driving a herd of stolen cattle through the same Guadalupe Canyon. Only one of the gang, a man named Earnshaw, got away.

See also: *Guadalupe Canyon Massacre.*

CLANTON, William (c. 1865-1881): Outlaw

The only Clanton to die at the O.K. Corral, young Billy Clanton was considered by many the bravest of the family. While the Earp supporters always sought to claim that Billy was 17 or 19 at the time of the O.K. Corral fight, the anti-Earps have tended to set his age between 13 and 15 at most and thus claim that Wyatt Earp killed a "baby." Billy Clanton was deserted by Billy Claiborne and his brother, Ike, and the McLowerys staggered off as they were hit. His right hand shattered by a shot, Billy shifted his gun to his left hand and kept fighting alone. He shot Virgil Earp through the leg. Then Wyatt Earp put the sixth bullet in Billy Clanton and he went down. Billy worked his way up to his knees and tried to level his .45, allegedly pleading, "Just one more shot, God,

just one more shot." Finally, he fell back to the dirt, and the Earps and Holliday all held their fire.

Billy Clanton's reputed last words were: "Pull off my boots. I promised my mother I'd never die with my boots on."

See also: *O.K. Corral.*

CLARK, James G. (1924-   ): Sheriff and smuggler

Using electric cattle prods on demonstrators during the Selma, Ala. desegregation protests of the 1960s, Sheriff James G. Clark of Dallas County became a symbol of resistance to black voting rights.

Following passage of the Voting Rights Act of 1965, Clark was defeated for sheriff. After that, he himself got into trouble with the law. In 1978 he was charged with marijuana smuggling after officials confiscated about three tons of the drug aboard a DC-3 that had landed in Montgomery, Ala. in May of that year. The marijuana, valued at $4.3 million, had been flown in from Colombia. Pleading guilty to the charge, Clark was sentenced to two years in federal prison. At the time of his sentencing in December 1978, four charges of fraud and one of racketeering were also pending against him, in an unrelated case in New York City.

CLARK'S Battalion: New Orleans posse

In 1800 Spain, which had held New Orleans and the rest of the Louisiana province for 30 years, ceded the area back to France. However, the French were slow taking possession, the reason becoming clear with the purchase of Louisiana by the United States in 1803. During that three-year period, and especially in the final year, law and order crumbled. The Spaniards remained in nominal control but had lost all interest in maintaining the peace. On November 3, 1803 Spanish troops sailed for Havana, leaving the city with no organized protection and facing the likelihood of full-scale rioting and looting by the lower and criminal elements.

To fill this vacuum, the American consul, Daniel Clark, organized a battalion of 300 men, Americans living in the city and Creoles. The battalion had no clear legal code and in effect meted out posse justice to offenders, utilizing pillories located on Chartes Street. Major offenders were warned they faced the American hangman as soon as full authority was established. With a few French officials, Clark supervised the imposition of several regulations that were in keeping with American law and provided residents with a foretaste of U.S. rule. Among the ordinances adopted were ones outlawing profanity and the driving of carts on Sunday. Other regulations established curfews for slaves and sailors, which banned them from the streets after 8 p.m. without a written pass from their owners or commanding officers. With the official takeover by the United States on December 17, 1803, these new laws-by-posse became permanent.

CLIFTON, Dan (?1865-1896?): Outlaw

Better known as Dynamite Dick, Dan Clifton was a small-time Oklahoma Indian Territory safe blower, holdup man and rustler who hooked up with the Doolin gang in 1892. He was involved in all the gang's jobs from then on and had three fingers shot off during the Doolins' famous battle with the law at Ingalls, Okla. in 1893. A reward of $3,500 was put on Dynamite Dick's head, and he became the most "killed" outlaw in America, as reward-hungry posses kept trying to pin his identification on any shot-up corpse. Some overlooked the matter of the three missing fingers, while the more knowledgeable would simply cut three off, alas often the wrong three.

In all likelihood, Dynamite Dick was tracked down in 1896 near Blackwell, Okla. and shot dead. While there were three fingers missing on the corpse, considerable speculation arose that the dead man was still not Dynamite Dick but another outlaw named Buck McGregg.

CLINE, Alfred L. (1888-1948): Bluebeard

One of the most successful criminals at marrying and murdering widows for their money was Alfred L. Cline, until the law cut off his career in California in 1945.

His modus operandi remained constant, and he is known to have killed eight unfortunate wives after he had convinced them to will their estates to him. Cline would take his brides on a lavish vacation and in some smart hotel get them to drink a glass of buttermilk that he had laced with a heavy amount of a sleep-producing drug. He would follow this up a few hours later with a fatal dose of the drug, but in the meantime he would call the house physician and inform him that "Mrs. Cline has had another heart attack." When he resummoned the doctor shortly thereafter, his wife would be dead, and the doctor, prepared for that event, would not be suspicious and would issue a death certificate, citing heart failure as the cause.

Eventually, many of the facts about Cline's crimes surfaced, but the law invariably foundered on one key element. Cline always had his wives' bodies cremated, a process that destroyed all evidence of the poison he had used. However, the authorities were able to prove that he had used forgery to get his hands on his wives' money and for this he was sentenced to 126 years in prison. Cline died in California's Folsom Prison in 1948.

CLUM, John P. (1851-1932): Indian agent and publisher

One of the most colorful men of the Old West, John Clum was born near Claverack, N.Y. At the age of 23 he was an Indian agent on the San Carlos Reservation, where he is generally credited with developing the concept of the Indian police. The principle of giving Indians armed authority was not one that

came easily to many whites, and Clum and other Indian agents who tried it found themselves involved in many imbroglios with the power structure. Of all the agents, Clum, not surprisingly, had the most effective Indian police force. He resigned from the Indian Service in 1878 because of the government's hardening line towards the Indians.

John Clum poses with some of his highly regarded Indian police.

In 1880 in Tombstone, Arizona Territory, he founded one of the West's most colorful and outspoken newspapers, the *Tombstone Epitaph,* which became known as the town's pro-Earp publication. Publisher Clum was often a more worthy citizen than the elements he supported at times—Earp and Doc Holliday, for instance, were little more than corrupt lawmen and murderers—and there is little doubt that his newspaper did much to bring law and order to the area. Selling out his interests in the *Epitaph* in 1882, Clum left the area after the death of his wife and daughter to become assistant editor of the *San Francisco Examiner.* He died in 1932, two years after making a sentimental return to Tombstone.

See also: *Wyatt Earp, Indian Police,* Tombstone Epitaph.

CLUTTER Family Murders: *In Cold Blood* case

The Clutter family murders in 1959 were a brutal, senseless affair that became the subject of Truman Capote's best-selling book *In Cold Blood.*

The Clutters were sought out, robbed and killed by two ex-jailbirds and vagrants named Richard E. Hickock and Perry E. Smith. Hickock had learned of the Clutters while sharing a prison cell with a convict named Floyd Wells, who had once worked for Clutter, a well-to-do wheat farmer in Holcomb, Kan. Hickock pumped Wells about Clutter's wealth and whether he kept a safe in his home and how much money he was likely to have on hand. When Hickock was paroled from the Kansas State Penitentiary, he hooked up with Smith and the two headed for the Clutter home. They invaded it on November 15, 1959. After terrorizing the family, the pair killed Clutter and his wife, Bonnie, both 45, daughter Nancy, 16, and son Kenyon, 15. Clutter's body was found in the basement of his home with his throat cut and shot in the head. His wife and two children had been killed with shotgun blasts at close range. All the victims were bound by the wrists.

When news of the murders reached the penitentiary, Wells went to the warden and told him of Hickock's interest in the Clutters. This put the police on Hickock's trail, and he and Smith were captured in Las Vegas. Both men made confessions, each trying to shift more of the blame on the other. While they had expected to find $10,000, they had netted less than $50 for the four murders. Smith said of Clutter: "He was a nice gentleman. . . . I thought so right up to the moment I cut his throat."

At the trial the jury was urged by the prosecuting attorney not to be "chicken-hearted" and to find them guilty of first-degree murder. The jury did so, and after a number of appeals, Hickock, 33, and Smith, 36, were hanged in April 1965.

COCKFIGHTING

A generally illegal but much-practiced sport, cockfighting was imported into the United States from the Spanish islands and Mexico. During the 19th century it became a common weekend entertainment in many parts of the South and West. Some cocks were armed with steel spurs to make their battles more bloody and furious.

Cockfighting has never been stamped out, and secret matches are still held in large cities for big-money prizes. Not long ago, police in Los Angeles broke up a cockfighting gambling ring and freed some two dozen cocks that had fought in matches for stakes of up to $10,000. Similar arrests have been made in Chicago and New York, where vacant buildings in deserted slum areas have been turned into exhibition halls. Cockfighting has outlasted dogfighting because it is easier to maintain secretly and because much of the action takes place in barrios, where police investigation is generally unpopular.

While local laws generally ban cockfighting, proposals in Congress have called for action on a federal level, which has brought protests from congressmen representing Mexican-American areas. A Texas congressman denounced a successful House vote to ban interstate transportation of birds and the use of the mails for the promotion of cockfighting, citing "the ethnic and cultural background of some of us."

COE, George Washington (1856-1941): Gunfighter

A sidekick of Billy the Kid, George Coe took part in most of Billy's battles during New Mexico's Lincoln County War in the late 1870s, barely escaping death when severely wounded in the gunfight at Blazer's Mill. He accepted amnesty when it was offered by the new governor of the territory, Lew Wallace, and thereafter lived a long and peaceful life, becoming the last survivor of that great commercial conflict for the wealth and riches of New Mexico.

In 1934 Coe had his reminiscences ghost-written in a book called *Frontier Fighter,* which offered a rather cleaned-up portrait of Billy the Kid. One observation said Billy was as fine as any "college-bred youth and with his humorous and pleasing personality got to be a community favorite. In fact, Billy was so popular there wasn't enough of him to go around."

COE, Phil (?-1871): Gambler and Wild Bill Hickok victim

A Texas dandy, Coe was the Hollywood prototype of the Western gambler, handsome and elegant with neatly trimmed beard, gold-headed cane and derby hat. His killing by Wild Bill Hickok tarnished the latter's reputation as a fair gunfighter more than any of Hickok's other shootings.

Little is known of Coe's origins because "he told as many stories about his past as there were cards in a deck," but he was a fixture on the gambling circuit of the 1860s and early 1870s and prospered. In 1871 Coe turned up in Abilene, Kan. with a vicious gunfighter named Ben Thompson and they opened the Bull's Head Tavern and Gambling Saloon. The establishment thrived, and this put the partners in conflict with Wild Bill Hickok, who, as town marshal, was also the protector of the Alamo, the leading gambling emporium in the town. Coe charged that his fellow Texans up on cattle drives were being cheated at the Alamo's tables while Hickok looked the other way; the marshal charged in turn that Coe ran a crooked game.

The tension was further heightened by what became known as the *Shame of Abilene*. Coe and Thompson had the front of their establishment painted with a huge bull, with even larger genitalia. If some considered the representation offensive, Coe and Thompson found it boosted business greatly. Within weeks, reports of the *Shame of Abilene* were even being carried in the Eastern press. Finally, Hickok, prodded by the more genteel elements as well as the other gambling interests, ordered Coe to remove the painting or at least reduce the size of the more offending parts to scale. When Coe refused, Hickok, armed with paint can and brush, did the job himself, revealing perhaps some overlooked talents.

There has been much speculation that the argument over the bull painting was the cause of the Hickok-Coe gun duel, but it appears more likely that the showdown stemmed from Hickok's desire to win control of the lion's share of Abilene's gambling business. The trouble came to a head on October 5, 1871, at a time when Ben Thompson, whose skills with a gun more closely approached Hickok's than did Coe's, was out of town. Coe was bidding a liquid farewell to a bunch of Texas cowboys. They wound up in front of the Alamo, where Coe fired a shot from his gun. Hickok hurried out of the saloon, there being an ordinance against carrying firearms inside the town limits. Putting away his weapon, Coe explained that he had just shot at a stray dog, and Hickok reprimanded him. Some anti-Hickok observers have suggested that Coe's explanation only infuriated Hickok more, since as marshal he collected 25 cents for each stray he killed and Coe was thus threatening to cut the marshal's paycheck. What happened next is a matter of dispute. The Texans all insisted that when Coe turned away, Hickok whipped out a pair of derringers and shot him. The other version was that Hickok did not shoot until Coe pulled his gun and fired point blank at him. In any event, Hickok's image as a gunfighter was soon tarnished by a charge that he was "trigger-happy." As Coe fell mortally wounded, Hickok heard loud bootsteps behind him and, thinking he was being attacked from behind, whirled and fired again. He shot his own deputy, Mike Williams, who was rushing to his aid. Williams died a few minutes later stretched out on a poker table in the Alamo, while Hickok continued to curse the dying Coe. One rather maudlin pro-Hickok recorder of the events added: "Tears are the safety valves of a woman's soul. Without them she could not survive. Sometimes they and strong men also. 'Jesus wept.' declares the Gospel. So did Wild Bill." In reality, there was little doubt Hickok was determined to kill Coe; he simply got more than he bargained for in the process.

See also: *Wild Bill Hickok*, Shame of Abilene, *Ben Thompson*.

COFFIN, Double-Decker: Mafia body disposal method

From the time of its first appearance in America during the 19th century, the Mafia has been most inventive in the ways it disposes of the bodies of murder victims; a great many are finally listed in official records as missing, instead of dead. Some victims have been fitted with "concrete overcoats" or ground up in garbage shredders. Top New York mafioso Tony Bender is believed now to be either part of a large Manhattan skyscraper or of the recently crumbling West Side Highway (an in-joke in certain Mafia circles is that "dagos make lousy roads").

Perhaps the quaintest of all body disposal devices is the "double-decker coffin." A murder victim is taken to one of the mob's cooperative undertakers who constructs a special panel in a coffin he has ready for an about-to-be-buried corpse. The unwanted murder victim is placed in the bottom of the coffin and a panel is put over the body. Then the right corpse is placed on top. After a properly mournful funeral, the two corpses are buried together. No undertaker has ever been convicted as a result of this method because he can always claim the mob must have dug open the grave after burial and put in the extra corpse. The undertaker cooperating with the mob on such a matter is assured of the proper financial reward because the crime family will see to it that he gets a good deal of their regular business thrown his way.

COHEN, Mickey (1913-1976): Gangster

One of the most shot-at gangsters of the 1940s and 1950s, Mickey Cohen was the gambling czar of the West Coast, succeeding to that position after the underworld execution of Bugsy Siegel, Cohen's mentor in 1947 by "persons unknown." Those unknown persons were members of the national syndicate. Cohen later did battle with them, especially the syndicate's Los Angeles representative, Jack Dragna, refusing to turn over a cut of the proceeds from his bookmaking operations despite a series of attempts on his life.

Cohen lived in a mansion surrounded with an electrified fence and spotlights. On two occasions his home was dynamited. While he survived both times, he bemoaned the loss of much of his 200-suit wardrobe in one of the blasts.

Noted for his colorful and fiery comments, Cohen told television interviewer Mike Wallace, "I have killed no man that in the first place didn't deserve killing by the standards of our way of life." When asked to name the California politicians who had once protected his gambling interests, he refused, stating, "that is not my way of life."

Cohen wasn't any more communicative when he appeared before the Kefauver Committee's hearings on organized crime in 1950. When asked by Sen. Charles Tobey, "Is it not a fact that you live extravagantly . . . surrounded by violence," Cohen responded: "Whadda ya mean, 'surrounded by violence'? People are shooting at *me.*"

When pressed on how he had obtained a $35,000 loan without putting up collateral from a Hollywood banker, Mickey quipped, "I guess he just likes me."

In 1958 Cohen, ever the publicity hound, gave the newspapers love letters written by actress Lana Turner to Johnny Stompanato, her gangster lover and a former Cohen bodyguard who was stabbed to death by Turner's teenage daughter. What upset Mickey was the fact that he had been stuck with the bill for Stompanato's funeral.

The Internal Revenue Service nailed Cohen twice for income tax violations. He served four years the first time and did 10 years of a 15-year term the second time. Released in 1972, he announced his intention to go straight. Cohen didn't have too much choice in the matter since he was partly paralyzed as the result of a head injury inflicted by a fellow convict in the federal penitentiary at Atlanta in 1963. In 1974 Cohen attracted attention by campaigning for prison reform and, later, by stating he had been in touch with people who knew the whereabouts of kidnap victim Patricia Hearst.

Cohen died of natural causes in 1976.

COLBERT, Chunk (?-1874): Gunfighter and outlaw

Chunk Colbert was a gunfighter credited with killing seven men, but he is best remembered for taking part in one of the most famed gun duels in the history of the West.

The man Colbert challenged in an obvious effort to become

known as one of the truly great gunfighters was an accomplished duelist and outlaw named Clay Allison, whose own killings eventually totaled somewhere between 15 to 21. Colbert rode from the Colorado to the New Mexico Territory just to face down Allison. Once there he invited Allison to dine with him at the Colfax County Inn. As the duel was immortalized by Hollywood and John Wayne, the pair, eyeball to eyeball, stirred their coffee and whiskey with the muzzles of their six-guns. Each reholstered their piece, still eyeing the other carefully, and started to eat. In a telltale sign, Colbert reached for his coffee cup with his left hand. Below the table he was moving up his gun with his right hand. Allison detected the move and went for his own gun. Desperate, Colbert fired before his gun had cleared the table top and the slug plowed into the wood. Allison shot him directly over the right eye, and then, the story goes, calmly proceeded to finish his meal as his foe's body was being removed.

Later, Allison was asked why he had sat down to eat with a man he knew was determined to kill him. "Because," he said, "I didn't want to send a man to hell on an empty stomach."

See also: *Clay Allison.*

COLEMAN, Edward (?-1839): Murderer

A fierce New York gangster, Edward Coleman became one of the city's most-hated murderers for killing one of New York's favorite street characters.

The Hot Corn Girls of the early 19th century were the predecessors of the hot dog and peanut vendors of today, but they also had a certain aura of romance about them. Appearing mostly in the Five Points section of early New York, the Hot Corn Girls sold hot ears of corn from wooden buckets that hung from their shoulders. All successful Hot Corn Girls were of striking beauty; they had to be because of the intense competition. They strode through the streets barefoot in calico dresses and plaid shawls singing:

> Hot Corn! Hot Corn!
> Here's your lily white corn.
> All you that's got money—
> Poor me that's got none—
> Come buy my lily hot corn
> And let me go home.

The young bloods of the city would vie for the favors of a Hot Corn Girl. Many duels were fought over them. The more artistic suitors celebrated their beauty in story and verse. If a man had an aversion for work and a handsome wife, he could live a life of leisure by sending her forth with a cedar bucket full of corn. Such a husband, however, might find he would have to trail behind her to fend off the blades who tried to flirt with his Hot Corn Girl.

Edward Coleman wooed and won a truly beautiful member of this elite group, one so fetching that she was called The Pretty Hot Corn Girl. He married her after winning battles with about a dozen other suitors. The marriage was a short one, though. Coleman became enraged when he found her earnings were less than he had expected. He beat her so badly

that she died. He was arrested, convicted and, on January 12, 1839, became the first man to be executed in the newly completed Tombs Prison, a punishment much applauded by a public who still knew the victim only by the name of The Pretty Hot Corn Girl.

COLL, Vincent "Mad Dog" (1909-1932): Gangster and murderer

Alternately known as Mad Dog and the Mad Mick, Vincent Coll stands as the best remembered of the so-called baby-faced killers of the 1930s. On another level, he was typical of the latter-day Irish gangsters who resisted the growth of organized crime, fighting a bloody war for an independent existence.

Some have described Coll as at least half-demented, with no regard for human life. Others have said he had no regard for even his own life, exhibiting a death wish as he invaded the far stronger gangland empires of Dutch Schultz, Legs Diamond and Owney Madden. With mindless nerve, he even accepted a commission to assassinate Lucky Luciano, Vito Genovese, Frank Costello and Joe Adonis. He was hired by Salvatore Maranzano, then the Mafia's "boss of bosses," who wished to rid himself of the young Turks he knew were plotting against him. Maranzano wanted the killings done by a non-Italian so that he could insist he was above the bloodshed. Coll drew a $25,000 advance and was on his way to Maranzano's office, where a trap was being laid for Luciano and Genovese. Luciano learned of the plot and had Maranzano killed first. When Coll got there, he found he had lost his murder contract, but being ahead $25,000, he walked off content.

Vince Coll emerged from the Irish ghetto of New York's Hell's Kitchen, where criminal activity was an accepted mode of behavior. In his early twenties, he and his brother Peter hired out as rumrunners to Dutch Schultz at $150 a week each. As he told his brother, the job was merely a way of learning the ropes before they either started up a bootleg empire of their own or simply took over the Dutchman's. Within a short time, Coll was demanding a cut of the action from Schultz, a proposal that was angrily rejected. The Coll brothers then started laying the groundwork for their own organization. As the fate of Vincent Barelli, a Schultz hood, and Mary Smith, Barelli's girlfriend, proved, Vince Coll was prepared to use gratuitous violence to accomplish his goal. The Coll brothers and Mary's sister, Carmine, had attended the same Hell's Kitchen grade school, and on the basis of this connection, Mary got Barelli to attend a meeting with the plotting brothers. When Barelli refused to desert Schultz, Coll shot him and Mary.

Schultz was unaware of the scheming and still regarded the Coll brothers as being in his stable. After Vince was arrested for violating the Sullivan Law against carrying weapons, Schultz put up $10,000 bail. He became duly incensed when Coll promptly jumped bail; as a moral lesson, the beer baron had Peter Coll murdered. This launched the bitter Coll-Schultz war, in which at least 20 gunmen were killed. An exact count was impossible since the Castellammarese War for control of the New York Mafia was raging at the same time and the police had difficulty figuring out which corpse resulted from which feud.

Even though he had less firepower, Coll held his own against the Schultz forces. Constantly pressed for cash, he raised it in desperate fashion by kidnapping mobster kingpins attached to the Legs Diamond and Owney Madden gangs and collecting huge ransoms for their freedom. Thus, Coll was soon being hunted by a large portion of the New York underworld. In July 1932 Coll won his sobriquet of Mad Dog when he tried to gun down several Schultz gangsters on East 107th Street. Riding by them in a car, Coll cut loose a machine-gun blast that missed the gangsters but hit five small children, aged five to seven, leaving them writhing on the ground, some shot as many as five times. Five-year-old Michael Vengalli died, most of his stomach blown away.

The public was indignant and orders went out to the police to bring in Mad Dog Coll dead or alive. Realizing he would be caught sooner or later, Coll kidnapped yet another Owney Madden aide and collected $30,000 in ransom. He used this money to hire the top lawyer of the day, Samuel Leibowitz, to defend him. Remarkably, Coll was acquitted of the murder charge after the masterful Leibowitz somehow seemed to make the eyewitnesses, rather than his client, the defendants. The Mad Dog was back on the streets.

Later, the underworld put a $50,000 reward out for the trigger-happy youth. Schultz gunners almost cornered Coll on four occasions but he fought his way to safety each time. Then one day late in 1932, Coll was in a drug store telephone booth talking to Owney Madden, threatening to kill him unless he was given money. Madden kept talking to him while the call was traced. Coll was still in the phone booth when a black automobile pulled up outside the drug store. One man stood outside on the street and another just inside the door. A third with something bulging under his overcoat strode towards the phone booth. Coll saw him as the man leveled a Tommy Gun at him. In his cramped position Coll was unable to react as the man squeezed the trigger.

At the autopsy 15 steel-jacketed bullets were removed from Coll's face, chest and stomach.

See also: *Samuel S. Leibowitz, Owney "the Killer" Madden, Salvatore Maranzano.*

COLLEGE Kidnappers: Chicago gang

During the early-1930s heyday of the kidnapping gangs, one combine that operated in unique fashion was the so-called College Kidnappers of Chicago. They specialized in snatching only underworld characters, who not only could afford to pay but also were not likely to complain to the police.

The gang got its name because most of its members were college graduates; the leader, Theodore "Handsome Jack" Klutas, was an alumnus of the University of Illinois. The modus operandi of the gang was to pick up gossip in underworld circles about who had made a big "score." They would

then kidnap the individual and release him only when they received a slice of the loot. Quite often, members of the Chicago mob were their victims, a pattern that earned the College Kidnappers the enmity of the Capone operation. But Klutas and his men had little fear of organized crime and continued their onslaughts, reportedly pulling in more than $500,000 dollars in ransom money between 1930 and 1933.

In 1933 a hot rumor, later proven to have some basis in fact, spread that the College Kidnappers had merged the Dillinger gang into their operations. Faced with this disturbing news, the Capone forces decided to try to buy off the kidnappers and persuaded one of the kidnappers, Julius "Babe" Jones, to approach Klutas to arrange a deal. Klutas told Jones he would consider it but, as soon as Jones left, ordered his assassination. The attempt was made by first stealing Jones' car and then faking a telephone call, allegedly from the Joliet police, to tell him that his car had been found and could be picked up at a local garage. Jones, an old hand at College Kidnapper tricks, was suspicious and drove by the garage dressed as a woman. As he expected, he spotted two gang members parked in a car opposite the garage, ready to gun him down when he appeared.

Now trapped between the College Kidnappers and the Capones, Jones could only turn to the police, informing them about a number of the gang's hideouts. One was a brick bungalow in Bellwood. When two squads of detectives stormed the bungalow, they captured two wanted criminals. One was Walter Dietrich, one of 10 convicts Dillinger had helped to break out of the Michigan City Prison. Dietrich refused to say where Klutas was or whether he alone or the rest of the Dillinger gang had joined the College Kidnappers. Meanwhile, acting on Jones' information, the police rounded up several other gang members, but not Klutas.

Later that same day a stakeout at the Bellwood bungalow paid off. A car pulled up and Klutas boldly strode up the walkway. As Klutas pushed open the door, four police officers trained guns on him, including Sgt. Joe Healy's machine gun. Healy said: "Hands up. Police officers."

Klutas, who had always vowed never to be taken alive, reached under his overcoat for a gun. Healy loosed a burst of machine-gun bullets into the gangster's chest. Klutas was thrown clear off the bungalow porch to the sidewalk. He was dead and the College Kidnappers were finished.

COLLINS, Dapper Don (1880-1950): Confidence man

The archetypal smooth operator who uses his charms to seduce women and defraud them of their wealth, Dapper Don Collins was a notorious rogue who, by his own admission, "could never pass up a score," large or small. He swindled women by reversing the old badger game, so that they were extorted when he was "arrested" by confederates posing as law officers. The police impersonators would say he was a Mann Act violator or suspected procurer for white slavers. To protect the honor of the woman, usually upper class and perhaps married, he would give the bogus officers all his cash, only to be visibly shaken when they announced it was not enough. The panicky woman, facing sure ruin if the case was publicized, could be counted on to contribute her money, jewelry and furs.

Born in Atlanta, Ga. as Robert Arthur Tourbillon, he affected a number of aliases for his various cons but became best known as Dapper Don Collins, because according to his confederates, he was a dandy who could "sweet talk a lady" or anyone else for that matter. He often used a phony police badge and pretended to be a police officer, one who, of course, was always open to a bribe. Dapper Don first arrived in New York around the turn of the century after an unrewarding circus career riding a bicycle around in a cage full of lions. He gravitated to the notorious Broadway poolroom of Curly Bennett, where he befriended most of the metropolitan underworld.

Dapper Don soon became a gang leader, forming the first of his blackmail rings for extorting money from women. Besides his various confidence games, he masterminded train robberies and drug-smuggling and alien-smuggling operations and later, with the onset of Prohibition, was a top bootlegger and rumrunner. Collins often used a luxury yacht for rumrunning and bringing in aliens. In one of his more audacious exploits, he once entrapped a society woman aboard the yacht by having phony law enforcement raiders seize him on Mann Act violation for transporting the woman from Connecticut for "illicit purposes." They shook the woman down for $7,000 in cash and diamonds. Before the raiders left the yacht, they seized three aliens Collins had brought into the country from a ship offshore. Dapper Don had already collected $1,000 from each of them, but now the "law officers" confiscated the rest of their personal fortunes as a payoff for not taking them into custody. Because Collins was fearful of overlooking some of their money, he even had his men take all the victims' luggage with them to search at their leisure.

While he bossed many of these grandiose schemes, Collins could not pass up even the smallest take. For a time, he headed a "punch mob" on Manhattan's West Side that specialized in looting nickels from pay telephones. One of his extraordinary cons occurred in 1920 during the hunt for a Railway Express agent who had skipped out of his job with $6,000. While police hunted the agent, Dapper Don came across him first. He immediately turned copper and swindled the thief out of his haul in return for letting him go free, appropriating as well the man's watch, ring and tiepin.

While Collins occasionally did time for various capers, he usually beat the rap for his blackmail exploits because his victims refused to testify against him. He retained the Great Mouthpiece, Bill Fallon, to defend him on a number of charges and usually went free. The pair were constant companions on Broadway.

According to Gene Fowler in *The Great Mouthpiece,* when Fallon was asked why he chummed with such a notorious individual, he replied: "Because he is a philosopher as well as the Chesterfield of crime. He performs in a gentlemanly manner. This first bit of philosophy he ever dropped in my company made me laugh and made me like him. We were discussing whether any man is normal; precisely sane; and what sanity consists of. Collins said: 'Between the ages of sixteen and sixty, no man is entirely sane. The only time any man between those ages is sane is during the first ten minutes after he has concluded the supreme love gesture. Fifteen minutes after, and the old insanity creeps back again'!"

Part of his success with the ladies stemmed from his reputation as the biggest spender and fashion plate on Broadway. It cost him plenty. What Collins netted from one gullible but adoring lady one day he might blow the next on another lady. Once Collins set up a Maryland matron and took off to Atlantic City with her. He was then to guide her to Washington for the kill. Instead, he stayed in Atlantic City for a week with her. At the end of that week of bliss, he kissed her goodbye and went to Washington alone. He had four confederates in this operation and had to pay them $350 apiece for a caper that was intended to net a $10,000 profit.

In 1924, with the police hunting him for a number of capers, Dapper Don transferred his operations to Europe and seduced several women in Berlin and Paris. In the French capital, he took up with Mrs. Helen Petterson, former wife of Otto Young Heyworth, and extracted money from her under a number of ruses. Moreover, during a New Year's party at the Hotel Majestic, he flipped her out of a third-floor window. She broke her leg in the fall, and Collins was hustled off to prison for that offense and failure to pay his hotel bill. Undaunted, Mrs. Petterson limped from her hospital room at Neuilly to visit Collins, announcing, "We are going to be married." However, some New York police officers were in France to pick up a suspect in another case and spotted Collins in the prison. They promptly arranged for his extradition to the States on a robbery charge. Dapper Don was brought home in grand style aboard the steamship *Paris,* sharing a fine stateroom with a New York detective. Passengers knew that one of the two was a crook, but most believed the detective was the guilty party.

Back home, Collins beat the rap but later did short stretches on a couple of other charges. Dapper Don then got involved in a liquor-smuggling operation with another top confidence operator, Count Victor Lustig, supplying the notorious Legs Diamond with booze. They worked a label-switching dodge that enabled them to cheat the gangster out of thousands of dollars. Eventually, Diamond found out about the swindle and the pair had to go into hiding. For a time, Collins left the country again, but in 1929 he came back and was caught swindling a New Jersey farmer out of $30,000. He was sent to prison for three years. When he came out, a lot of the old Dapper Don was gone, as indeed was the pre-Depression era that nurtured him. He was over 50, paunchy around the waist and looking tired, perhaps having lost some of his self-confidence. He told the press he was reforming.

That was impossible; he was just plain tired. In 1939 Dapper Don, then a drug addict, was far gone, and his swindles were petty. Long ago, Collins had learned the danger of going after small potatoes. Unlike big people, little victims scream.

He swindled an immigrant woman out of a few hundred dollars by pretending to be an immigration official and threatening to deport her husband. For this unimportant caper Collins drew the longest sentence of his career, 15 to 30 years.

The newspapers reported that Dapper Don started off on his train ride up the river as light-hearted and debonair as ever. But that was newspaper hyperbole. Collins was old and beat. "The only way I'll ever come out again," he told the officer escorting him, "is feet first."

He was right. He died in Attica Prison in June 1950 and was buried in a pauper's grave. No one attended the funeral.

COLLINS, John Norman (1947-): Michigan co-ed murderer

For a time it appeared that the murders of seven co-eds in the Ypsilanti area between August 1967 and July 1969 would never be solved. The victims had been shot, strangled or beaten to death and then sexually mutilated. There were no clues, and even the importing of Peter Hurkos, the Dutch "psychic detective," failed to provide any fruitful leads. With the seventh murder, that of 18-year-old Karen Sue Beckemann, the police had what appeared to be a logical suspect in 22-year-old John Norman Collins, an Eastern Michigan University student and motorcycle enthusiast. Karen Sue had been seen with him shortly before her disappearance, and other students told of hearing things Collins had said that hinted he might be the Michigan co-ed killer.

Collins was arrested but soon released because there was no solid evidence against him. Like so many other suspects, he seemed to be just another odd character caught up in the investigation. The eventual case against Collins resulted from a discovery made by a relative, his aunt, Mrs. Dana Loucks. Mr. and Mrs. Loucks had gone away on vacation and let Collins use their home. When they returned, Mrs. Loucks found some dark stains in the basement. She pointed them out to her husband, who was a member of the Ypsilanti police force. The stains proved to be blood, of the same type as that of Karen Sue, who had been killed while the Loucks were away. The police then searched the basement and discovered some male hair clippings, which matched hair clippings found on Karen Sue's underwear. It developed the Mrs. Loucks cut the hair of her two boys in the basement. Based on the hair clippings, the blood stains and Collins' admission that he had used the Loucks' basement during the time they were on vacation, Collins was brought to trial in Ann Arbor in 1970. He was convicted and given a life sentence.

COLLINS, Walter (1919-1928): Kidnap and murder victim

Nine-year-old Walter Collins suffered the sad fate of being kidnapped and murdered by a maniac on March 10, 1928, although his body was not found until the following year.

However, it was his widowed mother's fate rather than that of the unfortunate child's, that made Walter's case so bizarre.

When Walter disappeared, a nationwide search for him was launched, and some five months later, a boy who looked exactly like him was picked up in Lee, Mass. The boy was a runaway and readily identified himself as the missing Walter Collins. In the period before he was turned over to Mrs. Collins, someone, whose identity was never learned, coached him so that he could pass himself off as Walter. This meant knowing little details that allowed the boy to discuss Walter's past with relatives and friends. It took Mrs. Collins three weeks to become suspicious that the boy was not Walter. She then measured his height and found he was an inch and a half shorter than her son had been before he disappeared. Convinced she had an impostor on her hands, Mrs. Collins went to the police, demanding that this strange boy be taken away. The police promptly committed the woman to a psychopathic institution for observation. Mrs. Collins was kept there almost a week before doctors became convinced she was sane and released her. Finally, the boy confessed his impersonation. Mrs. Collins sued the authorities who had had her wrongly committed and was awarded $10,800.

COLOMBO, Joseph, Sr. (1914-1978): Murdered mafioso

There were those in the underworld who said that Joe Colombo, the head of one of the Mafia's biggest crime families, had to come to a bad end. He was a lightweight in a killers' world. Colombo's rise to power had been achieved through neither muscle nor brain power but by the simple expedient of being what was regarded as a "fink." When Joe Bananas made a powerful push in the 1960s to take over the whole New York Mafia, he planned the murder of the entire top echelon of the crime syndicate's ruling board. Bananas gave the assignment to his ally Giuseppe Magliocco, who had fallen heir to Joe Profaci's Brooklyn crime family, and Magliocco in turn ordered his ambitious underboss, Colombo, to carry out the hit contracts.

Colombo was probably too frightened to make the hits and also judged Magliocco a sure loser; so instead, he betrayed the plot to the leading would-be New York victims, Carlo Gambino and Tommy Lucchese. Eventually, the old guard won the ensuing Banana War, and Colombo was rewarded by being put in charge of the Profaci family. Colombo soon found he had his hands full trying to deal with an insurrection led by the upstart Joey Gallo and his brothers.

At the same time, Colombo went off on an ill-conceived program to improve the image of Italian-Americans by forming the Italian-American Civil Rights League. Colombo's idea was that this organization would make Italian-Americans proud of their heritage and that in unity they would be able to fight the authorities' alleged victimization of them. The league was also intended to fight the Italian gangster stereotype. Other Mafia leaders looked upon Colombo's efforts with distaste.

Mafia boss Joseph Colombo, Sr., holding umbrella, pickets FBI headquarters in 1971 as part of his Italian-American Civil Rights League activities.

They had long ago learned that denying the existence of the Mafia was another way of calling attention to it. Ignoring their displeasure, Colombo went ahead with a giant rally on June 29, 1970 at Columbus Circle. It was a smashing success, with 50,000 persons in attendance. And it was too powerful a demonstration to be ignored by the politicians. Even Gov. Nelson Rockefeller accepted honorary membership in the league, despite its Colombo imprint.

Joe Colombo came out of it appearing, to himself at least, a hero. He laid new plans for extending the league's power. Meanwhile, some of Colombo's lieutenants fretted over the declining revenues of the family while the chief spent ever more time pushing the league instead of minding criminal business. These men approached the other families who were upset by Colombo's activities, and they agreed that he had become more than a mere tribulation. The leading voice among them was Carlo Gambino, whose life had been saved by Colombo's finking. Gratitude was one thing and business another.

It was decided to let the Gallo forces have a shot at Colombo. Joey Gallo jumped at the chance. The second Unity Day rally of the league was set for June 28, 1971. Gallo knew he and his men could not get close enough to kill Colombo, but he had other sources of strength. Of all the Italian racketeers,

Joe Gallo was the only one who had genuine power in the black gangster movement in Harlem.

On the morning of the 28th, Joe Colombo showed up early at the rally, as the crowd was just starting to form. A black man, Jerome A. Johnson, wearing a newspaper photographer's badge neared. When he was within a step of Colombo, he pulled out a pistol and fired three quick shots into the gang leader's head. Instantly, Colombo's bodyguards gunned down the assassin.

Johnson died on the spot. Colombo did not, but he suffered such brain damage that he turned into a vegetable. He died seven years later in an upstate hospital.

See also: *Banana War, Crazy Joe Gallo.*

COLONEL Plug (?-1820?): River pirate

With Bully Wilson, Colonel Plug was one of the two most important pirates who preyed on boat traffic along the Ohio and Mississippi rivers. A bewhiskered giant whose real name was Fluger, Colonel Plug boasted he had been a colonel in the American Revolution. Plug's modus operandi was to hide aboard a flatboat that was tied up for the night. When it got going in the morning, he would dig out the caulking between the planks and bore holes in the bottom. Colonel Plug would time his work so that the boat would be scuttled opposite his hideout. His gang would row out to the flatboat in skiffs, supposedly coming to the rescue. The only person to be rescued would be Colonel Plug, of course, along with the cargo; the crew and passengers would be left to drown, or, if they resisted, to be shot. Colonel Plug was active for many years until, according to the legend, he bored too many holes one day and the boat he was sabotaging went to the bottom before Plug could climb out of the hold. At least, so the story was told in pirate circles, presumably accurate since suddenly Colonel Plug ceased to be a scourge of the rivers.

See also: *Cave-in-Rock Pirates, Piracy.*

COLONIAL Punishment

Punishment for crime tended to be less severe in Colonial America than in the countries from which most colonists had come. The New England colonies and the Quaker settlements in West Jersey and Pennsylvania had punishments that in general were less harsh than those used in New York and the South. In New England the main thrust of punishment came in the form of humiliation; thus when Mary Mandame of Plymouth became the supposed first female sex offender in 1639, she was required to wear a badge of shame on her left sleeve. Had she failed to do so, she would have been branded in the face with a hot iron, but the mere threat of this punishment brought compliance in almost all cases. Vagrancy brought punishment in the stocks, while the ducking stool was held ready for the scold. More serious crimes brought stricter penalties. Murder and witchcraft called for hanging, and burglars were branded.

The same crime called for far different punishments in various jurisdictions. Theft in New York was punishable by multiple restitution and whipping, but in numerous Southern colonies the death penalty was often exacted when the sum taken was more than 12 pence. In several New England settlements a gentleman could commit the following offenses and be fined a sum equivalent to $10: lie eight times; swear four times; beat his wife twice; or criticize a court once.

In the Massachusetts Bay Colony in the early 18th century punishment did not end with a mere flogging or confinement in the stocks. After initial punishment offenders were then required to wear on their arm or bosom for a year or many years a large letter cut from scarlet cloth. The letter identified the crime for which the offender had been punished, such as A for adultery, B for blasphemy, D for drunkenness, I for incest, P for poisoning, R for rape, T for thievery. However, it was soon decided that this punishment was too inhumane and it was abandoned.

Whippings were often carried to excess, with the result that the convicted person often was left crippled for life. In New England an attempt was made to prevent this abuse by limiting the number of lashes to 39, as called for under Mosaic law. Contrary to common belief, no one, not even a witch, was burned at the stake in New England. However, burning and quartering were practiced in New York and the South. In the

great Negro Plot of 1741 in New York, many blacks were put to the stake. Quartering was generally applied for treason and to blacks. In Maryland a black who murdered an overseer was punished by having a hand cut off, then hanging and finally quartering.

Perhaps the sternest punishments were carried out in Virginia. A slave who ran away might have an ear nailed to the pillory and then cut off. Criticism of the authorities in that colony meant an offender could be pilloried with a placard, lose both ears, do a year's service for the colony or have his ears nailed to the pillory. The most common punishment for the offense was being laid "neck and heels" in irons and then heavily fined. Virginia probably decreed more castrations of blacks than did any other colony.

See also: *Book Whippings, Branding, Flogging, Mary Mandame, Mutilation, Pillory, Salem Witchcraft Trials.*

COLT, John C. (1819-1842?): Murderer

John C. Colt was the central figure in a classic murder case in 1841 that started with a solution but concluded in a mystery.

Colt was a member of one of New York's millionaire merchant families and the brother of Samuel Colt, inventor of the Colt revolver and the Colt repeating rifle. At 22 John was tall, slim and handsome, with curly blond hair and steel gray eyes. The darling of society, he fancied himself a writer of sorts and numbered among his close friends Edgar Allan Poe, Washington Irving, James Fenimore Cooper, John Howard Payne, George Palmer Putnam and Lewis Clark.

Despite his literary bent, Colt had a quick, uncertain temper, and in a nasty argument he killed Samuel Adams, a printer he had hired to produce a book of his. Colt was tried speedily and sentenced to be hanged. There were those who said Colt would never hang, that his family was too powerful. Press exposes of Colt's treatment in the city's new prison, the Tombs, informed the public that Colt lived an exceedingly happy life for a condemned man. He had flowers on his table and a pet canary. A young Charles Dana reported: "In a patent extension chair he lolls smoking an aromatic Havana. . . . He has on an elegant dress-gown, faced with cherry-colored silk, and his feet are encased in delicately worked slippers." His food was "not cooked in the Tombs, but brought in from a hotel. It consists of a variety of dishes—quail on toast, game pates, reed birds, ortolans, fowl, vegetables, coffee, cognac."

The greatest concession to Colt's grand station was the permission granted by prison authorities that he be allowed to marry his fiancee Caroline Henshaw on the morning of November 18, the day of his execution. Newspaper announcements of the bizarre nuptials-gallows ceremony brought out thousands of thrill seekers who jammed Centre (later Center) Street at dawn. Miss Henshaw was forced to come by carriage to a side street entrance to the Tombs at about 11:30. During the actual wedding ceremony, carpenters assembling the gallows in the courtyard politely suspended their hammering, a fact a guard relayed to the crowd outside. The crowd moaned at that. It moaned again when word was passed, "They're married." Other news was passed as it happened. "The guests have gone. . . . There are silk curtains across the cell door. . . . They've ordered champagne. . . . They're testing the gallows!"

Shortly after 1 p.m. the new Mrs. Colt was advised that she had to leave, and she did so "smiling bravely." Later, there would be much conjecture over whether Caroline slipped her groom a large dagger with which he could stab himself in the heart and thus escape the noose. At 3:30 p.m. the Rev. Henry Anton, who had officiated at the wedding, was ordered to offer his final services to the condemned man. At that moment the tinder-dry wooden cupola atop the adjacent Hall of Justice mysteriously caught fire. Within three minutes smoke was pouring into the interior of the prison. Panic broke out and several guards raced out of the building. Convicts banged on their bars and begged to be let out, and some apparently were by the few remaining keepers. In the smoke-filled confusion, the Rev. Anton rushed up to Sheriff Monmouth Hart and cried: "Mr. Colt is dead! He has a dagger in his heart!"

Instead of proceeding to the cell, the sheriff rushed around in search of the doctor who was there to pronounce Colt dead after his now unnecessary execution. At 7 p.m. a hurriedly convened coroner's jury officially declared Colt had committed suicide. It was a remarkable hearing, with no official identification of Colt being made. Not even Rev. Anton was called to testify. The body was released and buried that same night in the yard of St. Mark's Church. Afterward, the recently widowed Mrs. Colt disappeared.

At first, the newspapers focused on the source of the death dagger, including in the speculation every member of the wedding party. Only when it later was conceded by officials that a number of prisoners had escaped during the fire, did it suddenly occur to anyone that Colt could have escaped in the confusion—if there was a body to substitute for him.

The *New York Herald* commented, "We have no doubt that Governor Seward will order an investigation at once into this most unheard of, most unparalleled tragedy." No investigation was ever held, however, although even George Walling, who was appointed chief of police shortly thereafter, gave considerable credence to the idea of a substitute corpse. So too did Colt's friends. In 1850 Edgar Allen Poe received an unsigned manuscript from Texas written in the unmistakable hand of John Colt. He took the manuscript to Lewis Clark, editor of *The Knickerbocker* magazine, and found Clark too had gotten a copy. They concluded it was Colt's way of letting them know he was alive and still trying for a literary career. Then in 1852 Samuel Everett, a close friend of Colt, returned from a visit to California and told others in the Colt circle of friends that he had met John Colt while horseback riding in the Santa Clara Valley. According to Everett, Colt lived in a magnificent hacienda with his wife, the former Caroline Henshaw.

Many students of crime dismiss the substitute corpse theory and regard Everett's story as apocryphal, insisting it was just an exotic fillip to an incredible tale. Others find the chain of events too mired in coincidence. That Colt should commit suicide just at the moment of a mysterious fire during which several prisoners escaped, they say, staggers the imagination. And why did the widowed Mrs. Colt disappear from New York City after her husband's death?

See also: *Tombs Prison.*

COLT .45: Early police weapon

Well into the 19th century, lawmen relied almost solely on nightsticks and muskets for weapons. In 1830 James D. Colt, while on a voyage at sea, whittled a wooden model of a new-style six-shot handgun. When he returned home, he started production but soon found that few law enforcement officers had much interest in the weapon. The one consistent buyer was the Texas Rangers. During the war with Mexico in 1846, the Texas Rangers refused to fight without their beloved Colts. This brought added fame to the Colt six-shooter and after the war most lawmen in the West used the weapon. They continued to do so until the first decade of the 20th century, when they switched to the smaller but potent .38-caliber Smith and Wesson, which most policemen in the rest of the country had already adopted as the basic firearm.

COMMISSION, The: Organized crime overseers

There is the mistaken impression that Organized Crime, in capital letters, is ruled by something called The Commission, also in capital letters, which is the ruling body of The Mafia. In point of fact, the Mafia is not organized crime (or the national crime syndicate) and above all, the commission does not rule over the forces of crime with the powers of life and death. Organized crime is not a monolith but rather a confederation of forces, and the commission is the body charged with seeing it remains no more than a confederation. It restrains itself from interfering with the internal operations of any member gang or crime family.

While the Mafia supplies many or most of the members of the commission, it does not totally control it, just as it does not fully control organized crime. The commission is composed of nine members drawn mostly from the 24 crime families that blanket the United States. While many of the commission members are rotated from this pool of 24 families, some non-Mafia members, especially Meyer Lansky, remain a regular and powerful participant in all syndicate discussions. For a time in the late 1940s and early 1950s the commission was dominated by the so-called Big Six, including Tony Accardo and Greasy Jake Guzik of the Chicago mob, the heirs of Al Capone. (While dominated by Mafia types, the Chicago mob, with its heavy Jewish and Irish membership, never really qualified as a Mafia crime family.) Frank Costello, the so-called Prime Minister of the underworld, who recognized the need for a broader base of support for the Mafia, was also one of the Big Six. Joe Adonis was another member, one whose power spread from Brooklyn to New Jersey and was closely tied to Costello's interests. The remaining two members were, like Guzik, Jews: Meyer Lansky and Abner "Longy" Zwillman.

Zwillman had been a Prohibition bootleg king who later infiltrated a number of legal enterprises and frequently played an important role in naming governors, attorneys general and mayors in New Jersey, political clout that made him vital to the commission. Lansky, of course, has for decades been vital to the syndicate in handling gambling enterprises for criminal elements in Miami, New Orleans, Las Vegas, the Bahamas, Saratoga, N.Y. and, in pre-Castro days, Cuba.

While Hollywood has never failed to portray the commission as ruthless and efficient, the group has by the very nature of its composition and assigned duties been somewhat less than all powerful. The commission's more notable failures include its inability to stifle the Profaci-Gallo war in Brooklyn and the more explosive Banana war, in which Joseph "Joe Bananas" Bonanno came close to becoming a new "boss of bosses." On the whole, however, the commission has undoubtedly done much to keep crime organized and operating in relative harmony.

See also: *Mafia*.

"COMPANY, Girls!": Brothel phrase

For over a century the traditional call of harlots to work in American houses of prostitution has been a madam's shout of "Company, girls!" Many historians of the subject have mistakenly credited the origin of the custom to a San Francisco madam named Tessie Wall; however, the call preceded Miss Tessie by at least three decades and appears to have been sounded first in San Francisco in a Sacramento Street brothel run by Madame Bertha Kahn. A large woman with a vibrant contralto voice, she would stride to the foot of the stairs and shout, "Company, girls!"

It had a certain genteel quality compared to such earlier calls as "All whores!" And in fact, Madame Bertha's establishment became one of the most popular of the 1870s. Her girls were dressed in red sandals, matching red velvet caps and long lacey white nightgowns. Unlike other bagnios, Madame Bertha's sold no liquor, and no obscene talk or rough conduct was permitted. Each bedroom bore a sign reading, "No Vulgarity Allowed in This Establishment." It is said that Madame Bertha also introduced to San Francisco charge accounts for regular customers. But she is best remembered for forbidding the prodding and feeling of the merchandise, which was the practice in other houses, and insisting her girls be refined in greeting company and in turn be treated as ladies by the company.

COMPUTER Crime

Computer crime is the least understood of all illegal activities because it is so new and steeped in a technology not as yet fully developed. The difficulty of detecting computer fraud has attracted many criminal minds. Some known swindles are monumental, such as the 64,000 fake insurance policies created between 1964 and 1973 on the Equity Funding Corp.'s computer. That operation involved $2 billion.

The main weakness in a computer system is that a criminal can perpetrate a fraud once he or she has learned the code or password that will activate the system. All a crook has to do is attach a typewriter-like keyboard terminal to an ordinary touch-tone telephone and issue instructions to the computer. In one case a bank employee simply programmed the firm's computer to divert over $120,000 from various customers' accounts to those of two friends. A clever scheme was pulled off by a programmer who ordered a computer to deduct sums from many accounts and credit them to dummy accounts, which he then emptied. In another case a bank employee embezzled more than $1 million to finance his betting on horse racing and basketball games. Ironically, his computer-based system for handicapping the horses proved nowhere near as efficient as his money diversion scheme.

With the discovery of each new method, computer practices are changed to prevent such fraud. Some sophisticated systems use fingerprints or voiceprints as a method of insuring their integrity, and the FBI has computer fraud experts who conduct training seminars for police officers and businessmen to combat this new type of crime. But it is obvious that computer fraud is itself a growth industry.

COMSTOCK, Anthony (1844-1915): Censor

The "great American bluenose," Anthony Comstock conducted a lifetime crusade against vice—as he saw it. He was responsible for the arrest of at least 3,000 persons for obscenity, destroyed 160 tons of "obscene literature" and got the Department of the Interior to fire Walt Whitman for publishing *Leaves of Grass* and the city of New York to ban Margaret Sanger's books on birth control. He proudly boasted that he had caused 16 persons to be hounded to death, either through fear or suicide, under his relentless attacks. He caused George Bernard Shaw to coin the word "Comstockery," which is defined in the *American College Dictionary* as "over-zealous censorship of the fine arts and literature, often mistaking outspokenly honest works for salacious productions."

At the age of 18, Comstock started his crusade against sin by breaking into a liquor store in New Canaan, Conn. and opening the spigots on all the kegs. Throughout the ensuing years, in concert with the Young Men's Christian Association, he launched a campaign against pornography. In 1873 he established the New York Society for the Suppression of Vice and labored as its secretary until his death 42 years later. In that same year Congress passed the Comstock Act, which banned obscene materials, including rubber prophylactics, from the mails. The Post Office appointed Comstock a special agent charged with enforcing the new law. As a result of his activities, publishers stripped their books of any explicit language, e.g., "pregnant" became "enceinte."

What constituted pornography or sin was determined by Comstock's fanatical puritanism. Female crusader Victoria Claflin Woodhull was hauled into court for what Comstock considered a "crime," her exposure of a love affair between clergyman Henry Ward Beecher and a parishioner's wife. In 1905 Comstock instituted actions against George Bernard Shaw's play *Mrs. Warren's Profession*. Shaw, who had already invented the word Comstockery, warmed to this opportunity to do battle with the censor, declaring: "Comstockery is the world's standing joke at the expense of the U.S. It confirms the deep-seated conviction of the Old World that America is a provincial place, a second-rate country town." The resultant publicity made the play a box office sensation. Such was also the case when Comstock leveled his sights at the innocuous nude painting *September Morn*, by Paul Chabas. The publicity generated by Comstock's blasts made the painting a monumental success, after it had been rejected as being too tame for a barber shop calendar.

In 1915 President Woodrow Wilson named Comstock the U.S. representative to the International Purity Congress in San Francisco. Although in failing health, Comstock was a fiery figure at the congress. But he lost a humiliating battle in that city's courts during the congress when he arrested some department-store window dressers for putting clothes on five bare wax models in full view of passersby. A San Francisco judge listened to the charges the next morning and promptly dismissed the case. "Mr. Comstock," said the judge, "I think you're nuts."

Comstock came back home and died shortly after, on September 21, 1915. He was buried in Brooklyn, New York City, his epitaph reading, "In memory of a fearless witness."

See also: *Madame Restell, September Morn*.

CONFESSIONS

In the "old days," as veteran policemen will admit, the standard way for the police to extract confessions was through the time-honored "third degree." In the 1920s one of New York's legendary cops, Johnny Broderick, imparted the keen deductive processes he used to solve a certain case. "Ah, it was nothing," he said. "All I did was bat around some guys until they told me what I wanted to know." Four decades before that, Chief Inspector Alexander S. Williams, better known as "Clubber" Williams, explained to his men the art of cracking cases with just three words, "Beat, beat, beat."

Some years ago a California police authority once listed the only three possible results of third-degree treatment: the suspect would finally confess to anything, guilty or not; he would go insane; or he would die. Since by the 1930s too much of this had occurred, a presidential fact-finding group known as the Wickersham Commission was assigned to investigate the extent of third-degree practices around the county. Its report of brutal treatment in 29 large cities from coast to coast led to such a public outcry that many police departments finally mended their ways, or at least, forced confessions dropped in a number of cities.

The pattern of reform however, was mixed, particularly because in some cities the practice was more entrenched than in others. Even in recent times the saying in Philadelphia was, "If you get arrested in this town, your only defense may be the telephone company." It was meant literally. According to official findings, one of the methods used by Philadelphia police to question a suspect was to put a telephone book on his head and then hammer on it. Somehow, guilty or not, the record shows quite a few suspects confessed under this treatment.

The record also indicates that telephone book interrogation was not the only one employed by the Philadelphia police. A case in point occurred in October 1975. At that time the family of Radames Santiago was on the alert because of several recent firebombings in their neighborhood and had stationed a 14-year-old youth to keep guard on their tiny porch during the night. At 3:20 one morning a Molotov cocktail, a bottle filled with gasoline and stuffed with a flaming rag, crashed through the window of the house. As the screams of Mrs. Santiago and her four children filled the night, a passerby, 26-year-old Robert "Reds" Wilkinson, returning home from celebrating his first wedding anniversary, rang a fire alarm. By the time the fire engines arrived, the screams had stopped—Mrs. Santiago and her children were dead.

It didn't take the police long to latch on to a suspect. According to an old axiom, an arsonist often turns in the alarm to his own handiwork. That, as far as the police were concerned, pointed the finger of guilt at Wilkinson. The only thing needed was that he be interrogated and make a confession. Wilkinson did not get the telephone book treatment. Instead, before each question someone slapped him hard across the face. Wilkinson, with no police record at all, insisted he did not do the firebombing. Another slap, another question. Then with each slap Wilkinson was warned that unless he confessed, "You'll never see your wife and baby again."

While this was going on, Mrs. Wilkinson was being abused in another room. A police officer constantly screamed at her: "We already know your husband did it. Tell us the truth, or you'll never see your baby again."

Hour after hour the slapping went on. And at the same time, seven other "witnesses" were also being verbally abused and beaten until they gave "evidence" against Wilkinson. They all fell in line, and after nine solid hours of punishment, Wilkinson did the only thing he was by then capable of doing: he confessed.

The case seemed air-tight. The culprit had confessed, and there was a host of witnesses against him. The 14-year-old boy who was standing guard positively identified Wilkinson as the firebomber. Wilkinson was sent to prison for murder and arson, but fortunately for him a later federal investigation cleared him of any involvement in the case. All the witnesses admitted they had been pressured by the police into giving false testimony. The 14-year-old guard had fallen asleep and was too ashamed to admit it; when the police informed him Wilkinson was guilty, he was all too willing to agree with them.

While third-degree confessions obviously still occur, they are definitely on the decline, as much because of the sloppiness of the method as due to public revulsion. J. Edgar Hoover once stated: "My indignation against the third degree arises from practical as well as humanitarian reasons. No matter how viciously they beat and abuse their suspects, the average third-degree officer manages to convict only about one out of every five prisoners whom he takes into court. That is a record of 20 percent efficiency."

In comparison, the FBI's record on confessions has always been phenomenal. An agency that gets about 97 convictions out of every 100 arrests, the FBI has actually gone into court with confessions in up to 94 percent of its cases during some periods. Yet, as American Civil Liberties Union counsel Morris L. Ernst, a veteran of countless battles involving violations of an individual's civil rights has stated, the charge of third degree "is almost never raised against the FBI."

What the FBI employs instead is a psychological approach, often using what is known as the "one-two" or "Mutt-and-Jeff" technique. A typical case was one in which the agency was called when a batch of rifles was stolen from an Army post. The military officers had a suspect, the only person who logically could have taken and disposed of the rifles with ease. But they had no proof. The agents knew that to get a confession, they had to find the emotional key to the suspect's mind. Usually, it's love or pride or even a happy memory of a childhood incident.

The agents tried one trick after another but couldn't get the suspect talking. Then the man was asked how long he had been in the Army.

"Nine years," the soldier answered with pride.

The FBI men knew they had their angle. Isn't it a joke, one of them said, how the Army couldn't even clear up a little matter like some missing rifles without having to call in the FBI. "Does this brass think all we have to do is stuff like this?" The conversation continued to set the pattern of thought that it was almost disloyal for anyone to put the Army in such a spot, making it a laughing stock. After about an hour or so, the FBI men left the room and told the company commander to go inside. The soldier saluted him and said: "Sir, I stole those rifles. I wouldn't tell those bastards, but I want to tell you."

Most police forces now use variations of the one-two or Mutt and Jeff to get confessions. The first detective to question the suspect will generally come on strong, talking tough and trying to antagonize or frighten him. His teammate then moves in gently, befriending the suspect. The second man stands out as a friend in a sea of foes and becomes, so to speak, the prisoner's father confessor. Sometimes the friendly detective pretends to be on the outs with the suspect's chief tormentor. He may, if the prisoner's condition has made him so gullible as to believe almost anything, suggest that the tough officer is out for his scalp, trying to boot him off the squad or even off the force. Both he and the suspect are thus kindred souls, oppressed by the same villain. The whole thrust of the approach is to find a way to "stick it to" the enemy detective. The friendly one tells the suspect, "If you are going to confess, say you'll only do it if *he* leaves the room." In the Mutt-and-Jeff technique, this brings

on a strong emotional response that can produce a fast confession before the feeling wears off.

Men who have succumbed to the Mutt and Jeff often wonder afterwards what made them "be sucker enough to confess." However, members of the psychiatric fraternity, realizing the effect of the technique, have invented the term "menticide" for this shrewd wearing down of a suspect's mind. Anyone, experts say, can be made to confess to anything if the pressure is great enough.

Even the new tightened rules that require officers to inform a suspect of his right to have counsel present during interrogation can be gotten around by the sort of emotional response evoked by this new-wave type of police questioning, a method that in large part has rendered the third degree obsolete.

See also: *Confessions, False.*

CONFESSIONS, False

In Chicago during the 1950s a pregnant woman was viciously slain and her body dumped in a snowbank. Almost immediately a factory worker came forth and confessed. He stood a good chance of becoming a modern-day lynching victim since a spirit of vengeance dominated the woman's neighborhood. That sentiment dissipated, however, when a 19-year-old sailor at the Great Lakes Naval Station also confessed to the slaying. This second confession turned out to be the real one.

In 1961 a young widow in New York tearfully told police she had killed her husband several years earlier. His death had been attributed to natural causes. The body was exhumed and an autopsy performed. The man had died of natural causes, and psychiatrists found the woman was merely suffering from delusions which stemmed from a guilt complex that she had failed to be a good wife to her late husband.

Both of these persons could easily have been convicted of the crimes to which they so eagerly confessed. Throughout hundreds of years of legal history, the confession has been viewed by the courts and society as the "queen of proofs" of criminal guilt. Yet, each year probably thousands of persons in this country confess to crimes that they did not, and could not, have committed. Why do they do it? Some are neurotics who will confess to any crime just for the excitement of being the center of attention; for example, more than 200 persons confessed to the Lindbergh baby kidnapping. Others are motivated by bizarre guilt feelings for some other incident, often trivial; they seek punishment, consciously or subconsciously, for a crime they did not commit.

Whenever legal experts discuss false confessions, the subject of the mutiny of the *Hermione* is raised. The *Hermione* was a British frigate captained by a harsh disciplinarian named Pigot. In September 1797 the seething anger of the crew erupted against Pigot and his officers. The men of the *Hermione* not only murdered the captain and the officers, they butchered them. The crew then sailed to an enemy port, but one young midshipman escaped and got back to England. He identified many of the offenders, and some of them were run down and hanged.

Many innocent sailors confessed to taking part in the *Hermione* mutiny. One Admiralty officer later wrote:

> In my own experience, I have known, on separate occasions, more than six sailors who voluntarily confessed to having struck the first blow at Captain Pigot. These men detailed all the horrid circumstances of the mutiny with extreme minuteness and perfect accuracy. Nevertheless, not one of them had even been in the ship, nor had so much as seen Captain Pigot in their lives. They had obtained from their messmates the particulars of the story. When long on a foreign station, hungering and thirsting for home, their minds became enfeebled. At length, they actually believed themselves guilty of the crime over which they had so long brooded, and submitted with a gloomy pleasure to being sent to England in irons for judgment. At the Admiralty, we were always able to detect and establish their innocence.

The last sentiment was, of course, self-serving and perhaps not shared by all. Sir Samuel Romilly related the fate of another seaman who confessed to taking part in the same incident. He was executed. Later, Sir Samuel learned that when the mutiny had taken place on the *Hermione,* the sailor was at Portsmouth aboard the *Marlborough.*

American criminal history is replete with persons confessing to crimes and indeed to noncrimes. The classic case of the latter occurred in Vermont during the 19th century, when two brothers, Stephen and Jesse Boorn, confessed in colorful detail the slaying of Russell Colvin, their brother-in-law. They were both sentenced to death, but Jesse, in recognition of the fact that he had confessed first, had his sentence commuted to life. Stephen's hanging was only postponed when Colvin fortuitously returned home after an absence of seven years, during which time he had had no idea that he had been "murdered."

Probably the great-granddaddy of all cases involving false confessions was the Los Angeles murder of Elizabeth Short in 1947. The case was to become famous as the Black Dahlia murder. The police took full written confessions from at least 38 suspects, and after more than 200 others had telephoned their admissions of guilt and offers to surrender, the police stopped keeping count of confessions.

In the Black Dahlia case the number of confessions was attributable to the sadistic nature of the crime. Such vile crimes invariably produce great numbers of confessions, as though the neurotic confessors literally beg for the spotlight of revulsion and contempt. Many, experts say, are made by persons propelled by a death wish and eager to find the most spectacular method of committing suicide, e.g., in the Black Dahlia case, going to the gas chamber. Others have different motivations. When a girl named Selma Graff was bludgeoned to death by a burglar in Brooklyn during the 1950s, the police got the usual rash of phony confessions. One of them came from a young ex-con out on probation for auto theft. He carried within him a vicious hatred for his mother, who was always so embarrassed by his criminal traits and who at the moment was threatening to notify his parole officer that he had been visiting bars. So he walked into police headquarters and gave himself up for the Graff killing. His story proved to be a hoax when he was unable to supply the murder weapon and could not describe the Graff home accurately. Finally admitting his falsehood, he said he gladly would have gotten himself convicted of the murder, even gone to the chair, in order to torment his mother.

Privately, even some former prosecutors say all confessions should be suspect, that it is illogical to expect that a police officer who has worked hard to extract a confession from a suspect will be just as diligent in his efforts to test whether the confession is true or not. More often, the police and prosecutors have clung to discredited confessions in an effort to convict someone who later proved to be an innocent man. A case in point was George Whitmore, Jr., the man who was wrongly accused of the notorious "career girl" sex slayings of Janice Wylie and Emily Hoffert in their Manhattan apartment in 1963. Whitmore-type incidents, especially repudiated confessions, were cited by the Supreme Court in the landmark Miranda decision, which led to curbs on police powers to interrogate suspects. Some attorneys, such as O. John Rogge, a former assistant attorney general of the United States and author of the book *Why Men Confess,* hold to the theory that no repudiated confession should ever be used in court. They believe that the Supreme Court is gradually moving, perhaps with some steps backward from time to time, in that direction. Quite naturally, prosecuting attorneys claim that such action will make convictions next to impossible to obtain.

See also: *Black Dahlia, Boorn Brothers, Harold Israel, Janice Wylie.*

CONNORS, Babe (1856-1918): St. Louis madam

Outside of the bagnios of New Orleans, no brothel contributed more to the arts than the famous St. Louis parlor of a plump mulatto madam named Babe Connors. More than most practitioners of her trade, Babe thought of her places, especially her famous Palace which she opened in 1898, not only as houses of sexual pleasure but also as centers of entertainment, mostly erotic of course, but musical as well. The Palace itself was a work of art, featuring magnificent crystal chandeliers, extremely expensive rugs, tapestries and objets d'art. Babe staged renowned shows in which her most lovely octoroons danced on a mirrored floor wearing elegant evening gowns and no underclothes. But the highlight of the show was always music and song. For years Babe presented the incredible old black singer Mama Lou. Mama, who wore the traditional calico dress, gingham apron and bright bandana, gave forth with famous downhome field songs and blues. Music-loving whites flocked to Babe Connors' establishment to listen to Mama Lou. Even the great Ignace Paderewski journeyed to hear Mama Lou and accompany her on the parlor piano in the early 1890s. Virtually all of Mama Lou's songs were obscene, but many provided the original melodies for such later hits as "Bully Song" and "Hot Time in the Old Town Tonight."

While Babe Connors' resorts, such as the Palace on Chestnut Street and the earlier Castle on Sixth Street, were among the most lavish in the country, racial law and custom restricted their profit level to about a third or less than what other great houses of the period netted. But even as $5 houses, Babe Connors' famed resorts produced revenues that made her among the most illustrious women of her kind and allowed her to live in fun-loving elegance. Her open carriage was one of the sights at Forest Park, where Babe, bedecked with feathered boa and parasol, rode by in regal splendor, nodding her head only at those gentlemen who acknowledged her first. In her later years Babe converted to Catholicism and, unlike most of her scarlet sisters, was permitted burial in consecrated ground.

CONSCIENCE Fund: Anonymous donation money

Every day the U.S. Treasury receives money, often anonymously, from persons who, having stolen or otherwise withheld money from the government, have become conscious-stricken and have decided to pay up. "Conscience money" is the popular term for these sums, although it enters the records as "Miscellaneous receipts: Moneys received from persons unknown." Sums received have varied from as little as one cent to $80,000.

One immigrant wrote that he had achieved success in his adopted country and was therefore upset because he had avoided a tax payment of $30 some 30 years previous. He enclosed $50 to cover the payment on the principal plus interest. Most contributors do indeed add the interest. Some go to unusual lengths to make sure their money goes where it truly belongs this time. One man, taking care that the money was not stolen in the mail or up on receipt, cut a total of $250 in half and sent the halves to two separate government bureaus with an explanation of his actions. Another sent in only a half of each bill and demanded a receipt for these before sending the other half.

Many of the donors to the conscience fund are former government employees weighed down by the knowledge that they illegally appropriated government supplies or money. Other persons confess failing to pay certain taxes and customs duties or even under-stamping mail. Remarkably, very few say their conscience money is to cover income tax underpayments.

The biggest contribution ever made came from an anonymous donor of a total of $80,000. Sending in $30,000 as his final installment, the person wrote:

> This amount makes a sum aggregating $80,000 which I have sent the United States, or four times the amount which I stole years ago. I have hesitated about sending all this money because I think it does not really belong to the government, but conscience has given me no rest until I have consummated the four-fold return like Zacchaeus, the Publican of old. That every thief may understand the awfulness of the sin of stealing is the sincere wish of a penitent. Let no one claim any of this amount on any pretext.

When details of this donation were printed, a woman wrote in to claim part of it. She said her husband, an habitual drunkard, was the anonymous donor and had sent in $15,000 too much. She demanded its return. Treasury investigators checked out the woman's claim and found it spurious.

No effort is made by the government to otherwise determine the identity of a donor. The official government position is that it will not prosecute persons making restitution. If requested, it will even mail a formal receipt—with no questions asked. This attitude of nonprosecution is not necessarily all that high-minded. It is recognized that if prosecutions were undertaken, the flow of conscience money would cease.

CONSIGLIERE: Mafia "hearing officer"

The press and various books revealing the "inside" story on organized crime have spread a fundamental misconception about the post of *consigliere* in the Mafia. He is often pictured as the operating brains of a crime family, the adviser to the Don, the master planner. The role is far less important. Originally, it was little more than a public relations invention of Lucky Luciano, probably the most brilliant leader the Mafia ever produced.

By 1932 Luciano had risen to the zenith of power, having engineered the murders of Giuseppe "Joe the Boss" Masseria and Salvatore Maranzano on the Night of the Sicilian Vespers. With these killings Luciano became in fact if not in name the new "boss of bosses," a position previously held by Masseria and then Maranzano.

It was now in Luciano's interests to bring the killings to a halt; he therefore announced the establishment of the position of *consigliere,* with one to be named in each crime family. The function of the *consigliere* was that of a hearing officer who would have to clear any plan to knock off a member of the Mafia before a hit could be made. Thus, it would be possible for everyone to get back to plucking the fruits of crime and to reduce intrafamily warfare. If he disapproved because the reasons for the killing were unjust, there would be no hit. It was a marvelous cosmetic device that gave Mafia members a sense of "law and order." In actuality, no hearing officer would ever dare interfere with the orders of the top bosses, and the record shows that none ever has. But the position hangs on to this day, having long ago served Luciano's purposes and fostered an image of himself as Lucky the Just.

CONTRACT: Mob killing assignment

The word "contract" has graduated from argot into common English. However, underworld murders by hire are arranged through an elaborate technique little understood by the general public. The importance of the use of a contract is the protection it affords the party ordering the execution. He is completely isolated from the trigger man, never talking to him about the job. Instead, he lets the contract to a second party. This person then selects the hit man, or killer. Even this person will sometimes have the order passed by another party. All negotiations are handled one to one, so that even if someone in the line of command eventually talks, the authorities still do not have the vital corrobative witness required to make a case against whomever he informs on.

This shrewd procedure protected Albert Anastasia, the Lord High Executioner of Murder, Inc., again and again. The same caution protected the planners of the October 1957 rub-out of Anastasia himself, even though the name of the man who ordered it was no secret to the police. Anastasia was eliminated as part of Vito Genovese's strategy to take control of the major portion of New York crime. In a cunning stroke, Genovese gave the contract to Carlo Gambino, the number two man in Anastasia's crime family. Gambino was ambitious and saw he would ascend to Anastasia's throne if the crime boss was eliminated. Gambino accepted the contract but in turn protected himself by passing it on to Joe Profaci, another top Mafia leader. Profaci then picked as hit men the three brothers, Crazy Joey, Larry and Albert "Kid Blast" Gallo. It has never been fully established whether Crazy Joey and Larry personally carried out the famed execution of Anastasia in a Manhattan hotel barber shop or whether they merely acted as spotters, pointing out the victim to the person whom they may have passed the hit contract to.

This near-scientific method of parceling out contracts explains why virtually all gang murders end up unsolved. In Chicago from 1919 until February 1, 1967, there were approximately 1,000 gangland executions, but only in 13 of these cases was there a conviction.

CONVICT Labor System

Throughout the years and in different jurisdictions, various forms of convict labor systems developed. In the earliest form, manufacturers supplied prisons with raw materials, supervised the work of the convicts and marketed the goods they made. The pay for the convicts' labor went to the state. Then some states switched to piece work, whereby the prison authorities supervised the work and got paid on delivery of the finished products.

Early in the 19th century leasing convicts for work outside prison walls became common, especially in mines and sawmills and for railroad construction. The employers paid a lump sum for the leased workers and were responsible for board and discipline. Excesses and abuses marked this system, as prisoners were generally overworked, underfed and often brutalized. The system continued to grow well into the latter half of the century, when union opposition became fierce and frequently turned violent, more against the outside employers than against the convicts, a notable instance occurring in Tennessee in 1891-92. Consequently, the convict lease system virtually died in the first decade of the 20th century.

Ironically, the working conditions of the convicts did not improve as the prisons switched to turning out goods themselves and, when this foundered because of business opposition, to manufacturing items solely for governmental use. The states proved to be harsh exploiters of convict labor. In the South especially, states found a new outlet for leasing, providing convicts to the counties for road construction. This produced the great excesses of the Southern chain gangs. Since World War II, when most chain gang abuses ended, convicts have labored producing goods for the use of the state and other political subdivisions. The prisoners are paid only enough to buy cigarettes or candy, an irritant said to be the cause of much convict discontent. Reformers insist this dissatisfaction will continue until prisoners' pay is raised enough to let them provide some assistance to their families.

See also: *Chain Gangs, Convict Lease Battles.*

CONVICT Lease Battles

Probably few methods of strikebreaking during the 19th century aroused the ire of unionists more than that of the convict lease system, whereby employers could rent convict labor from the state whenever faced with a work stoppage.

The procedure was in very wide use in Tennessee, where it always set off violent conflicts with civilian workers. One of the state's greatest confrontations was an escalating battle during 1891-92. In Briceville mine owners leased 40 convicts to take over a mine idled by a strike and had them rip down the miners' houses and erect a stockade for themselves. Ten days later, on July 15, 1891, 300 heavily armed miners overwhelmed the stockade, marched the convicts, their guards and some management officials to the railroad station and put them on a train to Knoxville. The following day the convicts were brought back, escorted by 125 militiamen led personally by the governor. Outrage spread through the surrounding area, and on July 20 a force of 2,000 miners confronted the militia and again succeeded in marching them and the convicts to the depot and sending them all back to Knoxville. The governor responded by sending in 600 militiamen, but a truce was agreed upon to allow the legislature to hold a special session for the purpose of repealing the convict lease law. Under lobbying by business interests, however, the legislators failed to act, and the miners returned to the use of force. In early October they evicted several hundred convicts and burned three stockades to the ground. In December the governor brought the convicts back and had Fort Anderson built. This was a permanent military barracks, guarded by 175 troopers and a Gatling gun and surrounded by trenches. Matters festered for the next several months, while the nation's attention focused on the great Homestead steel strike in Pennsylvania. In August 1892 similar trouble developed at the Oliver Springs mine in Anderson County. When miners marched on the convicts' stockade, the guards fired and several miners were wounded. Miners poured into the area, marched on the stockade again and forced the guards to lay down their arms. The strikers followed their usual practice of burning the facility to the ground and returning the convicts and their guards to Knoxville. The miners then marched on Fort Anderson and placed it under siege. The arrival of 500 soldiers routed the miners, and they were taken into custody and locked up in churches, schoolhouses and railroad cars. The revolt had been crushed but local juries soon released all the miners. It was clear that resistance was too great to the convict lease system and that it could not be made to work; soon thereafter, it was abolished.

COOK, David J. (1842-1907): Lawman

A remarkable Western crime fighter, Dave Cook never achieved the press of an Earp, Hickok or Masterson, but it was not for lack of trying. His memoirs, published in 1882 under the title of *Hands Up! or Twenty Years of Detective Work in the Mountains and on the Plains,* is an almost incredible account of robbery, shoot-outs and bloodletting that stakes his claim to being one of the most violent characters of the West, even allowing for a certain amount of exaggeration. Cook did make a total of 3,000 arrests, many, of course, for minor offenses, and that meant contending with a lot of quick tempers and quick triggers.

Cook was born in Indiana in 1842, and after working as a farmhand in the corn belt, he moved on to Colorado in 1859. Joining the Colorado Cavalry in the Civil War, he was assigned to detective duty tracking spies, gold smugglers and the like and earned himself enough of a reputation to become city marshal of Denver in 1866. Subsequently, he served as a federal marshal and later as a range private eye. Cook was credited with almost single-handedly wiping out the Musgrove-Franklin gang that terrorized Colorado in the 1860s, running down Musgrove in 1868 and holding him in jail to lure Franklin into a rescue attempt. Franklin arrived in Denver with that idea in mind, but Cook learned he was hiding out in the Overland Hotel and burst into his room to find the outlaw lying on the bed with nothing on except a pair of long johns and a gun belt. When Franklin went for his piece, Cook, to use his own words, sent "a ball crashing through his very heart."

If Cook had a failing, it appears to have been a singular propensity to lose his prisoners to lynchers. But that may have been one of his maxims for staying alive. Another was, "Never hit a man over the head with a pistol, because afterward you may want to use your weapon and find it disabled." Thanks to such rules, one of the most gunfight-prone lawmen the West ever saw was able to die with his boots off. He passed away on April 2, 1907.

See also: *Lee H. Musgrove.*

COOK, Dr. Frederick A. (1865-1940): Explorer and land fraud conspirator

Dr. Frederick A. Cook is most famous for his dispute with Commodore Robert E. Peary over who was the first to reach the North Pole. For a brief time, Dr. Cook was hailed throughout the world after announcing he had reached the North Pole. However, shortly thereafter, Peary made the same claim and labeled all of Cook's claims false. In the controversy that followed, Peary clearly gained the upper hand and Cook was to keep only a few believers. He returned home disheartened and

in disgrace, and things were to get worse for him. In the 1920s Cook's name was used to promote a Texas oil-land sale that was branded fraudulent. While there was much reason to believe that Cook was not an active member of the fraud, he had a famous name and thus made an excellent target. He was convicted of using the mails to defraud and sentenced to 14 years. After working as a prison doctor in Leavenworth, he was released in 1931. Considering that the lands in question were now selling at prices well above the so-called fraud figure, it would indeed have been unseemly to hold him longer. President Franklin D. Roosevelt granted Dr. Cook a presidential pardon shortly before the latter's death in 1940.

COOK, William (1929-1952): Mass murderer

Few mass murderers have ever gone on a worse bloodletting spree than the one 21-year-old Billy Cook launched on December 30, 1950. On that day, Cook, posing as a hitchhiker, forced a motorist at gunpoint to get into the trunk of his own car and then drove off. Over the next two weeks Cook went on a senseless killing rampage. He kidnapped nearly a dozen people, including a deputy sheriff; murdered six in cold blood, including three children; attempted other killings; and generally terrorized the Southwest border area.

A hell raiser as a child, Cook was in and out of reform schools. He sported a tattooed letter between the knuckle and first joint of each finger of each hand, and when he held his hands together, the letters spelled H-A-R-D-L-U-C-K, an obvious form of self-pity that in retrospect psychologists said fostered a feeling of persecution. He clearly turned this feeling outward, even shrieking to his lawyer in the San Quentin death house, "I hate them; I hate their guts—everybody!"

Cook exhibited that feeling from the moment he kidnapped his first victim, a motorist, near Lubbock, Tex. Luckily for the motorist, he was able to force open the trunk and escaped on a small road. Far less lucky was the family of Carl Mosser. Mosser, his wife, Thelma, and their three small children were on a motor trip from Illinois to New Mexico when they picked up the killer. Cook soon produced a gun and forced Mosser to drive on. Following the gunman's mercurial directions, they went to Carlsbad, N.M., to El Paso, to Houston. After a time, Cook shot and killed all five of them and, for good measure, the family dog. He dumped their bodies in an abandoned mine shaft just outside Joplin, Mo.

Eventually, the Mossers' car was found abandoned near Tulsa, Okla. The car was a complete shambles, the upholstery blood-soaked and ripped open by bullets. Then their bodies were discovered. But Cook left something in the car besides bullets, a receipt for a gun he had bought. The killer's identity was learned and a massive manhunt was launched. Cook headed for California and there kidnapped a deputy sheriff who had almost captured him. He forced the deputy to drive him around while he bragged about killing the Mosser family.

After a 40-mile ride in the deputy's car, Cook ordered the

lawman to stop. "Out," he ordered his prisoner. Then he forced the deputy to lie down in a gully and tied his hands behind him. "I won't bother to tie your feet because I'm going to put a bullet through your head anyway," Cook said.

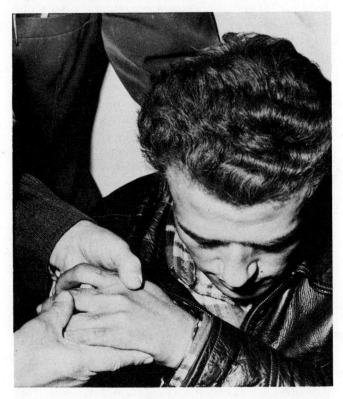

Police officers hold up left hand of mass murderer Billy Cook to show "Hard Luck" tattoo across his fingers.

The mass murderer was just having his joke. He drove off as the officer waited for the shot that would kill him. A short time later, Cook stopped another motorist, Robert Dewey, whom he did kill. With the alarm for him covering the Western half of the country, Cook headed into Mexico, kidnapping two other men. In the little town of Santa Rosalia, 400 miles below the border, Cook, with his hostages in tow, was recognized by the police chief. The officer simply walked up to Cook, snatched a gun from the killer's belt and placed him under arrest. Cook was rushed back to the border and turned over to FBI agents. On December 12, 1952 he died in the gas chamber at San Quentin for the Dewey murder.

COOKSON Hills, Oklahoma: Outlaw hideout

Ranking with such outlaw refuges as Hole in the Wall and Robber's Roost, the Cookson Hills of Oklahoma have harbored badmen of all kinds over the last two centuries.

With its endless peaks and twisted gullies, the Cooksons have served as the hideout for the Bandit Queen, Belle Starr, and, in this century, for public enemy Pretty Boy Floyd. In 1979 the hills again made the news when a 57-year-old Army

Air Corps deserter from World War II came out after hiding there for 36 years. Pvt. D. B. Benson had hidden in one abandoned shack or temporary shelter after another ever since going AWOL from the service in June 1943. From time to time he roamed the woods and mountains into Arkansas but was rarely seen. While newsmen were amazed at his feat, lawmen were not. "A lawbreaker can get lost in those hills for all his life and live off the land without ever being caught," one said.

COOLEY, Scott (1845-?): Texas Ranger and murderer

The man who ignited the Mason County War of 1875, Scott Cooley is often cited as the type of gunslinger who never should have been a Texas Ranger. To be fair to the Rangers, it should be pointed out that Cooley's major offenses occurred after he left that organization, where his record was nondescript. Cooley had been attracted to big money, which in Texas during the 1870s meant cattle money, and he became close with a number of cattlemen, including Timothy Williamson of Mason County.

In September 1875 Williamson was shot to death by a mob as he was being taken to jail for rustling by Deputy Sheriff John Worley. This was the official start of the Mason County War, although it might have ended there. Most similar wars in the Old West generally sprang from obvious monetary motives, such as cattleman vs. cattleman or vs. sheep man or vs. homesteader. If the Mason County warfare began that way, it soon became a matter of friends choosing sides. Williamson was Cooley's friend, and the latter blamed Worley for being involved in the killing. Riding to the lawman's home, he shot him dead and then cut off his ears, which he showed around as an example of what awaited all the anti-Williamsons in the county. Cooley was good to his word, and several more murders were attributed to him and his friends, just as others were linked to Williamson's enemies. About a year later, the Texas Rangers were sent in and the fighting ended. But Cooley never was brought to justice for his crimes. What happened to him is not known, although there was talk that he was killed in 1876. However, the record shows the Rangers continued to hunt for him long after that, without success.

See also: *Frank Jones, Mason County War, Texas Rangers.*

COONS, William (1838-1881): Murderer and Western lynch victim

The "stringing up" of William Coons, a relatively minor outlaw in the Old West, was, besides having a touch of rather macabre humor, illustrative of the region's theory and practice of lynching, which was that the man with the fewest friends got hanged more readily.

Coons, a homesteader, spent two years working his land in Lincoln County, N.M. without incident; the only bad mark against him during this time was a suspicion that he was doing a spot of rustling and hog stealing on the side. Then in 1881 Coons got into a dispute with John Flemming, a neighbor, over water rights. One day in April he rode over to Flemming's place and shot him dead. Since Flemming was hit in the chest, Coons claimed that Flemming had gone for his gun first. In point of fact, according to witnesses, Coons drew on Flemming and started shooting while his neighbor's back was turned. After Coons missed several shots, Flemming turned around and was hit full in the chest. However, when Sheriff Pat Garrett investigated, the witnesses couldn't be found, having fled out of fear of Coons. Flemming's friends started some lynch talk, but Coons had his supporters, and the matter became a Mexican standoff. The following month Coons celebrated his 43rd birthday with about a dozen supporters. Quite a few other apparent well-wishers showed up at Coons' home, and it appeared the Flemming people had decided to let the past be forgotten. When the Coons people were "plastered good," the Flemming forces all drew guns, herded the drunken celebrants into a bedroom and locked them up. Bill Coons suddenly found himself facing an impromptu court, with the evidence of the eyewitnesses now presented against him. He was found guilty and sentenced to be hanged forthwith from a tree outside his house. Since it was Coons' birthday, however, the members of the court and jury felt obliged to help the condemned man finish off the party's supply of whiskey. Then, in further deference to the occasion, an improvised band formed to play at the hanging. Since there were more Flemming supporters than Coons' men in Lincoln County, no arrests were ever made for the lynching.

See also: *Lynching.*

"COOPER, D. B." (?-?): Legendary airline hijacker

A hijacker who commandeered an airliner, collected a $200,000 ransom and then apparently parachuted to earth, "D. B. Cooper" achieved folk hero status in the Pacific Northwest. His daring 1971 exploit made him the perpetrator of the nation's only unsolved skyjacking. D. B. Cooper T-shirts were sold, and books about his crime were written. The community of Ariel, Wash., near the spot where Cooper was believed to have landed, has held annual daylong celebrations on the anniversary of the crime.

On Thanksgiving eve 1971, a man calling himself D. B. Cooper bought a ticket for a Northwest Orient Airlines flight from Portland, Ore. to Seattle, Wash. Once airborne, Cooper, wearing dark glasses, told a flight attendant he had a bomb in his briefcase and demanded $200,000 in $20 bills and four parachutes. After the plane, a 727 Trijet, landed in Seattle, the hijacker released the 36 passengers and all but three of the crew upon receipt of the ransom money. He then ordered the 727 be flown to Reno, Nev. When the plane landed in Reno, there was no trace of Cooper, but the rear exit door under the tail was open. The FBI theorized that Cooper, dressed only in a business suit and street shoes, jumped from the plane over southwest Washington into a howling wind and a freezing rain.

Did D. B. Cooper survive? Although the FBI never said so officially, it was known to have felt that the hijacker-extortionist had most likely perished in the plunge. However, no body has ever been found. The $200,000 in ransom had been paid in marked bills, none of which turned up until 1980, when a few thousand dollars was discovered partially buried along the north bank of the Columbia River near Vancouver, Wash. The bills had been dug up by children playing in the sand during a family picnic. It was unclear whether the money had been buried there or washed downstream years ago from a Columbia River tributary. While the find reinvigorated the investigation of the case, the true believers in D. B. Cooper refused to accept the theory that the money had been blown away when Cooper died on impact. They felt it could have been lost or, because it was a small portion of the loot, deliberately discarded by Cooper in an effort to make it appear he had not survived. Obviously, as far as the legend goes, until a body is found and identified, D. B. Cooper lives!

COOPING: Police sleeping on duty

Few rule infractions are more common on major city police forces than that of sleeping on duty.

In 1969 a major expose in New York City revealed that the custom was so ritualized that some officers showed up for the duty lineup armed with pillows and alarm clocks. Newspapers ran pictures of police officers sleeping in patrol cars in Brooklyn's Fort Greene Park. The practice is known as "cooping" in New York and has different names in other localities. In Boston on-duty catnapping is known as "holing," and in Atlanta policemen have been described as seeking out "pits," usually in lovers' lanes or in a tunnel under the city. An investigation of "huddling" in Washington, D.C. revealed that an harassed headquarters could only awaken drowsy officers by activating the shrill buzzers on their walkie-talkies.

Cooping has been a problem ever since there have been police forces in this country. The earliest form of protection in most cities in this country was a guardian of the peace, often a private citizen drafted for the chore, who was little more than a night watchman assigned to patrol a given area. He was provided with a small wooden shanty in which to take short respites from the weather, and of course, many slept on the job. It became a favorite sport of the young bloods of the 17th and 18th centuries to sneak up on such a cooper, bind the shed with rope and uproot it and then drag it away a goodly distance, much to the guard's embarrassment and disgrace among his neighbors.

The highest-ranking police officer ever charged with the offense of cooping in New York was a Brooklyn police captain, who was allegedly caught napping while on duty in 1980. Facing charges of "conduct unbecoming an officer," he submitted his resignation. Earlier that year a lieutenant was suspended for sleeping on duty, becoming for a time the highest-ranking officer caught cooping. Two months later, 11 officers in a station house were charged with snoozing on the job. In 1978 six other New York City officers had been found guilty of the charge and given fines ranging from $1,052 to $2,880.

While most officers deny it vehemently, some experts view the two-man police car as the worst invitation possible to cooping, since one officer can remain by the car radio while the other goes off to snooze.

COPELAND, James (c.1815-1857): Land pirate and hired killer

The most-feared outlaw in Mississippi during the 1840s, James Copeland bossed a vicious gang of "land pirate" highwaymen and hired killers, yet was welcomed within a certain strata of high society in the state. This resulted from his performing several "chores" for one of the state's most arrogant, powerful and corrupt families, the Wages, great landowners around Augusta.

Being under the protection of the Wages gave Copeland virtual immunity from the law, but he finally committed an act so brazen that he had to be arrested. When Gale H. Wages and another man were killed by one James Harvey, the elder Wages paid Copeland $1,000 to avenge his son's death. Taking on the chore eagerly, Copeland shot Harvey in the head on July 15, 1848. However, he was identified as the killer, quickly tried, convicted and sentenced to be hanged. That Old Man Wages had paid Copeland to do the job was common knowledge, but Copeland refused to say anything and for his silence won the full support of the Wages clan. He thus stayed alive for nine years, such being the power of the family. Even when he was finally executed on October 30, 1857, the famed land pirate said nothing to implicate any of the Wages in his crime.

COPPER: Slang for policeman

The origin of the word "copper," referring to a police officer, most probably goes back to Jacob Hays, the first high constable of New York City in the early 19th century, who introduced the badge system for policemen.

According to Detective Alfred Young, official historian of the New York Police Department: "The badge then was a five-pointed star. Different metals were used for different ranks. Brass was for patrolmen, silver for lieutenants and captains, gold for the commissioner. But everybody with a beef always went to the sergeant. He was the guy with the copper star. So whenever a problem came up, they just said, 'Take it to the copper,' and the name just sort of stuck."

COPPOLA, Michael "Trigger Mike" (1904-1966): Syndicate gangster

Trigger Mike Coppola was successful in the Luciano-Genovese crime family because he was a raging sadist and thus an excellent enforcer.

When Vito Genovese fled a possible murder rap and Luciano was sent to prison in the 1930s, Coppola ran much of the crime family's rackets, including the lush artichoke racket, levying an underworld tribute on the vegetable no Italian family wanted to do without, and a goodly portion of the Harlem numbers racket. He was said to net something around $1 million a year. An oft-told underworld tale concerns the time Coppola woke up in the middle of the night remembering he had left a package in the freezer of one of his favorite night spots. A hurried phone call brought the package to his door and he spent the rest of the night thawing out $219,000 of mob money, which he had to dispense in the morning.

There is considerable evidence that Coppola would do anything and kill anybody to advance his fortunes or protect himself. His first wife, according to the subsequent testimony of his second wife, Ann, happened to overhear her husband discussing with another gangster the impending murder of a Republican political worker, Joseph Scottoriggio. She was called to testify against her husband in the case but her appearance was postponed because of her impending pregnancy. She gave birth to a baby daughter and conveniently died afterward in her hospital bed. Coppola's second wife later charged that Trigger Mike had her killed to prevent her from talking.

Ann Coppola's marriage to Trigger Mike was a nightmare highlighted by mental and physical abuse. At their honeymoon party Coppola took a shot at her for the entertainment of the guests. In 1960 Ann discovered her husband was giving drugs to her teenage daughter by a prior marriage. She filed for divorce and testified in an income tax case against Coppola, who sent strongarm men to kidnap and beat her up. She was found badly mauled on an isolated beach, recovered and continued to testify against him. Finally, Trigger Mike gave in and pleaded guilty; he was sent to Atlanta Penitentiary.

Ann Coppola, who had squirreled away something like $250,000 of Trigger Mike's underworld money, fled to Europe to escape the mob's hit men. In Rome in 1962 Ann Coppola stopped running. She wrote a last letter to Internal Revenue, addressing certain portions of it to Attorney General Robert F. Kennedy. She penned a farewell to Trigger Mike as well, saying: "Mike Coppola, someday, somehow, a person or God or the law shall catch up with you, you yellow-bellied bastard. You are the lowest and biggest coward I have had the misfortune to meet." Then she wrote in lipstick on the wall above her hotel bed: "I have always suffered, I am going to kill myself. Forget me." She took a dozen sleeping pills and lapsed quietly into death.

Trigger Mike was released from prison the following year and died in 1966 of natural causes.

COPPOLINO, Dr. Carl (1933-): Murderer

Two of the most sensational murder trials in the 1960s involved Dr. Carl Coppolino, an anesthesiologist charged with murdering his wife and, in a separate case, a male patient with whose wife he had had an affair.

The doctor was the first alleged to have used succinylcholine chloride to commit a murder. The drug commonly was used during operations to keep patients' muscles from trembling; an excessive dose could paralyze the muscles of the lungs, causing death. However, saying that and proving it in court were two different matters because when injected into the body, succinylcholine chloride broke down into its component parts and, for all practical purposes, disappeared.

Coppolino had given up his practice in anesthesiology at the age of 30, retiring because of heart trouble. Although the insurance company in time would become suspicious that he was faking his ailment, it paid him benefits of $22,000 a year. Coppolino and his wife moved from New Jersey to Sarasota, Fla., where they lived rather comfortably. Carmela Coppolino was a doctor herself, and between her practice and Carl's insurance payments, they had no trouble making ends meet, including covering the cost of a new $65,000 insurance policy taken out on Carmela's life. In 1965 Carmela died. A local doctor who knew Coppolino was some kind of expert on heart problems accepted his word that Carmela had had such an ailment and put down heart attack as the cause of her death.

Perhaps the matter would have ended there had Coppolino not married a 38-year-old divorcee named Mary Gibson. Hearing of the marriage, an older woman named Marjorie Farber, a widow then living in Sarasota who had been a neighbor of the Coppolinos in New Jersey, came forward and accused the doctor of killing his first wife. He had also, she said, killed her husband in 1963. According to Marge Farber, she and Coppolino had carried on a torrid love affair, and because he was jealous of her husband, the doctor had murdered him. She said she had watched the whole thing. Coppolino gave Farber, a retired Army colonel, an injection of some drug that was supposed to kill him. When it failed to take effect quickly enough, the doctor took a bed pillow and smothered the unconscious man. The death was passed off as coronary thrombosis.

After an extensive investigation, Dr. Coppolino was indicted for murder both in Florida and New Jersey. He was tried first in the Farber case but won an acquittal. No trace of any poison had been found in the dead man's body and the only testimony against the doctor came from a scorned woman.

Florida authorities decided to press their case, which, on the surface at least, looked weaker. There was no eyewitness to the alleged crime, and there appeared to be no proof as to the cause of death. The Florida trial was dominated by scientific evidence. Dr. Milton Helpern, the New York City medical examiner, did an autopsy on Carmela's body and found that she had been in good health and had not suffered a heart attack. He also found that she had been given an injection in her left buttock just prior to death. Next, Dr. Joseph Umberger, the toxicologist in the Medical Examiner's Office took over, attempting to identify any poison in Carmela Coppolino's body. Dr. Umberger set about finding a method to identify the drug succinylcholine chloride—or its component parts—in the corpse in quantities or qualities that could only be explained by an injection. For six months he worked with tissue from the victim's liver, kidneys, brain and other organs and finally, using spectrography, found succinic acid, one of the components of the drug, in her brain.

Dr. Umberger was on the witness stand for two and a half days, mostly under withering cross-examination by the defense, which contended that succinic acid is present in every brain. Dr. Umberger agreed but pointed out that such acid is "bound," that is, tied to the proteins and perhaps other substances in human tissue. But the type of succinic acid Dr. Umberger had discovered in the woman's body was "unbound," or what he preferred to call "store-bought," and this could only have gotten there by injection.

Coppolino was found guilty of second-degree murder and given a life sentence.

CORBETT, Boston (1822-?): Killer of John Wilkes Booth

An Army sergeant named Boston Corbett, whose name has always figured prominently in logical or illogical Lincoln conspiracy plots, was one of the pursuers of John Wilkes Booth, the man who assassinated the President. When Booth was trapped in a tobacco-curing barn near Port Royal, Va., Corbett shot and killed him after the structure was set afire. Did Corbett shoot Booth because, as he claimed, God had told him to or because he was part of a conspiratorial cover-up, as some later investigators claimed? There is little doubt that Corbett suffered from serious disorders that led to further unstable behavior and criminality. He later castrated himself so that he might better "resist sin." After he fired two pistols into a crowded session of the Kansas legislature, Corbett was committed to a mental institution. He escaped and vanished from sight forever.

A soldier with mental problems, Boston Corbett was credited with shooting John Wilkes Booth after the assassination of President Abraham Lincoln, and since that time he has figured in a number of Lincoln conspiracy theories.

COREY, Giles (1612-1692): Salem witchcraft trial victim

Of all the victims of the Salem witchcraft hysteria, none died a worse death than 80-year-old Giles Corey. Corey made a strange martyr. Like most people of his day, he believed in evil spirits and had originally accused his wife of witchcraft. However, when he himself was accused in the madness, he protested by contemptuous silence. Under English law a defendant had three chances to plead, and if he did not, he or she could not be tried but was subject to a judicial sentence of death. Giles entered the court and stood mute, causing the judges to order a judicial finding. He was stretched out on the ground and weights were placed on his chest. Nevertheless, he refused to utter a word for the two days he suffered before dying. Only near the end did he gasp, "More weight!" so that he might die sooner. After Corey's death the townspeople's uneasiness about the trials turned to revulsion, and his demise hastened the end of the witchcraft trials.

Corey's fate has been portrayed in Arthur Miller's play *The Crucible* and in a ballad written in 1692. The latter goes in part:

> "Giles Corey," said ye Magistrates,
>   "What hast thou hearde to pleade,
> To those who now accuse thy soule
>   Of Crymes and horrid Deed?"
>
> Giles Corey he sayde not a Word,
>   No single Word spake he;
> "Giles Corey," sayeth ye Magistrates,
>   "We'll press it out of thee!"
>
> They got them then a heavy Beam
>   They layde it on his Breast,
> They loaded it with heavy Stones,
>   And hard upon him presst.
>
> "More weight!" now sayde this wretched Man,
>   "More weight" again he cryde,
> And he did not Confession make
>   But wickedly, he dyed.

See also: *Salem Witchcraft Trials.*

Further reading: *Capital Punishment, U.S.A.* by Elinor Lander Horwitz.

CORLL, Dean (1940-1973): Mass murderer

Many people who knew Dean Corll of Houston, Tex. thought of him as a friendly sort of guy, but there was another Dean Corll, a homosexual murderer of at least 27 young boys in that city's "crime of the century" during the early 1970s. Corll used two teenage boys, Elmer Wayne Henley and David Brooks, to steer young victims to him. They would get the victim drunk and then Corll would take over.

The victim would revive to find himself stripped naked, gagged and spread-eagled on a plywood plank. His legs and arms would be secured by handcuffs and nylon ropes. A radio would be going full blast and there would be plastic sheeting on the floor to take care of the blood. Sometimes Corll would kill his victim in as little as 10 minutes, but other times he'd stretch it out for as long as 24 hours or even more. On occasions, perversely, he would suddenly cut the boy loose and explain, laughing, that he was just kidding, seeing if he could scare the youth. But for the murder victims, there was a wooden "body box" on hand in which the slain boys were transported to a city boat shed, a Gulf Coast beach or a wooded area in East Texas for disposal.

On August 7, 1973, 17-year-old Henley shot and killed Corll in self-defense because of fear the sadistic murderer intended to turn on him and Brooks. The police investigation soon implicated Henley and Brooks in the murderous reign of terror, and the pair admitted they had been paid from $5 to $10 for each adolescent boy they had recruited for Corll. For their parts in the crimes, Brooks, convicted on one count, got life imprisonment and Henley, convicted on nine counts, got a total of 594 years. By then the Houston police had recovered somewhat from the criticism heaped on them when the murders were discovered. In most cases, when the victims were reported missing to the police, worried relatives had been informed they had probably run off and "joined those hippies in California."

Henley, who was not charged in the Corll killing, won a new trial in 1979 but was convicted for a second time.

CORNETT, Brack (1859-1888): Western outlaw

A little-remembered south Texas bank and train robber, Brack Cornett, a fast-shooting cowboy from Louisiana, deserves recognition as a criminal far ahead of his time. He was the most advanced of the Western outlaws at "casing" a job and plotting an escape route, especially compared to the prevailing criminal technique of shoot-'em-up-and-ride. Cornett would have his gang travel the escape route several times, noting each possible cut-off, a method not seen again in bank robbing until the 20th century days of Baron Lamm, John Dillinger and the Barkers. Because he was a pioneer, Cornett's modus operandi stood out like a sore thumb and led to his downfall. His gang was seen riding hell-for-leather near Pearsall, Tex. by a rancher who suspected they had just pulled something. He reported them but no crime had been committed and they were written off as some cowpokes in a hurry. When a train was robbed a few days later and the gang rode off hell-for-leather in the direction of Pearsall, the report was recalled. It took sheriff's deputies a while to track down some fast riders, but on February 12, 1888 they located Cornett hiding out on a ranch near Pearsall and, when he refused to surrender, killed him in a spirited gunfight.

CORONA, Juan (1934-   ): Mass murderer

A Mexican labor contractor who had started out as a migrant

fruit picker, Juan Corona was convicted of the murder of 25 migrant workers in 1970-1, becoming labeled as the greatest captured mass killer in California history. (There is speculation that the uncaptured "Zodiac Killer" may have killed almost twice as many people.)

All Corona's victims were transient laborers between the ages of 40 and 68. They had been mutilated, usually with a machete, and buried in peach orchards and along a river bank in Yuba County. Unfortunately for Corona, some of his bank deposit slips and receipts had apparently been found buried with some of the victims, leading the authorities directly to him.

Bloodstained weapons and clothing were found in his home, including two butcher's knives, a machete, a pistol, a jacket and some shorts. The most sensational evidence, however, was what the prosecution called Corona's "death list," a ledger containing the names of many of the victims with a date after them.

In January 1973 Corona was found guilty and sentenced to 25 consecutive life terms, a somewhat meaningless exercise in overkill since he technically would become eligible for parole in 1980. Later that year he was attacked in his prison cell and stabbed 32 times, causing him to lose the sight of one eye. In 1978 a new trial was ordered for Corona on the grounds that his lawyer had failed to provide him with an adequate defense by not presenting what the appeals court called an "obvious" insanity plea. The court emphasized it did not doubt the correctness of the guilty verdict, but it insisted Corona was entitled to an insanity defense. Corona was sent to a mental facility for observation to see if he could eventually be put on trial again. In the early 1980s he was still there and was found guilty again.

CORPUS Delicti

Technically, a corpus delicti refers to "the body of the crime," which in homicide cases means first that death has occurred and second that the death was caused by a criminal agency. Typical of the laws in other states, the New York Penal Law demands the following in all homicide cases: "No person can be convicted of murder or manslaughter unless the death of the person alleged to have been killed and the fact of the killing by the defendant, as alleged, are each established as independent facts; the former by direct proof, and the latter beyond a reasonable doubt."

Naturally, a number of murderers have escaped prosecution because they succeeded in getting rid of the body *without anyone seeing it*. The law is not required to produce the actual body, however, if it can produce witnesses who saw the body and can thus testify that a crime had been committed. In one case neighbors heard shooting in a Bronx luncheonette and saw several men carry a body from the establishment to a car. Although the body was never found, the testimony of the witnesses was sufficient to prove that a murder had occurred. A corpus delicti can also be proved if bone or body fragments necessary to human life can be identified.

CORTEZ, Gregorio (1875-1916): Fugitive

Mexicans in Texas still sing the "Ballad of Gregorio Cortez." In the song, the hero, pistol in hand, defiantly declares, "Ah, so many mounted Rangers just to take one Mexican!"

Cortez came to Texas with his family when he was 12. He worked as a ranch hand until he and his brother took over a farm. In 1901 the Karnes County sheriff came to arrest the brothers on charges of horse stealing. Gregorio Cortez denied the charges and refused to surrender. The sheriff opened fire and wounded his brother. Gregorio then shot and killed the sheriff. Fearing Texas justice, which was undoubtedly prejudiced in its treatment of Mexicans, Cortez fled. He was to fight off posse after posse, some with up to 300 men, that tried to take him. The chase covered more than 400 miles. During it he became a hero to his compatriots, fighting for his and their rights. A posse caught Cortez close to the Mexican border and in the ensuing gun battle he killed another sheriff.

The legal battle on Cortez' behalf lasted four years, with hundreds of Mexicans contributing to his defense fund. They looked upon Cortez' act as a protest against American injustice. He was cleared in the killing of the first sheriff but sentenced to life imprisonment for killing the second. Protests continued until in 1913, at the age of 38, he was freed. He died three years later but the "Ballad of Gregorio Cortez" preserves his memory.

CORTINA, Juan (1824-1892): Bandit and Mexican patriot

Juan Cortina, a Mexican born on the Texas side of the Rio Grande, was, in the view of Anglo Texans, one of the worst bandits that state had ever seen. In the Mexican view, he was a daring patriot unafraid to stand up to the *gringos* who stole everything the Mexicans had.

Cortina was heir to a huge spread that spanned both sides of the Rio Grande; as such, he became a leader of the Mexican community. Mexicans and Mexican property were fair game in Texas, and land grabbers began whittling away at the Cortina spread. By the time Cortina had reached manhood, he had killed a number of these land grabbers and there was a warrant out for his arrest.

Cortina was living on the family ranch near Brownsville, but although it was no mystery where he was, no one seemed too interested in invading that stronghold to take him. On September 13, 1859 he came upon the marshal of Brownsville brutally beating a former employee of the Cortina ranch. He wounded the officer and helped the beaten Mexican to escape. Brownsville boiled over this "greaser insult," and there was talk of going out and capturing Cortina. Instead, on September 28 Cortina, at the head of an army of 1,000 cutthroats, captured Brownsville. According to the Texan version, Cortina then summarily executed several men. The Mexican version was that the only killings occurred while Brownsville was being seized. What is not in dispute is that Cortina held the town for ransom, demanding $100,000 under threat of burning it to the ground. Eventually, influenced by less volatile members of his family, he relented, withdrawing to the town limits and keeping it under siege. A Brownsville citizen slipped through the cordon and summoned aid in the form of U.S. troops, Texas Rangers and civilian volunteers. Cortina and his men routed this force in a battle at Palo Alto, but by December 1859 he was compelled to keep constantly on the move, harassed by superior forces. Still, Cortina was able to capture Edinburg, and then Rio Grande City, from which he extracted a ransom of $100,000 in gold. By Christmas Day a large contingent of Texas Rangers was able to force Cortina across the border into Mexico, but neither the Rangers nor the U.S. Army was able to keep him from periodically raiding far into Texas over the next several years.

Cortina and his men were regarded by Texans as that state's worst cattle rustlers, making off with an estimated 900,000 animals in their raids. From the Mexican viewpoint, Cortina was merely making up in a small degree for the cattle previously stolen from Mexicans. During his later years in Mexico, Cortina's fortunes ran to extremes. He was a general in the army of President Benito Juarez and then served as military governor of the state of Tamaulipas. In 1875, with the emergence of the Diaz regime, Cortina was imprisoned and remained there until 1890. He lived out the last two years of his life in retirement on the border with Texas.

See also: *Leander H. McNelly.*

COSA Nostra

The Mafia, pure and simple, by another name: Cosa Nostra—literally, "Our Thing." For many years FBI chief J. Edgar Hoover insisted there was no such thing as organized crime or the Mafia. Says crime historian Richard Hammer, "In order to get Hoover off the hook, a new name had to be created, hence Cosa Nostra."

See also: *Mafia.*

COSTELLO, Frank (1891-1973): Prime Minister of the Underworld

No syndicate criminal in this country ever enjoyed as much political pull as did Frank Costello, who was the advocate within the national crime syndicate of the "big fix." He believed in buying favors and even paying for them in advance. Scores of political leaders and judges were beholden to him. An entire array of New York's Tammany Hall bosses "owed" him. They ranged from Christy Sullivan to Mike Kennedy, from Frank Rosetti to Bert Stand and from Hugo Rogers to Carmine DeSapio. Costello had done them favors, had raised money for them, had delivered votes that really counted. And when it came time to make appointments, Costello practically exercised the equivalent of the Senate's prerogatives to advise and consent. Tammany kingpin Rogers put it best when he said, "If Costello wanted me, he would send for me."

It was the same with judges. In 1943 Manhattan District Attorney Frank Hogan obtained a wiretap on Costello's telephone. Investigators were treated to this enlightening conversation on August 23 between Costello and Thomas Aurelio just minutes after the latter had learned he was getting the Democratic nomination to become a state supreme court justice:

"How are you, and thanks for everything," Aurelio said.

"Congratulations," Costello answered. "It went over perfect. When I tell you something is in the bag, you can rest assured."

"It was perfect," Aurelio said. "It was fine."

"Well, we will all have to get together and have dinner some night real soon."

"That would be fine," the judge-to-be said. "But right now I want to assure you of my loyalty for all you have done. It is unwavering."

Despite the disclosure of the wiretap, the grateful Aurelio went on to be elected to the judgeship after beating back disbarment proceedings. Clearly, when Costello said something was in the bag, it was in the bag.

Born Franceso Castiglia in Calabria, Italy in 1891, he came to New York with his family at age four. At 21 he had a police record of two arrests for assault and robbery. At 24 he was sentenced to a year in prison for carrying a gun. He did not return to prison for another 37 years. Beginning in the early days of Prohibition, his best friends were Lucky Luciano, a Sicilian, and Meyer Lansky, a Polish Jew. These three were to become the most important figures in the formation of the national crime syndicate during the 1930s. While Luciano and Lansky did most of the organizing among criminals, Costello's mission was to develop contacts and influence among the police and politicians. By the mid-1920s the trio's varied criminal enterprises, mostly bootlegging and gambling, were making them rich. To protect these interests, they were paying, through Costello, $10,000 a week in "grease" directly into the police commissioner's office. Within a few years, during the regimes of commissioners Joseph A. Warren and Grover A. Whalen, the amount rose to $20,000 a week. In 1929, just after the stock market crash, Costello told Luciano he had to advance Whalen $30,000 to cover his margin calls in the market. "What could I do?" Costello told Luciano. "I hadda give it to him. We own him."

No one ever questioned whether Costello always dispensed mob money the way it was intended. Costello was a man of honor on such matters. Besides, the results were there for the mob to see, with cases never brought to court, complaints dropped and so on.

Costello became the most vital cog in the national crime syndicate after the forceful purging of the old mafiosi or "Mustache Petes." The gangs cooperated and Costello supplied the protection. As part of his reward, Costello got the rights to gambling in the lucrative New Orleans area.

He was respected by all the crime family heads and was considered the Prime Minister of the Underworld, the man who dealt with the "foreign dignitaries"—the police, judges and politicos. Much has been made of the fact that Costello

At the pinnacle of his power during the Kefauver Committee hearings in the early 1950s, Frank Costello, as Prime Minister of the Underworld, was the mob's representative in dealings with politicians, judges and the police.

was not a murderer, but he sat in on all syndicate decisions concerning major hits, and while he may have often been a moderating force, he was a party to murder plans. His general reluctance to use violence was not due to squeamishness; it was just that he felt hitting a man over the head with a wad of greenbacks could be more persuasive than using a blackjack.

One of the prime accomplishments of the Kefauver investigation during the 1950s was the exposure of Costello's vast influence in government. While he insisted that only his hands be shown on television, that minor subterfuge could hardly cover up his activities. When he left the stand, Costello knew his term as Prime Minister was at an end. He was too hot for everyone, those who appreciated the mob's favors and the mob itself.

Through the 1950s, with Luciano deported to Italy, Joe Adonis being harassed and facing the same fate and Costello facing tax raps that would finally send him to prison, Vito Genovese moved to take over the syndicate. In 1957 Genovese engineered an attempt to assassinate Costello; he survived by perhaps an inch or two, his assailant's bullets just grazing his scalp. Later that same year Genovese arranged the rub-out of Albert Anastasia, the Lord High Executioner of Murder, Inc.

and a devoted follower of Costello and Luciano.

It looked like Genovese was in. Meanwhile, Costello really wanted out, to retire in peace and concentrate on his battles with the government about his citizenship and tax problems. But Genovese's blueprint for power was soon destroyed. Costello, Lansky, Carlo Gambino and Luciano masterminded a drug operation that involved Genovese. As soon as he was mired deeply in it, evidence was turned over to prosecutors, and in 1959 Genovese went to prison for a term of 15 years. He would die there in 1969. During this period Costello did a short stint in Atlanta Penitentiary, the same one Genovese was in; it was said the two had a sentimental reconciliation there. Genovese may have been sincere but Costello certainly was not. When he left prison, he felt no pangs of sorrow for Genovese.

Costello went into quiet retirement after that, living the life of a Long Island squire until his death in 1973.

See also: *Apalachin Conference, Carlo Gambino, Vito Genovese, Vincent "the Chin" Gigante, Kefauver Investigation, Meyer Lansky, Charles "Lucky" Luciano, Willie Moretti, Slot Machines, Wiretapping and Bugging.*

COSTER, F. Donald: See Philip Musica.

COTRONI Gang: Mafia's "body importers"

Based in Montreal, Canada, the Cotroni gang has a tremendous impact on crime in the United States, its main function being to import for the Mafia new blood, mainly Sicilians who have proved tougher and more reliable than second- and third-generation American recruits. The mass importation of native Sicilians was started in the 1960s by the late "boss of bosses" Carlo Gambino, who felt there was a need for tough young recruits still schooled in the old Mafia codes and, above all, "hungry" and not as anxious to move to the suburbs.

According to Canadian police, the Cotroni gang provides aliens with a pipeline into the United States for a fee that runs between $2,000 and $3,000. It is easy for aliens to get into Canada since the only thing needed for a three months stay without a visa is $300 in cash and a Canadian address where they can be reached. The Cotronis supply the addresses and have little trouble moving their immigrants across the border.

Many of the mobsters recently arrested by police have been new Mafia faces, all recent arrivals, which has led to fears that American police will lose track of mob operations as these unknown newcomers take on more and more of the Mafia's street duties.

COUNTERFEITING

Throughout American history there have always been people who have thought the best way to make money is, simply, to make money.

Mary Butterworth, the kitchen counterfeiter, may have been the first. This housewife with seven children operated a highly successful counterfeiting ring in Plymouth colony during the early 1700s.

The comparatively crude paper money used in Colonial times, "Continental currency," was so frequently and successfully faked that it gave rise to the saying, "Not worth a Continental." During the Civil War, it was estimated that a good third of the currency in circulation was "funny money." The counterfeiter's chore was made much easier because some 11,600 state banks across the nation designed and printed their own currency. Finally, in 1863 the nation adopted a uniform currency.

Counterfeiting today is hardly a lost art but few stay successful at it for very long. In 1976 the Secret Service made a record haul in the Bronx, New York City, arresting six suspects who had run off $20 million in what was characterized as "highly passable" bills. This followed on the heels of raids in Los Angeles that netted four men men with over $8 million worth of bogus bills. The main worry of the government today is that sophisticated new photographic and printing equipment will permit counterfeiters, as never before, to approximate the intricate whorls, loops and crosshatching that makes American paper money just about the most difficult in the world to imitate.

In a typical counterfeiting operation, distribution is handled by an army of wholesalers, distributors and passers. The standard breakdown calls for the counterfeiters to sell their output to wholesalers for 12 percent of face value. The wholesaler then has the job of reselling the bills to distributors for 25 percent. The distributors turn it over to street-level passers for 35 percent.

Although counterfeiting is punishable by up to 15 years in prison and a $10,000 fine and Treasury officials estimate that almost 90 percent of all bad-money makers are jailed in less than a year, counterfeiters, big and small, still keep trying their luck. There are those who will print fake $1 bills despite the rather high overhead involved. It took the Secret Service 10 years to catch up with a lone operator who passed fake $1 bills in New York. He was an elderly former janitor who circulated only eight or 10 ones every few days, making it a point never to pass them twice at the same place. He explained later that he "didn't want to stick anybody for more than a dollar."

Some even try their hand at counterfeiting coins, even though breaking even is nearly impossible in these inflationary times. In the past, however, coin counterfeiting was big business. In 1883 a deaf-mute named Joshua Tatum made a small fortune by slightly altering the original liberty head nickel and passing it for 100 times its real value. On the face of the nickel was a woman's head wearing a liberty headpiece. On the other side was the motto *E. Pluribus Unum* and a large V. The V, the Roman numeral five, was the only indication of the coin's value to be found on the nickel. Tatum noted that the liberty head nickel closely resembled in design and size the half eagle, or $5 gold piece, which was then in general circulation. The face of the latter also displayed a woman's head with a liberty headpiece. On the reverse side was the sign of value, Five D., indicating $5. About the only difference was the color: the nickel had a silvery appearance and the half eagle gold. Tatum began gold-plating nickels by the thousand and then buying 5¢ items all over the East Coast. Invariably, he got $4.95 in change. On occasion, a merchant would flip the coin over, note the V for five and assume it was a newly issued $5 gold piece. He couldn't prove it by Tatum, who was a deaf-mute. When Tatum was finally caught, the courts freed him because he was a deaf-mute. The authorities could never prove Tatum had ever asked for change, and there were no laws on the book prohibiting a person from gold-plating a nickel. The law was changed accordingly and an emergency session of Congress was called to alter the design of the nickel.

Students of the fine art of counterfeiting contend that the true craftsmen are all in their graves. There were, for example, artists like Baldwin Bredell and Arthur Taylor, who in the late 1890s turned out such perfect $100 bills that the government had to withdraw from circulation the entire issue of $26 million in Monroe-head bills. Sent to Moyamensing Prison, Bredell and Taylor astounded the experts by pulling off a money-making caper so amazing that Treasury Department experts at first refused to concede it possible. Within several months of their arrival in the prison, Bredell and Taylor began turning out counterfeit $20 bills at night in their cell. To do this, they needed to have supplies smuggled in. One of Taylor's relatives brought books and magazines on his weekly visits. These hid engraving tools, steel plates, files and vials of acids. Another smuggled in a kerosene lamp piece by piece and some magnifying glasses hidden in a basket of cookies. The printing press they needed was made to specifications the counterfeiters drew up and had smuggled out. Getting the press in was easy because it was the size of a cigar box. Since Bredell's wife was pregnant, she became just a bit more expecting. Inks were a different problem. With their former workshop under government padlock, there was no way to get the special bleaches and inks that were needed. One couldn't buy the proper ink legitimately without the government knowing about it. So the pair stole the bleaches they needed from the prison laundry and then their relatives started bringing fruits and flowers. From the dried fruits and berries and the green leaves of the flowers, they made their own ink.

Soon the Bredell-Taylor $20s—virtually as good as Uncle Sam's—started turning up. What the pair hadn't counted on was that John E. Wilkie, the chief of the U.S. Secret Service, would spot the work as being too good to be anybody's but theirs. Naturally, Wilkie assumed the plates had been prepared by the pair before their arrest and they were just being used now. So he put a watch on relatives of Taylor and Bredell, and after one was caught passing some of the fake $20s, Wilkie uncovered the whole story. The experts called in by the Secret Service scoffed at the possibility that Bredell and Taylor could have produced such work in prison. They insisted it could not have been done without a camera, a huge workroom and an eight-ton press. Only when the prisoners reenacted their feat were the experts convinced.

In recognition of their extraordinary talents, Chief Wilkie decided to help the pair get a new start in life when they were released. He got financial backing for a mechanical engraving machine Taylor had perfected, starting the ex-counterfeiter on the way to becoming a prosperous manufacturer. Bredell went on to establish a leading engraving and lithography plant and also became rich. The two master counterfeiters were lured away from their illicit activities the only way the government could think of—by making them rich, legally.

Today, there are no counterfeiting geniuses such as Taylor and Bredell or Jim the Penman, perhaps the only counterfeiter in history to make top-grade notes simply by drawing them. Using a fine camel's hair brush, he made phony bills by tracing them from genuine notes that he placed before a strong light. Criminal craftsmen of such caliber, to the U.S. government's relief, are a dying breed.

See also: *Mary Butterworth, "Count" Victor Lustig.*

Further reading: *Money of Their Own* by Murray Teign Bloom.

COUNTY Seat Wars: Midwest Boomtown Violence

Encouraged by unscrupulous speculators during the land boom in several Western states following the Civil War, fierce struggles broke out between various communities over the location of county seats. Obviously, the prestige of being the county seat would add to the value of a town's property and deadly wars were fought to win this distinction. Kansas alone had 28 of these disputes, and others cropped up in Nebraska and North and South Dakota. The ultimate decision on the location of a county seat was left to local elections, but both sides would use bribes, trickery and fraud to fix the results as well as hire professional gunmen to intimidate voters. Even civic-minded citizens resorted to importing gunslingers to protect the polls. Unfortunately, whatever the result, the losing side seldom accepted it. A common practice was to invade the winning town and simply attempt to steal the courthouse records, a typical case being the invasion of Cimarron by Ingalls forces in Gray County, Kan. In one case an attempt was made to jack up a wooden courthouse on rollers and physically cart away the entire building.

One of the bloodiest confrontations involved Hugoton and Woodsdale in Stevens County, Kan. The sheriff and three Woodsdale citizens were murdered by Hugoton men on July 25, 1888, and Woodsdale prosecutor Col. Sam N. Wood was assassinated in Hugoton in 1891. As was often the case in county seat wars, all murder charges eventually were dropped. In the end, Hugoton became the county seat. At Coronado in Wichita County, Kan., three Leoti residents died in a street battle in 1887, but not in vain; their community eventually won the war. Finally, bad economic times and the ensuing collapse of the short-grass land boom brought an end to the county seat wars.

See also: *Cimarron County Seat War.*

COURTRIGHT, Longhair Jim (1845?-1887): Western lawman and murderer

A prime example of a lawman gone bad, Jim Courtright, variously reported as being born in Iowa or Illinois between 1845 and 1848, was a popular two-gun sheriff in Fort Worth, Tex., but after two years on the job, he was fired in 1878 for drinking. Courtright bounced around to a few other jobs as a lawman, but his brooding nature was such that these rarely lasted for long. Eventually, he drifted into a job as a guard for the American Mining Co., in whose employ he killed two would-be robbers in 1883. News of this exploit reached the attention of a New Mexico rancher named Logan, who had been Courtright's old Civil War commander. Logan offered him a job as a ranch foreman, but Courtright's real assignment would be to rid Logan's range of squatters. He got off to a fast start by promptly shooting two unarmed nesters. Because there had been witnesses, Courtright was forced to flee. He was arrested in Fort Worth and held for extradition. Courtright knew the jail routine well, and after being smuggled a pair of pistols, he escaped, fleeing to South America. After three years he returned to face trial, but by that time the witnesses against him had scattered, and he was easily acquitted. Returning to Fort Worth, he set up the T.I.C. Commercial Detective Agency. Finding little demand for his services, Courtright used the agency as a guise to demand protection money from the town's various gambling halls and saloons. For this ploy to be successful, a 100 percent record of collection was necessary; it was Courtright's misfortune that an emporium called the White Elephant Saloon was run by a pint-sized gambler named Luke Short, one of the West's grand masters of the six-gun. On February 8, 1887 Courtright sent a messenger into the White Elephant demanding that Short step outside. Short did, and moments later, Courtright called out, "Don't try to pull a gun on me." Courtright clearly was laying the legal basis for a claim that he was acting in self-defense. The matter was academic, however. Courtright started to draw one gun, but Short shot his thumb off as he tried to trip back the hammer. This was not a trick shot; Short's aim was slightly off on his first blast. As Courtright went to pull his other gun, Short was on target with three more shots, two in the chest and one in the forehead.

See also: *Luke Short.*

COY, Bernard Paul (1900-1946): Bank robber and Alcatraz Prison Rebellion leader

Bernie Coy was 46, with 16 years more to go on a 25-year sentence for bank robbery, when he masterminded the famous breakout-rebellion attempt from Alcatraz in May 1946.

Regarded as little more than an ignorant Kentucky hillbilly, Coy initially was not considered smart enough to be the mastermind behind the escape attempt. During the 48-hour break attempt, prison officials were sure the leader of the plot was Dutch Cretzer, a former Public Enemy No. 4 doing a life sentence. Unlike Coy, Cretzer was a brutal killer and hard to control, but Coy needed him in the escape because of Cretzer's outside connections, who could arrange a getaway once they reached the mainland.

In fact, as a subsequent investigation proved, the entire escape plot was Coy's. He secretly designed and had built a bar spreader made from plumbing fixtures and valve parts and concealed it until the time of the break, both incredible accomplishments in security-conscious Alcatraz. With the bar spread, Coy was able to break into the gun gallery, where the only weapons in the cell block were kept, overpower the guard and arm his accomplices. There is no doubt the escapers, having turned loose a great number of other convicts to make things look like a prison riot rather than break, could have made it across the prison yard to the wharf and then aboard the prison launch. Coy's plan adhered to a strict timetable that took advantage of the very guard procedure designed to prevent escapes. His plan foundered, ironically, because one guard disobeyed the rules and failed to put the key to the last door back on its rack. He had it in his pocket and, when taken hostage, managed to hide it in a cell. The escapers took nine guards hostage, but because of one locked door, Coy's plan failed and the prison launch left the island before they had a chance to reach it. Although the break and riot lasted 48 hours, Coy lost control of his men, and Dutch Cretzer, who all

along chafed at taking orders from Coy, "a hick hillbilly," shot up the hostages while Coy was trying to negotiate over the phone with the warden. Throughout the remainder of the rebellion, Cretzer spent his time trying to find and kill Coy and Marv Hubbard, a con who supported Coy, while Coy tried to hunt down Cretzer. As Marines and the guards bombarded the prison with grenades and raked the cell blocks with rifle and shotgun fire, the grim duel continued. Although popular accounts to this day often insist that the three ringleaders joined together and fought the attacking guards to the death deep within the underground tunnels of the prison, the fact was that Cretzer killed Coy and then died in a final confrontation with a host of attackers, who also killed the wounded Hubbard.

See also: *Alcatraz Prison Rebellion, Joseph Paul "Dutch" Cretzer.*

CRABB, Christopher Columbus (1852-1935): "Solid man"

It is generally acknowledged that the most eminent and successful "solid man" in the history of American vice was Christopher Columbus Crabb, whom Chicago Mayor Carter Harrison, Jr. described as "an imposing looking rooster." Remarkably, Crabb was able to function as lover and financial manager for more than one madam at the same time.

Crabb was a $14-a-week clerk in Marshall Field's department store when he met Lizzie Allen in 1878. Lizzie was one of the city's top madams, operating brothels just a cut in quality below those of the famous Carrie Watson. Crabb had been a lover to several of Lizzie's prostitutes, and while he was not a pimp, the ladies lavished gifts upon him. At the age of 38, Lizzie had at last found her true love and promptly smothered Crabb with kindness.

Crabb was known as a square-shooter in Chicago vice circles, a man who could be trusted to handle madams or harlots' money. He was constantly urging various madams to give their workers a better break, and while he would be most helpful in initiating a new girl "into the business," he would just as willingly aid others who wanted to get out. While his affair with Lizzie Allen was blossoming, Crabb apparently played the same role with another madam, Mollie Fitch. When the latter died a few years later, she left Crabb $150,000. In 1890 Crabb and Lizzie spent $125,000 to build a large double house at 2131 South Dearborn Street, which was later taken over by the Everleigh sisters and became the nation's most famous bordello. Under Lizzie, the resort was called the House of Mirrors. When she retired in 1896, Lizzie signed over all her property to Crabb and died later that same year. Crabb buried her in Rosehill Cemetery and had her tombstone inscribed, "Perpetual Ease."

The press estimated that Crabb inherited well over $300,000 from Lizzie. He spent the later years of his life as a sort of elder statesman in vice circles, and when he died on January 5, 1935, he left an estate of $416,589.81, three quarters of which he bequeathed to the Illinois Masonic Orphans' Home.

See also: *Lizzie Allen, Everleigh sisters.*

CRAFT, Gerald (1965-1973): Kidnap victim

Although not very well known in white circles, the kidnap-murders of eight-year-old Gerald Craft and six-year-old Keith Arnold in Detroit on December 1, 1973 stand as the "black Lindbergh case."

Gerald Craft was actually a familiar face to most of the country's whites, being famous, if anonymously, for a television commercial in which he gobbled down big helpings of fried chicken with a devilish grin on his face. On that December 1, a Saturday afternoon, Gerald was playing football with a friend, Keith, in front of his grandmother's house when both suddenly disappeared. The next day a hoarsely whispered telephone call demanded a ransom of $53,000 for the return of the children. This was an amount the families could not pay. With the help of the Detroit police, a bogus package of ransom money was dropped at a designated spot, which the police staked out. Two men came to retrieve it but officers moved too slowly to capture them before they drove off. Two days later, the bodies of the two boys, both shot twice, were found in a field near Detroit's Metropolitan Airport.

The *Detroit News* offered a $5,000 reward for information leading to the capture of the kidnappers and set up a "secret witness" phone number for informers. Within a week the information received through this source led to the arrest of three 21-year-old men and a teenage girl and the solution of the case. The girl provided evidence that convicted the men, Byron Smith, Geary Gilmore and Jerome Holloway. All three were given mandatory life sentences.

As big a news splash as the kidnapping made in the black press around the country, few whites ever heard much about it.

CRANE, Stephen (1870-1900): Writer and police victim

Few writers have suffered as much harassment from the police as did Stephen Crane during the last four years of his life. Crane's troubles began in September 1896, when the author, already famous for his book *The Red Badge of Courage,* visited the vice-ridden tenderloin section of Manhattan to collect material for a series of sketches on the district. A tall, broad-shouldered policeman named Charles Becker walked up to a free-lance prostitute, Dora Clark, and started beating her to a pulp. Becker over the years was to become famous as "the crookedest cop who ever stood behind a shield" and in 1915 he died in the electric chair for the murder of gambler Herman Rosenthal. His prime concern during his days in the tenderloin was not to drive out the prostitutes but to make sure he got his share of their income.

Dora Clark was definitely not soliciting when Becker started roughing her up and arrested her. Crane, having witnessed the entire incident, so testified at her hearing. The Clark woman complained she had been subjected to Becker's constant ha-

rassment and demands for money. The judge chose to believe Crane over Becker and released the woman.

Becker was brought up on police departmental charges before Commissioner Frederick Grant, who at the time was considered one of the department's looser administrators and an opponent of reforms advocated by another commissioner, Theodore Roosevelt. Becker's defense tried to shift the case to one against Crane, accusing him of regularly consorting with prostitutes and of being an opium smoker. Despite attacks by the newspapers, Commissioner Grant allowed a long line of questioning on such points, causing the *Brooklyn Daily Eagle* to lament that "the reputation of private citizens is permitted to be assailed without comment or protest, while so much is done to shield one of a body of men that collectively was lately shown to be one of the most corrupt, brutal, incompetent organizations in the world." Other newspapers joined in observing that the rank treatment of Crane showed the police had hardly reformed since the revelations of their crookedness by the Lexow Committee two years previously.

Becker escaped without suffering any major penalties for his conduct, and the police thereafter kept up a steady campaign of intimidation and harassment against Crane. His rooms were raided, and police insisted they had found opium there. (The conventional wisdom was that they had brought the opium with them.) The police vendetta against Crane reached such intensity that the author was forced to flee the city for a time. As soon as he returned, the police resumed their persecution of him. When a policeman saw Crane at the theater with a woman, he loudly accused her of being a "goddam French whore" and only beat a retreat after realizing the other member of the Crane party was a priest.

By 1898 the malicious attacks on Crane again forced him to leave the city. When next he returned, there was no need for the police to reactivate their campaign a third time. Crane was dying of tuberculosis.

See also: *Charles Becker.*

CRATER, Joseph Force (1889-1937?): Missing judge

On August 6, 1930 a portly 41-year-old man wearing a high-collared shirt, brown pin-striped double-breasted suit and extremely polished and pointed shoes stepped into a taxi in front of a Manhattan restaurant, waved goodbye to a friend and rode off into history, to become known as America's greatest vanishing act. The man was New York Supreme Court Justice Joseph Force Crater. From that day forth, Crater was never seen again—alive or dead. His disappearance provided grist for the mills of jokers, playwrights, graffiti writers, cartoonists and amateur detectives over the next half century.

Crater was born in Easton, Pa., graduated from Lafayette College and earned a law degree at Columbia University. He established a successful New York practice and formed important political connections, later rising to the presidency of the Cayuga Democratic Club, an important part of the Tammany organization. In April 1930 Gov. Franklin D. Roosevelt appointed him to the New York Supreme Court.

Crater cut short a vacation in Maine to return to the city in order to take care of some business. He was seen in his court chambers on August 5 and 6 and had his aide cash two checks for him totaling $5,150. Later that day he met some friends at a restaurant and then stepped into the taxi and oblivion.

The investigation into his disappearance eventually mushroomed into a months-long grand jury probe that quizzed hundreds of witnesses but produced no leads to explain what happened to him. One theory was developed about why he had vanished. The grand jury uncovered considerable evidence of corruption in the Cayuga Democratic Club, which brought on the much-publicized Seabury probe.

Twenty-five years after Judge Joseph Force Crater's disappearance, his wife, since remarried, calls for a renewal of the hunt for him.

Meanwhile, the tantalizing mysteries of the case continued. Under New York City law, cabbies were required to keep records of all their trips, starting points and destinations. But despite many appeals from the police, a $5,000 reward offered by the city and a $2,500 reward offered by the *New York World,* the cabbie who picked up Judge Crater never came forward nor offered any information concerning the case. If he had, Crater's movements could have been traced at least one more step.

On countless occasions in the 1930s, the case seemed to be a fraction of an inch from being solved, but each lead fizzled. There was no limit to the type of leads the police ran down over the years. The missing Crater was identified wrongly as: a gold prospector in the California desert country; a human torch who died of self-inflicted burns in Leavenworth, Kan.; a

skeleton at Walden, Vt.; an unidentified murder victim in Westchester County, N.Y.; a man who hanged himself from a tree less than 15 miles from the Crater summer home at Belgrade Lakes, Maine; an amnesia victim in the Missouri State Insane Asylum; a sufferer of "daytime somnambulism."

Then again he was: a Hollywood race tout; a free-spending American tourist in Italy; an ill-shaven door-to-door beggar in Illinois ("I didn't pull his whiskers but I'm pretty sure they were false," one Chicago housewife bubbled to police.) Perhaps the best of all was the G.I. who returned from overseas in 1946 with the emphatic intelligence that Crater was operating a bingo game in North Africa for a strictly-Arab clientele.

Jokers, of course, got into the act. Assistant Chief John J. Sullivan was sitting at his desk one day when a call from Montreal was switched to him. A very calm voice said: "I can't tell you my name, because I don't care to get mixed up in it, but Judge Crater is now in room 761 at my hotel. I am in the hotel now, but I don't dare give you my name." In a matter of minutes Sullivan had the Montreal police breaking into the room of a honeymooning couple.

Throughout the country a number of dying bums felt compelled to make deathbed confessions, each admitting that he was the judge. One in the Midwest, who lived long enough for the police to question him, admitted finally that he was just trying to "get myself a decent burial instead of being laid in that pauper's plot all the other boys end up in."

In 1937 Judge Crater was ruled legally dead, and his widow remarried. At the time, it was estimated the hunt for Crater had expended 300,000 Depression dollars. Even by the 1950s the Judge Crater legend had not faded. Former Police Commissioner Edward P. Mulrooney, under whose supervision the case was first investigated, revealed he still carried a picture of Crater in his pocket at all times. "You never know but that someday you might run into him," he said. "I'd give my right arm to find him." During the following decade the police were still up to the search, digging up a Yonkers, N.Y. backyard in the hope of finding the judge's bones. Nothing came of it.

CRAZY Butch Gang

During the 1890s and first few years of the 20th century, the most efficient gang of young criminals in New York City was the Crazy Butch gang. Crazy Butch, the leader of the gang, had been tossed into the world at the tender age of eight. Renouncing his alcoholic parents, he never acknowledged his family name. After surviving for two years as a shoeshine boy, Crazy Butch became a pickpocket. When he was about 13, Butch stole a dog, which he named Rabbi, and trained it to steal handbags from careless women's hands. Rabbi would snatch a purse, race through the streets until it lost any pursuers and then meet Crazy Butch at Willett and Stanton streets, tail wagging and the purse clenched in his teeth.

In his late teens Crazy Butch switched his operation from a dog to a gang of 20 to 30 youths, whom he trained to prowl the streets snatching handbags and muffs. Butch would lead his minions down a street on a bicycle, bump into a pedestrian, preferably a little old lady, and alight to help her up while at the same time berating her as a careless walker. As people pressed in to see what was happening, Crazy Butch's boys would thread through the mob rifling pockets and purses. When the crowd was completely milked or a policeman appeared, Butch would apologize to his victim and pedal away. At the gang's headquarters, his proteges would turn in their spoils and Crazy Butch would reward each with a few pennies.

By the turn of the century, Crazy Butch and many of his followers had advanced to such adult occupations as musclemen, sluggers and, on occasion, paid murderers, often pursuing their criminal endeavors in bicycle teams. A subchief under the celebrated Monk Eastman, Crazy Butch held his followers, some 60 strong, always at the ready should they be needed to do battle with the Five Point's Gang of Paul Kelly, whose ranks already included a young hoodlum named Johnny Torrio and would soon be graced by such names as Luciano, Yale and Capone. Crazy Butch demanded his men be ready for action at all times. Once, hearing the Five Pointers were preparing an onslaught, Crazy Butch decided to test his boys' preparedness. So, one night Crazy Butch and three of his men charged up the stairs and into the hall of the gang's Forsyth Street headquarters, blazing away with two revolvers each. The gang members, who were boozing or playing cards, either went out the windows or down the backstairs. Little Kishky, who had been sitting on a window sill, was so startled he fell backwards out the window and was killed. Crazy Butch was furious; he wanted his men better prepared for action than that.

Crazy Butch survived a number of gun battles with the Five Pointers and other gangsters under Humpty Jackson, but his own gang and the great Eastman gang started falling apart at the same time. In 1904 both he and Eastman disappeared from the scene. Eastman was sentenced to 10 years in prison for robbery, and Crazy Butch was killed by Harry the Soldier in a fight over a girl, an expert shoplifter called the Darby Kid.

Crazy Butch is seldom remembered today in criminal histories, but he trained many of the early 20th century gangsters and especially the sluggers of the union wars. Big Jack Zelig had started out under Crazy Butch. In fact, that notorious bruiser had always quaked under Butch's rage.

See also: *Monk Eastman.*

CREDIT Mobilier Scandal: First great robber baron plot

A financial unit set up to finance the construction costs of the Union Pacific, Credit Mobilier was the cause of one of the greatest congressional scandals of the 19th century.

In order to get favorable legislation on land grants and rights-of-way, Credit Mobilier "sold" company stock at half price to key congressmen—"where it would do the most good." The chief bagman in the operation was Rep. Oakes Ames of Massachusetts, a principal officer of Credit Mobilier. When the *New York Sun* broke the scandal in 1872, it was determined that among those whose goodwill Ames had managed

to buy was Vice President Schuyler Colfax (who had been Speaker of the House at the time of his alleged involvement), Sen. Henry Wilson and Rep. James A. Garfield. A congressional committee investigating the case concluded that the Credit Mobilier stockholders, including the congressmen involved, had reaped $23 million in ill-gotten profits. Garfield survived the scandal and went on to be elected president in 1880. Ames, however, fell victim to a censure motion in the House and returned home to Massachusetts, broken-hearted but still maintaining his innocence.

Some later economic historians concluded that Credit Mobilier's profits totaled "only $13 million to $16 million" and were not "excessive" by the standards of the day. Ames is described by some of these historians as being guilty of no more than a "grievous error of judgment." Nonetheless, the label of "robber baron" has remained attached to him.

CREEP Joint: Crooked brothel

Much of the prostitution activity in San Francisco during the 19th century was conducted in what were called cribs or cowyard cubicles. When business was brisk, a customer was not permitted time to undress, even to remove his footwear. Instead, a piece of oilcloth was spread along the bottom of the bed to keep the man's boots from soiling the bedding. Of course, all customers were required to remove their hats, since no self-respecting prostitute would consider entertaining a man with his hat on.

One type of crib that never forbade the removal of clothing by customers was the so-called creep joint. Here men were encouraged to hang everything in a closet that was attached to the back wall of the crib. The back walls, however, were really doors, and while the customer was otherwise occupied, an accomplice of the woman would open the door and steal all the man's money and valuables.

Creep joints may or may not have originated first in San Francisco, but at least in that city the rip-off was carried out with a certain amount of style and a touch of sympathy; a dime was always left in the man's clothing for his carfare home. Few men ever taken in creep joints attempted to put up a fight. It was common knowledge that such cribs had a push-button alarm attached to a nearby barroom which, if activated, would bring the saloon bouncer and several other toughs over to manhandle the protesting victim.

See also: *Badger Game, Panel House.*

CRETZER, Joseph Paul "Dutch" (1911-1946): Bank bandit and murderer

One of the key figures in the Alcatraz Prison Rebellion of 1946, the Rock's greatest break-out attempt, Dutch Cretzer was the country's top bank bandit of the late 1930s and Public Enemy No. 4.

The Cretzer gang laid waste to banks all along the West Coast up to the time their leader was captured in 1939. Sent to the federal prison on McNeil Island in the state of Washington, Cretzer attempted an escape by crashing a truck through a gate but was caught. Brought to trial in Tacoma for the attempt, he was quickly found guilty and given five additional years. As he was being led from the court, Cretzer clubbed a federal marshal with his handcuffed hands, killing him. He then picked up the dead lawman's gun and leveled it at the judge, intending to use him as a hostage. But before he could reach the judge, a court bailiff returning to the room jammed his gun into Cretzer's neck and disarmed him. Cretzer was convicted of murdering the federal marshal but escaped the death sentence because his victim had actually died of a heart attack during the assault on him.

Given a life term, Cretzer was taken in chains to Alcatraz, where within nine months he attempted another escape. He and another convict, Crazy Sam Shockley, overpowered a guard and tried to drill through a barred window in a prison workshop. In a speedboat nearby, two men were fishing, or at least they appeared to be fishing. They were really Cretzer gang members, and under some canvas aboard the boat were four submachine guns. The drilling of the bars was unsuccessful, however, and the convicts were found by other guards.

Cretzer was put in solitary for the next five years, an unusually harsh punishment in any federal penitentiary other than Alcatraz. But even that didn't stop Cretzer from once more joining an escape attempt after he was returned to the main cell house in March 1946. He once told a Seattle detective who came to see him about a bank job he had pulled: "I can't stand living at Alcatraz. I was reared in San Francisco, and being able to see the city lights go on each evening from my cell . . . I can't stand that. I'll make a break from here one day. And if I don't get killed in the trying, I'll kill myself."

Within days of returning to the cell house, Cretzer threw in with a Kentucky bank robber named Bernie Coy who had plotted out the most intricate escape plan ever devised in the prison. Coy had designed and built a bar spreader made from plumbing fixtures and valve parts and had figured out a way to break into the cell house gun gallery, where the only weapons in the building were kept. This acquisition of weapons was the one thing no previous Alcatraz breakout attempt had ever achieved. Coy had planned out a minute-by-minute, step-by-step escape route that would get himself, Cretzer and four others through Alcatraz's tight security net, across the prison yard and to the wharf, where they would seize a prison launch when it was just about to sail. They could make the mainland quickly, and then Cretzer's gang would pick them up in fast getaway cars before the authorities would have time to react.

Cretzer went into the deal even though he had a problem accepting Coy, whom he regarded as a "hick hillbilly," giving the orders. The great Alcatraz Prison Rebellion started on May 2, 1946 when the six plotters took over the cell block and freed the prisoners to confuse matters for prison officials. Once armed, they quickly took nine guards hostage. Cretzer, without Coy's knowledge and despite orders against any killing, shot and killed another guard. The plotters almost made it to freedom, Coy's plan failing only at the last corridor door be-cause a guard had, against prison rules, kept the key to the door in his pocket instead of returning it to its proper peg. Coy's delicate timetable collapsed and the prison launch left the island before the escapers could locate the key.

Cretzer went wild at the plan's failure and during Coy's absence turned his guns on the nine hostages, killing only one but severely wounding several others. Thinking he had killed them all, Cretzer retreated into an isolated part of the prison. Three of the plotters then slipped back to their cells as Cretzer, Coy and another prisoner, Marv Hubbard, tried to devise alternate escape plans. In a bizarre development Cretzer stalked Coy and his friend Hubbard, determined to kill them, while they in turn hunted him. Meanwhile, the released prisoners started a full-scale riot, and alarmed officials called in sharpshooter guards from other prisons as well as a detachment of battle-outfitted Marines. The "battle of Alcatraz" raged for almost 48 hours, as hundreds of grenades and gas bombs were dropped through holes in the roof to try to subdue the rampaging convicts. During this time Cretzer moved deeper into the bowels of the prison, attempting to find a way out along the sewer lines. Coy and Hubbard made their way to the same area, and it was here that all three men would die. According to some accounts, guards cornered them and a fierce gun battle ensued. Fanciful stories of this hit-and-run confrontation have Cretzer cackling insanely as he fired at the pursuers and screaming, "Hey, this is fun!" with Coy responding, "Yeah, and there's more coming."

Nothing like this happened. In a darkened tunnel Coy walked right into Cretzer, who shot him dead. The maddened Cretzer also tried to kill Hubbard but was driven off by the guards. A short time later, Cretzer was trapped and shot to death. So was Hubbard. The great crashout attempt was over.

See also: *Alcatraz Prison Rebellion, Bernard Paul Coy, Sam Shockley, Miran "Buddy" Thompson.*

CRIME Clocks: FBI statistical device

Probably no FBI method of publicizing crime statistics is more controversial than its so-called crime clocks, whereby an anxious public is given such intelligence as "there is a rape in this country every (14, 13, 12) minutes" or "someone is robbed every (5½, 5, 4½) minutes" etc.

What is most severely criticized about these crime clocks is that each year the time between the occurrence of such offenses almost inevitably shrinks, indicating an apparently constant increase in crime. The fallacy in the presentation is that no allowance is made for a steadily growing population, which may well mean more crimes statistically but not necessarily proportionally. Perhaps an even more germane criticism is based on the fact that an enormous number of all violent crimes are committed by teenagers, and in periods of rapid growth of this age group, the crime clock figures present a far greater distortion.

Much better than crime clocks, insist some critics, would be comparative figures to indicate the risk of violent attack from strangers, which is one of the less likely hazards facing the average American. For instance, the risk of death from reported cases of willful homicide is about one in 20,000, and a scant 25 percent of such murders are committed by strangers, all the rest being the work of the victim's family or friends. An average American is about 15 times more likely to be killed in a car crash. Rather than reduce crime statistics to mere minutes or seconds, critics prefer to note that the average chance of one being the victim of a crime of violence is roughly once in 400 years.

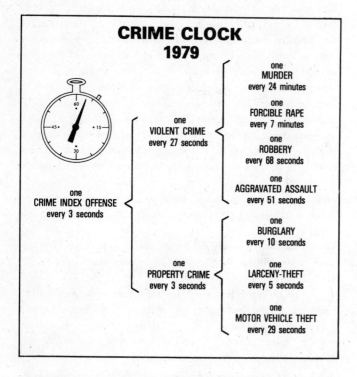

The FBI crime clocks have long been criticized for inaccurately indicating an apparently constant increase in crime.

CRIMMINS, Alice (1939-   ): Convicted child killer

One of New York's most lurid criminal cases started on July 14, 1965, when a 26-year-old mother and divorcee, Alice Crimmins, reported her two young children, four-year-old Alice Marie and five-year-old Edmund, were missing from her Queens apartment, apparently abducted. Both children were later found dead. The girl had clearly been murdered by strangulation, but the boy's body was too decomposed to ascertain the cause of his death.

However, the kidnapping theory was soon abandoned and investigators focused on the possibility that Alice Crimmins had killed her daughter in a fit of anger and then, with the aid of gangsters, murdered her son because he had witnessed the strangulation of his sister.

Originally tried in 1968 on a charge of killing her daughter, Alice Crimmins was found guilty of first-degree manslaughter in a trial spiced with lurid testimony about the defendant's extramarital affairs and "swinging" lifestyle. Many courtroom observers were surprised at the verdict and expressed the opinion that the manslaughter case had been rather weak and the woman had been convicted mainly because of her style of living, which much of the public found offensive.

Crimmins was sentenced to five to 20 years, but the guilty verdict was set aside after it was learned that several jurors had visited the scene of the alleged slayings on their own. When Crimmins was retried in 1971, she was charged with murdering both her daughter and her son. After a five-week trial she was convicted of manslaughter in the case of her daughter, for which she was given five to 20 years, and first-degree murder of her son, for which she drew life. An assistant district attorney was overheard to say he was "stunned" by the severity of the murder verdict. Eventually, higher courts threw out the murder conviction because of insufficient evidence but found there was "overwhelming proof" that Mrs. Crimmins had killed her daughter. As a result, her life sentence was lifted and she was left with the term of five to 20 years on the manslaughter count.

Early in 1975 newspapers reported that Crimmins was in a work-release program working as a secretary for an undisclosed Queens company while living in a Manhattan medium-security residential facility. She had also been allowed to marry Anthony Grace, a wealthy contractor who admitted he had been having an affair with her at the time of her daughter's death and on whose yacht she had been spending her summer weekends while on the work-release program. Later that same year Crimmins was granted a parole after serving the minimum five years of her sentence.

CRITTENDEN, Thomas T. (1832-1909): Missouri governor

The governor of Missouri during the last years of the Jesse James gang's reign, Thomas Crittenden clearly conspired with the Ford brothers to kill the noted criminal leader, an act that was to have a profound effect on his political career.

By 1882 the James gang was in disarray, most of its stalwart members either killed or jailed, and Jesse and Frank James were forced to rely on such less trustworthy accomplices as Dick Little and Bob and Charles Ford. By late 1881 Dick Little was secretly negotiating to surrender. Either through him or others, the Ford brothers had begun dickering with Gov. Crittenden about the $10,000 reward offered for Jesse James, dead or alive. They eventually met with Crittenden, and it later became a common belief that he actually gave the Ford brothers a written guarantee that they would be pardoned and given the reward money if they killed James. No such document ever surfaced, but when on April 3, 1882 Bob Ford shot the outlaw leader, Crittenden kept his part of the bargain, granting the Fords pardons and the reward money.

Crittenden clearly expected to be applauded for ridding the state of Jesse James and so was not prepared for maudlin support given to the murderous outlaw. "Good-Bye, Jesse!" wailed the *Kansas City Journal;* "Jesse By Jehovah," cried the *St. Joseph Gazette.* But the governor did not help his cause by telling the *St. Louis Republican* after the killing: "I have no excuse to make, no apologies to render to any living man for the part I have played in this bloody drama . . . I am not regretful of his death, and have no censure for the boys who removed him. They deserve credit, is my candid, solemn opinion. Why should these Ford boys be so abused?"

Such are not the statements of political heroes. When in 1882 Frank James stalked into the governor's office, unstrapped his guns and announced it was the first time he had done that since his days riding with Quantrill, the governor's stock plummeted further. Mobs cheered Frank James as he stood on train platforms on his way back to stand trial in Clay County. Crittenden was booed.

Crittenden had hoped to win another term as governor and then to pick up the mantle of the illustrious George Vest in the U.S. Senate, but the "James vote" was now against him, and his party refused even to renominate him for governor, leaving his political career in ruins. By contrast, when Frank James announced his support for Rough Rider Teddy Roosevelt after the turn of the century, the Missouri newspapers considered the endorsement important news and a boost for T.R.

See also: *Charles Ford, Robert Newton Ford, James Brothers, Dick Little.*

CROWLEY, Francis "Two Gun" (1911-1931): Murderer

Francis "Two Gun" Crowley was perhaps the nearest thing America produced to a 20th century counterpart of Billy the Kid. The only differences were that Crowley lived two years less and the Kid was never involved in as fierce a gun battle as Crowley was. In a short but violent criminal career, Crowley engineered a bank robbery, shot down a storekeeper in one of several holdups, was involved in the murder of Virginia Banner, a dance hall hostess who had turned down his partner-in-crime, and killed Frederick Hirsch, a policeman who had asked him for identification in a deserted spot near North Merrick, Long Island.

By then the newspapers had labeled the sallow-faced 19-year-old Two Gun Crowley, a reputation he would enhance in the most savage gun battle in the history of New York City. On May 7, 1931, in what was termed the "siege on West 90th Street," Crowley traded bullets with 300 police attackers from his hideout room, while his 16-year-old girl friend, Helen Walsh, and his partner, Rudolph Duringer, cowered under a bed. The police poured more than 700 bullets into the room, blasting away brick and mortar from the building's facade. In response, Crowley raced from window to window firing back and throwing tear gas cannisters lobbed into his room back to the street, where they overcame a number of his besiegers. Fifteen thousand persons jammed against police barricades, often seeming about to press through the barriers into the "no man's land" where the battle raged. More leaned out of neighboring windows, using pillows as armrests. It was violent Dodge City transferred to a Depression-weary Manhattan, an event to be savored. Finally, Crowley, shot four times and weakened by tear gas, was overwhelmed by a police assault squad that smashed through his door.

At his trial Crowley lived up to his press notices with an air of bravado, bantering with reporters, officers and the judge. He smirked when sentenced to the electric chair. In Sing Sing, Crowley maintained that attitude for a while. He fashioned a club out of a tightly wrapped magazine bound with wire from his cot and tried to slug a guard and escape from the death house. He set fire to his cell. He took off his clothes, stuffed the toilet with them and flooded the cell. Warden Lewis E. Lawes ordered Crowley be kept naked. Still, the youth looked for violence. He placed grains of sugar on the floor, and whenever a fly settled there, he would kill it and laugh.

Then slowly, Crowley changed. A starling flew into the cell and Crowley didn't kill it. He fed it, and each day the bird returned. "The prisoner had tamed the bird," Lawes noted. "But more surprising was the fact that the tiny bird tamed the bandit." The warden allowed Crowley all his former privileges, and they talked for hours. Lawes saw Crowley for what he was, a pathetic youth with a mental age of 10, born illegitimately and deserted by his mother. The only mother he had ever known was a woman who took him from a foundling home. He had had to work since the age of 12.

Shortly before he was to be executed, a press syndicate offered him $5,000 for his signature on a series of articles already written that purported to tell his life story. Crowley rejected the deal, telling Lawes, "If mother [meaning his foster mother] had that five grand when I was a kid, maybe things would have been different."

A few hours before he died, Crowley pointed to a large water bug running around his cell floor. "See that?" he said to Lawes. "I was about to kill it. Several times I wanted to crush it. It's a dirty looking thing. But then I decided to give it a chance and let it live." Lawes doubted if Crowley even grasped the significance of his remark.

He went to his death without the braggadocio of the newspaper-bred Two Gun Crowley. "Give my love to mother," he called out to Lawes as the hood went over his head.

CUNNINGHAMS' Revenge

In 1855 a band of 13 Mexican bandits, Juan Navaro's band, raided the Arizona ranch of Dave Cunningham and made off with his daughter, 15-year-old Mary. Cunningham and his two sons, John and Adrian, took up the pursuit and soon discovered the sad fate of the girl. She had been raped, and then she and her pinto pony had been forced over a precipice. The trail of the bandits showed they were headed for Mexico. The older Cunningham turned back. He had a wife and ranch to take care of. The two boys went on in what a president of the United States would later call "the most audacious feat ever brought to my attention."

They tracked Navaro's band to the town of Naco and then on to Agua Prieta, where the gang had taken over a cantina. One bandit came outside to relieve himself and the brothers stabbed him to death with their razor-sharp skinning knives. Soon, another bandit came out call to the first one. He met the same fate. Two other bandits emerged, accompanied by a woman. John jumped on one, neatly slitting his throat. Adrian, however, missed his man, who drew a long knife and gashed Adrian's arm before John came to the rescue and stabbed the bandit. The woman began screaming and the brothers fled. The remaining nine-man Navaro band did not give chase but rode off, after shooting up the town in anger. They obviously were not sure who or how many men had done the killings.

Eventually, after a run-in with the Mexican police, who were suspicious of their reasons for being in Mexico, the brothers again caught up with Navaro's band heading toward their home base at Chihuahua. They crept close to the bandits' sleeping camp and opened fire. The brothers did not know how many they had killed until dawn, when they found five corpses and the tracks of four horses. Navaro was among the missing. Now, however, Navaro knew he was being hunted and set a trap for the two brothers. One bandit rode ahead with the four horses while Navaro and the other two bandits waited in ambush. In the ensuing shoot-out two bandits were killed but Adrian was badly wounded in the leg. The brothers continued their pursuit with Adrian suffering in agony. Only Navaro and one other bandit were left. The Cunninghams had no choice but to make their way to Chihuahua openly, even though they knew Navaro would be waiting for them. Gangrene had infected Adrian's leg, and when they reached the town, a doctor said there was no alternative but amputation. Meanwhile, John Cunningham went out searching for the two bandits. He found them in a cantina. On the lookout for any American, they were instantly suspicious of him and may or may not have recognized him. When John walked out of the cantina, Navaro and the other bandit followed him. Outside, John Cunningham whirled, drew two six guns and opened fire. Both Mexicans dropped, and John stepped over them and fired several more shots into their bodies.

John Cunningham was arrested, but no charges could be pressed against Adrian. While they languished in Chihuahua, a detachment of U.S. cavalry under Maj. Ben Hunt, returning from a mission to Mexico City, passed through and heard of the affair. Maj. Hunt went to see the Cunninghams. The niceties of Mexican law did not impress Hunt; with a veiled threat of force, he secured the release of John Cunningham and returned the brothers to the United States. The Mexican government filed a protest, saying that what the brothers had done amounted to an armed incursion into Mexican sovereignty. A complete report of the affair was made to President Franklin Pierce, who decided that the Cunninghams would not be extradicted to Mexico. He called their bloody ride "the most audacious feat ever brought to my attention." Eventually, Mexico let the matter drop.

CURRY, Big Nose George (1841-1882): Outlaw and murderer

Often confused with Kid Curry (Harvey Logan), Big Nose George Curry (alias Flat Nose George Parrott, alias George Manuse) stands in his own right as not only a prolific stagecoach and train robber but also as the biggest cattle rustler of the 1870s in the Powder River region, Wyoming Territory. Harvey Logan, one of the most prominent of the Wild Bunch, was so taken with Big Nose's criminal career that he appropriated Curry as a nickname for himself.

Big Nose Curry was finally apprehended for the 1880 holdup of a Union Pacific train and the killing of two deputy sheriffs; he was sentenced to hang on April 3, 1882 in Rawlins, Wyo. A week before his slated execution, Big Nose broke out of jail but was immediately captured by a mob that, taking unkindly to condemned men escaping, resolved to hang him on the spot. Big Nose was ordered to climb a ladder set against a lamp post, put a rope around his own neck and jump. Big Nose did, but the rope broke. While some of the mob said another rope should be secured, others felt it wasn't worth the effort and shot Big Nose to death as he lay on the ground.

Even in death, Big Nose had a role to play. The local druggist, Dr. J. E. Osborne, who was also the coroner, performed an autopsy on the badman and in the process helped himself to some of his parts. He peeled off the hide from Big Nose's chest, tanned it and made a pair of slippers, which were still on display in a Rawlins bank during the 1970s. Osborne, who incidentally went on to become governor of Wyoming, fashioned other tanned hide from the outlaw into a tobacco pouch. When he had finished skinning Big Nose, Osborne dropped the rest of the corpse into a barrel of alcohol, put it out behind his premises and forgot about it. The barrel was rediscovered in 1950 and caused quite a stir until the dry bones therein were identified as the old badman Big Nose Curry.

CUSTOM House Place: Chicago vice district

Of all the "brothel streets" in Chicago during the 19th century, the one that gave the police the most trouble was Custom House Place. Besides the standard bordellos, the street contained an abundance of panel houses, where, by use of sliding panels, a male customer's possessions would be stolen while he was involved with a prostitute. A study in 1890 revealed there were almost 200 panel houses on Custom House Place, Plymouth Place and Clark and State streets, with the greatest number on Custom House Place.

Probably the most notorious business on Custom House Place was at No. 202, a resort that functioned as a standard brothel, as a panel house and as a meeting place for some of the worst female ruffians of the 1880s and 1890s. The house was run by Lizzie Davenport, probably the biggest operator of panel houses in the city and certainly the wealthiest. Among the women who headquartered at No. 202 were Emma Ford, her sister Pearl Smith, Flossie Moore and Mary White, better known as the Strangler. All these women functioned as panel house workers, street muggers and holdup artists. The Strangler was estimated by police to have stolen more than $50,000 in less than three years. Inside No. 202 it was quite common for 10 to 15 robberies to take place in a night. Because the house was subject to frequent police raids, Lizzie Davenport protected her ladies by installing a closet made of three-inch oak planks with a massive door, where they could hide. Detective Clifton Wooldridge became the darling of the press when he rousted the women by boring holes in the door and blowing pepper inside. Through such sterling police work, one of Chicago's most notorious houses was finally shuttered.

See also: *Emma Ford, Flossie Moore, Panel Houses, Clifton Wooldridge.*

CUTLER Lie Detector Decision

Although lie detector findings are generally not accepted as evidence in courtroom proceedings, based on a landmark decision in *Frye v. United States,* there has been an occasional ruling the other way. A breakthrough of sorts occurred in California in 1972. Raymond Christopher Cutler was stopped by a deputy U.S. marshal in the Los Angeles International Airport when the officer became suspicious of a suitcase Cutler was carrying. The marshal requested permission to open the suitcase for inspection and Cutler's response was to be a point of contention later. The marshal said Cutler had agreed and Cutler said he had not. In any event, the suitcase was opened and found to contain marijuana.

Cutler's defense was based on the claim that his luggage had been searched illegally since he had refused permission. With the consent of Superior Court Judge Allan Miller, both men, the defendant and the marshal, were subjected to lie detector tests. The examiner reported that Cutler's claim of having denied permission for his luggage to be searched was truthful, and on this basis the defendant was freed. Judge Miller ruled that since scientific tests had demonstrated the accuracy of lie detector equipment and techniques, rules preventing the use of lie detector findings as evidence should be changed. It was a surprising decision, one that sparked the district attorney's immediate notice of an intention to appeal. However, no appeal was made. It soon appeared, observers noted, that the decision in the Cutler case would have no impact on other cases, which provided more sweeping precedents.

Ironically, shortly after the Cutler decision California Gov. Edmund Brown, Jr. signed into law a bill that ran contrary to the spirit of the Cutler case. The law, referred to as the police officers' bill of rights, gave law enforcement officers the right to refuse to take a lie detector test without fear that such refusal could be held against them.

See also: *Frye v. United States, Lie Detector.*

CYCLONE Louie (1882-1908): Coney Island strongman and murderer

Using the name Cyclone Louie, Vach Lewis was a noted professional strong man who was always available for a hit assignment, thereby earning the title of the Coney Island Killer in the early 1900s. When two men were found strangled on the beach one morning with their necks virtually wrung like chickens, all Coney Island knew Cyclone Louie had done the deed. So too did the police, but two dancing girls and six other members of their family insisted the strong man had spent the entire night under their tender ministrations after he had allegedly wrenched his back while wrapping an iron bar around his neck. There Cyclone Louie lay moaning, too weak to unwrap the cursed metal. The police were forced to drop the charge against Louie, who shortly thereafter regained his strength and unbent the iron bar.

While Cyclone Louie's murder services involved a substantial fee, he rendered similar duty without charge for Kid Twist, the last great leader of the Eastman gang before it fractionalized upon his killing. The big, hulking Cyclone Louie followed Kid Twist around like a loyal dog, marveling at his mental superiority. There were those who said that Cyclone Louie would never meet his mental equal. But although he wasn't bright, Cyclone Louie was nonetheless useful to Kid Twist. One service he performed was the elimination of "the Bottler," the partner of Kid Twist and Kid Dahl in the operation of a profitable crooked card game in a Suffolk Street house on Manhattan's Lower East Side. Twist and Dahl had simply declared themselves in on the Bottler's operation and later decided to declare the Bottler out. Thus, at the time of the Bottler's murder Kid Twist was in the Delancey Street police station arguing with the desk sergeant for the release of a fellow gangster who had purposely got himself arrested, and Kid Dahl was in a Houston Street restaurant involved in a loud argument with the proprietor. With those alibis firmly in place, Cyclone Louie walked in on the card game and shot the Bottler dead in front of 20 players, each of whom later claimed either to have been elsewhere or, if they admitted being there, to have been looking in the other direction.

Cyclone Louie died in the service of Kid Twist on May 14, 1908 while making the rounds of Coney Island dives. The pair ran into a mortal enemy of Twist's, Louie the Lump, in one dive and ordered him to jump out the window, a rather unfriendly suggestion since they were on the second floor of the building. Louie the Lump was forced to leap but survived and, being a member of the Five Points Gang, quickly put in a call to Manhattan for reinforcements. Twenty gunmen answered the summons and stationed themselves outside the dive, where Twist and Cyclone Louie were drinking themselves senseless. When the pair emerged from the joint, Louie the Lump shot Kid Twist in the brain. Cyclone Louie tried to run for it but was cut down by a Five Point volley and tumbled dead atop his beloved mentor. Later, every Five Pointer involved insisted his bullet struck Cyclone Louie. The police do not seem to have made an accurate count of the bullets that brought about Cyclone Louie's demise. The only one ever arrested for the crime was Louie the Lump. The killer's lawyer made a fervent, if somewhat tortured, plea of self-defense, which evidently had some effect since Louie the Lump was sent to prison for a mere 11 months.

See also: *Kid Twist.*

Firing a shot into President William McKinley's stomach, assassin Leon Czolgosz cries, "I have done my duty."

CZOLGOSZ, Leon (1873-1901):
McKinley assassin

The crowd at the Pan-American Exposition in Buffalo, N.Y. at noon on September 6, 1901 was jubilant over the opportunity to meet William McKinley, the President of the United States, face to face. They queued up excitedly after the President had agreed to shake hands with all comers. At the end of the line was a dark little man of 28, his right hand swatched in a white bandage. When he was about sixth in line, the man lowered his head to keep from being spotted. He had lived in nearby West Seneca for some time and was known to police as a dangerous anarchist.

The President was smiling as he stepped toward Czolgosz. Czolgosz waited until he was just a few feet from the President and then flipped a pistol out from under the phony bandage and fired. The first shot hit a button and bounced away, but the second penetrated the President's abdomen. McKinley stiffened a moment but did not lose consciousness as guards and soldiers pounced on his attacker. "I done my duty," Czolgosz cried. A guard took careful aim and smashed his fist into Czolgosz' face. "Be easy with him boys," the President said weakly.

Eight days later, McKinley died of gangrene of the pancreas. Latter-day opinion contended that bungled medical care was as much the cause of death as Czolgosz' bullet. Nine days after the President's death, Czolgosz was put on trial, a matter in which the defendant took no interest. He said nothing to his court-appointed lawyers, refused to take the stand and showed no reaction when a verdict of guilty was announced. All he would do was affirm his anarchist beliefs, even though long before the assassination an anarchist publication, *Free Society,* had urged others to avoid him, denouncing Czolgosz as a dangerous crank and possibly a spy or police agent.

When Czolgosz went to the electric chair at Auburn Prison, he said: "I killed the President because he was the enemy of the good people—the good working people. I am not sorry for my crime." When he was placed in his coffin, sulfuric acid was poured on his body, and experts predicted his corpse would decompose in 12 hours.

After McKinley's death, the third presidential assassination in 36 years, the new President, Theodore Roosevelt, ordered the U.S. Secret Service to take over full responsibility for guarding the chief executive.

D

DALTON, J. Frank: See Jesse James—Impostors.

DALTON Brothers: Outlaws

The outlaw Dalton brothers might have become great bandits in the tradition of their cousins, the Younger brothers, who rode with Jesse James, had they not come into the Wild West just as it was taming down. Law and order were taking over, but the Daltons refused to believe it. They were driven to make a name for themselves.

Oddly enough, four of the brothers—Frank, Gratton, Robert and Emmett—first pinned on U.S. marshal badges for Hanging Judge Parker's court in Fort Smith, Ark., and Frank was killed in the line of duty. Evidently, the surviving brothers plus younger William were unimpressed by Judge Parker's hang-'em-high policies and decided to hit the outlaw trail. They headed for California, where they pulled a few small capers and then tried a train robbery in 1891. Bill was caught and sent to prison for 25 years. Grat was given the same sentence but escaped and rejoined Bob and Emmett, and they hightailed it back east.

In Oklahoma the trio started up a gang that took in such worthies as Charlie Bryant, Charley Pierce, George Newcomb and Bill Doolin, who was to become a more distinguished outlaw than any of the Daltons. They pulled a few minor jobs, during which Doolin was starting to think the Daltons were nothing like their kinfolk, the Youngers.

The brothers, for their part, were determined to do something big to make the West stand up and take notice of them, and they came up with the idea of the great Coffeyville Raid. They decided to hit the Kansas town and pull a double bank job, robbing two institutions at the same time. It made sense to them, one entrance into town, one escape from town and double profits. Six men started out on the raid, but Doolin pulled out when his horse went lame, perhaps thinking, What am I doing with clowns like these?

Contemporary rendering depicts the bloody demise of the Dalton gang in Death Alley, Coffeyville, Kan.

On October 5, 1892 the three Daltons plus Dick Broadwell and Bill Powers rode into the Coffeyville town plaza and set about holding up the Condon and First National banks. They had done no recent scouting and found the hitching posts in

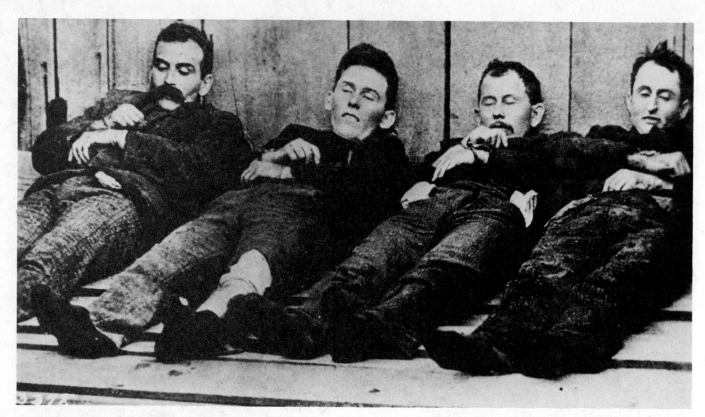

The end of the Daltons. Photo shows corpses of (left to right) Bill Powers, Bob Dalton, Grat Dalton and Dick Broadwell.

front of both banks had been removed because workmen were busy on the street. The bandits had to leave their horses in an alley—Death Alley, it would be called later—about a block away. They came out of Death Alley carrying Winchesters and broke off in two groups to head for the banks. The scene was noted by a local citizen, Alec McKenna, who thought he even recognized one or two of the men as Daltons. Watching from a distance, McKenna spotted weapons being pointed in one of the banks and sounded the alarm. The robbers still might have gotten away in time had they not had to wait around for a time lock to open one of the safes.

By the time the gang emerged from the two banks, half the town was armed and laying for them. In the next two hectic minutes, four citizens of Coffeyville died from the outlaws' gunfire, but the Dalton gang would ride no more. None of them survived the race through Death Alley, although they did make it to their horses. Charlie Connelly, the town marshal, traded bullets with Grat Dalton and both fell dead. Broadwell was shot out of his saddle and both Powers and Bob Dalton were gunned down by John Kloehr, a livery stable owner.

Only Emmett made it to the end of the alley and could have gotten away, but in a show of brotherly devotion, he turned back to try to save Bob, whom he idolized. Dying, Bob moaned: "Don't mind me, boy. I'm done for. Don't surrender! Die game!"

Emmett was still trying to pull Bob up in the saddle when he was felled by 18 buckshot in the back. Of the five, only Emmett survived. He was sentenced to life in the Kansas State Penitentiary. Ironically, his act of pointless heroism at Coffeyville gave the Daltons their greatest claim to fame.

In 1895 Bill Dalton, released from prison, was killed by a posse in Oklahoma Territory. Emmett Dalton was pardoned in 1907 and moved to California, where he prospered as a building contractor. He also did some writing for the movies and appeared in small roles in some of his own epics. His main literary work was entitled *When the Daltons Rode,* which appeared in 1931, six years before the last of the Daltons died. It purported to be a true account of the Daltons' activities but has never been regarded as overly accurate or incisive. The fact is the Daltons never understood they had been born a quarter of a century too late. Emmett showed that in 1910 when a New York reporter asked his expert opinion on how to keep the city cleansed of crime. The reformed outlaw earnestly advised, "Guard the entrances to the town."

DALY, John (1839-1864): Western outlaw

The head of perhaps the most vicious gang to terrorize the Nevada gold fields in the 1860s, John Daly, a young gunfighter from California who followed the gold trail, firmly believed in what might be called "criminal vigilantism." He felt that resistance by law-abiding elements called for their lynching. Because of these fear tactics, the Daly gang operated with a great deal of impunity and left a trail of robbery and murder from Aurora to Carson City. In 1863 one of Daly's confederates, Jim Sears, tried some horse stealing and was shot dead by an employee of William R. Johnson. Daly promptly held Johnson responsible for this act of resistance and prepared to exercise his form of vigilante justice. On February 1, 1864 Daly and three of his men cornered Johnson and made an example of him by cutting his throat and setting his body aflame. Daly later boasted of the work of "us vigilantes," but it developed that what he had accomplished was not the quashing of all resistance but the planting of a powerful suggestion. The Citizens' Protective Association was set up, and exactly one week after the Johnson assassination, Daly and three members of his gang, Johnny McDowell, William Buckley and Jim Masterson, were seized separately before they suspected what was afoot and were summarily hanged outside Aurora's Armory Hall.

DANCE Of Death: Famed multiple hangings

Probably no simultaneous public hangings in the 19th century produced more protests than the celebrated Dance of Death at Fort Smith, Ark. on September 3, 1875.

Six condemned men had been found guilty in Hanging Judge Parker's so-called Court of the Damned and were sentenced to die on a special 12-man gallows constructed by George Maledon, who became known as Parker's Lord High Executioner. This first multiuse of the gallows brought out a crowd of 5,000 eager citizens. Jamming into the fort compound, families came by the wagonload from as far as 50 to 60 miles away to witness the first dispensation of Parker-style justice. Youngsters mounted the walls of the fort for a better view; however, the more comfortable vantage points were reserved for gentlemen of the press from St. Louis, Kansas City, Philadelphia, New York and Boston, among others.

At exactly 9:30 a.m. the six men were brought to the gallows. One, a Cherokee named Smoker Mankiller, had been found guilty of killing his white neighbor but protested to the end that he had not done so, his unfortunate name notwithstanding. Sam Fooy, a half-breed who had murdered a school teacher during a robbery, had made peace with himself and was ready, even eager, to die. John Whittingham, who had clubbed and knifed a drinking companion to death, left behind a written condemnation of "demon rum." Edmund Campbell, convicted of a double-passion slaying, had nothing to say. James H. Moore, a horse thief and murderer, spotted a friend in the crowd, waved and called, "Goodbye, Sandy." And Dan Evans, who had killed an 18-year-old for his boots, surveyed the throng from the high platform and opined, "There are worse men here than me."

After prayers led by four local clergymen, Maledon slipped black masks over the men's heads and adjusted the nooses of specially ordered Kentucky hemp rope around their necks. He clambered down the 12 steps and pressed the trigger-release. Six bodies hurtled into an eight-foot drop. Not a single body twitched. All had died instantly of broken necks rather than suffering slow strangulation. Hangman Maledon was proud of his handiwork and certainly the local citizenry was satisfied both with the show and the demonstration of quick, unyielding justice.

The hangings received coast-to-coast newspaper coverage, and the reaction was generally far from laudatory. Newspaper readers were horrified over the simultaneous public hangings, although most probably, they would readily have accepted such executions if performed separately. Judge Parker bore the brunt of the public revulsion, being regarded as a monster who enjoyed wholesale executions and gaining for the first time the sobriquet of Hanging Parker, a name that would stick to him during the 21 years of his judicial reign. Despite the criticism, Parker and Maledon continued their brand of legal retribution, although never again would six doomed men do the dance of death at one time. Thereafter, the top number was five.

See also: *George Maledon, Isaac "Hanging Judge" Parker.*

DANIELS, James (?-1865): Murderer and vigilante victim

Called the "vigilante's experiment," murderer James Daniels was the first prisoner of the famous Montana Vigilance Committee of the 1860s to be turned over to the law instead of being promptly lynched. The experiment was not a glowing success and the vigilantes did not make the same mistake twice—at least not with the same man.

A bad-tempered Californian, Daniels stabbed to death a man named Gartley in a dispute over cards. When she heard of her husband's death, Mrs. Gartley suffered a fatal heart attack. Normally, Daniels would have faced quick vigilante action, but times were changing in the territory, and many citizens— even vigilance committee members—were convinced the politic thing to do was to hand over Daniels for trial in the regular courts of justice. And they prevailed.

In view of the extenuating circumstance—both men had gone after one another at the same time—Daniels was found guilty only of murder in the second degree and was sent to prison for three years. If that conclusion galled a number of citizens, it was nothing compared to the feelings aroused when Daniels was granted a pardon after only a few months. It appeared that the pardon may have resulted from a clerical error but the matter was soon academic. Daniels returned to the scene of his crime and made it clear he intended to wage war on the vigilantes who had brought him to justice. In Daniels' case such loose talk was a capital matter, and he was seized by vigilantes on his first night in Helena and hanged forthwith. It was a considerable length of time before the vigilantes decided their experiment with established justice was worth trying again.

See also: *Professor Thomas J. Dimsdale.*

DANIELS, Murl (1924-1949): Mass murderer

With another parolee, Murl Daniels committed a series of

senseless murders in Ohio in 1948, making him the quarry in what came to be labeled the "greatest manhunt in Ohio history."

Both Daniels, a psychopath, and his partner, John Coulter West, had done time at the Mansfield Reformatory, where, said Daniels, they had formed a compact that they would return someday to "take care" of one or more of the guards who had mistreated them. At the time, Daniels was serving a one-to 25-year term for a stickup and West, a feeble-minded man, was doing a one- to seven-year stretch for stealing tires off a truck. Some critics of the American justice and penal systems have said that Daniels never should have been paroled, while others have insisted that the state was negligent in permitting an inmate such as West to mingle with a dangerous psychopath like Daniels.

When the two were paroled, they teamed up to commit stickups throughout the Midwest, finally killing a tavern owner during a robbery. They continued to rove the Midwest, committing several more holdups before they remembered their compact about killing some of their former guards. They headed for Mansfield, especially determined to kill a guard named Harris. But they were unable to locate him. They then decided to get Harris' address from his superior, John Elmer Niebel, who was in charge of the reformatory farm. They awakened Niebel about midnight and decided they would have to hold him and his wife and daughter until after they had killed Harris. They took the three of them to a cornfield outside of town and ordered them to take off their clothes, in order to make it more difficult for them to give an alarm if they worked themselves loose from their bindings, but then the pair realized that they had neglected to bring any rope with them. So instead, they shot and killed all three and fled to Cleveland. When they were identified as the killers an intensive manhunt was mounted. Daniels and West raced around the state, killing a farmer to get his car and later a truck driver for his truck.

They almost made it out of the state with the truck, a haulaway carrying new Studebaker cars. They were waved through a number of police roadblocks until one sheriff realized that the truck was headed back towards the auto plant instead away from it. The two were ordered to stop and West started shooting, hitting a guard before he himself was killed. Daniels surrendered meekly and went to the electric chair on January 3, 1949.

DANITES: Alleged Mormon murder squads

There was a time when almost every anti-Mormon in the West was certain that the Mormon Church had a special terrorist killer squad charged with the violent eradication of all those who opposed the Mormons. According to the belief, Brigham Young had organized these Destroying Angels, or Danites, who operated as a separate cell of the church and took on all assignments involving death or violence. In an interview with Horace Greeley, Young emphatically denied their existence.

Real or not, the story of the Danites was widely believed, and every Mormon charged with a crime would be labeled a Danite. The belief, of course, kept anti-Mormonism at fever pitch for many years.

DANNAN, Emmanuel (1843-1851): Murder victim folk hero

Known as the "boy who wouldn't lie," eight-year-old Emmanuel Dannan became an instant Wisconsin folk hero when he was killed by his adopted parents, Samuel Norton and his wife, in 1851. Both of Emmanuel's English-immigrant parents died before he was five years old, and he was saved from the poorhouse by an uncle, who unfortunately died a year later. The Samuel Nortons then adopted the child.

Emmanuel was eight when he happened to see his stepparents murder a peddler. The Nortons ordered the boy to lie to the police, but he said he would not. He was hanged by his wrists from the rafters of the family's log cabin deep in the woods and beaten with willow switches for two hours. During his ordeal the only thing the boy would say was, "Pa, I will not lie!" After two hours the boy's spirit was still unbroken, but his body was and he died. The facts came out in an investigation, and the Nortons were both sent to prison for seven years, while Emmanuel's tale spread throughout the area.

There was talk of erecting a monument to his memory, and a total of $1,099.94 was collected, only to be siphoned off by a fund raiser. Over the years the story of Emmanuel Dannan's bravery became part of the state's folklore, and finally, on May 2, 1954 a monument was erected in his memory at Montello, Wis. The inscription read, "Blessed are they which are persecuted for righteousness sake, for theirs is the kingdom of Heaven." Since then, Truth Day in Montello has been celebrated every May 2.

DARROW, Clarence Seward (1857-1938): Defense lawyer

America's greatest lawyer, Clarence Darrow, had been practicing before the bar for 16 years when in 1894 he took on the case of a convicted murderer who was appealing to a higher court. Darrow lost and the man, Robert Prendergast, was hanged. He was the first—and last—Darrow client to be executed, although the famous lawyer represented more than 50 accused murderers, many of whom were definitely guilty.

Born in the Ohio farmlands in 1857, Darrow's formal education ended after he finished the equivalent of one year of high school. He continued to study law books at night, however, and saved up enough money to go to law school. In 1878 Darrow was admitted to the bar and soon became a political reformer, backing the ill-fated John Peter Altgeld's efforts in Illinois. Later, he was a well-paid corporation lawyer, but his natural sympathies lay with the working man, and in 1894 he rejected the business world to defend labor leader Eugene V.

Debs in connection with the Pullman strike. He earned the permanent enmity of business when in 1906 he successfully defended radical labor leader Big Bill Haywood on a murder charge. However, he was forced to plead labor men James McNamara and John J. McNamara guilty in the 1910 bombing of the *Los Angeles Times,* a decision that had a shattering effect on the Western labor movement. The unions refused to pay him his $50,000 fee in the case, and the prosecution, prodded by *Times* publisher and rabid anti-unionist Harrison Gray Otis, tried to convict him of jury tampering. Darrow beat the charges, but he never again took a labor-related case.

He continued to achieve considerable success, however, in leading criminal cases. Darrow's secret, he admitted, was his ability to pick a jury, which he considered the most important part of any case. "Get the right men in the box," he said, "and the rest is window dressing." Darrow would seldom accept a German or a Swede for a jury. A German, he felt, was too bullheaded and too "law and order" oriented and a Swede also too stubborn. His favorite jurors were Irishmen and Jews. Both, he felt, were highly emotional and easily moved to sympathy. He often said the perfect jury was six Irishmen and six Jews. "Give me that combination in the box," he remarked often, "and I could get Judas Iscariot off with a five dollar fine."

Darrow also preferred older men to younger ones. An older

man, he said, was more sympathetic to the jams other men got into. In important cases Darrow assigned investigators to look into the lives of prospective jurors and would come into court with a dossier on all the veniremen, aware of their foibles, their likes and dislikes and their prejudices. Through the years Darrow was never troubled by the testimony of experts against his clients. His handling of a medical witness called to testify that an accident victim would soon be up and around was typical; it ran:

> "You came here from out of town to testify for the company, Doctor?"
> "Yes."
> "And you had a nice trip?"
> "Yes, Mr. Darrow."
> "How much are you getting for testifying, Doctor—over and above the expenses of your trip?"
> "Three hundred dollars."

Darrow then turned to the jury, raised his eyebrows and, still looking at the jurors rather than the witness, growled, "That will be all, Doctor."

Once Darrow implied that an expert was a money grubber, he never deigned to concern himself with what the witness had to say—and usually neither did the jury.

There is no record of how much money Darrow made in a year. There were years when he made over $100,000, but

The Great Defender, Clarence Darrow, is shown in shirt sleeves, at the Monkey Trial. Standing behind him in light jacket is schoolteacher John Scopes.

others when, bogged down in cases with penniless clients, he netted very little. Even in what was perhaps his most famous case—that of thrill-slayers Nathan Leopold and Richard Loeb in 1924, two wealthy Chicago youths whom he saved from execution—his clients, the boys' parents, reneged on paying him the major part of his fee.

The Leopold and Loeb case showed Darrow's courtroom genius at its best, passing up a jury trial in favor of making his case to a judge. From experience, Darrow knew that while a juror might convict and thus doom a defendant if his vote was only one-twelfth of the decision, that same juror would draw back if his vote alone was the deciding factor. He shrewdly viewed the judge, a humane jurist, John Caverly, as no different than the average juror.

Although both sides presented expert psychiatric testimony, Darrow knew in the end that he would have to sway the judge with his summation, in part because he himself probably recognized his two clients were homicidal. Throughout the trial Darrow had had trouble keeping them from smirking in court and hamming it up for photographers outside the court. Public opinion had been against the two rich boys from the beginning and became even more so because of their mannerisms during the trial.

For two days Darrow summarized his case, maintaining his clients were not murderers but two boys who had taken a human life because they were mentally and morally sick, victims of complicated, often misunderstood forces, buried deep in their past. He ended by declaring: "Your Honor, if these two boys hang, *you* must order them to hang. It will be entirely up to *you*, Your Honor. There must be no division of responsibility here, Your Honor. The sentencing of these boys to die must be an act on *your* part alone. Such a sentencing must be your own cold, deliberate, premeditated act, without the slightest chance to shift any part of the responsibility. Your Honor alone stands between these boys and the trap door of the scaffold."

Darrow's gamble of bypassing a jury trial worked. The judge sentenced the pair to life imprisonment.

The following year Darrow won worldwide acclaim in Tennessee's famous Monkey Trial, in which he dueled with William Jennings Bryan over the theory of evolution. Darrow's client, a young schoolteacher named John Scopes, was convicted of teaching evolution, a decision that was almost inevitable considering the time and the place, and fined $100, but the famous lawyer clearly won the case against Bryan in the world of public opinion.

Darrow published his autobiography in 1932, six years before he died at the age of 81.

See also: *John P. Altgeld, William J. Burns, William D. "Big Bill" Haywood,* Los Angeles Times *Bombing, Leopold and Loeb, Massie Case, Mistaken Identity, Harry Orchard, Earl Rogers, John T. Scopes.*

DAUGHERTY, Roy (1871-1924): Outlaw

One of the few Western bank robbers to make the transition from riding a horse to driving an automobile in his line of work, Roy Daugherty, better known as Arkansas Tom, was born in to a very religious Missouri family; two of his older brothers became preachers. Leaving home in his early teens, he turned up in Oklahoma Territory and by 1892 was riding with the notorious Doolin gang.

He was with Bill Doolin and his men in the epic Battle of Ingalls on September 1, 1893 and was the only member of the gang captured there. While the other gang members were in Murray's Saloon, Arkansas Tom was sleeping in his room at the Pierce Hotel when a posse of 13 lawmen headed by Jim Masterson, Bat's brother, came thundering into town. When the shooting started, Arkansas Tom climbed up on the hotel roof for a better overview and from there killed Deputy Tom Houston and probably killed Deputy Ike Steel. His sharpshooting permitted the rest of the Doolin gang to fight their way out of town with only one man wounded, but Arkansas Tom was trapped on the hotel roof. An hourlong shoot-out ended when Tom Masterson got hold of several sticks of dynamite and threatened to blow up the entire building and Arkansas with it. Arkansas Tom laid down his arms and surrendered.

For his part in the Battle of Ingalls, Daugherty was sentenced to 50 years in prison, but he was paroled in 1910, in large part due to the efforts of his preacher brothers. Arkansas Tom vowed to go straight after that. Nonetheless, he took part in a bank job in Neosho, Mo. in 1916. Sent back to prison, he was not released until November 11, 1921. Arkansas Tom was soon identified as having been involved in another bank stickup, this time in Asbury, Mo., but he managed to stay out of the way of the law until August 6, 1924, when a young policeman recognized him in Joplin, Mo. Arkansas had managed the switch from horses to cars in bank robberies easily enough, but the switch in clothing fashions was more difficult for the old-fashioned gunfighter. Back in his younger days, Arkansas Tom was quite a fast draw, but in 1924 it wasn't common practice to walk around with hip holsters. While fast-draw Tom was trying to claw his shooting iron out of his back pocket, the policeman easily cut him down.

See also: *Doolin Gang; Ingalls, Oklahoma Territory, Battle of.*

D'AUTREMONT Brothers: See Edward Oscar Heinrich.

DAVIS, Angela (1944-): Political activist and accused murderess

Few political figures in recent years have been so enmeshed in a criminal case as black activist Angela Davis, a former acting assistant professor of philosophy at the University of California at Los Angeles. In 1972 Davis was charged with kidnapping, murder and conspiracy in connection with the highly publicized shoot-out at the Marin County Courthouse in San Raphael, Calif. in August 1970. Before she was brought to trial, Davis fled and was placed on the FBI's list of the 10 most-wanted fugitives.

Born in Birmingham, Ala., Davis took part, with her mother, in civil rights demonstrations during the mid-1950s. After graduation from Brandeis University and two years of postgraduate study in West Germany, she enrolled in the University of California at San Diego in 1967 to study under Marxist philosopher Herbert Marcuse. Growing more radical in her political beliefs, Davis became involved with a number of militant black organizations, including the Black Panthers. In 1968 she joined the Communist Party. The following year Davis was hired to teach four courses in philosophy at UCLA. Within a few short months she was dismissed from her position after her membership in the Communist Party was revealed by an ex-FBI informer. She won reinstatement under court order and in 1969-70 her courses were described as among the most popular on campus. The school administration monitored her classes and found them "excellent," but the Board of Regents, which included Gov. Ronald Reagan, refused to reappoint her.

What most upset the regents was her speeches in support of the Soledad Brothers, the name given to a group of black prisoners at Soledad Prison who had organized a Marxist revolutionary collective among the convicts. Three of the Brothers, George Jackson, Fleeta Drumgo and John Cluchette, were accused of murdering a white prison guard a short time after three other blacks involved in a fistfight had been shot dead by a tower guard, an action the local district attorney had labeled justifiable homicide.

Davis became a principal figure in the Soledad Brothers' Defense Committee, organized in support of the three prisoners. She established a clandestine correspondence with George Jackson even before meeting him. Eventually, the charges against Jackson, Drumgo and Cluchette were dismissed.

Meanwhile, after receiving threats against her life, Davis legally bought several guns for the defense of Soledad House, her base during the trial of the trio. On August 7, 1970 Jonathan Jackson, George's teenage brother, and Davis' constant companion during this period, took the guns Davis had purchased and entered the Marin County Courthouse, where a San Quentin prisoner, James McClain, was on trial for a prison stabbing. Jackson's plan was to free McClain and two other inmates there to testify in McClain's defense and to take white hostages who would be held as ransom for the release of the Soledad Brothers. Passing guns to the three convicts, Jackson supervised the taking of five hostages from the courthouse, including Judge Harold Haley and District Attorney Gary Thomas. A gunfight erupted in the parking lot and Judge Haley, Jackson and two of the inmates were killed, while Thomas was badly wounded and left permanently paralyzed.

Because the guns were owned by her, Davis was indicted on charges of murder, kidnapping and conspiracy. She went into hiding and became the object of a nationwide search. Two months later, she was captured by the FBI in a New York City motel and extradited back to California. While she was held without bail in California, a worldwide Free Angela movement sprang up. Finally, Davis was released on $102,000 bail.

During her trial, which finally began on February 28, 1972 after a series of procedural delays, the prosecution's case proved

to be astonishingly fragile, based on the premise that Davis' "passion for George Jackson"—who had been killed in August of the previous year while allegedly attempting to escape from prison—had led her to plot the courthouse kidnappings. The defense countered that there was absolutely no evidence linking Davis to the kidnapping or to the planning of it. On June 4, 1972 a jury of 11 whites and one Mexican-American acquitted her on all counts following 13 hours of deliberation.

DAVIS, Jack (?1845-1879?): Train robber

On November 4, 1870 Jack Davis, a leader of the Davis-Chapman gang, pulled the first train robbery in the Far West, holding up the Central Pacific's Train No. 1 near Verdi, Nev. The job netted more than $40,000.

As successful as he was at train robbing, Davis was a failure at most other criminal endeavors. He appeared as a not too successful gambler around Virginia City in the late 1860s. Davis was suspected of having taken part in some small-time stagecoach holdups but the charges never stuck. Early in 1870 he linked up with John Chapman, the superintendent of a Sunday school in Reno, and together they plotted to imitate the train-robbing exploits of the Reno gang of Indiana. Their first robbery was a success, but careless free spending by some of the gang eventually led to their capture. Davis was sentenced to 10 years and Chapman to 20.

Davis got out after serving less than six years and went back on the outlaw trail, joining up with a couple of young hard cases named Joel Collins and Sam Bass from Texas; the latter would go on to become a legend on his own. With a few other men, the trio went into the stagecoach-robbing business, a line that had never proved too remunerative for Davis. And it certainly would prove no different now. Western historians have delighted in telling of the gang's misadventures. The first stage they attempted to hold up just never stopped despite their murderous gunplay. The next two stages did stop, but the first was devoid of passengers, gold or cash. The second yielded only $30 from four flat-broke passengers; the road agents gave each $1 for breakfast money. Another stage robbery brought in a gold watch and $3. The one after that produced $6. The gang was clearly operating at a loss, and Davis suggested they try a train. Bass was dubious but did concede that Davis had a record of a big score in the train-robbing field.

Surprisingly, the gang executed a train holdup at Big Springs, Neb., on September 18, 1877 that was a crowning success, the loot totaling $60,000. The gang then scattered. Collins and two others were shot down in gunfights with the law, and only Davis, Bass and one other member avoided pursuers. Davis drifted on to New Orleans, where he presumably dropped his $10,000 share of the loot at the gaming tables. In any event, by 1879 he was back in Nevada robbing stagecoaches with his accustomed lack of success. In fact, his bad luck in this field may have resulted in his death. A bandit tried to hold up a stage at Willow station and wounded one of the guards. The other guard was Eugene Blair, a legendary Wells Fargo shotgun rider with an amazing record of dispatching road agents. He did so in this case with two hefty charges from a scattergun in the bandit's face, which made recognition of the outlaw impossible. Blair insisted he had a look at the man first and it was Jack Davis. However, there were reports as late as 1920 that Davis was alive in Nicaragua.

See also: *Sam Bass, John T. Chapman.*

DAY, Gertie (1895-1915): Murder victim

The 1915 murder of Gertie Day is memorable mainly because her killer was trapped thanks to his ignorance of the unusual properties of dynamite. Her killing followed the pattern of *An American Tragedy:* a young girl gets pregnant, tells her lover and is murdered by him. In Gertie's case her lover was more than two decades older, George Morton Field, the richest man in Mustoch, Kan., a small community 30 miles west of Atchison.

Field was also the religious leader of the community, having contributed generously to local church building funds. When a visiting preacher was not on hand, Field often gave the sermon from the pulpit. They were frequently of the fire-and-brimstone variety, promising damnation to all sinners. Field, however, was not one to heed his own dire warnings and seduced young, rosy-cheeked Gertie, whose full alto voice was the pride of the church choir.

Unfortunately, Gertie became pregnant and informed Field he had better find a solution to her problem. Gertie agreed to accept $2,000 and leave the area, but Field soon realized he would be open to blackmail from the girl and decided to kill her, thus protecting his good name for sure. He journeyed to Kansas City to purchase all the necessary ingredients for a bomb and then arranged a meeting with Gertie at the church late one night.

While Gertie awaited her $2,000, Field crept under the wooden church and planted his paper-wrapped homemade bomb. He returned home just as the bomb exploded, killing Gertie and totally demolishing the church.

Field felt free of suspicion, not realizing that he had unwittingly wrapped the dynamite bomb in paper on which he had started to compose a new church sermon. As is often the case in dynamite explosions, the material closest to the dynamite was not totally destroyed. Sheriff James R. Carter, a famous Kansas peace officer of the time, found enough of the sermon text to realize that Field was implicated, a fact confirmed when store clerks in Kansas City identified him as the man who had bought the makings of a bomb. Field was sentenced to life imprisonment and died in 1926.

DAYBREAK Boys: New York criminal gang

Although no member was much over the age of 20, the Daybreak Boys were among the most desperate New York gangs in the 1850s. It was said that no one could join the gang until he had killed at least one man, but this was an exaggeration since some members were as young as 12 or even 10 and hadn't yet advanced to homicide. However, once in the gang, such delinquents were quickly initiated in the practice. Police estimated conservatively that from 1850 to 1852 alone the gang committed at least 20 murders—and more likely over 40—and stole loot worth $200,000. What made the gang so fearsome was its habit of scuttling ships just to demonstrate its power and willingness to kill even when there was no hope for gain. The roster of leaders of the gang was a who's who of the most dangerous criminals in New York during the 1850s: Nicholas Saul, Bill Howlett, Patsy the Barber, Slobbery Jim, Cow-legged Sam McCarthy and Sow Madden.

In time, the depredations of the Daybreak Boys became so troublesome the police declared a virtual war on them and killed with an abandon that matched the tactics of the Daybreakers themselves. Three officers named Blair, Spratt and Gilbert killed 12 of the gang in various gun battles in 1858. By the end of 1859 the gang, having lost so many of its leaders, broke up, although individual members still remained dangerous criminals on their own for years afterward.

DE FEO, Ronald, Jr. (1951-): Mass murderer

In November 1974 Ronald De Feo, Jr. stunned Amityville, Long Island by shooting to death his mother, father, two brothers and two sisters as they slept. It marked the start of what can only be described as a "murder groupie" rage.

The type of killings De Feo perpetrated is hardly unusual on police blotters; yet his crime supposedly made the house haunted. The alleged ghostly experiences of its next owners were described in a book, *The Amityville Horror,* which became a best-seller.

As for De Feo himself, no more than a necessary prop in the ghostly tales that followed, he tried unsuccessfully to plead insanity and was sentenced in 1975 to a total of 150 years imprisonment.

DE KAPLANY, Dr. Geza (1926-): Murderer

Dubbed the Acid Doctor, Dr. Geza de Kaplany committed what one expert called "the most horrendous single murder in American history" and caused a further scandal when he was paroled. Dr. de Kaplany was an anesthetist at a San Jose, Calif. hospital. He wooed and eventually married his 25-year-old fiancee, Hajna, a part-time model and leading beauty of California's Hungarian community, largely on the basis of his professional status. The marriage proved a failure. Exactly why is not absolutely clear: according to the prosecution in the subsequent murder trial, de Kaplany was unable to consummate the marriage, but the defense contended his love had been rejected. For whatever reason, de Kaplany decided in his own words, "to ruin her beauty."

He assembled an elaborate torture kit in their honeymoon apartment and, on the evening of August 27, 1962, even stopped off to get a manicure so as not to puncture the rubber gloves he would wear. Exactly what de Kaplany did early the following morning, during what he called "my one-hour crack-up" is best left to the medical texts. In any event, neighbors in the building got annoyed by loud music from the de Kaplany apartment, and despite the music, they could hear some terrible wailing. The police were summoned, and they took Hajna away, her once lovely face and body now covered with third-degree, corrosive burns. Careless ambulance attendants burned their own hands moving her body.

The bedroom resembled a torture chamber, the bedclothes virtually disintegrated in acid. There were bottles of nitric, sulfuric and hydrochloric acids in a leather case. Also found were rubber gloves, a roll of adhesive tape and a note that read, "If you want to live—do not shout; do what I tell you; or else you will die."

Hajna did die but only after suffering excruciating pain for three weeks in a hospital, with her mother praying for her death and nurses unable to look at de Kaplany's handiwork.

During his trial, at which he pleaded both "not guilty" and "not guilty by reason of insanity," de Kaplany denied wanting to kill his wife, only to mar her looks. He was convicted and escaped with just one life sentence because the jury was assured by a spokesman for the state prison system that he would be classified a "special interest prisoner," that is, someone almost certain never to be paroled. To add to that precaution, the judge ordered that photographs of de Kaplany's wife's body be kept in his file. Later on, it was discovered the pictures had not remained there very long.

Many Californians were both amazed and shocked when they heard an announcement in 1976 that de Kaplany had been paroled and quietly put aboard a plane to Taiwan. Pressed for an explanation, the Adult Authority, the state parole board, said that de Kaplany had been released six months ahead of any possible scheduled parole because a missionary hospital in Taiwan urgently needed the skills of a cardiac specialist. Since de Kaplany was not a heart specialist but an anesthesiologist whose skills had wasted for 13 years and whose medical license had been revoked, the explanation seemed implausible. The uproar over, the parole of a murderer many people thought would never be released from prison was tempered only by the fact that he prudently had been sent out of the country.

DE PALMA, William (1938-   ): Wrong man

A former federal convict, William De Palma holds the record for receiving the highest compensation ever awarded to a man wrongfully convicted of a crime. The Whittier, Calif. native agreed on August 12, 1975 to a $750,000 settlement for 16 months wrongful imprisonment at McNeil Island Prison in Washington. De Palma had been found guilty of armed robbery and given a 15-year sentence in 1968 on the basis of forged fingerprint evidence.

DEAD Line: Fulton Street, New York City

Attempting to contain a growing wave of bank robberies in the financial district, Inspector Thomas F. Byrnes of the New York City police announced on March 12, 1880 the establishment of a "dead line" at Fulton Street. He said known criminals would be "dead," i.e., arrested, if they were found south of the line. The plan, like so many others by Byrnes, who was always more flamboyant than effective, proved to be a dud. But the officer is credited by some scholars with popularizing the word "deadline" in America.

DEAD Man's Eyes: Superstition

An old story has it that the last thing a murder victim sees is his killer and that this image remains imprinted on the retina. Some superstitious murderers have gone to considerable trouble to shoot out a victim's eyes in order to destroy such imaginary evidence. Monk Eastman, a famed gangster and murderer at the turn of the century, supposedly heard the theory discussed once and suddenly remembered it after his next murder. He thereupon reclimbed three flights of stairs and shot out the dead man's eyes.

The origin of the superstition is unknown, but it came into renewed vogue around 1900, when criminals had become impressed with such scientific advances as fingerprinting, which was making police detection more effective. Even now, there are a few reports of murder victims found with their eyes shot out each year.

DEAD Man's Hand: Aces and eights

A poker hand of a pair of aces and a pair of eights has been known in American culture as a "dead man's hand" ever since Jack McCall shot Wild Bill Hickok in the back of the head on August 2, 1876 as Hickok held those cards in a poker game in Carl Mann's saloon in Deadwood, S.D.

See also: *Wild Bill Hickok, Jack McCall.*

DEAD Man's Tree: Chicago "murder announcement" site

During the infamous Aldermen's Wars that wracked Chicago's 19th Ward, the so-called Bloody Ward, from 1916 to 1921, a poplar tree on Loomis Street in Little Italy became famous as the Dead Man's Tree. Both sides, those supporting John "Johnny de Pow" Powers and those backing Tony D'Andrea, took to announcing the impending death of a victim by posting his name on the tree, a notice that, if it did not completely shatter his nerve, at least offered the marked man an opportunity to set his affairs in order. In a majority of the 30 deaths that occurred during the wars, the victim's name had been written on the tree; none of these was ever solved.

See also: *Aldermen's Wars.*

DEAD Rabbits: Early New York gang

From the 1820s until their final decline in the 1870s, the Dead Rabbits were a huge gang of criminals who controlled much of the Lower East Side, excluding the Bowery, and achieved great renown as thieves and thugs. When they went on looting forays or to do battle with other gangs, their leaders carried a dead rabbit impaled on a pike. The Dead Rabbits were also noted political sluggers, supporting pro-Irish candidates. They were given credit for controlling the voting booths in 1856 when Tammany Hall's Fernando Wood was reelected mayor during an election in which at least 10,000 fraudulent votes were cast. Wood won by a little over 9,000 votes.

The main foes of the Dead Rabbits were the Bowery Boys, who were aligned with the anti-Irish Native American Party, and the two organizations, each with satellite supporters, fought many pitched battles. The greatest of these occurred on July 4 and 5, 1857, when the Dead Rabbits and the Plug Uglies and several other Five Points gangs marched into the Bowery to loot stores and do battle with the Bowery Boys. Armed with knives, pistols, clubs, iron bars and huge paving blocks, they attacked a Bowery Boys headquarters, putting a small contingent of the enemy to rout. When the news of the outrage spread, the Bowery Boys, in alliance with the Atlantic Guards and other gangsters determined to protect the sanctity of the Bowery, poured out of their holes onto Bayard Street to engage in the most desperate and largest free-for-all in the city's history.

The police made an early and feeble effort to control the fighting but merely took a few prisoners before wisely retreating. By this time the fighting forces had grown to an estimated strength of about 400 to 500 on each side. The *New York Times* reported:

> Brick-bats, stones and clubs were flying thickly around and from the windows in all directions, and men ran wildly about brandishing firearms. Wounded men lay on the sidewalks and were trampled upon. Now the Rabbits would make a combined rush and force their antagonists up Bayard Street to the Bowery. Then the fugitives, being reinforced, would turn on their pursuers and compel a retreat to Mulberry, Elizabeth and Baxter streets.

While the rioting was going on, other gangsters used the opportunity to attack households and stores along the Bowery and several other streets, and residents and storeowners had to barricade their buildings and fight off attacks with shotguns and pistols. In the afternoon a much larger force of police moved into the area and cleared the streets, forcing the rioters into the houses and up to the roofs. One gangster who refused to surrender fell from the roof of a house onto Baxter Street. As he lay there, his head in a pool of blood, his foes stomped him to death. As soon as the police retreated with more prisoners, the fighting resumed. It continued until three regiments of troops were brought into action the next day. At that point, eight rioters were dead and more than 100 wounded, half of whom required long hospitalization. More of their dead were carried off by both sides and it was common knowledge that several new graves decorated the underground passages and cellars of the Five Points and Paradise Square.

Small bands of the rioters continued battling for another week, while the general citizenry demanded something be done to curb the criminal elements. The Dead Rabbits resented descriptions of themselves as criminals and so informed the press. The *Times* reported:

> We are requested by the Dead Rabbits to state that the Dead Rabbit club members are not thieves, that they did not participate in the riot with the Bowery Boys, and that the fight in Mulberry street was between the Roach Guards of Mulberry street and the Atlantic Guards of the Bowery. The Dead Rabbits are sensitive on points of honor, we are assured, and wouldn't allow a thief to live on their beat, much less be a member of their club.

Nonetheless, several noted sluggers of the Dead Rabbits, and the Bowery Boys as well, were never seen alive again.

See also: *Bowery Boys, Roach Guards.*

DEATH Corner: Chicago murder locale

During the heyday of the Black Hand, this loose society of extortionists terrorized Italian communities in America, demanding money from designated victims and promising them death if they refused. The most dangerous locale in Chicago's Little Italy at this time was the intersection of Milton and Oak streets, nicknamed Death Corner because so many Black Hand victims were slain there. In one 15-month period, from January 1, 1910 until March 26, 1911, 38 Black Hand murders occurred there.

There never was one official Black Hand organization; rather the extortions and killings were carried out on a free-lance basis by various criminals. It is likely that some so-called Black Hand murders were really private affairs and disguised as Black Hand matters to confuse the police. Whatever the case, none of the 38 murders were ever solved, and there were many residents of Little Italy who would always go blocks out of their way to avoid passing Death Corner.

See also: *Black Hand, Shotgun Man, White Hand Society.*

DEBTORS, Imprisonment Of

The practice of imprisoning debtors was an English custom readily imported into the American colonies, and it also became common that such persons could be sold into service for periods of time in order to pay off their debts. However, this method of discharging debts was eliminated during the early years of the 19th century thanks to a backlash against the imprisonment of debtors that had started about 1775 (more than a century after similar outcries in England). By 1800 strong reform movements were active and some state legislatures passed poor debtor and insolvency laws that were liberal. "Prison limits" for debtors posting bonds sometimes extended throughout an entire county. Yet despite these improvements, the most common crime in America was debt, and more than 75,000 debtors a year were sent to prison for the offense. The amount owed had little to do with the sentence. A survey in one Pennsylvania penitentiary in 1829 revealed that there were almost 100 prisoners serving sentences for owing amounts of less than $1.

It became clear to reformers that the only true cure was the absolute and total ban on jailing debtors, and laws were passed totally banning imprisonment of debtors or at least greatly restricting the rules under which imprisonment was called for. In 1821 Kentucky became the first state to act, followed by New York a decade later. North Carolina, South Carolina and Florida were the last to act, constitutionally forbidding imprisonment for simple debt in 1868.

DEEP Nightstick: Secret informant

As famous as Deep Throat in the Watergate scandal was Deep Nightstick in a newspaper investigation of police brutality in Philadelphia during the mid-1970s. The investigation was given much of the credit for ending the mayoral career of controversial tough ex-cop Frank L. Rizzo.

In 1976 a new court reporter for the *Philadelphia Inquirer,* Jonathan Neumann, observed that although murder suspects routinely testified to brutal beatings by the police, officials never bothered to investigate. Later, Neumann, a former New Yorker, asked an editor about this strange situation and was told, "Welcome to Philadelphia."

Neumann and another young reporter, William Marimow, began digging into the subject of police brutality and produced a series of articles that would win them a Pulitzer Prize in 1978. Much of their information was to come from Deep Nightstick, a secret source with close ties to the police department who provided them with leads that kept their investigations on course. Checking the records of 433 homicide cases between 1974 and 1977, they found confessions and statements in 80 cases were thrown out because of illegal interrogations but no action had been taken against the policemen involved. By the time the pair won their journalistic prize, nine officers had been convicted, three had been acquitted, three were under indictment, seven were under arrest and two others had pleaded guilty to departmental misconduct charges.

In 1979 Mayor Rizzo tried to effect a change in the city charter that would allow him to run for a third four-year term in November 1979. However, the police brutality charges became a dominant issue in the campaign for the charter revision and Rizzo lost by a two-to-one margin.

See also: *Frank L. Rizzo.*

DEEP Throat: Watergate informant

Without doubt the most famous informer in U.S. history, Deep Throat, named after the title of what has been described as a landmark pornographic film of the early 1960s, remains unidentified. He was the chief source of *Washington Post* reporters Robert Woodward and Carl Bernstein during their investigation of the break-in at the Democratic Party's head-

quarters in the Watergate office complex, which toppled the administration of President Richard Nixon and sent a number of his top aides, including a former attorney general—the first ever—to prison.

DEFENBACH, Marie (?-1900): Murder victim

A young Chicago model named Marie Defenbach may have been the most gullible murder victim in American history. Marie got involved in a plot to bilk 10 insurance companies out of $70,000 by faking her own death. She named her three accomplices as beneficiaries and then moved into a boarding house under another name. According to the plan, the brains of the conspiracy, Dr. August M. Unger, would give her a special medicine that would induce a deathlike sleep and later he would revive her. Meanwhile, another body would be substituted for cremation. For her troubles, Marie was to get half of the $70,000, whereupon she would depart on a tour of Europe. Remarkably, Marie accepted the plan, not considering that her three accomplices would get twice as much money if they really killed her. On August 25, 1900 Marie took the medicine and died in severe agony 15 minutes later. Dr. Unger signed the death certificate. The three conspirators then proceded to collect all the insurance money. But an uncle of the girl investigated her disappearance and uncovered the bizarre plot with the aid of private detectives. One of the three killers turned state's evidence, and Dr. Unger and the third accomplice, Frank Brown, were sentenced to five years in prison for fraud. The murder itself could not be proved against them, however.

DEMARA, Ferdinand Waldo, Jr. (1921-1982): Impostor

Known as the greatest impostor in 20th century America, Ferdinand Waldo Demara, Jr. had a compulsion to impersonate people. A high school dropout. he was nonetheless able in the 1940s to masquerade successfully as a doctor of philosophy named Robert L. French and to teach college psychology classes. He also passed himself off as Cecil Boyce Haman, a zoology Ph.D.; a Trappist monk in a Kentucky monastery; a biologist doing cancer research in a Seattle, Wash. institution; a law student; a hospital orderly; an American soldier; an American sailor; a recreational officer at a maximum security prison in Texas; a two-time "convert" to Catholicism (although he was born a Roman Catholic); and a deputy sheriff.

Demara's greatest impersonation occurred during the Korean war, when he assumed the role of a lieutenant-surgeon with the Canadian Navy and successfully performed a number of major operations under severe battle conditions. Demara would bone up on medical books aboard ship and then remove tonsils, pull teeth and amputate limbs. In his most-accomplished operation, he successfully removed a bullet from within a fraction of an inch of the heart of a wounded South Korean soldier. When he finished the skillful operation, a small cheer went up from fascinated spectators.

However, news stories about the amazing medical lieutenant wired back to Canada finally resulted in Demara's exposure, and he was ordered back to Victoria. Incredibly, the Canadian Navy decided that Demara had enlisted under a false name; it didn't occur to them that he was not actually a doctor. As a result, he was merely discharged with all pay due him and asked to leave the country.

In 1956 Demara was caught posing as an accredited teacher at a school in Maine. He served a few months in jail for "cheating by false premises." His longest prison term for any offense was 18 months. Demara was the subject of a book and then a Hollywood movie starring Tony Curtis. When asked why he engaged in a lifetime of impersonations, Demara said, "Rascality, pure rascality."

DENNISON, Stephen (1909-   ): Candy thief

One of the most bizarre miscarriages of justice in American history occurred in 1925, when 16-year-old Stephen Dennison was sent to a reformatory for stealing a $5 box of candy in New York. Treated brutally in the institution, Dennison became known as a rebellious troublemaker. He was transferred to the state prison, and because of continuous minor infractions, he had years and years added on to his original sentence. Incredibly, Dennison ended up doing a total of 34 years for having committed no crime greater than stealing a box of candy. After he was finally found "buried alive" in a prison cell, he was released in 1959. It took Dennison seven years in the courts to win compensation: the New York Court of Claims granted him $115,000. The court said, "No amount of money could compensate Dennison for the injuries he suffered and the scars he bears." So it allotted him a little over $3,000 for each year he spent behind bars.

DENVER'S "Spiderman" Murderer: See Philip Peters.

DEPRESSION, The Great (1929-1940)

On the surface, it would seem that the underworld should have been a victim not a beneficiary of the Great Depression of the 1930s. Generally, this was not the case because the goods and services it provided—liquor, sex, drugs and gambling—all boomed when everything else went bust, avidly craved by Americans caught in the hopelessness of an economic system gone to pot.

While businessmen, small and large were ruined by "cash flow" problems and the banks were shutting down, the underworld was flush with greenbacks. Where could strapped businessmen readily get the money needed to tide them over? Only the underworld extended credit so generously, making loansharking one of organized crime's most lucrative fields. Moreover, during the 1930s the underworld's grip on corrupt unions strengthened, as workers, desperate to keep their jobs, willingly kicked in more dues and paid more assessments even if they knew the money went straight into gangster's pockets.

Al Capone played a role as a "socially responsible" gangster, taking care of many of Chicago's unemployed. A Capone storefront on State Street offered food and warmth for the destitute. It was, Capone informed reporters, his civic duty to do his share to help the jobless. Capone's Loop soup kitchen dispensed 120,000 meals at a cost of $12,000. On Thanksgiving Day, Capone proudly announced he was donating 5,000 turkeys.

Capone turned his famous soup kitchen into a great publicity campaign. As it turned out, the charity really hadn't cost him very much. Coffee roasters and blenders in Chicago had been leaned on to supply that commodity. Various bakeries were required to provide day-old doughnuts and pastries. The hearty meat dishes were gratis from the packinghouses, and the South Water Market Commission merchants pitched in the potatoes and vegetables. They were all assigned regular quotas, and those who objected that the amount was too much were informed the Big Fellow was very concerned that their trucks were not wrecked or their tires slashed.

Capone also knew how to squeeze a bit of profit out of all this unemployment. In December 1930 the price of beer to the speakeasies, which cost an estimated $4 a barrel to produce, was raised from $55 to $60, allegedly to help finance aid for the poor. The Loop's speakeasy operators were informed by Capone's salesmen, "The Big Fellow says we've all got to tighten our belts a little to help those poor guys who haven't got any jobs."

DERRICK, The Folsom: Prison torture

The "derrick" was used in various forms at many prisons but nowhere more freely than at California's Folsom Prison. Around 1900 it was estimated that an average of 10 men were on the derrick day in and day out the year round. Sentences on the derrick might be for as long as 50 hours, but the maximum length a man could stand it was about five hours a day; so, long sentences had to be stretched out over 10 days.

Located in the prison dungeon, the derrick was a block and tackle suspended from a balcony over the convict's head. The prisoner's arms would be yanked backward and a pair of handcuffs snapped on his wrists. Then a guard would pull a rope attached to the handcuffs, drawing the prisoner upward. When the victim's heels were just off the floor, the attendant would give the rope a sharp jerk and then tie it fast to a cleat on the side of the wall. The weight of the prisoner's body would make the handcuffs bite deeply into his wrists as he swung limply from the block and tackle. Then the guard would release an inch or so of slack so that the prisoner could get a steadying position, the tips of his shoes barely resting on the flagstones of the dungeon. Prisoners who had suffered on the derrick said later that after the initial pain they were overcome by a sense of reeling drunkenness, followed by the return of pain which steadily increased to an excruciating level.

A prisoner's ordeal on the derrick might continue for 2½ hours in the morning and then resume for 2½ hours in the afternoon. Once sentenced to punishment on the derrick, only severe medical reasons justified its interruption or suspension. A common ailment caused by the punishment was bleeding from a prisoner's kidneys. The prison doctor would be summoned when a prisoner's shoes were soggy with blood. This might gain the prisoner a three-day respite in the prison hospital, but he would then be returned to the dungeon to complete his punishment. The derrick remained in use at Folsom until 1911, when an outraged legislature outlawed all forms of corporal punishment at places of detention. However, it was believed that some limited forms of derrick punishment continued thereafter for a number of years.

DERRINGER

The derringer might be called the Saturday Night Special of the 19th century. The original $3 version was produced about 1850 by a Philadelphia gunsmith named Henry Deringer, Jr., who turned out some versions that were only 3¾ inches long and thus easily concealed by a professional gambler in his vest pocket or up his sleeve, an outlaw in his boot or a prostitute in her garter. Most were one-shot affairs and accurate only at a range of less than six feet, which was generally more than sufficient for its purposes.

Since Deringer had failed to patent his model, dozens of other gunsmiths began putting out imitations shortly after the appearance of what is now called the Deringer-derringer. The only thing these manufacturers did to conceal their theft was to add an "r" to the name of the weapon. One of the more popular competing models was E. Remington and Sons' over-and-under double-barreled version, which was in continuous production from 1865-1935.

Despite the fact that the derringer was tiny to hold, it had an unusually large caliber, .50 the largest and .41 the most common, and was thus a real killer at close range. The derringer inspired such other quaint weapons as the muff pistol and the pepperbox revolver in the constant hunt for sneakier ways to kill.

See also: *Muff Pistol, Pepperbox Revolver, Saturday Night Special.*

DESALVO, Albert H. (1933-1973): Boston Strangler

Between June 1962 and January 1964, a mass murderer who became known as the Boston Strangler killed 13 women in Boston, Mass. He used various devices to talk his way into the homes of women living alone and then sexually assaulted and strangled them. The first murder, that of 55-year-old divorcee Anna Slesers in June 1962, was typical. She was found sprawled on the floor of her apartment, strangled with the cord from her own housecoat. In some of the other cases, there was a hint of a robbery attempt, but police concluded this was merely a blind to cover up the clear sexual motivations of the murderer.

As the murders continued, a hysteria developed among Boston women, and many would never open a door to a stranger's knock. While the police pressed their hunt and brought in numerous suspects, the crimes continued up to January 1964, when they suddenly stopped without explanation. Then in October the Strangler struck again, molesting a young woman in her home after gaining entrance by pretending to be a detective. But although he threatened her with a knife, he left without killing her. The victim was able to identify her attacker as Albert DeSalvo, who had been released from prison in April 1962 after serving time for indecent assault. When his photograph appeared in the papers, scores of women reported to police that he was the man who had assaulted them.

The Boston Strangler, Albert DeSalvo, dances with senior citizen in a 1972 prison affair sponsored by a volunteer community agency "trying to show how both these neglected groups [senior citizens and prisoners] of people can help each other." DeSalvo was stabbed to death the following year by one or more of his fellow inmates.

There still was no direct proof that DeSalvo was the Boston Strangler until he made a confession, relating scores of details no one but the murderer could have known.

After his incarceration for life, a weird interest in the quotations of the Boston Strangler continued. Some, in letters by DeSalvo, were auctioned off, while others were recorded by reporters who had managed to have themselves confined in cells near him. Two sample quotes:

"Ha, they even know me in the Soviet Union."

"Boston people are sexpots, they all love sex. . . . Most broads are just waiting to get so-called raped."

Copies of a paperback about him, which DeSalvo attempted to slip to female visitors at the institution where he was confined for a time, were inscribed with the dedication, "Can't wait to get my hands around your throat."

Apparently, some of his fellow inmates at the Walpole State Prison, where he was confined in 1973, had somewhat similar feelings about him. He was found dead in his cell, stabbed 16 times by an unidentified convict or convicts.

See also: *F. Lee Bailey.*

DEVIL'S River Valley: Texas outlaw hideout

While Hole in the Wall and Robbers' Roost were the most-fabled outlaw hideouts in the West, neither was any meaner than Devil's River Valley in the alkali section of southwestern Texas. The *St. Louis Star* once reported of the refuge: "For many years it has been known to convicts from the Texas Penitentiary that if they could reach the Devil's River country after escaping there would be small danger of being recaptured. It is probable that no other portion of the West harbors so many notorious characters as this particular section. In fact, some of them boast that should they be arrested it would be impossible for the arresting officer to take them out on account of the intervention of friends." It was an unnecessary boast since no such attempt was ever made.

DEVINE, John: See Shanghai Chicken.

DEVOL, George (1829-1902): Riverboat gambler

With Canada Bill Jones, George Devol was probably the most talented of the riverboat gamblers, an expert not only at three-card monte but also at poker, seven-up and other card games, especially faro, in which he was the bank and could control the flimflamming. By his own estimate in his 1887 autobiography, *Forty Years a Gambler on the Mississippi*, he made more than $2 million but, like most others in his profession, could not hold on to it, losing most of it in casino faro games. He described himself as "a cabin boy in 1839; could steal cards and cheat the boys at eleven; stack a deck at fourteen . . . fought more rough-and-tumble fights than any man in America, and was the most daring gambler in the world." And the amount of exaggeration was not too great.

Devol's most constant partner was Canada Bill Jones, and the pair made a perfect team. Devol dressed like a fashion plate while Canada Bill acted and dressed like a lout with an intelligence level somewhere below that of moron. Together with Canada Bill and two others, Devol formed a riverboat combine that netted each of the participants $200,000 a year by the time the group broke up. While he was not, and most likely no one was, as great a manipulator at three-card monte as Canada Bill, Devol was nonetheless a master at card skullduggery. On one occasion, in a friendly poker game with four other gamblers he rang in four cold decks on the same hand and dealt each of the other players a set of four aces. He then sat back and watched the fireworks. Each of the gamblers felt he had been hit with a hand that comes once in a lifetime, and soon, everything the gamblers owned was in the pot. When the hilarious showdown came, it took them hours to sort out who owned what.

Like all cardsharps, Devol appreciated a sucker who lost magnanimously, but not surprisingly, he often met the opposite kind. A sore loser once pulled a gun on Devol, who extricated himself from the dilemma by "using my head." He butted his foe unconscious. Devol was probably correct when he said he engaged in more rough-and-tumble fights than any man in America. He usually did so as a "butter." Devol was the proud possessor of a massive, dome-shaped cranium that made an awesome weapon. Besides using it against sore-losing gamblers, he won many a bet in butting contests against various strongmen and circus performers, including the famed Billy Carroll of Robinson's Circus, billed as "the man with the thick skull, or the great butter." When Carroll recovered consciousness, he placed his hand on the gambler's head and said, "Gentlemen, I have found my papa at last."

After more than 40 years of gambling on the great rivers and in the Wild West, Devol married late in life. Between his wife and a militant mother-in-law, he was pressured to give up gambling and settle down in Cincinnati. In 1887 he published his memoirs. More or less retired from gambling, he sneaked away for an occasional poker game and allegedly slipped into Kentucky now and then to trim the racetrack suckers at monte. He celebrated his 60th birthday by winning a bet that he could batter an oak whiskey cask to splinters with his hard head. When Devol cashed in his chips in 1902, the *Cincinnati Enquirer* reported that he had won and lost more money than any other gambler in American history. Whether that was true or not, George Devol typified his lusty era.

See also: *William "Canada Bill" Jones, Three-Card Monte.*

DEWEY, Thomas E. (1902-1971): Prosecutor and near assassination victim

Thomas E. Dewey was only one of several prosecutors, especially in New York State, to use his crime-fighting prowess to advance himself politically, moving on to the governorship and twice running for president, in 1944 and 1948. Dewey had started off as a Wall Street lawyer, and observers would note that as a prosecutor of industrialists, businessmen and financiers, he showed limited brilliance and effectiveness. In prosecuting gangsters, however, the Dewey zeal was limitless and telling. In various roles—U.S. attorney, special prosecutor and district attorney—he clapped in prison the likes of Waxey Gordon, Louis Lepke, Gurrah Shapiro and Lucky Luciano.

Before he got Luciano, Dewey set his sights on Dutch Schultz, the king of Harlem policy rackets and numerous other criminal enterprises. Although the Dutchman was a brilliant criminal leader, he was also a bit of a flake, fond of solving pressing problems with a gun. When Dewey's investigators closed in on his operations, Schultz went before the national board of the crime syndicate to demand that the prosecutor be assassinated as a solution to both Schultz's present problems and the future ones of others. When the crime syndicate was formed, a firm rule was agreed upon, as Luciano stated it, that "we wouldn't hit newspaper guys or cops or DAs. We don't want the kind of trouble everybody'd get."

Led by the forces of Luciano and Lansky, the crime board voted down Schultz. "I still say he ought to be hit," the mad dog underworld leader is reported to have snarled in defiance. "And if nobody else is gonna do it, I'm gonna hit him myself."

At first, the syndicate decided that Schultz was simply blowing off steam, but then it was discovered in October 1935 that Schultz was setting an assassination plot in place. He had Dewey's Fifth Avenue apartment staked out by a man who posed each morning as the father of a child pedaling a velocipede. What could be less suspicious than a devoted parent strolling with his offspring? Dewey and the two body guards always at his side passed them without suspicion on their way to a nearby drug store, where Dewey made his first phone call of the morning to his office from one of several booths. He did not use his home phone for fear it might be tapped.

Once the "caser" with the child learned this, a murder plot was worked out; a killer carrying a gun with a silencer would be inside the drug store first and shoot Dewey when he entered one of the booths. Dewey's bodyguards waiting outside would not be aware of a thing as the killer walked out past them.

Schultz' mistake was involving Albert Anastasia in the plot. Anastasia was close to Luciano, and although he also favored killing Dewey, he would never betray Luciano. He passed the word about the plot to Luciano and others in the syndicate. Luciano was horrified. So were most of the others. An immediate trial was held and the death sentence passed on the absent Schultz. According to Martin A. Gosch and Richard Hammer in *The Last Testament of Lucky Luciano,* Meyer Lansky, while not casting a dissenting vote, told Luciano: "Charlie, as your Jewish *consigliere,* I want to remind you of something. Right now, Schultz is your cover. If Dutch is eliminated, you're gonna stand out like a naked guy who just lost his clothes. The way La Guardia and the rest of them guys've been screamin' about you, it's ten to one they'll be after you next."

Luciano allowed that Lansky could be right, but the syndicate had no other choice than to eliminate Schultz. The vote taken was unanimous. On October 23, 1935 Schultz was shot to death in a chop house in Newark, N.J.

Dewey did not learn of his "almost assassination" until 1940, when it was revealed to him by Murder, Inc. prosecutor Burton Turkus. Dewey listened impassively to the step-by-step details, but his eyes widened perceptibly when mention was made of the proud papa with the tot on the velocipede. After 5 years he apparently still remembered them.

By that time, as a result of Dewey's efforts, Lucky Luciano had been sent to prison for 30 to 50 years on a charge of compulsory prostitution, the longest sentence ever handed out for such an offense. After the end of World War II, Dewey backed a parole board's recommendation that Luciano be released, an action for which Dewey was roundly criticized by political opponents. The move was made because of Luciano's aid to the war effort, Dewey said, but it may also have been based to some degree on what had to remain an unspoken gratitude for Luciano's having saved his life. Perhaps somewhat ingraciously, Luciano to his dying day insisted there was yet another reason: the mob had contributed $90,000 in small bills to Dewey's campaign fund.

See also: *Louis "Lepke" Buchalter, Charles "Lucky" Luciano, Dutch Schultz, Jacob "Gurrah" Shapiro.*

DIAMOND, Jack "Legs" (1896-1931): Racketeer and murderer

Two things often said about Jack "Legs" Diamond, one of the most notorious gangsters of the 1920s, was that "the only woman who ever loved him was his mother and she died when he was a kid" and "the bullet hasn't been made that can kill Legs Diamond." Both were inaccurate. Although he was a brutal killer, quite a few women loved Legs, especially his wife, Alice, and his showgirl mistress, Kiki Roberts. While he was indeed called the Clay Pigeon of the Underworld, he was the ultimate proof that no one can live forever with bullets constantly being fired at him.

Legs' main problem in life was that almost everyone in the underworld hated him. He was a double-crosser, a chiseler, a man totally incapable of keeping his word. At various times, he fought with most of the leading criminals in New York, thinking nothing of continually increasing his roster of enemies.

Legs started out as a sneak thief in his early teens, heisting packages off the backs of delivery trucks and outracing pursuers, thus gaining his nickname. In the early 1920s Legs had moved up to work for Little Augie Orgen, the top labor racketeer in the city, after he arranged the death of Nathan Kaplan, better known as Kid Dropper. Little Augie turned over to Diamond his smaller bootlegging enterprises. It appears that Augie was the last important gangster Diamond was loyal to. He acted as his bodyguard and even took some bullets in his arm and leg when Little Augie was shot down on a Lower East Side street in 1927. That loyalty did not extend to seeking vengeance for the death of his boss, however, even though Diamond had recognized the killers—Louis Lepke and Gurrah Shapiro. When he got out of the hospital, he made peace with them. They got what they wanted—the labor rackets—and Diamond took over the rest of Little Augie's bootleg business and his narcotics trade.

Suddenly, Legs Diamond was a big-timer, a sport on Broadway. He even opened his own joint, the Hotsy Totsy Club, a second-floor bistro on Broadway in the 50s. The club provided Diamond with a cover, and he often invited underworld rivals to peace meetings there. Many of the overly trusting gangsters were murdered in a back room. In 1929 Diamond committed a murder that really demonstrated his recklessness and total lack of conscience. He and his lieutenant, Charles Entratta, murdered a hoodlum named Red Cassidy right at the bar in front of a number of employees and patrons. Diamond and Entratta were forced to flee. Then from hiding, they decided to eliminate the law's case against them. Four witnesses who had seen the killing were in turn murdered, three customers and the club bartender. Four other persons, including the hat-check girl, simply disappeared and were never heard from again. Apparently, Diamond and Entratta had no fear that the missing witnesses might suddenly turn up again because the two resurfaced, confident the police no longer had a case against them.

Legs Diamond, in pin stripes, was considered "unkillable" by the underworld and "unconvictable" by the law. The theory proved to be half true.

However, Legs' forced retirement caused complications. The notorious Dutch Schultz had moved in on Diamond's rackets while he was gone, and what the Dutchman took, he seldom gave back. It led to a full-scale war between the two. Schultz was never a popular figure with the rest of the underworld, but no one complained about his efforts to kill Diamond.

There were many who were convinced that Diamond couldn't be killed. It had always been that way. In October 1924 some unknown gunmen had peppered his head with birdshot and put a bullet in his heel. Diamond then drove himself to Mt. Sinai Hospital and had his wounds taken care of. The second near miss was the attack on Little Augie. Diamond had lost so much blood from wounds in his arm and leg that he was not expected to survive. The war with Schultz added to his battle injuries. Shortly after he killed a couple of Schultz' men in

October 1930, Legs was curled up in a cozy suite with show-girl Kiki Roberts when gunmen broke in and pumped five bullets into him. Kiki was unhurt.

Legs was rushed to a hospital and, to the amazement of doctors, survived. In April 1931 Diamond was ambushed as he left a roadside inn. He got a bullet in the lung, another in the back, a third in the liver and a fourth in the arm. Once again, surgeons gave up on him but again he recovered.

By this time, Diamond himself was convinced he couldn't be killed. He let it be known that once he was all better, he intended to take a bigger slice of the action in Manhattan. Legs indicated he was not satisfied with what he had gotten when criminal mastermind Arnold Rothstein was murdered and his empire divided. He served notice on Joey Fay that he wanted more of the nightclub rackets and on Waxey Gordon that he deserved more of the bootlegging and moonshining business.

All of this made it rather difficult to determine whose troops paid him a fatal visit on December 18, 1931. Diamond was hiding away in a room in Albany, N.Y. that only a few confederates knew about. He was sound asleep when two gunmen slipped into the room. One held him by the ears and the other shot him three times in the head. This time Diamond was absolutely dead.

See also: *Hotsy Totsy Club, Jacob "Little Augie" Orgen, Dutch Schultz.*

DIAMOND Switch: Confidence theft game

Considered to be the superstars of shoplifters, diamond switch experts, often women, victimize top jewelry stores by feigning interest in the purchase of a diamond. The thief will examine the stone and, when the salesperson's attention is distracted, substitute a worthless or inferior stone for the genuine article. The thief then makes a hasty exit before the switch is discovered.

The prowess of these operators was pointed out not long ago by a woman who had cheated two leading jewelry stores on New York's Fifth Avenue. Handsomely dressed in a fur coat, the woman considered the purchase of an $18,000 ring but after some thought decided it was too expensive. She handed the clerk back a cheaper diamond, one worth only about $7,500. Since the two stones were cut alike and determination of the full quality of the costlier diamond required more than examination by the naked eye, no suspicions were aroused until some time after the supposed customer had departed. Meanwhile, the same thief had entered a second store to inspect a $35,000 diamond, for which she neatly substituted the $18,000 stone. By the time both stores discovered their losses, the woman was long gone from Fifth Avenue.

DILLINGER, John Herbert (1903-1934): Public enemy

John Dillinger was the consummate public enemy, certainly the "superstar" gangster of the 1930s. But what is really amazing is that he achieved this status in a criminal career that spanned a mere 11 months, from September 1933 to July 1934. Dillinger and his mob—he actually was not the leader but merely a member among equals of the first so-called Dillinger mob—robbed between 10 and 20 banks. They also plundered three police arsenals, engaged in three spectacular jail breaks and fought their way out of police traps, murdering 10 men and wounding seven others in the process. This last fact was never considered very important by the public, just as Missourians did not hold such indiscretions against Jesse James a half-century earlier.

Dillinger captured the public's imagination with his style and verve; he displayed dash and derring-do in a spectacular but apocryphal "wooden gun" jail escape, he had a casual impudence toward authority and he often displayed a form of chivalry during robberies, especially flirting with older women bystanders, that turned him into a Depression-day Robin Hood. After all, he just robbed banks, not people, and on occasion told depositors to hang on to their money, that all the gang wanted was the bank's money. Undoubtedly, Dillinger was smart enough to understand such behavior stood him well with the public and could conceivably help him out of a tight spot someday.

Dillinger was a master bank robber. His gang's jobs were all well planned and timed to precision. During his nine-year stretch in prison for attempting to rob a grocer, he had learned the meticulous "Baron Lamm method" of bank robbery, named after a former Prussian army officer turned American criminal, which called for careful casing of a bank beforehand, pretested and timed getaway routes and the like. Dillinger followed the technique to the utmost detail but added his own daring touches. The day before one robbery, two of his men cased a bank posing as journalists and were taken on a grand tour of the institution by its chief officer. During another caper the townsfolk thought they were witnessing a rehearsal for the filming of a movie; a "movie director"—reputedly Homer Van Meter, the daring clown of the gang—had visited the scene the day before to publicize the event.

The product of an unhappy home life—John's mother died when he was three and his father subsequently remarried—young Dillinger became a juvenile delinquent. As a member of a youth gang called the Dirty Dozen, he was charged with stealing coal from the Pennsylvania Railroad's gondolas to sell to residents of his Indianapolis neighborhood; he was in the sixth grade at the time.

So far as the record shows, Dillinger did not get involved in serious crime until 1924, following a stint in the Navy from which he just "walked away." That year he and an older, more-seasoned criminal, Ed Singleton, attempted to rob a grocer whom they knew carried the day's receipts on him. The two men accosted their victim, B. F. Morgan, on a darkened street, and Dillinger, armed with a .32, struck him on the head with a bolt wrapped in a handkerchief. The grocer stayed erect and struggled, and Dillinger's gun went off. The hapless robbers then fled. Apprehended quickly, Dillinger drew a sentence of 10 to 20 years, although he had been assured by the local prosecutor that as a first offender, he would be treated lightly if he pleaded guilty. Dillinger's accomplice, 10 years older, was brought before a different judge and drew a far shorter sentence; he was released after doing two years. Dillinger ended up serving nine and the experience embittered him.

In 1934 Indiana Gov. Paul V. McNutt's secretary, Wayne Coy, would observe: "There does not seem to me to be any escape from the fact that the State of Indiana made John Dillinger the Public Enemy that he is today. The Indiana constitution provides that our penal code shall be reformative and not vindictive. . . . Instead of reforming the prisoner, the penal institutions provided him with an education in crime."

Doing time first in the Indiana State Reformatory at Pendleton and then in the state prison at Michigan City, Dillinger came in contact with criminals who became his mentors and later his accomplices, among them accomplished bank robbers like Harry Pierpont, John Hamilton, Homer Van Meter, Fat Charley Makley, Russell Clark and Walter Dietrich. Despite his youth and relative inexperience, Dillinger was accepted as a member of this clique of hardened criminals because of his personal trustworthiness and willingness to help other prisoners. These were qualities much respected by men behind bars, even causing Pierpont, the group's nominal leader, to overlook a failing in Dillinger which he tolerated in no other associate—having an "old lady" prison lover.

Several members of the Pierpont clique had unsuccessfully attempted to break out of the prison, leading most of them to conclude their only chance for escape was a scheme based on having aid from outside and making the proper payoffs inside. Dillinger, soon to be paroled, was designated the "outside man." As such, he would have to raise a lot of money and fast, and the group, which included a number of "jugmarkers" (men who had knowledge of good banks to be robbed), told him how to go about it. Pierpont and others also supplied him with names of trustworthy accomplices to use on various capers. Dillinger's duties were to get enough money to make the proper payoffs, buy guns, obtain getaway cars and clothes and find a hideout for the escapees. With only limited experience but a vast amount of criminal knowledge, Dillinger emerged from prison to become the greatest public enemy in the history of American crime.

He was released in May 1933, after a petition bearing the signatures of almost 200 residents of his adopted hometown of Mooresville, Ind., including that of his grocer victim, was presented to the governor. Dillinger immediately set about committing robberies to raise the funds needed for the mass escape. Many of his capers were pulled with criminals little more experienced than he was and were badly bungled, often clearing less than $100. But Dillinger kept trying for bigger scores and finally pulled off a bank robbery that netted $10,600, no small sum for a bank in a Depression-racked area, and then a payroll heist that yielded more than $24,000. He now had enough funds to spring the Pierpont group, being totally unmindful at the time that Capt. Matt Leach of the Indiana State Police had identified him as the busy holdup artist. Leach had an alarm out for Dillinger and had just missed catching him on a number of occasions.

Meanwhile, Dillinger gave a large part of the escape money to Mary Kinder, a 22-year-old woman whose brother was one of the convicts slated to be in on the escape and who would become Pierpont's mistress. The complete story about the Michigan City breakout of 10 convicts was never fully revealed. Payoffs were made, that much is certain. In addition, Dillinger traveled to Chicago, where through an intermediary he bribed the foreman of a thread-making firm to conceal several guns in a barrel of thread destined for the prison's shirt shop. The barrel was marked with a red X so that the escapees would recognize it.

On September 26, 1933 Pierpont and nine others took several hostages and made their way out of the prison, a feat that resulted in all sorts of political recriminations in Indiana. The new McNutt administration contended that holdover Republican guards or some who had been dismissed must have been involved, but the former Republican governor, Harry Leslie, blamed the breakout on the 69 new guards appointed by the Democrats. It mattered little to the Pierpont bunch. They were free. It mattered less to Dillinger. He had in the meantime been captured in Dayton, Ohio while visiting one of several new girl friends.

The Pierpont bunch were stunned when they learned from Mary Kinder that Dillinger had been arrested. There was no question of what they were going to do about it. Dillinger had kept his word and freed them and now they were going to free him. They planned a raid on the jail in Lima, Ohio where Dillinger was being held. Dillinger had been informed of the escape plot in advance and asked that another of his girl friends, Evelyn "Billie" Frechette, a half Indian in her mid-twenties, be waiting for him when he got out.

The grateful Pierpont would deny Dillinger nothing. Billie, the wife of a bank robber then in Leavenworth, was brought to an apartment in Cincinnati to await Dillinger's release. On October 12, Columbus Day, Pierpont, Makley and Clark broke into the Lima Jail, mortally wounded Sheriff Jess Sarber and freed Dillinger. On the way out of the jail, Dillinger paused to look at the dying sheriff, who had treated him kindly and whom Dillinger had developed an affection for, and said sharply to Pierpont, "Did you have to do that?"

Pierpont shrugged. He might not have taken such a rebuke from another man, but he genuinely liked and respected Dillinger.

The "Dillinger mob" was now ready for action, although at the time, it should have been called the "Pierpont mob." Dubbing it the Dillinger mob was the idea of lawman Matt Leach, who thought he might produce friction between the pair by making Dillinger into a greater criminal than he was. However, Leach's ploy failed. Nothing would come between Dillinger and Pierpont, and in fact, the latter wanted Dillinger to assume a more active leadership. He quickly grasped that Dillinger inspired confidence, trust and loyalty, vital qualities in a criminal organization, and could bring peace between feuding gangsters.

The mob pulled off a string of somewhere between 10 to 20 bank robberies; the number could not be determined because the gangsters never confessed which ones they had perpetrated and which were falsely attributed to them. This first so-called Dillinger mob functioned until January 1934, by which time the gang, after going to Florida for a rest, had moved to Tucson, Ariz. Several members were captured there by police work that was partly brilliant, partly pure luck and partly a result of tips from persons who recognized some of the gang from detective magazine pictures.

Dillinger was caught with Billie Frechette. Pierpont, Makley and Clark were taken with Mary Kinder and another woman. The three men were shipped to Ohio to be charged with the murder of Sheriff Sarber. Dillinger was flown to Chicago, where that city's entire "Dillinger Squad," 40 officers permanently assigned to the job of capturing him, and 85 other policemen met the plane. A 13-car convoy then took America's most famous prisoner to an "escape-proof" jail in Crown Point, Ind.

It was here that Dillinger was to electrify the nation with his famous "wooden gun" escape. According to the first version of the story, he used a knife to whittle a wooden gun out of the top of a washboard, colored it with shoe polish and used it to escape. But how did America's number one criminal get hold of a knife in jail? All right, change that to a razor blade. Both versions were sheer nonsense. Dillinger's wooden gun was a real one. The true story behind his escape from the Crown Point Jail was that his lawyer, an incredible rogue named Louis Piquett, had met with a prominent Indiana judge on the grounds of the Century of Progress in Chicago and handed over an envelope containing several thousands of dollars. In return, the judge agreed to smuggle a gun into the jail. Dillinger used the gun to capture and lock up several guards and then made his way to the warden's office, where he grabbed two machine guns.

He gave one of the machine guns to a black prisoner, 35-year-old Herbert Youngblood, and together they locked up several more officers; snatched the car of a lady sheriff, Mrs. Lillian Holley, from the jail parking lot; and made good their escape, taking two hostages with them. Dillinger later released the two hostages, giving one, an auto mechanic, $4 for his troubles.

Naturally, the supposed wooden gun escape made headlines. Sometime later, however, a secret investigation conducted by the Hargrave Secret Service of Chicago on orders of Gov. McNutt turned up the true story about the gun. McNutt and Attorney General Philip Lutz, Jr. decided not to reveal the information because they quite properly didn't want Dillinger to know that certain informants whom he might trust again in the future had talked to private detectives. By the time Dillinger was killed, the judge too had died and the findings about the gun never were made public.

Meanwhile, Dillinger basked in the glory of the wooden gun story and sought to perpetuate it. In a letter to his sister,

John Dillinger (second from left) is photographed at arraignment in Arizona, the last time he would be taken alive.

he told her not to worry about him and that he was "having a lot of fun." Concerning the gun, he added:

> . . . [the reports] I had a real forty five Thats just a lot of hooey to cover up because they don't like to admit that I locked eight Deputys and a dozen trustys up with my wooden gun before I got my hands on the two machine guns. I showed everyone the wooden gun after I got a hold of the machine guns and you should have seen *thire* faces. Ha! Ha! Ha! Pulling that off was worth ten years of my life. Ha! Ha!

Dillinger's intention obviously was to cover up the fact that a real gun had been smuggled to him and to satisfy his ego. It was not the only time he had done that. Dillinger had often tormented his chief pursuer, Matt Leach, with phone calls and letters. And on one occasion he supposedly sent a book entitled *How to Be a Detective* to the excitable Leach. When he was captured in Arizona, Dillinger had been asked if he had in fact sent the book. He replied, "I was there when it was sent." That too was sheer nonsense. The book had been sent to Leach as a practical joke by Jack Cejnar, the bureau chief of the International News Service in Indianapolis.

After their escape Dillinger and Youngblood immediately separated. Thirteen days later, on March 16, 1934, Youngblood was mortally wounded in a gun battle with lawmen in Port Huron, Mich. As evidence of the loyalty Dillinger in-

spired in men, the dying Youngblood falsely told police that Dillinger had been with him the day before.

Immediately, Dillinger put together the real Dillinger mob, including among others Van Meter, jugmarker Eddie Green, Hamilton, Tommy Carroll and a newcomer, a short, violent-tempered punk named Lester Gillis, better known as Baby Face Nelson. It took considerable skill on Dillinger's part to keep Nelson and Van Meter, and occasionally some of the others, from shooting at one another. Dillinger undoubtedly disliked Nelson but he needed him. Nelson was the sort who would never desert his post in a robbery, and Dillinger had to commit several robberies fast. He had to get money to provide a legal defense for Pierpont, Makley and Clark, who were to be tried for murdering Sheriff Sarber.

Dillinger sent the money, but it did little good. All three were convicted: Clark got life and the other two were sentenced to the electric chair.

Time was running out for Dillinger as well. The same month as his breakout from the Crown Point Jail, he barely escaped in a barrage of machine-gun fire during a confrontation with FBI agents in St. Paul. Dillinger was wounded in the leg, but Billie Frechette drove him to safety. The next month, April 1934, Dillinger and the rest of the mob were hiding out at Little Bohemia Lodge, a closed summer resort about 50 miles north of Rhinelander, Wis., when the FBI closed in. Warned by barking dogs, Dillinger and his men escaped. Baby Face Nelson killed Special Agent W. Carter Baum and wounded another agent and a local police officer. The FBI wound up capturing only three of the mob's women, who were found hiding in the basement. They also managed to shoot two innocent bystanders, a salesman and a Civilian Conservation Corps (CCC) cook, and kill another young CCC worker, all of whom they thought were escaping gangsters.

It was a debacle for the FBI and, in a sense, another laurel for Dillinger. Will Rogers got into the act, writing, "Well, they had Dillinger surrounded and was all ready to shoot him when he come out, but another bunch of folks come out ahead, so they just shot them instead. Dillinger is going to accidentally get with some innocent bystanders some time, then he will get shot."

Dillinger and Van Meter both submitted to plastic surgery to alter their faces and fingerprints. Neither job was overly effective. Ironically, Dillinger "died" on the operating cot. Given a general anesthetic, he swallowed his tongue and stopped breathing. One of the panicky outlaw doctors managed to pull out his tongue with a forceps and applied artificial respirations, and Dillinger started breathing again.

By this time Hamilton had died of wounds received in a shoot-out with pursuing officers, and while Dillinger was recovering from the plastic surgery, Tommy Carroll was killed near Waterloo, Iowa. The mob was falling apart, and Dillinger could only think of making a few big scores and then fleeing to Mexico.

Still, Dillinger's facial surgery gave him enough confidence to venture openly in the streets. Using the identity of Jimmy Lawrence, he took up with a 26-year-old Chicago waitress named Polly Hamilton. Polly shared rooms with a friend, Anna Sage, whose real name was Ana Cumpanis. Sage had come to America from Rumania just after the war and had operated whorehouses in Gary, Ind., and East Chicago, Ill. She had twice been convicted of operating a disorderly house but had won pardons from Indiana Gov. Leslie. Recently, however, Sage had been convicted a third time and Gov. McNutt had refused her request for a pardon. The Immigration Bureau was seeking to deport her as an undesirable alien.

Dillinger felt safe with Polly Hamilton and Anna Sage; he had never had trouble with women betraying him. It is doubtful that Hamilton knew his true identity, but Anna Sage soon discovered it. Dillinger felt comfortable talking to her. She was 42, an older woman and perhaps even a mother figure for him. Sage listened to his stories and ramblings and perhaps would not have informed on him merely because there was a $10,000 reward for his capture. But through a police contact in East Chicago, she made a deal with the FBI to betray Dillinger in exchange for a promise that the deportation proceedings against her would be dropped and the reward money would be given to her. Melvin Purvis, agent in charge of the Chicago office of the FBI, agreed to help with those matters as far as possible.

On July 22, 1934 Dillinger took the two women to a Chicago movie. Earlier in the day Sage had called the FBI to tell them about Dillinger's plans, but at that time she did not know which of two movies they would attend. The FBI staked out both and waited. As planned, Sage dressed in red so that the FBI men would recognize her. The agents at the Biograph Theater saw Dillinger and the two women enter. FBI Inspector Sam Cowley, in charge of the nationwide hunt for Dillinger, telephoned J. Edgar Hoover and the decision was not to try to take Dillinger inside the movie house but to wait until he came out. When Dillinger and the women walked out of the theater, Purvis lit a cigar, the signal that identified Dillinger. Then he called on Dillinger to halt. The gangster looked about suddenly, and he saw that his female companions had vanished. In that brief instant he must have realized he had been betrayed by a woman. He pulled a Colt automatic from his right pants pocket and sprinted for the alley at the side of the movie house. Three FBI agents fired. They wounded two women passing, but they also shot Dillinger. One bullet went through his left side, another tore through his stooped back and came out his right eye. Dillinger fell dead.

Within a few months the second Dillinger mob was completely wiped out. Eddie Green was shot by the FBI. A month after Dillinger died, Homer Van Meter was also killed in an alley, this one in St. Paul, after being betrayed by friends. In November, Baby Face Nelson killed two FBI agents but died himself of wounds received in the gun battle. Meanwhile, Pierpont and Makley attempted to escape from the death house at the Ohio State Prison in Columbus by imitating Dillinger's mythical wooden gun ruse. With guns carved out of soap, they succeeded in overpowering one guard and were trying to batter their way out through the door leading from the death house when a riot squad opened fire. Makley was killed and Pierpont wounded. A month later, Pierpont died in the electric chair.

See also: *John Herbert Dillinger—Double, Dirty Dozen Gang, Jug Markers, Herman "Baron" Lamm, George "Baby Face" Nelson, Public Enemies, Melvin Purvis, Ed Singleton, Wooden Gun Escapes, Herbert Youngblood.*

DILLINGER, John Herbert—Double

The death of John Dillinger in July 1934 marked the end of crime's greatest folk hero of the 20th century, and it was therefore hardly surprising that his death was not accepted by many. This has been a common behaviorial reaction. For decades there were people who believed Jesse James had not been shot by Bob Ford, that a substitute corpse had been used. And for decades one "real Jesse James" after another turned up. In the cases of the Apache Kid and Butch Cassidy, the weight of opinion seems to favor the theory that they survived their alleged demises, but the identification of their corpses was far more controversial.

The disbelief about John Dillinger started instantly after his death and continued for years. In a book entitled *Dillinger: Dead or Alive?* (1970), Jay Robert Nash and Ron Offen made perhaps the most complete case that the great public enemy had not been killed by FBI agents. Their basic premise was that the FBI had been duped into thinking the dead man was

Dillinger, and when the agency discovered otherwise, it could do nothing but develop a massive cover-up.

What makes this case less than totally acceptable is the number of people such a plot would have required. Certainly Anna Sage, "the woman in red," and her East Chicago police contact or contacts. And someone would have had to have planted a phony Dillinger fingerprint card days before the killing. According to this theory, "Jimmy Lawrence" was not a Dillinger alias but the name of a real minor hoodlum whose career was rather hazy.

Proponents of the fake Dillinger theory make much of glaring discrepancies found in Dillinger's autopsy report, which was allegedly lost for more than 30 years. For instance, in the report the dead man's eyes were listed as brown, Dillinger's were blue. But this was an autopsy performed in Cook County during the 1930s, a time when coroners' findings nationwide were notorious for being replete with errors. The autopsy was performed in a "looney bin" atmosphere. A reporter for the *Chicago Tribune* appeared in news photos propping up Dillinger's head and was identified as the "coroner." Even after the autopsy was performed, Dillinger's brain was actually "mislaid" for a time. If all errors made in autopsies of that period were taken seriously, probably just half the victims of violent deaths could really have been considered dead.

Another question that must be raised is how John Dillinger lived happily ever after and on what. By all accounts, he had less than $10,000 available to him for a final, permanent escape. Could he stay away from crime forever? And if he could not, would he not have been identified sooner or later? And what of Anna Sage? Despite promises made to her by the FBI, she was deported back to her native Rumania. She could undoubtedly have bought a reprieve from that fate had she come forward with the true facts about a Dillinger hoax.

In sum, the "Dillinger lives" theory appears to be a case of wishful thinking, one fostered by the fact that John Dillinger was too good—or too bad—to be allowed to die.

DIMSDALE, Professor Thomas J. (1831-1866): Vigilante chronicler

Just as John X. Beidler is remembered as the hangman of the famous Vigilantes of Montana, Professor Thomas J. Dimsdale stands as their authorized biographer.

A consumptive English professor and Oxford graduate, Dimsdale settled in Virginia City, Mont. in search of a healthful mountain climate. After running a private school for a time, he was named Montana's first superintendent of public instruction in 1864 by the territorial governor. In August of that year he also became editor of the *Montana Post,* the first important newspaper in the territory, and he regularly chronicled the doings of the Montana vigilantes, offering what folks considered "book learning" justification for rope justice.

When in 1865 a bully named James Daniels killed another man in a dispute over cards and the victim's wife died of a heart attack on hearing the news, Dimsdale approved the vigilantes' decision to turn the defendant over to the law for the exacting of justice. However, he was as incensed as the rest of the community when Daniels got only a three-year sentence and was pardoned after serving just a few months. The pardoned killer returned to Helena and went about threatening to take vengeance on the vigilantes who had caught him. As a result of this misbehavior, the vigilantes seized him a second time and hanged him without recourse to the courts. While Dimsdale agreed that the "politic and the proper course would have been to arrest him and hold him for the action of the authorities," he could not condemn the lynching. He wrote in the *Post:*

> When escaped murderers utter threats of murder against peaceable citizens, mountain law is apt to be administered without much regard to technicalities, and when a man says he is going to kill any one, in a mining country, it is understood that he means what he says, and must abide the consequences. Two human beings had fallen victims to his thirst of blood—the husband and the wife. Three more were threatened; but the action of the Vigilantes prevented the commission of the contemplated atrocities. To have waited for the consummation of his avowed purpose, after what he had done before, would have been shutting the stable door after the steed was stolen.

And, Dimsdale added, Daniels was hanged "not because he was pardoned, but because he was unfit to live in the community."

Dimsdale's articles in the *Post* provided an instant history of the vigilante movement and certainly the most authoritative accounts on the subject. In 1866 a large number of them were collected and published in book form under the title of *Vigilantes of Montana,* the first book published in the territory. Dimsdale died on September 22, 1866, at the age of 35, just after the book's appearance. Although copies of the original edition are extremely rare, the book was republished in 1953 by the University of Oklahoma Press.

See also: *James Daniels, Vigilantes of Montana.*

DIO, Johnny (1915-1979): Labor racketeer

Johnny Dio, whose real name was John DioGuardi, rose from the ranks of the old Murder, Inc. to become organized crime's most notorious labor racketeer. He was always believed to have been responsible for the acid blinding of labor columnist Victor Reisel in 1956. According to the police theory, Dio had ordered the acid blinding of Reisel because Teamster official Jimmy Hoffa had said in a moment of rage that something should be done about the labor writer's probing columns. Dio reputedly carried out Hoffa's wishes in order to curry favor with him. In any event, Dio was arrested; but the case never came to trial.

Years earlier Thomas E. Dewey, then New York's racketbusting special prosecutor, called Dio "a young gorilla who began his career at the age of 15." As a protege of the leaders of the old Brooklyn Murder, Inc. syndicate, Dio became an important mobster by the age of 20 and a gang chieftain at 24. In the mid-1950s Senate investigators named Teamster head Hoffa and Dio as the co-organizers of the paper locals of the union that eventually seized control of the lucrative airport trucking business in New York City. Finally, Dio was convicted and sentenced to 15 years in prison for stock fraud. He died in a Pennsylvania hospital after being moved there from the federal penitentiary at Lewisburg, Pa. Although he had been front-page copy for years, Dio's death escaped public attention for several days, even though a paid death notice appeared in the *New York Daily News*.

DIRTY Dozen Gang: Indianapolis kids' gang

In 1913 a spokesman for the Pennsylvania Railroad declared that a neighborhood kid gang in the Oak Hill section of Indianapolis was "the worst on our entire right-of-way," but at the time, he could hardly have known why. What started out as little more than a typical neighborhood gang of 10-year-olds had soon turned into a band of minor criminals. One of their biggest illegal activities was stealing tons of coal from railroad gondolas on the belt line that ran through the area and selling it at bargain rates to local homeowners and residents.

The Dirty Dozen were finally caught by railroad detectives. When hauled into juvenile court, all except one of them was frightened. The leader of the gang, chewing gum, faced the judge with arms folded and a slouch cap over one eye. Angrily, the judge ordered him to take the gum from his mouth and the cap from his head. With a crooked smirk, the youth did both and then stuck the gum on the cap's peak.

"Your mind is crippled," the judge said to 10-year-old John Dillinger.

See also: *John Dillinger.*

DIX, Dorothea Lynde (1802-1887): Prison reformer

In 1841 Dorothea Dix, a consumptive 39-year-old teacher went to the East Cambridge, Mass. House of Correction to teach Sunday school to the convicts and emerged to become the "angel of mercy" of prison reform. From that point on, she spent almost five decades of her life improving conditions for prisoners, the insane and the mentally ill. She found that prison inmates lived in the most inhumane conditions, chained naked and whipped with rods. She started a crusade, traveling the breadth of the country inspecting prisons, jails and alms-houses and presenting her findings to legislative bodies. She told about how convicts and those having committed no crime other than being insane were imprisoned in cages, cellars, stalls and closets. More than any one person, she effected enormous improvements almost everywhere she went.

There was only a brief hiatus in her reform work when she was appointed superintendent of women nurses for the North during the Civil War. Immediately after the war she resumed her prison reform crusade. She even journeyed to England and elsewhere in Europe, where her initiative and perserverance brought reforms in every country she visited. She died in Trenton, N.J. on July 17, 1887, active to the end stopping prison horrors wherever she found them.

DOANE Gang: Revolutionary war outlaws

The American Revolution was the first golden age for criminality in this country. The turmoil produced by the shifting fortunes of war created the ideal setting for bands of cattle rustlers, horse thieves and highway robbers. If a criminal stole from the British, he could count on the sympathies and sometimes even the active support of revolutionaries; if he preyed on known enemies of England, he was to the British a supporter of the Crown. Into this law enforcement vacuum stepped the notorious Doanes (sometimes called Doans), who left a trail of plunder through eastern Pennsylvania and parts of New Jersey.

Commanded by raw-boned Moses Doane, a fierce-looking man with long hair and a fur hat, the gang, composed of five of his brothers and as many as 10 to 15 others, became the terror of Bucks County, Pa. especially. Moses Doane declared himself a Tory so that upon the anticipated triumph of the British, he and his confederates would be labeled loyalists and free from the threat of punishment. On that basis, the Doanes stole only from the patriot side, but at no time was any of their loot delivered to His Majesty's forces. Their most daring robbery took place on a cold, windy night in October 1781, when 16 members of the gang boldly rode into Newtown, Pa. and headed directly for the home of John Hart, Esq., the treasurer of Bucks County, who was in the habit of hiding government funds in his home for fear of seizure by the British. Terrifying Hart and threatening his children, Moses Doane forced him to reveal the various hiding places of a total of about $4,500 in today's currency, then little short of a king's ransom. The robbery showed how proficient the Doane spy service was. Whenever and wherever in Bucks County a hoard of patriot money was to be found, the Doanes soon knew it. Tax collectors who changed their appointed rounds found that such intelligence was not long kept from the Doanes. Ironically, the Newtown robbery coincided with the collapse of Moses Doane's strategy of aligning himself with the British cause. Just three days previously, Cornwallis had surrendered at Yorktown, dooming the hopes of the Crown. The Doanes were now labeled outlaws by the recognized forces of law and order and were on the run. Their forays continued for several years, but they had few safe refuges other than caves, there being as many storied Doane cave hideouts in Pennsylvania as there were Jesse James caves in Missouri.

From 1783 on, wanted posters for various gang members dotted the Pennsylvania and New Jersey countryside. Before that, the Doanes had intimidated the local inhabitants by exacting vengeance on the nearest inhabitant to any wanted poster. If an individual didn't remove the poster, he faced a visit from the Doanes, one he would not forget—if he survived it. But by 1783 fear of the Doanes was fading, and additionally, some gang members, such as the fabled James "Sandy Flash" Fitzpatrick, had split off with gangs of their own. Fitzpatrick was hanged in 1787. On September 24, 1788 Abraham and Levy Doane, by then more critical to the gang than Moses, were executed on the Philadelphia Commons. A short time thereafter, Moses Doane was also caught and hanged.

See also: *James Fitzpatrick.*

DOAN'S Store

While much can be said about lawlessness in the Old West, the fact remains that overall the frontier was composed of honest folk, as exemplified by the existence of Doan's Store, located at the Red River crossing just north of Vernon, Tex. Founded in 1874 by two brothers, Jonathan and Corwin Doan, the store sold supplies and clothing on credit and loaned out money to hundreds and hundreds of trail drivers and cowboys, all without collateral and to many men who were complete strangers.

Author J. Frank Dobie insisted that in almost two decades of business, the Doan brothers never lost a cent to any of their customers and that cowboys would ride hundreds of miles to pay up their accounts. And of course, it was the very clear code of the West that Doan's Store could and would never be robbed and that anyone who did so would have no place to hide.

DOBBS, Johnny (?-1892): Bank robber and murderer

Johnny Dobbs was one of the most successful crooks in America during the 19th century. A colorful fence, bank robber and murderer, he was credited by authorities with netting himself at least $1 million over a 20-year criminal career.

During his youth Dobbs, whose real name was Michael Kerrigan, served in the Patsy Conroy gang of river pirates and then became a bank burglar of renown, working with the likes of Worcester Sam Perris, Shang Draper, Red Leary, Jimmy Hope, Jimmy Brady, Banjo Pete Emerson, Abe Coakley and the King of the Bank Robbers, George Leonidas Leslie, in whose murder Dobbs later participated. Dobbs played a key role in the celebrated $2.7 million robbery of New York's Manhattan Savings Institution in 1878. He reportedly took part in bank jobs all over the East that netted perhaps $8 million in loot.

With a portion of his revenues, Dobbs opened a saloon at 100 Mott Street, just a short distance from police headquarters, and blatantly operated there as one of the biggest fences in New York. He supposedly fenced over $2 million in hot money and securities, keeping about $650,000 as his own share. When asked once why crooks congregated right by police headquarters, he replied, "The nearer the church the closer to God."

Dobbs and his accomplices murdered Leslie because they believed the King of the Bank Robbers was informing on them in exchange for the opportunity to start a new life elsewhere. Although he was not convicted of the murder, Dobbs was sent to prison for a number of robberies and spent most of the 1880s in various institutions. A week after he was discharged from the Massachusetts State Prison, he was found lying in a gutter in New York City and taken to Bellevue Hospital's alcoholic ward. He died there broke on May 15, 1892. To pay for his burial, one of Dobbs' former mistresses pawned an expensive broach he had presented to her in happier days.

See also: *George Leonidas Leslie*

DOCTORS' Mob: Great New York riot

On a Sunday evening in April 1788, a strange and bloody riot developed after a young medical student, annoyed by several children peering in the window of the New York Hospital in lower Manhattan, picked up the arm of a corpse he had just dissected and pointed it at them. "This is your mother's hand, he yelled. "I just dug it up. Watch out or I'll smack you with it." Ironically, one child among those who scattered upon hearing that terrifying threat had just lost his mother. He rushed home and told his father of the event. The man rushed to the cemetery where his wife had recently been buried, and by the greatest of coincidences, the grave was open and the woman's body gone. In a rage, the man headed for the hospital, telling his friends on the way what had transpired. Within minutes he was joined by an angry mob of hundreds.

Armed with torches, bricks and ropes, the members of the mob screamed for the doctors to come out. Dressed in street clothes most of the physicians slipped out by mingling with the crowd. Frustrated, the mob stormed the hospital and wrecked tables holding valuable specimens. One doctor and three students who remained behind to try to stop them barely escaped with their lives and were put in jail by the sheriff to protect them.

The mob's fury was not spent and the rioters spilled back into the street looking for doctors. They attacked many doctors' homes. One of the homes was that of Sir John Temple, who was not a physician, but "Sir John" sounded like "surgeon." The medical student whose jest started the riot, John Hicks, Jr., was almost cornered in a physician's house but escaped over the rooftops.

On the following morning, April 14, authorities fully expected the riot to be over, but the mob's violence increased and scores of doctors were forced to leave the city. Later in the day a huge, ugly mob moved toward Columbia College in search of more grisly specimens and the "savage experimenters" who had gathered them. Several prominent citizens tried to intervene to end the madness. Alexander Hamilton was shoved aside. John Jay was knocked unconscious with a rock.

Meanwhile, Gov. George Clinton had called out the militia and prepared to use force to put down the violence. Baron Friedrich von Steuben, a hero of the Revolution and one of the most popular men in the city, begged the governor to hold off. Standing in front of the troops, he said he would try to dissuade the rioters. For his efforts the baron got hit on the head with a brick. In a quick turnabout, Steuben got to his knees and shouted, "Fire, Clinton, fire!"

The militia cut loose and 20 rioters fell in the first volley alone. In all, eight rioters were killed and dozens more injured.

Still, the riot continued until the morning of the 15th, when the mob was at last sated, and returning physicians could tend the wounded rioters. Laws were passed giving medical researchers access to the bodies of executed persons, but this hardly fulfilled the need, and grave robbing remained a serious problem for many years, although no more bloody riots such as the Doctors' Mob incident occurred.

DODGE City, Kansas

In 1872 the railroad gangs of the Atchison, Topeka and Santa Fe Railroad turned a small hole-in-the-ground oasis where whiskey peddlers camped into what became probably the biggest, bawdiest, brawliest train town America ever saw. Located on the Arkansas River a few miles from the military reservation at Fort Dodge, the new town sprouted makeshift saloons and gambling dens in dugouts or tents on both sides of the tracks. Soon, rickety buildings were going up. The place was christened Dodge City and labeled the "queen of cow towns," the "wickedest little city in America," the "Gomorrah of the Plains" and, perhaps most picturesque of all, the "beautiful, bibulous Babylon of the frontier." It was all these and more. The mecca of buffalo hunters and trail herders, Dodge City became a wanton paradise of gamblers, gunmen and harlots. As one journalist reported: "No restriction is placed on licentiousness. The town is full of prostitutes and brothels." Another quotable remark made by an observer was "All they raise around Dodge City is cattle and hell." The terms "boot hill" and "red-light district" were born there. Wyatt Earp, Bat Masterson and company, the lawmen of Dodge, were called the Fighting Pimps, which should explain some of what was allowed in Dodge. Through a man named Ned Buntline, Earp achieved his first nationwide fame in Dodge, although he killed but one man there. Buntline, a journalistic rogue, came to Dodge in 1876 and with his writings did for Earp what he also did for Wild Bill Hickok and Buffalo Bill. Earp, according to Buntline, was all good and Dodge was all bad. Buntline was wrong on the first item but at least half right on the second.

Good or bad, Dodge had to be because it was a vital cattle center. With the years, it tamed down as the West itself did. Today, it is still a cattle center of some 14,000 people.

See also: *Dodge City Peace Commission, Wyatt Earp, Luke McGlue, Red-Light District.*

DODGE City Peace Commission: Gunmen

The Dodge City Peace Commission was anything but what its name implied. It was a conglomeration of some of the toughest and meanest gunfighters of the West—Wyatt Earp, Luke Short, Doc Holliday, Bat Masterson, Shotgun Collins and others—who threatened to drown Dodge City in a sea of blood in defense of the institutions they held dear, namely gambling and prostitution.

During its early years Dodge City was dominated by a political group of saloon keepers, brothel owners and gamblers that became known as "the Gang." The Gang, especially under Mayor "Dog" Kelly, maintained their idea of a wide-open town by utilizing the guns of Earp, Masterson and Short. By the early 1880s times were changing in Kansas. For one thing, the forces of prohibition were gaining in the state, although not in Dodge. Still, there were reformers trying to change Dodge, primarily by warring on prostitution, the lifeblood of an open cattle town.

Members of the Dodge City Peace Commission were dedicated to preserving gambling and prostitution in Dodge City. Seated, left to right: Charles E. Bassett, Wyatt Earp, M. C. Clark and Neal Brown. Standing, left to right: W. H. Harris, Luke Short and Bat Masterson.

In 1883 the "reformers" under Lawrence E. Deger pushed through ordinances against prostitution and vagrancy, the latter instituted as a way of harassing gunfighters and gamblers. The first crackdown was made against the Long Branch Saloon, owned by Luke Short and W. H. Harris, two of the out-of-power Dodge City Gang. The reform party itself contained other saloon elements, especially those of A. B. Webster, who was the chief business rival of Short and Harris, and the new laws seemed to be enforced unevenly. Of course, the reformers could argue a start had to be made somewhere. Somewhere came with the arrest of three singers from the Long Branch, known as "horizontal singers," on prostitution charges.

Those arrests marked the start of the so-called Dodge City War. Luke Short was fighting mad at the arrest of his ladies and tried to shoot L. C. Hartman, the lawman who had taken them into custody. Hartman survived the fusillade only because he accidentally slipped to the ground. Short was later arrested for attempted murder and released on bond. When Mayor Deger learned that Short and a half dozen of his supporters were composing a "death list" and that some reformers were talking of setting up a vigilante group, he ordered Short and his men run out of town.

Short took his side of the argument to the governor and the newspapers. Both sides deluged the state capital with petitions supporting their views. Short threatened open warfare, and when the governor made it clear he would not send troops in to protect Dodge, Short acted. First Wyatt Earp and Bat Masterson, two of Short's oldest friends, showed up to lend a hand in Topeka and plan strategy. Suddenly, the citizens of Dodge found Doc Holliday was in town. And there were others to back up Holliday—Charlie Bassett, Neal Brown, Shotgun Collins, Rowdy Joe Lowe and others.

While a nervous governor sent in the adjutant general on a fact-finding mission, Earp and Masterson escorted Short into town. Hysteria started building. A local newspaper gave its readers some of the foreboding facts:

A brief history of these gentlemen who will meet here tomorrow will explain the gravity of the situation. At the head is Bat Masterson. He is credited with having killed one man for every year of his life. This may be exaggerated, but he is certainly entitled to a record of a dozen or more. He is a cool, brave man, pleasant in his manners, but terrible in a fight. Doc Holliday is another famous killer. Among the desperate men of the West, he is looked upon with the respect born of awe, for he has killed in single combat no less than eight desperadoes. He was the chief character in the Earp war at Tombstone, where the celebrated brothers, aided by Holliday, broke up the terrible rustlers.

Wyatt Earp is equally famous in the cheerful business of depopulating the country. He has killed within our personal knowledge six men, and he is popularly accredited with relegating to the dust no less than ten of his fellow men. Shotgun Collins was a Wells, Fargo & Co. messenger, and obtained his name from the peculiar weapon he used, a sawed-off shotgun. He has killed two men in Montana and two in Arizona, but beyond this his exploits are not known. Luke Short, for whom these men have rallied, is a noted man himself. He has killed several men and is utterly devoid of fear.

While there was considerable exaggeration in the biographies of many of the gunfighters, it was obvious the Short-Earp forces had the firepower to make the O.K. Corral fight a Sunday school outing by comparison. With each hour their legions grew. The citizenry learned of the arrival of gunmen now known only as Cold Chuck Johnny, Dynamite Sam, Black Jack Bill, Three-Fingered Dave, Six-Toed Pete and, most ominously, Dark Alley Jim. They began thinking that the militia would be unable to handle such skilled gunfighters even if it did intervene. Faced with this bleak outlook, the reformers in Dodge capitulated. Short and Harris were invited back to run the Long Branch as they had in the good old days. Prostitution was saved and Dodge City remained a wide-open town.

Later, seven of the Short supporters posed for a victory photograph and labeled themselves the Dodge City Peace Commissioners. Through the years, and especially thanks to Hol-

lywood, the impression took hold that the peace commissioners had something to do with peace and law and order.

See also: *Luke Short.*

DOGFIGHTING

Dogfighting is an illegal sport that is now almost completely eradicated in this country, unlike cockfighting, which continues. Nonetheless, it has a long and terrible tradition in America. Although illegal in almost every state, dogfighting contests were common in every part of the country during the 19th century, and thousands of dogs suffered horrible deaths. Dog stealing became a major criminal activity, as gangsters used every means possible to provide enough animals to keep up with demand. Most top fighting dogs were imported from England or bred from that country's stock. Championship battles often generated as much betting action as did prize fights. Some of the most infamous dogfighting arenas in the country were Hanly's Dog Pit and Bill Swan's Saloon and Rat Pit in New Orleans and Kit Burns' Sportsmen's Hall in New York.

Fights were not only staged between dogs but also with wharf rats which were brought in to battle dogs after being starved for a considerable length of time. Generally, fighting terriers could handle the rats but occasionally one would start to flee after taking several nips from the rodents. The rooting of the crowd would then shift in favor of the rats, as the spectators hoped to see an execution by them. In a contest at Bill Swan's establishment in 1879, a dog named Modoc killed 36 rats in two minutes and 58 seconds, but good as that was, it hardly equaled the record of a dog named Jacko, who in 1862 had killed 60 rats in two minutes, 43 seconds. The same year, Jacko set his all-time endurance record by disposing of 200 rats in 14 minutes, 37 seconds.

Probably America's greatest dogfight was that staged at the Garr farm near Louisville, Ky. on October 19, 1881. The battle was fought under *The Police Gazette's* revised rules for dogfighting with the purse of $2,000 being held by Richard K. Fox, the owner of that publication. While the match was illegal and in danger of being halted, the contest enjoyed such advance publicity that bets were made on it from coast to coast. The Ohio and Mississippi Railroad ran special excursion trains that brought dogfight fanatics from places as distant as New York and New Orleans. It became apparent that if authorities stopped the battle, they would face rioting in Louisville by disgruntled fans.

The contestants were New York's Cockney Charlie Loyod's brindled, white dog Pilot and Louisville's "Colonel" Louis Kreiger's white battler Crib. Because the fight was for the title of "American champion," the winner was required to kill his foe. Therefore, the brutal and inhumane fight lasted one hour and 25 minutes before Pilot emerged victorious. Pilot became as well known as the famous bare-knuckled boxing champion of the era John L. Sullivan.

By the turn of the century, interest in dogfighting had

given way to boxing, which had become somewhat more civilized with the introduction of boxing gloves and three-minute rounds.

DOLAN, Dandy Johnny (c.1850-1876): Gangster and murderer

One of the most imaginative and brutal gangsters of the 19th century, Dandy Johnny Dolan probably qualified as the Thomas Edison of the underworld. A renowned member of the Whyos, a gang that dominated crime in New York during the decades following the Civil War, Dolan came up with a host of innovative methods to maim and kill, his prize invention being a great advance in the technique of gouging out eyes. Dolan produced an apparatus, made of copper and worn on the thumb, that could do the gruesome job with dispatch. It served the Whyos well both in criminal endeavors and in battles with other gangs. Dolan also designed special fighting boots for himself with sections of a sharp axe blade imbedded in the soles. A simple stomping of a downed enemy produced an ending both gory and mortal.

Dolan's downfall came when James H. Noe, a brush manufacturer, caught him in the process of robbing his factory. The gangster managed to get away by using his terrible eye gouger on Noe and then beating his victim to death with an iron bar. Later, Dolan proudly displayed Noe's eyes to admiring members of the Whyos. The police did not catch Dolan with the eyes, but they did find him in possession of Noe's cane, which had a metal handle carved in the likeness of a monkey, as well as his watch and chain. This evidence was enough to doom Dolan, and he was hanged on April 21, 1876.

See also: *Whyos*.

DOLLAR Store: First "big store" swindle

In 1867 a stocky, red-whiskered, friendly man named Ben Marks opened the Dollar Store in Cheyenne, Wyo., where everything in stock sold for that price. Marks, however, was not interested in merchandising but in confidence games, and what he started would develop into the "big store," the grift that was to become the technique used in most great confidence rackets for the next 100 years.

In the windows of his store, Marks featured all sorts of useful price-worthy items, but sales proved few and far between since the pitch was used merely to draw gullible travelers and immigrants into the store. A pioneer exponent of three-card monte and other swindles, Marks had confederates operating several games complete with shills who appeared to be winning. Many a wagon train settler stepped into the store to buy a sturdy shovel and left minus most of his stake for a new life in the West. Ben Marks' cheating Dollar Store in time graduated into the big store concept, the phony gambling club, horse parlor or fake brokerage and other "stings" in which the gullible were separated from thousands of dollars. Ironically, among the scores of dollar stores that sprang up to imitate Ben Marks' pioneer venture was one in Chicago that grew into a great modern department store. Its founder had originally leased the building for a monte operation but discovered he could actually sell cheap and flashy goods at a dollar and make more profits than he could at monte.

See also: *Big Store, Three-Card Monte*.

DONAHUE, Cornelius "Lame Johnny" (1850-1878): Outlaw, lawman and lynch victim

Long an enigma in the Dakotas, Cornelius Donahue had the distinction of having Lame Johnny Creek in the Black Hills named after him, no doubt because of his other claim to fame, that of being the victim of one of the strangest lynchings in American history.

Donahue was a college-trained Philadelphian who went to Texas to satisfy his romantic dreams of being a cowboy. Because he suffered from a deformity that earned him the nickname Lame Johnny, he found that he commanded very poor pay and soon turned to stealing horses. When he pulled out of Texas in the mid-1870s, he was a much-wanted thief. Lame Johnny moved north to Deadwood in Dakota Territory and showed enough talent with a gun to become a deputy sheriff. Later, he worked for a mining company until he was recognized in early 1878 by a rider from Texas. Oddly, he was not sent back to Texas, probably because he had been so popular, but he lost his job and finally reverted to horse stealing, perhaps doing some stage robbing as well. In 1878 a livestock detective named Frank Smith caught Lame Johnny stealing horses from the Pine Ridge Indian Reservation. Smith and his prisoner boarded a stage bound for Deadwood, where he was to be lodged in jail, but on the trip the coach was halted by a masked man who rescued Lame Johnny. At least that's what was thought until Johnny was found hanging from a tree the next day. It appeared he had been spirited away and lynched by a mob of one. No one could figure it out. Perhaps, according to one theory, Lame Johnny had done something really terrible in Texas that merited his fatal treatment at the hands of a mysterious kidnapper. But the puzzle remained unsolved; the miners named a creek after Lame Johnny and let it go at that.

DONNER Party: Murder and cannibalism

The tragic fate of the Donner Party, a group of California-bound settlers who split off from a wagon train at Fort Bridger, Wyo. remains the ultimate horror story of America's westward migration.

Following the lead of George Donner, the 89-member caravan took the so-called Hastings Cut-off, a supposed shortcut that was instead to bring them to tragedy. Progress was slow through the rugged Wasatch Mountains and many of the settlers' horses and oxen died on the torturous trek. Bickering broke out and a number of killings resulted. One of the organizers of the group, James Reed, killed a young man named James Snyder in an argument. At first, the other members of the wagon train favored hanging Reed but later decided merely to banish him, and he was forced to leave behind his wife and children and continue on his own.

By the end of October 1846, the Donner Party was compelled to camp at what was then called Truckee Lake, now known as Donner Lake, because 20- to 60-foot snows had stopped the wagon train from making it through their last obstacle, the Sierra Nevadas. Desperately, the pioneers built shelters and tried to last through the winter by killing their remaining animals to augment the dwindling food supply. However, it soon became apparent that they would starve, and a party of 17 men and five women started out on foot to try to break out of the mountains and get help. One of them died along the way and the others ate his flesh to survive. Only two Indian guides refused to partake of the human flesh. They decided to leave the rest of the party, suspecting they would be killed next to provide more food, but were quickly located and murdered. Meanwhile, members of the party at Donner Lake started dying and the survivors there also resorted to cannibalism to keep themselves alive. Then the murdering started. No one ever found out who died naturally and who was killed.

Finally, the escape party made it through the mountains to an Indian camp and then to an outpost. Rescuers from the outpost set out back across the mountains. One of them was James Reed, who heroically led the largest rescue team and found his wife and two of his children (another child had died and was eaten). It was not until April 17, 1847 that the last of the travelers were saved; by that time, of the 89 emigrants only 45 still survived.

It soon became evident that a number of the dead had been murdered to provide food, while whole legs of oxen lay untouched in the snow not far away. The weakened pioneers had lacked the strength to dig up the meat. The villain of the party was made out to be Lewis Keseberg, who was found lying beside a simmering pot containing the liver and lungs of a small boy. Other parts of human flesh were scattered around the floor of his cabin, and a contemporary account described his "lair" as "containing buckets of blood, about a gallon, and parts of human flesh strewn all around."

After the rescue Keseberg was charged with committing six murders, robbing the dead George Donner of his gold and cannibalizing several bodies. Denying all the charges except that of cannibalism, he described what had happened: "Five of my companions had died in my cabin, and their stark and ghastly bodies lay there day and night, seemingly gazing at me with their glazed and staring eyes. I was too weak to move them had I tried."

He insisted he had resorted to flesh eating as a last desperate act.

I cannot describe the unutterable repugnance with which I tasted the first mouthful of flesh. There is an instinct in our nature that revolts at the thought of touching, much less eating, a corpse. It makes my blood curdle to think of it. It has been told that I boasted of my shame—said that I enjoyed this

horrid food, and that I remarked that human flesh was more palatable than California beef. This is a falsehood. It is a horrible, revolting falsehood. This food was never otherwise than loathsome, insipid, and disgusting."

A court freed Keseberg but he suffered the rest of his life from public disrepute. Whenever children saw him, they shouted: "Stone him! Stone him!" In a sense, Keseberg was the last victim of the ill-fated Donner Party.

DOOLIN, Bill (1863-1896): Outlaw leader

Probably the most popular of the Western outlaws with the public was not Butch Cassidy, Jesse James or Sam Bass but Bill Doolin, the leader of the Oklahombres of the 1890s.

An Arkansas-born cowboy, Doolin punched cattle in Wyoming and later in Oklahoma for the HX (Halsell) Ranch, the breeding ground for a lot of future badmen. Doolin hit the outlaw trail in 1891 with the Daltons. He enjoyed the easy money but clearly was never too sure how smart the brothers were. Doolin started out with the gang for the famed raid on Coffeyville, Kan., where the brothers sought to recapture the lost glory of the James boys and the Youngers by holding up two banks at the same time—a stupid play as far as Doolin was concerned. Fortunately, or conveniently, for him, his horse turned lame and he was forced to turn back. The Daltons were annihilated in Coffeyville, and Doolin alone went back to Oklahoma to form a new band of robbers.

The new Doolin gang reflected much of their leader's personality. They were friendly and fun-loving except when cornered—then they shot to kill. The gang even operated under a code of honor that barred shooting a tracking lawman in the back. Indeed, when the redoubtable lawman Bill Tilghman once appeared unexpectedly in the gang's camp, Doolin saved his life by telling his men to put down their weapons. Doolin knew the Oklahoma badlands section called Hell's Fringe like the back of his hand and always led pursuers on a merry chase there. He was aided too by his popularity with residents, counting on warnings from them whenever posses were in the area. Warned in time, Doolin and his men beat off and escaped a huge posse in the famed Battle of Ingalls in September 1893.

Early in 1894 Doolin married a minister's daughter and under her influence started to settle down to honest pursuits. The Oklahombres began splintering, individuals or pairs going their separate ways. But Doolin had too long a record, having committed too many robberies, for the law to forget him. Bill Tilghman captured him in a Eureka Springs, Ark. bathhouse after a fierce half-hour fight in which neither man used a gun. When Tilghman brought Doolin to Guthrie, Okla., 5,000 people crowded the town to greet Doolin. They all but ignored the brave marshal as they pressed in to touch the famed outlaw and ask him for autographs. Doolin was bigger than life, and he proved that by promptly escaping from the Guthrie jail, freeing 37 prisoners in the process.

Doolin fled to New Mexico, where, it was learned 40 years later, he was sheltered at the ranch of the famous novelist

Eugene Manlove Rhodes. There he saved his host from being killed by a wild horse. By 1896 Doolin and his wife had settled in a small house near Lawton, Okla.; at this point the outlaw was in very poor health due to consumption.

For years there have been two versions of Doolin's death. The original story was that Heck Thomas caught up with Doolin on a dark night as the outlaw walked down a road, cradling a Winchester in one arm while leading a wagon driven by his wife. Doolin fired first and Marshal Thomas blasted him to death with a shotgun.

Years later a second version surfaced. There had been no confrontation on a dusty road. Thomas had pushed through the door of the Doolin home to find the outlaw's wife in tears. Doolin was dead, she said. Thomas walked into the bedroom to find Doolin's still-warm body. He was dead and that meant no reward money. Quickly, Thomas leveled his shotgun and fired. Then, after concocting the story about a shooting on a road, he claimed a reward. It was not, however, an act of greed on Thomas' part. Like many other law officers, he respected Bill Doolin and did not wish to see his widow and young boy live in poverty. He gave the $5,000 reward money to the widow.

See also: *Doolin Gang; Ingalls, Oklahoma Territory, Battle of; Henry Andrew "Heck" Thomas; Bill Tilghman.*

DOOLIN Gang

While Western criminals were often the object of a great deal of hero-worship, one outlaw band that was genuinely respected during the 1890s, not only by the public but by law officers as well, was the Doolins of the Oklahoma Territory. Neither Bill Doolin nor any of the members ever claimed they "were forced into crime," admitting they were in it for the sheer devilry.

The gang was formed by Bill Doolin, who had ridden on a number of bank jobs with the Daltons, but unlike the Daltons, members of the Doolin bunch were good at their trade. They took their work seriously and practiced hard before a bank robbery, gunning a target tree as they rode past and dropping to one side of their mounts as they dodged imaginary bullets. They seldom had to hide in their home areas, such as Rock Fort and Ingalls, where friendly residents provided a network of spies that informed them whenever the law was coming. The gang clearly won the great Battle of Ingalls, beating a posse of about twice its size. Although some of the leading lawmen of the era, respected names like Tilghman, Madsen, Thomas, Ledbetter, Jim Masterson, captured a few gang members, the group, including Bill Doolin, dissolved of its own accord to follow more peaceful pursuits.

See also: *Roy Daugherty; Bill Doolin; Ingalls, Oklahoma Territory, Battle of; George "Bitter Creek" Newcomb; Rose of Cimarron.*

DOOR-KNOCKER Thieves: Colonial lawbreakers

One of the most prevalent types of theft in Colonial days was stealing brass knockers from the doors of fashionable homes. Professional criminals netted considerable profits from such crimes, disposing of their loot to receivers of stolen goods who transported the knockers to another colony for resale. Door-knocker thefts became such a rage that even well-to-do youths took up the crime as a form of sport, making it perhaps the first form of middle-class crime in America. A Philadelphia newspaper in 1773 reported that "wonton Frolicks of sundry intoxicated Bucks and Blades of the City" resulted in the theft of scores of brass knockers from various homes. That same year, in a story datelined Philadelphia, the *Newport Mercury* told of how "three of our Philadelphia Bucks, in the Night, lately attacked one of our Watchmen with swords" while he was attempting to prevent their nefarious deeds. However, "before he got relief they wounded him, of which Wounds he died. One of them made his escape, two were taken; one of those a reputable Merchant's Son in the City; the other a Merchant's Clerk, unknown to me. Various Opinions concerning them, what will be their fate. They are, I hear, loaded with Irons in the Dungeon."

The record appears incomplete regarding the ultimate fate of the perpetrators of this vicious crime, but knocker thievery finally was eliminated through the efforts of one Daniel King, who invented a knocker "the Construction of which is peculiarly singular, and which will stand Proof against the United Attacks of those nocturnal Sons of Violence."

DOTY, Sile (1800-1876): King of the Hotel Thieves

One of the great "lock men" of crime, Sile Doty was the first thief to develop the complete burglar kit. He bought locks by the dozen, took them apart, studied them and then designed skeleton keys to fit the various types. He also perfected a set of pliers that could be inserted in a door to turn a key on the other side. With these impressive improvements in the art of burglary, Doty was able to boast that he could break into any hotel room in any establishment in the country. In 1835, for example, Doty hit the United States Hotel in Detroit, which was then the state capital, and burglarized the rooms of about a dozen state legislators.

Because of his great success as the King of the Hotel Thieves, Doty in later years set up a criminal network that included crooked hotel managers and clerks, who steered him on to likely victims, and corrupt sheriffs and judges, who protected him in case of a hitch. With this apparatus in place, Doty branched into circulating counterfeit money, but his first love remained anything to do with locks. He designed handcuffs and sold them to sheriffs and then sold criminals special keys that could open the cuffs even while they were being worn.

Doty liked to claim he "made crime pay," but despite all his brilliance and his payoffs, he spent 20 years of his life—on and off—behind bars before retiring at 72 and writing his memoirs.

DRAFT Riots

Beginning early on the morning of July 13, 1863 and continuing for three more bloody days, great riots broke out in New York City, leaving, according to the best estimates, 2,000 dead and another 8,000 wounded. The cause of the rioting was indignation over President Lincoln's draft, fanned by racial hatred, Irish resentment at occupying the lowest level of the social and economic order and the greed of the great criminal gangs of the Bowery and the Five Points, which saw a chance to loot the city much as had been done during the earlier anti-abolitionist and anti-English Astor Place riots of the 1830s and 1840s.

There were minor disturbances of the peace in opposition to the draft in Boston, Mass., Portsmouth, N.H., Rutland, Vt. and Wooster, Ohio, but none approached the size or ferocity of the New York riots. There the city's poor, largely Irish, allied with the Democrats in opposition to the war, rioted to protest the draft, which they saw as trading rich men's money for poor men's blood through a provision in the law that allowed a potential draftee to buy out of the service for $300. Since this was a monumental sum to the Irish, it meant they had to do the fighting and dying in the conflict between the North and the South.

What had started out as violent protest against the draft turned by the second day into savage lynching of blacks—the cause of the war in the Irish poor's eyes—and wholesale looting, as rioters and criminals sought to seize armory supplies, overpowering and then torturing, mutilating and murdering defending soldiers. Some saw in the great riots a Roman Catholic insurrection, which they were not, although along with the "No Draft" signs were some that sang the praises of the Pope and proclaimed, "Down with the Protestants." Considerable church properties of various Protestant faiths were among the 100 buildings burned to the ground by the rioters, but none belonging to the Catholic faith were touched. Lone Catholic priests turned back rioters bent on looting and killing, but Catholic Archbishop Hughes refused to counsel the rioters to disband until the fourth day, when the violence had run its course. On that day he addressed a pastoral letter entitled "Archbishop Hughes to the Men of New York, who are called in many of the papers rioters." Later, the archbishop was to acknowledge that he had "spak too late."

The rioters were bent on mayhem and some of their crimes were heinous indeed. Policemen and soldiers were murdered, and the children of the rioters picked the bodies clean of every stitch of clothing, proudly wearing the bloodstained garments as badges of honor. Great throngs—estimated to be between 50,000 and 70,000 persons in all—stormed across Manhattan from the Hudson to the East rivers, looting stores, burning buildings and beating every black they saw. At least three black men were hanged before sundown of the first day, and thereafter, the sight of bodies hanging from lamp posts and trees were common throughout the city. The blacks' bodies were all viciously mutilated, slashed with knives and beaten with clubs. Often, they were mere charred skeletons, the handi-work of the most ferocious element in all early American riots—women. Trailing behind the men, they poured oil into the knife wounds of victims and set the corpses ablaze, dancing beneath the awesome human torches, singing obscene songs and telling antiblack jokes.

Burning of the Second Avenue Armory caused many deaths.

The black settlements were the scene of much of the violence, the target of those of the rioters more concerned with bloodletting than looting. A house of prostitution on Water Street was burned and its occupants tortured because they refused to reveal the hiding place of a black servant. In New Bowery three black men were cornered on a rooftop and the building set afire. For a time the men clung by their fingers to the gutters while the mob below chanted for them to fall. When they did, they were stomped to death.

Meanwhile, as other groups of rioters attacked armories in search of weapons and police stations in anger at the police resistance to them, a mob sought to destroy the offices of Horace Greeley's prodraft *New York Tribune*. They started several blazes that forced the staff to flee by the back stairway. Greeley was compelled to take refuge under a table in a Park Row restaurant. A police garrison of 100 men retook the newspaper's premises and extinguished the fires, and the following day 100 Marines and sailors took up guard in and around the building, which bristled with Gatling guns and a howitzer posted at the main entrance.

By late evening the mobs moved further uptown, leaving the scene behind them filled with numerous fires. At 11 o'clock a great thunder and lightning storm extinguished the blazes. Had it not, many historians believe the city would have been subjected to a conflagration far worse than the great Chicago fire a few years hence. Complicating the firefighting was the fact that several fire units had joined the rioters and others were driven away from many of the blazes by the rampaging mobs

Probably the greatest hero of the first day of the riots was Patrolman George Rallings, who learned of a mob's plan to attack the Negro Orphanage at 43rd Street and Fifth Avenue where 260 children of freed slaves were sheltered. He spirited the children away before the building was torched. Only one tiny black girl was killed by the axe-wielding rioters. Overlooked in the exodus, she was found hiding under a bed and axed to death.

The fighting over the ensuing three days reflected the tides of military battle, as first the rioters and then the police and various militia units took control of an area. A pitched battle that left an estimated 50 dead was fought at barricades on Ninth Avenue until the police finally gained control of the thoroughfare. Rioters captured Col. H. J. O'Brien of the Eleventh New York Volunteers, tied a rope around his ankles and dragged him back and forth over the cobblestones. A Catholic priest intervened long enough to administer the last rites and then departed. For three hours the rioters tortured O'Brien, slashing him with knives and dropping stones on his body. He was then allowed to lie suffering in the afternoon sun until sundown, when another mob descended on him and inflicted new tortures. Finally, he was dragged to his own backyard, where a group of vicious Five Points Gang women squatted around him and mutilated him with knives until at last he was dead.

Drawing shows the corpse of a policeman killed in the riot being abused by children and women following in the wake of the mob.

By the second day most of the rioters' fury was taken out on blacks, many of whom were lynched.

On July 15 militia regiments sent toward Gettysburg were ordered back to the city, and by the end of the 16th, the rioters had been quelled. The losses by various military units were never disclosed, but the toll of dead and wounded was believed to have been at least 350. The overall casualties in the riots, 2,000 dead and 8,000 wounded, were greater than those suffered at such famous Civil War battles as Bull Run and Shiloh; virtually every member of the police force had suffered some sort of injury. The number of blacks lynched, including bodies found and others missing, was believed to total 88. Property losses probably exceeded $5 million. Among the 100 buildings totally burned were a Protestant mission, the Negro Orphanage, an armory, three police stations, three provost marshals' offices as well as factories, stores and dwellings. Another 200 buildings were looted and partially damaged.

Even while the riots were going on and in the days following them, Democratic politicians seeking to embarrass a Republican president and a Republican mayor, demanded the police and troops be withdrawn from their districts because they were "killing the people." As a result of political influence almost all of the hundreds of prisoners taken in the last two days of the riots were released. This was especially true of the gang leaders of the Five Points and the waterfront who were caught leading looting expeditions during the fighting. In the end, only 20 men out of the thousands of rioters were brought to trial. Nineteen of them were convicted and sentenced to an average of five years in prison. No one was convicted of murder.

On August 19, the city now filled with troops, the draft drawings resumed and those who could not pay $300 were sent off to war.

DRISCOLL, Danny (?1860-1888): Gang leader and murderer

The last great New York ruffian gang of the 19th century was the Whyos, captained jointly in their heyday by Danny Lyons and Danny Driscoll. In the 1880s Lyons and Driscoll reportedly mandated that a potential member of the gang had to kill at least one man. It is perhaps fitting that this brutal pair were themselves hanged within eight months of one another.

Driscoll went first. In 1887 he and tough Five Points gangster, Johnny McCarthy, became involved in a shooting dispute over whom a young prostitute, Breezy Garrity, was working for. Breezy made the mistake of standing around to see who the winner would be, presumably to hand over to him her recent receipts. In the fusillade one of Driscoll's stray shots struck and killed her. It was clearly a case of unintentional homicide and by most measures of justice Driscoll should have escaped with something less than the ultimate penalty. However, the authorities had been after Driscoll for years on suspicion of several murders and were not going to allow a golden opportunity such as this to slip away because of legal niceties. The prosecution hardly had to remind the jurors of the many atrocities committed by the Whyos, since everyone living in New York ventured out in constant fear of these gangsters. Driscoll, screaming outrage and frame-up, was sentenced to death, and on January 23, 1888 he was hanged in the Tombs.

See also: *Danny Lyons, Whyos.*

DROP Swindle

A notorious con game employing a variety of techniques is the drop swindle. A "dropper" drops a wallet at the heels of a likely victim and then pretends to find it. The wallet is stuffed with counterfeit money. Pleading that he is in a hurry, the dropper offers to sell the wallet to the victim, saying something like: "There's a couple of hundred bucks in there. The guy who lost it will probably give half the dough as a reward just to get the rest of it and his IDs back. Tell you what, give me fifty and you can take care of returning the wallet to him and get the rest of the reward." Naturally, like most cons, this racket appeals to a victim's larcenous streak since he has the option of simply keeping the wallet. One of the most famous practitioners of this swindle was Nathan Kaplan, better known as Kid Dropper, who, after earning his nickname practicing the swindle in his youth, went on to become the most famous gangster in New York City during the early 1920s.

While the drop swindle is well worn, it remains viable. Almost any big city police force will handle a few dozen complaints of the scam annually, and of course, the unreported cases are undoubtedly far more numerous.

See also: *Kid Dropper.*

DRUCCI, Vincent "Schemer" (1895-1927): Bootlegger and murderer

One of the chief lieutenants in Dion O'Banion's North Side Gang during the 1920s, Drucci took charge of the Chicago outfit after O'Banion and his successor, Hymie Weiss, were assassinated by the Capone forces.

In one sense, Drucci was Capone's toughest rival in that opposing gang, because he was, as Capone put it, "a bedbug."

The Schemer had earned his nickname because of his imaginative but totally off-the-wall ideas for robbing banks and kidnapping millionaires. He was also a tough kill. In a street duel with ambushing Capone gunners, he traded shot for shot with them while giggling and dancing a jig to avoid the bullets that sprayed the pavement around him. When a police car appeared on the scene, the Capone gunmen sped off in their car, but the Schemer had not had enough. Despite a slight leg wound, he hopped on the running board of a passing car, poked his gun at the motorist's head and yelled, "Follow that goddamn car." Police had to drag him off the car. When questioned, Drucci claimed it was not an underworld battle but a stickup. "They wanted my roll," he said, flashing a wad of $13,500.

With Drucci at the head of the O'Banion gang, Capone had to beef up protection for himself, since the Schemer was capable of any wild plot to get at him. According to one unconfirmed story, Drucci actually cornered Capone alone in a Turkish bath and almost strangled him to death before the gang leader's bodyguards showed up. The Schemer escaped stark naked, hopped in his car and drove off.

Frustrated in his efforts to get Big Al, Drucci decided to hurt him as best he could. A few weeks later, he had Theodore "the Greek" Anton, the owner of a popular restaurant over a Capone headquarters, the Hawthorne Smoke Shop, kidnapped. Anton was an honest man who idolized Capone for what he considered the gangster's tenderheartedness, such as his practice of buying all a newsboy's papers for $20 and sending him home. Capone was eating in the restaurant when Anton was snatched by lurking O'Banionites. He understood what it meant and sat in a booth the rest of the evening crying inconsolably.

Anton's body was found in quicklime. He had been tortured and then shot.

Capone vowed to kill Drucci, but the next several murder attempts were made by the Schemer. As a matter of fact, the Capone gang never did get Drucci. He was arrested on April 5, 1927 for perpetrating some election day violence against reformers seeking to supplant the William Hale Thompson machine. Put in a squad car, Drucci got enraged because a detective, Dan Healy, had dared lay a hand on him. He screamed, "I'll get you for this!" and tried to wrestle the detective's gun away. The officer pulled his hand free and pumped four quick shots into Drucci's body.

The O'Banionites wanted Healy charged with murder. "Murder?" asked Chief of Detectives William Schoemaker. "We're having a medal struck for Healy."

The North Siders gave Drucci a marvelous funeral. He lay in state a day and a night in a $10,000 casket of aluminum and silver at the undertaking establishment of Assistant State's Attorney John A. Sbarbaro. The walls of the room were hidden by masses of flowers; the dominant floral design was a throne of white and purple blooms with the inscription "Our Pal." After Drucci was buried, his blonde wife declared proudly, "A cop bumped him off like a dog, but we gave him a king's funeral."

See also: *Samuel J. "Nails" Morton; Charles Dion "Deanie" O'Banion; Standard Oil Building, Battles of the; Hymie Weiss.*

DRUG Racket

The drug racket is among the most lucrative of all criminal activities. It has long attracted much of the Mafia's attention and is the prime activity of both the new black and Latin-American criminal combines. The potential profits involved are truly staggering. It is said to be one of the most tempting sources of potential police corruption. In the early years of his reign over the FBI, J. Edgar Hoover fought desperately and successfully to keep narcotics control out of the hands of his agency. He was known to have felt that corruption and bribery were virtually inevitable in the policing of this field.

It would be pure guesswork to attempt to put a total dollar value on the drug racket. According to the Drug Enforcement Administration, the average heroin junkie needs some 50 milligrams of the drug each day to satisfy his habit. A rule of thumb sets the average cost of such a habit at $65 a day or $24,000 a year. Since there are between 100,000 to 150,000 hard-core heroin users in the country, this aspect alone makes narcotics at least a $2.5 billion dollar business.

Of course, heroin is just a small part of the drug trade. The Senate Internal Securities Subcommittee has placed the number of regular pot users at over 10 million. Another 25 million have smoked marijuana at some time or other, indicating that public hostility toward marijuana today is probably not much more severe than that toward whiskey during Prohibition. This public acceptance has done wonders for the marijuana seller. He can charge excessive prices because he is dealing in an illegal product; yet the high public acceptance of the drug lessens the amount he must pay for protection and the risk he has to take.

The drug racket's profit margins up the distribution ladder work much like European value-added taxes but in vastly greater percentages. The importer goes out of the country and obtains five kilograms of "pure heroin," which really means about 80 percent pure, for a total price of $250,000. Adding quinine and milk sugar, he cuts the purity to 40 percent, doubling his supply. This he will sell at $65,000 a kilo, earning a profit of $400,000, or a gain of 160 percent on his investment. The heroin is passed on to the big supplier, who further dilutes the product, so that each kilo he has bought becomes 1.6 kilos. The drug is sold in quarter-kilo bags for $15,000 each, netting the big supplier a total of $300,000. From the supplier the heroin goes to the pushers, who then dilute the product to about five percent pure and retail the stuff in $5 and $10 units. The profit for the pushers is about $300,000. Thus, besides recouping the original investment, the five kilograms of heroin has produced a million dollars in illegal profits throughout the distribution pipeline.

DRUGS In Prisons

Perhaps the most constant cat-and-mouse game played in jails and prisons today involves the smuggling of drugs. New prisoners must be searched thoroughly to prevent illegal drugs from being slipped into penal institutions in the hair, ears or mouth. All body cavities and the groin area must be searched. Even if such searches were 100 percent effective, however, the flow of drugs into the jails still would be of flood-like proportions. Jail authorities have found prisoners trying to conceal narcotics by saturating handkerchiefs, pants pockets and shirts with them and then reironing. Relatives bringing a tie for a prisoner to wear to court may well have soaked it in a concentration of narcotics.

When female visitors are allowed to kiss prisoners, they sometimes pass packets of drugs by mouth. Prisoners have been known to swallow balloons filled with narcotics that can be retrieved after a bowel movement. Visitors have discarded cigarette butts filled with narcotics. There have been cases of narcotics being thrown over jail walls inside rubber balls or even dropped from low-flying helicopters.

Of course, prisoners have their own explanation for why some police guards are so determined to stop the flow of drugs into an institution. They say it is because these guards want to be the convicts' only—and high-priced—suppliers.

DRY Tortugas Prison

Although its correct name was Fort Jefferson, the most-dreaded federal prison of its day was generally called by the name of the Florida coral islet on which it was situated, Dry Tortugas. Built in 1846 originally as a fort, it turned out to be a fiasco—at a reported cost of $1 per brick—when it was determined that the water around it was too shallow for enemy ships ever to get within cannon range. The government then simply converted it into a prison, and Dry Tortugas became a hellhole for everyone in it, prisoners, guards, soldiers and officials. Mosquitoes swarmed over the place and were considered a terrible nuisance, but the yellow fever that abounded was never attributed to these insects. The prison was hit with periodic epidemics during which men often died faster than they could be buried.

The guards and soldiers stationed there treated the prisoners brutally, a behavior fueled in part by the terrible living conditions they themselves had to endure. It was an open secret that the government sent to Dry Tortugas those prisoners who deserved "special treatment." That certainly was the case with Dr. Samuel Mudd, the physician who set John Wilkes Booth's leg after he had assassinated Abraham Lincoln. Prison officials specifically instructed the guards to be exceptionally harsh with "that Lincoln murderer." Mudd, however, was to nurse the garrison and prisoners through a yellow fever epidemic and thereby win the gratitude of the officials. He was pardoned in 1869 after his humanitarian acts became known, and the resulting publicity about conditions in the hellhole led to its abandonment in the early 1870s. The prison became a national monument in 1934.

See also: *Dr. Samuel Mudd.*

DRYGULCH

The best location for killing a man in the West was at a place he would have to come to sooner or later, and in dry, arid country that meant a waterhole. The attacker could hide in the waterhole's protective cover and shoot the victim before he could quench his thirst. Even if he missed or only wounded the victim, the killer could hold the key ground until the man died or surrendered to get a drink, hence the origin of the term "drygulch."

DUGGAN, Sandford S. C. (1845-1868): Woman beater

Sandford Duggan was one of a hated breed in the West, a lawman turned outlaw and murderer. Yet his life ended swinging from a rope not because of the murders or holdups he had commited but rather for woman beating.

A Pennsylvanian who developed an itchy trigger finger after migrating west, Duggan was still in his teens when he murdered his first man in a Black Hawk, Colo. saloon. He got away before a miners court could convene and wound up in Denver, where he was soon living off the earnings of a young prostitute named Kittie Wells, who willingly supported him. Duggan banged her around regularly and one night he pistol-whipped her almost to death. Such actions toward women, respectable or otherwise, were not tolerated in the West, where families were in such short supply. Duggan was arrested before a lynching could be arranged, but the next morning a judge freed him on a technicality. A miners lynch mob formed immediately, but Duggan again avoided capture and made it out of town.

He fled east to Laramie City, a Union Pacific end-of-track town. Apparently in such urgent need of a lawman that they had no time to check into Duggan's background, the town's authorities named him marshal. However, in due course a traveler from Denver revealed the details of the Kittie Wells affair, and Duggan was stripped of his badge.

The facts of the case have been lost, but not long afterwards, Duggan was given 24 hours to get out of town. Once again, the alleged offense was woman beating. Duggan then rode the holdup trail until he was captured at Golden by Marshal Dave Cook, who took him back to Denver. This was a double stroke of bad luck for Duggan: he was hated in Denver and Dave Cook had the misfortune, or perhaps the knack, of often losing prisoners to lynch mobs.

That's exactly what happened to Duggan. He was dragged out of jail and quickly strung up from a cottonwood tree. Someone tacked a sign on his corpse that read, "woman beater."

DUKE'S Restaurant: Mob headquarters

If any building or place during the 1940s and 1950s could have been called the underworld's Capitol, it would have been Duke's Restaurant, 73 Palisades Avenue, Cliffside Park, N.J. It became a prime topic of inquiry during the historic Kefauver Committee's probe of organized crime in the early 1950s. Duke's was the meeting place, and safe sanctuary, for the leaders of the national crime syndicate. Presiding over all affairs at Duke's was one of the top leaders of crime in New York and New Jersey, Joe Adonis.

Casual visitors to Duke's, which was across the street from the popular Palisades Amusement Park, found it to be a typical Italian restaurant. It had a long bar and booths and served tasty meals. Most did not suspect that to the rear of the public dining area there was a sliding panel with an "ice box door," typical of the nearly indestructible and soundproof barriers used by illegal gambling establishments. Behind the panel there was what could be called the control room from which the Mafia and much of organized crime planned and directed their operations.

Much of the surveillance of Duke's was done by various federal agencies, mainly the Internal Revenue Service and the Bureau of Narcotics, and by Manhattan District Attorney Frank Hogan's staff. It was not an easy undertaking. These investigators found that once they had crossed the George Washington Bridge into New Jersey, they were shadowed, hounded, badgered and even picked up by various local police departments. A car of investigators parked outside of Duke's to keep an eye on the alleged diners entering and leaving were often harassed by police telling them to move on, even after they displayed their credentials. Duke's obviously was set in unfriendly territory for New York and federal investigators.

Meanwhile, inside the restaurant's chamber the likes of Adonis and Albert Anastasia presided over criminal activities, collecting the revenues from various enterprises, arranging "hits," handling "affairs at the table," which were trials of syndicate soldiers for various alleged offenses. On Tuesday, known as the "big day," the top leaders of crime in America came in for their "cabinet" meetings. During the late 1940s and early 1950s, when the syndicate's national commission was dominated by the so-called Big Six, the top men converged on Duke's. Flying in from the Midwest were Tony Accardo and Greasy Jake Guzik, the representatives of Chicago's Capone mob. The remaining four came from the East. They were Adonis; Frank Costello; Meyer Lansky, who could be coming from anywhere since he handled the mob's gambling interests in Saratoga, N.Y., Miami and Las Vegas; and Longy Zwillman, the boss of New Jersey, who had a powerful voice in naming the state's governors and, more importantly, its attorneys general.

Duke's even survived the prying of the Kefauver Committee. Gangster Willie Moretti insisted he went there for the food and ambience, which was, he said with a straight face, "like Lindy's on Broadway." Tony Bender took the Fifth Amendment rather than reveal if he had ever been in Duke's, insisting even a visit to a restaurant could be incriminating.

Duke's lost its significance when Adonis was deported in 1953. It was, in the words of one newspaperman, "something like the British burning the White House."

DUNCAN'S Saloon: Chicago pickpocket haven

From 1890 through most of the first decade of the 20th century, Duncan's Saloon on Chicago's State Street was the best-known hangout for pickpockets and professional tramps in the United States. The proprietor, Bob Duncan, had long been heralded by the Chicago press as the King of the Pickpockets, but he had retired from active duty to serve as a sort of unofficial greeter for traveling pickpocketing mobs. No less than 20 professional mobs headquartered at Duncan's place, not only for sociability but also because Duncan had developed considerable clout as a fixer with the police. Duncan supposedly could arrange matters so that an individual mob enjoyed free hunting in specified locales. Furthermore he could even fix it so that a police officer would be on hand to confuse victims.

Professional hoboes also used Duncan's place as a rendezvous and mail drop and always saved whatever money they had for a spree in the establishment. One of the most illustrious knights of the road to headquarter at the saloon was Wyoming Slivers. Slivers retired from the road life in 1896, when he married a rich widow in Minnesota. Mrs. Slivers died a couple of years later, leaving him a nest egg of $10,000. Slivers immediately repaired to Duncan's Saloon and, with about 20 of his cronies, staged a six-month spree with the money. Ten of the hoboes died of delirium tremens, and Slivers came through the orgy minus an ear and three fingers lost in fistfights.

Duncan's Saloon closed following one of Chicago's periodic graft investigations and it was believed that Duncan then returned to his light-fingered trade.

DURRANT, William Henry Theodore (1872-1898): Murderer

William "Theo" Durrant, who became famous in this country and Europe as the Demon in the Belfry for the murder of two young women in San Francisco in 1895, was as close to a real-life Jekyll and Hyde as America ever produced.

At 23 Theo was an excellent student in his senior class of Cooper Medical College and a dedicated member of the Emanuel Baptist Church, functioning as assistant Sunday school superintendent, Sunday usher, church librarian and secretary of the young people's Christian Endeavor Society. Whenever there were repairs to be made on the church, Theo could be counted on to offer his services. Several times a week, in his less sane moments, Theo patronized the notorious brothels on Commercial Street, regarded as far more degenerate than those elsewhere in the city. Theo's custom was to bring with him a sack or small crate containing a chicken or pigeon; during the high point of the evening's debauch, he would slit the bird's throat and let the blood trickle over himself. The only hint of Theo's other life was some gossip that he had attempted to kiss girls at church socials.

On April 3, 1895 Theo was seen entering the church with 18-year-old Blanche Lamont, a high school student who often spoke of becoming a teacher. Inside the church Theo excused himself, saying he had a chore to perform. He returned a moment later, stripped naked. When the girl resisted him, Durrant killed her in a frenzy, strangling her and mutilating her body. He then dragged the body up to the belfry and hid it. Two hours later, he calmly appeared at a Christian Endeavor meeting.

The Demon in the Belfry is depicted carrying a beautiful victim to his hiding place in the bell tower.

Theo was questioned when Blanche was reported missing, but he earnestly informed the police that it was his theory that white slavers might have kidnapped her and installed her in a brothel somewhere in San Francisco or perhaps shipped her to some faraway locality. Nothing much would have developed from the investigation had not Theo struck again that same month, killing 20-year-old Minnie Williams in the church after some naked trysts. Minnie, unlike Blanche, had responded to Theo's bizarre wooing, but he murdered her just as well. He slashed the body with a knife and left it hidden behind a door in the blood-spattered church library, where it was found the next day. The theory was that Theo might have told her about Blanche's murder, and Minnie responded by saying she was going to the police.

Again, Theo had been seen with a young woman who later disappeared or was murdered, but he denied any knowledge of the crime. However, police found Minnie's purse hidden in a suit pocket in his closet, and they finally trekked up to the belfry and found Blanche Lamont's body as well.

Theo's trial was a spectacle, perhaps the first to receive sensational "sob-sister" coverage. William Randolph Hearst's *Examiner* printed a front-page sketch of Theo's hands so that its readers could recognize the "hands of murder." A "sweet pea girl" appeared at each session of the court and offered Theo a bouquet of flowers. This was either a defense tactic or a newspaper trick to generate reader interest. In all, 125 witnesses testified, including Theo himself, who thought he had convinced the jury with his denials of guilt. He was nonetheless found guilty on the first ballot. Appeals delayed the execution for almost three years until January 7, 1898, when Durrant was hanged.

On the scaffold, Theo told the hangman, "Don't put that rope on, my boy, until I talk." The sheriff merely waved to the hangman to continue his work, and Theo was hanged without further ado. The newspapers were somewhat peeved at being deprived of some final words from the fiendish killer, but they were able to report one final macabre incident.

Theo's mother and father had apparently reveled in their notoriety during the trial. After the hanging they called for their son's body. While waiting in a prison anteroom, the couple was offered some food by the warden. When the body arrived, with Theo's face contorted in a hideous grimace, they sat eating not five feet from the open coffin. Hearst's newspaper reported that at one point Mother Durrant said, "Papa, I'd like some more of that roast."

DUTCH Henry (?-c.1930): Western horse thief

In the Old West, where stealing a man's horse was considered the equivalent of cutting off a man's legs, it was remarkable that a man like Henry Borne could live to a ripe old age as the King of Horse Thieves, with an estimated 300 men working for him in his prime.

Dutch Henry, whose real name was Henry Borne, was of German extraction. He first turns up as a member of the 7th Cavalry, which he quit in the late 1860s. Apparently, he had greater expectations in another line of work because he was soon arrested at Fort Smith, Ark. for stealing 20 government mules. Sentenced to a long term at hard labor in 1868, Dutch Henry broke prison three months later and went into the horse-stealing business in earnest. He soon was hiring men to steal whole herds at a time for him. No deal being too small for Dutch Henry, a thief with but a single pilfered animal would find him a ready, if tight-fisted, customer. Legends about Dutch Henry abound; one of the best-known tales concerns Henry selling a sheriff one of his own stolen horses.

Dutch Henry had his run-ins with the law but seemed to lead a charmed life. In 1874 he was wounded in a gunfight after being found in possession of a large number of stolen horses—but he was not prosecuted. Bat Masterson arrested Dutch Henry in 1878 and brought him to Dodge City for trial

only to see the horse thief beat the charge. The way Dutch Henry always told it, he was a victim just as much as the original owner of the property. Nobody really believed that, and a "Dutch Henry" became another name for a stolen horse. Eventually, the champion horse stealer's luck ran out, and authorities in Arkansas tied Dutch Henry to the long-escaped Henry Borne. Henry was sent back to prison, and other jurisdictions later seized him to serve terms in their area. As a result, Dutch Henry was out of circulation for well over 20 years. By that time the horse-stealing trade was in its decline, better law enforcement and something called the horseless carriage sealing its fate. Dutch Henry just faded away, although a number of old-timers insisted they saw him alive in Arkansas and elsewhere as late as 1930 and heard that he died shortly after that. Be that as it may, Dutch Henry's name lived on as a part of American culture, preserved in Hollywood movies as the favorite name used by uninventive screen writers for a villain and, almost always, for a horse thief.

See also: *Horse Stealing*.

DUTCH Mob: 19th century pickpocket gang

One of the largest gangs of pickpockets and muggers ever to operate in an American city, the Dutch Mob, under the cunning leadership of Little Freddie, Sheeney Mike and Johnny Irving, controlled the area just east of New York's Bowery from Houston Street to Fifth Street for about a decade beginning in 1867.

At its peak the gang consisted of 300 members, all professional pickpockets, who used varied methods to rob victims. A common practice would be to stage a street fight that attracted viewers who were then stripped of their wallets as they watched the action. In other instances a few of the gang would pick a fight with a victim and threaten to beat him up, but before they could, the cowed victim would be "rescued" by other members of the mob who would deftly pick his pockets while rushing him to safety. In time, the newspapers referred to the entire area from Houston to Fifth as "pickpocket paradise." Under a newly appointed precinct captain, Anthony J. Allaire, the police finally acted to clean up the district in 1877. Allaire's technique was simple enough; he sent in flying squads of police with orders to club anyone in the area resembling a pickpocket or mugger. The strategy worked and the Dutch Mob soon dwindled to a few. Irving moved into a new line of work, becoming a bank robber.

See also: *Pickpocketing*.

DYER, Mary (?-1660): Executed Quaker martyr

A Quaker who became a religious martyr, Mary Dyer may have been the only person ever executed in America simply to test a law. Dyer came to America about 1635 with her husband, William Dyer, and settled in Boston. In 1650 she went back to England on a visit and there was converted to Quakerism. When she returned to New England to spread the Quaker word, she was imprisoned in Boston and later banished. In 1657 Dyer was banished from the New Haven settlement. At this time the Massachusetts Bay Colony passed a law that made a visit following banishment punishable by death. Nevertheless, Mary Dyer returned to visit and minister to other jailed Quakers. She was arrested and condemned to death but was saved through the efforts of her son. In May 1660 Mary Dyer returned to Massachusetts once again, determined to see if the death penalty would ever be enforced and confident that it would not be. She was again seized and, on June 1, 1660, hanged on the Boston Common.

DYER Act: Auto theft law

Following World War I Congress became upset about the shocking growth of a new crime, automobile theft. The previous year 29,399 cars had been stolen in 21 cities, and 5,541 of them were never recovered. The theft problem already had proved too great for local authorities to handle, since they legally could not pursue a stolen vehicle across a state line. So, in an effort to curb car thefts, legislation was introduced making it a federal offense to transport a stolen automobile across a state line.

Although it produced a long debate over states rights, the National Motor Vehicle Theft Act, or Dyer Act, was passed in 1919. It hardly solved the problem, however, as the number of thefts mushroomed with the growth of automobile use. Between 1935 and 1955 an estimated four million vehicles were stolen; by 1975 the rate was up to one million per year.

The real impact of the Dyer Act was in its effect on the criminal justice system in general, bringing the FBI into areas of law enforcement never originally intended as part of its bailiwick. The public enemies of the early 1930s often needed to steal a car to pull off a bank robbery or some other crime and then escape across state borders. This provided the legal authority for the FBI to enter the chase.

See also: *Auto Theft.*

E

EARLE, Willie (1922-1947): Lynch victim

One of the most shocking cases of a Southern jury refusing to convict whites for the lynching of a black man occurred following the 1947 killing of 25-year-old Willie Earle in South Carolina.

Earle was picked up for questioning following the fatal stabbing of a cab driver near Liberty, S.C. He was taken to the Pickens County Jail, where he was interrogated and protested his innocence. Earle was not charged with the slaying but word spread of his arrest, and outraged cabbies gathered in Greenville to discuss the murder of a fellow driver. Soon, a large mob, armed with shotguns and knives, formed a convoy and headed for the jail. They broke into the jail and forced the jailer to open Earle's cell. Earle was dragged screaming to an automobile and taken in convoy to Saluda Dam, where he was "questioned" and "confessed." The prisoner was then driven to Bramlett Road in Greenville County and viciously put to death there. Earle was stabbed several times and one lyncher shattered the butt of his shotgun on the victim's skull. Others in the mob knife-gouged huge chunks of flesh from Earle's body. Only then was the pathetic prisoner finished off with several shotgun blasts. Satisfied, the lynchers drove home.

The killing shocked the nation and indeed most people in South Carolina. The FBI was called and cleared the jailer of violating Earle's civil rights, finding that he had not willingly released the prisoner. However, the agency cooperated with local authorities in identifying 28 persons among the lynch mob. Twenty-six of these confessed their part in the lynching. Gov. Strom Thurmond named a special prosecutor and pledged that justice would be done, a feeling, observers agreed, that was shared by most residents of the state.

Nevertheless, the result of the trial reflected the longstanding behavior of juries in cases where whites were accused of lynching blacks. The defense offered no testimony whatsoever, and despite the confessions, all the defendants were found "not guilty."

EARP, James C. (1841-1926): Brother of Wyatt

The eldest of the Earp brothers, James Earp came home from the Civil War in 1863 so severely wounded that he could not become a lawman like his other brothers. However, he was always linked to his brothers' shadier activities, generally looking after their gambling and saloon interests, while his wife ran an Earp-protected brothel. James died in San Francisco in 1926.

EARP, Morgan (1851-1882): Lawman

The brother of Wyatt Earp and participant in the famous, or infamous, gunfight at the O.K. Corral, Morgan Earp was an erstwhile lawman in his own right.

Born in Iowa, he started his career as a deputy town marshal in Dodge City, Kan. in 1876. He later worked in Dodge as a deputy sheriff and developed a reputation as an efficient gunman. Morgan Earp then moved on to Butte, Mont., where he became even more famous as a "town tamer." He apparently dispatched more than a few gunfighters, although the so-called classic gun duel he reputedly had with Billy Brooks in 1880 was no doubt fictional since Brooks had been hanged some six years earlier. If Earp killed a man named Billy Brooks, it was some nonentity. Later that year Morgan joined his brothers Virgil and Wyatt in Tombstone and became a shotgun rider on Wells Fargo coaches. In October 1881 the Earp and Clanton forces had their famous shoot-out at the O.K. Corral, and Morgan was wounded in the battle. He was still recuperating on the night of March 17, 1882 when he went to Bob Hatch's billiard saloon on Allen Street. Morgan was lining up a shot when a hail of .45 slugs smashed through the glass-windowed door and into his back, shattering his spine. He died about 30 minutes later on the sofa in Bob Hatch's office.

Within a short time of Morgan Earp's murder, Wyatt Earp gained vengeance by killing at least three men apparently involved in the crime, Deputy Sheriff Frank Stilwell, Wild Bill Brocius (although others besides Wyatt Earp are suspected of the Brocius killing) and Florentine Cruz, a Mexican-Indian half-breed who got $25 for holding the horses.

See also: *William L. Brooks, Virgil Earp, Wyatt Earp, O.K. Corral.*

EARP, Virgil W. (1843-1906): Lawman

After serving with the Union during the Civil War, Virgil Earp divided his time between being a prospector and lawman. In 1877, after serving as deputy town marshal of Dodge City, Kan., Virgil moved to Prescott, Arizona Territory to try the mining business. Because of his enthusiasm about the chances of becoming rich there, his brothers James and lawmen Wyatt and Morgan followed him. The brothers all settled in Tombstone, and in 1881 Virgil became temporary marshal when the former holder of the position died of "lead poisoning." During this period the growing conflict between the gambler forces in Tombstone, represented by the Earps, and the cowboy forces, represented by the Clanton family, climaxed in the gunfight at the O.K. Corral; the war continued long afterward.

Like his brother Morgan, Virgil was wounded at the O.K. Corral, and a few months later, he was the object of an ambush shooting. Hit by five shotgun blasts, Virgil was temporarily paralyzed and lost the use of his left arm permanently. When brother Morgan was murdered in February 1882, Wyatt put Virgil and his family on a train out of the state and he and young brother Warren concentrated on avenging the two crimes. Wyatt Earp succeeded but was also forced to flee Arizona. The Earps didn't return to the territory until around the turn of the century, and shortly after Warren Earp came back, he was murdered. It is said Virgil Earp exacted vengeance for that killing in due course. Virgil had by that time returned to Prescott, Ariz., where he was even asked to run for sheriff. He declined, and there was some speculation that he couldn't win with the Earp name. Virgil Earp died of pneumonia early in 1906.

See also: *Morgan Earp, Wyatt Earp, O.K. Corral.*

EARP, Warren B. (1855-1900): Lawman

The baby brother of the Earp family, Warren never achieved the fame or notoriety of Wyatt, Virgil or Morgan, arriving in Tombstone, Ariz. just after the gunfight at the O.K. Corral in 1881. He did serve, however, as deputy federal marshal for a while and aided Wyatt in the hunt for Morgan Earp's assassins. After the Earps left, or were run out of, Arizona in 1882, Warren went with them to California. In 1900 he returned to Arizona to become a cattle detective. It was not a wise move. A few months later, he was killed in Wilcox in a saloon gunfight with a man named Johnny Boyett. The shooting seemed linked with the troubles at Tombstone's O.K. Corral and the revenge slayings that followed the Morgan Earp murder.

Virgil Earp let it be known that he intended to kill the man responsible and he didn't mean Boyett. Chroniclers of the Earp family agree Virgil did just that in 1905, although the victim's identity was never officially revealed. The Earps had become a little more circumspect in taking their vengeance.

EARP, Wyatt Berry Stapp (1848-1929): Gunfighter, pimp, lawman

Few Western characters are credited with more heroic deeds than Wyatt Earp. His legendary stature, however, is almost entirely a product of the 20th century. Those who knew him best treated him differently. They drove him out of California for horse stealing; they fired him from his job as a policeman in Wichita for pocketing fines; they chased him out of Arizona after the gunfight, or slaughter, at the O.K. Corral and the ensuing murders. About the only place he wasn't kicked out of was Dodge City; he left voluntarily for not exactly heroic reasons.

Earp belonged to a clan of brothers: James, Virgil, Morgan and Warren. Natives of Illinois, the Earps moved to California in 1864 by wagon train. Wyatt's jobs there included stagecoach driver, bartender and gambler. In 1871 he was indicted for horse stealing, paid $500 bail and took off for greener pastures doing stints as a buffalo hunter. In Wichita, Kan. he became a lawman and, according to some biographers, performed many a valiant deed. But he apparently made no important arrests and eventually came under a cloud of suspicion when fines he collected never seemed to end up in the town treasury. He was dismissed from his post in 1874 and drifted into Dodge City, Kan., where he served as a deputy marshal from 1876 to 1879. Again, the legend tells how he cleaned up Dodge and gunned down many a varmint in the process. In reality, however, he had only one kill during all his years in Dodge, and that was of a drunken cowboy named George Hoy or Hoyt, who may or may not have been trying to gun down Earp for a bounty put on him by a Texas cattleman. The Dodge City cleanup by Earp and his friend Bat Masterson was strictly a part-time thing. Both supplemented their income working as card sharks and procurers and became known as the Fighting Pimps. Earp had a piece of the action in most of the whorehouses south of the "deadline," the railroad tracks that bisected Dodge. He probably was at least half owner of the brothel-saloon that belonged to his brother James. James' wife ran the brothel, while James took care of the gambling and saloon end of the business. The couple always trailed after Earp and set up shop wherever he was a lawman.

In 1879 Dodge City kind of settled down—meaning that the Earps' brothel profits weren't what they used to be—and Wyatt decided to try something more lucrative. He headed for the rich silver-strike area of the Arizona Territory. On the way, Earp stopped off in Mobeetie, Tex., where, with the aid of Mysterious Dave Mather, he perpetrated a gold brick swindle on gullible cowboys and was run out of town by Deputy

Sheriff James McIntire. Moving on to Tombstone, Wyatt set himself up as a saloon keeper. Brother James became a bartender, and several of the Earp women opened brothels. When Virgil was named temporary town marshal upon the death of the marshal, Wyatt became his deputy. When he later lost out on appointment to the sheriff's office of the newly created Cochise County, Wyatt consoled himself by becoming a part owner in the fabulously successful Oriental Saloon, amazingly without any monetary investment, a clear indication of his shakedown ability and the value attached to the protection he could offer such an establishment.

By early 1881 the Earps—four of the brothers now on hand in various capacities—became involved in a feud with the out-county cowboy element led by the Clanton family. The Earps drew to their banner a character as unsavory as any of the Clanton family killers, the murderous Doc Holliday. There are experts who insist the trouble between the two groups resulted from the Earps' rigid enforcement of the law, mainly to protect their casino and vice interests, and infringement on the Clanton ring's rustling and stage-robbing activities.

Really serious trouble broke out in March 1881, when the Kinnear and Co. stage was attacked and two men killed. Wyatt Earp went after the killers and named a trio of gunmen as suspects. In June, however, Doc Holliday was arrested as one of the suspects in the robbery and murders. The charges were dropped as unproven, but the incident sapped the Earps' popularity. More and more citizens believed the Earps were involved in various criminal activities, including stage robberies.

It was this climate of antagonism that actually led to the great gunfight at the O.K. Corral on October 26, 1881, in which three of the Clanton gang—the two McLowery brothers and Billy Clanton—were killed. The battle later brought fame to Wyatt Earp, then a deputy U.S. marshal, but the local Earp-supporting *Tombstone Epitaph* gave it only page-three coverage at the time, possibly because the Earps could have been brought up on murder charges for the killings. There were and still are considerable doubts about whether two of their opponents were even armed, but there is no doubt the Earps provoked the shoot-out.

The gunfight did not end the Earp-Clanton feud but merely intensified it. In its aftermath, Clanton supporters separately ambushed Virgil and Morgan Earp, fatally wounding Morgan. In revenge, Wyatt Earp shot and killed Frank Stilwell, who was known to have been involved in Morgan's death. He then led a posse that shot to death Florentine Cruz, another man involved in the ambush. It is unclear whether Wyatt also killed Curly Bill Brocius, the reigning head of the Clanton gang. With a warrant for murder hanging over his head, Wyatt was forced to flee Arizona, and the rest of the Earps followed.

In 1883 Earp turned up in Dodge City as part of the celebrated but short-lived Dodge City Peace Commission, really a terrorist action to force the return of gambling and prostitution interests to the town. It is interesting to note that the local newspaper did not remember Earp as the man who had "cleaned up" Dodge but as a man "famous in the cheerful business of depopulating the country."

In 1884 Wyatt was living in Idaho Territory, where he and his brother James operated a couple of saloons, and became involved in a combine that specialized in claim jumping. Shortly thereafter, Wyatt saw the merits of moving on to California, where he spent the rest of his days except for four years when he was a saloon keeper in Alaska during the gold rush. In the 1920s Earp hung around the movie lots of Hollywood, befriending Tom Mix and William S. Hart in an effort to get them to do his life story. Studio producers and directors exploited him for information about the Wild West days without ever paying him. In 1927 Earp finally began setting down the facts for an enthusiastic young writer, Stuart Lake, who produced a highly fanciful biography that established the ill-deserved legend of Wyatt Earp. Earp died on January 13, 1929, before the book appeared.

See also: *John Behan; Joseph Isaac "Ike" Clanton; William Clanton; Dodge City, Kansas; Dodge City Peace Commission; Morgan Earp; Virgil W. Earp; Gold Brick Swindle; John Henry "Doc" Holliday; William B. "Bat" Masterson; Mike Meager; Oriental Saloon and Gambling House; Johnny Ringo.*

EAST Texas Regulator War (1841-44): Vigilante conflict

The establishment of a Regulator vigilante movement in 1840 in Shelby County eventually resulted in turning much of eastern Texas into a battlefield. The need for vigilantes was as acute in Shelby County as anywhere in the West. The area was overrun with thieves, counterfeiters, murderers and corrupt county officials, who made law and order virtually impossible to maintain. Unfortunately, the leadership of the Regulators fell to Charles Jackson, a steamboat operator suspected of rather shady dealings, and it appears he created the Regulators as much for gaining personal control of the county as for ridding it of outlaws. When Jackson was cut down by an assassin, the leadership passed to Watt Moorman, a man with even less scruples than Jackson. Soon, the Regulators descended to the level of the outlaws they had been founded to drive out. In 1841 a countermovement of moderators appeared on the scene to curb the excesses of the Regulators, but both sides attracted criminal elements to their banners. While Regulators and Moderators theoretically battled outlaws and other villains, they began to spend more time warring with one another. In a short while, the entire county became involved; every man had to align with one side or the other and often found himself fighting with his neighbor or even his own relatives. To their credit, the Moderators cleaned their ranks of outlaw forces over the next three years, and by 1844 they were poised for a wholesale shooting war with the Regulators. President Sam Houston of the Republic of Texas prevented a certain bloodbath by sending in the militia, and the outbreak of the Mexican War further defused matters. In all, 18 deaths were officially attributed to the vigilante war; the number of severely wounded or permanently crippled was put in the hundreds. Thereafter, many blood feuds among Regulator and Moderator partisans continued for several decades and the hatreds kept alive lasted into this century.

See also: *Regulators and Moderators.*

EASTMAN, Monk (1873-1920): Great gang leader

There are those authorities on crime who consider Monk Eastman the greatest gangster this country ever produced. Historian Herbert Asbury called him "the prince of gangsters" and "as brave a thug as ever shot an enemy in the back."

Eastman was the boss of the last great primarily Jewish street gang in New York City, able to field 1,200 to 1,500 vicious gangsters on short notice. The Eastmans wiped out the remnants of the brutal Whyos, a truly murderous collection of thugs, near the end of the last century and were always ready to do battle with Paul Kelly's notorious gangsters, the great Italian Five Points Gang. After the turn of the century, the Five Pointers boasted on their roster such future devotees of mayhem and violence as Johnny Torrio, Al Capone, Lucky Luciano and Frankie Yale. Yet, in comparison to Eastman's crew they were choir boys.

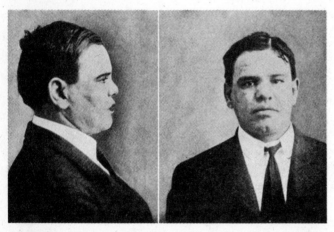

One of the most famous turn-of-the-century gang leaders, Monk Eastman once clubbed a hapless bar patron because "I had 49 nicks in me stick, an' I wanted to make it an even 50."

In appearance, Eastman looked precisely the way a gangster should—squat, massive, bullet-headed, with a busted nosed and a pair of cauliflower ears. And his behavior was worse than his appearance. He deserted his home area in the Williamsburg section of Brooklyn, where his respectable Jewish restaurateur father had set up a pet store for him, and headed for the crime-ridden fleshpots of lower Manhattan. He was to become a legend.

In the early 1890s Eastman became a bouncer at a rough dance hall, New Irving Hall, where a girl might well get raped by a number of the boys if not by her date. Eastman patrolled his domain with a huge bludgeon, a blackjack in his hip pocket and brass knuckles on each hand. He was always proud of the fact that during the six months of his reign no less than 50 men required the attention of surgeons and that jocular ambulance drivers refered to the accident ward of Bellevue

Hospital as the Eastman Pavilion. Eastman kept close count of the victims he clubbed and notched each assault on his club. One night an inoffensive little man was sitting at the bar drinking beer when Eastman walked up to him and cracked his scalp open with a mighty swipe. When asked why he'd done so, he replied, "Well, I had 49 nicks in me stick, an' I wanted to make it an even 50."

If that seemed a bit antisocial, at least Monk could pride himself on his near-Victorian treatment of women. He never once struck a woman with his club, no matter how trying she became. At most, he simply blackened her eyes with his hammy fist. "I only gave her a little poke," he would exclaim. "Just enough to put a shanty on her glimmer. But I always takes off me knucks first."

With behavior such as that, Monk Eastman became a legend on the East Side, and other young bloods took to imitating him in speech and manner. Of course, from such personal magnetism great leaders are born, and Eastman soon gathered around him a band of hoodlums eager to do his bidding. It didn't take long before he told them to go forth, beat up some citizens and bring back some money.

From then on, Eastman's gang grew rapidly. He and his men took over much of the crime on the Lower East Side, engaging in robberies, burglaries, assault, muggings and murder for pay. Eastman seized control of many of the gambling dens and houses of prostitution, and even individual street-walkers and hoodlums had to pay him for the privilege of operating in his turf. Although a crude savage, Eastman was smart enough to ingratiate himself with Tammany Hall and, in exchange for protection and a regular stipend, handled any chore required. On election day he furnished the largest contingent of voters, his own men, who voted early and often, and then blackjacked any honest citizen who was considering voting against Eastman's patrons. Whenever Eastman or his men got in trouuble, Tammany Hall lawyers appeared in court for them. Bail was posted and promptly forfeited until the case was expunged from the records.

As rich and powerful as he became, Eastman could never resist doing violence himself, sometimes even personally carrying out a blackjacking commission. "I like to beat up a guy once in a while," he used to say. "It keeps me hand in."

In one confrontation with the hated Five Pointers, Eastman was shot twice in the stomach and left for dead, but he climbed to his feet and staggered to Gouverneur Hospital, plugging a gaping wound with his fingers. Eastman hovered near death but, in keeping with underworld tradition, would not name his assailant. When he got out, Eastman personally shot the Five Pointer and dumped his body in the gutter.

In time, the Eastmans appeared to be winning the war with the Five Pointers and also routing the forces of another major gang leader, Humpty Jackson, but in 1904 Eastman caused his own downfall by holding up a expensively dressed young man who had overimbibed. It was a robbery Eastman did not have to commit but could not resist. Unfortunately for the gangster, the victim was a scion of wealth whose family had hired a Pinkerton to follow him for his protection. Seeing

Eastman accost the young man, the detective opened fire on him, and the gangster fled right into the arms of a policeman, who knocked him out before recognizing him.

If Eastman expected aid from Tammany, he was sadly disappointed. In view of the rising spirit of reform, the political bosses were happy for the chance to be rid of him. The great gangster was shipped off in ignominy to do 10 years in Sing Sing. When he was released, he found his power was gone. The Eastmans had factionalized a dozen ways, as the times would no longer support great street gangs. Eastman could not understand what had happened. But World War I proved to be a godsend for him and he went off to fight. When he returned, he was awarded a pardon by Gov. Al Smith, who signed an executive order restoring him to full citizenship.

In December 1920 Eastman was shot dead by a corrupt Prohibition agent with whom he was running a penny-ante bootlegging and dope-selling operation.

See also: *Crazy Butch Gang.*

EDWARDS Heirs Association: Swindle

As much as any of the incredible "heirs swindle," the one involving the so-called Edwards estate was among the most durable. Its operation was handed down from father to son and lasted for decades.

The swindle was the brainchild of Dr. Herbert H. Edwards of Cleveland, Ohio, who in the 1880s maintained with much fervor that he was a descendant of Robert Edwards, a Colonial merchant who had willed to his heirs 65 acres of Manhattan Island, right in the middle of which eventually had been erected the Woolworth Building. It was obvious that this bit of real estate had become one of the most valuable in the world. The Edwards estate was apparently worth not millions, but billions.

Dr. Edwards formed the Edwards Heirs Association, which was passed down from father to son, taking in $26 annually from each of thousands of people named Edwards as dues to fight for their legal rights. Naturally, every member of the association believed he would receive at least a thousand times what he had put in when a settlement was reached, an event that was always just about to be achieved. The association was also noted for having a great fete each year, which members attended by the hundreds, to celebrate the profits soon to come. The suckers even had their own anthem, which they sang with leather-lunged joy:

> We have rallied here in blissful state
> Our jubilee to celebrate.
> When fortune kindly on us smiled,
> The Edwards Heirs now reconciled.
> Our president deserves our praise,
> For strenuous work through dreary days,
> In consummating our affairs
> And rounding up the Edwards heirs.
>
> We're Robert Edward's legal heirs,
> And cheerfully we take our shares.
> Then let us shout with joy and glee
> And celebrate the jubilee.

Finally, after several decades of successful operation, the great swindle was smashed by the Post Office. The members of the association never saw any of the promised rewards, but they could at least recall their annual hangovers, perhaps still with some measure of fondness.

EGAN'S Rats: St. Louis gang

First organized in St. Louis about 1900 by Jellyroll Egan, the Rats became the most-feared gang in the city. Egan specialized in renting out his men as "legbreakers" to anti-union businessmen. When such activities became less profitable about 1920, Dinty Colbeck, who had taken over the reins from the late founder, turned Egan's Rats in new criminal directions. Operating out of a poolhall called Buckley's, Colbeck controlled bootlegging operations in the St. Louis-Kansas City area and masterminded a number of spectacular safecracking and jewelry thefts, many with the aid of the best safecracker of the 1920s, Red Rudensky.

Dinty Colbeck cut a flamboyant figure in St. Louis and paid enormous bribes to crooked politicians and policemen to allow his enterprises to operate without harassment. Approaching an officer on the street, he was known to pull out a big wad of bills and say, "Want a bribe, officer?"

Like many of the other independent gangs that had been given a new life by Prohibition, Egan's Rats could not cope with the changing crime scene of the post-bootlegging 1930s. Colbeck was killed by rival gangsters and the surviving Rats had to find new homes in other criminal combinations.

EINSTEIN, Isadore: See Izzy and Moe.

ELECTROLYTIC Marine Salts Company: See Gold Accumulator Swindle.

ELWELL, Joseph Bowne (1875-1920): Murder victim

Joseph Bowne Elwell was *the* bridge expert of the day and a notorious ladies man. He was the author of *Elwell on Bridge* and *Elwell's Advanced Bridge,* or so it seemed. In fact, the books were written by his wife, later ex-wife, Helen Darby, whose high social position gave Elwell entree into the world of society. This was vital for Elwell because the bridge books did not really bring in the kind of money needed to afford him the really good life. Elwell was basically a card hustler who milked the rich. With his ill-won wealth he established himself as one of them, becoming the owner of a racing stable, a yacht, an art collection and several cars.

Elwell was also the owner of what the tabloids referred to after his death as a "love index," a roster of 53 women, married and single, who boasted both high social affiliations and considerable allure. He maintained another list for male acquaintances and more run-of-the-mill females. Clearly, Elwell was a womanizer, a fact that proved to be something of a minor mystery in itself since after death he was revealed to have been toothless and bald, owning a collection of no less than 40 toupees.

Early one morning in 1920, just as dawn crept over Manhattan's West 70th Street, someone put a .45 caliber bullet into Elwell's head as he was reading a letter in his study. His housekeeper found him near death when she came to work; he was not wearing his toupee or his false teeth. The housekeeper, Marie Larsen, was a devoted servant who, while doctors labored over Elwell, hid a pink kimono she found in the house. Later, it was discovered but the young lady who owned it proved had an alibi for the time of the shooting. Almost all of the ladies on the love index and those in Elwell's larger file had been sound asleep at the time of the murder.

The newspapers had a field day with this first sex-and-murder scandal of the decade. All sorts of filmy underclothes were found secreted in Elwell's bedroom. It undoubtedly took a keen mind to remember which belonged to whom and perhaps a slip of this kind is what did Elwell in. All sorts of theories developed, featuring jealous women, their husbands or other lovers, gambling rings, gambling victims, mysterious spies (according to this postulation, Elwell, who had been a secret government agent in the war, was killed by spies he had uncovered) and even rival horse owners. One could have a pick of suspects and motives, but the public clearly preferred the idea that some fashionable matron (or her daughter) committed the murder for reasons of passion. Yet a .45 was hardly a woman's weapon and Elwell, a notoriously vain man, would never had admitted a female to his presence without putting in his teeth and donning his toupee. The answer to that argument was, of course, that a woman murderer might use a .45 and then remove his plates and wig precisely to make it look like the work of a man. Russel Crouse, the playwright and a former crime reporter, who had a keen eye for such things, once observed, " 'Cherchez la femme!' will echo every time the murder of Joseph Bowne Elwell is mentioned. And the fact that she will never be found will not still the whispers."

See also: *Charles Norris.*

EMBEZZLEMENT

The most enduring crime magazine article is probably the embezzlement story. There is something so eternal about the crime, probably because its root causes are deeply related to basic human failings. At times a writer will explain the motive for embezzlement in terms of the "three W's" or the "three R's"—it's all the same whether one speaks of wine, women and wagering or rum, redheads and race horses. The fact is that sex and greed can drive many people to steal large amounts of money, and they frequently do. Recent estimates place embezzlement losses at over $4 billion a year.

Typical embezzlers work at a bank or other business institution for years or even decades before they are finally exposed—if ever. As a cashier, John F. Wagner, was able to skim somewhat more than $1.1 million from the First National Bank of Cecil, Pa., by juggling the bank's books for at least a score of years until he committed suicide in 1950. The vice president of a bank in Baton Rouge, La. kept up his looting for a dozen years. When he was finally caught, he said: "I'm glad it's finally over. These past twelve years of living under the constant strain of wondering when I'd eventually get caught have cost me more than any amount of money could be worth."

Some embezzlers don't like the strain of wondering if and when the Federal Deposit Insurance Corporation auditors will come calling. Richard H. Crowe, an assistant branch manager of a New York bank, was that type. So he simply went to the vault one Friday in the late 1940s, stuffed $883,000 into a bag and went home to dinner. The following Monday he was nowhere to be found. However, such runaways are generally not difficult to find and often all the FBI has to do is determine where a man with a lot of extra spending money is most likely to turn up. Agents found Crowe in a plush bar in Daytona Beach, Fla.

Perhaps the classic bank embezzlement, with certainly the brashest motive of all, was that committed by bank president Ludwig R. Schlekat. Out of the $719,000 in cash supposedly on hand at the Parnassus National Bank of New Kensington, Pa., Schlekat managed to appropriate no less than $600,000, accumulating the sum over a 23-year period. When the shortage was found by bank examiners in 1947, it was determined that Schlekat had used $100,000 for his own better living. What had happened to the rest? Well, when Schlekat started working for the bank as an apprentice clerk at the age of 17 he had had only one ambition: to rise to bank president. After the bank's owner became eager to retire, Schlekat used the bulk of the $600,000 to purchase the bank through two nonexistent individuals who supposedly lived in Cleveland. Schlekat had simply used the bank's own money to buy the institution for himself. Then he had the bogus owners make him president. He was caught, tried and given a prison term of 10 years.

Generally, bankers and other business officials insist that people continue to embezzle because of the light sentences that are often imposed. It would be a somewhat more telling argument if all banks paid employees decent wages. In a classic case of that sort some years ago, federal Judge Frank L. Kloeb refused to sentence a cashier of an Ohio bank who had been convicted of embezzling $7,500 over a 10-year period ending in 1941. The judge hit the ceiling when he learned that the man had started as a cashier in 1920 at an annual salary of $1,080 and 22 years later he had been earning no more than $1,900 a year. The cashier had stopped his embezzlements as his salary started to rise faster and he was not found out until many years later.

The judge simply deferred sentencing indefinitely and refused even to put the cashier on probation, because that would have made him a criminal. "If I had the authority," the judge said, "I would sentence the bank officers and the Board of Directors to read the story of Scrooge at Christmas and think of the defendant."

Experts say women are just as likely to become embezzlers as men are. Bankers claim it is very common for middle-aged spinsters to resort to juggling the books. Having gone through life with perhaps little or no romance, such women may be desperate for companionship at this stage. In their eagerness to cement new friendships, they bestow gifts with reckless abandon. That old cliche of a shocked banker asking a trusted employee-turned-embezzler—"Was it a woman?"—definitely has its reverse—"Was it a man?"

As a rule, women are more generous with their loot than men. One trusted bookkeeper who stole $30,000 with the aid of some skillful record doctoring gave most of it to fellow employees in the form of salary increases.

The boom in computers in recent years has opened up new vistas for embezzlers. One bank employee developed a computerized money-diversion scheme to steal over $1 million, which he used to finance his gambling. It seemed he also had a computer system for handicapping the horses, but unfortunately for him, it was less efficient than his embezzlement operation.

Computer embezzlement has even become a problem within the Internal Revenue Service. One IRS computer programmer set up a system that funneled unclaimed tax credits into a relative's account, and another IRS programmer computer-transferred to his own account checks being held for taxpayers whose mailing addresses could not be determined.

In the pre-computer era it was estimated that there were at least 200 ways to embezzle money from a bank without danger of immediate exposure. Now, in an era of advancing technology, the ways cannot be counted. According to John Rankine, IBM's director of data security, "The data security job will never be done—after all, there will never be a bank that absolutely can't be robbed."

See also: *Computer Crime, John F. Wagner.*

EMMA Mine Fraud

In the West's great scramble for the riches of silver ore from the 1870s to the end of the 19th century, there was scant exploitation by legitimate mining interests of Utah's silver deposits. The origin of this strange diffidence toward a profitable opportunity was the notorious Emma Silver Mining Co. bubble, which had caused investors to lose millions, some in this country and even more in England.

With the first sign of a silver strike in Little Cottonwood Canyon in 1868, a mining speculator, James E. Lyon of New York, moved in to take effective control. He in turn had to yield a good deal of it to San Francisco mining interests, and they then brought in Trevor W. Park of Vermont and Gen. H. Henry Baxter of New York. To protect his interests, Lyon introduced Sen. William M. Stewart of Nevada into the combine, which by then had decided to sell stock in the mine in England. Important names were added to the operation. Professor Benjamin Silliman, Jr. of Yale, for a fee of $25,000, issued a favorable report on the mine's ore deposits. The board of directors of the British company included three members of Parliament, the U.S. minister to the Court of St. James and a former president of the New York Central Railroad, among others. Marketing of the company's stock was handled by Baron Albert Grant, a London financier of dubious ethical

standards but a brilliant salesman, who was paid a fee of £170,000 for his troubles. It was a small price since the income from floating the stock was something like £600,000. All the American operators did extremely well, with the possible exception of the original investor, James Lyon. His supposed protector, Sen. Stewart, was able to buy him out for £50,000, half of what Lyon had been promised.

For a time, even the English investors did well, as the stock in the Emma Silver Mining Company, Ltd., quickly moved from £20 to £50. Then a rival firm, the Illinois Tunnel Co., announced the Emma claim had not been recorded correctly and that the English company was mining the ore from the claim to pay the dividends on its stock. Even more shocking was the revelation that the owner of Illinois Tunnel was Trevor W. Park, who was also a member of the board of Emma Mining and who had made one of the biggest profits in the entire deal. All sorts of suits were then filed, especially after 1872, when Emma Mining announced its ore deposits had run out. In the end, everyone who had been in the original combine made and kept money and all the shareholders in Emma Mining lost their money except for a total of $150,000, which Park offered in 1877 for all outstanding shares. Park continued to mine Emma for a number of years and is believed to have made that money back easily. In any event, the Emma Mine scandal was to frighten off virtually all investment in Utah mines by outsiders for some three decades, and the fraud was often cited as an example of "Yankee ingenuity."

ESPINOSA Brothers: Murderers

In 1861 three Mexican brothers and some other kin invaded Colorado with the announced purpose of killing 600 Americans. This vendetta, they said, was to make up—at the rate of 100 to one—for the loss of life suffered by the Espinosa family during the Mexican War. By mid-1863 the three brothers, Felipe, Julian and Victorio, had managed to dispatch 26 Americans. Their typical victims were freighters, prospectors, sawmill workers or soldiers whom they had caught alone. While vengeance was supposedly the first order of the day, the Espinosas saw to it that their victims were also worth robbing; their soldier-victims, for instance, had generally been waylaid right after payday.

With 574 victims to go, Felipe Espinosa, the leader and most audacious member of the family, sent a message to the territorial governor, offering to quit the murderous campaign if the Espinosas were given a land grant of 5,000 acres and made captains in the Colorado Volunteers. Such an offer was hardly likely to be accepted, as Felipe most certainly knew, and probably represented a bold attempt to put the best possible face on the criminal acts. The governor responded by placing a reward of $2,500 on Felipe's head.

The killings went on and terror gripped the territory. Groups of vigilante miners rode hell-for-leather around the countryside trying to corner the Espinosas and hanged more than one suspect, even some who quite clearly were not Mexicans. Finally, however, they did catch Victorio Espinosa in the Fairplay-California Gulch area and strung him up. Later they staged a drunken celebration because they mistakenly believed their victim was Felipe, without whom the Espinosas were thought to be incapable of continuing their murderous activities.

When the terror did not end, it was obvious Felipe was still alive. He continued to elude posses of miners and Army patrols. Finally, the Army commissioned a storied scout named Tom Tobin to bring in the Espinosas with the aid of a 15-soldier detail. Late in 1863, Tobin successfully tracked down the remaining two Espinosa brothers, but at the last moment he slipped away from the troopers because he did not want to share the reward money with them. Tobin cornered Felipe and Julian Espinosa at Indian Creek and shot them dead before they could return his fire. He cut off their heads as proof he had gotten the right men and returned to Fort Garland to claim his reward. However, because of a shortage of cash in the territorial coffers, Tobin was given only $1,500 and some buckskins.

For several years pickled "Espinosa heads" were exhibited around the West. Long after, in 1955, Kit Carson, III labeled these exhibits, some still around, as fakes. Carson said Tom Tobin, his maternal grandfather, had always insisted the heads had been buried behind Fort Garland and never removed.

ESTES, Billie Sol (1925-   ): Con man

In the 1960s Billie Sol Estes, a flamboyant Texas "salesman" and political supporter of President Lyndon Johnson, became famous as the prototypical big-time swindler after being convicted of inducing farmers to invest in fertilizer tanks that never existed. He was sentenced to 15 years and paroled in 1971 after serving six years. Under the terms of his parole, Estes was not allowed to engage in promotional schemes, but almost immediately, he was implicated in some financial dealings that involved allegations of fraud. In August 1979 Estes was sentenced to two 5-year federal prison terms to be served consecutively following his conviction for bilking investors by borrowing money and using as collateral oil field cleaning equipment that was nonexistent. One of his victims, J. H. Burkett, an Abilene used-car dealer who lent Estes his life savings of $50,000 shortly after meeting him in 1975, said: "I met him in church, in Bible study in Abilene, and he struck me as a very nice guy. He seemed very humble, very earnest, remorseful. I was very impressed by him, and I still am, but in a different way. The man is the world's best salesman. Just go and meet him, and you'll find out. He'll sell you something."

Following his 1979 conviction Estes told the judge: "I love this country. I'd rather be in prison here than free anywhere else in the world." He said that whether or not he went to jail, he would pay the money he owed, including $10 million in back taxes, to the government. Estes claimed he had more than a million friends and could raise $10 from each of them. There were those who said he probably could.

Estes was always a spellbinder. In a 1961 interview he once outlined his personal philosophy, which apparently won him devoted followers. "You win by losing, hold on by letting go, increase by diminishing, and multiply by dividing. These are the principles that have brought me success."

EVANS, Charles (?-1875): Murderer

In another era or in another jurisdiction, Charles, or Daniel (as he was sometimes called), Evans might not have ended up on the end of a rope, thereby helping to make Isaac C. Parker's reputation as "the hanging judge."

Long known as a thief and horse stealer, Evans was arrested in April 1875 for the murder of an 18-year-old boy named Seabolt. The body was found in Indian Territory, Oklahoma, bootless and with an empty wallet nearby. Evans was arrested when he was found in possession of Seabolt's horse. At his trial he insisted he had bought the horse. Since all the evidence against him was circumstantial, he was found not guilty. However, the presiding judge who was resigning and leaving the area, failed to sign certain legal papers, so that Evans had to be held over for a new trial. In June he was brought before a new judge, Isaac C. Parker, who was later to become known as the Hanging Judge. Parker could have ruled that Evans was being exposed to double jeopardy, but such legalisms seldom influenced him and he ordered a trial.

Evans was sure of acquittal and came into court all dolled up to celebrate his forthcoming freedom. The dead man's father was in the courtroom, and when he looked down at the boots the defendant was wearing, he realized they were his son's. Judge Parker sentenced Evans to hang and no doubt noted to himself how a legal technicality had almost freed a guilty man.

See also: *Isaac C. "Hanging Judge" Parker.*

EVANS, Christopher (1847-1917): Anti-railroad outlaw

Called affectionately the Old Chief by many residents of the San Joaquin Valley, Chris Evans, together with the Sontag brothers, led the California Outlaws, a group of train robbers who carried on a fierce war with the Southern Pacific Railroad, looting its express cars but never victimizing any of its passengers.

A veteran of many gun battles with railroad and federal posses, Evans survived a number of wounds, including one that blinded his right eye, but kept up his relentless campaign against the railroad. After George Sontag was captured, Evans and John Sontag were forced up into the hills where they were finally cornered by a huge posse in the famous Battle of Simpsons Flat. The gunfight raged for eight hours, with Evans and Sontag dashing from tree to tree and holding off the army of pursuers. Two Tulare County deputies were killed and a number wounded, but in the end, John Sontag lay dying and Evans was "too filled with lead to run any more." Although expected to die, Evans survived and was lodged in jail in Fresno.

In his autobiography, written many years later, Ed Morrell,

a member of the outlaws who worked as a spy inside the ranks of railroad detectives, said that their boss, Big Bill Smith, decided it would be best if Evans died trying to escape, despite the fact that he could barely walk or ride. He ordered Morrell to go to Evans and arrange for a jail break, during which Evans would be shot. Morrell said he frustrated the plan by helping Evans to escape 24 hours ahead of schedule.

While Morrell carried, or half-dragged, Evans for weeks, Smith flooded the valley and surrounding hills with hundreds of agents. Eventually, the fugitives were forced to take refuge in a farmhouse. Although many residents of the area were sympathizers and hid them willingly, there was now a huge reward offered for their capture, and they were betrayed. Chris Evans was quickly sentenced to life imprisonment. So was Morrell, who later was subjected to brutal torture in prison. When word of Morrell's ordeal got out, he was pardoned in 1907 and became a national hero and a champion of prison reform. Evans was paroled in 1911 and quietly lived the last six years of his life with his family in Portland, Ore.

See also: *California Outlaws, Ed Morrell, Sontag Brothers.*

EVERLEIGH Sisters: Madams

Some experts on the subject insist there has not been a genuine bordello in America since 1910, when Chicago's Everleigh Club, run by sisters Ada and Minna Everleigh, shut its doors. And when it did, the sisters, still in their early thirties, retired with, among other things, $1 million in cash; perhaps $250,000 in jewelery, much of which had come from grateful clients; paintings, statues, rare books, rugs and other valuables for which they had paid $150,000; about 50 brass beds inlaid with marble and fitted with specially designed matresses and springs; and 25 gold-plated spittoons worth $650 apiece. For the Everleighs the wages of sin had been enormous.

Coming from a small Kentucky town, the Everleighs inherited about $35,000 between them. Everleigh was not their real name—it may have been Lester—but one they adopted in honor of their grandmother, who signed her letters, "Everly Yours." For a time the sisters joined a theatrical troupe while they looked for a nice town in which to invest their money. Early in 1898 they decided on Omaha, Neb., then readying for the Trans-Mississippi Exposition, which was expected to bring big crowds. At the time, Ada was 23 and Minna not quite 21, but they were hard-headed business women and cooly analyzed what type of business would please a fun-seeking exposition crowd. So they went out and bought a whorehouse, a field in which they had no experience. They brought in all new girls and charged the highest prices in Omaha. It worked during the exposition, but when the crowds left, the sisters found out there was no way the sports of Omaha were going to pay $10 for a girl and $12 for a bottle of wine. So they packed up and moved to Chicago. The sisters bought the lease to and girls at the brothel of Madam Effie Hankins at 2131-3 South Dearborn Street for $55,000. On February 1, 1900 they opened the incredible Everleigh Club. Describing it, the *Chicago Tribune* said, "No house of courtesans in the

world was so richly furnished, so well advertised, and so continuously patronized by men of wealth and slight morals."

On opening night the club took in $1,000. Never again were revenues so small, as word got around about the fabulous services offered. Separate soundproof parlors were called the Gold, Silver, Copper, Moorish, Red, Green, Rose, Blue, Oriental, Chinese, Egyptian and Japanese rooms and were appropriately furnished. The *Tribune* described the Japanese Room as "a harlot's dream of what a Japanese palace might look like." Every room had a fountain that squirted a jet of perfume into the air.

Quite naturally, the charges were hardly cheap for the era, ranging from $10 to $25 to $50, depending on how long a client wished to avail himself of a prostitute's company. The $10 price was really little more than the cost of admission; if a man failed to spend at least $50, he was told not to return. The costs of running such a magnificent house—which included a library, an art gallery, a dining room, rooms where three orchestras played and a Turkish ballroom with a huge indoor fountain—were enormous. Overhead ran to $75,000 a year, including $30,000 for servants, music and entertainment and probably protection, since the sisters were never bothered and the name of the club did not appear on the police lists of bawdy houses. Also on the payroll were 15 to 25 cooks. This was an excellent investment because, while a good sport might spend $50 or $100, and gentleman throwing a dinner party for a small group of friends (with wine at $12 a bottle) could easily run up a tab of $1,500 for an evening's fun.

Madame Minna met each visitor in the grand hallway, clad in a silk gown and bedecked with jewels, including a diamond dog collar. The sisters permitted no lineup of their girls but had them drift from parlor to parlor, talking to a man only after a formal introduction. Everleigh Club prostitutes were much sought after by other bordellos and a girl who made it in the club had her future assured in the business—if she did not go directly from the business to marriage of a wealthy patron.

"I talk with each applicant myself," Ada once explained. "She must have worked somewhere else before coming here. We do not like amateurs. . . . To get in a girl must have a good face and figure, must be in perfect health, must understand what it is to act like a lady. If she is addicted to drugs, or to drink, we do not want her." For the girls the work was lighter and the pay higher than elsewhere, so the sisters always had a waiting list of applicants. Those accepted got regular classes in dress, manners and makeup and had to read books from the establishment's library.

A man who partied at the Everleigh Club even once could boast of it for years. The real secret of the sister's success was their understanding of male chauvinism and fantasies. One much-appreciated gimmick used at times was to have butterflies to flit about the house. As a rival madam, Cleo Maitland, observed, "No man is going to forget he got his behind fanned by a butterfly at the Everleigh Club."

The list of celebrities who patronized the club was almost endless. Prince Henry of Prussia enjoyed a mighty orgy there in 1902, and repeat callers included John Barrymore, Ring Lardner, heavyweight boxing champion James J. "Gentleman Jim" Corbett, George Ade, Percy Hammond and Bet-A-Million Gates. One of the rave reviews of the establishment was offered by newsman Jack Lait, who said, "Minna and Ada Everleigh are to pleasure what Christ was to Christianity."

Other madams and whoremasters were jealous of the sisters' success and tried to fabricate charges of clients being robbed or drugged there, but the Everleighs paid the highest graft in the city and the authorities would not listen to such nonsense. One resourceful bordello operator, Ed Weiss, opened up next door to the Everleigh Club and put taxi drivers on his payrolls so that when a particularly drunken sport asked to be taken there, he would be deposited at the Weiss place instead without knowing the difference.

The great reform drive against vice in Chicago in 1910 forced the Everleigh Club to close. The sisters had no intention of doing battle with the authorities, who were under attack from do-gooders. Most Everleigh clients could not believe such a palace of pleasure would ever go out of business. The trauma was much worse for them than for the sisters, who took a year's grand tour of Europe and on their return settled in New York City in a fashionable home off Central Park. They lived out their lives in genteel fashion, Minna dying in 1948 and Ada in 1960.

See also: *Friendly Friends, Nathaniel Ford Moore, Weiss Club.*

EXECUTION, Methods Of

Aside from a few early and isolated instances of executions by crushing with weights, drawing and quartering or burning at the stake (these last two almost exclusively punishments reserved for blacks), the death penalty in America has been accomplished by four basic methods—hanging, the electric chair, the gas chamber and the firing squad.

These methods can be discussed in their general order of chronological usage and popularity.

Hanging

Allowing for possible changes and the reimposition of the death penalty following the Supreme Court's 1976 approval of executions, hanging is in vogue in a half-dozen states, although at one time its use was almost universal. The main argument against hanging is that it is far more cruel and painful than other methods; on the other hand, proponents of hanging argue that its very repulsiveness makes it more of a deterrent. Of course, were this latter viewpoint true, hanging should have eliminated murder and other capital crimes centuries ago.

Years of practice and refinement have gone into the technique in an effort to achieve what is known as a "clean" hanging. Here is how things go if a clean hanging occurs—which, according to experts, happens in a minority of the cases. First of all, there is no longer the embarrassment of the rope slipping from the crossbeam since it is now attached to a chain suspended from the gallows crossbeam. The noose is adjusted so that the knot is positioned extremely tightly behind the

victim's left ear, and a black hood is placed over his head so that witnesses will be spared the condemned man's final grimaces. In some states the hangman does not spring the trapdoor himself. His job is limited to fixing the knot, binding the legs together to prevent disconcerting kicking and centering the doomed man correctly over the trapdoor. Then he gives a signal and three men in a little booth on the platform each cut a string, only one of which springs the trapdoor. When the drop occurs, the knot ideally will strike behind the left ear, instantly knocking the doomed man unconscious. If things work to perfection, just the right number of small bones of the cervical vertebrae in the neck are broken so that the head is not ripped off. The bones should then collapse on the spinal cord, cutting off oxygen to the brain and paralyzing the rest of the body. Rapid brain death follows. This is what can be considered a "clean" clean hanging. It doesn't happen all that often. There are other hangings that are still clean enough.

Many printed accounts and renderings of 19th century hangings afforded that form of execution a romantic flavor devoid of reality.

In the average clean job, the victim's thrashing at the end of the rope lasts for but a few minutes. His wheezing can be heard but never reaches the fever pitch of a botched job. The stench, however, may be rather troublesome, since the victim often urinates, defecates and ejaculates at the same time. The resultant odors, mixed with an overwhelming one of perspiration, is somewhat sickening, especially as human waste runs down the victim's legs and drops to the floor. Finally, after a relatively short few minutes, the dying man's violent shudders subside and the rope stops dancing. There is one final jerk, just a bit of twitching and quiet.

So much for the good work. Former San Quentin Warden Clinton Duffy, who witnessed 60 hangings, describes most hanging as being of the less than clean variety. In a "dirty" hanging the condemned man will strangle to death slowly, a vile process that can take as long as a quarter of an hour. His wheezing is extremely loud, and indescribable, save to someone who has heard the hysterical squealing of a dying pig. The victim may even bob up and down on the rope like a yo-yo as he fights for air. Sometimes his legs, even when bound together, whip far out in search of a perch. It may become necessary for a guard to seize the man's legs and hold them steady so that his violent churnings do not break the rope, a development that might upset the witnesses. When death finally comes, it may be difficult to determine for whom the agony was worse—the condemned or the witnesses.

Of course, sometimes things get even messier. A poorly placed knot occasionally gouges out a chunk of the face and head and witnesses see this gory mess drop to the floor. When the noted outlaw Black Jack Ketchum was hanged in New Mexico in 1901, he shouted out as the hood went over his face, "Let her rip!" The rope did so, decapitating Ketchum as he hurtled into space.

The same thing happened during the 1930s in West Virginia when a wife murderer named Frank Myer was hanged. Myer was a bad hanging victim, being heavyset with short neck and what were described as "soft bones." When the trapdoor opened, Myer's body crashed to the concrete floor, followed by a second thud as his head landed nearby. Several of the witnesses got sick as the head rolled a few feet in their direction, and after the execution some of them allowed they would never again attend a hanging.

The sheer messiness of hangings finally led to the abandonment of the method by most states, which opted for either the electric chair or the gas chamber. One state, Utah, just couldn't sever its sentimental attachment to hanging, but it at least has offered the condemned a choice, the noose or the firing squad. The rope has lost out in that popularity contest as well.

Shooting

Most condemned men in Utah opt for the firing squad over hanging, two of the most illustrious examples being labor hero Joe Hill, almost certainly executed for a crime he did not commit, and Gary Gilmore, the first man executed after the Supreme Court's reimposition of the death penalty. In some respects, death by firing squad is the most "humane" method of all. The condemned man is strapped down in a chair against an oval-shaped canvas-covered wall. A doctor locates the heart precisely and pins a cloth target directly over it. Unless the victim objects, he is hooded.

Just 20 feet away in a canvas enclosure, five sharpshooters are given .30 caliber rifles, each loaded with a single cartridge. One, however, receives a blank so that each marksmen can later rationalize he did not do the killing. They place their weapons through slits in the canvas, and when the order is given, they fire in unison. Four bullets thump into the heart, making death virtually instantaneous and probably painless. With such a fine method for killing, it may be surprising that more jurisdictions haven't switched to death by shooting, but there are good reasons. One is the fact that the execution is bloody, and society generally does not like a mess around to remind it that a human being has just been slaughtered. But even more important is that sometimes the marksmen turn "chicken" or "cheat." If a marksman wants to make sure he

does not fire the fatal bullet, he will aim "off-heart" and thus be able to figure that the victim died long before his shot could have taken any effect. In 1951 the height of official embarrassment was achieved when all four marksmen hit the victim, Elisio J. Mares, on the right side of the chest. He bled to death slowly. Because of such inefficiencies, death by firing squad never will gain much popularity.

Electric Chair

When in May 1979 30-year-old John Spenkelink became the first man in over a dozen years to die in Florida's electric chair, there was some worry that "Old Sparky" as some called the venerable electric chair at the state prison at Raiford, might not be up to the task, having been in disuse for 15 years. The worry was groundless. Old Sparky worked beautifully. The Spenkelink execution was not without fault, however. A venetian blind was dropped over the window through which witnesses were supposed to watch Spenkelink being brought to the chair and strapped in. Evidently, he staged a battle royal with his guards. When the blind was opened, he was strapped down with a gag in his mouth. It was something that shouldn't happen. Death house guards are supposed to know how to handle a condemned man and be able to con him into dying easy, but Spenkelink had carried on in such macabre fashion that it was thought wise to spare the witnesses this sight. However, the guards too had had a 15-year layoff.

More than 1,000 men and women have gone to the hot seat since its introduction in 1890, and the history of electrocution

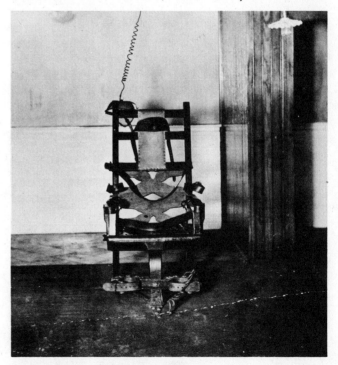

Early version of the electric chair.

is dotted with ghoulish and bizarre incidents. In Florida in 1926 a condemned man named Jim Williams was in the chair waiting for death when an argument broke out between Warden

John S. Blitch and Sheriff R. J. Hancock, each of whom insisted it was the other's duty to throw the switch. The argument went on for 20 minutes until poor Williams collapsed. He was carried back to his cell while the dispute went to the courts. Eventually, a ruling was made that the sheriff had to do the job, but by then the Board of Pardons decided Williams had done enough penance and commuted his death sentence to life imprisonment.

During World War II two convicted murderers, Clifford Haas and Paul Sewell, beat the death sentence when one state switched to electrocution from hanging. The War Production Board said the materials required for the chair could be better used fighting the Japanese and the Nazis and refused to grant a priority. No chair, no killing.

The usual electric chair has two legs in back and a heavier single leg in front, all bolted to the floor. The extrawide arms are fitted with straps to hold the arms of the victim rigid. Other straps go around his chest and abdomen. The wiring around the chair is covered with rubber matting. Actually, the electric chair is a rather simple contraption, as indicated by the fact that some Southern states have used portable or mobile chairs.

In Mississippi the chair was carried around in a van with its own generators and controls so that it could be brought into the courtroom where the defendant was convicted. A power line lead from the truck's generators into the packed courtroom. When a newsman once told U.S. Sen. Theodore G. Bilbo that the practice was little different than lynching, he responded, "Ah, this is pretty tame compared to a lynching."

Ideally, an electrocution is a three-minute drill, with the prisoner strapped into the chair quickly. Inexperienced guards practice with the straps in advance to avoid fumbling delays. The so-called humane character of electrocution is probably best measured by what the witnesses are spared rather than what happens to the condemned person. A tight mask is placed over the prisoner's face to hide the facial contortions when the "juice" is turned on. The mask is especially tight around the eyes to keep them from popping out of their sockets.

Two popular myths about the execution chamber almost never happen. There are no long goodbyes or last statements, although a famous gangster of the 1930s, Two-Gun Crowley, did manage, "Give my love to mother." And the lights never dim in the rest of the prison, because the chair is always powered by a separate source. Hollywood prefers the light-dimming routine because it gives a scriptwriter an opportunity to stage a prisoner protest or achieve special dramatic effect.

Once he is sure everyone is clear of the chair, the executioner throws a switch and the raging current pitches the victim against the bindings with terrible force. His hair stands up and his flesh turns the color of beets. If the executioner fails to flip the switch when the prisoner's lungs are empty, there is a "gurgling" noise as air is forced from the lungs by the shock of the current. The first jolt, executioners have learned by trial and error, should be 2,000 volts or slightly more, after which it is cut back to 1,000 volts to prevent what witnesses might take as unseemly burning of the body. At this stage the victim

may pass waste. The tradition of a last hearty meal for the condemned is truly a tribulation for the executioner. Almost certainly, mouth foam will seep out from under the hood. Often, the electrical jolt may be repeated to make sure the victim is dead. It is a worthwhile precaution. When Arthur Lee Grimes was executed in Alabama in 1954, the doctor found his heart still beating. He stepped back and waited for it to stop, but instead of expiring, Grimes started to shudder violently and thrash against the straps. He started to come back to consciousness, gasping and sucking in air. It took seven full minutes of juice, six massive jolts in all, to end his life.

Proponents of electrocution find such lapses as the Grimes execution lamentable, just as they did the world's first electrocution, that of William Kemmler in New York in 1890. In the 1880s a state legislative commission was established to decide if hanging should be abolished. After viewing a number of hangings, including that of a woman who slowly strangled to death, the members decided the noose had to go. But it is doubtful they would have conceived of the electric chair had it not been for a monumental battle over business profits. Thomas A. Edison and George Westinghouse were competing for domination of the then-budding electric power industry. Edison had developed the first electric power system in 1882 by the use of low-tension, direct current (DC). Two years later, Westinghouse came out with his alternating current (AC) system, which utilized light, easily installed wires compared to the expensive heavy-wire installation required for DC. Faced with an opposing product that was clearly superior, Edison decided his best hope lay in disparaging AC in the public's eye and dispatched a young engineer, Harold P. Brown, to stage shows around the country demonstrating the system's death-dealing potential. Brown shocked people by electrocuting stray dogs and cats and even horses. When he took his show to Albany, the special commission asked if he could kill an orangutan. He could and he did. The poor orangutan even caught fire, but that didn't deter the commission from coming up with the concept of an electric chair. A human being wasn't covered with hair and so was not likely to catch fire. The electric chair was born.

Kemmler's execution was not a happy one. A first jolt of 17 seconds failed to kill him and shocked doctors watched Kemmler's breast heave and his heart resume beating. Panic ensued in the execution chamber and finally the current was turned on again for another 70 seconds at 1,300 volts. Some of the witnesses fainted and another retched and bolted from the room. Finally, William Kemmler was good and dead. Unfortunately, the flesh on Kemmler's back was badly burned and his muscles carbonized. When his body was autopsied, a witness described his flesh as well-cooked beef.

Despite worldwide protests of the tortures involved in the new method of extermination, the electric chair was here to stay. In time, executioners learned to watch the condemned person's hands. When they turn pink, other parts of the body, nearer to the source of the electrical charge, are far darker and closer to being burned. Unfortunately, in later years "overburning" still occurred.

To the public there was something fascinating about botched-up jobs; thus when the first electrocutions of four murderers took place at Sing Sing in 1891, the roads from Ossining to the prison were jammed with tourists and sightseers hoping that something would go wrong. But the chair worked four times without a hitch. In 1903 disaster struck at Clinton Prison when one of three brothers executed, Fred Van Wormer, started to move in the autopsy room. A rush call brought the executioner, Robert P. Elliott, back to the prison. By the time he got there, Van Wormer had expired, but everyone agreed it made sense not to take any chances. The dead man was hauled back to the chair and given another 1,700 volts.

Survival after death in the electric chair has always been an intriguing idea. When Ruth Snyder was executed along with her lover Judd Gray for the murder of her husband, her lawyer sought a court order to prevent the performance of an autopsy on her body, a legal requirement to determine the cause of death. The lawyer planned to revive her with adrenalin. The idea was never tried out because the courts rejected the move. A number of condemned persons have swallowed all types of metal objects under the belief that somehow this would cause the electric chair to "short." In the 1950s a prisoner named Donald Snyder entered his Sing Sing death cell weighing 150 pounds and soon started eating and eating and eating. He had come up with the novel idea of getting too fat to fit into the chair. Weightwise he did remarkably, eventually tipping the scales at over 300 pounds. His request for the traditional last meal was, "Pork chops, eggs and plenty of 'em!" He spent his last few hours speculating with a guard how the newspapers would go wild when it turned out he couldn't be executed.

It remained for a New York tabloid to write finis to Snyder's bizarre plan: "The hot seat fitted him as though it had been made to order."

Contrary to all the evidence of botched executions, burnings, gasping for air and continuing heartbeats, there are many experts who insist that electrocution is immediate and painless. They can perhaps take comfort in the case of Harry Roberts, a New York slayer who informed the prison doctor as he was strapped into the chair: "Doc, my last act is going to be for science. We'll see how fast this juice really works. The moment I feel it, I'll wiggle this finger." It never wiggled.

A more or less authoritative source, depending on one's viewpoint, would be Dr. Harold W. Kipp, who, as chief medical officer of Sing Sing, attended more than 200 executions. Dr. Kipp said: "The effect of electricity is instantaneous brain death. What observers see are muscle contractions, not agony."

Not all medical authorities agreed with this enthusiasm for electrocution and the hunt was on for yet a new more humane method of killing. They found it in the gas chamber, and during the 1920s and 1930s it was hyped as truly superior to electrocution and hanging.

Gas Chamber

First employed in Nevada, the gas chamber was eventually adopted by eight other states—Arizona, Colorado, Maryland, Mississippi, Missouri, North Carolina, Wyoming and California. The most famous gas chamber is the one at San Quentin. Built in 1938, it has been the site of some of the nation's most dramatic executions, including those of Barbara Graham, Caryl Chessman and Burton W. Abbott, whose gassing in 1957 was almost stayed by an order of Gov. Goodwin Knight. When the phone call came from the governor's office, the gas pellets had already been dropped behind his chair. So the execution proceeded.

The gas chamber is designed with two chairs so that two executions can take place at the same time. (Double executions almost certainly guarantee newspapers good quotes. When kidnapper and murderess Bonnie Heady died in the Missouri gas chamber along with her partner, Carl Austin Hall, she asked guards not to strap in her man too tightly. "You got plenty of room, honey," Heady asked. Hall replied, "Yes Mama." Thus satisfied, the woman smiled and sat back to breathe the deadly fumes.) Under the chairs are shallow pans into which tubes from a small vestibule are fed a mixture of water and sulfuric acid. A lever is pulled and bags with 16 one-ounce cyanide pellets are dropped into the mixture. Fumes rise swiftly and the victim dies quickly—once in a while. Some reporters who have covered various types of executions regard the gas chamber as the most vile and inhumane of all.

Essentially, the victim strangles to death without the courtesy of a rope. He is forced to do it to himself as he battles for oxygen that is no longer there, except in a "frozen" state that is useless to the body. The condemned person is often told that as soon as he smells an odor resembling rotten eggs, he should count to 10 and then take several deep breaths. This, he is told, will cause him to pass out quickly and die without pain. It doesn't happen that way. Man's instinct, the body's instinct, is to live. The victim will gasp and wheeze, struggling for air. His mouth opens and shuts like a beached fish. Often, he screams or sobs. Choking, he thrashes about. He pulls on his bonds. Occasionally, it is said, a victim will break an arm free, usually in the process severing the skin, so that his blood may spurt over the windows through which the witnesses are watching.

The asphyxiation process is slow. The thrashing victim's face turns purple, his eyes bulge. He starts to drool. A swollen tongue hangs out. But death still hasn't occurred. The death process takes eight or nine minutes. The record, although statistics are not definitive on the matter, appears to be 11 minutes in a North Carolina execution.

Caryl Chessman's ordeal of dying in 1960 may not have been the most unusual but it received greater media coverage than most other executions. He tried to make his dying easy, inhaling as quickly and deeply as he could. By prearrangement with a newsman witness, Chessman was to signal if the pain became agony. Shortly after his ordeal began, Chessman looked towards the reporter and nodded his head vigorously, the signal the dying process was indeed agonizing. Finally, his head slumped to his chest and his tongue popped out.

A woman reporter on the scene described what happened next: "I thought he must be dead but no, there was another agonizing period during which he choked on the gas. And again. And then again. There was a long period, another deep gasp. At the fourth such straining, Chessman's head lolled in a half circle, coming forward so that he faced downward with his chin almost touching his chest. This must be the end. But the dying went on.

"A deep gasp, then his head came up for an instant, dropped forward again. After two or three deep breaths, which seemed something like sobs, a trembling set up throughout his body. Along the line of his broad shoulders, down the arms to his fingers, I could see the tremor run. Then I saw his pale face grow suddenly paler, though I had not thought that it could be after his 12 years in prison. A little saliva came from his lips, spotted the white shirt that a condemned man wears for his last appearance. Even more color drained from his face and the furrows in his head smoothed out a little. And I knew he was dead. . . ."

There seemed to be some sentiment among the witnesses to the Chessman execution that death in the gas chamber was not really the painless process it was billed as. None of the methods of executions used in this country really are. And the search for the perfect method continues.

Injection

The newest method of capital punishment in the United States is death by injection, or what the inhabitants of the death rows in the various states opting for it refer to sardonically as "the ultimate high." Under an Oklahoma law passed in 1977, death is to occur by the continuous intravenous injection of "an ultrashort-acting barbituarate in combination with a chemical paralytic agent." Death would be almost instantaneous, with the condemned man simply falling asleep and expiring. Offically, death would be attributable to coronary arrest.

In 1977 Texas joined Oklahoma in passing death-by-drug legislation, and Idaho and New Mexico followed later. Other states have considered similar action. Because of appeals on death sentences, no such executions had been carried out by mid-1981, although 200 men were under such sentence, and it was believed injection executions might not begin until well into the decade.

The routine, however, has been well planned. In the Oklahoma State Penitentiary at McAlester, there would be no more "last-mile" walk through the basement to the electric chair. Instead, the doomed man would be strapped onto a stretcher and transported, head propped up, to the third floor of the administration building to be executed there in view of about 30 persons. Among them would be six newsmen and five persons chosen by the condemned.

The executioner would be one of three unidentified medical technicians. They would stand behind a panel through which a tube would be passed and connected to the condemned person's arm or leg. The three technicians would inject a dark fluid into the tube, but none would know which of them was injecting the lethal substance.

In essence, this would be similar in approach to the firing squad technique of supplying one marksman with a blank. The argument has been made that execution by injection is more humane than any other method of legal killing, but it must be noted that as society becomes more "humane," the anonymity of the procedure increases to a point where the actual killing is done by only one man in three.

The American Medical Association passed a resolution in 1980 labeling participation in such executions by doctors unethical. However, in 1982 the first execution by injection was carried out in Texas.

In 1980 when some of the more rabid advocates of capital punishment, including some in Congress, proposed that the exacting of the death penalty be shown on television, opponents of capital punishment were appalled. Why, it is hard to understand. It was not the student demonstrations or the draft card burners who stopped the Vietnam war. Rather, it was television. Through the constant showing on the evening news of the blood and violence occurring in a senseless conflict, the American public sickened of that conflict. The same thing would happen after a dozen or so execution spectaculars were viewed on the home screen. The public turned against the death penalty from 1945 to the mid-1960s without being exposed to the full graphic horrors of executions. The impact of television showings are readily predictable—and not even the death penalty could survive the public's reaction to such exposure.

See also: *John X. Beidler, Capital Punishment, Caryl Chessman, Gary Mark Gilmore, Gee Jon, William Kemmler, George Maledon, Monsieur New York.*

EXECUTIONS, Public

From the time of the first execution in this country's history in 1630, that of John Billington, one of the original pilgrims on the Mayflower, Americans followed the European custom of public executions on the dubious theory that such legal killings would serve as a warning to others.

Throughout the years such public executions were no more than circuses, drawing proportionally a far greater audience than Sunday football games. In the Old West many hangings were reserved for the weekend so that as many people as possible would be free for the festivities. When in 1824 a hatchet murderer named John Johnson was hanged in New York City at 13th Street and Second Avenue, journals of the day reported that some 50,000 spectators attended the execution. Perhaps the most spectacular hanging in New York took place on Bedloe's Island, now the home of the Statue of Liberty, where the murderer Albert E. Hicks was executed on July 13, 1860 not merely for the edification of those squeezed on the island for the event but for thousands more who jammed aboard a mass of ships, from small craft to large excursion vessels, that filled the water around the island. Hawkers paddled in rowboats between the craft selling their wares.

In due course, many communities and many sheriffs banned public executions, finding that they could run a ghoulish sort of black market selling invitations to private executions at hefty prices. However, the custom of public executions stretched into the present century, even extending to electrocutions. In some states, primarily Southern ones, a portable electric chair was brought into the courtroom and the condemned man was executed there before as many spectators as could get inside. The current was fed into the courtroom from a van-type truck equipped with the necessary generators. A journalist once asked Mississippi Sen. Theodore G. Bilbo if he did not think such executions were little different than lynchings. "Ah," Bilbo replied, "this is pretty tame compared to a lynching."

The last public execution in the United States took place in Owensboro, Ky. in 1936, when a 22-year-old black named Rainey Bethea was hanged for the murder of a 70-year-old white woman. Some 20,000 persons crowded into the town for the big event, and when Bethea was pronounced dead, souvenir hunters fought over the hood that covered his head, ripped off pieces of his clothing and even tried to cut chunks of flesh from his hanging body.

See also: *Capital Punishment, Rainey Bethea, John Billington, Albert E. Hicks.*

EXTORTION: See Black Hand.

EYE Gouging

Eye gouging was a common crime in pre-20th century America, especially in the big cities, where Irish gangsters used the technique—often against Englishmen—and on the frontier, where it was a part of the so-called rough-and-tumble style of fighting and much used against the Indians. In his diary Maj. Eluries Beatty tells of witnessing one eye gouging in Louisville, Ky. In 1791: "One of these. . . . gougers, a perfect bully; all the country round stood in awe of him, for he was so dextrous in these matters that he had, in his time, taken out five eyes, bit off two or three noses and ears and spit them in their faces."

So despised did this cruel practice become that vigorous laws were passed in many jurisdictions specifically to combat it. In the Northwest Territory a law was promulgated stating:

"Whosoever . . . shall voluntarily, maliciously, and on purpose, pull out or put out an eye while fighting or otherwise . . . shall be sentenced to undergo confinement in jail . . . and shall also pay a fine of not less than fifty dollars and not exceeding one thousand dollars, one fourth of which shall be for the use of the Territory, and three fourths . . . to the use of the party grieved, and for want of means of payment, the offender shall be sold into service by the court . . . for any time not exceeding five years, the purchaser finding him food and raiment during the term."

Such punishment was perhaps the only reason a white man on the frontier could be sold into servitude.

Gouging was not easy to eradicate. As late as the 1870s a New York gangster named Dandy Johnny Dolan became celebrated for the invention of an improved eye gouger made of copper and worn on the thumb for instant use. Dolan was hanged in 1876, and for the next quarter century, magistrates meted out heavy penalties against eye gougers. The public became particularly exercised about the practice, and political leaders, who relied on and supported the great gangs of the city, passed the word that eye gouging was out. A criminal caught in possession of a pistol, two or three knives and a pair of brass knuckles had no great fear of the law provided he had the proper political protection, but if he was found with eye gougers, he would be abandoned by his patrons and given severe punishment. Over the years the practice of eye gouging faded away, proof perhaps that rigid enforcement of the laws could in fact eliminate a considerable amount of crime.

F

FAHY, William J. (1886-1943): Postal inspector and criminal mastermind

The robbery of the eight-car mail train of the Chicago, Milwaukee and St. Paul Railroad on June 12, 1924 at Roundout, Ill., proved memorable in the annals of the U.S. Postal Service for a reason greater than the mere fact that $2,059,612 in loot had been taken. It was a case that shook the service to its core.

What particularly upset the postal service was that the robbers, six masked men, had known precisely when the most loot would be aboard. Had they struck earlier or later, the amount would have been far less. The robbers clearly had good information.

Put in charge of the case was Bill Fahy, a slim, well-dressed postal inspector of 40 with a confident and alert attitude. He had cracked a number of tough cases as a member of both the Philadelphia and the Chicago offices and was considered the fair-haired boy of the service. If anyone could solve the Roundout mess, he could.

However, Fahy proved a total disappointment. His investigation was a disaster, following clues down one blind alley after another. Soon, the other agents on the case began striking out on their own investigations. They caught some professional thieves with a portion of the loot. They named the others involved and admitted the gang had inside information. The robbers had a contact in the postal service, but the six never knew his identity.

Suspicion centered on the 18 mail clerks aboard the train. Fahy and his men checked on all of them. But one of the captured gang members said their informer had made it clear he was running the show and was getting the biggest cut. It hardly seemed likely that a mere postal clerk could have that much muscle with a gang of professional criminals. Finally, the other investigators discovered that Fahy had been secretly trying to break down the witnesses' positive identifications of the criminals. That only made sense if Fahy was the inside man.

A trap was baited. Fahy was told a high postal service official was coming to town with a lead on where one of the fugitives of the gang was hiding. The fugitive was Jimmy Murray, the contact man in the gang who had dealt with the postal service insider. When Fahy heard the news, he went home and telephoned a certain C. Anderson at the Ambassador Hotel in Chicago. In a wire-tapped conversation he told Anderson to lie low, that someone was in town who apparently had a lead on his whereabouts. With that, Murray was nabbed, and so was Bill Fahy. Fahy was convicted along with the other robbers and sentenced to 25 years in prison.

He was released in 1937, still proclaiming his innocence and saying he had been "framed by my criminal and professional enemies." He had earlier rejected a commutation offered in exchange for an admission of guilt. Fahy said he was going to prove his innocence but he never did. He died in 1943.

FAKED Deaths: See Insurance Fraud—Faked Deaths.

FALL, Albert Bacon (1861-1944): Political grafter

The central figure in the Teapot Dome scandal, Secretary of the Interior Albert B. Fall was the most tragic figure in the Harding Administration. Unlike many of the other grafters, his motive was not so much avarice as a genuine need for money. There is evidence that he resisted temptation until he saw clear cases of corruption by Attorney General Harry M. Daugherty and the rest of the Ohio Gang.

Born in Frankfort, Ky. in 1861, Fall was forced by ill health to move to a Western climate. He taught school for a short time in Indian Territory in the Oklahoma area and then became a cattle drive rider, later trying his hand at mining and oil prospecting. In New Mexico he became a close friend of

Edward L. Doheny, was admitted to the bar and started to develop a huge ranch at Three Rivers, N.M.

Fall also turned to politics, holding several positions in the territorial government, and in 1912, after New Mexico had achieved statehood, he became one of the state's first two senators. In 1921 his friend Warren Harding named him to the cabinet as secretary of the interior. It was a welcomed opportunity for Fall, whose personal fortunes had sagged badly.

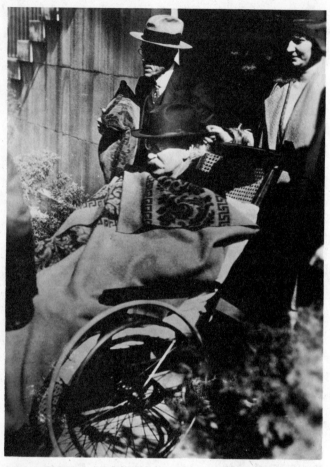

Albert Fall, secretary of the interior during the Harding Administration, was broken physically by the time of his conviction and imprisonment and remained an invalid the rest of his years

His ranch needed many repairs and improvements and all his properties were heavily mortgaged. In 1922 Fall secretly leased the Elk Hills, Calif. and the Teapot Dome, Wyo. oil lands, which were held by the government as a reserve in case of war, to Doheny's Pan-American Co. and Harry F. Sinclair's Mammoth Oil Co. It is doubtful if Fall would have done this had it not been for his long friendship with Doheny. Furthermore, Congress had authorized the leasing of the oil lands, although not the secret way Fall had gone about it or, of course, as a quid pro quo for bribes. Doheny gave Fall $100,000, and Sinclair arranged to have Fall receive a "loan" of $260,000 in Liberty Bonds.

The affair became public when a Wyoming oil man wrote his congressman demanding to know how Sinclair had leased Teapot Dome without competitive bidding. In the resulting senatorial inquiry the story of the payoffs to Fall was unraveled. Fall at first insisted that he had gotten the $100,000 as a loan from the eccentric millionaire Edward B. McLean. When McLean then surprised him by denying such a loan, Fall admitted getting the money "in a black bag" from Doheny.

Over the next several years Fall went on trial eight times, sometimes with Doheny or Sinclair and sometimes alone. On the witness stand, Doheny told a tale of how the two young friends started out together, with one eventually striking it rich in oil while the other had nothing but bad luck. "Why shouldn't I lend him $100,000 and tear his name off the note?" he asked. "He was an old friend." Then Doheny called the $100,000 "a mere bagatelle," and the newspapers and public were outraged. It was said that remark did more to doom Fall than any evidence against him. While the two oil men were finally acquitted of the charges against them (Sinclair did get nine months for contempt for having a Burns detective follow the jurors during one trial), Fall was convicted, drawing a year in prison and a fine of $100,000. The money penalty was dropped when Fall signed a pauper's oath, and because he was suffering from tuberculosis, he was allowed to serve his sentence in the New Mexico State Penitentiary, into which Fall, his face ashen, was carried on a stretcher. He came out of the prison an invalid, needing the constant attention of his family until he died poverty-stricken in El Paso in 1944.

See also: *Ohio Gang, Teapot Dome.*

FALLON, William J. (1886-1927): Defense attorney

William Joseph Fallon was New York's greatest criminal lawyer during the Roaring Twenties. Fallon was the Great Mouthpiece, as his biography by Gene Fowler was entitled, for pimps, madams, prostitutes, thieves, stock swindlers, second-story men, gangsters and murderers. Few Fallon clients ever spent a day in jail pending trial. Even if a Fallon client were not acquitted, he almost certainly benefitted from long delays due to hung juries. The novelist Donald Henderson Clarke called Fallon "the Jail Robber."

A large number of Fallon's cases never made it to a courtroom. Fallon paid off cops and bought people working in district attorneys' offices who could see to it that the evidence against his clients disappeared. On one occasion, during a court recess, the prosecutor was called to the telephone; he took along his briefcase, which contained the prosecution's case against the defendant. On the telephone, he was startled to hear an anonymous female voice inform him his wife was guilty of infidelity. The prosecutor walked out of the telephone booth in a daze and down the corridor. When he remembered his briefcase and went back for it, it had "disappeared." In court, Fallon demanded the trial continue; without the state's key evidence, his client was cleared.

Unlike those defense lawyers who never take on murder cases when the evidence is overwhelming, in order to protect their claim of never losing a client to the electric chair, Fallon took on any number of individuals who seemed doomed. Still, not one of his clients ever went to the chair. In 12 years before the New York bar, he defended about 100 murderers. About 60 percent of them were acquitted, and the rest got off with comparatively light sentences. Fallon's technique was to badger prosecutors and judges, confuse prosecution witnesses, and fool jurors. Above all, his specialty was producing a hung jury. He would address his entire summation to a single juror, picking out the one he judged to be most susceptible to such flattery. After some years a Hearst newspaper would point to Fallon's almost endless record of cases with juries hung by 1-to-11 votes. When he judged his skills were not winning the battle, Fallon was not above bribing a juror. He often paid them off in the courthouse elevator, giving them half in advance and half afterwards. He reputedly never made a second payment.

His courtroom performances were replete with trickery. In one case he defended a Russian who stood accused of arson and against whom the case looked strong indeed. The man twice previously had been convicted of setting fire to stores he had owned in attempts to bilk insurance companies. Fallon realized his only hope was to discredit the prosecution's witnesses. A fireman testified to entering the burning structure and smelling kerosene on a number of wet rags. Fallon insisted the rags were soaked with water and demanded the fireman submit to a test to see if he could tell the difference. The lawyer produced five bottles number 1, 2, 3, 4 and 5 and asked the fireman to sniff the contents of each and say if it was kerosene or water. The fireman sniffed bottle number 1 and announced it was kerosene. So too were bottles 2, 3, 4 and 5, he declared.

Fallon then took a sip of bottle number 5 and told the jury: "The contents of this bottle does not taste like kerosene to me. This bottle—this bottle that the gentleman on the witness stand would have you believe contains kerosene—doesn't contain kerosene at all. It contains water. When you get into the jury room, I wish you would all help yourself to a taste of its contents. If what you taste in the slightest resembles kerosene, I think it is your duty to convict my client. If what you taste is water, then it is your duty to acquit my client."

Fallon's client was of course acquitted because the liquid was pure water. What he had done was to have the fireman inhale deeply of the first four bottles all of which contained kerosene. Then when he sniffed the water, the fumes from the first four bottles were still in his nostrils.

In 1924 Fallon himself was brought to trial for allegedly bribing a juror in one of his 1-to-11 specialties. Reporters for Hearst's *New York American* had followed a number of jurors who had voted the Fallon way until they found one who was spending an unseemly amount of money after being the lone holdout in a jury hearing the case against two stock swindlers. It appeared Fallon had extracted $25,000 from his clients for the bribing of the juror, offered the man $5,000, given him $2,500 and kept the balance.

The juror confessed and Fallon was brought up on charges. The famous lawyer ran his own defense, even putting himself on the stand, and proceeded to make William Randolph Hearst, rather than William Joseph Fallon, the defendant. The lawyer insisted Hearst had trumped up the charges because he, Fallon, had gone to Mexico and uncovered the birth certificates of twins fathered by Hearst with a well-known Hollywood actress. While the jurors sat agog at the testimony, the prosecution tried to knock out all references to Hearst. But the point had been scored. It took the jury only five hours, with time out for dinner, to bring in a not-guilty verdict.

Fallon bounded out of his chair and thanked each juror, and then as the crowds of well-wishers thinned out, he approached the press table, where Nat Ferber, the *American* reporter who had dug up the case against him, was sitting. "Nat," he whispered, "I promise you I'll never bribe another juror!"

Actually, Fallon went on operating the way he always had for another couple of years, but by then drink was taking its toll. He died in 1927 of heart disease complicated by alcoholism. He was only 41.

FANNY Hill Case: American obscenity prosecution

The American edition of John Cleland's English classic of soft pornography, *Fanny Hill, or the Memoirs of a Woman of Pleasure,* became the subject of the first obscenity trial of a book in the United States.

In 1821, 71 years after *Fanny Hill* first appeared in England, printer Peter Holmes, the American publisher of the book, was found guilty of smut peddling. Three years later, the state got around to writing a law that defined and outlawed obscenity. In 1963 G. P. Putnam's Sons republished the work and was promptly taken to court. After winning in the first court and then losing in the second, *Fanny Hill* won her final emancipation by a vote of four to three in New York's Court of Appeals.

FARRINGTON Brothers: Outlaws

It has been estimated that at least 25 young Missourians turned to a life of crime when they saw the public adulation that was lavished on the James brothers. Two of these were the Farrington brothers, Levi and Hilary. Like the James boys, they were ex-Confederate guerrillas who had taken part in Quantrill's bloody raid on Lawrence, Kan. Later, they rode under George Todd. These two bearded, hardly literate giants witnessed what "ole Jesse and Frank were adoin" and saw no reason they couldn't do the same. They, however, lacked the flair of the James brothers, being nothing more than brutish killers, and never basked in the hero worship accorded to Jesse and Frank. Nonetheless, they were skillful riders and gunmen and their crimes cut a wide swath from Missouri and Tennessee down into Mississippi.

In 1870 they teamed up with another bloody pair, William Barton and William Taylor; flagged down the Mobile and Ohio flyer at Union City; and robbed the express car of $20,000.

As they continued their depredations and recruited new members to their gang, Pinkertons and express company detectives picked up their trail and finally cornered the gang in a hideout deep in the canebreaks at Lester's Landing in Mississippi. The raiders, headed by William Pinkerton, the son of the founder of the agency, and Pat O'Connell, considered the best express company detective of the time, captured five gang members after a gunfight but then discovered the Farringtons had pulled out two hours earlier. Weeks later, Pinkerton and O'Connell cornered Hilary Farrington in a farmhouse in Verona, Mo. and captured him after a daylong gun battle. Extraditing him to Union City, Tenn., his captors placed Hilary aboard the sternwheeler *Illinois*. When he attempted a nighttime escape, he fell overboard in a battle with William Pinkerton and was crushed to death by the vessel's stern paddle.

In 1871 Levi Farrington was taken by the Pinkertons during a hand-to-hand battle in the town square in Farmingdale, Ill. Crowds gathered, but unlike the admiration people showed for the James boys, they wanted to string Levi up. The Pinkertons held off the mob at gunpoint and got their prisoner back to Union City. They could have saved themselves the trip, however. A large band of nightriders seized Levi Farrington from the sheriff and hanged him from a tree near the main gate of the Union City cemetery.

FAUROT, Joseph A. (1872-1942): Father of fingerprinting

Joseph Faurot is regarded as the father of fingerprinting in the United States, although he was a lowly member of the New York Police Department when the system was introduced in St. Louis. However, it was Faurot's insistence on the system that shook up the brass of the nation's biggest, and often most complacent, police department and literally forced it into accepting the new scientific method.

Fingerprinting had been an attraction at the 1904 Louisiana Purchase Exposition in St. Louis, where it was demonstrated by experts sent from London's Scotland Yard. St. Louis police officials were so impressed they sent a man to London to study the method and subsequently installed the first American system. Meanwhile, a 32-year-old detective sergeant in the New York Police Department, Joseph Faurot, was bombarding his superiors with proposals that they adopt the system. Faurot finally prevailed upon Commissioner William McAdoo to grant him permission to go to London and study fingerprinting. When Faurot returned, he discovered McAdoo was no longer commissioner and that the current brass had little interest in new methods.

Faurot had realized the enormous value of fingerprinting in Europe and refused to stop lobbying for its use in New York. He got his first break when the suite of a socially prominent person in the Waldorf-Astoria was burglarized. Important pressure was put on the police to solve the theft, and Faurot was given permission to fingerprint several suspects. The prints were sent on to Scotland Yard, and in due course, one of the suspects was identified as Henry Johnson, an international hotel jewelry thief. Johnson was intensively questioned and finally confessed, leading officers to the hidden loot.

In 1908 Faurot used fingerprinting to crack a murder case. A nurse named Nellie Quinn had been choked to death in her room. By the time Faurot arrived, the policeman on the beat and several others had entered the premises, and since they understood nothing about fingerprints, they touched many things in the room. Fortunately, they had not touched a whiskey bottle on the table. Faurot confirmed this by matching the officers' prints against those on the bottle. Some of the prints were the nurse's but there was another set of fingerprints that could not be identified. After fingerprinting friends and neighbors of the slain woman, he discovered the owner of the prints—a man—on the bottle. Since the nurse had bought the bottle the evening of the murder, that placed the murderer in the murder room on the evening of the crime. Confronted with the evidence, the man confessed.

The shadow on Faurot's accomplishments in both cases was that convictions were obtained because of the culprit's confessions and not because of the fingerprint evidence. Until convictions could be obtained on the basis of fingerprint evidence, the technique had an uncertain future. The precedent-setting case turned out to be a prosaic burglary in 1911. A suspect taken into custody had an alibi, but Faurot's fingerprinting method identified him as the guilty party. The trial judge seemed dubious about the worth of fingerprint evidence. Faurot, however, offered a demonstration. While he left the courtroom, some 15 men in the room (various court attendants and lawyers) pressed their fingers on an ink pad and then put their prints on paper. One of the 15 then put his prints on a glass. When Faurot returned to the room, he quickly matched the prints on the glass with the correct set on paper. Both the judge and jury were impressed and the defendant was found guilty.

Fingerprint evidence had been tested by a court and accepted, and a new method of identification had been firmly established. Armed with this success, Faurot went on to establish the police department's fingerprint bureau and through the years provided the evidence that convicted thousands of criminals. By the time he retired in 1930, he had risen to the rank of deputy commissioner and had been acknowledged as the father of fingerprinting in the United States.

See also: *Fingerprinting*.

FENCE: Receiver of stolen property

Without fences to buy stolen goods, criminals would find many types of thefts unprofitable. Yet despite their key position in the world of crime, the receivers of stolen property seldom face much risk. During one year in New York state some 6,400 persons were arrested for criminal possession of stolen property, but only 30 of those arrested actually served time. This tolerance of fences is all the more incredible in light of the fact that many criminals work in collaboration with them and "steal to order" what the fence can resell at the time. Obviously, rather than just a passive link in the commission of a crime, the fence is often closer to being its mastermind. Unquestionably, fences enjoy most of the fruits of crime, generally paying the professional thief no more than 25 percent of the loot's value, and much less if the crime has generated "heat."

The operation of one California fence ring, which became the largest collector of stolen property throughout the entire state, was so lucrative that the head of the ring used mink stoles for rugs in his office and lined the dashboard of his car with other expensive stolen furs.

Fagin-type receivers of stolen goods appeared in America during earliest Colonial days; an individual named Silas is recorded as one of the pioneering practitioners in Massachusetts, being subjected to floggings, brandings and the stocks in the 1660s and 1670s. Possibly the most important stamping ground for fences in the 19th century was the so-called Thieves' Exchange in New York City during the 1860s, a dive located near Houston Street and Broadway. Each night criminals and fences would gather there to lift glasses in crooked camaraderie while dickering over price. The exchange operated with the connivance of the politicians and police, who were paid by the fences for the right to operate. Journalists of the period alleged that some important politicians and police officials even garnered commissions on a fence's gross business. Criminals with an illegal plan could even shop around for a fence to furnish the capital needed for the enterprise. Despite frequent exposes, the Thieves' Exchange prospered until the turn of the century, when police shut it down because of public outrage.

The most prosperous fence in American history was Fredericka "Marm" Mandelbaum, who from 1854 to 1884 so dominated the fencing racket that she has been described as the first in the country to put crime on a syndicated basis. She bossed the operations of several gangs of bank robbers, blackmailers and confidence men and even operated special schools for advanced courses in burglary and safe blowing. She also ran special classes for young boys and girls to learn the art of pickpocketing and sneak thievery. She enjoyed great esteem in the underworld as one who never betrayed a confidence. A leading thief, Banjo Pete Emerson, once said, "She was scheming and dishonest as the day is long, but she could be like an angel to the worst devil as long as he played square with her."

Marm's chief competitor was a stooped little man named Travelling Mike Grady, who went about the streets of New York with a peddler's box on his shoulder. It was always stuffed with such items as bonds, pearls and diamonds, all stolen and purchased from crooks by Travelling Mike, who never ventured forth with less than $10,000 in cash to buy purloined loot. It should be noted that neither Marm Mandelbaum nor Travelling Mike ended up in prison but rather lived out their time in lavish retirement, although Marm was inconvenienced to the point where she was forced to flee to the safety of Canada.

Today, police have found that maintaining their own fence operation and using undercover officers to pose as big-time buyers are excellent ways to round up professional thieves and recover stolen property. Such antifencing ruses are funded by federal grants from the Law Enforcement Assistance Administration. During the life of one such front in Washington, D.C. in the 1960s, the police took in a huge amount of stolen items at extremely low prices. Some of the loot included: televisions, radios, stereos, cameras, sound recorders, antiques, kitchen appliances, typewriters, calculators, guns, cars, credit cards, savings bonds and government checks. After many months of operation, the supposed fancers held a party to celebrate the success of their ring, and the thieves showed up in droves to take part. They arrived in luxury cars, many in black tie. As they passed from one room to the next, uniformed police placed them under arrest and hauled them off to jail. It was most disconcerting to the thieves, who thought all along they were working with Mafia figures.

See also: *Grady Gang, Fredericka "Marm" Mandelbaum, Sting, Thieves' Exchange.*

FENCE Stealing

Although widely practiced, the stripping of fences is hardly considered much of a crime and is often the work of children seeking supplies for building a clubhouse. But in past years it was a serious problem, being among other things a way to obtain firewood and a method to encourage a farmer's stock to "stray."

In this sense, fence stealing was considered a serious offense that called for very severe penalties. A 1659 ordinance in New Amsterdam reveals how stern the Colonial punishment for the crime was. It read, "No person shall strip the fences of posts or rails under penalty of being whipped and branded, and for the second, of punishment with the cord until death ensues."

FERGUSON Rangers: Texas Ranger cronyism

Probably the most-scandalized law enforcement agency in American history was the Texas Rangers from 1933 to 1935, when every officer in service was fired and replaced by cronies of newly-elected Gov. Miriam "Ma" Ferguson. The force thus became known as Ferguson Rangers. The Texas Rangers had made the mistake of becoming politicized to the extent of openly backing Gov. Ross Sterling in his race for reelection against former Gov. Miriam Ferguson. Ma Ferguson won and, as one of her first acts, dismissed all 44 rangers in service and put in her close political friends.

During the previous 15 years the Texas Rangers had received considerable criticism for the way they allegedly did and did not enforce law and order, but the record of the Ferguson Rangers made any previous abuses pale. Within a year a Ranger captain had been charged with theft and embezzlement, another had been convicted of murder and several others were found to have seized illegal gambling equipment and set up their own illicit betting enterprises. Undismayed by these scandals, Gov. Ferguson handed out special commissions, and in time, there were 3,000 active "Special Rangers," with the right to carry weapons and exercise other police privileges.

In 1935, following the succession of James Allred to the governorship the Texas Rangers lost their independent status and were made part of the Department of Public Safety. In a thorough housecleaning, their numbers were reduced to about 40.

See also: *Texas Rangers.*

FERNANDEZ, Manuel (?-1873): Murderer

A young troublemaker named Manuel Fernandez stabbed a Yuma, Ariz. storekeeper to death in December 1872. Yet, he avoided the obligatory and rapid lynching that normally would have followed, especially for Mexicans. Instead, he became the first man to be hanged legally in the Arizona Territory. By all accounts, the long waiting period was difficult to bear for a number of "rope-minded" citizens, but after Fernandez was duly and properly executed on May 3, 1873, the general opinion was that the delay hadn't "hurt too bad."

FERNANDEZ, Raymond Martinez: See Martha Beck.

FIELDS, Vina (?1865-?): Madam

The concept of the madam with the "heart of gold" is, of course, more fancy than fact; yet if one woman of that calling had to be singled out for the characteristic, it would be Vina Fields, a black madam who flourished during the last two decades of the 19th century in Chicago. About her, even the antivice muckraker William T. Stead conceded, "She is probably as good as any woman can be who conducts so bad a business."

Vina Fields maintained the largest brothel of the day in Chicago, one that generally had no fewer than 40 prostitutes and as many as 70 or 80 during the World's Fair of 1893. Madame Fields employed black harlots only but allowed patronage by whites only. From 1885 until just about the end of the century, she operated a fancy house on Custom House Place, and during that time, no man ever complained to the police about being robbed there. Vina insisted she never paid a penny in protection money, which may have been the only time she told a lie. Hers was the one house in Chicago where black prostitutes could count on getting a fair shake, drawing a far larger percentage of the take than elsewhere. Because of her generosity, she could also maintain strict discipline. In a famous book on corruption and vice, *If Christ Came to Chicago,* Stead wrote, "The rules and regulations of the Fields house, which are printed and posted in every room, enforce decorum and decency with pains and penalties which could be hardly more strict if they were drawn up for the regulation of a

Sunday School." Fields permitted no drunkenness, no soliciting from the windows and no overexposure in the parlors or hallways. She held a court every three days, and girls who had broken rules were fined, ordered to perform menial duties, banned from the parlor or, for major infractions, evicted from the house.

Stead further commented:

> Strange though it may appear, [she] has acquired the respect of nearly all who know her. An old experienced police matron emphatically declared that 'Vina is a good woman,' and I think it will be admitted by all who know her, that she is probably as good as any woman can be who conducts so bad a business. . . . She is bringing up her daughter who knows nothing of the life of her mother in the virginal seclusion of a convent school, and she contributes of her bounty to maintain her unfortunate sisters whose husbands down south are among the hosts of unemployed. Nor is her bounty confined to her own family. Every day this whole winter [1893-94] she had fed a hungry, ragged regiment of the out-of-work. The day before I called, 201 men had had free dinners of her providing."

There are many tales, though all unsubstantiated, about what became of Vina Fields in her later years.

See also: *William T. Stead.*

FINCH, Mrs. Barbara (1923-1959): Murder victim

The murder of Mrs. Barbara Finch by her California doctor husband and his mistress was one of the most sensational in recent decades. The case required three jury trials before a verdict was given.

Dr. Raymond Bernard Finch and his wife were prominent in social circles in Los Angeles and popular members of the Los Angeles Tennis Club. By 1957 the couple had drifted apart and Dr. Finch, using another name, rented an apartment where he regularly met with a 20-year-old married ex-model, Carole Tregoff. In 1958 Tregoff got a divorce, but Finch's wife refused to give him one.

Finally, she decided to seek a divorce. Under California divorce laws, when the grounds for divorce are desertion, cruelty or adultery, the courts can award all the property to the innocent party instead of dividing it equally. Suing on grounds of desertion, Mrs. Finch claimed all the property, including her husband's interest in a medical center, and demanded heavy alimony. If she won, Dr. Finch would have been left in virtual poverty.

Thereafter, according to later court testimony, Dr. Finch and Tregoff sought to obtain compromising evidence against the doctor's wife and, for that purpose, involved a petty crook named John Patrick Cody to make love to her. Later, according to Cody, he was offered money to kill Mrs. Finch. Cody said Carole Tregoff offered him $1,400 to shoot her. He claimed she stated, "If you don't kill her, Dr. Finch will . . . and if he won't, I'll do it."

On July 18, 1959 Dr. Finch and Carole Tregoff drove to the Finch home for a conference with Mrs. Finch. There was a shot, and Mrs. Finch lay dead on the driveway with a .38

bullet in her back. Dr. Finch's version was that during an argument his wife had pointed a gun at him and he had seized it and tossed it over his shoulder. The gun went off, he said, and fatally wounded his wife.

The prosecution's version was somewhat different. It claimed the pair had come to the Finch home with a so-called murder kit for the purpose of killing Mrs. Finch. The first plan, according to the prosecution, called for injecting an air bubble in her bloodstream; and if that failed, injecting a lethal dose of sodium seconal. An alternate plan, the prosecution contended, involved driving the unconscious woman over a cliff in back of the house. The prosecution contended the shooting was deliberate and presented scientific testimony that "the woman was in flight" when shot.

Dr. Finch took the stand and, with tears coursing down his face, gave a heartrending version of his wife's last words to him after the "accident." They were: "I'm sorry . . . I should have listened to you . . . I love you . . . take care of the kids. . . ." It was a rather novel defense, almost as though the victim was apologizing for being killed.

Nevertheless, the doctor's testimony was effective, resulting in a hung jury after eight days of deliberations. Finch and Tregoff, who had not spoken a word to each other throughout the trial, were retried a second time and again the jury failed to agree. On the third try, Dr. Finch was convicted of first-degree murder and Carole Tregoff of second-degree. Both were sentenced to life imprisonment. As they left the courtroom, Finch tried to kiss Tregoff but she turned away. Carole Tregoff was paroled in 1969; she never answered any of the many letters Finch wrote to her. Dr. Finch was freed in 1971.

FINGERPRINT Forgeries: See William de Palma.

FINGERPRINTING

The art of fingerprinting as a means of identification is a very old one. The ancient Chinese used a thumbprint in clay as an identifying seal, and a clay tablet in a British museum tells the tale of a Babylonian officer ordered to make arrests and obtain the defendants' fingerprints. In 1882 a geologist in New Mexico put his fingerprint on his claims and then signed his name across the print to protect against forgery. It was probably this incident that got Mark Twain to solve a crime through the use of fingerprints in a remarkable story called *Pudd'nhead Wilson*.

In the story, lawyer Pudd'nhead Wilson tells the jury:

Every human being carries with him from his cradle to his grave certain physical marks which do not change their character, and by which he can always be identified—and that without shade of doubt or question. These marks are his signature, his physiological autograph, so to speak, and this autograph cannot be counterfeited, nor can he disguise it or hide it away, nor can it become illegible by the wear and mutations of time. . . . This autograph consists of the delicate lines or corrugations with which Nature marks the insides of the hands

and the soles of the feet. If you will look at the balls of your fingers . . . you will observe that these dainty curving lines lie close together, like those that indicate the borders of oceans in maps, and that they form various clearly-defined patterns, such as arches, circules, long curves, whorles, etc., and that these patterns differ on the different fingers. . . . One twin's patterns are never the same as his fellow-twin's patterns. . . . You have often heard of twins who were so exactly alike that when dressed alike their own parents could not tell them apart. Yet there was never a twin born into this world that did not carry from birth to death a sure identifier in this mysterious and marvelous natal autograph.

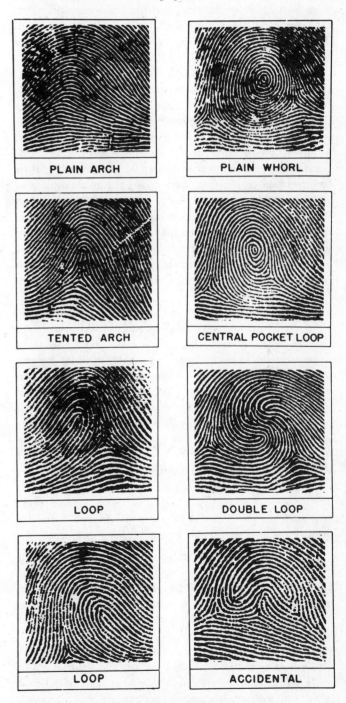

PLAIN ARCH **PLAIN WHORL**

TENTED ARCH **CENTRAL POCKET LOOP**

LOOP **DOUBLE LOOP**

LOOP **ACCIDENTAL**

An FBI sampling of fingerprint patterns.

Twain accepted the worth of fingerprints long before any police department in this country or elsewhere did. Beginning in the 1880s, the primary identification method used by all police agencies was a system developed by the French criminologist Alphonse Bertillon. The Bertillon system compiled information on several physical features of a subject based on the assumption that a combination of measurements, photos and other data would always be distinct for different individuals. It was a theory considered valid for only two decades, however. In 1903 two American criminals imprisoned in Leavenworth, one named William West and the other Willie West, were found to have the same Bertillion measurements. That discovery greatly undercut the validity of the Bertillon system. The fingerprints of the two Wests were taken and found to be totally dissimilar.

Scotland Yard pioneered development of a fingerprinting system in the late 1890s, and in 1904 a New York detective sergeant, Joseph A. Faurot, began to press for its adoption in this country, eventually becoming known as the father of American fingerprinting. Today, it is estimated that well over 1,000 fugitives a month are identified through fingerprint files. Unquestionably, numerous criminals would give the bulk of their loot to change their prints. That, however, is an almost impossible task, unless one is willing to destroy not only the prints but most of the fingers as well. Gangster John Dillinger paid a renegade doctor $5,000 to sear his prints with acid. Yet within a few agonizing weeks, after the doctor had wisely moved on, identical ridges grew back in place. After Dillinger was killed by FBI agents, identification of his body was a simple matter for fingerprint technicians.

The only American criminal known to have successfully obliterated his prints was a minor bandit named Robert James "Roscoe" Pitts, who accomplished the task in the 1940s. Once he became famous as the "man without fingerprints," however, he was a marked man. Whenever a robbery occurred in which no prints were found, Pitts automatically became a top suspect. He eventually was apprehended for a robbery and sent to prison for 20 years. While Pitts had eliminated his fingerprints, he had failed to prevent his identification. The doctor he used had erased his fingerprints down to the first joint, but when Pitts had been officially fingerprinted, the prints had inadvertently extended below the crease into the second joint. That area is not normally considered in the classification process, but it is actually just as unique as the primary, first-joint print. Pitts never would have been able to deny his identity.

The facts and fallacies about fingerprints are legion. Only in the movies do detectives pick up guns with handkerchiefs or by sliding a pencil under the trigger guard so as not to smudge fingerprints. Nor do killers wipe a "rod" clean after using it. In not one case in 1,000 will a usable set of prints be found on a gun.

Normally, the finding of a single fingerprint is useless since fingerprints must be classified by full sets and a partial would create an incredible search problem unless it belonged to a person who was already a suspect. Yet a single print found on a gas can put the FBI on the trail of Doc Barker and his gang, who had abducted a banker and released him. The banker remembered the men had refueled their car on the road with gas cans. The FBI found the discarded cans and got one clear impression, that of Doc Barker.

Once, a small portion of a print proved sufficient to doom a criminal in Alabama. A woman was criminally assaulted one night, fighting her attacker until beaten unconscious. When a doctor later treated her wounds, he found a small piece of skin lodged between her lower teeth. Under a microscope, its whorls suggested it might be a piece of a man's fingertip. A number of suspects were brought in and one had a bit of flesh torn from his left middle finger. The man, Major Preston, insisted he had injured his finger at work. His fingerprints were on file, however, and when the whorls on the bit of flesh were compared with the print of his left middle finger on the card, they matched exactly. Preston was convicted and executed.

Actually, duplicate fingerprints could possibly turn up. An expert once estimated the chances were "one in two quadrillion; a sum representing one million times the earth's population." Probably half the population of the United States have their fingerprints on file somewhere and thus could have their identities traced. An "inquiring reporter" once queried a half-dozen persons on the street about whether they had any objection to universal fingerprinting. Only two of the six didn't object, and one was a policeman. One of the others said, "Who knows, I might yet become another Dillinger . . . I wouldn't want my prints on file." Despite intensive campaigns, especially by the FBI, in favor of universal fingerprinting based on the value it has had in identifications following disasters, the American people have been notoriously unimpressed.

A not unfounded fear is the possibility of the planting of fingerprints. Experts have demonstrated how it could be done, and while some fingerprint men claim they can spot such plants, tests made to verify such claims have turned up a rating of less than 50 percent, statistically below even the law of averages.

See also: *Joseph A. Faurot, "West Brothers."*

FINK, Isidor (c.1899–1932): Suspected murder victim

The killing of Isidor Fink on March 9, 1929 in a tiny little laundry he operated on East 132nd Street in New York City has remained one of the most perplexing in the history of American crime. Alfred Hitchcock wrote about it and undoubtedly toyed with the idea of filming it but failed to come up with a logical solution. Ben Hecht wrote *The Mystery of the Fabulous Laundryman*, but that short story hardly pleased the locked-room addicts seeking a plausible explanation.

Fink kept the doors and windows of his one-room laundry locked at all times because of fear of robberies. A woman napping next door heard three shots in rapid succession and then something heavy, like a body, thud to the floor. She called police. When Patrolman Albert Kattenborn arrived, he found the door bolted and was unable to enter. He lifted a small boy up to the transom, but the boy found it locked. He smashed the glass, climbed inside and opened the door. Fink was dead on the floor. Patrolman Kattenborn let no one else enter and made the boy wait until detectives showed up. Fink had two bullet wounds in the chest and one in the left wrist. The immediate conclusion of the detectives was that he must have committed suicide since it was evident that no one could have gotten out of the room.

The problem with that solution was the suicide gun. It was nowhere to be found, and Fink had died almost instantly. The small boy was searched to make sure he had not secreted the weapon on his person. Then the police set about searching the room. Perhaps Fink had tied the gun to some sort of elastic device that pulled it out of sight. They literally ripped the room apart. No gun. No loose boards. No hidden panels. No trap doors. A squad of specially-picked sleuths was sent up from headquarters to solve the mystery. At first, they worked with vigor, then with some irritation and finally in total bewilderment. Reluctantly, the police accepted the fact that they had a case of murder, one that through the years became a favorite of the Sunday supplements. About the most profound conclusion ever to be drawn from the Fink case was the published comment of a detective after a year's work on the puzzle: "That damn two-for-a-cent mystery gives me the creeps!"

FIRE Bombing: See Apache Indian Job.

FISH, Albert (1870-1936): Mass murderer and cannibal

A harmless-looking house painter in New York City, Albert Fish was a degenerate who admitted molesting more than 400 children over a span of 20 years. Fish, labeled by the press as the "inhuman monster," was described by one shocked psychiatrist as a man of "unparalleled perversity. There was no known perversion that he did not practice and practice frequently."

Fish had a personal and married life that was odd, to say the least. He enjoyed sticking needles into himself, spanking himself with a nail-studded paddle or having children beat him until he bled. He appreciated children because of their innocence and because, as he once put it, "They don't tell." Certainly, the 15 to 17 children he murdered never told.

He got married when he was 28. It lasted for about 20 years before his wife ran off with a half-wit. She returned about a year later and asked to move back in with her lover. Fish said she could stay but her lover could not. Later, he discovered his wife had hidden her lover in the attic. He kicked him out and again told his wife she could stay, but she went off with her lover and Fish never saw her again. Fish had six children. They were aware their father was a bit peculiar, but he was kind to them and never beat them. The children had seen him use his nailed paddle on himself, but they assumed he must be sane, if somewhat eccentric, since they knew he had been under psychiatric observation a number of times and had always been discharged by the doctors.

His occupation as a house painter allowed him to move from town to town and gave him access to cellars and deserted buildings. By his own count, he committed offenses in at least 23 states. He had some close calls. In St. Louis Fish had almost been caught with a small boy he had been torturing for days but escaped just in time. There were narrow squeaks in Virginia and in Delaware and several in New York. Children disappeared with a kindly old man never to be seen again; others were found brutally mutilated. He was questioned several times but was never a serious suspect.

At a very minimum, he killed and ate at least 15 children. His last such victim apparently was a 12-year-old New York City girl, Grace Budd, whom he lured from her parents in 1928 by telling them he was bringing her to a party a friend was giving for a daughter. He cut up her body and cooked the parts in a stew with onions and carrots. It took him nine days to eat most of her. He buried what was left. It was six years before he was caught for that crime. The police were baffled by the case, but Fish could not resist writing Mrs. Budd to tell her what he'd done. He didn't sign the letter, but the police readily traced him. Fish acted as though he had been waiting for them for a long time. He immediately confessed and led them to a spot in White Plains where they found the girl's bones. He also confessed to a number of additional cannibal murders.

Fish's trial consisted of a long parade of psychiatric specialists. Only Dr. Frederic Wertham and two other defense experts insisted he was insane. Fish was judged guilty and sane enough to die in the electric chair. The prospect excited Fish. "What a thrill that will be if I have to die in the electric chair," he said with a broad smile. "It will be the supreme thrill. The only one I haven't tried." When he did go to the chair on January 16, 1936, he was described by the press as being positively joyful. He even helped adjust the electrodes when he was being strapped down.

The newspapers had one more ghoulish report for their readers. The first massive jolt of electricity failed to kill Fish. The theory was that the 400 plus needles he had inserted into his body over the years had apparently caused a short circuit. A second potent jolt was needed to complete the job.

FISHER, John King (1854-1884): Gunman and lawman

John King Fisher was one of the 19th century's controversial gunmen for whom Texas was famous or infamous, becoming a popular hero to some and a callous murderer to others. Fisher once shot a man in the head because he wanted to see if a bullet would bounce off his bald pate. Perhaps his mean streak was best illustrated by the sign he erected at a crossroads when he established his own spread in southern Texas: "This is King Fisher's Road—Take the other one." The sign became something of a landmark and was considered no idle threat. In 1878 Fisher said he was responsible for killing seven men in gunfights, not counting Mexicans.

Fisher's first scrape with the law occurred in 1870, when at the age of 16 he drew a two-year term for robbery but served only four months. Gaining a pardon, he worked as a cowboy for a few years and then started his own spread, which became headquarters for an unsavory crew of rustlers, killers and deadbeats. He formed an alliance with Mexican rustlers, but after a dispute on a division of the spoils, he pistol-whipped one, shot a second as he went for his gun and then gunned down two others who were just sitting on a fence. During Fisher's "ranching" days he reputedly formed a partnership with an *insurrecto* named Porfirio Diaz, who later became president of Mexico, whereby Diaz delivered stolen Mexican cattle to Fisher and received Fisher's rustled American beef. On both sides of the border there were stock buyers who were not particularly mindful of brands if they were from the other country.

Fisher frequently was arrested on murder charges and was subject to considerable Texas Ranger harassment, but he was inevitably found not guilty or the charges were dismissed for lack of evidence. Then King Fisher made a sudden transformation: he got religion and in 1881 became a lawman, appointed deputy sheriff of Uvalde County. There were those who insisted he backslid a bit now and then, but in 1883 he made plans to run for sheriff the following year. In March 1884 Fisher went to Austin, the state capital, on official business and ran into an old gunman buddy, the crazed Ben Thompson. The pair rode together to San Antonio, where they entered the Vaudeville Variety Theater, a gambling hall whose proprietor, Jack Harris, Thompson had murdered some two years previously.

Thompson and Fisher had a drink at the bar and then repaired to a box upstairs to watch the variety show. They were joined in the box by bouncer Jacob Coy and two of Harris' former partners, Billy Simms and Joe Foster. Thompson made several nasty remarks about the Harris killing and then playfully jammed his six-gun into Foster's mouth, whereupon bouncer Coy moved in and seized the cylinder. There was a moment of tense silence and Fisher made a remark about leaving before things got out of hand. Suddenly, there was a blaze of fire and Thompson was dead, with nine slugs in him. King Fisher went down in a hail of 13 bullets.

Some suggested that but for his chance meeting with Thompson, the reformed King Fisher would have lived out a full life as a respected rancher and lawman. Not everyone was sorry about Fisher's demise. A woman whose son Fisher had killed came to the Uvalde cemetery on every anniversary of her son's death, set a brush fire atop Fisher's grave and danced "with devilish glee" around it.

See also: *Ben Thompson.*

FITZPATRICK, James "The Sandy Flash" (c.1760-1787): Early highwayman

The first of America's "romantic" criminals, James Fitzpatrick was a handsome young Irishman who was for a time a member of the Doane gang, the first important band of criminals in this country, before splitting off to form his own gang in the early 1780s. Preying on wealthy landowners mainly in Chester and Delaware counties, Pa., he cut a dashing figure, so much so that he would become the "Sandy Flash" of Bayard Taylor's

Story of Kennett, a 19th century best-seller. By 1785 a reward of 200 pounds, a king's ransom in those days, was placed on the Sandy Flash, but fear of betrayal and arrest did not faze him. One day, with the kind of daring that Jesse James would exhibit a century later, Fitzpatrick calmly rode his big black stallion into the center of Chester, Pa. and took his meal at the Unicorn Tavern. Present at the bar were several members of the posses searching for him. Fitzpatrick bought drinks for his hunters, who regaled the tavern crown with what they would do to the Sandy Flash when they captured him. Fitzpatrick could get away with such feats of courage because, like Jesse James, he was a man without a face, with no unusual features by which to be recognized. However, his luck eventually ran out and he was cornered by a posse and taken prisoner. The fair maidens of two counties wept, we are told, when the Sandy Flash was hanged in the Old Chester Jail in January 1787.

See also: *Doane Gang.*

FITZPATRICK, Richie (1880-1905): Gangster and murderer

One of the few non-Jews to achieve high stature in the Eastman gang, the last great Jewish outfit to dominate crime in New York City, Richie Fitzpatrick, a lethal young Irishman, won the appreciation of leader Monk Eastman because of his great cunning at killing. Once assigned by Eastman to eradicate the owner of a Chrystie Street dive, Fitzpatrick pulled a cunning ruse long before the brothers Corleone thought of it in *The Godfather*—he had a gun planted in the toilet of the dive. Immediately suspect when he walked in, Fitzpatrick permitted himself to be searched and then informed the dive operator that Eastman had ordered him assassinated. He said he was defecting from the Eastman ranks and was thus willing to aid the dive owner. Fitzpatrick's story was accepted, and he joined in a round of drinks, swearing allegiance to his new allies. His next move was to heed the call of nature. When Fitzpatrick emerged from the toilet, he shot the dive operator dead and fled before his henchman could react.

When Eastman was taken by the law for a 1904 attempted robbery, the leadership of the gang fell to an uneasy combination of Fitzpatrick and Kid Twist, so named because of his criminal cunning. It was soon obvious that the pair would have to settle the leadership problem violently, and the gang began to divide into warring factions. The Kid suggested a peace conference in a Chrystie Street dive. Fitzpatrick accepted with alacrity, and the underworld awaited to see what deceit he would conceive to eliminate his foe. Unfortunately for Fitzpatrick the Kid too was noted for his trickery. As the talks began, the lights suddenly went out and a revolver blazed. When the police reached the scene, Fitzpatrick was alone in the back room with his arms folded across his chest and a bullet in his heart.

The underworld applauded the treachery; Kid Twist, the saying went, "had twisted first."

See also: *Kid Twist.*

The teeming Five Points in 1829.

FIVE Points: New York crime district

Every account of crime in old New York is replete with references to the Five Points and the gangs and crimes it spawned. It was the incubator of crime in the city for an entire century. Its early history was tame enough, being a relatively homey place at the junction of Cross, Anthony, Little Water, Orange and Mulberry streets. In the center of the Five Points was Paradise Square where the poor people of the city came for their fresh air and recreation. By the 1820s the area had turned first seedy and then vile, and the Five Points became a hellhole of impoverished humanity that produced crime in awesome, if predictable, numbers. By the time of the Civil War, the Points and Paradise Square area housed no less than 270 saloons, and many times that number of dance halls, houses of prostitution and green-groceries that dispensed more liquor than vegetables or other provisions. It was already described as a slum section far more wicked than even the Whitechapel district of London.

Perhaps Charles Dickens offered the most graphic picture of the district in his *American Notes:*

Let us go on again, and plunge into the Five Points. This is the place; these narrow ways diverging to the right and left, and reeking everywhere with dirt and filth. Such lives as are led here, bear the same fruit here as elsewhere. The coarse and bloated faces at the doors have counterparts at home and all the whole world over. Debauchery has made the very houses prematurely old. See how the rotten beams are tumbling down, and how the patched and broken windows seem to scowl dimly, like eyes that have been hurt in drunken frays. Many of these pigs live here. Do they ever wonder why their masters walk upright instead of going on all-fours, and why they talk instead of grunting?

So far, nearly every house is a low tavern, and on the barroom walls are colored prints of Washington and Queen Victoria, and the American Eagle. Among the pigeon-holes that hold the bottles are pieces of plate glass and colored paper, for there is in some sort a taste for decoration even here. And as seamen frequent these haunts, there are maritime pictures by the dozen; of partings between sailors and their lady-loves; portraits of William of the ballad and his black-eyed Susan; of Will Watch, the bold smuggler; of Paul Jones, the pirate, and the like; on which the painted eyes of Queen Victoria, and of Washington to boot, rest in a strange companionship. . . .

From every corner, as you glance about you in these dark streets, some figure crawls half-awakened, as if the judgment hour were near at hand, and every obscure grave were giving up its dead. Where dogs would howl to lie men and women and boys slink off to sleep, forcing the dislodged rats to move away in quest of better lodgings. Here, too, are lanes and alleys paved with mud knee-deep; underground chambers where they dance and game; the walls bedecked with rough designs of ships, of forts, and flags, and American Eagles out of number; ruined houses, open to the street, whence through wide gaps in the walls other ruins loom upon the eye, as though the world of vice and misery had nothing else to show; hideous tenements which take their names from robbery and murder; all that is loathsome, drooping and decayed is here.

This was the Five Points that gave New York such gangs as the Dead Rabbits, Chichesters, Plug Uglies and Roach Guards and, much later, the dreaded Whyos and the Five Points Gang. From the ranks of the Five Pointers came such fledgling gangsters as Johnny Torrio, Frankie Yale, Lucky Luciano and Al Capone, an impressive result of 100 years of crime breeding.

Today, the old Five Points section takes in parts of Chinatown and Little Italy and a large portion is taken up by Mulberry Park. Much of the area consists of decaying housing that the former residents of the Five Points would have considered luxury apartments.

See also: *Little Water Street, Old Brewery*

FIVE Points Gang: Pre-Prohibition New York gang

The last great pre-Prohibition gang in New York City was a 1,500-man collection of eye-gouging terrorists called the Five Points Gang. They carried on in the tradition of those 19th century cutthroats the Whyos and their predecessors, such as the Dead Rabbits. Bossed by an ex-bantamweight prizefighter, Paul Kelly (nee Paolo Antonini Vaccarelli), the gang's gunners and musclemen hired out to businessmen as strikebreakers or to other mobs as murderers for hire. Probably more modern-day gang leaders emerged from the Five Pointers than any other similar organization.

Kelly's headquarters was in his own New Brighton Dance Hall in Great Jones Street, one of Manhattan's more lavish fleshpots and a mecca for slumming socialites eager to meet a famous gangster. Kelly was an urbane man who spoke fluent Italian, French and Spanish, dressed like a fashion plate and had manners that fit easily into polite society. One of Kelly's top aides was a short youngster, Johnny Torrio, who was to become "the Brain" of the underworld. Under Kelly's direction Torrio developed a subgang called the James Street Gang. His recruits included such ambitious youths as Al Capone, Lucky Luciano and Frankie Yale. All of them were eventually moved up into the Five Pointers, which by 1915 was fast deteriorating because of a lack of rackets to sustain them. Kelly moved off to waterfront labor racketeering and Torrio and Capone to Chicago, while Luciano and Yale remained in New York. All achieved new power and authority through the fruits of Prohibition, a bizarre experiment that provided fresh impetus to gangsterism in America.

See also: *John Torrio.*

FLAKING: Police slang for frame-up

This is the term used by policemen and private detectives to describe the framing of an individual. When it is done, the police officers usually justify it as being a service to society; since the victim has committed so many other crimes, it hardly matters if the facts of a crime he is actually charged with are a fabrication.

Naturally, not all law enforcement officials engage in the practice. New York Deputy Chief Fire Marshal John Barracato relates in a book called *Arson!* about how he was urged to participate in a flaking by another fire marshal and refused. He says, "To me flaking was the most heinous violation of a cop's honor."

Flaking was heavily practiced in the heyday of union organizing in this country, when private detectives framed unionists, often based on the belief that unionism did a worker more harm than good, and that even if a unionist was not actually guilty of a certain act of labor violence, he was undoubtedly responsible for others.

FLAMINGO Hotel

Known as the casino that made Las Vegas, the Flamingo was the brainchild of mobster Bugsy Siegel. Siegel had come to the West Coast in the late 1930s to handle the mob's betting empire. During the war years he began envisaging a new gambling empire, one that could turn the Nevada sands into gold dust. Gambling was legal in Nevada, where the main attraction was Reno, offering diversion to passing tourists and individuals waiting for their divorce decrees. Siegel saw Las Vegas, then no more than a highway rest stop with some diners, gas stations and a sprinkling of slot machines, as a lavish new gambling oasis.

Bugsy had little trouble convincing Meyer Lansky, treasurer of the national crime syndicate, that his vision was a great idea, and several big city mobs laid out money to build a new casino-hotel, which was to be called the Flamingo, the nickname of Virginia Hill, Siegel's girl friend and the former bedmate of a number of top mobsters.

During the construction of the Flamingo, Siegel assured building contractor Del E. Webb, who had become nervous about the mob's involvement, that he had nothing to fear because "we only kill each other." At the time Bugsy didn't realize how accurate his statement would prove to be. In the short run, the Flamingo was a disaster, mainly because in the immediate post war years it was an idea ahead of its time. It would take considerable patience to make it a success, but Siegel had no time. Not only had he failed to produce the profits the mob expected on its $6 million investment, but it appeared he had been skimming off the construction funds. When Siegel refused to make good, indeed could not make good, he was rubbed out.

After Siegel's execution the mob continued to support the Flamingo and eventually saw it grow and prosper. The syndicate poured millions more into Las Vegas, building one successful casino after another.

See also: *Las Vegas, Benjamin "Bugsy" Siegel.*

FLOATERS: Murder victims

Almost every waterfront city in America during the 18th and 19th centuries came to know the term "floater," used to describe a corpse found floating in the water after meeting with foul play. It was a term imported from England to refer to such crimes, which were common along the Thames in London.

The "floater" capital of the United States was probably Buffalo, N.Y., the terminus of the Erie Canal beginning in 1825. The canal at Buffalo was probably the most crime-infested waterway in the country, and murder victims were dumped there with monotonous regularity. The primary source of this pollution was the dives of Canal Street, whose rear areas extended over the canal, supported by wooden dock pilings. Unsuspecting canalers and lakers were hustled to these places by shills to be trimmed with exorbitant prices. However, if a man had a bundle and was uncooperative about parting with it, he was fed enough knockout drops to put a team of horses to sleep.

He would be hauled into a back room, stripped of all his clothes and dumped naked down a slick wooden chute into the canal with hardly an incriminating splash. Not even the cold water would be enough to revive him, and he eventually would be discovered floating face down in the murky water. The police would know no more than that he had been killed in one of about 100 places on Canal Street and would close the file on the case by listing the victim as a "floater." In one week in 1863 no less than 14 floaters were fished out of the canal, five on one morning alone.

FLOATING Hog Ranches: Riverboat bordellos

While from time to time it may have existed in other countries, the floating brothel was fully developed on the Mississippi and later migrated to the waterways of the Far West.

The riverboat brothels made their first appearance along the riverfronts of New Orleans and Natchez-under-the-Hill, where the flatboat crews couldn't even wait to get ashore to enjoy feminine companionship. It was customary for flatboats to be sold once their cargoes were unloaded, and many were turned into bagnios, with prostitutes entertaining customers in narrow cubicles built into the cargo boxes. On occasion there was not even time for that and the harlots made ready for business on deck with only a tarpaulin cover.

When prostitutes started west, following the frontier, they shunned travel on horseback or by coach, which represented a waste of valuable time. Instead, a typical madam would travel overland with her girls until reaching the next waterway and then purchase any kind of available craft to do business while floating westward. Since the brothels of the West were called hog ranches, such boats were known as floating hog ranches; and it has been said that among the most-welcomed calls on parts of the frontier was one announcing, "Hog ranch a'coming!"

FLOGGING

Almost from the beginning, the whipping post was a common fixture in Colonial America. Since prisons did not come into being until much later, flogging or whipping became the most common form of punishment. Initially, "knout," which was made of knotted rawhide, was used but it was later replaced by several bound leather strips, referred to as the cat o' nine tails. The development of prisons did not result in a great decrease in floggings; since mere confinement was not regarded as a complete enough punishment, offenders got both flogged and imprisoned. Floggings were brutal affairs that often left the victim crippled or, at the very least, permanently scarred. The Quakers were the first to ban the practice, and after the Revolutionary War, reformers made some headway against the whipping post by calling it an "English" device.

Although the whipping post was condemned by reformers after the Revolution as an "English" device, its use continued in the 19th century and, to some extent, in more recent times.

The custom died slowly, however, always gaining new life along the frontier, where there was a need for a quick form of justice. In the mining camps of the West, justice had to be fast so that a man could get back to hunting for his fortune, and a malefactor faced either hanging or whipping (or, to a lesser extent, amputation). There simply were no other choices, and in that sense, the whip undoubtedly saved many men from the noose. Floggings virtually disappeared in the 20th century, although Maryland, which had abandoned flogging around the turn of the century, reinstituted it in 1933, at a judge's discretion, for wife beaters and Delaware continued its use prior to a prison sentence for a number of offenses. But while the custom died outside of prison, it remained a form of punishment for recalcitrant convicts. With the introduction of modern ideas of penology, floggings in prisons tended to be abolished, although a few institutions in the South have admitted its use and others are believed to practice it secretly.

FLORES, Juan (1835-1857): Outlaw and murderer

Unlike Joaquin Murieta, there was nothing fictional about Juan Flores, one of California's most spectacular and blood-thirsty villains. He was no more than a minor rustler and horse thief when he was put away in San Quentin in 1856. If he had served out his term, he probably would have remained a small-timer, but Flores and a number of other prisoners escaped. Their method of escape made Flores a well-known figure, held in awe by both the public and other outlaws.

Flores viewed the walls of San Quentin and decided escape that way was difficult and dangerous, if not impossible. But he soon found a weak spot in the prison's security. When the opportunity came, Flores and a group of followers stormed aboard a provision ship tied up at the prison wharf, took control of the vessel and managed to sail off, erratically, but successfully in the end.

The fugitives were unsophisticated, to put it kindly, since they seriously debated sailing their stolen vessel to Australia to "take over the country." Instead, the winds and tides settled the matter, and they landed farther down the California coast. Because of his new fame, Flores, now an outlaw leader, had little trouble recruiting a gang of 50 guns within a few days, including a fairly noted badman named Andres Fontes. From their hideout in the hills around San Juan Capistrano, the gang terrorized the area south of Los Angeles. They held up stagecoaches and mining supply wagons and invaded small towns to loot stores. Flores also led the gang in kidnapping or waylaying travelers and holding them for ransom. When a German settler wouldn't or couldn't meet his ransom demands, Flores paraded him into the plaza at San Juan Capistrano and summarily shot him to death as a warning to future victims to be more cooperative.

A posse headed by Sheriff James R. Barton went out after Flores in January 1857 and only three members of the posse came back alive. Sheriff Barton was not among them, having been gunned down by Fontes. Since the outlaw attacked Americans and Mexicans alike, he was soon hunted by posses of both nationalities. Led by Don Andres Pico, a 50-man Spanish-American posse armed with lances routed the gang in one encounter, killing and capturing several of its members, but both Flores and Fontes escaped. On February 1 Flores was finally run to ground by a 40-man posse headed by a Doc Gentry. Held prisoner in a ranch house, Flores broke free but, unarmed, was easily recaptured two days later. He was brought back to Los Angeles, and on February 14, by what was described as a "popular vote," the 22-year-old outlaw was sentenced to hang, the penalty being exacted forthwith. Fontes made it back to Mexico but soon died there in a gunfight.

FLOUR Riots: New York mob action

The Great New York Fire of December 1835 was largely responsible for bringing on the Panic of 1837, as banks failed and insurance companies went bankrupt, and set the stage for the bloody Flour Riots of 1837. Because many employers in New York could not rebuild, thousands were thrown out of work and economic activities ground slowly down. There was also a falloff in the supplies of food and by the autumn of 1836 the price of a barrel of flour had risen first to $7 a barrel and then to the unheard of sum of $12. Actual starvation developed in the slum areas of the Five Points and the Bowery as bread, a staple of the poor's diet, disappeared. By February 1837 the flour depot at Troy, N.Y. had on hand only 4,000 barrels of flour as opposed to the usual 30,000 and it was predicted the price would rise to $20 a barrel or more. New York newspapers denounced as gougers certain merchants who allegedly were hoarding great amounts of grain and flour, waiting for bigger profits.

On February 10 an enormous mob attending a meeting in City Hall Park moved en masse on the big wheat and flour store of Eli Hart & Co. on Washington Street. Despite defenses by the watchmen, the huge mob battered down the doors and began throwing barrels of flour, sacks of wheat and watchmen out the windows. Several watchmen were seriously injured, and the flour and wheat were spilled out of their containers and scattered by the rioters. They destroyed an estimated 1,000 bushels of wheat and 500 barrels of flour before they were driven off by a large contingent of police supported by two companies of national guardsmen. The rioters scattered, carrying off their dead and wounded. However, the mob simply poured across the city and launched a new attack on the store of S. H. Herrick & Co. Once again, a large amount of flour and wheat was destroyed before the rioters were dispersed. Ironically, very few of the mob made an attempt or even thought to carry off any of the precious flour. And the following day the price of flour increased another dollar.

The Flour Riots did little to alleviate the condition of the poor, who, like their counterparts a century later, simply learned to make do on less until the country emerged from its economic woes.

FLOYD, Charles Arthur "Pretty Boy" (1901-1934): Public enemy

Raised in the Cherokee Indian Territory of Oklahoma, Public Enemy No. 1 Charles "Pretty Boy" Floyd was probably the last of the great "social bandits" in America. Just as Billy the Kid was idolized by the poor Mexican herdsmen and villagers of New Mexico, and the James brothers could do no wrong as far as Southern sympathizers in Missouri were concerned, so too was Floyd, the Robin Hood of the Cookson Hills, the hero of the sharecroppers of eastern Oklahoma. As Pa Joad in John Steinbeck's *The Grapes of Wrath* said: "When Floyd was loose and goin' wild, law said we got to give him up—an' nobody give him up. Sometimes a fella got to sift the law."

Unlike other gangsters of the 1920s and the Depression era, Floyd was known as a hard worker who might never have gone wrong if he had been able to find legitimate work. In 1924 things were already tough for sharecroppers in eastern Oklahoma when Floyd married a 16-year-old girl. The following year, his wife pregnant, Floyd turned to crime, got caught pulling a $5,000 payroll robbery and drew a three-year sentence. Released after serving slightly half that time, he committed bank and payroll robberies on his own until hooking up with a few professionals. Working his way east, Floyd and another criminal were arrested in 1930 for the robbery of a Sylvania, Ohio bank, and Floyd was given 10 to 25 years. However, on his way to the Ohio State Penitentiary, Floyd leaped through an open train window, rolled down an embankment just 10 miles from the prison gates and escaped. His fame back in Oklahoma was now established, he would never spend another day behind bars during the rest of his short life.

Floyd made his way to Toledo, Ohio, where he joined forces with Bill "the Killer" Miller, who had been recommended as trustworthy. Floyd's idea was for the pair to go about robbing banks. Bill the Killer—the slayer of at least five men—was four years younger than Floyd but still regarded him as a young punk who needed "seasoning." Miller probably did more than anyone else to turn Floyd from a quick-triggered gunman into a future public enemy. Bill the Killer took Floyd to Michigan, where they limited themselves to $100 to $300 jobs, holding up filling stations and lone farmers. Only then did they move on to some small bank robberies.

By the time they reached Kansas City, the pair had enough of a poke to retire for a time to the splendor and safety of Mother Ash's place, a brothel of considerable standing. Some say it was from the ladies at Mother Ash's that Floyd first picked up his nickname Pretty Boy; others claimed the hill folk had so named him because in his teens he always went around with a pocket comb to neaten up his "slick as axle grease" pompadour. However it started, Floyd always hated the nickname. He did, however, love the girls at Mother Ash's, especially the madam's daughter-in-law, Rose. Bill the Killer was much impressed with Rose's sister, Beulah Bird. This proved to be a deadly double triangle because the sisters were married to Wallace and William Ash, the madam's sons, gangsters in their own right who doubled as bouncers at the establishment. Floyd and his partner solved the problem by murdering both brothers and setting off with the girls in tow on a string of bank robberies.

In Bowling Green, Ohio the quartet attracted police attention. Floyd shot and killed Chief of Police Carl Galliher and wounded another officer, but he was the only one to leave the scene of the shoot-out. Bill the Killer was fatally shot and the two girls were wounded.

Immediately after that incident Floyd returned to Oklahoma and hooked up with 40-year-old George Birdwell, an ex-church deacon turned outlaw. By this time Pretty Boy was regarded as a hero by many in the Cookson Hills and the surrounding area, who saw him as a modern Robin Hood. Rejoicing in this role, Floyd would sprinkle money out the car window as he and Birdwell and whatever aides they recruited rode off after robbing a small-town bank. And inside the bank, he always tried to locate and rip up any first mortgages he could find, hoping they had not as yet been recorded.

The Pretty Boy Floyd legend flowered best in his hometown of Sallisaw. Once he wrote the sheriff there: "I'm coming to see my mother. If you're smart you won't try to stop me." The sheriff was smart. On another occasion, apparently on a dare, Floyd returned home just to prove he could rob the bank there.

He casually stepped from a car with a machine gun tucked under his arm, and, recognizing some friends lounging outside the barbershop, waved to them.

"How de," one called. "What you doin' in town?"

"How you, Newt," Floyd replied. "Going to rob the bank."

"Give 'em hell," another admirer yelled. Floyd did.

Most Floyd-Birdwell forays were far from picturesque and harmless. They killed often during their robberies, but none of this tarnished Floyd's reputation. He remained a hero while public opinion blamed all the cold-blooded murders on Birdwell.

Late in 1932 Birdwell was killed pulling a bank robbery in which Floyd had not participated. After that, Floyd gravitated back to big-city crime in Kansas City. He became a prime suspect in the notorious Kansas City Massacre of June 18, 1933, in which four lawmen and their prisoner, Frank "Jelly" Nash, were machine-gunned to death. Floyd was incensed by the charge and wrote to the police and newspapers denying any complicity in the massacre. Subsequent disclosures combined with his uncharacteristically vehement denial indicated Floyd probably was innocent.

Innocent or guilty, Floyd had only a little over a year to live. Labeled Public Enemy No. 1, he reportedly was forced to disguise himself as a woman to avoid detection (he had attended Birdwell's funeral in such garb). For a short time, Pretty Boy apparently hooked up with the Dillinger gang, but he generally operated with his own gang, with Adam Richetti as his main partner.

Floyd avoided several police traps set after tips from informers, further building his legend. Meanwhile, his wife was cashing in on the legend: early in 1934 Mrs. Ruby Floyd and her nine-year-old son toured the country promoting a film called *Crime Doesn't Pay*.

In October 1934 Floyd and Richetti were spotted in a wooded area near Wellsville, Ohio. The local police captured Richetti, but once again Floyd escaped. With Richetti identified, FBI agents under Melvin Purvis descended on the area, determined to tighten the ring on Floyd. On October 22 Floyd was cornered in a cornfield near East Liverpool. He ran in a zigzag pattern across the field, hoping to throw off the lawmen's aim, but went down with eight bullets in him.

Purvis hovered over the dying gangster and said, "You're Pretty Boy Floyd." Even as his life ebbed away, the gangster took offense at the nickname. "I'm Charles Arthur Floyd," he snapped. Another agent asked if he took part in the Kansas

City Massacre. Floyd raised himself up and uttered several obscenities, adding, "I won't tell you nothing." He died almost immediately thereafter.

See also: *Kansas City Massacre, Bill "the Killer" Miller.*

FORD, Charles (1858-1884): Plotter in the assassination of Jesse James

While it was Charley Ford's brother, Bob, who killed Jesse James, there have always been those who felt that Charley deserves more infamy than he has received.

"I saw the governor," Charley testified at the inquest after James' murder, "and he said $10,000 had been offered for Jesse's death, I went back and told Bob and he said that if I was willing to go, all right. Then we saddled up and rode over to the Samuel place. . . ."

Thus did Charley outline the script for the killing of Jesse James. There is much to indicate that contacting Gov. Thomas T. Crittenden of Missouri was more Charley's idea than Bob's and many Missourians felt that older brother Charley knew how to manipulate his younger brother. Certainly, things did work out somewhat better for Charley, at least on the surface. He allowed Bob to get the credit, or discredit, for the assassination, but shared equally in the reward and enjoyed an equal share of the profits in their stage appearances as *The Outlaws of Missouri.* Yet, virtually all the boos, catcalls and ripe fruit were directed at brother Bob.

Charley was found dead in his Richmond, Mo. hotel room on May 6, 1884, a suicide, according to the coroner. Quite naturally, his death was thought to be an act of remorse by a man who had been denounced as having one of "the blackest hearts in Creation."

See also: *Thomas T. Crittenden, Robert Newton Ford, James Brothers.*

FORD, Emma (c.1870-?): Female crook

Detective Clifton Wooldridge, a turn-of-the-century historian of criminality in Chicago, described a black woman named Emma Ford as the most dangerous strong-arm woman in the city. In point of fact, it would be a close call between Emma and another black woman, Flossie Moore, with whom she maintained a sometimes-friendly, sometimes-unfriendly rivalry.

Emma was a highly successful pickpocket and panel-house worker, but her first love was always violent street muggings. Operating alone or teaming up with her sister, Pearl Smith, Emma would prowl Chicago's South Side and attack men with razors, brass knuckles, knives, guns and sawed-off baseball bats. One of her favorite tactics when a victim did not prove instantly submissive was to slash his knuckles with a razor. Emma Ford had an imposing air about her, being over six feet tall and weighing over 200 pounds. She had both strength and pantherlike agility. According to detective Wooldridge: "She would never submit to arrest except at the point of a revolver. No two men on the police force were strong enough to handle her, and she was dreaded by all of them." While incarcerated in Denver before coming to Chicago, she once seized a prison

guard by the hair, lifted him off the floor and plucked out his whiskers one by one. In the Cook County Jail she once held a guard submerged in a water trough until he almost drowned. On another occasion she badly scarred six other female convicts with a hot iron. Every time she was released from jail, the word would spread rapidly, and unhappily, throughout the Levee that "Emma Ford's loose again."

Emma terrorized the South Side area until 1903, when she vanished. Speculation had it that she had been set on by a half-dozen male toughs and sent to her reward, or had returned to Denver, or had gone to New York, or had found a "loving man" and gone off to raise a family. In any event, Chicago did not see her again.

See also: *Custom House Place, Flossie Moore, Panel Houses, Clifton Wooldridge.*

FORD, Robert Newton (1860-1892): Assassin of Jesse James

Bob Ford was the "dirty rotten coward who shot Mr. Howard" of American ballad folklore, Mr. Howard being the alias used in 1882 by the outlaw Jesse James.

At 22, Bob Ford was a minor member of the James gang as well as a cousin of the Jameses. At the time, the James gang had broken into factions and Jesse was in the process of reorganizing it to rob a bank in Platte City. Jesse didn't trust Bob Ford or his brother Charley, but he was scraping the bottom of the barrel for gunmen. It was a fatal mistake. The Ford brothers were in negotiations, either through Charley or through an intermediary, with Missouri Gov. Thomas Crittenden, who was offering them pardons and $10,000 in reward money for bringing in Jesse James dead.

When Jesse, or "Mr. Howard," welcomed the brothers into his home on the outskirts of St. Joseph, Mo., he did so wearing his gun harness, which he kept on till he finished breakfast. Then Jesse walked into the parlor to talk to the Fords, by this time a little more relaxed. He took off his holster and tossed it aside and then got up on a chair to straighten out a picture. It was a chance Bob Ford knew he would not likely get again. He drew his single-action Colt .44 and thumbed back the hammer. The slight sound was enough to make Jesse start to turn around. Ford's gun blasted and the famed outlaw tumbled to the floor, instantly dead. His wife, Zerelda, rushed from the kitchen to cradle the bloody head of her dead husband.

Ford said in a stunned voice, still unable to comprehend that he had killed the great outlaw, "It went off accidentally," to which Zerelda James replied, "Yes, I guess it did."

Charley Ford was already out the door to telegraph Gov. Crittenden. Ford quickly surrendered and was tried and convicted of murder. However, the governor, true to his word, pardoned both Fords and saw that Bob got his reward money. Crittenden was sure his actions in the matter would be applauded, but instead, public opinion turned on him, and his political career was wrecked.

Bob Ford and his brother hit the entertainment trail to tell the story of how Jesse James had been killed. Audiences flocked to see the act, mainly to hiss and boo Bob. In September 1882 the pair appeared at Bunnell's Museum in New York. The *Police Gazette* reported: "They will give exhibitions of how they did up Jesse James and sold his cold meat for the reward of $10,000. As the 'Jesse James Avengers' are said to be upon their track, the museum will be put in a state of defense. Manager Starr will wear an armor-lined shirt and will be seated on a Gatling gun while taking tickets. Any suspicious person attempting to pass him will be put on the deadhead list."

When Bob Ford, the slayer of Jesse James, began making personal appearances after the shooting, crowds turned out to hiss and boo.

A few years later, especially after Charley Ford committed suicide in 1884, Bob took heavily to drink—due to a guilty conscience, some said—and then married. He moved west and opened a saloon and gambling joint in Walsenburg, Colo. In 1892 the Fords were operating a new saloon-whorehouse in Creede, Colo., where they separated the miners from their silver. Mrs. Ford ran the sex side of the business while Ford handled the bar and the gambling. He also handled the rough stuff, especially from other gambling interests trying to drive him out. Chief among these was Jefferson "Soapy" Smith, a con man and killer who was to become famous later for his depredations in the Klondike.

On the afternoon of June 8, 1892, a man carrying a double-barreled shotgun stepped into Ford's tent saloon and, without a word, raised it up and blew the killer of Jesse James away. The man was Edward O'Kelly, who was related by marriage to the Younger brothers and thus sort of a kin to Jesse James. There was some question about whether that was the reason he had killed Ford or whether there was some private grudge between them or whether Soapy Smith had paid him to eliminate the competition. In any event, O'Kelly was sent to prison for 20 years. Since his act was rather popular, it was hardly surprising that he was granted a full pardon after serving just two years.

Nobody seemed to mourn the "dirty rotten coward who shot Mr. Howard," and Jesse James admirers, whose numbers were then legion, observed with some satisfaction that Bob Ford had not lived to be as old as his celebrated victim.

See also: *Thomas T. Crittenden, Charles Ford, James Brothers, Edward O'Kelly.*

FOREMAN, Percy (1904-): Defense attorney

Perhaps the greatest accolade that can be heaped on a defense attorney comes not from judges, prosecutors, students of the law or even grateful clients but from other defense lawyers. One who stands in the front ranks of the profession, Texas attorney Richard "Racehorse" Haynes says he has tried to pattern himself after his idol, Percy Foreman. In recent years any list of leading criminal lawyers would count Haynes, Edward Bennett Williams, F. Lee Bailey and, of course, Foreman on the fingers of the first hand.

Foreman, operating out of Houston, clearly deserves this distinction. In a legal career that has spanned five decades, he has represented more than 1,500 capital case defendants and has lost probably less than five percent to prison and only one to the executioner.

In the courtroom Foreman often comes across at first as a somewhat ridiculous-looking figure, a hulking six-feet four-inch 250 pounder with baggy pants. However, he certainly has done well by the vast majority of his clients, with his grandstanding methods getting many a defendant off when earlier courtroom wisdom had declared that a conviction was inescapable. In one case, Foreman's client was a woman who had killed her husband, a cattleman, because he had used a whip on her. Addressing the jury, the lawyer picked up the long black whip from the counsel table and cracked it continuously. When he finished, the jury was ready and willing to vote the lady a medal of honor.

It has long been Foreman's tack to save his client by focusing on the murder victim as a person most deserving of being killed. He worked wonders in the 1966 scandal-ridden trial of Candy Mossler by portraying murder victim Jacques Mossler as a "depraved" deviate who could have been killed by many different persons. Candy was acquitted and then engaged in a long and stormy quarrel with Foreman for the return of jewels she had given him as security. His final fee worked out to something like $200,000 and assorted baubles.

Over the years Foreman has taken all sorts of security for later payment of fees, including a few dozen pianos, five elephants and a pool table (fittingly, since the lady in the case said she shot her husband because he was always playing pool). While Foreman has always had a reputation for showing no mercy when billing the well-heeled, he has often represented penniless defendants without charge.

At times, Foreman, like most great defense lawyers, seems cynical about the law. He is fond of quoting Aaron Burr, who defined the law as "whatever is boldly asserted and plausibly maintained." However, Foreman, like his brethren of the craft, knows that it is the state which does most of the asserting, leaving the average defendant at a disadvantage.

What has made Foreman a great legal light has been his ability to understand human reasoning and communicate with jurors. That and, of course, the knack of picking the right jurors. He once said: "If you have a drunken-driver client, you ask a prospective juror if he's ever been a member of a temperance organization. If he simply says no, pay no attention. But if he says no and gives a little grin at the same time, grab him!"

FORMBY Gang: Chicago youth gang

Contrary to popular opinion, the term "Chicago gangster" did not first come into vogue with the appearance of the Capone mob in the 1920s but some two decades earlier, when young punks had virtually taken over the community. Typical gangs included the Car Barn Bandits, the Market Streeters, the Briscoes, the Feinberg gang, the Trilby gang, the Brady gang, and the Formby gang, perhaps the most brutal of all.

Not a single member of the Formby gang was 20 years old, yet they committed a number of the city's most vicious crimes, including murder. Headed by a trio of young toughs—David Kelly, 16, Bill Dulfer, 17, and Jimmy Formby, 18—the gang committed hundreds of burglaries and robberies. Formby and Dulfer were the top "gunners" of the gang; the former murdered a street car conductor in 1904 and the latter slayed two men while the gang held up a saloon. Dulfer boasted of gunning down both victims at the same time. "I didn't even have to aim to hit 'em," he said. "Just held a gun in each hand and let go. They both went down. I saw 'em fall, that was all I wanted." When he was captured by the police, he asked that he be charged with murder rather than robbery. "I'm a killer, not a robber," he insisted.

While Dulfer and Formby got long prison terms, the city's problem with their gang or others like it was far from over. In 1906 the *Chicago Tribune* reported the young gangster menace was worse than ever: "It is not unusual for a boy six years old to be arrested for a serious offense. Boys who should be at home learning their ABC's are often found with cheap revolvers and knives." In one police precinct, the newspaper found, arrests of boys under the age of 16 for serious crimes totaled about 60 per month.

The newspaper concluded, "Chicago is terrorized by . . . criminals who have helped to make the name 'Chicago' a byword for crime-breeding throughout the country." It was from these fields that the O'Donnells, the O'Banions, the Lakes, the Druggans and finally the Torrios and the Capones plucked so many of their members and perpetuated the concept of the Chicago gangster.

FORT Smith Elevator: Frontier newspaper

It has become common today to speak with disapproval of Judge Isaac Parker, better known as Hanging Parker, but it should be remembered that he was dealing in one of the most lawless areas of the country, the territory west of Fort Smith, Ark. The man reflected the times, and the support and adulation he enjoyed was considerable among those who wanted the territory "civilized." While Parker may have been attacked by the Eastern press, he had enthusiastic grass roots support. For example, it is hard to find a critical comment on the judge and the justice he dispensed at Fort Smith in the columns of the city's leading newspaper, the *Elevator*. Its comments proved that Parker was not an aberration but rather a reflection of the inhabitants' mood; his justice was their justice. When Lincoln Sprole was sentenced for the brutal double murder of a farmer and his young son, the *Elevator* commented, "It is only to be regretted that he has not two necks to break instead of one." It was the sort of statement Hanging Parker would make from the bench. The *Elevator* expressed wry satisfaction with Parker justice following the conviction of Crawford Goldsby, better known as Cherokee Bill, noting that the defendant had been found guilty of only one murder but was wanted in four other states for murder and adding, "He will hardly be wanted by any other state after they get through with him here."

When Cherokee Bill escaped the hangman because of appeals to the Supreme Court and eventually murdered a jailer, the *Elevator* ranted (some say the words were secretly written by Parker himself):

> For the benefit of those who may not understand why Cherokee Bill was not hanged (why he was allowed to remain alive long enough to commit another brutal murder), we will say that his case was appealed to the Supreme Court of the United States upon what is known in law as technicalities—little instruments sometimes used by lawyers to protect the rights of litigants but oftener used to defeat the ends of justice. It will remain there until the bald-headed and big-bellied respectables who compose that body get ready to look into its merits. . . .

See also: *Isaac C. "Hanging Judge" Parker.*

FORTUNE Society

Recognizing that one way to reduce crime is to maximize the opportunities for those who have been in trouble in the past, the Fortune Society, formed in 1967, is probably the most well-known ex-convict rehabilitation organization in America.

At the heart of the society's program is a one-to-one counseling program, ex-offender to ex-offender, that aims through tutoring programs to raise educational levels and encourage development of careers. Over 1,500 new persons each year come to the Fortune Society's offices in New York for help; of these about 100 are teenagers, most with arrest and conviction records.

The organization evolved from a 1967 off-Broadway play, *Fortune and Men's Eyes,* written by an ex-convict, John Herbert. The play's producer, David Rothenberg, developed a weekly forum to permit audiences to learn about prison life and problems. Ex-cons joined these theatrical forums, and they learned how little the "square world" knew about the prison experience. Members of the audience began inviting ex-convict panels to address their church or school groups. The Fortune Society at first operated out of a desk in founder and executive director David Rothenberg's office but by 1980 had offices on Park Avenue South with a full-time staff of 18 ex-cons and nine others plus hundreds of volunteers. The society has been successful in finding jobs for about 300 ex-offenders a year. It does not claim to have a magical formula for crime prevention and reduction but rather shares those experiences that have worked in practice. In many instances other programs and localities have utilized elements of the Fortune Society's program.

FORTUNE-TELLER Swindles: See Handkerchief Switch.

FORTY Little Thieves: 19th century juvenile gang

Of all the New York juvenile gangs of the mid-19th century, few equaled the viciousness of the Forty Little Thieves, who took the name of the first adult criminal gang in the city with a disciplined membership. The Forty Little Thieves were often used by grown criminals as lookouts or decoys or to enter places to be burglarized through openings that would not admit an adult, but the gang members, aged eight to about 13, committed a number of major crimes on their own, especially looting the wharves. Their leader was a tough little vixen named Wild Maggie Carson, a street orphan who supposedly took her first bath at the age of nine. Under her leadership the gang, according to the police, committed a number of murders, but none was ever proved.

In her 13th year, Wild Maggie went through a remarkable reformation when the Rev. L. M. Pease opened a mission in the Five Points section in 1850 for the very purpose of saving juveniles. Under Pease, Wild Maggie learned the joy of sewing buttons on shirts and she became as efficient a seamstress as she had been a mugger. When she was 15, Maggie was adopted by a good family, and she eventually married well. Wild Maggie was the exception rather than the rule, as most of the Forty Little Thieves grew up to join the great gangs of the Civil War era.

FORTY Thieves: 19th century New York gang

The first criminal gang in New York City with a disciplined membership and an acknowledged leadership was the Forty Thieves, a group of Lower East Side Irish immigrants who served as political sluggers as well as muggers and holdup men.

The gang, which was formed in the early 1820s, met regularly in a grocery speakeasy run by a colorful wench named Rosanna Peers on what is now Center Street. In that speakeasy their chieftain, Edward Coleman, would parcel out assignments and criminal beats to the stickup artists. Each man was expected to bring in a certain amount of loot and knew that if he consistently missed his quota, there were a number of younger criminals in the area eager for the opportunity to join the Thieves.

It was perhaps unrealistic to think that a gang of that size could maintain such discipline in an area as lush as early New York, and indeed, by 1850 the Forty Thieves had just about dissolved as a result of individual members striking out on their own or joining other bigger, more loosely organized gangs. Oddly, the name Forty Thieves then passed on to the Tammany Hall politicians, who by 1850 had begun their systematic looting of the city treasury. The Common Council of 1850 was given the sobriquet Forty Thieves, an affront to the remnants of the old gang of strong-arm robbers, who regarded themselves as much more honorable than politicians.

FORTY-TWO Gang: Chicago juvenile gang

Perhaps the worst juvenile gang ever produced by this country, the 42 Gang out of the "Patch," or Littly Italy, section of Chicago became a source of recruits for the Chicago mobs in the post-Al Capone era.

Even among the wild juvenile gangs of the 1920s, the 42ers were known as crazy, willing to do anything for a quick buck. They stripped cars, knocked over cigar stores, held up nightclubs, slipped into peddlers' stables and stole from their carts or killed their horses, hacking off the hind legs to sell as horse meat. Many neighborhood Italian girls idolized the 42ers, not only becoming their sexual playthings but also going along with them on their nightly crime capers to act as lookouts or "gun girls," secreting the gangsters' weapons under their skirts until needed so that the boys would be "clean" if stopped by police.

The gang derived their name from the story of Ali Baba and the Forty Thieves, which always fascinated them. In 1925 they decided to go Ali Baba two better and called themselves the 42 Gang, an exaggerated figure since at their "founding" meeting there were only 24 members. But in ensuing years their numbers did grow to about 42. The violence-prone gang committed any number of murders, including stoolies and policemen among their victims, but paid a high price. In 1931 University of Chicago sociologists conducted a study of the gang and came up with some staggering statistics. More than 30 of those considered to be the original 42ers had either been killed or maimed or were doing time for such crimes as murder, rape, armed robbery or other felonies.

In 1928, when a number of 42ers were confined to the boys reformatory at St. Charles, the institution's head, Major William J. Butler, received a long-distance phone call from Chicago. "This is the 42 Gang," he was informed. "Unless you let our pals go, we'll come down there and kill everybody we see. We've got plenty of men and some machine guns." Butler was inclined to laugh off the threat until Chicago police told him the 42ers probably meant it. The state militia was called out to guard the school, and Butler armed himself with a gun. A few days later, a 42er advance guard of three punks headed by Crazy Patsy Steffanelli was picked up outside the reformatory walls. Crazy Patsy readily admitted harboring plans to machine-gun his buddies to freedom. The incident brought forth a spate of stories about the 42ers, pointing out they should not be sent to St. Charles (an institution meant primarily for wayward boys rather than hardened criminals), even those of a tender age. The *Chicago Tribune* editorialized that the 42ers were a separate criminal class and should be sent either to such higher institutions as Joliet or to the electric chair.

The great ambition of the 42ers was to receive recognition from the big bootleggers and the Caponeites, and after a successful caper they would turn up in mob hangouts, dressed to the hilt and spending money like water. While the big bootleggers occasionally used them as beer runners or drivers, they still regarded the 42ers as "those crazy boys."

But even the Capone men could eventually be convinced by enough accomplishments. It was one of the "mooniest" of the gang, Sam Giancana, who finally made it into the syndicate, winning the support of its two top men, Paul Ricca and Tony Accardo, who took Giancana on as his driver. When Giancana finally proved he could curb his temper and wild behavior and be a disciplined, cunning gangster, he quickly moved up the organizational ladder, eventually becoming head of the entire outfit. And with Giancana's climb, the remnants of the 42 Gang were integrated into the mob.

See also: *Sam "Teets" Battaglia, Fiore "Fifi" Buccieri, Sam "Momo" Giancana.*

FOUNTAIN, Albert Jennings (1838-1896): Murder victim

The Wild West's most-celebrated unsolved murder was that of Colonel Albert Jennings Fountain and his eight-year-old son, who were killed on January 31, 1896 in New Mexico Territory.

A world traveler, former journalist and leading lawyer, Fountain had been appointed a territorial judge and during his judicial career had sent a number of well-connected men to the penitentiary. At the time of his murder, the judge was deeply involved in a Lincoln County grand jury investigation of cattle rustling that was expected to implicate certain prominent individuals. Returning to their home at Las Cruces, Fountain and his child disappeared along the Tularosa-Las Cruces road. Their bodies were not found for several days. Eventually, three men—Oliver Lee, William McNew and James Gililland—were charged with the murders but acquitted. In Lincoln County, there was a widely held suspicion, which persists to this day, that a political enemy of Fountain, a youthful Albert B. Fall, later to be involved in the Teapot Dome scandal, was implicated in the killings.

Had the Fountain murders occurred less than two decades before, at the time of the Lincoln County War, the incident would no doubt have erupted into another bloody frontier war, in which suspicions were investigated with six-gun and rifle. Historian W. Eugene Hollon theorized on this change in climate: "Maybe it was because the Southwest had finally reached the point in civilization where its people no longer would tolerate wholesale violence. And maybe too, in this corner of the vanishing frontier, the law had finally begun to arise over the ruin wrought by generations of lawlessness."

See also: *Albert B. Fall.*

Further reading: *The Life and Death of Colonel Albert Jennings Fountain* by A. M. Gibson.

FOUR Deuces: Capone mob gambling den

One of the most notorious "pleasure" joints run by the Capone mob was a four-story structure on Chicago's South Wabash Ave. The first floor was given over to a bar, and gambling activities occupied the next two. The fourth floor sported a lavish bordello. It was also the scene of numerous murders.

The Four Deuces was not without competition, especially from the nearby Frolics Club, which dispensed both liquor and women at lower prices. This unfair competition was dealt with in an imaginative fashion. One night when a murder occurred in the Four Deuces, the boys lugged the body over to the Frolics and stuffed it into the furnace. One of the Capone men then called the police with an irate complaint that the Frolics was running an illegal crematorium. The police rushed over and found evidence of a corpse in the furnace. The Frolics was promptly padlocked, and the authorities ripped it apart in search of more corpses. None were found, but the Frolics never reopened.

"FOUR Hundred" Assassination List: Secret Service suspects

In the social world, the Four Hundred is a reference to status, but the "400" listing put together by the Secret Service's Protective Research Section refers to the most active potential political assassins in this country. Obviously, the 400 is not a complete or definitive grouping, but it does represent an effort to glean the most likely candidates for political violence out of a computer listing of 30,000 suspects maintained by the Secret Service.

Most of the persons on the larger list have made verbal or written threats against the president or are suspect for some other reason. They are routinely checked on whenever the president visits their locality. Members of the 400 are subjected to closer scrutiny. Since they are often mentally disturbed or have a history of violence, every effort is made to keep them far away from a presidential appearance. If legal or family restraints prove ineffective, the 400 suspect is put under close surveillance, an operation which may require the work of as many as 15 agents on a 24-hour basis.

Watching the 400 to make sure they don't harm the president can be dangerous for the agents. Many of them are well known to the agents, and this familiarity is a danger in itself. A case in point occurred in 1979. That year the Secret Service had Joseph Hugh Ryan committed to a mental hospital outside Washington, D.C. after he tried to break through a gate at the White House. Following his release, Ryan turned up in the Denver, Colo. office of the Secret Service to complain that he was being harassed by agents. Stewart Watkins tried to calm him down, but when the agent moved close to him, Ryan drew a .45-caliber pistol from under his coat and shot Watkins twice, killing him. Another agent then shot Ryan dead as the killer tried to turn his weapon on him.

Of course, neither the 400 grouping nor the larger computer listing is foolproof. Sara Jane Moore did not qualify for either of them despite the fact that she had threatened to kill President Gerald Ford and had one of her guns confiscated by San Francisco police the day before she took a potshot at the President in 1975. Moore was interviewed by two Secret Service agents but found to be "not of sufficient protective interest to warrant surveillance." Although she had a long history of erratic behavior, her name was not put on the computer listing because of the fact that she was simultaneously an informer for the FBI, the San Francisco police and the Treasury Department's Bureau of Alcohol, Tobacco and Firearms. It is possible that the Secret Service considered Moore's "kookie behavior" merely a cover for her other activities.

See also: *Secret Service*.

FRANCIS, Willy (1930-1947): Double execution case

If everything had gone normally in the execution of Willy Francis in Louisiana, the only unusual note in the matter would have been that he had paid the supreme penalty at a rather young age. However, the Willy Francis case was to result in a landmark decision on what constitutes cruel and unusual punishment.

A 17-year-old boy, Francis was sentenced to the electric chair for a murder he had committed when he was 15. As it turned out, he went to the chair twice. The first effort was botched when a malfunction in the chair caused him to receive an insufficient electric shock. Willy was returned to his death cell. When the state of Louisiana prepared to electrocute him a second time, his lawyers appealed to the Supreme Court that subjecting the youth to a second ordeal in the chair was cruel and unusual punishment. The Supreme Court ruled by a vote of five to four that since the first unsuccessful electrocution was only cruel because of an accident, it "did not make the subsequent execution any more cruel in the constitutional sense than any other execution." In May 1947, about a year after the first try, the chair worked fine.

Further reading: *Death and the Supreme Court* by Barrett Prettyman, Jr.

FRANK, Leo (1884-1915): Lynch victim

Probably the most infamous anti-Semitic lynching in America

was that of Leo Frank, a 29-year-old Atlanta businessman. Frank, Brooklyn-born, a graduate of Cornell and president of the Atlanta chapter of B'nai B'rith, managed the National Pencil Co. factory for his wife's uncle. On Saturday, April 26, 1913, Confederate Memorial Day, the factory was shut but Frank was there catching up on paper work. At noon, as he later told police, 14-year-old Mary Phagan, all dressed up to go to the holiday parade, entered the plant to pick up her wages. Frank said she left immediately, but her body was found in the basement sometime after. She had been strangled and beaten. Penciled notes found by the body were supposedly written by the girl. One, addressed to "Mum," described her murderer as "a long, tall, sleam, black negro . . . that long tall black negro did buy his slef."

The next day Leo Frank was charged with the rape-slaying. James Conley, a semiliterate Negro employed at the factory made some startling accusations against Frank, among them that he had been summoned by the white man, shown Mary's dead body and told to carry it to the basement. In addition, he charged that Frank had ordered him to write the notes. At Frank's trial Conley also said that he had often seen Frank performing acts of sexual perversion with a number of young girls who worked at the factory.

Lynch-law pervaded the atmosphere during the 30-day trial. Mobs cheered the prosecutor and harangued the defense attorneys—"If the Jew doesn't hang, we'll hang you." A newspaper editorial declared: "Our little girl—*ours* by the eternal God!—has been pursued to a hideous death by this filthy perverted Jew from New York."

While the jury deliberated, crowds outside the courthouse kept chanting the "Jew monster" had to hang. Frank was found guilty and sentenced to death.

Leo Frank defense committees were formed in various parts of the nation. In Chicago 415,000 persons signed petitions asking Georgia's Gov. John M. Slaton to commute the death sentence, but the chief executive was also under considerable pressure, and threats of death, not to do so. The Frank defense brought in William J. Burns, perhaps the nation's leading detective, to investigate, and he turned up considerable proof of a police frame-up. The police would not open any of their records to Burns other than those he obtained with a court order; on one occasion Burns and his assistant barely escaped from a lynch mob determined to make the case against Frank stand. Ironically, this was perhaps the first murder case in the South in which the word of a black was taken over that of a white man.

Burns discovered a witness, a black woman, who had been Conley's lover from time to time, and she signed a statement that Conley had told her he had killed the white girl. She also had 100 sexually explicit love notes from Conley in which he had described himself performing the very acts he later accused Frank of. In response to the Burns findings, Gov. Slaton commuted Frank's death sentence; it proved to be an act of political suicide. "The Annie Maude Carter notes, which were not before the jury, were powerful evidence in behalf of the defendant," he wrote. "These letters are the most obscene and lecherous I have ever read."

A Northern newspaper editorial announced, "The reign of terror in Georgia is over." But it was not. On August 17, 1915, two months after the commutation, 25 members of a secret vigilante group—the Knights of Mary Phagan—entered the Milledgeville Prison Farm and, without any resistance from armed prison guards, took Frank away with them on a ghastly 175-mile ride to Marietta, the murdered girl's hometown. Leo Frank was lynched there before a howling, gloating mob. The lynchers then proudly posed for pictures around the hanging corpse.

Two months after the hanging, the Knights of Mary Phagan congregated on the top of Stone Mountain near Atlanta to burn a cross and sing a folk song that had materialized out of the tragedy.

> Little Mary Phagan
> Went to town one day,
> Went to the pencil factory
> To get her little pay.
>
> Leo Frank, he met her
> With an evil heart and grin. . . .

There are many versions of the verses that followed, and it is still sung today in rural pockets of Georgia.

See also: *William J. Burns.*

FRANKLIN, Rufus "Whitey" (1912-?): Bank robber and murderer

Whitey Franklin was probably America's most-mistreated federal prisoner, even more so than Robert Stroud, the Birdman of Alcatraz.

A lean, slow-talking Alabaman, he first ran afoul of the law in 1927, when at age 15 he was arrested for stealing a car and sentenced to a chain gang. He later served another year for carrying a gun and, before he was 18, drew a life sentence for murder. Having oversentenced him as a youth, the state of Alabama made up for it, in a manner of speaking, by paroling him from his life sentence after he had served about six years. A fully committed criminal by then, he was arrested for bank robbery within two months of his release and ended up at Alcatraz doing 30 years.

On May 23, 1938 Franklin led two other convicts, Jimmy Lucas and Tom "Sandy" Limerick, on a desperate and foolish prison escape attempt. In the process, Franklin apparently bludgeoned a guard to death with a hammer. The escape, however, failed. Limerick was killed, Lucas surrendered and Franklin ended up trapped on barb wire atop the prison's furniture factory roof with bullets in both his shoulders.

Franklin and Lucas were both tried for the guard's murder and, much to the disgust of Alcatraz guards, got life sentences instead of the death penalty. Although the prosecution had considerable circumstantial evidence that Franklin was the killer, the jury had some doubts and recommended a life sentence for both defendants.

Lucas suffered much harsh treatment through the years, but it was nothing compared to what Franklin received. He was put into an isolation cell, which convicts called the hole, totally cut off from all contact with the rest of the prison. It was always assumed by the rest of the prisoners that Franklin was beaten regularly by the guards and physically and mentally abused in many other ways. In 1946, following the great revolt at Alcatraz, an investigation of prison conditions found that Whitey Franklin was still in his solitary cell—after seven years and 21 days straight. His skin was dry and had a pasty look from his long years of confinement.

When reporters asked Warden James A. Johnston how long the prisoner would remain in solitary, Johnston (frequently described in magazines and newspapers as "stern but fair") replied, "As long as necessary for discipline." Sometime after the public revelation of Franklin's fate, he was transferred to an electrically locked isolation cell, where he would remain. He was fed the same prison fare as other convicts, a treatment he had not received earlier, and on rare occasions was taken for a walk in the exercise yard, but he never saw another prisoner and his guards did not say a word to him. In time, few of the Alacatraz prisoners even remembered him.

It must be assumed that Franklin is now dead, since it is doubtful he ever would have been granted a parole. In 1977 author Clark Howard, who was writing a book on the 1946 revolt, attempted to find out from the U.S. Bureau of Prisons if either Franklin or Lucas was still alive and, if so, still confined in prison or free. He was informed that neither man was within the federal prison system. Subsequent requests to determine whether they had died in prison brought no response.

See also: *James Lucas.*

FRANKS, Bobby: See Leopold and Loeb.

FRAZER-MILLER Feud: Texas lawmen's duels

One of the most-storied feuds in Texas involved two lawmen of the early 1890s, G. A. "Bud" Frazer and Killin' Jim Miller.

Frazer was elected sheriff of Reeves County in 1890 and shortly thereafter appointed Miller, a Pecos hotel owner, as his deputy. At the time, Miller already had the nickname of Killin' Jim, apparently having gunned down a number of men, but in Pecos he seemed to lead a respectable life. When Miller killed a Mexican prisoner in 1892, Frazer fired him. Miller claimed the Mexican had resisted arrest, but the real reason for the killing was that the prisoner knew Miller was engaged in mule stealing.

Frazer also had Miller charged with livestock theft, but since it was Miller's word against that of a "dead Mex," he was soon freed. Later that year Miller ran against Frazer for the sheriff's post but lost. A short while after, Miller was named city marshal of Pecos, and the feud between the two men festered. Finally, in a violent confrontation Frazer shot Miller in the arm in a duel on a Pecos street. Miller, his gun incapacitated, fired back but managed only to wing a spectator. Frazer then emptied his pistol into his foe's chest and walked away, certain he had killed him. He was rather surprised later to hear that Miller had recovered.

A few months afterward, Frazer lost his race for a third term and moved on to the New Mexico Territory. He returned in December 1894 and encountered Miller. The inevitable shoot-out occurred and Frazer again got the best of it, hitting Miller in the arm and leg. He then pumped two more shots into the wounded man's chest, but incredibly, Miller would not go down. Frazer fled the scene. It became a part of Texas folklore that Miller's life had been saved in the two duels because he had worn a hidden steel breastplate.

Frazer would have needed more than a breastplate to save him in the pair's third and final confrontation on September 14, 1896, when he was visiting his family in Toyah, Tex. Miller spotted Frazer playing cards in a saloon and blasted him with a shotgun from outside the door, blowing away most of his head and face. When Frazer's sister came at Miller with a gun, the gunfighter warned her, "I'll give you what your brother got—I'll shoot you right in the face!"

Miller was tried for Frazer's murder, but the first trial ended in a hung jury because of the argument that the victim had started the shooting feud more than two years earlier. In a second trial, however, Miller was convicted, but that verdict was set aside on appeal. No more legal action was taken against Miller, who went on to become one of the West's most-feared professional killers—he once boasted his victims totaled 51—until he was lynched in 1909 in Ada, Okla. after his murder-for-pay of another ex-lawman.

FRENCHY: See Old Shakespeare.

FRICK, Henry Clay: See Alexander Berkman.

FRIENDLY Friends: Chicago madams' association

In the early 1900s a group of "better class" madams in Chicago formed a trade society "to protect our interests," which meant, among other things, controlling prices and competition and, most importantly, seeing they got their money's worth for the protection they bought.

The Friendly Friends specifically did not invite the most successful madams of the era, the Everleigh sisters, to join. In fact, most of their proceedings were given over to investigating ways of eliminating the fabulous Everleigh Club, the city's most-renowned brothel, which took away so much of the "cream" of the business from their own fashionable establishments. The Friendly Friends were reportedly behind a number of plots to frame the Everleighs in various ways. When a young male member of a leading Chicago family accidentally shot himself in his home in 1905, a story spread that the man had really been the victim of a shooting in the Everleigh Club. The rumor was later put to rest after it was revealed that a

black vice operator, Pony Moore, had offered one of the Everleigh Club's courtesans $20,000 to sign an affidavit confirming the alleged shooting. It was generally agreed that most of the money for the bribe plus whatever went to Moore had come from the Friendly Friends.

The leaders of the society were madams Zoe Millard, Georgie Spencer and Vic Shaw. Madam Millard was the most disturbed of all by the Everleigh competition and once administered a frightful battering to one of her prize bawds for speaking nicely of the Everleighs. Madam Spencer was the hell raiser of the group, ready with a complaint to the police whenever anything occurred that displeased her. Her wrath intensified greatly when police pressure increased as a result of public indignation over the vice in Chicago's Levee area. "Redolent of riches and ablaze with diamonds," according to one account, she stormed into the office of police Capt. Max Nootbaar, hammered on his desk with her jeweled fist and declared: "Listen to me, policeman! I'm rich. I own a hotel that's worth forty-five thousand dollars. I own a flat worth forty thousand, and these stones I'm wearing are worth another fifteen thousand. I'd like to see you interfere with my business."

Capt. Nootbaar was that rare bird, an honest Chicago police officer, and he eventually drove Madam Spencer into wealthy retirement in California.

Of all the Friendly Friends, Vic Shaw held on the longest, trying to keep the society in business even after the shuttering of the Levee district. She continued later with a lavish call house on South Michigan Avenue. As late as 1938 when she was about 70 years old, she turned up operating a similar resort on the North Side.

See also: *Everleigh Sisters, Nathaniel Ford Moore.*

FRISCO Sue (1853-?): Stagecoach robber

Despite the Hollywood concept of the cowgirl hellion, the number of Western badwomen can be counted on one's fingers. The facts about even those who really existed have been steeped in the stuff of which legends are made. One of the real female villains was a lady known simply as Frisco Sue, a former San Francisco dance hall shill and prostitute, supposedly of breathtaking beauty.

In 1876, at the age of 23, Frisco Sue left for the Nevada gold fields, not to trim the miners, as other prostitutes did, but rather to reform herself. Sue decided she could escape her dreary profession by turning to a career of violent crime. Realizing she could not work alone, she shopped around for a suitable partner and finally settled on a minor road agent named Sims Talbot. If Talbot had any misgivings about working with a woman, Frisco Sue had, we are assured by various biographers of the day, all the necessary charms to make him forget them.

Sue's plans were to become very rich and transport herself to a new life in Europe, posing as an orphaned heiress. But that dream was to founder in the reality of her life of crime. The couple's first effort at stagecoach robbing netted them only

$500—Sue had rolled society drunks for more than that in her California days. She was furious, and Talbot had a hard time calming her down. But he quickly hit upon a daring scheme that appealed to her. Now that the stage had been robbed, Talbot explained, the line would be confident it would not be robbed again right away and would therefore put on board a valuable shipment. So the couple held up the same stagecoach on its return run. Talbot's strategic thinking was less than perfect: this time the stage carried two shotgunners. Talbot had barely time to announce, "Hands up!" when he was blasted out of his saddle, shot dead. Frisco Sue was captured and sent to prison for three years. The Western press would not let her legend die, however, and there was always a story about some blade's plans to bust the lady free. It didn't happen. Frisco Sue served her time and then disappeared. According to one oft-told tale, she was seen a number of years later in San Francisco, married to a millionaire, but then the West always liked stories that ended with a happy and ironic twist.

FRYE v. United States: Lie detector ruling

Almost without exception, courts have refused to accept lie detector findings as evidence in courtroom proceedings, generally falling back of the landmark decision in *Frye* v. *United States,* ironically one that would have saved an innocent man from prison had it gone the other way.

In 1920 Dr. Robert Brown, a leading physician in Washington, D.C. was shot to death in his office. An arrest was finally made about a year later. Police said a robbery suspect, a young black named James Alphonse Frye, had confessed to the murder. Before the trial Frye repudiated his confession, saying he had made it only because he had been offered half the reward if he was convicted. Frye's young lawyers asked Dr. William M. Marston, a pioneer polygraphist, to conduct a test with his newly perfected lie detector. Acting without fee, Marston did so and was surprised to find that his examination agreed with Frye's claims of innocence.

At Frye's trial the defense team tried to introduce Marston's evidence but was overruled by the judge. Even the offer to submit the defendant to a new test in the courtroom was rejected. Frye was found guilty, but only of second-degree murder; the jury had apparently been impressed by the mention of the lie detector test in open court. He was sentenced to life imprisonment. Appeals of the case resulted in a federal court ruling that lie detector findings were in a "twilight zone" and lacked reliability and validity.

Finally, after Frye had been in prison for three years, another man confessed to the murder of Dr. Brown, and after an intensive investigation, Frye was released. However, his freedom did not erase the federal appellate court decision that remains a legal precedent to this day.

See also: *Lie Detector.*

FUGMANN, Michael (1884-1937): Murderer

Veterans of the bloody coal mine union organizing days of the 1930s in Wilkes-Barre, Pa. still remember with horror the frightful Easter season of 1936, when wholesale death came through the mails.

The first of six Easter gifts, each apparently a box of cigars, came to the home of Tom Maloney on the morning of Good Friday. Maloney had left his position as a leader of a union of anthracite coal miners to join John L. Lewis' United Mine Workers of America. When Maloney opened the box, it blew up, killing him and his four-year-old son. Meanwhile, a second homemade bomb in a cigar box was being delivered via parcel post to 70-year-old Mike Gallagher, who died instantly when he opened it.

A third package was received by Luther Kniffen, former sheriff of Luzerne County, who made a mistake that saved his life. Inadvertently, he slit the box open from the rear, and, turning back the lid, found himself staring at two sticks of dynamite, a detonator cap and a trigger mechanism attached to the front of the lid. Authorities immediately sent out a citywide alert, and three other persons who had gotten cigar box-sized parcels in the mail notified postal officials. The boxes were opened under full precautions and discovered also to contain booby-trap bombs.

At first, there seemed to be little chance of finding the bomber. The cigar boxes were of a common type, and while dynamite and detonator caps might be traced in a big city, they were too readily available to be traced in a coal-mining area.

There was one clue, however, in the form of the small pieces of wood used in making the bombs. Just a few days before the bombings, Bruno Richard Hauptmann had been executed for the kidnap-murder of 20-month-old Charles Lindbergh, Jr. Probably the most damning evidence against him had been the testimony of Arthur Koehler, an expert on woods, who had traced one rung of the ladder used in the crime to the Hauptmann home. Koehler was summoned to Wilkes-Barre by postal authorities and asked to study the wood scraps. He soon traced the wood to the home of one of the many suspects in the case. Slats from which the bits of wood had been cut were found in the home of a miner named Michael Fugmann, an independent unionist opposed to the United Mine Workers. Found guilty of the crime, Fugmann went to the electric chair in June 1937, suffering the same fate as Hauptmann on much the same evidence.

See also: *Arthur Koehler.*

FUNERALS Of Gangsters

When Dion O'Banion, Chicago's notorious Irish gangster, went to his grave in 1924, a newspaper commented, "Presidents are buried with less to-do." His bronze and silver casket, made to order in Philadelphia and rushed to Chicago by express car, cost $10,000. Forty thousand persons passed through an undertaker's chapel to view the body as it "lay in state," as the *Chicago Tribune* put it.

To the "Dead March" from *Saul,* the pallbearers—triggermen Two Gun Alterie, Hymie Weiss, Bugs Moran, Schemer Drucci and Frank Gusenberg and labor racketeer Maxie Eisen, president of the Kosher Meat Peddlers' Association—bore the casket to the hearse. Close behind them came Johnny Torrio, Al Capone and their henchmen. Despite the solemnity of the occasion, police plainsclothesmen were still fearful of a shoot-out and circulated among the gangsters confiscating firearms.

The funeral procession was about a mile long, with 26 cars and trucks carrying flowers, including particularly garish ones sent by Torrio, Capone and the Genna brothers, all of whom probably had been involved in planning O'Banion's murder. Some 10,000 persons followed the hearse, jamming every trolley car to the Mount Carmel area, where the cemetery was situated. At the cemetery 5,000 to 10,000 more spectators waited.

"It was one of the most nauseating things I've ever seen happen in Chicago," commented Judge John H. Lyle, an honest Chicago jurist—somewhat of a rarity in that era.

The O'Banion funeral typified the gaudy gangster funerals of the 1920s. Similar, though not quite as lavish, treatment was given to any number of the O'Banion gang, as one after another went to his reward. Before the O'Banion funeral, with its 26-vehicle flower procession, a previously deceased member of the gang, Nails Morton, had been honored with 20 cars. When Hymie Weiss departed, the flower train dropped to 18 vehicles; a patient Bugs Moran had to explain to the grieving widow that since the passing of Morton and O'Banion, 30 others in the gang had expired, obviously reducing the number of donors and, consequently, the amount of flowers. After Schemer Drucci was shot dead by a police officer, his funeral was a touch less impressive than Weiss', although he still was buried under a blanket of 3,500 flowers. His widow commented, "A cop bumped him off like a dog, but we gave him a king's funeral."

Attendance at gangster funerals by public officeholders was more or less obligatory during this period. After all, the underworld had bought them and therefore, had a right to call on them. Thus, when Big Jim Colosimo, the great whoremaster and mentor of Johnny Torrio—who with Al Capone plotted his demise—was assassinated in 1920, the honorary and active pallbearers included two congressmen, three judges, a future federal judge, a state representative, 10 aldermen and a host of other politicians and community leaders. Mayor Big Bill Thompson sent personal representatives to express his heartfelt loss. It made sense, considering the fact that Colosimo's organization had piled up huge votes for Thompson and his Republican allies. In his eulogy of Big Jim, Alderman Bathhouse John Coughlin of the First Ward said: "Jim wasn't a bad fellow. You know what he did? He fixed up an old farmhouse for

broken-down prostitutes. They rested up and got back in shape and he never charged them a cent."

Into the 1930s the big gangster funeral was considered a must. "That's what buddies are for," one mobster explained to a reporter. However, by the time Al Capone died in 1947, low key was the vogue, and it has been basically that way ever since. The only untoward events at such affairs are scuffles between mobsters and reporters and photographers.

When Frank Costello died in 1973, his widow saw to it that his unsavory friends stayed away from the funeral. The burial ceremony was over in a few minutes. The only person to approach her was a cousin of Frank. Hat in hand, he whispered what she expected to be words of condolence. "What are you going to do with Frank's clothes?" he asked. Mrs. Costello walked on without bothering to answer.

FURY, Bridget (1837-1872?): Ruffian and murderer

With the exception of Mary Jane "Bricktop" Jackson, the toughest woman in New Orleans during the years just before and after the Civil War was a vicious free-lance prostitute, mugger and pickpocket known as Bridget Fury. Her real name was Delia Swift and she was born in Cincinnati. There, by the age of 13, she had become an accomplished criminal, working in a dance house where her father was a fiddler. When her father killed a girl in a fit of passion, Bridget moved on to New Orleans, where she plied her trade with a fighting fury that earned her her nickname and established her as a leading criminal of the French Quarter. For a time she teamed up with Bricktop Jackson and a few other vicious women in a gang that could best any group of sailor bullies.

In 1858 she murdered a man and was sent to prison for life but was freed in a general amnesty in 1862. Bridget immediately went back to her belligerent ways. After a few years she decided the violent life did not pay enough; so, with money raised from cracking skulls, she opened a brothel on Dryades Street in the late 1860s. In 1869 she was arrested on charges of robbing some $700 from two Texans visiting her house and was sent to prison for several months. Upon her release she found her brothel being run by others. A few years earlier Bridget Fury would have torn the place apart getting her due, but by then she was older and perhaps weary. Within another year she had turned into a gutter hag who was pulled in for drunkenness every two or three days. She was last seen around 1872 in such a state of deterioration that it was said she couldn't live more than a few weeks. The estimate was no doubt correct and after a brief time she was seen no more.

See also: *Mary Jane "Bricktop" Jackson*.

G

GACY, John Wayne (1942-): Mass murderer

Charged with 33 killings, more than any other mass murderer in American history, John Gacy was a building contractor who lived in a neat three-bedroom brick-fronted house in Knollwood Park Township, Ill., a Chicago suburb. During the period from 1972 to 1978, Gacy, who was in his thirties, murdered 33 boys and young men whom he had lured to his home with the promise of a job. After having sexual relations with them, he killed them and disposed of their bodies in a variety of ways.

Gacy was arrested in December 1978, when authorities traced a missing youth, 15-year-old Robert Piest, to his home. Twice-married, twice-divorced, he had come under suspicion after police learned that he had once served 18 months in an Iowa prison for sodomy with a teenage boy. By the time the killer was apprehended, however, young Piest was dead. Under questioning, following the discovery of three skeltons on his property, Gacy made a rambling statement. He had strangled the Piest boy and tossed his body in the Des Plaines River. Police began searching for victims and found three bodies in his garage, fished four out of the river and discovered 28 buried beneath the crawl space under his house. Of these, he was charged with a total of 33 deaths. It was clear that Gacy himself didn't know the exact count.

At his trial in March 1980, the chief issue was whether Gacy was a cold-blooded murderer who planned the killings or a mentally unbalanced man who lacked the capacity for understanding his actions. He was convicted and, on March 13, 1980, sentenced to the electric chair. At the time, the last execution in Illinois had occurred in 1962.

GALANTE, Carmine (1910-1979): Murdered mafioso

After the death of Vito Genovese in 1969, Carmine Galante was considered to be the most ruthless and brutal of Mafia leaders. It could only be guessed how many murders he had committed during a life of crime that dated back to 1921. He was known to have carried out many killings for Genovese, including the 1943 murder of radical journalist Carlo Tresca in New York. (Genovese was in Italy at the time and seeking to curry favor with Benito Mussolini, who was enraged by Tresca's antifascist activities.) Galante eventually became an underboss in the Joe Bananas family, specializing in narcotics trade.

He was finally sent to prison for 20 years on a narcotics charge. While serving time, he plotted to seize power from the other Mafia families in New York upon his release and was considered fearsome and capable enough to have done so. Even from prison, he ran the Bananas family, in which he had ascended to power in 1974, issuing orders to an estimated 200 members, among them many of the top gunners in the country.

The Bananas family had been nothing but grief for the other crime families in New York and elsewhere in the country. In 1964 its retired head, Joe Bananas, had plotted to eliminate virtually the entire governing board of the Mafia and take over. After waging a bloody five-year war, he gave up. Now, it appeared certain Galante would make the same try. Galante talked less than Bananas, believing the best policy was kill, kill, kill. Freed in 1979, he was gathering strength and making demands backed up with threats.

According to the underworld grapevine, a number of crime leaders held a meeting in Boca Raton, Fla. to decide the "Cigar" problem (Galante was noted for always having a large cigar in his mouth). Mob leaders not present were consulted about whether or not to issue a contract on him. Those said to have been involved included such big shots as Jerry Catena, Santo Trafficante, Phil Rastelli and Frank Tieri. Even the retired Joe Bananas was consulted and okayed the contract on Galante.

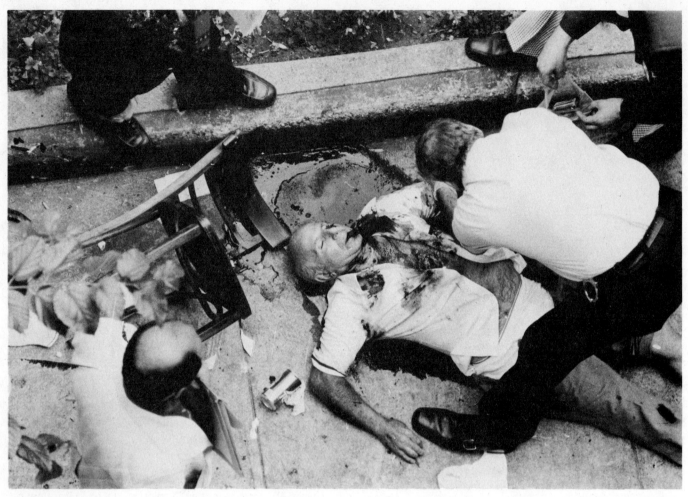

The assassination of mafioso Carmine Galante in the garden of a Brooklyn restaurant in 1979 was said to have solved the underworld's "Cigar" problem.

On July 12, 1979 Galante had just finished the main course of a meal in the outdoor rear area of an Italian restaurant in Brooklyn. His cigar was in his mouth and he held a glass of wine in his right hand. Three masked men suddenly came through the indoor restaurant into the courtyard.

"Get him, Sal!" one of the masked men said and a hood with a double-barreled shotgun stepped forward and fired two blasts into the gangster. Galante died with his cigar still in his mouth.

A joke that made the rounds in the underworld asked, What's the first thing Galante would do if he could come back to earth alive? Answer: Have dessert.

See also: *Vito Genovese, Carlo Tresca.*

GALLATIN Street: New Orleans crime area

From 1840 until 1880 Gallatin Street in New Orleans was described as having more crime per square foot than any street in America. Indeed, it had the distinction of not containing a single legitimate enterprise anywhere on its two-block length. Running from Ursuline Avenue to Barracks, it offered enough debaucheries from dusk to dawn to sate the country boys, city slickers, sailors and steamboat men seeking varied pleasures.

Such visitors, one historian noted, were in turn sought out by "a horde of harlots, sneak thieves, garroters who openly carried their deadly strangling cords, and footpads with slung shots looped about their wrists." There were barrelhouses where for five cents a man bought no mere glass of liquor but all the booze he could drink, dance houses that were also bordellos and sailors' boarding houses from which seamen were at times shanghaied. It was often said that a miracle man in New Orleans was one who could enter Gallatin at Ursuline with money in his pocket and emerge at Barracks with his cash and skull untapped. At times, the police entered the street by day in large armed groups but were nowhere to be seen after sunset.

Much of the mayhem on Gallatin Street was the work of the Live Oak Boys, a gang formed in 1858 by one Red Bill Wilson, a vicious thug who always concealed a knife in his bushy red beard. The Live Oak Boys were not a disciplined bunch. While they collected protection from virtually every house on the street, that was no guarantee they would not smash such a place to pieces when they had a mind to, which proved a rather common occurrence. Then too, they considered any payment they received from an establishment null and void if the proprietor of a rival business offered them a bounty to shut down the competition.

Despite such depredations, any resort on Gallatin was invariably a gold mine. Typical was Archie Murphy's, which in a decade of operation left the proprietor in a state a newspaper described as one of "extreme wealth." Murphy achieved that happy status by encouraging his girls "not to allow any sucker to get away." One of his more skillful harpies was Lizzie Collins. A foolhardy farmer once bragged to Lizzie that he had $110 in gold tied in a handkerchief around his leg. He shrewdly refused all drinks but jumped at Lizzie's invitation to go upstairs. As the couple entered Lizzie's room, three other harlots jumped on the man and held him while Lizzie poured whiskey down his throat. When the farmer was helpless, Lizzie retrieved the handkerchief with the gold and then called on the Murphy bouncers to toss the farmer into the alley. The farmer pressed charges and Lizzie was arrested, but the case was dismissed when the farmer could produce no evidence other than his word.

Lizzie Collins went on to suffer a bizarre fate. Years of drink addled her brain and she developed a mania for stealing items that Archie Murphy found little use for. Instead of taking a man's money, she would drug or knock him out and then cut all the buttons off his pants. Archie Murphy tried to get Lizzie to mend her ways, but he finally kicked her out. For some years thereafter, Lizzie stalked Gallatin Street practicing her strange pastime, becoming one additional peril for visitors to the street.

See also: *Bridget Fury, Mary Jane "Bricktop" Jackson, Live Oak Boys.*

GALLO, Crazy Joe (1929-1972): Brooklyn Mafia leader

Joseph Gallo was nicknamed Crazy Joe by rival Mafia figures who considered him "flaky" and hard to deal with. Crazy was all that and mean besides, but at the same time he was among the most perceptive of the new breed of underworld leaders. In the 1960s Crazy Joe recognized the changing tides in the underworld, the steady shift in power from Italian to black and sought to reach an accommodation with the emerging power structure, much in the fashion that Meyer Lansky had recognized the decline of Jewish gangsterism in the 1920s and allied with the Italian Mafia, under which he continued to prosper. In prison, Crazy Joe befriended black criminals. He attempted to break down convict color lines by having a black barber cut his hair; he became friends with Leroy "Nicky" Barnes and tutored him on taking over control of the drug racket in New York's Harlem and then far beyond; he sent released black prisoners to work. In all this, Crazy Joe realized nothing was permanent in crime. Years before, he had questioned the stranglehold the older underworld element had on various activities. "Who gave Louisiana to Frank Costello?" he once demanded in a conversation taped by law enforcement officials.

Crazy Joe started his criminal career at the age of 17, accumulating such charges as assault, burglary and kidnapping.

He moved up rapidly in the Carlo Gambino family and was believed to be the chief gunman in the murder of Albert Anastasia in 1957. Gallo went to war against the Profaci family, a war that took more than a dozen lives, because he felt the Gallos were entitled to a bigger slice of the rackets in Brooklyn. After Profaci died and Joe Colombo, Sr. became head of the Profaci family, the war continued. When Columbo was shot and "vegetabled," to use Gallo's term, the murderer turned out to be a black man, Jerome A. Johnson. Gallo was immediately brought in for questioning because of his ability to recruit black troops whenever he needed them. But nothing could be proved against him and he was released.

On April 7, 1972 Crazy Joe left the safe confines of his Brooklyn territory and went to Umberto's Clam House in New York's Little Italy to celebrate his 43rd birthday. It seemed safe. There was always a tacit agreement within the Mafia that no rubouts would take place in Little Italy. In Crazy Joe's case, however, an exception was made. The Gallo party was seated at two tables when a man walked in with a .38-caliber pistol in his hand. Women screamed and customers hit the floor as the killer opened up on Gallo. Gallo's two bodyguards fired back. In all, some 20 shots were fired before the assassin fled. Mortally wounded, Gallo staggered out the front door and collapsed and died in the middle of the street—one block from police headquarters.

See also: *Leroy "Nicky" Barnes, Joseph Colombo, Sr.*

GALLOWS Hill: Execution spot

A hill on the outskirts of Salem, Mass. was the site where a score of persons were hanged in 1692 during the witchcraft delusions. From that time on, it was known as Gallows Hill, even though during the period of public remorse attempts were made to give it another name. While there have been many other American towns with similarly named hills, Salem's has the distinction of being the oldest by far.

See also: *Salem Witchcraft Trials.*

GALLUS Mag (c.1860's): Female thug

Described by New York police as the most savage female ruffian of the period from just before to just after the Civil War, Gallus Mag was a towering six-footer known as the Queen of the Waterfront. Her antecedents were English, but little else was known about her. At times, she would refuse to give any information and, on other occasions, would provide varying and contradictory stories. Once when a saloon habitue asked Gallus Mag her age, she punished him for his nosiness by smashing his skull with a mallet, chewing off his ear and throwing him into the street.

Gallus Mag, who earned her nickname by wearing galluses, or suspenders, to hold her skirt up, held sway in the legendary Hole-In-The-Wall Saloon on New York City's Water Street, where she was a partner with One-Armed Charley Monell and acted as bouncer. The saloon was a "bucket of blood" where more men were said to have been robbed or killed than in any other watering hole of that era. Despite her duty to keep the peace, Gallus Mag was a prime cause of the violence. She would stalk the dive looking for trouble and was well prepared for it, with a pistol always tucked into her skirt and a bludgeon strapped to her wrist. Whenever she found a man violating the rules of the place, such as robbing a stranger without a permit from the management, whe would immediately crack him over the head. Her custom was to then seize the offender's ear between her teeth and drag him out the door. If her victim dared to struggle, she would bite his ear off. Gallus Mag became infamous for this act and kept all such severed ears in a huge jar of alcohol behind the bar, a trophy collection that was one of the more gory sights on the crime-ridden waterfront.

Gallus Mag's only real female competition was the notorious Sadie the Goat, so named because when she spotted a likely victim for a mugging she would lower her head and butt him in the stomach. A blow to the head would end the victim's resistance, and Sadie would rifle his pockets at leisure. One day Sadie attempted to butt her way to a victory over Gallus Mag, but a mallet proved more than a match for Sadie the Goat's skull. Gallus Mag chewed off her rival's ear, and Sadie fled the East Side waterfront in disgrace. The vanquished warrior later achieved great fame as the leader of the Charlton Street pirates on the West Side, who terrorized the Hudson River for many miles north of the city. When the Charlton Streeters were finally broken up, Sadie the Goat returned to the East Side and made her peace with Gallus Mag, accepting Mag's primacy as the queen of the area. This total surrender so impressed Gallus Mag that she magnanimously fished around in her alcohol jar of ears and returned Sadie's severed member to her.

Gallus Mag's reign on the East Side waterfront ran from the late 1850s to 1871, when the Hole-In-The-Wall was closed because of the numerous murders and other crimes committed there. Many tales circulated about Gallus Mag's subsequent fate: one that she found true love with a poor young man and another that she found true love with a rich old man. Whatever her fate, the waterfront was never the same after her reign.

See also: *Hole-In-The-Wall Saloon.*

GAMBI, Vincent (?-1819): Pirate

A contemporary—at times a follower and at times a foe—of Jean Lafitte, Vincent Gambi, a surly, hot-blooded Italian, was easily the worst cutthroat to sail the Gulf of Mexico during the first two decades of the 19th century. While Lafitte and many of the other pirates headquartering in the "pirates' home" of Barataria Bay and the islands off Louisiana were more or less privateers under commission to Cartagena, which was then revolting against Spain, Gambi often boasted he was a genuine bloody pirate, and he was. By 1810 he was known to have murdered a score of men with his favorite weapon, a broadax.

When Lafitte became the acknowledged leader of the Baratarian pirates about that time, Gambi was the only captain

who occasionally challenged his authority. Unlike Lafitte, Gambi wished to attack all shipping, including that of the United States, ignoring the consideration that American merchants were the prime purchasers of the Batarian freebooters' loot.

Once, Gambi attempted to overthrow Lafitte and had his lieutenant announce loudly, "The men of Gambi take orders only from Gambi!" Lafitte answered that display of dissension by drawing a pistol and shooting the man dead. Gambi immediately lost interest in any thought of revolt. Even after the Americans finally drove the pirates from their Baratarian bases in 1814, Gambi followed Lafitte in pledging to support Gen. Andrew Jackson at the Battle of New Orleans. Lafitte's motive was undoubtedly financial and political; Gambi's was simply to satisfy his urge for violence. He was credited with more killings than any other pirate taking part in the battle.

Following the successful conclusion of the war against the British, Gambi, like the other Baratarians, was granted a full pardon with all the rights of an American citizen, but by early 1816 he, Lafitte and many of the others had tired of New Orleans city life. Lafitte went off with perhaps 1,000 followers to found a community on an island that later became Galveston, Tex., but Gambi set off on his own to earn a new fortune and greater infamy as a pirate. He succeeded, plundering and sinking a score of ships over the next three years. In 1819 Gambi was slaughtered by his own men with his own ax as he slept on a pile of stolen gold, which, as was his wont, he had divided by a method that defied the standard rules of mathematics.

See also: *Jean Lafitte, Piracy, Pirates' Home.*

GAMBINO, Carlo (1902-1976): Mafia chieftain

Whether Gambino ever was the so-called boss of bosses, assuming the existence of any such character, is debatable, but he was without doubt the head of New York's most powerful crime family as well as the model for Mario Puzo's *Godfather.* Gambino, a youthful companion of Lucky Luciano and Meyer Lansky, rose through the underworld ranks to become the underboss to Albert Anastasia in the 1940s and 1950s.

It is generally believed that Vito Genovese ordered the execution of Anastasia after winning the approval of Gambino. From the time of Anastasia's murder in 1957 and the forced retirement of Frank Costello after a botched assassination attempt on his life, Genovese became the most powerful Mafia figure in New York, allegedly controlling all five major New York crime families. However, Genovese's reign was a short one. He was convicted in a narcotics case, which was reputedly "set up" by Costello, Lansky and Luciano, and sentenced to 15 years in prison. Although he continued to control syndicate operations from behind bars, several others, including Gambino, were able to increase their power. By the time Genovese died in prison of natural causes in 1969, Gambino had emerged as the strongest family leader in New York. By judicious alliances and killings, he eventually became the dominant chieftain of the five families, although it is doubtful he ever attained the fictional Godfather status.

The short, bulb-nosed Gambino, however, did display many of the personal traits of the Godfather. There was the same ruthless cunning, the Long Island retreat, the tomatoes planted in the garden and the excursions to fruit stands in Italian neighborhoods. Even in death, Gambino resembled the Godfather. After he died of a heart attack in October 1976, the hundreds of mourners at his funeral were cordoned off from reporters and strangers by hard-faced men who easily convinced onlookers that it would be impolite to intrude on the grief of the family, friends and associates of Carlo Gambino.

See also: *Albert Anastasia; Apalachin Conference; Joseph Colombo, Sr.; Vito Genovese.*

GAMBLER'S Belt

Employed by crooked gamblers in the 19th century, the so-called gambler's belt was a lethal body device of considerable firepower used to discourage any attempt by a victim to recover his losses forcibly.

The belt appeared in gambling dens in Philadelphia, Cincinnati and Chicago and proved popular on the Mississippi and in the West. In a typical version, a body belt was fitted with three small-caliber revolvers that could be fired simultaneously by operating a trigger mechanism hidden on the wearer's right side. Naturally, when fired, the device destroyed the wearer's trousers but did far worse damage to his foe, who would be struck by three shots in the abdomen. According to one account, an unnamed gambler in Nevada used such a belt to kill a miner objecting to his method of dealing, and the other miners gathered around, expressing wonder at the device's design. On reflection, they decided it gave the gambler an unfair advantage in the gunfight, so they marched him out to the street and hanged him.

GANGS And Gangsters

The terms "gangs" and "gangsters" are used in this book—and in almost every other book on the subject of American crime—in the loose modern definitions and not in their specific original meanings. Thus, Jesse James had a "gang," and John Dillinger had a "gang" and was a "gangster." Originally, and strictly, the words applied to 19th century organizations that were virtual armies. The Gophers, for instance, could field 500 fighting men, every one a fierce thug and eager killer. Yet, by the standards of the time, the size of the Gophers was unremarkable. Another New York gang, the Dead Rabbits, mobilized far greater numbers. So did other gangs in all parts of the country: the Sydney Ducks, Whyos, Bloody Tubs, Bowery Boys, Roach Guards, Potato Peelers, Plug Uglies and so on. In 1850 the New York police estimated the city gangs totaled about 30,000 men and women. These gangs consisted of bruisers, brawlers and thugs who could and did paralyze American cities when they rampaged. On a more routine basis, a gang might commit a dozen or more robberies of business places and homes each night, and some gangs were good for 30 to 50 street muggings every evening. They often killed, but simply in the course of business with little homicidal intent. If a victim had a weak skull, it was his misfortune. Eventually, many gangs found and met a demand in the market place for their murderous abilities. The Whyos, among others, rented themselves out as primitive forerunners of Murder, Inc., committing mayhem according to a set fee schedule.

In the same era there were specialized groups of more sophisticated criminals who perpetuated spectacular and amazing crimes. They were called "mobs" and ranged in number from as few as three or four individuals up to about 15 or so. By this usage, the 1930s saw the Dillinger "mob" in action.

True gangs are still with us, although but for a quirk of history they might well have vanished as they did in many other advanced countries. The true era of the great gangs ran 90 years, roughly from 1825 to 1915. They flourished almost unopposed until the Civil War, when they finally met some police effort to contain them. This was no easy task since many of the gangs had strong political connections as a result of their ability to provide votes for the political forces protecting them and, more importantly, to dissuade voters from opposing their patrons. Where the gangs were contained, it was basically through the raw force of police beatings and improved educational, economic and social conditions. By the second decade of the 20th century, the reform-minded citizenry in most big cities had brought about wholesale destruction of the gangs. In New York during 1914-15 some 300 gangsters, including the best-known underworld figures of the day were shipped off to prison. The great gangs crumbled. The Whyos were no more, and the last great New York gang, the Five Pointers, were losing the revenues required to keep a large criminal combine alive. After the World War I it seem doubtful if the big gangs could ever recover. But Prohibition provided the gangsters with a public-approved criminal activity, bootlegging, around which to regroup and which made the likes of Al Capone a hero worthy of being cheered at baseball games. The Mafia crime families were able to flourish and the national crime syndicate was born. They were so well organized that after the repeal of Prohibition they could move en masse into the new criminal activities of the 20th century. Thus, the traditions of the old gangs are preserved today in the various Mafia crime families, the new Purple Gang and the massive but less well-known black narcotics gangs.

GARCIA, Manuel Philip (?-1821): Murderer

As a murder, Manuel Garcia's crime was rather ordinary, but it led to the introduction of a new method of detection in this country that has been widely used ever since. Garcia killed Peter Lagoardette, a rival highwayman and burglar in the Norfolk, Va. area, in a feud over a woman. He had induced another bandit, Jose Castillano, to help him lure the victim to an abandoned house, where Garcia hacked Lagoardette to death and the pair cut up the body and burned it in the fireplace.

The job was so messy both killers had to leave their blood-drenched shirts behind.

When the neighbors were attracted by smoke coming from the chimney of an abandoned house, they investigated and found Lagoardette's partially burned torso and limbs. They also found the shirts, which were turned over to the sheriff. That lawman had been reading a recent newspaper account from England describing how a murderer's clothing had been traced through laundry marks. The same was done in the Lagoardette case, and the trail led straight to Garcia and Castillano. Apparently, it was the first time a laundry mark had been used to apprehend a murderer in the United States, and Virginia newspapers were at first ecstatic about the method and then somewhat somber as they speculated that many murderers henceforth would undoubtedly do their foul business in an undressed state. The two murderers were hanged in Norfolk on July 1, 1821.

GARDNER, Roy (1888-1940): Escape artist

As a criminal, Roy Gardner was less than a master, getting himself caught frequently. The problem for the law was not catching him but holding him. One of the leading columnists of the early 1920s, S. Jay Kaufman, wrote in the *New York World:* "There is no end of fascinating questions in the career of this extraordinary man. How often do we find a criminal who has taught Emerson and Thoreau, fought for liberty across the border, knocked down the great Jim Jeffries, written a book of scholarship that is a classic in its field? Roy Gardner is Renaissance man born too late in a world he never made. He is a man of whom they make legends, and we are in need of legends to brighten this dreary world."

Roy Gardner was America's greatest escape artist during the Roaring Twenties, and as he slipped in and out of the hands of the law, he produced one fantastic newspaper headline after another. Born in 1888, the son of a well-to-do Detroit businessman, Gardner appeared to have a brilliant future when he graduated from college with honors. He showed a strong literary bent and at a very early age became a faculty member of a Midwestern college. His record in the English department was outstanding and a work he published on 17th century literature was very well received.

By all rights, Roy Gardner should have become a fixture in the academic world and lived out a useful educational career, but youthful enthusiasm and a craving for adventure caused him to drop out. He went to Mexico to fight with the revolutionaries. In 1908 Gardner was caught bringing ammunition to the Carranza army and was sentenced to death after a summary government trial. He escaped from the military prison at Hermosillo before the execution could be carried out. Three other Americans escaped with him. Later, two were wounded and recaptured, but Gardner and the other American made it away clean.

Having no desire to return to the university life, Roy gravitated to the West Coast and took a fling at prizefighting becoming a sparring partner for James J. Jeffries. It was through his acquaintances in the boxing world that Gardner turned to crime. With two others, he pulled a $19,000 van robbery. Afterward, one of his accomplices was caught and he implicated Gardner, who spent two years in San Quentin as a result.

When he got out, he went straight and got married. Gardner opened his own welding shop in Oakland, Calif. and prospered until the shop burned to the ground. He had no insurance. Thereafter, Gardner went to Los Angeles and took a job as a welder. He also started to do some serious writing, but after a while, honest work ceased to interest him. He robbed a mail truck in San Diego, netting only a small sum of money, and was soon caught.

Gardner played the role of the flippant criminal, answering the judge with Shakespearean quotes and constantly showing off his literary knowledge. The judge was unimpressed and sentenced him to 25 years at the federal penitentiary on McNeil Island, Wash. Gardner was stunned at the sentence. Then he regained his composure. "You'll never get me there," he shouted as he was being led away. No one paid him any mind.

But Roy Gardner was right. He overpowered his train guards, seized their weapons and hopped off the train as it neared Portland, Ore. While a vast manhunt for him was launched in the Pacific Northwest, he went east through Canada, holed up in Minneapolis and eventually moved to Davenport, Iowa, where he took a job as a welding instructor. Soon, the old restlessness surfaced and he returned to Napa, Calif., where his wife lived under constant surveillance. He slipped past the stakeout to see her and sneaked away again. A neighbor spotted him and called the police, but despite an intensive hunt, with his picture splashed across the newspapers, Gardner escaped.

In May 1921 he robbed a Southern Pacific mail car of $200,000 in cash and securities. By not fleeing the area, however, he again proved to be a poor thief. Six days later, he was caught in a Roseville gambling room, betting big and bragging about how smart he was. When apprehended, Gardner had only a small amount of his loot and refused to say where the rest was.

Another 25 years was added to his sentence, and the law put him on a train for McNeil Island once more and once more failed to get him there. Already the newspapers had dubbed him the Escaping Professor and printed his boast that he would not be taken as far as Tacoma, Wash.

On the train Gardner asked his two guards for permission to go to the toilet. The officers, being cautious, accompanied him and kept another prisoner handcuffed to him. The four trooped to the men's room, one of the large types of the 1920s. Nothing untoward happened until they moved to the sink. Suddenly, using his free hand, Gardner pulled a gun from under the sink. He and the other prisoner, Norris Pryor, handcuffed the officers and taped their mouths shut with the tape that had been used to secure the gun in its hiding place. How it got there Gardner never revealed. As the train slowed in the Vancouver yards, Gardner and Pryor jumped off, disappearing in the misty rain.

Gardner's escape made headlines across the country, and he became one of the nation's most glorified criminals. Unfortunately for him, he became so recognizable that he was readily recaptured. The newspapers speculated about how far the law would succeed in transporting Gardner this time, but the authorities took no chances. He was shackled to two unarmed officers and guarded at a distance by two others. When he entered the prison, one journalist mourned "the end of a legend."

It wasn't. On Labor Day, 1921 Gardner was watching a baseball game from the bleachers of the prison ball field. As all eyes were focused on the field, he and two other convicts dropped through the bleacher seats to the ground. They cut through the barbed wire fence with wire cutters Gardner had stolen from the machine shop and raced for undergrowth 50 yards from the fence. If they made that, they would have a chance. The tower guards didn't see them until they were halfway there. In the fusillade of bullets that followed, Gardner's two companions went down. Gardner was wounded in the left leg but made the bushes. He hid out there until dark while guards searched for him and police craft circled the island. What they didn't know was that Gardner had retraced his escape route and was hiding out in the prison barn. He treated his wound which was not too serious, and milked a cow whenever he got hungry.

Gardner stayed hidden for 48 hours, by which time it was decided he had reached the mainland. Only then did he move to the water's edge, drift 2½ miles to Fox Island and from there swim to the mainland. He vanished for a few weeks and then was back in the headlines. Audaciously, he had addressed a letter to President Warren Harding offering a deal. He wanted his sentences suspended so that he could return to his wife and young children "to start life anew." In return, he promised to pay back to the government some $250,000 in loot, which he said he had salted away.

It made good newspaper copy but had no results. The President naturally ignored the offer.

Gardner was now 33 years old. Somewhere between his escape from the prison in September and November 15, all the fight went out of him. He tried to hold up a mail clerk on a train in Arizona but was easily overpowered. This time he was sent to Leavenworth, his sentence now having reached 75 years. He never escaped custody again. Gardner's reputation earned him a transfer to the new maximum security federal prison at Alcatraz in 1934, but he was sent back to Leavenworth two years later because of his good behavior. Two years after that, he was freed. The newspapers speculated investigators wanted him to lead them to his stolen money hoard, but the real reason for his release was his poor health. Thereafter, Gardner lived alone in a rundown hotel in San Francisco, his wife having died years before. In January 1940, at the age of 52, the Escaping Professor made his final break to freedom. He turned on the gas.

GARFIELD, James A.: See Charles Julius Guiteau.

GARFIELD Portrait Swindle

Shortly after the assassination of President James A. Garfield in 1881, some 200 newspapers carried an advertisement that was to become a minor classic swindle. The ad offered the grieving public what seemed to be a rare portrait of the dead President, stating:

> I have secured the authorized steel engravings of the late President Garfield, executed by the United States Government, approved by the President of the United States, by Congress and by every member of the President's family as the most faithful of all portraits of the President. It was executed by the Government's most expert steel engravers, and I will send a copy from the original plate, in full colors approved by the Government, postpaid, for one dollar each.

To every eager person sending a dollar, the swindler fulfilled his promises to the letter by mailing back an engraving of President Garfield on a 5¢ postage stamp.

Following the Garfield portrait swindle, con men went on to pull the same racket countless times in endless variations involving other notable persons and subjects that have appeared on commemorative stamps, sometimes also promising "suitable mounting," which meant putting the stamp on an index card.

GARMENT Area Crime: See Hijacking, Sneak Thievery.

GARRETT, Patrick Floyd (1850-1908): Lawman and killer of Billy the Kid

To sum up Pat Garrett's career as a lawman, he was at his best on a manhunt only when he killed from ambush, a trait he exhibited constantly while tracking his greatest prize, Billy the Kid. While stalking the Kid, Garrett, then sheriff of Lincoln County, plotted an ambush from the old hospital at Fort Sumner, New Mexico Territory, where the wife of one of the Kid's gang, Charlie Bowdre, was confined. When the gang appeared and Garrett thought he spotted the Kid, he ordered his men to open fire, but the wrong man, Tom O'Folliard, was mortally wounded. Four days later, Garrett set another ambush outside an abandoned rock house near Stinking Springs, N.M. He passed the word that the ambushers were to shoot Billy the Kid when he walked outside at dawn. As dawn broke, Charlie Bowdre came out, and since he was of the same general appearance and size as the Kid, Garrett signaled for the shooting to commence. Bowdre too was fatally wounded. It was a needless killing and a needless ambush. The Kid and his gang were trapped and eventually did the only thing they could do, surrender.

Garrett always thought ambush. When he caught up with Billy on July 14, 1881, following the young gunman's escape from custody, Garrett shot him to death as the unsuspecting outlaw walked into a darkened room in his stocking feet with his gun tucked in his belt. He then ran triumphantly out of the building shouting gleefully: "I killed the Kid! I killed the Kid!"

Pat Garrett's fanciful biography of Billy the Kid served to enhance his own reputation as well as that of the young outlaw.

Garrett gained nationwide fame for the killing, especially far from New Mexico, where he was not all that popular. In fact, he was denied renomination as sheriff by the Democratic political powers, who undoubtedly were not happy about the way he had killed the Kid from ambush. In addition, Gov. Lew Wallace appeared to have put obstacles in the way of Garrett's collecting the reward for Billy, and Garrett finally had to lobby in Santa Fe to get a special act through the state legislature awarding him $500.

There is reason to think Garrett lived in fear that some fan of the Kid would take revenge on him. When he became cattle boss on a large ranch, he ordered that no cowhand be allowed to carry a six-shooter. Several cowboys who resented the order said it was clearly given because Garrett was afraid to turn his back on them. In 1889 he ran for sheriff in Chavez County but lost, the stigma of Billy the Kid still clinging to him. Embittered, he pulled up stakes and moved to Uvalde County, Tex., where he befriended John Nance Garner, a future vice president of the United States then in his thirties and already a political power. With Cactus Jack's help, he was elected a county commissioner and held that post until 1897, when old friends in Dona Ana County got him to return to New Mexico. Garrett became sheriff of Las Cruces County and held the office for one term. When he was not renominated, he returned to ranching until Teddy Roosevelt, who admired law-and-order types, named him a customs collector in El Paso. For some unknown reason, he fell from presidential favor and was not reappointed in 1905. Following his return to farming, Garrett got involved in a feud and was shot to death in 1908. That killing, like many of Garrett's, was controversial. A neighbor, Wayne Brazel, admitted he had killed Garrett but said it was in self-defense, a version backed up by a witness, Carl Adamson. However, it was evident that Garrett had been shot in the back of the head while heeding a call of nature. There was considerable reason to believe that the real murderer was Killin' Jim Miller, a professional hired gun, and that he had been assigned the task by Adamson, who wanted Garrett's land. Officially, Brazel was charged in the killing and cleared.

Today, Garrett is remembered only for the killing of Billy the Kid and is generally better thought of than he was at the time. Part of the reason for this is Garrett's contribution to Western history, *An Authentic Life of Billy the Kid*, a book written in Garrett's name by an itinerant journalist, Ash Upson. In the preface Garrett assured his readers, "I am incited to this labor by an impulse to correct the thousand false statements which have appeared in the public newspapers and in yellow-covered cheap novels."

He nonetheless proceeded to deliver a version full of falsehoods. One piece of misinformation was that Billy the Kid had killed his first man at the age of 12 to avenge an insult to his mother. He was also mistaken when he said the Kid rescued a wagon train by routing marauding Indians with an ax, and Billy never rode 81 miles in six hours to get a buddy out of a Texas jail, as Garrett claimed. In praise of himself, Garrett loftily claimed credit for delivering to New Mexico "a season of peace and prosperity to which she has ever, heretofore, been a stranger."

See also: *Billy the Kid.*

GAS House Gang: 19th century New York gang

A vicious group of street thugs, the Gas House Gang originally controlled the Gas House district around New York's East 35th Street, but in an unusual criminal migration just before the start of the 20th century, the gang moved southward to take control of Third Avenue from 11th Street to 18th Street.

During their heyday over the next dozen or so years, the Gas Housers, numbering about 200, controlled the area with an iron fist, extracting tribute from saloon keepers and businessmen, running gambling games and so on. Whenever they failed to find enough entertainment and riches in their immediate neighborhoods, they would invade other gang precincts and take what they wanted. Usually, they met little resistance because other gangs, even larger ones, knew any war with the Gas Housers would be debilitating.

Essentially, however, the Gas Housers remained true street thugs, revelling most in muggings; in their prime they averaged some 30 street holdups a night. The term "Gas House Gang" entered the English vernacular as a description for a bunch of brawling rowdies; thus when some years later the St. Louis Cardinals baseball team developed into the rowdies of the diamond, they quite naturally became known as the Gas House Gang.

GEBHARDT, Dr. Fritz (1895-1935): Murder victim

The first murder verdict in America with an anti-Nazi tone was given in the case of Dr. Fritz Gebhardt, who in 1934 had met and wooed an American woman, Laura Parr, on a sea cruise. Within a year both were living in the Beekman Tower in New York City, Laura on the 19th floor and Gebhardt on the 21st.

On November 25, 1935 Gebhardt telephoned Laura and asked her to come to his apartment because he was feeling ill. When she arrived in her nightclothes, Gebhardt made a miraculous recovery. It was then that he suggested Laura engage in what she regarded as an immoral act. When she refused, according to her later testimony, he threatened her with a gun. Laura seized the gun and shot Gebhardt dead.

The press initially judged Laura guilty, labeling her the Icy Blonde. The *New York Daily Mirror* ran Laura's picture on the editorial page with the caption "With Such a Lady—Be Careful." The *New York World-Telegram* asked, "Can True Love Yield to Murderous Hatred?" Even the *New York Times* found interest in the case so intense that it devoted four columns to it just prior to the trial.

At the onset of the trial, public opinion was against Laura Parr, but this changed as her defense lawyer, the legendary Samuel Leibowitz, developed his case. The lawyer succeeded in putting on trial not only the victim, a German businessman, but the entire Nazi regime as well. In fact, while prospective jurors were being questioned, it appeared as though the accused was German philosopher Friedrich Wilhelm Nietzsche, then dead some 36 years. During the trial itself, for a time the real defendant seemed to be Field Marshal Hermann Goering. (During World War I Dr. Gebhardt had served with distinction in the Richtofen Squadron, where he became friendly with a young pilot named Hermann Goering.) Somehow even the personal peccadillos of brutal Brownshirt chief Ernest Roehm became part of the case, although there was no record of Roehm ever residing in the Beekman Tower.

By the end of the trial, the choice was clear; the jury could vote for the supermen of the German master race or for American womanhood. When Laura Parr was found not guilty, women spectators squealed in delight. "The defendant is discharged," the judge announced stiffly and left the bench. It was one of the few times in a New York court when a jury was not thanked by the presiding judge for its labors.

See also: *Samuel S. Leibowitz.*

GEIDEL, Paul (1894-): Longest-term convict

It is believed that no one ever served more time in an American prison than Paul Geidel, who was found guilty of the 1911 murder of a wealthy guest in a New York City hotel where he worked as a porter. Geidel, who was 17 years old at the time, was sentenced to 20 years to life in Clinton Prison. In May 1980, 68 years and seven months later, he was released from the Fishkill Correctional Facility, to which he had been transferred, and was sent to live out his remaining days in a nursing home.

GEIN, Edward (1906-): Murderer

Few murderers in the 20th century have evoked such horror as Ed Gein, a Wisconsin farmer, in the 1950s. Gein worked the family farm at Plainfield, Wis. with his brother Henry and his elderly mother, who always insisted that her two boys never marry. His mother died in 1945, and brother Henry followed her within a year, leaving Ed alone on his farm with his strange fantasies. Gein developed a strong interest in female anatomy and, greatly affected by Christine Jorgensen's successful transsexual operation, apparently wanted to change his sex. He developed a morbid need to acquire women's bodies in order to study the anatomical structure of female organs, and to satisfy that desire, he took to digging up female corpses from their graves.

To aid in this secret task, Gein recruited a lame-witted old farmer, assuring him that their ghoulish activities would advance the cause of science. The old man helped Gein bring the corpses to a shed next to his farmhouse. Here, Gein skinned the bodies and sometimes even donned the skin and walked around his house so clad for hours. He also kept parts of the bodies as trophies, mounting the heads, hearts, livers and sex organs. When the doting farmer was committed to an old-age home, Gein was faced with the task of gathering the corpses on his own—or finding some easier way to collect bodies than exhuming them from all those graves. Some time in the early 1950s, he apparently decided it would be simpler to kill fresh victims rather than go through all the trouble of digging graves.

Later, Gein would helpfully try to name his victims, but he suffered from a lack of memory on the subject and could recall only two for certain. In 1954 Gein walked into a bar run by 51-year-old Mary Hogan in Pine Grove and, seeing her alone, pulled out a pistol and shot her in the head. He piled her body on a sled and took her home. Subsequently, he accumulated some other bodies, although after his arrest he couldn't remember if he had killed them or dug them up. In November 1957 he killed Mrs. Bernice Worden, the operator of a hardware store in Plainfield. Ironically, the night before the murder Gein had mentioned to Mrs. Worden's son, who happened to be a deputy sheriff, that he would have to buy some antifreeze. The following evening the deputy went to his mother's store and found her missing. There was some blood on the floor and a half-written receipt for a purchase of antifreeze, and the cash register was gone.

Mrs. Worden's son remembered his conversation with Gein and the latter's farm was searched. There the authorities found all sorts of grim relics, including bracelets made of human skin, a sewn-up skull fashioned into a soup bowl and dozens of other gruesome remains from at least 15 bodies. Gein admitted the grave robbings and the murders but was most upset when accused of robbing the cash register from his last victim's store. "I'm no robber," he said indignantly. "I took the money and the register only because I wanted to see how the machine worked."

Gein was committed for life to an institution for the criminally insane. For some years the Gein farmhouse was regarded a place of horror until finally the local people burned it to the ground.

GELLER, Max: See Green Parrot Murder.

GEM Saloon, Gunfight At The

While the O.K. Corral is the most famous shoot-out site in America, far more deadly gun duels and killings took place at the infamous Gem Saloon in El Paso, Tex. It was here in January 1877 that Pink Higgins outdrew Merritt Horrell, chalking up another death in the Horrell-Higgins feud. But just as there was *the* gunfight at the O.K. Corral, so too was there *the* gunfight at the Gem, one that probably had more stock elements than any of a score of famous duels: right against wrong, a man bucking incredible odds, mistaken identity, black Western humor and a prime example of the art of gunfighting.

The duel or more correctly, duels were fought on April 14, 1884. On that day a gambler and dandy named Bill Raynor, who had gained his reputation as a gunfighter by planting eight foes in the ground, turned "mean" and walked through town looking for a fight. Given his reputation, he found no takers. After challenging every man in a barbershop, he moved on to the Gem. He sauntered into the saloon's gambling room and finally provoked one faro player, Bob Rennick, into demanding Raynor stop leaning on him. Raynor told him he was stepping out to the bar to have a drink and was then coming back in to kill him. The other players advised Rennick to move away from the table so they could continue their game in peace. Rennick checked his six-gun, moved to the wall and began watching the doorway. A minute or so later, Raynor

burst into the room, his guns blazing. Four shots splintered the chair Rennick had vacated; Rennick stepped out from the wall and answered with two shots that caught Raynor in the stomach and chest. Raynor staggered out to the street and collapsed in the arms of a noted visitor in town, Wyatt Earp, asking Earp to inform his mother that he had "died game."

Raynor was taken to the doctor's office, where his friend Buck Linn rushed to him, inquiring about who had shot him. Raynor gave a garbled answer that indicated the man who had gunned him down was Bob Cahill. Linn vowed to take vengeance on his friend's alleged assailant. When this news got back to the Gem, Cahill, an inoffensive gambler who had never shot a gun, became petrified. A friend named Dan Tipton handed Cahill a loaded .45 and Wyatt Earp gave him a fast lesson in gunfighting, to wit: stay calm, take plenty of time aiming and shoot for the belly button. This was standard advice, but observers could not tell how much of it the frightened Cahill had absorbed. Five minutes later, Buck Linn entered the saloon. After spotting the little gambler, he pulled his gun and fired four fast shots from a distance of 12 to 15 feet. All missed. Cahill aimed his .45 and sighted in on Linn's belt buckle when he was about eight feet away. His aim was high, and he shot Linn right through the heart.

Thus ended the Gem's most famous shoot-out, although Raynor did not expire for 48 hours. On the chance that he might recover, both Rennick and Cahill, who had pushed their luck to the limit, rode hard for Mexico. The two victors had popular support, one drunk at the bar proclaiming: "I'm damned glad Bill got it. He should have been killed years ago." From the silence that greeted his comment, the drunk realized there was still the chance that Raynor might recover. He added quickly, "If Bill gets well, what I said don't go." But Raynor, fortunately for the drunk, didn't make it.

The *El Paso Herald* stated: "The victims had no one to blame but themselves. Their train of life collided with loaded revolvers and they have gone down forever in the smash-up. Thus endeth the first chapter of our spring fights."

GEMSTONE: Watergate code word

The code word for the break-in at the Democratic National Committee's headquarters in the Watergate complex in Washington, D.C. was Gemstone. Five men were caught in the ill-conceived, still not fully explained operation that resulted in the toppling of the Nixon Administration, with Richard Nixon forced to resign the presidency and several of his top associates sent to prison.

GENNA Brothers: Prohibition-era Chicago family gang

The Genna brothers, known as the Terrible Gennas, were the first Chicago gang to jump into moonshining in a big way with the advent of Prohibition. Most of the brothers had been

Black Hand extortionists preying on the residents of the city's Little Italy section, but in 1919 they realized there was more money putting people to work producing illegal alcohol, and they turned Little Italy into one large cottage moonshining industry.

The brothers Genna—Bloody Angelo, Tony the Gentleman, Mike the Devil, Pete, Sam and Jim—had come to Chicago from Sicily in 1910. Five of them were typical Sicilian killers—haughty, vicious, treacherous, murderous and devoutly religious. They carried their crucifixes in the same pocket with their pistols. The "different" Genna was Tony the Gentleman, or, as he was sometimes called, Tony the Aristocrat. He studied architecture, constructed model tenements for poor Italian immigrants, was a leading patron of the opera and lived elegantly in a downtown hotel. Tony had strong personal convictions against killing and never did a job himself, although he attended all family councils at which rub-outs were planned. When Johnny Torrio and Al Capone were setting up their operation, the two feared the Gennas more than any other gang because they commanded the most savage set of killers. Among them were Sam "Smoots" Amatuna, the gangland dandy who loved music almost as much as he loved committing murder; Giuseppe "the Cavalier" Nerone, a university graduate and mathematics teacher turned gunman; and the celebrated murder duo John Scalise and Albert Anselmi, who introduced the practice of rubbing bullets with garlic in the hope of inducing gangrene should the victim survive the initial gunshot wound.

Combined with the Gennas' constant application of deadly force was their ability to corrupt the police. In 1925 a confession by their office manager indicated the brothers had on their payroll five police captains and some 400 uniformed officers, mostly from the Maxwell Street station, as well as many plainclothesmen from headquarters and the state attorney's office. The Gennas' booze-making operation grossed $350,000 a month, and the six brothers netted a clear monthly profit of $150,000. When Johnny Torrio brought most of the gangs together under one umbrella, the Gennas were the hardest to control. Ever devious, they constantly flooded other gangs' areas with their cheap booze, underselling them with terrible rotgut. A three-way competition soon developed among the Gennas, the North Side O'Banions and the Torrio-Capone mob.

Eventually the Gennas started getting picked off one by one, especially after Anselmi and Scalise deserted their banner to join the Capone forces.

Bloody Angelo Genna fell victim on May 25, 1925 to North Side gangsters who had followed his roadster through Chicago streets. When Angelo first became aware of them, he picked up speed. But in his desperate haste to get away, he smashed into a lamp post and was pinned behind the wheel, unable to do anything but watch as the pursuing black sedan glided to a stop by him and three shotguns blasted him apart.

Mike Genna vowed vengeance on the O'Banions who had done the job. The following month he and Anselmi and Scalise were out hunting for North Siders. What Mike Genna didn't

known was that he was being taken for a ride by the pair, who had secretly defected to Capone. The three got caught in a gunfight with police. Anselmi and Scalise killed two officers, wounded a third and fled, leaving a wounded Genna to be captured by police. As Mike Genna was being placed on a stretcher, he cut loose a powerful kick with his good leg and knocked out one of the attendants. "Take that, you dirty son of a bitch," he snarled. He died two hours later.

Tony the Gentleman, the real brains of the Terrible Gennas, realizing that Anselmi and Scalise had deserted, knew he was next. Just as he was about to leave the city, he arranged for a final meeting with his supporter Nerone on a darkened street corner. He did not know that Nerone also had defected. When Tony Genna emerged from his car, Nerone grasped his hand in a steel-like handshake. Just then one or two gunmen stepped out of the darkness and filled Tony with bullets. Tony the Gentleman lingered for days before dying.

The power of the Gennas was now broken. The three surviving brothers fled, Sam and Pete to hideouts outside Chicago and Jim all the way back to Sicily. In Palermo, Jim Genna got two years for stealing the jewels that adorned the statue of the Madonna di Trapani.

Eventually, the three brothers came back to Chicago but avoided the rackets. They ran an olive oil and cheese importing firm, finishing out their days in relative obscurity.

See also: *Anselmi and Scalise, Alphonse "Scarface Al" Capone, Maxwell Street Police Station.*

GENOVESE, Kitty (1935-1964): Murder victim

The events surrounding the murder of Kitty Genovese, a 28-year-old woman from Queens, New York City, were more bizarre than the brutal crime itself, in which a killer stalked and killed his victim in three separate attacks over a 35-minute period. The attacks occurred after 3 a.m. on March 13, 1964. The killer, 29-year-old Winston Moseley, walked away after first stabbing the woman on Austin Street in the middle-class section of Kew Gardens. As Kitty Genovese staggered around the short block toward the entrance to her home, her assailant returned in his car, looked for her in doorways, found her and stabbed her again. He drove off but in a few minutes came back to find the woman in a hallway at the foot of a staircase. He stabbed her a third time, fatally, and drove off.

The crime itself was not all that unusual. What made the Genovese case different is that at least 37 persons witnessed all or part of the attacks but not one of them called the police.

After the first attack, the victim shrieked: "Oh, my God, he stabbed me! Please help me! Please help me!" Lights went on in several apartments in a 10-story apartment house across the street. A man yelled out: "Let that girl alone!"

It was enough to make Moseley walk away. When he returned the first time and stabbed her again, Kitty Genovese screamed: "I'm dying! I'm dying!" Again lights went on and again windows went up. Many persons saw Moseley, but still no one called the police. After Moseley finished off his victim on the third try, the first call to the police was made.

Eventually, Moseley was caught and sentenced to the electric chair, which because of the law on capital punishment at the time, meant in effect a life sentence. What remained puzzling to police, newspaper reporters and psychologists was why nobody had called the police earlier. The man who finally placed the first call had done so with trepidation. Before he made the call, he telephoned a friend in Nassau County to seek his advice on what to do. After some deliberation it was decided he should telephone the police. The comments gotten from some witnesses were perhaps instructive of the noninvolvement instincts present in contemporary American society. Among the statements were: "I didn't want to get involved"; "Frankly, we were afraid"; "I didn't want my husband to get involved"; "I don't know"; "I was tired. I went back to bed"; "Get away or I'll throw you down the steps."

Another was possibly the most instructive: "The last time I complained to the police, I was sent to a concentration camp." Kew Gardens contained a high concentration of former victims of the Nazis in Europe, and a common characteristic of many was that the last thing one did was have anything to do with the symbols of authority.

GENOVESE, Vito (1897-1969): Mafia chieftain

Vito "Don Vito" Genovese was probably the most awesome of the Mafia dons. He is credited with being the moving force that put the Mafia in the narcotics business, a shift some others, such as Frank Costello and, despite the contentions of federal narcotics investigators, Lucky Luciano, strongly opposed. Genovese, who started out in the shadow of Luciano in the early 1920s, rose to the top of the syndicate crime empire by killing off his many rivals. He is known to have ordered the deaths of Willie Moretti in 1951, Steve Franse in 1953 and Albert Anastasia in 1957. He was the obvious mastermind behind the attempt on the life of Frank Costello, which eventually led to the latter's retirement.

Genovese was always a cunning criminal. Faced with a murder charge in 1937, he fled to Italy, where he ingratiated himself with Benito Mussolini despite the fascist leader's ruthless campaign to wipe out the Italian Mafia. Genovese became the chief drug supplier for Mussolini's foreign minister and son-in-law, Count Ciano. During the war, to further gain Mussolini's favor, Genovese ordered the execution of Il Duce's long-time nemesis, radical editor Carlo Tresca, in New York City, a hit carried out by a Genovese underling, Carlo Gambino.

In 1944, with the Mussolini regime crumbling, Genovese turned up as an interpreter for the Army's intelligence service. Due to his energetic and diligent efforts, a number of black market operatives were caught in southern Italy. However, the military's pleasure with Genovese's performance vanished when it was discovered that as he unearthed the black marketeers and put them out of business, he simply took over their rackets.

Genovese returned to the U.S. after the war, when the witnesses to the murder charge against him had been dealt with. He took control of the Luciano family and, with his mentor now in exile, set about making himself the dominant figure in the American underworld. To do that, he had to gain dominance over the five New York crime families, eliminate Frank Costello and lessen the influence of Meyer Lansky, all the while paying lip service to Luciano.

It took Genovese almost a decade to solidify his position to the point that he could attempt this takeover, in the process gaining needed revenues from the narcotics trade. By 1957 he was ready to move. He first ordered the execution of Costello, whose importance in the underworld had diminished as a result of the Kefauver hearings. The plot failed and Costello was only slightly wounded. A few months later, however, another of his assassination orders was spectacularly successful. Albert Anastasia was shot to death as he sat in a barber's chair in a New York hotel. At the time, Anastasia was Costello's most important ally, and without him the fabled Prime Minister of the Underworld appeared helpless.

Later that year Genovese sought to solidify his new power by calling the famed Apalachin Conference in upstate New York. That meeting ended in a fiasco when the state police raided it and took dozens of leading Mafia dons into custody. Genovese was not perceptive enough to realize the meeting had been sabotaged by enemies far smarter and craftier than he, including Costello, Lansky, Luciano and Carlo Gambino, the heir to the Anastasia crime family. Gambino and Lansky had cooperated with Genovese in the elimination Don Anastasia for their own reasons—Gambino to gain new power for himself and Lansky to eliminate the pressure the kill-crazy Anastasia was putting on him for a share of his vast Cuban gambling profits.

In these four, Genovese was facing the top double-dealers of the underworld. They understood better than Genovese that war between the two camps would be senseless, leading only to trouble for all. Instead, they plotted to eliminate Genovese by cunning and treachery. They decided to set him up for a federal drug bust, but the narcotics agents who were tipped off muffed the opportunity and Genovese slipped away. The underworld conspirators then arranged a trap that even allowed for the government's ineptitude. The four pitched in a $100,000 kitty and paid a minor Puerto Rican dope pusher named Nelson Cantellops to implicate Genovese in a deal. Although it was not logical that an unimportant street pusher like Cantellops would have the type of inside information to put away a power like Genovese, the government gladly accepted his testimony and convicted Genovese. In 1959 he was sentenced to the Atlanta Penitentiary for 15 years. According to underworld informer Joe Valachi, Genovese continued to direct the activities of his crime family from behind bars, but there is no doubt his influence lessened. Unquestionably, his effort to become the top boss of the underworld had been a disaster.

It was said that Genovese and Costello, sent to the Atlanta Penitentiary on tax charges, later held a tearful reconciliation in prison. If so, Genovese didn't understand the role Costello had played in his downfall; the facts of the plot were not revealed until Luciano broke his silence on the matter shortly before he died in 1962. When Genovese died in 1969, still a federal prisoner on a trumped-up charge, he was proof that mere brawn would never be enough to take over organized crime in America.

See also: *Albert Anastasia, Apalachin Conference, Frank Costello, Carmine Galante, Carlo Gambino, Peter LaTempa, Charles "Lucky" Luciano, Willie Moretti, Carlo Tresca, Joseph M. Valachi.*

GENTLE Annie: See Annie Stafford.

GENTLEMEN'S Riot

Easily the "classiest" riot in American history was staged in 1835 in Boston by the "broadcloth mob," a crowd of 3,000 wealthy and socially prominent men most of whom were dressed in broadcloth. On October 21 they gathered to protest a lecture by the famous English abolitionist George Thompson on behalf of the Boston Female Anti-Slavery Society. The mob planned to tar and feather the speaker, but Thompson had been forewarned and fled the city. The mob, angered at losing the victim, vented its frustration on William Lloyd Garrison, who published the antislavery newspaper *Liberator.* Garrison was bound with ropes and hauled away some distance, and by this time it was probably uncertain if the intent was a tar and feathering or a hanging. Garrison, however, was rescued by a number of friends and the police who carried him through the crowd to the city jail and kept him there overnight for protection. The disturbance became known as the Gentlemen's Riot. No convictions ever resulted.

GEORGE, Christian (?-1724): Cult leader and accused murderer

Christian George was one of the first to preach free love in the New World and died at the end of a rope because of it.

A religious fanatic from Switzerland, he preached his free love faith to the citizens of Charleston, S.C. He soon gathered a small sect of faithful believers and lead them to the Orange Quarter of South Carolina late in 1723 to set up a love commune. Among George's converts were a young couple, Peter and Judith Dutartre. The free love zealot apparently impressed the woman considerably with his gospel, so much so that she was soon pregnant with George's child. News of this "Devil's child" shocked the good burghers of Charleston, who, led by Justice Symmons, formed a posse to destroy George's love camp. Rather than submit to arrest, George ordered his followers to barricade their camp and resist. The Charleston forces stormed the commune's fortification but were beaten back. Then Peter Dutartre seized a musket and shot Justice Symmons dead. The next attack succeeded and the free love congregation was captured.

While the killing of Justice Symmons was a lone act by Peter Dutartre, the real quarry for Charleston justice was Christian George, who, it was feared, might lead other gullible persons from the path of morality. Dutartre, Christian George and a third cult member, Peter Rombert, were put on trial together, and after a two-day hearing all three were sentenced to hang. The verdict was carried out the following day. The citizens of Charleston then burned the love commune to the ground and returned to their own churches, content that morality had carried the day against the teachings of the Devil.

GIANCANA, Sam "Momo" (1908-1975): Syndicate leader

Considered by many to have been the most ruthless Mafia killer in the country, Sam "Momo" Giancana was for years the crime boss of Chicago and was suspected of involvement in various CIA plots to assassinate Cuban Premier Fidel Castro.

Giancana's arrest record dated back to 1925, when he was a gun runner for Al Capone. Unlike other crime bosses, whose arrest records were usually short, Giancana was a "doer," with over 70 arrests for everything from assault and bookmaking to bombing and suspicion of murder. He served prison sentences for auto theft, operation of an illegal still and burglary. During World War II he was asked by the draft board how he made his living; Giancana replied: "Me? I steal." He was rejected for service as "a constitutional psychopath."

According to well-publicized charges, Giancana was recruited in 1960 by the U.S. Central Intelligence Agency to "hit" Fidel Castro. Some say Giancana deliberately botched the assignment because he still had hopes of rebuilding the Mafia's gambling business in Cuba. In 1975 the Giancana-CIA connection talk was so widespread that the crime boss was about to be summoned before a Senate investigating committee. Before Giancana could appear, gunmen entered his fortress-like home in Chicago's Oak Park suburb and put seven bullets in him. CIA Director William Colby announced forthwith, "We had nothing to do with it." Newsmen contacting unofficial spokesmen for the syndicate got the same response from that source.

See also: *Anthony Joseph Accardo, Apalachin Conference, Fiore "Fifi" Buccieri, Forty-two Gang, Paul "the Waiter" Ricca.*

GIBBS, Charles (c.1800-1831): Pirate

Officially credited with the murder of 400 victims, a Rhode Islander named Charles Gibbs stands high on any list of American pirates, even if, as is probable, the total number of killings attributed to him was greatly exaggerated.

His modus operandi rarely varied. He would sign on a ship and pilfer what supplies he could whenever the vessel hit port. If he found the cargo aboard worthwhile, he would recruit a few other seamen aboard to join him, and they would murder the captain, first mate and whomever else in the crew they thought would harbor any feelings of loyalty. Since crews of the average vessel generally numbered less than 10, three or four murders usually were sufficient for Gibbs' purpose. When he was captured, Gibbs bragged that he often was able to keep all the booty for himself by frightening off the seamen who had helped him.

Gibbs' biggest haul was his last one, some $50,000 worth

of cargo seized from the *Vineyard*, which he had signed on in New Orleans on November 1, 1830 for a run to Philadelphia. Together with the ship's cook, Thomas Wansley, and three others, Gibbs murdered Capt. William Thornby and First Mate William Roberts off Cape Hatteras, N.C. After the mutineers landed, the three sailors who had joined Gibbs and Wansley went to the authorities, explaining they had agreed to join in the piracy only because they realized they would be killed if they had refused. Gibbs and Wansley were captured and convicted. Much to the delight of the press, Gibbs added one gory confession after another to his murderous exploits. Some were definitely true; others were somewhat doubtful. In any event, Gibbs achieved celebrity by the time he and Wansley were hanged on Ellis Island on April 22, 1831. Thousands watched the spectacle from pleasure boats and fireboats offshore.

GIGANTE, Vincent "The Chin" (1926-   ): Mobster

Vincent "the Chin" Gigante was a hulking 300-pound gangster generally credited as the hit man in the famous attempt to assassinate crime boss Frank Costello in 1957. According to popular theory, the hit was masterminded by Vito Genovese to seize the leadership of organized crime in New York. Gigante reportedly took target practice daily in a Greenwich Village basement in preparation for his big opportunity.

On May 2, 1957 Costello returned to his apartment building on Central Park West at the corner of 72 Street. As he did, a large black Cadillac pulled to the curb and a huge man got out and hurried ahead of Costello into the building. When Costello entered the lobby, the big man stepped from behind a pillar and produced a .38-caliber revolver. Just before firing, he called out, "This is for you, Frank."

At the sound of the man's voice, Costello turned, and by that movement saved his own life. The bullet tore through the right side of his scalp just above the ear. The fat man raced off for the waiting Cadillac, satisfied he had killed his target. Costello, although needing hospitalization, was not seriously hurt. Maintaining the underworld code, he refused to name his assailant. However, the apartment house doorman had gotten a good look at the blubbery gunman, and based on his evidence, an alert went out for the Chin. He was not readily found. According to the later statement of underworld informer Joe Valachi, "The Chin was just taken somewhere up in the country to lose some weight."

When that body beautifying was completed, Gigante surrendered, saying he understood the law was looking for him. It was thus a trim and slim Chin who went on trial for attempted murder, but Costello refused to identify him and the doorman either wouldn't or couldn't. The Chin left the court a free man.

It was supposedly the Chin's farewell to the big time, his last moment in the spotlight, but he was involved in a struggle far greater than himself. Powerful Mafia forces lined up on two sides—Genovese and his men on one side and the aging Costello, the deported Lucky Luciano and the crafty Meyer Lansky on the other. On the surface, peace was arranged. Genovese, who wanted Costello eliminated to ease his path to total power, agreed that Costello would no longer be threatened and would be allowed to retire on his racket revenues. Costello and his allies consented to the arrangement, and apparently to show good faith, the Chin was even invited to a number of Costello parties.

However, the Costello-Luciano-Lansky axis joined by the cunning Carlo Gambino were determined to get rid of Genovese and concocted a plot whereby he would be handed over to federal narcotics detectives in a tidy drug-smuggling plot. Part of the strategy called for the payment of $100,000 to a minor dope pusher, Nelson Cantellops, to implicate Genovese. Costello contributed $25,000 to the kitty with only one proviso: the Chin had to be involved as well. Everything went according to the script: In 1959 Genovese got 15 years, and 24 of his aides, including the Chin, received long prison terms as well.

In the 1970s various printed accounts claimed Gigante was still alive, although, according to underworld sources, suffering from a mental ailment and frequently regressing back to childhood. His brother, Mario Gigante, is reputedly still an important power in the old Luciano family, while another brother, Father Louis Gigante, is a politically active priest in the South Bronx, New York City.

See also: *Apalachin Conference, Frank Costello, Vito Genovese.*

GILLETTE, Chester (1884-1908): Murderer

Chester Gillette was the real-life Clyde Griffiths of Theodore Dreiser's classic novel *An American Tragedy.*

An ambitious factory worker who wanted to make it into high society, Gillette worked at his uncle's skirt factory in Cortland, N.Y. As the relative of a well-to-do businessman in town—Gillette had been deserted at the age of 14 by his own parents, who had gone off around the country to spread the Salvation Army gospel—he was accepted into local society and could look ahead to the time when he would marry a wealthy girl. Those future plans, however, did not prevent Gillette from partaking in the pleasures of the present, especially an affair with Billie Brown, an 18-year-old secretary at the factory.

Things went along well for the 22-year-old youth up to the time he received a letter from Billie saying she was pregnant. She did not ask Gillette to marry her but kept sending him heart-rending letters, which were intended sooner or later to persuade him to "do the right thing." Gillette ignored Billie's plight until she wrote warning him that she would tell his uncle. Seeing his world threatened, Gillette informed Billie he not only would do right by her but also intended to take her on a glorious holiday.

On July 8 the couple spent the night in Utica, registering in a hotel as man and wife, and from there moved on to the North Woods Section of the southern Adirondacks. After some time at Tupper Lake, they moved on to Big Moose Lake, where Gillette asked for "any old hotel where they have boats to rent." They were sent to the Glenmore Hotel, where Billie registered under her right name while Gillette used a phony. They got separate rooms.

On the morning of July 11, the couple took along a picnic lunch and a tennis racket and rowed out on the large lake. Chester Gillette was not seen again until almost 8 o'clock that evening; Billie Brown was never seen alive again. Her body washed ashore at Big Moose Lake on July 14. The medical report revealed that she had died from blows to her face, which had been badly battered, not from drowning. The same day, Gillette was arrested for murder at the Arrowhead Hotel on Eagle Bay, where he had since registered. Under some new-turned moss on the shore, the police found a buried tennis racket and asserted it was what Gillette had used to kill Billie. He denied it and told many conflicting stories. One was that Billie had committed suicide by jumping overboard; another was that the boat had capsized accidentally and that she had drowned after hitting her face on the side of the boat.

During Gillette's trial, which lasted 22 days, 109 witnesses appeared. So many of them came from the Cortland skirt factory that it had to shut down. Numerous women said they could not believe this charming, calm and handsome young man was capable of murder. From his cell Gillette sold photos of himself for $5 apiece and thus could afford to have his meals sent in from the local inn. Despite what his female supporters thought, the jury found differently, convicting him of premeditated murder. After more than a year of appeals, Chester Gillette went to the electric chair at Auburn Prison on March 30, 1908, refusing to admit his guilt.

GILMORE, Gary Mark (1940-1977): Murderer

In 1977 Gary Gilmore, age 36, became the first man to be executed in the United States in about a decade. His death followed the reinstatement of the death penalty, which had been outlawed in 1972, under constitutional limits set by the Supreme Court.

Gilmore had been convicted of murdering a Utah gas station attendant and a motel clerk in July 1976. His case attracted worldwide attention not only because his execution would mark the return of capital punishment but also because he disparaged groups and individuals opposed to capital punishment who tried to block his execution. One stay was granted by the Supreme Court on the request of Gilmore's mother. The High Court ruled that the state of Utah was required to prove the prisoner, who had twice attempted suicide in his cell, had been of sound mind when he waived his right to appeal his death sentence. In its final decision, however, the Supreme Court ruled five to four that Utah's capital punishment law was constitutionally sound.

While a last-minute effort was made to get the High Court to prevent his execution, Gilmore went to his death on January 17, 1977 before a firing squad in the Utah State Prison at Point of the Mountain. The condemned man spent his last hours with his family and attorneys and showed little tension until he learned that a federal judge had granted a restraining order delaying the execution. However, a few hours later, a federal appeals court reversed that order.

Meanwhile, as lawyers again petitioned the Supreme Court to halt the proceedings, Gilmore was removed from his cell to a warehouse on the prison grounds. He was strapped in a chair on a raised platform, and a black paper target with a white circle was pinned to his T-shirt directly over his heart. Asked by the warden if he had anything more to say, Gilmore responded, "Let's do it." At 8:07 a.m. five men armed with .30-caliber rifles fired from a cubicle 10 yards in front of Gilmore. One of the rifles contained a blank cartridge and each of the other four had a real bullet. All four bullets pierced Gilmore's heart, but he lived a full two minutes after the shooting.

The final Supreme Court ruling against Gilmore had been handed down at 8:04, just three minutes prior to the shooting. Prison officials later admitted the execution had taken place before they had received word of the verdict on the appeal to the Supreme Court.

Gilmore's life and execution were scrutinized in detail in a best-selling book, *Executioner's Song,* by novelist Norman Mailer.

See also: *Capital Punishment.*

GING, Katherine "Kitty" (1867-1894): Victim of hypnotic murder

Criminologists have often cited the killing of 27-year-old Kitty Ging in Minneapolis, Minn. in 1894 as an authentic case of hypnosis being used to cause a murder. The facts are hazy at best and certainly subject to various interpretations.

Early that year Harry T. Hayward, a smooth-talking local wastrel, had completed a course in hypnotism and tried out his techniques both on Kitty Ging and on Claus Blixt, a dim-witted building engineer and handyman. Eventually, Haywood induced Kitty to give him several thousand dollars, all her ready cash, so that he could "invest" it for her. How much of this was due to "hypnotic powers" and how much to the sheer weight of his personality cannot be measured. In any event, he also was able in time to get Kitty to make him the beneficiary of two $5,000 life insurance policies.

Meanwhile, Hayward was spending long sessions with Blixt too. "He always made me look into his eyes," the simple-minded Blixt later said. "He said that unless I looked into his eyes, I couldn't understand what he was saying." What Hayward was usually saying was that crime paid and was easy. Blixt insisted Hayward "induced" him to set fire to a vacant factory building on which Kitty Ging held a mortgage. She collected $1,500 in insurance and the money eventually found its way into Hayward's pockets. Since Hayward gave some of the money to Blixt, it was unclear how much of Blixt's acts had been due to his own greed and how much to Hayward's hypnotic powers.

Hayward now began to plot Kitty Ging's murder so that he

could collect her life insurance. Apparently, he had less than total confidence in his power to induce Blixt to carry out the crime because he first approached his own brother, Adry Hayward, to commit the murder while he established an iron-clad alibi. The astounded Adry rejected the proposition. He later said: "I don't know why I listened when Harry talked to me of this dreadful thing. He kept looking at me as he talked, and sometimes I felt as if I was being hypnotized. When I refused, he talked about getting Blixt to help him. He said Blixt was so simple-minded that he could easily be influenced."

Adry related his conversation with his brother to a lawyer friend of the family, who simply ignored the story as too preposterous until Kitty Ging's body, her head crushed in and a bullet wound behind her ear, was found on the evening of December 3, 1894. The lawyer then took his information to the Hennepin County district attorney's office, and Blixt and Adry and Harry Hayward were brought in for questioning. Hayward proved to be a tough man to crack, possessing a perfect alibi for the time of the murder: attendance at the Grand Opera House.

For a while, Adry attempted to shield his brother, and Blixt insisted he was not involved in any way. Finally, Blixt broke and admitted murdering Kitty Ging, arranging to do so at a time when Harry Howard had an alibi. He said that before his act he had spent several long sessions with Hayward during which he was told over and over again that murder was an easy crime to commit and get away with. After Blixt's admission, Adry talked, and finally, Harry Hayward confessed to masterminding Kitty's murder, saying his mistake "was in not killing Blixt, as I had originally intended."

Claus Blixt was sentenced to life imprisonment and Harry Hayward, "the hypnotic plotter," was condemned to die on December 11, 1895. His execution proved as bizarre as his crime. He promised to cause no trouble if the scaffold was painted bright red and the rope dipped in red dye. The authorities agreed to these requests but refused to allow him to wear red clothing or to use a red hood in place of the traditional black. On the scaffold Hayward recited a prayer and asked God's forgiveness for his sins. Then he shouted: "Don't pay any attention to that! I just said it to oblige one of my lawyers. I didn't mean a word of it! I stand pat. . . ."

At that moment the outraged executioner, without waiting for his signal, sprang the trap.

GLANTON, John J. (c.1815-1850): Scalp hunter and murderer

Of all the men who operated in the bloody business of scalp hunting, probably the most successful was a Tennessee-born thug who had escaped prison in Nashville in 1845 while doing time for murder and taken refuge in the Army during the Mexican War. When mustered out in 1848, he organized a band of those who were described in Texas as "border scum" and went into the scalp-hunting business in a big way. It was estimated that Glanton and his men took in about $100,000

for scalps, which meant slaughtering well over 1,000 Indians since the going rate for Apache scalps paid by the Mexican governor of Chihuahua was $100 for a male, $50 for a female and $25 for a child.

What spoiled their lucrative business was the discovery by both Mexican and U.S. authorities that they were taking a lot of "suspect" scalps, apparently lifted from the heads of Mexicans and Americans of a dark complexion. Rewards of more than $75,000 were posted on Glanton and various confederates, forcing the gang to flee west to the California border on the Colorado River. There, Glanton engaged in a running war with the Yuma Indians for control of ferrying operations across the river. Learning that the Indians charged covered-wagon immigrants a small sum to cross the river, Glanton realized he could exact exorbitant sums if he eliminated the Indian competition. Initially, the killing margin favored Glanton, but on April 23, 1850 a large force of Yumas overwhelmed Glanton and his men and killed all but three of them. The massacre of whites by the Indians brought an Army detachment to the scene to quell the "uprising," but when the victims were found to be Glanton and his men, peace was restored. When Fort Yuma was built later in the year, it was named in honor of the Indians who had wiped out one of the West's bloodiest gangs. The Yumas received no reward money, however. Paying a reward to Indians for killing whites, even those with a price on their heads, would have been regarded as an outrage.

See also: *Scalp hunting*.

GLATMAN, Harvey Murray (1928-1959): Rapist and murderer

By masquerading as a detective magazine photographer, Harvey Glatman, a particularly sadistic California murderer in the 1950s, got three young women to pose for the usual "bound-and-gagged" stuff and, after sexually abusing them and taking many pictures, strangled them to death. Glatman was the classic example of a mama's boy turned killer. He had previously done time in New York state for a string of "phantom bandit" attacks on lone women and been imprisoned in Colorado for aggravated assaults on women. After each run-in with the law, Glatman fell back on his aged mother, who paid for his psychiatric treatment for five years. In 1957 his mother gave him the money to attend a television repairman's school in Los Angeles and supplied him with funds to open a TV repair shop.

Glatman's murder victims were two young photographic models and an attractive lonely hearts club divorcee. On separate occasions he had succeeded in convincing 19-year-old model Judy Dull and 24-year-old model Ruth Rita Mercado that he was a photographer on assignment for a detective magazine. With his third victim, divorcee Shirley Bridgeport, he simply made a date. In each case, after gaining their confidence, he then lured the women to his home, pulled out a gun and tied them up. After sexually assaulting his victims, he took lewd pictures of them. Later, he drove each of the three women into the desert, where he inflicted additional perversities on them for many more hours before finally killing them.

"I used the same five-foot length of sash cord for all three," he later said, almost gloatingly. "I kept it in my car with the gun. . . . I made them lie on their stomachs. Then I tied their ankles together, looped the end of the cord about their necks and pulled until they were dead."

Two other women almost suffered the same fate. One escaped when she grew suspicious of Glatman's actions. The other, 28-year-old Lorraine Vigil, offered desperate resistance when he pointed a gun at her and tried to tie her up on the shoulder of the Santa Ana Freeway. Although shot in the leg, she managed to pull the gun from Glatman's hand and had it pointed at him when a highway patrolman arrived on the scene.

Glatman eagerly described his murderous acts and seemed to bear no remorse for them. His main concern was keeping his 69-year-old mother from attending his trial. "It would have been too hard on her," he said after his conviction. He refused to cooperate with lawyers trying to appeal his case, announcing in San Quentin's death row that he wanted to die. "It's better this way," he said. "I knew this is the way it would be." Glatman was executed in the gas chamber on August 18, 1959, undoubtedly pleased that a number of publications had engaged in spirited, if unseemly, bidding to publish the photographs he had taken of his victims.

G-MEN: Slang for F.B.I. agents

The use of the term "G-man" to describe an FBI man was bestowed, according to agency historians, by public enemy George "Machine Gun" Kelly when he was captured in 1933 in a Memphis boarding house. Trapped without his weapon, Kelly was described as screaming, "It's the government men— don't shoot, G-men, don't shoot!"

Actually, a Memphis police sergeant, W. J. Raney, was the man who broke in on Kelly and jammed a shotgun in his stomach. Kelly said, "I've been waiting for you." Additionally, some accounts indicate that during the 19th century members of the underworld referred to other government agents, notably the Secret Service, as G-men.

See also: *George R. "Machine Gun" Kelly.*

GOAD, John (?-1907): Gun-toting preacher

An itinerant Baptist preacher, John Goad roamed the Nevada gold camps in the 1870s lecturing against sin and crime and backing up his words with what was to become famous throughout the West as the "John Goad Bible."

In his preaching he would denounce the lawless element in the area by name and such denunciation often brought attempts at retaliation. As protection, Goad carried a loaded derringer in a hollowed-out Bible and would not hesitate to use it when the situation required. In a typical instance a local ruffian named

Mike Fink was hired by the drink-and-prostitution crowd in Carson City, Nev. to break up Goad's meeting and promptly got a ball in the chest for his troubles. That sort of gunsmoke preaching earned Goad proper respect in time, and when John Goad came to town, the lawless element made no effort to silence him.

GOHL, Billy (1860?-1928): Mass murderer

Billy Gohl undoubtedly belongs somewhere near the top of any list of the most deadly American mass murderers, having killed a minimum of 40 men and almost certainly many more.

Gohl was always mysterious about himself. He turned up in the spring of 1903 in Aberdeen, Wash. as a delegate of the Sailors' Union of the Pacific. Nobody among Aberdeen's 12,000 inhabitants knew him, and he seems to have told differing tales of his labor and maritime past, although that was not unusual in a wide-open town like Aberdeen. He was a squat, bull-necked man with a shaven head and an almost angelic-looking face. But everyone realized that Billy Gohl was a man who could take care of himself and that earned him respect in the Sailors' Union.

As a union official, Gohl performed all sorts of chores for seamen. The union office was generally the first stop for sailors from schooners and four-riggers arriving in port. The seamen would check with Gohl for mail and would leave their valuables with him when they went carousing. Since this would often be their first shore leave in months, their pay generally came to rather large sums. Union delegates always kept the money in the safe until the sailors called for it. Billy Gohl just kept it.

Gohl's technique was to murder a seaman as soon as he showed up, before he had time to make friends. He would look out the window to see if anyone had seen the man enter the union office; if not, and if the sailor had turned in enough cash or other valuables to make the effort worthwhile, Gohl would simply take a gun from his desk drawer and shoot the man through the head. From there on, Gohl had everything down to a science.

He cleaned the gun, searched the corpse for additional money and stripped the body of all identification. Gohl's office was on the second floor of a building whose rear extended out over the Wishkah River, which fed into Gray's Harbor. Supported by stilts, the house had a trapdoor with a chute leading to the water. Down the chute went the corpse to be carried away by the rapid river current. If and when the body bobbed to the surface, it would be miles out in the harbor.

After 1903 Aberdeen began to be known by sailors as a "port of missing men," but no one thought to attribute that sad turn of events to Billy Gohl. Between 1909 and 1912 a total of 41 "floaters" were fished out of the water. Most were believed to be merchant seamen, and the most upset man in town was invariably Billy Gohl, demanding the law do something. He was finally trapped when one of his victims was traced to his office and no further. Gohl had shot the man as soon as he entered his office. When he searched the body, he found a gold watch with the name August Schleuter of Hamburg, Germany engraved on it. Gohl decided it would be too incriminating to keep and returned it to the body. When the corpse drifted ashore, Gohl identified Schleuter as one of his men. It took the law weeks to find out the truth, which as good as convicted Gohl. It turned out the victim really was a Danish seaman named Fred Nielssen. He had bought a watch in Hamburg, and the name of the watchmaker was August Schleuter.

In 1913 Gohl was convicted of two murders but only laughed when asked to make a complete roster of his victims. He avoided execution because the year before, the state of Washington had eliminated capital punishment. Gohl's mass murder spree was used as an argument for its restoration, even though he had committed his murders while the death penalty had been in effect. In 1914 the death penalty was restored. Gohl died in prison in 1928.

GOLD Accumulator Swindle

A monumental fraud perpetrated on hard-headed New Englanders in 1897 involved a so-called gold accumulator, which allegedly mined gold from the ocean. The scheme was the work of a veteran English con man named Charles E. Fisher and a Connecticut Baptist minister named Prescott Ford Jernegan. Jernegan may well have been a dupe at the beginning of the operation but by the time it reached fruition he proved just as adept as Fisher at holding on to his ill-gotten gains.

Fisher, it seemed, had a secret invention to extract the gold eddying about in Passamaquoddy Bay near the town of Lubec, Maine. Fisher's gold accumulator was painted with mercury and another "secret compound" and lowered into the water. When the device was raised the following day, it was crusted with thin flakes of gold. Fisher and Jernegan demonstrated the device on several occasions to some extremely dubious Yankee businessmen, who insisted on guarding the scene of the demonstration all night to prevent any tampering. However, they were unaware that Fisher, who had been a deep-sea diver back in England, would swim to the accumulator during the night and plant the grains of gold.

Eventually, shares in the Electrolytic Marine Salts Co. were sold to a gullible public. The value of the initial issue of 350,000 shares a $1 a share soon climbed to $50 a share as New Englanders rushed to get in on a good thing. In addition, a grateful board of directors voted to give Fisher and Jernegan $200,000 each for their services. All this took place on the basis of $25,000 having been "mined," but it was apparent that the process could just go on forever. It went on only until Fisher quietly disposed of his shares of stock, added that money to his $200,000 and left for Boston "to get more supplies." He didn't return and suddenly the gold accumulator didn't accumulate any more gold.

The Rev. Jernegan announced he was off in search of Fisher and disappeared with his $200,000-plus as well. His search apparently took him to France, where he was later found living in luxury with his family. The irate board of directors of the marine salts company demanded the French government take him into custody. It did, but the minister was soon released. It was obvious that the $200,000 had been legally voted him and there was no way to force him to return it. All that appeared to have gone wrong was that an apparent gold-mining procedure had run dry.

Jernegan finally came back to America and actually returned $175,000 to the swindled stockholders. This represented what he said was left of the $200,000. He continued to live well thereafter in the Philippines and Hawaii, undoubtedly on the revenues from the sale of his bloated stockholdings. When Jernegan died in 1942, there was a report circulated that Charlie Fisher had been living in the South Seas as a rich American. According to the story, Fisher had been caught fooling around with the wife of a tribal chieftain and that he and she had been killed according to tribal custom. Apparently, the still-living investors in the Electrolytic Marine Salts Co. were determined to have their revenge, real or fancied.

GOLD Brick Swindle: Confidence game

The gold brick swindle is a hardy perennial that just will not die. The victim buys what he thinks are gold brick ingots and ends up with worthless lead or brass. Most big-city bunco squads handle several such cases each year.

The origin of the gold brick swindle is unknown but probably started in the California gold fields during the 1850s. Wyatt Earp and Mysterious Dave Mather got involved in the game in Mobeetie, Tex. in 1878, after Earp learned how well the racket worked in Kansas. A fabulous young swindler, Reed Waddell, brought the racket to New York in 1880 and trimmed some rather bright and supposedly sharp businessmen with it. Waddell's bricks certainly looked real, being triple gold-plated and marked in the manner of a regulation brick from the United States Assayer's Office, with the letters "U.S." at one end and, below that, the name of the assayer and the weight and fineness of the bullion. Waddell's operation included a phony assayer's office where the brick was supposedly tested. If the sucker hesitated, Waddell would get angry, pull a slug from the brick and insist the victim take it to any jeweler of his choice. As part of the ruse, Waddell had sunk a slug of pure gold into the center of the lead brick, but the trick always worked and his victim would become eager to buy. In all, he took in some $350,000 over the next dozen years. Another ring, headed by Tom O'Brien, netted $100,000 in just five months working the World's Fair in Chicago in 1893. Waddell and O'Brien then joined forces and took the scam to Europe, where O'Brien killed Waddell in an argument over the division of the proceeds from one of their swindles.

Perhaps the greatest swindle of this nature occurred in Texas, where from 1932 to 1935 two crooks, one posing as a minister, victimized a wealthy widow. They told her that gold had been buried in various spots on her vast ranch about 100 years earlier and that ancient maps to the locations could be bought from an old man in Mexico. The widow gave them enough money to buy one map, and sure enough, they came back with some gold bricks. Over the next three years the widow gave them $300,000 and they dug up what was allegedly $4 million in gold. Since at this time the hoarding of gold was illegal, the woman didn't dare attempt to cash in the bricks and therefore never learned they were fake. The con men's downfall came about because of their wild spending, which caused a government agent to investigate the source of their money. The swindle was thus uncovered, and the two crooks were sent to prison.

See also: *Reed Waddell.*

GOLDSBY, Crawford: See Cherokee Bill.

"GONE To Texas": Western saying

"Gone To Texas" was a euphemism that expressed one important motivation for the Western migration and a fact most people on the frontier knew: that a great many of those who went to Texas or elsewhere in the West were running from something. In fact, an early settler, W. B. Dewees, related in his memoirs that it was common to ask a man why he had fled his home. "Few persons feel insulted at such a question. They generally answer for some crime or other which they have committed. If they deny having committed any crime or say they did not run away, they are looked upon suspiciously."

An Easterner visiting Texas, Frederick Law Olmstead, wrote:

In the rapid settlement of the country, many an adventurer crossed the border, spurred by love of liberty, forfeited at home, rather than drawn by a love of adventure or of rich soil. Probably a more reckless and vicious crew was seldom gathered than that which peopled some parts of Eastern Texas at the time of its first resistance to the Mexican government. 'G.T.T.' (gone to Texas) was the slang appendage . . . to every man's name who had disappeared before the discovery of some rascality. Did a man emigrate thither, everyone was on the watch for the discreditable reason to turn up.

G.T.T. was the way of the rascal and the felon but it was also part of the way America was built.

GONZALES, Thomas A. (1878-1956): Medical examiner

Dr. Thomas A. Gonzales, chief medical examiner of New York City from 1937 to 1954, was recognized as one of the country's foremost forensic pathologists. His evidence convicted hundreds of murderers and saved a number of other innocent men, some of whom were accused of crimes that never happened. Often Dr. Gonzales needed only a moment's view of the corpse to tell immediately, for instance, that a husband who strangled his wife had tried to make it appear a case of suicide by gas inhalation.

Clearing an innocent suspect gave Dr. Gonzales the most satisfaction. Such was the case when an elderly tenant was found dead 15 minutes after he had had a heated argument with a muscular real estate agent over the rent and repairs. The old man's body was discovered just inside the door of his apartment, his face bruised and marked and his scalp deeply gashed. Several pieces of furniture in the foyer were overturned or moved out of position. Police learned of the angry dispute from neighbors and arrested the agent. He denied striking the old tenant, but the case against him was strong indeed. There was the confrontation, the obvious signs of a fight, a witness in the hallway who said no one entered the apartment after the agent left and the fact that the victim was dead just a quarter of an hour later.

Dr. Gonzales inspected the scene, diagrammed the position of the furniture and then performed an autopsy. As a result, charges against the real estate man were dropped. The old man had not been beaten to death. He had suffered a heart attack and stumbled around the foyer, displacing the furniture in his death throes. The diagrams of the furniture placement demonstrated how the old man had suffered each of the injuries he received.

Dr. Gonzales, a tall, spare man was one of the top assistants to Dr. Charles Norris, who founded the Medical Examiner's Office in 1918. He took over following Dr. Norris' death in 1935, first as acting head and later as the chief medical examiner, after outscoring all other competitors in the tests given for the position. During his career he testified in many famous cases in New York and elsewhere in the country and coauthored *Legal Medicine and Toxicology*, still regarded as a classic in the field. He often said only medicine could solve many cases.

One common puzzle in many violent deaths was whether the cause had been homicide or suicide. He once proved that a man who had allegedly stabbed himself through his shirt had actually been murdered. (Suicides, he found, almost invariably preferred to strip away their clothing before stabbing themselves.) In another case Gonzales solved a stabbing that had police baffled. A man was found stabbed through the heart in a third-floor bathroom that was locked from the inside. The only window had been painted shut. It was clearly a case of suicide except there was no knife. The case was a stumper for the detectives but not for the medical examiner. "Never mind what happened here," he told the police. "See if you can find out about a knife fight anywhere in the area." The police checked and found that the victim had been stabbed in an altercation. As Dr. Gonzales later explained, it was quite possible for a man stabbed in the heart to walk a block, climb a couple of flights of stairs, lock himself in a bathroom and then finally collapse. Such victims often head for the bathroom to clean themselves up, not realizing they have been fatally wounded.

Dr. Gonzales retired in 1954 and died two years later.

See also: *Charles Norris.*

GOOCH, Arthur (1909-1936): Outlaw and kidnapper

The first man ever to die under the so-called Lindbergh Law of the 1930s, which made kidnapping for ransom a capital offense even if no harm came to the victim, Arthur Gooch was considered by many persons to have gotten a "raw deal." On November 26, 1934 Gooch and a partner in crime were stopped by two police officers for routine interrogation at a Paradise, Tex. gas station. In an ensuing gunfight Gooch and his partner seriously wounded one officer and then forced the two lawmen to drive them across the state line into Oklahoma. There they ran into a force of federal agents involved in another case and a second gun battle broke out. Gooch's confederate was killed and Gooch himself captured. The officers were freed unharmed.

Federal authorities pressed for the death penalty in the Gooch case to determine the constitutionality of the law and to enhance its deterrent effects. However, the case was clearly not the right one to serve their purposes. Much to the chagrin of the authorities, a large part of the press ignored the trial. No one had been killed and no ransom passed. Nevertheless, Gooch was eventually convicted and sentenced to death.

Gooch's attorneys appealed the verdict to the Supreme Court on the ground that he had not committed a kidnapping for ransom and therefore should not have been sentenced to die. In February 1936 the Supreme Court held that the kidnapping of a police officer was adequately covered by the phrase "for ransom, reward, or otherwise." The precedent-setting aspect of the Gooch decision was compromised by the fact that although Gooch was executed on June 19—an event that drew relatively minor attention—it became quite common for juries in federal cases to recommend mercy when bringing in guilty verdicts for capital offenses.

See also: *Lindbergh Law*.

GOOD-TIME Laws

Good-time laws, by which a convict can appreciably reduce his sentence based on good conduct in prison, have generally not fulfilled their promise. The average good-time law prescribes the deduction of one month for the first year of satisfactory behavior, two months for the second and so on until, from the sixth year on, a convict can earn six months off his sentence for every year of good behavior. Unfortunately, such a formula is of more value to a long-term offender than to a short-termer, who is often a first offender and thus a more likely candidate for rehabilitation. In the eyes of convicts, good-time laws seem to be intended less to benefit the prisoner or his reformation than to assist the prison administration in extracting labor from convicts and maintaining discipline.

New York state appears to have started the first good-time law in 1817, under which a first-term convict doing up to five years could reduce his sentence by one-fourth. But there is no record of the system ever actually being used. Similarly, relatively unused statutes appeared over the next few decades in Connecticut, Tennessee and Ohio. The good-time principle gained a more effective foothold in Australia and France. But after the Civil War good-time laws spread rapidly, following the example of the "Irish system," by which a prisoner could win his freedom by earning a certain number of "marks," or credits. By 1868 24 states had passed such laws, and today they are the norm.

In addition to this reduction of sentence by statute, in most states convicts can earn "industrial good time" for taking part in prison industries and "merit good time" for especially good behavior such as taking part in medical experiments and the like. These reductions generally affect only the amount of the time served before an inmate is entitled to his first parole hearing rather than the sentence itself. Thus, when a prisoner is subsequently passed over for parole, he may feel he has been "conned" by the system. Reformers often criticize industrial good time on the grounds that many convicts apply for the benefits and accept shop work instead of training programs which develop the skills, the trades and, more importantly, the attitudes required to reintegrate them into society upon release.

Another problem with good-time laws is that convicts view the benefits as a right, especially in prisons where a new inmate is immediately credited with his maximum time off and then this figure is reduced whenever he violates prison rules. The practice can encourage prisoners to believe that society constantly discriminates against them by taking away good time, an attitude that is at least partially the cause of many prison riots.

GOPHERS: New York gang

One of the last of the all-Irish gangs of New York, the Gophers were the kings of Hell's Kitchen until they disintegrated in the changing society of the pre-World War era. The Gophers controlled the territory between Seventh and Eleventh avenues from 42nd Street to 14th Street. Brawlers, muggers and thieves, they gained their name because they liked to hide out in basements and cellars. With an ability to summon 500 gangsters to their banner, they were not a force to be dismissed lightly by the police or other gangsters.

They were such hell raisers and so fickle in their allegiance that no one could emerge as the single leader of the gang. Thus, the Gophers never produced a gangster with the stature of Monk Eastman, the greatest villain of the period. Among the most prominent Gophers, however, there were numerous subleaders, such a Newburg Gallagher, Stumpy Malarkey, Happy Jack Mulraney and Marty Brennan.

Another celebrated Gopher was One-Lung Curran, who in due course expired due to this deficiency. Once when his girlfriend wailed that she was without a coat for the chilly fall weather, Curran strode up to the first policeman he saw and blackjacked him to the ground. He stripped off the officer's uniform coat and presented it to his mistress, who, being an adept seamstress, converted it into a military-style lady's jacket. This event caused such a fashion sensation in Gopher society that thugs by the dozen soon were out on the streets clubbing and stripping policemen.

In brute power and violence, the police could seldom match

the Gophers. To do so would have accomplished little anyway, since the gang enjoyed a measure of protection from the ward's politicians, who found the Gophers of immense assistance during elections. They however, were too anarchistic to exploit this advantage to the fullest, feeling that with raw power they could achieve anything they wanted.

The Gophers had no reason to fear the police when they looted the New York Central Railroad freight cars along Eleventh Avenue. But while they might enjoy a measure of tolerance from public officials, they failed to grasp the extent of corporate power and the railroad's ability to field a virtual army against them. The New York Central's special force was staffed with many former policemen who had suffered insults and injuries from the gangsters and who were anxious for the opportunity to retaliate. Railroad property became a no-man's land, and the company detectives began to venture further afield to devastate Hell's Kitchen itself. The Gophers were smashed, their prestige savaged and their unity crushed. Gallagher and Brennan went to Sing Sing, and many others were killed or maimed. Factions of the Gophers joined other criminal combines, but these were organizations that specialized in purely criminal ventures and wasted neither time nor strength on unprofitable street bashings. An era of American criminality was ending.

See also: *Lady Gophers*.

GORDON, Captain Nathaniel (?-1862): Pirate

A big, bluff adventurer, Capt. Nathaniel Gordon plied the trade of piracy long after it had declined as a popular criminal endeavor. In the mid-1800s former pirates concentrated on smuggling slaves into the country, bringing in as many as 15,000 per year and reaping enormous profits. In the forefront of this activity were Gordon and his daredevil crew aboard the 500-ton *Erie*. How bloody a business they were engaged in is best revealed by the statistics concerning the cargo. The *Erie* regularly transported approximately 1,000 black captives, but because of the appalling conditions no more than 700 or so would survive the journey. Finally captured on a slave run by the American ship *Mohican*, Gordon was quickly convicted and sentenced to be hanged.

Since the last death penalty for piracy had been carried out some 40 years earlier, protestors insisted it was unfair to execute Gordon for a crime considered virtually extinct. His supporters petitioned President Abraham Lincoln for a pardon, but they failed to consider the political realities. With the nation at war over the matter of slavery, it would have been impossible for Lincoln even to consider pardoning Gordon while Northern soldiers were dying fighting the slave states. Gordon was duly executed in the Tombs in New York City on March 8, 1862. As one last token of fear of a disappearing breed of criminals, authorities packed the prison with armed guards to foil a buccaneer-style rescue attempt, which the newspapers insisted was sure to be made. Unfortunately for Gordon, there

were no pirates left. Nathaniel Gordon was the last man hanged for piracy in the United States.

See also: *Piracy*.

GORDON, Vivian (1899-1931): Murder victim

The murder of Vivian Gordon was one of New York City's gaudiest cases, so shocking that it wrecked the lives of several others and even led to the abrupt end of the corrupt administration of Mayor Jimmy Walker. At the same time, it brought to prominence Samuel Seabury, a lawyer and ex-jurist whose name was to become synonymous with governmental honesty and integrity as a result of the Seabury Investigations. Much of the evidence in the Seabury probe came from a number of "little black books" belonging to Vivian. In them she had kept a day-by-day account of her sexual and criminal doings, which included blackmailing several gentlemen. When revealed, they destroyed the personal and private lives of many men. They also destroyed Vivian's 16-year-old daughter.

Vivian Gordon was born Benita Franklin in Detroit, the daughter of John Franklin, former warden of the Illinois State Penitentiary in Joliet, and was brought up under strict supervision, which included being sent to a convent school in Canada. Eventually, she rebelled and ran away, determined to pursue an acting and modeling career, and later, she married briefly and had a daughter. In 1923 Benita was arrested for prostitution by Patrolman Andrew G. McLaughlin. McLaughlin was a crooked cop who was subsequently found to have banked—on a yearly salary of $3,000—an average of $1,500 monthly. Benita was hauled before a magistrate, H. Stanley Renaud, and became, allegedly, just one of 24 girls without legal representation whom Renaud wrongfully sentenced. Both McLaughlin and Renaud later became targets of the Seabury probe. Benita always insisted she was innocent of the McLaughlin charge, even in later years when, as Vivian Gordon, she was no longer innocent of very much.

Whatever validity her claim of innocence to that charge had, Vivian Gordon became a hooker, and while she branched out into numerous other illegal enterprises, such as being part backer in a stock swindle and financing bank robbery schemes, her steadiest scam was blackmailing men after taking them to hotel rooms. She kept a diary loaded with names, dates and details and put the bite on many an anxious gentleman. During much of her career Vivian worked with a particularly nasty individual named Harry Stein. Later, Stein would be charged with her murder but acquitted; convicted of another woman's murder and serve time for it; and finally executed in the electric chair for a robbery-murder.

While Vivian was living a purple present, she was determined to prove to her teenage daughter that she was a good woman. This and the fact that she felt she had been double-crossed by some politicians in a vice blackmailing scheme prompted her to take the story of her criminal life to the Seabury investigators. In a meeting with one of Seabury's young aides, Irving Ben Cooper, she laid out charges against the police vice squad, including a number of officers who were on her bribe payroll. She claimed her diaries contained explosive evidence against several important men, many of whom were public officials. Cooper listened to her shocking story and told her to gather up all her evidence and bring it to the probers the following week. Vivian said she would. On February 27, 1931 she was found dead in Van Cortlandt Park, strangled with a length of clothesline looped around her neck three times.

Her death became a sensation and loosed the Seabury Investigations with the full support of Gov. Franklin D. Roosevelt. Her diaries were found and led to explosive hearings. They revealed the names of officers on her payroll and, more importantly, the names of many public officials with indications of the prices for which they could be "bought." The ever-widening probe finally included Mayor Walker who was accused of being "on the take" from a number of business interests.

Under pressure, the police came up with a solution to the Gordon murder, charging Harry Stein and one Samuel Greenberg. They had witnesses who said Stein had tried to pawn Vivian's mink coat and diamond ring just a few hours after the murder. And they had the testimony of Harry Schlitten, who allegedly drove the death car, a Cadillac limousine rented by Stein for the occasion. According to Schlitten, Stein had told him that a party, who turned out to be Vivian Gordon, had to be killed to oblige another party and that Greenberg, posing as a diamond merchant to lure the victim along, would be picked up as they drove toward the Bronx. When Greenberg got in the car, Vivian supposedly said to him, "Where have you been all my life?"

The trio, sitting in back of the limousine, killed off a bottle of bourbon and then the men, said Schlitten, killed off the lady. He said Vivian struggled quite a bit and then he heard Stein say, "She's finished now." He looked back and saw Stein with his hand on the rope. They dumped the body in the park, the informer said, and drove back to Manhattan.

Not too surprisingly for the era, Stein and Greenberg were found not guilty. Their lawyer, the famous Samuel Leibowitz, went into one of his favorite routines, postulating a "police frame-up," which worked very well amidst the Seabury probe's constant revelations of police venality. Some detectives complained bitterly about Stein beating their "perfect case" and pointed out later that if he had been convicted, he wouldn't have been around to commit several other murders, one of which was to send him to the electric chair in 1955.

That was only one of the misfortunes to result from Vivian Gordon's murder. There was also the tragedy of Vivian's teenage daughter, Benita. Although teachers and classmates at her high school tried to shield her from the details, she read every line about the case in the newspapers. The girl became more and more withdrawn, but she too kept a diary. There were a series of pitiful entries, including one on March 1 that said, "I guess I will have to change my name."

Two days later, she made a final entry: "March 3, 2:15 P.M. . . . I'm tired . . . I've decided to give it all up . . . I am turning on the gas."

See also: *Seabury Investigation.*

GORDON, Waxey (Irving Wexler) (1888-1952): Prohibition beer baron

One of the top three or four Prohibition bootleggers, Irving Wexler, better known as Waxey Gordon, was a multimillionaire by the end of the 1920s and then fell to depths almost unparalleled in underworld history.

He got his nickname as a kid pickpocket because he could slip a mark's wallet out of his pocket as if it were coated with wax. Although still a small-timer, Gordon moved up in the underworld as a strikebreaker, whoremaster and, at times, a dope dealer.

As it did for so many other criminals of the era, Prohibition made Waxey Gordon a big-timer. First in junior partnership with Mr. Big, Arnold Rothstein, and finally in charge after buying Rothstein out, Gordon was one of the leading illegal liquor importers on the East Coast. His personal income ran somewhere between $1 million and $2 million a year, and he owned blocks of real estate in New York and Philadelphia. He also owned nightclubs, speakeasies, gambling casinos and a fleet of ocean-going rumrunners and lived in a castle, complete with moat, in southern New Jersey. His distilleries in Philadelphia cut, reblended and rebottled booze for dozens of leading bootleggers around the country. He was able to charge an arm and a leg for his supplies, often cutting himself in for a piece of his customer's action. Since one could not really hide major operations like distilleries and breweries, Gordon became probably the biggest graft-paying criminal in the East. When New Jersey reformers grew upset about the noise made by trucks rumbling out of his illicit breweries, Waxey paid off politicians so that his beer could be pumped through pressure hoses in the sewer systems of Elizabeth, Paterson and Union City.

Gordon was so powerful that he even forced his way into a "shotgun-partnership" with the Luciano-Costello-Lansky-Siegel forces in New York, although tension between himself and Lansky grew so intense that they would not even sit at the same table with each other. In the 1930s Gordon feuded with Dutch Schultz, and when it looked like the end of Prohibition was nearing, the two turned to open warfare for control of legitimate beer distribution rights in New York.

By this time, Gordon had won the title of New York's Public Enemy No. 1, an accolade belied by his short, dumpy appearance and the meager wisps of hair on his dome. Outside of Schultz, one of the most violence-prone gangsters of the era, few wanted to take on Gordon in gangland combat, especially since Waxey enjoyed extreme loyalty from his men, who refused to be bought out or to engage in takeover attempts.

There is little doubt that the Luciano-Lansky forces brought about Gordon's downfall by getting the law to do their dirty work for them. Gordon was tossed to the income tax wolves. Meyer Lansky's brother Jake and others, according to the underworld gossip, fed the tax men information about Gordon's operations. The government's case, presented by a young federal prosecutor named Thomas E. Dewey, showed that the Prohibition bootleg baron took in $2 million a year, all the while reporting a net income of just $8,125 annually. Convicted in December 1930, Waxey got 10 years, which finished him as a major underworld operator. Just as they were to do with others, the Luciano-Lansky forces moved to take over Gordon's rackets.

When Gordon was released from Leavenworth in 1940, he announced to reporters: "Waxey Gordon is dead. From now on, it's Irving Wexler, salesman." Actually, it proved to be Waxey Gordon, salesman, hawking one of his old lines, narcotics. In 1951 Gordon, now a small-timer, was nailed as he delivered a $6,300 package of heroin to a federal narcotics stool pigeon.

Among the arresting officers the aged gangster recognized police Sgt. Johnny Cottone. He broke down sobbing. "My God, Johnny," he pleaded. "Shoot me. Don't take me in for junk. Let me run, and then shoot me!" One of the old man's younger confederates started weeping too. He pulled $2,500 from his pockets and ripped two diamond rings off his fingers. "Take this," he cried. "Take me. Take the whole business. Just let Pop go."

To the end, Waxey Gordon enjoyed the loyalty of his men. In December the 63-year-old Gordon was sentenced to two terms of 25 years to life. He was sent to Alcatraz, a fate the aged criminal hardly deserved. Six months later, on June 24, 1952, he died there of a heart attack.

GORDON-GORDON, Lord (?-1873): Swindler

One of America's most audacious confidence operators was a Scotsman who, masquerading as Lord Gordon-Gordon, swindled some of America's greatest robber barons, including Jay Gould, out of $1 million in negotiable securities. Gordon-Gordon never revealed his real identity. Instead, he spread the word through intermediaries that he was the heir of the great Earl of Gordon, cousin of the Campbells, collateral relative of Lord Byron and proud descendant of the Lochinvar and the ancient kings of the Highlanders.

Gordon-Gordon's first known peccadillo occurred in 1868 in Edinburgh, where, under the equally fanciful name of Lord Glencairn, he swindled a jeweler out of £25,000. Then in 1871, as Lord Gordon-Gordon, he appeared in Minneapolis and opened a bank account with $40,000 from his jewelry swindle. He set up representatives of the Northern Pacific Railroad for a swindle by declaring he was in search of immense areas of good lands on which to settle his overpopulated Scottish tenantry. He suggested he could use upwards of a half-million acres, the very answer to the railroad's dreams. Since the company in its push westward was sorely pressed for capital, it did all it could to woo several millions from Gordon-Gordon. He was wined, dined and taken on lavish hunting expeditions. How much hard cash Gordon-Gordon managed to pocket was never known, but the "trinkets" given him in one instance were worth $40,000. After some three months Gordon-Gordon had picked out all the land he wished to buy,

and he told the railroad executives he was returning to New York to arrange for the transfer of funds from Scotland to make the purchase. He left Minneapolis not only with fond farewells but also with special letters of introduction from Colonel John S. Loomis, the line's land commissioner, to Jay Gould, then fighting for control of the Erie Railroad, and Horace Greeley, a stockholder in the Erie and a business associate of Gould.

Lord Gordon-Gordon portrayed himself as a potential savior to Gould, just as he had to the Northern Pacific. He let Greeley believe he was a substantial holder of Erie stock and also the holder of proxies from a number of European friends, enough to provide Gould with the margin of victory. But Gordon-Gordon has a price for his aid. He wanted the management of the railroad reformed and an active voice for himself, but, he generously added, he was prepared to leave Gould in charge. Gould was ecstatic—and grateful. He handed over to Gordon-Gordon $1 million in negotiable securities and cash in "a pooling of interests" that could only be considered a bribe.

Soon after this transaction, large chunks of stock began appearing for sale. Gordon-Gordon was quickly cashing in on his profits from the gullible Gould. Convinced he had been swindled, Gould sued Gordon-Gordon, who immediately threw in with Gould's business rivals. But time was running out for Gordon-Gordon. On the witness stand he cheerfully reeled off the names of important European personages he knew and represented in the Erie deal. Before his references could be checked, he decamped to Canada with a large portion of Gould's money.

When located in Canada, Gordon-Gordon had little trouble convincing the authorities there that he was a man of high breeding and that charges by various Americans, Gould in New York and railroaders in Minnesota, were ill-founded and malicious. He told people in Fort Garry, Manitoba that he intended to invest huge sums in the area and that the Americans were being vindictive because he would not utilize the funds in their country.

Convinced they would never get the scoundrel back to face charges by any legal means, a group of Minnesotan railroaders, perhaps financed by Gould, attempted to kidnap Gordon-Gordon. They actually snatched him in July 1873 and were only apprehended at the border by a group of the swindler's friends and a contingent of Northwest Mounted Police. The kidnappers, including two future governors of Minnesota and three future Congressmen, were clapped into prison and allowed no bail.

The Gordon-Gordon affair blew up into an international incident. Gov. Austin of Minnesota ordered the state militia to be ready to march and demanded the return of the kidnap party. Thousands of Minnesotans volunteered for an invading expeditionary force. Finally, negotiations between President Ulysses S. Grant and his secretary of state, Hamilton Fish, and Canadian Prime Minister Sir John MacDonald produced an agreement in the interests of international amity that allowed the raiding party to go free on bail. Gordon-Gordon was safe in Canada, since the treaties between the United States and that country did not provide for extradition for such minor offenses as larceny and embezzlement.

All might have gone well for Gordon-Gordon had not news of the incident reached Edinburgh. The owners of Marshall and Son, Jewelers became convinced that the description of Lord Gordon-Gordon matched that of the long-gone Lord Glencairn. They dispatched a clerk who had dealt with His Lordship to check up on Gordon-Gordon in person. He made a firm identification and the master swindler was ordered returned to England to clear up the matter. Gordon-Gordon undertook a legal battle, but when it was obvious he had lost, he shot himself to death.

GRABBERS: 19th century New York procurer gangs

Grabbers was the popular name given in the 1860s and 1870s to the procurer gangs operating in New York. The two most important gangs were those headed by Red Light Lizzie, perhaps the most-noted procurer of the time, and her principal rival, the brazen Hester Jane Haskins, also known as Jane the Grabber. Both gangs operated out of business offices and each month sent a circular out to clients advertising their newest wares.

Procuring was generally tolerated by the police so long as the grabbers followed the usual procedure of sending out "talent scouts" to outlying villages upstate and surrounding states to lure young girls to the metropolis with promises of high-paying jobs. The girls were then "broken into the life."

A "grabber scandal" of sorts erupted in 1875 when the Haskins woman began specializing in recruiting girls from good families, the better-paying brothel clients being much enticed by having the company of females of refinement. Too many girls disappeared, however, which created quite a stir. Jane the Grabber was arrested with a number of her minions and sent to prison. Upon their release they were "rousted" out of New York by the police apparently because of intolerance for procurers who could not understand certain class distinctions.

See also: *Procuring*.

GRADY Gang: 19th century sneak thief gang

During the 1860s the art of sneak thievery achieved new heights thanks to a New York gang of thieves masterminded by John D. Grady, better known as Travelling Mike.

Travelling Mike, perhaps the number two fence of the era, after the infamous Marm Mandelbaum, was a stooped, dour-faced little man who padded the streets winter and summer wearing a heavy overcoat and carrying a peddler's box on his shoulder. Mike's box did not contain the standard peddler's stock of needles and other small articles, but rather pearls, diamonds and bonds, all stolen property. He never ventured out with less than $10,000 with which to make his daily purchases from various criminals. Mike was frequently to be seen at the notorious Thieves' Exchange, near Broadway and Houston Street, where fences and criminals met each night and dickered openly in the buying and selling of stolen goods.

To drum up more business, Travelling Mike organized his own gang and planned their jobs. His most famous underling was "Billy the Kid" Burke, a brilliant sneak thief who was arrested 100 times before his 26th birthday but was still able to retire, according to legend, a wealthy man. Mike engineered a raid on the money hoard of Rufus L. Lord, a grasping and penurious financier of the day. Worth $4 million, Lord spent his time clipping coupons and counting his hoard of money in a dingy office at 38 Exchange Place. He was so miserly that he wore tattered and patched clothing and would not light his office with more than one candle at a time. Yet in business he was extremely cunning and was supposedly able to milk the last penny out of any adversary.

In March 1866 Travelling Mike approached Lord about securing a loan for an alleged business venture, and long discussions were held about terms. Finally, on March 7 the fence returned to Lord's office accompanied by his minions, Greedy Jake Rand, Eddie Pettengill, Hod Ennis and Boston Pet Anderson. When Travelling Mike offered to put up high-class security for the loan and suggested an interest rate of 20 percent, Lord bounded from his chair and seized him by the lapels, imploring him to close the deal immediately. While the anxious Lord was thus distracted, Boston Pet and Pettengill slipped in the darkness to the huge safe the financier often absentmindedly left open and made off with two tin boxes. Travelling Mike then agreed to close the deal and said he would return in an hour to sign the necessary papers.

When the gang opened the tin boxes, they counted loot totaling $1.9 million in cash and negotiable securities. Rand, Pettengill, Ennis and Boston Pet instantly joined Billy the Kid Burke in wealthy retirement, while only Travelling Mike continued in the rackets.

Mike did not consider the Lord caper his crowning achievement. He learned that his archrival, Marm Mandelbaum, had trailblazed a new business method in crime by forming a gang whose members were paid strictly on salary, with all the loot going to her. Travelling Mike, with devious acumen, approached her criminals and purchased much of their loot at extremely low prices. Since the gangsters would have netted nothing extra otherwise, both they and Travelling Mike profited. Only Marm was victimized. When she learned of the plot against her, she dissolved her gang and railed about the lack of honor among thieves, with Travelling Mike specifically in mind.

GRAHAM, Barbara (1923-1955): Murderess

Barbara Graham was a call girl and murderess who worked with a California gang of notoriously savage robbers and killers who often tortured their victims to extract loot from them. She was subsequently immortalized in *I Want to Live!*, perhaps the phoniest movie ever made about a female criminal.

Admittedly, Barbara was the product of an unhappy childhood. When she was two years old, her mother was sent to a reformatory for wayward girls, and Barbara was raised in a rather indifferent manner by neighbors. Later, mother and daughter were reunited, but Barbara ran away at the age of nine. Ironically, she ended up doing time in the same institution where her mother had been confined.

Barbara was drawn into organized crime circles in the 1940s. In 1947 she was a star call girl in San Francisco for Sally Stanford, the city's most infamous madam. Following her fourth marriage, to a man named Henry Graham, she gave birth to her third child and took up drugs. She also joined a murderous robbery ring headed by Jack Santos. Santos' gang included Emmett Perkins, second-in-command, a brute as vicious as Santos himself; John L. True, a deep-sea diver who later turned state's evidence; and Baxter Shorter, who eventually tried to turn state's evidence, was kidnapped and was never seen again.

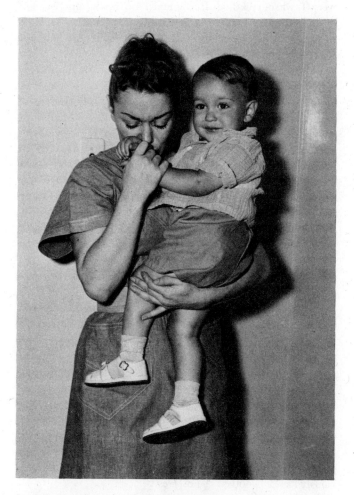

Barbara Graham, on trial for murder, posed for photographers with her 19-month-old son.

Among the crimes the gang committed were the December 1951 torture and robbery of a gold buyer, Andrew Colner, and his wife; the December 1951 murder of Edmund Hansen, a gold miner; the October 1952 murder of a grocer, Guard Young, his two little daughters and a neighbor's child; and the March 1953 brutal beating murder of Mrs. Mabel Monahan, a 63-year-old crippled Burbank widow believed to have had a large amount of jewels.

Of these crimes the only one that Barbara Graham was definitely tied to, primarily by True's confession, was the Monahan killing. She was to get the gang into the house by asking to use the telephone. According to True, the original plan called for the four men to crowd in as soon as the door was opened, tie up, gag and blindfold Mrs. Monahan and then ransack the house, grab the treasure and leave. The plan went awry when Barbara ran amok.

She struck the widow to the ground, seized her by the hair and began beating her over the head with the butt of the gun she was carrying. The old woman, bewildered and in agony, started moaning, "Oh, no, no, no!" One of the men egged Barbara on, "Give her more!" She did, cracking her skull and killing her. Later, a veteran prosecutor was to tell a jury the victim looked "as if she had been hit with a heavy truck traveling at high speed. The savage brutality of the attack is like nothing I have seen in 20 years of experience. I can scarcely believe that human beings could do that to an elderly woman against whom they had nothing, merely because they wanted money."

The gang, however, got no money. There was no large sum in the house and no valuable jewelry. They had simply been misinformed.

At her trial Barbara tried to prove her innocence by producing two alibis, both of which were probably false. Meanwhile, a police officer posing as an underworld agent offered to furnish her another alibi if she paid $25,000. Barbara agreed, and the plot was then exposed in court complete with taped recordings. Barbara lost her composure and cried out chokingly: "Oh, have you ever been desperate? Do you know what it means not to know what to do?"

On June 3, 1955 Barbara Graham, Santos and Perkins died in the San Quentin gas chamber. Barbara asked for a blindfold. "I don't want to have to look at people," she said bitterly.

In 1958 actress Susan Hayward won an Academy Award for her film portrayal of Barbara Graham.

GRAHAM, John Gilbert (1932-1957): Mass murderer

John Graham was a typical, if awesome, example of the plane saboteurs most active in the 1950s and 1960s who placed bombs on airliners to collect the insurance on a single passenger. He thought nothing of the fact that he had to kill 43 other persons because he wanted to murder his mother, Mrs. Daisy King of Denver, Colo.

On November 1, 1955 Graham placed a time bomb made with 25 sticks of dynamite in his mother's luggage before she boarded a DC-6B at Stapleton Airport. The plane was aloft only 10 minutes before it crashed in flames. When traces of a bomb device were found, suspicion soon focused on young Graham because he had attracted so much attention to himself in the terminal before flight time buying insurance policies on his mother's life from a vending machine. He had nervously spoiled a number of them and kept buying more, finally salvaging $37,500 worth.

When the FBI found material used to make bombs in his home, Graham confessed the plane sabotage. Public speculation as to how anyone would kill in such a manner and take the lives of so many innocents brought a simple explanation from a psychologist: "People actually have very few restraints concerning a person they have no intimate knowledge of. A mine disaster that claims 120 lives doesn't really impress many people. But should a neighbor fall from a ladder and die, the effect on these same people is tremendous."

Certainly, Graham showed no remorse about all his victims, being more concerned about his mother. Mrs. King had been going to visit her daughter in Alaska and, planning to go hunting, she had carried a box of shotgun shells on board the plane. Graham laughed, "Can't you just see Mother when all those shells began to go off in the plane?"

At his trial Graham, found sane but resentful of his mother's neglect when he was a child, recanted his confession but was convicted by the overwhelming evidence. He refused to take any steps to appeal his death sentence and went silently to the gas chamber on January 11, 1957.

GRAHAM-TEWKSBURY Feud: Sheepmen-cattlemen war

Some historians have insisted that the Graham-Tewksbury feud, sometimes known as the Pleasant Valley War, of 1886-92 was nothing more than a family feud; but the fact remains that it escalated into a great sheepman-cattleman confrontation which was to leave Arizona's Tonto Basin a "dark and bloody ground."

The Grahams and Tewksburys were both small-time ranchers who had built their stock with a "long rope," that is stealing their cattle rather than raising it. There is reason to believe the two neighboring families engaged in this operation as a joint enterprise, with all the stolen stock being hidden on Graham land. When it came time to divide their loot, however, the Tewksburys discovered the Grahams had registered all of them in their own brand. The Tewksburys were left a ranch without cattle, while the Grahams suddenly were able to move in big cattlemen circles.

Not surprisingly, some shooting resulted, but the leaders of each family, John D. Tewksbury and Tom Graham, argued for restraint. Still, the Tewksburys thirsted for revenge and finally came up with a reprisal that not only enraged the Grahams but all the other cattlemen in the basin. They made a deal with some big sheepmen to bring their flocks into Pleasant Valley in a deliberate effort to ruin the Grahams' grazing land. The conflict suddenly was bigger than a family feud, and all the cattlemen took up arms to drive out the sheepmen. Gunfighters lent their services to the side that reflected their economic interest. Not illogically, confirmed cattle rustlers joined in the fight against the sheep invasion since their livelihood, as well as that of honest cattlemen, was imperiled.

Initially, the war was limited to the killing of sheep, which were stampeded over cliffs, burned in the brush or shot to death by night-riding gunmen. Inevitably, human life was lost and the war escalated. Five cowboys called on the Tewksbury ranch in what was later claimed to be a peaceful visit. As they were leaving, two of them were shot dead by Jim Tewksbury, the deadliest of his family. Tewksbury claimed the two were in the process of turning and drawing on him. While Tom Graham still tried to stem the violence, another cattleman gunfighter attempted to kill Jim Tewksbury and paid with his life. When Billy Graham, 18, the youngest of the family, was gunned down by a deputy sheriff who sympathized with the Tewksburys, Tom Graham gave up and personally joined the fight, leading a raid on the Tewksbury ranch and offering a reward of $500 for every sheepherder and $1,000 for every Tewksbury killed. In the raid John Tewksbury, Sr. and Jr. and Bill Jacobs were murdered, but Jim, brother Ed and a number of supporters escaped. The cattlemen then allowed hogs to feed on two of the corpses.

Although from then on, the Tewksburys were outnumbered, they generally had the best of it, and more cattlemen than sheepmen died thereafter. In 1888 Jim Tewksbury died of consumption. Nonetheless, Ed Tewksbury had enough supporters to fight on until by 1889 only he and Tom Graham were left of their respective families. The sheep were driven out, but so was Graham, who remorsefully moved away from the valley. He returned in 1892 to settle some affairs and was ambushed and killed, some witnesses said, by Ed Tewksbury and John Rhodes. The case against Rhodes was not very strong and he was released, but Ed Tewksbury, the last survivor of the feud, was charged with murder. He was convicted but the verdict was thrown out on a technicality. The second trial ended in a hung jury, and finally, in 1896 the charges were dropped.

Until he died in 1904, Ed Tewksbury was a constable in Globe, Arizona Territory and deputy sheriff of Gila County.

The story of the feud has been told many times in many ways, including Zane Grey's rendition in his novel *To the Last Man*. But while the personal conflict of the Grahams and Tewksburys had provoked the war, the battle between cattlemen and sheepmen was repeated in many other areas of the country. This age-old conflict only ended when the cattlemen discovered they could indeed allow sheep to graze on the same lands with cattle if scientific agricultural techniques were applied. Then, ironically, the cattlemen began raising the previously hated "woolies" themselves.

See also: *Commodore Perry Owens.*

GRAND Central Fruit Stand Swindle

One of the most bald-faced swindles in history occurred in 1929 when two well-to-do Italian fruit dealers bought the rights to convert the information booth at New York's Grand Central Station into a fruit stand. It all began when a well-dressed stranger dropped into their bustling fruit store in mid-town and presented them with his card:

T. Remington Grenfell
Vice President
GRAND CENTRAL
HOLDING CORPORATION

Mr. Grenfell told the fruit dealers, Tony and Nick Fortunato, that they had been selected, after an intensive investigation, to be offered the rights to the information booth. He explained that the railroad was upset because too many travelers were jamming the big circular booth in the center of the station to ask unnecessary questions. So, it had decided to let the ticket sellers answer all questions and this opened up the information booth for commercial use, ideally as a fruit stand. The rental would be $2,000 a week with the first year's rent paid in advance. The $100,000 payment did not faze the Fortunato brothers—in 25 years in the country they had amassed a goodly fortune through hard work, without ever really catching on to the sharp American ways—but they did ask for time to think it over.

Mr. Grenfell was somewhat curt. He said that wouldn't be possible. He mentioned the name of a nearby competitor of the Fortunato brothers and said he was to get second option if they refused. Quickly, the brothers agreed. It seemed like a good opportunity. While $2,000 a week was certainly high rental, the traffic at Grand Central was enormous. Besides the ordinary fruit sales, travelers would undoubtedly be buying expensive baskets to give as gifts.

The brothers followed Mr. Grenfell into a building connected with Grand Central to the door of a suite of offices that bore the legend:

Wilson A. Blodgett
President
GRAND CENTRAL
HOLDING CORPORATION

They were ushered past a blonde secretary into Mr. Blodgett's office. Blodgett was a very busy man and could not spend much time on such a trifling matter. When the brothers again hesitated, Mr. Blodgett seemed to take it that they would have trouble raising the $100,000. Imperiously, he started to dismiss them, but thanks to Mr. Grenfell's intercession and the brothers' hasty assurances, he relented. It was agreed that the brothers would close the deal the following morning by presenting a certified check for the full amount.

The next morning the transaction went like clockwork. The check changed hands and the papers were signed. The brothers were to take possession at 9 a.m. on April 1, coincidentally April Fool's Day.

Shortly before the appointed hour, Tony and Nick Fortunato arrived at the station accompanied by a small gang of carpenters. Some remodeling was, of course, necessary to transform the information booth into a plush fruit stand. Eager to get started, the brothers ordered the carpenters to start doing the lumber work outside the booth. The puzzled information booth clerks wondered what was going on. At exactly 9 o'clock, Tony Fortunato approached the booth and ordered the clerks

out. The clerks then began asking the questions, with the indignant Fortunatos shouting answers. Railroad guards appeared, trying to clear away the carpenters, who were blocking travelers from getting to the information booth.

Finally, one hour and one melee later, the Fortunatos were escorted into the administrative offices of the New York Central Railroad. They flaunted their written contract but were told that there was no such thing as the Grand Central Holding Corp.

Undaunted, the Fortunato brothers promptly led the officials to the offices of that firm—or at least where the offices had been. The officials of the railroad tried to explain to them that they had been the victims of a confidence scheme. The brothers were convinced that a rich American corporation was trying to cheat two foreigners out of $100,000 and then lease the booth to another fruit dealer. In the end, they were forcibly ejected from the terminal. The brothers took their complaint to leaders of New York's Italian community, who complained to the police. But while the police had extensive files on confidence game operators, they could not identify Grenfell or Blodgett. It had been a perfect crime, one that many in the Italian community continued to believe had been cooked up by a rich corporation to take advantage of naive Italians. For many years thereafter, Tony and Nick Fortunato would come into Grand Central Station and glare at the poor information clerks, hurling insults of shaking their fists at them, thus becoming, after a fashion, another strange sight for tourists arriving in Gotham.

GRAND Street School: Criminal institution

Operations of Fagin-type schools for crime were common in 19th century America, but few achieved the stature of the so-called Grand Street School in New York City in the 1870s.

Run by the celebrated Marm Mandelbaum, the leading fence and perhaps the greatest criminal organizer of the era, the establishment was virtually within sight of police headquarters. Marm's staff of expert pickpockets and sneak thieves taught small boys and girls, many under the age of 10, the secrets of their profession, and there were also advanced courses in safecracking and burglars, confidence rackets and blackmail techniques.

No charges were levied for the instructions but virtually all the income from "class work" went to Marm and her cohorts. Upon completion of the courses, several of the more proficient students were put on straight salary, binding them to turn in everything they stole. Marm Mandelbaum abandoned this practice after she discovered that several of her top employees were instead selling a considerable portion of their loot to rival fences while still drawing their regular pay. This realization that there was no honor among thieves and Marm's conclusion that the crime school had become too blatant when the young son of a prominent police officer applied for training forced her to cease operations after a half-dozen years.

See also: *Fredericka "Marm" Mandelbaum.*

GRANNAN, Riley (1868-1908): Gambler and gunfighter

Although he was reputed to be fast on the draw, Riley Grannan is best remembered as a truly successful Western gambler, a brilliant student of horse racing and the inventor of modern form-betting. He once bet $275,000 on a horse and won.

Born in Paris, Ky. in 1868, Grannan arrived on the Western scene fairly late and soon grasped that with the closing of the frontier, the old style of the cheating gambler was outdated. He came up with the idea of establishing a gambling palace that could offer customers satisfaction for all their desires and, an idea still relatively unique for the West, honest gambling. For the locale of this great dream, Grannan picked out a plot of land at Rawhide, Nev. in 1907 and plunked down $40,000 for its purchase. There were those who considered it a foolish idea to try to build a great gambling center in the desert and they appeared to be right. When Grannan died suddenly in April 1908, he was flat broke, his dream having drained away virtually all his funds.

Four decades later, a leading hoodlum named Bugsy Siegel would come up with the same dream and lose millions of the crime syndicate's money building the Flamingo. Eventually, the gambling paradise of Las Vegas was to prove that Siegel, and Riley Grannan before him, were right.

GRANT, Joe (?-1880?): Billy the Kid victim

Joe Grant was a mean Texas gunman who "leaned on" Billy the Kid in a saloon at Fort Sumner, N.M. in January 1880 and was shot dead after falling for a clever ruse by the Kid. At least, that's the way the story is told in many of the more colorful biographies of Billy the Kid.

Over the years Joe Grant was built up from an unknown to a vicious gunman who drifted up from Texas for the specific purpose of ridding New Mexico of the Kid. But when he challenged Billy in that saloon, he did not exactly behave like a seasoned gunman. According to the legend, Billy smooth-talked him into showing him his gun, from which Grant had already fired a few shots. The Kid admired the .45 and—unknown to Grant—spun the barrel arround to an empty chamber. When the shooting started, Joe Grant was embarrassed to hear his gun click on the empty chamber, but his embarrassment was short-lived as the Kid gunned him down. Writer after writer has embellished the account, but more recently, experts, such as James D. Horan and Paul Sann, have argued that the so-called duel might well have been an "invention." And it may be that not only was the duel apocryphal, but so was Joe Grant himself, living—and dying—only in the legend of Billy the Kid.

GRANT, Ulysses S. (1822-1885): Traffic offender

Both before and after he entered the White House, Ulysses S.

Grant was a notorious speedster with horse and rig. On at least two occasions, Grant, while in command of the Union armies, was fined $5 in precinct court. Such an offense was not so readily handled during Grant's first presidential term. President Grant was apprehended in the nation's capital for racing his horse and buggy at breakneck speed on M Street between 11th and 12th. The arresting constable, a man named William H. West, was dragged some 50 feet after seizing the horse's bridle. When Constable West recognized Grant, he started to apologize, but the President said, "Officer, do your duty." The horse and rig were impounded for a time but finally returned to Grant when no charges were pressed. A constitutional dilemma developed, much as it would a century later in the Watergate scandal, about whether it was possible to indict a president without first impeaching him.

GRAVES, Thomas T. (1843-1893): Murderer

The murder of a rich elderly lady named Josephine Barnaby by Dr. Thomas Graves in 1891 ranked as New England's second most-celebrated mystery during the 1890s, surpassed only by the case of Lizzie Borden. What especially offended the Victorian mores of the day was that a physician had done in his patient for profit. It was something "doctors don't do," a contemporary account noted.

The estranged wife of a Providence, R.I. businessman, Mrs. Barnaby inherited a paltry $2,500 upon her husband's death. Dr. Graves, who had treated the woman for a number of years, masterminded Mrs. Barnaby's campaign to reverse the will and eventually succeeded. The grateful widow gave her doctor power of attorney over her finances, whereupon the good doctor proceeded to loot her assets.

To make the task easier, Dr. Graves prescribed long trips for his patient's health. The old woman eventually grew suspicious, and when she insisted upon returning home and taking charge of her own affairs, the doctor warned her that he might have her declared incompetent and put in a home for the aged. Initially, Mrs. Barnaby was too petrified to protest any further, but then she let the doctor know she was returning from California and planned to take care of her estate personally.

On her trip back home, Mrs. Barnaby stopped off in Denver, Colo. to visit with a friend, a Mrs. Worrell. When she arrived there, she was greeted with a package from the East. It contained a bottle of whiskey on which was pasted a note reading: "Wish you a Happy New Year's. Please accept this fine old whiskey from your friend in the woods."

The two women used the whiskey in mixed drinks, found it rather "vile" but downed it all. Both of them died six days later. When the gift of whiskey was discovered, one of Mrs. Barnaby's daughters financed an autopsy on her body that turned up evidence of poison. Suspicion soon centered on Dr. Graves, who was much reviled in the press despite his denials of the crime. But suspicion was one thing and proof another, and although Dr. Graves was arrested, he was soon released on

$30,000 bail. The lack of proof of any connection between the doctor and the poisoned whiskey made it appear that he would eventually be cleared, and numerous patients continued to visit him, declaring their belief in his innocence.

However, at Dr. Graves' trial the prosecution brought forth a newly discovered witness, a young man named Joseph Breslyn who told of Dr. Graves approaching him in November 1890 in the Boston train station and asking him to write a note, claiming he himself could not write. This was the note pasted on the poisoned whiskey bottle. Convicted, Graves was awaiting a retrial after a successful appeal when he committed suicide in April 1893 with poison smuggled into his jail cell.

GRAVES Of Criminals

The headstone and marble shaft stands on Plot 48 in Chicago's Mount Olivet Cemetery. An inscription reads:

QUI RIPOSA
Alphonse Capone
Nato: Jan. 17, 1899
Morto: Jan. 25, 1947

The tourists still visit the grave but there is no body. Even in death, Al Capone continues to be involved in deceit. When the Capone family realized, after Al's death, that the public would keep coming to the grave site to gawk, they secretly had the caskets of all the family's members moved across town to Mount Carmel Cemetery where the real graves are clustered around a granite slab, each headstone bearing the words "My Jesus Mercy."

A similar deception was practiced two decades earlier by the wife of Chicago gangster Dion O'Banion, who was murdered by Capone gunners. Originally, he was buried in November 1924 under a headstone bearing his name, in unconsecrated ground at Mount Carmel, as directed by Cardinal George Mundelein. A spokesman for the archdiocese explained: "One who refuses the ministrations of the Church in life need not expect them in death. O'Banion was a notorious criminal. The Church did not recognize him in his days of lawlessness and when he died unrepented in his iniquities, he had no claims to the last rites for the dead." In 1925 Anna O'Banion had the remains of her husband disinterred and reburied in consecrated ground under a granite shaft inscribed, "My Sweetheart." The cardinal was outraged when he heard of it and ordered the monument removed. He relented, however, about having O'Banion's body moved again and allowed it to remain, marked only by a simple headstone.

Most Mafia big shots, with few exceptions, prefer the same type of anonimity in death that they seek in life. The body of Thomas Lucchese reposes in Calvary Cemetery in Queens, New York City under a headstone with his name oddly misspelled Luckese, a version never used by the family. The theory is that it was his or the family's way of misdirecting the curious.

Another Queens cemetery, St. John's, has become known as the Mafia's Boot Hill. Charles "Lucky" Luciano (1897-1962) personally picked out his future resting place at St. John's in 1935. His Grecian mausoleum near the entrance (Section 3, Range C) provided the final resting ground for a number of his family who died before him. Twenty-five years after selecting the site, Luciano was fortunate to be able to be interred there. Since at the time of his death he was in exile in his native Italy, permission had to be obtained so that his body could be returned to the United States for burial.

Vito Genovese (1897-1969) also lies buried in St. John's. Once an ally of Luciano, he became his mortal enemy in later years. Now they are closer than ever. Genovese reposes very near Luciano (Section 11, Range E, Plot 9) in a simple tomb.

Also near the Luciano mausoleum is the Romanesque tomb of Joseph Profaci (1897-1962), former head of one of New York's five crime families. Profaci's resting place, another mausoleum, is the largest of all the dons, located on a circular road fronting the Cloister building that contains the body of Carlo Gambino, the model for Mario Puzo's *Godfather*. in a private family vault on the fifth floor. Among others buried at St. John's in more recent years are Joseph Colombo (1914-1978) and Carmine Galante (1910-1979).

Walkie-talkie-equipped keepers guard the privacy of all the underworld big shots at St. John's. Picture takers are given the bum's rush by guards, especially at the Luciano and Genovese grave sites, with the explanation that the families of the deceased do not appreciate such activities. One crime writer, Philip Nobile, advised readers recently that if they wished to "shoot" the Profaci grave, "do it from a moving car, a tactic perfected by the Mafia itself."

By comparison, it is relatively easy to snap pictures at other cemeteries, such as St. Michael's, also in Queens, where Frank Costello (1891-1973) lies. St. Michael's is nonsectarian, which is perhaps most fitting for Costello, the most "non-Italian" of the syndicate. Like that of Luciano, Costello's tomb is positioned just to the left of the main entrance, almost like a greeting to visitors.

Ironically, both Albert Anastasia, born Anastasio, (1902-1957) and Crazy Joe Gallo (1929-1972) lie buried in Brooklyn's Greenwood Cemetery, the former's death being the result of the latter's plotting. Guards at the cemetery will direct visitors to Gallo's grave. But then, Crazy Joe was always one of the more exhibitionist characters in the underworld.

Graves of criminals are probably raided more often than those of other people. When Billy the Kid was laid to rest in 1881, after being shot dead by Sheriff Pat Garrett, he was dressed in a borrowed white shirt by Deluvina Maxwell, the Indian servant girl who loved him, and buried under a wooden cross bearing the legend *"Duerme bien. Querido"* ("Sleep well, beloved"). But before long, the cross was carried off by ardent souvenir hunters. Today, Billy is buried in a common grave in Old Fort Sumner with two of his fellow outlaws, Tom O'Folliard and Charlie Bowdre. A stone marker with the inscription "Pals" identifies the trio and their dates. The grave is surrounded by a high wire fence, the only enclosure to successfully contain the Kid.

GRAY, Henry Judd: See Ruth Snyder.

GREAT Diamond Hoax

In 1872 two seedy prospectors named John Slack and Philip Arnold pulled off a monumental fraud, fooling some of the best business brains of this country and the diamond experts of Tiffany's.

Slack and Arnold visited the Bank of California in San Francisco and asked to have a leather pouch deposited in the vault. After first refusing to say what it contained, they finally shrugged and spilled out the pouch's glittering contents, a hoard of uncut diamonds. By the time they left the bank, the head teller was already in the office of the bank's president, William C. Ralston. A former miner himself, and probably selected by Slack and Arnold for that very reason, Ralston soon went looking for the two prospectors. His offer: to form a mining syndicate for harvesting the diamonds. Slack and Arnold conceded they could use some help but they were not about to reveal the source of the diamonds until they had cash in hand. The diamonds were sent over to a jeweler's office in San Francisco to determine their genuineness and the answer came back that they were indeed the real thing. Still, caution prompted Ralston and his associates to double-check with Tiffany's in New York. Tiffany's proved even more enthusiastic, suggesting the diamonds sent them meant that those in hand were worth at least $1.5 million.

Now convinced there was a pot of diamonds at the end of the rainbow, Ralston & Co.'s next step was to find a way to separate the diamond find from the grizzled prospectors. Slack and Arnold were first brought into the mining syndicate and then offered $300,000 apiece for their shares—provided they would reveal the source of the diamonds. The two prospectors rubbed their whiskers and said that was a good enough offer since they weren't the greedy kind. The fact that the mining company had in its possession an estimated $1.5 million in gems made it a very good deal for Ralston and the others, some might even say a swindle. That, of course, is the secret behind many a great swindle—the cheated must believe they are cheating the cheaters.

Before the money was turned over to the pair, they would have to prove the diamond field existed. This they agreed to provided the man sent with them to check its authenticity, mining expert John Janin, went and returned blindfolded. Slack and Arnold stated they would not reveal the field's location until they were paid. They traveled a day and a half by train and then two days by pack mule with Janin blindfolded all the way. What the mining expert found at the end of the trip made him ecstatic. There were diamonds all over the place, just below the ground, between rocks, in ant hills! When the three returned to San Francisco, Janin refused to make his report until he was permitted to buy into the mining corporation. That ignited the whole thing. A diamond craze hit the West. Ralston's company paid off the prospectors, who headed east, and then prepared to mine the diamond field before other fortune hunters found it. The company sent out phony search groups to mislead other prospectors. At least 25 expeditions were launched to find diamonds. However, before the Ralston combine could really get its operation off the ground (the company first wanted to set up its own, and the country's first, diamond-cutting industry in San Francisco), the bubble burst. A prominent geologist, Clarence King and two others set out to find the field. When they did, King quickly determined it had been "salted." Some of the diamonds found by King showed lapidary marks.

The news was electrifying. The *San Francisco Evening Bulletin* headlined the story:

THE DIAMOND CHIMERA
It Dissolved Like the Baseless
Fabric of a Dream
The Most Dazzling Fraud of the Age

Investigation in Europe revealed that Slack and Arnold had come to Amsterdam with $25,000 they'd won gambling and bought up a huge amount of flawed uncut diamonds. This was what they salted the desert with. Very few reputations came through the scandal unmarred. Charles Lewis Tiffany had to admit that his experts, who were the best in America, hadn't ever worked with uncut diamonds and thus simply were not aware how much of a raw stone was lost when fashioned into a jewel. Many of California's tycoons dropped huge amounts of money and Ralston's bank collapsed. Ralston committed suicide.

Slack and Arnold fared better. Private detectives found Arnold living quite happily in his original home in Elizabethtown, Ky. on his $300,000 take. The courts there did not look kindly on efforts to have him extradited to California. He and Slack were admired, even lionized, by much of the country. After all, even if they had taken some supposedly sharp tycoons for $600,000, hadn't those greedy men swindled them out of a "billion dollar" mine? Finally, in return for giving back $150,000 of his haul, Arnold had all charges against him dropped. Nothing more was heard of Slack for many years. Just before leaving California, he had told his friends that he intended to drink up his $300,000 or die in the effort. Then years later, he turned up as a well-to-do coffin maker in White Oaks, N.M.

GREAT Michigan "Free Land" Swindle

There have been any number of swindles involving the sale of vacation or retirement plots, but never has there been anything to rival the fantastic ripoff worked early in the 20th century by two colorful rogues, Colonel Jim Porter, a former Mississippi steamboat gambler, and his young assistant, who over the years would become famous as Yellow Kid Weil.

Colonel Porter had a cousin who was a county recorder up in Michigan and the owner of several thousand acres of undesirable or submarginal land. Porter and his assistant bought a large chunk of this land at $1 an acre and then set up a Chicago sales office, showing the usual artist's concept of a clubhouse, marina and other features that would be built. However, they said nothing was ready for sale yet. Meanwhile, Porter, posing as an eccentric millionaire, and Weil started ingratiating themselves with hundreds of people by giving away free lots. No one was immune to the offer. Porter on certain evenings would give away 30 to 40 lots to prostitutes, madams, waiters and bartenders. Weil even gave some to Chicago police detectives. But they admonished each recipient not to mention the gift because then everyone else would want one. Naturally, they would also inform the happy recipients that they should immediately write and have the transaction recorded at the county seat. The fee for this, it developed, was $30; it had been just $2 before the swindle, but Porter's cousin had raised the fee to $30 with the understanding that $15 of it would go to Porter and Weil, netting the pair $16,000, and the rest he would keep for himself. The operation was entirely legal since all they had done was give away some valueless land, and not taken a penny from any recipient.

GREEN, Eddie: See Jug Markers.

GREEN, Edward (1833-1866): Bank robber

In a sense, Edward Green, often mistakenly called America's first bank robber, represents a criminal trend that has come full circle. When Green, who was postmaster of Malden, Mass., robbed that town's bank on December 15, 1863, he was an amateur, it was his first crime and he did it on impulse. Today, that is the description of the average bank robber, the professionals having long since deserted the field.

Green, a cripple, visited the bank and discovered that the president's son, 17-year-old Frank Converse, was alone there. Green went home, returned to the bank with his pistol and shot Converse in the head, killing him. He then scooped up $5,000 in cash and ambled out. Behaving like the amateur he was, Green, who was deep in debt, suddenly paid all his bills; a heavy drinker, he drank even more and spent money lavishly. When the police brought him in for questioning, Green quickly confessed the robbery and murder and was duly hanged on February 27, 1866. Shortly after Green's bank robbery, the James and Younger boys, the Missouri badmen, went into the bank-robbing business and raised the crime to an art form in America.

See also: *Bank Robberies*

"GREEN, Ballad Of Baldy": Frontier song

Not too much is known about the life of Baldy Green, but his accomplishments were, in a manner of speaking, impressive. As a stagecoach whip, Baldy drove the trails of the Nevada gold camps for Wells Fargo in the 1860s. This was not a safe occupation, considering the number of highwaymen that plagued Wells Fargo. Many drivers got shot but never Baldy Green. It was said that Baldy was just about the most polite victim a stagecoach robber could wish for, and he became celebrated for his ability to throw his hands up and the strongbox to the ground in one motion.

According to one story, Wells Fargo finally fired Baldy while they still had some strongboxes left. While Baldy's fate is lost to history, his fame as a Wells Fargo driver was and is still celebrated in the rollicking "Ballad of Baldy Green."

GREEN Chair Curse: Chicago underworld superstition

One of the most colorful legends in crime is that of the Green Chair Curse, also sometimes referred to by the chroniclers of Chicago crime as the Undertaker's Friend. The curse was named after a green leather chair in the office of William "Shoes" Schoemaker, who became Chicago's chief of detectives in 1924. Several of Chicago's top gangsters were hauled into Schoemaker's office for grilling and ordered to sit in the green chair. Several of them died violent deaths shortly thereafter. This could hardly be considered a startling coincidence in view of the death rate in Chicago's gang wars during Prohibition.

The newspapers, however, quickly seized on a great story and belief in the curse of the green chair began to grow. In time, Schoemaker started keeping a record of the criminals who sat in the chair and later died violently. When the "inevitable" event occurred, Shoes put an X by the gangster's name. There were the bloody brothers Genna (Angelo, Tony and Mike), Porky Lavenuto, Mop Head Russo, Samoots Amatuna, Antonio "the Scourge" Lombardo, John Scalise, Albert Anselmi, Schemer Drucci, Zippy Zion, Pickle Puss DePro, Antonio "the Cavalier" Spano. Undoubtedly aprocryphal tales had it that other gangsters, including Al Capone, absolutely refused to sit down in the chair.

When Shoes retired in 1934, there were 35 names in his notebook and 34 had Xs after them. Only one criminal, Red Holden, was still alive and he was doing time in Alcatraz for train robbery. "My prediction still stands," Shoes informed reporters. "He'll die a violent death. Maybe it'll happen in prison. Maybe we'll have to wait until he gets out. But, mark my words, it'll happen."

Holden, however, outlived Shoes, who died four years later. The chair passed to Capt. John Warren, Shoes' aide, and he continued to seat an occasional hoodlum in it. By the time Warren died in September 1953, the green chair death rate was said to stand at 56 out of 57. Only Red Holden was still alive. He had been released from Alcatraz in 1948 and thereafter was involved in several shoot-outs, which he survived. Then he was convicted of murder and sent to prison for 25 years. On December 18, 1953, he died in the infirmary of Illinois' Statesville Penitentiary. The newspapers reported he was "smiling" because he had "beaten the chair"—the green one rather than the electric one.

Holden's passing set off a newspaper search for the illustrious green chair that had so cursed the underworld, but alas, it was no more. The chair was traced to the Chicago Avenue police station, where it had been confined to the cellar after Capt. Warren's death. When it was found to be infested with cockroaches, it was chopped up and consigned to the furnace before Holden died in his hospital bed. Otherwise, some claimed, Holden would never have escaped its curse.

GREEN Corn Rebellion: Antiwar movement

Antiwar sentiment during World War I was much more pronounced than it was during the Vietnam conflict, but it produced only one major and premeditated violent incident: the Green Corn Rebellion of eastern Oklahoma.

The organization behind the rebellion was the Working Class Union (WCU), a syndicalist movement associated with the Industrial Workers of the World, which was formed before the beginning of the war. In August 1917 several hundred angry WCU farmers assembled to march on Washington, take over the government and end the war. While they awaited the arrival of thousands of other antiwar, antidraft protestors to swell their ranks, the farmers subsisted on unripe green corn. They managed to cut some telegraph wires and tried unsuccessfully to blow up railroad bridges. Before the movement was fully mobilized, they were attacked and scattered by patriotic posses. A total of 450 farmers were arrested. Many were released, but the leaders drew prison sentences of three to 10 years and many lesser supporters were given 60 days to two years.

There were several shootings and hangings during the war period, but in all cases save the Green Corn Rebellion, the violence was initiated by supporters of the war.

GREEN Goods Swindle: Confidence game

The green goods game is an old swindle by which a victim is sold what he thinks is an extraordinarily well-executed set of counterfeit money, only to find out later he has bought a bundle of worthless paper.

The racket made its first appearance in 1869. The mark would be shown a batch of genuine bills, told they were perfect counterfeits and given the chance to buy them at an extremely reasonable rate. Invariably, the victim would jump at the opportunity, but just before the sale was completed, the money package would be switched for one containing cut-up green paper.

By the 1880s several green goods gangs flourished in this country. They set about picking their victims in a scientific manner. First, a list of people who regularly bought lottery tickets was compiled and scouts were sent out to determine whether they were likely to go for a dishonest scheme and whether they had the funds to make fleecing them worthwhile. In this fashion quite a number of small-town bankers and businessmen were targeted and then caught in the swindlers' net. Rather brazenly, the approach would even be made by

mail. One circular issued in 1882 read:

Dear Sir:

I will confide to you through this circular a secret by which you can make a speedy fortune. I have on hand a large amount of counterfeit notes of the following denominations: $1, $2, $5, $10 and $20. I guarantee every note to be perfect, as it is examined carefully by me as soon as finished, and if not strictly perfect is immediately destroyed. Of course it would be perfectly foolish to send out poor work, and it would not only get my customers into trouble, but would break up my business and ruin me. So for personal safety, I am compelled to issue nothing that will not compare with the genuine. I furnish you with my goods at the following low price, which will be found as reasonable as the nature of my business will allow:

For $ 1,200 in my goods (assorted) I charge $100
For $ 2,500 in my goods (assorted) I charge 200
For $ 5,000 in my goods (assorted) I charge 350
For $10,000 in my goods (assorted) I charge 600

Faced with the glowing prospect of making a considerable sum of money, very few carefully screened recipients of such letters notified the authorities. In a few rare cases the sellers of the "counterfeit" money were seized when they appeared to close the deal, but they were released when an examination showed their money was genuine. In one case a fast-talking swindler convinced a New England police chief that he represented a bank executive who was planning to offer an important position to a local banker but wanted to test his honesty first.

Among the swindlers who worked the green goods game over the years were Reed Waddell, Tom O'Brien, George Post, Pete Conlish, Yellow Kid Weil and Fred Buckminster. For a time the New Orleans Mafia pulled green goods swindles, and even Mafia godfather Carlo Gambino supposedly worked it several times. Although most victims never reveal that they have been swindled, police bunco squads get a few such reports each year.

See also: *Reed Waddell.*

GREEN Parrot Murder

The murder at the Green Parrot Restaurant and Bar on Third Avenue near 100th Street on July 12, 1942 was a run-of-the-mill crime, the slaying of the proprietor during an apparent holdup; yet it is remembered today by New York police as a case with a most unusual solution. Although there had been 20 patrons in the bar at the time of the shooting, none would admit seeing anything, insisting they had been at the far end of the bar or in booths lining the wall.

It was not unusual in this tough section of East Harlem to find such a group of uncommunicative witnesses. A few acknowledged that they had seen a man with a gun, heard a shot and ducked. When they lifted their heads, the patrons said, the man with the gun was gone, and owner Max Geller was lying on the floor behind the bar in a pool of blood. Had the man simply walked in, drawn a gun and shot the bar owner? Or had it been an attempted robbery? None of the witnesses was certain. Only one of them had yelled "Robber, robber,

robber!" And that was the establishment's green parrot, kept on a perch behind the bar.

The Green Parrot Bar was actually a community landmark because of the bird. It was a reason to bring guests and tourists to the place, for this was no ordinary talking pet with a few limited phrases but a crotchety old creature with the vocabulary of a longshoreman. An unsuspecting visitor might be told to offer the parrot a cracker. If he did so and expected a grateful reaction, he was sadly disillusioned. Such acts of friendship only provoked outrage from the bird, who would cut loose with a torrent of sulfurous language. But the creature was clearly the keen sort. Evidently, Geller had cried out "robber" during the attack on him, and the parrot had picked up the cry.

Knowing that a robbery had been attempted and finding a solution to the case were two separate matters, however. For almost two years the case remained unsolved, forgotten by almost everyone except Detective John J. Morrisey, who occasionally would return to the neighborhood in an attempt to dredge a forgotten fact from the memories of the witnesses. Finally, he learned that in addition to cursing the bird had been taught to greet several patrons by name. It was a long, tedious process but after a number of weeks the bird would pick up a patron's name and repeat it, appealing to the vanity of the customer.

The detective returned to the Green Parrot and tried to teach the bird his name and some other expressions. If the bird was smart, it was also stubborn and took weeks to pick up what the police officer taught it. Suddenly, Morrisey realized it was impossible for the parrot to have picked up the word "robber" after just hearing it once. No, the bird hadn't been saying "robber" but something else.

A short time later, Morrisey arrested Robert Butler, a former resident of the area, in Baltimore, Md., where he was working as a lathe operator. He had vanished from New York right after the Geller murder. As the case turned out, the bird had not been shrieking "robber," but had actually been repeating a name he had learned earlier: "Robert, Robert, Robert!" Butler was the only bar patron greeted by that name, and it was he whom the parrot had identified as the murderer. Indeed, he had not tried to commit a robbery but had shot Geller in a drunken rage because the bar owner had refused to serve him, claiming he was intoxicated when he entered.

On February 10, 1944 the only killer ever convicted because of a parrot was sentenced to seven to 15 years in Sing Sing.

GREEN Tree Dance House

The dime-a-dance halls of this century trace back to the much more bawdy dance houses of the 19th century. All such dance houses featured three attractions: liquor, women and, least important, dancing. Most dance houses would have at least 20 to 30 girls who not only were unsalaried but indeed had to pay rent for rooms or cubicles on the upper floors of the building. They made their living from the customers they could lure to their room to engage in paid sex or to be robbed. When business was especially good, harlots would be imported from a nearby brothel. The general rule was that the nearer the dance house was to the waterfront, the rougher and meaner it was. The Green Tree on Gallatin Street in New Orleans was a good example of one of the more-depraved dancehall establishments.

The Green Tree opened its doors in 1850. An old woman ran the place with a firm hand. The first floor of the establishment was divided into two rooms. The first room, much bigger than the second, sported a long bar, which could accommodate as many as 250 patrons elbow to elbow. A smaller room in back was for dancing and featured a piano and a fiddle, occasionally supplemented by a few brass instruments. At times, the bouncers would have to enforce a minimum of decorum on the dance floor, where some of the girls would try to stimulate business by suddenly whipping off their dresses and dancing in the nude. The clients would sometimes follow suit, and the bouncers would have to clear the floor of couples doing everything else but dancing.

The bouncers, as many as six at a time, were always armed at least with clubs and brass knuckles. Besides maintaining order in the back room, they were needed to handle trouble at the bar. They were not too concerned with ordinary fights or an occasional knifing, provided the culprit showed the decency to clean up afterward by dumping his victim or victims outside the premises. The bouncers main concern was to prevent physical damage to the house, and they would move in quickly and viciously the second any furnishings were splintered.

The history of violence at the Green Tree can be traced through the fate of its various owners. The first owner, the old woman, disappeared from the scene in the mid-1850s. Her place was filled by Harry Rice, who lasted until 1864, when he was almost stoned to death by a group of Union soldiers objecting to the high water content of the liquor served. It took a detachment of U.S. cavalrymen to save him, and Rice, maimed for life, closed shop. The resort was reopened the following year by Mary Rich, better known as One-Legged Duffy because of her wooden leg. She failed to last a year, being murdered on the premises by her lover, Charley Duffy, who not only knifed her to death but also smashed her skull in with her own wooden leg. Paddy Welsh, a veteran saloon keeper, took over but got in trouble with one of the worst criminal gangs of the district, the Live Oak Boys, who wrecked the dive, admonishing Welsh not to open up again. Welsh paid no heed to their warning, however, and a few days later, his body was found floating in the Mississippi.

William Lee, a former drum major in the U.S. Army, remained in New Orleans after the Civil War and eventually took charge of the Green Tree. He was stabbed to death by a gangster in an argument over a woman. The last owner of the Green Tree was Tom Pickett, who saw the place torn apart by Live Oak bullies in 1876. After brooding about the fact that it would take a fortune to try to refurbish the establishment, Pickett went out hunting with a revolver. He found several Live Oak men in a saloon and shot two of them dead. He was sent to the state penitentiary for life but escaped in 1885 when it caught fire. Pickett was later identified in New York, but the authorities apparently made no effort to return him to justice. As for the Green Tree, it became regarded as a jinx. When the premises next opened, it was a bakery.

See also: *Live Oak Boys.*

GREENLEASE, Robert C., Jr. (1947-1953): Kidnap-murder victim

The first major kidnapping of the post-World War II period was the abduction of six-year-old Bobby Greenlease, Jr., the son of a wealthy Kansas City, Mo. automobile dealer, on September 28, 1953. Using the ruse that the child's mother had suffered a heart attack and was calling for her son, one of the kidnappers, 41-year-old Bonnie Brown Heady, posed as the boy's aunt to get him out of the French Institute of Notre Dame de Scion, one of the city's most exclusive schools for small children.

She and her accomplice, Carl Austin Hall, the 34-year-old ne'er-do-well son of a respected lawyer and an alcoholic who had turned to crime, then drove the Greenlease boy across the state line to Kansas, where Hall attempted to strangle him in a field. The feisty youngster fought back fiercely, several times breaking from Hall's grasp and striking back. Finally, Hall drew a revolver from his pocket and shot the child twice.

The kidnappers put the corpse back in their car and later buried it in the garden of Mrs. Heady's home in St. Joseph, Mo. Then, by letter and telephone, they demanded and received $600,000 in ransom from their victim's frantic parents. It took several fouled-up efforts to get the money to the kidnappers, but the child was not returned. On October 6, 1953 the two were arrested by police in St. Louis after they had gone on a drunken spree and attracted the suspicions of a cab driver.

Justice came swiftly. They were found guilty the following month, and on December 18, 1953 they died together in the gas chamber. As they were strapped into their chairs, Bonnie Heady's main concern was that her lover not be bound too tightly. "You got plenty of room, honey?" she asked. Hall replied, "Yes, Mama." The gas was turned on and they died.

An unanswered question was what happened to that part of the ransom money which Hall had placed in two metal suitcases. After the pair's arrest the suitcases were brought to the Eleventh Precinct Station in St. Louis. When the money was counted, it totaled only $295,140. Since the couple had spent just a few thousand dollars, the FBI determined, the missing amount was $301,960. It was an open secret that the FBI suspected a member or members of the St. Louis police force, but no charges were ever lodged.

GUADALUPE Canyon Massacre

Actually, there was not one but two Guadalupe Canyon massacres, the second of which came close to being commemorated as a national holiday in Mexican border towns because so many *gringos* had been killed. The first massacre was the work of the notorious Clanton gang. In July 1881 Old Man Clanton, the leader of the outlaws, learned that a Mexican mule train was freighting bullion through the Chiricahua Range. Clanton scouted the area and decided the best place for his cutthroats to ambush the mule train was in Guadalupe Canyon. With about 20 men, among them Curly Bill Brocius, Johnny Ringo and several of Clanton's own brood, Old Man Clanton led an attack on the train when the 19 Mexican muleteers were in an exposed position. They killed several of the Mexicans and—on Clanton's orders—lined up the survivors and executed them. The gang escaped with $75,000 in loot and left a large section of the Chiricahua country mourning their dead.

Less than two weeks later, Old Man Clanton and five of his men attempted to drive a herd of stolen Mexican cattle through the same canyon, totally unmindful that the Mexicans might have learned something from their ambush. A band of relatives and friends of the massacre victims ambushed the small Clanton contingent, killing all but one of them, including Old Man Clanton.

While there was considerable rejoicing in Mexican adobes after the massacre of the *gringos,* the joy was short-lived. Later that same month Curly Bill Brocius, who had taken over the leadership of the gang, ambushed a Mexican trail herd in the San Luis Pass and killed six *vaqueros.* Eight others surrendered and were tortured to death by Curly Bill and his men.

See also: *Newman "Old Man" Clanton.*

GUITEAU, Charles Julius (1844-1882): Assassin of James A. Garfield

It is generally agreed that no assassin today could kill a president of the United States with the ease that Charles J. Guiteau, a disgruntled office seeker, shot President James A. Garfield in a Washington railroad station on July 2, 1881. First of all, it is doubtful an assassin could get as close as he got. Moreover, Guiteau fired and missed on his first shot: now, he would almost certainly be dropped before he had a chance to squeeze the trigger a second time.

Only after Guiteau's second shot did the President's guards pin his arms behind him and hustle him off to jail. It may have been the quietest assassination on record. But the President did not die immediately, lingering the whole hot summer with a bullet lodged so deep behind his pancreas that an operation to remove it was impossible. He finally died, after much suffering, on September 19, 1881.

"How could anybody be so cold-hearted as to want to kill my baby?" Garfield's mother asked.

Guiteau was eager to answer the question. He was busy in his jail cell writing his memoirs. He had had an erratic background as a sort of self-styled lawyer. Abandoning his wife, a 16-year-old waif he found in the streets, he had moved to Washington, D.C., where he did volunteer work for the Republican Party and picked up syphilis. When Garfield won the nomination, Guiteau mailed the candidate a disjointed speech he had written for Garfield to use and passed printed copies of it at meetings. Garfield never utilized the unsolicited speech, but Guiteau became convinced that his words provided Garfield with his margin of victory and thereby petitioned the newly elected President for the post of ambassador to France. He did not get it and resolved to gain vengeance by shooting Garfield. He bought a .44 caliber pistol and practiced shooting at trees along the Potomac. When he considered himself a credible marksman, he started dogging Garfield. When he was unsure of the President's schedule on a certain day, he simply asked the White House doorman, who told him. He once got near to Garfield in church but decided not to shoot because he feared others would be hit. On another occasion he passed up a golden opportunity to shoot the President because Mrs. Garfield was present, and Guiteau considered her "a dear soul."

Charles J. Guiteau shoots President Garfield in a Washington railroad station.

Shortly before he finally shot Garfield Guiteau visited the District of Columbia jail to see what his future accommodations would be like and concluded it was "an excellent jail."

Brought to trial two months after the President's death, Guiteau subjected the courtroom to venomous outbursts during the 10½-week trial. He leaped up and launched into long diatribes against the witnesses and called them "dirty liars." The prosecutor was alternately "a low-livered whelp" and an "old hog." At other times, he was most civil; after the Christmas and New Year's recesses, Guiteau assured the judge that he "had a very happy holiday."

When in his cell, Guiteau made a point of strutting back and forth behind the bars so that visitors and crowds outside could gawk at him. In his own defense, he told the jurors that God had told him to kill. "Let your verdict be, it was the Deity's act, not mine," he demanded. When he was found guilty, he shook his finger at the jury box and snarled, "You are all low, consummate jackasses!"

In the days before his scheduled execution, Guiteau was relaxed and unrepentant during his waking hours, but his jailers insisted he moaned all night and slept in terror with his blankets over his head. At dawn on June 30, 1882, the date of his execution, Guiteau insisted on shining his shoes. He ate a hearty meal and memorized a poem he had written to recite on the scaffold. Guiteau went silently to the gallows, but after mounting the scaffold, he wept for a moment and, as the hangman came forward, recited his verse. "I am going to the Lordy," it started.

Then Guiteau was gone.

GUNFIGHTING, Western

It happened just the way good Western gunfights were supposed to happen. One day in late 1876 Turkey Creek Jack Johnson got into an argument with a couple of card-playing miners in Deadwood and invited them outside to settle matters. The trio headed out to the cemetery followed by a large crowd. Each of Johnson's opponents strapped on an exra gunbelt as Johnson started toward them from one end of the cemetery. The pair started from the other end and at 50 yards began firing at Johnson. Before they had gone 10 yards, each of Johnson's foes had finished one six-shooter and shifted to the other. Johnson had not yet fired a shot. Finally, at 30 yards Johnson fired his first shot and killed one of the men. Johnson stopped walking and let his remaining opponent move closer to him. The man approached, firing three more shots. Then Johnson shot him dead. When they rolled the man over, his finger was still on the trigger of his cocked gun. Johnson had fired just two shots.

That was how gunfights were supposed to be fought in the Wild West, and once in a rare while, they were. Turkey Creek Johnson's feat is notable for its rarity. Wyatt Earp once expounded that fighting a duel was a matter of "going into action with the greatest speed of which a man's muscles are capable, but mentally unflustered by an urge to hurry or the need for complicated nervous and muscular actions which trick shooting involves." Earp's detractors, on the other hand, insist the controversial lawman seldom if ever lived up to those words, engaging instead in what amounted to cold-blooded murder without giving his opponent a chance. Few Western "gunfights" really fit the bill; most consisted of sneaking up behind a man and shooting him or drawing down on him at a bar without giving him the opportunity to go for his gun. Even when both sides were able to shoot it out fairly, what usually resulted was a wild shooting spree in which neither protagonist was hurt, although this was not always the case with onlookers. Such duels ended when the fighters simply ran out of ammunition. This was even true in cases where the opponents faced each other at almost point-blank range. In 1882 Cockeyed Frank Loving and Jack Allen fought a storied duel in Trinidad, Colo. in which they fired a total of 16 shots without drawing blood. The next day, however, Allen got Loving—coming up behind him and shooting him down in cold blood, some said.

Few supposedly great gunfighters deserved their reputations. Bat Masterson killed only one man and that in self-defense after being shot by a drunken, brawling cavalryman. Jesse James was a notoriously bad shot. He once fired at a bank cashier at point-blank range and missed. On another occasion, attempting to kill a train robbery victim, he fired six shots at the man from a close distance but failed to hit him once. Billy the Kid certainly did not qualify as a great gunfighter, and there is no evidence that he ever gave any of his victims, variously estimated from four to 21, any kind of chance to draw. The Kid also was not much of a two-gun man, as he is often portrayed. Not many were—since two guns with belt and cartridges weighed at least eight pounds.

Even gunfights fought on "fair" terms generally amounted to little more than murder, since it was usually evident beforehand which man was the better and quicker shot. A case in point occurred when a cowboy named Red Ivan dispatched a cardslick named Pedro Arondondo in Canon City, Colo. in 1889. Ivan accused the gambler of stacking the deck, which meant an automatic duel. Arondondo asked for a delay long enough to take care of a few matters. He bought himself a black suit and ordered a headstone with the inscription "Pedro Arondondo, born 1857—died 1889, from a bullet wound between the eyes fired by Red Ivan." Which is exactly what happened.

See also: *Gwin-McCorckle Duel, Cockeyed Frank Loving.*

GUNNESS, Belle (1859-?): Murderess

It would be difficult to estimate whether Belle Gunness or Jane Tappan holds the record as America's greatest murderess. The latter did not keep score, and the former just plain never told. The best estimate on Belle Gunness was given by Roy L'Amphere, a Canadian farmhand who became her on-and-off lover. He said she killed at least 49 persons—42 would-be husbands, two legal husbands, a young girl left in her care, three of her own children and an unknown saloon wench she'd hired as a servant and whose body she used as a stand-in corpse for herself.

Belle turned up in La Porte, Ind. at the age of 42 as the Widow Sorenson from Chicago. She was not the friendly sort and kept neighbors off her property with a high wire fence. All the local folks seemed to know about her was that she slaughtered hogs for a living. Actually, she also carried on another very profitable slaughtering business, that of killing off would-be suitors. She would place advertisements in matrimonial magazines announcing she was seeking a husband with two fine attributes. He had to be "kind and willing to help pay off a mortgage." The first man to answer an ad was an amiable Norwegian named Peter Gunness. Belle married him, insured him and then he died. One of Belle's children told a schoolmate that her mother had killed her father. "She hit him with a cleaver." But Belle explained her unfortunate husband had met his end when a meat grinder toppled off a shelf. Naturally, the widow Gunness was believed, children being given to overactive imaginations.

After that, Belle never bothered going to the trouble of marrying her mail-order suitors. She'd have them bring their money with them, and if they didn't have enough, she'd send them back home for more. Then she murdered them and buried them within a day or two on her farm. Once, according to L'Amphere, Belle got $20,000 from a victim, but in most other cases it was around the $1,000 mark. In all, it was estimated she collected well over $100,000 from 1901 until 1908, when her murder spree ended. It probably ceased because a relative or two of the murdered men began writing in an effort to locate their missing relatives. Belle must have concluded it was only a matter of time before the law would close in on her.

On April 28, 1908 the Gunness farmhouse burned to the ground. Inside were found the bodies of Belle's three children, aged 11, nine and five, and Belle herself. Well, it could have been Belle except the woman was shorter and weighed about 150 pounds while Belle was a good 250, at least. And to top it off, the head was missing. The head, of course, would have contained teeth that could have been traced. Belle was known to wear a false plate anchored to a tooth, and this was found in the ashes. The obvious conclusion was that Belle had even ripped out her anchor tooth and plate to deceive the law. No one was fooled, but that didn't do much good. Belle Gunness had disappeared. It was soon proven that mass murder had taken place on the Gunness farm. All or parts of the bodies of at least 14 different men were dug up before the law stopped looking. It would have been virtually impossible to unearth completely 40 acres of farmland. And there was already more than enough evidence to convict Belle, if she were ever found. She was not. Over the years various bulky ladies from coast to coast would be identified as Belle Gunness and then cleared with the law's apologies.

L'Amphere was sent to prison in 1909 for his part in the activities of the Lady Bluebeard of La Porte. He died there two years later after revealing all he knew about Belle's murderous activities. He said Belle was supposed to get in touch with him after she had settled elsewhere but she never did. About the only legacy Belle Gunness left was a bit of bad poetry written about her. The last stanza went:

> There's red upon the Hoosier moon
> For Belle was strong and full of doom;
> And think of all them Norska men
> Who'll never see St. Paul again.

GUZIK, Jake "Greasy Thumb" (1887-1956): Capone mob financial manager

A pimp in his early teens, Moscow-born Jake "Greasy Thumb" Guzik rose to become one of the most powerful men in the Chicago syndicate both during Al Capone's reign and for a quarter of a century afterward. During all that time, it is believed that Guzik never carried a gun. He was the trusted treasurer and financial wizard of the mob and, in the years after Capone's fall, was considered the real brains of the organization, along with Paul "the Waiter" Ricca. The intense loyalty Jake showed his fellow criminals was repaid many times over. He was the only man tha Capone ever killed for out of pure friendship.

It happened in 1924, just a few years after Guzik had joined the mob and was promoted to a high position because (so the story goes) without previously knowing Capone he had saved the mob leader from an ambush after accidently overhearing two hit men from a rival gang talking about the plot. One evening in May, Guzik got into an argument with a free-lance hijacker named Joe Howard, who slapped and kicked him around. Incapable of fighting back, Guzik waddled off to Capone and told him what had happened. Capone hunted down Howard and found him in Heinie Jacobs' saloon on South Wabash Avenue, boasting about how he had "made the little Jew whine."

When Howard saw Capone, he extended his hand and said, "Hello, Al." Capone seized his shoulders and, shaking him, demanded to know why he had assaulted his friend. "Go back to your girls, you dago pimp," Howard replied. Without another word Capone put six bullets in Howard's head.

After that killing—which required a considerable amount of fixing—Capone had in Guzik a faithful dog who remained loyal to him and who, it is said, did much to support him financially when Capone was in his deteriorating stage during his final years.

One of Jake Guzik's most important duties for the mob was acting as a bagman in payoffs to police and politicos, hence the origin of the nickname Greasy Thumb. Actually, the name was first applied to Jake's older brother, procurer Harry Guzik, of whom it was said that his "fingers are always greasy from the money he counts out for protection." Later, the title was transferred to Jake, whose thumb was much more greasy since he handled much more money. One of his chores was to sit nightly at a table in St. Hubert's Old English Grill and Chop House, where district police captains and the sergeants who collected graft for some of them could pick up their payoffs.

Other visitors to Guzik included bagmen for various Chicago mayors and their aides.

Like Capone, Guzik eventually was nailed on tax charges but handled his few years behind bars with aplomb and returned ready to take up his money chores. He was one of the hits, if not a very communicative one, of the Kefauver hearings with his refusal to answer because any such response might tend to "discriminate against me."

Guzik's position in the mob was never questioned, and all of Capone's successors—Nitti, Ricca, Giancana, Accardo, Battaglia—allowed Jake complete freedom to make the financial arrangements for the mob. When he died on February 21, 1956, he was at his table in the restaurant partaking a simple meal of lamb chops and a glass of Mosel while making his usual payoffs. He collapsed of a heart attack. During his services there were more Italians in the temple than ever in its history.

Jake was buried in an ornate bronze coffin that cost $5,000. "For that money," one of the hoods said, "we could have buried him in a Cadillac."

GWIN-MCCORCKLE Duel

Gun duels in the Old West seldom fit the picture portrayed by Hollywood. An excellent example was the gunfight between William M. Gwin, a judge, and Joseph McCorkle in California in 1855. The duel took place on a marsh north of the Presidio, some miles from the Gwin home on Jackson Street in San Francisco. Gwin arranged to have relays of horses ready for a messenger to carry the news of the gunfight to his wife. In due course, the messenger came riding down Jackson Street and rushed into the Gwin house reportedly shouting, "The first fire has been exchanged and no one is hurt!"

"Thank God!" Mrs. Gwin cried and dropped to her knees in prayer with the rest of her family.

Sometime later, the messenger dashed into the house again and yelled, "The second fire has been exchanged and no one is hurt!"

"Praised be the Lord!" Mrs. Gwin replied.

On the third occasion, the messenger knocked on the door, tendered his card and was brought into the parlor. When Mrs. Gwin greeted him, he said, "The third fire has been exchanged and no one is hurt."

"That's good," Mrs. Gwin said.

The next time, the messenger on arriving was asked to stay for dinner. He did, ate heartily and joined in the customary dinner table conversation. Then he announced in passing: "Oh, by the way, the fourth fire has been exchanged and no one is hurt. What do you think of that, Mrs. Gwin?"

"I think," the lady said, "that there has been some mighty poor shooting!"

The poor shooting continued and both emerged unscathed, a fact that, if nothing else, later allowed Mr. Gwin to become the first U.S. senator from California.

See also: *Gunfighting*

GYP The Blood (1889-1914): Gangster and killer

One of the most vicious gangsters in New York during the early 1900s, Gyp the Blood (real name Harry Horrowitz) worked on commission for Big Jack Zelig as a slugger, bomber and killer. He filled in slow periods as a mugger and, at times, as a bouncer in East Side dance halls, gaining the reputation as the best bouncer since Monk Eastman, which was high praise indeed. Having enormous strength, he boasted he could break a man's back by bending him across his knee, and he lived up to the claim a number of times. Once, he won a $2 bet by seizing an unfortunate stranger and cracking his spine in three places. Gyp the Blood truly loved violence; Gyp's explanation for his eagerness to take on bombing assignments was, "I likes to hear de noise."

When the violence business got a bit slow, Gyp the Blood formed his own gang, the Lenox Avenuers, who engaged in muggings, burglaries and stickups around 125th Street. Gyp the Blood and three of his underlings, Whitey Lewis, Dago Frank and Lefty Louie, murdered gambler Herman Rosenthal on July 16, 1912 because he had begun revealing to District Attorney Charles S. Whitman the tie-ins between gamblers and the police. All four were apprehended despite a police slowdown on the investigation. Gyp the Blood, in an effort to save himself, said they had been hired to do the killing by Big Jack Zelig at the behest of police Lt. Charles E. Becker. Zelig then talked about Becker, and although Big Jack was assassinated before he could testify in court, Becker was convicted and executed. Gyp the Blood and his three henchmen went to the electric chair on April 13, 1914.

See also: *Charles E. Becker, Lenox Avenue Gang, Big Jack Zelig.*

GYPSY Curse Swindle: Enduring con game

The Gypsy Curse is a concept that goes back many centuries in Europe and endures to the present in this country. Witch doctors have gouged the gullible since Colonial times, placing on or removing curses from believing victims.

The greatest practitioners of the art in the 20th century were two audacious swindlers, Mrs. William McBride and Edgar Zug, who produced terror in hundreds of people and then bilked them of fortunes. Dressed in weird ceremonial costumes, the pair told wealthy victims they, their property and money were under evil spells. Then they explained that Zug, as the sole living white witch doctor in the United States, could be the instrument of their salvation. "The only way to relieve this deadly spell," Zug would intone, "is to buy your way out of it. These evil spirits respect cash."

In 1902 Zug and Mrs. McBride put the curse on an elderly rich couple, Mrs. Susan Stambaugh and her palsy-ridden husband. "I see your profiles on the side of a distant mountain . . . and through the brains of these profiles, evil spirits have thrust long needles. This was done many years ago and the needles are now rusty. When these needles break, a day not long off, you both will die."

Upon hearing this prediction Mrs. Stambaugh fainted and her husband had a spasmodic fit. When they came to, Mrs. McBride had some good news; Edgar Zug could save them from their awful fate. There was a way Zug could convince the spirits to withdraw the fatal needles. Zug nodded but warned, "It will take money, a lot of money." Within seven days the scheming pair had stripped the Stambaughs of all their savings and the deeds to their many properties. Then Zug had some bad news for them. The spirits were not satisfied. "You are going to die," he intoned with an air of resignation, "unless you can come up with at least another five thousand." But there was then some good news; the Stambaughs would end up getting more back than they paid in through a hidden treasure that the spirits would reveal to them.

The now desperate but hopeful couple hysterically hunted for more money, trying to secure loans from friends. Finally, one of them revealed the reason for the cash and the Gypsy Curse swindlers were arrested and convicted of fraud. As they were being led from the courtroom, Zug cried, "That's what I get for being kind!"

Police report that variations of the Gypsy Curse swindle are still worked today on the elderly rich in almost every ethnic community in big cities.

GYPSY Swindles: See Handkerchief Switch.

H

HAHN, Anna (1906-1938): Mass poisoner

The first woman electrocuted in the state of Ohio, Anna Hahn specialized in being a companion to well-off elderly men who had no relatives, providing them with tender loving care and a little arsenic. After each one died, she either produced a will naming her the beneficiary or simply looted her victim's bank accounts before moving on to brighten up the last days of another old gentleman. Exactly how many men she killed is not known. Anna was not cooperative on the subject, and the authorities stopped exhuming bodies after they found five loaded with arsenic.

Anna Hahn arrived in Cincinnati from her native Fussen, Germany in 1927, married a young telegraph operator named Philip Hahn and opened a bakery in the "Over the Rhine" German district. Then Anna's husband became afflicted with a strange illness and finally was taken to a hospital by his mother over Anna's protests. In retrospect, it seemed likely that her husband was suffering from something he ate, but in any event, Anna Hahn took the opportunity to move in with a septuagenarian burgher named Ernest Koch, who seemed remarkably vigorous despite his age. Under Anna's ministrations that condition did not continue for long. On May 6, 1932 a much weakened Koch died. When his will was probated, Anna was bequeathed his house.

Anna's next victim was Albert Palmer, an aged and ailing railroad retiree who lasted almost no time at all. Anna avoided the embarrassing coincidence of twice being named heir to an old man's estate by simply borrowing Palmer's money before he died. She insisted on giving him an I.O.U. for the money, but after he expired, she simply tore up the note and no one was the wiser. Anna then sold the Hahn house and moved to another part of the city.

Next on her list was a man named Jacob Wagner, who left an estate of $17,000 to his "niece" Anna. She earned another $15,000 taking care of one George Gsellman for a few months until his demise. One who escaped her deadly attention was a man named George Heiss. As he revealed after Anna's arrest, Heiss became suspicious when flies sipping the beer she brought him kept flipping over and dying. He demanded that Anna share his stein, and when she refused, he ordered her from his house.

Not quite as careful was Anna's last victim, George Obendoerfer. Anna lured him to Colorado with a story about a ranch she had there. Obendoerfer never made it to the ranch however, expiring in a Denver hotel. In the meantime Anna had gained possession of his bankbook and looted it of $5,000. But when it came time to pay for Obendoerfer's burial, she refused, claiming she had just met him on a train and had pretended to be his wife at his suggestion. Police became suspicious when they discovered the bank transfer, and an autopsy was performed, revealing lethal amounts of arsenic in the dead man's viscera. Upon her return to Cincinnati, Anna was arrested. The bodies of four other of Anna's old gentlemen were exhumed and post mortems confirmed the presence of arsenic in each case.

After a sensation-packed trial a jury of 11 women and one man convicted Anna with no recommendation of mercy. She exhibited iron nerve until shortly before her execution on June 20, 1938. But when strapped into the electric chair, Anna broke and screamed hysterically. She regained her composure with the help of a prison chaplain. As she removed her hand from his, Anna said, "You might be killed, too, Father."

HAIRTRIGGER Block: Chicago "shoot-out" area

During the Civil War, Chicago gambling thrived as it probably did in no other city, North or South. In the gamblers' vernacular, the city was a "sucker's paradise," teeming with Army officers and, more importantly, paymasters, soldiers from the front with many months pay, speculators rich with war contracts and so on, all ready and eager to lose their money at cards. The center of the gambling industry, which was illegal but well protected through heavy payments to the police, was on Randolph and Clark streets, which contained palatial "skinning houses" for trimming the suckers. Naturally, with fortunes won and lost so easily, shootings and killings were common and probably far more frequent than could be found in any town of the Wild West. In fact, Randolph Street between Clark and State was commonly referred to as Hairtrigger Block because of the many shootings that took place there.

Some of the shootings were between professional gamblers themselves over matters such as possession of a "mark" or out of just plain nastiness. The most famous feud on Hairtrigger Block was between two big gamblers, George Trussell, the dandy of Gambler's Row, and Cap Hyman, described as "an insufferable egotist, an excitable, emotional jack-in-the-box." They could barely tolerate one another when sober, but when drunk they would immediately start shooting at each other; each probably shot at and was shot at by the other at least 50 times. Both, especially when intoxicated, were incredibly bad marksmen, and the usual damage was to windows, bar mirrors and street signs. So long as the shooting was confined to Hairtrigger Block, the police did not intervene; unfortunately, the two gamblers often staggered off to other areas in search of each other and continued their shooting sprees, leading the *Chicago Tribune* to declare that "the practice is becoming altogether too prevalent in this city."

In 1862 Hyman once staggered into the lobby of the Tremont House hunting for Trussell, fired several shots and allowed no one to leave or enter the hotel for an hour. Hyman was frequently arrested and fined for his forays, and after paying the penalty, he would meticulously deduct the amount from his usual police payoffs. Whenever a Trussell-Hyman duel started, the inhabitants and habitues of Hairtrigger Block immediately wagered on which one would be killed. As it turned out, neither of the two ever prevailed over the other. Trussell was shot to death by his mistress in 1866; Hyman went insane and died in 1876.

See also: *George Trussell.*

HALBERSTAM, Dr. Michael: See Bernard Charles Welch, Jr.

HALL, Lee (1849-1911): Texas Ranger

One of the most famous Texas Rangers, Lee Hall started out as a schoolteacher in Texas after relocating there in 1869 from his native North Carolina. Two years later, he made the rather unlikely switch to the post of city marshal of Sherman. He subsequently served as a deputy sheriff and in 1876 joined the Texas Rangers. Assigned to clamp down on the brutal Taylor-Sutton feud, Hall gained wide acclaim for fearlessness, once entering unarmed into a room full of the feuding cowboys and marching out seven men wanted for murder. In 1877 Hall was promoted to captain, and within two years he and his men had

made some 400 arrests and successfully quelled the murderous feud.

Hall ran up an enviable record of capturing lawbreakers; he was involved in tracking down and shooting the noted outlaw Sam Bass. In 1880 Hall resigned from the Rangers to become a successful rancher. For two years he harbored an ill young man named Will Porter on his ranch, where Porter gathered much of the material for the stories he would write under the name O. Henry.

In 1885 Hall was made an Indian agent, but he was removed in 1887 on trumped-up graft charges. It took him two years to clear his name. Later, Hall held various law enforcement positions and in 1899 served as an Army officer in the Philippines. After contracting malaria there, he was forced to resign from the Army. Hall died in 1911.

HALL-MILLS Murders: Unsolved double killing

It was once said that no American murder case had more words written about it than did the unsolved Hall-Mills case of 1922. On September 16 the bodies of a man and woman were found in a lovers lane in New Brunswick, N.J., with cards and personal letters strewn around them. The contents of the letters and the identity of the couple caused a sensation. The man was the Rev. Edward Wheeler Hall, 41, Rector of St. John's Episcopal Church, and the woman was Mrs. Eleanor Mills, 34, a member of his flock, a choir singer and the wife of the church sexton. The letters had been written by Mrs. Mills to the pastor; they would become some of the juiciest newspaper reading of the 1920s. Hall had been shot with a bullet in the head, and Mrs. Mills had suffered three such wounds and her throat had been cut for good measure. Someone had arranged the bodies in delicate intimacy in keeping with the tone of the letters.

Nothing much came of the case despite its explosive nature. The local police insisted they were stumped. Then in 1926 the *New York Daily Mirror* uncovered a secret witness whose testimony resulted in the indictment of Mrs. Frances Stevens Hall, seven years the pastor's senior and a woman of position and wealth, for the two murders. Also indicted were Mrs. Hall's two devoted brothers, William and Henry Stevens, and her cousin, Henry de la Bruyere Carpender, a member of the New York Stock Exchange. According to the *Mirror* the four had bribed witnesses and the police and had soft-soaped the local prosecutor to avoid arrest in 1922.

When the trial of Mrs. Hall and her brothers began, 300 reporters from around the nation and the world were on hand. Sixty wires were required to handle the incredible flow of words going out to a waiting public. Five million words were transmitted the first 11 days and a total of nine million during the 18 days of the trial. Even the august *New York Times* had four stenographers on hand so that its readers would not lose a precious syllable of testimony.

In the trial it was alleged that Mrs. Hall had been trying to catch her husband in a compromising position with the choir singer. The star prosecution witness was 56-year-old Mrs. Jane Gibson, called the Pig Woman because she raised Poland China pigs. She was dying of cancer and testified from a hospital bed with a nurse and doctor in attendance. Mrs. Gibson said that as she was passing the murder spot, De Russey's Lane, she recognized Mrs. Hall and her brother Henry in the bright moonlight among a group of four figures huddled around a crab-apple tree, under which the bodies were later found. She heard snatches of conversation, she testified, such as "explain those letters," and someone being hit continuously. "I could hear somebody's wind going out, and somebody said, 'Ugh.'"

Then Mrs. Gibson said a flashlight went on and she saw two men wrestling. The light went out and she heard a shot. Had she heard a woman's voice? "Yes. One said, 'Oh, Henry,' easy, very easy; and the other began to scream, scream, scream so loud, 'Oh my, oh my, oh my.' so terrible loud." The Pig Woman testified she had heard three shots and then mounted her mule Jenny and rode away as quickly as she could.

Clearly, the main thrust of the prosecution's case depended on the credibility of the Pig Woman. All through her testimony her aged mother sat in a front row muttering, "She's a liar, she's a liar, she's a liar." Mrs. Hall's defense team, called the Million Dollar Defense (actually their fee came to $400,000), found small discrepancies between the Pig Woman's testimony before a grand jury in 1922 and her current testimony. But they impugned her supposedly superior memory by getting her to testify that she couldn't remember when she had married, if she had been divorced, if she had remarried and if she knew the names of a number of men.

As the Pig Woman was removed from the courtroom, she shook a finger at Frances Hall and cried, "I've told the truth, so help me God, and you know it, you know it."

Henry Stevens presented evidence that he was bluefishing in Barnegat Bay the weekend of the murder and produced witnesses to back him up. Mrs. Hall took the stand and testified in an icy calm that earned her the journalistic sobriquet the Iron Widow. When asked if Mr. Hall was "a loving, affectionate husband," she answered, "Always." She denied all involvement in the murders.

After only five hours of deliberations, the jury acquitted Mrs. Hall. Her brothers were cleared as well and the indictment against Carpender was thrown out. Mrs. Hall and her brothers sued the *Daily Mirror* for $3 million and accepted an out-of-court settlement.

HAMER, Frank (1884-1955): Texas Ranger and killer of Bonnie and Clyde

The most legendary Texas Ranger of the 20th century, one who would have fit the mold even a century earlier, was Frank Hamer. He is best remembered, if in a distorted fashion, as the killer of Bonnie Parker and Clyde Barrow. His career started when portions of the West were still wild, with cattle rustlers, horse thieves, bank robbers on horseback, six-shooters

and "walkdowns" in dusty cowtown streets. It lasted through the gangster era of the late 1920s and early 1930s, with speeding black sedans and chattering Tommy Guns. Hamer spanned both eras and remained a top-notch officer through the 1940s, when the development of sophisticated methods of crime detection began making old-style criminal operations all but obsolete. Before his long and distinguished career ended, he was involved in over 50 gunfights, was wounded 20 times and was ambushed four times. On two occasions he was shot up so badly that his assailants left him for dead. It was the criminals who ended up dead—100 of them, according to some biographers. Others place the estimate lower, anywhere from 40 to 55. Even Hamer probably didn't know the exact number.

In 1906 Frank Hamer became a Texas Ranger after some stints as a cowboy. Although only 22, he soon demonstrated he could get the job done on lone assignments, the way the Rangers generally operated. In 1907 he was sent to clean up Doran, Tex. It was typical of the towns that had sprung up during the turn of the century oil boom—rough, dirty, jerry-built, boisterous, with more than its share of toughs, con men, fancy women, card sharks and other ruthless characters out for a dishonest buck. Unlike the other towns, most of the vice in Doran was controlled by one man, a clever, vicious operator named Haddon Slade. Criminals who wanted to "work" in Doran either worked directly for Slade or kicked in a healthy percentage of their take for what Slade called "franchise rights." He was so sure of himself that he even had his men murder the local sheriff.

Hamer was sent in to solve that killing and at 23 he probably looked like easy pickings, although Slade no doubt knew better than to murder a Ranger unless he could come up with a good story. Apparently, he tried his best. There was evidence he planned to shoot Hamer from ambush, use the Ranger's gun to kill two of his own men and then plant the gun he used to murder Hamer on one of them. This would leave everything tidy for the law. But the plot backfired when Hamer spotted Slade and dropped him with three bullets in the chest. With Slade gone, Doran was an easy place to tame. Over the years Hamer gained a reputation for catching bank robbers, once tracking three robbers to a job and killing two of them as they tried to shoot their way out. Although wounded in the leg, Hamer marched the surviving bandit to the local jail before taking what he called a "medical laydown."

Hamer's most bizarre case involved one of the state's scandals: the killing of innocent men by local Texas law officers to collect bounties for dead bank robbers. The bounties were the ill-conceived idea of the Texas Bankers Association to stop a rising tide of bank thefts. The bankers group posted the following notice in every bank in the state:

REWARD
$5,000 for *Dead* Bank Robbers
Not One Cent For Live Ones

In no time at all, bank robbers started turning up dead as a result of this throwback to the bounty system of the Old West. Frank Hamer was appalled at the practice. He started a lone investigation that shocked the state with the discovery that local lawmen, hungry for reward money, had actually formed murder combines and sought out drifters and other homeless men to kill. Law enforcement officials expressed disbelief over his findings, and the Texas Bankers Association refused to withdraw the reward system. Finally, Hamer took his charges to the newspapers. The resulting stories broke the scandal wide open and led to the filing of charges against some of the murder ring leaders. Hamer arrested them and they subsequently confessed.

In 1934 Hamer resigned from the Texas Rangers because it was being corrupted by the cronyism of controversial Gov. "Ma" Ferguson, who had just taken office. He went to work as a plant security specialist at a salary of $500 a month, a considerable sum at the time, but he soon left to join the Texas Highway Patrol at $150 a month. Unlike the Rangers, the Highway Patrol was not under the governor's tight control. He was offered a very special assignment—capture the notorious outlaws Bonnie and Clyde.

The highly popular movie *Bonnie and Clyde* portrayed Hamer as a not-too-bright "flatfoot", who viciously gunned down the handsome, daring Clyde Barrow and the beautiful Bonnie Parker. Nothing could have been further from the truth. Hamer took the assignment because Clyde Barrow had killed a number of his fellow law officers. Methodically, he learned all he could about the two desperadoes, from first-hand sources, from people who knew them and from newspaper stories of their bloody deeds. In his own words: "On February 10th, I took the trail and followed it for exactly 102 days. Like Clyde Barrow, I used a Ford V-8, and like Clyde, I lived in the car most of the time."

Hamer decided that Barrow "played a circle from Dallas to Joplin, Missouri, to Louisiana and back to Dallas." Occasionally, he would leave his beat, but he would always come back to it, as most criminals do. "It was necessary for me to make a close study of Barrow's habits. I have never seen him and I never saw him until May 23rd."

On May 23 Hamer's persistence finally paid off. An informer told him the couple, driving a gray Ford sedan, would travel a certain road. With some other officers, he set up a secret roadblock, and when the car appeared, Hamer sprang the trap.

"At the command of 'stick 'em up,' both turned," Hamer recalled. "But instead of obeying the order . . . they clutched the weapons which they held in their hands or in their laps. When the firing started, Barrow's foot released the clutch, and the car, in low gear, moved forward on the decline and turned into the ditch on the left."

Before the pair ever got a chance to lift their weapons, the officers had sent a hail of rifle bullets and shotgun blasts into the car. Clyde Barrow and Bonnie Parker were wiped out.

About a year later, Ma Ferguson's control on the Texas Rangers having been loosened by the voters, Hamer returned to the Rangers, serving until his retirement in 1949. He died July 10, 1955 at home in his bed in Austin.

See also: *Bank Robberies—Bounties. Bonnie and Clyde.*

HAMILTON, Ray (1912-1935): Robber and murderer

Remembered best as a part-time accomplice of Bonnie and Clyde, Hamilton had a career in crime that was in many respects more spectacular than that of Clyde Barrow, with whom he started off as a juvenile criminal in the sneak thief Square Root Gang in Houston, Tex. From that time on, Hamilton would be linked with Bonnie and Clyde in several short but bloody stints.

In 1932 Hamilton served time with Barrow at the Eastham Prison Farm in Texas. Two years later, Bonnie and Clyde broke Hamilton, Henry Methvin and Joe Palmer out of the prison. However, as a trio, Bonnie, Clyde and Hamilton could not continue for long. A major reason was sexual jealousy. When the three traveled together, it was Hamilton who slept with Bonnie Parker. This was not, as portrayed in the movie *Bonnie and Clyde,* because Clyde Barrow was impotent, but rather because he was homosexual, a preference he developed at Eastham. At times, Hamilton also slept with Barrow. Such an arrangement couldn't last, and Hamilton would keep dropping in and out of the menage.

Hamilton's crime record, which began in earnest in January 1932—when he was 19—and lasted a short three years, was awesome. Alone or with Barrow or other accomplices, Hamilton held up at least two dozen places, including seven banks, two oil refineries, a packing plant, a post office and even the National Guard Armory at Fort Worth, where he stole boxes of shotguns, automatic rifles and machine guns. Although apprehended a number of times, he escaped two road traps "no human could escape," as one reporter described them, including one manned by a posse of 20, all of whom he disarmed and whose leader he took with him as a hostage. Even when Hamilton was caught, holding him was another matter. In all, he escaped four times, and thus, while he had committed several murders, it took five trials to get him convicted and sentenced to the chair for just one of them. In 1934 Hamilton broke out of the death house in the state penitentiary at Huntsville, Tex. After a 10-month manhunt he was recaptured and, on May 10, 1935, executed.

See also: *Bonnie and Clyde.*

HAMS: Smuggling technique

"Hams" were first used during Prohibition by rumrunners bringing their contraband to shore. If they found themselves pursued by the Coast Guard, the smugglers would jettison gunny sacks, or hams, containing several bottles of liquor wrapped in straw. Attached to each ham was a bag of salt and a red marker. Weighted by the salt, the ham would sink to the bottom. When the salt melted sometime later, the red marker would float to the surface. Then the danger above would have passed and the smugglers could return to retrieve the treasured hams. The ham remains a favorite method of narcotics smugglers.

HAND, Dora (?-1878): Murder victim

Dora Hand (also known as Fannie Keenan) was called the First Lady of Dodge City when it was truly the Gomorrah of the Plains. Her early life was shrouded in mystery, although the West had no trouble coming up with an impressive set of "facts." She was allegedly from a most genteel family in Boston, had been educated in Europe and had enjoyed a brilliant operatic career before coming to Dodge City, where she had been brought by Mayor James H. "Dog" Kelley to oversee his whorehouse operations.

Chronicler Stuart Lake described her in these words:

Saint or sinner, Dora Hand was the most graciously beautiful woman to reach the camp in the heyday of its iniquity. . . . By night, she was the Queen of the Fairybelles, as old Dodge termed its dance-hall women, entertaining drunken cowhands after all the fashions that her calling demanded. By day, she was the Lady Bountiful of the prairie settlement, a demurely clad, generous woman to whom no appeal would go unheeded.

Once, Dora Hand had been a singer in Grand Opera. In Dodge, she sang of nights in the bars and honkey-tonks. On Sundays, clad in simple black, she crossed the Dead Line to the little church on the North Side to lead the hymns and anthems in a voice at which those who heard her forever marvelled. A quick change of attire after the Sunday evening service, and she was back at her trade in the dance hall. . . .

At least 12 men supposedly died fighting one another to win Dora's heart in Dodge and in her previous ports of call, Abilene and Hays. Her main man in Dodge was the mayor himself, who exhibited a rather violent jealousy when other suitors tried to show their affections. This led to a smoldering feud with young James Kennedy, son of Mifflin Kennedy of Texas' King Ranch. Finally, one night when Kennedy became particularly attentive to Dora in the Alhambra, Dog's showcase establishment, Kelley tossed him out. Kennedy left town, vowing revenge. In October 1878 Kennedy attempted to make good on his threat, sneaking up on Dog's frame house and pumping a couple of shots in the direction of the mayor's bedroom. Unfortunately for Kennedy, Dog Kelley wasn't even there at the time. But Dora was asleep in the bed and was killed instantly. Kennedy rode out of town without knowing the damage done by his bullets.

Sheriff Bat Masterson quickly organized a posse that included Wyatt Earp, Neal Brown, Bill Tilghman and Charlie Bassett. The posse ran Kennedy to earth; Masterson put a rifle slug through his right arm, shattering it, and Earp shot the fugitive's horse from under him. Kennedy cursed his captors, swore to get even and then asked if he had killed Kelley. When told that Dora Hand had been his victim, he turned morose and said he wished the posse had killed him.

Dora was given a lavish funeral, some say the best Dodge ever had. The procession was certainly an unusual one, consisting of dance hall girls, gunslingers, saloon keepers, gamblers, cowboys and even some of the more respectable ladies of the town. Epitomizing the ways of the frontier, a minister admonished, "He that is without sin among you, let him first cast a stone at her."

The overwhelming sentimentality, however, did not carry over to the cause of justice. While Kennedy's remorse had its limits, his wealthy father's purse had none. The best lawyers were hired and much was made of Kennedy's shattered arm, now four inches shorter. The defendant went free for "lack of evidence," and a father took his errant son home.

See also: *William B. "Bat" Masterson.*

HANDKERCHIEF Switch: Gypsy bunco operation

A famous confidence game dating back as far as gypsy fortune-tellers, palmists and card readers, the handkerchief switch has been used to bilk thousands of gullible Americans out of millions of dollars annually.

At first, the victim is told his fortune for a small fee, during which the fortune-teller gauges his or her gullibility and means. The victim is then told that the fortune-teller's power of prayer will solve his or her problems. The prayer must be accompanied by the burning of a candle, and the size and price of the candle determine how long these potent prayers will continue. Once a likely prospect has been found, the fortune-teller informs the victim that evil spirits are within him or her, and must be routed. The victim may be asked to bring a raw egg on the next visit, at which time the fortune-teller, by sleight of hand, breaks the egg, displaying a black mass inside. This, the victim is informed, constitutes the evil spirits that transfer their potent bad luck on everything the victim comes in contact with.

By further prayers, the fortune-teller discovers the reasons these evil spirits remain in the victim's body. It is because of the money the victim has. If he or she gets rid of the money, the evil spirits will depart. The victim is then instructed to bring a large sum of money, preferably in big bills. The fortune-teller places the money in a very large handkerchief, which is then folded up and sewn together at the ends. In the process, another stuffed handkerchief is substituted while the victim is not looking, and the substituted handkerchief is buried in a cemetery, flushed down a toilet or thrown in a river or the ocean. Sometimes the victim himself is permitted to throw the handkerchief in the ocean or to flush it down the toilet. Occasionally when the money is to be flushed down a toilet, the use of the handkerchief is discarded, and the victim is permitted to watch the roll of money flush away. In such cases, the toilet's plumbing has been altered so that the money is trapped in the pipes, to be extracted later.

HANKS, O. C. "Camilla" (1863-1902): Train robber

As a member of the Wild Bunch, Camilla or, as he sometimes was called, Deaf Charley Hanks was considered to be the best and most fearless train robber of the gang. As Kid Curry once said, he could rob a train "as slick as a whistle." Butch Cassidy would think nothing of having Hanks cover all the passengers in a train car alone, feeling certain no one could get the drop on him. One story tells how a passenger did get the drop on him, leveling and cocking a Derringer at Hanks as he was going up the aisle collecting loot. When the passenger ordered Hanks in a low menacing hiss to drop his piece, the outlaw turned and fired first. The tale may be a bit overdramatized, since Hanks was deaf in his right ear and later said he'd heard neither the command nor the gun being cocked.

In 1892 Hanks was captured after robbing a Northern Pacific train at Big Timber, Mont. and drew a 10-year term at Deer Lodge Penitentiary. Released on April 30, 1901, Hanks headed for Hole in the Wall country, located Butch Cassidy at Brown's Hole and went back in the train-robbing business. Hanks took part in every job the Wild Bunch pulled over the next year and accumulated a big pile of cash. He headed for Texas to do some wild living. He got into a saloon brawl, and when the law wondered where his money had come from, Hanks went for his gun. A lawman named Pink Taylor was faster, and on October 22, 1902 the slickest of the train robbers was shot dead.

See also: *Wild Bunch.*

HARDIN, John Wesley (1853-1895): Gunfighter and murderer

John Wesley Hardin was one of the dedicated gunfighters of the West who delighted in showing a gun full of notches. In his case the boast was deserved. By his own count Wes Hardin killed 44 men. Some historians credit him with 40, and even the most skeptical will grant him 34 or 35.

Hardin started killing in his native Texas in 1868 at the age of 15. He shot a black who had taken his new citizenship rights too seriously, a not unpopular crime of that era. Then he gunned down three Yankee soldiers who came after him for the shooting. Hardin went on the run and received the ready assistance of most folks who knew him. By 1871, at about 18 years of age, he was a trail cowboy driving cattle from Texas to Kansas and his murder toll stood at about a dozen, give or take a corpse or two. Many of his victims had died in face-to-face confrontations, but Wes was certainly not fussy about putting a slug in a man's back. Around Abilene he knocked off another eight or so and for a time escaped the wrath of Marshal Wild Bill Hickok, who clearly wanted no trouble with this fast-drawing young hellion.

When Hardin killed a man in his hotel, however, Hickok came after him. Hardin later claimed the man had tried to knife him because he had made some big gambling winnings the night before. The other version was that Hardin had shot him because his snoring in the next room had disturbed the gunfighter's sleep. Fleeing out a second-story window in his long johns, Hardin avoided being arrested by Hickok. On the trail he trapped three members of a posse sent out by Hickok, and in a rare gallant gesture, Hardin refrained from killing them. Instead, he made them strip off their pants and sent them back toward Abilene in that condition. Through the years Hardin supported himself mostly by gambling and only occasionally by punching cattle. A man who was especially fast

on the draw had a way of facing down an opponent in a disputed hand. If a man got into a lone game of poker with a young feller who he later learned was the notorious Wes Hardin and was then informed that a straight beat a flush, why that was an unarguable proposition as long as Hardin had his gun. And Hardin always did, and did something about it if anyone tried to take it away from him. In his memoirs he wrote of an incident in Willis, Tex.: "Some fellows tried to arrest me for carrying a pistol. They got the contents of it instead."

In 1874 Wes Hardin celebrated his 21st birthday by shooting Deputy Sheriff Charley Webb of Brown County between the eyes. By now his murder toll stood somewhere between 35 or 36 and 44. Hardin himself was no authority on the matter, preferring to ignore some of his back-shooting escapades. With a $4,000 price on his head, the gunfighter decided to head for points east. He moved through Louisiana to Alabama and into Florida. He gambled and drank but avoided killing anyone, so as not to mark his trail. Despite his care, Hardin was captured by Texas Rangers aboard a train at Pensacola Junction on August 23, 1877.

Back in Texas, Hardin got only 25 years instead of the death sentence, a fact that produced a bitter protest from a condemned gunman, William P. Longley. He had only killed half as many men as Hardin—at most—and he was due to be hanged. Where was the justice in that, Longley demanded in a death cell letter to the governor. The governor didn't bother to respond and Longley was hanged, while Hardin went to prison.

Hardin studied law behind bars, and when he was released in 1894 with a full pardon, he set up a law office. However, he did most of his lawyering in saloons and at the gaming tables. In El Paso he gained the enmity of a nasty old lawman, John Selman, who was a sterling advocate of the principle that one shot in the back was worth more than two up front. On August 19, 1895 Hardin was standing at the bar, being his loud and boisterous self, when Constable Selman walked in and put a bullet in the back of his head. Selman was acquitted, claiming self-defense. He said it had been a fair fight since Hardin had seen him in the mirror. They might not have bought that one even in Texas had not Wes Hardin been the notorious character he was.

See also: *Jack Helm, John Selman, Sutton-Taylor Feud.*

Further reading: *The Life of John Wesley Hardin* by John Wesley Hardin.

HARE, Joseph Thompson (?-1818): Highwayman

At the beginning of the 19th century the most-celebrated highwayman in America was Joseph Thompson Hare, who led a gang of cutthroats along the Natchez Trace and the Wilderness Road for years. Not only was Hare uncommonly successful, pulling some most lucrative robberies, he was also an elegant dresser and a dandy who excited the public's imagination.

Born in Chester, Pa., Hare grew up in the slums of New

York City and Baltimore and then went to sea. When his windjammer docked in New Orleans, Hare, never having seen a city at the same time so vile and so enticing, jumped ship. He soon became an accepted and successful member of the New Orleans underworld and in time ventured out on the Natchez Trace, where he became notorious for his "stand and deliver" escapades. He was a legend on the Trace, a phantom the law could not catch since, despite his fame, there was no firm description of him. He frequently returned to New Orleans without hindrance to sample its fleshpots until the time he once more needed loot to sustain his life as a rogue and blade.

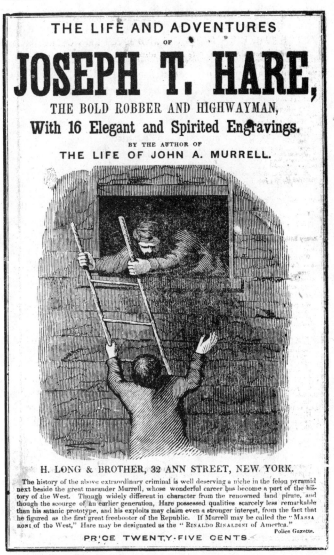

THE LIFE AND ADVENTURES
OF
JOSEPH T. HARE,
THE BOLD ROBBER AND HIGHWAYMAN,
With 16 Elegant and Spirited Engravings.
BY THE AUTHOR OF
THE LIFE OF JOHN A. MURRELL.

H. LONG & BROTHER, 32 ANN STREET, NEW YORK.

The history of the above extraordinary criminal is well deserving a niche in the felon pyramid next beside the great marauder Murrell, whose wonderful career has become a part of the history of the West. Though widely different in character from the renowned land pirate, and though the scourge of an earlier generation, Hare possessed qualities scarcely less remarkable than his satanic prototype, and his exploits may claim even a stronger interest, from the fact that he figured as the first great freebooter of the Republic. If Murrell may be called the "MASSARONI of the West," Hare may be designated as the "RINALDO RINALDINI of America."
Police Gazette.

PRICE TWENTY-FIVE CENTS.

Joseph Thompson Hare's career inspired many literary efforts, which usually included his advice to others to avoid the ways of the highwayman "as it is a desperate life, full of danger, and sooner or later it ends on the gallows."

When he was finally captured in 1813, Hare expected to be hanged but got off with only a five-year prison term. When he was released, he returned immediately to his highwayman's career. Robbing the Baltimore night coach near Havre de Grace, Md., he netted $16,000, a tremendous haul for the period. Two days later, he was apprehended in a fashionable tailor shop in Baltimore while purchasing a coat, which he described in his memoirs as "in the style of an officer's, at the price of $75, very dashy." Hare was hanged in Baltimore on September 10, 1818, leaving his diary in his cell. It ended with a somber warning for readers not to take to the highway "as it is a desperate life, full of danger, and sooner or later it ends on the gallows."

HARGRAVES, Dick (1824-1882): Gambler and killer

Probably the epitome of the Mississippi gambler, Dick Hargraves cut a dapper and deadly figure on the river in the 1840s and 1850s.

A fashion plate who ordered boots from Paris and clothing from his native England, Hargraves came to New Orleans at the age of 16 and went to work as a bartender. He turned to professional gambling after winning $30,000 in a legendary poker game. Thereafter, he was a fixture on the river, where he became famous as an honest but pitiless gambler. Since at least 90 percent of all Mississippi gamblers were dishonest operators, Hargraves prided himself on being "square" and always felt that characteristic made it totally unnecessary for him to feel any sympathy for those he won money from. He supposedly shot at least eight or 10 men who sought vengeance after losing their money and often all their possessions to him. At the peak of his prosperity, Hargraves was worth an estimated $2 million.

As the best-known gambler in New Orleans, it was inevitable that women would be attracted to Hargraves. One of his numerous affairs resulted in scandal and death rivaling a Greek tragedy. Hargraves became involved with a banker's wife and was challenged to a duel by the enraged husband. He killed the banker with dispatch, and when the dead man's brother warned he would shoot the gambler on sight, Hargraves met him at a Natchez-under-the-Hill gambling den and killed him in a desperate battle. When Hargraves returned to New Orleans, the banker's widow stabbed him and then committed suicide. He recovered from his wounds and married a girl whose life he had saved in a fire. Tired of river gambling, he joined a filibustering campaign to Cuba and during the Civil War served as an officer in the Union Army. After the war Hargraves, a wealthy but ill man, moved to Denver, where he died of tuberculosis in 1882.

See also: *Riverboat Gamblers.*

HARPE Brothers: 18th century highwaymen

For more than 50 years during the latter part of the 18th century, the Natchez Trace, which was little more than a narrow path from Natchez to Nashville, was probably the most crime-infested area in America.

Among the bandits who roamed the Trace and the Wilderness Road were two brothers, Micajah and Wiley Harpe, better known as Big and Little Harpe. There is no accurate record of how many men, women and children the Harpes butchered in the 1790s, but it was well up in the scores. In 1799 a large posse of frontiersmen cornered the Harpes in the Ohio wilds. Little Harpe escaped but Big Harpe was shot from his horse and, while still alive, had his head cut off by a man whose wife and children he had slaughtered; Big Harpe was 31 at the time. After his escape Little Harpe, two years his brother's junior, joined up with the bandit gang of Samuel Mason, a strange character who had turned to outlawry in middle age after being a soldier and justice of the peace in Kentucky. Mason would boastfully carve on a tree at the scene of one of his many murders, "Done by Mason of the Woods."

Late in 1803 Little Harpe, now going under the name of Setton, and Sam Mays, another member of the Mason gang, axed their chieftain's head off. They packed it in clay and went to Natchez to claim a reward. Unfortunately, while waiting for their money, they were accused of stealing horses and Setton was identified as Little Harpe. Little Harpe and Mays were hanged at Greenville, Miss. on February 8, 1804. Their heads were cut off and Harpe's head was stuck on a pole and displayed on the Trace to the north of the town. May's head was placed on view to the south of town, a warning to other outlaws that the murderous days of the Natchez Trace were coming to a close.

See also: *Sam Mason.*

HARPER, Richard (?-c.1839): Early Chicago thief

The record is unclear concerning Chicago's first thief, or, more correctly, the first to get caught. His name was listed as Richard Harper and he was lodged in the city's first jail, constructed in 1833 of "logs firmly bolted together."

Various historical accounts differ on Harper's background and crimes. One describes him as a young loafer from Maryland, but another relates he was a young man of considerable education and breeding who was brought down by a devotion to whiskey. All sources agree he enjoyed stealing better than working. In 1833 Harper was put up for sale under the Illinois vagrancy law, making him the first white man in the area to be auctioned. That act caused considerable controversy, but despite strong feelings on the subject, no one in the large crowd would raise the 25¢ bid made by George White, the Negro town crier, and Harper was led away by his new owner at the end of a chain. One historian reported that he escaped that very night and was never seen again. However, Chicago's first directory, published in 1839, contained the listing "Harper, Richard, called 'Old Vagrant.'"

HARRIS, William And Emily: Kidnappers of Patricia Hearst

The bizarre hunt for kidnapped heiress Patricia Hearst ended on September 18, 1975, when Hearst and 32-year-old Wendy Yoshimura were captured by the FBI in an apartment in the Mission District of San Francisco. About an hour earlier, William and Emily Harris, 30 and 26 respectively, were picked up on a street corner by FBI agents. The Harrises were considered to be the last of the Symbionese Liberation Army, a radical terrorist group that had taken Hearst from her Berkeley, Calif. apartment in February 1974. Some three months after her abduction, Hearst renounced her parents and said she was joining her SLA captors.

It appeared the Harrises had been with Hearst during virtually the entire period of her kidnapping and witnessed her startling behavioral conversion from prisoner to willing partner. In the San Francisco apartment agents found a portion of William Harris' autobiography describing the Hearst abduction and her later transformation to a willing member of the SLA, a development that startled the Harrises. The manuscript quoted Hearst as labeling her parents racists.

In August 1978 the Harrises pleaded guilty to "simple kidnapping" rather than to the more serious charge of "kidnapping for ransom and with great bodily harm." Before they were sentenced in October, William Harris accused Patricia Hearst and her family of "lies, distortions and exaggerations" about her life with the SLA. He said: "She was not brainwashed, beaten, tortured or raped. She was not coerced into rejecting her family and remaining with the people of the SLA." This had been Hearst's defense at her own trial on charges of taking part in a bank robbery with other SLA members.

With credit for time served and good behavior, the Harrises were assured of being released in 1983.

See also: *Patricia Hearst.*

HARRISON, Carter (1825-1893): Corrupt Chicago mayor

In a city where crooked politicians were the rule, Chicago Mayor Harrison Carter, who served five separate terms in the 19th century, was perhaps the most audacious of the lot. While newspapers were constantly exposing Harrison's involvement in the ownership of many vice properties and connected him with known criminals and corrupters, Chicago voters kept right on electing him to office.

Born in Kentucky in 1825 and a graduate of Yale, Harrison came to Chicago in 1850 and quickly made a fortune in real estate, becoming a financial and political power. Elected mayor, he soon realized he could rent out a number of his properties for three or four times their former rental values by giving them over to saloon, gambling and prostitution enterprises. In 1877 the *Chicago Times* pointed out that an entire block occupied by buildings housing every sort of vice activity was owned by "Our Carter." Despite this intelligence, the voters of Chicago promptly reelected Harrison on his next try for the mayorality.

Harrison's close connections with the underworld started in the 1880s, when he formed a working relationship with Mike McDonald, the crime king of Chicago. McDonald handled the "fix," charging most criminals a percentage of their take in exchange for a guarantee of immunity from official persecution. Gamblers, vice operators, swindlers, pickpockets and other crooks were allowed to keep from 40 to 65 percent of their take, with the rest going to McDonald, who in turn paid off the police, judges, aldermen and other city officials and supplied bribe money to fix juries. Describing this arrangement, the famed muckraker William T. Steed wrote: "Many people had a finger in the pie before the residue reached Mr. Harrison. But however many there were who fingered the profit en route, there was enough left to make it well worth the Mayor's while."

As part of the agreement between Harrison and McDonald, the latter retained an important say in the police department, replacing an honest police chief, Simon O'Donnell, with the more compliant William J. McGarigle. In 1882 McGarigle was shifted to the wardenship of the Cook County Hospital, where he then hired McDonald's contracting firm to paint a public building for $128,500. A number of bribes were given to aldermen to approve the deal and the paint job was done—with a mixture of chalk and water. When the scandal broke, McGarigle left town without packing a bag, and a number of aldermen were sent to jail. McDonald and Harrison were unscathed, however.

Harrison was elected to his fifth term in office by promising Chicagoans an open town for the Columbian Exposition of 1893. And he certainly kept his promise, simultaneously insuring that the public was fleeced as expeditiously as possible by the underworld with, above all, no scandal to taint the good name of the Fair and the city. Typical of these arrangements was the one made with the pickpockets via McDonald. Under an agreement reached by the politicians and the pickpockets, whose negotiations were handled by Eddie Jackson, the dean of the dips, no Fair visitor was to be robbed at the entrance gates, since if they were, they would have no money to spend inside. The terms of the agreement required that a pickpocket seized at the gate return the loot to the victim if he could be found; if not, the money went to the police. Regardless of what finally happened to the loot, the pickpocket would be required to pay the arresting officer $10 for his release. This was a harsh measure, but as a sop to the pickpockets, they were promised that any thief arrested in the downtown area between 8 a.m. and 4 p.m. would be released when brought to the Central Station House.

With such arrangements the Fair was a bonanza for the underworld as well as the business interests of Chicago. On American Cities Day, October 28, 1893, three days before the Fair closed, Harrison delivered a speech at the fairgrounds and then returned home ahead of his family and servants. When he went to answer his door bell, Harrison was shot dead by a disgruntled office seeker named Prendergast. The public display of grief was overwhelming, and Harrison was given a funeral that rivaled anything since the grand passage of Abraham Lincoln's body. Over the next two decades the late mayor's son, Carter Harrison II, held sway in Chicago, much of the time as mayor, while McDonald and his successors in the underworld noticed little change in their relationship with City Hall.

See also: *Biler Avenue, Michael Cassius "Mike" McDonald.*

HARSH, George S. (1907-1980): Murderer and war hero

Once sentenced to death for a senseless "thrill killing," George S. Harsh went on to become a much-storied World War II hero and an author and spokesman against capital punishment.

In 1929 Harsh and Richard G. Gallory confessed to the shooting of a drugstore clerk during an Atlanta holdup that the newspapers called a thrill killing. The two were also charged in six other robberies and the killing of another clerk. Both defendants came from wealthy and socially prominent families. Harsh's family put up an elaborate and expensive defense, including testimony from 12 psychiatrists that he suffered from "psychological irresponsibility and hereditary taints." Harsh was nonetheless found guilty and sentenced to die in the electric chair, but this was later commuted to life imprisonment on a Georgia work gang. In 1940 he was granted a parole after helping to save a fellow inmate's life by performing an appendectomy on him.

Harsh joined the Royal Canadian Air Force. Shot down by the Germans, he was captured and sent to a Nazi prison camp. He played a key role in the tunnel breakout of 126 Allied soldiers from the camp, 50 of whom were later apprehended and executed. The movie entitled *The Great Escape* was based on this incident. Harsh was eventually freed from captivity, and after the war he turned to writing about his life and his moral redemption, relating his experiences in a book entitled *A Lonesome Road.* He also crusaded against capital punishment, writing in 1972: "Capital punishment is a law zeroed in on the poor, the underprivileged, the friendless, the uneducated and the ignorant. I was convicted of a senseless crime and sentenced to die in the electric chair. This sentence would have been carried out had I not come from a white, wealthy and influential family. This Mosaic law of death is drawn from the worst of all human motives, revenge."

Harsh died on January 25, 1980 in Toronto, Canada.

HART, Brooke (1911-1933): Kidnapping and murder victim

The kidnap-murder of a 22-year-old hotel and department store heir in California in 1933 probably triggered more official approval of vigilantism than any other crime in this century.

Brooke Hart was seized by two 24-year-old youths of comfortable middle-class backgrounds, John Maurice Holmes and Thomas H. Thurmond, the latter having no criminal record at all. The pair abducted Hart as he left the family's department store in San Jose on November 9 and, using the victim's car, drove to the San Mateo-Hayward Bridge. Hart was knocked unconscious and his body, weighted down with cement blocks, heaved into the bay. Hart regained consciousness on hitting the water and, screaming, tried to stay afloat whereupon Thurmond shot him several times until his body disappeared. An hour later, the kidnappers were on the telephone to the victim's father, Alex Hart, demanding a ransom of $40,000 for the safe return of his son. Several more calls were necessary to arrange a pickup spot for the money, and on November 15 police traced a call to a San Jose garage and arrested Thurmond while he was still on the phone with the elder Hart. Thurmond confessed and named Holmes as his accomplice, each man accusing the other of devising the plot and committing the murder.

On November 24, young Hart's body washed ashore and the San Jose community, especially the college students who knew Hart as a recent graduate, were enraged. By that evening crowd of 15,000 had gathered outside the jail where the two quarreling killers were being held in separate cells. The college students took up a cry of "We want a touchdown," a chant that chilled not only the prisoners but Sheriff William Emig as well. He called Gov. James "Sunny Jim" Rolfe requesting troops, but his plea was rejected. Gov. Rolfe insisted there was no need. For the next several hours local and state police held off the crowd, which was growing bigger and more ugly by the minute. They held them back with high-powered hoses and tear gas but the mob continued to surge toward the jail. Alex Hart appeared on the scene and begged the would-be vigilantes to leave, but he was ignored. Not long before midnight, the mob moved in, battered down the jail door and poured past the handful of police guards. Holmes was attacked in his cell, stripped of his clothes and beaten so badly an eyeball dangled from its socket. When the mob located Thurmond's cell, they found it empty. Then while everyone grew silent, they could hear labored breathing and spotted him hiding in the pipes over the cell's toilet. Thurmond was beaten badly, dragged outside to a park and hanged from a tree. A pleading Holmes was hanged next, while the crowd chanted, "Get that ball!"

Authorities never charged anyone in the lynchings, although many identifications could have been made. Newspapers in California and the rest of the nation condemned the lynchings, but it was clear the popular and official California reaction approved of the acts. Gov. Rolfe described the lynchings as "the best lesson ever given the country. I would pardon those fellows if they were charged. I would like to parole all kidnappers in San Quentin and Folsom to the fine patriotic citizens of San Jose."

Thomas Thurmond's body dangled from a tree after he was dragged from his cell by angry Californians and hanged. Gov. Sunny Jim Rolfe called the lynching "the best lesson ever given the country."

HART, Gene Leroy (1944-1979): Wrong man

A full-blooded Cherokee Indian and an escaped convict, Gene Leroy Hart became an Oklahoma folk hero in his successful battle against charges that he killed three Girl Scouts in 1977. Serving sentences totaling 140 years for rape, kidnapping and burglary, Hart escaped from the Mayes County, Okla. jail in 1973. He was still at large on June 13, 1977 when three Girl Scouts—Lori Lee Farmer, Michele Guse and Doris Denise Milner, aged 8, 9 and 10—were sexually assaulted and beaten to death at a camp near Pryor. Within two weeks of the crime, law enforcement officials announced that Hart was their principal suspect. Many local people believed in Hart's innocence, and they helped him to continue to hide out from the law. Finally, after a 10-month manhunt that attracted a small army of police officers and civilian volunteers, Hart was caught.

Brought to trial for the murders, Hart had to defend himself against a case that was both highly technical and circumstantial. During his trial, Oklahoma's longest, his family and friends held support meetings for him and raised money for his defense by selling chili suppers. After a former jailer testified that some of the state's evidence against the popular Indian had been in officials' possession up to three years before the crime was committed and other Girl Scouts identified photographs of a convicted Kansas rapist as looking like the murderer, Hart was acquitted in March 1979. While he went back to prison, his supporters held a champagne celebration. On June 4, 1979 the 35-year-old Cherokee died of a heart attack after jogging in the prison yard. An estimated 1,000 mourners attended the funeral of the man whose case was said to have done much to further the cause of Indian rights. However, even as Hart was being buried, officials insisted they had new evidence that proved his guilt.

HART, Pearl (1878-?): Last stagecoach robber

Pearl Hart was a failure at stagecoach robbing, but she did have the distinction of taking part in the last stage robbery in the United States.

Pearl, who described herself as "slightly married," had left her husband in her native Canada and headed for the Wild West at the age of 20, having devoured all the tales about Jesse James and Butch Cassidy. She was determined to become the greatest woman outlaw in history. Slinging hash in an Arizona mining camp, she met up with Joe Boot, a cash-short miner, and convinced him there was more money in robbing stage coaches than in mining. Apparently, Pearl didn't even know that Wells Fargo had by that date stopped shipping money in stage strongboxes. On May 30, 1899 Pearl and Boot held up the Benson-Globe stage. As Joe Boot collected the loot from the three passengers—a traveling salesman, $390, an Eastern dude, $36 and a Chinese man, $5—Pearl, her long brunette locks stuffed under a hat, trained a six-gun on the driver and

the victims. As the pair took off, Pearl, elated at their magnificent take of $431, broke into song, her spirits undampened by a sudden rain squall. Then the last of the stagecoach robbers got lost. After traveling three days and nights in the rain, they finally lay down to sleep, and that was how the law found them. Taken to Florence by Sheriff William Truman, they were greeted by a large crowd. A reporter asked Pearl, "Would you do it again?" Giving him a "savage look," she snarled "Damn right, podner."

Joe Boot was sentenced to 35 years. Being a woman, Pearl got only five years. She was the only female inmate at the Yuma Territorial Prison and became quite an attraction. Sunday visitors often asked her to pose for pictures in the jail yard and she always obliged. Released after doing almost 2½ years, Pearl toured theaters billed as the Arizona Bandit, with her record somewhat embellished. Pearl's footlight glory lasted about a year, and then nothing was heard of her until 1905, when she was arrested in Deming, New Mexico Territory for conspiring to rob a train. Released for lack of evidence, she dropped out of sight. In 1924 Pearl, now a white-haired little woman in her late forties, turned up at the Pima County Courthouse and asked to be allowed to look around for old time's sake. Treated as a celebrity, Pearl Hart got the grand tour and then vanished again, this time for good.

HARTLEY Mob: 19th Century New York gang

Probably the most colorful of New York's 19th century gangs was the Hartley Mob, which dominated an area around Broadway and Houston Street. Numbering in its membership some of the city's most cunning thieves and vicious killers, the Hartley Mob thrived in the 1870s. Even the contemporary Whyos, probably the worst of gang of the century and often described as the forerunners of Murder, Inc., made it a practice of not tangling with the Hartley Mob.

The gang's criminal technique was daring and original. While an obliging traffic officer would hold up the flow of other vehicles, the very well-armed gangsters, dressed in solemn black, would transport their stolen goods hidden behind the drapes of a hearse and on the floors of accompanying funeral carriages. The Hartleys discovered the combat uses of the hearse in a noted battle with a vicious Five Points gang, which had been encroaching on their territory. The Five Pointers stationed themselves on Mulberry Street to take the onslaught of the Hartleys but respectfully parted ranks to allow a hearse and some funeral carriages to pass. They were then overwhelmed from behind by two dozen Hartley Mob battlers who swarmed out of the vehicles.

The Hartley Mob was too mean and deadly a gang to last. Unlike other gangs, the mob saw no need to seek political protection, and within a few years most of the members were imprisoned.

HARVEY, Captain Julian (1916-1961): Mass murderer

At first regarded as the fortunate sole survivor of a cruising yacht that had sunk, a 45-year-old adventurer, Captain Julian Harvey, was later unmasked as the perpetrator of one of this country's worst mass murders at sea.

On November 13, 1961 Harvey was rescued from a dinghy, which also contained the drowned body of a little girl. Harvey explained he was the skipper of the ketch *Bluebelle,* which had caught fire and sunk the day before some 50 miles from Nassau. He said that because of the flames he had been unable to save any of his passengers, Mr. and Mrs. Arthur Dupperrault, their 14-year-old son Brian, their 11-year-old daughter Terry Jo, their seven-year-old daughter Renee or his own 34-year-old wife Mary, although he was able to fish Renee's dead body from the water.

There seemed little reason to doubt the captain's story, despite the fact that he had taken out a $20,000 double-indemnity life insurance policy on his wife shortly before the *Bluebelle* sailed from Fort Lauderdale, Fla. on November 8 with the Dupperrault family as passengers. Then, 3½ days after Harvey was rescued, 11-year-old Terry Jo Dupperrault was found floating on a cork raft. The story she told was far different from Harvey's tale. She revealed that Harvey had slaughtered her parents and brother and his own wife. She saw the bodies of her mother and brother covered with blood "all over." Harvey had left her on the deck of the sinking ketch after opening the sea cocks, but she managed to escape on a raft before the craft went down.

Harvey was attending a Coast Guard hearing into the sinking when word came that the girl had been rescued. He walked from the room, shaking his head. He went back to a Miami motel and killed himself by slashing his veins with a razor blade. Subsequent inquiry revealed Mary Harvey had been the second wife of Julian Harvey to die in a violent accident. In 1949, while he was an Air Force lieutenant colonel, Harvey crashed the car he was driving through a bridge railing into a Florida bayou. He told investigators he was thrown free but his wife, Joan, and her mother, Mrs. Myrtle Boylen, were trapped and drowned.

As he had requested in a suicide note, Harvey was buried at sea by friends. A blue ribbon emblazoned with gold letters read, "Bon voyage, Julian."

HASTINGS, Mary (1863-?): Madam

A young prostitute from Brussels, Belgium with previous experience in Paris, Toronto, British Columbia, San Francisco, Portland and Denver, Mary Hastings arrived in Chicago at the age of 25 and immediately set about earning her reputation as the worst madam in the city's history. She boasted that her first bordello at 144 Custom House Place contained only harlots who were thrown out of "decent houses." To satisfy some customers' desires, however, she hired procurers to kidnap girls as young as 13 from other cities. Frequently, she would go on such forays herself, returning with girls between 13 and 17, whom she had lured to Chicago with the promise of jobs. Once the girls were safely confined in one of her houses, they would be subjected to a process of brutalization and rape to introduce them to "the life." In one typical case, three young girls were locked in a room overnight with six men. Those girls Madam Hastings had no need for in her own houses she would sell to other establishments for sums varying from $50 to $300, depending on their age and beauty.

Madam Hastings bought police protection by paying cops on the beat $2.50 a week plus free drinks, meals and girls whenever they desired. Naturally, the payoffs to ward politicians and the higher brass at the Harrison Street police station were much higher. When she once complained that the charges were excessive, a police captain stormed back, "Why, damn you, what are you made for but to be plundered?"

While virtually all the police accepted bribes for overlooking mere prostitution, many refused to be bought when the offense involved was the forceful procuring of young girls. In 1895 hard evidence against her was finally supplied by four girls from Cleveland who had escaped a Hastings house by climbing down a rope made of sheets and reached a police station. A raiding party crashed into the house and freed five other girls. After bail was posted by her "solid man," Tom Gaynor, Madam Hastings was indicted. She promptly fled to Canada, and the bail was forfeited. When she returned, however, strings were pulled, and the funds were returned to Gaynor. Then Madam Hastings decamped again for Canada, this time signing over all her property to Gaynor so that it could not be seized by the courts. By mid-1897 she was able to return once more because the witnesses against her had scattered. However, when she tried to reclaim her brothels, Gaynor threw her out on the street, to the cheers of the inmates. Finally, he let her have $200 and Mary Hastings left the city for good.

HATFIELDS And McCoys: Mountaineer feud

America's classic mountain feud between the Hatfields in West Virginia and the McCoys in Kentucky was in many respects an extension of the Civil War. The Hatfields, under the leadership of young Anderson "Devil Anse" Hatfield, had sided with the South, while the family of Randolph McCoy took up the Union cause. Both families rode with border guerrilla bands and built up a hatred that would long outlive the war.

After the war, although relations were strained, there was no important confrontation until 1873, when Randolph McCoy accused Floyd Hatfield of stealing a hog. The case finally came for adjudication before Parson Anse, a Baptist minister who dispensed justice in the backcountry. Mountaineers streamed to the trial, all armed with long knives, or "toothpicks," and long-barreled rifles. Supporting the Hatfields were the Mahons, Vances, Ferrels, Statons and Chafins. On the McCoy side were the Sowards, Stuarts, Gateses, Colemans, Normans and Rutherfords. Six supporters of each side were placed on a jury and it appeared matters would be deadlocked. However, one of the jurors, Selkirk McCoy, who was married to a Hatfield, voted in favor of the Hatfields, breaking the tie. He pointed out that both men had presented sound arguments but in the final analysis possession was what counted and there did not seem to be enough grounds to take the hog away from Floyd Hatfield.

The decision ended the legal battle but ill feelings festered. It was only a matter of time before violence erupted. The first to die was Bill Staton, a Hatfield supporter who had vowed to kill McCoys. How many died after that was never accurately counted; both clans were close-mouthed on such matters, but the bloodbath escalated. When Ellison Hatfield, a brother of Devil Anse, was shot by McCoys in an election day dispute in 1882, the Hatfields took three McCoy brothers hostage and warned them they would die if Ellison died. Two days later, Ellison died and the three McCoy brothers were tied to papaw bushes along a stream and shot to death.

Word about the various murders seeped out to the cities of Kentucky, and the governor of the state finally posted rewards for the capture of any Hatfields. Since the majority of the Hatfields and their supporters lived in West Virginia, and the McCoys and their followers mostly resided in Kentucky, the matter soon flared into a dispute between the two states. In 1888 the Hatfields, who resented the fact that the McCoys kept trying to bring in the law, decided a major drive was necessary to eliminate their foe. A large Hatfield contingent attacked the home of Randolph McCoy. Wearing masks, they yelled out, "Come out, you McCoys, and surrender as prisoners of war!" When the call went unanswered (Randolph McCoy was not present), they shot in the windows and set fire to the house. Randolph's young daughter ran out and was slain. Then his son Calvin emerged and went down in a fusillade. Old Mrs. McCoy tried to run to her daughter and was clubbed over the head and left for dead. This would be the last great reprisal in the feud.

Newspapers all over the country reported the atrocity. Kentucky law officers made several raids into West Virginia, and at least two Hatfield clansmen were killed and nine others captured. West Virginia appealed to the Supreme Court to have the captives returned. The High Court handed down a quick decision stating the law provided no method of compelling one state to return parties wrongfully abducted from one another state. Of the nine, two were executed and the others sent to state prison.

By 1890 the feud was about over. A year later, Cap Hatfield wrote a letter to a local newspaper stating the Hatfields were declaring a general amnesty and that "the war spirit in me has abated." Shortly thereafter, Devil Anse came out of hiding, finally sure no Kentucky lawmen would be waiting to apprehend him.

By the time Devil Anse died in 1921 at about 100 years of age, the two clans had intermarried frequently. In the younger generations the feud was nothing more than ancient history, like the Civil War itself.

HAUN'S Mill Massacre: Anti-Mormon killings

For about three decades from the time of the establishment of the Church of the Latter Day Saints by Joseph Smith in 1830, the history of Mormonism was one of persecution and murder, first in New York state, then in Ohio and later in Missouri. It was common for Mormons to be beaten, robbed, tarred and feathered, whipped and killed. On October 30, 1838 a group of 200 Missourians under the leadership of Nehemiah Comstock attacked an encampment of Mormons at Haun's Mill. The death toll was about 20, with many more seriously wounded. Men, women and children were among the victims. One victim was a small boy who had sought refuge with other children in a blacksmith shop. When he was found, the child begged for his life. But a gun was placed to his temple and his brains blown out; the killer bragged of his deed long after. The attackers threw the corpses down a well and then plundered the camp. Not only were there no prosecutions following these killings, but Gov. Lillburn W. Boggs shortly thereafter announced, "The Mormons must be treated as enemies, and must be exterminated or driven from the state for the public peace." The Haun's Mill Massacre, as well as the murder of Joseph Smith, set the precedent for 1857 slaughter of more than 120 wagon train emigrants by a Mormon attacking party in the Mountain Meadows Valley, Utah Territory.

See also: *Mountain Meadows Massacre, Joseph Smith.*

HAUPTMANN, Bruno Richard: See Lindbergh Kidnapping.

HAVANA Convention: Underworld conference

Probably the most important underworld conference in the post-World War II period was the Havana meeting in December 1946, convened to heal the rifts that were appearing in the national crime syndicate. With Lucky Luciano in exile in Italy, serious rivalries developed as Vito Genovese attempted to extend his power over the New York crime families. Luciano had left Frank Costello in charge of his crime family, just as he had been during the period when he was serving time in American prisons. Genovese, who had recently been returned to the United States from his self-imposed exile in Italy to face a murder charge (which he had beaten), was attempting to fill the Luciano vacuum.

The Luciano-Meyer Lansky combination had called the meeting to bring about order and to reassert the former's position of control. Luciano clearly felt he could bide his time in Havana for a couple of years while he waited for the proper political strings to be pulled so that he could come back to the United States.

Among those present at the conclave were Costello, Tommy Lucchese, Joe Profaci, Genovese, Joe Bananas Bonanno, Willie Moretti, Augie Pisano, Joe Adonis, Giuseppe Magliocco and Mike Miranda, all from New York-New Jersey; Steve Magaddino, from Buffalo; Carlos Marcello, from New Orleans; Santo Trafficante, from Florida; and Tony Accardo and Charlie and Rocco Fischetti, from Chicago. Also present, although in nonvoting roles (this was essentially an Italian Mafia conference), were Meyer Lansky and the syndicate's partner in New Orleans, Dandy Phil Kastel, both Jews. Another attendee was a popular young singer, an Italian-American from New Jersey named Frank Sinatra, whom Luciano would describe as "a good kid and we was all proud of him."

Sinatra was not there to take part in the deliberations. He had come with his friends the Fischetti brothers to be the guest of honor at a gala party. As such, he provided good cover for the many Italian mobsters in attendance, giving them an alibi, if necessary, for being in Havana.

The conference proved less than a total success for Luciano in many respects. Genovese actually had the nerve to suggest privately to Luciano that he "retire" from the syndicate. Luciano handled this effrontery by easily facing down Genovese, but he soon learned his word was no longer law.

Luciano effectively blocked Genovese from taking more power and stifled Genovese-inspired complaints about Albert Anastasia, the Lord High Executioner of the mob, who was accused of becoming kill crazy. Anastasia apparently was advocating the assassination of Bureau of Narcotics Director Harry Anslinger. Luciano evidently curbed Anastasia but did not "defang" him, realizing he would be a valuable weapon in any future war with Genovese.

However, Luciano lost on another important issue, narcotics. Like Lansky, Costello, Magaddino and a few others, Luciano wanted to take the syndicate out of the narcotics business, but the profits were so enormous that many important crime chiefs would not or, perhaps because of opposition from their own underlings, could not give up the trade. Luciano was forced to leave the decision up to the individual crime families.

Another serious matter of business for the convention was the passing of the death sentence on Bugsy Siegel. A longtime underworld partner of Luciano and, in particular, of Lansky, Siegel had squandered huge sums of money building a great financial lemon, a Las Vegas gambling casino-hotel called the Flamingo. Besides being a bad businessman, Siegel was suspected of also being a crook, skimming off money the mob had put up to construct the hotel. It was Lansky's motion that sealed Siegel's doom: "There's only one thing to do with a thief who steals from his friends. Benny's got to be hit."

In due course, Siegel was hit.

Luciano had taken up residence in Cuba with two passports (the extra was in case one was taken from him) made out in his real name, Salvatore Lucania, but his presence in Cuba could not be kept secret for long and he was soon found out. It was Luciano's belief that Genovese had tipped off the U.S. government. Finally, the Cuban government, despite its gambling operation arrangements with the mob, was forced to make Luciano return to Italy. The crime leader's dream of returning to the United States was permanently shattered, and slowly over the years his influence over criminal matters in America waned.

HAWTHORNE Inn: Capone's Cicero headquarters

Located at 4833 22nd Street, the Hawthorne Inn was the Capone headquarters in Cicero, Ill. A two-story structure of brown brick with white tiles set in the upper face, it was completely redone on Capone's orders. Bulletproof steel shutters were affixed to every window, armed guards were posted at every entrance and the entire second floor was refurbished for Capone's private use. Eventually, the Hawthorne Inn was a regular stop for sightseeing buses, whose conductors referred to it as the Capone Castle.

On September 20, 1926 it almost became Capone's tomb. Eleven automobiles packed with gangsters loyal to Hymie Weiss, the successor to Capone's late rival and assassination victim Dion O'Banion, drove slowly past the inn and fired more than 1,000 bullets at the building, as shoppers and lunch-tour promenaders screamed and ducked for cover. Capone, eating in the restaurant on the ground floor, was raising a cup of coffee to his lips when the Thompson submachine guns began blasting. He was saved by a quick-thinking bodyguard, Frankie Rio, who knocked him to the floor. After the attack bullet holes were found in 35 automobiles parked at the curb. Inside the inn, doors and woodwork were splintered, plate glass and mirrors shattered, plaster torn from the walls and office and lobby furniture ripped apart.

Mrs. Clyde Freeman, sitting with her infant son in a car that took 30 bullets, was hit by a shot that plowed a furrow across her forehead and injured her eyes. Capone paid doctors $5,000 to save the woman's sight.

Capone refused to name any suspects in the shooting, but he told reporters: "Watch the morgue. They'll show up there." Twenty days later Hymie Weiss turned up at the morgue.

HAYMARKET Affair: Terrorist bombing

One of the most tragic instances of labor turmoil in this country was the Haymarket affair in Chicago on May 4, 1886. Fifteen thousand workers jammed Haymarket Square in a rally to demand shorter work hours, condemn police brutality and protest the killing of a worker four days earlier in a strike-breaking battle at the McCormick-Harvester plant. Suddenly, as Samuel Fielden, a 40-year-old teamster who had immigrated to the United States from England, was speaking, 180 police officers appeared and one of the officers in charge said, "In the name of the people of the State of Illinois, I command this meeting immediately and peaceably to disperse."

Fielden responded, "We are peaceable."

As he and other speakers began to descend from the truck wagon being used as a podium, a dynamite bomb flew through the air and exploded in front of the police. Several fell. The police reformed and started firing. Those workers who had guns fired back. In all, seven policemen, and two civilians died and 130 others were wounded.

The public uproar against anarchists and Reds was instant and widespread. The color red was cut out of street signs, and the press all around the country attacked anarchists, socialists and aliens, especially Germans since most of the speakers were German.

Nine men, most of them speakers at the rally, were indicted for murder; they were: Albert Parsons, Samuel Fielden, Michael Schwab, August Spies, Adolph Fischer, Oscar Neebe, George Engel, Louis Lingg, who was charged with making the bomb, and Rudolph Schnaubelt, who was reported to have thrown it. Parsons and Schnaubelt disappeared before the trial opened; the latter was believed to have gone back to his native Germany.

When the trial began on June 21, 1886, Parsons, who had been in hiding in Wisconsin, walked into the courtroom and sat down with the other defendants. A veteran of the Confederate Army from Alabama, he had long alienated his socially prominent family by embracing radical causes. He later explained his reappearance by saying, "They will kill me, but I could not bear to be at liberty, knowing that my comrades were here and were to suffer for something of which they were as innocent as I."

With the aid of the prosecution, Judge Joseph Eaton Gary refused to bar from the jury one individual who had a relative among the dead policeman and another who had been a close friend of one of the officers. The strategy was to force the defense to use up its challenges on such potential jurors and then it would be forced to take whomever was offered. The jurors selected were all either businessmen or white-collar workers; none was an industrial worker.

The prosecution's case was exceptionally weak. It presented no evidence concerning who had thrown the bomb, nor did it connect the unknown bomb thrower to any of the speakers at the rally. Amazingly, Judge Gary ruled that it was not necessary for the prosecution to identify the bomb-thrower or even to prove that the murderer had been influenced by the anarchist beliefs of the defendants.

All the defendants were found guilty. Neebe was sentenced to 15 years imprisonment and the remaining eight were sentenced to death. The verdict was hailed throughout Chicago and the nation, although not in foreign countries and U.S. labor circles. But with delays in the execution, public opinion started to shift and pressures for a commutation began building. Finally, Fielden and Schwab's sentences were reduced to life imprisonment, but the other five were still scheduled to hang.

The day before the executions Louis Lingg placed a small bomb in his mouth and blew off half his face, dying 6½ hours later. The next day the remaining four, Parsons, Engel, Schwab and Spies, died on the scaffold. They shouted anarchist slogans and Parsons said: "Will I be allowed to speak, O men of America? Let me speak, Sheriff Matson! Let the voice of the people be heard!" The executioner at that moment sprang the trap.

In 1892 John P. Altgeld, a wealthy property owner, was elected governor of Illinois. He ordered a complete study made of the Haymarket affair and trial and then condemned Judge Gary for unfairness. He pardoned the three defendants still alive, Fielden, Schwab and Neebe, declaring them and their executed comrades innocent. Altgeld was severely criticized for his act by most newspapers, many of which pointed to his own German birth. Earning the sobriquet of John "Pardon" Altgeld, his political career was wrecked.

Perhaps the real vindication of the wrongfully hanged men came in the next century, when labor finally achieved the prime objective of the Haymarket rally—the eight-hour day.

See also: *John P. Altgeld.*

HAYNES, Richard "Racehorse" (1923-   ): Defense attorney

Without a doubt, the most colorful defense lawyer practicing today is a square-jawed Texan named Richard "Racehorse" Haynes. Nothing quite like him has been seen in a courtroom since the days of such legendary figures as Bill Fallon, Clarence Darrow or Moman Pruiett. If anything, he may be more successful than all of them. Noted for his lurid defenses in murder trials, which are generally marked by some very rich defendants on one side and some very damning evidence on the other, Racehorse, who was given the nickname by his high school football coach for his moves on the field, is now regarded by many as America's premier criminal defender. In any event, he may well be the highest paid. Based in Houston, Haynes does not reveal his fees, but at least two of his cases supposedly commanded million dollar sums. Randolph Hearst for a time considered employing Haynes to defend his daughter Patty but settled on F. Lee Bailey, in part, it is believed, because Bailey's charges were much lower.

Haynes insists he is "worth every dollar" he charges. With a smile he says, "What's money when you're faced with spending 25 years to life in the Crossbar Hotel?"

Few deny that Haynes is now "the best lawyer money can buy," but a prosecutor who has dueled with him in the courtroom is less than enthused, commenting: "He's good, he's very good. But on account of him, there are a couple dozen people walking free in Texas who wouldn't blink before blowing somebody's head off. He's a menace to society."

Haynes' response is the one always used by defense attorneys: "I sleep fine at night. It isn't my job to be judge and jury, but to do the best I can on behalf of the citizen accused."

Texas citizens successfully defended by him have included the late Dr. John Hill, the defendant in the Houston case made famous by the bestselling book *Blood and Money,* and oilman T. Cullen Davis, the richest man in America ever tried for murder. Davis was charged with staging a shooting spree in his $6 million family mansion during which his 12-year-old stepdaughter and his wife's lover were killed, his estranged wife was severely wounded and a family friend was crippled. Despite the fact that three eyewitnesses named Davis as the killer, Haynes won an acquittal for him, with the jury deliberating a mere four hours. Later, Haynes' client beat additional charges, considered ironclad by the prosecution, and left court a free man.

While Haynes is regarded as a master of the theatrical defense, the fact is he solidly grounds his cases in scientific analysis and often can pick apart prosecution testimony on ballistics, pathology, stains, hair and other supposedly damning evidence. Haynes was involved in the first case allegedly solved by the use of nuclear techniques. In that case scientists had analyzed the hairs of a dead woman by nuclear activation and linked the victim's strangle murder to an aircraft mechanic. The scientists were awarded medals for their accomplishment, but at the subsequent trial Haynes proceeded to debunk their findings and got the judge to bar the evidence as failing to meet the court's standards for scientific proof. As a result, the jury ended up voting nine to three for acquittal.

Another Haynes' feat still commands awe in Texas legal circles. He defended a man accused of battering a woman to death with a replica of a sword and spiked-ball and chain. Although his client had confessed and signed a statement and blood on his clothes matched the type of the victim, Haynes produced a hung jury at the first trial and won an acquittal at the second.

The key to most of Haynes' defenses revolves around jury selection. "I can usually raise real doubt in the minds of at least a couple of jurors if I've picked the jury right." Haynes uses social scientists and psychologists to profile the ideal juror in any given case. In the first Cullen Davis trial, he spent $30,000 for a jury study and utilized the services of a Ph.D. in psychology when making the actual jury selections.

In 1971 Haynes won freedom for two Houston police officers accused of violating the civil rights of a black man by kicking him to death in the station house. They had arrested the man for "stealing" a car that turned out to be his own. The lawyer got the trial moved out of Houston to New Braunfels, Tex., a conservative German-American community. "I knew we had that case won when we seated the last bigot on the jury," he told a reporter at the end of the trial.

Haynes takes no more than 15 percent of the cases brought to him, often basing his selection on the degree of challenge they offer. The high fees he commands allow him to take other cases at no charge. He once won freedom for a motorcycle gang accused of punishing an errant female member by nailing her to a tree. A typical Haynes case is far from the Perry Mason variety, in which a dramatic last-minute act of deduction frees the defendant. "My clients admit they pulled the trigger, plunged the knife, swung the club," he says. "I have to show why, because sometimes the pulling, plugging or swinging

was justified. When all else fails, I just ask the jury for mercy. They usually oblige me."

A Haynes defense seldom relies on a single factor to sway a jury. He tends to develop several possible scenarios for a jury to pick from, and in his summation he follows the argument he feels has the best chance of working. Haynes once outlined his defense strategy for an American Bar Association seminar in New York. "Say you sue me because you say my dog bit you. Well, now this is my defense: my dog doesn't bite. And second, in the alternative, my dog was tied up that night. And third, I don't believe you really got bit. And fourth, I don't have a dog."

HAYWOOD, William D. "Big Bill" (1869-1928): Radical and labor leader

Big Bill Haywood, a leader of the radical labor movement during the most turbulent era in the history of American unions, was tried for murder in a case considered to be the most important judicial confrontation between capital and labor in this country.

Haywood, a miner, cowboy and homesteader in his youth, joined the Western Federation of Miners in 1896 and quickly rose to position among the nation's union leaders. In 1905 former Gov. Frank Steunenberg was assassinated by a bomb. The confessed assassin, Harry Orchard, insisted he was carrying out Haywood's orders, as he said he had done in many previous acts of terrorism and murder. In a 1906-07 trial Haywood was charged with two others, Charles H. Moyers and George A. Pettibone, of conspiring in the bomb assassination. The 78-day courtroom drama had numerous stars: besides Haywood and Orchard, there were Clarence Darrow, the defense attorney, and future Sen. William E. Borah, prosecutor. The state's case was that Steunenberg had been murdered in retaliation for his antilabor actions during a strike in the Coeur d'Alene mines. Considered a classic today, Darrow's defense shredded the prosecution's case of any supporting evidence other than Orchard's confession, which had been written with the assistance of the Pinkertons. In his summary, Darrow conducted a eulogy on the righteousness of labor as opposed to the evils of capitalism. The defendants were acquitted.

From 1905 to 1917 Haywood remained the most charismatic labor leader in America and had a devoted following. He was arrested in the 1917 Palmer Raids and convicted of sedition, a vague charge most legal scholars agree would never be upheld today. He was sentenced to Leavenworth Penitentiary but on appeal was released on $30,000 bail. Haywood jumped bail and fled to Soviet Russia in 1921. He spent his last few years lonely and sick in Moscow, where on May 18, 1928, after a party at the home of foreign correspondent Eugene Lyons, he died.

See also: *Clarence Darrow, James McParland, Harry Orchard, Palmer Raids, Pinkerton's National Detective Agency, Frank Steunenberg.*

Charles Moyers, Big Bill Haywood and George Pettibone (left to right) were acquitted of conspiracy in the bomb assassination of former Idaho Gov. Frank Steunenberg.

HEARST, Patricia (1955-   ): Kidnap victim

Few crimes in recent history were as sensational and involved as many bizarre twists as the kidnapping of Patricia Hearst, who was taken from her Berkeley, Calif. apartment on February 5, 1974 by members of the Symbionese Liberation Army (SLA), a radical terrorist organization.

At first, the kidnappers offered to return the 19-year-old heiress if her father, newspaper publisher Randolph Hearst, would start a food program for the poor in the San Francisco Bay area. Later, however, a tape-recorded message from Patty said she had "chosen to stay and fight" with the SLA for the "freedom of the oppressed people." She adopted the SLA name of "Tania" and was subsequently linked to the armed robbery of a San Francisco bank on April 15. Hearst refused to believe his daughter was acting of her own free will, but photographs of the bank robbery and reports by eyewitnesses indicated she "absolutely was a participant." In later tapes sent by the SLA, Patty ridiculed the idea that she had been brainwashed.

Meanwhile, law enforcement authorities pressed their hunt for the handful of SLA members and cornered six of them in a Los Angeles hideout on May 17. All six including Donald DeFreeze, alias "Field Marshal Cinque," the alleged leader of the group died in an ensuing gun battle and fire. Actually, subsequent evidence indicated the real leaders were a dynamic female trio Patricia Soltysik, Nancy Ling Perry and Camilla Hall, all of whom perished with guns in their hands during the desperate shoot-out. Fears that Patty was among the dead proved unfounded, and although she was still missing, she was indicted on a charge of bank robbery.

Finally, 19 months after her original kidnapping, Patty Hearst was captured in a hideout in San Francisco. With her was 32-year-old Wendy Yoshimura, who had joined her after she had gone into hiding. The hunt ended with Patty telling FBI agents, "Don't shoot. I'll go with you." Just an hour earlier agents had arrested William and Emily Harris, the last remaining members of the SLA group that originally seized Patty.

At Patty's trial, defense attorney F. Lee Bailey stressed the brutality of the kidnapping by the SLA and claimed she had endured hardships and constant terrorization during her captivity. He argued the bank robbery had been staged by the SLA just to make Patty believe she could not return to society. The lawyer also said that DeFreeze had familiarity with brainwashing techniques and "knew just enough about this process to start it moving" on "a particularly vulnerable, frightened 19-year-old girl."

In her own testimony Patty said her early treatment by her abductors had included a number of death threats. She insisted she had been forced to have sexual intercourse with DeFreeze and another SLA member, William Wolfe. The prosecution presented psychiatric testimony to refute any contention that Patty had been anything but a "voluntary member of the SLA." Dr. Joel Fort cast doubt on her tale of sexual abuse while with the SLA, noting that she had been "sexually active at age 15," and Dr. Harry Kozol described her at the time of her kidnapping as a "rebel in search of a cause."

Patty Hearst was found guilty of the bank robbery charge and sentenced to seven years imprisonment. She served a total of 28 months, including time in prison before and after her trial. William and Emily Harris were given 10 years to life for the kidnapping.

When Patty Hearst was released, she married and settled into what was described as a very establishment life style.

See also: *Dorothy Allison, F. Lee Bailey, William and Emily Harris.*

HEATH, John: See Bisbee Massacre.

HECHT, Ben (1894-1964): Crime reporter

Many of the fascinating facts that typified novelist and playwright Ben Hecht's writing were drawn from his earlier experiences as a Chicago crime reporter. He started out as what was called a "picture chaser" for the *Chicago Journal*, assigned to acquire, by any means possible, photographs of ax murderers and the like and their victims, sometimes pilfering them from the family mantelpiece. Before long he advanced to reporter, which in the Chicago journalism of the day did not require an undue concern for accuracy.

Hecht became expert at writing stories that began, e.g., "If Fred Ludwig is hanged for the murder of his wife, Irma, it will be because of the little gold band he slipped on her finger on his wedding day, inscribed with the tender words, 'Irma—Love Forever—Fred.'"

If Hecht and his favorite crony, Charles MacArthur of the rival *Examiner* and later the *Daily News*, sometimes purpled their facts, they also solved many a case that had the police stumped. It was basically Hecht who cracked Chicago's famed Case of the Ragged Stranger, in which a pregnant woman named Mrs. Ruth Wanderer was shot by a ragged stranger as she and her husband were returning from a movie the night of June 21, 1920. At the time, her husband, Carl, according to his statement, was carrying the Colt .45 service automatic that he had kept upon discharge from the Army after World War I, and he blazed back at the attacker. A total of 14 shots were fired, and when the smoke cleared, Mrs. Wanderer was dead and so was the ragged stranger. Only Carl Wanderer was unscathed.

Wanderer was celebrated in the press and by a public fearful about the rise in violent crime. But Hecht and MacArthur both were skeptical. MacArthur traced the gun found on the ragged stranger back to a relative of Carl Wanderer's. That man, a cousin, had given it to Wanderer. Hecht in the meantime befriended Wanderer and learned much of his private life, including that he was a homosexual who was appalled at the thought of being father to a woman's baby. When Hecht found letters Wanderer had written to a male lover, the husband confessed he had tricked an unidentified stranger, whom he had met in a skid row bar, into waiting in the vestibule for him. When he and his wife arrived, Wanderer pulled two guns and opened up on both his wife and the stranger.

Ironically, the two reporters spent much time with Wanderer in the death house at the Cook County Jail, playing cards with him (and winning his money), and prevailed upon him to read attacks on their city editors as his last words on the gallows. The reporters forgot that a condemned man is bound hand and foot when hanged. At his execution Wanderer could only glance unavailing at the speeches strapped to his side. Shrugging at the reporters, he did the next best thing he could think of, bursting forth in a rollicking version of "Dear Old Pal O' Mine."

After the trap was sprung, MacArthur turned to Hecht and said, "You know, Ben, that son of a bitch should have been a song plugger."

Even after Hecht went on to bigger and better things as an author, playwright and screen writer, his Chicago crime-writing days came back to haunt him. In Hollywood during the early 1930s Hecht wrote the screenplay for *Scarface*, starring Paul Muni, for Howard Hughes' studio. One night there was a knock at his hotel room in Los Angeles, and two sinister-looking gentlemen confronted him with a copy of the screenplay.

"You the guy who wrote this?" one said, brandishing the script.

Hecht couldn't deny it.

"Is this stuff about Al Capone?"

"God, no!" Hecht assured them. "I don't even know Al." He rattled off the names of Chicago underworld characters he had known—Big Jim Colosimo, Dion O'Banion, Hymie Weiss.

His visitors seemed satisfied, one saying: "O.K. then. We'll tell Al this stuff you wrote is about them other guys." As they started to leave, however, the other one had a thought. "If this stuff isn't about Al Capone, why are you calling it *Scarface?* Everybody'll think it's him."

"That's the reason. Al is one of the most famous and fascinating men of our time. If you call the movie *Scarface*, everybody will want to see it, figuring it's about Al. That's part of the racket we call showmanship."

"I'll tell Al. Who's this fella Howard Hughes?"

"He got nothing to do with it. He's the sucker with the money."

"O.K. The hell with him." And Capone's men left placated.

HEDGEPETH, Marion (?-1910): Outlaw

Marion Hedgepeth did not have the look, or the name, of a

Western outlaw, but, as Robert Pinkerton noted, "He was one of the really bad men of the West." Immaculately dressed (his "Wanted" posters observed that his shoes were usually well polished) in a well-cut suit and topcoat with his hair slicked down under a bowler hat, Hedgepeth often looked like easy pickings to other gunfighters. But he was exceedingly fast on the draw, once killing a foe who already had his gun out before Hedgepeth even started to draw.

Not much is known about Hedgepeth's early life except that he ran away from his Missouri home in his mid-teens and became a cowboy in Wyoming and a holdup man in Colorado during the 1880s. He killed men in both states. By 1890 he was the leader of a small band of train robbers known as the Hedgepeth Four. The other members of the group, all daring and cunning killers, were Albert D. Sly, Lucius Wilson and James Francis, better known as "Illinois Jimmy." They pulled their first train job in Nebraska, netting only $1,000, but a week later, they knocked off a train in Wisconsin and got away with $5,000. Eventually, the gang made its biggest score in a train robbery at Glendale, Mo., making off with $50,000. Hedgepeth became something of a new folk hero in the area, which was Jesse James' old stamping grounds.

The gang scattered after that hit, but the Pinkertons eventually ran Hedgepeth to earth in San Francisco in 1893 and brought him back to Missouri for trial. The dapper outlaw became the toast of St. Louis, and dour-faced lawmen were forced to fill his cell with flowers sent by feminine well-wishers. His popularity with women did not prevent him from being found guilty and drawing a 25-year prison term.

While awaiting transfer to the penitentiary, Hedgepeth shared a cell with a man called H. H. Holmes, whose real name was Herman Webster Mudgett. Holmes was being held on a swindling charge, but what was not known then was that he was also the worst killer of women in America's history. In his "murder castle" in Chicago he may well have killed 200 women, collecting on the insurance policies and obtaining the dowries of many of them. Holmes offered Hedgepeth $500 if he could put him in touch with a "shrewd lawyer." Hedgepeth did and Holmes was eventually sprung from jail, but not before he had made some incriminating statements to Hedgepeth. The outlaw might have kept Holmes' secrets had he gotten the $500 promised him, but Holmes, no spendthrift, never paid him the money. Hedgepeth wrote a letter to the St. Louis police chief in which he exposed an insurance plot in Philadelphia that Holmes was involved in. The authorities checked on it and discovered Holmes had killed a man named Herman Pitezel there. They took Holmes into custody and then discovered his wholesale murders in Chicago.

Meanwhile, Hedgepeth was sent to the pentitentiary. For 12 years committees, most composed of women, mounted efforts to win his freedom, pointing out he was a "friend of society" because his actions had resulted in the capture of the terrible woman killer Holmes. Finally, Hedgepeth was pardoned in 1906.

A happy Hedgepeth said he was going to live an honest life thereafter and went to Nebraska, where he immediately started blowing safes. He was caught in 1907 and got 10 years but was released after doing less than two. In late 1908 he formed a new gang but they were a pale imitation of the old Hedgepeth Four. After a few minor jobs the outlaw pulled out and went on his own. By this time he was suffering from the ravages of tuberculosis, however, and no longer resembled the old bandit dandy. On January 1, 1910 he walked into a bar in Chicago and threatened the bartender with a six-gun while he proceeded to clean out the cash register. A passing policeman saw him through the window and rushed in with pistol drawn.

The officer shouted, "Surrender!"

Hedgepeth coughed and replied, "Never!"

Both fired at the same time. Hedgepeth, weakened by his illness, missed, probably for the first time in his life. The policeman's shot caught Hedgepeth in the chest and spun him around. Hedgepeth fell to his knees, raised his gun by instinct and, holding it with both hands, fired again. A bullet went through the officer's coat. Hedgepeth died still firing his weapon.

See also: *H. H. Holmes.*

HEINRICH, Edward Oscar (1881-1953): Criminologist

Known by the press as the "Edison of crime detection," Edward O. Heinrich trailblazed in the use of scientific methods in criminal detection. A criminologist in private practice and a lecturer on the subject at the University of California at Berkeley, he was utilized by police departments all over the country. Over a 45-year career, he was credited with solving 2,000 major and minor mysteries. He did so by being a master of all trades; he was a geologist, a physicist, a handwriting expert, an authority on inks and papers and a biochemist. He was fond of saying that no criminal ever departs the scene of his crime without leaving several clues and that it was up to a scientific investigator to find and interpret them correctly. He proved a number of alleged suicides to be murders and a number of suspected murders to be suicides or accidents. His work in the investigation of the 1916 Black Tom explosion, which he was able to lay at the door of a German sabotage ring, brought him considerable fame, as did his presentation of scientific evidence in the bestial sex murder involved in the Fatty Arbuckle case.

Probably his most famous case, because it demonstrated his deductive powers so well, was the attempted robbery of a 1923 Southern Pacific Railroad mail train and the resultant quadruple murders. On October 11 the train with its coaches filled with passengrs was moving slowly through a tunnel in the Siskiyou Mountains of southern Oregon when two men armed with shotguns climbed over the tender and ordered the engineer and fireman to halt as soon as the engine, tender and next car, the mail car, cleared the tunnel. They followed instructions and watched helplessly as a third man appeared outside the tunnel with a bulky package, which he carried to the side of the mail car. Running back to a detonator, the man set off an enormous explosion. The mail car and its contents were consumed in flames, which obviously ruined the robbery attempt. It also incinerated the lone mail clerk inside the car.

Before the trio left, they cold-bloodedly shot down the engineer, fireman and a brakeman who had come forward through the tunnel to investigate th explosion.

The attempted train robbery, reminiscent of the Wild West days, became front-page news as railroad police, postal detectives, sheriff's deputies and other lawmen converged on the scene. Posses set out to track the bandits but came up empty. All that was found was a detonator with batteries, a revolver, a pair of well-worn and greasy blue denim overalls and some shoe covers made of gunnysack soaked in creosote, apparently to keep pursuing dogs off the criminals' scent.

As days and weeks passed with no discernible leads, the authorities asked Heinrich to help. He was sent the overalls for examination with information that a garage mechanic who worked not far from the tunnel had been taken into custody because his work clothes appeared to have the same greasy stains. Heinrich started out with a magnifying glass and microcopic examination of the garment and its "contents," such as scrapings of the grease stains and lint and other tiny items from the pockets.

The first thing he discovered was that the garage mechanic should be released. "The stains are not auto grease," he said, referring to the overalls from the scene of the crime. "They're pitch from fir trees." Then he went on to stun detectives with a full description of the man they sought: he was a left-handed lumberjack who'd worked the logging camps of the Pacific Northwest. He was thin, had light brown hair, rolled his own cigarettes and was fussy about his appearance. He was five feet ten and was in his early twenties.

All of Heinrich's conclusions were backed up with solid evidence which he had "properly interpreted." He had quickly identified the grease as being fir stains, and in the pockets of the overalls he had found bits of Douglas fir needles, common to the forests of the Pacific Northwest. The pockets on the left side of the overalls were more heavily worn than those on the right. In addition, the garment was regularly buttoned from the left side. Therefore, the wearer obviously was left-handed. From the hem of a pocket, Heinrich extracted several carefully cut fingernail trimmings. Such manicuring was somewhat incongruous for a lumberjack unless he was fastidious about his appearance. The scientist found a single strand of light brown hair clinging to one button. More than merely determining the suspect's hair coloring, however, Heinrich used his own techniques to make a close estimate of the man's age. Heinrich also found one other clue, which other investigators had totally overlooked. Using a delicate forceps, he was able to dig out from the hem of the narrow pencil pocket a tiny wad of paper, apparently rammed down inadvertently with a pencil. The paper appeared to have gone through a number of washings with the overalls and was blurred beyond all legibility, but by treating it with iodine vapor, Heinrich was able to identify it as a registered-mail receipt and establish its number.

The receipt was traced to one Roy d'Autremont of Eugene, Ore. In Eugene authorities found Roy's father, who, it turned out, was worried about his twin sons, Roy and Ray, and another son, Hugh, who had all disappeared on October 11,

the date of the train holdup. Inquiries about Roy showed he was left-handed, rolled his own tobacco (confirming Heinrich's findings of tobacco samples) and was known to be fussy about his appearance. Authorities later said Heinrich had virtually furnished them with a photograph of the suspect.

Following Heinrich's cracking of the mystery, one of the most intensive manhunts in American history was launched. Circulars were printed in 100 languages and sent to police departments throughout the world. Records of the men's medical histories, dental charts and eye prescriptions were supplied to doctors, dentists and oculists. Finally, three years and six months after the crime, Hugh d'Autremont was captured in Manila, the Philippines. In April the twins were found working in a steel mill in Steubenville, Ohio under the name of Goodwin. All three were convicted and given life imprisonment.

Edward Heinrich returned to his laboratory, where he continued to supply his expertise to police forces faced with baffling crimes until his death in 1953.

HEIRENS, William (1929-): Murderer

Beginning at the age of nine, William Heirens committed hundreds of thefts, most often slipping into women's bedrooms and stealing their underthings, which he would later fondle in his room. He dressed in women's clothing and stared at pictures of Nazi leaders for hours. At the age of 13 he was arrested on a charge of carrying a loaded pistol. In his home police found an impressive arsenal of weapons. Heirens was sent to private home for correction. Since he was an above-average student, he was enrolled in Chicago University at the age of 16. But he continued to commit burglaries.

In March 1945 he disturbed a sleeping woman, Mrs. Josephine Ross, slit her throat and stabbed her several times. Three months later, another victim saw him but he merely knocked her out. In October he killed Frances Brown, shooting her twice and stabbing her. Her body was draped over the tub in the bathroom; the top part of her pajamas was around her neck and a long breadknife was stuck in her neck just below the left ear.

Young Heirens knew he was being overwhelmed by madness. On the wall of Miss Brown's living room, he scrawled in bright red lipstick: "For heavens sake catch me before I kill more I cannot control myself"

Unfortunately, the police did not catch William Heirens until after he committed his most shocking crime, kidnapping six-year-old Suzanne Degnan from her home and slaughtering her in January 1946. He dismembered the body and scattered the parts in Chicago sewers.

While his killings were gory almost beyond description, he had always cleaned the blood off his victim's body. Both Miss Brown and Mrs. Ross had been washed clean. The parts of the child, which were found inside bags, had also been immaculately washed.

Heirens was caught the following June 26 by a caretaker and a tenant in an apartment complex he was trying to enter.

For a time he denied the killings, insisting they had been done by one George Murman, who psychiatrists discovered was his alter ego. Even when Heirens made a full confession, he seemed less remorseful about the murders than the fact that his school grades were only average. "I should have been a 'B' level student," he said, "but my grades slipped due to my messing around and cutting up."

Judged insane, Heirens was sentenced to three consecutive life terms with a provision that he never be paroled.

HEITLER, Mike "De Pike" (?-1931): Brothel keeper and murder victim

A wizened, ageless brothel keeper who looked something like a Surinam toad, Mike "de Pike" Heitler could be described as Chicago's "grand old man" of merchandised vice, with a career that spanned about half a century.

Heitler got his nickname de Pike, from the fact that he ran the cheapest fancy house in Illinois, and hence was a piker. But Mike actually prided himself on being the first to introduce modern assembly line methods in the world's oldest profession. He operated a 50¢ house at Peoria and West Madison. The customers stood in line at the foot of the stairs and handed Mike half a dollar, which he rang up on a cash register. When a girl came downstairs with a satisfied customer, Mike gave her a brass check that she could redeem for two bits, and then the man at the head of the line took her back upstairs.

Helping de Pike keep the traffic moving was another quaint character, Charlie "Monkey Face" Genker. Monkey Face would scurry up the doors of Heitler's houses and poke his homely face through the transom to urge the prostitute and her customer to hurry up. The sudden appearance of that monkey face proved disconcerting to many customers, and the more knowledgeable regulars would go through their paces quickly in hope of beating Genker to the punch.

Heitler operated with certain peacefulness for many years, aside from an occasional arrest and conviction for white slavery, but he lost much of his personal clout when Al Capone tightened his hold on the entire prostitution racket in Chicago and the surrounding area. Heitler's choice was either to come in as a paid employee or simply be declared "out." Through the 1920s his position continued to deteriorate as Capone turned more to Harry Guzik to look after prostitution operations. Smarting over this lack of respect, which he considered his due, Heitler took to informing on other Capone activities.

He told Judge John H. Lyle about the mob's part-time headquarters in a resort called the Four Deuces. As recounted in *The Dry and Lawless Years,* Heitler told the judge:

> They snatch guys they want information from and take them to the cellar. They're tortured until they talk. Then they're rubbed out. The bodies are hauled through a tunnel into a trap door opening in the back of the building. Capone and his boys put the bodies in cars and then they're dumped out on a country road, or maybe in a clay hole or rock quarry.

Heitler made the mistake of passing on information to oth-

ers who evidently were not as hostile toward Capone as he assumed. He wrote an anonymous letter to the state-attorney's office revealing many secrets about the Capone brothel empire. Not long afterward, the letter turned up on Capone's desk. Heitler was summoned to appear before the mob leader at his office in the Lexington Hotel. Capone insisted only Heitler could have imparted the specific information and told him, "You're through."

Still, Heitler continued to write letters. In one, which he gave to his daughter, he named eight Capone figures as being responsible for the murder of *Chicago Tribune* reporter Jake Lingle. Unfortunately for Heitler, he apparently gave another copy of the letter to the wrong people and on April 30, 1931 his charred remains were found in the smoldering wreckage of a suburban house.

HELLIER, Thomas (?-1678): Murderer

Long before Nat Turner's 1831 slave uprising, a bonded white man struck fear into the hearts of Virginians by killing his masters. Because of his act, he later became, in a manner of speaking, a local tourist attraction.

A lifelong troublemaker and thief, Hellier was finally sold into bondage in early 1678. He passed from one owner to the other, eventually becoming the property of a gentleman farmer named Cutbeard Williamson, who had a plantation appropriately dubbed Hard Labour. The place was true to its name, Hellier discovered, and in a fit of vengeance he entered his master's mansion late one night and axed to death Williamson and his wife and the couple's maid.

Hellier fled but was soon captured by other farmers. He was hanged on August 5, 1678 at Westover, Va., and his body was chained to a giant tree that overlooked the James River, to be viewed not only by all travelers on the waterway but, most importantly, by other bonded servants being barged upriver. The body remained a gruesome sight for a number of years until it deteriorated completely.

HELL'S Kitchen: New York crime area

Hell's Kitchen, known for a time as New York City's most crime-ridden area, was originally a notorious pre-Civil War dive, but after that conflict the name was applied to a large area to the north and south of 34th Street west of Eighth Avenue. The dominant gang of the area was the original Hell's Kitchen Gang, bossed by one of the true ruffians of the late 1860s and 1870s, Dutch Heinrichs. According to one contemporary account, Heinrichs and his toughs exacted tribute from every merchant and factory owner in the district. The gang thought nothing of breaking into private houses in broad daylight and beating and robbing pedestrians at will. About 1870 Heinrichs absorbed the Tenth Avenue Gang led by Ike Marsh, the mastermind of New York City's first train robbery, and quickly grasped the wisdom of raiding the railroads. Thereafter, much of the gang's activities focused on looting the Hudson River Railroad yards and depot on 30th Street.

The railroad hired its own detectives to try to curb the gang's activities. When that action proved insufficient, it began to pay bounties to police officers for each arrest of a Hell's Kitchen gangster. Under this steady harassment, Heinrichs was finally sent to prison for five years. Even though the power of the original Hell's Kitchen Gang eventually waned, the area remained a stronghold of other gangs well into the 20th century. Only the advent of Prohibition caused these gangs to lose their distinctive neighborhood character, as they spread their activities over more of the city.

See also: *Tenth Avenue Gang.*

HELM, Boone (1824-1864): Killer and vigilante victim

The tales told about Boone Helm describe him as one of the grisliest and most-depraved killers ever to set foot on the Western scene. Among his multitude of crimes, he once killed a companion as they crossed the mountains in deep snow and then ate his flesh. When drunk he could be coaxed to talk about it and he would freely admit the act. "You don't think I was damned fool enough to starve to death, do you?" he would snarl. While the vigilantes of the 1860s would later receive considerable criticism for being "excessive" in their hanging, there was never a harsh word said about their elimination of Helm.

A vacant-faced Missourian who somehow inspired fear just by the way he could look at a person, Helm committed his first murder at the age of 27, stabbing a man to death in a drunken dispute. Deserting his wife and young daughter, Helm fled to Indian Territory in the vicinity of what is now Oklahoma, where he was captured and returned to Missouri. His trial was postponed three times because of the difficulty of finding material witnesses. Helm claimed he had acted in self-defense and wondered out loud how the witnesses against him would feel when he was acquitted. The three main witnesses apparently gave some thought to this prospect and finally decided that they hadn't seen a thing.

Deserting his family a second time, Helm next turned up on Oregon, where, despite an unsavory record of violence, he was hired by Elijah Burton to guide a small party through the mountains to Salt Lake City. The trek was disastrous, as Helm was anything but a competent guide. Along the way, members of the group dropped out to await warmer weather, but Burton himself pressed on with Helm, not realizing he would be killed and eaten by his scout. When Helm arrived in Salt Lake City, he looked rather well-fed. He did not remain there long enough for firm suspicion to be established against him, however. After killing a gambler in a particularly brutal fashion, he was driven out of town.

Nothing was heard from Helm until he turned up on San Francisco, where he slaughtered a customer in a brothel parlor who had insisted he should be served before Helm. The eager lover was hacked to death with a variety of hatchet and bowie knife blows, causing the establishment's madam to complain that her parlor looked like a butcher shop. Helm committed his next murder in Idaho and then drifted into Canada, where the law became suspicious of him after he had gone trapping with a man named Angus McPherson and returned alone with a rich load of furs. However, since nobody could be found, the authorities were forced to release him. Helm was then escorted to the Montana border.

In Montana he joined up with Henry Plummer's murderous gang of road agent killers known as the Innocents. Helm became one of Sheriff Plummer's deadliest gunmen and was probably responsible for a dozen slayings. When the vigilantes finally rode against the Innocents, one of their main targets was, of course, Helm. Captured on the morning of January 14, 1864, he was hanged along with four others that same afternoon. Helm had never shown any pity for his victims and showed none for himself. "I have looked at death in all forms and I am not afraid to die," he said. He scorned those of his companions who pleaded for mercy. As George Lane swung from the gallows, he commented, "There's one gone to hell." When Jack Gallagher strangled to death, he called out: "Kick away, old fellow. My turn next. I'll be in hell with you in a minute!"

HELM, Jack (c.1838-1873): Lawman and murderer

A captain of the Texas state police and sheriff of DeWitt County, Jack Helm has been called "the most cold-blooded murderer ever to wear a badge." The contention is debatable, but there is no question that killings happened fast when he was around.

The facts about Helm's early life are hazy, but he fought on the side of the Confederacy and, during that conflict, killed a black man on the spot for whistling a Yankee tune. In the early 1870's Helm was a captain in the Texas state police and commanded a force, official and unofficial, of 200 men, whom he involved on the side of the Suttons in the bloody Sutton-Taylor feud that engulfed DeWitt County. In 1873 Helm's men arrested two Taylor supporters, brothers Bill and Henry Kelley, on a minor charge of disturbing the peace, but the two captives never reached town. Their bodies, riddled with bullets, were found in a clearing near their ranch. Helm's deputies said they had been shot trying to escape, while Helm said he hadn't seen a thing. Because of the furor the newspapers raised, Gov. E. J. Davis dismissed Helm from the state police force, but he remained sheriff of DeWitt County.

Helm might have continued as the biggest gun in the Sutton-Taylor feud but for the appearance in 1873 of John Wesley Hardin. Wes Hardin was distantly related to the Taylor clan but close enough to join in the killing. He shot down Helm's deputy and almost got Helm on a couple of occasions. The sheriff apparently saw the handwriting on the wall and tried to negotiate a truce. One armistice meeting ended in a free-for-all that left two Sutton men dead. In another one, held in a saloon, Hardin drew his guns and backed out on Helm simply because he didn't trust him. The final confrontation occurred in a blacksmith's shop. There are many versions of what happened: according to one, it was to be an unarmed truce meeting. In any event, the three participants, Helm, Hardin and Jim Taylor were all armed to the teeth. Helm apparently pulled a knife and stabbed Taylor, and then Hardin produced a hidden shotgun and cut Helm to the floor with a double blast. Taylor then produced a six-gun and finished off the dying sheriff with three shots to the head.

Thus, as Hardin stated later in his memoirs, died a man "whose name was a horror to all law-abiding citizens." The authorship of this statement was rather ironic, but the sentiment was not entirely inaccurate.

See also: *John Wesley Hardin, Sutton-Taylor Feud.*

HELTER Skelter: Manson murder code

Originally the title of a rock song by the Beatles, "Helter Skelter" took on a grim meaning within the notorious Charles Manson "family." In August 1969 the words were found printed in blood outside of the home of two of the Manson family's murder victims, Leno and Rosemary LaBianca. The words meant, according to Manson, that blacks were destined to rise up and wipe out the entire white race, with only Manson and his family permitted to survive.

See also: *Charles Manson.*

HENDRICK'S Lake: Pirate treasure trove

Of all the tales about buried or lost pirate treasure, perhaps the most dependable is one that claims $2 million in silver lies somewhere at the bottom of Hendrick's Lake in Texas. It was the loot of Jean Lafitte, the French pirate who ravaged the Gulf of Mexico in the early 1800s. In his last apparent act of piracy before settling down to the staid business of smuggling and slave trading, Lafitte seized the silver aboard the Spanish brig *Santa Rosa.* He then had it transported to what is now Galveston and there loaded onto wagons to be sent to St. Louis for disposal. Lafitte entrusted this task to Gaspar Trammell, an aide who generally handled fencing operations.

The silver convoy made it as far as Hendrick's Lake, a small body of water fed by the Sabine River, when 200 Mexican troops searching for the loot cut the pirates off. Trammell knew he and his men faced certain death but resolved at least to prevent the enemy from getting the silver. Under cover of night he had the heavily ladened wagons shoved into the lake, where they sank quickly in some 50 feet of water with a 15-foot mud bottom. In the ensuing battle Trammell and all but two of his men apparently were killed. These two, a man named Robert Dawson and another who remains unidentified, escaped being slaughtered by the cavalrymen by slipping into the cold water of the lake and breathing through reeds. The troops made a half-hearted effort to retrieve the silver and then pulled out.

Robert Dawson reached St. Louis and related what had happened to the loot, and the other man returned to Lafitte with the same intelligence. Lafitte reportedly made an effort to salvage the treasure but gave it up as a hopeless task. The Mexican government also tried until they became involved in other troubles with Americans who had settled in Texas. Thereafter, nothing was done about the lost silver for perhaps half a century, when treasure hunters again took up the hunt. In 1927 a fisherman snagged his line on something in the lake and pulled a silver ingot to the surface. In all, he salvaged four bars of the Spanish silver. Each year thereafter, fortune seekers have continued to search, but the only thing found since then was an iron rim believed to have been one of Trammell's wagon wheels.

Lafitte's loot is still in the lake, now more valuable than ever since the value of silver has increased to the point that the treasure would be worth, depending on the fluctuation of price, somewhere between $20 million and $50 million.

See also: *Jean Lafitte.*

HENDRICKSON, John, Jr. (1833-1853): Poisoner

A lame-brained youth, John Hendrickson, Jr. is nonetheless given credit as the first American murderer to make use of what was at the time a little-known vegetable poison, aconitine, to get rid of his young wife in 1853.

John Hendrickson had married his 19-year-old fiancee Maria and taken her to live with the other seven members of his family in Bethlehem, N.Y. In almost no time, Maria was ordering not only John but the rest of the family about. Members of the Hendrickson family told John he would have to get rid of her. Whether they meant murder can be disputed, but that is what young John did. The family thereafter tried to cover up the poisoning but authorities ordered an examination of the body and found evidence of the substance. Because it was doubted that a dimwit like John could have carried out such a plot on his own, all the Hendricksons came under suspicion and talk pervaded the community of a family of poisoners. In the end, however, only John was prosecuted, and on March 6, 1853 he was hanged.

HENLEY, Elmer Wayne, Jr.: See Dean Corll.

HENRY Street Gang: Chicago gang

The most prosperous and vicious of the criminal gangs in Chicago during the last two decades of the 19th century was the Henry Street Gang, bossed by Chris Merry, who was finally hanged in the 1890s for kicking his invalid wife to death. The *Chicago Tribune* labeled Merry "one of the worst criminals that ever lived in Chicago."

Merry was ostensibly a peddler but his wagon was little more than a ready container for stolen goods. The Henry Street Gang would simply ride along Maxwell and Halstead streets in broad daylight taking anything they wanted from stores and outside stands. Eventually, the gang moved on to bigger things and developed the "kick in." With a half-dozen thieves in his wagon, Merry would drive to a store selected for a robbery. One man would stay in the wagon holding the reins while two others stood on the sidewalk brandishing revolvers, threatening passersby and looking out for police. Meanwhile, Merry and the other gangsters would kick in the door of the store and cart off the loot, holding the store employees at bay with their guns until ready to take off at breakneck speed in the wagon.

Merry was a huge bull of a man with enormously long arms and huge hands and feet. He was usually sullen and morose but was given to terrible fits of anger. At such times, as the *Tribune* described him, he was "a demon unleashed, and acted more like a mad animal than like a human being." When Merry engaged in physical combat, he used his teeth, fists, feet and any weapon that was handy. He permanently maimed or disfigured many men who had dared to challenge him. The police generally left Merry alone, although they frequently suspected him of specific crimes. When it became necessary to bring Merry in, a squad of at least six or eight men was sent on the difficult mission.

With Merry's trial and ultimate execution, the Henry Street Gang broke up and, oddly, the kick-in technique more or less disappeared for better than a quarter of a century. It was reintroduced with the automobile by John Dillinger and other gangsters.

HERRIN Massacre: Labor dispute

The Herrin Massacre gave Williamson County, Ill. its nickname Bloody Williamson. On June 22, 1922, 47 nonunion scabs brought in to operate a strip mine during a coal strike were besieged by several hundred union men and surrendered under a promise of safe conduct. Instead, they were herded to an area outside Herrin and told to run for their lives under a fusillade of fire. Twenty-one of the scabs were killed and many others wounded: many women and children allegedly took part in the slaughter. A large number of arrests were made and several accused strikers were tried on charges of murder and other crimes. After a five-month trial all were acquitted. It was apparent that because of public opinion in the county no guilty verdicts would ever be returned, and the charges against all the other indicted individuals were dropped.

HERRING, Robert (1870-1930): Outlaw

To this day in the Wichita Mountains of Oklahoma, treasure seekers still hunt for the "traitor's gold." The traitor was Bob Herring, a Texas outlaw with an incorrigible habit of betraying his accomplices. While still a teenager, Herring and two other youngsters once robbed a herd of Mexican horses and drove them to New Mexico for quick sale. Along the way, he kept cutting horses from the pack and trying them out, saying he

wanted to keep the fastest one for himself. His reason became clear when the trio sold the herd. Herring simply grabbed the money, hopped on his fast horse and galloped off into the sunset.

In 1894 Herring hooked up with Joe Baker, an active outlaw on the Texas trail, and two of his sidekicks, known only as Six Toes and Buck. The quartet pulled a number of minor jobs and a major one that netted them $35,000 in gold. Herring put the gold in his saddlebags and rode off once more. Joe Baker was enraged and swore he would catch up with the dishonest crook, a chase that became known in Texas as the "Herring hunt."

Baker ranged as far north as Montana in his search for Herring but couldn't resist such distractions as horse stealing and was shot dead during one such misdeed. Six Toes also met an untimely end when he tried to break out of a jail where he was being held for a minor offense. All of which calmed Herring's nerves enough for him to return to Texas. He settled down in Dallas, sure that the otherwise anonymous Buck was no longer tracking him. Buck wasn't, but a few years later, in 1899, Buck and Herring bumped into each other in Dallas. During a rather heated argument, Herring offered to take Buck to the hidden loot in Oklahoma. Apparently, Buck did not relish the thought of many nights sleeping on the trail with Herring and decided he'd just as soon have his revenge. In the shooting melee that followed, Buck was killed. It is entirely possible that Herring could have successfully pleaded self-defense but for the fact that he also had killed two innocent bystanders in the battle. Herring was sentenced to 35 years, talking for years afterwards about getting out and retrieving his buried loot. However, he never had the chance, dying in prison in 1930, his 30th year behind bars. The secret of the "traitor's gold" died with him.

HICKMAN, Edward (1904-1928): Kidnapper and murderer

In the years before the Lindbergh baby was kidnapped, the abduction of 12-year-old Marion Parker was considered the most heinous. Little Marion was kidnapped near her Los Angeles suburb home on December 15, 1927 by Edward Hickman, a 23-year-old college student who later claimed he did it to cover his tuition costs. Hickman then sent Perry Parker, the girl's businessman father, a ransom note demanding $7,500. The note was signed, "The Fox." Several other notes followed, with "DEATH" elaborately scrawled across the top of them. There was also a letter written by little Marion that read:

> Dear Daddy and Mother:
>   I wish I could come home. I think I'll die if I have to be like this much longer. Won't somebody tell me why all this had to happen to me? Daddy please do what the man tells you or he'll kill me if you don't.
>   Your loving daughter,
>   Marion Parker
>   P.S. Please Daddy, I want to come home tonight.

The first effort by Perry Parker to pay the ransom failed because of the kidnapper's caution, and there followed another letter from the child.

Dear Daddy and Mother:

Daddy please don't bring anyone with you today. I am sorry for what happened last night. We drove right by the house and I cryed all the time last night. If you don't meet us this morning, you'll never see me again.

Love to All,

Marion Parker

Accompanying this note was one from the kidnapper that advised, "If you want aid against me, ask God, not man."

By the time Parker received the notes it was too late to receive aid from any quarter. Hickman had strangled Marion immediately after she wrote the letter and then, inexplicably, cut off her limbs and almost severed her head. The following morning Parker drove to an appointed rendezvous on the outskirts of Los Angeles to exchange the money for his daughter. Hickman drove his car up next to Parker's and, holding a blanket-wrapped figure, said he would take the money and then leave the girl farther along the road. Parker threw the money into the kidnapper's car and after a moment's delay proceeded up the road until he saw the blanket-wrapped bundle. He jumped from his auto and anxiously unwrapped the blanket to find the grisly remains of his daughter.

Hickman was not able to enjoy the fruits of his gruesome crime for long. He drove to Seattle, Wash. where local police, armed with a description of the kidnapper given by Parker and flashed across the country, noticed his free-spending activities and arrested him. Hickman did not deny the crime and was put on a train for the trip back to Los Angeles. Thousands of curious onlookers gathered at each station stop to catch a glimpse of the vicious murderer. Hickman waved to them. Some simply gawked, but others waved back.

Along the way, Hickman made two superficial attempts to take his own life in the train's washroom, which authorities later insisted were merely efforts to lay the ground work for a plea of insanity. That was how Hickman pleaded, but he failed to convince a jury. He was hanged at San Quentin on October 19, 1928.

HICKOK, James Butler "Wild Bill" (1837-1876): Gunfighter and lawman

In some respects James Butler "Wild Bill" Hickok was a genuine Western hero despite the fact that he was a master of the art of back-shooting as he demonstrated in his great gun battle with the "McCanles Gang" in 1861. However, most of his so-called great accomplishments, except for those during his tour as an Army scout, were provably false. Sifting out the truth from Hickok's tall tales could occupy a lifetime. As a scout in 1868, he saved 34 men in an Indian siege in the Colorado Territory by riding through the attackers' ranks to get help. But he did not, as he boasted to the Eastern press,

knock off 50 Confederate soldiers with 50 bullets fired from a new-fangled rifle.

Born in Troy Grove, Ill. in 1837, Hickok was originally called "Duck Bill" because of a long nose and protruding lip. Once he had demonstrated his great ability with a gun, however, the other young blades thought it wiser to call him Wild Bill.

Wild Bill Hickok's reputation as a fearless lawman was built on the numerous ridiculous stories told of him by dime novel writers who overlooked his many less laudable traits.

The Hickok legend began in 1861, when, as was described later in a ridiculous profile in *Harpers Monthly*, he wiped out the so-called McCanles Gang of nine "desperadoes, horsethieves, murderers and regular cutthroats" in "the greatest one-man gunfight in history." In fact, there was no McCanles gang. Dave McCanles was a rancher who was owed money by a freighting company for which Hickok was working. With his 12-year-old son in tow, McCanles, probably unarmed, came to the branch office at Rock Creek Station, Neb. for his money. Two of his ranch hands, most certainly unarmed, waited outside. An argument ensued inside the building between the manager and McCanles; Hickok, hiding behind a calico curtain, shot the rancher dead. The two ranch hands outside the building were then killed by other members of the depot crew; one possibly was shot by the depot manager's wife. McCanles' 12-year-old son survived only by running away.

Hickok was charged with murder, but the boy was not permitted to testify and the charge got lost in the shuffle.

A few years later, Hickok demonstrated he did have great shooting ability by gunning down Dave Tutt in a face-to-face duel at a distance of 75 yards. As his fame in that exploit spread, the Hickok legend grew and was expanded on with every retelling. Tutt, like McCanles, became a savage outlaw, when in fact he and Hickok had been friends since youth and their quarrel was over a girl.

In 1869 Hickok was elected sheriff of Ellis County and promptly killed two men in Hays City, the county seat. One of these killings was a remarkable performance. He had his back turned on a troublemaker named Sam Strawan when the latter started to draw. Hickok whirled, drew and shot first, killing Strawan. That November, in spite of these accomplishments, Hickok was voted out of office, apparently for taking more graft from brothels and gaming saloons than the average sheriff.

Hickok left town but returned in July 1880 and promptly got into a drunken brawl with five cavalry troopers. He shot two, one fatally; the others backed off. Hickok fled town again.

In April 1871 he was hired as city marshal of Abilene, Kan. with orders from the city fathers to clean up the town. Wild Bill did some shooting, but basically, he found it more gratifying to take protection money from gamblers and pimps rather than to interfere with their business. He spent his afternoons at the card table and almost every night in the town's red-light district.

In October 1871 Wild Bill got into a gunfight with a gambler named Phil Coe and mortally wounded him. As Coe fell, Hickok's deputy, Mike Williams, came rushing through the crowd, guns drawn, to help Hickok. Hearing Williams' footsteps, the marshal whirled and fired off two quick shots before he saw who it was. Williams died instantly of two bullets in the head. That was all the citizens of Abilene could take and within a few weeks Wild Bill was fired and forced to leave town. Although his record in Abilene actually was a sorry one, it is still sighted today as one of the greatest reigns by a lawman in the history of the West.

The remaining five years of Hickok's life were pretty much downhill. He joined Buffalo Bill Cody's Wild West Show for a time but found the work both tiresome and degrading. He quit and tried his hand at prospecting and gambling, not having too much success in either. He was arrested several times in the Wyoming Territory, said a newspaper report, "as a vagrant, having no visible means of support."

In June 1876 Hickok turned up in Deadwood, Dakota Territory with Calamity Jane, an amazon whore. Hickok, who had accumulated a spot of cash, ensconced himself at Mann's Saloon Number 10 along the main street. On August 2, 1876 Wild Bill was playing poker and mulling over what to do with his hand—two pairs, aces and eights—when a saddlebum named Jack McCall slipped up behind him and shot him through the brain. Thereafter, the hand of aces and eights became known as a "dead man's hand." McCall claimed he was avenging his brother, whom he said Hickok had killed. Asked why he

hadn't met Hickok face to face, McCall shrugged. "I didn't want to commit suicide," he said.

See also: *Phil Coe, Dead Man's Hand, Jack McCall, McCanles Gang,* Shame of Abilene, *Samuel Strawan.*

HICKOCK, Richard E.: See Clutter Family Murders.

HICKS, Albert E. (?-1860): Gangster and murderer

One of New York's most legendary thugs in the 1850s was Albert Hicks, a free-lance gangster who eschewed working with any of the great gangs of the period because he felt he could fare better as a lone wolf criminal. The record bears out his judgment; he lived a carefree existence and never appeared to worry about money. The police suspected Hicksie, as he was called, of a number of robberies and possibly a dozen murders but, as he often said, "suspecting it and proving it are two different things." His reputation was such that when he was working a certain street along the waterfront, gangs of footpads knew they would be wise to move elsewhere.

"Hicksey" was a free-lance killer whom even the organized waterfront gangs steered clear of.

Remarkably, Hicksie's downfall came about simply because he was not recognized by a Cherry Street shanghaier in whose establishment he had wandered dead drunk. The crimp operator put laudanum in his rum, and when Hicksie awakened the next morning, he was aboard the sloop *E. A. Johnson*, headed for Deep Creek, Va. on an oyster run. After ascertaining that the captain, named Burr, had a money bag along to pay for his cargo, the unwilling sailor resolved to murder the skipper and the other crewmen, two brothers named Smith and Oliver Watts. He did so in particularly bloody fashion, decapitating two of them and dazing the other and then chopping off that victim's fingers and hands as he clutched the rail in a futile attempt to avoid being thrown overboard.

After looting the sloop and letting it drift off, Hicksie returned to Manhattan with quite a substantial booty. Soon, he fled the city for Providence, R.I. with his wife and child. But he left a trail. Having flashed large sums of money, he came under suspicion when the bloodstained *Johnson* was discovered and put under tow five days after the murders. Hicksie was located in Providence and found in possession of the personal belongings of the captain and one of the Watts brothers.

He was tried for piracy and murder on the high seas and sentenced to be hanged on July 13, 1860. About a week before his scheduled execution, he made a full confession to the warden of the Tombs. Hicks was certainly one of the most-celebrated villains of the day and his confession made him all the more infamous. There was a steady stream of visitors to the Tombs to see the noted blackguard shackled to the floor of his cell. For a small fee paid to the jailers, a visitor was permitted to speak a few words with the murderer.

Among those calling on Hicksie was Phineas T. Barnum, the great showman, whose American Museum enjoyed enormous popularity. Barnum told the flattered villain that he wished to obtain a plaster cast of his head and bust for display in the museum. After haggling the entire day, Hicksie agreed to pose for $25 and two boxes of 5¢ cigars. After the cast was made, the magnanimous Barnum returned with a new suit of clothes, which he traded to Hicks for his old suit, with which he wished to adorn a display dummy. Later, Hicks complained to the warden that Barnum had cheated him, that the new suit was shoddy and inferior to his old one.

Hicks was to be hanged on Bedloe's Island. He was ushered from the Tombs to the mainland dock by a fife and drum corps and a procession of carriages full of dignitaries. Thousands lined the procession route and cheered Hicksie, who graciously waved back to them. His only protest was that his suit did not fit, for which he cursed Barnum, but the warden informed him there was no time for alterations.

It was estimated that at least 10,000 persons witnessed the execution on Bedloe's Island. The scaffold was positioned only 30 feet from the water and hundreds of boats, from small craft to large excursion vessels formed a solid line offshore. Hicksie's body was left suspended for half an hour and then cut down and transported back to Manhattan. His corpse was buried in Calvary Cemetery, but within a matter of days it was stolen by ghouls, who sold it to medical students more than willing to pay a premium for the chance to study the brain of such a notorious and bloodthirsty criminal.

HIGGINS, John Calhoun Pinckney "Pink" (1848-1914): Rancher and gunfighter

A fiery Texas rancher of the "I am the law" school, John Calhoun Pinckney "Pink" Higgins was probably as mean and sadistic as Print Olive, perhaps the West's most notorious big-spread owner. Higgins had the good sense to confine his excesses to Texas, which tolerated a lot from the high and mighty. Olive, also a Texan, made the mistake of shifting his operations, including his practice of "man burning," to Nebraska, a state that eventually sided with the homesteaders.

In the art of killing, Higgins was cut from the Olive mold. Typical was his treatment of a cowboy he caught butchering one of his cows just after he had shot it. Higgins gunned him down with a Winchester at 90 yards, disemboweled the dead animal and stuffed the would-be rustler's corpse inside. He then rode to town and informed authorities of a miracle he had just witnessed: a cow giving birth to a man.

From the time he was a young man, Pink exhibited a penchant for direct action. He was twice wounded by Indians and was an officer in the Ku Klux Klan. When he started his own ranch, he was brutal in his treatment of rustlers or those he considered rustlers. Pink also was the key figure in the bloody Horrell-Higgins feud that shook Lampasas County in the 1870s. On the surface, the feud started after the owners of a huge neighboring spread, the Horrells, killed three lawmen, including one of Pink's kin. But the real reason was the disappearance of cattle. When the fighting broke out, Pink took up his Winchester without hesitation. He gunned down Zeke Terrell, a rider for the Horrells, and then gave him the cow-birth treatment. Next, he shot Ike Lantier, another Horrell cowboy, for having the temerity to use the same water hole for watering his stock. Higgins' most callous act in the feud was the murder of Merritt Horrell as he sat in a saloon. Horrell was unarmed when Higgins marched in through the back door and pumped four slugs into him without giving his foe a fighting chance.

Lampasas became a regular battleground for the feudists, with Higgins and his men ambushing the Horrells as they rode in. A major shoot-out occurred in the town on June 14, 1877, when Higgins and three of his men took on seven of the Horrells. The gunfight lasted for several hours. It finally ended when the townsfolk convinced both sides to stop shooting and ride out their separate ways, but not before Higgins' brother-in-law died in the fighting. The following month Higgins led all his riders in an attack on the Horrell ranch. The siege ended after 48 hours, as the Higgins men started running low on ammunition.

The Texas Rangers arrived in the region in July and prevailed upon Higgins and the Horrells to sign a treaty, bringing peace to the county. Despite his excesses, Higgins did not suffer any major loss of popularity, since the Horrells were not exactly models of virtue. Two of the brothers, Mart and Tom Horrell were lynched the year after the truce for some other indiscretions they were suspected of having committed.

Higgins' last known killing, one of his fairest, occurred in 1903, when Pink met up with Bill Standifer, a longtime opponent of his. Both expert riflemen, they exchanged shots at a distance of 60 yards. Standifer hit Higgins' horse, but Pink put a Winchester bullet through his foe's heart. Higgins died of a heart attack in 1914.

See also: *Horrell-Higgins Feud.*

HIGHBINDER Societies: Chinese gangs

Highbinder societies were strong-arm groups that engaged in blackmail, kidnapping and murder on assignment. These gangs never achieved the power or influence of the Chinese tongs, although their hatchet men were often hired by the tongs. Little Pete, the infamous Chinese tong warrior, started his career as a member of the Gin Sin Seer highbinders, but because of his cunning and ability, he soon moved up to the Sum Yop tong.

See also: *Little Pete, Tong Wars.*

HIJACK: Word origin

During Prohibition, when the commandeering of trucks loaded with illegal booze became a common occurrence, the usual greeting given by an armed gunman sticking up was a terse "High, Jack"—meaning raise your hands high, Jack; hence "hijack."

HIJACKING

In its various forms, hijacking goes back to early Colonial times, but it hit a peak during Prohibition, when the stealing of liquor shipments by one gang from another reached bloody and epidemic proportions. Today, hijacking is a highly professional art committed by gangs that limit their criminal activities to this one lucrative field. The theft of entire shipments of television sets, refrigerators, furs, clothing, cigarettes, drugs, oil and liquor is handled with smooth efficiency based on precise advance planning. By surveillance or bribery, a hijack gang will learn a truck's schedule and type of cargo and plan exactly when and how to steal that cargo. One Chicago gang had special "scouts" to tip them off about valuable shipments, and its "work cars" were equipped with high-powered engines, police radios and switches to extinguish rear lights when desired. A special "crash car" was utilized to cut off the arrival of police during the operations.

Usually, hijackers are thought to work on lonely stretches of road in the middle of the night, but some of the lushest operating areas for these thieves are crowded business centers in broad daylight, a typical example being New York's garment district. Two members of a hijacking mob will climb up to the cab of a truck, perhaps when it is halted at a red light or still parked at the curb on a side street, and force the driver and his helper to get out at gunpoint. They will be ordered to walk quietly to a car right behind the truck. Inside the car, the driver and helper are bound and blindfolded. They are then driven off to some quiet spot to cool their heels for three or four hours while one of the hijackers drives the truck away, empties its load into another truck—or a warehouse—and finally disposes of it. Once the job is over, the driver and helper are released.

A particularly daring breed of hijacker is the so-called switch man. This operator drives through the garment district in his own truck looking for another truck that the driver has had to park and leave for some reason. The switch man generally likes to see the driver go into a luncheonette where he will be sure to stay for several minutes. While the driver is gone, the switch man and a helper or two will clean the truck out in a matter of minutes and load the contents in their own truck. The switch man, of course, does not operate like the sophisticated crook of the more traditional hijacking gangs, but he does get the job done.

Another approach has been perfected in recent years by a New York area crook who takes jobs with parcel delivery companies under assumed names. His first day on the job, he is given a truck full of merchandise and sent out on his assigned rounds. It is the last the delivery service sees of the driver or the merchandise. All that is ever recovered is an abandoned delivery truck.

Overall figures on hijacking indicate it is a relatively "low incidence, high profit" crime. Losses, according to insurance officials, probably exceed $100 million a year, but estimates are inexact because of the difficulty of determining whether an actual hijacking or a case of employee theft has occurred. When an area experiences a sudden increase in hijackings, insurance firms and associations may send in undercover agents who use trucks as bait. A single arrest can cause hijacking in an area to cease for a considerable time, as apparently the news spreads rapidly. Similarly, insurance groups sometimes pass the word among truckers that an area is under surveillance, and as a result complaints of hijackings usually decrease. In such cases it is suspected that the drivers themselves are doing the looting and decide to "cool it" for a while.

Probably the greatest hijacking gang in history was Detroit's Purple Gang, which during Prohibition sent convoys of liquor from Canada across the border into the United States and hijacked the trucks of rival shippers to augment their supply. Police believe that remnants of the old Purples are still responsible for much of the hijackings in Michigan and neighboring states.

HILL, Joan Robinson (1930-1969): Alleged murder victim

One of the most notorious, headline-provoking murder cases in modern American history was the alleged "murder by omission" of beautiful and wealthy Joan Robinson Hill by her husband, a leading plastic surgeon in Houston, Tex. After he walked out free as a result of a mistrial, he was assassinated by a paid gunman, which kept the case boiling for years.

Joan Robinson was the daughter of oil multimillionaire Ash Robinson, a man who epitomized Texas-style money and power. Robinson was highly influential in state politics and had the ability to get what he wanted. But few things meant as much to him as Joan. She had been through a couple of marriages when she met Dr. John Hill in 1957. The two were married in a mammoth, Texas-sized wedding paid for by Ash Robinson. Hill's career kept him away from his wife a good deal, but

Joan, an accomplished horsewoman, didn't seem to mind and old Ash was perfectly happy because he still had his daughter around so much of the time.

By 1968, however, the marriage was breaking up. Joan became aware that Hill was seeing other women. They argued often. In March 1969 Joan grew ill, and after considerable delay her husband put her in a small hospital, which didn't have the facilities to handle what developed into a very serious condition. During the course of her treatment, she had a sudden heart failure and died. The following morning a most peculiar event occurred. When doctors arrived to perform an autopsy, they found the body had been sent to a funeral home "by accident." Upon reaching the funeral home, they discovered the body had already been drained of fluids and was partly embalmed, making a really thorough autopsy most difficult. Back at the hospital a brain said to be Joan Hill's showed signs of meningitis, but there was some reason to suspect it was not Joan's brain since the brain stem in the body failed to produce the same symptoms.

From the time of Joan's funeral, old Ash Robinson pressured the district attorney to get a murder charge brought against Hill. In addition, Robinson had a parade of his important friends approach the DA with the same demand. Then, three months after the death of his first wife, John Hill married a woman with whom he had been linked while his marriage to Joan was disintegrating. That galvanized Robinson to further action. He hired detectives to follow Hill and lined up medical testimony, even bringing in the New York City medical examiner to reexamine the body. Two grand juries were convened but both refused to indict Hill. A third grand jury, however, received some additional material. By that time, Hill's second wife, Ann, had divorced him and testified Hill had confessed to her that he had killed Joan. Moreover, she claimed Hill had tried to kill her on more than one occasion. Hill was indicted for murder by neglect, technically "murder by omission," in that he willfully denied his wife adequate medical attention.

Hill's murder trial ended in a mistrial when his second wife blurted out that Hill had told her he had killed Joan. Such a statement could not be permitted in court, since under the law she could only testify about the period before she married Hill.

Before a new trial could be held, Dr. Hill married a third time. Just after returning from his honeymoon in September 1972, he was shot and killed by an assassin wearing a Halloween mask. The murderer was identified as a young Houston hood, Bobby Vandiver, who had brought along a prostitute to keep him company while he waited to ambush Hill in the latter's home. Vandiver confessed he had gotten $5,000 for the job and his story implicated a number of people, among them Ash Robinson. The killer said that Ash had let it be known he would pay for the execution of his ex-son-in-law and that his intermediary in the hit contract was a Houston woman named Lilla Paulus, a former prostitute and madam. The Paulus woman was indicted, but before her trial began, Bobby Vandiver was killed while attempting to escape jail. Despite this development, Paulus was convicted on the testimony of the young prostitute who had accompanied Vandiver. The prostitute,

however, could produce no admissible evidence linking anyone else to the crime. Lilla Paulus was sentenced to life imprisonment but refused to implicate anyone else in the murder.

Following the verdict, Ash Robinson continued to deny to the press any involvement in Hill's murder. He successfully fended off a civil suit against him by the Hill family, and it appeared that with Joan Robinson dead, John Hill dead and Ash Robinson growing old, the Hill-Robinson murders were destined to remain one of the most bizarre mysteries of modern times. In 1981 a four-hour mini-series dramatization of the case was shown on television; it had already been the subject of a best-selling book, *Blood and Money* by Thomas Thompson. Joan Robinson was played by Farrah Fawcett, and the actress, or her publicity agent, took special pains to let it be known that Ash Robinson, the surviving principal in the case and then 84 years old, had voiced his "casting approval" of Farrah as the "ideal choice" to play his deceased daughter. Rumor also had it that Robinson had suggested he portray himself in the film.

HILL, Joe (1879-1915): Labor organizer and alleged murderer

A handsome Swedish immigrant, Joel Hagglund became the troubadour of the Industrial Workers of the World, a radical labor union founded in 1905. Soon the songs of "Joe Hill" were known throughout America. He composed many of the Wobblies' favorite songs and is perhaps most famous for the refrain of "pie in the sky" in "The Preacher and the Slave."

In 1915 two Salt Lake City policemen were shot in a grocery store holdup. Hill was charged with the crime, convicted and sentenced to die. The verdict was most controversial and the IWW and the rest of the American left considered it a frame-up. Just before he was executed by a Utah firing squad, Hill wired Big Bill Haywood, the head of the IWW: "Don't waste any time in mourning. Organize."

HILL, Virginia (1918-1966): Syndicate girl friend and bag woman

Mistakenly dubbed the Queen of the Mob by newspapers in the early 1950s during the Kefauver Committee hearings into organized crime, Virginia Hill was no more than a trusted bedmate to many of the syndicate's top gangsters and a bag woman for the mob, delivering funds to secret Swiss bank accounts or elsewhere as instructed. From the time she arrived in Chicago to be a cooch dancer in the 1934 World's Fair Virginia took a series of husbands and lovers. First came Joe Epstein, the bookmaking king and tax expert for the Capone mob, followed by the brothers Fischetti, Tony Accardo, Murray Humphreys, Frank Nitti, Joe Adonis, Frank Costello, and lastly her true love, Benjamin "Bugsy" Siegel.

Virginia was truly in love with Siegel, yet was conveniently away in Europe when the Bug was shot to death in her living room by an underworld assassin in 1947. After his death she still spoke lovingly of Siegel (he had named the Flamingo Hotel in Las Vegas in honor of her nickname) without being critical of the syndicate, which had ordered his execution because his Las Vegas deals had cost them a fortune.

Virginia Hill, the so-called Queen of the Mob, added a touch of glamour and, at one point, violence to the Kefauver hearings.

She provided the Kefauver hearings with one of its high points as she parried questions about why so many gangsters gave her money. (It was strictly because of her personal charms, she said.) She also added some off-the-stand excitement by tossing a right cross to the jaw of reporter Marjorie Farnsworth of the *New Jork Journal American* and screaming at other reporters: "You goddamn bastards. I hope an atom bomb falls on all of you."

After that dramatic peak in her life, Virginia took a new husband and wandered the pleasure spots of Europe. According to some, she oversaw the Swiss bank accounts of several mobsters. It is generally believed that Virginia supplied much of the funds that allowed Lucky Luciano to live out his exile in Italy in comfort.

But Virginia missed the action of the old mob days and hated growing old. She attempted suicide a number of times, and finally, in March 1966 she swallowed a large number of sleeping pills and lay down in the snow outside Salzburg, Austria to watch the clouds as death closed in on her.

See also: *Bagman, Flamingo Hotel, Kefauver Investigation, Benjamin "Bugsy" Siegel.*

HINCKLEY, John W., Jr. (1955-   ): Accused assailant of Ronald Reagan

On March 30, 1981 Ronald Reagan became the eighth sitting president of the United States to be subjected to an assassination attempt and the fourth—after Andrew Jackson, Harry Truman and Gerald Ford—to survive. Reagan was shot by a 25-year-old drifter, John W. Hinckley of Evergreen, Colo., as he left the Washington Hilton Hotel, where he had addressed a labor audience. The assailant was seized immediately after having fired four to six shots from a .22-caliber revolver, a type known popularly as a Saturday Night Special. The President was hit by a bullet that entered under the left armpit, pierced the chest, bounced off the seventh rib and plowed into the left lower lobe of the lung. Reagan froze for a moment at the door of his limousine and then was brusquely pushed inside the car by a Secret Service agent. Remarkably, the President did not realize he had been shot but thought he had simply been injured when shoved into the car. Only upon arrival at the hospital was it determined that he had been shot.

Also wounded were three others: the President's press secretary, James S. Brady; a Secret Service agent, Timothy J. McCarthy; and a District of Columbia police officer, Thomas K. Delahanty. All three survived, although Brady remained hospitalized for many months after the assassination attempt.

Hinckley turned out to be the son of an oil executive who had grown up in affluence in Dallas and moved with his family to Colorado in 1974. He had attended Texas Tech University on and off through 1980 but never graduated. At times he had traveled across the country, and in 1978 he had enrolled himself in the National Socialist Party of America, generally known as the Nazi Party of America. A spokesman for that organization said the group had not renewed Hinckley's membership the following year because of his "violent nature."

Hinckley had evidently flown from Denver to Los Angeles on March 25 and then boarded a Greyhound bus for Washington the following day, arriving March 29, the day before the attack. Following Hinckley's arrest for the attack on President Reagan, it was discovered that he had been in Nashville, Tenn. on October 9, 1980, when then-President Jimmy Carter was there. Hinckley was arrested at the airport in Nashville when X-ray equipment disclosed he had three handguns and some ammunition in his carry-on bag. The weapons were confiscated and he paid a fine of $62.50. Despite his arrest, federal authorities did not place Hinckley under security surveillance thereafter. Four days after his release, Hinckley turned up in Dallas, where he purchased two .22-caliber handguns in a pawnshop. One of these weapons was alleged to have been used in the attack on Reagan.

A bizarre sidelight to the case was the discovery that Hinckley had been infatuated with movie star Jodie Foster, then a student at Yale University. He had written her several letters, and an unmailed letter dated March 30, 1981, 12:45 p.m.—

one and three-quarter hours before the attack—was found in his Washington hotel room.

It read:

Dear Jody,

There is a definite possibility that I will be killed in my attempt to get Reagan. It is for this very reason that I am writing to you now.

Hinckley went on to say he loved her and that

although we talked on the phone a couple of times, I never had the nerve to simply approach you and introduce myself . . . Jody, I would abandon this idea of getting Reagan in a second if I could only win your heart and live out the rest of my life with you, whether it be in total obscurity or whatever. I will admit to you that the reason I'm going ahead with this attempt now is because I just cannot wait any longer to impress you. I've got to do something now to make you understand in no uncertain terms that I am doing all this for your sake. By sacrificing my freedom and possibly my life, I hope to change your mind about me.

It appeared that Hinckley had been influenced in his alleged actions by the film *Taxi Driver,* in which Jodie Foster plays a child prostitute. At one point in the film, the protagonist, a taxi driver, is planning to assassinate a presidential candidate.

In August 1981 Hinckley was indicted by a federal grand jury in Washington, D.C. on charges of attempting to kill President Reagan as well as the other three men. The FBI reportedly concluded that Hinckley had acted alone. In a verdict that shocked the nation, he was acquitted by a jury on grounds of insanity. He was then committed to a mental institution.

HITE, Wood (1848-1881): James gang outlaw

A cousin of Jesse and Frank James, Wood Hite was shot and killed in 1881 in what has been characterized by some as a "dress rehearsal" for Jesse James' murder some four months later.

Born in Logan County, Ky. in 1848, Hite rode with the James gang from 1870 until 1881. By that year the gang was in disarray. Many of its key members had been killed or imprisoned while others had apparently contacted law enforcement officials about betraying Jesse James in return for leniency. In 1881 Hite had the misfortune to choose the home of a relative of Bob Ford, James' eventual assassin, as a hideout. Also seeking refuge there was Dick Little, another gang member who like the Fords, was seeking to turn traitor. According to certain accounts Hite somehow got wind of the plot or came to suspect that the Fords and Little were planning to turn him in. He accused them of it and died in a blazing gun battle in the kitchen. Other accounts, such as that of contemporary James biographer Frank Triplett, insist the killing was more dastardly: "Creeping one night lightly to his room, Dick and Bob Ford put a pistol to his head, and he was soon weltering in his gore."

Jesse James partisans have since maintained that had Hite

managed to get his information to Jesse, the latter would have trusted the Ford brothers even less than he already did and thus might have saved his own life.

See also: *Jesse James. Dick Little.*

HOBBS, James (1819-1879): Scalp hunter

Together with James Kirker, James Hobbs was a partner in America's most lethal scalp-hunting team.

As a boy Hobbs was taken prisoner by Indians and instead of being killed was adopted by them. Thereafter, he seems to have had a love-hate relationship with the Indians, living with them, marrying them, deserting them, scalping them for bounties and aiding them against other white men. Hobbs had the same sort of attitude towards whites. He might help them against Indians, or if they happened to be dark-skinned and dark-haired, he was just as likely to scalp them since their hair would be indistinguishable from that of an Indian and would bring the same bounty.

Hobbs left his original tribe, the Comanches, in 1839 and became a trapper and hunter of both buffalo and scalps. He formed an alliance with another scalp hunter, James Kirker, and together they took scalps by the hundreds. In one Indian village, aided by Shawnees friendly to Hobbs, they lifted 300 scalps. Eventually they accumulated an extremely valuable load, which they took to Mexico to turn in for a bounty. Kirker stole the down payment they received for the scalps and deserted Hobbs, but in time Hobbs received the balance of the money due from the Mexican authorities, which made him a wealthy man. He also gained added fame when he started killing Navajos, much to the Mexicans' delight. Later though, Hobbs joined the American cause in the war against Mexico and came out of the conflict a captain. He then headed for the gold fields of California, getting as far as Yuma Indian country. He settled with the tribe for a while, and in 1850 he even helped them to dispose of a vicious scalp hunter named John Glanton. Hobbs lived out his life in this contradictory fashion, sometimes scalping Indians and sometimes joining their cause, until his death in Grass Valley, Calif. in 1879.

See also: *John Glanton. James Kirker. Scalp Hunting.*

HOCH, Johann (1855-1906): Mass murderer

In 1905 Chicago police inspector labeled a Chicago packing house employee named Johann Hoch "the greatest mass murderer in the history of the United States." No accurate list of victims could ever be compiled so, the claim cannot be verified statistically, but Hoch's record was certainly formidable in many respects. From about 1890 until 1905 it was estimated that he married bigamously as many as 55 women. The lucky ones he robbed of all their possessions and deserted; the unlucky ones he not only robbed but poisoned as well. While the more sensationalist newspapers placed his murder toll at about 25, diligent police work determined the number to be about 15. He was convicted of only one homicide, however, that of his next-to-last known bride, 46-year-old Marie Walcker, the owner of a small candy shop. His other 14 unfortunate spouses all died rather quickly after exchanging vows with him. All their bodies were found to contain traces of arsenic, but virtually all embalming fluid at the time contained some arsenic, and Hoch always saw to it that each of his dearly departed was very heavily embalmed.

Hoch located his victims by simply advertising in German-language newspapers. The ad that attracted Mrs. Walcker read:

> WIDOWER, quiet and home-loving, with comfortable income and well-furnished house wishes acquaintance of congenial widow without children. Object, matrimony. Write Box B-103.

Mrs. Walcker did write and within days became Mrs. Hoch. She managed to live only a month following the wedding, taken mysteriously ill shortly after she'd transferred all her life savings to her husband. In keeping with Hoch's record of the most marriages in the shortest period of time, he promptly married his widow's sister four days later. He did not kill her, but instead took her money and ran. Unaware of his intentions, Hoch's new wife reported him missing. In the ensuing police hunt, Hoch's picture appeared in newspapers around the country and woman after woman came forward to say he, under the name of Hoch or various other aliases, was her husband as well. Other persons came forward to identify Hoch as the short-term husband of a departed member of their family. Hoch was finally located in New York City as he was popping his favorite question to the landlady of a boarding house.

By this time, authorities were convinced they had a monstrous mass murderer on their hands. The newspapers named him Stockyard Bluebeard, a reference to his sometime work in Chicago packing houses. Arsenic traces were found in a number of Hoch's dead wives, and he was returned to Chicago to be tried for Marie Walcker's death. It was a prudent choice, the one case in which Hoch could not use his pat defense that the traces of arsenic in the dead body came from the embalming fluid. By this time science had made advances in the undertaking field, and the newest embalming agents contained no arsenic. The undertaker who'd embalmed Marie Walcker had switched to one of the new fluids just two weeks before. That fact and the testimony of several of Hoch's wives about how he had absconded with their money—one told of him stealing off in the night, even taking the gold bridgework she had left in a water glass beside her bed—sealed the verdict against the defendant. He was hanged on February 23, 1906 before 100 witnesses at the Cook County Jail.

Forty-nine years later, some very old human bones were found in the wall of a cottage where Hoch had lived. The police had searched the premises at the time hoping to find evidence of additional killings by Hoch but had discovered nothing.

HODGES, Thomas: See Tom Bell.

HOFFA, James R. (1913-1975?): Labor leader and alleged murder victim

Theoretically, the disappearance in 1975 of former Teamster labor boss James R. Hoffa is still under investigation by federal and local law enforcement agencies in Michigan. Actually, the handful of FBI agents still assigned to the Hoffa case do little more than check out an occasional lead. In fact, the FBI considers the case—one of murder—solved.

Hoffa had for decades been a controversial union leader, one with established links to organized crime. Yet despite his underworld connections and a long list of nefarious dealings, he remained immune to prosecution until he became the target of Robert F. Kennedy, first as chief counsel to the Senate Select Committee on Improper Activities in the Labor or Management Field, more popularly known as the McClellan Committee, and later as attorney general.

Subjected to a persistent "Get Hoffa" campaign by Kennedy, the labor leader was finally brought to trial in 1962 for demanding and receiving illegal payments from a firm employing Teamsters. The result was a hung jury, but Hoffa was later convicted of attempting to bribe one of the jurors and sentenced to eight years. In 1964 he was also convicted of misappropriating $1.7 million in Teamster pension funds. Finally entering prison in 1967, Hoffa served a total of 58 months.

In 1975 Hoffa was in the midst of a struggle to retake control of the union from his former protege, Frank Fitzsimmons. His sentence had been commuted in 1971 by President Richard Nixon with the provision that he stay out of union politics for 10 years. He was challenging that legal stipulation and, perhaps more critically, the will of various organized crime fiefdoms within the Teamsters whose leaders did not want a strongman like Hoffa back in power, fearing he would upset or take over their operations.

On July 30, 1975 the 62-year-old Hoffa left his suburban Detroit home and drove to a restaurant, Manchus Red Fox, allegedly to meet a member of the Detroit underworld, a Detroit labor leader and a power in New Jersey Teamster affairs. Hoffa arrived for the meeting at 2 p.m.; at 2:30 p.m. he called his wife to tell her the others had not yet shown up. That was the last ever heard from him. He was seen getting into a car with several other men in the restaurant parking lot about 2:45. According to the most popular police theory, he was garroted and then his body was run through a mob-controlled fat-rendering plant that was later destroyed by fire.

The government's list of suspects, gathered through information received from underworld characters and convicts seeking to reduce their own sentences, has long included reputed Pennsylvania crime kingpin Russell Bufalino, Anthony "Tony Pro" Provenzano and two of his underlings, Gabriel Briguglio and Thomas Andretta. Another suspect, Gabriel's brother Salvatore Briguglio, was reported to be talking to the FBI when he was shot to death in front of a New York City restaurant in March 1978. According to the FBI scenario, Tony Pro set up the so-called peace meeting with Hoffa and instead ordered him murdered. Provenzano denied even being in Detroit on the date of the Hoffa disappearance and produced an alibi that placed him in Hoboken N.J., visiting various union locals.

One of the more curious aspects of the case is the question of why, if he had ordered Hoffa's execution, would Tony Pro link himself to the murder by setting up a meeting with the victim, a fact that Hoffa had made known to a number of individuals. Even more confusing is why Hoffa's killers would pick him up some 45 minutes late, an unlikely display of tardiness for mob hit men. However, the FBI's theory, backed up by such facts as the finding of traces of Hoffa's blood and hair in the back seat of the abduction car, appears more convincing than any other plausible explanation. One Teamster foe of Hoffa under suspicion told investigators, with a perfectly straight face, he had it on good authority that the missing union leader "ran off to Brazil with a black go-go dancer."

Since the former union leader's disappearance, those suspects mentioned most often have either started serving sentences or been convicted of other crimes, some on evidence uncovered during the Hoffa investigation. But convictions in the Hoffa case clearly will depend on the authorities' ability to get some lower-level hoodlum in organized crime to talk or the possibility that one of the conspirators will say the wrong thing to the wrong person. Otherwise, the authorities have no court case. "We all know who did it," one unidentified Teamster vice president has been quoted as saying. "It was Tony with those guys of his from New Jersey. It's common knowledge. But the cops need a corroborating witness, and it doesn't look like they're about to get one, does it?"

HOFFMAN, Harold Giles (1896-1954): Governor and embezzler

One of the most flamboyant politicians in recent American history, Harold G. Hoffman lived a double life, that of an elected public official and an embezzler, whose total depredations remain undetermined. At the high point of his career, in 1936, he was boomed by New Jersey Republicans for president of the United States. At the low point in his life, in 1954, investigators closed in on him and he became an almost certain candidate for prison.

Hoffman was an Army captain in World War I, a small-town banker, mayor of South Amboy, assemblyman, congressman, state commissioner of motor vehicles and, lastly, governor of New Jersey. At the age of 33, he began looting money. By the time he left the governorship in 1937, he had stolen at least $300,000, a considerable sum in Depression dollars. He spent the last 18 years of his life juggling monies in order to cover his embezzlements.

As near as could be determined, Hoffman started stealing from his South Amboy bank, dipping into dormant accounts to keep up his free-spending ways. Whenever an inactive account became active, Hoffman was able to shift money from another quiet account to cover his looting. Some of Hoffman's stolen funds went to promote his political career. Eventually, he reached Congress. Happily, Washington was not too far away from South Amboy, so he could keep a lid on things at the bank. When Hoffman suddenly left Congress to take the post of state commissioner of motor vehicles, which to many seemed a political step-down, some observers theorized that the move was part of Hoffman's plan to eventually run for governor, but the real reason was that he needed access to public funds. Sooner or later, an examiner might discover the shortages at the bank; so it was extremely advantageous for Hoffman to be able to juggle the funds of the motor vehicle department. When money had to be at the bank, it was there; when it had to be in the state coffers, it was there. In the process, more and more stuck to Hoffman's fingers.

When Hoffman won the governorship at the age of 39, he enjoyed wide popularity in his state and grew to be a national political power. However, he became a center of controversy in the sensational Lindbergh kidnapping case. His interference and attempts to reopen the investigation after Bruno Richard Hauptmann was convicted brought him widespread criticism. When he granted Hauptmann a few months' reprieve, he provoked a storm of criticism. He would never again be elected to any public office. Upon completing his term, Hoffman was named director of the unemployment compensation commission, an agency with a budget of $600 million, and he was able to continue his money-juggling operations.

While still governor, Hoffman had become president of the Circus Saints and Sinners, a group devoted to the twin duties of providing help to old circus folk and providing themselves with a good time. Hoffman became known as a boisterous buffoon, but inside he must have been a frightened, lonely man trying to keep his crimes hidden.

In 1954 newly elected Gov. Robert B. Meyner suspended Hoffman pending investigation of alleged financial irregularities in his department. Exorbitant rentals were apparently being paid for some department offices, and the state's attorney general subsequently found that favored groups stood to make nearly $2 million from a modest investment of $86,854. Other irregularities appeared in the purchase of supplies.

Hoffman put up a joyous front. The day following his suspension he appeared before the Circus Saints and Sinners. Harry Hershfield, the famous wit, cracked, "I knew you'd get into trouble in Jersey, fooling with a Meyner." Hoffman answered, "I can't even laugh." And he broke into raucous laughter.

The next two months, however, were lonely ones for Hoffman as he waited for the ax to fall. One morning in June he got up in the two-room Manhattan hotel suite provided by the Saints and keeled over with a fatal heart attack.

Later, more and more facts came out. The state became concerned when they discovered Hoffman had deposited $300,000 of public money in his own bank in a non interest-bearing account. Officials then learned that not only was the interest missing but so was the principal.

Hoffman had written a confession to one of his daughters to be opened only upon his death. It said, ". . . until rather recently I have always lived in hope that I would somehow be able to make good, to get everything straight."

See also: *Lindbergh Kidnapping, Ellis Parker.*

HOLDBERG Technicality: Legal technicality

Much has been made of criminal cases being thrown out on technicalities, sometimes with sound legal justification but sometimes for what seem the most absurd of reasons. Probably the leading example of the latter was a criminal case in Illinois in 1919 in which a man named Goldberg was indicted on 50 criminal counts and convicted on all of them. However, the conviction was reversed on appeal and the case remanded because on one of the 50 court documents, the defendant's name was spelled Holdberg instead of Goldberg, a simple typographical error. To this day a discussion of the Holdberg Technicality is part of the regular course work at a number of law schools.

HOLE, The: Prison punishment cell

Known by various names in different penal institutions, the hole is reserved for "incorrigible inmates." Few persons have ever understood the horrors the hole represented until the courts in recent years started taking up the question of whether such cells were unconstitutional. They have steadily rejected the claims of prison administrators that such cells are a necessary part of institutional discipline.

The strip cell at California's Soledad Prison was one that the courts have closed down. Each such cell measured eight feet four inches by six feet, with side and rear walls and floor of solid concrete. One prisoner, cited in a court case, spent his first eight days totally naked, sleeping on the floor with only a stiff canvas mat that "could not be folded to cover the inmate." The only other furnishing was a toilet which was flushed by a guard outside the cell, once in the morning and once at night. The cell was without light or heat and was never cleaned, so that the floors and walls were "covered with the bodily wastes of previous inhabitants."

A federal court found solitary confinement cells at New York's Dannemora Prison little different, although the cells did have sinks ("encrusted with slime, dirt, and human excremental residue"). The court also found that the prisoners were kept entirely nude for days while the windows just across from the cell were left wide open during the night—even in subfreezing temperatures.

A University of Connecticut professor of law, Leonard Orland, has a program in which his students are sent to prison for a weekend as part of their class work. He himself once spent 24 hours in the hole in a Connecticut institution. His cell was a windowless four by eight foot steel box, with a single light bulb and a small peephole controlled from outside. He was not alone in the cell—there were three cockroaches in the sink. In his book *Prisons: Houses of Darkness,* Orland described his experience as being confined in a "very small stalled elevator." And he added:

> Its effect on me was devastating: I was terrified; I hallucinated; I was cold (I was nude and the temperature was in the low 60's). When the time came for my disciplinary hearing, I was prepared to say or do anything not to return to the hole. And yet I could not have experienced a tenth of the desperation of those men for whom the situation is a genuine one.

HOLE In The Wall: Western outlaw stronghold

Probably the best known of all the Western badman hideouts, Hole in the Wall was located in Wyoming some 50 miles south of Buffalo and about a day's ride from Casper. East of the Hole lay the lush grazing lands of the Powder River country.

At first strictly a refuge for outlaws, particularly horse thieves and renegade Indians, Hole in the Wall soon became a haven for unemployed cowboys, especially after the drought of 1883. For a while, it appeared that Hole in the Wall was getting bigger and badder, but in reality, it was being civilized. Some of the cowboys did pilfer a cow or two, but they were homesteading the land and slowly pushing the badmen out. Still, people spoke of something called the Hole in the Wall Gang, a band that never existed. There were many gangs that periodically headquartered at Hole in the Wall, but the concept of a specific "gang" was an oversimplification. Certainly, there was little loyalty among the resident thieves, as full-time and part-time bandits shifted allegiance from one outfit to another whenever a new leader looked like he was about to produce something worthwhile. In time, Butch Cassidy lost his taste for Hole in the Wall and hid out thereafter in Brown's Hole or Robber's Roost. When the Hole in the Wall Gang is mentioned, what is meant is the Wild Bunch, of which Cassidy was the acknowledged leader. Other Hole-in-the-Wallers included the Black Jack Ketchum gang and the Laughing Sam Carey gang.

Laughing Sam might well be considered the founder of the outlaw community at Hole in the Wall, turning up there some time before 1880. Carey, a mean-streaked bank robber and train robber who killed a number of men, fled to the Hole whenever a posse was closing in on him. Somehow he never had trouble recruiting renegades and cowboys to follow him on forays, even though he was not really a very successful bandit. Once when he and his gang attempted to hold up the Spearfish Bank in South Dakota, Laughing Sam was the only one to get away alive, and he was badly shot up. He struggled back to Hole in the Wall, where a cowboy took three slugs out of him. Ten days later, he was off again with a full complement of men to hold up a train. As Butch Cassidy is supposed to have said to the Sundance Kid, "Kid, there's a lot of dummies at Hole in the Wall."

See also: *Brown's Hole, Robber's Roost, Wild Bunch.*

HOLE-IN-THE-WALL Saloon: 19th century New York dive

One of the toughest saloons in New York City between the 1850s and the 1870s was the legendary Hole-In-The-Wall, located at Dover and Water streets in the heart of the crime-ridden Fourth Ward. A stranger happening into the Hole-In-The-Wall, operated by One-Armed Charley Monell, could be mugged while standing at the bar. If he survived, he was tossed out into the street; if he was wise, he dusted himself off and left without further protest. When such an assault proved fatal, the mugger was expected to bring a cart to the side door after dark and carry the corpse away.

The dive was famous for its two women bouncers, Gallus Mag and Kate Flannery. Gallus Mag would have been enough on her own. A six-foot Englishwoman of undetermined age, she earned her nickname because she wore galluses, or suspenders, to hold her skirt up. She always carried a pistol in her belt and a bludgeon strapped to her wrist. While she was expert with either weapon, Gallus Mag's routine method for maintaining order in the dive was to beat a troublesome customer to the floor, grab his ear with her teeth and drag him to the door. If the man still resisted, Gallus Mag would bite his ear off. She kept these trophies in a jar of alcohol behind the bar.

It was at the Hole-In-The-Wall that one of the underworld's most infamous duels was fought in 1855 by Slobbery Jim and Patsy the Barber, two vicious members of the violent Daybreak Boys. The pair had mugged a portly immigrant by the seawall at the Battery, knocking him unconscious and relieving him of all his wealth, 12 cents. Then Slobbery Jim lifted the unconscious victim over the wall and deposited him in the harbor, where he drowned. The two killers adjourned to the Hole-In-The-Wall to divide their loot, such as it was. Since he had done the heavy labor of lifting the victim over the wall, Jim insisted he should get eight cents. Certainly, he would not settle for less than seven cents. Patsy the Barber was furious, pointing out that he had done the original clubbing of the victim and was thus entitled to an equal share.

The dispute turned violent when Slobbery Jim bit down and chewed on Patsy the Barber's nose. Patsy promptly drew a knife and stuck it in Jim's ribs. The blow had no effect on Jim, however, and the pair wrestled on the floor. The fight went on, incredibly, for some 30 minutes without interference from Monell or Gallus Mag or anyone else, since this, after all, was no drunken brawl but a professional dispute. The battle finally ended in Slobbery Jim's favor when he got hold of the knife and slashed his opponent's throat. As the blood gushed from the wound, Jim proceeded to kick the Barber to death. It was the last seen of Slobbery Jim, who fled the city and was not heard of again until the Civil War, when some New York soldiers insisted they'd seen him in the uniform of a Confederate Army captain.

The Hole-In-The-Wall was too deadly a place even for the Fourth Ward and it was finally shut down by the police in 1871 after the occurrence of seven murders in two months; no one knew how many other unreported slayings had happened there.

See also: *Gallus Mag*.

HOLLIDAY, John Henry "Doc" (1852-1887): Gunfighter and dentist

Suffering from tuberculosis, John Henry "Doc" Holliday, an Atlanta, Ga. dentist, came west in 1873 seeking to extend his life span after being given no more than a year or two to live. He practiced dentistry now and then when he could be coaxed

out of a saloon but spent most of his time gambling, usually as a house gambler, and gunning men down. Of the so-called Dodge City Gang, Doc Holliday was one of the few genuine killers, unlike Wyatt Earp, who exaggerated his kill record, and Bat Masterson, who only killed once. Doc killed often and cruelly. During the infamous gunfight at the O.K. Corral, in which he stood with the Earps, Holliday pulled a shotgun out from under his long coat and blasted Tom McLowery, who stood by his horse unarmed except for a rifle in his saddle scabbard.

Friends of the Earps never approved of their association with Holliday, whom they considered a pathological killer, but the Earps appreciated a man who was always there when they needed him. Holliday first met Wyatt Earp during the latter's days as a lawman in Dodge City, and Earp credited Doc with saving his life once when he was surrounded by a bunch of gunslinging Texas cowboys. From then on, the friendship was never to be broken. In 1879 Holliday left Dodge at about the same time as Earp departed. He ran a saloon for a time in Las Vegas, New Mexico Territory by the rule of the gun. When a love-struck former Army scout named Mike Gordon tried to lure one of the saloon's prostitutes away to a better life, Holliday shot him dead.

When Wyatt Earp located in Tombstone, Doc Holliday drifted in and took a job as a gambler-bouncer at the Oriental Saloon, a lavish gambling joint in which Earp had an interest. Holliday rode out of town a lot—coincidentally while he was out riding, stagecoaches seemed to get robbed quite frequently. In March 1881 the Kinnear and Co. stage was held up near Conception. Holliday was suspected of having pulled the job, and the Earps were suspected of having planned it. The charge may have been false and spread by the Earp-hating Clanton gang, but it was indicative of Holliday's low esteem among the public.

In Griffin, Tex., Holliday got into an argument over cards with a man named Edward Bailey and killed him with a bowie knife. Doc was arrested by the town marshal. The town of Griffin having no jail available, he was locked up in a hotel room. By early evening the locals were getting liquored up and talking about a lynching. Big Nose Kate Elder, a prostitute and longtime girl friend of Holliday, heard the rumblings and distracted the forming mob by setting fire to a shack. While the crowd was busy with the fire, Kate helped her lover escape.

Kate's devotion to Holliday rose and fell depending on how much he beat her. At the time of the Kinnear stagecoach robbery, Doc had been particularly unkind to her so she signed a statement that he had pulled the job and committed the murders involved. After the Earps got her away from their enemy, Sheriff John Behan, and put her in a cell in Tombstone to sober up, she retracted her statement and said her fancy man was innocent. Later, Holliday reputedly married her, a fortuitous arrangement since a wife could not testify against her husband.

After the O.K. Corral battle, Virgil Earp was injured and Morgan Earp killed by Clanton men. Holliday rode with Wyatt Earp to gun down the suspected assassins. In the Hollywood version of what followed, one Clanton supporter is depicted sneaking up on Earp in the train yard at Tucson to shoot him in the back. In truth, Earp, Holliday and three other horsemen ran the Clanton supporter down in the Southern Pacific yards and pumped 30 bullets into him. Two days later, Holliday helped corner another Clanton follower, Florentino Cruz, and executed him with 10 or 12 shots.

Over the next few years Holliday drifted around the West gambling and gunfighting, but it was apparent he was losing his big battle in life. He entered a sanatorium at Glenwood Springs, Colo. in the spring of 1887 and lasted another six months. Just before he died, on November 8, 1887, he downed a large glass of whiskey, looked at his bootless feet and said, "I'll be damned!" He had fully expected—and perhaps hoped—to die with his boots on. He was 35.

See also: *Dodge City Peace Commission, Wyatt Earp, O.K. Corral, Oriental Saloon and Gambling House.*

HOLMES, Alexander William (1812-?): Sailor accused of murder

Alexander Holmes was a robust, handsome Finnish seaman who became involved in one of the greatest legal decisions in American history.

Holmes's ship, *William Brown,* hit an iceberg in April 1841 on its voyage from Liverpool to Philadelphia. In the rush for the two lifeboats, far fewer than could accommodate all those on board, the captain and eight seamen took refuge in one, a jolly boat, while First Mate Francis Rhodes, Holmes and seven other sailors crammed 32 passengers and themselves into the other, a longboat designed to carry 20 persons. The survivors then watched the *William Brown* go under, as they listened to the pitiful cries from the four men, eight women and 19 children stranded on board.

The two boats drifted together for a while until Capt. George L. Harris cut the jolly loose, saying he was going to try to make Newfoundland. He ignored pleas from Rhodes to take a few more from the longboat aboard the jolly. Instead he told Rhodes he was in charge and to do whatever he had to do but "only as a last resort."

At dusk it started to rain and the seas began to rise. Finally, giant waves battered the longboat. All aboard bailed water, which rose steadily to within four or five inches of the gunwales. It was soon evident that another giant wave would capsize the boat. Rhodes, who seemed about to collapse, said to Holmes, "We must go to work." Holmes looked away. Another wave slapped at the boat. "Men, fall to work or we will all perish," Rhodes screamed hysterically. This time Holmes motioned to another seaman and together they seized a passenger, Owen Riley, and heaved him overboard. Then a second man went. A third asked to be allowed to pray first and then let himself be thrown over the side. Several women clawed their way to the far end of the boat to get further away from Holmes. Even though the craft had been lightened by some 500 pounds, it still sat perilously low in the water. A man named Frank Askins was heaved overboard, and immediately, his two screaming sisters followed him. Later, there would be

a dispute about whether Holmes had ordered them cast overboard or whether they had hysterically jumped after their brother. In the next 10 minutes, eight more men were jettisoned.

By morning the longboat was riding easier, now weighing a full ton less. Then crewmen found two more male passengers hiding under women's skirts. Holmes ordered them forward to bail. After a while, the sea grew rough again and the danger of sinking returned. Without a word, Holmes and three sailors seized the two men and cast them over the side. "How cruel, how cruel!" a voice moaned. It was Rhodes. He was no longer capable of clear thought after nine hours of killing. It was obvious that Seaman Holmes was in charge of the craft. Some sailors wanted to throw some of the women over, but Rhodes stopped them, saying, "No, we will go before the women."

A little after 9 o'clock, the sun appeared in brightening skies, and Holmes said to the passengers, who still eyed him warily: "Be of good cheer. There will be no more killing. We will all live or perish together." An hour later, they were picked up by a passing schooner bound for Le Havre. After reaching Le Havre, the survivors were put on another vessel and sent to New York. When they got there, they discovered that Capt. Harris and the jolly boat had made it safely and the news of their survival and the ordeal had preceded them. Public debate was raging over whether or not the frightful events aboard the longboat had been justified.

Newspapers throughout the country demanded murder trials be held. The *New York Courier* wrote, "Every soul aboard that boat had the same right to such protection as she afforded as the mate and the seamen and until a fair and equal chance was given by lot for a decision as to who should be sacrificed, no man could throw his fellow man overboard without committing murder." And the *Philadelphia Public Ledger* declared, "No human being is authorized to kill another in self-preservation unless against an attempt of that other to kill."

U.S. Attorney William Meredith brought murder indictments against Rhodes and Holmes in Philadelphia. Capt. Harris was allowed to leave and immediately shipped out. Rhodes disappeared and was believed to have left with Capt. Harris. Only Holmes surrendered to face trial. The prosecution, aided by the testimony of three women, hammered away at the point that no seaman had died and no lots had been drawn. However, most of the survivors testified in Holmes' behalf. The defense was headed by David Paul Brown, the Clarence Darrow of his day, who was hired to represent Holmes by the Female Seamen's Friend Society. Brown hit hard at the prosecution charges:

Whoever heard of casting lots at midnight in a sinking boat, in the midst of darkness, of rain, of terror, and of confusion. This case, in order to embrace all its horrible relations, ought to be decided in a longboat, hundreds of leagues from shore, loaded to the very gunwales with 41 half-naked victims, with provision only sufficient to prolong the agonies of famine and of thirst, with all the elements combined against her, leaking from below, filling also from above, surrounded by ice, unmanageable from her condition and subject to destruction from the least change of wind and the waves—most variable and most terrible of all elements. Decided at such a tribunal, nature would at once pronounce a verdict not only of acquittal but of commendation.

Following an eight-day trial, the case went to the jury. After 16 hours the jury advised the court it couldn't agree and was sent back for more deliberations. Ten hours later, the jury returned a verdict of guilty, with a recommendation of mercy. By this time, public opinion had shifted entirely in Holmes' favor. Before he was sentenced, even the *Philadelphia Public Ledger*—the very newspaper that had once said, "An act of greater atrocity could scarcely be conceived of"—now warned that an effort would "be made to have him pardoned by the President if anything more than a nominal sentence be passed upon him."

Holmes got six months and was fined $20, and even this light sentence brought many protests. He served his time and then disappeared back to sea. His six-month punishment established the precedent that a sailor "is bound to set a greater value on the life of others than on his own."

HOLMES, H. H. (1858-1896): Mass murderer

His real name was Herman Webster Mudgett, but he became infamous as H. H. Holmes—probably the greatest mass killer in American history. At various times, he admitted killing anywhere from 20 to 27 persons, being a master of inconsistency, and undoubtedly he murdered many more. Some wild-eyed biographers credit him with killing 200 women in his "murder castle" in Chicago during the 1890s, while a more reasonable count would fall somewhere between 40 and 100.

If there was any question about his arithmetic, there was none about his dedication. Holmes killed with a bizarre fervor to make the last possible cent out of his victims, mostly marriage-starved women whom he murdered for their money. He kept a keen eye out for newspaper ads requesting skeletons, and when he found such an ad, he would scrape his latest victim's bones clean and sell the skeleton to an interested medical student or institution.

As a medical school student, Herman Mudgett had always shown the greatest interest in bodies, more so in those of women than those of men. However, he lost interest in his studies of female anatomy and in time, despite a marriage before he was 20 and a second bigamous one before he was 30, became adept at such additional careers as horse thieving, forging and swindling. He finally went into murder in a big way. With the proceeds from his various crimes, he built a massive "hotel" in 1892 at Sixty-third and Wallace, in anticipation of the Columbian Exposition the following year.

The first floor consisted of stores and the second and third floors of about 100 rooms. Holmes used several as his office and his living quarters. The remaining rooms were for guests, many of whom were never seen alive again. A newspaper subsequently described one of the rooms as an "asphyxiation chamber" with "no light—with gas connections." The room had no windows; the door was equipped with stout bolts; and the walls were padded with asbestos. All Holmes had to do was get a victim in the room and turn on the gas. Most of the rooms featured these gas connections and certain ones had false-bottom floors, which covered small airless chambers. Some of the rooms were lined with iron plates and some had blow-torchlike appliances. Various rooms had chutes that carried human cargo to the basement. Here, Holmes maintained a crematory, complete with vats of corrosive acid and quicklime pits. The pits later yielded up bone and skull fragments of many women he had held prisoner and killed. All the "prison" rooms had an alarm that buzzed in Holmes' quarters if a victim attempted to break out. The evidence indicated that he kept many of the women prisoners for months before he decided to dispose of them.

Holmes obtained most of his victims through ads offering good jobs in a big city or through offers of marriage. If the offer was for a job, he would describe several in detail, and a young woman on her first visit would select the one she wanted. Holmes then sent her home to pack her things and withdraw all her money from the bank since she would need the money to get set up. He would require that the woman not reveal his name to anyone and he would not tell her where the job was until she returned with her money, claiming he had business competitors who were trying to steal his clients. When the woman returned and Holmes was satisfied she had revealed nothing about him, he would take her prisoner. If he was not satisfied, he would say the job had been canceled and send her away. Those whom he offered to marry got the same sort of line. If they came back with less than all their worldly goods, Holmes would use various types of torture apparatuses to make them reveal the whereabouts of their remaining valuables. He then would imprison the women while he went to get their property.

Amazingly, Holmes was able to keep his wholesale murder operation secret for four years. His trouble started when he got involved in an insurance swindle with a shady character named Benjamin F. Pitzel. To pull it off, they both traveled around the country, and in the process Holmes was arrested in St. Louis. He revealed part of the insurance scam to a cell mate, a notorious bank robber named Marion Hedgepeth. Holmes offered Hedgepeth money to put him in touch with a good lawyer. Hedgepeth obliged and Holmes got out, promptly forgetting to pay Hedgepeth. He went to Philadelphia and met up with Pitzel. The two had a falling out and Holmes killed his partner in crime. About this time, Hedgepeth decided his former cell mate had stiffed him and told the authorities what he knew. Holmes was captured and the Pitzel murder discovered. When Chicago police searched his "hotel," the results were awesome.

Before he was hanged in Philadelphia on May 7, 1896, for the Pitzel murder, since that city refused to surrender him to Chicago for his more gruesome deeds, Holmes made a number of confessions concerning the women he had killed. He accepted an offer of $5,000 from a Chicago newspaper for his story and then perversely concocted a death list that included several women who were still alive and omitted others who had been identified among his victims.

See also: *Marion Hedgepeth*.

HONEYMOON Gang: 19th century New York gang

One of the most brutal New York gangs in the mid-1800s was the Honeymoon Gang, whose members were considered so beyond the pale that they were denied protection by the politicians who took care of most other organized gangsters because of their value as electoral enforcers.

By 1853 the Honeymooners had so terrorized the East Side's 18th Ward that it became literally unsafe to walk there. Every evening the gang would place their men at each corner of Madison Avenue and 29th Street and attack every well-dressed citizen who came along. At midnight the Honeymooners' "basher patrol" would adjourn to a drinking establishment to spend a portion of the night's ill-gotten gains.

The Honeymooners were not molested by police until George W. Walling was appointed captain of the district in late 1853. Organizing the city's first Strong Arm Squad, he picked out his six burliest men, put them in plain clothes and sent them into the Honeymooners' turf armed with locust clubs. The beefy officers simply walked right up to the gangsters and battered them senseless before they could bring their own bludgeons and brass knuckles into play. A few nights of this treatment convinced the Honeymooners to evacuate their ambush posts. But this did not satisfy Walling, who then provided every policeman on his roster with the identifications of all the Honeymooners. Whenever one was sighted, he was attacked and beaten mercilessly. Within two weeks the Honeymoon Gang vanished, its members scattering to other wards where police tactics were not so rough.

See also: *Strong Arm Squad*

HOODLUM

Hoodlum is as American as apple pie. The word refers to a member of any gang of thugs. The explanations for its origin are varied and many, but there is no doubt that the term was first applied to the San Francisco underworld in the late 1860s. One theory holds that the term was initially used to describe several vicious brothers whose name was Hoodler and that the name was corrupted into "hoodlum" with the passage of time. Another explanation is that it arose from the street thugs' practice of turning up the collar and lapels of their jackets to act, as much as possible, as a hood while they stalked and molested their victims.

The *Los Angeles Express* of August 25, 1877, seemed to offer the most plausible theory:

> A gang of bad boys from fourteen to nineteen years of age were associated for the purpose of stealing. These boys had a rendezvous, and when danger threatened them their words of warning were 'Huddle 'em! Huddle 'em!' An article headed 'Huddle 'Em' describing the gang and their plans of operation, was published in the *San Frncisco Times*. The name applied to them was soon contracted to hoodlum.

HOODOO War: See Mason County War.

HOOK Gang: 19th century New York waterfront gang

The Hook Gang was composed of thugs who worked the East River area around the Corlears' Hook section of New York from the late 1860s to the late 1870s.

Known as the daffiest of all river pirates, the Hookers were captained by Terry Le Strange, James Coffee, Tommy Shay and Suds Merrick. Neither the gang nor its individual members thought any job was too big for them. Coffee and Shay once rowed up to the boat of an eight-man rowing club and, with guns leveled, ordered them to head for the Brooklyn shore. When they got within 50 yards of shore, they forced the rowers to jump and swim for it and headed back to Manhattan with their prize boat. Long before the rowers got back to sound the alarm, the pair had transported the outsized craft to the Hudson docks and sold it to the skipper of a canal boat.

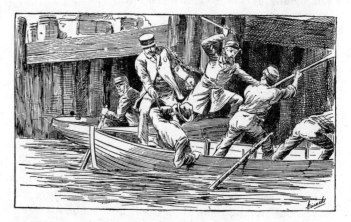

The Hook Gang, 19th century river pirates, fought pitched battles with police for over a decade before finally being driven from the East River.

Another gang member, the redoubtable Slipsey Ward, finally overstepped himself when he mounted the deck of a schooner at Pike Street and attempted single-handedly to overpower the crew of six. He had downed three before he was stopped; he ended up with a long sentence at Auburn Prison for this crime. On more than one occasion, the Hookers would pull a number of wagons up to a likely boat in dock and, after simply cordoning off the street, loot it at their leisure. Once, an officer a few blocks away saw their barricades and, thinking there was some authorized work going on, helpfully diverted traffic onto a side street.

In a manner of speaking, the Hookers had no one to blame but themselves for their eventual demise. It all started when one of their number, Nigger Wallace, tried to rob three men in a rowboat. They turned out to be three detectives taking the sun on their day off and Wallace ended up dunked and towed off to jail. This started the police thinking that if they had some decoy craft on the river, they could catch the pirates in their act. Thus, in 1876 the Steamboat Squad was organized. By the end of the decade, the police had cleared the Corlears' Hook area. Many of the Hookers were imprisoned, others scattered and the rest shifted their activities to safer, onshore thefts and burglaries.

See also: *Suds Merrick, Steamboat Squad.*

HOOVER, Herbert: Al Capone's nemesis

"That bastard," Al Capone was to repeat many times after his conviction on income tax charges. "That bastard got me." He was referring to President Herbert Hoover; underworld opinion held that Capone had been railroaded because of the personal vindictiveness of a bitter president of the United States. According to mob legend, Hoover had come to hate Capone for either of two reasons or both. One was that shortly after his victory over Al Smith in the 1928 election, Hoover had visited the J. C. Penney estate on Belle Isle in Florida, not far from the Capone retreat on Palm Island. As the story went, there was so much shouting, females screaming and shooting during the night from the Capone compound that Hoover could not fall asleep, and he vowed to crush the mobster once he took office. According to the second story, Hoover watched in chagrin as a crowd of newsmen in a Miami hotel lobby deserted the President-elect for what they regarded as a more important interviewee, Capone.

In fact, both stories are apocryphal, but it is true that Hoover had determined to bring down Capone, whom he regarded as a blot on the national honor. The method used was suggested to Hoover by Colonel Frank Knox, publisher of the *Chicago Daily News,* who came to him in despair over the unwillingness or inability of local and state authorities to jail Capone. He suggested to Hoover that the best way to catch the mobster was to charge him with two federal offenses: bootlegging and income tax evasion.

Thereafter, Hoover hounded the Treasury Department to eliminate Capone. Andrew Mellon, who was secretary of the treasury at the time, later recalled the activities of Hoover's so-called Medicine Cabinet, a small group of high officials the President invited to the White House each morning to toss around a medicine ball. "Every morning when the exercising started, Mr. Hoover would bring up the subject," Mellon said. "He'd ask me, 'Have you got that fellow Al Capone yet?' And at the end of the session, he'd tell me, 'Remember now, I want that Capone in jail.' "

In another era, or in another economic climate, Herbert Hoover might well have won the reelection just for successfully putting Capone behind bars. But not in the early 1930s. The public clearly agreed with a minor Capone follower quoted by the press as saying, "President Hoover should be worrying more about putting people to work than sending a simple bootlegger to prison."

HOOVER, J. Edgar (1895-1972): FBI director

For better or worse, the history of the Federal Bureau of Investigation can be told in the life of its longtime director, J. Edgar Hoover. Hoover more than typified the agency, he was in a very real sense *the* FBI. The agency's successes were attributable to him, just as its excesses and abuses often resulted from his personal failings. Despite scandals that were revealed after Hoover's death, such as the agency's deliberate attempts to destroy individuals not accused of crimes by leaking damaging information—sometimes true, often false—about them, the FBI is recognized as one of the most brilliant and efficient investigative forces in any country.

It was not always that way, especially when Hoover joined the U.S. Department of Justice in 1917 as a young attorney. The agency, then known as the Bureau of Investigation, was a disorganized body of about 200 poorly supervised agents, some political hacks, others outright crooks. The agency was virtually worthless in any battle against crime and proved totally incapable of preventing sabotage during World War I. The great sabotage and espionage ring organized by German Ambassador Johann von Bernstorff had almost a free hand to operate in this country. Defense plants were wrecked and wheat fields in the West set afire. The great "Black Tom" explosion in New York Harbor destroyed the nation's biggest arsenal, producing a tremendous roar heard more than 100 miles away.

Hoover rose rapidly in the ranks and became special assistant to Attorney General A. Mitchell Palmer. Despite his later denials, Hoover played a vital role in the Palmer Raids inspired by the post war Red Scare. He planned and executed mass raids against aliens, built up a card file on 450,000 radicals and organized his first informer network, a technique Hoover developed to the level of a science, far better than any other American law official.

By 1924 the Bureau of Investigation was mired in scandal, much like the late Harding Administration. Hoover was named to head the agency and cleanse it. To his credit, he did so with ruthless efficiency, forcing out scores of incompetents and cheats and establishing professional standards for agents, such as the requirement that new recruits have training as either lawyers or accountants. During the 1930s Hoover toughened the FBI into a highly mobile crime-busting organization. He laid heavy emphasis on scientific detection methods and established the FBI Laboratory. The FBI National Academy was formed to train local police officers in the newest law enforcement techniques.

In 1933 Hoover launched a highly publicized war on the so-called public enemies—Dillinger, the Barkers, Alvin Karpis, Pretty Boy Floyd, Baby Face Nelson, Machine Gun Kelly and others of their ilk, all 20th century versions of the desperadoes of the Old West. They were relatively easy targets, certainly compared to the Mafia and the emerging national crime syndicate formed by the great ex-bootlegging gangs of the Prohibition era. Since he was a Republican holdover in a Democratic administration, Hoover needed some sort of spectacular display. Speaking of the campaign years later, a high ex-FBI official, William C. Sullivan, said, "The whole of the FBI's main thrust was not investigation but public relations and propaganda to glorify its director."

Hoover needed all the public relations he could get in the

1930s. When John Dillinger was killed, a conservative Virginia newspaper editor assailed the FBI's work on the case. "Any brave man," he editorialized, "would have walked down the aisle and arrested Dillinger . . . why were there so many cowards afraid of this one man? The answer is that the federal agents are mostly cowards."

Later it was revealed that the Secret Service was secretly investigating the conduct of FBI agents in the Dillinger case and the case of another gang member, Eddie Green, who had been described as shot while attempting an armed escape from FBI custody. Green was found to be unarmed, however. Clearly, the Secret Service was trying to show that the G-Men were trigger-happy amateurs at best. In 1936 Hoover himself came under rigorous attack in Congress. Sen. Kenneth D. McKellar of Tennessee grilled him at an appropriations hearing about his background and experience, bringing out the fact that Hoover had never personally handled an investigation or made an arrest.

Hoover reacted to this attack on his courage and competence the following month by personally arresting public enemy Alvin "Creepy" Karpis in New Orleans. Karpis was later to insist that Hoover had hidden out of sight until after other agents had seized him in a car and called to Hoover that it was safe to approach. On the other hand, Don Whitehead in *The FBI Story* credited Hoover as having "reached into the car and grabbed Karpis before he could reach for a rifle on the back seat." There is some question about this accomplishment, since the car had no back seat. The arrest proved to be a bit of a fiasco when none of the dozens of agents present could carry out Hoover's orders to "put the handcuffs on him." None of them had thought to bring along handcuffs.

In 1939 Hoover's FBI was handed the responsibility of guarding the nation against sabotage and subversion. It was these wartime duties, carried out with efficiency, that did the most to upgrade Hoover's image to one of unquestioned authority and wisdom. By 1943 Sen. McKellar was calling him a "grand man."

In the post-1945 Cold War years, Hoover rediscovered the Red Menace that had launched his career. The FBI's war on the Communist Party reached the stage of the ridiculous when agency informers in the organization probably outnumbered bona fide members. As the party dropped in size and influence, Hoover assured conservatives this merely indicated that the members were going underground and that more concentrated efforts—and larger budgets—were needed to combat the remaining threat. Hoover long ago had discovered that while conservatives might bewail the crime menace, their hold on the purse strings did not loosen much to combat such danger. However, given a good Red Scare, the money simply gushed forth.

In all, Hoover served under eight presidents, none of whom dared take the political consequences of attempting to oust him. Few attorneys general, technically his superiors, countered his views, especially in the 1940s and 1950s. The first to give Hoover genuine orders was Robert Kennedy in 1961, when he insisted the FBI concentrate on battling organized crime, truly an affront to its director, who for years had denied the existence of organized crime and the Mafia. Critics of Hoover said he took this tack because fighting the syndicate was not an easy matter, certainly more difficult than battling the great threat to the Republic posed by car thieves, probably 90 percent of whom were joyriding teenagers.

In the early 1960s it was clear that President John Kennedy wished to replace Hoover, who had reached retirement age, but having been elected by a thin majority, he felt incapable of withstanding the political repercussions. Undoubtedly, though, Kennedy planned to oust him if reelected to a second term. After Kennedy's assassination Lyndon Johnson is said to have exploited his power to force Hoover to step down by demanding the director perform illegal political investigations for him. According to ex-FBI official Sullivan, "There was absolutely nothing Johnson wouldn't ask of the FBI, and Hoover hotfooted it to Johnson's demands."

By the time he reached his late sixties, Hoover had turned crotchety and vindictive, launching secret operations against real and perceived personal enemies, including a particularly vicious campaign to discredit Martin Luther King based on sexual misbehavior. A lifelong bachelor, Hoover was never tainted by any innuendos of sexual improprieties.

Perhaps the best example of the tenor within the FBI in this period occurred during a top-level FBI meeting in 1968 presided over by Clyde Tolson, the number two man in the agency and Hoover's alter ego. When Robert Kennedy's name came up, Tolson declared, "I hope someone shoots and kills the son of a bitch." Shortly thereafter, someone did.

By 1970 President Richard Nixon had resolved to get rid of Hoover. The President invited him to the Oval Office to inform him that his tenure was at an end. Sullivan, who obviously was Nixon's man within the FBI, wrote in his *The Bureau—My Thirty Years in Hoover's FBI* that Hoover "started talking non-stop. It was his usual line of conversation, starring Dillinger, Ma Barker and a cast of thousands, and he kept talking until the President ended the interview.

"Assistant Attorney General Robert Mardian called me later and said: 'Christ almighty, Nixon lost his guts. He had Hoover there in his office, he knew what he was supposed to tell him, but he got cold feet. He couldn't go through with it.'"

Later, when Hoover forced Sullivan out of the FBI, Nixon, Mardian, John Mitchell, John Ehrlichman and Bob Haldeman determined that Hoover would go after Nixon's reelection. Hoover died, however, in May 1972, six months before the election. Had he lived, he undoubtedly would have survived this new threat to his reign, as his would-be purgers became immersed in the Watergate scandal, from which none would survive politically. They would have needed Hoover more than he would have needed them.

After Hoover's death and especially after the disclosure of his latter-day excesses, such as the notorious COINTELPRO program aimed at punishing Hoover targets who were neither convicted nor even suspected of illegal activities, some of his critics demanded Hoover's name be taken off the new FBI headquarters building. It was a senseless exercise. To separate

Hoover from the FBI in such fashion would be a silly attempt to rewrite history. The FBI itself, not the building, was Hoover's monument. The agency in 1972 was and, indeed, still is—"warts and all"—the embodiment of J. Edgar Hoover.

See also: *Briefcase Agents, Cosa Nostra, Alvin "Creepy" Karpis, Gaston Bullock Means, Palmer Raids, Melvin Purvis, Clyde A. Tolson.*

HOPE, Jimmy (1840-?): Police fixer and bank burglar

One of the most important underworld figures of the 19th century, Jimmy Hope was a crooked ex-cop in New York who handled "the fix" for the Shang Draper-George Leonidas Leslie mob of bank burglars.

Maintaining a fifth column of crooked officers within the New York Police Department, Hope could get the law to do anything he wanted, an ability he demonstrated stunningly in the great $2,747,000 looting of the Manhattan Savings Institution in 1878. In preparation for that job, he paid off many of the officers in the Detective Bureau just as he had in the past. Ordered to ensure the bank watchman would not interfere, Hope determined that the man could not be bribed. He solved the dilemma by having him hired away to a better-paying job on the recommendation of several police officers. When Manhattan Savings officials asked the police department to suggest a replacement, Hope saw to it that a 60-year-old Irishman named Patty Shevlin got the job. Shevlin was perfect. Whenever safecracker George Leonidas Leslie wanted to study the layout of the bank or the safe, Shevlin was told to take a nap in the basement and stay there until morning.

Hope also arranged that on the day of the burglary, Sunday morning, October 27, the policeman on the beat, John Nugent, would remain at a suitable distance away from the bank, yet close enough to guard the retreat of the burglars and, if necessary, to delay or mislead pursuit. As it was, the mob had so much loot packed in their small satchels that Nugent had to be summoned to carry one of them.

It took almost a year for the police to make arrests in this case. Two of the gang, Abe Coakley and Banjo Pete Emerson, were acquitted, but Bill Kelly and, ironically, Jimmy Hope were convicted. Patrolman Nugent was said to have won his freedom by bribing a juror, but within a few months he was convicted and sent to prison for highway robbery. Kelly and Hope got long prison terms. When the ex-fixer was set free near the turn of the century, he quickly disappeared.

See also: *George Leonidas Leslie.*

HORN, Tom (1860-1903): Hired killer

In recent years there have been efforts by some writers and even by Hollywood—in a 1980 movie—to "rehabilitate" Tom Horn, probably the most callous hired gun and bushwacker the Old West ever saw. Much is made of Horn's early years and his heroism as an Army scout under the celebrated Al Sieber and as a lawman and cowboy. Some of the more unquestioning also applaud his four years as a Pinkerton, although during that period he can only be described as a roving gun for the agency, with a toll of victims reputedly amounting to 17. Horn quit the Pinkertons, announcing he "had no more stomach for it." Agency apologists said that indicated he found the job too boring; others thought it meant Horn felt he was underpaid for the work. Immediately thereafter, he offered his lethal services to Wyoming cattlemen. There was no one Tom Horn wouldn't kill for $500. "Killing men is my specialty," he once remarked. "I look at it as a business proposition and I think I have a corner on the market."

Born in Missouri in 1860, he left home at about age 13, after an altercation with his father, and headed west. A tough, headstrong youth, he is believed to have had a row with Billy the Kid and slapped his face. No one was ever to accuse Horn of lacking guts. At 15 he was a stagecoach driver and from 1875 to 1886 he worked off and on for Al Sieber, chief Army scout at the San Carlos Indian Reservation. It was Horn who arranged the final surrender of Geronimo to Gen. Nelson Miles in 1886. After that, he became a deputy sheriff in the Arizona Territory.

By the time he went to work for the Pinkertons, he had quite a reputation, one that only worsened while he served in the agency. He ached with the desire for big money, but his only real talent was his skill with guns. The law paid peanuts, the Pinks somewhat more. The real money lay in working directly for the big cattlemen, settling old scores for them and eliminating small ranchers and rustlers (in Cheyenne's cattle baron circles the two terms were used interchangeably). Members of the Wyoming Cattlemen's Association bid high for Horn's services and Horn gloried in their attentions. He smoked their cigars, drank their liquor, backslapped with them and murdered for them.

Horn was a tidy butcher and regarded his assassinations as works of art. Testimony at his later trial would reveal how even in a driving rain, he waited for hours chewing on cuds of raw bacon, to get the one sure shot at a victim. After the kill he always left behind his trademark, a small rock under the victim's head, so that there could be no argument over who had carried out the assignment.

Horn once even offered his deadly services to Wyoming Gov. W. A. Richards. The governor, who owned a large ranch in the Big Horn country, was fearful of having the gunman seen at his office in the state capital, so he used the premises of the state Board of Livestock Commissioners. Another big stockman, William Irvine, who took part in the meeting, later recollected:

> The Governor was quite nervous, so was I, Horn perfectly cool; told the Governor he would either drive every rustler out of the Big Horn County, or take no pay other than $350 advanced to buy two horses and a pack outfit; that when he had finished the job to the Governor's satisfaction he should receive $5,000 because, he said in conclusion, "Whenever everything else fails, I have a system which never does." He placed no limit on the number of men to be gotten rid of.

Irvine said the governor clearly got cold feet when Horn matter-of-factly made his murder proposition. The killer saw this immediately and tactfully ended the discussion by saying: "I presume that is about all you wanted to know, Sir. I shall be glad to hear from you at any time I can be of service."

Horn's murder dealing became so well known that rustlers and other desperadoes often cleared out of an area when he appeared on the scene. But the small rancher, his entire life tied up in his meager holdings, could not. And if a big cattleman said a small rancher was rustling his cattle, that was good enough for Horn.

Because of his powerful connections, Horn was considered immune from the law. But in 1901 he murdered a 14-year-old boy, Willie Nickell, from ambush. Hired to shoot the boy's sheepman father, Horn mistook the youth for the father in the early dawn light. The case remained unsolved until Joe Lefors, a deputy U.S. marshal who led the famous pòsse that chased Butch Cassidy and the Sundance Kid, took over the investigation. He wormed his way into Horn's confidence, and when the latter was drinking heavily, he got him to boast of his killings, including the Nickell affair, while hidden witnesses and a stenographer listened.

Horn was thrown in jail. When he sobered up, he insisted he had merely been telling tall tales and accused the stenographer of adding statements he had not made. Horn had brilliant legal talent defending him at his trial, with some $5,000 donated to his defense fund by an unknown "admirer." However, the case against him was overwhelming and he was sentenced to hang.

While he awaited execution, people wondered if Horn would start naming all his powerful employers, and it appears that employers wondered too. In August 1903 someone smuggled a pistol to him, and he escaped with another prisoner. He was quickly recaptured, however, and spent much of the rest of his time hurriedly penning his memoirs, leaving out, of course, all references to his murderous "range detecting." With the streets of Cheyenne patrolled by militiamen, Tom Horn was hanged on November 20, 1903, his lips still sealed.

A Wyoming cattleman was to recall, "He died without 'squealing,' to the great relief of many very respectable citizens of the West."

In recent years some effort has been made to discredit the Lefors testimony. Dean Krakel, Horn's chief biographer and author of *The Saga of Tom Horn*, insists the Horn confession was a frame-up and would be inadmissible in modern courts and that Horn was innocent of the Nickell shooting.

See also: *Range Detectives*.

HORRELL-HIGGINS Feud

One of Texas' bloodiest feuds, the Horrell-Higgins conflict broke out in central Texas in 1873 over charges of cattle rustling around the frontier town of Lampasas, northwest of Austin. Suspicion centered on the men of the Horrell spread. When the sheriff attempted to arrest one of the Horrell men, he was promptly killed. A squad of state officers were dispatched to Lampasas to take care of the Horrells, once again with fatal consequences for the law officers. A group of Horrells

were found in the Gem Saloon and ordered to give up their guns and surrender. Shooting broke out immediately. When the gunsmoke cleared, four officers lay dead or dying. Only Mart Horrell, who was wounded, was arrested. However, when he was placed in the jail at Georgetown, his friends and brothers broke in and freed him. The Horrells then moved their herds into New Mexico to avoid further problems with the Texas authorities.

Finding themselves ensnarled in similar rustling disputes in New Mexico, the Horrells returned to Texas, where two of them were tried and acquitted in the killing of the four law officers. Meanwhile, new suspicions about the Horrells rustling cattle were voiced, especially by the Higgins clan, which had lost a considerable amount of stock. Pink Higgins led his family in a war against the Horrells. Higgins, a fiery gunfighter, threatened to wipe out every Horrell. In January 1877 Pink killed Merritt Horrell at the Gem.

With all sorts of legal charges against both clans, someone broke into the courthouse one night in July 1877 and removed the records of all pending criminal cases. The families then prepared to settle the matter between themselves. Later that same month the two factions fought a bitter gun battle for several hours in the streets of Lampasas. At least one innocent bystander was among those killed.

Finally, in July the Texas Rangers moved into the area in force. A detachment under Sgt. N. O. Reynolds entered the Horrell ranch house before dawn and captured the family and its supporters without a fight. Other Rangers simultaneously captured the Higgins clan. Realizing that a few prison sentences would hardly end the shooting, the Rangers had long discussions with each group. Eventually, members of both families signed a formal peace treaty. Such agreements had been tried in other feuds without success, but in this case all the participants faithfully observed the treaty and the Horrell-Higgins feud ended.

See also: *John Calhoun Pinckney "Pink" Higgins*.

HORSE Poisoners

Common during the early decades of this century in New York, horse poisoning was one of the most-detested of all crimes, viewed with horror by the public, the police and even much of the underworld. The horse was the lifeline of many businesses, such as the produce, ice cream, beer and seltzer trades. Businessmen faced with stiff competition would often hire gangsters to destroy the competition's trade. The simplest way to do this was to poison a rival's horses, thus destroying his distribution system. It was a common sight on the Lower East Side to see a produce seller with two dead horses desperately trying to sell his stock at half price to clamoring housewives before it was all ruined.

By 1913 three gangs of horse poisoners under the leaderships of Yoske Nigger, whose real name was Joseph Toplinsky, Charley the Cripple, whose real name was Charles Vitoffsky, and Johnny Levinsky dominated the field. They would steal or poison horses to order. Unlike their clients, these three did not engage in cutthroat competition among themselves. Instead they divided the field into separate monopolies, with Yoske Nigger handling the produce markets, truckmen and livery stables; Charley the Cripple the seltzer and soda water dealers and manufacturers; and Levinsky the ice cream trade. Whenever an order came in from some area not covered by this jurisdictional agreement, the three handled the matter jointly.

A defecting member of one of the gangs finally revealed to the police the trio's scale of fees:

Shooting, fatal	$500
Shooting, not fatal	$100
Poisoning a team	$50
Poisoning one horse	$35
Stealing a horse and rig	$25

The first two items, of course, referred to human victims and were much higher than the rates a client could find elsewhere. Since many gangsters at the time hired out to do a murder for as little as $10 to $20, it was not surprising that most of the trio's business was limited to horses. Yet the horse poisoners were hated by other gangsters who had no qualms about shooting humans but found the poisoning of dumb beasts despicable.

Eventually, the three poisoners felt the full wrath of the law when a chicken dealer named Barnett Baff was shot to death in 1914. According to the police theory, Baff's competitors had paid the staggering sum of $4,200 for his violent demise. This money, was supposedly given to Levinsky, Yoske Nigger and Charley the Cripple, who divided it up after paying a mere $50 to the actual hit man. Under close surveillance and harassment by the police, the trio abandoned their poisoning practices and retired to reputable business lives in the wilds of Brooklyn, remaining honest, it was said, until the bootlegging era beckoned them back to criminality.

HORSE Stealing

As an old quip has it, "One day the first man tamed the first horse; the next day another man stole it." Certainly, horse stealing was one of the most prevalent crimes in Colonial America, and horse thieves flourished during the Revolution, selling animals to both sides and often the same beasts at that. However, horse stealing in America is most often associated with the West, where it was considered a crime without equal. Stealing horses was regarded as murder, and indeed, it often amounted to as much since a man without his horse in open spaces was at the mercy of the elements or of Indian raiders as well as vulnerable to death by starvation or thirst.

T. A. McNeal in *When Kansas Was Young* summed up the utter necessity of a horse:

A horse was about the only means of conveyance, and in the cattle business it was essential. It was necessary, too, to let the horses run on the range unguarded. The cattlemen reasoned that unless the men who lusted for the possession of good horses were restrained by fear of prompt and violent death, no man would be sure that when he turned his horses out at night he would be able to gather any of them in the morning.

In 1878 a Houston, Tex. newspaper bemoaned the fact that 100,000 horses had been stolen in the state during the preceding three years.

It further estimated that 750 men are regularly engaged in this business and that not more than one in ten is ever captured and brought to justice. By common practice in the rural districts, every man caught is either shot on the spot or hanged to the nearest tree. No instance is yet recorded where the law paid the slightest attention to lynchers of this kind. It is conceded that the man who steals a horse forfeits his life to the owner. It is a game of life and death. Men will pursue these thieves for 500 miles, go any length, spend any amount of money to capture them, and fight them to the death when overtaken. That they will be totally exterminated admits of no doubt. The poor scoundrels cannot last long when the feeling of all civilization is so much aroused against them as it now is in Texas.

When vigilantes in Fort Griffin hanged a horse thief from a pecan tree and put a pick and shovel there for anyone with a mind to bury him, a correspondent for the *Dallas Herald* recorded the event and added: "So far, so good. As long as the committee strings up the right parties, it has the well wishes of every lover of tranquility."

Lynching of horse thieves became common throughout the entire West, but it was not a very effective deterrent. The horse thieves thrived. One, Dutch Henry, known as the King of the Horse Thieves, had some 300 men working during one period for him. Because horses could easily be recognized on sight by former owners, thieves would often drive them hundreds, even a thousand miles, to sell them. The famed Horse-Thief Trail ran from Salt Lake City in the north to the Mexican border in the south without ever once following the frequently used commercial trails. Horse thieves worked both ends of their run: a gang stealing horses in Texas would drive them to Kansas and in Kansas collar a herd and drive it back to Texas.

Perhaps the futility of using the death penalty as a deterrent is illustrated by the history of this crime. Even the threat of hangings on the spot did not deter horse thieves from stealing thousands of horses each year. Their ranks were slowly thinned only after the development of efficient range detective methods and, more importantly, after the invention of the horseless carriage.

See also: *Dutch Henry, Horse-Thief Trail, Henry Tufts.*

HORSE-THIEF Trail

In the post-Civil War West it was possible for outlaws to drive stolen horses all the way from Salt Lake City, Utah through Arizona, New Mexico and Texas to Mexico without once running into the law or an honest rider. The route they followed was the famous but unmarked Horse-Thief Trail, and any man who knew the entire route had his fortune made, the only source of danger being other horse thieves.

HOT Corn Girls: See Edward Coleman.

HOT Springs, Arkansas: See White Front Cigar Store.

HOTSY Totsy Club: New York speakeasy

Among all the notorious New York speakeasies that thrived during Prohibition, none had a worse reputation than the Hotsy Totsy Club, a second floor joint on Broadway between 54th and 55th streets. Although Hymie Cohen fronted as the proprietor, a big chunk of the place was owned by gangster Legs Diamond. Diamond utilized the club to hold court and directed several rackets from there. He also used it as an execution site. Many crime figures whom Diamond wished to prevail upon would be invited there for some revelry and a business discussion. If they failed to go along with Diamond's view of things, they were murdered in a back room and later carried out "drunk."

The Hotsy Totsy's bloodiest claim to fame came in 1929, when Diamond and sidekick Charles Entratta gunned down a hoodlum named Red Cassidy. Also killed in the wild shoot-out at the bar was an innocent bystander, Simon Walker, who nonetheless happened to be wearing two loaded revolvers in his belt. Unlike the pair's other murders in the club, a great number of witnesses were present during the shooting causing Diamond and Entratta to flee.

From hiding, Diamond directed a reign of killings to clear his name. That meant the bartender had to be rubbed out, along with three customers who had seen what had happened. The cashier, a waiter, the hat check girl and another club hanger-on disappeared, although their fate was not entirely a mystery to police or the newspapers. But suspicions meant little. Diamond and Entratta surrendered and were charged with the killings at the club. But they were soon freed because the authorities had no witnesses to present evidence against them.

See also: *Jack "Legs" Diamond.*

HOUNDS: 19th century San Francisco anti-foreigner gang

Officially bearing the high-sounding title of the San Francisco Society of Regulators, the Hounds, as they were more commonly called, were a collection of young thugs organized to contain the peril to Anglo-Americans presented by Spanish-Americans in San Francisco in 1849.

Under the pretense of a fiery patriotism, flamed by the influence of the Know Nothings, the Hounds set about driving the foreigners out of the gold fields, a goal that had a good deal of public support. They beat, stabbed and shot helpless Mexicans and Chileans whenever they had the chance and extorted money and gold from those few who had managed to accumulate any wealth. Officials made no effort to stop these outrages until the Hounds got the idea that the good people of San Francisco should pay them for their protection of the community. Then no man's property or life—be he Spanish or Anglo-American—was safe. The Hounds roamed the streets in bands, robbing stores and pedestrians in broad daylight. Merchants trying to stop them were stabbed. The gang victimized saloons, gorging themselves on the best of food and drink and telling the proprietor to collect from the city as they walked out. If there were objections, the building was set on fire. The Hounds increased their atrocities against the "greasers" and blacks. They cut off the ears of a black man who had accidentally brushed a Hound in passing. A Mexican who talked back to a Hound had his tongue ripped out by the roots.

Using a patriotic pretense, the Hounds first attacked Hispanics in San Francisco and then turned their violence on whites as well.

In the summer of 1849 the Hounds, in full battle array—almost all were veterans of the Mexican War—made their most violent onslaught against the Mexican tents and shanties. The authors of a contemporary account wrote:

> These they violently tore down, plundering them of money and valuables, which they carried away, and totally destroying on the spot such articles as they did not think it worth while to seize. Without provocation, and in cold blood, they barbarously beat with sticks and stones, and cuffed and kicked the offending foreigners. Not content with that, they repeatedly and wantonly fired among the injured people, and amid the shrieks of terrified women and the groans of wounded men, recklessly continued their terrible course in different quarters, wherever in fact malice or thirst for plunder led them. . . . There were no individuals brave or foolhardy enough to resist the progress of such a savage mob, whose exact force was unknown, but who were believed to be both numerous and desperate.

This outrage at last galvanized the whole town. Money was collected for the relief of the destitute Spanish-Americans and 230 volunteers were deputized to round up the Hounds. Many of the gang immediately fled the city, but 20-odd Hounds, including one of their leaders, Sam Roberts, were taken. Several witnesses, including a number of injured Spanish-Americans who later died, testified against the prisoners. Roberts and a man named Saunders were sentenced to 10 years at hard labor, while others drew shorter punishments. But within a few days political supporters of the gang won their release and none of the sentences were ever carried out. However, the Hounds were too frightened ever to reorganize and within a short time virtually all of them left the area.

HOUSE Of All Nations: Celebrated brothel

While the Everleigh Club was undoubtedly Chicago's, America's and perhaps the world's most famous brothel, another, much more reasonably priced contemporary at the turn of the century was almost as well known in the Windy City. It was the celebrated House of All Nations, a bordello on Armour Avenue that was considered a must stop for on-the-town sports.

The House of All Nations was famed for two qualities: its employees allegedly came from all parts of the globe (or at least could affect the proper accents) and they came in different price ranges. There was both a $2 and a $5 entrance, and in typical whoredom flimflammery, the ladies of the house all worked both entrances, dispensing the same services for either price tag. One commonly held belief in Chicago was that Oriental prostitutes working in the house plied their profession during the winter months clad in long underwear because they were unable to take the chilly Chicago climate. The practice gave the Oriental harlots an added "exotic" quality that made them even more popular, but it should be noted that for a small additional fee they would strip down to the skin and brave the elements.

The House of All Nations was shuttered prior to the start of World War I, a victim of the great vice cleanup of the notorious Levee section on Chicago's South Side.

HOUSTON, Temple L. (1860-1905): Criminal lawyer

The son of Texas patriot Sam Houston, Temple Houston became one of the West's most colorful lawyers. Tall, with hair down to his shoulders, he cut a flamboyant figure in long Prince Albert coats, white sombreros and ties fashioned out of rattlesnake skin.

As a courtroom orator, Houston had few equals. Defending a prostitute named Millie Stacy for plying her trade in 1899, he mesmerized the jury with oratory. Proclaiming that, "where the star of purity once glittered on her girlish brow, burning shame has set its seal forever," he begged the all-male jury to let Millie "go in peace." They did.

Some of his tactics were most unusual. Representing a man who had shot first when facing a skilled gunfighter, Houston, in an effort to demonstrate the speed the victim possessed, whipped out a pair of Colt .45s and blazed away at the judge and jury. When peace was restored, the lawyer got around to mentioning that the guns had been loaded with blanks. It was an effective demonstration, but the jury still convicted his client. Undismayed, Houston argued for a new trial on the grounds that when the jurors had scattered after he started

shooting they had mingled with the courtroom crowd and therefore could no longer be considered sequestered. The lawyer won his appeal and the eventual freedom of his client.

Houston was himself an expert gunman and easily outpointed Bat Masterson in a shooting contest. Besides being called on many times to lead posses after criminals, he fought several duels and never sustained a wound. Once, he got into a saloon shoot-out with another lawyer at the conclusion of a trial and killed his opponent. He then defended himself successfully in court, pleading self-defense.

Temple Houston died of a stroke in Woodward, Okla. A newspaper called him "a mingling of nettles and flowers" and observed that the Southwest "probably will never see his counterpart."

HOWARD, Joseph: See Civil War Gold Hoax.

HOWE And Hummel: Shyster lawyers

Howe and Hummel were easily the grandest shysters ever to seek out a loophole, suborn a witness or free a guilty man. Practicing in New York from 1869 to 1906, they made a mockery of the law. Rotund, walrus-mustached William F. Howe was a great courtroom pleader who could bring sobs to any jury. Young Abe Hummel was a little man who was marvelously adept at ferreting out loopholes in the law, to the extent that once he almost succeeded in making murder legal.

At the age of 32, Howe came to America from England, where his career as a medical practitioner had terminated in a prison term for performing an illegal operation on a woman patient. He studied law and within three years he opened up shop on New York's Centre (later called Center) Street. Howe was an instant success because of his resonant voice and a face that could turn on and off any emotion he wished to display for a jury. Years later, David Belasco, the theatrical producer, watched Howe's tearful performance winning an acquittal for a woman who had shot her lover full of holes. "That man," he said, "would make a Broadway star."

In the late 1860s Howe hired young Abe Hummel as his law clerk and in almost no time promoted him to partner. Anyone so adept at finding holes in the law was too good to lose. One case that illustrated Hummel's ability involved a professional arsonist named Owen Reilly. Hummel suggested they save the prosecution the trouble of a trial by pleading Reilly guilty to attempted arson. Only after the plea was accepted did anyone notice that there was no penalty for the crime of attempted arson. However, the statutes did say that the sentence for any crime attempted but not actually committed was to be one-half of the maximum allowable for the actual commission of the crime. Since the penalty for arson at the time was life imprisonment, obviously the defendant's sentence had to be half a life. Howe made nonsense of that standard.

"Scripture tells us that we knoweth not the day nor the hour of our departure," he told the judge. "Can this court sentence the prisoner at the bar to half of his natural life? Will it, then, sentence him to half a minute or to half the days of Methuselah?" The judge gave up and set Reilly free; the state legislature rushed to revise the arson statutes shortly thereafter.

On another occasion the pair almost managed to make murder legal in New York state. It happened in November 1888, when a client named Handsome Harry Carlton was convicted of having killed a cop. Since the jury failed to recommend mercy, the death penalty was mandatory. Little Abe studied the statutes very carefully and pointed out to Howe that in the month of November there was no death penalty for murder on the books, the state having abolished hanging the previous June, with the provision that it be replaced by the electric chair. The new death-dealing apparatus was to start functioning on the following January 1, and as Hummel noted, the law specifically said that electrocution should apply to all convictions punishable by death on and after January 1.

When Carlton came up for sentencing, early in December, Howe objected as the judge prepared to pronounce the death penalty. In fact, he objected to any sentence being passed on Carlton. If the jury had recommended mercy, Carlton could be sentenced to life imprisonment, the lawyer noted. "However, my client has been convicted of first-degree murder with no recommendation of mercy and there is no law on the books covering such a crime.

He then read the precise language in the new law and concluded that all the judge could do was turn his client free. Nonplussed, the judge delayed sentencing while the case moved to the state supreme court. Quite naturally, Howe and Hummel's contention made headlines across the country. In New York the public reaction was one of utter shock. According to the lawyers' contention, anyone committing murder between June and the new year could not be executed. Other murderers confined in death cells clamored to be released on the ground that they were being wrongfully held and could not be executed.

The district attorney's office vowed to fight the matter, and Inspector Thomas Byrnes of the New York Police Department's Detective Bureau pledged to the public that his men would continue to clap murderers behind bars, law or no law.

In the end, Howe and Hummel lost out on their interpretation; the high court ruled that no slip in syntax could be used as an excuse to legalize murder. Harry Carlton swung from the gallows two days after Christmas, a nick-of-time execution. However, if Carlton had lost out, Howe and Hummel did not; their crafty efforts brought many felons and murderers to their office door.

Buoyed by the publicity, the two shysters coauthored a book entitled *In Danger, or Life in New York: A True History of the Great City's Wiles and Temptations.* They explained in the preface that it was published in the interest of justice and to protect the innocent from the guilty, but what they actually turned out was a primer on every type of crime—blackmail, house burglary, card sharping, safecracking, shoplifting, jewel thievery and, of course, murder.

It became an immediate best-seller, with book store owners noticing a lot of traffic in their shops by persons who did not appear to be frequent book buyers. The book became required reading for every professional or would-be lawbreaker, from streetwalkers to killers. More and more when Howe and Hummel asked a new client, "Who sent you?" the stock reply was, "I read about you in the book."

No one ever computed exactly what percentage of murderers Howe and Hummel got off scot-free, but a prosecutor once estimated it was at least 70 percent, and "90 percent of them were guilty."

Whenever they had a client who was obviously as guilty as could be, the pair went into their bandage routine, having the defendant appear swathed in yards of white bandage, as though to suggest so frail a mind that his brains might fall out at any moment. One contemporary account tells of a Howe and Hummel client who simulated a village idiot's tic by "twitching the right corner of the mouth and simultaneously blinking the left eye." As soon as he was cleared, the defendant's face "resumed its normal composure, except for the large grin that covered it as he lightly removed the cloths from about his forehead." Another client, whose supposedly blithering insanity was accompanied by muteness and an ability to communicate only by sign language, seized Howe's hand gratefully when the verdict was announced in his favor and boomed, "Silence is golden."

The pair did not always resort to such trickery. When it was more convenient, they simply bribed witnesses and appropriate officials to get records changed; yet somehow they never ran into deep trouble until after Howe died in 1906. The following year Hummel was caught paying $1,000 to facilitate a divorce action. He was sentenced to two years in prison. Released at the age of 60, Hummel retired to Europe and died in London in January 1926, a regular to the end in the visitors' section during trials at the Old Bailey.

See also: *Handsome Harry Carlton,* In Danger, *Fredericka "Marm" Mandelbaum.*

HOYT, George (?-1877): Wyatt Earp victim

George Hoyt, a Texas cowboy and alleged outlaw, was killed by Wyatt Earp in Dodge City, which in itself was a distinction. Despite the reputation he gained there as a gun-toting lawman, Earp killed only one man in Dodge City, and his chief deputy, Bat Masterson, killed none. The fact that Earp and Masterson were nicknamed the Fighting Pimps perhaps indicates what they meant by "cleaning up" the town. Not that Earp's brand of justice didn't include plenty of violence, especially against cowboys, for whom he always showed considerable contempt. Earp proudly recalled, "As practically every prisoner heaved into the calaboose was thoroughly buffaloed (crowned with a revolver barrel) in the process, we made quite a dent in cowboy conceit."

One cattleman subjected to this treatment was Tobe Driskill. Following his experience Driskill supposedly put, in true Texas style, a $1,000 reward on Earp's head. There was some indication that a couple of drunken cowboys tried to collect that reward, but they missed Earp and he missed them. Finally,

HURRAHING THE TOWN 353

George Hoyt gave it a try. Hoyt was allegedly a wanted outlaw in Texas, and as a further inducement to kill Earp, Driskill is said to have promised to use his influence in order to get the charges against Hoyt dropped. On July 26, 1877 Hoyt rode into the town's plaza and fired six shots at Earp, who was standing in front of the Comique Theater, where Eddie Foy was at the moment singing "Kalamazoo in Michigan." Three of the bullets whizzed by Earp and plowed through the door of the theater and into the audience section, hitting nobody but causing Foy to drop flat on his face. Hoyt's mount bucked furiously, making him a poor target, but Earp still spilled the cowboy in the dirt with his third shot. Hoyt lingered a month before dying and never told Earp who had hired him to do the job.

HUGHES, John R. (1855-1946): Texas Ranger

Illinois-born John Hughes was one of the most productive of all Texas Rangers. He compiled an outstanding record of captures, even crossing the Rio Grande, with or without permission, to bring back an outlaw. In 1877 Hughes gave up running his Texas horse ranch after he had been forced to go after a gang of six rustlers who had taken his stock. He killed four of them and captured the other two, but he also realized that as the sole operator of his ranch, he would continue to suffer losses from his herd. Hughes eventually decided that if he had to chase rustlers, he might as well get paid for it, and he joined the Rangers.

By 1883 Hughes had risen to captain, a high rank in the law organization, and single-handedly had brought in the notorious outlaw Juan Perales. Over the years he was also responsible for wiping out such gangs as the Ybarras, Friars and Massays. Hughes ended his career in 1915 at the age of 60 and died in 1946.

HUMMING Bird, The: Prison torture

It is perhaps futile to attempt to single out the most hideous and brutal torture ever practiced on the inmates of prisons in the United States, but "the humming bird" was certainly among the worst. This innocuous-sounding name was applied to a technique that involved placing a prisoner, chained hand and foot, in a steel bathtub filled with water. He was then rubbed down with a sponge attached to an electric battery. According to one description of the torture's agonizing effects, "Two or three minutes and the victim is ready for the grave or the mad house."

Bloody riots at the Oregon State Prison at Salem during World War I were in large measure aimed at eliminating this cruel instrument of torture. Needless to say, the leaders of riots were subjected to the humming bird, although its use in Oregon prisons was discontinued shortly thereafter.

HUNT, Sam "Golf Bag" (?-1956): Capone mob enforcer

Together with Machine Gun McGurn, Sam "Golf Bag" Hunt was perhaps the toughest of the Capone mob enforcers, or "blazers," as they were more commonly called. Placed on the Chicago Crime Commission's list of the city's public enemies, Hunt was often described as the killer of no less than 20 men. He got his nickname as a result of one of his more colorful assassinations, the victim of which remains a mystery.

One day in 1927 a Chicagoan was taking an early morning stroll along Lake Michigan's beautiful South Shore when the boom of shotgun blasts disturbed the tranquil air. He hurried in the direction of the shots and found a corpse, so recently rendered dead that blood was still oozing forth. The morning stroller rushed to a telephone and informed the police. The officers who responded came across Hunt and McGurn less than a half mile away. When asked about the golf bag he was carrying, Hunt gave a reasonable explanation: "Jack and I were going out to play a little golf."

This answer, however, did not prevent the policemen from peering into the bag and finding among the golf clubs a semi-automatic shotgun. The weapon was still warm, a fact that convinced the police they had a hot clue. But it didn't turn out that way. The good citizen led them to the spot where he had found the body, but it was no longer there. Either the dead man had walked away or he had been carted away, and all that remained was a splatter of blood on the dewy grass.

In any event, there was nothing to link Hunt to a crime, and the only thing he was tagged with was a permanent nickname. The athletically-inclined assassin outlived his mentor Capone and most of the other blazers, dying in 1956 in his late fifties.

HURRAHING The Town: Cowboy custom

In the quiet lives of Western town dwellers, one of the most disruptive events was when the cowboys came into town, "yippeeing" their ponies along the plank walks and into the saloons. These "ruffians" on horseback would later ride out of town firing their six-shooters in the air. Undeniably there was gunplay, drunken brawling and wanton vandalism, the same that existed back east in the infamous dives of New York, Cincinnati and Chicago, where huge street gangs literally would take apart a saloon or a whole row of saloons when the notion struck them. Indeed, Western cowboys, even when "hurrahing the town," were restrained by comparison.

Historian Ramon F. Adams describes the practice from the cowhand's perspective:

Let's follow a newly paid-off puncher with $100—three or four months' pay—burning a hole in his pocket. First he visits a barber, has a tangle of beard removed and his hair cut. Then he drops into a dry goods store and buys himself a new outfit. Now he is ready to celebrate. The saloon men, the gamblers, the pimps, are all waiting to filch his hard-earned pay. The bartender sets out a bottle of cheap frontier whiskey, "two bits a throw." A little heady after a few drinks, the puncher heads for the poker table, where a flashy gambler is waiting with his marked cards. Our puncher watches the dealer's pile of chips grow and his own melt away. Convinced he is being robbed, he can't prove it. Finally, pockets empty, he pulls away from the table, mounts his pony, races up and <u>down</u> the street and blazes a few indignant shots at the stars. Then, with a yell, he spurs the pony and gallops out of town, heading for the security of his cow camp. And yet, because of this type of conduct, he became known to the Easterner as a bloodthirsty demon, reckless and rowdy, weighted down with guns and itching to use them.

Writers of the day insisted the cowboys were semisavages and lionized the likes of Hickok, Earp, Masterson and Holliday —the men who regarded the gamblers, whoremasters and saloonkeepers as clients and the cowboys as foes. Wyatt Earp especially held the cowboy in contempt. For some time he operated a con game with Mysterious Dave Mather in Mobeetie, Tex. selling phony gold bricks to gullible trail hands.

See also: *Wyatt Earp, Gold Brick Swindle.*

HYPNOTISM And Crime

Can a person under hypnosis be made to commit murder or another crime? For years the possible use of hypnotism in murders and other crimes has been a subject of debate in scientific circles, with the weight of opinion apparently slowly shifting to the side of those who think it possible. Even legal authorities have admitted the need to deal with the problem. In the 1950s a New York prosecutor, Assistant District Attorney Sheldon S. Levy, raised the possibility of law-abiding citizens being hypnotized against their will and made, by various means, to commit acts they would not do if they had their usual control over themselves. Writing in the *Journal of Criminal Law,* he quoted findings of some psychologists that "a hypnotist who really wished a murder could almost certainly get it."

Of course, it has never been proven that a hypnotist can actually get another person to commit a murder for him, since such a test, obviously, cannot be carried out. Yet numerous stage hypnotists have demonstrated the ability to get people to commit other crimes against their conscience. In a well-publicized demonstration at New York City's Carnegie Hall, one hypnotist called several people to the stage and induced them to rob members of the audience when they returned to their seats. He did so by hypnotizing them and giving them cards that read: "You must raise money for a charity that will save hundreds of children from starvation. The people from whom you are taking things are wicked and do not deserve their ill-gotten gains. You cannot possibly be caught."

The hypnotized persons returned to their seats without the audience being informed about what they had been instructed to do. When they were told to return to the stage, they had with them a number of wallets and a woman's handbag, all stolen without the victims' knowledge.

The note, according to student of hypnotism, had broken down all mental resistance by the subjects. While no one can be forced to perform an act that he knows is wrong, they say, he can be induced to commit an illegal act if he is convinced it is right. The note had the added value of assuring the subjects they would not be caught, thus overcoming any fear factor. Similarly, in tests at various universities hypnotized subjects threw sulfuric acid into a person's face, which unknown to them, was protected by an invisible sheet of glass. Some subjects threw the acid with an obvious pleasurable display of violence, while others shuddered and only threw it after considerable hesitation.

Disbelievers say such experiments prove nothing because the subject, although in a trance, is still aware that the experiments are being conducted in a laboratory or entertainment atmosphere and thus knows he will not be permitted to do anything wrong. Since a hypnotized person "knows" he won't be called upon to commit murder, he will pick up a gun and fire it, reasoning the weapon will be loaded with blanks. Assistant District Attorney Levy countered this view by pointing out that all a hypnotist bent on homicide would have to do was convince a person that he was merely undergoing a psychological test and that the gun contained blanks and then substitute real bullets.

Occasionally newspaper stories report a person's claim that he or she was hypnotized into committing a crime, but there is no recent record of any such story being accepted. Indeed, the California Supreme Court once said that "the law of the United States does not recognize hypnotism."

One classic murder case that seems to come closest to proving the murder by hypnosis theory occurred in Minnesota in 1894. Harry Hayward was a young blade about Minneapolis who was known as a lady's man as well as a hard-drinking, heavy-gambling, all-around sport. He was also a student of hypnotism, having taken a course on the subject. Some students of crime are convinced that he used this power to win the favors and money of Katherine Ging and to get her to assign her insurance—$10,000 worth—over to him.

Hayward was also practicing his power of hypnosis on a local handyman named Claus Blixt, whom he convinced to carry out relatively minor crimes, such as burning down a small factory on which Kitty Ging held a mortgage. Kitty collected the insurance money, and Hayward collected from her. Soon, the lady was down to no assets but her life insurance. For days Hayward talked to the handyman, always making him look into his eyes as he spoke. Hayward later confessed, "I would repeat over a few times how easy it was to kill someone, and pretty soon he would be saying right after me, 'Sure, that's easy; nothing to that.'"

Whether the handyman was actually under hypnosis at the time he murdered Kathering Ging or whether his will to resist the idea had simply been broken by suggestions made during earlier trances was never made clear. But either way, Blixt committed the murder while Hayward was miles away establishing an alibi. Hayward was later hanged for the killing, but the handyman, a relatively pathetic character, was allowed to plead guilty and drew a lesser sentence.

Another supposed hypnotic murderer, convicted in 1894, was Dr. Henry Meyer, who left a string of corpses from New York to Chicago. Before setting himself up as a doctor in the Middle West, Meyer had studied hypnotism in Leipzig, Germany under Professor Herbert Flint, one of the celebrated mesmerists of the era.

Meyer murdered several persons to collect on their insurance polices. He killed his first wife and then the husband of another woman so that he could marry her. When he saw a chance to kill his second wife for $75,000, he conceived a murder plan involving hypnosis. Meyer chose as the tool of his plot a plumber named Peter Bretz, an ideal hypnotic subject who soon fell under his spell. He convinced the plumber that he was in love with Mrs. Meyer who apparently was ready herself for an affair of the heart, and should run away with her. Britz was to take the second Mrs. Meyer to Arizona, offer to show her the Grand Canyon and, when nobody was around, shove her over the canyon lip. The plumber and the intended victim had actually reached the Grand Canyon when he broke out of the spell. The couple then returned to Chicago and revealed the plot to authorities. But since the authorities at that time could not possibly get a grand jury to swallow such a tale, Meyer went free to commit another murder before being brought to justice. Students of hypnotic crime insist the Meyer case deserves closer study. Basically, despite the claims of some believers in the feasibility of hypnotic murder, the justice system continues to ignore the question.

See also: *Katherine "Kitty" Ging.*

HYPNOTISM And Detection

Experts agree that hypnotism, if properly used, can play an important role in fighting crime, far greater than the potential danger that it may be employed in the commission of crimes. In the 1976 kidnapping of 26 children in a school bus in Chowchilla, Calif. hypnosis helped the bus driver remember part of the license plate number of a van used in the kidnapping so that the police were able to trace the vehicle to the criminals. New York police made an arrest in the murder of a young female cellist at the Metropolitan Opera House after a ballerina who had seen a man with the musician was enabled by hypnosis to give a description for a police sketch. Part of what convinced police that Albert DeSalvo was the Boston Strangler was his description under hypnosis of gory details concerning the sex murders and the tortured thoughts that made him commit his terrible crimes.

Similarly, hypnotic examination of a young man, Allen Curtis Lewis, who had admitted to pushing a young woman, Renee Katz, onto the New York City subway tracks in 1979 as well as of a Connecticut teenager, Peter Reilly, who had confessed murdering his mother helped clear them, revealing, among other things, how their confessions had been produced by subtle coercion.

There are, however, a number of obstacles to widespread police use of hypnosis. One is that attempts have been made to interrogate suspects under hypnosis against their will. The second objection is that hypnotized persons do not necessarily give reliable information. In the $2.7 million Brinks robbery during the 1950s, police traced a license plate number furnished under hypnosis only to find it belonged to a college president who had an iron-clad alibi not only for himself but for his car as well. In another case a man charged with the murder of a child supplied "hypnotized" evidence that indicated his wife, rather than he, was the guilty party. However, discrepancies turned up indicating that the suspect had used the opportunity to try to shift the guilt away from himself.

A classic example of the perils of accepting as legal evidence a confession obtained by hypnosis is the case of Camilo W. Leyra, Jr., who was convicted and sentenced to death for the 1950 hammer slaying of his 74-year-old father and 80-year-old mother. He was released from the death house in 1956 after an appeals court overturned his conviction for a third time because the only evidence against him was his original confession obtained through hypnosis. Stated the New York Court of Appeals:

> The prosecution has produced not a single trustworthy bit of affirmative, independent evidence connecting the defendant with the crime. Under the circumstances, a regard for the fundamental concept of justice and fairness, if not due process, imposes upon the court the duty to write finis to further prosecution against the defendant. . . . It seems quite probable that both the police and the District Attorney, relying too heavily on the confessions that they had obtained. . . failed to do the essential careful and intensive investigation that should be done before a defendant is charged with a crime, certainly one as serious as murder.

Despite the dangers of misuse, there is little doubt that the practice of hypnosis will continue to grow. In New York City the technique was used in about 400 cases between 1976 and 1980. Many of the cases were homicides, and all the subjects were either victims or witnesses. The New York Police Department has firm rules against using the method on any person even slightly suspected of being guilty of the crime. In Los Angeles, the police have 11 officers trained in hypnosis and have used the method in 600 cases. In 90 percent of the cases the hypnotic probes were said to have provided information that led to an arrest.

I

ICE Pick Kill: Murder technique

Long a favorite rub-out method of Mafia hit men, the so-called ice pick kill is employed to make a murder victim's death appear to be the result of natural causes. Generally, the victim is forced into a men's room or some isolated place, and while two or three of the hit men hold him still, the killer wielding the ice pick jams the weapon through his eardrum into the brain. The pick produces only a tiny hole in the ear and only a small amount of bleeding, which is carefully wiped clean, but massive bleeding occurs in the brain, causing death. Examination of the victim by a doctor generally results in a finding that the person has died of a cerebral hemorrhage. Only expert medical examiners are capable of uncovering murder. When a gangland murder victim is found with numerous ice pick wounds, police generally theorize the victim struggled so much that the normally meticulous execution proved impossible and the victim was simply ice-picked to death.

IDA The Goose War: New York underworld feud

If Homeric Greece had its Helen of Troy, the New York underworld had its Ida the Goose. Despite her rather unromantic name, the only one that has come down through posterity, Ida the Goose was a noted beauty, a maiden whose favors were traditionally reserved for the leaders of the notorious Gopher Gang of Hell's Kitchen. Ida was the last woman, so far as is known, to have caused a full-scale gang war over an affair of the heart.

In the early 1900s the Gophers were one of the most prominent gangs of the city, especially following the fractionalization of the powerful and bloody Eastman gang as a result of the imprisonment of their leader, Monk Eastman. One group of Eastmans, perhaps 400 to 500 strong, rallied to the banner of Chick Tricker, who maintained his headquarters at his own

Cafe Maryland on West 28th Street. The Tricker gangsters engaged in all sorts of criminality from robbery to homicide. Their main battles generally were fought against other former members of the Eastman gang who had joined up with Big Jack Zelig or Jack Sirocco. Tricker hardly wanted an additional war with the Gophers, but he proved powerless against the momentum of events that bore down on him.

It started when a tough Tricker gangster, Irish Tom Riley, who, despite his name, was probably a Spanish Jew, won the heart of Ida the Goose and lured her from the bosom of the Gophers to the Cafe Maryland. The enraged Gophers sent a delegation to retrieve their lost princess, but both she and her new lover refused to agree to her return to Hell's Kitchen. Tricker merely shrugged. He would not order the surrender of Ida, since that would represent a loss of face. Over the next several weeks the Gophers and the Trickers had numerous hand-to-hand confrontations, including a few nonfatal stabbings, but after a while finally it appeared the Gophers had lost interest in launching a total war to regain Ida the Goose.

Thus, it was a surprise when on a snowy night in October 1909 four Gophers brazenly strolled into the Maryland and ordered beer at the bar. About a half-dozen Trickers, their noted leader absent, sat at tables eyeing the intrusion with both shock and disbelief. Had Tricker himself been present, he probably would have ordered an immediate attack on the hated intruders. As it was, only Ida the Goose spoke up with indignation. "Say! Youse guys got a nerve!"

The Gophers silently drained their mugs and then one said, "Well, let's get at it!"

They whirled around, each man holding two revolvers, and opened fire. Five of the surprised Trickers went down, several mortally wounded. Only Ida's lover was unscathed, and he scrambled across the floor and dove under his lady's voluminous skirts. The Gophers made no move to shoot him, instead watching Ida the Goose to see what she would do.

The lady surveyed the scene a moment, shrugged and contemptuously raised her skirts. "Say, youse!," she said. "Come out and take it!"

Trembling on his hands and knees, her lover crawled out to the middle of the floor. Four revolvers barked and he fell dead with four slugs in him. One of the Gophers strode forward and put another bullet in his brain. The four assassins then turned and walked out to the street, followed at a respectful distance by Ida the Goose. She fully understood the honor bestowed on her by having been the cause of such a great battle and it was said that she nevermore strayed from her place of adornment in Hell's Kitchen.

See also: *Kiss of Death Girls.*

IMMIGRATION, Illegal: See *Pollos.*

IN Danger: **Primer for criminals**

Probably no book ever published in America was more blatantly an instruction guide to criminality than *In Danger, or Life in New York: A True History of a Great City's Wiles and Temptations,* which appeared in 1888. The book was signed, "Howe and Hummel, the Celebrated Criminal Lawyers." Howe and Hummel indeed were celebrated attorneys and probably the most corrupt New York has ever seen. As they declared in a moral-toned preface, the two wrote the book after being moved by a clergyman's sermon in which he had declared, "It had been well for many an honest lad and unsuspecting country girl that they had never turned their steps cityward nor turned them from the simplicity of their country home toward the snares and pitfalls of crime and vice that await the unwary in New York." That was the last piece of high-minded drivel to appear in the book, the rest of which was given over to a detailed guide on what to steal and how.

By way of invitation, Howe and Hummell wrote of "elegant storehouses, crowded with the choicest and most costly goods, great banks whose vaults and safes contain more bullion than could be transported by the largest ships, colossal establishments teeming with diamonds, jewelry, and precious stones gathered from all the known and uncivilized portions of the globe—all this countless wealth, in some cases so insecurely guarded."

Having thus whetted the appetites of novice and would-be criminals, they hastened to add that "all the latest developments in science and skill are being successfully pressed into the service of the modern criminal." The ever-helpful authors went into detailed technical descriptions of various devices used by jewel thieves and shoplifters, such as "the traveling bag with false, quick-opening sides . . . the shoplifter's muff . . . the lady thieves' corsets." There were instructions for making one's own burglar tools and descriptions of the methods used in various skin games and the mathematical formulas used for rigging cards. And did crime pay? Howe and Hummel never said so in so many words, but, e.g., of shoplifting they stated, "In no particular can the female shiplifter be distinguished from other members of her sex except perhaps that in most cases she is rather more richly and attractively dressed."

The great shysters also touted certain legal services available at "what we may be pardoned for designating the best-known criminal law offices in America."

In Danger was severely criticized by the police and denounced from the pulpits, but each fresh denunciation merely produced more sales of the book.

See also: *Howe and Hummel.*

INDIAN Police

One of the few techniques of self-government introduced by the white man to the Indian that had a modicum of success was the Indian police force and court system. The system proved popular with the Indians themselves because it took them away from the white man's justice, which for the red man simply did not exist.

The first to experiment with the concept of Indian police were Gen. George Crook and Indian agent John P. Clum, both of whom persisted despite being called the "Indian lovers." Even the anti-Indian Interior Department saw that the Indian police had value because they relieved the government of the need and expense of supplying troops to preserve peace on the reservations. Indians charged with committing crimes against other Indians were brought to Indian courts for trial and given justice that average Indians would accept as valid.

Clum made the most effective use of Indian police, and with their aid he brought in Geronimo in April 1877, scoring a great coup. Shortly thereafter, he informed the government he was prepared to supervise all the Apache in Arizona without the help of Army troops provided he be allowed to raise two companies of Indian police. The government, however, would not accept the proposal because it was assuming a more restrictive policy, including forced migration of the Indians. During those later migrations the loyal Indian police were treated as roughly and unfairly as any other Indians. By then Indian police were hated by most other Indians. From a certain perspective, they played the same sort of role performed by the police of the Warsaw ghetto during World War II. Certainly, the murder of Sitting Bull in 1890 by a number of Indian police was done at the instigation of white men wishing to avoid any direct involvement.

See also: *John P. Clum.*

INFANTICIDE

Next to spouse slaying, the most common type of murders within families is infanticide. It is estimated that parents kill about 600 or 700 children a year, or about three percent of the total murder toll. However, if killings not reported as murders could be counted, the infanticide rate would probably be much higher.

Very few cases of infanticide are committed by fathers, but experts agree this is simply because they have far less contact with babies than mothers have. Mothers who murder their offspring usually suffer from emotional disturbances and build up to the deed over a long period of time. Generally, less severe forms of child abuse provide warning signals of the impending tragedy. Some mothers become fearful of the possibility of what they might do to their children and have themselves committed. A California mother recently signed herself into Napa Hospital after trying to kill her two tiny sons. She received some therapy and was sent home. Later she killed both boys and then failed in a suicide attempt.

Judith Catchpole may or may not have been the first woman tried for infanticide in America, but she did establish a first of a kind. While surviving details of the case are somewhat sketchy, it is known that in September 1656 the first all-female jury in the colonies was empaneled in the General Provincial Court at Patuxent, Md. to hear evidence concerning the charge that she had murdered her child. Catchpole claimed she had never even been pregnant, and after hearing her evidence, the jury acquitted her.

In a bizarre case in Maryland in 1976, a 19-year-old mother killed her baby boy as she was dressing him to go to church service, while a young woman friend watched in horror. The mother started screaming she could see the devil trying to enter her baby and she tried to stop him by slapping the child and scratching at his navel—while he screamed in agony—and, finally, wringing the baby's neck. When the mother appeared in court five months later, all the parties—prosecution defense and psychiatrists—agreed she had been insane at the time of the act, and an insanity plea of not guilty was accepted. However, when the judge asked for testimony on her current condition, psychiatrists would not certify her as insane, and she was freed. Yet, the horror of society toward the crime of infanticide was exhibited in the legal treatment accorded to the woman friend who had watched the killing. Because she had not attempted to stop the mother's insane acts, for whatever reason, she was sentenced to a 7-year prison term.

When fathers do commit infanticide, the victim is almost always a boy, rarely either a daughter or a baby. The underlying motive may be an attempt to gain supremacy in the household, but occasionally, the motive has been monetary. On Halloween night 1974, in Pasadena, Tex. Ronald O'Bryan poisoned his eight-year-old son, Tim, with cyanide to collect the boy's $65,000 life insurance policy. O'Bryan was sentenced to the electric chair.

Because of the close-knit relationships involved and the horror of the crime, experts agree that a large number of infanticide cases are hushed up by families which, having one loss, see nothing to be gained from having another. Thus, it is generally believed that the rate of infanticide is greatly understated. Society also simply ignores other forms of infanticide. In a recent and already classic study of the subject, *Infanticide: Past and Present*, Maria W. Piers refers to babies who are "forgotten," or left behind, by their young mothers immediately after delivery. This happens especially in impoverished sections. Piers states: "Many of them probably assume that their babies will survive, but the assumption is incorrect. Because of insufficient hospital staff and the inefficiency of adoption procedures, human babies die in misery from sheer neglect, while authorities avert their eyes."

INFORMER: See Squealer.

INGALLS, Oklahoma Territory, Battle Of

One of the great gunfights of the West, the Battle of Ingalls on September 1, 1893 added significantly to the folklore of a dying era. The battle resulted from a disastrous effort by the law to capture the Bill Doolin gang, a hell-for-leather outfit that probably enjoyed greater down-home esteem than was ever achieved by the James gang or Butch Cassidy's Wild Bunch.

One of the gang's many headquarters was the clapboard town of Ingalls, some 10 miles east of Stillwater. In Ingalls they felt safe because the locals were friendly and sympathizers would hurry in with reports whenever a posse approached.

On the night of August 31, the U.S. marshal's office in Guthrie got a tip that the Doolin gang was carousing in Ingalls, and the following day a posse of marshals slipped into town in a covered wagon to wipe out the gang in one swoop. The lawmen might have succeeded in their mission had not one of the gang, Bitter Creek Newcomb, spotted them as he came out of Murray's Saloon. There is some indication that Newcomb had been tipped off. What followed was the celebrated Battle of Ingalls, which proved to be a resounding triumph for the outlaws. Three deputy marshals were killed, while all of the gang survived and only one of them, Arkansas Tom, who was asleep in his hotel room at the time, was captured as the rest were escaping, Bill Dalton's horse went down. Bill Doolin rode back for him, and the two of them shared the same mount in a daring dash to freedom. The most amazing escape of all, however, was Bitter Creek Newcomb's, who for a time was literally enveloped in mushrooming dust caused by the posse's bullets. He was wounded but survived to get away, an accomplishment so incredible that a very special savior was invented for him. The legend developed that Newcomb had lived through the battle because a daring young lass who loved him came charging to his rescue with an extra gunbelt of ammunition, that she shielded him with her own body and that she even provided protective fire for him. The best evidence is that there was no girl involved in any way in the fighting but the myth grew nonetheless.

The Battle of Ingalls became the Doolin gang's greatest feat, the lore of it persisting even after the outfit had disbanded and each member had been blasted into extinction. They sang praises of the great fight, and song and story recorded the heroic love of Newcomb and the "Rose of Cimarron," who supposedly had saved his life.

See also: *Bill Doolin, George "Bitter Creek" Newcomb, Rose of Cimarron.*

INNOCENTS: Western outlaws

A particularly inappropriate name, the Innocents were members of the most efficient gang of the frontier West, bossed by a magnetic personality, Henry Plummer, doubling as the Montana sheriff whose duty it was to contain the sudden rampage of criminality. The full story of the Innocents can never be told since it is impossible to pinpoint each of the hundreds of crimes they committed; the murders attributed to the band have been fixed by most historians at 102.

In 1862 Plummer, a lawman in California until he got into trouble because of a couple of messy murders and other, lesser infractions, drifted into what is now southwest Montana, where gold had been discovered. He assembled a large group of outlaws, including a number he had used in previous criminal endeavors in Idaho. Most were in their teens or early twenties. Plummer himself, a handsome rogue who had a way with women, was only 25 or so. Some historians have insisted that the Plummer gang was composed of murderous juvenile delinquents. But this overlooks the fact that it was traditional in the West for men to hit the outlaw trail at an extremely young age.

The Innocents operated with a certain childlike fervor and enthusiasm, terrorizing stagecoaches and miners hauling ore in and out of Bannack. Since at one time the Innocents totaled over 100 men, they needed secret ways of identifying themselves to one another and thus wore red bandanas with special sailor knots. They used a secret handclasp and the password "innocent" when meeting, under the assumption that saying such a word could hardly imply any kind of guilt.

The only recourse for the victims of the Innocents was the local sheriff, Henry Plummer, who, while sympathetic, seemed incapable of stemming the criminal tide. The Innocents, however, were too vast an organization not to spring leaks, and in time, suspicion spread to Plummer himself. A Montana vigilante movement sprang up, and in a six-week period in late 1863 and early 1864, they hung no less than 26 outlaws, including Plummer, who met his doom on a scaffold he had built himself as part of his legal duties. The rest of the gang scattered, although some others were to receive the same rough-hewn justice throughout the rest of the year.

Over the years Henry Plummer and his Innocents became the inspiration of a near-endless string of stories, books and movies depicting the nefarious activities of a crooked sheriff unmasked in the dramatic denouement.

See also: *Bannack, Montana; Thomas J. Dimsdale; Boone Helm; Haze Lyons; Henry Plummer; Cyrus Skinner, Vigilantes of Montana, Erastus "Red" Yager.*

INSANITY Defense

Most jurisdictions have statutes that protect insane or incompetent persons from criminal prosecution, but the legal responsibility of such persons varies considerably from place to place. Courts recognize that a person afflicted with insanity or a mental disorder may not be responsible for his actions and therefore not liable to prosecution. However, the legal tests for insanity have long been the subject of much confusion. Some states apply the "wild beast test," which requires that to be judged insane, the defendant must be so devoid of reason that

he no more knows what he is doing than would an infant, a brute or a wild beast. Others call for a "delusion test," whereby an accused criminal must be shown to have been suffering from delusions before he can be cleared of responsibility. A little over half the states abide by *M'Naghten Rules,* which hold an accused not responsible if he "was laboring under such a defect of reason, from disease of the mind, as not to know the nature and the quality of the act he was doing, or if he did know it, that he did not know he was doing what was wrong."

Some states adhere to the "right and wrong test," which centers on a defendant's ability to tell right from wrong. Another standard used is the "irresistible impulse test," which requires that in order to be considered sane there needs to exist, in addition to the capacity for intellectual judgment, the possibility of doing what is considered right and to refrain from doing what is thought to be wrong.

A striking case was that of William Milligan who was charged in 1977 with raping four Ohio State University coeds. Milligan was found to have 10 distinct personalities, and only one of which was criminal. The four coeds had the misfortune of meeting the wrong one of the 10. He was found not guilty by reason of insanity and shipped off to a mental institution. Similarly, Howard Unruh, the New Jersey mass murderer who killed 13 neighbors and strangers in the streets of Camden in 1949 never faced trial for his crimes. Instead, he was sent to the Trenton State Hospital where some three decades later he was described as quiet and withdrawn, a man in his late fifties who mostly reads or sits around.

The law's treatment of insane persons charged with crimes has been the subject of much criticism because such persons are frequently released from confinement. If it were merely a simple choice of finding a murderer, for instance, either guilty and sending him to prison or finding him insane and sending him to a mental institution, such criticism would be muted. However, the decision is not always so clear-cut. A not unusual case, which occurred in California in 1976, involved a mother who had killed her baby in a religious frenzy. She pleaded guilty on the ground of insanity, a contention of considerable merit considering her many previous acts of crazed violence. It appeared logical that she would simply be sent to a mental institution when the judge accepted her plea. However, while a number of mental experts agreed the woman had been of unsound mind when she killed her infant, the preponderance of opinion on her "current condition" was that she was not certifiably insane. Under the circumstances, the judge was forced to release her and, legally, could not even require her to undergo psychiatric treatment.

Because of numerous publicized cases of this type, jurors have developed a form of "sophistication," rightly or wrongly, leading to their refusal in many cases to bring in a verdict of insanity for fear the defendant might at some later date be inflicted upon society again. As a result, several observers agree, obviously insane persons are being convicted and placed in prison, a terrible ordeal both for the person and the institution.

A typical example of this sort was mass murderer Herbert

William Mullin, who, between October 1972 and February 1973, killed at least 13 persons. Mullin called his victims "sacrifices" and killed them because he was convinced their deaths were necessary to ward off a predicted cataclysmic earthquake in California. Mullin's record showed five previous hospital releases after he had voluntarily committed himself each time. The jurors were described as fearful of what would happen if they judged him insane and he was later discharged from the hospital for the sixth time. Consequently, they were said to have ignored all the evidence concerning his mental condition when they brought in a guilty verdict, requiring him to be sent to prison.

Perhaps because of this trend, the courts in recent years have become more concerned with protecting the rights of allegedly insane persons charged with crimes. Juan Corona was convicted in 1972 for the murders of 25 itinerant farm workers, whose mutilated bodies had been found in shallow graves in the peach orchards around Yuba City, Calif. However, in 1978 the courts ordered a new trial for Corona on the ground that his attorney had failed to provide him with proper representation. Corona had a history of hallucinations and mental illness, but his lawyer had refused a psychiatric examination for him and presented no witnesses on the subject of his mental state. The appeal judges made it clear they did not doubt the evidence against Corona, but ruled he was entitled to mental competency hearings. At the time of the ruling, a number of California legal authorities predicted Corona would never be returned to prison. Because of the state of the law on insanity questions, a number of new cause celebres will no doubt emerge in the coming years.

INSULL, Samuel (1860-1938): Stock manipulator

Among the most grandiose swindlers of the 20th century, Samuel Insull built up a multibillion-dollar Midwest utility empire, one of the great financial marvels of the 1920s, by merging troubled small electric companies into an apparently smooth-running combine. He was hailed by the nation's press as the financial genius of the age, and lucky was the banker from whom Mr. Insull deigned to borrow money.

Clearly outdoing even Horatio Alger, Insull began his career as a 14-year-old dropout in his native London and rose to the pinnacle of high finance. He first worked as an office boy for $1.25 a week and later became a clerk for Thomas A. Edison's London agent. He was so impressive that he was recommended to Edison as a youth worth bringing to America, and the great inventor made him his secretary in 1881; Insull was 21 at the time.

Soon, Insull was handling the organization of several Edison companies and by 1902 he was president of Chicago Edison. In 1907 he merged all the electric companies there into Commonwealth Edison. He then struck out on his own, joining small, often poorly run utilities into one operation. By the 1920s he was among the nation's richest men, worth $100 million, and people felt they were making the smartest investment in America when they purchased his stock.

The secret of Insull's success was to have one of his electric companies sell properties to another of his companies at a handsome profit over the original cost. The second company would not be hurt because it would later sell other properties to yet another Insull company. Thus, even in 1931, at the depths of the Depression, Insull's Middle West Utilities group reported the second most profitable year in its history. Of course, by this time Insull had to do more than sell properties to himself. He started cutting depreciation allowances in his various utilities or eliminating them entirely.

Then Insull had to spend huge sums—which he took in from gullible investors—to fight off takeover bids from other Wall Street operators eager to latch onto a strong financial organization. The problem was that if a takeover occurred the buyers would soon discover that Insull had done it all with mirrors. The swindler spent $60 million in the battle and won, but his financial empire was now so weak the bubble had to burst. The collapse came in June 1932, with investor losses estimated at $750 million.

Broke at the age of 72, Insull fled to Paris, where he lived on a yearly pension of $21,000 from a few companies of his that hadn't gone under. Facing extradition back to the United States on embezzlement and mail fraud charges, the old man left France and went to Greece. The Greek government let him stay a year but then bowed to U.S. pressure and ordered him out. For a time Insull drifted about the Mediterranean in a leased tramp steamer, but he finally had to put in at Istanbul for supplies. The Turks arrested him and shipped him back home for trial.

Because Insull's financial capers were so involved and often fell into areas where the law was not really clear, the government failed to prove its charges and he was able to go back to Paris. He dropped dead on a street there at the age of 78. At the time, he had assets of $1,000 cash and debts of $14 million.

INSURANCE Frauds—Faked Deaths

Cases of "dead men" turning up alive are common in insurance company fraud files, although the industry has never seen the virtue of publishing any statistics on the subject. There is, of course, even less information on those who have gotten away with such fraud. One of the most-publicized disappearance frauds of all was perpetrated in the 1930s by John H. Smith, who had once run for governor of Iowa. Smith made it look as if he had been burned to death in an auto accident, substituting an embalmed body in his fire-gutted car. Mrs. Smith later confessed her husband had faked his own death to fleece an insurance firm out of $60,000 stating, "Under our plan, I was to collect the insurance or accept it when the insurance company paid it to me, and then meet John when he got in communication with me, which might be from one to two years."

Smith might have gotten away with his plot had he not developed a roving eye. He committed bigamy during his disappearance by marrying an 18-year-old Kansas farm girl. That was something Mrs. Smith hadn't agreed to, and since her wounded pride meant more to her than $60,000, she screamed for the law as soon as she learned what her husband had done.

Probably the longest successful insurance disappearance was pulled off by socially prominent Thomas C. Buntin of Nashville, Tenn. who vanished in 1931. Shortly thereafter, Buntin's 22-year-old secretary also disappeared. Buntin had $50,000 in insurance, and after waiting the customary seven years, the insurance company paid off the claim. However, the firm, New York Life, did not close the case. It kept up a search for Buntin, and in 1953—some 22 years after he vanished—the company found him living in Orange, Tex. with his ex-secretary under the name Thomas D. Palmer. For 22 years the couple had posed as Mr. and Mrs. Palmer and had even raised a family.

A trust fund had been established with the money from Buntin's insurance policy and there was still $31,000 left when he turned up alive. The insurance company immediately launched legal action to get the money. As for Buntin, he obviously had not benefitted personally from the fraud. What was the reason? Very often a husband wishing to leave his wife and knowing he cannot expect a divorce will use a disappearing act to get out from under. Along with acquiring his freedom, the man can feel he has discharged all his duties as a husband and father by defrauding an insurance company into providing for his family. In the end, Buntin and his former secretary suffered no penalties from the law. In fact, after they were exposed, their neighbors sent them flowers.

Of course, producing a dead body will make a faked death even more convincing, but this often entails murder. In the 1930s Philadelphia's notorious Bolber-Petrillo murder ring specialized in killing off husbands so their wives could claim the insurance. Occasionally, they worked with a loving couple who wanted to enjoy the fruits of the husband's life insurance policy while he was still alive. In such cases the ring would kill an itinerant stranger and use him as a stand-in corpse for the husband.

Another famous insurance fraud murderer was Charles Henry Schwartz, a sort of mad scientist. When Schwartz ran his business into the ground in the 1920s, he looked for someone to use as a substitute corpse so that he could collect $200,000 in insurance. He settled on a traveling evangelist, Warren Gilbert Barbe, and murdered him in his Berkeley, Calif. laboratory. Since Barbe didn't look much like him, Schwartz worked hard on his substitute. Because Schwartz had a scar on his own chest, he burned away a section of Barbe's chest. He pulled out two teeth from the murdered man's upper jaw to match his own missing teeth. To take care of the difference in eye color between the two, Schwartz punctured his victim's eyeballs, and then for added protection, he blew up the laboratory. Despite all this, the corpse was soon identified as someone

other than Schwartz and the latter was exposed. To avoid imprisonment he committed suicide.

Beyond doubt the prize victim of all insurance swindles was a beautiful but gullible model named Marie Defenbach. She was persuaded by a Dr. August M. Unger to join him and two accomplices in a fraud in which she was to take out $70,000 worth of life insurance and then fake her own death. The men were to be her beneficiaries and were to give her half the money. Dr. Unger assured Marie he would personally handle her "demise." He would give her a special medicine of his own that would induce a deathlike sleep. Later, the doctor convinced her, she would be revived in the back room of an undertaking establishment and spirited away, with an unclaimed body left in her place for cremation. If Marie had had any sense, she would have realized that it would save the man a lot of bother and money if they just fed her some old-fashioned poison. But Marie was already mentally counting her loot.

On the evening of August 25, 1900, Marie blithely informed her Chicago landlady she was feeling ill, and she sent a messenger to get her some medicine. Fifteen minutes after taking it, she died in terrible agony. In due course, the true nature of Marie's death was uncovered by a suspicious uncle, whose investigation finally led to the arrest and conviction of the culprits.

In a curious sidelight to insurance frauds, the man responsible for the fact that few insurance company investigators carry weapons while on the job was a New Jersey man named J. R. Barlow, who had a wife and a $200,000 life insurance policy. One day he swam out from a beach and never swam back. His wife reported him as missing and applied for the insurance. The insurance company was suspicious, however, and after an intensive investigation traced Barlow to Mexico. When he was confronted by an insurance agent, Barlow turned violent, and in the ensuing struggle the investigator was forced to shoot him. Ironically, the insurance company was then compelled to pay off on his death. Soon after, the company issued a rule forbidding investigators to carry weapons.

See also: *Warren Gilbert Barbe, Bolber-Petrillo Murder Ring, Marie Defenbach.*

INTERROGATION Methods: See Confessions.

IRVING, Clifford (1930–): Howard Hughes book forger

In 1971 writer Clifford Irving pulled off what was undoubtedly the most celebrated literary hoax of the 20th century when he swindled the McGraw-Hill Book Co. out of $765,000 for a fake autobiography of billionaire recluse Howard R. Hughes. Irving also conned Life Magazine, which planned to print excerpts of the book with 20 pages of handwritten letters by Hughes. After examining the letters, a number of handwriting experts had declared all of them to be genuine.

Together with a friend who was a children's book author, Richard Suskind, Irving wrote an engrossing 1,200 page book, which veteran newsmen who had long covered the enigmatic Hughes found to be most "authentic." The scheme was so daring and so outrageous it was widely accepted even after Hughes said in a telephone call from his hideaway in the Bahamas that he had never met with Irving and that the work was "totally fantastic fiction." Irving's hoax was finally wrecked

Clifford Irving's phony biography of Howard Hughes earned him a dubious distinction from *Time* magazine.

when a Swiss bank broke its vow of secrecy to reveal that a $650,000 check from the book publisher to Hughes had been cashed in one Swiss bank by "H. R. Hughes" and deposited in another under the name "Helga R. Hughes"—actually Irving's wife.

On March 13, 1972 Irving pleaded guilty to federal conspiracy charges. He was forced to return what was left of the publisher's money and was sentenced to 2½ years in prison. He served 17 months.

In 1977 Irving was asked by the editors of the *Book of Lists* to compile a list of the 10 best forgers of all time. He listed Clifford Irving as number nine.

ISRAEL, Harold (1901-): Wrong man

One of America's most famous "wrong man" murder cases wrecked the elective political career of a prosecutor named Homer S. Cummings in the 1920s. The case was the murder of a popular minister in Bridgeport, Conn.

In 1924 an unidentified person shot Father Hubert Dahma, pastor of St. Joseph's Episcopal Church, in the back of the head, throwing the city into an uproar. Both the city government and a local newspaper offered rewards, and the public demanded the police come up with a solution to the crime. This they appeared to do by arresting an itinerant young man, 23-year-old Harold Israel. After many hours of questioning, Israel made a confession. He later tried to retract it but there was no denying that when apprehended, he had been carrying a gun of the same caliber as the murder weapon. In addition, police had the testimony of a ballistics expert that Israel's gun had been the murder weapon.

Since Father Dahme was one of Bridgeport's most popular citizens, the pressure on prosecutor Cummings was enormous. There was press speculation that a conviction in the case would earn the state's attorney a sure nomination for governor. Cummings was a former chairman of the Democratic National Committee, keynote speaker at the 1920 national convention in San Fancisco and, indeed, Connecticut's favorite son for the presidential nomination. Under the circumstances, it would have been quite logical for Cummings to have accepted the sure conviction handed him. Amazingly, he did not.

Even though the public defender announced that Israel would plead guilty by reason of insanity, Cummings had strong misgivings about the case. The prosecution regarded some of the witnesses who had sworn Israel was the priest's killer as less than reliable. When he checked the area where the murder had occurred and where the witnesses said they had been standing, he determined it would have been too dark for them to recognize anyone. Cummings also had his doubts about the ballistics expert, who struck him as overly anxious to help the police solve the crime. He asked six other experts in the field to make their own findings without telling any of them that others were doing the same work. All six agreed that Israel's gun had not fired the fatal bullet.

When Israel's case came to trial, Cummings made an opening presentation outlining the findings that had weakened the prosecution's case. He then calmly proceeded to load the so-called murder gun. He aimed it downward at a 45 degree angle—the position the murder gun had been in—and pulled the trigger. Nothing happened. The gun, Cummings explained, had a defective firing pin and would not fire when held in that particular position.

On Cummings' motion, Israel was released. The prosecutor personally escorted the happy youth to the train station and saw him off to his home in Pennslyvania. It's possible that Cummings felt his presence was necessary to keep the police from rearresting Israel.

Years later, the Israel case was made into a movie called *Boomerang*. While Cummings won considerable praise in many circles for his work in the case, he did not get quite as much as he deserved in his native state. When Israel was cleared, Cummings' chance for the governorship fizzled. In 1933, however, he was named by President Franklin D. Roosevelt to be attorney general. As for Israel himself, he faded into obscurity, to which Cummings felt he was entitled. Still, Cummings wondered if his clearing of the young man had paid off and in the late 1930's he ordered the FBI to make a secret check on him. The agency reported that Israel was a respectable miner in Pennsylvania, a married man, the father of two children and a pillar of the Methodist Church.

ITALIAN Dave Gang: 19th century New York pickpocket gang

From the 1840s to the 1860s the most notorious Fagin in America was the New York criminal mastermind named Italian Dave. He always had some 40 or so boys aged nine to 15 whom he instructed in the art of pickpocketing and sneak thievery. He provided the boys with room and board in an old tenement on Paradise Square and conducted daily classes in various techniques of theft. They were shown how to pinch articles from store windows and counters, how to beg and, with the aid of fully dressed dummies of men and women in various positions, how to pick pockets and snatch purses and muffs. Whenever a boy fumbled his assignment, Italian Dave would ceremoniously dress himself in a policeman's uniform and work him over with a nightstick. Other thieves and gangs would rent out squads of boys for specific criminal assignments such as lookouts, with all money paid directly to Italian Dave.

Dave took advanced students out into the streets himself and would point out victims to be robbed, observing his pupils' modus operandi with a most critical eye. When a student failed to use a club on a mugging victim with sufficient stunning effect, Italian Dave would step forward and demonstrate how to do it properly. His most apt pupils deserted him within a couple of years because he was so miserly, giving them only pennies out of what they stole. However, long after Italian Dave passed from the scene, his pupils continued to benefit from his harsh lessons; among his students were master pickpockets Blind Mahoney and Jimmy Dunnigan and the redoubtable gang leader Jack Mahaney, who later became known as the American version of Jack Sheppard, the famous British escape artist, because of his ability to escape from custody.

See also: *Jack Mahaney.*

IVERS, Alice: See Poker Alice.

IZZY And Moe: Revenue agents

Prohibition brought many things to the American scene: speakeasies, rot-gut liquor, gangsters, hijacking and "the ride." But Prohibition had its comic side as well, as demonstrated by the merry antics of those dry clowns Izzy and Moe. They were the greatest and wackiest Prohibition agents of all time and they fit right into the Roaring Twenties. The newspapers gave front-page coverage to their capers, one joyously announcing, "IZZY IS BIZZY AND SO IS MOE." Hundreds of hilarious newspaper stories were written about the pair and a great many of them were no doubt true.

In 1920 Isadore Einstein was a short, smiling cherub of 225 pounds who worked as a clerk for the New York Post Office. Previously, he had been a dry goods salesman. One day Izzy showed up at the Federal Prohibition Bureau headquarters and announced his availability. That got a laugh. "Izzy," one official said, "you don't even look like a Prohibition agent." On reflection, it was decided that Izzy might thus be handy to have around and he got the job. A product of the polyglot Lower East Side, he could speak fluent Yiddish, Hungarian, Polish, German and Italian.

Bizzy Izzy and Moe, as the newspapers dubbed them, were the clown princes of Prohibition enforcement, using many disguises to make their busts.

Bureau officials figured the worst that could happen was that a few tough assignments would send Izzy in hasty retreat back to the Post Office. They decided to send him out to hit a 52nd Street speakeasy. A dozen agents had previously tried and failed to bust the place. A few had gotten past the front door but they were served nothing stronger than beer because they couldn't produce a regular customer as a sponsor.

Izzy talked his way into the speakeasy, waddled up to the bar, plunked down his newly acquired badge and said to the bartender, 'How about a good stiff drink for a thirsty revenue agent?"

The bartender nearly doubled up with laughter. "Get a load of this funny fat man!" he called to his customers. Then, fingering Izzy's badge, he asked, "Where did you buy this?"

"Give me a drink and I'll take you to the place sometime," Izzy replied.

The bartender obliged. So did Izzy. He took the man down to the Revenue Office.

Izzy's superiors were stunned . . . and immediately assigned him to another tough case. Izzy made that pinch as well.

After a few weeks on the job, Izzy started to miss his old coffeehouse buddy, Moe Smith. He asked if they had a job for Moe as well. The only trouble was, Izzy noted, that Moe didn't look like an agent either; he was fat like Izzy. Moe got the job and the pair worked as a team, a sort of Laurel and Hardy of the Revenuers—except both were Hardy. They were so effective that some speakeasies posted pictures of the two, but that proved futile. The pair disguised themselves with false whiskers and noses. On occasion they wore blackface. Once, they donned football uniforms to bust a joint serving the thirsty athletes playing in Van Cortlandt Park in the Bronx. To crack a Coney Island speakeasy in midwinter, Izzy went swimming with a polar bear cub and was then carried quivering into the establishment by a solicitous Moe. "Quick," Moe cried, "some liquor before he freezes to death." A tenderhearted bartender complied and was arrested.

Another time, the pair marched into a speakeasy arguing loudly about the name of a particular revenue sleuth. Was it Einstein or Epstein? The bartender agreed it was Einstein. Nonsense, said Izzy, and bet the bartender double the price for two drinks. The bartender won the bet and got pinched.

Because they needed to produce liquor served them as proof of a crime, Izzy and Moe designed special funnels to be strapped inside their vests. One time, they started out at 5 a.m. and made 24 arrests by 9 a.m., just working up an appetite for breakfast. The pair's all-time record was 65 raids in one day.

Their standard line when making a pinch was "Dere's sad news here." Over a five-year period their combined score was five million bottles of liquor confiscated, 4,392 persons arrested and convictions achieved in 95 percent of their cases, which was 20 percent of all the successful illegal liquor prosecutions in the New York district. Everybody loved Izzy-and-Moe stories. Stanley Walker once said, "Izzy and Moe almost made prohibition popular."

Once Izzy met his namesake—Albert Einstein. He asked him what he did for a living. "I discover stars in the sky," the scientist replied. "I'm a discoverer too," Izzy said, "only I discover in the basements."

Izzy and Moe became so famous that other bureaus began asking for the pair's help in busting some problem spots in their cities. In Pittsburgh they made a pinch within 11 minutes of leaving the train depot. In Atlanta it took 17 minutes and Chicago and St. Louis 21. They set their record in New Orleans: 35 seconds.

Unfortunately, Izzy and Moe were called on the carpet often because of their penchant for publicity. They were warned that the service had to be dignified in its procedures. Finally, in November 1925 the boys turned in their badges. Izzy explained, "I fired myself," because they were to be transferred away from their beloved New York to the wilds of Chicago. Bureau officials insisted they had been dismissed "for the good of the service."

Both men went into the insurance business and soon numbered among their clients many of the people they had arrested for liquor violations. Izzy even published an autobiography, *Prohibition Agent Number 1,* which didn't sell very well.

See also: *Prohibition.*

J

JACKSON, Andrew: Victim of assassination attempt

On January 3, 1835 the first attempt on the life of a United States president took place when Andrew Jackson was attacked in the rotunda of the Capitol while attending the funeral of a South Carolina congressman, Warren Ransom Davis. A house painter named Richard Lawrence stepped up to President Jackson and, at a distance of six feet, fired two pistols at him. Both misfired and Jackson's would-be slayer was seized. Lawrence, who believed he was the rightful heir to the English throne, was committed to an insane asylum.

JACKSON, Eddie (1873-1932): Pickpocket

Among authorities on the subject, there are those who say that Eddie Jackson was the most proficient pickpocket America has ever produced. Jackson lifted his first poke when he was 14 and is said to have been the greatest "kiss-the-sucker" operator of all times. Kissing the sucker is walking right up to the victim, bumping him in front and lifting his wallet from his inside coat pocket in one quick motion. It is not a technique that many pickpockets, or "dips," like to employ since there are far easier and safer methods. Of course, Jackson used other techniques as well. Generally operating with three or four accomplices, he would use his nimble fingers to lift a victim's money while the others jostled him and diverted his attention. He usually worked Chicago's Loop district, often making as much as $1,500 a week, an incredible sum for the 1890s and early 1900s.

Jackson kept a famous lawyer and politician, Black Horton, on retainer, and when he and his mob were working, they would report to Horton every hour. Whenever they failed to report, Horton immediately hurried to the police station with bail money and a writ of habeas corpus. Over a career that spanned 40 years, Jackson was arrested some 2,000 times.

Pickpockets are subject to frequent arrests, especially on loitering charges but he generally avoided prosecution by giving back a portion of his loot. He was only convicted twice, sentenced once to 10 days and another time to a year. In later years the "Jackson touch" abandoned him and he died a pauper in 1932.

JACKSON, Frank (1856-?): Texas outlaw

In the folklore of Texas outlaws, Frank Jackson is remembered for his refusal to betray his legendary outlaw chief, Sam Bass, and perhaps more importantly, as a man whose loyalty was probably rewarded with the secret of Bass's hidden treasure troves.

Born in Llano County, Texas. in 1856 and orphaned when he was seven, Jackson grew up with relatives, training as a tinsmith. The occupation held little attraction for the youth, and by 1876 he was working as a cowhand at the Murphy Ranch in Denton County. From time to time, the Murphys harbored the notorious outlaw Sam Bass. Making the outlaw's acquaintance, Jackson quickly enlisted in the gang, thereafter taking part in all the gang's Texas train robberies.

Bass accumulated a considerable amount of his loot in the form of $20 gold pieces and buried it in several places in the hills and hollows northwest of Dallas. Frank Jackson's last ride with Sam Bass occurred in July 1878, when he, Bass and Seaborn Barnes attempted to hold up a small bank in Round Rock. They were betrayed by another gang member, Jim Murphy of the ranching family. Barnes was killed and Bass badly wounded in the ensuing gun battle. With Jackson's help Bass was able to ride out of town. The next day trackers found Bass dying in a woodland. For 24 hours lawmen questioned the outlaw, trying to get him to reveal his accomplices on various robberies and the hiding places of his loot before he died. Bass kept his silence to the end, and Frank Jackson was never seen again. The circumstances fueled speculation in Texas cow coun-

THE ATTEMPTED ASSASSINATION,
OF THE PRESIDENT OF UNITED STATES, JAN. 30.1835.
As the Funeral Procession of the Hon. Warren R. Davis, was about moving from the Capitol of the United States Richard Lawrence, a supposed maniac, rushed from the crowd, and snapped two heavily loaded pistols immediately at the body of President Jackson, both of which Providentially missed fire! Lawrence was instantly arrested by persons present, examined by Judge Cranch, and committed for trial.

Andrew Jackson remained convinced that the attempt on his life by an insane house painter was inspired by his political foes.

try that Bass must have encouraged the steadfast Jackson to leave him to die and told him where the gang's accumulated loot had been buried. Jackson was presumed to have retired from the outlaw trail a wealthy man.

See also: *Sam Bass, Jim Murphy.*

JACKSON, Humpty (?-1914): New York gang leader and murderer

One of New York's most-feared gang leaders at the turn of the century, Humpty Jackson was an odd combination of cold-blooded murderer and bibliophile. A man with a superior education, although a hazy past, he bossed some 50 gangsters, many of whom later became notorious in their own right. Among them were Spanish Louie, Nigger Ruhl, the Grabber and the Lobster Kid.

Humpty was never without a book on his person. His favorite writers were Voltaire, Darwin, Huxley and Spencer and he often read various tomes in Greek and Latin. His scholarly pursuits, however, did not carry over into his professional life, which was thoroughly dedicated to crime. He always carried three revolvers in his person—one in his pocket, another slung under his hunchback, which is why he was called Humpty, and the third in a special holder in his derby hat.

Jackson's headquarters was an old graveyard between First and Second avenues bound by 12th and 13th streets. Sitting on a tombstone, he would dispense criminal assignments to his thugs. If a customer wanted someone blackjacked or otherwise assaulted, he or she simply approached Humpty and for $100, in the case of blackjacking, he would see the job was done. Naturally, Jackson never soiled his own hands on such chores but merely handed them out to one of his men. Similarly, he would plan burglaries or warehouse lootings but seldom lead the forays himself. Nevertheless, Jackson was a man with a volatile temper who committed many acts of violence, which earned him more than 20 arrests and convictions. In 1909 he was sentenced to 20 years for ordering the execution of a man he'd never met. He died behind bars in 1914.

See also: *Spanish Louie.*

JACKSON, Mary Jane "Bricktop" (1836-?): Female ruffian and murderess

Nicknamed Bricktop because of her flaming red hair, Mary Jane Jackson was reputedly the most vicious street criminal, male or female, New Orleans has ever produced. Any number of the Live Oak gangsters, the city's toughest gang, backed off from confrontations with her. In about a decade of battling, Bricktop Jackson never lost a fight, killed four men and sent at least two dozen more to the hospital, from which many emerged permanently maimed. When she took up living with a notorious criminal named John Miller, the pair became known as New Orleans' toughest couple.

Born on Girod Street in 1836, Bricktop, a husky, well-endowed girl, became a prostitute at age 13. The next year she attained a measure of security when a saloon keeper took her as his mistress. When he tired of her after three years and threw her out, she charged into his saloon and gave him a fearsome beating, sending him to the hospital minus an ear and most of his nose. Bricktop then entered a Dauphine Street whorehouse, where, while she gained a following with the customers, she terrified the other girls. She was turned out of the Dauphine street establishment and subsequently, several other brothels. Bricktop was headed for the dance halls of New Orleans' toughest thoroughfare, Gallatin Street, and got a job with the redoubtable Archie Murphy in his notorious Dance-House. Nothing was considered too rough for Murphy's place, but Bricktop Jackson proved the exception to the rule. She had to be forcibly evicted from there as well as many other tough dance houses, whose owners had foolishly thought they could control her. Bricktop finally became a free-lance prostitute and street mugger. In 1856 she killed her first man and in 1857 her second; one had called her a "whore" and gotten clubbed to death for the insult, and the other, Long Charley, had been cut down with Bricktop's made-to-order knife following an argument over which way he would fall if stabbed (the nearly seven-foot-tall Charley was reported to have fallen forward when Bricktop tested her hypothesis.)

One of Bricktop's more famous murders occurred on November 7, 1859, when she visited a beer garden with two other vicious vixens, America Williams and Ellen Collins. A man at the next table, Laurent Fleury, objected to Bricktop's language and told her to shut up. Bricktop cursed even more and threatened to cut Fleury's heart out. Fleury, who had not recognized the scourge of Gallatin Street, slapped her. In a second the three women were all over him and the luckless Fleury disappeared in a mass of flailing hands, swirling skirts and flashing knives. Joe Seidensahl, the owner of the beer garden, tried to come to his rescue but was driven back, severely cut up. A Seidensahl employee shot at the women from a second floor window, but they drove him off with a barrage of bricks. By the time the police arrived, they found Fleury dead and his pants pocket cut out. The pocket, with money still inside, was found tucked under Bricktop's skirt. She was locked up in Parish Prison but eventually freed when an autopsy failed to show the victim's cause of death. Bricktop's lawyer contended he had died of heart disease.

It was in Parish Prison that Bricktop Jackson met a man who was, for the time, the love of her life, a jailer and ex-criminal named John Miller. The pair became a colorful item, even by Gallatin Street standards. Miller had lost an arm in a previous escapade and now walked about with a chain and iron ball attached to his stump, which made an awesome weapon. The couple supported themselves by close teamwork based on their respective skills. Bricktop would start up a romance with a stranger in a French Quarter dive and repair to the back streets with him. The man would end up with a very sore skull, no recollection of what happened and empty pockets.

The romance between Bricktop and Miller was marred by a dispute over who was the master of their nest. One day in 1861 Miller came home and decided to bullwhip Bricktop into subservience. She snatched the whip away from him, however, and gave him a bloody beating. He lashed out with his iron ball but she seized the chain in midair and began dragging him around the room. Miller pulled out a knife and slashed at Bricktop, who bit the knife free, grabbed it and then stabbed her lover five times. It was a fatal end to their relationship and one that caused Bricktop to be sent to prison for 10 years. She was released after only nine months when Gen. George F. Shepley, the military governor of the state, practically emptied the penitentiary with blanket pardons. Upon her release, Bricktop Jackson disappeared from New Orleans, a loss that went totally unlamented by honest and dishonest citizens alike.

See also: *John Miller.*

JACKSON-DICKINSON Duel

In the famous, or infamous, duel between Andrew Jackson and Charles Dickinson in 1806, there was no quarter given. Although Dickinson was considered to be the best shot in Tennessee, Jackson had challenged him after he had made disparaging remarks about Jackson's wife, Rachel. The duel was fought at a range of 24 feet. Dickinson got off the first shot, which crashed into Jackson's chest, missing his heart by only an inch. Blood gushed through his clothes, but Jackson managed to keep his feet, though unsteadily. He took dead aim at Dickinson, who broke and ran from the line of fire. The seconds ordered Dickinson back to his previous position, as the dueling code required, and he stood awaiting Jackson's shot with his arms crossed to protect his heart. Jackson aimed a bit lower at his target and fired, hitting Dickinson in the groin. Death came slowly and excruciatingly to Dickinson. Jackson carried the lead ball he had received until the end of his days, it being too close to the heart to be removed.

JAMES Brothers

The James brothers, especially Jesse, who was born in 1847, were probably the best-known outlaws in America, leading a gang of robbers from 1866 to 1882, when Jesse was assassinated for the reward on his head. Since then his niche in American folklore has remained secure, perhaps typified by a ballad that surfaced instantly after his death. It started:

> Jesse James was a lad who killed many a man.
> He robbed the Glendale train.
> He stole from the rich and he gave to the poor,
> He'd a hand and a heart and a brain.

Jesse James was the American version of Robin Hood, as the loving tales told about him reveal. He was the holdup man who stole money from the wicked banker about to foreclose and gave it to the poor widow to pay off her mortgage (and then—perhaps to embellish the fantasy—he restole the money from the banker). He fought for the oppressed, saved the frail from the bully and so on. But the truth is that he and his brother Frank, four years his elder, never once gave a penny to the poor. What they stole they kept. They were ruthless, desperate men who killed anyone who got in their way.

Yet they were popular. Reflecting the political alignment of a border state in the aftermath of the Civil War, Jesse became a hero to the defeated Rebels and those who had sympathized with the South and was invariably described as having been driven to his crimes because of persecution by Northerners, particularly businessmen. Ex-Unionists and abolitionists called the Jameses and their frequent allies, the Youngers, murderers and thieves and said they were deserving of hanging.

The James boys were born in Clay County, Mo., the sons of a preacher, the Rev. Robert James, who died when Jesse was three. During the Civil War, Frank joined Quantrill's Raiders and continued to ride with him even after it became apparent he was nothing more than a plunderer and butcher. In 1864, at the age of 17, Jesse hooked up with Confederate guerrillas under Bloody Bill Anderson and took part in the Centralia massacre that year, in which he is reputed to have brutally murdered a Union officer.

Jesse came out of the war badly wounded and was nursed back to health by a cousin, Zerelda Mimms, whom he would eventually marry. Even though the conflict was over, neither the James boys nor Cole Younger and his brothers saw any reason to stop their looting. They formed a gang and robbed $17,000 from a bank in Liberty, Mo. on February 13, 1866, killing a bystander in the process. It is known that they committed a number of additional bank robberies, but later practically every bank job in Missouri from 1866 to 1869 was attributed to them. There is no doubt that the James-Younger gang robbed the bank at Gallatin in 1869, since all of them were well identified. After that, they ranged as far afield as Alabama and Iowa. Jesse often provided a touch of verve to the capers. Once, they hit a bank while a political rally was taking place, and Jesse, on the way out, stopped in front of the crowd and ernestly informed them he thought there might be something wrong back at the bank. Perhaps their most audacious outing

occurred at a fair in Kansas City where Jesse and his men rode right up into a crowd of 10,000 people and robbed the box office of $10,000. Many persons thought it was all part of the show until a little girl was shot.

What made the James boys popular in much of Missouri was their harassment of railroad officials, perhaps the most-hated group in the state because of their seizure of private lands under condemnation orders, for which they paid a mere pittance. The gang's first known train robbery was in 1873, when they derailed the Chicago and Rock Island express near Adair, Iowa. As happened during many of their jobs, someone died during the holdup, in this case the engineer when the train derailed.

Cole
Younger

Jesse
James

Frank
James

Bob
Younger
(rear)

The alliance between the James brothers and the Youngers eventually foundered over Jesse's readiness to sacrifice any member of the gang as the price for escape.

The James-Younger move into train robberies put them in the big time and the Pinkertons on their trail. In January 1875, the Pinkertons were convinced the James brothers were holed up in their mother's home and laid siege to it. In an effort to flush them out, the detectives threw in a bomb—the agency later insisted it was only a flare—and when the smoke cleared, the brothers' 9-year-old half-brother, Archie, was dead and their mother, Mrs. Zerelda Samuels, had had most of her right arm blown off. The incident stoked great resentment toward the Pinkertons and brought forth a rash of sympathy for the James boys, not only in Missouri but throughout the country. Lost in the shuffle of support for the outlaws was an recollection of their own long list of victims. The bungling Pinkertons had done as much as anybody to make them respectable.

In 1876 disaster struck the gang when they attempted to rob the First National Bank of Northfield, Minn. Of the eight gang members, including the James brothers and three Younger brothers, only Jesse and Frank escaped when things went wrong and the citizenry came out shooting. The rest were either killed, captured there or in the ensuing chase.

For the next three years the James boys were relatively inactive, living off accumulated loot, but in 1879 Jesse reconstituted the gang. Although he didn't feel comfortable with some of the new men, including Bob and Charles Ford, he made do. After two more murders by the gang in 1881, the state of Missouri posted $5,000 rewards on each of the brothers. The Fords then made a deal with Gov. Thomas Crittenden to assassinate Jesse James for a $10,000 reward.

On April 3, 1882 Jesse summoned the Fords to his home in St. Joseph, where he was living under the name of Howard, to plan their next job. When Jesse climbed up on a chair to straighten out a picture, Bob Ford shot him dead.

The James legend didn't die with Jesse. He was lionized by much of the press. The *Kansas City Journal* headlined his death with a mournful farewell: "GOODBYE JESSE."

He was buried in a corner of his mother's yard and later an inscription was put on the marker:

> Jesse W. James,
> Died April 3, 1882.
> Aged 34 years, six months, 28 days.
> Murdered by a coward whose name is not worthy
> to appear here.

Of course, few killers ever get their names inscribed on the headstones of their victims. But no matter, a legend was being constructed, one that continues to the present day.

In October 1882 Frank James, tired of running, walked into Gov. Crittenden's office and surrendered his guns. He too was now part of the legend, and he was treated like one. Mobs cheered him as he stood on train platforms during a trip back to Clay County to stand trial for a couple of murders. The authorities were wasting their time; there was no way Frank James was going to be convicted. He was then shipped to Alabama to stand trial for a robbery charge but was found not guilty. Missouri tried again on another robbery count. Again he went free.

Thereafter Frank James lived in retirement from crime, working at a number of jobs, such as a horse race starter, shoe salesman and farmer. He died in 1915, a much respected citizen.

See also: *Thomas T. Crittenden; Charles Ford; Robert Newton Ford; Wood Hite; Jessee James—Impostors; Northfield, Minnesota Bank Raid; Allan Pinkerton; Younger Brothers.*

JAMES, Jesse—Impostors

Almost from the time Jesse James was laid in his grave, impos-

tors came forth claiming to be the real Jesse James, insisting he hadn't been shot at all. Most were proven liars and disappeared. Oddly, the last one seemed to be the most convincing. In 1948 a man named J. Frank Dalton, citing his age at 101, claimed to be the real Jesse James. At the time he was bedridden in Lawton, Okla.

Rudy Turilli, a noted authority on Jesse James, asserted that Bob Ford hadn't killed Jesse but rather another member of the gang, Charlie Bigelow. According to this theory, Bigelow looked like Jesse, having often passed himself off as the famous outlaw. He was due for extinction anyway because he was suspected of being an informer. Among those involved in the hoax, said Turilli, were James' mother and wife, the Ford brothers and even Gov. Thomas Crittenden, who, he alleged, was a longtime friend of the James family.

Much of the speculation that Jesse James was not killed by Bob Ford stemmed from the fact that the only known photograph taken after his death failed to show that the tip of his left-hand middle finger was missing.

In 1966 Turilli published a booklet, in cooperation with the Jesse James Museum of Stanton, Mo. entitled *I Knew Jesse James*, relating how he had found Dalton in Oklahoma through a tip. Turilli rounded up two of Jesse's old cronies: 108-year-old James R. Davis, a former U.S. marshal, and 111-year-old John Trammell, a black who had cooked for the James gang. Both men identified Dalton as Jesse James. Dalton was interviewed by dozens of reporters; writer Robert Ruark spent three days with Dalton and the other old-timers and was absolutely convinced that Dalton was no hoaxer.

One of those not convinced was Homer Croy, among the more reliable of Jesse James' biographers. He visited Dalton before the old man had a chance to school himself on all the details of Jesse's life that unbelievers might ask about. When Croy asked him who or what was Red Fox, Dalton identified the name as that of a scout for Quantrill, a part Indian. Actually, Red Fox was Jesse's race horse.

The real stumbling block, however, was the fact that the tip of Dalton's left-hand middle finger was intact. Supposedly, Jesse accidentally had blown part of that finger off while cleaning his pistol during the period in the Civil War when he rode with Bloody Bill Anderson, though some experts are unsure whether the fingertip was really shot off or not. Turilli challenged anyone to produce a photo of Jesse showing a missing fingertip. Probably because of the dearth of photographs of Jesse James, the challenge went unanswered. However, at the coroner's inquest into Jesse James' death, several witnesses testified they recognized the dead man as James, including Sheriff James H. Timberlake of Clay County, who knew well what Jesse looked like. Timberlake, who had last seen the outlaw in 1870, said he recognized Jesse's face. And he stated, "He had the second joint of his third finger shot off, by which I also recognize him." Other witnesses besides Timberlake mentioned the missing part of the finger.

J. Frank Dalton died on August 16, 1951, just short of Jesse James' 104th birthday.

See also: *Al Jennings*.

JENNINGS, Al (1864-1961): Alleged outlaw

One of the classic frauds in American crime writing is the effort to paint Al Jennings as the "last of the Western outlaws." He was not, despite a famous lurid article on his career in the *Saturday Evening Post* and a Hollywood movie about him and the so-called Al Jennings gang, whose rampage one authority described as "the shortest and funniest on record."

Jennings grew up one of the four sons of a frontier judge in the Oklahoma Territory. In later years he said he began his life of crime at the age of 16, but we have only his word for it. No court or law enforcement records list any charges against him or against his brothers, who, he stated were his partners in crime. The fact that all four were admitted to the bar tends to cast suspicion on Jennings' later claims. Two of his brothers did end up in a murderous affair, but as victims rather than perpetrators. Ed and John Jennings got into a saloon dispute with flamboyant lawman-gunman Temple Houston in 1894. Ed was shot dead while John was badly wounded and died a short time later.

People who didn't know Al Jennings—and thus were unaware that he was a notoriously poor shot—expected him to go after Houston. He never did. Instead, he and brother Frank hit the outlaw trail together with three stumblebums. The road

agents "ran riot" for 109 days, during which they abandoned two efforts to hold up trains before finally robbing a Rock Island train on October 1, 1897. This achievement, on which Jennings subsequently built his reputation, netted the five outlaws $60 apiece. Four of the gang, including Al and Frank Jennings, were arrested single-handedly by lawman Bud Ledbetter without firing a shot. When he cornered the two brothers, he told them to drop their guns and tie themselves up. They did.

For their trivial crime the Jennings brothers got life sentences, this was a period when long sentences were meted out and later reduced (the pardon business was thriving and lucrative). Al did five years and Frank seven. After that, both returned to the straight life, Al even running unsuccessfully for governor of Oklahoma. He also hit the lecture circuit, far from Oklahoma, where folks knew better about his wild and wooly past. The *Post* article eased his way into Hollywood, where filmmakers and afterward, the filmgoers simply ate up the tales of his fanciful life of crime. Highly intelligent, Jennings proved a huge success as both an author and a film producer.

In 1948 Jennings was able to carry his outlaw hoax a little further. In that year 101-year-old J. Frank Dalton turned up, announcing he was the real Jesse James. He was brought together with 85-year-old Jennings, who said: "Boys, there isn't a bit of doubt on earth. It's him. It's Jesse James." Of course, Jennings had never even met Jesse James. It was the reverse side of the pot calling the kettle black. When he died in 1961, the obituary writers paid due tribute to Al Jennings, "last of the Western outlaws."

See also: *Jesse James—Impostors*.

JEWETT, Helen (1813-1836): Murder victim

The murder of Helen Jewett in 1836 remains one of New York's most infamous unsolved cases, particularly since it was all too evident that the public didn't want the case solved. Helen Jewett at the time was the city's most desirable and most sought-after prostitute, always the "star woman" in whatever scarlet establishment she deigned to grace, and she was, according to one contemporary biographer, "kind to excess to all who required her assistance." However, she did have a troubling side to her nature, being quick to defend her rights whatever the consequences.

When a drunken British naval officer ripped up all her dresses and drowned her pet canary, she hauled him into court and collected damages. And when a wealthy rake got annoyed with her and knocked her down in a theater, she promptly had him arrested for assault and battery, charges ladies of her profession seldom brought, regarding such affronts as one of the perils of the profession.

Raised in a New England foster home under the tutelage of a kindly judge, she had grown up in an atmosphere of music, literature and the social graces that undoubtedly put her a cultural cut above most of her customers. Helen handpicked many of her lovers. If a man proved attractive to her, she would attempt to seduce him by missive. Taking a liking to an actor she had seen in *Othello*, she wrote:

> Othello is in my opinion a great lout and a great fool, and has not one half so much to cry about as Iago. . . . I should like to see you in Damon or in Romeo. I should like above all things to be your Juliet, or to rehearse the character with you in private, at any rate. I have some notions on the philosophy of her character and likewise on that of Romeo, which would perhaps amuse you.

In 1834 Helen enticed a young rake named Richard P. Robinson into her regular army of admirers. Like many other blades of the day, he conducted much of his night life under an alias, that of Frank Rivers, but as his affair with Helen bloomed, he readily revealed to her his true identity. Robinson also developed a jealous streak, the thought of her having an interest, other than financial, in any other man obsessed him. Of course, Robinson never gave a thought to marrying Helen, and when he decided to wed a respectable young lady of considerable means, a second note of friction entered his relationship with the haughty harlot.

For whatever reason, at 3 o'clock on Sunday morning April 10, 1836, Robinson entered Mrs. Rosina Townsend's famed brothel, where Helen Jewett was in residence. He was wearing his usual flashy visored cap and billowing Spanish cloak, so that Madam Townsend and another prostitute readily recognized him. What they didn't know was that Robinson carried a hatchet under the cloak. Helen Jewett was found brutally murdered several hours later, her skull savagely hacked in.

Helen Jewett's death exposed New York's false morality. At first, the newspapers treated the murder as a sensational affair, but it soon became evident that nobody wanted Robinson arrested, including the police and several important protectors of Madam Townsend. Robinson apparently felt so safe that he did not bother to flee the city. Finally, after what can only be described as a lethargic investigation, he was arrested.

A public cry of sympathy went up, with one newspaper regretting that so young a person as Robinson should be sacrificed for ridding the city of so great a disgrace to her sex." A Methodist minister pleaded from the pulpit for mercy for him, and young rakes adopted a new heroic dress, striding up Broadway in "Frank Rivers" caps and "Robinson" cloaks and chanting, "No man should hang for the murder of a whore."

No man did. Robinson's trial was a five-day farce, with most newspapers printing nothing but laudatory comments about the accused and somber warnings to prostitutes to stay away from the City Hall area because of threats of violence. By his attitude, it was clear Mayor Philip Hone considered the accused innocent; he later wrote in his diary, "He certainly looks as little like a murderer as any person I ever saw."

During the trial prosecution witnesses who had furnished damaging evidence against Richardson, both regarding the murder and his general dissolute life, became shaky in their testimony. A grocer named Robert Furlong gave the defendant a dubious alibi, but his subsequent suicide somewhat spoiled the effect. Just to make sure nothing went wrong, a few of Robinson's more ardent supporters bribed at least one juror.

The effort proved unnecessary, as a not-guilty verdict was quickly brought in. That evening Robinson was honored at a great celebration.

Obviously, good had triumphed over evil, although James Gordon Bennett's *Herald*, which alone held Robinson guilty wrote:

> The evidence in this trial and the remarkable disclosure of the manners and morals of New York form one of those events that must make philosophy pause, religion stand aghast, morals weep in the dust, and female virtue droop her head in sorrow.
>
> A number of young men, clerks in fashionable stores, are dragged up to the witness stand, but where are the married men, where the rich merchants, where the devoted church members who were caught in their shirts and drawers on that awful night? The publication and perusal of the evidence in this trial will kindle up fires that nothing can quench.

Nonetheless, the good burghers of New York had an unsolved mystery on their hands and obviously preferred it that way. After Richard Robinson was freed and left the city, rumor had it that he became a desperado along the Mississippi.

JEWISH Mafia

There has been a long-standing argument over whether or not the Mafia, Italian style, exists. Of course, the real argument lies in the definition of the term Mafia and how close a relationship can be assumed to exist among various "crime families." Certainly, in a looser context, there is an Italian Mafia, and years ago there was a Jewish Mafia. Like the Italian Mafia, there were Jewish gangs that cooperated with one another, and this did not change just because a Monk Eastman or a Jack Zelig, to name two brutes, or an Arnold Rothstein, to name a brain, were removed from the scene. Meyer Lansky was able to put the pieces back together again and lead a new Jewish Mafia in cooperation with the Italian Mafia. Lansky first did some missionary work around the country, bringing in the Moe Dalitz forces from Cleveland and the Purple Gang from Detroit, among others. Then he organized a convention of East Coast forces at the Franconia Hotel in New York City on November 11, 1931. Those attending included Bugsy Siegel, Joseph "Doc" Stacher, Louis "Lepke" Buchalter, Hyman "Curly" Holtz, Jacob "Gurah" Shapiro, Philip "Little Farvel" Kovalick, Louis "Shadows" Kravitz, Harry Tietlebaum and Harry "Big Greenie" Greenberg.

The conference closely followed a revolutionary change in the operation of the Italian Mafia. Just two months earlier, Lucky Luciano had effectively seized control of the Italian underworld by the assassination of Salvatore Maranzano, the so-called boss of bosses. Luciano's plan, which was at least 50 percent Lansky's idea was to establish a new "combination," or national crime syndicate. Lansky's job was to bring in the Jewish mobsters, and the final scene in that act was the Franconia conference, which established the firm rule that "the yids and dagos would no longer fight each other."

The new "interfaith" combination was to be paramount. If there were any doubters, they were converted when one of the

Franconia participants, Big Greenie, was eliminated by Bugsy Siegel, filling a contract that came down from the national board of the syndicate. When Siegel was later erased for defying the same board, his erstwhile tutor and partner Lansky would simply say with a shrug, "I had no choice."

JOE The Boss: See Giuseppe "Joe The Boss" Masseria.

JOHNNY Behind The Deuce (1862-1882): Gambler and killer

One of the West's most colorful and deadly gamblers, Johnny Behind the Deuce won a fortune at cards, killed several men, was saved from a lynch mob by Wyatt Earp and went to his own reward in a blazing gunfight—all before he reached his 21st birthday.

Nothing is known of his early life, but Johnny turned up in Tucson, Arizona Territory in early 1878 at the age of 16, giving his surname, at various times, as O'Rourke and his Christian name as either Michael or John. He worked as a hotel porter and seemed to spend all his free moments learning to manipulate a gun and a deck of cards. By 1880 he was famous throughout the territory as Johnny Behind the Deuce, a hard man to beat at any game of cards. In time, a suspicion developed that as he sat in the saloon gambling, Johnny would watch for a man passing out from drink and then leave the table for a short period. When the drunk sobered up the next day, he would find his belongings had been burglarized. Hardly anyone accused Johnny Behind the Deuce of such crimes, since he had already demonstrated a deadly knack for dealing with critics.

In January 1881 in Charleston a miner named Henry Schneider dared to call Johnny a thief when he found his poke had disappeared from his shack. He died with a bullet between the eyes after, Johnny Behind the Deuce alleged, drawing a knife. Marshal George McKelvey hustled the gambler off to Tombstone before the miners could start thinking of a lynching. Upon his arrival in Tombstone a crowd quickly gathered but a shotgun-armed Wyatt Earp held them off long enough for the prisoner to be moved to Tucson, where he was able to break out of jail. Since Johnny Behind the Deuce often dealt in the Oriental Saloon, of which Earp owned a piece, it is very likely that the latter felt he owed the young gambler something.

What happened next is guesswork, but a popular theory that summer was that the fugitive gambler came across the notorious Johnny Ringo, Wyatt Earp's mortal enemy, sleeping off a powerful drunk under a gnarled oak in Turkey Creek Canyon. Johnny Behind the Deuce supposedly figured he owed Earp one, so he shot the outlaw through the head. Whether true or not, the story was generally believed by Ringo's gunfighter friends. One of these, Pony Deal, got into a card game with Johnny Behind the Deuce in Sulphur Springs Valley. After a few hands Deal called Johnny a four-flusher, cheater and murderer. Angered, the gambler went for his gun, but Deal outdrew him and shot him dead.

See also: *Johnny Ringo.*

JOHNSON, George (?-1882): Lynch victim

Since George Johnson was lynched for a murder that didn't happen, his case pricked the conscience of Tombstone, Ariz. Not that Johnson didn't deserve hanging, as old-timers would relate years later, but it didn't seem quite just.

In October 1882 Johnson held up, or at least attempted to hold up, the Tombstone-Bisbee stage, firing a shot to bring it to a halt. Inside the coach one of the two passengers, Mrs. M. E. Kellogg, felt her husband slump down beside here when the shot was fired. He was dead. The woman screamed, and that frightened the would-be bandit's horse, which then bolted, unseating its rider. Johnson lost his weapon on hitting the ground and then did the only thing he could do under the circumstances: he ran off on foot.

The stage driver jumped down and seeing that Mr. Kellog was dead, unhitched two horses. He put the new widow on one horse and sent her back to Tombstone to request aid while he took off after the bandit on the other. Mrs. Kellogg got back to Tombstone in hysterical shape but was able to tell the sheriff what had happened. He and a doctor headed for the scene of the crime. Meanwhile, the stage driver ran Johnson to earth and brought him back to town. Unfortunately for Johnson, they came back by a different road and missed the sheriff.

By the time the sheriff, the doctor and the corpse returned, they found Tombstone justice had been done. Johnson had been strung up by a lyncher mob. The sheriff was angry and the doctor upset, and for good reason. The dead man had not been shot at all. He had suffered a heart attack and died when the stagecoach was stopped. George Johnson had not killed anyone; he hadn't even robbed anyone. Under the circumstances a necktie party did seem somewhat extreme. Business in the saloons and brothels reportedly was a bit subdued that night. Conscience finally got the better of folks and a collection was taken up. The sum of $800 was presented to Johnson's widow to ease her loss. In addition, the words "Hanged By Mistake" were put on his tombstone.

JOHNSON, John (?-1824): Murderer

John Johnson's crime in 1824 was in many respects a most pedestrian murder; at the same time it was probably the most publicized homicide in New York City's history.

When Johnson's roommate, James Murray, collected his pay, Johnson decided to appropriate it. Splitting Murray's skull with an ax he packed the dead man in a blanket and lugged his grim load toward the harbor to dispose of it. On the way he was challenged by a suspicious police officer. Johnson dropped his gory bundle and ran, managing to elude capture.

Stuck with a corpse they could not identify, officials ordered the dead man put on display at City Hall Park in the hope that someone would recognize it. For days an estimated 50,000 persons made the trek to view the body, many of them using the occasion as an excuse for a picnic in the area. Finally, a neighbor identified Murray and the police quickly arrested Johnson. His execution was held at Second Avenue and 13th Street on April 2, 1824. Due the previous publicity the murder had attracted, the execution drew a crowd of 50,000.

JOHNSON, Mushmouth (?-1907): Gambler

Perhaps the most successful black gambler in America, John V. "Mushmouth" Johnson dominated black gambling enterprises in Chicago from the mid-1880s until his death in 1907. Johnson, a flamboyant man with the obligatory cigar in mouth, controlled the city's policy racket, as well as scores of faro, poker and crap games in the black sections. His influence also extended over the Chinese quarter, where he charged all gambling enterprises a fee for protection. Mushmouth had considerable clout with the law as a result of his ability to deliver large blocks of black votes in elections.

Generally believed to have been a native of St. Louis, Mushmouth Johnson first appeared on the Chicago scene as a waiter at the Palmer House in the 1870s. In the early 1880s Andy Scott hired him as a floor man in his gambling emporium on South Clark Street and soon became so impressed with Mushmouth's abilities that he gave him a small interest in the operation. Mushmouth decided that what Chicago needed was a good nickel gambling house. A few years later, he opened his own place at 311 South Clark and did a thriving business with tables that catered to all races, offering bets as low as 5¢ in any of the games. Mushmouth sold off his interest in the place in 1890 and opened a saloon and gambling hall at 464 State Street, which operated without interruption for the next 17 years despite reform waves that shut down other gambling resorts at various times.

Together with two other big-time gamblers, Bill Lewis and Tom McGinnis, Mushmouth opened the Frontenac Club on Twenty-second Street. The club catered strictly to whites, and to be admitted, one was required to display a certain amount of cash. The fact that the Frontenac excluded blacks did not hurt Mushmouth's standing with his fellows; on the contrary, his success in the white world was a matter of black pride.

A total nongambler himself, Mushmouth is generally believed to have accumulated a quarter of a million dollars, a sizeable sum for any man in that day and a colossal sum for a black man. Yet, shortly before his death in 1907, Johnson told a friend he had only $15,000, all the proceeds of his saloon business, and that he had lost money on his gambling ventures through the years. He said that he had spent $100,000 on fines and that police protection had always drained him, claiming, "I have had to pay out four dollars for every one I took in at the game." Johnson also implied he had been forced to pay more than his white counterparts because of the color of his skin.

When the claim gained currency following Mushmouth's death, an unnamed police official was outraged, denouncing Mushmouth Johnson as a "whiner" and a "damnable liar." It was unclear whether the official objected to Johnson's statement that he had paid for protection or, simply, that he had been discriminated against in the rates charged.

JOHNSON County War: Range conflict

In 1892, under the guise of driving out "rustlers," the great cattle barons of Johnson County, Wyo. waged a war of extermination against small ranchers and homesteaders. There is no question that the big stockmen, mostly absentee owners residing in Cheyenne and members of the Wyoming Stock Growers' Association, had been losing cattle and that some had been taken by the "long rope," which was the traditional way most ranchers got started, picking up mavericks on the open range, and, indeed, the way most of the big stockmen themselves had gotten started. However, there were other reasons for the losses, including poor management and overstocking of the ranges, prairie fires, grass-destroying grasshoppers and bad weather. Traditionally too, many foremen on absentee-owner ranches built up small herds of their own and blamed the shortages on outside rustlers.

The stockmen followed the usual procedure of sending in "range detectives" to kill a few rustlers but found the results in Johnson County unsatisfactory. Whenever a small rancher or homesteader was arrested on rustling charges, a friendly jury of homesteaders invariably released him. The stockmen soon discovered, howeever, they could control not only the state administration, which they already owned, but the press as well. Their new-found power came about after a posse of cattlemen lynched a prostitute named Cattle Kate because she apparently had accepted beef from cowboys in payment for services rendered, and the beef the stockmen alleged, was stolen. To avoid any legal repercussions as a result of the lynching, they claimed Cattle Kate was a "bandit queen" who had masterminded a vast rustling operation. The press eagerly accepted the story and printed ridiculous accounts about the depredations of Cattle Kate. Encouraged by the public relations coup, the cattle barons decided to launch a full-scale war of extermination by going into the county in force with an army of gunmen to wipe out their arch enemies, one or two at a time.

For a period of a few months, members of the Wyoming Stock Growers' Association were invited to forward the names of deserving victims to the secretary of the organization. The executive committee then selected who would go on the death list (it was later estimated that a total of 70 victims were chosen), and sent 46 "regulators" under command of Colonel Frank Wolcott and Frank H. Canton, a wanted murderer, into the county on a brutal murder mission.

Their first victims were two small ranchers, Nick Ray and Nate Champion who were killed in cold blood. Sickened by the murders, a doctor and one of the reporters accompanying the invaders left the expedition. But the shootings delayed the murder army and word spread of their presence. They soon found themselves besieged by a possee of 200 county residents.

The stockmen's army was forced to seek refuge in a ranch 13 miles south of Buffalo. They faced certain extinction until the U.S. Cavalry rode to their rescue. The killers then laid down their arms, surrendered to the Army and were escorted back to Cheyenne. The local sheriff, Red Angus, unsuccessfully requested that the invaders be turned over to his custody. Had they been, there undoubtedly would have been 40-odd lynchings that evening.

The Johnson County "war" ended in a total disaster for the stockmen, who spent the next few years attempting to conceal their culpability. When a muckraker of the period, Asa Mercer published *The Banditti of the Plains* the following year, the cattle barons used their power to have the book suppressed; its plates were destroyed and Mercer was even jailed for a time for sending "obscene matter" through the mails. Copies of the book were torn up and burned and even the Library of Congress copy vanished.

While the stockmen had failed to exterminate the homesteaders of Johnson County, none were ever prosecuted for their offenses.

See also: *James Averill,* The Banditti of the Plains, *Frank M. Canton, Cattle Kate, Nathan D. Champion, Red Sash Gang.*

JOHNSTON, James A. (1876-1958): Warden of Alcatraz

In 1934 James A. Johnston, a veteran penologist, was appointed by the U.S. Department of Justice to be the first warden of a new maximum-security minimum-privilege federal prison on Alcatraz Island in San Francisco Bay. Johnston had previously served as warden of both Folsom and San Quentin prisons, California's toughest, but he had a reputation as a reformer. As such, his appointment caused something of a surprise. Old prison hands wanted someone tougher in the job, and many of Johnston's supporters were perplexed that he had accepted the post, which, by the nature of the prison had to be a repressive one.

From the beginning, Alcatraz was Johnston's creation; he personally designed the cell blocks and composed the most restrictive regulations ever used in a federal prison in the United States. In the popular press, Johnston was referred to as being "tough but kindly." The convicts thought differently, however, calling him Saltwater Johnston because they considered him as bitter as salt water.

The rules that Johnston laid down were so severe that they are credited with having driven any number of convicts "stir crazy." For the first four years a rigid "rule of silence" prohibited the convicts from speaking a word in the cell blocks, in the mess hall or at work. A single word uttered without permission meant instant punishment, often in solitary confinement for periods up to several months. It was an abrupt change for a warden who in a dozen years had reformed San Quentin in more ways than had been accomplished in the previous 50. There, he had introduced individual treatment of convicts, established honor camps, abolished corporal punishment and did away with the ugly striped prison uniform. At Alcatraz the hole became a standard punishment. In the cramped space a convict slept on concrete and received only water and four slices of bread a day. Solitary was a little better, since the prisoner got a bunk and one regular meal a day.

During the so-called Alcatraz Prison Rebellion of 1946, really just an escape attempt by six convicts, Johnston proposed an all-out attack on the cell blocks by armed guards and grenade-tossing Marines. When his superior in Washington, Bureau of Prisons Head James Bennett, said he was worried about "what public reaction will be if a large number of innocent inmates are unnecessarily killed," Johnston responded rather stiffly, "Mr. Director, there are no *innocent* inmates in here."

The investigation following the 1946 rebellion revealed that one prisoner had been held in total isolation for more than seven years. Johnston bristled when asked how much longer the man would remain there and said, "As long as necessary for discipline." The warden insisted that the FBI agents preparing a murder case against three members of the six-man escape team interview them in the dungeon, relenting only when the officers explained that any statements they got from the prisoners under those conditions might not be admitted in court.

There is little doubt that Johnston was personally brave. Even in periods of unrest—and Alcatraz was almost constantly beset by strikes, sit-ins and riots—Johnston always entered the dining hall alone and unarmed; of course, machine-gun toting guards patrolled the catwalk outside. He would taste the soup and then take his position by the door, exposing his back to the convicts marching out. During a strike in September 1937, a young convict known to be mentally deficient attacked the 61-year-old warden, battering his face in, knocking out several teeth and stomping on his chest before guards could tear him away. It was a week before Johnston could get out of bed. His assailant went to the hole for a long stay. As a lifer, he faced death for attacking a prison officer, but the warden never brought charges.

Johnston retired as warden in 1948, a man who had believed in rehabilitation but who had during 14 years molded a prison incapable of rehabilitating anyone. Summing up his tenure, he said: "Atlanta and Leavenworth had sent me their worst. I had done my best with them." Johnston died at the age of 82, having outlived many a younger con who had sworn to celebrate on the day the warden died.

See also: *Alcatraz Prison, Alcatraz Prison Rebellion, Atlanta Boys Convoy, Rufus "Whitey" Franklin, Rule of Silence, Robert Stroud.*

JOHNSTOWN Flood Looting

The flood that struck Johnstown, Pa. in 1889 was easily the worst disaster to occur in the United States during the late 19th century. When a 100-foot-high earthen dam broke, the resulting cataclysm killed at least 2,000 people—an average of about one out of every 10 persons living in the way of the flood—and bodies were still being found as late as 1906. However, much as the public was upset by the tragedy and the almost certain criminal negligence in the construction and supervision of the dam, it became more outraged by the looting, especially of the bodies of dead victims, that took place in the aftermath of the disaster.

As soon as the waters started to settle, hordes of looters descended on the scene to pillage business establishments and to strip the dead of cash, watches, wedding rings and the like. Dozens of looters were arrested, but they were the lucky ones. Outraged citizens killed others on the spot.

A Miss Wayne from Altoona, Pa. reported she was swept off a ferryboat by the rampaging waters and ended up on a beach, where she awakened to find herself stripped naked by looters. She feigned death and watched bands of thieves "slice off with wicked knives" the fingers of women to get their rings.

"DEATH TO THE FIENDS!" A contemporary sketch revealed the swift justice meted out to looters and mutilators of the dead at Johnstown in the aftermath of the great flood there.

So outraged was the citizenry over this story that many persons lost interest in rescue work and set out in vigilante style to hunt for looters. One looter captured with a ring-bearing severed finger in his pocket was summarily drowned. Others were shot. Even the police, overburdened with rescue work, were caught up in the frenzy of catching looters. A publication of the period reported:

> A trap was laid for a crook undertaker, who was robbing the bodies in the Fourth Ward morgue. A female was brought in, and before it was dressed for burial a diamond ring was placed upon one of her fingers, and the pseudo undertaker was assigned to take charge of the body. He was detected in the act of stealing the jewelry, and was promptly arrested by the chief of police.

JON, Gee (?-1924): First gas chamber victim

In 1924 Gee Jon became the first man to die in the gas chamber in Carson City, Nev. Reformers in that state were sure they had come up with a humane execution method when they pushed through a bill to have condemned men killed by poison gas that would be piped into their cells. The idea was that the execution would take place while the prisoner was asleep, so that no prior notice would have to be given. Jon, the first man facing such a fate, would thus be spared the macabre preparations for the execution as well as having to await a preestablished time of death. However, these well-laid plans had to be scrapped because prison officials couldn't figure out how to carry out such an execution without having the gas spread and kill off a considerable number of the prison population. An airtight chamber was then constructed and Jon had to endure all the frightful preparations the reformers had hoped to spare him. He was led into the chamber with a stethoscope attached to his chest and strapped into a chair under which cyanide pellets tied in a gauze sack hung on a hook. The chamber was cleared and a lever was pulled allowing the cynanide "eggs" to drop into a pan filled with a mixture of water and sulfuric acid. Within a matter of seconds, deadly fumes rose and, in a short time, the condemned man's heartbeat stopped. An effusive Carson City reporter informed his readers that Nevada had moved "one step further from the savage state."

See also: *Execution, Methods of*.

JONES, Frank (1856-1893): Texas Ranger

One of the most colorful and storied Texas Rangers, Frank Jones had become a Ranger in his native Texas at the age of 17 and a hero in the organization at 18. Sent after a gang of Mexican horse thieves, Jones saw the two Rangers accompanying him cut down in an ambush. Carrying on alone, he killed two of the enemy and took one prisoner. Later, as a sergeant, he led a seven-man force after a group of rustlers. In a bitter gunfight three Rangers were killed and Jones and three others were captured. Then, in an act of heroism befitting the storybook reputation of the Texas Rangers, Jones managed to seize the rifle of one of the rustlers and shoot his five captors dead. In 1880, as a captain, Jones was sent out with a murder warrant to arrest the notorious Scott Cooley, the instigator of the Mason County War of 1875. In a rare failure, Jones did not find Cooley (no one ever did and there is some reason to believe Cooley was dead at the time), but he did turn up three other desperadoes, one of whom he gunned down, the others he captured. After a while, Jones killed a rustler in a stand-up gun duel in a saloon, and in another barroom shoot-out he wounded and captured a notorious gunman named Tex Murietta. The list of Jones' daring accomplishments lengthened until June 29, 1893, when he went after a father-son outlaw team named Olguin. In a withering gun battle Jones, long regarded as "unkillable," was riddled with bullets. Ironically, the gunfight took place on an island in the Rio Grande that was actually on the Mexican side of the border, where the Olguins were immune to Texas justice.

See also: *Scott Cooley, Mason County War.*

JONES, William "Canada Bill" (?-1877): Gambler

Probably the greatest three-card monte cheater this country has ever produced and a fine all-round gambler, Canada Bill Jones cut a mangy figure along the Mississippi in the middle of the 19th century. In his autobiography *Forty Years a Gambler on the Mississippi,* George Devol, another legendary gambler, described Canada Bill as

> a character one might travel the length and breadth of the land and never find his match, or run across his equal. Imagine a medium-sized, chicken-headed, tow-haired sort of a man with mild blue eyes, and a mouth nearly from ear to ear, who walked with a shuffling, half-apologetic sort of a gaint, and who, when his countenance was in repose, resembled an idiot. His clothes were always several sizes too large, and his face was as smooth as a woman's and never had a particle of hair on it.

> Canada was a slick one. He had a squeaking, boyish voice, and awkward gawky manners, and a way of asking fool questions and putting on a good natured sort of a grin, that led everybody to believe that he was the rankest kind of sucker—the greenest sort of country jake. Woe to the man who picked him up, though. Canada was, under all his hypocritical appearance, a regular card shark, and could turn monte with the best of them. He was my partner for a number of years, and many are the suckers we roped in, and many the huge roll of bills we corralled.

Normally, three-card monte favored the dealer two-to-one, but Canada Bill seldom gave a sucker such a decent break. He was probably the century's greatest manipulator of cards and could show a victim two aces and a queen and then, virtually in the act of throwing the cards, palm the queen and introduce a third ace so that the sucker could never find the queen. About 1850 Canada Bill formed a partnership with Devol and two other talented gamblers, Tom Brown and Hally Chappell. The larcenous quartet operated on the Mississippi and Ohio and other navigable streams for close to a decade. When the partnership dissolved, each man's share of the profits was more than $200,000.

As quickly as both he and Devol made their money, however, they squandered it, both being suckers for faro. Canada Bill, who truly loved gambling for its own sake, was the originator of what was to become a classic gamblers' comment. He and a partner were killing time between boats in a small Mississippi River town when Bill found a faro game and started to lose consistently. His partner, tugging at his sleeve, said, "Bill, don't you know the game's crooked!"

"I know it," Bill replied, "but it's the only game in town!"

When river traffic dwindled and then virtually disappeared by the start of the Civil War, Canada Bill shifted his operations to the rails. The railroads, however, did not always exhibit the same tolerance for gamblers that the riverboats had, and three-card monte players were ejected when spotted. In 1867 Canada Bill wrote to one of the Southern lines offering $25,000 a year in exchange for the right to operate without being molested. He promised to give the railroad an additional percentage of the profits and said he would limit his victims to very rich men and preachers. Alas, his offer was refused.

Alternately flush and broke Canada Bill continued his itinerant gambling style until 1874, when he settled in Chicago and, with Jimmy Porter and Charlie Starr, established some very lucrative and dishonest gambling dens. Within six months he was able to pull out with $150,000, but in a short time, he lost his entire poke at faro. Canada Bill worked Cleveland a bit, winning and then losing, and in 1877 he wound up in Reading, Pa., an area noted as a refuge for gamblers. While down on funds he was committed to Charity Hospital and died there in 1877. He was buried by the mayor of the city, who was later reimbursed by Chicago gamblers for the cost. As two old gambling buddies watched Canada Bill's coffin being lowered into the grave, one offered to bet $1,000 to $500 that the notorious cheat was not in the box.

"Not with me," the other gambler said. "I've known Bill to squeeze out of tighter holes than that."

See also: *George Devol.*

JUANITA (1828-1851): First woman hanged in California

The hanging of a Mexican woman named Juanita, who comes down through history by that name alone, in the town of Downieville, Calif. in 1851 brought denunciations of American border justice from as far away as England.

Downieville was at the time a mining camp full of violent miners and harlots of all ages and hues, but Juanita was unquestionably the prize beauty. One account testifies: "Her dusky hair, long and glossy, was pulled low over delicate olive features and knotted loosely at the nape of her graceful neck. It gave her a Madonna-like expression. No doubt, many a rough miner stood in awe of her beauty and bared his head in reverence mingled with a certain human admiration." But she also had some faults, being described as, among other things, "a live volcano, an enraged lioness, a fighting wildcat."

In mid-1851 Juanita found true love with a young Mexican miner and set up housekeeping. She was henceforth not available as in the past. On the Fourth of July a celebrating miner named Jack Cannon came knocking on Juanita's door, brandishing a bag of gold dust. Juanita screamed at him in Spanish to let her alone. Cannon ignored her protestations and forced his way into the cabin, actually smashing the cabin door from its hinges. A knife flashed in the Mexican girl's hand, and Cannon fell bleeding to death on the floor.

Cannon was known in the camp as a rowdy, but he was a popular one, and an angry crowd soon gathered and began talk of lynching. Juanita was dragged to Craycroft's saloon for what was supposed to be a trial, but in the meantime some of her clothing had been dipped in Cannon's blood so that her crime would be more evident. A "prosecutor" was appointed to present the case, and a young unidentified lawyer who had journeyed over the mountains from Nevada to hear the Fourth of July speeches in Downieville was permitted to defend Juanita. While the "trial" proceeded, a number of miners argued over whose rope should be used for the girl's execution. When the young attorney started making a strong case of self-defense, he was knocked off the barrel he was standing on and flung out to the street. The jury then was ready to bring in a verdict, which, of course, turned out to be guilty.

Then a Dr. C. D. Aikin, who had come to the camp only weeks before, interrupted the proceedings to declare he was treating Juanita for pregnancy. An angry murmur arose in the crowd, which numbered in the hundreds. Three other local medical men were charged with examining the girl and came back to announce the claim was a hoax. Dr. Aiken quickly was held in contempt for his humane effort to save the girl and was given 24 hours to get out of town or be hanged himself.

Juanita was dragged back to her cabin and given an hour to prepare for her fate, while a crowd gathered outside the cabin and started shouting curses at her and stoning the flimsy structure. A priest was not allowed to go to her. After the hour was up, Juanita was marched to Durgan Bridge, from which a noose hung out over the wide Yuba. Extending from the bridge was a six-foot plank, on which the condemned woman was to stand. As she took her position, Juanita was silent, unlike during her courtroom appearance when she voluably had attacked the kangaroo proceedings in Spanish. Now she merely observed the crowd and smiled in contempt. When she spotted a friendly face, she called out, "Adios, amigo, adios." Then the plank was kicked out from under her.

When news of the execution reached the outside world, the press from one end of the country to the other condemned the bloodthirsty affair. Even the *Times of London* printed severe and caustic criticism of the manner in which border justice had been dispensed. Juanita was described as the first and only woman ever hanged in California, which was not true. Many Mexican and Indian women had been hanged but hers was the first to follow a "trial."

JUDD, Winnie Ruth (1909-   ): Murderess

Winnie Judd was called the Tiger Woman by a devoted press, which kept her supplied with clippings for 40 years after her conviction in the trunk murders of two young women in Phoenix, Ariz.

Winnie had been friendly with 27-year-old Agnes LeRoi, a nurse who worked at the same medical clinic as herself, and Hedvig Samuelson, with whom Agnes shared an apartment, and often stayed with them. On October 16, 1931, screams were heard coming from the apartment. The next day Winnie showed up for work but Agnes did not. On October 18 Winnie went by train to Los Angeles with a large trunk and a small one. Upon her arrival she asked a baggage room employee to help her load them in her car. The employee noticed a dark red fluid dripping from a corner of one of them and demanded to know what was inside, suspecting the trunks might contain contraband deer meat. Winnie said the keys were in the car and went to get them. She drove off, but the baggage clerk managed to write down her license number.

When authorities opened the trunks, they found the body of Agnes LeRoi in the large one and most of the dismembered body of Hedvig in the smaller one. She had been cut up to make her fit. An alarm went out for Winnie, who finally surrendered five days later after an appeal from her Los Angeles husband, from whom she had been separated for some time.

Winnie Ruth Judd (center), the trunk murderess, being returned to prison after one of her many escapes.

The public was enthralled by the trunk murderess, but it was difficult to tell whether people were more taken by the grisliness of the crime or letters that Winnie had written but never sent to her husband, which revealed strange heterosexual, bisexual and homosexual activities that were common at the LeRoi-Samuelson apartment.

Winnie insisted she had killed in self-defense after Hedvig pulled out a gun and shot her in the hand following a bitter argument. She said she had struggled for the gun, managed to wrest it from Hedvig and in the ensuing melee shot both women. At her trial the prosecution made the point that no one had noticed the gun wound in Winnie's hand until two days after the killings.

Winnie was found guilty and sentenced to hang, but the governor granted her a stay and a sanity hearing 72 hours before her scheduled execution. At the hearing the Tiger Woman put on a show that delighted the newspapers. She clapped, laughed and yelled at the jury. She got up once and told her husband she was "going out the window." Winnie's mother testified that she herself was feeble-minded and that her daughter had "been more or less insane all her life." Her father produced a family tree that traced insanity back 125 years to Scotland. Winnie emphasized the point by ripping at her hair and trying to pull off her clothes. She finally had to be removed from the hearing room and ultimately was judged insane and sentenced to life imprisonment in the state mental institution.

When she arrived at the institution Winnie no longer acted crazy. She was quiet, helpful and plotting. She fashioned a dummy of herself, put it in her bed and escaped. She was found some days later, and it was discovered that strangers had helped her on a number of occasions.

Winnie was brought back and tightly confined. It did no good. Over the years she escaped seven times, each time sparking headlines. One of her escapes lasted six years. It got so that in newsrooms on dull news days an editor would say, "Well, maybe Winnie Ruth Judd will escape again." One of the more sensational crime publications warned its readers. "When you read this story, the country's cleverest maniac may be at large again, perhaps walking down your street, or sitting next to you!"

In 1969, after one of her long-term escapes, attorney Melvin Belli fought Winnie's extradition from California to Arizona, but Gov. Ronald Reagan ordered her returned. Doctors then ruled Winnie was perfectly sane and she was sent to prison. In 1971 Winnie won a parole. She was then in her 60s and no one seemed to be upset about the Tiger Woman being on the loose, possibly because she had had so much free time before.

JUDICIAL Corruption

The roster of corrupt judges in the American judicial system is, sadly, a long one. It is least serious in the federal judiciary. As Donald Dale Jackson states in *Judges* (1974), "Manton, Kerner, Ritter, perhaps three dozen others in the history of the republic is not bad." But Jackson goes on to add: "Corruption in state courts is oceanic in comparison to federal courts. Salaries are lower, prestige is lower, and inevitably the quality declines. Most important, the state courts are too often havens for failed politicians and mediocre lawyers. Character, given these limitations, is a sometime thing."

Unscrupulous judges have for generations taken advantage of the opportunity to milk estates through their authority to appoint special guardians and appraisers. This practice can profit a judge's political allies, personal friends, members of his family and others. Some have believed in garnering the rewards more directly. Clem McClelland, a probate judge in Harris County, Tex. even went so far as to set up a dummy corporation, the Tierra Grande Corp. in which his appointees could buy stock and thereby contribute to his personal fortune. The judge was finally convicted of stealing $2,500 from an estate in his court and in 1965 was sentenced to 10 years imprisonment.

About the same time as the McClelland affair broke, the judicial system of Oklahoma was rocked by a scandal involving four justices of the state's nine-man Supreme Court. In his confession one of the jurists, Nelson S. Corn, said he and three other members of the court had shared $150,000 for reversing a tax decision against an investment company. Corn and Justice Earl Welch avoided impeachment by resigning. Another judge died before the plot was revealed and the fourth, Justice

Napoleon Bonaparte Johnson, a part-Cherokee honored as Indian of the Year in 1964, was impeached by the state senate. Perhaps the most sordid testimony of the investigation occurred when Corn was asked if there had been any year during his 24 on the bench when he had failed to take a bribe. He answered, "Well, I don't know."

Perhaps the most prolific fixer ever to preside over a court was the late New York Circuit Judge Martin T. Manton. Manton's method of trying a lawsuit was to decide in favor of the highest bidder. He told one prospective victim, "While I'm sitting on the bench, I have my right and my left hand." This particular victim, who happened to be as underhanded as Manton himself had the judge's fix offer wire-recorded. After Manton heard the recording, he rushed back to court and handed down the required verdict for not so much as a thin dime. Manton was not caught on that particular caper, but he was on some 17 others. He served a prison term, was disbarred and died in disgrace.

The last federal judge impeached and removed from office by the U.S. Congress was Halsted L. Ritter in 1936. Among other charges brought against him were continuing to practice law while serving on the federal bench and giving his former law partner an excessive $75,000 fee as receiver of a Palm Beach hotel and taking in exchange a kickback of $4,500. He also accepted a number of other kickbacks and appointed his sister-in-law manager of a bankrupt hotel where he then received free room and board and other services. Ritter had failed to report any of these items on his income tax returns.

Removed from office, Ritter ignored the removal order of the Senate and refused to leave his office until forcefully ejected by a U.S. marshal.

See also: *Martin T. Manton, Halsted Ritter.*

JUDSON, Edward Z. C. (1823-1886): Writer and rioter

While Edward Judson is best remembered as Ned Buntline, the author of those hokey, bloodcurdling dime novels that brought fame to Buffalo Bill Cody and Wild Bill Hickok, he also had a long record in the annals of crime. Among other things, he killed a a cuckolded husband in a messy love triangle, was shot at while on the witness stand by his victim's brother, narrowly escaped a lynching and was imprisoned for his part in inciting New York's notorious Astor Place Riots of 1849.

Born in Stamford, N.Y. in 1823, he went to sea at the age of 10 as a cabin boy after quarreling with his father, a minor writer named Levi C. Judson. He returned to land at the age of 20 and, almost overnight, became a writer. By late 1843 he was publishing a gutter journal in Nashville, Tenn. called *Ned Buntline's Own*.

In Nashville, Judson had an affair with a married woman whose husband Robert Porterfield, came after him with a gun. While he was testifying at a hearing into the killing in magistrate's court, the dead man's brother fired three shots at him, all of which gave him skin burns but did no other damage.

Judson was released but the local citizenry felt that justice had not been done and pursued him to his hotel. He was forced to jump from a third-floor window to escape his pursuers, a leap that gave him a permanent limp. Judson was then put in jail for his own protection until the lynch mood subsided. Later on, he wrote that lynchers took him from his cell and actually strung him up, leaving him for dead, and that some friends cut him down before he expired. This, however, might well be taken with the same skepticism due when reading his writings on the heroics of Cody and Hickok. Lynchers seldom left a body before it was stone-cold dead, and sporting bets were usually made over when the victim would twitch his last twitch.

A few years later, Judson moved to New York City, where he became a writer and henchman for the notorious political leader and rogue Captain Isaiah Rynders. In 1849 Judson was sent to prison for his part in the Astor Place Riots, in which 23 persons had been killed mainly because of the anti-British hysteria whipped up by Rynders and Judson. When Judson came out of Blackwell's Island after serving his one-year term, he published a book called *The Convict's Return or Innocence Vindicated*. After that, the rest of Judson's life was free of rascality and criminality—except for the hyperbole of his dime-novel writings.

See also: *Astor Place Riots*.

JUG Markers

When the desperadoes of the 1920s and 1930s turned to bank robbing as a major occupation, a need developed for the services of a "jug marker," a caser who would know which bank to rob and when. The great bank robber Baron Lamm, who first organized bank gangs into specialized, militarylike units, was his own jug marker, considering it the most important role in the operation. A good jug marker not only learned the particulars of a bank's security system but also ascertained who had responsibility to open which safe and when, as well as what day of the week the most money would be on hand.

John Dillinger's favorite jug marker was Eddie Green, although he sometimes utilized the brash Harry Pierpont who once cased a bank by interviewing the president in the guise of a newsman. Green was perhaps the most thorough at his trade. He kept an "active list" of banks and checked back on them to see if anything had changed since his last go-round. Even while in jail he was able to sell his information to bank-robbing gangs and to receive a share in the profits. When he joined the Dillinger gang, Dillinger asked him to name a good bank. Green cited one in Sioux Falls S. D. and started rattling off details. The gang then went out and robbed it.

On some jobs Green went so far as to find a reason for visiting bank officials in their homes just to study them more carefully, to be able to judge how they would act under stress. Green found the First National Bank of Mason City, Iowa for the Dillinger mob and discovered the bank's vault contained more that $240,000. Through no fault of Green's the gang botched the operation and got only $52,000. Green was shot dead by FBI agents in St. Paul, Minn. in April 1934. His

death put a considerable crimp in Dillinger's short-lived operations thereafter.

With Dillinger's demise, Baby Face Nelson emerged as the great bank-robbing public enemy. Nelson's idea of jug marking was to charge through a bank's front door blazing away. Obviously, an era in bank robbing was ending. Following Green's death probably the greatest jug marker, and some say the only really good one, to appear on the scene was Slick Willie Sutton. In the late 1960s and through the 1970s, the impulsive amateurs took over and, as Sutton noted, "jug marking plain went to hell."

JUKES : Alleged criminal clan

For many years the Juke clan of New York state was regarded as the most-depraved family in America, having produced, from the mid-1700s to the 1870s, seven generations of rapists, thieves, prostitutes, disease carriers and murderers. Begun in the 1870s, criminal-genealogical study—*The Jukes, A Study in Crime, Pauperism, Disease and Heredity* by Richard L. Dugdale—established, to the author's satisfaction, that criminal traits could be inherited just as much as hair coloring.

Dugdale started his study with a mid-18th century Dutch tavern keeper he called Max, who was well known as a gambler and drinker and was the father of two sons. The sons in turn married two illegitimate sisters, whom Dugdale described as harlots. He dubbed one of these sisters, "Margaret, mother of criminals" and indicted her as "the progenitor of the distinctly criminal line of the family."

Dugdale traced 540 "blood relatives" and 169 others related by marriage or cohabitation. Of these, 140 were criminals and offenders of various stripes, almost 300 were wards of the state and the remainder generally a debased, foul and diseased lot. Dugdale enraged his readers by estimating that the price of imprisonment, public assistance and the like had cost the taxpayers something like $1.3 million.

During the early 20th century, critics began to question Dugdale's research methods and findings. The famous prison reformer Thomas Mott Osborne marveled at Dugdale's supposed ability to trace family bloodlines among the illegitimately born. Not a scientific researcher but merely a functionary of the Prison Association of New York, Dugdale seemed to rely very heavily on reciting the criminal backgrounds of various unnamed wretches who, he was satisfied, were related to the original Margaret. Osborne soon became convinced that Dugdale had simply operated under the assumption that every criminal he happened upon must have been a Juke and every Juke was probably a criminal. The shoddiness of Dugdale's research was shown by some of the "criminals" he unearthed: "a reputed sheep-stealer"; a man "supposed to have attempted rape"; an "unpunished and cautious thief"; "a petty thief but never convicted"; and a particularly offensive lad about whom it was "impossible to get any reliable information, but it is evident that at nineteen he was a leader in crime."

Many sociologists attached the Juke thesis, but it received a new lease on life when in 1916 Arthur H. Estabrook took up the Dugdale mantle, claiming that since the 1870s the Jukes had continued to spawn more criminals and unworthies. Estabrook admitted there was a lot of "good" Jukes around but insisted that since in recent years the Jukes had taken to marrying outside the breed, the theory of hereditary criminality and immorality was not weakened. Today, Dugdale and Estabrook alike enjoy little support because of their failure to give any weight to the influence of cultural and environmental factors on the development of criminal behavior.

JULIAN Street: Cripple Creek Colorado vice center

Cripple Creek, the last of the Colorado gold towns, was as wicked as any of its predecessors and perhaps even a bit more open about it. Train travelers passing through the town were treated to a full view of Myers Avenue and its "line," replete with such signs as "MEN TAKEN IN AND DONE FOR." A leading turn-of-the century journalist, Julian Street, exposed the shame of Myers Avenue to a national audience in a searing article in *Colliers* magazine, calling the thoroughfare a disgrace to the entire country. The outraged city fathers of Cripple Creek fought back by bestowing a special honor on the journalist: they renamed Myers Avenue "Julian Street."

JUMP, John (?-1943): Murder victim

When one December morning in 1943 the dismembered body of John Jump was found on the train tracks near Fort Valley, Ga., the authorities' first theory was that the man had obviously been drunk and fallen in front of the train. However, the police soon discarded this theory and began looking for a murderer.

Inspection of the Jump home showed that the kitchen walls had recently been washed halfway to the ceiling and chemical tests revealed blood stains on the walls. Finally, Jump's young widow admitted killing him, claiming self-defense. After splitting the victim's head open with an ax, she cut the body in three parts and in two trips in the dark, carried the pieces to a desolate section of train tracks.

Given a long prison term for second-degree murder, she might well have gotten away with the crime but for one glaring miscalculation. There were three sets of tracks on the right-of-way where the body was found, but she had chosen to place its parts on the one set of tracks over which no train had run for eight months.

JUVENILE Delinquency

In one sense, juvenile delinquency was not a problem in early Colonial times. Until the Revolution settlers in this land lived under English common law, which held that juvenile offenders from the age of seven were accountable for their acts and could face the same penalties imposed on adults for various offenses. While a judge had discretion to determine the culpability of children between seven and 14 years of age, there were numerous executions of children as young as one eight-year-old hanged for burning a barn with "malice, revenge, craft and cunning." One well-known case was that of 12-year-old Hannah Ocuish, hanged for the murder of a six-year-old child. A contemporary account, which in tone approved of the execution, did comment that "she said very little and appeared greatly afraid, and seemed to want somebody to help her." Protests that she was too young to die drew very little public support.

An early 19th century woodcut depicts Boston authorities in pursuit of suspected youthful thieves who flooded the town. Not even the sight of a hanging figure (in background) could deter the juvenile criminals, many of whom were homeless.

Still, the punishment of juveniles was much more lenient in the colonies than in England. Corporal punishment and incarceration were gradually replacing the hangman's rope, especially in the post-Revolutionary War period. The Society for the Prevention of Pauperism was established in New York in 1817 to improve the lot of "those unfortunate children from 10 to 18 years of age, who from neglect of parents, from idleness and misfortune have . . . contravened some penal statute without reflecting on the consequences, and for hasty violations, been doomed to the penitentiary by the condemnation of the law." Funded by private donations the House of Refuge was established in 1825 in New York to admit children convicted of crimes and those so destitute or neglected that they were in imminent danger of becoming delinquent. This marked the first time that children and adults were jailed separately.

By today's standards, the House of Refuge was a harsh institution, but it merely reflected the general practices of the day, when children were often put in irons, whipped, placed in solitary confinement, forced to survive on a reduced food supply and subjected to the silent treatment. The institution had the right to act as a parent for neglected or criminal children, and parents who objected were generally unable to win the release of their offspring. Houses of refuge were set up in Boston and Philadelphia, and both instituted reforms in treating juveniles. Boston prohibited corporal punishment; Philadelphia housed each child in a cell of his own. By 1834 the New York House took the revolutionary step of accepting black children. In 1856 the first girls' reformatory, the Massachusetts State Industrial School for Girls, opened.

In the 1860s an ill-fated experiment was attempted with "ship schools," whereby young offenders were sent to sea on special vessels. Disciplinary problems, heavy operating expenses and protests from adult seamen fearful of losing jobs dealt the ship schools a quick death. In the 1870s and 1880s the so-called child-saving movement started under the leadership of a number of women's clubs. As a result of such efforts, separate courts for juveniles were established in 1899 in the states of Illinois and Rhode Island and the city of Denver, Colo.

The first federal effort to combat juvenile delinquency came with the establishment of the Children's Bureau in 1912. Under federal encouragement many states and large cities opened special reformatories for juveniles. These institutions did not solve the juvenile delinquency problem or clarify how juveniles could be rehabilitated through confinement. To this day, brutality, homosexuality and rioting remain ever present problems. Following the new approaches to aiding troubled juveniles expounded by John Dewey, Karen Horney, Carl Rogers, Erich Fromm and others, a new era of get-tough approaches to juvenile delinquency began in the 1970s.

The new public attitude was bolstered by such horrors as New York City's "laugh killing" in July 1978, the senseless slaying of a 16-year-old seminary student by a 13-year-old boy, a tragedy some experts say will have as great an impact on America's attitude toward juvenile crime as any offense has ever had. The killing took place in front of Teachers College at Columbia University when the 13-year-old and a 15-year-old companion came up to the seminary student, Hugh McEvoy, and a friend, Peter Mahar, 15, who were sitting on a railing. According to later testimony, the 13-year-old boy asked McEnvoy, "What are you laughing at?"

Mahar replied, "We're not laughing at anything."

With that, the 13-year-old pulled out a .22-caliber pistol, placed it to McEvoy's head and pulled the trigger. McEvoy was fatally wounded.

Under the existing law, the 13-year-old, who had a record of 10 arrests, nine within the previous 18 months, could only be tried in family court and receive a maximum sentence of 18 months in a "secure facility," with the option that his sentence could be renewed. After the first 18 months the 13-year-old would automatically be able to receive home passes and furloughs. The uproar over the laugh killing brought speedy passage of what some reporters called "Carey's law," named after New York Gov. Hugh L. Carey, which allowed juveniles to be tried for murder like adults and to be sentenced to life in prison. It was predicted that the laugh-killing law would spread throughout the country.

The chief deficiency in any serious study of juvenile delinquency (as pointed out in the entry on Age and Crime) is the absence of reliable statistics concerning juvenile crime in the 19th century, or even the first three decades of the 20th until the first appearance of the FBI's *Uniform Crime Reports*. Even use of the *Uniform Crime Reports* is not that helpful and can cause misleading conclusions about a "juvenile crime wave" based on increase in juvenile arrests. Certain types of crimes both violent and nonviolent, are typically juvenile offenses and explode upward when a crop of baby boom youths hits the crime-prone ages.

See also: *Age and Crime, Ship Schools, Walsh School Feud.*

K

KANSAS City Massacre

Just as the St. Valentine's Day Massacre in 1929 marked the turning point in the public's tolerance of Al Capone, so too did the Kansas City Massacre signal the beginning of the end to the public's glorification of the early 1930s gangsters. Ironically, while the massacre was considered a gangland depredation perpetrated by public enemies, it may well have been something entirely different—a political rub-out.

Ostensibly, the crime was an effort to free a federal prisoner, gangster Frank "Jelly" Nash, whom FBI agents had captured in Hot Springs, Ark. and were escorting to Kansas City, Mo. on June 17, 1933. Nash knew a lot about instances of corruption, certainly about political-criminal relationships in Hot Springs and more importantly, in Kansas City, where the Boss Pendergast machine's ties with the underworld had reached shocking proportions. There were powerful forces who wished Nash out of the law's hands—one way or another. That was accomplished in particularly bloody fashion.

As the officers and Nash piled into a car at Union Station, a large man carrying a machine gun appeared—it wasn't clear from where—and yelled, "Get 'em up!" Two other gunmen showed up and, for a moment, Nash thought his deliverance was at hand. Suddenly, the trio cut loose a fusillade of bullets, spraying the car and Nash. The supposed object of a rescue died screaming: "For God's sake! Don't shoot *me*."

With Nash died four lawmen, and two others were wounded. One FBI agent survived by feigning death.

The identities of the murderous threesome became a matter of some dispute. Several witnesses thought the machine gunner was Charles "Pretty Boy" Floyd, but during this period *every* maching-gunning was thought to be Floyd's. It was firmly established that one of the trio was Vern Miller. If another was in fact Pretty Boy Floyd, then the third had to be his sidekick Adam Richetti. That was the FBI's position.

Floyd, a fugitive on the run, was furious over this charge against him and wrote indignant letters to authorities and the newspapers vehemently denying any involvement. The fact that he never showed such indignation over other crimes ascribed to him led some to think he might be innocent. Certainly, he was not worried that the crime would send him to the gas chamber; the law already had enough on him to execute him several times over.

Five months later, Miller's bullet-riddled and mangled nude body was found on the outskirts of Detroit. Speculation arose that he had been punished for botching the Nash rescue or, after having murdered Nash intentionally, had been killed to prevent him from ever revealing who had ordered the attack. Floyd was killed by FBI agents in October 1934, and Richetti was captured that same month. With his dying breath Floyd refused to admit involvement in the Kansas City Massacre, and Richetti continued to deny it until his execution in 1938. In addition, most of the witnesses failed to identify him as one of the gunners.

In 1954 an underworld informer named Blackie Audett presented a new theory—or facts, as he insisted. Audett said he himself had seen the killers escape and he identified them as Miller, Maurice Denning and William "Solly" Weisman. It developed that two weeks after Miller's corpse had been discovered, the body of Weissman also had been found on the outskirts of Chicago. He had been murdered in the same fashion as Miller. Denning was never seen again after the massacre either dead or alive and could be assumed to have been murdered. Audett added a bizarre fillip. He claimed everyone in the Kansas City power structure seemed to know about the impending killings. He said he had been invited by City Manager Henry McElroy's daughter to come down to the station with her to witness the event. McElroy was Pendergast's "front man" in Kansas City.

"Me and Mary McElroy watched the whole thing from less than fifty yards away," Audett claimed. If true, Audett's charges give a distinct political flavor to the massacre. They also show that Floyd and Richetti were innocent and that more shocking things than a mere underworld massacre happened in the Kansas City of that era.

See also: *Charles Arthur "Pretty Boy" Floyd, Frank "Jelly" Nash.*

KARPIS, Alvin "Creepy" (1907-1979): Public enemy

None of the public enemies of the 1930s upset FBI Director J. Edgar Hoover more than did Alvin "Creepy" Karpis. Hoover always referred to him as a "rat," and Karpis sent word to the head G-Man that he intended to kill him the way his agents had killed Freddie Barker and his mother Ma Barker, during a famous shoot-out in Florida in 1935. According to Karpis, Ma Barker was never a criminal mastermind but just a dumpy little middle-aged woman trying to take care of her wild—and murderous—boys as well as she could. That same year Karpis resurrected the virtually defunct art of train robbery, holding up a train in Garrettsville, Ohio, partly because he knew it would be regarded by Hoover as a personal affront. Once a crime had been wiped out, no one was supposed to bring it back.

A Montreal-born, Kansas-raised gangster, Karpis met Freddie Barker in prison, where the former was doing a term for safecracking. Barker brought him home to Ma Barker, who took an instant liking to the sallow, dour-faced, "creepy"-looking Karpis, and treated him like another son, probably because Freddie was the only one not imprisoned or dead at the time.

As some of the other sons came back from prison, the Barkers and Karpis organized a formidable gang. They robbed a number of banks and in 1933 kidnapped a St. Paul brewery millionaire, William Hamm, for whom they got $100,000 in ransom. Six months later, the gang abducted a Minneapolis banker, Edward Bremer, and netted $200,000. The FBI fostered a myth that Ma Barker was the brains of the gang, a claim for which there is no evidence whatsoever. It is also doubtful any criminal as capable as Karpis would have taken orders from a middle-aged woman. Karpis' version of the real Ma Barker was that she "just didn't have the brains or know-how to direct us on a robbery. It wouldn't have occurred to her to get involved in our business, and we always made a point of only discussing our scores when Ma wasn't around. We'd leave her at home when we were arranging a job, or we'd send her to a movie. Ma saw a lot of movies."

When Freddie Barker, along with Ma, was fatally shot in 1935, the Barker-Karpis mob was finished. Doc Barker had been captured shortly before and was already in Alcatraz. Karpis carried on with minor criminals, robbing a train that was supposed to have a $200,000 payroll on board but had only $34,000.

During a Senate committee hearing in April 1936, Sen. Kenneth D. McKellar of Tennessee subjected Hoover to a savage grilling about the performance of the FBI and the director's own competence, stressing the point that Hoover had never made an arrest. After the hearing Hoover vowed to take Karpis personally.

When word was received the following month that Karpis was holed up in New Orleans, Hoover flew to the scene to be in on the arrest. FBI agents swarmed all over Karpis' car and captured him as he was about to drive away from the house. Hoover himself announced that he was under arrest. "Put the handcuffs on him," Hoover snapped, but among the horde of agents not one had remembered to bring handcuffs. An agent had to pull off his necktie to tie Karpis' hands.

According to Karpis' memoirs, published in 1971, his arrest, which had made Hoover a national hero, was not quite as heroic as it was made to appear. In *The FBI Story,* which is at least a semiofficial history of the agency, author Don Whitehead states that Hoover grabbed Karpis before he could reach for a rifle on the back seat. Yet the car Karpis was captured in was a 1936 Plymouth coupe, which, as he asserted, had no back seat.

"The most obvious flaw in the FBI story, though," Karpis wrote, "lies in Hoover's own character. He didn't lead the attack on me. He hid until I was safely covered by many guns. He waited until he was told the coast was clear. Then he came out to reap the glory. . . . That May day in 1936, I made Hoover's reputation as a fearless lawman. It's a reputation he doesn't deserve."

Sentenced to life imprisonment, Karpis entered Alcatraz in 1936 and remained there until transferred to the McNeil Island Penitentiary in Washington in 1962. When transferred he had served more time on the Rock than any other inmate. In January 1969, after doing almost 33 years, Karpis was released on parole and deported to his native Canada. His book appeared in 1971. In the late 1970s he lived in quiet retirement in Spain.

See also: *Arizona Clark "Kate" or "Ma" Barker, Barker Brothers, J. Edgar Hoover.*
Further reading: The Alvin Karpis Story by Alvin Karpis with Bill Trent.

KEARNEY, Patrick: See Trash Bag Murders.

KEATING-HOLDEN Gang: 1930s St. Paul gang

Perhaps the most brutal gang of kidnappers, bank robbers and murderers to operate during the 1920s and early 1930s was the Keating-Holden mob, sometimes called the St. Paul Outfit.

Longtime holdup men in Chicago before moving to St. Paul, Minn., Francis Keating and Tommy Holden had a habit of surrounding themselves with criminals who were considered flaky—and thus more likely to be feared by helpless victims. The gang was forced into temporary retirement in the late 1920s, when Keating and Holden were sentenced to 25 years at Leavenworth for a $135,000 mail robbery. By using stolen trustee passes, the pair escaped on February 28, 1930. They may have been supplied the passes by a minor criminal named George Kelly, later famous as Machine Gun Kelly, eager to do a favor for a couple of big-timers. Keating and Holden promptly returned to St. Paul and reorganized their old gang. Among its members were the likes of Frank "Jelly" Nash, who was to die in the Kansas City Massacre, Alvin "Creepy" Karpis, Harvey Bailey, Shotgun George Zeigler, Verne Miller and Freddie Barker. For sheer flakiness the last three could hardly be surpassed. According to underworld legend, Keating and Holden were suspicious when considering Miller for membership since he had once been a sheriff. As a test of his trustworthiness, Miller was told to work over a hood whom the gang leaders did not particularly like. Miller promptly kidnapped the hood, drove him out to the country and broke all of his fingers. Then he let the man go. Keating and Holden were duly impressed that Miller was a "nut" and deserving of membership in the gang.

The reconstituted gang terrorized parts of the Midwest for about a year and a half until Keating, Holden and Bailey were captured on July 7, 1932, while playing golf at the Old Mission Golf Course in Kansas City. But what the arresting team of FBI agents and city police didn't realize was that the trio had teed off as a foursome. Jelly Nash, a terrible golfer, was trailing far behind. By the time he played through 18 holes, he could only wonder what had happened to his comrades.

Holden and Keating returned to prison under life sentences and their gang disintegrated, but three surviving members—Alvin Karpis, Freddie Barker and Shotgun Ziegler—went on to form the infamous Barker-Karpis gang of bank robbers and kidnappers.

KEELER, Leonarde (1903-1949): Lie detector expert

The father of the polygraph, Leonarde Keeler was considered the nation's foremost authority on deception tests. His version of the lie detector was developed in collaboration with Dr. John A. Larson, a pioneer criminologist who was once a policeman in Berkeley, Calif. and later assistant state criminologist of Illinois.

The pair met when Keeler was a student at Stanford University working on a machine of his own. Keeler gladly became Larson's junior partner and the two developed a lie detector that was embraced by August Vollmer, the founder and chief of Berkeley's celebrated "scientific police department."

Their first lie detector used pens to record on a moving strip of graph paper the variations of a suspect's blood pressure, pulse and respiration. Keeler later added galvanic skin response, measured by electrodes attached to the fingertips, which are said to show evidence of perspiration when a person is answering falsely or is under emotional stress.

Keeler's record of success as a lie detector expert was probably unequaled. In many cases his expert testimony led to the freeing of defendants either already convicted or facing certain guilty verdicts.

Keeler, like many other supporters of the polygraph, insisted that when the testing was done by skilled interrogators, his method of detecting lies was far more reliable than the testimony of eyewitnesses. At the time of his death he was bitterly disappointed that the polygraph had failed to gain widespread judicial recognition, although he himself was frequently called to testify as an expert witness. Unlike certain other exponents of the polygraph, Keeler did admit the machine could be "beaten" and that he himself could do so.

See also: *Lie Detector*.

KEELY, John E. W. (1827-1898): Swindler

Few swindlers have ever deceived their victims and the public longer than ex-carnival pitchman John Keely of Philadelphia. In 1874, he convinced four top financiers, Charles B. Franklyn, an official of the Cunard steamship line, Henry S. Sergeant, president of the Ingersoll Rock Drill Co., John J. Cisco, a leading banker, and Charles B. Collier, a lawyer, that he could convert a quart of water into enough fuel to power a 30-car train a mile a minute for 75 minutes. Over the next 24 years he held frequent demonstrations in his workshop that seemed to confirm he was about to revolutionize the entire field of energy. The previously mentioned foursome organized the Keely Motor Co. and over the years advanced him large sums of money for his research. Company stock was traded on exchanges in this country and Europe and Keely proved adept at getting money out of people besides his primary backers. Clara Jessup Moore, a wealthy widow, not only invested an estimated half-million dollars in Keely's so-called invention but also authored a book entitled *Keely and His Discoveries*. At one stage, John Jacob Astor "wanted in" to the tune of $2 million.

The Scientific American attacked Keely's claims as ridiculous, but this did nothing to cool the ardor of thousands of investors. Finally, after Keely's death in 1898, investigators dismantled his house and found Keely's mysterious force was nothing more than compressed air. Buried under the kitchen floor of the house was what *The Scientific American* in its February 4, 1899 issue described as "a steel sphere forty inches in diameter, weighing 6,625 pounds." This sphere was "an ideal storage reservoir for air . . . at great pressure." The compressed air traveled upward to a second-floor workshop, where Keely gave his demonstrations, through steel and brass tubes nine inches in diameter with a three-inch bore, strong enough to withstand the tremendous pressure. Between the ceiling of the room on the first floor and the floor of the workshop was a 16-inch space "well calculated to hide the necessary tubes for conveying the compressed air to the different motors with which Keely produced his results." It was a setting in which "for a quarter of a century the prince of humbugs played his part." Concealed in the walls and floor of the workshop were spring valves that could be operated by foot or elbow to "run" a motor whenever desired. Clearly, the whole setup was similar to the fun and mystery houses Keely had seen during his carnival days.

KEENE, John (?-1865): Murderer

Had there been a 10 Most Wanted List during the Civil War,

John Keene most likely would have made both the Union and Confederate rosters, each for a different set of crimes.

Keene's early background is unknown, but before the outbreak of hostilities he was working in Memphis, Tenn. Immediately after Fort Sumter, he joined the Confederate Navy and was assigned to a ram. Hardly the material with which wars are won, Keene's first hostile action was directed against his own captain, whom he brained with a marlinespike.

Viewing his act as a sort of informal resignation, Keene went on the run. While being hunted by the Southern authorities, Keene allegedly killed a man or two along the way. He eventually made his way back to Memphis, which at the time was in the hands of the Union. This circumstance provided Keene with a new lease on life, but in almost no time, he killed a man named Dolan and was again forced to flee. Changing his name to Bob Black, Keene organized a gang of highway robbers and terrorized the Tennessee countryside, with Union troops in constant pursuit.

Finally captured by Union forces, Keene broke out of the guardroom and headed north. For a while, Keene-Black ran a saloon in St. Paul, Minn. which was little more than a cover for fencing and other criminal activities. When the law closed in on him, he took the only escape path open to him—west. Not surprisingly, he fell in with the wrong sort of people, got in trouble in Salt Lake City and had to make for Montana. There he had a minor association with those notorious outlaws the Innocents, but the Montana Vigilantes soon ordered him out of the territory.

Instead of leaving Montana directly, he headed for Helena, where a short time later he spotted a former acquaintance named Harry Slater sleeping off a jug or two outside a saloon. Back in Salt Lake City, Slater had made it clear that he disliked Keene and intended to do something about it. Keene, a man who always believed in seizing an opportunity, shot the sleeping Slater dead. He was apprehended for the crime and brought before a miners court, which dispensed justice with lightning rapidity. They gave him an hour's grace and then hanged him high from a giant pine.

KEFAUVER Investigation: Organized crime hearings

Probably the most important probe of organized crime in America was that conducted by the 1950-51 Senate Special Committee to Investigate Crime in Interstate Commerce, more commonly known as the Kefauver Investigation. Because the hearings appeared on television, the investigation drew more public attention and had far greater impact than other such probes. Scores of crime figures and politicians came under the camera's gaze as the hearings moved from one major city to another. Headed by Democratic Sen. Estes Kefauver of Tennessee, the five-man panel included fellow Democrats Herbert O'Conor of Maryland and Lester C. Hunt of Wyoming and Republicans Alexander Wiley of Wisconsin and Charles W. Tobey of New Hampshire. Brought before them by chief counsel Rudolph Halley were more than 600 witnesses, including underworld figures from minor hoods to major racketeers and public servants from policemen to mayors.

The Kefauver Committee hearings made the phrase "taking the Fifth" part of the American vernacular, as many witnesses invoked the constitutional right against self-incrimination, although not always eloquently. Gambler Frank Erickson took the Fifth "on the grounds it might intend to criminate me" and Jake "Greasy Thumb" Guzik of the Chicago syndicate felt that his replies could well "discriminate against me."

In Chicago viewers watched police Capt. Dan Gilbert, chief investigator for the state attorney's office in Cook County and often referred to as "the world's richest cop," admit his office had not raided Chicago bookie joints since 1939. In the New York area the cameras focused on New Jersey top underworld fixer Longie Zwillman, from whom former Republican Gov. Harold G. Hoffman had personally solicited support in 1946. Three years later, Zwillman had offered to give $300,000 to the Democratic candidate for governor, Elmer Wene, in exchange for letting him name the state's attorney general. The offer had been refused.

In Louisiana the committee turned up county sheriffs and other lawmen who refused to enforce gambling laws because they insisted their communities would die without gambling revenues and that thousands of people, many old and underprivileged, would lose their jobs in the illegal casinos. By coincidence, these same sheriffs and marshals somehow had gotten very rich, as had the New Orleans chief of detectives, who—on a salary of $186 a month—managed to squirrel away some $150,000 in a safe-deposit box. In Detroit the committee found some important mob figures, such as Joe Adonis and Anthony D'Anna, maintained important business concessions with the Ford Motor Co. despite their notorious backgrounds. The panel charged that a meeting between D'Anna and Harry Bennett, at the time Henry Ford's chief aide, was held at the latter's request

to instruct him [D'Anna] not to murder Joseph Tocco, who had a food concession at a Ford plant. . . . Bennett entered into an agreement that D'Anna would refrain from murdering Tocco for five years in return for the Ford agency at Wyandotte. As a matter of record, Tocco was not murdered until seven years after this meeting. Also as a matter of record, D'Anna did become a 50 percent owner in the Ford agency at Wyandotte within a matter of weeks after the meeting.

The highest entertainment point of the hearings occurred in New York City, where Virginia Hill, the lady friend of a number of top mobsters and reputed bag lady for the mob, provided a bit of comic relief as she denied any knowledge of the mobsters' business. She also contributed a touch of violence when, leaving the hearings, she threw a right cross to the jaw of reporter Marjorie Farnsworth. Turning the remaining horde of reporters and photographers, she screamed: "You goddamn bastards. I hope an atom bomb falls on all of you."

Frank Costello added to the drama at the hearings when he refused to give testimony before the television cameras and threatened to walk out. He finally testsified after it was agreed his face would not be shown: the cameras instead focused on his hands, making them the most famous pair of hands on television. The committee looked closely into Costello's far-flung criminal activities: his interests in gambling rackets and casinos in Louisiana, his connection with a harness racing track, from which he received an annual stipend to keep bookies off the premises; and his power in Manhattan politics, which included the ability to name judges to the bench. When asked why Tammany boss Hugo Rogers had once said, "If Costello wanted me, he would send for me," Costello stated he was totally mystified.

When the questioning got too tough, Costello staged a famous walkout, and by the conclusion of his testimony, it was obvious that he would never return to his high position in the underworld syndicate. He had been too badly damaged by evidence presented in the probe and was faced with constant legal battles. He was sentenced to 18 months for contempt and later did another term for income tax evasion.

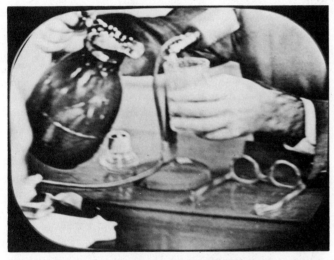

The most famous television view of the Kefauver Committee hearings into organized crime was that of Frank Costello's hands. The underworld boss refused to allow his face to be shown on camera when he testified.

Probably even more damaged by the hearings was former New York City Mayor William O'Dwyer, who came out of the inquiry a symbol of civic corruption. Accommodation with organized crime was a hallmark of O'Dwyer's reign both as mayor and earlier as district attorney in Brooklyn. Indeed, even before the hearings the revelations concerning O'Dwyer's association with criminal elements forced him to resign the mayoralty to seek the relative sanctuary of the ambassadorship to Mexico.

The committee produced evidence that O'Dwyer was friendly with top mobsters Joe Adonis and Costello and had often visited the latter's home. Sworn testimony that envelopes of money were passed to O'Dwyer by leaders of city unions brought hazy or contradictory recollections from the ex-mayor. In its report the panel excoriated O'Dwyer:

> A single pattern of conduct emerges from O'Dwyer's official activities in regard to the gambling and waterfront rackets, murders and police corruption, from his days as district attor-

ney through his term as mayor. No matter what the motivation of his choice, action or inaction, it often seemed to result favorably for men suspected of being high up in the rackets. . . . His actions impeded promising investigations. . . . His defense of public officials who were derelict in their duties and his actions in investigations of corruption, and his failure to follow up concrete evidence of organized crime . . . have contributed to the growth of organized crime, racketeering and gangsterism in New York City.

When the investigation ended, the Kefauver Committee offered a number of suggestions to tighten up the laws against racketeers and crooked politicians. Among the recommendations adopted were the formation of a racket squad in the Justice Department, increased penalties for the sale of narcotics, various curbs on gambling and the dissemination of gambling information and increased efforts to deport gangsters. Cynics claimed that within a few months the syndicate was running as smoothly as ever, but this was not so. There were several far-reaching changes. Costello's power was broken; Adonis was deported (voluntarily to avoid prison); gambler Willie Moretti was executed by his comrades, who feared his bantering testimony indicated that mental illness was loosening his tongue; and reform movements gained in a number of cities. While the underworld was hardly destroyed, it was badly wounded. Furthermore, the FBI, which had for years denied the existence of a "Mafia" or of "organized crime" at last joined the battle against them.

KEHOE, Andrew: See Bath, Michigan School Bombing.

KEHOE, Jack: See James McParland, Mollie Maguires.

KELLEY, Daniel (?-1884): Western outlaw

Daniel Kelley was a Western outlaw who was captured in a standoff with a barber.

Kelley was one of five holdup men who staged Arizona's infamous Bisbee Massacre, a robbery in 1883 in which four innocent bystanders, three men and a woman, were killed. The massacre sparked one of the West's greatest manhunts, with each of the five men eventually tracked down. Kelley got as far as Deming, N.M., by then sporting a heavy beard. He visited a barber shop to have his heavy stubble removed, not knowing that he had been identified as one of the murderers and his identity telegraphed throughout the Southwest. When the barber, Augustin Salas, set about shaving off the beard, he recognized Kelley and immediately planted the razor across his throat and yelled out for a passersby to go for help. For several minutes the two waged a strange duel, with the barber holding the razor to Kelley's Adam's apple and the latter fingering his revolver, until the outlaw was taken into custody.

It is a part of Western folklore that the circumstance of

Kelley's capture spawned the term "close shave," but the claim is probably disputable. In any event, Kelley was hanged on March 8, 1884.

See also: *Bisbee Massacre.*

KELLY, George R. "Machine Gun" (1895-1954): Public enemy

Of all the public enemies of the 1930s, George "Machine Gun" Kelly enjoyed the best press. Everyone insisted he was a very bad man, especially his wife Kathryn and the FBI's J. Edgar Hoover, but calling Kelly Public Enemy No. 1 was an insult to hundreds of far more dangerous criminals. One candid profiler called him "a good-natured slob, a bootlegger who spilled more than he delivered," referring to his criminal activities before he met and married the flamboyant Kathryn Shannon. She gave him his reputation, making him into something supposedly big in big-time crime, but the fact is that Kelly never fired a shot at anyone and he certainly never killed anyone, a remarkable statistic for a public enemy dubbed Machine Gun.

Kelly met Kathryn in Oklahoma City, where he was already out of his element just trying to make it as a simple bootlegger. She had excellent underworld connections thanks to a "fugitive farm" her parents ran on their small Texas ranch, where criminals on the run could hide out for a price. Determined to make Kelly into a fearless crook, Kathryn gave him a machine gun as a gift and had him practice shooting walnuts off fence posts. It must have been exciting for Kelly, who already had a "bum ticker." Kathryn passed out cartridge cases in underworld dives, remarking, "Have a souvenir of my husband, Machine Gun Kelly." Machine Gun, she would say, was at the moment "away robbing banks."

Machine Gun did break in with a few small bank holdup gangs and took part in some capers in Mississippi and Texas. Fortunately for Kelly, he never had to prove his mettle under fire, since the jobs went off smoothly. Soon, Kathryn insisted they go big time like some other mobs and get into kidnapping. They formed a kidnap gang with a rather mild-mannered middle-aged crook named Albert Bates. The two men, armed with machine guns, broke into the home of millionaire oil man Charley Urschel in Oklahoma City. The Urschels were playing cards with a neighboring couple. Kelly, not exactly a master at planning a job, hadn't the least idea which one was Urschel, never having seen or even obtained a picture of him. When no one would say who Urschel was, the kidnappers were forced to take the two men. After they drove for a while, Kelly had both men produce their wallets and identified Urschel. He tossed the other, Walter Jarrett, out on an empty road.

After a number of false steps and missed signals, the kidnappers collected $200,000 in ransom. Once they had the money, Kathryn demanded they protect themselves by "killing the bastard," but Kelly, in the one time he stood up to his wife, convinced the others in the gang that their victim should be freed or it would "be bad for future business."

The FBI ran the gang to earth thanks to victim Urschel,

who turned out to have a brilliant memory. Although he had been kept blindfolded throughout his ordeal of several days, he was able to remember so many details that the agents soon identified the place where he had been held as the ranch of Kathryn's parents in Texas. Once the gang members were identified, they were readily captured. Bates was picked up in Denver. Kelly and Kathryn were cornered a little later in a hideout in Memphis. According to the version later given by Hoover, Kelly cringed in a corner of the room, hands upraised, and pleaded: "Don't shoot, G-men—don't shoot." This dramatic incident supposedly gave the FBI agents their popular name. The tale was sheer hogwash, however. The name "G-men" had been used years earlier to describe government workers and agents, and Kelly was actually captured by Detective Sgt. W. J. Raney and Detectives A. O. Clark and Floyd Wiebenga of the Memphis Police. After the three broke down the bedroom door, Raney shoved a shotgun into Kelly's paunch, and Kelly said, "I've been waiting for you all night."

Shipped off to Alcatraz under a life sentence, Kelly soon became known as the easy-going man he always had been (Pop Gun Kelly to some) and was eventually transferred out of that prison of toughs to Leavenworth, where he died of a heart attack in 1954. Kathryn Kelly was released from her life sentence in 1958 and faded into oblivion with her aged mother.

See also: *G-Men.*

KELLY, Honest John (1856-1926): Gambler

For a quarter century beginning in the late 1890s, John Kelly was known as the most honest gambling house operator in the country, an attribute that did not stand him well with the police, since he was famous for refusing to pay for protection.

Honest John earned his sobriquet when he was a baseball umpire. In 1888 he refused a $10,000 bribe to favor Boston in an important game with Providence. Thereafter, he became the darling of the big gamblers and was trusted to be the dealer in games where tens of thousands of dollars were riding on a turn of a card. In the late 1890s Honest John opened his own gambling house in New York City and became so prosperous that he soon had operations at several locations, all renowned for being totally honest. His best-known house was a brownstone at 156 West 44th Street, where he fought many battles with the police, boasting he constantly had to buy new doors and windows to replace those smashed by indignant detectives. The worst raid occurred in 1912, when the police descended on the gambling house with crow bars and fire axes and smashed doors, windows, gambling equipment and furniture. The raid succeeded only in making Kelly a hero to the public, and when he opened the Vendome Club on West 141st Street, his business boomed. After Kelly closed the West 44th Street brownstone, the police remained convinced he was still operating it for gambling purposes and stationed an officer at the front door. Sightseeing buses took visitors past the brownstone, and guides pointed out the gambling house that wouldn't pay off the police. The guides insisted patrons entered it through trapdoors from other buildings, but further police raids never uncovered any gambling. In the early 1920s Honest John sold the building to a Republican Party organization and relocated to Palm Beach, Fla. where he operated a place with only limited success because of his refusal to pay protection. He died on March 28, 1926.

KELLY, Joseph "Bunco" (1838-1934): Shanghaier and murderer

Oddly, the two greatest shanghaiers in America were named Kelly—Shanghai Kelly and Joseph "Bunco" Kelly. At age 26, Joseph Kelly of Liverpool, England set up in Portland, Ore. in 1859 and for the next 35 years made thousands of men into unwilling seamen, filling orders from crew-short sea captains. Totally without conscience, he hesitated at sending no one to sea, recruiting his victims from anywhere along the waterfront. He often used two doxies, Liverpool Liz and Esmeralda, as sex lures to coax drunks from Erickson's Saloon, where it took 15 men to tend the block-long bar, or from the Paris House, the city's biggest brothel, or from Mark Cook's Saloon. If such tactics failed, he simply bludgeoned hapless passersby and carted them off to a ship ready to sail.

Kelly sometimes had trouble acquiring accomplices, and for good reason. After once receiving an order for 10 men, he and two assistants deposited eight drunks into a ship's hold. "Here," said the skipper, "I need ten men, I told you."

Kelly nodded, battered his two aides senseless and collected for a full consignment. The profitability of the procedure was unassailable: in addition to collecting a fee for his assistants—as well as the other shanghai victims—he also saved the money he would otherwise have had to pay them.

Kelly picked up his nickname Bunco for another of his double-dealing deeds. He would bring an apparent victim wrapped in a blanket aboardship and deposit him directly in a bunk, telling the captain, "drunkenest sailor I ever seen." Kelly would collect his $50 stipend as the ship set sail. Not until the next morning would the angered captain discover Kelly had slipped him a cigar store Indian instead of a drunken sailor.

Bunco's biggest coup occurred when he came across 24 waterfront bums either dead or dying in the basement of an undertaking establishment, where they had partaken of barrels filled with embalming fluid under the illusion they were inside the next building, which was a saloon. At the time Bunco found them, he had an order outstanding for 22 shanghai victims at $30 a head. The master of the craft was extremely pleased when Kelly oversupplied the order by two, and gratefully handed him $720 for the bunch. The next day the red-faced captain had to dock in order to unload 14 corpses and another 10 men whose lives could be saved only by energetic stomach pumping. The captain vowed never again to do business with Bunco Kelly, but he probably broke his resolutions, since in Portland a ship's master almost had to deal with Kelly, even if wisdom required a close inspection of any goods purchased from him.

Despite actions by the police, which varied from largely indifferent to modestly determined, Kelly continued his nefarious trade until 1894, when he was apprehended for murdering a retired saloon keeper, 73-year-old George Washington Sayres. Kelly denied the charge, claiming it was a frame-up by competitors who wanted to take over his business. "I am being tried not as the person who killed poor old George Sayres," Bunco said in a statement. "I am being tried for all the crimes ever committed in the North End. I am on trial because I am operating a successful sailor's boarding house—the finest on this coast. I am being tried because I have no influence with the city's politicians. I had nothing against George Sayres."

That last statement, at least, was accurate. The jury concluded Kelly had committed the murder for $2,000 given him by Sayres' enemies.

Kelly did 13 years in the Oregon State Penitentiary and was released in 1907. He got a newspaperman named John Kelly, no relation, to help him write a book, *Thirteen Years in the Oregon Pen,* in which he continued to proclaim his innocence. Kelly left Portland in 1909 and eventually was said to have ended up in South America, where, as proof of the adage that only the good die young, he lived until the ripe old age of 96.

See also: *Shanghaiing, Shanghai Kelly.*

KELLY, Shanghai (1835-?): Shanghaier

Without doubt the most-feared name wherever Pacific sailors gathered in the 19th century was that of Shanghai Kelly, a stubby, red-bearded Irishman who became the most prodigious shanghaier on San Francisco's Barbary Coast.

Kelly maintained a saloon and boarding house at 33 Pacific Street. There is no way to precisely estimate how many men passed through his notorious shanghai pipelines but it was at least 10,000. He got the best deal from shipmasters because he generally provided bona fide sailors rather than unsuspecting landlubbers who happened to stumble along. Not that Kelly didn't turn a dishonest dollar in his shanghai operations whenever he could. Occasionally, among a boatload of drugged victims, Kelly would toss in a corpse or two. Since the usual transaction only allowed time for a head count of men in various degrees of stupor, it is easy to see how a captain might not discover he had been "stiffed with a stiff," as the saying went, until he was well out into the Pacific. Police could only wonder how many murder victims were turned over to Kelly to be disposed of for a price, thus providing him with a double fee. The master shanghaier knew that such a corpse would receive a quick and unrecorded burial far out at sea.

Feared as he was, Kelly still had no trouble keeping his boarding house stocked with sailors, many of whom knew the fate that lay in store for them. The popularity of Kelly's place rested on his reputation of providing free women to go along with his free liquor. To many a sailor the price of their next voyage was little enough to pay. Once, in the 1870s, though Kelly received an order for 90 sailors at a time when he was understocked. Chartering a paddle-wheel steamer, he announced he would celebrate his birthday with a picnic at which there would be all the liquor a celebrant could drink. Naturally, there was an admission charge, since Kelly firmly believed in getting all he could out of any deal. He kept a close count of the willing celebrants clamoring aboard and as soon as the number reached 90 the gangplank was pulled up and the steamer paddled off. Barrels of beer and whiskey were opened and the happy picnickers toasted Kelly's health. Of course, all the drink was heavily drugged and within a couple of hours everyone aboard except Kelly and his men was sound asleep. The paddle steamer pulled up to the two ships that had ordered crews, and Kelly handed over the agreed-on number to each and collected his pay. On his way back, he rescued survivors from the *Yankee Blade* which had sunk off Santa Barbara. Luckily for Kelly, the landing of the rescued men caused a great stir and nobody noticed that his picnic guests were missing. Of course, he would have felt even luckier if he had been able to sell the rescued seamen as well.

Kelly was active in his trade till near the end of the 19th century, when he faded from sight.

See also: *Joseph "Bunco" Kelly, Shanghaiing.*

KEMMLER, William (1861-1890): First victim of electric chair

The first man to die in the electric chair, William Kemmler was an illiterate Buffalo, N.Y. huckster who took an ax to his mistress, Tillie Ziegler. His case became a cause celebre only because of the novel method of execution ordered for him.

On death row Kemmler became a minor pawn in a major economic battle between two industrial giants, Thomas Edison and George Westinghouse. Edison had developed the first electric power system through the use of low-tension direct current (DC). Westinghouse then devised his alternating current (AC) system, which was much superior because it was easier and less costly to install. Edison sought to discourage the use of AC by pointing out its death-dealing potential. His arguments were so telling that Westinghouse's system was adapted for use in the new electric chair. Fearful that the use of AC for executions would affect its general acceptance by the public, Westinghouse waged a long, expensive campaign to save Kemmler from death. He hired top legal talent, including Bourke Cochran, then considered the leading lawyer in the country, and spent well over $100,000 in a losing cause.

While an appeal was sent to the Supreme Court for a ruling on the constitutionality of the punishment, Edwin F. Davis, the electrician at Auburn Prison, started building the chair in the institution's woodworking shop. Although authorities tried to keep the work a secret, newspapers presented diagrams that closely resembled what the real chair looked like. The papers also hastened to inform their apprehensive readers that the contraption "was not at all uncomfortable to sit in." Finally, on August 6, 1890, Kemmler went to the chair. As one observer wrote later, "His manner indicated a state of subdued elation, as if he were gratified at being the central figure of the occasion." The execution was botched badly. After the current was turned off, Kemmler's body moved and frantic officials

rushed to apply more current. Newspaper comment on the execution was universally unfavorable. The *Buffalo Express* predicted in an editorial, "Kemmler will be the last man executed in such a manner."

See also: *Execution, Methods of.*

KEMPER, Edmund Emil, III (1948-   ): California's "coed killer"

In 1972 and 1973, 25-year-old Edmund Kemper, a 280-pound, six-foot-nine giant, terrorized Santa Cruz County, Calif., particularly female students at the Santa Cruz campus of the University of California. Kemper killed six women, decapitating them and performing sex acts that could not be fully reported in the newspapers.

Kemper had an earlier history of murder. In 1964, at the age of 16, he was living with his grandparents when he started wondering what it would be like to shoot his grandmother. So he did. Then he shot his grandfather and called his mother to inform her that both her parents were dead. Judged insane, Kemper was confined at the Atacadero State Hospital. In 1969 the medical board at the institution found him "fully recovered," and he was released over the strenuous objection of the prosecuting attorney in his case.

Apparently free of antisocial tendencies, Kemper expended considerable effort to have the record of his earlier murder sealed and convinced four psychiatric specialists to support him in court. During his last two psychiatric interviews, the head of his most recent victim was in the trunk of his car parked just outside the psychiatrist's office.

Because Kemper's mother worked for the university, Kemper was able to obtain a school parking sticker, which allayed any suspicions of hitchhiking coeds when he offered them a ride. Kemper always kept large cellophane bags in his car so that if he killed and dismembered a girl, the upholstery would not be stained. He safely delivered many more girls than he actually killed, making certain not to harm any who had been seen getting into his car. Kemper generally decapitated the victims with a power saw and kept some of the bodies in his room for a day or two before disposing of them.

On April 20, 1973 Kemper bludgeoned his mother to death as she slept and dismembered her body, severing her hands and throwing them into the garbage disposal. He shoved the headless torso into a closet and then invited over a woman neighbor, his mother's best friend, and strangled her also. He threw her body in with his mother's and went to a local bar called the Jury Room, where he often drank with a number of off-duty police officers. After a time, Kemper got in his car and drove off. Three days later, in Pueblo, Colo., he called Santa Cruz police, who still knew nothing of the murderers, and gave himself up, warning he might kill more unless he was taken.

Convicted of eight counts of first-degree murder, Kemper was asked what he considered to be a fit punishment. He replied, "Death by torture." He was sentenced to life imprisonment and first became eligible for parole in 1980.

KENNEDY, John F.: See Lee Harvey Oswald, Jack Ruby.

KENNEDY, Robert F.: See Sirhan Bishara Sirhan.

KERRYONIANS: 19th century New York Irish gang

Among the gangs of the Five Points, the worst crime district in 19th century New York City, were the Kerryonians, who were organized around 1825. A collection of thugs, pickpockets, thieves and murderers no better than the Plug Uglies, Chichesters, Roach Guards or Dead Rabbits, the Kerryonians, natives of County Kerry, Ireland, had one distinction: they made it a rule only to victimize Englishmen, or at least individuals who looked English. Eventually, absorbed into other gangs, the aging Kerryonians had their last hurrah during the infamous Astor Place Riots of 1849 protesting an appearance by the eminent British actor William C. Macready.

See also: *Astor Place Riots.*

KETCHUM, "Black Jack" Tom (1862-1901): Train robber and murderer

Black Jack Ketchum and his brother Sam were Butch Cassidy's chief rivals as leaders of the various Hole In the Wall gangs in the 1890s. It was a situation that bewildered Cassidy, since he regarded the Ketchums as about the most stupid outlaws he'd ever met. And it was hard to fault his logic: after all Black Jack often beat himself over the head with his own six-shooter when things went wrong. Yet somehow Ketchum managed to blast his way into prominence in the annals of outlawry, so that when he was hanged even the *New York Times* felt the event deserved special coverage, a fortuitous decision since the affair proved memorable.

Tom and brother Sam rode out of their native Texas Panhandle in the early 1880s and made their way north, punching cattle and doing various odd jobs, until they reached New Mexico, where the brothers turned to crime. They held up a store-post office in Tucumcari, and when the angry owner, Levi Herzstein, took up their trail, they murdered him. The Ketchums next turned up in Hole in the Wall country in Wyoming and soon led a number of other outlaws on various robbery sprees. Late in 1898 Black Jack and his men robbed a train, the Twin Flyer, near Twin Mountains, New Mexico Territory of less than $500. If the robbery hadn't exactly been lucrative it had at least worked. Convinced he had a winning formula, Black Jack stuck up the same train at the same spot three more times, the last on July 11, 1899. But on that day the law was ready. A posse captured most of the robbers at Turkey Canyon, near Cimarron. During the gun battle Sheriff Edward Farr of Huerfano County, Colo. and W. H. Love of Cimarron were killed. Although shot through the shoulder

Ketchum escaped capture, but only for a few days. He was caught and brought to trial in Santa Fe.

The apprehension of the most-wanted man in the Southwest aside from Butch Cassidy caused a sensation, and newspapers from coast to coast covered Ketchum's trial. He was found guilty of "attempted train robbery." Since the penalty for that offense was death, indicting him for murder had been considered unnecessary. Delays in the case put off Black Jack's hanging until April 26, 1901. Ketchum watched the building of the scaffold for his hanging outside his cell window. "Very good, boys," he yelled to the workmen when it was completed, "but why don't you tear down that stockade so the boys can see a man hang who never killed anyone."

The execution of Western outlaw Black Jack Ketchum achieved a particularly awesome climax.

On the day of his execution, the condemned man "leaped" up the gallow steps, the *Times* correspondent reported. Black Jack helped in adjusting the noose around his neck and said cheerfully, "I'll be in Hell before you start breakfast." After the black cap was placed over his head, Ketchum called out "Let 'er go."

The trap was sprung, but the weights had been amateurishly adjusted and Ketchum's head was torn from his shoulders. Later, some writers found it necessary to improve on the ghoulish story, so they changed Black Jack's last words to "Let her rip!"

See also: *Sam Ketchum.*

KETCHUM, Sam (1860-1899): Train robber and murderer

Sam Ketchum, the brother of the infamous "Black Jack" Tom Ketchum, basked in his younger brother's glory and, in fact, was considered by some lawmen to be the real Black Jack. Actually, he was little more than a follower of his brother, as he demonstrated after Black Jack's capture in July 1899. Black Jack had daringly and stupidly held up Train No. 1 at Twin Mountains, N.M. four different times. He was finally caught. That left Sam in charge of the gang back in Hole in the Wall. It was an awesome responsibility for him since he had to plan a robbery without his brother's guidance. In what stands as a monument to outlaw obtuseness, Sam Ketchum came up with a grand scheme: the gang would hold up Train No. 1 at Twin Mountains. On August 16, 1899 the last of the Ketchum gang staged the suicidal undertaking. Sam Ketchum was shot by conductor Frank Harrington. With pursuers hot on his trail, he made it to a ranch, where a cowboy amputated his shotgun-shattered arm. It was a botched job and his captors could not save him from dying of blood poisoning.

See also: *"Black Jack" Tom Ketchum.*

KEY Racket: B-Girl swindle

The so-called key racket, where a bar-girl gives a customer the supposed key to her apartment in exchange for cash, is still practiced.

Shortly after its birth in San Francisco, it reached the proportions of a minor industry in that city. The practice began in the Seattle Saloon and Dance Hall, perhaps the lowest dive on San Francisco's Barbary Coast after the earthquake of 1906. The second floor of the Seattle was an assignation floor, where the 20-odd "waiter girls" could adjourn with customers. The ladies developed a lucrative sideline making dates to meet drunken customers after the Seattle closed at 3 a.m. In this scam a woman would promise to spend the night with a customer but only if the meeting were kept secret from her boyfriend, who met her each night after the saloon closed and escorted her home. It would therefore be impossible for the customer and the woman to leave the resort together. Instead, she would offer to sell the man a key to her flat for a price ranging from $1 to $5, depending on what she thought the traffic would bear, so that he could join her an hour after closing. If the customer objected that he was paying for a pig in a poke, the woman would counter that since she did not know him, she would be stuck with the expense of changing the lock on her door if he didn't show up. To a man with a liquor-logged brain, the argument often made sense. After handing over the cash, the customer would write down the woman's address, which would be some nearby building but, of course, not the one where she really lived.

Some popular waiter-girls at the Seattle often sold a dozen keys a night. The custom was soon picked up in most of the other Barbary Coast resorts, so that on a typical night, long after the dance halls closed, scores of furtive figures would be seen staggering through the streets, key in hand, trying to find a door that would open. For a time, watching the "key men" became a slumming sport for those San Franciscans who were rather proud of their city's reputation as the vilest this side of decadent Paris. The lucrative practice continued for about a year until the police cracked down on it as a result of newspaper exposes that published hundreds of complaints from reputable householders plagued by drunks trying to unlock their doors.

"KICKING The Habit"

The term "kicking the habit" refers to the process drug addicts undergo to conquer their addiction to narcotics. In the first days of withdrawal, an addict suffers only minor symptoms, such as yawning, watery eyes, running nose and sweating. During the peak period of withdrawal, which starts 48 to 72 hours after the last dose, the addict becomes irritable and restless. He is unable to sleep and has no desire to eat. He suffers gooseflesh, tremors and severe sneezing and yawning. Then he is wracked by nausea and vomiting and often suffers stomach cramps and diarrhea. The addict alternately feels flush and chilled and enormous pain builds up in the bones and muscles of the back and in the extremities. Usually, he will experience muscle spasms and kicking movements, hence the expression kicking the habit. Even when this period of suffering subsides, there is no guarantee that the addict is cured, as restoration of physiological and psychological equilibrium vary in individual cases.

KID Curry (1865-1904): Robber and murderer

Perhaps the most feared of the Wild Bunch, Harvey Logan, better known as Kid Curry, probably killed more lawmen than any other Western outlaw. He killed and wounded several law officers in the Wyoming, Arizona and Utah territories. Before he joined the Wild Bunch he had killed eight men in street gunfights. As a Buncher, he had to be contained by Butch Cassidy or his murder toll would have been much higher.

One of four Logan brothers, Harvey hailed from Missouri. At 19, he and two younger brothers and a cousin headed for Wyoming, where the four became rustlers, soon gathering enough stock to start their own ranch. Harvey learned the art of rustling from Big Nose George Curry, who was the top stock thief in Wyoming's Powder River region during the 1870s.

Harvey so admired Big Nose that upon his lynching in 1882, he adopted the older man's surname as his own, becoming known as Kid Curry. In the mid-1890s Kid Curry turned up at Hole in the Wall, the notorious outlaw hideout, and hooked up with the Wild Bunch. Cassidy liked Curry's raw nerve and dependability, but he often found it necessary to put himself between the Kid and train guards to prevent needless slaughter.

When Cassidy and the Sundance Kid decided in 1901 that the West was getting too hot and opted for South America, Kid Curry promised to join them but instead went on robbing banks and trains to become the most-hunted outlaw in the country. He worked his way east as far as Knoxville, Tenn. where he got involved in a shoot-out with the police, wounding three of them, and although wounded himself, he managed to escape. Tracked by a posse using bloodhounds, he was captured 20 miles outside the city.

Placed in the Knoxville Jail pending transfer to an "escape-proof" prison in Columbus, Ohio, he executed one of the most sensational jail breaks in criminal history. He used a noose he made of wire from a broom to strangle a jail guard, tied up two others, and forced another to saddle him up a horse, on which he made his escape. Where Curry went is a matter of some dispute. Some say he went on to South America and joined up with Cassidy and Sundance. Others, including the Pinkertons, insisted he returned to the West and formed up a new gang in Colorado. According to this theory, over a period of 12 days he traveled 1,400 miles, hooked on as a ranch hand with a brand new identity, formed a gang, robbed a train and spent two days on the run before being trapped by the law.

Curry was cornered near Glenwood Springs. Rather than be captured again, he put a bullet through his head. The Pinkertons identified the dead man as Kid Curry. Others, including a number of deputies and chief agent Canada of the Union Pacific, objected. The dead man's picture was taken back to the jail in Knoxville, where those guards who had been in daily contact with the jail's most famous prisoner unanimously agreed it was a photo of Kid Curry. A federal court ordered the case "closed by virtue of suicide."

See also: *Big Nose George Curry, Wild Bunch.*

KID Dropper (1891-1923): New York gangster chief

For a time in the early 1920s, the premier gangster in New York City was Kid Dropper, born Nathan Kaplan, who literally murdered his way into the position of top labor slugger-extortionist during the post-World War I period. He had come a long way from his lowly position as a minor ally of the last great New York criminal gang before the advent of Prohibition, the Five Pointers.

In his youth he earned the sobriquet Kid Dropper from his scam of dropping a wallet filled with counterfeit money on the street. He would then pick it up in front of a potential victim, pretend it was an accidental discovery and, claiming to be in a great hurry, offer to sell it to the mark, who in turn would be able to return it to its rightful owner for a reward or keep it.

As late as 1911, when he was sentenced to seven years in prison for robbery, Kid Dropper was not considered a major criminal. When he came out, however, there was a void in the labor slugging field left by the passage from the scene of

Dopey Benny Fein and Joe the Greaser Rosensweig. Kid Dropper organized a gang with another Five Pointers alumnus, young Johnny Spanish, a vicious killer with perhaps more nerve than the Dropper. Previously, they had had a falling out over a woman and Spanish had done seven years for shooting her. That rift indicated the two could not work together for long, especially since each obviously intended to become "top dog."

Soon, a war broke out between the two rivals, and both fielded platoons of killers. Bullet-ridden corpses became commonplace, particularly in the garment district. The war was concluded on July 29, 1919, when three men, one always presumed to have been the Dropper, walked up behind Johnny Spanish as he left a Second Avenue restaurant and emptied their revolvers into his body.

Thereafter, the Kid headed all the important labor slugging rackets in the city, working either for the unions or the employers or both. Between 1920 and 1923 the Dropper was responsible for at least an estimated 20 murders. He became a notorious sight along Broadway in his belted check suit of extreme cut, narrow pointed shoes, and stylish derby or straw hat slanted rakishly over one eye, and at all times he was surrounded by a bevy of gunmen.

By 1923 the Dropper was beset by new and even tougher opponents than the late unlamented Johnny Spanish. They were headed by Jacob "Little Augie" Orgen, a bloodthirsty gangster with such supporters and "comers" as Jack "Legs" Diamond, Louis "Lepke" Buchalter and Gurrah Shapiro. The Dropper's men and Little Augie's followers began open warfare over control of the wet wash laundry workers and were soon involved in wholesale shoot-outs all around the town.

Finally, in August 1923 Kid Dropper was picked up on a charge of carrying a concealed weapon and hauled into Essex Market Court. The arrest of the great gang leader attracted a large number of newsmen and onlookers. When the Kid's arraignment was transferred to another court, he was led to the street by a phalanx of policemen. As he was entering the car, a minor and particularly lamebrained hoodlum named Louis Kushner jumped forward and shot him through the windshield. Kushner had been properly "stroked" by the Little Augies gang into believing that such a daring act would make him an important gangster and member of their outfit.

The Dropper crumpled up inside the car, while his wife fought her way through the police guards wrestling with Kushner. "Nate! Nate!" she cried. "Tell me that you were not what they say you were!" Instead, the Kid managed only to moan, "They got me!" and died.

Kushner in the meantime announced triumphantly: "I got him. I'd like a cigarette."

In due course, Kushner got 20 years and Little Augie absorbed the Dropper's illicit enterprises. He held them only until 1927, when he too was violently removed from power, apparently by Lepke and Shapiro, who then took over the union rackets.

See also: *Drop Swindle, Labor Sluggers War, Jacob "Little Augie" Orgen, Johnny Spanish.*

KID Twist (1882-1908): New York gang leader

Long the right-hand man of Monk Eastman, perhaps the most notable Jewish gangster in American history, Kid Twist succeeded to the leadership of the Eastmans when the Monk was sent to prison in 1904. The Eastmans were the last Jewish gang to dominate crime in New York City. Eastman showed great pride in the Twist because he never failed to carry out a murder assignment, the total variously estimated at between 10 and 20, and could be counted on to perform any other important job.

Born Max Zweiback, or Zwerbach, he was aptly nicknamed Kid Twist becuase of his treacherous nature, which he demonstrated in dealing with another Eastman lieutenant, Richie Fitzpatrick, in the struggle for the Eastman throne. Fitzpatrick was an accomplished killer in his own right and was not prepared to settle the question of succession by any method other than a test of arms. The Kid suggested a conference to settle all differences, and Fitzpatrick agreed to a meeting in a Chrystie Street dive. The talks had barely begun when the lights went out and a revolver blazed. When the police arrived, no one was in the place save Fitzpatrick, who lay dead on the floor with a bullet in his heart and his arms folded on his chest. Kid Twist sent flowers to the funeral and wore a mourning band on his sleeve for months thereafter. The underworld toasted the Kid's finesse and acknowledged his leadership of the Eastmans.

Had a matter of the heart not distracted him, Kid Twist's savage cunning probably would have maintained the 1,200-man Eastman gang's supremacy over the various Irish gangs, the new Italian Mafia gangs and Paul Kelly's Five Pointers, which already included the likes of Johnny Torrio and would soon add such luminaries as Al Capone and Lucky Luciano. The Twist took time out from the systematic murder of Fitzpatrick's top supporters to fall in love with Carroll Terry, a Coney Island dance hall girl of striking beauty. It so happened that Carroll was also being pursued by Louis Pioggi, better known as Louie the Lump, one of the Five Pointers' more vicious killers.

Since Louie the Lump was rather undersized, Kid Twist took to battering him around at times when Louie could not draw his gun because of the number of Eastmans on hand to blast him. The rivalry between the two reached a climax on May 14, 1908, when the Kid found the Lump in a second-floor Coney Island dive. He decided to torment Louie. "Carroll says you is an active little cuss, always jumpin' around," the Kid remarked. "Let's see how active youse is, kid. Take a jump out of the window!"

When Louie the Lump hesitated, Kid Twist and his companion, Cyclone Louie, a local strongman and hired killer, moved menacingly toward their weapons. Louie jumped and landed on all fours, avoiding serious injury. Determined to exact vengeance, he hurried to a telephone and called Five Pointer headquarters to report Kid Twist was about with only one companion for protection. Within the hour, 20 Five Pointer gunmen appeared on the scene. Given the honor of gunning down the hated foe, Louie the Lump shot Kid Twist through the brain when he eventually came out of the dive. Cyclone Louie tried to run, but a hail of Five Pointer bullets sent him spinning down atop his fallen chief. Just then Carroll Terry came rushing out and the love-thwarted Louie shot her in the shoulder and watched her collapse next to her dead lover.

The death of Kid Twist was to have profound effects on the New York underworld over the next few years as the Eastman gang broke into factions. Ethnically, the top position in the underworld would pass to the Italian gangsters and to the next generation of Jewish gangsters, such as the 1920 Bug and Meyer gang, headed by Bugsy Siegel and Meyer Lansky, who found it more profitable to work in concert with other ethnic groups than to oppose them. None of this was foreseen in 1908, however, when New York City seemed delighted to have the likes of Kid Twist depart the scene, a sentiment expressed rather obviously by Louie the Lump's punishment for two counts of manslaughter: 11 months in the Elmira Reformatory.

See also: *Cyclone Louie, Richie Fitzpatrick.*

KIDD, Captain William (1645?-1701): Pirate

Probably more songs, legends and ballads have been composed about Capt. William Kidd than any other villain on land or sea, but more recently, some biographers have attempted to paint him as more sinned against than sinning, a man virtually forced into piracy. The facts are that Capt. Kidd was indeed a pirate and that he killed ruthlessly in the course of his criminal pursuits.

Born in Scotland sometime around 1645, Kidd started out as a peaceful trader and shipowner. After settling in America in 1690, he distinguished himself routing French privateers marauding the coast in the New York area. For this the state assembly awarded him a citation and a cash bounty of 150 pounds. Capt. Kidd settled down in New York, marrying a wealthy widow and becoming a leading citizen and church member.

In 1695 a private syndicate authorized by King William III of England and several leading Whigs commissioned Kidd as a privateer to run down pirates preying on British shipping and to attack French vessels of commerce, with the prizes going to the syndicate. Capt. Kidd set sail for the East Indies in 1696 aboard his *Adventure Galley*, but he was stymied by a severe shortage of enemy shipping. According to some historians, his crew, composed mostly of wastrels, sea rats and cutthroats, virtually forced him into attacking friendly ships. Kidd did indeed attack his own nation's shipping and kept the lion's share of the booty for himself.

Kidd returned to New York in 1698 with a shipload of gold, jewels and silks, some of which he buried on Gardiners Island, off Long Island.

Kidd was confident that his privateer's commission would shield him from a charge of piracy, but news of his acts reached London and charges were lodged against him, partly at the instigation of the Tories, who were eager to find fault with their Whig enemies. Kidd was sent back to England, where he probably could have gotten off lightly and perhaps even scot-free if he had agreed to implicate his Whig associates. Instead, he insisted on both their innocence and his own. Numerous deserters from his crew were brought forth to testify against him, no doubt embellishing their testimony with fanciful accounts of his cruelty. At his trial Kidd declared: "I am the innocentest person of them all. Only I have been sworn against by perjured persons." He was hanged on May 23, 1701.

Part of Capt. Kidd's booty was found on Gardiners Island, but treasure hunters have continued to hunt there ever since. Legend has it that more of Captain Kidd's treasure is still buried in such places as Deer Isle, Maine: Clarke's Island in the Connecticut River; Stratford Point, Conn.; Rye Beach, Fishers Island and Capt. Kidd's cave on the lower Hudson River, all in New York; and Block Island, R.I., where through the years some old coins have been found.

See also: *Piracy.*

KIDNAPPING

Kidnapping for ransom was hardly an American invention, the practice dating back to ancient times. However, probably nowhere else was the crime committed as frequently as it was in the United States during the early 1930s, typified best by the Lindbergh baby kidnapping in 1932.

Although there were many early kidnappings in America, especially of children—girls for the purposes of prostitution—and free blacks, the first major kidnapping for ransom case in this country is generally regarded to have been that of four-year-old Charley Ross, who was abducted on July 1, 1874. Technically, the case was never solved and "little Charley Ross," which became a household phrase, was never found. It is almost certain that he was murdered by his kidnappers, two notorious criminals named William Mosher and Joey Douglass and an ex-policeman named William Westervelt.

The question kidnappers always face is whether or not to kill the victim. When the victim is murdered the crime usually occurs immediately after the abduction. Conversely, the victim's family must decide whether or not to pay the ransom, since paying may only lead to the killing of the victim. A general rule of thumb is that a so-called amateur kidnapper will tend to kill the victim, but a true professional will let him or her live, realizing that murdering the victim lessens the chance of collecting a ransom for the next kidnapping. This perspective evolved in the 1920s, when organized criminals were kidnapped by other organized criminals and held for ransom. Killing the victims under such circumstances would have eliminated the "goose that lays the golden eggs." Underworld ransom kidnappings were very profitable because the racketeer-victims seldom were able to appeal to the law for assistance. Equally important, such victims hardly wished to let it be known that they had been unable to defend themselves. As a result, their kidnappers received scant public attention. Around 1930 organized kidnap rings started to victimize private citizens, and the public not only grew aware of kidnappings but demanded the authorities put a halt to them. The FBI's success in smashing several kidnapping gangs did much to alter that agency's tarnished image.

Major Kidnappings in American History

1900: Edward A. Cudahy, Jr., 16, in Omaha, Neb. Released after $25,000 ransom paid. Pat Crowe confessed but acquitted.

1927: Marion Parker, 12, in Los Angeles, Calif. $7,500 ransom paid but victim had already been murdered and dismembered. Edward Hickman convicted and executed.

1932: Charles A. Lindbergh, Jr., 20 months, in Hopewell, N.J. $50,000 ransom paid but victim had already been murdered. Bruno Richard Hauptmann convicted and executed.

1933: William A. Hamm, Jr., 39, in St. Paul, Minn. Released after $100,000 paid. Alvin "Creepy" Karpis convicted and sentenced to life.

1933: Charles F. Urschel, in his forties, in Oklahoma City, Okla. Released after $200,000 paid. Kathryn and George "Machine Gun" Kelly and four accomplices convicted and sentenced to life.

1936: Charles Mattson, 10, in Tacoma, Wash. $28,000 ransom demanded but never collected. Victim found dead. Case remains unsolved.

1937: Charles S. Ross, 72, in Franklin Park, Ill. $50,000 ransom paid but victim then murdered. John Henry Seadlund convicted and executed.

1953: Robert C. Greenlease, six, in Kansas City, Mo. $600,000 ransom paid but victim had already been murdered. Carl A. Hall and Bonnie Brown Heady convicted and executed.

1956: Peter Weinberger, 32 days old, in Westbury, N.Y. $2,000 ransom demanded but not paid. Victim found dead. Angelo John LaMarca convicted and executed.

1963: Frank Sinatra, Jr., 19, in Lake Tahoe, Calif. Released after $240,000 ransom paid by father. John W. Irwin, Joseph C. Amsler and Barry W. Keenan convicted and sentenced to prison.

1968: Barbara Jane Mackle, 20, in Atlanta, Ga. Released after $500,000 paid. Gary Steven Krist and Ruth Eisemann-Schier convicted and sentenced to prison.

1974: Patricia Hearst, 19, in Berkeley, Calif. $2 million ransom paid but victim not released and later charged with joining her captors. Except for William and Emily Harris, all of victim's kidnappers killed in gun battle with police. Harrises convicted and sentenced to 10 years to life.

1976: 26 children and bus driver in Chowchilla, Calif, Ransom demanded but victims escaped. Frederick Newhall Woods, IV, James Schoenfeld and Richard Allen Schoenfeld convicted and sentenced to life.

See also: *College Kidnappers; Individual listings under names of victims or kidnappers except Frank Sinatra, Jr. and Peter Weinberger.*

KIDNAPPING Of Free Blacks

Throughout the decades preceding the Civil War, kidnapping of free blacks in the North and shipping them to the South to be sold as slaves was a thriving criminal enterprise. Kidnapping rings operated with impunity despite laws in Southern states prohibiting the practice. Such laws were mere shams since blacks were disqualified as witnesses and thus could not incriminate their captors. Entire families were abducted but many kidnap rings preferred dealing only in children and young women because such captives could be more easily contained. Some enterprising kidnappers used the ruse of marrying mulatto women and then selling them off as slaves at the first opportunity. Unscrupulous federal magistrates cooperated in schemes to seize blacks and transport them to the South under the pretext of enforcing the fugitive slave laws.

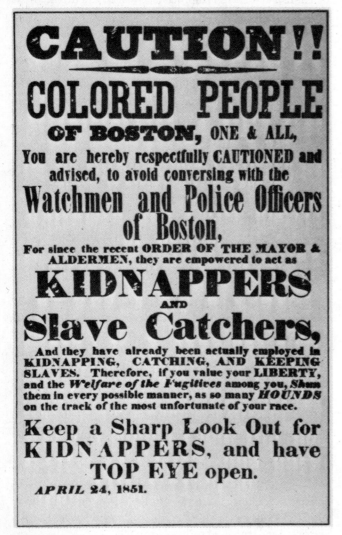

CAUTION!!
COLORED PEOPLE
OF BOSTON, ONE & ALL,
You are hereby respectfully **CAUTIONED** and advised, to avoid conversing with the
Watchmen and Police Officers of Boston,
For since the recent **ORDER OF THE MAYOR & ALDERMEN**, they are empowered to act as
KIDNAPPERS
AND
Slave Catchers,
And they have already been actually employed in **KIDNAPPING, CATCHING, AND KEEPING SLAVES.** Therefore, if you value your **LIBERTY**, and the *Welfare of the Fugitives* among you, *Shun* them in every possible manner, as so many *HOUNDS* on the track of the most unfortunate of your race.
Keep a Sharp Look Out for KIDNAPPERS, and have TOP EYE open.
APRIL 24, 1851.

An 1851 proclamation warned free blacks of the activities of "slave catchers."

KILPATRICK, Ben (?1865-1912): Last of the Wild Bunch

In addition to being the handsomest of the Wild Bunch and a ladies' man, Ben Kilpatrick, known as the Tall Texan, was lightning quick on the draw and, as Butch Cassidy said, absolutely fearless. He was also to meet an ignoble end because he tried to carry on a form of outlawry whose day had past, when all the other Bunchers were dead, imprisoned or wisely retired.

Kilpatrick rode into the famous outlaw hideout Hole in the Wall about 1890. Thereafter, he scourged the Southwest, often with fellow Texans the Ketchum brothers and then more and more with Cassidy's Wild Bunch. When at times he suddenly would disappear, his fellow outlaws knew he had lost himself in the fleshpots of the West and would return only when his money ran out. Usually, he came back with a mistress in tow. His last was the celebrated Laura Bullion, alias Della Rose, the Rose of the Bunch.

During a bank or train robbery, Cassidy always preferred to station Kilpatrick at his back, knowing he could be counted on to carry out his assignment and stick to his post no matter what complications arose. His steel nerve was not necessarily matched by his brainpower, however; in November 1901, after taking part in the robbery of a train at Wagner, Mont., Kilpatrick took the Rose to St. Louis on a spree, expending Bank of Helena (Mont.) currency, which was very uncommon in Missouri, like water. Local police and Pinkertons crashed into their hotel room and found $7,000 from the Wagner job. Kilpatrick confessed to taking part in the train robbery and was sent to the federal penitentiary at Atlanta, Ga. Della Rose got five years as an accomplice of the gang.

As Kilpatrick left the penitentiary on June 11, 1911, he told prison mates he intended to resume his outlaw ways. But the Wild Bunch was gone. Cassidy and Sundance had vanished, apparently in South America; Kid Curry was dead; Elzy Lay had reformed; and Matt Warner had even turned lawman. In addition, his woman Della had disappeared. The days of the Wild Bunch were over, and the West was no longer the place it had been.

Nonetheless, the Tall Texan teamed up with another outlaw, Ed Welch, alias Howard Benson, and set out to bring back the good old days. They pulled a couple of minor stick-ups just to get in shape. Then on March 14, 1912 they boarded the express car of the Southern Pacific's Sunset Limited and quickly got the drop on the Wells Fargo messenger, David Truesdale. In the old days express guards were generally cowed by bandits and offered no resistance, but times had changed. When Welch moved into the baggage car for a moment and Kilpatrick turned his gaze for a split second, the guard picked up an ice mallet and slammed Kilpatrick in the head, killing him with one blow. He then picked up Kilpatrick's rifle and when Welch stepped back into the car, he shot him dead. For a time Truesdale enjoyed great national notoriety and newspaper cartoonists reveled in caricaturing Kilpatrick's humiliating end.

See also: *Butch Cassidy, David A. Truesdale, Wild Bunch.*

KING, Dot (1894-1923): Murder victim

The murder of playgirl Dot King in New York in 1923 was

the classic Broadway drama which, as Russel Crouse wrote, "might easily be credited to a hack and his typewriter. Its characters are creations at a penny a word—the Broadway butterfly, the 'heavy sugar daddy,' the dark, sinister lover, the broken-hearted mother, and even the Negro maid, for comedy." Countless books on the "sins of New York" have described the Dot King case with varying degrees of accuracy.

Born into an Irish family living in an uptown slum, Anna Marie Keenan married a chauffeur when she was 18 but dumped him shortly afterwards as she began making it big as a model. To fit her new image, she changed her name to Dot King and, with her stunning looks, natural blonde hair and sparkling blue eyes, became a hostess in a plush speakeasy. It was here that she met "Mr. Marshall," the sugar daddy who made her the envy of her night club coworkers. Within a year after she met Mr. Marshall, he had showered some $30,000 in cash and jewelry on her.

On March 15, 1923 Dot King was found dead on her bed, at first glance an apparent suicide. An empty bottle of chloroform lay nearby, and the telephone had been shifted away from the bed as far as the cord would stretch. On closer inspection, the police noticed Dot's arm was twisted behind her back as if it had been put in a hammer lock, and the suicide theory was discarded for one of murder. But who had done it? There were many suspects, but the most logical one was the missing Mr. Marshall, whom the victim's maid described and who had written scores of "spicy" letters. One, which the newspapers delighted in publishing, read: "Darling Dottie: Only two days before I will be in your arms. I want to see you, O, so much, and to kiss your pretty pink toes."

And there was Dot's "kept" man, a Latin named Alberto Santos Guimares, upon whom the Broadway butterfly seemed to bestow gifts with almost the same frequency as she received them from Mr. Marshall. Police soon had evidence that Guimares, who apparently survived by petty swindling and exploitation of women, repaid Dot for her generosity by beating her up regularly. As a suspect, however, Guimares had drawbacks. He claimed that at the time of the murder he was in the arms of another woman, a leading socialite who backed up his story. If the tabloid readers suffered any disappointment over that development, they were overwhelmingly compensated by the identification of Mr. Marshall, who had already revealed his identity to the police. They had tried to shield him because they accepted his word that he had nothing to do with the murder—and because he was someone worth protecting. However, an enterprising newspaper reporter learned who he was.

His name was J. Kearsley Mitchell, the wealthy son-in-law of E. T. Stotesbury, the most prominent millionaire on Philadelphia's Main Line. Gossip writers ran amok with tales of twisted passions and plots of blackmail. Had Kearsley wanted to leave Dot and was she blackmailing him? The police said no, but their theories weren't respected since they had admitted attempting to hide Kearsley's identity to protect the millionaire's socially prominent wife and their three children from scandal.

Eventually, the police fell back to a theory that was safest of all, although devoid of social scandal, lurid romance and the like. It was that Dot had been the victim of robbers who had chloroformed her a bit too thoroughly. About a year later, another Broadway butterfly, Louise Lawson, suffered the same kind of death. Police learned that Louise, whose apartment, like Dot's, was stuffed with cash and baubles from an admirer, had opened the door to two men who said they had a package for her.

Undoubtedly, a woman—like Dot King—who had a sugar daddy would almost certainly open her door for someone saying he was bearing gifts. Of course, the public did not like the robbery theory. They much preferred a story of Main Line society, twisted and violent jealousy, and since the Dot King case remained unsolved, they never had to abandon that version.

See also: *Charles Norris*.

KING, Kate (1842-?): Quantrill's mistress and madam

The young woman who was soon to become the mistress of Confederate guerrilla leader William C. Quantrill was about 20 when she was kidnapped by the Raiders in Missouri. The facts of her life and even her identity are uncertain; her name was either Kate Clarke or Kate King, the name she was to use later in life. Young Kate willingly became Quantrill's lover, living in the brush with him. When the rebel raider was taken prisoner by Union forces in May 1865, he made out a will that gave Kate half his estate, mostly the loot from the war.

Kate took her good fortune to St. Louis and opened a fashionable brothel. According to a piece of the folklore passed on about Kate, she allegedly shot a client who had referred to the late Quantrill as a butcher. Kate is said to have attended a number of annual reunions of veterans of Quantrill's Raiders, where she would hand out her business card, before she married a man named Woods and passed into obscurity.

KING, Martin Luther, Jr.: See James Earl Ray.

KIRKBUZZER: Pickpocket

Nineteenth century America produced a special breed of pickpocket called a kirkbuzzer, whose modus operandi was picking pockets in church. Andy Craig, a noteworthy Chicago pickpocket, was considered a past master of the art. In his somber Sunday best, he would go through a church crowd, psalm book in hand, relieving at least a half dozen of the worshipers of their money purses. For a time Craig organized a group of kirkbuzzers, but in 1893 he gave up this racket as part of a deal between the underworld and the city's politicians that gave certain dips the pickpocketing rights to the World's Fair of 1893 in return for their promise that they would no longer victimize churchgoers. Soon kirkbuzzers around the country were forced to give up their church beats once police came to regard their activities as exceeding normal criminality and verging on blasphemy. According to some old-time pickpockets, the first "BEWARE OF PICKPOCKETS" signs appeared on church fronts.

KIRKER, James (1810-1852): Gunrunner and scalp hunter

In the history of scalp hunting, James Kirker stands as one of America's greatest mass murderers, taking an estimated 300 scalps personally and a great number more in alliance with another Indian killer, James Hobbs. There was perhaps some mitigating explanation for Kirker's crimes in that his parents had been killed by the Apaches in what is now Arizona while he was in his teens; he spent the decade in a private war with them. When in 1837 Kirker heard about scalp hunters killing 400 Mimbreno Apaches in one swoop and taking a fortune in scalps, he realized he wasn't getting full mileage out of his scalp taking. In 1842 he teamed up with James Hobbs to lift scalps on a wholesale basis but left the partnership to run guns to Chief Mangus Colorado of the Apaches. That activity ended when the Mexican governors of Sonora and Chihuahua placed a reward of 10,000 pesos on his head. Deciding that scalp hunting was safer, Kirker again hooked up with Hobbs, who had been living with the Shawnees and had recruited a band of these Indians to help him take Apache and Navaho scalps. In one village alone, the Kirker-Hobbs forces took 300 scalps. The partners then hauled the scalps to Chihuahua to collect the bounty. To hide his identity, Kirker shaved off his beard and dressed differently. The total reward came to some 23,000 gold pesos. Since the local treasury at that moment held only 2,000 pesos, they were given a written receipt for the balance. Kirker seemed nervous about the arrangement, no doubt realizing that Hobbs could turn him in and take the whole 23,000 pesos, a kingly sum, for himself. So he slipped off to California with the 2,000 pesos, which was more than enough money to allow him to retire from running guns and lifting scalps. Kirker settled down near Mount Diablo and proceeded to drink himself to death, dying of alcohol poisoning in 1852.

See also: *James Hobbs, Scalp Hunting.*

KISS Of Death: Mafia execution signal

The kiss was always important in the Mafia. During the old days in New York, it was considered a form of greeting whenever one member met another. The custom was ordered stopped by Lucky Luciano on his ascendency to power in 1931. "After all," he is alleged to have declared, "we would stick out kissing each other in restaurants and places like that." The kiss of death, however, was never too popular in this country because all it accomplished was to alert the potential victim; the practical American Mafia found that symbolism had little to recommend it. The kiss of death was given occasionally, however,

when the real purpose was to demonstrate the power of the one either doing the killing or ordering the killing. Vito Genovese used the kiss of death while behind bars in the federal penitentiary at Atlanta to prove that he was still the "boss of bosses." That strategem backfired when Genovese told another prisoner and soldier in the Mafia, Joe Valachi, that he wanted to give him a kiss for "old time's sake." All the convicts took that for what it was, a death sentence, because Valachi was widely suspected of being an informer for the Federal Bureau of Narcotics. Valachi was not, or so the official record states, but, realizing that Genovese was marking him for death, he took refuge in solitary confinement and there, supposedly for the first time, considered becoming an informer. When he finally did, Valachi rocked the criminal structure of the country.

See also: *Vito Genovese, Joseph Valachi.*

KISS Of Death Girls: Underworld jinxes

A traditional underworld archetype is the kiss of death girl, a sobriquet newspapers apply to women whose lovers seem to die at a much more frequent rate than the mortality tables and laws of chance would allow.

The origin of the term "kiss of death" girl is not clear. There is some indication that the first such female was Ida the Goose, an inamorata of the New York City underworld in the early part of this century who provoked the 1909 Ida the Goose War between the Gophers and the equally murderous Chick Tricker gang. Ida the Goose, a noted beauty despite her rather unromantic name, was the plaything of one Gopher Gang captain after another, generally upon the demise of a prior lover. Her crowning kiss of death caper occurred when, after defecting to the Tricker ranks, she was reclaimed by the Gophers after they assassinated her Tricker gang lover along with several of his fellow gang members in a celebrated cafe shoot-out.

Another famous lady who jinxed her lovers was Mary Margaret Collings, dubbed Kiss of Death Maggie by an appreciative Chicago press during the Capone era. The lady had the misfortune of losing no less than six husbands, underworld characters all, either in gang battles or confrontations with the police. It got so that guests at her weddings made wagers on how long her newest spouse would last. One reporter calculated that "six months was about par for the course."

The most famous of the breed was Evelyn Mittleman, who was labeled the Kiss of Death Girl of Murder, Inc. because of her love affair with Pittsburgh Phil Strauss, the organization's most-dedicated killer. Actually, Evelyn just seemed to be a luscious blonde who attracted men who were equally attracted by violence. At an early age, Evelyn, who came from the Williamsburg section of Brooklyn, New York City, attracted the attention of newsmen covering the breeding spots of criminality. When the Murder, Inc. investigation broke in 1940, Eddie Zeltner, a columnist for the *New York Daily Mirror,* wrote: "I knew Evelyn ten years ago, when she was barely sixteen, a gorgeous blonde who used to come from Williamsburg to Coney Island to swim, and dance in the cellar clubs which are grammar schools for gangsters."

When she was 18, Evelyn was in California with a fellow named Hy Miller, who was enamored of her. One night at a dance another man was struck by her looks. A violent disagreement ensued between him and Miller, who lost Evelyn and his life that very night. The same sort of thing happened a couple of years later back in Brooklyn. She was then dating one Robert Feurer when she caught the eye of Jack Goldstein, a Brownsville gangster involved in the wholesale fish market racket. Goldstein promptly killed Feurer when the latter objected to his attention to Evelyn. Thereafter, Goldstein proudly paraded around with Evelyn in tow until one day they happened to pass a Brownsville poolhall and were seen by Pittsburgh Phil. Phil liked what he saw and said so. Goldstein took exception to the remark and complained about his behavior. Phil quickly went back inside the poolhall and emerged with a billiard cue. He gave Goldstein a vicious going over, completely altering his features and his romantic notions about Evelyn.

Goldstein did not come around much after that, but it was not until four years later that he succumbed to the kiss of death curse. He was murdered by Pittsburgh Phil, but it was not over Evelyn's affections. A contract was put out on him because of his racket activities, and a number of killers headed by Phil, were assigned to the hit. The hit men were ordered to hammer Goldstein into unconsciousness, but not to kill him, and to bring him directly to Phil, who insisted on drowning Goldstein personally.

Pittsburgh Phil proved to be Kiss of Death Evelyn's last victim. She was the final visitor in his death cell before he was executed in 1941. Thereafter, Evelyn, the greatest of the kiss of death girls, faded into obscurity.

See also: *Ida the Goose War.*

KISSING

From time to time, kissing has been considered a crime in certain jurisdictions of the United States and there are still various laws on the books forbidding this nefarious practice. Thus, in Indiana it is illegal for a man with a mustache to "habitually kiss human beings" and in Cedar Rapids, Iowa the kissing of a stranger is clearly a crime. A health ordinance in Riverside, Calif. bars kissing on the lips unless both parties first wipe their lips with carbolized rosewater.

These legal restrictions on kissing have long been thought humorous since the mores of the country changed and attitudes on kissing altered. All of which no doubt would be of small comfort to a Captain Kemble, who was placed in the public stocks in Boston in 1656 for kissing his wife in public on the Sabbath. The only extenuating circumstance the captain could present, which was promptly rejected by the law, was that he had just returned from a three-year voyage at sea.

KITTY And Jennie Gang: Chicago two-woman gang

From 1886 until the turn of the century, Chicago men were menaced by what the police called the Kitty and Jennie Gang. Actually, the "gang" consisted of only two members, Kitty Adams and Jennie Clark, but their depredations befitted a criminal combine much larger in size. Kitty Adams first appeared in Chicago around 1880. She was the wife of a noted pickpocket, George Shine, but soon tossed him over and won a reputation of her own as the Terror of State Street. Although white, she did a short stint in a black brothel and there mastered the use of the razor, a weapon she always hid in the bosom of her dress and used when the need arose. Once when a lover of hers became overbearing, she whipped out her razor and sliced off both his ears.

About 1886 she set up a streetwalker's crib in the Levee, Chicago's segregated vice area, but really supported herself as a footpad. She started working with a very attractive young woman named Jennie Clark, who would pick up men on the streets and lead them into alleys. Here, Kitty Adams would seize the victim and put a razor to his throat while Jennie took his valuables. Between 1886 and 1893, Kitty and Jennie staged, at a minimum, 100 such robberies a year. Finally, in 1893 a victim was able to shake off enough of his fright to testify against Kitty Adams and she was sent to Joliet Prison.

Jennie Clark instantly petitioned Gov. John P. Altgeld for a pardon on the ground that Kitty was dying of tuberculosis. Altgeld ordered an investigation, and when Kitty appeared before the Board of Pardons, she had cut her gums with a toothpick so badly that she spat and coughed blood at a rate that convinced the board's members she would soon die. The pardon was forthcoming and Kitty returned to Jennie. The pair were soon back in action.

In 1896 they were both arrested for robbing a man. Kitty jumped bail, but Jennie appeared for trial before Judge James Goggin, a jurist noted for making astounding decisions. In the Jennie Clark case, Judge Goggin made his celebrated ruling that a man who went to the Levee deserved to get himself robbed. Jennie was released and the fugitive warrant against Kitty was withdrawn. Two years later, Kitty was caught again and this time a more tradition-bound jurist sent her back to Joliet, where ironically, she died of tuberculosis. Without Kitty Adams as a confederate, Jennie Clark faded from the crime records.

KLUTAS, Theodore "Big Jack": See College Kidnappers.

KNAPP, Captain Joseph (c.1770-1830): Murderer

The conviction and execution of Captain Joseph Knapp in Massachusetts in 1830, following a trial in which Daniel Webster personally led the prosecution, deeply divided public opinion. Although there was no doubt about Knapp's guilt, he could have gone free had he not refused to testify against his brother. As it was, both brothers were executed.

Joseph Knapp, his brother John Francis Knapp, Richard Crowinshield and, most likely, his brother George Crowinshield had conspired to rob a retired sea captain, Joseph White, of his hoarded wealth. One or more of the four entered the old man's bedroom and clubbed and stabbed him to death. The Crowinshield brothers, who both had unsavory reputations, were immediately suspected and taken into custody. While in jail, they revealed their part in the crime to another prisoner, who, upon his release wrote a letter to the Knapp brothers, demanding money from them. The authorities, watching the released convict, seized the letter and, in time, got Joseph Knapp to confess under a promise of immunity provided he would testify against the others. Learning of this development, Richard Crowinshield, the main culprit and the actual murderer, hanged himself in his cell. George Crowinshield went free despite Joseph Knapp's testimony, at which point the authorities insisted Joseph testify against his brother John. Joseph refused to do so, but his brother was found guilty and hanged anyway. Webster then declared that Joseph Knapp had lost his immunity because he had failed to aid in the conviction of his brother. He therefore prosecuted Joseph Knapp, and he too was convicted and hanged, despite considerable outcry from those who felt that since John Knapp had been found guilty and executed without his brother's testimony, it was vindictive to prosecute Joseph.

KNAPP Commission: New York police corruption investigation

Like earlier investigations of the New York City police, the Knapp Commission (1970-72), appointed by Mayor John Lindsay, found corruption and bribe taking in the department. Police officers had accepted bribes, the commission reported, from organized crime, particularly for narcotics and prostitution violations. Even building contractors declared that bribes to police added a full five percent to construction costs. Testimony was given that one policeman had held out $80,000 worth of heroin and $127,000 in currency when he seized a large amount of the drug. A rogue cop, William Phillips, who had been caught accepting bribes and trying to fix court cases, was recruited by the commission and supplied with a tape recorder; the evidence collected by Phillips indicated that New York police officers took at least $4 million in bribes annually.

The Knapp Commission did not win unanimous approval, however. Some civil libertarians attacked it, charging that much of the testimony was tainted by use of methods that violated the privacy and rights of the persons being investigated. Many hours of the hearings were wasted on debates over the "rotten apple" defense offered by the police establishment. Police Commissioner Patrick V. Murphy, who had been outspoken in opposition to police corruption, insisted the commission had gone too far and was ruining the reputation of

thousands of honest officers. He attacked the use of Phillips as a witness, denouncing him as a rogue cop caught in the act and "squirming to get off the hook." The same criticisms, however, certainly did not apply to two honest officers, Sergeant David Durk and Detective Frank Serpico, who gained considerable recognition for their roles in the investigations.

It is difficult to gauge the work of the Knapp Commission based on indictments of police officers because the police department and various New York district attorneys moved at about the same time, often claiming their actions were based on independent investigations. However, 37 Brooklyn plainclothesmen were indicted by the Kings County district attorney, and 19 officers in the Bronx were indicted or brought up on criminal charges for operating a "pad," through which regular payments were received from area gambling establishments and divided into a monthly "nut" of $800 per officer. Within two days of the opening of the commission's hearings, 113 plainclothesmen were transferred.

However, more important than the number of convictions is the ultimate effect of the commission's efforts to promote honesty and counter graft within the police department. In its final report, made public in 1972, the commission stated:

> The present situation is quite like that existing at the close of previous investigations. A considerable momentum for reform has been generated, but not enough time has elapsed to reverse attitudes that have been solidifying for many years in the minds of both the public and the police.
>
> After previous investigations, the momentum was allowed to evaporate.
>
> The question now is: Will history repeat itself? Or does society finally realize that police corruption is a problem that must be dealt with and not just talked about once every 20 years?

Not unexpectedly, newspapers conducting surveys about a year after the hearings reported plenty of quotes from cabdrivers, small businessmen and the like that indicated little had changed. That sentiment could in part be attributed to the general cynicism of the average New Yorker about any kind of official honesty. About a decade later, knowledgeable newsmen more or less agreed that while corruption and graft still existed, abuses definitely had not reached pre-Knapp Commission levels and that in terms of big-city police corruption, New York City was probably cleaner than other metropolitan forces.

See also: *Rotten Apple Theory.*

KNUCKLE Voice: Convict communication system

A sound language now used in nearly all jails of the world, the "knuckle voice" was introduced in America late in the 19th century in the dungeon at San Quentin Prison by Ed Morrell, generally considered to be one of the most remarkable prisoners in the history of the United States. Morrell, sentenced to life in solitary confinement in the dungeon, did not invent the system, having learned it from an escaped convict from Russia, where it was first used by Nihilist prisoners being held in the

St. Peter and Paul fortress in St. Petersburg. The code used in the knuckle voice was based on a pattern called the Siberian Square

	1	2	3	4	5	6
1	A	B	C	D	E	
2	F	G	H	I	J	
3	K	L	M	N	O	
4	P	Q	R	S	T	
5	U	V	W	X	Y	Z

The vertical numbers indicate the number of knuckle raps that precede a short pause, the horizontal numbers indicate the number of raps that follow this pause. Thus, the code for letter A is one rap, pause, one rap. Letter B is one rap, pause, two raps. Letter F is two raps, pause, one rap. Letter 0 is three raps, pause, five raps. Letter Z is five raps, pause, six raps.

Morrell needed several months to teach the system to Jake Oppenheimer, who was the only other man in the history of San Quentin to be sentenced to life imprisonment in solitary confinement. Oppenheimer was 13 cells away from Morrell in the dungeon and at first could neither grasp what the tappings meant nor understand the code. Finally, after many months, he solved the puzzle and the two rapped away to each other. It was years before the guards realized the men were communicating, assuming instead that both of them had simply gone crazy.

When Morrell was later freed from solitary confinement and returned to the general prison population, he taught the knuckle voice code to other convicts, and the system quickly spread to virtually every prison in the country.

See also: *Ed Morrell.*

KOEHLER, Arthur (1885-1967): Wood detective

Shortly after Bruno Richard Hauptmann was convicted in the 1932 kidnap murder of the Lindbergh baby, Edward J. Reilly, the chief defense counsel, told an interviewer: "We would have won an acquittal if it hadn't been for that guy Koehler. What a witness to ring in on us—somebody they plucked out of a forest. Do you know what he is? He's a—a xylotomist." While the dictionary defines a xylotomist as one who studies wood anatomy and is proficient in the art of preparing wood for microscopic examination, the lawyer said the word as if he were mouthing an obscenity.

Arthur Koehler was not an obscenity but the nation's foremost wood detective. Until his retirement in 1948 Koehler spent 36 years with the U.S. Forest Service including 34 years at the famous Forest Products Laboratory in Madison, Wisc., where he was the chief wood identification expert for the gov-

ernment. While Hauptmann's counsel had not heard of him, law officials in the Midwest had long relied on Koehler to crack perplexing criminal cases. His evidence was vital in convicting a Wisconsin farmer named John Magnuson for the 1922 dynamite-by-mail murder of Mrs. James A. Chapman and the crippling of her wealthy farmer husband. Fragments of the wood portions of the bomb were given to Koehler, who identified the pieces as elm. Although the suspect denied he had elm lumber on his farm, the police swept up wood shavings from the floor of his workshop. Koehler identified the sweepings as particles of elm and matched up their cellular structure with the wood used in the construction of the bomb. Magnuson was convicted.

Koehler's reputation in the Midwest became so great that on one occasion the mere mention that he was being brought into an investigation caused an arsonist to confess. In another case his testimony trapped a tree rustler who had made off with a huge amount of choice logs. Koehler traced the logs back to a certain valuable timberland and even identified which log was cut from which tree by matching saw cuts and the structure of the annual rings to the tree stumps. He also was instrumental in convicting Michael Fugmann, a triple murderer whose bomb packages had terrorized a Pennsylvania coal mining town during a union dispute in 1936.

In the Lindbergh case Koehler presented the damning evidence that one of Hauptmann's tools had been used to construct the kidnap ladder and that one of the ladder's rails came from Hauptmann's home. Despite many subsequent attempts by certain writers to prove Hauptmann's innocence, Koehler's expert evidence has never been successfully challenged.

Koehler had spent 18 months tracing the wood used in the kidnap ladder. At one point, about six months before Hauptmann's capture, he was so close on the trail of the culprit that the two men were in the same lumberyard at the same time. Hauptmann, apparently warned by instinct, had fled the yard, leaving behind a 40¢ plywood panel he had paid for. If one of the yard employees had mentioned the matter to Koehler, it is conceivable that the Lindbergh case would have closed six months earlier in a most dramatic fashion.

See also: *Mrs. James A. Chapman, Michael Fugmann, Lindbergh Kidnapping.*

KORETZ, Leo (1881-1925): Swindler

A contemporary of Charles Ponzi, Leo Koretz is not as well remembered today as a notorious swindler, certainly not as well as he should be. True, Ponzi is believed to have netted something like $7 million while Koretz appears to have stolen a mere $5 million. But Koretz carried off his scheme for much longer and, unlike Ponzi, who preyed to a great extent on unsuspecting immigrants, Koretz robbed the elite of the Chicago business world. In fact, Koretz' depredations may well have been greater than Ponzi's since a number of businessmen were known to have taken their losses in silence, fearing that any revelation that they had been swindled would damage their reputations as shrewd businessmen.

Koretz' scam was based on stock in the Bayano Timber Syndicate of Panama, which had supposedly garnered a fortune in mahogany from its vast land holdings and then discovered oil on its property. Koretz started selling stock in Bayano in 1917. Within no time at all the company was rewarding its stockholders with a quarterly dividend of five percent on their original investment. In reality, there was no Bayano Timber Syndicate. The swamp land it allegedly held was owned by the Panamanian government, since no one had any interest in mining or having anything to do with its only known commodity, mosquitos.

Koretz' ignorant stockholders were happy with their dividends. Of course, in theory, he had to pay the investors their dividends out of their original investments, creating the same kind of impossible pyramid structure that eventually brought Ponzi to grief. The more cunnning Koretz solved that troublesome matter by encouraging his investors to take their dividends in additional stock, each certificate as worthless as the originals.

The stockholders adored Koretz, even as the news of Ponzi's fraud was breaking; in fact, they started calling him "Lovable Lou . . . Our Ponzi." They regarded him as the first true financial genius to come down the pike since John D. Rockefeller. Once, Koretz was feted at a sumptuous dinner at Chicago's Congress Hotel. Sitting next to him was Arthur Brisbane, William Randolph Hearst's top editorialist and himself a big Koretz sucker. During the dessert, newsboys broke into the hall with an extra announcing, "Leo Koretz' oil swindle." For a moment everyone was stunned. Then Brisbane rose laughing. He had had phony newspapers printed up as part of the evening's entertainment. Then, embracing Koretz, he shouted, "Mr. Koretz is a great and honorable financier!" Everyone learned differently at the end of 1923, when his great hoax was exposed.

In 1922 a large group of happy stockholders thought it was about time that they visited the company's vast holdings. Koretz succeeded in stalling them for almost a year, but when they sailed from New York in November 1923, Koretz knew his time had run out. Taking $5 million with him, he fled to Canada and assumed an identity he had established there years ago as Lou Keyte. What brought Koretz down was his diabetes, for which he had to take insulin, then a rare and expensive commodity. He was traced thanks to his dependency on the drug and finally arrested in Halifax.

In the ensuing investigation, it was found that his elderly mother had invested $50,000 in his scheme and his brother $140,000. Even his secretary had parted with $3,000. Koretz said he had accepted the investments because he didn't know how to turn them down without arousing suspicion.

Koretz spent only about a month behind bars for his crimes. He induced a lady friend to bring him a five-pound box of chocolates. He ate the entire box on January 9, 1925 and promptly keeled over dead, certainly one of the most bizarre prison suicides in history.

KOSTERLITZKY, Colonel Emilio (c.1853-1928): Mexican police official

Although Col. Emilio Kosterlitzky was only a Mexican police official he had an important effect on Mexican-U.S. relations. Born in Russia, Kosterlitzky emigrated to the United States to join the Army. By 1873 he had moved on to Mexico, where he enlisted in the cavalry as a private. A soldier of exceptional ability, he rose rapidly to become the commander of the dreaded *la cordada,* an elite cavalry unit that patrolled the Arizona and New Mexico borders. He worked closely with various American law officers and especially the Arizona Rangers, helping them to round up a great many wanted renegades.

Kosterlitzky commanded the buckskin-clad *rurales,* cutthroat troops many of whom were ex-bandits, welding them into the only effective police force on the Mexican border. The colorful colonel, noted for leading his troops on a striking white charger, ruthlessly enforced the federal policy of Porfirio Diaz, not only doing battle with bandits and Indians but suppressing the peons. Kosterlitzky endeared himself to American peace officers by often arranging to hand over wanted men without protracted legal hearings. It is suspected that he often exported some of Diaz' political problems by turning over revolutionary peons to American lawmen as supposed transnational bandits.

After the fall of Diaz in 1911, the *rurales* became an isolated force without government approval, but Kosterlitzky maintained order among them for a number of months until it became apparent they could not stand against the nation's social revolution. Finally, he fled across the border at Nogales, placing himself under American protection. Because of his strong support among U.S. lawmen, there was no chance that Kosterlitzky would be returned to the Mexicans, and in fact, he worked several years for the Department of Justice in Los Angeles up to his death in 1928. During those years he remained a thorn in relations between the two countries.

KRIST, Gary Steven (1945-   ): Kidnapper

The kidnapping of 20-year-old Barbara Jane Mackle, the daughter of a Florida real estate developer, on December 17, 1968 was one of the most bizarre plots in the history of American crime. Her kidnappers, Gary Steven Krist and Ruth Eisemann Schier, buried her alive in a nine-foot pit inside an elaborate coffin-like box for three days while they negotiated a $500,000 ransom. The woman's prison box was equipped with light, a fan and two flexible tubes extending to the surface that allowed her to breathe. She was also suppled with a small amount of food and water. After 83 hours the ransom was paid and agents in Atlanta were notified the victim could be found in a box in a pine forest in Gwinnett County, Ga. By the time Mackle was rescued, the light had failed and her food and water were about gone.

The kidnappers had dropped a suitcase and abandoned a blue 1966 Volvo near the first spot where the ransom money was to be picked up. The car and the suitcase were traced to George C. Deacon, which turned out to be an alias for Gary Steven Krist, an escaped convict from California. The FBI also ascertained the Krist was associating with 26-year-old Ruth Eisemann Schier, and both were put on the FBI's 10 Most Wanted list, making Eisemann Schier the first woman fugitive to gain that distinction. Krist was apprehended in an alligator-infested Florida swamp with almost all of the ransom money still intact. Eisemann-Schier was caught when her fingerprints were sent to the FBI for a routine check after she had applied for a nursing service job.

Eisemann Schier was sentenced to seven years in prison and Krist was given life. In May 1979 he was granted a parole which drew considerable adverse criticism from the press as well as the judge and prosecutor in the case. Under the conditions of his parole, Krist had to live in Alaska, where his family ran a fishing village at Sitka. Krist praised the parole board's "courage" in releasing him, saying they recognized the remorse he had felt during his 10 years behind bars. "I've learned that a conscience can be a bigger burden than anything anyone else can put on you," he said. He also made a public statement to Barbara Mackle: "Thank you for not opposing my parole and having the Christian charity to forgive me for something I did that was unforgivable."

KU Klux Klan

As a movement, or more correctly, three different movements, the Ku Klux Klan dates back to 1866, when it was organized in Pulaski, Tenn., in response to radical Reconstruction. By their night-riding tactics against blacks, the white-hooded Klansmen did much to bring about the "redemption" of Southern state governments by white conservatives. Officially, the original Klan disbanded in 1869, but it did not die in most areas until years later, when this recapture of political power was completed.

The second and largest Klan was formed in Atlanta, Ga. in 1915 by Colonel William J. Simmons. It remained largely a local antiblack movement until 1920, when two professional publicity agents, or hustlers, Edward Y. Clarke and Mrs. Elizabeth Tyler, launched a nationwide membership drive under the slogan of "native, white, Protestant"—an effective rallying cry during a period of rampant nationalism, red-baiting and

Despite continuing instances of violence and killings, by the 1950s the Ku Klux Klan had lost some of its former fearsomeness, as some blacks in the South showed up at rallies to watch the festivities.

xenophobia. By 1925 total Klan membrship stood between four and five million and fiery crosses, the symbol of the movement, appeared in every part of the country. So did the whip and the rope, by which the Klan's moral position was enforced with floggings and lynchings. Among those facing the often fatal wrath of the hooded terrorists were blacks, Jews, Catholics, bootleggers, pacifists, Bolshevists, internationalists and evolutionists. Despite numerous exposes, the Klan became a potent political force and in many states, such as Oklahoma, Texas, Louisiana, Maine, Kansas and Indiana, unscrupulous politicians rose to power as "Klan men." Many of their administrations, especially in Indiana, proved unusually corrupt and did much to discredit the movement. By 1928, when the Klan abandoned its secrecy, the organization's power was in rapid decline.

The third Klan was born in the 1950s in response to the civil rights movement. It was actually a proliferation of competing Klans that independently engaged in a certain amount of unrestrained terrorism in the rural and small-town Black Belt South. By the mid-1960s many of these Klans had been brought more or less under control without ever having achieved anywhere near the murderous impact of their predecessors.

In 1969 seven Klan leaders were jailed for contempt of Congress for refusing to bare details about membership. In 1978 and 1979 there was a resurgence of violent-type Klan activities in the Northeastern states as well as the South.

The modern Klan is divided into three main groups: Robert Shelton's United Klans of America, headed by Robert Shelton, which is believed to be the largest of the three groups and the most secretive of the hooded organizations; David Duke's Knights of the Ku Klux Klan, which is reportedly the fastest-growing organization; and Bill Wilkerson's Invisible Empire, Knights of the Ku Klux Klan, the most violent of the three. While there is intense rivalry between the Klan leaders and a lack of cohesive ideologies, the trinity still maintains a certain bond because of the unifying belief in white supremacy.

Wilkinson, a 37-year-old former electrical contractor and a onetime associate of David Duke, runs his Invisible Empire out of Denham Springs, La. He flies his private plane from state to state to appear on radio shows, organize demonstrations and recruit new members. A former Navy man, Wilkinson has spearheaded drives to recruit members among U.S. Navy personnel and he claims that a KKK incident aboard the *U.S.S. Concord* involved sailors who were "and still are my men." In Decataur, Ga. about 100 Wilkinson men disrupted a parade sponsored by the Southern Christian Leadership Conference and it was at an Invisible Empire rally in Plains, Ga. that a drunken opponent of the Klan drove a car through the demonstrators, injuring several.

See also: *Leo Frank, Madge Oberholtzer.*

KUSZ, Charles (1849-1884): Murder victim

Journalism in the Old West was without doubt one of the more dangerous professions, given as it was to personal reporting and a readership who took things personally indeed. In that context it was perhaps amazing that Charles Kusz, a rabble-rousing bigot, lived as long as he did.

A native New Yorker, Kusz came west at the age of 26 to strike it rich. Within five years, he made $150,000 mining in Colorado. Kusz then moved on to Manzano, New Mexico Territory, where he founded a newspaper. It was an extraordinary publication even for the West. Perhaps its title, *The Gringo and the Greaser,* tells it all, but it should be noted that in addition to a strong dislike for many cowboys and *all* Mexicans, Kusz also passionately hated Roman Catholics, rustlers and the educational structure of the area. He constantly exercised his First Amendment rights to express his hatreds in diatribes published in the paper, which incidentally was printed entirely in italics.

Kusz' journalistic efforts lasted for about four years until he was assassinated on March 26, 1884 by two rifle shots through a window of his home while he was eating dinner. Motive became a key factor in the Kusz murder, but when the law got around to eliminating those not likely to have a motive, they still had enough of the community left to constitute a fairly complete census. Not surprisingly, the case was never solved.

L

LABOR Sluggers War: Thug rivalry

About 1911, as unionization efforts in New York intensified, especially in the needle and allied garment industry trades, both labor and management started utilizing thugs to achieve their goals, providing the underworld with a lucrative source of income. This produced a strange underworld conflict rooted as much in class loyalties and political philosophy as in the desire for illicit revenues. Union leaders hired thugs to blackjack and murder strikebreakers and to convince recalcitrant workers to join the unions. Employers hired the gangsters to guard strikebreakers, slug union pickets and raid union meetings.

A number of gangs vied for the labor slugging business, but all clearly preferred working for the unions rather than the employers. In some cases this was undoubtedly because the unions often paid better than the employers, but it was also due to the fact that most of these labor sluggers were Jews and Italians, just as were the workers of the area. There was an inclination to help your own as long as it wasn't too unprofitable.

By about 1912-13 the labor slugging trade was dominated by an alliance of gangs headed by Dopey Benny Fein and Joe the Greaser Rosensweig. So feared was Dopey Benny that some employers once offered him $15,000 to remain neutral in a strike. Deeply offended, he replied he would accept no offer from them and stood ready to provide his gangsters to the union because his heart was always with the workingman. In fact, this was not always the case. Dopey Benny and Joe the Greaser divided up lower Manhattan into districts and assigned a vassal gang to each, and it was possible to see their men in one district supporting the union while those in another engaged in antilabor skull bashing.

In the process of establishing their monopoly, Dopey Benny and Joe the Greaser froze several rival gangs out of working for the unions. Finally, the leaders of these gangs, including Billy Lustig, Pinchey Paul, Little Rhody, Punk Madden, Moe Jew-

bach, and others, banded together to declare war and establish their right to support unionism. In late 1913 the two sides staged a running gun battle at Grand and Forsyth streets. Surprisingly, no one was killed, although many store windows were shot to pieces and business was generally brought to a halt.

Later battles resulted in fatalities and, more commonly, maimings. Eventually, one of the dissident leaders, Pinchey Paul, was murdered and Nigger Benny Snyder, a Fein-Rosensweig henchman, was accused of the killing. While in jail Nigger Benny concluded that he was being abandoned by the Fein-Rosensweig forces and confessed to the murder, saying it had been assigned to him by Joe the Greaser, who had tipped him $5 upon its successful completion.

In time, the dissidents were wiped out in a series of gunfights outside of various factories, but the victors had their own problems. Dopey Benny was arrested on a murder charge, and Joe the Greaser got sent away for 10 years. Benny recognized his predicament and decided to make a pitch for leniency by informing on his labor connections and fellow sluggers. On the basis of Dopey Benny's statements, 11 gangsters and 23 union officers were indicted, but in the end, none were convicted. Under his deal with the law, Benny was tried on only one murder charge and was released when the jury failed to reach a verdict.

However, Dopey Benny's power was broken, as was that of his rivals. Because of the disclosures, a number of unions thereafter refused to hire sluggers. As a result, the New York labor scene was relatively peaceful through the war years until about 1920, when the notorious Kid Dropper, formerly Nathan Kaplan, reorganized the slugger trade with those unions still willing to use such methods. In 1923 the Kid's power was disrupted by a challenge from forces aligned with Jacob "Little Augie" Orgen.

Little Augie won this second sluggers war by arranging the assassination of Kid Dropper while he himself was under police guard, thereby becoming the new king of the labor sluggers. Two other men allied with Little Augie at this time were Louis "Lepke" Buchalter and Gurrah Shapiro, both would rise high in the ranks of the national crime syndicate established in the 1930s. Lepke, in fact, became head of that organization's enforcement arm, Murder, Inc.

Little Augie milked the labor slugging racket as well as he could, although fewer unions were willing to resort to his organizing tactics, until he began shifting his operations into bootlegging. He rejected a suggestion from Lepke that if the unions would not use sluggers, then the gangsters should move and physically take over union locals, milk the members with heavy dues and extort tribute from employers to insure against strikes. Little Augie, faced with tightened police surveillance, looked upon this as a high-risk operation. Besides, he saw he could earn enough from bootlegging to retire a rich man in a few years. So he ordered Lepke to cease such activities.

In 1927 Little Augie was machine-gunned to death either by Lepke and Shapiro or by bootlegging rivals whose customers he had stolen. Lepke soon became the king of the labor extortion racket in New York.

See also: *Kid Dropper, Nobles, Jacob "Little Augie" Orgen.*

LADY Gophers: New York female gang

Often referred to by the press as the ladies auxiliary of the Gophers, an early 20th century gang that controlled Hell's Kitchen in New York City, the Lady Gophers were officially known as the Battle Row Ladies' Social and Athletic Club. Its members were the first organized gang of women to engage in what may be called the "social crimes" of the 20th century.

The Lady Gophers fought side by side with the Gophers in many battles against the police. Their leader, Battle Annie, was said to have been the sweetheart of practically the entire Gopher Gang, 500 strong. In many respects, she was much smarter than her male counterparts. Known as the Queen of Hell's Kitchen, Battle Annie soon saw the special uses for an army of gangster women. She approached both labor unions and employers who had started to hire gangsters and explained the value of utilizing women sluggers. Thereafter, for a number of years Battle Annie enjoyed a handsome living supplying female warriors to either side in local industrial disputes. Her women might appear on the scene posing as either the enraged wives of the strikers or as the wives of the strikebreakers—sometimes even playing both roles—and end up scratching, biting and clawing the picketers, the strikebreakers or both.

The Lady Gophers failed to survive, however, when the male Gopher Gang disintegrated between 1910 and 1912.

See also: *Gophers.*

LAFITTE, Jean (1780-1826): Pirate

Probably no man in the annals of American crime is more controversial than Jean Lafitte. He can and has been described as a villain, pirate and murderer, yet there are others who have portrayed him as a much misunderstood man, a true patriot, a gentleman-smuggler, in an era when such a combination was possible a legally sanctioned privateer. At the far end of his spectrum of admirers was a former president of the Louisiana Historical Society who insisted "there is no character to compare him with except that of Robin Hood, whom he surpassed in audacity and success."

No one is certain of Lafitte's birthplace, but the present consensus is that he was born in 1780 in Bordeaux, France. It is still in dispute whether his father was a footloose sea dog or a titled aristocrat. There is also a wide discrepancy about Lafitte's appearance. One historian insists he wore a beard clean shaven from the front of his face, i.e., no mustache; another pictures him as a tall, handsome man with a mustache. He is also depicted as rather slight of build with almost feminine hands and feet or as a huge man with an appearance most harsh.

One certainty is that Jean and his brother, Pierre, turned up in New Orleans in 1806, after having accumulated considerable funds (preying on ships in the Indian Ocean or, again according to another version, pimping for a number of years in Paris). The brothers Lafitte opened a large mercantile establishment that was rather obviously devoted to the sale of smuggled goods. They had as partners some of the most prominent millionaires in the city, and Lafitte maintained close connections with the "privateers" sailing under the commission of the so-called Republic of Cartagena, which the Spaniards still considered a part of the Spanish empire. About 1809 Lafitte went to sea, taking a commission as a privateer from Cartagena; his brother was left in charge of operations in New Orleans. Lafitte took charge, by both persuasion and raw power, of all the privateering vessels operating out of Barataria Bay and the island of Grand Terre off the Louisiana coast. Among those privateers or pirates who fell under his sway were Captain Dominique, Rene Beluche, Cut Nose Chighizola and Vincent Gambi, the mad killer of the Gulf whose allegiance to Lafitte was often tenuous and stormy.

Under Lafitte's command, the pirates thrived as never before. Grand Terre, the home of some 500 ruffians and perhaps another 200 whores who catered to them when they came ashore, became a great trading center. Merchants from New Orleans and other Southern cities flocked there, via a tortuous two-day journey by pirogue and barge through marshes and bayous, to buy goods stripped from the holds of plundered Spanish merchantmen. Soon, more cargo came into New Orleans from Grand Terre than from any other source. For a time the U.S. authorities allowed the trade, which was certainly good business for the Louisiana merchants, but the government eventually came to realize that the illicit trade was greatly reducing the tax revenues from incoming goods that would normally go to national and local coffers. In late 1813 the government served notice on Lafitte that the pirates would have to leave. He gave some thought to resistance, but he faced a major problem with his men: many of his captains wanted to strike at all shipping, including that owned by Americans. Lafitte had to use brute force to suppress such sentiments, publicly shooting down Vincent Gambi's top lieutenant for questioning his orders. When U.S. troops moved into the Baratarian islands in 1814, Lafitte wisely ordered his men to flee without shooting back.

Lafitte returned to New Orleans, spurning the courtship of the British, then at war with the United States. Instead, he brought Gen. Andrew Jackson intelligence about the British plans to attack New Orleans and offered his services and those of pirates in fighting them off. With considerable doubts, Jackson accepted the offer and Lafitte and his crews performed in the victory over the British. In the aftermath of the war, Lafitte and his Baratarian crews won full pardons and the opportunity to remain in the United States with all the rights of citizenship.

Lafitte stayed ashore about a year, but wearying of a land existence he and most of his old comrades sailed off to start a new pirates' colony along the shore of what was then northeastern Mexico. In 1816 Lafitte and 1,000 followers set up a colony on a small island they called Galveztown, which was to become Galveston, Tex. Resuming his privateering against the Spanish, Lafitte seized $2 million in silver from the brig *Santa Rosa*. It was a colossal haul and Lafitte's last act of piracy. Unfortunately some of his associates were to lose the silver hoard in a lake during a confrontation with Mexican troops.

Lafitte continued his career as a smuggler, mostly bringing in slaves to Louisiana, by then against the law but still a thriving business in the South. He seldom bought his slaves at the markets in Cuba, preferring to steal them from Spanish ships. By 1819 Lafitte had lost control of some of the pirates, who started attacking American shipping, and a large number of them were caught and hanged that year in New Orleans despite his intercession. After two more years of depredations, the Americans became exasperated with the pirates, and U.S. naval forces dispersed the Galvezton colony. Lafitte was still considered a hero in New Orleans and could have returned there, as did some of his men, but he sailed off in search of a site for yet another colony further down the Mexican coast. With his ship *Pride*, he continued smuggling but the facts about the last few years of his life are hazy. He was perhaps murdered by his own men or was killed in a sea battle with a British man-of-war or died of fever somewhere in the West Indies. The most meticulous research indicates he probably passed away alone, forgotten and bitter in the Yucatan village of Teljas in 1826.

Lafitte could have died an honored and revered hero in New Orleans. His aide Captain Dominique lived out his remaining years in that city, a popular figure in the cafes and coffeehouses. Although he died poor in 1830 at the age of 55, on the day of his death the city's flags were lowered to half-staff and all business places were shut. Dominique's funeral was given full military honors. New Orleans honored its pirate heroes and has lionized Lafitte ever since.

See also: *Vincent Gambi, Hendrick's Lake, Piracy, Pirates' Home.*

LAGER Beer Riot

The so-called Lager Beer Riot, also known as the German Riot, in Chicago in 1855 was that city's first great mob disturbance. The cause of the riot was the city's attempt to enforce the Sunday closing law for saloons and increase their license fees from $50 to $300 a year, exacerbated by an antiforeign attitude, which in Chicago at the time meant antiGerman. The Germans, clannishly isolated on the North Side, stuck to their own language, maintained their own schools and newspapers and, of course, had hundreds of their own beer gardens. The Sunday closings and fee increases were but a prelude to a vote that summer on a drastic prohibition law. The German populace, especially the saloon keepers, saw the moves as an effort to destroy their rights. "The excitement throughout the city ran high," a contemporary historian wrote, "but the *Nord Seite* was in a perfect ferment. Meetings were held, speeches made, resolutions adopted, and pledges registered that the Germans of Chicago would die, if need be, rather than submit to this outrage upon their rights." Because they were likewise affected, the Scandinavians and Irish residents joined the German protest. The first Sunday the closing law was enforced, the German beer gardens and saloons were shut down tight by the police but American-owned bars on the South Side were allowed to carry on business via their side and back doors. The following Sunday the German saloon keepers opened for business and refused to shut down; 200 of them were immediately arrested. Later, they were freed on bail and representatives of the city and the German district agreed to a single test case that would be binding on both sides. The trial opened on the morning of April 21, 1855. As the contemporary account continues:

> The liberated saloon-keepers had collected their friends on the North Side, and, preceded by a fife and drum, the mob, about five hundred strong, had marched in solid phalanx upon the justice shop, as many as could entering the sacred precincts. After making themselves understood that the decision of the court must be in their favor if the town didn't want a taste of war, they retired and formed at the intersection of Clark and Randolph Streets, and held possession of these thoroughfares to the exclusion of all traffic. Crowds gathered from all sections of the city, friends and enemies, and the uproar was deafening.

The mob retreated after a brief but bloody fight with a score of police that left nine prisoners in custody. By 3 o'clock the protesting mob had reached 1,000 men, armed with rifles, shotguns, knives and clubs, and they advanced again, this time to be met by 200 police, who had formed a solid line across Clark Street. Amidst cries of "Shoot the police!" the mob attacked, firing guns, and the police returned the fire. Officially, only one German was killed, a police officer had his arm blown off by a shotgun and perhaps 20 others were seriously wounded. The mob carried off many of their own injured and the *Chicago Times* reported, "A few days later there were several mysterious funerals on the North Side, and it was generally believed that the rioters gave certain victims secret burial."

In all, 60 prisoners were taken by the police in what came to be called the Lager Beer Riot. Of these, 14 were brought to trial. Eventually, two Irishmen named Halleman and Farrell were convicted of rioting. A 19th century historian summed up the public reaction: "It seemed little less than a travesty on justice that in a sedition notoriously German, the only victims should be two Irishmen." The two men were granted new trials but they were never held. By then the powerful prohibition forces no longer cared. The temperance movement was gaining around the country, and an easy victory was expected in the Chicago balloting. Instead, the vote went antiprohibition by a huge margin. Many voters said they had been fearful of lawless German reaction to a "yes" vote, but Chicago was apparently thoroughly "wet" in sympathy. In any event, the Lager Beer rioters had won.

LAHEY-CLAFFEY Feud: New Orleans family rivalry

Rivaling in many ways the more famous feud of the Hatfields and McCoys, two clans, the Laheys and the Claffeys, each composed of several families, kept the so-called Irish Channel, the district where Irish immigrants concentrated in New Orleans in the 1840s, in turmoil for more than two decades.

The newspapers of the day reported several alleged causes of the feud, but simply stated, it was bad blood that led to the many killings and maimings. When violence broke out between the clans, who both lived on Corduroy Alley, no one was safe. In 1861 the *True Delta* described the area:

> St. Thomas Street is keeping up with its ancient reputation, especially that portion of it which boasts of Corduroy Alley. The inhabitants of the Alley appear for the most part to be an intemperate and bloodthirsty set, who are never contented unless engaged in broils, foreign or domestic, such as the breaking of a stranger's pate or the blacking of a loving spouse's eye. These are the ordinary amusements of the Alley. . . . Honest people, doubtless, live on St. Thomas Street, but they must have a hard time of it if they manage to keep their skulls uncracked and their reputations unstained.

On July 4 of that year, Bill Claffey, the leading thug of his clan, decided to wipe out the Laheys in one drunken onslaught. He stabbed several Laheys as well as a half-dozen innocent bystanders with a long razor-sharp knife before being shot by a policeman whom he had attacked. It was said that several of the wounded Laheys died later, but the clans were generally close-mouthed about such matters. The Civil War effectively ended the feud, as several of the most aggressive young men on both sides entered the Confederate Army. Apparently, the police then launched a crackdown on both clans, making arrests for the slightest provocation, with the result that many of the families moved from the area. Corduroy Alley was not completely tamed, but it was possible for a stranger to make it through without being caught in a flurry of brickbats.

LAMM, Herman K. "Baron" (?1890-1930): Bank robber tactician

America's most brilliant bank robbery planner, one whose

technique John Dillinger studied intently, was a young ex-German army officer, Herman K. Lamm, who brought Prussian precision and discipline to the art.

Shortly before World War I, Lamm was caught cheating at cards and forced out of his regiment. Emigrating to the United States, he put his military training and study of tactics to the best possible use as a holdup man in Utah. He was caught in 1917 and sent to prison for a short stretch. In prison he worked up what became known as the Baron Lamm technique of bank robbery.

It was Lamm's belief that a bank job required all the planning of a military campaign, with a full range of options to allow for unforeseen developments. When he got out of prison, Lamm organized a bank robbery gang and drilled the members in a fashion that would have done a Prussian sergeant proud. He always spent many hours in a bank before robbing it, drawing up a detailed floor plan, noting the location of the safes and whose duty it was to open them. Then the Baron put his men through a complete series of rehearsals, sometimes even using a full mock-up of the bank's interior. Each man was given a specific assignment, a zone of the bank to survey for possible trouble and an exact time schedule for his duties. Lamm's cardinal rule was that the job had to performed on schedule and the gang had to leave the bank at the specified time no matter how little or how much loot had been collected.

The next phase of the operation, the getaway, received meticulous attention from the Baron. He always obtained a nondescript model car with a high-powered engine and his driver was usually a veteran of the race tracks. Lamm pasted a chart on the dashboard for the driver to follow. The escape route, with alternate turns and speedometer readings was marked block by block. Before the robbery Lamm and the driver clocked the route to the second under various weather conditions.

From the end of World War I until 1930, Baron Lamm's men were the most efficient gang of bank robbers in the business, pulling dozens of jobs without a hitch. Finally, things went wrong during the robbery of the Citizens State Bank of Clinton, Ind. on December 16, 1930. The gang successfully robbed the bank of over $15,000, but when they got to the getaway car, the driver noticed the local barber approaching the bank with a shotgun. The barber, who was one of thousands of Indiana vigilantes organized to help police fight the growing number of bank holdups, was coming to investigate the presence of four strangers in the bank. The driver panicked and pulled a quick U-turn that caused the car to jump a curb and blow a tire. Lamm and his men were forced to seize another car, which, unfortunately for them, had a secret governor installed by a man to prevent his elderly father from driving recklessly.

They switched to a truck but it had very little water in the radiator; so they commandeered another car, which happened to be down to just one gallon of gas. The gang was cornered in Illinois by a horde of 200 police officers and vigilantes. In the wild gun battle that ensued, Lamm and the driver were killed. Another member of the gang, 71-year-old Dad Landy shot himself rather than spend his final years in prison. Two others, Walter Dietrich and Oklahoma Jack Clark, were caught and sent to prison.

In prison the two were permitted to join the Dillinger mob and escape with them under one proviso: they had to provide the details of Baron Lamm's technique. It was a system Dillinger used extensively throughout his career.

See also: *John Dillinger.*

LAND Frauds

The Western land frauds of the late 19th and early 20th century remain one of the great raids on the public purse in the history of the United States. Almost 40 million acres of valuable public land were set aside as forest reserves and the General Land Office was put in charge of protecting this natural treasure. Almost immediately, land office agents began peddling the rich forest acreages to private parties, who then turned around and made a quick killing reselling the property to lumber companies.

By the time of Theodore Roosevelt's administration, these land looters had become so influential in Congress that they were able to strip the Department of Justice of an investigative force charged with collecting evidence against the wholesale frauds. Finally, however, an investigation launched by Secretary of Interior Ethan A. Hitchcock uncovered the manipulations carried out by members of the General Land Office, including the agency's own detectives. Much of the evidence in the land frauds cases were gathered by William J. Burns, then the star agent of the Secret Service, and in a total of 34 cases that went to trial, 33 ended in conviction. Among those convicted were U.S. Sen. John H. Mitchell and Rep. John N. Williamson, both of Oregon. Sen. Mitchell appealed his conviction but he died in 1905 before his case was reviewed by a higher court. The Senate departed from custom and did not adjourn its session or send a delegation to Mitchell's funeral.

In later years some of the prosecutions were found to be politically tainted and corrupt. Many charges were brought against Burns, among them that witnesses had been intimidated into providing perjured testimony. In 1911 a report made to President William Howard Taft by Attorney General George W. Wickersham said there was no doubt that Burns had stage-managed the selection of jurors. Although the same accusation was made against the flamboyant Burns in numerous cases over the years, there is little doubt about the guilt of most of those charged in the land frauds.

See also: *William J. Burns.*

LANSKY, Meyer (1902-1983): Syndicate leader

Despite a rash of publicity before his death, Meyer Lansky remained the most shadowy of the organized crime leaders. Yet he was, next to Lucky Luciano and perhaps even ahead of him, the godfather of the national crime syndicate that emerged in the early 1930s as the successor of the warring Prohibition gangs as well as of the old-line Mafia, headed by the so-called Mustache Petes, particularly Giuseppe "Joe the Boss" Masseria and Salvatore Maranzano. Of course, the Mafia still exists today but its present shape and prosperity were as much influenced by Lansky, a Jew from Grodno, Poland, as by the Sicilian Luciano.

They made a perfect pairing: the well-read, studious Lansky, who could survey all the angles of any situation, and the less-than-erudite Luciano, who nonetheless possessed a magnificent flair for organization and the brutal character to put any plan into operation.

Not that Lansky was less given to violence. Together with "Bugsy" Siegel, he formed the Bug and Meyer gang, the most vicious of the Prohibition mobs, working alternately as booze hijackers and protectors of liquor shipments for bootleggers who were willing to meet their price. The Bug and Meyer boys were also available for "slammings" and rub-outs for a fee and were the forerunners of Murder, Inc., the enforcement arm of the syndicate. Indeed, Lansky probably had as much to do with forming Murder, Inc. as anyone, proposing the enforcers to be put under the command of a triumvirate composed of Louis Lepke, Albert Anastasia and Bugsy Siegel. Other leaders of the emerging national crime syndicate objected to the kill-crazy Siegel, feeling he would be too loyal to Lansky and more likely give the latter too powerful a weapon should the confederation fall apart in a war of extermination. Bugsy was removed from the murder combine, but Lansky's influence was not lessened. It is said no major assignment for Murder, Inc. was ever approved without consulting him, including the elimination of Siegel in 1947 for spending too much of the syndicate's money on his Las Vegas hotel operation. "I had no choice," Lansky reportedly told friends. Other versions say he pushed hard for a vote to kill his former partner, although he did suggest the mob hold execution of the verdict in abeyance while pressure was put on Siegel to produce profits from his Las Vegas ventures.

Luciano and Lansky together had planned the formation of a new syndicate as early as 1920, when Luciano was in his early 20s and Lansky was only 18. Together they survived the crime wars of the 1920s by shrewd alliances, eliminating one foe after another, even though they lacked the firepower of other gangs. When Luciano-Lansky effected the assassination of Masseria and Maranzano, they stood at the pinnacle of power in the underworld. Not even Al Capone thought of challenging them.

As Luciano later said, "I learned a long time before that Meyer Lansky understood the Italian brain almost better than I did. That's why I picked him to be my *consigliere.* . . . I used to tell Lansky that he may've had a Jewish mother, but someplace he must've been wet-nursed by a Sicilian." Luciana often said that Lansky "could look around corners," i.e., anticipate what would happen next in underworld intrigues, and that "the barrel of his gun was curved," i.e., he knew how to keep himself out of the line of fire. Through the years these were Lansky traits.

He never begrudged Luciano the top role, realizing that with it went the obvious dangers of notoriety, such as losing one's cover and becoming an inviting target for the law. Lansky preferred the safety of the shadows and for years avoided almost all publicity. As late as 1951, when his name popped up during the investigation of bookmaking czar Frank Erickson, the *New York Times,* despite one of the best news libraries in the world, did not know who he was, identifying him in print as "Meyer (Socks) Lansky," mistaking him for Joseph (Socks) Lanza, a waterfront gangster. During the Kefauver Investigation, Lansky was considered so unimportant that he was not even called to testify. Nor was he mentioned in the committee's first two interim reports. Only in the final report did the Senate investigators correct their oversight and declare: "Evidence of the Costello-Adonis-Lansky operations was found in New York City, Saratoga, Bergen County, N.J. New Orleans, Miami, Las Vegas, the west coast, and Havana, Cuba."

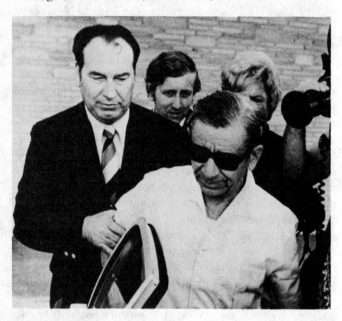

Although forced to return to the United States after being denied permanent sanctuary in Israel, Meyer Lansky, aging and ill, successfuly fought off several legal efforts in the 1970s to jail him.

Finally, Lansky's role as "the brains of the combination" became known. The "little man," as he was called by his underworld associates, held together Luciano's crime empire when he went to prison in the late 1930s. Lansky was the money man trusted to hide or invest millions for the syndicate, and he saw to it that Luciano got his share of the profits even after he was deported to Italy. It was Lansky who opened up what was for a time the syndicate's greatest source of income, gambling in Havana. He alone handled negotiations with dictator Fulgencio Batista for a complete monopoly of gambling in Cuba. Lansky was said to have personally deposited $3 million in a Zurich, Switzerland bank for Batista and arranged to pay the ruling military junta, namely Batista, 50 percent of the profits thereafter.

In the rise and fall of underworld fortunes, Lansky survived because he was considered too valuable to lose. Thus, he could agree with Vito Genovese that Albert Anastasia should die and

later take part in an incredible conspiracy that would deliver Genovese to the Feds and still enjoy immunity from retribution.

Lansky's arrest record over the years was minor-league stuff. It was not until 1970 that the federal government made a concerted effort to get him on income tax charges and deport him as an undesirable alien. In 1970 Lansky fled to Israel, settling in the plush Dan Hotel in Tel Aviv and claiming Israeli citizenship under the Law of Return which offers citizenship to anyone born of a Jewish mother. Lansky invested millions of dollars in the country to win public support, but he proved an embarrassment to the Israeli government. After a long battle in the courts and intense debate by the public, Lansky was forced to leave Israel.

In 1973, after undergoing open heart surgery, Lansky was brought up on income tax charges in Miami, Fla. but, much to the government's chagrin, was acquitted. In December 1974 the federal government abandoned its efforts to put the then 72-year-old organized crime legend behind bars. Although he faced other charges for violations of state laws, it was generally conceded he would never go to prison.

After a lifetime in crime, Lansky was the last major figure left of the original syndicate. David Harrop, author of *America's Paychecks: Who Makes What* (1980), placed Lansky's personal wealth at somewhere between $100 million and $300 million. No wonder Lansky could once say of the crime syndicate he had helped found, "We're bigger than U.S. Steel."

See also: *Frank Costello, Thomas E. Dewey, Jewish Mafia, Las Vegas, Charles "Lucky" Luciano, Benjamin "Bugsy" Siegel.*

LARN, John M. (?-1877): Crooked sheriff

A man with a murky past, John M. Larn showed up in Fort Griffin, Tex. about 1870 and went on to become famous as that state's notorious "outlaw lawman."

Larn didn't talk much about his previous history when he signed on as a cow puncher. He prospered in Fort Griffin, eventually marrying his boss' daughter. By early 1876 Larn was regarded as one of the more substantial citizens of Shackelford County and, as such, rode with other men of property in Texas' most active and effective vigilance committee. He is believed to have been the man in charge of a vigilante group who strung up a horse thief from a pecan tree and then left a pick and shovel underneath the swaying corpse for anyone who might want to dig his grave.

In April 1876 Larn was elected county sheriff and for a time he seemed to do a good job. Meanwhile, his ranching enterprise thrived, especially after he signed a contract to deliver three steers a day to the military garrison at the fort. Neighboring ranchers noticed their herds dwindling while Larn's seemed to stay as large as ever. He resigned from office under pressure, but the cattle disappearances continued. Vigilantes began watching the Larn ranch, and finally, in June 1877 a nester found a water hole near Larn's slaughter pens where the former lawman was dumping the branded hides of the stolen cattle. Larn shot the nester but the man escaped.

Larn was arrested by his successor in office, Sheriff William Cruger, and placed in a flimsy jail in Albany. Because of rumors that his supporters intended to break him out, the sheriff had the local blacksmith shackle the prisoner's legs to the cell floor. The Fort Griffin vigilantes did not think the peril of Larn's possible escape had been sufficiently eliminated, however; just before midnight on June 23, 1877, they overpowered the jail guards. But the shackles frustrated their plan to string Larn up. So instead, they finished off the outlaw lawman with a firing squad execution in the jail cell.

LAS Vegas

Las Vegas was built on mob money. During World War II it was a jerkwater town with a few greasy spoons, filling stations and some slot machine emporiums. Gangster Bugsy Siegel first conjured up the idea of Las Vegas as a glittering gambling mecca in the desert. Using $6 million in mob funds, he built the Flamingo Hotel, which was initially a bust, largely because it took time to build up public interest. The mob was upset with Siegel due to the lack of return on its investment, and when it learned that Bugsy had pocketed some of the construction money, he was killed.

Nonetheless, the Bug's idea still made sense. Slowly, the Flamingo began to flourish and once the public accepted the idea of trekking through the desert to dice and roulette tables, one casino after another sprang up. State authorities adopted strict oversight measures to ensure the new casinos would not fall under mob domination, but to little avail. Syndicate money was traced directly to many major gambling establishments. Meyer Lansky financed much of the Thunderbird. Although some others fronted as its proprietors, the Desert Inn was largely owned by Moe Dalitz, head of the syndicate's Cleveland branch. The Sands was controlled—from behind the scenes—by Lansky, Joe Adonis, Frank Costello and Joseph "Doc" Stacher. The Sahara was launched by the Chicago mob—the Fischetti brothers, Tony Accardo and Sam Giancana. The Dunes was a goldmine for New England mafioso Raymond Patriarca.

When Frank Costello was shot in 1957, police found tallies in his coat pockets that matched the revenues of the Tropicana for a 24-day period. Up until then, presumably only the Nevada Gaming Control Board was unaware that the Tropicana provided a great source of income for Costello and his New Orleans partner, Dandy Phil Kastel. The word on Caesar's Palace was that almost everyone in the mob had a piece of it. Comedian Alan King said of its decor: "I wouldn't say it was exactly Roman—more kind of early Sicilian."

The value of Las Vegas to organized crime is difficult to measure. Its casino-hotels made huge profits, and when some of the revenues were skimmed off the top so that taxes would not have to be paid on them, the take was much greater. It was later alleged that in an eight-year period Lansky and some of his associates skimmed $36 million from the Flamingo alone. In addition, the vast exchange of money across the gaming

tables offered a perfect opportunity to launder funds from other, illegal enterprises. Jimmy Hoffa invested Teamsters' pension funds in the hotels in the form of interest-free "loans" that were never paid back, providing the mob with additional capital.

One thing Vegas proved was that given the opportunity to run a gambling setup honestly, the mob would still operate it dishonestly. Despite the huge profits, by the mid-1950s the mob had started selling off some of its properties to individuals and corporations. In the 1960s billionaire Howard Hughes started buying one casino after another.

In the early 1970s the mob's interest in Vegas was reportedly at a low point, but by the close of the decades, many observers concluded, mobsters were returning to the scene.

See also: *Flamingo Hotel, Benjamin "Bugsy" Siegel.*

LASER Detection

Probably the most striking advances in criminal investigation methods until the year 2000 will come from laser technology, which has already helped solve a number of crimes. Laser light can pick up fingerprints that chemical powders can't. Two men who recently robbed a New York City bank wore ski masks to hide their faces and plastic gloves to prevent fingerprint identification. Nonetheless, their prints were identified by use of a laser beam. In 1980 the FBI used laser beam technology to find 215 sets of fingerprints that standard methods of detection had failed to reveal.

When the two New York bank robbers fled with their loot, they used a stolen car for the getaway and then transferred to a second car. In the process one of the robbers discarded his plastic gloves on the floor of the first car figuring the static electricity on the gloves would prevent the detection of any fingerprints. But that was before the era of the laser. Light directed inside the fingers of the gloves revealed a perfect set of prints and subsequently led to the robbers' apprehension and conviction.

The FBI's 215 fingerprint findings by laser led to positive identifications in 45 cases. One suspect left his prints on plastic electrician's tape in a bomb threat case and another on the plastic stock of a sawed-off shotgun.

Perhaps an even more exotic use of laser light was involved in the Case of the Purloined Bicentennial Coin Collection. A rare silver certificate in the middle of the coin collection had been taken along with the coins. No fingerprints were found but the laser brought out the outline of the missing bill and was even able to "read" the shadows of the serial numbers. With that information the bill was traced and recovered along with the stolen coins.

Although the laser has been used regularly as a clue detector since the mid-1970s, it has never been tested by the judicial process, because there has never been need for a test. All of the suspects identified by use of the laser have confessed to their crimes and pleaded guilty.

LATEMPA, Peter (1904-1945): Vito Genovese murder victim

The death of Peter LaTempa in 1945 ranks second only to the demise of Abe Reles, the Murder, Inc. informer, in 1941 as an example of the long reach of the Mafia. Crime kingpin Vito Genovese had fled from New York to Europe in 1937 to avoid being charged with the murder of Ferdinand Boccia. He was finally returned in 1945, after he was found working for the U.S. Army in Italy. The key witness linking him to Boccia's murder was Ernest "the Hawk" Rupolo, who had gone to the authorities with the story because he was in trouble for other offenses. However, lacking supporting circumstantial evidence, the law needed at least one other witness. That man was Peter LaTempa, a small-time hoodlum who had witnessed the Boccia killing. Under pressure, LaTempa finally implicated Genovese, but only after he knew that the crime leader had left the country and was unlikely ever to be prosecuted.

With Genovese's unexpected return, LaTempa, figuring the best place to be was in jail, asked to be placed in protective custody. He was lodged in a Brooklyn prison. On the evening of January 15, 1945 LaTempa swallowed some of the pain-killing tablets he regularly took for a stomach disorder and went to sleep. He died in his sleep. An autopsy revealed he had taken enough poison "to kill eight horses." It was never established who had arranged to put the poison in the bottle of tablets, but logic pointed to Genovese. Without LaTempa's testimony, the evidence against him was insufficient to warrant a trial. Not only had the government obligingly brought him back to the United States but now it had to release him, setting the stage for his eventual emergence as the top figure in the Mafia.

See also: *Vito Genovese.*

LATIMER, Robert Irving (1866-1946): Murderer

It was hardly surprising that after Robert Irving Latimer murdered his 60-year-old mother on the family estate in Jackson, Mich., the newspapers in due course would refer to him as Bungling Latimer. Latimer had constructed what he considered a brilliant murder plot so that he could inherit the family fortune and collect this insurance. On the morning of January 25, 1889, Latimer was seen, as per plan, leaving Jackson on his way to Detroit. Later that night he slipped back into Jackson, murdered his mother and returned to Detroit. It was a simple enough alibi: he couldn't possibly kill his mother if he was in Detroit at the time of her death. That was the plan, but Latimer bungled it from start to finish.

Shortly after he checked into a hotel in Detroit, a porter saw him slipping out a back door, which struck the man as a strange move for a newly arrived guest. Then Latimer took a Michigan Central train to Ypsilanti, where he caught another train to Jackson. By not taking a direct train to Jackson, Latimer risked being remembered by not one but two conductors. (And both did.) After locking up the small family dog in a room, something only a nonstranger could have done without causing the dog to bark, Latimer killed his mother and slipped back to the train station under cover of darkness. On the return trip to Detroit the bungling murderer got into a shouting match with a conductor because at first he was unable to get a sleeper. The following morning Latimer went to a barber shop next to his hotel. The barber noticed that his shirt cuffs were missing and that there was blood on his coat. Furthermore, the chamber maid had found Latimer's bed unslept in; he had not even thought to rumple it. Latimer was convicted and sentenced to life imprisonment, still proclaiming his innocence for years afterward. A cartoonist aptly characterized Latimer painting a sign reading, "I WENT THIS WAY."

Latimer was doing life in the Michigan State Prison when he became a cause celebre for those who wanted to introduce the death penalty in Michigan. A model prisoner, he became a trusty and was put in charge of the prison pharmacy. On the night of March 26, 1893, he served a couple of guards a midnight lunch of sardines and lemonade. To the lemonade he had added prussic acid and opium, obtained from the pharmacy. Within 20 minutes one guard was unconscious and the other, George Haight, dead. Latimer escaped and went to the home of relatives expecting to be hidden, only to be turned away. Recaptured a few days later, he insisted that he had not meant to kill the guard, that he had unwittingly put too much prussic acid in the drink. Latimer was saddled with another life sentence, which capital punishment proponents thought insufficient. They asked what would happen if he murdered another guard; under the law, he could only be given yet another life term.

However, the death penalty storm passed, and Latimer went back to being a model prisoner. Ironically, he was popular with the guards, who felt he had simply made a miscalculation. By 1907 he had been made a trusty again and put in charge of landscaping the prison grounds. In the mid-1920s Latimer, who had progressed to the position of "senior con," often was interviewed by the press about his two murders and his attitude toward the newer convicts, who, he said, lacked the class and style of the old boys. Later on, when the prison was to be moved to a new location, he protested having to leave. His cell, fixed up as a library with many plants and a desk, was his home. He asked to be permitted to stay. Considered harmless, Latimer was appointed a watchman for the deserted prison. Finally, after spending 46 years in prison, Latimer was released in 1935. Picked up as a vagrant a few times, he was taken into a state home for the aged and died there in 1946.

LAWES, Kathryn (1885-1937): Angel of Sing Sing

No fiction writer would ever dare to invent a character like Kathryn Lawes, the so-called Angel of Sing Sing and pass off as plausible the tear-jerking story of her death. It simply would not be believed.

The first wife of Sing Sing Warden Lewis E. Lawes, Kathryn was the mistress of the prison on the Hudson for 17 years after Lawes took over. She was known to the prisoners as a kind, understanding woman who wrote letters for them, helped many of their families and cared for them in the prison hospital. Her deeds became so legendary that she was considered an angel of mercy.

In 1937 Kathryn Lawes was killed in an automobile accident. The prisoners of Sing Sing were stunned, and their grief was real. There was genuine anguish among them when it was announced her funeral would take place in a church outside the prison walls. A committee of prisoners went to Warden Lawes to protest and insist on the convicts' right to pay their last respects.

Lawes was willing to gamble on his men. He had in the past allowed many prisoners to go home on emergency visits without escorts, a practice that had left him open to possibly ruinous criticism if anything had gone wrong. The warden took a much greater risk now by declaring he would comply with the prisoners' request

The night before the funeral, the south gate of Sing Sing swung open and out trudged a silent procession of murderers, swindlers, thieves and crooks of all kinds—marching out of the prison to the warden's house, a quarter of a mile away. There were no guns trained on them and not a single guard accompanied them; yet not one man strayed from line, nor looked for the chance to escape. When the men entered the house, they silently passed the bier, many uttering a short word of prayer, and then walked outside, reformed their ranks and marched silently back to their prison.

See also: *Lewis Edward Lawes.*

LAWES, Lewis Edward (1883-1947): Warden of Sing Sing

Probably the most reform-minded and certainly the best known of all prison wardens in America, Lewis E. Lawes was in charge of Sing Sing Prison in Ossining, N.Y. for 21 years, where he became a strong voice for the philosophy that prisons should try to rehabilitate prisoners.

The son of a prison guard, Lawes became one himself at the age of 22, but unlike the old-time guards and most of the new ones, he viewed and studied penology as a science and soon rose through the system building a reputation as a realistic reformer. In 1915 he became superintendent of the New York City Reformatory, and in 1919 Gov. Alfred E. Smith named him to the difficult position of warden of Sing Sing.

Within a short time, Lawes accomplished the near impossible in penology, gaining the respect of both the guards and the convicts. He rapidly reduced the incidence of corporal punishment. Lawes once said:

> It became quickly apparent to me that under conditions as they were, the prison warden, to be effective, would have to constitute himself not as an instrument of punishment but a firm, frank friend in need. He would have to stretch humanitarianism to the limits of the law, with a stiff punch always in

reserve. I have been charged, since my incumbency, with being too kind. I wish I could plead guilty to the accusation, but my sense of duty will not permit it. My job is to hold my men and, as far as possible, to win them over to sane, social thinking. And I judge the effectiveness of that job not so much by obedience to rule, for rules can be enforced, but by the humor of the general prison population.

Lawes set up a system for prisoner self-government which for him had a very precise meaning—the government of self. Under Lawes, the prisoners' Mutual Welfare League was charged with regulating the leisure hours of the inmates, subject only to the warden's approval. But unlike methods used in other prisons, the prisoners did not have power over other prisoners, a sure way to create friction. Machinery was established whereby a convict with a pressing problem could get to see him. Lawes placed great trust in the convicts, often allowing them leave to visit home for a funeral or to go to the bedside of a dying relative. They were honor-bound to return, and they did. Lawes often loaned money to prisoners being discharged, and almost always they would return it, some coming to the prison gate years later with the money. Lawes could thus dedicate one of his books "to those tens of thousand of my former wards who have justified my faith in human nature."

Although he was forced to officiate at many executions, Lawes was a bitter foe of capital punishment and toured the country campaigning to abolish it. He opposed the death penalty because of the infrequency and the inequity of its application and martyrdom it provided a convicted murderer. He felt all these problems weakened the entire structure of social control and actually encouraged the desperate criminal toward the extreme penalty. "He knows," Lawes said, "that his gamble with the death penalty is safer than with a long term in prison for a lesser offense."

When Lawes retired in 1941, he had held the post for 21 years, longer than any other warden. His predecessor had lasted only six weeks.

See also: *Francis "Two Gun" Crowley, Kathryn Lawes.*

LAY, Elza, Or Elzy (1868-1934): Wild Bunch outlaw

Called "the educated member of the Wild Bunch" by Butch Cassidy, slim, handsome, "Boston-educated" Elzy Lay was the man responsible for planning the most successful of the gang's bank and train robberies. He was the outlaw closest to Cassidy, far closer than was the Sundance Kid, despite popular legend. In fact, in a 1975 book, *Butch Cassidy, My Brother,* Cassidy's last surviving sister, Lula Parker Betenson, insisted that most episodes in the movie *Butch Cassidy and the Sundance Kid* really involved Lay rather than Sundance. But, she asked, "who would go to a movie entitled Butch Cassidy and Elzy Lay?"

Lay was born in MacArthur, Ohio and was not "Boston-educated," as many writers have stated. In fact, there is no record of his ever having been to Boston. Furthermore, it has never really been established whether he went to college or was merely smarter than the rest of the Wild Bunch. Of all the members of the Bunch, it was always evident that neither Cassidy nor Lay were killers by nature. They had met while doing ranch work in Wyoming. Both were looking for excitement and became lifelong friends. They pulled many two-man holdups. Whenever they separated, Lay would team up with the Black Jack Ketchum gang and pull other jobs, although Ketchum never really appreciated that Lay would be considered the mastermind of the band.

Lay's last holdup with the Wild Bunch was the robbery of a Union Pacific train at Wilcox, Wyo. on June 2, 1899. On July 11, 1899, Lay, as part of the Ketchum gang, robbed the *Texas Flyer* at Twin Mountains, N.M. They were pursued by a posse headed by Sheriff Ed Farr, who was killed in a gun fight at Turkey Creek Canyon, N.M., with the fatal shot attributed to Lay. The Ketchum gang then split up, and Lay headed south. On August 17, 1899 he was cornered by another posse near Carlsbad, N.M. and captured following a spirited battle. He was sentenced to life imprisonment at New Mexico State Penitentiary. In prison he underwent a complete reformation and won a governor's pardon in 1906.

After his release Lay went straight. For a while, he operated a ranch for the father of a girl he married and then became interested in oil geology. He found what he thought was a large oil deposit and claimed the land, but he eventually had to give it up because of the high production costs involved. Standard Oil of California took over the claim and struck oil.

There has been considerable speculation about whether Butch Cassidy ever visited Lay after his return from South America (many historians now doubt the story of his and the Sundance Kid's death in Bolivia in 1909) and several persons in Baggs, Wyo. insisted they saw Cassidy and Lay together on many occasions in 1929-30. Lay refused to admit anything, even under the coaxing of Western novelist Zane Grey. Just before Lay died on November 10, 1934, however, he told his wife, "Mary, get hold of Zane because I'm not going to live much longer." He died before Grey reached him.

See also: *Butch Cassidy, Wild Bunch*

LE ROY, Kitty (1850-1878): Woman gambler

Along with Madame Moustache, Kitty Le Roy represented the best of the West's woman gamblers. Texas-born Kitty first came to public attention as a jug dancer in Dallas at the age of 10. Over the next decade her beauty bloomed, and she became the toast of Dallas. Her attractiveness and personality helped her win a role in local society comparable to that played by Lily Langtry in Victorian London. Kitty also took up a theatrical career but eventually gave up the stage in favor of working as a faro dealer, an occupation in which she became most proficient. As the profession demanded, Kitty became accomplished at pistol shooting and scored many a deliberate near-miss to settle disputes at the gambling table. She reportedly was always armed with several bowie knives and revolvers and, in fact, had an arsenal of 12 knives and seven guns. By the time

she was 26, Kitty had run through four husbands. She married the first because he was the only man in town sporting enough to let her shoot apples off his head as she galloped by on horseback. She supposedly ran him out in favor of a wealthy German; she chased the latter away when he ran out of funds. Sometime later, Kitty shot up an admirer who annoyed her with his persistence. Fickle or guilt-stricken, she married her victim a few hours before he died of his wounds.

In 1876 Kitty moved to Deadwood, Dakota Territory with another spouse and opened the Mint Gambling Saloon. The Mint was known to be a regular calling point for the likes of outlaw Sam Bass and Wild Bill Hickok, both of whom Kitty is said to have entertained on a number of occasions. Kitty's husband killed her and himself in 1878, presumably out of jealousy.

LEATHERHEADS: First New York police

The first policemen of post-Dutch New York City were little more than watchmen. Called leatherheads because of their heavy leather helmets, which were rather similar to those of today's firemen, they patrolled the streets at night to enforce a rigorous curfew. After 9 o'clock anyone caught outside his house without a plausible reason automatically was considered to be of "bad morals" and locked up until daylight on general principle. In fact the main duty of the watch was to sing out each hour that all was well, for the most part, which it was in 18th century New York.

There were a few watch houses that served as area headquarters and some sentry boxes that provided shelter from time to time during the long cold nights. The leatherheads, of which there were no more than 30 or 40, supervised by a high constable, were never accused of being overly bright, overly sober or overly alert. They were, in fact, very prone to sleeping on duty, and it was a favorite sport of the roisterers of the era to hunt for one dozing in his sentry box, lasso the box and drag it through the streets, whooping over the plight of their trapped victim.

While such antics were often the worst lawlessness to be reported on many evenings, New York in that era was not entirely crime-free. There were hangings enough for drunken murderers, forgers, counterfeiters and others found guilty of the long list of capital crimes, including church robbery. But the fact remained that New York was a sleepy little town, only reaching 50,000 inhabitants in 1799. The crime pace quickened early in the next century with the appearance of the great criminal gangs, and a more professional police force than the leatherheads was needed to cope with the new lawlessness.

LEBLANC, Antoine (?-1833): Murderer

Although the claim may be dubious, Antoine LeBlanc is generally known as the fastest murderer in America.

LeBlanc arrived from France on April 26, 1833, and by May

2, 1833 he had committed three murders. Upon his arrival he had gone to work on the estate of the Sayre family in rural New Jersey and apparently could not cope with his lowly position which required him to sleep in the woodshed. On May 2 LeBlanc crept up on Mr. and Mrs. Sayre, battered them to death with a shovel and buried their bodies under a pile of manure. LeBlanc thought the Sayre's black maid was away, but when he discovered her presence in the attic of the house, he murdered her as well. He did not immediately flee the area, believing he could remain a while and say that his employers had gone away for a short time. The more scandalous purveyors of the news in that era later reported that LeBlanc, a tall, handsome rogue, entertained a number of young ladies in the Sayre home. In any event, friends of the missing couple found the bodies and captured the Frenchman. He was quickly tried and convicted and hanged on September 6, 1833 on the Morristown green before a crowd of 12,000. It is unclear how many were attracted by his savage crimes and how many by his romantic reputation since, as one historian of the day related, of those in attendance "the majority were females."

LECHLER, John (?-1822): Murderer

As the odd man out in a tawdry love triangle, John Lechler of Lancaster, Pa. killed his wife, Mary, and her lover's wife, Mrs. John Haag, in 1822. He would not be worthy of note save that the facts in the case were so bizarre the area's newspapers conducted what was apparently the first "poll" ever taken on the public's reaction to a trial verdict.

Mary Lechler's morals were never too high. When John Lechler returned home and found her in bed with neighbor Haag, he threatened to kill the two of them. The shaking Haag offered to buy him off with a promissory note. After some haggling over the amount, Lechler accepted the settlement but flew into a rage some days later when Haag refused to honor his commitment. Lechler rushed home and strangled his wife until she was unconscious and then hanged her in the attic. Armed with two pistols, the doubly cheated husband went to Haag's home and called on him to come out. When Haag refused, Lechler fired through the door, fatally wounding the cowering Mrs. Haag rather than her husband. Lechler was convicted and hanged in Lancaster on October 25, 1822.

The sentence in the case evoked considerable public debate. Readers of several publications cast a divided vote on the appropriateness of the death penalty. Although the farming community strongly believed in the sanctity of written contracts, and many of its members were sympathetic to Lechler's outrage a majority of the readers questioned favored his execution. Their attitude probably was best summed up by a farmer who said, "If he'd killed Mr. Haag instead of the missus, I would say he would have deserved a less severe sentence."

LEE, John D.: See Mountain Meadows Massacre.

LEIBOWITZ, Samuel S. (1893-1978): Defense attorney and judge

A flamboyant lawyer who built his reputation with highly remunerative defenses of gangsters, Samuel S. Leibowitz ran up an amazing record: he represented 140 persons charged with murder and lost only one to the electric chair. However, he won international fame for his defense of the Scottsboro Boys, nine young blacks charged with the rape of two "Southern ladies"—actually hobo-style prostitutes—aboard a freight train in Alabama in 1931. In a total of 10 trials and retrials, the stirring defenses by the "New York Jew nigger lover," as he was called by many citizens and much of the press in the South, resulted in the dropping of charges against four of the nine and played a huge part in winning paroles for four others; the last, Haywood Patterson, the alleged ringleader, escaped but eventually was captured and sent to prison for another crime. One of Leibowitz' most important accomplishments was winning a Supreme Court decision that the exclusion of blacks from jury service was unconstitutional, a finding that over the years was to have a profound effect on the administration of justice in the South.

Leibowitz was born in Rumania and came to the United States at the age of four. He worked his way through law school and became a lawyer in 1916. Within a few years he established himself among criminal defendants as a miracle lawyer, with a knack for assembling "friendly juries" and an ability to demolish eyewitness testimony.

Leibowitz firmly believed in prescreening jurors, an entirely legal procedure few defense lawyers bother with because of the expense and tediousness of the research involved. Leibowitz wanted to know how many times each prospective member of the panel had served on a criminal case jury, how they had voted and much about their personal life and beliefs, and he was usually blessed with high-paying clients who had no trouble financing such research. The prosecution, aided by the vast investigative machinery at its disposal has always engaged in the screening of potential jurors, often to a far greater extent. Once Leibowitz had the background information, picked jurors whom he felt would be sympathetic to the defense and disposed of those more likely to vote for conviction. Even district attorneys admitted no lawyer could pick a more "friendly" panel than Leibowitz.

Leibowitz generally had contempt for eyewitness testimony, knowing how faulty it could be. He firmly believed circumstantial evidence was, on the whole, more dependable. Out of court, Leibowitz delighted in exposing the unreliability of eyewitness evidence, staging events to show the contradictory stories told by witnesses. In one classic demonstration he performed at legal seminars and at law school lectures, Leibowitz would ask regular smokers of Camel cigarettes, "Is the man leading the camel or sitting on its back?" In one typical result, two out of five said the man was leading the camel, two out of five that he was sitting on the camel and only one in five correctly stated there was no man in the picture.

In his famous defense of Vincent "Mad Dog" Coll, a gangster who had gunned down five children on a Manhattan street, one of them fatally, Leibowitz got his client off by shifting the focus of the trial to eyewitnesses of the tragedy until it almost seemed as if they were the defendants.

Leibowitz successfully represented many of the top mobsters of the day, once rather easily getting Al Capone acquitted of a murder charge. He secured acquittals for Pittsburgh Phil Strauss, Abe Reles, Buggsy Goldstein and Bugsy Siegel, admittedly before the existence of Murder, Inc. and he turned down a $250,000 fee to defend Louis Lepke when that investigation was breaking in 1939. By that time Leibowitz had tired of the role of defense attorney and was seeking appointment to a judgeship.

Attorney Samuel Leibowitz (left), shown with one of the Scottsboro Boys, was famous for losing only one client to the electric chair out of 140.

When in 1940 the Democratic Party of Brooklyn proposed him for judge of the King's County Court, his nomination brought forth vigorous opposition. "Elect Leibowitz and he'll open the doors of the jails," his political opponents cried. "He'll turn loose every crook who comes before him."

It was a fear never realized. He turned out to be what is known as a "hanging judge," meting out extremely harsh sentences to professional criminals. On his retirement from the bench in 1970, eight years before his death, he observed, "I was tough with hardened criminals, toughness is all they understand."

Still, Leibowitz remained true to his belief in the right of every defendant to proper counsel.

In a typical scene in his court, a defendant would be brought up on robbery and assault charges.

"Let's see now," the judge would say. "You first appeared in juvenile court when you were fifteen. Since then you've been charged with crime, twelve times; everything from petty larceny to manslaughter. You've been convicted four times, and you've spent ten years behind bars. Bail is fixed at fifty thousand dollars. Have you got a lawyer?"

"I got no money to pay a lawyer," the defendant would reply.

"You need a good lawyer," Leibowitz would declare. "I'm going to appoint the best defense lawyer I know to represent you, without pay."

That was the law, according to Sam Leibowitz.

See also: *Vincent "Mad Dog" Coll, Dr. Fritz Gebhardt, Mistaken Identity, Scottsboro Boys.*

LENNON, John: See Mark David Chapman.

LENOX Avenue Gang: New York gang of burglars and killers

One of the most ferocious New York City gangs of this century was the Lenox Avenue Gang, formed as an independent venture by Gyp the Blood, the chief underling of Jack Zelig. They operated around 125th Street, terrorizing the neighborhood with daytime muggings, nighttime burglaries and killings-for-pay around the clock.

As the gang's chief, Gyp the Blood was a natural at his calling and could bring out the worst in any recruit. Jacob "Whitey Lewis" Seidenshner had been a third-rate boxer, but under Gyp the Blood's patient instructions, he became a master of the blackjack, neatly denting a skull without causing fatal results when they were unwanted or unpaid for. Louis "Lefty Louie" Rosenberg was mainly a pickpocket but with Gyp's guidance, became renowned as an expert gunman. Francesco "Dago Frank" Cirofisi was the meanest of the mob, more vicious than even Gyp the Blood himself, which was saying a lot. Dago Frank sneered at any job that didn't promise at least some likelihood of shooting. Val O'Farrell, one of the city's most famous police detectives, labeled Dago Frank "the toughest man in the world." Police laid six killings directly to Frank but could prove none of them in court, and had no idea how many others he had committed. Dutch Sadie, Dago Frank's girl-friend, was the main female member of the Lenox Avenuers. She carried a large butcher knife in her muff and would come howling to help Dago Frank whenever an intended mugging victim offered serious resistance. Her bloodcurdling shrieks were enough to freeze most men into total inaction.

The Lenox Avenue Gang came to an abrupt end in 1914, when Gyp the Blood, Lefty Louie, Dago Frank and Whitey

Lewis all went to the electric chair as the triggermen in the murder of gambler Herman Rosenthal.

See also: *Charles E. Becker, Gyp the Blood, Jack Zelig.*

LEOPOLD And Loeb: Thrill murderers

One day in May 1924 two youths, the sons of two of Chicago's wealthiest and most illustrious families, drove to the Harvard School for Boys in the suburb of Kenwood, Ill. to carry out what they regarded as the "perfect murder." Eighteen-year-old Richard "Dickie" Loeb, the youngest graduate of the University of Michigan, was a postgraduate student at the University of Chicago, and 19-year-old Nathan "Babe" Leopold, a Phi Beta Kappa from Chicago, was taking a law course there. The pair had perpetrated several minor crimes before they decided to commit the perfect murder. The killing, they felt, would be fun and an intellectual challenge, one worthy of their superior mental abilities.

Working out their plot for seven months, they picked as their victim 14-year-old Bobby Franks, the son of millionaire businessman Jacob Franks and a distant cousin of Loeb. The Franks boy who was always flattered when the pair took note of him, happily hopped into their car when they pulled up in front of his school. They drove the boy to within a few blocks of the Franks residence in fashionable Hyde Park and then grabbed him, stuffed a gag in his mouth and smashed his skull four times with a heavy chisel. Following the murderous assault Leopold and Loeb casually motored to some marshy wasteland and carried the body to a culvert along tracks of the Pennsylvania Railroad. After dunking the boy's head under swamp water to make sure he was dead, they poured hydrochloric acid on his face to complicate identification and then stuffed the body in a drain pipe.

Satisfied with their work, the pair repaired to Leopold's home, where they played cards and drank liquor. At midnight they called the elder Franks and informed him he would receive instructions on how to ransom his missing son. By the time their typewritten note demanding $10,000 was received, workmen had found the boy's body. Despite their self-proclaimed mental abilities, the two young killers weren't very good criminals. They were easily caught. Leopold had dropped his eyeglasses near the spot where the body was hidden and police checked the prescription until it led back to him. Furthermore, the ransom note was traced to Leopold's typewriter.

Dickie Loeb broke first, and then Leopold confessed as well. A shocked city and nation fully demanded and expected that the pair would be executed.

The parents of the two called in famous lawyer Clarence Darrow to defend them. For a fee of $100,000 Darrow agreed to seek to win the best possible verdict, one that would find them guilty but save them from execution. The trial began in August. Both sides produced psychiatrists to prove or disprove their mental competence. Darrow had less trouble with the opposing psychiatrists than he did with his clients, who turned the court proceedings into a circus. They clowned and hammed through the sessions, and the newspapers caught their frequent smirks in page-one pictures. The public, always against the two "poor little rich boys," became even more hostile.

Still Darrow prevailed. He put the human brain on trial and presented evidence that Leopold was a paranoiac with a severe manic drive; Loeb was pictured as a dangerous schizophrenic. He derided their supernormal intelligences and portrayed them as having the emotional capacities of seven-year-olds. For two days Darrow talked. "Do you think you can cure the hatreds and the maladjustments of the world by hanging them?" he asked the prosecution before Judge John R. Caverly, chief justice of the Criminal Court of Cook County, who was hearing the case without a jury. "You simply show your ignorance and your hate when you say it. You may heal and cure hatred with love and understanding, but you can only add fuel to the flames with cruelty and hating."

Then Darrow wept. In macabre detail he described how the state planned to hang the defendants. He invited the prosecution to perform the execution. Even the defendants were gripped by Darrow's presentation. Loeb shuddered, and Leopold got hysterical and had to be taken from the courtroom for a time. The lawyer refused to let up. He wept for the victims and he wept for the defendants and he wept for all other victims and defendants. In the end, Darrow won. Sentenced on September 10, the defendants got life for the murder of Bobby Franks plus 99 years for kidnapping him. Ironically, Darrow was paid only $40,000 of the much larger fee due him, and most of that only after he had dunned the two families a number of times.

The public was not through with Leopold and Loeb, however. There were subsequent exposes of the favored treatment they received in prison. Unlike many other prisoners at Joliet, each was put in a separate cell. They were provided with books, desks and filing cabinets. Loeb kept two canaries. They ate in the officers' lounge, away from the other prisoners, and had their meals cooked to order. They freely visited one another and they were allowed to keep their own garden.

Over the years Loeb became an aggressive homosexual, noted for pursuit of other convicts. In January 1936 he was slashed to death in a homosexual brawl.

Leopold, on the other hand, made tremendous adjustments in his behavior. Nevertheless, his appeals for parole were rejected three times. During his fourth appeal poet Carl Sandburg pleaded his case, saying he would be willing to allow Leopold to live in his home. Finally, in March 1958 Leopold was paroled. He said: "I am a broken old man. I want a chance to find redemption for myself and to help others." He published a book, *Life Plus 99 Years,* and went to Puerto Rico to work among the poor as a $10-a-month hospital technician. Three years later, he married a widow. Leopold died of a heart ailment in 1971.

See also: *Clarence Darrow.*

LEPKE, Louis: See Louis "Lepke" Buchalter.

Thrill killers (at left) Richard Loeb (left), who would later be killed in prison, and Nathan Leopold were saved from execution by the efforts of defense attorney Clarence Darrow. Leopold (at right) in 1957 shortly before he won parole.

LESLIE, Frank "Buckskin" (1842-?): Gunfighter

The prototype Western gunfighter who took his calling seriously, paying loving care to his guns and always practicing his aim, Frank "Buckskin" Leslie, was a pitiless gunslinger officially credited with some 10 to 14 kills.

A mystique has developed around Leslie. He has been described as a man who was never crossed twice by the same person. When the much-feared Johnny Ringo impertinently asked Leslie, "Did you ever shoot anybody in front?" Leslie had nothing to say. He still had nothing to say when they found Johnny Ringo resting under a tree with a bullet in his head, and nobody asked him any impertinent questions about that, although he remains the only suspect in Ringo's murder.

Little is known of Leslie's early life because of his habit of telling contradictory stories about himself—he was born in Kentucky or he was born in Texas; he studied pharmacy or he studied medicine in Europe. In the 1870s Leslie served as an Army scout in several Indian campaigns, and in 1880 he turned up in Tombstone, Ariz. with enough funds to open the Cosmopolitan Hotel. He had a reputation as a gunfighter and in June he demonstrated his prowess by killing a man named Mike Killeen in a dispute over Killeen's wife. A few months later, Leslie married the widow.

At this time, Tombstone was immersed in the Earp-Clanton

feud. Leslie's position in the matter is unclear. More often than not he appears to have sided with the Clantons, but according to the record, he shot up more Clantons than Earps. One Clanton gunner who made the mistake of crossing Leslie was Billy Claiborne. Claiborne, a survivor of the gunfight at the O.K. Corral, had been insisting everyone call him Billy the Kid, in honor of that late lamented outlaw, and had gunned down three men for laughing when he demanded they address him this way. In November 1882 Leslie was working at the Oriental Saloon as a barman-bouncer when Claiborne walked in one day and told him what he wanted to be called. Leslie just gave him a sour look. Claiborne then ordered him to step outside. Leslie did, shot Claiborne dead and returned to the bar.

Leslie was a maverick in the Earp-Clanton disputes and a gunfighter pure and simple. He strode the streets with his pistol lodged in a quick-fire rig, attached by a stud to a slotted plate on his gun belt so that it could be fired by swiveling it from the hip. He also used his wife for target practice, tracing her outline with bullets along a wall in their home. This may explain why the marriage didn't last. Leslie formed a relationship with one of the town's leading whores, Mollie Williams, but that affair didn't survive either. He shot her dead in 1889.

Leslie was sent to prison for killing Mollie but was paroled in 1896. After that, he traveled to the Klondike, and when he showed up in California in 1904, he had quite a poke. He apparently drank up most of that money and then worked as a bartender in a number of saloons. From 1913 to 1922 he operated a pool hall in Oakland, but thereafter, Leslie fades into obscurity. Some say he ended up working as a janitor, and there were many reports that he committed suicide, but the facts are not clear one way or the other.

See also: *Billy Claiborne, Oriental Saloon, Johnny Ringo.*

LESLIE, George Leonidas (1838-1884): King of the Bank Robbers

Unquestionably, the greatest bank robber (although, strictly speaking, most of his capers were burglaries) of the 19th century, notwithstanding the likes of Mark Shinburn, George Bliss and other notables, was George Leonidas Leslie, who New York Superintendent of Police George W. Walling held to be the mastermind of 80 percent of all bank thefts in America from 1865 until his violent death in 1884. Leslie's gang, according to Walling, stole somewhere between $7 and $12 million. In addition, this criminal genius was called in as a consultant on bank jobs by underworld gangs all over the country. His consultation fees ranged from $5,000 to $20,000, payable in advance regardless of the take.

Leslie was contemptuous of most criminals, regarding them as too stupid to make crime pay to its full potential. Typical was the Ace Marvin gang in San Francisco. In late 1880 they gave him $20,000 to help plan a bank job. The plan was to rob a bank over the weekend so that the theft would not be discovered until Monday; that was the only part of the caper Leslie liked. All the rest was awful. Ace Marvin was not a bank man but rather a jack of all crimes who thought a bank job would be a great way to make a big score. Leslie shook his head at such amateurism. Then too, Ace's "pete" man if allowed to follow his blasting technique, probably would blow half the town into the Bay. And Marvin didn't even have a fix in with the law. Leslie generally preferred to have a police license before he staged a heist. It made things simpler for everybody, and besides, the law came rather cheap. Finally, Marvin had not adequately planned the getaway. Leslie liked things laid out so that the escape route went down a narrow street where a carriage could be pulled out at just the right time and left in the way of any pursuers.

After listening to Ace's exposition of the robbery, Leslie junked the whole thing. He conceived a plan that called for the thieves to enter the bank not once but twice.

One night Leslie, Ace and six henchmen, including a skilled locksmith, forced the lock on the bank's side door and entered. The locksmith immediately set about replacing the lock on the door with a duplicate so that there would be no evidence of any forced entry. Meanwhile, Leslie carefully pried the dial off the safe lock with a small file. It was difficult work because he had to avoid leaving any marks or scratches. At last, the dial popped off. Then Leslie drew out a weird looking instrument made of thin steel wire, arranged it inside the surface of the dial and then replaced the knob securely on the safe.

Even Ace Marvin understood. "Well, I'll be," he said. "That wire is going to cut out grooves under the dial every time the combination is worked!"

Leslie nodded pridefully. He explained the device was called the little joker. If Leslie had not invented it, he certainly refined it and used it to perfection. "The deepest cuts will indicate the numbers of the combination. You just won't know which order the numbers are in and will have to try all the various possibilities, but there can only be a few dozen, so you'll have the right combination in a matter of minutes."

The next morning Leslie hopped a train back to New York. When he got home, he read in the newspapers about a $173,000 burglary of a bank in San Francisco. Leslie shook his head in disgust. Everyone had estimated the loot would be well over $200,000. If he had run the job, he would have counted the money on the spot and finding it short, he would have left it in the safe and returned another time, especially since it was only a few weeks until Christmas. If Marvin had waited a while bank deposits by businessmen would have soared. In fact, Leslie might have broken in three or four times before making the haul. But Ace Marvin was not George Leslie; he just wasn't in the same class.

That year, 1880, Leslie was at the height of his fabulous career. He had come a long way since graduating from the University of Cincinnati with high honors. Everyone knew he would go far but they assumed it would be in architecture, the field in which he had earned his degree. He was born in 1838, the son of a well-to-do Toledo brewer who put him through college and set him up in an office in Cincinnati. In 1865 both Leslie's mother and father died, and he closed his office in Cincinnati, perhaps because of the resentment there by people who considered him a war slacker, and went to New York.

With his experience and background, Leslie could have walked into almost any architect's office and secured a good position. Instead, in almost no time at all, he was knee-deep in crime. Demonstrating a remarkable knack for pulling bank capers, he soon gathered around him such desperate and cunning criminals as Gilbert Yost, Jimmy Brady, Abe Coakley, Red Leary, Shang Draper, Johnny Dobbs, Worcester Sam Perris, Banjo Pete Emerson and Jimmy Hope. He pulled off bank jobs of an unprecedented magnitude, among them the theft of $786,879 from the Ocean National Bank at Greenwich and Fulton streets and $2,747,000 from the Manhattan Savings Institution at Bleecker Street and Broadway. The take in the Ocean Bank robbery would have been even higher had not his men left almost $2 million in cash and securities on the floor beside the vault. The gang also wandered afield to pull off such lucrative capers as the burglaries of the South Kensington National Bank in Philadelphia, the Third National Bank of Baltimore, the Wellsbro Bank of Philadelphia and the Saratoga County Bank of Waterford, N.Y.

Despite all his jobs, Leslie never spent a day behind bars. When in trouble, he was represented by Howe and Hummel, the notorious criminal lawyers, to whom he once paid $90,000 to square a charge. His fame spread, both in police circles and in the underworld, and he sat in the place of honor at the dinner parties given by Marm Mandelbaum, America's most notorious fence, through whom Leslie laundered great sums of cash and securities. At the same time, Leslie led a double life, posing as a man of inherited means who, with his family background and education, was readily accepted in New York society. He held memberships in prestigious clubs and was known as a bon vivant and man about town. He could be seen at openings of art exhibits and theater first nights and gained quite a reputation as a bibliophile, possessing an excellent collection of first editions and being frequently consulted by other collectors.

Leslie seldom associated with fellow criminals except when planning jobs or visiting the Mandelbaum mansion, but he did have a way with their women. With his wife ensconced in Philadelphia, he carried on numerous affairs in New York with women belonging, in one way or another, to other criminals, most notably Babe Irving, the sister of Johnny Irving, and Shang Draper's wife, and lavished much time and money on them.

It was probably his amatory activities that proved to be the death of him, although some of Leslie's capers started going awry about a year before he was killed. He was known to have become quite rattled after J. W. Barron, cashier of the Dexter Savings Bank of Dexter, Maine, was killed in one of his ill-fated schemes. When several criminals were arrested for the Manhattan Bank job and police gained knowledge about the Dexter matter, many felt Leslie had arranged the leaks to protect himself.

Early in May 1884 Leslie returned to Philadelphia and told his wife he planned to get out of crime and that they would move elsewhere to start a new life. He admitted he was worried about being assassinated. Against his wife's protests, however, he returned to New York City. She would never again see him alive.

During the last week of his life, Leslie was seen on a number of occasions in different locations. He seemed to make a point of never sleeping two nights at the same place.

On May 29 Leslie stopped in Murphy's Saloon on Grand Street and was given a letter addressed in woman's handwriting. He read it and said something about doing an errand "over the water," meaning Brooklyn. On June 4 his decomposing body was found at the base of Tramps' Rock, near the dividing line between Westchester and New York counties. He had been shot in the head.

The murder was never officially solved, although the accepted theory is that he was killed by Shang Draper, Johnny Dobbs, Worcester Sam Perris and Billy Porter, all residents of the Williamsburg section. Furthermore, it seems probable that Draper's woman was forced to write the letter that lured Leslie to his death. Clearly Leslie had gone off in expectations of a pleasant tryst. There were no bloodstains on his clothing when his body was found, and he had apparently been dressed after his death. The King of the Bank Robbers, the man who had stolen millions, was buried in a $10 plot in Cypress Hill Cemetery, a fate little better than that of the city's paupers.

See also: *Bank Robberies, Johnny Dobbs, Jimmy Hope, Little Joker, Fredericka "Marm" Mandelbaum.*

LEVINE, Peter (1926-1938): Kidnap-murder victim

The second oldest unsolved kidnapping—after the Charles Mattson abduction— carried in the FBI's files, the Peter Levine case began in New Rochelle, N.Y. about 3:30 p.m. on February 24, 1938, when the 12-year-old boy left school and started home. At 5 o'clock his mother received a telephone call informing her that her son had been kidnapped and that she should go to a vacant house in town for further instructions. Under the front door of the house, the distraught mother found a note that said her son was safe and demanded a ransom of $60,000.

Four days later, the Levines received a letter telling them the money was wanted quickly. A penciled note on the back of the letter in Peter's identifiable scrawl read: "Dear Dad, Please pay, I want to come home. I have a cold. Your son, Peter." After two more days a third note, reducing the demand to $30,000, directed that someone other than the parents should bring the ransom money to a certain spot in nearby Mamaroneck. Two intermediaries made four trips with the money along the route indicated but they were never met by the kidnapper.

The boy's father made several appeals over the radio and in the newspapers to the kidnapper for additional communications, but there was no further word. After three months the headless body of a boy floated ashore in New Rochelle from Long Island Sound. It was identified as that of Peter Levine.

A team of 30 FBI agents closely investigated dozens of suspects. Nine persons were convicted of attempted extortion, posing as the kidnappers and promising to return the boy if money was paid. But the real perpetrator was never caught. The closest identification the authorities ever made was the kidnapper was likely to be a man with an Italian or German accent.

LEWIS, Vach: See Cyclone Louie.

LEXOW Committee: New York police corruption investigation

In the first major investigation of a police department in the United States, the Lexow Committee of 1894 uncovered mass corruption in New York City. Later inquiries in that city as well as in other major cities proved this to be the norm rather than the exception.

Corruption in the New York Police Department was revealed to be handled by a highly organized machine called the system. The study showed the system flourished under both parties but had become most blatant under the Tammany Hall reign of Richard Croker. Anyone opposing the system—businessman, private citizen or honest policeman—was "abused, clubbed and imprisoned, and even convicted of crime on false testimony by policemen and their accomplices." Great steamship companies and even lowly pushcart peddlers were required to pay graft.

Naturally, the underworld was a prime source of funds; the committee set the figure at $7 million annually. By allowing streetwalkers and thieves to operate on their beat, crooked patrolmen and detectives earned more in graft than in salary, and the revenue dishonest officials received from gamblers, illegal liquor dealers and brothel keepers produced a corps of millionaires. Fixed set monthly levies ran as follows: saloons, $2 to $20; poolrooms (actually horsebetting parlors), $200; policy shops, $20 on each of the 1,000 in operation; brothels, a minimum of $5 per prostitute; new brothels, $500 to open. The graft was broken down so that the patrolman or detective-collector got 20 percent; the precinct commander pocketed 35 to 50 percent and the inspector took the balance. Appointments to the police force did not come cheaply, especially considering the value of the 19th century dollar. Becoming a patrolman cost $300 and an equal sum was necessary to be promoted to roundsman; making sergeant cost $1,600; and reaching the heights of captaincy required as much as $15,000.

While the head of the Lexow Committee was State Sen. Clarence Lexow, a Republican, the general success of the group was attributed to the work of its counsel, John W. Goff, a Democrat. The following November the Republicans, out of office for many years, were swept into full power in both the city and state because of public revulsion over the disclosures. Inspector Alexander "Clubber" Williams, often called the most dishonest cop in America (he insisted he became wealthy by speculating in real estate in Japan), was eventually forced out. Many reforms were instituted, but it soon became obvious that although camouflaged, the system continued, subsequently as revealed by the Charles Becker-Herman Rosenthal murder case of 1912, the Seabury Investigation of the 1930s and the Knapp Commission of the early 1970s.

See also: *Alexander S. "Clubber" Williams.*

LIE Detector

The lie detector dates back to 1921, although man's effort to expose liars is centuries old. Some ancient peoples used tests based on principles that are considered at least somewhat sound even today, and that, indeed, provide the basis for the modern lie detector. In parts of the Orient a suspect was given a handful of rice to chew. If he could spit it out, he was innocent. If it remained dry and he could not spit it out, he was guilty. The reasoning was that fear caused by guilt would dry up his flow of saliva.

The technique Solomon used when two women claimed the same child would be hard to beat. He reasoned that the real mother would rather deny her claim than have her child killed. But most other tests of long ago were brutal and senseless. Tibet had a quaint custom of detecting liars in cases where two individuals made conflicting claims. Two stones, one white and one black, were put in a pot of boiling water. The two disputants plunged their arms in, and the individual who got the white stone was declared the honest one. If nothing else, the system probably cut down the number of lawsuits. Medieval methods were as brutal and relied even more on chance. In

the trial by water, the suspect, tied with rope, was thrown in a vat of holy water. If he sank, he was innocent. If he floated, it was reasoned that the holy water had refused to receive him, and he was declared guilty. Trial by fire took a little longer. The suspect, after appropriate church rituals, either drew a stone from a pot of boiling water or carried a hot stone for a prescribed number of feet. After the ordeal his hand was bandaged by a priest, and if after ten days the wound was healing cleanly, he was declared innocent. If the wound festered, he was guilty. One wonders how many germs convicted innocent men in those unhygienic days.

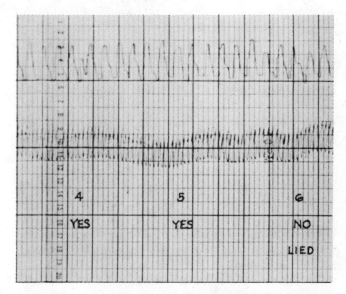

Chart of a lie detector test demonstrates why a trained expert is needed to interpret polygraph results.

By these standards, the present-day lie detector is a scientific marvel. Much scientific research on the detection of lying was carried out both in Europe and the United States by scientists and criminologists, such as the Italians Cesare Lombroso and Vittorio Benussi and Americans William Moulton Marston and Fr. Walter G. Summers of Fordham University. The first practical lie detector fashioned for police work was ordered by August Vollmer, the legendary police chief of Berkeley, Calif. In 1921 he assigned a colleague, John A. Larson, followed later by Leonarde Keeler, to develop what has become known as the polygraph, a machine that measures various bodily reactions to questions requiring a yes or no answer. Among the measurements graphed were variations in blood pressure, breathing, pulse and electrodermal response, a minute electrical discharge from the skin. Simply stated, changes in the norm of these indicators show a subject is lying, according to the test.

Lie detector experts like to cite the many instances when a lie detector test ferreted out a guilty man and produced a confession. They are somewhat more reticent about discussing well-known failures. A case in point was Paul Joseph Altheide, age 26, who was charged with murdering a tailor in Phoenix, Ariz. in the 1950s. Altheide claimed to have been 500 miles away in Texas at the time. A lie detector test indicated he was lying when denying his guilt. This more than satisfied the law but did not satisfy a reporter, Gene McLain of the *Arizona Republic,* who went to Texas and eventually turned up witnesses who proved Altheide's innocence. He was released after spending 137 days in jail for a crime he had not committed. His incriminating polygraph test had clearly dissuaded the law from making further efforts to clear him. In a number of other cases, suspects have been cleared by lie detector tests only to be proved guilty later by other evidence.

Lie detector proponents like to proclaim their tests are 97 percent accurate with a three percent "gray area," in which the operator cannot form a definite conclusion. However, at least two independent studies, one by the Stanford Research Institute and the other by the Massachusetts Institute of Technology, put the accuracy figure at 70 percent.

The lie detector does not blow a gasket or flash "tilt" when a suspect is caught in an untruth. It isn't that simple. Leaders in the field, like John Reid, operator of the nation's largest commercial polygraph agency, have long regarded the machine itself as only one component of three needed to get at the truth: the polygraph, an operator who can interpret it correctly and a foolproof questioning technique. The importance of this last point has been shown often in cases where a rapist was asked if he had raped the victim and was able to deny it successfully, having rationalized in his own mind that all he had used was "excessive persuasion." Polygraph experts say the question in such cases should be worded to ask if the suspect has had "sexual intercourse" with the victim, since the machine merely records whether the suspect *thinks* he's lying. However, even this formulation of the question may not be sufficient. Some men do not consider themselves to have had sexual relations if they have failed to achieve an orgasm.

Similarly, a farmer once "beat" the machine by denying that he had stolen some barbed wire. What had happened was that the roll of barbed wire had been lying around unused for months, and when the farmer appropriated it, he was, in his own mind, merely putting it to good use instead of letting it rust.

Many guilty parties have been able to beat the machine through a concerted effort. The late polygraph expert Leonarde Keeler admitted he could beat his own machine. Lesser intellects than Keeler have also been successful. Gerald Thompson, who confessed to and was later executed for the murder of Mildred Hallmark, passed a lie detector test with flying colors. When his questioner specifically asked him, "Did you kill Mildred?" he just concentrated on another Mildred and denied it.

Another murderer, Chester Weger, who killed three wealthy matrons in Starved Rock State Park, Ill. in 1960, later claimed he had twice passed polygraph tests by first swallowing a lot of aspirins and washing them down with Coca-Cola. The late director of the FBI, J. Edgar Hoover, frequently denounced the lie detector (although the agency now relies on it to an increasing extent), once commenting: "The name lie dector is a complete misnomer. The machine used is not a lie detector. The person who operates the machine is the lie detector by

reason of his interpretation. Whenever the human element enters into an interpretation of anything, there is always a possibility of error."

No more than a handful of states have laws requiring the licensing of polygraph operators. In most states a person can become an "expert" by buying a machine and a handbook telling him how to use it. There are no accurate estimates of how many persons in the country regularly give lie detector examinations, but the figures are well into the hundreds, perhaps thousands. It has been estimated that at least 80 percent of these are "unqualified." An acknowledged leader in the field grudgingly concedes that competent operators probably comprise anywhere from 10 to 40 percent of the total. Most unqualified operators, who don't know how to interpret a chart and really don't care, are what is known in the trade as "sandbaggers," relying on coercion and bluster to get a confession. "I know you done it," they say. "The machine says so, so come clean, you sonovabitch!"

One prominent lie detector operator tells of another "expert" who worked for several Midwestern police departments. He was called in to doublecheck the other man's findings and came to the exact opposite conclusions in 12 cases. This writer once interviewed a so-called expert who was often consulted by police departments in the East. He sported a business card that showed he was a man of many talents. The card read: "Hypnotist —Relieve Insomnia—Stop Smoking—Stop Drinking—Many Other Benefits." And in addition to his lie detector work, he was also licensed as a private eye.

Generally, lie detector findings have not been admitted, save in rare instances, as evidence in trials. Objecting to this practice, lie detector proponents cite the 1920 landmark murder case of a Washington, D.C. physician that resulted in the conviction of a young black, James Alphonse Frye, despite attempts by the defense to present testimony by Dr. William Marston about findings of a polygraph test given to Frye. Marston's findings indicated Frye was innocent, but the test results were barred as evidence and he was convicted. Later on, another man was found to be the real murderer and Frye was freed. The ruling barring lie detector evidence in the Frye case stood, however, and since then courts have repeatedly refused to admit polygraph findings. An exception was a 1972 case in California in which a judge permitted lie test evidence that a man accused of possession of marijuana had refused police permission to search his suitcase. The judge declared that lie detector equipment and techniques had improved so much that rules against the use of evidence obtained by polygraph should be changed. The ruling, however, proved to be an isolated one and gained little acceptance.

See also: *Cutler Lie Detector Decision, Frye v. United States, Leonarde Keeler, Chester Weger.*

LIGHTFOOT, Captain (1775-1822): Irish and American highwayman

Michael Martin was only 17 in his native Ireland when he ran away from home and turned to a life of crime, becoming the infamous Captain Lightfoot. After fleeing he made an attempt at reform but soon resumed his criminal career, becoming the most-hunted outlaw of the post-Revolutionary period.

Following a 16-year career in Ireland and Scotland as Captain Lightfoot, Martin found the countryside teeming with troops determined to put an end to highway robbery. On April 12, 1818 he made it aboard the brig *Maria* shortly before he would have been cornered by pursuers. On June 17 Lightfoot landed in Salem, Mass., where he decided to live out his days in honest toil. However, efforts to make a go of it working a farm and, later, operating a small brewery failed, thanks to what he later told a biographer was the sharpness of Yankee tradespeople.

Following an unhappy love affair, Lightfoot returned to his former occupation as a highwayman. Over the next three years he became the scourge of all New England, committing one holdup after another. No traveler was safe anywhere in New England and even far into Canada. Indians too fell victim to Lightfoot's call to "stand and deliver." On the road to Boston, he committed his most famous crime. When a young woman passenger on a coach tried to hide her watch, Lightfoot doffed his hat and said, "Ma'am I do not rob ladies," making him a Robin Hood figure in the story telling at country taverns. In time, it finally dawned on authorities that the scoundrel was Europe's notorious Captain Lightfoot, and efforts to catch him intensified. The highwayman was finally captured in a stable near Springfield by a slow-closing ring of posses. In October 1821 Lightfoot was sentenced to death, but the next day he escaped by sawing through his chains with a file supplied by a friend. However, he was quickly recaptured, and this time the chains were forged to his ankles and wrists and attached to his cell floor.

Lightfoot was now a national legend. In interviews his jailers praised his quiet bravery, and the balladmakers were composing tributes to the "brave Captain Lightfoot" even before he was dead. A writer, Frederick W. Waldo, was permitted to stay with him long enough to gather material for a full-length biography, *Captain Lightfoot, the Last of the New England Highwaymen*. He was described as "calm and serene" at his execution on December 22, 1822; when the hangman fumbled with the noose, he gallantly assisted by putting the rope around his own neck. He also relieved the sheriff of the task of dropping the handkerchief as a signal to the hangman. Captain Lightfoot held the handkerchief aloft in his hand and, as the crowd hushed, let it flutter free. Before it came to earth, Lightfoot had swung to his death.

LIME Cell: Prison torture

One of the most hellish tortures ever used in American prisons was the so-called lime cell, which remained quite popular in a number of institutions well into the 20th century. A prisoner would be led to a cell where the white coating of lime was some three inches thick. A guard would sprinkle the cell with a hose, resulting in a white mist from the exploding chloride of lime filling the cell, and then the prisoner would be shoved inside.

The convict would clutch his burning throat with both hands, reeling and toppling to the floor. He would claw at the walls, trying to struggle back to his feet. One convict who underwent this ordeal graphically described it as feeling as if he were in the middle of a volcano. Cramping pains tore at his bowels and his breath seemed to sizzle. When he was pulled from the cell, he had to be hosed down to stifle the burning fumes. The misery never lasted more than five or six minutes, but sometimes a severely punished convict would be given the lime cell treatment for as many as 10 days in a row. At the end of this ordeal, the mucous membranes of his mouth, nose and throat would be seared, his voice reduced to a whisper and his eyebrows and eyelashes completely burned off.

Despite official denials, the lime cell remained a favored form of punishment in a great number of prisons until recent years, when nationwide prison reform supposedly ended the inhuman practice. Yet reports indicate it is still practiced in isolated instances.

LINCOLN, Abraham (1809-1865): Assassination victim

By present-day standards, the protection of Abraham Lincoln at the time of his assassination in 1865 bordered on the criminally negligent. On the night of April 14 President and Mrs. Abraham Lincoln attended the performance of *Our American Cousin* at Ford's Theater in Washington, D.C. Attending with them as substitutes for Gen. and Mrs. Ulysses S. Grant, who had canceled (because Mrs. Grant could not abide Mrs. Lincoln), were the daughter of Sen. Ira Harris and his stepson, Maj. Henry Rathbone. Earlier that day the President had asked the War Department to provide a special guard. Oddly, the request was refused, a matter of considerable puzzlement to historians. The only presidential bodyguard that night was a shiftless member of the Washington police force, who after the start of the performance, incredibly left his post outside the flag-draped presidential box to adjourn to nearby Taltavul's tavern for a drink.

While there, he may well have rubbed elbows with another imbiber, John Wilkes Booth, who had been drinking heavily for several hours, determined that tonight he would kill Lincoln. At 26 Booth, a noted Shakespearean actor, had long made no secret of his Southern sympathies. The War Department undoubtedly knew of his drunken boasting about a plot to kidnap Lincoln and drag him in chains to Richmond, where he would be held until the Union armies laid down their arms. As a matter of fact, Booth and a small group of conspirators had waited in ambush about three weeks earlier to attack the Lincoln carriage outside the city limits but were thwarted by the President's change of plans.

After that failure Booth shifted to the assassination attempt. The plan called for him to kill Lincoln while other members of the group simultaneously attacked Vice President Andrew Johnson and various Cabinet members.

Four of those charged with the crime, Mrs. Mary Surratt, Lewis Paine, David Herold and George Atzerodt, were hanged, although to the end most people expected Mrs. Surratt's death sentence to be commuted.

At 10 o'clock Booth left the bar and went to the theater, pausing long enough to bum a chew of tobacco from a ticket taker he knew. In the foyer of the theater Booth caught the eye of actress Jennie Gourlay, who later recalled he had appeared pale and ill and distraught with "a wild look in his eyes."

Booth entered Lincoln's unguarded box, leveled his one-shot Derringer behind the President's left ear and pulled the trigger. As Lincoln slumped, Booth cried out, *"Sic semper tyrannis"* ("Ever thus to tyrants"), dropped his gun and pulled a dagger. He slashed Maj. Rathbone as the officer lunged for him. Booth hurtled the rail of the box in what he undoubtedly visualized as a dramatic appearance on the stage, shouting, "The South is avenged." However, his spur caught in the flag outside the box and he almost fell on his face. Somehow he kept his footing and limped on a fractured left leg across the stage and out into the street. There he mounted his horse and rode off.

Were it not for his leg injury, Booth might have made good his escape, crossing the Potomac and losing himself among the soldiers being demobilized following Lee's surrender. But the pain slowed his flight. He met up in Maryland with David Herold, another of the conspirators, who had failed in a simul-

taneous attempt on the life of Secretary of State William Seward, and the pair located Dr. Samuel Mudd. After Mudd set Booth's leg the two left the doctor's home and made it to the Potomac River awaiting an opportunity to cross into Virginia.

Meanwhile, the hunt for the assassin was pressed, some observers said later with considerable incompetence. Certainly, greed for the reward money being offered and hysteria hindered the search, and it was not until April 26 that the fugitives were cornered in a tobacco shed on a farm near Port Royal, Va.

The commander of the Union troops, a Lt. Baker, ordered the pair to surrender or the building would be set on fire. Booth called out, "Let us have a little time to consider it."

Five minutes later Booth declared: "Captain, I know you to be a brave man, and I believe you to be honorable; I am a cripple. I have got but one leg; if you withdraw your men in one line one hundred yards from the door, I will come out and fight you."

Baker rejected the offer and Booth then shouted, "Well, my brave boys, prepare a stretcher for me."

Then the soldiers heard loud voices from the shed and Booth's voice could be heard saying: "You damned coward, will you leave me now? Go, go; I would not have you stay with me." Then Booth yelled, "There's a man in here who wants to come out."

A trembling Herold surrendered himself.

The structure was set afire, and the troopers could see a dark figure hobbling about. Suddenly, there was a shot—possibly by Booth himself and possibly by a Union zealot, a soldier named Boston Corbett—and Booth fell. Soldiers rushed into the barn and pulled Booth outside.

"Tell mother I die for my country," Booth whispered before breathing his last.

Even before Booth's death, the government had implicated eight other persons in the assassination—Herold, George A. Atzerodt, Lewis Paine, Mary E. Surratt, her son John H. Surratt, Edward Spangler, Dr. Mudd and Michael O'Laughlin. All except John H. Surratt, who eluded capture, were tried before a military commission, on the ground that Lincoln was the commander-in-chief and had fallen "in actual service in time of war." The trial, which ran from May 9 to June 30, was a bizarre spectacle conducted under decidedly unfair conditions and amidst postwar hysteria. Somehow the defendants were linked to the deeds of the Confederate government and Jefferson Davis. Many of the charges dealt with such irrelevancies as starvation of Union prisoners in notorious Andersonville Prison and the plot to burn New York City.

At the same time, important witnesses were never called to testify. John F. Parker, who negligently left Lincoln unguarded, was not summoned (nor was he dismissed from the police force or even reprimanded). Even men who had harbored Booth for a week after the assassination were not forced to appear. Most observers felt that the case against Mrs. Mary Surratt was singularly weak, depending largely on the word of a known liar and an infamous drunkard. Her sole offense seems to have been owning the rooming house where much of the plotting had taken place.

Nonetheless, Mrs. Surratt was sentenced to hang along with Paine, Herold and Atzerodt. Mudd, Arnold and O'Laughlin received life sentences and Spangler got six years. The executions were carried out on July 7, 1865, ironically with umbrellas held over the prisoners' heads on the gallows to protect them from the sweltering sun. To the very end, it was thought that Mrs. Surratt would be pardoned. Paine told the executioner: "If I had two lives to give, I'd give one gladly to save Mrs. Surratt. I know that she is innocent, and would never die in this way if I hadn't been found at her house. She knew nothing about the conspiracy at all. . . ." However, there was no last-minute reprieve and the four were executed at the same moment.

The hunt for John Surratt became a world chase and he was finally located in Italy serving in the Swiss Guards. Brought back to trial in 1867, when the hysteria had died down, Surratt went free when the jury could not agree on his guilt.

The weakness of the case against the imprisoned men also became apparent in time, and by March 4, 1869 President

Andrew Johnson had pardoned all of them except O'Laughlin, who had died in prison in 1867.

See also: *Boston Corbett, Dr. Samuel A. Mudd.*

LINCOLN, Abraham: Defense attorney

Attorney Abraham Lincoln of Illinois "rode the circuit" around Springfield in the practice of his profession. While most of his cases were civil, involving land disputes, livestock claims and financial matters, he also defended a number of clients on criminal charges. Most of these cases involved prosaic allegations, such as theft, drunkeness and the like, but he conducted a murder defense that brought him statewide fame.

William "Duff" Armstrong was accused along with James Norris of killing James "Pres" Metzker in a drunken brawl near Havana, on August 29, 1857. It was established beyond doubt that Norris had hit Metzker with an ox-yoke. Tried separately, he was convicted and given eight years in the penitentiary. However, young Armstrong denied he had struck the victim another deadly blow with a slung shot, insisting he had done all his fighting with his fists.

"Riding the circuit" made young Abraham Lincoln one of the best-known lawyers in downstate Illinois.

Lincoln took the case without fee because, as he would tell the jury, the defendant was the son of Jack and Hannah Armstrong, who had provided the now-famous lawyer with a home when he was "penniless, homeless, and alone." The inference

Lincoln would make was that such a fine couple could not possibly have raised a killer.

The trial opened in Beardstown, Ill. on May 7, 1858. The prosecution's case was based primarily on the testimony of a house painter named Charles Allen, who said he had seen every detail of the murder, which had occurred at 9:30 in the brilliant light of a full moon. Lincoln took Allen over the details of the crime several times, drawing from the witness again and again a description of the brilliant moonlight that had enabled him to see the events so clearly. Then Lincoln produced a farmer's almanac and turned to the page for August 29, the day of the murder. It showed that the moon had been just past its first quarter, providing little help for the witness. In addition to discrediting Allen's testimony, Lincoln stressed that the mark on Metzker attributed to Armstrong's lethal blow could have been caused by the victim falling to the ground after being struck by Norris.

As the jury filed from the courtroom, Lincoln is reported to have turned to Mrs. Armstrong and said, "Aunt Hannah, your son will be free before sundown." The acquittal came quickly. When it did, Lincoln said thoughtfully, "I pray to God that this lesson may prove in the end a good lesson to him and to all."

LINCOLN, Abraham: Target of body snatchers

After Abraham Lincoln was buried in 1865, authorities found it necessary to move his casket 17 times, mainly to prevent it from being stolen and held for ransom. That feat was almost achieved in 1876 by Big Jim Kenealy and his gang of counterfeiters. They concocted a weird plot to steal the body, rebury it elsewhere and then return it in exchange for money and the release of the outfit's master engraver, Ben Boyd, then doing 10 years in prison. Their plot was foiled when an informer working on counterfeiting matters infiltrated the gang and tipped off the Secret Service.

The would-be body snatchers were thwarted just as they were moving the casket, then kept in a mausoleum in a lonely section of forest two miles outside of Springfield, Ill. Nevertheless, the gang succeeded in eluding the Secret Service agents who swooped down on them. After 10 days all were rounded up, but Kenealy suddenly had a surprise for the authorities. He had previously determined that there was no law on the books making it illegal to steal a dead body, not even that of a martyred president. However, all the gang members were convicted and given the maximum sentence, one year in prison, for attempting to steal a coffin.

For the next two years the casket remained hidden under a pile of scrap lumber until it was moved again. Finally in 1901, it was locked in a steel cage and buried 10 feet below the floor of a national shrine in Springfield.

LINCOLN, Warren (1870-1941): Murderer

When Chicago defense lawyer Warren Lincoln retired to the pleasant surroundings of Aurora, Ill. just after reaching 50, he was anticipating a happy existence. But the faults of his wife, Lena, which Lincoln had ignored as long as he had the hustle and bustle of criminal court life to distract him, now became his obsession in the solitude of Aurora. She opposed, not necessarily in order, liquor, tobacco and sex. In short, she was a bore. Adding to his misery was Byron Shoup, his brother-in-law, who moved in as something of a permanent guest. Since Lincoln was used to the workings of a criminal mind, it was perhaps inevitable that he should come to think of murdering the two of them. No doubt, he felt he could get away with it. In Chicago he had once won acquittals for five very guilty murderers in a row. One day both Lena and Shoup were missing. Lincoln sadly told friends that his wife had left a letter saying she was running off with another man. That being the case, Lincoln said, he had ordered Shoup out of the house. Lincoln then went back to tending his garden. He used lots of fertilizer much of which he mixed himself. His special mixture contained a great deal of ashes, including those of Lena and Shoup.

In time, suspicions were voiced and Lincoln was caught in a number of lies concerning his missing wife and brother-in-law. Police dug up his garden searching for their bodies but found nothing.

The only parts of Lincoln's victims that he hadn't burned were their heads, which he'd planted in flower boxes on his porch and later covered with cement. But Lincoln wasn't worried about any trace of the heads, since he had covered them with quicklime. Eventually, the police dug up the flower boxes and found two perfectly preserved heads. Unfortunately for Lincoln, he once had employed a rather dim-witted greenhouse helper who had mistakenly transposed a barrel of quicklime with a barrel of slaked lime. Instead of covering the heads with quicklime, which would have disintegrated them quickly, Lincoln had covered them with slaked lime, which acted as a preservative. He was sentenced to life in Joliet Prison and died there in 1941.

LINCOLN County War

While the Lincoln County War is most remembered because of the prominence it provided to Billy the Kid, the conflict itself had much greater significance. Indeed, it was a full-scale war conducted by rival banking, mercantile and ranching interests with insignificant cowboys comprising most of the casualties. There were passions and personal hatreds involved that gave it aspects of a blood feud: such was the case for Billy the Kid as the result of the cold-blooded murder of his adopted father, a newcomer from England who had joined one side in a quest for the wealth of the county and indeed much of the New Mexico Territory.

Lincoln County was a remote and extremely lawless section of the territory when one of the West's greatest cattlemen, John Chisum, pushed his herds into the area in the early 1870s and preempted huge sections of government land. At the time, the area was economically dominated by a hard-nosed businessman named Lawrence G. Murphy, who ran a huge mercantile store in Lincoln called The House. Because of the economic importance of his store, Murphy virtually named public officials and lawmen. He later sold his business to two tough Irishmen James J. Doland and James H. Riley, who forcefully increased The House's predominance in the county.

The key to power in the county lay in control of government contracts for supplying beef to Army posts and Indian reservations. Through The House's close ties with influential territorial officials in the capital—the notorious Santa Fe Ring—the profits on such contracts were kept at enormous levels. The Santa Fe Ring was comprised of corrupt Republican officeholders, while the owners of The House, Dolan and Riley, headed a county Democratic machine. Their alliance was probably the first proof that Republicans and Democrats could work together if there were profits to be gained.

John Chisum resented this control of the cattle marketing business by mere merchants and formed an opposing alliance with lawyer Alexander McSween, a former Murphy adherent, and John Tunstall, a young, ambitious Englishman who had established a large ranch. It was Tunstall who recruited Billy the Kid as a cowboy and gunman. In the ensuing conflict a number of small ranchers were caught in the middle. Many resented Chisum for seizing public lands and thus lined up with The House, but others who detested the businessmen, to whom they sold their cattle at low prices and under harsh credit terms, sided with Chisum and the insurgents.

The owners of The House held most of the trump cards, including Sheriff William Brady, a puppet who willingly harrassed their opponents, charging the cattle barons with innumerable offenses. Tunstall countered by opening a rival store in Lincoln that offered better terms to farmers and small ranchers, so that more of them rallied to the Chisum-McSween-Tunstall banner. In early 1878 Sheriff Brady was ordered to execute an arrest warrant against Tunstall. He handed the job over to a posse of hastily deputized gunmen, remaining conveniently in the background. The posse rode out to the Tunstall spread and, catching the Englishman helpless on foot, shot him to death.

Much has been made of Tunstall's death turning Billy the Kid into a killer. Such a conclusion, of course, ignores the fact that Billy was already a murderer, but after the Tunstall slaying his homicidal activities had a "purpose." The Kid pledged to avenge Tunstall's death. The two members of the posse who had done the actual shooting, William Morton and Frank Baker, were caught by a rival posse of "regulators," which included Billy the Kid. The pair surrendered on the posse leader's promise that they would be returned to Lincoln alive. Along the way, Morton was allowed to mail a letter to a relative in Virginia. It said in part, "There was one man who wanted to kill me after I had surrendered and was restrained with the greatest difficulty by others." That man was Billy the Kid, and he wasn't about to keep his guns holstered through the long trip. On the third day the Kid shot down both Morton and Baker as well as a member of the posse who evidently had tried to protect the prisoners.

With Tunstall dead, Billy the Kid transferred his loyalties to McSween and became the gunfighting leader of the faction. In the spring, he led his forces in a memorable battle against Brady and his men at Tunstall's store and killed the sheriff. In July the two factions fought a four-day pitched battle, with the Kid and his forces barricaded in McSween's adobe house in the center of Lincoln. On the fifth day most of them escaped, but lawyer McSween was shot dead.

With the death of McSween, the owners of The House and the Santa Fe Ring won the Lincoln County War. Chisum remained a powerful cattle baron but never achieved the complete domination of the Pecos Valley he so desired. With the end of the war, Billy the Kid lost his "purpose" but went right on killing.

See also: *Billy the Kid, John Tunstall.*

LINDBERGH Kidnapping

No kidnapping in American history achieved more notoriety or produced more public clamor than the abduction of the Lindbergh baby in 1932. By its very nature, the crime inspired an incredible array of swindles, hoaxes and controversies. At the time, the depths of the Depression, Charles A. Lindbergh— Lucky Lindy—was a hero in an era of few heroes. He had enjoyed that stature since his epic flight from New York to Paris in May 1927. "Lindbergh," Frederick Lewis Allen was to write in his book *Only Yesterday,* "was a god"—and indeed he was. Consequently, the kidnapping of 20-month-0ld Charles A. Lindbergh, Jr. from the family's home near Hopewell, N.J. was little short of sacrilege, a crime that outraged the public far more than even the Leopold-Loeb case of the previous decade.

The night of the crime, March 1, was particularly windy, and after Mrs. Lindbergh and the baby's nurse, Betty Gow, put the child to bed, the nurse remained with him until he was asleep. A short while later, Lindbergh heard a noise, but not hearing it again, he and his wife dismissed the sound as the wind. At about 10 p.m. the nurse, making her customary check, found the baby's bed empty. Searching around the house, Lindbergh discovered a homemade wooden ladder with a broken rung outside the nursery window, and he called the police.

Near the window sill he found a note written in broken English that indicated the writer might be German.

> Have fifty thousand dollars ready, 25,000 in twenty-dollar bills 15,000 in ten-dollar bills, and 10,000 in five-dollar bills. In 4-5 days we will inform you where to deliver the money. We warn you for making anyding public or for notify the police The child is in gut care Indication for all letters are signature and three holes.

But by that time the authorities had already been called in, and inevitably, the press and the nation soon learned of the crime. From then on, the case was nothing short of a three-ring circus. Everyone from the well-intended to a legion of crackpots and hoaxers got into the act. Police on various levels

Symbols show location of the Lindbergh baby's room (A) and areas where kidnapper's ladder (B) and baby's bedding (C) were abandoned.

jockeyed for position in the investigative process. No one was clearly in charge, except possibly Lindbergh himself, who was impressed by certain investigators and unimpressed by others.

Initial theories about the crime revolved, quite naturally, around the possibility that the underworld was responsible for the kidnapping. Hearst columnist Arthur Brisbane championed the idea of releasing the notorious gangster Al Capone from prison to help find the child and return him to the Lindberghs. Since Brisbane had only a short time before he had to square a $250,000 tax claim, he quite possibly felt a sort of kinship with another man convicted on income tax charges. Within federal law enforcement circles, it was suggested that the aid of Lucky Luciano should be sought. Officially at least, nothing became of these proposals, although there is considerable reason to believe that the Capone mob had set about framing an ex-convict, Robert Conroy, who had labored on the fringe of the outfit. He was found shot dead in August and there was later speculation that the mob had intended to pin the kidnapping on Conroy with manufactured evidence.

About a month after the abduction, a retired school principal, Dr. John F. "Jafsie" Condon, published a letter in the *Bronx Home News* in New York City offering to act as go-between in the return of the missing baby. Probably much to his surprise and that of the editor, the offer was accepted. A letter from a man who became known as Cemetery John provided facts that only the kidnapper could have known. A meeting was held in a cemetery between Jafsie and John, who raised the ransom demand to $70,000. John promised to send the baby's night clothes to prove he was the real kidnapper. Further negotiations dropped the ransom back down to $50,000.

At another meeting, with Lindbergh on hand, Jafsie handed over the money; all the bills had been marked, including $20,000 in gold certificates. The kidnapper said the baby could be found on a boat at Martha's Vineyard, Mass. A frantic Lindbergh rushed there but found no boat and no child. He had been duped.

On May 12, 1932 the body of a baby, identified by Lindbergh as his child, was found in a shallow grave just a few miles from the Lindbergh home. The ransom money eventually trapped the kidnapper, Bruno Richard Hauptmann, in September 1934, when an alert filling station attendant recognized a gold certificate given him by a customer as one of the marked bills and noted down the man's car license number. Hauptmann was traced through the license and over $11,000 of the ransom money was found in his garage. A U.S. Forestry Service "wood detective," Arthur Koehler, eventually identified the lumber yard that had cut the wood used to make the kidnap ladder and matched a rung of the ladder to a board in Hauptmann's attic.

Hauptmann's trial was held in January 1935 in Flemington N.J. amidst a carnival atmosphere. Crowds stayed up all night to get seats in the courtroom, vendors sold Lindbergh baby dolls. During the trial Jafsie Condon identified Hauptmann as Cemetery John, and Lindbergh, who had been present at the second meeting with the kidnapper, identified the voice. A number of handwriting experts linked the kidnap notes to the defendant, and wood expert Koehler's testimony proved unshakable.

After he was taken into custody, Bruno Hauptmann consistently maintained he was innocent of the kidnapping.

Hauptmann was convicted despite his continued pleas of innocence. Yet there were many who felt Hauptmann had not been the only one involved in the plot. Among those dissatisfied with the verdict was New Jersey Gov. Harold Hoffman, whom others would accuse of using the case as a launching pad for a possible presidential bid. Gov. Hoffman clearly had need to move up higher in government so that he would have greater authority to conceal his current and past embezzlements of public funds. Gov. Hoffman stayed Hauptmann's execution to hear what was considered evidence of a new solution, but nothing developed. He also fired H. Norman Schwarzkopf as superintendent of the New Jersey State Police, calling the Lindbergh case "the most bungled police job in history." That assessment was not shared by many others, including Lindbergh, who remained a firm friend of the lawman.

For a time, until Hauptmann's capture, Dr. Condon was suspected of being a confidence operator who had swindled Lindbergh out of the $50,000 ransom money. Gaston B. Means, a notorious political rogue who had for years operated in the shadowy fringes of law enforcement agencies in the federal government, swindled a scatter-brained socialite, Mrs. Evalyn

Walsh McLean of Washington, D.C., out of $104,000 on the premise that he would use his underworld connections to retrieve the missing child. In another bizarre episode, one of the most-fabled detectives of the era, Ellis Parker, was convicted of kidnapping and torturing a disbarred lawyer, Paul H. Wendel, and of forcing him to confess that he and others and not Hauptmann were involved in the kidnapping. Both Means and Parker died in prison on charges arising out of the Lindbergh case.

Perhaps the most bizarre aspect of the case was the long hours before Hauptmann's execution on April 3, 1936. A leading news commentator of the day, Gabriel Heatter, offered a play-by-play, minute-by-minute radio commentary to a public eager to hear about the final act in the drama and to learn whether Hauptmann would talk and implicate others during his final minutes. Hauptmann did not, denying his own guilt to the end.

A crowd stayed up all night to get seats in the morning at the Hauptmann trial.

Over the years many efforts have been made to shed more light on the case, including numerous attempts to portray Hauptmann as a mere scapegoat. The most formidable effort was a 1976 book by Anthony Scaduto, *Scapegoat, The Lonesome Death of Bruno Richard Hauptmann,* in which the author presents many contradictions in the evidence. According to the Scaduto thesis, police faked evidence against Hauptmann, and prosecution witnesses, state attorneys and even Hauptmann's own defense lawyers took part in distorting or suppressing evidence. However, despite the unearthing of considerable discrepancies, Scaduto failed to present solid proof that Hauptmann was the victim of a miscarriage of justice. Similarly, recent efforts to prove a New England man to be the "real" Lindbergh child—not at all an uncommon occurrence in celebrated cases of this type—have foundered.

See also: *Harold Giles Hoffman, Lindbergh Law, Gaston Bullock Means, Ellis Parker.*

LINDBERGH Law

The Federal Kidnapping Statute, enacted in June 1932 as a reaction to the kidnapping of the Lindbergh baby and popularly known as the Lindbergh Law, declares it a federal offense to take a kidnapped person across a state line for the purpose of ransom, reward "or otherwise." In the 1930s the last stipulation proved to be a powerful weapon against bank robbers and escaped convicts because they often took hostages with them. By treating the hostages well, however, the outlaws frequently defused much of the public's outrage, and the locally-directed hunts for them were often ineffective.

Twenty-four hours after a kidnapping, a legal presumption is made that the victim has been transported out of the state, permitting the FBI to enter the case. However, if it becomes apparent that no state line has been crossed, the FBI will drop its active involvement. An amendment to the Lindbergh Law states that it is a federal offense to kidnap a foreign official or an official guest of the United States whether or not the victim has been taken across a state line.

See also: *Arthur Gooch.*

LINGLE, Alfred "Jake" (1892-1930): Reporter and murder victim

When Alfred "Jake" Lingle, a police reporter for the *Chicago Tribune,* was murdered on June 9, 1930, it became one of the city's most sensational crimes, uniting the local newspapers in a joint denunciation of the murder of a courageous reporter who had waged a relentless battle against the underworld. But this unity soon fell apart as the newspapers turned on each other.

The cause of this dissension was the double life of Jake Lingle, whose peculiar style of living somehow had never provoked the suspicion of his employers. Despite the fact that his highest salary as a legman was only $65 a week, Lingle owned both a house in Chicago and a summer bungalow in Indiana. He wintered with his family in Florida or Cuba and owned a Lincoln, for which he employed a chauffeur. He kept a room for himself in the Stevens Hotel on Michigan Avenue and was an inveterate gambler, sometimes betting as much as $1,000 on a single horse race.

Lingle's explanation for his life-style was that he had inherited $50,000 or $160,000 (his stories varied) and that before the market crashed he had sold a lot of stocks for triple the price he had paid for them in 1928.

Lingle's value as a *Chicago Tribune* reporter lay in his friendship with both the underworld and the law. He could get stories from the Bugs Moran North Siders, from the Capone people and from the police. He was especially close to Police

Commissioner William P. Russell, their friendship dating back to Russell's days as a patrolman. He and Lingle went to sporting events and the theater together; they golfed together; they borrowed money from each other. Later on, people began to speak of Lingle as "Chicago's unofficial chief of police."

On June 9, 1930 Lingle left the *Tribune* city room after informing his editor he was going to try to contact Bugs Moran about a gang war story. A few minutes later, he was seen at "the corner," the intersection of Randolph and Clark streets, a meeting place for gamblers, mobsters and racetrack touts. Then he headed down Randolph to catch a train to the track. He stopped to buy a racing form and headed through the pedestrian street tunnel, carrying the paper under his arm and puffing on a cigar. Suddenly, a nattily dressed young man pushed through pedestrians and got behind Lingle. Coolly, he took a revolver from his pocket, leveled it at the reporter's head and pulled the trigger. Lingle pitched forward dead, still clutching the paper and the glowing cigar.

Immediately after the murder, Lingle became a national hero. Harry Chandler of the *Los Angeles Times,* president of the American Newspaper Publishers' Association, eulogized him as a "first line soldier," and Chicago newspapers and other civic groups posted rewards totaling $55,725.

However, almost immediately upon the launching of an investigation, Lingle's image began to tarnish. Evidence showed that he was a fixer of enormous power who could barter gambling and liquor-selling rights because of his police connections. "I fix the price of beer in this town," he boasted. He not only knew the Moran forces well, he had secret partnerships with some of the local brothel keepers, shaking them down, nonetheless. At the time of his murder, Lingle was wearing an expensive diamond belt buckle presented to him by Al Capone. But the evidence showed he had double-crossed Capone on various deals and had shaken down a number of Capone's followers. He also had promised favors to several political leaders, presumably for handsome payoffs, and then failed to deliver.

It developed that almost anybody who was anybody in the Chicago underworld hated Jake Lingle. When the facts about Lingle started to emerge, the *Tribune's* publisher Colonel Robert McCormick, was stunned, and then, reacting to taunts from other papers, he editorialized, "There are weak men on other newspapers." The *Tribune* ran a 10-part series by a St. Louis reporter, Harry T. Brundige, that named some of these errants of the competition. There was Julius Rosenheim, a legman for the *Chicago Daily News* who had been hit by gangsters a few months earlier. He had blackmailed bootleggers, brothel keepers and gamblers by threatening to expose them in his newspaper. And there were many others, some working closely with the North Side Gang, others running their own rackets in league with gangsters, still others who junketed to Miami and Havana with Capone and so on.

McCormick had his men dig desperately into probate court records to prove that Lingle had inherited much of the wealth he had spent so lavishly. But it turned out that what he had inherited from his father was not $50,000 or $160,000 but a mere $500.

Four months later the newspapers reported, almost with relief, that police had charged one Leo V. Brothers with the murder. A 21-year-old St. Louis labor terrorist and gangster, Brothers previously had been arrested on arson, bombing, robbery, and murder charges. He was convicted on the basis of eyewitness identifications by four persons and was sentenced to 14 years, which most newspapers denounced as a ridiculously light sentence, insisting that powerful forces had been operating in Brothers' behalf. Certainly, Brothers, although penniless, had mounted a high-pressure and high-priced defense with a staff of five legal experts. There were even hints that Brothers was not the guilty party but had been paid to take the fall thereby diffusing public concern over the case. When Brothers heard the sentence, he smirked, "I can do that standing on my head."

As it turned out, he only had to do eight years before his release, after which he faded into obscurity. Right up until his death in 1951 he refused to say who had paid for his legal defense and, indeed, who had hired him to kill Chicago's tainted knight of the press.

LITTLE, Dick (1852-?): James gang outlaw

In the betrayal of Jesse James, Dick Little played almost as important a role as the Ford brothers did. Shortly before Jesse's assassination, Little sent his mistress to Gov. Thomas T. Crittenden to negotiate his surrender. There is no question that the discussion included a bargain to involve the Fords in betraying Jesse James.

Little, whose real name was reported as Liddil or Liddell, was born in Jackson County, Mo. in 1852. He joined the James gang late, after the disastrous Northfield, Minn. bank raid had decimated the band's original ranks. Following that debacle James was forced to work with "second-raters," such as the Fords and Little, men who felt no great devotion to him. When Wood Hite, another member of the gang, became suspicious of the loyalty of Bob Ford and Dick Little, Little murdered him, later explaining to James that there had been an argument about the division of the proceeds from a small robbery they had pulled together.

When Little surrendered to the law, the story made news throughout Missouri, but it was nothing compared to the headlines a few days later when Jesse James was shot. The James family never had any doubts about the role Little had played in Jesse's assassination. At the inquest into James' death, newspapers reported, the moment of highest drama came when Jesse's mother, Mrs. Zerelda Samuel, confronted Little.

"Oh you coward, you did all this," she was quoted as crying. "You brought it all about. Look upon me, you traitor. Look upon me, the broken-down mother, and this poor wife and these children. Ah, you traitor, better for you that you were in the cooler where my boy is than here, looking at me. Coward, that you are, God will swear vengeance upon you." While listening to this diatribe, Little covered his face with his hat.

After the James killing, Little was sent to an Alabama prison for eight months, as much for safekeeping as anything else. In 1883 he was brought back to Missouri to testify in the trial of Frank James, who had since surrendered. By that time public sentiment was so much against Gov. Crittenden, the Fords and Little that the jury acquitted Frank James on all counts.

A short time later, Little and Bob Ford bought a saloon in Las Vegas, N.M. Business was bad, however, since as one historian observed, "Even the rough frontier town objected to a Judas drawing its beer or pouring its shots of whiskey." Bob Ford went on from there to meet his own assassination, but Dick Little's trail simply disappears.

See also: *Thomas T. Crittenden, Charles Ford, Wood Hite, James Brothers*.

LITTLE, Joan (1954-   ): Accused murderer

In a murder case that indicated the profound changes occurring in the administration of justice in the South, Joan Little, a young black woman convict, was acquitted by a jury in North Carolina of charges that she had murdered her jailer, 62-year-old Clarence T. Alligood, on August 27, 1974.

During her trial, which attracted international attention, Little graphically described an oral sex act she said Alligood had forced her to perform while he held an ice pick to her face in her cell at the Beaufort County Jail. She stated that she had been able to seize the ice pick when the jailer's grip loosened on it and that she had stabbed him with it 11 times when he tried to get up from the bunk where he had been sitting, with Little on her knees before him. She then escaped from the jail, where she had been serving seven to ten years for breaking and entering, and surrendered eight days later to the state Bureau of Investigation with the stipulation that she not be returned to Beaufort County. The prosecution insisted she had lured the jailer into her cell and killed him in an escape plot, but the jury of six white and six blacks returned a not-guilty verdict in just 78 minutes.

Sent back to serve her original sentence, Little escaped from a prison for women in Raleigh in 1978 and fled to New York. Before being apprehended and extradited to North Carolina she worked for the National Council of Black Lawyers. Civil rights advocates opposed her return to North Carolina, fearing that she would suffer mistreatment. In June 1979 Joan Little was paroled and returned to New York to work as a file clerk in a law firm.

LITTLE Joker: Safecracking device

Perhaps the most amazing gadget used by 19th century bank thieves was the little joker, invented by either of two of the most-esteemed criminals of the day, George Bliss or George Leonidas Leslie.

According to Bliss, he designed a steel wire contraption that could be fitted inside the combination knob of a bank safe. He related that after breaking into the bank,

> All I had to do was to take off the dial knob of a lock, adjust the wire on the inside surface of the dial, and replace the knob; returning later to the bank. The lock in the meantime having been used by the bank people to open the vault or safe, I had only to remove the knob and examine the marks made by the wire, and I had the combination numbers. All that remained between me and the right combination was to figure out the order in which the numbers were used, and that was not difficult.

It took almost 10 years before the police and the safe manufacturers discovered the technique and new dial knobs were designed. For many years Bliss and Leslie engaged in a feud over who had invented the joker. The dispute remains unresolved, neither of them having patented the invention.

See also: *Safecracking*.

LITTLE Pete (1864-1897): Tong warrior

With the possible exception of Mock Duck, the resourceful tong warrior who dominated the West Coast, Fung Jing Toy, or Little Pete, as the English-language press dubbed him, may have been the greatest fighter in America's Tong wars. Coming to the United States at the age of five, he was raised in the tong way of life and death. From the balcony of his San Francisco home at Washington Street and Waverly Place, he watched the great fight between the Suey Sings and the Kwong Docks in 1875. He is said to have plotted then how the tide of battle could have gone differently; at the time he was 10.

By 1885 Fung Jing Toy was Little Pete, a man of considerable wealth accumulated by peddling opium, dealing in female slaves, running gambling enterprises and filling murder contracts. He soon became the owner of a shoe factory on Washington Street, which gave him honest cover in the eyes of the law. Meanwhile, he had become a legend in San Francisco's Chinatown. On contract, he once chopped down a high-ranking member of the Suey On Tong. Immediately, the Suey Ons sent three warriors after him to avenge the killing. They cornered him in an alley and one swung a hatchet down on his skullcap, but instead of Little Pete collapsing, there was just a metallic clang. His assailants then swung at his chest and again drew clangs rather than blood. The attackers' puzzlement didn't last long, for Little Pete drew his own hatchet and quickly dispatched two of them. The last one fled. Following the attempted assassination, word quickly spread that Little Pete was indestructible. In fact, he wore a coat of chain mail and inside his hat was a curved sheet of steel fitted around his head.

By the time he was 25, Little Pete controlled the Sum Yop Tong, bringing it immense wealth, much at the expense of the Sue Yop Tong, which had previously been the major power in Chinatown. This brought about one of San Francisco's bloodiest tong wars, in which Little Pete directed his forces with the

genius of a Napoleon. He is believed to have been responsible for the death of at least 50 rival hatchet men.

Little Pete slept in a windowless room, and on each side of his bolted door was chained a vicious dog. In addition, a minimum of six heavily armed hatchet men were nearby at all times. When he went out, he wore his suit of chain mail and employed a bodyguard of three white men, one in front, one beside him and one bringing up the rear. The whites were symbols Little Pete found useful. It implied to his enemies that he had great influence with white law authorities, which indeed he had. His payoffs to the political leaders of San Francisco, especially to Christopher A. Buckley, the blind political boss of the city, were said to be enormous.

Some of the hatchet men taken into custody for the murder of Little Pete. Even Little Pete's coat of mail (center) failed to prevent his assassination.

Little Pete's end came in a moment of carelessness. On the evening of January 23, 1897, he went to a barber shop. He had left his home hurriedly with only one bodyguard and then sent this man to buy him a newspaper. Two hired killers, Lem Jung and Chew Tin Gop, entered the shop as Little Pete was bending his head under a faucet so the barber could wet his hair properly for plaiting. Lem Jung shoved the barber aside, grabbed Little Pete by the hair and jammed the muzzle of his revolver down the back of the tong leader's neck, inside the coat of mail. He pulled the trigger five times, and Little Pete hit the floor dead, with five bullets in his spine. His murderers fled to Portland, Ore., where they were greeted as great warriors, and then went back to China to live out their lives in luxury on the blood money they had received.

See also: *Tong Wars*.

LITTLE Water Street: New York vice district

Historians generally agree that the single most notorious street in early 19th century New York was Little Water Street, in the crime-infested Five Points section. Many an outsider who entered Little Water Street was never seen again, being killed and robbed and then buried in the walls of wretched tenements or in underground passages connecting them. A more dismal thoroughfare could hardly be imagined, the filth in the street generally reached shoe-top depth. On Little Water Street one found houses with such sinister names as Gates of Hell and Brick-Bat Mansion. In his description of the Five Points, Charles Dickens wrote of "hideous tenements which take their names from robbery and murder."

A mid-19th century book, *Hot Corn,* by an anonymous author takes the reader on a tour of Little Water Street, advising one to

> saturate your handkerchief with camphor, so that you can endure the horrid stench, and enter. Grope your way through the long, narrow passage—turn to the right, up the dark and dangerous stairs; be careful where you place your foot around the lower step, or in the corners of the broad stairs, for it is more than shoe-mouth deep of steaming filth. Be careful, too, or you may meet someone, perhaps a man, perhaps a woman, who in their drunken frenzy may thrust you, for the very hatred of your better clothes, or the fear that you have come to rescue them from their crazy loved dens of death, down, headlong down, those filthy stairs. Here, one would find as many as four or five couples living in a single, squalid room, wearing, eating, drinking nothing that most of them did not steal.

LIVE Oak Boys: New Orleans gang

Probably the outstanding example of the mindlessly brutal criminal organizations that plagued America's big cities during the mid-19th century was the Live Oak Boys of New Orleans. Lasting about a generation, most of them met a bitter fate.

Formed about 1858 by Red Bill Wilson, a vicious thug who always concealed a knife in his bushy red beard, the Live Oakers were not a gang in the usual sense of the word. There was no recognized leader, no regular organization and no division of loot. They often committed crimes on the spur of the moment, allying themselves with whatever other Live Oakers happened to be handy, and each kept what he stole. Sometimes they even stole from one another. In 1867 this unwholesome trait cost the gang two of its most-noted brutes.

Live Oaker Henry Thompson had been asleep at the shipyard the gang utilized as a rendezvous (the shipyard owner had long since desisted from trying to evict them because of their threat to burn the place down) when he awoke to find fellow Live Oaker Jimmy O'Brien, with whom he had tied on a drunk the night before, searching his pockets. Thompson started struggling, whereupon O'Brien jammed a knife into his heart and continued the search, being rewarded with a few coins. Unfortunately for the latter, a black and a small boy had witnessed the murder, and O'Brien was sent to the penitentiary, where he later died.

The Live Oakers devoted their nights to robbing and killing. They were feared throughout the city for their vicious forays, but most of their activities were confined to Gallatin Street and the surrounding area; in its dives they loafed, slept and planned their crimes. They were particularly the bane of dance house proprietors, raiding at least one such establishment almost nightly, either out of sheer deviltry or because they had been hired to do so by a business rival. When the Live

Oakers stormed a place brandishing the oaken clubs that gave them their name, bartenders, customers, musicians and bouncers quickly repaired out the rear exit and harlots fled upstairs. They then would take apart the establishment at their leisure, smashing furniture, gouging up the dance floor, destroying the musical instruments and, quite naturally, emptying the till and carting off all the liquor they desired.

The only place safe from their depredations was Bill Swan's Fireproof Coffee-House on Levee Street. Swan was a former member of the gang who had acquired enough money to go into business. His resort enjoyed the protection of the Live Oakers, partly for old time's sake but also because Swan always provided the gang with free drinks.

Among the more notable members of the Live Oak Boys, in addition to Red Bill Wilson, Bill Swan, Henry Thompson and Jimmy O'Brien, were Jimmy's brother Hugh and his two sons, Matt and Hugh, Jr.; Crazy Bill Anderson; Jack Lyons; the three Petrie brothers, Redhead, Henry and Whitehead; Yorker Duffy; Barry Lynch; Jack Lowe; Tommy Lewis; Charley Lockerby and his son Albert; and Billy Emerson. Most of these were either killed, sent to prison or became drunken derelicts.

The most ferocious of all was Charley Lockerby, a short, powerful man who was credited with several murders. He was mortally wounded in a gun duel with a saloon keeper named Keppler, whom he killed. Doctors at Charity Hospital marveled over how long Lockerby lasted despite his fatal head wound. Hugh O'Brien was killed after robbing a fisherman of a rowboat and setting out on the Mississippi with the whiskey-besotted idea of becoming a pirate.

In a way, the lucky ones were those of the gang who were killed or imprisoned. With the passage of years the others turned into derelicts. While in earlier days there was no record of the New Orleans police standing up in combat to the Live Oakers, that changed as the gang members aged and turned helpless. In 1886 the *New Orleans Picayune* made the following comment about Crazy Bill Anderson, who generally was arrested for drunkeness 10 or 12 times a month:

> Now he is handled without gloves by the police, and is kicked and cuffed about like any other common drunkard. Yet, there was a day . . . when the police really feared to approach him with hostile intentions, and it usually occupied all the time, strength and attention of four able-bodied policemen.

By the late 1880s it was common for the young toughs of the city to seek out old Live Oakers to beat and torture. In time, only Bill Swan, the entrepreneur of the bunch, remained of a gang known as the terror of New Orleans for almost three decades.

See also: *Gallatin Street, Green Tree Dance House.*

LOANSHARKING

After gambling, loansharking is probably the most profitable activity of the Mafia today. Known in the underworld as shylocking or six for five, the loanshark racket generally nets its operators 20 percent profit—per week. For every $5 borrowed the amount that must be repaid the following week is $6, or $1 if the borrower wishes just to pay the interest and not retire the principal. The standard short-term Mafia loan is for six weeks, which means the borrower must pay back a total of $11 dollars for each $5 borrowed: 120 percent interest for 42 days. Generally, the borrower must have permission to extend the payment date of the loan. One investigation in New York found that some syndicate loans brought back as much as 3,000 percent interest. Naturally with such profit margins, some loan sharks have been tempted to reduce their rates to stimulate business. In Dallas, Tex. in 1938 a loan shark was found to be making loans to destitute customers for only 585 percent annually. One man borrowed $20 to pay a medical bill and was charged $2.25 in weekly interest. Nine years later, he had paid a total of $1,053 and still owed the original $20.

While the Mafia first viewed loansharking as a way to victimize the poor or gamblers having a bad run of luck at a dice game, they soon discovered that it was easy to find potential victims among businessmen. A neighborhood store owner with his bank credit overextended and in need of quick cash often had no choice but to deal with a loan shark. Today, however, the Mafia's thrust is to use the racket to gain a foothold in legitimate businesses. A garment manufacturer may guess wrong on the season's line, a home builder is caught in a credit squeeze, a Wall Street securities house is hit in a sudden shift in market prices—the short-term solution is offered by the mob; in return, a piece of the business is demanded. Once the Mafia has an investment in a legitimate company, it protects it to the limit, perhaps terrorizing the competition or at least obtaining an advantageous labor contract through its connections with corrupt union officials.

At times, the gangsters may decide to simply loot a company, an operation perfected under the aegis of a cunning Mafia operator named Joseph Pagano. In the 1950s a large meat wholesaler got into financial trouble and had to borrow mob money. In time, he was forced to accept Pagano as the firm's new president "to safeguard the loan." Pagano's people bought up a huge amount of poultry and meat on credit and then resold it at cut-rate prices, collecting $1.3 million. Having milked the company and its suppliers the mob simply ordered the firm to go into bankruptcy.

LOCKSTEP Surveillance: Harassment technique

Although illegal, lockstep surveillance, or rough shadowing, as it is sometimes called, is a form of harassment frequently practiced against important members of organized crime.

One of the most famous recent incidents of this harassment involved the late boss of the Chicago mob Sam Giancana. Since the old days Giancana had been known as Mooney, which meant he at times acted erratically. Hoping to make him lose his control and commit mistakes, FBI agents subjected Giancana to a 24-hour "rough."

Everywhere Giancana went he was followed. FBI cars were constantly parked outside his house, even when his daughters were having girl friends over to visit. There were times on the golf course when as many as six FBI agents watched him putt and often deliberately tried to upset his game with caustic remarks. In one effort to shake off his followers, the crime boss slipped into a church. The FBI men followed and verbally abused him when he exhibited rustiness on what to do during the services, taking his cues on when to stand, sit and kneel from his neighbors. The agents would whisper to him: "Kneel, asshole. . . . Sit down, asshole."

In desperation, Giancana took the FBI to court to force them to stop lockstepping him. Amazingly, he won, and the FBI was enjoined from practicing the technique. The decision, however, was later vacated for technical reasons, and lockstepping continues today. Important gang figures do not generally go to court to challenge the treatment because they will be required to testify that none of their activities warrants police surveillance. Having so testified, they can be cross-examined on their activities and alleged criminal acts, thus opening the door to a possible perjury conviction.

The courts are more inclined to protect a private citizen from any form of rough shadowing and have often upheld complaints of this type. Still, such cases do occur. One classic example involved the late author Iles Brody, whom private detectives jostled in crowds and awakened with mysterious midnight phone calls. They had been hired to do so by rich friends of the Duke and Duchess of Windsor in an attempt to prevent the publication of Brody's gossipy book *Gone With the Windsors*.

LOGAN, Harvey: See Kid Curry.

LOHMAN, Ann Trow: See Madame Restell.

LOMBARDO, Antonio "The Scourge" (1892-1928): Capone aide

Part of Al Capone's success as a crime boss rested on his ability to obtain advice and support from men more brilliant and cunning than himself. Antonio "The Scourge" Lombardo, an urbane, level-headed Sicilian who had prospered in Chicago as a wholesale grocer, was a typical example. Capone followed much of Lombardo's advice following the departure of Johnny Torrio, his original mentor, and eventually made the Scourge his *consigliere*. Lombardo played a key role in arranging a famed peace conference that led to a brief period of tranquility in the Chicago underworld. He counseled Capone to seek accommodation with the North Siders, a predominantly Irish gang, even after the murder of their leader, the celebrated Dion O'Banion, by Capone gunners. To bring about peace between the two mobs, Lombardo told the North Siders he would arrange to have O'Banion's killers, the murderous team of Albert Anselmi and John Scalise, turned over to them. But

Capone rejected this deal, declaring "I wouldn't do that to a yellow dog." The everplotting Lombardo promptly turned this rare show of mercy into a propaganda coup, declaring it proved that "Big Al's the best buddy any of his boys could ever hope to have."

Still, overall, Capone followed Lombardo's advice and even picked up his practice of using court tasters; Lombardo was so fearful of being fed poison in his food that he always insisted on having an underling sample his meals before he ate them. In 1925 Capone rewarded Lombardo for his faithful service by making him, through gangland muscle, president of Chicago's huge branch of the Unione Siciliane. Despite his close ties to Capone and the fact that he had ordered many a man's death, Lombardo received rather fine press. In honor of his appointment, he issued a glowing testimonial to himself:

> Chicago owes much of its progress and its hope of future greatness to the intelligence and industry of its 200,000 Italians, whose rise in prestige and importance is one of the modern miracles of a great city.
>
> No people have achieved so much from such small beginnings, or given so much for what they received in the land of promise to which many of them came penniless. Each life story is a romance, an epic of human accomplishment.
>
> Antonio Lombardo is one of the most outstanding of these modern conquerors. . . . He was one of hundreds who cheered joyously, when, from the deck of the steamer, they saw the Statue of Liberty, and the skyline of New York, their first sight of the fabled land, America. With his fellow countrymen he suffered the hardships and indignities to which the United States subjects its prospective citizens at Ellis Island without complaint, for in his heart was a great hope and a great ambition.
>
> Mr. Lombardo . . . accepted the hardships as part of the game, and with confidence in his own ability and assurance of unlimited opportunities, began his career. . . ."

Such glowing testimony did not prevent Lombardo from falling victim in the vicious battle between Capone's followers and enemies for control of the criminal-dominated fraternal organization. On September 7, 1928 Lombardo was gunned down on Madison Street in the midst of a dense crowd of shoppers and office workers, two dum-dum bullets ripping away half his head. If it was any comfort to Lombardo, Capone saw that the Aiello mob, "the dirty rats who did the job," paid for it.

LONELY Hearts Murders: See Martha Beck.

LONERGAN, Wayne (1916-   ): Murderer

In one of New York City's most sensational murder cases, Patricia Burton Lonergan, a 22-year-old heiress to a $7 million brewery fortune, was murdered in her bedroom on October 24, 1943. She had been strangled, bludgeoned by a pair of antique candlesticks and left naked on her bed.

Two months earlier, her husband had departed for his native Canada to join the Royal Canadian Air Force. However, it was discovered that he had been staying in a friend's apartment in New York City on the weekend of the murder. He was traced back to Toronto, arrested and returned to New York. At first, Lonergan, a bisexual, insisted he had spent the time in New York hunting for soldiers, but after 84 hours of interrogation he supposedly confessed that he had gone to Patricia's apartment and, after a quarrel, killed her, throwing his bloodstained uniform into the East River. His confession received a terrific play in the press, in part because of the concurrent admission that he had taken part in sex orgies.

The case against Lonergan was not the tightest on record. The police had neglected or failed to get Lonergan to sign his so-called confession. Moreover, there was no conclusive proof to show that he had visited the apartment or handled the candlesticks. Some legal observers felt he was convicted as much because of bisexuality as because of the evidence. The jury found him guilty of second-degree murder and he was sentenced to 35 years to life. After doing 21 years in Sing Sing, Lonergan was paroled in 1965 and deported to Canada.

LONG, Huey (1893-1935): Assassination victim

The powerful Kingfish of Louisiana politics, first as governor and then as a U.S. senator, flamboyant Huey P. Long, was shot to death in 1935. At the time, he was among the most-beloved and most-hated men in the state and nation. His supporters called him "the one friend the poor has," while his foes considered him a "demagogue," a "madman" and the "destroyer of constitutional government." One group that was solidly in Huey's camp was the underworld, with whom he could always reach accommodation. When New York City Mayor Fiorello La Guardia started busting up the syndicate's slot machines, Long told Frank Costello, in effect, to bring his business down. The underworld shipped in one-armed bandits by the thousands, making New Orleans the illegal slot machine center of the country. The payoffs supposedly contributed the grease that kept the Long machine running.

On September 8, 1935, Long, although a U.S. senator at the time, was attending a special session of the Louisiana House of Representatives in Baton Rouge. As he walked down one of the Capitol corridors with five bodyguards in attendance, a 29-year-old man, Carl Weiss, who was considered a brilliant medical doctor, stepped from behind a pillar and shot Long with a .32 caliber automatic. The Kingfish screamed and clutched his side as he ran down the hall. His bodyguards knocked Weiss to the floor, shooting him twice. As he struggled, a fusillade of 61 shots turned his white linen suit red with blood.

Weiss died on the spot. Long lived about 30 hours, as doctors vainly struggled to save his life. Weiss' exact motive for killing was never learned, other than that he and his family had long hated the Kingfish. However, there was another version of the assassination: Weiss had not killed Long at all.

There were two variations of this theory. According to one of them, a cut on Long's lip had come from a punch in the mouth Weiss had given him. The enraged bodyguards, so the story goes, pulled their guns and started shooting wildly, and one of their shots fatally wounded the Kingfish. After killing Weiss, they took his gun and fired it. Since the bullet that killed Long passed right through his body, it was impossible to tell which of the many discharged bullets was the fatal one. In the other variation, Weiss had intended to kill Long but was gunned down before he could get off a shot. In either case the consensus was that Long's aides and bodyguards had put the blame on Weiss to protect themselves.

Long was buried on the landscaped grounds of the capitol he had built. A novel based on his career, *All the King's Men,* won the Pulitzer Prize, and the movie version won an Academy Award in 1939.

Further reading: *The Day Huey Long Was Shot* by David Zinman and *The Huey Long Murder Case* by Hermann B. Deutsch.

An artist's conception of the assassination of the Kingfish.

LONG, Steve (?-1868): Lawman and thief

A man with an obscure past, six-foot six-inch Big Steve Long drifted into Laramie, Wyo. in 1867. Having the reputation of a gunman, Long rather quickly was made a deputy marshal. He soon became known as one of the bloodiest lawmen in Wyoming history, killing eight men in a two-month period. On October 22, 1867 four boisterous cowboys decided to roust four greenhorn Easterners. Although they had no guns, the newcomers were not cowed by their foes, wading into them with fists flying. Long arrived on the scene and demanded a halt to the action. When the participants ignored him, he drew his two .44s and began pumping shots into the battling horde. When the smoke cleared, two cowboys and three of the newcomers lay mortally wounded.

Despite all of Deputy Marshal Long's firepower, Laramie remained a lawless place, and local vigilantes had to take over some of the more important functions of the law, which Long seemed unable to manage. The reason for his inefficiency became evident the following year when it was discovered that the deputy marshal was moonlighting as a highwayman. In October 1868 Long was wounded by a prospector he tried to waylay. He made it back to town and had his wounds treated by his fiancee, a young lady proud of having a law officer for her future husband. When she discovered the cause of his wound, however, she immediately informed the vigilantes and the following day Long was hanged from a telegraph pole. Apparently retaining some fondness for him, she erected a marker to his rather tarnished memory.

LONGBAUGH, Harry: See Sundance Kid.

LONGLEY, William P. (1851-1877): Gunfighter and murderer

Among Western gunfighters, William "Wild Bill" Longley probably stands second only to another Texas killer, Wes Hardin, in total "notches." Hardin had an estimated 40 and Longley, by his own admission, had 32.

Like Hardin, Longley had a pathological hatred for blacks, Yankees and carpetbagging lawmen. At the age of 15, he killed his first victim, a black state policeman who had asked Bill in an "arrogant manner" to identify himself. After that, he gunned down another black lawman and a Yankee sergeant. Then he rode with Cullen Baker's so-called Confederate Irregulars, who were really just a bunch of farm looters. After a year Wild Bill left the gang and headed west, traveling from the Rio Grande to the Black Hills and out as far as Wyoming. Almost everywhere he went he managed to shoot someone.

Although a much-hunted man, Longley slipped back into Texas in 1875 and murdered Wilson Anderson of Evergreen, who, Longley was convinced, had shot a cousin of his. He managed to elude capture for more than two years but was finally apprehended in 1877 and taken to Giddings, Tex., where he was convicted and sentenced to death. While the decision was being appealed, Longley wrote an angry letter to the governor demanding to know why Wes Hardin was sent to prison for "only twenty-five years" for his many murders while he, Longley, was doomed to the gallows. The governor did not respond. The night before he was hanged, Longley told a guard about many of his killings. "He said that he didn't regret killing but one man," the guard later reported. "They were in camp together and Bill said it seemed like the feller was watching him. He said he had had a hard day and he was sleepy, but he wasn't going to sleep with the feller watching him. Well, he said, that kept up until midnight, when he got plumb tuckered out, so he got up and shot the feller in the head and went to sleep. The next day he found out that the feller was on the dodge just like him, so he always felt sorry about killing him."

Longley was his cool, dapper self mounting the gallows. He surveyed the crowd of 4,000 and said, "I see a good many enemies around, and mighty few friends." After the execution a number of the witnesses found amusement in the observation that Longley's head could be rotated until his billy-goat beard rested between his shoulder blades.

See also: *Cullen M. Baker.*

**ADVENTURES
—OF—
BILL LONGLEY**

Captured by Sheriff Milton Mast and Deputy Bill Burrows, near Keatchie, Louisiana, in 1877, and was executed at Giddings, Texas, 1878.

BILL BURROWS - LONGLEY - SHERIFF MAST

By Henry C. Fuller
Nacogdoches, Texas

The life story of Bill Longley became a best-seller in Texas.

LOOMIS Gang: Criminal family

For the better part of the 19th century, crime in upper New York state, especially in the Mohawk and Chenango valleys, was dominated by a sinister family gang, the large Loomis brood. Indeed, had Richard L. Dugsdale focused on the Loomis clan rather than the largely fanciful Juke family in his controversial theory that immoral behavior could be passed on genet-

ically from one generation to the next, his detractors probably would have had a much tougher time demolishing his position.

The Loomis family's roots in the area were planted by George Washington Loomis, Sr. who was forced out of Vermont in 1802 by a posse cleansing the area of horse thieves. In 1812, just before he went off to war, Loomis married Rhoda Marie Mallett, a young school teacher. Rhoda's father was an illicit distiller and forger, so that both sides of the Loomis family contributed to its later criminal tendencies. Rhoda mothered 12 children and served as the female Fagin for her brood. As her devoted son, Washington Jr. (born 1813), better known as "Wash," lovingly said, she approved of the children "stealing little things—and as long as we were not caught it was all right. If we got caught we got licked."

By the 1840s Wash was the leader of a great crime family, giving orders to brothers Grove, Bill, Wheller, Denio and Plumb and sister Cornelia. Three other sisters engaged in minor criminality, such as luring strangers into traps where they would be waylaid and robbed, but Cornelia was a true hellion who could ride and jump horses and shoot as well as any of her brothers.

The headquarters for the family's illegal enterprises was the miasmal Nine-Mile Swamp, from which no posse was ever able to dislodge them. From here, they could strike out on criminal raids, terrorizing communities, murdering, burning and robbing. As a sideline the family masterminded the distribution of counterfeit money. To their banner the Loomis brothers and sisters recruited a strong band of escaped fugitives and runaway slaves and ran massive sheep-, cattle- and horse-stealing operations.

In 1857 a large posse of citizens enraged by the gang's ever-growing operation, bore down on the Loomis farmhouse and seized most of the family. Huge quantities of stolen goods were found behind trapdoors and in sealed-off rooms. More than a dozen sleighs were needed to haul off the evidence to Waterville, where members were arraigned on larceny charges. Those Loomis brothers who had not been apprehended led the gang in a night raid on the courthouse to burn the records and resteal much of the evidence. Some witnesses against the Loomis brothers disappeared and were not released until the arrested members of the family were freed, there no longer being any case against them.

When Grove Loomis was grabbed a short time later for running the gang's counterfeit money distribution network, newspapers in Utica reported that the local district attorney carried the evidence on him rather than leave it unguarded in his office. So the gang simply kidnapped him, took the evidence and beat him severely. Without the evidence, Grove had to be released.

In 1858 the gang's first important nemesis appeared. He was James L. Filkins, a blacksmith who had been elected constable of the town of Brookfield. More than anyone else, he was responsible for destroying what had become one of the most powerful gangs in the nation. Even when his fellow citizens wouldn't back him up, he tackled the gang alone, more than once using his fists to subdue a Loomis.

At first, the Loomis gang regarded Filkins as little more than a nuisance, even though he constantly raided their farmhouse. They were too busy running a massive horse-stealing venture, especially when the price of horses escalated with the outbreak of the Civil War. The gang shipped hundreds of horses, suitably disguised, to markets in Albany, Scranton, Pa. and various places in Canada, where they commanded top prices. To dispose of their other loot, they ran "thief boats" along the Erie Canal and down the Hudson River to New York City, where such famous fences as the notorious Marm Mandelbaum handled their resale.

When another mass trial for several members of the gang was scheduled in the North Brookfield Courthouse, the Loomis clan fell back on "smoking" to solve the problem. The courthouse was set afire and the fire hoses cut. The evidence burned, and once more, several Loomis boys and their followers walked away free. Afterward, another set of indictments and evidence on still other charges were kept in a safe in the town clerk's office in Morrisville. It was burglarized and the papers burned right in the town clerk's own potbellied stove.

By 1865 Constable Filkins decided extralegal means were needed to destroy the gang. He organized a vigilante committee and they descended on the Loomis farmhouse. A hand-to-hand battle ensued, and Wash Loomis was literally stomped to death. The vigilantes thought they'd also killed Plumb and tossed his body on a fire outside the house as they left. Ma Loomis pulled Plumb from the flames, and although he was badly seared, he survived. Denio and Plumb took charge of the gang and it was soon operating as ruthlessly and efficiently as it had under Wash. In 1867 the vigilantes staged another raid. This time, they hung Plumb and Grove by their hands over a fire until they confessed their crimes. The vigilantes then rousted the women from the Loomis house and burned it to the ground. In the ensuing confusion, Grove slipped away while Plumb was taken off to a jail.

In 1870 Grove Loomis died, but the gang, led by Denio continued operating into the 1880s, when both Denio and Plumb died. Cornelia took charge of the gang then, masterminding its still vast operations, especially horse and sheep stealing. She died in 1897 and a few months later the gang's great foe, Constable Filkins, also passed away. It didn't matter; the Loomis gang was just about finished. By 1911 the last of the minor Loomises disappeared from the valley, 99 years after George Washington Loomis, Sr. started raising his brood.

LOS Angeles Times Bombing

In 1910 few cities in the United States had a more firmly anti-labor climate than Los Angeles, Calif. One reason for this was the labor-baiting views of Harrison Gray Otis and his *Los Angeles Times*. Otis was the prime mover behind the Merchants and Manufacturers Association, which was violently opposed to labor unions and the closed shop and proudly proclaimed, "We employ no union men."

It was an era when many segments of the labor movement believed that the only answer to such intransigence was bombs and dynamite. For protection, Otis strapped a small cannon to his car's running board.

On the morning of October 1, 1910, the *Times* was hit by an explosion. The entire south wall of the Broadway Street side of the building crumbled, and the second floor collapsed under the weight of linotype machines and crashed down on office workers below. The first floor then smashed into the basement, shattering the building's gas mains and heating plant. Flames soon turned the structure into an inferno. Printers, clerks, reporters, editors, typesetters, old scrubwomen, young copy boys—21 in all—died, and at least an equal number suffered permanent injuries.

An enraged city demanded a solution to the crime. Mayor George B. Alexander brought in the famed private detective, William J. Burns, to aid in the investigation. Eventually, although under attack by some officials, union leaders, rival newspapers and others, Burns solved the case through clues found in other bombs delivered to Otis' home and the home of the secretary of the Merchants and Manufacturers Association. He arrested Ortie McManigal, an Indianapolis resident, James B. McNamara; and his brother John J. McNamara, secretary-treasurer of the International Union of Bridge and Structural Iron Workers. In addition, two anarchists named David Caplan and Matt A. Schmidt were not caught until 1915. Burns struck a deal with McManigal under which he would testify against the McNamara brothers.

The arrest of the McNamaras mobilized organized labor against what they considered to be an outrageous antilabor plot. American Federation of Labor President Samuel Gompers hired Clarence Darrow, fresh from successes defending Eugene Debs of the Railroad Brotherhoods and Big Bill Haywood of the Industrial Workers of the World (IWW), to conduct the brothers' defense. Darrow proceeded to call the McNamaras "pawns in a vast industrial war," victims of a "capitalistic conspiracy." He said the great frame-up was being financed by "the steel trust with its gold." The labor unions even utilized what was at the time still a novelty, the motion picture, and produced a movie about the McNamaras and their plight. Buttons were sold proclaiming, "THE McNAMARAS ARE INNOCENT." There were torchlight parades and rallies.

Burns countered by saying, "If Mr. Gompers will just sit down with me, at his convenience, I am certain I can convince him this is strictly a criminal case and does not concern organized labor. If need be, I will even show him evidence that cannot be made public as yet."

Gompers spurned the offer, reminding reporters that private detectives had often planted evidence and bought false confessions in the past to discredit unions. Nevertheless, by the time the trial opened, Darrow realized the McNamaras were guilty and sure to be convicted. His options were to fight a hopeless case in order to protect the union movement or to plead the defendants guilty in the hope of saving their lives. He chose the second course, which had a devastating effect on the Western labor movement. Gompers considered Darrow a traitor, and most of the country was numbed with shock.

James McNamara got life (as did Caplan and Schmidt after they were apprehended), but John J. McNamara got 15 years because he could not be linked directly to the Los Angeles bombings. Having won their case against union violence, the Otis forces then decided to try to eliminate Darrow's future service as a labor defender. He was charged with attempting to bribe a juror.

Darrow was alone, having lost his support from the unions, indeed not having received even his $50,000 fee in the case. However, following a trial that lasted several months, thanks to a prosecution strategy to stretch out the time in order to drain Darrow's dwindling finances, the master of the courtroom was acquitted after making a moving summation, lasting a day and a half, in his own defense. Undaunted, the prosecution simply indicted him for the attempted bribery of a second juror. This case ended in a mistrial when the jury failed to reach a verdict. The state had no interest in attempting to prosecute Darrow yet another time and settled for an agreement whereby Darrow promised never to practice law in California again.

Some historians consider the case Otis' greatest triumph. Although Darrow was to win many a great legal battle thereafter, he never defended another union man.

See also: *William J. Burns, Clarence Darrow.*

LOVEJOY, Elijah (1802-1837): Abolitionist and murder victim

Few murder victims have ever encountered the merciless hatred reserved for abolitionists by proslavers who felt their way of life threatened.

Typical was the fate of abolitionist Rev. Elijah P. Lovejoy, who was lynched by a proslavery mob in Alton, Ill. on November 7, 1837. As editor of the *Alton Observer,* Rev. Lovejoy had written, "Abolitionists, therefore, hold American slavery to be a wrong, a legalized system of inconceivable injustice, and a SIN . . . against God."

A "posse" upholding "law and order" broke into the newspaper's office, seized the printing press and threw it into the river, set the building aflame and shot Lovejoy. The next day the posse returned for Lovejoy's mutilated corpse and dragged it through the streets to the cheers of crowds of proslavers. In the final analysis, Lovejoy's martyrdom advanced the abolitionist cause.

LOVING, Cockeyed Frank (1854-1882): Gambler and gunfighter

A cockeyed gambler who worked the Colorado circuit, Frank Loving went down in history as the victor in one of the West's most famous gun duels, one that went far to establish the myth that triumph belonged to the man who fired slowly and last.

The gunfight was the culmination of a long-standing feud over a woman between the gambler and Levi Richardson, a hard case reputed to have killed three men. On April 5, 1879 words turned to lead at Dodge City's Long Branch Saloon. Richardson, being the much faster draw, started firing first, fanning his pistol as the pair waltzed around a gaming table and a stove. With the men so close together that their pistols almost touched—Richardson got off some five shots but, except for one shot that scratched his opponent's hand, did no more than hit the wall.

There is some confusion about Loving's shooting, but apparently, his first three shots also hit nothing but wall. Finally, at a distance of no more than a couple of feet, he found the mark with three shots, and Richardson dropped, fatally wounded. Loving hung around Colorado bars for the next three years, telling of his exploit and expounding his theory that a "cool head" will always prevail in a gunfight. In April 1882 in Trinidad, Colo. he met up with a former lawman named Jack Allen. In one duel the pair exchanged 16 shots and every one missed. When they met again the next day Allen shot first and more accurately and Cockeyed Frank fell dead, although he lives on today as the epitome of the great Western duelists.

See also: *Gunfighting.*

LOWE, Joseph "Rowdy Joe" (?1846-1899): Gunfighter and brothel keeper

Rowdy Joe Lowe was a tough and mean gunman, brothel and saloon keeper and gambler. As a procurer, he could well be described as the Lucky Luciano of the Plains. He and his wife, known as Rowdy Kate, ran what was described as the vilest dive in the cow camps. While Kate reputedly gave an occasional stray girl money to go back home in order to escape a life of shame, Rowdy Joe could never be accused of such softheartedness.

Little is known of Lowe's early life except that he was probably born in Illinois in 1846. Various historical accounts place him in Quantrill's guerrillas during the Civil War and in the Texas Rangers in 1866. There are doubts about these stories but none that Lowe deserved his nickname of Rowdy. Once in a saloon battle between Lowe and another man, the local lawmen intervened and demanded the two apologize to one another. Lowe told his opponent: "Come here. I want to kiss and make up." He promptly bit off the end of the man's nose.

In 1869 Lowe was run out of Ellsworth, Kan. where he had been operating a combination saloon and brothel, on suspicion that he had donned a mask and held up customers after they left the dive. Two years later, Lowe and his wife opened a wicked dive in Newton, Kan. Killings and shootings were frequent there, and in 1872 Rowdy Joe shot and killed Jim Sweet, who had been paying too much attention to Rowdy Kate. The Lowes then moved on to Delano, Kan. and opened another establishment. Among the new admirers of Rowdy Kate, there was another saloon keeper named E. T. "Red" Beard, whom Lowe killed in a 50-shot duel, thus wiping out in one swoop a romantic and business rival. Because of confused and contradictory testimony about what had happened,

Lowe was acquitted of the murder but lesser charges were then brought against him. The Lowes got out of town fast. After that, they plied their trade in bad whiskey, bad women and crooked cards in such places as Fort Worth and Fort Griffin, Tex. Dodge City, Kan., Tombstone, Ariz., and several boom camps that sprang up and later disappeared when the veins ran dry.

In the early 1880s Lowe was reported killed several times, once while robbing a train, once by outlaws, and once by scalp-taking Indians. All these reports were erroneous. He turned up in Kansas in 1880s to help Luke Short and Wyatt Earp make their play during the Dodge City War. Lowe finally came to a much-deserved violent end in 1899, when E. A. Kimmel, an ex-policeman, shot him in a Denver saloon over an old grudge. It is part of Western folklore that after Rowdy Kate buried her husband, she moved on to San Francisco, married a millionaire railroad tycoon and became an honored member of Nob Hill society.

LUCAS, James (1908-?): Bank robber and murderer

Jimmy Lucas, once described as "the most vicious slugger on the Rock," typified the "new social order" that developed in Alcatraz after it was set up as a superprison for supercriminals. Famous criminals, such as Al Capone, Machine Gun Kelly, Alvin Karpis, became minor characters while toughs such as Lucas became kings of the Rock. Lucas won his fame in a confrontation with Capone.

One day a number of convicts including Capone, were lined up at the barber shop. After a while, the famous mobster got tired of waiting and moved to the front of the line, just ahead of Lucas, a mean Texas bank robber doing 30 years.

Lucas was not impressed by Capone and said, "Hey, lard ass, get back at the end of the line." Capone put on a mean look and said, "You know who I am, punk?" Lucas was enraged. He grabbed the scissors from the convict cutting hair and stuck the point into Capone's fat neck. "Yeah," he said, "I know who you are, greaseball. And if you don't get back to the end of that fucking line, I'm gonna know who you *were*." Capone went to the back of the line and never again acted like anything but just another con on the Rock.

In 1938 Lucas, Whitey Franklin and Sandy Limerick took part in one of the most daring and brutal escape attempts from Alcatraz. After murdering a guard, they climbed to the roof of the furniture work shop and tried to storm a gun tower. Limerick was killed, Franklin wounded and Lucas surrendered when he saw the situation was hopeless.

Franklin and Lucas were convicted and sentenced to life for the murder of the guard. Franklin, who had done the actual killing, spent the next seven years in solitary confinement without a break until the Alcatraz Prison Rebellion of 1946. After the revolt was squelched, he was returned to solitary. Lucas was treated mildly better, although he too did long stretches in solitary and following the trio's escape attempt was subjected to what was called "the worst grilling in Rock histo-

ry" to try to make him reveal who else had been involved. Although his reputation had been tarnished badly in the prisoners' eyes because he had given up without a fight, Lucas won back their esteem when he refused to talk.

Subsequently, Lucas and Franklin became nonpersons in the federal penal system. In addition, Franklin was to become the most ill-treated prisoner on the Rock, even more so than the Birdman of Alcatraz, Robert Stroud. However, Stroud, who had also killed a federal prison guard, was too famous to be turned into a nonperson. Both Lucas and Franklin are probably dead. It is doubtful if either was ever paroled. In 1977, in response to queries by author Clark Howard, the U.S. Bureau of Prisons simply stated that neither man was at the time incarcerated within the federal system. If by some chance Lucas was free, the bureau was not about to admit it.

See also: *Rufus "Whitey" Franklin.*

LUCCHESE, Thomas "Three-Finger Brown" (1903-1967): Top Mafia leader

Of the five crime families in the New York area established after the murder of the last boss of bosses, Salvatore Maranzano, the Gagliano-Lucchese combine was always recognized as the most efficient and relatively peaceful crime family, especially after the death—from natural causes—of Tom Gagliano and the coming to power of underboss Thomas Lucchese. Lucchese was also known as Three-Finger Brown—after a leading pitcher of the same name—ever since 1915, when he had lost three fingers in an accident.

The generally peaceful development of the Lucchese family was rather remarkable considering its leader's penchant for violence during his early years. In the 1920s he had served as a bodyguard for Lucky Luciano when both were working under Giuseppe "Joe the Boss" Masseria and he became Luciano's favorite killer. He murdered several Maranzano men during the war for control of the New York Mafia and is believed to have been involved in a total of 30 murders, although his only important arrest was for grand larceny in 1923.

After Luciano had Masseria assassinated and made a shaky peace with Maranzano, he used Lucchese as the fingerman in Maranzano's murder on September 10, 1931. From the lowly status of a Sicilian gunman, Lucchese thus rose to the high councils of the modern Mafia. One of the most popular crime bosses, he exerted great power in the garment industry rackets and ran smooth operations in the narcotics, gambling, loan-sharking and construction rackets. As a corrupter, he was the equal of Frank Costello and had friends and connections at all branches and levels of local government. When the mob wished to make its desires known to judges and legislators, Lucchese was the most important pipeline. Of all the Mafia leaders, he was probably the best at remaining out of the limelight. When Lucchese died of cancer, his funeral was one of the biggest in underworld history, with a turnout of over 1,000 mourners, including politicians, judges and businessmen as well as hit men, loansharks, narcotics peddlers and Mafia leaders. Because it was known that the FBI and police were going to monitor the funeral on film, the Lucchese family let out word they would not be offended if important mafiosi stayed away. Many did but sent emissaries to deliver their money envelopes out of respect. Despite the warning, others, including Carlo Gambino, then the most powerful boss in New York, Aniello Dellacroce, Crazy Joe and Vincent Rao, insisted on coming in person to show how much they thought of Lucchese. Perhaps what they respected most about him was that for the last 44 years of his life he had never seen the inside of a courtroom.

See also: *Charles "Lucky" Luciano, Salvatore Maranzano, Giuseppe "Joe the Boss" Masseria.*

LUCIANO, Charles "Lucky" (1897-1962): Syndicate leader

Charles "Lucky" Luciano is generally regarded as the most important figure in the development of organized crime, even more important than Al Capone. As the guiding genius along with Meyer Lansky, Luciano, by a campaign of double-dealing and, where necessary, murders, cleansed the Italian underworld of its narrow-minded old-line leaders and took it into alliances with other ethnic groups. Thus, in the early 1930s he established the national crime syndicate that has dominated many aspects of American life ever since. Despite public misunderstanding of the subject, Luciano's creation is not the Mafia, but something even bigger and more powerful. In a manner of speaking, he can be credited with killing off the Mafia.

Luciano was born Salvatore Luciana in the Palermo area of Sicily. He came to this country in 1906 at the age of nine and was arrested at 10 for shoplifting. At this tender age he started a racket that would later produce millions for him; for a penny or two a day, he offered younger and smaller Jewish kids his personal protection against beatings on the way to school. Of course, he slugged those who would not pay. One runty little Jewish kid who wouldn't pay was a youngster from Poland, Meyer Lansky. At first the two fought and then they became the best of friends, a relationship that was to continue long after Luciano had been sent into exile.

By 1916 Luciano was a full-fledged member of the notorious Five Points Gang and was listed by police as the prime suspect in a number of murders. Early on, Luciano developed an unabiding hatred for the "Mustache Petes," the old-timers who ruled the Mafia gangs, and by the 1920s he was plotting their elimination. At that time, Luciano was already an important figure in the underworld, a power in bootlegging rackets in cooperation with Lansky and his erstwhile partner Bugsy Siegel as well as Joe Adonis, Vito Genovese and, especially, Frank Costello. Costello put him in contact with other ethnic gangsters (much to the displeasure of the Mustache Petes): Irishmen like Big Bill Dwyer and Jews like Arnold Rothstein, Dutch Schultz and Dandy Phil Kastel. What impressed Luciano most about Costello was the way he could buy protection from city officials and the police, which Lansky had for years stressed to Luciano was an absolute requirement for a successful underworld existence.

By the late 1920s Luciano had risen to the number two position in the family of Giuseppe "Joe the Boss" Masseria, the top Italian gangster of the era. Luciano detested Joe the Boss' Old World ways, steeped in the rituals of the Sicilian Mafia that stressed "respect" and "honor" for the chief and distrust and hatred of all non-Sicilians. The things Luciano respected and honored were ways to earn more money from crime, and in Masseria's prejudice against other gangsters, Sicilian as well as non-Sicilian, he saw an unconscionable obstacle to achieving greater profits. Instead of cooperating with other criminals to make more money, Joe the Boss fought them, even waging old-fashioned feuds with fellow Sicilians based on which town or village they had come from.

In 1928 the Castellammarese War broke out between the forces of Joe the Boss and those of the second most powerful mafioso in New York, Salvatore Maranzano, and over the next two years dozens of gangsters on both sides were killed. While the fighting was going on, Luciano was cementing relationships with the younger, second-line leadership within the Maranzano camp, and it soon became clear that both groups were merely waiting to see which of the two leaders would die first so they could make plans to get rid of the other.

When after a time neither had been assassinated, Luciano took matters into his own hands. Three of his men and Bugsy Siegel on loan from Meyer Lansky, shot Joe the Boss to death in a Coney Island restaurant after Luciano had stepped into the men's room. Luciano then became number two man under a seemingly grateful Maranzano, who proclaimed himself the "boss of bosses" of New York. Actually, Maranzano intended to make himself the supreme boss of the entire Mafia in the U.S. and, to that end, drew up a death list of those who would have to be eliminated because they stood in his way. The top name on the list in Chicago was Al Capone, in New York, Luciano.

Unfortunately for Maranzano, Luciano anticipated his actions, in fact learned of them in advance, and avoided walking into a death trap in the gang leaders' office, where he and his aide Vito Genovese had been summoned for a conference. Maranzano had arranged for a homicidal Irish gunman, Mad Dog Coll, to assassinate the pair in his office. Instead, moments before Coll arrived to set up the ambush, four of Lansky's gunmen, pretending to be law officers, entered the office and shot Maranzano to death.

In a practical sense, Maranzano's death marked the end of the "old Mafia," at least in the United States. It has long been rumored that Luciano followed up the assassination with the murders of 40 other "Mustache Petes" across the country, but no list of victims was ever compiled and probably no such deluge of killings was necessary. In the years prior to Luciano's revolt, many of the old-timers had already passed away: either as the result of natural causes or assassinations.

The remnants of the old Mafia were incorporated into a new national crime syndicate, a more open society that combined all the ethnic elements of organized crime. The new syndicate included among its directors Lansky, Joe Adonis, Dutch Schultz, Louis Lepke and Frank Costello. There was no boss of bosses, although Luciano was really the boss in everything but name. The syndicate moved to control the bootlegging, prostitution, narcotics, gambling, loansharking and labor rackets.

Luciano was at the top of the heap, becoming a dandy dresser and a well-known sport along Broadway. He still looked menacing, however, thanks to a famous scarring he had received in 1929, when knife-wielding kidnappers severed the muscles in his right cheek, leaving him with a drooping right eye that gave him a sinister look. Luciano told various stories about how he was kidnapped and by whom, alternating culprits from gangland rivals (including the Maranzanos), to drug smugglers who thought he knew about a big incoming shipment and wanted to hijack it, to rogue cops who tried to get information from him by torture. More likely than any of these stories was a theory that he had been kidnapped by a policeman and his sons because he had been playing around with the cop's daughter. Since he had survived a "ride," something few gangsters ever did, he was nicknamed Lucky.

Lucky Luciano's downfall started in 1936, when special prosecutor Thomas E. Dewey succeeded in getting him convicted on prostitution charges, which the underworld has always insisted were a "bad rap," claiming Dewey had framed the case with the perjured testimony of pimps and whores who would say anything to avoid going to jail themselves. The conviction was especially ironic in view of the subsequent disclosure that Luciano had had Dutch Schultz murdered because that flaky and brutal gang leader had been planning to assassinate Dewey. The prosecutor had been putting heavy pressure on the syndicate in general and on Schultz in particular, and the latter appeared before a board meeting of the syndicate to demand that Dewey be eliminated. Luciano led the opposition to Schultz' demand, insisting Dewey's death would cause more problems that it would solve. When the enraged Schultz insisted he would go it alone in the "hit," Luciano pressed for a vote to kill the Dutchman for the good of the syndicate. It was done.

Luciano got 30 to 50 years for the prostitution charges, the longest sentence of its type ever given to anyone. Nevertheless, he continued to run syndicate affairs from his cell until he was paroled in 1946 for his so-called war services, especially for ordering security tightened on the mob-controlled New York waterfront (which was true) and for enlisting the aid of the Mafia in Sicily during the Allied invasion (which was nonsense). Upon his release, Luciano was deported to Italy. He was able to sneak back to Cuba for a time to continue his involvement in American criminal affairs, and at a top conference there in 1947 he approved the execution of Bugsy Siegel for looting the mob's funds while constructing his dream, the Flamingo Hotel, in the hopes of making Las Vegas a plush gambling mecca. When his presence in Cuba was revealed, Luciano was forced to return to Italy because of protests from the U.S. government. He continued to issue orders and receive his cut of racket funds through underworld couriers, including Virginia Hill. With the assassination of Albert Anastasia and the attempted assassination and forced retirement of Costello in 1957, Luciano lost two of his most ardent supporters within the syndicate. Genovese turned against him and there is reason to believe he even planned to eliminate him.

Lansky remained semi-loyal, seeing that syndicate money continued to be funneled to Luciano—but in decreasing amounts.

Luciano was in no shape to mount a serious protest, having suffered a number of heart attacks in his later years. Gradually, he began to reveal to journalists his version of many of the past criminal events in the United States. In 1962 he died of a heart attack at the Naples airport. Finally, Luciano was permitted to come back to America—for burial in St. John's Cemetery in New York City.

See also: *Joe Adonis; Albert Anastasia; Anthony "Tough Tony" Anastasio; Atlantic City Conference; Bagman; Broadway Mob; Louis "Lepke" Buchalter; Castellammarese War; Frank Costello; Thomas E. Dewey; Vito Genovese; Havana Conference; Meyer Lansky; Thomas "Three-Finger Brown" Lucchese; Salvatore Maranzano; Giuseppe "Joe the Boss" Masseria; Murder, Inc.; Mustache Petes; Night of the Sicilian Vespers; S.S.* Normandie; *Arnold Rothstein; Dutch Schultz; Seven Group; Benjamin "Bugsy" Siegel; Ciro Terranova.*

LUETGERT, Adolph Louis (1848-1911): Murderer

Few murders have ever shocked the citizens of Chicago as much as the gruesome killing in 1897 of Louisa Luetgert by her husband, Adolph, the owner of a leading sausage-making business.

Luetgert had emigrated from his native Germany in the 1870s and, over the years, had acquired three distinctions: he made just about the best German sausages in the city; he was a man of enormous appetite and considerable girth, weighing about 250 pounds, and he had sexual appetites that equalled or exceeded his culinary one, having three regular mistresses at the time of his wife's demise and a bed installed at his plant for his many trysts.

Luetgert was relatively happy except for one thing: his hefty wife, Louisa. She annoyed him, so much so that he often felt, as he told one of his lovers, "I could take her and crush her." Actually, as the police were to surmise in 1897, he probably stabbed her to death with a huge knife. That much is conjecture because almost nothing of Louisa's body was ever found. After Adolph killed her, he did something that was to damage the sale of sausage meat in Chicago for a long time. He melted her body down in a vat at his meat plant and made her part of his sausages.

Louisa turned up missing on May 1, 1897. Adolph told her relatives that he had hired private detectives to find her and that he would not go to the police because, as a prominent businessman, he could not afford to have any scandal. Eventually, his wife's relatives went to the police, who in turn searched Adolph's sausage factory. After several searches the police emptied one of many steam vats and found some pieces of bone, some teeth and two gold rings, one a wedding band with the initials "L.L." engraved on it. Both rings belonged to Louisa Luetgert. Although Adolph insisted the bone fragments were animal, analysis identified them as human. The wedding ring was even more damning because the sausage maker's wife suffered from swollen joints in some of her fingers and had been unable to remove the ring for years. However, as the police theorized, she could have been melted out of it.

Luetgert's trial was sensational, although most unsavory. The evidence against him was formidable, especially when one mistress after another took the stand to testify against him. Convicted, Luetgert was sentenced to life at Joliet Prison, where he died in 1911.

LUFTHANSA Robbery

The biggest holdup in the history of American crime occurred on December 11, 1978, when six or seven men wearing ski masks and armed with shotguns and automatic weapons staged a bold pre-dawn raid on the Lufthansa Airlines cargo facility at New York City's Kennedy International Airport and made off with $5.85 million in cash and jewelry. Although the caper has not been completely solved, authorities have made a number of arrests and pieced together a scenario of the daring heist, which has since resulted in a trail of corpses.

Investigators now know through certain confessions that the robbers had inside aid and information. Louis Werner, a Lufthansa cargo agent, was convicted and sentenced to 16½ years in prison for giving the robbers crucial inside assistance. Because of fear of retribution, Werner has refused to give testimony against others involved in the crime. Within a year after the crime, authoritative counts of persons rubbed out because they had knowledge of various aspects of the caper rose to a

minimum of nine and perhaps as many as a dozen.

The crime, authorities are certain, was planned at Roberts Lounge, a bar near the airport where known cargo thieves, airline cargo handlers and undercover cops congregated to drink and bet on horses. The bar's ownership has since changed hands but its current customers still gossip about the huge theft and whisper alleged new revelations about it.

There seems little doubt that the crime was a "Mafia operation," planned by members of the crime family of the late Tommy Lucchese. According to the FBI, the Lucchese group supervised the plot and then handled the disposition of the money and jewels. It is said the mob secured the cooperation of the inside employees by the standard Mafia method of encouraging them to gamble beyond their means, then pressuring them to pay up, lending them money at exorbitant rates and finally pointing out they could cancel their debts and come out ahead by helping pull off the heist.

While only 10 persons are believed to have been directly involved in the robbery, the circle of those who took part in the overall operation may amount to as many as 30 or 35. A key suspect in the investigation has been James "Jimmy the Gent" Burke, the former operator of Roberts Lounge. Shortly before the Lufthansa job, Burke was released from prison, where he had been serving time for another cargo caper. He reputedly was the "coach" on the job, tirelessly training the holdup men during methodical rehearsals of the robbery. Burke

An aerial view of the route taken in the Lufthansa heist, the biggest holdup in American history.

refused to answer any questions about the heist and eventually was returned to prison for parole violation.

Other leading suspects are Thomas DeSimone, believed to have been one of the holdup men, and a big-time bookmaker named Martin Krugman, who is said to have passed on the idea of the scheme to the men who carried it off. Both DeSimone and Krugman are missing. Some law officials believe they are dead, but others are doubtful and point out that no effort was made to hide other victims' bodies, probably indicating the mob wanted the various deaths to act as a deterrent to those who might talk.

The only murder victim whose identity the killers tried to conceal was Theresa Ferrara, a 27-year-old part owner of a Long Island beauty shop who had shared a house with an associate of Burke. Her dismembered body washed ashore near Toms River, N.J. and could only be identified by X rays.

Police thought they had a major break in the case when they got a tip that another body was buried in the yard behind Roberts Lounge but when they dug up the ground, they found only the body of a horse. A year after the robbery, FBI agent Steve Carbone was optimistic about eventually breaking the case. "It took the Brink's people five years to solve that case, so we still have four to go," he said. "We're very confident."

LUPO The Wolf (?1870-1944): Black Hander and murderer

From the 1890s until 1920, Ignazio Saietta, better known as Ignazio Lupo, or Lupo the Wolf, was the most important Black Hander in New York City. The Black Hand was not an organized society but a mixed bag of amateur and professional extortionists who terrorized various Italian communities throughout the United States, threatening victims with death unless they paid to stay alive. The victims would receive letters demanding money and at the bottom of the letter there would usually be the outline of a hand that had been dipped in black ink, a sign sure to produce icy terror. Lupo the Wolf fostered and perfected the Black Hand technique, promoting himself into the embodiment of evil in the Italian section of Harlem.

Lupo came from Sicily as a grown man and soon won a reputation as one of the most desperate and bloodthirsty criminals in the history of American crimes. His followers knew they had to kill without questioning his authority, so terrified were they of him. It was the custom in Italian Harlem for a resident to cross himself on the mere mention of Lupo's name and extend his fingers to ward off the spells of this evil creature. Many of Lupo's killings took place in the infamous Murder Stable at 323 East 107th Street, where eventually the bodies of some 60 murder victims were found. Some of these were individuals who had refused to meet Lupo's Black Hand demands, but more were victims of murder-for-pay jobs done for other gangs, secret societies or private individuals who had contracted with Lupo for an old-country vendetta killing.

Included among the victims were gang members who had strayed, such as the 18-year-old stepson of Giuseppi Morello,

Lupo's chief ally. The youth was tortured and slaughtered because he was suspected of having betrayed the gang's counterfeiting activities. Using fear and intimidation, Lupo continued to operate through the first two decades of the 20th century seemingly immune to arrest for his various murders and extortions. Finally, in 1920 Secret Service agents caught him in a counterfeiting plot in which dollars were forged in Sicily and then smuggled into this country.

Lupo the Wolf was sent to prison for 30 years. Released in the late 1930s, he emerged to find much of the criminal world altered. Black Hand operations had long since ceased because of the increased sophistication of the Italian community whose members now would go to the law if pushed. There was no longer any room for Lupo in other rackets. Mafia racketeers had joined in an organized crime confederation that used murder only as a last resort and in accordance with sound business procedures. Clearly, Lupo the Wolf, with his crude methods, did not belong, and he was so informed. Terror and murder as he practiced them would only cause serious legal and political problems for the organization and simply would not be tolerated. Lupo took the warning to heart and went into retirement until his death in 1944.

See also: *Black Hand, Murder Stable.*

LUSTIG, "Count" Victor (1890-1947): Con man

Probably the only confidence operator who could be classed as the equal of the legendary Yellow Kid Weil was "Count" Victor Lustig, a remarkable rogue who not only pulled the most outrageous swindles of the 1920s and 1930s but also constantly courted danger by victimizing the top gangsters in America, including Al Capone and Legs Diamond.

Born in 1890 in what is now Czechoslovakia, Victor Lustig soon established himself as the black sheep of the family (although when he became a successful international confidence swindler, his brother Emil followed in his footsteps).

Lustig pulled a number of swindles in Europe as a young man and was hunted by police in several countries. Consequently, he came to the United States just after World War I and immediately emerged as the leading practitioner of the "money-making machine" swindle. A sucker would be informed that the Count had discovered a secret process for making real currency out of plain paper that he fed into a machine. He demonstrated the process several times, although what came out were other genuine bills that he had secreted in the machine earlier. As outrageous as the dodge was, Lustig had such a gift for grift that he sold the machine—often for sums up to and even exceeding $10,000—to bankers, businessmen, madams, gangsters and small-town lawmen.

An incorrigible rascal, Lustig believed in flimflamming as a matter of principle, and no one was exempt. He originated one of the con man's favorite petty swindles, that of "tishing a lady." Lustig was a habitue of brothels and paid extremely well, at least in a manner of speaking. Upon taking leave of a lady, he would produce a $50 bill, fold it up, lift up her skirt and pretend to tuck it in her stocking. Actually, he would palm the bill and stuff in a wad of tissue paper. Then the Count would explain to the woman that it was trick money and that if she removed it before morning, it would turn to tissue paper. The lady would promise to leave it there but after Lustig's departure she would eagerly retrieve her pay—and indeed, it had turned to tissue paper!

In the mid-1920s Lustig returned to Europe and twice succeeded in selling the Eiffel Tower. He had read in the newspapers that the great tourist attraction was in need of repairs and would be very costly. The Count had a brainstorm. When he arrived in Paris, he sent out letters to six leading scrap metal dealers inviting them to a secret government meeting in a luxury hotel. Lustig introduced himself as "deputy director-general of the ministry of mail and telegraphs," and explained to the dealers that since it was too costly to repair the Eiffel Tower, it would have to be torn down and sold for scrap. However, the government was fearful of public reaction, so the plans had to be kept secret. Then when the government announced how much money would be saved, the public would accept the idea.

The dealers were invited to bid for the scrap metal from the tower. All turned in secret bids. Then Lustig informed one of the dealers that for a fee his bid would be accepted. The dealer paid eagerly, and Lustig immediately fled to Vienna. When the story of the swindle failed to make the newspapers, he realized the dealer had been too frightened or too ashamed to go to the police. So he returned to Paris and swindled another dealer. This one, however informed the law when he realized he had been taken and Lustig realized he couldn't sell the Eiffel Tower again and returned to America.

For a time Lustig operated in the worthless security field, selling bogus paper that he often presented as "stolen." He found a number of underworld buyers who agreed to take the hot stuff off his hands for as little as 10¢ on the dollar, with the idea of holding it several years before disposing of it. Among those so taken were Big Bill Dwyer, Nicky Arnstein and Legs Diamond, who actually thought he was buying some retirement security. Oddly, when the gangsters found out they had been taken, they could do nothing because Lustig said he would spread the word on how they'd been suckered, making fools of them. Even the maniacal Diamond saw the humor of the situation and left Lustig alone.

The Count once swindled Al Capone out of $5,000 and the famous gangster never realized he had been taken. Lustig asked Capone for $50,000, promising to double it in 60 days in a scam he was working. Capone gave him the money, warning what he did to welchers and swindlers. Lustig simply put the money in a safe-deposit box for the allotted time and then dolefully informed him his plan had failed and he had not made any money. Capone was about to explode, thinking he had been taken, when Lustig returned his $50,000, keeping up a spiel of apologies. Capone was not prepared for this situation. Initially figuring Lustig had swindled his money, he now was faced with the obvious fact that the Count was playing square with him.

"If the deal fell through," Capone said, "you must be down on your luck." He peeled off five $1,000 bills and handed them to Lustig. "I take care of guys who play square with me." The Count gratefully left with the $5,000, which was what he was after from the beginning.

One of the Count's prize patsies was a renowned madam of the period, Billie Scheible, operator of a string of very plush houses in Pittsburgh and New York. He once sold the madam a moneymaking machine for $10,000 after telling her he was too impatient with it since it could only turn out one $100 bill every 12 hours. When Billie determined she had been hoaxed, she had some of her strong-arm boys run the Count down in Philadelphia.

Lustig refunded Billie's $10,000 and then turned on the charm full voltage to sell her $15,000 in worthless securities. "The Count had a way with him," Billie once explained.

Since many of Lustig's swindles involved money schemes, it was only natural he would also venture into counterfeiting. But counterfeiting was another matter and the Count, who had never done time for any of his cons, was caught in 1935.

On September 1, the day before he was supposed to go on trial in New York City, Lustig, using a rope fashioned from nine bed sheets tied together, climbed out a lavatory window of the Federal House of Detention and started his escape descent. Part way down, Lustig noticed lunch-hour pedestrians watching him. Immediately, he began to go through the motions of cleaning the window. Down he went, floor by floor, scrubbing every pane he passed. When he hit the sidewalk, he ran. It was several minutes before one puzzled onlooker approached the small wicket in the formidable jail doors and asked, "Do you know your window cleaner has run away?"

The Count's fantastic escape made headlines throughout the country, as did the ensuing manhunt for him. Billie Scheible was questioned but knew nothing. Perhaps Arthur "Dapper Don" Collins did. Collins, reputed to be one of the country's greatest con men, had been pals with Lustig before his arrest. But he was not too helpful either. It turned out Lustig had swindled him out of several thousand dollars and, quite naturally, failed to keep in touch.

Finally, Lustig was run to earth in Pittsburgh. He was convicted and sentenced to 15 years for the counterfeiting charge and five more for his escape. He died in prison in 1947.

See also: *Money-Making Machine.*

LYNCH, William (1724-1820): First lyncher

The origin of lynching has been attributed to many persons named Lynch, some who did the hanging and some who were hanged. Many texts credit a Virginia planter, Colonel Charles Lynch, who with his brother founded Lynchburg, as the first lyncher. His activities, however, seem to have been limited to the flogging of criminals and Tories during the American Revolution; there is no evidence that he ever hanged anyone by extralegal means. Most likely, the first lyncher was another Virginian named Lynch, Captain William Lynch, who used the rope to cleanse Pittsylvania County of a ruffian element. In a sense, Captain Lynch did only what the community required, since in the frontier the law was either weak or entirely lacking.

Writing in 1836, Edgar Allen Poe discovered the date the first lynching organization was formed when he found a compact signed by Lynch and a number of his supporters. It read:

Whereas, many of the inhabitants of Pittsylvania . . . have sustained great and intolerable losses by a set of lawless men . . . that . . . have hitherto escaped the civil power with impunity . . . we, the subscribers, being determined to put a stop to the ubiquitous practices of those unlawful and abandoned wretches, do enter into the following association . . . upon hearing or having sufficient reason to believe, that any . . . species of villainy (has) been committed within our neighborhood, we will forthwith . . . repair immediately to the person or persons suspected . . . and if they will not desist from their evil practices, we will inflict such corporeal punishment on him or them, as to us shall seem adequate to the crime committed or the damage sustained. . . . In witness whereof we have hereunto set our hands, this 22nd day of September, 1780.

The compact did not specifically mention hanging but hangings occurred, especially after floggings had stimulated confessions, true or imaginary. The hangings were carried out indirectly, as described by an acquaintance of Lynch:

A horse in part became the executioner . . . the person who it was supposed ought to suffer death was placed on a horse with his hands tied behind him and a rope about his neck which was fastened to the limb of a tree over his head. In this situation the person was left and when the horse in pursuit of food or any other cause moved from his position the unfortunate person was left suspended by the neck—this was called "aiding the civil authority."

See also: *Lynching*.

LYNCHING

The extent of lynching in the United States had never been accurately measured. Before 1882 there were no reliable figures at all. Since then the records have been reasonably accurate. Statistics compiled at Tuskegee Institute indicate that from 1882 to 1936 at least 4,672 persons were lynched in this country; of this total, almost three quarters, or 3,383, were blacks, and 1,289 were whites. Between 1886 and 1916 lynch mobs killed a minimum of 2,605 blacks, and in 1892 alone the figure was 160.

By the 1890s the frontier was being tamed and lynchings in the West started to decline, but in the South they started to increase. In that decade 87 percent of all lynchings occurred in the South; from 1930 to 1937 the South had 95 percent of all lynchings. While the standard assertion in the region was that lynchings were necessary to protect white womanhood, less than 30 percent of black lynch victims during the seven-year period were accused, let alone proved guilty, of rape or attempted rape.

Obviously, these figures give an incomplete picture of the extent of lynching. Omitted entirely is any reference to Chinese or to Indians, probably the most common victims of lynchings in the West. While the literature and history of the West describe the lynching of murderers, claim jumpers, rustlers and thieves, it has always been members of minority groups who have most felt the lynch mob's wrath. The early German settlers seem to have had a particularly strong bent for lynching Indians. In 1763 German settlers, fired up by the passions of the French and Indian War, butchered 20 peaceful Conestoga Indians, many women and children, near Lancaster, Pa.

This lynching, hardly the first to occur in the colonies, preceded the activities of two Virginians, Colonel Charles Lynch and Captain William Lynch, both of whom are credited in various texts as being the first lyncher and the one who lent his name to the practice. The evidence appears to favor William Lynch.

A contemporary drawing of the lynching of two black men and three black women for the killing of a white man in Greenville, Ala. in 1895. One account assured readers that the 100 men in the lynching party were "all cool and brave."

Whoever deserves the credit, lynching became a widespread practice in America, employed for whatever reasons the lynchers thought just. The Vicksburg Volunteers in the 1830s used it to get rid of the gamblers who were driving the residents of that Mississippi port city to poverty with their crooked games. The Vigilantes of San Francisco did much to clean up San Francisco, ridding the city of a number of cutthroats and crooked politicians. Probably the greatest lynching rampage in the West occurred in the 1860s, when the Vigilantes of Montana wiped out the Innocents, a massive outlaw gang run by a sheriff, the notorious Henry Plummer. During six weeks in late 1863 the vigilantes hanged an estimated 26 Innocents as well as the sheriff himself. Many lynchings were probably stage-managed by private detectives, railroad detectives and range detectives, who would take suspects into custody and make a point of jailing them in an area where the feeling of the community ran high against the detainees. Their apparent strategy was to fan the public's ire and then stand to one side as a lynch mob took over.

The various Ku Klux Klans that were established starting in 1866 aimed to keep the South under the control of white Protestants. Naturally, blacks were the most frequent victims of the Klan, but others who felt the whip and the hangman's rope included Jews, Catholics, bootleggers, pacifists, "Bolshevists," internationalists and evolutionists. While hangings and shootings were the most common methods of lynching in the South, methods of shocking cruelty were often used. In 1899 thousands of whites took special excursion trains to Palmetto, Ga. to watch a black man being roasted alive.

Two of the most outrageous lynchings of this century involved white victims. One was Leo Frank, a pencil company executive in Georgia who was lynched in 1915. Frank was taken from a prison where he was serving a life sentence for the murder and rape of a young girl, a crime of which he was almost certainly innocent. What he was not innocent of was being Jewish and rich. Frank was hanged by vigilantes calling themselves the Knights of Mary Phagan, the name of the girl whom Frank had been convicted of murdering. Shortly thereafter, most of the Knights were initiated into a "reincarnated" Invisible Empire of the Knights of the Ku Klux Klan.

The other shocking case occurred in the aftermath of the 1933 kidnap-murder of California department store heir Brooke Hart in 1933. A huge mob broke into the jail in San Jose where Hart's two confessed murderers, John Maurice Holmes and Thomas Harold Thurmond, were being held, and hanged the pair after brutally mistreating them. The tenor of the times was best articulated by Gov. James "Sunny Jim" Rolfe, who announced the lynch mob provided "the best lesson ever given the country. I would pardon those fellows if they were charged. I would like to parole all kidnappers in San Quentin and Folsom to the fine patriotic citizens of San Jose."

But despite such publicized mob executions of whites, the vast majority of lynching victims in the 20th century have been blacks. From its inception in 1909, the National Association for the Advancement of Colored People fought mob violence and campaigned for a federal antilynching law, but congressional action was always frustrated by filibusters in the Senate. About 1935 the number of lynchings started to decrease, and by 1952-54 there was, for the first time in the nation's history, a three-year period without a reported lynching. Since then there have been some lynchings, but by and large, they have become a thing of the past. While no antilynching statute has ever been adopted, the 1968 Civil Rights Act, which makes it a federal offense for two or more persons to join in a conspiracy to violate a citizen's constitutional rights whether or not death occurs, has been considered effective in preventing lynchings.

See also: *Bishee Massacre, William Coons, George Johnson, William Lynch.*

LYNDS, Elam (1784-1855): Sing Sing's first warden

He was regarded in his day—not particularly an era of enlightenment in the treatment of convicts—as the wickedest warden ever to run an American penitentiary, and still today, many historians trace almost every evil committed in the history of American penology to Elam Lynds, the first warden of Sing Sing. If that was perhaps too sweeping a judgment, it can at least be said that whatever evil he did not originate, he most certainly refined. A full century after Lynds' reign, another warden of Sing Sing, Thomas Mott Osborne, wrote, "We are just now getting rid of the Lynds' influence." And another, Lewis E. Lawes, added, "Bit by bit, one reform at a time, the memory of Captain Lynds is being scrubbed out of the stones at Sing Sing."

The atrocities committed in the new prison Lynds built with convict labor at the village of Sing Sing, N.Y. in the 1820s gave the community such a bad reputation that the local citizens changed the village's name to Ossining.

It was Lynds who originated the use of striped uniforms and who developed the technique of lockstepping (close marching) convicts. He initiated the practice of having prisoners pass each other with downcast eyes so that no inmate would come face to face with another; of prohibiting prisoners from talking, in or out of their cells; and of making prisoners perform hard labor from dawn to dusk. Above all, he believed in the whip. "Whip 'em till they drop," he commanded his guards until he won the sobriquet the Whip of Sing Sing.

Born in 1784 in Litchfield, Conn., Lynds entered military service while in his teens. By the beginning of the War of 1812, he had gone from private to lieutenant and was subsequently promoted to captain for valor in action. After the war the government cut the size of the Army and Lynds was mustered out. Finding a job suited to his talents, he became principal keeper of the new state prison at Auburn, N.Y. The warden was a political appointee with no background in penology and he turned over the running of the institution to Lynds, who immediately introduced a series of severe practices. One that he was not allowed to implement was the equipping of all guards with rawhide whips so that they could mete out instant punishment. In 1821 the warden died and Lynds succeeded him, initiating the darkest period in penal history. Auburn Prison became known as the harshest in the country, which made Lynds the darling of the prison discipline societies throughout the nation and their allies in the legislature.

Lynds gave them exactly what they wanted. The New York legislature approved a plan that allowed Lynds to pick 80 prisoners to be kept in solitary confinement in the first of 550 individual cells being constructed at the prison. The inmates were to remain there for the entire duration of their sentences. If any of them broke their silence, they tasted Lynds' whip. Within the first two years of this cruel experiment, only two of those among the 80 who were not lucky enough to win their freedom survived, the rest either died or went hopelessly insane.

Lynds transferred more men into the newly completed cell blocks—the first of their kind in the world and upon which all others have been patterned. Six days of the week the men were allowed out of their cells from dawn to dusk to do hard labor and then returned to their unlit, unheated and unsanitary confines for the long silent night. The seventh day they were kept locked up the entire 24-hour period.

The Rev. Louis Dwight, head of the Boston Prison Discipline Society, wrote admiringly of Lynds' concept of labor, beatings and silence:

> The whole establishment, from the gate to the sewer, is a specimen of neatness. The unremitted industry, the entire subordination and subdued feeling of the convicts, has probably no parallel among an equal number of criminals. In their solitary cells they spend the night, with no other book than the Bible, and at sunrise they proceed in military order, under the eye of the turnkeys, in solid columns, with the lock march, to their workshops; thence in the same order, at the hour of breakfast, to the common jail, where they partake of their wholesome and frugal meal in silence. Not even a whisper is heard through the whole dining area. The convicts are seated in single file, at narrow tables, with their backs towards the center, so that there can be no interchange of signs. If one has more food than he wants, he raises his right hand, and the waiter changes it. When they have done eating, at the ringing of a little bell, of the softest sound, they rise from the table, form the solid columns, and return under the eye of their turnkeys to the work-shops . . . .
>
> At the close of day, a little before sunset, the work is all laid aside at one and the convicts return in military order to the solitary cells; where they partake of the frugal meal, which they are permitted to take from the kitchen, where it was furnished for them, as they returned from the shops. After supper, they can, if they choose, read the Scriptures undisturbed, and then reflect in silence on the errors of their lives. They must not disturb their fellows by even a whisper. : . . The men attend to their business from the rising to the setting sun, and spend the night in solitude."

Despite such glowing testimonials, there were several critics who were appalled at the sufferings of the prisoners and Lynds' dedication to whipping. In one case he actually flogged a prisoner 500 blows. He lashed convicts who had fits and those who were insane. Indeed, there is no way of knowing how many men went insane because of Lynds' brutal practices.

The huge increase in insanity cases and suicides plagued Lynds. Prison reform associations were springing up and all railed against his oppressive rule. They were especially revolted by one case in which a guard, acting on Lynds' orders, entered the cell of a woman prisoner, one of 100 kept in the segregated south wing of the prison, and whipped her severely. Within a month she died. When her body was later shipped to a medical college, it was ascertained that her death had not been from natural causes. Finally, even Lynds' devoted supporters in the legislature couldn't protect his Auburn post. They arranged for him to be put in charge of the construction of a new prison at Sing Sing on the Hudson River. The transfer proved irresistible when Lynds pledged to build the prison free of cost to the state.

The site at Sing Sing was picked out because it was accessible by boat and had large quantities of marble rock and good building stone that were not difficult to quarry. Lynds arrived there in the spring of 1825 with 100 prisoners from Auburn. All the convicts were given striped uniforms, the first time such outfits were used. Lynds decided on the uniforms because they would stand out against the background of trees if any prisoners tried to escape.

It took the work force three years to complete the prison, constructing individual cells for themselves and for 400 other convicts and a chapel room for 900 more. It was quite an accomplishment. The convicts had labored without an enclosing wall and yet none had escaped. Lynds had driven them hard, never coddled them. During the winter months the men worked fewer hours because there was less daylight. Since they worked less, Lynds cut their food rations, reasoning they did not need the same level of nourishment. Of course, the government had provided the same amount of rations. Lynds had simply sold the "surplus" to outside merchants, a practice he was to continue during his long reign and which was to supplement his $1,000 annual salary and make him a rich man.

And Sing Sing was built without cost. While quarrying stone for building their own cells, they were also cutting beautiful slabs of light gray stone, almost like granite, for sale to state and local communities all over New York and New England. State legislative inspectors were so thrilled by the pay-as-you-go construction of the prison that they ignored additional tons of stone continually stacked on the river's bank for shipment to private builders at special cut-rate prices.

Lynds was given a free hand in the prison he had built, and he, in turn, loosed his guards on the inmates. "Punish! Punish!" he ordered them. "I don't believe in reformation of an adult criminal. He's a coward, a willful lawbreaker whose spirit must be broken by the lash. Why is it that one guard, armed with a whip, can control twenty convicts? They are afraid of him. I'll teach them to fear my guards. And all of them, guards included, to fear me. That is the only way to conduct a prison."

Lynds personally met every new batch of prisoners shipped up from New York City. He would look over the commitment papers to find the new arrival with the worst record, pull that man out of line and have him strapped to the whipping post. He would then lash him 10 times. Such was the greeting newcomers received in Lynds' grim fortress on the Hudson.

"You'll be back for more," Lynds told a man who had assaulted a brutal guard at Newgate Prison in Greenwich Village, from where he had been transferred. "I know my men." Thereafter, Lynds found special cause for singling out the convict for punishment. One day at the rock quarry, the man found lasting freedom from the whip by refusing to run when some explosives were set off.

Such was the fear that Lynds could inspire. For no matter what the prisoners thought of him, he was no coward, as he proved constantly by parading in their midst.

Once when Lynds learned the prison barber, a murderer named Wilde, was threatening to kill him if he ever got the chance to put a razor to his throat, he sent for the barber. Leaning back in his office chair, he told Wilde to shave him. By the time the shave was completed, the barber was a nervous wreck. Lynds laughed. "I know you threatened to kill me, Wilde," he said. "But I knew you wouldn't. Unarmed, I'm stronger than you are with a weapon. Now get out."

If Lynds was a terror to the prisoners by day, he was far worse by night. Two French writers, G. de Beaumont and A. de Tocqueville, who visited Sing Sing related in their famous book, *On the Penitentiary System of the United States*, published in 1833, how Lynds, a barrel of a man, prowled on tiptoes through the silent galleries of the prison, at night, his ever present whip in hand, listening for violators of the no-whispering rule:

> It was a tomb of living dead. . . . We could not realize that in this building were 950 human beings. We felt we were traversing catacombs. A faint glow from a lantern held by an inspector on the upper galleries moved slowly back and forth in the ghostly darkness. As it passed each narrow cell door we saw, in our imagination, the gateway to a sepulcher instead. . . . The watchman wore woolen moccasins over his shoes to deaden even the faint scrape of his shoes on the gallery floor. There was not a sound.

Not a sound until some unfortunate cried out in anguish when his cell door was thrown open and that awesome whip cracked. Some prisoners, apparently guilty of no more than talking in their sleep, told later of being jarred awake by the first slash of rawhide.

Eventually, Lynds was removed from his post, but it was not because of his unhumane treatment of convicts. Rather, it was due to financial and other forms of malfeasance. It was found that contractors who supplied the food for the inmates billed the prison for a certain quality of meat but supplied a much cheaper grade. Lynds insisted on half the difference in value as his kickback. Another revelation was that the garbage swill from the convicts' food was sold to pig farmers, but since they insisted on a certain quality, Lynds dumped part of the prisoners' rations directly into the garbage.

Perhaps the most telling case against him was made by Colonel Levi S. Barr, an ex-Army officer and lawyer who was sent to Sing Sing for three years. His accusations against Lynds took on added weight when, after his release, he proved the criminal charges against him had been unwarranted. "In my three years of confinement," he declared in a petition to the legislature, "I ate no butter, cheese, milk, sugar, no turnips, beets, carrots, parsnips or vegetables of any kind save potatoes, no soups or strengthening drinks. . . . I have gladly eaten the roots of shrubs and trees that I dug from the ground in which I labored. . . . I saw no exception among individuals around me. . . . There were some who told me they ate the clay they worked in. . . . It at least filled their stomachs."

Additional charges were brought by John W. Edmonds, an inspector of prisons, who uncovered evidence that some prisoners had thrived, enjoying double food rations provided they had the money to pay the warden for them. It was also discovered that Lynds had hushed up several escapes. Inmates who had broken out were still carried on the books.

Lynds finally was forced to resign in 1845. He lived out his remaining years in comfortable retirement, buying a fashionable home and making numerous business investments, all presumably financed by savings from $1,000-a-year salary. While the man died in personal disgrace, his penal beliefs and practices lived on after him and many would say they have yet to be totally eradicated.

LYONS, Danny (1860-1888): Murderer

A leading member of the Whyos, easily the most murderous gang in New York City during the late 19th century, handsome Danny Lyons was available to do any job at a price. He would blacken both eyes of a victim for a $4 fee, break his leg for $19, shoot him in the leg for $25 or "do the big job" for $100 and up. A strutting rooster, he kept three women in prostitution on the streets: Lizzie the Dove, Bunty Kate and Gentle Maggie. When they failed to bring in the revenues that Lyons felt were necessary to maintain him properly, he recruited a fourth Kitty McGown. But Kitty already had a lover, Joseph Quinn, who vowed to get Lyons for stealing his inamorata and meal ticket. The two prowled lower New York for months and on July 5, 1887 their paths finally crossed. They blazed away at each other, and Quinn dropped with a bullet in his heart.

Lyons went into hiding but was caught some months later and hanged on August 21, 1888. In underworld circles there was much denunciation of the execution for what was considered a bum rap. The story was that Quinn had shot first, and Lyons had merely acted in self-defense. Certainly, the authorities had been hoping to get a noose around Lyons' neck and such a God-sent opportunity was not to be lost because of a quibble over who had shot first.

Kitty McGown and Bunty Kate immediately found themselves new protectors, but Lizzie the Dove and Gentle Maggie put on widow's black and canceled all business engagements while they went into mourning. One night toasting their departed lover in a Bowery dive, they got into a heated argument over which of them he had loved more and whose sadness was greater. Gentle Maggie won the argument by plunging a cheese knife into Lizzie the Dove's throat. As she lay dying, Lizzie told her rival, "[I will] meet you in hell and there scratch your eyes out."

See also: *Danny Driscoll, Whyos.*

LYONS, Haze (1840-1864): Road agent and murderer

A minor member of Sheriff Henry Plummer's huge gang of crooks, Haze Lyons ended up celebrated because of a sentimental ballad bewailing his misfortunes.

A young cowboy, Lyons made his way from California to Montana and there joined Plummer's gang of Innocents, who plundered the area in robberies plotted by the sheriff himself. Lyons did whatever ordered, no less so when told to help take care of Sheriff Plummer's deputy, Bill Dillingham, a peace officer suffering from a terminal incorruptibility. However, Lyons and two other Plummer gunmen botched the job and were caught. Lyons tried to argue that he was just an innocent bystander but was quickly tried and convicted before a miners court and sentenced to hang. The rope was round his neck when someone started reading aloud a last letter he had been permitted to write to his mother. It was a sentimental bit of prose that, it is said, reduced the tough miners to tears. The miners untied Lyons' hands, put him on a horse and told him to "git" back to mother. Lyons made the mistake of going only as far as Bannack and reporting back to Plummer. He pulled some more jobs for the sheriff and just a few months later, on January 14, 1864, was taken prisoner by vigilantes who were not impressed by sentimental letters. They hanged him the same day. Much was made of the gunman who wouldn't go home to mother. A ballad celebrated his fate, but the verse is lost, as is, perhaps more sadly, that heartrending letter that saved a killer's life, at least for a time.

See also: *Innocents, Henry Plummer.*

M

MACCORMICK, Austin H.: See Welfare Island Prison Scandal.

MCCALL, Jack (1851-1877): Killer of Wild Bill Hickok

Jack McCall is remembered as one of the two meanest and vilest assassins in Western history, the other being Bob Ford, "the dirty coward" who shot Jesse James. McCall arrived in Deadwood, Dakota Territory in the spring of 1876, using the name of Bill Sutherland, probably because he was suspected of having stolen range stock in Nebraska. He was a cross-eyed, broken-nosed, whiskey-besotted saddle tramp who was always getting into scrapes. It was said he got his cross eyes in a dispute with a sheriff whom he went after with a couple of .45s. The lawman simply picked up a hefty piece of lumber and cracked him over the head, rendering him unconscious for 24 hours and leaving him with scrambled eyes thereafter.

Wild Bill Hickok, himself a notorious back-shooter, drifted into Deadwood about a month after McCall. They apparently got to know each other over the town's poker tables. Thus, it came as a shock when on August 2, 1876 at about 4 p.m., McCall walked into Carl Mann's Saloon Number 10, stepped up behind Hickok, who was playing cards, and put a bullet through his head. Hickok slumped forward dead, still clutching his cards, a pair of aces and a pair of eights, thereafter to be known as a "dead man's hand."

As soon as everyone realized what had happened, there was a mad rush for the exits. McCall tried to shoot twice at the fleeing figures, but his gun misfired both times. He rushed out the door and hopped on the first horse he saw. Unfortunately for McCall, its owner had slackened the saddle cinch because of the heat, and he was sent sprawling in the dust. He ran into a butcher shop to hide, but someone stuck a rifle in his back and forced him out.

McCall faced a miners court the following day and pleaded self-defense. He also said he was avenging the death of his brother, whom Hickok had killed. By a vote of 11 to one the jury declared him not guilty and set him free, indicating despite what the makers of the Hickok legend have said, how people really felt about Wild Bill.

McCall quickly left town, ending up in Laramie, Wyo., where he often bragged of killing Hickok in a duel. Finally, he was arrested for the Hickok killing by a federal marshal and brought to trial at Yankton, Dakota Territory. McCall's protest that he'd "done been tried" was ignored, since miners courts had no official standing. In a real court of law there was not much chance of his being found not guilty on the grounds of self-defense. His claim about avenging his brother's death wasn't too effective either after it was established he had three sisters but no brother. There was some speculation that McCall felt Hickok had cheated him out of $25 in a card game, but that was doubted on the ground that McCall rarely possessed such a bountiful sum. Some evidence indicated that the pair had had words over whether McCall owed Hickok 25¢. That may well have been the real motive for the shooting. McCall was asked why he had shot Hickok from behind rather than face-to-face. For that at least, he had a perfectly logical answer, "I didn't want to commit suicide."

On March 1, 1877 McCall was hanged and buried with the rope still around his neck.

See also: *Wild Bill Hickok.*

MCCANLES Gang: Wild Bill Hickok foes

The Wild Bill Hickok legend began in Rock Creek, Nebraska Territory in 1861, when he wiped out the "McCanles gang" of nine "desperadoes, horse-thieves, murderers and regular cutthroats," as *Harper's Monthly* called them, in "the greatest one-man gunfight in history." In the battle Hickok supposedly made use of a six-gun, rifle and bowie knife and took 11 bullets in his own body.

The true facts were a little less spectacular than the magazine reported, however. The so-called McCanles Gang actually consisted of David C. McCanles, a 40-year-old rancher who had sold his previous homestead to a stage and freight company for use as a relay station, and his 12-year-old son, a cousin and a youthful employee. The four went to the company's office in the McCanles' former home to demand the payments beyond the first, which were long past due. In charge of the station was a man named Horace Wellman, who had as his assistant a 24-year-old stock tender named James Butler Hickok. McCanles, who was something of a community bully and appears to have had some conflict with Hickok over a woman, demanded to see Wellman, informing Hickok that if he didn't send him out he would come in after him. Hickok entered the depot and in a few minutes McCanles was summoned to follow. There is some dispute over whether McCanles was even armed at the time and over why he would have brought his young son along if he expected a shoot-out. While McCanles was belaboring Wellman, Hickok apparently shot the rancher while hiding behind a calico curtain. McCanles' son rushed into the building and cradled his dying father in his arms while the other two young men, both almost certainly unarmed, were murdered, one hacked to death with a hoe and the other killed by a shotgun blast. Both were killed by other members of the relay station crew. The McCanles boy avoided being murdered only because he was fast afoot. There is no indication that the "McCanles forces" ever fired a shot, and Hickok certainly was not wounded.

Hickok, Wellman and a man named J.W. "Doc" Brink were charged in the three deaths, although there was considerable evidence that Mrs. Wellman was responsible for at least one of the killings. The record doesn't reveal whether they were ever brought to trial. Well into the 20th century, each time a new scrap of evidence was discovered by historians, the facts of the McCanles killing were dredged over again and again. At no time, has Hickok ever come out looking heroic. Still, the myth of a "McCanles gang" persists.

See also: *Wild Bill Hickok.*

MCCARTY Gang: Wild Bunch outlaws

The McCartys were a flaky band, fitting in well with Butch Cassidy's Wild Bunch, with whom they often rode. On March 30, 1889 Tom McCarty, Cassidy and an unidentified member of the gang walked into the First National Bank of Denver, where McCarty told the bank president he had just overheard a plan to rob the bank.

"My God," the bank officer cried. "How do you know about this plot?"

"Because I planned it," McCarty said. "Hands up!"

The McCartys fared well under Cassidy's wing, but when they struck out on their own in 1893, it was a different story. They bungled a holdup of the Merchant's Bank in Delta, Colo. Overhearing cries for help, a young hardware store owner, W. Ray Simpson, instantly seized a rifle and some shells and stepped out to the street. In an incredible display of shooting, Simpson blasted the top of Bill McCarty's head off, put a bullet through the heart of Fred McCarty, Bill's son, and killed Tom McCarty's mount. Still, this last McCarty managed to get away. He later sent a messenger to inform Simpson he was going to come back to kill him.

Simpson's response was laconic. McCarty's messenger left Delta bearing a small piece of cardboard, about the size of a playing card, with 10 bullet holes in it. The card read, "Made at 225 feet." Tom McCarty never returned to Delta to settle the score.

MCCONAGHY, Robert (1810-1840): Mass murderer

Robert McConaghy's 1840 crime—the murder of his wife, his mother-in-law and four of her other children in a mindless frenzy—won enormous notoriety thanks to a best-selling publication that focused on the bizarre events at his execution.

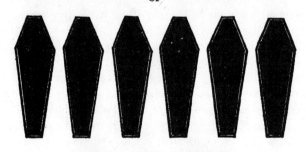

TRIAL, CONFESSION AND EXECUTION

OF

ROBERT McCONAGHY,

FOR THE

Murder

OF

SIX

OF

HIS RELATIVES

IN BROAD DAY-LIGHT.

McConaghy was executed a few weeks since, and did not make his Confession until he was once suspended; the rope broke and let him down, after which he made a full Confession.

Price 12½ cents.

McConaghy went on his murder spree on May 30, 1840. Throughout his trial, he refused to admit his guilt, but he was nonetheless convicted and sentenced to hang. On November 6, 1840 McConaghy mounted the gallows at Huntington, Pa. The large crowd in attendance gasped loudly when the rope broke. McConaghy, in a state of shock, was carried up the scaffold again. The ordeal proved too much for him, and he started babbling out the full confession he had refused to make earlier. This time the rope held. The drama of McConaghy's execution inspired a pamphlet about his case.

Although priced at a not-inexpensive 12½¢ a copy, it was one of the biggest-selling pamphlets of the decade.

MCDONALD, Michael Cassius "Mike" (1832-1907): Gambler and fixer

Chicago gambling, confidence swindling, vice and the political fixing during the 30 years after the fire of 1871 starred Michael Cassius McDonald.

A professional gambler while still in his early teens, Mike became the King of the Bounty Jumpers during the Civil War, heading an organized gang of crooks who reaped a fortune collecting bounties for enlisting in the Union Army and promptly deserting to repeat the process elsewhere. McDonald masterminded the movements of his men, keeping track of their "enlistments" on a large war map. He came out of the war with a stake large enough to open a gambling house at 89 Dearborn Street.

In 1869 McDonald swindled $30,000 out of an assistant cashier who, in turn, was embezzling money from the large company he worked for. McDonald was arrested for the swindle but beat the rap by hiring scores of witnesses to testify that his gambling place ran honest games and that his victim had begged him, with tears in his eyes, to be allowed to play. However, the trial drained McDonald's finances, and he was unable to keep up protection payments to the police, which resulted in raids on his establishment several times a week. The experience left him with a hatred for policemen, which continued into his later life when he was the greatest fixer in the city and even named police chiefs. Years after, a patrolman came to him and said: "We'd like to put you down for two dollars, Mike. We're burying a policeman."

"Fine!" Mike replied. "Here's ten dollars. Bury five of 'em!"

Like all other gambling and vice operators, McDonald was wiped out by the Chicago Fire, but because he was one of the quickest to get back in business, he was able to "build a poke" before the police became organized enough to collect protection payments again. By 1873 he and two partners had opened a four-story resort in a building that would later become the home of the Hamilton Club. The first floor was a top-notch saloon; the second floor housed McDonald's office and a large set of gambling rooms. The third and fourth floors were run by his wife Mary, who rented furnished flats to select gamblers and bunco men, such as Kid Miller, Snapper Johnny Malloy,

Dutchy Lehman, Jew Myers, Charley Gondorf, Boss Ruse and Black-Eyed Johnny. Another of his cronies, Hungry Joe Lewis, took Oscar Wilde for several thousand dollars during the English writer's tour of the United States in 1882. The same year two others, Johnny Norton and Red Jimmy Fitzgerald, swindled diplomat Charles Francis Adams out of $7,000.

In this famous resort, called The Store, McDonald uttered a number of phrases that were to become part of the American vernacular. When a partner objected that his plans were too lavish and that they would never attract enough customers, McDonald replied, "There's a sucker born every minute." While later writers would attribute the remark to P.T. Barnum, it was McDonald who coined it as well as another equally famous saying: "Never give a sucker an even break."

By 1880 McDonald's stature had grown to the extent that he controlled all vice operations except for prostitution, a business activity he found repulsive. "A crook has to be decent to work with Mike," a friend of his once explained. And working with Mike meant making good money. McDonald moved into politics, refining the political fix to a fine art. A criminal wishing to operate freely had to pay Mike as much as 60 percent of his take, which was then divided among the police, various city officials and judges and McDonald's own syndicate. McDonald became close friends with such Chicago mayors as Harvey Colvin and Carter Harrison. During the terms of these two mayors, Mike's minions were allowed to run wild. In 1882, during one of the mayoral reigns of Carter Harrison, McDonald flexed enough muscle to have Superintendent of Police Simon O'Donnell, who was both honest and efficient, reduced in rank to captain and replaced by his own man, William J. McGarigle. McGarigle later had to skip town following the disclosure of a cleaning and painting swindle of a governmental building that netted McDonald's company $67,000. While some of the governmental grafters went to prison, McDonald remained untouched.

McDonald continued to control the Chicago rackets until the turn of the century, pulling in his horns whenever a reform administration came in and then swinging back into action when the heat was off. After accumulating several million dollars, he started to lose interest in his business because of marital problems. In the mid-1880s his wife ran off with a minstrel singer. McDonald finally tracked her down in San Francisco and brought her home, but in 1889 she took off again, this time with a Catholic priest who used to say mass at a private altar in the McDonald mansion. The lovers went to Paris, where they lived for six years until the priest entered a monastery and McDonald's wife returned to Chicago to operate a boarding-house. Mike meanwhile had obtained a divorce and married Dora Feldman, four decades his junior. In the ninth year of this second marriage, Dora shot and killed a young artist named Webster Guerin, who, it developed, had been her secret lover during almost all of the marriage. The now-retired political fixer never recovered from the shock of the disclosure and his wife's comments to the press that she had always disliked him; he died on August 9, 1907. Nevertheless, McDonald had left his second wife a large portion of his estate and had set up a special defense fund of $40,000 for her murder trial. Chicago being Chicago, Dora McDonald was acquitted in 1908.

See also: *Bounty Jumping, Carter Harrison.*

MCGLUE, Luke: Fictitious thief

During the boom years of Dodge City, Kan., from about 1877 to 1887, the nefarious Luke McGlue committed more crimes in the "wickedest little city in America" than anyone else. If a man had his hotel room looted, it was most likely the work of Luke McGlue. If a man's luggage disappeared, it was that damnable Luke McGlue again. If a man's trousers disappeared while he was visiting a harlot in a crib, she would tell him—with a straight face—it was the work of Luke McGlue. Luke McGlue specialized in robbing greenhorns or constantly playing practical jokes on them, and they would leave town happy to have seen the last of him. Well, not literally, since they had never seen Luke McGlue. Nor could they have. Luke McGlue didn't exist. He was invented by the denizens of Dodge City as an explanation for the many practical jokes and petty thefts greenhorns were subjected to. Even Wyatt Earp assured such victims he was on the lookout for Luke McGlue and would deal with him severely when he caught him.

MCGUIRK'S Suicide Hall: New York underworld dive

Few dives on New York's Bowery ever descended to the depths of McGuirk's Suicide Hall, the favorite haunt of the lowest female criminals and prostitutes around the turn of the century.

Men were permitted in Suicide Hall, and if they were fortunate enough not to be drugged and robbed, they could very likely find sexual companionship for as little as a nickel. Gangsters low on their finances, however, were always welcomed as patrons and fawned over by women desperate to obtain a sponsor or protector. The place teemed with "lush workers" (women who robbed drunks), pickpockets, purse snatchers, burglars, panhandlers, beggars, drug addicts and female thieves of all descriptions.

The only real competition Suicide Hall faced for the patronage of these dregs of female humanity was Mother Woods' on Water Street. The two establishments often engaged in price wars and sought additional business by permitting almost any unwholesome activity on their premises. Suicide Hall won out, allowing McGuirk to make his famous boast that more women had killed themselves in his place than in any other house in the world. After seven years of existence, the establishment passed from the scene in 1902, a victim of constant police raids and better economic conditions, which reduced female criminality and generally destroyed the low Bowery dives. The Suicide Hall building later housed the Hadley Rescue Mission.

MCGURN, Machine Gun Jack (1904-1936): Hit man

Machine Gun Jack McGurn was the kind of subject Hollywood embraced for its gangster movies of the 1930s. James De Mora was 19 when his father was murdered in Chicago's Little Italy. Legend has it that the son soaked his hands in his father's blood and vowed vengeance. He started practicing to take his revenge by shooting birds off telephone wires with a Daisy repeating rifle.

Meanwhile, he tried boxing, becoming a reasonably good welterweight, under the name of Jack McGurn. When it was apparent he didn't have the stuff of a top-notch fighter, McGurn's manager dropped him, and he went back to hunting his father's killers, whose identities were, in fact, hardly a dark secret. McGurn's father had been an alcohol cooker for the vicious Genna gang, which controlled illegal booze production in Little Italy. When he made the mistake of supplying alcohol to the competition, he was killed. Young McGurn could hardly expect to learn which Genna gunmen had done the job, so he decided to kill any and all Genna men. The best way to do that was to join the Capone outfit, which sooner or later would have to make war on the Gennas.

McGurn became one of Capone's most reliable hit men, exceedingly proficient with a machine gun, hence he was called Machine Gun McGurn. The police supposedly attributed 28 killings to McGurn, including about six of the Genna gang. In the hand of each of these, McGurn had placed a nickel to show his contempt for the dead men, lousy nickel-and-dimers. His devotion to killing for Capone knew no limits. He is said to have personally held the heads of Albert Anselmi, John Scalise and Hop Toad Guinta as Al Capone battered their brains out with an Indian club at a famous party thrown in their honor. He also is generally believed to have been one of the machine gunners and certainly one of the chief planners of the St. Valentine Day's Massacre. But charges against him had to be dropped when Louise Rolfe, a showgirl, insisted he had been with her at the time of the massacre, thus winning her fame as the Blonde Alibi. Later, the police were able to prove the story was false and charged McGurn with perjury, but he beat that rap by marrying Louise Rolfe, who, as his wife, could not be forced to testify against him.

McGurn was a great nightclub crawler. With the shoulders of his suit heavily padded and his hair pomaded, he did his best to look like Rudolph Valentino. He so prospered in his criminal endeavors that he soon owned a number of Loop nightclubs. One of his entertainers was a young comer named Joe E. Lewis, who eventually deserted him to work in a rival club. A week later, Lewis was waylaid by three of McGurn's men. Two of them pistol-whipped him while the third worked him over with a knife, carving up his face and slashing his throat and tongue. Somehow Lewis survived. He had to learn to talk all over again, and it was 10 years before he once more rose to the top of his profession.

After Al Capone was convicted of income tax evasion, McGurn went into a slow decline. By 1936 things had really gotten tough for him. He was being edged aside by other Capone gang members and his nightclubs had folded because of the Depression. On February 13, the eve of the anniversary of the St. Valentine's Day Massacre, McGurn was in a bowling alley with two other men when three gunmen entered. The trio drew their guns, as did the two men with McGurn. All five turned their weapons on him and opened fire. In his right hand they pressed a nickel, perhaps indicating McGurn's killing was an act of revenge for his earlier slayings of Genna gang members. On the other hand, the fact that the murder occurred on the night before the anniversary of the massacre may mean it was the work of Bugs Moran and remnants of the O'Banion gang. Then again, both touches could have been deliberately staged by the Capone mob to cover their tracks. In any event, neither the police nor the public seemed too concerned about who had been responsible.

See also: *St. Valentine's Day Massacre.*

MCINTYRE, Charles (1858-1874): Lynch victim

Lynched at the age of 16, Charles McIntyre may have been one of the youngest labor union martyrs in the country's history, but he is little remembered, mainly because he didn't live long enough to accomplish much.

A native of Pennsylvania, McIntyre was working in the Nevada mines at 16. He was also making noise about the miners organizing into a union, and for that he earned the enmity of mining interests. On May 20, 1874 McIntyre was in the company of a friend, John Walker, who wounded a man named Sutherland in a gunfight. Although McIntyre had been hardly more than a disinterested spectator, he was placed in the Belmont, Nev. jail along with Walker. Eleven days after their arrest the pair broke jail and hid out in an abandoned mine shaft. They were found two days later, and about midnight of June 2 a mob stormed the jail and hanged McIntyre and Walker in their cell. The hangings, credited to the 301 Vigilante Movement, stand out as flimsy cases even for lynch justice. Walker's victim had not died and, of course, McIntyre had not killed or robbed anyone; in fact, he had done nothing worse than break out of jail, which was seldom regarded as a hanging offense. The miners speculated that McIntyre had brought on the vigilante action because of his organizing talk, but that speculation was done in whispers.

MCKINNEY Touch: Sadistic trademark

A Western term that for the most part became extinct when the frontier tamed down, the McKinney Touch, was named after James McKinney, who won fame from Leadville, Colo. to California's San Joaquin Valley as, for want of a better description, a mad buttocks mutilator.

Born in Illinois in 1861, McKinney is officially credited with killing his first man in Leadville. In a display of gratuitous sadism, he then shot off the nipples of his victim's girl friend.

Moving westward, he introduced the McKinney Touch when he deliberately decorated a cancan dancer's rump with bullet ridges. In California he whittled off a bit of a schoolteacher's ear and knifed two lawmen, the last offense earning him seven years in San Quentin. Within a short time after he got out, McKinney had refined his trademark to the point that folks started calling it the McKinney Touch. On December 13, 1901 McKinney shot and killed a man named Sears. When a lawman hearing the shooting bounded out of an outhouse gun in hand, McKinney sent him scurrying with two shots that grazed his rump. Amazingly, McKinney was held blameless in these shootings: it was ruled he had acted in self-defense when Sears tried to kill him and that he had taken due care not to maim the officer when he came at him without first ascertaining the facts.

That was the last time the McKinney Touch was considered a mere prank. After he killed a man named William Linn and wounded two lawmen, McKinney fled California with a posse hot on his heels. He crossed into Mexico but soon returned to California and killed two prospectors. The law knew the killings were McKinney's work because of where the two had been shot. Finally, on April 18, McKinney was cornered in a Chinese opium den in Bakersfield, Calif. City Marshal Jess Packard and five deputies stormed the den. When the smoke cleared, McKinney, Marshal Packard and Deputy Marshal William Tibbett, the father of Lawrence Tibbett, the future Metropolitan Opera star, lay dead.

MCLOWERY Brothers: Clanton gang members and O.K. Corral gunfight victims

The McLowery, or McLaury, brothers were important members of the Clanton gang, which terrorized parts of Texas, the Arizona Territory and Mexico in the 1870s. Both ended up shot to death in the famed gunfight at Tombstone's O.K. Corral.

The elder brother, Frank, was as mean and vicious as Old Man Clanton and Curly Bill Brocius, taking particular delight in torturing to death Mexican mule pack drivers after the gang robbed them of their silver. Tom McLowery, the tamer of the pair, was never tied to any particular killings, although he joined the Clantons in many cattle-rustling operations.

In the gunfight at the O.K. Corral, the Earps concentrated most of their early firepower on Frank McLowery, since he was considered by far the most dangerous opponent. There has been much dispute over whether or not Tom McLowery was even armed when the shooting started, although somehow he did obtain a gun during the next 30 seconds. It is unclear whether he had a concealed weapon or whether a weapon was passed to him by a comrade. After the fatal shootings the McLowerys and Billy Clanton were laid out in caskets at the undertaker's under a large sign that read, "MURDERED IN THE STREETS OF TOMBSTONE."

See also: *O.K. Corral.*

MCNAMARA Brothers: See *Los Angeles Times* Bombing.

MCNELLY, Leander H. (1844-1877): Texas Ranger

A sickly law officer who often had to direct his men from a wagon bed, Leander McNelly nonetheless was one of the most-fabled and fearless of the Texas Rangers.

A former captain in the Confederate Army during the Civil War, he later served in the Texas State Police. When the Texas Rangers were reorganized in 1874, he won command of the Special Battalion, which was charged with running down rustling rings and international smugglers and assigned whatever unusual missions came up. For this task McNelly recruited an unusually tough band of Rangers, who were willing "to follow him to hell and back if we can make it."

McNelly's assignments were, first, to cool the bitter Sutton-Taylor feud in De Witt County and then, to do battle with the American outlaws infesting the Nueces Strip near the Mexican border. In that area McNelly also faced the Mexican bandit army of Juan Cortina, which had plagued Texas for some 15 years.

In June 1875 Cortina's men stole a large herd of cattle from the King Ranch and headed for the safety of the border. McNelly and his men caught up with them, killed 12 of the rustlers and headed the cattle back north. Later on, determined to break Cortina's hold on the border, McNelly took 36 Rangers across the Rio Grande in an illegal invasion. The Rangers and Cortina's men fought several engagements, including one in which the Rangers routed a band of 300 Cortinastas. McNelly's daring raid was given credit for ending large-scale rustling sorties into Texas by Mexican outlaws.

McNelly then turned his attentions to other outlaws, but tuberculosis compelled him more and more to direct his troops from a wagon bed. In February 1877 he was forced to resign and he died on September 4 of that year.

See also: *Juan Cortina, Sutton-Taylor Feud, Texas Rangers.*

MCPARLAND, James (1844-1919): Undercover detective

Probably no private detective was more hated by the radical labor movement in America than Irish-born James McParland, who gained credit as the man who broke the secret labor society known as the Mollie Maguires.

McParland emigrated to the United States in 1863. After working as a coal company wagon driver, he joined the Pinkerton National Detective Agency in the early 1870s. After distinguishing himself in a number of cases, McParland was assigned to a case that eventually would bring him worldwide notoriety. The Pinkertons were hired by the Philadelphia and Reading Railroad to help crush a secret labor society known as the Mollie Maguires, which was terrorizing the railroad's coal fields. These agitators had taken the name of an earlier Irish land reform group called the Mollie Maguires.

Allan Pinkerton sent McParland into the anthracite-mining region of eastern Pennsylvania with orders that he infiltrate the Irish-Catholic community there. The undercover man gained membership in the fraternal Ancient Order of Hibernians, some of whose lodges in the area were under the control of the Mollies. He gained the confidence of the Mollie leadership and was able to make daily spy reports on their activities, which included sabotage against the coal operators and, occasionally, murder. In all, McParland was responsible for the conviction of more than 60 men, including Mollie chief John "Black Jack" Kehoe and 10 other of the 19 men who were hanged.

The hardest moment for McParland during a series of sensational trials in 1876-77 came when defense attorneys forced him to admit that he knew of planned murders and did nothing to prevent them, although he had ample time to do so. McParland's defense, which at least satisfied the antilabor forces, was that he feared he would have been assassinated if he had tried to prevent the killings. McParland was lionized in a number of contemporary books and other accounts of his exploits, and in later years the McParland legend was further enhanced by Sir Arthur Conan Doyle, whose melodramatic *The Valley of Fear* was based on the detective's work.

After the destruction of the Mollie Maguires, McParland became the head of the detective agency's Denver office. Following the turn of the century, he starred in his second world-famous labor case, which involved the prosecution of the labor leadership of the Western Federation of Miners and the Industrial Workers of the World. After the 1905 murder of Frank Steunenberg, ex-governor of Idaho, McParland uncovered two informer-assassins, Steve Adams and Harry Orchard, whose statements led to the arrest of union leaders William D. "Big Bill" Haywood, Charles H. Moyers and George A. Pettibone. Later, Adams withdrew a confession he had made involving the trio and insisted his false statements had been Pinkerton-inspired. Clarence Darrow, presenting the defense, made a shambles of the prosecution's case and Orchard's written confession, which included a number of inked corrections, many believed to be in McParland's hand. In the end, all the defendants were acquitted, and only Harry Orchard was condemned to death (his sentence was later commuted to life imprisonment).

Whatever excuses could be made for the loss of the case—and the Pinkertons and McParland had many—the fact remained that the Orchard-Haywood case could hardly be viewed as a great success. So of his two great labor cases McParland won one (the Mollie Maguires) and lost one (Orchard-Haywood). Sixty years later even that score had to be revised. In January 1979 John Kehoe was granted a full state pardon a century after his hanging, a sort of final determination that the Mollie Maguire leader had been subjected to a frame-up by detectives and spies in the employ of the mining company.

See also: *William D. "Big Bill" Haywood, Mollie Maguires, Harry Orchard, Pinkerton's National Detective Agency, Frank Steunenberg.*

MCPHERSON, Aimee Semple (1890-1944): Evangelist and alleged kidnap victim

For a decade before 1926, Sister Aimee Semple McPherson was America's most successful, if controversial, female evangelist, billing herself the World's Most Pulchritudinous Evangelist, until a bizarre "kidnapping" started her career in decline.

Born near Ingersoll, Ontario, Sister Aimee married a Pentecostal evangelist, Robert Semple, with whom she served as a missionary in China. When he died, she returned to the United States and remarried. She left her second husband, Harold McPherson, in favor of a life of preaching that took her all over the United States, Canada, England and Australia. When she finally settled in Los Angeles, she was without funds but had a large, devoted following, which she organized into a religious movement called the International Church of the Four-Square Gospel. The church appealed especially to transplanted Midwesterners and Southerners who had difficulties coping with California life.

Raising $1.5 million from her devout followers, Sister Aimee built the huge Angelus Temple, where 5,000 of the fervent could attend her meetings, which featured faith healing, adult baptism by immersion, an aura of hope and Cecil B. DeMille-style spectacle. Sister Aimee would appear in a white silk gown, her hair adorned with flowers and colored lights dancing on her figure. A 50-piece band played patriotic songs and rousing religious music. Sister Aimee's lectures were broadcast live from the group's own radio station in the church. The sheer size of the operation required a weekly payroll of $7,000.

As well known as Sister Aimee was, she became even more famous in the spring of 1926, when she went to a lonely section of beach near Venice, Calif. and disappeared after being seen entering the water. Her mother, active in the temple, summoned the faithful and bade them to pray for her. "We know," she said, "she is with Jesus." Besides praying, the faithful kicked in $25,000 as a reward for anyone helping Sister Aimee to return. About 100 of her devoted followers hurled themselves into the waters where Sister Aimee had disappeared. One drowned and another died of exposure. A young girl became so distraught at the loss of her spiritual mentor that she committed suicide. A plane scattered lilies over Sister Aimee's watery departure spot.

Then, 32 days after her disappearance, Sister Aimee limped out of the desert near Douglas, Ariz., the victim of an alleged kidnapping. She said that while she was on the beach, her secretary having returned to a nearby hotel, she was kidnapped by a couple and a second man who said they wanted her to say prayers over a dying baby. Instead, they drugged her and imprisoned her in a hut in Mexico. They told her that if she didn't raise a half-million dollars in ransom, they would sell her to a Mexican white slaver. One of the men burned her with cigars when she would not answer all his questions. On June 22 the trio had gotten careless in their vigil and Sister Aimee was able to slip away, hiking for 13 hours across the desert to Douglas, Ariz.

While several of the faithful gathered outside the hospital, Sister Aimee showed burns on her fingers and assorted bruises and blisters she said she had gotten while tied up and during her long trek to freedom. The story did not sit too well with many, however. Her shoes and clothing didn't seem scuffed enough for such a hike across sun-baked sands, and some thought it odd that after such an ordeal Sister Aimee hadn't even asked for a drink of water.

Los Angeles District Attorney Asa Keyes investigated and was dubious, so dubious that in due course he indicted Sister Aimee and her mother for obstruction of justice because of their story of the "disappearance" and "kidnapping." Keyes produced evidence that while the evangelist's flock was praying for her return, the good Sister was trysting with the married radio operator of her temple, Kenneth G. Ormiston, at various hotels. At her trial Sister Aimee announced, "I am like a lamb led to slaughter," and she blamed her troubles on "the overlords of the underworld." Keyes ignored such comments and called to the stand a parade of hotel maids, house detectives and others who identified Sister Aimee as the woman who accompanied Ormiston on various stopovers while the nation puzzled over her disappearance.

Keyes also had flushed Ormiston out of hiding in Harrisburg, Pa. Previously, he had supposedly mailed an affidavit to Keyes admitting to the hotel trysts but insisting his companion was really "Miss X" whom he would not embarrass by identifying. The district attorney had been unimpressed by the paper since it bore a signature that closely resembled the hand of Sister Aimee. However, Keyes failed to call the radio operator to testify, and midway through the trial he suddenly moved for an acquittal. Keyes never explained why, but it is worth noting that in later years the district attorney himself went to prison for taking bribes in a number of strong cases that had been dropped or plea-bargained.

Officially cleared, Sister Aimee returned to her spiritual work, but the ardor had gone out of many of the faithful. She took to touring Europe and the Orient but never fully recaptured a style one historian described as fusing "economies and ecstasy, showmanship and salvation, carnival and contrition." Sister Aimee later had a short marriage with a radio man named Dave Hutton and then dropped from public view. In September 1944 she died in Oakland, Calif., apparently from an overdose of sleeping pills.

MACKLE, Barbara Jane: See Gary Steven Krist.

MAD Bomber: See George Peter Metesky.

MADDEN, Owney "The Killer" (1892-1964): Bootlegger and murderer

The transformation of Owney "the Killer" Madden from a vicious young thug, who was called "that little banty rooster out of hell," into a sleek, dapper sophisticate of crime was truly remarkable. During the early 1900s Madden was known as a heartless, mindless murderer. He killed his first victim at the age of 17 and had done in five by the time he reached 23. During the 1920s and 1930s he was one of the top bootleggers and gang leaders in New York, a debonair character who was still capable of murder—but with a certain flair.

Owney came to New York from his native Liverpool, England when he was 11 and soon enrolled in one of the major gangs of the day, the Gophers. He ran up a total of 44 arrests in his youthful escapades without ever doing any time in prison. In the process he became accomplished with a slung shot, a blackjack, brass knuckles and his favorite weapon, a piece of lead pipe wrapped in a newspaper. Because of his callousness and daring, Madden quickly gained the nickname the Killer and advanced to the leadership of the gang. In that exalted position he raked in an estimated $200 a day for the robberies, labor beatings, killings and intergang attacks he planned. By the time he was 20, he was receiving extortion money from scores of merchants eager to pay "bomb insurance" to avoid having their storefronts blown out.

The police charged but couldn't prove that Madden had killed his first man, an Italian, for no other reason but to celebrate his rise to power in the Gophers. Some of his homicides, on the other hand, resulted from affairs of the heart. When he learned in 1910 that an innocuous clerk named William Henshaw had asked one of his girls for a date, Madden followed him onto a trolley car at Ninth Avenue and West 16th Street and shot him in front of a dozen other passengers. Before departing the trolley, he paused to toll the bell for his victim. Henshaw lived long enough to identify Madden, who was captured after a chase across several roof tops in Hell's Kitchen. He was not convicted of the murder, however, since all the witnesses thought it wise to vanish.

In November 1912 a youthful Owney the Killer almost had his career cut short during a confrontation in a dance hall with 11 gunmen from the rival Hudson Dusters. When he tried to outdraw and outshoot the bunch of them, he ended up with five bullets in his body. Rushed to the hospital, Madden refused to tell the police who had shot him. "It's nobody's business but mine," he said.

By the time he got out of the hospital, his men had knocked off six of his assailants. However, Owney the Killer had other pressing problems to deal with. Little Patsy Doyle had moved to take over the Gophers, spreading the false word that Owney was crippled for life. Little Patsy was motivated by more than blind ambition; the Killer had appropriated his woman, Freda Horner, and made Patsy a laughing stock. Little Patsy played tough, shooting up a number of Madden loyalists. In due course, Owney ended Little Patsy's bid for power and his entire insurrection by filling him with bullets. For this offense Madden was imprisoned in Sing Sing from 1915 to 1923.

By the time Owney the Killer got out of prison, he had undergone a sort of metamorphosis. He had attained a measure of finesse and respectability. Owney went into rumrunning and into the coal and laundry rackets, proving such a dependable crook that Tammany's Jimmy Hines stood behind him. Owney the Killer moved in the top criminal circles with such ascending powers of the 1920s as Lucky Luciano, Dutch Schultz, Frank Costello, Waxey Gordon, Longy Zwillman, Louis Lepke and the Bug and Meyer team of Bugsy Siegel and Meyer Lansky. Despite his rise in status, Madden had not lost his instinct for violence. When Mad Dog Coll was running around Manhattan kidnapping and murdering top criminals, it was Owney who kept him talking on the telephone one day until gunmen arrived to cut off the Mad Dog's connection.

In the 1930s Madden moved into the world of sports, promoting the dim-witted Primo Carnera into the heavyweight boxing championship. Carnera ended up stone broke, but Madden was said to have made a million, taking a 100 percent cut of the Italian fighter's earnings.

Owney was picked up in 1932 for a parole violation, but after a short stay in prison he was back on the town. The police kept the heat on him with all sorts of minor arrests until in the mid-1930s he decided to retire. If 20 years earlier a veteran cop had been asked what young punk would most assuredly end up on a slab in the morgue, more than likely he would have picked Owney the Killer. Instead, Madden retired to the good life in Hot Springs, Ark., a famous underworld "cooling-off" spot where his protection by the local law was to become legendary. The local cops performed heroic work keeping him from being annoyed by pesky journalists. If they didn't, Owney warned them, he would have them transferred and broken. By the time he died in 1964, Owney the Killer had almost achieved the stature of a Southern gentleman.

See also: *Vincent "Mad Dog" Coll.*

MADSEN, Chris (1851-1944): Lawman

A Dane who led a truly adventurous life, Deputy Marshal Chris Madsen became one of the West's legendary peace officers as one of the Oklahoma Territory's famed Three Guardsmen, along with Heck Thomas and Bill Tilghman.

Madsen was a far more honest and productive lawman than the likes of Wild Bill Hickok or Wyatt Earp. Born in Denmark in 1851, red-haired, cherubic-faced Madsen served in the Danish Army, fought with the forces of Italian rebel Garibaldi and for the French Foreign Legion before the lure of gold brought him to America in the 1870s. He joined the 5th Cavalry and took part in a number of Indian campaigns before pinning on a nickel-plated deputy's star in the Oklahoma Territory.

As a law officer in what was called the worst badlands in America, Madsen became the scourge of rustlers, whiskey peddlers, thieves, train robbers and murderers. Either by himself or working with others, he played a key role in rounding up members of the Dalton gang, killers Kid Lewis and Foster Crawford and train robber Henry Silva. In the campaign against the Doolin gang, the three Guardsmen were each assigned a portion of Bill Doolin's known territory and given the task of cleaning it up. Madsen got much of the credit for running down and killing two of Doolin's worst toughs, Tulsa Jack Blake and Red Buck Waightman.

In 1898 Madsen resigned his post to join Teddy Roosevelt's Rough Riders. Although he contracted yellow fever in Cuba, he was able to resume his law enforcement career after the war until 1907, when Oklahoma became a state. Afterward, he settled in Guthrie, Okla., and lived to the rip old age of 92. He died on January 9, 1944 as the result of a fall, a far more peaceful end than many of his friends and enemies experienced.

See also: *Henry Andrew "Heck" Thomas, Three Guardsmen, Bill Tilghman.*

MAFIA

Referred to by several names, the Mafia first became known to American officials in New Orleans during the 1880s, when some mafiosi murdered the city's chief of police. The society had been founded in Italy some six centuries earlier to fight the oppression of the French Angevins. Its slogan then was *Morte alla Francia Italia anela!* ("Death to the French is Italy's cry!) The word "Mafia" was taken from the first letters of each word of the slogan. The Mafia turned to crime in the 19th century, sometimes victimizing wealthy landowners but more often hiring out to them as oppressors of the peasants. The society spread to the rest of Italy and, to a lesser extent, to other European countries. Its arrival in the United States came in two great waves, the first during the last two decades of the 19th century and the other in the 1920s, after Benito Mussolini declared war on the Mafia and forced hundreds of criminals to flee the country.

The first known Mafia victim in America was a Neapolitan named Vincenzo Ottumvo, who was killed in New Orleans while playing cards on January 24, 1889. He was the victim of Sicilian gangsters in what was the opening of a bloody war between Neapolitans and Sicilians for control of the New Orleans waterfront. When the police—or at least some of the top brass—seemed to be favoring the Neapolitan element, the city's police chief, David Hennessey, was ambushed and shotgunned to death in 1890. A grand jury considered the evidence in the case and found that "the existence of a secret organization known as the Mafia has been established beyond doubt."

Nineteen Sicilians were indicted for conspiring to murder Hennessey. However, a Mafia reign of terror silenced most of the 60 witnesses scheduled to testify at the trial, with the result that none of the accused was found guilty. After the trial the defendants were returned to their cells awaiting final disposition of their cases.

Public outrage, fueled by anti-Italian feelings in general, mounted to fever pitch. Headed by 60 of New Orleans' most prominent citizens, mass protests were held, and finally a mob of several thousand marched on the parish prison and killed 11 of the defendants. Newspapers headlined the "Destruction of the Mafia," a somewhat overly optimistic statement. Part of the Mafia simply went underground for a time while other important elements moved on to different cities, establishing "beachheads" in a number of Southern cities and as far north as St. Louis. Still others moved to New York. The Mafia was neither destroyed nor contained by the bloody events in New Orleans.

In city after city the police proved incapable of stopping Mafia gangsters, in part from pure ignorance, if not indifference, to most matters Italian. A few urban police forces organized Italian squads to oversee the sprouting Little Italy sections, but even these units made only limited headway because of the attitude of the Italian immigrants toward police, whose help they shunned. In the old country the police were ineffective against the Mafia. Could the American police be any better? Thus the Mafia was able to grow.

Many mafiosi became Black Hand extortionists, threatening death to those who would not pay for protection. Others committed various forms of robbery and mayhem—almost always against Italian victims, especially newly arrived immigrants. The son of an immigrant-criminal once explained this propensity:

> Can you imagine my father going uptown to commit a robbery or a mugging? He would have had to take an interpreter with him to read the street signs and say 'stick 'em up' for him. The only time he ever committed a crime outside Mulberry Street was when he went over to the Irish section to steal some milk so my mother could heat it up and put it in my kid brother's ear to stop an earache.

As early as the first decade of the 20th century, the U.S. government began trying to deport Mafia criminals. Lt. Joseph Petrosino of the New York Police Department's Italian Squad did considerable work along these lines until he was murdered by gangsters in Italy in 1909.

In New York City the Manhattan Mafia fought a bloody war in 1916-19 with the Brooklyn Camorra, the main Neapolitan underworld organization. Under the leadership of Don Pelligrino Morano, the camorristi controlled most of the Brooklyn waterfront rackets and extracted protection money from Italian businessmen, including storekeepers and ice and coal dealers. Mafia gangsters ran similar extortion rackets in Manhattan, chiefly in the Greenwich Village and East Harlem areas. Whenever either side made a move into the other's territory, the killing would start.

The leader of the Manhattan Mafia, Nicholas Morello, thought it was foolish for the two sides to carry on their bloody Old World rivalry, and when Morano suggested a peace conference, Morello agreed. It was held in a cafe on Brooklyn's Navy Street. Morello was still suspicious of Morano and thus showed up with just a bodyguard and not his top lieutenants, on the assumption that their absence would frustrate an assassination plot. Although Morano was disappointed when he saw Morello's top guns were missing, he nonetheless had a five-man execution squad cut the pair down after pledging eternal peace.

Morano's strategy backfired. In this case witnesses actually talked. Several camorristi went to the electric chair and Morano was sentenced to life imprisonment. After the gang leader's trial the *Brooklyn Eagle* reported: "Morano was surrounded by a dozen Italians who showered kisses on his face and forehead.

On the way to the jail other Italians braved the guard and kissed Morano's hands, cheeks and forehead."

The war continued, but without Morano's cunning leadership, camorristi were murdered by the dozens. By 1920 many of the gang's surviving members gave up the struggle and even joined various Mafia outfits. In a sense, the 1920s was the heyday of the old Mafia, but already new problems were arising. The aging leaders of the Mafia continued to follow the society's old-fashioned customs. Fundamentally, this meant limiting their activities to exploiting Italians. Young Mafia members saw that the gravy lay in broadening the base of criminal activity and forming alliances with other ethnic gangster groups, mostly with the still potent Irish gangs and the great Jewish gangs of the 1920s.

The last of the big-time "Mustache Petes" were Giuseppe "Joe the Boss" Masseria and Salvatore Maranzano, who sought to eliminate Joe the Boss in order to establish himself as the "boss of bosses" of the Mafia. Maranzano fought a bitter war against Masseria, which he won in 1931, when underlings of Joe the Boss, led by Lucky Luciano, murdered their leader and made peace. The peace lasted only a few months until Luciano, working in cooperation with non-Italian gangsters, mainly Meyer Lansky, successfully directed the liquidation of Maranzano. Luciano and Lansky then brought together various criminal elements—Italian and non-Italian—from around the country and formed the national crime syndicate.

The fall of the last "Mustache Petes" could be regarded as the end of the old Mafia and the establishment of the new one, which reached new levels of wealth as the most dominant force within the national crime syndicate. In the next few decades the Mafia prospered as never before, meeting little opposition on the federal level. For years FBI Director J. Edgar Hoover denied the existence of the Mafia, claiming that it was a mere figment of the imagination of crime writers. In a sense, informer Joe Valachi got Hoover off the hook by referring to the new Mafia as Cosa Nostra, "Our Thing." Hoover readily conceded there was a Cosa Nostra, neglecting to explain why he had failed to note that point all the years he had insisted there was no Mafia.

Today, the Mafia has some 5,000 men, just as it had during the time Hoover was saying it didn't exist, belonging to 24 separate organizations, or "crime families," located in major cities around the country. New York City has five families, which generally function independently of each other and in relative peace, except when the leader of one family attempts to enlarge his territory at another family's expense or even tries to take control of all five families, as the late Carmine Galante did in 1979. As a result of his efforts, Galante was shot dead by hit men in the garden of a Brooklyn restaurant before the last course of his meal.

By the late 1960s a third great wave of mafiosi had begun to arrive from the old country, this one fostered by the crime bosses in America, who had come to realize that a new infusion of toughness was needed to keep the Mafia going. Too many second- and third-generation Italians were proving incapable of serving as soldiers. Crime family head Joseph Bonanno (Joe

Bananas) was particularly irate on two occasions when soldiers begged off assignments because they had promised to spend the evening with their wives. As more and more aliens were imported to staff Mafia operations in the 1970s, police were forced to admit they were losing touch with mob operations.

See also: *Cosa Nostra; Charles "Lucky" Luciano; Mafia, Jr.; Mafia Families; Mafia, New Orleans Mass Execution of; Salvatore Maranzano; Giuseppe "Joe the Boss" Masseria; Morello Family; Mussolini Shuttle; Mustache Petes.*

MAFIA Families

Any discussion of the Mafia in America soon boils down to the question of whether or not there is a "boss of bosses." There does not appear to be, and such discussions often beg the more serious question as to who is the acknowledged boss of each of the various crime families around the country.

In New York City the authorities label the five local families by the names of their long-ago or more recent leaders, even though they may now be dead. A discussion of the current leaderships often entails getting into a morass of partial or inaccurate information and guesswork. Thus, it is generally said that the five crime families in New York are the Genovese (nee Luciano) family, the Gambino (nee Anastasia) family, the Profaci family, the Bonanno family and the Lucchese (nee Gagliano) family.

In other localities there tends to be just one Mafia family in operation and it is easier to identify the boss. In 1978 the FBI's list of crime leaders, subject to attrition through assassination, retirement and death due to old age or other ailments (heart disease is definitely a peril of the profession) included:

Baltimore: Frank Corbi
Binghampton, N.Y.: Anthony Frank Guarnieri
Boston: Raymond Patriarca, also believed to control all of New England
Buffalo: Joseph Angelo Tieri
Chicago: Anthony Accardo (retiring); Joe Aiuppa (in charge)
Cleveland: James Licavoli
Denver: Clarence M. Smaldone
Detroit: Anthony Zerilli
Kansas City: Joseph N. Civillo (in prison); Carlo De Luna and Carlo Civillo (contending)
Las Vegas: Tony Spilotro
Los Angeles: Louis Dragna
Milwaukee: Frank Balistrieri
New Orleans: Carlo Marcello
Niagara Falls, N.Y.: Benjamin Nicoletti
Philadelphia: Angelo Bruno
Pittsburgh: Sebastian La Rocca
Rochester, N.Y.: Sam J. Russotti
Rockford, Ill.: Joseph Zammuto
St. Louis: James Giammanco
San Francisco: Anthony Lima
Syracuse, N.Y.: Joseph Falcone

In addition, Miami and Atlantic City are considered "open cities," with many forces active. In Miami the Genovese and Gambino families are prominent. In Atlantic City the Gambino and Bruno families are active.

MAFIA Gun

The date of the first appearance of the Mafia in this country was not fixed by identification of any specific individuals but rather by the appearance of a typically Italian shotgun, which became known to the New Orleans police as the "Mafia gun." It was first used in 1869 by what the *New Orleans Times* called a group of "notorious Sicilian murderers, counterfeiters and burglars, who, in the last month, have formed a sort of general co-partnership or stock company for the plunder and disturbance of the city." This "co-partnership" consisted of four Italian mafiosi who had been driven out of Palermo by the Sicilian police. They came to New Orleans and established a Mafia branch after a savage war against a number of gangsters from Messina who were trying to organize crime in the delta city.

The war was won by a number of efficient assassinations committed with a unique shotgun, one with the barrels sawed off to about 18 inches and the stock sawed through and hollowed out very near the trigger. The stock was then fitted with hinges, so that the gun resembled a jackknife, and was carried inside a coat hanging on a hook. It had a certain, if messy, fatal effect up to a distance of 30 yards.

As the executions with the weapon continued and the authorities learned more about the Sicilian version of the Mafia, the weapon was christened the Mafia gun. Because a slaying with such a gun was instantly labeled a Mafia job, the organization in time greatly reduced its reliance on the weapon in favor of more American murder techniques.

MAFIA, Jr.: Young Mafia recruits

Following in the wake of the first criminal gangs to appear in America were "junior contingents," youth gangs, such as the Little Dead Rabbits and the Little Forty Thieves, whose members eagerly awaited the opportunity to move up to the "big boys." Oddly, the great gang of today, the Mafia, no longer seems to have this abundant pool of youthful reserves.

As late as the early 1960s, the newspapers still wrote feature stories about a "Mafia, Jr.," comprised of youngsters schooled by the mob to step into the rackets. Indeed, there had been a Mafia youth auxiliary from virtually the beginning of the century. Mafia leaders of the 1930s, such as Lucky Luciano, Frank Costello, Al Capone, and Joe Adonis, had been weaned in the old Five Points Gang. There were always juvenile toughs eager to do gangsters' bidding in the hopes of stepping up. The mob leaders actively searched out such young talent.

A case in point was Harry "Pittsburgh Phil" Strauss. The word got around about him when he was a 16-year-old student at Brooklyn's Jefferson High School in New York City. Jefferson was scheduled to play an important basketball game in the Bronx against James Monroe High School, which had a star player named Hank Greenberg, destined to become one of the top baseball players of all time. Strauss went to the Bronx with the bright idea of perhaps knifing Greenberg so he wouldn't be able to play. Although he wasn't able to pull off the assault,

young Harry became the talk of the Brownsville section of Brooklyn. The story reached Louis Capone, Louis Lepke's right-hand man in Brooklyn, who related it to his boss. Lepke mentioned the story to Albert Anastasia, and everyone got a big laugh out of it. The word came back to Capone to "keep your eye on that kid. We might be able to use him." Strauss eventually became the star killer of Murder, Inc.

For years the New York Mafia could recruit all the eager punks it needed from Bensonhurst, Brownsville and the Bath Beach districts of Brooklyn, drawing most of its new blood, quite naturally, from the Italian population and, by necessity, from the Jewish population as well. By the 1960s all this had changed. Mafia leaders were bewailing the fact that the native-born youths were not good enough to keep the crime families functioning and that the organization was hurting. By 1971 some two-thirds of the 5,000 Mafia members identified in the McClellan Committee reports less than a decade before were in jail, facing trial or dead. The youthful hoods put in charge of Mafia operations were proving totally inept. Crime boss Carlo Gambino complained that most of the young Italian-American criminals seemed primarily interested in moving to the suburbs.

The Mafia was forced to go back to Sicily for new recruits, picking up youths who still believed in the old Mafia traditions and who could and would follow orders. Some 300 young Sicilians were smuggled into New York via South America, while a much larger number came in from Montreal via a pipeline run by the Cotroni gang.

However, if today's Mafia, Jr. speaks more *Scidgie,* the Sicilian dialect, than English, it is as much the fault of the crime elders as it is of the easy life. Contrary to popular belief, nepotism is virtually nonexistent in the Mafia. The dream of virtually every mob parent is that his children will become lawyers, doctors or legitimate businessmen; few will allow their offspring to mix in Mafia matters. There are of course the exceptions, like Bill Bonanno, the son of Joe Bananas, and Tony Zerilli, the son of Detroit boss Joe Zerilli. Far more common, though, was the experienced Carlo Gambino, who set up his sons in a legitimate trucking business. It was accepted in the mob that the elder Gambino would have had their legs broken if they had done anything illegal.

See also: *Cotroni Gang.*

MAFIA, New Orleans Mass Execution Of

While it is difficult to determine with certainty, the first significant appearance of the Mafia in America seems to have been in New Orleans during the late 1800s. Between 1888 and 1890 the New Orleans Mafia achieved so much power that its members were able to terrorize much of the city, committing an estimated 40 murders without serious opposition. During this period Antonio and Carlo Matranga, two top Honored Society members from Palermo, Sicily took control of the Mississippi River docks. Tribute had to be paid to them before a freighter could be unloaded. However, the Matranga operations were challenged by the Provenzano brothers, leaders of another Mafia group.

War broke out between the two groups and killings along the docks became a regular occurrence. The police appeared unable to stop the slaughter until flamboyant Chief of Police David Peter Hennessey personally took charge and launched an investigation. Soon, the Matrangas found themselves pressured everywhere by the police while the Provenzanos were left relatively unbothered, raising some question about the fairness of Hennessey's investigation. The Matrangas sent warnings to the chief to lay off. When that tactic failed, they tried to bribe Hennessey. The police leader rejected the offer, convincing the Matrangas that the Provenzanos had offered him more and that Hennessey was determined to have a piece of the riverfront rackets for himself.

At this stage the Mafia in America had no real understanding of what they could get away with and what they couldn't. Back in Sicily they had killed their enemies, each other and any government official who had dared to interfere. They resolved to do the same to an American police chief if it became necessary.

Ironically, Hennessey's fatal provocation occurred when police conducting a routine murder investigation charged two Provenzano brothers with involvement in the killing of a Matranga gangster whose head had been cut off and stuffed in a fireplace. Seeing a great opportunity to eliminate their hated rivals, the Matrangas hired some of the leading lawyers of the city to aid the prosecution. Then Chief Hennessey interfered. He announced to the press that he had uncovered the existence of a criminal society known as the Mafia in the city and said he planned to introduce his evidence at the Provenzanos' trial. On October 15, 1890 Hennessey left the Central Police Station and started for his home. He was cut down by a shotgun blast a half block from his house. Hennessey managed to get off a few shots at several of his assailants as they fled. When asked who had shot him, he whispered, "Dagoes," collapsed and died.

Hennessey was an enormously popular official despite his flamboyance—or because of it—and his murder outraged the city. A grand jury was convened and announced that "the existence of a secret organization known as the Mafia has been established beyond doubt." Nineteen members of the Mafia were indicted as principals and conspirators in the police chief's murder, but their trial proved to be an affront to any concept of justice. A large number of the 60 potential witnesses were intimidated, threatened or bribed and several members of the jury were later found to have taken bribes as well. Despite overwhelming evidence against at least 11 of the defendants, all but three were acquitted, and the jury could not reach a verdict on these three.

All the defendants were returned to the parish prison to await final disposition of their case and release. The Mafia organized victory parades and celebrations in the Italian section, but there was a cry of public outrage and protest meetings in other parts of the city. Two days after the verdicts, a mob, several thousand strong, headed by 60 leading citizens, marched on the jail. They had a death list composed of the 11 defendants against whom the evidence had been the strongest;

yet the mob was under instructions not to touch those defendants, including the Matranga brothers, against whom the legal case had been weakest. Two of the mafiosi were dragged out to the street and hanged from lamp posts. Seven others were executed by firing squads in the yard of the women's section of the prison, and two others were riddled with bullets as they hid in a doghouse built for the jail's guard dog. The lynch mob contained a large number of outraged blacks, making it perhaps the most unusual lynching ever to take place in the South. While some newspapers denounced the hangings, the citizens of New Orleans were, on the whole, rather proud of their accomplishment and a new song by a popular poet named Fred Bessel became a best-seller. Entitled "Hennessey Avenged!" the song started:

> Chief Hennessey now will lay at rest, his soul will be at ease,
> It would be useless without their lives his spirit to appease,
> They have killed and robbed among themselves, that all of us do know,
> They cannot do it among us, for our power we now do show. . . .

It concluded:

> Great praise is due those gentlemen whom we all do know,
> Who called upon the citizens for them their power to show.
> No more assassins we will have sent from a foreign soil,
> In New Orleans we've proved to all we're honest sons of toil.

One of two men hanged by a New Orleans mob determined to wipe out the Mafia.

In an interview with the *St. Louis Globe Democrat*, Mayor Joseph Shakespeare declared: "I do consider that the act was—however deplorable—a necessity and justifiable. The Italians had taken the law into their own hands and we had to do the same." Resolutions endorsing the lynchers were adopted by the Sugar Exchange, the Cotton Exchange, the Stock Exchange, the Mechanics', Lumbermen's and Dealers' Exchange and the Board of Trade.

Seven mafiosi were executed by citizens firing squads in the yard of the women's section of the New Orleans prison.

For a time the lynchings threatened international complications. Italy recalled its ambassador, severed diplomatic relations with the United States and demanded reparations and punishment for the lynchers. Eventually, the matter was settled when Washington agreed to pay $25,000 to the dead men's relatives in Italy.

Meanwhile, newspapers announced, "The Mafia Exterminated." The report was a bit exaggerated, although it took some two decades before the New Orleans Mafia regained full strength.

MAGRUDER, Lloyd (1823-1863): Murder victim

The motive for the killing of Lloyd Magruder was a common one, greed. But the murder case was to become famed in the literature of psychic happenings, since the crime could be said to have been solved as the result of a dream.

Magruder was a mule train operator who traveled the Montana-Idaho gold camps in the early 1860s. His closest friend was Hill Beachy, a lifelong acquaintance who ran a hotel, the Luna House, in Lewiston, Idaho Territory. In October 1863 Magruder set out back through the Bitterroot Mountains to pick up a new load of gold. His party consisted of five muleteers, including a man named Bill Page; three guards, David Howard, Chris Lowery and James Romaine; and two prospectors. As the party crawled into their sleeping bags one night, the three guards killed Magruder, the two prospectors and four of the teamsters—all except Bill Page. Page was not part of the murder plot, but the three killers decided they needed someone to lead them through the snow-driven passes.

Bad weather forced them, against their plan, to come into Lewiston. There, they ran into Hill Beachy, who looked at them with amazement. Several nights earlier, Beachy had had a horrifying dream that some men had killed Magruder out on the trail. The men who had just come into town looked like the killers in the dream. Of course, Beachy felt silly; he had no proof that Magruder was even dead and could hardly go to the law with a demand that the men be held. So, he watched them leave Lewiston.

A few days later, someone found a few of Magruder's pack animals shot to death. They also discovered Magruder's six-gun and some other personal effects. Beachy was now convinced the men he'd seen were Magruder's killers, since they had ridden into town from the same direction Magruder would have been traveling. Even if they had not seen Magruder, they should have at least noticed the dead pack animals. Getting himself deputized, Beachy swore out warrants for the arrest of the four men and tracked them through Washington Territory, Oregon and into California, where he finally caught up with them and brought them back to Idaho. He coaxed Page into testifying against the other three. Page was given his freedom, but on March 4, 1864 the rest were hanged in a ravine outside Lewiston before a crowd of 10,000, most of whom wanted to see the outcome of the "dream murder."

Much was made of the psychic import of Hill Beachy's dream. Yet the area around where the killings had occurred was violent country, rife with murders; e.g., one band of holdup men committed over 100 murders there in less than a year. Given those grim circumstances, nightmares like Hill Beachy's must have been common enough occurrences.

MAHANEY, Jack (1844-?): Thief and great escape artist

One of the most colorful and famous American criminals in the 19th Century, Jack Mahaney was called the American Jack Sheppard because of his constant and daring escapes from captivity. Twice he was locked up in Sing Sing and twice he escaped. He also escaped from New York City's Tombs Prison on two occasions and broke out of several other Eastern prisons. Several times he leaped from speeding trains and somehow avoided what seemed certain death without even suffering serious injury. His numerous exploits made him one of the regulars to grace the illustrated covers of the *National Police Gazette*.

Born to a wealthy family in New York in 1844, he was sent to boarding school at the age of 10, where he was an "undisciplined terror" despite numerous floggings. Jack ran away from the boarding school and joined up with a gang of notorious young dock rats. Caught by the police, he was sent to the House of Refuge and promptly made his first escape from incarceration, taking a dozen youths with him.

Eventually, Mahaney came in contact with Italian Dave, an infamous Five Points Fagin who gave him a liberal education in crime. In a rickety tenement on Paradise Square, Italian Dave ran his own boarding school for some 40 youths, instructing them in the art of sneak thievery. The boys, aged nine to 15, learned how to pick pockets with the aid of fully dressed dummies. Italian Dave quickly came to regard young Mahaney as his prime pupil and allowed him privileges extended to no other youth. Mahaney was permitted to accompany Italian Dave on his more important jobs. On other occasions they would walk the streets together and young Jack was given the opportunity to pick out a logical mugging victim. If the master approved, they would fall on the unfortunate pedestrian, rob him and adjourn back to Paradise Square.

Young Jack soon tired of working with Italian Dave because of the latter's unwillingness to share the loot, and he severed connections with the Fagin. Italian Dave was supposedly shattered by the loss of his protege and tried to win Mahaney back by offering him 10 percent of all future earnings, a truly magnanimous gesture, at least by Dave's standards. However, Jack Mahaney was ready for bigger and better things, first organizing his own gang of butcher cart thieves and then becoming an accomplished burglar and all-around crook. It was in this period that he achieved his fame as a great escaper, becoming a hero to the urchins of the New York slums. In later years, Mahaney joined a group of confidence men and appears to have adopted a number of aliases, so that his subsequent exploits are shrouded in mystery.

See also: *Italian Dave Gang.*

MAIMING

One of the most willful and vicious crimes, maiming has a long history in America. The early Irish gangs of the 1820s were notorious for not only robbing Englishmen but cutting off their ears or noses as well. If the gang members were in a more bestial mood, they might blind the victim or cut out his tongue. Eye gouging became an art form in the underworld and many criminals carried special devices to pluck out eyes with studied efficiency. The Whyos, a New York gang of the late 19th century, hired out for maiming jobs as well as murder. For a trifling $15 a client could arrange to have an enemy's "ear chawed off," certainly an economic alternative to the staggering $100 fee for "doing the big job," murder.

Black Hand extortionists in big-city Italian communities seldom killed the first time a blackmail victim refused to pay. Instead, they would chop off one of the victim's fingers or the finger of a relative of his. Organized crime long used maiming as a "convincer." In his youth, Tony Accardo, a Chicago crime boss, was nicknamed Joe Batters for his proficiency with a baseball bat, one of the favorite arguments used during the Prohibition era to sell mob beer and liquor. The Green Ones, the Mafia branch in Kansas City during Prohibition, were dedicated bat maimers, even working over victims with clubs after they had been shot dead.

Entertainer Joe E. Lewis was the victim of an underworld maiming when he switched from one Prohibition nightclub to another. The offended owner of the club he left, Machine Gun Jack McGurn, demanded he return; when he refused, three of McGurn's men burst into Lewis' hotel room and pistol-whipped him. One of them drove a knife into his jaw and then forced it upward along his face to his ear. Lewis was stabbed a dozen times, his throat and tongue severely gashed. For many months the comedian could barely speak at all and the pummeling administered to his head left him unable to recognize words. Through an incredibly determined effort Lewis learned how to talk and sing again, although it took him 10 years to regain his top form.

Labor columnist Victor Riesel was blinded with acid in 1956 on the orders of gangster Johnny Dio, who at the time was seeking to curry favor with Teamster leader Jimmy Hoffa. The acid thrower was identified as Abraham Telvi, but he never got a chance to admit anything. He was found lying on a street in New York City's Lower East Side with a bullet hole in the back of his skull.

Just as some gangsters become accomplished hit men, others become specialists at delivering beatings that leave the victim maimed but still alive. There have even been cases of such underworld maimers losing their fee because the victim inadvertently died; a maimed victim is often considered a better advertisement for cooperation with the mob than is a mere corpse.

In New York state anyone who permanently injures, disables or disfigures another is subject to imprisonment for up to 15 years. Maiming oneself to escape performing a legal duty, such as military service, or to escape or protest odious prison work assignments is also a felony. Often with the passage of time, the victim may recover from his disability or disfigurement, in which case the offender cannot be convicted of maiming but rather of a lesser charge of assault.

MAISON Coquet: "Legal" bordello

Around 1800 the Maison Coquet, a lavish gambling den and brothel, opened on Royal Street in the center of New Orleans, advertising itself on street corner placards as operating with "the express permission of the Honorable Civil Governor of the city." In point of fact, the so-called legal status of the establishment was accomplished more by daring than decree. At the time, New Orleans was in the process of being transferred from Spanish to French rule, creating a power vacuum. The Spanish owned but no longer reigned, and the French were doubtful of their status. It may well be that bribes were paid to someone, but in any case, the resort opened and operated with impunity.

When the American flag was raised over New Orleans in December 1803 following the Louisiana Purchase, the Maison Coquet was an established reality, as were a number of other fancy brothels. By their simple, though dubious, assertion of official recognition, the Maison Coquet and its imitators established a quasi-legal existence that gave New Orleans the nearest thing to legalized prostitution anywhere in America. So firmly rooted was this tradition that it did not disappear until World War I.

See also: *Prostitution.*

MAJCZEK, Joseph (1908-   ): Accused cop killer

On December 9, 1932 two men holding up a small grocery store in Chicago shot and killed a police officer named William Lundy. In due course, two men, Joe Majczek and Theodore Marcinkiewicz, were convicted of the crime and sentenced to life imprisonment. They would have stayed in jail had it not been for Joe's mother, Tillie. She scrubbed floors to raise money to fight for her son's release. When she had saved $5,000, she appeared at the *Chicago Times* to place an ad reading, "Five thousand dollars reward for killers of Officer Lundy on December 9, 1932. Call Gro-1758, 12-7 p.m." Classified tipped off the city desk that Tillie might be worth interviewing and the newspaper sent a reporter to see her. The story led to a full-scale investigation that finally established Joe's innocence and showed he had been the victim of an official frame-up. The police had gotten the woman owner of the grocery to identify Majczek and Marcinkiewicz by threatening to arrest her for selling liquor. She later admitted she had no idea what the two robbers looked like. The police, it developed, were under pressure at the time to solve murders because the Chicago World's Fair was to open the following year and a poor police record might discourage visitors. Naturally, if any case should be solved it was that of a cop killing. Finally, after 12 years behind bars, Joe Majczek was freed and awarded the sum of $24,000 for the miscarriage of justice —$2,000 for each year in prison. Ted Marcinkiewicz was not released until 1950 and he never got a penny. The Majczek story was used as the basis for the movie *Call Northside 777*.

MALCOLM X (1925-1965): Murder victim

The murder of Malcolm X in New York City on February 21, 1965 remains steeped in controversy, although three men were convicted of the killing and sent to prison for life. Within the black community there remains a conviction that the police investigation was superficial, that one or more of the men charged were not the right men and that the crime itself may not have been the work of the Black Muslims or not of that group alone.

Malcolm X had risen to become the second most powerful figure in the Nation of Islam, at the time the official name for the Black Muslim separatist movement. He had been converted to the Black Muslims 15 years earlier while serving a prison term for burglary. A glib and powerful speaker, Malcolm X clearly represented a threat to the leader of the movement, Elijah Muhammad, and to his presumptive successor and son-in-law, Raymond Sharrief.

In 1964 Malcolm split away and formed his own group, the Organization of Afro-American Unity, after being suspended from his post by Elijah Muhammad. Tension built up between the two groups, and a week before his assassination Malcolm X' home was bombed. The next Sunday, February 21, he arrived at a mosque in Harlem to deliver a speech. As he stepped before the audience of 400, a disturbance broke out near the front rows. One man yelled to another, "Get your hands off my pockets—Don't be messin' with my pockets!"

As four of at least six bodyguards moved forward, Malcolm X said, "Now, brothers, be cool." At that moment another disturbance erupted further back in the audience. A smoke bomb was set off, and at that instant a black man with a sawed-off shotgun charged toward the stage and blasted Malcolm X in the chest. Two other blacks rushed forward with handguns and fired several bullets into the black leader's prone body.

For a moment the audience and most of Malcolm X' bodyguards froze and the killers raced off. One of the assailants, however, was shot in the thigh by a bodyguard. As he dropped at the front stairway exit to the ballroom, members of the audience surrounded him and started beating him until he was rescued by police officers.

Immediately after the assassination, the police, the media and Malcolm X' supporters believed the killing was the work of the Black Muslims, and a Muslim mosque was burned in retaliation. However, the assailant trapped at the scene, 22-year-old Talmadge Hayer, married and the father of two children, could not be identified as a Black Muslim. Two other men arrested later by the police and tried with Hayer were Black Muslims, but both denied any involvement. Hayer admitted his guilt and said he had three accomplices, whom he refused to name, but declared neither of the other two defendants, Norman 3X Butler, 27, and Thomas 15X Johnson, 30, were part of the plot.

After a while, most blacks agreed that Butler and Johnson were the wrong men, since both were well-known Black Muslims and, as such, would have had difficulty penetrating the security at the mosque. In addition, Norman 3X Butler had been treated at Jacobi Hospital in the Bronx on the morning of the assassination for thrombophlebitis; he had had his right leg bandaged and had been given medication. Some observers who claim no real investigation was made find the idea of a physically impaired assassin being used in the plot unbelievable. Oddly, several of those present, including three of Malcolm X' lieutenants and bodyguards, vanished.

MALEDON, Ann (1877-1895): Murder victim

Annie Maledon was an 18-year-old hangman's daughter who was killed in a lover's quarrel that provided Hollywood filmmakers with the basis for an endless variety of dramatic situations.

Annie's father was George Maledon, the fearsome executioner for Hanging Judge Parker, who presided over the federal court in Fort Smith, Ark. and later administered justice in the rough-and-tumble Indian Territory. Annie died with a bullet in her spine, the end result of an ill-fated love affair with a married adventurer named Frank Carver. There was an argument, a desperate struggle and finally a gun went off. Judge

Parker was incensed at the killing and forthwith sentenced Carver to hang. A grim George Maledon started oiling up his rope and thousands prepared to attend the festivities, which were sure to provide some moments of high drama. At the last minute, however, the execution was canceled. Carver's death sentence was thrown out on appeal as being excessive for what did not appear to be premeditated murder.

Judge Parker was outraged by the reduction of Carver's sentence to a prison term. He had looked forward to seeing Carver swing for killing little Annie, who had played with the two Parker boys in her childhood. Maledon too was enraged. And the community had lost a wonderful Sunday afternoon's entertainment and could only speculate whether Maledon would have done his usually brilliant job of dispatching a victim with merciful quickness, or whether in this one case the hangman's handiwork would have resulted in what was referred to as the long twitch.

See also: *George Maledon.*

MALEDON, George (1834-1911): Hangman

The saying around Hanging Judge Parker's court in Fort Smith, Ark. was that Parker sentenced men to death and George Maledon "suspended sentence." Maledon was Parker's executioner and, during their 21-year association, hanged almost all of the 88 men Parker sent to their doom. Maledon's ambition knew no bounds. He constructed a 12-man gallows for special no-waiting occasions, although the most ever to "stretch rope" at the same time was six, in the notorious Dance of Death, a multiple execution that brought vigorous criticism to both Parker and Maledon for being excessively bloodthirsty and gave the former his nickname the Hanging Judge.

Born of German immigrant parents, Maledon left the industrial grime of Detroit to seek a new occupation. He found it as an officer of the Fort Smith Police Department. During the Civil War, Maledon joined the Union Army and afterward held a number of lawman jobs, including that of a deputy U.S. marshal working out of Fort Smith. He distinguished himself by volunteering to act as hangman whenever there was an execution, a service that earned him extra pay. When federal Judge Parker arrived in 1875, Maledon's future was assured. The hangman got what he considered a good fee for his services, $100 a man, minus the pittance it cost him to bury the dead.

Maledon went about preparing for an execution like a craftsman, oiling his specially purchased ropes and stretching them with sandbags to even them out and thus guarantee a good knot. He could always be counted on for some quotable comments, such as: "I never hanged a man who came back to have the job done over. There's no ghosts hanging around the old gibbet."

Maledon regarded multiple hangings as a special challenge, demanding a certain drop that would dispatch all the victims with the same lethal quickness. He never quite understood the outrage of much of the rest of the country, especially the Eastern press, whenever he staged one of these multiple dances

of death. But he also could not understand why much of the community shunned him nor why even some of his own family shrank from him. Mrs. Maledon was most upset by his labors and would not let him post press clippings and photographs of the men he killed in the living room.

After Judge Parker died, Maledon continued to work as an executioner for a few more years and then retired, taking his ropes, traps, photographs and newspaper clippings on the road for the curious to see. He also tried his hand at farming but was a failure at it. He died on May 6, 1911.

See also: *Dance of Death, Ann Maledon, Isaac C. "Hanging Judge" Parker.*

MALLOY, Indestructible Mike (1872-1933): Murder victim

Perhaps the most durable American murder victim, Indestructible Mike Malloy was an unheralded barfly who achieved fame and earned his nickname posthumously. He was selected to be murdered in 1932 by a Bronx, New York City insurance murder ring headed by a speakeasy operator named Tony Marino. Marino was assisted by his barkeep, Joe Murphy, and two others, Frank Pasqua and Dan Kriesberg. They had killed their first victim the previous year, a young blonde named Betty Carlsen. Marino had befriended Betty, who was down on her luck. He brought her into the speak, gave her drinks on the house and even set her up in a room nearby. Betty had never been treated so well. She couldn't do enough to thank Marino, even signing some papers so he could run for public office. Actually, what she signed was an insurance policy naming her newly found benefactor her beneficiary. One frigid night Betty passed out in the speakeasy and the boys carried her back to her room, laid her out on the bed naked, poured cold water over her and left the window wide open. When she was found dead the next morning, the coroner declared her death the result of pneumonia compounded by alcoholism. The boys collected $800, not an inconsiderable sum in that Depression year.

Then the murder ring started glad-handing Mike Malloy, a derelict more accustomed to getting the bum's rush whenever he entered the speakeasy. Now, he was greeted like an old buddy. They gave him a back room to sleep in so that he would not have to freeze in some drafty hallway. By the way, did Mike think it was a good idea for Marino to run for office? Absolutely. Mike's life was soon insured for a total of $3,500 under a double-indemnity clause. The boys shrewdly figured they would not avail themselves of that provision but settle for $1,750, thus allaying suspicions.

At first, the four tried to get Malloy to drink himself to death, but the more he drank the more he seemed to thrive. Since that method appeared to offer only bankruptcy for Marino, they switched to giving Malloy some "new stuff" that had come in, actually automobile antifreeze, which of course was poisonous. After consuming some of the new stuff, Malloy commented that it was quite smooth. A couple of hours later, Mike collapsed on the speakeasy floor and they dragged him out back to let him expire in privacy. An hour later, a beaming—and thirsty—Malloy was back at the bar. Over the succeeding days the boys kept lacing his drinks with ever stronger doses of antifreeze and finally, in desperation, with turpentine. Malloy downed shot after shot and lived. Even when the four took to using diluted horse liniment laced with rat poison, nothing happened. They had to wonder what Malloy had been drinking all his life.

The boys decided nothing liquid would kill Malloy. They switched to food and started giving him raw oysters, tainted and soaked in wood alcohol. Malloy downed two dozen at once and gave the treat his approval. "Tony," he told Marino, "you oughta open up a restaurant, you know first-class food."

After several days of tainted oysters followed by rotten sardines, with which Malloy always requested some of that "new booze," the plotters were ready to throw caution to the wind. They got him drunk and then lugged him to Claremont Park, where they stripped off his coat, opened his shirt, poured a five-gallon can of water on him and dumped him in a snowbank.

The next day the boys scanned the newspapers for a report of a corpse being found in the park, but there was nothing. Pasqua, sneezing fiercely as a result of his battle with the elements while carrying Malloy to the park, was most upset. Finally, that evening Malloy appeared wearing a new suit. He explained he had really tied one on the previous night and wound up practically clothesless in the park. But it had all turned out well. The police had found him and had a welfare organization outfit him with new clothes before he was released to the world.

Truly desperate, the would-be murderers hired a criminal who was working as a cab driver to kill their seemingly indestructible victim. Once again, they got Malloy into a drunken stupor and then took him at 3 a.m. to the deserted intersection of Gun Hill Road and Baychester Avenue. They held him upright as the cab driver backed his taxi up and then roared forward at 45 miles per hour. At the last instant they jumped back leaving the weaving Malloy standing in the path of the oncoming cab. When struck by the vehicle, Mike catapulted into the air. To make absolutely sure that he had done the job right, the cabbie backed his taxi over Malloy's prone body.

This time their victim was surely dead. But nothing appeared in the newspapers. They visited the morgue looking for his body. No Malloy. They contacted the hospitals. No Malloy. In fact, Malloy didn't show up again for three weeks. When he did, he said he had been in the hospital after having a car accident. The hospital had listed him under the wrong name. Seeing how downcast his friends were, Mike assured them he was all right, that he had suffered a concussion of the brain and had a fractured shoulder. "But I'm all right," he said, "and I sure could use a drink."

At this point, the boys were beyond desperation. They even contacted a professional hit man about machine-gunning Malloy on the street. The explanation would be that he was a poor unfortunate caught in the cross fire of a gangland battle. Unfortunately, the hit man wanted $500 for the job and the boys were getting close to having a losing proposition on their hands as it was. The plan was abandoned. The four decided that only straightforward murder would work. They rented a furnished room for Malloy and, on February 22, 1933, ran a hose from a gas jet to his mouth and held it there until he stopped breathing.

Unfortunately for the killers, they had to get a corrupt doctor to sign a phony death certificate citing lobar pneumonia as the cause of death.

By now there were just too many people involved in the plot. A cab driver was complaining to friends that he had been hired to run down a guy and had been paid so little it failed to cover the cost of fixing the dents in his cab. A gunmen told of losing out on a hit contract with some pikers. The police got wind of an insurance ring killing people in the Bronx and started checking around. They learned of an Irishman being buried within four hours of his death. And without a wake? That was unusual. They exhumed the body and started asking questions. Everybody started talking—the doctor, the cab driver, the hit man, even the undertaker. When accused, each of the four murderers tried to shift the blame to the remaining three. On various dates in June and July 1934, the four—Marino, Pasqua, Kriesberg and Murphy—died in the electric chair at Sing Sing, none of them nearly as well remembered as Indestructible Mike Malloy.

MANDAME, Mary (c.1639): Pilgrim sex offender

Mary Mandame of the Plymouth colony was the first American woman to be forced to wear a mark on her clothing for a sex offense. Specifically, she was charged in 1639 with "dallyance diverse tymes with Tinsin, an Indian" and "committing the act of uncleanse with him." Her punishment was to be whipped through the streets of Plymouth and thereafter to always wear a badge of shame on her left sleeve. Since Mary Mandame's name does not appear again in historical records, it would seem that she obeyed the terms of her punishment. Had she not, she would have been branded in the face with a hot iron. In 1658 the punishment given to Mary was extended to wives found guilty of committing adultery. This cruel punishment became the basis for Nathaniel Hawthorne's *The Scarlet Letter* (1850).

See also: *Colonial Punishments.*

MANDELBAUM, Fredericka "Marm" (1818-1894): Fence

The most notorious fence, or receiver of stolen goods, in the 19th century was Fredericka Mandelbaum, better known to the underworld as Marm because of her often maternalistic attitude toward criminals. Indeed, the sobriquet Ma Crime, as she was called by the press, was well justified since, unlike the fences of today who insulate themselves from the actual commission of crimes, she was an active plotter and bankroller of many of the great capers of the period.

It would be difficult to put a dollar value on the loot Marm handled in her three decades of activity, from 1854 to 1884, but it certainly was in the tens of millions. In fact, it could be said that Marm Mandelbaum, rather than the later-arriving Lucky Luciano and Meyer Lansky, first put crime in America on a syndicated basis. She angeled, or bossed, the operations of several gangs of bank robbers, blackmailers and confidence men, gave advanced courses in burglary and safe blowing and outdid Dickens' Fagin with a special school for teaching little boys and girls how to be expert pickpockets and sneak thieves.

Fredericka came to America from her native Prussia in 1849 with her rather meek husband, Wolfe, whom she supposedly had induced to embezzle funds from his employer. Arriving in New York City, they bought a home and dry goods store at 79 Clinton Street in the teeming Kleine Deutschland section of Manhattan's East Side. Wolfe Mandelbaum would have been content to be an honest businessman, but Fredericka soon began dabbling in stolen goods, and by 1854 the store was nothing more than a front for her illegal operations. Soon, she required several warehouses in Manhattan and Brooklyn in which to keep her stolen articles and remove their labels, trademarks and other means of identification. She retained the famous criminal law firm of Howe and Hummel to keep herself and her growing legion of thieves out of serious trouble. Other flunkies handled her direct payments to the police.

Upon her arrival in New York, Fredericka weighed 150 pounds, a weight she was to double as she grew in stature, literally and figuratively, in the underworld. She had a sharply curved mouth, unusually fat cheeks, small, beady black eyes, bushy brows and a high, sloping forehead. She generally wore a tiny black bonnet with feathers over her mass of tightly rolled hair. Although far from a raving beauty, she was lovingly regarded by the underworld. One leading thief, Banjo Pete Emerson, was quoted as saying, "She was scheming and dishonest as the day is long, but she could be like an angel to the worst devil as long as he played square with her."

While she was undoubtedly the leading criminal in America during the latter part of the 19th century, Marm was—by her own standards—a lady. She was treated with respect by the ruffians with whom she dealt on a daily basis. Vile language was definitely not permissible. A party at the Widow Mandelbaum's—Wolfe died in 1874—was definitely the highlight of the underworld social season, and Marm was not above, or below, playing gracious hostess to the better half of town, whose homes and purses her thugs robbed regularly. Her parties were also attended by judges, police officials, politicians and the like. Marm, ever on the lookout for ways of improving the social life and mores of the underworld, judiciously mixed into these gatherings the best of the criminal lot. Thus, at the dinner table the wives of a judge and an important City Hall figure might well find themselves flanking someone like Mark Shinburn, a burglar of distinction and one of Marm's favorites. Shinburn insisted that he was an aristocrat at heart and detested associating with crooks even for business reasons.

Marm took an intense interest in all her flock, constantly trying to improve them in mind and manners. When it came

to finances, however, she dropped any pretensions of being a lady and was as tight-fisted as they came, seldom if ever granting a thief more than 10 percent of the value of any stolen article he sold her. Yet, after completion of a deal, Marm might turn right around and hand that same individual several hundred or thousand dollars for a needed operation or as a retirement kitty. It was Marm who counseled Shinburn to save his money, go back to Europe and live out his life in luxury. Buying himself a title with a portion of his loot, Shinburn became Baron Shindell of Monaco and lived aristocratically ever after.

A dinner party at Marm Mandelbaum's was always a high point in the New York underworld's social life.

Following the Civil War Draft Riots in New York, Marm was the biggest receiver of the goods looted, much of which she disposed of as far away as Chicago; fittingly enough, a good portion of the loot taken during the Chicago Fire a few years later ended up in Marm's New York warehouses.

Besides Shinburn and Emerson, some of the top criminals who worked at her beckon were George Leonidas Leslie, the King of the Bank Robbers; Sheeny Mike Kurtz, burglar extraordinary; Shang Draper, master of the panel game rackets; Ned Lyons; Johnny Dobbs; Jimmy Irving; and Bill Mosher and Joe Douglas, these last two the confessed kidnappers of little Charley Ross. There was no loot Marm could not handle, including stolen horses shipped in by the Loomis gang from upstate New York.

Marm became the queen mother of the leading lady crooks. There were Queen Liz and Big Mary, the top shoplifters of the day and instructors in one of Marm's schools for the underworld juniors; Black Lena Kleinschmidt, blackmailer, pickpocket and sneak thief; Sophie Lyons, wife of bank robber Ned Lyons and a renowned con lady; Old Mother Hubbard; Kid Glove Rose; Little Annie; and Ellen Clegg. Marm liked all these ladies because they shared her desire for respectability and because, above all, they recognized her as their social queen. Only Black Lena ever challenged Marm's position. It happened when Marm started courting the rich. Black Lena moved to Hackensack, N.J., posed as the wealthy widow of a

South American mining engineer and began giving elaborate functions that rivaled Marm's.

Although the social columns of the day referred to Black Lena as the Queen of Hackensack, she continued to spend two days a week in New York working her illegal trade to replenish her coffers. She was finally dethroned when she wore an emerald ring that one of her dinner guests recognized as having been stolen from a friend's handbag. Marm read the news of Black Lena's arrest and exposure with pure delight. "It just goes to prove," Marm told the tittering ladies of her court, "that it takes brains to be a real lady."

Marm's own fall from grace came in 1884, a seemingly unlikely event considering the amount of protection money she paid the police. Her problem came in the form of one Peter B. Olney—a sort of oddity for his day—a district attorney without a price. Convinced the police would never catch Marm, Olney turned to the Pinkertons. After four months of intensive work, one of the agents gained her confidence by posing as a thief. Soon after, thieves working with Marm stole a supply of silk from the store of James A. Hearn and Sons on 14th Street, but the bolts had been secretly marked by detectives. Later the same night a task force of Pinkertons smashed through the doors of Marm's house and found the stolen silk. But that was nothing compared to what else they found. As one reporter put it:

> It did not seem possible that so much wealth could be assembled in one spot. There seemed to be enough clothes to supply an army. There were trunks filled with precious gems and silverware. Antique furniture was stacked against a wall and bars of gold from melted jewelry settings were stacked under newspapers. There were scales of every description to weigh diamonds.

Marm, her son Julius and her clerk Herman Stroude were clapped behind bars. It was the first and only night Marm spent in jail. The following day she posted $21,000 bail and got her lawyer Bill Howe working on a fix so that she could continue operations. However, Tammany Hall was having problems with reformers and Marm was advised her day was over. She shrugged, gathered up what was believed to be $1 million in cash and fled. When she didn't show up for her trial, the newspapers berated the police for not keeping her under constant surveillance.

The Pinkertons were put back on the job and within a month they located her in Toronto, Canada, but under existing extradition laws, she could not be forced to return to the United States. She did come back twice, however. In disguise and weeping profusely, she turned up in 1890 for the funeral of her daughter in Kleine Deutschland. The local papers learned of it, but the police professed to be skeptical—until Marm was safely across the border again.

In 1894 Marm came back to New York for burial, dead at the age of 76. The newspapers reported that several of the mourners at the cemetery had their pockets picked.

See also: *Grand Street School, Howe and Hummel, George Leonidas Leslie, Mark Shinburn.*

MANN Act: White slavery control statute

The White Slave Traffic Act, introduced in 1910 by Rep. James Robert Mann of Illinois and popularly known as the Mann Act, outlawed the transport of women across state lines for immoral purposes. The direct cause of the legislation was the disclosure that a Chicago vice couple, Alphonse and Eva Dufaur, had imported 20,000 women and girls into the United States to stock their many brothels. The first prominent person to run afoul of the act was Heavyweight Champion Jack Johnson, the first black to hold the heavyweight boxing title, who in 1912 persuaded a white woman, whom he later married, to leave a house of prostitution where she was working and travel with him to another state. Johnson was sentenced to one year in prison but fled the country after posting bail. He finally returned in 1920 to serve his time.

While the Mann Act has been successfully used to prosecute a number of minor criminals over the years, it has not been an unqualified success. Some enterprising prostitutes turned it into a valuable blackmail foil, and the act failed miserably in stopping the prostitution activities of the Capone mob. With the decline of prostitution as an organized crime activity, the result of changing sexual mores rather than effective law enforcement, the Mann Act has been relegated to relative unimportance.

See also: *Procuring.*

MANSON, Charles (1934-   ): Murder cult leader

The highly publicized leader of a "family," or self-aggrandizing cult, Charles Manson burst on the California scene in shocking style, even in a state long thought inured to bizarre bloodletting. On August 9, 1969 Charles "Tex" Watson and three female accomplices, Patricia Krenwinkel, Susan Atkins and Leslie Van Houten, entered the Beverly Hills estate of film director Roman Polanski, who was away at the time, and murdered his pregnant wife, actress Sharon Tate, and four others—Abigail Folger, heiress to the Folger coffee fortune; Voyteck Frykowski, a Polish writer and producer, who was living with Folger; Jay Sebring, a hair stylist; and 18-year-old Steven Earl Parent. The five were shot, stabbed and clubbed to death, with Sharon Tate begging to be allowed to live for the sake of her unborn baby. The killers used the victims' blood to scrawl crazed slogans and words like "Pig" and "War" on the walls. During the slaughter Watson kept screaming, "I am the devil and I have come to do the devil's work!"

Two nights later, the shocking process was repeated at the home of Leno and Rosemary La Bianca; they were butchered and the same sort of bloody messages were scrawled all over their home.

The murderers were soon traced back to the Manson family. Manson, at 34, had done time in several prisons and reform schools for such charges as procuring and forgery. After his last release from prison, he had set up a sort of commune for a cult of shiftless hippies and drifters at the Spahn Ranch outside Los Angeles, once a filming location for Hollywood studios. At

Charles Manson (right) and two of his female cultists, Patricia Krenwinkel (left) and Leslie Van Houten, were in a jovial mood at a court appearance after their arrest. All were convicted of murder.

the ranch the cult practiced free love, experimented with drugs and conducted pseudo-religious ceremonies built around Manson as a Christ-like figure. When Manson ordered guerrilla tactics, his followers practiced guerrilla tactics, and when he told them to kill, they killed.

After their capture none of the actual killers or Manson, who had directed them, showed any sign of remorse over the horrifying crimes. At their trial—during which a number of Manson's shaved-head female followers kept daily vigil outside the courthouse—the prosecutor called Manson "one of the most evil, satanic men who ever walked the face of the earth." For a time the three women defendants offered to admit their guilt if Manson was declared innocent. Manson waved off their offer, telling the court: "I have done my best to get along in your world, and now you want to kill me. I say to myself, 'Ha, I'm already dead, have been all my life . . . I don't care anything about any of you."

All were found guilty and sentenced to die, but they were spared the death penalty because of the Supreme Court ruling outlawing capital punishment and were given life instead. They have been eligible for parole since 1978. In 1980 Manson was turned down on his third annual application for parole. The parole board advised him to train for a trade as part of his rehabilitation, but Manson said: "I'll stay here forever. I'm too old. I can't do too much. I like to sit around, smoke grass, read the Bible now and then."

See also: *Helter Skelter.*

MANTON, Martin T. (1880-1946): Crooked judge

The only federal judge ever imprisoned for corruption, Martin T. Manton was something of a courtroom wunderkind. When Woodrow Wilson named him district court judge, he was, at the age of 36, the youngest federal jurist in the country. Within a year and a half he had moved up to the appellate court; in 1922 it was said that he missed an appointment to the Supreme Court by an eyelash. Over a 10-year period Manton produced 650 opinions, an output very few judges have ever equaled. However, it developed that his opinions were for sale. Soliciting a bribe in one case, Manton was quoted as saying, "While I'm sitting on the bench, I have my right hand and my left hand."

In 1939 Manhattan District Attorney Thomas E. Dewey accused him of taking bribes with both hands and even employing an agent to negotiate the sale of verdicts. The charges against Manton were considered so incredible that he had no trouble convincing Judge Learned Hand and two former presidential candidates, Al Smith and John W. Davis, to appear as character witnesses at his trial. Nonetheless, he was found guilty. Pleading his own appeal before the Supreme Court, Manton came up with a novel argument: "From a broad viewpoint, it serves no public policy for a high judicial officer to be convicted of a judicial crime. It tends to destroy the confidence of the people in the courts." The High Court was unimpressed, however, and turned down his appeal. Manton served 19 months at the federal prison in Lewisburg, Pa. and died a broken man in 1946.

See also: *Judicial Corruption*.

MARANZANO, Salvatore (1868-1931): Mafia "boss of bosses"

For four months in 1931, Salvatore Maranzano was probably the most important criminal boss in the United States, even more important than Al Capone, whom Maranzano put on a list of mobsters to be eliminated in order to solidify his authority throughout the entire country. Maranzano founded what came to be known as the Cosa Nostra.

Maranzano was a "Mustache Pete," an old-line Mafia leader who held to the criminal society's traditions of "honor" and "respect" for the gang boss and bloody feuds with foes of decades past. Nevertheless, he had modern ideas about crime and wanted to institutionalize it in America—with himself on top. If he had survived 1931, organized crime in America today would operate much differently.

Maranzano had come to the United States late in his criminal career, around 1918, but he had been an established mafioso in Sicily (he had fled because of a murder charge and because the older Mustache Petes resented his new ideas and probably would have killed him if he had stayed). His magnetism quickly made him a gang power and he surrounded himself with gangsters from his home town in Sicily, Castellammare del Golfo. College-trained and originally a candidate for the priesthood, he was a far cry from the standard mafiosi. Within a few years he had grown so powerful he was becoming a threat to the acknowledged Mafia boss of New York, Giuseppe "Joe the Boss" Masseria.

Masseria was a glutton, both in personal habits and in the way he ran criminal affairs, demanding enormous tribute from his subchiefs. Maranzano shrewdly used the resentment this produced to lure many leading gangsters away from Joe the Boss. But he could not bring in the biggest prize, a rising young mobster named Lucky Luciano, a brilliant strategist whose reorganization of much of Joe the Boss' empire resulted in greatly increased profits.

When Maranzano seemed to be getting too strong, Joe the Boss declared war on him. The police, having no way of separating gang war killings from other underworld executions, never knew how many men died in what was called the Castellammarese War; the toll between 1928 and 1930 may well have been 50. Because he could field probably 200 more gunmen than his foe, Joe the Boss did not take the threat seriously at first. But Maranzano kept winning defections by promising Masseria men a better share of the loot if they joined him.

While Maranzano and Masseria fought their two-sided war, a third side was developing. Luciano had been cultivating the younger gangsters within the Maranzano forces, telling them an entirely new crime setup, one that would really bring in big money. He had developed contacts with the Jewish gangs that would lead to the formation of a new crime syndicate and end the Mafia's internecine struggles as well as its battles with other ethnic groups involved in crime. Luciano, through Frank Costello, had also established rapport with the New York police, sending $10,000 a week directly to police headquarters (the sum was doubled in the late 1920s), and he could thus supply better protection than either Joe the Boss or Maranzano.

For a time Luciano had hung back waiting to see which of the two leaders would eliminate the other. When a stalemate developed, he decided to help matters along by getting rid of Joe the Boss, who would be easier to kill since he trusted Luciano. On April 15, 1931 Luciano and Masseria had lunch in a Coney Island restaurant. About 3:30 p.m. Luciano went to the men's room. Just then four assassins stepped up to Masseria and fired a fusillade of 20 shots at him, hitting him six times. Joe the Boss lay dead.

Luciano had handed the crown to Maranzano. Now, he bided his time to allow Maranzano to think he was secure. As a supposed act of gratitude, Maranzano gave Luciano the number two position in his new organization. In a memorable conclave he summoned 500 gangsters to a meeting in the Bronx and outlined his great new scheme for crime. The New York Mafia would be divided into five major crime families, with a boss, a sub-boss, lieutenants and soldiers. Above them all would be a "boss of bosses"—Salvatore Maranzano. He called this new organization La Cosa Nostra, which meant nothing more than "Our Thing." Years later, the phrase "Cosa Nostra" would be used to get J. Edgar Hoover out of a bad hole of his own making. For decades Hoover had insisted there was no such thing as organized crime and no Mafia. Oh yes, he was able to announce, there was a Cosa Nostra.

While Maranzano was constructing his new empire, he was aware that not all those under him were loyalists. He knew better than to trust the ambitious Luciano, who was too worldly and was setting up a partially non-Italian power base. Maranzano composed a death list that, when carried out, would guarantee his rule. On that list were Luciano, Costello, Vito Genovese, Joe Adonis, Willie Moretti, Dutch Schultz and the "fat guy" in Chicago, Al Capone, who was friendly with Luciano.

It would be a prodigious undertaking to eliminate them all, and Maranzano realized it would be dangerous to trust other Italians with the task—whomever he picked might be a secret ally of Luciano. So, he decided to have the job handled by a non-Italian. He enlisted the notorious young killer Vince "Mad Dog" Coll and arranged for him to come to his office in the Grand Central building at a time when Luciano and Genovese would be present. Coll was to kill them and then get as many of the others on the list as possible before the murders became known. Maranzano gave Coll $25,000 as a down payment and promised him another $25,000 upon successful completion of the assignment.

The boss of bosses then invited Luciano and Genovese to a meeting in his office. Unaware how many gunmen Luciano had won over to his cause, Maranzano made the mistake of trusting a gangster named Tommy Lucchese, who had been a secret friend of Luciano for years and his chief spy in the Maranzano organization. Lucchese learned of the murder plot and warned Luciano. On the day set for the meeting, Lucchese innocently dropped into Maranzano's office a few minutes before Luciano and Genovese were due. Just then four men walked in flashing badges and announced they had some questions to ask. The four were Jewish gangsters Luciano had borrowed for the plot because they were unknown to Maranzano and his bodyguards. On the other hand, since the gunmen did not know Maranzano, Lucchese was there to ensure they got the right man.

The phony officers lined the bodyguards up against the wall and disarmed them. Then two went into Maranzano's office and shot him to death. The assassins charged out, as did the bodyguards after ascertaining their boss was dead. On the way down the emergency stairs, one of them ran into Mad Dog Coll coming to keep his murder appointment. Appraised of the new situation, Coll exited whistling. He had $25,000 and nothing to do for it.

The death of Maranzano meant a new deal for crime in America. The forces of Luciano, Meyer Lansky and Dutch Schultz would form a national crime syndicate. Over the years Schultz would be killed by the others, but the apparatus was there to stay.

See also: *Castellammarese War, Vincent "Mad Dog" Coll, Thomas "Three-Finger Brown" Lucchese, Charles "Lucky" Luciano, Giuseppe "Joe the Boss" Masseria, Mustache Petes, Night of the Sicilian Vespers, Joseph M. Valachi.*

MARIN County, Calif. Courthouse Shooting: See Angela Davis.

MARIS, Herbert L. (1880-1960): Defense attorney

A Philadelphia lawyer whose cases became the basis of a television series called "Lock-Up," Herbert L. Maris cleared an estimated 500 unjustly convicted persons during a half-century career. His record was probably one of the best arguments for abolition of the death penalty because it highlighted the grave possibility of judicial error. Time after time he demonstrated how often justice erred, freeing men originally sentenced to death but lucky enough to win a commutation to life. Only after Maris took their case was justice finally rendered and wrong man after wrong man set free. Almost every convict in Pennsylvania recognized his name. Maris became known as "a lifer's last hope."

Such was the situation in what came to be called the Case of the Beer Bottle that Never Was. It started one evening on a Philadelphia street corner when a young man met his girl friend, allegedly had an argument with her and hit her across the back of the neck with a beer bottle. The prosecution produced three witnesses who said they had observed the assault. The jury ignored the man's story that he had merely embraced the girl and was stroking the back of her neck when suddenly she lurched against him and collapsed on the sidewalk, blood spurting from her mouth. In a matter of seconds the girl had died.

The supposed killer was sentenced to life imprisonment and served three years before he got in touch with Maris. The lawyer soon demolished the case that had sent the man to prison. With the aid of the coroner's report, he showed that the girl had died of an aneurysm in the aorta; in this heart condition the blood vessel can burst, fatally, at any moment, and shock or excitement can cause the rupture.

Checking the court transcript, Maris found that the judge and district attorney had accepted the testimony of the witnesses at face value, and the court-appointed defense counsel hadn't challenged anything the witnesses had said. The findings of the coroner's report simply had not been considered at the trial.

Then Maris broke down the witnesses one by one, establishing that none of them had heard what the couple had been saying, thus none could really swear there had been an argument between the two. And no one had seen a bottle in the man's hand. The witnesses "thought" he had something in his hand. One state witness, coached to elaborate on the incident, had testified that the man had struck the girl with a beer bottle. Yet no beer bottle had been found.

In case after case Maris proved the so-called beer bottle murder was hardly a unique miscarriage of justice. He constantly cited instances of where official indifference, incompetence, suppression of evidence or even the invention of evidence that had resulted in the conviction of innocent men.

A farmer from near York, Pa. was given the death penalty, later commuted to life, and did 10 years before Maris cleared him of a murder charge. It turned out that two local constables and two civilians had decided it would be fun to "arrest" the farmer, ride him off 18 miles and force him to walk home. But the farmer, thinking it was a kidnapping, shot and killed one of the constables. When the joke turned into tragedy, the survivors decided to cover the matter up by stating that at the time of the shooting, the farmer was being arrested on a warrant for stealing a calf. The warrant the slain constable was allegedly carrying was produced in court and the farmer was convicted.

Maris proved the warrant hadn't been prepared until three months after the killing. In addition, he found that the prosecutor had managed to introduce the phony warrant in court without naming the complainant. When that man was questioned, he denied having had a calf stolen. He had not come forward at the time of the trial, he stated, because he didn't even know he was involved.

Maris declared, "I am convinced, on the basis of my long experience, that the guilt of fully 20 percent of those in our prisons is extremely doubtful," and he liked to say he always had at least 10 cases on hand in which the convicted individuals were "absolutely innocent." Even in his late seventies, he still put in 80- or 90-hour weeks trying to help as many of these unjustly convicted persons as he could, often without fee.

MARTIN, Michael: See Captain Lightfoot.

MARTIN-Tolliver Feud

Far more disruptive to the life of its community than the more famous Hatfield-McCoy feud, the dispute between the Martins and the Tollivers, which had begun as an election argument, in Morehead, Ky. erupted into bloodshed in 1884, when Floyd Tolliver shot John Martin. Before the law could act, Martin shot Tolliver to death. While Martin was being held under arrest, members of the Tolliver clan killed him. For the next three years a bloody feud enveloped Rowan County. The resulting anarchy provoked an exodus of hundreds of residents from the county; the county seat at Morehead saw its population drop from 700 to 300. Because of close marital ties, the Logan family was drawn into the struggle on the side of the Martins. By 1887 the death toll stood at 23, with the number of wounded kept secret by the close-mouthed clans. The feud ended on June 22, 1887, when Daniel Boone Logan led a large Martin-Logan force into Morehead and, in a pitched battle, killed the Tolliver leaders.

MASON, Sam (c.1755-1803): Highwayman and murderer

A brawling river man who for a time had been one of George Rogers Clark's rangers, Sam Mason was the greatest terror of the Mississippi, beginning in 1800. He collected a large gang of cutthroats, who seldom let a robbery victim live to tell about it. Mason would often leave his trademark at the scene of the crime, carving on a tree, "Done by Mason of the Woods."

Like the Harpe brothers, a pair of brutal killers of the same era, Mason often killed indiscriminately. But he might turn around and let his next hapless victim go with no more than a boot in the pants. The governors of both the Louisiana and the Mississippi territories put him at the head of the list of wanted men. Mason was captured early in 1803 but escaped before he was identified.

Meanwhile, a bearded man named Setton joined the Mason gang and took part in a number of forays and killings. Mason did not know it, but Setton was the much-sought Little Harpe, whose older brother, Big Harpe, had been captured by the law and executed earlier that year. There was a handsome reward out for Mason and Harpe-Setton had designs on it. One day in late 1803, Harpe, with the aid of another gang member named Sam Mays, waited until Mason was separated from the rest of his men and then tomahawked him to death. Harpe and Mays took Mason's severed head to Natchez to claim their reward. Unfortunately, Little Harpe was recognized and they, like their victim, ended up with their heads cut off.

See also: *Harpe Brothers.*

MASON County War: Western feud

Although not as bloody as the Graham-Tewksbury feud in the Arizona Territory, the Mason County War in Texas was another violent confrontation in which the underlying causes (cattle rustling) soon were forgotten, swept aside by blind passion, hatred and brutality, with friends coming to the aid of friends.

The first victim of the 1875 war was Tim Williamson, a cattleman not averse to shooting his enemies or mixing cattle from other herds together with his own stock. Arrested for stealing livestock, he was on his way to jail when a mob of his enemies abducted him and shot him to death despite the efforts of John Worley, a deputy sheriff of Mason County. Worley's attempt to save Williamson did not impress a number of the deceased's friends, especially Scott Cooley, an ex-Texas Ranger turned gunman who had worked for Williamson and other cattlemen for some time. Cooley, who had developed a warm friendship with Williamson, became convinced that Deputy Worley had conspired in the mob killing. He took his revenge by not only shooting the lawman but cutting off his ears as well. Cooley exhibited his grim prize, promising publicly to kill every man involved in the Williamson murder. When Cooley and a number of friends killed Daniel Hoerster on suspicion of being part of the mob that had attacked Williamson, full-scale war broke out. Unable to corner Cooley, his enemies set upon two friends of his, the brothers Elijah and Pete Backus, and hanged them from a tree. Cooley's forces dispatched a pair of mob law advocates, Pete Bader and Luther Wiggins. The other side then shot to death Moses Beard, a Cooley man. By that time the conflict had been named the Hoodoo War. In all, the eye-for-eye struggle officially resulted in the killing of at least a dozen men and the wounding of many more. There is little doubt that some other killings were wrongly attributed to unknown desperadoes and road agents.

After more than a year, the war came to an abrupt end when a company of Texas Rangers was sent into Mason County to prevent further bloodshed. Cooley, the main instigator, disappeared, and only a few minor characters had to face charges. One of these was a then little-known friend of Cooley's, Johnny Ringo. Ringo had killed an anti-Williamson man after the latter had invited him to sit down and eat with him. Jailed for murder, Ringo broke free from his cell in Lampasas and quickly left Texas.

See also: *Scott Cooley, Johnny Ringo.*

MASSERIA, Giuseppe "Joe the Boss" (c.1880-1931): Mafia leader

Joe the Boss Masseria was the undisputed boss of the New York Mafia in the 1920s, a rank he achieved by knocking off a number of rivals for the throne. Masseria had come from Sicily in the early years of the 20th century with solid Mafia connections. He soon teamed up with Lupo the Wolf, often regarded as the cruelest mafioso in the country and the owner of the infamous Murder Stable in East Harlem where his foes or victims were hung on meat hooks.

Masseria looked like a round little cherub except for his cold eyes, which betrayed a fearsomeness that made him a worthy partner of Lupo. When the pair made extortion demands of Italian immigrants, their victims paid whether they could afford to or not. In 1920 Lupo went to prison on a counterfeiting charge and Masseria fell heir to his operations, the most important of which, with the onset of Prohibition, was control of the liquor stills and wine-making vats that were common in many Italian households.

The revenues from bootleg booze made Masseria richer than any Mafia leader before him, and he moved quickly to consolidate his power. Whenever any leader appeared to be gaining strength, Joe the Boss had him killed. He too was the subject of numerous assassination attempts. Once, two gunmen sent by his archrival, Umberto Valenti, shot at him as he left his Manhattan apartment on Second Avenue. Joe the Boss darted into a millinery shop, trailed by the gunners, whose bullets shattered windows and mirrors and hit Masseria's straw hat twice. But they missed the Italian gangster, who thereby gained the mystique of being able to dodge bullets.

In due course, Joe the Boss announced he wanted to make peace with Valenti and asked for a conference to discuss terms. The pair met in an Italian restaurant on East 12th Street and Masseria pledged his loyalty to his new "brother." As they left the restaurant, Masseria draped his arm over Valenti's shoulders. On the sidewalk Joe the Boss suddenly moved away and Valenti was cut down by a hail of bullets.

Masseria ruled supreme for several years until he received a challenge, the most serious of all, from Salvatore Maranzano, who wanted to be the "boss of bosses." Masseria was upset by the effrontery—after all, he was Joe the Boss. Soon, war broke out and bodies littered the streets in all the boroughs of New York.

Masseria felt secure. He had twice as many gunners as Maranzano had and some very able assistants as well. His top aide was Lucky Luciano, and among others were Joe Adonis, Frank Costello, Carlo Gambino, Willie Moretti and Albert Anastasia. And under them was a host of savage killers. Masseria especially liked Anastasia, who shared his own instincts for solving matters by murder, but he had to admit Luciano was his most cunning assistant, a brilliant planner and organizer. All these young hoods had one problem: they kept telling him the gang had to abandon the ways of the old country and make deals with other ethnic gangsters, like the Irish and the Jews. Luciano insisted everyone could make more money if they cooperated, and he and Adonis were working their bootleg rackets with the Bug and Meyer gang—Bugsy Siegel and Meyer Lansky. Joe the Boss did not trust Siegel and Lansky, and he bridled at working with Dutch Schultz, even if he had converted to Catholicism. Moreover, he disliked the fact that Costello was paying off all the politicians. It was all right to bribe an official now and then when needed, but one should not "sleep with them" all the time. The politicians would

eventually corrupt you, Masseria felt, even though Luciano insisted it was the other way around.

Joe the Boss didn't realize that these younger mafiosi hated him as intently as they hated Maranzano. They looked forward to the day when they would be rid of all the "Mustache Petes," as they disdainfully called old country mafiosi. They even had secret contacts within the Maranzano organization, especially with Tommy Lucchese and Tom Gagliano, intended to stop the senseless killings between the groups so that everyone could just concentrate on making money.

Luciano counseled the others to bide their time until either Masseria killed Maranzano or vice versa, but by 1931 both leaders were still around and others were doing the dying. That year Luciano decided something had to be done. Since it would be easier to kill someone who trusted him rather than one who did not, he decided Joe the Boss would have to die first. On April 15, 1931 Luciano suggested to Masseria that they drive out to Coney Island for lunch. Joe the Boss agreed and they dined at a favorite underworld haunt, Nuova Villa Tammaro, owned by Gerardo Scarpato, an acquaintance of a number of gangsters. During lunch Joe the Boss gorged himself, and after the rest of the diners cleared out, he and Luciano played pinochle while owner Scarpato went for a walk along the beach.

About 3:30 p.m. Luciano went to the toilet. As soon as he left, four men came marching through the door. They were Vito Genovese, Joe Adonis, Albert Anastasia and Bugsy Siegel, loaned especially for the operation by Meyer Lansky, who was destined to become Luciano's closest associate. All pulled out guns and fired at Masseria. Six bullets hit home, and the reign of Joe the Boss came to an abrupt end.

In newspaper reports of the sensational assassination, Luciano told the police he had heard the shooting and, as soon as he had dried his hands, went out to see what was going on. Actually, Luciano's recollection was not accurately reported, possibly a form of self-censorship by the press. What he told the police was: "I was in the can taking a leak. I always take a long leak."

In any case, the first significant step in the Luciano-Lansky plan to establish a new national crime syndicate had been completed.

See also: *Castellammarese War, Thomas "Three-Finger Brown" Lucchese, Charles "Lucky" Luciano, Salvatore Maranzano, Mustache Petes.*

MASSIE Case: Hawaiian murder case

Few criminal cases provoked as much racial hatred in the 1930s as Hawaii's Massie Case. Thalia Massie, the pretty wife of a young U.S. naval officer, Lt. Thomas H. Massie, was allegedly raped by five Hawaiians in Honolulu in 1931. News of the alleged crime led to racial tensions between Hawaiians and Americans and American sailors rioted in the streets. Thalia Massie was the daughter of socially prominent Mrs. Grace Fortescue of Long Island, N.Y., who promptly rushed to her daughter's side. Five beach boys were arrested and charged with the rape, but the case against them was weak. After the jury became deadlocked, a mistrial was declared. More battles between Hawaiians and Americans immediately broke out.

At this stage Mrs. Fortescue and Lt. Massie decided to take matters into their own hands, and together with two sailors, E.J. Lord and A.O. Jones, they made plans to force a confession out of one of the defendants. They grabbed Joseph Kahahawai right off the street and shoved him into a car. But a friend of Kahahawai had witnessed the abduction and provided police with the car's license number. About an hour and a half later, police located the vehicle bound for Koko Head, a bluff overlooking the sea. Inside they found Lt. Massie, Mrs. Fortescue, the two enlisted men and the body of Joe Kahahawai. He had been shot in the chest.

An investigation revealed the four had taken the man to the Massie home and questioned him there about the rape. Someone had shot him, but the four insisted they were in a "daze" and didn't know what had happened.

All four were charged with murder. The charge created such a sensation in Honolulu that a Marine detachment was assigned to maintain order. Reaction on the mainland was also strong. One day Mrs. Fortescue received what was described as a boatload of flowers from well-wishers. A Hearst newspaper headlined the case, "The Honor Slaying," and the American press in general reported all sorts of atrocity stories, later proved to be false, of rapes and assaults that had, according to a Hearst report, "forced decent white folks to take up arms to protect the honor of their women."

Mrs. Fortescue hired the aged Clarence Darrow to represent herself and the other three defendants, in what was to be one of the most sensational trials of the century. Darrow's task was enormous. He tried to establish that Lt. Massie had been suffering from "temporary insanity" but he would not admit that Massie had fired the fatal shot. In the end, the jury of five whites, three Europeans, three Chinese and one juror of mixed white-Oriental ancestry was partly swayed by Darrow's tactics and voted only a manslaughter conviction. The native population was satisfied when the defendants were all given 10 years, but the sentence caused an explosion back in the States.

Various congressmen demanded a presidential pardon be issued. A military boycott began, damaging the local economy, and soon, the territorial governor and Darrow engaged in intense negotiations over the sentences. In the middle of their talks, the governor received a call from President Herbert Hoover. The end result was one of the strangest sentencing agreements in American judicial history: the governor ordered the prisoners brought into court and had them "held" one hour before he commuted the remainder of their sentences. Part of the agreement called for the Massies and Mrs. Fortescue to leave the islands immediately.

Officially, the case ended there, but on reflection, much of the public decided the original rape case was not all it had seemed. Thalia Massie's gynecologist was quoted as saying, "If I had . . . to tell everything I knew . . . it would have made monkeys out of everybody." Two years after the incident the Massies were divorced. Lt. Massie eventually remarried and left the Navy for private business. Thalia Massie's later life included several suicide attempts and hospital confinements. She finally remarried before committing suicide in 1963.

MASTERSON, Edward J. (1852-1878): Lawman

Ed Masterson, Bat Masterson's older brother, enjoyed far more respect as a lawman than did Bat, who mainly was respected for his gunslinging prowess. Ed was inclined to rely more on talking than on gunfighting to uphold the law. It was a point of dispute between the brothers, with Bat insisting a lawman must inspire fear and, to that end, use his gun often.

Ed, like his brother, worked at a number of jobs before turning up as assistant city marshal of Dodge City, Kan. in 1877. There, he followed, as much as possible, a policy of keeping his gun holstered. Late that year he was wounded in the chest while arresting a drunken Texas cowboy named Bob Shaw in the Lone Star Dance Hall. Before the year was out, Ed had recovered sufficiently to take over as city marshal. Clearly, the citizens of Dodge City appreciated Ed's style of settling things peacefully, unlike the style of brother Bat, who in the meantime had been elected sheriff of Ford County, which included Dodge.

Ed Masterson's term of office was to last a little over four months, during which time he cajoled cowboys out of "hurrahing the town" and organized a "vagrant patrol" to arrest tramps, who then worked off their jail time by cleaning rubbish that accumulated on the streets. Ed Masterson was obviously a different kind of lawman.

Late on the evening of April 9, 1878, Marshal Masterson hurried over to the Lady Gay Dance Hall to try to disarm two drunken cowboys, Jack Wagner and Alf Walker. His gun, as usual, was in its holster. As both cowboys leveled their guns at him, Ed seized one of them and pinned him to a wall. Just then Bat Masterson came charging across the Sante Fe tracks to the rescue, taking a quick shot at the other cowboy. Finally, Ed Masterson felt he had no choice but to draw, and as he did, so did the cowboy he had been holding. In the next two seconds the two Mastersons shot both cowboys fatally, but Ed Masterson also suffered a mortal gunshot wound, which the *Ford County Globe* reported, was fired from such close range that "his clothes were on fire from the discharge of the pistol, which had been placed against the right side of his abdomen and 'turned loose.' "

Ed Masterson's funeral was one of Dodge City's biggest. All businesses were closed and draped in mourning. The Dodge City Fire Company, to which Ed belonged, conducted the funeral. A choir stood by the marshal's coffin in the parlor of the fire company and sang somber dirges. It was said that every buggy and wagon in workable condition joined the cortege to Masterson's burial site in the military cemetery at Fort Dodge. The entire city council preceded the hearse, with Bat Masterson riding directly behind it. Behind Bat rode the 60 members of the fire company.

It was an outpouring of respect that Dodge City never gave

another law official, and one that the city never would have given Bat Masterson, who was voted out of office the following year.

See also: *William B. "Bat" Masterson.*

MASTERSON, James P. (1855-1895): Lawman and gunfighter

The youngest of the three Masterson brothers, Jim Masterson engaged in far more shooting scrapes than his more famous brother, Bat, and was a more-accomplished lawman as well. Like Bat, he generally used his guns to serve the important political powers as a law officer in Dodge City and Ford County, Kan.

When not working as a law officer, Jim frequently operated saloons, in which capacity he had a number of gun battles with clients and partners alike. In one such confrontation, Jim shot and killed Al Updegraff, a bartender hired by his partner. As a result of this fray, both Jim and Bat, who also took part in the proceedings, were forced to leave Dodge City. However, Jim went on to hold a variety of law enforcement jobs, including that of U.S. marshal. In 1889 Jim was working in Ingalls, Kan., as a "deputy sheriff," i.e., hired gunman, during that town's bloody war with Cimarron over which would become the county seat.

In the early 1890s Masterson played a key role in cleansing the Oklahoma Territory of numerous outlaws and performed heroically against the Doolin gang at the famed Battle of Ingalls. Shortly thereafter, he developed "galloping consumption" and died in 1895.

See also: *Cimarron County Seat War; Ingalls, Oklahoma Territory, Battle of; William B. "Bat" Masterson.*

MASTERSON, William B. "Bat" (1853-1921): Gunfighter and lawman

There probably have been more lies told about Bat Masterson's gunfighting than that of any other Wild West character. A Kansas newspaper said of him in 1884: "He is credited with having killed one man for every year of his life. This may be exaggerated, but he is certainly entitled to a record of a dozen or more. He is a cool, brave man, pleasant in his manners, but terrible in a fight." However, even that newspaper's tally of Masterson's victims was more than a bit excessive; he actually killed only one gunfighter, Mel King, who outdrew him in a dance hall brawl and hit him with a near fatal shot before Bat gunned him down. Bat undoubtedly would have been killed had not a dance hall girl named Molly Brennan shielded him with her own body, absorbing a fatal shot, a situation for which Hollywood would be eternally grateful.

However, Masterson cannot be dismissed as merely a dapper fop. He was a genuine hero in which 35 buffalo hunters made a famous stand at the Battle of Adobe Walls, against 500 attacking Indians, and as a lawman, he was an effective peacemaker. So demonstrably fast on the draw, he simply was not challenged by other gunfighters. Masterson showed his great sharp

shooting ability when he captured Spike Kennedy, the murderer of Dora Hand, knocking him off his horse with a rifle shot at what was described as a huge distance. As sheriff of Ford County, Kan., Masterson was part of the Dodge City Gang of Mayor James H. "Dog" Kelley and Marshal Wyatt Earp and he was not above taking his cut of the revenues from various vice operations, figuring such rewards came with the job. In fact, he was voted out of office because the citizens felt he was too free and easy with public money, having somehow managed to spend the then-staggering sum of $4,000 for five months' care and feeding of seven prisoners.

Bat Masterson was credited with "having killed one man for every year of his life." His actual number of gunfight victims amounted to one.

After his Dodge City days Bat drifted around the West, often showing up to help out Wyatt Earp or Luke Short whenever they needed it. His reputation always preceded him. Far more than even Earp's or Doc Holliday's, Bat's appearance was an invitation to silence and respect. This was partly due to sheer showmanship and his ability to tell a tall tale or two. When he didn't, friends of his would. A certain Dr. Cockerell once told the *New York Sun* how Bat had shot seven men dead in just a few minutes. He also described how Masterson had killed a Mexican father and son badman team and put their bodies in a sack. Dr. Cockerell, however, went on to tell how Bat had lost out on the reward for the pair because, after a ride of two days, the sun had "swelled and disfigured the heads so that they were unrecognizable, taking advantage of which the authorities refused to pay the reward."

A myth about Masterson which has persisted up to the present is that he carried a walking stick, or "bat," hence his nickname, which served either as a repository for a secret gun or as a club. Actually, his use of the walking stick was restricted to his later gambling days and did not account for his sobriquet, which he coined himself because he could not abide his given name of Bartholomew, which he officially changed to William Barclay.

In later years the once hard-drinking Masterson became an ardent prohibitionist and, as a special officer, even tried to close down the Dodge City saloons. This odd conversion occurred in 1885, just a year after Masterson, as one of the so-called Dodge City Peace Commissioners, had—by threat of force—brought back Luke Short to that town and reopened Dodge to all matters of vice and prostitution. Masterson's conversion did not last long; by 1886 he was working with Short at the White Elephant Saloon in Fort Worth, Tex.

Later, Masterson moved to Colorado, where he occasionally wore a badge but spent most of his time as a gentleman gambler and sport. He continued to drink heavily, and in 1902, no longer the expert gunman, he was run out of Denver by force. He went to New York City, where President Theodore Roosevelt, who had met him years before, appointed him a deputy U.S. marshal, a desk job entailing no old-style gunslinging. When President William Howard Taft refused to reappoint him, Masterson, through the intercession of Alfred Henry Lewis, established a name for himself as a writer, turning out a series of articles on his gunslinger acquaintances. Lewis later helped him become sports editor of the *New York Morning Telegraph*.

In a sense, Masterson achieved a greater measure of respectability than any of his gunfighter pals. In 1921 he died of a heart attack working at his desk on his next column. It read: "There are many in this old world of ours who hold that things break about even for us. I have observed, for example, that we all get about the same amount of ice. The rich get it in the summer-time and the poor get it in the winter."

See also: *Molly Brennan; Cimarron County Seat War; Dodge City, Kansas; Dodge City Peace Commission; Wyatt Earp; Dora Hand; Edward J. Masterson; James P. Masterson; Notched Weapons; Theodore Roosevelt.*

MATHER, Cotton (1663-1728): Promoter of Salem witch trials

The American Colonial clergyman Cotton Mather, it has been said, was simultaneously the most intelligent and the most stupid man this country has ever produced. He was the author of no less that 450 books on many erudite subjects, but he was also obsessed by witches. With his fiery sermons, Mather was probably the man most responsible for the Salem witchcraft mania of 1692. He encouraged the persecutions, which finally ended only because of public revulsion. Among the many contributions Dr. Mather made on the general subject of witchcraft was the theory that the devil spoke perfect Greek, Hebrew and Latin, but that his English was hampered by an odd accent.

See also: *Salem Witchcraft Trials.*

MATHER, Mysterious Dave (1845-?): Lawman and outlaw

Mysterious Dave Mather, one of the most cold-blooded gunmen in the West, was the epitome of the lawman-outlaw, serving as marshal of several frontier towns and spending as much time in their jails.

Little is known of Mather's life before he reached the age of 28 except that he was from Massachusetts and appears to have been, as he claimed, a direct descendant of Cotton Mather. Mather earned his nickname Mysterious not so much because his escapades were unknown but because it was a mystery how he got away with so many of them. It was pretty well established that Mather became involved in cattle rustling in 1873. The following year in Dodge City, Kan. he worked sometimes as a gambler and sometimes as a peace officer. Dave kept drifting in an out of Dodge City over the years and ran up quite a record as a killer and a lawbreaker in general. It was often said—and believed—that he once killed seven men in a single gunfight, but the facts are hard to pin down.

In one of his law-abiding phases, Mather headed a vigilance committee that strung up horse thieves. Operating on the other side of the law, he and Wyatt Earp ran a con racket in 1878 in which they sold "gold bricks" to gullible cowboys in Mobeetie, Tex. The following year Mather was accused of train robbery but the charge was dropped because of insufficient evidence. Mysterious Dave was again on the side of the law in 1880, aiding Las Vegas Marshal Joe Carson battle the Henry gang. In the gunfight, in which the marshal was killed, Mather shot dead one of the gang and wounded another, who was taken off to jail. Three days later, he killed a third member. When the last two gang members were rounded up and put behind bars, Mather led a lynch mob to the local jail and there they dispensed rope justice to the three survivors of the gang. Within a few months Dave left the Las Vegas scene following accusations that he had engaged in "promiscuous shooting." After some drifting and apparently more lawbreaking, he took a job as assistant marshal in El Paso, Tex., but he found the remuneration poor and turned to procuring for a time. Mather was slightly wounded one day for reasons that are unclear. Either because he had tried to skip out with a prostitute's entire wages or because he had attempted to hold up a whorehouse, he was shot and butcher-knifed by an angry madam. In any event, he returned to law work in Dodge City as assistant city marshal.

In February 1884 Mather lost his position following an election, and he suffered the added annoyance of being succeeded in the job by Tom Nixon, with whom he had never gotten along. By this time Mysterious Dave had set himself up in the saloon business, the same activity Nixon engaged in after his normal working hours. The two got into a price war over beer, and when Mather got the best of it, Nixon used his law enforcement job to cut off his competitor's beer supply. The conflict eventually led to a gun battle, but it appears that the immediate cause of the shooting was Dave's attention to Nixon's young wife. As Mather came out of his saloon on July

18, 1884, Nixon took a shot at him and fled, thinking he had killed his quarry. But Mysterious Dave had been hit by nothing worse than flying splinters. Nixon was arrested, but Mather refused to press charges, preferring to exact private justice. Three days later, on July 21, 1884, Nixon was lounging in front of a Front Street saloon. The last words he heard were a whispered "Hello, Tom." Then Mather put four bullets in Nixon's back, killing him instantly.

Mysterious Dave was brought to trial for the murder. In a verdict that could happen only in the American West, he was acquitted on grounds of self-defense. After all, Nixon had started the shooting three days earlier.

The following year Mather killed a man and, in a separate shooting, wounded two others. He was finally run out of Dodge by the town's fearless marshal, Bill Tilghman. Moving on, Mather did short stints as city marshal in a couple of small towns in Kansas and Nebraska. After that, his trail disappears. According to unconfirmed accounts, he served in the Canadian Mounties, but other reports say he became an outlaw up north. There was a story that he was alive in Alberta, Canada as late as 1915. Mather's final years remain a mystery.

See also: *Wyatt Earp, Gold Brick Swindle.*

MATTRESS Girls: Prostitutes

Almost from its founding, New Orleans became the sex capital of America and the mecca for countless traveling prostitutes seeking to make a living in the world's oldest profession. Competition was so intense and the houses so crowded that many prostitutes could not find lodgings and took to carrying a mattress on their heads, ready to set up for business in an alley or open field. Some of them branched out from New Orleans, trekking up the Mississippi or westward with their trusty mattresses on their heads. The call "Mattress girl a-comin' " often caused considerable excitement. In time, reform elements in various communities, including New Orleans, either drove such prostitutes away or into houses where it was felt they belonged, and a quaint, if demeaning, custom vanished from the scene.

MATTSON, Charles (1926-1937): Kidnap-murder victim

Few kidnap-murder cases upset America as much as that of 10-year-old Charles Mattson. With Christmas just two days past, three of the Mattson children and a young playmate were happily planning the rest of the holiday season in the Tacoma, Wash. home of Dr. W.W. Mattson. As the children—the three Mattsons, Charles, 10, William, 14, and Muriel, 16, and their visitor, Virginia Chatfield, 16—talked, they were unaware of a shadowy figure watching them from the darkness outside the French doors. Suddenly, the intruder, a scarf masking his face, pushed through the glass doors and entered the room, brandishing a .38 revolver.

At first, the man demanded money, but when the children told him they had none, he announced, "All right, I'll take the kid." As he seized Charles, his scarf dropped and the other children saw a coarse-featured man of 25 to 35 years old with a break in the bridge of his nose. He was about five feet eight and wore a tan checked cap, dark trousers and a zippered jacket. He readjusted the scarf and then backed from the room, holding his prisoner. Just before he left, he threw a prepared ransom note on the floor, indicating that kidnapping was his intention from the first.

The note, prepared with what appeared to be a toy printing set, demanded a $28,000 ransom. Charles Mattson was never to be seen alive again. Negotiations for the child's release were carried on through personal ads in the newspapers. The parents were harrowed not only by the kidnapping but also by unrelenting coverage of the press, radio and newsreels. In fact, some authorities have always felt the circus-like atmosphere created by the media finally panicked the kidnapper into killing his young victim.

On January 11, 1937 a rabbit hunter found little Charles' body in an open field near Everett, Wash. Bits of orange pulp were found in the child's mouth, indicating that the killer had murdered the boy as he was eating.

In the ensuing years the FBI questioned some 26,000 suspects in the case but failed to come up with a solution. Among the 400 kidnap cases the FBI has investigated since given that duty in 1932, the Mattson case is one of only four that the agency has failed to solve. Ironically, young Charles had been a playmate of George Weyerhaeuser, who had been kidnapped in 1935 but released when his father, wealthy lumberman John Philip Weyerhaeuser, paid a $200,000 ransom. In that case the kidnappers were captured and convicted. After Charles Mattson's death Weyerhaeuser established an endowment in his memory at the Children's Orthopedic Hospital in Seattle.

MAURY County, Tennessee Jail Fire

One of the most bizarre jail fires in American history occurred on June 27, 1977 at the Maury County Jail in Columbia, Tenn. The fire was all the more tragic in that it took place during visiting hours.

A juvenile prisoner started the fire in his cell. As the plastic padding in the young arsonist's cell burned, it produced cyanide and carbon monoxide gases, which were quickly transmitted to all parts of the jail through the ventilation system. As the poisonous smoke came pouring out of the air ducts into the prisoners' cells, panic ensued and visitors stampeded blindly through the corridors. When a prison guard realized what was happening, he hurried to unlock the cell block doors, but he was bowled over by the panicked visitors and the keys disappeared among the shuffling feet. There was another set of keys in the jailer's office but no one had the presence of mind to locate them. By the time the cell doors were battered open, 42 persons, virtually all prisoners or their relatives, had died from the poisonous fumes. In some cases entire families were wiped out; one inmate, for instance, died along with his parents, his wife and his sister. Ironically, many of the prisoners had not even been convicted but were awaiting trial.

MAXWELL Street Police Station: Chicago's most corrupt precinct

When in the early 1920s Charles C. Fitzmorris, Chicago's chief of police, publicly stated, "Sixty percent of my police are in the bootleg business," he was not referring to the Maxwell Street police precinct in the heart of Little Italy. There, the percentage was placed, according to a popular saying, at 110 percent, which was not a mathematical impossibility. Chicago's Little Italy at the time was the heart of the city's bootleg alcohol production and was for thousands of immigrant families a sort of cottage industry that earned them a rather fine living. This racket was controlled by the notorious Gennas, a family of five ruthless brothers. The Gennas induced Italian families to set up portable copper stills in their kitchens or the back rooms of their stores for extracting alcohol from corn sugar. In return, they received a set fee of $15 a day, far more than immigrants could make as simple laborers. Those families that refused usually changed their minds quickly when they received Black Hand threats. So pervasive was the "alky cooking" that all of Little Italy was enveloped in the stink of fermenting mash.

It was an activity that could hardly be kept secret from the police of the Maxwell Street precinct, a matter the Gennas easily handled with bribes. There was plenty of money available for police graft, since a home still could produce 350 gallons of raw alcohol a week for considerably less than $1 a gallon and the Gennas, after processing the alcohol further in their plant at 1022 Taylor Street, sold the product wholesale for $6 a gallon.

The Maxwell Street cops got their cut out of this huge gross, being paid $10 to $125 a month depending on their importance and length of service. There were regular payoffs to some 400 officers plus larger stipends for plainclothesmen, detectives attached to the state attorney's office and five police captains. All day on the monthly payday, police officers would troop in and out of the Taylor Street plant, many openly counting their graft on the street. The Gennas found they had to contend with a particularly venal form of police dishonesty, officers from other precincts showing up and pretending to be from the Maxwell Street station, hence the 110 percent figure. The local police brass solved this dilemma by furnishing the gang with a list of badge numbers to check all claims against. Because an occasional Genna truck would be seized by police in other parts of the city while making deliveries, the Maxwell Street precinct also supplied police escorts through such dangerous zones. The police tried to shut down those alky cookers not working for the Gennas but were generally put off when the independents insisted they were operating Genna stills. To solve that problem, the Gennas supplied the police with a complete list of their stills. Whenever a private operation was unearthed, the police would move in with axes and destroy it,

often alerting the newspapers in advance so that the precinct's aggressive fight against crime would be publicized.

See also: *Genna Brothers.*

MEAGHER, Mike (1844-1881): Kansas lawman

Michael Meager and his twin brother, John, came to America from their native Ireland with their father, Timothy, and settled in Kansas. Both brothers became local lawmen. Mike eventually won fame as the marshal who taught Wyatt Earp all he knew.

Mike served several years as city marshal of Wichita with John as his deputy. John later was elected sheriff but quit after one year to follow the gambling trail, eventually becoming the owner of several saloons. After a short stint as a deputy U.S. marshal tracking down horse thieves, Mike again became city marshal of Wichita, which had grown into a rip-roarin', shot-em-up cattle town in need of taming. One of his deputies was Wyatt Earp. Meagher managed to quiet Wichita down and reduce the size of his force at the same time.

In 1877 Meagher shot and killed Sylvester Powell, who had wounded the marshal while resisting arrest. The killing weighed on Meagher, and he decided not to run for reelection later that year. All through Wichita's worst shooting years, Meagher had kept order without ever having to kill a man, but now his record had been bloodied. Killing was not something Meagher was proud of, a feeling he failed to instill in Wyatt Earp. Meagher moved on to Caldwell, Kan. and was its mayor for a time. He quit politics to open a saloon. When murders became common in Caldwell, the townspeople asked him to take the marshal's job, but Meagher refused, telling them he no longer wanted to be a lawman. He would, however, leave his saloon to put on a badge temporarily when the marshal called for help. On one such mission in 1881, Meagher was murdered by an unidentified gunman.

MEANS, Gaston Bullock (1880-1938): Swindler and rogue

In the pecking order of J. Edgar Hoover's pet hates, Gaston Bullock Means stood close to the top of the list and deservedly so, since Means was perhaps the most outrageous figure to appear on the Washington scene in the 20th century.

At one point this rogue of unsurpassed effrontery stood almost at the top of the list of future candidates to become head of what was then called the Bureau of Investigation, later renamed the Federal Bureau of Investigation. He was, in William J. Burns' words, "the greatest natural detective ever known." The word "detective" easily could have been replaced by such terms as con man, swindler, hoaxer, spy, influence peddler, blackmailer and, quite possibly, murderer. His depredations were astonishing. Only Gaston Means, for instance, could do more to besmirch the administration of Warren G. Harding than the Ohio Gang and Teapot Dome. Always the opportunist, he made more money out of the Lindbergh kidnapping than did Bruno Hauptmann.

Means, born in North Carolina in 1880, had a most-undistinguished record as, among other things, a towel salesman and sometimes lawyer. When he joined the Burns Detective Agency in 1910, it was in this period that Means so impressed Burns, using such standard private detective cons as "secret informants" and other phony methods indicative of investigative prowess to impress his superior.

In 1915 Means left the agency for bigger and better things, becoming bodyguard and financial overseer for madcap heiress Maude R. King. There is strong reason to suspect that Means gained Mrs. King's confidence by arranging to have a thug fake a robbery attempt on her and some friends on a Chicago street, a crime frustrated by the gallant appearance of Means. In no time at all, the con artist was managing the woman's financial affairs and by 1917, he had bilked her out of some $150,000. Even as flighty a person as Maude King eventually got a bit upset about her losses, but Means solved this problem by taking her on a hunting trip to North Carolina. Mrs. King, unaccustomed to such sport, was shot to death on the trip. Means was tried for murder but acquitted; the conclusion was that the woman had committed suicide.

Means' activities were not confined to swindling heiresses. During World War I he hired out as both a secret agent for the Germans (with duties to disrupt British shipping) and at the same time, as a counterspy for the British against the Germans. Eventually—before the United States entered the war—Means severed his German connections, probably less because of patriotism than because of the difficulty he encountered in collecting his pay. Quite naturally, he shifted his activities to U.S. Army Intelligence.

When the Harding Administration came to power in 1921, Burns brought his old friend Means into the Bureau of Investigation, which enraged Hoover, who was made assistant director of the agency. Although the bureau was rife with bribe takers during this period, Means upgraded the graft system to a fine art. He was also busy, as he subsequently revealed, in the employ of Mrs. Harding, secretly investigating her husband's love affairs and paternity situation. For a time Means came under such a cloud that he was dropped from his job, but he was quickly reinstated as an "informant" through Burns' good offices. A short time later, Means was indicted for a scheme in which he had swindled a number of bootleggers by telling them he was collecting graft for Secretary of the Treasury Andrew Mellon. During a Senate committee investigation, Means told how he had acted as a go-between in the payment of $50,000 to an associate of Attorney General Harry Daugherty to have a $6 million government suit against an aircraft concern killed.

In this same period Means was also busy attempting to blackmail the Hardings for $50,000 with the accusation that the President had fathered a child by Nan Britton, an undistinguished young poetess from Ohio. After Harding died in office, Means tried to make his money by coauthoring a book with Nan Britton entitled *The President's Daughter*. Eventually,

Means went to prison for his bribery scams. When he emerged in 1930, he further pursued his literary career with a scandalous best-seller, *The Strange Death of President Harding*, in which he implied Mrs. Harding had poisoned her husband.

Means capped his career of unbridled roguery by concocting a swindle to capitalize on the Lindbergh baby kidnapping. He convinced another flighty heiress, Mrs. Evalyn Walsh McLean, that through his underworld contacts he could recover the child. Mrs. McLean gave him $100,000 for the ransom and $4,000 for his own expenses. The child was not recovered, and Means did not give back the money, instead telling the woman one preposterous story after another. He finally insisted he had returned the money to an associate of Mrs. McLean, but his story was proved false and he went to prison for 15 years.

When Means suffered a heart attack in 1938, Hoover dispatched FBI agents to his prison hospital bed to learn the whereabouts of Mrs. McLean's money. Means gave them a puckish smile and died.

See also: *Lindbergh Kidnapping*.

MEDICAL Quackery

In a century that has seen monumental strides in pharmaceuticals, general medicine and surgery, medical quackery has become among the most lucrative criminal activities in the United States. The public wastes hundreds of millions and probably billions of dollars each year on "miracle" and "sure-cure" medicines, cosmetics, drugs and therapeutic devices. Particularly victimized are persons who have incurable diseases and those with great fear of going to doctors.

Typical cures are those that will grow hair on a bald head and renew sexual vigor in older men. In fact, there are nostrums for every human ailment from hemorrhoids to cancer. Devices offered include a magnetized copper bracelet with magical powers against rheumatism and arthritis, an electric rolling pin that melts fat and a plug-in vibrating cushion that cures arthritis and varicose veins. Concentrated seawater, according to those who sell it, will do away with such varied ailments as diabetes, baldness and cancer, among other things, while offering our bodily glands "a chemical smorgasbord."

One of the more unique instruments sold some years ago was a set of two small rubber hammers for people tired of wearing glasses all the time. They were instructed to tap their eyes with the hammers 200 times a day as a method of "strengthening" them. Then they were to put a mask over their eyes for total relaxation and rest. When the mask was removed, quite a few of the victims sported two perfect black eyes. But the promoter even turned this development into a plus by insisting that the discoloration indicated the victim was eminently susceptible to the treatment and that if the hammers were used on the male genital organs, such tapping would increase virility.

Probably the biggest con man in the cancer field was Norman Baker, who battled postal inspectors with every available legal delaying tactic for almost a decade before he was put out of business. Baker's empire mushroomed to include a number of hospitals and radio stations, and he even published a newspaper in Iowa. It was charged that he fed his patients large amounts of flavored waters and acids as a cancer cure. Since he gave the patients in his hospitals no substantial foods, his operating expenses were greatly reduced. In the process, a great many of his patients, understandably, died, but Baker was nonetheless able to accumulate millions of dollars. His achievement was even more monumental considering the punishment he later received: four years imprisonment and a $4,000 fine.

According to postal inspectors, the two main obstacles to successful prosecution of medical quacks are the fact that potential chief witnesses against them often die before the case reaches court and the mistaken belief of many of their victims that they are getting treatment the "medical interests" and the American Medical Association in particular conspire to keep from the public.

MELDRUM, Robert (1865-?): Hired killer

Famed, not entirely accurately, as a "hired killer who never was caught," Robert Meldrum was, next to Tom Horn, probably the most notorious gunman employed by what Westerners called "the interests," generally meaning ranchers and mine operators who wanted troublesome nesters and activists neutralized. As was common in such matters, the case or cases against Meldrum were always shrouded in mystery and controversy. When he arrived in Baggs, Wyo. in 1899, Meldrum had the reputation of a paid killer. According to local tales, he was a New Yorker, the son of a British Army officer. The following year Meldrum was appointed town marshal of Dixon, Wyo., quite possibly based on his supposed ability to handle troublemakers. During the course of his duties there, he won fame for killing Noah Wilkinson, a Texas outlaw with a price on his head.

In 1901 Meldrum quit being a lawman in favor of more lucrative work as a guard at the Smuggler Union Mine in Telluride, Colo., which was having strike troubles. Shortly after Meldrum's appearance, a number of the strikers were assassinated, and it was suspected that Meldrum had done the killings. He also had dealings with Tom Horn, another paid killer of the interests. A popular notion was that Meldrum helped Horn with a number of range assassinations. When Horn was hanged for his crimes in November 1903, there was speculation that his silence had saved Meldrum from a similar fate.

Over the next four years Meldrum had two brushes with the law: once, in 1904, when he killed a miner, apparently for the offense of smuggling whiskey into the workings in violation of company rules; and again, in 1908, when he killed another miner, a man named Lambert, who was considered a troublemaker. The first matter did not even reach the indictment stage and the second resulted in a not-guilty verdict. In 1910 Meldrum, back in Baggs, committed a "personal" killing shooting down John "Chick" Bowen because of the attention Bowen was paying to Meldrum's common-law wife. The personal

nature of the killing did not prevent a number of ranchers from raising Meldrum's $18,000 bail, which he promptly jumped. Six years elapsed before Meldrum surrendered to stand trial, and there was considerable speculation that his friends among the ranchers and mine operators had made a deal for him. That theory seems to have been borne out by Meldrum's relatively light sentence of five to seven years for a reduced charge of manslaughter. After serving only three months, he was paroled into the custody of an obliging rancher.

Following that experience Meldrum's gunslinging days appeared at an end, as much due to the general taming of the area as to his own advancing years. For a time he ran a saddler's business in Walcott, Wyo., but he was still known as a man with a violent temper and one to stay clear of. Meldrum's business burned down in 1929; some said the fire was the result of one of his rages and others claimed it was the work of enemies. Shortly thereafter, Meldrum disappeared from sight.

"MERRICK, Pulling a Dick": Saying for a lucky survival

In Missouri the saying "pulling a Dick Merrick" was more popular in the 1860s and 1870s than the expression "a Frank Merriwell finish" was in the 1920s and connoted an even more miraculous conclusion to a tight situation.

In 1864 Dick Merrick and Jebb Sharp were convicted and sentenced to hang in Jackson County for the robbery and murder of a horse trader named John Bascum. It was a period of no-nonsense treatment of murderers, and the execution was scheduled to be held the day after the jury's verdict. Early that morning the condemned pair were rousted out of their jail beds and duly dispatched. On returning to the jail, Deputy Sheriff Clifford Stewart was stunned to find Merrick and Sharp sitting in their cell. It took a few hours for the sad truth to be uncovered. During the night two drunks had been heaved into a cell to sleep off their inebriation, and it was they who had been taken to the scaffold. Since the pair were still so boozed up, they were in no condition to protest, indeed to comprehend, what was being done to them. Quickly, the matter was rushed to the sentencing judge, who ruled that since the men had not been hanged at the prescribed time, they had to be released. Merrick and Sharp wasted no time raising dust on the trail, leaving behind only the folklore about "pulling a Dick Merrick."

MERRICK, Suds (?-1884): Burglar and river pirate

For most of the 1860s and into the 1870s, Suds Merrick was one of the most-renowned river pirates in New York City. He was one of the coleaders of the Hook Gang, which plundered the East River docks and cargo boats moored there. The Hookers were at least 100 strong, and many of their crimes were masterminded by Merrick.

In 1874 Merrick, Sam McCracken, Johnny Gallagher and Tommy Bonner boarded the canal boat *Thomas H. Brick,* tied up the captain and set about looting the cargo at their leisure until they were surprised by police. Merrick escaped by diving overboard, but his three accomplices were captured and sentenced to long terms at Auburn Prison.

After the incident, Merrick fell into disfavor with the Hookers, who were suspicious about the affair. Some thought Merrick must have been in trouble with the law and set up the trio in exchange for his own freedom. Since there was no proof of this, he was simply allowed to resign from the gang. For the next 10 years Merrick operated as a lone wolf, carrying out numerous burglaries and muggings. He was ignored by the rest of the Hookers, and there is no record of other criminals attacking him, which indeed would have been a foolhardy enterprise since Merrick was virtually unbeatable in a fight at anything near even odds. He never ventured abroad without a knife and gun and generally wore brass knuckles or carried a blackjack up his sleeve. In 1884 he was found murdered in the Bowery. There were no clues as to who might have done the killing, and the police seemed singularly unconcerned about solving the case, considering the murder a definite civic improvement.

See also: *Hook Gang.*

METESKY, George Peter (1903-): New York's "Mad Bomber"

Starting in 1950, New York's mysterious Mad Bomber terrorized New York City for eight years, planting 32 homemade bombs in train stations and movie theaters, including Radio City Music Hall. The bombings injured 15 people and created a period of anxiety that was said to have hurt Manhattan's theater business as much as television did.

Actually, the Mad Bomber had gone through an earlier period of maniacal bombings in 1940-41, virtually all of them duds. Then a decade later, the Bomber started up again, this time more efficient in his production of explosives. The bombings were followed by notes that ranted about the local utility company, Consolidated Edison. He often signed these notes "Fair Play." Metesky set off bombs in Radio City Music Hall, Grand Central Station, Penn Station and several theaters. A train porter at Penn Station was permanently crippled by one of his bombs and seven persons suffered serious injuries from a blast in a theater.

The hunt for the Mad Bomber got nowhere for years until he wrote a letter to a newspaper in which he once more castigated Consolidated Edison and charged the company had caused him to contract tuberculosis. Finally, a close study of the firm's records turned up a former employee, George Peter Metesky, who in 1931 had had an accident working for the company and had previously made a claim of having developed tuberculosis on the job.

Metesky was taken into custody at his home in Waterbury, Conn. and accused of attempted murder. The assortment of charges against Metesky made him liable to a total of 1,235 years imprisonment, but he was found criminally insane and incarcerated in a mental hospital in New York state. Pronounced cured some 15 years later, Metesky was set free in 1973 and had the charges against him dropped. A bachelor in his seventies, Metesky went home to take care of his ailing sister and later rejected a marriage proposal from a pen pal.

MICKEY Finn: Knockout drink

Named after a Chicago barkeep, a Mickey Finn is a drink used to put a victim into a state of collapse so that he can be robbed. Mickey Finn did not originate the drink but bought the recipe of a secret voodoo mixture that could be added to alcohol and water.

Finn, who operated the Lone Star Saloon and Palm Garden on Chicago's notorious Whisky Row during the Gay Nineties, ordered his employees to give the drink to any lone customer. Two of the employees, Isabelle Ffyffe and Gold Tooth Mary Thornton, eventually testified before a special crime commission. Gold Tooth Mary, so named because her single tooth was crowned with the precious metal, explained the potency of the drink: "When the victims drink this dopey stuff, they get talkative, walk around in a restless manner, and then fall into a deep sleep, and you can't arouse them until the effect of the drug wears off." While so incapacitated, the victim would be lugged into the back room, where Finn, in an odd ritual, would be waiting in a derby hat and a clean white apron to "operate." The victim would be searched to the skin for valuables, and if articles of clothing were deemed to have any worth, they too would be taken. The victim would then be dressed in old rags and dumped in an alley. When he awoke, he seldom had any recollections of what had happened. Eventually, Finn lost his license and was put out of business. He thereupon sold his secret recipe to several other eager saloon keepers and use of Mickey Finns soon spread throughout the country.

MIDNIGHT Rose's: "Office" of Murder, Inc.

Midnight Rose's was a seedy little Brooklyn candy store, at the intersection of Saratoga and Livonia avenues under the elevated New York subway tracks, where probably more murders were planned than anywhere in the world. In the late 1930s the store was owned by a woman who kept it open 24 hours a day and was thus called Midnight Rose. Early in the morning and late at night, the gunmen, knife specialists and garroters of Murder, Inc. gathered on the corner and in the store. Midnight Rose's was the assembly room and dispatch office for homicide specialists who worked out the details for the elimination of an estimated 300 to 500 victims.

See also: *Murder, Inc.*

MIDNIGHT Terrors: Gay Nineties New York gang

One of the most mindless, vicious street gangs in New York in the 1890s was the Midnight Terrors, named for their nocturnal muggings. Overflowing with self-esteem, the Terrors decided to form a baseball team. They raised money for uniforms and equipment in their home territory, the First Ward, by robbing and beating anyone who seemed likely to have money; as one of the Terrors said, "Dat's de way we was to get the uniforms for de ball club."

The Terrors enjoyed considerable freedom from a police department not eager for confrontations as long as they confined their depredations to their own area and to their "own kind." The Terrors, however, carried their actions to the public parks and even to their baseball games. Watching them was not the safest activity for a baseball fan, as some of the bench warmers would circulate in the crowd looking for potential mugging victims. The Terrors disappeared around the late 1890s, victims of their own crude operating methods, which resulted in their repression.

MILLER, Bill "The Killer" (1905-1931): Partner of Pretty Boy Floyd

A remarkable young criminal, William Miller, better known in the underworld as Bill the Killer, molded Charles "Pretty Boy" Floyd into a future public enemy.

It was not an easy task, since Floyd, four years older than Miller, was a trigger-happy punk who preferred to shoot first and think afterward. In 1930, after jumping out of a train window while en route to the Ohio State Penitentiary, Floyd made his way to Toledo to hook up with Miller, who had been recommended by another criminal as a man who could be trusted. Floyd immediately suggested they start robbing banks. However, the younger hood was dubious. Floyd's past criminal record was hardly inspiring. In 1925 he had been caught following a $5,000 holdup of a paymaster and had served 15 months. Earlier in the current year, 1930, Floyd had been convicted of bank robbery and sentenced to 10 to 25 years. It was while on his way to serve this sentence that Floyd had staged his escape. In between these two relatively big but bungled crimes, he had been arrested several times on such charges as vagrancy and possession of firearms.

Bill the Killer on the other hand, was a young Missouri gangster with a rather amazing record. Before meeting Floyd, he had killed five men and had broken out of prison. Furthermore, in 1929 in Detroit, he pulled off one of the most incredible escapes on record. Charged with the murder of Detective Frank Tradeau, he was in a long line of prisoners all handcuffed together. Suddenly, he ran out of the line with his handcuffs dangling on one wrist and made a clean getaway. It was never learned how he had gotten himself free from the manacles.

Miller finally agreed to join up with Floyd, but he decided they needed considerable "seasoning" to work as a team. The pair moved on to Michigan, where they stuck to small scores, holding up farmers and filling stations. In no case did their take come to more than a couple of hundred dollars. They pulled three minor bank holdups in the northern part of the state and then headed for safety in Kansas City, where they holed up at Mother Ash's place, a whorehouse of some standing. At this establishment love came to both men, Floyd falling for Mother Ash's daughter-in-law, Rose, and Miller for Rose's sister, Beulah Bird. The fact that Wallace Ash was married to Rose and his brother, William, had been keeping company with Beulah didn't prevent the two young hoods from marching the women out of the house under Mother Ash's hateful glare. Wallace and William Ash, besides being bouncers at their mother's establishment, were deeply involved in Kansas City crime and announced they planned to kill Floyd and Miller. A short time later, Wallace Ash received a telephone call from a woman asking him and William to rendezvous with their two former loves. The brothers left for the appointment. When next seen again on March 25, 1931, they were lying in a ditch beside a burning automobile; each had a bullet in the back of his head. According to a weeping Mother Ash, Miller and that "pretty boy" had killed her sons.

Miller and Floyd went back to bank robbing, hitting three banks in Kentucky for sums of $4,000, $2,700 and $3,600. With their lady friends in tow, they then repaired to Bowling Green, Ohio to enjoy the loot. When they attracted too much attention buying suits and dresses, especially with Floyd flashing a fat roll of bills, Chief of Police Carl Galliher was notified and he and an assistant, Ralph Castner, investigated. They found Miller and the two women about to enter a store. Pretty Boy Floyd was stationed across the street, on Miller's theory that it was always a good idea to have someone maintaining watch even when they were relaxing.

When Galliher ordered Miller to stop, the gangster dropped to the ground so that Floyd would have a clear view of the officers. Pretty Boy opened up with a pair of pistols and Castner fell dead. Miller then tried to run to Floyd's side but Chief Galliher shot him through the neck, killing him instantly. Floyd drove the police chief to cover with a barrage of shots, broke for his car and sped out of town. After the battle Miller and Castner lay dead and both women were wounded. From then on, Floyd would have to make his legend without instructions from his young tutor, Bill the Killer.

See also: *Charles Arthur "Pretty Boy" Floyd.*

MILLER, John (1829-1861): New Orleans criminal and jailer

One of the most colorful, if deadly, scourges of antebellum New Orleans was John Miller, a one-armed brute with a chain and iron ball attached to the stump that was left of his other arm. It proved to be a most effective weapon in his criminal endeavors.

Miller was born in Gretna, across the river from New Orleans, and became that community's principal ruffian. So far as can be determined, he never did an honest day's work in his life, making enough by venturing over into the French Quarter two or three times a week to fall on some unsuspecting visitor and make off with his purse.

In 1854 Miller branched into fight managing, taking under his wing a heavyweight named Charley Keys, who soon became the champion of the Gretna side of the Mississippi. He arranged a bout between Keys and Tom Murray, the so-called bruiser of Gallatin Street. Miller wagered a considerable sum on his man, who was soon being belted mercilessly by Murray. It became apparent that if the fight continued, Murray would surely win. Realizing this, Miller stuck a knife into Murray's chief backer. A general riot ensued, enabling Miller to keep his money but resulting in the loss of his left arm. After the riot he attached a chain and iron ball to the remaining stump of his left arm, and with a knife in his right hand, he was as fearsome an opponent as one could meet in the back alleys of the city. He proved this in 1857, when he killed a man in a fight. Since Miller was "disabled," he got only two years for this offense. If that struck the citizenry as unusual, it didn't compare to the stir caused by what happened to him when he completed his term in the parish prison. In an ironic turnabout arranged by the parish politicians of the day, Miller was kept on as a prison guard. While some claimed that there had been a genuine "reformation of his character," Miller's case was widely credited as a prime cause of the creation of the New Orleans Vigilance Committee for the purpose of "freeing the city of thugs, outlaws, assassins and murderers."

Miller left his position more or less voluntarily, having discovered there his true love, a prisoner named Mary Jane Jackson, better known in the vicious slums and dives of the city as Bricktop Jackson, who was also doing a stint for murder. When she was released, the couple repaired to a love nest in Freetown. A mean street fighter, Bricktop gave away nothing in a match with any of the tough bullies of Gallatin Street. While there is no absolute proof that she was the toughest female in the city, there is no doubt that as a couple Bricktop and Miller were unequaled in viciousness by any other husband-wife team in the city. A half-dozen Live Oak gangsters were known to have backed off from a battle with Bricktop Jackson and Miller, swinging his iron ball.

In keeping with Miller's past history, there is no record of the couple ever supporting themselves honestly. They would strut through the French Quarter arm in arm, with many a man staring at Bricktop, who was a most attractive woman. Finally, Miller would leave her alone, and it was usually just a matter of moments before she would attract a male admirer. She and her new friend would then be seen departing for a destination unknown but reasonably deduced. When next seen, if ever, the gentleman involved would be sporting a very bruised head, not surprising considering the bruising potential of an iron ball.

The love of Bricktop Jackson and John Miller ended on December 5, 1861, when Miller came home with a cowhide whip and announced to the entire neighborhood that Bricktop was in need of a thorough thrashing. It soon became clear which of the pair was the toughest. Bricktop took the whip away from him and beat him unmercifully. Miller tried to brain her with his iron-ball, but she grabbed the chain in midair and pulled him around their living quarters. In desperation, Miller drew a knife and tried to slash her. Bricktop wrestled the knife free and, shoving him against the wall, stabbed her lover five times. Miller was dead when his body hit the floor.

The *New Orleans Picayune* commented, "Both were degraded beings, regular penitentiary birds, habitual drunkards, and unworthy of any further notice from honest people." Bricktop Jackson served nine months for the killing.

See also: *Mary Jane "Bricktop" Jackson.*

MILLER, William F. (1874-?): Swindler

A 24-year-old Brooklyn, New York City bookkeeper, William F. (520%) Miller was one of the greatest swindlers this country has ever produced. Charles Ponzi did nothing but lift Willy Miller's modus operandi; and while the latter could not be credited with having originated the idea of robbing Peter to pay Paul, he certainly carried it to dizzying heights during 11 incredible months in 1899, while he trimmed an array of suckers out of well over $1 million.

For years Miller was an insignificant bookkeeper who tried in vain to make a killing in the stock market. He made small investments, in the hundreds of dollars, with money borrowed from friends in his community. Miller was good for it, though, and always repaid his debts promptly—by the simple expedient of borrowing a slightly larger sum elsewhere. It took Miller some time to figure out this robbing-Peter-to-pay-Paul tactic was one of the great secrets of high finance.

One day he posted a sign in his window:

WM. F. MILLER
Investments
The way to wealth is as plain as
the road to market.—B. Franklin

Miller was a great admirer of Benjamin Franklin.

By the following Sunday everyone in the neighborhood had seen the sign and Miller was asked about it in the adult Bible class he ran at the local church. With a very earnest expression he said, "It's not fair that the Morgans and the Goulds and the Vanderbilts are making so many millions when us little people are making so little—and I've decided to do something about it."

Then he confided a great secret. Everyone knew he was always hanging around Wall Street. Well, he had learned the investment secrets used by the big boys. Naturally, he couldn't tell what they were, but he was now in a position to pay 10 percent interest on money invested with him. A few persons expressed interest, since that rate was substantially more than what the banks were paying.

"You don't understand," Miller said matter-of-factly. "I don't mean ten percent a year. I mean ten percent a week."

"Holy smoke!" one parishioner exclaimed. "That's 520 percent a year!"

"I suppose it is," Miller said modestly.

Now, many of his students were impressed and wanted to invest right on the spot. Righteously, Miller said he wouldn't take any investments on the Sabbath. The next night when he got home from work, there was a line of investors waiting at his door. True, many had only tiny sums, undoubtedly cautious about so remarkable an investment opportunity. Miller took many amounts of less than $10, but he told each investor to return in one week for their first interest payment.

Sure enough, after seven days an investor who had given $10 got $1 back as interest. By the time 10 weeks passed, all the original investors had made back initial investments and were still drawing more. All of these people were investing larger sums now, as were others who had joined the eager procession as soon as Miller started making payments.

Miller's fame spread far beyond his Brooklyn community. He was known as 520% Miller and money flowed in much more rapidly than he was paying it out. Some investors thought they were being rather shrewd by promptly reinvesting their interest as soon as Miller handed it to them. In 11 glorious months Miller trimmed his suckers for well in excess of a million dollars. According to some later accounts, while he lived high on the hog, he managed to salt away $480,000 and possibly more, considering that in one month in 1899 he made an estimated $430,000 profit.

But Miller never did get to enjoy his money. The great con man was himself conned out of half of the $480,000. A fixer named T. Edward Schlesinger told Miller that for a cut of the take, he would show him how to keep the law off his neck. Gullible Miller, the genius swindler, dutifully handed over the money. Schlesinger, however, didn't offer Miller any foolproof method to avoid legal harassment. He simply took his $240,000 and caught a fast boat for Europe, finishing out his days in Baden-Baden.

Miller's turn at playing the sucker would come again. His second bit of gullibility resulted from his meeting with a slick lawyer named Robert Ammon. He hired Ammon to give him legal advice on how to stay out of jail once it became known that when new investments stopped coming in, Miller would be unable to pay any more juicy 10 percent dividends.

Ammon's advice was that Miller leave the country. As for the $240,000, Miller said he had left, Ammon suggested he leave it with him "because if you are caught and have the money in your possession, it would be proof of your guilt."

Miller went to Canada after getting Ammon's firm promise that he could have his money sent to him whenever he wanted it. He never did get a penny of the loot he left with Ammon and was eventually caught and sent to prison, but only for 10 years, a surprising ending to one of the most fabulous crime careers in American history. Well, maybe not quite the ending. Miller was sent to Sing Sing, where he finally was able to make a deal with the law to get out of prison in 1907, having served only five years. The authorities were very much interested in lawyer Ammon and Miller told everything he knew about him. Ammon screamed that Miller had given him nowhere near $240,000. In any event, Ammon went to Sing Sing and Miller got out. He returned to Brooklyn and, for a time, worked again as a bookkeeper. But after a few years Miller just sort of faded away, perhaps going off to enjoy the underestimated fruits of his crime.

MINA, Lino Amalia Espos Y (1809-1832): Impostor and murderer

An impostor for whose favor much of early 19th century Philadelphia society vied, Lino Amalia Mina was a young man who passed himself off in that city as the son of the Spanish governor of California. He claimed to be stranded without funds until the arrival of a clipper rounding the Cape. Of the several important families that offered to house him, Dr. and Mrs. William Chapman won out. Dr. Chapman's wife, Lucretia, was overjoyed; she was very socially conscious and she thought having Mina as a houseguest would be a triumph. Within a week Mina's presence developed into a triumph in more ways than one. The servants saw Mina kissing Mrs. Chapman on a number of occasions, and the 41-year-old matron offered no resistance at all. If Dr. Chapman noticed anything, he said nothing, and within another month he was not able to say anything.

Mina went to a Philadelphia pharmacy and bought a huge amount of arsenic—for "stuffing of birds." Four days later, Dr. Chapman suddenly became ill and died. Two weeks after the funeral, Mina and the widow Chapman traveled to New York and were married. When they returned home, valuables in the mansion started disappearing. So did much of Lucretia's jewelry, and Mina set about cleaning out certain bank assets. He also posed as Dr. Chapman to complete certain financial dealings. This brought him to the attention of the authorities. Now suspicious, they ordered an autopsy performed on Chapman's body. Massive amounts of poison were found, and both Mina and Lucretia were charged with murder. Mrs. Chapman wept at the trial, insisting she had been totally taken in by Mina. A male jury was swayed and freed her but condemned Mina to death.

It was reported that a number of important personages attended Mina's hanging, perhaps more incensed over how the cad had bamboozled the city's high society than over the murder he had committed.

MINER, Bill (1847-1913): Stagecoach and train robber

Although he had one of the longest careers of any stagecoach and train robber, running from the 1860s until 1911, colorful Old Bill Miner seldom gets the recognition he deserves in histories of American crime. He was, so far as can be determined, the man who invented the phrase "Hands up!"—an Americanism as distinctive as the English road agent's order "Stand and deliver!"

At the age of 13 young Bill ran away from his Kentucky family, which his footloose father had abandoned a few years earlier, and went West to become a cowboy. He ended up in the California gold fields, but the only place he ever searched for gold was in the pokes he stole from sleeping miners. In 1863 he did a stint as an Army dispatch rider and then set up his own business as a mail rider. Bill made good money carrying the mail but invariably spent more than he earned. By 1869 he had hit the outlaw trail (although he may have been at it as early as 1866), robbing a stagecoach near Sonora, Calif. of a few hundred dollars. Pursued by a posse, Bill was captured when his horse dropped dead in his tracks. He probably avoided being lynched only because he looked so young; prudently, he announced his age as 16.

Bill was sentenced to 15 years in San Quentin. Behind bars he became an avowed religionist and in 1879 the authorities released him early for good behavior. But instead of leading a saintly existence thereafter, Miner headed for Colorado and became a train robber. He and a hard case named Bill Leroy made a daring duo, notching up a long string of train and stagecoach holdups until Leroy was captured in a gun battle with vigilantes and strung up. Bill fought his way free in the same gunfight, leaving three bullet-ridden possemen behind him. That brush with death had a sobering effect on Miner, who promptly made for San Francisco and from there to Europe, where he became a free-spending tourist on the proceeds of his Colorado crimes.

Miner actually plotted out some train robberies in England but wisely decided his American style would stand out too much and assure his apprehension. He bounced around the continent for a while and finally wound up in Turkey, where he joined up with desert bandits in the slave trade. When the law started looking for a light-haired American, Bill hightailed it for Africa, finding his way to South Africa. In Capetown he considered the idea of holding up a diamond train, a thought he abandoned, as he said in his memoirs, "when I saw they [the guards] would be too much for me."

The next stop was South America and a stint at gunrunning, but Miner hankered for the Western outlaw trail and by November 1881 he was back in business in California as a road agent, holding up the Sonora stage for $3,000. Pretty soon, Bill had posses on his trail again and fled to Colorado, where he pulled another holdup before returning to California to rob the Sonora stage once more, this time with a partner named Jimmy Crum. They were caught shortly thereafter and Miner was sent back to San Quentin under a 25-year sentence. He emerged from prison in 1901, again a reformed man determined to follow the Good Book. By 1903 he and two others were holding up trains in Oregon and Washington. With the law hot on his trail, Old Bill moved into Canada to continue his unlawful activities. He was finally arrested there after a train robbery and, at the age of 60, was put away for life. When he heard the sentence, Bill just smirked at the judge, declaring, "No jail can hold me, sir." He was right. A year later, in August 1907, Miller tunneled under the prison fence and escaped.

For the next four years Old Bill, now stoop-shouldered and white-haired, pulled off several bank and train jobs in Washington and Oregon. The Pinkertons sent out an alert for his apprehension, figuring he would be easy to catch since there weren't too many stoop-shouldered, white-haired old codgers robbing trains and banks. By February 1911 Bill had worked his way to White Sulphur, Ga., where he led a gang of four others in the holdup of the Southern Railroad Express. Even though he had put some 3,000 miles between that robbery and his previous job, Old Bill was identified and eventually run down in a Georgia swamp by a Pinkerton-led posse.

Once more, he received a life sentence, this time at the state penitentiary at Milledgeville, Ga. On three occasions in 1911-12, Old Bill escaped, but he was soon recaptured each time. When caught the last time, he was up to his waist in swamp water with bloodhounds baying at him, Bill confided to his captors, "Boys, I guess I'm getting too old for this sort of thing."

He returned to the prison and spent his final year and a half tending a flower garden and dictating his adventures to a detective who had come to admire the incorrigible old crook. One day he told a fellow prisoner he had a plan for getting out, but he died peacefully while asleep in his cell in late 1913.

MIRANDA Decision: Prisoner's rights ruling

Probably no Supreme Court ruling has been more bitterly attacked by law enforcement officials than the Miranda decision, which mandated new procedures for interrogating prisoners. For years the courts decided the validity of confessions on a case-by-case basis, taking into account the individual circumstances. Then on June 13, 1966 in *Miranda* v. *Arizona,* the High Court changed that approach.

In 1963 an unemployed 22-year-old man named Ernesto Miranda was arrested for stealing $8 from a bank employee in Phoenix, Ariz. While in custody, he was picked out of a lineup by a young girl who said he had kidnapped and raped her. Miranda at first denied the charge, but two steady hours of police interrogation produced a written and signed confession by the suspect. The Supreme Court threw out this confession because the police had failed to advise Miranda of his right against self-incrimination under the Fifth Amendment.

In its decision, the court laid down certain rules the police had to follow in questioning suspects. Failure to follow four basic rules, said the court, meant that a confession made by a suspect could not be used against him even if it appeared to be voluntary. First, the prisoner taken into custody must be advised he has the right to remain silent. Second, he must be informed that if he says anything, it can and will be used against him. Third, he must be advised of his right to have a lawyer present while he is being questioned. Finally, he must be told that if he cannot afford a lawyer, the court will appoint one before he is questioned.

Additionally, on the matter of counsel, the defendant can indicate "at any stage of the process that he wishes to consult with a lawyer before speaking (or continuing to speak)."

Quite naturally, the police strenuously attacked the new rules for questioning prisoners as placing an impossible burden on them during a "national crime crisis." Voting in the minority on a more recent Miranda-type decision, Chief Justice Warren Burger called the majority opinion "weird" and "intolerable" and said it punished the public "for the mistakes and the misdeeds of law-enforcement officers." Most legal experts agree that future court rulings may dilute certain aspects of the Miranda decision but that the main thrust of guaranteeing the rights of arrested persons could not be totally reversed. The need for this guarantee is itself somewhat dubious in light of the aftermath of the Miranda decision, something seldom mentioned by opponents. Despite the quashing of the confession, Miranda was later convicted of the rape charge and sentenced to a 20- to 30-year term. Later freed on parole, he was killed in 1975 in a brawl in a Phoenix bar.

MISCEGENATION

The prohibition of and criminal penalties against interracial marriage were largely American ideas. England, for instance, had no such bans when it colonized America. The concern that developed in the colonies sprang not only from revulsion at the idea of marriage between black slaves and whites (especially indentured white women) but also from the economics of the situation, since children of such a union were free under the law.

Maryland and Virginia adopted antimiscegenation laws in the 17th century and other colonies soon followed suit. The typical law prohibited only interracial marriages that included a white person and one of another color, not those involving, for example, an Indian and a black. By the 1950s about 30 states carried such laws on the books, but court rulings therafter began stripping them away on constitutional grounds. Finally, in the 1967 Loving decision the U.S. Supreme Court declared unconstitutional laws that restricted, solely on the basis of race, a person's "fundamental freedom" to marry. The High Court ended antimiscegenation laws once and for all by declaring it would only uphold racial classifications when they were "shown to be necessary to the accomplishment of some permissible state objectives independent of the racial discrimination which it was the object of the Fourteenth Amendment to eliminate."

MISSISSIPPI Bubble: 18th century fraud

Although the fraudulent Mississippi Bubble was developed in France and felt most there, the scourge of criminality it introduced into the New World left its mark for decades to come.

The Bubble was a swindle conceived by a resourceful and unscrupulous Scot named John Law, who founded the Mississippi Company in 1718 to extract the supposedly vast riches of French Louisiana and convinced the French government to back his scheme. With the aid of the French regent, Law soon had all of France caught up in a frenzy of speculation. Frenchmen invested their entire savings in the glorious company that was to yield enormous riches, and the national currency was inflated to further the bogus operation. In fact, a few who sold at the right time made 36 times their investment. Unfortunate-

ly, most held out for more. Not only was there no more, there was just plain nothing, except Law's lavish promises. Millions of Frenchmen were wiped out, and France itself tottered on the brink of ruin. Law, disguised as a beggar, barely escaped the country before being lynched.

But what of Louisiana itself? In its zeal to reap the wealth of this new land, the government had peopled it with a type of colonial not found anywhere else in the New World, at least not in comparable numbers. Historian Albert Phelps noted:

> The government went boldly to the task of ransacking the jails and hospitals. Disorderly soldiers, black sheep of distinguished families, paupers, prostitutes, political suspects, friendless strangers, unsophisticated peasants straying into Paris, all were kidnapped, herded, and shipped under guard to fill the emptiness of Louisiana. To those who would emigrate voluntarily the Company offered free land, free provisions, free transportation to the colony and from the colony to the situation of their grants, wealth, and eternal prosperity to them and their heirs forever; for the soil of Louisiana was said to bear two crops a year without cultivation, and the amiable savages were said so to adore the white man that they would not allow these superior beings to labor, and would themselves, voluntarily and for mere love, assume all the burden of that sordid necessity. . . . And now the full tide of the boom began to reach Louisiana. The emigrants, hurried out to fill seignorial rights, began to arrive in swarms and were dumped helplessly upon Dauphin Island. . . . Crowded, unsheltered and unfed, upon that barren sand heap, the wretched emigrants sickened, grew discontented, starved and died. . . ."

The seed of the Mississippi Bubble planted in Louisiana, particularly in New Orleans, bloomed into a level of criminality that for the next 100 years was unmatched in any locale on the North American continent.

MISTAKEN Identity

The annals of crime are filled with cases of mistaken identity, pointing up the unreliability of eye witness testimony.

Christopher Emanuel Balestrero was arrested on the eye witness testimony of four women clerks at a New York insurance company that he had twice robbed the office. He was finally cleared when the real robber confessed the crimes along with 26 others. Alfred Hitchcock made Balestrero's story into a movie, *The Wrong Man.* However, as a case of mistaken identity, it was hardly startling. A far more incredible case involved a man named Hoag who arrived in Haverstraw, N.Y., where he acquired a job, a large circle of friends and a wife. Six months later, he got out of town fast when he was revealed to be a bigamist who had a spouse in another city. Some two years after his departure a man named Parker settled in Haverstraw and suddenly found himself identified as Hoag and brought to trial. The prosecution presented more than a dozen witnesses who identified him as Hoag. Hoag's former boss recognized Parker as his onetime employee and Mrs. Hoag positively identified him as her husband. Winding up her testimony, Hoag's wife declared that her husband had a long red scar on his right foot. Parker immediately took off his shoe and rolled up his pants leg. There was no scar. Naturally, the case was dismissed. "He lies like an eyewitness" is a common saying around courtrooms. The statement is, as the late Judge Jerome Frank noted in his book *Not Guilty*, a study of 36 cases in which innocent men had been convicted, "made in jest. But it does point up an important fact: Any witness, being human, may be fallible.

"Eminent lawyers and judges have expressed awareness of this fact. A well-known judge said, 'It has been profoundly observed, that of all the various sources of error, one of the most copious and fatal is an unreflecting faith in human testimony.' Another judge wrote: 'It must be admitted that at the present day the testimony of even a truthful witness is much overrated'."

Certainly overrated was the testimony of five bank tellers who agreed that Bertram Campbell was the forger who passed worthless checks for more than $4,000. After Campbell served three and a half years and emerged from prison a broken and sick man, it was discovered that the real forger was a professional check passer named Alexander D. L. Thiel, whose appearance could not be regarded as very similar to Campbell's (see comparison photographs under Bertram Campbell).

How could five honest persons make such an error? There is a case on record of a man being convicted as a swindler on the testimony of 19 eyewitnesses and later proved innocent. There have been numerous instances of police "helping" a witness make an identification by combing the suspect's hair the way the witness described it. Or they let the witness see the suspect before he or she was put in a lineup. One of the four women who testified against Manny Balestrero picked him out of a lineup that included the woman's own husband. Nor do the cards have to be so strongly stacked against a defendant. If a witness picks out a possible suspect from a police mug shot and then confronts him or her in person, is the witness identifying the person from his or her memory of the crime or from the memory of the mug shot?

A famed private detective, John Terry, who often worked for defense lawyer Sam Leibowitz, a master at breaking down witnesses who had made positive identifications, once observed: "Eyes make a helluva lot of mistakes. Put a man in handcuffs and to a witness he immediately looks like a guilty man. A witness is in an abnormal state of mind during a robbery and it's the same thing when he goes into a station house. The average person isn't around jails all the time. In that atmosphere, plus seeing a man in handcuffs, he could name anyone a crook."

A lawyer particularly distrustful of eyewitness identifications was Clarence Darrow. He would question a witness very closely for several minutes and suddenly turn his back on him. Then he'd snap, "All right, let's just test your memory. You've looked at me for some time now. Is the scar on my face on the left or the right cheek?" Often the witness made a guess—and the wrong one. Darrow had no scar.

Rape victims, not surprisingly, make very poor eyewitnesses. In Chicago a woman guest in one of the better hotels was slugged in her darkened room and raped "by a big giant of a man at least six feet three inches in a bellhop's uniform." That was all she could tell about her assailant. John E. Reid, inventor of the Reid Polygraph, tested the bellhop most matching the victim's description and cleared him. Seven other bellhops were also tested and cleared. Reid then asked the hotel manager if there were any bellhops he hadn't seen.

The manager said he hadn't bothered to send him one. Reid demanded to know why, and the manager replied, "Because Shorty is Shorty."

Reid nonetheless tested Shorty and got a confession. He was the rapist—five feet two inches.

See also: *Bertram Campbell*.

MOB Pistol

A four-barrel flintlock pistol of foreign make, the mob pistol was much used in the first half of the 19th century, as its name implies, to quell mobs. All four barrels were fired at once and covered such a broad range that there was always an excellent chance that someone would be hit by one of the balls. The gun found its way to California thanks to sailing masters who used the weapon to tame mutinous crews. When sailors abandoned their ships to hunt for gold there, a number of guns, quite naturally, went with them. The gun apparently violated the "code of the West" and was not much used in gunfights. It was deemed acceptable, however, for use in attacks on the mining camps of "greasers," or Latin Americans, who seemed to have arrived at the promising sites first, and a great many fell dead under its terrifying blast.

MOCK Duck (1878-1942): Tong leader

Recognized as the greatest tong warrior ever to appear in any American Chinatown, Mock Duck became the top Chinese gangster in the nation, exerting power from New York to Boston and all the way to San Francisco. He led the upstart and relatively small Hip Sing Tong in their great battles against the On Leong Tong, the rich and powerful society that dominated Chinese rackets, especially opium, gambling and prostitution, until Mock Duck's appearance in New York City in 1900.

To wrest control of the rackets, the rotund, 22-year-old Mock Duck had to topple the near-legendary Tom Lee, who had cultivated a reputation as the unofficial mayor of Chinatown. Tom Lee was celebrated in the white press because of his massive payoffs not only to the police but to newspapermen as well. With no more than a handful of supporters, Mock Duck approached Tom Lee and blandly informed him that he desired half the revenues from all gambling and singsong girl (prostitute) operations, adding, "If this is not agreeable with your honorable self and that of your wonderous tong, we shall have to fight."

Tom Lee stared at Mock Duck for a long time, then laughed and walked on without saying a word to this upstart. By that evening all Chinatown was laughing over Mock Duck's impudence.

Mock Duck waited only 48 hours before demonstrating he was very serious about his demands. A fire started in an On Leong boarding house on Pell Street, killing two tong members. Tom Lee could not be absolutely sure this was the work of Mock Duck and his Hip Sings, but he could be certain of who was responsible for the next attack. An On Leong member walking on Doyers Street was set upon by a pair of Hip Sing *boo how doys,* or hatchet men. The next day his head was found in the gutter.

Tom Lee countered with orders to kill all Hip Sings, especially Mock Duck. What followed was an incredible series of survivals by Mock Duck that was to win him the nickname Clay Pigeon of Chinatown and to convince many Chinese that he was truly unkillable. Two On Leongs waylaid him late one night, jabbing daggers into his shoulders. Mock Duck lunged free, shot them both and ran back to the Hip Sing battle headquarters on Pell Street with the two knives still embedded in him.

In the next assault the On Leongs used guns. Mock Duck was walking out of Hip Sing headquarters when an On Leong gunman grazed his coat with one shot and hit him square in the midsection with another. Remarkably, Mock Duck escaped injury, as the bullet struck his belt buckle.

After these two attacks Mock Duck took to wearing a bulletproof vest made of chain mail. Now, he was a match for the *boo how doys.* Whenever he met three or four enemy hatchet men, he would go into a squat, clamp his eyes shut and start blazing away with two pistols. As a terror tactic, the routine was unbeatable. Mock Duck was not a very accurate shot, but that was the beauty of his tactic. If he had taken careful aim and fired, the *boo how doys* might have moved in on him without fear, figuring that with his poor marksmanship, he never would hit them. But with his eyes shut and both guns singing in mad tattoo, their fate was in the hands of luck. Invariably, they broke ranks before the unorthodox assault and fled. Indeed, the gods seemed to be on the side of Mock Duck. Despite his wild shooting—high, low and to the side—he almost always drew blood from his foes.

In desperation, Tom Lee placed a $1,000 bounty on Mock Duck's head and lesser sums, all the way down to $25, on the heads of lesser Hip Sings. This action set off a war among the Chinese the likes of which had never been waged in America. Mock Duck proved to be the better strategist. He formed an alliance with the Four Brothers, one of the oldest and most-respected family guilds in China. In America the family guilds had been undermined by the tong organizations, a fact that annoyed many members of the Four Brothers. After Mock Duck promised them renewed cultural power once the On Leongs were eliminated, the Four Brothers joined the battle.

Mock Duck added to his fighting power by importing two incredible *boo how doys* from San Francisco. One was Sing Dock, among the most fiendish killers the tong wars ever produced. The other was Yee Toy, a pasty-faced little executioner often called "the girl face." Many a hatchet man met his end because he did not regard the one with the effeminate features as much of a threat. It was estimated that Sing Dock and Yee Toy

murdered close to 100 men in the tong wars. They followed Mock Duck unquestioningly. Yee Toy later killed Sing Dock in a private quarrel, only to be stabbed to death himself a year later by his best friend, who had been bribed by the On Leongs.

Mock Duck had other weapons in his arsenal. While Tom Lee had the police on his side, Mock Duck keenly realized that with New York in a spasm of reform, the crusading Rev. Charles Parkhurst made a better ally. He went to see Parkhurst and told him that as a decent Chinese trying to make an honest living, he was being persecuted by the gangsters of Chinatown. He described the terrible gambling dens and singsong girl houses. Parkhurst was enraged and forced the authorities to raid every address furnished by Mock Duck. One On Leong establishment after another on Pell and Doyers streets was hit. Mock Duck cunningly outmaneuvered Tom Lee by not giving Parkhurst information on the locations of On Leong establishments on Mott Street. Thus, Tom Lee realized he could not loose the police on Hip Sing places, for Mock Duck would then turn the white crusader on his Mott Street dens, which at the time were the On Leongs' prime source of income.

Tom Lee was totally outfoxed and finally solved his problems by going on an extended vacation. In 1906 a truce was arranged but it lasted only about a year, giving Mock Duck the opportunity to consolidate his power. Then he struck again. Tom Lee returned to try to rally the On Leongs but lost what remained of his influence after their decisive defeat during the great war of 1909-10.

Mock Duck was now the supreme power in Chinatown. However, occasional bad luck dogged him. In 1912 an On Leong hatchet man invaded a Hip Sing gambling house on Pell Street while Mock Duck was conducting tong business in the basement. Two plainclothes police detectives walking by a short while later heard the sounds of shooting.

Rushing into the basement, the officers found Mock Duck sitting at a table reading a Chinese pamphlet on the origins of feudalism. Another Chinese stood nearby with his hands up his sleeves. A third sat at the table opposite Mock Duck with his head slightly bowed, as if in deep thought. Mock Duck allowed he had heard some shots but said he had just entered the place by the back door. The second Chinaman was equally evasive. The officers turned to the third man but he wouldn't talk either—he couldn't, having expired with a bullet in his heart.

The police couldn't prove that Mock Duck had killed the On Leong warrior but they were able to pin something on him. In his pockets they found a mass of slips of paper with Chinese characters on them and proved in court that these were policy slips.

Mock Duck was convicted and served two years in Sing Sing. When he came out, the invigorated On Leongs struck with full fury. Numerous attacks on Mock Duck failed. The police arrested him on several occasions and he was accused of murder a dozen times, but the charges were always dropped for lack of evidence. In 1918 Mock Duck disappeared, leading to conflicting reports that he had retired from the rackets or that he had been murdered. Both stories were proved erroneous when he reappeared in 1921, announcing a new peace in Chinatown. He did the same thing in 1924 and 1928.

It was clear that Mock Duck's enemies, within Chinatown and without, could not depose him. Finally, however, in 1932, U.S. officials, together with representatives of the Chinese government, prevailed upon him to make peace. By that time Mock Duck was ready to retire, satisfied that the affairs of Chinatown had become so institutionalized that his followers could no longer be overthrown.

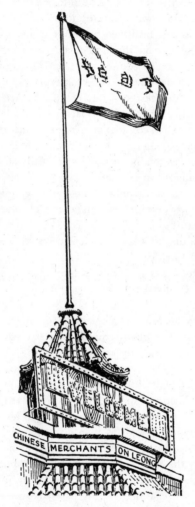

Although the meaning was lost on the white man, the flag of truce atop the On Leong Tong House on Mott Street signaled peace between the On Leongs and Mock Duck's Hip Sings.

Mock Duck left Chinatown, taking up residence in a lavish home in a remote section of Brooklyn. Until his death in 1942, he returned to Chinatown once a week to visit a relative who ran an importing firm on Pell Street. He arrived in a chauffeured limousine, which waited with motor running while Mock Duck joined his kin in partaking of tea and dried octopus flakes. Always, about 10 young Hip Sing stalwarts stood guard outside until he left. The protection was not necessary,

however, for even the On Leongs had long realized that Mock Duck was indestructible.

See also: *Bloody Angle, Tong Wars.*

MOLASSES Gang: 19th century New York hoodlums

The Molasses Gang, composed of relatively small-time thugs, operated in New York City for a half-dozen years starting in 1871 and are best remembered for their comic behavior. Captained by Jimmy Dunnigan, they never rose beyond the level of sneak thieves and till-tappers who victimized small store owners. After several members of the gang entered a store, one would remove his soft hat and ask for it to be filled with sorghum molasses. The explanation would be that it was a bet on how much the hat would hold. When the hat was filled, the thugs would clap it on the proprietor's head and pull it down over his eyes, practically blinding him. While the proprietor wrestled with that sticky problem, the gang would leisurely loot the establishment.

Other gangs regarded the Molasses Gang as flaky and undependable men, who might just walk away in the middle of an important caper if they thought of something more entertaining to do. By 1877 the law had had enough of the gang's outrageous behavior and clapped the last of them in jail.

MOLINEUX, Roland B. (1868-1917): Accused murderer

The least-remembered figure involved in the murder of Mrs. Katherine Adams, which proved to be one of New York's most sensational and most enduring mysteries, was the victim herself. All she did was drink some poison, die and get buried. Instead, the "Molineux Case" was named after the handsome and dashing young man who, depending upon which verdict one believes, either did or did not poison the elderly widow.

In 1898, at the age of 30, Roland Molineux moved with grace and ease in the city's high society. He was the son of Brigadier Gen. Edward Leslie Molineux, who had served with considerable honor in the Civil War and was a leading citizen of Brooklyn and a power broker within the Republican Party. With an excellent education behind him, Roland had a brilliant future as a chemist. He also possessed considerable charm— attested to by the fact that he had been named correspondent in a divorce case at the tender age of 15.

A fine physical specimen, Molineux was a member of the Knickerbocker Athletic Club and national amateur horizontal bar champion. Because of his social standing and athletic prowess, he exerted considerable influence on club affairs and usually got his way. One member he apparently didn't get his way with was Henry C. Barnet, who annoyed Molineux by courting a young lady named Blanche Cheeseborough even after she had become engaged to Molineux. However, in November 1898 Barnet died under mysterious circumstances. There was rumor that he had taken poison sent to him through the mail, but nothing came of the charge and Molineux and Blanche were married.

Meanwhile, Molineux developed a new feud, this time with Harry Cornish, the athletic director of the club. Actually, they had been at odds for a couple of years, mainly because Cornish did not seem to show the proper deference to the officious Molineux. Then Cornish bested Molineux in a weightlifting tournament, and the angry Molineux went to the club's board of directors and demanded Cornish be fired for various offenses. The board rejected Molineux' demands and the young athlete resigned in a huff.

On December 23, 1898 Cornish received a bottle of Bromo Seltzer in the mail from an anonymous donor. He considered it the work of a club wag, twitting him not to overdrink during the holidays. On December 28 Mrs. Adams, his landlady, complained of a splitting headache and the helpful Cornish fixed her a Bromo. She drank it and complained of its bitter taste. Cornish took a tiny sip and said he noticed nothing. Moments later, Mrs. Adams writhed in agony on the floor and died a half hour later. Cornish became deathly ill from his small sip.

Cornish had retained the wrapping the Bromo Seltzer had been mailed in, and suspicion soon centered on Molineux when a number of handwriting experts identified the writing on it as his. Other handwriting samples linked him to the poison that apparently had been sent to Barnet. Molineux was charged with the Adams killing, and press indignation and public hysteria ran high against him by the time he was brought to trial. The trial lasted three months and cost a staggering $200,000. Five hundred potential jurors were questioned before 12 could be selected. After eight hours of deliberation they found Molineux guilty and he was sentenced to die.

At this point Molineux' father financed a massive appeal effort. John G. Milburn, the Buffalo lawyer in whose home President William McKinley had died of an assassin's bullet, finally won a retrial on the ground that the judge had allowed the jury to hear evidence about the Barnet matter although it had no bearing on the case under consideration.

During his 18 months on death row Molineux had written a book of prison tales called *The Room with the Little Door*, which critics hailed as the work of a most sensitive and gifted writer. By the time the new trial began, the public atmosphere had changed. The previous hysteria had faded and Molineux was now viewed as a talented man of letters. The defense marshaled just as many handwriting "experts" on its side as the prosecution had in the previous proceedings, not a difficult accomplishment considering the state of that art at the time. Molineux' lawyer also produced a woman named Anna Stephenson, the wife of a policeman, who said she had been at the General Post Office when the poison was originally mailed. She assured the court she had seen a man mail a package addressed to Harry Cornish at the Knickerbocker Club and that man was not Molineux. In fact, the man had looked something like Cornish himself.

It turned out the woman could not see very well, but she insisted her vision had been perfect in 1898. Her husband was called to the stand and he advised the jurors to pay his wife no mind. The jury did not follow his advice and acquitted Molineux in four minutes.

Molineux was now a greater celebrity than ever. Newspapers hired him to write about other murder trials and he published a number of books. In the meantime, his wife, who had stood by him during his ordeal, divorced him. Later, she tried to appear in vaudeville as Blanche Cheeseborough Molineux, but her former husband took legal action to prevent it. In 1913 Molineux wrote a play, which David Belasco produced, called *The Man Inside*, about a reformed criminal. During its run Molineux, demonstrating his own ordeal had not left him unscathed, caused scenes at the theater and had to be ejected on a number of occasions.

Later that year he was committed to an asylum, where he died in 1917. Upon his death a police official declared the Adams murder had been considered closed since the time of Molineux's second trial.

See also: *John F. Tyrrell.*

MOLLIE Maguires: Secret labor terrorist organization

A secret organization of Irish immigrant miners in the anthracite region of Pennsylvania, the Mollie Maguires fought against what some experts have described as perhaps the worst working conditions in 19th century America. Taking their name from an old-country group of anti-landlord agitators in the 1840s led by a widow named Mollie Maguire, the Pennsylvania version, also known as the Buckshots and the Sleepers, undoubtedly used illegal means, including terror, sabotage, intimidation and murder of police and mine officials, to attain their goals.

In 1874-75 the Mollies conducted their devastating Long Strike against the mines, and the owners determined to destroy their influence forever. An undercover Pinkerton detective, James McParland, was sent into the coal fields to gain evidence against the Mollie Maguires, or, from the Mollies' point of view, to act as a provocateur.

McParland's testimony in a series of trials from 1875 to 1877 led to the conviction of more than 60 Mollies, including 19 men who were hanged on murder charges. According to McParland, he was present when a number of murders were planned by the Mollies but did nothing to warn the intended victims, although he had had ample time to do so. McParland's explanation was that he himself would have been murdered if he had warned them.

The testimony given by McParland proved sufficient to destroy the Mollies, although a considerable number of observers believed much of it was tainted. Three decades later, McParland was less successful in his investigation of the murder of ex-Gov. Frank Steunenberg of Idaho. The detective had been instrumental in bringing murder charges against three radical union leaders: Big Bill Haywood, Charles Moyers and George Pettibone. The famous lawyer Clarence Darrow made a shambles of the charges by showing that the written confession of the prosecution's main witness, Harry Orchard, contained many corrections in McParland's handwriting.

Thus, throughout the 20th century there were many moves to clear the Mollies who had been convicted on McParland's evidence. In 1979 Jack Kehoe, the leader of the Mollies, was granted a full state pardon, a century after his hanging.

See also: *James McParland.*

MONA Lisa Swindle

Probably the most audacious—and still unsolved—art swindle ever perpetrated in this country was the sale of six copies of the famed *Mona Lisa* to American art collectors in 1911-12.

In 1908 an international art crook, using a variety of aliases, came to America and befriended a number of millionaire art collectors. He made separate secret agreements with six of them to sell each one the *Mona Lisa* if he could steal it from the Louvre Museum in Paris. Meanwhile, he had an expert art forger make six copies of the Da Vinci masterpiece and had the fakes stored in New York. Then in 1911 the genuine *Mona Lisa* was stolen by a Louvre employee named Vincent Peruggia, who kept the painting in his apartment for two years. To this day it is unclear whether the art crook had arranged this theft or whether it happened coincidentally while his own plans were afoot. In any event, Peruggia was arrested in Italy in 1913, when he attempted to sell the original for $95,000. In the meantime, the cunning art crook had sold each of the six millionaires a copy of the masterpiece, collecting a total of $2 million. At his trial in Florence, Peruggia based his defense on patriotism, claiming he merely wanted to return the painting to the land of its creator, and got off with a mild sentence of a year and 15 days in prison. The art crook who had swindled the six American collectors was never caught.

MONEY-MAKING Machine: Swindle

A racket that dates back to the 19th century is the "money-making machine," which is sold to a victim with a bizarre tale that it can duplicate a bill of currency so exactly that no expert can tell the real from the fake. The only thing that is different is the serial number, which the machine changes with a special "scrambling" device. However, this particular part of the process is very slow, and it takes the machine six hours to complete the entire procedure for duplicating a single bill. The swindler demonstrates the machine by placing a plain piece of white paper on a tray inside the machine and closing it up. He then places a genuine bill in another compartment of the machine and inserts it into the machine. Then he and the victim remain by the machine until the entire procedure is finished. After the six hours have elapsed and the victim is convinced that no trickery has taken place in the meantime, the genuine bill is removed and the tray in which the plain paper was inserted is opened. Inside is a new, apparently perfect bill. The victim is advised to take the bill to a bank and change it. He does and it is readily accepted. Naturally, the victim is now most eager to

buy the machine. The swindler is at first loathe to sell it, but he does allow that he is impatient with the machine because it takes so long to produce a new bill. At the rate of only four in a 24-hour period, the machine will produce just $400 a day at most. Perhaps if he got a good offer. . . .

There are cases of the machine being sold or leased for as much as $50,000. The deal is closed as soon as the gullible buyer brings the money. The swindler leaves and the eager victim waits for his first new bill. It comes out right on schedule. Merrily, he puts in another plain sheet of paper. Six hours pass . . . out comes the same blank piece of paper. The victim tries it again but gets the same results. Finally, it dawns on him that he has been conned. By that time, of course, the crook has had a minimum of 12 hours to get away. The secret of the money machine is the tray in which the plain paper is loaded. As the swindler closes the tray, he presses a pin that drops a false top which holds a real bill previously concealed there. When the tray is opened six hours later, this is the bill that appears.

In the 19th century, money-making machines were quite the vogue both in America and England. As late as the 1930s, one American operator, "Count" Victor Lustig, is reputed to have made well over a million dollars with the scheme. Even today, police bunco squad experts estimate that the swindle is worked hundreds of times annually in this country. Bankers, stockbrokers and other professional men are the usual victims. Because of the advances made in photocopying techniques, authorities say, supposedly sophisticated individuals are now more likely to become victims.

See also: *"Count" Victor Lustig.*

MONK, Maria (1817-1849): Anti-Catholic hoaxer

One of the most infamous impostors of her time, a young girl named Maria Monk became a rallying point in the 1830s for American Protestants against what was regarded as the evils of popery, fanning emotions that were later exploited fully by the Know-Nothings. Maria arrived in New York in January 1836 in the company of a Canadian clergyman, the Rev. W. K. Hoyt, who told all who cared to listen that he had saved her from a life of sin in the famous Hotel Dieu nunnery in Montreal. More likely, Rev. Hoyt had, as Maria was to admit in moments of candor, met her following a street corner solicitation.

The pair had with them the first draft of what they claimed was Maria's memoirs of her years as a novice and nun at the Hotel Dieu. When published under the title of *The Awful Disclosures of Maria Monk,* it was to say the least most shocking in its charges. According to Maria, the remote cellars of the nunnery were strewn with the bones of nuns who had resisted the advances of amorous priests. She said the sisters were called upon nightly by priests from a nearby monastery, who ventured through subterranean passages to conduct their amorous and abusive exercises. Maria had a tiny tot with her whose origin she traced to these nocturnal visits from the neighboring clergyman. A later investigation by Canadian authorities turned up rather convincing evidence that the gentleman who had fathered the child—though not in the nunnery—was a Montreal policeman.

Maria and Hoyt found as sponsors for the book the Society for the Diffusion of Christian Knowledge, especially its president, Dr. W. C. Brownlee, pastor of the Collegiate Dutch Reformed Church and himself the author of a militant anti-Catholic best-seller, *Popery.* Dr. Brownlee thought so highly of this supposed refugee from a nunnery that he took her into his own house under the care of his wife, leading in time to complaints by the Rev. Mr. Hoyt that Maria was a "damned jilting jade."

By that time Maria was worth fighting over; her book sold an astonishing 20,000 copies almost immediately. Anti-Papists could delight in a variety of chilling charges; for example, one nun's punishment for some minor infraction was to be stretched out on a mattress

> with her face upwards, and then bound with cords so that she could not move. In an instant, another bed [mattress] was thrown upon her. One of the priests, named Bonin, sprang like a fury first upon it with all his force. He was speedily followed by the nuns until there were as many on the bed as could find room, and all did what they could do, not only to smother, but to bruise her. Some stood and jumped upon the poor girl with their feet: and others, in different ways, seemed to seek how they might beat the breath out of her body. After the lapse of fifteen or twenty minutes, Father Bonin and the nuns ceased to trample on her and stepped from the bed. They then began to laugh. . . .

Maria assured her readers "speedy death can be no great calamity to those who lead the lives of nuns," and she offered to visit the Hotel Dieu "with some impartial ladies and gentlemen, that they may compare my account with the interior parts of the building, and if they do not find my description true, then discard me as an impostor."

Her challenge was not taken up, but in time even firm believers in Maria developed doubts. Maria's mother in Montreal denied that her wastrel daughter had ever entered a nunnery. Moreover, she insisted that she had been visited in 1835 by the Rev. Mr. Hoyt, who offered her $500 to say such were the facts. Eventually, Dr. Brownlee concluded he had been hoodwinked; not only did the girl's story appear contradictory but she had also run off in the meantime with his young clergyman protege, John J. L. Slocum. In 1836 Slocum brought suit against the publishers of the book for Maria's share of the royalties, all of which had been appropriated by the Society for the Diffusion of Christian Knowledge. The resulting trial clearly demonstrated Maria's story to be a hoax.

This, however, did not stop Maria. In August 1837 she turned up at the house of a Dr. Sleigh, a Philadelphia clergyman, and told a tale of being kidnapped by a group of priests and held captive in a nearby convent. She had escaped, she said, by promising one of the priests that she would marry him. The result of all this was, of course, a sequel to her first book, *Further Disclosures of Maria Monk.*

The second publication also did rather well, but Maria evi-

dently saw little of the financial rewards. Slocum persuaded her to sign over to him a number of rights to both publications and he then decamped for London to arrange for their foreign publication.

Maria's life plunged downward. She became a habitue of the dives of the Bowery, a drunken hag before she was 30. She was confined in jail for picking a man's pocket in 1849 and died that year at the age of 32, although her true identity went unnoticed for some time. But *The Awful Disclosures of Maria Monk* has outlived her. To date, well over 300,000 copies have been sold.

MONKEY Trial: See John T. Scopes.

MONSIEUR New York (c.1822-?): Hangman

The most famous American executioner of the mid-19th century was "Monsieur New York," that state's official hangman, whose true identity was a closely guarded secret. For years newspapers referred to him by that nickname or a more prosaic one, George. He was considered a master of his craft, and one of the few executioners of the era who could dispatch a condemned person with a minimum of disconcerting suffering, prolonged strangling or, the most embarrassing of circumstances, unwarranted decapitation.

Monsieur New York got his start in the profession in the early 1850s, when he approached the sheriff of New York and offered to carry out the hanging of a black convicted of murder. At the time, he was about 30 years old and a butcher's assistant at the Washington Market. He had read about and sought to emulate Jack Ketch, the renowned high executioner of Great Britain. Because the previous hangman had abruptly walked away from the job, a not uncommon occurrence, since few could cope with the public attitudes and comments once they were identified, George's offer was accepted. The job was his, subject of course to a demonstration of his efficiency.

Observers described the execution as a "beautiful job" and George was named a deputy sheriff, although only a handful of officials knew his real identity. As he performed further commendable jobs, his fame spread and Monsieur New York was soon in demand in many parts of the country. His standard fee was $100 per execution plus all expenses, which often included a carpenter's charge for constructing the proper gallows and the price of a sound rope. Newspapers in communities he visited somberly informed their readers that "his daily visits to the slaughter-house had made him familiar with the use of the windlass to the perfection of an application for the humane accommodation of the law-breaking community."

Even the Army made use of Monsieur New York's unsurpassed abilities, calling on him in 1861 to execute one Capt. Beale, a Confederate officer charged with nefarious activities, and a Capt. Kennedy, a Union officer who had burned down a hotel in New York. Like many artists, Monsieur New York had a temperament and in 1869, in a moment of pique, refused to do any hangings for the current sheriff. As a result, the *Police Gazette* reported, "the departure of John Real was sadly bungled." Needless to say, the sheriff placated his star hangman shortly thereafter.

Possibly because of rivalry, neighboring New Jersey for a time refused to avail themselves of Monsieur New York's services. During this period one Bridget O'Brien was scheduled to die in New Brunswick for the murder of her mistress. While the master hangman was professionally ignored, he was extended the courtesy of an invitation to the hanging.

"Boys, that Jerseyman will make a mess of the job," was his immediate comment when he viewed the gallows; disaster loomed, he warned.

"What are you trying to do, you damned fool!" he cried out in dismay when he saw how the Jersey hangman was handling the rope. "Then," one account of the event stated, "unable to restrain himself, the scientific strangler pushed his way through the crowd and saw to it that Bridget was sent out of this vale of tears in as laudable style as conditions would permit and the hand of an artist could assure."

In the 1880s, Monsieur New York's last decade of service, a newspaper revealed he lived with his family in a house near the East River in the vicinity of 125th Street and that he was a member of the Methodist Church. The neighborhood was rife with speculation about his identity and many a family man, determined to lay to rest any suspicions about himself, made it a point to be seen on a street in his neighborhood whenever an execution was taking place downtown. To the end, the identity of Monsieur New York remained a secret.

MOONERS: Moon-affected criminals

An official publication of the New York City Police Department reads: "Mooner. A mentally disturbed person who is activated during a full moon."

It is neither a novel nor a new belief. Sir William Blackstone, the great British jurist, was the first to define the mooner theory in legal terms.

> A man who is a lunatic or *non compos mentis* is one who hath understanding, but by disease, grief or other accident, hath lost the use of his reason. A lunatic is indeed properly one that hath lucid intervals, sometimes enjoying his senses and sometimes not, and that frequently depending upon the change of the moon.

And backing up these two authoritative views is the experience of numerous cops on the beat who believe that a full moon spells trouble for them. At the time of the full moon, it invariably seems that more screwballs and more drunks are abroad, more family quarrels erupt and more false fire alarms are sounded. Veteran newspapermen claim that during the full moon a higher percentage of crackpots turns up in city rooms with tips of zany stories. A survey made in Connecticut showed that during the period of the full moon some types of crimes increased by as much as 200 percent. Violent robberies rose about 100 percent and breaking and entering went up some 78 percent. Drunk cases doubled and fatal accidents quintupled.

Arsonists are notoriously affected by the full moon. Some years ago investigators for the National Board of Fire Underwriters solved a mysterious string of fires in a Pennsylvania town by tracking the cycle of the moon. Explaining the firebug's capture, the investigators remarked, "The majority of the fires set by this man falls within the full-moon cycle, and his apprehension was brought about by surveillance based on the theory that the person responsible for the fires would set another during the next full moon."

This country's classic moon murderer was DeWitt Clinton Cook, who by the age of 20 had committed 300 burglaries and numerous attacks on women in California. During Cook's crime rampage a leading expert on abnormal behavior, police psychiatrist Dr. J. Paul de River, warned the authorities they were dealing with a mooner whose "attacks on women will continue every month until he is caught." On February 24, 1939, the night of a full moon, Cook killed Anya Soseyeva, a pretty young drama student at Los Angeles City College. He was not captured until a moon burglary in August. When Cook was caught, Dr. de River diagnosed him as "a nocturnal prowler who likes to wander in lonely places at night."

While more and more evidence accumulates indicating that "moon madness" may be a genuine affliction, jurors are not prepared to hand down insanity verdicts on such ground. Cook went to the gas chamber, and the Pennsylvania arsonist, a 24-year-old fireman, was sentenced to 30 to 60 years.

MOONEY Case: Labor frame-up

The Mooney case, which was to become a labor cause celebre for more than two decades, began in deadly violence on July 22, 1916 during a Preparedness Day parade in San Francisco. A bomb exploded on the sidewalk, killing outright or mortally wounding 10 persons and injuring 40 others. Among those charged with the bombing were two labor organizers, Thomas J. Mooney and Warren K. Billings. During a strike in 1913, Mooney, his wife, Billings and two others had been arrested on a charge of unlawful possession of explosives. In a subsequent trial Mooney had been found not guilty while Billings had been sent to prison for two years. Thereafter, Mooney was marked as an agitator.

Following the Preparedness Day parade massacre, the case against Mooney was extremely weak but both he and Billings were found guilty. Mooney was sentenced to death; Billings drew life imprisonment. Their trial had taken place during a period of mounting anti-Red sentiment. Revelations in 1918 that much of the testimony against Mooney had been perjured and that other evidence was highly questionable eventually caused even the trial judge to join in the long fight to clear him. President Woodrow Wilson prevailed on Gov. William Stephens to delay the execution, and the governor eventually commuted Mooney's sentence to life imprisonment. Labor unions and other organizations kept up the battle for Mooney. One California governor after another was petitioned for either a rehearing or a pardon. Finally, in January 1939 Gov. Culbert

For two decades demonstrations such as this one in Detroit marked efforts to free labor organizer Tom Mooney.

L. Olson, shortly after being inaugurated, pardoned Mooney and later that year released Billings by commuting his sentence. Upon his release Mooney declared he probably had been more valuable to the labor movement behind bars than he could have been if he had stayed out of prison. Mooney died in 1942 at the age of 59 and Billings in 1972 at age 79.

MOORE, Flossie (1866-?): Female mugger

Described by a police biographer as "the most notorious female bandit and footpad that ever operated in Chicago," Flossie Moore, a black woman, appeared in the Levee and other vice districts in Chicago in the late 1880s and soon was making much more money than any of her male counterparts. She openly declared that a holdup woman in Chicago had to make at least $20,000 a year or be a disgrace to the profession. Flossie did considerably better than that, earning $125,000 from late 1889 to mid-March 1893, when she was sent to Joliet Prison for five years for a particularly vicious mugging of an elderly farmer who had been visiting the city.

Flossie considered herself the black queen of crime in Chicago and got extremely jealous when her rival for that crown, a strong-arm woman named Emma Ford, made a bigger score. Often, the next man down the street had to pay for that. As befitting a crime queen, Flossie always carried a huge roll of bills in the bosom of her dress and another in a stocking, sported a white lover named Handsome Harry Gray, to whom she gave an allowance of $25 a day, an astonishing figure for the era, and appeared at balls staged by brothel keepers in gowns costing $500 and more. To handle her legal problems, she paid a lawyer $125 a month, but the man had to work for his money. Flossie was arrested as often as 10 times in a single day, and in one year alone she was scheduled for trial in criminal court three dozen times. Once when fined $100, she laughed at the judge and said: "Make it two hundred. I got money to burn!"

When she was sent to Joliet in 1893, Flossie quickly proved to be the most uncontrollable woman ever imprisoned there, twice almost killing a matron and serving a good portion of her sentence in solitary confinement. Flossie Moore returned to Chicago after serving her sentence but soon complained she was a marked woman, constantly watched by the police. About

1900 she left Chicago for New York; thereafter, no more is known of her.

See also: *Custom House Place, Emma Ford, Panel House, Clifton Wooldridge.*

MOORE, Lester (?-?): Mystery subject of epitaph

Lester is a real question mark. Did he ever live? More importantly, did he ever die? No devotee of graveyard humor is unfamiliar with the inscription on Lester's tombstone in the Boot Hill Cemetery at Tombstone, Ariz. It reads:

> Here lies
> Lester Moore
> Four slugs
> From a forty-four
> No Les
> No More

According to one story, a Wells Fargo guard was responsible for sending Lester to his poetic reward, but there seems to be no written record of that fact. Western historian Denis McLoughlin destroys a humorous, if morbid, bit of Americana by suggesting that no one is buried there, pointing out, "The aroma of the prankster emanates from this plot of ground; no date of death accompanies the verse, and had the latter originated during Tombstone's lead-swapping period, '*four balls from a .44*' would have been apt for the time."

MOORE, Nathaniel Ford (1883-1910): Suspected murder victim

Few deaths aroused as much gossip and scandal in Chicago as that of playboy Nathaniel Ford Moore, the 26-year-old son of James Hobart Moore, president of the Rock Island Railroad and one of the nation's most influential capitalists. There were many back in 1910 who firmly believed Nathaniel Moore had been murdered and that belief persists to this day.

Young Moore supposedly found a check for $100,000 under his breakfast plate on his 21st birthday and became a playboy that night, visiting Chicago's and America's most-renowned and fabulous bordello, the Everleigh Club. For the next five years he was a regular there. His final visit was the night of January 8, 1910, when he showed up drunk. The strict rule of the Everleigh Club prohibiting the admittance of any customer in an inebriated condition was relaxed in Moore's case. However, one of the Everleigh sisters, Minna, refused to allow him to be served any more wine, which set off an argument between her and one of her girls, Moore's favorite, whom the playboy always tipped lavishly. The harlot marched out of the Club, vowing vengeance on the Everleighs.

Moore himself left about 1 a.m. About 30 hours later, at dawn of January 10, Minna Everleigh received a telephone call from the harlot who had paraded out of the club in such a rage. Tearfully, the girl told Minna that Moore had died in a fashionable brothel run by Madam Vic Shaw. She also imparted the intelligence that Madam Shaw and some other madams along South Dearborn Street, members of the Friendly Friends, a society of brothel owners who constantly plotted against the Everleigh sisters because their club siphoned off so much of the "playboy money," had come up with a bizarre plot to plant Moore's body in the Everleigh Club furnace.

Minna Everleigh, accompanied by some supporters, marched on the Shaw brothel and forced her way in. She confronted Madam Shaw, who finally admitted to the presence of young Moore's corpse. Minna insisted the police be called and stood by while the young heir's body was removed to the family's Lake Shore Drive home, rather than her furnace. According to Minna Everleigh, Moore had died of a murderous overdose of morphine in his champagne, but the official investigation indicated death was due to heart disease. The investigation's finding, however, did not stop the whispering that there had indeed been a murder but that the family had used its power to limit the scandal to the proportions it had already achieved. The facts were never fully established to everyone's satisfaction.

The furnace plot became a part of Chicago folklore, adopted by the Capone gang for use when an unwanted stiff had to be removed from a mob resort called the Four Deuces. The boys would haul the corpse to the cellar of a competing establishment and put it in the furnace. Then the manager of the Four Deuces would complain to the police that the competition was running an illegal crematorium. In the ensuing investigation the rival resort would be so ripped up by police looking for additional "bodies" that it could never reopen.

See also: *Everleigh Sisters, Four Deuces, Friendly Friends.*

MORAN, George "Bugs" (1893-1957): Gangster

By 1927 Al Capone's control of Chicago crime, including bootlegging, was almost complete. The only major force still in his way was the bloodied but still powerful O'Banion gang from the North Side. O'Banion and his successor Hymie Weiss had already departed the scene in a hail of Capone bullets and the next boss, Schemer Drucci, was killed by a policeman. That left George "Bugs" Moran as the only North Sider tough enough to continue the battle against the Capones, and in fact, he was still capable of forcing Big Al to stay under cover for fear of attack.

Bugs earned his nickname for his flaky behavior as the sometimes clown prince of the gang, but he was also committed to violence. O'Banion's North Siders pulled no shooting caper in which Moran did not participate. He was the first to put a bullet in the head of a riding academy horse the O'Banions snatched and "executed" after it had thrown and killed their celebrated compatriot Nails Morton. He was also the gunman who rushed across the street to finish off Johnny Torrio after Torrio had been hit four times out of a barrage of shots fired at his limousine. But Bugs' gun misfired and Torrio survived. Moran was also in the lead car when the North Siders made their famous 11-car convoy attack on the Hawthorne Inn in Cicero, pouring 1,000 bullets and shotgun slugs into the building in a vain effort to assassinate Capone.

Upon his assumption of the gang's leadership, Moran continued his policy of frequently making peace with Capone but breaking it several hours later. Moran's hatred for Capone was almost pathological. He considered Capone a lowly type and never could resist taunting him in public. Bugs held to the high moral tone of the O'Banions, permitting no whorehouses to operate in the gang's territory. He told of Capone's frequent entreaties for permission to introduce prostitution, offering to pay Moran 50 percent of the profits. "We don't deal in flesh," Moran thundered. "We think anyone who does is lower than a snake's belly. Can't Capone get that through his thick skull?"

Before turning 21, Moran had committed 26 known robberies and served three prison sentences. O'Banion loved Moran like a brother, mainly because he had a similarly murderous "wit." Once, Moran ran into Judge John H. Lyle, one of Chicago's few honest and courageous judges of the period, at a baseball game and said: "Judge, that's a beautiful diamond ring you're wearing. If it's snatched some night, promise me you won't go hunting me. I'm telling you now I'm innocent."

This puckish style made Moran good copy for the newspapers and gained him acceptance by the public as sort of a jolly good killer, with far more enviable characteristics than Capone. And probably more citizens were rooting for Moran to win the war of survival with Capone. As a matter of fact, each managed to survive the onslaughts of the other. Moran's closest call was the infamous St. Valentine's Day Massacre.

In early 1929 Capone used a Detroit front man to pretend he had a load of hijacked booze available. Moran agreed to take delivery of the shipment at the gang's headquarters, a garage at 2122 North Clark Street, on the morning of February 14, 1929. Arriving a little late for the transaction, Bugs noticed three men dressed as policemen and two others in plain clothes entering the premises. Figuring it was a police shakedown, Moran hung back, waiting for the law to depart. Minutes later, machine-gun fire erupted inside the garage, leaving six gangsters and an innocent bystander dead. Moran took off.

The St. Valentine's Day Massacre decimated the North Side mob. Although Moran vowed vengeance, wailing, "Only Capone kills like that," his power was gone. The North Siders fell apart, some drifting away, others joining Capone. Moran may have had one small victory thereafter. He has often been credited, although the fact has never been established, with the assassination seven years later of Machine Gun Jack McGurn, a Capone enforcer popularly believed to have been one of the perpetrators of the massacre.

After that, Moran's crimes turned petty. He was involved in a number of burglaries about on a par with his teenage capers. In 1946 he and two others robbed an Ohio bank messenger of $10,000, a sum that the former millionaire bootlegger would have looked on as pocket money in his palmy days. Arrested by the FBI for the job, Moran served 10 years. On his release from prison, he was rearrested for an earlier bank robbery and sent to Leavenworth, where he died of cancer in 1957. Unlike his compatriots, O'Banion, Weiss and Drucci, who had all been given lavish gangster funerals, Moran was buried in a plain wooden casket in a potter's field west of the prison's walls.

See also: *Louis "Two Gun" Alterie, Alphonse "Scarface Al" Capone, Hawthorne Inn, Samuel J. "Nails" Morton, Charles Dion "Deanie" O'Banion, St. Valentine's Day Massacre, Hymie Weiss.*

MORAN, Dr. Joseph Patrick (1895-1934): Underworld's doctor

A promising young Illinois doctor, Joseph Patrick Moran wrecked his career through drinking and performing abortions. He was sent to prison in 1928 following the death of a girl on whom he had performed an abortion. In Joliet, Moran befriended a number of leading gangsters and removed a bullet that one of them had been carrying around for 10 years. When he was released, convicts with strong political connections sent him to a Chicago ward committeeman who arranged to get him a new medical license. He became the doctor for a Teamsters local involved in labor racketeering wars and treated many members for bullet wounds sans the obligatory report to the authorities. He also treated wounded holdupmen and other criminals sent to him by former Joliet cell mates.

By the early 1930s Moran was known as the underworld's family doctor and did considerable work for the Barker-Karpis gang as well as for the Dillinger mob. He performed especially painful plastic surgery operations on Alvin "Creepy" Karpis and Freddie Barker, leaving the pair in agony for weeks but hardly altering their appearances other than to give them a number of new facial scars. Moran also attempted to remove their fingerprints but after a few months the same whorls reappeared. Operating in unsanitary hotel rooms and cellars, Doc Moran's patient survival rate was naturally less than that of the average medical man, but he saved the life of many a hoodlum and murderer and thus was seldom begrudged his fee, which was almost never less than $1,000 and often two or three times that amount.

In the end, Moran's drinking habit did him in again. He needed several shots before he could probe a wound. The most pointed critique of his ability was made by the notorious Shotgun George Zeigler, who said: "I can't shoot straight when I'm pie-eyed. It stands to reason that a doctor can't cut straight when he's that way." Zeigler was rather upset because a gunman buddy of his had died after gangrene set in following an operation performed by Doc Moran.

Still, under the theory that even an incompetent sawbones was better than none, the Barkers took Doc Moran on the lam with them after the FBI identified him not only as an underworld medical man but also as one of the handlers of the ransom money in the Edward George Bremer kidnapping. Unfortunately for Moran, one night in 1934 he got drunk at the Casino Club near Toldeo, Ohio and informed members of the gang: "I have you guys in the palms of my hand. One word from me and your goose is cooked."

A doctor who drank and sometimes botched operations was one thing but a doctor who drank and sometimes botched operations and had a loose lip as well was quite another. The gang quieted the Doc down and later he left the club with two of them for a cooling-off boat ride on Lake Erie. Doc Moran was never seen again. As Freddie Barker later informed an associate: "Doc will do no more operating. The fishes probably have eaten him up by now."

MORAN, Thomas B. "Butterfingers" (1892-1971): Pickpocket

Thomas "Butterfingers" Moran picked his first pocket at the age of 14 and then went on to pick an estimated 50,000 more over the next 65 years, winning the title King of the Pickpockets.

What made him exceptional was that he eschewed working with a gang, which meant he had no "framers" to distract his victims while he pulled his light-fingered routine. Furthermore, Moran, unlike most pickpockets, had taught himself his trade. "All you gotta do," he once said, "is do it." He did it first in 1906 on the day of the great San Francisco earthquake. "Nobody was worried about getting their pockets picked then, and I picked several and got myself all the confidence I needed for the rest of my career."

Moran's career took him to all the 48 states and Canada, and he was caught in every one of them, doing short stints that added up to about seven years of imprisonment. However, he seldom was caught more than once in a state, and out of 50,000 "scores," some 60 "wrong ones" did not add up to a bad record. His nickname Butterfingers was really meant as a compliment, since he could "slide in and out of a pocket like pure butter."

Moran never tried to make big scores around banks and in business districts, because he knew police surveillance was tougher there. Instead, he would work race tracks, subways, buses. One of the best spots, he reported, was union meetings since "everyone's a brother there." Moran's most impressive talent was his ability to "kiss the sucker," which means lifting a victim's wallet from his inside coat pocket while facing him. It is the hardest maneuver for a pickpocket to pull but it is also the one that a victim least expects because he considers his wallet invulnerable inside his coat pocket.

Moran's last arrest was in 1970, when he was 78 years old. When he was released, police noted he had only $2 in his pocket. He shrugged and said: "I'll get on a bus and get out of this town and get off with some sucker's wallet. I've never worried about money. I can get some anytime." Shortly before his death in a charity ward in Miami, Fla. on September 14, 1971, he said he was going to the races the next day because he was "feeling lucky."

See also: *Pickpocketing.*

MORELLO, Nicholas (1866-1916): Mafia leader and murder victim

The leader of the New York mafiosi during the first of the Mafia wars, Nick Morello was a crafty and brilliant gang leader, one of the first to conceive the idea of a great criminal syndicate, each of its elements at peace with one another and in control of all the rackets in the country. But in spite of his goal, Morello, the last of that notorious family to come to power, found himself at war with the Brooklyn camorristas, immigrant criminals from the Camorra gangs of Naples. While the Sicilian mafiosi controlled the rackets of East Harlem and Greenwich Village in Manhattan, the camorristas, under Don Pelligrino Morano, had consolidated their power in Brooklyn, collecting protection money from Italian storekeepers, ice and coal dealers and sundry businessmen as well as controlling the Brooklyn docks.

The conflict between the two organizations ostensibly flared because of an attempt by the Morano forces to move into the East Harlem rackets, but it was more likely a continuation of a bloody Old World rivalry. Morello believed it was silly to keep fighting such battles and sent out peace feelers. The Morano forces spurned these offers, and by 1916 tensions between the two syndicates had become so intense that no mafioso or camorrista would dare set foot in the other's territory.

Finally, Morano abruptly sent word that he had seen the merit of Morello's idea for an armistice. Morello was cautious about accepting Morano's invitation to come to Brooklyn for a peace conference. It took six months for Morello to show up, and he failed to bring his top aides, as Morano had suggested. When Morello and his bodyguard stepped out of their car in front of the meeting place, a cafe on Brooklyn's Navy Street, Morano was clearly disappointed, but he decided to make the best of a poor situation. He gave an order and a five-man execution squad stepped forward and cut down the pair in broad daylight.

Later court testimony revealed Morano had done the job in such a brazen fashion because he was under the assumption that the payoffs he had made to a New York police detective, Michael Mealli, had "cleared the operation with the cops." Some of the killers talked, and Morano and a number of his top aides went to prison for life. When his sentence was pronounced, the *Brooklyn Eagle* reported, "Morano was surrounded by a dozen Italians who showered kisses on his face and forehead. On the way to the jail other Italians braved the guard and kissed Morano's hands, cheeks and forehead."

With Morello dead and Morano in prison, the first Mafia war ended and with it the dreams of Nick Morello for a "great combination" of the gangs. The Italian underworld was forced to continue its pattern of Old World organization, but a number of new faces in the gangs had heard Morello and listened. One of these was Salvatore Luciana, then only a young thug in the Five Points gang. He would Americanize his name to Charles "Lucky" Luciano and he would Americanize the Mafia 15 years after Morello's murder.

See also: *Mafia, Morello Family, Mustache Petes.*

MORELLO Family: Early Mafia gang

It is difficult to decide whether Giuseppe Esposito or the Morello family was the first to introduce the Mafia to this country. Both Esposito and the Morellos were vicious killers. Esposito had the greater range, with his activities stretching from New York to New Orleans, more because of the pressure of police pursuit than by design, while the Morellos had the more firmly established power base in New York. The Morellos were a cunning and vicious clan of brothers, half-brothers and brothers-in-law from Corleone, Sicily. They were numerous enough by themselves to constitute a Mafia "family."

The head of the clan was Antonio Morello, the eldest brother of the main branch of the Morello family; Antonio was credited with some 30 to 40 New York murders in the 1890s. Another brother, Joe Morello, killed often and ghoulishly and eventually became the boss of the New York Mafia. Their younger brother Nick died in 1916 in a war with the Neapolitan gangs, the Camorra, that controlled crime in Brooklyn. Other important members of the Morello gang included Ciro Terranova, an important mafioso until the 1930s, and his brother-in-law, the notorious Lupo the Wolf, until 1920 the most-feared gangster in all the Italian communities of the city.

The early crimes of the Morellos included Black Hand terrorism, contract killings, waterfront thefts and counterfeiting. The Secret Service found it difficult to break up their counterfeiting operation because it was carried out in Sicily, with the bills being shipped over hidden in legitimate freight. The Morellos could easily retrieve the caches of bogus bills through their control of the docks.

A great number of the Morellos' descendants are involved in New York-New Jersey Mafia rackets today.

See also: *Lupo the Wolf, Nicholas Morello, Ciro Terranova.*

MORETTI, Willie (1894-1951): Syndicate chief

An important syndicate figure, Willie Moretti was a power in New Jersey gambling operations who, near the end of his life, provided some comic relief at the Kefauver Committee hearings into organized crime.

A boyhood friend of Frank Costello, Moretti was, in his younger days, as tough as any gangster. By 1943, however, he was starting to act strangely, exhibiting the first signs of mental illness brought on by syphilis, for which he never had been treated. Moretti loved to gamble and began talking wildly about betting and winning millions of dollars on horses that didn't exist in big races that were never run. He rambled on about syndicate affairs that shouldn't have been mentioned in public. Some of the Mafia capos, those otherwise loyal to Costello, began to grumble that Willie was a threat to everyone.

Costello had been best man at Willie's wedding and had a genuine affection for him. He prudently decided to head off trouble by getting Moretti out of the line of fire, sending him on a long vacation out West with a male nurse. While Willie was away, he pleaded regularly with Costello, in conversations wiretapped by the police, to be allowed to return. Costello refused and continued to protect Willie from himself. Only when he became less voluble was he allowed back.

When Moretti was called before the Kefauver Committee to testify in 1950, pressure built up for his assassination, but

Costello again prevented it. After much stalling Moretti finally appeared before the Senate committee and proceeded to talk and talk and talk. However, he really said very little, aside from offering the probers such pearls of wisdom as, "They call anybody a mob who makes six percent more on money" and, on gangsters he knew, "well-charactered people don't need introductions." He also patiently explained to the senators that he could not be a member of the Mafia because he didn't have a membership card.

Protected by Frank Costello even after his testimony at the Kefauver Committee hearings into organized crime, Willie Moretti finally fell victim to a mob "mercy killing."

Moretti left the stand with the praise of the committee ringing in his ears. Sen. Estes Kefauver commended him on his forthrightness and Sen. Charles Tobey found his frankness "rather refreshing." "Thank you very much," Willie replied to the praise. "Don't forget my house in Deal if you are down on the shore. You are invited."

While Willie had handled himself to the mob's satisfaction, his condition further deteriorated in 1951. He became friendly with a number of New Jersey newspapermen and was threatening to stage a press conference to talk about gambling in New Jersey. One who considered Willie dangerous was the ambitious Vito Genovese, who saw in the elimination of Moretti a chance to enhance his own position, with his men taking over Willie's operations and thus eroding the power of Genovese's prime enemy, Costello. He argued Moretti was losing his mind and was endangering the entire organization. "If tomorrow I go wrong, I want you to hit me in the head too," Genovese said. Finally, even such a Costello loyalist as Albert Anastasia was convinced that a "mercy killing" was necessary for the sake of both Willie and the syndicate.

On October 4, 1951 Willie sat down in a New Jersey restaurant with four men. When the waitress stepped into the kitchen, they were chatting amiably in Italian. Suddenly, she heard several gunshots. She peered through the swinging doors. All the customers but one were gone. Willie Moretti, 57, lay dead on the floor, his left hand on his chest. Moretti's assassination, like virtually all syndicate rub-outs, remains unsolved.

MORRELL, Ed (1871-1946): Convict and prison reformer

While it may be presumptuous to single out any one man as the most-tortured prisoner in the history of American penology, that distinction has frequently been assigned to Ed Morrell, the so-called Dungeon Man of San Quentin. He had been the youngest member of a gang known as the California Outlaws, which made war on the land-grabbing Southern Pacific Railroad in the 1880s and 1890s. Many of Morrell's torturous experiences in Folsom and San Quentin prisons formed the basis of Jack London's *The Star Rover*.

Pennsylvania-born Morrell arrived in California in 1891. He found injustices in the area little different from those he had witnessed in his own anthracite region of Pennsylvania, where the Mollie Maguires, a secret labor terrorist society, came into existence. The beautiful San Joaquin Valley of California appeared to offer hope for a new life. Instead, he found, as in his native state, law and order were on the side of money and might. Life in the valley was a bitter experience. Land agents working for the railroad were swindling the settlers with the help of the law. Anything perpetrated by the gunmen of the railroad, popularly called the Octopus, was considered legal, including such atrocities as the Slaughter of Mussel Slough, in which seven settlers had been shot and killed in 1880. The result was a virtual civil war. Railroad undercover agents moved in among the settlers to spy on them and report any troublemakers, who were dealt with brutally. Under the circumstances, it was inevitable that an organization like the California Outlaws would spring up in the valley. They existed solely to steal from the Southern Pacific Railroad, robbing its express car but never victimizing any of the passengers or stealing the mail.

Bribes and threats were made to area residents in an effort to force them to betray the Outlaws. The gang countered by planting 20-year-old Ed Morrell as their own spy in the employ of the notorious railroad detective Big Bill Smith. In time, the ranks of the gang dwindled down to 25 men, 24 regular Outlaws, headed by Chris Evans and the Sontag brothers, George and John, plus Morrell. When Evans was finally captured, a conspiracy was hatched to have the badly wounded Outlaw leader killed attempting to escape, and Smith assigned Morrell a key role in the plot. Instead, Morrell staged a real escape for Evans and went with him. Morrell carried, or half-dragged, Evans through the valley and surrounding hills for weeks, with hundreds of railroad agents, Pinkertons and Wells Fargo men in pursuit. They were sheltered by one hill family after another but finally betrayed by a man enticed by the big reward offered for them. Both were captured and Evans was

sentenced to life. All Morrell was guilty of was aiding Evans to escape, an offense normally punishable by just a few years in prison. Smith, however, pointed out that Morrell had taken the police chief's revolver during the escape, which constituted robbery. As a result, Morrell was sentenced to life at hard labor in Folsom Prison. Folsom at the time was known as the private lockup of the Southern Pacific. The warden of Folsom was a former railroad detective, as were many of the guards. Sometime later, it was discovered that the warden was still carried on the railroad's payroll despite his state position.

Folsom was a mankiller with a blood curdling, awesome history. Many convicts not tough enough to endure its brutal labor conditions and tortures were known to have deliberately charged the armed guards or even hurled themselves into the surging waters of the American River to achieve at least a more merciful death.

Morrell was assigned to rock pile work under the sweltering sun and supervised by guards who went out of their way to discipline him for imaginary infractions. Finally, for stepping out of line in formation, a minor infraction at best, Morrell was given 50 hours on the derrick. Few men at Folsom were given 50 hours of this treatment, the usual punishment calling for 10 hours spread over a two- or three-day span. The derrick was a block-and-tackle contraption whereby a prisoner was suspended with his arms bound behind his back and the tips of his shoes barely resting on the dungeon floor. The pain, needless to say, was excruciating and often resulted in severe bleeding from the kidneys. For that reason a prisoner normally would be subjected to no more than to two 2½-hour sessions a day. On one occasion Morrell's punishment lasted for 13 days because he bled so badly he could not do the full five hours a day.

Punishment after punishment was heaped on Morrell and the warden informed him he would never get any respite until he revealed the identities of the California Outlaws still at large. Morrell endured his punishment and said nothing. Once, the California Outlaws bribed a guard to look the other way so that Morrell could escape. Another guard learned of the plot and alerted the warden, who decided to let Morrell make the attempt and stationed guards outside the wall to gun him down. But Morrell never came out. The warden's wife, known as the Angel of the Prison, saved him. She had overheard her husband's plan and sent word to Morrell through another convict. Morrell had to endure additional tortures because he would not reveal details of the escape plan or say who had warned him.

For this stubborness Morrell was subjected to a number of sessions in the "lime cell," a fiendish torture chamber lined with a coating of lime. A guard would hose down the walls and a white mist from the exploding chloride of lime would fill the cell. Tossed inside, the prisoner would feel as though his throat was on fire and would actually think his breath was aflame. Once subjected to 10 days in a row of such punishment, Morrell ended up with his eyebrows and eyelashes completely burned away, and his nose, throat and mouth so seared that his voice was reduced to a faint whisper.

Through all these ordeals, Morrell's spirit never broke and he even organized other escape attempts and riots. Finally, he was transferred to San Quentin. There too, Morrell was subjected to very special treatment. When he arrived, he was given 20 days in solitary for "looking at" a guard. The day after he was released, he was sent back for 30 more days on a complaint from the same guard.

Morrell was regularly punished with the "San Quentin overcoat," which resembled a supertight full-length straitjacket. The overcoat was a coffin-shaped piece of coarse, heavy canvas with brass eyelets along the sides and two inside pockets for the hands. First, Morrell would be wrapped in a blanket, not to ease the pain but rather to avoid leaving too many marks and bruises in case he died and also to make the overcoat fit more tightly. Then the garment was fitted around him and laced tight.

Later, in his autobiography, *The 25th Man,* Morrell described his first experience in the overcoat:

> Jungle travelers have described the awful agony of a native victim being squeezed to death by a giant boa-constrictor. It is all too terrible for the human mind to contemplate, but even this inconceivable spectacle must pale before the death terrors of the jacket.
>
> I had not been in it fifteen minutes when pain began shooting through my fingers, hands and arms, gradually extending to my shoulders. Then over my whole body there was a prickling sensation like that of millions of sharp needles jabbing through the tender flesh. . . . Hour after hour I endured the pain and as the time passed the anguish became more and more unbearable. I slept neither night nor day, and how slowly my torture went on when all was silent in the prison! The hours dragged as if weighted with lead.
>
> Now a new horror came. The bodily excretions over which I had no control in the canvas vice ate into my bruised limbs. My fingers, hands, and arms grew numb and dead.
>
> Thus I suffered incessantly for four days and fourteen hours. . . . Released from its pressure I attempted to gain my feet, but was too weak. My limbs were temporarily paralyzed. After a time, mustering all my strength, I reached a sitting posture and finally managed to drag off my saturated clothes.
>
> "What a sight I beheld! My hands, arms, and legs were frightfully bruised. My body was shriveled like that of an old man, and a horrible stench came from it.

After enduring this punishment, Morrell was framed on a charge of having a gun smuggled in to him for an escape. For this alleged infraction he was ordered to spend the rest of his life in solitary confinement in San Quentin's dungeon. There was only one other prisoner undergoing the same treatment there, Jake Oppenheimer, who was known as the Tiger of the Prison Cage.

The two, who had never seen each other, were separated by 13 cells, but they eventually learned to communicate using a form of "knuckle talk," with various knocks on the steel walls indicating different letters. It was the first use of such a method of communication in an American prison and has since been adopted in almost every prison in the world.

In 1903 San Quentin's most brutal and villainous warden, Martin Aguirr, disgraced by prison scandals, was forced to resign. The next warden learned from the captain of the yard, John C. Edgar, that Morrell had been framed on the gun charge and made an investigation. As a result, Morrell, now famed as the Dungeon Man, was returned to the general prison population. In 1906 Edgar became warden and worked unceasingly for Morrell's release. Edgar did not live to see the fruition of his efforts, but two years later, the acting governor, Lt. Gov. Warren Porter, personally came to San Quentin to present a pardon to Morrell.

It was a different San Quentin that Ed Morrell left. The new warden, John E. Hoyle, was the first of California's progressive penologists, and his term marked a new era in the treatment of prisoners, one made possible by the publicity given to Ed Morrell. For the first time the American public took an interest in the administration of prisons and demanded humane treatment for inmates.

Morrell became a national hero. He lectured on prison reform, arguing primarily for the abolition of corporal punishment. He organized the American Crusaders to promote changes in the administration of prisons nationwide. He spoke before the legislatures of California and Pennsylvania and, in 1918, became the only ex-convict ever to be called to Congress to advise on inmate labor problems. Jack London's *The Star Rover* and Morrell's own autobiography further popularized the man on whom was visited almost all forms of evil practiced in America's prisons. Much of the improvement later achieved in the nation's prisons was due to Morrell's dogged determination to survive the whip, the dungeon, the derrick, the lime cell and the San Quentin overcoat. He died in 1946.

See also: *California Outlaws, Christopher Evans, Folsom Derrick, Knuckle Voice, Lime Cell, Sontag Brothers.*

MORSE, Charles W. (c.1860-1942): Swindler

One of the most proficient American swindlers and confidence operators was Charles W. Morse, a Midwesterner who pulled off hundreds of crooked deals and bilked victims out of millions of dollars with every conceivable financial scam.

His greatest coup occurred two years after he was arrested, for the first and only time, in 1910 and sentenced to 15 years for tampering with the books of the Bank of North America. In 1912 President William Howard Taft granted him a full presidential pardon after government physicians reported he was dying of Bright's disease. To the amazement of the medical men, the cunning swindler thrived and lived for 30 years after his release. It was finally discovered he had faked the symptoms of the disease with a special concoction composed mainly of different soaps.

MORTON, Samuel J. "Nails" (?-1924): Chicago mob gunman

Nails Morton was a top gun in the Dion O'Banion gang, which from 1920 to 1924, the year of O'Banion's death, fought the Italian mobsters even. Morton was held in awe by other Chicago mobsters because in World War I he had won the Croix de Guerre in France and received a battlefield-promotion to first lieutenant.

Morton was an inventive sort of killer, but he was to become more noteworthy because of the way he died and the act of revenge that followed. Nails was fond of horseback riding in Lincoln Park, "where the society swells ride." One day, in what the mob considered vicious treachery, a horse threw him and kicked him to death. The O'Banion gang took the required vengeance. Four of them, Bugs Moran, Schemer Drucci, Little Hymie Weiss and Two Gun Alterie, went to the riding stable and, with drawn guns, snatched the animal. After leading it to the spot where Morton had been killed, the animal was dispatched, in proper underworld style, with four slugs in the head, the incident later forming the basis for an episode in Mario Puzo's *The Godfather*.

See also: *Dion O'Banion*.

MOSSMAN, Burton C. (1867–1956): First head of Arizona Rangers

One of the Southwest's most successful ranchers, Burt Mossman was also one of its most illustrious lawmen, as the first head of the Arizona Rangers.

Born in Aurora, Ill., he was ramrodding his first spread in the New Mexico Territory by the age of 21. Nine years later, he was manager of the huge Hash Knife ranch, containing 60,000 cattle. He proved to be an action-oriented manager who cleared the Hash Knife range of rustlers. In 1901 Gov. Nathan O. Murphy named Mossman the first captain of the newly organized Arizona Rangers, specifically assigned to clear the state of rustlers and, above all, to "get Chacon." Augustine Chacon, a Mexican killer, was said to have notched his gun 30 times in shooting frays on both sides of the border.

Getting Chacon was not easy, and Mossman first had to take care of business closer at hand. In one stand-up gun duel he killed a vicious robber and killer named Juan Saliveras. In other exploits he rounded up a number of rustling gangs and chased several more far out of the state. Then in a daring mission in 1902, Mossman went to Mexico and managed to bring Chacon back to the hangman after wheedling his way into the bandit's confidence and suggesting a raid on the San Rafael ranch in the Arizona Territory.

Later in that year Mossman resigned his post to return to ranching, which was now a much safer activity in the area thanks to him and his rangers. Mossman was one of the Southwest's biggest ranchers until he retired in 1944. He died at Roswell, N.M. in 1956.

See also: *Burt Alvard, Arizona Rangers*.

MOTHER Carey's Chickens: Slang for brothel inmates

One of the most popular terms for referring to a brothel inmate, the phrase set off a hunt by some social historians and writers to find the original Mother Carey, who was assumed to be a Western madam since the term originated in the West. The term "Mother Carey," however, seems to be a corruption of *mata cara*, meaning dear mother.

MOUNTAIN Meadows Massacre: Religious mass killing

One of the worst crimes in Mormon history occurred on September 7, 1857, when a westbound wagon train of 140 men, women and children was attacked by Indians at Mountain Meadows, Utah Territory.

Some fanciful accounts contend that the attackers were not Indians at all but disguised white Mormons. There is little doubt, in fact, that some Mormons were acting in concert with the Indians. After about 20 of the emigrants had been killed in the first assault, the battle was interrupted by the arrival of Mormon Bishop John D. Lee, who was also Indian agent for the area, with a large group of his men and some Indian auxiliaries. Lee offered to escort the wagon train to Cedar City, Utah provided they would lay down their arms. The wagon train party gratefully agreed. However, as soon as the emigrants had put down their weapons, Lee and his men, in collusion with the attacking Indians, shot down all the men, including the wounded. The killing of the women and children was left to the Indians. Only 17 very young children, too young to bear witness, were spared in the massacre.

When Brigham Young learned what had happened, after being told false versions by Lee, he decided to do nothing to aid the authorities in their investigation, out of fear that all the men of the Mormon community would be implicated. Later, he excommunicated Lee and several other leaders of the massacre. It took the federal government 18 years to gather enough evidence to bring Lee to trial in July 1875. On March 23, 1877, having been found guilty, Lee was taken to the site of the massacre and executed there by a firing squad.

See also: *Haun's Mill Massacre*.

MUDD, Dr. Samuel (1833–1883): Alleged Lincoln assassination conspirator

A Maryland practitioner, Dr. Samuel Mudd became implicated in the Lincoln assassination conspiracy after he set the leg of John Wilkes Booth during the latter's flight from Washington. Although Mudd was in no way involved in the crime, as was proved in later years, the hysteria of the times resulted in a vengeful trial in which Mudd was convicted of conspiring to kill the President. He was sentenced to life imprisonment in what was at the time the nation's most-dreaded federal prison, Fort Jefferson in the Dry Tortugas off Florida, where he was subjected to vicious treatment by his guards. Under orders from superiors, the guards kept Mudd chained to the floor of his cell and abused him regularly.

The Dry Tortugas Prison, as it was called, was a pesthole of illness and the scene of frequent yellow fever epidemics. Fol-

THE SCENE OF THE MOUNTAIN MEADOWS MASSACRE, UTAH TERRITORY.—[FROM A RECENT SKETCH.]

Even 15 years after the Mountain Meadows Massacre, the Eastern press continued to fuel the hysteria over the slaughter.

lowing a particularly deadly outbreak in 1867, in which another of the convicted Lincoln assassination conspirators, Michael O'Laughlin, and all the Army surgeons died, Dr. Mudd surprised officials by offering to treat the prisoners, soldiers and guards. Mudd treated the prison population throughout the epidemic, even after contracting the disease himself.

Because of his humanitarian efforts and a four-year campaign by his wife, Mudd was released from prison in 1869 and returned to Maryland. In recent years an effort was made to obtain a complete pardon to clear his name, and in 1979 President Jimmy Carter sent a telegram to Dr. Richard Mudd, grandson of Dr. Mudd, affirming his belief that his grandfather had been unjustly convicted. President Carter regretted that the military commission's guilty verdict was not one that could be set aside by a president.

See also: *Dry Tortugas Prison, Abraham Lincoln.*

MUFF Pistol

In the 19th century, gunmakers produced a whole series of .22 caliber firearms seldom longer than three or four inches. Because a lady could easily conceal one in her muff, they were known as muff pistols. Of course, not too many ladies carried these weapons but quite a few female criminals, such as Babe Irving of New York and Kitty Adams of Chicago (who often stuffed two in her muff), did. The muff pistol fell into general disrepute because of newspaper campaigns that blamed them for fostering criminality, much like the drives launched in the 1970s against the so-called Saturday Night Special.

MUGGING

The crime of mugging—sneaking up on a hapless victim, incapacitating him and robbing him—is as old as man himself. Practitioners of the art in early America were called footpads, because they padded out the soles of their shoes or boots with cloth or some other material to deaden the sound of their footsteps.

The term "mugger" itself appears to have originated in the 1830s in Buffalo, N.Y. on Canal Street, one of the most vile of all the sin streets of the 19th century. Crime ran rampant on Canal Street after the completion of the Erie Canal, and violence was always considered the quickest and easiest solution when a gentleman ran so short of money that he could not even afford to buy a mug of beer. He would simply walk out into the darkness of Canal Street and waylay, or "mug," an unsuspecting passerby.

See also: *Canal Street*.

MULLIN, Herbert (1947-): Mass murderer

Voted most likely to succeed by his 1965 high school class, young Herbert Mullin went on to become a college dropout, dope addict and all-round weirdo. Late in 1972 he went on a four-month murder spree, during which he killed at least 10 persons because he somehow believed this would prevent a major earthquake popularly, if not scientifically, predicted to happen in early 1973. According to his later confession, Mullin said that he had been telepathically "ordered" to kill and that only human sacrifices could prevent the impending tragedy. He stated, "I'm a scapegoat person made to carry the guilt feelings of others. . . . Every day people die. There's a steady flow of death in order to keep the coast free of cataclysmic earthquakes and the earth in orbit."

Declared legally sane, Mullin was found guilty of murdering three women, one man and six boys in the Santa Cruz Mountains of northern California and was sentenced to life imprisonment. He was not tried for three additional murders to which he confessed, including that of a Catholic priest in Los Gatos, Calif., whom he had stabbed to death, he said, after having second thoughts about a confession he had made to him.

MULLINEN, Joe (?-1781): Colonial Robin Hood bandit

A daring Colonial bandit, Joseph Mullinen clearly got his inspiration from the tale of Robin Hood; he stole from the rich and gave to the poor, at least to some extent. Mullinen began his depredations in southern New Jersey around the start of the American Revolution. He made gifts of part of his loot to the needy, seeking to build up a sympathetic network of well-wishers who would help him avoid the law. It worked for several years, as he made his forays out of the Pine Barrens, a 1,000-square-mile wilderness of woods and swampland, his own Sherwood Forest. Mullinen kept the major portion of his loot and, as we know from his confederates, buried it in various spots in the Pine Barrens.

A womanizer and drinker, Mullinen might have avoided capture had he not been so dedicated to having a good time. He was apprehended at a barn dance in New Columbia, N.J. and in August 1781, hanged. Those attending his execution came not so much to see him swing as in the hope that at the last minute he might reveal the hiding places of his booty. He did not, however, and New Jerseyites have gone on Mullinen treasure hunts right up to the present day.

MUNICIPAL Brothel: San Francisco bordello

The nearest thing to a governmental whorehouse in America was San Francisco's infamous Municipal Brothel in the early part of the 20th century. Because it soon became common knowledge that virtually all of the profits of the establishment flowed into the pockets of city officials and their political sponsors, the famous house, officially known just as 620 Jackson Street, soon won its more recognizable name. Saloon keepers and other businessmen who sought political favor advertised the brothel to customers. When strangers in town asked policemen where women could be found, they were obligingly directed to it; an officer who failed in that assigned task could count on being transferred to a less favorable beat. The house was a regular stop for Jackson Street trolleys, and if no ladies were aboard, the conductors shouted, "All out for the whorehouse!"

The brothel was first opened in 1904 as a three-story affair with some 90 cubicles. Recruitment of women was the duty of Billy Finnegan, a veteran character in San Francisco vice. He rented out space at a daily rate ranging from $2 to $5 per crib with a guarantee of immunity from arrest. After the place was destroyed by the earthquake and fire of 1906, a four-story and basement structure containing 133 cribs and a saloon was erected in its place. The prices varied according to floor and the beauty of the individual women. The basement was given over to Mexican harlots, who charged 25¢. The first, second and third floors were occupied mostly by American and French women, with the prices rising from 50¢ to 75¢ and up, to $1 on the third floor, which was populated exclusively by what customers were assured were "genuine Frenchies." The fourth floor was given over to black prostitutes at 50¢.

Not only were the inmates protected from arrest under the political rule of Boss Abe Ruef and his puppet mayor, Eugene Schmitz, but most other brothels in the immediate area were shuttered to guarantee a good return for the political figures. Testimony before a grand jury in December 1906 established that Herbert Schmitz, the Mayor's brother, owned a one-quarter interest in the brothel and that, despite their denials, both the mayor and Ruef took a cut of the profits, in Ruef's case $250 a week. The indictment of Mayor Schmitz, Boss Ruef and several members of the Board of Supervisors, whom Ruef himself described as "being so greedy for plunder that they'd eat the paint off a house," led to the fall of the administration in 1907. None of the indictments in the case was acted upon, although Ruef eventually went to prison for bribery.

Despite the wave of reform that hit San Francisco, the brothel continued to operate for a time, but from early 1907 it was subjected to many police raids, under pressure from a grand jury and the newspapers. The pervasiveness of the bribery involved was indicated by the fact that at first the harlots were simply driven off rather than arrested. When they finally were arrested, they were permitted to post small bonds, which they promptly forfeited. In September 1907 Chief of Police William J. Biggy visited the resort personally and ordered it closed when he found it swarming with boys as young as 14 years of age. The following year Chief Biggy crossed San Francisco Bay in a police launch to attend a conference. Later, he reembarked and was never seen alive again. His body was found floating in the bay a week later.

With Biggy's death, efforts were made to reopen the brothel but they were soon abandoned because of the opposition of a crusading priest, Father Terence Caraher, the *San Francisco Globe* and the new chief of police, Jesse B. Cook, formerly an acrobat and tumbler with the troupe of Renaldo, Cook and Orr.

MURDER

Official FBI statistics shows that something like 19,000 or 20,000 murders are committed in the United States each year. The figures are not to be taken seriously, however, since such a raw compilation has little to do with the actual murder rate. As far back as 1953 William F. Kessler, M.D., and Paul B. Weston, a deputy inspector in the New York Police Department, said in their authoritative study *The Detection of Murder:* "Nowhere in the world is the investigation of unexplained or unexpected death so casual and haphazard as it is in the United States." They pointed out that murder is proved in only one-third of one percent of all unexplained and unexpected deaths. The ambiguous "fell, jumped or pushed," and "apparent suicide" are standard newspaper terms that undoubtedly cover a multitude of sins.

How many mass murderers walk free among us? How long do they get away with their crimes? Among the greatest *known* mass murderers in recent years has been John W. Gacy, an Illinois building contractor, who from 1972 to 1978 murdered 33 boys and young men he had lured to his home. After having sexual relations with his victims, he killed them and buried most of them in the crawlspace under his house. Of course, none of Gacy's victims caused a "recount" of the murders reported for the years in which they died. Such recording problems indicate how it is almost impossible to put a handle on the true number of murders committed in a year.

Who gets caught? Dr. Alan R. Moritz, longtime head of Harvard's Department of Legal Medicine, says, "Usually only the stupid ones are caught and convicted." Certainly, it is difficult to argue with estimates that for every murder discovered, there is another that is not even noticed. The *Journal of the American Medical Association* states, "With reasonable certainty it may be said that several thousands of murders pass unrecognized each year in the United States." In Virginia, which is considered to have one of the best medical examiner systems in the nation, it has been estimated that there are at least 50 murders a year that pass as natural deaths. Unquestionably, murders are more readily recognized in states like New York and California, but in a great many states, especially those still saddled with a nonscientific, often politically dominated coroner system, the procedures used in determining the cause of deaths are woeful. Some coroner's offices are as competent as any medical examiner's office, but in many parts

of the country there is no requirement that the coroner even be a medical man. Some are dentists or undertakers or political hacks. Thus, death certificates contain, as surveys have shown, such comments as "Could be diabetes or poison," "Died in a shanty," or "The deceased died suddenly. Might be heart trouble."

Some states do not specifically require that the coroner be able to read and write. A university study once discovered a report by a coroner, presumably the highest medical man in the county, that read, "So far as I could ascertain, I found She came to her death from A natur cause comely called hart failure, and I found no cause to suspect any foul play."

Ignoring the ineptitude of certain coroner systems, a number of actual cases have perplexed medical examiners over the years. A 60-year-old New York man was sitting on his porch one day, minding his own business, when he suddenly slumped down and died. His grieving relatives told the medical examiner what had happened. "He suffered an attack and apparently struck his head on the stoop when he pitched over." It made sense, a natural death with no blood spilled.

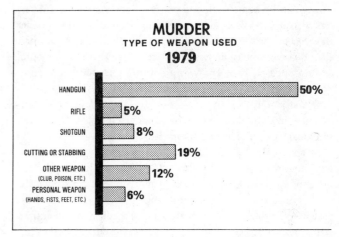

Statistics clearly demonstrate that hand guns are the murder weapon of choice.

That conclusion might have stood if the man's killer had not confessed. He was a mentally deranged man with a 20-year record in psychiatric institutions. He was caught in a spree of shooting people through windows with a .22 caliber rifle. After his apprehension he kept upsetting the police by insisting he had killed a man even though they had no such murder victim. He repeatedly furnished the date and place of the crime but nobody would believe him. Finally, a check was made. The 60-year-old man's body was dug up and an autopsy performed. Only then was a .22 caliber bullet found deeply imbedded in the dead man's brain.

There is a cynical police saying that goes, "If there ain't no murder suspect, well then there might not have been any murder." That sentiment may explain why the "cleared by arrest" record in murder cases is so superior to other types of crimes. While the police make an arrest in only one out of five crimes in general, the arrests in murder cases are better than 70 percent, an average undoubtedly helped by the fact that investigators simply fail to recognize many violent or unexpected deaths as murder.

In some instances they may simply not *want* to recognize a death as a possible murder. Such was the case with Mrs. Jeanne Brown, about age 30, in New York City. She was found dead, her jugular vein cut, sitting on the floor propped up against her bed. There were a number of empty beer bottles and one empty whiskey bottle in the room. Although the telephone wires had been ripped from the wall, no signs of a struggle were evident. At the time of her death, Jeanne's husband was aboard a ship in the Persian Gulf, and the police found no indication that she had ever entertained any male visitors while her husband was away. The woman had a history of alcoholism and had been under treatment a few months earlier.

The medical examiner first labeled the case a "definite homicide" and later a "possible homicide." However, the police and the district attorney did not agree. First of all, they had no suspect. They said the woman had had a past history of ripping telephone wires from the wall. As the police reconstructed the case, the woman had been drinking and had a beer can opener in her hand when she ripped out the telephone wires. As she jerked the wires free, her arm swung around and the opener slashed her throat. Not realizing how badly she had been hurt, she grabbed some facial tissues, placed them against the wound and dropped off to sleep. Within 30 minutes, she had bled to death.

It was a convenient theory. But the fact remains the woman's death could have been an accident, it could have been suicide or it could have been murder.

In an equally baffling case, in Milwaukee, Wis., a despondent housewife apparently crawled inside an oil furnace, let the door swing shut, then used a cord and rubber band device she contrived to turn on the controls and cremate herself. At least that was the theory, one that the county medical officer admitted was possible but added he could not rule out the possibility of a bizarre murder. It was not the usual sort of suicide, especially not for a woman. Usually, women suicides prefer sleeping pills or gas. A furnace death is almost always a case of murder.

Either of these two cases could have been a suicide or a murder and so could dozens of other violent, unexplained or sudden deaths that occur daily. There can be little doubt that some are murders.

Police in a large Eastern city know of one case recorded as accidental death that was really murder—yet the murderer remains forever free. The victim was found in a pool of blood diluted with whiskey on the landing at the top of a flight of stairs. He was lying on his left side. There were pieces of shattered glass sprinkled about in the slowly coagulating blood. The first detectives on the scene quickly theorized what had happened: "The fellow is coming up the stairs and trips and falls. The broken bottle cuts him up."

The medical examiner arrived and soon agreed with the comment that "here's one guy who died of booze the hard way."

The body was carted off to the morgue, an autopsy was performed, the blood and glass on the landing cleaned up and the case marked closed. When the man fell, the official view went, the weight of his body caused several glass fragments to lacerate the left armpit and death resulted from loss of blood.

It took a year for the truth to surface. One night a woman, the dead man's part-time lady friend, got drunk and boasted how she had killed him. She said she had grasped the bottle of whiskey she was bringing home for them by its neck and smashed it against the stair railing. As the man raised his arm to hit her, she rammed the jagged end of the broken bottle into his armpit and just took off.

As Kessler and Weston noted: "She was never prosecuted. There were no eye-witnesses, no fragments of glass, and no testimony as to the location of the various fragments. No one had ever processed the larger pieces of glass for fingerprints, no one had bothered to photograph the scene—in fact no one had bothered to conduct anything more than a cursory investigation."

Thus another murder failed to make the crime tables. Murder remains a most serious problem, and undoubtedly far more serious than official statistics would indicate.

Some crime writers have said that murder is more diverse and complicated than any other offense. That is hardly the case. Rather it is one of the most monotonously consistent. Often the method of murder tells who did it. A single girl is stabbed two dozen times in a murderous frenzy. The police know immediately to look for her boy friend or a secret admirer. If she is married, they zero in on her husband. If he is cleared, they then start looking for a lover. Not long ago in New York City a young mother was stabbed to death in her hospital bed. Was there a maniac loose in the hospital? That frightening theory was played up in the newspapers until police arrested a young man who lived across the street from the woman. He had been secretly enamoured of her for a long time.

Murder is largely a family affair. In his book *Crime in America,* former U.S. Attorney General Ramsey Clark warns, "If you are afraid of being murdered, there is more safety in deserting your family and having no friends than in additional police, who rarely have the opportunity to prevent friends and relatives from murdering each other."

While Americans are concerned about being murdered by a stranger, the truth is that murders committed by persons unknown to the victim account for no more than 20 percent of all homicides. Perhaps two-thirds of all aggravated assaults are committed by relatives, friends or neighbors of the victim. Murder is a crime of hate and to hate someone it is helpful to know the person.

When John Godwin, the author of *Murder USA,* asked a veteran New York City patrolman what was the most dangerous situation facing a police officer, the patrolman unhesitatingly replied, "Trying to stop a family brawl on a hot night." In fact, out of every five officers killed in the line of duty, one dies as a result of intervening in a domestic dispute.

Not surprisingly most in-home homicides take place in the bedroom (where there is often a gun handy) or in the kitchen (where there is always a knife). The basic disputes are, of course, over money and sex and often follow considerable drinking. Quite naturally, most domestic murders occur on a Saturday and in the hot summer months.

Handguns are by far the most common murder weapons, used in about 50 percent of all such cases. Adding in shotguns and rifles, guns account for perhaps 65 percent of all killings. Part of the debate over gun control is whether guns or people kill people. The fact is that the National Rifle Association notwithstanding, *people with guns* kill people.

It is popularly thought that murder is currently at its highest rate ever in this country. But it is not very likely. While statistics are limited, there is little doubt that murders were more frequent in the 19th century, especially when the great street gangs were springing up in the 1820s and in the period from the 1860s to the 1880s. Then murders seemed to slack off until the 1920s and 1930s, when they increased again. The first fairly reliable nationwide statistics date from 1933; the murder rate then was 14 percent higher than in 1967. Since that time murders have increased ever so slightly. The rise may be because more murders are being detected or reported to the police than an increase in violence.

Murders are much more frequent in the United States than in the nations of Western Europe or in Japan, which have more homogenous societies and are thought to be less subject to the pressures of industrial life. However, this country's murder rate is considerably lower than that of the Latin American countries, where the warmer climate is considered a contributing factor.

One of the most popular, if fruitless, pastimes of crime buffs is to try to figure out who was the greatest mass killer in American history. As mentioned earlier, John Gacy stands high on the list with 33, but no one is sure of his actual total. Some supporters of Belle Gunness, the Lady Bluebeard of La Porte, Ind., credit her with 40, but others place her total at 14 to 17. Probably the top killer of all was H. H. Holmes, the keeper of the notorious Murder Castle in Chicago during the 1890s. Estimates of his kill count range from 20 to 200; all of his victims were women. Holmes complicated matters by taking delight in misleading the police. He confessed killing women who later turned up alive and denied murdering others who had been found dead. In any event, it seems likely he dispatched somewhere between 40 and 100.

Of course, that is hardly a record if one considers John A. Murrel, who may have killed hundreds of kidnapped black slaves. He was in the business of stealing and selling slaves, but he sometimes got confused and sold slaves back to the same parties he had stolen them from. Whenever Murrel found himself in doubt about where he had gotten certain slaves from or had to dispose of those he couldn't sell quickly, he drowned them in the river.

John Billington is generally recognized as America's first murderer. At least he was the first found guilty of murdering a white man. Billington was one of the original band of 102 pilgrims on the *Mayflower*, a rowdy who many said would come to a bad end. He did in 1630, when he waylaid and killed a fellow settler and was duly hanged.

MURDER, Incorporated: Syndicate's professional hit squad

Murder, Inc., a gang of professional killers who carried out homicides on assignment in the 1930s, was hardly a new criminal idea. Professional killer gangs existed in the American underworld in the 19th century and murders were committed for pay, with prices generally ranging from $100 down to $5 and even $2. But the Brooklyn "troop" of killers, dubbed by the press Murder, Inc., was an elitist outfit. Not available for hire by outsiders, they were solely at the disposal of the emerging national crime syndicate formed primarily by Lucky Luciano and Meyer Lansky, an ethnic conglomerate composed of "young Turk" mafiosi and the great Jewish and, to a lesser extent, Irish gangs that blossomed in the Prohibition era. The purpose of the new syndicate, especially after Repeal, was to divide up such criminal activities as gambling, loansharking, labor racketeering, prostitution and narcotics in some sort of acceptable and orderly fashion. Of course, what was acceptable to one gang was not necessarily acceptable to others and thus there developed a need for an enforcement arm to put muscle in the national board's edicts.

Murder, Inc. killed only for business reasons and was never to be used against political figures or reporters—Meyer Lansky and Moe Dalitz, then the criminal power in Cleveland, were most insistent on this point—because of the public stir and "heat" such assassinations caused.

A whole new vocabulary was developed by the troop of killers. The assassins accepted "contracts" to "hit" "bums." Perhaps the most significant term was "bums," meaning marked victims. Psychiatrists could see in this a rationalization for the killers' crimes, one that allowed them to regard victims as subhumans deserving of dying. Thus, a Murder, Inc. killer could, as happened, go directly from a cold-blooded killing to the bedside of a dying grandparent and weep real tears over the sad event.

Operating commanders of the troop were Albert Anastasia, its so-called Lord High Executioner, and Louis Lepke, the nation's number one labor racketeer and a member of the crime cartel's national board. However, none of the estimated 400 to 500 murders committed by the outfit was ever allowed to proceed without the concurrence, or at least the absence of any negative votes, of other top executives, especially Luciano, Lansky, Joe Adonis and Frank Costello. Bugsy Siegel probably best summarized the top gangsters' attitude toward Murder, Inc. as merely a necessary business device when he told construction executive Del Webb he had nothing to fear from the mob because "we only kill each other."

Directly below Anastasia and Lepke were a number of lieutenants, such as Louis Capone (no relation to Chicago's Al), Mendy Weiss and Abe "Kid Twist" Reles. Instructions on a specific contract generally were only given to one underling, who then passed the word on, so that no legal proof of the top men's involvement could be found. Some of the quaint killers of the mob included Vito "Chicken Head" Gurino, who sharpened his shooting skills by blasting off the heads of chickens;

Frank "the Dasher" Abbandando; Happy Maione, who wore a permanent scowl; Buggsy Goldstein; Blue Jaw Magoon; and, the most notorious of all, Pittsburgh Phil Strauss. Pittsburgh Phil was the troop's most prolific and resourceful killer and was named in 58 murder investigations around the country. His actual kill toll was most likely about twice that figure. The boys would hang around a certain 24-hour candy store in the Brownsville section of Brooklyn called Midnight Rose's, awaiting assignments, and then hit the trail for wherever in the country their victim happened to be. More often than not, the assigned killer had never before met the "bum," creating a difficult situation for the police. Murder by a stranger with no personal motive presents a puzzle that is seldom solved.

Probably the most famous victim of Murder, Inc. was top gang lord Dutch Schultz, himself a founding member of the crime syndicate. In 1935 Schultz had become the chief target of special prosecutor Thomas E. Dewey and responded with a demand to the national board that Dewey be hit. This was in direct defiance of the founding rules that no politicians were to be murdered. When Schultz' demand was rejected, he stormed away, vowing to handle the job himself. Immediately, a contract was voted on Schultz to prevent him from carrying out his desperate and dangerous-for-business plot.

In 1940 Murder, Inc. came apart when a number of lesser mob members were picked up on suspicion of various murders. Abe Reles got the idea that somebody would talk and implicate him, so he started singing first. He eventually gave details of some 200 killings in which he had either participated or had knowledge of. In the ensuing investigation several top killers went to the electric chair, including Pittsburgh Phil, Mendy Weiss, Louis Capone, Happy Maione and Frank Abbandando. Also executed was Lepke, the only top-level syndicate leader to suffer that fate.

In November 1941 Reles was still doing his canary act and was considered the key witness in a case against Bugsy Siegel and Albert Anastasia, but before he could testify, he "went out the window" of a Coney Island hotel, where he was being held under police protection. Whether Reles' death was suicide, accident or murder has never been established, although in his later years Luciano insisted that he gave the orders from his prison cell to kill Reles before he doomed Siegel and Anastasia and that money was paid to certain members of the New York Police Department to make sure "the canary who could sing couldn't fly."

Of course, Murder, Inc. did not end with the breakup of the Brooklyn troop. The syndicate has kept right on ordering contracts and having them filled.

See also: *Frank "the Dasher" Abbandando, Albert Anastasia, Louis "Lepke" Buchalter, Midnight Rose's, Pittsburgh Phil, Abe Reles, Dutch Schultz, State Street Crap Game.*

MURDER Stable: Early Mafia burial site

The accidental discovery of the infamous Murder Stable in New York City in 1901 drove home to Americans that there was a "Mafia" or a "Black Hand," or at least some kind of organized gang of Italian criminals.

In the spring of 1901 the U.S. Secret Service began investigating rumors of an anarchist plot to kill President William McKinley. Among those asked to aid in the investigation was a New York police detective named Joseph Petrosino, who would become legendary for his battles with the Mafia and with various Black Handers. Petrosino reported there was no organized conspiracy but there was much talk among anarchists of an individual possibly attempting such an assassination. McKinley was killed by such an "independent," Leon Czolgosz, in Buffalo, N.Y. some three months later. During the course of the investigation, Petrosino and the Secret Service had stumbled onto the so-called Murder Stable, a property located in Italian Harlem at 323 East 107th Street. Digging up the premises, they found the remains of approximately 60 murder victims. The property was owned by one Ignazio Saietta, better known in Italian crime circles as Lupo the Wolf. When it became apparent the victims had been killed as part of an effort to consolidate Italian control of the waterfront, the Secret Service dropped out of the investigation. It was left to local officials to contain Lupo and the notorious Morello gang he worked with. Lupo successfully insisted he was just the landlord and knew nothing, and he remained an awesome figure in the New York crime scene for another two decades.
See also: *Lupo the Wolf.*

MURIETA, Joaquin (c.1830-1853 or 1878): Bandit

The greatest desperado of the early gold rush days in California may have been the Mexican-born Joaquin Murieta, or Murrieta or Muriati. There is considerable confusion about his last name and indeed even over whether such a person existed, notwithstanding the fact that his pickled head was later brought in by California Rangers.

The Murieta legend seems to be a mixture of fact and folklore. The most likely version is that Murieta was born about 1830 of Spanish parents near Alamos, Mexico and studied in the Jesuit school there. He took up arms in a revolt against the Mexican government by many of his native Sonorans as well as Mayo and Yaqui Indians. In 1848 Murieta, now married, joined thousands of Sonorans on a trek to California to escape their war-ravaged province.

Murieta apparently turned to crime after seeing the way the Americans, who had won California in the Mexican War, treated his countrymen. After supposedly being run off a number of gold claims, he vowed vengeance, organized a gang of cutthroats and outlaws and cut a swatch of terror through California. In 1853 the state legislature established the California Rangers and commissioned them to bring in not one but five "Joaquins": Joaquin Ocomorenia, Joaquin Valenzuela, Joaquin Botellier, Joaquin Carrillo and Joaquin Murieta. The Rangers, under Capt. Harry Love, set forth on their mission, inspired by the $1,000 reward posted for Murieta's capture. Love and his men did have an encounter with Manuel "Three-

Fingered Jack" Garcia and killed him and another unidentified Mexican. The more Love contemplated this second man the more he reckoned he was the notorious Joaquin. Garcia's mutilated hand and "Joaquin's" decapitated head were placed in jars of preserving fluid and transported to San Francisco.

Joaquin Murieta was a major attraction both in life and after his apparent death.

Although newspapermen were skeptical of the claim, the governor was impressed and paid out the reward. After that, the head of Joaquin and the hand of Garcia went on tour around the country. Murieta's head was on display until it was destroyed in the San Francisco earthquake of 1906.

Of course, the Mexicans of California never acknowledged that the head was that of the celebrated Joaquin. They said he escaped his pursuers and eventually settled down to a life of farming in Sonora, where he died in 1878. To the Mexicans his looting and killing of Americans were not acts of banditry but of active warfare against a foreign invader. In the barrios of California, Murieta is still referred to as *el Patrio,* or the Patriot, perhaps on the assumption that if he had not existed, he should have.

MURPHY, J. Reginald (1935-): Kidnap victim

J. Reginald Murphy, editor of the *Atlanta Constitution,* was kidnapped on February 20, 1974, ostensibly by members of a right-wing group called the American Revolutionary Army, and held for $700,000 ransom. Murphy was abducted by a man calling himself Lamont Woods, who had contacted the newspaper with a request for help in anonymously distributing $300,000 worth of fuel oil to the needy. Murphy met with Woods to sign papers for the fuel distribution. As they drove outside Atlanta, Woods pulled a gun and told the editor: "We're going to straighten out this damn country. We're going to stop these lying, leftist, liberal news media." Despite talk about an American Revolutionary Army with 223 members and chapters in the Southeast and Northeast, Woods appeared to be acting alone as he held Murphy captive for three days until the newspaper paid the $700,000 ransom.

Murphy was released on February 23 and six hours later William A. H. Williams, a building contractor in Lilburn, Ga., was arrested in his home, where the authorities found suitcases containing the ransom money. Williams turned out to be the fanciful Lamont Woods. He had been linked to the kidnapping even before Murphy's release because of a tip the FBI received from a man to whom Williams had tried to sell $300,000 worth of nonexistent fuel oil the previous December. Williams was sentenced to 40 years imprisonment.

MURPHY, Jim (1861-1879): Outlaw and informer

Just as Missourians built a legend around Jesse James, Texans made a folk hero of Sam Bass, their renowned train robber of the 1870s. Similarly, Texans had their own Bob Ford ("the dirty little coward that shot Mr. Howard and laid Jesse James in his grave") in the person of Jim Murphy, who betrayed Bass. As one Texas Ranger put it, Murphy was a "veritable Judas in every sense of the word."

One of two sons of Henderson Murphy, a Denton county rancher, Murphy was close to the Bass gang of outlaws, so close that on six different occasions he made overtures to the law to turn in Bass for various considerations. Meanwhile, the

Murphy family harbored the gang from time to time, and on May 1, 1878 father and sons were arrested because of this and charged with being accessories after the fact in Bass' robbing of the U.S. mails. Murphy won his release from Ranger Capt. Lee Hall by agreeing to turn Bass in.

Murphy had no trouble throwing in with Bass and took part in planning a robbery of a bank in Round Rock, Tex. On the way to Round Rock, Murphy slipped away long enough to wire the Rangers about the gang's plans. The gang was ambushed, and although he escaped for a time, Bass was mortally wounded. The following day, July 20, 1878, Bass was found in a woodland and brought back to Round Rock, where he died the next morning. Before he died, Bass was questioned about his accomplices but refused to betray them, saying: "It is agin my profession to blow on my pals. If a man knows anything, he ought to die with it in him."

The contrast between Bass' dying words and Jim Murphy's actions made the latter as unpopular as Bob Ford was to become. Even Ranger Hall labeled him a traitor. Murphy was to outlive Sam Bass by less than a year. He returned to Denton County and his family was released from jail, but he found hatred wherever he went. Often, he was so overcome with fear that he asked to sleep in the local jail for his own protection. He died in June 1879 after swallowing some very poisonous eye lotion. Considering that his death was most painful and slow, it seemed likely that taking the lotion was not Murphy's idea. A few years later, a ballad writer produced an epitaph for Murphy:

> And so he sold out Sam and Barnes and left
>   their friends to mourn,
> Oh, what a scorching Jim will get when Gabriel
>   blows his horn!
> Perhaps he's got to heaven, there's none of us
>   can say;
> But if I'm right in my surmise, he's gone the
>   other way.

See also: *Sam Bass.*

MURPHY Game: Confidence swindle

Originally conceived during the 19th century as a sex swindle, the Murphy game has changed with the times. It was apparently named after an engaging rogue named Murphy who had the face of a pimp a man could trust. In the swindle the con artist would describe the delightful and talented young lady he had in store for the lascivious pigeon. Then the "pimp" would convince the pigeon to leave the money for the whore with him so that the woman would not be liable to a bust for accepting money in exchange for services rendered. The pigeon would be sent up the stairs of a building to a non existent apartment, and by the time he returned to the street, either puzzled or enraged, the Murphy man had disappeared.

Today, the original Murphy game is fast dying out but a substitute sex object has been found in the form of what is often called the "$75 Sony Trinitron." A pair of hustlers will start patronizing a bar, actually several in different parts of town, and one will make a big show of delivering to the other

an expensive radio or other electronic item for something like a dime on the dollar. Then the boys will let slip that the seller has a contact at a wholesaler's warehouse and can get almost anything. But right now he has a big deal cooking. The inside man at the warehouse has found a way to cover up the disappearance of 10 Sony Trinitrons in perfect condition. The only thing is that he has to move them all at once. Naturally, all the barflies are interested when they hear the price for the $600 sets is only $75 apiece, or $750 for all 10.

Naturally, the deal falls in place and the suckers are taken to the warehouse in a rented van. The con artist collects all the money and disappears into the warehouse to make the payoff and have the sets brought out on the loading platform. The suckers in the van wait and wait and wait. What else can they do? Go into the warehouse and ask, "Where's that crooked employee of yours who's going to heist ten Trinitrons for us?" Meanwhile, the con artist has long since disappeared via another exit.

MURREL, John A. (1794-?): Mass murderer

Murrel has often been described as the most extraordinary criminal America has ever produced. Certainly, as a wholesale murderer, not even H. H. Holmes or Murder, Inc.'s Pittsburgh Phil was a match for him, even taking into account their highest estimated kill totals. Murrel may have killed over 500 victims.

With his brother, Murrel owned a very profitable plantation in Tennessee, which he used as a cover for his activities. Murrel found he could make it more profitable by stealing slaves, whom he would then resell. If he couldn't make a fast sale on a slave or if he had stolen the same slave so often that another sale might be dangerous, he would have the slave murdered. Murrel became known as a rich, if eccentric, visitor to the gambling dens and bordellos of New Orleans. Actually, he would be on scouting missions looking for money-ladened travelers who would be leaving the city along the Natchez Trace. When they left, Murrel left and only Murrel would be seen again. His technique for getting rid of a victim was to disembowel him, fill his stomach cavity with sand and stones and sink his body in a creek or river.

But even Murrel's estimated 500 killings was minor compared to what he had in mind. He concocted an incredible scheme, probably the most grandiose ever developed by a criminal mind. It called for fomenting a slave rebellion; while the authorities would be battling to quell it, Murrel and 500 underworld confederates would sack New Orleans, Nashville, Memphis, Natchez and a number of other cities. He actually planned to establish an underworld empire in the captured cities and become the supreme ruler, with New Orleans as the capital. The trouble with the scheme was that it involved too many people and too many mouths. The slaves had to be drilled for their uprising and some were overheard discussing the plot. Various criminals were also overheard discussing their part in the bizarre operation. Then a man named Virgil Stewart, whom Murrel thought he had convinced to join his "army," defected and talked to authorities. Following Stewart's disclosures, Murrel was taken into custody. By this time it was too late to stop the uprising, which was scheduled for July 4, 1835, but without Murrel's leadership the campaign foundered. Authorities easily contained outbreaks in the criminal districts of Nashville, Memphis and Natchez. In Tennessee about 20 slaves and 10 white men were hanged for their part in the conspiracy.

After the grandiose plan collapsed, Murrel sulked in prison under a 10-year sentence. He served his term, but by the time of his release, he had degenerated to the level of an imbecile. When last seen, he was a derelict in the Gut, the red-light district of Memphis.

MUSGROVE, Lee H. (?-1868): Outlaw leader

The Musgrove gang of road agents and livestock thieves plundered the Colorado Territory in 1867-68. The group was noted for a barbarity that was even more pronounced in their leader, Lee Musgrove, a native Mississippian who had cut a wide trail of violence when he came west in the 1850s.

Settling first in the Napa Valley of California, Musgrove developed a reputation as a mean man with a gun. He was suspected of a number of robbery-murders, but it was a killing in 1863 over "a matter of honor"—a man who did not share Musgrove's rabid Confederate sympathies—that forced him on the run. Musgrove moved on to Nevada but had to flee again after two more killings. Musgrove then operated as an Indian trader and alleged dealer in stolen goods in the Idaho Territory. When he notched another victim, he headed for the Wyoming Territory, where he organized a gang of cutthroats whose holdups and stolen beef and horse flesh operations ranged from Kansas to Texas. At least a dozen killings were attributed to the gang, but their days were numbered when a Colorado lawman named Dave Cook started tracking them. Cook chipped away at the outfit, dispatching permanently or arresting them one after the other.

Cook followed Musgrove to the Wyoming Territory and finally nailed him in the midst of preparations for a job. After Musgrove was tucked away back in Denver, Cook learned that the outlaw chief's top sidekick, Ed Franklin, had escaped from Fort Sanders, Wyoming Territory, where he was being held after attempting to make off with a herd of Army mules.

Cook figured rightly that Franklin would head for Denver to try to free his boss and intercepted him in the nearby mining camp of Golden. Lying in his hotel bed wearing only his long johns and gun belt, Franklin was just able to jump off the bed before Cook sent a bullet through his heart.

Franklin's failure to free Musgrove was to prove fatal to the latter. A mob of heavy drinkers got to thinking that other members of Musgrove's gang surely would try the same things. Under the circumstances, the logical thing to do was to string up the outlaw leader before such a tragedy could befall the town, and on November 23, 1868 Musgrove was duly dispatched without benefit of a court conviction. Cynics were to observe that some cattle interests had fired up the mob because they believed such drastic action was the best answer to livestock thievery. Other suspicious souls were to point out that Dave Cook himself had an amazingly consistent record of losing his prisoners to lynch mobs.

See also: *David J. Cook.*

MUSICA, Philip (1877-1938): Swindler

As a 20th century swindler, Philip Musica in many ways surpassed the great Charles Ponzi. He stole more money, and while Ponzi lasted only a matter of months, Musica lasted years. In his prime he was a pillar of society, a patron of the arts, a bosom friend of the great tenor Enrico Caruso and a charming, cultured gentleman. On Wall Street he was known as a financial genius, in the midst of the Morgans, Astors and Rockefellers. Not at all bad for a man who had previously been, among other things, an ex-convict, stool pigeon, swindler, forger, rumrunner, smuggler, bootlegger, gunrunner, hijacker and briber. With a record like that, it might seem odd that Musica was able to make *Who's Who in America,* but then again, that illustrious publication is better known for judging people for what they appear to be rather than what they are.

Musica had qualified for *Who's Who* under one of his other identities (he used several during a long criminal career).

It was his final and greatest identity, that of F. Donald Coster, about whom the book of the nation's notables declared:

COSTER, Frank Donald, corpn. official; b. Washington, D.C., May 12, 1884; s. Frank Donald and Marie (Girard) C.; PhD., U. of Heidelberg, 1909, M.D., 1911; m. Carol Jenkins Schiefflin, of Jamaica, L.I., N.Y., May 1, 1921. Practicing physician, N.Y. City, 1912-14; pres. Girard & Co., Inc. (succession to Girard Chem. Co.), 1914-26; pres. McKesson & Robbins, drug mfrs., since 1926; also pres. McKesson & Robbins, Ltd.; dir. Bridgeport City Trust Co., Fairfield (Conn.) Trust Co. Methodist. Clubs: New York Yacht, Bankers, Lotos, Advertising (New York); University, Black Rock Yacht (Bridgeport); Brooklawn Country. Home: Fairfield, Conn. Office: McKesson & Robbins, Inc., Bridgeport, Conn.

In 1883 six-year-old Philip Musica came to America from Italy with his parents, and by the time he was in his early twenties, he had become the most Americanized of all the children as well as the active head of the family. He kept telling Papa Antonio that things were different here than in the old country and that there were different standards of ethics. Quickly, he involved his father and a number of brothers and sisters in dishonest schemes, starting off with an imported cheese business made all the more lucrative by bribing customhouse weighers. Soon, the Musicas could afford a mansion in the fashionable Bay Ridge section of Brooklyn, complete with landscaped grounds, horses, stables and a carriage house. In 1909, however, the roof fell in on Musica's financial empire. Several customhouse weighers confessed to taking bribes and young Musica was sentenced to a year in prison. He served only a few months, however, before winning a presidential pardon, apparently because he came across as somewhat gallant, shielding his father from a jail term by accepting all the blame himself.

Once freed, Musica moved immediately into a new line of business, that of importing human hair from Italy to supply the needs of American females. By 1913 he had established a thriving business and was once more a leader in Italian-American social and financial circles. Then the William J. Burns Detective Agency dug up evidence that Musica had swindled 22 banks out of $1 million by taking loans on hair shipments based on phony invoices. When the cases of supposedly long hair were opened, they were found to contain tissue paper and short hair, worth no more than $1 a box and known as trash in the field.

The entire Musica family was captured in New Orleans shortly after boarding a liner for Honduras. One of Musica's sisters tried to throw overboard $18,000 she had stashed in her girdle. Musica had $80,000 in cash and $250,000 in other money instruments on him. Again, he accepted full blame for the swindle. He was lodged in the Tombs Prisons in New York City because he promised to make full restitution and said that from there he could better help authorities round up his assets. While in prison, Musica endeared himself to a succession of prosecutors by becoming a professional stool pigeon who spied on other prisoners. It paid off. In 1918 these grateful officials got him a suspended sentence for the hair fraud.

That was the last seen of Philip Musica until he emerged from his final cover, F. Donald Coster, in 1938. Musica became "William Johnson," an "investigator" for the district attorney's office, a career that was cut short when he was indicted for perjury in a murder trial in which he had testified against two men. William Johnson promptly disappeared.

He was replaced by "Frank Costa," a copartner in a firm called the Adelphi Pharmaceutical Manufacturing Co., which was entitled to 5,000 gallons of alcohol a month during Prohibition for production of its hair tonics and the like. The innovative Mr. Costa so scented and colored Adelphi's products that running them through a simple still would return them to high-proof straight alcohol. Cut with water and spiked with the proper coloring and flavoring and presto—"great stuff right off the boat." Eventually, Adelphi's real business was discovered by revenue agents and one of the owners was caught, but not Costa, who disappeared.

Musica reemerged as F. Donald Coster, president of Girard and Co., and obtained a new alcohol license. By this time Papa Musica was dead and Philip was the acknowledged leader of the family. Because he was still being hunted on the perjury charge, Philip severed all ties with his Musica past. Girard was the new family name he gave to Mama Musica and her daughters—save for one, who, in Philip's words, "disgraced our whole family by running off and marrying a gardener." Girard and Co. also gained three new officials, "George Vernard," "George Dietrich" and "Robert Dietrich"—really Musica's three brothers, Arthur, George and Robert.

By 1925 F. Donald Coster had become a man of high socie-ty, more than 13 years after Philip Musica had cavorted about so flashily. Of course, "Doctor Coster" was nothing like Philip Musica. He was starting to gray on top and in his trim mustache, and he was American-born and a Methodist now, not Italian and a Catholic.

In 1926 he moved to the pinnacle of the Wall Street heap by buying the 93-year-old drug firm of McKesson and Robbins. He did so after obtaining a loan against Girard and Co., an easy matter since its books, thanks to bootlegging activities, were in excellent shape. Once in control of McKesson and Robbins, Coster swung a stock flotation and money flowed in. A large portion of this new money was used to establish a Canadian "crude drug" department. It was Coster's master swindle. George Vernard became fiscal agent and representative in charge of the department, which proved to be the world's easiest job. The Canadian crude drug department consisted of large inventories of drugs in half-a-dozen warehouses. But there were no drugs and no warehouses in Canada. There was just George Vernard—and he wasn't even Vernard. Unwittingly, through its new owner the reputable McKesson and Robbins "bought" drugs from phantom companies and shelled out hard cash, which wound up in the pockets of F. Donald Coster. Receipts, inventories, invoices, bills of lading and the like from the crude drug department carried the names of Coster, Vernard and Dietrich, and no questions were asked.

The Depression of 1929 hit McKesson and Robbins as hard as most companies but the firm continued to look robust because of its inventories of crude drugs, which rose in value by several million dollars. Coster became known as the wizard of the drug field. "No one can match Coster when it comes to crude drugs," honest directors of McKesson told one another.

Up in Fairfield, Conn., Coster relaxed in the splendor of his 16-room mansion and aboard his 135-foot ocean-going yacht. He contributed lavishly to charity and even established a free heart clinic in Bridgeport, Conn. out of his own money. Why not, there was plenty more where that had come from. But beneath the facade of luxurious tranquility, Coster was troubled. Business was crashing downward and more and more he had to cover up his lootings with forgeries. By 1935 he was paying $25,000 a year in blackmail money to those who knew him as Philip Musica and Frank Costa. Then there were reports that he used McKesson facilities to smuggle guns and munitions to Franco Spain. Franco received rifles packed in cases labeled, "Milk of Magnesia." However, there were indications that Coster was rather impartial. He appeared to be selling to the Loyalists as well, although there were also reports that the Franco forces were informed—for a price—where the Loyalists' shipments were going so that they could seize them, allowing Coster to collect twice.

Coster's undoing came from two quarters. First, he took to adulterating his own drug products, and in September 1938, agents of the Pure Food and Drug Administration seized some of the firm's adulterated quinine in New Jersey and New York. Meanwhile, the business recession of 1937 had battered the firm and Julian F. Thompson, a Wall Street figure whom Coster had hired as the window-dressing treasurer (George

Dietrich was assistant treasurer and handled all illegal matters), demanded that Coster reduce the crude drug inventories to give the company more cash assets. Coster stalled. He couldn't produce something out of nothing. After a year of stalling. Thompson launched a quiet investigation of his own and found that an alleged $21 million worth of inventories carried no insurance. Checking further, he discovered they weren't insured because they didn't exist.

Thompson took his findings to the New York Stock Exchange and early in December 1938 all trading in the firm's stock was halted. Each of McKesson's 82 vice presidents shuddered, but none more than George Vernard and George and Robert Dietrich. The master swindler remained calm as story after story about him hit the newspapers. Inevitably, tips about Coster came in and authorities took a deep interest in his past. On December 14 Coster was fingerprinted in his home. "This is a pesty business," he grumbled.

Within 24 hours newspapers revealed the life story of Philip Musica, a long-vanished swindler and perjurer. On December 16 government agents arrived at his house to place him under arrest, but he had shot himself to death in the bathroom.

Musica left two notes, one to his wife pleading for her forgiveness and the other, eight pages long, trying to rationalize his underhanded dealings.

McKesson, he insisted, would have gone into receivership in 1930 and 1932 had he not bolstered its paper profits. He asserted all the alleged "lost" millions were merely fictional "profits to save the company . . . what is missing is the alleged profits plus expenses and blackmail money paid to maintain it. . . ."

"As God is my judge," he concluded, "I am the victim of Wall Street plunder and blackmail in a struggle for honest existence. Merciful God bring the truth to light! F. D. Coster."

For their part in the swindle, Musica's three brothers got off with mere three-year sentences, possibly because not all of Coster's claims were hogwash. True, he had indeed siphoned off $8 million or $10 million for his own use, but the rest of the "loot" probably never existed, being mere figure juggling to keep up the firm's profit margins. The conventional wisdom on Wall Street was that without Coster's shady dealings McKesson and Robbins would have been forced into bankruptcy years earlier and the stockholders wiped out. Instead, the firm weathered the storm and the stockholders had been both robbed and saved.

MUSSOLINI Shuttle: Deportation of mafiosi

As a result of Benito Mussolini's war on the Sicilian Mafia and other gangsters in the 1920s, perhaps hundreds of young mafiosi were forced to scurry to the safety of the United States, where they provided fresh blood for the criminal legions of the "Mustache Petes," who had begun emigrating to America around the 1890s. Journalists named this mass deportation effort the Mussolini Shuttle.

Mussolini's campaign against gangsters cost him heavily in support from Americans of Italian descent, who saw the new criminal migrations as fostering more crime in their communities and stirring fresh anti-Italian feelings among the general populace.

See also: *Mustache Petes*.

MUSTACHE Petes: Old-line mafiosi

The early leaders of the Mafia in America were called "Mustache Petes" by younger Italian gangsters, a term coined to deride their elders' inability to adapt to the new society and their insistence on extraction of "respect" from those beneath them. These old-line criminal leaders were eliminated by the rising young gangsters of the 1920s and 1930s, Lucky Luciano, Frank Costello, Joe Adonis, Vito Genovese, Albert Anastastia, Tommy Lucchese and others.

There can be little doubt that their forceful elimination was a sign of progress for the Italian underworld. The younger gangsters felt the Mustache Petes had to go for Italians to become powerful and perhaps even to dominate crime in America, a situation eventually accomplished when the national crime syndicate was formed in the 1930s. What especially upset these younger criminals was that the older mafiosi insisted on exploiting only their Italian compatriots and distrusted other ethnic criminals as well as politicians. The Luciano types understood the need to work with Jewish gangsters, such as Meyer Lansky and Bugsy Siegel, the heads of New York's Bug and Meyer Gang, and such other non-Italian groups as Cleveland's Mayfield Road Gang and Detroit's Purple Gang. The old Morello-Lupo the Wolf-Joe the Boss Masseria-Salvatore Maranzano approach of bleeding the Italian communities was by nature limited since the Italians as a whole were the poorer "outs" of American society.

As these old-time leaders fell or were pushed from power and were succeeded by the "new-breed" Italian leaders, a more-Americanized and a more lucrative Mafia emerged.

See also: *Mafia, Night of the Sicilian Vespers, Mussolini Shuttle*.

MUTILATION: Punishment method

Mutilation was certainly never used to punish criminals in the United States to the extent it was used in Europe. However, the practice was not totally uncommon, especially in New England and the South. For contempt of court or perjury, the punishment in both areas could be losing part of an ear or having one's tongue pierced with a hot iron. In Colonial Virginia one convicted of slander might have his or her tongue bored through with an awl, while the possible punishments for criticizing the Colonial authorities included losing both ears or, for lesser offenders, having one's ears nailed to a pillory. A runaway slave often received the latter punishment, which produced enormous pain but allowed the slave owner's property to remain pretty much intact. Castration was a penalty reserved for a slave found guilty of attempting to rape a white woman.

The frontier West used mutilations in a more practical sense, often coupling such punishments with expulsion from the area in cases where the death penalty was judged too harsh. Many Three-Fingered Jacks got that way as a result of the actions of vigilante tribunals. A Nevada miners court once needed to protect the community from a miner who would start shooting indiscriminately when drunk. Because the offender was otherwise rather popular, hanging was deemed inappropriate; instead, the trigger finger on each of his hands was cut off. He was thereafter referred to as Eight-Fingered Bill.

Branding the face was practiced legally as late as 1844, although ranchers continued to use it long after as an extralegal punishment for rustlers, considering it a "humane" alternative to lynching. A rancher's brand on a thief's face identified him as a cattle rustler and warned him to stay away from that range or face the rope the next time.

N

NASH, Frank "Jelly" (1884-1933): Gangster and Kansas City Massacre victim

Frank "Jelly" Nash was one of the most-accomplished robbers and murderers of the early 20th century and had a remarkable ability to gain his freedom from prison one way or another. In his hometown of Hobart, Okla. people thought Nash would have a brilliant future if he could conquer a violent temper. As it was, he could not. Implicated in a murder in 1913, Nash was put on trial but acquitted. He then murdered a witness who had testified against him in the trial, and for that, he was sentenced to life imprisonment. Early in 1918 his sentence was commuted to 10 years and in July he was granted a full pardon. Within a short time, Nash robbed the Corn State Bank in Corn, Okla. He was apprehended and sentenced to 25 years at McAlester Penitentiary. Remarkably, the former lifer got another reduction in sentence. On December 29, 1922 the governor signed an order commuting Nash's 25-year sentence to a mere five years, and the next day he was freed.

Over the next eight months Nash is believed to have committed a number of murders and robberies. On August 20, 1923 he took part in the holdup of a mail train in Osage County, Okla., during which he brutally assaulted a mail custodian. On March 3, 1924 Nash was sent to the federal penitentiary at Leavenworth; back in Hobart there was general agreement that Nash would receive no political clemency at the federal level. Nash did not, but he did enjoy some unusual privileges despite his past record. He became a model prisoner and was made a trustee. After being given an outside assignment in October 1930, he simply walked away from the prison.

Exactly what Nash did after his escape is not clear. He is known to have spent considerable time in Chicago and to have become involved in the affairs of the Capone mob. There is some evidence that he also got involved in Kansas City rackets, sometimes with elements tied to the Pendergast machine and sometimes with those operating without political support.

Nash was almost bald, with only a fringe of hair around his head, and had very distinctive features: prominent ears, a pointed chin and a large, hooked nose. He attempted to alter his appearance by getting a nose job, which bobbed off a bit of the hook. He grew a bushy mustache, wore glasses and put on a toupee. He also got married, unconcerned that there already was a Mrs. Nash. He and his young bride moved to Hot Springs, Ark., then considered to be the country's safest haven for criminals. Nash, apparently under police protection, seemed to be working various rackets and would occasionally venture out of town for a robbery.

On June 16, 1933 two FBI agents and the police chief of McAlester, Okla., Otto Reed, captured Nash in Hot Springs and spirited him out of town, realizing that if he was turned over to local authorities he would probably "escape" immediately. The gangster was escorted to Kansas City, where a very special welcome awaited him, the infamous Kansas City Massacre. As several officers and Nash climbed into an automobile at Union Station, a large man carrying a machine gun ordered them to "get 'em up!" Two other gunmen appeared and suddenly the three opened up, spraying the car thoroughly. Nash died screaming, "For God's sake, don't shoot *me!*"

Also killed were four lawmen, and two others were wounded. One FBI agent survived by playing dead. It has been debated for years whether the shooting was an attempt to free Nash or to kill him because of information he could give the government. The identity of the murderers remains in dispute as well.

See also: *Kansas City Massacre, White Front Cigar Store.*

NATCHEZ-UNDER-THE-HILL: Mississippi vice center

One of the most crime-ridden river ports of 19th century America, Natchez-under-the-Hill was separated from the tamer part of the city, which was located on a high bluff. Because of this separation, the under-the-hill district was not subject to the same type of reform movements that had swept the better part of town in previous years. Simply stated, there was "no reason for decent folks to go down to that hell." Providing the coarse rivermen with whatever they wanted and could pay for, lower Natchez shocked the few decent visitors who ventured into it. One John Bradbury said in 1810, "For the size of it there is not perhaps in the world a more profligate place." Another described it as "the safest place in America to kill another human being with no threat of retribution." Gamblers and prostitutes always did a thriving business, with as many as 150 flatboats and keelboats tying up there on an average day in 1808. Baby girls were said to have been born in certain whorehouses and grown up there to become working prostitutes by the age of 12. Some of these unfortunate girls reportedly never even saw upper Natchez, knowing no more of the world than the rough rivermen who stormed ashore each day.

Among the most famous citizens of Natchez-under-the-Hill were a tavern owner named Jim Girty and his paramour, Marie Dufour, the leading madam of the town. Girty was regarded by rivermen as unkillable, having survived a number of gun and knife fights. Legend had it that Girty's chest was not ribbed but solid bone that deflected pistol ball or blade. Marie Dufour was also known for her prowess in battle. She invariably won wrestling contests with rivermen, the loser taking a traditional dunking in the Mississippi. Despite her ruggedness, Marie was also known for her womanly charms and ran *the* high-class house of prostitution in Natchez. The couple came to a tragic end when Girty proved not completely unkillable, being shot down from ambush after a gambling dispute. Marie Dufour rushed to his side and, finding him dead, committed suicide by shooting herself in the mouth.

In 1835 vigilantes tried to clean up lower Natchez, driving off and killing a number of gamblers, while many of the prostitutes escaped with the rivermen aboard their flatboats. However, immediately after each raid the gamblers and the harlots set up business again. Such occasional forays by the outraged citizens were not likely to drive out criminal elements when vice could make its organizers rich in just a year or two. Some prostitutes who knew how to save money soon had enough to buy themselves a flatboat and sail down to New Orleans in comfort, where they would set up a floating bordello and, perhaps in due course, open a lavish house in the French Quarter.

Natchez-under-the-Hill continued in its violent ways until the Civil War, but the decline of the steamboat cut off its lifeblood, and it gradually became just another prosaic and dreary river port with no more than legends to remind visitors of its tawdry past.

NATHAN, Benjamin (1813-1870): Murder victim

The murder in 1870 of philanthropist Benjamin Nathan, described inaccurately as "the richest man in New York," remains to this day a tantalizing unsolved crime.

At 6 a.m. on July 28, 1870, Washington Nathan went downstairs in the family mansion at 12 West 23rd Street for a drink of water to soothe his regular hangover. He passed his father's bedroom, looked in and received, presumably, a shock. Benjamin Nathan lay dead on the floor, his features and clothing covered with blood and gore. He had been repeatedly struck on the head with an 18-inch carpenter's "dog." A safe in the room had been opened and there were signs of a struggle. There were also indications that the killer, rather than hurrying from the place after the crime, had leisurely washed up in a basin on the dresser. The murderer had not been very neat, leaving a bloody handprint on the wall.

While within 24 hours rewards totaling $47,000 were offered, the case was never solved. Police suspicion centered on dissolute Washington Nathan, who was known to have had terrific rows with his father over his lavish spending, but a case against him could never be proved. Washington was provided with an alibi for part of the time when the murder may have been committed by a "lass of the pavements," as the papers called her.

In 1879 Washington Nathan, still keeping up his dissolute ways, was paying court to an actress named Alice Harrison when a former inamorata named Fanny Barrett, who had followed him, whipped out a revolver and shot him in the neck. When it appeared that Washington would require an operation to remove the bullet, and Chief of Police George W. Walling worked out a plan to have him questioned after the operation as he was coming out of the anaesthetic in the hope he would say something about his father's murder. But the bullet came out by itself, thwarting that strategy.

A much better technique became apparent too late, some three decades after the murder, when incredulous New York police were prevailed upon by Scotland Yard to take the thumb smudge of a man arrested for a New York hotel theft and send it to London. There, it was matched up to a print found on a jewel case in a robbery. Some New York police historian then remembered the bloodstained prints of all five fingers on one hand of Nathan's murderer had been left on the wall but, the fingerprinting detection method had not yet been developed.

NATION, Carry A. (1846-1911): Saloon smasher

Carry Nation's saloon-smashing crusade was inspired by the Brahma Bull and Red Hot Bar in Richmond, Tex., where her second husband, David Nation, was badly beaten by hard-drinking patrons. This caused such revulsion in 53-year-old Carry that she went on her famous bar-smashing campaign in Kansas, where the couple had moved after the ugly event. She had had an earlier tragic experience with demon rum when her first husband had died of alcoholism within two years of their marriage.

On June 5, 1900 Carry wrapped a number of stones and bricks in old newspapers and drove her horse and buggy 20 miles to Kiowa, Kan. She entered one saloon and announced,

"Men, I have come to save you from a drunkard's fate!" She thereupon set out to smash every bottle in the place and finished up by destroying the bar's mirror and front glass window. She went through Kiowa like a tornado, destroying six saloons. Amazingly, no one thought of having her arrested, apparently because Kansas was, in law if not in fact, a dry state. Carry then moved on to Wichita, where, among others, she wrecked the elegant bar located in the basement of the Hotel Carey. "Glory to God," she announced to stunned onlookers, as she went about her work. When she finished, she said, "Peace on earth, good will to men." This time, Carry was arrested. She promptly drew a large number of supporters, who pointed out that the saloons she had smashed were all illegal. She was thereupon released.

Carry Nation spread her wrath throughout Kansas and then beyond the state's borders. When she arrived in a town, many saloon keepers immediately closed down. One did try to stop her at gunpoint, but she swung a hatchet at his head and the man dropped his weapon and ran. Carry was arrested more than 30 times but paid her fines with a shrug, financing their cost by selling souvenir hatchets bearing her name.

Now famous, Carry launched a new career as a public speaker (she climaxed her speeches by leading members of the audience on a saloon-busting expedition) and began publishing a weekly newspaper called *The Hatchet*. She became a leader of the Women's Christian Temperance Union, whose militant marching song was "A Saloonless Nation in 1920." Carry's most famous raid was in Washington, D.C., where she wreaked havoc in the Union Station bar with her three trusty hatchets, dubbed Faith, Hope and Charity.

Worn out from a decade of intense activity, Carry Nation collapsed while making a speech in Eureka Springs, Ark. and died in a hospital in Leavenworth, Kan. on June 9, 1911. While others could claim greater credit for bringing about Prohibition in 1919, Carry Nation had established the militant tone of the campaign.

NATIONAL Association For The Advancement Of Colored People: See Springfield, Illinois Race Riot.

NATIONAL Motor Vehicle Theft Act: See Dyer Act.

NEAGLE, David (1847-1926): Saloon keeper and lawman

Although little more than the typical gunman-lawman of the West, David Neagle became famous for a landmark U.S. Supreme Court decision, *In re Neagle,* which has been described as "the most relevant utterance of the court on the extent of executive authority under the Constitution."

Boston-born Neagle grew up in the San Francisco Bay area. He dropped out of school in 1860, when he was 13, and headed for mining camp country. While a teenager he became proficient with a six-shooter and pursued a checkered career as a gunman, miner, gambler, saloon keeper and lawman. In 1880 Neagle served as a deputy sheriff in Tombstone, Arizona Territory during the period of the Earp-Clanton feud. Although his boss, Sheriff John Behan, clearly sided with the Clantons, Neagle managed to hold to a neutral line. After the Earps were forced to leave Tombstone, Neagle became city marshal. Beaten in a race for sheriff late in 1882, he moved on to other boom towns.

Neagle later became a lawman in San Francisco and, in 1888, got involved in the famous Hill-Sharon-Terry-Fields case, one of California's wildest legal battles. Originally, the dispute centered on whether or not Sarah Althea Hill was married to William Sharon, a millionaire and senator from Nevada. The dispute continued even after Sharon's death and Sarah's marriage to flamboyant David Terry, one of her attorneys and a former, controversial member of the California Supreme Court. When a court decision went against Mrs. Terry, a melee broke out in court, and as Sarah was being ejected into the hallway, David Terry drew a knife to come to her aid. Among those disarming Terry was David Neagle. The case had been tried by an old political rival of Terry, Stephen J. Field, an associate justice of the U.S. Supreme Court.

Terry subsequently made several threats against Field's life, and when Field returned to California the next year, Deputy Marshal Neagle was given the job of protecting him. On August 14, 1889 Terry confronted Field at the Lathrop railroad station. In the ensuing argument Terry threatened the jurist and Neagle shot and killed Terry. Neagle was charged with murder but was freed after a habeas corpus hearing. Afterward, Field presented Neagle with a gold watch for having killed Terry.

California appealed the freeing of Neagle and the case went all the way to the U.S. Supreme Court with the state insisting that its homicide laws gave it jurisdiction over the case. The opposing claim was that under a broad interpretation of the law, Neagle had not acted improperly in killing Terry, since he was a deputy marshal, despite the fact that no federal statute authorized marshals to protect judges. The High Court's decision upholding Neagle's freedom greatly enhanced the authority of the executive branch by declaring that the word "law" could be interpreted to mean "any obligation fairly and properly inferable" from the Constitution.

Neagle remained a lawman in the area for another decade and then faded into obscurity, but the legal decision named after him heralded, under Theodore Roosevelt, the development of the strong presidency.

NELSON, Earle Leonard (1892-1928): Mass murderer

For almost a year and a half, Earle Leonard Nelson terrorized the nation with a series of vicious rape-murders. His official murder toll between February 1926 and June 1927 stands, by most counts, at 20.

Born in 1892 in Philadelphia, Nelson was orphaned at an early age and raised by an aunt. He suffered a head injury in a childhood accident that would cause him intense pain from time to time. As a teenager, he exhibited a streak of meanness and violence usually directed at children or women. At other times, he became a Bible fanatic, spending hours either reading the Bible alone in his room or loudly lecturing others with long quotations from it. His aunt would point to his devout character whenever one of his more antisocial peccadilloes got him in trouble with the law. Nonetheless, in 1918 he was placed in a home for mental defectives after raping a young Philadelphia girl. Nelson promptly escaped but was soon caught and placed on a state prison farm. He escaped from there but was captured again and this time was sent to the state penitentiary, from which he quickly escaped yet again.

That was the last time the law would have him in its hands for nine years. In 1919, under the alias of Roger Wilson, he married a young schoolteacher. Life for Mrs. Wilson was a horror; Nelson lectured her constantly from the Bible and accused her of consorting with other men. She finally had to be hospitalized because of a nervous breakdown. Nelson visited her in the hospital and had to be ejected fron the building when he was caught trying to rape her in her bed. Thereafter nothing was heard from or of him for seven years. Considering his prior record and his bloody record afterward, if he was entirely law-abiding during that time, it would have been one of the greatest self-rehabilitative efforts in the annals of crime.

On February 20, 1926 Nelson entered a San Francisco rooming house in search of lodgings. As the landlady, Mrs. Clara Newman, ushered him up the stairs to the third floor, a murderous urge overcame Nelson. He strangled the woman with her own pearl necklace before they even entered a room. Then he dragged her body into an empty room, raped the dead woman and left. Over the next few months Nelson strangled, killed and raped three other landladies in the San Francisco-Oakland area. By now the police had a description of the killer as a short, blue-eyed, dark-complexioned man. But they didn't catch him.

Nelson moved on to Portland, Ore., where in two days he killed two more landladies. A few weeks later, he killed another landlady. Then he went back to San Francisco for his next murder, after which he returned to Portland and killed again. Nelson moved towards the East Coast, killing more women all the way to Philadelphia. By June 1927 authorities all over the country were hunting for the man who had definitely murdered 20 landladies and was strongly suspected of having killed two others.

Feeling the pressure of the police hunt, Nelson fled into Canada and took lodging in a rooming house in Winnipeg. His landlady remembered him as a very devout gentleman who always carried a Bible. Nelson did not kill his landlady, realizing that would only open up his trail again, but the blood urge in him could not be stilled. Within a few days of his arrival in Winnipeg, the city was rocked by two murders. One was of a teenaged girl living in the same house as Nelson. In another section of town, the raped and strangled body of Mrs. Emily Paterson was found by her husband.

Nelson had killed them both, but this time he left a trail that could be followed. He had stolen a number of items from the Paterson home and left some of them at a second-hand clothing dealer where he purchased a change of clothes. A description of the killer led to his capture within four miles of the border, which he was preparing to recross to evade pursuit.

Although the vast majority of Nelson's crimes were committed in the United States, he was tried, sentenced to death and, on January 13, 1928, hanged in Canada. On the gallows the man whose aunt had predicted he would grow up to become a minister turned biblical one final time. "I am innocent," he said. "I stand innocent before God and man. I forgive those who have wronged me and ask forgiveness of those I have injured. God have mercy!"

NELSON, George "Baby Face" (1908-1934): Public enemy

None of the "public enemies" of the 1930s more thoroughly deserved the description "mad dog" than did George "Baby Face" Nelson. All the gangsters of the 1930s, Dillinger, the Barkers, Pretty Boy Floyd and others, killed to escape capture, but Nelson was addicted to violence, much as were Bonnie and Clyde. Even the latter were a bit more restrained, frequently turning from murderous to maudlin because of a potential victim's white hair. Nelson was vulnerable to no such sentimentalism, as demonstrated by his approach to bank robbery, which was to come through the door shooting and then simply force the lucky survivors to hand over the loot. Once when Dillinger henchman Homer Van Meter, a believer in a slightly more thoughtful approach, laughed sarcastically at Nelson's ideas on a robbery, only the quick intervention of John Dillinger prevented Baby Face from punishing such disdain with a sub-machine gun.

Chicago-born Lester J. Gillis, a name he discarded as too "sissy," preferred to be known as Big George Nelson, a ludicrous sobriquet considering his five-foot five-inch stature. Behind his back he was called Baby Face Nelson. He started his criminal career in 1922, when he was sent to a home for boys after being arrested for auto theft. Paroled in April 1924, he was in and out of custody thereafter for parole violations and other crimes. By 1929 Nelson was working for the Capone mob as a goon in the union field. Apparently he took the work too earnestly and was dismissed as unreliable because he sometimes killed when he was only supposed to injure.

Nelson was caught pulling a bank job in 1931 and got one year to life. He escaped from a prison guard in 1932 while being escorted back to the penitentiary from Wheaton, Ill., where he had been tried for another bank robbery charge. Now accepted as a "big-timer," something he always wanted, Nelson hooked up with the Dillinger mob. Dillinger was not overly fond of Nelson and his quick temper and even quicker trigger finger, but when several of his gang, including Harry Pierpont, Russell Clark and Charlie Makley, were clapped behind bars, he was forced to make do. Inevitably, Dillinger's capers became bloodier after the arrival of Nelson, who often needlessly shot down bank guards and bystanders.

As his victim toll mounted, Nelson grew to resent the fact that Dillinger got more notoriety than he got and that the latter had a bigger price on his head. He did all he could to change that. In the famous shoot-out at the Little Bohemia Resort in northern Wisconsin in April 1934, Nelson separated from the rest of the Dillinger gang and shot it out at close quarters with FBI agents, killing Special Agent H. Carter Baum and escaping in an FBI Ford.

Later, Nelson rejoined Dillinger and they pulled several more capers. By now, Dillinger wanted no more of Baby Face but was so "hot" himself that he had no chance of recruiting new help. On the night of July 2, 1934 Dillinger was shot dead by FBI men outside a Chicago movie house. Thereafter, Nelson, who had not been with Dillinger that night, became Public Enemy No. 1. His reign, however, was destined to be short.

Just as Dillinger fell, so did other members of the gang. Tommy Carroll was killed in a gunfight in Iowa and in separate incidents in St. Paul, Minn., G-men caught up with Eddie Green and police gunned down Homer Van Meter. The only support Nelson had left was his wife, Helen, and his longtime faithful sidekick, John Paul Chase. Still, the insane Nelson decided to become the greatest criminal the country had ever known, one who would make the public forget about the fabled Dillinger. He started organizing a gang with the intention of robbing every day for a month straight.

That grandiose scheme never came to fruition, however. On November 27, 1934 two FBI agents, Sam Cowley, who played a key role in catching Dillinger, and Herman E. Hollis, came upon Nelson, his wife and Chase in a stalled car near Barrington, Ill. Hollis, armed with a shotgun, crouched behind an FBI car while Cowley rolled into a nearby ditch with a submachine gun. Nelson opened up with his trusty submachine gun

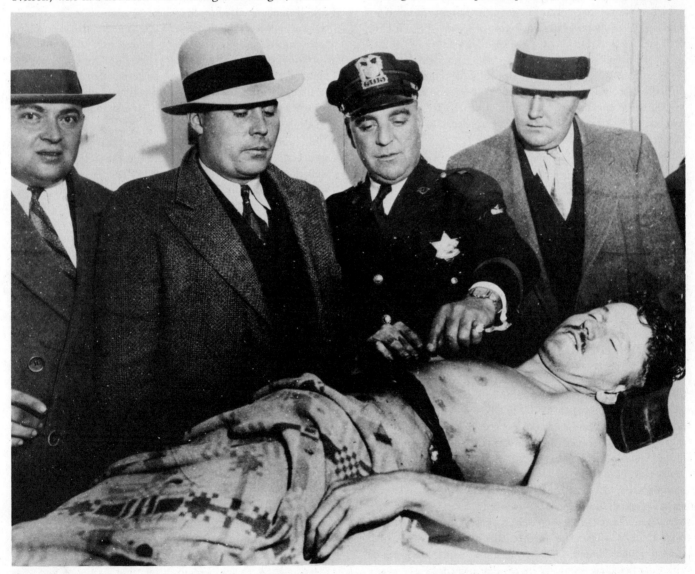

Photo shows Baby Face Nelson's bullet-riddled corpse on an undertaker's slab in Niles Center, a suburb of Chicago.

while Chase started firing an automatic rifle. As the wild gunfight began, Helen Nelson ran for cover and several highway construction workers hugged the ground.

Finally, Nelson grew impatient with the standoff, stood up erect and announced, "I'm going down there and get those sons of bitches."

He strode forward, his weapon spewing bullets.

"It was just like Jimmy Cagney," one of the workers later recalled. "I never seen nothing like it. That fellow just came right a'coming at them two lawmen and they must of hit him plenty, but nothing was gonna stop that fellow."

From his place in the ditch, Cowley fired desperately as Nelson advanced. The gangster took a bullet in the side but came plodding on. He sprayed the ditch with bullets, cutting Cowley almost in half, even as he absorbed more lead himself. Then Nelson turned his fire on Hollis. The agent dropped his empty shotgun and ran for cover behind a telegraph pole, where he drew his pistol. Hollis scored several hits on Baby Face before being fatally shot in the head.

Nelson walked to the FBI car, got in and backed it up to his wife and Chase, who loaded their arsenal inside. "You'll have to drive," Nelson told Chase. "I've been hit."

He had been hit—17 times.

The next day Nelson's body, stripped nude to prevent quick identification, was found in a ditch some 20 miles away. He got the same mawkish coverage from the press that Dillinger had received. An interview with Helen Nelson, who had surrendered two days later, read in part:

'Baby Face' Nelson died in the arms of his wife with a smile on his lips, but with tears in his eyes for his two young children.

Those were the high-lights of a thrilling story told by Nelson's pretty widow, in which she gave a heart-broken account of his death at the hands of federal agents.

Such journalistic excess greatly upset the FBI's J. Edgar Hoover, but he could revel in the knowledge that the last important member of the Dillinger gang had been eliminated. Chase was captured a short time later in California and sent to prison for life.

See also: *John Dillinger.*

NELSON Tombstone: Libelous epitaph

When H. Lawrence Nelson of Raleigh, N.C. was killed in 1906, his friends and relatives had inscribed on his tombstone: "H. LAWRENCE NELSON, born Dec. 16, 1880. Murdered and robbed by Hamp Kendall, Sept. 25, 1906."

Indeed, a farmer named Hamp Kendall had been convicted of the crime and sentenced to life imprisonment. However, 11 years later, in 1917, Kendall was pardoned; the real murderer had confessed. Then began the great Battle of Nelson's Tombstone. Kendall petitioned the courts to have the offending tombstone altered, but the courts said they had no jurisdiction. County officials declined to take action, pointing to a state law that made it a felony to tamper with a tombstone. The Board of Deacons of the church that owned the graveyard property also insisted they had no power to act. Kendall then

appealed to the governor, stating, "No man can stand under the scandal of this tombstone in the town where he is making an honest living." He was informed that it was not a state matter and had to be handled by county or city authorities. After years of trying, Kendall finally succeeded in convincing the legislature to pass a law declaring illegal "any tombstone which charges anyone with a crime." In 1950 the accusing inscription was removed, clearing Kendall's name 33 years after he was pardoned for the crime.

NESS, Eliot (1902-1957): "Untouchables" leader

One of the most-storied law officers in American history, Eliot Ness was the young head of the so-called Untouchables. This 10-man team has been credited in the more melodramatized crime histories in print and on television with laying waste to Al Capone's underworld empire in Chicago. No doubt Ness and his raiders caused the Capone organization grievous financial harm and serious inconvenience, but the claims made by the lawman and his eager biographers were a bit bloated. Certainly, the Untouchables never dried up Chicago or put the mob out of business. In fairness, however, Ness did justify his reputation as the head of an incorruptible unit of officers in an era when honest law enforcers were not easy to find.

A University of Chicago graduate, Ness was 26 years old in 1928 when he was placed in charge of a Prohibition detail specifically created to harass Capone. At the time, he knew full well the dishonest and venal record of the Prohibition agents who had worked under the Treasury Department until responsibility for enforcing the law was shifted to Justice. Ness weeded through hundreds of files before he came up with nine agents who had "no Achilles' heel in their make-ups." All were in their twenties and were experts in such activities as wiretapping, truck driving and, especially, marksmanship. These men were dedicated to their task, defied all threats and violence and proved unbribable. They were dubbed the Untouchables by the underworld, which was shocked to come across law officers who could neither be bought nor frightened.

Ness, who reveled in personal publicity, informed the press whenever a major raid on a brewery was planned. The horde of cameramen who descended on the scene often got in the way, but Ness' superiors did not interfere. The resultant coverage showed the citizenry and members of the underworld that Capone was not invulnerable. The Untouchables also distracted Capone while other revenue agents infiltrated his organization to gain the evidence of income tax evasion that eventually resulted in his conviction.

After the fall of Capone, Ness became the Justice Department's chief investigator of Prohibition violations in the Chicago area and later in the "moonshine mountains" of Tennessee, Kentucky and Ohio. In 1935 a reform administration in Cleveland, Ohio installed Ness as its new Public Safety Director. Cleveland was then mired in crime, and its police force was generally acknowledged to be "on the pad," i.e., taking graft from the underworld. A vicious gang known as the Mayfield Road Mob controlled gambling operations, bootlegging and prostitution, which blighted virtually every neighbothood in the city. The building trades were being strangled by labor racketeers. Violence was endemic; gang killings and the one-way ride were almost as prevalent as they had been in Chicago during its worst period.

Ness quickly established a new environment in the city and rooted out corruption in the police department, ordering mass transfers and firing officers for such offenses as taking bribes or being drunk on duty. During his six-year tenure, Ness was the object of shootings, beatings, threats and an attempted police frame-up. In the end, he won the battle of Cleveland, changing it, as one crime historian put it, "from the deadliest metropolis to 'the safest big city in the U.S.A.'" The Mayfield Road Mob was crushed, and such Syndicate big shots as Moe Dalitz were forced to move their gambling operations outside the city limits to the surrounding counties and eventually, because of continuing pressure, into northern Kentucky.

Ness left his Cleveland post during World War II to become federal director of the Division of Social Protection for the Office of Defense. After the war he went into private business until his death in 1957.

NEUTRAL Ground: Crime area during American Revolution

During the American Revolution probably the most crime-ridden and violent area in the colonies was a section of Westchester County in New York, the so-called neutral ground between the American lines to the north and the British forces in New York City to the south. While both sides occasionally ventured into this no-man's land, it generally was left to be ravaged by "cowboys," who rode for the British, and "skinners," who rode for the Americans. Both groups, composed mainly of rough farmhands, lived off the land by stealing horses and cattle and whatever else the local populace had to offer at the point of a musket. The word "cowboy" derives from these rugged and often vicious fighters and meant "thief" as much as anything else.

Further reading: *Neutral Ground* by Frank Hough.

NEW Orleans Axeman: Uncaptured mass murderer

From 1911 to 1919 New Orleans was plagued by a series of gruesome murders. Most of the victims were Italian grocers and/or their relatives. The murderer had a set pattern, always chiseling in through a door panel and wielding an axe as a murder weapon, very often one that was found on the premises. In all cases, the bloodstained axe was left behind.

In 1911 there were six axe murders, the victims being three Italian grocers and their wives. The next murderous onslaught came in 1918. The first victims were Mr. and Mrs. Joseph Maggio, who owned a small grocery business and lived over the store. A bloodied axe was found outside their back door. Despite the similarity to the earlier murders, the police decided their best suspects in this attack were two of Maggio's brothers who had been living with the couple, and they arrested both. Meanwhile, the press became convinced that the various murders had been committed by one axeman. This theory was bolstered when the Maggio brothers produced alibis and were released.

On June 28 there was another axeman attack; the victims were grocer Louis Besumer and a Mrs. Harriet Lowe, who were living together as man and wife. Each survived the onslaught, Besumer suffering a deep gash on his head and Mrs. Lowe a more serious skull wound. Besumer was released from the hospital the next day. Then the case became slightly twisted. The newspapers, which had thought Louis Besumer to be Italian, discovered he was Polish, spoke several languages fluently and received considerable mail from abroad. In 1918, a war year, that meant Louis Besumer might not only be the vicious Axeman but a German spy as well; at the time there was little distinction drawn in New Orleans between Poles and Germans. Mrs. Lowe compounded the mess by declaring from her hospital bed, "I've long suspected that Mr. Besumer was a German spy." The police arrested Besumer.

The next day the woman made a new statement: "I did not say Mr. Besumer was a German spy. This is perfectly ridiculous." The police released Besumer.

About a month after the attack, Mrs. Lowe died, mumbling rather incoherently about Louis hitting her with an axe. Besumer was rearrested.

That same night the Axeman struck again. Edward Schneider returned home to find his pregnant wife lying unconscious on the bed in a pool of blood. Mrs. Schneider recovered and recalled seeing the dark form of a tall, heavyset white man wielding an axe. She remembered the axe coming down at her. On August 10 Joseph Romano was fatally wounded by an axe assailant, who was seen fleeing by the victim's young niece. This time the Axeman had varied his pattern somewhat: Romano was not a grocer but a barber. Otherwise the technique was the same, with a door panel chiseled out and the death weapon abandoned nearby.

A wave of hysteria swept New Orleans, especially in the Italian section and most especially among grocers. Families set up night watches, and the police received constant calls from nervous grocers who reported seeing a man with an axe near their home. On March 10, 1919 the Axeman struck again, severely wounding Charles and Rosie Cortimiglia and killing their two-year-old daughter, Mary. All the usual signs were present, but in this instance one of the victims announced she knew the identity of the assailant, or, more properly, the assailants. Mrs. Cortimiglia said the murderous attack was the work of 69-year-old Iorlando Jordano and his son, Frank, rival grocers from down the street. The police, happy to have a positive identification, arrested both Jordanos despite Mr. Cortimiglia's vehement statements that the rival grocers were not the attackers.

All this gave the police too many Axemen in custody. Poor

Louis Besumer was still incarcerated, awaiting trial. When his case came up in April, the prosecution looking rather inept as it attempted to introduce hearsay and rumor as evidence. Federal agents testified they had no facts linking Besumer to cases of espionage. In her lucid moments Mrs. Lowe had indicated Besumer had not attacked her; only when delirious had she stated otherwise. Louis walked out of court a free man, not a killer, not a spy and, certainly, not the Axeman.

By now the entire city was seized by an "Axeman craze." People held Axeman parties, and a new song, "The Mysterious Axeman's Jazz," became a local bestseller. Then the *New Orleans Times-Picayune* received a letter signed, "The Axeman," announcing that he planned to stalk the city on the night of March 19 and that he loved jazz and would not invade any house playing such music. On the 19th, bars and nightclubs were packed, and the city echoed to the sound of thousands upon thousands of record players blaring at full blast. The sound must have mellowed the Axeman into passivity; at least no one was axed to death that night.

In May 1919 the Jordanos came to trial. They were convicted solely on Mrs. Cortimiglia's testimony, even though her husband, now separated from her, repeated his story that the Jordanos had not attacked them. Frank Jordano was sentenced to hang and the elderly Iorlando drew a life term. There were some in New Orleans who felt the Axeman terror had ended. But on August 10 a grocer named Steve Boca was attacked. A few weeks later, in another apparent Axeman attack, someone started working through a door panel of the home of an Italian druggist. The assailant fled when the druggist fired a revolver. The following night a 19-year-old woman was found wounded and unconscious in her bed and an axe was discovered outside her window. She recovered but could not say who had attacked her.

The last suspected attack by the Axeman occurred on October 27, 1919, when Mrs. Mike Pepitone, the wife of yet another Italian grocer, walked into her bedroom and found her husband dead, with his blood stains all over the walls and ceiling. She started screaming, and the Axeman, who was still in the room, rushed out past her.

The more recent assaults made it appear that the Jordanos, convicted in the Cortimiglia case, quite possibly were not responsible for the Axeman rampage. Then in December, Rosie Cortimiglia rushed into the city room of the *Times-Picayune* in tears, dropped to her knees and admitted she had lied about the Jordanos. Within a few days they were released.

Happily for the police, the Pepitone murder, was the last foray of the mysterious Axeman. Aside from the Jordanos, the sum of their detective work in about a half-dozen cases had been to arrest whomever had discovered the body or bodies. Then a new development took place 2,000 miles away in Los Angeles. A man named Joseph Mumfre was shot dead by a woman who turned out to be Mrs. Mike Pepitone. She announced that Mumfre was the Axeman and had killed her husband. The police checked Mumfre's record, which showed he had constantly been in and out of prison around New Orleans but had always been on the loose when an Axeman killing took place. Still, the police had been burned too often to label the Axeman case closed. The Los Angeles authorities were unimpressed with Mrs. Pepitone's tale and charged her with Mumfre's murder. Sentenced to 10 years imprisonment, she was paroled after doing three.

Did the Mumfre killing solve the Axeman case? Or was there more than one Axeman, up to a dozen or so, each stealing the idea from the other? Or was it all a Mafia plot aimed at extorting money from members of the Italian community in New Orleans? None of these questions has ever been answered.

NEW Orleans Procuresses

Even in cities that openly allowed prostitution in the 19th century, the crime of procuring was frowned upon even by the corrupt police who took bribes from brothel owners. Many officers in such wide-open cities as Cincinnati and Chicago never thought twice about breaking up a procuring ring preying on young innocents. The exception to this rule was post-Civil War New Orleans, where the procuring trade was largely in the hands of women who seemed to have little or no trouble with the law despite the particularly unsavory character of their profession, giving rise to the term "New Orleans procuresses."

The activites of the procuresses went back a long time in the city's history, but they received little public attention until 1845, when it was revealed that Mary Thompson was doing a thriving business selling virgins out of a cigar store blind on Royal Street. She sold these inexperienced girls for sums of $200 to $400, depending on their looks. In March 1845 she became friendly with 15-year-old Mary Fozatte and gave her presents of clothes, toy jewelry and candy. Then she sold the girl to an elderly gentleman for $350. As she was taking her merchandise to a house on Burgundy Street, young Mary broke away and ran home. Most indignant, the procuress charged the girl with stealing. The case against her was dropped, however, and in turn, she was awarded $50 damages. The police, as one writer put it, "told Mary Thompson that if she tried to sell another girl she might be punished."

In the post-Civil War era the procuresses were kept busy supplying girls for houses of prostitution in several cities besides New Orleans: Atlanta, Memphis, Galveston and a number of other Southern cities. They took orders for "stock" and "fresh stock," which meant inexperienced children worth very high fees. In the late 1860s a schoolteacher-procuress, Louisa Murphy, had a set price of $800 for a young girl.

By the 1880s the procuresses operated with increasing boldness. Such notables as Miss Carol, Mother Mansfield, Spanish Agnes, Emma Johnson and Nellie Haley, called the Queen of the Procuresses, sent out mail circulars of their stock. By that time the competition was so fierce that the price for virgins sometimes dropped as low as $50.

Spanish Agnes got into only minor difficulties when in 1890 police discovered she had sold the owners of a Galveston brothel two girls who had been reported missing by their parents. In a newspaper interview, Agnes said:

> I frequently receive orders from the keepers of fashionable places. These ladies ask me to send them girls, or women for that matter. I always prefer to have experienced women than virtuous girls, because there is less fear of trouble. I am in correspondence with women like Molly Waters and Abbie Allen of Galveston; these people write to me for girls. Some time ago I received an order from Miss Abbie Allen to send her some girls, and soon after Miss Lena Smith informed me that she could secure two nice young girls. . . . I do not like to have anything to do with innocent girls. . . . Not a very long time ago a mother brought her three daughters to me and offered them for sale. Two, she said, were bad, and the youngest still unacquainted with vice and the wickedness of the world. She demanded $25 for the girls, and expressed her belief that she ought to get more for the guileless maiden.

The procuress added she bought all three girls and realized a substantial profit.

In 1892 a newspaper reporter doing an expose on the work of procuresses approached Emma Johnson about buying a 15-year-old girl, then demurred at making the actual purchase. The Johnson woman was incensed: "You're a fool! The girl's a virgin! You'll never get another chance like this in New Orleans!"

There was no record of Emma Johnson coming to grief because of the revelations, and in fact, the New Orleans procuresses continued to prosper until 1917, when Storyville and much of the brothel operations in New Orleans were shut down by the military as a wartime health measure.

NEW York Fire Of 1835: Looting spree

The New York Fire of December 16-17, 1835 produced an orgy of looting as well as the saying, "I'm a firefighter and well-to-do, thank you."

The fire started in a five-story building on Merchant Street in the fledgling financial district. By the time the alarm was sounded at 9 a.m. on the morning of December 16, it had already spread to surrounding buildings. Most of the city's 49 engines and six hook-and-ladder units responded, but because of the weather they faced a brutal task. The temperature was 17° below zero, and hydrants had frozen solid, while the engine pumps froze over with ice unless constantly heated. The ice covering the river was broken through and bucket brigades formed, but these efforts were unavailing. By 11 p.m. the fire had swept into Water and Pearl streets and Exchange Place, the home of the stock exchange at the time. Within another hour 13 acres of Manhattan were ablaze, and the glow could be seen as far away as Philadelphia.

By the early morning hours of December 17, the tenement dwellers and criminals of the Bowery and the Five Points had descended on the scene and engaged in incredible looting. While Marines from the Navy Yard dynamited buildings to form firebreaks around the financial district, many of the firefighters joined the looters and were seen carrying goods out of burning shops and disappearing. Looters made off with hoards of clothing, jewelry and furniture, which had been heaped in the street without adequate guards. Thugs set afire those buildings that weren't already burning to cover their criminal activities. A group of irate citizens caught one thug as he was firing a store on Broad Street and hanged him from a tree. It was three days before harried police got around to cutting down the frozen body.

The fire was finally contained at the end of the second day, but by that time much of New York was in ruins. Almost 700 buildings were gutted and losses, estimated at $22 million, bankrupted most insurance companies and were credited with bringing on the Panic of 1837.

During the week following the blaze, the police staged numerous raids on the hovels of the poor and criminal classes of the Bowery and Five Points districts, repossessing huge amounts of loot. Moving vans were required to handle the booty in several individual buildings. No raids, however, were made on the homes of firefighters, although Fire Chief Handsome Jim Gulick was dismissed for failing to curb the spreading of the fire or the illegal activities of many of his men. However, when the firefighters threatened to go on strike, the fire-panicked city reinstated him. In the Bowery and Five Points a bitter greeting came into vogue: "I'm a firefighter and well-to-do, thank you."

NEW York Lottery Swindle

One of the earliest lottery swindles in America was unearthed in New York in 1818, when it was found that lottery operators had arranged for certain numbers to win in return for kickbacks from the pre-arranged winners.

The lottery, much of whose proceeds were allegedly slated for the unfortunate, was exposed by Charles Baldwin, the editor of the *New York Republican Chronicle,* who wrote:

> It is a fact that in this city there is SWINDLING in the management. A certain gentleman in town received intimation that a number named would be drawn on Friday last and it was drawn that day! This number was insured high in several different places. A similar thing had happened once before in this same lottery; and on examination of the managers' files the number appeared soiled as if it had been in the pocket several days. . . .

Baldwin was sued for libel by several of the operators and a select committee was appointed to look into the matter. What they found was that one of the complainants, John H. Sickles, was a secret supplier of the lottery forms and had provided certain politicians with the winning numbers in advance. By using political figures in the scheme, Sickles and others assured that the lottery would enjoy general governmental approval and support. Based on these findings, Baldwin was acquitted and became famous as the first of New York's journalistic muckrakers.

NEW York World's Fair Bombing

A baffling bombing case, one that the New York police spent more man-hours on than any other, was the attempt to blow up the British Pavillion at the New York World's Fair on July 4, 1940. Two days earlier, on a Tuesday, an anonymous telephone call warned a telephone operator of the coming explosion, and immediately, a dozen extra detectives were placed on duty at the building. On Wednesday afternoon, a pavillion employee noticed a suitcase in the engine room but disregarded it because, incredibly, he had not been made aware of the warning. At about 4 o'clock Thursday afternoon, the man saw the suitcase again, but this time, passing closer to it, he heard a ticking sound coming from inside and informed officials. Within minutes four members of the New York police bomb squad arrived on the scene and carried the suspect suitcase to an open field, where two minutes later, as they started to inspect it, the case exploded, killing two of the officers, Detectives Joseph J. Lynch and Ferdinand A. Socha, and wounding the other two. Despite endless hours of police work tracking down every possible lead, the case remained unsolved. To this day, a reward of $26,000 awaits the person who can supply information leading to a solution of the case.

NEWCOMB, George "Bitter Creek" (?1866-1895): Outlaw

Handsome, extravagantly mustached George Newcomb was perhaps the most devilish member of that often likable bunch of hell raisers the Doolin gang and also the tragic hero of the supposedly authentic tale of the Rose of Cimarron.

Newcomb appears to have been born in Kansas. He left home early, moving to Texas, where he herded cattle for rancher John Slaughter and was known as Slaughter's Kid. In the 1880s Newcomb drifted into the Cherokee Strip, working as a cowboy and then becoming an outlaw. He rode with the Daltons near the end of their days and then with Bill Doolin, who had been a part-time member of the Dalton gang. During one train robbery Newcomb put three lawmen-guards out of commission, allowing him and his accomplices to get away safely with their booty.

Newcomb always had a way with the ladies and was noted for singing his own verse:

> I'm a wild wolf from Bitter Creek,
> And it's my night to howl.

It was apparently such sterling talents that turned the head of 15(?)-year-old Rosa Dunn, whom he met at a dance, and the pair soon became lovers. Young Rosa was often in the company of various members of the Doolin gang, and she evidently was the legendary Rose of Cimarron, who allegedly intervened to aid the gang when they were ambushed at the famous Battle of Ingalls in the Oklahoma Territory. When Newcomb took a bullet in the leg during that conflict, Rosa supposedly brought him more ammunition, shielded his body with hers and helped him escape. Aside from the fact that Newcomb was wounded and escaped, little of the legend is true. According to most trustworthy accounts by various combatants, neither Rosa nor any other Rose of Cimarron was on hand to perform "angel of mercy" rescue.

However, probably because of his legend rather than his criminal deeds, Bitter Creek Newcomb soon sported a $5,000 reward on his head. In May 1895 Newcomb, with fellow outlaw Charlie Pierce, returned to Cimarron River country to visit his Rosa. An added inducement may have been the fact that Rosa's brothers owed him $900. Arriving at the Dunn ranch, the two had barely dismounted when Rosa's two brothers opened up on them, dropping both men in their tracks. When the Dunns moved in on their victims, they found Pierce still breathing and immediately shot him again.

The following morning the Dunn brothers had loaded the two apparent corpses on a wagon and were heading for Guthrie, Okla. to collect the reward money when Bitter Creek started moaning and asked for a drink of water. The Dunns responded with another bullet, this time a fatal one.

See also: *Doolin Gang; Ingalls, Oklahoma Territory, Battle of; Rose of Cimarron.*

NEWTON Massacre: Kansas shoot-out

The great Western shoot-outs were seldom calculated, eyeball-to-eyeball confrontations but rather spontaneous explosions of violence. Certainly, such was the case with what became known as the Newton Massacre. The trouble developed in early August 1871, when ex-railroad tough Mike McCluskie shot and killed a gunfighter named Willie Wilson, apparently in an argument over who was buying drinks for whom. McCluskie was warned that Wilson had a lot of friends who would be looking for vengeance, but he just shrugged.

On August 11 McCluskie was in a saloon-dance hall in Hide Park, Newton's bordello area, talking to some railroaders for the Atchison, Topeka and Santa Fe. A group of Texas cowboys headed by Hugh Anderson, the son of a wealthy cattleman, stormed in, firing as they came. Anderson shot McCluskie in the neck, but the latter lived long enough to get off a shot that wounded Anderson. For a moment there was a shocked silence in the place and then a frail-looking youth of no more than 18 got up from a table, picked up both Anderson's and McCluskie's guns and walked to the door. He locked it and whirled around shooting. In less than two minutes four of the Texas cowboys were dead and several others wounded. By the time the smoke cleared, the youth, known only as Riley and dying of tuberculosis, had vanished, leaving the citizens of Newton with a roomful of corpses. It was, in the words of a local newspaper editor, "worse than Tim Finnegan's wake."

NICKNAMES, Criminal

More than the rest of us, criminals often pick up colorful nicknames, many of which spotlight their illegal activities or, in effect, describe their modus operandi. Thus, the Snowman is a notorious New York dope peddler. Bunko is an ace con man. And Kissing Sam is a pickpocket who can perform the toughest trick in that line of work, lifting a victim's billfold from an inside coat pocket while staring him right in the eye, close enough, in fact, to kiss him.

Years ago, Billy the Clock was an arsonist who developed a

special celluloid timing device to touch off fires, and slow-paying clients of a New York loan shark called Gas Pipe Sam Bianculli soon found out, to their regret, how he had earned his nickname. Waxey Gordon, who grew up to become one of the most powerful bootleg kings, traced his nickname back to his youthful days as a dip, slipping in and out of people's pockets as though his hands were coated with tallow. Jack "Legs" Diamond gained his monicker as a youth by displaying a speedy grab-and-run technique in New York's fur and garment district.

Other nicknames are bestowed in deference to a prominent personal characteristic or appearance. Duck Walk was a Chicago gun moll whose strut was greatly affected by the two .38s she kept holstered to her knees. "Tough Tony" was tough, and Nails was as hard as same. Vince Coll, a wild killer, certainly earned the sobriquet Mad Dog. Scarface Al Capone got his scar, and his resulting nickname, from a fight with a Brooklyn longshoreman, although he always attributed it to a bayonet wound he suffered in combat during World War I, a distinction the military records did not bear out. Golf Bag Sam Hunt, a Capone gunman, got his tag because of his habit of packing an automatic shotgun with his golf clubs. The accuracy of some nicknames in describing those honored by them has been debatable, to say the least. If Slick Willie Sutton, for example, was so "slick" why did he spend most of his adult life behind bars.

Prostitution has proved a rich source of quaint nicknames over the years. Jennie the Factory was a New York brothel inmate whose name described her productivity. Mike "de Pike" Heitler was a top brothel keeper who earned the label de Pike because he ran the cheapest fancy house in Illinois and was thus considered a piker. Actually, Mike de Pike resented being so dubbed because he thought of himself as a skilled manager who had been able to hold prices down by the introduction of modern, assembly-line business methods. Also appropriately named was Mike's assistant, Monkey Face Charlie Genker, who, in addition to being no beauty, matched the agility of the jungle creature for whom he was named by scampering up doors and peering over transoms to encourage the ladies and their customers to speed things along.

Women have won their own share of underworld nicknames. Over the year there have been numerous Kiss of Death girls, such a Mary Margaret Collins, who was labeled Kiss of Death Maggie by reporters because she had run through six husbands, all killed in battles with either the underworld or the police. Several other women who traveled in similar company found themselves tagged with the same nickname. Louise Rolfe won fame in the press as the Blonde Alibi during the trial of Machine Gun Jack McGurn for murder. McGurn insisted he had been on an amorous trip out of town with Louise, a nightclub entertainer. The alibi won him his freedom, but the prosecution later found proof that McGurn had been lying and indicted him for perjury. Louise was slated to be the chief witness against him, and his conviction seemed certain. But McGurn solved that problem by making Louise his permanent Blonde Alibi; he married her, confident in the knowledge that a wife could not be forced to testify against her husband.

Many criminal nicknames have stemmed from a single but dramatic incident. "Titanic" Thompson was a con man operating aboard the *Titanic* when it sank in 1912. Thompson and three of his confederates, who had been fleecing passengers in card games, managed to get aboard lifeboats and survive the tragedy. Thompson not only put in maximum claims for lost baggage and valuables but also obtained the names of deceased passengers so that fellow con men could make bogus claims. Before Lucky Luciano achieved his high status in organized crime, he earned his nickname by supposedly surviving a "ride" given him by a rival gang. Yet there is some suspicion that Luciano had never been marked for death by other gangsters but had been kidnapped and beaten by a family whose daughter he had dishonored. According to this theory, when he was finally let go, he contacted Meyer Lansky and together they concocted the tale about Luciano surviving an underworld hit because they felt a reputation for invincibility would be helpful in winning the respect of other criminals.

Several underworld nicknames have been highly laudatory, such as Frank (the "Prime Minister") Costello's and Johnny ("the Brain") Torrio's. Complimentary in its own fashion was the sobriquet, Hot Stove given to Jimmy Quinn, an ex-convict whose record did not prevent his election as a Chicago alderman in the early part of this century. Quinn was, as a saying of the day had it, "so crooked he'd steal a hot stove."

But some criminals have deeply resented their nicknames. Benjamin "Bugsy" Siegel's friends called him Ben; he would go bugs if anyone called him Bugsy to his face. Charles "Ice Wagon" Connors was equally annoyed by his nickname, which was given after he smashed a robbery getaway car into an ice truck.

Harry Guzik, a longtime procurer and the man who handled payoffs to the police for the Capone mob, was called Greasy Thumb Guzik because, according to his version, he had to peel off so many bills from the huge roll he always carried that he could never get the grease off his thumb. The Chicago police had another, more self-serving explanation for the origin of his handle. It went back to his days as a waiter, when he couldn't seem to serve a plate of soup without getting his thumb in it. Whichever the case, when Harry died, the newspapermen transferred the nickname to his younger brother Jake, who became the top payoff man for the syndicate. Some nicknames are just too good to die.

NIGHT Of The Sicilian Vespers: Alleged Mafia killings

The purge of the old Mafia's "Mustache Petes" that began during the Castellammarese War was completed on September 10, 1931 with the assassination of Salvatore Maranzano, the "boss of bosses." An old myth repeated by a number of crime historians, including former Attorney General Ramsey Clark, was that on the same day no less than "forty members of La Cosa Nostra died by gunfire" around the country. It makes for an intriguing tale, but Lucky Luciano, the supposed mastermind behind this rash of killings, which came to be called the Night of the Sicilian Vespers, often challenged anyone to present a list of supposed victims and his challenge was never answered.

The only killings that could be tied in with Maranzano's were those of Jimmy Marino, a Maranzano underling who was shot six times that afternoon as he stood in the doorway of a Bronx barbershop, and Louis Russo and Sam Monaco, whose bodies washed ashore in Newark Bay three days later. The men, who were identified as Maranzano faithfuls, had had their throats cut and their heads crushed. They were wrapped in sash cord and weighted with sash weights.

Later, informer Joe Valachi asked Vito Genovese why these men had been killed. He was told that when a "big boss dies, all his faithful have to go with him."

See also: *Castellammarese War, Charles "Lucky" Luciano, Salvatore Maranzano, Mustache Petes.*

NINETEENTH Street Gang: Pro-Catholic New York gang

In the 1870s a pack of juvenile criminals, whose members continued in the gang until they reached their mid-twenties, terrorized New York City's Poverty Lane, the area from 19th to 34th streets around Second Avenue. The leader of this band, called the 19th Street Gang, was an incredibly mean punk named Little Mike. What made this gang of pickpockets, sneak thieves and muggers unique was its unswerving religious affiliation. Violently pro-Catholic, it often attacked Protestant missions and schools. But the gang's main purpose was stealing and its members victimized cripples, blind men and children as well as storekeepers. The only defense against these attacks was for a potential victim to prove he was Catholic. Thus, a man being waylaid might be asked to give his baptismal name, recite his catechism, name his parish priest or reveal his Easter duty. Even this was not always a complete defense. As Little Mike is quoted as having said to one victim: "You're a good Catholic all right, but we haven't made a score in a long time. We're taking half your money." Happily for the public, the gang faded away by the mid-1880s.

NITTI, Frank (1884-1943): Capone mob lieutenant

The importance of Frank Nitti, whom Al Capone supposedly chose as his successor when he went to prison, has been highly exaggerated; in fact, his greatest claim to fame probably was the television show "The Untouchables," which often cast him in the role of the mob's mastermind. Yet when the national crime syndicate was being established in the early 1930s, its founders dealt with Paul "the Waiter" Ricca as the head of Chicago's Capone mob—without Nitti's knowledge. No one thought it important that he be informed.

Born in 1884, Frank Nitti was a barber whose customers included a number of crooks. He became a fence, eventually getting involved with the Capone forces at the onset of Prohi-

bition. He was a skillful organizer and Capone relied on him to see that his orders were transmitted and carried out. After Big Al's fall, the newspapers hailed Nitti as the new boss of the Capone mob. Nitti probably thought he was, but men like Ricca, Tony Accardo, Jake Guzik, the Fischetti brothers, Murray Humphreys and others were not going to follow him.

However, Nitti was valuable as a front man, someone who could take the heat from the authorities. In 1932 two police officers, under orders from Mayor Anton Cermak, shot and severely wounded Nitti. Cermak was determined to wrest control of Chicago from the Capone mob and replace it with his own group of criminals, headed by Teddy Newberry.

Although near death at one point, Nitti survived and the legend about him grew. When the mob became deeply involved in its shakedown of the film industry, Nitti's name was often used by Willie Bioff and George Browne to frighten movie moguls. Finally, federal rackets investigators succeeded in getting Nitti, Ricca and several others indicted. Ricca, who with Accardo was more openly assuming leadership of the Capone mob, demanded that Nitti "take the rap," but Nitti refused. He had served 18 months in the early 1930s for income tax violations and he was terrified by the thought of going back behind bars.

"Frank, you're asking for it," Ricca is said to have raged at him during a gang conference in Nitti's home.

Ricca's words, Nitti knew, were as good as a death sentence. The next day, March 19, 1943, Nitti took a walk along some railroad tracks. He drew a pistol from his pocket and shot himself to death.

NOBLES: Labor musclemen

During the heyday of union organizing, especially in the needle and allied garment industry trades, it became common for both fledgling unions and employers to hire thugs to win their battles. Employers used goons to guard strikebreakers, slug union pickets and raid union meetings; the labor unions used them to blackjack and murder strikebreakers and pressure those workers who did not wish to join the union. Yet even these thugs had some loyalty, and although they seldom let their feelings interfere with business, they basically considered themselves in sympathy with the workers.

During this period a group of workers in New York haunted the employment agencies of the Bowery and Sixth Avenue looking for work as strikebreakers, since the pay for such efforts was much higher than normal wages. Ironically, the thugs assigned to protect these strikebreakers held them in such ill repute that they referred to them as "finks." They, on the other hand, considered themselves so superior, despite their evil work, that they called themselves "nobles."

These nobles so preferred practicing their art on behalf of the unions, which generally paid better than the employers, many of whom were penny pinchers, that from 1913 to 1915 they engaged in open warfare among themselves for the right. This conflict came to be known as the Labor Sluggers War.

See also: *Labor Sluggers War.*

NO-MAN'S Land: Outlaw refuge area

Through a boundary quirk in the latter part of the 19th century, an area of some 800 square miles just north of the Texas Panhandle was neither incorporated into the states of Texas, Colorado or Kansas nor included within the territorial limits of New Mexico or the Indian Territory, which eventually became part of Oklahoma. Thus, outside the law enforcement jurisdiction of either white or Indian law, it was referred to as No-Man's Land and became a safe refuge for wanted men, such as Ned Christie and various other outlaws. No-Man's Land was eventually eliminated in 1890, not as an anti-outlaw measure but rather as a consequence of the Oklahoma land rush, which also resulted in the taking of the Cherokee Strip from the Indians.

NORCROSS, Henry L.: See Russell Sage.

NORFLEET Manhunt

In 1919, while stopping at a Dallas hotel, a Texas rancher named Frank Norfleet was taken by a group of confidence men. Using a variation of the "big store" racket, they roped Norfleet in by letting him "find" the lost wallet of an obviously rich man. When Norfleet returned the wallet, he was offered a $100 reward, which he refused. The wealthy man, a supposed speculator on the Dallas Cotton Exchange, then said that he would invest the money for him and let him have the winnings. Soon, Norfleet's "winnings" totaled $73,000. However, it developed he had to post some $45,000 as security before he could get his money. Norfleet was "put on the send," i.e., sent back home to empty his savings account and put a mortgage on his ranch. He returned with the money and gave it to the five crooks, who soon decamped with it.

Norfleet so far had behaved like the ideal sucker, but he didn't continue to. Vowing vengeance, he went after the gang. After raising another $30,000, he spent the next four years on a private manhunt, running down the confidence men one by one. His prize catch was the gang's leader, Joe Furey, a legendary swindler. In Denver, while on the trail of another of the crooks, W. B. Spencer, Norfleet infiltrated a phony stock exchange operation and gathered evidence that led to the arrest and conviction of three dozen con men. But his quarry was not among them. He later caught up with Spencer in Salt Lake City. When caught, Spencer complained bitterly, "None of us had a minute's peace since you got on our trail."

Also caught in the Norfleet net were two lawmen who provided protection for confidence operators. In all, Norfleet covered 40,000 miles and spent $30,000 in his four-year vengeance hunt. The Texas legislature took note of the plucky rancher's tenacity and daring and appropriated a small amount of expense money for him, but the action was ruled illegal. The matter was taken under advisement in 1923 by the governor and the legislature, seeking to find some way to reimburse Norfleet. In 1960, at the age of 95, Frank Norfleet said whimsically, "Far as I know, the thing is still 'under advisement.' "

NORMANDIE, S.S.: Sabotage case

On the night of February 11, 1942 a spectacular fire at a pier in the Hudson River lit up the blacked-out skies of New York. The blaze was aboard the French luxury liner S.S. Normandie, interned after the fall of France and in the process of being converted into a troopship. The vessel burned for days, finally listing and turning on its side. There was much speculation about the cause of the fire, ranging from worker carelessness to possible Nazi sabotage. The truth was not revealed until more than three decades later, when the posthumous memoirs of Lucky Luciano explained that the ship had been sabotaged by the underworld.

The motive behind the act was to establish a climate of fear that would force the military authorities to request aid from the then-imprisoned Luciano in return for certain considerations. During the early months of the war, Navy intelligence was all over the New York waterfront seeking the aid of workers in protecting ships and cargo. The first man to see the opening this could provide Luciano was Albert Anastasia, Luciano's longtime doting underling. Albert consulted with his brother, Tough Tony Anastasio, and then brought the plan to Frank Costello, who immediately presented it to Luciano in Dannemora Prison. Luciano agreed that if the Normandie burned, the Navy, fearful of similar acts, would be forced to ask the underworld to help guard the waterfront. And that would mean dealing with Luciano.

The result was predictable. Years later, Luciano said: "That god-damn Anastasia—he really done a job. Later on, Albert told me not to feel too bad about what happened to the ship. He said that as a sergeant in the Army he hated the fuckin' Navy anyway." The reaction by the Navy and Washington was equally predictable. Almost instantly, Operation Underworld was launched, with the intention of enlisting underworld leaders to help the war effort. The Navy soon found final approval for such a plan lay in Luciano's prison cell, and the gang leader exacted a price for his cooperation, demanding to be moved from "Siberia," as Dannemora was known in prison circles. He was transferred first to Sing Sing and then to Great Meadow Prison, considered the most pleasant of all the state's penal institutions.

It must be recorded that for the balance of the war the New York waterfront remained immune to any major security problems. After the war the rest of Luciano's price was met. On January 3, 1946 Thomas E. Dewey, the man who had put Luciano away for 30 to 50 years on a charge of compulsory prostitution, announced his approval of Luciano's release provided he was deported. Operation Underworld, born in a flaming ship at a New York pier, was concluded successfully, at least from the underworld's point of view.

See also: *Anthony "Tough Tony" Anastasio, Charles "Lucky" Luciano.*

NORRIS, Charles (1867-1935): Medical examiner

Charles Norris, New York City's first medical examiner after

During World War II the burning of the S.S. *Normandie* was considered by many to be Nazi sabotage. Later revelations indicated it was more likely a case of Mafia sabotage, part of a successful effort to "spring" Lucky Luciano from prison.

the city abandoned the outdated and generally inept coroner system in 1918, became a living legend who inspired an endless amount of material for feature writers. He was a reliable source for authors of crime material based on facts and was the model for the brilliant, philosophical medical wizard of many a detective novel. Despite numerous difficulties, both financial and political, Norris created the nation's model medical examiner's office. As a pathologist, he provided evidence that altered many a police investigation.

When Joseph B. Elwell, a famous bridge expert, was found slain in his West 70th Street apartment, the death was described as a suicide until Dr. Norris ordered a detailed study of the body at the morgue. He then determined that Elwell had been shot by a revolver held directly in front of his forehead, in a position that would have made it impossible for the victim to have pulled the trigger. In the Dot King murder case a few years later, Dr. Norris not only deduced the cause of death as chloroform asphyxiation but also supplied police with the information that whoever had applied the chloroform had exceptional strength and that "the position of the body suggests that a hammerlock hold had been applied."

Both the Elwell and King murders remained unsolved. But in hundreds of other homicides Dr. Norris gave expert testimony that resulted in guilty verdicts.

In a number of other cases, he saved innocent men. In 1919 Mrs. Bessie Troy was found dead on the sidewalk in front of her apartment on Amersterdam Avenue. Her husband, Michael, was charged with murder on the complaint of Bessie's relatives that he had flung the body from a window to cover up her killing. Dr. Norris was able to testify that the woman had been alive when her body hit the pavement, and her husband went free.

In an even more bizarre case, in 1926, a policeman on patrol along the waterfront noticed a man carrying a heavy bundle, which he flung into New York Bay. The officer stopped the man, who insisted the bundle had contained only old clothes, but the officer had the bundle fished from the water. It contained parts of a woman's body. The man, Francisco Trapia, was taken back to his flat, where the rest of the body was found. Trapia immediately confessed that he had killed the woman after a long drinking bout. By the time Dr. Norris arrived, he had been taken away.

"No doubt about this one, is there, Doc?" an officer greeted the medical examiner.

Dr. Norris viewed the scene with an experienced eye, observed the cherry-red color of the remaining torso and agreed, "No doubt at all," he said, "But it isn't murder, you know."

Dr. Norris quickly determined that death had resulted from

carbon monoxide poisoning caused by fumes from a faulty kitchen stove in the one-room flat. As Norris reconstructed the events, Trapia awakened from a drunken sleep (before he too was killed) and found the woman's body. He remembered slapping her about and assumed he had killed her. He then decided to get rid of the body.

It was one of the few cases in which the police took a case to court in opposition to the medical examiner. They had, they felt, a perfect case, complete with a confession. However, based on Dr. Norris' testimony, the defendant was cleared, or at least almost. He was charged and convicted of transporting a body through the public streets without a license.

A volatile individual, Dr. Norris zealously guarded his domain from political encroachments. He announced his resignation on a number of occasions, the last time in 1932, when Acting Mayor Joseph V. McKee ordered a 20 percent cut in his office's budget. Public outrage mounted, Mayor McKee retreated and Dr. Norris returned. He died in 1935 at the age of 67 while still in office.

NORTH, John (?-1835): Alleged Vicksburg insurrection leader

Although John North may never have planned the capture and sacking of Vicksburg, Miss. in 1835, he was definitely caught up in the hysteria over a plot that year by John A. Murrel to combine a slave uprising with the takeover by lawless elements of several Southern cities. North would have been the logical man to handle such a plot in Vicksburg, being the big man of the Landing, the pesthole that held most of the city's large criminal element. North ran a dishonest gambling house and saloon-brothel in the Landing area and controlled many criminal endeavors. Word got out that on July 6, 1835 he was going to unleash a large army of thieves and gamblers to loot the city. Whether the rumor was true or false, vigilantes struck first and routed the criminals of the Landing. Whether they really broke up a budding revolt or simply got rid of a festering criminal mob is debatable, but in any event, they hanged undesirables by the dozen. North fled but was captured the next day and hanged on a hill above the city, with most of the citizens in attendance. His body was left hanging with a "fixed" roulette wheel tied to it, an indication that dishonest gambling may well have been just as much cause for capital punishment as leading an insurrection.

See also: *John Murrel, Vicksburg "Volunteers."*

NORTHFIELD, Minnesota, Bank Raid: James gang's downfall

The 20-minute raid on the First National Bank of Northfield, Minn. on the afternoon of September 7, 1876 marked the virtual end of the James brothers' gang. Ironically, the gang had originally intended to hold up the First National Bank at Mankato, Minn., but street repairs outside the bank had caused a last-minute change in plans.

Riding south, the eight members of the gang—Jesse and Frank James; Cole, Jim and Bob Younger; Charlie Pitts, Clell Miller and 19-year-old Bill Chadwell—stormed into Northfield, never expecting to find strong resistance from honest citizens who were not awed by the "greatest revolver fighters in the West." Inside the bank, cashier Joseph Heywood insisted that the safe could not be opened because of a time lock. Jesse accused him of lying and pistol-whipped him to the floor. Then one of the clerks made a mad dash out the back door, escaping with a wound in his arm from a bullet fired by Pitts.

That shot alerted the citizenry. Rather untypical for a Western town of the era, Northfield had a limited number of firearms. A citizen named Elias Stacy, grabbed a shotgun loaded with only bird shot and blasted one of the lookouts, Miller, off his horse. His face bloodied, Miller remounted and charged at Stacey. Meanwhile, a medical student on vacation from the University of Michigan, Henry Wheeler, had located a carbine and taken a position in a second-floor window of the Dampier Hotel. When he saw Miller trying to ride Stacy down, he shot him out of the saddle, this time fatally.

Inside the bank the bandits prepared to flee, but on the way out, Jesse James paused long enough to place his revolver to the temple of cashier Heywood and blow his brains out. Amidst chaos and gunsmoke the desperadoes fought their way out of town, but not before young Chadwell was shot through the heart by the town's hardware merchant, A. E. Manning. Manning also hit Cole Younger in the shoulder and Bob Younger in the thigh.

As the gang thundered out of town, Bob Younger's horse was shot dead, leaving the dismounted outlaw screaming: "Hold on, don't leave me! I'm shot." Cole Younger wheeled his horse and reached Bob just as the latter had his left elbow shattered by a load of buckshot. Cole pulled his brother up on his mount and raced to catch up with the rest of the fleeing bandits. Following in their heels, citizens who lacked firearms threw rocks at the raiders.

Only two of the gang had been killed but the battle was not over. Aroused posses were formed throughout the state, and the route the bandits were traveling was reported by telegraph. Somewhere along the getaway trail, the James brothers split off from the Youngers and Charlie Pitts. Some of the friendlier Jesse James historians claim this was a deliberate tactic to split the pursuers, but it is more likely that Jesse and the slightly wounded Frank James resented the fact that the badly bleeding Youngers were slowing the flight. Jesse supposedly made a remark about "finishing off" the seriously injured but was faced down by the Youngers and Pitts.

A few days after the split, the Younger group was cornered in a thicket of willows and plum trees. In the ensuing battle Pitts was killed and the three Youngers all received multiple bullet wounds. Finally, only Jim Younger, with five wounds, remained standing, and he cried out: "The boys are all shot to pieces. For God's sake, don't kill me!"

The brothers were taken into custody and felt certain they would all be lynched. They weren't and seemed almost relieved when sentenced to life in the state prison.

Jesse and Frank made good their escape but the James gang

The disastrous bank raid in Northfield, Minn., as depicted in a contemporary print, marked the destruction of the James-Younger gang, although Jesse James stayed alive and free for another six years.

was finished. Thereafter, Jesse formed a second gang but was forced to accept such unreliables as Bob and Charlie Ford, who later killed him. The new gang did pull off a few more train robberies but the glory years were over. For the next six years their main accomplishment was evading capture, a feat they admittedly carried out with considerable flamboyance, adding greatly to the James brothers' legend. However, the disastrous Northfield bank raid remained proof that their day had ended.

See also: *James Brothers, Younger Brothers.*

NOTCHED Weapons

Western gunmen supposedly notched their six-guns after each killing, but actually very few of them ever did. Openly advertising their criminal record would have served only to attract the attention of the law or vigilantes. Many guns, however, were notched after a gunfighter's death to enhance his reputation. One celebrated fake is a Colt .45 initialed "W. B.," which allegedly belonged to Billy the Kid. Bat Masterson, among others, did a thriving business in notched guns, selling them to admirers even after he came to New York to finish out his days as a sports writer for a newspaper. He combed hock shops for suitable guns on which to carve 20 or more notches. Today, there are scores of collectors who own a notched six-gun "belonging to Bat Masterson."

One true tale of a notched weapon concerns the legendary turn-of-the-century New York City gangster Monk Eastman, who began his career as a bouncer in an East Side dance hall. Eastman enforced the peace with a huge bludgeon and he proudly notched it every time he laid open the skull of a rowdy customer. One evening Eastman approached a quiet little man drinking a beer at the bar and cracked him over the head. As they carried the man out, Eastman was asked why he had made the unprovoked attack; he replied, "Well, I had forty-nine nicks in me stick, an' I wanted to make it an even fifty."

NUMBERS Racket

The numbers game remains without doubt the biggest and most profitable racket of all. It is estimated that at least 20 million people a day engage in this illegal activity and that the total annual take is in the billions, with organized crime reaping a quarter billion in profits in New York City alone. The numbers game is not an American invention, having been played, in one form or another, in England since the 18th century. So-called policy shops, where people went to play the numbers, showed up in the United States in the 1880s. One New York operator, Al Adams, had about 1,000 policy shops in the city, and his bribery payments to Boss Tweed's Tammany Hall were said to be enormous. With his protection thus assured, Adams not only ran the game but rigged the results as well. After he finally went to prison following the removal of Tweed by a reform movement, the winning numbers were most often based on Treasury Department figures, released daily by telegraph, offering players the assurance that the results could not be fixed.

The term "policy" derived from the penny insurance that was then highly popular—both were a cheap gamble on the future. Each day the winning number was a three-digit figure and a bettor was allowed to pick any three numbers from 000 to 999. The payoff usually was based on odds of 600 to one. Since the mathematical odds against winning were 1,000 to one, the operator's potential profit margin was far higher than in any other gambling venture.

Over the years this huge cut has allowed numbers operations to support an entire bureaucracy, from the "banker" on top down through operators, distributors, agents and runners. Only the bottom two rungs face any risk of arrest, and even then it is the duty of the higher-ups to see that underlings are immediately bailed out, that the fix is put in to prevent convictions and, at worst, that the families of those sent to prison are provided for.

Because numbers could be played for as little as a nickel (and in some places a penny), the game naturally was embraced by the poor. From the turn of the century on, New York's Harlem has been the most lucrative area for the numbers racket. One Harlem operator, Madam St. Clair, offered a policy wheel that allegedly also provided a magical potency to the players. After it became known that the racket had made her a millionaire, she required several bodyguards.

Prohibition beer boss Dutch Schultz was responsible for organized crime's takeover of the numbers racket. He moved into Harlem, which then had some 30 competing policy banks, with his accustomed fierceness, terrorizing individual bankers into paying him protection and then simply announcing he was assuming control of their business. After Schultz was murdered on orders from a new crime syndicate formed by Lucky Luciano and Meyer Lansky, the numbers racket was run by Vito Genovese, Luciano's aide.

So lucrative has the numbers racket been that probably as many murders can be laid to conflicts generated by it as can be attributed to the old bootleg wars. Numbers money is most likely still the greatest source of illegal payoffs to the police and politicians in most parts of the country.

Today, the numbers racket is undergoing an ethnic revolution. Using increasing force, black racketeers have pushed the Mafia out of numbers operations in New York's Harlem and Brownsville sections and several similar ghettos around the country.

See also: *Albert J. Adams, Otto "Abbadabba" Berman.*

O

O'BANION, Charles Dion "Deanie" (1892-1924): Gang leader

Of all the Prohibition-era Chicago gangsters, Dion O'Banion is credited with the greatest number of remarkable traits. Indeed, he may have been the most pious killer in that city of gangsters, carrying his rosary with him on murder assignments. He was a cheerful swashbuckler who was never without a carnation in his buttonhole and three pistols tucked away in special pockets of his expensive made-to-order suits. Although labeled by Chief of Police Morgan Collins as "Chicago's arch-criminal" and declared the murderer of at least 25 men, a figure that may have been underestimated by 35 more, O'Banion, at the pinnacle of his power, was celebrated by the Democrats, who reveled in his ability to get out votes until he switched to the Republicans for more money. A contemporary joke asked, "Who'll carry the Forty-second and Forty-third wards?" The answer was, "O'Banion, in his pistol pocket."

The more cynical members of the city's press corps saw O'Banion as a man of humor. One of his funnier stunts, at least from Dion's viewpoint, was his shotgun challenge. The gangster would fill a shotgun with hard-packed clay and then wager an unsuspecting victim that he could not hit the side of a barn some 30 feet away. Naturally, the challenge would be accepted and O'Banion would load the weapon, hand the gun to the sucker and move far away. When the man pulled the trigger, the backfire would cause him to lose an arm or an eye or perhaps most of his face. The gang boss would still be laughing about it the next day.

O'Banion, the son of a Chicago plasterer, grew up in a section of Chicago's North Side known as Little Hell. He was an altar boy and a choir boy at Holy Name Cathedral, but outside the church he learned the law of the street jungle in a tenement district jammed with unruly saloons and whorehouses. Thanks to his voice, trained in church, he launched on a career as a singing waiter in a number of tough dives, including McGovern's Cabaret at Clark and Erie. While bringing tears

Dion O'Banion and his bride on their wedding day. Deanie was a devoted husband and churchgoer as well as a bootlegger and murderer.

to the customers' eyes with sentimental ballads of the old country, he would pick their pockets. After hours, young Deanie was a street mugger. While pursuing this trade one night, the 16-year-old met a youthful Lou Greenberg, who was destined to become the multimillionaire owner of the Seneca Hotel on Chicago's Gold Coast, when both sprang out of the shadows to crack the skull of the same victim. A moment of suspense followed as each of the attackers tried to decide who would get the proceeds of the mugging. With the wisdom of Solomon, they divided the loot evenly and formed an alliance for the rest of the night, sharing the revenues from additional skull rappings of unsuspecting revelers.

The O'Banion-Greenberg combine continued for several months until Deanie was convicted of robbery in 1909 and was sent to Bridewell Prison for three months. In 1911 Deanie was arrested for carrying concealed weapons (a set of brass knuckles, a revolver, a sheath knife and a leather blackjack) and sent away for another three months. It was the last sentence O'Banion ever served, although he was arrested often thereafter. He learned how to work the fix, Chicago style, and spent the required funds to pay off police officers, prosecutors and judges.

Quickly, O'Banion progressed from street mugging and robbery to slugging newspaper dealers for Maxie Annenberg, Moe Annenberg's brother, when Maxie was circulation manager for the *Chicago Tribune*. After learning the techniques of this brutal trade, O'Banion abandoned the *Tribune* for a higher-paying position with the Hearst papers. At the same time, he became adept at safecracking, picking up that art from the top man of the era, Charlie "the Ox" Reiser. He got caught cracking safes a few times, but he was so prized by his newspaper employers that on at least one occasion an executive of Hearst's *American* put up $5,000 bail to secure his release on a safe-cracking charge.

By the time Prohibition arrived, O'Banion had formed an impressive gang on the North Side, including such stalwarts as Bugs Moran, Frank Gusenberg, Two-Gun Louis Alterie, Dapper Dan McCarthy, Hymie Weiss and Schemer Drucci (the only Italian O'Banion ever liked and vice versa). The O'Banions, who were primarily Irish, ran the 42nd Ward and soon formed an alliance with the Jewish gangsters of the old 20th Ward, especially those attached to Nails Morton. Morton's demise in a riding accident resulted in the O'Banions' execution of the horse that had thrown him.

Seeing the profits Prohibition promised even before the law went into effect, O'Banion began hijacking booze while its distribution and sale was still legal. At first, O'Banion saw no great economic rewards in making his own booze. "Let Johnny Torrio make the stuff," he was quoted. "I'll steal what I want of it." However, as soon as he realized that thievery would never be enough to take care of the demand in the North Side, he started buying up some of the area's best breweries and distilleries.

As O'Banion started making his own liquor instead of stealing Torrio's, a major irritant between the North Siders and the Torrio-Capone mob was removed. As aggressively as the Italian gangsters sought to take over Prohibition rackets in Chicago and much of the surrounding suburbs, they were very content not to tangle with the North Siders, who were known, justifiably, as fierce killers. O'Banion could have continued operating in peace, even though his refusal to allow any bordellos on the North Side angered the Torrio-Capone combine and cut the Chicago underworld's revenues by millions of dollars annually. O'Banion was too pious to allow the sale of bodies,

although he had no qualms about filling them with bullets.

While he tolerated a wide variety of other ethnics within his own gang, O'Banion bore an unabiding hatred for Sicilians. He robbed and murdered bootleg liquor deliverers employed by the Terrible Gennas, a brutal family of Sicilians who organized moonshining as a cottage industry in Little Italy and worked closely with Torrio. O'Banion listened to and often agreed with Torrio's appeals for peace and tranquility to allow all elements of the underworld to make their profits without harassment, only to resume hijacking the supplies of the other gangs almost immediately thereafter.

The final affront to the Torrio-Capone forces came when O'Banion, announcing his retirement from the rackets, sold an illegal brewery to Torrio for $500,000. Literally just minutes after the transaction was completed, federal agents swooped down on the brewery, closed it and seized Torrio for violation of Prohibition laws. Torrio, who later received a nine-month sentence, was out the $500,000, which O'Banion refused to return even after it was learned that he had received advance warning of the raid. When Hymie Weiss advised O'Banion to make peace with Torrio and Capone and the Gennas, O'Banion, with huge contempt, rejoined, "Oh, to hell with them Sicilians."

The phrase made war inevitable, although Mike Merlo, an important Italian political figure and head of Unione Siciliana, prevailed for a time in his efforts to achieve a peaceful solution. However, when Merlo died a natural death on November 8, 1924, no one else was capable of maintaining peace among the various factions—the Italians, the Jews, the Irish, the Poles, the Greeks, the blacks—reaping profits from Prohibition. O'Banion did not understand how rapidly his opponents would strike.

Deanie ran a florist shop on North State Street, directly opposite the cathedral where he had once been an altar boy as well as a choir boy, partly because he wanted a legitimate front and partly because he genuinely loved flowers and found he could make a small fortune supplying them for many gangland funerals.

Merlo's death supposedly cast a pall over underworld activities and O'Banion busied himself supplying wreaths for the funeral, some of his creations selling for hundreds or thousands of dollars. On the night of November 9, O'Banion received a telephone order to prepare a special wreath for the following morning. The next morning three men, all apparently unknown to O'Banion, entered the flower shop. "Hello, boys," Deanie said. "You from Mike Merlo's?"

The man in the middle, decked out in an expensive overcoat and fedora, nodded and grasped O'Banion's hand in a firm handshake, so firm that O'Banion could not pull free. Immediately, the man's two companions pulled out pistols and pumped several bullets into the Irish gangster. The last shot, through the left cheek, was fatal. O'Banion was given one of the grandest underworld funerals in Chicago's history.

The O'Banion murder was never officially solved, although the killers were identified as two Capone gunmen named Albert Anselmi and John Scalise and the man with the firm handshake as Frankie Yale, imported specially for the job by Torrio and Capone.

The Torrio-Capone combine fought many bloody battles with the remaining O'Banions until the new leaders, first Weiss and then Drucci, came to violent ends. However, in the process Johnny Torrio was badly wounded and retired back to Brooklyn. The O'Banion gang's last leader, Bugs Moran, saw his power broken by the Capone-ordered St. Valentine's Day Massacre in 1929. The North Siders were finished and Chicago belonged to Big Al.

The O'Banion assassination marked the beginning of the great Chicago gang wars of the 1920s and led to the eventual dominance of the Windy City by Al Capone. But the real importance of O'Banion's death was that it and the resulting battles came to be viewed by the Chicago underworld as senseless bloodletting which prevented the formation of a national crime syndicate in which all factions—Italians, Irish, Jews—could achieve enormous profits.

See also: *Louis "Two Gun" Alterie, Anselmi and Scalise, Alphonse "Scarface Al" Capone, Vincent "Schemer" Drucci, George "Bugs" Moran, Samuel J. "Nails" Morton, Charles "the Ox" Reiser, John Torrio, Hymie Weiss.*

OBERHOLTZER, Madge (1897-1925): Murder victim

While the death of 28-year-old Madge Oberholtzer was billed in the newspapers as the KKK's sex scandal murder, its real significance was that it resulted in a landmark legal decision which ruled the defendant was guilty of murder even though his victim had died as the result of a suicide attempt.

Thirty-four-year-old David Curtis Stephenson was a maverick member of the Ku Klux Klan who rose to Grand Dragon of the Realm of Indiana. He feuded with the Klan's Imperial Wizard, Hiram Evans, and led his group out of the national organization. Stephenson was accused of skimming off a portion of membership fees collected from 300,000 Klansmen and of immoral behavior.

On March 15, 1924 he and two other men kidnapped 28-year-old Madge Oberholtzer of Indianapolis, drove her to a railroad station and put her in a private berth aboard a train, where Stephenson, who had been sexually attracted to the woman for some time, stripped, beat and raped her.

The three men and their captive left the train at Hamilton, Ind. and registered at a hotel. Because she was in severe pain, Oberholtzer got one of the men to let her buy some medication in a drug store. She then swallowed six bichloride of mercury tablets in an attempt to commit suicide. On March 17 the kidnappers brought their victim, now extremely ill, back to her parents' home. They explained her bruises by saying she had been involved in a car accident. Oberholtzer recovered from her wounds but died the following year from the effects of the poison she had swallowed.

Stephenson and his two accomplices were charged with murder, although the woman had clearly died as a result of her own suicide attempt. The prosecutor, however, argued that by

their acts "D. C. Stephenson and his cohorts became murderers just the same as if they plunged a dagger into her throbbing heart." Stephenson's accomplices went free but the KKK leader was sentenced to life imprisonment, his unusual conviction upheld by higher courts.

O'BRIEN, John Patrick (1873-1951): New York mayor

In 1932 John P. O'Brien became a one-year mayor of New York City, having succeeded Jimmy Walker, who resigned in disgrace. O'Brien was another of the corrupt pre-La Guardia chief executives who took orders from Tammany leaders like James J. Hines and Albert Marinelli, who in turn got their orders from Prohibition gangsters. Thus, when the new mayor was asked who his new police commissioner would be, he said, "I haven't had any word on that yet."

In 1933 O'Brien was succeeded in office by Fiorello La Guardia and underworld payoffs to City Hall and to the police commissioner's office ceased, with "business as usual" not returning until the corrupt administration of William O'Dwyer in 1945.

O'CONNOR, "Terrible Tommy" (1886-?): Escaped murderer

Although the electric chair became the mode of execution in Illinois in 1928, the scaffold it replaced remains stored in a basement room of the Chicago Criminal Courts Building, available for a final hanging should an escaped murderer ever be caught. His name is Terrible Tommy O'Connor, a convicted murderer who in 1921 escaped custody just four days before his scheduled execution by feigning illness and, while being taken to the prison medical office, pulling a gun that apparently had been smuggled to him. Since then the authorities have been required by a court order to retain the gallows until the gangster's fate has been definitely determined.

For a time after his escape Terrible Tommy probably received more newspaper coverage than any other gangster except Al Capone. Speeches bemoaning his escape were made in the U.S. Senate and there were serious proposals that the Army be used to hunt him down, but despite the uproar, Tommy was never caught. Through the years newspapers have run feature stories on the manhunt and on the rope that still awaits O'Connor. If he is still alive and if he is ever caught, Terrible Tommy's advanced age (he would be in his nineties) and the Supreme Court's ban on executions ordered before 1972 make his hanging rather unlikely.

According to a stipulation made by the Illinois legislature at the time the electric chair was adopted, the gallows will one day be removed from its storage room and set up in the galleries of the Chicago Historical Society. But before it can become an exhibit of grim things long past, the death of Terrible Tommy must be a certainty. The law remains bound to enforce the court's sentence: "You shall hang by the neck until you are dead."

O'CONNOR'S Gunners: Police machine gunners

In 1927, when Chicago gang killings were at their peak, the new chief of detectives, William O'Connor, felt obliged to offer some measure of reassurance to the public; so he announced the formation of an armored car force to do battle with gangsters. He recruited volunteers from the ranks of policemen who had seen action during the war and could handle machine guns.

His orders to the squad—probably the height of irresponsibility even for those zany times were:

> Men, the war is on. We've got to show that society and the police department, and not a bunch of dirty rats, are running this town. It is the wish of the people of Chicago that you hunt these criminals down and kill them without mercy. Your cars are equipped with machine guns and you will meet the enemies of society on equal terms. See to it that they don't have you pushing up daisies. Make them push up daisies. Shoot first and shoot to kill. If you kill a notorious feudist, you will get a handsome reward and win promotion. If you meet a car containing bandits, pursue them and fire. When I arrive on the scene, my hopes will be fulfilled if you have shot off the top of their car and killed every criminal inside it.

Some observers wondered about the possibility that O'Connor's Gunners, as they were called, might kill some innocent bystanders. It proved to be a groundless fear, as did any fears among gangsters; the Gunners were seldom in the right place at the right time.

OCUISH, Hannah (1864-1876): America's youngest execution victim

Because records on criminal matters prior to the 20th century were not adequately kept, it is difficult to determine with certainty the youngest person ever executed in America. But it may well have been Hannah Ocuish, a 12-year-old girl with Indian blood who was tried in 1876 for murder in New London, Conn. and sentenced to death.

The girl, living on her own after having been long abandoned by her parents, was apprehended for killing six-year-old Eunice Bolles after the younger child had accused her of stealing strawberries. Despite a defense based on her tender age, Hannah was quickly convicted and hanged on December 20, 1786. A reporter on the scene noted "she said very little and appeared greatly afraid and seemed to want somebody to help her."

O'FOLLIARD, Tom (1859-1880): Accomplice of Billy the Kid

Like Charlie Bowdre, Tom O'Folliard is more famous for the company he kept both before and after death than he is for his crimes. O'Folliard is buried along with Bowdre and Billy the Kid in a fenced-in grave at old Fort Sumner, New Mexico Territory under a granite marker inscribed, "PALS."

O'Folliard, born in Uvalde, Tex. in 1859 and orphaned the following year when both his parents died of smallpox, was raised in a number of foster homes. At the age of 17 he went off on his own to New Mexico. Early in 1878 O'Folliard met up with Billy the Kid and from then until his death he faithfully followed the Kid.

O'Folliard may have been as accomplished a killer as Billy the Kid. He and the Kid took part in innumerable gunfights after which it had been impossible to determine whose bullet had killed whom. O'Folliard was a member of the ambush committee that gunned down Sheriff William Brady, the Sheriff of Lincoln County, N.M. on April 1, 1878; although Billy the Kid was officially charged with the crime the fatal bullet could have been O'Folliard's.

O'Folliard was so closely identified with Billy's saga that he was to share his young mentor's fate, being shot in the dark by the crafty lawman Pat Garrett. Garrett had laid plans to ambush Billy the Kid one night in December 1880, when the Kid would be leading his outlaw band. At the last moment, the Kid dropped off from the lead position and ordered O'Folliard to take his place while he went for a chew of tobacco. Garrett and his men opened up on O'Folliard, sure they were aiming at Billy the Kid. After a murderous volley O'Folliard lay dead in the winter snow. The Kid outlived his follower by a mere seven months. Then he too was killed in the dark by Garrett.

See also: *Billy the Kid, Charlie Bowdre.*

OHIO Gang: Harding Administration grafters

Without doubt, the so-called Ohio Gang, a group of political cronies from Ohio who put Warren G. Harding in politics and eventually in the White House, took more from the public coffers in their two-year and five-month stay in Washington than any other corrupt group in American history. Including Teapot Dome, their total depredations have been estimated to total as much as $300 million, or five to 10 times what the Tweed Ring made off with.

The unofficial head of the Ohio Gang was President Harding's attorney general Harry M. Daugherty, who had guided Harding's political career from 1900 until his triumphant arrival in Washington in 1921. The Ohio Gang, as the group was soon labeled, let it be known that they had come to Washington for only one reason, to make money. A price tag was placed on everything they controlled. Judgeships, lucrative Prohibition-agent jobs, public lands and oil reserves were all up for sale. Bribes and payoffs were made at the House on 16th Street. The Little Green House on H Street featured poker games, bathtub gin and women to convince the dubious to join the graft game.

Daugherty and his Ohio henchman, Jess Smith, are believed to have a hand in every payment of graft, and there is little doubt that Harding knew much and suspected more. "My God," he told William Allen White, "this is a hell of a job. I have no trouble with my enemies. I can take care of them all right. But my damn friends, White, they're the ones that keep me walking the floor nights."

Harding didn't really spend much time walking the floors; he sat in on the poker games. Actually, the President didn't know how to control Daugherty and was a little afraid of him. Daugherty knew of Harding's illegitimate child and he had also advanced him $100,000, which he dropped in the stock market. As the stocks dipped, Daugherty's hold on Harding tightened.

The Ohio Gang's plundering was so massive that scandals started to break even before Harding died in 1923. There were rumors of frauds in the Veterans Bureau running as high as $200 million. Eventually, Colonel Charles R. Forbes was sent to prison for taking kickbacks from contractors building veterans hospitals. Jess Smith, the Ohio Gang's bagman, killed himself and the newspapers speculated whether it was because of pangs of conscience or whether he had been murdered to ensure his silence. Albert B. Fall, Harding's secretary of the interior, served his time for his part in the Teapot Dome Scandal along with oil man Harry Sinclair. Harry Daugherty narrowly escaped conviction in a bribery complicated case involving the alien property custodian. In the final analysis, the Ohio Gang could not have functioned if Harding had been a strong president, but Daugherty probably would not have promoted him if he had possessed that potential. As Sen. Frank Brandegee of Connecticut said at the time of his nomination, Harding was "no world-beater but he is the best of the second-raters."

See also: *William J. Burns, Albert Bacon Fall, Teapot Dome.*

OHIO State Penitentiary Fire

The most tragic fire in American penal history occurred at the Ohio State Penitentiary in Columbus on April 21, 1930.

The ancient, fortress-like institution was situated in the downtown area and was vastly overcrowded, holding 4,300 convicts in accommodations originally designed for 1,500. Coping with this situation and a recent rash of escapes had made the administration and guards extremely edgy. Recognizing that such conditions could not continue, the state had begun construction to expand the facility, which left many of the cell blocks filled with scaffolding and littered with piles of tar paper and wood scraps. After the prisoners had returned to their cells following the evening meal, flames suddenly spouted from the construction rubble and flashed up the scaffolding. Within seconds the top two tiers of the six-tier cell block were enveloped in fire and smoke.

Dumbfounded by the conflagration and somewhat suspicious that it was part of a planned breakout, the guards failed to open the cell doors. The warden, Preston Thomas, shared their suspicion and his first call for help did not go to the fire department but to the National Guard, whose aid he requested to help contain the prisoners. Were it not for a passerby outside the prison who sounded the alarm, there is no telling when the fire department would have been called.

Finally, faced with a fire of frightening proportions, the warden ordered the cell doors opened, but the intense heat warped the locks and the keys would not open them, leaving the prisoners trapped in their cages. Finally, one convict managed to force his door open and, seizing a sledge hammer, started smashing other cell doors open. Some 135 prisoners were freed in this manner before the flaming roof crumbled. A total of 320 men were burned alive.

In the prison yard guardsmen with drawn bayonets broke the freed prisoners into small groups that could be watched easily. Meanwhile, a new panic developed outside the prison walls, as those prisoners' relatives who lived in Columbus attempted to storm the jail to save the threatened men. Soldiers had to be sent to all entrances to keep people from breaking into the prison. If authorities did a poor job saving lives, they did an excellent one maintaining security. Only one prisoner escaped; after obtaining some civilian clothes, he managed to walk off with some onlookers. Three and a half hours after the fire started, it was brought under control.

The public uproar over the tragedy continued for many months. It was found that the prison guards had not been trained to handle such emergencies—at all. Not a single fire drill had been held, and scores of fire regulations had simply been ignored. There were a number of cries for the dismissal of Warden Thomas, but in the end, no action was taken. The warden and his superiors insisted the fire had been started by the prisoners, but evidence indicated the real cause had been an electrical short circuit.

O.K. Corral: Famous gunfight scene

There have probably been more exaggerations and lies told about the gunfight at the O.K. Corral in Tombstone, Arizona Territory on October 26, 1881 than about any other shoot-out in the history of the West. Undoubtedly, the biggest lie of all was that the Earps—Wyatt, Virgil and Morgan—and Doc Holliday were heroes of the day in some sort of "moment of truth." Anti-Earp observers, then and now, have regarded the shootings at the O.K. Corral as outright murder, and one has to conclude that what happened was indeed more homicidal than heroic. Popular versions of the event often put guns in the hands of men who more than likely had none and insist that some men fired their guns before they themselves were hit when in fact they had never drawn them.

The gunfight was in part an outgrowth of a long-smoldering feud between the Clanton gang and what should be called the Earp gang, the same bunch that the citizens of Dodge City referred to as the Fighting Pimps. The out-country Clanton cowboys were not welcome in Tombstone except to be taken in the gambling joints and whorehouses either run or protected by the Earp crowd.

In previous months tensions had increased as more and more people in the town started to suspect that the Earps and Holliday, despite Virgil's position as town marshal, were behind a series of stage robberies and other crimes. Holliday had actually been indicted for a particularly vicious Wells Fargo stage robbery in which two men had been killed, but he was released for lack of evidence. Wyatt Earp saw in that robbery an opportunity to be elected sheriff of Cochise County—the region's prime graft position—if he could pin the charges on others and, in the process, clear Holliday of suspicion.

It was this motivation, rather than alleged desire to clean up a rash of livestock rustling, in which the Clantons were clearly involved, that led directly to the confrontation at the O.K. Corral. One man had been captured and charged with the stage robbery but he had escaped under unusual and suspicious circumstances. The Earp brothers declared three known outlaws were responsible for the crime and, thereafter, conducted an intensive hunt for them. After failing to find the three, Wyatt went to Ike Clanton, the most important of the clan, and offered to give him the $6,000 reward money posted by Wells Fargo in return for his help in capturing the outlaws. All Earp wanted was the credit.

A deal was apparently struck whereby Clanton was to betray the hunted men, but it collapsed when the three outlaws were killed, one ambushed along with Ike's father while on a cattle-rustling foray into Mexico and the other two during an attempted store robbery in New Mexico. Now, the secret negotiations between Wyatt and Ike posed a danger to both of them. Wyatt attempted to extricate himself by having acquaintances spread the story that Ike had tried to sell out his friends; Ike charged Wyatt with fabricating and circulating the story and vowed vengeance.

What followed were a number of clashes and near gun battles involving adherents of both factions until the morning of October 26, when the Earps "buffaloed," i.e., pistol-whipped the heads of, both Ike Clanton and Tom McLowery, a member of the Clanton gang. Clanton was then hauled into court, had his weapons confiscated and was fined $25.

The stage was thus set for further violence. In court Morgan Earp had taunted Ike Clanton, offering to pay his fine if Ike would agree to fight him. The reason was obvious. Few of the Clantons or their associates were considered adept in the use of handguns, while certainly all the Earps and Holliday were.

Thus, on October 26, having learned that Ike Clanton and Tom McLowery were rendezvousing near the O.K. Corral with Billy Clanton, Ike's younger brother; Frank McLowery, Tom's older brother; and Billy Claiborne, another Clanton gunman, the three Earps and Holliday came hunting for them, determined to disarm them because, they claimed, the Clantons wanted to kill them. On their way to Fremont Street, where the corral was situated, Virgil Earp deputized Holliday, thus making the shotgun he carried beneath his white duster a legal weapon. The four men ignored the pleas of Sheriff John Behan, who was friendly with the Clantons, to stop and allow him to get the Clantons' guns and persuade them to leave town.

The gunfight, or slaughter, lasted a mere 30 seconds. It started with Virgil Earp's somewhat confused command to the Clantons: "Give up your arms or throw up your arms!"

In answer, Billy Clanton and Frank McLowery touched their weapons but did not draw. "Hold," Virgil cried, "I don't mean that. I have come to disarm you."

At that moment Tom McLowery threw open his vest and declared: "I have nothing." Pro-Earp historians later insisted Tom really had a gun concealed on his person, but if he had, he never shot any of his enemies with it. The best evidence indicates that he and Ike Clanton, as Ike claimed, had no weapons.

In any event, the shooting started, although who shot first is another matter of dispute. Some say Billy Clanton drew and fired at Wyatt Earp first. If so, it was a remarkable feat by the youth, outdrawing the great Earp. And if he did shoot, he missed. More likely, Wyatt drew first and, ignoring Billy Clanton, who was a mere six to eight feet from him, fired at Frank McLowery, considered to be the only adequate gunslinger among the Clantons. Earp's shot hit McLowery in the stomach and he staggered toward the street with his gun still holstered.

At this point, Billy Clanton was definitely shooting at and definitely missing Wyatt. Meanwhile, Tom McLowery, seeing his brother hit, took cover behind Frank's horse. Billy Claiborne, who was farthest from the action, kept it that way by dashing to the safety of Fly's Photograph Studio after firing off a few shots into the street. Indeed, many historians consider Claiborne's activities so peripheral they do not include him in their description of the gunfight.

The second man to go down was Billy Clanton, shot by Morgan Earp, first in the right wrist and then in the chest. He hit a wall and slid slowly to the ground but, in the process, managed to shift his pistol to his left hand. Half-lying, half-sitting, he rested the gun barrel across his arm and kept shooting. Meanwhile, Ike Clanton grabbed Wyatt Earp's arm and tried to wrestle away his weapon. Wyatt shoved him aside and said, "Go to fighting or get away," a fair enough challenge if Ike had been armed.

Ike took it as an invitation to race for Fly's, as Doc Holliday sent a shotgun blast after him. The shooting caused Frank McLowery's horse to shy and then burst out into the street, exposing Tom McLowery as he tried to get Frank's rifle out of the saddle scabbard. Holliday had missed Ike but he didn't miss Tom. Doc's buckshot ripped into Tom's chest, and he stumbled to the street and collapsed, dying.

Now, only Billy Clanton and Frank McLowery were left. Somehow the latter, despite his stomach wound, stood erect and as his horse rushed by, he attempted to pull his rifle out of its scabbard. But like his brother, he failed and finally drew his pistol. By this time Holliday was almost upon him, having discarded his shotgun in favor of a six-shooter. The two fired simultaneously and Holliday went down, hit in the hip. Morgan Earp then shot Frank just below the ear, finishing him off. At the same instant, Billy Clanton shot Virgil Earp in the leg and then turned his fire on Morgan Earp, hitting him in the shoulder.

Billy tried to rise to his feet but shots fired by Wyatt and the downed Morgan sent him crashing to the ground again. Even as he lay dying, he kept trying to cock his six-shooter. "Give me some more cartridges," Billy begged photographer Camillus Fly, who had rushed to the scene. Fly solemnly pulled the pistol from his weakening hold. Until he expired,

Billy kept pleading for one more shot at the Earps.

The gunfight was over, to be embellished by historians in succeeding decades. It did not enjoy so fine a reputation for gallantry at the time, however. In fact, the *Tombstone Epitaph,* the pro-Earp newspaper, reported the event on page three and devoted less than two full columns to it. The story failed to preempt the item in the opening column, which reminded the readers that the Knights of Pythias were meeting that night at 7:30 for regular drill, or such newsworthy notes as "Winter underwear, of every conceivable kind, at Glover's."

Clearly, the *Epitaph* played down "YESTERDAY'S TRAG-EDY" because it felt the Earps and Holliday could well face murder charges. Indeed, when the three corpses—the two McLowerys and Billy Clanton—were laid out at the undertaker's, a huge sign was placed over the caskets reading, "MUR-DERED IN THE STREETS OF TOMBSTONE."

Eventually, Wyatt Earp and Doc Holliday were brought up on murder charges, but they were cleared by a justice of the peace, ending the legal bickering. The shoot-out, however, did not help the Earps' standing in the community, which was already divided in its opinion of them. Virgil Earp was fired from his post and, in time, the Earps, after being subjected to a number of assassination attempts, one of which (against Morgan) was successful, finally pulled out—some would describe it as ran out—of Tombstone.

Nonetheless, the legend of the gunfight grew over the years, enhanced greatly by the colorful, if fanciful, 20th century writings of Walter Noble Burns and Stuart N. Lake, who elevated the killings into an epic moment of heroism in the history of the West.

See also: *John Behan, Buffaloing, Billy Claiborne, Joseph Isaac "Ike" Clanton, William "Billy" Clanton, Morgan Earp, Virgil W. Earp, Wyatt Earp, John Henry "Doc" Holliday, McLowery Brothers.*

O'KELLY, Edward (?-1904): Murderer of Bob Ford

Bob Ford, the "dirty rotten coward who shot Mr. Howard," i.e., Jesse James, outlived that noted outlaw by 10 years. In 1892 he was running a tent saloon in Creede, Colo. when, on the afternoon of June 8, a woman came into the tent collecting money to bury a local girl who had committed suicide. Ford donated $10. As the woman left, a man carrying a double-barreled shotgun stepped inside and let Ford have it with both barrels, killing him instantly. The murderer turned out to be Edward O'Kelly (sometimes listed as Edward O. Kelly), who was related by marriage to the Youngers and thus, in a way, kin to Jesse. Whether O'Kelly killed Ford to avenge his murder of Jesse is open to question. There was some talk that Ford had accused O'Kelly of stealing his diamond stickpin, but whatever the cause, O'Kelly killed the man who had killed Jesse James and was therefore a hero to some. He was sentenced to 20 years in the Colorado State Penitentiary. Because of his popularity, the sentence almost immediately was reduced to 18 years, and in 1894 he got a full pardon. In all, he

had served just two years for murdering Bob Ford. O'Kelly didn't seem to understand that killing Ford might be tolerated but committing other criminal acts would not be. He was shot dead by a police officer during a holdup in Oklahoma City in 1904.

See also: *Robert Newton Ford.*

OLD Brewery: Tenement of death

No other building in America, perhaps the world, had as many murders committed within its walls—a police estimated average of one killing a day for 15 years, or well over 5,000—as a 19th century New York tenement called the Old Brewery. Built in 1792 as Coulter's Brewery in the old Five Points section of lower Manhattan, it produced a beer famous throughout the Eastern states. Condemned for use as a brewery in 1837, it was transformed into a filthy tenement of 100 rooms, housing at least 1,000 persons. The building was five stories in height but only three floors had windows; many rooms had no windows and received neither sunlight nor fresh air. Some children born there literally did not see the outside world until their early teens.

In this nightmare existence, men, women and children committed murder and were, in turn, murdered, their bodies often left to rot or buried under the floors or in the walls. The occupants were divided about equally between blacks and immigrant Irish. All the basement rooms were occupied by blacks, many of whom had white wives, while the Irish tended to populate the upper floors. On the first floor was a large room called the Den of Thieves, where more than 75 men, women and children, black and white, lived without furnishings of any kind or any conveniences. Many of the women were prostitutes who entertained their customers there, at least the brave ones who risked entry.

Throughout the upper floors ran a long corridor, aptly called Murderers Alley, that led off to the individual rooms. In the 1850s, 26 people dwelled in one room no more than 15 feet square. In this room a little girl was once foolish enough to show a penny she had begged and was promptly stabbed to death, her body shoved in a corner for five days until her mother dug a shallow grave in which to bury her. In 1850 an investigator discovered not one of the occupants had been outside the room for a week, although some had stood in the doorway waiting to attack a more fortunate dweller passing through the alley with food.

Throughout the Old Brewery every imaginable criminal roamed—thieves, pickpockets, whores, murderers. Twenty-four hours a day there were fierce fistfights and drunken orgies; screams of luckless victims and cries of starving children; and men, women and even children writhing on the floor with delirium tremens.

While the police knew murder was common and that many wanted criminals hid out in the Old Brewery, they seldom entered its vile confines; when they did, they went in groups of 40 or 50. If only five or six policemen entered together, they knew they might never emerge alive. More than likely, they would be murdered and every stitch of clothing stripped from their bodies.

Just as the police could not enter safely in small groups, the building's residents could not leave safely in daylight hours, unless they took some underground tunnels that snaked out through the Five Points. So greatly were these residents hated and feared that a denizen leaving the Old Brewery in daylight would be pelted with brickbats thrown by pedestrians determined to drive him or her back inside. Many of the inhabitants of the Old Brewery had previously been persons of some importance. It was said that the last of the Blennerhassetts, the second son of Harman Blennerhassett, who had joined Aaron Burr in the great conspiracy to establish a Western dictatorship, vanished into the Old Brewery never to be seen again. He and other persons of some consequence soon sank to the level of the rest of the residents, living and dying amidst the violence, insanity and sexual promiscuity that were accepted facts of life within the Old Brewery.

Probably more murders were committed within the walls of the Old Brewery, a five-story tenement that had windows on only three floors, than in any other building in the United States.

Occasionally, missionaries tried to alter conditions in the Old Brewery, but being mostly Protestant, they were driven away by the Irish inhabitants who considered them heathens. Finally, the Missionary Society, with money from a fund drive headed by Daniel Drew, succeeded in buying the building for $16,000; the city contributed $1,000 towards the purchase. In December 1852 the society asked the police to drive the inhabitants out so that the building could be razed in preparation for the construction of a mission house. The police had to fight many battles at close quarters to clear out the residents and gangsters, and at least 20 wanted murderers fell into their net. Children, never having seen the light of day, blinked in terror when brought outside. As the building was ripped down, laborers carried out several sacks filled with human bones that they had found inside the walls, beneath the floorboards and in the cellars.

Although the destruction of such buildings was hardly a solution to the problem of city slums, the Old Brewery was beyond redemption.

See also: *Five Points*.

OLD Shakespeare (?-1891): Alleged American victim of Jack the Ripper

Incongruous though it may seem, the killing of an aged alcoholic prostitute in a run-down New York hotel became one of the 19th century's most-celebrated murders.

Old Shakespeare was an otherwise unidentified Bowery habitue who won her nickname for her ability to quote the bard once she had consumed sufficient drink. Whatever slight fame her literary knowledge had brought her was eclipsed by the notoriety over her violent end. On April 24, 1891 Old Shakespeare's mutilated body was found in her locked room, Room 31, in the squalid East River Hotel off the Bowery, where she had registered as "Carrie Brown," one of several names she had used for business purposes.

The newspapers jumped at the opportunity to headline the case as the "arrival" of Jack the Ripper in New York, direct from his awesome string of brutal killings in London. These headlines presented a direct challenge to New York Police Department's Chief Inspector Thomas F. Byrnes, who had previously chided Scotland Yard for failing to apprehend the mass murderer of London. If Jack the Ripper committed a murder in New York, Byrnes had declared with his typical bombast, he would be apprehended and imprisoned within 36 hours. That being the case, the pressure was on Byrnes' police to solve the Old Shakespeare murder forthwith. So they quickly arrested Ameer Ben Ali, an Algerian Frenchman generally known as Frenchy.

The case against Frenchy was circumstantial at best, consisting of little more than opportunity and the fact that bloodstains had been found on both sides of the door to his room, which was directly across the hall from Room 31. Frenchy was convicted of second-degree murder despite his protestations of innocence and sentenced to life imprisonment. He served 11 years before a group of citizens dug up evidence that proved he was the wrong man. First, they produced witnesses who said there were no bloodstains on Frenchy's door until many hours after the murder had been discovered. Furthermore, no effort had been made to find the key to the locked door of Room 31 or the man who was known to have accompanied the victim to her room late the night before. The committee of citizens found that this missing companion had been recognized from newspaper descriptions as a man who lived in a New Jersey boarding house. He had disappeared but in his bureau drawer a bloody shirt and a key to Room 31 had been discovered. Frenchy, who was clearly innocent, was released and immediately sailed back to his native Algeria. Thus, New York's Jack the Ripper case remained just as unsolved as any of its London counterparts.

See also: *Thomas F. Byrnes*.

O'LEARY, Big Jim (c.1860-1926): Chicago gambler

Jim O'Leary, the son of the Mrs. O'Leary of cow and Chicago Fire fame, grew up to be one of the city's most prominent gamblers and a millionaire. He started out as a handyman for the bookmaking syndicates, quickly learned the ropes and soon made a try at operating a gambling resort of his own. Its blueprints called for stockades, barbed-wire fences, alarm boxes, lookout posts for armed sentries, cages for ferocious watchdogs and a whole network of tunnels. Situated in Long Beach, Ind., 23 miles from the center of Chicago, the ambitious resort failed to draw the crowds O'Leary hoped for and it folded.

O'Leary moved back to the Windy City and opened a gambling house on South Halsted Street near the stockyards. He then set up a string of bookie operations and poolrooms. Big Jim, as he became known because of his stature in the business, fostered the idea of a floating gaming resort. He outfitted the steamboat *City of Traverse* as the first vessel in American history strictly devoted to gambling. Each afternoon about 1,000 horse players came aboard for a leisurely sail on Lake Michigan and remained out on the lake until all the day's races were run. Results were flashed to the boat by wireless. The police finally grounded the *City of Traverse* by arresting passengers as they disembarked and by scrambling the wireless messages giving the odds and results of the races.

O'Leary returned to his South Halsted Street house determined to make it the premier gambling resort in the country. It certainly became one of the most lavish, complete with a restaurant, a Turkish bath, bowling alleys and a billiard room. But its main attraction was the horse parlor, outfitted with plush couches and chairs, servants to provide refreshments and charts showing the odds and results of every race in the United States and Canada. Action was also taken on every other kind of sporting event as well as on elections and even the weather. Big Jim once won a $10,000 bet that there would be 18 days of rain during the month of May.

What was amazing about O'Leary was that he prospered without the usual payoffs to the police. He once was quoted by a newspaper reporter as saying: "I could have had all kinds of it, [protection] but let me tell you something. Protection that you purchase ain't worth an honest man's dime. The police is for sale, but I don't want none of them." His South Halsted Street resort boasted massive iron-bound oaken doors layered over with zinc and were, as Big Jim put it, "fire-proof, bomb-proof and police-proof." During the gamblers' war of 1907, the doors held against bombs from rival operators. At times the police did breech the doors with sledge hammers and axes and even arrested some of O'Leary's bookies and customers, but usually the reward for their efforts was hilariously anti-climatic. Once they found the grand betting parlor devoid of furniture save for a kitchen table at which an old man was sitting reading a prayer book. When the police took to axing through his inner walls looking for hidden rooms and exits, Big Jim countered by loading the walls with red pepper. When the police axes penetrated the wall's zinc covering, they were so blinded by the pepper that several required long hospital treatment for inflamed eyes. When Big Jim O'Leary died in 1926, he was a millionaire several times over and perhaps as famous in Chicago as the family cow.

OLINGER, Robert (1841-1881): Victim of Billy the Kid

A killer both with and without a badge, Bob Olinger has come down in the folklore surrounding Billy the Kid as the young outlaw's least lamented victim. Most folks seemed to agree that Olinger deserved to be shot.

A drifter from Ohio, Olinger punched cows all around the New Mexico Territory until, in 1876, he got the job of town marshal in Seven Rivers. When word soon got around that Olinger was working with outlaws, he was back punching cattle. As a lawman, Olinger developed a knack for gunning down men from ambush, and it is generally believed he used the same method to commit a few murders for personal reasons. His dispatch of Pas Chavez in Seven Rivers in 1878, was an exception. The pair had had a violent confrontation about a week earlier, and when they met on the town's main street, Olinger indicated all was forgotten and he extended his hand. When Chavez held out his hand, Olinger suddenly pulled him off balance, stuck his revolver into Chavez' stomach and pulled the trigger. Chavez died cursing him.

Despite Olinger's unsavory background, Pat Garrett had no compunctions about enlisting him as a deputy. When Billy the Kid was captured in 1881, Olinger was assigned to guard him in jail. Olinger evidently regarded this assignment as an opportunity to attain lasting glory by killing Billy during an escape attempt, and he went out and bought a brand new breech-loading shotgun. Taunting the Kid, he advised him to try to escape and take a fatal load of buckshot, an easier death than he faced shortly at the hands of the hangman. Just to add to the provocation, Olinger marked off the days on a calendar until Billy's hanging date and then waved the shotgun in his face and again urged him to try to escape.

As it turned out, on April 28 Billy the Kid did attempt to escape, successfully. While Olinger was across the street taking his meal at La Rue's Bar, Billy somehow got hold of a revolver and gunned down his other guard, J. W. Bell. Olinger heard the shots and came running across the street. By this time Billy had grabbed Olinger's shotgun and was waiting in a second-floor window. As Olinger came into view, Billy called out cheerfully, "Hello, Bob!" Olinger barely had time to look up at his executioner before Billy cut loose with both barrels, dropping his tormentor in his tracks. Billy hurled the shotgun at the dead man, shouting, "You won't follow me any more with that gun!" Billy the Kid then rode off to freedom.

See also: *Billy the Kid.*

OLIVE, Isom Prentice "Print" (1840-1886): Murderer

The epitome of the arrogant big rancher, Texas-born Print

Such was the mystique surrounding Billy the Kid that his murder of lawman Bob Olinger, shown in a contemporary print, was rather popular.

Olive and his brother Bob owned one of Nebraska's greatest spreads. For many years he was a law unto himself, directing a brutal war against the homesteaders who, in his view, were crowding his range. Print Olive cut fences, destroyed crops and employed a cowboy army of over one hundred to terrorize the homesteaders, but the state of Nebraska kept siding with these settlers, a development that made the Olive brothers even more violent.

In November 1878 Bob Olive was killed in a shoot-out with two homesteaders, Luther Mitchell and Ami Ketchum. The two men were arrested but, while being taken to a hearing, were handed over to Print Olive's men in exchange for cash. They were brought to the Olive ranch, where Print meted out his own version of frontier justice, shooting, hanging and—after dousing them with whiskey—burning them. For this outrage, which earned Print Olive the label "man burner," the cattle baron was brought to trial and, along with one of his chief aides, Fred Fisher, was sentenced to life imprisonment. When Olive's private army of cowboys threatened to break him free, President Rutherford B. Hayes, at the behest of the governor of Nebraska sent in several companies of mounted soldiers. Still, Print Olive bragged he would not remain in prison, and he proved right. Within two years, during which he spent $250,000 in legal fees, he was released and a new trial was ordered. It was never held, however, because the witnesses had "scattered."

Print Olive soon moved on to Colorado, where he gained a reasonable amount of acceptance over the next few years. However, his code remained as violent as ever. In 1886 in Trial City, Colo. Olive came across a former cowhand employee named Joe Sparrow, who owed him $10. Olive demanded the money in a saloon confrontation. When the smoke cleared, the cattle baron was dead.

OMERTA: Mafia code of silence

Omerta is, we are told, the time-honored underworld code of silence dating back to the birth of the Mafia in Sicily in the 13th century. The Mafia was formed to rid the island of the Spanish and French invaders who looted the Sicilians' homes and villages. However, this secret society soon began committing its own crimes and, later on, hired out to wealthy landowners who wanted to terrorize the farmers. The Mafia grew in power until it began to corrupt the government of Sicily and then that of Italy. The Mafia was able to rule because it was prepared to kill and was protected by the code of *omerta*.

The code forbade all members to say anything to the authorities or to call on the police for help in settling accounts against others. They had to handle such matters themselves. However, far more importantly, *omerta* sealed the lips of victims and witnesses alike. This was the real power of *omerta* in Sicily, a power the Mafia brought with it to America. It was through this code of silence that the Mafia and various Black Hand extortionists could victimize hapless Italian immigrants. For a minor violation of *omerta*, the penalty might be a slit tongue; for a major violation, it was a slit throat or a bullet-riddled body.

In America, *omerta* has become almost totally reserved for

Mafia victims and those of its lower echelon who believe it really exists. Nearly everything we know about the Mafia comes from only one source: the Mafia itself. The organization was quick to learn that one of the simplest ways to get rid of criminal competition was to "rat" to the police. The cops would break up the rival gang and the Mafia could then step in and take over. Mafia leaders, schooled in treachery, learned to break *omerta* to suit their own purposes. On one occasion Lucky Luciano, having been caught with some narcotics, is known to have "squared" the matter with the police by fingering a big load of drugs that a rival mob was moving. It was such maneuvers that enabled Luciano to become the biggest of the big crime bosses.

While it is true that the mob punishes many informers with death, it is equally true that far fewer corpses are found with a canary stuffed in their mouth, or their genitals cut off and similarly placed than was the case a few decades ago. In recent years informers have been treated more gently, if they have value. A case in point was Jack Mace, reputedly the biggest mob fence in the East. He supposedly got in trouble with the law in New York and squared accounts by fingering some crooks. A few New York gangsters exacted punishment by putting him in the hospital for a long time. He was not killed because he was considered too valuable. Mace had, after all, moved millions of dollars in mob money and he had all the connections. Furthermore, he had made a great deal of money for the underworld, and since it has always honored money more than *omerta*, he was merely taught a lesson for his infraction.

The extent to which *omerta* has collapsed within the Mafia and, for that matter, outside of it is attested to by the fact that during the late 1970s the federal government had under its protection about 700 informers, including many Mafia men of the Joe Valachi stripe. *Omerta* obviously doesn't exert the power it once did. As Vinnie Teresa, the biggest Mafia informer since Valachi, said, "But looking back on my life with the Mafia members, I realize now that *omerta*—the code—was just a lot of bullshit."

ONE-ARMED Bandits: See Slot Machines.

O'NEIL, Jack (?-1898): Innocent execution victim

On January 7, 1898 Jack O'Neil was hanged for the murder of Hattie McCloud at Buckland, near Shelburne Falls, Mass. To the end, O'Neil insisted he was innocent and that he was the victim of anti-Irish bigotry. Going to his death, he said, "I shall meet death like a man and I hope those who see me hanged will live to see the day when it is proved I am innocent—and it will be, some time."

Just a few months after the execution, a Shelburne Falls soldier fighting the Spanish in Cuba with the Sixth Massachusetts Militia confessed to the McCloud murder and cleared O'Neil. An ace reporter of the day, Eddie Collins, interviewed the soldier and arranged to have him sign a death bed confession. He flashed the story to Dan W. Gallagher of the *Boston Post*. By that time, of course, it did O'Neil little good. Gallagher had already covered his execution. But O'Neil's dying words proved true.

O'NEILL, William O. "Buckey" (1860-1898): Lawman and Rough Rider

Generally regarded as one of the best lawmen the West ever produced—a rather remarkable achievement for a peace officer who never killed a man in the course of his duties—Buckey O'Neill has been described by Western author William McLoed Raine as "the most many-sided man Arizona ever produced." Making his way west in 1879 from his native Washington, D.C., O'Neill, in a short, crowded life, became famous as a gambler, lawyer, journalist, lawman, judge, mayor, conservationist and soldier. His nickname Buckey derived from his habit of constantly bucking the odds at the faro tables.

O'Neill's first experience as a lawman was his tour as a part-time deputy to City Marshal Henry Garfias in Phoenix. One day when a dozen Texas cowboys "treed" Phoenix, i.e., ran citizens of the town up trees by shooting at their heels, Garfias tossed O'Neill a badge and the two went out to restore order. Garfias killed two of the troublemakers, while O'Neill, perhaps shooting a bit more carefully, wounded two others.

After becoming one of the Arizona Territory's youngest lawyers, publishers and judges, O'Neill was elected sheriff of Yavapai County in 1888. During his one-year term crime in the area declined. Even more remarkably, the year passed without a single fatal shooting by anyone connected with the sheriff's office. When four ex-Hashknife Ranch cowboys turned train robbers, O'Neill went after them with a posse whose members understood there would be no killings unless absolutely necessary. The four were tracked down after a 600-mile chase that ended in a nonfatal shoot-out in the Utah Territory.

After his term as sheriff, Buckey O'Neill conducted some highly valuable explorations of the Grand Canyon, discovered a copper mine and ran several Populist political campaigns that culminated in his election as mayor of Prescott, Arizona Territory in 1898. He left that office to become a Rough Rider with Teddy Roosevelt in the Spanish-American War. After serving heroically in the skirmish at Las Guasimas, he was shot dead by a sniper at San Juan Hill on July 1, 1898. Roosevelt wrote glowingly of Buckey O'Neill on several occasions, and undoubtedly, his exposure to O'Neill led to his later patronage of other former Western lawmen, such as Pat Garrett and Bat Masterson, neither of whom were nearly as deserving as the remarkable Arizona sheriff.

ONE-WAY Ride: Underworld euphemism

Hymie Weiss, the number two man in Dion O'Banion's gang, which dominated Chicago's North Side in the early 1920s, has been credited with coining this quaint underworld euphemism. In 1921 Steve Wisniewski offended the O'Banions by hijacking one of the gang's loaded beer trucks. Weiss was given the duty of imposing the proper punishment. He invited Wisniewski for a drive in the country by Lake Michigan, from which the latter never returned. Later, Weiss bragged to friends, "We took Stevie for a ride, a one-way ride."

OPERATION Underworld: See S.S. *Normandie.*

ORCHARD, Harry (1866-1954): Murderer

Either Harry Orchard, whose real name was Albert E. Horsley, was the greatest labor assassin in history or he cooperated in a monumental conspiracy with the Pinkertons to frame America's radical labor leadership and save himself from execution in the process.

Orchard was convicted of the 1905 murder of ex-governor Frank Steunenberg of Idaho, and his confession made nationwide headlines when he insisted he had killed Steunenberg on specific orders from William D. "Big Bill" Haywood, a leader in the Western Federation of Miners, and others. Orchard eventually admitted he was a paid labor bomber and had often bombed and killed on union orders, specifically Haywood's. Organized labor has always scoffed at Orchard's confession, pointing out he was assisted in preparing it by Pinkerton detective James McParland of Mollie Maguire fame. In any event, the trial of Haywood, Charles H. Moyers and George A. Pettibone foundered when the prosecution failed to corroborate Orchard's charges. Furthermore, another man, who had admitted taking part in the murder, Steve Adams, repudiated his own confession, which he said was Pinkerton-inspired. The Haywood trial in 1907 won fame for Clarence Darrow, who, as defense attorney, charged the prosecution with attempting to turn a murder case into a condemnation of the American labor movement.

Harry Orchard alone was convicted and sentenced to hang, but his sentence was commuted to life imprisonment. Years later, he would transmit a message to William A. Pinkerton requesting aid in winning a parole. Pinkerton refused, a startling move since the agency generally attempted to win freedom for its informers whether or not their testimony had helped win the conviction of others. In an internal agency memo Pinkerton wrote, "I know that McParland always thought Orchard should have been released for testifying, but I still regard Orchard as a cold-blooded murderer who killed many innocent persons and who testified only to save his own skin." Orchard died in jail on April 13, 1954.

See also: *Clarence Darrow, William D. "Big Bill" Haywood, James McParland, Frank Steunenberg.*

OREGON Boot: Shackle for prisoners

The so-called Oregon boot was a cruel device that made the Oregon State Prison one of the most feared by 19th century criminals. Invented by Warden J. C. Gardner, who required that all prisoners wear it during their entire term, the contraption, which weighed over 15 pounds, consisted of a heavy iron band that fastened around the leg above the ankle and held in place by a steel ring with a pair of braces that were attached to the heel of the wearer's boot. While it no doubt cut down on escape attempts, it could also produce permanent deformities on those serving long terms.

Warden Gardner patented the device in 1866, firmly expecting other prisons to adopt the shackle. He was surprised when none did, most considering it too sadistic. After another decade, as a result of mounting criticism, the device was only applied to the more desperate criminals in the Oregon State Prison. Slowly and quietly, the use of the Oregon boot tapered off and finally ended even in the state that gave it its name.

ORGEN, Jacob "Little Augie" (1894-1927): Gang leader and killer

Jacob "Little Augie" Orgen was one of the last big-time independent gangsters to fall victim to the national crime syndicate. When Little Augie was assassinated in 1927, his union racketeering in New York's garment district was taken over by the notorious Louis Lepke. Lepke refined the racket into a smoother and more professional operation and gave it syndicate support, cutting in such Italian gangsters as Tommy Lucchese, Luckie Luciano, Joe Adonis and Albert Anastasia and such non-Italians as Meyer Lansky and Bugsy Siegel. Little Augie had failed to appreciate such grandiose schemes, a shortsightedness that may well have proved to be the death of him.

Jacob Orgen was the son of highly religious Jewish parents, whom he shamed by becoming a labor slugger for Dopey Benny Fein shortly before the outbreak of World War I. Dopey Benny, the top labor racketeer of his day, carried out sluggings and murders both for unions seeking to recruit new members and terrorize strikebreakers and for employers attempting to intimidate workers and introduce strikebreakers. By 1915 effective police action had put Dopey Benny out of business, and for about four years thereafter, the labor slugging racket almost ceased. During that period of tranquility Little Augie returned to the bosom of his family and was accepted as a reformed sinner.

In 1919 Orgen, tired of leading an honest life, organized a gang called the Little Augies. At that time, labor slugging, which had recently resurfaced, and extortion of employers were controlled by the premier New York gangster of the day, Kid Dropper, who had attained his success after a savage war that culminated in the assassination of another leading mobster and killer, Johnny Spanish. Kid Dropper was notorious for not sharing any of his income and for leaving only scraps for the Little Augies of his entourage.

Augie learned the virtue of patience, slowly gathering around him some of the future big-name criminals of the era. Among those who flocked to his banner were Jack "Legs" Diamond, Gurrah Shapiro and Louis Lepke. By 1923 the Little Augies initiated open warfare with the Droppers, fighting vicious gun battles with them to control the wet wash laundry workers and, later, other groups of employees. In strength, firepower and reputation, Kid Dropper seemed invincible, but Orgen finally emerged victorious after convincing an unimportant and gullible hood named Louis Kushner that he could become a leading member of the gang by killing the Dropper. Kid Dropper, then in police custody for a minor charge, was being transferred by car from one court to another when Kushner walked up to the vehicle and shot Dropper through the windshield.

Little Augie and his lieutenants were arrested for the murder, but Kushner insisted he had done the the whole thing on his own and proudly went off to prison for 20 years. Augie immediately took over the union slugging racket. However, after assuming power, he was constantly harassed by the police. Moreover, the racket was becoming less lucrative, as more sophisticated union leaders moved away from using such brash violence to achieve their goals. Lepke, who had gauged this decline, strongly urged Little Augie to move from working for unions and employers to seizing control of locals, milking their treasuries and exacting tribute from employers who wished to avoid strikes or operate nonunion shops.

Lepke saw the potential for untold riches in this method of operation, but Little Augie was moving more into bootlegging and was even thinking of retiring within a few years, with the hope that he could again win favor with his parents and family. He gave Lepke strict orders to stay away from union rackets and stick to bootlegging. Augie probably saw little reason to fear Lepke as long as he had the murderous Legs Diamond as a trusted bodyguard, but in October 1927 he was murdered as he was walking on Norfolk Street with Diamond at his side. It is to this day unclear whether Lepke was behind the murder or whether it was the work of bootlegging rivals.

Little Augie was buried in a satin-lined red coffin bearing a silver plate that read:

JACOB ORGEN

Age 25 Years

Actually, the gangster was 33 years old, but his father had considered him dead since 1919, the year he organized the Little Augies.

See also: *Louis "Lepke" Buchalter, Kid Dropper, Labor Sluggers War.*

ORIENTAL Saloon And Gambling House

Tombstone, Arizona Territory was long known as the nastiest mining town the frontier ever saw, and in Tombstone the place to go for drinking, fighting and shooting was the Oriental Saloon and Gambling House. One Western chronicler estimated that "200 men held their last drink, poker hand or conversation in and around the Oriental's precincts before being carted off to a resting place in Tombstone's Boot Hill, their corpses filled with various bullet and buckshot holes." While it might be difficult to verify such an estimate, there is no doubt that the Oriental was the site of some of the West's most memorable, if pointless, gun duels. A case in point was the time Johnny Ringo invited Louis Hancock to have a drink with him. "All right," Hancock said, "I'll have a beer." Whereupon Ringo replied: "No man drinks beer with me. I don't

like beer." It was teeth-gritting time. "Well," Hancock said, "I like beer." And Ringo responded, "I don't." Hancock faced Ringo menacingly. "Barman," he said, "I'll have a beer." The two went for their guns and Hancock lost. They buried the loser holding a bottle of beer. Some historians have questioned that last touch, but Westerners liked their anecdotes tidy and the ending provided a nice conversation piece for the Oriental.

The Oriental's history began when Jim Vizina set up for business in a canvas tent with two wagonloads of whiskey. He later erected a building, which he eventually rented to Mike Joyce, who gave the Oriental a lavishness seldom found in Western saloons. The main gambling hall and bar were decorated sumptuously and a piano was hauled all the way from Denver through blazing heat, storms, flash floods and Apache country.

After being shot in the arm by Doc Holliday, Joyce sold out to a sharp operator named Lou Rickabaugh, who then gave Wyatt Earp a one-quarter interest in the Oriental. This was not as unselfish an act as it seemed. Once the deal was struck, Rickabaugh did not have to worry about getting shot up by Earp's friend Holliday or about providing security for the Oriental, which came under Earp's protection. The barman was a skilled gunslinger named Buckskin Frank Leslie. Two other proficient gunmen, Bat Masterson and Luke Short, ran gambling tables, and the Earp brothers and Holliday were often on the scene.

Clara Brown, a famous reporter of the era, visited Tombstone in 1880 to describe it from a woman's point of view. She called the town a hellhole but she was ecstatic about the Oriental. She wrote: "The Oriental is simply gorgeous. The mahogany bar is a marvel of beauty, the gaming rooms carpeted with Brussels, brilliantly lighted and furnished with the latest reading matter and fine writing materials for its patrons. Every evening there is the music of a violin and a piano, and the scene is most gay." Clearly, she was happy to find one haven amidst the wretchedness of Tombstone. The very day after Miss Brown left, the entertainment at the Oriental picked up. Rog King called Johnny Wilson a liar, as they stood at the bar, and emphasized his point by putting a .45 slug through Wilson's forehead.

The Oriental was such a prize money-maker it required firepower to keep it. In an attempt to seize control of the establishment, Johnny Tyler sent one of his ace gunslingers, Charlie Storms, to the Oriental for the express purpose of getting into a shoot-out. Storms picked on Luke Short, a little man but one of the West's deadliest duelists. They stopped outside where Storms announced, "I'll give you the first shot." That was just what Short had in mind, having already emptied his holster as Storms was uttering his offer. He fired three shots and then stepped over Storms' body on his way back into the Oriental to resume dealing faro. Shortly thereafter, Tyler learned of Earp's interest in the Oriental and backed off from further efforts to take over.

The Earps and Doc Holliday left Tombstone shortly after the gunfight at the O.K. Corral. Contrary to common belief today, it was not a voluntary departure, especially since it meant giving up the Oriental, but they were given strong hints to "git" and they got. The day of the vigilantes had not yet passed.

When the silver ran out, the Oriental died along with the town. The population of Tombstone dropped from 15,000 to a few hundred and the deserted saloon was stripped clean.

See also: *Wyatt Earp; Luke Short; Tombstone, Arizona Territory.*

OSBORNE, George O. (1845-1926): Father of Prison Reform

The first prison warden to make wholesale changes in prison conditions, not simply to reduce cruelty but in an attempt to reform inmates was George O. Osborne. Warden of the New Jersey State Prison for more than 20 years in the late 19th and early 20th centuries, Osborne inaugurated a number of reforms that were widely adopted in succeeding years. Among these were establishment of prison schools with practical courses, improvements in the parole system and more emphasis on religious life. Osborne was perhaps the first warden to eliminate a number of dehumanizing practices found in virtually all prisons: the ball and chain, shaved heads, striped uniforms and so-called dark cells, or dungeons. Osborne's work earned him the title Father of Prison Reform. He died in retirement in Florida.

OSBORNE, Thomas Mott (1859-1926): Prison reformer

Perhaps the greatest prison reformer in America in the 20th century, Thomas Mott Osborne was a successful manufacturer who left the business world to campaign for prison reform. "The prison must be an institution where every inmate must have the largest practical amount of individual freedom because," he said, quoting British statesman William Ewart Gladstone, " 'it is liberty alone that fits men for liberty.' "

Osborne was appointed to the New York State Commission on Prison Reform in 1913. To gain a better appreciation of the prisoners' lot, he spent a week inside Auburn Prison as inmate "Tom Brown." The following year he was appointed warden of Sing Sing, whose administration was subject to political influence and intrigue. Because he altered the status quo, Osborne's enemies had him indicted on a charge of perjury and neglect of duty, but the case was dismissed and he triumphantly returned to his post. At Sing Sing, Osborne introduced the Mutual Welfare League, which was to be widely imitated. Under it prisoners established their own system of discipline, were paid for their work and received improved recreational and job-training services. While Osborne's pioneer work drew praise from other penologists, he was constantly subjected to political criticism for "coddling criminals" and in 1917 he resigned his wardenship. Ironically, when Lewis E. Lawes became warden of Sing Sing, he instituted almost all of Osborne's ideas.

Osborne's three books, *Within Prison Walls* (1914), *Society and Prisons* (1916) and *Prisons and Common Sense* (1920), which answered the "coddling" charge, are considered classics of prison reform literature. One of Osborne's greatest contributions was his critical analysis of Richard L. Dugdale's famous but highly suspect study of the Juke family, in which Dugdale attempted to prove his theory of hereditary criminality. After Osborne's death in 1926, his work was continued by the Osborne Association of New York, a national organization dedicated to prison reform.

See also: *Jukes.*

OSTER Gang: Counterfeiters

Among the great counterfeiting operations in this country, perhaps the most durable was a New Orleans band formed in 1872. The gang, which lasted almost 50 years, was organized by Phil Oster, who started counterfeiting money in his mid-twenties and was still at it in his mid-seventies. He was arrested many times, but invariably, within 24 hours of gaining his freedom, he would be back in business. Oster's last appearance in New Orleans, shortly before his death, took place in November 1917, when the Secret Service caught him with some excellent counterfeiting apparatus in his room on Bourbon Street. The old counterfeiter told a newspaper reporter:

I've been in the penitentiary five times. I've been pardoned as many times, and I'm proud of my record. I started making counterfeit money forty-five years ago. It took 'em fifteen years before they got me, and after I had made and spent enough money—if I had it now, well, there would be few, if any, men in New Orleans more wealthy.

OSWALD, Lee Harvey (1939-1963): Assassin of John F. Kennedy

At 12:30 p.m. on November 22, 1963, President John F. Kennedy was shot to death in Dallas, Tex. with a mail-order rifle belonging to Lee Harvey Oswald. Oswald was an employee of the Texas School Book Depository and, as such, had access to a sixth-floor window that provided a perfect vantage for the sniping. As the motorcade passed, Oswald apparently fired three times, killing Kennedy and badly wounding Texas Gov. John B. Connally, who was sitting directly in front of the President in the executive limousine.

Ever since, there has been a dispute over whether or not Oswald was the only gunman and whether additional shots were fired by others. Critics of the Warren Commission, which investigated the assassination and concluded that Oswald had acted alone, have insisted, with varying degrees of plausibility, that the commission's reconstruction of the events was based on fallacies and physical improbabilities such as the commission's theory that a single bullet hit both Kennedy and Connally.

After the shooting Oswald concealed his rifle among some crates and casually walked from the building. He went home, secured a pistol and went out again. When stopped by Dallas policeman J. D. Tippit, Oswald shot the police officer four times, killing him. He took refuge in a movie house without purchasing a ticket and was apprehended there by police officers. When approached by the officers, he pointed his gun at them but it misfired.

Oswald consistently denied having killed either Kennedy or Tippit, although several witnesses identified him as Tippit's killer and his palm print was found on the weapon used to kill Kennedy. A check into Oswald's background produced a picture of a misfit and an apparent on-again, off-again believer in communism. He had received a hardship discharge from the Marines in 1959 because of an injury his mother had suffered, but he did not stay home long to help her. Instead, he traveled to the USSR using funds the source of which has never been identified. He gave up his American citizenship, went to work for the Soviets on radar installations and married the daughter of a KGB colonel. After two and a half years Oswald tired of life in the Soviet Union and decided to move back to America with his family. After obtaining a loan from the U.S. State Department, he returned and settled in New Orleans, where he seems to have divided his political affiliations between such diverse groups as the right-wing China Lobby and the left-wing Fair Play for Cuba Committee. He also had links with persons who were known conduits for arms and money provided by the CIA to counterinsurgency forces. Thus, Oswald may have been a Soviet agent, a CIA agent or plant or just a plain kook.

Oswald did not live long enough to provide an answer to that question or why he had killed the President. Two days after his apprehension he was shot to death by Jack Ruby, a Dallas nightclub operator, as police were transferring him to the county jail. The murder was shown live on television, as the media covered Oswald's movements. That such a valuable prisoner could be so easily assassinated was shocking and led to a bitter denunciation of Dallas law officials.

While the Warren Commission found that Oswald had acted alone in his assassination of the President and that Jack Ruby similarly had killed Oswald on his own, the controversy was not stilled. Dozens of books have been written attacking the conclusions of the commission, all pushing various conspiracy theories. New Orleans District Attorney James Garrison put forth the most fantastic claims of a vast plot to eliminate Kennedy from power.

In December 1978 the House Select Committee on Assassinations issued a report that challenged the Warren Commission's findings. Much of the committee's conclusions that Kennedy "was probably assassinated as a result of a conspiracy" was based on a study of the noises in Dallas' Dealey Plaza at the time of the murder. The acoustical study led the probers to conclude "the evidence established a high probability that two gunmen fired" at Kennedy that day. The panel said, however, that it was "unable to identify the other gunman or the extent of the conspiracy." Another conclusion, based on the evidence available, was that the Soviet Union, Cuba, organized crime or anti-Castro groups had not been involved. The committee flatly stated that none of the U.S. intelligence agencies—the CIA, the FBI or the Secret Service—were implicated. However, the agencies were criticized for their failings prior to and at the time of the assassination and during the ensuing probes.

Thus, the Kennedy assassination continues to tantalize students of the event. The story remains rife with gaping holes and contradictions and coincidences of staggering proportions, not the least of which was the fate of so many material witnesses in the affair. In the three years following the Kennedy and Oswald murders, no less than 18 key witnesses died. Six were shot to death, two committed suicide, three died in car accidents, one was killed by a karate chop to the neck, one bled to death from a throat slashing, three suffered fatal heart attacks and two expired from other natural causes. The reserved London *Sunday Times* engaged an actuary to determine the mathematical probability of this happening. He concluded the odds were 100,000 trillion to one.

See also: *Jack Ruby.*

OUTLAW Exterminators, Inc.: Western bounty hunters

Five hard-riding, fast-shooting bounty hunters, dubbed Outlaw Exterminators, Inc. by the press because they never brought 'em back alive, contributed greatly to clearing the Arizona Territory of badmen in the 1870s and 1880s as anyone.

Clay Calhoun and Floyd Davis were deputy sheriffs, but the other three members of the group were part-timers—Ben Slack and Dick Hunter, cattlemen, and Fred Beeber, a bartender—who laid aside their mundane jobs whenever the prospects of a nice reward thundered across the mesa. Since rewards at the time were paid on a "dead or alive" basis, the Exterminators decided "dead" was easier and just as profitable.

The band's prize catch was probably bad John Allman, so-called Cavalry Killer who went on an orgy of murder in the Arizona Territory in 1877. When Clay Calhoun brought in Allman, the body contained four bullet holes: one in the groin, stomach, chest and mouth. The holes were in such a perfect line that Calhoun's story about a shoot-out was almost certainly a fabrication. More likely, the bounty hunter had killed Allman while the outlaw was asleep. But like the dozen-odd other victims of the Exterminators, Allman was not exactly popular and nobody worried much about such details. Despite numerous gunfights and the fact that they made a lot of enemies, the Exterminators lived out full lives, the last survivor, Clay Calhoun, dying on November 21, 1948, at the age of 97.

See also: *John Allman.*

OWENS, Commodore Perry (1852-1919): Lawman

As a flamboyant lawman, Commodore Perry Owens—with blonde locks reaching almost to his waist, a wide-brimmed sombrero, hand-tooled chaps, a long-barreled Colt .45 and a gunbelt that held a double row of ammunition—put even Wild Bill Hickok to shame. At gun play, he surpassed anything the more famous Hickok ever achieved; in one classic Arizona gun battle, Owens killed three men and wounded another in less than a minute.

Born in Tennessee in 1852, he was christened in honor of naval hero Commodore Oliver H. Perry. After spending his youth in Indiana, he drifted west in his late teens to follow the cattle trails. By the time he rode into Apache County, Arizona Territory in 1881, he was a skilled gunman. Having earned a reputation for honesty, he was named sheriff in 1886. Apache County was rough country, an area of big cattle ranches like the Hashknife whose men enjoyed taking apart saloons, and the home of a tribe of Navaho, who engaged extensively in horse stealing. While he was able to keep both these elements under control, Owens had a major problem in quelling the Graham-Tewksbury feud.

On September 4, 1887 Owens rode into Holbrook in search of Andy Blevans, a member of the Graham faction who was wanted for horse stealing. When Owens found him on his porch and told him he was under arrest, Blevans ran in the house, slamming the door behind him. Andy fired one shot through the door before the sheriff's fatal answering blast knocked him across the room. Owens jumped from the porch just as brother John Blevans charged around the side of the house firing at him. The sheriff felled John with one shot and pivoted in time to shoot Moses Roberts, a brother-in-law of the Blevans, through the head. Almost at the same time, Sam Houston Blevans, the youngest of the three brothers, came out the door, but Owens cut him down before he could level his six-shooter. Of Owens' four victims, only John Blevans survived; he was sent to prison for five years.

The bloody shoot-out gained Owens a fine reputation, but over the next few years the public's opinion of him changed. The day of the gunfighter was passing, and a man who could or would kill so quickly and so efficiently was more to be feared than honored. In 1896 Owens quit, disgusted over the new attitude toward him. He lived out his days working nondescript jobs and drinking heavily. He died on May 10, 1919.

See also: *Graham-Tewksbury Feud.*

P

PACKER, Alfred (1842-1907): Cannibal

The person who became famous in Colorado as The Man Who Ate Democrats made his first recorded appearance on the Western scene as a prospector in southwestern Colorado; he was in his mid-twenties at the time. In 1873 Alfred Packer guided a party of 20 men from Salt Lake into the rugged San Juan Mountains. Described as a "tall man, with long, dark curling hair, dark mustache and goatee, deep set dark grey eyes," Packer had a reputation of knowing Colorado as well as any man. Thus, it was surprising that, having brought the party to Chief Ouray's camp on the Uncompahgre, near the Los Pinos Indian Agency, Packer rejected the chief's advice against pushing on through the heavy snows. Because they offered to pay him well, Packer continued the trek with five men, Israel Swan, Frank Miller, Shannon Bell, George Noon (or Moon) and a man named Humphrey.

Some weeks later, Packer staggered back to Los Pinos, claiming his five companions had abandoned him when he became footsore and snowblind. Suspicion, however, buzzed around Packer. He was found in possession of a Wells Fargo draft belonging to one of his companions as well as the gun and skinning knife of another member of the party. He seemed to have money enough to spend freely at the bar. Perhaps the most damning comment reported came from Chief Ouray, who looked at Packer and grunted, "You too damn fat."

Months later, search parties turned up the bodies of the five missing men. Four had had their skulls crushed, apparently while they slept, and the fifth appeared to have been shot after a struggle. Four of the skeletons had been totally stripped of flesh and the other was partially so. According to one of several stories that Packer then told, 60-year-old Swan had been the first to die of starvation when the party ran out of food, and the others had eaten him to stay alive. Next, Shannon Bell, Packer related, killed Humphrey to replenish the group's food supply. Then Miller was murdered, and a few days later, Bell shot Noon. When Noon was finished, Bell tried to kill Packer, but the latter got him first. Packer said he carved off strips of Bell's flesh to provide him with enough food to make it back to the agency.

Packer was found guilty of murder and sentenced to 40 years at hard labor. So awesome was his crime that he became a legend celebrated in story and song as The Man Who Ate Democrats, an accolade given him by the judge who leaned down from the bench and cried, "Packer, you depraved Republican son of a bitch, there were only five Democrats in Hinsdale County, and you ate them all!"

Packer served 17 years before being released. He died in 1907 at the age of 65.

PALMER Raids: Roundup of alleged Red subversives

Two headlines run by the *Boston Herald* in 1920 probably best reflected the anti-Red hysteria then sweeping the United States. They were "BOLSHEVIST PLAN FOR CONQUEST OF AMERICA!" and "BRIDE THINKS REDS KIDNAPED MISSING GROOM." In the post-World War I period, violent strikes swept the country and bombs were mailed to many prominent citizens, most of whom had a well-known antipathy toward organized labor. One bomb was sent to the attorney general, A. Mitchell Palmer. Although it exploded harmlessly on his stoop, Palmer swore revenge, determined to quash the impending "Bolshevik revolution."

On New Year's Day 1920 Palmer, who harbored strong presidential ambitions, utilized the wartime Sedition Act to authorize hundreds of agents to invade homes and union halls in 33 U.S. cities. More than 4,000 persons—American citizens and aliens alike—were swept up in the net. In some places individuals were kept in jail for up to a week without being charged. In Hartford, Conn. people who came to visit those arrested as suspected subversives were also placed under arrest, on the theory that they too were likely to be revolutionaries or "Bolshies."

Palmer enjoyed considerable popular support but soon became embroiled with the legal community and various members of the Wilson Administration over the capriciousness of his acts. Secretary of Labor William B. Wilson, authorized under the Sedition Act to deport anarchists or other advocates of the violent overthrow of the government, demanded fair hearings for the accused. The result was that the overwhelming majority was released because of the total lack of evidence. Although Palmer had assured the public that an insurrection was virtually at hand, the menacing horde had yielded but three pistols and nary a bomb. Undeterred, Palmer pressed on with his fight, warning that radicals were planning a nationwide uprising on May Day, 1920. When the day passed quietly, Palmer's star began to wane, although he continued to make loud noises for many months and was instrumental in the deportation of some 600 aliens, including anarchists Emma Goldman and Alexander Berkman.

Historians Charles and Mary Beard in *The Rise of American Civilization* offer two conclusions concerning the Palmer Red Raids:

> The first is that not a single first-class German spy or revolutionary workingman was caught and convicted of an overt act designed to give direct aid and comfort to the enemy. The second is that, as in England during the period of the French revolution, the occasion of the war which called for patriotic duties was seized by emotional conservatives as an opportunity to blacken the character of persons whose opinions they feared and hated.

See also: *J. Edgar Hoover.*

PANAMINT City, California: Lawless mining town

Born in the California silver boom of 1872, Panamint City had four lusty years of existence, during which it became known as a suburb of hell.

Located in a box canyon in the Panamint Mountains just west of Death Valley, Panamint was virtually inaccessible other than by a narrow trail between towering walls of rock. But for the silver find, it would never have existed. Wells Fargo soon wished it didn't exist; stages and bullion shipments were held up with such regularity that finally even that hardy express company declined to handle Panamint's business. In time, the locals solved the problem by casting the bullion into gigantic balls that could only be moved down the canyon at an extremely slow pace. Seizing the bullion in this form was pointless, since robbers couldn't move the loot fast enough to evade capture.

Panamint, set between confining canyon walls, was a one-street town about a mile long. Within its narrow boundaries all the evils of a wild mining town were contained. There were at least 40 gambling halls and a somewhat greater number of saloons, with much of the rest of the real estate taken up by institutions such as Madame Martha Camp's fancy bordello and an uncounted number of cribs operated by free-lance bawds.

Legend has it that Madame Camp's establishment had a silver plaque to mark the spot where a character names Barstow expired from three bullet wounds inflicted by Bill McAllister, the owner of the Snug Saloon, in a dispute over who would be the first to enjoy the favors of one of the madam's new arrivals. The Oriental and Dexter saloons were famous for their shoot-outs. Patrons of the adjoining establishments had to face the disconcerting possibility that lead fired in one saloon might penetrate the walls and kill an imbiber in the other. To solve this problem, the two managements jointly installed a wall of sheet iron between their premises so that a man hit in the Oriental could be sure it was Oriental lead and vice versa.

The silver boom in Panamint was short-lived, the veins starting to run out in 1875. In 1876 a flash flood destroyed the town.

PANEL House: Brothel specializing in robbing customers

The panel house, a bordello designed more for robbery than for prostitution, may not have been an American invention, but its operation was certainly raised to a fine art in this country. In these dens, sliding panels were installed in doors and walls so that a prostitute's customer could be robbed while he was otherwise occupied. A chair for the customer's clothing would be placed right near a panel. If the man deposited his clothes elsewhere, a hooked pole was used to retrieve them. One advantage of the operation was that the prostitute normally could not be charged with robbery, since she clearly had not done the robbing.

A 19th century print warns readers to beware of panel houses.

A New York and Philadelphia madam named Moll Hodges, who operated during the 1850s and, 1860s, is generally credited with becoming the first panel house operator. In 1865 Lizzie Clifford, a former employee of Moll Hodges in New York, opened a panel house in Chicago, and by 1890 there were an estimated 200 such establishments in that city. A police report in 1896 calculated the amount of money stolen in Chicago panel houses at $1.5 million a year. For several years complaints of such robberies came in at the rate of 50 to 100 every 24 hours. The establishments were finally eliminated around 1900 thanks to the efforts of a single Chicago police detective, Clifton Wooldridge, a colorful and resourceful character who cam up with the idea of arresting the property owners who rented buildings to the panel houses operators. No property owner appears to have been imprisoned, but as police bore down on them, the practice came to a quick end.

See also: *Creep Joint, Custom House Place, Clifton Wooldridge.*

PANZRAM, Carl (1891-1930): Mass murderer

Among America's most vicious mass murderers, Carl Panzram was a study in hatred and violence, a self-confessed killer of 21 persons and sodomizer of at least 1,000.

Panzram's first arrest came at the age of eight, when he was charged with being drunk and disorderly in his native Minnesota. Many of his early years were spent in correctional facilities, where the brutal treatment he received almost guaranteed that his vicious instincts would blossom. By the time he completed a term in Fort Leavenworth Prison in 1910, he said, "All the good that may have been in me had been kicked and beaten out of me long before." Thereafter, Panzram spent his life robbing, sodomizing and killing his victims. He did time in various institutions and frequently escaped.

Panzram said, "I don't believe in man, God nor devil. I hate the whole damned human race including myself." Many of his crimes were done in revenge for the treatment he had received behind bars. At the Montana State Training School he had been beaten on the bare back, legs and buttocks with a baseball bat; at Leavenworth Prison he had been chained across the chest and by the arms and left dangling for hours; at the Oregon State Prison he had been chained naked to a wall and given the water hose treatment with such force that his eyes blackened, his genitals swelled enormously and his body welted all over. Also at Oregon he had been tortured with the "humming bird," which involved placing an inmate in a steel bathtub filled with water, chaining him hand and foot and rubbing him down with a sponge electrified by a battery.

If such treatment was intended to reform Panzram, it failed miserably. Each time he got free, he robbed, sodomized and murdered.

Finally in 1928 Panzram was sentenced to Leavenworth for burglary and murder, whereupon he announced, "I'll kill the first man who bothers me." On June 20, 1929 Panzram bashed in the skull of the prison laundry foreman. Sentenced to death for the murder, he was incensed when the Society for the Abolishment of Capital Punishment sought a commutation for him, citing as one of its arguments Panzram's previous mistreatment. Panzram wrote to President Herbert Hoover insisting on his "constitutional rights" to be hanged. As for the reformers, he said, "I wish you all had one neck, and I had my hands on it. . . . I believe the only way to reform people is to kill them."

On September 5, 1930 Panzram went to the gallows. When the hangman asked him if he had anything to say, he replied: "Yes, hurry it up, you Hoosier bastard! I could hang a dozen men while you're fooling around!" He spat twice at his executioner before the trap was pulled.

PARDON And Amnesty

The power to pardon or offer amnesty or commutation of sentence, resides with the president of the United States and the governors of the states, within their specific jurisdictions, although in a number of states the pardoning power is shared between the chief executive and a council or board of pardons.

Commutation, or the reduction of a sentence to a less severe one, is the most common modification of a criminal penalty, but it does not wipe away guilt in the eyes of the law. In the past, many governors have used this power to change death sentences to life imprisonment. A pardon, on the other hand, excuses the person from all penalties and often indicates removal of guilt and restoration of the full rights and privileges of citizenship. President George Washington extablished the broad precedent when he granted a blanket pardon, or amnesty, to all those involved in the Whiskey Rebellion provided they swore allegiance to the government. In individual cases James Madison pardoned, reluctantly, Jean Lafitte and all his pirates who could prove they had fought with Andrew Jackson at the Battle of New Orleans; Warren G. Harding pardoned labor leader and Socialist Eugene V. Debs, who was imprisoned for opposing World War I; and President Gerald Ford granted a full pardon to former President Richard M. Nixon for all federal offenses he might have committed in office. President Ford also offered limited amnesty to about 28,500 Vietnam war draft evaders provided they return to the United States and perform up to two years of some community work. Some observers feel the latter move was intended to make the Nixon pardon more acceptable.

In the past pardons were most frequently used as a way to rectify judicial wrongs, offering the simplest way for innocent persons to be restored to freedom and the rights of citizenship. In practice, pardons have been used as a method of extending mercy to convicted persons believed to have suffered sufficient punishment. At times, this use of pardons had brought charges of corruption or misuse of power. Such misuse was alleged against retiring Gov. Ray Blanton of Tennessee in January 1979, during the final days of his administration, when Blanton outraged the public and stunned state officials by granting pardons to or drastically reducing the sentences of 52 prisoners, including 24 convicted murderers.

Among those released were a 32-year-old man who had shot his ex-wife and her lover 18 times, reloading his two-shot derringer eight times to do so; two men who had tortured a cabbie for a whole night before shooting him to death, and a woman who had poisoned her mother and father-in-law by spiking their Jell-O with arsenic. Because it was feared that Blanton would release even more felons, Lamar Alexander, the governor-elect, took office three days earlier than had been scheduled. Meanwhile, Nashville's country music industry memorialized Blanton's deeds in a tune that swept Tennessee:

> Pardon me, Ray
> Are you the cat that signs the pardons?
> 'Cause you're an old friend of mine
> Just put your name on the line.
> Double-murder and rape
> That's all the jury put me in for.
> And I'm sure you'll agree
> They took advantage of me.

PARISH, Frank (?-1864): Outlaw

When the Montana Vigilance Committee was in its prime, Frank Parish was one of its less important victims, but one whose final word spoiled the intended effect of his execution.

The vigilantes had no evidence connecting Parish with any crimes, but they nonetheless voted to hang him one day in January 1864 along with five other proven criminals. In their deliberations the vigilantes thought it would be wise to hang one man with a bad reputation even though he was not known to have committed any crimes. Such a "preventive hanging" would serve as an example for others, they reasoned. Since Parish associated with the wrong sort of people and was an "outsider," he was regarded as well cast for such an object lesson. The point of the plan, however, was lost when Parish used his last moments to confess his sins, including livestock theft and a $2,500 stagecoach robbery the year before. To their disappointment, the vigilantes discovered they were hanging just another guilty man.

See also: *Vigilantes of Montana.*

PARKER, Bonnie: See Bonnie and Clyde.

PARKER, Ellis (1873-1940): Detective

Often referred to as the county detective with a worldwide reputation and the Cornfield Sherlock, Ellis Parker, as chief of detectives of Burlington County, N.J., was one of this country's leading investigators. Over a career that spanned four decades, he solved thousands of crimes—226 murder mysteries out of 236—using a combination of scientific detection methods and brilliant deductive reasoning. His reputation was such that homicide investigators in all parts of the country asked his advice when stumped on a case. Often, Parker would decide during the early part of an investigation who the guilty party was and stubbornly pursue only that party. In his stubbornness he was almost always right, but his career was to end in shambles because of one case in which he was wrong.

One of Parker's key tenets was that professional criminals always have alibis whereas innocent persons often do not. He once quickly solved the murder of a soldier at Fort Dix, N.J. in a case that involved well over 100 soldiers as likely suspects. Three months after the soldier's disappearance, his body was found. After it was established that he had been murdered, the soldiers in his outfit were asked to come up with alibis and only one was readily able to do so. Parker found it difficult to believe anyone could remember what he had been doing that far back. So he immediately concentrated on that soldier, produced holes in his alibi and developed enough evidence to charge him with the crime and obtain a confession.

In 1920 Parker solved the David Paul murder, a case that students of crime consider to be a classic example of detective logic. When Camden County, N.J. authorities couldn't solve the case, they asked Parker to help. Paul, a 60-year-old runner for a Camden bank, had disappeared with a pouch containing about $100,000 in cash and securities; the logical assumption was that he had absconded. His friends said they had not seen him since the night before his disappearance. Then, 11 days after his disappearance, Paul's body was found in a shallow grave near a stream. Mysteriously, while the ground around the corpse was dry, Paul's overcoat and clothing were sopping wet. He had been shot through the head, and a medical examination showed he had been dead from 48 to 72 hours. It now appeared that Paul actually had absconded with the money and was later killed for it by others or that he had been kidnapped at the start but was kept alive for eight or nine days before being killed.

Stubbornly, Parker refused to accept this latter theory. He was convinced Paul had been murdered eight or nine days earlier than the date set by the medical examination and soon came to believe the solution lay in Paul's wet clothes. At this point the police theorized that Paul's killers, probably unsure about whether the gunshot had killed him, had made certain he was dead by "drowning" his body in a nearby stream, Bread and Cheese Run. Parker found that illogical and stupid and said so. Finally, he discovered there were a number of tanning factories upstream from where the body was found. That gave him the key. He had a chemical analysis made of the water from the stream and learned it had a high percentage of tannic acid, enough to act as a preservative on a human body, so that after a week or more in the water it would show hardly any sign of decomposition.

Now, Parker could zero in on Paul's friends, especially on two men named Frank James and Raymond Schuck, both of whom had alibis for the time when the medical examination estimated the murder had taken place. James had been in a convention in Detroit and Schuck had gone downstate to stay with friends for several days. It was another case of criminals having alibis, according to Parker's pet theory. But they had no alibis for the real time of death, which they had gone to such great lengths to try to hide. That and the fact they had spent a considerable amount of money right after Paul's disappearance strengthened the case against them. Both later confessed and went to the electric chair.

The Lindbergh kidnapping proved to be Parker's last case. A vain man, he was offended when authorities who had so often relied on him failed to ask for his help in solving the nation's most important case. Partisan politics in the state administration and in the state police force were partly responsible. Parker brooded over this snub and then exploded to reporters about the incompetence of the investigation. When Bruno Hauptmann was arrested for the kidnapping, Parker stubbornly held to the theory that he was the wrong man and that the real culprit was a Trenton man named Paul Wendel.

In his investigations Parker had often broken into the homes and offices of suspects in the search for clues. In the Lindbergh case he went even further, actually kidnapping Wendel and holding him captive in various hideaways in Brooklyn, New York City and parts of New Jersey until he extracted a "confession." In court Wendel was able to repudiate the so-called confession, and Parker was open to a federal charge of abduction. He was convicted and sentenced to six years in federal prison and died in confinement in 1940, while a number of his admirers were conducting a campaign to get him a presidential pardon.

See also: *Harold Giles Hoffman, Lindbergh Kidnapping.*

PARKER, Isaac C. "Hanging Judge" (1838-1896): Jurist

The famous "hanging judge" of Arkansas, Isaac Parker was named to the federal bench in 1875 by President Ulysses S. Grant after serving four years as the Republican congressman from Missouri. During the first session of his court, which lasted eight weeks, he tried 91 defendants, including 18 for murder. Of the latter, 15 were convicted, and of these, eight got long prison terms, one was shot trying to escape and the remaining six were sentenced to death. When pronouncing the death sentences, Parker bowed his head and declared: "I do not desire to hang you men. It is the law." Then he started weeping. In time, people came to realize that Judge Parker really enjoyed weeping.

The jurisdiction of his court was the Western District of Arkansas, including the crime-ridden Indian Territory. Over the next 21 years, Parker would sentence 172 persons to death, 88 of whom were executed. Parker's will in the remaining cases was frustrated by presidential pardons and by the acts of other judicial officials. His record of imposing the death sentence was unequaled by any other jurist. Those defending Parker have always claimed that his was a rough jurisdiction and, consequently, a rough court. While 88 men were hanged, no less than 65 of his deputy marshals, "the men who rode for Parker," were killed in the performance of their duty. As a judge, Parker leaned more toward the Bible's eye-for-an-eye precept than toward the finer points of American jurisprudence.

He clearly let everyone in his court, especially the jurors, know where he stood during a case. "I have been accused of leading juries," he once remarked. "I tell you a jury should be led! If they are guided they will render justice. They must know that the judge wants enforcement of the law." Parker's juries certainly knew. The conviction ratio in his court, again a record, was about 8,600 convictions to 1,700 acquittals, or an astonishing 5 to 1.

The one charge he was absolutely rigid on was murder. While hanging was not the only possible sentence for this offense, it was the one Parker insisted on. He would, of course, weep while passing sentence and then weep again as he watched the hanging from the window of his chambers—but he always watched. It would be difficult to read through Parker's sentencing speeches without detecting a strong sense of sadism. Multiple hangings became common and thousands flocked to see three, four, five or even six men do their "dance of death" under the watchful eye of George Maledon, Parker's trusty hangman. Such exhibitions brought Parker nationwide publicity; what surprised him was that very little of it was favorable. His court was referred to as the Court of the Damned, and legal authorities demanded his conduct be tempered.

After 1889 the Supreme Court for the first time allowed appeals from Parker's Indian Territory court, and the results were astonishing. Of 46 doomed persons whose cases reached the High Court, 30 were found to have had unfair trials; of these, 16 were later acquitted and the rest received only prison terms. At one point the Supreme Court informed Parker that the rules of evidence were the same in all parts of the country, despite his well-known concern for rigorous law enforcement in his particular jurisdiction. Angrily, Parker responded, in an interview in the *St. Louis Globe-Democrat,* "During the twenty years that I have engaged in administering the law here, the contest has been one between civilization and savagery being represented by the intruding criminal class." Parker railed on, expressing criticism still heard today, about "the laxity of the Courts" and the Supreme Court's preoccupation with the "flimsiest technicalities." In a sense, Parker was in the same category as the old gunfighter of the West, who also could not see that his day had passed.

Even as Parker held their life in the balance, prisoners began to sneer back at the judge. In 1895 he was about to embark on one of his dramatic death-sentence pronouncements when the defendant, a bandit named Henry Starr, broke in:

> Don't try to stare me down, old Nero. I've looked many a better man than you in the eye. Cut out the rot and save your wind for your next victim. If I am a monster, you are a fiend, for I have put only one man to death, while almost as many men have been slaughtered by your jawbone as Samson slew with the jawbone of that other historic ass.

Parker was struck speechless, for in a sense what had just happened reflected the change in his court over the past two decades. He sentenced Starr to death, but the case was later reversed by the Supreme Court. Finally, in 1895 Congress had had enough and removed the Indian Territory from Parker's jurisdiction. Parker became ill and died before the formal transfer of authority took place.

In the Fort Smith jail news of his death was greeted with jubilation: yet a number of distinguished citizens throughout the country came forward to praise Parker as the greatest judge in the history of the West. Among those with the highest praise for the Hanging Judge were the Indians under his jurisdiction, and a chief of the Creeks attended his funeral. The Indians, like many whites of earlier years, understood the justice Parker imposed.

See also: *Dance of Death, Ann Maledon, George Maledon.*

PARKER, William H. (1902-1966): Los Angeles police chief

For 16 years, until his death in 1966, Chief William H. Parker led the Los Angeles Police Department, shaping it into what many reformers regarded as the nation's preeminent law enforcement agency. Although he was a crusty cop and often accused of "shooting from the lip," Parker was, in his time, probably the most-respected law enforcement official in the country after J. Edgar Hoover, and his views on law enforcement, *Parker on Police,* became required reading for officers in all parts of the country.

Parker, a tea-totaler and nonsmoker, joined the force at the age of 25 and later won a law degree studying at night. Not well liked by other officers in what was then a pretty loose department, Parker nonetheless rose rapidly, becoming chief in 1950. It was a position with less than glowing prospects; the average tenure of his predecessors was 18 months. Parker lasted 16 years, through three city administrations, and was still going strong when struck by a fatal heart attack.

He did much to raise the level of professionalism and efficiency of his officers. Parker set a minimum IQ of 110 for members of the force. A survey in 1965, a year before his death, showed the department had one officer with a doctorate, 15 with master's degrees, 15 with law degrees, 208 with bachelor's degrees, 228 with two-year college certificates, 375 with police academy diplomas and 2,000 officers taking college courses. This was a level of educational achievement that few police departments of any size had attained. Chief Parker created TV's "Dragnet" image and firmly believed his men were carrying it out.

After the Watts riots Martin Luther King remarked that "there is a unanimous feeling that there has been police brutality," a statement that incensed Parker. In 1962 a Civil Rights Commission delegation investigating the riots was unable to cite any specific evidence of flagrant physical brutality by the police. A frequent charge by blacks at the time was that most of the officers were Southerners, but in fact, the vast majority were from the West Coast.

Chief Parker produced a wholesome improvement in his police department and thanks to his efforts the Los Angeles police were rated near the top of any list of good big-city police forces.

PARKHURST, Reverend Charles H. (1842-1933): Reformer

In the 1890s the chief spokesman against all forms of urban vice, especially police corruption, was the Rev. Charles H. Parkhurst, head of the Society for the Prevention of Crime in New York City.

After preaching in New England for a number of years, Parkhurst became pastor of the Madison Square Presbyterian Church in 1880. He attracted very little attention until 1892, when he delivered a blistering sermon against New York City's municipal government in general and Tammany Hall in particular, denouncing the men who ran them as "a lying, perjured, rum-soaked and libidinous lot." Parkhurst also lashed out at the police department for giving protection to and making profit from the city's racketeers, gamblers and prostitutes. He thundered, "While we fight iniquity, they shield or patronize it. While we try to convert criminals, they manufacture them."

When the *New York World* printed almost the entire sermon, Parkhurst's charges took the city by storm. Astonishingly, much of the newspapers' comments about him were unfavorable. The press and various public officials demanded substantiation of his charges, and the following week, when he was hauled before a grand jury, he was ridiculed because he could not present legal evidence to back up his charges. In the end, the grand jury denounced the clergyman for making unfounded charges.

The experience, however, did not silence Parkhurst, who was determined to gather all the evidence he needed by going disguised into the devil's den. With the aid of a private detective, Parkhurst transformed himself into a dandy who could pass without suspicion. The private detective who accompanied Parkhurst related, in a pamphlet called *The Doctor and the Devil,* that "Dr. Parkhurst was a very hard man to satisfy. 'Show me something worse,' was his constant cry. He really went at his slumming work as if his heart was in his tour." A case in point was Parkhurst's visit to Hattie Adams' brothel on 27th Street near Fifth Avenue, where he and the detective hired five girls to perform a "dance of nature." Parkhurst and the detective seemed to get into the spirit of things by engaging in a game of leapfrog with the young ladies, an incident that caused considerable consternation among Parkhurst's parishoners and led to a ribald tune that became extremely popular. It went:

> Dr. Parkhurst on the floor
> Playing leapfrog with a whore,
> Ta-ra-ra-Boom-de-ay
> Ta-ra-ra-Boom-de-ay.

The detective provided earnest assurances that the clergyman removed none of his clothing other than his hat and permitted none of the usual variations in this form of recreation. Indeed, during most of the exercise, the detective assured his readers, "the Doctor sat in a corner with an unmoved face, watching us and slowly sipping at a glass of beer."

When on Sunday March 13, 1892 Dr. Parkhurst preached his second sermon on vice and corruption, he was armed with a number of affidavits from private detectives to back up his charges. Despite the feelings of some that he had demeaned his cloth by his visits to such awful dens of iniquity, his charges could not be ignored and led directly to the famed Lexow and Mazet committees, which based much of their evidence on Parkhurst's findings. In the wave of reform, 14 police officers were indicted or dismissed and many more resigned. Reformers swept into office over Tammany Hall candidates, but the movement proved short-lived. By 1897 Tammany forces were back in power, and they celebrated their victory with an all-night torchlight parade, featuring anti-Parkhurst signs and snake-dancing men and women who chanted, "Well, well, well, reform has gone to hell!"

Parkhurst continued his fight against crime, vice and corruption, and his efforts were very much responsible for the removal from office of Chief of Police Big Bill Devery. Parkhurst retired as a preacher in 1918, and in 1930, at the age of 90, he was honored by a gathering of leading new reformers. He called for the overthrow of the "new Tammany," which he denounced for being as corrupt as the forces he had exposed in the 1890s. Parkhurst lived long enough to watch the Seabury Investigations confirm his charges. He died in 1933 after plunging from his second-floor bedroom window while sleepwalking.

PARKS, Robert F. (1910-1950): Alleged murder victim

Police files are filled with examples of attempts to make murders seem like accidents, but there also have been cases in which accidents have appeared to be murders, resulting in the near conviction of innocent persons. The death of Robert F. Parks in 1950 is often cited by criminologists as a case in point. On the night of February 13 police in Luray, Va. were summoned to the Parks home, where they found Parks, a former Army captain, dead in a bedroom, an open door of which led to the dining room. He had been shot, and because of the absence of powder burns and the direction in which the bullet had entered his body, it appeared that Parks couldn't have shot himself. A bullet had gone through his right arm, passed through his heart and halted in his right side. In the dining room the police found an automatic pistol lying against the far wall from the bedroom door. A cartridge case had jammed in the gun.

Given the circumstantial evidence, the tale Mrs. Parks told was not very convincing. "I was in the kitchen," she said, "when I heard the shot. I ran to the bedroom and Bob was standing there. He looked at me and said, 'Honey, the gun backfired.' And then he fell."

Because the statement didn't square with deductions the police had made about the shooting and because evidence was found that the couple had had violent arguments on a number of occasions, Mrs. Parks was charged with murdering her husband. In all likelihood, the case would have been handled as a typical domestic quarrel leading to homicide had not a sharp-eyed policeman noticed a fresh dent on a metal grille over a hot-air duct in the doorway between the two rooms. The brown paint on the grille had been chipped, and there was brown paint on the rear of the gun slide.

The police sent everything—gun, bullet, cartridge case and grille—to the FBI laboratory. There, experiments showed that the gun would go off if it was dropped on the rear part of the slide and hammer if that part of the gun hit against something. The brown paint on the grille and the gun slide proved to be identical, and the indentations in the grille could have been made by the rear sight and knurling of the hammer. When scientists fitted the rear sight and hammer into the

markings on the grille, it was obvious that in the Parks home the gun would be pointing in the direction of the bedroom where Parks had been standing.

The truth was now apparent. Parks had managed to kill himself accidentally. In an apparent fit of temper, he had thrown the gun against the grille and it had fired, hitting Parks. The gun had then dropped to the floor and slid across the dining room, coming to rest against the far wall from the bedroom.

The murder charge against Mrs. Parks was dismissed.

PAROLE

Of the 200,000-plus adults confined in the nation's prisons about 140,000 are eligible for parole in any given year. Approximately 50,000 are granted parole annually, and almost two-thirds will be paroled before completion of their sentences. Parole is, in a manner of speaking, American in origin in that English felons, beginning in the 1650s, were granted early release from their prison sentences provided they went to America, where they were sold to the highest bidders as indentured servants. In effect, this was a parole system. Our contemporary parole system developed out of the concept of "good time" laws, which shortened prisoners' sentences for good behavior. This led to the introduction of indeterminate-term sentences (e.g., one to 10 years) with the opportunity for release before completion of the sentence. Under this system, which began about 1870 and still exists, the prisoner was required to adhere to certain rules after his release and was subjected to supervision.

Within a half century the system of parole became an ingrained part of all American prison systems. Invariably, when concern over crime has risen, attacks on the parole system have increased. Edward R. Hammock, chairman of the New York State Parole Board, says the public has a "silly notion" that such a board "releases criminals back into the community willy-nilly. It's not true but we're still getting the blame for the fact that people don't feel safe on their streets and in their parks."

Experts insist the idea that parolees commit a great number of new crimes is false. In New York state in 1979 only 3.4 percent were returned to prison for committing new crimes while on parole. Another 8.5 percent were sent back for parole violations. This compares favorably with the overall figure of 30 percent of all ex-prisoners being sent back to prison within five years of their release. Despite these statistics, the parole system is under stronger attack now than at any time during the last 50 years. There has been an obvious shift in national opinion about the method and purpose of sentencing. Concluding that prisons simply do not rehabilitate, more and more judges, prosecutors and even penologists now insist that if criminals cannot be reformed, they should be given uniform, predictable jail sentences and kept off the streets until they have paid for their crimes. Of course, this theory raises the problem of prisons becoming even more crowded and more costly to maintain without much assurance that the public will really be any safer. By 1980 the number of inmates in state prisons had doubled in less than 10 years. "But we're still scared to get on the subway at night," chairman Hammock noted.

In the final analysis, the parole system will probably survive because of recognition that its screening process and supervision of released convicts provides a measure of control over ex-prisoners that would be abolished by a system of fixed jail terms.

See also: *Probation.*

Further reading: *Crime and Punishment* by Aryeh Neier, *Encyclopedia of Criminology* edited by Vernon C. Branham and Samuel B. Kutash.

PARROT Pimp

For some 25 years around the end of the 19th century, Carrie Watson's brothel at 441 South Clark in Chicago was famed for its beautiful inmates, its luxurious trappings and its high prices. So renowned was the resort that Carrie Watson never had a need to advertise. There were no red curtains on the windows and certainly no red light over the doorway. However, Miss Watson did feel a need to add a touch of homey distinction to her premises, so she placed an expensive trained parrot in a cage outside the door. This hustler, who soon was dubbed the Parrot Pimp, would beckon: "Carrie Watson. Come in, gentlemen."

PARSLEY Racket: Underworld extortion method

One of the underworld's fastest growing, if little-known, rackets is the parsley shakedown. For years in New York many Manhattan restaurants have been forced to buy mob parsley to use as a garnish for their meals. In addition to serving it with meats and salads, they have been under considerable pressure to put it in some mixed drinks as well.

As the price was jacked up from 5¢ to 40¢ a bunch, some restaurateurs found their parsley tab amounting to $150 a month. In the early 1980s a number of restaurant owners hit on a money-saving tactic. Since most diners simply shoved aside the greenery, they ordered busboys to put the parsley aside, and then it was washed for reuse.

This affront to good health and the Mafia caused considerable anguish to a 75-year-old mafioso known to New York restaurateurs as *Un Occhio,* or One Eye, a name given him because of an injury suffered back in 1934 in the bombing of an East Side bakery. *Un Occhio,* who handled both parsley and murders for the mob out of his East Harlem headquarters, walked into a few restaurants and expressed outrage at this disgraceful recycling of parsley. On the spot one steak house owner ordered 150 new bunches. *New York Daily News* columnist Jimmy Breslin commented, "That night, as they will forever, the steak house and all other midtown restaurants served meals that appeared to be growing lawns."

There has never been much doubt that New York's fondness for parsley will eventually spread around the country. At the same time the mob squashed the parsley rebellion in Manhattan, the Montana State Crime Control Commission was investigating the bombings of two restaurants in Butte. The commission reported it had intelligence that a New York "parsley king" was involved in the bombings.

Un Occhio is reported to control vast acres of parsley in Ventura County, Calif. that can be cut five times a year, enough to feed not only New York but a green-hungry nation.

PAT Lyon At The Forge: Painting of accused criminal

Virtually none of the visitors to Boston's Museum of Fine Arts who pause to admire an early 19th century painting, *Pat Lyon at the Forge,* by John Neagle, are aware that the blacksmith it portrays was, in his time, famous as one of America's first "wrong men," accused of a crime he did not commit.

Pat Lyon was a leading Philadelphia-area blacksmith who did many jobs for local banks and wealthy citizens, designing strongboxes and repairing locks and bars. Shortly after he performed this latter task for a Philadelphia bank, it was entered surreptitiously and looted.

The police could think of only one likely suspect, blacksmith Lyon. Despite his anguished denials, he was thrown into jail on the theory that he alone could have gotten by those locks and bars. After three months the real criminals were caught and Lyon was released. But he had much to be bitter about. There were still whispers that he must have been involved, and he discovered his business suffered because of this rumor. Finally, after enduring the malicious talk for some years, he brought suit against his more virulent defamers. The courts ruled in the blacksmith's favor, and he was granted $9,000 in damages.

It was an enormous sum of money in that day, and Lyon could have retired on his fortune, but he found a better use for a large portion of his new-found wealth. He commissioned John Neagle, the finest portrait painter he could locate, to paint the real Pat Lyon, an honest blacksmith toiling at his honest labors. *Pat Lyon at the Forge* is the way this wrongly accused man wished to be remembered by posterity.

PATRIARCA, Raymond L. S. (1908-   ): New England Mafia boss

The Mafia boss of New England, Raymond Patriarca is probably almost as feared as Vito Genovese was; like Genovese, he was able to keep running his crime empire even while serving time in prison for his part in a murder conspiracy in the early 1970s.

He is regarded as totally ruthless, as he demonstrated during the Irish wars in Boston when a young upstart Irish gangster named Bernard McLaughlin tried to muscle in on the mob's loansharking rackets. McLaughlin and his supporters were totally eradicated. On one occasion, Patriarca allegedly even threatened his own brother with death because, while in charge of mob security, he had failed to catch an FBI bug planted in Patriarca's office.

As a young gangster, Patriarca showed a remarkable ability to avoid trouble with the law, only going to prison once, for armed robbery in 1938. He was sentenced to five years but won a pardon after serving only 84 days. The resulting newspaper publicity forced an examination of the facts surrounding the pardon. It was found that a key factor behind the pardon was an imploring letter from one Father Fagin, who turned out to be a nonexistent priest. Patriarca was ordered back to prison to do his time.

During the 1940s and 1950s, Patriarca set about building his crime empire from his base in Providence, R.I., concentrating on vice, gambling and loansharking enterprises. Remarkably, as his empire grew over the next 25 years, he was seldom mentioned in the press. Finally, though, because of Joseph Barboza, a hit man turned informer, Patriarca was convicted of conspiracy to commit murder for ordering an underling in 1966 to kill Rocco DiSiglio, a young mafioso who was fingering mob crap games for a stickup gang.

After a number of appeals he went to prison in 1970 to serve five years. During that time Patriarca continued to run Mafia affairs in New England, and he reputedly warned other Mafia bosses to stay out of his area. They did.

PATTERSON, Nan (1882-?): Accused murderer

The 1904 case, one the New York newspapers dubbed The Girl in the Hansom Cab, had everything the readers of the new yellow journalism could want: a Floradora Girl, at the time the most dazzling of Broadway figures; a big-spending gambler and race horse owner; a jealous wife, and a murder mystery.

Gorgeous Nan Patterson was Floradora Girl, not a member of the original sextette but a replacement for one who had married a millionaire. All Floradora Girls, the public believed, were destined to marry millionaires. Nan, a doll-faced, stage-struck young thing, had made it to the Great White Way after eloping in her teens. She later fell for, instead of a millionaire, a married gambler, Francis Thomas Young, known to his friends as Caesar. Young, who was what might be called a cad, and Nan were constantly seen together at the races, at gambling spas and at all the top hotels and restaurants. However, Young also had a wife, whom he wouldn't or couldn't give up. He kept his wife in one New York hotel and Nan in another on the same block. It made the gambler's life a hectic one. He paid for Nan's divorce, and in 1904 he finally decided to divorce his wife and run off with Nan. But his wife talked him out of that plan and the couple reconciled. Feeling she could win back her husband from Nan by separating them, she convinced Young to sail to Europe with her on June 4.

The day before his departure, Young spent his time with Nan Patterson. The pair drank heavily and quarreled, Nan still trying to get him to change his mind. Early the following morning, they had a make-up breakfast and entered a hansom cab for a ride down Broadway. Suddenly, there was the sound of an explosion inside the cab. Nan was heard to cry out: "Look at me, Frank. Why did you do it?"

What Nan Patterson claimed Young had done was shoot himself in the chest, out of anguish over having to leave her. It was a peculiar story in that, as newspaper sketches would explain to their eager readers, Young would have had to have been a contortionist to have inflicted the wound that had killed him. In addition, somehow the dying man had managed to put the gun back in his pocket.

Nan was arrested for murder. The state's version was that she had pulled out a gun, and when Young grabbed it, she had pulled the trigger. During two sensational trials Nan took the stand and stuck to her story despite vigorous cross-examination. In neither case could the prosecution get better than a hung jury, and speculation arose that the state simply would never be able to get a jury of 12 men to visualize a smoking pistol in such a lovely woman's hand. The district attorney's office tried a third time, with the same predictable result. In her prison cell Nan was deluged with messages of sympathy and not a few offers of marriage. It was all too much for the authorities. Ten days after the third trial, the judge granted a motion that she be discharged, and a crowd of 2,000 persons cheered her as she was released. Children sang in the streets:

> Nan is free, Nan is free,
> She escaped the electric chair,
> Now that she's out in the open air.

That night Nan Patterson got gloriously drunk at one plush Broadway spot after another. She soon was offered starring roles in top musicals, but her career collapsed when theatergoers discovered she had no acting or other talent. Nan then reconciled with her ex-husband and they remarried. However, the union again soon ended in divorce, and The Girl in the Hansom Cab just faded away.

PEACEMAKER, The: Wild Bill Hickok's gun

Certainly one of the most-storied weapons of the Old West was Wild Bill Hickok's Peacemaker, a single-action Colt, serial no. 139345. Wild Bill reportedly killed 14 men with the gun in the two years he owned it before his death on August 2, 1876, when Jack McCall shot him in the back of the head while he was playing poker in Deadwood, Dakota Territory. Hickok's personal belongings, including the Peacemaker, were sent to his sister, Mrs. Lydia M. Barnes of Oberlin, Kan.

Over the next six years nothing was heard about Wild Bill's famous pistol. On the night of July 14, 1882, it was fired in a darkened room in old Fort Sumner, New Mexico Territory and a youthful man lay dead on the floor. The dead man was Billy the Kid. The man holding the Peacemaker was Sheriff Pat Garrett. Legend has it that when Hickok was killed by McCall, Billy the Kid had been riding to Deadwood with the intention of forcing a duel with Wild Bill. In an extraordinary coincidence, the gun that might have killed the Kid then was responsible for his death six years later. It turned out that Wild

Bill's sister had given the Colt to a family friend, Pat Garrett, who wore it while hunting down Billy the Kid.

When Garrett retired from law enforcement, he gave the weapon to Fred Sutton of Oklahoma City, a collector of historical firearms. Since then the Peacemaker has passed from one eager gun collector to another, becoming perhaps the most famous gun in Western history.

PEACH, Arthur (?-1638): Murderer

The first white man executed in America for the murder of an Indian, Arthur Peach was, according to a contemporary account, a "lustie and desparate yonge man" who murdered an Indian youth of the "Narigansett" tribe returning from the Massachusetts Bay Colony with cloth and beads he had acquired in trade. Three runaway servants had helped Peach commit the crime; two of them were caught with him. The capture of Peach and his two confederates led to an argument about whether three white men should be executed for the killing of one Indian. Gov. William Bradford wrote that during the affair "some of the rude & ignorante sorte" among the colonists raised the question as to whether "*any* English should be put to death for the Indians."

It was finally decided that Peach and his confederates should die, and most certainly, the decision was not made on moral grounds alone. The more level-headed colonists warned that if the crime was not quickly avenged, "it would raise a war." The authorities invited a number of Indians to the hanging, "which gave them & all the countrie good satisfaction." It was an application of justice seldom repeated over the next 250 years in this country.

PEACOCK, Dr. Silber C. (1896-1936): Murder victim

Few murdered persons have ever been more unjustly maligned than was Dr. Silber C. Peacock, a successful and wealthy Chicago pediatrician who was killed on the night of January 2, 1936.

Dr. Peacock had left his home at 10:05 p.m. to answer what was to prove to be a fake emergency call about a sick child. Hours later, he was found dead in his Cadillac, shot, slashed and viciously clubbed. Dr. Peacock did not appear to have been robbed of his money or valuables (it was subsequently discovered that $20 had been taken), and the public and the newspapers soon began a series of speculations about him. Among other things, he was said to have been the victim of a narcotics robbery, a leading narcotics dealer, the keeper of a secret love nest, a habitue of underworld dives and a society abortionist. All these allegations eventually proved groundless. For example, the charge of keeping a "swank love nest," as one newspaper put it, started because his wife could not identify an apartment key that was found in his possession at the time of his death. Eventually, the police discovered it was the key to the apartment of the parents-in-law of a Chicago deputy coroner, who, during his investigation, had somehow inadvertently dropped it among the effects found on the dead man.

Finally, 10 weeks after the slaying, four young men were arrested and confessed to the murder. They had plotted to rob a physician, selected Peacock's name out of hundreds of doctors listed in the classified telephone directory and lured him to his death with a telephone call. When he had resisted, they killed him and fled. Three of the culprits—Emil Reck, Robert Goethe and Durland Nash—went to prison for 199 years plus four consecutive terms of one year to life. The fourth, 17-year-old Mickey Livingston, drew a 30-year sentence.

PEDIGREED Dog Swindle

A short con, or quick hustle, the pedigreed dog swindle is less important for its own sake than it is for the more lucrative swindles it fathered.

The 19th century victim of such a caper was often a bartender, who was approached by a strange customer with a dog, most often a mongrel terrier. The customer would explain that the dog was a prize winner and produce some impressive-looking papers to prove the point. "Look," he might say, "this dog is really valuable and I have an important meeting with some bankers and I can't take him with me. I'll give you ten dollars to watch him for a couple of hours."

Naturally, the bartender would agree. After the dog owner left with a final word about how valuable the dog was, another customer would walk in. He would pretend to be very impressed by the dog, declaring he really liked the animal and that his kids would be wild about it. After this buildup he would offer the bartender $50 for the animal. The bartender would explain the dog was not his, but the man would only grow more insistent, raising the offer to $100. Patiently, the bartender would refuse and keep refusing as the ante was raised. Finally, the customer would say, "Listen, I'll stop conning you. I know my dog flesh. That's a valuable dog. If you'll sell it, I'll go to five hundred dollars."

By now the bartender would be in agony, turning down such an offer. The customer would then say, "Look, I'm from out of town. If you can swing a deal for me for the dog, I'll give you the five hundred, but I have to catch a train in an hour and I'll stop back just before I have to leave."

A half an hour later the dog's owner would reappear, looking downcast, and order a drink. The bartender would serve him, asking if anything was wrong. Sorrowfully nodding, the dog owner would explain that his business deal had fallen through. "I was really counting on that deal, now I don't know what I'll do."

The bartender, trying to curb his enthusiasm, might then offer to help the poor dog owner. He had taken a liking, he would explain, and was willing to pay $100 for it. The dog owner wouldn't consider it, again pointing out how valuable the animal was. The bartender would have to raise the bid to $300 before the owner would agree to part with the valuable animal, but only with the proviso that he could buy the dog back the following month for $400 if he solved his financial problems. That detail wouldn't worry the bartender. He could always say the dog had been trampled by a horse.

The bartender would take the money from the register and exchange it for the mutt. Now, with the original owner gone, he only had to wait for the return of the prospective buyer to realize a $200 profit. Of course, this proved to be a wait considerably longer than the dog's life span.

The pedigreed dog swindle was a favorite with the short con operators for decades, and eventually, it evolved into a bigger con, with the profits increasing 10- to 100-fold. The victim changed from a bartender to a greedy banker or businessman, and instead of selling a pedigreed dog, the con man would offer a gold mine or some oil stock, invariably worthless, which, for some reason, he could no longer keep.

PEEL, Fanny (1828-1858): Famous 19th century prostitute

Perhaps the most famous 19th century American prostitute was "the notorious Fanny Peel," as the New Orleans newspapers labeled her.

The daughter of a Troy, N.Y. clergyman and a graduate of the Troy Female Seminary, she had been "soiled" at the age of 15 and thereafter became a prostitute, at the time virtually the only fate possible for one so ruined. After working in a number of brothels, her uncommon beauty attracted the attention of a rich man and he made her his mistress. Thereafter, she became the mistress of a number of millionaires from New York to Chicago, acquiring a considerable fortune for herself in the process.

In 1857 Fanny came to New Orleans rich enough to employ a coachman, a free black. Ever on the lookout for more money, she sold him as a slave to a Louisiana planter and entered a fashionable brothel on Dauphine Street. She was soon hailed by the press as easily the most beautiful courtesan ever to appear in New Orleans. Disenchantment set in rather quickly, however, as Fanny rejected the money of the city's leading bloods, declaring the men visiting the brothel were not good enough for her. Finally, she was dismissed by the brothel and left New Orleans for Mobile, Ala., where she died the following summer.

PENDERGAST, Thomas Joseph (1872-1945): Kansas City political boss

For several decades Boss Tom Pendergast of Kansas City ran a political machine whose record for graft, fraud, strong-arm tactics and murder probably surpassed that of any other machine in the country. During the underworld meetings of the 1920s and 1930s that culminated in the formation of the national crime syndicate, Pendergast was the only political boss invited to take part in the deliberations. Generally, he was represented in crime circles by the king of Kansas City's North Side wards, Johnny Lazia. Pendergast, who became a power in state and national politics, once said, "People work for a party because they can get a job or get a favor."

The Pendergast machine was first organized around the turn of the century by Tom's older brother James, a former saloon keeper who built a base in the Catholic blue-collar wards of the city. When James died in 1910, Tom took charge and slowly extended his influence throughout the city. By the 1920s he was in firm control. He quickly converted Kansas City into a truly open town, parceling out control of horse racing wires, liquor, vice and gambling. In 1922 Pendergast launched the political career of Harry S Truman by aiding his election as county judge. Later on, many opponents of Truman attempted to tar him with the Pendergast brush, failing to understand that most political machines utilize a few incorruptible types to provide a touch of class to their operation. Almost inevitably, these individuals are backed, as Truman was, for positions such as U.S. senator or others of little importance to a machine compared to those at city hall or at the state house.

While the Pendergast machine mainly achieved its goals by fraud, it made use of violence if deemed necessary. When Lazia was convicted of tax evasion in 1934 and was threatening to inform on the machine, his lips were sealed by machine-gun bullets in an execution almost certainly ordered by the Pendergast forces. It has long been theorized that the infamous Kansas City Massacre in June 1933 was actually a planned rub-out of Frank "Jelly" Nash, the man whom the machine-gunning gangsters were allegedly trying to free. Nash knew the ins and outs of the machine as well as all facets of crime in Kansas City; if he had talked, many important figures would have faced jail. While the FBI charged the crime to Verne Miller, Pretty Boy Floyd and Adam Richetti, considerable evidence developed later indicated the agency was wrong and that the real killers were Miller, Maurice Denning and William "Solly" Weissman. The bodies of Miller and Weissman turned up later that year but Denning disappeared. It seemed evident that they were killed not because they had murdered Nash but because they knew who had ordered his execution. This version was backed up by the later statements of underworld figure Blackie Audett, who said that almost everyone in power in Kansas City knew about the impending rub-out. At the time, one of Pendergast's closest associates was City Manager Henry McElroy. Audett stated that Mary McElroy, Henry McElroy's daughter, knew about the shooting hours before it occurred and, in fact, invited him to come with her to Union Station to watch the execution. He said they had witnessed the massacre from about 50 yards away. Even if Audett's story was apocryphal, it still captured the flavor of Pendergast's domain, where anything could happen.

For a time it seemed Tom Pendergast's hold on Kansas City's politics and underworld was untouchable, but the federal government started a massive crackdown in the late 1930s, thanks to the machine's effrontery in the 1936 elections. Although the city had a population of under 400,000, it managed to come up with an astonishing total of about 270,000 registered voters. Federal Judge Albert L. Reeves ordered a grand jury investigation, stating:

I can't sit quietly in my district here, charged with responsibility as I am, and allow my fellow countrymen who stand for the law, and the citizens who stand for the law, to witness some man going with dripping fingers to the ballot box. A corrupt vote is akin to a gun pointing at the very heart of America.

The FBI uncovered damning evidence of vote theft, stuffed ballot boxes and intimidation of voters. There was clear proof that erasures had been made on ballots. Indentations on many ballots revealed they had been marked one on top of the other. One precinct captain, complaining about his hard day, stated: "I've been in the basement and those damn Republicans certainly write heavy. It was a tough job erasing."

No less than 256 Pendergast followers were convicted in the vote fraud case, marking the beginning of the end of the Pendergast machine. The boss himself was convicted of tax evasion in 1939. Although he served only a year, his control over Kansas City was broken. He died in 1945.

See also: *Kansas City Massacre.*

PEONAGE

As a method of forced labor to pay off debts, peonage continued in the United States after the end of slavery. The system, introduced in the New World by the Spaniards was applied in both North and South America. Well into the 20th century it was possible for an employer in some states in this country to swear out a warrant against a poor, unsophisticated workman, arrange his release on bail and force him to work on a plantation or farm under the threat of being sent back to prison. In certain states employers were allowed to pay off a prisoner's fine and then require him to work off the debt. The federal government finally moved in to protect the civil rights of such laborers.

The case that probably caused more public revulsion over the practice and led to a major crackdown occurred in Georgia in 1921. A farm owner, John S. Williams, "bought" black prisoners from state and county road gangs and bound them to work out the so-called purchase price on his farm. When agents of the Bureau of Investigation (the forerunner of the FBI) started probing into Williams' operations, evidence indicated he had killed at least a dozen of the ex-prisoners in an attempt to eliminate witnesses who might testify against him. He was convicted of murder and imprisoned for life. To this day reports of peonage continue to turn up in connection with various share-cropping systems in the South.

The newest form of peonage involves the illegal importation of Mexican workers. Produce growers of California's lush San Joaquin and Imperial valleys pay smugglers to bring in the illegal aliens at so much a head. These smugglers also collect money from the aliens, who are unaware they are being sold into a form of near-slavery. The growers and ranchers find these imported workers to be docile and pliant. They are totally isolated on the farms and remain under the threat of arrest and deportation. They are not permitted to read newspapers and are generally worked 10 to 12 hours a day for incredibly small pay and their keep.

Prosecutions for this crime have been virtually nonexistent, certainly in view of the scope of the activity.

See also: Pollos.

PEPPERBOX Revolver

The pepperbox revolver was one of the most popular small handguns of the 19th century, generally selling for about $5.75, which today would be considered the price range of a Saturday Night Special. Only two and a half to three inches long, this multibarrel weapon generally came in two styles: stationary barrels with a rotating firing pin or with barrels that revolved into a position over the firing pin. The caliber of the gun varied from .22 to .36, the larger size certainly enough to blow much of a victim's head off at close range. Christian Sharps produced the most popular pepperbox, a four-barrel model, in 1859; over a 20-year period Americans bought 150,000 of them. While the weapon was very inaccurate beyond a few feet, holdup artists found sticking four barrels into a victim's face was a most effective convincer.

As a result of the 1968 Gun Control Act, a 20th century copy of Sharps' four-barrel model using .22-long ammunition and selling for under $30 was placed on the embargo list.

See also: *Derringer, Saturday Night Special.*

PERCY, Valerie (1945-1966): Murder victim

Senatorial candidate Charles H. Percy's 21-year-old twin daughter Valerie was killed in the family's mansion in Kenilworth, Ill. on September 18, 1966. At about 5 a.m. that morning Percy was awakened by his wife's screams. He immediately turned on a switch that set off a piercing burglar alarm atop the 17-room suburban home and rushed to Valerie's bedroom, where he found the girl still alive but mutilated by numerous stab wounds. She died shortly thereafter. Hearing a noise, Valerie's stepmother had investigated and come upon a shadowy intruder standing over the girl's bed. He had shined a flashlight in the woman's face and, while she was temporarily blinded, successfully made his escape.

The case shocked the country and for a time its political impact in the Senate race between Percy and 74-year-old Senate Democrat Paul Douglas was hard to gauge. Some political observers concluded the tragedy produced a significant sympathy vote for Percy that helped him win the election although Douglas later admitted that Percy had already pulled ahead of him in the summer.

From the beginning, there appeared to have been a sexual motive behind the Percy murder, indicating the act of a person harboring a strong sexual animosity toward the girl. Over the next several years the case remained unsolved despite Sen. Percy's offer of a $50,000 reward and an intensive police investigation, in which 14,000 persons were questioned and 1,317 leads followed up. A total of 19 confessions were made—all false. A youth in Tucson, Ariz. confessed to the murder in October 1966 but later denied it. In 1971 police in South Yarmouth, Mass. reported that a 24-year-old man had admitted committing the Percy killing and 17 other murders as well. Confession number 18, another phony, was made by a 26-year-old suspect in a Las Vegas murder case. The final one came from a 27-year-old man in Miami, who not only claimed he had killed Valerie but John F. Kennedy, Robert F. Kennedy and Martin Luther King as well.

By 1973, the authorities considered the murder solved, although they agreed there would probably never be a prosecution. Reporter Art Petacque of the *Chicago Sun-Times* broke the case by obtaining a statement from a Mafia operative, 58-year-old Leo Rugendorf, who oversaw the activities of a gang of cat burglars that had robbed the homes of wealthy people all over the country. Rugendorf, near death from heart disease, fingered burglars Francis Hohimer and Frederick Malchow, who had plunged to his death from a railroad trestle in 1967 after escaping from a Pennsylvania prison. Hohimer at the time was doing 30 years in the Iowa State Penitentiary for armed robbery.

Rugendorf said Hohimer told him shortly after the murder: "They'll get me for the Valerie Percy murder. The girl woke up, and I hit her on the top of the head with a pistol." In addition, the reporter was able to get corroboration of Rugendorf's claim from Hohimer's younger brother, Harold, who reported Frank was "real nervous and uptight" the day after the murder. Harold said his brother had told him he "had to 'off' a girl."

Harold Hohimer further stated: "I asked him why he had to do someone in, and he said it was because the girl made a lot of noise and they got in a fight. I asked him, 'What score are you talking about?' and he said, 'It's all in the newspapers and on the radio today.' He was talking about the Valerie Percy thing."

Yet another acquaintance of Frank Hohimer claimed Frank had told him two weeks before the murder that he had cased the Percy mansion and intended to rob it. After maintaining his silence for a while, Frank Hohimer consented to answer questions put to him by Petacque and investigators. He denied killing Valerie and denied being in the Percy mansion. Instead, he accused Malchow of the murder, stating that on the morning of the crime Malchow had come to his flat in blood-soaked clothes.

In 1975 Frank Hohimer wrote a book about his criminal past, *The Home Invaders*, admitting a number of burglaries, including a robbery of Elvis Presley's mansion in Memphis, but holding to his version of the Percy murder.

Without physical evidence linking Malchow or Hohimer to the murder, officials admit, there is no chance anyone will ever be prosecuted for the murder of Valerie Percy. The offer of $50,000 reward has been withdrawn. Reporter Petacque won a Pulitzer Prize for his work on the story.

PERKINS, Josephine Amelia (1818-?): Horse thief

Following a series of misadventures in her native England, a young woman named Josephine Amelia Perkins arrived in New York in the 1830s without any money or a place to stay and only the clothes on her back. She immediately stole a horse, thereby taking the initial step toward becoming notorious as America's first female horse thief. In 1839 she published

her confession, which included the following description of herself:

> A young woman, who, in early life was deservedly esteemed for her exemplary behavior, yet for three years last past (friendless and unprotected) has been unhappily addicted to a criminal propensity, more singular and surprising in its nature (for one of her sex) than can be found on record; in the commission of which, she has been four times detected, twice pardoned on account of her sex, once for reasons of supposed insanity, and the fourth and last time, convicted and sentenced to two years imprisonment in Madison county jail, Kentucky. Annexed is a well-written Address to Parents and Children.

She did not total up her thefts but they apparently numbered in the hundreds.

Since horse-theft was considered no minor crime, Perkins apparently decided any future infractions would bring severe punishment, and so far as the record shows, she appears to have retired from the profession in 1841.

PERRY, Oliver Curtis (1864-1930): Train robber

Train robbery was often thought of as a Western crime, but probably the greatest train robber of all practiced his art in the East. His name was Oliver Curtis Perry and he was described by the *New York World* as "one of the most spectacular train robbers the country has ever known." The accolade was well-deserved. Perry was a former Wyoming cowboy who had come east to make his dishonest fortune. In a series of incredible one-man capers, he displayed a daring never equaled by any other train robber.

Perry, who claimed to be a descendant of Oliver Hazard Perry, the hero of the Battle of Lake Erie in 1812, committed his first train robbery on September 29, 1891. With a small saw, he cut out a square in the wooden end of the express car of the New York Central's Fast Flyer No. 31 out of Albany and crawled through a pile of packages to overpower the messenger inside. After tying the messenger up, he broke open the safe and took $5,000 in cash and $3,000 in jewelry. Then, hanging by one hand, sawed through the air hose between the express car and the adjoining car, bringing the crack train to a halt. Perry jumped down and fled into the nearby woods, making good his escape.

Pinkerton detectives learned the identity of the robber when he turned up in Rochester spending too much money in saloons and whorehouses and dropping boastful hints. Knowing Perry's identity and catching him, however, were two different matters. The Pinkertons just missed catching him after each of two more robberies he pulled.

Perry's wildest train robbery took place near Lyons, N.Y. in 1892, a spectacular attempt that even Hollywood would have rejected as too far-fetched. Having learned that a New York Central train departing Syracuse on September 20 would contain $100,000, he somehow got on top of the icy roof of the train's express car during the height of a hailstorm, slid down a rope and kicked in a side window. Firing a shot over the head of the messenger in the car, he jumped through the window.

In a savage fight Perry pistol-whipped the messenger into unconsciousness, but not before his victim managed to pull the bell rope. The bandit worked feverishly at cracking open the safe until he was interrupted by an investigating conductor. Perry fired a shot at the conductor and fled, stopping just long enough to rifle the unconscious messenger's pockets and empty the petty cash box.

A newspaper sketch illustrates one of Oliver Curtis Perry's most spectacular train robberies.

Flinging open the door, he jumped out of the train, which had ground to a stop near Jordan, N.Y. He intimidated the crew and passengers with several more shots and ordered the train to move, warning that otherwise he would shoot to kill. The train picked up speed and headed for Lyons, N.Y. When it got there, a 50-man posse was formed to return to Jordan and hunt for the train robber. Just as the posse was about to leave on a special train, the conductor who had interrupted Perry in the express car spotted him moving briskly through the station. After he had ordered the train to pull out in Jordan, Perry had hopped aboard the last car and pretended to be a passenger. But for the conductor noticing him, he would have made good his escape in Lyons.

Perry wasn't through yet. He raced through the train yards,

with the posse after him, and jumped aboard a freight engine already moving out under a full head of steam. He forced the engineer and fireman to jump and took off with the throttle wide open. His pursuers mounted a faster engine on a parallel set of tracks and gave chase, quickly closing ground on him. As they neared several members of the posse opened up with pistols and shotguns. Perry threw his engine in reverse and headed in the opposite direction. As the two engines passed each other, Perry exchanged shots with the posse men, who then put their engine in reverse. Again the two cars met, with more shots exchanged. Perry's engine and that of his pursuers flew back and forth through the train yards, bullets filling the air. Finally, the steam supply in Perry's locomotive dropped and he was forced to make a run for the woods.

The posse chased Perry into the swamps. He probably still would have escaped had not another posse under Wayne County Deputy Sheriff Jeremiah Collins cut him off. Interviewed by a reporter after his capture, Perry said, "I had to take a bold stroke with big chances and I guess I lost."

He was sentenced to 49 years in Auburn Prison. Even following his confinement the press continued to fawn over him, quoting Pinkertons Superintendent George Bangs' description of the Lyons caper as "the most daring train robbery attempt in criminal history. I would call Perry the nerviest outlaw I ever heard of. There are few western badmen who possessed his courage."

In prison, Perry was deluged by mail from women, including many proposals of marriage. One even sent him a saw hidden inside a Bible. After causing a number of disturbances, he was removed to the State Hospital for the Criminally Insane at Matteawan. In 1895 Perry received another saw hidden in a Bible from the young lady who had sent him the same type of gift while he was in Auburn. He sawed through the bars of his cell and, after releasing a number of other prisoners, slid down 80 feet of drainpipe to freedom.

With no money and a huge posse tracking him, Perry made his way to New York City and then slipped aboard a ferry to Weehawken, N.J. The town policeman there caught him as he huddled sick and hungry over a small fire.

Perry was sent to the maximum-security prison at Dannemora, but he still dreamed of making another escape. After several futile efforts he was put in solitary confinement, where he was to remain for a quarter of a century. In 1920, having long since given up hope of escaping, Perry constructed a device consisting of a block of wood and two nails and used it to pierce both of his eyes. Permanently blinded, he dictated a letter to his lawyer: "I was born in the light of day, against my will of course. I now assert my right to shut out that light. In plain words I wanted to tear out my eyes."

Perry tried to starve himself to death during his last six years but was kept alive by forced feedings until he passed away in 1930. In those final years he refused to say a word to his guards. It was a gruesome end for a man who, according to the *New York World,* had "electrified the nation with his daring exploits."

PERRY, Phenie (1917-1937): Murder victim

Few killers have ever gone to such great lengths to frame someone else for their crime as 23-year-old Arthur Perry did for the murder of his 20-year-old wife, Phenie. In the event his wife died, Perry stood to collect $1,000 in insurance money, a not inconsequential sum in the Depression year of 1937. A passing pedestrian found the body of Phenie Perry in a lot on 157th St. in Jamaica, New York City. Her dress was torn down the front and her knees were dirt-smeared and scarred. She had been bludgeoned and kicked to death, and her body lay in a pool of blood. There were plenty of footprints belonging to the murderer. Better yet, there was even one of his bloodstained shoes.

All this was part of Arthur Perry's unique plot. The Perrys shared a home with another couple, the Ulysses Palms. Perry had decided to frame Palm, a church deacon, precisely because he was an unlikely suspect and an illogical choice for anyone to attempt to frame.

First, he forged a love letter to his wife and signed Palm's name to it. In the letter Palm demanded that Phenie Perry be nice to him. It was an excellent forgery and respected handwriting experts would dispute whether Palm or Perry had written it. On the night of the murder, Arthur Perry put on a pair of shoes he had stolen from Palm and waylaid Phenie as she was coming home from a movie. He did it at a time when he knew Palm was home alone, while Mrs. Palm was visiting friends on church business. After killing his wife, Perry left one of Palm's shoes at the scene of the crime. He also had stolen some papers and personal letters from Palm as well as one of his shirts. He then ripped the pocket from the shirt and planted it and the papers under the body so that it would appear Phenie Perry had ripped off the pocket in her death struggle. All Perry had to do then was slip back home with one shoeless foot and plant the remaining shoe and the torn shirt in one of Palm's closets while he was sleeping.

It was an intricate and cunning plot and it almost worked. At first, investigating officers had little doubt that Palm was their man. The only thing that bothered them was the deacon's strong denials and his spotless reputation. That made them look at Arthur Perry a little more closely, and they eventually found evidence that he had staged the murder to make it look like the act of his neighbor. Perry had slipped on one minor point, which proved enough to send him to the chair. Dirt particles on his sock were found to match a sample of dirt taken from the scene of the murder.

PETERS, Frederick Emerson (1885-1959): Check passer

Probably the most prolific passer of bad checks in American history, Frederick Emerson Peters, starting at age 17, cashed thousands of bad checks all over the United States, using hundreds of different names. One of his favorite ploys was to pose as the son or some other relative of a well-known figure,

especially Theodore Roosevelt, whose appearance he could somewhat emulate. He would engage a shopkeeper in conversation, casually let drop his identity and then make a purchase with a check for a somewhat larger amount. Few small shopkeepers, impressed by having a celebrity as a customer, would turn him down; in fact, any number of them would eventually frame the bad check and proudly recall the time they "got took by Teddy Roosevelt's kid."

Asked once why he continued to write bad checks after a number of convictions, Peters shrugged and said it was so easy that it would take the "rock-like willpower of the Sphinx to resist such temptation." He stated his record achievement was to pass 30 worthless checks in one day in a small Indiana town whose name he could no longer remember. Much of his life was spent behind bars; during those tours he often helped establish prison libraries. One day while he was making his check-passing rounds in New Haven, Conn., he suffered a fatal stroke; Peters was 74 years old at the time. He was given a pauper's funeral, although it was observed that with some advanced warning he could have given the undertaker a handsome check.

See also: *Check Passing.*

PETERS, Philip (1868-1941): Murder victim of Denver's Spiderman

On the evening of October 17, 1941, a Denver, Colo. couple became worried about an elderly neighbor, Philip Peters. They broke into his home and found him murdered. It turned out to be one of the most bizarre cases in that city's history, with the killer to become famous as the Spiderman of Moncrieff Place. What the police couldn't figure out was how the murderer had escaped. All the doors and windows had been locked from the inside, but no one was found hiding in the house.

About a month earlier, 59-year-old Theodore Coneys, a tramp who had known Peters years before, approached the house to beg for food. Just then Peters came out and entered a car to visit his sick wife in the hospital. Coneys slipped into the house to steal money and food but made an opportune discovery: a trapdoor, only about 2½ times the size of a cigar-box lid, which led to a narrow attic cubbyhole. Rounding up a pile of rags, some food and an old crystal radio, Coneys settled into his newly found hiding place.

He planned to become a permanent uninvited boarder. Whenever Peters left the house, Coneys would descend from his attic hideout and eat, bathe and shave, using Peters' razor. On October 17 Coneys was in the kitchen eating. He thought Peters had gone out, but the old man was just taking a nap. Suddenly, the kitchen door popped open, and Peters stood there gaping. Coneys panicked. He grabbed an iron stove shaker and attacked Peters, who was screaming and had obviously not recognized him. Peters collapsed on the floor dead.

Coneys did not flee the house, feeling he had nowhere to go. He climbed back up into his hiding place and was there when the murder was discovered and the police searched the house. The officers had noticed the trapdoor but decided a man could not fit through it. They were partially right: an average-sized man couldn't but a thin man—like Coneys—could.

When Mrs. Peters returned from the hospital, she and her housekeeper kept hearing strange sounds in the house, and the tale soon spread in the area that the house was haunted. One night the housekeeper caught a glimpse of a shadowy figure creeping around. She convinced herself that it was Mr. Peters' ghost and talked Mrs. Peters into moving.

Even with the house vacant, Coneys did not leave. The electricity was left on and he had stored up some food and could get water by scraping snow from the gutters. Often, a passerby would notice an eerie light coming from the top of the house, but whenever the police investigated, they found nothing, as Coneys, hearing them arrive, would flip off the tiny light he maintained in his lair. The police were sure children were playing in the house and deliberately attempting to frighten passersby. Still they made periodic checks on the house and on July 30, 1942 two detectives heard a lock click on the second floor. They charged upstairs just in time to see the legs of the Spiderman slip through the trapdoor.

The most bizarre case in Denver's history was solved, and Coneys was sent to the penitentiary for life.

PHILADELPHIA Anti-Catholic Riots

Perhaps one of the worst series of anti-Catholic riots in the United States took place in Philadelphia over a two-month period in 1844.

The initial battles erupted on May 3, when several thousand Protestants, calling themselves Native Americans, attempted to stage an Anti-Catholic street rally in the Irish section of Kensington. Forced out by the Catholics in the first round of fighting, the Protestant mob stormed back into the area on May 8, setting fire to a number of houses, churches, a Catholic rectory and a schoolhouse. The violence was finally controlled after the cavalry was called out and martial law declared. During the next several weeks sporadic fighting broke out, and there was much ill-feeling on the part of the Native Americans, who resented the fact that the military was being used to protect the Catholics. The Nativists and the Army fought the final battle of the conflict on July 4, with each side making use of batteries of cannon. The soldiers proved better cannoneers, scattering the Nativists. The next day a dazed city totaled up the casualties in the two-month confrontation: 30 dead, 150 wounded and 220 families burned out. The financial losses were put in the millions of dollars.

PHILLIPS, David Graham (1868-1911): Murder victim

David Phillips, one of the most popular novelists of the first decade of the 20th century, achieved posthumous fame as the only writer ever to be murdered because of a character he created.

One day late in 1910 a neurotic 21-year-old member of Philadelphia society, Fitzhugh Goldsborough, picked up one of Phillips' novels, *The Fashionable Adventures of Joshua Craig,* which was plotted largely around a scatterbrained, selfish young socialite. Goldsborough had an elder sister, a frivolous member of Phildelphia society who seemed to match Phillips' character in one unflattering detail after another. He also had an explosive temper and had often come to blows with persons who had said anything he took to be unkind about his sister. Goldsborough whipped himself into a murderous frenzy over Phillips' apparent insult.

On January 23, 1911 Phillips left his Gramercy Park apartment in New York City; as he walked through the park, he was confronted by a disheveled, haggard-looking young man. Fitzhugh Goldsborough pulled out a pistol and screamed, "Here you go!" and then shot the author several times. As Phillips fell to the ground mortally wounded, Goldsborough glanced at horrified passersby and said, "Here I go!" He put the gun to his temple and pulled the trigger, killing himself. Police soon uncovered the motive for Goldsborough's act, but never found any indication that the victim had ever known or even heard of the murderer's sister.

PICKPOCKETING

It happens very quickly. The "stall" bumps the "mark" and makes him look his way. The second that happens the "hook," or "mechanic," comes along on the other side and "fans" his pockets. The hook immediately "dukes the poke" to the "caretaker," who starts traveling.

There in a nutshell is a typical pickpocketing operation. It can happen on a subway platform, in a crowd at a racetrack or any place else a victim can be easily jostled.

It's really quite simple. The first man bumps into or may even speak to the victim to distract him. The second man, the actual pickpocket, expertly brushes the victim's pockets to locate his wallet in the event the trio hasn't already spotted its location, as is more often the case. Once the pickpocket takes the wallet, he has committed a crime, and the evidence is on him. If he is inexpert in his movements, the victim will notice and probably grab him and start yelling. So, almost in the same motion, the pickpocket passes the wallet to the third man, who is never close enough to the victim to come directly under suspicion. It is the third man's assignment to get away quickly with the loot.

There are many different pickpocketing operations. One that is often used in subways involves a caretaker who is also an initial spotter, noting in which pocket a potential vicitm has placed his wallet or roll of bills. A good place to make this observation is the token booth. The spotter follows the victim to the platform and stuffs an envelope into the same pocket in which the victim has his money. This signals the stall and the mechanic, who wait for the train to pull into the station before making a move. As the train doors open, the stall, often a fat man, crowds in front of the victim, blocking his entrance, and the mechanic comes up behind him. The stall stops dead in his tracks, as though realizing he is about to get on the wrong train. As he turns to get off, there is a pileup and the victim, nailed between the stall and the mechanic, is stripped clean.

The handoff is made to the caretaker and the three take off. The victim rides away on his train, probably cursing out that stupid fat man under his breath. He will curse even more when he discovers he's been robbed, but by that time he will be far from the scene of the crime.

It is very difficult to estimate how much money is lost to pickpockets. Authorities in New York City roughly estimate the losses there are probably at least $1 million annually. Not everyone reports such a theft; many victims never know they've had their pockets picked, believing they simply lost their money through carelessness.

PICKPOCKETS

The New York City Transit Police Pickpocket Squad is one of the finest in the nation. But our transit system is about the world's largest, and presents unparalleled opportunities for pickpockets. You can stop most pickpockets by being aware of their existence and taking these simple precautions.

HOW TO RUIN A PICKPOCKET'S DAY.

1 Carry your wallet inside coat or side pants pockets—never in back pants pockets.

2 Use handbags that close tightly, and carry them securely.

3 Beware of loud arguments or commotion. Incidents can be staged to distract you while your pocket is picked.

4 If you're jostled in a crowd, be aware that a pickpocket might be responsible.

5 Avoid crowding in the area of the subway car doors when entering or exiting. Doing this will minimize the chance of your losing your property to a pickpocket.

A PICKPOCKET GLOSSARY.

Breech	Side pants pocket.
Bridge	Left or right front pocket.
Cannon	Individual who removes property from pockets.
Dick	Pickpocket detective.
Dip	Placing hand in pocket or purse.
Framing	Using two or more stalls to distract victim.
Lush-worker	Victimizes sleeping drunks.
Mark	Victim.
Prat	Rear pants pockets.
Stall	Accomplices of pickpocket who distract victim.
Tip	A crowd.
Whiz	Organized group of pickpockets.
Wire	The pickpocket.

WHAT TO DO IN AN EMERGENCY.

If your pocket is picked, call out immediately to warn the driver or conductor and everyone else that there's a pickpocket on board. Don't be afraid to shout.

Some tips from the New York City Transit Police Pickpocket Squad on foiling light-fingered thieves.

The bluebloods of pickpocketing are the "live cannons," or "pit workers," who can flip your wallet out of your "pit," or pocket, as easily as they can peel a banana. The best of them can "kiss the sucker," which means face the victim directly—close enough to kiss him—and lift his wallet from his inside coat pocket, the hardest location of all. Naturally, in such an operation the pickpocket needs some "togs," or cover for his nimble hands. It may be a coat over his arm, a package or a newspaper.

When a top cannon starts losing his "grift sense," or nerve, he has to limit his action to that of a "moll buzzer," one who specializes in opening women's handbags and lifting a wallet or change purse. The lowest a pickpocket can fall is to the ranks of a "lush worker," i.e., one who rolls drunks who have passed out or, if need be, conked out.

According to police, few women make good pickpockets. Most women pickpockets are lush workers, but some are good moll buzzers. The reason for this is that in most cities there are laws against jostling, a must for a dip. "If a guy jostles a woman, she thinks he's on the make," one detective says. "She screams and the dip's facing a morals charge. A woman bumps a woman and they both let it pass with maybe an icy stare."

There is no such thing as a pickpocket who doesn't get caught. They are usually arrested scores of times, but seldom with the loot in their hands. So they are generally convicted of no more than jostling and usually they plea-bargain for a suspended sentence or possibly a small fine.

Perhaps the dean of pickpockets was Thomas "Butterfingers" Moran, who died in 1971. He stole an estimated $500,000 over a career of more than four decades. He also had the distinction of being arrested in every continental state of the union plus Canada.

Some rules for foiling pickpockets that were developed by the New York City Transit Police Pickpocket Squad are shown in the accompanying illustration.

To this should be added one more: beware of "BEWARE OF PICKPOCKETS" signs. Dips deliberately hang around these signs because many persons will automatically touch their money or wallet when they see such a warning. It is thus a boon for pickpockets.

See also: *Dutch Mob, Eddie Jackson, Thomas B. "Butterfingers" Moran.*

PIERRE Hotel Robbery

The greatest hotel robbery in history was that of the stately Hotel Pierre on New York's Fifth Avenue in the early morning hours of January 2, 1972. Six robbers with dyed hair and wearing false beards and mustaches and rubber noses stole, according to most estimates, $4 million in jewels, cash and securities from 54 safe-deposit boxes. An assistant district attorney felt as much as an additional $4 million in cash might have been taken and not reported by the victims.

At 3:45 a.m. the robbers pulled up in a limousine at the side entrance of the hotel and stepped to the door. They stuck a .38 into the doorman's chest, pushed their way inside, where they rapidly rounded up 18 hotel employees who were on the ground floor and pushed them into an office near the room containing the safe-deposit boxes. Each employee was handcuffed and bound and their mouths taped. The side door was left locked so that any late-arriving guests would have to use the Fifth Avenue entrance to enter the hotel.

At that late hour, only three hotel guests came into the area where the robbery was taking place; they too were bound and gagged and shoved in with the other prisoners. No shots were fired at any time and none of the prisoners were hurt. After two hours of steady labor the satisfied thieves walked out with their loot. Had they had more time they could have opened the remaining 146 boxes, which would have made the haul even more monumental. Still at the rate of at least $2 million an hour, their time was rather well rewarded.

Although the robbery has never been solved, the police did capture one man in possession of approximately $1 million worth of the stolen gems and another when he attempted to pass a smaller amount of the jewels to a fence who made the mistake of dealing with an FBI informant. However, the two could not be connected with the actual robbery and were liable to conviction only for possession of stolen property, a minor charge. Both men plea-bargained for second-degree burglary and got off with very short sentences.

The police have never identified the rest of the robbers, and it is now too late. The statute of limitations has passed.

PIGEON Drop: Con game

Probably the most-practiced confidence game of all time, the so-called pigeon drop comes in many varieties but all follow a basic pattern. Con man number one finds a wallet, purse, attache case or even a paper bag apparently filled with money. An unsuspecting victim standing nearby witnesses the discovery. Just then con man number two appears and claims he is also entitled to a share of the booty as much as the other two. If it hasn't occurred to the victim as yet, he now realizes he ought to share in the proceeds. An argument ensues about whether they should divide the money immediately or first check to find out if it is stolen. Con man number one says his "boss" has police connections and can check. This is done by phone and the report comes back that the money was probably dropped by some big gambler or tax evader and that the three should share it. The "boss" offers to hold the money until all three can produce a substantial amount of their own money to demonstrate that they are acting in good faith and are responsible enough to keep the secret. Con man number two, apparently determined not to be cut out of the deal, produced a large sum of money on the spot to prove his reliability. Con man number one and the victim then hurry off to get their money. When the victim returns and hands over his share, it is the last he sees of the two con men or the "boss."

While the plot appears almost incredible, it must be remembered that the acting is high powered; in particular, the bickering between the two con men makes the victim fearful he will be "left out" unless he abides by all the conditions of the agreement. The reliability of the employer—in some scams he is alleged to be a police detective—is the convincer. The money involved is always so great that the victim wants to believe. In a 1979 incident in the Bronx, New York City, two sisters in their sixties leaped to their deaths in a joint sucide after realizing they had been swindled out of their life savings of $17,000 by a version of the pigeon drop.

MISS PIGGOTT Special: Knockout drink

During the 1860s and 1870s a ferocious old woman known only as Miss Piggott operated one of the worst saloon-boarding houses on San Francisco's Barbary Coast, from which men were regularly shanghaied for long sea voyages. The secret of her success was the Miss Piggott Special, which was generally enough to lay any man low. She employed a runner to lure likely victims into her Davis Street saloon, where they would be served the Special, a drink composed of equal parts of gin, whiskey and brandy with a liberal lacing of laudanum. Such a drink would almost instantly leave a man shivering and defenseless, whereupon Miss Piggott would reach over the bar and clout the helpless man with a club. The victim would always be positioned over a trapdoor, and as he crumpled to the floor, Miss Piggott would push a lever that would open the trap and send the victim hurtling down to the basement onto a mattress, generously provided to safeguard the merchandise. When the man awoke, he would find himself aboard a ship standing out to sea from the Golden Gate, usually with no memory of what had happened to him. Regulars at Miss Piggott's saloon were aware of where the trapdoor was and never stood on it, because it was understood that anyone fool enough to do so deserved to be dropped. Even when Miss Piggott passed from the scene in the 1870s, the Miss Piggott Special lingered on for many years as a tool of most shanghai operators until the advent of the more powerful Mickey Finn.

PILLORY: Colonial punishment method

Within the first year of its establishment, every new colony in America is believed to have used the pillory as a form of punishment. Usually consisting of a wooden frame with boards containing holes through which were placed the head and hands, and sometimes the legs, of an offender, it became one of the most common methods of punishing criminals in early America. New Orleans had two such devices, used, in turn, by the Spanish, French and Americans. One was the standard head and hands arrangement; the other held only the fingers of one or both hands with the first joints bent. A convicted man sentenced to the pillory sat on a platform, usually with a sign dangling from his neck that read:

My name is ————.
I am a thief [or whatever].
I stole from ————.
Sentenced to ———— days' exposure at the pillory.

Someone undergoing such punishment was subjected to the ridicule of the town, and it was common practice for young boys and various riff-raff to hurl rotten fruit or garbage at the prisoner. The pillory fell into disfavor first in the South, where it was considered bad form to allow blacks to see whites so abused. Generally speaking, it continued as a punishment for whites until about 1839. New Orleans abandoned the practice in 1827 for whites but used it to punish blacks for another two decades.

See also: *Colonial Punishment.*

PINEAPPLE Primary: 1928 Chicago election

A rash of political violence marred the 1928 Republican primary in Chicago, one that the press dubbed the "Pineapple Primary" because of the wholesale use of "pineapples," or bombs, to intimidate voters and office seekers alike. Professional terrorists were employed by both sides, with the Capone gang supplying many or most of the tossers. The homes of candidates were bombed and several campaign workers killed.

In the primary, Sen. Charles S. Deneen's wing of the party opposed the faction headed by Mayor Big Bill Thompson and State's Attorney Robert E. Crowe. The latter forces, combined with those of Gov. Len Small, who was known as a friend of mobsters, controlled much of patronage jobs in the state. On March 21, 1928 cafe owner and racketeer Diamond Joe Esposito was killed by a bomb. Esposito, the power behind the Genna bootlegging gang, was also close to Sen. Deneen. On the day of Esposito's funeral, bombs were placed at the homes of Sen. Deneen and Judge A. Swanson, Deneen's candidate for state's attorney.

In addition to attracting worldwide attention, the violence of the Pineapple Primary roused Chicago voters the way no other of the city's recent disruptive elections had, and the Deneen forces won easily despite Al Capone's backing of the Thompson-Crowe machine. It was a stunning upset and one that sobered Capone. In the autumn of that year, crusader Frank J. Loesch, the 75-year-old president of the Chicago Crime Commission, called on Capone in an effort to ensure peaceful elections. He asked the gangster if the Pineapple Primary indicated what would happen in the general election.

Capone's response was flamboyant and arrogant. "I'll give you a square deal if you don't ask too much of me."

"Now look here, Capone," Loesch said. "Will you help me by keeping your damned cutthroats and hoodlums from interfering with the polling booths?"

"Sure," Capone responded. "I'll give them the word because they're all dagos up there, but what about the Saltis gang of micks on the West Side? They'll have to be handled different. Do you want me to give them the works, too?"

If Capone was trying to shock Loesch, he failed. The crusader said that would make him very happy.

"All right," Capone said. "I'll have the cops send over squad cars the night before the election and jug all the hoodlums and keep them in the cooler until the polls close."

Capone, who had often bragged, "I own the police," kept his word. On election day, police squad cars toured the polling places, and there was not a single irregularity. Actually, there was little need for Loesch to make the appeal, which only gave Capone a chance to grandstand, since the candidates were all anti-Thompson and thus anti-Capone. The mobster was merely making the best of a bad situation. Besides, he knew his position would not be significantly altered by the election; he would remain top man in Chicago until federal agents nailed him for income tax evasion.

PINKERTON, Allan (1819-1884): Private detective

Although he was later to epitomize the establishment private detective, Allan Pinkerton, the founder of the agency that still bears his name, was something of a revolutionary in his youth. An agitator for labor reforms in Scotland, he evaded arrest only by emigrating to America at the age of 23. Settling in Kane County, Ill. he supported himself as a cooper while becoming an ardent abolitionist and an important cog in the "under-ground railroad" that smuggled runaway slaves to Canada. Pinkerton joined the Chicago police force and was appointed its first detective. Gaining fame in a number of cases, including the smashing of a large counterfeiting ring, he opened his own agency in 1850.

As a private detective, Pinkerton developed new police methods and techniques. He devised what was in effect the first rogues' gallery, compiling detailed descriptions of known criminals, including physical characteristics, peculiarities, background, friends and hideouts. He also devised methods of psychological warfare to use against offenders. Brought in to solve the 1856 murder of a bank teller, Pinkerton assigned a detective very similar in looks to the dead man to shadow a suspect named Drysdale. Faced with the constant sight of what appeared to be the man he had killed, Drysdale finally confessed and then, still shaken, committed suicide.

Pinkerton won a contract with the Illinois Central Railroad to supply it with guards and, in the process, became acquainted with its lawyer, Abraham Lincoln. At this time Pinkerton probably could have been described as being to the left of Lincoln. In 1859 John Brown hid out in his home with 11 runaway slaves. Pinkerton gained national fame when he uncovered a plot to kill Lincoln on a train scheduled to take Lincoln to Washington for his first inauguration and outwitted the plotters by putting Lincoln on an earlier train. He was then put in charge of Civil War secret service operations under Gen. George B. McClellan.

After the war Pinkerton came to be regarded as the ally and tool of big business interests in the North, especially by the unreconstructed Confederates of the border states and by workingmen attempting to organize. Pinkerton's men were also involved in unsuccessful hunts for the James-Younger gang. The James gang killed a Pinkerton spy trying to infiltrate the group, and in 1874 a top Pinkerton agent, Louis J. Lull, and Sheriff Ed Daniels of Osecola, Mo. died following a shoot-out with the Younger Brothers. Pinkerton earned the personal enmity of Jesse James when in 1875 his agents, thinking they had found the gang's hideout, open fired on a cabin and killed Jesse's eight-year-old half-brother and wounded his mother. On one occasion James went to Chicago expressly to kill Pinkerton but gave up when he was unable to corner the detective alone. James later said, "I known God some day will deliver Allan Pinkerton into my hands."

After Pinkerton died in 1884, the firm continued under the leadership of his sons, William and Robert.

See also: *William D. "Big Bill" Haywood, Tom Horn, James Brothers, James McParland, Mollie Maguires, Harry Orchard, Allan Pinkerton, Reno Gang, Charles Siringo.*

PINKERTON'S National Detective Agency

Started in 1850 by Allan Pinkerton, Pinkerton's National Detective Agency remains the premier organization of its type in the United States. Its organizational structure was used as a model for the Federal Bureau of Investigation.

Initially, the Pinkertons handled cases that were criminal in nature and were called on by many communities whose own law enforcement capabilities were limited, corrupt or incompetent. In later years the agency accepted labor-management assignments. As numerous court cases were to prove, Pinkerton agents employed by management did not hesitate to promote violence that would discredit unions and frame and convict union leaders. Included among the agency's more unsavory episodes were Jay Gould's use of dozens of spies to break a strike against his Texas and Pacific Railroad in 1888; the infiltration of the mine workers organization at Coeur d'Alene, Idaho by agent Charles Siringo in 1894; and the efforts of the Pinkertons to involve labor leader William "Big Bill" Haywood in the murder of ex-Gov. Frank Steunenberg of Idaho in 1905. Finally, after a 1937 resolution by Congress declared labor spying unfair and illegal, the agency officially abolished its industrial division.

PIPER, Thomas W. (1849-1876): Mass murderer

In the 1870s, about 90 years before the Boston Strangler began his rampage, a mass murderer terrorized the city of Boston with a series of sex-related murders.

He committed four brutal murders and raped a number of young girls. The first victim was a girl named Bridget Landregan, who was attacked as she passed some bushes lining a snow-covered road on the night of December 5, 1873. The killer had clubbed her to death and was about to attack her body when a passerby happened along. The murderer, with black cloak flowing, fled. Later that same night, apparently the same assailant beat another girl bloody and raped her before being frightened off. Again, he was described as a black, batlike figure with a flowing cape. At the time, Boston Chief of Police Savage remarked to the press, "It was unseemly queer that only the nicest and most modest young ladies seem to get themselves raped."

When this fiend in black later killed two other girls, one in her own bedroom, the police and the public knew they had a real crime wave on their hands. As hysteria gripped the city, Chief Savage issued an order that all lone men seen wearing cloaks about the streets after dark were to be stopped and questioned, and for the following season opera cloaks fell out of fashion among the young blades of the town.

It was only after the killing of yet a fourth victim, a five-year-old girl named Mabel Hood Young, that the strange killer was found. His identity was a terrible shock to proper Bostonians. Little Mabel was murdered in the tower of the old Warren Avenue Baptist Church, and the murderer, 26-year-old Thomas W. Piper, the church sexton, had been seen taking her there. After the girl's body was discovered, Piper was arrested and soon confessed not only Mabel's murder but the previous murders as well.

Piper was tried and convicted only for the murder of little Mabel and sentenced to hang; he had in the meantime retracted all his confessions. Before he died, Piper once more admitted his crimes to Chief Savage, who asked him to commit them to paper. "I'll be hanged if I will," Piper snapped. Then he was hanged. There was no doubt Piper was the mass murderer, for the brutal killings by a man in a black cape ceased after his execution. In due course, opera cloaks returned to favor.

PIPERS: Police spies

The use of spies within police departments has been a rather common practice. Generally, such operators are referred to as "shoo flies" by police officers. In Chicago, however, they have been known as "pipers."

The origin of the term goes back to 1903, when the Chicago City Club brought in Capt. Alexander Piper of the New York Police Department, a former U.S. Army officer and future deputy police commissioner of New York, to conduct a secret study of the local force. The study, released to the newspapers on March 19, 1904, found that on the whole, the Chicago police force was both insufficient and inefficient. Many policemen were declared unfit for work "by reason of viciousness and bad habits." Ten percent of police personnel were either too fat or decrepit for active duty. Even worse, Piper concluded, the force was operating with no discipline, officers were afraid of crooks and lacked the intelligence to cope with criminal minds and many officers loafed and spent most of their tours of duty in saloons or soliciting bribes.

Under such severe criticism police officials gave Piper authority to establish a spy system within the department to root out wrongdoing. The work of these undercover operatives, who became known as "pipers," was hardly an unqualified success. While a few dishonest officers were identified, the pipers were often tricked by frame-ups of honest cops, who were then thrown off the force so that they would no longer interfere with various "fixes." Capt. Piper left Chicago hoping that curing the ills of the New York police would prove an easier task.

PIRACY

Piracy plagued the United States from early Colonial days until almost the middle of the 19th century, when its practitioners were finally eliminated not so much by legal suppression as by advancing technology. Fast-moving steamships simply proved too large and quick for pirate attack.

Boston-based Dixey Bull, who raided the Massachusetts coast during the 1630s, is regarded as the first American pirate, and the 1632 expedition that unsuccessfully tried to catch him was the first effort by colonists to deal with piracy. Colonial sea lanes were a natural preying ground for pirates and the North American coastline provided an endless number of islands where the pirates could find sanctuary. Furthermore, Colonial merchant vessels were, at best, lightly armed. During wartime the governors of various colonies licensed privateers to plunder enemy ships, and these violent men simply continued their activities against friendly shipping when peace arrived. Others, like Capt. William Kidd, who were commissioned to hunt down pirates simply turned to the activity themselves, finding it far easier to prey on helpless shipping than risk death in battle against genuine pirates. Pirates received aid from corrupt Colonial governors, who offered their protection in exchange for a portion of the booty taken. Typical was the arrangement between the notorious Blackbeard (Edward Teach) and Carolina Gov. Charles Eden. Blackbeard was finally rooted out of his sanctuary on Ocracoke Island when Gov. Alexander Spotswood of Virginia, whose shipping the pirate often attacked, commissioned an expedition against him. Blackbeard was killed in 1718.

The early 18th century was the golden era of piracy along the North American coast, marked by the activity of Kidd, Stede Bonnet, the so-called Gentleman Pirate, and Capt. Calico Jack Rackham, whose crew featured two infamous woman pirates, Anne Bonney and Mary Read. The two women, who fought alongside the men, were finally captured by a British government ship in October 1720. Rackham was hanged but both women escaped the noose by claiming, falsely, to be pregnant, a condition that legally precluded their execution. Read, however, died of "prison fever" in her cell.

A new wave of piracy developed in North American coastal waters during the post-Revolutionary period, especially by privateers once again turned pirate. The actions of French "privateers" led to an undeclared naval war with France in the late 1790s. In the early 1800s the Gulf of Mexico was the preying ground of a number of pirates, the best known being Jean Lafitte, who received a pardon for his role in defeating the British at the Battle of New Orleans in 1815. However, a number of Lafitte's followers continued to plunder American shipping. Between 1814 and 1825 they and other pirates mounted over 1,500 attacks on U.S. ships, operating from the Gulf islands, Cuba and Puerto Rico. By 1827 they were finally driven from the last of their Caribbean strongholds by the U.S. Navy. Thereafter, thanks to the arrival of steamboats, piracy steadily diminished, although the last American pirate, Capt. Nathaniel Gordon, was hanged as late as 1862.

See also: *Blackbeard, Major Stede Bonnet, Cave-in-Rock Pirates, Charlton Street Gang, Colonel Plug, Vincent Gambi, Captain Nathaniel Gordon, Captain William Kidd, Jean Lafitte, Pirates' Home.*

PIRATES' Home: Corsair refuge

During the early years of the 19th century, an entire section of Louisiana shoreline, especially the many islands in the Bay of Barataria as well as the island of Grand Terre, became known collectively as Pirates' Home. Headquartered here were pirates, privateers and smugglers, including not only the legendary Jean Lafitte but also Rene Beluche, Dominique You (Captain Dominique), Cut Nose and the bloodthirsty Vincent Gambi. The Bay of Barataria afforded them a safe anchor for their ships from which they could sweep out and attack Spanish vessels in the Gulf of Mexico. U.S. shipping was not molested since Americans were the prime buyers of the stolen loot. Merchants from New Orleans and other Southern cities trekked regularly

to Pirates' Home to buy the expensive merchandise at bargain prices. The high point of local pirate activity occurred from 1810 to 1813, but in the following year the U.S. Army destroyed the pirate settlements. This action was not taken to accommodate other seagoing nations but because the illicit trade in Pirates' Home was materially reducing the governmental tax-revenues on incoming goods. Afterward, only those pirates who fought with Jean Lafitte at the Battle of New Orleans were allowed, for a time, to operate off the American coast.

See also: *Vincent Gambi, Jean Lafitte.*

PITTSBURGH Phil (1908-1941): Murder, Inc.'s top hit man

Probably the most prolific and certainly the most cold-blooded professional hit man this country has ever seen, Harry Strauss, better known as Pittsburgh Phil, was the top killer of the national crime syndicate's enforcement arm, Murder, Inc. So far as is known, Strauss was never in Pittsburgh in his life, having been born and bred in Brooklyn; he just liked the sound of the name. He also liked committing murder; he often volunteered for murder contracts, as Brooklyn District Attorney William O'Dwyer once said, "sometimes just for the lust to kill."

"Like a ballplayer, that's me," he once told a friend, explaining his enthusiasm. "I figure I get seasoning doing these jobs. Somebody from one of the big mobs spots me. Then, up to the big leagues."

And that's just what happened. He made it into the Murder, Inc., and it got so that whenever a call came in from one of the out-of-town mobs for someone to fill a special "contract," Phil was almost always the one requested. Phil would pack his briefcase with a shirt, a change of socks, underwear, a gun, a knife, a length of rope and an ice pick—he was an artist at a multitude of murdering methods—hop a plane or train to his port of call, pull the job and catch the next connection back to New York. More often than not, Phil didn't even know the name of the person he had killed, and generally it didn't matter to him. It was the killing that counted. If, by chance, he was curious about or particularly proud of a job, he would buy an out-of-town paper when he got back to New York and read all about it.

When the Murder Inc. story broke wide open in 1940, O'Dwyer's staff had concrete evidence linking Phil to 28 killings. In addition, an equal number of murders had been positively identified as Phil's work by law enforcement officials from Connecticut to California. And those were just the known killings. A present-day crime historian gives serious credence to an estimate that Phil killed at least 500 persons from the late 1920s until 1940. The figure is sheer nonsense, but there seems little doubt his total kills probably exceeded 100. This is an incredible figure, especially considering the next two most active killers in the "troop"—Kid Twist Reles and Happy (so called because of his surly expression) Maione, probably did no more than 30 apiece.

Phil was the dandy of the troop. His love affair with Evelyn

Mittleman, a Brooklyn beauty who was to be dubbed the Kiss of Death Girl, was one of the underworld's more touching affairs, climaxed by Phil's eradication of a rival for her affection. Tall, lean and handsome, Phil was a fashion plate. He wore the best suits $60 could buy—$60 in Depression times—and became known to the police and his colleagues alike as the Beau Brummel of the Underworld. Phil and his dandy dress, in fact, were what led to Police Commissioner Lewis J. Valentine's famous "muss them up" orders against hoodlums. One day the commissioner had come over to Brooklyn to look at a lineup and blew his top when he saw Phil standing against the white wall radiant in a well-fitting Chesterfield, pearl-gray fedora, blue shirt with tie to match, blue striped suit and gleaming black shoes. "Look at him!" the commissioner raged. "He's the best dressed man in the room and he's never worked a day in his life!"

The commissioner was wrong about that. Phil was working very hard. In fact, he had the Brooklyn police toiling over one of his murders at that moment. The victim was George Rudnick, whom labor extortionist Louis Lepke had suspected of being an informer.

After getting a contract to hit Rudnick, Phil and a few of his confederates snatched the suspected stoolie one afternoon as he walked along Livonia Avenue. It was a short drive to the execution chamber, a garage at Atlantic Avenue and Eastern Parkway. A few hours later, Rudnick's body turned up in a stolen car on the other side of the borough.

Deputy Chief Medical Examiner Dr. Edward Marten's autopsy report detailed Phil's savagery.

> This was a male adult, somewhat undernourished; approximate weight 140 pounds; six feet in height. There were 63 stab wounds on the body. On the neck, I counted 13 stab wounds, between the jaw and collarbone. On the right chest, there were 50 separate circular wounds. He had a laceration on the frontal region of the head. The wound gaped, and disclosed the bone underneath. His face was intensely cyanic, or blue. The tongue protruded. At the level of the larynx was a grooving, white and depressed, about the width of the ordinary clothesline. When the heart was laid open, the entire wall was found to be penetrated by stab wounds. My conclusion was the cause of death was multiple stab wounds, and also . . . asphyxia due to strangulation.

When the Purple Gang in Detroit marked a local gangster, Harry Millman, for death, they found him hard to kill; one attempt failed, and Millman thereafter was on his guard. Outside talent was needed and Pittsburgh Phil was one of two killers sent from Brooklyn. Millman was in a crowded restaurant eating dinner one evening when two men walked in, fired 12 slugs into him, wounding five other diners in the process, and paraded out. Sweet, direct and simple was the way Pittsburgh Phil liked it.

Phil could, at times, carry out a job with a touch of poetic irony. Walter Sage ran the syndicate's coin machine racket in the Catskills until he became what the mob called a trolley car conductor, shortchanging the organization on its profits. Phil ice-picked him 32 times. He got rid of the body by lashing it

to a pinball machine and dumping it in a lake. Phil was very proud of that touch. "It's a symbol," he asserted proudly.

A week later, however, the grisly package rose to the surface because of buoyancy from gases in the decomposing body. As Phil learned, perforations made with a small weapon, like an ice pick, are virtually sealed by blood pumping from a still-beating heart. "How about that," Phil philosophized. "With this bum, you gotta be a doctor, or he floats."

So far as is known, Phil failed on only one job. Traveling to Florida to fill a contract, he followed his intended victim into a movie theater, where the man sat down in the last row. Rather than use a gun, which would attract attention, Phil secured the fire ax kept in a glass case. However, by the time he'd gotten the ax, his intended victim had moved ahead several rows. Angered, Phil walked out. As he complained later to the troop, "Just when I get him set up, the bum turns out to be a goddamn chair hopper."

Usually, though, he could get the job done regardless of any obstacles. In another Florida hit assignment, the victim was a Mafia old-timer who couldn't speak a word of English. That didn't faze Phil at all. Conversing with the man in sign language, Phil showed him his briefcase of weapons and led him to believe he'd come to kill someone else and wanted advice. The old-timer picked a rope and showed the hit man a dark street where the killing could be done safely. Phil strangled him there and went home.

How long Phil would have gone on with his killing had Kid Twist Reles not turned stoolie is something awesome to contemplate. Today, it seems incredible he could have operated for a decade without getting caught. Reles talked because he figured the law was closing in and if he didn't, someone else in the troop would and he would get the chair.

Reles later horrified a Brooklyn jury with a description of how Phil had killed one Puggy Feinstein. Puggy was decoyed to Abe Reles' house, where Phil was hiding behind the door, his trusty ice pick in hand. When Puggy walked in, Phil threw him on the couch and went to work with the pick. Puggy, fighting for his life, managed to bite Phil's finger. Enraged by such foul play, Phil yelled: "Give me the rope. I'll fix this dirty bum."

Reles then described Phil's mastery of the art of rope murder.

> I give Phil one end of the rope, and I hold the other end. Puggy is kicking and fighting. He is forcing his head down, so we can't get the rope under his throat. Buggsy [Buggsy Goldstein, another of the murder troop] holds his head up, so we can put the rope under. Then me and Phil exchange ends . . . cross them, so we make a knot . . . a twist. Then we cross them once more. Then we rope around his throat again, to make two loops.
>
> Buggsy gets Puggy by the feet, and me and Phil get him by the head. We put him down on the floor. He is kicking. Phil starts finishing tying him up . . . [and] gets his feet tied up with the back of his neck. He ties him up like a little ball. His head is pushed down on his chest. His knees are folded up against his chest. His hands are in between. The rope is around

his neck and under his feet. If he moves the rope will tighten up around his throat more.

And so Puggy Feinstein died with Phil kicking him for biting his finger. "Maybe I am getting lockjaw from being bit," Phil yelled defensively.

Later, they dumped Puggy's body in a vacant lot and set it ablaze. But even after the boys adjourned to Sheepshead Bay for a seafood dinner, Phil was unhappy about his finger and barely finished his lobster.

The break in the Murder, Inc. case came when a few minor hoods were arrested and started talking. Phil, Reles, Maione and Goldstein were picked up on suspicion and the word went out that one or the other was "ratting." None had, but Reles decided to tell all, and when he did, Murder, Inc. was smashed. Big shots like Louis Lepke, Mendy Weiss and Louis Capone were to die in the electric chair before Reles' trilling came to a sudden end when he "went out the window" of a Brooklyn hotel while under police guard. Pittsburgh Phil was also doomed. He and Buggsy Goldstein were indicted for the Puggy Feinstein murder.

The authorities secured five more murder indictments and, if necessary, were ready to try him on those as well. It wasn't. Since he had no real defense, Phil did the next best thing: he feigned insanity. He refused to shave or change his clothes. When put on the witness stand and asked to give his name, he merely licked his lips. Sent back to the defendant's chair, he spent most of the rest of the trial nibbling on the leather strap of a lawyer's briefcase. It was a great act. The newspapers loved it. The jury didn't. They found him guilty.

Phil kept up his crazy act in the death house in the hope of winning a commutation. It wasn't until his last day that he gave up the act, combed his hair and became his old swaggering self. He said goodbye to Evelyn, the Kiss of Death Girl. On June 12, 1941 Buggsy Goldstein went to the chair. Moments later, at 11:06 p.m., Phil followed him. The best enforcer the syndicate ever had was dead.

Only later was it revealed that prior to his trial Phil had offered to turn state's evidence if he was allowed to talk to Reles first. The request was rejected. The authorities had no intention of letting Phil get in the same room with informer Reles. It was a wise precaution. As Phil said on his last day in the death house, he really had no intention of singing. "I just wanted to sink my tooth into his jugular vein. I didn't worry about the chair, if I could just tear his throat out first."

No one doubted he would have tried to.

See also: *Kiss of Death Girls; Murder, Inc.; Abe "Kid Twist" Reles.*

PLACE, Etta (?1880-?): "Associate" of Wild Bunch

Probably the most beautiful woman in the outlaw West, Etta Place was described in a Pinkerton dossier as an "associate of outlaws." More precisely, she appears to have been associated with two prime members of the Wild Bunch, Butch Cassidy and Harry Longbaugh, the Sundance Kid, although most of her affections seem to have been reserved for Sundance. She was tall and stately with raven black hair. Even the other women at Robber's Roost commented on her beauty when she first appeared there during the winter of 1896-97. Some historians insist she was a schoolteacher at the time she first met Butch and Sundance and rode with them on the outlaw trail. That hardly seems likely considering that she was, by fairly reliable accounts, born in or near Denver about 1880, making her a bit young for that profession. According to other historians, Etta was a former prostitute from Fanny Porter's bordello in Fort Worth, Tex., a far more logical place than a schoolhouse for Cassidy and Sundance to find a female companion.

Etta Place and the Sundance Kid posed for this formal portrait in New York City before sailing to South America.

Etta is credited with having been an expert rider and a first-rate shot with both a Colt .45 and a Winchester. She rode with the gang on a number of jobs but hung back from direct involvement. Her total devotion to the pair may best be illustrated by the fact that she always tagged along with them on their fleshpot forays, waiting dutifully in a hotel room for their return. Her forgiving or unjealous nature is further attested to by the Sundance Kid's known propensity for "catching cold," a whorehouse euphemism for contracting venereal disease, and Etta's understanding aid in caring for him during such periods of illness.

In 1901, with the law hot on their trail, Cassidy and Sundance decided to leave outlaw country and, with Etta in tow, headed first for New York City and then, the following year, for South America. From here on, the Cassidy-Sundance-Place story is conjecture. One account has Etta sticking with the pair for some time while they hit the South American bandit trail and finally returning to New York to get medical treatment for "acute appendicitis"—quite likely an ailment more social in nature. The Sundance Kid supposedly accompanied her to New York but returned to Cassidy in time for the two of them to get killed in a battle with Bolivian soldiers. In this version, Etta Place simply fades away.

Another version states that she stuck with the pair until she and Sundance got separated from Cassidy with no way of resuming contact. Years later, according to Butch Cassidy's sister, Lula Parker Betenson, the outlaw returned to the West and drifted down to Mexico. One day he was sitting in a bar in Mexico City when suddenly he felt a grip on his shoulder. His first thought was that after all this time the Pinkertons had finally run him to earth, but he turned to see . . . Etta Place. The same old Etta, beautiful as ever, and living in Mexico City with Sundance. The three old Wild Bunchers had a long, happy reunion, if one chooses to believe this story.

See also: *Butch Cassidy, Sundance Kid, Wild Bunch.*

PLASTIC Surgery For Criminals: Criminality "cure"

Many criminals, such as John Dillinger, Alvin "Creepy" Karpis and several of the Barkers, among others, have attempted to alter their appearance by undergoing plastic surgery so as to avoid detection. Overall, these attempts have been failures, but plastic surgery has been used quite successfully to rehabilitate criminals, both professionals and amateurs.

Does an ugly face or a disfigured body help mold an ugly character? Ever since the time of Homer, poets and novelists have contended as much and today psychiatrists and criminologists tend to agree. One leading department store in New York City employs a psychiatrist to examine persons caught shoplifting provided they are not known professional crooks. Very often, these persons are respectable middle-aged women with no economic pressures forcing them to steal. This is not an unusual phenomenon, according to psychiatrists. Shoplifting, they recognize, is largely a woman's crime that often stems from psychological problems related to a growing dissatisfaction with marital relations. As a wife grows older and wrinkles start to develop, they theorize she may feel she is losing her husband and turn to shoplifting as an exciting way to forget her gnawing self-doubts.

The New York department store psychiatrist frequently gives such women what may seem like odd advice: have your face lifted. "Where such recommendations are followed, I have never heard of the woman reverting to shoplifting," the psychiatrist observes.

For many years a unique plastic surgery program run by Dr. John Pick has been instrumental in rehabilitating inmates in the Illinois prison system. The theory is that a new face makes a new man, and the records of hundreds of released convicts bear out that claim. On average, only about one in 25 returns to prison, an impressive record compared to the general rate of recidivism. Typical of those Dr. Pick has reformed through surgery was a man who had led an entirely respectable life until he lost his nose in an accident. He soon wound up in prison. Then there was the man with a broken nose and mastiff jowls who took to crime after his seven-year-old son remarked: "Daddy, you look just like a bad man. Why don't you change your face?" Pick did precisely that at Joliet, and Daddy is now a law-abiding delicatessen owner.

When Dr. Pick first started taking a day off from his lucrative private practice in the 1940s to help out convicts while testing his theory that ugliness breeds crime, he met considerable official indifference. Most prison officials were concerned with only three things, in the following order: keeping prisoners safely behind bars; controlling unruly prisoners, and rehabilitating prisoners, very often with programs that had been scaled down as a result of insufficient funds.

Fortunately, the warden of Joliet at the time Dr. Pick began his work was James E. Ragen, then regarded as one of the most-enlightened wardens in the country. Ragen gave Pick his full support and cooperation. The doctor's first patient was a youth who was born with upside-down ears. It seemed hardly surprising that someone with such a disfigurement would wind up a criminal. Pick's surgery was a success and the young man, for the first time, lost his hostility toward society. Once the door of Joliet swung open for him, he never returned.

"Ultimately, of course," Dr. Pick once recalled, "the fellows down at Springfield [the state capital] heard about the project and began to wonder if we were lifting faces and changing fingerprints. Naturally, we take careful before-and-after pictures, recording all changes in appearance."

The project won over the doubters as its astounding results gradually became more evident. Warden Ragen, for one, reported that convicts who had undergone plastic surgery became much more manageable prisoners.

The files at Joliet bulge with hundreds of testimonials from released prisoners. Some typical messages have been: "I have a new life," "Nobody laughs at me any more" and "I can hold a good job now."

Once asked why he had ever started his prison work, Dr. Pick explained:

First of all there was a chance to make a contribution to society which also might bear scientific fruit. Then there was a sense of guilt. I long ago became convinced that the reasons why a man becomes a criminal rest only half within himself. The other half of the story is within society. We do nothing about the fact that society rejects the deformed, but at least we owe them understanding.

Of course, Dr. Pick did not always succeed in bringing about a reformation of his patients. Sometimes the physically improved criminals went right back to their wrongful ways, and formerly ugly criminals who had worked as sneak thieves and burglars were able to promote themselves into dapper confidence operators and rubber check artists. This did not destroy Dr. Pick's basic beliefs, however, nor alter the fact that most of his operations were successful. Among those criminals who did not reform, physical disfigurement was obviously not the basis for their criminal behavior.

Still, Dr. Pick realized his work was to some extent too little and certainly too late. Physical disfigurements, he found, weigh most on children from six to 16 and this is the critical period in determining whether or not a child goes bad. "The reform school is the place to begin," he once said. "We could hope thus to stop a criminal career right at the start."

A survey conducted in the 1950s by Dr. Anna Brind, a consulting psychologist on the staff of the American Institute of Family Relations, supports Dr. Pick's observations. Brind made a detailed analysis of the cases of 180 children who were suffering from personality disorders. All of them had a facial disfigurement of one sort or another. In 85 percent of the cases, it was concluded that facial defects were the main cause of the children's misbehavior.

It should be noted that Bonnie Parker of Bonnie and Clyde fame was often called horse face when she was a girl, and as a child, Pretty Boy Floyd had sought to dandify himself because he was unhappy about his appearance. Had Pretty Boy Floyd actually been pretty he might never have become a public enemy.

The unfortunate aspect of the Illinois plastic surgery rehabilitation program is that to this day it remains almost unique despite a long record of remarkable achievement.

PLEA Bargaining

The principle of plea bargaining, the reduction of a criminal charge to a lesser offense in exchange for a guilty plea, has long been accepted in the criminal justice system, although not without misgivings by many judges, prosecutors, defense lawyers and defendants.

The Supreme Court has in effect approved of the process. In a 1970 case it said:

> For a defendant who sees slight possibility of acquittal, the advantages of pleading guilty and limiting the probable penalty are obvious—his exposure is reduced, the correctional processes can begin immediately, and the practical burdens of a trial are eliminated. For the State there are also advantages— the more promptly imposed punishment after an admission of guilt may more effectively attain the objective of punishment; and with the avoidance of trial, scarce judicial and prosecutorial resources are conserved for those cases in which there is a substantial issue of the defendant's guilt or in which there is substantial doubt that the State can sustain its burden of proof. It is this mutuality of advantage that perhaps explains the fact that at present well over three-fourths of the criminal convictions in this country rest on pleas of guilty.

Against this might be the view of Alice in Wonderland, who was offended by the Queen of Heart's logic that the sentence should come first and the verdict and trial later. What is plea bargaining other than setting the sentence first with the trial and verdict not simply postponed but eliminated

from the process? In effect, plea bargaining is seldom a "bargain" for either side; usually, the prosecution has the best of it because it can set the standards to be applied in each case. It does not bargain if it does not want to, and the system allows a prosecutor to insist one defendant must be brought to trial while another is not. Even if the decisions in both cases are right, only one side is making them.

In every jurisdiction in the country the percentage of felony cases reduced to misdemeanors is enormous, but this does not necessarily indicate excessive leniency is the rule in prosecutors' offices. To induce plea bargaining, many district attorneys deliberately file excessive charges against a defendant to frighten him. Another trick used by prosecutors is to ask for extremely high bail, because it is well established that a prisoner kept in jail for a time is more likely to accept a lesser charge. And a system geared to plea bargaining arrangements actually is more prone to convict innocent persons. An innocent man, opponents of plea bargaining argue, is even more frightened of the prospect of going to jail that a guilty person and will tend to grasp at any offer that suggests the possibilty of a mere suspended sentence. It has been shown that fear of the death penalty has led innocent suspects to plea bargaining.

In recent years probably a majority of judges, prosecutors and defense attorneys have felt that plea bargaining is a poor practice, but they also feel trapped by the sheer volume of cases and the shortage of courts and personnel.

In 1980 it was revealed that more than 99 percent of all persons subjected to felony arrests in New York state—not an atypical jurisdiction—never served a day in a state prison. The chance of a given felony arrest ending in a sentence to state prison was put at about one in 108. The year before in New York City, 88,098 felony arrests out of a total of 104,413 were dismissed by district attorneys or treated as misdemeanors. In trying to determine who is to blame for the excessive use of plea bargaining, disputes have broken out between prosecutors and the police. District attorneys insist police tend to "overcharge" (one explanation for this practice is that officers win promotions for felony arrests, not for misdemeanor arrests), while the police deny this and point to the classification by prosecutors of certain offenses as "technical felonies," which are charges the DAs simply refuse to prosecute.

A spokesman for the Queens County district attorney in New York City said: "Every felony is not a felony when someone looks at it in detail. A judgment has to be made. How serious was it? Does the guy have a record? All this has a bearing on it."

Yet essentially, in deciding not to prosecute certain charges, i.e., technical felonies, the district attorney is substituting his judgment of what constitutes a crime for that of the legislature. Asked to justify this, Manhattan District Attorney Robert M. Morgenthau stated: "We try to make the best use of limited resources. The public does not benefit from presenting a case to the grand jury, getting an indictment and having it end up as a misdemeanor plea."

Clearly, the trend throughout the nation is more and more toward plea bargaining. A typical case might be that of a burglar caught breaking into a building with the intent to steal silver. Facing a charge for which he could be sentenced to seven years in prison, he would probably be allowed to plead guilty to trespass and possession of burglar's tools, both misdemeanors, and get off with no more than a few months in jail. Only the most enthusiastic supporter of plea bargaining would argue that such an arrangement would "more effectively attain the [State's] objective of punishment."

Further reading: *Crime and Punishment* by Aryeh Neier.

PLUG Uglies: 19th century New York gang

One of the very first gangs spawned by the notorious Five Points section of New York, the Plug Uglies were fierce both in action and in appearance. They looked like tall, black-clad versions of Uncle Sam. Some writers insist they maintained membership standards on height that prohibited anyone who was not at least six feet tall. More likely, it never occurred to a short thug to try to become a Plug Ugly. The gangsters got their name because of the hugh plug hats they wore, which, stuffed with wool and leather scraps, was pulled down over the ears to serve as a most effective helmet. Nothing could stir quite as much fear in 1825 New York as the sight of an approaching Plug Ugly looking for trouble or loot. In one hand the giant gangster might carry a brick, in the other a heavy bludgeon. He would have a pistol tucked in his belt and he would be wearing heavy hobnailed boots, ideal for trampling a fallen victim or enemy gangster.

The Plug Uglies remained awesome figures in the New York underworld for decades, taking an active part in the Civil War Draft Riots of 1863. They began disappearing toward the end of the 19th century, being merged into the then dominant gangs, such as the Whyos and the Five Points Gang.

See also: *Draft Riots, Gangs and Gangsters.*

PLUMMER, Henry (1837-1864): Renegade lawman

Probably the inspirational protagonist of more tales, novels and films than any other American, Henry Plummer was the original devious sheriff unmasked at the end of a drama as the villainous leader of the badmen. However, few novelists or screenwriters have dared to ascribe to their characters all the villainies attributable to Plummer himself. While not all of Plummer's depredations have been unearthed, the popularly held belief that he personally killed 15 men may be reasonably accurate. There is little doubt that his gang of outlaws—most of whom were several years younger than Plummer, who was only in his mid-twenties—killed 102 victims during its brief existence.

Plummer was a handsome, well-spoken and ingratiating young man who had a magnetic effect on the pioneer people of several regions. When he ran away from his New England home at age 15, Plummer showed little of his future tendencies. He worked his way to California, where he went into partnership in a bakery. In 1856, when he was only 19 years old, he became marshal of Nevada City, Calif. While in office he killed an irate husband who objected to the young lawman having an affair with his wife and was sentenced to 10 years in prison. Within a year Plummer had wrangled a pardon and went back to the bakery business. His troubles with the law multiplied as he continued sweeping ladies off their feet and committing various mayhems. He apparently robbed a Wells Fargo office in Washoe and eventually murdered another man. He was apprehended but escaped by bribing a jailer before being brought to trial.

Plummer moved on to Oregon, where he is believed to have shot a sheriff to death. He later carried out a number of criminal and amorous affairs in Washington and then turned up in Orofino, Idaho, where he definitely took part in the murder of a man. In the spring of 1861 Plummer worked in a gambling emporium in Lewiston, Idaho but spent his spare time recruiting a band of thieves and road agents. As the gang's depredations grew, the local citizenry organized a vigilance committee, of which Plummer was a leading member. In an effort to break up the vigilantes, Plummer had one of their leaders assassinated.

In the fall of 1862, Plummer shifted his base of operations to Bannack, Mont., where miners were making rich strikes. Portraying himself as a fearless vigilante from Lewiston and a former lawman in California, Plummer was soon elected sheriff. As the Plummer gang, or Innocents, as they were called, increased its activities, the sheriff somberly erected a scaffold from which to hang malefactors. The few who were executed by Plummer were not his henchmen, some of whom served as deputy sheriffs. The Innocents were such a huge organization that not every member knew all the others, so that they had to operate with secret identifications and handshakes. Some worked only as spies, learning which stagecoach or wagon carried loot worth robbing and marking them with coded symbols.

Plummer soon expanded his operations into Virginia City, becoming the town's marshal by forcing the previous holder of the post to flee the area. Plummer's fatal flaws, which were shared by his gang, were that he operated with what one historian called "an almost juvenile fervor" and that he failed to cover his tracks sufficiently. The end came when a former confederate, Jack Cleveland, attempted to blackmail Plummer into giving him a large portion of the profits from the gang's lucrative crimes. Plummer gunned him down in a saloon but didn't realize he was still breathing. A local butcher, Hank Crawford, took Cleveland to his home, where, over the next several hours the dying outlaw whispered a number of facts about Plummer.

Crawford, in turn, began whispering these same facts to others until Plummer drove him from the area. Soon, the settlers of the Bannack and Virginia City area formed another vigilance committee, one that did not include Sheriff Plummer in its counsels. What followed was one of the most notable outbreaks of lynch law in America. From late 1863 through the end of the following year, the Vigilantes of Montana hanged dozens of Innocents and other suspected criminals. Oddly, even when some of his key men were strung up, Plummer himself made no effort to flee, apparently convinced he could brazen it out. A theory embedded in Montana folklore holds that Plummer made a deal, or thought he made a deal, with some of the leading vigilantes: immunity in exchange for a portion of the outlaw loot. If that was the case, he was double-crossed.

On January 10, 1864 a weeping Plummer and two of his henchmen were hauled to the very gallows the rogue lawman had built himself. Plummer begged for mercy, pleading that instead of hanging, he should have his tongue cut out and his legs or all his limbs cut off and be left in a cabin in the hills. Unimpressed, the vigilantes placed a rope around the neck of each man, hoisted them on their shoulders and flipped them into the air; they slowly strangled to death.

See also: *Bannack, Montana; Thomas J. Dimsdale; Innocents; Vigilantes of Montana.*

POKER Alice (1851-1930): Gambler and madam

One of the few great female gamblers of the West, Poker Alice Ivers was also one of the few gamblers who was an accomplished gunfighter.

Born in England the daughter of a schoolmaster, Alice came to America with her family at the age of 12 and married an engineer named Frank Duffield in Colorado Territory when she was 19. Her husband died in a mining accident the following year, and Alice began supporting herself by teaching school. She also took up poker and was soon dealing cards in a saloon on a percentage basis. Any traces of schoolmarm decorum soon vanished completely as she began toting a gun and smoking big black cigars. She became famous for two sayings "I'll shoot you in your puss, you cheating bastard!" and "I never gamble on Sundays."

Poker Alice, as she was by then known, worked the railroad gambling circuit, beating fellow travelers in high-stake card games. She later settled in Creede, Colorado and dealt cards in a saloon belonging to Bob Ford, the man who killed Jesse James. From there Poker Alice moved on to Deadwood, S.D., where she demonstrated her shooting prowess one night when a drunken miner accused another dealer, William Tubbs, of cheating and went at him with a bowie knife. Poker Alice drew her gun and fired, shooting the miner in his arm and knocking the knife from his hand.

Alice and Tubbs were married in 1899 and retired from gambling to run a chicken farm until 1910, when Tubbs died of pneumonia. Poker Alice then took up her gun, cigars and cards and headed back for the gaming tables, opening her own place near Fort Meade, S.D. Realizing that men do not live by gambling alone, she stocked the second floor with ladies who offered other diversions. Poker Alice's place was a gold mine, relying on a clientele of soldiers from the fort. But Alice held to her old-fashioned ways. On Sundays drinks were served but there was no gambling and the ladies upstairs did no entertaining. It was this reluctance to be completely accommodating that got Poker Alice in trouble. One night in 1920 a bunch of drunken soldiers tried to break into her place after closing time. Alice fired through a door and a soldier fell dead. She was tried and found guilty of killing the soldier, but the judge let her go, saying, "I cannot find it in my heart to send a white-haired lady to the penitentiary." Once outside the court and beyond the judge's view, Poker Alice lit up a victory cigar.

The Army was not so compassionate, however, and declared Alice's place off limits. That and Prohibition drove Poker Alice out of business and she retired to a ranch to smoke cigars and recall the good old days. She died in 1930.

POLICE

The colonies and later the young nation muddled through with rather amateurish crime-fighting methods until the 1830s, when in city after city near anarchy forced the introduction of more professional techniques. The police department system that developed at this point was intended to battle mob rule rather than what is recognized as ordinary, or pedestrian-type, crime: theft, mayhem and murder.

The first policing procedures adopted by the colonies were patterned after the English parish constable system. In England noblemen appointed constables, that country's first local law enforcement figure, to police rural parishes. The counties traditionally were policed by a sheriff.

From 1608 to 1783 American sheriffs and constables were large landowners appointed by the Colonial governors. Many of them had the added duty of being the chief local financial officer, who collected taxes and other fees and kept 10 percent of the proceeds as recompense. This method of policing was sufficient only until the crime problem started to increase. In Boston additional means of policing proved necessary in the 1630s, when the first night watch was formed, consisting initially of a military officer and six soldiers. Later, the night watch was expanded and, probably as an economy measure, was staffed with citizens appointed by the town government. Philadelphia and New Amsterdam armed their night watches with rattles, probably the first effort at crime prevention, rather than crime detection. The *ratelwacht,* or rattlewatch, as the patrols came to be known, used their rattles not so much to corner felons as to warn of their own presence and thus, hopefully, put any nocturnal marauders to flight.

These methods continued to be used throughout the 18th and into the 19th century, although some localities hired their night watchmen and supplemented them with special "day forces" to assist the constable. Of course, more stringent measures were adopted in areas where the crime problem became more acute. In Virginia's backwoods frontier during the 18th century, the practice of lynching won its name as a result of the activities of Colonel William Lynch, whose band of law enforcers exacted their own punishment, including the ultimate penalty, on a number of evildoers.

Overall, however, through the 17th century criminality was not a major problem in most localities. In New Amsterdam the first recorded police activity was by one Johan Lampo, a provincial Dutch authority who had arrived in 1620. His first known arrest was the collaring of a pig thief. In post-Dutch New York the first salaried officers on the night watch were known as leatherheads, because of the heavy leather helmets they wore, similar in style to those worn by today's firemen. The leatherheads were supposed to patrol the streets but some spent far too much time in their sentry boxes.

This relatively peaceful era ended a few decades into the 19th century with the appearance of the first great city gangs, mostly immigrant Irish toughs jammed into the new slums. New York's Cherry Street, where George Washington and John Hancock had strolled so peacefully just a few decades earlier, was now the domain of criminals. These gangs made the area unsafe not only by night but by day as well. In the mid-1830s riots took place in city after city. There were food riots, election riots and the first mob attacks on abolitionists. At the same time, Catholic immigrants fought Protestant nativists in street battles that lasted for days. Since the constables and watches could not cope with such anarchy, professional police forces came into being.

These new police were generally a ragtag, motley crowd. Law enforcement jobs were given strictly on a political basis, and officers usually served only a one-year term and could thus be fired at whim by local aldermen. No training was given to them and they usually had no uniforms, which were considered too European and undemocratic in style. An officer could only be recognized by the badge he wore, and when prudence dictated, he could hide the symbol of his authority. These policemen were, at best, only marginally more successful than their predecessors, and it was not until the 1850s that reform movements succeeded in making police forces efficient and effective crime fighters. In 1855 the Boston Police Department was reorganized and reformed into what became a fairly efficient organization.

The evolution of the police department in New York City was somewhat more troubled. The Municipal Police were formed in 1853 but by 1857 they were considered so corrupt and inefficient that the state legislature set up a new force called the Metropolitans. Many officers remained loyal to the Municipals, who refused to disband, and soon, they and the Metropolitans faced each other in open warfare on the streets, much to the benefit of criminals and the detriment of the public. The rivalry between the two forces led to a great battle at City Hall, in which 52 officers were injured. Public pressure and a Supreme Court decision finally led to the disbanding of the Municipals.

State police forces held sway for the next 13 years, with such cities as Baltimore, St. Louis, Kansas City, Detroit, Cleveland and Chicago utilizing state-controlled police. Eventually, local forces reappeared in virtually every jurisdiction in the country.

Often in the West formal policing methods were unavailable and citizens banded together to protect their lives and property through such institutions as miners courts and vigilante committees, both of which dealt out instant justice. Many of the latter groups were not lynch mobs but honest men forced to take collective action. Later on, more formal policing took place under the leadership of such legendary law officers

as Wyatt Earp, Bat Masterson, Wild Bill Hickok, Pat Garrett and others, whose achievements were often wildly exaggerated. Many lawmen habitually crossed over to the outlaw trail and back again, their final reputations often being determined on which side of the law they were operating at the time of their demise.

Women were slow to enter police work and were initially restricted to police matron duties. Lucy Gray, the first Los Angeles police matron, was a pioneer woman in the criminal justice system. By the 1880s Gray, who had come west with her family in a covered wagon, had set up a police department position to aid women and children, both victims and offenders, who were not getting appropriate care. Fearless and kind, she was renowned for her ability to calm unruly prisoners and eventually earned the title of City Mother. Technically, she was not a policewoman, although she performed many of the duties associated with that job.

The first uniformed policewoman in the United States, and most likely in the world, was Mrs. Alice Stebbins Wells, who joined the Los Angeles police force in 1910. Within six years 16 other departments that had monitored the Los Angeles experiment hired policewomen. Buffalo hired the first black policewoman in 1924. (There seems to be no accurate record of where the first black policeman appeared.)

Police scandals and reform movements have occurred in almost every major city. In New York, investigations of the police department take place about once every generation; the next one should be due about 1990. Two future U.S. presidents led local police reform movements and occupied law posts themselves, Grover Cleveland in Buffalo, N.Y. and Theodore Roosevelt in New York City.

Lewis J. Valentine stands out as a towering figure in uprooting corruption in the New York Police Department during the tenure of Fiorello La Guardia. William H. Parker, head of the Los Angeles force for 16 years until his death in 1966, is credited by many reformers with building the nation's preeminent law enforcement agency and substantially raising the professional quality of his men. Undeniably, J. Edgar Hoover accomplished miracles in upgrading the FBI to a position of national respect from the morass of venality, corruption and incompetence that characterized the agency during the Wilson and Harding administrations, when it was known as the Bureau of Investigation.

Despite many continuing charges of police corruption and brutality, there is little doubt that the policeman of today is far superior, professionally and morally, to his counterpart of earlier years. Much of today's abuse of power by the police is directed at such ethnic groups as blacks and Hispanics, but the fault may lie less in the role of the policemen than in the prejudice and indifference of society in general.

See also: *Boston Police Strike; Cooping; Deep Nightstick; Knapp Commission; Leatherheads; Lexow Committee; William H. Parker; Pipers; Police Riots of 1857, New York; Policewoman, First Killed; Policewomen;* Ratelwacht; *Rotten Apple Theory; Seabury Investigation; Lewis J. Valentine.*

POLICE Dogs

It is estimated that about 400 police agencies in the United States employ police dogs, or K-9 squads, as they are popularly known. The first use of dogs in police work occurred in Ghent, Belgium in 1900. Since then the duties of police canines have expanded. Each year "pot hounds" for the U.S. Customs Service sniff out a minimum of $100 million to $200 million in contraband narcotics. Intrepid, a golden retriever, became the Florida drug-sniffing champion by uncovering $16 million worth of drugs in Dade County in less than two years.

The most-used breed of police dog is the German shepherd, which has an excellent nose and can pick up scents as tiny as one-millionth that discernible by a human. Dogs have a better record of locating explosives than do bomb-detecting machines, and at a total cost of about $4,000 for training and $3 or $4 per day for maintenance, they have proved to be a bargain for cost-conscious police departments, which have also found that a policeman accompanied by a dog is a far greater crime deterrent than two officers. The armed forces use a great number of dogs for sentry duty and department stores keep them to sniff out thieves who try to hide until after closing time, loot the store and slip out the following morning.

POLICE Riots Of 1857, New York: Warring police forces

The Police Riots of 1857 in New York between two rival forces of law officers climaxed several months of terror in New York City during which policemen battled policemen while criminals attacked citizens with impunity. Even when apprehended, a criminal could escape if a member of the rival police force happened on the scene and got into an altercation with his counterpart.

The Municipal Police was formed by the state legislature in 1853, but within four years, during the second term of Mayor Fernando Wood, it was considered so chaotic and corrupt that the legislature intervened to abolish the force it had created. In its place the state lawmakers installed the Metropolitan Police, with the governor appointing a board of five commissioners, who in turn named a superintendent, Frederick Talmadge. The new Metropolitan Police Board then called on the mayor to disband the Municipals. Mayor Wood refused, however, even after the Supreme Court ruled in May 1857 that the law creating the new force was constitutional. Superintendent George W. Matsell of the Municipals stood by the mayor, as did 15 captains and 800 patrolmen.

Things came to a head when Capt. George W. Walling, who had pledged his loyalty to the new force, was sent to place Mayor Wood under arrest. When Wood refused to submit, Walling tried to take him in by force, but with 300 Municipals inside City Hall, he had no chance and was tossed into the street. Immediately thereafter, a troop of 50 Metropolitans marched on City Hall, a striking image in their plug hats and frock coats. The Municipals swarmed out of the building and attacked them and the battle was on, eventually extending to the corridors of the City Hall. Finally, the Metropolitans were routed. In all 52 policemen were injured, one Metropolitan was so badly beaten he was invalided for life.

The mayor and his police supporters held out until the members of the Metropolitan Police Board used the power granted them to call out the National Guard. The Seventh Regiment surrounded City Hall. Only when a platoon of infantry with fixed bayonets marched into the building and surrounded Mayor Wood in his office did he submit to arrest. He was released on nominal bail on a charge of inciting to riot and returned to his office.

The Metropolitan Police battled the Municipal Police in several bloody confrontations in New York City during 1857.

Confrontations continued the entire summer, with each of the two forces attempting to carry out its functions. The public itself was to bear the heavy brunt of the dispute. When a Municipal arrested a criminal, a Metropolitan would come along and release him and vice versa, as the feud became more important than the protection of the citizenry. While the police argued the criminals simply went about their business. Pedestrians were held up on Broadway in the middle of the day, while rival officers attacked each other with clubs to determine who had the right to interfere. Soon, large gangs of thieves plundered stores and other places of business and robbed passengers on stagecoaches in the city's midst. The gangs turned on each other, fighting for the robbing rights in certain areas, and a great battle between rival gangs broke out in the Bowery. A handful of Metropolitans tried to stop the fighting but were severely beaten. The Municipals simply said the battle was none of their business, leaving it to the Metropolitans.

Whenever a Metropolitan arrested a criminal and succeeded in bringing his charge to the police station, he would find an alderman and magistrate who supported the mayor waiting there to hold an immediate hearing and release the prisoner on his own recognizance. Officials who favored the Metropolitans did the same thing in Municipal station houses.

Such was the public outcry over this breakdown in police protection that an appeal of the Supreme Court decision was rushed into court. When the original decision was upheld, Mayor Wood abolished the Municipals. Several months later, about 50 of the officers, both Municipal and Metropolitan, who had been injured in the City Hall riot filed suit against the mayor. Each received a judgment of $250 but Mayor Woods never paid. Finally, the city paid the claims, together with the legal costs involved.

POLICEWOMAN: First killed in line of duty

Not for 64 years after Mrs. Alice Stebbins Wells became the first uniformed policewoman in the United States was a female officer killed in the line of duty. In September 1974 Gail A. Cobb, 24, a member of the District of Columbia police force, was shot and killed by a robbery suspect whom she had pursued into a garage. Officer Cobb's distinction was based on FBI files that dated back only to 1960, when apparently it was first deemed possible that a policewoman might someday be killed. Only in recent years has it become more common for policewomen to be assigned to general "line" duty.

POLICEWOMEN

While some use was made of women police matrons in the 19th century, police officials generally were greatly biased against female officers. Indeed, authorities usually reacted with horror to such suggestions, not merely because women were considered too "weak" for such work but also because of the opinon that they would be "too sympathetic" to defendants. When they finally made the ranks, policewomen proved such fears groundless.

A former social worker, Mrs. Alice Stebbins Wells, became the first uniformed policewoman in the United States, and probably the world, when she joined the Los Angeles Police Department on September 12, 1910. Her chief duties consisted of enforcing the regulations concerning "dance halls, skating rinks, penny arcades, picture shows and other similar places of public recreation." Other duties specifically assigned to her were "the suppression of unwholesome billboard displays, searches for missing persons, and the maintenance of a general information bureau for women seeking advice within the scope of police departments." The official enthusiasm over having a policewoman on the force was reflected in a regulation that read: "No young girl can be questioned by a male officer. Such work is delegated solely to policewomen, who, by their womanly sympathy and intuition, are able to gain the confidence of their younger sisters."

Mrs. Wells encountered difficulty when she attempted to ride free on street cars, as the city's police officers were entitled to do. She was constantly accused by conductors of misusing her husband's badge and was threatened with arrest if she did so again. To rectify this problem, she was issued "Policewoman's Badge No. 1" and allowed to design her own official uniform. Mrs. Well's performance was watched closely by other law enforcement agencies, and because of her record 16 other police departments added women in the next six years. In 1924 Buffalo hired the first black policewoman.

Some sources list a Mrs. Marie Owen as the first policewoman, hired by Superintendent Morgan A. Collins of the Detroit Police Department in 1893. However, the Detroit police have no record of Superintendent Morgan A. Collins much less a Mrs. Owen.

POLLARD, Edward (c.1845-1885): Murder victim

The biggest mistake Edward Pollard and George Brassfield ever made was taking on two hired hands, James Lamb and Albert O'Dell, at harvest time in 1885 on the farm they leased together in Lebanon, Indian Territory (later Oklahoma). Had the ensuing events occurred in a major city and enjoyed massive news coverage, it would have doubtless have become a legendary American murder case.

Mrs. Pollard took Lamb as a lover and Mrs. Brassfield couldn't stay away from O'Dell. The affairs could not be kept secret in an area where everyone knew everyone's business, and finally, Brassfield took off, leaving his wife and his share of the farm to O'Dell. Edward Pollard was more stubborn and refused to leave, remaining "in possession of his chattels, if not his wife."

On December 30, 1885 a preacher was called to the Pollard home to marry Lamb and Mrs. Pollard, the women explaining her husband had deserted her and "would not be back." The preacher refused to perform the marriage under those circumstances, and the next day the two couples left the area. Two months passed before the murdered body of Edward Pollard was found in a shallow grave off the trail, and warrants were issued for the two farm hands and the two errant wives. The quartet were found 50 miles away at Buck Horn Creek, where they had set up house. Both women were pregnant by their lovers.

O'Dell and Lamb had been close throughout their period of courtship and crime, but now each hired his own counsel. The two men were tried before the famous Hanging Judge, Isaac C. Parker, who seemed as much taken aback by their outrageous romantic behavior as by the murder. Each defendant's lawyer seemed to be prosecuting the other defendant along with the prosecution, which was armed with the testimony of the two women. Sitting in judgment of them, Hanging Parker was determined to see legal vengeance wrought. It was a case with no defense, and both men were hanged together on January 14, 1887.

POLLOS: Illegal Mexican immigrants

Pollos, or chickens, are impoverished migrants attempting to sneak into the United States. The name was given to them by border bandits, who consider the migrants no more than chickens to be plucked and, at times, slaughtered.

Most *pollos* attempt to enter the country through the so-called corridor, a stretch running 5½ miles along the California border from the San Ysidro-Tijuana port of entry to the Pacific Ocean. Since the chain-link fence separating the two countries is full of holes, three times as many illegals get in as are captured by the border patrol. However, evading the bor-

U.S. border guards comfort two *pollos* stranded in the Arizona desert by alien smugglers.

der patrol hardly means the *pollos* have made it. Far greater danger is posed by the border bandits, young Chicanos from San Diego and Los Angeles who waylay the migrants in the corridor at night. These bandits are out to seize the migrants' money and pitifully small possessions, knowing the *pollos* can hardly call on the authorities for protection.

Border crossings by *pollos* are carefully organized affairs. They pay a "coyote" in Mexico to arrange for their transportation and for a "mule," or guide, to lead them. The coyote often collects another bounty of about $15 a head from California growers to deliver the migrants straight to their farms where they are paid wages well under the legal minimum. Again, the *pollos* can hardly complain to the authorities, since the alternative is deportation.

Before the *pollos* reach this stage of exploitation, they first face the treachery of the mule. He too looks for an extra payment and will often lead them to an ambush by the border bandits in return for a portion of the loot. These robberies are generally brutal affairs, marked by bone-breaking, pistol whippings and an occasional fatal knifing. In a recent two-year period the reported crimes in the corridor included 251 robberies, seven rapes and seven murders. Of course, the unreported crimes are many times greater.

See also: *Peonage.*

POLYGAMY

Few marital practices have engendered more violence in America than that of polygamy as engaged in by the Mormons. It resulted in the mob murder of Joseph Smith in 1844, after that Mormon leader had enunciated the religious concept of pluralism. Actually, what Smith had advocated was polygyny, plural marriage for men only, which he saw as a solution to the problems of adultery and prostitution. The 1856 Republican platform called for the elimination of "the twin relics of barbarism," slavery and polygamy, and a number of laws were passed calling for heavy fines and long prison sentences against practitioners of polygamy.

Between 1885 and 1900 more than 1,000 Mormon men were convicted of the crime of polygamy. The practice did not cease until the closing years of the 19th century, when court tests upheld laws that disincorporated the Mormon church, forcing Mormon President Wilford Woodruff to issue a manifesto directing church members to cease engaging in pluralism. Certain fundamentalist Mormon sects, officially excommunicated, have continued the custom in isolated parts of Utah and Arizona. However, some recent, and no doubt exaggerated estimates, have claimed that perhaps 30,000 Mormons today live in secret polygynous marriages despite the ever present threat of fine and long imprisonment.

See also: *Joseph Smith.*

POMEROY, Jesse H. (1860-1932): Murderer and prisoner

Jesse Pomeroy's prison sentence is often cited as one of the cruelest ever imposed in this country. Convicted of murder at the age of 16, young Pomeroy of Boston was sentenced to be hanged, but after two years of controversy the sentence was commuted to life imprisonment in solitary confinement. The stipulation of solitary confinement was to satisfy those who wanted to exact the death penalty because of Pomeroy's long record of previous offenses. He spent 41 years in solitary before finally being permitted to mingle with the general prison population. Although still imprisoned, Pomeroy was, in a sense, reborn when he came out of solitary into the new world of electricity, moving pictures, the automobile, the phonograph and the telephone.

PONVENIR Massacre: Murder of Mexican-Americans

The Ponvenir Massacre was probably the worst instance of police murder in American history, an early equivalent of the more recent police Death Squads in Brazil. During World War I the exposure given to such alleged plots as the Plan of San Diego and the Zimmerman Note, both calling for Mexican uprisings and the annexation of portions of the United States and both almost certainly hoaxes, created hysteria among superpatriotic vigilante groups, particularly in the Texas borderlands and especially among the Texas Rangers. A virtual reign of terror was launched against local Chicanos. The lowest estimate of the number of Mexicans killed was 500, and some counts put the death toll at 5,000.

In 1919, acting on charges brought by State Rep. J. T. Canales, a Texas House-Senate committee found that the Texas Rangers had widely violated the civil rights of Mexicans, entered private houses illegally, made improper arrests, killed needlessly while making arrests and executed prisoners. An uncontested charge was that the Rangers had executed five prisoners arrested after a train robbery near Brownsville. The local sheriff managed to save the lives of two other prisoners by refusing to turn them over to the Rangers. In Cameron County the sheriff had threatened to arrest any Texas Ranger who illegally took firearms belonging to a Chicano without just cause. The most serious charge of all involved the massacre in the little village of Ponvenir in Big Bend country.

On December 25, 1917 between 40 and 50 bandits raided Brite's store, located outside Ponvenir, killing two Mexican passengers and the driver of a stagecoach when they happened along at the wrong moment. The bandits also attempted to raid a ranch house but were repelled, suffering heavy losses. The Texas Rangers were called in to investigate and supposedly learned that Chicanos in the village of Ponvenir were wearing new shoes of the same type stolen from Brite's store. Capt. J. M. Fox then organized a group consisting of eight Rangers and four civilians to conduct a raid on the village.

It was later determined that the raiders had terrorized the town. While getting drunk, they had rounded up 25 men and tortured them. In addition, the raiders had commissioned professional Mexican bravos to shoot a couple of villagers and worst of all, had brought together 15 unresisting villagers and massacred them.

The Rangers' version differed considerably. They stated that after they had taken a number of prisoners, other Chicanos had opened fire on them from the cover of brush, beginning an all-night firefight. By morning the Chicanos had disappeared. The Rangers claimed they had then gathered up some stolen goods as evidence and returned to their headquarters. They said they were not in a position to know if they had killed anyone during the long fight but assumed they had. The Texans had suffered no losses themselves.

The Rangers' defense was one that very few could swallow. Although no murder charges were ever brought against any of the raiders, Capt. Fox and all his men were dismissed from the Rangers.

See also: *Texas Rangers*.

PONZI, Charles (1877-1949): Swindler

Among the greatest swindlers ever to prey on the American public was Charles Ponzi—ex-dishwasher, ex-forger, ex-alien smuggler—who came to America from his native Italy in 1899. And for a time, he was also the most-beloved, especially among those who got in early on his fantastic scheme and actually made money. Once when Ponzi was being hauled before an official hearing to explain his money-trading operations, he was cheered by crowds in front of the State House in Boston. A voice from the crowd called out, "You're the greatest Italian of them all!"

"No, no," Ponzi responded, "Columbus and Marconi. Columbus discovered America. Marconi discovered the wireless."

"Yes, but you discovered money!"

That last claim was to prove debatable indeed. Not that Charles Ponzi didn't have money-making acumen. He discovered he could buy up international postal-union reply coupons at depressed prices in some foreign countries and sell them in the United States at a profit of up to 50 percent. It was, in fact, a classic get-rich-slowly operation, and as such, it bored Ponzi. So he figured out a better gimmick. He simply told everyone how he was making the money and said he needed a lot of capital to make a lot of money. For the use of their funds, he offered investors a 50 percent profit in three months. It was an offer they couldn't refuse, and the funds just came rolling into Ponzi's Boston office. In a short time, he had to open offices in neighboring states.

When Ponzi actually started paying out interest, a deluge followed. On one monumental day in 1920, Ponzi's offices took in an incredible $2 million from America's newest gamblers, the little people who squeezed money out of bank accounts, mattresses, piggy banks and cookie jars. There were days when a Ponzi office looked like a hurricane had hit it. Incoming cash had to be stuffed in closets, desk drawers and even in wastebaskets. Of coures, the more that came in, the more Ponzi paid out. In that sense, Ponzi was merely following the example of the legendary Billy "520 percent" Miller who had pulled the same caper in Brooklyn, New York some two decades earlier.

As long as investors kept pouring in new funds, Ponzi could continue to pay the interest on the old funds. After about six months the newspapers started to investigate his operation, but he was able to buy more time by hitting them with huge lawsuits. Meanwhile, Ponzi became a great dandy. His wardrobe consisted of 200 suits; he sported more than two dozen diamond stickpins; and he owned an elegant mansion. But Ponzi's bubble had to burst. The *Boston Post* dug up his past record, which showed he had spent time in prison in Montreal for forgery and in Atlanta for smuggling aliens. It was enough to make large numbers of eager investors hesitate to put in more money; the moment that happened, Ponzi's fragile scheme collapsed, since it required an unending flow of cash. His books, such as they were, showed a deficit of somewhere between $5 and $10 million, or perhaps even more. No one ever knew for sure.

Ponzi went to federal prison for four years for using the mails to defraud and was then sentenced to seven to nine years in Massachusetts for theft. When he emerged from prison in 1934, he was sent back to Italy. At this point the picture of Ponzi blurs. Some accounts, apparently not all fanciful, have him furnishing his "financial genius" to the Mussolini regime. If he did, the Fascists obviously did not profit from the experience, for within a few years Ponzi had to leave the country. He ended up in Rio de Janeiro, working for an Italian company until 1939, when the war put him out of work. Ponzi's last years were filled with extreme privation. He became partially blind and paralyzed and ended up in the charity ward of a Brazilian hospital, where he died in January 1949.

POPULATION Density And Crime

A person living in an American city of 250,000 or more has a three to 10 times greater chance of being a crime victim than someone living in a rural area. This is hardly surprising since urban life in the United States is more and more one of anonymity, crowded living conditions and a spirit of alienation. Middle-class flight from the inner cities to the suburbs results in an eroded tax base and forced cuts in police protection, as the crime problem worsens. Naturally, crime is most pervasive in the ghetto sections. In the 28th precinct in New York's Harlem section, about one out of every 500 residents will become a homicide victim. The nationwide ratio is one in 10,000.

Cities in all modern societies, in this country and abroad, have always been the breeding ground for crime. Comparisons between 19th and 20th century crime rates in the United States are hampered by the lack of anything near reliable crime figures for the period before the 1930s. The one thing that is apparent even from fragmentary figures, however, is that there is *less* crime in the cities of today compared to those of yesterday. In 1862 New York City, then comprising only the island

of Manhattan, had a population of about 815,000. In that year the police arrested 82,072 men and women and estimated the number of criminals residing in the metropolis at between 70,000 and 80,000. Both the arrest total and the estimated number of criminals represented almost 10 percent of the entire population. If that percentage held true today, the term "crime wave" would not be adequate to describe what American cities would be facing.

Crime in New York and in other major cities has merely reflected the activity of the criminal element in the ghettos. In an attempt to categorize the Draft Riots of 1863 as strictly a criminal matter—a contention that need not be accepted—historian Herbert Asbury argued that the reason the rioters were mostly Irish was "simply because the gangsters and the other criminal elements of the city were largely of that race." Then, as now, it was the ghettos that produced crime, and the shifting ethnic and racial composition of their occupants determined the ethnic and racial composition of criminals as a whole. Today's ghetto residents are blacks and Hispanics and, to a large extent, so are the cities' arrestees.

Former Attorney General Ramsey Clark notes in his book *Crime in America* that on the average an American is likely to be the victim of a violent crime only once in 400 years, but that the estimated figure for a resident of the black ghettos is once in 80 years, or five times more probable. However, since ghetto crime is vastly under-reported, Clark raises the possibility that a slum dweller may well be a violent crime victim about once every 20 years.

By contrast a white middle-class urban dweller, living in a good section of the city, will probably be a violent crime victim only once in about 2,000 years, and among the upper middle class and rich suburbanites, the odds dip to once in 10,000 years. Ironically, it is the perception of crime by these latter two groups that leads to the heralding of "crime waves." Today, much of white New York eschews traveling in the city's subways. Yet it has been established that the subways are safer than the city streets and a person is far less likely to be murdered, robbed, assaulted or raped on a subway platform than above ground.

Fear of crime is said to be the prime reason for middle-class flight from the cities to the suburbs (actually, such factors as soaring rents and housing costs, racial bias and filth are also major considerations). If so, the migration is proving to be a mistake. The suburbs are becoming less and less havens from crime, and murders in even rural areas are rising so rapidly that they now run only about 20 percent below the figures for the standard metropolitan statistical areas. Clearly, where a person lives affects his or her vulnerability to crime, but the tensions that produce crime, especially violent crime, are becoming universal.

See also: *Race and Crime.*

PRAIRIE Queen: Fancy Chicago brothel

In the 1850s Chicago was still a frontier town, a fact apparent in the rough quality of its brothels along Wells Street. A few more pretentious houses appeared, but none to match the luxurious bordellos that would soon become a municipal legend. The first of the fancy brothels opened in 1854, was the Prairie Queen on State Street, run by Eleanor Herrick, more generally referred to as Mother Herrick, a mainstay in Chicago's red-light district for 30 years. Besides such attractions as plush carpeting and melodeons in the parlors, the Prairie Queen was renowned for its entertainment. There was dancing every night, of a type shocking to Chicago's more genteel element, and a special erotic show once a week. In a further effort to attract clients, the Prairie Queen added regularly scheduled prizefights, fought with bare knuckles and for a purse of $2 and a night with one of Mother Herrick's ladies. The police had been ignoring the dancing and the erotic shows, but the fights were too much to be tolerated. On June 3, 1857, they swept down on the Prairie Queen and arrested the two fighters, Billy Fagan and Con McCarthy, on that night's card and shut down the brothel for going too far.

See also: *Sands, Whore War.*

PRESCOTT, Abraham (1816-1836): Murderer

Eighteen-year-old Abraham Prescott was a New Hampshire youth who committed an ordinary crime of passion and then made legal history with the first claim of sleepwalking as a defense.

On June 23, 1833 Mrs. Sally Cochran rejected Prescott's advances, and the enraged youth beat her to death with a stake. He was quickly identified and arrested as the killer. At his trial Prescott's defense lawyers announced the defendant was a confirmed somnambulist and that whatever he had done had occurred while he was asleep. News of the claim evoked general outrage. Of course, this was an era when any defense based on lack of mental competency received short shrift. Not surprisingly, the jury quickly rejected the defense and found Prescott guilty. However, because of the novelty of the claim, Prescott's lawyers were able to keep the case on appeal until the first days of January 1836.

At last, Prescott was slated to die, and a great mob attended his scheduled execution. When a short time before the start of the proceedings it was announced that the condemned man had been granted a temporary stay of execution, the crowd rioted, resulting in a number of injuries. Prescott was moved to Hopkinton, N.H., where authorities decided public tranquility superseded legal precedents and niceties; so on January 6 Prescott was hanged.

PRISONER—Longest Term: See Paul Geidel.

PRISONS And Prison Riots

One of the first institutions brought to the New World was the jail, a place where lawbreakers could be held while awaiting trial and punishment, which for about 150 offenses was death. Lesser crimes were punished by whipping, branding, maiming or public humiliation. The jail was basically not a place where prisoners were kept for punishment. In fact, the idea of a penitentiary or state prison was a purely American invention that was to have a profound effect on correctional policy in this and many other countries.

The first state prison was the notorious Newgate, established at Simsbury, Conn. in 1773. It was actually an abandoned copper mine in which prisoners were chained together to live and labor some 50 feet beneath the earth. Many of the prisoners were Tories incarcerated there during the Revolution. The first prison riot at Newgate occurred in 1776, when prisoners set fire to a massive wooden door in an attempt to reach a drainage channel that led to freedom. The riot failed, as smoke filled the mine, choking a number of prisoners to death and disabling the rest.

Newgate set the pattern of hellhole prisons in this country. Almost immediately, prison reformers appeared, but it is debatable whether their early efforts to achieve humane treatment of those imprisoned benefitted or harmed prisoners. The first reform of prison practices was attempted in 1790 at Philadelphia's Walnut Street Jail, which was renovated through the efforts of a group of Quakers called the Philadelphia Society to Alleviate the Miseries of Public Prisons, an organization that exists to the present day as the Philadelphia Prison Society. A 19th century historical account describes the unreformed Walnut Street Jail in its early days as a scene of "universal riot and debauchery . . . with no separation of those accused but yet untried, nor even of those confined for debt only, from convicts sentenced for the foulest crimes . . . no separation of . . . age or sex, by day or night."

After the jail was remodeled in 1790, men and women for the first time were housed separately in large, clean rooms. Debtors were segregated from other prisoners, and children were removed from the jail entirely. Hardened offenders were placed in solitary confinement in a "penitentiary house" and prisoners were given work and religious instruction. Within a short time, however, the Walnut Street Jail became overcrowded and a new institution had to be built.

About the same time, two new prisons were built, which were soon to function as the models for what became known as the Pennsylvania and Auburn prison systems. Eastern Penitentiary was built at Philadelphia in 1829 to further the Quaker idea of prisoner isolation. Prisoners were confined in windowless cells about eight by 12 feet with running water and toilet facilities. Each prisoner had his own "exercising yard," about eight by 20 feet, surrounded by a high brick wall. The walls between the cells were thick and virtually sound proof, so that an inmate never saw another inmate, only a few guards, chaplains and an occasional pious person who came by to pray and offer spiritual advice. Needless to say, great numbers of prisoners went insane under the Pennsylvania system, but that did not stop it from becoming popular both elsewhere in the United States and around the world.

Also in 1829, a rival system ,which eventually gained wider

acceptance, was launched with the building of a new prison in Auburn, N.Y. The trouble with the Pennsylvania system, said the New York prison experts, was that the convicts spent too much time praying and working alone and thus could not "pay for their keep" through convict labor. At Auburn the prisoners were permitted to work together by day fulfilling convict labor contracts, but in all other aspects the isolation of the Pennsylvania system was maintained.

Inmates were forbidden ever to talk to one another, even when working together in the prison's shops. The prisoners marched in lockstep, their gaze always downward. In Warden Elam Lynds, the system had a devoted champion. Lynds felt the purpose of the system was to break the prisoners' spirits. He personally flogged prisoners and urged his guards to treat the men with contempt and brutality. A typical, and sometimes lethal, punishment instituted by Lynds was the water cure. The punishment consisted of fastening a prisoner's neck in an iron yoke and then pouring a stream of icy water on his head. In a variation of the water cure, the prisoner was shackled naked to a wall and a high-pressure water hose was turned full blast on his back. The man was plastered to the wall by the force of the water and the pain was almost unbearable. However, the torture left no marks.

The Auburn system was rapidly adopted throughout America because it was more economical to operate than the Pennsylvania system. In Auburn the cells were only seven feet high, seven feet long and 3½ feet wide. As the Auburn system spread, the methods of repression mushroomed. The striped uniform was introduced at Sing Sing, and floggings, the sweatbox, the straitjacket, the iron yoke, the thumbscrew and the stretcher became widespread. The latter device had a number of variations. A man could be handcuffed to the upper bars of his cell so that his toes barely touched the floor, and usually he would be left that way the entire day. In another version, inmates had their ankles chained to the floor and their wrists tied to a rope that was passed through a pulley attached to the ceiling. When the rope was pulled, the prisoners were stretched taut. Some prisons built sweatboxes right into the cell door, actually a double door in which a prisoner could be placed in a space so small that he could barely move. In other prisons this type of sweatbox was not considered stern enough. It was, after all, much more effective if the sweatboxes were placed near a fireplace so that the suffering could be intensified.

The Auburn system was based on cruelty and repression, with the idea that such treatment would reform the prisoners. It was a failure, but some of the Auburn system's practices have been adopted in varying degrees by more modern prisons.

In the post-Civil War period, however, penologists did begin experimenting with the new ideas. In 1870, mainly through the efforts of penologists like Enoch Cobbs Wines and others who formed the American Prison Association, the reformatory system came into being. Because of these penologists the Elmira Reformatory opened in New York in 1876. Although the reformatory plan was originally intended for all ages, at Elmira it was limited to prisoners between the ages of 16 and 30. The chief principle of the Elmira system was reformation, rather than expiation of guilt, and it was hailed as the greatest advance in penology since the substitution of the prison for the medieval method of maiming and/or execution.

Prisons, whether of the old wooden variety or the more modern type, have had the same general effect—nonreformation of the convict.

When a prisoner entered Elmira, he was automatically placed in the second of three grades. If and when he showed improvement, he was moved to the first grade, and upon continued improvement he won parole. If he turned out to be a troublemaker, he was dropped to the third grade and had to work his way back up. Many of the prisoners were sentenced to indeterminate terms so that they could be afforded the full benefit of the reformatory concept.

By the turn of the century, 11 states had adopted the reformatory system, but by 1910 this innovation was all but dead. Most guards and even wardens proved incapable of administering a complex grading program, and in the majority of systems, the advancment of prisoners was based on favoritism or their ability to get along in the institution rather than their progress in achieving a full-scale reformation. As a result, most reformatory graduates went out and committed new crimes.

Today, many prisons retain the name of "reformatory" but are merely part of the general prison system. Despite the claims of penologists, there has been little general advance in prisons since the introduction of the reformatory. Currently, prisons are divided into three classes: maximum security, medium security and minimum security. Because of reform wardens like Thomas Mott Osborne and Lewis E. Lawes, both of Sing Sing, who had an impact on penological theories, much of the blatant cruelty and squalor of the 19th century prisons has been considerably reduced. Still, extremely punitive concepts have persisted, as indicated in the 1930s by the establishment of Alcatraz as a "super prison" for the worst federal prisoners, an American Devil's Island. It proved a total failure. According to some estimates, almost 60 percent of the inmates went stir crazy there. Alcatraz unquestionably left its mark not only on many of the prisoners but on many of the guards as well. The prison soon lost its original purpose as a place of confinement for escapers and other troublemakers and became a place to lodge inmates simply deemed deserving of harsher treatment, such as Al Capone and, later on, Morton Sobell, of the Rosenberg atom bomb spy case. By 1963 Alcatraz was abandoned, having proven an unqualified failure.

Yet there are those who consider the entire American prison system a failure. Overall, various critics have charged, prisons have failed to reform criminals or even to act as a deterrent crime. Moreover, prisons are generally conceded to be schools for crime, where lesser offenders learn from their "betters." It is this last fact that makes unfeasible the idea of simply using prisons as places of confinement and retribution. Sooner or later, prisoners must be released, if for no other reason than a shortage of space.

And without rehabilitation programs the problem of prison riots would increase manyfold. Such riots have become commonplace in the 20th century, evidenced especially in the three great waves—1929-32, 1950-56, 1968-73—of prison rebellion. The most tragic riot, if indeed it was one, occurred at the Ohio State Penitentiary in Columbus on April 21, 1930. More than 300 prisoners died in a fire that, prison officials claimed, was started by inmates. More likely, an electrical failure caused the fire, which the prison guards were poorly trained to handle. Certainly, there was reason enough for a riot, since the prison was jammed with 4,300 inmates in accommodations designed for 1,500.

The worst riot of the 1950s occurred at the overcrowded Southern Michigan State Prison at Jackson. Guards were seized as hostages and prisoners roamed the prison setting fires and smashing thousands of windows. The damage toll was put at $2.5 million.

The worst two-year span of prison rioting occurred in 1970-71. Among the major disturbances were the following:

January 1970: Soledad Prison, Salinas, Calif. Three black convicts and a white guard killed during a race riot among prisoners.

July 1970: Holmesburg Prison, Philadelphia, Pa. Eighty-four prisoners and 29 guards injured in riot with pronounced racial overtones.

October 1970: Tombs Prison, New York, N.Y. Convicts hold 26 hostages to protest overcrowded conditions.

November 1970: Cummings Prison Farm, Grady, Ark. About 500 convicts riot to demand separate facilities for whites and blacks.

August 1971: San Quentin, Calif. Three inmates, including black militant George Jackson, and three guards killed in what was described as an escape effort.

September 1971: Attica Prison, Attica, N.Y. Thirty-two prisoners and 11 guards being held hostage killed by prison guards and state police rescuers in aftermath of four-day protest over prison conditions.

Various studies indicate that there are many causes for prison riots, some of the main ones being inconsistent sentencing and parole policies; prisoner-perceived unfair sentencing; overcrowding; pent-up anger; racial tensions; public and official indifference to conditions; idleness; lack of rehabilitative programs; and most recently, the activity of radical and revolutionary groups in the inmate population that regard all convicts as political prisoners.

See also: *Alcatraz Prison, Alcatraz Prison Rebellion, Attica Prison Riot, James A. Johnston, Lewis E. Lawes, Elam Lynds, Ohio State Penitentiary Fire, George O. Osborne, Thomas Mott Osborne, Sentencing of Criminals, Welfare Island Prison Scandal.*

PRISONS—Good Time: See Good-Time Laws.

PRIVATE Eye: Slang for private detective

The term "private eye" originated from the symbol of Pinkerton's National Detective Agency, founded in 1850, which featured an eye and the slogan "We never sleep." As the fame of the agency spread, criminals began expressing fear of the "Eye" and later of the "private eye," as distinguished from the eyes of the police.

PROBATION

It would seem that probation, rather than imprisonment, is the standard method of punishment used in this country; far more people are on probation than behind bars.

The father of the probation movement was a wealthy Boston businessman named John Augustus, who, because of his interest in drunkards, persuaded a judge in 1841 to release a "common drunkard" in his custody. Augustus took him home, gave him clothes and found him a job. Weeks later, Augustus returned to court with the man, now totally changed in both appearance and manner, and the judge, thoroughly impressed, released the prisoner from the charge with a fine of 1¢.

Over the last 18 years of life, Augustus won probation for almost 2,000 persons. At first, he labored solely on the behalf of drunks but then expanded his activities to include defendants charged with more serious crimes. Augustus' record was superb, far better than those achieved by later probation programs. Less than a dozen of his charges ran away and only a few committed new crimes. Another Bostonian, Fr. Rufus W. Cook, and a Philadelphian, William J. Mullen, who eventually worked as a prison agent for the Philadelphia Prison Society, became leading exponents of probation.

Probation departments today generally claim a rehabilitation success rate of more than 70 percent. The National Probation and Parole Association states:

> Far more effective than deterrence as an objective of sentencing is rehabilitation, the satisfactory adjustment of the offender to law-abiding society. Whether it takes the form of probation—proved to be the most practical approach where circumstances warrant its use—or of commitment and ultimately parole, it is based on the principle that the best way to protect society is to change convicted offenders into law-abiding citizens.

Not all observers accept in full the rehabilitative value attributed to probation. Aryeh Neier, executive director of the American Civil Liberties Union, notes:

> There is no evidence that probation rehabilitates people any more than if people were simply left alone. Probation is punitive, however, and its principal use should be as an alternative to prison for people who have committed minor crimes and who deserve some punishment.

One of the actual motives for granting probation is to reward police informers. But it is also used to allow the probationer to work and provide restitution to the victim for his or her loss or injury or to keep the prisoner's family intact and off the charity rolls.

Probation is considered an effective way to promote guilty pleas, and most judges agree it is necessary to provide them with a way to invoke a relatively mild form of punishment for first offenders. Above all, probation is necessary to reduce prison overcrowding. The cost is about one-tenth that of maintaining him or her in a penal institution. This last fact alone should guarantee the system a future.
See also: *Parole.*

PROCURESSES: See New Orleans Procuresses.

PROCURING

A double standard toward vice held by much of society views prostitution itself tolerantly but regards procuring, the recruitment of girls and women to serve as prostitutes, a vital part of the overall business, as far more unwholesome. In almost every major city in the United States during the 19th century, vice operators had no trouble paying off crooked police officers, and, indeed, entire police units and departments for permission to run houses of prostitution, but the enforcers of the law were less accommodating when it came to allowing procurers

to supply young girls for these establishments. Some corrupt officers who accepted payoffs for almost anything else rebelled when happening upon "break-in" houses, where male specialists indoctrinated, by repeated rapes, young victims lured to the big city by the promise of well-paying jobs.

In New York's so-called Grabber Scandal in 1875, the notorious Hester Jane Haskins, better known as Jane the Grabber, was arrested by enraged police because she was recruiting girls from the better portion of society to satisfy the demands of higher-priced bordellos patrons for young ladies of refinement and education. Jane the Grabber had been allowed to operate for years, recruiting gullible girls right off the boat or from upstate farm country and publishing a monthly circular that advertised her wares to whorehouse clients. But when she started kidnapping the daughters of the well-to-do, she was carted off to prison.

Procurers emerged in America shortly after the arrival of the white man. Their first victims were Indian maidens, who were bought or stolen from their tribes to be used as prostitutes. Soon, they flourished in every port city, attracting an endless stream of young girls and women, including those who spoke not a word of English. Other procurers, operating sometimes in gangs, worked the Ohio and Mississippi rivers, again either kidnapping or buying young females from their impoverished parents and selling them down river at the infamous flatboat auctions in Natchez and New Orleans. Perhaps the most famous of the procurer gangs was the one led by white slaver Sam Purdy, whose heyday was around the start of the 19th century. By 1805, however, the gang was wiped out as a result of assassinations carried out or instigated by a colorful reformer named Carlos White, the scourge of fleshpots from St. Louis to New Orleans.

In the 19th century New Orleans was probably the most tolerant of procurers with several of that city's famed procuresses being allowed practically a free hand in recruiting and despoiling young virgins, some barely in their teens. The New Orleans procuresses supplied not only houses of prostitution in the French Quarter and elsewhere in the city but also bordellos in Atlanta, Memphis, Galveston and a number of other Southern cities. In their lavish brochures "fresh stock" indicated inexperienced girls, who thus commanded the highest prices. In time, fierce competition drove the prices of a virgin down as low as $50, but by the late 1860s Louisa Murphy, a schoolteacher-procuress, was commanding $800 for a young girl. Murphy had little trouble with the police whom she paid off regularly. Similarly, Nellie Haley, considered the Queen of the Procuresses in the 1880s, was never arrested in New Orleans; later in her career Nellie did run afoul of the law when she attempted to ply her trade in Chicago.

Chicago gave a mixed welcome to procurers; many operated without interference but others were harrassed whenever certain policemen experienced a sudden infusion of righteousness. Still, Chicago's vice trade required so many women that procurers operated there with or without approval, and the city became the supply point for many other cities in the Midwest.

Some procurer gangs dealt solely in foreign women, among them the band headed by French Em Duval and her husband. The Duvals ran their own brothel in Chicago on Armour Avenue but maintained a stockade outside the city on Dearborn Street, where women shipped in from New York were kept awaiting sale to buyers. The stockade had barred windows and the inmates were not permitted any street wear until they were being transported to the brothel which had purchased them. The Duval operation was broken up in 1908 by federal authorities utilizing immigration statutes, the only legal weapon available for use against vice operations prior to the Mann Act.

Another important procurer mob of the era was the Dewey Hotel Gang, considered the most efficient operation in the city. The gang, comprised of Russian Jews, specialized in providing, not surprisingly, Russian Jewesses, a prize attraction in American bordellos. The gang maintained break-in rooms and a stockade on the top floor of a hotel on Washington Boulevard. They held regular auctions, at which women were stripped and inspected by brothel keepers and sold to the highest bidders. At an auction in 1906, 25 women were sold for sums ranging from $25 to $100 apiece. This sale did not constitute the gang's total profits, however, since for a considerable time thereafter each woman had to turn over her share of the money she earned to the procurers.

No account of procuring in this country would be complete without mentioning Harry "Greasy Thumb" Guzik and his wife Alma, perhaps the most proficient procurer couple in America. One of five brothers who as youngsters earned nickels running errands and hustling for Chicago prostitutes in the Levee district, Harry was a full-time pimp before he reached his teens. After getting busted early in his career, he started paying off virtually every politician and policeman who came into view. A ward politician once said, "Harry's fingers are always greasy from the money he counts out for protection." Thus, he won the nickname Greasy Thumb.

Harry eventually accumulated a string of whores in the Levee and married one of them, Alma. Thereafter, the couple became the chief procurers for all the important brothel operators in the city, men like Big Jim Colosimo and women like Victoria Moresco.

Harry and Alma combed the rural areas of Illinois, Indiana and Wisconsin in search of new girls, particularly those who dressed "city style" and obviously wanted no part of farm living. After finding a likely prospect, Harry would go to bed with her and be joined by Alma. Afterwards, Alma would regale Harry about being a cheapskate and insist he give the girl $10. Later the girl would be invited to visit Chicago. Once again, she would end up in bed with the couple, but this time a male friend of Harry's would show up and the threesome would become a foursome. Upon leaving, Harry's friend would insist on giving Alma and the girl $10 each. Generally, by the next day the girl was working in a whorehouse. The Guziks sold each recruit for $100 plus expenses and a percentage of the girl's future earnings. They often procured some 10 girls a month in an attempt to keep up with the demand for "fresh bodies."

In 1921 the Guziks had trouble convincing a farm girl to turn prostitute; so they made her a prisoner, took away her clothes and had her forcibly indoctrinated. After many months the girl got word out to her family and was rescued by her brothers. The couple tried to fix things by bribing the father of the girl, now a mental and physical wreck, not to press charges. But the attempt didn't work and they were convicted and sentenced to the penitentiary. Out on bail while the case was being appealed, the Guziks stepped up their recruiting activities to raise a large sum of money. These funds found their way to Illinois Gov. Len Small, who abruptly granted them a full pardon before the judicial process was completed.

After Harry Guzik joined the Capone syndicate, he was put in charge of prostitution and procuring and became the chief funnel for much of the mob's payoffs to police and politicians. Eventually, brother Jake Guzik handled even bigger payoffs for the Capone gang, and upon Harry's death the Greasy Thumb monicker passed on to him.

Two Chicago newspapermen once overheard a conversation between Guzik and a young Willie Bioff, then primarily a procurer known for slugging whores who attempted to hold out on him. It was Guzik's observation that "they're so dumb (prospective prostitutes) you have to teach them never to give away what they can sell." The pair then discussed the best technique for convincing women to "go horizontal." The first step was to seduce a woman, then lavish money on her and finally wake up one morning and declare bankruptcy. Bioff told Guzik: "Then I hint that if she really loved me, she'd lay a friend of mine who wanted to give me a hundred dollars if he could just get in her pants once. She always cries. She always tells me she loves me and she could not possibly lay anybody else. But I tell her I wanted to buy such wonderful things for her—and here we are without even breakfast money. She comes around."

"And," rejoined Harry Guzik, "once she's laid one other guy for money, she's hooked. After that you can put her right into a house and she'll turn over her earnings to you every night. If she tries to hold out, you just slap her around a little."

A mistaken belief today is that most procurers are black, a perception fostered, according to Richard Milner, coauthor of *Black Players,* perhaps the most definitive study of black pimps, by the fact that the blacks are primarily street operators and thus more visible than white procurers. In New York the role of black procurers in recruiting runaway girls around the Port Authority bus terminal on Eighth Avenue has been the subject of numerous studies.

According to Milner, most important procurers are whites. It is they who recruit women for the legalized whorehouses in Nevada and for the "massage parlors" in various major cities. By abandoning the streets to the blacks, the same as has occurred in drug distribution, the white procurers have been able to shift attention away from their activities.

See also: *Beckett Sisters, Willie Morris Bioff, Grabbers, Joseph "Rowdy Joe" Lowe, Mann Act, New Orleans Procuresses, Prostitution, Sam Purdy, White Slave.*

PROFACI, Joseph (1896-1962): Mafia family head

Of all the long time crime family bosses of the New York Mafia, the least Godfatherly was undoubtedly Joe Profaci, one of the original five bosses who formed the modern Mafia after the assassination of the boss of bosses, Salvatore Maranzano, in 1931.

A vicious young gunman, Profaci became the head of the Mafia family in Brooklyn while in his twenties and ruled it in the strict old Sicilian manner, requiring every member of the family to kick in $25 in monthly dues to him. In theory, this was to build a slush fund to take care of legal fees, bribes and support money for a soldier's family in the event he was sent to jail. It was an old custom that had long been abolished in other families, but Profaci, a multimillionaire with a huge mansion on a 328-acre estate on Long Island, complete with hunting lodge and private airport, could not resist gathering up extra pennies in this fashion. The gang boss ran all the rackets hard and leaned on his men for a heavy percentage of their illegal profits. In other families the smarter operators cut the head of the family in for a slice of whatever racket they ran, but it was offered as a form of "affection" or a "token of respect." Profaci demanded it, and he demanded plenty.

Profaci was able to run his family with an iron hand because he killed ruthlessly whenever anyone objected to his techniques. For years Brooklyn was littered with corpses of those who did not play according to Profaci's rules.

But while the Brooklyn underworld knew the dark side of Profaci, the respectable community had a different view of him. Probably more than any other top mafioso, Profaci was a religious man. He regularly attended St. Bernadette's Catholic Church in Brooklyn and even had a private altar built in his cellar so that mass could be celebrated at family gatherings by a priest who was a close friend of the Profacis. In 1949 a group of leading Italian-Americans petitioned Pope Pius XII to confer a knightship on Profaci, a "son of Sicily" who had become America's leading importer of tomato paste and olive oil and who, as the principal owner of more than 20 other prominent businesses, was a kindly employer of hundreds of his fellow countrymen. Profaci was also cited as a generous donor to many Catholic charities. The petition was denied after Miles McDonald, the Brooklyn district attorney, pointed out to the Vatican that Profaci was a top racketeer, extortionist, murderer and Mafia leader.

While this may have left Profaci disappointed, it did not dampen his religious zeal. When a young thief stole a jeweled crown from St. Bernadette's, an act that in his eyes was probably the greatest possible sacrilege not only against the church but against the mob itself, the word was passed that the crown had to be returned or blood would flow. The thief returned the crown but first removed a few diamonds. Thus, the matter remained a capital offense, and a death sentence was issued and carried out. Vincent Teresa, the biggest Mafia informer since Joe Valachi, summed up the rationale: "If Profaci hadn't had the kid put to sleep, Profaci would have lost a lot of prestige in the community. After all, he owned Brooklyn, he was the boss."

During the last three years of his life, from 1960 to 1962, the Brooklyn Mafia boss was involved in the famed "mattress war" with the Gallo brothers, young upstart members of the family who resented Profaci's greed and the fact that he had not rewarded them for services rendered, especially carrying out the execution of the dreaded Albert Anastasia on orders passed down from Vito Genovese. The Gallos were under the assumption that this hit would entitle them to a piece of Brooklyn's gambling and narcotics action. Finally, open warfare broke out when the young rebels kidnapped five of Profaci's leading gang members. They were returned when Profaci promised to deal with the Gallos' complaints. Instead, in typical Profaci manner, he attempted to have them killed. In the later warfare far more Gallo men were murdered than were Profaci gangsters, but the aging Profaci did not live to see the eventual demise of the Gallos. He died in 1962 of quickly advancing cancer, and his family was eventually taken over by Joseph Colombo.

See also: *Crazy Joe Gallo.*

PROHIBITION

"Goodbye John. You were God's worst enemy. You were Hell's best friend. . . . The reign of tears is over." Using those words, the Rev. Billy Sunday held a mock funeral in Norfolk, Va. for John Barleycorn when the 18th Amendment took effect on January 16, 1920. The supporters of Prohibition were confident that it was the panacea for all the social ills in America. In retrospect, Prohibition accomplished the exact opposite. As far as crime was concerned, the cure proved far worse than the ailment; in part, this was because Prohibition simply wouldn't work and, to a larger extent, because it fostered corruption. Law enforcement agencies became open to bribes to an extent unheard of even in the less than pristine years that preceded it. Worse yet, Prohibition was the midwife of organized crime in America.

The great gangs of America—born in the 1820s and continuing up to World War I—operated in two major fields, committing various forms of violent crimes and acting as bully boys for the political machines of the big cities. By 1914 these violent gangs had just about been wiped out. In New York City the 1,500-member Eastman gang was in disarray, with their leader in prison. The Eastmans' arch rivals, the Five Pointers, were scattering and their leader Paul Kelly, understanding that an enlightened public would no longer tolerate gang violence in elections, moved into relatively minor labor racketeering activities. Prostitution, another gang operation, was also in decline. During World War I the federal government shuttered the country's most infamous vice centers, especially those in San Francisco, New Orleans and Chicago.

However, now the huge profits of illegal activities spawned by Prohibition gave criminal organizations a new lease on life. Across the country 200,000 speakeasies sprang up and giant bootlegging organizations were required to supply them. In

New York City alone, 15,000 saloons were replaced by 32,000 speakeasies. Bootleggers and rumrunners brought in liquor from outside the borders. The production of alcohol became a cottage industry in many cities, producing foul odors that lay heavy over entire neighborhoods.

The Purple Gang of Detroit, up until then more interested in robberies and murders, became one of the most important of the Prohibition gangs, controlling much of the liquor supplies smuggled in from Canada. In Cleveland, the violent Mayfield Road Gang emerged as an extremely potent force, and of course, Chicago's Al Capone gained recognition as the nation's most prominent Prohibition gangster. It has been estimated that Capone himself made $60 million from bootlegging and rumrunning.

With the incredible profits from Prohibition rackets, the mobs found they could corrupt federal agents, police, politicians and judges to an extent never before considered possible. In fact, in the pre-Prohibition era it was the politicians who controlled the gangsters. With their newfound wealth the gangsters were able to reverse this role; they now gave the orders and the politicians jumped.

Disrespect for the law grew as it became fashionable for respectable citizens to drink bootleg liquor in their homes and in speakeasies. After all, President Warren G. Harding paid lip service to Prohibition while turning the White House into a private saloon. It was widely and correctly assumed, that

most Prohibition agents themselves violated the law and accepted enormous bribes. The Treasury Department reported that between 1920 and 1928 the government fired 706 agents and prosecuted another 257 for taking bribes. Head T-man Elmer L. Irey called the agents a "most extraordinary collection of political hacks, hangers-on and passing highwaymen." In New York, Capt. Daniel Chapin ordered a lineup of all agents and announced, "Now everyone of you sons of bitches with a diamond ring is fired." Half were.

By 1928 a large segment of the population realized that Prohibition had to be abolished. New York Gov. Al Smith, a vocal opponent of the 18th Amendment, won the Democratic nomination for president. Smith lost but Prohibition was doomed, although it lasted another five years. In 1931 President Herbert Hoover established a bipartisan panel, the Wickersham Commission, to study the question. It found that Prohibition was unenforceable but still suggested it be maintained. Finally, in 1933, with the Democrats in power, Prohibition was repealed by passage of the 21st Amendment.

The effects of Prohibition however, did not end with its repeal. The great gangs that had fed on it were so big and powerful and had such excellent political connections that they simple moved into new rackets, especially those that enjoyed considerable public approval, such as gambling. With the end of Prohibition, the national crime syndicate was organized to

Good old "mountain dew" was a problem in backwoods America before, during and after Prohibition.

save the mobs from destruction. The expertise the criminals gained during that era has helped them to thrive ever since.

See also: *Bootlegging, Izzy and Moe, Carry A. Nation.*

During Prohibition, the well-shoed lady could carry a tube of liquor in her heel for emergency partying.

PROSTITUTION

Prostitution came to America with the white man; the Indians had never heard of the custom, but they were soon to learn it. The first colonists in Massachusetts and Virginia tried to suppress the practice, and Virginia had a set policy of shipping back to England any arriving females believed to be prostitutes. However, when in the early 1700s both the English and French began sending over their bawds along with criminals, vagrants and beggars, the New World was simply overwhelmed. Soon, New York, New Orleans and other port cities sported large European-style brothels. By the time of the American Revolution, some leaders considered the fight against prostitution hopeless. To Benjamin Franklin and Thomas Jefferson it was an inescapable aspect of life. In his proposal for the establishment of the University of Virginia, Jefferson boldly included a house of prostitution, arguing a well-regulated house would be better than the unregulated ones that would otherwise develop. But he was forced to drop that part of his proposal.

As the nation moved west during the 19th century, prostitution became more tolerated in "man's country," and indeed, it was much more of a civilizing force there than in all the large Eastern cities, where prostitution was tolerated and even encouraged by the politicians and police because of the tremendous graft involved. Scarlet women first tamed the rough miners of the West, who visited not only for the pleasures of the flesh but to have their socks mended and buttons sewed on as well.

A look at the numbers quickly reveals why prostitution was

inevitable in the West. In San Francisco, after gold was discovered, the population consisted of 65,000 men and only 2,500 women, and those figures were hardly as disparate as the ones in other communities. In 1880 Leadville, Colo. had an even poorer male-female ratio than San Francisco and boasted a bordello for every 148 inhabitants. The town that was an exception to the rule was Salt Lake City, where the Mormon male and female populations were almost even and there was no prostitution.

With the influx of "respectable women," advocacy or tolerance of prostitution was replaced in some Western towns by active opposition. In Denver an ordinance was passed requiring prostitutes to wear yellow ribbons on their arms as a mark of shame. The city's madams ordered their women to wear nothing but yellow, from bonnets to shoes, and to carry yellow parasols. It created such a bizarre sight that the law had to be rescinded.

In other cities and towns prostitution was deeply rooted and appreciated. A Topeka newspaper commented on the attitude in Ellsworth, Kan.:

> The city realizes $300 per month from prostitution fines alone. . . . The city authorities consider that as long as mankind is depraved and Texas cattle herders exist, there will be a demand and necessity for prostitutes, and that as long as prostitutes are bound to dwell in Ellsworth it is better for the respectable portion of society to hold prostitutes under restraint of law."

Tokens like these were used as currency in the pleasure houses of the Old West. (From the Milner Collection.)

When the noted muckraker Julian Street witnessed blatant prostitution on Market Street in Cripple Creek, Colo., he wrote a scathing denunciation of the town in *Colliers* magazine. In response, the city fathers changed the name of the bawdy thoroughfare to . . . Julian Street. But in a sense, that was open prostitution's last hurrah. The celebrated madams of the 19th and early 20th century were passing from the scene— Julia Bulette of the Comstock, Tessie Wall and Madame Atoy of San Francisco, Josie Arlington of New Orleans, the Everleigh

Sisters of Chicago, Mattie Silks and Jennie Rogers of Denver and Babe Connors of St. Louis.

While these women gave the illegal activity a certain glamour and mystique, they could not hide the grim reality of prostitution, its almost exclusive reliance on exploiting poorer girls, often immigrants who spoke no English. They lived drab lives, often entertaining as many as 50 men a day and ending up with very little money after paying off madams, pimps, drug pushers, and the police. A great myth was that many prostitutes eventually married and settled down to raise families, but these were the exceptions. The more common experience was for such women to deteriorate, moving lower down the scale of whorehouses as their bodies and looks showed the ravages of years at the profession. When they were unacceptable to the madams of brothels, they were thrown out to survive as best they could as streetwalkers. Suicide exceeded alcoholism and drug overdoses as a cause of death among prostitutes. In Denver it was common for at least two or three girls a week to take poison.

A Depression-era sign that was a bit more blatant than most.

The passage of the Mann Act in 1910, forbidding the transportation of women across state lines for immoral purposes, marked the swing of public opinion in favor of suppressing prostitution. Over the next seven years law enforcement agents closed down most organized vice areas in big cities. Naturally, such moves didn't wipe out prostitution, and houses of ill repute continued to thrive although in lesser numbers. They still exist in some big cities, sometimes in the form of "massage parlors" or "rap studios," but the trade no longer draws the traffic it once enjoyed. Some modern madams attribute the decline to the Sexual Revolution, specifically objecting to the amateurs who are "killing business by giving it away."

Occasionally, a madam has been lionized in recent years, as was the case with Polly Adler, whose doings and quotes were dutifully reported by the Broadway columnists of the 1930s and 1940s. In 1980 a lesser madam in Sault Ste. Marie, Mich., Ethel Brand, received nationwide publicity—and an increase in patronage—when it was revealed that she paid all taxes due on her income and that of her women.

The only state that allows prostitution is Nevada, which had outlawed the practice for a time during and after World War II. Now, it is considered one of the state's most important tourist attractions. In 1980 Joe Conforte, the owner of the state's most famous brothel, the Mustang Ranch, sold it to Madam Gina Wilson for a reported $19.8 million. Even allowing for considerable hype in the price quoted, it is evident that the wages of sin remain most rewarding.

See also: *Polly Adler, Josie Arlington, Chicken Ranch, "Company Girls!", Babe Connors, Everleigh Sisters, Floating Hog Ranches, Mann Act, Procuring, Red-Light District, Matty Silks, Storyville, White Slave.*

PROSTITUTION—Legal: See Maison Coquet.

PROSTITUTION, Male

It is perhaps one of the archetypal male fantasies that there be houses of prostitution staffed by male harlots who would service female clients. The first such brothel for this purpose was Aunt Josie's Place in San Francisco. In 1906 Aunt Josie, an old black madam, opened her unique brothel on Mason Street, in what was known as the Uptown Tenderloin area. Madam Josie hoped to attract the ladies of society as clients but appears to have had only limited success despite a relatively lavish two-story setup with great guarantees of privacy, including the furnishing of silk masks to clients so that even the lady's partner did not have to see her face unless she wished it.

Customers were offered a book of photographs of male harlots along with related copy that supplied pertinent physical statistics. Once the woman made her selection, the lover was then summoned to the house by telephone or runner. The fee for his services was set at $10, two to 40 times the going rate in female brothels. Quite naturally, the story spread that many of these men refused to take any money, feeling their reward was already sufficient.

It was never determined how many women availed themselves of the exotic offerings of Aunt Josie's place other than female prostitutes who enjoyed the idea of having their usual role reversed. The brothel closed in 1907 mainly because of threats from pimps who said their girls were spending too much of their (the pimps') money on such silly diversions, whereupon Aunt Josie ended her experiment and converted her place into a more normal house of sin.

In more recent times male prostitution has continued to a minor extent. Advertisements in the underground press in such cities as New York, San Francisco and Las Vegas offer male prostitutes for women, usually on an outcall arrangement, but these are more often homosexual operations. In the 1930s Hollywood was reputed to have a number of gay houses, but in actuality, gay prostitution activities are generally more suited to "bath houses" than to brothels as such. While Hollywood has contributed films about the male prostitute who services women, the fact remains, as Aunt Josie discovered, that this type of brothel product just won't sell.

PROWLING Brigades: Civil War plunderers

Probably the worst crime wave ever to hit the Southern states occurred during the Civil War, when groups of deserters and draft dodgers hid out in the hills and survived by burning, plundering and confiscating the property and livestock of Confederate citizens. While virtually all Southerners, the members of these so-called prowling brigades occasionally took in a stray Union deserter as well. They maintained a number of strongholds, especially in western North Carolina and Alabama, and were very active in the wake of Sherman's march through Georgia. Many of the prowling criminals were able to go back to their homes after the war by simply posing as returning soldiers or former prisoners of war, but others chose to head for the outlaw trails of the West.

PRUIETT, Moman (1872-1945): Criminal lawyer

There are those who maintain that Moman Pruiett was the greatest criminal lawyer this country has ever produced, far superior, they say, to Clarence Darrow. It was a sentiment Pruiett himself always shared. He was an ex-convict who had never spent a day in law school; in fact, his formal education, accomplished in his boyhood, added up to a mere nine months. He became a lawyer without passing a bar examination, but his record shows that out of 343 defendants charged with murder—the majority of whom he later freely admitted had been guilty as could be—won acquittals for 303. Of the other 40, only one was given the death sentence, and afterward, Pruiett went to Washington to present President William McKinley with a phony record of the case and had his client's sentence commuted to life.

In the Oklahoma-Texas panhandle, where Moman Pruiett set up practice, families would travel from miles around to attend court when he was slated to be the defense counsel in a murder case. And Old Moman, as he became affectionately known, never disappointed his fans, always putting on a good show. At the beginning of a trial, Moman made an impressive appearance, nattily dressed in a custom-tailored suit with a high bat-wing collar. But by the time he reached summation, one of his contemporaries recalled, he was partly disrobed, his collar was always awry and his disheveled hair fell over his forehead to meet his bushy eyebrows. His piercing black eyes automatically sought and stared unwaveringly into a juror's eyes, holding them until Moman felt that he controlled the person. He reenacted death struggles with grunts and shouts. While explaining how one of his clients had killed a rival, supposedly in self-defense, he lunged at the jury with a metal-tipped pencil as he claimed the victim had done with a knife at the defendant. Several jurors were so under Moman's spell that they became convinced he had a knife and bolted out of the jury box in fright. On returning, they promptly brought in a verdict of not guilty.

Pruiett was born prematurely on a steamboat on the Ohio River in 1872. His childhood was troubled and at the age of 16 he was convicted of forging bills of lading in connection with a freighting job he had. He served six months and then he and his mother moved to Texas. Two years later, he was convicted of rolling a drunk for $3,000, a charge Pruiett insisted to his dying day was false. He was convicted and sentenced to five years in prison. The 18-year-old was stunned at the verdict. He shook his fist at the judge and jury and cried: "You'll all regret this. I'll empty your damned jails, and I'll turn the murderers and thieves loose in your midst. And I'll do it in a legal way."

Pruiett served two years before his mother's tearful pleas to the governor won his freedom. Upon his release he went to work for some lawyers. A federal judge took an interest in his case, became convinced he was innocent and, because of his work in lawyers' offices, granted him permission to practice law before the federal courts, not an unusual procedure in the 19th century. Young Pruiett then won the right to practice in state courts and launched what was to be an astounding 50-year legal career. Throughout it his credo was to win his cases, no matter how. In a candid autobiography published shortly before his death, *Moman Prueitt, Criminal Lawyer,* he admitted faking evidence, jury tampering and suborning perjury. More than once, he was forced to flee a town to escape an angry mob because he had succeeded in acquitting an obvious killer. But Pruiett did not always have to utilize trickery and illegal means; he was extremely well versed in the law and knew the intricacies of every legal argument.

In the 343 murder cases he handled, Moman never pleaded a client guilty. When Clarence Darrow waived a jury trial and admitted the guilt of Leopold and Loeb, Pruiett snorted derisively. He said he would have taken the case to a jury. "I would have got them off with a defense of temporary insanity mixed up with a few other things."

Among the other defenses used by Pruiett was justifiable homicide. When Lottie Baker shot her husband for carrying on an affair with another woman, Moman defended her right to shoot him. He crouched before the jury box, holding an imaginary pistol. "I'd have taken my gun and shot him through the heart," he cried. "As he fell to the earth, I would have placed my ear over his bloody bosom and listened with relish and satisfaction while I heard his soul yelping its way into hell." He ended his summation on his hands and knees, head cocked sideways, with an ear over an imaginary bosom. His client was found "free of guilt."

Insanity was Moman's favorite plea and he got scores of killers off with such a defense. One prosecutor refused to release a prisoner after Pruiett had won him an acquittal. "If he's crazy, then he belongs in an institution," the prosecutor told Pruiett. Moman was flabbergasted. "You know that defense is just so much words," he said, making it clear he felt the prosecutor wasn't playing fair. Contradiction didn't really bother Pruiett. A week after he convinced one jury his client was insane, he went back to the same courtroom and proved to another jury the man was absolutely sane.

While awaiting a verdict in another case, Pruiett admitted

his client was a murdering maniac and a menace to peace and safety. "Then he ought to be hanged," a listener noted.

Pruiett shook his head. "If the jury says you're not guilty when you are, why then you're not guilty."

He would use any means to gain a not-guilty verdict. In one case he had the defendant's half-sister seduce a juror to win an acquittal. He could always spot the troublesome juror. Once hearing that a jury was deadlocked 11 to one for acquittal, he smuggled a note to the recalcitrant juror, allegedly in the hand of the juror's employer, reading, "Don't hold out any longer, turn the poor devil loose." The juror did.

In another case Pruiett defended a woman who was accused of shooting her husband, a popular Klansman, on a Miami street. After allowing the jury to be packed with members of the Ku Klux Klan, he put his client on the stand and had her reveal her husband was born in Sicily. That statement brought the xenophobic Klansmen to attention. Then the woman told how her husband, this alien, had beaten her and sent all her money to his relatives back in Sicily. During his summation Pruiett argued it was the duty of American manhood to protect American womanhood from the alien beast. He ended his summation by shouting the secret password of the Klan, "All's well on the Potomac."

The jury freed the woman, only learning much later that the victim's body had been shipped back to his birth place in Davenport, Iowa, to be buried by his Anglo-Saxon family.

Pruiett became rich in his practice. The woman who had killed her Klansman husband willed him her home and her husband's life insurance policies. He received a 1,600 acre farm for winning another acquittal and stocked it with 200 head of cattle given him by a couple whom he had defended from a charge of poisoning their own child. In another case he demanded $25,000 from a man accused of killing his father. The client at first offered him $10,000 but finally agreed to a sporting proposition. If Pruiett got him off scot free, the lawyer would get $40,000. If the man were found guilty and got any kind of a sentence, the lawyer wouldn't get a dime. Pruiett got the full $40,000. Yet, while he relished a high fee, he never forgot his oath to "empty your damned jails." The same week he collected the $40,000, he provided his services free to a prostitute who had killed a lover. She too went free.

Moman never kept track of how much money he earned. He lived lavishly, provided for his parents and his own family in grand style and was always a sucker for a touch. Many of the clients he defended for free ended up putting the bite on him after the trial. When a hurricane hit Florida and the land boom there collapsed, Pruiett lost almost all of his considerable fortune. He returned broke to Oklahoma, where a short time later, he was accused of trying to shake down a wealthy hotel owner. He was disbarred, but in 1935 the Oklahoma Supreme Court changed the penalty to a one-year suspension. Pruiett, however, never practiced again. Wracked by illness, he lived out his last years in frugal retirement, alleviated only by the publication of his autobiography in 1944, a year before his death.

PSYCHIC Detection: See Dorothy Allison.

PUBLIC Enemies

A term invented by J. Edgar Hoover, director of the FBI, the "public enemies" were little more than armed stickup men of the 1930s who had thousands of predecessors in the big-city gangsters of the previous century and those who rode on horseback in the Wild West. To magnify such creatures into supervillains took the cooperation of a story-hungry press. Many crime experts view the immediate post-Prohibition period as marking the breakup of the old bootleg mobs and the formation of the new criminal syndicate. Had the full energies of the FBI at the time been devoted to the more difficult task of containing this emerging element, it has been argued, the effectiveness of organized crime today would be greatly reduced, if not eliminated.

Instead, Hoover and his men concentrated on the likes of John Dillinger, a holdup man of considerable flair to be sure but hardly the menace to society that the syndicate was (and is). The total loot accumulated by the Dillinger mob probably came to far less than $300,000—the Chicago syndicate made that in a day. Clyde Barrow and Bonnie Parker were the bloodiest of the public enemies, killing 13 to take the highest estimate; yet Al Capone was responsible for killing 500 victims, directly or on his orders, but was not troubled by the FBI. While the likes of Baby Face Nelson, Pretty Boy Floyd, the Barkers and Alvin "Creepy" Karpis were being either killed or imprisoned by the FBI, mobsters like Frank Costello, Lucky Luciano, Louis Lepke, Albert Anastasia and Meyer Lansky were consolidating their power, claiming more victims in a month than all the public enemies managed in their criminal careers.

Possibly the closest the FBI came to nailing an organized crime figure was the case they made against Roger "the Terrible" Touhy, who was convicted of kidnapping in the early 1930s. However, the agency work in trapping Touhy proved futile years later when the courts freed him, labeling the kidnapping charge an underworld fabrication accomplished with connivance of the victim.

"PULLING A Dick Merrick": See "Merrick, Pulling a Dick"

PURDY, Sam (?-1805): White slaver

The most notorious white slaver operating in America at the beginning of the 19th century, Sam Purdy has been given credit by some writers with being the originator of the phrase "sold down the river" referring to the practice of "stealing" young girls along the Ohio and upper Mississippi and selling them down river, especially at Natchez. The most infamous of these sales took place on flatboats with spirited bidding from bordello keepers and "floating hogpen" operators. Not all the girls sold had been kidnapped; many were purchased from their impoverished farmer parents. Purdy, an unscrupulous Kentuckian, was the king of the trade, specializing in particularly good-looking girls and commanding sums well in excess of the average $125 price. In one case Purdy's ring of procurers, which included Lou Evans, Blackie Coe, James Feeney, Johnny Gaines, Joe Bontura and Tommy McMurren, collected the astonishing sum of $1,650 for an 18-year-old girl.

Purdy finally ran afoul of a reformer named Carlos White, who effectively destroyed his operations by rescuing a number of girls, including the famed Beckett sisters, whom he spirited out of a New Orleans den of iniquity known as The Swamp. How rough reformer White got is a matter of conjecture, but in 1805 Sam Purdy was found stabbed to death in his own bed. After that, one after another of the Purdy gang was shot to death, either in bed or from ambush. The exception to this bloodbath was 60-year-old James Feeney, who was given a 10-year jail term after being hauled into court by White. The Purdy white slavers having been eliminated, Carlos White moved to the Louisiana countryside and established a sprawling cotton plantation, which, it must be noted, was worked by black slaves.

See also: *Beckett Sisters.*

PURPLE Gang: Detroit bootlegging gang

One of the most vicious bootlegging mobs of the Prohibition era, the Purple Gang, under the notorious Abe Bernstein, dominated the rackets in Detroit. In the city's bootleg wars the gang was responsible for upwards of 500 killings. Detroit was an important prize because it was the funnel for supplies of liquor coming in from Canada.

The killers of the Purple Gang became legendary as the most proficient in the underworld, and three of them, George Lewis and the brothers Phil and Harry Keywell, were believed to have been borrowed by Al Capone for use in the St. Valentine's Day Massacre in 1929. In addition to bootlegging, which earned the gang millions of dollars, the Purples' major interests included extortion, hijacking and jewelry thefts plus an occasional foray into another city to pull off a big robbery.

When the national crime syndicate was formed in the 1930s, the Purple Gang was invited to join. It was strictly an invitation, since the gang was considered too dangerous to be forced into anything. The Purples accepted willingly and assumed a strong position in the crime cartel's gambling empire.

PURPLE Gang: Modern New York gang

A new crime gang that arose in Manhattan in the late 1970s, the Purple Gang, named after the Prohibition mob of the same name, has reached the point of becoming New York's sixth crime family.

A decade earlier, its members had been no more than teenage errand boys for major narcotics traffickers, but they had organized, according to a 1976 report by the Drug Enforcement Administration, with an "enormous capacity for violence" and a "lack of respect for other members of organized crime." The gang, with an estimated strength of 110, is an outgrowth of an Italian-American youth gang from Pleasant Avenue, an underworld stronghold in East Harlem, that served as a link between the old-line crime families and the new black gangs that had taken over the street sale of drugs.

Law enforcement agencies fear that the Purple Gang will declare war on both the Mafia families and the blacks and seek to establish supremacy in New York and, in fact, on the entire East Coast. In December 1977 the *New York Times* attributed to the gang the following activities: (1) large-scale distribution of drugs in Harlem and the South Bronx; (2) muscle jobs for two organized crime families' extortion networks; (3) the murder, and often the dismemberment of 17 individuals with criminal backgrounds, including two police plants; and (4) international gunrunning, with alleged ties to Latin-American terrorists.

Membership in the gang is restricted to young Italian-Americans who were raised on Pleasant Avenue between 110th and 117th streets. This membership policy is much more restrictive than those of the five established New York crime families and could have an explosive impact within the crime establishment, even leading to warfare with Mafia groups who seek to import new blood from Italy.

PURSE Snatching

Purse snatching is an increasingly common crime. There an estimated 50 to 100 purse snatchings each month in the New York City subways, the number often swinging widely because of the depredations of a single teenager. When such a professional is in custody, the snatchings decrease by more than 50 a month. One of the favored techniques is to stand between two subway cars and, as the train starts pulling out of the station, reach out and pull free a woman's purse.

Recently, a crime analysis officer for the New York Police Department found that purse stealing in Manhattan's top restaurants was up 35 percent over the previous year. When a woman puts her purse on a vacant chair at a table or at her feet beside her chair, she is inviting a purse snatcher to take it. Purse snatchers often work in pairs. When a target in a restaurant is sighted, one of the them will create some kind of disturbance to gain the victim's attention. While the woman is looking away from her table, the actual snatcher will lift the purse. A popular technique is for the thief, man or woman, to carry an umbrella with the curved handle down. The umbrella handle suddenly hooks the bag and in an instant it is on the thief's wrist, or under the coat over his arm if he is a man, and on its way out of the restaurant. Police advise that women in restaurants keep their purses either on their laps or on the floor between their legs.

Other purse snatchers who operate in theaters are called "seat tippers," victimizing women who put their purses down on an adjacent empty seat. Yet others specialize in snatching purses from ladies' rooms. When a woman is in a toilet stall, her purse should never be placed on the floor or hung on the coat hook on the door. Thieves simply dive under the door and grab the purse on the floor or stand on the toilet in the next stall and reach over and take the purse off the hook. The snatcher has ample time to escape since the victim can't immediately pursue the thief.

PURVIS, Melvin (1903-1960): FBI agent

In 1934 Melvin Purvis, the young special agent in charge of the Chicago office of the FBI, was voted eighth in a *Literary Digest* poll of the year's outstanding world figures, coming in ahead of Rear Adm. Richard E. Byrd and Secretary of Labor Frances Perkins. He was hailed by the *New York Times* as the nemesis of public enemies. Purvis captured more public enemies than any other FBI man, directing the hunts that netted such gangsters as Baby Face Nelson, Verne Sankey, Thomas H. Robinson, Jr. and Pretty Boy Floyd. He won the most acclaimed, however, as the man who set the trap for John Dillinger outside a Chicago movie house on July 22, 1934. It was Purvis who called out, in his famed squeaky voice, "Stick 'em up, Johnny, we've got you surrounded." As Dillinger went for a gun in his trousers pocket, he was shot to death by FBI agents.

As acclaimed as he was, Purvis' years with the FBI, from 1927, after a brief law career in his native South Carolina, until 1935, were not always happy ones. He had his share of failures and his ego, as towering as that of his superior, J. Edgar Hoover, put him in constant conflict with the director. Of all the regional offices of the FBI, the Chicago office was the only one that did not begin its press releases with the obligatory "J. Edgar Hoover announces. . . ." Purvis' name was substituted for Hoover's in such releases.

This competition between Purvis and Hoover developed after Purvis was appointed to the Chicago office in 1932, following five years of duty in various field offices. Chicago was the hub around which both the great Prohibition gangs and the more flamboyant of the desperado-type "public enemies" worked. The latter were typified by members of the Dillinger gang and the Terrible Touhys. The Touhys' leader Roger Touhy, represented one of Purvis' greatest failures. In 1933 Purvis arrested Roger Touhy and three henchmen for the $100,000 kidnapping of St. Paul millionaire brewer William Hamm, announcing, "We have an ironclad case." A jury acquitted them, however, and later, the Hamm job was found to be the work of the Barker-Karpis gang.

Immediately after that failure, Purvis charged Touhy and his men with kidnapping a mysterious figure, Jake "the Barber" Factor. "This case," Purvis said, "holds a particular interest for me because it represents a triumph of deductive detective work. We assumed from the start, with no material evidence, that the Touhy gang was responsible for the crime."

Some observers were not sure whether Factor had really been kidnapped or not. Touhy was sentenced to 99 years in prison, and it was not until many years later that the truth came out: the Capone mob had faked the Factor kidnapping in order to use the FBI to get rid of Touhy, an uncooperative competitor.

Probably Purvis' most trying experience was the famed shoot-out between FBI agents and the Dillinger gang at the Little Bohemia resort in Wisconsin in April 1934. In the gun battle an FBI agent was killed by Baby Face Nelson and a local police officer was wounded. All the agents captured were three of the gang's molls, but they shot two innocent bystanders, a salesman and a Civilian Conservation Corps (CCC) cook and killed another young CCC worker.

The day after the debacle newspapers demanded Purvis' badge. Somberly, he offered his resignation, which Hoover refused to accept, as much to save the agency as Purvis. Even when Purvis did trap and kill Dillinger, he and the FBI were subjected to considerable abuse. A Virginia newspaper editor commented: "Any brave man would have walked down the aisle and arrested Dillinger . . . why were there so many cowards afraid of this one man? The answer is that the federal agents are mostly cowards."

It was a bad rap on Purvis, who frequently had exhibited (and would continue to exhibit) great personal courage—trading shots with Baby Face Nelson; dragging then-Public Enemy No. 1 Verne Sankey out of a Chicago-area barbershop with lather still in his ears; stalking Pretty Boy Floyd across an open corn field; tackling, together with another agent, gangster Volney Davis as he was about to drive off in a stolen car. However, it was not unwarranted criticism that led to Purvis' resignation from the FBI in July 1935.

There is little doubt that this departure was the result of continuing friction with Hoover, especially in the aftermath of the Dillinger case. Dillinger had been betrayed by a madam named Anna Sage, "the Lady in Red," who had made a deal with the FBI to deliver Dillinger in exchange for a promise that a deportation move against her would be dropped and that the reward money would be given to her. Purvis agreed to help her on these matters. She got most of the reward money but was deported despite Purvis' intervention. It was widely believed that Hoover had not joined in the effort to save the Sage woman so that Purvis would be placed in an awkward position. Hoover was also believed to have been behind the decision by Attorney General Homer Cummings to prohibit the making of a Hollywood movie about Purvis' career. When Purvis tendered his resignation "for purely personal reasons," Hoover had to issue a denial that a rift existed between them.

After that, Purvis picked up some quick money organizing the Melvin Purvis Junior G-Man Corps for a breakfast cereal firm, an act that further strained relations with Hoover.

Purvis also wrote a book on his FBI career entitled *American Agent,* fully demonstrating the ill feelings between him and Hoover by never mentioning the director's name. Hoover did not get a chance to answer in kind until 1956, with the appearance of *The FBI Story,* a best-seller by Don Whitehead. The book is as near to an "authorized" history of the agency as has ever been written and one that Hoover obviously exerted considerable control over. In Whitehead's book Hoover's pride and prejudices show through. For example, Hoover hated William J. Burns, his predecessor in the Bureau of Investigation, which was replaced by the FBI. Whenever Whitehead touches on Burns' many successes, credit is given only to some unnamed former Secret Service operative. It would have been impossible to drop all reference to Purvis in discussions about the agency's war on the public enemies but the agent's name is omitted from the extremely thorough index.

During World War II Col. Melvin Purvis was assigned to the U.S. Army War Crimes Office. In November 1959 Roger Touhy was released from prison following a ruling by a federal judge that the kidnapping charge against him had been a fabrication of organized crime. Twenty-three days after he was freed, Touhy was murdered by underworld assassins. A few months later, on February 29, 1960, Purvis, who had been practicing as a lawyer, committed suicide in his home in Florence, S.C. At the time he was 56 years old and had been in poor health.

See also: *John Dillinger, Charles Arthur "Pretty Boy" Floyd, Roger "Terrible" Touhy.*

PURVIS, Will (1874-1943): Wrong man

Will Purvis' escape from execution in Mississippi in 1894 has long been cited by opponents of capital punishment as an example of the danger of error in dealing out the death penalty.

A 19-year-old farmer in Mercer County, Miss., Purvis was arrested and charged with the murder of Will Buckley in what appeared to have been an internal dispute within the White Caps, a Ku Klux Klan-type organization of the period. Purvis had joined the White Caps some three months before Buckley was shot to death. After Buckley's murder blood hounds traced a cold trail to near the Purvis farm. Jim Buckley, the dead man's brother, identified Purvis as the murderer, and he was indicted and quickly found guilty.

Purvis' execution by hanging was scheduled for February 7, 1894, and on that day about 3,000 persons jammed the area around the scaffold to watch the events. Many in the crowd, however, still insisted Purvis was being executed for a crime he had not committed and were there to show their support for him. At the moment a preacher implored heaven, "God save this innocent boy," the hangman severed the rope holding the trapdoor shut, but Purvis just tumbled to the ground below, as the rope around his neck unwound.

His hands still tied, Purvis jumped back up the gallows steps, crying, "Let's get this over with!" Officials were about to oblige, but the crowd grew unruly. The preacher asked for a show of hands of "all who are opposed to hanging Will Purvis a second time." A sea of hands rose and hundreds of men moved forward menacingly. Purvis was then returned to his jail cell.

After a time, the Mississippi Supreme Court ruled that Purvis had to be executed, but before the second attempt could be made, friends of the condemned man helped him to escape. He remained in hiding until 1896, when a new governor, A. J. McLaurin, took office. McLaurin had campaigned on a promise to reduce Purvis' sentence to life imprisonment. In 1898 Purvis was pardoned when Jim Buckley admitted he was not sure Purvis had been the killer.

Then in 1917, 24 years after the murder, an old man named Joe Beard came forward at a religious revival meeting to purge his soul before taking to his deathbed. He said he and another White Capper, Louis Thornhill, had been chosen by lot to kill Will Buckley. Beard offered enough independent proof to indicate he had information about the crime that only the real murderer or murderers would have. In 1920 the Mississippi legislature awarded Will Purvis $5,000 compensation "for a great wrong done you" and removed "all stain and dishonor from your name."

PYRAMID Schemes: Confidence racket

Among the oldest con games, pyramid rackets have been used to swindle millions of dollars annually, employing everything from dollar bills in chain letters to more sophisticated schemes that sell franchises to unsuspecting individuals who then must sell more franchises to other victims and so on. In theory, pyramid schemes can continue on indefinitely, but in reality, the bubble eventually collapses from the sheer weight of the numbers involved.

A typical operation was the pyramid financial scheme that swept California in the late 1970s, leaving a trail of broken families and wrecked friendships. In the scheme each player paid an entry fee of $1,000. Then that player was required to bring in two new players, who contributed $1,000 apiece. Half of this amount, or $500, went to the top of the pyramid while the remaining $500 from each of the two newer players went to the player who recruited them. Thus, the first player got his money back and then waited to move up another rung on the pyramid as each of the second two players recruited two more players so that they could recover their original $1,000 investment. As each such step on the pyramid was mounted, the initial player moved from the number 16 rung, to the number eight rung, to the number four rung, to the number two rung and finally, to number one rung. Upon reaching number one or top, rung the player received the money that accumulated at the top for him, $16,000.

While it might seem simple for each player in a pyramid scheme to induce two others to join, the mathematics soon become astronomical. In essence, each player on the number 16 rung is responsible for the creation of two new pyramids and this progression of twos keeps getting bigger and bigger, for there are 16 players on the bottom rung, and it takes 32 players to get them to advance to the next rung. Each of these 32 players must now recruit two players, or a total of 64. The 64 then must recruit a total of 128. The total jumps to 256, at which point the first set of 16 players have reached the top of their pyramids. However, for the next set of players who started on the 16 rung, the total of new recruits needed jumps to 512, and for the next group the number required is 1,024.

It is thus apparent why, by June 1980, the mass pyramid craze in California collapsed. Even that state ran dry of enough gullible people to keep the scheme going. A member of the state attorney general's office reported that a number of operators had been arrested attempting to start new pyramids in New York, Florida and Canada. Ironically, such pyramid rackets even attract sophisticated victims who fully understand that a scheme must eventually collapse. No matter what the actual stage of recruitment is, they are told they are "getting in at the start, so there's no way you can lose."

R

RABLEN, Carroll (1895-1929): Murder victim

The murder of Carroll Rablen in 1929 resulted in one of California's most sensational murder trials, so sensational it had to be held in an open-air dance pavillion to accommodate all those eager to attend.

Carroll Rablen of Tuttletown, Calif. was deaf because of an injury received during World War I. His wife Eva was a vivacious, fun-loving woman who enjoyed dancing. While Carroll didn't dance, he took her to affairs and didn't object to her dancing with other men. On April 29, 1929 the couple went to the town's weekly ball. Carroll stayed outside in their car while Eva went inside to enjoy herself. About midnight Eva pushed through the crowd to bring her husband a cup of coffee and then returned to the dance. Moments later, Carroll was writhing in agony on the floor of the car; his cries brought his father and several others to his side. He complained of the way the coffee had tasted. A doctor was summoned but Carroll died before he arrived.

Carroll's father was sure Eva had poisoned her husband for his insurance, but when the contents of the dead man's stomach were sent to a chemist for analysis, no trace of poison was found. However, a subsequent search of the dance hall area uncovered a bottle marked, "Strychnine." The bottle was traced to a pharmacy in a nearby town, where records showed it had been bought by a Mrs. Joe Williams, allegedly to kill some gophers. The druggist identified Eva Rablen as Mrs. Williams. She was charged with her husband's murder and her trial drew one of the largest crowds ever to attend a formal judicial hearing in the state. The weakness in the prosecution's case was that no poison had been found in Carroll Rablen's body. Consequently, the prosecutor called in one of the most famous chemists in the nation, Dr. Edward Heinrich, who was recognized as a brilliant forensic expert.

Heinrich found traces of strychnine in the dead man's stomach as well as in the coffee cup. He also theorized that since Eva Rablen had carried the coffee through a packed dance hall, she might have spilled some on the way. An appeal for help produced a woman who remembered that Eva had bumped into her and spilled coffee on her dress. The coffee stains on the dress also contained traces of the poison. Faced with this damning evidence, Eva Rablen changed her plea to guilty and was sentenced to life imprisonment.

RACE And Crime

Even a cursory study of criminal statistics makes it apparent that blacks, comprising only 11 percent of the population, commit a high proportion of most crimes, especially those of a violent nature. Despite their inferior numbers, blacks commit more murders than whites (generally about a five to four ratio), more robberies (a five to three ratio) and more rapes (a 10 to nine ratio). On a proportional basis, blacks also commit more aggravated assaults, burglaries, larceny-thefts and car thefts. Probably the only serious crime with a low black participation is kidnapping. These figures, however, are based on arrest records as compiled by the FBI, and most crime experts admit that blacks are arrested more frequently and on less evidence than whites and are more often victims of mass, or sweep, arrests. On the other hand, it is well-established that violent crime is less frequently reported in the ghetto than elsewhere, and since this is clearly black-committed crime, the aforementioned black-white ratios should probably be more pronounced than they are.

The figures do not prove that blacks are any more crime-prone than other ethnic groups. They are simply behaving the way every other ethnic group behaved when it dominated the ghettos. The Irish were the main residents of the big-city ghettos in the 19th century, and they were far and away the prime perpetrators of crime. Until late in the century, most of the great gangs were Irish. When the Irish were replaced or supplemented in the ghettos by the Italians, Jews and Poles, these ethnic groups were responsible for most of the crime.

Perhaps the most salient point about any study of ethnic crime is that whoever occupies the ghettos commits the crimes *and almost always against their own kind*. The Jews victimized Jews; Italians victimized Italians. This was somewhat less true of the Irish, who brought with them certain basic hatreds that put them in conflict with many "native Americans," which in the early 19th century often meant those of British descent.

Today, ethnic or racial crime follows the same pattern. Blacks victimize blacks; Hispanics victimize Hispanics. This is not necessarily what the media reports, for the simple reason that black victimizing black is not considered important, but black victimizing white—especially in a white-oriented media—is.

While it is widely reported that more than half of all murders are committed by blacks, it is seldom added that nine times out of 10, the victims are also black. The statistics of ghetto crime, now and in the past, are frightening. Among young blacks aged 10 to 14, homicide is the second leading cause of death, exceeded only by motor vehicle accidents. From ages 15 through 34 homicide is the number one cause of death among black males. It is also the leading cause of death among black females between 15 and 29.

Overall, a ghetto black male is 10 times more likely to be murdered than a white man. A black female is five times as likely to be raped as a white woman, and both black males and females are four times as likely to get assaulted than are whites of either sex.

As John Godwin notes in *Murder U.S.A.*:

> The newspapers of both races tend to skirt the psychic impact of this black-on-black carnage, albeit for different reasons. The white press knows that its readers worry about black crime only when it affects *them*. Black papers prefer to dodge the issue because they consider it "too sensitive"; they fear it may cause further stigmatization of their race. Together they have created what resembles a conspiracy of semi-silence surrounding one of the most explosive problems of our time. They are chiefly responsible for the wondrous ignorance of most whites concerning the terror haunting black communities— terror far starker than what they suffer.

While it is difficult for white America to reject the contention that blacks are simply more "criminal," the fact is that the black experience to a great extent mirrors that of other ethnic groups in earlier periods, typically the Irish and Italians before they left the ghettos. It is readily apparent that the black crime rate varies with socioeconomic status and geographic region. As Peter W. Lewis and Jack Wright, Jr., professors of criminal justice, state in *Modern Criminal Justice:* "Criminologists generally consider race to be a significant factor in the explanation of crime rates insofar as it affects the nature of social experience and social interaction."

See also: *Population Density and Crime.*

RAGEN, James M. (1881-1946): Gambling czar and murder victim

From 1940 to 1946 James M. Ragen was the most powerful man in gambling in America, having taken control of the horse-racing wire business following the imprisonment of Moe Annenberg. Ragen waged war with the Chicago syndicate and held his own for a time until he became the victim of a mob execution.

Like many other members of the Chicago underworld in the early years of the 20th century, Ragen got his start as a circulation slugger for the *Chicago Tribune* during the period of the great newspaper wars, when Max Annenberg, Moe's older brother, was circulation manager. Among Ragen's coworkers were such criminals as Dion O'Banion, Frankie and Vince McErlane, Walter Stevens, Mossy Enright and Tommy Maloy— part of the roster of killers who kept the city of Chicago bloody for decades thereafter. Ragen managed to outlive most of his fellow sluggers and future gang bosses while maintaining a certain independence from the Capone mob.

When Moe Annenberg went to prison in 1940, the federal government was sure that the dismantling of his Nation-Wide News Service would be a crippling blow to illegal race horse betting throughout the country. But Ragen quickly moved in to fill the void. His Continental Press Service became the dominant racing wire in the nation, providing the latest results from scores of tracks directly to thousands of bookie joints. The Chicago mob had never tried to move in on Annenberg, perhaps because he was considered too powerful or because of some secret accommodation, but it soon informed Ragen they were dealing themselves in.

Ragen had survived the Chicago scene too long to just give up his business, even when he was offered a fine price to sell out. He told acquaintances he knew the ways of the mob, that even if he sold, he would not be permitted to live to enjoy his profits. Under Bugsy Siegel the mob set up Trans-American Publishing and News Service and forcibly gained control of the California market, supplying bookies with the necessary racing information for $100 a day. Ragen, however, held on to the rest of the country, and it soon became apparent that the only way to take over his empire was to kill him. In June 1946 he was hit by a fusilade of bullets from a passing car, but he survived and was rushed to a hospital.

From his hospital bed Ragen accused the mob of trying to eliminate him in order to assume control of his racing wire. His accusations proved an embarrassment to the mob. In September he died, apparently of his wounds. An autopsy later revealed he had been poisoned by mercury. The mob obviously had found a way to penetrate Ragen's around-the-clock police protection, and his death was listed as a gangland slaying. Several leaders of the mob were questioned, especially Jake Guzik, but nothing much developed from the investigation.

Ragen's murder became just another digit added to the column of unsolved gangland killings, which, during a period of a little over three decades, totaled more than 970.

See also: *Moses L. Annenberg.*

RAGEN'S Colts: Chicago gang

One of Chicago's huge Irish gangs, Ragen's Colts, achieved their height of power during the first two decades of the 20th century. The gang's fate was typical of the pattern of absorption of Irish gangs into what became part of the national crime syndicate.

Dominating Chicago's South Side around the stockyards, the Colts were political sluggers, racists, jingoists, bootleggers and killers. Formally called Ragen's Athletic and Benevolent Association, the gang started, as did a number of others in that era, as a baseball team. Frank Ragen was the star pitcher and also the star political operator. He soon was offering the gang's services to Democratic Party candidates throughout the entire city. With the Colts' muscle and firepower, elections proved easy to win and many members of the City Council and state legislature owed their victories to the gang. "When we dropped into a polling place," one Colt bragged, "everybody else dropped out."

By 1902 Ragen's Colts numbered 160, and by 1908 the gang's motto was "Hit Me and You Hit 2,000." Over the years the gang launched the careers of aldermen, sheriffs, police brass, county treasurers and numerous other officeholders as well as some notable ballplayers. Ragen himself became city commissioner. However, the Colts' main product was accomplished criminals. Its notables included Gunner McPadden, who committed a long string of homicides; Harry Madigan, the owner of the notorious Pony Inn, a Cicero saloon, who was charged—but never tried because of the Colts' political connections—with several kidnappings and assaults during various elections; Dynamite Brooks, another saloon keeper who often killed in a drunken rage; Danny McFall, who was made deputy sheriff, in the mysterious ways of Chicago politics, despite having murdered a couple of business competitors; Stubby McGovern, a deadly triggerman whose assignment to a hit was a guarantee of success; Yiddles Miller, a boxing referee and notorious white supremacist who once called the members of the Ku Klux Klan "nigger lovers"; and Ralph Sheldon, a fearless bootlegger and hijacker.

In addition to furnishing political strong-arm services and running a number of South Side rackets, the Colts took it upon themselves to defend the white race, provoking a great race riot in 1919. It started one day when a black youth swimming off a South Side beach encroached on segregated waters. He was stoned and drowned by white bathers. As tensions mounted between the races on the South Side, members of Ragen's Colts baited blacks. Later that night the Colts stormed through the Black Belt, shooting blacks on sight, firing and dynamiting homes and looting shops. Black war veterans dug out their service weapons and returned the fire. Rampaging blacks overturned autos and streetcars carrying whites and destroyed property belonging to whites. Before the fury on both sides subsided from sheer exhaustion after four days, 20 whites and 14 blacks were dead and the injured toll stood at 1,000, about equally divided between the races.

After the riot the Colts turned to more profitable pursuits, namely bootlegging, although a contingent of the gang under Ralph Sheldon exhibited little interest in making booze, preferring simply to hijack it from others. Despite having to fight a number of bootlegging wars with the gang, Al Capone showed

considerable patience toward the Colts and eventually a large portion of the gang was absorbed into his organization. The descendants of the original Colts are important members of organized crime today.

RANGE Detectives: Hired guns

They were known as range or cattle detectives or stock inspectors, but most Westerners simply called them hired guns. They enforced the rules as laid down by their employers, the big ranchers who wanted the range cleared of "rustlers," and a rustler was anyone the boss labeled as such. In the infamous Johnson County War, every small rancher and nester on the range who ever roped an unmarked maverick was considered a rustler, or bandit, to be killed on sight, and common whores were lynched as "bandit queens."

The stockmen who employed these hired guns, of course, had money and influence. They could fix matters if a so-called stock inspector did anything that the law took exception to. Equally important, they could pay very well. Range detectives earned $100 to $150 a month, which was two to three times what a deputy U.S. marshal could hope to earn. In some cases the pay went as high as $250 a month, plus bonuses for every horse thief or cattle rustler that was convicted. And if a suspect was arrested and somebody organized a necktie party for him, the bonus came through all the quicker. With these premium pay scales the stockmen got the best gunslingers money could buy, including the notorious Tom Smith; Frank Wolcott; Frank Canton (a wanted killer gone "respectable"); Pat Garrett, the slayer of Billy the Kid, and former Texas Ranger John Armstrong, the captor of Wes Hardin.

The most notorious range detective of all was Tom Horn, a former roving gunman for the Pinkertons. His score in four years with the detective agency was put at 17. When he later showed up in Wyoming, he denied having killed anyone for the detective agency and, at the same time, offered his services to Wyoming cattlemen, pegging his rate at $500 for each rustler shot. He was finally hanged for killing a 14-year-old boy while on an assignment to kill the boy's father. A leading Wyoming cattleman paid him tribute: "He died without 'squealing,' to the great relief of many very respectable citizens of the West."

See also: *Frank Canton, Tom Horn, Johnson County War.*

RAPE

Statistics on rape are probably the least reliable of all crime figures. According to the FBI's *Uniform Crime Reports,* the rate of forcible rape virtually doubled from 1970 to 1979. This finding, however, is probably unreliable, as is the FBI's report of 75,989 such offenses per year. The figure is generally regarded as a gross underestimate. In fact, rape is so consistently underreported that all such statistics are meaningless. It may well be that the entire doubling of the rape average during the 1970s is attributable to the fact that more women have been reporting such offenses, mainly because many police departments now have more sympathetic rape squads and complaints are more frequently handled by female officers.

Still, even with these improvements, the fact remains that the vast majority of rapes are not reported. Among the main reasons are the public embarrassment facing the victim if she presses charges and a fear, often not unfounded, that the offender will take revenge. It is therefore hardly surprising that some rapists commit hundreds of rapes before ever being arrested. Of rapes reported to the police, about half are "cleared by arrest." Of these, approximately three out of five are brought to trial and about half of the defendants are found guilty of rape or a lesser charge.

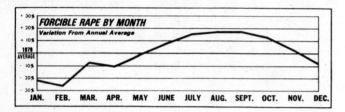

The incidence of rape, as a graph for an average year illustrates, increases as the temperature rises.

Despite talk of a new attitude on the part of the police, they still are often suspicious of rape claims, feeling there is frequently a hazy line between a woman's "yes" and "no" and "please." In about 15 percent of all cases reported, according to law enforcement officials, the charge of forcible rape is ultimately determined to be unfounded. Some of these cases involve complaints made by jilted sweethearts, and others are charges lodged by prostitutes who have not been reimbursed for services rendered.

The public's greatest misconception about rape concerns the reasons behind it. Many people view the rapist as someone overcome with sexual desire. Others believe the fault lies with

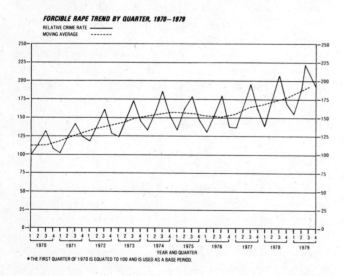

The apparent doubling of forcible rape cases through the 1970s, as shown in the FBI's *Uniform Crime Reports,* may well be attributable to the increasing willingness of women to report this crime.

the victim: she was dressed too seductively; or she "asked for it"; like all women, she wanted to be raped. On the contrary, rape is basically a crime of violence, a hostile attack, motivated by a desire to hurt and humiliate. Sex is only the weapon. When someone asks, "What kind of creep would be turned on by an 80-year-old woman?" he or she is missing the point. As targets of violence, anyone can be a rape victim—children, mothers, grandmothers.

Another false notion is that rape only happens in certain high-risk situations—walking alone at night, going alone to a bar, hitchhiking. While rapes do occur in such situations, they also take place in ordinary, seemingly safe places. One-third happen in or near the victim's home. Rapists are not always strangers to the victims. In over one-third of the cases reported, the rapist is an acquaintance, neighbor, friend or relative. It is suspected that an enormous number of such cases are never reported to the police, and many, in fact, are not even revealed to other members of the victim's family.

The public tends to remember rape cases involving celebrities, such as Hollywood's Fatty Arbuckle or Errol Flynn; those with a bizarre or unusual twist, such as the crimes of William "Theo" Durrant; or those with racial overtones, such as Hawaii's Massie case or Alabama's Scottsboro Boys case. Readily forgotten are rapists responsible for committing literally hundreds of rapes. Among the less-publicized rapes are those of black women, who are five times more likely to be raped than white women.

One typical mass rapist was Colorado's Richard Turner, who ran up a string of rapes in the mid-1970s before being convicted of the rape and brutal assault of two teenage girls. In 1976 he murdered a family of five and raped the three female members—the mother and her two young girls—before or after killing them. Turner always committed his crimes under the influence of liquor and it was clear his real desire was to hurt people.

See also: *Rosco "Fatty" Arbuckle, Richard Turner.*

RATELWACHT: First American police force

On August 12, 1658 New Amsterdam established the first police force in America. Called the *ratelwacht,* or rattlewatch, because of the rattles they carried as signal devices, members of this force were little more than night watchmen. They were paid 24 stuyvers, or about 50¢ a night, with the levy for their services collected each month from the city's inhabitants. A guard caught sleeping on duty was fined 10 stuyvers, and there were varying penalties for such on-duty offenses as swearing, drinking and fighting.

RAWLEY, R. C. (?-1864): Montana vigilante victim

The life and death of R. C. Rawley, which is believed to have been an assumed name, provides a good example of the virtue of knowing when to keep one's mouth shut. Rawley arrived in Alder Gulch, Montana Territory in late 1863 and became a habitue of the town's saloons. Allegedly, he had been a merchant elsewhere and was looking for a business to buy. Actually, it seems quite likely that he functioned as a spy for Sheriff Henry Plummer and his Innocents, who ravaged the area with their robberies and murders. Rawley made a wise move when he disappeared a few months before Sheriff Plummer was hanged by vigilantes in January 1864. In September Rawley returned, satisfied that the Montana Vigilantes had finished their grisly business. He guessed right; the vigilantes had forgotten their earlier suspicions about him. For two months Rawley drank unmolested in saloons in Bannack and Virginia City. Unfortunately for him, however, his elbow bending loosened his tongue, and he made some tactless comments about the "strangling bastards" who'd killed Plummer. Now *that* was a capital offense and Rawley was seized and hanged from the same gibbet where Sheriff Plummer had swung.

RAY, James Earl (1928-   ): Assassin of Martin Luther King, Jr.

On April 4, 1968 the Rev. Dr. Martin Luther King, Jr., the acknowledged leader of the black civil rights movement and an advocate of Gandhian principles of nonviolent resistance, was in Memphis, Tenn. to lend support to a controversial strike by the city's sanitation workers. That evening King stepped out onto the balcony of his room at the Lorraine Motel and was shot and mortally wounded by an assassin firing from a bathroom window of a nearby rooming house. A 30.06-caliber rifle bullet struck King in the right side of the jaw, penetrated his neck and severed his spinal cord. The force of the bullet was so powerful it ripped his necktie completely off his shirt.

Items left by the assassin were traced to cities as far away as Los Angeles and Atlanta. Through fingerprints the murderer was identified as a white man named James Earl Ray, a minor criminal who had no apparent reason for killing King. After the murder Ray fled to Canada and in May he went to London on a Canadian passport, showing a remarkable sophistication at eluding capture. He took a mysterious side trip to Lisbon, came back to London and was about to fly to Brussels when he was apprehended on June 8. He was returned to the United States in July.

Over the years Ray has continued to be a controversial figure. Certainly, a number of details appear to indicate the existence of a broad plot to kill King. Some have even claimed that the FBI was involved in his death and that Ray was merely a scapegoat. Nothing of the sort has ever been proved, although there is no doubt that the agency did much to besmirch King's character both before and after his death.

A retired FBI man who had worked in the agency's Atlanta office at the time of the King assassination told of deep anti-King feelings prevalent there and how one agent literally had leaped for joy when he learned King had been killed. The FBI was forced to admit it had wiretapped King's home and sent Mrs. Coretta King letters that implied her husband was involved sexually with several other women. When King was scheduled to receive the Nobel Peace Prize in 1964, the FBI had even sent a letter to him intimating he should commit suicide before the award was given. It read in part: "King—there is only one thing left for you to do. You know what it is. You have just 34 days in which to do it. It has definite practical significance. You are done. There is but one way out. . . ."

J. Edgar Hoover had been incensed by the thought of King getting the Nobel Peace Prize and had called him "the most notorious liar in the country." Hoover had authorized the investigation of King's sex life and ordered many of the illegal harassments used against him. The director had even inspired a news story that caused King to switch from his initial choice of a white-owned hotel to the Lorraine Motel, where he was shot.

James Earl Ray seemed too much of a misfit to be involved in so monumental a case as the King assassination. A 10th-grade dropout, he held nothing but menial jobs until 1946, when he joined the Army. He was discharged in December 1948 for "ineptness and lack of adaptability to military service." After that, he had a string of arrests for some bush-league armed robberies, small-time smuggling and burglaries. He also served three years for forgery. He broke out of the Missouri State Prison in April 1967 but was considered such an unimportant criminal that the reward for his capture amounted to only $50. While Ray was being hunted for the King murder, his father insisted that if he had done the job, "he couldn't have planned it alone; he wasn't smart enough for that."

After he was apprehended and brought back to the United States, Ray pleaded guilty to murdering King and drew 99 years. Within 24 hours he attempted to reverse his plea and insisted on dropping his original attorney, Percy Foreman, and getting a new lawyer. He maintained he was innocent and that "Raoul," a shadowy figure known only to Ray, had sent him to Memphis to take part in a gun-smuggling operation and had passed him money and orders. He said he did not know who had killed King.

During hearings on the King murder held by the House Select Committee on Assassinations in 1978, a St. Louis man, Russell G. Byers, told the panel he had been offered $50,000 in late 1966 or early 1967 to arrange King's death. He said the offer had come from two men, John Kauffmann and John Sutherland, acting on behalf of a group of businessmen. Both Kauffmann and Sutherland were now dead and their widows said they did not believe they could have taken part in such a plot. It developed that the FBI had been aware of Byers' allegations in 1973, but the information had not been passed on to agents investigating the King assassination. A spokesman for the FBI said that the handling of the information was in "violation of established rules and procedures," but that the bureau was satisfied a simple misfiling had occurred through "administrative error," rather than a deliberate attempt to block the investigation. Since the agent responsible for handling the information had retired, there was, the spokesman said, no need for a formal inquiry into the matter.

In any event, Byers said he suspected that Sutherland and Kauffmann had planned to recruit him as a dupe who would take the blame for the murder but not actually carry it out. Byers' story prompted House investigators to look for links between Byers or Kauffmann and Sutherland and Ray's escape from the penitentiary in April 1967. The committee heard testimony that Ray had committed the murder in the hope of collecting a $50,000 bounty, and in December 1978 it concluded there was a "likelihood" of a conspiracy. The panel found that "no federal, state or local government agency was involved in the assassination of Dr. King," although it did say the Domestic Intelligence Division of the FBI was guilty of "gross" abuse of its legal authority in its surveillance of King and that the Justice Department had "failed to supervise adequately" that division.

James Earl Ray remains the only person ever convicted in the King murder case and has been behind bars since 1969 save for a three-day period when he escaped from prison. On that occasion his escape lacked the financing and planning which had marked his flight following the murder of King and he was quickly retaken.

RAYNOR, William P.: See Gem Saloon.

READING Game: Famous illegal crap game

The biggest crap game in the history of gambling on the East Coast, and perhaps in the country, was the so-called Reading Game, operating out of Philadelphia from 1959 to 1962, when the Federal Bureau of Investigation finally smothered it.

Each night big gamblers from all over the East would gather at a restaurant in the heart of Philadelphia. There, they would be picked up by "luggers" and driven 50 miles to Reading, where a million dollar dice game was played on three high-rolling "California tables."

A reformed hood later commented: "Everybody made a buck on that game. They rented their limousines from a funeral director, because they only used them from ten at night until seven in the morning." He indicated how much freedom organized crime had in Philadelphia at the time, stating: "They even had a cop out in front of the restaurant—he'd blow a whistle like a hotel doorman to signal a limo when he had a full load coming in for the game. It looked like opening night on Broadway. The cops never touched them."

REAGAN, President Ronald: See John W. Hinckley, Jr.

REAVIS, James Addison (?-1908): Swindler and Baron of Arizona

A former St. Louis streetcar conductor, James Addison Reavis went on to become the most colossal swindler-forger in Ameri-can history, laying claim in 1881, as Baron de Arizonaca and Caballero de los Colorados, to 10.8 million acres of the Arizona Territory, including all of its largest city, Phoenix. As such, his claims were recognized as legitimate for over a decade, and he would point out to railroad executives, mine owners and big ranchers that they were trespassing on his property. However, he was willing to discuss rents. The tab for the Southern Pacific's right-of-way was set at $50,000 annually.

The origin and intricacies of Reavis' amazing fraud were never fully learned because he steadfastly refused to make a confession. However, it was revealed that as a youth in the Confederate Army, he had developed a knack for forging his commanding officers' signatures. After the Civil War, while working as a streetcar conductor in St. Louis, he used his skillful writing ability to forge a fraudulent real estate document that earned him a large sum. He moved west before he could be caught.

In Santa Fe Reavis got a clerical job in the records division of a special governmental commission that handled claims on property annexed by this country following the Mexican War. A treaty settlement required the United States to honor all legitimate claims of Spaniards and Mexicans and return to them the title of their lands. It was in this office that Reavis laid the groundwork for his incredible claim. He learned the pure Spanish used on ancient documents and eventually produced one that indicated he was the undisputed owner of a grant given by the Spanish crown in 1758 to a nobleman, Miguel Silva de Peralta de la Cordoba, for military services rendered in the New World. In addition, Reavis presented himself as the husband of the last of the mythical Peraltas, a young woman he found working as a serving girl on a California ranch. The girl became convinced she really was a long-lost Peralta.

Government experts and others studied Reavis' documents, which he had forged, and checked them against historical records, which he had doctored over a five-year period, in Madrid, Seville and Mexico City. They concluded his claims were valid. As a result, until he was exposed in 1894, Reavis collected some $10 million in rent from hundreds of companies and thousands of families.

Finally, two tiny errors he had made were discovered. Reavis had used old inks and had found paper that appeared to be old, but a printer who was suspicious of him discovered that the watermark on the paper had not been designed until 1878. In addition, part of Reavis' hoax rested on proof that a pair of Peralta twins had been born long ago near San Bernardino, Calif. Their births were listed in the birth register at the Mission of San Salvador. Somehow Reavis had removed an entire page from the register and forged a substitute that included the names of the twins in place of the names of two other babies. What Reavis did not know was that births were also recorded each day in a separate volume that was kept hidden. Instead of the names of the twins, the secret volume listed two different names.

Reavis fought the case against him with the great wealth he had accumulated, but in the end, he was convicted and went to prison for six years. When he came out, he was a broken man, with no money left from his years of lavish living. He returned to Phoenix, once the scene of his great criminal triumph, as a vagrant. Until his death in 1908, he spent most of his time in the library reading old newspaper accounts of himself during his period of grandeur.

RECIDIVISM

A massive study by the FBI of almost 88,000 persons arrested in 1966 and 1967 revealed that at least 82 percent had been arrested previously, 70 percent had been convicted previously and 46 percent of those convicted had been imprisoned for three months or more. Among those arrested for murder, rape, robbery and felonious assault, 75 percent had already been convicted of a crime. Other studies also showed a high repeater rate. Eighty-five percent of male felons imprisoned in California in 1969 and the same percentage imprisoned in Massachusetts in 1971 had been in correctional institutions before.

By contrast, most studies of recidivism among parolees put the repeater rate at 25 percent. However, this is not considered a reliable calculation since it represents only those cases of recidivism known to parole officers, and in many areas the parole staff simply does not have the manpower needed to assemble complete information. In states where there is more supervision, the percentage of reported crime repeaters increases significantly.

All agencies involved in various forms of custody, prisons, probation or parole, experience a large number of recidivists, a situation that often provokes public cries for "throwing the book" at criminals and the elimination of parole. Objective studies comparing the recidivist rate among like groups of prisoners serving long and short terms have been difficult to set up. However, a landmark decision of the U.S. Supreme Court presented a unique opportunity for analyzing just such a situation. The court, in *Gideon* v. *Wainwright,* threw out the convictions of more than 1,000 indigent Florida prisoners on the ground that they had not been represented by lawyers. The Florida Corrections Department used this special situation to set up two groups of 110 recently released inmates, the first 110 being composed of those who had completed their original sentence and the other 110 being composed of inmates who had been abruptly released far short of their original sentences as a result of the Gideon decision. Care was exercised to match up the individual characteristics of the members of the two groups as much as possible. In the 28 months following their release, 25.4 percent of those who had fulfilled their sentences had committed another crime. During that same period the prisoners freed by the Gideon ruling showed a repeat crime rate of only 13.6 percent.

Many who considered long imprisonment as the answer to the recidivism problem have, in the words of Leonard Orland, professor of law at the University of Connecticut, found the "logical conclusion of this research . . . shocking." The researchers at the Florida Corrections Department concluded, "Baldly stated, it is that if we, today, turned loose all the inmates of our prisons without regard to the length of their sentences and, with only some exceptions, without regard to their previous offenses, we might *reduce* the recidivism rate over what it would be if we kept each prisoner incarcerated until his sentence expired."

Clearly, studies in the future need to focus on the repeat crime rates under programs of amnesty and pardon.

RED-LIGHT District: Name for vice areas

The custom of calling a place of prostitution a red-light house appears to have started in Dodge City, Kan., one of the most wide-open towns in the Old West. It was the custom of train crews of the Santa Fe to leave their red lanterns outside when entering a Dodge City bordello so they could be located quickly in case of an emergency. The enterprising brothel keepers soon realized this was excellent advertising comparable to the flashing neon lights of the 20th century—and the red-light custom spread quickly, becoming a national code. It was one of the few early American customs to work its way from west to east.
See also: *Prostitution.*

RED Light Saloon

Called "violent, obscene and godless" and the "worst whorehouse in Kansas," Caldwell's fabled Red Light Saloon had a mere two-year run, but for sin and violence its record was hard to match anywhere in the West. Two town marshals were murdered on its premises while a third was killed as he staggered from it after a night of carousing.

Mag and George Woods, who had run an establishment of low repute in Delano, arrived in Caldwell in 1880 and opened a two-story saloon, dance hall and bordello on Chisholm Street. Just so there would be no doubt as to the entertainment offered, they called the place the Red Light. The first floor was occupied by a saloon and ballroom and the couple's living area in the rear; the entire second floor was given over to the resident whores.

Caldwell was a wide-open town but the blatant violence of the Red Light was too much even for it, and numerous attempts were made to shut the establishment down. While sharpers skinned cowboys inside, women lured some of them outside to be knocked unconscious and robbed. The whores of the Red Light were as hard a bunch as could be found in any resort in the West. Once after a cowboy was shot and killed at the bar, a harlot who had entertained him earlier stripped off his bandana and dipped it in his blood. Although she had bewailed the fact that he had paid her so poorly, she seemed placated because "now I have a souvenir from the cheapskate."

In August 1881 a cowpoke named Charlie Davis rode into town to savor the pleasures of the Red Light. During the evening he got into an argument with one of the bawds. George Woods intervened and Davis put a pistol to his chest and shot him dead. Davis rode off and was never caught, even though a tearful Mag Woods put a $500 reward on his head.

Compared to his wife, George Woods had been relatively inoffensive, and after his death the Red Light became an even worse den of sin without his restraining influence. On June 22, 1882 two celebrating cowboys killed young Marshal George Brown when he came after them. It was the last straw as far as Caldwell was concerned. A regular headline in the *Caldwell Standard* was, "The Red Light Must Go." The new marshal was given authority to clap down on bawdy entertainment in the saloons, mainly the Red Light, and an ordinance was passed allowing the local courts to run undesirables out of town. Mag Woods realized it was only a matter of time until she was banished, so one August morning in 1882 she sold off all her liquor and fixtures, boarded up her resort and headed for the train station with her women and bartenders, amid jeers from the townspeople. The citizens, however, did not have time to give her a final hoot as her train pulled out. Suddenly, they were aware of flame and smoke and had to rush back to contain the fire Mag Woods had set to burn down the Red Light. Her vengeance was not all that successful: the saloon burned to the ground but the fire was extinguished before more than minor damage occurred to the buildings surrounding it.

RED Sash Gang: Alleged rustling gang during Johnson County War

The Red Sash Gang remains a controversial subject in Wyoming to this day, but the weight of evidence seems to indicate it was a figment of the imaginations of the Pinkertons and the great cattle barons of the lush Cheyenne Club to justify a bloody effort to clear the Johnson County range of plows and barbed wire. According to the charges, a small rancher named Nathan Champion, later murdered by the cattlemen's hired guns, was the head of a gang of rustlers who wore red sashes around their waists, a rather silly practice since it would only have helped to identify them.

See also: The Banditti of the Plains, *Frank Canton, Nathan Champion, Johnson County War.*

REED, Ed (1871-1895): Murderer

Although he was never convicted of the crime, there is little doubt that Ed Reed murdered his own mother, Belle Starr. Reed was the offspring of a common law union between Belle and Jim Reed, an outlaw-lawman who rode with the infamous Tom Starr. Like both his parents, Ed Reed was a bad character. He was an alcoholic at 13, a bootlegger at 14, a horse thief at 15 and the murderer of his mother from ambush at 18. The crime most probably resulted from their incestuous relationship, although some folks said it was due to the fact that Belle was always whipping Ed because of his dishonesty.

At 20 Reed was doing time in prison for horse stealing. Within three years, in one of those minor miracle conversions in the Old West, he turned up as a deputy marshal at Fort Smith. His most famous accomplishment as a lawman was the killing of two former deputy marshals for the crime of being drunk. At age 24 lawman Reed was shot dead in a drunken tavern brawl.

See also: *Jim Reed, Belle Starr.*

REED, Jim (?1845-1874): Outlaw

Jim Reed is remembered as one of the many "husbands" of Bandit Queen Belle Starr, but of the two Reed was much more the outlaw. Belle was infatuated with him, as she later was with so many others, mainly because she simply adored badmen.

Born in Vernon County, Mo., Jim Reed was occasionally a lawman, but more often an outlaw who rode with old Tom Starr's band of killers. After he started living with young Myra Belle Shirley, Reed killed a man named Shannon, and he, Belle and their young daughter fled to California. There, Jim supported his family and a newborn boy named Ed (who 18 years later was suspected of murdering his mother) by the best trade he knew, highway robbery. Finally identified in a stagecoach holdup, Reed took his family back east. He and two other outlaws made a big score by torturing an old Creek Indian until he revealed where he'd hidden a $30,000 gold hoard. With that loot Reed took Belle to Texas, where she first began playing the role of the Bandit Queen. Belle opened a livery stable while Jim rode off to Oklahoma Indian Territory with the Tom Starr gang of horse thieves. The result was that Belle always carried a handsome supply of stock.

Reed was killed in August 1874 by Deputy Sheriff John T. Morris of Lamar County, Tex., who shot him in the back. Just a few years earlier, Morris had been Reed's partner in various stock thefts and stagecoach robberies. After she buried Reed, Belle parked her two young children with relatives and rode off to enhance her own legend.

See also: *Ed Reed, Belle Starr, Tom Starr.*

REED, Nathaniel "Texas Jack" (1862-1950): Train robber

Texas Jack Reed was one of a very few Western badmen who had more than modest success, especially in later years after his reformation.

A long-haired Arkansas youth, Reed turned outlaw at the age of 23 after punching cattle for a few years in the Oklahoma Territory. To go along with his new-found profession, he adopted an alias, Texas Jack. He was successful from the start, joining in with several others to hold up the express car of a train in Colorado, earning some $6,000 for his first criminal effort. By comparison, the notorious Reno gang of train robbers netted less than $2,000 per man in their inaugural caper. From then on, Texas Jack pulled a few bank and stage robberies in Texas interspersed with other lucrative holdups in the Arizona Territory, Colorado and California.

After a decade of criminal activity, Texas Jack finally came to grief during an attempted train holdup in the Oklahoma Territory. Instead of looting what they expected would be $60,000 in the express car, he and accomplices Buzz Luckey, Tom Smith, Tom Root and a few others were greeted by an ambush party under the command of Deputy U.S. Marshal Bud Ledbetter. Texas Jack was badly shot up in the fracas and limped home to Arkansas. Root and Luckey stopped to battle pursuers a short time later and killed lawman Newton LaForce.

When they were captured, however, Root turned informer, leading to a murder charge against Luckey and the capture of Texas Jack.

Luckey was sentenced to death by Hanging Judge Parker and Texas Jack faced a stiff sentence, which was put off while Luckey's appeal was heard by the U.S. Supreme Court. Luckey's murder conviction was overturned, and he was convicted solely of involvement in the train robbery. Texas Jack got a lighter sentence than Luckey because he had not been present at the time of the LaForce killing.

Jack served only about two years before being released on parole. He did not go back to the outlaw trail, instead setting out with a crime-does-not-pay roadshow entitled *Texas Jack, Train Robber.* It was even more profitable than his crime career, and the reformed outlaw followed that up with an autobiography. *The Life of Texas Jack* sold 70,000 copies, and Nathaniel Reed became living proof that there were indeed ways to make crime pay. The redoubtable Texas Jack died in 1950 in Oklahoma City.

REES, Melvin David (1933-1961): Mass murderer

In the late 1950s Melvin David Rees, a professional musician, terrorized Maryland and Virginia with a total of nine murders, most accompanied by sexual assault on his women victims.

In June 1957 near Annapolis, Md., Rees drove alongside a car bearing an army sergeant and his girl, Margaret Harold, and forced their car off the roadside. When Rees tried to caress the woman, she resisted and he shot her. The sergeant bolted and, after running about a mile, reached a farmhouse, from which he called the police. They found Margaret Harold's body and the car, but no trace of the deadly marauder, whom the sergeant had described as tall and thin-faced. Nearby, the police found the basement walls of an unoccupied cinderblock building literally papered with pornographic photographs. They theorized that the murderer might have been using the basement building as his hideaway.

The Harold murder was still unsolved in January 1959 when a 29-year-old truck driver, Carroll Jackson, driving his wife and two young children home after a stay with relatives, was forced by another car to the side of a road near Fredericksburg, Va. The driver ordered the family at gunpoint to climb into the trunk of his car and drove off with them. Two months later, the body of Carroll Jackson was discovered in some underbrush. There was a bullet in his head. The Jacksons' 18-month-old girl was found suffocated under her father's body. A few weeks after that discovery, the bodies of Mrs. Jackson and her four-year-old daughter were found near the scene of Margaret Harold's death. The child had died of a fractured skull while Mrs. Jackson had been strangled, after having been repeatedly raped.

A massive manhunt followed, based on the description given in the Harold killing. Finally, the widespread publicity produced information from a Norfolk, Va. man who said he suspected a young musician named Melvin David Rees had

committed the murders because of things Rees had said to him. Rees was arrested in West Memphis, Ark., where he was working as a piano salesman. He denied the charges but was identified by the army sergeant in the Margaret Harold case. When investigators searched the home of Rees' parents near Washington, D.C., they turned up the murder gun and long, written accounts of his treatment of Mrs. Jackson before he murdered her. He had killed the woman in a most brutal fashion. Other evidence linked Rees—now known in the press as the Sex Beast—to four other murder victims not originally connected with the Harold and Jackson cases. Marie Shomettee, 16, and Ann Ryan, 14, both of whom had been sexually assaulted and murdered near College Park, Md., and Shelby Jean Venable, 16, and Mary Elizabeth Fellers, 18, whose naked bodies had been found floating in Maryland rivers.

For his Maryland crimes Rees got a life sentence, but he was then tried in Virginia for the Jackson family killings, found guilty and executed in 1961.

REGULATORS And Moderators: Historic vigilante factions

One of the earliest forms of vigilantism in America appeared in the backwoods of South Carolina in 1767 following a militia campaign against the Cherokee Indians. A great number of poorer settlers and farmers who had been uprooted by the conflict turned to various forms of disobedience against authority, including outlawry. This soon aroused the ire of many of the large property owners, who determined to bring about a return to tranquillity by organizing as "regulators" and summarily executing several of the "troublemakers." While other men of wealth and standing shared a common hatred for the backcountry settlers, the violent behavior of the Regulators and the fact that they acted without legal authority frightened them into organizing as "moderators." The Moderators also operated outside the law but substituted the lash for the hangman's rope. Colonial justice never brought a single Regulator or Moderator to the dock, and by the time the American Revolution began, the backcountry had been violently pacified by their efforts.

Throughout the history of America, the establishment of Regulator groups in various parts of the country has often resulted in the formation of Moderator groups. The most prominent cases were in eastern Texas in 1840-44, southwestern Missouri in 1842-44 and southern Illinois in 1846-50. At times the struggle between the two groups became so intense that shooting erupted between them, and the lawbreakers were virtually ignored; in fact, especially in eastern Texas, the lawbreakers would often join one side or the other.

See also: *East Texas Regulator War.*

REISER, Charles "The Ox" (1878-1921): Safecracker and killer

Charlie "the Ox" Reiser led a Jekyll-and-Hyde existence. Under the name of Shopes he was known as a reliable family man and a friendly landlord. Yet the underworld and the police regarded him as the premier safecracker in America during the early 20th century. He was also a brutal killer and indoctrinated many of the notorious Chicago gangsters of the 1920s into the ways of big-time crime, among them Dion O'Banion, Bugs Moran, Hymie Weiss and John Mahoney.

The Ox, a mountain of a man, could single-handedly shove a safe from one end of a room to the other. He was a brilliant "peterman," or handler of nitroglycerine. Reiser first ran afoul of the law in Chicago in 1903, when he was charged with safecracking. Out on bail, he killed the witnesses against him, and the case was dropped. In 1905 he was arrested again. The witness disappeared and there was no case. He beat another rap in 1907 and then was convicted of assault with a deadly weapon and did 30 days. In 1909 police from Seattle, Wash. apprehended him on a charge of burglary and murder. Thereafter all the witnesses died, and Reiser returned to Chicago.

During World War I he became friends with O'Banion and used that deadly Irishman and a number of his pals in several safecrackings. All this time, Reiser was living a double life under the name of Shopes and pouring his ill-earned money into real estate, becoming the owner of a large apartment building. He was known to tenants as a prince of a landlord; while he expected his rent, he did not hound a man if he got a little behind. He was considered to be a fine husband to his second wife. His first wife had not fared so well. Reiser boasted to his underworld acquaintances that when the woman had threatened to get the law after him, he promptly beat her to death. The coroner's jury thought she had died of asphyxiation.

Clarence White, who aided the Ox in the cracking of a Standard Oil Co. safe, was invited by the police to come in for questioning. White said he would but first telephoned the Ox, who rushed right over to White's apartment and shot him through the heart, making it look like a suicide. This intelligence came from another errant gang member, John Mahoney, who turned informer after being caught cracking safes on his own. Mahoney provided considerable evidence against Reiser, all of which proved useless when Mahoney was murdered in April 1921.

On October 10, 1921 the Ox entered the premises of a cold storage firm, planning to bust open its safe after first killing the watchman. He shot the watchman but took two bullets himself, one through the lung. Reiser was hospitalized and charged with murder. He became the subject of some bizarre newspaper stories, in which reporters informed their readers that if Reiser was convicted, his property would be confiscated and turned over to some of his past robbery victims. Although untrue, the stories may in some way have contributed to Reiser's death. His wife, who found the prospect of his property being confiscated rather souring, showed up at his hospital room and was admitted even though the police guard stationed outside the room had been instructed to let no one enter. A few moments later, there was "a rattle of shots." Mrs. Reiser-Shopes tearfully related that her husband had committed suicide. One thing was certain: the Ox was very dead, with 10 bullets in him.

Understandably, the police found the death suspicious, especially since Reiser had had both his right hand and his left arm broken in the storage firm robbery, making use of a gun rather difficult. Murder charges were brought against the widow, but Chicago being Chicago, a coroner's jury ruled Reiser's death a suicide after all. Reiser's estate of over $100,000 went to his wife.

See also: *Charles Dion "Deanie" O'Banion.*

RELES, Abe (1907-1941): Murder, Inc. killer and informer

What was so amazing about the criminal career of Abe Reles, better known as Kid Twist within Murder, Inc., was how long he remained out of serious trouble despite the fact that he personally took part in at least 30 murders. Until the Kid started "singing," the law did not even know about Murder, Inc., the enforcement arm of the national crime syndicate that committed an estimated 400 to 500 murders during roughly the decade of the 1930s. Once Reles went into what was called the most famous "canary act in underworld history," goggle-eyed investigators cleared up no less than 49 murders in Brooklyn alone, some of which they hadn't even known about. Reles was in a position to know. He was a second-rung leader of Murder, Inc., ranking just below the top leaders of the extermination "troop": Louis Lepke and Albert Anastasia. As an underworld stoolpigeon, he was much more highly placed than Joe Valachi, for instance.

Reles' police rap sheet in 1940 listed 42 arrests over 16 years, including many charges of assault, robbery, burglary, possession of narcotics, disorderly conduct and murder (only six). He had done six minor stretches but had never once talked to the authorities. However, when he was picked up in 1940, along with a number of other major and minor members of Murder, Inc., on a homicide charge, he feared someone else would talk. The Kid decided to save his own skin by talking first.

Reles revealed that he and other members of the troop, such as Pittsburgh Phil, Happy Maione, Dasher Abbandando, Chicken Head Gurino and Buggsy Goldstein, were given assassination assignments not only in New York but elsewhere around the country, at times not even knowing the identities of their victims. He made a deal with the prosecutors that he would walk away clear from any murder he had participated in provided he furnished them with all the details including the names of his accomplices, an easy task for the Kid since he had the most phenomenal memory of any informer prior to John Dean.

It was Reles' testimony that doomed Abbandando and Maione for the brutal killing of a loan shark named Whitey Rudnick. They had stabbed him more than 60 times, cracked open his skull and then, just to be sure, strangled him. With a perfectly straight face, Kid Twist said Rudnick had deserved his fate: he had been a stoolpigeon.

Reles gave chilling testimony against Pittsburgh Phil, who

also took part in Rudnick's murder plus perhaps 100 others, and Buggsy Goldstein that sent them to the chair for the vicious garroting of a minor gambler named Puggy Feinstein. He provided key information about Charlie Workman, accused of murdering Dutch Schultz, so that when Workman heard all the testimony against him, he switched to a plea of guilty to get a life sentence instead of the electric chair.

The Kid's testimony helped build a successful case against the great crime boss Louis Lepke as well as underlings Mendy Weiss and Louis Capone, who were accused of murdering a garment industry foe named Joseph Rosen, even though Reles was no longer around to testify by the time of their trial.

Reles appeared at a number of trials for more than a year, during which time he was kept under protective custody in the sixth-floor wing of the Half Moon Hotel in the Coney Island section of Brooklyn. Then, in the early morning hours of November 12, 1941, despite the fact that he was always guarded by six officers and never left alone in a room even while he slept, Reles jumped, fell or was tossed out the window to his death. Several sheets tied together were found, and the police theorized that Reles had climbed out the window to escape; to climb down one floor in order to play a prank on his guards; or to commit suicide, although the sheets were hardly necessary for that option. One problem with all the police theories was that the Kid's body had landed a good 20 feet away from the wall of the hotel building.

Twenty years later, an ailing Lucky Luciano, the chief founder of the national crime syndicate in the early 1930s, stated that Frank Costello had arranged for Reles' demise and that $50,000 had been distributed within the police department to have Reles sent out the window. The murder had been necessary because at the time the Kid was about to give information that would have doomed two leading underworld leaders: Albert Anastasia and Bugsy Siegel. Subsequently, William O'Dwyer, then Brooklyn district attorney and later mayor of New York City, received much criticism for failing to proceed with the prosecution of Anastasia in what was described as a "perfect case" based on Kid Twist's testimony. O'Dwyer claimed that case "went out the window" along with informer Reles.

In 1945 a Brooklyn grand jury charged that there had been "negligence, incompetence and flagrant irresponsibility" in O'Dwyer's handling of the Anastasia prosecution. The jury stated O'Dwyer was

> in possession of competent legal evidence that Anastasia was guilty of first degree murder and other vicious crimes. The proof admittedly was sufficient to warrant Anastasia's indictment and conviction, but Anastasia was neither prosecuted, indicted nor convicted. . . . The consistent and complete failure to prosecute the overlord of organized crime . . is so revolting that we cannot permit these disclosures to be filed away in the same manner the evidence against Anastasia was heretofore "put in the files."

Other ugly rumors swirled around Reles' death, including the charge by Ed Reid, a prize-winning reporter for the *Brooklyn Eagle*, that "Reles served several purposes besides being a fount of information about gang activities. Some of the infor-

Informer Abe Reles jumped, fell or was pitched out a sixth-floor window of a Coney Island hotel.

mation he gave out was used by unscrupulous persons connected with law enforcement in Brooklyn—to shake down gangsters."

In any event, Reles did not live long enough to fulfill his potential as a stoolpigeon. While Murder, Inc., or at least its Brooklyn branch, was destroyed, the crime syndicate continued in business.

See also: *Louis "Lepke" Buchalter; Murder, Inc.; Pittsburgh Phil.*

REMUS, George (1874-1952): Murderer

Often cited as one of the most farcical murder trials in American history, the conviction of George Remus for the murder of his wife, Imogene, in Cincinnati on October 6, 1927 should have been a cut-and-dried affair.

When Remus finished a prison term in the federal penitentiary at Atlanta for bootlegging, he returned home convinced his wife had been unfaithful during his years behind bars. So he shot her. As a lawyer, albeit disbarred, Remus insisted on his right to handle his own defense and won the judge's agreement despite his plea of not guilty on the basis of his own insanity.

While the prosecution paraded alienists to the stand to testify to Remus' sanity, the defendant set about proving, by his own behavior and by the testimony of his witnesses, that he was insane. The jurors were treated to the spectacle of a defendant getting his witnesses to say he was deranged and dangerous. In the end, they were convinced by his performance, taking only 19 minutes to bring in an acquittal by reason of insanity. The prosecution was not caught off guard by the verdict, however, moving quickly to get the judge to commit Remus to a state asylum on the basis of his witnesses' testimony that he was dangerously insane.

The Remus case was to have one more astonishing twist. Just four months later, Remus stood before the Ohio Court of Appeals, proved he was totally sane and walked out a free man.

RENO Gang

The Reno brothers—Frank, John, Simeon and William—led a gang of about two dozen outlaws, who had previously limited their activities to saloon holdups, burglaries and highway robberies on the first train robbery in this country, near Seymour, Ind., on October 6, 1866, taking $10,000 from the express car. Over the next two years they robbed a number of banks and trains; in 1868, e.g., they boarded a train as it paused to take on water at a whistle stop outside Marshfield, Ind., and seized the unheard of sum of $96,000, much more than Jesse James and his gang ever got.

While many later train robbers developed a romantic air about them and achieved an uncommon popularity with the public, such was not the case with the Renos. They tended to be too brutal and too kill-crazy. Relying on sheer terror, the Renos operated rather openly around Seymour and often met in the train station. Private detective Allan Pinkerton and six of his men managed to arrest John Reno during a lightning

attack at the station and hustle him aboard an outbound train. When the rest of the gang realized what had happened, they jumped on another train and forced the engineer to give chase. The frantic race continued into Illinois, where Pinkerton was able to divert his prisoner to authorities and John Reno was sent to prison.

In March 1868 Pinkerton tracked the gang after a bank robbery and, with a huge posse, surrounded them at Council Bluffs, Iowa. After their apprehension the prisoners were jammed into a small local jail, but they escaped on April 1, after painting the words "APRIL FOOL" on the side of the building.

Outraged at the law's inability to contain the Renos, and agreeing with the *Seymour Times* that "Seymour has a carnival of crime," a number of citizens formed a vigilance committee. Shortly afterward, the Pinkertons nabbed three of the gang—Lefty Clinton, Volney Elliott and Charlie Roseberry—and were moving them by rail to Seymour when the train was flagged down by masked vigilantes, who seized the prisoners and hanged them from the nearest tree. The Renos were outraged and sent threats to known vigilance committee members and accused the Pinkertons of having cooperated with the lynchers.

Meanwhile, the Pinkertons tracked down the rest of the Reno brothers and several other gang members in Indianapolis and Canada and brought them back to stand trial. They were first placed in the Jackson County Jail, but because of vigilante rumblings, they were shifted to the more substantial Floyd County Jail in New Albany. The fugitive members of the gang declared open war on suspected members of the Southern Indiana Vigilance Committee. There were night ambushes, beatings, unspeakable tortures and mutilations. Messages attached to rocks thrown through windows of local and state officials' offices warned, "If the Renos are lynched you die."

Such moves did not deter the vigilantes, and on December 11, 1868—the Night of Blood as it became known—100 masked vigilantes took over the town of New Albany, wounded the sheriff, dragged Carl Anderson and Frank, William and Simeon Reno from their cells and hanged them from an iron ceiling beam in the jail. After the vigilantes left, Simeon Reno revived and, clawing at the rope, tried to pull himself up to relieve the pressure on his neck. The other prisoners screamed for the jailers but all had fled. Simeon Reno kept up his struggle for almost half an hour until his strength gave out and he slowly strangled to death.

In the meantime the vigilantes pulled out of New Albany by train, giving a local official a cell key so that the wounded sheriff could be freed and treated by a doctor.

Ten days after the Night of Blood, the vigilance committee issued a warning:

> We are well aware that at the present time, a combination
> of the few remaining thieves, their friends and sympathizers,
> has been formed against us, and have threatened all kinds of
> vengeance against persons whom they suppose to belong to
> this organization. They threaten assassination in every form,
> and that they will commit arson in such ways as will defy
> detection. They carrying out in whole, or in part, of each or

any of these designs, is the only thing that will again cause us to rise in our own defence. The following named persons are solemnly warned, that their designs and opinions are known, and that they cannot, unknown to us, make a move toward retaliation.

Wilk Reno, Clinton Reno, Trick Reno, James Greer, Stephen Greer, Fee Johnson, Chris. Price, Harvey Needham, Meade Fislar, Mart Lowe, Roland Lee, William Sparks, Jesse Thompson, William Hare, William Biggers, James Fislar, Pollard Able.

If the above named individuals desire to remain in our midst, to pursue honest callings, and otherwise conduct themselves as law abiding citizens, we will protect them always.—If however, they commence their devilish designs against us, our property, or any good citizen of this district, we will rise but once more; do not trifle with us; for if you do, we will follow you to the bitter end; and give you a "short shrift and a hempen collar." As to this, our actions in the past, will be a guarantee for our conduct in the future.

That marked the end of the Reno menace.

RESTELL, Madame (1812-1878): Madame Killer

"The wickedest woman in the city," Ann Trow Lohman, better known as Madame Restell, was New York's most infamous abortionist in the 19th Century.

Born in poverty in England, she emigrated to the United States in 1831 with her first husband, a tailor named Henry Summers who died two years later as a result of yellow fever, typhoid and alcoholism. In 1836 she married "Doctor" Charles R. Lohman, a former compositor who had prospered as a quack physician selling medication that supposedly inhibited conception and aborted unwanted fetuses. Soon, Lohman's new wife turned up in newspaper advertisements as "Madame Restell, female physician and professor of midwifery."

Madame Restell opened an establishment on Greenwich Street where she sold various contraceptive devices, performed abortions and delivered babies who were later put up for adoption by their single mothers. To stay in business, Madame Restell paid enormous sums to the police. The superintendent of police, George W. Matsell, was widely believed to have been on her payroll. Concurrently, Matsell's private company was proprietor of the *National Police Gazette*, which regularly ranted about Madame Killer and her establishment. Clearly, Matsell used his publication as leverage to raise the ante on his bribes. Madame Restell became so notorious that while Boss Tweed allowed her to operate, he refused, in a rare burst of virtue, to take her money and declined invitations to parties at her lavish Fifth Avenue mansion.

Madame Restell prospered despite her numerous expenses. It was said, for example, that more than 100 wealthy men paid regular tribute to her establishment for the right to send young girls there for various forms of "treatment." She was arrested on a number of occasions, especially when a young girl sent to her died from an abortion, but she never served more than a year in prison for any offense. A far more serious threat to her were the angry mobs that frequently gathered outside her establishment and threatened to destroy it. Whenever she went forth in her carriage, street boys followed it shouting: "Yah! Your house is built on babies skulls!"

While Madame Restell could hardly stand as a tragic heroine, she was probably less of an abortionist than a purveyor of contraceptives and the operator of an undercover maternity hospital and adoption center. In the 19th century there was a great semantic confusion concerning abortion and contraception, both officially viewed as the same evil.

After her husband died in 1876, Madame Restell led a lonely life. Because of her notoriety she was abandoned by her brother and a step-daughter by her first marriage. She lived for the affection shown her by her two grandchildren, for whom she entertained high social ambitions. She was elated when her granddaughter married extremely well in 1878.

The following month, however, Madame Restell was trapped by Anthony Comstock of the New York Society for the Suppression of Vice, who purchased a number of contraceptive items from her. He then had her arrested for possession of articles used for "immoral" purposes. Facing a sensational trial and fearing the publicity would lead to estrangement from her grandchildren, Madame Restell climbed into her bathtub and slit her throat with a carving knife. She left an estate of $1 million, a stupendous sum for that era.

REYNOLDS Gang: Colorado outlaws

The Reynolds gang, a moderately successful group of Civil War bandits, or Confederate "irregulars," won a permanent niche in Colorado folklore in part because of the belief that they buried a great treasure but also because of the way they were eradicated. As historian Henry Sinclair Drago put it, their execution "stands as one of the blackest pages in Colorado history."

Jim and John Reynolds, two brothers, first appeared on the Colorado Territory around Bayou Salado (South Park) about 1863. Although they never worked, they always seemed to have good horses and money, and the suspicion grew that they were highwaymen. There was no hard evidence against them, but since the Reynolds were from Texas, it seemed like a good idea to put them in an internment compound in Denver for Confederate sympathizers. The brothers soon escaped and returned to their native Texas, where they came up with the idea of functioning as Confederate irregulars in the Colorado Territory, stealing gold for the cause.

Whether the Reynolds gang, which consisted of 20 members, ever intended to turn over any loot to the South is moot. Their first strike on the Santa Fe Trail netted some $40,000 in gold. Then the gang moved into Colorado's Spanish Peaks section. Here, Jim Reynolds mumbled something about the loot belonging to Jeff Davis, a contention disputed by most of the gang. In the end, about a dozen men pulled out, each taking his own share. According to some accounts, the Reynolds brothers buried the balance of the gold; other reports maintain it was divided among the remaining members of the gang. The Reynolds outfit pulled several more robberies with moderate success, including a stagecoach holdup that yielded $10,000 in gold dust.

In the late spring of 1864 the gang was badly shot up; one man was killed and Jim Reynolds and four of his men were captured. Only John Reynolds and Jake Stowe got away. Tried in Denver, Jim Reynolds and his four accomplices were sentenced to life imprisonment (the death sentence was not considered because the gang had never killed anyone). They were kept in jail in Denver until the middle of the summer, although local authorities expressed the fear that Southern sympathizers might try to break them out.

In August, Col. John M. Chivington of the 3rd Colorado Cavalry took charge of the prisoners and had them tried secretly. They were sentenced to be hanged as conspirators against the United States. However, because the military tribunal feared it was exceeding its authority, an announcement was made that the prisoners would be sent to Fort Leavenworth, Kan. for a review of their case. A troop of the 3rd Cavalry under Capt. George Cree set off with the prisoners on August 19.

A few days later, Capt. Cree returned to report the five prisoners had been shot trying to escape. The truth came out when Dick Wooten, the famous scout, discovered the bodies of the five men lashed to trees and filled with bullet holes near the ghost town of Russelville, Colorado Territory. Capt. Cree then tried to explain his actions by claiming he'd been given oral orders to shoot the prisoners at the first opportunity. That claim was not believed because it obviously reflected on Chivington, a fine officer and also a Methodist preacher. Three months later, after Chivington's infamous massacre of Cheyenne Indians at Sand Creek, a wave of revulsion over the barbarous execution of the Reynolds gang had swept the territory.

A final chapter in the Reynolds gang saga occurred in 1871, when John Reynolds returned to the Colorado Territory, it was said, to retrieve the gang's hidden loot in Spanish Peaks and Handcart Gulch. He committed a number of additional holdups and was finally mortally wounded, but not before allegedly imparting the secret of the hiding places to his companion, a two-bit outlaw named Brown. Since he died a drunken vagrant in the Wyoming Territory, it's almost certain Brown never found the loot.

Thus, the story of the Reynolds gang remains both a blot on the history of Colorado and a tantalizing tale of lost treasure. On this last point, Perry Eberhart was to write, about a century after the Reynolds gang rode, in *Treasure Tales of the Rockies:* "Fortune hunters have torn down fences and fence posts, trampled fields and dug holes up and down three gulches. They [the Colorado natives] wish they had never heard of 'The Bold' Reynolds and his infernal treasure."

RICCA, Paul "The Waiter" (1897-1972): Chicago mob leader

For 40 years after the fall of Al Capone in 1931, the newspapers argued about who was in charge of the Chicago mob, with speculation centering first on Frank "the Enforcer" Nitti, followed by Tough Tony Accardo, Sam "Momo" Giancana and Paul "the Waiter" Ricca.

Ricca was a power even in the Capone days, with Big Al standing up as best man for him at his wedding in 1927. In the mid-1930s Nitti assumed control, but Ricca's influence continued to grow and by about 1939 he had gained the leadership. Within the Chicago syndicate power always fell to the man strong enough to seize and hold it, not only by force, but by sheer personality. That was Al Capone's strong suit; it was Ricca's as well. He could dominate almost any planning session of the mob and was regarded, along with Accardo and Jake "Greasy Thumb" Guzik, as one of the most intelligent and cunning mobsters.

Ricca's power was based on force. He had a long string of syndicate killers allied with him, many of them psychotics who would do anything to curry his favor. And Ricca never hesitated to use violence. It was not so much his ability to order executions but the quiet manner in which he did so that made him so feared. "Make'a him go away," he would order softly and the object of his rage was a dead man.

Ricca came to America in 1920. In 1917 he had been sentenced to 2½ years in prison in Ottavino, Italy, near Naples, for the murder of Emilio Parrillo. The chief witness against him was Vincenzo Capasso. The first thing he did when he got out was kill Capasso. Then he fled. Ricca was tried in absentia for the murder and given a 21-year sentence. Arriving in Chicago, he worked first as a theater usher and then did a short stint as a waiter. He earned his nickname the Waiter not so much because he had briefly waited on tables but because that occupation was cited in testimony at immigration hearings to prove he was a worthwhile citizen and not a criminal. Ricca and Capone had mutual friends in Italy, and Capone soon took Ricca into his organization.

Throughout his career Ricca was known as a great fixer. He paid off politicians at almost every level of government. Although he went to prison several times, Ricca always seemed to get off with very short sentences. Along with almost the entire top leadership of the Chicago mob, he went to prison for the huge shakedown of the motion picture industry in the early 1940s. Ricca and most of the others were sentenced to 10 years in 1943 but released in August 1947 because of the intercession of Attorney General Tom Clark. The early paroles enraged the Chicago newspapers, which published Ricca's claims that his influence reached into the White House. Printed accounts had Ricca telling his lawyers to find out who had the final say in granting him a speedy release, adding: "That man must want something: money, favors, a seat in the Supreme Court. Find out what he wants and get it for him."

Granted that several of the Chicago newspapers were bitter enemies of President Harry Truman, the facts were that Attorney General Clark had allowed the early parole of Ricca and the others to go through and that Clark was appointed to the next opening on the Supreme Court. In 1952 the *Chicago Tribune* called for Clark's impeachment because of his "utter unfitness for any position of public responsibility and especially for a position on the Supreme Court bench." The editorial went on to state: "We have been sure of [his] unfitness ever since he played his considerable role in releasing the four Capone gangsters after they had served the bare minimum of their terms."

In any event, Paul Ricca was back in circulation and became the real power in the Chicago underworld. While he was in prison, Tough Tony Accardo had visited him in his cell by masquerading as his attorney. Accardo had kept Ricca informed of syndicate activities and had gotten his decision about whether to go ahead or to pull back. After his release Ricca, when he was so inclined, allowed Sam Giancana to give syndicate orders but later took away that power. In its hearings on organized crime, the Kefauver Committee in 1950 labeled Ricca "the national head of the Crime Syndicate" and the McClellan Committee in 1958 referred to him as America's "most important" criminal. Ricca's testimony on the witness stand before each committee was punctuated by frequent citings of the Fifth Amendment.

In 1957 Ricca was stripped of his citizenship and two years later he was ordered deported. Ricca started all sorts of appeals and delaying actions. He got a court stay on deportation to Italy by bringing an action before an Italian court, demanding that his Italian citizenship be dropped. In what can only be described as an incredible action, the Italian government decided that Ricca was such a despicable character and had been so unwholesome of behavior in America that it did not even want him back to serve out his old murder sentence, presumably because he would contaminate its prisons. Immigration authorities then ordered Ricca to find a country to which he wished to be deported. Ricca dutifully obeyed and sent letters to more than 60 countries, supposedly seeking asylum but always including a packet of news clippings to indicate how undesirable he was in the United States. No country expressed any willingness to accept him. The government was still trying to get rid of Ricca when he died in 1972 at the age of 74.

See also: *Frank Nitti*.

RICE, William Marsh (1816-1900): Murder victim

One of Texas' more famous millionaires, William Marsh Rice had but one ambition in his later years: to give his adopted state, which had made him rich, an institution of higher learning as a memorial to himself. His life was ended by a bizarre murder plot to rob his estate, most of which was intended for the founding of that institution.

Rice had garnered a fortune in oil, land and hotels. At the age of 80, he had buried two wives, had no children and was living alone in New York. He hired 23-year-old Charles F. Jones as a combination nurse and secretary and by 1900 he so trusted Jones that he allowed him to handle all his banking affairs.

At the time, Rice was involved in a legal dispute over part of his fortune. Before his second wife died, she made up a will disposing of half of Rice's money, to which she was entitled under the community property law in Texas, where the couple had been living. Rice countered that he was actually a resident of New York and only visited Texas and that therefore all the money rightfully was his. Nonetheless, he made out a will leaving almost all of his estate to establish "The Rice Institute." One of Rice's adversaries was a brash Texas lawyer with a shady past, a man named Albert T. Patrick, who went to New York to gather proof that Rice's claim of residency in that state was a fraud. In fact, Patrick had something else in mind. He was out to get the Rice millions for himself. After promising secretary Jones a fortune, he drew him into the plot.

Although Rice had made a will in 1896 for the establishment of the school, Patrick set about producing a new will that would name him the chief beneficiary. In this new will Rice's relatives would receive much more money, making them far more likely to support it than the original. He also left $5,000 to each of the prospective trustees of the new school, whom Rice had named in the authentic will. "They'll be glad to forget about the school," Patrick told Jones. "Every man has his price. You know, any man in Houston can be bought for five thousand dollars."

On September 24, 1900 Patrick sent an office boy to Rice's bank with a check for $65,000. It was made out to Abert T. Patrick but endorsed by Albert T. Patrick. Because of the faulty endorsement, it was rejected. When the boy returned with the correct endorsement, the bank became suspicious and called Rice to verify his signature. Jones answered the phone call and said the check was authentic, but he was nevertheless asked to put Mr. Rice on the phone. The secretary replied that Rice was not available. Later that same day the bank called again; this time Jones said his employer had died.

As a matter of fact, Rice had been dead when the check was first presented for payment. Jones had tiptoed into Rice's room while he was asleep and covered his face for 30 minutes with a sponge soaked in chloroform. Then he called Patrick, who in turn arranged for a Dr. Walter Curry to examine the body. Dr. Curry signed a death certificate that declared Rice had succumbed to "old age, weak heart and collocratal diarrhea with mental worry."

Meanwhile, Patrick informed Rice's bank that he held another check for $65,000 as well as an assignment of all his bonds and securities. The bank wondered why Rice had left everything to Patrick. Patrick said: "Frankly, the old gentleman admired me. He was just stuck on me. He thought I was the most wonderful man in the world. Said he never met anyone he liked better."

Nevertheless, the bank and a number of Rice's relatives and proposed trustees of the school insisted on a post-mortem, which revealed traces of mercury in the dead man's organs and congestion of the lungs caused by "some gas or vapor." On October 4 Patrick and Jones were arrested on charges of forgery and confined in the Tombs Prison. Patrick, who until then had exercised considerable authority over Jones, ordered his accomplice to confess to the murder and assume the entire guilt. Jones slit his throat with a pen knife and spent two weeks recuperating in Bellevue Hospital.

When he was returned to the Tombs, Jones first stated that Patrick had administered the fatal chloroform to the old millionaire. Then he admitted he had done it after Patrick had showed him a picture of his two smiling daughters and said he could not kill anyone.

Patrick was brought to trial for murder in January 1902. The proceedings lasted 10 weeks and the testimony filled 3,000 pages. Jones turned state's evidence and, in exchange, was not charged with anything. He spent five days on the witness stand. Patrick was convicted and sentenced to death in the electric chair.

Patrick's long fight for freedom has been described as one of the blackest chapters in New York's legal history. A wealthy brother-in-law reportedly poured thousands into the battle. Patrick spent four years and seven months in the death house, during which time he saw 17 others go to the chair. Finally, in December 1906 Gov. F. W. Higgins commuted his sentence to life imprisonment. Patrick, the star boarder on death row, announced: "I refuse to accept the governor's commutation. I propose to continue my fight for freedom."

He shuttled back and forth to various courts with all sorts of arguments. In one court he argued that he was legally dead and, as such, could not be kept in Sing Sing. It could be that everyone wearied of the entire matter, but in any event, on November 28, 1912 Gov. John A. Dix gave Patrick a complete pardon, noting in a brief comment that "an air of mystery has always surrounded the case." The governor's act was, to say the least, controversial, but so was the fact that Jones, the actual killer, had not even been tried for the murder.

In a certain sense, all the parties in the case came out fairly well off. Rice Institute was endowed and grew to be the nation's wealthiest school on a student per capita basis. Patrick eventually became a man of property before he died in 1940 at the age of 74. Ironically, even Jones ended up with a fair sum of money, which he inherited from his family. When he committed suicide in 1954 at the age of 80, his neighbors in Baytown, Tex. had no idea he was *the* Jones who had been involved in the Rice murder. However, it was not a guilty conscience that prompted him to take his life but fear of becoming an invalid and dependent on strangers.

See also: *John F. Tyrrell.*

RICH Men's Coachmen's Club: Criminal organization

One of the strangest criminal organizations in history was the Rich Men's Coachmen's Club, which appeared in Chicago in the 1880s. Among the city's coaching set the true sign of social importance was to have English grooms and coachmen, since English fashion still represented the ultimate authority in the Gem of the Prairie. The social order became somewhat scrambled as many of these English grooms and coachmen who flooded Chicago attempted to exploit and bully their employ-

ers, getting away with such behavior, because the crowning disaster in the city's society was to lose one's English servant.

The field became so lush that a number of Yankee imposters posed as Englishmen to get coachmen's jobs. A leading faker of this ilk was one John Tilbury, who won a position with Victor Fremont Lawson, the owner of the *Chicago Daily News.* Tilbury's real name was James McGraw and he really hailed from New York City, but he affected a perfect accent and had provided himself with impressive forged credentials. Tilbury saw there were enormous opportunities for dishonest coachmen if their activities could be properly organized.

He formed the Rich Men's Coachmen's Club, headquartered in Lawson's barn, where both business and social meetings were held. The latter activities included drinking and carousing and betting on dog and cockfights. Business meetings consisted of reports on mansions that could be burglarized; valuable dogs that could be stolen and sold, trained as fighters or returned to their owners for ransom; and family secrets that could be used for blackmail. Honest servants of rich families were appalled by the actions of Tilbury's gang. They informed their employers and wrote anonymous letters to the police accusing various coachmen of being former inmates of British jails or deserters from the British Army. However, most employers refused to believe such charges against their coachmen, restrained by their own pride in having British servants or the threat of blackmail. Nonetheless, Lawson may have breathed a sigh of relief when Tilbury left his employ to join the staff of Mrs. Hollis M. Thurston, a leading figure in Chicago society. No doubt Mrs. Thurston was proud of her catch of a coachman who claimed to be a former guards officer and the disinherited member of a titled family.

Some three months later, Tilbury had gathered enough dirt on the Thurston family to approach his mistress and inform her he wanted $12,500 to remain silent about certain family scandals. Mrs. Thurston was made of stern stuff and informed private detectives, who seized Tilbury at the mansion as the blackmail money was paid to him. The detectives then turned him over to the police. When the story broke in the newspapers the next day, the *Chicago Times* reported: "Chicago society has turned white with dread."

At Tilbury's trial, Mrs. Thurston was subjected to a withering cross-examination, which attacked her conduct and character. In the end, Tilbury was freed on the ground that the private detectives hired by the woman had violated his rights. However, the police thereafter hounded Tilbury and some other crooked coachmen until they finally left town and the Coachmen's Club was dissolved.

RICHARDSON, George: See Springfield, Illinois, Race Riot.

RIDE: See One-Way Ride.

RIDLEY, Edward Albert (1847-1933): Murder victim

Few unsolved murders in America have provoked as much speculation as that of 86-year-old millionaire Edward Albert Ridley.

A New York real estate tycoon, Ridley maintained his office in the subcellar of a garage on Allen Street. In 1931 Ridley entered his office and found the body of Herman Moench, 60, his bookkeeper and rent collector for some 30 years. Moench had been shot twice but the police were unable to learn the identity of his killer or killers. Then two years later, on May 10, 1933, business associates of Ridley found that the millionaire's office phone was not being answered. They investigated and discovered the bodies of Ridley and Lee Weinstein, Moench's successor. Weinstein had been shot seven times and Ridley had been beaten to death with a stool. Ballistics tests revealed the same weapon that had killed Moench two years previously had also killed Weinstein. The murders of Moench, Weinstein and Ridley, who left an estate of $3 million, have never been solved.

"RIGHT To Bear Arms": Gun owners' slogan

Opponents of gun control legislation frequently cite what they insist is a fundamental right guaranteed by the Constitution: "the right to bear arms." However, few constitutional scholars find any such "right" in the document, insisting that meaning is derived only when the words are taken out of context. The Second Amendment reads: "A well regulated Militia, being necessary to the security of a free State, the right of the people to keep and bear Arms, shall not be infringed." Historian Irving Brant notes:

> As the wording reveals, this article relates entirely to the militia—a fact that was made even clearer by a clause dropped from Madison's original wording: "but no person religiously scrupulous of bearing arms should be compelled to render military service in person." It was made clearest of all in the congressional debate on the amendment. Why was a militia necessary to "the security of a free state"? Elbridge Gerry asked and answered that question: "What, sir, is the use of the militia? It is to prevent the establishment of a standing army, the bane of liberty." Thus the purpose of the Second Amendment was to forbid Congress to prohibit the maintenance of a state militia. By its nature, that amendment cannot be transformed into a personal right to bear arms, enforceable by federal compulsion upon the state.

Of course, if the opponents of gun control laws really feel there is merit in their claim, there are any number of gun restrictions on the law books that could be challenged, thus allowing a final determination on the matter by the courts.

RILEY, James "Butt" (1848-?): San Francisco hoodlum

Butt Riley grew up as a hoodlum in New York and then, after a stint as a sailor, ended up in San Francisco, where police soon labeled him King of the Hoodlums. Certainly, he was one of that city's principal, if less sophisticated, criminals. He never led any specific gang, but most of the city's toughs would flock to join him whenever he called.

James "Butt" Riley was frequently used by contemporary newspaper artists as a model for what the "more exquisite-type" hoodlum looked like.

Riley was known as a vicious fighter who was always armed with a long knife, brass knuckles, a slungshot and a hickory bludgeon. However, his principal weapon was his head, which he claimed had the thickest skull in Christendom. He would disable a foe by charging him and butting him in the stomach or on the chin, rendering the man helpless. When Butt Riley led raids on Chinese opium houses or slave dens, he always batted the doors down with his head, and when his men grabbed a Chinese victim, Riley would see how far he could butt him. Records were kept on such matters, and according to them, Riley once butted a 160-pound man exactly 10 feet. Riley has been described as an extraordinarily handsome man, and it is a matter of record that he was eagerly sought after by prostitutes and that when he bestowed his favors, the usual procedure was reversed and he collected a fee. He even sold female admirers his photograph for 25¢; for his favorite harlots only, a photo of him in the nude was available for 50¢. It was quite common for clients of some of the city's most popular prostitutes to find themselves making love under an autographed picture of the King of the Hoodlums. Riley would have new photos taken of himself each week and on Mondays he would make a picture-selling tour of the red-light areas, his merchandise in a black satchel slung over his shoulder.

In 1871 Riley butted the wrong victim, a 22-year-old carriage painter named John Jordon, who took two vicious butts to the stomach and then pulled a revolver and shot Riley in the chest. Doctors at the county hospital said the wounds were fatal but Riley recovered. Unfortunately, his health was poor thereafter, and he lost the strength and beauty the harlots admired. He also lost his standing with the hoodlums and degenerated to a common housebreaker. In 1876 he was caught breaking into a house and sent to San Quentin Prison for 15 years. After that San Francisco's King of the Hoodlums disappeared.

RINGO, John (?1844-1882): Outlaw

Little is known of the early life of outlaw Johnny Ringo, who, with the possible exception of Curly Bill Brocius, was the most dangerous member of the Clanton gang, the bitter foe of the Earps in Tombstone, Arizona Territory.

Ringo, whose real name may have been Ringgold, is believed to have been the black sheep of a leading Southern family and is definitely known to have been college educated. Cultured, able to quote Shakespeare at length (in their desire to make the "good guys"—the Earps—good and the "bad guys"—the Clantons—bad, some historians of the Tombstone legend transferred this literary attribute to Doc Holliday), Ringo epitomized the ideal gentleman outlaw. He was known to be a man of his word, and when he promised to surrender to the law, he did so. However, none of these laudable characteristics prevented Ringo from being a murderous bandit. His record, though shadowy at times, included participation in Texas' bloody Hoodoo War in the 1870s, during which he did his share of killing as a sidekick of the notorious Scott Cooley.

Later, as a member of the Clanton gang, Ringo ran up a string of vicious and often senseless killings. One Louis Hancock came to a bad end in a Tombstone saloon for having the temerity to order beer when Ringo offered to buy him whiskey. Ringo participated in the bloody Guadalupe Canyon Massacre of Mexican silver miners by the Clantons, took part in the attempt on the life of Virgil Earp and was the lookout when Morgan Earp was assassinated. He was the only member of the Clantons with the nerve to challenge Doc Holliday to a one-on-one duel, a confrontation prevented by the arrival of lawmen. In the Tombstone area's twisted political setup, Ringo was a sheriff's deputy in the posse that chased the Earps out of the county for the last time.

Despite his rather checkered and deadly career, Ringo won a sort of admiration from Tombstonians as a brooding, silent and tragic loner with a past that probably outshone his present and future. That future seemed to be short in 1882 when Ringo turned more dependent and started drinking heavily. Early in July of that year, Ringo went off on a long drinking bout with Frank Leslie, a gunman with a reputation for killing a number of Clanton supporters. The two had not been on friendly terms earlier, particularly after Ringo had asked Leslie, "Frank, did you ever shoot someone not in the back?"

Ringo was soon found dead in Turkey Creek Canyon with a bullet in his head. Leslie was a prime suspect, although offi-

cially the death was classified as a suicide, an odd verdict since no powder burns were found around the entrance wound. Pony Deal, an outlaw friend of Ringo's, felt the likely murderer was a gambler named Johnny Behind the Deuce and shot him to death in retribution. Years later, Wyatt Earp claimed he had killed Ringo for his involvement in the plots against his brothers, but most historians have written off Earp's claim as the words of a "blowhard" who was in Colorado when Ringo died. In any event, the true story of Ringo's demise remains as steeped in mystery as much of his earlier life.

See also: *Joseph Isaac "Ike" Clanton, Guadalupe Canyon Massacre, Johnny Behind the Deuce, Frank "Buckskin" Leslie.*

RITTER, Halsted Lockwood (1868-?): Impeached judge.

As of 1981, the last federal judge to be impeached and removed from office by Congress was Halsted L. Ritter, who had supplemented his $17,300 salary with kickbacks.

After appointment to the bench by President Calvin Coolidge in 1929 despite bipartisan opposition, Ritter continued to practice law, receiving a $2,000 fee from the Mulford Realty Corp., which had considerable holdings in his Florida judicial district. He gave his former law partner, A. L. Rankin, an excessive $75,000 fee for acting as receiver for a bankrupt Palm Beach hotel. In return, Ritter accepted $4,500. Other kickbacks on receiverships netted him at least $7,500. In one case he made his sister-in-law manager of another bankrupt hotel and then received free room and board as well as valet service there. Ritter, however, neglected to report any of these "supplementals" on his income tax returns and was eventually charged with tax evasion for the years 1929 and 1930.

In 1936 Ritter became the 13th government official in American history to be impeached by the House of Representatives, which passed seven articles of impeachment against him. In the Senate, he escaped conviction on the first charge by one vote. Acquitted of the next five articles by larger margins, he was then narrowly convicted of an omnibus charge, including major features of the previous six charges, and thus removed from office. But by a unanimous vote of the Senate he specifically was not "disqualified from holding any office of honor, trust, or profit under the United States."

Ignoring the order of the Senate, Ritter refused to leave his office and had to be ousted by a federal marshal. He took his case to the U.S. Court of Claims, declaring his ouster unconstitutional because he had been convicted on a composite charge but cleared on the individual counts. His petition was denied. Ritter faded into obscurity thereafter and no public announcement was made of his death, which apparently occurred some time in the 1950s.

See also: *Judicial Corruption.*

RIVERBOAT Gamblers

During the heyday of the riverboat on American waterways in the mid-19th century, it was estimated there were between

2,000 and 2,500 riverboat gamblers plying their trade. The first of the breed had appeared along the Mississippi near the beginning of the century. Far from the courtly gentlemen of Hollywood legend, they were tough, slovenly dressed characters who serviced the rugged flatboat sailors of the day both ashore and afloat. These gamblers were murderous types who would often kill those they couldn't cheat.

When the first steam packets appeared on the river to cater to higher strata of society, professional gamblers were not wanted and were usually heaved over the side or stranded on some lonely shore or sandbar. Slowly, the boat operators began to realize that during a long card session, players tended to spend huge sums on liquid refreshments. During one poker game in 1858 the liquor tab for the players came to $791.50. Soon, the gamblers, now often done up in exquisite finery, were welcomed with great respect and many owner-captains would not cast off until they were sure there was one aboard.

There is little doubt that some gamblers paid off captains for the privilege of being allowed to practice their art. Naturally, such overhead required most card sharks to ensure that winning wasn't left to mere luck or skill. One contemporary expert on the subject estimated that of the 2,000-odd gamblers, he could think of only four who were honest all the time.

Tom Ellison, a gambler turned honest in his later years, said:

> I've seen fellows pick every card in a pack, and call it without missing once. I've seen them shuffle them one for one all through from top to bottom, so that they were in the same position after a dozen shuffles that they were in at first. They'd just flutter them up like a flock of quail and get the aces, kings, queens, jacks and tens all together as easy as pie. A sucker had no more chance against those fellows than a snowball in a red-hot oven. They were good fellows, free with their money as water, after scheming to bust their heads to get it. A hundred didn't bother them any more than a chew of tobacco would you.

Ellison told of a planter who lost

> his whole tobacco crop in one night and get up and never mind it particularly. Many a time I've seen a game player just skin off his watch and ring and studs and play them in. Men often lost their goods playing in their way bills. I've seen them betting a bale of cotton at a crack, and it wasn't at all uncommon to hear an old planter betting off his Negroes on a good hand. Every man who ever ran on the river knows that these old planters used to play in their lady servants, valuing them all the way from $300 to $1,500. I saw a little colored boy stand up at $300 to back his master's faith in a little flush that wasn't any good on earth.

Few riverboat gamblers exercised their dishonesty alone. They either paired up or operated in groups of up to half a dozen. Often, one member of a crooked combination would disembark at a stop to be replaced by another gambler coming aboard there, thus allaying any suspicions that might be building up among the victims. A common procedure would be for a confederate to stand among the interested spectators and signal his partners what cards the suckers held. This trickery, known as "iteming," might be achieved by puffing on a cigar

or by scratching certain parts of the anatomy to indicate certain hands. One such confederate used a walking stick as a signal, indicating various hands by the angle of the stick. Perhaps the most ingenious was a gambler's partner who played coded snatches of music on a violin while masquerading as a half-wit.

Among the top riverboat gamblers were Canada Bill Jones, perhaps the greatest practitioner of three-card monte; George Devol; and Dick Hargraves, the richest of the square gamblers. Another honest gambler was John Powell, the beau ideal of his river colleagues. Tall, handsome and always strikingly, though not vulgarly, dressed, Powell was well educated and a close friend of Andrew Jackson and Stephen A. Douglas. Although he turned down a chance to run for Congress from his native state of Missouri, Powell took a keen interest in politics. His advice was sought frequently by Louisiana politicians when he was ashore in the lavish home he maintained in New Orleans.

Powell once took part in a three-day poker game aboard the steamer *Atlantic*, during which he won more than $50,000 from a rich Louisiana planter named Jules Devereaux. It was said that in his most successful years—from 1845 to 1858—he netted at least $100,000 a year. In the fall of 1858 Powell won $8,000 from a young Englishman, who turned up on deck the next morning, shook hands with fellow passengers and, putting a pistol to his temple, blew his brains out. The gambler was so unnerved by the event that he sent the $8,000 and the lad's luggage (he had won that as well) to his family in England and retired from gambling for an entire year. When he returned to the river, his luck and skill deserted him and he went through his entire fortune within a year. Powell died in extreme poverty a few years later, a symbol to other gamblers of the perils of a guilty conscience.

See also: *James Ashby, George Devol, Dick Hargraves, William "Canada Bill" Jones.*

RIZZO, Frank L. (1920-   ): Philadelphia police chief and mayor

A longtime police chief who became mayor of Philadelphia for eight years, Frank Rizzo built, nurtured and protected that city's police force until some regarded it as one of the toughest and most effective crime-fighting forces in the country while others, including officials of the Justice Department, regarded it as "the most brutal in the nation."

The son of a policeman, Rizzo left high school without graduating and joined the force in 1943, becoming—in his own words—"the toughest cop in America." Immensely popular with the public because of his outspoken calls for law and order, he moved steadily up the ladder to the post of commissioner and in 1972 became mayor, the first incumbent police chief ever elected to that office.

Although the department then came under the nominal rule of Joseph F. O'Neill, in fact it remained the exclusive province of Rizzo. "When it comes to the police department," Rizzo said, "I'll be there to defend them even if they make errors in judgment. Nobody will get to them while I'm mayor." Included among the "errors in judgment" charged against the police was a record of interrogating suspects in a way that produced confessions out of innocent men. According to sworn testimony, police interrogators would put a telephone book on a suspect's head and then hammer on it. In some cases questioning would continue for 24 hours straight, with many suspects allegedly beaten in the back, ribs, kidneys and genitals.

A few of Rizzo's pithy comments reflected his regime's attitude toward law and order. When a mentally retarded white man was proved to have been wrongfully convicted of murder because of police intimidation and beatings, Rizzo kept the guilty officers on duty, saying, "These were good men who did nothing wrong." When 10 policemen broke nightsticks over a prostrate black man, Rizzo was led to a whimsical observation: "It's easy to break some of these nightsticks nowadays." During a religious pilgrimage to Rome in the midst of student riots, he drew worldwide attention when he invited Italian officials to send some of their police to Philadelphia for training on such disturbances. "We'll show them how to eat those guys up," he said, adding in Calabrese, *"Spacco il capo!"* Roughly translated the phrase means, "Break their heads."

Re-elected easily to a second term in 1975, Rizzo moved in 1978 to put through an amendment to the city charter that would have allowed him to run for a third term the following year. At first, his proposal was considered a shoo-in, but as the campaign progressed, the issue of police brutality came to the fore. Rizzo's proposal lost by two to one.

See also: *Deep Nightstick.*

ROACH Guards: Early 19th century New York City gang

Originally formed in the 1820s as a street gang that protected certain New York liquor sellers in the Five Points section, the Roach Guards were Irish toughs who would often rampage through the city committing robberies and murders.

When not working as murderers and thieves, the Roach Guards fought pitched battles with other gangs, especially the hated Bowery Boys and the Dead Rabbits, the latter being an offshoot of their own organization. The Roach Guards, who could call on perhaps 500 warriors, even had a battle uniform consisting of pantaloons with a blue stripe. The Dead Rabbits were a group of dissidents who wanted a more-disciplined attitude toward organized crime activities and more onslaughts into the Bowery area. Of about equal size, the two gangs fought many great "slugger battles," but whenever some hated outside gang would invade the Five Points, they would immediately unite against the new threat. The Roach Guards started to decline in importance in the 1850s and failed to survive the Civil War as an important gang.

See also: *Dead Rabbits.*

ROAD Agent Spin: Gunman's trick

A Western gunman's deadly deception when surrendering his shooting iron, the "road agent spin," or "border roll," involved extending the weapon butt first but keeping the index finger in the guard and suddenly spinning the gun back into firing position. It was not an easy maneuver and many who tried fumbled it and lost their lives in the process.

Perhaps the most famous feat of this type—real or imaginary—involved the notorious Texas killer Wes Hardin and Marshal Wild Bill Hickok of Abilene. According to the legend, Hickok found Hardin and some buddies playing tenpins in a bowling alley. Seeing the the Texan was wearing pistols in defiance of a local ordinance, Hickok ordered Hardin to surrender them, at the same time drawing his own six-gun.

"I said all right," Hardin recalled later, "and pulled them out of the scabbard, but while he was reaching for them, I reversed them and whirled them over on him with the muzzles in his face, springing back at the same time. I told him to put his pistols up, which he did."

Hickok's more ardent admirers were enraged that someone could make such a claim about their hero, but the story may well have been true. Hardin apparently wore his guns quite a bit in Abilene and evidently the marshal never, or never after that incident, attempted to take them from him.

ROBBER'S Roost: Western outlaw hideout

Along with Hole in the Wall and Brown's Hole, Robber's Roost was one of the nearly impregnable hideouts used by the bandits of the West.

Located in Wayne County in southeastern Utah, Robber's Roost lay high on a plateau on the summit of the San Rafael Swell. Bounded on the east by the Green River, it was a desolate and arid place with no more than four or five springs where water could be obtained. Other than the Green River, there were only two routes into Robber's Roost: by way of Hanksville and the other from Dandy Crossing. It was futile for lawmen to enter Robber's Roost, because their quarry, perched in their vantage point, would have too much advance warning and the chances of even a large party making it out safely were poor. Bandits could enter the roost, lick their wounds and plan new jobs in safety.

Among the many leading bandits who often made Robber's Roost home were Butch Cassidy, the Sundance Kid, Black Jack Ketchum, Elza Lay, Bob Lee, George Curry, O. C. Hanks, Harry Tracy, Dave Lant and the Logans of Missouri.

See also: *Hole in the Wall.*

ROBERT'S Hill Stagecoach Robbery: Biggest holdup until Great Brink's Robbery

Stagecoach robberies were common in the Old West, but the really successful jobs, including the greatest of all, were the holdups of "six-horse limiteds" carrying gold dust—a cargo that shippers tried to keep secret—to the mint in San Francisco.

A special 10-horse limited belonging to the Oregon and California Stage Co. left Jacksonville, Oregon Territory in May 1857 carrying the almost unheard-of sum of $500,000 in gold dust. The company's deception, or attempted deception, was even more elaborate than usual in such cases: while the stage was scheduled to arrive in San Francisco, it would instead head for Portland, and from there the cargo, and the fooled passengers as well, would be sent on by boat to San Francisco.

The added horsepower would make the stage almost immune to road agents trying to catch it in the open expanse of the Rogue River Valley, especially since it would be driven by the legendary Jack Montgomery, just about the best driver in the business. As added protection, extra guards had joined the stage outside of Jacksonville, so as not to attract attention. The only danger would be in hill country, where an ambush was possible.

By the time the stage thundered towards Robert's Hill in the middle of the night, only 10 minutes away from the Mountain House Stage Station, Montgomery and the guards relaxed. The road on Robert's Hill was too narrow to allow for an ambush; and once down the hill the stage would again be in open country and unstoppable under Montgomery's drive.

But at the bottom a band of road agents waited while one of the gang climbed high above the road. As the stage passed beneath him, the man detonated a large explosive charge that set off an avalanche of rock and dirt, burying the horses. Montgomery managed to save his own life by dropping the reins, kicking the boot cover loose, drawing his knife and cutting the driver's belt—all in one motion. He leaped clear and tumbled down a steep grade, a lighted cigar still clenched in his teeth. His shotgun rider was a bloody, mangled corpse and the hind-boot guard was thrown clear but left unconscious. Three of the passengers were killed while the rest were also knocked unconscious.

As the road agents charged up Robert's Hill, only Montgomery was in any shape to offer resistance. As the driver later revealed, he fired until he ran out of bullets and then he fell silent, as several road agents came down the grade looking for him. One stumbled over him in the darkness, and the pair struggled until Montgomery jammed his still burning cigar into the man's eye. As the bandit screamed in agony, Montgomery pulled a knife from his boot and plunged it between the man's shoulder blades. The stage driver then tossed himself further down the grade. The other outlaws found their comrade and threw him across one of the team mules they had brought to haul off the gold.

By the time Montgomery reached the stage station and a posse could be mounted, it was dawn and the road agents and their mules had vanished. The bandits' trail lasted only a short distance before the mule tracks divided in several directions, moving into hill country. The gold or parts of it could have gone in all, several, few or only one of the directions the tracks indicated; there was no way of telling and the robbers got away clean.

The Robert's Hill holdup galvanized the citizens of Oregon and, as much as any single event, led to the formation of the famed Oregon Vigilantes. Far more secretive than other vigilante groups, the Oregon Vigilantes were noted for meting out swift and terrible punishment and never revealing their deeds. There are few written accounts of their acts. Rumor had it, however, that the Robert's Hill bandits were eventually caught and punished.

According to the story, in 1869 some Umpqua Indians reported to the vigilantes that a group of suspicious-looking whites were holed up in a cave in the Siskiyou Mountains. The vigilantes caught them and a fair amount of gold dust in their possession. The suspects claimed they had accidently stumbled across the hoard in the cavern. However, according to a long-held theory, the road agents had buried their loot in several spots and would return from time to time to retrieve parts of it. What really doomed this band was the fact that one of them was missing an eye, as though it had been burned out, perhaps with a cigar. That was proof enough for the vigilantes and they strung up their prisoners on the spot.

The story may well be apocryphal. What is certain is that the Robert's Hill stage robbery was the largest of its kind and held the record as the most lucrative armed holdup in this country for 90 years until the Brink's job in 1947.

ROBLES, Richard: See Janice Wylie.

ROGERS, Earl (1870-1922): Defense lawyer

One of the most colorful defense lawyers ever to grace a courtroom, Earl Rogers compiled an enviable record of 183 acquittals in murder cases against less than a score of convictions and became known as an attorney who had a penchant for freeing murderers. In California courtroom circles the saying went, "A guilty man is guilty unless he hires Earl Rogers." Some prosecutors, no doubt in part out of pique, insisted that around the turn of the century Rogers seldom went to a murder trial without having bribed at least one juror on a murder panel. When he secured an acquittal in a case that the prosecution had considered ironclad, an assistant prosecutor is said to have cracked, "The bastard has bought all twelve this time!"

Rogers did play fast and loose with facts and evidence and could drive judges and prosecutors wild by the way he juggled testimony; swiped or switched incriminating exhibits; and went through fits of anger, passion, hysteria or ecstasy, as the situation required, to divert the attention of the jury from important elements of the case. However, he was also a brilliant lawyer, quick, sharp, resourceful. When he was sober, which probably was less than half the time, he was virtually unbeatable. As Bill Fallon, at the time noted as the Great Mouthpiece of Broadway, put it, "Even when he's drunk, Earl Rogers is better than any other stone-sober lawyer in the whole damned country."

Fallon no doubt was attracted to his West Coast colleague because of their great similiarities. He, like Rogers, was addicted to the good life, liquor and the ladies, and both had the oratorical ability to cast a spell over jurors. But Rogers went one step better than Fallon: he really studied his cases and his juries. He was a pioneer in compiling files on prospective veniremen and generally knew plenty about a prospective juror before he even asked him a question. Often he ingratiated himself with a juror-to-be by asking him not a single question, as though he found the man's appearance and demeanor most acceptable.

Rogers had a knack for throwing the prosecution off the scent by sometimes querying a prospective juror about a phase of the case that he intended to ignore. While the prosecution scurried about gathering facts on that element, Rogers struck elsewhere.

There never was a client too venal for Rogers to defend or for whom he would not try every trick, honest or not, to win an acquittal. Once, Rogers conned a jury into releasing a procurer who had murdered his wife, and then brushed away the man's ardent thanks. "Get away from me, you slimey pimp," he said. "You know you're guilty as hell!"

Another of his defendants was a man named William Alford, who had shot and killed a prominent attorney, Jay E. Hunter, after an altercation in an office building corridor. Alford, who was seen by several witnesses standing over the victim with the smoking gun in his hand, quickly confessed to the police. Then Rogers, a young lawyer still in his twenties and much in need of clients, entered the case. He had not graduated from law school, having first worked as a reporter on several California papers and then served an apprenticeship with a law firm. Admitted to the bar in 1897, he took cases most lawyers refused to handle, considering them lost causes. Rogers quickly gained a reputation by pulling miracles in a number of them, including the Alford case. Preparing for the trial, he studied medical texts day and night and consulted with a number of doctors about a man's insides. He even visited a hospital to examine a human stomach in a glass jar.

Alford retracted his confession. It had, Rogers announced, been beaten out of him. The lawyer did not bother to dispute the prosecution's contention that bad blood had existed for some time between the victim and the defendant. What he demanded was that the victim's stomach be brought into court. Why was that necessary? the judge asked.

"Why, to prove that the state's case is false. My client, Your Honor, was not standing when he shot Hunter. He was lying face up on the floor. Hunter knocked him down with the heavy cane he always carried and was leaning over beating him when my client shot in self-defense."

When the victim's stomach was presented in court, Rogers demonstrated to the somewhat awed jurors how the bullet could have entered the victim's navel and traveled upward through the intestines if the man had been bent over administering a beating to his poor client. The prosecution made the mistake of trying to counter Rogers' claims, so that in the end the jury was so fascinated about how the killing could have occurred that it did not consider how it had occurred. Self-defense was the verdict.

Rogers had his own way of riding roughshod over opposing witnesses, in an era when restraints on lawyers were somewhat less strictly enforced than in later years. Often, he would ask a witness if it were not a fact that he was in the pay of the district attorney. When the witness indignantly denied the accusation, Rogers would then mention a name and ask if it was not true that the witness had been convicted under that alias in another state on some charge in "the year of 1904."

The witness would scream a denial, and Rogers would say: "My mistake. I meant 1905."

Another denial and Rogers would ask, "1906?" Yet another denial and Rogers would smile. "1907?"

The point was driven home to the jury that somehow the witness was unsavory, without the presentation of any facts to substantiate the implication.

One time, Rogers accused William J. Burns, founder of the Burns International Detective Agency, of pulling a sword out of a cane as he was cross-examining him. Rogers was standing near Burns and Burns shifted in the witness chair, causing the cane he carried to rise in the air a bit.

"Your Honor!" Rogers shouted. "The witness has a sword in that cane!"

Burns was stunned, too stunned to respond as Rogers continued: "Make him open that cane, Your Honor! Make him take out the sword and give it to the bailiff."

Burns surrendered his cane, finally finding words to deny the preposterous charge.

Rogers shrugged. "My mistake," he said. "But he does carry a sword in a cane that looks just like this one." Then Rogers glanced at the jury. He had scored points with a very silly charge.

Rogers was just as flamboyant in his private life as he was in court. He affected wine-red dressing gowns. In restaurants he selected his own steaks and mixed his own salads. He used perfume. By 1911, however, he was more a drinker than a bon vivant, but his reputation was still great enough that Clarence Darrow hired him as his main defense counsel when he was brought to trial in the aftermath of the *Los Angeles Times* bombing case, in which 21 persons had died. Darrow was accused of having his associate, Bert Franklin, offer a $5,000 bribe to a juror. Under pressure from Burns detectives, Franklin, a former law officer who had set up an agency to investigate prospective jurors, said he had done so on orders from Darrow.

The case reeked of frame-up, and Rogers jumped at the chance to defend the great Darrow. "I've been slipping somewhat," he told acquaintances, "and I need Darrow almost as much as he needs me. Selecting me to defend the nation's acknowledged premier criminal lawyer will eventually place me in Darrow's class."

As it was, Darrow got off, but it is a moot question as to who was responsible. Darrow and Rogers feuded constantly about courtroom tactics and the former became upset with Rogers because of his constant drinking and the fact that he acted like a lawyer who considered his client guilty. By the end of the trial, Darrow had taken over much of his own defense and made an eloquent 1½ day summation in his own behalf that is generally credited with winning him an acquittal. Yet Rogers added a terse few sentences to the jury that obviously made a most telling point. He said:

Will you tell me how any sane, sensible man who knows anything about the law business—and this defendant has been in it for thirty-five years—could make himself go to a detective and say to him: just buy all the jurors you want. I put my whole life, my reputation, I put everything I have into your hands. I trust you absolutely. I never knew you until two or three months ago and I don't know much about you now. But there you are. Go to it.

That made for a solid one-two punch that brought victory, but the two lawyers parted less than friends. Thereafter, Rogers scored more courtroom wins but took some losses as well, especially when he was "on the sauce."

Late in 1918 his second wife left him because of his drinking, the second spouse to do so, and the rest of the way was downhill. Sometimes, Rogers had funds after a legal victory but more often he did not. In one of his last notable wins, he cleared a man charged with willfully avoiding the draft during World War I. The man had gone to a professional nurse who was a scout for an optometrist who specialized in supplying glasses that weakened rather than improved the sight of wealthy cowards.

The optometrist and the nurse were tried along with the alleged draft dodger but the pair had their own counsel. When Rogers finished with the jury, they agreed with him that it was not his client's fault he went to an eye man who was so incompetent that he was fitted incorrectly. Why he had gone to the optometrist to get his vision improved so he could fight for his country. The jury cleared the defendant but convicted both the optometrist and the nurse.

In Rogers' last trial he lost his client to the gallows. A few days later, he was picked out of the gutter dead drunk and sent to an institution. When he came out, he opened a shabby little law office but was evicted for nonpayment of rent. In February 1922 Rogers died. He was living in a cheap lodging house on the edge of Los Angeles' Chinatown. A few minutes before he died, he had bummed a quarter from the house clerk to get a drink.

See also: *Clarence Darrow.*

ROGERS, George W. (1898-1958): Hero and murderer

Few men have gone from such heights of heroism to depths of villainy as dramatically as George Rogers. He first achieved national fame when the luxury liner *Morro Castle* caught fire enroute back to New York from Havana, Cuba on September 8, 1934. One hundred thirty-four passengers perished. Rogers, the ship's radioman, sent the SOS that brought help and saved many lives, remaining at his post with flames licking close to him and his shoes actually starting to smoke. He suffered superficial but very painful burns. When Rogers returned to his hometown of Bayonne, N.J., he was greeted by a brass band, heaped with flowers, embraced by the mayor and presented with a $200 gold medal.

Rogers was hired by the Bayonne police force as an assistant to Lt. Vincent J. Doyle, chief of the police radio bureau. Four years later, he was on his way to prison after seriously wounding Doyle with a planted bomb in an effort to take over his job. Labeled a "psychopathic personality" by a psychiatrist, Rogers got 12 to 20 years. In 1942 he was released from prison because his skills as a radio technician were needed by the armed forces to aid the war effort. However, once the services got a look at Rogers' record, they refused to take him. Never-

George Rogers (right) emerged as the hero in the *Morro Castle* tragedy, having to be dragged from his wireless key aboard the burning ship. He testified against William Warms (left), the acting captain, and the chief engineer, both of whom were sentenced to prison but subsequently had their verdicts reversed. Later evidence also pointed to Rogers as the real villain in the ship fire.

theless, the disgraced hero was permitted to remain on parole.

In sentencing Rogers for the attack on Lt. Doyle, the judge accused him of having "the mind of a fiend," and after his release the former hero went about proving him right. In 1953 in Bayonne Rogers murdered 83-year-old William Hummel, to whom he owed $7,500, and Hummel's 58-year-old unmarried daughter. Just before the killings, Hummel had been pressing him for the money because he was preparing to retire to Florida. Hummel had drawn his savings from a bank and had $2,400 in his home when he and Rogers had an argument about the debt. Rogers picked up a footstool and crushed the old man's skull with it. He then went upstairs and did the same to Hummel's daughter, who was unaware of what had happened.

Well-known to the Bayonne police, Rogers, who had been deeply in debt just before the murders, was quickly identified as the slayer of the Hummels when he went on a spending spree with the stolen $2,400. For the second time Rogers was sent to the New Jersey State Prison at Trenton, this time for life, which proved to be a little over four years. He died there of a heart attack on January 10, 1958. Obituary writers at the time felt obliged to repeat the facts about his heroism aboard the *Morro Castle*, but a 1972 study of the disaster, *Shipwreck: The Strange Fate of the Morro Castle* by Gordon Thomas and Max Morgan Witts, produced some very damning evidence which indicated that Rogers, the much-acclaimed hero, may well have been the villain behind it all. They suggested he had poisoned the ship's captain and then started the fatal fire with a small time bomb. His supposed heroism at the radio, according to their version, had been nothing more than a cover-up.

ROGERS, Mary Cecilia (1820-1841): Murder victim

Twenty-one-year-old Mary Cecilia Rogers was a celebrated New York murder victim in 1841 who gained immortal fame as the model for the victim in Edgar Allan Poe's classic story *The Mystery of Marie Roget*. Mary, a beautiful woman, worked as a clerk in a tobacco shop and it seemed that Poe and several other famous literary lights patronized the place just to exchange a few words or a smile with her. Among them were James Fenimore Cooper and Washington Irving. Fitz-Green Halleck was so taken with her that he wrote a poem to her loveliness.

On Sunday morning July 25, Mary left her mother's boarding house on Nassau Street to visit her sister. Three days later, her body was found in the Hudson River near Hoboken. The case was never solved, although there were several theories about the murder. According to one popular version, Mary had been abducted, raped and strangled by one or more unknown assailants. Another theory had her going aboard a ferry to Hoboken with "a dark complexioned young man," perhaps a naval officer, who choked her to death for some unexplained

reason. Yet another theory was that she had died during an illegal abortion and her body had been dumped in the river. An autopsy performed by a coroner indicated she had been sexually attacked several times just prior to her death and before that time she had been "of chaste character." Later, the coroner was to say the autopsy had been rushed and not performed under optimum conditions and that some of his findings might have been wrong. Exactly which ones it was never made clear.

Very little was revealed by the so-called police investigation of the affair. First, the New York police didn't even want to investigate the murder because the body had been found in New Jersey and was thus none of their affair. New Jersey felt the body had simply been dumped there and it was New York's problem. Such was the sorry state of the police system at the time. The city had no real crime-fighting forces. At night, the streets were patrolled by leatherheads, who were little more than night watchmen and not even very effective at that, earning a little over $1 a day. During the day protection was provided by roundsmen, who were unsuccessful stevedores, wagoneers, laborers and porters and certainly not criminologists. They got no salary at all, making their living from the fees they received serving legal papers and from the rewards they might get from robbery victims whose property they recovered. Murder cases got short shrift from the roundsmen since there was no profit in them unless the city or some private party posted a reward.

In the case of Mary Cecilia Rogers, the newspapers caused such a storm of protest that the roundsmen were forced to make an investigation. Not surprisingly, they made no arrests. The closest they came to a solution was bringing in for questioning a young married man who had picked up a girl, taken her to Staten Island, caused her to miss the last ferry back by manipulating her watch and then made some advances. The young lady spurned him, and he left her peevish with frustration. After the murder was revealed, he told a friend he feared the girl might have been Mary Cecilia Rogers and that he was fleeing the city because he didn't wish to get involved. He was apprehended and returned to New York, but the real lady of that misadventure came forward and cleared him, quite proud that the newspapers had duly informed their readers of her most honorable behavior.

A year after the murder Poe published *Marie Roget,* setting the story in Paris. He solved the Roget murder with some brilliant deductive processes that had little relevance to the Rogers case, although several of the characters were clearly copied from real life. Later on, Poe's editors appended a footnote to the story claiming that the author's version was fully confirmed in the Rogers case by two subsequent confessions. In fact, there never were any confessions worthy of belief. Over the years interest in the case was revived periodically whenever a principal or assumed principal died or otherwise came to public attention. When Mary's employer in the cigar store died, it was revealed that he had said he knew the identity of her killer. But it turned out Mary's ghost had been the source of his information and the octogenarian was more than a touch senile.

While the Mary Cecilia Rogers case remained unsolved, it had an important impact on New York. The stir over the lack of effective police protection and the inefficiency of the rounds-man system sparked a reform movement. By 1845 the police force was entirely reconstituted. It did not become a totally efficient operation at once, but at least a start was made in the development of a professional police system.

See also: *Leatherheads, Roundsmen.*

ROGER'S Barracks: Underworld refuge and vice area

In the 1850s a diminutive Englishman from Yorkshire, Roger Plant, came up with the idea that what Chicago needed was the Compleat Underworld Refuge, which he set about establishing at the northeast corner of Wells and Monroe streets. He started with just a single two-story house and then expanded straight down the block, adding one rookery after another until he had what a journalist of the day called the "very core of corruption." By the mid-1860s Plant's dives lined both sides of the street for almost a block. The police came to call the conglomeration Roger's Barracks. Journalist Frederick Francis Cook described it as "one of the most talked about if not actually one of the wickedest places on the continent" and as "a refuge for the very nethermost strata of the underworld—the refuse of the Bridewell."

A tunnel led from Roger's Barracks under Wells Street to the various underworld strongholds between that street and the Chicago River. All sorts of stolen goods were funneled through it and out the various dives. It was said that the underworld's first bomb was manufactured in a room in the barracks, leading the *Chicago Times* to comment in December 1870, "Such a discovery in a civilized community seems almost incredible, but there is not the slightest doubt of its truth."

Plant collected exorbitant rents for making his premises available for such nefarious purposes, but he also garnered considerable revenues from so-called straight rackets, including dance halls, brothels and deadfalls, i.e., saloons that specialized in robbing strangers. Special cubicles were rented out to streetwalkers, male degenerates and procurers, who would have young girls raped in the cells by a half-dozen men as a preparation for their assignment to bordellos.

Plant weighed barely over 100 pounds but was known as a vicious fighter. Although always armed with knife, pistol and bludgeon, his favorite weapon was his own teeth, which he would readily use on a foe's ears or nose with maiming efficiency. The only person Plant could not control was his wife, a fearsome creature of 250 pounds who would often pick him up with one hand and spank him with the other. Mrs. Plant ran the family's brothel interests and lent a hand herself during peak hours. She also produced an estimated 15 children, all of whom were cunning little rascals credited by journalists with being able to pick a pocket almost before they could walk.

Roger's Barracks was seldom bothered by the police because, as Cook recorded, "Roger paid his toll with exemplary regularity." By 1870 Plant had collected a fortune, and he abruptly shuttered all his establishments and moved to the country to become a gentleman of leisure and patron of the turf. The Plant children, however, appear to have carried on the criminal tradition of the family, several finding their way onto the police blotters for robbery and sundry other crimes while in their teens. In 1894 English journalist William T. Stead published the *Black List* of Chicago property, which named Roger Plant, Jr. as the operator of three saloons and two bordellos and listed two sisters, Daisy and Kitty Plant, as the operators of adjoining brothels on South Clark Street. It was said that a secret passage allowed harlots to pass from one of these establishments to the other as needed and that it was quite possible a customer venturing from one place to the next might well find himself being entertained by the same female clad in a different colored wig.

ROOSEVELT, Theodore (1858-1919): Would-be assassination victim

On October 14, 1912 Theodore Roosevelt, then running for the presidency as the Bull Moose candidate, left a dinner at Milwaukee's Hotel Gilpatrick to deliver a campaign speech at the Milwaukee Auditorium. As he entered an open car, a plump, short little man with receding light brown hair stepped to within six feet of him and fired a .38 Police Positive. The bullet hit Roosevelt in the chest, and he lurched into the back seat of the car. When the assailant leveled his gun for a second shot, an associate of Roosevelt, Elbert E. Martin, downed him with a flying tackle. Several policemen pounced on the would-be assassin and dragged him off.

Fortunately for Roosevelt, the bullet had penetrated a metal spectacles case in his breast pocket and gone through a 50-page speech manuscript that had been folded twice. It had then smashed into a rib but most of its lethal force had already been spent.

Roosevelt's assailant was a 36-year-old ex-saloon owner named John Nepomuk Schrank, who was suffering from a severe mental illness. On September 15, 1901, the day after William McKinley had died of an assassin's bullet and Roosevelt succeeded to the presidency, Schrank dreamed that McKinley's ghost came to him and accused Roosevelt of the murder. From that day on, Schrank hated Roosevelt, and when Roosevelt dared to run for what Schrank considered to be a third term, he loathed him even more. Then one night in 1912 McKinley's ghost reappeared in Schrank's dreams and begged him not to let a "murderer" become president. Schrank determined to kill Roosevelt, and he left his home in New York and followed the candidate around the country. He got close enough in Chicago and Chattanooga to get in a shot, but he lost his nerve. In Milwaukee his nerve did not fail him.

The bullet had entered Roosevelt's chest so deeply that doctors decided against removing it and the ex-President carried it in his body until his death from natural causes in 1919.

He said the bullet bothered him no more than if he were carrying it in his vest pocket. Schrank was declared insane and spent the rest of his life in mental institutions in Wisconsin. When Theodore Roosevelt died, Schrank said he was sorry because "he was a great American." However, when Franklin Delano Roosevelt ran for a third term in 1940, Schrank was enraged. He told doctors that if he were free he would shoot this Roosevelt also. Schrank died of a heart ailment on September 15, 1943, exactly 42 years after he first dreamed of McKinley's ghost.

ROOSEVELT, Theodore: New York police commissioner

Theodore Roosevelt's reputation as a reformer originated during his three years as a police commissioner in New York City, from 1895 to 1897. He was instrumental in rooting out departmental corruption in the entrenched, politically protected regimes of Chief Inspector Alexander S. Williams and Big Bill Devery, who for a time even held the post of chief of police. Roosevelt won acclaim for starting the process of promotion based on merit rather than politics, a revolutionary idea in 19th century New York. He also pioneered a bicycle squad, a telephonic communications system and special training for new recruits, another unheard-of procedure. Later, Roosevelt lent powerful support to the Pennsylvania State Constabulary, which was to become the model for modern state police organizations. In 1908, as President, he set up the Bureau of Investigation, the forerunner of the FBI.

An admirer of men of action, Roosevelt made some lamentable mistakes, for example, naming Pat Garrett, the killer of Billy the Kid, to the post of customs collector. Garrett was murdered in 1908. In 1905 he had tried to appoint the aging Bat Masterson to the post of U.S. marshal for the Oklahoma Territory. Masterson, who realized the President did not understand that an era had ended, declined the offer as diplomatically as possible. "I am not the man for the job," he wrote Roosevelt, ". . . and if I were marshal some youngster would try to put me out because of my reputation. I would be bait for grown-up kids who had fed on dime novels. I would have to kill or be killed. No sense to that. I have taken my guns off, and I don't ever want to put them on again."

ROSE, Della (1873-?): Dance hall girl and Wild Bunch companion

Della Rose was more of a hard-riding lass than Etta Place, the companion of Butch Cassidy and the Sundance Kid (Harry Longbaugh). She shared a sleeping bag with many a Hole-in-the-Waller after her husband, real or assumed, Edward Bullion, brought her to the outlaw hideout in 1889.

Della was a veteran dance hall girl from the Wyoming Territory. Her real given name was Laura, and she had grown up near Austin, Tex. She had six brothers, at least two of them rustlers, and three sisters. Her mother was an industrious, God-fearing ranch widow who in one letter complained she could not cope with her litter. "I can't stand another minute of it," she wrote Laura, whom she regarded as the prize of the brood, perhaps indicating the extent of her ordeal.

Shortly after taking up residence in the Hole, Della started making the rounds with the boys, Bullion either disappearing or getting lost in the shuffle. Around 1896 she made a permanent alliance with a bank robber named Bill Carver, who had recently joined up with the Wild Bunch. Thereafter, she and Carver rode side by side when the gang went out on raids. This happy partnership ended abruptly in April 1901, when Carver was killed in Sonora, Tex.

Della grieved suitably for some weeks before attaching herself to another Buncher, the Tall Texan, Ben Kilpatrick. This romance was definitely the real thing, but it was to last only until November of that year, when she and Kilpatrick were caught in a St. Louis hotel room with $7,000, what was left of their share of the loot from a Wild Bunch train robbery in Montana. Kilpatrick got sentenced to 15 years and Della to five. Naturally, the Rose of the Bunch promised the Tall Texan she would be waiting for him upon his release. That turned out to be in 1911, but by that time Della Rose had just faded away.

See also: *Ben Kilpatrick*.

ROSE Man Of Sing Sing (1858-1930): Editor and murderer

Warden Lewis E. Lawes once described murderer Charles Chapin as "among the outstanding personalities of Sing Sing's prison population." Chapin has gone down in prison folklore as the Rose Man of Sing Sing. For 20 years before he entered prison, Chapin was known as the most autocratic and tyrannical city editor in the New York newspaper industry, famed as the *New York Evening World* executive who would fire a reporter on Christmas Eve. Once when his men uncovered a murder that had been labeled an accident, he chortled that it had "been a good day. . . . I've started a man on the way to the electric chair."

Staffers repaid Chapin in kind. When he was reported as too ill to come to work one day, a member of his staff, reporter Irvin S. Cobb, volunteered, "I hope it's nothing trivial."

Chapin loved to hobnob with the extremely wealthy and lived far beyond his means; early in his life he ran through $50,000 left to him by his great-uncle, Russell Sage, the famous Wall Street financier. Chapin lost far more than he could afford in the stock market, and in the summer of 1917 he was faced with a mountain of debt. He was also not in the best of health and worried about leaving his wife, Nellie Beebe, penniless. He had been married to her for 35 years and had been an affectionate, though neither a faithful nor a particularly thoughtful, husband.

Chapin took his wife on a trip to Washington, D.C. after borrowing a revolver from an aide to the New York City police commissioner. He planned to put a gardenia in his buttonhole, escort his wife to a musical show and then kill her and himself. However, he lost his nerve and the couple returned to

New York. Somehow, Chapin survived another year on his job while his financial situation worsened. He had owned a car, a yacht, even a couple of race horses, but they were all gone now. He managed to hold off creditors only by borrowing heavily from his employer, Joseph Pulitzer.

Finally, one night in September 1918 he shot Mrs. Chapin in her sleep, putting the revolver to her head as they lay in bed together. In the morning Chapin dressed and set off for Central Park, where he was determined to shoot himself. Instead, he wound up the next day in Prospect Park reading his own press notices after his wife's body had been found. Then he surrendered, telling police: "This is the first time in five years that I have been happy. The sooner I go to the electric chair the better."

Chapin did not get the chair but rather 20 years to life in Sing Sing, where he was to become a most unusual prisoner. He was made editor of the prison newspaper, *The Star of Hope*, later called *The Bulletin*. It became a prison version of the flamboyant *World*, filled with spicy confessions of Sing Sing inmates. Among the typical stories was one of a bigamist named Wilson who had had seven wives at the same time. Chapin urged Wilson to keep his tale "heavy on the human interest; tell 'em all about love." Chapin headlined the account, "The Man with the Seven Wives." Wilson told too much and a stir was created in Albany, the state capital. *The Bulletin* folded, and Chapin was out of his last editorial job. However, he claimed proudly that under his tenure circulation of the prison newspaper had soared.

Warden Lawes kept a file of letters he received about Chapin, few of which were favorable. One read:

> I knew Mr. Chapin long and from a certain angle intimately in the years he was at the *New York World*. That is, I knew intimately the anguished stories of the hundreds and thousands of young writers whose lives he made a living hell. He was the worst curse our reportial craft ever enjoyed. I·used to think him a sort of devil sitting on enthroned power in the *World* office and making Park Row gutters flow red with the blood of ambitious young men. If you enjoy him I hope you keep him long and carefully.

Yet over the years Lawes and his wife and, indeed, the inmates of the prison saw a different Chapin. Although for a time despondent at losing his prison newspaper, he came to the warden with another suggestion, asking that he be allowed to replace the gravel, cinders and crushed rock on some of the prison grounds with "a little garden." Lawes agreed but said there were no funds available. That was no problem for Chapin.

He wrote to garden magazines and soon bone meal, fertilizer, rose plants, tulip bulbs and hundreds of pounds of seed rained down on Sing Sing from manufacturers and suppliers. Chapin grew rose plants, cannas and dahlias all over the prison, even around the death house. Both Ruth Snyder and Judd Gray paused in turn to inhale the fragrance of Chapin's roses before entering the death house in 1928.

Some of Chapin's old co-workers visited him in prison and stared in disbelief at the gardens of the now-famed Rose Man of Sing Sing. Cobb, Arthur Brisbane and others made the trek up the Hudson to visit and marvel at the new Chapin, a man whom scores of convicts now called Uncle Charlie. Horticulturists visited Sing Sing to view Chapin's work. So did Adolph Lewisohn, the philanthropist, who then sent a truck load of plants from his own gardens.

Then in 1930, while a new drainage system was being installed in the prison, a steam shovel gutted much of Chapin's beloved gardens. In *20,000 Years in Sing Sing* Lawes wrote: "I think it affected him deeply. He was never the same. He was suddenly the helpless invalid, unable to carry on."

Chapin died on December 13, 1930. His last words to Lawes were: "I want to die. I want to get it over with."

Lawes got scores of letters from journalists around the country who had once served under Chapin. After his death, none were critical of him. One wrote, "As an old *Evening World* man who owes whatever success he has attained to the fact that he received his early training under the greatest newspaper general in the world, I send you this word in memory of Charles Chapin."

ROSE Of Cimarron: Western outlaw heroine

Fabled in story and song, the Rose of Cimarron provided sundry joys and a touch of glamour to the Oklahoma Territory's Doolin gang. She became a legendary figure following the Battle of Ingalls on September 1, 1893 by going to the aid of her lover, Bitter Creek Newcomb, after he had been downed with a leg wound. Most sources claim she dashed to his side with a new supply of ammunition and/or shielded his body with her own as lawmen tried to finish him off. According to other reports, she picked up a gun and covered Bitter Creek as he hobbled to safety. There are many more versions, some who were there in the thick of the fighting even contending that there was no woman on the scene at all.

Such doubts have never dampened the enthusiasm of the myth makers and balladeers, and they have trotted forth several likely females as the genuine Rose. One was named Rose O'Leary, who has been characterized variously as a tough Western gun moll or a tender angel of mercy. Then again, the Rose of Cimarron was said to have been Rosa Dunn, who at least had some connection with the Doolin gang and supposedly lost her virtue to Bitter Creek Newcomb when she was 12, 13, 14 or 15 years old or thereabouts, according to various chroniclers.

Bitter Creek Newcomb himself gave some credence to the heart-rending tale of the Rose of Cimarron when, some 20 months after the gunfight, on May 2, 1895, the much-hunted outlaw returned to the Dunn Ranch on the Cimarron River to visit with Rosa. Here, the tender tale ends in harsh reality. Bitter Creek was shot dead by Rosa's brothers, who then claimed the $5,000 reward on his head. Rosa went off and married another beau.

See also: *Ingalls, Oklahoma Territory, Battle of; George "Bitter Creek" Newcomb.*

ROSELLI, John (1905-1976): Mafia leader

Like his mentor, Chicago mafia boss Sam Giancana, John Roselli was tied closely, by his own admission, to CIA plans to assassinate Fidel Castro of Cuba, who had closed down the mob's gambling operations in Havana upon taking power. Roselli at the time was running the swank Sans Souci gambling casino in that city. In July 1975 he testified before a special hearing of the Senate Intelligence Committee that he and Giancana had been recruited to kill the Cuban leader, something he looked upon as a "patriotic" endeavor. According to his testimony, both poisoned pills and poisoned cigars had been considered by the CIA, but for some reason the mobsters had bungled the mission. Roselli's testimony came five days after Giancana was murdered in his Oak Park, Ill. home. Apparently, Roselli felt he was safe about implicating the CIA but refused to discuss Mafia matters.

Being one of the more adventurous of the Mafia leaders, Roselli had long been successful at carrying off daring missions. In the late 1930s Roselli, as the Chicago mob's Hollywood man, had extorted $1 million from movie companies by threatening to have a Mafia-controlled stagehands union slow down production. He did three years in prison for that caper but remained a Hollywood luminary, helping to produce some crime films, such as *He Walked by Night*. Despite his past, Roselli made it into the Friars Club, much to the regret of a number of other members. In 1968 he and four others were convicted of swindling a number of Friars, including singer Tony Martin and comedians Phil Silvers and Zeppo Marx, out of some $400,000 in a typical Mafia crooked card game. Observers on an upper floor used peepholes to read the cards the players were holding; they then signaled key information to a confederate in the game, who picked up the messages on equipment he wore in a girdle under his clothes.

After his CIA testimony Roselli laughed at his lawyer's advice to hire a bodyguard. He still apparently was supervising the Chicago mob's gambling interests while living quietly in Plantation, Fla. "Who would want to kill an old man like me?" he said. Whoever did went about it in the classic manner. Sometime in the summer of 1976, he was killed and his body was sealed in an empty 55-gallon oil drum. Heavy chains were wrapped around the drum and holes punched in its sides. It was dumped in the waters off Florida and should have stayed down indefinitely, but decomposition of the body produced gases that lifted the drum to the surface.

See also: *Sam "Momo" Giancana.*

ROSS, Charles Brewster (1870-?): Kidnapping victim

When four-year-old Charley Ross was taken from his Philadelphia home on July 1, 1874 and held for ransom, it was the first case of this type to achieve nationwide notoriety; "poor little Charley Ross" soon became a household phrase.

The boy's wealthy father, Christian K. Ross, received a note demanding $20,000 and immediately contacted the police,

although he had been cautioned not to. Ross then entered into tortuous negotiations with the kidnappers, who set up three separate meetings over the next few months to collect the ransom. The criminals did not keep any of these appointments, apparently because they correctly suspected the police had set traps.

"What happened to poor Charley Ross?" became one of the most haunting and persistent questions of the late 19th century.

Meanwhile, New York City police identified a known criminal, William Mosher, as one of the kidnappers by matching his handwriting with that on the ransom notes. On the night of December 13, 1874, Mosher and another notorious burglar, Joey Douglass, were both fatally wounded while attempting a burglary in Brooklyn. Before dying, Mosher admitted the kidnapping and named Douglass as an accomplice. He would not reveal the whereabouts of the child, however. Suspicion now centered on William Westervelt, an ex-New York policeman with an unsavory reputation. Westervelt was soon identified as the man seen near the Ross home before the crime who had asked numerous questions about the financial worth of Christian K. Ross. Despite this evidence, Westervelt would admit nothing about the kidnapping, even after being found guilty of charges related to the abduction and sentenced to seven years.

Upon his release Westervelt faded into obscurity, but the Ross case would not, despite underworld rumors that Westervelt had definitely been in charge of holding the child and, as the hunt had intensified, had panicked and drowned the boy in the East River. The Ross family spent the next 20 years tracking down leads, spending a fortune on some 500 separate journeys. But the era's most haunting question, "What happened to poor little Charley Ross?" remained unanswered.

William Mosher and Joey Douglas were both shot in a burglary attempt in Brooklyn. Before dying, Mosher admitted the pair had been involved in the Ross kidnapping, but he would not reveal the whereabouts of the child.

ROSS, Mrs. Hannah (c.1880s): Medium

Fake spirit mediums have used many tricks to make "spirits" appear before gullible victims, but none have matched the feat of a noted Boston medium, Mrs. Hannah Ross, in 1887. She actually seemed to make a long-dead baby materialize literally in the flesh. Mrs. Ross would seat herself in a cabinet in a darkened room and call the baby back from the beyond, and sure enough the baby's image would appear at the front of the cabinet. The grieving and awestruck parents of a departed baby would be able not only to see their baby but touch and kiss it as well. The baby would actually appear to be alive. And for good reason, as reporters from a Boston newspaper and the police discovered when they uncovered Mrs. Ross' act. She had a baby's face painted on her breast and would poke her breast through a slit in the curtain on the cabinet. With this exposure of her racket, Mrs. Ross decamped from the Boston area, undoubtedly to ply her trade in another venue.

ROTHSTEIN, Arnold (1882-1928): Gambler and fixer

He was Mr. Big, the Brain, the Big Bankroll, the Man Uptown and the Fixer. Arnold Rothstein was all of that and more, the man to see on Broadway for about a decade and a half until his murder in 1928. Operating strictly in the background, Rothstein may well have been the leading criminal in America at the time, but he always managed to avoid trouble with the law. At various times he bankrolled the operations of such criminal kingpins as Waxey Gordon and Legs Diamond, and he was one of the early tutors of such young underworld types as Lucky Luciano, Meyer Lansky and Frank Costello. He preached to them the virtues of forming alliances independent of ethnic consideration and of remaining behind the scenes to pull the strings and, above all, taught them the ins and outs of the political fix.

Rothstein was known on Broadway as the man who could fix anything. His political and police contacts were the best and he could clear almost any nefarious activity with the right powers. He proved his mettle during Prohibition, when for a fee he would fix almost any bootlegging rap. He was close to Tammany boss Charley Murphy and his heirs. In fact, during the Rothstein years, of the 6,902 liquor-related cases that went before the New York courts, 400 never made it to trial and another 6,074 were dismissed. The largest individual credit for these incredible statistics went, of course, to A. R., as knowing court observers referred to Rothstein.

For a time A. R. was the biggest illegal importer of Scotch whiskey in the country, an activity he often pursued in partnership with Charles A. Stoneham, sportsman and owner of the New York Giants baseball team. Baseball was, in a manner of speaking, one of Rothstein's passions, especially considering his involvement in the so-called Black Sox Scandal in 1919, when several players of the Chicago White Sox succeeded in throwing the World Series to the underdog Cincinnati Reds. It has never been clear whether Rothstein financed the big bribe and betting coup through ex-featherweight boxing champion Abe Attell or turned down the deal when it was offered to him and then, knowing the fix was in, simply bet $60,000 on Cincinnati and won $270,000.

That was always A. R.'s way—staying in the background while taking a major portion of the loot. Realizing early in Prohibition that bootlegging was too big to be dominated by one man or one gang, he took control of the importing racket, the safest part of the business and one in which he could also insulate himself from arrest. He closed deals with European distilleries and made himself immune to gangland assassination—if he was killed, the flow of good liquor would stop. A. R. made himself too valuable to be allowed to die.

He kept the various gangs happy by cutting all of them in for a share of the supplies, especially filling the needs of Luciano and his young associates. Luciano saw firsthand how Rothstein separated himself from personal involvement and paid heed to Rothstein's lectures on the need to remain less visible. It was A. R. who got Luciano to drop the loud dress, which marked, for example, members of Chicago's Capone mob, in favor of the refined attire of a gentleman. It was no simple task. Once, Rothstein told Luciano, "I want you to wear something conservative and elegant, made by a genteel tailor."

Luciano was taken aback. "What the hell are you talkin' about?" he said. "My tailor's a Catholic."

Still, Luciano paid Rothstein a noteworthy compliment: "If Arnold had lived a little longer, he could've made me pretty elegant; he was the best etiquette teacher a guy could ever have—real smooth."

By the mid-1920s Rothstein was probably completely out of the booze racket—selling out for a huge sum—save perhaps for lending money to a bootlegging operation or arranging a fix. He immersed himself in his first love, gambling, operating a number of betting parlors in many of the city's best speakeasies.

For some reason Rothstein seemed to come apart in 1928. Physically, he started to deteriorate, and as a gambler, he suddenly became a heavy loser. From September 8 to 10 A. R. took part in a fabulous poker game with two gamblers from California, Nigger Nate Raymond and Titanic Thompson, and lost $320,000. The story shocked Broadway but not nearly as much as the news that Rothstein then refused to pay up, claiming the game had been fixed. The word that A. R. was welching really shook up the town.

On November 4, 1928 Rothstein sat in Lindy's restaurant making election bets. He wagered almost $600,000 that Herbert Hoover would beat Al Smith and that Franklin Roosevelt would win the governorship. In a few days he would have collected more than enough to pay off his poker losses, and indeed, he could have anyway, since he held assets, mostly in real estate, totaling $3 million. In any event, later that night A. R. was shot to death at the Park Central Hotel.

The prime suspects were Thompson and Raymond. But both of them had perfect alibis and were never prosecuted. Yet on Broadway there was no doubt who had been behind Rothstein's murder.

See also: *Black Sox Scandal.*

ROTTEN Apple Theory: Police corruption

Following any exposure of widespread police corruption a standard defense offered is that such evildoing is the work of no more than "a few rotten apples" in an otherwise good barrel. However, most major investigations of police corruption have found that the opposite was true.

In New York the Lexow Committee of 1894-95 discovered graft to be part of the system itself rather than the acts of individual wrongdoers. A generation later, the Seabury Investigation reached the same conclusion. In 1950 the Kefauver Committee revealed an unchanging pattern of graft and payoffs by criminals to law enforcement officials. Twenty years later, New York's Knapp Commission found police corruption widespread instead of merely the product of a few rotten apples. The commission found almost all policemen accepted various favors as a "natural prerequisite of the job." Some officers were found to be "grass eaters," i.e., they took payoffs under the right circumstances, and others "meat eaters," i.e., they aggressively sought out shakedown situations. Within the Narcotics Division extortion had been developed to a fine art, with a number of officers automatically sharing in a "score" whenever a drug dealer was victimized. Indeed, the general understanding among Greenwich Village dealers was that a bust could be "squared" by the police appropriating two-thirds of a pusher's inventory and allowing him to keep one-third. The police share was then funneled back into trade through other pushers. As has generally been the case, gambling payoffs involved the most-sophisticated system, with specific amounts paid to individual officers according to rank.

The New York story has been constantly retold elsewhere.

In 1973 the Police Foundation, attempting to measure the extent of police corruption throughout the country, ordered a clipping service survey. In two months, clippings accumulated from 30 states reported allegations of corruption at all levels, in small-town, suburban, big-city, county and state police forces. In Philadelphia it was reported that police felt they were "operating in a world where 'notes' are constantly floating about, and only the stupid, the naive, and the fainthearted are unwilling to allow some of them to stick to their fingers."

Not unreasonably, police sometimes attempt to justify corruption by pointing out that police graft is a trifling part of a pattern that includes much greater graft taking by public officials in such fields as building permits, liquor licenses, zoning ordinances, franchises, condemnation cases, land and waterfront leases and the like. It is clear that elimination of police corruption would require a general improvement of ethics at all levels of public government.

See also: *Kefauver Committee, Knapp Commission, Lexow Committee, Seabury Investigation.*

ROUGH And Ready, California: Lawless mining town

Rough and Ready was a wild mining camp in California's Grass Valley that more than lived up to its name. It was probably the most rebellious of the gold towns that sprang up in the California Mother Lode country in 1849.

The Rough and Readyites believed in only two things: gold and the gun. Nothing took precedence over the former. On one occasion the townspeople had gathered on the local cemetery hill to bury a recently departed citizen when the gravedigger revealed a high amount of "color." The burial service was instantly forgotten as the mourners hustled about staking out claims amid the graves and heaving out corpses that interfered with their hunt for gold.

In 1850, before the Civil War, Rough and Ready "seceded" from the Union. What upset the populace was not the slavery issue but rather the fact that nearby Nevada City had been named the seat of Nevada County, a distinction Rough and Ready had wanted. To show their displeasure, the citizens drove all federal employees out of town, destroyed the post office and all its mail and burned all governmental furnishings. Eventually, the Rough and Readyites got over their pique and accepted the return of federal authority. The U.S. Post Office Department, however, was not about to let bygones be bygones and refused to furnish the town with a mail-handling facility for an entire century, finally relenting in 1954.

See also: *County Seat Wars.*

ROUNDSMEN: Early detectives

The first nighttime police protection in American cities was provided by watchmen, who in most places were referred to as leatherheads because of the leather helmets they wore. These leatherheads were only capable of watching property and perhaps apprehending a criminal in the performance of a crime. Solving crimes was supposed to be the work of the day men, or roundsmen, as they were called. These men were considered detectives, or plainclothesmen in the sense that they did not wear helmets that would have identified them as police officers. But they certainly were not detectives in the modern sense of the word, being seldom able to solve a real crime and, in fact, having little incentive to do so.

The average roundsman was no more than an unsuccessful stevedore, porter, cartman or laborer, and he drew no pay. While a leatherhead was paid about $1 a night, a roundsman was expected to earn his keep strictly from the fees he garnered for serving legal papers and from rewards posted by citizens for the return of stolen property. But since roundsmen rarely solved crimes, collecting such rewards by legitimate means proved difficult. Most roundsmen overcame their problem by forming alliances with gangs or individual thieves. First, the criminals would steal some goods and then the victim would post a reward for the return of the loot. The roundsman would magically recover the goods and collect the reward, which he would then split with the thieves. This, to a very large extent, was the basis of law and order in the 18th and 19th Century in most American cities.

Under such a system the crime of murder got a low priority since rewards were rarely posted in such cases and someone would have to be arrested. In that era most murderers who were caught either were captured in the commission of their crime or had murdered someone from a family that could afford to post a reward. Occasionally, a case got enough publicity to make its solution worthwhile. After all, if a roundsman could find a murderer, an unlikely prospect, he might be counted on to serve a summons on some elusive bounder.

When a crime did receive widespread publicity, it often served to underscore the incompetence of the roundsmen. Such was the case in the famous New York murder of Mary Cecilia Rogers in 1841, an incident later immortalized in American literature when Edgar Allen Poe used it as the basis of his brilliant story *The Murder of Marie Roget*. Poe solved his mythical case; the New York authorities failed miserably with the real one. The public at last came to understand that the roundsmen system hardly ensured the maintenance of law and order, and by 1845 reformers had entirely revamped the police force. Other cities copied the New York system and the day of the modern policeman dawned as the era of the roundsmen dimmed.

See also: *Leatherheads, Mary Cecilia Rogers.*

RUBINSTEIN, Serge (1909-1955): Financier and murder victim

In 1955 financial wizard and convicted draft dodger Serge Rubinstein was not considered a very likable person. In fact, the government was trying to deport him as an undesirable. Someone considered him even less desirable and on January 27 bound and strangled him to death in his luxurious five-story home on New York's Fifth Avenue.

A White Russian emigre, he burst upon the American scene a few years before World War II as the enfant terrible of the financial world and fattened an already swollen personal fortune by destroying, through devious means, a succession of companies and their stockholders. He was forced to take time from that unsavory activity to do 2½ years in prison for failure to serve in the Army during World War II, having falsely claimed Portuguese citizenship.

Upon his release Rubinstein went right back to his financial double-dealing. In 1949 he was indicted for stock fraud, mail fraud and violation of the Securities Acts. It was charged that he had made $3 million profit by buying Panhandle Producing and Refining stock at less than an average of $2 a share, driving the price up with false rumors and having the company pay dividends it hadn't earned and then, after he had liquidated his holdings, selling short when the public found out the truth and the stock started to fall. After a vigorous two-year battle, Rubinstein was acquitted of stock fraud and was ready for more capers.

He also led the life of a man-about-Manhattan, recruiting a large selection of lady friends, most of whom had keys to his home and whom he would often summon in the middle of the night to make a quick visit.

Early on the morning of January 27, 1955, Rubinstein returned home with a blonde he had taken to dinner. After a short time the blonde left. Apparently, Rubinstein read for a while and then telephoned another blonde acquaintance and asked her to come over. The woman, roused from her sleep, said she was too tired.

Excluding his murderer or murderers, the second blonde was the last person Rubinstein spoke to in his life. A little after 8 a.m. Rubinstein's butler brought a breakfast tray to his bedroom and found him dead. Clad in black silk mandarin pajamas, he lay sprawled on his back, his hands and feet bound with Venetian-blind cord. Strips of wide adhesive tape were plastered across his mouth and wound around his throat. It was obvious he had been strangled and the early theory was that the adhesive tape had done the job, perhaps inadvertently. At first, it was thought Rubinstein had been the victim of a kidnap attempt and had been killed in error. However, the autopsy showed he had died by manual strangulation. He had been throttled by someone with powerful hands.

Police developed many theories. One postulated that business enemies had been responsible; another claimed it had been "a mob job—a syndicate job"; yet another attributed the murder to a robbery attempt gone awry. The previous August, Rubinstein had filed charges against three men for attempting to extort $535,000 from him. In all, the police questioned literally thousands of persons whose names Rubinstein had written in several loose-leaf notebooks. It appeared he was in the habit of writing down the name of every person he met who might ever be useful to him, either for business or pleasure. Business contacts, friends, enemies, associates, prison mates and girl friends, both past and present, were hauled in and interrogated, all to be caught in the limelight of intensive newspaper coverage.

The more sensational newspapers had a field day with several of the murdered man's lady friends because of his written comments about them or because of the fact that he seemed to have kept a number of them under surveillance. In one case Rubinstein had even hidden a small battery-operated transmitter under a woman's bed to record her bedside conversations. Later, he had confronted her with the recording of her amorous conversation with a date. When the story of the recorder broke in the newspapers, the girl said, with a certain ingenuousness, "Now everyone in New York knows my bed squeaks."

Despite a flurry of investigative activity, the murder remained unsolved.

RUB-OUT: Slang for a killing

Although well known as the underworld term for gangster killings, the word "rub-out" goes back much further in American history. According to Samuel Eliot Morison's *The Oxford History of the American People,* the term was used by white trappers in the early 1800s, with the same meaning it has today. Presumably, since rub-out connotes a certain disdain or lack of respect for the victim, it may be that it was first applied to the killing of Indians.

RUBY, Jack (1911-1967): Killer of Lee Harvey Oswald

Even as the nation was still in shock over the assassination of President John F. Kennedy, millions watched on television as the President's accused killer, Lee Harvey Oswald, was shot to death in the Dallas, Tex. city jail on November 24, 1963. The murderer was 52-year-old Jacob Rubenstein, better known as Jack Ruby, a local nightclub operator.

Oswald, flanked by lawmen, was being escorted through the basement of the municipal building to a waiting armored truck that was to take him to the county jail when Ruby stepped out from a cluster of newsmen, thrust a snub-nosed .38-caliber revolver at Oswald's left side and fired a single shot. Clutching his side, Oswald slumped to the concrete floor, writhing in pain. He lost consciousness without saying a word and 86 minutes later, at 1:07 p.m., he died while undergoing emergency surgery.

Ruby was described as an ardent admirer of President Kennedy and his family who had become distraught about his murder. In the ensuing controversy over the assassination and whether or not Oswald had acted alone, as the Warren Commission later found, Ruby was pictured as a player involved in an intricate plot to kill Kennedy and, later, to silence Oswald, who may have been the actual killer or merely a scapegoat. Despite several scenarios arriving at these various conclusions, no positive link between Oswald and Ruby has ever been established.

Ruby was convicted of Oswald's murder. While awaiting a retrial on appeal, he was transferred in December 1966 to a hospital where he was found to be suffering from cancer. He died the following January 3 of a blood clot in his lung.

That same day a three-minute conversation between Ruby and his brother Earl tape-recorded in the hospital in December was made public. In it Ruby said he had known that Oswald was going to be transferred to the county jail the morning of November 24 but added that his presence at the jail was due to his having made an "illegal turn" behind a bus that put him in the jail parking lot. He said he had no recollection of the moment he shot Oswald. "It happened in such a blur . . . before I knew it . . . the officers had me on the ground."

Ruby angrily denied a rumor that he had met Oswald at his nightclub before the assassination, saying, "It's a fabrication." He told his brother he always carried a gun because of various altercations he had had in his club and because he carried fairly large amounts of cash at times.

Ruby's demand that he be given a lie detector test to prove he had acted alone in the murder of Oswald was denied because, it was said, his physical condition would make such a test valueless.

See also: *Lee Harvey Oswald.*

RUDABAUGH, Dave (1841-1886): Western outlaw

One of the few outlaws ever to ride with Billy the Kid on a more or less equal basis, Dave Rudabaugh began his criminal career while still in his teens, first in his native Missouri and then in Kansas. In the 1870s, while doing a bit of cattle rustling and highway robbery, Rudabaugh hit on a lucrative career holding up the construction-gang pay trains of the Atchison, Topeka and Santa Fe Railroad. Finally tracked down in 1878 through combined manhunts led by Wyatt Earp and Bat Masterson, Rudabaugh won his freedom by implicating his accomplices and then moved on to Texas and the New Mexico Territory. Together with Billy Wilson, a Texas outlaw who later won a presidential pardon from Theodore Roosevelt and lived out his days as a lawman, Rudabaugh formed the Dodge City gang, committing a number of crimes in Texas and the New Mexico Territory.

In 1880 Rudabaugh joined up with Billy the Kid, considering himself the Kid's equal. Both were captured together at Stinking Springs, New Mexico Territory, in December 1880, and both were to make separate escapes, the Kid eventually being killed by Sheriff Pat Garrett. Rudabaugh was sentenced to 40 years imprisonment, but an old murder indictment was still pending against him and he faced the possibility of being hung. He solved that problem by tunneling his way out of jail in San Miguel on December 3, 1881.

Crossing the border into Mexico, Rudabaugh organized a gang of *gringos* and Mexicans that terrorized the province of Chihuahua for the next five years. On February 19, 1886, he and his band made the mistake of trying to victimize the village of Parral, whose citizens, in an uncommon display of resistance, met them with gunfire. Rudabaugh was shot dead. In a subsequent town fiesta, his head was cut off and stuck up on a pole.

Rudabaugh, like many other criminals in American history, was resurrected by the popular imagination. In his case, the tale was that just one of his men had been killed in Parral and that he had returned north of the border and lived out his days as an honest rancher in Oregon. Similar stories have also been told about Jesse James and John Dillinger, among others.

See also: *Billy the Kid, Pat Garrett, Billy Wilson.*

RUEF, Abraham (1864-1936): Political boss

Abe Ruef, the political boss of San Francisco in the early 1900s, ran his domain as a "wide open city" that rivaled such bastions of sin and corruption as New Orleans and Chicago.

Born of moderately wealthy French-Jewish parents, Ruef was a brilliant student, graduating with high honors from the University of California at age 18. He earned a law degree and then entered politics as an enthusiastic Republican reformer. However, witnessing the depredations of machine rule during the period of the Southern Pacific Railroad's domination of California, he soon lost his reformer zeal and turned opportunist.

In 1901 Ruef gained leadership of the newly formed Union Labor Party and seized control of the city government, installing musicians union head Eugene E. Schmitz as mayor. Then the Ruef machine proceeded to loot the city in every way possible. Boss Ruef even described his hand-picked members of the Board of Supervisors as "being so greedy for plunder that they'd eat the paint off a house." Of course, he did all right himself. Typical was the graft derived from a "cowyard" on Pacific Street, which housed 48 prostitutes in little cribs and was operated by six politically connected individuals, including a cousin of the mayor. The operators paid city officials $440 a week for protection and Ruef $250 a week.

Ruef apportioned grafting rights in almost every field of endeavor, with much of the vice operations run by one of the San Francisco underworld's most colorful, if distasteful, characters, Jerome Bassity. The political boss handled the more important illegal revenue sources personally. As investigations by reformers, such as special prosecutor Francis J. Heney and his assistant, Hiram Johnson, and by private undercover operatives of William J. Burns showed, Ruef received incredibly large lawyer's fees from public utilities and doled out part of these funds to most of the supervisors.

The final destruction of the Ruef machine must be credited to the newspapers and, especially, to editor Fremont Older of the *San Francisco Bulletin,* which ran almost daily exposes of local government machinations. In 1908, with a reform administration now in power, Ruef was convicted of bribery and eventually served time in San Quentin from 1911 to 1915. He had been sentenced to 14 years but his term was considerably shortened because of the intercession of the *Bulletin,* which by then was convinced of his reformation. The newspaper published his jail cell memoirs, entitled *The Road I Traveled; an Autobiographic Account of My Career from University to Prison, with an Intimate Recital of the Corrupt Alliance between Big Business and Politics in San Francisco.* Upon his release from prison Ruef entered the real estate business.

The destruction of the Ruef machine presaged the abandonment of San Francisco's gold-rush tradition, which had required it to be a wide-open town. The Barbary Coast soon withered away.

See also: *Jerome Bassity.*

RULE Of Silence: Prison disciplinary method

Probably the harshest form of discipline ever attempted in American prisons was the so-called rule of silence, which was first enforced at Auburn Prison in the 1830s and later refined at Alcatraz Prison in the 20th century.

As originally practiced, the rule of silence was imposed on inmates when they were let out of their cells by day to work in the shops. Maintaining silence, they had to march in lockstep with downcast gaze. Violators of the rule were flogged. But at least prisoners were allowed to talk in the cell blocks.

Such was not the case at Alcatraz, where it was first used in 1934 as a punishment for problem prisoners. The rule of silence was to be so enforced that it was conceivable a convict could forget what his own voice sounded like. Prisoners could not talk in the dining room; they could not talk in the work shops; they could not talk in the cell blocks. The attempt was ludicrous; prisoners still found ways to talk to one another despite the risks of punishment, which could take the form of being sent to the hold.

But the prisoners could use the rule of silence against the authorities at critical times. During an early escape attempt at Alcatraz, one convict hit a prison guard over the head with a hammer seven times, and then two others dragged the bleeding, dying victim across the floor into a corner, where they covered him with some old work clothes. A half-dozen other convicts were present at the time, but none stirred or said a word. They were obeying prison rules.

Within four years of its opening, Alcatraz greatly modified the rule of silence, as a number of areas were eliminated from the no-talking restriction. Still, long periods of silence were enforced and Alcatraz maintained its premier spot as the hellhole of federal prisons, where enforced monotony drove many inmates insane.

See also: *Alcatraz Prison.*

RUM Row: Bootleg fleet

With the onset of Prohibition in 1919, the easiest way to smuggle liquor into the United States was along the Atlantic coastline, especially from Maine to New Jersey. Vessels carrying liquor could drop anchor just outside the three-mile limit, where they were safe from government interference, and await the arrival of smaller, speedier boats to take on their illicit cargo and make a fast dash for shore. These little craft were known as rumrunners and engaged in many duels with government gunboats known as rumchasers. Meanwhile, the long line of liquor-laden vessels, often stretching for miles, rolled on the swells awaiting completion of unloading. This line of vessels, everything from old fishing boats to luxury yachts and cruisers, became known as Rum Row, always visible and embarrassing proof that Prohibition was unenforceable.

RUPOLO, Ernest "The Hawk" (1908-1964): Genovese murder victim

Before his last arrest in 1958, Vito Genovese slowly schemed and murdered his way to the top post in the Mafia following the deportation of Lucky Luciano. He achieved his position with little interference from the law because very few individuals were ever willing to testify against him. One who did testify was a lowly New York hoodlum named Ernest "the Hawk" Rupolo, whom Genovese had hired to carry out the murder of Ferdinand Boccia in 1934. Harassed by the numerous charges lodged against him, Rupolo implicated Genovese, who fled the country in 1937. Finally brought back to stand trial in 1945, Genovese beat the rap after the only witness other than Rupolo who could tie him to the crime, Peter LaTempa, conveniently swallowed some poisoned pills in his jail cell. The crime boss was released for lack of evidence and that left Rupolo, as the boys said, "with the meat in his mouth and the sauce on his shirt."

As a reward for his useless testimony, Rupolo was set free, but the authorities warned him that he was practically committing suicide by leaving prison. For years Rupolo led a terror-filled life, never knowing when Genovese would take his vengeance. Within the Mafia it was recognized that Genovese was delaying the death sentence just to increase Rupolo's suffering. Finally, in August 1964 Rupolo disappeared. On August 27 his mutilated corpse washed ashore from New York's Jamaica Bay; his body was pockmarked with ice pick holes and the back of his head had been blown away. Not surprisingly, the case has remained unsolved.

RUSSIAN Bill (1855-1881): Outlaw

William Tattenbaum was a colorful character who turned up in Tombstone, Arizona Territory in 1880 claiming to be the son of Countess Telfrin, a wealthy Russian noblewoman. He also said that as a young lieutenant he had deserted the Czar's Imperial White Hussars when faced with a court-martial for striking a ranking officer. Decked out in the finest and flashiest Western clothing and gear, Tattenbaum was quickly dubbed Russian Bill by the citizens of Tombstone, who did not believe a word he said about himself. Nevertheless, Russian Bill managed to ingratiate himself with Curly Bill Brocius, the head of the notorious Clanton gang, and rode with the outlaws for about a year. There is no record of Russian Bill engaging in any overt banditry and he seems to have served mainly as a "horse holder," but Curly Bill insisted on keeping him around so that he could watch him groom his own hair for hours "just like a Chinaman" and listen to him quote the classics. Russian Bill comes down to us, thanks to Hollywood depictions, as a comic character. Quite possibly to escape that very reputation in Tombstone, he struck off for the New Mexico Territory on a horse-stealing enterprise of his own. The result was not a happy one, as he was soon captured by the Law and Order Committee of Shakespeare, New Mexico Territory. Russian Bill and another malefactor named Sandy King were given a fast trial by the committee in the banquet room of a local hotel. In keeping with the group's reputation for quick justice, he was hanged from a beam in the room without further ado.

In 1883 inquiries from the Countess Telfrin about her son confirmed that all of Russian Bill's tales had been true. The town of Shakespeare was a mite chagrined about having hanged "an honest-to-God son of a countess." To spare the Countess' feelings and a troublesome investigation by Washington, it was duly reported to the authorities that Russian Bill had met with an accidental death.

RUSTLING: See Cattle Rustling, Horse Stealing.

S

SACCO-VANZETTI Case: Murder trial and conviction of anarchists

No murder trial in America has ever caused more worldwide turmoil than that of Nicola Sacco and Bartolomeo Vanzetti, two acknowledged anarchists who were convicted of being members of a five-man bandit gang that held up a shoe factory in South Braintree, Mass. on April 15, 1920. The gang robbed the factory's $15,776.51 payroll and killed the paymaster and a guard. Sacco and Vanzetti were found to be in possession of two guns, and supposedly expert ballistics testimony tied their weapons to the crime.

In retrospect, no fair judging of the facts can deny that the two men were prosecuted more for their politics than their alleged crimes; they were foreign-looking, Italian-looking, and worst of all, they were anarchists. After one of the most unfair trials in American history, Sacco and Vanzetti were found guilty on July 14, 1921 by a jury sitting under Judge Webster Thayer, a rock-ribbed pillar of Back Bay aristocracy and opponent of anything he deemed radical, and sentenced to death. Out of court the judge often referred to the defendants as "dagos" and "sons of bitches." During a Dartmouth football game he asked a friend, "Did you see what I did to those anarchist bastards?"

Ignored at the trial were instances of possible perjury committed by state police officers and strong indications that the crime had been committed by members of the Boston Mafia, a version alleged by a professional criminal during Sacco and Vanzetti's years in the death house and later confirmed by underworld informer Vinnie Teresa, a New England gangster whose information to authorities in recent years has probably exceeded in importance that supplied by Joe Valachi.

Despite all the prosecution's claims, its tenuous case against the defendants centered on the testimony of two ballistics "experts." One expert was state police Capt. William Proctor, who demonstrated on the stand that he could not even take apart and reassemble Sacco's pistol. Proctor said that one of the

The trial and execution of Nicola Sacco (front right) and Bartolomeo Vanzetti (front center) caused more national and international turmoil than any other murder case in American history.

murder bullets had markings "consistent with being fired by that pistol," but he later admitted in an affidavit that he merely had meant the bullet "could" have been fired by Sacco's weapon—but that he did not believe it had been. He also revealed that he had been coached by the prosecution.

The state's other ballistics authority was Charles Van Amburgh, who presented much of the damning evidence against the defendants. By 1924 Van Amburgh was exposed in other cases as an expert witness who fitted his testimony to the needs of the prosecution if he thought other evidence had already proved the defendant guilty. Many ballistic experts and legal authorities were certain that in one case he knew he was giving false evidence but felt it did not matter because he was convinced of the defendant's guilt. Later, the defendant was proved totally innocent.

The real question surrounding the case is not whether a certain bullet was fired from a certain gun barrel—the subject of much scientific inquiry over the years—but, more basically whether the evidence against the pair was rigged by the substitution of a bullet.

None of this mattered at the time, however. More significant was the tenor of the era, which dictated the verdict that was reached. One of the witnesses made a sworn statement that before the trial the man later picked to be foreman of the jury had said, "Damn them, they ought to hang anyway."

Subsequent accusations about doctored evidence, testimony by phony experts and the like led to worldwide demonstrations against the verdict and the death sentence. Finally, in 1927 Gov. Alvan Tufts Fuller appointed a special commission to study the case. It included Abbot Lawrence Lowell, president of Harvard University; Dr. Samuel Stratton, president of the Massachusetts Institute of Technology; and Robert Grant, an ex-probate judge.

Armed plainclothes guards, such as this one, ringed the Massachussetts court during the Sacco-Vanzetti trial to repel any "attack by anarchists."

The Lowell Commission studied the official record of the trial, which some witnesses protested contained errors made by the court interpreter in translating key testimony, and heard some prosecution witnesses recant their original statements to the jury. However, in the end, the commission found nothing

to indicate a miscarriage of justice, although it seemed rather upset by Judge Thayer's "grave breach of official decorum."

The governor accepted the Lowell Commission findings and, on August 10, 1927, granted a legal 12-day reprieve to allow for final, though obviously futile, legal moves. Around the world the protests turned violent. Forty persons were hurt in a demonstration in London and there were disorders in front of the U.S. consulate in Geneva. Street fights broke out in Paris and an American flag was burned in Casablanca. Other riots occurred in Berlin, Warsaw, Buenos Aires, Brest, Marseilles and various localities in Japan, Mexico, Argentina and Cuba. Among the voices raised in protest were those of George Bernard Shaw, H. G. Wells, Romain Rolland, John Galsworthy, Anatole France and Albert Einstein. Up to the last minute throngs marched in Boston and New York.

On August 23, 1927 Sacco, the factory hand, and Vanzetti, the fish peddler, were executed.

Their deaths did not still the controversy about the case. It would be impossible to compile a complete bibliography of all the books and magazine and newspaper articles written about the case. In 1977 Sacco and Vanzetti had their names cleared in a special proclamation signed by Massachusetts Gov. Michael S. Dukakis.

SAFECRACKING

Few crimes have gone into such a precipitous decline in recent years as that of "box busting" or safecracking. It's not difficult to see why given the following recent news items:

● In New York a safecracking gang used too much explosives trying to blow a safe and set off more than two dozen alarms in surrounding buildings.

● In the Chicago area a so-called torch man burned his way into four safes in a row and succeeded in burning the money inside all of them to a crisp.

● In New Jersey a pair of "yeggs" worked over a safe with acetylene torches for three hours and managed to weld the safe permanently shut.

Yeggs is the word generally used to describe the crop of modern-day safecrackers, shadows of the old-timers who accomplished crooked miracles and had safe makers and law enforcers in a state of nervous anxiety for decades.

There indeed have been safecrackers who could open some safes by manipulation, and there have always been fewer manipulation-proof safes than manufacturers have claimed. There are a few men with such skills today, but there is no need for them to be dishonest. They command top fees performing legal "safecrackings," such as opening safes for tax officials investigating evasion cases and for estates when the deceased has failed to leave a record of the safe combination. Of course, it takes years of practice and an intimate knowledge of combination locks—thousands of them—to be successful at manipulation. On the outside of a safe there is a knob and dial and inside the lock a set of metal disks, or tumblers. The tumblers have a small cut out of them and revolve on a spindle controlled by the knob. When the correct combination is dialed, the slots fall in line and a metal level drops into the opening and releases the bolt mechanism, allowing the safe to be opened. Good safes have at least 100 numbers on the dial and four tumblers, creating some 100 million combination possibilities. Spending one minute on each combination possibility of a four-tumbler, 100-number lock, a safecracker could take something like 200 years to get the right one. As a result there are indeed few Jimmy Valentines in real life.

Through the years the safe maker and the safecracker have battled for the technical advantage. When combination locks were first introduced a century or so ago, crooks developed the "drag," a screw setup that mashed the walls around the lock. Safe manufacturers got around this by strengthening the walls. The box busters retaliated with the "jackscrew," a rig that by the turn of a screw forced the safe door with a series of steel wedges of varied thicknesses, from the thinness of a razor blade to the thickness of a fist, until the door popped from its hinges. The manufacturers responded by making doors that shot bolts into the jamb of all four sides and devising dovetailed arrangements joining the door to the jamb to block the wedges. The crooks' countered with an air pump that distributed a fine grade of gunpowder all around the crack of the door. The air pump was placed at the bottom of the door and a funnel of powder at the top and then the rest of the crack was puttied up. When the pump sucked air from the safe and created a vacuum, the powder was sucked around the crack. A pound of powder set off by a cap blew the door.

A top safecracker, Langdon Moore, developed a safe-busting tool consisting of a back brace with adjustable extension legs. The brace was bolted to the floor and adjusted to dial height, and a crank with a one-quarter inch diamond-pointed drill was then fitted into a head piece at the top of the legs. The drill could bite through two inches of solid chilled steel and lock casing in about a half hour. Using a small bellows, a charge of powder was blown through the hole into the lock, a short fuse was attached and lighted. There would be a very dull blast, and the door would swing open.

No less inventive and a little more subtle was safecracker George Bliss, who found an easy way to open safes. He would remove the dial knob of a lock, adjust a tiny instrument of thin steel wire inside the surface of the dial and replace the knob. Some days later, he would return to the safe and remove the knob. By examing the marks made by the wire, he could determine the combination numbers and then had only to try them in different order until he found the correct sequence—all in a matter of minutes.

For a time safe makers were sure they had come up with an uncrackable box nicknamed the cannonball. The money container was a large egg-shaped compartment attached to a lower stand of four-foot-thick steel. The door consisted of 12 steel plates, each two inches thick and bolted to another. Instead of swinging open, the door "unscrewed" when the wheel attachment was turned according to the combination. The way the door was made, it was impossible to penetrate the first door to place explosives inside. The cannonball was the bane of safecrackers for years until perhaps the greatest safecracker of all,

Herb Wilson, recalled his Boer War days in South Africa and the way soldiers would break open large ostrich eggs found on the veld. "With a small hatchet we'd crack the shell on the large end, going completely aroung the egg. Then one last blow with the hatchet, a little pressure with one hand while the other seized the opposite end of the egg, and the two pieces came apart as the contents went into the frying pan."

Wilson imagined the cannonball as a giant ostrich egg. Using a specially designed oxygen-acetylene torch, he cut a one-inch groove around the big end of the "egg," pouring cold water on the heated metal. Holding the edge of a specially-made hatchet in the groove, he had an accomplice bang the hatchet with an eight-pound copper hammer (copper against steel makes little noise). Once a full circle had been completed, Wilson took aim with the hatchet and delivered a sharp blow to the groove at the top of the safe. Just as happened to ostrich eggs, the big end of the cannonball safe cracked off. Wilson's largest bust netted $170,000.

For Wilson safecracking was an art, a compulsion. The same was true of Dion O'Banion, a top Chicago mobster of the 1920s who made millions annually out of bootlegging and other rackets. O'Banion had started as a safecracker and could never give it up, even when he no longer needed the money. Captured on one such a caper (which he promptly bought his way out of), O'Banion was asked why he bothered. "Aw," he said, "it's like playing the horses. Once it's in your blood you can't give it up."

The old-fashioned approach to safecracking has not entirely disappeared. When the Mosler Safe Co. put out a booklet titled "What You Should Know About Safes," it got a request for a copy from a man whose return address was TSPF, Snipe, Tex. TSPF stood for Texas State Prison Farm, and the man was a safecracker still trying to further his knowledge of the field. Unlike the new yeggs, however, he is of a vanishing breed. The old-timers complain the new crop just don't take the trouble to really learn their trade properly.

See also: *Bank Robberies, George Leonidas Leslie, Little Joker.*

SAGE, Russell (1816-1906): Would-be murder victim

On December 4, 1894 a bearded stranger entered the offices of Russell Sage, the financial tycoon. He carried a carpetbag containing, he informed a secretary, bonds from John D. Rockefeller for personal delivery to Mr. Sage. There was a small meeting going on in Sage's office, but Mr. Rockefeller's bonds were always welcome and the messenger was ushered in. Silently, the bearded man handed Sage a typewritten note that read: "I hold in my hands ten pounds of dynamite. If I drop it on the floor it will tear the building to pieces and everyone with it. For $1,250,000 it shall not drop. Yes or no?"

Sage reacted with the ruthlessness for which he was infamous. He grabbed one of his low-paid clerks, shoved him toward the bearded man and, at the same time, broke for the door. There was a deafening explosion. A secretary and the bearded stranger were killed. Five others, including the clerk

Sage used as a human shield, were badly injured. The clerk later sued Sage and was awarded $40,000.

The only clue the police had was the head of the bearded stranger, but they could not identify him. Investigators theorized that there was a gang of mad anarchists on the loose aiming "to rid the country of millionaires." Meanwhile, Ike White, a legendary reporter for the *New York World* sifted through the wreckage and found a button. He washed it off and determined it bore the identification of a Boston tailor. In time, White was able to identify the bomber as Henry L. Norcross, a frustrated inventor. The *World* broke the story with a huge picture of the bearded head and a one-word headline: "IDENTIFIED!" It was one of the most sensational scoops in American newspaper history.

See also: *Ike White.*

ST. Paul Layover: Hideout arrangement for criminals

From the beginning of the century to the 1930s, St. Paul, Minn. was regarded as the safest hideout town for American criminals, even better protected than such places as Hot Springs, Ark. and Joplin, Mo. Some insisted that this distinction was of enormous benefit to local citizens, since for 30 years St. Paul was free of gangland violence and robberies.

Around the turn of the century, Police Chief John J. O'Connor let it be known to out-of-town criminals that they were welcome to "lay over" in St. Paul and spend their money freely. The only proviso to the St. Paul Layover, as it became known, was that no crime of any sort was to take place in the city. As a result, the city's crime statistics were absolutely unbelieveable. Burglaries were almost nil, and St. Paul was one of the few cities during the era where lone women could walk the streets late at night without fear.

When an out-of-town criminal visited the city, he reported to Paddy Griffin's lodging house on Wabasha Street, where he was assigned a place to stay at a healthy rental. Griffin kept Chief O'Connor informed on all visitors, and the chief saw to it that the criminals did not misbehave and, just as importantly, were not subject to any police interference. O'Connor's operation was made possible by the political clout of his younger brother, Richard O'Connor, the boss of the city and state Democratic Party. Richard O'Connor was known for his dedication to protecting the poor, something the layover system complemented.

It is believed the O'Connor brothers never accepted any protection money from these out-of-town criminals, content to run the system simply for the satisfaction expressed by the public at living in a crime-free community. The O'Connor family income came from the saloon business—they were the official and unofficial owners of an entire string—and from a well-regulated prostitution industry that paid large sums to the police for the privilege of operating without harassment. A particularly lavish brothel was allowed to conduct business directly behind police headquarters.

The golden era of the layover system ended around 1920.

By then Dapper Danny Hogan had taken over Griffin's role and ill health had forced Chief O'Connor to retire. Richard O'Connor shifted his interests to national politics, paying little attention to St. Paul matters. The layover system was so ingrained, however, that it continued even under a police chief who opposed it; the operation was supervised by other brass, and incoming criminals now checked in at the Green Lantern saloon on Wabasha Street, within sight of the state capitol.

Hogan's supervision of the layover system came to an explosive conclusion on December 5, 1928, when a bomb went off as he stepped on the starter of his car. He was succeeded by his ambitious partner, Harry Sawyer, who indeed had a motive to dispatch Hogan. Hogan's death marked the end of the peaceful era of the layover system, and once the lid came off, the violence continued. Sawyer lacked the muscle Hogan had used to maintain the peace and soon was making less and less out of layover revenues. Outside elements no longer saw any reason to exempt St. Paul from criminal endeavors, and in time, Sawyer joined with various underworld gangs in planning many local capers. He threw in with several kidnap mobs that worked the St. Paul area and later went to prison on a life sentence for his part in the Barker-Karpis gang's kidnapping of banker Edward Bremer. With his departure the St. Paul Layover passed into memory.

ST. Valentine's Day Massacre: Gangland killings

No underworld atrocity, not even the Kansas City Massacre, in which a number of lawmen were killed in an allegedly botched attempt to rescue an arrested gangster, ever upset the public more then the St. Valentine's Day Massacre in Chicago on February 14, 1929. There is no doubt that the crime, technically never solved, was the work of the Capone mob, although none of the actual killers, except for Fred "Killer" Burke, could be definitely linked to the job.

The massacre was the outgrowth of a long-standing war between the Capone mob and the heirs of the North Side Gang organized in the early 1920s by Dion O'Banion. By 1929 a number of the North Siders, including O'Banion, had been killed and only George "Bugs" Moran remained to oppose Capone's take over of the gang's lucrative area.

The North Siders were set up for the kill by a Detroit gangster who told Moran he had a load of hijacked booze available. Moran agreed to take delivery of the stuff at the gang's headquarters, a garage at 2122 North Clark Street. Early on Valentine's Day, a group of five men, three in police uniforms, pulled up in front of the garage in a black Cadillac, similar to the unmarked cars used by police, and rushed into the garage. Quickly, they lined the men they found there against a wall: six Moran henchmen—Adam Heyer, John May, brothers Frank and Pete Gusenberg, Al Weinshank and James Clark—and Dr. Reinhardt H. Schwimmer, an optometrist and something of a gangster groupie who just happened to be on hand. Then two of the raiders cut loose with Thompson submachine guns, killing all seven.

The St. Valentine's Day Massacre shocked the nation as few other Capone mob excesses had. So great was the public interest in the massacre that many helpful publications ran an upside-down version so readers could identify the dead without having to turn their newspapers around.

The only foul up was that the killers had not gotten Moran. He and two others, Willie Marks and Teddy Newbury, had just rounded a corner near the garage when they saw what appeared to be policemen entering it. Figuring it was a police shakedown, they remained out of sight, waiting for the officers to leave. When the machine gunning started, they fled.

The killings broke the power of the North Siders, and all Moran could do was wail, "Only Capone kills like that."

Actually, it was a long time before the theory that Capone had ordered the massacre won acceptance. There was much public speculation that the killings had been the work of real policemen. The Chicago police were held in such disrepute the Frederick D. Silloway, the local Prohibition administrator, was quoted as telling the press:

> The murderers were not gangsters. They were Chicago policemen. I believe the killing was the aftermath to the hijacking of 500 cases of whiskey belonging to the Moran gang by five policemen six weeks ago on Indianapolis Boulevard. I expect to have the names of these five policemen in a short

time. It is my theory that in trying to recover the liquor the Moran gang threatened to expose the policemen and the massacre was to prevent the exposure.

The next day Silloway retracted the charge, insisting he had been misquoted, certainly a monumental misquotation if there ever was one. His superiors in Washington transferred him out of Chicago as a sop to the local authorities, but a cloud of suspicion continued to hang over the police. The country's leading authority on forensic ballistics, Major Calvin H. Goodard, was brought in from New York to clear up the situation. He announced that according to his tests the bullets used in the massacre had not been fired from any machine gun in the possession of the Chicago police, still not a definitive exoneration. Almost a year later, the police located the murder weapons in the home of a professional killer, Fred Burke. In April 1930 Burke was captured in Michigan. Instead of being brought to trial in Illinois for the massacre, where if convicted he could have gotten the death penalty, he was tried in Michigan for the murder of a policeman and sentenced to life there.

This led some underworld sources to whisper that the Illinois authorities had been fearful of trying him because testimony would have revealed the weapons had been planted in his home.

Despite such accusations, the St. Valentine's Day Massacre was a Capone operation. Through the years a changing cast of characters has been listed as the actual killers. Almost certainly, the chief planner of the job was Machine Gun McGurn, one of Capone's most-trusted henchmen.

Chicago, in its own style, memorialized the massacre. The garage on North Clark became a tourist attraction. Newspapers printed close-ups of the corpses upside down so that readers would not have to turn the page around to identify the victims. In 1949 the garage was bought for use as an antique furniture storage business and in 1967 it was finally ripped down. However, the bricks from the bullet-pocked wall were saved for posterity by a Canadian businessman. In 1972 he opened a night spot with a Roaring 20s theme and rebuilt the wall, for some odd reason, in the men's room as a tourist attraction. Three nights a week women patrons were allowed to enter that sanctum for a quick peek. The club continued for a few years, and then the businessman supposedly put the bricks in storage, preparing to market them together with a written account of the massacre for $1,000 apiece. Of course he couldn't possibly afford to sell the bullet-scarred bricks at that bargain price.

See also: *Anselmi and Scalise, Alphonse "Scarface Al" Capone, Machine Gun Jack McGurn, George "Bugs" Moran.*

SALEM Witchcraft Trials

The witchcraft executions in Salem, Mass. in 1692 were not the first in America—a witch was hanged in Charlestown in 1648 and another in Boston in 1655—but they were the most awesome. It all started when a group of young girls suddenly gave every evidence of having been bewitched. Ten girls, aged nine to 17, gathered in the kitchen of the Rev. John Parris' house and listened to the stories of his West Indian slave, Tituba. Although Tituba had been converted to Christianity, she had grown up steeped in the secrets of magic and voodoo. She taught the girls fortune-telling and palm reading and told bloodcurdling tales of spells and murder. The stories seem to have had a terrifying effect on the girls, who grew up in a particularly God-fearing society. Little Elizabeth Parris, the minister's daughter, awoke one night in a screaming frenzy and insisted there were awful creatures in her room. The doctor was called and he quickly gave his diagnosis: an evil spell had been cast on the child. Someone in Salem was practicing witchcraft. The news rocked Salem. Then the other girls who had been involved in the meetings with Tituba began having seizures. It has long been debated whether the girls were simply pretending or had actually deluded themselves into thinking they had been bewitched. Perhaps with most, what had started out as a way to get attention developed into a form of hysteria. All the girls no doubt believed in witchcraft, as did the townspeople, who were also mindful of the Biblical injunction, "Thou shalt not suffer a witch to live."

At first, three women—Tituba, Goodwife Osburn and Sarah Goode—were charged, and the mad frenzy of the witch hunt began. Trials were held and a number of men and women were accused of practicing witchcraft. When the impact of what was happening hit her, one of the girls, Mary Warren, confessed that it was all pretense. But the other girls then accused her of witchcraft and said they had seen her ghost. Mary withdrew her confession, but no one had believed her in any case because of the fact that she had been bewitched. Far more impressive to the people of Salem was the spectacle of the other girls proving their affliction by convulsing on the floor of the courtroom, biting their arms and screaming, and accusing witch after witch.

A five-year-old girl, Dorcas Goode, confessed to being a witch and admitted keeping a black snake as a familiar spirit. Little Dorcas was kept in heavy chains in jail for eight months. The restraints were considered necessary to keep her from casting evil spells. She was the daughter of Sarah Goode, who had been hanged, along with Tituba and Goodwife Osburn, after denying she was a witch. Only those who denied being witches were executed. Although some who confessed died in jail, all the others who admitted being witches were eventually released. In all, 19 persons were hanged and one, 80-year-old Giles Corey, was pressed to death when he refused to plead guilty or not guilty.

By September 1692 the witch delusion had faded away. People had become concerned that innocent persons had been executed. The girls continued their hysterics but were generally ignored. One of them, Anne Putnam, declared that she had accused guiltless persons and had her confession read from the pulpit. As opinion turned against the girls, judges and jurors publicly declared they had been mistaken. The jurors signed a declaration that they had been "under the power of a strong and general delusion." For many years thereafter a day of repentance and fasting was held in Salem.

See also: *Giles Corey, Gallows Hill, Cotton Mather.*

SALTING: Mine swindle

Easily the most prevalent form of larceny in the Old West and later, in Alaska was the "salting" of worthless mining i.e., making an area of land appear to be rich in gold ore or other minerals. As Mark Twain once put it, "There was nothing in the shape of a mining claim that was not salable."

There were many ingenious ways to salt an area, a quite common one being to shoot gold dust into the ground with a shotgun. This method worked well in mine shafts, where the gold specks would convince a potential buyer/victim that a particular vein was not as yet played out. Shotgun salting on the surface could only be successful if some way was found to induce a sucker to search in the right area; salting a huge area would have been an expensive proposition.

According to one California mining legend, some prospectors stuck with a poor-paying claim devised an ingenious scheme to unload it on a group of Chinese fortune hunters. Unable to guarantee that the would-be buyers would look in the right spots, the miners hid one of their number in a gulch with a dead snake. When the Chinese arrived, the miners suggested areas for them to search, and as was to be expected, the potential victims, wary of a salting plot, said no and pointed into a far corner of the claim. As they approached the spot, the miner with the snake heaved it out of his hiding place. Quickly, a miner with the Chinese leveled his shotgun and shot the reptile. The fortune hunters became convinced of the miners' trustworthiness, for not only had they been saved from the snake but, after digging the area, they also found strong traces of gold.

One of the greatest silver saltings ever was that of a worthless hole called the North Ophir in the Comstock field in Nevada. During the 1860s great nuggets of silver turned up there and stock belonging to the North Ophir claim went through the ceiling. The bogus claim's promoters had cut silver dollars into pieces, pounded them into lumps, blackened the lumps and then salted the claim. The bubble burst when a "nugget" turned up with "ted States of" printed on it.

Many miners, looking ahead to the day when their claims would be played out, used a special technique to prepare a salting for a future sucker. Since in the last century gold salts were widely used in the patent medicines miners took religiously for kidney ailments brought on by heavy drinking, they would urinate over large stretches of their claim so that traces of gold would still show up when they were ready to move on.

No tale was too tall for gold salters. A Calistoga Springs, Calif. promoter advertised that the local water was so rich in tiny particles of gold that he was filtering $5 to $10 worth out of each barrelful. While so-called flour gold was sometimes so fine that it would float in water, the Calistoga Springs water had none—except what this promoter had put there. It remained for Mark Twain to demolish the scam as only a master storyteller could. In response to an account about the claim, Twain wrote:

> I have just seen your dispatch from San Francisco in Saturday evening's Post. This will surprise many of your readers but it does not surprise me, for once I owned those springs myself. What does surprise me, however, is the falling off of the richness of the water. In my time the yield was a dollar a dipperful. I am not saying this to injure the property in case a sale is contemplated. I am saying it in the interest of history. It may be that the hotel proprietor's process is an inferior one. Yes, that may be the fault. Mine was to take my uncle (I had an extra one at that time on account of his parents dying and leaving him on my hands) and fill him up and let him stand fifteen minutes, to give the water a chance to settle. Well, then I inserted an exhaust receiver, which had the effect of sucking the gold out of his pores. I have taken more than $11,000 out of that old man in less than a day and a half.
>
> I should have held on to those springs, but for the badness of the roads and the difficulty of getting the gold to market, I consider that the gold-yielding water is in many respects remarkable, and yet no more remarkable than the gold-bearing air of Catgut Canyon up there toward the head of the auriferous range. This air, or this wind—for it is a kind of trade-wind which blows steadily down through 600 miles of richest quartz

croppings—is heavily charged with exquisitely fine, impalpable gold.

> Nothing precipitates and solidifies this gold so readily as contact with human flesh heated by passion. The time that William Abrahams was disappointed in love he used to sit outdoors when the wind was blowing, and come in again and begin to sigh, and I would extract over a dollar and a half out of every sigh.
>
> I do not suppose a person could buy the water privileges at Calistoga now at any price, but several good locations along the course of Catgut Canyon gold-bearing trade-winds are for sale. They are going to be stocked for the New York market. They will sell, too.

Twain was right; almost any kind of salting plot would work because of the irresistible lure of easy treasure that had affected Western prospectors ever since the gold rush of 1849.

See also: *Great Diamond Hoax.*

SAMOOTS, Sam: See Samuzzo "Samoots" Amatuna.

SANDBAR Duel: Birthplace of bowie knife

Probably the most famous, and certainly the bloodiest, duel ever fought on the Mississippi was the so-called Sandbar Duel of September 19, 1827. Although many men died the battle is remembered chiefly as marking the debut of the bowie knife.

In August of that year a duel was arranged between two Natchez men, a Dr. Maddox and Samuel Well, to be fought on the Vidalia sandbar in the Mississippi near Natchez. Each combatant appeared with a number of supporters, all heavily armed. The duelists fired two exchanges without suffering injury, but before the affair could be ended, heated quarrels started among the supporters of the two men. Suddenly, mass shooting broke out. One of the participants wounded by the gunfire was frontiersman Jim Bowie. Although badly hurt, Bowie drew a homemade knife, fashioned either by himself or his brother Rezin, and killed Major Norris Wright, a local banker with whom he had been having a financial dispute. In all, six men died and 15 others were severely wounded in the post-duel melee, but the main notoriety went to Bowie and his fearsome weapon, with which he had so efficiently, as one account stated, "disemboweled" his opponent.

See also: *Bowie Knife.*

SANDS: Chicago vice area

In the 1850s the worst vice district in Chicago was called the Sands, lying just about where the Tribune and Wrigley buildings are now situated. At the time, the Sands consisted of about 40 buildings, every one of which was a brothel, a gambling den, a thieves' hideout or a saloon partly used for prostitution. The *Chicago Tribune* called the Sands

> the vilest and most dangerous place in Chicago. For some years past it has been the resort or hiding place of all sorts of criminals, while the most wretched and degraded women and their

miserable pimps [are] there in large numbers. A large number of persons, mostly strangers in the city, have been enticed into the dens there and robbed, and there is but little doubt that a number of murders have been committed by the desperate characters who have made these dens their homes. The most beastly sexuality and darkest crimes had their homes in the Sands. . . .

Typical of the establishments found there was a saloon-bagnio operated by Freddy Webster. It was noted for both its viciousness and vileness. One of Webster's inmates was a prostitute named Margaret McGuinness, who was described as never having been sober or out of the house in five years and never having had clothes on in three years. She entertained anywhere from 15 to 40 men a night. When she died on March 8, 1857 of "intemperance," hers was the seventh death to occur in the Sands in the previous seven days.

The Sands, or at least its women, were the cause of the so-called Whore War of 1857, when a group of madams on State Street attempted to lure away some of the area's star prostitutes. Led by a brutal young prostitute, Gentle Annie Stafford, the forces of the Sands prevailed.

Numerous political figures vowed to wipe out the Sands but never did, mainly because its inhabitants insisted they would fight to the death to remain there. Finally, in 1857 Mayor Long John Wentworth accomplished the deed on a day when all the men and many of the women had left the Sands to attend a great dog fight at a nearby racetrack. Accompanied by some 30 policemen and two horse-drawn wagons loaded with hooks and chains, the mayor ordered the flimsy structures of the Sands pulled down. As the work progressed, a fire company arrived and destroyed several shanties with streams of water. Some of the buildings were burned, and by the time the inhabitants of the Sands returned, they found nothing left but rubble and ashes. The area eventually became a prime business location, but whether the destruction of the Sands represented civic progress is debatable. Its several hundred undesirable residents simply spread themselves around Chicago.

See also: *Annie Stafford, Whore War.*

SANDY Flash: See James Fitzpatrick.

SANGERMAN'S Bombers: Bombers-for-hire gang

While bombings in late 19th and early 20th century America were always considered the work of foreign elements, such as Black Hand extortionists or black-bearded anarchists, the fact is that the bombers were just as often dyed-in-the-wool Americans.

The first criminal gang of bombers was Chicago's Sweeney gang, which carried out wholesale bombing attacks during and after World War I until its members were arrested by police in 1921. Sweeney's Bombers, as the newspapers labeled them, were succeeded by Sangerman's Bombers, who raised the practice to new technical heights, carrying out terrorist labor bombings as well as selling their services to politicians

and elements of organized crime. The kingpin of the operation was Joseph Sangerman, a leading manufacturer of barber shop supplies as well as head of the barbers' union. The Illinois Crime Survey called him "the directing genius of the bombing trust, the contractor of bombing." As an officer in the barbers' union, he began by hiring bombers to discipline barber shop owners who refused to operate their stores in accordance with union rules. Finding that his gang could do a job effectively and escape detection, he began to accept commissions in other fields. Arrested in 1925, Sangerman admitted to police that he maintained a full-time staff of six bombers, including one woman, and that his rates ran from $50 to $700 a job.

One star member of Sangerman's crew was George Matrisciano, described as the best bomb maker in Chicago's history. Matrisciano always carried two sticks of dynamite in his pockets. When several indictments were drawn against him, fear grew that he might talk, as Sangerman had, and he was killed, according to the crime survey, by "the guns of the officers of the barbers' union."

With the breakup of Sangerman's Bombers, the incidence of bombing in Chicago started to decline. The bombings in the 1916-21 Aldermen's Wars and the 1928 Republican primary proved to be too loud in more ways than one. As the Capone mob and its successors learned, bombings were spectacles that drew too much attention. The gun, knife and ice pick were more pedestrian but, in the long run, safer.

See also: *Aldermen's Wars, Pineapple Primary, Sweeney's Bombers.*

SATURDAY Night Special: Cheap handgun

Saturday Night Special is the name applied to the small, easily concealed, usually illegal handguns that have been used in millions of crimes by persons, including youths, who cannot afford to spend more than $5 or $10 for a weapon.

Its birthplace was Detroit, Mich., one of the nation's most violent cities but not necessarily one where guns were easy to purchase. In the late 1950s and early 1960s mayhem-minded Detroiters began making one-hour car trips to Toledo, Ohio, a gun buyer's paradise where weapons could be bought at shoeshine stands, filling stations, candy stores and even flower shops. Harassed Detroit lawmen found that the purchases made during these trips were often used in stickups on Saturday nights and thus dubbed the weapons Saturday Night Specials.

It is wrong to try to categorize these handguns as merely cheap foreign imports, since many of them are produced by American gun manufacturers.

Testifying before a Senate committee in 1971, New York City's police commissioner, Patrick V. Murphy, spoke of the perils of Saturday Night Specials and other guns as well.

What kind of guns are used by our criminals? . . . Of the 8,792 illegal weapons seized by the New York City Police Department in 1970, 24 percent of them were classified by our ballistics section as of this type. In one recent sixteen-month sampling we were able to establish that such weapons, retailing for as little as five or ten dollars, were used in at least 36 murders, 68 robberies, and 117 felonious assaults.

There is absolutely no legitimate reason to permit the importation, manufacture, or sale of these weapons, or their parts. They are sought only by people who have illicit motives, but who may have some difficulty securing a better gun. . . .

But Saturday Night Specials are only one part of the handgun problem, and by no means the most significant part. Most of the guns we seized are quality weapons manufactured by reputable foreign and domestic companies. . . .

See also: *Derringer, Muff Pistol, Pepperbox Special.*

SCALICE, Frank "Don Chreech" (1894-1957): Mafia underboss.

The number two man in Albert Anastasia's New York crime family, Frank Scalice died in a web of Mafia intrigue that probably will never be unraveled.

As second in command to Anastasia in what had originally been the Mangano crime family, Scalice became most active in recruiting new members into the Mafia beginning in 1954, when the "books," or membership rosters, were opened for the first time since the early 1930s. It was later charged that Scalice was taking kickbacks of up to $50,000 from successful applicants. When Anastasia heard the accusations against his aide, he immediately ordered his murder, and Scalice was cut down by four bullets in the neck and head as he stood in front of a Bronx fruit store. Anastasia's motive for acting with such unseemly haste apparently was due to a widely circulated rumor that he himself was getting a cut of Scalice's kickbacks.

One theory has it that Scalice was innocent of the charge and that it resulted from a frame-up by Vito Genovese, then involved in a struggle with Anastasia for the top position in the New York Mafia. Genovese is believed to have formulated the plot to discredit Anastasia, but the latter simply outwitted him by killing Scalice. In any event, the official police report on the slaying summed up the only hard facts ever determined about the crime: murder bullets were "fired by two unknown white males who fled in an automobile."

See also: *Vito Genovese, Albert Anastasia.*

SCALISE, John: See Anselmi and Scalise.

SCALP Hunting

Contrary to what has now become the widely accepted view, American Indians did not learn scalping from white settlers. But while they indeed started the practice, the introduction of steel knives and tomahawks by Europeans made scalping easier and helped spread the custom. Scalp hunting became a business when whites introduced a system of paying for scalps as a way of getting rid of hostile or unwanted Indians. The bounties offered at various times by Colonial governments and then by Mexican and U.S. government agencies in the West were pretty much standard: $100 for a male Indian scalp; $50 for a female; $25 for a child. Naturally, such a system was an invitation to commit wholesale slaughter. One of the more terrible instances occurred in 1837, when a scalp hunter named James Johnson devised a scheme whereby the Mimbreno Apaches were invited to a lavish feast in the town plaza of Santa Rita del Cobre, just south of the Rio Grande. After the Indians had been plied with food and whiskey and were no longer alert, two howitzers as well as rifles, pistols and bowie knives were used to slaughter them. Four hundred scalps were taken.

Besides Johnson, probably the most proficient of the Western scalp hunters were John Glanton, James Kirker and Jim Hobbs, none of whom was known to be above taking the hair of Mexicans or dark-skinned Americans. Operating under the doctrine of Manifest Destiny, government bounty payers seem to have been not very particular.

See also: *John Glanton, James Hobbs, James Kirker.*

SCHMID, Charles Howard (1942-): Mass murderer

Often called the Pied Piper of Tucson, Charles Schmid was 22 years old in 1964 when he led a weird clique of admiring young people on forays of rape and bizarre behavior, ending in a series of meaningless murders.

Even in his high school days Schmid behaved strangely Only five feet three inches, he padded his cowboy boots to make him taller, dyed his red hair black, wore cosmetics and designed a phony mole on his face to make him look meaner. He told wild tales that somehow made him very popular, attracting a number of girls who prostituted themselves to provide him with money. One girl went to work in his parent's nursing home and faithfully deposited most of her week's pay in Schmid's bank account.

Schmid rented a cottage on the outskirts of Tucson, bought a beat-up car and became a fixture of the Speedway Boulevard area, a strip that attracted race-happy motorcyclists, souped-up car enthusiasts and rock-and-roll music lovers. On May 31, 1964 Schmid was drinking with two young friends, Mary French and John Saunders, when he announced he felt like killing a girl. "I want to do it tonight," he said. "I think I can get away with it!"

Mary French invited 15-year-old Alleen Rowe to join them late that night and they went for a drive in Schmid's car. After stopping in the desert, Mary stayed in the car while Schmid and Saunders took the girl to a secluded spot. Schmid raped her and then casually told Saunders to "hit her over the head with a rock." Saunders started to obey but the horrified girl ran off. After catching up with her, Schmid knocked her to the ground and smashed her skull in with a rock. They buried the girl in a shallow grave and went off to do some more drinking.

In August 1965 a girl friend of Schmid's, 17-year-old Gretchen Fritz, disappeared with her 13-year-old sister, Wendy. Like Alleen Rowe, the Fritz girls were listed as runaways by the police, but a short while later, Schmid boasted to a friend, Richard Bruns, that he had strangled both sisters and thrown their bodies into a ditch. Since Bruns refused to believe the story, Schmid showed him the corpses.

Bruns kept silent about the matter for a while until he got it into his head that Schmid was going to kill his, Bruns', girlfriend. He started having nightmares about Schmid and finally went to the police. Schmid was arrested on November 11, 1965, as were French and Saunders, The latter two turned state's evidence against their bizarre hero. Schmid got 55 years for the rape-murder of Alleen Rowe and the death sentence for the slayings of the Fritz girls. French got four to five years and Saunders life imprisonment for their parts in the Rowe crime. When the Supreme Court abolished capital punishment, Schmid was resentenced to two terms of life imprisonment.

On November 11, 1972 Schmid escaped from the Arizona State Prison along with another triple murderer, Raymond Hudgens. The pair held four hostages on a ranch near Tempe, Ariz., and then separated. Both were recaptured within a few days and returned to prison.

SCHULTZ, Dutch (1902-1935): Underworld leader

Among the great underworld leaders spawned by Prohibition, Dutch Schultz was one of the flakiest, probably the cheapest and often the most cold-blooded. In the end, he had to be executed by his fellow gangsters because he threatened the status quo established between organized crime and the law. Born Arthur Flegenheimer in the Bronx, New York City, he tended bar and had only a minor criminal record until the mid-1920s, when he formed a gang and took over much of the beer trade in the Bronx. Tough, aggressive and probably keener in his appreciation of potential sources of illicit revenues than even Lucky Luciano, he was the first to see the fortune to be made out of the numbers racket in Harlem. He moved in on the independent black operators there and, using force and violence, turned them into his agents in a new multimillion dollar racket. Through a mathematical genius named Otto "Abbadabba" Berman, he figured out a way to fix the numbers game so that the smallest possible payout was made when someone hit.

Few other gangsters, including most of his own men, either liked or respected him, but they feared him. Schultz was a miser who paid his gangsters as little as he could get away with, and he would almost fly into a rage whenever he was asked for a raise. The only man in the organization he paid really well was Abbadabba, who got $10,000 a week, though only after he threatened to take his mathematical skills elsewhere.

Schultz never spent more than $35 for a suit or $2 for a shirt. "Personally," he once told an interviewer, "I think only queers wear silk shirts. I never bought one in my life. A guy's a sucker to spend fifteen or twenty dollars on a shirt. Hell, a guy can get a good one for two bucks!"

Lucky Luciano once said of him: "Dutch was the cheapest guy I ever knew. The guy had a couple of million bucks and he dressed like a pig, and he worried about spending two cents for a newspaper. That was his big spending, buying the papers so's he could read about himself."

Schultz was somewhat of an expert on newspapers. He admitted that he took the name of Dutch Schultz because "it was short enough to fit in the headlines. If I'd kept the name of Flegenheimer, nobody would have heard of me." Once, he raged at Meyer Berger, the star crime reporter of *The New York Times*, because Berger had described him as a "pushover for a blonde."

Actually, only one offense truly enraged Schultz. His famous "mouthpiece" Dixie Davis, later said of him: "You can insult Arthur's girl, spit in his face, push him around—and he'll laugh. But don't steal a dollar from his accounts. If you do, you're dead."

Among those who did and died for it was the murderous Jack "Legs" Diamond, who became known as the underworld's clay pigeon in his wars with various gangsters, especially Schultz. When Diamond expired in an upstate New York hotel room with several bullets in his head, Schultz was quoted as saying, "Just another punk caught with his hands in my pockets." Vincent "Mad Dog" Coll, a former underling with a fiery temper and raging ambitions, also challenged Schultz. Coll staged wholesale raids on Schultz' beer drops and policy joints, and while he matched the Dutchman at killing, he was forced into hiding by the Schultz organization's superior firepower. On February 8, 1932 he ventured forth to use a telephone booth and was gunned down by Schultz' machine gunners.

After that, no one really wanted to take on Schultz. He would fight to the last man and had powerful political protection, mainly through Jimmy Hines, the Tammany boss who would later go to prison for his protection of the Schultz forces. Although Luciano, Meyer Lansky and the other founders of the national crime syndicate dealt the Dutchman in, considering him too powerful to leave out, they secretly sought to get rid of Schultz because they considered him too erratic and because they wanted to take over his lucrative beer and policy rackets. While Schultz was awaiting trial after being indicted on tax charges, Luciano and his associates moved quickly to take over his rackets through the cooperation of Schultz' top aide, Bo Weinberg. Amazingly, Schultz beat the case against him and returned to reclaim his domain. Rather than fight him, the syndicate leaders gave back large chunks they had gobbled up, explaining they had been simply minding the Dutchman's holdings in his absence. Schultz was almost forgiving, but not towards Weinberg. Shortly thereafter, Weinberg became a permanent missing person. According to one underworld report, Schultz personally put a bullet in his head, but in another version Weinberg was fitted with a "cement overcoat" and dropped—still alive—into the Hudson River. Either story could be true.

Schultz' demise came about because of his desire to get rid of special prosecutor Thomas E. Dewey, whom Gov. Herbert Lehman had appointed in 1935 to investigate racketeering and vice. When Dewey started cracking down on the mobs, particularly on Schultz and his gang, the Dutchman, seeing his revenues decline, went before the national board of the syndicate to demand that Dewey be assassinated. The proposal was quickly turned down by Luciano, Lansky, Louis Lepke, Costello and others, who were convinced it would bring an avalanche of police pressure on the entire underworld.

Undeterred by the strong vote against him, Schultz stormed out of the meeting, defiantly declaring: "I still say he ought to be hit. And if nobody else is gonna do it, I'm gonna hit him myself."

When the syndicate learned Schultz was really going ahead with the plot and had even picked a murder site, they quickly put out a quick contract on him.

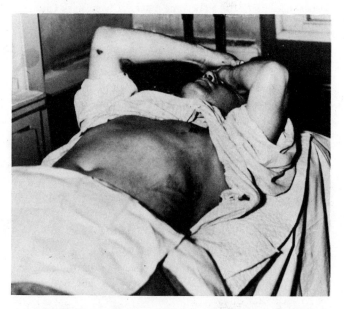

Dutch Schultz lingered for two days after being shot, but he did not name his killers. Instead he talked mostly gibberish, including some mysterious mumblings about all the money he had hidden.

On October 23, 1935 Schultz, Abbadabba Berman and two bodyguards, Abe Landau and Lulu Rosenkrantz were in a favorite hangout, the Palace Chop House and Tavern in Newark, N.J. Schultz left his three henchmen sitting at a table in the back and went into the men's room. While he was in there, two gunmen entered the Palace. One of the two burst into the men's room and shot to death a man standing at a urinal, not realizing the victim was Schultz. He then charged at the table where Berman and the two bodyguards were seated and, with two guns blazing, killed them all. Only at that point did the gunmen discover that Schultz was not among the three. However, when they checked the men's room, they found Schultz was the man who had been shot simply to ensure that the pair were not surprised from behind. The gunman who had done all the shooting lifted a considerable amount of cash from Schultz' pockets and then fled.

Schultz lingered in a hospital for two days before dying. Eventually, one of his killers was identified as Charles "the Bug" Workman. He was tried and sentenced to 23 years for the crime.

See also: *Otto "Abbadabba" Berman, Meyer Berger, Thomas E. Dewey, Charles "Lucky" Luciano, Jacob "Gurrah" Shapiro.*

SCHUSTER, Arnold (1928-1952): Murder victim

In February 1952 Arnold Schuster, a 24-year-old Brooklyn clothing salesman, made the front pages of newspapers from coast to coast after he spotted the notorious bank robber Willie "the Actor" Sutton while riding on a New York City subway. He followed Sutton out of the subway, watched him enter a garage and then notified the police. Sutton was captured on the street as he was removing the battery from his stalled car. On March 9, 1952 Arnold Schuster was back on the front pages: a gruesome picture displayed his corpse lying on the Brooklyn street where he lived. He had been shot four times: twice in the groin and once in each eye.

An unsuccessful police manhunt was organized for a 37-year-old murderer and escaped convict named Frederick J. Tenuto after he was tentatively identified by a witness who had seen the assassin leaving the site of the crime. Tenuto was already on the FBI's list of the 10 most-wanted criminals. Years later, an unexpected source, Mafia informer Joe Valachi, confirmed that Tenuto had killed young Schuster on orders from the Mafia's most-feared executioner, Albert Anastasia. Watching Schuster being interviewed on television after Sutton's capture, the crime boss had become enraged and had exploded, "I can't stand squealers!" He ordered Schuster executed for informing on Sutton, even though the bank robber had no connection with organized crime. Anastasia removed any risk of being connected with the Schuster murder by having Tenuto assassinated.

At the Mafia's famous Apalachin meeting in November 1957, Vito Genovese justified the barber shop killing of Anastasia on the grounds of his maniacal rages and his capacity to have almost anyone murdered at any time. The Schuster killing was clearly one of the things Genovese had in mind.

See also: *Albert Anastasia, Apalachin Conference, Willie "the Actor" Sutton, Frederick J. Tenuto.*

SCHWARTZ, Charles Henry: See Warren Gilbert Barbe.

SCOLDS

Punishment of women for being common scolds, i.e., vituperative females who rebuke others so rudely and loudly that they frequently disturb the public peace, was long practiced in America right up to the middle of this century.

A typical example was Anne Royall of Washington, D.C., who in 1829 was made to pay a $10 fine and post a $50 good-behavior bond. In 1947 a woman in Greensburg, Pa. was forced to pay court costs and was given a suspended sentence for being a scold. That same year three sisters in Pittsburgh were sent to jail on scolding charges for terms ranging from three to 23 months.

SCOPES, John T. (1900-1970): Monkey trial defendant

In 1925 John T. Scopes, a 24-year-old biology teacher in Dayton, Tenn., violated state law that forbade the teaching of "any theory that denies the story of the Divine Creation of man as taught in the Bible, and to teach instead that man has descended from a lower order of animals." Since there was no question that by teaching evolution Scopes had broken the law, he played only a minor role in the ensuing criminal trial, which pitted three-time presidential candidate William Jennings Bryan, age 65, against defense lawyer Clarence Darrow, age 68.

The trial became a worldwide media event, as more than 100 journalists descended on the small hamlet to watch the philosophical battle, which reached its highest drama when Darrow called the great believer, Bryan, to the stand. Bryan based his testimony on a literal interpretation of the Bible, accepting the creation of Eve from Adam's rib. When Darrow asked, "Did you ever discover where Cain got his wife?" Bryan answered, "No, sir; I leave the agnostics to hunt for her." As Darrow proceeded with questions about the origins of the earth and the ages of rocks, Bryan was reduced to shambling contradictions, finally falling back completely on fundamentalist beliefs.

By the time the 11-day trial ended, newspapers around the nation and around the world were treating Bryan with contempt. Nonetheless Scopes was convicted and fined $100, and fundamentalists cheered the news that the monkey was on the run. The decision was later reversed on a legal technicality, and the authorities didn't dare bring the matter to court again.

Bryan was shocked at the scorn heaped on him and drowned his sorrow in food. Five days after the trial, he sat down to a breakfast that consisted of a large stack of hot cakes soaked in syrup, six fried eggs, three thick slices of ham, an immeasurable amount of fried potatoes, seven corn muffins and six cups of coffee with sugar and cream. Then he died.

Darrow was quite solicitous of his rival's death and mumbled a few words of respect until a reporter told him, "They say that Mr. Bryan died of a broken heart and that you were the cause of it."

Darrow snorted. "Broken heart, hell," he snapped. "He died of a busted belly."

See also: *Clarence Darrow.*

SCOTTO, Anthony M. (1934-   ): Union leader

Anthony M. Scotto emerged as a force in New York longshoremen's union affairs during the 1960s after the death of Anthony "Tough Tony" Anastasio, to whom he was related by marriage. At the time, Scotto was hailed as a new-breed leader who would bring respectability to waterfront unionism. It was not to be so. In 1979 federal investigators, insisting labor racketeering was still a way of life on the waterfront, arrested Scotto, then general organizer of the AFL-CIO International Longshoremen's Association and president of the union's Local 1814 in Brooklyn, one of the top three posts in the 100,000-member union, representing dock workers from Maine to Texas. He was charged with labor racketeering.

In November, Scotto was convicted of taking more than $200,000 in cash payoffs from waterfront businesses despite his claim that he had "never taken a cent" for himself from anyone. He insisted he had accepted a series of political contributions, not payoffs, totaling $75,000, which he claimed he then gave to New York Lt. Gov. Mario M. Cuomo for his unsuccessful 1977 bid to become mayor of New York City and to New York Gov. Hugh L. Carey for his successful 1978 campaign to win reelection.

In 1980 U.S. District Judge Charles E. Stewart, Jr. sentenced Scotto to five years in prison and fined him $75,000. The judge said he had been "extremely impressed" by letters from prominent politicians and labor and business leaders requesting leniency for Scotto, who could have gotten 20 years. Among those who had testified as character witnesses at his trial were Gov. Carey, and two former New York mayors, Robert Wagner and John V. Lindsay. Convicted along with Scotto was his father-in-law, Anthony Anastasio, the late Tough Tony Anastasio's nephew.

SCOTTSBORO Boys: Accused rapists

The greatest civil rights battle of the 1930s was the Scottsboro Case, in which nine black youths, aged 13 to 20, were tried and convicted of raping two "Southern ladies" aboard a freight train in Alabama in 1931.

The incident started on a Memphis-bound freight train when the nine blacks got into a fistfight with a number of white youths also riding the rails in search of work. The blacks defeated the whites and tossed them off the slow-moving train. One of the whites reported the clash to authorities and the order was given to "round up every Negro on the train and bring them to Scottsboro."

The freight was halted and the nine youths were taken in by deputies. Also netted were two white females clad in overalls: Victoria Price, 19, and Ruby Bates, 17. Fearing they would be charged with vagrancy, the two declared they had been gang-raped by a dozen blacks, three of whom had jumped from the train. The nine were tied together and hauled to Scottsboro to await Alabama justice, while Victoria Price and Ruby Bates were transformed into the epitome of Southern womanhood. As the story spread, the youths were nothing but "black brutes" who had, among other things, chewed off one of Ruby Bate's breasts.

A whirlwind trial took place within 12 days of the alleged crime. During the trial the defendants were under constant threat of being lynched and National Guardsmen were sent to protect them. Lawyers were finally provided for the nine on the day the trial began; one of the counsels appeared to be drunk during the entire proceedings. At one point in his presentation to the jury, the prosecutor declared, "Guilty or not, let's get rid of these niggers." The jury voted guilty despite medical evidence that while both females had had sexual intercourse, the acts had not occurred as recently as the day of the alleged incident and there was none of the usual signs indicating force had been used. Eight of the nine were sentenced to death, and the youngest, aged 13, was given life imprisonment because of his age, although seven jurors had voted for his execution.

In the succeeding months and years the Scottsboro case was in and out of various courts, with the defendants now represented by attorney Samuel S. Leibowitz, the "New York Jew nigger lover," as he was called. The original verdict was thrown out by the Supreme Court in 1932 on the basis that the defendants had been denied adequate counsel.

Several trials ensued involving various of the defendants. In that of Clarence Willie Norris, Leibowitz charged that Victoria Price was a prostitute, and Ruby Bates admitted no rapes had occurred. Nevertheless, Norris was convicted. Leibowitz then succeeded in getting several of the convictions set aside by winning a Supreme Court decision that the exclusion of blacks from jury service was unconstitutional. More trials followed. The so-called ringleader, Haywood Patterson, was convicted and given 75 years.

Meanwhile, international protests mounted. Albert Einstein and Theodore Dreiser were in the forefront of the protests. Europeans stoned a number of U.S. consulates and an American bank in Cuba was bombed. Finally, the state, under intense pressure from the public and the press, dropped charges against four defendants, and by the 1940s four more had been paroled. In 1948 Patterson escaped from prison and fled to Michigan, where two years later he was convicted of manslaughter in the stabbing death of a black man. He died in prison in 1952.

By 1980 Norris was the only Scottsboro boy known to be alive. He had jumped parole in 1946, escaped to Ohio and eventually moved to New York. In July 1976 Norris, still a fugitive under Alabama law, applied to Gov. George Wallace for a pardon, which was granted in October. When he went to Alabama early in 1977 to accept his pardon, Norris was hailed by blacks and a great many whites as something of a hero. A few months later, the Alabama House Judiciary Committee voted down a bill to pay him $10,000 compensation.

See also: *Samuel S. Leibowitz.*

SEABURY Investigation: New York corruption probe

In 1930 a former jurist, Samuel Seabury, took leave from his lucrative private legal practice to launch a series of probes into New York City's scandal-wracked administration, the first important such probe since the much-heralded Lexow Committee investigation of 1894-95. Essentially, the Seabury Investigation arrived at the conclusion that little had improved in a generation, that graft taking, for instance, was a common practice within the police department rather than the acts of a few corrupt officers, or "bad apples."

Seabury's probe of the vice squad was sidetracked for a time when the leading potential witness, a high-priced prostitute

and blackmailer named Vivian Gordon, was found strangled to death in Van Cortlandt Park after she had started providing investigators with extensive evidence of corruption. Eventually, 20 members were dismissed.

Seabury determined that bribery of public officers was vital to obtaining special privileges for waterfront leases, bus franchises and variances from building zoning law and in condemnation cases, and was needed to conduct many other activities as well. Day after day the Seabury hearings exposed payoffs, venality and crime, linking the worst criminal elements with the political powers of Tammany Hall, various police commissioners and, especially, Mayor Jimmy Walker. Magistrates squirmed as they tried to explain the special considerations shown to gambling figures and others possessing good political connections.

Gov. Franklin D. Roosevelt was accused in some quarters of giving Seabury less than full support, causing Walter Lippmann to write, "Franklin D. Roosevelt is no crusader." Roosevelt at the time was campaigning for the Democratic nomination for president and was wary of offending Tammany. While denouncing civic crime, Roosevelt said he did not feel a strong enough case had been made against Mayor Walker to warrant executive action on his part. However, once the nomination was locked up, with the support of Tammany's Jimmy Hines, Roosevelt reversed himself and fully backed Seabury, declaring that Walker and all other city officeholders had to answer all questions put to them or get out of office.

Seabury hauled a parade of city officials and politicians before the committee and grilled them relentlessly. Caches of money, clearly bribes, turned up all over, and many were linked to the mayor. Walker appeared in the hearing room and brashly announced, "Little Boy Blue is going to blow his horn—or his top." He did neither, proving to be an unimpressive witness as one juicy piece of evidence after another was placed before him.

Walker was forced to admit that at one time he had shared a joint bank account with a broker who had made a $246,692 cash deposit to the account, allegedly the profits from stock transactions, although there was no evidence of this. Later, the mayor had withdrawn the money and put it in his safe. "Not in a tin box," he said, not without a measure of charm. What happened to the money? he was asked. He and his wife had "just spent it."

As more and more evidence piled up against Walker, he lost a lot of his jauntiness. When Roosevelt gave strong indication he was preparing to remove the mayor from office, Walker acted quickly, sending off a telegram to Albany: "I HEREBY RESIGN AS MAYOR OF THE CITY OF NEW YORK . . . JAMES J. WALKER."

The Seabury probe was credited with paving the way for the reform administration of Mayor Fiorello La Guardia. After the investigation Seabury returned to private practice. He died in 1958.

See also: *Vivian Gordon, James J. Walker.*

SECRET Band Of Brothers: Reputed 19th century crime syndicate

The first "Mafia" in the United States may not have been the one that originated in Sicily but a mysterious organization said to have started in the 1830s. Not much is known about it other than what appeared in a modest book published in 1847, *The Secret Band of Brothers* by Jonathan F. Green, who could be described as 19th century Joe Valachi. According to Green's thesis, this secret band was set up and run almost exactly the way Valachi would describe the operations of the Cosa Nostra more than 100 years later. The band had initiation rituals, codes and orders that had to be obeyed without question. Within the ruling organization there were grand masters and vice-grand masters and, above all, a boss of bosses called the worthy grand. The group, Green said, was "pledged to gambling, thievery and villainy of all kinds" and members "wandered from place to place, preying upon the community in the character of barkeepers, pickpockets, thieves, gamblers, horse players, and sometimes murderers." Orders from the top were written in secret ink and left at message drops in caves and hollow trees.

Among those who believed the story of this secret band was Horace Greeley, who employed Green as the chief undercover agent for his New York Association for the Suppression of Gambling. Green was a reformed gambler and passer of "queer," or counterfeit money. The Secret Service considered him reliable enough to use as a plant in New York's Tombs Prison to seek evidence about counterfeiting.

The Secret Band of Brothers was never fully exposed, but that does not necessarily cast doubt on Green's story. It must be remembered that in this period there was no national police organization to counter such a group and that local police organizations, even if not corrupt, were not equipped to handle such a task. If Green fantasized his secret band, he was a clairvoyant of some skill, given what is known today about the workings of organized crime.

SECRET Service: Federal law enforcement agency

The fastest-growing federal law enforcement unit, the Secret Service is charged with protecting the president of the United States, detecting and arresting counterfeiters and guarding the buildings and vaults of the Treasury Department, of which it is a branch.

Created in 1865 to combat counterfeiters, the Secret Service was the first general law-enforcement agency of the federal government. Abraham Lincoln approved the establishment of the organization during his last cabinet meeting. At various times the service took on added duties, battling opium smuggling, the Ku Klux Klan, extortion rackets, espionage rings and land frauds and even foiling a plot to steal Lincoln's body from its tomb. These duties were transferred over the years to newer agencies, leaving the Secret Service solely concerned with anticounterfeiting activities until 1901, when presiden-

tial protection was added to its chores in the aftermath of the McKinley assassination.

In succeeding years the agency's presidential protection function was expanded to cover the president-elect, the president's immediate family, the vice president and vice president-elect, the former presidents and their wives and widows and their children until they reach the age of 16. In 1968 Secret Service protection was extended to include major presidential and vice presidential candidates and, in 1971, the protection of visiting heads of state and other foreign dignitaries.

As such, the Secret Service is seemingly immune from budget-cutting efforts. In 1963, when John F. Kennedy was assassinated, the Secret Service had 389 agents and a budget of $5.4 million. In 1980 it had 1,552 agents and a budget of $157 million. The agency's Protective Research Section processes some 14,000 cases a year, and in 1978, a typical year, it made 406 arrests and secured 351 convictions or commitments of persons found guilty of threatening the lives of the people—chiefly the president—whom the section is assigned to protect.

Much of the service's time is consumed checking on potential assassins from a computer list of about 30,000 "risk types" and an even more closely screened roster of "400" prime suspects. Before the president visits a city, the agency checks on each of the "400," many of whom are mentally disturbed and/or have a history of violence, and puts several under 24-hour surveillance, which may require the use of 14 or 15 agents full time.

The Secret Service had successfully guarded all presidents in its care until the Kennedy assassination in 1963, after which it was severely criticized by the Warren Commission for being ill prepared in manpower and facilities to handle presidential protection under complex modern conditions. This resulted in rapid increases in budget and staff.

Today, the agency considers its protective procedures about as foolproof as they can be made.

The president is often shielded by bulletproof glass shields on stands and the floor of his review stand is fitted with heavy armor plating to protect against bombs. Helicopters fly overhead to keep the sky safe and to watch for rooftop snipers. Secret Service agents have perfected a car with bulletproof hood, windows and tires and now arm themselves with powerful miniature walkie-talkies, .357 magnum revolvers and Israeli-made Uzi submachine guns or M-16 rifles. They are regularly schooled by psychiatrists on the profile of an assassin, although until the two attacks on Gerald Ford in 1975 the classes did not cover females.

Before the president goes near any water, military frogmen check undersea for bombs and the Coast Guard provides vessels for offshore patrols. A week before any presidential visit to a city, agents pour into the area to construct a "sanitized zone." They work out routes where motorcades can flow freely with a number of sudden turnoffs, should they prove necessary, and crowds can be easily observed. Travel time is computed and the number of men needed to watch rooftops and windows is estimated. Agents closest to the president memorize the faces of "400" suspects believed to be in the area so that they can spot them in a crowd. To prevent the crowd from knowing where agents are looking, they often wear sunglasses, even during heavy rain.

The agency probably feels it can handle threats close to the president as well as those from rooftops. As in the case of Oswald, the biggest danger is spotting a window sniper in time.

White House protection is generally considered to be impregnable. Agents closely examine all food and packages that enter the White House and scrutinize the long lines of tourists. The visitors are constantly watched by TV cameras buried in the ground, hidden under bushes and disguised as lanterns. There is no way anyone can slip across closed-off sections of the White House lawn—seismic sensors planted in the grass will pick up even a baby's footsteps. Ever since a helicopter unexpectedly came down on the South Lawn, White House police have been armed with Redeye shoulder-fired antiaircraft guns. All the White House gates have been reinforced ever since an intruder crashed through them one Christmas. And if things ever got really serious, there is a bomb shelter in the East Wing and a tunnel leading from it to a helicopter waiting nearby for sudden evacuation.

Proof of the thoroughness of White House protection was furnished in 1950, when an attempt was made on the life of Harry Truman. At the time Truman was staying across the street in Blair House while repairs to the White House were being made. Two Puerto Rican terrorists, Oscar Collazo and Griselio Torresola, tried to storm Blair House and kill Truman. They managed to kill one guard and wound two others before Torresola was killed and Collazo was brought down wounded. However, the would-be assassins had failed to penetrate even the outer rim of presidential protectors. Had they gotten into Blair House, they would have had to kill at least 20 agents before reaching the president.

The ability of the Secret Service to dictate to a president what he can and cannot do is more myth than reality. Presidents are generally strong-willed individuals used to having their own way, at times forcing agents to cope with situations as best they can. After the two attempts on his life, Gerald Ford proved more amenable to Secret Service dictates, but other presidents have been notoriously uncooperative. Most guilty of wading into crowds on the spur of the moment was Lyndon Johnson. Even Truman, no paragon of security-consciousness himself while in office, lectured Johnson on his lack of cooperation with the guards assigned to protect him. When John Kennedy was shot, no agents were perched on his automobile because of his request. Had they been there, they conceivably could have blocked the assassin's line of vision to the President.

While it is hardly ever discussed, many agents come to realize that some presidents exhibit latent hostility towards their protectors simply because they resent their constant presence. Even Calvin Coolidge was known to play cruel jokes on the Secret Service.

During his early days in the White House, Coolidge happened to poke behind some curtains and noticed a button on the wall. He pressed it and sat down at his desk to see what would develop. Suddenly, the door flew open and a flock of agents bounded into the room. Coolidge looked up innocently and asked what the rumpus was all about. The men mumbled their apologies and left.

Coolidge had happened on to an alarm the agents had installed throughout the building to signal danger. He immediately pressed the button again. Over the next week, one remembered by the service as a nightmare, he tormented his guards, making the puffing agents charge and recharge into his office while he kept a straight face. Finally, a suspicious agent stayed behind out of sight and watched the President in action. The agent said nothing to Coolidge, but the wires to the button were cut. Thereafter, whenever Coolidge pushed the button, nothing happened, much to his disappointment. And that, at least according to Secret Service folklore, is why Silent Cal never smiled again during the rest of his White House years.

See also: *Assassination, Counterfeiting, "Four Hundred" Assassination List.*

SEDUCTION

Generally speaking, there are relatively few prosecutions today for the crime of seduction, which is the act of persuading a chaste female to have sexual intercourse under a promise of marriage or by means of a fraudulent representation.

In recent years seduction prosecutions have declined as a result of the Sexual Revolution. In addition, the crime is effectively and legally erased if the man marries the woman. When a man has taken this escape hatch, however, the courts have been loath to release him from his commitment even if he subsequently was able to prove fraud. In cases where the man suddenly developed proof that he was not the only recipient of the woman's favor, the courts have generally held that only a fool involved in an illicit relationship would believe he was the sole individual so favored.

A New Jersey court used a different rationale in the case of an ex-prostitute who had convinced a man to marry her by telling him that she had been chaste and that he had seduced her. After the marriage the man discovered the truth, but he failed to make legal headway in having the union dissolved. The court declared:

> Certainly it would lead to disastrous consequences if a woman who had once fallen from virtue could not be permitted to represent herself as continent and thus restore herself to the rights and privileges of her sex, and enter into matrimony without incurring the risk of being put away by her husband on discovery of her previous immorality. Such a doctrine is inconsistent with reason and a wise and sound policy.

Obviously, seduction cases are shunted off court calendars as expeditiously as possible and simply not permitted to return.

SELMAN, John (1839-1896): Gunman and lawman

Many Western historians have puzzled over the fact that lawman John Selman, with an estimated 20 kills to his credit, never won the mass recognition given to other gunfighters. It may be that his record was just too unsavory to gain admirers, even of the perverse sort who honored badmen, such as Jesse James or Billy the Kid, or lawmen of questionable character such as Wyatt Earp or Wild Bill Hickok.

Selman's most famous kill, which was also typical of his others, was the assassination of the notorious gunfighter Wes Hardin in an El Paso, Tex. saloon in 1895. Selman, then a town constable, walked up behind Hardin, who was standing at the bar, and shot him in the back of the head. At the time, Hardin possessed a full pardon and was not wanted for any crime. According to Selman's novel defense, Hardin had seen him in the mirror, and since the constable was fearful that Wes would whirl and draw, he simply shot first. With that flimsy explanation, Selman managed to beat a murder rap.

Sometime lawman, sometime badman John Selman shot Wes Hardin in the back of the head. The shooting proved to be a solid case of "self-defense."

With or without a badge, Selman boasted a long line of such murders. When he was not working as a lawman, he was generally committing crimes. After growing up in Arkansas and Texas, Selman tried ranching, first in the New Mexico Territory and then in Texas. In Fort Griffen, Tex. Selman became acquainted with such frontier gunmen as Wyatt Earp, Doc Holliday, Bat Masterson, Killin' Jim Miller, Pat Garrett and Jesse Evans. He also became an aide of Sheriff John Larn, whose previous occupation was cattle rustling, and the pair hit it off famously. In a typical case Selman handled for Larn, he shot to death a man named Hampden in a "gun duel." Since Hampden was half-deaf and unarmed at the time, it was mur-

der rather than a duel. Selman had called on Hampden to stop, and when he kept on walking, the lawman emptied his pistol into him.

When Larn retired from office, the pair started a ranch in partnership and build up their herd by the simple and inexpensive method of lassoing other ranchers' mavericks. Eventually, Larn was arrested and lynched for these transgressions. Selman fled.

After that, he organized a gang known as Selman's Scouts and hired out to ranchers who wanted their range cleared of rustlers. They would do an excellent job and then with the field to themselves, start their own rustling operation. When Army pressure caused the gang to break up, Selman shifted to West Texas, where he organized another gang of robbers and rustlers. He was arrested in June 1880 along with his brother, Tom Cat Selman, who was subsequently lynched. On his way back to Shackleford County for trial, he bribed his guards and escaped.

Selman fled to Mexico and moved between that country and the New Mexico Territory until 1888, when he learned the old charges against him in Texas had been dropped. He returned to wide-open El Paso, where he stayed relatively honest for a while, leading cattle drives and working in a smelter. He successfully evaded an attempt on his life and, on the basis of being such an upright citizen, was elected constable in 1892, a job he was to hold for the rest of his life, which wasn't for very long.

On April 5, 1894 Selman and Frank Collinson encountered Deputy U.S. Marshal Bass Outlaw and the trio repaired to Tillie Howard's well-known sporting house for some free entertainment, which their high station entitled them to. Outlaw was mean when drunk and he was almost always drunk; in the whorehouse he went wild, put a gun against the head of Texas Ranger Joe McKidrict and shot him twice. Then he started shooting blindly, hitting Selman in the leg twice. Selman shot the crazed lawman in the chest and Outlaw staggered off to die. It was just about Selman's most popular kill.

The following year Selman gunned down Wes Hardin, although that killing wasn't popular. After beating the charges against him he continued as constable until April 1, 1896, when he got into a dispute with yet another lawman, George Scarborough. The pair stepped out into an alley and Scarborough shot him dead. Ironically, the shooting was reminiscent of duels Selman had won—no gun was found on the dead man—and it too was listed as "justifiable homicide."

That didn't seem to upset folks too much. Most felt that Old John had simply been paid back for some of his previous duels. It might also be noted that Scarborough got his in 1900, when he was killed by Kid Curry of the Wild Bunch.

See also: *John Wesley Hardin.*

SENTENCING Of Criminals

The sentencing of convicted persons remains to this day one of the most trying procedures of the criminal justice system. Perhaps no other aspect—interrogation, arrest, trial or conviction—of the system is more rife with error and lack of balanced judgment than the sentencing process. Some judges sentence "long" and others "short." In *Crime in America* former Attorney General Ramsey Clark offers some illustrations of inequality in sentencing, often in different courtrooms in the same courthouse:

> Two boys fail to report for military induction—one is sentenced to five years in prison, the other gets probation and never enters a prison. One judge sentences a robber convicted for the third time to one year in prison, while another judge on the same bench gives a first offender ten years. One man far more capable of serious crime than another and convicted of the same offense may get a fine, while the less fortunate and less dangerous person is sentenced to five years in the state penitentiary. One judge, because of his personal values, thinks homosexuality the most heinous of crimes and gives long sentences. Another hates prostitution. A third judge would never jail juveniles for either offense. Some judges regularly give juvenile offenders prison terms for first-offense car theft, while others turn them over to the custody of their parents.

Inevitably involved in the process are diverse judicial temperament and philosophy as well as varying geographical attitudes. Willard Gayling, in his book *Partial Justice,* relates a story often told by Judge Edward Lumbard:

> A visitor to a Texas court was amazed to hear the judge impose a suspended sentence where a man had pleaded guilty to manslaughter. A few minutes later, the same judge sentenced a man who pleaded guilty to stealing a horse, and gave him life imprisonment. When the judge was asked by the visitor about the disparity between the two sentences, he replied, "Well, down here there is some men that need killin', but there ain't no horses that need stealin.'"

Certain crimes draw varying penalties depending on the economy of the area. Thus in Oregon, Gaylin, notes, 18 of 33 Selective Service violators were let off with probation and none of the others got a prison term of more than three years. Yet, in southern Texas, a defense-oriented state, 16 of 16 got prison terms, 14 of them the maximum five years allowed under the law.

One of the leading voices against the disparity of prison sentences was James V. Bennett, director of the Federal Bureau of Prisons for 27 years. He cited an almost endless string of unfair sentences. In one case a 32-year-old unemployed man whose wife had just suffered a miscarriage forged a government check. Despite the fact that he had no previous criminal record, he was sentenced to 15 years. In his memoirs, *I Chose Prison,* Bennett quoted the judge in that case as saying, "This court intends to stop the stealing and forging of government checks." Yet that same year, another federal judge in the same circuit gave a defendant just 30 days for a like crime.

In an attempt to answer such inequities, Bennett was instrumental in the establishment in 1959 of "sentencing institutes," where judges could exchange views on sentencing theories. There have been other limited advances. In *Crime and Punishment* Aryeh Neier, executive director of the American Civil Liberties Union, notes, " 'Sentencing councils' are another relatively recent innovation. The councils bring together probation officers and judges in an area to review recommendations for sentences by trial judges before the sentences are imposed. While the trial judge can reject the views of his colleagues, the discussions tend to circumscribe extreme disparities in sentencing." Unfortunately, Neier adds, such programs are only moderately popular in the federal court system and are not used "in most court systems where the great majority of criminals are sentenced."

There was a period recently when indeterminate sentencing was viewed by reformers as the only viable alternative to sentencing inequities. Ramsey Clark was a promoter of the idea as late as 1970. Since that time the idea of sentencing without a fixed term has fallen into disfavor, although it lifted a great burden off many judges. In 1976 Alan M. Dershowitz, professor at Harvard Law School, wrote: "The era of the indeterminate sentence . . . is quickly drawing to a close. Reaction is beginning to set in.

Many criminologists now agree that indeterminate sentences actually tend to result in longer prison terms than most judges would mete out and that the disparity in sentencing is often increased rather than reduced. Additionally, such sentences tend to give correctional officials too much control over prisoners' lives and are psychologically dangerous to many prisoners because they can never be sure when they will be released. These factors are often cited as the reason behind many prison riots.

The most recent proposal calls for the abolishment of the federal parole system and a reduction in the sentencing latitude given judges. Under this proposal, probably best articulated by former Attorney General Edward H. Levi, a permanent federal commission would establish sentencing guidelines for judges. In 1976 Levi said, "If a judge decided to impose a sentence inconsistent with the guidelines, he would have to accompany the decision with specific reasons for the exception, and the decision would be subject to appellate review."

Of course, even without such a system, appellate review of a sentence is possible, but it is extremely rare. "When it happens," notes Neier, "it is generally because judges have gratuitously offered their reasons for particular sentences and included impermissible considerations, as when a New Jersey judge cited an antiwhite poem by LeRoi Jones [Imamu Baraka] as the reason for giving him an extended prison term."

In other cases judges have refused to give shorter sentences or probation because a defendant insisted on a jury trial. It is obvious that justice often goes awry the first instant society attempts to apply fitting punishment. Few experts on crime today would deny that an unfair sentence started John Dillinger down the road to becoming Public Enemy No. 1. In 1924 Dillinger and an older man, Ed Singleton, were quickly apprehended attempting to rob an Indiana grocer. The 21-year-old Dillinger pleaded guilty and drew a sentence of 10 to 20 years, although he had been assured by the local prosecutor that as a first offender, he would be treated lightly if he entered a guilty plea. Singleton, 10 years older than Dillinger, was brought before a different judge and drew a far shorter sentence; he was released after doing two years. Dillinger ended up serving nine years. As Wayne Coy, a state official said in 1934: "There does not seem to me to be any escape from the fact that the State of Indiana made John Dillinger the Public Enemy that he is today. . . . Instead of reforming the prisoner, the penal institutions provided him with an education in crime."

SEPTEMBER Morn: "Pornographic" painting

In the early years of the 20th century the most famous American "pornographic" painting was born. It was *September Morn*, a picture of a somewhat immodest young lady taking a bath in a pond. Alas, *September Morn* really wasn't a very notable work of art, being a lithograph turned out for a brewer's calendar, but it fell victim to, and became famous because of, Comstockery, the puritanical view of Anthony Comstock, the "great American bluenose" and head of the New York Society for the Suppression of Vice.

In fact, the guiding genius behind making the work a commercial success was Harry Reichenbach, the great publicist. Reichenbach was just beginning his career when he was hired by a Fourth Avenue art dealer to promote a picture of a naked girl taking a bath in a pond. The dealer was stuck with 2,000 prints and had not made a single sale. Reichenbach telephoned Comstock, passing himself off as a minister, and said he had to report a disgraceful situation, the painting of a naked woman. "She's in the window of an art store on Fourth Avenue, and little boys are gathering around there to look at her."

Reichenbach rounded up several boys and gave them a quarter a piece to stand in front of the art store and gape at the picture. Comstock arrived and nearly choked in rage. "Remove that filthy picture!" he fumed, and when the dealer refused, he commenced legal action.

Comstock lost the legal case because even in that era the picture was found to be about as suggestive as one of a baby in a family album. But the censorship effort against *September Morn* made it a national issue. It became the source of songs and jokes as well as the target of attacks by reformers. Over seven million copies were sold at a dollar a piece, and to this day enjoys good sales.

See also: *Anthony Comstock.*

SEVEN Group: Forerunner of the National Crime Syndicate

The bootleg wars of the 1920s were the bloodiest underworld battles in American history, with a death toll that climbed into the thousands. In many parts of the country, peace came with the establishment of the Seven Group.

During the first years of Prohibition various underworld mobs faced a scramble for liquor and had to constantly protect their supplies from being hijacked by other gangs. What was needed was an organization that would set up a central liquor buying office, which would handle all orders for booze and give everyone a fair share. This system would reduce the bloody competition for supplies and cut down on the enormous ex-

pense involved in protecting booze shipments, and the organizations could then easily handle any free-lance hijackers who might still try to operate.

It is not clear who originated the idea of the Seven Group, but among those pushing it in 1927 were Lucky Luciano, Meyer Lansky, Arnold Rothstein and Johnny Torrio. As originally constituted, the Seven Group were made up of seven distinct power groups. The seven were Luciano and Frank Costello from Manhattan; Joe Adonis from Brooklyn; Longy Zwillman from Long Island, N.Y. and New Jersey; Meyer Lansky and Bugsy Siegel, the bootleg "enforcers"; Waxey Gordon and Nig Rosen from Philadelphia; Nucky Johnson from Atlantic City; and Torrio, who came out of retirement to act as an adviser and counselor.

As the Seven Group quickly proved its viability, it attracted other gangs around the country, such as those headed by Moe Dalitz in Cleveland; Danny Walsh in Providence and King Solomon in Boston. Even Al Capone saw the value of the setup, but the bloodletting in Chicago had gone on too long to be halted by reason. In much of the country, excluding Chicago, a new peace was achieved among the 22 gangs that joined the Seven Group.

However, the historic importance of the Seven Group was that it represented the first real step in establishing nationwide criminal links that would lead, in just a few years, to the creation of the national crime syndicate. The Atlantic City Conference of 1929, at which plans for new criminal enterprises following the end of Prohibition were first discussed, would never have been held were it not for the success of the Seven Group, which was regarded by the conferees as a model for future cooperation.

See also: *Atlantic City Conference.*

SHAME Of Abilene: "Pornographic" painting

In the days before *September Morn* was to become the most notorious painting in America, the *Shame of Abilene* was the West's most shocking work of art and one that indirectly added a notch to the gun of Wild Bill Hickok, the famous lawman of Abilene, Kan.

In 1871 two of the West's most colorful characters, Ben Thompson, a pathological gunman, and Phil Coe, a dapper Texas gambler, arrived in Abilene and opened the Bull's Head Tavern and Gambling Saloon. The establishment was typical of the town's other recreational outlets except for its facade. The owners of the Bull's Head had a representation of a giant bull painted across the front of the building. It was a bull of monumental proportions, with certain anatomical features enlarged even beyond the enormous scale of the rest of the painting.

The fame of Abilene's bull spread with telegraphic speed, and cowboys from hundreds of miles around spurred to Abilene to see the big bull and tarry at the saloon's gambling tables. By the time news of the *Shame of Abilene* had reached the East, the more straight-laced elements of the town had demanded that the marshal do something about it. Wild Bill had words with Coe, Thompson being out of town at the time, and gave the gambler 24 hours to remove the bull, or at least the objectionable parts. Coe stood pat. The following day, armed with a can of paint and a brush, Hickok painted over the offending section of the picture.

Decency prevailed but bad blood remained. Within days, on October 5, 1871, a shoot-out of sorts developed between Coe and Hickok. It was no contest; Coe was fatally wounded. Puritans and defenders of Wild Bill Hickok have always claimed the cause of the gunfight was the painting. Another group has held that other, monetary reasons caused the battle and that it was pure murder on Hickok's part.

See also: *Phil Coe, Wild Bill Hickok, Ben Thompson.*

SHANGHAI Chicken (1839-1871): Shanghaier's runner

The most famous of the runners who supplied bodies for the shanghaiers of San Francisco was Johnny Devine, better known as the Shanghai Chicken.

Little is known of the Shanghai Chicken except that he was born in New York and was shanghaied at age 18, turning up two years later in San Francisco, where he became an ornament of the waterfront. He quickly emerged a jack of all crimes, working industriously as a pickpocket, sneak thief, burglar, footpad and, eventually, pimp. He also hired out as a maimer and hit man for anyone who would pay his price, which was around $50. Although he was arrested seven times during his first nine months in San Francisco, he served no more than 50 days in jail.

With a record like that it was inevitable that Devine would soon attract the attention of Shanghai Kelly, probably the greatest kidnapper of sailors the world has ever known. In a few short years the Shanghai Chicken rose to be Kelly's chief of staff. He was one of the few in the trade who violated the rule that forbade stealing another runner's captives. Once, he tried to hijack a drunken sailor from Tommy Chandler, a particularly rough runner for Shanghai Brown. Chandler, a brute of a man, flattened the Chicken with a mighty punch to the jaw. The Chicken climbed to his feet and felled the sailor with a slungshot and then pulled a pistol and put two bullets into Chandler, leaving him incapacitated for months. The Chicken then lugged his prize off to Shanghai Kelly's boarding house.

In 1869 the Shanghai Chicken met his match in the person of Big Billy Maitland, another one of Shanghai Kelly's rivals. In an altercation at Maitland's saloon, Big Billy came after the Chicken with a knife; when the latter raised his arm to protect himself, Maitland neatly slashed off his hand at the wrist. Big Billy then tossed him out of his saloon. The Chicken brushed himself off with his one good hand and then screamed out to Maitland: "Hey, Billy, you dirty bastard! Chuck out me fin!"

Maitland flipped the severed hand out to the sidewalk, and the wounded Chicken staggered to Dr. Simpson's drugstore at Pacific and Davis, where he flung the gory hand on the counter. "Say, Doc," he said, "stick that on again for me, will you?"

He fainted before he could be informed that surgery had not yet advanced to that level of sophistication. The Chicken recovered from his wound and medical men attached a large iron hook to the stump of his left arm. Thereafter, he became an even more dangerous battler on the waterfront. While he earlier had earned the name of the Shanghai Chicken for some unknown reason, the hook now allowed him to fight in the manner of a battling cock. Keeping his hook honed to needle sharpness, the Chicken could cut open a foe with one quick thrust. But after his injury he drank so heavily that Shanghai Kelly fired him. Ever looking for ways to make an extra dollar, Kelly promptly attempted to shanghai the Chicken. Kelly's men got the Chicken as far as the boat landing, where he broke his bonds and started slashing away with his iron hook. The kidnappers fled, many bleeding profusely. The Chicken then made off with Kelly's boat and sold it to another shanghaier.

As a loner, the Chicken now had to make a living by rolling drunks and committing small thefts. He made the mistake of thinking a German sailor wouldn't resist; when the sailor did, he shot and killed him. The Chicken stowed away on a steamer scheduled to leave San Francisco but was discovered before the ship sailed. He was still wearing the victim's cap, since he had left his own hat at the murder scene. The Shanghai Chicken was hanged in 1871.

See also: *Shanghai Kelly, Shanghaiing.*

SHANGHAI Kelly: See Kelly, Shanghai.

SHANGHAI Smoke

In the heyday of the San Francisco shanghaiers, various potions were used to knock out likely victims. Most, like the Miss Piggott Special, were concoctions of various whiskeys and brandies with a goodly amount of opium or laudanum added. It remained for the legendary Shanghai Kelly to come up with something really novel, in the form of a cigar known as the Shanghai Smoke, which he had specially made for him by a Chinese cigar maker. Heavily laced with opium, it rapidly dulled the senses of a potential victim to the point that he could be led into an alley and waylaid, eliminating the need to lure him into a saloon and thereby saving time. The Shanghai Smoke became very popular on the Barbary Coast until cigars became so notorious that men would not accept a stogie unless the donor would smoke one also. Ultimately, the widespread wariness led to the Shanghai Smoke's decline in popularity.

SHANGHAIING

The custom of kidnapping seamen to fill out a ship's crew was practiced worldwide, but nowhere was the art so perfected as along the San Francisco waterfront.

In early times there were no ships sailing directly from San Francisco to Shanghai and back to San Francisco; the round trip involved a long dangerous cruise, which became known as a Shanghai voyage. When a man in San Francisco was forcibly impressed into a ship's crew, he was thus described as being "sent to Shanghai." This in time was shortened to just plain shanghaied.

By 1852, 23 known gangs in San Francisco were engaged in the shanghai trade. Some, of course, would waylay men foolish enough to walk the shadowy waterfront alone, but few shanghai gangs would wait so patiently for a fly to enter their web. The gangs employed runners to board incoming ships and induce sailors to come to boarding houses they operated. As the *San Francisco Times* of October 21, 1861 reported:

> They swarm over the rail like pirates and virtually take possession of the deck. The crew are shoved into the runners' boats, and the vessel is often left in a perilous situation, with none to manage her, the sails unfurled, and she liable to drift afoul of the shipping at anchor. In some cases not a man has been left aboard in half an hour after the anchor has been dropped.

The runners would all carry the standard gear of their trade: a pair of brass knuckles, a blackjack or slungshot, a knife, a revolver, obscene pictures, several bottles of rum and whiskey spiked with Spanish fly and a flask of liquid soap. If the runners swarmed aboard at meal time, the soap would be slipped into soup or stew simmering on the galley stove. When this awful mixture was served, the seamen would be disgusted and much more receptive to the runner's spiel. First, the runners would offer the sailors some doctored liquor. After that began to take effect, the seamen would be shown obscene pictures and given an enticing, graphic description of what awaited them at a certain boarding house as well as the brothels of the Barbary Coast.

Usually, this was enough to convince at least one sailor, and he would be ushered to a runner's boat, where the boatman would give him more to drink. If the sailor showed signs of wavering or attempted to fight, the runner and boatman would club him into silence. Sailors who insisted on staying with their ship were often brass-knuckled or threatened with knives or guns. Often competing runners would settle on the same sailor and each would seize an ear with his teeth and bite down until the frightened man shouted out the boarding house he wished to go to. It was considered a serious violation of the runner's code for one runner to steal another's victim.

Some captains would try to protect their crew, but they were helpless when as many as a score of armed men stormed aboard. In addition, shipmasters were often warned by "certain interested parties," as the *San Francisco Times* put it in 1861, meaning the politicians and city officials who received payoffs from the boarding house masters, to look the other way or they would not be allowed to raise a crew when they were ready to sail.

Once a sailor reached the boarding house, his bag of possessions would be locked up and he would virtually be held prisoner until he was resold to an outgoing vessel. Captive sailors were sold whiskey laced with opium to keep them docile and, on occasion, prostitutes would be brought in to service them; the boarding house master would get a percentage of the prostitutes' fees and whatever they could steal from the sailors. A shipmaster would pay the boarding house master between $25 and $100 for each crewman he supplied plus a customary two-months' advance salary to cover the seaman's bill in the boarding house. There was seldom any money left over for the sailor when the boarding house master figured out the bill.

Shanghaiing could exist on such an organized basis only because most sailors were brutalized men, long subjected to harsh treatment aboard ship and thus conditioned to receiving the same when ashore. Finally, with the rise of unions and a federal law against shanghaiing, the vicious practice began to disappear after 1906.

See also: *Joseph "Bunco" Kelly, Shanghai Kelly, Miss Piggott Special, Shanghai Chicken, Shanghai Smoke.*

SHANNON, Robert K. G. "Boss" (1877-1956): Criminal hideout proprietor

For the gangsters of the 1920s and 1930s in need of a safe refuge after a prison escape or a big job, the man to see was Robert K. G. Shannon in Wise County, Tex. The so-called boss of the county, Shannon was a gifted political operator who could deliver votes on demand and thus generally had the run of the county. He established his comfortable Paradise ranch as an underworld haven, charging felons hefty sums for the use of a hideout where no local law officials would snoop.

Boss Shannon was the stepfather, late in life, of Kathryn Kelly, and it was through his connections with the underworld that Kathryn's husband, George "Machine Gun" Kelly, finally made it into big-time crime. Shannon's ranch was used to hide Charles Urschel, kidnapped and held for a $200,000 ransom by the Kelly couple and Albert Bates. During this time Shannon irritated Kelly and Bates by giving refuge to three prison escapees, thus endangering a big-money operation for "small potatoes." Bates and Kelly were able to roust two of the fugitives by simply ordering them to leave but were less successful with the third, a leading public enemy named Harvey J. Bailey, who was suffering from a leg wound. Heavily armed, Bailey informed them he was not yet in shape to leave. The kidnappers then tried a different tack, giving Bailey $1,000 traveling money. Bailey took the money and said he would leave when he was able. He was still there when Bates and the Kellys pulled out.

Shannon was so awed by the big-time kidnapping operation that he refused to take any money for providing the kidnappers with a hiding place, saying it would be wrong to take from "family." Later, Shannon and his wife, Ora, Kathryn Kelly's mother, drew life sentences for their part in the crime. Eventually, Shannon's sentence was reduced to 30 years. In 1944 he was pardoned by President Franklin Roosevelt on the grounds of ill health and advanced age. He died at the age of 79 on Christmas Day 1956 at a hospital in Bridgeport, Tex.

See also: *George "Machine Gun" Kelly.*

SHAPIRO, Jacob "Gurrah" (1899-1947): Labor racketeer

One of the most fearsome of all labor racketeers, Jacob "Gurrah" Shapiro worked New York's garment industry in the 1920s and 1930s with all the finesse of a gorilla run amok. Shapiro was the chief lieutenant of Louis Buchalter, better known as Louis Lepke. The pair had met as teenagers in 1914, when they attempted to rob the same pushcart one day on the Lower East Side. It was the beginning of a murderous friendship. Lepke relied on Shapiro's muscle and Shapiro certainly needed Lepke's brain.

Lepke's plan, developed in the early 1920s, called for the pair to move into the union field and terrorize certain locals by the judicious or even indiscriminate use of beatings and murders. The next step would be to seize control, which would put them in a position to take kickbacks, or skim dues, from union members and then extort big payoffs from garment manufacturers who wanted to avoid strikes. At the same time, Lepke and Shapiro joined with the top labor racketeer of the day, Jacob "Little Augie" Orgen, to provide strikebreaking crews for employers. When Little Augie was assassinated in 1927 (according to one account, Shapiro was behind the wheel of the assassins' car when Augie was machine-gunned to death on the street), Lepke and Shapiro inherited a major part of the labor extortion racket.

Always, Lepke supplied the strategy and Shapiro the brawn. He was a lumbering hulk, growling orders in rasping bursts of sound. His stock phrase was, "Get out of here," but in his guttural snarl it came out "Gurra dahere." So his acquaintances took to calling him "Gurrah."

Although Gurrah became enormously rich in the rackets, he could never forsake the jobs of the blackjack, the knife, the gun, the bottle of acid—the "persuaders" used by labor racketeers. He was always in the forefront of the skull smashers when anyone tried to organize a legitimate rival union.

When Lepke led his forces into the emerging national crime syndicate, organized mainly by Lucky Luciano, he was put in charge of Murder, Inc., the enforcement arm of the syndicate. His chief aides were Shapiro and Albert Anastasia. Gurrah handled a number of assignments personally and spent the rest of his time searching for the proper young talent to carry out other murders. When racketeer Dutch Schultz, a genuine devotee of violence, went before the syndicate's ruling board in 1935 to propose killing an ambitious special prosecutor named Thomas Dewey, only Gurrah and Anastasia sided with him. Luciano and Lepke rounded up the votes against the proposal arguing that such a murder would generate too much heat. Gurrah immediately fell in line behind his mentor, as did Anastasia. That left only Schultz holding to the insane plot, but he insisted he would carry out the job alone. As a result, Schultz was wiped out by syndicate killers.

Later, Gurrah saw the syndicate's decision not to kill Dewey as folly, especially when the special prosecutor turned on the Lepke-Shapiro union rackets. In 1936 Gurrah was sentenced to life for labor racketeering and in 1944 Lepke went to the chair for murder. During Lepke's trial Gurrah had managed to smuggle a message to him from the federal penitentiary at Atlanta. Its sulfurous introduction recalled Schultz' 1935 plan to assassinate Dewey and it ended with a triumphant "I told you so."

The embittered Gurrah died in prison in 1947, still convinced his only failing was not being violent enough.

See also: *Louis "Lepke" Buchalter, Dutch Schultz.*

SHEELER, Rudolph (1916-   ): Victim of false confession

When Officer James T. Morrow was shot and killed by an unknown gunman, on November 23, 1936 the Philadelphia homicide squad swung into action to solve the cop killing. They demonstrated a remarkable ability to extract confessions from a number of suspects. First to confess was a man named Joseph Broderick, but on second thought, the police released him and arrested George Harland Bilger, a criminal well known to them. Obligingly, Bilger also confessed and was sent off to the penitentiary. After about three years the police had another thought: they decided a mad-dog gunman named Jack Howard was the killer. However, they could not extract a confession, since sometime previously Howard had been shot dead in a gun battle with a detective. Thereupon the police apparently concluded that Howard had had an accomplice, one Rudolph Sheeler, who at least was still alive.

Sheeler vanished into the recesses of police headquarters. A week later he confessed and was in due course sentenced to life imprisonment. After that, Bilger was pardoned and released.

It took Sheeler 12 years to clear himself. After seven years in prison, he told the institution's chaplain how he had been battered with questions for hours on end until he could no longer stand it. Sheeler's wife had produced records that proved her husband was at work in New York at the time of the killing in Philadelphia. The priest promptly passed the facts on to the authorities, but they took no action. Sheeler stayed in jail for five more years until he won a new trial through the efforts of a University of Pennsylvania criminal law professor named Louis B. Schwartz. Finally, in 1951 Sheeler got a directed verdict of not guilty from Judge James Gay Gordon, Jr., who called the case "a black and shameful page in the history of the Philadelphia police department and an ominous counterpart of what occurs daily behind the Iron Curtain."

Further reading: *Not Guilty* by Judge Jerome Frank and Barbara Frank.

SHEEP Killing

Some of the bitterest conflicts in American history were the sheepmen-cattlemen wars that embroiled the West well into the 20th century, spawning a rich trove of literature and films. However, it is doubtful that many more than 20 or 30 murders can be attributed to such range wars. The true barbarity of the struggle was the incredible slaughter of sheep. Essentially, the conflict was started by cowmen who were determined not to be "sheeped out"; the sheep allegedly destroyed the grass and polluted the streams to the detriment of cattle and horses. The cattlemen wouldn't listen to the claims of sheepmen that with proper management both animals could be grazed on the same land without problems. Instead, they launched terror raids in which sheepmen were driven off and sometimes killed, but primarily they focused on the sheep themselves. The animals were shot, clubbed, stabbed, dynamited, poisoned, burned, drowned and stampeded over cliffs, a tactic called rimrocking.

In the 1880s, Charles Hanna, who had introduced sheep to Texas, one morning found his entire herd of 300 dead with their throats cut, and in the Arizona Territory cattlemen drove some 4,000 sheep into the Little Colorado River, causing hundreds to perish in quicksand. In Garfield County, Colo. raiders stampeded 3,800 sheep over a bluff into Parachute Creek in 1894. In another raid in that same county, only one sheep survived the slaughter of a flock of more than 1,500. The greatest killings occurred in Wyoming, where raiders once slaughtered 12,000 sheep in a single night. At Tie Siding the raiders set fire to the wool of 2,600 sheep, killing virtually all of them. In 1905 the secretary of the Crook County Sheep Shooters Association in Oregon boasted that the group had slaughtered 8,000 to 10,000 sheep the previous season and promised they would improve on that record in the year ahead. The same year, 10 masked Wyoming raiders shot or clubbed to death more than 4,000 sheep belonging to Louis Gantz. They destroyed the sheepman's wagons and provisions and tied two sheepdogs to the wagons and burned them to death. Gantz did not attempt to prosecute the raiders, knowing they would not be convicted in a Wyoming court.

By 1909 public opinion had started to turn against the raiders. After a score of them attacked a herd of 5,000 sheep, murdering three herders and killing dogs and sheep with kerosene and fire, Herbert Brink and six others were indicted. Four confessed and Brink was sentenced to death, but his punishment was later reduced to life imprisonment. Organized sheep killing nonetheless continued for a number of years until cowmen finally discovered that sheep could indeed share the same range with cattle. The sheep actually improved the sod with their hoofs, and their droppings fertilized the ground. The cowmen started raising sheep along with their cattle and found them an economic lifesaver in the years beef prices fell.

SHELL Game: Swindle

The shell game—under which of the three shells is the pea?—is as old as America itself. Gambling authority John Scarne insists the first "thimble-rigger," as an operator of the shell game was called, arrived on these shores shortly after the *Mayflower*. The game itself is much older and was no doubt practiced by crooked gamblers in ancient Egypt and perhaps earlier in other places. Alciphron of Athens wrote an excellent description of the cups and balls, a forerunner of the shell game, in the 2nd century A.D.

In its standard form the game can never be won by the sucker, since the pea is not under any of the shells when he is making his selection. After the operator clearly places the pea under one shell and starts shifting all three around, he gingerly lifts the shell so that the pea is stuck between the back of the shell and the table top (generally a felt surface). He then pops the pea out between his thumb and first finger, and when he takes his hand away, his finger is covering the pea. After the sucker makes his pick of the shells and loses, the operator pulls the other two shells back towards him as he turns them over, in the process slipping the pea under one of them and announcing, "If you'd picked this shell, you would have been a winner."

The principle of the shell game is never to allow the sucker to win even once, the theory being that a loser will become more desperate and bet even greater amounts in a futile effort to get even. The greatest thimble-riggers were such 19th century gamblers as Canada Bill Jones ("Suckers have no business with money, anyway"), who is reputed to have won the deeds to several plantations with the shell game, and Soapy Smith, who made a fortune with the game before being shot dead by a vigilante in Alaska in 1898. There is only one recorded case where Smith lost at a shell game. A knowledgeable victim placed a gun on the little table, made a huge bet and announced he was wagering on which two shells the pea was not under. He turned them over himself and, naturally, found no pea. "I reckon there's no need to turn over the last shell," he said, taking his money. Smith folded up his table and left.

There have been numerous exposes of the shell game, the first by a reformed Mississippi gambler named Jonathan F. Green, who, beginning in 1843, wrote several books on cheating. Despite this exposure, the shell game has continued to prosper and can still be seen at carnivals, horse races and other sporting events and, in recent years, on the streets of major cities. The shell game is often played in New York's Wall Street area, especially on paydays.

See also: *William "Canada Bill" Jones, Soapy Smith.*

SHEPPARD, Samuel H. (1924-1970): Accused wife murderer

A leading osteopath in the Cleveland area, Dr. Samuel Sheppard was convicted of murdering his wife, Marilyn, on July 3, 1954 after a sensational trial that attracted national and international attention.

Marilyn Sheppard had been slain with more than 25 blows to the head in the upstairs bedroom of the couple's suburban home, which fronted on Lake Erie. She was 31 at the time and four months pregnant. Dr. Sam, as the newspapers labeled him, said he had been awakened by his wife's screams and the sounds of a terrible fight. When he came to his wife's aid, he said, he had been knocked unconscious by a "bushy-haired stranger."

The murder took on a sex scandal tone when Sheppard admitted he had been having an affair with Susan Hayes, a young, attractive medical technician at Bay View Hospital, where the doctor worked. Both Dr. Sam and Miss Hayes admitted their relationship on the witness stand. Probably this fact as much as any of the evidence resulted in a guilty verdict and a life sentence for Sheppard. Meanwhile, many voices were raised proclaiming Dr. Sam's innocence. Newspapers and magazines took up the crusade, as did the noted mystery writer Erle Stanley Gardner. With the aid of a new lawyer, F. Lee Bailey, Dr. Sam was released from the Ohio State Penitentiary in 1964 pending a new trial. The Supreme Court upheld his release, sighting "prejudicial publicity" and a "carnival atmosphere" at the first trial.

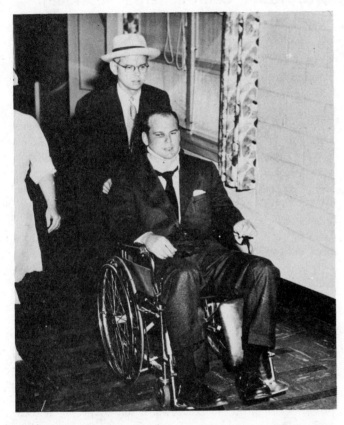

Sam Sheppard had to be wheeled to his wife's funeral with his neck in a brace, allegedly the work of a "bushy-haired stranger" who had murderd his wife. Sheppard was convicted of her murder but cleared 12 years later.

Bailey kept his client off the stand at the second trial, which was held in 1966, and attacked the prosecution's case as "ten pounds of hogwash in a five pound bag." The jury agreed, finding Dr. Sam innocent 12 years after his first conviction.

Following his acquittal, Sheppard married a woman who had befriended him by mail during his time in prison, and regained his medical license. However, in 1968 Sheppard's second wife sued for divorce, saying she feared for her safety living with him. Subsequently, Dr. Sam turned professional wrestler, but his health began to fail and he died in 1970. The murder of his first wife remains unsolved.

SHERIFF'S Ball: Hanging

Before the Civil War many executions gave local sheriffs in big cities the opportunity to make considerable sums of money.

The sheriff or other high officer charged with sending out invitations to hangings, called sheriff's balls, would sell tickets for on-the-scaffold or front-row seats to scalpers who would resell to the highest bidder, often for sums of $5 to $25, a significant amount of money in the period. It became customary for underworld friends of the condemned man to buy these choice tickets, either to pay their final respects to a fellow criminal or to ensure by their presence that the condemned man would not offer a last-minute confession naming them.

The hanging of Albert Hicks, a noteworthy murderer, in New York City on July, 13, 1860 was one such ball for which tickets went at a premium. Some 10,000 onlookers watched the hanging, mostly from boats since the execution site on Bedloe's Island was less than 30 feet from shore. Another lucky 1,000 got invitations to the island, many of which were sold through scalpers. It was said that the federal marshal, Capt. Isaiah Rynders, who was in charge of the arrangements, made a profit well in excess of $1,000 after paying out all commissions to his agents.

SHINBURN, Mark (c.1833-?): Aristocrat of bank burglars

Perhaps the most colorful of all New York criminals in the 1860s, Mark Shinburn was a dapper bank burglar who complained at length that he was at heart an aristocrat and that he was repelled by the crooks with whom he was forced to associate. Shinburn was a particular favorite of Marm Mandelbaum, the great fence, and would attend her famous dinner parties, where she entertained society's better half with a number of underworld personalities mixed in for spice. Shinburn always acquitted himself perfectly when the wife of a judge or an important City Hall figure happened to be sitting next to him. He would inform them, with somber earnestness, that he was involved in banking.

Some of Shinburn's crimes were truly spectacular. After he and a confederate robbed a bank in Saint Catharines, Ontario, they found all routes across the border blocked by Canadian police. The only unguarded point was a half-constructed suspension bridge over Niagara Falls. The pair started across on a snowy and sleety night after tying ropes around their waists and securing another rope to a girder. If one slipped off, his partner was to try to pull him back, but if the task proved impossible, each agreed to cut the other loose, letting him drop into the chasm below rather than letting him remain suspended in the air to freeze to death. Twice Shinburn slipped over the side but was pulled back to safety by his partner. Amazingly, the pair made it across to American soil and escaped.

Shinburn was also a member of the infamous Bliss Bank Ring, which corrupted the New York Police Department Detective bureau and paid off officers following every big caper pulled by the gang. However, Shinburn did not like sharing in big operations because he wanted to accumulate as much loot as he could in the shortest possible time in order to return to his native Prussia. He engaged in several two-man jobs, the largest being a $170,000 Maryland bank caper with gang leader George M. Bliss, one of the few criminals he respected. Shinburn then announced his retirement from crime and, after being bid a fond farewell from Bliss and Marm Mandelbaum, set sail for Europe.

Using some of his loot, Shinburn managed to buy a title and became Baron Shindell of Monaco. He lived quite well for many years, but his lavish life style eventually took its toll and he was forced to return to crime. He was caught attempting to rob a Belgium bank and imprisoned. When finally released he managed to scrape up enough money to return to the United States, where he apparently intended to return to his version of the bank business. However, he soon discovered that some of his real estate holdings' in Chicago had grown enormously in value, and he was once more able to retire in luxury under another assumed name. Since no more was heard of him, it is assumed his second retirement was permanent.

See also: *Bliss Bank Ring, Fredericka "Marm" Mandelbaum.*

SHIP Schools: Confinement method for juvenile delinquents

At the beginning of the 1860s, a new experiment aimed at rehabilitating young male juvenile delinquents was tried. It was felt that what these errant youngsters needed was the discipline and training of military life, not in any army-style camp but at sea, aboard a ship, from which there obviously could be no escape. On these so-called ship schools, boys under the age of 16 divided their time between studying and working. At the latter their time, according to one contemporary account, was spent in "domestic employments; in repairing sails and rigging; in going through sheet and halyard, brace and clewline, and the technical language of sailors; in short, in becoming practical seamen."

The ship schools proved to be disasters. There were rumors of these young gangsters often seizing control of the vessels, putting into shore and staging mass escapes. The system limped on into the post-Civil War period before being abandoned because of the disciplinary problems, enormous operating expenses and anger over honest adult seamen being thrown out of work.

See also: *Juvenile Delinquency.*

SHIRT Tails: Early 19th century New York gang

One of the meanest and most brutal of the early gangs to appear in New York City in the 1820s was the notorious Shirt Tails. So called because they wore their shirts outside their trousers in the Chinese style, the Shirt Tails never looked as violent as, for instance, the Plug Uglies, who carried brickbats and clubs and glared menacingly from under their plug hats. But in a murderous brawl or street mugging the Shirt Tails were just as well armed and just as deadly as other gangs. They had discovered that concealing their weapons under their long shirt tails did much to allay the suspicions of would-be victims. It is doubtful that the average Shirt Tail would venture abroad with less than three or four weapons on him. Fierce battlers, whose total number was somewhere in the low hundreds, the Shirt Tails finally disappeared as an organized force before the Civil War. The members joining other gangster organizations.

SHOCKLEY, Sam Richard (1909-1948): Bank robber and murderer

One of the first two men to die in San Quentin's gas chamber, Crazy Sam Shockley was executed for his role in the famous Alcatraz Prison Rebellion of 1946.

By any norm, Sam Shockley was crazy. No authoritative estimate was ever made of the percentage of Alcatraz prisoners who were insane or went stir crazy while there, but interviews with former inmates show that they considered at least 60 percent to have been deranged. It is amazing that Shockley—who believed the police had given him stomach cancer by using special light rays on him and who constantly heard "radio voices" in his head—was ever sent to Alcatraz at all and even more so that he was not transferred to an asylum.

In 1938 Shockley, a farm laborer, had robbed $2,000 from a bank in Paoli, Okla. and kidnapped the bank president and his wife to use as hostages during his escape in their car. Shockley had a special need for hostages since he didn't know how to drive. He released the couple unharmed eight hours before he was caught. Convicted of bank robbery and kidnapping, he drew a life sentence and was sent to Leavenworth. There, doctors determined he had an IQ of 54, the level of an eight-year-old. He frequently erupted in throwing, yelling and breaking fits, there by earning the nickname Crazy Sam. It was decided he was incapable of coping with the stress of a normal prison environment; so Leavenworth solved the problem by sending him to Alcatraz.

In 1941 Crazy Sam joined the one convict who had befriended him, Dutch Cretzer, a former Public Enemy No. 4, in an unsuccessful escape attempt. For the next five years Crazy Sam was in and out of solitary confinement. In 1946 he participated in the great escape attempt organized by Bernie Coy and Cretzer. The would-be escapers took nine guards hostage, and when it was apparent the escape was going to fail, Crazy Sam and another convict, Buddy Thompson, goaded Cretzer into shooting the hostages. Cretzer shot several, killing one. Later court testimony revealed that Crazy Sam cackled for joy over the shooting. Both Coy and Cretzer were killed in the breakout attempt.

Thompson and Shockley were tried and sentenced to death for their parts in the escape and murder. As they left the courtroom, Shockley grinned moronically at reporters and said confidently: "They'll never gas me. I'm crazy." He died on December 3, 1948, along with Thompson, to the disgust of his fellow prisoners, who regarded Sam as insane even by Alcatraz standards.

See also: *Alcatraz Prison Rebellion, Joseph "Dutch" Cretzer.*

SHOPLIFTING

Shoplifting is a major problem in all types of retail stores. Its precise extent is difficult to measure, complicated by the fact that "inventory shrinkage" also results, to a great extent, from employee theft. In 1970 J. Edgar Hoover called shoplifting "the fastest growing larceny in the country," and most recent estimates put the take at upwards of $2 billion a year. Undeniably, shoplifting arrests have soared, but this is more due to an attempt to discourage additional practitioners of the art by having offenders arrested and publicizing arrests. Previously, most stores preferred not to make arrests, letting the offender off with a stern lecture and, in many cases, even urging him or her to return as an honest customer.

There are two basic types of shoplifter: the professional and the amateur. The professional steals for profit and generally has a fence waiting to take the loot of his hands. The professional concentrates on higher-priced, resalable items and can cause a store heavy losses, but it's the amateur who gives retailers the greatest headaches. No one can say how many Americans indulge in shoplifting, either regularly or occasionally. Stores in college towns know to beware of student shoplifters late in the month, when many students are low on funds and awaiting their next allowance check from home.

There have been some attempts at estimating the percentage of pesons who enter the larger department stores in a city in order to steal something. In one survey in New York City, it was found that about one person in 10 who were followed swiped something. However, the study was conducted by a private security agency offering its shoplifting prevention services to stores; so it could well have had a vested interest in the results. Since the average shopper may well visit three or four stores on a shopping expedition, the one in 10 ratio would have a devastating effect on mercantile operations.

Women shoplifters outnumber men by four or five to one. Some shoplifters are said to net as much as $1,000 a week. Well known to New York police is a female "booster" who dresses herself exclusively in originals hand-picked at the very best stores. "I always wear my boosting drawers"—king-sized bloomers slung by suspenders under her full skirt—"just in case I see something I want," she has been quoted as stating. Like many other ladies of her profession, she sells to fences—and to individual customers who have placed specific orders with her.

While professionals steal for profit, amateur shoplifters steal for their own use—or for family or friends—and the profit motive never enters into it. They steal for "kicks," to balance the budget, to "get back" at the store for some previous unsatisfactory purchase or simply to get back at the "Establishment." Quite logically, shoplifting thefts increase dramatically in periods of high inflation. To the shoplifter some items are just not worth the purchase price.

The most popular shoplifted merchandise are clothes, especially sportswear and knits, portable TV sets, fur coats, air conditioners, radios, small electrical applicances, liquor, cosmetics and health products.

For a time during the height of the miniskirt craze, fashions were in favor of the store, since the short skirts cut down on "legging," sticking small items under the skirt between the legs and walking out of the store. Among professionals, this dodge is known as the crotch walk.

Store detectives are particularly on the lookout for women carrying shopping bags, especially empty ones, large handbags and umbrellas. Also subject to close scrutiny is a woman pushing a baby carriage, a convenient conveyance for hauling away a goodly amount of loot. Next under suspicion are young persons, teenagers and subteens. The average young person, like many parents, sees nothing wrong in stealing from a big store. If caught, he or she usually acts like it's a joke; if the store does decide to prosecute, most judges will let the offender off with a reprimand, particularly for a first offense.

While many stores have adopted a new "get tough" policy, others are reluctant to take a shoplifter to court. For one thing, it means the store detective or guard who made the arrest must be away from the job to testify, thus leaving the store that much shorter of protection. However, the main worry is false arrest suits. Juries are notoriously sympathetic toward false arrest plaintiffs, and awards have gone as high as $100,000. Even the fact that more than 40 states have changed their shoplifting laws so that shoplifters can be picked up inside the store by detectives, instead of being followed out to the street, has not resulted in many convictions. It remains difficult to prove to a jury that the person had not intended to pay for the merchandise. A particularly telling defense is a woman's claim of having become so exasperated over her inability to get the attention of a salesperson that she walked out without paying for the item she wanted.

Still, there have been some successful prosecutions. Take the case of the four Hoboken housewives who ventured to New York City each week for lunch and matinee. They also set aside an hour or so of their outing for shoplifting. All were prosperous-looking matrons and thus drew no suspicion for some time, but they were finally caught in the act. All were from comfortable backgrounds and could easily have paid for the items they stole. Their defense was that the store would hardly be affected by their pilfering. All were convicted and given jail sentences.

In recent years shoplifters have been foiled by various electronic transistorized plastic devices attached to store items. These devices set off buzzers and blinking lights when a customer attempts to wander off with the goods. Some stores have found that many customers resent such devices and complain they prevent them from trying on clothing properly to judge how the items look and fit. In deference to this complaint, the devices are sometimes attached to a garment's edge. Resourceful shoplifters have used razors to snip them off.

The traditional protection against shoplifting has been the old-fashioned convex mirror. It is, however, a method that often helps a thief more than it hinders him. Some thieves insist they will not steal in a store without such mirrors. Merchants tend to overlook the fact that while the mirror will let them see what a peson is doing, the shoplifter can just as well look up and see whether the merchant is watching.

Cases of family "togetherness" in shoplifting are an old story, with all the children, from the youngest to the oldest, "working" a store while mom or dad wait outside in the getaway car. Recently, a member of Atlanta police larceny unit said: "Men haul women around in cars, park and wait while the women shoplift. Then take off on the double when the women get back with the loot."

Perhaps the greatest shoplifting family in history was the White, or Weiss, family of Chicago, which from the 1890s to World War I was probably the most proficient clan in the business. One member of the family, Eva Gussler, was in charge of teaching the children to steal as soon as they could walk. A typical dodge involved a woman member of the family strolling through a store with a little child hidden under her long skirt. When the woman found an item worth stealing, she'd knock it to the floor and the child would retrieve it and slip it into specially sewn pockets in the lining of the skirt.

Things have not changed much since then. In San Francisco gaping store detectives recently watched two shoplifting mothers showing their little daughters "how to roll a suit" so that it would be as compact as possible.

See also: *White Family*.

SHORT, Elizabeth: See Black Dahlia.

SHORT, Luke (1854-1893): Gambler and gunfighter

Luke Short, an undersized gambler, legitimately won the sobriquet the Undertaker's Friend by being one of the quickest, trickiest and meanest gunfighters who ever settled an argument with a fast draw—fair or otherwise. Once, a man he was arguing with objected when Short put his hand under his coat. Short said: "I'm not trying to pull a gun. I haven't got a gun there, see!" Then Short pulled a gun and shot the man dead.

Luke Short was one of the Dodge City Gang, headed by Wyatt Earp and Bat Masterson, which either controlled or protected much of the vice in the Gomorrah of the Plains. After growing up in Texas, he hit the cowboy trail at about the age of 16 and by 1876 he had become a bootlegger, selling whiskey to the Sioux Indians—a federal offense. It was also a deadly profession, and Short had to kill at least six men defending his self-proclaimed franchise. He was finally put out of business by the Army and barely escaped a troop of arresting soldiers.

With a little distance and time behind him, Short turned Army scout. Tiring of that occupation, he took to the gambling tables at Leadville, Colo. In a manner of speaking, he came up with one of the surer winning systems. When he won, he collected; when he lost, he welshed; when men he owed money to protested, he outdrew and killed them.

In late 1879 he drifted into Dodge City, Kan., where he befriended Wyatt Earp, and when Earp later moved on to Tombstone, Arizona Territory, Short ended up there as a dealer at the Oriental Saloon. Short did his share of gunfighting at the saloon, and seldom needed help. Once, though, a hard case named Charley Storms called Luke a cheat and got the drop on him. Bat Masterson intervened and got Storms to leave the place peacefully. Later that afternoon Storms returned and, before Short noticed his presence, walked up to him and began tracing the outline of Short's mustache with his .45. Short watched his tormentor through slitted eyes, and then in a lightning movement that was to make him a shooting legend, he whipped out his Colt and fired three bullets into Storms, who died without being able to squeeze the trigger.

In 1881, weary of dodging lead for small pay, Short went back to Dodge City, where in time he purchased the Long Branch Saloon and turned it into one of the town's great moneymakers, offering everything a man could possibly want: liquor, gambling and women. About this time a "reform" movement took over the government of the town. The first thing it ordered was a ban on women employees in saloons. Such a law would have had the effect of putting Short out of business, especially since the ordinance was not enforced against saloons owned by the so-called reform element.

Short tried to fight the enforcement of the law the way he fought everything—with his gun. However, he and his supporters, clearly outnumbered, were run out of town. The angry Short lodged a complaint at the state capital, Topeka. When he got no satisfaction from the governor, he started sending wires around the West. Soon, the townspeople nervously watched the arrival of a stream of Short's friends—Earp, Masterson, Doc Holliday, Charlie Bassett, Shotgun Collins, Neal Brown and others—all gunmen.

Dodge City panicked. Short's enforcers adopted the name of the Dodge City Peace Commission, but in fact, they threatened war. Each day more fierce gunmen came to town to back up the "commissioners," who had taken such effective control of the town that folks said not even the state militia could dislodge them. While a nervous governor hesitated, the Dodge City reformers caved in. They "invited" Luke Short to reopen the Long Branch and run it the way things had been run before.

After a time Short sold out and took his gambling business to Fort Worth, Tex., where he ran the White Elephant Saloon and a number of other places in outlying sections. When gambling was declared illegal, Short became the most prosperous of the underground gambling house owners. In 1887 Longhair Jim Courtright, a former city marshal in Fort Worth and by then head of his own detective agency, started shaking down saloons and gambling places for protection payoffs. Despite Courtright's reputation as a top gunslinger, Short laughed him off and easily beat him to the draw. He shot off Courtright's thumb as Longhair Jim tried to trip back the hammer of one of his guns. When Courtright attempted to draw his other gun, Short killed him with three shots.

In 1890 Short had to defend his empire against a local saloon owner named Charles Wright. As Wright came at him with a shotgun, Short put the challenger out of commission by shooting him in the wrist. In 1893 Short died of natural causes; he was 39 years old.

See also: *Longhair Jim Courtright, Dodge City Peace Commission*.

SHORTCHANGE Artists

Shortchanging has long been a highly developed American swindle. As late as 1900 it was common among a number of small circuses traveling the country not to pay ticket sellers and in fact to charge them as much as $35 a week for the job because it gave them such a lucrative opportunity to short-change the excited patrons. Police bunco squads have estimated there are as many as 5,000 professional shortchange artists who frequently take jobs as cashiers, ticket sellers, bartenders, checkout clerks and check cashers simply because of the opportunities for stealing these jobs afford. However, probably an even more common form of shortchanging involves cheating clerks in stores.

The classic con of this type is the twenty and one. It calls for a gypster to make a purchase in a store for less than 50¢ and pay with a $20 bill. He starts talking about something: the weather, the news, anything. When the clerk puts the change down, it's usually in a standard form: a $10 bill, a five, four singles and a dollar in silver. The crook then makes another purchase of 10¢ or so, paying for it with a quarter from the silver change lying on the counter. He has made no effort to pick up the paper money. While this is going on, the slickster finds an apparently overlooked $1 bill in his pocket. He tells the clerk he's sorry for having forced him to change a twenty when he had the single. The customer then acts as though he is going to pick up the $10 bill from the paper money while putting down the single, but he does neither and continues talking.

Next, he shoves the $10 in bills across the counter and requests a $10 bill in exchange for the pile. When the clerk gives him the $10 bill, the con artist pretends he's going to leave. At this point the customer seemingly has been gypped out of $9. Most of the time the clerk doesn't even realize he or she is shorting the customer. And it makes no difference if they do or not, for at that moment the gyp pretends to have discovered the error. He asks the clerk to check on the money he has given him. The clerk does so and, red-faced, realizes the customer is right. Psychologically, the clerk has been put on the defensive, as the mistake is obvious. The gyp brushes off the matter but keeps up a steady flow of words to further confuse the clerk.

Now, he once more withdraws a dollar bill from his pocket and this time puts it on the bills on the counter and says: "Actually this whole mixup is my fault. I never should have given you the twenty in the first place. Here's twenty in change. You give me back the twenty and we'll be square." By this time the clerk, either still embarrassed or exasperated, is ready to do anything to be rid of the troublesome customer. He usually will hand over the twenty at this point, completely forgetting about the $10 the gyp has already picked up. Only a very alert clerk can keep up with such banter and not be talked out of the money. Even if the clerk does so, he does not accuse the customer of trying to swindle him, since the customer has already demonstrated his confused state of mind by almost getting gyped out of $9.

Despite the fact that security firms urge stores to educate employees to this most basic shortchanging racket, it remains perhaps the most successful of all such stings, with a success rate of far better than 50 percent. It accounts for a large amount of the estimated $500 million a year taken by all types of shortchangers.

SHOTGUN Man (?-?): Unidentified Black Hand hit man

America's best-known murderer, in the sense that literally thousands of people could have identified him—but didn't—was Chicago's infamous Shotgun Man, an assassin who worked for Black Hand extortionists. If the police were aware of his name and identity, no case could be built against him, and little of his past was known in Chicago's Little Italy, even though he openly plied his trade there. Most Black Hand gangs did not do their own killings but farmed them out to free-lance hit men who owed no loyalty beyond doing the job they were paid for. Between January 1, 1910 and March 26, 1911, the Shotgun Man killed 15 Italians and Sicilians on orders from various Black Handers. By comparison, the total number of unsolved Black Hand murders during that period was 38. In March 1911 the Shotgun Man assassinated four victims within a 72-hour period, all at the intersection of Milton and Oak streets. Before and after his killings he walked freely through the streets of Little Italy, his gun always for rent to the highest bidder. Although he was well known, no one in Little Italy identified him to the Chicago police. It was generally believed that the Black Handers who hired him had considerable political influence and that if arrested, the Shotgun Man would be back on the streets within a short time, a prospect likely to give any potential informer second thoughts. Black Handers supposedly paid the Shotgun Man extremely well for his services, since he made a fearsome walking advertisement for them. It may have been that he had accumulated all the wealth he wanted or just that the Black Hand menace was starting to recede anyway, but after a period of eight or nine years the Shotgun Man left Little Italy.

See also: *Black Hand, Death Corner.*

SIEGEL, Benjamin "Bugsy" (1906-1947): Syndicate leader

"We only kill each other," the notorious Benjamin "Bugsy" Siegel once told construction tycoon Del Webb. Whether or not Webb took this assurance on the mores of syndicate gangsterism at full value is not known, but Siegel's own life and death certainly gives his statement some credence. Bugsy Siegel was simultaneously the most colorful, the most charming and the most fiery-tempered of all syndicate killers. As the saying went, he charmed the pants and panties off Hollywood, while at the same time functioning as a mob killer. It was an incredible act right up to the moment he got his head blown open by three 30.30 caliber bullets from a hit man's rifle.

Bugsy grew up on the crime-ridden Lower East Side and formed an early alliance with a runty little youth four years his senior, Meyer Lansky, already a criminal genius in his teens. By 1920 the Bug and Meyer Gang was running gambling games, stealing cars and getting into bootlegging. On occasion the gang hijacked booze shipments from other outfits until Lansky and Siegel realized it was a lot easier to hire out their gunmen as protectors for these shipments. They soon began working with rising young Italian gangsters such as Lucky Luciano, Joe Adonis, Frank Costello and Tommy Lucchese. The gang provided much of the muscle and, in Lansky's case, the brains for Luciano's big push to topple the old "Mustache Petes" of the Mafia: Giuseppe "Joe the Boss" Masseria and Salvatore Maranzano.

The emerging national crime syndicate assigned Siegel to carry out numerous murders aimed at gaining control of the important avenues of crime. He was so enthused about killing, he was called "Bugsy," but not in his presence. Face to face, he was just plain Ben.

Bugsy was sent to California to consolidate the syndicate's West Coast operations. There, in his quieter moments, he was a genuinely suave, entertaining sort, hobnobbing with Hollywood celebrities and becoming close friends with such personalities as Jean Harlow, George Raft, Clark Cable, Gary Cooper, Wendy Barrie, Cary Grant and many others, some of whom invested their money in his enterprises. Siegel sometimes left his "class" friends at a party to go on a murder mission, which he did one night in 1939 when he, Frankie Carbo, later the underworld's boss of boxing, and Murder, Inc. wheelman Allie Tannenbaum assassinated an errant criminal named Harry Greenberg, better known as Big Greenie.

Big Greenie had had the death sentence passed on him by the syndicate board in New York. When Greenie fled to Los Angeles, it was decided to "let Ben handle it." Siegel was happy to, doing the job personally, although he was only supposed to arrange matters. Los Angeles County Deputy District Attorney Arthur Veitch later explained why Siegel had to lend a hand personally: "In gangster parlance Siegel is what is known as a 'cowboy.' This is the way the boys have of describing a man who is not satisfied to frame a murder but actually has to be in on the kill in person."

Others would say Siegel's craziness explained his bizarre actions. For example, there was the time he and one of his mistresses, Countess Dorothy diFrasso, trekked to Italy to sell Benito Mussolini a revolutionary explosive device. While staying on the diFrasso estate, Siegel met top Nazi officials Hermann Goering and Joseph Goebbels. According to underworld legend, Bugsy took an instant dislike to the pair—for personal rather than political reasons—and planned to knock them both off, relenting only because of the countess' frantic pleas. When the explosive device fizzled, the Bug returned to Hollywood.

His main syndicate business was running the rackets and directing narcotics deals on the West Coast as well as overseeing the delivery of West Coast racing results to East Coast bookmakers. In the process Siegel dreamed up the idea of turning Las Vegas into a legal gambling paradise. He talked

the syndicate into investing some $6 million in the construction of the first truly posh legal gambling establishment in the United States, the Flamingo (which was the nickname of Siegel's mistress, Virginia Hill). Unfortunately for Bugsy, he was a man ahead of his time, and the Flamingo proved to be a financial white elephant. Reportedly, the syndicate demanded he make good its losses, but Bugsy was guilty of more serious infractions than just losing the mob's money. He had skimmed off the Flamingo's construction funds and had been dipping into its gambling revenues.

The syndicate passed the death sentence on Siegel, the key vote being cast by Meyer Lansky, Bugsy's lifelong buddy ("I had no choice," Lansky reputedly said later). Lucky Luciano approved the decision at a 1947 conference in Havana, Cuba. On June 20 Siegel was sitting in the living room of the $500,000 Beverly Hills mansion of Virginia Hill, who had been sent on a syndicate mission to Europe, when a killer pumped nine shots through the window. Three hit Siegel in the head, killing him instantly.

See also: *Flamingo Hotel, Havana Convention, Virginia Hill, Meyer Lansky.*

SILENCE In Prisons: See Rule Of Silence.

SILKS, Mattie (1847-1929): Madam

One of the "grand madams" of American prostitution, Mattie Silks brought "class" to harlotry in Denver, a city whose fleshpots for a time rivaled those of New York, New Orleans, Chicago and San Francisco. By 1911 her House of Mirrors, at 1942 Market Street, was almost as famous in the West as was Chicago's Everleigh Club in the Midwest and points east. At that time, Mattie was in her sixties and considered one of Denver's most famous, if perhaps not most upstanding, citizens.

Other than that she was born in Indiana, little is known of her early years, including her real name, which she never revealed to anyone. It is established that she "turned tricks" in Springfield, Ill. while still a teenager. Thereafter, she traveled the Western mining camp route, going to wherever the discovery of gold or silver allowed men to enjoy some leisure entertainment. About 1876 Mattie, at the age of 29, decided there was much more money to be made in operating houses of pleasure than in handling all the business personally. She opened her first whorehouse in Denver and kept at it for the next four decades. Each time she opened a new house it was a step up in grandeur, climaxing in the House of Mirrors, a three-story mansion that included four parlors, a ballroom and 16 bedrooms. Its prize attraction was the main parlor of mirrors, with floor-to-ceiling mirrors on all sides and a large crystal chandelier. A five-piece black orchestra offered every kind of music from the classics to ragtime.

Mattie offered clients a small but select group of "boarders," never more than a dozen, and competition for employment at one of her houses was intense. Although she may or may not have first coined the phrase, her credo definitely was that each of her women had to "be a lady in the drawing room and a whore in the bedroom." Consequently, her boarders were not permitted to smoke or curse and they were never allowed to sit on a customer's lap in the grand parlor or any of the other open rooms. A customer was to be treated like a gentleman and shown the same respect he would receive at home from his wife and children. Only in the upstairs bedrooms could Mattie's women play the role of whore.

After retiring, Mattie, at age 79, granted a newspaper interview, in which she stated:

> I went into the sporting life for business reasons and for no other. It was a way for a woman in those days to make money, and I made it. I considered myself then and I do now—as a businesswoman. I operated the best houses in town and I had as my clients the most important men in the West.
>
> I kept the names of my regular customers on a list. I never showed that list to anyone—nor will I tell you the names now. If a man did not conduct himself as a gentleman, he was not welcome nor ever permitted to come again. My customers knew I would not talk about them and they respected me for this. . . .
>
> My houses were well kept and well furnished. They had better furnishing than any of my competitors—gilt mirrors, velvet curtains.
>
> I never took a girl into my house who had no experience of life and men. That was a rule of mine. . . . No innocent young girl was ever hired by me. And they came to me for the same reasons that I hired them. Because there was money in it for all of us.

By this time, 1926, the former Queen of the Red Lights had achieved dowager status. She died three years later.

SILVER, Frankie (?-1831): Murderess

Although many historians refer to Mary Surratt of the Lincoln assassination conspiracy as the first white woman hanged in America, that fate befell Frankie Silver some 35 years earlier in North Carolina.

Frankie hacked her husband to death with an ax as he slept before the fireplace. She then cut up his body into small pieces, burned all she could and stuffed the unburnable portions into a hollow log.

Mounting the gallows, she showed little remorse. In fact, she munched on a slice of cake and held up the execution until she had eaten every last crumb.

SILVER Street: Capone mob stronghold

For several decades one of the most vice-ridden streets in America was Silver Street in Hurley, Wis. Starting in the 1920s, the Capone mob ran a crime school there that thrived as long as the organization remained a power in B-girl bars and brothels. Silver Street was largely given over to honky-tonks in which teenage girls, imported from Canada and elsewhere in the Midwest, were taught the fine arts of "mooching and dipping." From there they were sent out to underworld dives all over the country.

Some of the girls were lured from Canada by the promise of dancing jobs. When they got to Silver Street, they were told the jobs were gone. Stranded without return fare home, the girls were ripe for offers to pick up some change drinking with honky tonk customers. After a time it was suggested to the girls that if the customers were drunk, they wouldn't notice someone picking a few bucks from their wallets. A woman "dip" taught the girls in dressing rooms backstage how to "swift dip" a man's wallet—taking it, removing the money and returning it to his pocket. The girls who proved to be apt pupils were taught the subtle uses of the Mickey Finn. Those with less intelligence were forced to become prostitutes.

Especially eyed as promising recruits were young runaway girls, who were suckers for a get-rich-quick line. Many were held as virtual slaves, kept in tow by their mob masters as long as they were productive. Some became strippers on the underworld's burlesque lounge route. Attempts to leave were met with violence, usually simple beatings or knifings but sometimes acid in the face, if the girl was to be made into an example for others. Eventually, most of the girls were put on dope to make them more compliant.

The heirs of the Capone mob have long since abandoned Silver Street, not because of a reform drive or their own consciences but as a result of the changing nature of vice, which largely has moved away from whorehouses to independent call girl operations that are much more difficult to control.

See also: *Prostitution.*

SING Sing Prison: See Lewis E. Lawes, Elam Lynds.

SINGLETON, Ed (1893-1937): John Dillinger's first partner

A small-time hoodlum and drunk, Ed Singleton was young John Dillinger's first partner in crime and a man whose treatment by the law probably did much to turn Dillinger into a public enemy.

In 1924 the 30-year-old Singleton talked 20-year-old Dillinger into attempting to rob a 65-year-old grocer named Frank Morgan, whom John had known since childhood. Together they slugged Morgan, but when the elderly man fought back, they ran. Eventually, both were caught. Dillinger was tried first and sentenced to 10 to 20 years in prison. Singleton later claimed he was drunk and was released after serving only a two-year term. Dillinger brooded in prison about the lighter sentence given to a man 10 years his senior and the acknowledged planner of the crime.

When Dillinger became a leading gangster, Ed Singleton gained a measure of fame as the public enemy's first partner. In 1937 Singleton, in a drunken stupor, fell asleep on a railroad track and was run over.

See also: *John Dillinger.*

SIRHAN, Sirhan Bishara (1944-   ): Assassin of Robert F. Kennedy

The early morning of June 5, 1968 was a moment of triumph for Sen. Robert F. Kennedy, brother of President John F. Kennedy, who had been assassinated in 1963. He had just won the California presidential primary, defeating Sen. Eugene McCarthy, and emerged for the first time as the likely winner of the Democratic nomination. That evening he delivered a victory speech in Los Angeles' Ambassador Hotel. After the speech the senator was walking toward a rear exit when a 24-year-old Palestinian, Sirhan Bishara Sirhan, approached carrying a Kennedy campaign poster, behind which he had concealed a .22-caliber eight-shot Iver Johnson pistol. He fired several shots at Kennedy, three of which hit home. Two struck Kennedy in his armpit and would not have been fatal. The third entered the side of his head behind the right ear. Kennedy fell, mortally wounded, while his assailant was wrestled into submission by the senator's bodyguards, including former sports stars Rafer Johnson and Rosey Grier. As they did so, Sirhan wildly emptied his weapon into the crowd, wounding five persons.

Kennedy died at 1:44 the following morning.

Sirhan was proud of his act. He joked with police officers, made them taste his coffee to make sure it was not poisoned and even spoke sorrowfully about how violent the society had become. He was particularly upset about the terrible things the Boston Strangler had done.

Meanwhile, some witnesses claimed 10 shots had been fired, leading to speculation that Sirhan might not have acted alone. A possible explanation was that some of Kennedy's bodyguards' guns had been accidentally discharged in the melee.

During Kennedy's speech, a campaign worker, Sandy Serrano, stepped out onto a hotel balcony to escape the smoke and heat. While she was there, two men and a young woman in a white polka-dot dress went by her into the building. Later, after the shooting, the trio rushed out and Serrano was "nearly run over." The woman wearing the polka-dot dress shouted, "We shot him!" When Serrano asked whom they had shot, the woman replied, "We shot Kennedy!"

The police eventually turned up a woman named Cathy Fulmer, but Serrano was unable to identify her as the one in the polka-dot dress. Fulmer was found dead in a motel room some days after Sirhan was convicted of the assassination.

Sirhan freely confessed his act and was convicted and sentenced to death, a fate he escaped when the Supreme Court abolished capital punishment in 1972. In the streets of Arab capitals throughout the Middle East, posters appeared hailing "Sirhan Bishara Sirhan, a commando not an assassin." "Commando sources" were quoted as saying the posters were designed to convey the idea that in shooting Kennedy, Sirhan was acting on behalf of all dispossessed Palestinians by striking at a supporter of Israel—Kennedy.

Currently, Sirhan remains in prison, actively pursuing a parole.

SIRINGO, Charles Angelo (1855-1928): Range detective

Regarded by many, including Butch Cassidy, as the greatest of the Pinkerton detectives, Charles Siringo started working as a cowhand in his native Texas at the age of 13. At 22 he first exhibited his taste for manhunting by going out alone in search of a 17-year-old killer known as Billy the Kid. He was forced to abandon the chase after being separated from his money at a gaming table. It was back to the range for Siringo, followed by two dull years working as a grocer in Kansas. Then, on a visit to Chicago, Siringo was told by a blind phrenologist that his skull indicated he had the makings of a detective; shortly thereafter, he joined the Pinkerton agency.

Siringo proved to be a masterful bloodhound with an incredible record of getting his man. He tracked desperadoes through blizzards and across scorching deserts; he lived with moonshiners; he masqueraded as a wanted man to persuade Elfie Landusky, a Hole in the Waller, to tell him the hiding place of the notorious Harvey Logan; he infiltrated the union involved in the Coeur d'Alene labor riots of the 1890s, escaping assassination by minutes.

After 20 years with the Pinkertons, Siringo retired to write about his experiences. He turned out a number of fairly successful books but died "in poor circumstances" in Los Angeles in 1928. He had always worked as a loner, and he died the same way. Perhaps the title of a pamphlet he wrote summarized his views most succinctly: *Two Evil Isms: Pinkertonism and Anarchism.*

See also: *Butch Cassidy, Harvey Logan, Pinkerton's National Detective Agency.*

SKAGGS, Elijah (1810-1870): Crooked gambler

Few dishonest gamblers or swindlers went through more pains to learn their craft or left such a mark as did a 19th century Kentuckian named Elijah Skaggs. In fact, before the Civil War the term "Skaggs patent dealer" came to mean any practitioner of fraud and deception at a gaming table.

Before reaching the age of 20, Skaggs had determined to become the country's greatest dishonest gambler. He worked hard at his ambition, learning various card tricks and studying other successful dishonest gamblers until he learned their tricks. If he could not discover their techniques, he would pull them aside and offer them large sums of money to teach him. If they refused, seeking to protect their secrets, he would threaten to expose them to their victims.

In time, Skaggs became a master, perhaps the greatest of his profession. He traveled the Mississippi from St. Louis to New Orleans and soon had a gang of confederates working the river boats with him, fleecing the gullible. Biographers agree that Skaggs' income at times hit $100,000 a month, especially after he began operating crooked faro games.

By the mid-1840s Skaggs was a millionaire and retired,

clearly knowing when to quit. He had become notorious; it was said that no honest man was allowed to leave one of his games a winner. At 37 Skaggs became a gentleman planter in Louisiana. During the Civil War the master gambler made his worst bet, investing heavily in Confederate bonds, and lost his entire fortune. He died an impoverished alcoholic in Texas in 1870.

SKINNER, Cyrus (?-1864): Outlaw

One of the most important members of Sheriff Henry Plummer's gang of Innocents during the days when they terrorized what is now Montana, Cy Skinner was a California and Idaho area saloon owner whom Plummer imported in the early 1860s to open a similar business in Bannack. The clapboard saloon Skinner bought became a meeting place for the Innocents, but it also served Plummer in a more practical sense. It was an ideal place to learn when gold was being shipped out from the mines by wagon or stagecoach. A bit too much liquor would loosen a man's tongue, and Skinner would hear enough to tip off the Innocents. Because of the importance of Skinner's information, there has been a tendency among some writers to refer to him as the brains behind Plummer, but that description is not accurate.

Skinner himself seldom went on jobs, but on one occasion he learned, on very short notice, about a shipment which sounded so lucrative that he joined an Innocent named Bob Zachery in holding up the stagecoach and murdering the driver; the loot was $250,000 in gold.

Skinner was a cold-blooded character. When another gang member shot a friendly Bannack Indian, Skinner promptly lifted the dead man's scalp and displayed it over the bar to add atmosphere.

It is inexplicable why Skinner remained in the Bannack area after Henry Plummer was hanged by vigilantes on January 10, 1864. As the lynching continued, it was obvious that some of the condemned men would talk and implicate the saloon keeper. Apparently, Skinner thought he could brazen it out. The vigilantes came and got him the morning of January 25 as he was sunning himself in front of his cabin. Despite his insistence that all they had was a "heap of suspicions" but no proof, the vigilantes thought otherwise and led him to the gallows the same day. Faced with imminent death, Skinner broke and ran, begging his captors to shoot him rather than subject him to the often lingering death by the rope. They dragged him back and hanged him.

See also: *Innocents, Henry Plummer.*

SKULL, Sally (1813-1867?): Multiple murderess

Her name was Sarah Jane Newman, but through a succession of marriages—or as near as it got to that in the Wild West—she became Sarah Jane "Doe"-Robinson-Skull-Doyle-Watkins-Harsdoff. However, she was generally called Sally Skull, the surname of one of her several husbands who came to mysterious and/or violent ends.

In 1821 Pennsylvania-born Sally and her family settled in what would become the state of Texas. By the age of 13 the future Sally Skull had blossomed enough to catch her first husband, whose name is unrecorded. So is his fate. Sally said he went off to fight Indians. Whatever the reason for his departure, he was never seen again. Her second husband was one Jesse Robinson, who married Sally in 1838 and left her bed and board in 1843, describing her as a "common scold" and a woman with a violent temper apt to shoot a little too close to him. Sally found her next husband within a few months, a horse trader named George Skull. He set Sally up on a ranch near Goliad, Tex., where the couple ran a profitable horse business and Sally became one of the area's more colorful sights, sporting her six-gun and bullwhip. George Skull disappeared but no one ever knew exactly when. All of a sudden he just wasn't around and hadn't been for some time. Sally simply said she wasn't going to talk about him. In 1852 John Doyle became another of Sally's ill-fated husbands. Folks said it was kind of predictable what would happen to him after blonde Sally was seen in the company of the famed Mexican bandit chief Juan Cortina. In any event, Doyle took to drinking and one day, presumably liquored up, fell into the Nueces River and drowned. For some reason rumor spread that Sally had drowned him in a barrel of whiskey.

During the Civil War, Sally Skull sported a new husband, whom she referred to as Mr. Watkins, but he didn't last long enough for the locals to learn his first name. Mr. and Mrs. Watkins went on a trip to Corpus Christi, where Mr. Watkins was shot to death by his spouse. There was some dispute about whether Sally had shot him because she thought he was an intruder or out of annoyance at his having the temerity to awaken her. But the lady's account of what had happened was taken and Sally Skull was free to marry again. In 1867 she married William Harsdoff. The couple set off for Mexico on a combination honeymoon and horse-buying trip and were never seen again. Some months later, the badly decomposed body of a woman was found on the road the pair had taken. It was never officially identified as that of Sally Skull, and it may well be that her saga did not end there.

SKYJACKING

Although skyjackings occurred elsewhere in the world as early as the 1930s, the crime did not become a problem in the United States until the early 1960s, when hijackers forced a number of planes to be flown to Cuba. Often, these skyjackings were for political reasons, but a number of criminal fugitives looked upon Cuba as a logical place of refuge. Invariably, the crews and passengers of skyjacked planes were well treated by the Cubans, although Premier Fidel Castro imposed a steep landing fee for all such aircraft.

Countermeasures were soon taken, and laws were passed making it illegal to carry a weapon onto a passenger plane. Some airlines placed guards on planes, and the Federal Aviation Administration ordered cockpits locked during flight. Soon, the number of skyjackings dwindled, but a new rash erupted in 1968-69, when a total of 63 attempts were made. Not all attempts were Cuba-bound; some were extortion plots calling for the payment of a huge sum of money in exchange for the safety of the passengers and plane. One extortion sky-jack that has become legendary was made by a man known only as D. B. Cooper, who took control of a November 1971 Northwest Orient Airlines flight out of Portland, Ore., and demanded a $200,000 ransom. When the plane landed in Seattle, Wash. the $200,000 was sent aboard and the 36 passengers were released. Cooper then ordered the plane to fly to Reno, Nev., and somewhere in the flight he parachuted to earth with the money. The case remains unsolved.

Because of a new outbreak of plane hijackings in the late 1960s, "sky marshals" were introduced on many flights and a program was launched to detect weapons and explosive devices carried by passengers, either on their person or in their hand luggage. In 1969 airline pilots staged a strike and demanded that there be an air travel boycott of countries allowing sky-jackers to enter. A 1973 U.S.-Cuban agreement aimed at stopping air piracy was the most effective measure of all. Castro voided the pact in October 1976, charging the CIA was involved in the bombing of a Cuban passenger jet. In 1980 there was a fresh spate of skyjackings to Cuba, these by Cuban refugees disenchanted with their life in America.

See also: *"D. B. Cooper."*

SLADE, Joseph "Jack" (1824-1864): Murderer

When sober, Jack Slade was a vicious killer; drunk, he was considerably worse. Born in Illinois the son of a congressman, Slade had to flee west after killing a man during an argument. Thereafter, he left a trail of corpses wherever he went. He worked on and off as a stagecoach driver, a station agent for the Central Overland and, finally, a district superintendent for that line. But his main occupation was killing. Some biographers insist that Slade was a regular Jekyll and Hyde, being one of the kindliest men around when sober. The truth is that his killings were only a little less cruel when he was not under the influence. A typical sober killing was that of a teamster named Andrew Farrar, who pulled a gun on Slade one day when the latter entered a saloon. Farrar could have shot him dead at that point, but he let Slade taunt him with the accusation that he was too cowardly to fight with his fists. Farrar rose to the bait and flipped his gun aside. As he was rolling up his sleeves, Slade shot him dead.

Alcohol seemed to make Slade go crazy. He once got intoxicated and shot up the Army post at Fort Halleck, Colorado Territory, sending armed soldiers ducking for cover. Worse than that, Slade under the effects of whiskey, engaged in acts of unparalleled cruelty. One of his victims was a larcenous Frenchman named Jules Beni, who had tried to kill Slade and made the mistake of failing. Slade caught up with Beni and tied him to a fence post. Between swigs on a bottle of whiskey, he shot Beni full of holes, aiming at his legs and arms to keep his victim alive. When finally he tired of the game, Slade

jammed his gun into Beni's mouth and pulled the trigger. He then cut off Beni's ears, one of which he reputedly used as a watch fob. He sold the other as a souvenir for drinking money.

Even Mark Twain recorded some of Slade's exploits in *Roughing It.*

> Slade was a matchless marksman with a navy revolver. The legends say that one morning at Rocky Ridge, when he was feeling comfortable, he saw a man approaching who had offended him some days before—observe the fine memory he had for matters like that—and, "Gentlemen," said Slade, drawing, "it is a good twenty-five yard shot—I'll clip the third button on his coat!" Which he did. The bystanders all admired it. And they all attended the funeral too.

Slade had the misfortune of performing some of his unwholesome deeds in Montana vigilante country, where the practitioners of the noose had cleaned out the Plummer gang and were looking to find other guests of honor for their necktie parties. Slade was warned to "get his horse and be gone," but he failed to heed the warnings, apparently figuring his reputation was enough to scare off any attackers. On the night of March 3, 1864 he went on one of his monumental drunks and shot up a good deal of Virginia City.

A group of vigilantes rushed him and tied him up, and within three hours he was convicted and ordered to be hanged forthwith. When the scourge of the West learned his fate, he crawled around on his hands and knees, crying: "My God! My God! Must I die? Oh, my poor wife, my poor wife! My God, men, you can't mean that I'm to die!"

Despite his pleas, Slade was hanged, and by the time his wife got to him, he had been laid out to "cool" in a hotel. The widow packed Slade's body in a tin coffin filled with raw alcohol and set out for Illinois to bury him at his birthplace. By the time the Widow Slade and the coffin got to Salt Lake City, however, the body was decomposing and giving off an awful odor. So Jack Slade was buried in the Mormon Cemetery.

See also: *Jules Beni.*

SLAUGHTER, John (1841-1922): Cattleman and lawman

One of Arizona's storied lawmen, John Slaughter was also an enormously wealthy cattleman and living proof of an old Western axiom that if you put a man with much to lose in charge of enforcing the law, the law gets enforced.

Slaughter was born in the Republic of Texas. After 18 months of fighting for the Confederacy, he was discharged for medical reasons. Those reasons, however, did not prevent him from serving six years with the Texas Rangers, during which he won some measure of fame for honesty and efficiency. He was known for his ability to tell a badman to move on and be obeyed. Slaughter took up ranching in Texas and then moved west to start what would become the 100,000-acre San Bernardino Ranch in southeastern Arizona.

In dealing with rustlers, Slaughter was his own law, burying a notorious "herd cutter" named Bittercreek Gallagher where he gunned him down on a prairie in the New Mexico Territory. In 1886 Slaughter formed a partnership with George W. Lang, and their ranching enterprises boomed. He also established a very profitable packinghouse in Los Angeles. The same year, he became sheriff of Cochise County, Arizona Territory, which contained violent Tombstone. The area had already experienced problems with lawmen: the Earps had been run out of Tombstone in the aftermath of the gunfight at the O.K. Corral, and their enemy Sheriff John Behan took off rather than face a grand jury indictment charging theft of county finances.

Slaughter brought a breath of honesty to the office and soon proved his effectiveness as a lawman. His message to outlaws that they were no longer welcome was simply, "Git." When Ike Clanton, the last important member of the Clanton gang, returned to Cochise County, it was Slaughter who invited him to leave. Clanton departed, only to continue his cattle-rustling activities in Apache County, where he was killed. Outlaws Cap Stilwell and Ed Lyle were two others who left rather than face Slaughter's wrath. It must be noted that the Tombstone area was taming down by the time Slaughter took office, but he certainly sped up the process.

When two Mexican outlaws, Guadalupe Robles and another known only as Deron, robbed a train near Nogales, Mexico, killing three crewmen and making off with $15,000, they decided to hide out up north. They made the mistake of picking Cochise County, where they were shot dead by Slaughter and his chief deputy, Burt Alvord, who cornered them in the Whetstone Mountains. Alvord proved to be one of Slaughter's mistakes. At the time, he was, as one writer later described it, "casting a crooked shadow" and would become one of the leaders of the Alvord-Stiles gang of train robbers while serving as a lawman, although by then Slaughter had put down his badge. Upon his retirement in 1890 he was appointed honorary deputy sheriff of the county and held that post until his death in 1922.

SLAUGHTER Housers: 19th century New York gang

By the late 1840s New York's Fourth Ward was known as the worst hotbed of crime in the city. In large part, it was run by criminal gangs, one of the most prominent and vicious being the Slaughter Housers. Before the Revolution the area had been the finest residential section of the city, containing the mansions of the great merchant families. But the wave of immigration that followed forced these aristocrats northward and their residences were replaced by shabby tenements where poverty and crime were a way of life. Police entered the Fourth Ward only in groups of a half dozen or more and well-dressed strangers proceeded at their peril. In similar sections of the city, such strangers could count on being robbed—in Slaughter Houser territory they would be lucky to escape with their lives. The Slaughter Housers would try to lure a passing stranger into a dive where he could be robbed and, often, murdered at leisure. But if he would not follow them, they in turn would

follow him until he passed below an appointed window, from which a woman would pour a bucket of ashes on his head. As the victim choked, several of the gangsters would shove him through an open cellar door. The victim would be killed or knocked unconscious, stripped of his clothes and tossed naked back on the sidewalk.

A gangster who set the tone of the Slaughter Housers was George Leese, described by a reporter of the day as "a beastly, obscene ruffian, with bulging, bulbous, watery-blue eyes, bloated face and coarse swaggering gait." Besides his career as a murderous mugger and river pirate, he was a sporting gentleman, serving as an official bloodsucker at illegal bare knuckle prize fights staged in the Fourth Ward's larger dives and entertaining the crowd at rat fights by biting off the head of a mouse and/or rat for anyone offering a quarter. While he never matched the legendary Jack the Rat at that enterprise, Leese still made quite a bit of money. The practice reinforced the perception of the Slaughter Housers as monsters, which secured their role as kings of the Fourth Ward until the end of the Civil War, when police action finally drove most of the criminals from the area.

SLAVE Murderers

The record of murders committed by slaves in America before the end of the Civil War is hazy and inaccurate. In Virginia, however, efforts were made to compile complete statistics, which probably have some validity as a guideline for an overall view. Between 1780 and 1864 the following murder convictions of slaves were tabulated by the type of victim:

Master	56
Mistress	11
Overseer	11
Other whites	120
Free Negroes	7
Other slaves	85
Children killed by mother	12
Victim not described	60
Total	362

These figures include the 57 whites slain in Nat Turner's rebellion of 1831.

See also: *Nat Turner, Denmark Vesey.*

SLEEPWALKING And Crime

Sleepwalking is one of science's deepest mysteries. It has been estimated that as many as two million Americans walk in their sleep, engaging in all sorts of activities, from writing letters, reading books and driving automobiles to robbing houses, committing murder and taking their own lives. It has been demonstrated that a sleepwalker can kill and then awaken unaware of what he or she has done.

In a classic case early in this century, a 16-year-old Kentucky girl shot and killed her father and six-year-old brother and wounded her mother during the night while in a somnambulistic trance. The girl, who had a long history of somnambulistic behavior, had suffered a nightmare that intruders had broken into the house and were going to kill her family.

She had gotten out of bed, gone downstairs through the living room and kitchen into the pantry, where she placed a chair by a closet so that she could reach the top shelf, the place her father kept two revolvers. Then she had gone upstairs, entered her parents' bedroom and opened fire—at her family. Based on the testimony of doctors, the girl was acquitted of homicide charges.

Writing in the legal journal *Case and Comment*, Dr. Edward Podolsky, a member of the psychiatric staff at Kings County Hospital in Brooklyn, New York City, cited the case of a Mt. Vernon, N.Y. man who shot and killed his wife while in a somnambulistic state. Brought to trial, the man swore to the jury that he had been sleepwalking and that he hadn't awakened until several hours after the slaying. The jury appeared unconvinced until several doctors testified the man's claims were not illogical, that a somnambulist can indeed sleep through virtually anything.

This fact is further attested to by the odd case of a civil engineer in Denver. He stabbed himself four times in his sleep and bled to death. Just before he died, he awakened and told his wife about a weird dream he had had. He had dreamed he was surrounded by enemies who were trying to ruin him and that finally an evil spirit persuaded him to kill himself in order to spite them. The man had thereupon sliced himself up. Remarkably, he had not been disturbed by the excruciating pain he had inflicted upon himself.

But can a person who would not kill when awake commit murder during a sleepwalking session? According to Podolsky:

> During somnambulism the individual commonly lives through a vivid experience, little or not at all related to his surrounding, and therefore hallucinatory in character. Although such persons appear to be walking in their sleep, they are not really asleep.
>
> While it is necessary for a person to have consciousness before any cortical function is possible, it is not necessary to have complete awareness. During somnambulism activity is so completely organized that it can function without awareness. There is a complete disassociation of behavior patterns from the patterns of awareness. The disassociation is in that part of the brain known as the diencephalon.
>
> Automatic movements occur in a pathological sense without the subject's being aware of their meaning, and even without his being aware of their happening at all. They have not the full cooperation of the personality and do not involve interest and attention. They may, in fact, when generalized, occur in the complete abeyance of the normal personality.

And Dr. Lewis R. Wolberg, a New York psychiatrist has noted:

> A sleepwalking person has enough discrimination to perceive right from wrong. Unless he harbored a murderous hostility he would not kill, even when sleepwalking. This hostility might be so deep he would be unaware of it, of course. It would be transmitted more easily when he was partially conscious.

Another expert, Dr. Abraham Weinberg, has written: "True somnambulists have no recollection of an incident when they awake, but at the time they are aware of what they are doing."

Some persons are capable of fighting off urges toward klep-tomania while awake but not when they are asleep. In one such case a sleepwalker would constantly steal his roommate's wallet in his sleep. If he were staying in a hotel, he would wander through the corridors asleep looking for an open door so that he could enter a room and pilfer something.

The extent to which a sleepwalker will break away from his moral code is best illustrated in the case study of a pastor compiled by the 19th century neurosurgeon Baron von Krafft-Ebing, who did much psychiatric research in the realm of somnambulism. Charged with having caused the pregnancy of a teenage girl, the pastor was acquitted after proving that he was a sleepwalker and that the forbidden relationship had taken place while he was in such a state. In another case a monk dreamed he had gotten out of his bed, walked down the corridor to the room of his prior, stabbed the prior three times and returned to his own bed. The next morning the monk excitedly ran to the prior's room and was relieved to see him alive. He told him of his dream, adding that he had dreamed that the prior had killed his mother and voices had called on him to take revenge. The prior told the astounded monk that he hadn't been dreaming, that he had indeed entered the room and gone through the actions he'd described. Fortunately, the prior had been unable to sleep and had been reading at his desk when the monk entered, walked to the bed and stabbed the rumpled blankets. Of course, to a psychiatrist, the monk's attempt to kill the prior was a subconscious expression of hostility. Because the monk was bound by the commandment "Thou shalt not kill" his subconscious had produced a justification for his violence, i.e., the prior's alleged murder of his mother.

Apparently, the first legal case in the United States in which a sleepwalking defense was upheld was that of Albert J. Tirrell, a very improper Bostonian and the black sheep of his wealthy family, in 1845. He slit the throat of his mistress, Maria Bickford, in a rooming house and then tried to burn the place down. Tirrell had been seen leaving the room moments before the fire broke out. Later, friends of his had seen him walking around in a sort of daze, mumbling to himself, "They broke in and tried to murder me . . . someone came into my room and tried to murder me . . . I'm in a scrape."

When Tirrell was brought to trial for murder, he maintained he knew nothing of what had happened. Provided with the top lawyers of the day, his defense was that he must have killed Maria Bickford during a sleepwalking hallucination and his attorneys had doctors testify that he was a chronic somnambulist. It took the jury just two hours to find him not guilty. Public opinion subsequently turned against Tirrell's novel defense and his family had him committed to an institution.

Controversy still surrounds the Tirrell case. Was sleepwalking the cause of his act or had he merely been intoxicated and killed the girl in a drunken rage? Only a few sleepwalking defenses have been offered over the years, and in those that succeeded, the defense generally had proved the existence of a long history of the disorder prior to the crime.

See also: Maria Bickford.

SLICKERS: Missouri vigilantes

In 1845 Lincoln County, Mo. was the most crime-ridden county in the state, mainly because gangs of horse thieves and counterfeiters came up with a way of thwarting arrest or, in the event of an arrest, conviction. The technique involved engaging obliging witnesses beforehand to provide the lawbreakers with alibis for the time of the crime. As a result, subsequent prosecutions proved futile.

Finally, the citizens of the county formed a vigilante group that called on suspected criminals and their backup witnesses and, if they decided the individuals were guilty of crimes, proceeded to "slick them down" with hickory sprouts, "slick" being slang for thrash. The punished individuals were then given a specified time to leave the county, generally no more than a few hours. The so-called Slicker Campaign of 1845-46 spawned an opposition group called the Anti-Slickers, but the vigilante movement proved an eminent success, probably the most successful ever in this country. It took only a few hangings to convince the county's troublesome characters that a slicking was a clear and pressing reason "to pull up stakes fast."

SLOT Machines

With the end of Prohibition, gangsters who had engaged in bootlegging went into slot machines in a big way. These so-called one-armed bandits provided much of the revenue needed to hold criminal organizations together in the post-Prohibition era.

The American slot machine dates back to 1887, where a skilled German mechanic in San Francisco made a machine that took in and paid out nickels. It quickly became popular and was set up in saloons around the city. The house take-out was usually set at 25 percent. Since gambling devices could not be patented, the mechanic's idea was lifted freely. In Chicago, Herbert Mills began making machines for distribution throughout the country, and by 1906 he was known as Mr. Slot Machine. A slot machine is a very complicated mechanism, with over 600 parts, including one very reliable apparatus whose adjustment determines the house percentage.

The biggest Mafia operator of slot machines in the 1930s was Frank Costello, who saturated New York City with them. Each Costello machine sported a special sticker, which protected it wherever it was set up. If a freelancer tried to install machines without Costello stickers, the color of which changed regularly, they would be subject to attack by the mob or to police seizure. Police officers who made the mistake of interfering with the operation of Costello's machines could count on departmental harassment, such as transfer to the far reaches of Staten Island.

Costello's hold on the New York slot machine racket was secure during the administration of Mayor Jimmy Walker, but when reformer Fiorello H. La Guardia became mayor, an all-out war was launched against the machines. Costello used all his political pull to get a court injunction restraining La Guardia from interfering with the slots, but the Little Flower simply ignored the order and sent special squads of police around town to smash the machines. Costello did not know how to react to this "illegal" behavior by the mayor and eventually pulled his valuable machines out of the city. He found a new location for them—thanks to an invitation from Gov. Huey Long of Louisiana—and set up a slot machine empire in New Orleans. Years later, when an aggressive and ambitious young hood named Joe Gallo demanded, "Who the hell gave Frank Costello New Orleans?" the answer was, of course, "ole Huey did."

Today, slot machines are legal only in Nevada and Atlantic City, N.J. For some reason, a myth persists that the casinos pay off at 95 percent. The actual payoff is much nearer to 75 percent. What the casinos generally do is put one 95 percent pay off machine in a line to draw in the suckers. Sometimes a player will work three machines at once. What money he gets back from the middle one is quickly swallowed up by those on the left and right.

SLUNGSHOT: Mugger's weapon

A most brutal weapon favored by 19th century footpads and muggers, the slungshot consisted of a weight of shot or other heavy material attached to a flexible handle or strap. When swung, the weapon picked up tremendous force and would invariably lay a victim low, sometimes even killing him.

Slungshot gangs controlled many streets in several large cities. One of the most fearsome of such groups was the teen-age killer gang of Quincy, Ill. in the 1850s, whose members made up for their lack of size and age by such effective use of the weapon that they drove other criminal outfits from the scene. Changing gentlemen's fashion led to the decline of the weapon, since its concealment required the suits and long coats popular in the last century. During that era no underworld dandy would venture abroad without a slungshot to complement a brace of pistols.

SMACK Game: Matching coin con

Among the most enduring of all con games is one called "smack." It involves two swindlers and a victim and is often worked at bus and train stations, airports and bars.

Con man A joins con man B, who has already lined up a victim, and suggests they pass the time matching coins for drinks or smokes. Soon, they are playing for money. The game calls for each to flip a coin with the odd coin the winner, such as one tails collects from two heads and so on. When con man A goes off to the men's room for a moment, con man B informs the victim how much he dislikes A and suggests they cheat him. Con man B says that whatever he calls, heads or tails, the sucker should call the opposite. That way A has to lose to one of them.

What happens, of course, is that A does lose each flip but most of the time B wins the money, especially on large bets, and thus collects not only from A but from the sucker as well. Suddenly, A gets suspicious and declares he thinks B and the sucker are cheating him. Both B and the sucker deny the charge, but A is not satisfied. If they aren't working together, he says, he would like them to leave in different directions. Con man B gives the sucker the high sign and whispers to him a place where they can meet nearby. The sucker goes off gleefully, looking forward to the division of the loot. Naturally, B never shows, and when the sucker returns to the scene of the swindle, A has disappeared as well. It is a great learning experience for most victims.

SMALL, Len (1862-1936): "Pardoning Governor" of Illinois

It would be futile to attempt to single out the most dishonest politician ever to hold office, but Len Small, governor of Illinois during the 1920s, stands as the most blatantly corrupt. A Kankakee farmer and puppet of Chicago Mayor Big Bill Thompson, Small took office in 1921 and was indicted a short time later for embezzling $600,000 during his previous term as state treasurer, an activity that before and after Small was a time-honored tradition in Illinois.

Facing trial, Small said he had an abiding faith in the jury system. As it turned out, he had very good reason to. While his lawyers fought the standard courtroom defense, Small's behind-the-scenes support came from Walter Stevens, then regarded as the dean of Chicago's gunmen; Jew Ben Newmark, a former chief investigator for the state's attorney who found greater prosperity as a counterfeiter, extortionist and all-around thief; and "Umbrella Mike" Boyle, a corrupt Electrical Workers' Union official. This trio successfully molded the jurors' opinions with bribes and, when that technique did not work, with threats against them and members of their family. Small was acquitted.

Duly grateful, the governor shortly thereafter was able to repay his debt to the three by granting all of them all pardons for sundry offenses—Boyle and Newmark for jury tampering and Stevens for murder. Thereafter, Small ran up a pardon-granting record unparalleled in American history.

During his first three years in office, he pardoned about 1,000 felons. And that was only the warm-up. Over the next five years Small freed another 7,000 on a strictly cash basis. A longtime Chicago newspaperman, George Murray, explained the operation most succinctly:

> The Republican party machinery of the state was then in the hands of Len Small as governor, Robert E. Crowe as state's attorney of Cook County, and William Hale Thompson as mayor of Chicago. . . . When Crowe would convict a wrong-doer the man could buy a pardon from Small. Then Small and Crowe would split the take and Crowe would go into court for more convictions. The voters returned this team to office year after year.

That incredible electoral streak came to an end in the infamous Pineapple Primary of 1928. Despite the support of the Capone mob, the Small-Crowe ticket went down to a resounding defeat, as enraged voters turned out in record numbers. "It was purely a revolt," concluded the Illinois Crime Survey, "an uprising of the people, expressing themselves through the ballot. The birth of 'Moral Chicago' was hailed throughout the world."

The accolade may have been somewhat overly enthusiastic but with the removal of Small from office, the citizens of Chicago and the rest of Illinois could at least entertain the hope that a convicted felon might actually be required to put in some time behind bars.

See also: *Pineapple Primary.*

SMITH, Edgar Herbert (1933-   ): Murderer

Probably few "wrong man" cases have taken as many twists as that of Edgar Smith, who was sentenced to death for the 1957 bludgeon murder of a 15-year-old New Jersey girl, Victoria Zielinski. Smith established a longevity record on death row, 14 years at Trenton State Prison. During that time he never ceased proclaiming his innocence and soon started a correspondence with conservative columnist William F. Buckley, Jr., which eventually totaled some 2,900 pages. Buckley encouraged Smith to write an impressive book, *Brief Against Death,* in his cell. The book, aided by Buckley's columns, made Smith a national cause celebre. Smith followed up with a second book, *A Reasonable Doubt,* which made belief in his innocence still more compelling.

Finally, in 1971 Smith won a new trial, at which he admitted his guilt and was sentenced to 25 to 30 years for second-degree murder. With time credited for good behavior, he was released on probation. As he left the prison, Smith was picked up by Buckley's car and driven to New York, where before TV cameras he again assured people he was innocent of the killing. His second trial had come about as the result of plea bargaining, which he was convinced was the only way he could get out of prison. "It was a difficult choice," he said, "but I wanted to be free."

Smith set to work writing his third book, *Getting Out,* in which he stated in the prologue:

> In the Prologue to *Brief Against Death,* I ended with the question: "Did Justice triumph?" Today, four years later, my fight ended and my freedom a reality, that question remains as valid as when it was first asked.
>
> *Did* Justice triumph?
>
> Each reader will have to find his own answer.

As it turned out, readers had to wait until October 1976 to make up their mind. In that month San Diego, Calif. police began a hunt for Smith to answer charges of assault, kidnapping and attempted murder. Smith had forced a young woman into his car at knifepoint, and when she fought him, he stabbed her. The women kept on battling and finally hurled herself out of Smith's car onto the freeway. Smith then drove off.

About a week later, Smith telephoned Buckley from Las Vegas. The columnist was out, so Smith left a number where he could be reached. Buckley promptly notified the FBI and Smith was arrested in a hotel room.

Taken into custody, Smith readily admitted his assault on

the San Diego woman and then added a bombshell. He admitted he really had murdered Victoria Zielinski 19 years earlier. "For the first time in my life, I recognized that the devil I had been looking at the last forty-three years was me," he said. I recognized what I am, and I admitted it."

Smith was sent back to prison for life.

SMITH, James Monroe "Jingle Money" (1888-1949): College president and embezzler

A member of the Huey Long regime, Dr. James Monroe Smith, president of Louisiana State University, was credited by that state's press with making education profitable—for himself—and won the journalistic sobriquet Jingle Money Smith.

Born in Jackson Parish, La. in 1888, Smith served as dean of the College of Education at Southwest Louisiana Institute from 1920 to 1930 and as president of LSU from then until 1939. For part of his academic years, he was an adviser and lackey to Huey Long. As it developed after his tenure at LSU, Smith could have taught the state's political dictator a few things about making money. While serving at the university, Smith had become known as a rather wild liver and free spender.

In 1939 Dr. Smith resigned his post and fled the state as an investigation began delving into missing school finances. In due course, the sum was found to be extensive, and by the time Smith was found hiding out in Canada, he had been dubbed Jingle Money Smith. He was arrested on a charge of embezzling $100,000 in university funds and was indicted on 36 counts, which indicated the theft was far greater. Convicted on the $100,000 embezzlement charge, Smith was sent to the penitentiary. He was released in February 1946 in poor health and died on May 26, 1949.

SMITH, Jefferson Randolph "Soapy" (1860-1898): Con man

An incorrigible con man and gambler, Jefferson "Soapy" Smith worked his trade—everything from three-card monte, the shell game and various other scams—throughout the West and in the goldfields of Alaska, areas where the suckers were plentiful but could prove unforgiving.

Soapy got his nickname from one of his famous cons. It involved selling soap to the hicks in the cow towns, where Smith would stand on a soap box and announce that several of the bars of soap he was selling had a $10 or $20 bill inside the wrapper. The suckers would rush to buy, especially after one buyer, one of Smith's shills, waved a $20 bill and yelled he had just pulled it out of a wrapper.

Soapy was in his early teens when he ran away from his Georgia home and ended up in Texas punching cows. He was separated from six months' pay by a shell game artist. Far from taking it badly, he decided to learn that con himself, eventually teaming up with a venerable old con man named V. Bullock-Taylor. When Bullock-Taylor died, Smith became the king of the con circuit throughout the West. He opened up a gambling hall in Denver that became famous for never giving a sucker an even break and recruited an organization that enabled him to control virtually all the city's con rackets, including gold brick swindles and phony mining stock. Later, he moved the center of his operations to Creede, Colo. to take advantage of the silver wealth pouring into that town. Smith took over most of the rackets there with only some opposition from saloon keeper Bob Ford, the assassin of Jesse James. Eventually, it was said, Soapy forced Ford to accept him as a secret partner. After Ford was killed by a man named O'Kelly, it was said that Smith had paid for the job.

Eventually, the silver ran out and Soapy and his gang headed for the Alaskan gold fields, setting up in Skagway to trim the miners just arriving and the big-strikers on the way home. Soapy's capers in Skagway became legendary. He trimmed suckers in his gambling saloon, robbing many of valuable claims. Too greedy to pass up any form of revenue, he set up a sign over a cabin that read "Telegraph Office" and charged $5 to send a telegram to anywhere and another $5 to receive a reply. Miners flocked to send out messages and paid their money for responses, never learning there were no telegraph wires out of Skagway.

Soapy also ran an "Information Office" to provide newcomers and travelers with whatever intelligence they needed. Inquirers imparted more information to Soapy's men than was wise and Skagway burglars and footpads became famous for their clairvoyance in locating sums of money. On some nights Skagway had as many as a dozen holdups, virtually all executed by Soapy's men. One of Soapy's most famous swindles involved a man of the cloth who was seeking funds to build a church. Smith was the first to contribute, giving the surprised clergyman $1,000. With the impetus from Soapy's contribution, the clergyman collected a total of $36,000, only to have it all stolen. Soapy thought 36 to one was a rather good return on his initial investment.

Efforts to control Smith's avarice were unavailing as he took control of the town, naming his own marshal and judges. A vigilance committee, called the Committee of 101, plastered up signs reading:

NOTICE
To all gamblers and bunco men:
We have resolved to run you out of town and make
Skagway a decent place to live in. Take our
advice and get out before action is taken.

Soapy laughed at the warning and promptly formed his own Committee of 303 to indicate he had the power and was not about to relinquish it. The Committee of 101 quickly lost heart and failed to act. In July of 1898, however, Soapy's men robbed a miner of $2,500 in gold in a daylight mugging that sparked an instantaneous uprising. With the men of the Committee of 101 in the lead, hundreds of angry miners armed with picks and shotguns stormed into Soapy's saloon. Soapy tried to con his way out; the vigilantes listened for a while and then shot him to pieces. Most of Soapy's supporters were rounded up and what would have been Alaska's greatest lynching was prevented only by the arrival of U.S. infantry troops and the establishment of martial law.

With Soapy dead, the citizens enjoyed telling tales of his wild cons and observing how fitting it was that someone had ceremoniously tossed three shells and a pea into his grave as he was being lowered into it.

SMITH, Joseph (1805-1844): Mormon leader and murder victim

Joseph Smith has been described as America's most charismatic religious leader. Certainly, as the founder of the Mormon Church, he inspired great love in some and incredible hatred in others. The hatred ended in his brutal murder.

Smith claimed he had received divine revelations when he was 15 and living with his family in Manchester, N.Y. The revelations continued through the 1820s until he published *The Book of Mormon* in March 1830. The following month he officially established the Mormon Church. Mormon beliefs stirred anger in virtually all non-Mormon religious circles, and Smith and his followers were forced to move constantly, from New York to Ohio, to Missouri and to Illinois. In various communities anti-Mormonism culminated in virtual civil war, as mobs attacked Mormon settlements, leaving a trail of arson, rape, pillage and murder. Gov. Lillburn W. Boggs ordered the Mormons out of Missouri under threat of annihilation, and Smith barely escaped execution there. The Mormon leader then established a community in a new city called Nauvoo in an area north of Quincy, Ill. Rumors about the practice of polygamy plagued the Mormons, particularly after Joseph Smith openly advocated the practice in 1843. In 1844 a split developed in the church, and a splinter group started publication of a newspaper attacking Smith, who in turn ordered its printing presses destroyed. Rioting followed, and Smith and a number of followers were jailed in Carthage, Ill. on charges of polygamy, arson and treason. Late on the afternoon of June 27, 1844, an angry mob broke into the jail and shot Joseph Smith and his brother Hyrum, patriarch of the church, to death.

See also: *Polygamy.*

SMITH, Moe: See Izzy And Moe.

Joseph Smith, the founder of the Mormon Church, was murdered along with his brother by an angry Illinois mob opposed to his religious teachings and practices.

SMITH, Perry E.: See Clutter Family Murders.

SMITH, Thomas "Bear River" (1830-1870): Lawman

As a town tamer of the Old West, Tom "Bear River" Smith had few equals. He had, for instance, tamed Abilene, Kan. before Wild Bill Hickok appeared on the scene, and he did it with his fists rather than the two guns he carried. Such titles as "Bear River Smith: Two-Fisted Marshal of Abilene" have appeared from dime novel days down to today's adventure magazines.

Smith's early history is clouded, although most of his biographers say he was a New York City policeman for six years in the 1850s or early 1860s and that he learned how to use his fists on a rough Bowery beat. Some writers describe Smith performing heroically in the New York Draft Riots of 1863, while others have him moving west before the Civil War. Beginning in 1865, Smith's trail becomes clear. He worked for a number of freighting outfits in the territories of Utah, Colorado and Wyoming until 1868, when he turned up as a construction worker in Bear River, Wyoming Territory, the "end of track" of the Union Pacific Railroad. The railroad workers were, of course, "hell on wheelers" and friction inevitably developed between them and the more conservative "townies," who soon organized a vigilance committee. When the vigilantes seized three railroaders and seemed intent on hanging them, Smith led a railroader counterattack. They set the jail on fire and then trapped most of the vigilantes in a store. A peace parley was held, but it ended abruptly when Smith shot a man named Nuckles, who may or may not have tried to shoot him first. In the ensuing battle 14 men were killed and Smith was badly wounded before the U.S. Cavalry from Fort Bridger restored order. He was never tried for his offenses, and after the battle the nickname Bear River stuck to him. The Union Pacific showed its appreciation by giving him the job of end-of-the-track marshal.

In 1869 Smith took on the marshal's job at Kit Carson, Colorado Territory, where he won the praise of Billy Breakenridge, another famous lawman, as "the bravest man I ever had the pleasure of meeting." By this time Smith had developed the practice of never using his guns. As the fame of Bear River Smith spread, the mayor of Abilene, Kan. appointed him marshal of that turbulent town. Smith immediately made his mark by declaring it illegal to carry a gun within the town limits and using his fists to enforce the edict. Within a few months Abilene experienced a startling transition. The Texas cowhands who used to shoot up the town were tamed, and Smith gained their admiration and respect. Had Bear River Smith's tenure lasted, Abilene's mention in chronicles of the lawless West might have been only a footnote. On November 2, 1870, as a favor to a neighboring sheriff, Smith rode out of Abilene to arrest a nester named Andrew McConnell on a murder charge. He found the wanted man with his partner, Moses Miles, but never got within fist range of them. The two men cut Smith down with rifle fire, and as he lay dying, they nearly decapitated him with an ax.

With Bear River Smith's death, Abilene returned to its bloody ways and remained so until Hickok arrived on the scene in 1871.

SMITH, Thomas L. "Pegleg" (1801-1866): Mountaineer, thief and swindler

One of the legendary mountain men who roamed the American West a law unto themselves, Pegleg Smith could also be described as a slaver, thief, rustler and con man. William Caruthers in *Loafing Along Death Valley Trails* says:

> Smith may be said to be the inventor of the Lost Mine, as a means of getting quick money. The credulous are still looking for mines that existed only in Pegleg's fine imagination. . . . [He] saw in man's lust for gold, ways to get it easier than the pick and shovel method. . . . When his money ran out he always had a piece of high-grade gold quartz to lure investment in his phantom mine.

Born in Crab Orchard, Ky. on October 10, 1801, Smith ran away from home in his teens. After a stint of flatboating on the Mississippi, he headed for St. Louis, where he worked for a fur merchant and met such trappers and mountaineers as Jim Bridger, Kit Carson and Milton Sublette. When Alexander Le Grand made his first expedition to Santa Fe, Smith went along and got a taste of living in the wild, an experience he found most satisfying. He picked up several Indian tongues and, like the majority of mountain men, some Indian enemies. One shot him just below his right knee, which was how Smith acquired his peg leg. He remained as good a horseman as ever despite his handicap, and during most of the 1830s was one of the most successful of the fur trappers.

Near the end of the decade, the value of pelts dropped through the floor and Smith went into a more nefarious trade, stealing Indian children and selling them to wealthy Mexicans looking for slaves. In time, the Indians were on the lookout for this mysterious child stealer with a wooden leg; so Smith moved on to California, where for the next decade he became an accomplished horse thief, one time leading a group of 150 Utah Indians across the Sierra Nevada into California, where they stole several hundred horses. With two other famous mountaineer scouts, Old Bill Williams and Jim Beckwourth, Pegleg Smith formed one of the biggest horse-stealing rings California ever saw. In time, pressure from the law became so intense that they disbanded.

Following the discovery of gold in California, Smith developed his mining swindle, insisting that he had found rich samples of gold-bearing black quartz before he had to flee from vicious Indians somewhere in the Chocolate Mountains or the Santa Rosa Mountains or the Borego Badlands. The locale kept changing as Pegleg changed his story, but the gullible still listened; some staked him while others bought maps showing the alleged location of the gold. Even after Smith died in the county hospital in San Francisco in 1866, men kept searching for the Lost Pegleg Mine and they still do today, a lasting tribute to the old reprobate's snake-oil charm.

See also: *Jim Beckwourth, William S. "Old Bill" Williams.*

SMITS, Claes (?-1641): First white murder victim in New York

The first murder in what is now New York occurred either in 1626 or 1641, depending on whether or not Indians are counted as murder victims. In 1626 an unidentified Indian started out for a Dutch trading post in New Amsterdam with a string of pelts for sale. He was accompanied by his young nephew. At Fresh Water Pond they came across three Dutch farm laborers chopping wood. The Indian made the mistake of showing off his furs, and with typical greed, the trio quickly dispatched him with an ax and took the furs, while the victim's young nephew ran off. This is the first recorded account of blood being spilled in the colony of New Netherland. Although it would have been a simple matter for the authorities to solve the murder, there appears to have been no consensus that a crime had been committed, since the dead man was only an Indian.

Thus, Claes Smits, a white man who was murdered in 1641, was considered the first genuine homicide victim. Ironically, Smits' murder had a direct relationship with the one 15 years earlier, for the culprit was the nephew of the murdered Indian. He too had been on his way to the settlement to trade some furs when he came upon the hut of a Dutch settler—Smits— who, as coincidence would have it, was also chopping wood. Smits, a wheelwright, took an interest in the pelts and brought out several blankets and, apparently, a hatchet to trade for the furs. The Indian noticed, perhaps mistakenly, a similarity with previous events and quickly axed and slew Smits.

This act, of course, was a genuine murder, considering the color of the victim's skin, and the Dutch authorities demanded that the Indians turn over the killer to face punishment. The Indians refused, declaring Smit's killer had merely followed tribal law and avenged the death of his relative after the whites had refused to act. The result of the dispute was a full-scale Indian war, in which many on both sides died, a tragedy that could have been avoided had Dutch officials taken the position in 1626 that a murder had occurred.

SMOKY Row, New Orleans: Prostitution area

Possibly the worst center of prostitution in New Orleans' French Quarter in the 1870s was a short row of dilapidated old houses on Burgundy Street between Bienville and Conti, which teemed with black prostitutes. The press was constantly printing warnings to visitors of the city to avoid the area and reported on the brawling and violence of such battling bawds as One-Eyed Sal, Fightin' Mary, Gallus Lu and the redoubtable Kidney-Foot Jenny. These women would often fight one another over a potential customer; if the gentleman made the error of trying

to settle the argument by making a selection, he would very likely end up being savaged by the other woman.

The whores of Smoky Row came in all sizes and ages, from 10 to 70 and wore only loose Mother Hubbards cut very low. When not entertaining a customer or fighting each other, they sat in rocking chairs in the doorways, chewing tobacco and smoking pipes. When a man passed, they tried to drag him inside, and if he resisted, they grabbed his hat. When the man went after it, one of the women would very often blind him with a well-aimed spit of tobacco juice and another would club him unconscious. He was then robbed of all money and things of value and tossed out on the street. Smoky Row continued in its wicked ways for about 15 years until 1885, when numerous complaints and a growing list of missing men forced the police to clean out the area. After the harlots were driven out, police searchers discovered piles of men's clothing and bloodstained wallets. They dug up the backyards of the houses in search of corpses but found none, concluding the code of Smoky Row called for all dead victims to be removed and buried in other parts of the city.

SMUGGLING: See Hams.

SNEAK Thieves

There is no way to measure the extent of sneak thievery or to describe the many techniques sneak thieves use, but it is safe to say that the great majority of people have no idea how skilled most professional sneak thieves are. A few examples from the "sneak thief paradise," New York's garment district, will demonstrate the skills involved, especially those of the "packies," "readers" and "slashers."

A packy is a sneak thief who has "rhythm," or the ability to steal directly under the noses of workmen and guards. Many of them are drug addicts (knowledgeable observers say addicts make the best packies.) A police detective once told the story of a packy with amazing timing who beat four men loading a truck.

> This guy watches the movements of the four men very careful-ly, timing them. They were working in a rhythm, and you actually see this packy swaying to it. Then, at just the right moment, he stepped in and beat them for a package. A few minutes later, when I told them what he'd done, they could hardly believe it.

Since the value of a package may range from $20 to $750 or more, a first-rate packy can obviously earn himself a decent living, but it is an ability few thieves possess.

Less proficient than a packy but skilled in his own right, a reader relies more on acting ability than on timing and dexter-ity. This type of sneak thief spots a likely-looking package in the hands of a delivery boy, reads the address on it and gets there first. When the boy arrives, the reader is waiting in front of the building, often in shirt sleeves with a pencil over his ear, anxiously pacing back and forth. When the readers sees the delivery boy, he goes into his act, demanding: "Where the hell have you been? Do I have to wait all day for one little package?" The reader complains that unless the service gets better he is going to take his business elsewhere, or else he declares he may call the boy's boss to complain he's too slow. He grabs the package away from the boy, signs a receipt for it, bawls the kid out a little more and then stalks into the building. The delivery boy naturally figures he's done his job. Meanwhile, the reader heads out the back door with a package that may contain expensive fur collars, meaning about $1,000 or $2,000 profit for a couple of minutes of playacting.

A slasher, by comparison, is a bush-league thief, but not without talent. He walks behind the big dress racks as they are pulled through the streets of the garment district. At the proper moment he slashes the canvas cover on the rack and yanks out an armload of dresses. He does it so neatly and quickly that the man pulling the rack never suspects anything has happened.

SNYDER, Ruth (1895-1928): Murderess

Ruth Snyder, a wife who, with her lover, murdered her husband, became probably the most reviled woman of the 1920s; even her death in the electric chair was subjected to indignity. Her sin was not so much being a conspirator in the murder plot but being the active planner and the more active participant in the crime. Her trial was so spectacular that the press contingent included such unlikely personalities as Mary Roberts Rinehart, David Belasco, D. W. Griffith, Billy Sunday, Peggy Hopkins Joyce, Dr. John Roach Straton, Aimee Semple McPherson and even Will Durant, then at the top of the best-seller list with *The Story of Philosophy*.

Albert Snyder never realized how many close calls he had at the hands of Ruth. She had resolved to kill him in 1926, a year after she met corset salesman Judd Gray and found true happiness in an adulterous affair. Gray, not the strongest of personalities, called her "queen," and "my momsie." She referred to him as "lover boy."

Ruth took out a $48,000 life insurance policy on Snyder with a double-indemnity clause. Then she set about trying to kill him, but he seemed to live a charmed life. Twice, she disconnected the gas while Snyder slept and slipped from the room, but both times her husband awoke and saved himself from asphyxiation, never even suspecting his wife. Another time she closed the garage door while he was inside with the automobile's motor running. He nearly fell victim to carbon monoxide poisoning but managed to survive. On two occasions she put bichloride of mercury in his whiskey, but he poured the stuff out, commenting that they had to change bootleggers. Twice she added powerful narcotics to his medicine while he was ill, but he still recovered.

In February 1927 Ruth convinced Gray to help her murder her husband. Gray hid in a bedroom closet before the Snyders returned home one night, and after Snyder fell asleep, he slipped out and hit him over the head with a sash weight. But the blow woke Snyder up. He struggled with Gray and cried out for his wife to help him. Ruth came to the aid of her lover, picking up the sash weight and hitting her husband again. As

he slipped into unconsciousness, Ruth chloroformed him and strangled him with picture wire. Finally, Albert Snyder was dead. Gray then tied Ruth up and when the police arrived, she told them she had been attacked by burglars.

The police became suspicious because her bindings had been tied rather loosely, as though not to cause her discomfort. When they found Gray's name a number of times among her possessions, they decided to tell her Gray had been arrested and had confessed. The trick worked and she talked. Hearing that Ruth had confessed, Gray admitted his part in the murder. Both attempted to make the other the principal party in the murder, but it was well established that the credit belonged to Ruth Snyder.

Millions of newspaper readers hung on every word in the case of Ruth Snyder and Judd Gray until their execution.

Both were convicted and sentenced to death in the electric chair, a fate they met on January 22, 1928 at Sing Sing Prison. Just as the executioner pulled the switch on Ruth Snyder, photographer Thomas Howard, sitting in a front-row seat, crossed his legs and snapped a picture with a camera strapped just above his ankle. The next morning the *New York Daily News* devoted the entire front page to the horrifying shot of the current coursing through Ruth Snyder's body, perhaps the most famous picture in tabloid journalism.

SOCCO The Bracer (1844-1873): Gangster

One of the leaders of the notorious Patsy Conroy gang that terrorized New York's East River docks in the 1860s and

1870s, Joseph Gayles, better known as Socco the Bracer, was described by a police inspector as the most ferocious thug on the docks. Socco was generally conceded to have killed more than 20 men and always prowled the streets with at least two guns and an assortment of knives. According to waterfront legend, Socco once was so disappointed with the loot he and three other Conroys netted during a raid on a brig that he lashed the lone seaman on watch to a sea chest, gagged him and heaved him overboard after filling the sea chest with several small sacks of sugar. "If the sugar melts fast, you'll be all right," he said. It didn't.

Socco the Bracer came to a fitting end on the night of May 29, 1873, when he and two other pirates, Bum Mahoney and Billy Woods, attempted a raid on the brig *Margaret*, which was tied up at Pier 27 waiting to take on cargo. While ransacking a sea chest, they made such a racket that the captain and two crewmen awakened. In a bitter fight the looters were forced over the side to their boat and they rowed off in the mist. However, as they neared shore, two policemen patrolling the river in a rowboat spotted them and exchanged fire with Socco the Bracer. One of the officers' bullets hit Socco in the chest and he collapsed in the boat. Mahoney and Woods kept to the oars, rowing to the middle of the river, where they decided to lighten their load by tossing Socco overboard.

Socco the Bracer swam back to the rowboat, clung to the gunwales and begged his companions to haul him back aboard. Woods told Mahoney to crack the wounded man one on the knuckles, but Mahoney, in a fit of tenderheartedness, pulled the wounded gangster in. However, before the boat had gone another 50 feet, Socco the Bracer expired, and his two disgusted accomplices once more heaved his body over the side. The corpse floated to shore four days later at the foot of Stanton Street.

SOLEDAD Brothers: See Angela Davis.

SON Of Sam (1953-   ): Mass murderer

Few cases of mass murder have ever generated the level of hysteria produced by the notorious "Son of Sam" killings, which terrorized New York City from July 1976 to August 1977. During that period the killer fired a total of 31 bullets into 13 young women and men, killing six and severely wounding seven in eight separate attacks. Generally, the victims were young girls or couples parked in cars at night.

At first, the murderer was labeled the .44 Caliber Killer because of the weapon he used. Later, he started writing letters to newspapers and signing them Son of Sam, which became his new nickname. Sam, the killer wrote, was the person really responsible for the crimes because he kept ordering him, the Son of Sam, to do his bidding. Next he asserted "demons" were responsible. The city was in a state of terror. Son of Sam's first female victims were brunettes, so thousands of women became blondes. But then he killed a blonde. His victims had long hair, so women with long hair cut their hair short. Son of Sam then shot women with short hair. Parents who had pre-

viously lost control of their teenage daughters suddenly reasserted that control and refused to let them out at night.

Vigilantism ran amok. In Brooklyn a burglar was caught carrying a large-caliber gun. A mob formed, and a noose was hung from a lamp post. It took a dozen police officers to rescue the hapless burglar. Another man caught speeding in a yellow Volkswagen was hauled into the street and nearly beaten to death—all because rumor had it that Son of Sam had driven a yellow Volks. Mob rule was starting to take over; Mayor Abe Beame subsequently admitted he had been just about ready to call for the National Guard to maintain order.

As the hysteria mounted, the newspapers set about making Son of Sam even larger than life. When the anniversary of the killer's first attack neared, the press was filled with speculation about whether he would observe the date with more killings. "DEATHDAY," one newspaper proclaimed. "Tell Us Sam, What Have You Planned for Us Tonight?" another echoed. Two days later, the killer struck again.

Subsequently, the police publicly expressed gratitude to the newspapers for cooperating with them on the release of information. Actually, they were stunned by the coverage given to the case, much of it fanciful. Police activities that never happened were reported to a breathless public.

Then on August 10, 1977, just 11 days after he had killed his last victim, 20-year-old Stacy Moskowitz of Brooklyn, and blinded her escort, Robert Violante, Son of Sam was captured.

His name was David Richard Berkowitz, a mailman and former city auxiliary policeman. At the time of his arrest, he was carrying the .44-caliber Bulldog revolver he used in his eight attacks. Berkowitz' capture resulted from seemingly unrelated clues—a parking ticket issued the night of July 30-31 in the vicinity of the Moskowitz murder, threatening notes he had sent to his Yonkers neighbors, and information provided by a neighbor, Sam Carr, who was believed to be the "Sam" referred to by the Son of Sam. Carr's dog had been wounded April 27 by a .44-caliber bullet, two days after Carr had received threatening letters.

Berkowitz pleaded guilty to the crimes, and three state supreme court justices, from the different counties—Bronx, Queens and Kings (Brooklyn)—where the murders had been committed, followed each other to the bench in one court to pass sentences on him. For the murders in their jurisdictions, they each passed terms of 25 years to life, the maximum allowed under the law, and additional sentences were added for the seven attempted murders. All three justices said they wished they could pass harsher sentences, and made some of the sentences consecutive, but under the law the sentences had to be merged into a cumulative penalty not exceeding 30 years. This meant the then 25-year-old murderer had to be released when he was 54 years old.

Plans were made to allow publication of an "official biography," with the full authorization of the surviving victims and the families of the dead as well as the courts. The author, Lawrence Kausner, was to receive $150,000 in salary and expenses, his agent $25,000 and a conservator appointed to manage the killer's affairs $75,000. Beyond the $150,000, all

John Sontag, one of the leaders of the California Outlaws, lies mortally wounded after an eight-hour gunfight with a railroad posse.

the author's future royalties would go to the conservator and two charities. It was estimated that $10 to $11 million would accrue from book and movie sales, and all funds received by the conservator would be turned over to the court to be given to the surviving victims and the families of the dead.

When Berkowitz heard of this arrangement, he announced from behind bars, that he would not cooperate "in any way" with the book or movie project. He said, "Maybe after some disturbed person sees the movie, he too will go out and kill some people and then someone will make a movie about him, then another and another."

In any event, Berkowitz was not going to be able to claim any share of the future proceeds. The state legislature passed the "Son of Sam Law," which prohibited a criminal from profiting financially from his crimes.

SONTAG Brothers: Train robbers

George and John Sontag, one-time owners of a quartz mine in California, became train robbers bent on carrying out a vendetta against the Southern Pacific Railroad. There is some dispute about whether the Sontag brothers committed train holdups at Kosota, Minn. and Racine, Wis. in the spring of 1892, but there is no disagreement that they, together with Chris Evans and a gang known as the California Outlaws, held up a number of Southern Pacific trains.

The Sontags and Evans have been described as common criminals, but that is not entirely true. The California Outlaws came into existence because of the avarice of the railroad, particularly its practice of virtually stealing the property of small landowners for railroad rights-of-way. In none of their robberies did the Outlaws take any money from passengers nor did they touch the U.S. mails. Their sole loot was always the contents of the train safe in the express car.

The Sontags' exploits in eluding huge posses of railroad detectives, generally with the aid of the local residents, made them a part of California folklore. Finally, after another train robbery, the Sontags and Chris Evans were cornered in the high country. Evans and John Sontag shot their way out, killing a deputy sheriff, but George Sontag was captured and given a life sentence at Folsom Prison. Evans and John Sontag kept up their war with the railroad and the Pinkertons by stopping stagecoaches to see "if there are any detectives aboard we can kill." In June 1893 a large posse located the robbers' hideout and an eight-hour battle, later known as the Battle of Sampson's Flats, ensued. When the smoke cleared, John Sontag was shot full of holes and bleeding profusely and Evans was also badly wounded. Evans recovered to be sentenced to life imprisonment, but John Sontag died of his wounds on July 3. When George Sontag got news of his brother's death, he led a revolt at Folsom and was shot down trying to scale the wall.

See also: *California Outlaws, Christopher Evans, Ed Morrell.*

SPANISH, Johnny (1891-1919): Gangster and murderer

Johnny Spanish was one of the bloodiest criminals during the first two decades of the 20th century.

A Spanish Jew (his real name was John Weyler), he is said to have been involved in a murder at the age of 17. For a time he operated as an independent slugger and killer, taking on all assignments, until he finally formed his own gang, which was attached to New York's notorious Five Pointers.

Spanish reportedly always ventured forth with two revolvers stuck in his belt and, on serious missions, two more in his coat pockets. When staging a holdup, he often had an accomplice, a man weighted down with additional guns who acted strictly as a weapons bearer.

Johnny Spanish gained considerable underworld fame for his daring, a classic example being the robbery of a saloon on Norfolk Street belonging to Mersher the Strong Arm. Spanish gave notice that he would appear at a certain time to empty the till, and he turned up on the dot with his trusty gun bearer. The daring Spanish did exactly what he said he would, shooting out the mirror over the bar as he entered and pistol-whipping several customers who objected to contributing their wallets.

In 1909 Spanish became fast friends with Kid Dropper, destined to be for a time the leading gangster in New York. They committed a number of jobs together before becoming deadly enemies when the Dropper stole the affections of Johnny Spanish's girl friend. In order to provide for the woman of his affections, Spanish determined to take over the stuss games on the Lower East Side, then a popular form of illegal gambling. In his efforts to absorb one such operation with his usual fast shooting, Spanish killed an eight-year-old girl who happened to be playing in the street. He was forced to flee the city for several months until things quieted down. When he returned, he was chagrined to find that the woman he had done the shooting for had left him for Kid Dropper.

Determined to take vengeance, he snatched the woman off the streets one night and drove to a marsh near Maspeth, Long Island. There, he put her up against a tree and fired several shots into her abdomen, which he considered appropriate revenge since she was pregnant at the time. The woman was found alive but unconscious several hours later and, in the meantime, had given birth to a baby with three fingers shot off. For this offense Spanish was sent to prison in 1911 for seven years. His only solace was that about the same time Kid Dropper also was put away for seven years on a robbery count.

Remarkably, when both were freed in late 1917, they hooked up again as partners in crime. However, the inevitable jealousies soon surfaced and the pair and their followers split into separate gangs, each determined to take over what was virtually the sole source of income for organized criminals at the time: labor racketeering and slugging. Each gang sought to service the unions who wanted strikebreakers maimed or killed or the employers who wanted union pickets and organizers eliminated. Both the Dropper and Johnny Spanish fielded large contingents of gunmen to control the rackets and a shooting war broke out that led to dozens of deaths. Johnny Spanish was suspected of carrying out a number of torture-murders himself.

On July 29, 1919 the Dropper forces learned that Spanish was dining in a Second Avenue restaurant without his usual collection of bodyguards. When Spanish stepped into the street, three gunmen, one said to be Kid Dropper himself, emptied their revolvers into his body. With Johnny Spanish's demise, Kid Dropper became the top racketeer in New York City, a position he held until 1923, when he too was assassinated.

See also: *Kid Dropper, Labor Sluggers War.*

SPANISH Louie: (?-1900): Thug and hit man

Few New York gangsters have ever inspired the awe that a strange individual known only as Spanish Louie did at the turn of the last century. Spanish Louie was a trusted underling of a colorful gang leader named Humpty Jackson, who presided over a collection of thugs headquartered in an old graveyard between First and Second avenues in the block between 12th and 13th streets. Humpty Jackson was a mysterious figure with a hunchback (under which he concealed a gun). His gang was a substantial power on the East Side, responsible for a large number of robberies and burglaries as well as beatings and murders on assignment. Jackson would take on a beating or murder mission and parcel it out to one or more of his 50 thugs. It is believed he handed most of the difficult murder assignments to Spanish Louie, who accomplished them with closed-mouth efficiency.

Little was known of Spanish Louie's background. While he talked of noble Portuguese and Spanish ancestors, some speculated that he was really an Indian. His knowledge of weapons indicated that he had served in the Army or Navy, and while Spanish Louie hinted so himself, he never divulged any specifics. He was always armed with a brace of revolvers and was referred to by a writer of the era as the most artilleried man in gangland. He also wore two scabbards containing eight-inch daggers concealed in his trousers. Spanish Louie always dressed in funereal black—jacket, trousers, neck-high sweater topped off with a large sombrero. When he stalked the streets, he cut an awesome figure. It was an outfit well calculated to strike fear in men and a different emotion in women. When he was not at work, Spanish Louie always seemed to have at least three beautiful women in tow and was never short of spending money.

One day his bullet-ridden body turned up on 12th Street. While his murder was never solved, there was speculation that he had either been killed in a dispute with another gang member, the Grabber, over the spoils of a crime or that Humpty Jackson had done him in for botching a murder assignment in Chinatown. In his pockets he had $70, in one shoe $700 and in the other a bank book from the Bowery Savings Bank showing $3,000. The only mystery about Spanish Louie that was ever solved was the matter of his forebearers. His body was claimed by a tight-lipped man from Brooklyn and taken off for an orthodox Jewish burial.

See also: *Humpty Jackson.*

SPANISH Prisoner Swindle

The Spanish Prisoner Swindle has been worked in America for at least 150 years. Most common now is a version initiated in a letter describing an alleged prisoner held captive in Mexico or Cuba. If he is a Cuban prisoner, he is in a Castro prison, a pity since he is a rich man who, before his incarceration, smuggled out of the country something like $250,000, which is now concealed in the false bottom of a trunk laying unclaimed in a U.S. customs house. The trunk can only be claimed by the writer of the letter, or perhaps his 18-year-old daughter. For a mere pittance, say $5,000 or $10,000, the prisoner could bribe his way out of prison and he and his daughter could escape Cuba to claim his fortune.

The letter also contains an offer that is difficult to refuse. If the recipient of the letter will send the bribe money to the address mentioned in the letter, generally a box number in Miami, not only will he get his money back within a month—when the prisoner gets to the United States—but he also will be rewarded by an additional $100,000 or so. Sometimes the letter is more pathetic. The prisoner writes that there is no way he can escape (the letter has been smuggled out at great risk) but by sending the bribe money, the recipient can enable the prisoner's young daughter to escape Cuba and claim the cache in the trunk.

Such letters are sent out by the hundreds and a large number of victims fall for the story. Of course, no money is sent to them, no prisoner escapes from Cuba and no trunk is claimed from customs. The Postal Service has issued constant warnings about the Spanish Prisoner Swindle without much success. Whatever the current situation, the confidence operators come up with a story to match it. In recent years the scam involved Mexican, Cuban or Turkish prisoners. During the 1930s it was Jewish prisoners in Nazi Germany. At least once, letters describing the plight of an "American prisoner" who had hidden $3 million in South America were sent to wealthy Latin Americans. In this particular case the operator employed six typists in New York to pound out letter after letter to be sent to Latin America.

SPECK, Richard Benjamin (1942-   ): Mass murderer

A drifter often high on both alcohol and drugs, Richard Speck was apparently in that condition on July 13, 1966, when he found himself in front of a row house serving as a nurses' dormitory for the South Chicago Community Hospital. After forcing his way into an apartment shared by nine student nurses, he committed one of Chicago's most heinous mass murders. Armed with a knife and a pistol, he trapped six nurses present and tied them up. He waited until three other nurses returned home and bound them also. Then after taking

their money, he led eight of the nurses, one at a time, from the room where they were being held and killed them, strangling five and stabbing three. He sexually assaulted one of his victims. The eight were Gloria Jean Davy, Suzanne Bridget Farris, Merlita Gargullo, Mary Ann Jordan, Patricia Ann Matusek, Valentina Pasion, Nina Jo Schmale and Pamela Lee Wilkening. The ninth, 23-year-old Corazon Amurao, managed to hide under a bed and was overlooked. Four hours she cowered there, not knowing what had happened to her roommates or whether the assailant had left. When an alarm clock went off at 5 a.m., the apartment was still. Two hours later, the terror-stricken woman finally crawled out from her hiding place. She found three bodies in the next room and ran screaming from the apartment.

Speck avoided arrest for a number of days until he attempted to slash his wrists and was taken to a hospital, where he was identified as the mass murderer. He was sentenced to the electric chair, but when the Supreme Court voided the death sentence in 1972, he was resentenced to eight consecutive terms of 50 to 150 years. Facing a possible total of 1,200 years in prison, Speck seemed to have received the longest sentence in history. By 1976, however, he was eligible for parole, and although turned down, he was entitled to a review of his case each year thereafter.

SPIDERMAN Of Denver: See Philip Peters.

SPINELLI, Juanita "Duchess" (1889-1941): Murderess

The first woman to be executed legally in California, Juanita Spinelli, dubbed the Duchess of Death by the newspapers, set up a school in California to train young men for crime and masterminded their criminal activities.

Until her middle years Juanita Spinelli's life is shrouded in mystery. She claimed she was born in a hobo jungle to a drifter and a runaway Sioux Indian girl. Her mother died in childbirth and her father disappeared. It is unclear who raised her, but it is known that she was married once or twice.

Her police dossier began in 1935, when she acted as "finger-woman" in a laundry union strike. She informed on a strike-breaker she knew was wanted by the police. At the time, she was living with Michael Simone, a Detroit hoodlum who served as a bodyguard for some of the city's leading gangsters.

While Simone's employers were not directly affected by Juanita's informant role, they felt uncomfortable about having a female stoolpigeon around. Sensing she was not wanted, Juanita moved on to California. There, she struck up an acquaintance with a young San Francisco car thief named Gordon Hawkins, moved in with him and began giving instructions to Hawkins and some of his friends on how to become big-time gangsters. Among her prize pupils were 23-year-old Albert Ives and 18-year-old Robert Sherrard, a fugitive from a mental institution. In time, she brought in Mike Simone from Detroit to act as her chief lieutenant in the gang.

At first, Juanita, now called Duchess by Hawkins, masterminded small operations—auto thefts, easy burglaries, rolling helpless drunks. Then they moved on to stickups. On April 8, 1940 Simone, Hawkins, Ives and Sherrard held up Leland S. Cash, the 55-year-old manager of a roadside barbecue stand. When they announced it was a robbery, Cash, who was hard of hearing, reached for his hearing aid, and Ives, panicking, shot him fatally in the stomach. The quartet escaped with the paper bags Cash was carrying, which they supposed contained the receipts for the day. Actually, the bags only held some extra meat that the victim was taking home.

The Duchess was furious about the needless murder and then even more furious when Sherrard started showing signs of "coming apart." Fearful he would talk about the murder, she ordered him killed. The gang knocked Sherrard out with a Mickey Finn, dressed him in swimming trunks and dumped him off a bridge. According to the Duchess, there was a good chance the police would mark the death down to accidental drowning. To be on the safe side, she moved her brood to Reno, where they pulled a few more jobs. Meanwhile, Ives began getting shaky, and he grew even more nervous when the Duchess started intimating he might be disposed of next. Deciding it was only a matter of time until he too was killed, Ives managed to slip away from the mob long enough to inform the police about the gang's murderous activities.

In the ensuing investigation, every male member of the mob tried to implicate everyone else, especially the Duchess, who sneered at their cowardice. In the end, Duchess Spinelli, Simone and Hawkins were sentenced to die in the gas chamber. Ives was judged insane and committed to a mental institution. He died in 1951.

Duchess Spinelli managed to delay her execution for a year and a half with appeals, including one to Gov. Culbert Olson requesting life imprisonment on the grounds that no woman had ever been legally executed in the state. The governor found the appeal without merit, and the Duchess prepared for death by putting a "curse" on the authorities, the judge and the jurors. She told reporters, "My blood will burn holes in their bodies, and before six months have gone by, my executioners will be punished."

However, an hour before she died on November 21, 1941, the Duchess relented, saying, "I have asked God to forgive them."

SPIRITUALISM

The birthplace of modern American spiritualism, the belief that the dead can communicate with the living through physical phenomena, was Hydesville, N.Y.

In 1848, 15-year-old Margaret Fox developed the ability to snap her big toe so loudly that it resembled a sharp rap on wood. She and her younger sister Kate kept the ability a secret and decided to play a prank on their parents. One night they called their mother and father to their bedside and said they could not sleep because of some strange rappings. The girls said they were sure the sounds were being made by the ghost of the former owner of the house, who had been murdered. Kate shut her eyes and went into a sort of trance and asked if the ghost was in the room. Margaret answered yes by snapping her toe twice under the blankets (one snap meant no). Mr. and Mrs. Fox excitedly put more questions to the strange spirit and got answers via the girls. The parents concluded their daughters had supernatural powers.

News spread rapidly through the surrounding area and hundreds of people descended on the Fox home seeking to get in touch with deceased relatives. By now the hoax had gotten so big that the girls dared not confess. They ended up becoming famous mediums for the next 40 years. Meanwhile, other charlatans readily came up with various methods of producing rappings from the dead and the principles of spiritualism became firmly imbedded in popular belief. Not even a confession by the Fox sisters in 1888 about their toe trick could stop the growth of this new racket.

Spiritualism caught on in America because it coincided with a loss of faith in authoritarian religious doctrine thanks to the profound impact of 19th century science. Evidence became more and more a requirement and spiritualists seemed to satisfy that criteria through rappings, "spirit lights" and the "materialized spirit."

Some fakers carried off particularly bald-faced swindles. Typical of these charlatans was Mrs. Hannah Ross, the most popular medium in Boston during the 1880s. Her greatest trick was to make a long-dead baby materialize before her gullible victims' eyes. Eventually, Mrs. Ross's con was revealed by an enterprising reporter. She would seat herself in a cabinet in a dark room and allegedly go into a trance. Then she would expose one of her breasts through a slit in the curtain surrounding her and the dead baby would seemingly appear. On her breast she had painted the face of an infant.

Converts from around the world flocked to spiritualism in the late 19th and early 20th century. Among them were William Gladstone, Sir Arthur Conan Doyle, John Ruskin and Alfred Russel Wallace. In the late 19th century leading mediums became important international figures despite the fact that exposure of their frauds increased. Henry Slade, the slate-writing medium, was one of the most famous exposed.

Probably the greatest American spiritualist was Daniel D. Home, who was one of the first to adopt the tapping trick of the Fox sisters. Leaving his home in Waterford, Conn. in 1850 at the age of 17, Home was one of the earliest swindlers to cash in on the spirit communication craze. He went to Europe in 1854 and, over the years, conducted thousands of seances, many by invitation in royal courts and the houses of nobility. At the court of Emperor Napoleon III of France, Home pulled off one of his most acclaimed performances. Knowing for a certainty that the empress would want to communicate with her departed father, Home smuggled in a rubber replica of the dead man's right hand. On touching it in the dark, the empress "recognized it at once" because of the missing third finger.

One of Home's greatest tricks, which convinced many of his supernatural powers, was having a chair he was sitting in rise and carry him around the room over the heads of his guests. Home retired in 1871 an extremely wealthy man. While all of his supposed psychic powers have been exposed as tricks, true believers in spiritualism still celebrate him as the greatest medium of all time.

See also: *Hannah Ross*.

SPOONER, Bathsheba (1746-1778): Murderess

Bathsheba Spooner, the Tory Murderess, was convicted and sentenced to death in 1778 in the first capital case tried in American jurisdiction in Massachusetts, and quite possibly, her subsequent ill fate was the result of her lowly political repute. Not that Bathsheba was innocent of the charges against her. She admitted conspiring with and assisting her lover and two escaped British soldiers in the murder of her husband, the elderly Joshua Spooner, but she most likely would have earned herself a lesser punishment had she possessed more revolutionary fervor.

Bathsheba was the daughter of Timothy Ruggles, chief justice of the Massachusetts Court on Common Pleas under crown rule. With the onset of the Revolution, Ruggles had been forced to flee to Canada. Bathsheba remained behind in that fateful year of 1776 and married 63-year-old Joshua Spooner, a retired merchant. Although old Spooner was rather apolitical, he was soon branded as a Tory sympathizer because of his marriage to the daughter of a leading Tory. It was not a situation to his liking and probably explained why he was so happy when he came home one day in the winter of 1778 to find his 31-year-old wife had taken in Ezra Ross, a handsome 20-year-old soldier in the Revolutionary Army who had been wounded in the chest during a recent campaign. Ross had literally collapsed outside the Spooners' door in the hamlet of Brookfield, near Worcester. With his wife, a suspected Tory, now nursing a Revolutionary hero, Spooner knew that the wagging rebel tongues would still.

Of course, his wife's care for the soldier had little to do with political sentiments; within a few months she would inform her recuperating patient that she was "with child." Bathsheba also told young Ross they would have to kill her husband before he learned of their affair and cast them both out of his lavish keep. Ross agreed to her suggestion in the abstract, but in practice he proved unavailing. She suggested poisoning her husband, but Ross, who said he could face any man musket to musket, backed off from such a low deed. Then Spooner had to journey to Boston to look after his investments and Ross went with him. Bathsheba's lover was supposed to kill her husband on the return trip and blame the murder on the British, but the pair returned together.

By this time Bathsheba Spooner had decided her young lover just wasn't going to do her bidding; so she recruited two passing British soldiers to carry out the plot. Whether James Buchanan and William Brooks were deserters or escapees from Revolutionary custody was of small consequence to Mrs. Spooner. The important thing was that they were willing to perform any deed which would earn them some gold. With Buchanan and Brooks backing him, Ross waylaid Spooner as he

came staggering home one midnight from Ephraim Cooley's tavern. The three clubbed the old man to death and dumped his body into a well at the side of the house.

A maid fetching water the next morning discovered the bucket covered with a film of blood and sounded the alarm. Old Spooner's body was raised and it was found to be devoid of purse, snuff box, silver shoe buckles and watch. Obviously, he had been murdered and robbed. Perhaps if they had kept a low profile, Ross, Brooks and Buchanan might have escaped detection, but with foolish abandon, they took to wearing their loot, and within days the trio was arrested. Servants in the Spooner household then came forth with tales of having heard the three in conspiratorial conversations with Mrs. Spooner. One servant, coachman Alexander Cumings, said he had come into the parlor and observed the men burning their clothing, which appeared to be bloodstained in the fireplace. The victim's money box lay open on the table and its contents divided up in neat piles.

It was, to say the least, a rather open-and-shut case, especially when Bathsheba confessed she had masterminded the murder of her husband to keep him from learning of her affair with young Ross. The case was tried by William Cushing, chief justice of the Massachusetts Supreme Court and later a member of the U.S. Supreme Court, and prosecuted by Robert Treat Paine, a signer of the Declaration of Independence. Defense attorney Levi Lincoln, who was to become attorney general under Thomas Jefferson, came up with the rather novel defense that since the plot had been so openly planned and botched, Bathsheba must have been "insane." He added that because only one of the three men had struck the fatal blow, the jury could not convict more than one of them and, lacking absolute proof against any of the three, it would have to release them all. Unmoved by the defense attorney's arguments, the jury found the four guilty. They were all sentenced to be hanged.

The sentences were scheduled to be carried out on June 4, 1778 but were postponed through the intercession of the Rev. Thaddeus MacCarty, a Worcester minister, who visited the condemned woman in her cell to discuss her spiritual future. Mrs. Spooner once more admitted her part in the crime but for the first time confessed the full story, including the fact that she was pregnant. If that were so, and the Rev. MacCarty was certain it was, both English law and custom forbade her execution. Urged on by MacCarty, the Massachusetts Council granted a stay until July 2 and ordered that "two men midwives and twelve discreet lawful matrons" conduct an examination "by the breast and by the belly" to determine the accuracy of the claim.

Their unanimous finding was that Bathsheba Spooner was not pregnant, which led MacCarty to charge that their opinion had been colored by their political sympathies. He empaneled his own jury of three men midwives and three lawful matrons. After they conducted an examination, all the men and one of the women declared Bathsheba was pregnant, but the two other women said she was not. In any event, the MacCarty panel had no legal standing, and even Bathsheba gave up the fight.

> She made a final request in a letter to the council
>
> that my body be examined after I am executed by a committee of competent physicians, who will, perforce, belatedly substantiate my claims. I am a woman, familiar with my bodily functions, and am surely able to perceive when my womb is animated. The midwives who have examined me have taken into greater account my father's Royalist leanings than they have the stirrings in my body which should have stirred their consciences. The truth is that they want my father's daughter dead and with her my father's grandchild.

Thousands attended the four hangings in Worcester on July 2, the dispute over Bathsheba's condition still raging. The crowd did not disperse until later that afternoon when a committee of surgeons completed an autopsy and rather reluctantly made their report public. In the executed woman's womb they had found "a perfectly developed male foetus, aged between five and six months."

Some latter-day historians have insisted that the Spooner case was so etched on the conscience of the citizens of Massachusetts that never again was a female condemned to death in the state, with or without a plea for mercy because of pregnancy. That theory is certainly open to debate, but one definite result of the affair was that certain male midwives and discreet lawful matrons needed a lengthy period of remorse before they could once more walk the streets of Worcester without downcast eyes.

SPRINGFIELD (Illinois) Race Riot

Probably no false rape story in American history had as much impact as one told in 1908 in Springfield, Ill. After a white woman claimed she had been raped by a black named George Richardson, whites rioted and 4,200 militia had to be called in to stop the violence. Richardson was spirited out of town to save his life, but during the two days of rioting—August 14 and August 15—two blacks were lynched, six other blacks were killed and over 70 blacks and whites were seriously wounded. Some 2,000 blacks fled the city. The instigators of the riot never were punished, although a number of people were arrested and indicted.

George Richardson also went free after his accuser admitted to a special grand jury in 1909 that it was a white man who raped her, although she refused to identify him. Prompted by the Springfield riot, a biracial group, including William Dean Howells, Jane Addams and W. E. B. Du Bois met in New York City the following year and agreed to form the National Association for the Advancement of Colored People.

SQUEALER: Slang term for informer

There are many theories on the origin of the slang term "squealer" as a synonym for informer. The simplest is that a lawbreaker squeals like a pig when caught, and in this squealing he often names his accomplices. Another theory traces the origin of the term to the case of an unfortunate stock thief who was making

off with a pig when the animal's squeals betrayed him. Whatever the etymology of the word, squealers are the chief source of information by which crimes are solved.

No matter how necessary informers may be to police, the public has never thought highly of them. In the 1870s four members of a gang that had robbed a train in Kansas were convicted on the testimony of a fifth member, Dave Rudabaugh. The *Kinsley Graphic* was much taken with the ethical question involved, commenting: "Rudabaugh testified that he was promised entire immunity from punishment if he would 'squeal,' therefore he squole. Some one has said there is a kind of honor among thieves. Rudabaugh don't think so."

In an infamous holdup in the Arizona Territory in 1883 called the Bisbeen Massacre, the mastermind of the operation, John Heath, turned informer to save himself and named his five confederates, all of whom were hanged. As a reward for his assistance, Heath was let off with a life sentence, a decision that did not sit well with the local populace. A large mob overwhelmed Heath's jailers before he was due to be shipped off to the penitentiary, and a short time later, the squealer's dead body was found dangling from a telegraph pole.

Over the years law enforcement officials have come to rely heavily on informers. Detective Lt. Jack Osnato broke the Murder, Inc. investigation by coaxing leads out of minor killers in the group until the trail led to Abe Reles, probably the most important informer in the history of American crime. In 1941 Reles "went out the window" of a sixth-floor hotel room, where he was being kept under police protection.

More recent informers have fared better. The celebrated Joe Valachi died in prison of natural causes in 1971. Vinnie Teresa, the New England Mafia songbird, remains hidden under the Justice Department's Witness Relocation Program, and is probably the informer most wanted by the underworld, with a reputed price of $500,000 on his head.

By 1976 the controversial relocation plan, sometimes called the Alias Program, had hidden away under new identities an estimated minimum of 2,000 witnesses and members of their families. Its origin and procedures have never been discussed in Congress, and critics have charged that the program's protection of witnesses is less than efficient. Indeed, in one incredible blunder a witness and several members of his family were given new identities and issued new Social Security cards—in *sequential* numbers. A private investigator tracking the witness eventually found him after hearing a story about a husband and wife who had sequential Social Security numbers. In other cases witnesses have walked away from their covers, finding them ineffective.

See also: *Abe Reles, Vincent Charles Teresa, Joseph M. Valachi.*

Further reading: *The Alias Program* by Fred Graham.

STACHER, Joseph "Doc" (1902-   ): Syndicate leader

Born in Poland in 1902, Stacher came to the United States at the age of 10. A few years later, he was a minor-league pushcart thief in Newark, N.J. During this period he formed friendships with future leading Jewish gangsters, such as Longy Zwillman and Meyer Lansky. In the 1920s Stacher ran many of Zwillman's gambling enterprises and in 1931, at Lansky's behest, brought together a number of the top New York Jewish gang figures for a conference at the Franconia Hotel, which resulted in the merger of the Jewish Mafia and the Italian Mafia into a new national crime syndicate. Lansky then assigned Stacher to handle gambling activities on the West Coast and in the Caribbean. Later, he oversaw gambling in Las Vegas for Lansky and was connected with such casinos as the Sands and the Fremont.

Federal agents finally nailed Stacher for income tax evasion, and he was sentenced to five years. Although the government wanted to deport him, the law prohibited sending anyone to an Iron Curtain country. As a Jew, Stacher was entitled, under the Law of the Return, to go to Israel. The gangster accepted this form of exile and emigrated in 1965. Scores of other mobsters of Jewish descent followed him. Lansky himself tried to emigrate to Israel in 1971, but he proved to be too notorious and was expelled. Doc Stacher was allowed to remain.

See also: *Jewish Mafia.*

STAFFORD, Annie (1838-?): Chicago madam

Annie Stafford, better known as Gentle Annie in her younger, more voluptuous days, was the leading fighter in Chicago's Whore War in 1857, representing the forces of the Sands, a sinkhole of vice, against an incursion by the madams of the better State Street district, who were looking for attractive talent to stock their house with. Annie at the time was merely a 50¢ prostitute in the house of Anna Wilson, but she nevertheless took on the brunt of the fighting, which eventually resulted in a victory for the Sands area. Somewhere along the line Annie got tired of doing all the work while others were making the money. She resolved to become the madam of her own establishment, and by the early 1860s she was running what she described as a "classy place with 30 boarders."

For close to two decades Annie was a principal figure in Chicago vice and her lovelife and business enterprises were duly recorded by the newspapers. Annie had been the longtime mistress of Cap Hyman, a leading Chicago gambler, who enjoyed her company and charms but didn't see the need for making it legal—until one September day in 1866 when Annie stormed into his gambling house carrying a rawhide whip. She found Hyman sleeping on a sofa, threw him down the stairs and chased him up the street, her whip cracking on his shanks with every stride. Shortly thereafter, Cap Hyman proposed marriage. The wedding was an elegant affair that attracted not only the Chicago underworld but also representatives from as far away as Cincinnati and New Orleans. Immediately following the ceremony, Cap Hyman announced he was giving his wife a very special present, a tavern outside the city limits called Sunnyside, which would be turned into "a high-toned roadhouse."

The opening of Sunnyside was a gala event, with guests of honor including city and county officials, young businessmen with sporting interests, big-time gamblers and reporters from each of the newspapers. Also invited were other leading Chicago madams, while some three dozen of Annie's young ladies were trained thoroughly on the proper etiquette for the occasion. The reporters were brought to Sunnyside in a huge four-horse sleigh.

Frederick Francis Cook, there as a reporter for the *Chicago Times,* reported that the festivities started in a most decorous fashion. "You were ceremoniously introduced, engagement cards were consulted, and all the rest of the little formalities that distinguish like functions in the *haut monde* were strictly observed. Yes, the make-believe was quite tremendous." One young redheaded lady of Annie's staff walked around looking gentlemen in the eye and asking, "Who's your favorite poet? Mine's Byron."

The tone couldn't last. Before the night had finished, case after case of champagne had been consumed, Cap Hyman had shot out the lights, Annie had had to reprimand other madams for passing out business cards, and several harlots had set up business on a free-lance basis in a number of the upstairs rooms.

While Sunnyside was a great social success, it flopped as a commercial enterprise. Annie Stafford noted that gentlemen just wouldn't travel that far even for high-class strumpets. So the couple returned to their Chicago haunts. In 1875 Cap Hyman suffered a complete physical and mental collapse. He died the following year, with Annie at his bedside. Annie continued to run a brothel until about 1880, when she dropped from sight.

See also: *Sands, Whore War.*

STANDARD Oil Building, Battles Of The

Probably more than any other events, the two so-called Battles of the Standard Oil Building in 1926 were what people thought of when they heard the words "Chicago gangsters."

On the morning of August 10 Hymie Weiss and Schemer Drucci, who took control of Dion O'Banion's North Side Gang after O'Banion's assassination, were on their way to make a payoff to Morris Eller, political boss of the 20th Ward, in order to secure protection for their numerous speakeasies. The meeting was to take place at 910 South Michigan Avenue, the new 19-story Standard Oil Building. Just as the pair reached the bronze Renaissance-style doors of the building, four Capone gunmen, the North Siders' sworn enemies, jumped from a car and charged at them. Seeing the attackers' drawn guns, Weiss and Drucci ducked behind a parked car and pulled their own weapons from shoulder holsters. The area, which at that hour teemed with pedestrians, erupted in gunfire. One pedestrian was hit in the volley of 30-odd shots, as bystanders either dived for cover or stood frozen with horror.

Weiss started to retreat from car to car, but Drucci headed for his hated foe. The Capone gunmen backed off to a sedan parked on the other side of the avenue and then pulled away, with a still-angry Drucci firing after them. He jumped on the running board of a passing car, put his gun to the driver's temple and ordered, "Follow that goddamn car." Just then a police flivver pulled up and officers yanked the crazed Drucci to the pavement.

Drucci told the police there had been no gang battle, that it had merely been a case of some punks "trying for my roll." The police brought Louis Barko, whom they had recognized as one of the Capone gunners, before Drucci for identification. In keeping with underworld tradition, Drucci shrugged, "I never seen him before." Barko and all other suspects were released.

Five days later, on August 15, Weiss and Drucci were again attacked at almost the same spot. This time they were driving in a sedan when rival gangsters trailing in another auto opened up on them. Although their car was riddled with bullets, the two gangsters were not hit. They dashed from their car to the sanctuary of the Standard Oil Building, firing wild shots over their shoulders.

On September 20 Weiss and Drucci retaliated with the famous attack on the Capone headquarters at the Hawthorne Inn in Cicero. A convoy of eight cars loaded with gunmen poured lead into the building in a vain effort to kill Al Capone. In addition to wounding some pedestrians, the gunmen shot Louis Barko in the shoulder. Later, police picked up Drucci on the suspicion that he had fired the shot which downed Barko. When asked if he could identify Drucci as his assailant, Barko returned a past favor by announcing, "Never saw him before."

About this time Lucky Luciano, Capone's Brooklyn schoolmate, visited Chicago on crime business. "A real goddam crazy place!" he told associates upon returning to the quiet of New York. "Nobody's safe in the streets."

See also: *Vincent "Schemer" Drucci, Hymie Weiss.*

STAR Route Frauds

One of the greatest frauds in U.S. postal history involved the so-called Star Routes, roads built in the 19th century West for mail delivery via wagon and horseback. The situation was ripe for fraudulent claims and a combine of crooked Postal Department officials, contractors, subcontractors and politicians set up a vast conspiracy. The combination lobbied for congressional appropriations to start new and useless routes and upgrade old ones. One road was improved for faster travel at a cost of $50,000 despite the fact that its use brought in only $761 in postal income annually. A single fraudulent affidavit, unopposed by postal officials, netted one contractor $90,000. A later investigation of the road improvement claims made by another contractor, John M. Peck, revealed that to equal the distance he claimed could be traveled in a day a man would have to ride for 40 hours.

Probes by congressional investigators, special agents and Pinkerton detectives resulted in more than 25 indictments. Trials held in 1882 and 1883 uncovered frauds related to 93 routes. However, not a single conviction was obtained. It was estimated that the government had been defrauded out of at least $4 million.

STARKWEATHER, Charles (1940-1959): Mass murderer

Charley Starkweather, Nebraska's mass murderer of the 1950s, killed his first victim on December 1, 1957. On that day the red-haired youth robbed a gas station attendant, Robert Colvert, at gunpoint in Lincoln, drove him to an open area outside the city and executed him with several shots in the head. He did nothing more for almost two months until January 21, 1958, when he drove to the home of 14-year-old Caril Ann Fugate.

Finding the girl not at home, he sat down to wait for her, toying with a .22 hunting rifle he had brought with him. Caril's mother, Velda Bartlett, yelled at him to stop fooling around with the weapon—whereupon he shot both her and Caril's stepfather, Marion Bartlett. When Caril Ann came home, Starkweather went to her two-year-old sister's bedroom and choked the child to death. He then dragged the parents' bodies outside and put Marion Bartlett's corpse under newspapers and rags in the chicken coop and Velda's in an abandoned outhouse. He dumped the child into a cardboard box and then went into the kitchen, made some sandwiches and joined Caril to watch television.

They put a sign on the door reading: "STAY AWAY. EVERYBODY IS SICK WITH THE FLU. MISS BARTLETT." When Caril's older sister came by and wanted to help, Caril Ann sent her away. Later, Caril Ann's lawyer would argue she had saved her sister from being killed by Starkweather, who was lurking behind the kitchen door as the two sisters talked.

Caril's older sister told her husband, who became suspicious and notified the police. When two officers came to the house to investigate, Caril Ann told them everyone inside was sick. They left. Two days later, Caril turned her grandmother away, and she went to the police. The police returned to the house and found it empty. They then searched the premises and found the three bodies.

An alert went out for Starkweather and the girl, and in the following week of terror, Little Red, the bow-legged teenager who modeled himself after movie star James Dean, played the role of a murderer without a cause, shooting and stabbing seven more people to death. When his car got stuck on a muddy road, a high school couple stopped to lend a hand, Starkweather shot them to death and he and Caril Ann transferred to the victims' car. He then shot a friend, August Meyer, for his guns and ammunition.

Back in Lincoln, Starkweather and Caril Ann entered the house of wealthy steel executive C. Lauer Ward and marched his wife and housekeeper upstairs. The two women were tied up and gagged and then Starkweather stabbed them to death. When Ward returned home, he was murdered before he had time to take off his coat.

The couple took Ward's smooth-running Packard and drove to Wyoming. Twelve miles outside of Douglas, they came upon shoe salesman Merle Collison catnapping in his new Buick at the side of the road. Caril Ann slipped into the back seat while Starkweather walked over to the driver's side of the car and shot the sleeping victim nine times in the head. It was his last killing. Thinking someone was in trouble, an oil company worker named Joe Sprinkle stopped to offer a hand. When Starkweather leveled a rifle at Sprinkle, the oil worker charged him and struggled for possession of the weapon. By luck, a deputy sheriff happened by and Caril Ann ran to him, screaming: "It's Starkweather! He's going to kill me. . . ."

Starkweather managed to break free, jump into the Packard and speed off. After gunning his car to 110 miles an hour and crashing through one roadblock, he was finally stopped when officers shot out his windshield.

Starkweather blandly announced he had killed everyone in "self-defense" and tried to defend Caril Ann. "Don't take it out on the girl. She had no part of it." He claimed she was a hostage. But when the girl started calling him a killer, he changed his attitude. "She could have escaped any time she wanted," he said. "I left her alone lots of times. Sometimes when I would go in and get hamburgers, she would be sitting in the car with all the guns. There would have been nothing to stop her from running away. One time she said that the hamburgers were lousy and we ought to go back and shoot all them people in the restaurant."

"After I shot her folks and killed her baby sister, Caril sat and watched television while I wrapped the bodies up in rags and newspapers. We just cooked up that hostage story between us."

Starkweather was condemned to death and Caril Ann Fugate was sentenced to life imprisonment, tearfully proclaiming her innocence as she left the courtroom. Starkweather went to the electric chair on June 25, 1959, after turning down a request from the Lions Club of Beatrice, Neb. that he donate his eyes to their eye bank following his death.

"Hell no," he said. "No one ever did anything for me. Why in the hell should I do anything for anyone else?" The 19-year-old's execution took four minutes.

Caril Ann Fugate was released on parole in 1977, considered completely rehabilitated.

STARR, Belle (1848-1889): Bandit Queen

Although the Eastern press dubbed her the Bandit Queen, the Lady Desperado and the female Robin Hood, Belle Starr was simply a hatchet-faced horse thief, a frontier fence and, whenever times got tough, a whore. It seems likely that naive makers of legends often confused her with Belle Boyd, the truly heroic Confederate spy.

Born Myra Belle Shirley in Carthage, Mo., or thereabouts, to "Judge" John Shirley (her father's judgeship may have been a product of her imagination) and his wife Elizabeth, Belle associated with some pretty mean characters in her teens. Her brother Ed Shirley rode with the James-Younger gang, and Belle formed a rather close attachment to some of the boys. Her first illegitimate child was a daughter named Pearl, born after a brief courtship by Cole Younger. After that, Belle took up with another badman, Jim Reed, by whom she had another child, a boy named Ed, who was born after the couple had trekked to California, where Reed engaged in highway robbery.

After a while, there was a price on Reed's head, and he headed back east with his family.

With $30,000 in loot, Reed took Belle to Texas, where she opened a livery stable and ranch and played her role of Bandit Queen. As a member of old Tom Starr's gang, Jim rustled horses in Indian Territory in what is now Oklahoma, and Belle's stable always had a fine supply of stock.

Belle Starr's reputation as the Bandit Queen was born in the pages of the sensationalist Eastern press, which portrayed the hatchet-faced horse thief and, when times were tough, prostitute as a comely, hell-for-leather lass.

Reed was killed in 1874 by a lawman who had previously ridden the outlaw trail with him. From 1875 to 1880 Belle was the acknowledged leader of a rustler band that forayed out of Indian Territory (Oklahoma). She had a succession of lovers but seemed most fond of her first love, Cole Younger. Cole, however, vanished from her life following the ill-fated bank raid at Northfield, Minn. in September 1876. Shot up in the raid, he was captured soon after and sentenced to life imprisonment.

Belle consoled herself with others. In 1876 another "husband" started making the rounds with Belle. He was a flat-faced Indian, half-breed or white man—there are conflicting stories—with the odd alias of Blue Duck. Subsequently, a lot of tales were told about this period in Belle's life. She supposedly rode with Blue Duck on rustling sprees, although there is no proof of that, and she was later said to have killed a Dallas lawman, a story without foundation.

In any event, before long Blue Duck was replaced by Sam Starr, with whom Belle broke tradition by legally marrying. Sam, a Cherokee, was apparently the son of horse thief Tom Starr, and after the marriage Belle resumed selling stolen livestock. Soon, the U.S. government had a $10,000 reward out for the capture of Sam and Belle Starr "dead or alive." This would seem to indicate that Belle was a genuine outlaw. However, in 1883, when they were captured and hauled before Hanging Judge Parker, who was notorious for handing out stiff sentences, Parker gave Belle only a six-month prison term, indicating she was probably guilty of no more than being a receiver of stolen beef and horseflesh. Sam Starr got a year. When he came out of the penitentiary, he found his wife had changed. She was now a celebrity. Richard Fox's *Police Gazette* had immortalized her as a "female Robin Hood and a Jesse James." Much was made of her past relationship with Jesse James, whom she knew from the old days and to whom she had evidently offered a refuge on her ranch around 1881. Belle got a job in a Wild West show playing the part of an outlaw who held up a stagecoach, which carried among its passengers none other than Judge Parker. Goggle-eyed audiences ate up this presentation with the same gusto they accepted the public-relations build-up of Buffalo Bill.

All this upset Sam Starr, but he may have been more hurt by the fact that Belle had a long line of lovers. He shot one of them and disappeared for a time. By 1886 the two were back together in the horse-stealing business. Taken into custody, Belle granted long interviews to the press, in which she indicated she wasn't worried about going before Judge Parker again on a rustling count. She proved right, as the judge released her for lack of evidence. Belle rode out of town, smiling graciously at the citizens of Fort Smith.

That Christmas, Belle became a widow when Sam Starr got into a drunken shoot-out with an Indian deputy. Both men died of their wounds. With Sam gone, Belle was no longer the Bandit Queen. She had a number of lovers, at least some of whom came cash in hand. Her last was an outlaw Creek Indian named Jim July. When he was charged with larceny, Belle talked him into surrendering at Fort Smith, pointing out that since the case against him was very weak, Judge Parker would have to set him free.

Belle rode with him to Fort Smith. Returning home alone she was bushwhacked on a lonely road near Eufaula, Indian Territory (Oklahoma) on February 3, 1889. A neighbor of hers, Edgar Watson, with whom she was on bad terms, was accused of the crime, but the charges were eventually dropped. Most historians now agree she was probably murdered by her 18-year-old son, Ed Reed, whom she alternately attacked with a bull whip and made love to in an incestuous relationship.

However, Belle Starr went to her grave with her Bandit Queen reputation firmly established. Belle's daughter Pearl had a short elegy inscribed on her tombstone that read:

> Shed not for her the bitter tear,
> Nor give the heart to vain regret,
> 'Tis but the casket that lies here,
> The gem that fills it sparkles yet.

See also: *Ed Reed, Jim Reed, Tom Starr.*

STARR, Henry (1873-1921): Bank robber and murderer

The last of the Starrs, a remarkable criminal clan that included Tom, Sam and by marriage, Belle Starr, Henry Starr was born in Indian Territory in what is now Oklahoma on December 2, 1873. For a time he appeared to be the "good Starr," avidly reading the classics and shunning such vices as smoking and drinking. In 1891, however, he was arrested for trading whiskey to the Indians, and after that, he was charged with stealing horses. Finally, he started his own Starr gang in late 1892 and pulled off several train and store robberies. During the course of one escape from the law, Starr killed Floyd Wilson, one of Hanging Judge Parker's deputies, a crime for which he was captured in 1893. On October 20, 1894 Starr was sentenced by Parker to be hanged, but a series of appeals kept putting off the execution and, it was reported, "gave Judge Parker fits."

In 1921 the last of the Starrs, Henry, parked his car—instead of tethering his horse as his forebears had done—held up an Arkansas bank and got himself shot to death.

After a string of reversals and new trials, the authorities acquiesced to a prison term for Starr. He served less than five years before being pardoned by President Theodore Roosevelt, a stroke of good fortune that Starr celebrated by sticking up a bank in Bentonville, Ark. By 1909 he was in custody again and throughout the next decade he was in and out of prison for various offenses. Remarkably, in 1919 Starr won another pardon. For a while, he seemed to have found a new career, appearing in a number of movies that, in one way or another, had the same theme: crime does not pay. In between movie chores, Starr, as it happened, was still robbing banks. On February 18, 1921 he parked his car, which he now used instead of a horse, in front of the People's Bank at Harrison, Ark. and tried to rob the bank at gunpoint. Banker W. J. Myers' answered Starr's demands with a shotgun blast that ended his career on and off the screen. He died of his wounds four days later.

STARR, Tom (1813-1890): Outlaw and murderer

A full-blooded Cherokee Indian, Tom Starr was among the West's most violent characters, and he certainly passed along his bad traits, fathering a bloodthirsty brood of eight boys and two girls, who—with their children and cousins and nephews—formed the "Starr clan gang."

"Uncle Tom" Starr was easily the most vicious. Born in Tennessee, Tom was brought by his parents to the Indian lands of what is now Oklahoma. In his twenties, he was a strapping six feet seven inches and an expert with a bowie knife, a skill that came in handy in the factional warfare that beset the Cherokee nation. When Tom Starr killed a rival tribesman named David Buffington, nothing much happened to him; no one seemed capable of doing anything about it. For no apparent reason, Tom burned a whole family to death in 1843. By then he had become a full-time outlaw, leading a mixed group of Indians, whites and half-breeds on many murderous horse-rustling raids. In 1845 his enemies attacked the Starr homestead and slaughtered his father and 12-year-old brother, Buck. Starr dropped his desperado career temporarily and went about taking fatal vengeance on the 32 raiders involved. He is said to have killed all of them, save those lucky enough to die of other causes before he could get to them; Starr was not a man who believed in ending an enemy's life quickly.

Having avenged his kin, Starr went back to crime for profit. It was considered an honor by outlaws of any race to be accepted into the Starr band. Among those accepted was Jim Reed, whose younger paramour would later become known as Belle Starr when she married Uncle Tom's son, Sam. Until his retirement from active criminal behavior in the 1880s, Uncle Tom's territory, now a part of Adair County, Okla., was considered to be the most unsafe in the entire region, although Starr often struck deep into Texas on criminal forays. Overall, he is believed to have personally killed more than 100 men. When he died in 1890, members of his clan insisted to journalists that he was a delightful old man "full of fun and eager to josh folks."

See also: *Jim Reed, Belle Starr.*

STARVED Rock State Park Murders: See Chester Weger.

STATE Street Crap Game

Few gambling operations were more important to organized crime than Brooklyn's State Street Crap Game, operated by the mob in the 1930s. It was located in a building just off the busy corner of State and Court streets in downtown Brooklyn, New York City. No nickel-dime setup, it attracted men of considerable wealth and prominence and was said to have been responsible for "sucking in" politicians and police brass, in time making them beholden to the underworld when they suffered big losses. The game was also one of the most important methods of financing Murder, Inc., the national crime syndicate's assassination "troop." The killers of Murder, Inc. did not receive a fee for each job but were paid on retainer and given rights to certain crooked operations. Abe "Kid" Reles aided by Pittsburgh Phil, one of the two most important hit men in the organization, was declared the official shylock of the game; his aides would circulate among the players, fists full of money, making loans at a mere 20 percent—per week.

It has been estimated that the play each night probably exceeded $100,000. Reles' nightly profit from the shylock operation was generally between $1,000 to $2,000. Druggists, clothing merchants, liquor store proprietors, dentists and shoe manufacturers were found to be paying incredible amounts of "or else" interest. In a manner of speaking, they were actually bankrolling the operations of Murder, Inc. When Reles started singing to the authorities, it was said the loss of the State Street game was almost as troublesome to the mob as was the exposure of Murder, Inc.

STEAD, William T. (1849-1912): Journalist

During the 19th century citizens of Chicago launched several reform movements aimed at cleaning up that city which was considered the most crime-ridden in the nation. But Chicago's greatest reform wave of all was started by an English muckraking journalist, William T. Stead, in 1893.

Before his arrival in this country, Stead enjoyed a reputation as an uncompromising investigative gadfly. In 1885, to expose prostitution in London, he bought a 13-year-old girl for £10 and placed her in a brothel. Although his purpose was to expose the evils of prostitution in a series of articles, he was sent to prison for the act. That experience did not curb Stead's enthusiasm for exposing evil, after visiting the 1893 World's Fair in Chicago, he remained to expose graft, corruption and vice in the city. Thousands thronged to his platform speeches, and in 1894 he published *If Christ Came to Chicago,* which became a runaway best-seller, eager readers subscribing to 70,000 copies before publication and buying 140,000 immediately thereafter. Stead named names long considered above reproach in his *Black List,* which showed who owned, rented and paid taxes on property used for illicit purposes.

He highlighted evidence of the extent of political corruption with a quote from a corporation lawyer: "There are sixty-eight aldermen on the City council, and sixty-six of them can be bought; this I know because I have bought them myself."

Readers were shocked when they read the following description of City Council graft:

> How much does it cost to pass a franchise through the City Council? There is no set price, because one franchise may be worth more than another. The highest price ever paid for aldermanic votes was a few years ago when a measure giving valuable privileges to a railway corporation was passed in the face of public condemnation. There were four members of the Council who received 25,000 dollars each, and the others who voted for the ordinance received 8,000 dollars each. An official who was instrumental in securing the passage of the measure received the largest amount ever given in Chicago for a service of this kind. He received 100,000 dollars in cash and two pieces of property. The property was afterward sold for 110,000 dollars. In one of the latest "boodle" attempts the aldermen voting for a certain franchise were supposed to receive 5,000 dollars each. One of them, however, had been deceived and was to get only 3,500 dollars. When he learned that he had been "frisked" of 1,500 dollars he wept in anger and went over to the opposition, assisting in the final overthrow of the steal.
>
> The "5,000 dollars per vote" is the high-water mark in the Council for the last four years. During 1891 and 1892 there were a dozen ordinances which brought their "bits," yet in one case the price went down to 300 dollars. In spite of what has been said of the good old times these two years were among the most profitable ever known in criminal circles.
>
> When it becomes necessary to pass an ordinance over the Mayor's veto the cost is 25 per cent more than usual.

The upshot of Stead's disclosures was the formation of the Civic Federation of Chicago, the city's first important reform organization to enjoy wide public support. Stead remained a thorn in the side of corrupt politicians and vice operators for close to two decades until his death aboard the *Titanic* in 1912.

See also: *Vina Fields.*

STEAMBOAT Squad: 19th century New York police unit

Until the mid-1870s river pirates were the scourge of both the Hudson and East rivers in New York City. They preyed on cargo craft tied up at piers, boarded boats in the river and even sailed up the Hudson for many miles to loot riverfront businesses, stores and homes. In 1876 the New York Police Department organized the Steamboat Squad, first using the steamboat *Seneca* and, after that proved successful, then several others, to patrol the rivers in search of gangsters. When pirates were spotted, a score or more of officers hidden in the cabin of a police steamer would set forth in rowboats to run them down. The story was often told of one small police boat being boarded by four river toughs in search of loot and ready to clout the few crew members. But when the hapless quartet opened the cabin door, they suddenly found themselves surrounded by two dozen club-wielding officers.

Later, steam launches were added to the fleet of the harbor police, which subsequently developed into the present-day Marine and Aviation Division, a unit recognized as probably the most efficient in the police department. Several high officers during the early years of the Steamboat Squad were dispatched to other cities to demonstrate their effective techniques. Within a few years the death knell was sounded for the long-lived profession of river piracy, a crime that had plagued the country since early Colonial days.

See also: *Hook Gang.*

STEUNENBERG, Frank (1861-1905): Idaho governor and murder victim

Had union leader Big Bill Haywood been convicted of the bombing murder of Frank Steunenberg, a former Democratic governor of Idaho, there is little doubt that the history of the American labor movement would have been quite different.

A native of Keokuk, Iowa, Steunenberg was chosen governor of Idaho in 1896 and reelected in 1898. As the state's chief executive he earned the enmity of the union movement for his probusiness actions during the bitter labor struggle in the Coeur d'Alene mines. After retiring from public office, Steunenberg devoted himself to the lumber company that eventually grew into Boise Cascade.

Late in 1905 Steunenberg was assassinated by a bomb placed in his home by Harry Orchard, a labor activist whose real name was Albert E. Horsley. Orchard, some say in exchange for a promise of leniency, named Big Bill Haywood, a leader of the Western Federation of Miners, as a conspirator in the assassination. The trial of Haywood attracted national and international attention and pitted prosecutor, and future senator, William E. Borah, against the renowned defense lawyer Clarence Darrow. Darrow scored a stunning victory that gave new strength to the union movement in the West. Orchard, a killer whose main claim to fame was his role in the "get-Haywood" effort, served a life sentence.

See also: *Clarence Darrow, William D. "Big Bill" Haywood, Harry Orchard.*

STEVENS, Walter (1867-1939): Hit man

One of the most proficient killers in a city of killers, Walter Stevens was known as the Dean of Chicago Gunmen.

Stevens turned up first in Chicago shortly after the turn of the century as a slugger and killer for Mossy Enright's union-busting mob. After Enright was murdered in 1920, Stevens became a free-lance hit man, often renting his guns out to Johnny Torrio and Al Capone. There was direct evidence linking Stevens with more than a dozen murders (although it was believed he had committed at least 60), but he only went to prison for one, the killing of a policeman in Aurora, Ill. However, he was pardoned shortly after his incarceration by Gov. Len Small, evidently for past services rendered. Years before, Small had been accused of embezzling more than $500,000 while serving as state treasurer. Stevens bribed and threatened a number of jurors and Small was acquitted.

While Stevens can only be described as ferocious in his profession—he once did a killing as a favor for a mere $50—he displayed an entirely different manner in his home life. Well-educated, he enjoyed the works of Robert Burns, Robert Louis Stevenson and Jack London. He neither drank nor smoked until he was 50, and for 20 years he took excellent and doting care of his invalid wife. He adopted three children and gave them a good education. Stevens was also a prude. He censored his children's reading material, tearing out pages of books that he considered immoral. When he found stage plays and movies not up to his puritanical standards, he ordered his children not to attend them. His daughters were not allowed to wear short skirts or use lipstick or rouge.

After an attempt was made on his life, Stevens retired, earning the same description as Johnny Torrio: "He could dish it out but he couldn't take it." Still, no one ever said it to Stevens' face during the last dozen years of his life.

STEWART, Alexander Turney (1803-1876): Grave-robbing victim

The nation's most sensational grave robbery was the removal of the bones of A.T. Stewart, two years after he died in 1876, from the churchyard of the venerable St. Mark's-in-the-Bouwerie in New York City. Since Stewart was the greatest of the merchant princes of his era and a multimillionaire, the grave ghouls demanded a ransom of $200,000 for the return of the body. Negotiations over the ransom continued for two years through newspaper personal columns until finally the ghouls agreed to accept $20,000.

Body snatchers turn over a bag containing the bones of the late merchant prince A.T. Stewart for $20,000 ransom.

The transaction was made at midnight on a lonely country road. The chief ghoul, using the assumed name of Henry Romaine, and two others took the money in exchange for a bag of bones, which were later definitely established as Stewart's. The identities of the grave robbers were never learned, although various police authorities claimed the crime was the work of either the notorious bank robber George Leonidas Leslie or the fence Travelling Mike Grady.

The Stewart family reburied A.T. Stewart's bones in the mausoleum of the Cathedral of the Incarnation in Garden City, Long Island, protected thereafter by an intricate burglar alarm system.

STILES, Billie (?-1908): Lawman and outlaw

Along with Burt Alvord, another law officer, Billie Stiles headed the notorious Alvord-Stiles gang, which terrorized the Southwest around the turn of the century. Both used their lawman positions as cover for their nefarious activities.

Very little is known of Stiles' early life except that he was born in the Arizona Territory in the 1870s and was said to have killed his father at the age of 12, an event that eventually had an ironic sequel. Handy with a gun, Stiles hired out as a deputy to various lawmen until he became an assistant to Burt Alvord, marshal of Wilcox, Arizona Territory. Both men had experience in chasing train robbers and both had the idea that it was an easy crime to commit. The pair recruited a gang of hardened gunslingers, including such leading desperadoes of the area as Three-Fingered Dunlap, Bob Brown, Bravo Juan Yaos and George and Louis Owens.

The gang thrived on a number of train robberies and other holdups until 1900, when they were all identified as perpetrators of a Southern Pacific train robbery near Cochise on the previous September 9. All the gang members denied their guilt except Stiles, who admitted his part in the crime and was released on his offer to testify against the others. However, he soon slipped into the county jail, wounded the jailer and released his confederates.

Stiles and Alvord returned to the outlaw trail and avoided capture for three more years. Finally retaken, they escaped again and tried to cover their trail by faking their deaths; they even shipped coffins supposedly bearing their remains to Tombstone. However, the Arizona Rangers continued their pursuit of the pair, finally cornering them on an illegal raid into Mexico. Alvord was wounded and captured in a gunfight but Stiles got away. Eventually, Alvord went to prison for two years and then vanished from the scene.

In January 1908 a Nevada deputy sheriff named "William Larkin" shot and killed a fugitive from justice. When the officer rode back to his victim's house, the dead man's distraught 12-year-old son seized a shotgun and shot Larkin dead with a double blast. Larkin was subsequently identified as the wanted Billie Stiles, a man who had killed his own father at the age of 12.

See also: *Burt Alvord.*

STILES, William C. "Bill" (1850-1939): James gang outlaw

Bill Stiles was the last surviving member of the James gang.

Part of the 150 cars, vans and trucks swept up in a recent "sting" operation by Indiana state police.

Born in New York, Stiles, by his own admission, spent his youth rolling drunks. He then journeyed west, free-lancing along the outlaw trail until 1876, when he joined the James gang. Some historians insist that Stiles was killed on September 7, 1876, when the James-Younger gang was cut to pieces in the raid on the First National Bank of Northfield, Minn. The man killed was not Stiles but Bill Chadwell, a youth of 19 who had joined the gang only a few weeks before. There was some confusion thereafter about whether Bill Chadwell and Bill Stiles were one and the same.

Sometime after the breakup of the James gang, Stiles worked his way east. In 1900 he was sent to Sing Sing for killing an unarmed man in New York City. Released in 1913, he kept his James gang membership a secret until shortly before his death in Los Angeles on August 16, 1939, when he made a confession. The facts he told about his past life seem to stand up, one of the few cases of a long-lost old-timer's tale doing so.

See also: *Northfield, Minnesota Bank Raid.*

STING: Undercover law enforcement operation

The definition of the word "sting" has undergone a number of changes through the decades. In the 1970s it came to mean undercover operations by law enforcement agencies to gather evidence against criminals, such as phony fencing setups or offers of political payoffs to government officials.

In the 1812 edition of J. H. Vaux's *Glossary of Cant,* the verb "to sting" is defined as "to rob or defraud a person or place." By the 1880s the term was obsolete in Britain, but according to Eric Partridge's *Dictionary of the American Underworld,* it survived in America as a noun meaning "a cheat, a swindler" or a "criminal coup," especially one involving a sudden, brilliantly successful move.

The word gained considerable prominence as a result of the 1973 film *The Sting,* in which Paul Newman and Robert Redford played confidence men operating in Chicago.

Sting soon became a media buzz word. It was first used in its most recent meaning to describe a warehouse fencing operation run by the District of Columbia Police Department in which undercover officers bought a wide range of stolen goods from criminals. Eventually, about 140 persons were arrested. Between 1973 and 1980 there were 93 federally assisted stings in 47 cities, in which local police departments made 7,134 arrests and recovered $236 million in stolen goods.

See also: *Fence.*

STOCK Thefts

It is probably accurate to say that all stock thefts, except for an isolated instance or two, in the United States are sponsored by organized crime. Syndicate gangsters alone have the know-how and technical ability to launder and disseminate stolen negotiable securities. The extent of underworld activity in this field was revealed during hearings of the Senate Permanent Investigations Subcommittee in 1971, when witnesses testified that

$400 million in securities had been stolen without detection in the two previous years. Murray J. Gross, an assistant district attorney for New York County, said that organized crime operated its "virtual monopoly" in the disposition of stolen securities often in collusion with certain New York banks. According to the prosecutor, some banks added stolen securities to their assets to improve their financial position, and loan officers were bribed to take stolen securities as collateral for loans. It was also reported that some small brokerage houses, generally the over-the-counter variety, were suspected of being "created and controlled" as conduits for organized crime. Knowledgeable crime observers have often noted organized crime's ability, through its loan-sharking activities, to force financially distressed Wall Street firms to do its bidding.

STOMPANATO, Johnny (1926-1958): "Justifiable homicide" victim

The death of Johnny Stompanato, a 32-year-old ex-bodyguard for gambler Mickey Cohen, in April 1958 was labeled a case of "justifiable homicide," harkening back to Hollywood's real-life murder and scandal days in the 1920s and 1930s. For a year prior to Stompanato's death, he had been the romantic interest of Lana Turner, at 38 still one of Hollywood's most glamorous actresses. Then, as the saying went, Turner "didn't pick up his option."

On the night of April 4 Cheryl Crane, the 14-year-old daughter of Lana Turner and Stephen Crane, the second of Turner's four husbands, was present when an argument broke out between her mother and the gangster. As the girl later related to police:

I was in my room talking to mother when he came in and began yelling at her. She told him "I don't want to argue in front of the baby."

Then mother and he went into mother's room and I went to the door to listen. He kept saying that he was going to have her cut and disfigured. I thought he was going to get her.

I ran downstairs to the kitchen and grabbed the first big knife I could find and raced back upstairs.

I stood outside the bedroom door, right around the corner.

Then I heard him say, "I'll get you if it takes a day, a week or a year. I'll cut your face up. I'll stomp you. And if I can't do it myself I'll find somebody who will—that's my business."

I went into the room and I said, "You don't have to take that, mother." Then I pushed the knife into his stomach with all my might.

The husky gangster crumpled without a word, according to both mother and daughter.

At a coroner's inquest, a week later, Lana Turner was the star performer, describing the killing as well as her relationship with Stompanato. The gangster had been advised to get out of England in 1957 after he had threatened Turner with a razor. Despite this difference, the pair reconciled, and shortly before Stompanato's death they had returned from a two-month stay in Acapulco, Mexico.

The actress said:

. . . I swear, it was so fast. I truthfully say I thought she had hit him in the stomach.

As best I remember, they came together. But I still never saw the blade. Mr. Stompanato grabbed himself here [indicating the abdomen].

And he started to move forward, and he made almost a half-turn and he dropped on his back and when he dropped, his arm went out, so that I still didn't see that there was blood or a wound until I ran over to him and I saw his sweater was cut.

And I lifted the sweater up and I saw this wound. I remember only barely hearing my daughter sobbing. And I ran into my bathroom which was very close. And I grabbed a towel. I didn't know what to do. Then I put a towel on Mr. Stompanato.

A medical report indicated the knife had severed the aorta and that the victim had died within minutes.

After hearing the evidence, the coroner's jury returned a verdict of justifiable homicide.

Cheryl Crane was a heroine, Lana Turner was a heroine and Johnny Stompanato was memorialized by Hollywood screenwriters who found ways to incorporate the drama into movie scripts.

See also: *Mickey Cohen.*

STONE, John (1806-1840): Murderer

John Stone, Chicago's first legally executed man, couldn't claim he hadn't been warned. In 1839 the *Chicago American,* perhaps reacting to a Jackson, Mich. newspaper's comment that "the population of Chicago is said to be principally composed of dogs and loafers," issued a warning to "suspicious loafers about the city," including Stone, that they "had better, as soon as possible, make themselves scarce, or the city watch will be at their heels." Stone had already made quite a mark as a "loafer" since arriving in Chicago in 1838. He had served prison sentences in his native Canada for robbery and murder and in New York for horse stealing. In Chicago he occasionally worked as a wood chopper but spent much of his time in the city's liquor groceries and in a particularly frowned-upon establishment, the city's first billiard hall, one flight above Couch's Tavern at Lake and Dearborn streets.

Almost a year to the day after the newspaper warning, Stone was arrested for the rape and murder of a Cook County farmer's wife, Mrs. Lucretia Thompson. A 19th century historian summed up the case against Stone and the verdict at his trial, noting:

A bit of flannel torn from a shirt which was proved to have belonged to the accused and which was found near the body of the victim, the burning by him of the clothes worn in the earlier part of the day of her disappearance, the club used as the instrument of killing to which still adhered, when found, a bunch of her hair, and a remembered threat by him against her virtue, sworn to by a single witness, in the absence of any circumstances pointing toward any other neighbor, were deemed sufficient to warrant a verdict of murder in the first degree. Nor has there been any doubt of its justice, although John Stone stolidly asserted his innocence to the last.

On July 10, 1840, handcuffed and chained, Stone was placed in a wagon and escorted by 260 mounted men under the command of Colonel Seth Johnson, who "appeared in full uniform," to a spot on the lake shore about three miles from the court house, where he was hanged before a large and festive group of spectators. The *American* described the event in full detail:

> The execution took place about a quarter after three. The prisoner ascended the scaffold, dressed in a loose white gown, and with a white cap upon his head, as is usual in such cases. He evinced much firmness upon the gallows, under the circumstances, and in the presence of the spectators (among whom we regretted to see women enjoying the sight) he persisted to the last in the assertion of his innocence—which declaration was publicly made in his behalf by the Sheriff, together with his acknowledgement, as requested, of the satisfactory manner in which he was treated in the jail. He stated that he was never in the house of Mrs. Thompson, and did not see her on the day she was murdered. He also stated that he believed two individuals were engaged in the murder, but on being asked if we knew them, he replied in substance, that if he did he would swing before their blood should be upon him. The Rev. Mr. Hallam, Isaac R. Gavin, Sheriff, and Messrs. Davis and Lowe, deputies, attended the prisoner on the scaffold. The Sheriff seemed particularly affected, even unto tears. After the beautiful, solemn and impressive services of the Episcopal Church for such occasions had been performed by Mr. Hallam, and the appropriate admonitions bestowed, the death warrant was read by Mr. Lowe, the knot adjusted, the cap pulled over the face of the prisoner, and he was swung into another world. After he was hung until he was "dead, dead," a wagon containing a coffin received his body, which was delivered by Drs. Boone and Dyer, pursuant to the order of the court, for dissection. It is supposed that he died from strangulation and that his neck was not broken in the fall, which was about four feet.

STORYVILLE: New Orleans red-light district

For 20 years, from 1897 until 1917, Storyville in New Orleans was the most famous red-light district in the United States.

Long before Storyville emerged, New Orleans had achieved the "almost universal reputation as the promised land of harlotry," as social historian Herbert Asbury put it. Prostitutes from all over the country flocked there. Eventually, the entire citizenry realized that unless prostitution was somehow suppressed or regulated, the entire city would become one vast brothel. However, all the proposed solutions were shot down in the cross fire between what might be called the brothel lobby and the equally powerful lobby representing the clergy and respectable Southern womanhood, which argued that a law licensing prostitutes would legitimatize vice. Finally, in January 1897 the City Council adopted an ordinance introduced by Alderman Sidney Story, a leading broker, that provided for the containment of prostitution in a prescribed area. After considerable maneuvering, including lawsuits by landlords in other parts of the city who would be left tenantless if the harlots moved elsewhere, a quasi-legal red-light district was estab-

lished. It consisted of five blocks on Customhouse, Bienville, Conti and St. Louis streets and three on North Basin, Villere, Marais, North Franklin, North Robertson and Treme streets. As a result, a total of 38 blocks was to be occupied exclusively by brothels, assignation houses, saloons, cabarets and other types of businesses that depended on vice for their prosperity. It was Alderman Story's misfortune that the area took his name.

Inside of a year Storyville became the top attraction of the city. Tours took visitors "down the line" so that they could see the richly furnished parlors of the plush, even palatial mansions of sin. Inside the cabarets they could be shocked by the bawdy shows and dancing and later they could peek through the shutters of the hundreds of cribs in the cheaper houses where naked girls lay waiting for customers. Actual pleasure seekers could find houses to meet any purse. In most of the crib-type brothels, flimsy one-story wooden shanties, the price varied from 25¢ up to $1. These establishments dominated St. Louis and Franklin streets and others could be found on Conti, Customhouse and North Robertson. A step up in class, $2 and $3 houses were located on Villere, Marais, Customhouse and North Liberty streets. Most of the $5 establishments were on North Basin Street. A good number of them were imposing mansions, where liaisons were conducted with great ceremony and elegance. Customers were expected to refrain from any rudeness or bawdy behavior and no drunken gentlemen were accommodated. Naturally, these finer houses sported such trappings as rooms with mirrored walls and ceilings, ballrooms with fine hardwood floors and curtained platforms for special circuses, indecent dancing and other forms of erotic entertainment. Top houses had bands, consisting of two to four musicians, who played in the ballrooms from about seven o'clock in the evening until dawn. It was these musicians who created jazz in the brothels on North Basin Street.

Storyville even developed its own newspapers. One such publication was the *Mascot*. A 5¢ tabloid that appeared weekly starting in 1882, the *Mascot* was a vigorous weekly on the liberal end of the political spectrum. While it devoted considerable space to crime and scandal in the vein of the *Police Gazette,* the newspaper also performed valued service in exposing high-level corruption. In the 1890s, however, the *Mascot* shifted more toward a Storyville orientation, instituting a column called "Society," which consisted of personal items about prostitutes, a sort of harlot gossip column. The column reported such news as:

> Madame Julia Dean has received a draft of recruits, and the fair Julia is bragging loudly of her importation. She seems to forget that the ladies played a star engagement here last winter at Mme. Haley's, and they all carry their diplomas with them.

> It is safe to say that Mrs. (Madeleine) Theurer can brag of more innocent young girls having been ruined in her house than there were in any other six houses in the city.

> Several amateurs have been enjoying quite a good time of late in the residence at the rear of a grocery store on Derbigny Street.

The *Sunday Sun* was perhaps more explicit in covering bawds. The following excerpts were taken from the column "Scarlet World":

> Miss Josie Arlington is suffering with a bad cold, but she is on deck all the same attending to business.

> Jessie Brown is expecting two girls from Atlanta, Ga.

> Stella Clements, who now calls herself Stella Moore, has taken the name of a performer in Haverly's Minstrels. Are you going to do the couche-couche, Stella?

> Lou Raymond, better known as Kackling Lou, ought to attend to her own business and quit poking her nose into her neighbors' affairs. The way Kackling Lou has put the devil in a couple of young girls, who were doing nicely with a neighbor of hers, was a caution. Such conduct on the part of a woman as old as Kackling Lou is most mortifying. Now will you be good, you naughty old girl, and attend to your own business?

Storyville's most famous publication was the *Blue Book*. It was published regularly from 1902 on and had a complete list of all prostitutes in residence in Storyville. The girls were coded by race, sometimes listed alphabetically and sometimes by street. There was a special listing of "Late Arrivals." The publication was 40 to 50 pages in length and sold for a quarter. It was on sale at hotels, railroad stations and steamboat landings and was of course available in saloons. The *Blue Book* was read as much for its advertisements as for its editorial content. The ads went straight to the point:

> Martha Clark, 227 North Basin. "Her women are known for their cleverness and beauty. Also, in being able to entertain the most fastidious of mankind."

> Diana and Norma, 213-215 North Basin. "Their names have become known on both continents, because everything goes as it will, and those that cannot be satisfied there must surely be of a queer nature."

> Eunice Deering, corner of Basin and Conti Streets. "Known as the idol of the society and club boys. . . . Aside from the grandeur of her establishment, she has a score of beautiful women."

> The Firm, 224 North Villere Street. Kept by Miss Leslie. "The Firm is also noted for its selectness. You make no mistake in visiting The Firm. Everybody must be of some importance, otherwise he cannot gain admittance."

> Mary Smith, 1538 Iberville. "A pleasant time for the boys."

Taps was sounded for Storyville when America entered World War I. The Army and Navy issued orders forbidding open prostitution within five miles of any Army cantonment or Navy establishment. Federal agents visited Storyville and ordered it closed. When New Orleans Mayor Martin Behrman went to Washington to lodge a protest, he was told that if the city didn't close Storyville, the Army and Navy would. After all manner of legal appeals—by city officials, madams, whores— failed, a final appeal was made to the Supreme Court, but it too was rejected and Storyville passed into history.

See also: *Josie Arlington.*

Further reading: *The French Quarter* by Herbert Asbury.

STOUDENMIRE, Dallas (1845-1882): Lawman

Dallas Stoudenmire is one of the best real-life examples of a Western lawman who came to be feared by the citizens he was supposed to protect, inspiring scores of novel and movie plots thereafter.

A former Texas Ranger, Stoudenmire became city marshal of El Paso in 1881 at the height of that community's boomtown violence. He quickly established his reputation as a lawman who shot first and talked afterward. In one case Stoudenmire avenged the shooting of a constable by gunning down his killer, John Hale, a partner of the Manning brothers, who controlled much of the town's saloon business. In the melee Stoudenmire also killed George Campbell, another friend of the Mannings, although Campbell had cried out he didn't want to fight. And somewhat embarrassingly, the marshal also fatally shot an innocent bystander. Despite this last mishap, the city fathers for some time approved of their new marshal, who gained the reputation of the toughest lawman in Texas.

Stoudenmire continued to turn El Paso into a shooting gallery and his private feud with the Mannings erupted into a number of gunfights. The lawman turned into a brooding drinker who frequently shot up the streets. Some citizens began to see the choice between the marshal and the Mannings as "picking between two hells." In April 1882 Stoudenmire and the Mannings signed a "truce," but even that pact, which was doomed to failure, did not save the marshal's job; he was forced to resign the following month. Two months later, he bounced back with a deputy U.S. marshal's badge.

Stoudenmire's hatred for the Mannings continued to fester until September 18, when a barroom dispute broke out between Stoudenmire and George "Doc" Manning. Manning shot first and wounded Stoudenmire, who then wrestled his enemy out into the street, bear-hugging him so that he could not shoot again. Finally, Stoudenmire was able to draw a small belly gun and shoot Doc Manning in the arm. Meanwhile, James and Frank Manning came charging up and James Manning pulled a .45 and shot the struggling Stoudenmire in the head, killing him. Doc Manning then straddled the corpse and viciously pistol-whipped it until lawmen pulled him away. In the subsequent legal proceedings all the Mannings were cleared of any wrongdoing by pleading self-defense.

STRANG, Jesse: See John Whipple.

STRANGLERS: Lynch law group

While the term "stranglers" was at times used to describe any lynch mob or vigilante group, it was the official name of one of the smallest group of Regulators ever organized. Headed by a Montana rancher named Granville Stuart, the Stranglers had a total membership of only 14. Nevertheless, between mid-1884 and the winter of 1886, the Stranglers hanged no less than 70 rustlers. This occurred during a period when vigilante justice was no longer accepted as it had been some years earlier. Very few of the Stranglers were ever identified, but they obviously included some of the "best folks" in Montana, meaning the ones who had the most to lose to rustlers. Stuart never officially admitted his role as a Strangler, but his reputation as one certainly didn't do him much harm, as he went on to pursue a successful political career.

See also: *Regulators and Moderators.*

STRAUSS, Harry: See Pittsburgh Phil.

STRAWAN, Samuel (1845-1869): Gunfighter

If, as some historians insist, few of Wild Bill Hickok's killings amounted to anything less than cold-blooded murder, at least Sam Strawan can be remembered as one of Hickok's more deserving victims. Strawan was gunned down in what has been called more than a fair fight—Hickok's back was turned as Strawan drew on him. Hickok, however, drew faster, whirled and shot his foe dead.

Strawan was known in Hays City, Kan. as a deadly killer and gunfighter. He not only ignored the formation of a vigilance committee and an order to leave town but pistol-whipped a leading vigilante, Alonzo B. Webster. Yet when Hickok was named sheriff in August 1869, Strawan departed. On September 27 Strawan ended his exile by riding into town with 18 other cowboys and taking over John Bitter's Leavenworth Beer Saloon on South Fort Street. The gunfighter announced he was going to "kill someone tonight just for luck." When Hickok arrived on the scene, the drunken cowboys had taken most of the saloon's glasses out to the street. Smilingly, Hickok retrieved them, saying, "Boys, you hadn't ought to treat a poor old man in this way."

Strawan followed Hickok into the saloon and said he was going to break every glass in the place. "Do," Wild Bill retorted, "and they will carry you out."

According to some reports, Hickok then turned his back on Strawan and faced a mirror. When he saw Strawan draw, he pulled his gun, turned and fired first. Other witnesses say Hickok was not facing a mirror but "sensed" Strawan was about to draw and drew, whirled around and fired before his victim could. If this were the case and Strawan had not gone for his gun, Hickok undoubtedly would have suffered nothing more than embarrassment, as he had in a number of his other quick-triggered gun "duels."

See also: *Wild Bill Hickok.*

STREET, Julian: See Julian Street.

STRONG-ARM Squads

It has been an age-old tactic of police forces faced with a serious outbreak of crime to resort to strong-arm methods. Possibly the first strong-arm squad in this country was organized by Capt. George W. Walling of the New York Police Department in 1853. Capt. Walling had long noted that the average city thug would seldom fail to flinch before a policeman armed with a heavy locust club and that what a criminal most feared was a thorough thumping. Walling decided to use a tactic he called "preventive patrolling," ordering his men to club known gangsters on sight.

The first targets of preventive patrolling were a notorious East Side gang, the Honeymooners, who were so brazen that they took control of the intersection of Madison Avenue and 29th Street from dusk to midnight and simply attacked every prosperous-looking man who came along. Walling put his patrolmen in plain clothes and sent them into Honeymooner territory for a pre-emptive strike. It worked like a charm, and within a matter of weeks the Honeymoon Gang disappeared from the area, because to stay meant being beaten with clubs.

Capt. Walling then used his men, now dubbed the Strong Arm Squad, against the English and Irish rioters of 22nd Street. That slum street between Second and Third avenues was the sight of as many as a dozen fights an evening, with the denizens swarming into the street to do battle at the slightest excuse. Police would only enter the area in groups of three or more. Plagued by newspaper demands that something be done to protect innocent pedestrians, Walling one night massed a large troop of men out of sight and waited for a big battle to break out. When one did, the strong-armers waded in, clubbing Englishmen and Irishmen indiscriminately. When the police left the street, scores of rioters lay bleeding on the ground. After that, 22nd Street was a safe and peaceful thoroughfare.

The public approved of Walling's action, and he eventually went on to serve as the city's superintendent of police from 1874 to 1885. However, his strong-arm tactics eventually fell into disrepute, although his theories were carried on by the likes of Alexander "Clubber" Williams, who, like so many strong-armers, was to prove somewhat inept at separating the innocent from the guilty.

See also: *Honeymoon Gang, Alexander "Clubber" Williams.*

STROUD, Robert Franklin (1887-1963): Murderer and Birdman of Alcatraz

Probably the most famous prisoner in the history of the federal prison system, Robert F. Stroud, the Birdman of Alcatraz, was the subject of a book, a movie and numerous magazine and newspaper articles about both his accomplishments behind bars and the kind of treatment he received on "the Rock."

A 19-year-old pimp in Juneau, Ala., Stroud shot dead a local bartender who had not only refused to pay for services rendered but had beaten up one of his prostitutes. Stroud drew 12 years in prison, first at McNeil Island and later at Leavenworth. In March 1916, shortly before he was scheduled to complete his sentence, Stroud got into an altercation with a prison guard in the mess hall and stabbed him with a knife. The guard died. There was a controversy over whether Stroud had acted without provocation, as the authorities claimed, or whether the guard had been about to club him, as Stroud said and many of the 300 other prisoners agreed. It was also uncertain whether the guard died of the stab wounds or as the result of a heart condition.

In any case, Stroud was tried and sentenced to death. After Stroud's mother pleaded with President Woodrow Wilson for clemency, Wilson, at the behest of Mrs. Wilson, commuted Stroud's sentence to life imprisonment with the stipulation that he would spend all his remaining years in solitary confinement. In his Leavenworth isolation cell, Stroud gained his Birdman nickname for writing two books on bird diseases and establishing a makeshift laboratory. He developed into one of the country's genuine authorities on bird ailments.

As the years passed, moves to win his release were launched by thousands of supporters, including veterinarians, bird breeders and poultry raisers. However, Stroud had killed an officer of the federal prison system, and government authorities were committed to keeping him behind bars and in isolation for life. There is no doubt that had Stroud been given his freedom, morale among the prison guard cadre would have sagged badly, perhaps affecting the entire operation of the system.

In 1934 Alcatraz Prison opened as the ultimate cage for super criminals. It soon housed convicts deemed to be the most troublesome and dangerous and those considered most likely to attempt an escape. In 1942 Stroud was ordered, on 10-minutes notice, to prepare to leave Leavenworth. He was not permitted to take his laboratory, his birds or his books. Since Stroud seemed unlikely to try to escape or to lead a riot, his transfer to Alcatraz smacked of official sadism. Ironically, Stroud became famous as the Birdman of Alcatraz, although he never conducted any of his bird studies there, since he was confined under conditions that prevented him from carrying on such work.

At Alcatraz, Warden James A. Johnston seems to have done what he could to lighten Stroud's burden, at least permitting him to have books and writing material and to communicate with his publisher. Stroud busied himself on a mammoth history of the federal prison system. In 1946 Stroud got out of his isolation cell for the first time in 26 years during the famous Alcatraz rebellion, during which six convicts attempted the most dramatic and bloody escape ever from the Rock. In the riot that ensued, Stroud was released into the cell block. He took no part in the violence and was, in fact, instrumental in getting the authorities to stop their bombing of the cell block by giving the warden his word that none of the prisoners in the block had guns. Even this deed, along with a new rash of news stories about him, did not help Stroud's plight. He was returned to solitary confinement, and in 1948 a new warden, E. B. Swope, who succeeded Johnston, tightened the reins on Stroud, so that he could no longer keep in touch with his supporters or write any more business letters.

The fight for the Birdman, now in his sixties, went on, but his health was shattered. Finally, in 1959, after a string of illnesses, the Birdman was transferred to the Federal Medical Center at Springfield, Mo. His isolation remained as complete as ever. He died in 1963 at the age of 76. He had spent 56 years behind bars, most of them in isolation. The U.S. Bureau of Prisons never permitted the release or publication of his massive study of the federal prison system.

STRUCK, Lydia (1833-1879): Poisoner

Madame Van der Linden, the Leiden poisoner, between 1869 and 1885 attempted, according to the record, to kill 102 persons and successfully poisoned at least 27. Helen Jegado of France officially did in 26 and may well have finished off another dozen or so. In the United States, Jane Toppan nursed and poisoned at least 31 persons in her care, and her final toll may have been over 100. Lydia Struck had a mere eight confirmed poisonings and three more probables. But while she didn't come close to breaking the record, for sheer callousness Lydia may well be at the head of the list.

Lydia's first victim was her husband of 17 years, a rogue cop fired from the New York City Police Department for cowardice. Edward Struck devoted full time to drinking, and when he drank, he got mean, and when he got mean, he beat Lydia. After one of his tears, Ed Struck grew morose and screamed that he was no good and would kill himself someday. Lydia promptly went out and got some arsenic to use as rat poison. Ed Struck died. Apparently, he had gone out of his mind in a fit of remorse and poisoned himself. All the neighbors said that was what had happened and the police agreed. Even the insurance company that carried a $5,000 policy on him as a policeman paid without question.

Lydia took the four young Struck children to live in Connecticut. Since they reminded her of her unlamented husband, she poisoned each of them. The children's deaths attracted no attention since Lydia claimed no insurance on them and was new to the state. After that, Lydia became a nurse for Dennis Hurlbut, a 75-year-old Bridgeport widower who said that if she married him, he'd leave her his entire estate. They were married and Hurlbut lasted only 14 months. It was arsenic that did him in, but no one suspected that anything other than old age had finished him off.

Lydia's next husband was Horatio Sherman of Derby, Conn. In a way, this was a misstep for Lydia. She was sure Sherman was a man of property and considerable wealth. Only later did she learn that he had married her for her money. Moreover, he drank. Even worse he had two children who drove her crazy. Lydia poisoned the children first. Then she poisoned Sherman as well. There was no profit in these last three murders and Lydia simply moved into the home of an apple farmer as a housekeeper. The arrangement soon turned amorous and Lydia was considering a proposal of marriage when the police located her. Somehow they had gotten suspicious about the deaths of Sherman and his two children happening so close together and had exhumed the man's body. His vital organs were sent to Yale University and found to be loaded with arsenic.

Lydia confessed all eight murders. For some reason she would admit the murders of the six children, Struck and Sherman but not that of old Hurlbut, even though he too had suffered the fatal effects of arsenic. She kept insisting he might well have taken the arsenic "accidentally." Authorities suspected Lydia of dispatching three other men, but she would not confess to those crimes either and there was little point in pursuing the matters. More than enough evidence had been accumulated against her. She was sentenced to life at the Connecticut State Prison at Wethersfield and died there of cancer in 1879, her sixth year of confinement.

SUBMACHINE Gun: See Chicago Piano.

SUICIDE Hall: See McGuirk's Suicide Hall.

SUICIDE Investigations

One of the first tasks for police investigating a mysterious or unexplained violent death is to determine whether it is an accident or a case of suicide or murder. Police use their own brand of intuition to come up with the likely answer, aided by the knowledge that suicides tend to act in predictable ways. A man's body is found on a sidewalk outside a tall building, his glasses smashed with slivers of glass imbedded in his face. Murder or suicide? Almost certainly, it is murder. Police know that genuine suicides will invariably take off their glasses before jumping. If they fell with their glasses on, it is because they were pushed.

A man is found in his bathroom with a long butcher knife in his chest, the blade penetrating through the front of his shirt. Suicide or murder? Again, it's probably murder. Suicides don't stab themselves through their clothing. A man will remove his shirt or at least pull it back out of the way. Women who commit suicide by stabbing themselves also will strip bare to the waist or perhaps leave on only a bra. Women rarely stab themselves with long-bladed knives. A female suicide will tend to use a small knife and stab herself 20 or 30 times in the stomach until she passes out from loss of blood and finally dies.

SUMNER, Charles (1811-1874): U.S. Senator and assault victim

The halls of Congress have been the scene of numerous acts of violence, most perpetrated by outsiders, of course. Perhaps the most criminal attack by one congressman upon another occurred in 1856 in what was, in a personal sense, a preview of the coming Civil War. On May 19 Sen. Charles Sumner of Massachusetts delivered a fiery attack on the proslavery forces, charging that Sen. Andrew P. Butler of South Carolina had embraced "the harlot, Slavery" as his "mistress." Three days later, Rep. Preston S. Brooks, Butler's nephew and also a native of South

Carolina, strode onto the Senate floor to avenge the insult to his uncle. As Sumner sat at his desk writing, Brooks charged at him and proceeded to beat him over the head with the heavy cane he was carrying. Sumner toppled to the floor under the savage barrage, tearing the desk from its moorings as he struggled to move away. Brooks pounded on Sumner's head until his cane broke. Two Georgia senators watching nearby were reported to have chuckled at the attempted murder. Sumner survived the assault, although he was nearly blinded in one eye and was disabled for a number of years. As for Rep. Brooks, he was showered with gifts of canes and whips from Southern admirers. From that date until Secession, many congressmen appeared on the legislative floor armed with pistols or bowie knives or both.

SUNDANCE Kid (1863-1911?): Wild Bunch outlaw

Hollywood has given us a romantic picture of Butch Cassidy and Harry Longbaugh, the Sundance Kid, as being two of the closest buddies in the outlaw West, but in fact, Cassidy was often ill at ease with Sundance. He preferred the company of such stalwarts as Elzy Lay and Matt Warner. Both were genuine wits, a trait Sundance also displayed but only when sober. Unfortunately, when he was drunk, he was very mean. And Sundance was often drunk.

At the age of 14, Longbaugh was arrested for horse stealing and spent a year and a half in jail in Sundance, Wyoming Territory. Upon his release he was dubbed the Sundance Kid and continued his outlaw ways, becoming a regular resident of such criminal hideouts as Robber's Roost and Hole in the Wall. By 1892 Sundance was an accomplished train robber. A few years later, he was working on the Bar FS ranch in Wyoming where he became acquainted with Butch Cassidy. The pair often talked of going legitimate as big ranchers. When instead Cassidy organized his Wild Bunch, Sundance eagerly joined up.

After each robbery the gang would ride hell-for-leather to Fannie Porter's gaudy bordello in Fort Worth, while angry posses would continue to search for them up North. Fannie considered Cassidy a wild one but, on the whole, well behaved. The same could not be said of Sundance. Sober, he was charming, but once he started drinking, he would often lock himself in the brothel for days and shoot up the place. Fanny became particularly angry with him when he shot down the expensive chandelier she had installed in her parlor. After Sundance sobered up the next morning, he sheepishly dug into his pockets to pay for the damages.

In late 1896 Sundance met up with Etta Place, who some say was a former schoolteacher. More likely, she was one of Fanny's "soiled doves." Etta was a fine horsewoman and an excellent markswoman. Thereafter, she rode with the Wild Bunch and is believed to have acted as lookout in a number of robberies. There are those who say she divided her favors between Cassidy and Sundance, but the latter was clearly her top choice. She was most understanding of the ways of her man and even rode with him and Butch on their forays to Fannie's place. When Sundance "caught cold," i.e., contracted venereal disease, as he often did, Etta nursed him.

In 1901 the Wild Bunch was falling apart. Many had been caught and others shot. Cassidy realized the old days were over. The telegraph, the Pinkertons and the steady advance of civilization spelled the end for the hell-raising cowboy-bandit. So, Cassidy, Sundance and Etta Place headed for South America. It is known that they remained there until 1907, reportedly trying for a while to go straight but soon hitting the outlaw trail, with Etta an active participant in some of the jobs. Then the record begins to peter out. Etta became ill and Sundance took her back to the States for medical treatment, dropping her off in either New York or Denver, and then presumably returning to South America to rejoin Cassidy. For some time it was generally believed that Sundance and Butch were killed in San Vincente, Bolivia in 1911 after hijacking a money-laden mule train. However, since there is some evidence that Cassidy later turned up in the United States and visited often with his family in Utah, that theory has been revised. Perhaps Cassidy survived and only Sundance was killed. According to this version, Sundance had been so shot up by attacking Bolivian soldiers that he gave Cassidy his money belt to give to Etta Place and then had Butch finish him off. However, Butch Cassidy's sister, Lula Parker Betenson, in a book entitled *Butch Cassidy, My Brother* (1975), insisted her brother told her Sundance had not been killed and had subsequently joined up with Etta Place in Mexico, where Cassidy later met up with the couple for a happy reunion.

See also: *Butch Cassidy, Etta Place, Wild Bunch.*

SUNSET Laws

During the Reconstruction era, a number of unscrupulous white men financed a crime wave in Southern states by establishing stores whose real purpose was to receive stolen corn, cotton and other farm products from thieves, mostly blacks and poor whites, in exchange for whiskey, cheap jewelry and sweets. The thefts became so prevalent that Southern lawmakers finally passed statutes, which became known as Sunset Laws, that forbade any trading or purchase of farm products after sunset unless a full written, witnessed record of the transaction was made. Since these laws made the movement of such products after dark automatically suspect, they effectively reduced the thefts that were driving farmers into bankruptcy.

SUTTON, Willie "The Actor" (1901-1980): Bank robber

One of the most-storied criminals of modern times, Willie "the Actor" Sutton started committing burglaries at the age of 10 and went on to be known as the Babe Ruth of Bank Robbers. When asked why he robbed banks, Sutton replied, "Because that's where the money is," although some claim that the explanation was actually supplied by a journalist. He earned his nickname the Actor because of the many disguises he used in holding up banks. On his capers, which netted him an estimated $2 million over 35 years, he masqueraded as a postman, messenger, window cleaner and even bank guard and police officer. "I love it," Sutton wrote in his memoirs, *Where the Money Was.* "I was more alive when I was inside a bank robbing it than at any other time in my life."

Although he committed numerous crimes from the age of 10 to 25, Sutton managed to stay out of prison until 1926, when he was sent to Sing Sing for four years on a burglary conviction. Upon his release he decided to make a career in armed robbery and led many of the country's most spectacular bank robberies, all committed with far more care and precision than those pulled by the Dillinger mob. However, as if to belie his reputation as a master thief, he was caught quite often but was able to achieve a new dimension of fame by his ability to break out of jail.

A legend in his own lifetime, bank robber and prison escaper Willie Sutton was lionized in his later years. Hospitalized in 1970, he got hundreds of get-well cards from his fans.

Sutton escaped from Sing Sing and from Holmesburg Prison near Philadelphia, though his most famous breakout scheme was unsuccessful. In 1941 he fashioned a plaster head that looked very much like him, and planned to leave it in his bunk while he escaped. Although guards discovered him working on his dummy face and braiding a rope from string to scale the prison wall, they allowed him to continue his efforts until he was almost finished, on the theory that if they stopped him, he would merely start on another plot.

In 1951 Sutton was placed on the FBI's list of the 10 most wanted criminals and was captured the following year after being spotted on a Brooklyn street by a young salesman named Arnold Schuster. In a bizarre twist, Schuster was murdered by a gunman hired by crime overlord Albert Anastasia, who, although he did not know Sutton, was enraged at Schuster for squealing. Sutton was appalled at the act, mainly because he realized public anger over the killing would doom him to a longer prison sentence. He was right; he drew a term of 60 years to life.

Released from prison in 1969, Sutton became a consultant to banks on security matters. He signed with the New Britain Bank and Trust Co. in Connecticut to promote its new photo credit card. "Now when I say I'm Willie Sutton," he said during a television commercial, "people believe me." Looking back, the Actor agreed that his way of life had robbed him far more than he had robbed banks. He had spent 33 of the 43 years from 1926 to 1969, the prime of his adult years, in prison. Sutton died November 2, 1980 in Spring Hill, Fla., where he had lived in retirement.

See also: *Arnold Schuster, Frederick J. Tenuto.*

SUTTON-TAYLOR Feud

One of Texas' bloodiest feuds was that between the Suttons and the Taylors. It started in the 1840s, when the two families were neighbors in South Carolina and, occasionally, a member or members of one family would kill someone from the other family. Ironically, both clans pulled up stakes in the 1860s and picked DeWitt County, Tex. as a new home, ending up as neighbors and fellow cattlemen. For a time nothing more lethal than a stray bullet or two passed between them, but in 1868 the feud was rekindled in earnest when Bill Sutton, at the time a deputy sheriff, shot to death Charley Taylor, who was suspected of stock theft. Six months later, he caught Buck Taylor in a saloon in Clinton and gunned him down. The fighting now broke out in earnest, with the county's gunfighters dividing equally into armed bands of about 200 each. Despite the efforts of the Texas Rangers, the feud could not be contained for another six years, during which a number of famous partisans took up one banner or another. The Suttons rallied to their cause Indian fighter Joe Tumlinson, cattleman Shanghai Pierce and the notoriously brutal lawman Jack Helm. The Taylors attracted the violent Clements brothers (Mannen, Gyp, Jim and Joe) and their even more violent cousin, John Wesley Hardin.

Hardin killed Helm in 1873 in a gun duel that was actually closer to an execution. In the various battles at least 40 men died in DeWitt County and adjacent Gonzales County. The Suttons suffered their most grievous loss in 1874 when Bill Sutton was killed. Bill and Jim Taylor had learned that Bill Sutton was aboard a steamboat about to leave Indianola for a trip to New Orleans. The Taylors rode onto the pier and dashed aboard, confronting Sutton and a friend, Gabe Slaughter, as they stood on deck with Sutton's young wife and child. As Mrs. Sutton looked on aghast, Jim Taylor shot Sutton in the head and heart and Bill Taylor fatally wounded Slaughter in the head.

The Taylors escaped, but the following year a band of Sutton supporters cornered Jim Taylor and two companions on a drinking expedition and literally cut them to pieces in a hail of bullets. After that, the fighting between the families petered out, most of the best fighters having been killed. Finally, in the late 1870s Bill Taylor left Texas for Indian Territory, where he became a law officer and later died in a gunfight with a criminal.

See also: *Jack Helm, John Wesley Hardin.*

SWAMP Angels: New York gang

Just prior to and during the Civil War, the Swamp Angels were among the most prolific waterfront thieves in New York. Rendezvousing in the sewers under Cherry Street, they would work their way to the East River docks, loot cargo and carry it back underground directly to the headquarters of a fence, where they would sell the stolen property before it was even missed. The police tried to contain the Swamp Angels by posting sharpshooters on the docks. Eventually, officers had to descend into the sewers to do nightly battle with the gang. Regular sewer patrols finally cramped Swamp Angel operations, but the waterfront was a big place, and the gang simply shifted to hijacking cargoes on the streets as they were being delivered to or coming from the piers.

The Swamp Angels were never conquered. They simply changed in composition through the years, so that by the 1920s their descendants were running the notorious White Hand Gang, still looting the docks as well as battling with Italian gangsters.

SWEARINGEN, George (?-1829): Murderer

An early Maryland murder, which is still the subject of dispute, had all the ingredients of a spicy love triangle. It involved the local sheriff, George Swearingen, his wife and Rachel Cunningham, described as the loveliest harlot in Washington County.

Complaints against Rachel Cunningham were so numerous that the sheriff was forced to call on her several times to advise her to leave the district. Each time, however, Swearingen became less insistent, and soon the pair were carrying on a torrid affair, which quickly became common knowledge in the county. The sheriff, an extremely wealthy landowner, totally neglected his business affairs as well as his wife. No amount of urging from friends could make him give up his new-found love.

One day early in 1829 Swearingen went out riding with his wife along the Hagerstown Road. He returned bearing her body across his mount. Swearingen insisted that his wife had been thrown from her horse and killed.

The story did not go over well in the community. The authorities questioned the sheriff closely about the matter. One night Swearingen picked up Rachel Cunningham and the pair disappeared. Eventually, they were found living in New Orleans and extradited to Maryland. Although the evidence against Swearingen was insubstantial, he was convicted of murder and hanged at Cumberland, Md. on October 2, 1829, probably as much for his scandalous behavior as for the alleged homicide.

SWEENEY'S Bombers: Gang of hired bombers

Criminal bombings in America were probably first practiced by Black Hand extortionists preying on Italians in the big cities and then by rival gamblers in numerous wars between them. However, these were merely the efforts of individual criminals who used bombs just as they would guns or any other death-dealing weapons. The first organized, professional band of bombers was probably a gang in Chicago called Sweeney's Bombers.

The head of the gang was a mean character named Jim Sweeney, who during World War I bossed a gang of bombers and sluggers ready to take on any job for a price. The Sweeney gang was hired frequently during Chicago's laundry union organizing disputes. In 1921 Andrew Kerr, a member of the International Union of Steam and Operating Engineers, confessed that the Sweeney gang had been used to bomb four laundries against which the engineers were conducting a strike. He revealed the membership of Sweeney's Bombers, including Sweeney, Soup Bartlett, the gang's explosive expert, and Con Shea, its labor agitator, whose duty it was to solicit business. Kerr revealed that the union had assigned him to see that the Sweeney outfit carried out all jobs effectively. In one instance Kerr gave the names of 25 individuals to be slugged and the addresses of seven laundries to be bombed. The gang completed the entire mission. For his part Kerr received only the regular $15 strike benefit paid by the union. Kerr's testimony led to the destruction of the bombing outfit; Sweeney and Bartlett were sentenced to long prison terms at Joliet.

SWOPE, Colonel Thomas B. (1825-1909): Murder victim

An elderly multimillionaire, Colonel Thomas B. Swope was the central figure in a bizarre 1909 murder plot that shocked Kansas City, Mo.

Swope, a bachelor, lived in a mansion with his brother's widow, a nephew and four nieces. A fifth niece had just moved into her own home nearby, having married a Dr. B. C. Hyde. Dr. Hyde had obviously thought he was marrying into money, so one can understand his sudden dismay when he learned that Swope was preparing to change his will, leaving most of his money to charity. A man of quick action, Hyde gave both Swope and his lawyer such a fast-acting poison that the two

men immediately "died of heart failure." Hyde, escaping suspicion for this strange double death, was not satisfied with just his wife's share of the Swope fortune, however, and calmly prepared to murder the other young heirs so that his wife would also inherit their shares of the estate. Before the authorities stopped him, he had fatally poisoned one and almost killed the other four with typhoid germs.

Although the evidence against Hyde was staggering, he was able to avoid conviction in three sensational trials. Found guilty the first time, Hyde won a reversal on technical grounds. The second trial ended in a mistrial and the third in a hung jury. Finally in 1917, the indictment against Hyde was dismissed and he quickly departed, never having spent a single day in prison for one of the most diabolical schemes of the era.

SYDNEY Ducks: San Francisco gangsters

Of all the riff-raff that poured into San Francisco in 1849 after the discovery of gold in California, probably the worst of the lot were former inmates of the penal colony in Australia. They set up their own section, which became known as Sydney-Town. It served as the city's biggest haven for burglars, thieves and killers. Of this section, the *San Francisco Herald* said:

> There are certain spots in our city, infested by the most abandoned men and women, that have acquired a reputation little better than the Five Points of New York or St. Giles of London. The upper part of Pacific Street, after dark, is crowded by thieves, gamblers, low women, drunken sailors, and similar characters, who resort to the groggeries that line the street, and there spend the night in the most hideous orgies. . . . Unsuspecting sailors and miners are entrapped by the dexterous thieves and swindlers that are always on the lookout, into these dens, where they are filled with liquor—drugged if necessary, until insensibility coming upon them, they fall an easy victim to their tempters. In this way many robberies are committed, which are not brought to light through shame on the part of the victim.

Whenever a particular brutal crime occurred in San Francisco, it was labeled, not unreasonably, the work of the Sydney Ducks with the saying "the Sydney Ducks are cackling in the pond." Between 1849 and 1851 more than 100 murders were attributed to them, and they were known to have started many conflagrations that almost consumed the city. This latter tack was essentially a burglary technique. The Ducks would set fire to a number of buildings, and while all attention was diverted to the fires, they would set about looting a nearby section.

Finally, in 1851 the citizens of San Francisco had enough, and the first of the city's great vigilante movements hanged four leading Ducks: James Stuart, better known as English Jim, John Jenkins, Samuel Whittaker and Robert McKenzie. The result of the hangings produced panic in Sydney-Town, and Ducks left the city in droves. Those who remained operated their dives and houses of prostitution with much greater respect for local mores.

T

TABLE: Mafia court of inquiry

When a member of the Mafia is tried for his alleged misdeeds, it is called "going to the table." A typical trial involves charges that one Mafia soldier has cheated another in some joint criminal enterprise or that a mafioso has violated the "no-hands" rule, whereby no member is permitted to use his hands on another. Although the latter charge may seem ludicrous and trifling for an organization that specializes in cold-blooded murders, it must be remembered that maintaining peace is vital in a place like New York City where there are five Mafia families in operation. Competition is very serious and potentially explosive, and petty quarrels could provoke major gang wars.

Each side at the table may be represented by its "rabbi," Mafia lingo for an informal lawyer. The verdict rendered is generally accepted as fair. Fair or not, it is final. In one such trial gang leader Albert Anastasia ruled that a mobster was to sell his share in a restaurant to his partner for only $3,500 because he had been stealing money from the business. When the alleged embezzler started to protest, Anastasia cut him off. "I have decided. Take what I allow, or take nothing."

Even major offenders are given a trial, but they are usually not present for the proceedings or the sentencing, since the mob has never felt it necessary to give a doomed man advanced warning. Bugsy Siegel was sentenced to death in absentia because, among other things, he had rejected an order from the mob to return several million dollars that he had squandered in building the Flamingo casino-hotel in Las Vegas. After the sentence was passed, Siegel's long-time companion in crime, Meyer Lansky, was reported to have said, "I had no choice"—the verdict was final.

A famous table hearing was held after the murder of Crazy Joe Gallo in Umberto's Clam House in New York's Little Italy in 1972. Carlo Gambino, who had ordered the assassination, was infuriated at the messy, saloon-style nature of the execution and demanded the hitman, to this day unidentified, be brought to the table. According to subsequent underworld gossip, the gunman explained he had faced unexpected problems. Gallo had not followed the Mafia custom of seating himself facing the door, which the killer had every right to expect. As a consequence, the killer said, he was forced to start shooting before he was sure which man at the table was his target. The fault clearly was Gallo's. The court of inquiry accepted the excuse, and the defendant was let off with no more than a harsh reprimand.

TABORSKY, Joseph (1923-1960): Murderer

On October 7, 1955 Joseph Taborsky walked out of the death house at the Connecticut State Prison in Wethersfield a free man; in convict parlance, he beat the big one.

In 1951 Taborsky was convicted of murdering a West Hartford liquor dealer named Louis Wolfson after his brother Albert confessed that the two of them were responsible for Wolfson's death. Albert got life because he had testified against his brother, while Joseph was sentenced to the electric chair. Joseph protested he was innocent and his brother was insane; he was half right. Albert soon had to be transferred to a state hospital because of his bizarre behavior. Meanwhile, appeals had kept Joseph Taborsky alive, and now news that his brother had been committed to a state hospital brought forth demands for a new trial from all over the state. When the state supreme court ordered the case retried, Joseph had to be freed—without the testimony of Albert Taborsky there was no case.

Joseph Taborsky shook hands with the people who had fought to free him and bylined his story in a national magazine.

In Connecticut a new murderous crime wave soon dominated the headlines. There was a rash of holdup-shootings that Connecticut police dubbed the Chinese Executions. A 67-year-old Hartford tailor was lucky. On December 15, 1956 a young bandit waving a gun robbed him and then shot him in the back of the neck before leaving. Miraculously, after a delicate operation, the tailor survived. The victims who were struck down 30 minutes later weren't so lucky. Edward Kurpiewski was stuck up in his gas station, ordered into the rest room and made to kneel. Then a bullet was fired into his head. It was Daniel Janowski's misfortune to drive up to the station just as this brutal act was completed. After his wallet was taken, he was ordered into the gas station storeroom, ordered to kneel and shot to death. Eleven days later, liquor dealer Samuel Cohn died the same way. Ten days after that, Mr. and Mrs. Bernard Speyer were killed when they walked into a North Haven shoe store. The owner nearly suffered the same fate when he wrestled with the two gunmen rather than get on his knees. He was battered unconscious, but his assailants fled without finishing him off. Three weeks passed and then a Hartford druggist, John Rosenthal, was slain the same way as the other murder victims.

Finally, the police arrested two men: Arthur Culombe and Joseph Taborsky. The shoe store owner made an identification, and the police got a confession. Taborsky snarled his admission to the six murders, and he had one more to confess: the murder of Louis Wolfson—the crime which he had been cleared of in 1955. Taborsky died in the electric chair in 1960.

TANNER, John (1780-?): "White-Indian murderer"

One of the most tragic figures in American history, John Tanner was captured by Indians as a youth. When he tried to return to white society after 30 years, he was regarded as an outcast both by whites and Indians. He was constantly accused of crimes, including murder. Although he was innocent, Tanner may have been secretly assassinated because of these suspicions.

At the age of nine, Tanner was captured by a Shawnee looking for a child to replace his dead son. Adopted by an Indian woman, he underwent a complete transformation, becoming in effect an Indian. He even forgot his original name and lost the ability to speak English. He fathered several children by two Indian wives but was eventually driven by some inner compulsion to return to his original world. Searching in Kentucky and Ohio, he finally located several relatives who had tried to find him through the years.

Tanner traveled back and forth between the whites and the Indians trying to arrange for his children to live with him. However, he succeeded in convincing only two daughters and his second wife to join him. Tanner settled in Mackinac, Mich. for a time but was unable to find work. In 1828 he moved to Sault Ste. Marie, where he became an interpreter for U.S. Indian Agent James Schoolcraft. Tanner, however, remained an outcast in both worlds: the Indians regarded him as a renegade and the whites suspected him of being steeped in the violent ways of the Indians. Whenever a mysterious crime occurred in the town, Tanner became the first suspect.

Eventually, his eldest daughter was taken from him by legislative order, and his wife returned to her tribe. Tanner then married a white woman, but this marriage ended with the woman claiming Tanner's living habits were intolerable and violent.

In 1846 Schoolcraft was murdered, and Tanner soon became the prime suspect. He fled the community, and troops and vigilantes scoured the countryside looking for him. According to one rumor, some vigilantes caught up with Tanner and decided to kill him secretly to end their "white-Indian" problem. Another story was that he returned to the Indians. In any event, Tanner remained a wanted man for several years until finally an army officer confessed that he had killed Schoolcraft in an argument over a woman. If John Tanner was still alive and heard that he had been cleared, he did not choose to return to the white world.

TAR And Feathering

Although it was never a legal form of punishment, tar and feathering—pouring molten pitch over a person and then covering him or her with feathers—has a long history in America, practiced especially by mobs against those who violated community standards. It was the treatment given to many Tories at the start of the Revolutionary War and to an occasional abolitionist in the ante-bellum South.

Perhaps the most famous incident involved Capt. Floyd Ireson, who, according to a New England legend, was tarred and feathered by the women of Marblehead for his refusal to go to the rescue of seamen in distress. In the West tar and feathering was considered to be the proper punishment for wife beaters (followed by banishment from the community, if deemed necessary), for whiskey peddlers who sold to the Indians and for card sharks who won with monotonous regularity. Of course, if the latter were actually caught cheating, they were more likely to receive sterner punishment, such as the rope or at least a spray of buckshot. By the turn of the 20th century the practice had just about vanished, although it was resurrected from time to time by white racists in the South.

TATUM, Joshua: See Counterfeiting.

TAYLOR, Arthur: See Counterfeiting.

TEAPOT Dome Scandal

The term "Teapot Dome" has become a catch phrase for governmental corruption and graft taking. Early in the ill-fated Harding Administration, Secretary of the Interior Albert B. Fall declared that the oil reserves at Teapot Dome, Wyo. and Elk Hills, Calif., which had been set aside for use by the U.S. Navy, were being drained by adjacent commercial operations and that consequently they should be leased out to private interests. It so happened that Fall had a number of close friends who would benefit from this decision, and in 1922, without allowing competitive bidding on the property, he secretly signed lease contracts with Edward L. Doheny and Harry B. Sinclair, two oil millionaires known for their freewheeling tactics. The two oil men, who figured to clear as much as $100 million from their leases, found ways to show their gratitude. Doheny slipped Fall $100,000 in a black bag, while Sinclair used a roundabout method to see that the secretary got a $260,000 "loan" in Liberty Bonds.

After the press and a senatorial inquiry headed by Thomas J. Walsh of Montana dug out the facts, the government canceled the leases, a decision eventually upheld by the Supreme Court. Oil man Doheny shocked the nation by dismissing his $100,000 payment as "a mere bagatelle." Criminal cases involving Doheny and Fall and Sinclair and Fall were tried but resulted in acquittals, although Sinclair was given nine months for contempt of court and Fall, tried separately, was found guilty of bribery charges and drew a one-year prison term. It can be argued that Fall was made the "fall guy" for all the scandals of the Harding Administration, in which even larger sums were siphoned out of the Treasury.

See also: *William J. Burns, Albert B. Fall.*

TEETH-MARK Evidence

In 1980 Theodore Bundy, suspected of killing and mutilating perhaps more than 30 young women across the country, was convicted of the brutal slayings of two Florida State University sorority sisters and sentenced to death. Perhaps the most damning evidence against him was the testimony of dental experts that only Bundy's scraggly teeth could have made the wounds found on the buttocks of the two coeds.

This was not the first case in which the testimony of forensic dentists was admitted in evidence. So far about a dozen states—among them New York, Florida, California, Maryland, Illinois, Texas, California and Connecticut—and the District of Columbia permit such testimony. Dr. Duane T. DeVore, a professor of oral surgery at the University of Maryland, is considered one of the pioneers in the use of teeth-mark evidence in criminal cases. Dr. DeVore says that while bite marks are not as reliable as fingerprints, they usually provide a good idea of who did the biting—or at least who did not—a fact that can be just as important. It is also possible, according to the dental expert, for forensic dentists to determine the general time a bite mark was inflicted and the positions of the bodies during an attack, frequently essential in corroborating the testimony of a defendant or a witness.

Dr. DeVore has helped convict some defendants and acquit others. In one case a defendant pleaded not guilty in a Maryland murder case until Dr. DeVore gave him a dental examination. The impression of the suspect's teeth matched the photographs of teeth marks found on the victim's body. The defendant shifted his plea to guilty.

TELEVISION Quiz Show Scandal

In 1959 the television broadcast industry was rocked by a quiz show scandal when it was established that many big-money winners had been provided with the answers to questions. Several recent highly acclaimed winners were exposed as frauds, perhaps the most shocking being Charles Van Doren, a 33-year-old Ph.D. who came from one of the nation's top intellectual families.

Van Doren, a $5,500-a-year instructor at Columbia University, had won $129,000 on NBC's "Twenty-One" after having been supplied with a trumped-up script in advance. Later, Van Doren, said he had been convinced to take part in the quiz show because it would be a boon "to the intellectual life, to teachers, and to education in general." He added, "In fact, I think I have done a disservice to all of them."

On the basis of his new fame as a quiz winner, Van Doren got a $50,000-a-year post with NBC, but in the aftermath of the exposures he lost that position as well as his teaching job at Columbia.

In the ensuing investigation New York District Attorney Frank Hogan found that of 150 persons who had testified before a grand jury about the quiz fixes, about 100 had lied. From 1959 to 1962, 18 contestants who had "won" from $500 to $220,500 on now-defunct quiz shows pleaded guilty to perjury and were given suspended sentences, although they could have been fined and imprisoned for three years. The punishment seemed sufficient, considering the fact that nothing was done to the corporate sponsors, some of whom, according to confessions by the shows' producers, had decided whether a contestant would be bumped or allowed to survive as a contestant.

Abroad the scandal generally was viewed as demonstrating a failing in American life. France's *France-Soir* saw a parallel between Van Doren's confession and Vice President Nixon's campaign-fund confession and observed: "In America, more than anywhere, contrition is a form of redemption. A sinner who confesses is a sinner pardoned." Nixon would survive to be pardoned again, but Van Doren never returned to public life.

TEN Most Wanted List: FBI fugitive roster

Started in 1950, the FBI's Ten Most Wanted list was designed to aid in capturing the country's leading fugitives through extensive publicity. In its first 30 years, the list resulted in well over 300 arrests.

Typical was the case of William Raymond Nesbit, a member of the original "class of 1950." Wanted for robbery and the murder of his partner, whom he allegedly blew up in a powder shack with 3,500 pounds of dynamite, Nesbit went to prison for murder but escaped. He was caught hiding out in a cave by the Mississippi River at St. Paul after being recognized by some boys playing in the area who remembered seeing his wanted picture in the newspapers.

Henry Randolph Mitchell was the only one of the original "Tenners" who was not caught. He was removed from the list when a federal warrant against him was dismissed in 1958. Many criminals were truly terrified of having their names on the list. Put on the list in 1953, armed robber John Raleigh Cooke told FBI agents after being caught that his capture was a "relief." Francis Laverne Brannan, a 1962 listee wanted for

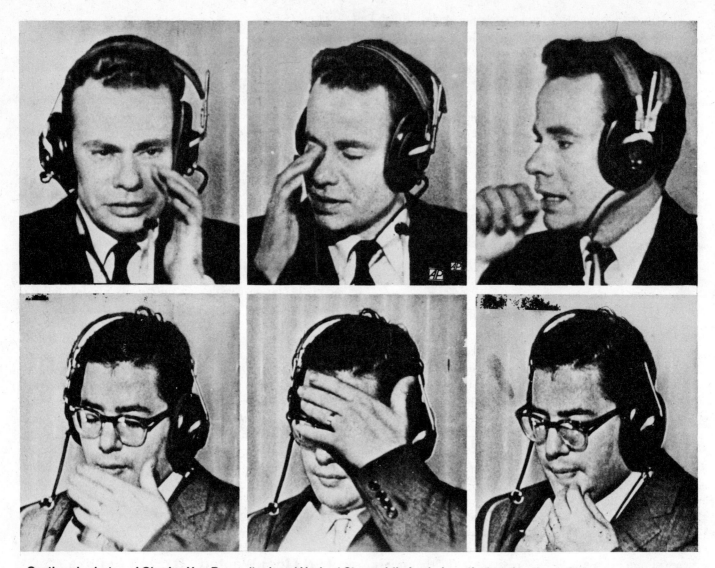

On-the-air photos of Charles Van Doren (top) and Herbert Stempel (below) show them going through the prearranged quiz show charade that made Van Doren for a time the most celebrated "egghead" in the nation.

the shotgun slaying of an elderly widow, called the Miami FBI office after making the roster and said, "Come and get me, I'm tired of running."

A composite profile of the average Top Tenner would be a 37-year-old, five-foot nine-inch, 167-pound male. The average stay on the list before capture is 145 days. Most Top Tenners have lengthly criminal records, have served prison terms and have in the past benefited from some form of judicial leniency.

In the 1950s the FBI arrested about 15 Top Tenners a year, but during the early 1970s there was only a total of 12 arrests in four years. In an attempt to improve its efficiency rate, the FBI in 1970 unofficially adjusted the list so that it contained 16 names instead of 10; if any of the 16 was caught, the agency could claim it had captured a Top Tenner. The reason for the FBI's declining score was that the list became dominated with radical fugitives who could effectively vanish into an organized underground.

Cynics have pointed out that the idea of a Most Wanted list came about in 1950 merely as a response to the Kefauver Committee investigation, which at the time was laying waste to J. Edgar Hoover's long-espoused denial of the existence of organized crime and the Mafia. The Ten Most Wanteds were thus offered up as proof that the FBI was a premier crime-fighting organization. Whatever the motives for establishing the list, with a total of 300-plus captures, it must be regarded as an effective publicity device for battling crime.

TENDERLOIN: New York vice area

Every major American city had or has a tenderloin district where crime and vice thrive, but the original term applied to an area in New York City. During the greater part of the 19th century, New York City, by most estimates spawned more crime and vice than any other city in the United States and possibly as much as the rest of the nation combined. And New

York City at the time consisted only of Manhattan Island. In the post-Civil War 1860s and the 1870s, some 20,000 full-time professional prostitutes worked the tiny island, and there was at least an equal number of part-timers. Together these two groups accounted for five percent of the population, or one out of every 20 inhabitants. In 1866 Bishop Matthew Simpson of the Methodist Church lamented in a sermon that the city harbored as many harlots as Methodists. One could speak of the lewdness, vulgarity and crime in Chicago and San Francisco, but nothing could compare to Manhattan Island, with its 5,000 open brothels and assignation houses. In some areas of the city brothels and other dives, such as groggeries, concert saloons and dance halls, often numbered as many as 10 per block.

The worst section of all was the Tenderloin, comprising just a part of what was the 29th Police Precinct, covering the area between 24th Street and 40th Street from Fifth Avenue to Seventh Avenue. By the 1890s the Tenderloin was bursting at its seams and by general acceptance, was extended north to 48th Street and as far west as Ninth Avenue.

Twenty straight blocks of Sixth Avenue, then New York's wickedest street, were lined on both sides with nothing but gin mills, dance halls, brothels and other low resorts. Day and night the streets were jammed with streetwalkers and crooks of all sort. So many live sex shows abounded that competition forced down the price of admission from $5 to 50¢. A Brooklyn preacher was so horrified with what he witnessed on Sixth Avenue that he dubbed it "Satan's Circus." In time, it was estimated that one half of all the buildings in the district were given over to some sort of vice.

Illicit fortunes were made in the Tenderloin by landlords, madams, pimps, sneak thieves, pickpockets, footpads, swindlers, burglars, holdup men, murderers and, of course, policemen. In 1876, after long service in relatively quieter precincts, Capt. Alexander "Clubber" Williams took command of the 29th and told a friend: "I've been transferred. I've had nothing but chuck steak for a long time, and now I'm going to get a little of the tenderloin." The new meaning stuck as a description for any area devoted to vice with the connivance of the police. Williams put police graft on a more organized basis than had ever been achieved before. He retired in 1895 under pressure from reformers, including police Commissioner Theodore Roosevelt. By that time Williams was a millionaire.

See also: *Alexander S. "Clubber" Williams.*

TENTH Avenue Gang: New York train robbers

Two years after the Reno Gang staged the first train robbery in America in 1866, a vicious gang imitated the crime in New York City.

The Tenth Avenue Gang had operated since 1860 under the leadership of Ike Marsh as typical burglars and holdup men. Determined to stage a train robbery because they were "as good as those cowboys," Marsh and a number of his men boarded a Hudson River Railroad train at Spuyten Duyvil, at the northern end of Manhattan in 1868, and forced their way into the express car. Binding and gagging the guard, they threw off an iron box that contained about $5,000 in cash and bonds.

For a time after that caper, the Tenth Avenue Gang was the toast of the underworld. But with a vengeful railroad flooding the city with detectives bent on smashing the gang, Marsh and his men eventually disbanded and sought refuge within the much bigger and more powerful Hell's Kitchen Gang.

See also: *Hell's Kitchen.*

TENUTO, Frederick J. (1915-1952?): Murderer

In 1952 a young Brooklyn man named Arnold Schuster became a short-lived public hero when he recognized Willie "the Actor" Sutton and notified the police, who promptly arrested the notorious bank robber; two and a half weeks later, Schuster was shot to death on the street where he lived. His killer is believed to have been Frank J. Tenuto, at the time a 37-year-old murderer and fugitive from justice who was on the FBI's list of the 10 most-wanted criminals.

Tenuto had his first run-ins with the law at the age of 16, with several arrests as a "suspicious person." At 18 he was put on probation for three years after being convicted of robbery and burglary. Arrested again, he was sentenced to 10 years in the industrial school at Huntington, Pa. He was in and out of prison several times in the 1930s and in 1940 he was convicted of the hired killing of a Philadelphia man. Sentenced to 10 to 20 years, he escaped two years later but was quickly recaptured. In 1945 Tenuto broke out again and enjoyed a month's freedom before being caught in New York. Sent to Holmesburg Prison on the outskirts of Philadelphia, he escaped once more in 1947 with four other men, one of whom was Sutton.

After that, Tenuto, ironically known as "the Angel" or "St. John," turned up in Brooklyn underworld haunts sporting two guns under his belt and boasting that the only way he would ever be retaken by the police was to be "shot in bed." Around this time, Tenuto apparently came under the wing of gang leader Albert Anastasia, the Lord High Executioner of the Mafia. When Sutton was caught in 1952, Anastasia, who had no connection with the bank robber, flew into a murderous rage at the "stoolpigeon"—Schuster—who had turned him in. Anastasia ordered Schuster killed, and Tenuto carried out the assignment.

It was a foolish thing for Anastasia to do, since he could in no way profit from Schuster's murder and simply left himself open to a possible homicide charge. According to underworld reports, Anastasia decided to make amends for his foolhardy action. He ordered Tenuto killed so that he could never be connected to the Schuster case. Tenuto's body was never found; one version states that he was given a "double-decker funeral"—that is, placed in a coffin with an about-to-be-buried corpse—and buried.

See also: *Arnold Schuster.*

TERESA, Vincent Charles (1930-   ): Underworld informer

Joe Valachi is generally considered to have been the most important underworld informer since Abe Reles. The Mafia, however, may well have a different idea about who deserves that distinction. When Valachi started telling what he knew about organized crime, the Mafia set a $100,000 price on his head. When Vinnie Teresa, who had previously been the number three Mafia man in New England, began talking to the authorities a few years after Valachi, the figure was set at $500,000. The price was about right. While Valachi presented a lot of generalized information, Teresa's evidence was harder and more valuable in court. Because of his testimony, some 50 mob figures were either indicted or convicted and valuable information was gathered on hundreds more.

Teresa described the activities of the Mafia from his home area of Massachusetts all the way to the Bahamas. He was the first informer to detail the extent of mob fixes of horse races at New England tracks, and he cleared up several murders that had baffled the authorities. He also did something that few informers had ever dared to do: he testified in court against the much-feared Meyer Lansky. Teresa was able to reveal many Mafia secrets because in his racket activities he had filled the mob's coffers with an estimated $150 million. By his own calculation he ran through $10 million during a 28-year career in crime.

Since completing his testimony in the early 1970s, Teresa has been hidden away under the Justice Department's Witness Relocation Program, no easy task when the man being hidden is a 300-pounder with a heart condition. In his first three years in hiding, Teresa and his family had to move five times. There are still prosecutors who want to use his testimony and there is still a $500,000 price on his head.

TERRANOVA, Ciro (1891-1938): Mafia leader

An imposing Mafia figure when the Morellos and brother-in-law Lupo the Wolf controlled organized crime in New York, Ciro Terranova went on to make his fortune in New York in two main rackets: numbers, as a junior partner of Dutch Schultz, and artichokes, as "the Artichoke King," a name given him by the newspapers. Informer Joe Valachi said, "He tied up all the artichokes in the city. The way I understand it he would buy all the artichokes that came into New York. I didn't know where they all came from, but I know he was buying them out. Being artichokes, they hold; they can keep. Then Ciro would make his own price, and as you know, Italians got to have artichokes to eat."

Terranova was at the zenith of his power during the 1920s but went into a slow decline after the Maranzano-Masseria war of 1930-31, when Lucky Luciano emerged as the new power. Luciano and his assistant Vito Genovese regarded Terranova as a coward and as someone, as Valachi explained, who could be "stripped [of power] . . . a little at a time."

Luciano's contempt for Terranova was based on the latter's performance in the assassination of Giuseppe "Joe the Boss" Masseria in 1931, which Lucky had engineered. On the day of the planned execution, Luciano, who was Joe the Boss' top assistant, Genovese and Terranova set out with Masseria for a Coney Island restaurant, where the latter was to be killed. During the ride Terranova, who was driving, became so nervous he almost gave away the plot and had to be relieved at the wheel by Genovese. It may even be that Terranova was supposed to have been one of the assassins who entered the restaurant later in the afternoon and gunned down Joe the Boss as he sat alone at a table waiting for Luciano to return from the men's room. The killers were Genovese, Joe Adonis, Albert Anastasia and Bugsy Siegel.

For a time Terranova retained his power, and when Schultz was murdered on orders from the new national crime syndicate, he moved to take full charge of the Dutchman's numbers racket in Harlem. It was at this point that Terranova was informed by Luciano and Genovese that he was now in retirement. Too weak to protest, Terranova retired, and three years later, according to Valachi, "he died from a broken heart." With Terranova's death, the old Morello gang, the first Mafia family established in New York, broke up; its members were absorbed by other groups within the crime syndicate.

See also: *Lupo the Wolf, Morello Family.*

TEXAS Rangers

The Texas Rangers date back to 1826, when Stephen Austin first proposed keeping "twenty to thirty Rangers in service at all times." Over the years the Rangers have become the most-storied, if controversial, lawmen in the country. The heroic side of the legend is captured in a frequently told tale set in a variety of towns in which a riot broke out; a lone Ranger was sent in to handle matters. When local officials saw a single Ranger ride into town, they expressed alarm. "Why," said this fabled Ranger, "there's only one riot, isn't there."

The Rangers early activities often involved actions against Indians or Mexicans. Indeed, they showed a remarkable inability to recognize the U.S.-Mexican border, often foraying into Mexico in pursuit of their quarry. During its Wild West period, the force had many heroes and villains and members who turned villain later. The heroes included Ben McCulloch, Big Foot Wallace, Frank Jones, John Coffee Hays and Leander McNelly. Also in its ranks were Bass Outlaw, who was indeed to live up to his last name, the psychotic Ben Thompson and the brutal Scott Cooley.

The Rangers were disbanded in the period immediately following the Civil War but were reestablished in 1874. Over the next decade and a half they reached their peak of acclaim, running to earth such outlaws as King Fisher, Sam Bass and Wes Hardin.

In the 20th century the Texas Rangers came under fierce criticism from a number of different sources. They were described as antiblack, anti-Chicano and antilabor. In 1919 a state House-Senate committee found that the Rangers had consistently violated the civil rights of individuals and groups, killed unnecessarily while making arrests and murdered prisoners. One of the worst offenses was the Ponvenir Massacre during World War I, in which a Ranger captain and eight of his men killed 15 or more Mexicans in cold blood. Although no criminal charges were brought against them, the nine were dismissed from the force.

In the 1930s the Rangers had become so politicized that the entire force was fired by incoming Gov. Ma Ferguson because they had openly supported her opponent. They were all replaced by Ferguson appointees, who brought the agency its greatest disrepute with an unparalleled record of corruption, theft, embezzlement and murder. The only Ranger to escape Ma's revenge was Frank Hamer, a tough lawman who had taken leave to go on special assignment hunting Clyde Barrow and Bonnie Parker. Hamer and Ranger Manny Gault were members of a party of six lawmen who literally "ventilated" Bonnie and Clyde in a roadside ambush in August 1935.

In 1935 Ma Ferguson's successor cleaned out the Ferguson Rangers and reconstituted a professional force as part of the Department of Public Safety. Later, it was returned to independent status, but the agency did not remain free of criticism. In 1967 the state AFL-CIO demanded the Rangers be abolished, insisting that instead of fighting smugglers and cattle rustlers, they spent too much time operating as tax-supported strikebreakers. During the effort by Cesar Chavez and his United Farm Workers to lead a strike of melon pickers in Texas, two strike leaders suffered brain concussions after an encounter with the Rangers. Besides the concussions, the men had bruises on their bodies and backs, had their fingernails ripped away and suffered deep cuts. The official Ranger explanation was that the men had hurt themselves by bumping into each other while trying to escape arrest. The Supreme Court upheld a three-judge federal court that had ruled against the Rangers in a suit brought by the union. The lower court had concluded, "It is difficult indeed for this court to visualize two grown men colliding with each other so as to cause such injuries." It was perhaps a sign of the times that in the 1970s a candidate for governor could run an extremely strong, if losing, race on a platform calling for the abolition of the Texas Rangers.

See also: *Ferguson Rangers, Lee Hall, Frank Hamer, Leander H. McNelly, Ponverir Massacre.*

THAW, Harry Kendall (1872–1947): Murderer

At first, quite a few people felt that railroad heir Harry Kendall Thaw did what was right and proper when he shot Stanford White, the distinguished architect, on the roof garden of New York's Madison Square Garden in 1906. Revelations showed that millionaire White had a hobby of seducing young girls. One of his amusements, it would be alleged, was having them put on little girls' dresses and cavort, legs flying, on a red velvet swing in a heavily curtained, lavishly decorated

miniature Taj Mahal he maintained on the West Side.

One girl White so despoiled was the beautiful Evelyn Nesbit, who became his mistress at the age of 16, by which time she had already posed for Charles Dana Gibson's painting *The Eternal Question* and had adorned the chorus of many hit shows, including "Floradora." Then in 1905, at the age of 19, Evelyn left White to become engaged to Thaw, whom she married the following year. Thaw was the wastrel heir of a Pittsburgh railroad tycoon who had reduced his allowance to a paltry $2,000 a year. However, he had a doting mother who gave him another $80,000 so that he could pursue the wild life. Among other bad habits that would soon become public knowledge, Thaw maintained an apartment in a New York brothel where he would entice young girls under the promise of winning them a show business career. Once he had them in the apartment, Thaw often would whip the girls, a treatment he soon inflicted on his new bride. Thus, there emerged a bizarre triangle: a lascivious architect with 50 elegant New York City buildings to his credit and a lascivious wastrel with $40 million in his future contending over gorgeous Evelyn, destined to become the fantasy idol of millions of American men and boys. Irvin S. Cobb was to describe her to enthralled newspaper readers as having "the slim, quick grace of a fawn, a head that sat on her flawless throat as a lily on its stem, eyes that were the color of blue-brown pansies and the size of half dollars, a mouth made of rumpled rose petals." Was it any wonder that the assassination of Stanford White enjoyed as much publicity as had that of President William McKinley a few years earlier?

At age 34 Thaw was no doubt going slowly mad. On a European cruise he finally cracked up and beat Evelyn until she "confessed" all her past sins with White. To stop the whippings, Evelyn was later to admit she told Thaw even more than had happened.

Thaw was now totally insane with jealousy. He forbade his wife to mention White by name but instead refer to him as "the Bastard" or "the Beast." Being rather on the genteel side, Evelyn more often simply called him "the B." Then on the evening of June 25, 1906, Thaw and his wife were attending a musical at the dinner theater on the roof of Madison Square Garden. Also in the audience was Stanford White. Suddenly, Thaw arose from his seat and strolled through the audience to within four feet of White. He drew a revolver and fired two times at the architect's head, killing him instantly. As the victim slumped to the floor, Thaw fired a final shot into his shoulder. Then he announced with evident satisfaction: "You deserve this. You ruined my wife."

Thaw unloaded his weapon, scattering the cartridges onto the floor, and held the gun aloft, indicating he meant no harm to others. He was quickly arrested and hustled off to jail.

While awaiting trial, Thaw had all his meals catered from Delmonico's, and his mother announced she was prepared to spend a million dollars to save her son. She hired the famous California trial lawyer Delphin Delmas to defend him. Even before the opening of the trial, Delmas began spreading stories that transformed bounder Thaw into a defender of American womanhood. Various of White's escapades with teenage girls were leaked to the press and the Rev. Charles A. Eaton, who numbered John D. Rockefeller among his parishioners, delivered a sermon in Thaw's defense. "It would be a good thing," Rev. Eaton said, "if there were a little more shooting in cases like this."

District Attorney William Travers Jerome, the uncle of Winston Churchill, saw what the defense was trying to do and reacted with an angry declaration that he would personally try the case. "With all his millions," Jerome roared, "Thaw is a fiend. In the conduct of his trial, I shall prove that no matter how rich a man is, he can't get away with murder in New York County!"

Tickets to the sensational trial were scalped at $100, and 80-odd world famous artists and writers, including Cobb, Samuel Hopkins Adams and James Montgomery Flagg, covered the proceedings. The prosecution's case was brief and simple: Thaw had shot and killed White. The high point for the defense came when Evelyn took the stand and, as the saying went, told all. Dressed in a plain blue frock with a white collar, big schoolboy tie and black velvet hat, she told, in dewy innocence, of the bizarre love games she played with White, often wearing a little girl dress with her hair hung back. It was a tale that would have enraged a statue. She sobbingly told of her ultimate deflowering, which White had accomplished by giving her drugged champagne that rendered her helpless. In rebuttal, the prosecutor elicited damaging testimony from a leading toxicologist, Dr. Rudolph Witthaus, who pointed out that Evelyn's story of the drugged champagne was dubious. No drug known to science would have worked as rapidly as she described without also killing the victim.

But what was such evidence worth against the word of Evelyn Nesbit—"a wounded bluebird, a soiled Broadway sparrow," as the press referred to her.

A group of alienists examined Thaw and pronounced him legally sane, but throughout the trial he alternately scribbled incoherent notes to his lawyers, cried like a baby and flew into rages until his eyes bugged out and "his face would turn purple."

In a flowery summation, defense attorney Delmas told the jury that his client had been temporarily seized by *dementia Americana . . .* that species of insanity which makes every home sacred . . . makes a man believe that his wife is sacred. . . . Whoever stains the virtue of his wife has forfeited the protection of human laws and must look to the eternal justice and mercy of God. . . ."

The gentlemen of the jury could not agree on a verdict. A year later, a new trial was held. Prosecutor Jerome decided his previous tactic of attacking Evelyn's rape story had boomeranged, so this time he stipulated she spoke the truth. Evelyn looked more lovely and Thaw acted more mad. The jury returned a verdict of "not guilty, on the ground of his insanity at the time of the commission of the act."

Thaw, however, did not go free. He was declared criminally insane and imprisoned for life in a mental institution at Matteawan, N.Y. His mother spent tens of thousands of dollars on legal hearings trying to win his freedom. Then in 1913 Thaw escaped from the asylum, fled to Canada and was finally retaken. While he was on the loose, Evelyn Nesbit announced: "Harry Thaw has turned out to be a degenerate scoundrel. He hid behind my skirts through two dirty trials and I won't stand for it again. I won't let lawyers throw any more mud at me." She then signed a contract to appear in vaudeville at $3,500 a week.

A battery of lawyers kept Thaw from going back to Matteawan and in 1915 a court declared him sane. The following year he celebrated his new freedom by horsewhipping a teenage boy. Before going off to the asylum once more, Thaw divorced Evelyn. He emerged from Matteawan in 1922 and embarked on a new career of wild living. Evelyn Nesbit continued to appear in vaudeville for many years and, sporadically, in some less austere night clubs and gin mills. She eventually retired to a career in ceramics in California. Harry Thaw continued to roam the world, spending his millions, until his death in 1947.

THIEL, Alexander (1890-1956): Forger

The bible of criminology, *Fundamentals of Criminal Investigation* by Charles E. O'Hara, labels Alexander Thiel "probably the most accomplished forger of modern times." It was an accolade few police authorities would dispute. From the 1920s to 1943 Thiel, known throughout the country as "Mr. X," was thought to be the head of the nation's most prolific gang of check forgers. Only after he was apprehended did the police discover that Mr. X had no gang, that he was a loner who netted something like $600,000 to $1 million, in an era when a dollar was worth five to 10 times what it is in the 1980s.

What made the authorities sure they were dealing with a gang of criminals was the fact that Thiel was an expert at several different criminal crafts. The man who passed the checks, a dapper look-alike of actor John Barrymore, was a master forger capable of imitating a real signature from memory. Thus, whenever a bank teller requested that he sign the back of a withdrawal slip to verify his endorsement of a check, he always duplicated the signature down to the dotted i's. Certainly, the second-story man in the mob was a specialist who knew how to break into a business office without leaving a trace. Once inside, he would locate a blank check ledger and rip out a page from near the back of it. He would then stamp the stubs: "Defective Checks. Removed by Printer." Thus, even if the missing checks were noticed, the explanation was readily at hand. Generally, however, the missing checks weren't noticed until they were cashed and Mr. X and his "gang" were long gone. Thiel himself handled every step of the operation, including the second-story work. "Accomplices mean extra tongues that can wag," he told police, a philosophy that permitted him to avoid detection for almost a quarter of a century.

Thiel was born in Chicago in 1890, one of six children. When he was 14, his father, a reasonably successful architect, was wiped out in the bank crash of 1904. That experience was to shape Thiel's criminal future. As he later told the authorities, "Right then and there I decided banks and bankers were all a bunch of no-goods and someday I was going to get even with them." He was a delinquent in his teens and was sent to reform school after being caught in a burglary.

In his twenties he was a card dealer and croupier at illegal gambling joints, where he discovered his superior forging ability by sheer luck. A heavy gambler committed suicide; almost by impulse, Thiel hurriedly scrawled out an I.O.U. chit for $2,500, using as a model a marker the gambler had given him earlier in the evening. He tossed the chit into his money box and pocketed $2,500. His employers never suspected a thing, figuring the dead gambler had obviously killed himself because he had lost more than he could afford.

Thiel decided it would be a lot healthier to swindle banks than gambling-joint operators, who tended to be most unforgiving about such matters. He quit the job and went into the bad paper business.

In his first big caper Thiel managed to acquire some blank checks belonging to New York real estate millionaire Messmore Kendall. It was three weeks before Kendall and his bank realized the millionaire's account had been looted of $162,000. That haul set Thiel up in a style of living to which he was to remain accustomed for about 20 years, although he never again pulled a job on such a grand scale. He came to realize that passing checks of $50,000 or more was too dangerous. Thereafter, he kept his forged checks within a range of $5,000 to $15,000 and simply cashed more of them.

Thiel started living the good life and became a fixture in New York nightclub society. He was a regular at the Stork Club when it was still a speakeasy, where he was known by sight, if not by reputation, by host Sherman Billingsley. However, he had a strong drug habit, one that had started when he was a teenager in reform school, and needed to cash thousands of dollars worth of bad checks annually just to cover his addiction.

By the late 1930s Mr. X was being sought by police all over the country. Under the name of George Workmaster, a real stockbroker, Thiel cashed checks totaling $4,160; again, an alert went out for the John Barrymore look-alike. This time the police got their man—or at least thought they had after five witnesses identified Bertram Campbell as the forger. Campbell was sent to prison for five to ten years, despite his anguished claims of innocence. Alex Thiel read newspaper accounts of the supposed criminal career of Bertram Campbell with mixed feelings. It took the pressure off him but, at the same time, he felt sorry for the man.

Thiel wrote a letter to District Attorney Thomas E. Dewey, whose office had prosecuted Campbell, informing him an innocent man had been convicted. He also wrote several letters to newspapers. But, of course, Thiel was not about to come forward and the suspicion grew that a friend of Campbell was perpetrating a hoax in the hope of getting him off. Finally, Thiel tried another tack. He resumed pulling more of his Mr. X capers. Still, the authorities refused to believe they had the wrong man. They formed the theory that Campbell had merely been a front man for a "syndicate" of check forgers and that the gang was still in operation. No one person could pull so many jobs by himself, they maintained.

So, while Campbell rotted in jail, Thiel went on forging checks. He was finally caught, ironically, because of his drug addiction. In 1945 Thiel was "taking the cure" at the United States Hospital at Lexington, Ky. Two New York detectives visited the institution in search of wanted check passers, since drug addiction was recognized as common in that particular profession. Going through pictures of the inmates, they ran across a photo of a John Barrymore look-alike and remembered the Campbell case. Thiel was brought back to New York and confronted with the witnesses in the Campbell case, who admitted they had identified the wrong man. He then confessed to being Mr. X, and cleared Campbell. When the two men were brought together, Thiel said, "I'm sorry for all the trouble I've caused you."

Campbell, in spite of his eight-year ordeal, showed no sign of anger. He simply replied, "I suppose you couldn't help it."

Within a few months, Campbell won a full pardon, and a short while later, he was awarded $115,000 for his wrongful conviction. Eighty-two days after getting the award, Campbell died.

Thiel drew jail terms totaling nine years. Freed in his mid-sixties, he went back to Chicago and, for a time, faded into obscurity. Then he forged a check for $100. When located by police, he was in bed near death. The master forger told the cops, "Give me a pen and a blank check and I'll square my bill with the undertaker now."

See also: *Bertram Campbell, Check passing.*

THIEVES' Exchange: New York criminal district

No extensive thievery is ever possible without an outlet for the criminals' plunder. Receivers of stolen goods, or fences, have always existed but perhaps nowhere quite as blatantly as in New York's notorious Thieves' Exchange, in the Eighth Ward near Houston Street and Broadway, during the last third of the 19th century.

Each night criminals and fences would gather over drinks to dicker about the price of stolen loot with virtually no attempt at subterfuge. There was little need since all the important fences paid regular stipends to the police for the right to operate in the Thieves' Exchange. It was said that major politicians and top police officials were even granted commissions on the fences' gross business.

A criminal down on his luck could shop around at the Thieves' Exchange for a fence who would supply him with funds in exchange for first option on his future loot. Fences would also listen to specific criminal plots to decide whether or not to supply financial backing.

There was little that could not be handled in the way of loot, big or small, at this criminal marketplace. When in the 1870s a gang stole $50,000 worth of needles and thread from the warehouse of H. B. Caflin and Co., they had little trouble finding an instant buyer for the goods at the Exchange. By the final two decades of the century, the Thieves' Exchange began crumbling under the assault of police reform movements. The fences, of course, did not disappear; they simply scattered.

See also: *Fence.*

THIRD Degree

Use of the third degree, whether in the form of brute force or the more subtle torture of protracted questioning or other psychological pressures, by the police to gain confessions has declined greatly in recent years.

In the heyday of the third degree, many police departments had their own favorite ways of extracting confessions from suspects they deemed guilty of an offense. A standard device was the rubber hose, which can inflict terrible pain but leaves no marks. The "water cure" had the same merit; a suspect would be forced to lie down and water would be poured slowly into his nostrils. The victim either suffocated or confessed. Another method was to drill into the nerve of a suspect's tooth. In his memoirs a police captain described a technique whereby officers would deliver

> a sharp but not heavy blow on the skull, repeated at regular intervals, so that the regularity of the blows arouses anticipation which increases the torture; assuring the suspect that he will not be hurt, then suddenly felling him with a blow from behind with a club or a slab of wood, followed by further sympathy and reassurance when the man revives, only to have the same thing happen again, the man never seeing who strikes him. . . ."

Widespread use of third degree methods undoubtedly resulted in the wrongful conviction of countless suspects. A report by a committee of the American Bar Association in 1930 stated, "For every one of these cases which . . . find a place in the official reports, there are many hundreds and probably thousands, of instances of the use of the Third Degree in some form or other." In 1947 President Harry Truman's Committee on Civil Rights arrived at the same conclusion.

Apologists for the third degree have often insisted its use is "rare" and it is never directed against "decent" persons. In fact, especially in lurid cases where the public demands a solution, the third degree has been used on prominent and respectable people, although, as the Truman committee put it, "Most of the victims . . . are ignorant, friendless persons, unaware of their rights and without the means of challenging those who violate those rights." Roscoe Pound, former dean of Harvard Law School, once emphasized, "No rich man is ever subjected to this process to obtain proof in violation of anti-trust legislation, and no powerful politician is thus dealt with to obtain proof of bribery and graft."

The main impetus for improvements in the treatment of suspects springs from the 1966 Miranda decision handed down by the Supreme Court. Under Miranda the police are required to warn a suspect that he has the right to keep silent; that anything he says can and will be used against him; that if he wishes, he has the right to have his attorney present during any interrogation; and that if he has no attorney or cannot afford one, a lawyer will be appointed to represent him.

Despite the Miranda ruling, the third degree is still practiced in some jurisdictions. In the late 1970s the Philadelphia police were often accused of using excessive force at the time of arrest, a sort of pre-third degree treatment considered helpful in getting a suspect to confess. The city's police officers were found to have engaged in marathon interrogations, in some cases breaking down the resistance of the innocent as well as the guilty. It was revealed that the force also employed the old-fashioned physical third degree, in the form of the "telephone book treatment," whereby a Philadelphia telephone directory was placed on a suspect's head and beaten upon with a steel hammer until his memory improved.

See also: *Confessions, False; Miranda Decision.*

THOMAS, Henry Andrew "Heck" (1850-1912): Lawman

If one man could be given credit for cleaning up the Oklahoma badlands, he would have to be Heck Thomas, one of the West's most remarkable lawmen. Actually, Thomas would probably have preferred to be remembered as one of the Three Guardsmen, a trio comprised of himself and two other illustrious deputy U.S. marshals, Chris Madsen and Bill Tilghman, although there is no doubt that Heck was the key planner. Among the outlaws Thomas tracked down were Sam Bass, the Daltons and the Doolin gang.

Born in 1850 in Athens, Ga. to a family with a distinguished military tradition, young Heck served as a courier in A. P. Hill's division of Stonewall Jackson's corps; he was 12 years old at the time. A year later, he was mustered out of the Confederate Army when he almost died of typhoid fever. After the Civil War Heck joined the Atlanta police force. Wounded in one of the city's numerous race riots, he won a reputation as a fearless fighter. After becoming bored with his job, he moved to Texas with his wife in 1875 and went to work as an express car guard for the Texas Express Co. During a train robbery in 1876 he prevented holdup men from getting $22,000 by hiding the money in an unused heating stove in the express car. Promoted to detective by the company, he led posses that ran to earth several members of the Sam Bass gang. Tiring too of this work, Thomas became a bounty hunter, his most notable catch being a pair of murderous brothers, Jim and Pink Lee, whom he killed in a shoot-out that established his reputation of always giving a wanted man a chance to surrender first. The Lees declined the offer.

Later that year Thomas became a deputy marshal for Hanging Judge Parker's court in Fort Smith, Ark. His job was to round up badmen in the Indian Territory and bring them to Parker for trial. When Thomas wasn't traveling alone, he rode with another deputy and drivers for two or three "prison wagons," each capable of holding about eight prisoners. On his first trip with a partner, Thomas brought in eight murderers, one horse thief, an illegal whiskey trader and seven other offenders. He soon became famous for the number of his catches. Working alone during the week after Christmas 1886, Thomas brought in four murderers. Not surprisingly, most of the territory's renegades soon recognized him on sight and sought to stay clear of this big man with the flowing brown mustache "who looked easy but fought hard."

During the late 1880s Thomas and Chris Madsen were given the task of running down the Dalton gang. The Daltons made a strenuous effort to avoid confrontations with the two lawmen. Thomas pushed the gang so hard that they decided to pull one big job in order to get enough money to flee to South America. On October 5, 1892 the Daltons staged their famous raid on Coffeyville, Kan. and were almost completely wiped out trying to rob two banks at once. Thomas, hot on the gang's trail, arrived in town just after the shooting. Even though he had taken no actual part in gunning down the Daltons, a Coffeyville banker awarded him $1,500 after the raid for bringing about "the extermination of this gang."

Next, Thomas, Madsen and Bill Tilghman went after the Doolin gang. Although Bill Doolin had been a member of the Dalton gang, he had missed the Coffeyville raid and had thereafter formed his own outfit. Thomas captured or killed several of the Doolin gang in various gunfights. He was also given official credit for finally killing Bill Doolin, supposedly in a nighttime gunfight in 1896. Years after, an apparently more accurate version of what had happened surfaced. Thomas had located Doolin's house and found the outlaw's wife weeping over his corpse, which was laid out on a bed. Doolin had just died of consumption. Without a moment's hesitation, Thomas leveled his shotgun and let the corpse have both barrels. He later told of having shot Bill Doolin as the outlaw went for his gun, and collected a $5,000 reward. Thomas gave the money to Doolin's widow, a penniless woman who had reformed her husband and made him give up his life of crime.

Later, around the turn of the century, Thomas tamed Lawton, Oklahoma Territory, became a hunting companion of Teddy Roosevelt and finally retired in 1909 following a heart attack. He died on August 15, 1912, five years after the territory he had tamed became a state.

See also: *Bill Doolin, Chris Madsen, Three Guardsmen, Bill Tilghman.*

THOMPSON, Ben (1842-1884): Gunfighter, murderer and lawman

English-born Ben Thompson was one of the West's more pathological gunfighters (perhaps only trailing his younger, even more trigger-happy brother, Billy), equally mean and murderous whether or not he was wearing a badge.

Raised in Austin, Tex. Thompson's first recorded scrape with the law occurred when he shot a black youth. In a significant departure from the normal judicial custom of the period, he was sent to prison under pressure from the local citizenry, indicating the low repute in which he was held. With the outbreak of the Civil War, Thompson joined the Confederate Army. Aside from the fact that he fought more with his comrades than against the common foe, his service was undistin-

guished. He was charged with a couple of killings but nothing came of the accusations.

After the war Thompson was accused of another shooting. While in jail in Austin, he bribed two guards, and he, the guards and five others headed for Mexico to join up with the forces of Emperor Maximilian. When Maximilian was executed in 1867, Thompson fled back across the border, barely avoiding capture by the forces of Juarez. In Texas he was acquitted of an old murder charge but soon got two years for another shooting.

Ben Thompson's death toll may have reached 32; he was just as likely to commit murder with his badge on as with it off.

Pardoned in 1870, Thompson hit the gambling trail and eventually opened a saloon and gaming establishment in Abilene in partnership with a gambler and old army buddy, Phil Coe. Thompson had a few confrontations with Wild Bill Hickok, but despite some tough talk, neither seemed anxious to have a showdown. No less an authority than Bat Masterson erased any doubt about who would have won. He considered Thompson the best gunfighter of all. "Others missed at times," he wrote later, "but Ben Thompson was as delicate and certain in action as a Swiss watch." The facade of the Thompson-Coe establishment boasted a representation of an enormous bull whose sexual organs were of an even greater dimension than the rest of its parts. Citizens dubbed the painting the *Shame of Abilene* and pressured Marshal Hickok to do something about it. When Thompson was out of town, Hickock got into an argument with Coe, supposedly over the painting, and killed him in a gun duel. Shortly thereafter, Thompson sold out his interest in the saloon and left Abilene, having suffered an accident in a wagon that left him with a broken leg.

Thompson returned to Kansas in 1873 and took part in several killings. In one incident Billy Thompson gunned down a sheriff in Kansas and Ben helped his brother get away. Thereafter, Ben Thompson kept on gambling and killing, pausing in 1879 to hire out his gun to the Santa Fe Railroad during its war to gain rights-of-way through Royal Gorge.

In late 1879 he returned to Austin with quite a stake from his gambling and gunfighting days. He opened a string of gambling houses and then, despite his unsavory record, ran for marshal. After being defeated once, he was elected to the post in 1880. Thompson gave the town quite satisfactory law enforcement for a time. The crime rate dropped dramatically and so did the number of arrests. Thompson's very appearance kept things peaceful. Overlooking his habit of getting drunk and shooting out the street lamps when things got too quiet, the voters reelected him in December 1881. However, when Thompson shot and killed an old foe, Jack Harris, in San Antonio in 1882, the citizens of Austin felt that he had gone a bit too far, and he was forced to resign. Thompson stood trial for the Harris killing but was acquitted on a plea of self-defense. When he returned to Austin, his supporters gave him a spontaneous parade of welcome.

Although no longer the town's lawman, Thompson still cut such an awesome figure that other badmen stayed clear of him and the community. Soon, he began to crave action. In March 1884 he met King Fisher, deputy sheriff of Uvalde, who was in Austin on official business, and the pair went on a drunk that took them to San Antonio. There, they entered the Vaudeville Variety Theatre, a gaming joint that the late Jack Harris had partly owned. Thompson and Fisher repaired to an upstairs box from which to watch the show. A short time later, two of Harris' former partners, Billy Simms and Joe Foster, entered with the establishment's bouncer, Jacob Coy. The five had a drink together, with the conversation quickly turning to Harris' death and Thompson viciously taunting the partners about it. As words got heated, he playfully, in a style of play only Thompson was capable of, jammed his six-shooter into Foster's mouth. Bouncer Coy grabbed the cylinder of the revolver and there was a scuffle. Suddenly, gunfire erupted and both Thompson and Fisher fell dead, shot down by Simms, Foster and Coy as well as three gunmen they had stationed in the next box. Thompson took nine bullets and Fisher 13. Fisher had not fired a shot and Thompson only one, which obviously made the killings self-defense, at least according to the official ruling.

See also: *Phil Coe, John King Fisher,* Shame of Abilene, *Billy Thompson.*

THOMPSON, Billy (c.1845-1888?): Gunfighter

The trigger-happy brother of Ben Thompson, one of the West's most notorious gunmen, Texas Billy Thompson was the more cold-blooded, if less efficient, murderer. On several occasions it was only Ben's intervention that saved Billy from retribution by his enemies or the law. Billy's family came to Austin, Tex. from Yorkshire, England when he was a small child. Growing up in the shadow of his brother, Billy was often moved to gunplay to prove he was worthy of as much attention as Ben.

After a number of shooting scrapes in the Confederate Army, from which Ben always rescued him, Billy turned gambler upon resuming civilian life and spent most of his free time either drinking or trying to shoot someone. In 1873 Billy shot and killed Sheriff C. B. Whitney in Ellsworth, Kan. "For God's sake, Billy," Ben reproached him, "you've shot our best friend."

"I don't give a damn," Billy retorted. "I would've shot if it had been Jesus Christ."

With the help of Ben and some friends, Billy got out of town. Once clear of pursuit, he lay down on the sod and fell into a drunken sleep. When he awoke, he rode back to Ellsworth and found Ben. His brother hid him for five days and then smuggled him out of town again. Billy then made his way to Buena Vista, Colo., where he was hailed as a hero and elected mayor by the outlaw element. Meanwhile, the governor of Kansas posted a reward for him in connection with the Whitney shooting, but he was not apprehended until three years later, when he wandered into Texas and was captured by Texas Rangers. Shipped back to Kansas for trial, Billy was found not guilty. It was said that Ben Thompson made a number of threats and spent a huge sum of money to get the not-guilty verdict.

Billy then traveled a bit, usually under his brother's wing. He was in San Antonio in 1884 when his brother was gunned down there by longtime enemies. Billy rushed to his dead brother's side and, although grief-stricken, made no effort to seek vengeance. After walking the streets in sorrow for several days and nights, he pulled out of San Antonio. There was speculation that without his brother's protection, Billy wouldn't last long. But he did commit another murder in Corpus Christi and managed to hole up in El Paso for many months. What happened to Billy after that is not certain, the most common rumor was that he was shot dead in Laredo about 1888.

See also: *Ben Thompson.*

THOMPSON, Gerald (1910-1935): Rapist and murderer

Few capital cases in recent history have degenerated into the kind of circus that took place during the rape-murder trial of Gerald Thompson in Illinois in 1935. Angry mobs paraded through Peoria threatening to lynch him, and at one point the defendant had to be secretly shipped out of town until the local citizenry quieted down.

People were incensed by his cold-blooded murder of young Mildred Hallmark as well as his long string of rapes carried out with weird, almost assembly-line efficiency. As far as the authorities were able to determine from the victims who finally came forward, Thompson raped 16 young women between November 1934 and June 1935, ending with the Hallmark murder. However, Thompson once confessed to a friend that he had actually averaged better than one rape a week for well over a year.

In his brutal series of crimes, Thompson followed the same modus operandi. He would pick up a girl in his car and imprison her there. The rapist had rigged up a clever wiring system from the battery to the car door handle so that if his victim attempted to flee, she would be literally jolted back into his arms. With a pair of scissors on hand, he would cut away the victim's clothes and then rape her. Finally, he would switch on his car lights and force the naked girl to get in front of his car, where he would make her perform sexual acts with him in strange positions while a self-timing camera clicked away. These pictures were later used to blackmail his victims into keeping quiet about their experience.

Unlike his other victims, Mildred Hallmark fought back viciously, and in the struggle the rapist brutally beat her and stabbed her several times with the scissors. He then dumped her naked body in a local cemetery. Thompson went about his normal work as a toolmaker at the Caterpillar Tractor plant in Peoria. One of his coworkers was John Hallmark, the father of the murdered girl, and when a collection was taken up to buy flowers for Mildred, Thompson made a large contribution.

Several suspects were questioned by police. After six days they focused on Thompson because of an anonymous tip. Apparently, the informer was one of his many rape victims who had also been attacked in the same cemetery and remembered that her rapist had been armed with a pair of scissors. A search of Thompson's home, which he shared with his grandmother, turned up direct evidence linking him to the murder: bloodstained trousers and a bloodstained car cushion from his auto, samples from which matched the victim's blood type. The police also found hundreds of obscene photos of Thompson with his other rape victims as well as a diary in which he had recorded the identities of his last 16 pickup victims with a description of what had occurred.

An army of newsmen descended on Peoria for Thompson's trial, as did hundreds of angry Illinoisans who were determined to see that Thompson died, whether legally in the electric chair or at the end of a lynch rope. Despite such threats, Thompson's trial was held and he was quickly convicted. He died in the electric chair on October 15, 1935.

THOMPSON, Miran Edgar "Buddy" (1917-1948): Robber and murderer

Buddy Thompson was one of the most dangerous and daring lone wolf criminals of the late 1930s and early 1940s. A confirmed criminal, Thompson while in his early twenties, left a trail of crimes through his native Oklahoma, Texas, New Mexico, Colorado, Kansas, Mississippi, Alabama and Georgia. Arrested eight times, he engineered eight successful jailbreaks.

His most stunning crime followed the death of his brother, Blackie Thompson, a fugitive from a Texas penitentiary, at the hands of an Amarillo police officer. Thompson sought out the officer and sat waiting for him at the soda counter of a drug store. When the officer noticed Thompson and thought he recognized him from a number of wanted posters, he approached him and asked for identification. Instead, Thompson opened his jacket to reveal an automatic tucked in his belt. He ordered the officer to draw.

It was crazy, something out of a Western movie. "What is this?" the officer asked. "Do I know you or something?"

"No, and you ain't never going to," Thompson said coldly. "You can draw or not, but when I count three I'm going to start shooting. One. Two. Three."

The officer drew but much too slowly. Thompson shot him twice, killing him.

Thompson fled Texas, kidnapping a motorist and forcing the man to drive him to Oklahoma. A month later, he was captured. Found guilty of killing the police officer, Thompson was sentenced to life imprisonment, a light sentence that infuriated Texas officials. They turned him over to federal officers, hoping that under the Lindbergh Law he would get the death sentence for kidnapping. But because the motorist had been released unharmed, Thompson got a 99-year federal sentence and ended up in Alcatraz.

Thompson's reputation preceded him to "the Rock," and Bernie Coy, actively plotting the Alcatraz rebellion-escape, was eager to include a man with a record of eight successful jailbreaks. The Alcatraz break of May 1946 foundered at the last minute because of a single missing key, which prevented the escapers from getting to a police launch that would have taken them to the California mainland, where getaway cars were waiting. When Thompson saw the plot had failed, he realized the only officers who could identify him as being in the break were the nine guards held hostage in two prison cells. Thompson goaded another leading member of the escape team, Dutch Cretzer, a former Public Enemy No. 4, to gun down the nine, against Coy's specific orders. Cretzer did so, and then Thompson slipped back to his cell block, not realizing that Cretzer's fusillade had killed only one officer; the rest were badly wounded or playing dead. After the revolt was crushed and Cretzer and Coy killed, Thompson thought he was home free, only to be accused by the eight surviving guards. Along with Sam Shockley, another participant in the attempted break and a pathetically insane inmate, Thompson was executed in San Quentin's new gas chamber on December 3, 1948, the first to die by that method in California. As the door to the chamber was being pneumatically sealed, Thompson said to Shockley, "I never thought this would really happen."

See also: *Alcatraz Prison Rebellion, Sam Richard Shockley.*

THREE Guardsmen: Western law officers

Three deputy U.S. marshals who carved out illustrious careers were known in folklore as the Three Guardsmen. Enforcing the law for Hanging Judge Parker's court in Fort Smith Ark. Heck Thomas, Chris Madsen and Bill Tilghman were instrumental in running to ground members of the outlaw gangs of Sam Bass, the Dalton brothers and Bill Doolin. In the process they gained well-earned reputations as being fair, brave and incorruptible, rare traits among Western lawmen.

Unlike many other peace officers, they even won respect from the outlaws they hunted. Bandit leader Bill Doolin reportedly refused to allow his men to gun Tilghman down from ambush, saying the officer was "too good a man to be shot down like that." Hollywood's numerous Western versions of the Three Musketeers in the 1930s and 1940s owed more to the careers of the Guardsmen than to the Dumas tale.

See also: *Chris Madsen, Henry Andrew "Heck" Thomas, Bill Tilghman.*

THREE-CARD Monte: Gambling con game

Three-card monte is a classic card gyp, whose history in America goes back to the early 1800s. Every few decades it enjoys a big revival because a new crop of suckers has grown up. Since the late 1970s, practitioners of the trade have been flooding most big American cities. On almost any weekday as many as a half-dozen street games may be in progress at one time, for example, on New York's fashionable West 57th Street from Fifth Avenue to Carnegie Hall.

The idea in three-card monte is to guess which of three face-down cards is the red queen. It looks easy: the dealer shows the winning card, then he does a fast shuffle and places the three cards face down; pick a card and put your money on it. The average victim will watch for a time and invariably spot the correct card every time. Other players try and win at times and lose at other times. These losing efforts are particularly exasperating to the potential victim who recognizes the correct card. Generally speaking, all these early players, winners and losers, are shills for the operation who try to coax outsiders to play. When an outsider does play, the dealer becomes extremely adept at his art and lays the cards out in a way that not only prevents the sucker from spotting the queen but makes another card appear to be the queen.

There are endless variations to the game. A victim may suddenly notice the corner of the queen is bent so that it can be easily identified. When the victim bets, the quick-fingered dealer will first straighten that corner and fold a losing card instead. Sometimes a victim will spot the correct card and try to put down say $50. One of the shills will quickly lay down $100 on a losing card and the dealer will take his bet and tell the victim, "Sorry, only one card can be bet a game." Should the victim protest his bet was down first, the other supposed bettor will insist his was. The dealer will throw up his hands in disgust and say, "I don't know whose bet was down first, so all bets are off. New deal."

THREE-FINGER Brown: See Thomas Lucchese.

TILGHMAN, Bill (1854-1924): Lawman

A two-fisted, fast-shooting lawman, Deputy Marshal Bill Tilghman was one of the most-respected law officers the West ever produced. He once brought in the noted badman Bill Doolin without firing a shot. Together with deputy marshals Chris Madsen and Heck Thomas, Tilghman formed what was popularly known as the Three Guardsmen, a trio of law officers that did more to clean up the Oklahoma badlands than any number of 50-man posses.

Born in Fort Dodge, Iowa on July 4, 1854, William M. Tilghman developed a quick draw but also learned that a man could sometimes use his fists faster than his gun. By the age of 23 he was proving that as a deputy in Dodge City under Sheriff Charlie Bassett. Tilghman, rather than Wyatt Earp, who later became town marshal, established—and enforced—the no-guns-in-Dodge rule. He did it by proving that he was better in a fistfight or a gunfight than any quick-tempered cowboy.

Tilghman held various lawman posts in Dodge, including that of chief of police during the late 1880s, and then became a federal deputy marshal. In 1890 he brought in Kid Donnor, a psychotic young killer who had terrorized the bad lands around the Wichita Mountains for two years, after tracking him for three months. It took him a month to catch up with John Braya, who had murdered an entire family west of Oklahoma City.

Tilghman's next assignment, with Madsen and Thomas, was to get the Doolin gang. While he helped arrest several of them, he earned a reputation for never killing unnecessarily. After shooting and almost killing one gang member, Bill Raidler, Tilghman nursed the outlaw until he was able to travel and then brought him in. While he stalked the Doolins, they knew he played fair and they did too. Once, he walked into a farmhouse where members of the gang, including their leader, were hiding. Several guns were aimed at Tilghman from behind drawn drapes, but Doolin would not let his men gun down the lawman, saying he was "too good a man" for a fate like that.

Tilghman eventually captured Doolin in Eureka Springs, Ark. Most Western lawmen would have shot Doolin first and then asked him to surrender, but Tilghman took him alive. Doolin was lodged in a wooden jail in Guthrie, from which he soon escaped. Later Heck Thomas caught up to the bandit and filled him with lead, perhaps after Doolin was already dead.

Tilghman became sheriff of Lincoln County, Oklahoma Territory in 1900 and chief of police in Oklahoma City in 1911. Three years later, he retired at the age of 60. In 1924 Gov. M. E. Trapp induced Tilghman to take up a badge again to clean up the oil-boom town of Cromwell. Tilghman, at age of 70, accepted the assignment but it was to be a fatal one. After bringing a large measure of order to Cromwell in two months, he was shot in the back by a drunken Prohibition agent, and died without knowing what had happened to him.

See also: *Bill Doolin, Chris Madsen, Henry Andrew "Heck" Thomas, Three Guardsmen.*

TILL, Emmett (1941-1955): Murder victim

Following a rumor that he had whistled at a white woman, a 14-year old black youth named Emmett Till was kidnapped sometime around August 28, 1955 from his uncle's home in Le-Flore County, Miss. On August 31 the youngster's body, tied in barbed wire, was fished from the Tallahatchie River. Two white men were eventually charged with the murder but were found not guilty by an all-white jury. Till's death inspired at least one of the protest songs of the civil rights movement during the early 1960s and was frequently cited by the leaders of the movement as symbolic of the double standard of American justice.

TIN Cup, Colorado: Lawless mining camp

It has been said that law and order developed in Western mining camps as bricks and stone began to be used for construction, giving such places a sense of stability. Tin Cup in Gunnison County, Colo., which remained a tent and shack town for all of its existence, certainly could be cited as supporting evidence. Law and order in Tin Cup was, at best, a sometime thing. One jest had it that Tin Cup pinned a badge on a marshal as a prelude to burying him. From 1881 to 1883 three marshals, Frank Emerson, Harry Rivers and Andy Jameson, were shot to death, and a fourth, Samuel Mickey, was shot at and cut up so often that the pressure of daily survival became too much for him and he finally had to be carted of to an insane asylum.

The only lawman to last was a Kansan named David Corsaut. Named marshal number five in 1883, he was famed for shooting "on suspicion." Mining camp justice was violent but impatient. If the guilty man was found, he was quickly strung up; if the guilty man got away, the crime was as likely to be quickly forgotten.

A gambler hit town once and died in a fight at a gambling table, holding a poker hand in his left hand and a shooting iron in his right. The boys buried him that way and nobody worried about going after his killer. There was gold to be panned and mined and time was short. When the gold ran out, the tents came down, the shacks were deserted and a very crowded boot hill was left to the wind and the dust.

TINKER, Edward (?-1811): Insurance swindler and murderer

The first captain of an American cargo ship known to have attempted insurance fraud by sinking his own vessel, Edward Tinker got caught up in his own plotting and finally had to resort to murder. Tinker sold off his cargo and then scuttled his schooner off Roanoke Island, Va., planning to claim the cargo had gone down with the ship. Two members of his crew, named Durand and Potts, readily joined his plot but a third, known as Edwards, expressed some trepidation. Tinker lured Edwards on a duck-hunting expedition and murdered him, weighting down the body with rocks and heaving it into the sea. The corpse, however, was carried back to shore by the tide, and Tinker, as the last person seen with the seaman, was arrested.

The captain then wrote a letter to his coconspirator Durand offering him money if he would testify that Potts had killed Edwards and had sunk the vessel earlier. Tinker explained to Durand that the worst that could happen to him if he was convicted of perjury was that a bit of his ear would be lopped off, the punishment for false swearing at the time. Durand, now terrified of Tinker's plots, feared that if he refused, Tinker would approach Potts with a plan to put the blame on him. The worried seaman solved his dilemma by revealing the letter to the authorities, and the scheming Tinker was convicted of murder and hanged at Cateret, N.C. in September 1811.

TIRREL, Albert: See Maria Bickford.

TOBACCO Night Riders: Farmer terrorists

During the first decade of this century, hundreds of tobacco farmers in Kentucky and Tennessee turned to violence to try to break the monopolistic hold of the tobacco companies, climaxing in the Black Patch War of 1906-09.

In the early 1900s the farmers formed cooperatives to fight for better prices; those growers who refused to join the campaign had their crops and barns burned. In 1906 more direct action was taken, as armed, mounted Night Riders, also known as the Silent Brigade, swept into the market towns and burned down the tobacco companies' warehouses in Elkton, Hopkinsville, Princeton and Russelville, Ky. Leaders of the farmers' association denounced the terrorist acts, at least officially. Although numerous arrests were made, there were no convictions. The tobacco interests charged that judges and jurors acquitted the defendants because of threats or other forms of influence, while supporters of the farmers insisted the acquittals merely reflected the community's backing of their actions.

Finally, thanks to heavy pressure from Kentucky Gov. Augustus Willson, several of the Night Riders were convicted and imprisoned, while others were successfully sued in the courts. Tainted by the criminal behavior of a number of their members, the cooperatives dissolved during the succeeding decade. Nevertheless, the tobacco firms increased their payments to the farmers.

TOLSON, Clyde A. (1900-1975): Associate and friend of J. Edgar Hoover

Longtime assistant to FBI Director J. Edgar Hoover, Clyde A.

Tolson had served as confidential secretary to three secretaries of war before joining the bureau in 1928. He became Hoover's alter ego and was eventually named associate director of the agency. The two men, both bachelors, dressed alike in conservative suits, lunched and dined together almost daily, went on vacations together and regularly attended the races together. Hoover would start each day by picking up Tolson in his chauffeured, bullet-proof limousine on the way to work. Tolson called Hoover "Eddie," and some said he never took his eyes off the director in public. Not surprisingly, it was whispered that the two were homosexual lovers, charges that Hoover described as coming from "public rats," "guttersnipes" and "degenerate pseudo-intellectuals."

When Hoover died in 1972, he left virtually all his $551,500 estate to Tolson, a situation that reportedly caused considerable bad feelings in the FBI heirarchy. Tolson resigned from the agency two days after Hoover's death.

Ironically, the Hoover-Tolson relationship stories have lived on, even after Tolson's death in 1975. In 1979 author Truman Capote, asked to name for *The Book of Lists 2* the persons whose lives he would have most wanted to live in past incarnations, listed Hoover and Tolson as one selection.

See also: *J. Edgar Hoover.*

TOMBS: New York City prison

New York City's original prison was built in 1838 on marshland that had been filled in to provide work for the poor, who had threatened to riot and revolt following the business collapse of 1807-08. The draining and filling of the swamp took many years to complete. When it was finished, it covered an area bounded by Mulberry, Lafayette, White and Leonard streets. Most of the landfill was then occupied by the Criminal Courts Building and the Tombs Prison. The official name of the prison was the Halls of Justice, but it was popularly referred to as the Tombs because its design had been copied from that of an ancient mausoleum, which a Hoboken man, John L. Stevens, had illustrated and described in a book, *Stevens' Travels*, that he wrote after touring Egypt.

From the first, the Tombs was rocked by scandal. Conditions for the average prisoner were described as "harsh and bleak and cold and damp," and calls for the prison's closing appear to have started around 1850 (and were finally heeded about a half century later). However, the first public scandal at the Tombs was not over ill treatment of the many but because of tender treatment of the few. In 1841 a young playboy named John G. Colt was lodged there on a murder charge. Colt and his family knew all the right people. His brother was Samuel Colt, inventor of the Colt revolver and the Colt repeating rifle. Among John Colt's close friends were Washington Irving, James Fenimore Cooper and John Howard Payne, author of *Home, Sweet Home.* Therefore, it was not surprising that Colt received very special treatment even after being sentenced to death. Charles A. Dana, then a reporter working for the *Tribune*, wrote of Colt's cell life:

Let us take a stroll through Murderer's Row in the Tombs and glance in on homicide Colt. . . . As the keeper swings open the door of Colt's cell the odor of sweet flowers strikes you. It is no delusion, for there they are in a handsome vase upon the center table. That handsomely dressed little lady with the golden hair and the sorrowful face whom we passed on the stairs has just left them. Tomorrow they will be replaced by fresh ones.

The table itself is a pretty one; there is nothing handsomer in Washington Square. It is of exquisite workmanship, and is covered with a dainty cloth. In a gilt cage hanging against the wall is a canary. . . . A pretty set of swinging shelves, suspended by silken cords, catches the eye. Here are to be found the latest novel, the freshest magazine. Pictures here and there break up the dull wall into gorgeous color. You tread on roses, for the cold stones are concealed by rare Kidderminster.

And Colt, how is with him? . . . In a patent extension chair he lolls smoking an aromatic Havana . . . He has on an elegant dress-gown, faced with cherry colored silk, and his feet are encased in delicately worked slippers. His clothes are neat and up in style to the latest fashion plate. To one side of him is his bed, a miracle of comfort.

When he is tired of reading or smoking or sleeping he takes a stroll in the yard. His toilet takes considerable time. Finally he appears, booted and gloved. He may have his seal-skin coat on, or he may appear in a light autumn affair of exquisite cut and softest tint. In his hand is a gold-headed switch, which he carelessly twirls during his promenade.

Then comes his lunch; not cooked in the Tombs, but brought in from a hotel. It consists of a variety of dishes—quail on toast, game pates, reed birds, fowl, vegetables, coffee, cognac. Then it is back again to his easy chair with book and cigar.

The public uproar over that revelation was nothing compared to the one that came about as the result of a fire in the Tombs. In the confusion during the fire Colt—or someone else—was found lying on his bed with a knife through his heart. The official verdict was that Colt had committed suicide. Several prisoners had escaped during the fire, and most people believed Colt had too, a theory that facts uncovered afterward seemed to confirm. The body on the bed probably had been a stand-in. The public demanded that the prison's top personnel be replaced and, later, that the Tombs be shut down.

Escapes from the Tombs were common in subsequent years and exposes of mistreatment of minor prisoners appeared regularly. Finally, a new Tombs was built in 1902. Through the years it too was the subject of a number of newspaper exposes, again because of its inhuman living conditions and its security problems. Finally, in 1974 the second Tombs was closed after a federal judge held it to be uninhabitable.

See also: *John C. Colt.*

TOMBSTONE, Arizona Territory

The "town too tough to die" was born when a grizzled long-haired prospector named Ed Schieffelin found silver ore on the borders of the Grand Canyon in 1877. He was alone in Apache country when military scouts from Fort Huachuca ran across him. "Whaddya doin' here?" a soldier asked. "Prespectin'," answered Schieffelin. The soldier laughed and said, "All you'll ever find in them hills is your tombstone." So Schieffelin named his claim Tombstone, and a town grew out of the bedrock, one that was to be described as "hell's last wide open resort under the western sky."

By 1881, the population of Tombstone had grown to 10,000, and it had become a mecca not only for miners but for gamblers, rustlers, desperadoes and killers of all stripes. Twice, President Chester A. Arthur sent special messages to Congress about the brutal conditions there and in 1882 he was forced to threaten the town with martial law. No other town in the West could claim a citizenry comparable to the roll of inhabitants—good and bad—who made Tombstone the town too tough to die. Over the years it was populated by the Earps, the McLowerys, the Clantons, Doc Holliday, Frank Leslie, Luke Short, Johnny Ringo, John Clum, Curly Bill Brocius, Sheriff John H. Slaughter, Deputy Sheriff Billy Breakenridge, Sheriff John Behan, John Heath, Pony Deal, Mike Kileen and Bat Masterson.

Tombstone didn't die from an excess of violence but because, after something like $30 million had been stripped from its bountiful hills, the veins ran out and the population faded away. Today there are 1,200, most devoted to keeping the town alive as a tourist attraction.

TOMBSTONE Epitaph: Newspaper

Known as the "law-and-order" newspaper of Tombstone, the *Epitaph* founded in 1880 by a former Indian agent named John Clum, certainly played an important role in ridding Tombstone, Arizona Territory of the lawless cowboy element. But whether this opposition to the cowboys represented a real stand for law-and-order or an alliance with the other lawless element in the town, the gambling interests, remains an open question. In any event, Clum's *Epitaph* could be counted on to support Wyatt Earp in all matters. As a newspaper in one of the Old West's most violent towns, the *Epitaph* gave the most comprehensive coverage to holdups, rustlings, gunfights and murders of any publication of its era. However, given Tombstone's bustling activity, it became necessary for the paper to file all minor killings, stabbings, robberies and brawls in a daily catch-all column entitled "Death's Doings."

Publisher Clum sold his interest in 1882, apparently feeling it wise to leave town about the same time the Earp brothers left, not entirely willingly. The *Epitaph* continued publishing and still appears today in what is now the tourist town of Tombstone.

See also: *John P. Clum, Wyatt Earp,* Tombstone Nugget.

TOMBSTONE Nugget: Newspaper

Just as the *Tombstone Epitaph* represented the Earp forces in Tombstone, the *Nugget,* started in 1879, had a strong "cowboy" bias. While, for instance, the *Epitaph* described the gunfight at the O.K. Corral as a fair match between the Earps and the Clantons, the *Nugget* reported it as a case of outright murder.

Thus, readers in Tombstone could pick sides between the newspapers, whose locations across the street from each other was appropriate for their typesetting shoot-outs. The *Nugget* died in May 1882, the beginning of the end of the cowboy era. See also: *Wyatt Earp,* Tombstone Epitaph.

TOMMY Gun: See Chicago Piano.

TONG Wars

The origins of the tongs date back roughly 2,000 years. In ancient China the tongs were bandit or rebel organizations. When first imported into the United States, they served as mutual aid societies. Unfortunately, aiding someone meant attacking someone else and the result was the great tong wars in American cities.

From about the 1860s more than 30 tongs appeared and prospered along the West Coast. San Francisco's Chinatown supported six great tongs. As the Chinese migrated east so did the tongs. Almost all these organizations derived their main incomes from such illegal enterprises as opium dens, gambling, smuggling of aliens, especially slave girls, and prostitution. The tongs tended to concentrate on the same illegal activities, making conflict inevitable. This gave rise to numerous small strong-arm gangs, or enforcers, known as highbinder societies, which were composed of hit men available for hire to tongs that wanted the competition eliminated. The Chinese called these fighting men *boo how doy* and the American newspapers dubbed them hatchet men, in honor of their favorite weapon. The tong wars raged on and off for more than 50 years, occasionally over the loss of face but far more often over the loss of profits. Great wars were fought at different times between the tongs, although tongs not infrequently changed from one side to the other. It made no matter, skulls were still split and pitched battles fought, while the white man's law proved incapable of stopping them.

When the tong wars got completely out of hand, white society tried unique tactics to restore the peace. After the great tong warrior Fung Jing Toy, better known as Little Pete, was assassinated in San Francisco in 1897, his tong, the Sum Yops, was decimated by the Sue Yops. Finally, some white Americans appealed to the emperor of China, Kwang Hsu, for help, and he called in the great Chinese statesman Li Hung Chang. "The matter has been attended to," Li Hung Chang reported in due course. "I have cast into prison all relatives of the Sue Yops in China, and have cabled to California that their heads will be chopped off if another Sum Yop is killed in San Francisco." Suddenly, one of the greatest tong wars ended. The Sue Yops and the Sum Yops signed a peace treaty that was never violated.

By 1922 the San Francisco Police Department had learned how to apply pressure to the Chinese community as a whole and in that year the presidents of the six great tongs put their signatures on a treaty of lasting peace.

As fierce as the San Francisco tong wars were, they were equaled in intensity and bloodshed by numerous battles in

New York City, especially the Hip Sings and On Leongs. One war in 1909-10 over the murder of a beautiful slave girl called Bow Kum, or Little Sweet Flower, resulted in 350 casualties. Lesser wars occurred in Boston and Chicago.

See also: *Ah Hoon, Bloody Angle, Bow Kum, Highbinder Societies, Little Pete, Mock Duck.*

TOPPAN, Jane (1857-1938): Mass murderess

As a mass murderer or murderess, nurse Jane Toppan has never received the recognition which she deserved, although she may well have killed 100 victims. One observer who did give her an appropriate amount of attention was Ellery Sedgwick, the distinguished editor of the *Atlantic Monthly*, who protested: "When it comes to evaluating the histories of famous murderers, Jane Toppan has never received proper recognition. Without the slightest doubt, she outranks both Bluebeard and Jack the Ripper." Sedgwick's interest in Toppan stemmed from the fact that he had been nursed by her through a siege of pneumonia and allowed to live. Many other of her patients did not survive her ministrations.

Nurse Toppan's poor record with patients did not become apparent for about 15 years, since at the time it was considered normal for sick people to die. In fact, Toppan had a reputation among doctors around Lowell, Mass. as one of the community's finest and most capable nurses. She was also for a period head nurse at Massachusetts General Hospital until administrators discovered her certificate was forged and that she was not even a graduate nurse.

Jane Toppan poisoned numerous patients with her own recipe of morphine and atropin, a mixture that prevented doctors from suspecting morphine poisoning because instead of the victim's eye pupils being contracted, as happens with morphine, they would be dilated. Her confession, made after she had taken poison herself in a futile suicide attempt, read: "Everybody trusted me. It was so easy. I felt strange when I watched them die. I was all excited and my blood seemed to sweep madly through my veins. It was the only pleasure I had."

The first step in her usual ritual was to help build up the patient so that the doctor would be encouraged. Then once the physician stopped making regular visits, she would sit at the patient's bedside and feed him or her a little of the poison brew, increasing the dosage each day. The patient's breath would grow short and painful. Then his body would be seized with convulsions, then become lax, then chill and then go into convulsions again. As the climax approached and the patient neared death, Jane would become more and more excited. "It wasn't my fault," she later said. "I had to do it. They hadn't done anything to me and I gained nothing from their deaths except the excitement of watching them die. I couldn't resist doing it."

Finally traced through some prescriptions she had forged to purchase the necessary ingredients for her poison, Toppan attempted suicide but was saved by quick medical attention.

However, she was told that she was dying and, in that belief, made her confession:

Yes, I killed them. I'm going to die and I can't face my Maker with this on my conscience. I killed Mattie. Then I killed Annie. I told her father it was suicide. It was poison. I killed Mr. Davis. And I killed Mrs. Mary Gibbs. . . . Oh, I killed so many of them.

In all, she rattled off the names of 31 victims, whose poisonings were later confirmed. The relatives of several dozen others whom she had nursed until their death refused permission to have autopsies performed, so that it was never determined how many of them were also her victims, although the conventional wisdom put the figure at about 100. At Toppan's trial her pugnacious defense lawyers would concede only 11 murders, but such disclaimers meant little, especially when the defendant told a horrified courtroom, "This is my ambition—to have killed more people—more helpless people—than any man or woman has ever killed."

Finally, the prosecution agreed to accept a plea of not guilty by reason of insanity when the defense consented to a stipulation that no request for parole would ever be made, even if she was pronounced sane at some future time. On June 23, 1902 Jane Toppan was sent to the State Hospital at Taunton, Mass. for the remainder of her natural life. That proved to be another 36 years. She died there in 1938 at the age of 81.

TORRIO, John (1882-1957): Underworld "brain" and Capone mentor

Everyone who ever worked with Johnny Torrio called him the Brain. He had taught Al Capone all he ever knew, and he was sought out for advice by Lucky Luciano. In time, the whole underworld would refer to him by that nickname, just as in his youth he was called Terrible Johnny. Both sobriquets were well deserved.

Born in Sicily in 1882 and brought to New York at the age of two, Torrio grew up on the rough Lower East Side. While he was still in his teens, he was a subchief of Paul Kelly's huge Five Points gang, one of the city's two most powerful (the other being the Eastmans), and a head of a subgang, the James Streeters. Torrio's name in that period never made a police blotter but his reputation in the underworld grew. He was cold, cruel and cunning, and when he fought, he used his fists, feet, knives and guns. Although small, he was mean and tough enough to be a bouncer at Nigger Mike's on Pell Street, one of the wildest joints in Manhattan (coincidentally, Irving Berlin got his start there as a singing waiter).

By 1912 the Bowery no longer drew the money it once did and Torrio opened a bar and brothel for the sailor trade in the even tougher Brooklyn Navy Yard district. Now and then he hired one of his James Street gang youngsters, a big, coarse hoodlum named Al Capone, as a strong-arm man. Torrio, not satisfied with just the whore business began handling other enterprises from hijacking to narcotics. He talked about how crime should and could be made into a big business. He had developed finesse and vision, and Terrible Johnny was being replaced by the Brain.

In 1915, when he was 33, Torrio got an offer from Big Jim Colosimo, his uncle by marriage and the biggest whoremaster in Chicago, to come out and help him with his business. He took over running Big Jim's flesh-peddling joints, everything from such landmarks as the House of All Nations to the low-cost Bedbug Row joints. Late in 1919 Torrio sent for Capone, figuring he needed Al's muscle for what he had in mind—bootlegging. The only problem was that Big Jim wasn't interested, a situation that steamed Torrio. Hadn't he reorganized the whore business and increased the net enormously? Big Jim nodded, but that was the problem. Torrio had made him so much money, Colosimo couldn't seen the need for any more.

Torrio realized that Colosimo was a drag on the organization and had to go, but neither he nor Capone could handle the job without being suspected. Another old buddy from Brooklyn, Johnny Yale, was brought in to assassinate Colosimo. With Big Jim erased, Torrio stepped in, and anyone who objected had to face Capone. Torrio set about creating a new crime empire. He dreamed of combining all the Chicago gangs under one umbrella and giving each its own area to milk without any competition. He called in the leaders of the other gangs: the Italian gangs, the North Side Irish, the South Side Poles. They'd all make millions and actually live to enjoy their fortunes, Torrio told them. Then he dropped his voice ever so slightly and said that if they didn't join the new syndicate, he would kill them, sooner or later.

These gang leaders were hard men, but most of them were persuaded, perhaps with a little force tossed in. Some, especially the Irish gangs, said they would but didn't. War soon developed with the tough North Siders, headed by Dion O'Banion. The Italian Genna gang was a tribulation as well, its members falling one by one. But the big roadblock was O'Banion. Then the Irishman called Torrio; he wished to end the war. In fact, he was getting out completely and wanted to sell the Sieben Brewery. Torrio jumped at the chance. A half-million dollars was a reasonable price to get rid of the murderous O'Banion. A week after the deal was closed, federal agents raided the brewery, and Torrio realized he had been taken. O'Banion had inside information on the raid and stuck Torrio with the loss.

For one of the few times in his life, Torrio lost his cool. He raged around his office brandishing a gun and screaming he'd see O'Banion in hell. Torrio kept his word. Frank Yale was sent for again. Yale and two other hoods, Albert Anselmi and John Scalise, walked into O'Banion's flower shop, which he ran as a legitimate sideline, to order flowers for an underworld funeral. As Yale shook hands with O'Banion, Anselmi and Scalise drew guns and shot the Irishman to death.

Capone was ecstatic; Torrio was not. He knew the gang wars would now intensify. O'Banion's men would want vengeance, and the longer they held out, the more others would think of rebelling. Hymie Weiss, one of O'Banion's top aides, tried to assassinate Torrio while the latter was riding in his limousine.

The chauffeur and Torrio's dog were killed, but all Johnny got were two bullet holes in his gray fedora.

Torrio raced to kill Weiss before he could mount another assassination attempt, but Hymie stayed out of sight. On January 24, 1925, Torrio was ambushed in front of his apartment house. He was hit with a shotgun blast and then another gunman pumped four slugs into him, in his chest, arm and stomach. Torrio hovered between life and death for 10 days while an army of 30 hoods, captained by Capone, threw a security net around the hospital where he was staying.

As Torrio recovered, he had time to take stock of his situation. He was 43 years old, had managed to stay alive for five years at the top of the Chicago gangland hierarchy, no small accomplishment, and he was a millionaire. Torrio decided to get out, telling Capone: "It's all yours, Al. I've retired."

Torrio walked away from the greatest crime setup ever established, one that allowed him to say, "I own the police force." The former chairman of the board took off to laze under the Mediterranean sun for a while and then retired in Brooklyn. No one ever knew if he really had retired completely. Luciano and the emerging national crime syndicate often asked him for advice, as did Capone. It is known that his counsel was sought before the decision was made to hit Dutch Schultz because of his idiotic plan to assassinate prosecutor Thomas E. Dewey. There were reports that some Murder, Inc. hits also required his approval. Torrio denied it all and said he just wanted to die in bed.

Some gangsters have died in barbershop chairs. Johnny Torrio, at age 75, had a heart attack in one in April 1957, an unlikely end for one who had ruled from the center of a violent world.

See also: *Atlantic City Conference, Alphonse "Scarface Al" Capone, Five Points Gang, Genna Brothers, Charles Dion "Deanie" O'Banion.*

TOUHY, Roger "Terrible" (1898-1959): Bootlegging king

A powerful bootlegging king in the greater Chicago area whom the Capone mob took years to dislodge, Roger Touhy in some respects resembled a businessman with a keen appreciation of the value of strong public relations. As far as the entire underworld was concerned, the Terrible Touhys' hold on the Chicago suburban area of Des Plaines was so complete and backed with such firepower as to be unchallengeable. Despite press coverage that often portrayed him and his gang as among the most vicious in the Midwest, the fact is that Touhy was never more than a middle-class type bootlegger who employed no more muscle than was necessary to see that all the saloons and speakeasies in his area bought and used Touhy beer and booze exclusively.

Touhy produced a superior beer, and his kegs, made at his own cooperage, were leak-proof, a fine selling point at the time. Touhy, as much as Johnny Torrio and Al Capone, realized that the way to achieve preeminence in a criminal endeavor was to corrupt the local politicians and police, and he was a past master of the art. In addition to providing the customary cash payoffs Touhy rewarded the local politicos and police brass with bottled beer brewed especially for them and often bearing their own personal labels. Kinky-haired, beady-eyed and with a hawklike-face, Touhy had the perfect appearance for toughness. There is considerable evidence that Al Capone personally feared him, and he is said to have been the only gangster who ever made Al back down in a confrontation. Touhy had sold the Capone mob 800 barrels of his superior brew at a special price of only $37.50 a barrel (it cost him $4.50 to $5.50 a barrel to produce), and as was his habit, Capone tried to beat down the price some $1,900 by claiming 50 of the barrels had leaks. Touhy put on his famed hard stare and said firmly, "Don't chisel me, Al." Capone paid in full.

Roger was the leader of the Terrible Touhys, a family of six brothers who entered a life of crime after starting out in respectable circumstances. Their father was a Chicago policeman, and many of their playmates on the West Side were later to become police officers. In the early 1920s Roger Touhy went into the trucking business "strictly legit"—until the revenues proved insufficient. Touhy then started filling the trucks with beer, and profits soared.

Touhy took control of the Des Plaines area in the northwest section of Cook County. Since he filled a vital need, he was far from frowned upon. He further solidified his popularity with the local citizens by keeping brothels out of the area. Whenever a group of mobsters attempted to open a roadside whorehouse, Touhy would relieve the local police of the need to handle the situation, sending in his own toughs to wreck the place. Even when Capone personally noted that Des Plaines was "virgin territory for whorehouses," Touhy's answer was his typical hard-eyed stare, which convinced Capone to drop his plans.

Touhy's headquarters always had the appearance of an armed camp. When rivals made rumblings about moving in, Touhy would invite them for a visit, and they invariably would gawk at walls lined with submachine guns. Little did such visitors know that the arsenal had been borrowed from cooperative local police just for the occasion. While a conference was being staged, one Touhy underling after another would march in and receive orders to "bump off" someone. Touhy's visitors would be suitably impressed and leave with the overwhelming conviction that war with the Touhys was a foolhardy undertaking. At various times two of Capone's gunners, Frank Nitti and Murray "The Camel" Humphreys, returned from the Touhy base thoroughly shaken and convinced that the Capones could not hope to handle the Touhys.

None of this prevented the Capone mob from continuing its efforts to take over, however, even when Big Al was sent to prison. Having ruled out direct action, the mob is believed to have used another favorite method to get rid of a problem— tricking the law into doing it for them. First, Touhy and several of his gang were arrested for the kidnapping of William Hamm, Jr. The FBI insisted it had a strong case against Touhy, but a jury thought differently, finding him not guilty. Later, an embarrassed FBI switched the charge to the actual perpetrators, the Barker-Karpis gang.

Then FBI agents arrested Touhy for the alleged 1933 kidnapping of Jake "the Barber" Factor, an international con man with ties to the Capone mob, choosing in the process to ignore word from the underworld grapevine that the abduction had been a put-up job masterminded by Factor and the Capone mob. In what would prove to be a terrible blot on a remarkable career, Melvin Purvis, the FBI special agent who later captured John Dillinger, among others, proclaimed the arrest of Touhy in the Factor case as a hallmark of detection. "This case," he said, "holds a particular interest for me because it represents a triumph of deductive detective work. We assumed from the start, with no material evidence, that the Touhy gang was responsible for the crime."

After the first trial ended in a hung jury, Touhy was convicted in a second trial and sentenced to 99 years in Joliet; he was led from court crying frame-up. The Capone mob moved instantly into Des Plaines.

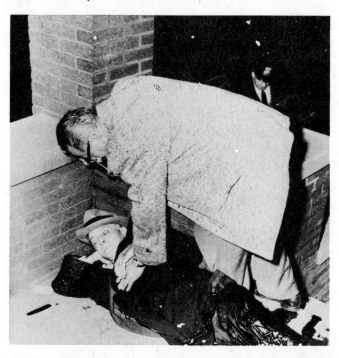

Roger "Terrible" Touhy lies dying after being shot by underworld assassins following his release from prison, where he had served 25 years as the result of a frame-up. "I've been expecting it," he said. "The bastards never forget."

In 1942 Touhy broke out of prison but was retaken in a short time and given an additional sentence of 199 years.

He continued to protest his innocence, a claim that several newspapermen took up, and in the 1950s he won a rehearing on his original conviction. After an intensive 36-day inquiry, Judge John H. Barnes ruled that Factor had never been kidnapped but had disappeared "of his own connivance." The judge went on to attack many key parties in the case, including the FBI, the Chicago police, the state's attorney and the Capone mob. He further noted that despite the FBI's classification of Touhy as a major criminal, he had never been listed by the Chicago Crime Commission on its roster of public enemies. Furthermore, the judge noted, Touhy had never even been linked to a capital case.

In 1959, after almost a quarter of a century behind bars for a crime that had never happened, Touhy was released. He collaborated on a book about his life entitled *The Stolen Years*. It was a quick job and for good reason. Twenty-three days after his release, Touhy was gunned down on a Chicago street. As he lay dying the former gangster muttered: "I've been expecting it. The bastards never forget."

It was an open secret in the underworld that the killing had been carried out by Murray "the Camel" Humphreys. Six months after the Touhy murder, Humphreys bought 400 shares of First National Life Insurance Co. stock at $20 a share from John Factor, Touhy's old nemesis. Eight months later, Humphreys sold the shares back to Factor for $125 a share, realizing a profit of $42,000 in capital gains. The Internal Revenue Service later moved to declare this sum income for services rendered, making the profits subject to straight income tax.

This was not the only unusual happening following Touhy's murder. Early in 1960, a few months after the slaying, retired FBI man Purvis committed suicide.

TOURBILLION, Robert Arthur: See Dapper Don Collins.

TOWN-SITE Frauds: 19th century swindle.

One of the most prevalent rackets of the 19th century was the Western town-site fraud, whereby gullible Easterners were swindled by land sharks into investing their money in property glowingly described in phony prospectuses.

Typical was the Nininger swindle. The city of Nininger, Minnesota Territory in the 1850s, as depicted on large and beautifully engraved maps printed by one Ingenuous Doemly, was a well-built metropolis expected in due course to house some 10,000 people. It had a magnificent courthouse, no less than five churches and was jammed with warehouses and stores to service the surrounding area. Packet companies kept the levee loaded with freight. Here truly was a growth area in God's Country if ever there was one. And to still any remaining doubts, one only had to peruse the *Nininger Daily Bugle*. Of all the phony attributes of Nininger, at least the *Daily Bugle* did actually exist, although it appeared weekly or biweekly or triweekly depending on how energetic its publisher was at any particular moment. The paper was loaded with local advertising—dry goods stores, hardware stores, groceries, millinery shops, blacksmith shops, shoe stores, all obviously thriving. Each issue carried accounts of a new store opening, complete with a total of its receipts for the day. It was very impressive fiction. As a contemporary account put it: "Every name and every business was fictitious, coined in the fertile brain of this chief of all promoters. It was enough to deceive the very elect—and it did. When the Eastern man read that there were six or eight lots, lying just west of Smith & Jones's drygoods store, on West Prairie Street, that could be had at a thousand

dollars per lot if taken quickly, and they were well worth twice that money on account of the advantageous situation, they were snapped up as a toad snaps flies on a summer day." In fact, some plain prairie land two miles from the river to which the anonymous promoters had not even bothered to obtain title, went for as high as $10,000 per acre. "If the editor or the proprietor had been found in Nininger in the following spring when the dupes began to appear, one or two of the jack oaks with which the city lots were plentifully clothed would have borne a larger fruit than acorns. Even the printer who set the type was forced to flee for his life."

An even more tragic swindle was the so-called Rolling Stone colony, also in Minnesota Territory. When some 400 purchasers, mostly from New York, arrived in Rolling Stone in the spring of 1852, they expected to find a thriving metropolis with library, lecture hall, a large greenhouse, a hotel, a large warehouse and a fine dock. That was how they had described the area to steamboat officers, who said they had never heard of such a place. The colonists, however, had produced maps supplied them by one William Haddock and from the maps the boatmen had pinpointed the location some three miles above Wabasha Prairie, on Sioux Indian land. Having insisted on being put ashore there, the colonists built sod houses for themselves or burrowed shelters in the river banks, but sickness came and many died through the summer and autumn. With the onset of winter, more died and the area was abandoned.

TRACY, Harry (?1876-1902): Desperado and murderer

In 1902 virtually the whole country went, as one editorialist put it, "wild about Harry." Harry was Harry Tracy, desperado, Hole in the Wall outlaw, bank robber, train robber, murderer and escapee. When he was finally shot down in 1902, after having killed eight men in a bloody chase across Washington and Oregon, his coffin was torn to pieces by avid souvenir hunters. His funeral drew a mob that was to rival Rudolph Valentino's in ardor. Tracy was a national hero. An editorial writer for the *New York World* carried this "wild about Harry" adulation to an extreme, writing of him: "This bad man who single-handed has for 30 days 'stood off' the State of Washington, its sheriffs, posses and bloodhounds, is undoubtedly a captain of industry—in his peculiar branch of it deserving a badge for superior criminal courage, something corresponding to the Victoria Cross or the Congressional Medal."

Despite such raves, Harry Tracy really was a rotten character. He most likely was born sometime around 1876, possibly in Pittsville, Wis. or Poughkeepsie, N.Y. It is known that he spent his younger days in Boston where he so intimidated policemen that they refused to attempt to arrest him single-handedly, or, as the joke went, without police protection. In the mid-1890s Tracy headed west, pulled a number of robberies and went to prison for burglary in Utah. In 1897 he escaped with another prisoner and joined the Wild Bunch at one of the famous outlaw hideouts, Brown's Hole. The boys welcomed Harry, but they soon changed their minds. He was surly, sullen and tight-lipped and readily exhibited a murderous nature. Even the tough men in the Hole made a point of avoiding him.

Tracy rode for a time with Butch Cassidy and the Wild Bunch and was sometimes called the Mad Dog of the Bunch, but he preferred to team up with the more ruthless killers in the Hole. He was apprehended a couple of times for murder, but on each occasion, while authorities in Colorado, Utah and Wyoming argued about who should have custody of him, he escaped, adding to his legend as a great escapee. After Tracy and a convict named Dave Merrill broke out of prison in Oregon, he married Merrill's sister. In their escape the pair had shot two guards to death and used two wounded ones as shields to get across a bridge outside the prison. Then Tracy finished off one of the guards but ignored the other, who played dead.

Tracy and Merrill engaged in a number of petty crimes to raise money and then pulled a bank robbery. On the run, they hid out in a barn near Puget Sound, where Harry came across a story in a newspaper that reported Merrill had once informed on him in an effort to get a lighter sentence, an incident Tracy had been unaware of. He laid down the newspaper, reached over and choked his partner in crime to death.

In a fishing village, Tracy commandeered a motor launch at gunpoint and ordered the captain to take him to Seattle. On the way he told the seaman at the helm to pass close to McNeil Island Penitentiary which stood out in the Sound, because "I want to pick a few guards off the wall."

Tracy thought better of that when he realized the guards would likely shoot back. In Seattle, Harry tied up the captain and his crew and walked inland, away from the city. He encountered a 21-man posse during a rainstorm and fought them to a standstill, escaping after killing a deputy sheriff and wounding three other pursuers.

Over the next several days Tracy happened on several young ladies who willingly provided him with food and a place to hide, apparently finding more reasons to be wild about Harry than those mentioned by the newspapers. He forced his way into the farmhouse of Mrs. R. H. Van Horn and made her cook him a meal, warning her politely to keep silent and make no outcry.

"I will today—but not tomorrow," she said.

When a butcher boy made a delivery, the woman managed to whisper "Tracy," and the boy notified the law. As Harry slipped out of the house that night and mounted a wagon, a posse closed in on him. Tracy jumped off the wagon firing with uncanny accuracy. He killed three men, two with shots in the brain and another with a slug in the heart, and slipped away in the confused gunfire.

The hunt for Tracy continued through July and into August 1902, with the gunman several times getting the best of posses. On August 5 lawmen learned Tracy was hiding at the Eddy Ranch near Davenport, Wash. and flushed him out of a barn there. Shooting as he ran, Tracy was hit in the leg by a chance rifle shot. He hobbled 75 yards to the edge of a wheat field. Bleeding profusely, he hid behind a rock and exchanged volley after volley with the lawmen. Shortly before night fell, a bullet tore into his thigh. The posse formed a cordon around the field to make sure he wouldn't slip out in the darkness. It was a needless precaution; Tracy couldn't move. As dawn was breaking, Harry raised his gun to his head and pulled the trigger. The lawmen waited until full daylight before carefully approaching. They found Harry Tracy dead.

See also: *Wild Bunch.*

TRAFFICANTE, Santo (1915-   ): Mafia leader

One of the most shadowy but certainly one of the most powerful leaders in the Mafia and the national crime syndicate, Santo Trafficante is the reputed underworld boss of Tampa, Fla. and long regarded to be deeply involved in many of organized crime's endeavors, including gambling and narcotics. At one time he was overlord of the mob-owned casinos in pre-Castro Cuba. Because of his eminence in the Mafia and his longtime close association with Meyer Lansky, it is often said that no important underworld event takes place without Trafficante's knowledge or approval. Accordingly, he was reportedly consulted before Carmine Galante was murdered in 1979.

Any plan by the CIA to utilize the underworld to assassinate Fidel Castro had to have involved Trafficante. Under pressure of a court order granting him immunity from prosecution for anything he might say but threatening him with contempt if he didn't talk, Trafficante admitted to a congressional committee in 1975 that he had recruited other mobsters, such as John Roselli, in the early 1960s to carry out assassination attempts on Castro's life. "It was like in World War II," he said. "They tell you to go to the draft board and sign up. Well, I signed up." Of course, Trafficante had a grudge against Castro for shutting down the casinos in 1959. According to the mobster, he and his fellow underworld conspirators considered "poison, planes, tanks. I'm telling you, they talked about everything." Eventually, they settled on poison pills, but that plot failed.

It has long been a theory among many researchers looking into the assassination of John F. Kennedy that the CIA-Trafficante efforts to kill Castro may have triggered a Castro retaliation against the President.

In 1978 Trafficante testified before a House assassination committee looking into the Kennedy murder. The committee was especially interested in a sworn statement made by Cuban exile leader Jose Aleman to committee investigators that months before the Kennedy assassination Trafficante had told him, "Kennedy's gonna get hit." However, in public testimony, Aleman, admitting he was fearful of Trafficante's wrath, remembered the matter differently. What the mobster probably meant, Aleman testified, was that Kennedy would be hit by Republican votes in 1964—not bullets. Trafficante denied he had made the comment.

See also: *John Roselli.*

TRAIN Robberies

Train robbing is a particularly American crime. While train robberies have occurred in many other countries, the United States provided far and away the most favorable ground for the crime, with its vast open areas along railroad rights-of-way, which gave the thieves ample opportunity to escape without being seen by witnesses.

The first reported train robbery of any magnitude occurred in 1866 between New York and New Haven when an Adams Express car on a New York, New Haven and Hartford Railroad train was looted of $700,000. The first actual holdup of a train in the United States, and perhaps the world, was pulled the same year by the Reno gang near Seymour, Ind., where they stopped and boarded an Ohio and Mississippi Railroad train and robbed $10,000 from the express car. They tried to break open the safe but were forced to give up. News of the Renos' deed had an electrifying effect; no one had ever thought of holding up a train before but now an epidemic of train robberies quickly broke out. Other bandits held up a train in Indiana and seized about $8,000. Jealous of their reputation and enraged by their imitators, the Renos organized an outlaw posse, captured two of their rivals and turned them in.

Train robbing became a big business from coast to coast. In the South there were the Farrington brothers and in the Midwest the much-storied James gang. The latter robbed many trains but never came close to equaling the Renos' biggest job, pulled on May 22, 1868, when they stole $96,000 from a train near Marshfield, Ind. In the East the Tenth Avenue Gang preyed on trains even within the city limits of New York. In the Far West there was the Jack Davis gang and Butch Cassidy and the Wild Bunch. In California, Chris Evans, the Sontag brothers and the California Outlaws carried on a private war with the Southern Pacific. Train robbers were frequently lynched, so often, in fact, that some observers have suggested these actions were encouraged by agents of the railroads who were determined to wipe out the crime by dispensing quick, if extralegal, justice.

The last of the train robbers can't be named in an absolute sense as isolated crimes have continued well into this century, but perhaps the last to rob trains on a regular basis was Old Bill Miner. His holdup days ran from the Civil War until 1911, when he was caught in a Georgia swamp after leading a five-man gang on a holdup that netted $3,500 from the Southern Railroad Express near White Sulphur. "I'm getting too old for this sort of thing," he told his captors. The truth was that technology more than the aging of the old-time train robbers was making the crime much more difficult. Trains were faster, news of robberies clicked over the telegraph wires and swift cars could hasten pursuit across a much more populated landscape.

One of the last major American train holdups occurred in November 1935, when a gang headed by public enemy Alvin "Creepy" Karpis, a leader of the Barker-Karpis gang, robbed a train at Garrettsville, Ohio of $34,000. The loot was much smaller than Karpis had expected, but the robbery had its compensations. As he wrote later: "I thought of the great bandits of the old West, the James brothers, the Dalton boys, and all the rest of them. They knocked over trains, and I was going to pull the same stunt." Karpis also admitted a contributing motive was his belief that resurrecting the crime would give FBI Director J. Edgar Hoover fits. It did.

See also: *Eugene "Captain Gerald" Bunch, California Outlaws, James Brothers, Bill Miner, Oliver Curtis Perry, Reno Gang, Tenth Avenue Gang, Wild Bunch.*

TRANSPORTATION: Exportation of criminals to America

While it is a common belief that the American colonies were populated by persons fleeing political or religious persecution in Europe, the fact is they were peopled as much by the dregs of English jails. The British crown looked upon the American colonies as a convenient dumping ground for criminals and the solution to the English crime problem. During the last four decades of the 17th century, almost 5,000 convicts were transported to America. During the next century the traffic increased enormously; from 1745 to 1775 almost 9,000 convicts were landed in just one port, Annapolis, Md. The local populace could have hardly been pleased when out of one shipment of 26 prisoners, five were convicted murderers.

In Virginia the local citizenry fought back by inspecting incoming female prisoners, and if they had become pregnant on the ship crossing, they were sent back to England on the ground that it was necessary to stamp out promiscuity in the colony. It was often suspected that the British authorities simply reshipped the women to another colony. Other protests took the form of pamphlets tracing the criminal deeds of the new arrivals. Much was made of the case of Thomas Lutherland, a convicted felon sent to New Jersey as a bound servant. Within days of his arrival he was convicted of stealing and punished. That did little to cure him, however, and a short time later, he murdered a boat trader and hid the victim's goods in his home.

Parliament turned a deaf ear to these protests, as it did to an official resolution by the Virginia House of Burgesses declaring that "the peace of this colony be too much hazarded and endangered by the great numbers of felons and other desperate villains sent hither from several prisons in England."

In the half century before the American Revolution, a total of 30,000 convicted felons were deposited in the colonies. The flow only stopped when America broke with England, which in turn merely shifted the bulk of its criminal exports to Australia.

Ironically, the flow of thugs from England went on unabated following independence. Mixed in among those Europeans fleeing to America to start a new life were a great number of criminals seeking to escape arrest in Britain and Ireland. Many newcomers flooded American cities and, instead of finding jobs, found only privation and slums at best the equal to those they had fled. The occupants of the crowded slums banded together and, by the 1820s, formed the first outlaw gangs, becoming the forerunners of organized crime in America.

Juvenile Delinquents

Almost as prevalent as the English custom of transporting adult criminals to America was the even more heinous practice of shipping over juvenile delinquents. There were many in the colonies who welcomed receipt of such wares under the theory that cheap labor was needed and the lash had more effect on young criminals than on the more-seasoned variety. In 1619 the Virginia Company, which prized child labor, eagerly sought to import children from London. That city seized upon the offer and promptly set out to rid its back streets, hovels, jails and poor houses of paupers, vagrants, petty thieves and orphans. The following year a law was passed permitting the deportation of children without their approval, and large-scale abductions became commonplace in every part of London.

In America the children were apprenticed until they were 21, when, in principle, they were to be freed and given cattle, corn and some public land. In practice, there was no real guarantee that their masters would set them free at the end of their apprenticeship. In addition, the youths were often subjected to cruelty by their masters, who had the law on their side. Thus, children found guilty of lying, swearing, fighting, cheating, stealing and running away were liable to added restraints that could delay their freedom, even though most of these offenses were not punishable if committed by adults.

TRAPMAN: Mob security expert

Not many years ago, long after the mob had disposed of the Flamingo Hotel in Las Vegas, the new owners discovered a secret safe in the hotel floor. It had undoubtedly been built many years earlier by Bugsy Siegel, the explosive partner of Meyer Lansky who had been murdered because he had defied the national crime syndicate. Obviously, Siegel had kept large amounts of money hidden there, but when the safe was found, it contained nothing. Since Siegel had died suddenly, it was hardly likely he had time to make a last-minute withdrawal. Speculation had it that either someone else knew of the existence of the safe or that a "trapman" had talked.

The trapman is one of the most important specialists used by the mob, as vital as hit men and respectable front men. The trapman's function is to build traps, or secret panels or hidden safes, for mob leaders. Knowledgeable police insist no important national crime figure is without one or more traps in his home. Organized crime leaders do not believe much in safe-deposit boxes or, contrary to public opinion, in Swiss bank accounts. They rely on hidden compartments where they can store cash, records and even guns on short notice. Underworld traps have consisted of walls that slide open or even panels in swimming pools.

Trapmen are generally not syndicate or Mafia members, but rather legitimate contractors, although they are often relatives of Mafia figures. Pledged to secrecy, a trapman in Los Angeles may be flown to Chicago or New York to install a special trap.

Only he and the man hiring him will ever know the secret of the trap. The trapman has two reasons for keeping the secret: he is extremely well paid and he wants to stay alive.

Persons other than crime leaders use trapmen for illegal purposes. Professional men, such as doctors and dentists, are notorious for installing traps in their homes to hide their "tax-free" funds. Of course, since they do not have access to the same trapmen who service the Mafia, they generally use the contractors who build their homes. The underworld is aware of this practice and makes a special effort to get a loan-shark hold on building contractors. Then in exchange for information about a trap, a contractor's loan is discounted against a portion of the money taken in a robbery of the trap.

Traps are often of extremely clever design. One technique is to place a trap behind another trap. Another is to hide a trap in the basement of a house but install its trigger mechanism in the attic, so that chances of accidental discovery are virtually nil. A unique deception is a fireproof panel built into a stove.

The only time a trapman is permitted to talk is if the party who has hired him suddenly dies, a not infrequent event in the underworld. Since the secret of the trap would otherwise be buried with the dead man, the trapman is permitted to tell the secret to the deceased's associates. If the trap has not already been cleaned out, the trapman is entitled to a portion of the cash found.

TRASH Bag Murders: California homicide wave

The first of the bodies in one of America's most bizarre murder sprees turned up on Christmas Day 1972; shortly thereafter, plastic-bagged bodies or parts thereof began appearing along the California coastline. Some dismembered parts were discovered in garbage bins, and others were found in ditches along the roadside and on freeway shoulders, obviously hurled from a car. A plastic-wrapped head turned up on a recycling plant's conveyer belt and a left leg was found in a junk heap outside a Sunset Beach saloon. By July 1973 the police had tied five homicides to the Trash Bag Murderer, and over the next four years that number more than quadrupled. Finally, in July 1977 a 38-year-old bearded, bespectacled ex-aerospace worker named Patrick Kearney surrendered to the authorities. Five months later, he pleaded guilty to 21 murders.

Kearney never revealed any motive for the killing spree, and no effort was made in court to discover one. There were seven other murder charges pending against Kearney, but authorities did not proceed on them. If they had, he could have been convicted of a total of 28, which at the time would have made him one of the worst mass murderers in American history. Kearney was given two concurrent life sentences for his crimes.

TRESCA, Carlo (1875-1943): Syndicalist editor and murder victim

For years the 1943 assassination of syndicalist editor Carlo Tresca on New York's Fifth Avenue has been listed as a great unsolved political murder. It has never been a mystery in Mafia circles, however. Tresca, as the underworld has always known, was gunned down on orders transmitted from Italy by a leader of the American Mafia. Tresca's anti-Fascist, anti-Communist Italian-language weekly, *Il Martello,* earned him the enmity of both Rome and Moscow. Thus, when the editor went down under a volley of gunfire after stepping out of his office on January 11, speculation arose that he could have been killed by either the left or the right.

He was most likely killed to satisfy the wish of Benito Mussolini, whose hatred for Tresca dated back a long time.

Tresca was born in Pulmona, Italy to a wealthy land-owning family, and, as a youth, gravitated to "lost causes" of the left. After serving as editor of the Socialist Party's newspaper, he was forced to flee the country. In Geneva, Switzerland in 1904 Tresca met another young man who had a reputation for being as much of a hothead as he was, Benito Mussolini. At the time, Mussolini regarded Tresca as not enough of a radical; Tresca regarded Mussolini as a charlatan, a judgment confirmed by subsequent events.

Tresca would later spend much of his energy fighting Mussolini's regime in Italy. The record indicates that Mussolini had put Tresca's name on a death list in 1931, but it was a dozen years before something was done about it. The agent of Mussolini's bidding was Vito Genovese, who had been forced to flee the United States in the 1930s to escape a murder indictment. Arriving in Italy, Genovese knew that Mussolini had vowed to wipe out the Mafia in that country, so he decided his personal comfort and safety required that he ingratiate himself with the Fascist cause. Genovese, who had left America with several million dollars, contributed $250,000 to build a Fascist Party headquarters. When World War II broke out, he further demonstrated his devotion to Mussolini by supervising—and partially financing—the construction of a munitions factory. The Italian leader personally bestowed the title of *commendatore* on the American gangster.

Another of Genovese's ploys to establish himself with the power elite was to supply Mussolini's son-in-law and foreign minister, Count Galeazzo Ciano, with narcotics, and in this way the gangster also became one of the country's richest narcotics dealers. When Mussolini raged to him about Tresca's anti-Fascist activities in New York, Genovese grandly informed the Italian leader that he would solve the problem. He then sent word through Mafia circles that Tresca was to be hit.

The contract was carried out by Carmine Galante, who, although later to become one of the top Mafia leaders in the country, was described in an account at the time as "a petty Brooklyn hoodlum." Witnesses were able to record the license number of a Ford sedan used in the assassination: 1C-9272. That number led to an ironic discovery. About two hours before the Tresca assassination, Galante, a parolee, was making his weekly report to his parole officer in downtown Manhattan. It was common practice for parole officers to trail parolees out of the office in the hope of seeing them consorting with other criminal types. Galante was followed to a car, which he entered and drove off. His parole officers could not

tail the car because of restrictions placed on such activity by the wartime gasoline shortage. All he could do was take down the license number: 1C-9272.

Picked up as a material witness in the Tresca murder, Galante denied everything. He had not entered any such car, he said. He had taken the subway uptown and was at a Broadway movie at the time of the killing, and besides, he asked, "Who is this guy Tresca? Never even heard of him."

Since no witnesses could identify the gunman, the link to Galante and the car was not enough to bring about a prosecution. When Genovese returned to the United States after the war, he had little to fear from the by then stale murder investigation.

See also: *Carmine Galante, Vito Genovese, Wall Street Explosion.*

TRIAL By Touch

As late as the end of the 17th century, American colonists employed the medieval custom of trial by touch in murder cases. It was believed that if the accused was the murderer, the corpse would give some signal.

In a typical trial held in Virginia in 1663, several members of a family were accused of having killed a former black servant. On orders from the court each of the defendants touched Uncle Joe's body, and since it "gave no sign," they were found not guilty. However, in the trial of a man accused of murdering John Clark, a boat trader in New Jersey, who was found dead and his supplies stolen in 1691, the results were somewhat different. The corpse was brought forth in court and the defendant, Thomas Lutherland, was ordered to touch it. It was firmly believed that the corpse would bleed if Lutherland was guilty. It did not, but Lutherland was hanged anyway because the victim's goods had been found in his home.

TRI-STATE Gang

If the Dillinger mob was noted for its members' loyalty to each other, the Tri-State Gang, a more typical criminal combination of the 1930s, won notoriety for the opposite. Based in Philadelphia and led by Robert Mais, Walter Legenza and Anthony Cugino, known as Philadelphia's Public Enemy No. 1, the Tri-Staters became famous for the short-lived careers of many of their members, most of whom were victims of internal assassinations. Cugino was particularly adept at this pastime, killing, at various times, four of his men and two of their girl friends.

Cugino's career in crime began at the age of 12, when he was sent to a reformatory. In 1919, barely out of his teens, he committed a $35,000 jewel robbery and, when caught, was sent to prison for 15 years. In prison he killed his cellmate, but he drew no added penalty for the act because he successfully claimed he had acted in self-defense. Released in 1930, Cugino hooked up with Mais, Legenza, Salvatore Serpa, Eddie "Cowboy" Wallace, John Zurkorsky and others to form a holdup and counterfeiting gang called the Tri-Staters. Together with Serpa, Wallace and Zurkorsky, Cugino stole a plant payroll and shot down a police officer guarding it.

A few months after the robbery, Cugino and Serpa, suspecting their partners in crime might betray them to the police to save themselves, took Wallace and Zukorsky for a ride. Riddled with bullets, the pair were dumped on a roadside and left for dead. Wallace was dead but Zukorsky staggered upright, hailed a car and was taken to a hospital. From the hospital he called Camden, N. J. police and begged them to go to a rooming house to save two girls with whom he and Wallace had been living. Detectives were too late. They found that the young women, Florence Miller and Ethel Greentree, had just left with two men whose descriptions matched those of Cugino and Serpa. Three weeks later, the bodies of the women were found in a shallow grave in a cornfield near Downington, Pa.

Sometime later, Cugino assassinated another gangster, Johnny Horn, who had two marks against him: Cugino suspected him of possible duplicity and regarded him as a rival for a certain young woman's attention. The only members of the gang Cugino seemed to have any loyalty toward (he later also stabbed Serpa to death in Chicago) were Mais and Legenza. When they were convicted and awaiting execution in Richmond, Va. for killing a mail-truck driver during a robbery, Cugino sent them two pistols hidden in a baked turkey. The pair broke out, murdering a guard in the process, and rejoined Cugino.

Back in business, the Tri-Staters robbed $48,000 from an electric company office in Philadelphia. Soon, Mais and Legenza were scouring the city's underworld for a certain hoodlum they believed had betrayed them, but they were informed on by certain other gang members who feared their vengeance would get out of hand. Returned to Richmond, Mais and Legenza were electrocuted. Meanwhile, Cugino shifted some of his operations from Philadelphia to New York, fearing he too would be betrayed. He still returned to Philadelphia, however, to recruit new Tri-Staters for jobs and to eliminate "weak links" in the operation. He also shot dead Anthony "Musky" Zanghi after a quarrel about how the spoils from a counterfeiting operation were to be divided.

It was the Zanghi murder that doomed Cugino. Convinced that Cugino now believed in nothing but "kill, kill, kill," several gangsters informed Philadelphia police that the gang leader hung around New York's theatrical district a great deal, especially the area of Seventh Avenue and 47th Street. Cugino was captured there just after midnight on September 8, 1935.

Questioned for 15 hours straight, Cugino laughed at police efforts to tie him to a large number of robberies as well as eight murders. Finally, he made some damaging admissions concerning the murder of a New York police detective, James J. Garvey, in 1934. Cugino never paid for any of his crimes, hanging himself in his cell later that night. With his death, the Tri-State Gang, perhaps the most devious and treacherous criminal organization ever, disintegrated.

TRUESDALE, David A. (1881-1948): Wells Fargo messenger

Just before World War I, the most famous Western character was neither a lawman nor an outlaw but an unimposing 31-year-old Wells Fargo messenger named David A. Truesdale. Bars and saloons, east and west, saluted him with the "Truesdale Special." What Truesdale had done to gain such fame was "cash in the chips" of the last active member of Butch Cassidy's Wild Bunch, the Tall Texan, Ben Kilpatrick.

On March 13, 1912, Kilpatrick and a confederate, an ex-convict named Ed Welch, halted the Sunset Limited of the Southern Pacific at Dryden, Tex. by posing as Union Pacific detectives. While Kilpatrick covered Truesdale, the Wells Fargo messenger in the express car, Welch went about looting the mail car. But the Tall Texan got careless and took his eyes off Truesdale. As the messenger later described the events to the *New York Herald:*

> They thought they were such smooth workers at the game. But it made me sore the way they acted, so I decided to take some of the conceit out of them. By a ruse I made the bigger one (Kilpatrick) look the other way; then I struck him on the head with the ice mallet. I picked up his rifle and killed the other one as he walked out of the mail car toward me.

Only afterward did the plucky Truesdale learn that the tall one was Ben Kilpatrick, one of the slickest bandits ever to ride with Butch Cassidy and Black Jack Ketchum. Did that scare him now that he knew who his victim was? He replied, "I am more worried about what to do with the vacation and the reward the company has given me than I am about killing those two."

Of course, Truesdale's moment of glory was short-lived, and the Truesdale Special enjoyed only a brief popularity. A wicked concoction of whiskey and gin (or whatever hard liquor happened to be handy) with just a dash of soda, it offered little to all but the hardiest of imbibers; its usual effect could well be described as being hit over the head with a mallet.

In 1930 Truesdale's feat got a replay when it was discovered that he was still waiting for his reward. The neglected payment was finally made and Truesdale, like the badmen of the West themselves, faded into obscurity.

See also: *Ben Kilpatrick, Ed Welch.*

TRUMAN, Harry S (1884-1972): Intended assassination victim

On November 1, 1950 a uniformed White House guard, Donald Birdzell, was at his post in front of Blair House, across the street from the Executive Mansion, where President Harry S Truman was staying while repairs were being made at the White House. Suddenly, Birdzell heard a faint, metallic click and turned his head. Ten feet away, a neat, dark man in a pin-striped blue-green suit was silently and carefully aiming a German F-38 automatic pistol at him. It went off just as Birdzell jumped for the street—a prescribed Secret Service action to draw fire away from the house where the President was staying so that he would not catch a stray bullet. The first assault on a president of the United States in his Washington residence was underway.

Birdzell landed on the streetcar tracks on Pennsylvania Avenue, turned and began firing back. The gunman put a bullet in his leg, dropping him to one knee. Another slug ripped into Birdzell's good leg and he pitched forward. As other guards and Secret Servicemen went into action, a second attacker darted up to the guard at the west sentry booth, pulled out a Luger and began shooting at point-blank range. A uniformed sentry, Leslie Coffelt, went down with bullets in the chest, stomach and legs. He died a short while later. Plainclothesman Joseph Downs toppled over, shot in the stomach.

There was one last burst of gunfire. The wounded Birdzell, stretched out flat with his pistol held braced at arm's length on the pavement before him, shot the first gunman in the chest as he frantically tried to reload. The would-be assassin sprawled out, his hat awry, his heels kicking. The second gunman lurched backward over a low boxwood hedge, dead with a bullet through his ears.

In the heavy silence that followed, Secret Serviceman Floyd Boring saw President Truman in his undershirt peering out the window of an upstairs room, where he had been napping.

"Get back, Mr. President!" Agent Boring shouted. "Get back!"

Truman stepped back while a few Secret Service agents converged on the scene. Most remained at their posts, on guard against further attacks.

Would-be presidential assassin Oscar Collazzo lies wounded at the foot of the steps to Blair House.

The wounded gunman was identified as Oscar Collazo and his dead partner as Griselio Torresola. In Torresola's pocket were found two letters from a fiery Puerto Rican nationalist, Pedro Albizu Campos.

While newspaper front pages were filled with details of the assassination attempt, a key factor failed to get the prominence it deserved. Although Torresola and Collazo started with the assassin's greatest asset—the element of surprise—they failed to penetrate even the outer rim of presidential protectors. Backing up the uniformed White House police was an agent sitting in a nearby office building with a clear view of Blair House. His duty was to drop any attacker who made it to the doorway of Blair House. However, even if the attackers had gotten through the door, they would have faced an agent

stationed inside the entrance with a submachine gun in his lap.

There was another agent on the stairway, one in front of Truman's door and others in surrounding rooms. It was estimated that the assassins would have had to kill at least 20 Secret Servicemen before getting within sight of the President.

How much faith President Truman placed in the Secret Service was pointed up by the fact that a few hours after the attack he delivered a speech and unveiled a statue before a large crowd in Arlington—all as though nothing had happened.

Collazo recovered from his wounds and was convicted and sentenced to death for the murder of Coffelt. President Truman commuted his death sentence to life imprisonment. On September 6, 1979 President Jimmy Carter, "for humane reasons," commuted his life sentence to time served and on September 10 he was released from prison.

TRUSSELL, George (1833-1866): Gambler and murder victim

Known as "a shrewd, cunning Yankee from Vermont," George Trussell was the dandy of the Chicago gamblers during the Civil War and, as such, the idol of the young sports of the city. Contemporary accounts described his good looks. He was, according to one, "tall, straight as an arrow, and might have stood as model for one of Remington's Indian-fighting cavalry officers."

Trussell first appeared in Chicago working as a bookkeeper and then as a bank teller, but he was discharged from that job for gambling. He then worked as a "roper," or victim hunter, for a faro operation and soon had his own gambling business. By 1862 he was operating two gambling houses, one on Dearborn Street and another on Randolph. From then until 1866 Trussell was at the peak of his power. He was said to be—and indeed claimed to be—the most generous dispenser of bribes to accommodating police.

Trussell constantly walked around armed and is noted for having used his weapon on sore losers who had been taken in his games, which may not have always been operated in accordance with the official rules. In addition to protecting himself against irate losers, he needed to carry a weapon because of what became known as the Hairtrigger Block feud, which he carried on with a rival gambler, Cap Hyman. This was a bullet-pocked yet somewhat humorous duel that went on for years whenever the two got drunk, which was quite often. Bets were always made in gambling circles on who would be killed by whom. As it turned out, Trussell was shot to death, but by a different party.

Since it was almost obligatory that a gambler of Trussell's station take a mistress from among the madams of the city's brothels, Trussell selected Irish Mollie, whose real name was Mary Cossgriff. For two years the affair flourished, as Trussell took his Mollie on daily carriage rides around the city, appeared with her at the theater and racetracks and continually showered her with gifts. In 1866 Irish Mollie found herself competing with an unusual rival. Trussell had acquired a half interest in

Dexter, a famous trotting horse, and was spending more of his time with the horse than with Mollie. Taunted by her friends that she was losing out to a horse, Mollie's devotion to her lover turned to insane jealousy and led to bitter quarrels between them. On September 4, 1866, enraged because her lover had forgotten their dinner engagement, Mollie walked into the bar of Seneca Wright's saloon on Randolph Street ("in a gorgeous white moire dress, with a light shawl thrown over it, and seemed as if she had just come from some dancing party," according to the *Chicago Tribune*). When Trussell told her to go home she pulled a revolver from under her shawl and shot him in the side. As Trussell tried to run out a side exit, Mollie shot him again. The gambler staggered into Prince's livery stable, where Mollie followed him and shot him a third time. Trussell fell dead, and Mollie prostrated herself over his body and sobbed: "Oh, my George! My George! He is dead!"

Irish Mollie was convicted of manslaughter and given a rather mild sentence of one year in prison, which would seem to indicate that the courts did not regard the loss of Trussell as a major civic tragedy. Before serving a day of her sentence, Mollie received a pardon from the governor and returned to her bordello. She never laid claim to Trussell's estate, which was considerable, even though she contended she had been legally married to him. Friends say it was because she was too grief-stricken at the loss of her lover to concern herself about his money, but more likely her pardon had been granted on the condition that she make no claim to his property.

See also: *Hairtrigger Block.*

TRUTH Serum

Although they have been touted in the past as the surest method for both lie and crime detection, the so-called truth serums have proved far from practical for legal purposes. Aside from the constitutional problems raised, the fact remains that none of the truth serums, such as scopolamine, sodium amytal, phenobarbital solution, sodium pentothal and others, has ever been scientifically accepted as a reliable and accurate technique for learning the truth. The theory behind truth serums is that they relieve the subject of inhibitions, so that he or she will make true statements. Although these drugs are used in the field of psychiatry, any attempt to use them on a person suspected of a crime, especially in light of the Miranda decision, which protects a prisoner's legal rights, draws almost universal opposition from defense attorneys. Not only is it necessary to get a suspect's permission to use such drugs, but he must also grant a written release of liability to the interrogator and the attending physician in case of unfavorable reaction. It is a level of cooperation few prisoners will accede to.

Even some of those who see value in truth serums for purposes of interrogation, such as criminologist LeMoyne Snyder, object to the use of the drugs alone. They see them as a complement to the lie detector, with neither a valid substitute for the other. Not surprisingly, the Nazis made considerable use of truth serums to interrogate suspected underground agents and other enemies, but the reliability of the results was at best

mixed and the drugs never replaced ordinary torture as the most effective method of interrogation.

TUB Of Blood Bunch: Post-Civil War New York criminals

One of the great "cleanups" of gangsters in New York occurred shortly after the Civil War, when the police started to force criminal gangs out of the Fourth Ward. The majority of these criminal elements moved northward along the East River into the Corlears' Hook district. Perhaps the worst of all were those who congregated in a notorious dive called the Tub of Blood. Some belonged to organized gangs but most were vicious loners who owed allegiance to no one and gave none. Even celebrated thugs like those of the Patsy Conroy gang steered clear of the Tub of Blood Bunch, which included such unsavory characters as Skinner Meehan, Dutch Hen, Jack Cody, Sweeney the Boy, Brian Boru and the celebrated Hop Along Peter.

It was said that Sweeney the Boy and Brian Boru had not slept in a bed in a house for 20 years. By day and late evening they could be found in the Tub of Blood and at night they would adjourn to a marble yard, where they slept. They never had a change of clothes, simply robbing or killing a hapless pedestrian when the clothes they were wearing bored them or got too dirty. The eventual fate of Sweeney the Boy is unknown, but Brian Boru suffered the misfortune of falling asleep in the marble yard one night in such a drunken stupor that he was unable to defend himself. The next morning he was found literally half eaten by the huge gray dock rats that often ranged blocks from the waterfront in search of food.

Probably the oddest of all the Tub of Blooders was Hop Along Peter, a certifiable half-wit, but nonetheless a vicious thug. Other gangsters utilized Hop Along Peter as a lookout because of his habit of flying into a fury whenever he saw a policeman's uniform and attacking its wearer. This readily afforded the other gangsters sufficient time to make their getaway. Hop Along Peter was, for a period of almost two decades, the most notorious cop fighter on the East Side. When he disappeared in the 1880s the police do not seem to have searched too hard or lamented too long, just as few cops—or criminals—were grief-stricken when the Tub of Blood eventually shut down for lack of patronage.

TUCKER Telephone: Prison torture

Any belief that brutality and torture had disappeared from the American prison system by the mid-20th century was dispelled in the late 1960s following probes of conditions at Arkansas' Cummings and Tucker prison farms. While all sorts of charges were made and perhaps only partially verified, the investigation established that a particularly awesome torture device, the "Tucker telephone," was used at the institutions. It was composed of an old telephone, a heavy duty battery and the necessary wiring. A convict would be stripped and one end of the wire fastened to his wrist or ankle and the other end to his penis. Electric shocks would be sent coursing through his body until the agony drove him to unconsciousness.

At the time this torture instrument was in use in Arkansas, the only other official authority in the world known to be employing a similar device was SAVAK, the Iranian secret police.

TUFTS, Henry (1748-1831): Horse thief

Henry Tufts was the first American criminal to write an autobiography, appropriately titled *The Autobiography of a Criminal,* which became, one presumes unintentionally, a manual for horse thieves.

Tufts was the compleat horse thief, developing what was then an unmindful criminal endeavor into a highly skilled profession. He carried an assortment of tools with which to break into locked barns, including corrosives that could soften or eat through iron and, concealed in the soles of his shoes, saw blades, which he also used to saw his way to freedom whenever he was apprehended stealing a horse. Tufts always brought along a variety of paints with which to disguise a stolen steed, and often a black horse he had sold to some unsuspecting buyer would turn chestnut after about a week.

Born in Newmarket, N. H. in 1748, Tufts stole his first horse at age 16. At 18 he performed the unique feat of stealing and selling the same dog three times in one day. But it was the Revolutionary War that really catapulted Tufts into big-time horse stealing, as both sides paid dearly for horses and asked no questions about their source. This was fortunate for Tufts, who often lost track of whether he was selling certain animals to the side he had stolen them from or to their enemies. Whenever constables or sheriffs were hot on his trail, Tufts would elude capture by enlisting in the Continental Army only to desert and return to the horse thief trail once the chase cooled.

In time, Henry Tufts gained the reputation of being the greatest knave and most arrant horse thief in New England. Finally, he retired from the profession in 1807 and, under another identity, published his autobiography. The work permitted him to reenter society as a reformed rogue truly regretful of a misspent life. No one seems to have been too upset or even aware that his autobiography was being used as a primer for would-be horse thieves, who learned from Tufts, for example, how to fashion cork shoes covered with sole leather that could be attached to a horse's hooves to eliminate the sound of its footsteps.

Tufts remained a respectable citizen for the rest of his days, save for a minor lapse here and there. Shortly before he died in 1831, he expressed sadness over the state of the horse-stealing profession. Even such awesome penalties as the lash and branding had failed to halt the crime, and now hanging was becoming the newest punishment. Old Tufts found the situation "most discouraging."

TUNSTALL, John Henry (1853-1878): Murder victim

It was the death of a wealthy young Englishman, John H.

Tunstall, that is said to have turned Billy the Kid from a rustler into a mean killer. Tunstall, a much-traveled entrepreneur, arrived in Lincoln, New Mexico Territory in 1876 and was soon embroiled in the Lincoln County War, one of the major violent commercial clashes in America, with the wealth of the entire territory as the spoils.

Tunstall had bought a large ranch and aligned himself with Alexander McSween, an ambitious lawyer, and John S. Chisum, a wealthy cattleman, against the forces of Lawrence G. Murphy, James J. Dolan and others of the so-called Santa Fe Ring, prominent Republicans attempting to dominate every aspect of economic life in the New Mexico Territory, including the revenues from very lucrative government beef contracts. Soon, a war broke out between the two groups, with the fighting done by cowboys such as Billy the Kid.

Artist Charles Russell depicts Billy the Kid executing two of the men who murdered his mentor, John Tunstall; the pair had surrendered on the promise that they would be brought back alive to Lincoln, New Mexico Territory.

The Kid was riding for Murphy until, at some point, he met Tunstall and switched sides. Although Tunstall was not much older than the Kid, Billy seemed to regard him as a father, and Tunstall said of him: "That's the finest lad I ever met. He's a revelation to me every day and would do anything on earth to please me. I'm going to make a man out of that boy yet." Quite predictably, latter-day Freudians have seen more to this odd relationship between an unschooled, undisciplined, homeless boy and a cultured foreigner in tweeds, but hard facts about what was to prove their brief encounter are missing.

Through a blatantly political move, Tunstall's business rivals had obtained a court order to seize some of his horses in payment for an alleged debt. When the Englishman refused to comply with the order, the ring's puppet sheriff, William Brady, sent an 18-man posse to seize the horses. When Tunstall rode up to the lawmen to protest their presence, he was ordered to dismount and hand over his pistol. As he complied, he was shot in the head by Deputy Billy Morton, becoming the first victim of the Lincoln County War.

The Kid, who witnessed the killing from a distance, was deeply affected. "He was the only man that ever treated me like I was free-born and white," he said. And when his mentor's body was being lowered into the grave, Billy vowed: "I'll get every son-of-a-bitch who helped kill John if it's the last thing I do."

It was an oath the Kid was quite successful in keeping. There are those who say that Billy was by nature and inclination a killer. In any case, Tunstall's murder made him a killer with a mission.

See also: *Billy the Kid, Lincoln County War.*

TURLEY, Preston S. (?-1858): Murderer

"Never hang a preacher" became a pre-Civil War saying in Charleston, Va., which is now West Virginia, following the execution of an ex-minister of the Baptist Church, Preston Turley, in 1858.

Demon rum had led to Turley's being defrocked, and from there on, it was straight down. One night in 1858 both Turley and his wife, Mary Susan, came home drunk. Suddenly, Turley began quoting scriptures and then strangled his wife to death while their three children watched. He disposed of the body in a nearby river, somehow not expecting his children would say anything about the murder. They did, however, and Turley was convicted and given the death sentence.

On September 17, 1858 Turley mounted the scaffold. He was given the right to make a final statement, which he turned into a harangue that lasted three and a half hours. Turley lectured on the wages of sin and the evils of drink, so much so that one account speaks of some members of the audience drifting away—that in a day when executions were considered highly entertaining. We are informed that the ex-minister was visibly saddened when the hangman approached, ending his lecture. He was also disappointed that his children were not present. In one note from his death cell, he had written them, "Don't you want to go and see Pa hung?"

TURNER, Nat (1800-1831): Leader of slave uprising

In the bloodiest slave uprising in this country, Nat Turner, a 31-year-old slave foreman in Virginia who was permitted by his owner to perform as a black preacher, led a band of about 70 or 80 blacks on a 48-hour rampage that took the lives of 57 whites.

General Nat, as his followers were to call him, later confessed he had begun plotting his rebellion when,

> on May 12, 1828, I heard a loud noise in the heavens, and the Spirit instantly appeared to me and said the Serpent was loosened, and Christ had laid down the yoke He had borne for the sins of men, and that I should take it on and fight against the Serpent, for the time was fast approaching when the first should be last and the last should be first. . . .

At 2 a.m. on August 22, 1831, Turner and six other black slaves entered the mansion of Turner's owners, Mr. and Mrs. Joseph Travis, and hacked the couple to death in their bed. For the next two days the killing continued, the slave leader murdering only one victim, a frightened woman he battered to death with a fence post.

In his confession Turner stated:

> As I came round to the door I saw Will pulling Mrs. Whitehead out of the house, and at the step he nearly severed her head from her body with his broad axe. . . . We proceeded to Mr. Levi Waller's. . . . I took my station in the rear, and as it was my object to carry terror and devastation wherever we went, I placed 15 or 20 of the best mounted and most to be relied on in front, who generally approached the houses as fast as their horses could run, this was for two purposes, to prevent the escape of and strike terror into the inhabitants—on this account, I never got to the houses, after leaving Mrs. Whitehead's, until the murders were committed, except in one case. I sometimes got in sight in time to see the work of death completed, viewed the mangled bodies as they lay in silent satisfaction, and immediately started in quest of other victims. Having murdered Mrs. Waller and 10 children, we started for Mr. William Williams'—while engaged in killing him and two little boys that were there, Mrs. Williams fled and got some distance from the house, but she was pursued, overtaken, and compelled to get up behind one of the company, who brought her back and after showing her the mangled body of her lifeless husband, she was told to get down and lie by his side, where she was shot dead. . . .

Within two days whites began a massive counterattack. Posses of 2,000 local militiamen scoured the area, aided by a force of 800 federal troops. The succeeding reign of terror claimed an unknown number of blacks, somewhere between 100 and 200. Some were killed on suspicion of being in on the plot, but others were slaughtered, decapitated and had their heads posted on roads merely as a warning to other blacks. Of the actual rebels, a handful escaped the area entirely, many were killed and a total of 55 captured, including Nat Turner, who was caught some two months after the uprising. Seventeen were hanged, 12 were "transported" and 20 were found not guilty. The others died of their wounds before being tried.

See also: *Slave murderers.*

TWEED Ring

The Tweed Ring—or, more accurately, the Hall-Connolly-Sweeny-Tweed Ring—stands as the greatest example of civic corruption in American history. Estimates of the loot the ring took from the New York City treasury between 1865 and mid-1871 have been placed as high as $200 million.

The Tweed Ring reached its zenith of power on January 1, 1869, when the city's robber barons appeared to be unassailable. William Marcy Tweed, the boss of Tammany Hall, had placed his man, John T. Hoffman, in the governor's seat so that there would be no state interference in city affairs. And in the metropolis, the ring members—Tweed, president of the Board of Supervisors; Mayor A. Oakley Hall, known as the Elegant One; City Comptroller Richard B. Connolly, called Slippery Dick; and City Chamberlain Peter B. Sweeny, alias Bismarck or Brains—ran the city as if it were their personal fief.

As a rule of thumb, the spoilers determined they would steal one dollar for every two paid out by the city. This, of course, meant stealing in myriad ways, including fraudulent bond issues, the sale of all sorts of franchises and the granting of tax forgiveness acts and other favors in return for cash payments. Merchants and contractors could not hope to have dealings with the city unless they paid huge bribes. Even these tributes failed to satisfy the ring, whose arrogance and greed led them to award grants from the city treasury to non-existent hospitals and charities.

The Tweed Ring might have held power almost indefinitely given its control of the police, the district attorney's office and the courts and its influence over most newspapers. Even the opposition Republican Party and various reform groups were neutralized by Tweed's tactic of putting scores of their leaders on the payroll. The ring also controlled the underworld. The muscle of the great gangs of the period was at the disposal of Tweed and his cohorts in exchange for protection of the criminals in their illegal endeavors. During elections the gangsters brought out those who would vote right and scared away those not likely to. Tweed became legendary for his mass production of voters. On one occasion, with the aid of a corrupt judge, Tweed in 20 days naturalized 60,000 immigrants; few of them knew the nature of the oath or a word of the English language. When election day arrived, Tweed hacks showed them how to vote.

Two things finally dislodged the Tweed Ring from power: an incorruptible reform movement, headed by Samuel J. Tilden, and the near bankruptcy of the city as a result of the group's depredations. No treasury could forever survive paying out $10,000 for $75 worth of pencils, $171,000 for $4,000 worth of chairs and tables and $1,826,000 for plastering a municipal building, a job later estimated to be worth no more than $50,000.

No amount of power could have kept Tweed from being indicted once authorities discovered his own illegal profits totalled $12 million. The first trial of the Tammany leader ended in a hung jury, a number of jurors having been bribed. During the retrial the prosecution took the unprecedented action of having each juror watched by a plainclothesman, each of whom was watched by another police detective, who in turn was watched by a private detective. Each of these watchers were required to send in a daily report so that any variation in any surveillance account would immediately become apparent. Tweed was convicted and given a 12-year prison term and a number of Tweed Ring judges were impeached. It was obvious that Tweed and the judges were being made the scapegoats.

On appeal Tweed's sentence was reduced and he was released in 1875. Then the state instituted an action against him to regain the money he had stolen, and when he was unable to furnish bail, he was incarcerated again. In December 1875 Tweed fled the Ludlow Street Jail and made his way first to Cuba and then to Spain. Ironically, he was recognized from a Thomas Nast cartoon, taken into custody and returned to the United States.

In 1876 Tweed found himself once more confined in the Ludlow Street Jail. In failing health, he made a partial confession and offered to reveal everything if he was simply allowed to die outside of prison; amazingly, his offer was not accepted. Tweed died in jail in 1878 and with him the full secrets of the Tweed Ring.

TYRRELL, John F. (1861-1955): Examiner of questioned documents

More than a mere handwriting expert, he was, as numerous biographers and journalists have referred to him, "Mr. E.Q.D." John F. Tyrrell was, until his death in his active 90s, America's leading examiner of questioned documents. For well over half a century, Tyrrell appeared in some of the nation's most famous criminal trials and produced compelling testimony that aided in bringing about guilty verdicts. He could identify handwriting—as well as papers and inks—with unerring accuracy. In addition, he was able not only to trace typed documents to a specific machine but often identify the typist by his or her individual methods of stroking the keys.

Early in the century, in one of Tyrrell's most bizarre cases, he developed the evidence that sent two identical-twin forgers to prison. The Longley brothers, Lloyd and Leon, of Milwaukee, Wis., specialized in writing rubber checks. They not only looked alike, dressed alike and wrote alike but made use of the same signature—L. Longley. Whenever one L. Longley was passing rubber, the other L. Longley would be establishing a firm alibi. For every witness who identified the bum check passer, there were a dozen reputable witnesses who could place L. Longley on the other side of the city when the crime had occurred. It was Tyrrell who established the existence of the two Longleys and sorted out one signature from the other so that both brothers went to prison—separate ones since two men who looked, acted and wrote alike could wreak a unique form of havoc within the walls of the same penal institution.

As a youth in Milwaukee, Tyrrell exhibited a flair for handwriting, and right out of school, he was hired by an insurance company to use his skill addressing envelopes. Young Tyrrell began contributing squibs and sketches to the *Penman's Art Journal*, then edited by William Kinsley, one of the 19th century's few handwriting experts. Kinsley had once testified in a forgery trial, during which the defense attorney, seeking to trip him up, put before him a large batch of similar-looking handwriting samples and challenged him to pick out the three written by the defendant. Kinsley did so and won great notoriety for the feat. He then ran a contest in his magazine challenging his subscribers to do the same. There were only two winners: Tyrrell and another young handwriting buff, Albert S. Osborn of Rochester, N.Y., who was also destined to become a leading expert in the field and, with Tyrrell, one of the founders of the American Society of Questioned Document Examiners in the next century.

Impressed by Tyrrell's skill, Kinsley began recommending him to authorities as a competent handwriting expert. Meanwhile, Tyrrell had risen to the position of clerk in his employment and started studying signatures of documents received by the insurance firm. He was able to spot several as forgeries, particularly those on medical examination forms. Checking on his findings, the insurance company discovered that a number of insurance applicants were in poor health and were using healthy stand-ins in the examinations. Tyrrell's handwriting detective work put a stop to the practice.

Tyrrell received national attention when he testified as an expert in the sensational trial of Roland B. Molineux in 1899. Molineux was accused of sending poisoned Bromo Seltzer to an enemy, Harry Cornish. Cornish did not use the medication but gave some to his landlady, Mrs. Catherine Adams, who died of cyanide of mercury poisoning. Tyrrell, Osborn and Kinsley all testified for the prosecution and identified as Molineux' handwriting the writing on the poison package and on letters sent to several manufacturers requesting sample powders.

Tyrrell's testimony was the most spectacular of the three. For the first time he demonstrated his courtroom technique, which involved making large, rapid freehand reproductions of all disputed writing. At first the jury could perceive no difference. Then Tyrrell would show tiny variations that pinpointed the writer's specific style. Newspapers promptly dubbed him the Wizard of the Pen.

Molineux was convicted but the case was thrown out because of legal errors. He was retried later by a judge who refused to admit any nonsense, such as testimony from handwriting experts. Without such expert testimony, Molineux was acquitted. He later turned homicidal and died in an insane asylum.

Shortly after Tyrrell appeared in the Molineux case, he testified in another affair that proved even more sensational, the murder of eccentric millionaire William M. Rice in a plot by a corrupt Texas lawyer, Albert T. Patrick, to steal Rice's fortune. Tyrrell proved forgery by showing that Rice's signature on each of four pages of a purported will were identical in every detail, proof that they had been traced. Patrick was convicted.

Thereafter, Tyrrell was called in on almost every major case in which there was a questioned document or sample of handwriting. He solved the dynamite murder of Mrs. James A. Chapman in Marshfield, Wis. in 1922, a case in which Tyrrell had nothing more to work on than a bit of dynamite-charred wrapping paper with part of the address written on it.

In the celebrated case of Leopold and Loeb, defense attorney Clarence Darrow decided to plead the two "poor little rich boys" guilty to kidnap-murder charges only after he heard Tyrrell's evidence linking them to a typewritten ransom note.

Tyrrell was among the battery of experts called in to testify in the Lindbergh baby kidnapping, and he examined all 15 ransom letters. He often painted an amusing portrait of the various handwriting experts during the trial, most of whom refused to discuss their theories, secretly guarding their diagnoses. Tyrrell's evidence was generally regarded to be the best.

Tyrrell frequently said the attempt to forge an old document was often filled with too many boobytraps for the average criminal, or even the skillful one. One resourceful heir to a rich man's fortune sought to improve his minor inheritance manyfold by claiming to find a will, yellowed with age, in a book. The plotter had gone to great pains to make the paper look old and then botched up his hard labors, Tyrrell found, by composing the will on a typewriter with a typeface that had not been designed until some 15 years after the date of the will.

Tyrrell was still being consulted by authorities and other experts until his death at the age of 94.

See also: *Mrs. James Chapman.*

U

UNDERHILL, Wilbur (1901-1934): Bank robber

As a gangster roaming the Cookson Hills of Oklahoma, Wilbur Underhill, was second in fame only to Arthur "Pretty Boy" Floyd. Actually, he robbed dozens more banks than Floyd did, becoming known as the Tri-State Terror for his forays in Oklahoma, Arkansas and Kansas.

Underhill had been responsible for robbing an unknown number of small-town banks in the late 1920s until he was finally caught and imprisoned at the Kansas State Penitentiary. In September 1933 he broke out of prison with two other inmates, Bob Brady and Jim Clark, and made for the Cookson Hills. Brady and Clark then went their separate ways, which promptly led to their capture by the law, while Underhill joined forces with the Ford Bradshaw gang. Within a short time, Underhill became the real leader of the gang, in fact if not in name, as the group hit bank after bank. The loot was never enormous; in a typical robbery, in November 1933, the gang netted about $13,000 from a bank in Okmulgee, Okla. A short time later, Underhill decided he had enough money to take a vacation from his criminal activities in order to marry his childhood sweetheart over the year-end holidays.

On New Year's Day 1934 FBI agents, having traced the movements of Underhill's bride, surrounded the couple's honeymoon cottage in Shawnee, Okla. and called on the bank robber to surrender. Underhill's answer came from two handguns, and an incredible battle raged for the next 30 minutes, during which at least 1,000 bullets were fired into the cottage. Finally, Underhill, armed with a shotgun and wearing nothing but his long underwear, charged out shooting. Although bleeding from a dozen wounds, he somehow broke through the cordon of lawmen, raced down the street and dove through a store's plate glass window. The officers found him passed out inside the store. He died from his wounds five days later.

UNIFORM Crime Reports

Since 1930 the FBI has issued the *Uniform Crime Reports (UCR)*, which categorize "crimes known to the police" and arrest statistics. Just as it is charged that the Dow Jones averages don't measure total stock activity and trends, the same can be said about the *UCR*. The reports use seven felonies to gauge the distribution and trend of crime in the United States; they are murder, forcible rape, robbery, burglary, larceny, aggravated assault and auto theft, probably the seven crimes most likely to be reported to the police.

When the *UCRs* first appeared, there was much criticism of the quality of the data, which were based on the dubious figures supplied by local law enforcement agencies. Over the years the FBI has pressured local agencies to supply more accurate figures. There is little doubt the *UCRs* have led to improved law enforcement. For many years it was common for the police in New York City to discard a huge number of complaints in order to make their percentage of arrests look better. If a case appeared relatively easy to solve, it was filed; if it seemed like a hard one, it was discarded and naturally no work was done on it. In some cases citizens checking on the status of their complaints were ordered out of a station house. Because of the FBI's refusal to accept New York crime figures, reforms were finally instituted by the police in that city.

While the *UCR* figures are now accepted as being more authoritative than in the past, conclusions should be drawn from them only with extreme care. For instance, according to the *UCRs*, bank robberies in 1932 totaled 609, with the dollar losses amounting to $3.4 million. In 1975 there were 4,180 bank holdups, with the loot totaling $18,179,000. Yet, crime experts would say that bank robbery is much less of a problem now than it was in the Dillinger days. Allowing for inflation, population growth, the proliferation of bank branches that are more vulnerable to robbery, the sudden drop in liquor hijack-

Mass killer Howard Unruh after he surrendered.

ing as a criminal activity, better crime reporting and other factors, it would appear that crime has not made the dramatic gains which the raw figures would indicate.

Similarly, the annual murder rate, according to the most recent figures, now runs around 20,000. This figure, of course, represents *reported* and *detected* murder cases. A few decades ago it was estimated that for every murder reported another went undetected. Since then better scientific detection methods and the replacement of untrained coroners with professional medical examiners have no doubt led to the discovery of more murders. On the other hand, improved medical skills and techniques have saved the lives of many persons subjected to homicidal attacks. On balance, one cannot state responsibly that the murder rate has increased in recent years. Undue weight given to *UCR* statistics can often result in a "crime crisis" that is more apparent than real.

The value of the FBI statistics are not utterly worthless, as some critics have said. But neither are the critics of the *UCR* system "illogical and inane," as the late J. Edgar Hoover was prone to charge.

UNRUH, Howard (1921-   ): Mass murderer

A quiet 28-year-old Bible reader who had become infatuated with guns while serving in the Army, Howard Unruh killed 13 people in 12 minutes because he felt his Camden, N.J. neighbors were laughing at him behind his back.

On September 5, 1949 Unruh stepped from his home at 3202 River Road. Dressed in a tasteful brown tropical-worsted suit, white shirt and striped bow tie, he entered John Pilarchik's shoe repair shop at exactly 9:20 a.m. He approached within three feet of Pilarchik, who was hunched over nailing a heel to a shoe, pulled out a 9-mm Luger and shot him in the chest, killing him instantly.

Holding his pistol at the ready, Unruh calmly stepped back out in the morning sun, turned left and entered Clark Hoover's barber shop next door. Mrs. Edward Smith was in the barber shop with her young son and daughter. Her six-year-old boy, Orris, was sitting on a wooden hobby horse while Hoover cut his hair. Mrs. Smith, her daughter and two other boys waiting to have their hair cut hardly glanced at Unruh, thinking he was another customer. Unruh approached Hoover and said quietly, "I've got something for you, Clarkie."

Then as one would brush a branch aside, Unruh shot the little Smith boy through the head and chest. Now he could see Hoover better and killed him with shots to the head and body. Ignoring the screaming mother clutching the body of her dead son, Unruh turned and walked out to the street. When he didn't find druggist Maurice Cohen in his store, the crazed killer went upstairs to his living quarters and shot him to death. Unruh also gunned down pedestrians, motorists and three-year-old Tommy Hamilton, who was peeking out a window of his home. He shot 17-year-old Armond Harris in the right arm after slugging him with the pistol barrel. As his potential victim lay senseless, Unruh pulled the trigger again but there was only a harmless click. Although he had more ammunition in his pocket, he simply shrugged and trotted back home. The massacre, which claimed 13 lives, was over by the time police cars skidded to a stop on the street. Sixty policemen and detectives then laid siege to the Unruh home with pistol, rifle and submachine-gun fire. Unruh fired back only a few times. He was otherwise occupied.

During the siege his telephone rang. Unruh picked it up and calmly said, "Hello." At the other end of the line was Philip Buxton, assistant city editor of the *Camden Courier-Post*, who had decided to call the Unruh home after hearing about the rampage. He came up with one of the most bizarre interviews in history.

"Is this Howard?" Buxton asked. He could hear the shooting in the background.

"Yes, this is Howard. What's the last name of the party you want?"

"Unruh."

"Who are you and what do you want?"

"I'm a friend, and I want to know what they're doing to you."

Unruh's voice was steady. "Well, they haven't done anything to me yet, but I'm doing plenty to them."

"How many have you killed?"

"I don't know yet—I haven't counted them, but it looks like a pretty good score."

"Why are you killing people?"

"I don't know. I can't answer that yet, I'm too busy. A couple of friends are coming to get me."

Buxton heard the line click. He dialed the number again but there was no answer. Inside the Unruh home, tear gas cannisters were exploding. Unruh parted the curtains, raised his arms and said he was coming out. He walked out to face the muzzles of several dozen guns. "I'm no psycho," Unruh said in a formal tone. "I have a good mind."

His final score fell far short of what Unruh apparently had intended. Except for some ragged shooting by Unruh, the death toll could have been at least 30. There were a lot of people he still wanted to kill. "I'd have killed a thousand if I'd had bullets enough," he said.

Medical experts did not agree with Unruh's evaluation of his mind. Never tried for murder, he was judged incurably insane and committed to a mental institution, where he remains as this is written.

UNWRITTEN Law: Defense against murder charge

A notion long honored in American justice, although certainly not supported by statute, is that a man who has been cuckolded and murders his wife or her lover is somehow exempt from paying the penalty for his crime. This notion or custom, "the unwritten law," was if not first established firmly rooted in the shocking Sickles-Key affair of 1859, often described as "the case that wrote the unwritten law."

In 1859 the Honorable Daniel E. Sickles was a congressman from New York with a brilliant future ahead of him. His wife was the former Teresa Bagioli, the daughter of a renowned Italian operatic maestro, and he was a protege of President James Buchanan. Through an anonymous letter, he discovered his wife was being unfaithful, meeting regularly in a house on Washington's 15th Street with Philip Barton Key, district attorney for the District of Columbia and the son of Francis Scott Key, the composer.

Sickles determined the accuracy of the charge and then ordered his wife from his home after making her write a confession of her adulterous behavior. The next morning, February 27, 1859, Sickles was being visited by two close political friends when he looked out the window to see Key parading back and forth across the street, raising and lowering a handkerchief three times, the signal he used to summon Mrs. Sickles. Obviously, Key was unaware that anything untoward had happened concerning his liaison with Sickles' wife.

Abruptly, Sickles left the house and his guests. In a little park nearby, he confronted Key and shouted, "Key, you scoundrel, you have dishonored my house—you must die!" With that Sickles produced a Colt revolver and shot his wife's lover.

Key sank to the ground, wounded. Sickles pulled the trigger a second time but the weapon misfired. He produced another gun, a derringer, and shot Key a second time. Then he pointed the Colt at the fallen district attorney again, whereupon Key, in a weak voice, cried: "Don't shoot me! Please don't shoot me!" Sickles shot him once more, killing him.

Sickles returned home, washed up and then walked to the home of the attorney general and surrendered. The news of the murder and its motive caused a sensation. Sickles was not lodged in a cell but allowed to occupy a comfortable room in the warden's quarters. Among the steady stream of well-wishers to call on him were many members of the Cabinet, and it was rumored that President Buchanan sent words of support.

Sickles was indicted and selection of a jury began on April 4, 1859. In the three weeks it took to select a jury, over 200 talesmen had to be dismissed after expressing approval of the shooting. During the trial Sickles' lawyers invoked the unwritten law, insisting a husband had the *right* to kill an interloper in his marriage. The defense offered another relatively new defense, claiming their client had become "temporarily insane" at the sight of Key.

All the prosecution could do was argue that it was against the law to go about murdering people whatever the provocation. It was no contest. Eleven of the 12 jurors said afterward that they didn't even want to leave the jury box, but one did. He prayed in a corner for divine guidance and then joined the other 11 in bringing in a verdict of not guilty.

Sickles went on to become a Civil War hero, losing a leg at Gettysburg. It should also be noted that a few years after his unwritten law acquittal, he took his wife back. To criticism of that, Sickles retorted: "I am not aware of any statute or code of morals which makes it infamous to forgive a woman."

Since Sickles' time, the unwritten law had been more talked about than invoked, as most lawyers regard the temporary insanity plea a much surer strategy. But some defense lawyers have used it often. When a judge once told Moman Pruiett, a famous attorney during the first half of the 20th century, "Moman there ain't no unwritten law," the courtroom wizard replied, "There is if the jury says there is."

V

VALACHI, Joseph M. (1903-1971): Informer

Although not a very important member of the crime organization he identified as the Cosa Nostra, Joe Valachi remains to this day one of the few Mafia members who violated *omerta*, the organization's code of silence. In September and October 1963 the gravel-voiced, swarthy, chain-smoking killer held much of the television public enthralled as he related the inner workings of organized crime, the Mafia and the national crime syndicate to the Senate Permanent Investigations Subcommittee headed by Sen. John L. McClellan.

"Not since Frank Costello's fingers drummed the table during the Kefauver hearings," *The New York Times* noted in an editorial, "has there been so fascinating a show."

The tale Valachi told was a bloody one, including several murders that he himself had committed in the struggle for power within the New York Mafia, which controlled much of the underworld operations not only in New York City but in other parts of the nation as well. During his long criminal career Valachi had worked for Salvatore Maranzano from the late 1920s until the latter's death in 1931 and then for the Lucky Luciano family, whose leader had masterminded Maranzano's demise. Valachi, whose police record started when he was 18, was a "soldier," or "button man," whose duties included acting as a hit man, enforcer, numbers runner and drug pusher until 1959, when he was sentenced to 15 to 20 years on narcotics charges.

Valachi was sent to the federal penitentiary at Atlanta, where he was a cell mate of Vito Genovese, who had become the head of the Luciano crime family and, after Luciano's deportation to Italy according to Valachi, the "boss of bosses" within the Mafia. In 1962, Valachi later revealed, Genovese, after being falsely told that Valachi was an informer, gave him the "kiss of death" in their cell to let him know that he, Genovese, had ordered his murder. Valachi was terrified and subsequently mistook fellow prisoner Joe Saupp for Joe Beck (Joe DiPalermo),

whom Valachi identified as the man assigned to kill him. Valachi killed Saupp with an iron pipe. After receiving a life sentence for that murder, he decided to turn informer and get federal protection.

When Valachi "sang" for the McClellan Committee, he was guarded by some 200 U.S. marshals. The Mafia was said to have placed a $100,000 price tag on his head. But to the man who admitted participating in five killings the bounty on his life came as no surprise. "You live by the gun and the knife and you die by the gun and the knife," Valachi said.

While not everything Valachi testified to was new, he had, by the time he was through informing, helped to identify 317 members of the Mafia. Attorney General Robert F. Kennedy called Valachi's testimony "a significant addition to the broad picture" of organized crime. "It gives meaning to much that we already know and brings the picture into sharper focus." However, other law enforcement officials and some persons with underworld connections derided much of Valachi's testimony as little more than good theater, at least half erroneous and even ludicrous. Many doubted the description of Genovese as the boss of bosses, insisting there was no such animal and if Genovese ever achieved that level of power, he never held it for any length of time. Some said the very expression "La Cosa Nostra" was generally unknown in syndicate circles, or was at best no more than a propaganda slogan aimed at the soldiers on the lowest level of organized crime. The Cosa Nostra label proved exceedingly valuable to the FBI's J. Edgar Hoover, who for decades had insisted there was no such thing as a Mafia or organized crime in America. Suddenly, and with a straight face, Hoover could assert that the FBI knew all about the Cosa Nostra and that "agents have penetrated its workings and its leadership" for "several years."

Yet there can be no doubt that Valachi's testimony, supplemented by his memoirs, *The Valachi Papers* (1969), had a devastating effect on many mafiosi. It greatly reduced the importance of the Genovese family and loosed a new violent power struggle within the Mafia.

Once Valachi had completed his testimony, he became the most carefully guarded inmate in the federal prison system. He was moved several times before being confined in September 1968 in the La Tuna Federal Correctional Institution at El Paso, Tex. He died there on April 3, 1971. To this day it is not difficult to find underworld characters who insist that Valachi did not die, that the death report was "a con to let the Feds hide him on the outside."

See also: *Vito Genovese.*

VALENTINE, Lewis J. (1882-1946): New York police commissioner

Police commissioner of New York from 1934 to 1945 and known during his 42 years in the department as the city's "honest cop," Lewis J. Valentine paired perfectly with Mayor Fiorello H. La Guardia in the latter's efforts to "run out the bums and rats." Valentine had previously seen his fortunes rise and fall depending on the extent of corrupt political and/or criminal influences that infected various city administrations. Joining the force as a patrolman in 1903, he made sergeant after 10 years and later became a lieutenant on the "confidential squad," charged with rooting out corrupt and graft-taking members of the department.

However, while Richard E. Enright was commissioner, Valentine fell from grace and was continually passed over for captain despite achieving the highest score on civil service examinations. He was transferred to the wilds of Brooklyn to satisfy Tammany Hall, which was upset by his constant raids on politically protected gambling operations. Later, under Commissioner George V. McLaughlin, he returned to favor and was promoted to captain, deputy inspector, inspector and deputy chief inspector within a year. He became even more famous for his gambling raids and his incorruptibility. When Grover A. Whalen was named police commissioner by Mayor Jimmy Walker, Valentine was broken to captain and once more returned to Brooklyn. Years after, it would be revealed that Whalen's office received $20,000 a week from the forces of Lucky Luciano, probably the city's most powerful Valentine hater.

Shortly after La Guardia took office, he named Valentine police commissioner. While Valentine's "rough on rats" program occasionally upset civil rights advocates, a spirit of reform swept through the police department. "I'll promote the men who kick these gorillas around and bring them in," Valentine said, "and I'll demote any policemen who are friendly with gangsters." In his first six years he fired 300 policemen, officially rebuked 3,000 and fined 8,000.

Valentine was given credit for filling the higher ranks of the police department with more honest men than ever before in New York's history. Under his command the time-honored police practice of "proving" efficiency, whereby citizen's complaints were simply left unrecorded in order to achieve a higher "solved" record, was eliminated.

Valentine deserved most of the credit for forcing Murder, Inc.'s Louis Lepke to surrender, although J. Edgar Hoover grabbed the limelight. Valentine applied such heat to the underworld that the gangster barely had enough time to breathe, and he warned that he intended to keep it up until the mobs realized control of their operations would be threatened unless Lepke surrendered. When some civil liberties groups protested to Mayor La Guardia that such police harassment was unconstitutional, the Little Flower summoned Valentine to the meeting and said, "Lewie, these people claim you violate the Constitution."

Valentine replied, "So do the gangsters." And on that note La Guardia sent the protestors on their way.

Paying a unique compliment to Valentine during the 1945 mayoralty campaign, all three major candidates for the office publicly promised to retain him in his post. When William O'Dwyer won, Valentine chose instead to retire. He signed a lucrative contract to function as "chief investigator-commentator" for the "Gang Busters" radio show and he made several movie shorts on crime prevention. However, Valentine soon tired of that career and accepted an offer from Gen. Douglas MacArthur to reorganize the Japanese police department along the lines of the New York department.

Valentine returned to this country in 1946, resumed his radio career and wrote his autobiography, *Night Stick.* He died in December of that year.

VALENTINE'S Day Massacre: See St. Valentine's Day Massacre.

VALLEY Gang: Early 20th century Chicago gang

Chicago's Valley Gang was an Irish precursor of Al Capone's mob and later merged into the latter's operations.

What was to become a gang of hardened criminals in this century started out in the 1890s as a neighborhood play group on Fifteenth Street in the Bloody Maxwell section of the city. In the 1900s the Valley Gang began committing burglaries, picking pockets and, later, hiring out for murders. Around the time of World War I, the gang was under the leadership of Paddy Ryan, better known as Paddy the Bear thanks to his physique, who controlled much of the crime in Bloody Maxwell from a saloon he ran on South Halsted Street. Paddy the Bear was killed in 1920 by Walter Quinlan, known as the Runt. After serving only a few years in prison for the crime, the Runt was released and opened a saloon that became a rendezvous for trigger men and gangsters. When on one occasion the police raided the Runt's saloon, they collected a dozen automatic pistols, two machine guns and 10 bulletproof vests. The Runt's defiance of the Valley Gang ended when he was killed by Paddy the Fox, Paddy the Bear's son.

The most important leaders of the Valley Gang took over in 1920. They were Frankie Lake and Terry Druggan, who moved the gang into bootlegging and rum running. In time, the gang was the most prosperous criminal combine in Chicago. Even the lowliest members rode in Rolls-Royces. Naturally, such wealth gave the mob considerable leverage with the law in Chicago. In 1924 Lake and Druggan were sentenced to a year in prison for contempt of court, a punishment that proved to be laughable. A newspaper reporter who went to the county jail to interview Druggan was told, "Mr. Druggan is not in today."

The reporter said he would speak to Frankie Lake instead. The response was: "Mr. Lake also had an appointment downtown. They will be back after dinner."

The reporter's inquiry led to a major newspaper investigation, which revealed that, in consideration for $20,000 paid in bribes, Lake and Druggan were entitled to certain special privileges. They were permitted to dine regularly in the finer Loop restaurants and spent more time in their own apartments than they did in their cells. They came and went as they pleased and used the death cell in the jail as an office, where they met with their troops to give them instructions. The sheriff and jailer were later sent to prison for conniving in this arrangement.

The Valley Gang in subsequent years was absorbed into the Capone operation, in which its members continued to thrive. The Capone men always cited the Valley Gang as proof that Big Al took good care of the gangsters who joined him willingly.

VAMPIRES: Vice extortionists

Among the more loathsome types of extortionists prevalent in big cities during the 19th century were the "vampires," who made their living by victimizing men seen coming from a house of assignation. Vampires were generally young thugs who would follow a man back to his residence and then threaten to stand in front of his house chanting he "has just come from a whorehouse, just come from a whorehouse." In most vice districts the vampires were finally wiped out by the bordello operators themselves, who came to realize such activities were bad for business. They also took offense when vampires tried to extort money from some housewife-inmates returning to their own neighborhoods, where no one knew of their secret occupation.

In Chicago in the 1870s a particularly successful band of vampires was crushed because they harassed patrons of a large bagnio on Biler Avenue belonging to one Dan Webster. Unfortunately for the vampires, they did not know that the secret landlord of the building, and most likely Webster's partner, was Michael C. Hickey, the superintendent of police. The vampires deserted the area when they found that police would lay for them and give them a severe clubbing whenever they came within a block or two of Webster's place.

VASQUEZ, Tiburcio (1835-1875): Bandit

Tiburcio Vasquez, who terrorized California in the 1870s, was a far more proficient robber and killer than the legendary Joaquin Murieta, and unlike Murieta he enjoyed the protection of his own people, mainly because they saw his acts as revenge for their treatment at the hands of the Anglos.

A thief since his teens who had been in and out of prison several times, Vasquez launched a five-year reign of terror after his release from San Quentin in 1870. Together with a large band of men, he carried out scores of robberies of stores, stagecoaches, and travelers. After the gang killed three unarmed men during an invasion-robbery of the town of Tres Pinos, he became the state's most-hunted man.

In one of his most daring raids, Vasquez robbed the hotel and all the stores in the town of Kingston, after his men first had tied up all the male citizens they found in the streets.

The reward on him was raised again after the Kingston raid. But he was finally betrayed, not for money but for love. One of his own men, Abdon Leiva, caught Vasquez, a prolific womanizer, with his wife. After waiting a while, Leiva surrendered to the sheriff and told him where Vasquez could be found. A large posse cornered Vasquez in Cahuenga Pass (now Hollywood). Although wounded in the battle, the outlaw was taken alive. This may be attributed to the reward, which offered $3,000 for him alive but only $2,000 dead.

Transferred to jail in San Jose, Vasquez was honored by his people, as thousands came to visit him. A large number were women, but it was clear he enjoyed great affection as a champion of the Mexican community. Certainly Vasquez thought of himself in that light, declaring before he was hanged on March 19, 1875: "A spirit of hatred and revenge took possession of me. I had numerous fights in defense of what I believed to be my rights and those of my countrymen. I believed we were being unjustly deprived of the social rights that belonged to us."

VESEY, Denmark (1767-1822): Slave uprising leader

As a champion of black slaves in this country, Denmark Vesey had greater potential to lead a successful rebellion against white slave masters than Nat Turner was to have nine years later.

Certainly Vesey enjoyed the support of many more desperate slaves. He had become a freedman some 22 years earlier after winning a lottery and purchasing his liberty from his owner for $600. Later, while working as a carpenter, he plotted with Peter Poyas and several other blacks to foment an uprising of all slaves in Charleston, S.C. Slaves from up to 100 miles away joined the plot, making it impossible to keep secret. The uprising was planned for July 2, 1822, but more than a month before that date an informer told the authorities of the plan. Vesey and Poyas were arrested, but they denied all charges. When a third man, a slave, voluntarily surrendered after hearing he was wanted, the authorities tended to doubt the report, and all three were released.

Vesey then ordered the date of the insurrection moved forward to June 16, but once again the authorities were tipped off, this time on the night before the scheduled uprising. When the authorities found black sentinels already on guard at various points, they knew the report was accurate. Vesey, Poyas and 33 slaves were hanged and some 43 other slaves banished, dashing Vesey's bold plan to take control of Charleston and slaughter all slave holders.

See also: *Slave Murderers, Nat Turner.*

VICKSBURG "Volunteers": Vigilantes

In 1835 the irate citizens of Vicksburg, Miss. formed a law-and-order group and cleaned out the Landing area, which was controlled by an army of whoremasters, con men and gamblers. Theoretically, the Volunteers acted following the great hysteria that gripped the South as a result of John Murrel's grandiose plot to take over a number of Southern cities with an army of criminals aided by rebelling slaves. While some local criminals were undoubtedly involved in the plan, how anyone could have believed that the rich gambling elements would have participated much less benefited is a mystery. Yet, the Volunteers didn't discriminate when they swept into the Landing area and dragged known gamblers and hustlers from their saloons and gambling dens, hanging them by the dozen. Among those lynched were gambler John North and several of his aides, including Sam Smith, Dutch Bill, D. Hullum and a steerer known as McCall. North was notorious for having swindled a number of local residents out of their farms and land holdings through his crooked faro tables and roulette wheels. His victims were prominent among the Volunteers, and when he was hanged, his body was left on display for a considerable time with a crooked roulette wheel tied to it.

See also: *John North.*

VIGILANTE Noose: Warning symbol

The vigilante noose became a warning symbol for other potential malefactors following a great many vigilante hangings in the Old West. After a troublemaker was "strung up," he often was buried with one end of the rope still around his neck and the other end running out of the grave as a warning to others. The proponents of this device insisted it worked well and, as one put it, "don't stink up the air with a corpse hanging around for days."

VIGILANTES Of Montana

One of the most notable American outbreaks of vigilantism occurred in late 1863 and 1864 in the Montana Territory. Its aim was to wipe out an outlaw scourge that had brought most commerce, particularly the shipping of ore, almost to a standstill.

The vigilante activity focused on a notorious gang of killers and cutthroats surreptitiously headed by Sheriff Henry Plummer. Called the "Innocents," this criminal group in time had come to number over 100 members. Plummer, who was extremely persuasive and charismatic, was able to diffuse the vigilante movement for a while, but eventually, the activities of the Innocents became too blatant. Many of the gang's members were publicly identified, and Plummer himself was revealed as the brains behind their operations. At that point the vigilante movement formally organized under a covenant which read:

> We the undersigned uniting ourselves in a party for the laudible purpos of arresting thievs & murderers & recovering stollen propperty do pledge ourselvs & and our sacred honor each to all others & solemnly swear that we will reveal no

secrets, violate no laws of right & and not desert each other or our standerd of justice so help us God. As witness our hand and seal this 23 of December A D 1863.

The Montana Vigilantes never wore masks, were not night-riders and generally afforded a suspect a reasonable opportunity to prove his innocence. They also attempted to warn a malefactor to clear out of the territory before he faced sterner action. A paper bearing the numbers 3-7-77 was usually tacked on a suspect's dwelling as a warning to leave. The exact meaning of the numerals is no longer known, but those who took heed were spared the rope.

WARNING!

WARNING!   WARNING!

FOOT-PADS, THIEVES AND DANCE-HOUSE LOUNGERS MUST GET OUT OF LAKE CITY AND STAY---OTHERWISE HANG.

The Foot-pads who are known to be in this city are hereby warned to leave immediately and

SAVE THEIR NECKS!

The proprietors of the Dance Houses are notified to close them immediately, and saloon keepers are notified that they will be held accountable for any injuries that may occur to persons or property. Miners are requested to go to their respective places of work and remain there. Parents are enjoined to keep their children off the streets at night.

By order of **THE VIGILANTES.**

Vigilante groups in the Old West usually issued a warning—once—before acting.

The vigilantes struck late in 1863. In six weeks an estimated 26 Innocents, including Plummer, were hanged. The reign of vigilante terror continued for another year, during which several other outlaws were hung without any evidence of a miscarriage of justice. The vigilantes sported their own historian, Thomas J. Dimsdale, an Oxford graduate and English professor whose chronicle of the movement was published in a book entitled *Vigilantes of Montana.* It was perhaps the most-impassioned tract ever written in support of lynch law. The "best" people of the territory were involved in the vigilance movement, including Nathaniel Pitt Langford, the father of Yellowstone National Park; Colonel Wilbur Fisk Sanders, later one of Montana's first U.S. senators; and Nelson Story, one of the state's leading businessmen and ranchers.

A later Montana vigilance movement was launched in 1884 against cattle rustlers but was labeled by some as being no more than a murderous tool of the big ranchers and stockmen against homesteaders. Such criticism never sullied the 1863-64 movement. As Wayne Gard pointed out in *Frontier Justice,* "Their work had made it easier to set up effective courts and law enforcement agencies when the territorial government was formed a few months later."

See also: *Bannack, Montana; John X. Beidler; Thomas J. Dimsdale; Innocents; Frank Parish; Henry Plummer.*

VIGILANTES Of San Francisco

The first justice in the gold camps of California was administered by miners courts. As crime increased, virtually every community of any size in the territory developed its own similar vigilance committees. Of these, the most notable was the one set up in 1851 in San Francisco, where crime was running rampant. In June of that year a former Mormon elder named Samuel Brannan organized the San Francisco Committee of Vigilance, which was unique for groups of its type in that it afforded each accused man a formal and reasonably fair trial before hanging him. Its first act was to hang an Australian highwayman caught in the act of robbing a safe. The local police chief attempted to rescue the condemned man but was shoved aside by the vigilantes to a roar of approval from the thousands who jammed the streets to see the execution. By August three more of the city's leading lawbreakers received similar treatment before the committee officially disbanded.

By 1855 crime had soared again in San Francisco, and Brannan called for a new vigilance committee. Joining him were such prominent citizens as William T. Coleman and Leland Stanford, who later became governor and eventually U.S. senator. The first victims were two men who had killed a U.S. marshal. They were given an "orderly and dignified trial" and then hanged from the second story of the vigilantes' headquarters. This was followed by two of the state's most-celebrated hangings, that of an English criminal, Joseph Hetherington, and a New York hoodlum, Philander Brace.

Whenever a hanging took place, an English journalist reported, the hills were aswarm with humanity. "They seemed to cluster like bees on a tree branch, and for the purpose of seeing a criminal convulsed and writhing in the agonies of violent death! This desire seemed to pervade all classes of Americans in the city."

In defense of the vigilantes, it must be said that their second appearance was caused by corrupt city officials who had literally turned San Francisco over to the criminals. With the election of an honest city administration, the second committee dissolved after staging a triumphal parade through the streets with 5,000 marchers. The San Francisco Committee

achieved worldwide fame, and for the first time, lynch law on the American frontier escaped universal condemnation. Even *The Times* of London noted it was "seldom self-constituted authorities retire with grace and dignity, but it is due to the vigilante committee to say that they have done so."

VIKING Murders

If you grant the Vikings really were the first European discoverers of America, there can be little doubt that they were also the first white men to commit murder in the New World.

According to the Viking sagas, Leif Ericson and his brother Thorvald Karlsefni started a colony in the New World around 1,000 A.D. and almost immediately came face to face with a group of nine Indians. Instantly, they killed eight of them. Even if, as was to become an American custom, killing Indians didn't count, the Vikings still deserve a first for homicide. Freydis, Ericson's half-sister, and her husband murdered her two brothers and several others in the colony. Freydis personally axed five women in the group to death when her husband refused to do the deed himself. The survivors then returned to Greenland with an agreed-upon story that the others had chosen to remain in the New World.

VIRGINIA City, Montana: Lawless mining town

No list of the most murderous towns in America, would be complete without the mining camp of Virginia City in what is now Montana.

Gold was discovered along Alder Gulch in 1863, and within weeks an estimated 10,000 miners had created the mining town of Virginia City. Like all mining towns, it was plagued by violence, in this case supplemented by the depredations of outlaw Sheriff Henry Plummer and his Innocents. Virginia City had the distinction of having 190 murders within a six-month period. Statistically, the figure worked out to a four percent chance that a man would meet a violent end there within a year and that over a 25-year period he was almost certain to contract lead poisoning.

Perhaps, it was fortunate that the placers started running out within just a few years and Virginia City began a steady decline toward becoming a ghost town. Today, with its ghost town features well preserved, it is the state's top tourist attraction.

See also: *Innocents, Henry Plummer.*

VOICEPRINTS: Identification method

Almost certainly in future years, despite misgivings by civil rights proponents, a national computerized file of sound spectograms or voiceprints will join the archives of fingerprints. Slowly, voiceprints are gaining legal recognition, although not without judicial objections. Advocates insist that for purposes of identification they are as reliable as fingerprints and far more reliable than handwriting comparisons. They insist that no two voices have ever been found to be exactly alike.

The developer of the technique, Lawrence G. Kersta, described his methods before the Acoustical Society of America in 1962. At the time a Bell Telephone researcher, Kersta insisted that after studying thousands of voiceprints, he concluded that no two human voices were exactly alike, not even those of identical twins, and that it was impossible to fool the spectograph by disguising a voice. Voiceprinting involves the use of a tape recorder and a spectograph, a device that turns speech sounds into visible disgrams, much as electronic impulses are turned into pictures for television. In one of Kersta's early tests, involving 25,000 spectographs, researchers were able to make a correct identification of the speaker with an accuracy rate of over 97 percent. Kersta has since held that with properly trained technicians accuracy would approach 100 percent.

Police have successfully used voiceprints in cracking cases involving telephone extortion demands and obscene phone calls. The findings of voiceprint experts have been allowed as evidence in some court proceedings but not permitted in others. Following the Watts riots, the Columbia Broadcasting System decided to air a TV program in California entitled "Watts: Riot or Revolt," which included an interview with a 19-year-old black youth who admitted taking part in the riot. As he was interviewed, the youth's identity was carefully concealed by camera angles and lighting. However, police obtained a sound spectrograph of the interview and, based on Kersta's findings, eventually made an arrest. Kersta was permitted to testify in court and the youth was convicted and sentenced to a term of one to 10 years. In October 1968 the California District Court of Appeals reversed the verdict, finding: "Kersta's admission that his process is entirely subjective and founded on his opinion alone, without general acceptance within the scientific community, compels us to rule that voiceprint identification has not reached a sufficient level of scientific certainty to be accepted as identification evidence in a case where the life and liberty of a defendant may be at stake."

Later that same year a New Jersey court permitted the introduction of voiceprint evidence in support of the defense, although the judge indicated he would forbid such evidence if presented as proof of guilt. Kersta's testimony in the case was instrumental in gaining the acquittal of a man convicted in a lower court of making obscene telephone calls.

In 1978 courts in Maine allowed spectrographic examiners to testify, applying ordinary evidentiary standards, which call for weighing the reliability and relevancy of the evidence against its tendency to prejudice, mislead or confuse a jury. That same year the U.S. Court of Appeals for the Second Circuit made a similar decision. On the other hand, Maryland's highest court, at about the same time, ruled out the use of voiceprint tests. Still, legal experts tend to believe the thrust is toward eventual acceptance of voiceprints as evidence in legal cases.

Perhaps the most famous use of voiceprints occurred in the case of Clifford Irving's forged biography of Howard Hughes. Although he denied the biography was authentic, Hughes refused to appear in public to attack the book. He did, however, agree to a telephone interview with seven newsmen who had known him. After he had answered their questions, all the newsmen were satisfied that the man they had talked to was Howard Hughes. Anticipating Irving's certain claim that the man was an imposter, the prosecution retained Kersta and another voiceprint expert, Dr. Peter Ladefoged, to judge the authenticity of the voice after studying sound spectrographs of the telephone conversation and comparing them with those of earlier recordings made by Hughes. Irving later confessed his hoax.

Nevertheless, the possibility of a computer bank of voiceprints has caused apprehension in many quarters. Opponents of the idea cite a report published by the *New York Post* in 1973 that the FBI, acting on behalf of the CIA, had asked a radio station, WMCA, which featured a "call-in" program, to record all incoming phone calls critical of President Richard Nixon and his associates. Although the station denied there was such a blanket demand, it said that it recorded all conversations and that the CIA had requested a recording of a specific conversation about the administration that was of a threatening nature. It remains clear that voiceprinting probably involves more "police state" potential than most other methods of identification.

Further reading: *Voice Printing* by Eugene Block.

VOLLMER, August (1876-1955): Berkeley, California police chief

The father of the modern scientific police force, August Vollmer is generally acknowledged today as having been America's most far-sighted and influential police chief. As chief of police in Berkeley, Calif. from 1905 to 1932, he created a department far ahead of its time. Though not a scientist, he steeped himself in all the latest scientific developments and looked for ways to apply them to police work. He even anticipated police radio communications before the introduction of the radio, devising a method whereby patrol cars could answer emergency calls with incredible speed for that era. Vollmer had special signal lights connected to police headquarters installed at all major intersections. When a crime was telephoned in to headquarters, the signal lights in the area of the crime were blinked on and off. Officers seeing the flashing lights would immediately telephone in for instructions on where to go.

Considering his later distinguished career, Vollmer had an unimpressive background. He had been a Philippine Scout in the U.S. Army and later a postman in Berkeley before becoming a police officer. Once on the force, his rise was meteoric. After he became chief, Vollmer recruited only the best possible candidates for job openings on the force. He had the advantage of having to maintain only a small department, for a long time just a few more than 30 men, and thus could, as he said, "be fussy." Most of the recruits he picked had at least some college background in the sciences. Early on in his post, he said: "We believe in employing every method known to modern science that will keep us at least one jump ahead of the criminal—not one jump behind." Under Vollmer's guidance the country's first formal training school for policemen was established in

Berkeley in 1908. His crime laboratory, though modest in size, became famous as one of the most efficient in the nation, and was consulted by many other departments on matters of identification and development of clues.

Every new scientific development interested him. He was particularly intrigued by the experiments being done in the area of lie detection and assigned a colleague, John A. Larson, to construct a lie detector that the department could use. Larson produced the first polygraph, and when Larson moved on to other law enforcement positions, Vollmer had a brilliant student at the University of California, Leonard Keeler, perfect the device and develop what became known as the Keeler Polygraph.

Vollmer credited many of his solutions to crimes to the fact that he simply was well read in the police sciences. Once, he solved a case without ever leaving his office. At a conference with some of his officers who were making no headway in solving an outbreak of arson cases in a certain neighborhood, Vollmer leaned back in his chair and said: "Well, I'd check the neighborhood very thoroughly. Ring doorbells. I'd look for a feeble-minded person, preferably one who hasn't been living in Berkeley very long and who might be homesick."

Without understanding why, the officers followed Vollmer's instructions and solved the case. A feeble-minded youth who had recently moved to California to live with relatives readily confessed to setting the fires. When the officers later expressed their amazement to Vollmer, he showed them a book, *Criminal Psychology* by Hans Gross, an Austrian criminologist, and had them read a chapter on nostalgia. Gross expounded on a theory that when a feeble-minded person is uprooted and moved to a new environment, he often becomes homesick. Somehow, he tends to relieve this feeling by starting fires.

After retiring from his post in 1932, Vollmer was active as a writer and lecturer on police work. Perhaps the best measure of his contribution to police work was that in the 1940s there were 25 police chiefs around the country who at one time had served under him in Berkeley.

WADDELL, Reed (1859-1895): Swindler

Among the most successful American swindlers to operate both in this country and in Europe during the last century, Reed Waddell was an artful practitioner of the green goods racket and without doubt the greatest of all at the gold brick swindle.

Some historians erroneously credit Waddell with originating the gold brick game in New York in 1880, but there is ample evidence that the racket was pulled before that. It is known, for instance, that Wyatt Earp and Mysterious Dave Mather were selling "gold bricks" to gullible cowboys in 1878 in Mobeetie, Tex. Even though Waddell did not invent the game, he certainly made it pay off more than anyone else had.

The son of a very rich and respectable Springfield, Ill. family, Waddell refused to go into the family business and instead gravitated to gambling circles. In 1880 he turned up in New York with the first gold brick to be offered for sale there. The brick was actually a lead bar covered with three platings of gold and containing a slug of solid gold in the center. Waddell would tell a potential sucker that he was forced to sell the brick. He would then guide the victim to an accomplice posing as an assayer, who would declare the brick pure gold. If the victim was still dubious, Waddell would impulsively dig out the slug of real gold in the center and insist the man take it to a jeweler himself for another test. When the assay turned out positive, the sucker was hooked. Waddell sold his first lead brick for $4,000, never got less than $3,500 and often made twice that price.

Another of Waddell's cons was the green goods swindle. In this scheme Waddell would show a sucker some real money, tell him it was counterfeit and then offer to sell him a large batch of the bills at bargain prices. Once the sucker was convinced the merchandise was absolutely undetectable, he would eagerly agree to make a big buy. At the time of the transaction he would again be shown real money, but at the last moment the package containing the bills would be switched for a similar-looking one in which there was nothing but cut-up pieces of green paper. From 1880 to 1890 Waddell took in more than a quarter of a million dollars with these two schemes before switching exclusively to gold bricks, a scam whose advantage was the great time lag before the victim realized he'd been taken. Waddell found Europe, especially Paris and London, an ideal locale for pulling the gold brick swindle. In March 1895 he was killed by another swindler named Tom O'Brien in a dispute over the split in one of their capers.

See also: *Gold Brick Swindle, Green Goods Swindle.*

WAGNER, John F. (1893-1950): Embezzler

It has been said that the motives for most embezzlers are one or more of the three R's: rum, redheads and race horses. What made one of this country's greatest embezzlers so different was that he was motivated by none of the three.

John F. Wagner was the cashier of the First National Bank in the little coal town of Cecil, Pa. When the bank examiners came calling one Monday morning in 1950, they found Wagner sprawled dead on the floor next to the vault, a bullet in his head. Soon, they discovered why. The 57-year-old Wagner, a resident of Cecil all his life, was short the sum of $1,125,000.

But the motivation for the embezzlement remained a puzzle, since Wagner didn't wench, drink or gamble. In fact, he only owned two winter suits, one of which he was buried in. The examiners solved the puzzle when they found a note in Wagner's handwriting. "The reason for the shortage was because of paying checks that were not good." Appended to the note was a list of persons who had defaulted on their loans or had written scores of rubber checks. Townspeople had an explanation for Wagner's downfall: he was a complete soft touch who never could turn away a friend in need.

Authorities went about trying to make as many people as possible meet their debts. But for Wagner, it was too late.

See also: *Embezzlement.*

WAITE, Dr. Arthur Warren (1887-1917): Murderer

In 1916 Dr. Arthur Warren Waite, a leading New York dental surgeon and a brilliant germ culture researcher at Cornell Medical School, committed two of this country's most-celebrated poison murders. He is remembered, however, not so much for his deeds as for his style, which, if nothing else, proved that a knowledge of medical science doesn't necessarily make a person an efficient killer.

Dr. Waite was an exceptionally handsome man in his late twenties. Tall, athletic and debonair, he had made a considerable impact on New York's Upper West Side society. An expert tennis player, he won several tournaments; Franklin P. Adams and other well-known tennis addicts considered him to be the best player on the local courts. Waite was also devoting a good deal of attention to making himself a millionaire. That he figured to do by wiping out his wife's parents, millionaire drug manufacturer John E. Pick and his wife of Grand Rapids, Mich. When the Pecks, in their seventies, passed away, Waite's wife stood to inherit approximately $1 million.

Mrs. Peck came to visit the Waites for Christmas in 1915. Waite took his mother-in-law out driving with the windshield open in a pouring rain so as to bring on pneumonia. He put ground glass in her marmalade. He sprayed her throat with bacteria and viruses known to cause influenza, anthrax, diphtheria and streptococcus. Some of Mrs. Peck's friends commented on how well she looked, and she did have a nice rosy-cheeked face. Finally, however, the old woman died on January 30, 1916, with doctors attributing her death to kidney disease. Waite wasn't at all sure whether she had died because of or in spite of what he had given her, but he was determined that no one else would know either. He had his mother-in-law cremated, which he said was her last request.

Mr. Peck, saddened by his wife's death, came to visit the following month. While consoling him, Waite filled his galoshes with water, dampened his bed sheets while he slept, opened a container of chlorine gas in his bedroom while he slept and even fed him a mixture of burned flypaper and veronal. When Peck developed a sniffle, Waite gave him a nasal spray laced with tuberculosis bacteria. Nothing happened.

Becoming desperate, he gave the old man 18 grains of arsenic, presumably enough to kill a team of horses. Peck took to bed but did not die. Finally, Waite took a pillow and smothered him to death. That, of course, worked, and Waite went out celebrating with his mistress. He was seen by a woman friend of the family, who thought it was callous of him to be carrying on in such fashion with his father-in-law's body not even cold. In an anonymous letter to the authorities, she accused the dentist of poisoning Mr. and Mrs. Peck. Large amounts of arsenic were found in Mr. Peck, and police investigators traced the poison to Waite, who finally confessed his entire plot.

Waite died in the electric chair at Sing Sing on May 24, 1917. He was annoyed when guards came to escort him to the death chamber because they interrupted his reading of a vol-

ume of Robert Browning's poetry. Waite marked with a pencil the last lines he had read:

> "Life's a little thing!
> Such as it is, then,
> pass life pleasantly. . . ."

WALKER, James J. (1881-1946): Mayor of New York

New York's inimitable Night Mayor, Jimmy Walker was the most important municipal chief executive ever forced from office on corruption charges. The silver-tongued politician became mayor in 1925 and soon demonstrated that he enjoyed the high life as well as the night life of New York far more than the grueling detail of running the world's richest city. In many respects the glib Walker was right for a fun-loving New York saddled with a Prohibition law that wouldn't work and a wild prosperity that wouldn't last. Under Walker the city sunk to new lows of corruption, with the mayor himself accepting money in both hands.

At the time Walker took office, the Luciano-Costello forces were making their first weekly graft payments to the police commissioner's office, initially $10,000 and within a few years $20,000. For this sum the gangsters' operations were allowed to function without interference as long as no innocent civilians were harmed and sometimes even if they were. Now and then, following negotiations between a police official and Luciano, a "raid for show" would be carried out, with attention given to ways of limiting the damage.

These payoffs were never traced to Walker, since he collected what was considered a better class of money. None of the graft taking and corruption became public knowledge until the various Seabury probes began in 1930, by which time Walker had won reelection, defeating a popular reformer, Fiorello La Guardia, by a huge margin. New York loved their Night Mayor, who paraded down Broadway and could be seen almost every night in the classier speakeasies in town, such as the Central Park Casino. Besides being the Night Mayor, Walker was also the Late Mayor, never arriving at City Hall before noon and almost never being on time for an appointment.

Perhaps the grimness of the onsetting Depression doomed Jimmy Walker as much as the probings of Samuel Seabury, but those investigations certainly took the bloom off his administration. Seabury started out focusing on the misdeeds of the New York Police Department, especially its vice squad, which concentrated on making the city safe for hookers. There were shocking tales of reputable housewives being blackmailed by cops, who told them they would have to pay money or face vice charges that would wreck their lives and marriages. Before she was murdered, a prostitute-madam-blackmailer named Vivian Gordon made even more shocking revelations about police misdeeds.

As the Seabury inquiry widened, the spotlight shifted to general municipal corruption until Walker himself was caught in the glare in 1932. He was summoned to take the stand before the Hofstadter Joint Legislative Committee, counseled by Seabury. It proved to be a difficult and embarrassing day for Walker. He denied allegations by Seabury that an accountant named Russell T. Sherwood—who could not be located—was his front man. It was shown that Sherwood had banked over $700,000 and had on one occasion, just before Walker sailed on a trip to Europe, withdrawn $263,838. Finally, the mayor was forced to concede that over a four-year period he had pocketed $432,677. Nor could Walker satisfactorily explain how he had earned $26,000 in oil stock deals with taxi-cab mogul J. A. Sisto without ever investing a penny of his own money. Evidence was presented that J. Allan Smith, a contact man for a bus company in search of franchises, staked Walker to a $10,000 letter of credit for a European vacation and came through with another $3,000 when the mayor ran over his expense budget. Then there was the $246,000 profit in a joint stock account with Paul Block, a Brooklyn publisher and financier. Block's testimony hardly helped Walker's case; the publisher said his 10-year-old son had once noted that the world's richest city paid its mayor a trifling pittance ($40,000 a year), so Block determined "to make some money for Jimmy."

During the Seabury Investigation, New York's "Night Mayor" of the 1920s, James J. Walker, was forced to make damning admissions about his huge secret income and subsequently resigned from office.

Armed with this testimony, Seabury took the case against Walker to Gov. Franklin D. Roosevelt. Walker beat the prosecutor to the punch on September 1, 1932 by wiring Roosevelt: "I HEREBY RESIGN AS MAYOR OF THE CITY OF NEW YORK . . . JAMES J. WALKER."

He then promptly sailed for Europe in the company of his showgirl-mistress. Walker did not return to America until 1935, when the heat from the investigations had cooled and he was certain he would no longer be prosecuted. The ex-mayor found New York in a forgiving mood and he enjoyed considerable popularity. He reminded the city of a time that was

colorful, sometimes charming and even elegant, although extremely corrupt. Walker represented the "good old days." It was hard to hate a man who had taken a ton of money and had now rather obviously run through it. Jimmy Walker simply was Jimmy Walker. Even such a hard-nosed exponent of honesty as Mayor La Guardia understood that. He appointed his predecessor to a $20,000 a year job as head of industrial and labor relations with the cloak-and-suit industry. Walker was still remembered fondly for years after he died in 1946.

See also: *Vivian Gordon, Seabury Investigation.*

WALKER, Jonathan: Last legal branding victim

Branding for criminal offenses was a common punishment in America from the 17th century until 1844, when Jonathan Walker became the last man to be judicially branded. He had the initials SS, for slave stealer, burned into the palm of his right hand. Walker had been convicted of attempting to help slaves escape to the Bahamas. Walker's experience was the inspiration for John Greenleaf Whittier's abolitionist poem "The Man With the Branded Hand."

See also: *Branding.*

WALL, Tessie (1869-1932): San Francisco madam

The best-known parlor house madam in San Francisco from 1900 to 1917, Tessie Wall was described as a "flamboyant, well-upholstered blonde." Her most famous brothel, at 337 O'Farrell Street, was regarded as the Golden Gate City's greatest fun palace. She stocked it with beautiful, slightly plump girls, remarkably all of them blondes. She charged what was then an outrageous price, $20, for an assignation. But the clients seemed to feel it was worth it and said Tessie Wall's services were "super." Overnight guests could expect to find their clothes pressed and shoes shined when they awoke in the morning. Those who were not staying and had to get back across the bay to Oakland would be interrupted by Tessie and informed, "You just have time to catch the last ferry."

As was true of many famous madams, Tessie Wall in later life was invested with perhaps more colorful accomplishments than she deserved, such as the journalistic credit for inventing the phrase, "Company, girls!"; those words were probably first uttered by an earlier madam, Bertha Kahn. In Tessie's case, this sort of embroidery was pointless since her own legitimate achievements were quite sufficient to make her famous. An incredible drinker, she once drank boxer John L. Sullivan under the table. Tessie was amazingly generous with the police and generally led off the Grand March at the annual policemen's ball on the arm of Mayor Sunny Jim Rolph. She started things rolling at such affairs by slapping a $1,000 bill down on the bar and shouting, "Drink that up, boys!"

Long married to Frank Daroux, a gambler and owner of a number of brothels, she resisted his entreaties that she leave the business and become a country housewife on a lavish estate that he had bought for her in San Mateo County. Once, Tessie told him, "I'd rather be an electric light pole on Powell Street than own all the land in the sticks." After Daroux finally divorced her, Tessie begged him to return. When he refused, she sent word to him that she would fix him so no other woman would ever want him. She did her best to keep her word in the summer of 1916 by firing three bullets into his body from a .22-caliber revolver. When the police arrived, she was standing over him crying, "I shot him because I love him—damn him!"

Daroux survived, and although the shooting permanently weakened him, he refused to testify against Tessie and she was released. Tessie retired from the business in 1917 during a wartime wave of reform that wiped out the Barbary Coast and most of the sordid features of her bailiwick, the so-called Upper Tenderloin, which was the city's best theater and restaurant district. Years of wild living and gambling had reduced her fortunes considerably, but she had enough left to establish herself comfortably in a nice flat on Eighteenth Street, taking with her many of the furnishings from her O'Farrell Street place, including a needlepoint wall motto that read, "If every man was as true to his country as he is to his wife—God help the U.S.A." Tessie died in April 1932.

WALL Street Explosion: New York bombing

Probably the most intensive police hunt in New York's history followed an explosion on Wall Street at noon on September 16, 1920.

On that day a horse-drawn wagon containing a concealed bomb was left in front of the U.S. Assay Office, opposite the J. P. Morgan Building. As during any other weekday lunch hour, clerks, stenographers, bankers, brokers and messengers choked the narrow streets. The only out-of-the-ordinary activity was the transfer by workmen of gold ingots, worth $15,000 each, to the Assay Office from the U.S. Sub-Treasury building next door.

At 12:01 p.m. the bomb exploded, killing 30 persons and injuring another 300. The pavements were littered with people writhing in agony or deathly still. Many had had limbs ripped off. A number of those still able to walk hobbled to nearby Trinity Church to take refuge. Bomb fragments rained into the House of Morgan, killing one employee inside. Other financial houses were badly damaged. Panic ensued in the New York Stock Exchange, as brokers racing for exits collided with one another, tumbling into heaps.

The disaster sent a shudder throughout New York and, as news wires crackled, stunned the entire nation. There was near unanimous opinion that the explosion had been the work of anarchists or other radical terrorists. Instantly, various public and financial buildings and men of great wealth were placed under heavy guard. In Chicago police cordoned off the Stock Exchange and other buildings in the La Salle Street sector. Similar measures were taken in Philadelphia and Boston. In New York a force of 30 private detectives guarded the J. P.

Morgan home on Madison Avenue, and pedestrians were not permitted to pass in front of the mansion. Forty armed guards ringed the Pocantico Hills estate of John D. Rockefeller.

William J. Flynn, chief of the Secret Service, announced: "This bomb was not directed at Mr. Morgan [who at the time was in Scotland] or any individual. In my opinion, it was planted in the financial heart of America as a defiance of the American people. I'm convinced a nationwide dynamiting conspiracy exists to wreck the American government and society."

A large number of suspects were questioned, including the anti-Communist Carlo Tresca and his group of Italian "terrorists." Tresca was later cleared, as were others, mostly foreigners deemed to have a hatred for Wall Street and what it represented. After a time some theorized that the dynamiting was the work of criminals who had planned a bold robbery of the gold bullion. According to this theory, having been slowed by traffic, the thieves were forced to flee the wagon because the bomb had already been activated and was about to go off.

Nothing much came of that theory either. In fact, all the massive investigation ever turned up was a horseshoe. Although it was traced to the manufacturer, the shoe produced no lead to the identity of the owner of the horse and wagon.

WALLACE, George W.: See Arthur Herman Bremer.

WALSH, Johnny "The Mick" (?-1883): Gang leader and murderer

Leader of the Walsh gang, a power on New York's Bowery in the 1870s and early 1880s, Johnny "the Mick" was a brutal gangster known to kill not only his victims but also any other crooks daring to operate on what he regarded as his turf.

The Walshers carried on a war with the Dutch Mob, a rival outfit of sneak thieves, muggers and pickpockets, for supremacy along the Bowery. Walsh personally feuded on a number of occasions with Johnny Irving, one of the Dutch Mob's leaders, and at least three times, the pair engaged in knife fights without doing one another serious damage. The police, for their part, did not interfere in the battles between the two gang leaders. Superintendent of Police George W. Walling was quoted as saying that only good could come of the bad blood between the pair; his words proved prescient. One day in late 1883 Johnny the Mick was standing at the bar of Shang Draper's notorious saloon on Sixth Avenue when Johnny Irving walked in with a friend, Billy Porter. The two gangsters stood glaring at each other for several moments. Suddenly, Johnny the Mick drew a pistol and shot Irving dead. Immediately, Billy Porter drew a gun and killed Johnny the Mick. Whereupon Shang Draper pulled a gun and shot Billy Porter. Porter survived, and no charges were pressed against him or Draper, each of whom claimed he was "keeping the peace." The police were satisfied, being rid of both Johnny Irving and Johnny the Mick.

See also: *Johnny Irving.*

WALSH School Feud

Undoubtedly, the most remarkable schoolboy feud in American history occurred in Chicago at the Walsh School on Johnson Street. A war between two rival gangs of schoolboys broke out in 1881 and continued for almost three decades, during which several boys were killed and more than a score were shot, stabbed or severely beaten with clubs or brickbats. A number of pitched gun battles were fought both inside and outside the school by the two gangs, which were known as the Irishers and the Bohemians, although ethnic origin was not the real touchstone of allegiance. Place of residence was the important factor, with boys living east of Johnson Street constituting the Irishers and those west of Johnson making up the Bohemians.

For years the boys came to school armed with revolvers and knives and on many occasions they would take pot shots at one another in the classrooms. Some of these little gangsters were only 10 years old and so small that they had to use both hands to even lift their weapons to firing position. The last major gunfight between the rival gangs occurred in December 1905, when 25 Irishers and an equal number of Bohemians blazed away at each other outside the school until police arrived. Finally, authorities launched daily searches of all pupils going into or leaving the school and confiscated all weapons found. This continued for several years until the level of violence dropped.

WARD, Return J. M. (?-1857): Murderer

Return Ward's execution was said to have attracted the largest crowd to attend a hanging in pre-Civil War Ohio. His crime was regarded as so heinous that the jury found him guilty without allowing him to finish his testimony.

A hulking lout, Ward had often mistreated his wife, Olive, until she finally left him. Early in 1857 she succumbed to his pleas and returned to him, much against the advice of friends and neighbors. When Olive was not seen for 24 hours, a horde of neighbors descended on the Ward home and accused Ward of killing his wife. They could not, however, find her body. The people were entirely right in their suspicions but had not thought to look under the couple's bed, where Ward had stowed his wife's freshly killed body when he heard the crowd approaching.

As soon·as everyone left, Ward dragged his wife's corpse into the kitchen, cut up her body with a carving knife and an ax and threw it piece by piece into the fireplace. The next day Ward cleaned out the hearth and placed the ashes outside the house. Neighbors keeping watch immediately searched the ashes and found the dead woman's jaw bone.

Ward was brought to trial within the week, and the multitude that descended on the trial scene in Sylvania expected a hanging forthwith. They were not disappointed, as the trial got no further than Ward's claim that he had killed his wife by accident and in panic had cut up her body. He was going into a detailed description of burning the corpse when the jury simply announced it would listen no more and was prepared to bring in a verdict. They then sentenced Ward to death. While legal scholars in later years might cite the Ward case as an example of an illegal verdict and a "legal lynching," Ohioans of the day felt justice had been served quite well.

WARDE, John (1912-1938): Suicide victim

Probably no suicide has ever been matched for drama, suspense and the ghoulish interest of the American public as that of 26-year-old John Warde in New York on July 26, 1938.

Warde, who two years earlier had been confined for a time in a mental hospital following a suicide attempt, was in room 1714 of the Gotham Hotel at Fifth Avenue and 55th Street when he told his sister, Katherine, "I'm going out the window." Before she could prevent him, he climbed out on a ledge 18 inches wide and 160 feet above the street. For 11 hours he stood there deciding whether or not to jump and warning police he would leap if any of them came near him. The structure of the building made it impossible for firemen to trap him with a large net, and as the drama continued, a huge crowd gathered to watch. Press photographers, newsreel cameramen and radio commentators set up shop on the street and in offices around the hotel, and the entire nation listened anxiously to reports of every move the slender, curly haired man made. Many of the spectators on the street called on Warde to jump.

Patrolman Charles V. Glasco, sitting on the window ledge with a noose around one leg, seemed to develop a rapport with the disturbed man and kept him talking about everything from sports to poetry while trying to lure him close enough so he could grab him. But as the night wore on, Warde still refused to come to safety. Finally, as Patrolman Glasco left his perch to make room for a boyhood friend of the would-be suicide, a roar went up from the crowd below. Warde had jumped. He landed on the hotel marquee and then bounced to the street, dead before he hit the ground. It was later estimated that the news media had spent $100,000 to cover the event.

WAREHOUSE Brothel

A newspaper article in early 1857 referred to a notorious establishment called the Warehouse Brothel as the most-depraved dive in Chicago; it became even more infamous for what was labeled in retrospect the Little Chicago Fire.

Housed on the second floor of a brick warehouse at 109 South Water Street, the brothel had a large population of resident prostitutes and a long row of cubicles that were rented to streetwalkers. Because of complaints by neighbors, the police raided the warehouse brothel almost continually to break up boisterous drunken orgies. On October 19, 1857 a drunken prostitute kicked over a lamp and in the quick-spreading fire 23 persons died and the brothel and surrounding property valued at a half-million dollars were destroyed. All the victims were either male customers or residents of the area. Being trained, thanks to previous police raids, to make quick escapes, none of the harlots died in the conflagration. It was several days before talk of lynching the harlots died down. After the Great Chicago Fire in 1871, the Warehouse Brothel tragedy was often referred to as the Little Chicago Fire.

WARNER, Matt (1864-1938): Bank robber and lawman

Willard Erastus Christianson was the hell-raising son of a Mormon bishop who became known as Matt Warner, or the Mormon Kid, a close companion of Butch Cassidy and the other Wild Bunchers.

They say young Warner would not have gone wrong if he had not gotten into a fight in 1878 in which he thought he had killed his opponent. Only 14 at the time he ran off and fell in with rustlers. Later, he worked with outlaws out of Robber's Roost in the Utah Territory and eventually met up with Butch Cassidy. In 1889 Butch, Matt and Tom McCarty held up the Telluride Bank in Colorado, making off with $31,000. After that, Butch, Matt and others earned quite a living robbing banks and rustling cattle and horses.

In the early 1890s Warner used some of his loot to open a saloon in Star Valley, an area on the Wyoming-Utah border. A bit of a wit, he covered the back of the bar with the most expensive wallpaper ever used, stolen bonds and bills, in the center of which was a $10,000 note that the gang had obviously reckoned they would never be able to cash.

In 1892 Warner and George McCarty were arrested in Ellensburg, Wash. for a bank robbery in Roslyn, Wash. While they were in jail, other Bunchers supplied them with tools and pistols, and two days before their trial the pair broke out and got as far as the livery stable, where McCarty was winged. Warner got off a shot that wounded an attacking citizen before the pair was forced to surrender. Remarkably, Warner and McCarty beat the bank robbery charge and were set free, their escape try overlooked because innocent men were sometimes allowed to attempt desperate measures in that era.

In 1896 Warner was arrested for a bank job and faced certain conviction. Cassidy immediately rounded up the Wild Bunch for a raid to free him. After word of the raid was passed to Warner, he talked Cassidy out of the attack on the ground that it was too risky. Instead, Cassidy had the boys rob a bank and contributed a large portion of the proceeds from the robbery to Warner's legal defense. Warner got off with just five years, on the whole a rather light sentence.

By the time Warner got out of prison, the Wild Bunch had busted up, Cassidy and the Sundance Kid fleeing to South America, where they continued in the robbery business. Warner settled in Carbon County, Utah, was elected justice of the peace and became a deputy sheriff. He worked as a policeman in Price, Utah, moonlighting on the side as a bootlegger. At the age of 74, Warner died a much-respected citizen.

There were reports that in his later years Warner often visited with Butch Cassidy, who, according to these reports, had not died in South America as the Pinkertons claimed. If he did see Cassidy, Warner carried that secret with him to the grave.

See also: *Butch Cassidy, Wild Bunch.*

WATERED Stock: Swindle

"Watered stock" is the term used to describe a stock swindle in which the assets of a company, real or imagined, have been exaggerated to attract gullible investors.

The term is believed to have originated out of a time-honored tradition in cattle country. Unscrupulous stockmen would drive their animals to market while giving them all the dry feed stuff they could hold down. Just before reaching the selling yards, the cattle would be allowed to drink all the water they wanted. Since the animals were sold by weight, the watered stock brought in considerable extra profits.

WATERFORD Jack (1840-?): Chicago streetwalker

Chicago's most industrious, wealthiest, and, paradoxically, most honest streetwalker in the last century was, as the *Chicago Times* called her, "a notorious old jade known as Waterford Jack." She was also known as the Millionaire Streetwalker and boasted that she had walked the streets every night, regardless of weather, for 10 years, accommodating from five to 25 men a night at prices ranging from $1 to $10.

In 1875 Waterford Jack decided to put streetwalking on a structured level, organized a band of streetwalkers and rented living and working space on the top floors of office buildings in the business district. She became the girls' manager and business agent, seeing to it that they kept themselves attractive and clean and, each day at "shape-up," assigning them to the areas they were to work. The choice girls were sent to the hotels and railroad stations.

Every night the streetwalkers would turn over their earnings to Waterford Jack, who would give each a small amount of spending money for food and clothing. After paying for police protection and, when needed, the services of bondsmen and lawyers, she would subtract a small cut for herself and bank the rest in trust for the girls. Apparently, none of the streetwalkers ever feared that Waterford Jack would steal any of the money and, indeed, she never did. Several, in fact, had enough saved for them to open their own brothels. Waterford Jack entertained no such desires, saying simply she would retire when she had saved $30,000. A red-light newspaper, the *Chicago Street Gazette* reported in 1877:

> Waterford Jack has $22,000 in the bank, every cent of which she had picked up (so to speak) on the streets of Chicago. Jack (her right name is Frances Warren) has made money. It is said to her credit that she never stole a cent and was never drunk in her life. She is a pug-nosed, ugly-looking little critter, but for all that she has prospered in her wretched business, and now stands before the world the richest street-walker in existence.

When Waterford Jack faded from sight in 1880, vice society in Chicago knew she had achieved her magic number of $30,000.

WATSON, Ella: See Cattle Kate.

WATSON, J. P. (1870-1939): Bluebeard

As a one-man murder machine, J. P. Watson, America's premier Bluebeard, ranks with the world's worst. He had all the charm and verve of France's Henri Landru, the killing efficiency of Germany's Peter Kurten and the utter lack of morals of Gilles de Rais of the 15th century, who is regarded by historians as the original Bluebeard.

Watson killed more women than most of his European rivals, although the exact number is undetermined. He is known to have married at least 40 women and killed at least 25 of them. The rest got off with just losing all the money they had given to Watson in their blind passion to marry him. Several of his wives followed him from one end of the country to the other, and even after he was sent to prison for murder, they remembered him wistfully for his passionate poetry and the grace with which he had wooed them. They were lucky he had not tired of them, but many others were not so lucky. Watson bashed in about a dozen skulls and wrung an equal number of pretty necks. He hid his victims so well that none were ever found except one, whose whereabouts he eventually revealed voluntarily.

Watson was born Charles Gillam in Paris, Ark. He ran away at the age of 12 and, thereafter, always used the pseudonym of J. P. Watson, varying the first name to whatever struck his fancy. He killed his first woman in 1893, a passionate hillbilly girl who had run off with him and then announced she was pregnant. After she mentioned marriage, Watson fed her poison and took off with her possessions. After that, he never murdered another woman before marrying her. Years later, he said he felt his victims were entitled to a measure of happiness before he separated them from the living.

By 1913 Watson had married 10 women and killed four of them. Then he started getting serious about his calling. To attract victims, he advertised:

> *Gentleman:* Neat appearance, courteous disposition, well-connected in business, has quite a little property, also connected with several corporations and has a substantial bank account. Would be pleased to correspond with refined young lady or widow, object matrimony. This advertisement is in good faith, and all answers will be treated with respect.

Watson leafed through hundreds of responses to pick out likely victims. Between about 1915 and 1920 he confined his amorous and murderous activities to the West Coast, from Vancouver, British Columbia to southern California. He dumped wives in such scenic spots as Idaho's Lake Coeur d'Alene and Seattle's Lake Washington. Others went into fast-running rivers. Watson never understood why some murderers had their corpses refloat to the surface. When he weighted a body down, it stayed down. The same was true of the many corpses he buried. He buried them deep, no shallow graves that animals or heavy rains would uncover.

Watson's downfall came about as a result of suspicions that had nothing to do with his murderous activities. One of his wives became suspicious of his constant traveling and, thinking he was two-timing her, hired private detectives to follow him. He was caught by police with a huge amount of loot from previous victims, including at least a dozen diamond rings from different-sized fingers.

Yet, even when the authorities knew they had a master bluebeard on their hands, they could not bring murder charges against Watson. Not a single body could be found. Then while he was in custody in California, the body of a woman turned up in Plum Station, Wash. Watson had done some burying there and he worried that the corpse was one of his victims. So he made a deal with the Los Angeles district attorney to reveal the hiding place of one of his victims provided the DA guarantee him no worse than a life sentence and fight any extradition effort. Since without a body there was no case, the DA consented. The deal was made and Watson led officers out to the desert where he had buried Nina Lee Deloney.

Afterward, Watson confessed to eight other murders and hinted at many more. His confession created a firestorm throughout the country. Dozens of people wrote asking for information on missing loved ones. Watson shunted such requests aside, saying he couldn't be expected to remember every woman he had married or exactly what had become of them.

In 1920 Watson was convicted and drew a life sentence. He died in San Quentin on October 15, 1939. Ironically, his murder confession had been uncalled for; the corpse found in Plum Station proved not to be one of his.

WE Boys Mob: Swindlers

One of the most audacious group of swindlers in America was the so-called We Boys Mob of the 1920s, who consistently hoodwinked the supposedly cynical and savvy journalists of the nation's newspapers. The gang, often no more than two fast talkers, would hit a newspaper city room with a sad tale about the death of some "old-time newspaperman," a story that was fictitious but profitable. The spiel would go something like: "We boys are getting together to see that he gets a decent burial and have something in the pot afterward for the widow, and knowing how all you guys feel about the boys in the business, we were sure all of you would like to make a small donation to build the kitty." There were just a few news rooms exempt from such flimflams, which would only be discovered when the old reporter would one day saunter into the office. The racket died after newspapers ordered much closer checking of facts whenever the death of a journalist was reported.

WEBSTER, John White (1791-1850): Murderer

A crime that might have been spawned by the imagination of an Edgar Allen Poe and has been called "America's classic murder" occurred in Boston on the afternoon of November 23, 1849. Dr. George Parkman, for whom the Parkman Chair of Anatomy had been established at the Massachusetts Medical College, called on Dr. John White Webster at the school to demand repayment of a loan. Dr. Webster (MA, MD, Harvard) who led a rather notorious wild life, said he could not make payment, whereupon Parkman shouted, "I got you your professorship and I'll get you out of it." In a rage Webster grabbed a heavy piece of kindling wood and smashed Parkman in the head. Parkman fell to the floor. When Webster examined him, he found Parkman was dead. The confrontation took place in a laboratory in the basement of the medical college building.

Webster dragged the body into an adjoining room and placed it in a huge sink. He then climbed in the sink and calmly began dissecting the corpse. When he finished, he incinerated the pieces in his assay oven. Some larger pieces he put in a vault used for storing the bones of dissected bodies.

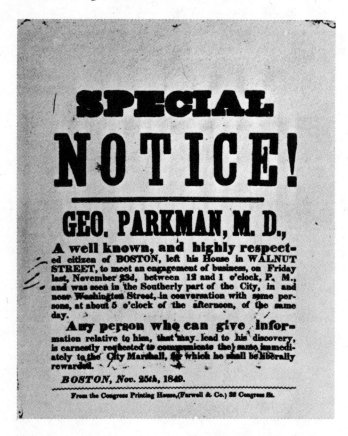

A city marshall poster asking for information concerning the whereabouts of Dr. George Parkman before his grisly fate was determined.

Quite naturally, the disappearance of Dr. Parkman caused a considerable stir and the college posted a reward of $3,000 for the apprehension of his apparent abductors. One of the few leads in the case came from Dr. Webster, who told of Dr. Parkman coming to visit him and accepting a $483 payment on his loan. The authorities theorized that the money provided a possible motive for robbery and continued their search. They did not suspect Dr. Webster. However, a college janitor named Ephraim Littlefield did. He had noticed that on the afternoon of the disappearance the wall behind Dr. Webster's assay oven had been very hot. When he later mentioned the fact to Dr. Webster, the latter seemed nervous and said he had been doing

some experiments. The next day, in an uncharacteristic gesture of generosity, Webster gave the janitor a Thanksgiving turkey, but the gift only heightened Littlefield's suspicions. A week after the disappearance, he used a crowbar to take some bricks out of Webster's vault and found a fleshy pelvis and parts of a leg. When the police were summoned, they made other grisly finds, including the most incriminating, that of Parkman's teeth in Webster's oven.

The trial of Dr. Webster in 1850 was a sensation. Among those testifying were Oliver Wendell Holmes, who by then occupied the Parkman Chair, Drs. W. T. G. Morton and C. T. Jackson, the discoverers of ether, and Jared Sparks, president of Harvard. Newspapers as far away as New Orleans sent special correspondents, and instant booklets relating the testimony appeared. Since an estimated 60,000 persons showed up to view the trial, the judge ordered that spectators could sit in the balcony for only 10 minutes at a time.

Webster pleaded not guilty and insisted the cut-up parts belonged to a routine cadaver, but the clinching evidence against him was the positive identification of Parkman's teeth by dentists. After an 11-day trial Webster was found guilty. Prior to his hanging on August 30, 1850, he made a full confession.

WEGER, Chester (1939-   ): Murderer

The savage robbery and murder of three well-to-do Chicago matrons in Starved Rock State Park, Ill. in March 1960 attracted nationwide attention. In investigative circles it is remembered as one of the most embarrassing cases in the annals of scientific detection. Police laboratory tests that should have pointed to the killer did not, and the murderer, 21-year-old Chester Weger, managed to do what many experts had claimed was the impossible, beating the lie detector, not once but twice.

The bodies of the women, Mrs. Lillian Oetting, Mrs. Mildred Lindquist and Mrs. Frances Murphy, wives of prominent businessmen, were found bound with twine and hidden in a cave. Nearby was a bloodied tree limb, some four inches thick, with which their killer had battered them to death. During the long investigation hundreds of persons were questioned. For a time the most promising suspect was Chester Weger, a dishwasher employed at the park's lodge. He was reported to have had a scratched face on the day the women had been murdered.

When police interrogated him, they discovered he had a bloodstained leather jacket, which they immediately sent to the police laboratory. While tests were being made on the jacket, Weger agreed to submit to a lie detector examination. The conclusion was that he was telling the truth when he denied any connection with the brutal crime. Then the laboratory analysis of the jacket found the stains were animal blood, as Weger had claimed. Authorities, reluctant to give up on the youth as a suspect, gave him another lie detector test. Once more, he passed with flying colors.

Weger was dropped as a suspect, as were all other local persons, and the police concluded that the women had been the victims of a transient thief. Two local deputies, Wayne Hess and William Dummett, were not convinced, however. They went back to the twine used on the women, which was originally thought to be of too common a type to be traced. The officers found the twine was a 20-strand variety and compared it with the twine used at the Starved Rock Lodge; it too had 20 strands. The lodge had bought the twine from a Kentucky manufacturer, who informed the officers that very few of his customers purchased that kind of twine. The lodge, in fact, was the only one in Illinois.

The deputies again centered their investigation at the lodge. Since the original investigators had casually dismissed the twine as a clue, the two deputies wondered if perhaps the rest of the inquiry had been just as poorly handled. Among other clues, the officers secured Weger's jacket again but this time sent it to the FBI Laboratory in Washington. Technicians there identified the stains as being human blood and most likely from the same group as that of one of the victims.

Weger was once more a suspect, but there was the troublesome matter of the lie detector tests. A top expert, John Reid of Chicago, was called in to perform a new test. This time the machine clearly indicated Weger was lying when he denied committing the murders. Meanwhile, Hess and Dummett had searched the records of previous crimes in the area and found a case in which a girl had been raped not long before the triple murders. The victim had been tied up with twine exactly like the cord used in the murders. Given a number of photographs of various men, she readily picked out one of Weger as her attacker.

Confronted with this new evidence plus the revised blood analysis and the incriminating polygraph findings Weger confessed. On March 4, 1961, Weger's 22nd birthday, he was convicted of the three murders and was later sentenced to life imprisonment.

Reid was asked how he could account for two previous failures by the lie detector before he, unlike the previous examiner, was able to get the incriminating results. "Simple enough," he said. "It's all a matter of technique—in knowing how to conduct such an experiment effectively." Weger himself had an entirely different rationale. "Before the tests," he said, "I just swallowed a lot of aspirin and washed it down with a bottle of Coke. That calms a guy down, you know. Why I didn't do that before this other guy tested me I'll never know."

See also: *Lie Detector*.

WEIL, Joseph "Yellow Kid" (?1875-1976): Con man

Joseph "Yellow Kid" Weil probably invented and practiced more swindles than any other confidence operator in the history of American crime and was most certainly the greatest con man of the 20th century. The only many to come close to him was Fred "the Deacon" Buckminster, who ironically started out in life as a plainclothes policeman in Chicago working on the vice and bunco squad.

In 1908 Buckminster had a warrant to pick up Weil after a

waterproofing cover he had been paid to paint on some city buildings washed off with the first rains. As Buckminster was escorting Weil to the precinct house, his prisoner handed him a wad of bills. Buckminster counted $10,000. "How'd you get this?" he asked. Weil said from his swindles. Buckminster weighed the money in one hand and his badge in the other. He pocketed the money, tossed away the badge and shook hands with the Kid. They became partners in scams for the next quarter century.

Even in his twenties Weil could affect a most earnest and dignified appearance. At the turn of the century he and Colonel Jim Porter, a former riverboat gambler, carried off what became known as the Great Michigan "Free Land" Swindle. Weil introduced Porter around as an eccentric millionaire who was giving away free lots. The pair gave the lots to prostitutes, madams, bartenders, waiters and even Chicago policemen. The two then opened a sales office and showed the usual artist's concept of a huge vacationland planned for the area, provided the supposed millionaire didn't give all the lots away before it was completed and ready for sale. Whenever Porter would give away some lots—which he and Weil had purchased at $1 an acre—Weil would sidle up to the sucker and beg him not to tell anyone else or everyone would be wanting free lots. He also advised the recipients of the land to make sure they had the transaction recorded at the county seat in Michigan. That was the key to the swindle. The recording fee was $30 and the recorder happened to be Porter's cousin. Previously, the fee was $2 but Porter's cousin had raised it with the understanding that $15 would go to Weil and Porter and he would keep the rest. Weil and Porter made just over $16,000 from this neat little flimflam.

In another of his great cons Weil posed as mining engineer Pope Yateman, who reportedly had garnered a fortune in Chile. Yateman was written up in *McClure's* magazine under the title "$100,000 A Year," together with a large picture of him. For a price a crooked printer who specialized in "first editions" of famous books agreed to substitute Weil's picture for Yateman's and reprint the required pages. Weil rebound the pages into actual copies of the magazine and then toured the Midwest trimming the gullible. He and a confederate would zero in on a rich man eager to invest in mining ventures and then Weil's confederate would mention the article in *McClure's*. Unfortunately, the confederate would say, he had no copies of the magazine, but "I'm sure you'll find one at the local library."

The swindlers had, of course, pinched the library copy and substituted a doctored one. The gullible victim would rush to the library, find the article with Weil's picture and be totally convinced. As soon as Weil milked a huge investment from the sucker, his confederate would retrieve the doctored copy of the magazine and return the original. As Weil often recalled later, "You can imagine the victim's amazement after being swindled, to go to the library and look up that article only to find that the picture did not resemble me at all!"

One of Weil and Buckminster's greatest coups was renting a vacant bank in Muncie, Ind. and stocking it with con men and their lady friends to act as depositors so that the pair could con financiers into investing in the bank.

Born in Chicago in 1875, Weil started hanging out in underworld dives early in life, almost always with a copy of the *New York Journal*, which contained his favorite comic strip, "Hogan's Alley and the Yellow Kid." Soon, all the crooks in town started calling Weil the Yellow Kid. He married young and had a devoted wife who spent most of her years trying to get him to go straight. Weil often tried for her sake, but even his honest efforts proved tainted. He once attempted to make a living selling a Catholic encyclopedia; using the name Daniel O'Connell, he told a priest in Flint, Mich. that the Holy Father, Pius X, had expressed the wish that at least 2,000 copies be placed in homes in Flint. The priest bought a set, and on the strength of that, Weil sold 80 more sets, earning $1,600 in commissions. Then the priest learned of Weil's imposture and canceled his order. Weil went back to his basic con rackets, selling phony stock and running phony boxing matches and horse races.

Although extremely glib, Weil, like other con men, was frequently arrested. Usually, he beat the rap because almost always his victim was put in a position of having been knowingly involved in a crooked scheme. "I never cheated an honest man," Weil often proclaimed, "only rascals." Still, he was convicted several times and did a number of stretches in prison. In 1934 Weil announced he had retired from the swindle game. Of course, he was lying. He had by then made some $8 million through his cons and was not about to give up the game.

Weil was always ready to lend a hand to a parish for a fund drive. One day he was walking down a Chicago street with a certain monsignor discussing a fund drive when a member of the police confidence squad stopped him and questioned him on his activities. Weil insisted he was on the level. The monsignor joined in to back him up, whereupon the detective turned on him and said, "You, aren't you ashamed to be wearing the cloth for a swindle?" The officer took both of them in and held them for questioning.

In 1948 the Kid decided to write his memoirs with Chicago journalist W. T. Brannon, once again announcing he was going straight. He proceeded to sell the movie rights to his autobiography to Brannon and then to a Hollywood studio.

One of his last attempted coups was to try to establish a little independent republic on a small island made of fill, somewhere in Lake Michigan. His object, he told Saul Bellow in a magazine interview, was to make himself eligible under the foreign aid program.

Weil died February 26, 1976. Newspapers listed his age as 100, a goal he often said he planned to attain. Quite a few printed records, however, indicated Weil was really born in 1877 rather than 1875, as he claimed in his later years.

See also: *Fred Buckminster, Great Michigan "Free Land" Swindle.*

WEISS, Hymie (1898-1926): Gang leader

The man who succeeded the assassinated Dion O'Banion as head of Chicago's North Side Gang during Prohibition, Hymie

Weiss continued O'Banion's gang war with the forces of Al Capone. Chicago police credited Weiss with being the one responsible for building O'Banion's bootlegging business into the empire it became. He was more thoughtful, forward-looking and resourceful than the headstrong O'Banion and used reason and bribery more freely than "Deanie" had. Despite the fact that he, like many gangsters, especially members of the North Side mob, regularly attended Mass and was never without crucifixes and rosaries in his pockets, he had a brutal and ugly disposition. He also carried a gun or two and killed without qualm or pity.

Weiss' real name was Earl Wajciechowski, which was soon changed upon his family's arrival in the United States from Poland. He was an accomplished crook in his teens, doing duty as a burglar, car thief, hired slugger and killer for labor unions and as a safecracker. The last skill won him a spot in the O'Banion gang, which specialized in jewel thefts and other safecracking jobs. The Irish gang leader toasted Little Hymie as the "best soup artist in Chicago." With the onset of Prohibition, O'Banion moved into bootlegging, and Weiss acted as his right-hand man in convincing saloon keepers of the value of O'Banion's merchandise.

Weiss wept openly at O'Banion's grave when the latter was buried in November 1924, following his murder by Capone's gunmen. Although Capone boldly appeared at the services with six bodyguards, Weiss kept the O'Banions in line, having promised the Irishman's widow there would be no violence until their beloved Deanie was under ground. Besides, there were 100 detectives on hand to maintain the peace. A reporter asked Weiss if he blamed Capone for O'Banion's death. The gangster threw up his hands in mock horror and said: "Blame Capone. Why Al's a real pal. He was Dion's best friend, too."

Weiss maintained the fiction of peace with Capone for almost two months, even banishing Two Gun Alterie from the gang because he kept publicly threatening Capone with vengeance. Meanwhile, Weiss lined up more gunners and bided his time. On January 12, 1925 Weiss, Schemer Drucci and Bugs Moran followed Capone's black limousine until it parked in front of a restaurant at State and Fifty-fifth streets. As they drove slowly by, they raked the vehicle with 26 pistol and shotgun blasts, wounding the chauffeur but missing two bodyguards in the back seat. Capone had stepped into the restaurant 15 seconds earlier.

Weiss' most famous attempt to kill Capone occurred in Cicero on September 20, 1926, when 11 automobiles filled with his gangsters drove past the Hawthorne Inn and poured more than 1,000 bullets and slugs from shotguns, handguns and machine guns into the establishment. A Capone bodyguard and an innocent woman bystander were shot, but Capone again escaped injury.

Three weeks later, On October 11, 1926, Weiss himself was on an undertaker's slab, his wiry body having been ripped open by 10 machine-gun bullets as he crossed the street to his headquarters above O'Banion's flower shop at 738 North State Street. His bodyguard, Paddy Murphy, was killed instantly by the same fusillade, which came from a second-floor room rented by the assassins the day after the Cicero raid. Three others walking with Weiss were wounded.

Weiss was 28 at the time of his death and had a fortune conservatively estimated at $1.3 million. His funeral was lavish, although his wife complained he had only 18 truckloads of flowers while O'Banion had been honored with 26 and a previously departed gangster, Nails Morton, had merited 20. It had to be explained to her that since the onset of the war with Capone, some 30 of Hymie's friends had abruptly departed the world, greatly reducing the number of available flower donors.

See also: *Alphonse "Scarface Al" Capone; Vincent "Schemer" Drucci; Hawthorne Inn; George "Bugs" Moran; Samuel J. "Nails" Morton; Charles Dion "Deanie" O'Banion; One-Way Ride; Standard Oil Building, Battles of the.*

WEISS Club: Chicago brothel

Located right next door to Chicago's opulent Everleigh Club, perhaps the most lavish brothel the world has ever seen, the Weiss Club operated in a strange, if luxurious, anonymity. The Everleigh sisters always credited the Weiss Club with being the only establishment that provided their resort with genuine competition. Yet, the name of the Weiss Club was unknown to all but a few vice insiders, and most of the patrons who sampled the pleasures offered there, came away believing that they had been in the Everleigh Club.

The club, located at 2135 South Dearborn, was run by Ed and Aimee Weiss. Ed Weiss was a seasoned "male madam" in Chicago, having operated some of the city's worst dives. He had "stepped up in class" in 1904, when he married Aimee Leslie, one of the most beautiful courtesans of the Everleigh Club. It was probably Aimee's idea to buy the brothel next door later that year and turn it into an imitation of the Everleigh Club. They were able to get it for a song from Madam Julia Hartrauft, who had just been robbed of over $3,000 by stickup men. Madam Hartrauft took the couple's money and left the area, bemoaning the lack of law and order in Chicago.

The Weiss Club was done up with luxurious appointments and stocked with women who would have been at least runners-up at the Everleigh and thus could command high fees. However, the real reason for the success of the resort was the fact that Ed Weiss shrewdly put most of the vice area's cabbies on commission. Whenever one of them picked up a fare who asked for the Everleigh Club and seemed too drunk to know where he was going, the cabbie would simply bring him to the Weiss establishment. Invariably, the customer would enter the club, be properly entertained and leave all the while thinking it was the Everleigh.

Both the Everleigh Club and the Weiss Club went out of business about the same time in 1911 during a crackdown on vice ordered by Mayor Carter Harrison, Jr. In an attempt to recapture the old glory, Weiss leased the building of the shuttered Everleigh Club in 1913, making preparations to pay the police $25,000 a year for protection, but the deal never came off because of continued antivice campaigns. Although Weiss remained a force within the Capone brothel empire into the 1920s, his dream of a grandiose new Everleigh-Weiss Club never came true.

See also: *Everleigh Sisters.*

WEISS Family: See White Family.

WELCH, Bernard Charles, Jr. (1940-   ): Master thief and murderer

Described by police as a one-man crime wave, Bernard C. Welch, Jr. was a remarkable master thief whose career ended in December 1980, when he was apprehended for the Washington, D.C., murder of Dr. Michael J. Halberstam, a noted cardiologist and author. Through the years since 1965, when he was 25, Welch was arrested a total of 25 times but avoided confinement on a number of occasions by jumping bail or escaping detention. His main activity was burglary, and often when free on bond, he went about committing additional thefts. He specialized in stealing furs, art objects, rare coins and silverware. Wherever he went, Welch lived in style, paying cash for luxurious houses, in one case almost $250,000 up front.

It can only be guessed how much money Welch made from 1965 to 1980 despite several years in prison during that time; it may have been anywhere from $10 to $20 million. Francis M. Mullen, assistant director of the Federal Bureau of Investigation, said of him after his capture in 1980:

> Welch has operated as a one-man crime cell; that's why he has been so hard to catch. . . . He has been so smart, melting much of the stuff to prevent it from being traced. He was a loner, so that it reduced the chance of someone close turning him in. He specialized in burglary, the type of crime hardest to solve. He was lucky, he never walked into one of our sting operations. And he was talented and well-trained.

From 1974—when he escaped from New York's Dannemora Prison by hiding on the grounds following a softball game and scaling a 25-foot fence after dark—to 1980, Welch was perhaps the FBI's most-sought criminal, with 15,000 circulars describing him and his method of operation distributed to police.

During those six years Welch continued his big-money capers and lived high on the hog, finally winding up in Great Falls, one of the more affluent suburbs of Falls Church, Va. He lived with his common law wife and three children in a $245,000 house, into which he poured an estimated $750,000 worth of improvements, including a huge indoor swimming pool and an environmental room that allowed for alteration of temperature and humidity to simulate both Arctic and Saharan conditions as well as everything in between. He surrounded his home with a security system, which, one newspaper noted, "the Central Intelligence Agency, 10 miles down the road, might envy." Spotted under the eaves of the home were a host of remote-controlled closed-circuit television cameras that swept the tree-decorated lawn in all directions. Weight sensors could detect footsteps on the grass and microphones in the outside walls would signal any attempt to enter.

Welch simply informed his neighbors, to whom he proudly exhibited his personal art collection, that he was a stockbroker (so successful that he had no need to take on any new clients). He also maintained a summer home in Duluth, Minn. and told a different story there about his profession. He was a fur dealer to the nation's wealthiest.

On the night of December 5, 1980, Welch burglarized four affluent homes in the Washington, D.C. area before invading the house of Dr. Halberstam. When Halberstam unexpectedly confronted him, Welch violated his cardinal rule against violent crime and shot the doctor. Halberstam managed to get in his car and was driving to a nearby hospital when he saw his assailant and swerved his car to hit him. Halberstam died on the operating table a short time later.

After Welch's apprehension, his Virginia home was located and searched. It took some 20,000 pages to catalogue the stolen loot found in his basement, more than 50 boxes and crates. About 2,000 burglary victims from the D.C. area were invited to try to claim over $4 million in stolen goods recovered by the police.

In May 1981 Welch was sentenced to nine consecutive terms of life in prison. He would be eligible for parole in 143 years.

WELCH, Ed (?1865–1912): Western outlaw

A man of many aliases (Howard Benson, H. O. Beck and Ole Hobeck, among others), Ed Welch has often been described as the last member of the Wild Bunch to be gunned down in action. He was not, although his craving to join that legendary outlaw gang did get him killed.

Welch was doing time in Atlanta, where his cell mate was none other than Ben Kilpatrick, the Tall Texan, of the Wild Bunch. When both were released on June 11, 1911, Welch tagged after Kilpatrick in the hope of joining the Bunch. They got as far as Texas and discovered there was no more Wild Bunch, no more Hole in the Wall Gang, no more Black Jack Ketchum gang. Kilpatrick couldn't find any important badmen to team up with, so he told Welch he would allow him to be his partner despite doubts about trusting his life to an older man whose reflexes might not be quick enough in a pinch.

The pair staged a few small robberies for stake money and then hit a Southern Pacific train at Dryden, Tex. on March 13, 1912. They stopped the train by claiming to be railroad detectives, and entered the express car and got the drop on the Wells Fargo messenger. While Welch was collecting loot, it was Kilpatrick's reflexes that failed. His attention strayed and the messenger struck him a killing blow with a mallet. The messenger then picked up Kilpatrick's weapon and shot Welch, who lived only long enough to regret his ambition to run with the big-timers.

See also: *Ben Kilpatrick, David Truesdale.*

WELFARE Island Prison Scandal

In 1934, as New York Mayor Fiorello H. La Guardia's newly appointed corrections commissioner, Austin H. MacCormick uncovered scandalous conditions in the prison system on Welfare Island. Built in 1826, the Welfare Island institution was by that time no longer fit for human habitation. It had an "anti-reformer" reputation and was, without doubt, the most bizarre prison this country had seen in a long time. The 1932 murder of convict George Holsoe, better known as Horseshoes, was a case in point. Horseshoes headed one of two prison gangs seeking to control the narcotics business in the institution. A peace conference was called to settle the dispute. Since it was a summit meeting of sorts, it was held in the warden's office. But the conference was a flop. The anti-Horseshoes forces, headed by a well-known hoodlum, Joie Rao, showed up with knives (made to order in the prison's machine shop), and suddenly, Horseshoes lay bleeding to death all over the warden's rug. A general melee followed, with the rival gangs running wild in the prison. Before the dispute was brought under control, 200 policemen had been sent into the prison, with fireboats circling offshore and police planes flying overhead.

The outburst drew front-page coverage. Grand juries were convened and witnesses called, but Horseshoes' murder remained unsolved. Things soon returned to normal on Welfare Island, which in theory was a tough prison but in reality was a "country club for gangsters." Like several other prisons, many of the inmates received too little food and almost no heat in the winter while certain kingpins lived in grand style. Rao and about 30 of his cohorts, for example, resided in prison cells with doors that could be lifted off their hinges. This convenience meant they didn't have to wait for a guard to open the door when they felt like going for a stroll.

Commissioner MacCormick learned about this and more on January 24, 1934, when he ordered Warden Joseph A. McCann to his downtown office on a ruse that he had some new appointments to announce. When the warden got there, he was shunted into a car, one of a convoy of vehicles carrying 30 policemen and 25 keepers from other institutions over to Welfare Island for a raid that was dubbed Operation Shakedown. MacCormick wanted Warden McCann along so that he could keep an eye on him.

Operation Shakedown was to shock New York City and the nation. When the raiders swept into the prison, they located Rao not in his nominal cell residence but in the hospital building, where he had usurped an entire floor for his own use. The floor was off limits to anyone who was actually sick. As a matter of fact, when found, Rao was being shaved by his personal barber. Many other residents on the floor were Rao henchmen. Those who weren't had to pay $75 a week for the privilege of staying there, which came with all the luxuries, including the best food cooked by the best chefs available. Rao had his meals served to him on the finest china and dined regularly on such fare as lobster, chicken, shrimp, nuts and fruit. Naturally, his private chef prepared the meals. Rao kept a wardrobe of a dozen suits, and whenever he didn't wish to have his wife trek all the way over to the island for dinner, he would dress up and sojourn to his favorite restaurant in Manhattan. The privileged convict maintained his own garden on prison grounds, complete with a private guard, where trespassing by either convicts or guards was strictly forbidden. Rao also kept a milch goat—which of course required a private shepherd, whose main duty was to keep the goat out of the flower garden.

Rao pretended to be a pigeon enthusiast, perhaps in the style of a nobleman with his falcons, but with the practical advantage of providing him with a way to import narcotics into the prison.

If Rao lived in the splendor befitting an Oriental potentate, Ed Cleary, the number two con in the prison, was not far behind. He also had hospital headquarters, in the Dormitory Hospital in another building. Cleary was listed as a "day nurse," which apparently entitled him to keep a stiletto stuck in the wall over his bed. An animal lover, Cleary had a pet police dog, which he kept chained to his bed. He brazenly named it Screw Hater, with no objection from the guards.

With Rao and about 80 of the top cons in the 1,700-inmate prison confined in a special wing, Operation Shakedown proceeded. Storming through the cells, the raiders tossed out all the contraband they found: knives, lead pipes, meat cleavers, rugs, surgeon scalpels, table lamps, electric grills, huge chunks of uncooked meats, dozens of loaves of bread, canned goods, razors and even tin poker chips made to order in the prison machine shop. Several walking sticks led one reporter accompanying the raiders to conclude that "some aristocrats must be living here."

The bulk of the cells, however, were found to be bare, and bitter inmates eagerly told reporters of the strangle hold the "convict politicians" had on the food that was rightfully theirs.

"All the food you wanted was available from the mob," one of them said. "The prices were steep, but it made life here better than in any other prison—if you could pay the price. The mob controls the distribution of the meat, so most of us guys ate nothing but meatless stew. For a fee, the guys who have the dough got regular meat delivery, guaranteed fresh, right to their cells."

Regular delivery entitled a prisoner to have a little electric stove so that he could cook his own steak and onions the way he preferred. Each inmate with a stove received a monthly electric bill, which he paid to the cell block bagman for the privilege of cutting in on a hot wire running through the cells. The bill was higher if a prisoner kept a radio.

"It was the same way with the milk," another convict said. "The big boys would let it stand around till the cream all came to the top and skim it off. For a buck a week you got a half pint delivered to your cell each morning. The rest of us got the bluest milk you ever saw in the mess hall.

"It was a good setup for about 300 cons who, I swear, ain't never been in the mess hall since they been here. They used to laugh at all us others. They said at least we could smell the odor of good food."

The prison guards themselves were demeaned because they had to take orders from important cons. Realizing this, the prisoner elite made life more bearable for them by providing 250 pounds of boneless beef to the keepers' mess each day.

This broke down to five pounds per day per guard. The mob wanted the keepers to eat well but made one proviso: the guards had to be careful not to spoil the leftovers, which once more became mob property. For a preferment fee of $2 a week, any con still suffering hunger pangs after eating the regular mess hall fare could slip into one of the keepers' chairs, while it and the food were still warm, and partake of the remains of steak dinners and other fine meals.

In the ensuing days more scandals came to light. The mob even ran a special lingerie and accessory concession to service the homosexual population, and there was a special method for reducing one's sentence by "buying out" at the rate of $100 for each month's reduction.

In the wake of the raid, Warden McCann was relieved of all duties, but MacCormick realized that Welfare Island was totally unfit to be a correctional institution. In 1935, with a new penitentiary on Rikers Island ready for full occupancy, demolition work began on the old prison. After serving as corrections commissioner for six years, MacCormick became research director of the Osborne Association of New York, a national organization dedicated to correctional reform.

See also: *Thomas Mott Osborne.*

WELLS Street: Chicago vice zone

In its frontier days Chicago made more of an effort than most towns to fight the establishment of vice, but it was a losing proposition. In 1835 the town's Board of Trustees established a fine of $25 for anyone found guilty of maintaining a brothel. In 1838 the fine was raised, but with little effect. Brothels were in open operation on Wells Street between First and Jackson. Although they were rough, shabby dives, they heralded the beginnings of one of the largest red-light districts the country has ever seen. By 1870 Wells Street had become such a pest hole that the Board of Alderman changed the name of the thoroughfare to Fifth Avenue, so as to no longer defame the memory of Capt. Billy Wells, the famous Indian fighter for whom the street had been named. Things did not improve until after the turn of the century, when the name Wells Street was reapplied.

WELSH, Leila (1921-1941): Murder victim

The murder of Leila Welsh in Kansas City, Mo. at about 3 a.m. on March 9, 1941 remains a classic unsolved case. The 20-year-old woman's head had been crushed with a blunt instrument and she had been stabbed several times with a razor-sharp knife. The police could find no leads—other than dozens deliberately left by the murderer. To confuse investigators, he had littered the room and the backyard with phony clues. First, there was a man's shirt and trousers that were readily traced to a very prominent citizen. They had been put into a garbage can by the man's servant and later retrieved by the killer. Then there was a butcher knife bearing fingerprints of yet another man, who turned out to be innocent. The knife, in any event, was not the murder weapon. A stonemason's hammer found at the scene proved not to have been the heavy instrument used to crush the victim's skull. Bloody gloves were discovered; it developed they had not been worn during the crime but had merely had blood smeared on them afterward. Over 50 cigarette butts were found; they evidently had been gathered from ashtrays all about town. A book of matches with a telephone number written inside led police to yet another innocent man. Eventually, the police did make an arrest, but the accused man easily won acquittal when brought to trial.

WEST, Little Dick (c.1870-1898): Western outlaw

As an outlaw, Little Dick West seemed to carry a curse. Every criminal gang he joined in his checkered career soon lay in ruin, but that is what gave him his claim to fame in a fittingly short-lived ballad called "The Luck of Little Dick."

Little Dick's earliest bad luck was being orphaned or abandoned as a child, no one ever knew which. He was found in Indian Territory by cowboys and raised by them on the Oscar D. Halsell HX ranch on the Cimarron River. That was another piece of bad luck since the Halsell spread was rather noted for spawning criminals, and Little Dick was inevitably educated in a life of crime. In the summer of 1892 Little Dick West joined the Dalton gang, just a few months before that outfit's disaster at Coffeyville. Then West became a member of the Doolin gang, but by 1895 that outfit ceased to exist. Afterward, Little Dick outdid his past failures by joining the Jennings gang, a laughable criminal organization that committed only one robbery, for which West's cut came to $60. Following Al Jennings' capture, Little Dick decided the time had come for him to go it alone. He pulled a few minor jobs before being gunned down by a posse near Guthrie, Oklahoma Territory on April 7, 1898.

See also: *Dalton Gang, Doolin Gang, Al Jennings.*

"WEST Brothers": Criminal look-alikes

One of the modern criminologist's primary investigative tools is the fingerprint, thanks, in part, to the case of Willie West.

In 1903, when the fingerprinting system was relatively new and little used, the primary system of identification was one developed in the 1880s by the French criminologist Alphonse Bertillon. This system measured various physical features of a subject based on the principle that each person would have a different set of measurements.

But that year a strange coincidence occurred which shook confidence in the validity of the Bertillon system. A new prisoner was brought to Leavenworth, Kan. to start his sentence at the federal prison there. Part of the normal processing included photographing and the taking of the prisoner's Bertillon measurements. The prison clerk responsible for this process was surprised to see William West enter the room. He did not recall that West had been released from the prison. Already having West's measurements, he felt that it was not necessary to take them again. But when the prisoner vehemently denied that he had been there before, it was then determined that

William West was, in fact, still serving a life sentence for murder.

The measurements of the new man, Willie West, were taken and compared to those of William West. They were identical. A fingerprint expert was called in to take the prints of the two men. They were found to be totally different. So, fingerprints proved to be the only means by which the two men could be distinguished.

The "West Brothers" case provided a shot in the arm for the new fingerprinting system. Sing Sing Prison in New York switched to it that same year. In 1904 Leavenworth received a sum of $60 to fund a changeover to fingerprinting and about the same time St. Louis adopted it. The War Department began fingerprinting military personnel in 1905.

See also: *Fingerprinting.*

WET Stock: Stolen cattle

Many of today's great cattle fortunes were built by herds of "wet stock." The owner of a big spread would announce he was going to Mexico to buy cattle and his riders would be put on double or triple pay because of the "danger" involved. It was a shopping trip for which no money was needed, since the rancher would merely locate a large herd of cattle, stampede it away from its Mexican guards and drive the animals to the border, crossing the Rio Grande in the middle of the night. Mexican troops and cowboys might follow the rustlers' tracks to the river but would hesitate to cross; the United States was intolerant of Mexicans retrieving their stolen property by force on the American side of the border. When the American rustlers felt there was a real chance that the Mexicans might continue the pursuit, the cattle would be driven straight to Kansas for sale. The profits would then be used to make legitimate purchase of American stock.

Occasionally, American rancher-rustlers would make an actual money offer to a Mexican owner. The price, of course, would be insultingly low, but the Mexican would look at the American army of cowboys and judge for himself whether it was prudent to accept some money or none at all.

See also: *Cattle Rustling.*

WHALE Barroom: San Francisco dive

During the 1870s and 1880s the Whale, run by Johnny McNear, was probably the toughest barroom ever to thrive on San Francisco's Barbary Coast. It was *the* rendezvous for members of the local underworld. If the police were searching for a burglar, footpad or murderer, they had good reason to look for him at the Whale, but to get him out required a large force of men and probably involved a gun battle.

One Whale alumnus was Cod Wilcox, who once blithely stole a sloop and became an important pirate in San Francisco Bay before finally being sent away to San Quentin Prison for 20 years. Tip Thornton, however, perhaps best typified the clientele of the Whale. Acknowledged to be one of the deadliest fighters on the Barbary Coast, he always carried a long knife with a narrow blade as sharp as a razor. Whenever Thornton got into a fight, his sole strategy was to slice off his foe's nose. If he couldn't manage a nose, he'd settle for an ear. Patrons of the Whale used to keep score of the number of noses and ears Thornton severed in and around the Whale, but the count was lost when it got up near 40.

Finally, Thornton cut off a nose too many, and Officer Jack Cleary, one of the very few policemen who ever entered the Whale alone, went to the saloon to arrest him. Cleary had to take care of the bartender and about six other customers before he finally dragged Thornton off at the end of a pair of handcuffs. Thornton was sent to San Quentin and somehow the Whale was never quite the same again.

WHIPPING: See Flogging.

WHIPPLE, John (?-1827): Murder victim

John Whipple had the misfortune of being married to a most promiscuous woman, a problem that worsened in 1825 when he took on Jesse Strang as a hired hand on his estate in Albany, N.Y. Whipple's wife, Elsie, soon lured Strang into her bed and, among other things, suggested they could have more time together if he would kill her husband. At first, the pair fed Whipple doses of arsenic but apparently without visible results. Then Elsie bought Strang an expensive rifle so he could shoot her husband through the window as he was preparing for bed. After practicing for months with the rifle to perfect his aim, Strang shot Whipple to death on the night of May 7, 1827. The conventional wisdom was that the shot had been fired by a passing drunk, and a coroner's jury, which included Strang among its members, found that the murder had been committed by "persons unknown." Imprudently, Strang all but moved in with the grieving widow, setting tongues wagging and arousing suspicion. The two were arrested and Strang, a rather weak individual, soon confessed the plot to the Rev. Lacey, rector of St. Peter's Church. Strang was convicted at his own trial after admitting his guilt and stating that Elsie Whipple had put him up to the murder. He had hoped to save himself from the gallows by testifying against Elsie at her trial, but he was not permitted to take the stand. She was found not guilty. So, Jesse Strang was hanged on August 24, 1827, found guilty of conspiring to commit murder with his lover, while Elsie Whipple went free, found not guilty of having conspired to commit murder with her lover.

WHISKEY Rebellion

Angry grain farmers in the four western counties of Pennsylvania rose up against the Excise Act of 1791, which put a tax on that region's most profitable product, rye whiskey, in the so-called Whiskey Rebellion, providing the first test of the enforcement powers of the federal government.

After failing to get legal support to block the tax, the Whiskey Boys turned to violence in the summer of 1794. They burned the home of General John Neville, the regional inspector for the tax, and carried out many acts of violence, culminating in a defiant march on Pittsburgh. Finally, in the autumn of that year President George Washington federalized the state militia and sent 13,000 soldiers into the rebellious counties to end the violence and enforce the tax. Some of the leaders of the Whiskey Boys were forced to flee into the Spanish lands of Mississippi when the troops, under the command of Secretary of the Treasury Alexander Hamilton, wiped out further resistance and rounded up 20 violators for trial in Philadelphia. Eventually, the offenders were freed and the tax itself repealed in 1802, but by then most of the small distillers had been put out of business by a combination of the tax and competition from larger distilleries.

WHISKEY Ring: Tax evasion conspiracy

The Whiskey Ring conspiracy during the administration of Ulysses S. Grant was one of the 19th century's biggest political scandals. In that the motivation of the politicians involved was principally the reelection of the President, the scandal had a number of parallels with the Watergate affair during the Nixon Administration.

The plot involved a group of Western distillers who conspired with corrupt officials in the Internal Revenue Service to evade payment of the whiskey tax. Because of their close connections with Grant, the members of the ring appeared immune to prosecution. However, Secretary of the Treasury Benjamin H. Bristow moved in May 1875 to indict more than 230 persons. A total of 110, including four government officials, were convicted. The court cases disclosed evidence that part of the illegally withheld monies went directly to the Republican Party for use in the campaign to reelect Grant to a second term in 1872. More money went to finance a third-term effort, but by then Grant's private secretary, General Orville E. Babcock, was under indictment and there were strong indications that the President himself was involved. General Babcock, however, was found not guilty, and the public appeared to dismiss any possibility that Grant was personally tainted.

WHITE, Dan (1946-   ): Assassin

A double assassination that triggered an unusual outbreak of public violence was the killing on November 27, 1978 of San Francisco Mayor George Moscone and Supervisor Harvey Milk by former Supervisor Dan White. The murder of Milk, an avowed homosexual, had far greater impact than that of Mayor Moscone.

White, a 32-year-old former policeman and fireman, had been an elected supervisor until he resigned because he found his $9,600 salary was not enough to support his wife and infant child. Under pressure from some of his constituents, White asked the mayor to reappoint him. At first, Moscone agreed, but later he changed his mind. Only an hour before the mayor was scheduled to announce a replacement for White, the distraught ex-supervisor went to Moscone's office and shot him four times. White then walked to the supervisors' chambers on the other side of City Hall and killed Milk, who had opposed his returning to the board.

White was quickly taken into custody, offering no resistance. At his trial the defense contended that when he committed the murders, White had been suffering from diminished mental capacity because of personal and financial pressures. On May 22, 1979 the jury cleared White of premeditated murder, finding him guilty of manslaughter. The verdict shocked much of the San Francisco citizenry, especially the city's large gay community. The day of the verdict thousands of homosexuals rioted in the streets to protest the alleged leniency shown the killer, which they said never would have been granted had not Supervisor Milk been a gay. Mob violence aimed at homosexuals has occurred fairly frequently in American history, but this was one of a handful of occasions when homosexuals themselves rioted.

White was sentenced on July 3, 1979 to seven years and eight months in prison, the maximum term permitted by the jury's verdict.

WHITE, Isaac DeForest "Ike" (1864-1943): Crime reporter

Ike White of the *New York World* was among the best crime reporters this country has ever produced. A thorn in the side of the police, he often solved cases in the columns of his newspaper when the official investigation had barely begun.

In the murder of one Melody Brown, White arrived on the scene even before the police and found the woman's body hanging from a rafter. When the law arrived and started musing about the possibility of suicide, White disappeared, suspecting it was a case of murder. From the building superintendent he learned that the woman had a boy friend who worked as a janitor in a building some blocks away. He found the dead woman's boy friend sitting on the front stoop, talking to neighbors. "It's no good, George, you didn't do a good enough job of hanging Melody," White told him. "We revived her and she told us everything."

There was a period of silence and then the man said: "Thank God. I must have been crazy to go that wild. I don't really hate her. . . . I'm sorry." The *World* published the interview with the murderer while the police were still pursuing their suicide theory.

White solved many other mysteries, including the identity of the "bearded stranger" who made the bomb attack on financier Russell Sage in 1891. He also brought to bay a notorious murderer named Dr. Robert Buchanan. When White died in 1943, one obituary credited him with being the greatest crime reporter in the history of American journalism and "perhaps the best detective this city ever had as well."

See also: *Dr. Robert Buchanan, Russell Sage.*

WHITE Caps: Vigilantes

The White Cap vigilante movement started in Indiana in the 1880s and, for a time, enjoyed considerable popularity in many rural parts of the country. While certain White Cap organizations may have exhibited anti-black or anti-Mexican attitudes, by and large the whole movement was aimed at taming "white trash." White Caps focused their attention on shiftless characters, prostitutes, drunks and men who did not support their families, and generally attempted to reform them by application of a whip. These organizations are regarded as links between the first Ku Klux Klan, which was started after the Civil War, and the second Klan, which was organized during World War I.

WHITE Caps (Gorras Blancas): Mexican vigilante society

Unlike the other victims of ethnic discrimination and exploitation in this country, the Mexicans of the Southwest formed a vigilante group to battle the encroachments of the Anglos, especially in the New Mexico Territory. They were led by educated, English-speaking Mexicans who had lived in the Anglo world and had learned how to fight back. One of these leaders was Juan Jose Herrera, who had witnessed the tactics labor had used against the railroads and mining companies in Colorado, which included violence, sabotage and murder. When he returned to the New Mexico Territory, Herrera helped found the *Gorras Blancas* or White Caps, and taught them to employ the same tactics against the Anglos who were discriminating against Mexicans, cheating them and illegally fencing in the lands so that small Mexican farmers could not survive. By 1888 the White Caps had about 1,500 members and were frightening Anglo elements throughout the territory by cutting fences, considered a major offense in the area, and destroying railroad property. Murders and other acts of violence were charged to them, although it is likely that they were blamed for many things they were not guilty of. The ranks of the White Caps started crumbling because of spies working within their structure and a decision by their leaders to shift their attention to the political arena. The Mexican White Cap movement is not to be confused with other White Cap movements, which were somewhat akin to the Ku Klux Klan.

WHITE-COLLAR Crime

Despite America's growing concern about what is regarded as a surge in crime, one sort of criminal activity, easily the most pervasive and probably the one with the greatest impact on people's everyday life, is usually ignored. It is "white-collar crime," which can be defined as the criminal activities of middle- and upper-class citizens, generally college-educated, who steal in their occupational roles in government, the professions and business.

The crimes include embezzlements, antitrust violations, business swindles, graft taking, income tax evasion, stock frauds, defrauding the government, violations of pure food and drug laws, consumer frauds and union-management collusion. It is impossible to measure the actual extent of white-collar crime. For example, based on arrest records, well over 10,000 embezzlement cases are believed to occur each year. However, many experts are convinced that less than one embezzler in 10 is ever reported to the police or prosecuted. The President's Commission on Law Enforcement and Administration of Justice estimated that $200 million is embezzled each year, and embezzlement is a minor offense in the white-collar crime field.

President Lyndon B. Johnson commented in 1967, "The economic cost of white-collar crime—embezzlement, petty theft from business, consumer frauds, anti-trust violations, and the like—dwarfs that of all crimes of violence."

Edwin H. Sutherland, a sociologist who coined the term "white-collar crime," wrote in 1940:

> The financial cost of white-collar-crime is probably several times as great as the financial cost of all the crimes which are customarily regarded as the crime problem. An officer of a chain store in one year embezzled $600,000, which was 6 times as much as the annual losses from 500 burglaries and robberies of the stores in that chain. Public enemies numbered one to 6 secured $130,000 by burglary and robbery in 1938, while the sum stolen by Krueger is estimated at $250 million; or nearly 2,000 times as much.

Some major white-collar criminals who have been convicted and sentenced in recent years include Billie Sol Estes, who developed a multimillion dollar scheme to swindle money from farmers for nonexistent fertilizer tanks; Eddie Gilbert who fled to South America after stealing $1,953,000 from a company of which he had been president; and Tony DeAngelis, who raised $150 million by showing creditors fraudulent and forged warehouse receipts for vegetable oil that did not exist. In the field of influence peddling, Robert G. "Bobby" Baker went to prison for his illegal activities while secretary to the Democratic majority in the U. S. Senate under President Johnson. From 1955 until he resigned in 1963, Baker's net worth grew from $11,000 to $1.7 million. Other political influence cases have involved former New York City Water Commissioner James L. Marcus and former Democratic leader Carmine DeSapio. White-collar crime convictions even reached the office of the vice president when Spiro Agnew pleaded no contest to an income tax evasion charge after being forced to resign his vice presidency in 1973.

In addition, there is an almost endless amount of white-collar crime committed by officials of some of the biggest corporate entities in this country. Generally, their punishment is hardly commensurate with their offenses. Yet, while the effect of white-collar crime on the public purse is obviously enormous, very little demand for reform is heard from the public, especially the articulate middle and upper classes.

In *The Thief in the White Collar* by Norman Jaspan, an expert in the field of security, and Hillel Black, the authors cite a case that perhaps typifies the extent of the problem.

> In one suburban store recently we found 29 part-time employees involved in theft. Two were elementary school principals, one a parochial school principal, another a credit manager of a large company, another an insurance adjuster and so on.
>
> The merchandise they voluntarily returned exceeded $50,000. Total loss to the store—over $200,000. Most of the thieves held two jobs so they could afford to live in the new suburban

area surrounding the store. The store carried items they needed in their new homes. As they helped each other steal, one would say to the other, "Be my guest."

WHITE Family: Chicago family gang

The White gang, also called the Weiss gang, was an incredible family of Chicago criminals.

In the 1860s the six sons and two daughters of the Widow Margaret Weiss all married into the Renich family of 10 daughters and two sons. The offspring of these marriages intermarried and near the turn of the century the tribe, bolstered by some cousins and other relatives, had grown to about 100 persons, every one of whom, the police claimed, was a criminal. Indeed, at any given moment in the 1890s at least 20 of the family were behind bars. During that decade the boss of the tribe was Mrs. Renich's sister, Eva Gussler, also known as Eva the Cow. One of the best shoplifters and pickpockets in Chicago, Eva the Cow assigned all the members of the tribe to specific criminal duties.

She also supervised the instruction of the young, seeing that they were schooled in the techniques of stealing as soon as they could walk. A typical use of children by the tribe was revealed in 1903, when Mary Boston and her five-year-old niece were apprehended for shoplifting in a department store. The woman was wearing a large dress with big pockets sewn into the lining. Her technique involved walking slowly through the store with the little girl under her skirts and knocking items to the floor so that the child could retrieve them and slip them into the hidden pockets.

As late as the beginning of World War I, members of the family were still being arrested, and a few of the men eventually joined the bootlegging gangs in the 1920s.

WHITE Front Cigar Store: Underworld hangout

With the possible exception of the Brooklyn candy store of Murder, Inc. fame, the White Front Cigar Store in Hot Springs, Ark. was perhaps the most notorious underworld hangout of the 20th century. Such an establishment was possible only in a "safe city," and in the 1920s and 1930s Hot Springs was the safest, with criminals even more immune from arrest there than they were in St. Paul or Kansas City, two other notorious criminal havens. All important underworld elements coming to "Bubbles," Hot Springs' underworld slang name, knew they had to report to the White Front. Whenever a sinister type arrived, he could simply tell the taxi driver, "Take me to the cigar store." The cabbie knew which one he wanted.

The White Front was run by Richard T. Galatas, who acted as liaison between all hoodlums and Dutch Akers, the local chief of detectives, a tall, slender man with stooped shoulders who shuffled around town with a remarkable ability to see no evil. The chief of police, Joseph Wakelin, ran probably the most lax police department in the country. He let Dutch Akers operate freely and for good reason. Akers collected a rakeoff from every prostitute in town and split that and the graft from the city's numbers racket with Galatas. As a sideline, Akers also sold police guns and equipment to gangsters with the only proviso being that they be used elsewhere.

When a gangster showed up at the White Front, Galatas would introduce him to Akers and explain that the town was wide open to all visiting hoods as long as they did not attempt to undercut local operations. Among the underworld characters to pass through the White Front pipeline were such killers as Owney Madden, Frank "Jelly" Nash, Alvin "Creepy" Karpis, many of the Barkers, the elite of Chicago's Capone mob and Detroit's Purple Gang, and Lucky Luciano.

The FBI, which considered the Hot Springs police force one of the most untrustworthy in the country, kept the White Front under almost constant surveillance. On June 16, 1933, agents spotted killer, bank robber and escapee Jelly Nash lounging in front of the cigar store. They trailed him to a horse parlor, where he was placed under arrest and speedily rushed out of town. When news of the arrest reached the White Front, Galatas immediately called Akers to notify him of the "federal snatch." Akers put out an all-points bulletin stating a man had been kidnapped in Hot Springs and "taken for a ride" by persons unknown. The agents successfully escaped the Galatas-inspired net and got their prisoner as far as Union Station in Kansas City, where three underworld machine gunners allegedly attempting to free Nash killed him and four officers and wounded two others in a savage crime that came to be known as the Kansas City Massacre. With that massacre, Galatas was forced to flee Hot Springs and the White Front went out of business. Caught the following year, Galatas was convicted and sent to Alcatraz for harboring an escaped prisoner, Nash.

See also: *Kansas City Massacre, Frank "Jelly" Nash.*

WHITE Hand Gang: New York waterfront criminals

The last Irish gang of importance to flourish on the New York waterfront, the White Handers terrorized the Brooklyn Bridge and Red Hook sections of Brooklyn after World War I. The gang collected tribute from barge and wharf owners; those who refused to pay were beaten or stabbed and their craft or wharves looted, burned or wrecked. The White Handers also required that longshoremen pay them for the right to work. Besides these criminal pursuits, the gang dedicated itself to keeping the docks clear of Italians, or "dagoes," as they would have said.

Gang members were exceedingly violent and they would often kill one of their own if they saw a reward in it. The number two man in the gang, Vinny Meehan, was knifed to death by a jealous underling who wanted his crown. Until 1923 the gang was led by Wild Bill Lovett, a pinch-faced gangster who looked harmless even as he killed people. Lovett was shot to death from ambush. It was suspected that the murder was the work of Italian dock gangsters, but it was just as likely the work of Richard "Peg Leg" Lonergan, who subsequently seized leadership of the outfit. A pock-faced killer—the police attributed 20 murders to him—Lonergan would maim

any Italian terrorist exacting extortion money on his docks and then charge the hapless victim double for having the effrontery to tred on Irish turf.

On December 26, 1925 Lonergan led a half dozen of his men into the Adonis Social Club, a South Brooklyn saloon controlled by Italian gangsters. Although the Irish thugs were greatly outnumbered, Lonergan sneered at the Italians, including a rather chubby one with a long scar on his face. When he spotted two Irish girls dancing with Italians, Lonergan ordered them out of the place and told them to "get back to the white men."

Suddenly, the lights in the establishment went out and flashes of gunfire blazed in the darkness. When the lights were switched back on, Lonergan and his two top lieutenants, Aaron Harms and Needles Ferry, lay dead on the floor with several bullets in their heads. Their colleagues had fled. It took the police some time to discover that one of those present during the shooting at the club was Al Capone, back from Chicago on a social visit to his old home ground. Capone denied having anything to do with the killings, saying, "I never met an Irishman I didn't like." A cynical newsman added the phrase "to kill" at the end of the sentence.

Leaderless, the White Handers disappeared from the waterfront within another three years.

WHITE Hand Society: Italian law-and-order group

Black Hand extortionists operated in virtually every Little Italy community in the United States, threatening to maim or kill victims and/or their families unless they paid tribute. Nowhere were the ravages of the Black Hand worse than in Chicago. Year after year during the early 20th century, anywhere from 25 to 50 Black Hand murders occurred in the city. As the *Chicago Daily News* noted: "A detective of experience in the Italian quarter estimates that ten pay tribute to one who is sturdy enough to resist until he is warned by a bomb. . . . Well informed Italians have never put the year's tribute to the 'Black Hand' at less than half a million dollars." Finally, the Italian community itself organized to battle the Black Hand criminals, forming in 1907 the White Hand Society, an organization of upstanding Italian business and professional men sponsored by the Italian Chamber of Commerce, the Italian newspapers and several fraternal groups.

The White Hand Society actually supplied its own police force and money to carry out the prosecution of Black Handers. White Hand detectives worked together with the police and even traveled to Italy to gather evidence of gangsters' criminal records and thus subject them to deportation. The society found it often had to contend not only with governmental indifference to the plight of Little Italy's residents but with the fear and the entrenched mores of the Italian immigrants. A typical problem was cited by the *Chicago Record-Herald* in an editorial in 1911:

> A murder was committed here in Chicago, and the detectives, native and Italian, were set to work on the case. They

succeeded in learning who the murderer was, but in spite of nets and traps, weeks passed in a vain hunt for him. Finally an Italian saw the "wanted man" leave the home of the brother of the murdered man. When the police summoned the brother to explain the strange affair he declared that the murderer had been wounded and that he and his family had shielded and nursed the wretch back to life in order to kill him and thus duly and personally avenge the death of the beloved brother. This sort of story would astonish one in a melodrama; what are practical policemen in real life to make of it? How could it have occurred to them to look for the criminal in the home of the victim's own devoted brother?

Still, the White Handers performed laudable service in battling the extortionists while giving as much protection as possible to witnesses and the families of victims. Several murderers and extortionists were convicted and sent to prison thanks to the efforts of the White Hand Society, almost all of whose officers and members were themselves threatened with death. Unfortunately, nearly every convicted Black Hander was pardoned almost as soon as he entered prison, such being the corrupt quality of Illinois politics in that era. Soon, they would be back practicing their same criminal activities. In 1912 Dr. Joseph Damiani, the president of the White Hand Society, told the *Record-Herald* that his members "were so discouraged by the lax administration of justice that they were refusing to advance further money to prosecute men arrested on their complaints." After late 1912 nothing more was heard of the White Hand Society. The Black Hand racket continued unabated until about 1920, when a combination of factors—crackdowns by law enforcement agencies, the shifting of gangsters into more lucrative bootlegging activities and a growing sophistication on the part of the Italian community in reporting threats to police—led to its demise.

See also: *Black Hand.*

WHITE Slave: Girl forced into prostitution

The origin of the term "white slave" is often associated with Mary Hastings, a Chicago madam in the 1880s and 1890s. Hastings prowled the Midwest in search of seducible young girls between the ages of 13 and 17. After luring them to Chicago with the promise of a good job, Madam Hastings would quickly lock them in a top-floor room of her establishment and abandon them to professional rapists. Finally, one young victim managed to toss a note out a window to a passer-by; it read, "I'm being held as a slave."

The police raided the establishment and freed the girl. The incident inspired a newspaper reporter to coin the phrase "white slave." Madam Hastings suffered no bad effects as a result of the raid, continuing in business for several more years until her activities got too unsavory even for Chicago's graft-hungry police and she had to flee the city.

WHITMAN, Charles (1942-1966): Mass murderer

On August 1, 1966, an enthusiastic Charles Whitman, user of guns, concluded 24 hours of killing by turning the University of Texas campus into a shooting gallery from his vantage atop a 307-foot observation tower, murdering a total of 18 people and wounding 30 others in a 96-minute rampage.

Whitman, a crewcut 24-year-old ex-Marine who maintained a near straight-A average at the school, was later described by his psychiatrist as an all-American boy. On July 31 Whitman typed a note declaring: "I am prepared to die. After my death, I wish an autopsy on me to be performed to see if there is any mental disorder." Then he stabbed his mother with a butcher knife and shot her in the back of the head. A few hours later, after feeding the dog, he picked up his wife from her job at the telephone company and brought her home. Sometime during the night he killed her with three knife wounds in the chest.

On August 1 Whitman hauled a footlocker containing a rifle, a shotgun, a revolver, two pistols and 700 rounds of ammunition to the observation tower, killing a woman at the information desk and then two tourists who happened to come along. Now, he prepared to shoot down at the students swarming over the campus during lunch hour. First, though, he set out his other supplies: sandwiches, Spam, fruit cocktail, Planter's peanuts, water containers, a transistor radio, a roll of toilet paper and a plastic bottle of Mennen spray deodorant.

Then he started shooting. His aim was phenomenal; at a typical distance of about 300 yards, he hit his target on at least one in every three shots. In one case he shot a pregnant student right through her stomach shattering the skull of her unborn baby. Almost 50 persons were hit by Whitman's shots and their bodies lay strewn over the grassy campus. Police efforts to dislodge him failed, as did an attack from a low-flying plane. Finally, officers led by Austin patrolman, Ramiro Martinez, charged up the barricaded stairway and shot Whitman to pieces. Officer Martinez was wounded in the shooting.

Later, an autopsy showed that Whitman had a tumor in the hypothalamus region of the brain, but doctors doubted the condition had caused his violent behavior. Sen. Ralph Yarborough said the man's actions were the result of TV violence, and Gov. John Connally demanded stiffer penalties for insane criminals.

WHITMAN, John Lorin (1862-1926): Jailer

Nicknamed the Boy Guard, John Lorin Whitman won fame with both the convicts of Illinois and the public, no mean accomplishment in an era when "coddling" convicts was not exactly popular.

Whitman was named a guard at the Cook County jail in Chicago, Ill. when he was 28 years old, but he was so young in appearance and slender in build that the prisoners looked on him as a mere boy and, for some reason, became very affectionate and protective toward him, giving him no trouble when he was on duty. Whitman, in turn, developed a kindly, compassionate and humane attitude toward prisoners that most of the other guards could not understand. It was not lost on his superiors, however, and Whitman was promoted to jailer, in

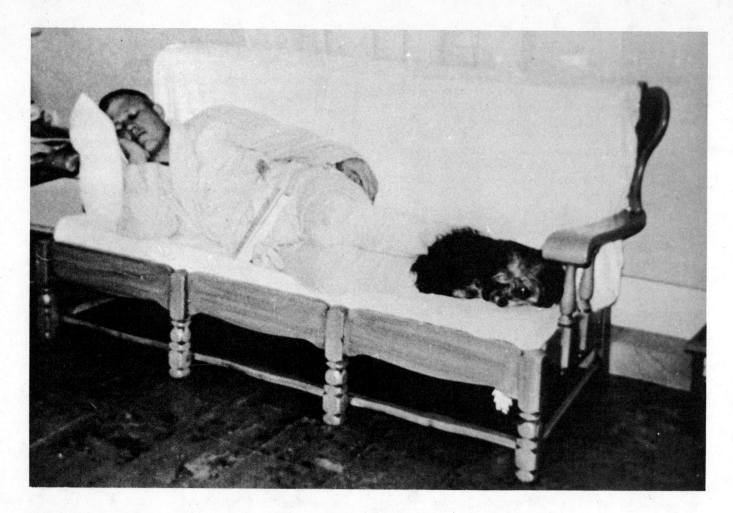

A photo found in a camera belonging to tower murderer Charles Whitman shows him asleep on a couch with his pet dog at his feet. It was believed that his wife took the shot just a few days before his murderous spree.

which position he was able to introduce a number of beneficial reforms in the running of the prison.

In 1907 Whitman was appointed superintendent of the House of Correction in Chicago, where he again instituted a program noted for its kindness and understanding. As a result, the prison had far fewer inmate problems than other penal institutions. Until his death in 1926, Whitman was always affectionately referred to by the convicts as the Boy Guard.

WHITMORE, George, Jr.: See Janice Wylie.

WHITNEY, Richard F. (1888-1974): Financial manipulator

Richard Whitney, former president of the New York Stock Exchange, earned himself two quite different nicknames during his checkered career. The epitome of conservative respectability, he was charged by the Bankers' Pool with handling the purchase of millions of dollars in stock on Black Thursday in 1929 in an effort to reinforce public confidence in the market; for his efforts he became known as the Strongman of Wall Street. In 1938 it was discovered that Whitney had misappro-

priated the securities of the clients of his bond company to cover his own losses. Renamed the Wolf of Wall Street, Whitney was sent to Sing Sing. He served three years and never returned to the Street, disappearing from sight for a time and then turning up as the manager of a fiber mill in Florida. He died in obscurity in 1974 at the age of 86.

WHORE War: Chicago prostitutes' feud

Jurisdictional disputes as well as ownership of "goods" have always dogged organized prostitution, but never has the business been more marked by violence than during the so-called Whore War in Chicago in 1857.

Pitted against each other were the forces of the Sands, the lowest center of vice in the city, and those representing the more "refined" houses of State Street, such as Julia Davenport's Green House and Mother Herrick's Prairie Queen. The spark that ignited the war was a provocative act by Mother Herrick, who lured away from the Sands the fairest specimen in Madame Anna Wilson's brothel with an offer of more money and a clean dress. Madame Wilson operated the only 50¢ brothel in the Sands, twice the standard rate for that area, and, as such, was considered the natural leader of the bordello forces there. Several pitched battles with harlots and pimps on each side were fought on city streets, as newspapers duly warned their readers to seek cover whenever a large gang of "strumpets and their men" appeared.

The Sands' forces had an advantage in having on their side a pugnacious young prostitute named Annie Stafford. Totally misnamed Gentle Annie, she was recognized as one of the most brutal fighters in Chicago, male or female. The war continued indecisively for a number of months until April 3, when Gentle Annie, with the aid of a number of henchwomen and their pimps, made a surprise attack on the Prairie Queen. They battered down the door, destroyed furniture and forced customers to flee in varying states of dishabille. Mother Herrick and her supporters were beaten, and Gentle Annie marched back in victory to the Sands, personally driving before her the stolen harlot as well as Mother Herrick's prize prostitutes as the spoils of victory. The State Street houses never again tried to raid the Sands.

See also: *Prairie Queen, Sands, Annie Stafford.*

WHYOS: Last great 19th century ruffian gang

A ruffian gang that was to dominate the New York crime scene for two decades after its formation in 1874, the Whyos recalled all the viciousness of such early marauder bands as the Chichesters and the Dead Rabbits. They, like their predecessors, were Irish to the core, but whereas the early gangs reveled in robbing, assaulting, maiming and killing Englishmen, the Whyos would victimize anyone. In fact, the gang functioned as a primitive Murder, Inc., ready to perform any sort of mayhem for a set fee. When one of the top Whyos, Piker Ryan, was apprehended in 1883, he had in his possession what the newspapers called the "official" Whyo price list for services. It read:

Punching	$2
Both eyes blacked	$4
Nose and jaw broke	$10
Jacked out [knocked out with a blackjack]	$15
Ear chawed off	$15
Leg or arm broke	$19
Shot in leg	$25
Stab	$25
Doing the big job	$100 and up.

So powerful were the Whyos that they exacted tribute from many other gangs for permission to operate. The names of Whyo members constituted a full roster of the most vicious thugs of the period: English Charley, Denver Hop, Hoggy Walsh, Big Josh Hines, Fig McGerald, Bull Hurley, Dandy Johnny Dolan, Baboon Connolly, Googy Corcoran and Red Rocks Farrell.

Big Josh, who had the franchise for collecting protection money from the various stuss games, an illegal form of gambling of the era, would parade from one game to another armed with two revolvers to take out the Whyos' portion of the revenues. When some of the stuss operators complained he took too much, Big Josh peevishly told a detective: "Them guys must be nuts. Don't I always leave 'em somethin'? All I want is me share!"

Because membership in the Whyos meant higher income, the more lethal criminals in the city naturally gravitated to it. In the 1880s the gang's two most-celebrated leaders, Danny Driscoll and Danny Lyons, enforced an edict reserving membership only to those who had killed at least one man. Both Driscoll and Lyons were hanged in 1888. Driscoll had been convicted of shooting to death a young prostitute and Lyons of killing another gangster in a street shoot-out. Shortly after Lyons' death, two young prostitutes—Gentle Maggie and Lizzie the Dove—who had toiled hard and long to keep him in the style to which he had become accustomed got into a boisterous argument about which of them missed Lyons the most. Gentle Maggie won the dispute by slitting Lizzie the Dove's throat.

The Whyos headquartered at a low Bowery dive aptly called the Morgue, whose proprietor proudly boasted his liquid refreshments were equally potent as either a beverage or an embalming fluid. It was at the Morgue that one of the gang's most brutal members, Dandy Johnny Dolan, would often display proof of his latest crime. In addition to flashing the appropriate bankroll, he would display his victim's eyes, which he carried around in a pocket. Dolan was the inventor of a new and efficient eye gouger, an apparatus worn on the thumb and available for instant use. He also designed special fighting shoes with sections of a sharp ax blade imbedded in the soles, so that a Dolan stomping was always particularly gory.

The Morgue was the scene of the Whyos' last battle. The gang members were notorious for fighting as much among themselves as with their victims. It started when Denver Hop and English Charley got into an argument over the division of some loot. Suddenly, both started shooting, and soon, at least 20 other Whyos joined in the gun battle. No one was injured, however, since all were drunk; the press reported that the proprietor felt the Whyos had been rather silly to expect to hit anything after imbibing his liquor.

The incident perhaps best explained why the Whyos were to disappear from the scene. While they were certainly the most efficient killers and maimers in town, they did not understand the full value of political influence. A powerful gang, the Eastmans, that came to the fore upon their decline was just as brutal, but its members learned to work with the Tammany Hall powers, providing efficient services at election time. The Whyos simply wanted to crack skulls and, as such, fell victim to the changing times. Without political protection, they were open to arrest and imprisonment.

See also: *Dandy Johnny Dolan, Danny Driscoll, Danny Lyons.*

WICKERSHAM Commission: Law observance unit

The National Commission on Law Observance and Enforcement, popularly known as the Wickersham Commission, was appointed by President Herbert Hoover in 1929. It was headed by George W. Wickersham, a lawyer who had been attorney general in the Taft administration. The commission delved into a number of subjects, such as the cost of law enforcement, the third degree, and other lawless police practices, juvenile delinquency and the belief that criminals were mostly foreign-born. The conclusion was that law enforcement was totally inadequate and that the cost of crime had hit the then-staggering figure of $1 billion a year.

However, the Wickersham report on Prohibition captured the most attention, as a majority of the commission declared the Noble Experiment a disaster and called for its repeal. Wickersham and three commission members favored a continued test of the program, but in 1932 he changed his position and urged the sale of alcoholic beverages under regulation. Wickersham's new stand was considered by many to be the death knell for Prohibition.

WILCOXSON, Bobby Randell "One-Eye" (1929-): Bank robber and murderer

An efficient and brutal bank robber, One-Eye Wilcoxson was known as the John Dillinger of the 1960s. While both men planned their robberies meticulously, Dillinger carried his off with a certain lightheartedness, but Wilcoxson was deadly serious. Wilcoxson killed cold-bloodedly; whereas it must be said that Dillinger killed only when he felt his own life was in imminent danger. While casing the Kings Highway branch of the Lafayette National Bank in Brooklyn, New York City, Wilcoxson made it a point to talk with the bank guard while he was eating in a diner across the street from the institution. He jokingly asked the guard, 52-year-old Henry Kraus, what he would do "if I walked in to hold up the bank." The guard smiled and said he would shoot him. One-Eye reported to his confederates that the guard would be a danger because he was a "Wyatt Earp type."

Two weeks later, on December 15, 1961, Wilcoxson and a partner, Peter Curry, walked into the bank. Wilcoxson spotted guard Kraus sitting in a chair, stepped up to him and pulled out a revolver. "Well, here I am with a gun," he said and shot the guard in the chest. When Kraus tried to rise, Wilcoxson shot him three more times, killing him. One-Eye then announced it was a stickup, and he and Curry seized more than $32,000. As they were leaving the bank for a getaway car driven by Albert Nussbaum, a police officer, Salvatore Accardi, appeared on the scene and opened fire. The policeman missed, but One-Eye didn't. His first shot hit the officer in the leg and his second penetrated Accardi's badge and sent him hurtling through the bank's outer glass door to the sidewalk. Later, Wilcoxson said he would have continued firing at the policeman except that he thought the cop was dead. Miraculously, the bullet that hit Accardi in the chest had become embedded in the officer's overcoat, and although stunned, he was not seriously hurt.

Born in Duke, Okla. the son of itinerant farm workers, Wilcoxson had been in trouble most of his life. He lost his right eye sometime during his boyhood but never talked about it. From the age of 10 he worked the California lettuce fields and by 1953 he had become a "boss" fruit picker. At this point in his life Wilcoxson had a wife and daughter and was frequently in trouble with the law for such offenses as wife beating and car theft. He wound up in Chillicothe Prison in Ohio on an auto theft conviction. In prison he met Curry and Nussbaum, and the three teamed up when they were released in 1959. On December 5, 1960 Wilcoxson and Nussbaum held up a bank in Buffalo and followed that up with another robbery in the same city the following month. It is not known how many bank robberies Wilcoxson pulled. He eventually pleaded guilty to the felony-murder of Kraus and seven bank robberies, in which the total loot taken was $205,873.

Wilcoxson's downfall came when Curry surrendered to police after the murder of Kraus, saying he hadn't counted on any killings when he agreed to take part in the bank robbery. Curry identified Nussbaum and Wilcoxson as his confederates. FBI agents captured Nussbaum in Buffalo on November 5, 1962 and learned that Wilcoxson was traveling with a 19-year-old woman and her baby. The agents traced them to Baltimore, where they were living in a rented house directly across the street from one FBI agent and half a block away from another. A week later, Wilcoxson was captured as he was carrying the baby to a station wagon. Suddenly, 30 agents moved in on him and three tackled him, pulling the baby away. Wilcoxson was quickly subdued, unable to draw the gun tucked in his belt.

Wilcoxson and Curry were sentenced to life imprisonment and Nussbaum got 20 years.

WILD Bunch: Outlaws

The term Wild Bunch is often used to describe the last great gang, an organization in the loosest sense of the word, that forayed out of such outlaw strongholds as Hole in the Wall, Robber's Roost and Brown's Hole. More specifically, the Wild Bunch came to represent the train-robbing, bank-busting, hell-raising outlaws who followed the celebrated Butch Cassidy. At any particular time the Wild Bunch generally consisted of no more than 10 members, but over the years the cast of characters totaled more than half a hundred. Among the famous gunmen who rode with the Bunch were the Sundance Kid (Harry Longbaugh), Kid Curry (Harvey Logan), Harry Tracy, Matt Warner, Elzy Lay and Ben Kilpatrick, the Tall Texan. The Bunch had more than its share of camp followers, but only two of these women ever rode out of the gang's hideouts on raids. They were Della Rose (the Rose of the Bunch) and Etta Place, both prostitutes, although some historians have described them differently, especially Etta, the companion of both Cassidy and the Sundance Kid, who was depicted as a school teacher in a late-1960s Hollywood movie. Etta was extremely understanding and even accompanied the boys back to Fort Worth, Tex. on their regular visits to Fanny Porter's bordello, her alma mater.

Such close-knit companionship was common in the Wild Bunch, whose members were noted for their absolute loyalty

Five of the Wild Bunch posed for this photograph in Forth Worth, Tex. in 1901 and sent a copy with a note of thanks to a Nevada bank they had recently held up. Left to right, bottom: the Sundance Kid (Harry Longbaugh), Ben Kilpatrick and Butch Cassidy; top: William Carver and Kid Curry (Harvey Logan).

to Cassidy and to one another. There is no record of Bunchers deserting one another in time of danger, a common practice among outlaw bands. By about 1902 the Wild Bunch was finished, having flourished for less than a decade, with most of the members dead or behind bars and Butch, Sundance and Etta living in South America. According to one story, Cassidy and the Kid died in a shoot-out with Bolivian troops, but in another version they survived and were reunited years later in Mexico. A third report has only Sundance living through the battle in Bolivia.

The last Buncher to attempt a return to crime was Ben Kilpatrick, who, after doing nine and a half years for a train robbery, informed a newspaper editor that he had reformed, was going to get himself a flock of sheep and prove he could be an upright citizen instead of an outlaw. Shortly thereafter the Tall Texan was killed trying to rob a train. As the editor summed up, "Alas, for good intentions."

See also: *Butch Cassidy, O.C. "Camilla" Hanks, Hole in the Wall, Kid Curry, Ben Kilpatrick, Elzy Lay, McCarty Gang, Etta Place, Della Rose, Sundance Kid, Harry Tracy, Matt Warner.*

WILDE, Oscar: See Banco.

WILLIAM Brown: **See Alexander William Holmes.**

WILLIAMS, Alexander S. "Clubber" (1839-1910): Police officer

Clubber Williams, a New York City police officer, is remembered for a number of reasons. A tough character capable of holding his own against any collection of criminals, Williams was the originator of the famous observation, "There's more law in the end of a policeman's nightstick than in a decision of the Supreme Court." He also coined the word "tenderloin," meaning a lush vice area. However, his most remarkable achievement was accumulating something in excess of $1 million from the time he started in 1866 as a patrolman until he retired in 1895 as an inspector, making $3,500 a year. The exact sum was never pinned down, since Clubber was not too precise in his testimony before investigating committees. Suffice it to say he was probably one of the most-crooked cops the city and the nation has ever seen.

Alexander S. Williams was a Nova Scotian by birth and served his youthful years at sea, becoming a ship's carpenter. At the age of 27 he found himself in New York flat broke. He became a police officer, not a difficult task in those days, the Metropolitan Police Department having a great number of vacancies. Not without reason, the public viewed the police as little better than the criminals they were supposed to be suppressing. At best most police officers were inept, at worst corrupt.

After two years in a quiet part of town, Williams was transferred to the area around Broadway and Houston Street, the stomping ground of many of the city's toughest gangs, including criminals who sportingly kept close count of the number of officers they maimed or killed. Williams was cut of a different cloth than most of their victims, however. Two days after he was assigned his post, he selected two of the most-feared toughs in the neighborhood and deliberately started fights with them, promptly battering them unconscious. He heaved them through the plate glass window of the Florence Saloon, a leading criminal haunt. Immediately, six friends of the disabled thugs issued forth to teach Williams a lesson, but he stood his ground and cut them down with his nightstick. Thereafter, he was said to have had at least one fight a day for almost four years. His prowess with the nightstick became so famed that he was hailed as Clubber Williams.

In September 1871 Williams was promoted to captain and put in charge of the 21st Precinct, the heart of the old criminal-infested Gas House district. He immediately went forth patrolling the streets alone, "invoking the gospel of the nightstick," as a doting writer of the era put it. The next day he took a dozen of his brawniest men and organized a special strong-arm squad. Up and down the district the band roamed, clubbing thugs.

While some objected to his violent methods and the occasional skull rapping of an innocent citizen, most of the public praised Clubber and said the city needed more men like him. Whenever delegations of important citizens and clergymen came around to protest clubbing excesses, Williams had a most impressive way of showing how well his techniques had cleaned up the area. Taking his gold watch and chain, he would hang them on a lamp post at Third Avenue and 35th Street and then lead the do-gooders on a casual walk around the block. When they got back, the watch and chain would still be hanging there.

Williams tamed the 21st and, later, the 8th and 4th precincts. In 1876 he was shifted to the 29th, the Tenderloin, as he was to call it. After hearing of his transfer, Captain Williams walked around with a huge smile on his rugged face. Asked by a friend the reason for this merriment, he replied, "I've had nothing but chuck for a long time and now I'm going to get the tenderloin."

Until that time Williams was relatively honest by departmental standards. He had, it was true, created a personal benevolent society to which businessmen contributed about one-third the tribute they had been paying protection racketeers (those that didn't pay continued to be harrassed by the criminals), but overall, Williams' former commands just didn't offer great graft possibilities. The Tenderloin was another matter. The area between 24th and 40th streets from Fifth to Seventh avenues contained so much vice it won the name of Satan's Circus. It was once estimated that at least half the buildings in the district were given over to some form of lawlessness. Sixth Avenue was lined with virtually nothing but brothels, dance halls, saloons and gambling joints.

By nature, Williams was not opposed to brothels and the like; they were "fashionable," he often said. What he objected to was that police grafting in the area was such a sorry, catch-as-catch-can spectacle. He assigned brothels a regular payoff rate, determined by the number of prostitutes and customers and the prices charged. Several years later, a woman who owned a chain of such houses testified that she had paid Clubber $30,000 a year in protection money. For others, Williams instituted a $500 initiation fee and monthly charges of $25 to $50. More than 600 policy shops paid Williams' command an average of $15 a month each; $300 was the fee collected from poolrooms (which were basically gambling establishments); and even larger sums were extracted from luxurious gambling joints.

A person opening any kind of business in the Tenderloin district was immediately visited by one of Williams' officers and told how much he'd have to pay if he wanted to do anything not quite legal. Even if the man was interested in operating an honest enterprise, he had to make some payment as a matter of principle.

Williams' chief source of revenue during his Tenderloin reign came from the whiskey business. Together with two partners, he produced a cheap rotgut and had his men force all the area's saloons to take so many cases of the brew a month. It was either that or be forced out of business by one police raid after another.

By the mid-1880s Williams had been brought up on brutality or graft charges 18 times and cleared 18 times. Finally, though, the stench got so bad that the Tammany-dominated police brass had to root Clubber out of the Tenderloin by promoting him to the rank of inspector, in charge of almost the entire East Side of Manhattan. Now the third-ranking member of the department, Williams immediately summoned all his captains and gave them strict quotas on how much graft they were expected to collect and what share they were to give him. A captain who wanted to remain honest was threatened with being busted in rank and returned to a beat.

Williams' arrogant behavior made him a target for such crusading newspapers as The Herald, The Tribune and The World. Particularly active against Williams was Lincoln Steffens, the great muckraking reporter, who pointed out that while Clubber got so much credit for cracking the skulls of gangsters and thugs, the fact remained that he and his command were far more active in bashing the heads of strikers, most particularly Russian Jews, for whom Williams had a never-explained antipathy. It was said that a Russian Jew brought into a station house when Clubber was present never left without a bandage on his skull and a limp.

Of course, mistreatment of foreigners and "anarchists" did not necessarily cost Williams much in the way of prestige among upright citizens, but he eventually ran afoul of the Rev. Charles H. Parkhurst, who, as head of the New York Society for the Prevention of Crime, started a crusade to get Williams, digging up evidence against him that was presented to the famed Lexow Committee of 1894.

The inspector's entire graft setup was laid bare before the legislative investigating committee. Capt. Max Schmittberger, who had been a sergeant in the Tenderloin, admitted he had collected money from gamblers and keepers of disorderly houses and given it to Williams. Other officers testified to paying Williams as much as $15,000 for promotions. Individual citizens came forth with tales of Williams' corruption; one family, after protesting to Williams about the noise from a nearby bordello, had found themselves evicted.

Inspector Williams took the stand, the picture of innocence. Yes, he had allowed some naughty places to stay open, because sin was fashionable. But, of course, he only allowed "those that were in good taste." No, he could not remember which particular houses had stayed open and which had been forced to close, and since he was bad at numbers, he couldn't estimate how many places he'd actually put out of business.

Yes, he did have several bank accounts; he was a thrifty man, not given to extravagant living. Yes, besides a town house he owned a magnificent country estate at Cos Cob, Conn. No, he couldn't recall how much it had cost him, but shown receipts in the committee's possession, he had to agree that the dock he'd had built for his private yacht had cost $39,000.

All that on his annual $3,500 salary? No, he had made some excellent investments in real estate in Japan. The committee was never able to locate a map showing the places Williams had mentioned. Despite all the testimony against him, Williams survived the inquiry without even a reprimand from the police department.

Still, the Lexow revelations spelled his end. A reform ticket was elected and a three-man board of police commissioners was established. It was presided over by reformer Theodore Roosevelt. Some students of history say that Clubber Williams was the inspiration for Roosevelt's "Speak softly and carry a big stick." But if Roosevelt did have a certain admiration for Williams' ability to cow the underworld, he also believed it was possible to have a police force that was both tough and honest.

On May 24, 1895 Clubber, realizing there was little point in clinging to his job while constantly under Roosevelt's eye, resigned. He lived out the next 15 years of his life in most comfortable retirement.

See also: *Lexow Committee, Tenderloin.*

WILLIAMS, Edward Bennett (1920-   ): Defense lawyer

F. Lee Bailey, one of the most famous lawyers in the country once said, "If I ever got in trouble, he's the one I'd want representing me." Bailey was referring to a burly Washington lawyer with the face of a middle-aged cherub, Edward Bennett Williams. Even men who despise Williams, and that includes many prosecutors, rival lawyers and even former attorneys general such as Robert F. Kennedy, have admitted he may be the best lawyer in the tradition of Clarence Darrow in recent decades.

Williams is not a "scorecard"-type lawyer, with X number of defendants of whom only a minute percentage go to prison. His success record was once estimated to be about 70 percent, an amazing figure for a lawyer whose clients have included Sen. Joseph McCarthy, Jimmy Hoffa, Adam Clayton Powell, Bobby Baker, Frank Costello, Aldo Icardi, *Confidential* magazine, and assorted admitted gamblers and accused Russian spies. Costello probably best summed up the attitude of Williams' clients toward the lawyer when he said: "What I like about Ed Williams is that he'll go up against any of 'em—J. Edgar Hoover, Bobby Kennedy, even President Johnson. He doesn't pull back. He's not afraid."

Opponents naturally see him in a different light; he has been called everything from "ruthless" and a "hypocritical trickster" to "the biggest egotist in the law since William Jennings Bryan" and "a man who would have defended Eichmann if there was enough money in it."

Some years ago Williams had a favorite riposte for his critics: "I'm called the Burglar's Lobby in Washington because I defend people like Frank Costello. The Sixth Amendment of the Constitution guarantees the right of legal counsel to *everyone*. It does not say to everyone *except* people like Frank Costello."

Once when Williams was defending Jimmy Hoffa during Robert Kennedy's tenure as attorney general, Kennedy said he'd "jump off the Capitol dome" if he lost the case. When Hoffa was acquitted, Williams offered to provide Kennedy with a parachute, thus ending a long friendship between the two.

Some of his opponents charge Williams with perverting the Constitution; he sees what he does as defending it. He probably has done more to restrain overzealous congressional committees than any other lawyer. One example was the case of Aldo Icardi, accused of committing one of the most vicious murders in World War II. On a 1944 Office of Strategic Services (OSS) mission, Icardi and OSS Maj. William V. Holohan parachuted behind enemy lines in northern Italy. Holohan, who had taken along a large number of gold coins for use on the mission, disappeared. Six years later, his corpse was fished out of an Italian lake.

Williams told an interviewer:

> Shortly thereafter, a Pentagon press release charged Icardi with Holohan's murder. Five years after that, a Congressional committee called Icardi to testify, and he denied committing the crime. He was promptly indicted on eight counts of perju-

ry, which, if conviction resulted, could potentially have forced him to spend forty years in prison. So I went to court and proved, to the satisfaction of the judge, that two members of the Congressional committee had called Icardi not for any valid legislative purpose, but because they were deliberately looking for a perjury indictment against him. In effect, here were two Congressmen assuming the triple roles of prosecutor, judge, and jury—yet every schoolboy knows that our freedom as a nation is protected by a delicate separation of powers between the legislative, judicial and executive branches of government. In acquitting Icardi, the court clearly defined the line between Congress as a lawmaker and Congress as a grand jury.

In his continuing battle against government prosecutors Williams once made shambles of a Treasury agent who had meticulously prepared an income tax case against Adam Clayton Powell. The agent withered under Williams' fire, admitted errors in the government's calculations and acted more like a defendant than like the prosecution's leading witness. In the end, the judge threw out two counts against Powell and the third and final count ended in a hung jury—a remarkable conclusion considering Powell had paid only about $900 in taxes on a gross income of $70,000.

Williams has long been a thorn in the side of police investigators engaged in illegal eavesdropping, winning a Supreme Court landmark decision against the practice in the early 1960s. The case involved three gamblers who ran a $40,000-a-day sports betting parlor in a row house on 21st Street, N.W., Washington, D.C. The police moved into the house next door and drove a spike into the common wall between the two buildings. The spike, part of an electronic listening device, was inserted into a duct, converting the entire heating system into a sort of microphone, which allowed police to record scores of conversations involving gambling transactions. Based on that evidence, the three gamblers were convicted and given long prison terms. Williams took over the case and argued before the Supreme Court that the police eavesdropping was "more subtle and more scientifically advanced than wiretapping" and was the grossest sort of violation of the rights of the defendants to be secure from unreasonable searches and seizures. It was no different than the police smashing into a house in the middle of the night without a search warrant. The Supreme Court threw out the convictions.

Williams has never seen the contradiction in defending—at approximately the same time—Sen. McCarthy and several of the Hollywood writers accused of communism during McCarthy's heyday in the 1950s. Certainly, McCarthy wanted Williams because he wanted the best possible defense in his fight to escape Senate censure, but the case against him was ironclad and Williams lost.

Williams undoubtedly took the McCarthy case because he had an abiding hatred for the encroaching power of the congressional investigative committees and what he has called "the legislative lynch." He later told a reporter: "When Estes Kefauver first ran roughshod over the rights of the hoodlums in 1950, the country was amused. Then the leftist intellectuals, who didn't spring to the defense of the hoodlums, found

that their turn was next. While this was going on labor thought it was funny but they soon discovered that they were being clobbered." In 1961 Williams was further amused to hear spokesmen for the business community deploring the abuse of business by congressional committees. He commented: "Nobody cares until it hurts him. That's why I'm interested in stopping such chain reactions—back where they hit the weak and the degraded—before they get started."

In recent years Williams has often visited law schools to try to convince young lawyers and students to take up criminal law, to concern themselves with human rights instead of property rights. "You look at the curricula of the top law schools," he once noted, "and you find that they are steeped in such courses as Real Property, Taxes, Estates, and Torts, all of which are required subjects. You generally find that Criminal Law and Constitutional Law are elective courses, which very few students take."

WILLIAMS, William A. H.: See J. Reginald Murphy.

WILLIAMS, William S. "Old Bill" (1787-1849): Mountaineer and thief

Old Bill Williams has been immortalized in the names of the Bill Williams River, the Bill Williams Mountain and the town of Williams, Ariz., but what the names do not reveal is that the mountain man was a scalp hunter, a horse thief and a cannibal.

Ginger-haired Williams was born in Rutherford County, N.C. but grew up in southeastern Missouri. In 1806 he stole a horse and moved west to become a trapper. From 1813 to 1825 he lived among the Osage Indians and, later on, scouted for the U.S. Army. In the 1830s Old Bill was taking quite a few scalps for bounties and for a time he teamed up with the notorious scalp hunters James Hobbs and James Kirker. He was reputed to have explained to them that taking scalps could be dangerous and that it was much safer to raid Indian villages when the braves were away, kill some squaws and steal the village's scalp trophies. The trophies could be sold to scalp buyers who would be none the wiser.

In the 1840s Old Bill teamed up with the mulatto mountaineer Jim Beckwourth and Pegleg Smith to form the biggest horse-stealing gang in California, driving their booty into what is today Utah, where they sold the horses to emigrants heading West, ranchers and traders. When vigilante action against the gang got too intense, Old Bill went back to scouting. In 1848 he acted as a guide for Gen. John C. Fremont on a railroad survey expedition. The trip turned into a disaster and 11 men died in the freezing weather and deep snows of Colorado's La Garita Mountains. Old Bill was accused of incompetence and cannibalism and as a result, was fired by Fremont. In March 1849 Williams was killed by Ute Indians taking vengeance for killings he had perpetrated against their people the year before.

See also: *Jim Beckwourth, Thomas L. "Pegleg" Smith.*

WILSON, Billy (1858-1911): Outlaw and sheriff

Originally a member of Billy the Kid's gang, Billy Wilson went on, with the aid of President Theodore Roosevelt, a noted Wild West fan, to begin a new life as a sheriff.

Wilson rode out of his native Texas with gunfighter Dave Rudabaugh about 1877. When Rudabaugh joined up with Billy the Kid, Wilson followed and became one of the Kid's most trusted aides. Wilson may have assisted Billy the Kid in gunning down James Carlyle and he certainly was with him on numerous other forays. He was also in the December 27, 1880 shoot-out at Stinking Springs, New Mexico Territory, where both he and the Kid were taken prisoner. Wilson was separated from Billy and sent to prison at Mesilla, New Mexico Territory, from which he tunneled his way to freedom. By that time the Kid had been finished off by Sheriff Pat Garrett. What Wilson did over the next few years is not known. But by 1886 he was working as a cowhand for the Hashknife Outfit under the name of Anderson. He then settled down in Terrell County, Tex. married and became a successful rancher. All the while, Wilson-Anderson lived with the fear that some day his New Mexico past would be discovered by visiting lawmen. Yet when the job of county sheriff was offered to him in 1900 he found it impossible to turn down. Shortly thereafter, while in El Paso, Sheriff Anderson was recognized by former lawman Garrett as the long-missing Billy Wilson. Garrett, a close friend of Theodore Roosevelt, who had appointed him collector of taxes for El Paso, did not expose Wilson. Instead, he persuaded the President and the governor of the New Mexico Territory to pardon Wilson for past crimes. The pardons were granted without revealing Wilson's new identity, and he was able to continue on as Sheriff Anderson until 1911, when he was shot dead by a lawbreaker.

See also: *Billy the Kid, Dave Rudabaugh.*

WILSON, Bully: See Cave-In-Rock Pirates.

WILSON, Frank J. (1887-1970): Secret Service agent and enemy of Al Capone

While Frank J. Wilson served as chief of the Secret Service from 1936 to 1947 and was regarded generally as the best man to have served in the post up to that time, he was best remembered as the federal agent who got Al Capone.

Wilson was assigned to catch Capone by Elmer I. Irey, chief of the Internal Revenue's Enforcement Branch, who saw the opportunity to prosecute the gang leader under a 1927 Supreme Court decision that made illegal income subject to income tax. However, it was no simple matter to prove Capone had a gross income of over $5,000, then the standard exemption, for the several years he had filed no return. Big Al had no property in his own name, maintained no bank accounts, endorsed no checks and gave no receipts. This meant Wilson had to gather evidence against him based on an analysis of his "net worth" and "net expenditure."

Wilson succeeded in planting agents on the periphery of the mob's activities and, finally, within it. The heat on Capone got really intense; a tipster reported, "The big fellow's eating aspirin like it was peanuts so's he can get some sleep." Finally, against the judgment of others in the mob, Capone imported five gunmen from New York and gave them a contract to get Wilson. Federal agents tried to put pressure on Capone to pull out the hit men, but he disappeared, forewarned by local police that the feds were hunting him. A message was given to Johnny Torrio, Capone's old mentor, who was in town at the time, that if the gunmen were not withdrawn within 24 hours, agents would start stalking them. With the planned rub-out of Wilson thus exposed, cooler heads among the mob's ruling circle prevailed on Capone to call off the killers. Torrio telephoned an agent and said, "They left an hour ago." The plot was Capone's last attempt to avoid apprehension. Eventually, Wilson presented an air-tight case against Capone that was to send him to prison, permanently removing him from running crime in Chicago.

Wilson went on to further successes. He was the federal representative in the Lindbergh baby kidnap case, and it was upon his insistence that the serial numbers of the ransom money were recorded, a tactic which resulted in the capture and execution of Bruno Richard Hauptmann. From 1936 to 1947 Wilson headed the Secret Service. During his tenure, for the first time in American history, the flood of counterfeit money was reduced to a mere trickle and the crime was virtually wiped out. He also developed presidential security measures that were to become standard procedures. Wilson retired in 1947 and died June 22, 1970.

Further reading: *Special Agent* by Frank J. Wilson and Beth Day.

WILSON, Tug (?1862-1934): Hoodlum

A ferocious rowdy and easily the most notorious hoodlum in New Orleans after the Civil War, Tug Wilson was a throwback to an earlier, more uncivilized era. From the time he first appeared in the French Quarter about 1881 or 1882, he became one of the most-publicized ruffians in the city and was a familiar sight in the saloons, red-light districts and speakeasies right up until the time of his death in 1934.

Wilson's heyday was during New Orleans' most corrupt period, the last two decades of the 19th century. He was arrested more than 100 times a year throughout most of this time. Wilson had enormous strength. Of only average height but stocky, he once broke the doors of five jail cells one after another. Why the police bothered to arrest him during this period is something of a mystery, since he actually served very little time, constantly being sprung by politicians who found his services invaluable. Wilson always wore a plug hat and a long coat, in the pockets of which he stored broken mugs and beer bottles for use as weapons. He was particularly fearsome on election day, intimidating voters and, on some occasions, entering polling booths with them to make sure they voted right.

Despite the introduction of some reforms in the city in the early 20th century, Wilson's brawn was still much in demand in the red-light areas during Prohibition. Shortly before he died, he was still a much-feared bouncer in speakeasies; he was in his seventies at the time of his death.

WINCHELL, Walter (1897-1972): Gossip columnist

A controversial gossip columnist and influential radio commentator, Walter Winchell played an important role in a number of crime stories. He was on speaking terms with several leading gangsters and, at the same time, a close friend of FBI Director J. Edgar Hoover. Even his detractors had to admit Winchell scored numerous crime scoops. He was the first to link Albert Anastasia to the murder of a private citizen, Arnold Schuster, after Schuster had spotted bank robber Willie Sutton and tipped off the police. He came up with a number of scoops in the Murder, Inc. case, and because he was trusted by the underworld, he was chosen to arrange the details of the surrender of Louis "Lepke" Buchalter to Hoover in 1939. Lepke was driven to Fifth Avenue and 28th Street, where he got out of a car and walked over to one in which Winchell was sitting behind the wheel. Winchell stared at Lepke intently for a moment, turned to his stocky companion in the back and said, "Mr. Hoover, this is Lepke."

Hoover nodded, opened the rear door and motioned for Lepke to get in. Lepke later said he had wanted Winchell to act as intermediary to guarantee he would not be shot down while surrendering.

In his later years Winchell ranted in his column over the level of street crime in New York City and told friends he would not venture out after dark without carrying a gun. Winchell, the King of Broadway, felt hostage on the streets that had been his beat for so many years.

WIRETAPPING And Bugging

Any figures on the extent of wiretapping and electronic eavesdropping, or bugging, are as unreliable as even the most suspect crime statistic. With regularity, various government spokesmen appear before congressional committees and state that a small, specific number of taps are presently in place. This presupposes both an honest count and the sudden abandonment of an enduring tactic practiced by officials who simply do not wish to be informed when a wiretap of dubious merit is put into operation. The former point is often gotten around without really telling a lie. While the House Judiciary Committee was considering the impeachment of President Richard Nixon, it was revealed that the late J. Edgar Hoover would regularly have several FBI taps disconnected just before he was to make his annual report to Congress on the number of taps presently in operation. Afterward, the taps could be turned on again.

Electronic eavesdropping has become so sophisticated that it is now extremely difficult to find wiretaps and bugs. American embassies around the world operate under the assumption that all telephones are tapped and the embassy itself bugged. Even organized crime is sophisticated enough to realize that the old hoodlum technique of holding conversations in bathrooms with all the water faucets turned on no longer works. While the "whoosh" of running water may drown out human voices, an eavesdropper can now filter out the interfering frequencies so that the voices come through clearly over the remaining frequencies. A wiretap can be placed so far away from the target telephone that only the most intensive hunt can locate it. The CIA in recent years even bugged telephone connections between the Kremlin and Soviet leaders riding in their limousines.

With all this new expertise available, it would perhaps be the height of gullibility to think it will not be used except under the firmest restraints. When a local police department has advanced wiretap capability, often it is used by rogue officers against narcotics dealers not to make drug arrests but to estimate what the size of their bribe should be. It is well established that in past years in New York City certain officers charged with cracking down on gambling set up wiretaps on bookmaking operations to make sure they were being told the correct gross figures of the business and thus were getting the right percentage in bribes.

In its own way the underworld has often appreciated the joys of wiretapping. Frank Costello for years had his own wiretapper, a colorful character named Gerard "Cheesebox" Callahan. Callahan, a renegade New York Telephone Co. employee, was Costello's personal "wire man," an electronic genius who not only fooled the police but underworld bookmakers as well.

Cheesebox got his name from a wooden cream cheese box he used to house his devices in order to mislead the law. The cheesebox was a glorious device, one that allowed a Costello bookie to supply his customers with a telephone number in the Bronx that when dialed was automatically transferred to another phone in Brooklyn, the real location of the bookmaking operation. Meanwhile, the police having wiretapped the line and traced it to the Bronx, broke into an apartment expecting to find an active bank of phone men sifting through betting slips. All they found was a cheesebox with some strange gear inside. Of course, the Bronx drop was watched by a bookmaker's scout, who reported the police raid to the gamblers. By the time the law located the Brooklyn base, the operation had long ago cleared out and reestablished with perhaps a Manhattan cheesebox drop feeding into a Queens location, or some other variation.

In addition to employing Cheesebox to help him stay one step ahead of the authorities, Costello found it very profitable to use him for "busting out" other bookmakers. A bookmaker's service line, Nationwide News at the time, would be tapped so that the results of a certain race could be held up for a minute or so, allowing Costello or his agents inside the bookmaking establishment to get down a late bet. Cutting in on the line, Cheesebox would imitate the announcer's voice running down the late odds and—by code words—reveal the winner. Then the regular transmission of the race, which had been recorded, would be broadcast and Costello would win big.

Some wiretapping exploits have become instant legends. Often mentioned is the job performed by a New York wiretap expert for a Midwestern union leader who was being investigated by two separate law enforcement bodies. For three days the expert checked the union president's home and office and removed no less than seven installations for microphones. Working secretly at night, the wire man also ripped out all the phone cables at union headquarters, rewired the entire telephone system (some 86 lines with 600 connections) and fed all the lines into one sealed terminal box. He gave the only key to the union president.

The union leader was duly impressed and ordered wiretaps set up on a dozen of his underlings whose loyalty he doubted. The listening post for all these calls was set up in his private office.

This did not complete the wiretapper's chores, however. When a grand jury decided to question eight union lieutenants, the expert designed special eavesdropping and recording devices that worked through wristwatch microphones and shoulder-holster recorders. Outfitted with this gear, the union men entered the supposedly secret chambers of the grand jury and told their tale. Playing back the recordings later, the union president was gratified to hear that all his aides had been completely loyal to him.

Wiretapping abuses are so widespread that they probably can no longer be controlled. The Watergate disclosures revealed widespread unauthorized or illegal taps during the Nixon Administration. Hoover's activities in this regard, such as the wiretapping of Martin Luther King, Jr., pre-dated the Watergate abuses.

For what the claims are worth, over a seven and a half year period, the American Telephone and Telegraph Co. revealed it had discovered 1,457 wiretaps on customers' telephones, 1,009 of which were illegal. According to the company, the largest number of taps involved matters of marital discord. However, it should be noted that most telephone companies tend to check with federal and local police authorities to make sure they are not interferring with an investigative tap so that the AT & T estimate need not be regarded as completely accurate. Also, most of the taps found by the telephone company are by mere happenstance and on complaint of a telephone user. When the wiretapped victim suspects nothing, the tap is almost never found.

The practice of wiretapping is common among all the nation's investigative bodies. Virtually every federal investigative agency—the FBI, the CIA, the Defense Intelligence Agency, the Secret Service, the Drug Enforcement Administration, the Bureau of Alcohol, Tobacco and Firearms, to name only the more prominent ones—has eavesdropping capabilities. So too do state police units and city and county agencies. The "leakage" of such expertise into the private detective market is known to be large.

The federal government not only engages in questionable wiretapping but is also responsible for spreading the practice in nonfederal jurisdictions. The Law Enforcement Assistance Administration funds about three-quarters of local police purchases of surveillance hardware, and some of its outlays go to police agencies without statutory wiretap authority.

WITCHCRAFT

Belief in witches and witchcraft was extremely widespread in 17th century America. The colonists brought this belief with them from the Old World.

Margaret Jones was executed in the Massachusetts colony in 1648, and Mary Parsons of Springfield was later indicted for witchcraft but was executed for the murder of her child. There were other cases in the 1650s. In 1688 Goody Glover was executed in Boston, largely on the testimony of a 13-year-old girl named Martha Goodwin. The case was closely studied by Cotton Mather and the techniques of prosecution were subsequently followed in the Salem witchcraft persecutions. Popular myth to the contrary, no one was burned at Salem. Eighty-year-old Giles Corey was pressed to death under an old English law that called for that punishment if a suspected witch refused to plead guilty or not guilty. In all, 19 persons were hanged and many other imprisoned in Salem as a result of the hysterical accusations of a number of young girls. Finally, saner attitudes called a halt to the persecutions. The judge and 12 jurists involved in the witchcraft trials publicly repented their acts and asked for forgiveness.

Although the Salem experience did not halt witchcraft cases in this country, it undoubtedly reduced them to a mere handful, such as in Virginia in 1706 and in North Carolina in 1712. The last case appears to have occurred in Rhode Island in 1728, but the record of the incident is sketchy.

See also: *Giles Corey, Cotton Mather, Salem Witchcraft Trials.*

WOOD, Isaac (?-1858): Mass poisoner

The largest all-in-the-family poisoning plot in American history was perpetrated by Isaac Wood at Dansville, N.Y. in the 1850s.

The first to die was Isaac's brother David, who owned a huge estate in the area. David Wood was struck down unexpectedly by a strange malady in May 1855. Before the year was out, his wife Rhoda and his three children had died of the same strange sickness. Isaac Wood had slowly poisoned all five so that he could gain control of the estate; he accomplished that goal by acting as administrator. Isaac then took his wife and child to live in New Jersey, where he murdered them as well. Now a rich man, he moved on to a new life in Illinois.

Before leaving for Illinois allegedly to bear his grief alone, Wood had leased his brother's home to a tenant named Welch. Shortly after the murderer departed, Welch found three packs of arsenic in the barn. The arsenic had been wrapped in legal papers that assigned Isaac Wood full authority over the estate after the death of his brother and his family. That link and the fact that all of Isaac Wood's relatives had died under similar circumstances were sufficient evidence to doom him. Wood was brought back to New York, tried and hanged on July 9, 1858 at Geneseo.

WOODEN Gun Escapes

Probably nothing is quite as romantic in underworld folklore as a criminal's escaping from prison armed with a fake gun. Few such escapes have excited the public's imagination more than John Dillinger's from the "escape-proof" jail at Crown Point, Ind. on March 3, 1934. In actuality, although the fake gun tale was accepted blindly by most newspapers, Dillinger used a very real gun. The full story of the intrigues behind this wooden gun hoax is told elsewhere in this book. Here, it is sufficient to point out that the Dillinger story, like almost all such reports, was a lie.

One of the few authenticated wooden gun breakouts was pulled by a Cherokee strip outlaw, Ben Cravens, shortly after he was sent to the Kansas State Penitentiary in January 1897 to serve a 20-year term. Cravens was confined for only a short time before he fashioned a wooden gun, covered it with silver paper and bluffed his way past a legion of guards. It is highly likely that Dillinger, who was an avid reader of Western outlaw literature, learned of the wooden gun caper from accounts of Cravens' career.

While Dillinger never used a wooden gun to escape from jail, his fake exploit did serve as inspiration for two of his most loyal gang members, Harry Pierpont and Charles Makley, who attempted to escape from the death house of the Ohio State Prison just a few months after Dillinger's death. They used pistols carved out of soap to overpower one guard and were smashing through a door leading from the death house when other guards opened up on them. Makley was killed and Pierpont was wounded, but he recovered sufficiently to die in the electric chair a month later.

See also: *John Dillinger.*

WOODS, Frederick Newhall, IV: See Chowchilla School Bus Kidnapping.

WOOLDRIDGE, Clifton (1850-1915): Police detective

Undoubtedly the most colorful police officer in American history was Clifton Wooldridge, "that damned little flycop," as the Chicago underworld dubbed him. Wooldridge, who ornamented the city's police force from 1888 until 1910, made a total of 19,500 arrests, averaging almost three a day every day of his career. At any given time there were hundreds of criminals in Joliet Prison who had been put there by Wooldridge. He recovered hundreds of thousands of dollars in stolen property in the days when an American dollar would buy more than one hearty steak dinner. He personally closed a hundred panel houses, rescued a hundred teenage girls from brothels and white slavery, broke up a hundred phony matrimonial agencies

and refused hundreds of bribes from $500 to $5,000. In the process he was shot at on 44 occasions, was wounded 23 times and wounded exactly twice that number of criminals. Although a crack shot, he never once shot to kill, only to wound. "A policeman's duty is to preserve order, not to kill," he proclaimed—and he meant it.

Originally an office clerk, Wooldridge was in his thirties when he joined the police department. As a police officer, he quickly proved his worth and was made a detective within a year. In many respects he was a comic character, a merry extrovert given to boast and bombast. In his memoirs, *Hands Up! In the World of Crime,* Wooldridge billed himself as "the World's Greatest Detective, the Incorruptible Sherlock Holmes of America," adding, "No braver, more honest or efficient police officer ever wore a star or carried a club." He was probably right. Sometimes his acts were on the zany side. To give an example, a strong-arm character named Adams once lacerated a few citizens and boasted he ate cops for breakfast. Wooldridge took him into custody forthwith and lowered the thug's standing in the underworld several notches by making the crook carry him piggyback seven blocks to the lockup. Adams had little choice in the matter since Wooldridge held the butt end of his revolver a few inches from the brute's skull and threatened to sock him if he so much as stumbled.

Despite this light-hearted approach to law enforcement, Wooldridge was all he claimed to be: the toughest, strictest and most successful detective on the force. He was positively fearless. When a murderer named Henry Foster barricaded himself in a saloon and kept officers at bay by shooting through the door, Wooldridge pulled out his gun and picked up a piece of plank for a shield. Then, screaming at the top of his lungs, he barreled into the saloon and charged right at Foster, who was behind the bar guzzling from a bottle. Panicking, Foster dropped the bottle and did the only thing he could think of doing under the circumstances: he put his gun to his head and pulled the trigger. However, he was so rattled by the sight of Wooldridge that he failed to aim correctly and only received a scalp wound. He died on the gallows July 1, 1895.

Wooldridge was the most energetic campaigner against vice in the Windy City, an unlikely role for an officer during an era when it was rare to find a Chicago mayor or chief of police who wasn't also the landlord of buildings given over to prostitution or gambling. Because of his law enforcement activities, Wooldridge on one occasion was ordered transferred to a quiet residential area, but the newspapers intervened and the order was rescinded. In 1896 a committee from the Civic Federation, armed with evidence furnished by Wooldridge, called upon Mayor George B. Swift to demand he enforce the regulations against bawdy houses. The committee said that the prostitutes were a menace to society and that young boys, drawn to the area by curiosity, could see orgies talking place through the windows.

The mayor, accompanied by Chief of Police J. J. Badenoch, toured Custom House Place and was duly shocked. His Honor ordered the brothel keepers to paint their windows and keep them closed. However, Wooldridge kept plugging away at the issue, and when the houses were finally shut down in the early 1900s, the newspapers gave him much of the credit.

Wooldridge's tiny form became the most-hated sight in the red-light districts. He closed down places no other officer dared touch. In the case of Big Susan Winslow, he made an arrest no other officer could figure a way of making. Big Susan ran a bawdy house in a two-story wooden structure on Clark Street, which was the source of countless complaints to the police, including many from men who were robbed there. Over five years a total of 20 warrants were issued for her arrest. Yet every officer who tried to arrest her gave up, unable to figure a way to get Susan out of the house.

Big Susan was aptly named; she weighed 450 pounds and was wider in every direction than any door or window in her dive. The police never figured out how she got in there in the first place.

Wooldridge drove a patrol wagon through an alley to Big Susan's back door. Standing outside the house, he read a warrant to her as she cackled away. Then Wooldridge removed the back door of the house from its hinges and sawed out the frame and about two feet of wall. He put two oak planks, 16 feet long and a foot wide, between the door sill and the rear end of the patrol wagon. The detective then unhitched one of the patrol wagon horses, attached a rope to its collar and tied the other end of the rope around Big Susan's waist. "Giddap!" he shouted and the horse pounded forward, pulling Big Susan out of her chair. As she slid up the planks, Susan began to shriek; Detective Wooldridge had somehow neglected to get dressed lumber. Big Susan suddenly decided to be cooperative and waddled painfully the rest of the way up the planks and into the wagon. During the ride to the station she lay prone on a bed inside the wagon while one of her girls sat beside her consolingly pulling splinters out of her bottom.

"After this," Wooldridge later noted, "the police had no more trouble with Susan Winslow."

In addition to such light-hearted triumphs, Wooldridge deserved credit for putting a number of big-time procurers, including the notorious Mary Hastings, out of business and behind bars. It can only be estimated how many girls he thus saved from white slavery.

For 22 years Clifton Wooldridge went on entertaining the public with his crime-smashing exploits which included the solving of many murders. In one such case a bartender named Reilly murdered a saloon keeper with the aid of the latter's wife and then tried to pass it off as a stickup murder. Suspicious of the pair's story, Wooldridge broke down the widow by presenting her with proof that the bartender, with whom she was in love, often spent his nights at the home of a certain Mrs. O'Brien. Shocked into a jealous rage, the widow confessed and implicated her lover in her husband's murder. Not until later did Wooldridge get around to explaining that Mrs. O'Brien was the bartender's mother, having reverted to her maiden name.

While Wooldridge was known to be tough on wrongdoers, he was a soft touch for any reformed criminal. He once explained: "There are only two ways of making a criminal reform. One is

a helping hand, the other a hard rap on the skull." When Wooldridge retired from the force in poor health in 1910, a Chicago newspaper observed: "His retirement marks the end of one of the most amazing and accomplished records in the history of the police system. It is also sad to see the end of such a source of levity in the grim business of crime battling."

WYLIE, Janice (1942-1963): Murder victim

The gruesome murders of Janice Wylie, the 21-year-old daughter of author Max Wylie and niece of writer Philip Wylie, and her roommate, 23-year-old Emily Hoffert, on August 28, 1963 shocked New York City, and caused a legal controversy for years thereafter.

The bodies of the two women were found bound together in their Manhattan apartment. Both had numerous stab wounds and Janice Wylie had been eviscerated. The newspapers depicted the murders as a ritualistic sort of sexual crime. Eight months after the murders the police charged a semiliterate 19-year-old black named George Whitmore, Jr. with the crime. He had been arrested in the Brownsville section of Brooklyn on a charge of attempted rape, which, said the police, he admitted along with the murder of a woman in Brooklyn and the Wylie-Hoffert homicides. A few weeks later, Whitmore repudiated the three confessions, insisting he had been beaten and otherwise coerced into making them. In all, he was brought to trial four times on various charges.

In his own version of how he was made to confess, Whitmore, whose IQ was at various times estimated to be between 60 and 90, wrote: "I am the kind of boy that like to have fun. . . . I don't like to be hurt nor me hurt anyone witch I'd never did. But when I first came to New York I was aquised of doing things I know nothing about."

Whitmore said that when he denied the attempted rape in the Brooklyn precinct house, he was "hit many times." He went on:

Then I was so squared that I was shakeing all over. And before I know it, I was saying yes. I was so squared if they would have told me name was tom, dick or harry I would have said yes. . .

Then I was asked about the killing in the city on 88 St. But I was squared in to saying yes. They would say George Didn't you do so and so here and so and so there. I wouldnt say anything.

They would would say shour you did. Then they would write it down. And go over it with me. Then call in some more men, and ask me the same quition again. I would just repeat what I just learned. . . .

I got enemies witch I never had. But I hope some time he or she will soon find out that I was the wrong boy. God will see to it. . . . God knows that I didnt do these things, and if I keep praying he will help me. . . .

Just bying here it can chang your life it can make you want to make something of your life when you get out it can also make you relazice many other things to. You learn to to fell sorry for other people as well as your self. So take it from me and witch what you are doing. I am a boy who never been in trouble before and went to jail for non-thing. . . .

In 1965 Whitmore was cleared in the Wylie-Hoffert homicides following a confession made by Richard Robles, a 22-year-old drug addict who was subsequently convicted and sentenced to life imprisonment. Whitmore's experiences, especially the discredited confessions, were cited by the Supreme Court in the landmark Miranda decision, which led to curbs on police powers to question suspects, and by the New York legislature in a 1965 statute that largely abolished capital punishment.

Whitmore was also cleared of the third murder accusation after newspapers turned up evidence that the white detectives had been biased against him and the Manhattan and Brooklyn district attorneys' offices found proof that he was innocent. However, he was still convicted three times of the attempted rape charge. In 1973, after Whitmore had served a total of four years in prison, it was found that the prosecution had withheld from the defense evidence which would have cleared him in the rape case as well.

Whitmore filed suit against the city in 1973 charging false arrest and wrongful imprisonment, but in 1979 a judge ruled that the statute of limitations in the Wylie-Hoffert case had run out by 1973 and that in the rape case there was no proof of "actual malice" on the part of the Brooklyn district attorney's office. The judge said he felt an "emotional strain" in ruling against Whitmore and suggested that the wrong-man victim seek redress from the legislature, which had the power to grant him a financial settlement.

See also: *Confessions, False.*

Y

YAGER, Erastus "Red" (?-1864): Outlaw

Red Yager was the 19th century Western precursor of such 20th century underworld informers as Abe Reles and Joe Valachi. Yager's squealing caused the downfall of the notorious sheriff-outlaw Henry Plummer and his gang of Innocents, which plagued what is now southwestern Montana in the early 1860s. Red's fate was also indicative of the riskiness of seeking clemency in the American West by turning informer.

A thin little man with a wild mop of flaming red hair and whiskers, Yager probably never killed anyone, but the vigilantes nevertheless suspected him of a number of crimes. As a consequence, he was taken prisoner in late December 1863, and he admitted carrying messages to road agents who held up stages, bullion wagons and individuals carrying large sums of money. Yager revealed to the vigilantes the structure of the outlaw organization and how orders were passed down from Sheriff Plummer, who masterminded the depredations of the outlaws while he was supposedly trying to root them out. He also told them the gang's password, "innocent," and identified a total of 26 key gang members. This intelligence enabled the vigilantes to destroy the gang.

After Yager finished telling what he knew, there was some inclination to show him leniency, but it was noted that his life had already been extended a full week from the time he should have been strung up. A solemn vote indicated that that was leniency enough, and on January 4, 1864 Yager was hanged from a cottonwood tree in Stinkingwater Valley.

See also: *Innocents, Henry Plummer.*

YALE, Frankie (1885-1927): Gangster

Brooklyn-born gangster Frankie Yale's two dearest friends were Johnny Torrio and Al Capone. Torrio brought his trusted buddy Yale out to Chicago twice to carry out two of his most important hits, on Big Jim Colosimo and Dion O'Banion; Capone sent his killers east to New York to knock off Yale.

In his teens Yale was a partner with Torrio in the old Five Points gang and was said to have killed close to a dozen men by the time he was 20. Around 1908 he and Torrio operated a Black Hand extortion racket in Brooklyn, threatening immigrant Italians with death unless they paid protection money. The pair also ran a bar and brothel in Brooklyn, where Yale hired Al Capone as a bouncer. Yale maintained the establishment after Torrio and Capone both moved on to Chicago.

In the early 1920s Yale moved into the big time on several fronts. He built up major bootlegging and rum running operations and took over control of the national Unione Siciliane, the powerful Sicilian fraternal organization that in large part was turned into a criminal-front organization. He also ran protection rackets and forced New York tobacconists to order the cheap cigars he manufactured; to add insult to injury, Yale's face appeared on each cigar box. As a result, in Brooklynese "a Frankie Yale" meant any kind of product that was overpriced and lousy. When police demanded to know how Yale made his living, he would say blandly, "I'm an undertaker."

Torrio used Yale to kill O'Banion because he was unfamiliar to the Irish mobster and could thus approach him in his flower shop without arousing suspicion. As Yale shook hands with O'Banion, he gripped the Irishman's gun hand so that he couldn't draw his weapon while two of Capone's trusty gunmen, John Scalise and Albert Anselmi, pulled out their pieces and shot him to death.

In 1927 Capone, almost regretfully, decided to have Yale knocked off for two reasons. First, he interfered with the running of the huge Chicago chapter of the Unione Siciliane, whose members' alcohol-cooking operations Capone wanted to control. Yale was trying to get part of the chapter's moonshining profits sent to the national organization, and under Capone's puppet president, Antonio Lombardo, those contributions had dwindled to nothing. More importantly, Capone suspected Yale, who was the Chicago mob's biggest East Coast supplier of imported liquors, was hijacking truckloads of booze he had already sold to Big Al and selling the same booze to him a second time.

Capone sent in a spy named James De Amato to find out. Yale found De Amato out and had him shot down on a Brooklyn street, but not before the spy had confirmed Capone's suspicions. Capone sent Yale an anonymous warning, "Someday you'll get an answer to De Amato."

On July 1, 1927 Yale was driving along 44th Street in Brooklyn when gunmen in a black sedan crowded him to the curb and machine-gunned him to death. What really upset New Yorkers about the incident was that it was the first underworld killing with a submachine gun. It was to be the first of many.

See also: *Dion O'Banion, John Torrio.*

YELLOW Henry Gang: New Orleans criminals.

One of the most vicious gangs in New Orleans during the 1870s and 1880s was a group of murderers, thieves and cutthroats bossed by Yellow Henry Stewart.

Stewart earned his nickname because he was afflicted with malaria, which he was convinced, rightly, would shorten his life span. As a result, he was unbridled in his lawless fury. He would as soon kill a victim as manhandle him, and he was equally feared by other criminals and by the police.

In 1877 Yellow Henry inherited the leadership of the gang that took his name when the former leader, Turpo, went to jail for murder. The new leader brought to his banner some of the most desperate criminals that New Orleans ever produced, including Joe Martin, probably the most expert garroter in the city's history; Crooked Neck Delaney, certainly a top-class performer in the same line as Martin; Tom McDonald, better known as Tom the Dog; Prussian Charley Mader, who wore a false beard and a mask whenever pulling a job; George Sylvester; Garibaldi Bolden; the murderous Haley brothers, Red and Blue; Pat Keeley; and the notorious Frank Lyons, who won fame as a police killer.

Yellow Henry attracted these supporters because of his ability to plan successful capers for the gang, including burglaries, holdups and protection rackets. Finally, Yellow Henry and three of his men were caught and sent to the penitentiary in 1884 for the robbery of a Julia Street sail maker. The brutal gang leader died there of malaria in July 1886.

Frank Lyons, in prison at the time, escaped in 1888 and proceeded to reorganize the Yellow Henry gang. He was apprehended again and returned to prison. In an act incomprehensible but typical of Louisiana in that era, Lyons won a pardon in 1890 from Gov. Francis T. Nicholls. The Yellow Henry gang arose once more, this time until 1892, when Lyons was sentenced to prison for killing a policeman, an act that brought down the full wrath of the police on the Yellow Henrys, breaking them up permanently.

YORKY Of The Great Lakes: Murderer who became a legend

For over a century now Yorky Mickey the Clam Man has scoured the Great Lakes on a mission of murder, and, the story goes, he will not give up until vengeance is his.

Yorky Mickey was a real person well-known to the denizens of Buffalo's Canal Street vice area, a jutting piece of land segregated from the rest of Buffalo by 40 feet of murky water called the Erie Canal. In the 1860s and 1870s Yorky ran a clam stand there that offered two main attractions. Yorky, a man of amazing strength, could crush a man's fingers with his grip and often did. Patrons flocked to his stand to watch in wonder as he opened clams with his fingers. After a patron filled up on clams, he could avail himself of the stand's second attraction: women. Yorky was also a procurer, leasing out women by the evening. It was a good deal for his patrons because Yorky was an honest man and never allowed his women to rob a customer.

Everyone liked Yorky and they were happy for him when love came into his life. He fell for one of his own women, a lass known as the Thrush, and they had a wedding that Canal Street—indeed the entire Great Lakes—long remembered. The Thrush, who was famed for her figure, performed at times as a singer in a bar called the Peacock. Her voice was not particularly good but no one seemed to notice.

It was in the Peacock that the pair joined in tragic wedlock. All Canal Street was there—the leading prostitutes, the rival saloon owners, the sporting men and the cooperative politicians. Liquor and beer flowed freely and food was plentiful. A brass band blared without letup. Finally, Yorky and his lady were married by a Canal Street character named Preacher Dobie, a minister who had deserted his flock for the ways of the fleshpots. Preacher Dobie ran through the words in a drunken stupor, but then everyone else was drunk as well—Yorky, his bride, and the guests.

The newlyweds were hustled to the bar as soon as the ceremony was over and served more liquor. Yorky was so happy he couldn't seem to get enough. As a result, the Thrush was being deserted by her groom only minutes after their marriage. The more Yorky drank the less likely it appeared he would be leaving soon. At first the Thrush didn't seem to mind. She had no aversion to the brew herself, but the more she drank, the more her eye would rove.

The Thrush drank until her eye settled on a rakish young sailor who'd just wandered into the Peacock. The fact that the Thrush was garbed in a wedding dress did not deter the young sailor. He was right off his ship, his pockets bulged with a month's pay and he ached to spend some of it. Yorky was so far gone he failed to notice his bride and the sailor slip out of the Peacock.

It took another two hours before Yorky noticed his bride's absence. He stormed forth to look for her, and his anger soared when he heard from others that she had been seen carousing with a young sailor. Yorky lurched from bar to bar, clenching his powerful fists tighter each passing minute. Finally, he found the Thrush. She was sprawled in a drunken stupor on the bed of the two-room flat Yorky had furnished for her. Her lipstick and clothing were in disarray and there was some money pinned to the rumpled pillow.

Later, when others ventured into the flat, they found the Thrush still lying on the bed, but her head had been twisted and she looked like a chicken whose neck had been wrung. She was dead and Yorky was gone.

He was never seen again on Canal Street, but lakers coming in from other ports reported having observed him scouring all the ships of the Great Lakes looking for the young sailor. A couple of times, it was said, Yorky had just missed catching his man.

Apparently he never did. Even today when a dim light is seen in the mist over the Great Lakes, there are some lakers who say it is Yorky still hunting for the sailor who seduced his new bride.

YOUNGBLOOD, Herbert (1899-1934): Fellow escapee of John Dillinger

When public enemy John Dillinger made his fabled "wooden gun" escape from the supposed escape-proof jail in Crown Point, Ind. on March 3, 1934, the only prisoner who accepted his offer to join in the breakout was a black man, named Herbert Youngblood, who was being held on a murder charge.

Having escaped in the sheriff's car with two hostages, Dillinger and Youngblood threw the hostages out when they reached isolated country. Then Dillinger ordered Youngblood to hide down between the seats, since the two of them together, one white and one black, could be easily identified.

The pair soon separated, but their brief contact evidently made a deep impression on Youngblood, who was destined to live only 13 more days. On March 16 he was cornered by three deputy sheriffs in a tobacco store in Port Huron, Mich. Youngblood managed to kill one of the lawmen and wound the other two, but he himself took six bullets. Just before he died, he confessed that Dillinger had been with him the previous day.

Youngblood's dying words triggered a manhunt in the area for Dillinger, and there were soon reports of the noted fugitive crossing the St. Clair River into Canada with two other men. At the time, Dillinger was hiding out with his girl friend, Billie Frechette, in apartment 303 of the Lincoln Court Apartments in the exclusive Hill section of St. Paul, Minn. Undoubtedly, Youngblood misled the authorities because he figured he owed John Dillinger a favor.

See also: *John Dillinger.*

YOUNGER Brothers: Outlaw band

Certainly just as daring, violent and cold-blooded as the James brothers, the Younger brothers terrorized Missouri and the surrounding states until the ill-fated Northfield Bank Raid in 1876 broke the power of the James-Younger gang.

The four outlaw Youngers were part of a family of eight sons and six daughters born to Henry W. and Bersheba Younger; the rest of the Younger children grew up to be law-abiding citizens. Cole (born 1844), Jim (born 1848), John (born 1851) and Bob (born 1853) killed their share of Union soldiers during the Civil War, especially after their father was murdered by Union irregulars in 1862. Bob was only 12 when he took part with his older brothers under Quantrill in the sacking of Lawrence, Kan.; John was just 10 when he helped brother Jim kill four Union soldiers. When he was 15, John, with no assistance, killed a man who had hit him over the head with a dead fish. He was brought to trial but acquitted on the ground of "self-defense."

The Younger brothers—left to right: Jim, Bob and Cole—with sister Rhetta.

Bob and John Younger, however, could not match the charm, cunning or deadliness of their elder outlaw brothers, Cole and Jim. Cole, the big bluff sort, was noted for his sense of humor and his way with the ladies. Among his many loves was Myra Belle Shirley, later famous as Belle Starr, who had a daughter by him. With his mannerisms and acting ability, Cole was able to assume almost any identity. Once while hiding from the law in Texas, he sang in a choir and worked as a government census taker.

Jim was regarded as the most handsome of the lot, easygoing, readily influenced by Jesse James, but in the end, he brooded about his misbegotten life and put a bullet in his brain.

The Youngers got together with the Jameses in 1866, when

Frank James introduced Cole to Jesse. It marked the beginning of a bloody decade in the Midwest. The six formed the nucleus of a gang that carried out numerous bank and train robberies, killing at least 10 persons and possibly many more, since it was never established which robberies could be attributed to the gang and which could not. After the robbery of a bank in Gallatin, Mo. in 1869, the Youngers were identified as colleagues of the James brothers. In 1872 Bob Younger took part, under Jesse's leadership, in a daring raid on the box office of the Kansas City fairgrounds.

In 1874 Jim and John Younger tangled with three lawmen and killed two of them: Louis J. Lull, a Pinkerton captain of detectives, and Sheriff Ed Daniels of Osceola, Mo. The lawmen, however, shot John to death and wounded Jim Younger, but he managed escape, leaving behind the bullet-riddled corpse of brother John.

The three remaining Youngers had only two years of freedom left, although during that time and thereafter they enjoyed great notoriety. Much of their fame derived from an 1875 book by John T. Appler called *The Guerillas of the West; or, The Life, Character and Daring Exploits of the Younger Brothers.* Although some parts of it were accurate, other sections were complete fabrication, such as the recounting of an episode during the Civil War when Cole supposedly decided to test out a new Enfield rifle on 15 Union prisoners. Told the rifle could fire a mile, Cole allegedly said that one bullet should be able to kill at least 10 men. According to Appler, he lined up the prisoners one behind the other and kept firing until all were dead.

In 1876 the James-Younger gang robbed a stagecoach in Texas and later a bank in Otterville, Mo. They then headed up into Minnesota, where they robbed a bank in Northfield on September 7, 1876. Up until then the gang seldom encountered much trouble from local citizens while pulling a job, but the Northfield residents were of a different cut. Alerted by gunfire inside the bank, the local citizens rushed out with guns and rocks to stop the bandits. Two of the robbers were killed before the gang could get out of town, and the rest were badly shot up. Bob's elbow was shattered and he was hit in the thigh. Cole took a bullet in the shoulder and Jim had his jaw nearly blasted away. Jesse and Frank James received lesser wounds.

Over the next several days the bandits could not shake pursuing posses. When Jesse suggested to Cole that they put Jim Younger out of his misery because he was slowing their flight, Cole and his brothers faced the two James boys down. Jesse and Frank James split off and threaded their way through the posses, while the three Youngers and the remaining member of the gang, Charlie Pitts, continued on together.

Finally, on September 21 the four were cornered in a thicket of willows and plum trees. Pitts was killed and the three Younger brothers were literally shot full of holes. Yet when they were being escorted in a wagon to the nearest town, Cole Younger, despite 11 bullet wounds, startled a group of gaping women by standing up and bowing to them.

All three Youngers were sentenced to life in prison. Bob Younger, who became a model prisoner, died there of tuberculosis in 1889. Jim and Cole Younger were finally freed in 1901. Unable to find suitable work and despondent, Jim shot himself to death in 1902. Ironically, Cole at the time was selling tombstones for a living.

In 1903 Cole published his autobiography, *The Story of Cole Younger,* and reunited with Frank James in a Wild West show. They split up after a few years, some said because of ill feelings stemming from the Northfield raid, with Cole continuing to tour with carnivals as a solo act. He died in 1916.

See also: *James Brothers; Northfield, Minnesota, Bank Raid; Belle Starr.*

YULCH, Adam (1885-1950): Laundry-mark expert

The practice of tracing criminals through laundry marks existed long before Adam Yulch set up a complete Laundry-Mark Identification Bureau in New York's Nassau County Police Department during the 1930s, but acting-Captain Yulch's success in the field made him nationally and internationally famous as the "laundry-mark hawkshaw."

Yulch made his first laundry-mark arrest in 1936 following the robbery of a bank messenger. One of the criminals left a jacket in the getaway car that had a faded dry-cleaning mark on an inside sleeve. Handed the assignment of finding the cleaner, Yulch covered every cleaner, laundry and tailor on Long Island, and then in New York City. Finally, he hit pay dirt in Westchester County at a wholesale cleaner. The mark was traced to a local tailor, who at first could not remember the customer. Yulch prodded the tailor's memory by pointing out the customer was probably a dandy dresser who got his clothes pressed often and who was around a lot in the daytime. Now the tailor remembered. The dapper holdup man was located and the robbery was solved.

When the next case with a laundry-mark clue turned up, the Nassau police immediately turned it over to Yulch. He realized then he should have kept records of all the marks of tailors whom he'd called upon in the previous case. Yulch started assembling such information on 3x5 index cards, organizing what was to become the most complete identification bureau in the country.

To the untrained eye one laundry mark looks like another, but the scrawl is a code that allows a cleaner and his wholesaler to quickly identify the store, the route and, in some cases, even the name of the customer. Laundries use a similar coding system, and many use invisible ink. Slowly, Yulch collected codes from every state in the union and, in time, became so familiar with those in his area that he could read them easily without even referring to his files.

In another case Secret Service agents raided a counterfeiting printing plant but failed to catch the suspect, who escaped through a hidden exit. He had been shaving at the time they arrived and had left his shirt behind. The agents brought the shirt to Yulch, who merely glanced at it, gave them an address and told them the man they wanted was in apartment 3-B.

The agents were startled but rushed to the place and captured the suspect busily packing his bags to flee. Yulch understood the laundry's code mark on the shirt, which, in addition to its own indicator, listed the customer's address and apartment number.

Yulch's Laundry-Mark Identification Bureau was always available to other law enforcement agencies, and Yulch helped a number of state police organizations set up their own systems before his death in 1950. He even organized one for the Royal Canadian Mounted Police. Decades later, the Nassau County bureau was still regarded as the best in the country.

YUMA Penitentiary

Easily the most-feared and hated prison in the Old West was the penitentiary built at Yuma, Arizona Territory in 1876.

Rehabilitation of prisoners was not one of Yuma's objectives. The overriding concern of the prison was restraint—restraint of the prisoners from escaping, rioting or creating any sort of a problem. Inmates were allowed to work and exercise during the daytime, but at night, when the blistering heat of the desert sun gave way to the chilling cold, the convicts were chained to the stone floors of their cells from dusk to dawn. Corruption and brutality were practiced by the guards until this hellhole of a prison was abandoned in the early 20th century. It is now a museum. In a sense, Yuma Penitentiary had at least one claim to innovation. So many escapes were attempted there that it became the first prison to be equipped with Gatling guns.

Z

ZANGARA, Joseph (1900-1933): Assassin

Virtually every presidential assassination or attempt has produced speculation of a deeper and more insidious plot. Joseph Zangara's attempt to kill Franklin D. Roosevelt on February 15, 1933 in Miami is unique in that the conspiracy theory posits the president-elect was not even the target and that Zangara, in fact, killed the man he was supposed to, Mayor Anton J. Cermak of Chicago. According to the majority of experts, the idea that Zangara was a Capone hit man is nonsense. Nevertheless the theory has long been held by many crime historians and Chicago journalists. A leading expert, Judge John H. Lyle, probably as knowledgeable as any non-Mafia man on the subject of Chicago crime, emphasizes "Zangara was a Mafia killer, sent from Sicily to do a job and sworn to silence."

Before the shooting, Cermak had been trying to get rid of the Capone mob so that gangsters under his control could take over crime in Chicago, and a current journalistic theory held that he had fled to Miami because he feared the Capones were going to assassinate him. The fact that Zangara had won several pistol-shooting awards when he was in the Italian Army and that he fatally wounded Cermak without even hitting Roosevelt provided additional weight to the theory that the intended victim of the assassination was Cermak. However, when Zangara opened fire on the car carrying Roosevelt and Cermak, he hit four bystanders, casting doubt on his ability as a marksman.

If Zangara kept his silence in a monumental criminal plot, he had not maintained his peace on political matters since his arrival in the country in 1923. Employed off and on as a mill hand in New Jersey, he had railed about "capitalist presidents and kings." According to his later confession, he would have been just as likely to have tried to kill Calvin Coolidge or Herbert Hoover as Roosevelt; he happened to select FDR only because he was in Miami when Roosevelt was there. "I see Mr. Hoover first I kill him first," he said at his trial. "Make no

Joseph Zangara was almost stripped of all his clothing by those who seized him after his unsuccessful attempt to assassinate President-elect Franklin D. Roosevelt.

difference. Presidents just the same bunch—all same." Zangara clung to that line to the day of his execution. Of Cermak, he said, "I wasn't shooting at him, but I'm not sorry I hit him."

Zangara claimed he might have tried to kill King Victor Emmanuel III had he remained in the Italian Army.

In the death chamber Zangara said: "There is no God. It's all below. . . . See, I no scared of electric chair." Sitting down in the chair, he glared at the witnesses with contempt. "Lousy capitalists." His last words were: "Goodby. *Addio* to all the world. Go ahead. Push the button."

See also: *Anton J. Cermak.*

ZELIG, Jack (1882-1912): Gang leader and murderer

Big Jack Zelig assumed the leadership of the New York criminal empire that had been held first by Monk Eastman and then by Kid Twist. A handsome, brutish killer, Big Jack's services were always available for hire to any bidder, high or low. There is no record of the gang leader ever turning down any job of violence. A Zelig henchmen once gave the police Big Jack's price list:

Slash on cheek with knife	$1 to $10
Shot in leg	$1 to $25
Shot in arm	$5 to $25
Throwing a bomb	$5 to $50
Murder	$10 to $100

If the fee for murder seemed a bit low, it must be remembered that such contracts normally included "fringe benefits," i.e., whatever valuables were found on the victim. Judiciously, Zelig would wait until a businessman, e.g., was making a deposit at the bank before killing him. A common workman would get his on payday. In one case Zelig held off on the murder of a victim until he ventured abroad to do his Christmas shopping.

Zelig, whose real name was William Alberts, was born in Norfolk Street in 1882 to respectable Jewish parents. He ran away at 14 and joined a juvenile gang of pickpockets under the leadership of the colorful Crazy Butch. Zelig soon figured out that the boy pickpockets did all the dangerous work but Crazy Butch took virtually all the loot. He deserted the Fagin and became very successful on his own as a "lush worker," rolling drunken men on the Bowery and in Chatham Square. With his childish face and appearance, he was seldom suspected of pickpocketing. And when his youthful appearance was not enough, Zelig could turn on the tears. One man from whom Zelig had stolen a wallet and a diamond ring was so overcome with remorse at having accused him that he bought the baby-faced thief a new suit of clothes and "forced" money on him.

By the time he was in his twenties, Zelig had moved on to muggings and murder for profit, but he never forgot the virtue of tears. Whenever he was arraigned—a frequent occurrence—he hired a frail and consumptive girl to come timidly into the courtroom and weepingly plead with the magistrate, "Oh, Judge, for God's sake, don't send my boy husband, the father of my baby, to jail!" The agony in the young "wife's" voice worked wonders for a number of years: Zelig would be released with a warning to go home to his wife and baby, of whom he had neither.

In the early 1900s Zelig attracted the attention of Monk Eastman and soon became one of his most dependable henchmen. When Eastman went to prison a few years later, Zelig remained loyal to Kid Twist, Eastman's successor, carrying out a number of murder assignments. After Kid Twist died in a gangland assassination in 1908, Zelig took over control of a large part of the old Eastman gang, while others left to follow the banner of Chick Tricker or Jack Sirocco. Most of the gangsters went with Zelig because he was a genius at organizing criminal activities and getting the most revenues out of them.

At heart, Zelig remained a bully and a brute. Seeking to impress a new sweetheart although short of cash, he marched into an East Side bordello with her and held up the madam for $80. The madam had the effrontery to complain to the police, and Zelig was arrested. Because of previous arrests, Big Jack faced a long prison term; so he sent word to Tricker and Sirocco to return the money to the madam and frighten her into refusing to testify. The pair deliberately did not carry out his orders, hoping Zelig would be sent away and they would inherit his crime empire. Big Jack finally got another gang leader, Jimmy Kelly, to carry his message to the madam, and when the case came up in court, the woman insisted Zelig looked not a bit like the man who had robbed her. Big Jack was released and vowed war on Tricker and Sirocco.

In the ensuing battles at least a score of gunmen on both sides died. In an awesome display of shooting, Zelig shot and killed a hired gunman, Julie Morrell, sent after him by his foes. Zelig's friends got Morrell drunk and he staggered out onto the dance floor of the Stuyvesant Casino shouting: "Where's that big Yid Zelig? I gotta cook that big Yid!"

Suddenly, Zelig spoke sharply from a table across the dance floor and the dancers scattered. Just then the lights went out and a single shot was fired. When the lights went on, Morrell lay dead on the floor and Zelig was gone. He had shot Morrell through the heart in the dark.

By this time Zelig was offering protection to many of the top gambling clubs in Manhattan. Finally, he was hired by police Lt. Charles E. Becker for a very special job, that of assassinating a gambler named Herman "Beansie" Rosenthal. Becker and Rosenthal had been partners, but when Becker had failed to protect Rosenthal in the way he wished, Rosenthal decided to blow the whistle on the payoffs delivered by the gambling interests of the city to the political and police powers. Zelig collected $2,000 for murdering Rosenthal. In a division of the spoils that was generous for Big Jack, he passed on $1,000 to four of his killers—Gyp the Blood, Whitey Lewis, Dago Frank and Lefty Louie—who did the actual work. After the killings, they appeared to have gotten away clean, since the investigation of the matter was in the hands of Lt. Becker himself. However, a reform district attorney named Charles Whitman launched his own investigation and easily found witnesses who identified the four murderers.

Gyp the Blood soon confessed. He said he had been hired by Big Jack Zelig and named Becker as the man behind the entire operation.

Zelig also broke the underworld code of silence, testifying before the grand jury on Becker's links to the crime. On October 5, 1912, the day before he was to appear in court, Zelig was gunned down on a Manhattan trolley car by Red Phil Davidson. The police department was sure the murder of Zelig was related to his feud with the Sirocco and Tricker forces. Everyone else in New York felt it had something to do with his forthcoming testimony against Becker. As it turned out, even without Zelig's testimony, there was more than enough evidence to convict the four gunmen and Becker as well. All eventually died in the electric chair.

See also: *Charles E. Becker, Gyp the Blood.*

ZERILLI, Joseph (1897-1977): Syndicate leader

Perhaps the closest thing in real life to the public's perception of a Mafia "godfather," Joseph Zerilli was the crime boss of Detroit for decades and the last survivor of that city's violent Prohibition-era gang wars.

Born in Terrasini, Sicily, he immigrated to the United States in 1914 and started working as a pick-and-shovel laborer. He quickly gravitated into criminal activities and worked his way up to an important position in the Purple Mob, eventually becoming the leader of an illegal operation that took in profits estimated at $150 million a year from such activities as bookmaking, numbers, loansharking, prostitution, extortion, narcotics and labor racketeering. Zerilli lived in a $500,000 home on a 20-acre suburban estate and always insisted he was just a businessman-baker.

While he was known to have been involved in a great many crimes, including murder, Zerilli was convicted of criminal charges only twice. In 1919 he paid fines for carrying concealed weapons and for speeding. As the highest-ranking mobster in Detroit, Zerilli was due to attend the infamous Apalachin summit meeting of syndicate leaders in 1957, but he turned back when he got word that a police raid was underway.

In his early seventies Zerilli retired from crime family business and turned over control to his son, Tony, one of the few Mafia cases where a son succeeded a father in the role of gang leader. However, the elder Zerilli returned to active control in 1975, when his son received a four-year prison sentence for conspiring to obtain a hidden interest in a Las Vegas casino.

Zerilli was implicated in the 1975 disappearance of James R. Hoffa, the former president of the International Brotherhood of Teamsters. When Hoffa disappeared, he was reported to have been on his way to meet Anthony Giacalone, Zerilli's top lieutenant. Zerilli provided the police with no information concerning the case. When he died October 30, 1977, a high police official observed he probably carried more criminal secrets to the grave than any crime leader who had passed away in the past decade.

ZIEGLER, Shotgun George (1897-1934): Gangster

Perhaps the best educated and certainly one of the smartest of the 1930 gangsters, shotgun George Ziegler (whose real name was Fred Goetz) was for a time the mastermind of the Barker-Karpis gang and was a chief planner in the kidnapping of wealthy Edward George Bremer of St. Paul, Minn. in 1934. He was also for a time one of Al Capone's most-trusted trigger men, remaining a prime suspect in the famous St. Valentine's Day massacre of the Bugs Moran gang.

During World War I, Ziegler had been a second lieutenant and pilot. In 1922 he graduated from the University of Illinois, where he had been a football player and an excellent golfer. Famed FBI agent Melvin H. Purvis said of him, "His character was one of infinite contradictions; well mannered, always polite, he was capable of generous kindnesses and conscienceless cruelty." It may well be that Ziegler became a criminal almost accidentally after being arrested on a rape charge. He jumped bail before his trial and, not wishing his parents to lose the money, decided to get it back quickly. He attempted to hold up a doctor he knew always carried large sums of money. When the physician drew a gun he had permission to carry, Goetz blasted him to death with a shotgun, launching his career as Shotgun George Ziegler.

When next heard of he was a gunman with the Capone mob in Chicago. Besides the St. Valentine's Day killings, Ziegler was credited with six to 10 other mob murders. From time to time he disappeared from the crime scene. During those periods he actually worked as an engineer; he had studied engineering in college. But he regularly departed from the straight life to win fame as one of the best artisans at "cracking a bank" while a member of the Midwest's Keating-Holden gang.

In 1933 Ziegler turned up in the Barker-Karpis mob, where his intelligence soon propelled him into a position of leadership. He picked Bremer as a likely kidnap victim, a caper that netted the gang a $200,000, ransom. Most of the money was turned over to Ziegler, who stashed it in a garage belonging to his wife's uncle, where it was to be left to "cool." That proved to be a fatal error on the Barkers' part. While they trusted Ziegler totally, he was slowly losing his mind. He began to talk wildly in underworld circles, loudly proclaiming credit for the Bremer job. The Barkers realized Ziegler had to be silenced, and on March 22, 1934, just two months after the Bremer kidnapping, four shotguns blasted Ziegler as he stepped out of his favorite cafe in Cicero, Ill. Ziegler fell dead, most of his head blown away. With Ziegler gone, only his widow knew where the ransom money was hidden. Ma Barker was able to cajole the grieving but trusting widow into turning over the money, insisting Ziegler had undoubtedly been killed by enemies from his Capone days. What couldn't be undone was the information the FBI had gained from Ziegler's corpse. On his body were membership cards to the Chicago Yacht Club and the Mohawk Country Club of Bensenville, Ill. Police then found his address and the names and addresses of many members of the Barker-Karpis mob. The Barkers were forced to scatter, all soon to fall victim to the law. Ma Barker and son Fred were killed in a famous shoot-out in Florida the following year.

See also: *Barker Brothers, Dr. Joseph Patrick Moran.*

ZODIAC Killer: California mass murderer

Starting in California in 1966 and extending over the next several years, a weird mass murderer, who became known as Zodiac because of the letters and cryptograms he sent to newspapers, killed a number of victims, mostly young girls, because, he said, he was "collecting slaves for my afterlife." There is considerable dispute over the number of persons Zodiac killed, since he did not claim credit for some murders he definitely committed and the police failed to find the bodies of many he claimed to have killed.

The first murders he acknowledged were those of two high school teenagers, who were parked on a lonely road outside Vallejo, Calif. on December 20, 1968. Carrying a .22-caliber pistol, a lone figure moved to the car and aimed it at the head of 17-year-old David Faraday. Three bullets smashed into Faraday's skull before he could react. Sitting next to the driver, 16-year-old Bettilou Jensen screamed and then bolted from the car. She didn't get far. The attacker dropped her with five bullets. Both youngsters died. The following July 4 Zodiac struck again, killing a young girl sitting in parked car in a public park near Vallejo. Her 19-year-old companion survived despite four bullet wounds. The killer had shined a flashlight into their car, temporarily blinding the youth, so that he could give only a sketchy identification of the attacker: a fairly heavy man with glasses.

In one of Zodiac's more gruesome killings, he stabbed Cecelia Shepard in the back 24 times, cutting the outline of a bloody cross. The best description of Zodiac was obtained when he killed a part-time college student working as a cab driver in San Francisco. He had shot him from the back seat and set about cleaning up the taxi, presumably to eradicate his fingerprints. Then he cut off a piece of the victim's bloody shirt—to enclose in a future letter to a newspaper—before leaving. Zodiac was seen by witnesses, and with their aid the police put out a composite description of him: a man of 35 to 45, five foot eight inches with short brown-reddish hair and wearing thick glasses.

Zodiac's letters to the police and to the newspapers continued throughout the early 1970s, although some were believed to be fakes. The San Francisco police attributed no more than six murders to Zodiac, although his own count eventually reached 37. A possible confirmation of Zodiac's total came in 1975 from Don Striepeke, sheriff of Sonoma County. Striepeke used a computer study of murder records in the state attorney general's office as the basis for a theory that about 40 murders in four Western states could be traced to one killer, perhaps Zodiac. The officer found in these murders what he regarded as threads of similarity, and he even theorized that the murderer was using a huge letter "Z" mapped over several Western states as a blueprint for where to commit his crimes. Since the mid-1970s nothing more has been heard from Zodiac, the most common police theory being that he is either dead or confined in some mental institution.

ZWEIBACH, Max: See Kid Twist.

ZWILLMAN, Abner "Longy" (1899-1959): Crime syndicate leader

A graduate of the bootleg racket in Brooklyn, New York City, Longie Zwillman emerged as one of the most powerful crime leaders in the country, a member of the Seven Group, the forerunner of the national crime syndicate that began in the 1930s.

Zwillman, an associate of Meyer Lansky, Frank Costello and Willie Moretti, was instrumental in the new combination's successful efforts to take over Dutch Schultz's empire. In the process Zwillman became the undisputed boss of crime in New Jersey, where he operated on a grand scale. When considerable heat was put on the syndicate as a result of the Lindbergh baby kidnapping, Zwillman relieved the pressure by posting a large reward for the kidnapper. His political power in New Jersey was impressive. In 1946 Republican Gov. Harold G. Hoffmann personally asked Zwillman's aid. Three years later, the mobster let it be known to the Democratic candidate for the governorship, Elmer Wene, that he would contribute $300,000; all he asked in return was the right to name the state's attorney general. Wene declined the offer.

In the early 1950s Zwillman moved much of his millions into legitimate enterprises and attempted to create the image that he was a civic-minded citizen by donating $250,000 for a slum clearance project in Newark. However, his new image didn't hold up very well when the McClellan Committee's rackets investigation in the late 1950s began focusing on his activities. Subpoenaed to appear before the committee and being hounded by an IRS probe, Zwillman seemed to be a beaten man.

He also had his problems within the syndicate. He had guessed wrong by supporting the aging Frank Costello when other forces in the organization wanted to retire him. Zwillman then guessed wrong again by siding with Albert Anastasia against Vito Genovese. Other crime leaders began edging into his New Jersey rackets.

Given the sum total of the pressures on him, it was not terribly surprising that Zwillman committed suicide on February 27, 1959, just prior to his scheduled appearance before the McClellan Committee. Perhaps the only troubling detail about Zwillman's suicide was the way he had done it. Apparently, he had managed to strangle himself with a plastic rope in the basement of his luxurious $200,000 mansion in West Orange, N.J. That clearly seemed the hard way of committing suicide; moreover, there were unexplained bruises on his body and indications that his hands had been tied with wire. Nonetheless, the official verdict was suicide.

Zwillman's death undoubtedly brought considerable relief to the members of the crime syndicate, especially Meyer Lansky, who feared Zwillman was growing too old to take the pressure and might turn informer.

SUBJECT INDEX

Since *THE ENCYCLOPEDIA OF AMERICAN CRIME* is arranged alphabetically and is thoroughly cross-referenced, this index is intended to serve a limited purpose. Index headings cover only geographic locations (major cities and states), types of crimes and criminals and other broad subject categories, such as **INVESTIGATIVE TECHNIQUES** or **PRISONS AND PRISONERS**. These broad headings permit the reader to trace the history of crime in a particular locale as well as to gain a general overview of a subject.

Ruef, Abraham
Small, Len
Tweed Ring
Walker, James J.

PUNISHMENT—*See also* PRISONS AND PRISONERS

Book Whippings
Branding
Capital Punishment
Carlton, Handsome Harry
Castration as Punishment
Colonial Punishment
Debtors, Imprisonment of
Execution, Methods of
Executions , Public
Flogging
Lynching
Mutilation
Pillory
Sentencing of Criminals
Tar and Feathering
Transportation
Walker, Jonathan

RACKETS—*See also* CONS AND CON ARTISTS

Accident Faking
Badger Game
Baker Estate
Begging
Carnival Gyps
Circus Grifting
Creep Joint
Insurance Frauds—Fake Deaths
Key Racket
Panel House
Shortchange Artists
Vampires

RAPE

Arbuckle, Roscoe "Fatty"
Rape
Scottsboro Boys
Thompson, Gerald
Turner, Richard

REFORM MOVEMENTS AND INVESTIGATIONS

Andrews Committee
Bank Robberies: Bounties
Comstock, Anthony
Dix, Dorothea Lynde

Kefauver Investigation
Knapp Commission
Lexow Committee
Nation, Carry A.
Parkhurst, Reverend Charles H.
Seabury Investigation
Stead, William T.
Wickersham Commission

RHODE ISLAND

Graves, Thomas T.

RIOTS AND MASS KILLINGS

Allen Massacre, The
Astor Place Riots
Bath, Mich.
Chinese Riots
Chivington, John M.
Cincinnati Riots
Doctors' Mob
Draft Riots
Flour Riots
Gentlemen's Riot
Guadalupe Canyon Massacre
Haun's Mill Massacre
Haymarket Affair
Herrin Massacre
Holmes, Alexander William
Jackson, Edward Z. C.
Lager Beer Riot
Mountain Meadows Massacre
Philadelphia Anti-Catholic Riots
Ponvenir Massacre
Springfield (Illinois) Race Riot
Tobacco Night Riders
Whiskey Rebellion

ROBBERIES

Bisbee Massacre
Brink's Robbery
Lufthansa Robbery
Pierre Hotel Robbery
Robert's Hill Stagecoach Robbery

SAFECRACKING

Leslie, George Leonidas
Little Joker
Reiser, Charles "the Ox"
Safecracking

SLAVERY AND ABOLITIONISM

Abolitionist Riots
Bras Coupe
Gentlemen's Riot
Kidnapping of Free Blacks
Lovejoy, Elijah
Slave Murderers
Turner, Nat
Vesey, Denmark

SOUTH CAROLINA

Earle, Willie
George, Christian
Vesey, Denmark

SOUTH DAKOTA

Calamity Jane
Dead Man's Hand
Hickok, James Butler "Wild Bill"
McCall, Jack
Poker Alice

SWINDLES AND SWINDLERS—*See* CONS AND CON ARTISTS

TENNESSEE

Animal Lynching
Jackson-Dickinson Duel
Maury County, Tennessee Jail Fire
Scopes, John T.
Tobacco Night Riders

TEXAS

Baker, Cullen M.
Ball, Joe
Bank Robberies: Bounties
Bass, Sam
Bean, Roy
Brennan, Molly
Brownsville Affair
Bunch, Eugene "Captain Gerald"
Cooley, Scott
Corll, Dean
Cornett, Brack
Cortez, Gregorio
Cortina, Juan
Courtright, Longhair Jim
Devil's River Valley
Doan's Store
East Texas Regulator War
Estes, Billie Sol

TRAIN ROBBERIES AND ROBBERS—See also WESTERN OUTLAWS AND GUNFIGHTERS

TRIALS—See WRONGFUL CONVICTIONS AND CAUSE CELEBRES

UNSOLVED MURDERS

UTAH

VERMONT

VIGILANTES AND VIGILANTE VICTIMS

VIRGINIA

WASHINGTON, D. C.

WASHINGTON STATE

WEAPONS

PHOTO CREDITS
(The numbers refer to pages.)

364.973   9/28/94
Sif   Sifakis, Carl
           The encyclopedia
           of American crime

DATE DUE

DEC 2 1 199			
MAY 0 5 1995			

DEMCO